PENGUIN HANDBOOKS

THE PENGUIN GUIDE TO BARGAIN COMPACT DISCS

EDWARD GREENFIELD, until his retirement in 1993, was for forty years on the staff of the *Guardian*, succeeding Neville Cardus as Music Critic in 1975. He still contributes regularly to the record column which he founded in 1954. At the end of 1960 he joined the reviewing panel of *Gramophone*, specializing in operatic and orchestral issues. He is a regular broadcaster on music and records for the BBC, not just on Radios 3 and 4 but also on BBC World Service, latterly with his weekly programme, 'The Greenfield Collection'. In 1958 he published a monograph on the operas of Puccini. More recently he has written studies on the recorded work of Joan Sutherland and André Previn. He has been a regular juror on International Record awards and has appeared with such artists as Dame Elisabeth Schwarzkopf, Dame Joan Sutherland and Sir Georg Solti in public interviews. In October 1993 he was given a *Gramophone* Award for Special Achievement and in June 1994 received the OBE for services to music and journalism.

ROBERT LAYTON studied at Oxford with Edmund Rubbra for composition and with Egon Wellesz for the history of music. He spent two years in Sweden at the universities of Uppsala and Stockholm. He joined the BBC Music Division in 1959 and has been responsible for such programmes as *Interpretations on Record*. He has contributed a 'Quarterly Retrospect' to *Gramophone* for a number of years, and he has written books on Berwald and Sibelius and has specialized in Scandinavian music. He has written a monograph on the Dvořák symphonies and concertos for the BBC Music Guides, of which he was General Editor for many years. He has translated Erik Tawastsjerna's three-volume definitive study of Sibelius. In 1987 he was awarded the Sibelius Medal and in the following year was made a Knight of the Order of the White Rose of Finland for his services to Finnish music. He has also edited *Guides* to *The Symphony* and *The Concerto* (OUP) and has recently completed a short biography of Grieg (Omnibus Press).

IVAN MARCH is a former professional musician. He studied at Trinity College of Music, London, and at the Royal Manchester College. After service in the Central Band of the RAF, he played the horn professionally for the BBC and travelled with the Carl Rosa and D'Oyly Carte opera companies. Now director of the Long Playing Record Library, the largest commercial lending library for classical music on compact discs in the British Isles, he is a well-known lecturer, journalist and personality in the world of recorded music. As a journalist, he contributes to a number of record-reviewing magazines, including *Gramophone*, where his regular monthly 'Collector's Corner' deals particularly with important reissues.

The Penguin Guide to Bargain Compact Discs

Completely revised and updated

Ivan March, Edward Greenfield and Robert Layton

Edited by Ivan March

PENGUIN BOOKS

PENGUIN BOOKS

Published by the Penguin Group
Penguin Books Ltd, 27 Wrights Lane, London W8 5TZ, England
Penguin Putnam Inc., 375 Hudson Street, New York, New York 10014, USA
Penguin Books Australia Ltd, Ringwood, Victoria, Australia
Penguin Books Canada Ltd, 10 Alcorn Avenue, Toronto, Ontario, Canada M4V 3B2
Penguin Books (NZ) Ltd, Private Bag 102902, NSMC, Auckland, New Zealand

Penguin Books Ltd, Registered Offices: Harmondsworth, Middlesex, England

This edition first published 1998
10 9 8 7 6 5 4 3 2 1

Set in 8/9.5 pt PostScript Monotype Times New Roman
Typeset, from material supplied, by Rowland Phototypesetting Ltd, Bury St Edmunds, Suffolk
Made and printed in Great Britain by Clays Ltd, St Ives plc

Contents

Foreword

Bargain and mid-priced records have been around since the earliest days of stereo LP; after they first arrived in 1983, compact discs were able to hold their premium-price monopoly for only some three years. Mid-priced reissues then began to appear on the major labels, soon to be followed by new, digital recordings from enterprising smaller companies like Pickwick (now Carlton), which were later to drop to the bargain-price range. In 1986–7, manufacturing costs began to fall dramatically and the way was now clear for the arrival of a super-bargain CD label which was to alter profoundly the whole basis of marketing classical music on compact disc. The story of how Naxos came into being is worth telling.

I: The coming of super-bargain CDs and the story of Naxos

Klaus Heymann, its founder, had begun his music business at the start of the 1970s with a small distribution company in Hong Kong, first importing hi-fi equipment, then promoting classical concerts sponsored by the manufacturers. Soon he was also importing records, and it was a short step for his company, Pacific Music, to move on to actually making recordings and eventually to establishing its own classical, premium-priced label, Marco Polo. Through his association with the Hong Kong Philharmonic Orchestra, Heymann had met and married the distinguished Japanese violinist, Takako Nishizaki, and an additional incentive for going into the record business was to feature her as a soloist on quality recordings which would promote her career in the West. She began by recording the complete works of Fritz Kreisler, then suddenly she became a star in China through her recording (in 1978) of the *'Butterfly lovers' Violin concerto*, which has since become one of the biggest crossover hits of all time and has sold millions of copies on the Chinese mainland (most of them pirated).

Over the next decade, Marco Polo became a respected minor label offering lesser-known symphonic repertoire, composed between 1850 and the early part of the twentieth century. To service the label, production plants for manufacturing CDs were set up in both Hungary and Slovakia (Bratislava). It was towards the end of the 1980s, with a successful trial release (at budget price) of some licensed recordings from Germany, that Heymann recognized the enormous potential of a quality budget classical label. He was not alone. The modest-sized LaserLight series already existed, its list including several very successful CDs, as did the Hungaroton White Label catalogue, which was however dogged by uncertainty of availability.

From the start, Heymann envisaged a planned repertory, high quality control, and entirely digital recordings made with young or unknown artists, and with orchestras which had had no proper exposure in the world market. He had not far to look: they were already available, in Bratislava and in Budapest; and that is the reason why all early Naxos recordings came from Slovakia and Hungary.

The cautious initial strategy was to issue only fifty titles as a first release, since Heymann thought that his venture would have a limited life. He felt sure that the major manufacturers would respond immediately, entering the budget market with famous names, determined to put him out of business. But they didn't take seriously the threat he posed and, by the time they did, Naxos had established itself firmly as the world's leading budget label. In its first year, 1987, Naxos was to issue 100 releases; 1.5 million CDs were sold through chain stores . . . and that is where we came into the picture.

Here it is necessary to introduce William Hall, musically erudite and an avid record collector, who lives in Hertfordshire. He is Edward Greenfield's cousin, and he acts as our ears and eyes in the marketplace; for he is able seemingly to find out about new ventures even before they have happened! It was Cousin Bill who discovered some of those early Naxos CDs in the Enfield branch of Woolworths.

Among them he was agreeably surprised to find a series of Beethoven *Sonatas* recorded by an excellent pianist who was totally unknown to him: Jenö Jandó. Not only were they well recorded, the performances were spontaneous-sounding and musically very impressive. 'He didn't over-pedal,' was Cousin Bill's critical comment. He told EG about them (who passed the information on to your Editor) and eventually, in November 1989, Bill wrote for a catalogue to the British distributor for the Pacific Music Company, one Peter Smith, who worked out of his home in Brixham, Devon. (The distribution was later to move north-east to Sheffield, where it was run very efficiently for some years by a husband-and-wife team, both musicians, Rona and David Harrison.)

Review copies were then sought, and EG introduced Jandó's Beethoven and other Naxos CDs to readers of his weekly record review in the *Guardian*. Subsequently, in October 1990, the Editor discussed the implications of the arrival of Naxos in his 'Collector's Corner' column in *Gramophone*. By then the first five CDs of Jandó's complete series of the Mozart *Piano concertos* had arrived, and his even more impressive pairing of Rachmaninov's *Second (C minor) Piano concerto*, coupled with the *Rhapsody on a theme of Paganini*. They were very well accompanied, the Mozart by an excellent Hungarian chamber orchestra, the Rachmaninov by the Budapest Symphony Orchestra under György Lehel. These records were not only of high musical and technical quality, they also had proper documentation (a surprisingly rare feature in the bargain arena). Retailing at that time at around £4 each, they seemed incredibly inexpensive.

In November, 'Collector's Corner' found space for an outstanding Naxos collection of Telemann's concertante works from the Capella Istropolitana of Bratislava, conducted by Richard Edlinger, and this was to be the first Naxos CD to be given a Rosette in the *Penguin Guide* – squeezed in at the last minute as the 1990 edition went to press.

Jandó's cycle of the Beethoven *Sonatas* had to wait until June 1991 before it could be fully covered in 'Collector's Corner', and until the autumn of that year to be included – with other Naxos releases – in the Penguin 1991 *Yearbook*. But before then we had begun to discover the other remarkable early Naxos venture: the projected complete recording of the Haydn *String quartets* by the Kodály Quartet.

The Editor first reviewed the six quartets of Opp. 71 and 74, plus Haydn's quartet version of *The Seven Last Words of our Saviour on the Cross*, with considerable enthusiasm in the main review columns of the February 1991 *Gramophone*, suggesting that the performances and recordings were 'in no way inferior to those one might find on the major companies' premium-price labels', and this assessment was fully confirmed when our 1992 (first) *Penguin Guide to Bargain Compact Discs and Cassettes* was also able to include Opp. 54/55 and the splendid set of the six *Erdödy Quartets*, Op. 76, to which we also gave a Rosette.

The direct result of this combined coverage was that Naxos CDs began to appear for the first time on the shelves of the big record stores, and from then onwards the label never looked back. The name of the Greek island where Theseus abandoned Ariadne to the mercies of Dionysus has now become very familiar to the purchasers of classical records.

A decade later, as can be seen in the following pages, the label has spread to cover a wide range of repertoire, from standard classics to early vocal music – the latter beautifully sung in a remarkably consistent series from the Oxford Camerata, directed by Jeremy Summerly. From recording the string quartets of Haydn (and other classical masters) and the complete works of Chopin (with Idil Biret), Naxos is ambitiously beginning a projected complete survey of the piano music of Liszt. A great deal of baroque repertory is also to be covered, from Albinoni's *Oboe concertos* with Anthony Camden to the projected 500 or so concertos of Vivaldi!

Moreover, the source of Naxos repertoire is no longer confined to Eastern Europe. English, Irish and Scottish orchestras are being used for a distinguished 'British composers' series. Andrew Penny is recording the Malcolm Arnold symphonies in Dublin (with the composer's imprimatur), David Lloyd Jones is embarking on the symphonies of Bax with the Royal Scottish National Orchestra, while Paul Daniel has already given us a superb account of Walton's *First Symphony* with the Northern Philharmonia of England.

Having already established Jandó's international reputation, Naxos is bringing further artists of distinction before the public: Laurence Cummings in the harpsichord music of François and Louis Couperin; the Vlach Quartet playing Dvořák; Vera Tsu (born in Shanghai) immediately establishing her credentials in a distinctive pairing of the Goldmark and Korngold *Violin concertos*; Einer Steen-Nøkleberg offering a comprehensive survey of the complete piano music of Grieg; the splendid cellist Maria Kliegel in the music of Kodály (and others); and Philip Thomson in Liszt. Mendelssohn's piano works bring the more familiar name of Benjamin Frith, and the *String Symphonies* arrive elegantly from the Northern CO under Nicholas Ward, while the Eder Quartet seem equally at home in Mozart or Shostakovich.

Today, Naxos CDs cost around £5 (in the USA $5.50) a disc, and in 1997 the catalogue had expanded to over 2,000 titles, and 16 million CDs were sold.

II: The other super-bargain labels

Until now, easily the most important of Naxos's direct competitors has been ASV's Quicksilva label, which has an impressive and growing catalogue of over 200 CDs. Although not all are digital, the coverage includes a first-class recording of Bach's *Flute sonatas* from William Bennett and George Malcolm, a fine cycle of the Beethoven symphonies from the Northern Sinfonia of England under Richard Hickox, John Lill's bold integral series of the Beethoven *Piano sonatas*, the four Brahms and four Schumann symphonies from the Royal Liverpool Philharmonic under Marek Janowski, a splendid complete account of Handel's *Water music* by the ECO under George Malcolm, a stimulating batch of Haydn *String quartets*, recorded live by the Lindsay Quartet at the Wigmore Hall, a highly recommendable pairing of Mendelssohn's *Scottish* and *Italian Symphonies* from the Orchestra of St John's, Smith Square, conducted by Mark Lubbock, music of Palestrina and Schütz from the Pro Cantione Antiqua, and two outstanding collections: '*The Splendour of Baroque Brass*' (from the London Gabrieli Brass Ensemble) and '*Für Elise*', Alan Schiller's delightful recital of romantic piano music, ideal for a late-evening reverie. But the highlight of the whole catalogue is surely Gordon Fergus-Thompson's coverage of the piano music of Debussy, beautifully played and recorded, and offered complete on four discs, a true bargain of the highest quality.

More recently, the Quicksilva label has been concentrating on new digital recordings of chamber and instrumental music, many of which have been very successful. The most notable is an outstanding new version of Schubert's greatest chamber work, the *C major String quintet*, by the Locrian Ensemble, which can be compared with the famous old Saga Aeolian record in its intensity of concentration but which has the advantage of digital background silence.

Other bargain-basement labels have arrived (and mostly departed). Those which have survived tend to remain on the periphery of the marketplace. The most useful of these are Discovery (now distributed by Koch) and Deutsche Harmonia Mundi's 'Baroque Esprit' series. Discovery concentrates, quite successfully, on offbeat repertoire, the highlight of an enterprising list being an absolutely complete recording of Walton's *Façade*, a disc to recommend to all collectors; while the Baroque Esprit series offers an outstanding single-disc collection of concertante works for two keyboard instruments, notably C. P. E. Bach's *E flat Double concerto for harpsichord and fortepiano*.

More recently, Polygram have inaugurated (in the UK but not in the USA) a super-budget label called Belart, which features reissued mono as well as stereo recordings, derived mainly from the back-catalogues of Decca/London and Philips. Easily the most important of the mono reissues is Sir Adrian Boult's pioneering Decca set of the Vaughan Williams symphonies which, as performances, have never been surpassed and still sound amazingly good. But Belart have also recently introduced an intriguing series of solo recitals from major British singers, including Sir Geraint Evans, Felicity Palmer, Sir Peter Pears, and – most notably – Owen Brannigan ('*A life of music*' is an unmissable disc), while couplings of songs by Butterworth and Finzi sung by Benjamin Luxon and the Vaughan Williams *Songs of travel* coupled with rare Parry repertoire from Robert Tear also stand out.

But the time was clearly ripe for a major competitor to Naxos to appear; the UK-based BMG/Conifer/RCA group could fill that role. In the last two years BMG has made a determined foray into the classical super-budget arena. RCA's Navigator series arrived first, concentrating on the UK market and drawing repertoire from the RCA and Russian Melodiya back-catalogues. These CDs immediately competed on price (they were priced at a very slightly lower cost than Naxos) and usually on quality too. Some of them offer really excellent value, notably a superb Julian Bream guitar recital of the music of Albéniz and Granados. As with Quicksilva, many of the Navigator recordings derive from analogue sources.

Clearly Navigator is not the complete answer, but perhaps Arte Nova is. This newest super-budget label originated in Germany two years ago, and it was launched in the UK by BMG towards the end of 1996 and in the USA soon afterwards (where, so far, it has made only a modest impact). Like Naxos, Arte Nova has relied on talented young artists and little-known orchestras, often with unlikely names, like the Putbus Festival Orchestra which (conducted by William Keitel) has already given us a splendid set of the complete symphonies of Schubert, and the Orquesta Filamonica de Gran Canaria. This is not – what its name might imply – a pick-up holiday-resort ensemble, but one of the oldest philharmonic orchestras in existence, recruiting players from all over the world. We were surprised by the quality of their ensemble in an impressive coupling of the *First* and *Sixth Symphonies* of Sibelius conducted by Adrian Leaper, which can stand comparison with the most illustrious alternative versions.

The Jena Philharmonic under David Montgomery has provided worthwhile records of music as diverse as the *Second* and *Fourth Symphonies* of Howard Hanson and an imaginative compilation of the music of Villa-Lobos, including the *Bachianas brasileiras No. 2* with its piquant portrait of '*The little train of the Caipira*'. Equally unlikely repertory for a German-based label is an Elliott Carter collection, confidently played by what is described as the SWFSO under Michael Gielen, including the *Piano concerto* (with Ursula Oppens) and the *Concerto for orchestra*. It is this same orchestra and conductor who offer one of the Arte Nova catalogue's highlights, a work in which they are obviously completely at home: Zemlinsky's *Lyric Symphony*; the results are first class in every way. Opera is the most difficult of all the recording genres to bring off successfully on a small budget (as Naxos have often discovered), but Arte Nova have scored a bull's-eye with their Linz recording (after a series of live performances) featuring a cast of talented young singers in Mozart's *Die Entführung aus dem Serail* under Martin Sieghart.

Like Naxos, Arte Nova is strong in the field of instrumental and chamber music. We are reminded of the artistry of Riccardo Castro (winner of the 1993 Leeds International Piano Competition) with a complete set of the Chopin *Nocturnes*, beautifully played and recorded, while an excellent young ensemble, who have named their group Opus 8, after Brahms's *First Piano trio*, offer a fine recording of this work, both as we know it today and in Brahms's (1854) original version. But the finest of the Arte Nova chamber-music discs so far is a captivating account of the Kreutzer *Septet*, a deliciously ingenuous and tuneful work based on the Beethoven *Septet*. It could not be presented more stylishly or spontaneously, and the recording is in the demonstration bracket. It carries the first Arte Nova *Penguin Guide* Rosette.

All Arte Nova recordings that we have encountered are digital and usually of good quality – but, alas, documentation is sparse and too often inadequate, especially where translations and texts are needed. Already there are several hundred Arte Nova discs, and BMG say they are investing heavily in future recordings, relying on a marketing strategy which aims 'to build confidence from critical endorsement of its repertoire'. We shall see.

III: The response of the major companies: bargain and mid-priced CDs, Duos and Doubles

Although, as we have suggested, no immediate reaction came from the major companies, during the 1990s they became increasingly aware of how competitive the marketplace for lower-priced CDs was becoming, and they reacted accordingly.

In the UK Polygram group, Decca re-vamped the bargain Eclipse label to offer top-quality, digital CDs with cassette equivalents; DG followed suit with the Classikon label, not entirely digital but offering very attractive repertoire, at a similar price. Philips kept in line, but perhaps less enthusiastically, with what has now become their bargain Virtuoso series. (Curiously, these three labels are available in the USA only as imports.) Each company in the group has also maintained and expanded its mid-price repertoire.

Comparatively recently, EMI have reduced the cost of their lower-mid-price Eminence label in order to combine it with the Classics for Pleasure budget series, and both catalogues are being re-packaged. The major EMI Classics mid-priced label (UK prefix CDM) remains unaltered.

Harmonia Mundi, Sony and Warner Classics (Teldec and Erato) have all continued both their mid-price and budget series. Chandos felt able to resist the temptation to create a bargain label, but they have introduced a quality mid-price series at the top end of the price-range.

Carlton confusingly uses two different price structures for their bargain CDs; but they had the good fortune to acquire the rights to distribute a fascinating list of 'BBC Radio Classics', emanating from the BBC Archives. Then, just as we were going to press, the BBC (extraordinarily) withdrew all but half a dozen of one hundred titles; the remaining few are all of music by British composers, plus 'The last night at the Proms'.

Among other smaller labels are Tring (which started as a super-budget series but soon switched to normal bargain price), which is notable for the introduction of two new pianists, Ronan O'Hora and Michael Roll; and Millennium, which offers interesting mono and early stereo recordings from the old Westminster catalogue.

The trump card, however, was dealt by Philips, when in June 1993 their Classics label introduced the Duo series: two CDs, generously full and cunningly packaged, back to back, in a single jewel-case, offered for the cost of a single premium-priced disc. It was a brilliant marketing ploy. Repertoire was skilfully selected, and the result was a runaway success – and deservedly so. Philips have recently celebrated sales of 5 million Duos (10 million CDs).

Needless to say, all the other major labels swiftly jumped on to the bandwagon. DG and Decca followed with Doubles (in the USA the Decca series is affectionately known as Double Deckers and they feature a London bus as their logo); French EMI introduced the elegantly named Rouge et Noir label; British EMI presented fortes (in the USA more appropriately called Double fortes); and Finlandia instituted their brilliantly conceived 'Meet the Composer' series, introducing the music of many little-known Finnish musicians, including Jukka Linkola, Magnus Lindberg, Leevi Madetoja and Aarre Merikanto, plus the more familiar Selim Palmgren. RCA chose the name 'Twofer' (ouch!), Warner Classics came up with Ultima (works drawn from both the Erato and Teldec catalogues). Even Hyperion, who hitherto had shunned the very idea of bargain reissues, produced their neatly packaged Dyads. Later, EMI were to go one better with Seraphims – two CDs for the price of a single *medium-price* disc, and this idea was taken up by both Carlton and Virgin Classics.

But the key to making a two-disc set value for money is to ensure that the two discs *match*, both in the chosen repertoire and in excellence of performances and recording. That was something Philips Duos got right from the very start; but not all the other labels have been so successful; in particular Carlton have often joined together performances of uneven quality and repertory which refused to twin up convincingly.

French Harmonia Mundi then went one better with Trios: three linked CDs in a slip-case (offered at bargain price in the UK but – where available – at mid-price in the USA) and as a counter-balance they instituted their super-budget Solo series, offering the collector a single work playing for about half an hour. On the face of it, this seems a very sensible idea, but one which may or may not catch on.

Last, but by no means least, came the bargain boxes – from all sources and in all price-ranges. The repertoire is almost always excellently chosen and the boxes are often unbeatable value for money; moreover, for the serious collector, since the individual discs are often paper-sleeved (with no obvious detriment) the boxes are very economical both financially and in terms of shelf-space. Leading this field is Nimbus, whose larger super-bargain offers are very inexpensive indeed, yet they include some really excellent recordings, from Bernard Roberts's integral set of the Beethoven *Piano sonatas* and the Franz Schubert Quartet of Vienna's admirable survey of the late quartets of Mozart to a very generous Tippett compilation and a rewarding survey of early English choral music from the Christ Church Cathedral Choir, directed by Stephen Darlington.

Preface

The oldest and truest adage in the world of recorded music is that newer is not necessarily better. Many of the greatest and most rewarding performances belong to the analogue stereo-LP era, and these records can offer an illusion of realism to compare with almost anything achieved more recently. One thinks, for example, of Previn's 1974 EMI recording of Britten's *Four Sea interludes* from *Peter Grimes*, still unsurpassed for its atmospheric realism

Moreover, with much more sophisticated remastering techniques we are now able to enjoy older recordings of outstanding musical quality from the early mono-LP and 78-r.p.m. eras. Indeed, some of the 78-r.p.m. transfers from Mike Dutton, the leading genius in this field, are little short of miraculous in restoring all the warmth and fullness which characterized the originals, with added clarity of focus.

There is, for instance, a superb Beecham disc which includes his most famous 78 record: Chabrier's *España*, together with his breathtaking account of Tchaikovsky's *Francesca da Rimini* – both with the LPO. But perhaps the finest example is the Dutton transfer of Sir Malcolm Sargent's first complete mono set of Handel's *Messiah*. Recorded in 1946, it had ideal soloists and the Huddersfield Choral Society, heard within the excellent acoustics of Huddersfield Town Hall; it originally appeared on countless 78s, and it has been directly transferred from those shellac originals. The result is aurally astonishing. One soon forgets its elderly provenance and simply sits back to enjoy the singing and playing.

Dutton has also revealed the superb quality some of the mono LPs on the old EMI Parlophone label featuring lesser-known conductors like Basil Cameron, Fistoulari, John Hollingsworth and Gaston Poulet. But it was Walter Legge and the Columbia label which gave us Karajan's early Philharmonia recording of Britten's *Variations on a theme of Frank Bridge* (now available in a new EMI transfer), which has a perfection of ensemble and a sonority of string-tone that still astonish; as a performance it is unsurpassed.

Sony are also continually remastering their early catalogue with great success, notably recordings from Bernstein, Copland and Szell, plus Igor Stravinsky's authoritative interpretations of his own music. But perhaps the greatest sonic improvement on this label has come with the reissue of Ormandy's glorious pioneering stereo recordings of the three Rachmaninov symphonies with the Philadelphia Orchestra. Sony are looking further back still for their latest, handsomely packaged (if rather expensive) Heritage series, which includes not only the legendary recordings of the Beethoven *String quartets* from the Budapest Quartet, made between 1940 and 1945, but also Mitropoulos's riveting 1951 set of Berg's *Wozzeck*.

RCA have also reprocessed treasurable 'Living Stereo' reissues from Rubinstein and Van Cliburn; the achievements of Fritz Reiner in Chicago and of Munch in Boston have been supplemented by a lively series of 'Pops' from the late Arthur Fiedler, who in the 1930s, '40s and '50s was directing the USA's equivalent in Boston of Sir Henry Wood's Promenade Concerts in London.

The operatic field has continued to expand, not only with complete recordings and highlights, but also with recitals. The complete Callas Edition has reappeared on EMI, while the CPO label has licensed recordings from EMI/Electrola to produce a fascinating mid-price sequence of lesser-known German operas and operettas (including rare works by Mendelssohn and Schubert). Naxos, never content to rest on its laurels, has supplemented its new opera recordings with a historic series which, drawing on the archives of the Metropolitan Opera in New York, features the starry casts on the Met. roster in the 1930s and '40s.

Chandos, sponsored by the Peter Moores Foundation, continues its excellent mid-price series of operas sung in English, of which Opera North's production of Mussorgsky's *Boris Godunov* is the finest example so far. Only a single disc of highlights is offered but, with John Tomlinson in his very finest form in the title-role, and with Paul Daniel conducting a responsive Leeds choral group and the Northern Philharmonia Orchestra, this disc can stand alongside the competing Russian versions of Mussorgsky's masterpiece.

The various 'editions' centred round a single composer continue to proliferate. Bach's orchestral, keyboard and organ music, plus the major choral works and cantatas, are all grouped in various boxes, but DG's Beethoven Edition obviously takes pride of place, even if it is better approached selectively, rather than as a complete package (or 'suitcase' – for that is what the entire compilation resembles).

Chopin, Handel and Haydn (with the complete symphonies, piano trios, string quartets and masses) are also well covered in different ways, and there are most impressive surveys of the complete music of Dowland, the secular music of Dufay, and even a five-disc set of Mozart's concert arias, while the recent bicentenary celebration of Schubert's birth, and the centenary of the death of Brahms have both brought prolific reissues, many of considerable interest. Perhaps most impressive of all is the Philips Vivaldi Edition in two Volumes, totalling 19 CDs in all.

Among instrumentalists, while Casals is not neglected, the huge Heifetz Edition remains the most remarkable achievement. RCA have been continuing to reissue the individual records separately, including the important stereo recordings of the major concertos. The great violinist hoped that his final reputation would be consolidated by his recordings, and he emerges as peerless among his contemporaries. He can still teach present-day virtuosi a thing or two, although the separate achievements of David Oistrakh and of Isaac Stern (also given editions of their own) are not diminished.

Among the pianists, the quite different achievements of Argerich, Brendel, Horowitz, Kempff and Sviatoslav Richter are properly represented, and admirers of Glenn Gould will find that his unique brand of pianism, complete with vocal obbligato, is not forgotten. How could it be? And by drawing on Melodiya's Russian archives, a whole host of little-known Russian pianists have appeared, many of real distinction.

The Beaux Arts Trio, the Alban Berg and Juilliard String Quartets are among the chamber groups individually celebrated and, while the range and breadth of Julian Bream's Guitar Edition stands supreme, it is good to welcome the playing of a remarkable new Cuban guitarist, Manuel Barrueco.

Gustav Leonhardt is an all-rounder: keyboard and string player, and director of the period-instrument ensemble which bears his name. He has been generously treated by Teldec, with a 21-disc coverage which fully documents his achievement in pioneering authentic performances of baroque music during the 1960s; Decca and EMI meanwhile have jointly reissued both David Munrow's stimulating musical explorations with his Early Music Consort of London, and key recordings from the Choir of King's College, Cambridge, under Sir David Willcocks, Philip Ledger and Stephen Cleobury.

In the upper firmament of conductors, Karajan, Monteux, Stokowski and Toscanini are celebrated in some depth and, while Neeme Järvi joins Mravinsky in Leningrad, many other famous names are represented by satisfactory two-disc portraits.

Among singers, the art of such luminaries as Victoria de los Angeles, Dame Janet Baker, the pioneering counter-tenor Alfred Deller, Dietrich Fischer-Dieskau, Kirsten Flagstad, Leontyne Price, Dame Elisabeth Schwarzkopf, Dame Joan Sutherland and Renata Tebaldi is generously featured, either in their own edition or in groups of single CDs. And there are other enticing vocal collections in plenty.

But for many collectors it is the Doubles and Duos which offer the most tempting repertoire of all. The Philips Duos now offer nearly 200 titles, ranging from the Quartetto Italiano's complete Beethoven string quartets and Alfred Brendel's recordings of the named Beethoven piano sonatas to the latter's favourite Mozart piano concertos and his outstanding set of Schubert's *Impromptus* and *Moments musicaux*. The Beaux Arts Trio, Arthur Grumiaux and I Musici are all well represented, as are the Royal Concertgebouw Orchestra under Haitink in Debussy, Mahler and Richard Strauss, and Sir Colin Davis in Haydn's *London Symphonies*.

Decca's listing, equally strong, is perhaps most notable for Ashkenazy's contribution in the solo piano works of Beethoven, Chopin and Scriabin, and in the concertos of Mozart, Rachmaninov and Prokofiev. There is a unique collection of Brahms's vocal and choral music (including the *Alto rhapsody*), superbly sung by the San Francisco Chorus and Orchestra under Blomstedt, and some fine opera and ballet recordings, notably Karajan's *Tosca* and Maazel's Cleveland recording of Prokofiev's *Romeo and Juliet*. On Decca's associate label, Oiseau-Lyre, Christopher Hogwood and his Academy of Ancient Music contribute the orchestral and chamber music of C. P. E. Bach, a splendid coupling of Schubert's *Octet* and the *Trout* quintet, and they are joined by Simon Standage in a refreshing period-instrument set of Mozart's five violin concertos.

DG Doubles include Kempff in Beethoven's late piano sonatas, Zukerman and Barenboim happily combining in the Brahms *Viola* and *Violin sonatas*, Karajan in the four Brahms symphonies and at his most dramatic in the Liszt symphonic poems and the complete overtures and preludes of Verdi. Sinopoli directs Mahler's *Seventh Symphony*, paired with Bryn Terfel's *Kindertotenlieder*, and there are two outstanding recitals of Schubert Lieder from Gundula Janowitz with Irwin Gage.

Because of the Rouge et Noir series, EMI Doubles are particularly strong in French music, especially chamber works, but there is plenty of standard repertoire, including Gilels in the Beethoven concertos, Jochum's Brahms symphonies, the keyboard suites of Handel played by Gavrilov and Sviatoslav Richter, Liszt's orchestral music from Masur, and liturgical music by Rachmaninov and Tchaikovsky, while Previn conducts the LSO in Prokofiev's complete *Cinderella* ballet as well as *Romeo and Juliet*. The recent Virgin super-bargain Doubles also have fine recordings of chamber music and Lieder (alas, poorly documented), besides reminding us of the special artistry of Stephen Hough in the two Brahms *Piano concertos* and the solo piano music of Liszt.

The comparatively small group of Hyperion Dyads makes up in quality for any deficiency in quantity, ranging from Roy Goodman's Bach *Brandenburg concertos* and *Orchestral Suites* and the Brahms *String quartets* and *Piano quintet* from the New Budapest Quartet (with Piers Lane), to distinguished recordings of Handel's *Messiah* and Monteverdi's *Vespers* from The Sixteen, under Harry Christophers.

RCA Twofers are not yet prolific either, but two fine examples are provided by Claus Peter Flor's Bamberg Mendelssohn compilation, which includes the *Overtures* as well as the *Midsummer Night's Dream* incidental music, and an impressive set of the Suppé *Overtures* from Gustav Kuhn and the RPO, which includes many novelties.

The repertory offered by the Warner Classics Ultima label is rather more uneven, but it does bring a first-class grouping of the concertos of Poulenc, recorded in Rotterdam under James Conlon, not to mention the symphonies of Clementi, Honegger and Roussel (the latter two sets conducted by Dutoit), an enterprising collection of the orchestral music of Milhaud and a memorable coupling of the two Liszt concertos, played with tremendous gusto and panache by Boris Berezovsky, supplemented by the sonata and other works in the capable hands of Elisabeth Leonskaya.

Mercury's 'Living Presence' series has many fine recordings to offer, but none is more stimulating or individual than the Double containing Dorati's 1965 recordings with the LSO of the first three Tchaikovsky symphonies, of which only No. 1 has ever been issued before in the UK.

Turning back to single discs, one can only revel in the huge range of Renaissance, Baroque and early Classical repertoire (often with a French accent) which has found its way on to Harmonia Mundi's bargain Musique d'Abord and mid-price Suite series. And one must not forget the continuing reissues in DG's mid-price 'Legendary Performance' Originals, which now include mono recordings such as Markevitch's remarkable pioneering versions of the *Third* and *Fourth Symphonies* of Berwald with the BPO.

Decca's 'Classic Sound' series also features a number of very desirable reissues, recently including the Melos Ensemble's beautiful collection of French chamber music with its Elysian account of Ravel's *Introduction and allegro for harp, flute, clarinet and string quartet*, and Monteux's delectably spirited VPO performances of Haydn's *Surprise* and *Clock Symphonies*.

In the last couple of months before we had to go to press, a brand-new mid-price label was launched by Britain's commercial classical radio station, Classic fM. With the advantage of a captive audience of some 5 million listeners, such a venture seemed automatically set to succeed. Nevertheless the joint brain-child of Robert O'Dowd and Alison Wenham, with Simon Foster initially managing the artists and repertoire, has got off to a very impressive start. The first release of 21 CDs and cassettes includes an elegantly spontaneous triptych of Mozart wind concertos (from Joy Farrall, Nicholas Daniel and Kate Hill, with the Britten Sinfonia conducted by Nicholas Cleobury), an outstanding concertante Gershwin collection, including the *Rhapsody in blue* (from the brilliant young American pianist, Michael Boriskin, with the Eos Orchestra under Jonathan Sheffer), the Sinfonia Varsovia and Lord Menuhin playing a rumbustiously witty collection of Rossini overtures, string quartets by Borodin, Dvořák and Shostakovich (from the Chilingirians), the Ulster Orchestra under Dmitry Sitkovetsky in Mendelssohn's *Scottish* and *Italian Symphonies*, clarinet concertos by Spohr and Weber from Andrew Watkinson with Roy Goodman's Hanover Band, and Vernon Handley directing the BBC Concert Orchestra in a lively collection of British light music.

Ivan March (Editor)

Introduction

The object of *The Penguin Guide to Bargain Compact Discs* is to give the serious collector a comprehensive survey of the finest bargain and mid-priced recordings of permanent music on CD (and, where available, on cassettes). As many lower-priced records are issued almost simultaneously on both sides of the Atlantic and use identical international catalogue numbers, this *Guide* should be found to be equally useful in the UK and the USA. The internationalization of repertoire and numbers now applies to almost all CDs issued by the major international companies and also by many smaller ones. Where bargain recordings available in England are not issued in America (and *vice versa*), this will be indicated.

The sheer number of records of artistic merit now available causes considerable problems in any assessment of overall and individual excellence. While in the case of a single popular repertoire work it might be ideal for the discussion to be conducted by a single reviewer, it has not always been possible for one person to have access to every version, and division of reviewing responsibility becomes inevitable. Also there are certain works and certain recorded performances for which one or another of our team has a special affinity. Such a personal identification can often carry with it a special perception too. We feel that it is a strength of our basic style to let such conveyed pleasure or admiration for the merits of an individual recording come over directly to the reader, even if this produces a certain ambivalence in the matter of choice between competing recordings. Where disagreement is more positive (and this has rarely happened), readers will find an indication of this difference in the text.

We have considered (and rejected) the use of initials against individual reviews, since this is essentially a team project. The occasions for disagreement generally concern matters of aesthetics, for instance in the manner of recording-balance, where a contrived effect may trouble some ears more than others, or in the matter of style, where the difference between robustness and refinement of approach appeals differently to listening sensibilities, rather than involving a question of artistic integrity. But over the years our views seem to grow closer together rather than to diverge; perhaps we are getting mellower, but we are seldom ready to offer strong disagreement following the enthusiastic reception by one of the team of a controversial recording, if the results are creatively stimulating. Our perceptions of the advantages and disadvantages of performances of early music on original (as against modern) instruments seem fairly evenly balanced; again, any strong feelings are indicated in the text.

EVALUATION

Most recordings issued today by the major companies are of a high technical standard and offer performances of a quality at least as high as is experienced in the concert hall. In adopting a starring system for the evaluation of records, we have decided to make use of from one to three stars. Brackets round one or more of the stars indicate some reservations about its inclusion, and readers are advised to refer to the text. Brackets round all the stars usually indicate a basic qualification: for instance, a mono recording of a performance of artistic interest, where some allowances may have to be made for the sound-quality, even though the recording may have been digitally remastered.

Our evaluation system may be summarized as follows:

*** An outstanding performance and recording in every way.

** A good performance and recording of today's normal high standard.

* A fair performance, reasonably well or well recorded.

Our evaluation is normally applied to the record as a whole, unless there are two main works or groups of works, and by different composers. In this case, each is dealt with separately in its appropriate place. In the case of a collection of shorter works we feel that there is little point in giving a separate starring to each item, even if their merits are uneven, since the record has to be purchased as a complete programme.

ROSETTES

To a very few records we have awarded a Rosette: ❁.

Unlike our general evaluations, in which we have tried to be consistent, a Rosette is a quite arbitrary compliment by a member of the reviewing team to a recorded performance which, he finds, shows special illumination, magic or a spiritual quality, or even outstanding production values, that places it in a very special class. Occasionally a Rosette has been awarded for an issue that seems to us to offer extraordinary value for money, but that presupposes that the performance or performances are outstanding too. The choice is essentially a personal one (although often it represents a shared view) and in some cases it is applied to an issue where certain reservations must also be mentioned in the text of the review. The Rosette symbol is placed before the usual evaluation and the record number. It is quite small – we do not mean to imply an 'Academy Award' but a personal token of appreciation for something uniquely valuable. We hope that, once the reader has discovered and perhaps acquired a 'rosetted' CD, its special qualities will soon become apparent.

DIGITAL RECORDINGS

Nearly all new compact discs are recorded digitally, but an increasingly large number of digitally remastered, reissued analogue recordings are now appearing, and we think it important to include a clear indication of the difference:

Dig. This indicates that the master recording was digitally encoded.

LISTINGS

Our listing of each recording first indicates its category, as follows:

(M) Medium-priced label
(B) Bargain-priced label
(BB) Super-bargain label

See below for price structures for CDs and cassettes in the UK and the USA.

LAYOUT OF TEXT

We have aimed to make our style as simple as possible, even though the catalogue numbers of recordings are no longer as straightforward as they once were. So, immediately after the evaluation and before the catalogue number, the record make is given, often in abbreviated form. In the case of a set of two or more CDs, the number of units involved is given in brackets after the catalogue number. Cassette numbers, if they exist, are denoted by being given in *italic type*.

AMERICAN CATALOGUE NUMBERS

The numbers which follow in square brackets are US catalogue numbers, while the abbreviation [id.] indicates that the American number is identical to the European, which is usually the case. Even RCA has moved over to completely identical numbers, although a few earlier issues have an alphabetical prefix in the UK which is not used in the USA. Where a record is available in the USA but *not* the UK *it will appear in square brackets only*, and that applies especially to RCA's Basic 100 series and EMI's Red Line Classics.

There are certain other small differences to be remembered by American readers. For instance, a CBS/Sony number could have a completely different catalogue number on either side of the Atlantic, or it could use the same digits with different alphabetical prefixes. Both will be clearly indicated. EMI use extra digits for their British compact discs; thus the British number CDM7 63351-2 becomes CDM 63351 in the USA (the -2 is the European indication that this is a compact disc). Prefixes can alter too. The British EMI forte CZS5 68583-2 becomes Double forte CDFB 68583 in the USA; and Virgin Classics VBD5 61469-2 becomes CDVB 61469. We have taken care to check catalogue information as far as is possible, but as all the editorial work has been done in England there is always the possibility of error; American readers are therefore invited, when ordering records locally, to take the precaution of giving their dealer the fullest information about the music and recordings they want.

The indications (M), (B) and (BB) immediately before the starring of a disc refer primarily to the British CD, as pricing systems are not always identical on both sides of the Atlantic. But if there is a difference in price for the American issue, that is indicated within the square brackets, e.g.:

(B) *** EMI CD-EMX 2055 [(M) id.].

This means that the disc is on a bargain label in the UK but is at mid-price in the USA.

When CDs are imported into the USA, this again usually involves a price difference e.g.:

(B) *** Decca Eclipse Dig. 448 710-2 [(M) id. import].

This means that the disc is on a bargain label in the UK and is a mid-priced import in the USA. (When mid-priced CDs on the smaller labels are imported into the USA, they often move up to the premium-price range.)

Where no American catalogue number is given, this does not necessarily mean that a record is not available in the USA; the transatlantic issue may not have been made at the time of the publication of this *Guide*. Readers are advised to check the current *Schwann* catalogue and to consult their local record store.

ABBREVIATIONS

To save space we have adopted a number of standard abbreviations in listing orchestras and performing groups (a list is provided below), and the titles of works are often shortened, especially where they are listed several times. Artists' forenames are sometimes omitted if they are not absolutely necessary for identification purposes. Also we have not usually listed the contents of operatic highlights and collections; these can sometimes be found in *Classical Catalogue*, published by RED Publishing Ltd (Paulton House, 8 Shepherdess Walk, London N1 7LB).

We have followed common practice in the use of the original language for titles where it seems sensible. In most cases, English is used for orchestral and instrumental music and the original language for vocal music and opera. There are exceptions, however; for instance, the Johann Strauss discography uses the German language in the interests of consistency.

ORDER OF MUSIC

The order of music under each composer's name broadly follows that adopted by *Classical Catalogue*: orchestral music, including concertos and symphonies; chamber music; solo instrumental music (in some cases with keyboard and organ music separated); vocal and choral music; opera; vocal collections; miscellaneous collections.

Classical Catalogue now usually includes stage works alongside opera; in the main we have not followed this practice, preferring to list, say, ballet music and incidental music (where no vocal items are involved) in the general orchestral group. Within each group our listing follows an alphabetical sequence, and couplings within a single composer's output are *usually* discussed together instead of separately with cross-references. Occasionally and inevitably because of this alphabetical approach, different recordings of a given work can become separated when a record is listed and discussed under the first work of its alphabetical sequence. The editor feels that alphabetical consistency is essential if the reader is to learn to find his or her way about.

CATALOGUE NUMBERS

Enormous care has gone into the checking of CD catalogue numbers and contents to ensure that all details are correct, but the editor and publishers cannot be held responsible for any mistakes that may have crept in despite all our zealous checking. When ordering CDs, readers are urged to provide their record-dealer with full details of the music and performers, as well as the catalogue number.

DELETIONS

Compact discs regularly succumb to the deletions axe, and many are likely to disappear during the lifetime of this book. Sometimes copies may still be found in specialist shops, and there remains the compensatory fact that most really important and desirable recordings are eventually reissued, often costing less!

EMI's Special UK Import Service, which began in the UK in August 1995, means that the whole EMI international bargain catalogue is available to UK customers. CDs which are available only through this service are indicated with the abbreviation SIS. EMI suggest that dealers should be able to obtain these special import discs quite quickly, and such records will no longer cost more than those in the standard UK catalogue. This does not affect the American equivalent issue where indicated as available.

Polygram have now followed suit with their own import service, and these CDs are indicated with the abbreviation IMS. Polygram, however, do currently make an extra charge for those discs which have to be obtained from Germany or Holland.

COVERAGE

As the output of major and minor labels continues to expand, it will obviously be impossible for us to mention every bargain CD that is available, within the covers of a single book; this is recognized as a practical limitation if we are to update our survey regularly. We have to be selective in choosing the discs to be included (although on rare occasions a recording has been omitted simply because a review copy was not available); anything which eludes us can always be included next time. However, we do welcome suggestions from readers about such omissions if they seem to be of special interest, and particularly if they are inexpensive.

ACKNOWLEDGEMENTS

Kathleen March once again zealously checked the proofs for errors and reminded us when the text proved ambiguous, clumsily repetitive in its descriptive terminology, or just plain contradictory, occasionally removing reviews that had somehow appeared twice!

Barbara Menard and Roy Randle contributed to the titling – never an easy task, and especially complicated in the many boxed anthologies involving a bouquet of different performers. Alan Livesey also cast an eagle eye over the proofs, in particular looking for mistakes in the musical listings; he also helped with both titling and retrieval of earlier material (connected with reissues) especially in the hectic period immediately before we sent off our final copy. Our team of Penguin proofreaders have once again proved themselves indispensable.

Grateful thanks also go to all those readers who write to us to point out factual errors and to remind us of important recordings which have escaped our notice.

The American Bargain Scene

CDs are much less expensive in the USA than they are in Great Britain and because of this (so we are told), many bargain recordings available in England are not brought into the USA by their manufacturers. This applies especially to the Polygram group, so that Decca Eclipse, DG Classikon and Philips Virtuoso labels have to be imported by the major US record stores and mail order outlets. What this means is that, while almost any recording mentioned in these pages will be available in the USA, sometimes it will cost more than the buyer might reasonably expect. Alas, this applies in particular to many of the Dutton transfers of old recordings, which are listed at full price in America, although the CDEA series is at mid-price.

Fortunately the two super-budget catalogues, Naxos and Arte Nova, are distributed directly in the USA; and other super-bargain labels such as EMI Eminence, Classics for Pleasure, Discover and ASV Quicksilva cost much the same on both sides of the Atlantic. This also applies to many of the bargain boxes.

Duos and Doubles, where available, remain at two discs for the cost of one premium-priced CD in both countries, and here US collectors have a price advantage. However, according to *Schwann*, many excellent mid-priced discs are not issued in the USA, and it may not prove very economic for American collectors to try to obtain them by mail order unless the recording is of extra special interest.

The RCA Basic 100 series and EMI's Red Line Classics are specifically selected for the US market. We have tried to include the best of them but have ignored some of the others, where the performances and recordings seem uncompetitive.

From your many letters, and from visiting record stores in the USA, we know that our *Penguin Guide* is read, enjoyed and used as a tool by collectors on both sides of the Atlantic. We also know that some of you feel that our reviews are too frequently orientated towards European and British recordings and performances. In concentrating on records which have common parlance in both Europe and the USA, we obviously give preference to the output of international companies, and in assessing both performers and performances we are concerned with only one factor: musical excellence. In a 400-year-old musical culture centred in Europe, it is not surprising that a great number of the finest interpreters should have been Europeans, and many of them have enjoyed recording in London, where there are four first-class symphony orchestras and many smaller groups at their disposal, supported by recording producers and engineers of the highest calibre.

However, the continuing re-emergence of earlier recordings by major American recording orchestras and artists is slowly redressing the balance. Our performance coverage in the present volume – helped by the huge proportion of reissued older records – certainly reflects the American achievement, past and present; with the current phenomenal improvements in transferring technology, we hope that more of the early recordings made by the great names from America's musical past will enjoy the attention of the wider public.

Price Differences in the UK and USA

Retail prices are not fixed in either country, and various stores may offer even better deals at times, so our price structure must be taken as a guideline only. The Vanguard CD label (except for the 8000 Series, which retails at around $15) is now mid-price in both the USA and UK. Harmonia Mundi's Musique d'Abord label (prefix HMA) is described as budget – which it is in the UK – but the American list-price is $9.98.

Comparable Prices in the UK and USA

Duos and Doubles, Delos Doubles, Double Deckers, Double fortes, Dyads, Finlandia 'Meet the Composer', Warner Ultimas where available (although they cost less west of the Atlantic) are two-for-the-cost-of-one-premium-priced-disc the world over. CfP and Carlton Doubles, EMI Seraphim and the new Virgin Classics Doubles are two-for-the-price-of-one-mid-priced-CD. Here are comparative details of the other price-ranges:

(M) MID-PRICED SERIES (sets are multiples of these prices)
Includes: Avid; Carlton 30366 series; Chandos (Collect; Enchant); Classic fM (UK only); CPO/EMI Operas (UK only); Decca/London; Delos; DG (including Originals); Dutton CDEA (USA only); Dutton CDAX, CDK, CDLX (UK only); EMI (Classics and Références); Erato/Warner (UK), Erato/WEA (USA); DHM; Harmonia Mundi Musique d'Abord (USA), Suite; Mercury; Oiseau-Lyre; Philips; RCA Gold Seal and Living Stereo; RCA Melodiya; Revelation; Saga; Sony; Sony Heritage (upper mid-price); Teldec/Warner (UK), Teldec/WEA (USA); Tring (USA only); Vanguard; Virgin.

UK
CDs: under £10; more usually £9
Cassettes: around £5
USA
CDs: under $13; usually under $12
Cassettes: $5–$6.50 – but very few are available

(B) BARGAIN-PRICED SERIES (sets are multiples of these prices)
Includes: Calliope Approche (UK only); Carlton (30367, 30368; more expensive: 30369, 30371); CfP; Debut; Decca Eclipse (UK only); DG Classikon (UK only); Dutton CDEA (UK only); Eminence (UK only); Harmonia Mundi Musique d'Abord (UK only); Solo; HMP; Millennium (UK only); Naxos Opera; Philips Virtuoso (UK only); Sony Essential Classics; Tring (UK only).

UK
CDs: £5.50–£7.00
Cassettes: around £4
USA
CDs: under $7
Cassettes: around $4

SPECIAL SETS: Decca/London, DG, Nimbus and Philips (as indicated); EMI CZS multiple sets are also within the bargain range in the UK but may cost rather more in the USA.

(BB) SUPER-BARGAIN SERIES – CDs
Includes: Arte Nova; ASV Quicksilva (UK only); Deutsche Harmonia Mundi Baroque Esprit; Discover; LaserLight; Naxos; Polygram Belart; RCA Navigator (UK only).

UK
CDs: £5; some (including Navigator) cost slightly less
USA
CDs: $5–$6

(In some cases, equivalent cassettes are available, usually costing slightly less than bargain cassettes.)

AN INTERNATIONAL MAIL-ORDER SOURCE FOR RECORDINGS IN THE UK

Readers are urged to support a local dealer if he is prepared and able to give a proper service, and to remember that obtaining many CDs involves expertise and perseverance. However, because of the recent recession many specialist sources have disappeared and, for that reason, if any difficulty is experienced in obtaining the CDs you want, we suggest the following mail-order alternative, which offers competitive discount, operates world-wide and is under the direction of the Editor of *The Penguin Guide to Bargain Compact Discs*, whose advice on choice of recordings is always readily available to mail-order customers:

Squires Gate Music Centre (PG Dept)
Rear 13 St Andrew's Road South,
St Annes on Sea, Lancashire FY8 1SX
England
Tel.: (0)1253 782588; Fax: (0)1253 782985

This organization patiently extends compact disc orders until they finally come to hand. A full guarantee of safe delivery is made on any order undertaken. Please write for further details, or make a trial credit card order, by fax or telephone.

❁ The Rosette Service

Squires Gate also offers a try-before-you-buy weekly loan service (within the UK only) so that customers can try out at home rosetted recordings, plus a hand-picked group of recommended key repertoire works, for a small charge, without any obligation to purchase. If a CD is subsequently purchased, it will be discounted and the trial charge waived. Full details sent on request.

Squires Gate Music Centre also offers a simple three-monthly mailing, listing a hand-picked selection of current new and reissued CDs, chosen by the Editor of the *Penguin Guide*, Ivan March. Regular customers of Squires Gate Music Centre, both domestic and overseas, receive the bulletin as available, and it is sent automatically with their purchases.

AN INTERNATIONAL MAIL-ORDER SOURCE FOR RECORDINGS IN THE USA

American readers seeking a domestic mail-order source may write to the following address, where a comparably expert and caring supply service is in operation (for both American and imported European labels). Please write for further details (enclosing a stamped, self-addressed envelope if within the USA) or make a trial order by letter, fax or phone to:

Serenade/Classical Choice (PG Dept)
122 South 21st Street
Philadelphia, PA 19103
USA
Tel.: (215) 665-1170; Fax: (215) 665-8076
Tel.: (for US orders only) **1-800-648-2224**
Internet: http://www.cdchoice.com
e-mail address: cdchoice@pobox.com

Regular customers of Serenade/ClassicalChoice, both domestic and overseas, can also on request receive a periodic mailing, with a hand-picked selection of current new and reissued CDs chosen by the Editor of the *Penguin Guide*, Ivan March.

Abbreviations

AAM	Academy of Ancient Music
Ac.	Academy, Academic
Amb. S.	Ambrosian Singers
arr.	arranged, arrangement
ASMF	Academy of St Martin-in-the-Fields
(B)	bargain-price CD
(BB)	super-bargain-price CD
Bar.	Baroque
Bav.	Bavarian
BBC	British Broadcasting Corporation
BPO	Berlin Philharmonic Orchestra
BRT	Belgian Radio & Television (Brussels)
Cal.	Calliope
CBSO	City of Birmingham Symphony Orchestra
CfP	Classics for Pleasure
Ch.	Choir; Chorale; Chorus
CO	Chamber Orchestra
COE	Chamber Orchestra of Europe
Col. Mus. Ant.	Musica Antiqua, Cologne
Coll.	Collegium
Coll. Aur.	Collegium Aureum
Coll. Voc.	Collegium Vocale
Concg. O	Royal Concertgebouw Orchestra of Amsterdam
cond.	conductor, conducted
Cons.	Consort
DG	Deutsche Grammophon
DHM	Deutsche Harmonia Mundi
Dig.	digital recording
E.	England, English
ECCO	European Community Chamber Orchestra
ECO	English Chamber Orchestra
ENO	English National Opera Company
Ens.	Ensemble
ESO	English Symphony Orchestra
Fr.	French
GO	Gewandhaus Orchestra
HM	Harmonia Mundi France
Hung.	Hungaroton
[id.]	same record number for US and European versions
IMS	Import Music Service (Polygram – UK only)
L.	London
LA	Los Angeles
LCO	London Chamber Orchestra
LMP	London Mozart Players
LOP	Lamoureux Orchestra of Paris
LPO	London Philharmonic Orchestra
LSO	London Symphony Orchestra
(M)	mid-price CD
[(M) id. import]	mid-price; same catalogue number only available as an import
Mer.	Meridian
Met.	Metropolitan
min.	minor
MoC	Ministry of Culture
movt	movement
N.	North, Northern
nar.	narrated
Nat.	National
NY	New York
O	Orchestra, Orchestre
OAE	Orchestra of the Age of Enlightenment
O-L	Oiseau-Lyre
Op.	Opera (in performance listings); opus (in music titles)
orch.	orchestrated
ORR	Orchestre Révolutionnaire et Romantique
ORTF	L'Orchestre de la radio et télévision française
Ph.	Philips
Phd.	Philadelphia
Philh.	Philharmonia
PO	Philharmonic Orchestra
Qt	Quartet
R.	Radio
RLPO	Royal Liverpool Philharmonic Orchestra
ROHCG	Royal Opera House, Covent Garden
RPO	Royal Philharmonic Orchestra
RSNO	Royal Scottish National Orchestra
RSO	Radio Symphony Orchestra
RTE	Radio Television Eireann
S.	South
SCO	Scottish Chamber Orchestra
Sinf.	Sinfonietta
SIS	Special Import Service (EMI – UK only)
SNO	Scottish National Orchestra
SO	Symphony Orchestra
Soc.	Society
Sol. Ven.	I Solisti Veneti

SRO Suisse Romande Orchestra
Sup. Supraphon
trans. transcription, transcribed
V. Vienna
Van. Vanguard
VCM Vienna Concentus Musicus
VPO Vienna Philharmonic Orchestra
VSO Vienna Symphony Orchestra
W. West
WNO Welsh National Opera Company

Abel, Carl Friedrich (1723–87)

Overtures: in C, Op. 1/2; in C, Op. 5/4; in D, Op. 7/3; in G, Op. 14/5; Symphonies: in E flat, Op. 4/3; in B flat, Op. 12/2.
(M) ** Van. Dig. 99703. Il Fondamento, Paul Dombrecht.

It was Abel who (as impresario) joined forces with J. C. Bach in London between 1765 and 1781 to give a series of concerts which put the symphony, as developed from the Italian overture, firmly on the map. However, on the evidence here, his own music (especially in the three-part overtures) is pretty thin and full of routine gestures. Il Fondamento, directed by Paul Dombrecht, give faithful period-instrument performances but fail to make a very enticing case for this repertoire. They are acceptably recorded.

Adam, Adolphe (1803–56)

Le Diable à quatre (ballet): complete.
(M) *** Decca (IMS) 444 111-2. LSO, Richard Bonynge (with MASSENET: *La Navarraise: Nocturne. Don César de Bazan: Sévillana. Les Erinnyes: Invocation;* BIZET: *Don Procopio: Entr'acte to Act II;* GOUNOD: *Le Tribut de Zamora, Act III: Danse grecque* ***).

Adam's *Le Diable à quatre* was recorded in a vintage period (1964) and, as the opening Act immediately demonstrates, produces Decca's top ballet quality, with glowing horns and woodwind, and wonderfully vivid detail. This was the seventh of Adam's thirteen ballets, arriving in 1845, four years after *Giselle*, and when Richard Bonynge points the elegant writing for the strings so seductively, it makes a splendid entertainment. Moreover, for this reissue Decca have found five equally winning *entr'actes* from their vaults (bringing the playing time up to 75 minutes), and these pieces are even more melodically characterful than the main work. Bonynge clearly relishes all these items and presents them with characteristic polish and spontaneity. The 1971 Decca sound is every bit as warm, richly hued and immediate as the complete ballet.

Giselle (older European score; complete).
(M) **(*) Mercury 434 365-2 (2). LSO, Fistoulari – OFFENBACH: *Gaîté parisienne;* Johann STRAUSS: *Graduation ball.* *

Giselle (ballet): complete.
(B) *** Decca Double Dig. 452 185-2 (2) [id.]. ROHCG O, Richard Bonynge.
(BB) *** Naxos Dig. 8.550755/6 [id.]. Slovak RSO, Mogrelia.

Giselle (1841) is the first of the great classical ballets. Andrew Mogrelia's complete recording uses the normal performing edition, including interpolated scenes by Friedrich Burgmüller, and by Minkus, which means that it offers some 1 hour 54 minutes of music. The orchestral playing has grace and elegance and plenty of life: the brass are not ashamed of the melodrama. The recording is resonantly full and warm in ambience, yet well detailed. Bonynge's performance on Decca is just that bit more strongly characterized and the Decca sound has a slightly sharper profile. That remains first choice (at Double Decca price), but this Naxos set costs slightly less.

Mercury's complete recording of *Giselle*, like Mogrelia's on Naxos, draws on the score which was in general use before the war and which incorporates music that is not by Adam at all. Fair enough, but this means that with Fistoulari there are some eighteen minutes of the score to take over to a second CD. Fistoulari was a great ballet conductor and the LSO play superbly for him: there is drama in plenty, while in the gentle lyrical music his magical touch consistently beguiles the ear. Moreover, in its CD format the early stereo sounds remarkably modern, and the over-resonant bass response which disfigured the LPs has been tamed, so that the sound-picture is resonantly full without an exaggerated imbalance. The snag is that the quite logical fill-ups of the Offenbach/Rosenthal *Gaîté parisienne* and the Offenbach/Dorati *Graduation ball* were among Mercury's least successful Minneapolis recordings, dry and lustreless, greatly detracting from the appeal of this reissue. We hope that Mercury will decide to recouple *Giselle*.

Adams, John (born 1947)

Shaker loops.
✿ (M) *** Virgin/EMI CUV5 61121-2 [CDM5 9610-2]. LCO, Warren-Green – GLASS: *Company* etc.; REICH: *8 Lines;* HEATH: *Frontier.* ***

The inspired performance by Christopher Warren-Green and his London Concert Orchestra is full of imaginative intensity, and understandably it received the composer's imprimatur. It is part of a well-conceived programme of minimalist music, almost all of which is worth returning to. Adams's four-part *Shaker loops* works within its minimalist 'straitjacket' with the utmost imagination and emotional resource. The title refers both to the weird practices of the religious group of that persuasion and to the musical devices of trills and shakes; the loops are its melodic basis. The outer movements are highly animated and strong in dynamic graduation; the inner movements are haunting, from the 'slow languid glissandi' of the *Hymning slews* to the more tangible *Loops and verses*. Outstandingly vivid recording.

Addinsell, Richard (1904–77)

Warsaw concerto.

(B) *** Ph. Virtuoso Dig. 411 123-2; *411 123-4* [id.]. Misha Dichter, Philh. O, Marriner (with Concert of concertante music ***).

(M) *** Decca Dig. 430 726-2. Ortiz, RPO, Atzmon – GERSHWIN: *Rhapsody* **(*); GOTTSCHALK: *Grand fantasia* ***; LITOLFF: *Scherzo* ***; LISZT: *Hungarian fantasia*. ***

Richard Addinsell's pastiche miniature concerto, written for the film *Dangerous moonlight* in 1942, is perfectly crafted and its atmosphere combines all the elements of the Romantic concerto to great effect; moreover it has a truly memorable main theme. It is beautifully played here, with Marriner revealing the most engaging orchestral detail. The sound is first rate and the Virtuoso reissue has an attractive new livery.

The alternative from Cristina Ortiz is a warmly romantic account, spacious in conception, with the resonant ambience of Walthamstow Assembly Hall providing beguilingly rich string-timbres. If the couplings are suitable, this is a rewarding collection, more substantial than Dichter's. The recording is first class.

Alain, Jehan (1911–40)

Complete organ music

Vol. 1: *Ballade en mode phrygien; Choral cistercien; Choral phrygien; Climat; 2 Danses à Agni Yavishta; Deuxième Fantaisie; Le jardin suspendu; Litanies; Monodie; Petite pièce; Préludes profanes 1–2; Suite; Variations sur un thème de Clément Jannequin.*

(BB) *** Naxos Dig. 8.553632 [id.]. Eric Lebrun (Cavaillé-Coll organ of the Church of Saint-Antoine des Quinze-Vingts, Paris).

Vol. 2: *Aria; Berceuse sur les deux notes qui Cornent; Choral dorien; 3 Danses; Grave; Intermezzo; Lamento; Postlude pour l'office des Complies; Prélude et fugue; Première Fantaisie; Variations sur l'hymne 'Lucis Creator'.*

(BB) *** Naxos Dig. 8.553633 [id.]. Eric Lebrun (Cavaillé-Coll organ of the Church of Saint-Antoine des Quinze-Vingts, Paris).

Jehan Alain was killed in action in the early days of the Second World War, thus cutting short a career which had already shown enormous promise. Had he lived, his reputation may well have rivalled that of Duruflé or Messiaen. As it is, his output reveals a distinctive and powerful voice. Although his sister, Marie-Claire Alain, made an authoritative three-LP set of his work on the organ in the early 1970s, only excerpts from it are currently available – in a five-CD compilation issued to mark her seventieth birthday. Eric Lebrun is the next keeper of the flame, and he is completely attuned to Alain's sound-world. His Cavaillé-Coll at the Church of Saint-Antoine des Quinze-Vingts in Paris is ideal, though the reverberant acoustic and the reticent balance result in less detailed textures and a less vital presence than in Marie-Claire Alain's old LPs. Readers who have yet to discover this music should lose no time in making its acquaintance: Alain's writing has virtuosity and harmonic resource to commend it. Try *Le jardin suspendu*, which has a Messiaen-like atmosphere. These performances are thoroughly recommendable and at the price make a splendid bargain.

Albéniz, Isaac (1860–1909)

Iberia (Books I–IV) complete (orch. Arbós and Surinach).

(M) **(*) Telarc Dig. 2CD-80470 [id.]. Cincinnati SO, Jesús López-Cobos.

The four Books of piano pieces (with three in each), which make up Albéniz's *Iberia*, were written between

1906 and 1908 and are regularly heard and recorded in their original format. But this is the recording première of the complete orchestral version. Fernández Arbós first scored *Evocación* and *El Corpus en Sevilla* from Book I, following with *El Puerto* and *Triana* from Book II, and *El Abaicin* from Book III. But it is good at last to have the whole work, with the remaining pieces skilfully orchestrated by Carlos Surinach. Jesús López-Cobos is thoroughly at home in this repertory, and the Cincinnati orchestra responds to his flexible rubato very persuasively; the Mediterranean atmosphere is agreeably sultry, especially in the opening *Evocación*, with some lovely warm Cincinnati string-playing. The rhythms too are often nicely bounced, and there is some delightfully pointed wind-playing in *El Puerto* and *Triana*. The 'Fête-Dieu' climax of *El Corpus en Sevilla* is very spectacular indeed, with the bass drum coming through as one expects from this label; and many will like the relative lack of garishness here. The closing *Eritaña* (from Book IV) is attractively light-hearted, and the wind-playing is most engaging, but the end effect is a shade easy-going, and at other times the playing, though warmly committed, could ideally be more gutsy. The Telarc recording is sumptuous, with plenty of weight in the bass, and there is a pleasing overall bloom. But the balance is relatively close and at times one longs for more transparent and subtle textures – and indeed for a little more glitter. The set comes with two discs costing the same as one premium-priced CD, but with a total playing time of only 82 minutes, so we are not really convinced that it should be included in a bargain survey.

Iberia: Triana; Fête-dieu à Seville. Navarra (all orch. Arbós).
(M) *** RCA 09026 62586-2 [id.]. Chicago SO, Reiner – FALLA: *El amor brujo* etc.; GRANADOS: *Goyescas: Intermezzo.* ***

This vintage Reiner collection of Spanish music is especially notable for the remarkably idiomatic account of these Albéniz pieces. The Latin passion of the climax of *Navarra* is matched by the climax of *Fête-dieu à Seville*, in which Reiner captures the boisterous vulgarity of a Spanish religious procession with superb aplomb. Vintage Chicago recording from 1958, still sounding amazingly ripe and vivid.

Rapsodia española (arr. Halfter).
(B) *** Decca Eclipse Dig. 448 243-2; *448 243-4* [(M) id. import]. Alicia de Larrocha, LPO, Frühbeck de Burgos – RODRIGO: *Concierto de Aranjuez* etc.; TURINA: *Rapsodia sinfónica.* ***

Albéniz's *Rapsodia española*, originally written for solo piano but heard here in Cristobal Halfter's arrangement for piano and orchestra, is a chimerical piece constructed fairly loosely from a series of contrasting Spanish dances. Alicia de Larrocha's performance is both evocative and dazzling, and she is given splendid support by Frühbeck de Burgos and brilliant Decca sound.

Suite española (arr. Frühbeck de Burgos).
(M) *** Decca 448 601-2. New Philh. O, Frühbeck de Burgos – FALLA: *El amor brujo* *** (with GRANADOS: *Goyescas: Intermezzo* ***).

Albéniz's early *Suite española* offers light music of the best kind, colourful, tuneful, exotically scored and providing orchestra and recording engineers alike with a chance to show their paces, the sound bright and glittering, and fully worthy of reissue in Decca's Classic Sound series.

GUITAR MUSIC

Cantos de España: Córdoba, Op. 232/4; Mallorca (Barcarola), Op. 202. Suite española: Cataluña; Granada; Sevilla; Cádiz, Op.47/1–4.
✿ (BB) *** RCA Navigator Dig. 74321 17903-2. Julian Bream (guitar) – GRANADOS: *Collection;* RODRIGO: *3 Piezas españolas.* *** ✿

Julian Bream is in superb form in this splendid recital (apparently his own favourite record), vividly recorded in the pleasingly warm acoustic of Wardour Chapel, near his home in Wiltshire. The CD is electrifying, giving an uncanny impression of the great guitarist sitting and making music just beyond the loudspeakers. The playing itself has wonderfully communicative rhythmic feeling, great subtlety of colour, and its spontaneity increases the impression that one is experiencing a 'live' recital. The performance of the haunting *Córdoba*, which ends the group, is unforgettable. The new super-bargain Navigator reissue includes additionally the *Tres piezas españolas* of Rodrigo. This is perhaps the finest single recital of Spanish guitar music in the catalogue and, at its new price, a bargain of bargains.

Suite española, Op. 47 (extended suite, arr. Barrueco).
(M) *** EMI Dig. CDM5 66574-2 [id.]. Manuel Barrueco – TURINA: *Guitar music.* ***

Although written for the piano, the *Suite española* sounds equally effective (if not more so) in transcription for guitar, especially in the hands of a master-guitarist. Manuel Barrueco is certainly that, and his arrangements of the complete extended suite are very welcome indeed. (The original suite of four pieces was extended by the publisher with the addition of four more movements, taken from the composer's other music.) Barrueco's playing combines warmth with a pleasing intimacy and a natural, relaxed sense of spontaneity. The more famous evocations which Bream also plays, *Castilla*, *Granada* and the closing *Sevilla*, are subtle in nuance and colour, while the vibrant *Asturias* brings a haunting, improvisational feeling in its calm middle section. The recording is beautifully judged, not over-projected.

Azulejos; Cantos de España (Preludio (Asturias); Oriental; Bajo la palmera (Cuba); Córdoba; Seguidillas (Castilla)). Malagueña; Mallorca (Barcarola); La Vega; Zambra Granadina; Zaragoza.
(M) *** EMI CDM7 64523-2 [id.]. Alicia de Larrocha.

Dating from 1959, this recital is another stimulating example of the younger Alicia de Larrocha playing with enormous dash and a glowing palette – the famous *Córdoba* is full of atmospheric poetry, helped by the warm bass resonance of the recording. Several of the items included as separate pieces were added by the composer's publishers to fill out the *Suite española*, and the opening *Preludio* (*Asturias*) of the *Cantos de España* has great fire. De Larrocha's glittering articulation in the *Seguidillas* (*Castilla*) and the brilliant *Zaragoza* is equally arresting, and the wide pianistic range of the extended *La Vega* brings playing that is both ruminative and dazzling, although the recording jangles at climaxes. Otherwise it is well focused and realistic.

Iberia (complete); *Suite española* (excerpts): *Granada; Cataluña; Sevilla; Cádiz; Aragon; Navarra. Pavana capricho, Op. 12; España (6 Hojas de album): Tango* (only); *Recuerdos de viaje: Rumores de la caleta; Puerta de Tierra.*
(M) *** EMI CMS7 64504-2 (2) [id.]. Alicia de Larrocha.

The EMI set offers de Larrocha's earliest stereo recording of Albéniz's great piano suite, *Iberia*, made for Hispavox in 1962. The younger de Larrocha is far tougher, more daring, more fiery and if anything even more warmly expressive than she was later. The EMI discs include the haunting *Tango*, deliciously done, the most celebrated of all Albéniz's music, making this a more popular collection.

Iberia (complete); *Navarra*.
(B) *** Decca Double 448 191-2 (2) [id.]. De Larrocha – GRANADOS: *Goyescas*. *** ✿

Alicia de Larrocha's second analogue set of *Iberia* was made in 1972, a decade after her earliest stereo version for Hispavox. As in that version, she plays with full-blooded temperament and fire, and although there are occasional touches of wilful rubato her natural overriding spontaneity carries the day, both here and in *Navarra*. The piano recording is excellent in its realism, and the Double Decca reissue, coupled with Granados's *Goyescas*, makes a formidable bargain, for on both artistic and technical merits *Iberia* loses little ground to her later, digital set which has rather more subtlety.

PIANO MUSIC

Suite española, Op. 47.
(BB) **(*) ASV Quicksilva CDQS 6079 [(M) id.]. Alma Petchersky – FALLA: *Fantasía bética* (with GRANADOS: *Allegro de concierto*). **(*)

Alma Petchersky plays engagingly and with a natural spontaneity that gives pleasure. The recording is generally faithful, without being in the top bracket. At super-bargain price this is worth considering.

Albert, Eugen d' (1864–1932)

(i) *Piano concertos Nos. 1 in B min., Op. 2; 2 in E, Op. 12. Overture: Esther.*
(BB) **(*) Naxos Dig. 8.553728 [id.]. (i) Joseph Banowetz; Moscow SO, Dmitri Yablonsky.

Best remembered for his opera, *Tiefland*, and a handful of piano pieces, Eugen d'Albert was a commanding virtuoso, acclaimed by Liszt, a composition-pupil of Sullivan and a protégé of Hans Richter. He played the Brahms concertos under the composer's own baton and succeeded Joachim as the director of the Berlin Hochschule für Musik, where his pupils included Backhaus and Dohnányi. The *Piano concerto No. 1 in B minor* comes from 1884, when he was nineteen, and it was dedicated to Liszt. It is an unusual work in one movement lasting about three-quarters of an hour. D'Albert's is a cultured rather than a distinctive voice, and his material is not perhaps strong enough to sustain its length, though it is a far from negligible work. Its companion here is the *Concerto No. 2 in E major*, another one-movement piece, albeit in four sections, written in 1893. The Naxos recording offers a bonus in the form of the overture (in reality more like a symphonic poem) *Esther*, composed midway between the two concertos in 1888. The debts to Liszt and Wagner are extensive. Good playing from Joseph Banowetz and good orchestral support, though the recording is on the dry side.

Die Abreise.
(M) **(*) CPO/EMI CPO 999 558-2 [id.]. Prey, Edda Moser, Schreier, Philh. Hung. O, Janos Kulka.

Eugen d'Albert wrote this charming one-acter, *Die Abreise* ('The Departure'), in 1898, five years before his most celebrated opera, *Tiefland*. Gilfen, bored with his wife Luise, plans to depart on a journey, but the machinations of his friend Trott alert him to the dangers, and it is Trott who departs. With delicate orchestral writing, it tells the story deftly in 20 brief sections of melodic conversation – though, unlike the other CPO reissues of EMI recordings in the series, there are no separate tracks after the overture. The absence of tracks also makes it harder to follow the synopsis in the booklet, provided instead of a libretto. Nevertheless this is a first-rate, highly enjoyable performance, recorded in 1978 with three outstanding and characterful soloists. Warm, clear EMI sound.

Albinoni, Tommaso (1671–1751)

Adagio in G min. for organ and strings (arr. Giazotto).
(M) *** Sony Theta SMK 60161. La Grand Ecurie et la Chambre du Roy, Jean-Claude Malgoire – Concert: ECO, Leppard: *'Music of the Baroque'*. ***
(B) *** Carlton Dig. PCD 2001 [(M) id.]. Scottish CO, Laredo (with String masterpieces ***).
(M) *** DG 449 724-2 [id.]. BPO, Karajan – RESPIGHI: *Ancient airs* etc. ***

Malgoire and his authentic string group (with a sonorously balanced organ contribution) give an impressively dignified account of a justly attractive piece that can too readily sound inflated. The slightly astringent quality to the string-timbre means that the climax is full-blooded without becoming too opulent. This comes as the final item in a generous concert of Baroque lollipops, stylishly played on modern instruments by the ECO under Raymond Leppard.

The bargain-priced, digitally recorded Carlton account is strongly contoured and most responsively played by the Scottish Chamber Orchestra under Jaime Laredo.

Karajan's view is stately and measured, and the Berlin Philharmonic strings respond with dignity and sumptuous tone. The anachronism of Giazotto's arrangement is obviously relished, and this is certainly a reasonable way of approaching it. The remastered recording sounds very good.

12 Concerti a cinque, Op. 5.
(M) *** Ph. Dig. 442 658-2 [id.]. Pina Carmirelli, I Musici.

This fine body of concertos has variety and resource to commend it. I Musici, with Pina Carmirelli as the solo player, are every bit as fresh as the music, and they are accorded altogether first-rate sound. This is one of the best sets of its kind among recent reissues; those prepared to explore these concertos will be well rewarded.

Concerti a cinque, Op. 7/1, (i) *2; 3,* (i) *6; 8;* (i) *Sinfonia in G* (arr. Anthony Camden).
(BB) *** Naxos Dig. 8.553002 [id.]. Anthony Camden; (i) Alison Alty, L. Virtuosi, John Georgiadis.

Concerti a cinque, Op. 7/4, (i) *5; 6,* (i) *11; 12;* (i) *Op. 9/12.*
(BB) *** Naxos Dig. 8.553035 [id.]. Anthony Camden; (i) Alison Alty, L. Virtuosi, John Georgiadis.

Concerti a cinque, Op. 9/2, (i) *3; 5, 8,* (i) *9; 11.*
(BB) *** Naxos Dig. 8.550739; *4.550739* [id.]. Anthony Camden, (i) Julia Girdwood, L. Virtuosi, John Georgiadis.

It would appear that Anthony Camden and the London Virtuosi conducted by John Georgiadis are working their way through the Albinoni concertos, and this Naxos series looks set to upstage the opposition, good though that is. The London Virtuosi use modern instruments, but their playing is fresh and refined and the digital recording is natural and beautifully balanced. The calibre of Anthony Camden's solo contribution is readily shown in slow movements, matched by Georgiadis's rapt, sensitive accompaniments. How exquisite is the solitary solo entry in the brief central movement of the *C major Double concerto*, Op. 7/2, while the warmly serene string-playing in the *Largo* of Op. 7/8, where the soloists are silent, is hardly less beautiful. Camden opens the *Adagio* of Op. 9/5 with a long controlled crescendo on a sustained note which is beautifully managed, while in Op. 9/6 the two oboes carol gently together. On the first disc Camden's excellent colleague is Julia Girdwood, but for the two other collections Alison Alty takes over and the partnership seems even more felicitous, with the two instruments quite perfectly blended. Also included is a *Sinfonia* arranged by Camden as a sinfonia concertante. It opens with a delightful theme which recalls *'Come landlord fill the flowing bowl'* and the finale is a sunny fugue in which a droll bassoon makes the third entry after the two oboes. This series can be strongly recommended on all counts.

(i) *Concerti a cinque, Op. 7/2–3, 5–6, 8–9, 11–12;* (ii) *Adagio in G min.* (arr. Giazotto).
(B) *** DG Classikon 439 509-2 [(M) id. import]. (i) Holliger, Elhorst, Bern Camerata; (ii) Lucerne Festival Strings, Baumgartner.

The playing of Heinz Holliger, Hans Elhorst and the Bern Camerata is refined, persuasive and vital, and the CD could hardly be more truthful or better detailed. This excellent collection has now been relegated to DG's bargain Classikon label and the famous *Adagio* (in a perfectly acceptable performance under Baumgartner) has been added to tempt a wider public. Let us hope it does so.

Concerti a cinque (for oboe and strings) in B flat; D, Op. 7/3 & 6.
(B) ** EMI CfP CD-CFP 6048 [(M) id. import]. Sydney Sutcliffe, Virtuosi of England, Davison – VIVALDI: *Oboe concertos.* **

A nicely stylish pair of performances from Sydney Sutcliffe that cannot be faulted, with a beautifully sprung, crisp accompaniment from Arthur Davison. The 1971 recording has the pleasing ambience of Barking Assembly Hall, yet is crisp, clean and clear and, with a fetching sleeve, this disc will give much pleasure if not taken all at one sitting. The reason for withholding the third star is the playing time (35 minutes), which seems short measure, even for a bargain disc.

(i) *Concerti a cinque, Op. 9/1–12;* (ii) *Adagio in G min. for organ and strings* (arr. Giazotto).
(B) *** Ph. Duo 456 333-2 (2) [id.]. (i) Felix Ayo, Heinz Holliger, Maurice Bourgue; (i; ii) Maria Garatti (harpsichord or organ); I Musici.

Albinoni's set of 12 Opus 9 concertos are delightful and inspired throughout. They are all included on this Philips Duo in excellent recordings from 1966–7. They are played with much finesse and style, which comment also applies to the famous Adagio, here sounding less inflated than usual and all the more effective in consequence. Ayo, Holliger and Bourgue are on top form throughout, and so are the Philips engineers.

Concerti a cinque, Op. 9/2, 5, 8 & 11.
(M) *** Virgin/EMI Veritas (SIS) Dig. VER5 61152–2 [CDM 611522]. Hans de Vries, Alma Musica Amsterdam, Bob van Asperen – TELEMANN: *Oboe concertos.* ***

Hans de Vries plays a baroque oboe, made by Gottlob Crone in Leipzig around 1735, and produces a most appealing timbre, while his technique is remarkably assured and true. There are several fine collections of Op. 9, but none more authentic than this. There is one cavil: the solo balance seems a shade too forward, even though the interaction with the strings (which are well in the picture) is effectively managed. The accompaniments are as alert and stylish as the solo playing and there is not a trace of vinegar in the string-timbre.

12 Concerti (Opera decima), Op. 10.
(B) *** Erato/Warner Ultima 0630 18943-2 (2) [(M) id. import]. Piero Toso, Giuliano Carmignola, Sol. Ven., Claudio Scimone.

Although the existence of this set of concertos was long known and was listed by the Amsterdam publisher, Le Cène, their rediscovery is comparatively recent. They came to light as late as the 1960s, when Michael Talbot found them in a Swedish library at the castle of Leufsta. They were immediately recorded by I Musici but now appear in a more recent (1979) two-record set from I Solisti Veneti. Four of the set are violin concertos (Nos. 6, 8, 10 and 12) and three are concerti grossi with a small concertino group (2, 3 and 4), while the remainder are without soloists and have non-fugal last movements. They were composed in the mid-1730s, 13 years after Op. 9 and after the composer had been absorbed by operatic ventures. They are of special interest, both in showing the development of the solo violin writing by the side of his earlier sets, and for their participation in the gestation of the string sinfonia (all the works are in the three-part format of the Italian overture – quick–slow–quick). But it is for their lyricism and warmth that these concertos will be cherished, readily demonstrated by the lovely slow movement of the *D major Violin concerto* (No. 6) or the serene *Adagio* of the *C major Concerto grosso* (No. 3) and the gracious, imitative Minuet finale of the same work. They radiate simple vitality and love of life and a youthful exuberance that belies the composer's age. The playing is warm and musical, and the recording is made in an ample acoustic. Some may prefer more sharply etched detail (particularly in the concerti grossi), but the resonant string-timbres are agreeably natural and immaculately transferred to CD.

Il nascimento dell'Aurora (*festa pastorale*; complete).
(B) **(*) Erato/Warner Dig. 4509 96374-2 (2) [(M) id.]. Anderson, Zimmermann, Klare, Browne, Yamaj, Sol. Ven., Scimone.

Written as a court celebration, probably on the birth of Princess Maria-Theresa, daughter of Charles VI of Austria, *Il nascimento dell'Aurora* makes a substantial and attractive two-hour stage entertainment or 'festa pastorale'. This well-balanced live recording, made in Vicenza, Italy, puts forward a persuasive case despite some roughness in the choral singing (which is particularly distracting in the first chorus) and some intrusive audience applause. Soloists are first rate and the orchestra generally stylish. The CD transfer is excellently managed. With full libretto and translation included, this is well worth exploring.

Alkan, Charles (1813–88)

Piano concerto, Op. 39 (orch. Klindworth); *Concerti da camera Nos. 1 in A min., Op. 10; 2 in C sharp min.; 3 in C sharp min.* (reconstructed Hugh Macdonald).
(BB) *** Naxos Dig. 8.553702 [id.]. Dmitri Feofanov, Razumovsky SO, Robert Stankovsky.

Alkan's Op. 39 consists of twelve *Etudes*, of which Nos. 8–10 comprise the *Concerto for piano*. The first movement alone runs to 1,342 bars, more than in Beethoven's *Hammerklavier*, and (to quote Allan Ho's notes) 'poses special problems of endurance as well as myriad technical difficulties'. Performances of all three movements are rare nowadays and none was given in Alkan's lifetime. However, the first movement was championed by the conductor and pianist, Karl Klindworth, perhaps best known to pianists for his edition of works by Chopin. A life-long champion of Alkan, he made a transcription of the movement for piano and orchestra in 1872 while he was teaching in Moscow and, thanks to Hans von Bülow, he sent this to the composer. Klindworth called the piece *Allegro de Concert* and, whether at the instigation of Alkan himself or on his own initative, made extensive changes in his final revision of 1902. A contemporary critic summed it up as 'a concert piece by Klindworth based on Alkan . . . because Mr Klindworth expanded the first movement of a very extensive concerto into an independent work. Alkan's work is only the core from which the rather long work developed.' In a useful note (incidentally the notes are copious and exceptionally good) the soloist, Dmitri Feofanov, answers objections to the Klindworth or 'Alkan de-Alkanized', as he puts it: 'the whole point of the *Concerto* was unmercifully to imitate a concert with a single performer: the wild touches are gone, the development shortened, everything is proper'. However, he was eventually won over and certainly wins over the listener.

Earlier in his career, Alkan himself had composed three concertos for piano and orchestra, the *First* in 1831 when he was seventeen, and the *Second in C sharp minor* two years later for a visit to London. A *Third* does not survive, but Hugh Macdonald, best known as a Berlioz scholar, argues convincingly that the *Andante romantique* of 1873 corresponds to a contemporary description of the piece. Feofanov does a heroic job in the Klindworth and shows a sympathy with Alkan that the Slovak-based Razumovsky Orchestra and Robert Stankovsky obviously share. Good recording makes this well worth anybody's money.

Barcarolle; Gigue, Op. 24; Marche, Op. 37/1; Nocturne No. 2, Op. 57/1; Saltarelle, Op. 23; Scherzo diabolico, Op. 39/3; Sonatine, Op. 61.
(B) *** HM HMA 190 927 [id.]. Bernard Ringeissen.

Bernard Ringeissen could be more flamboyant but he is fully equal to the cruel technical demands of this music. The recording, from the beginning of the 1970s, is first class.

Allaga, Géza (1841–1913)

Concerto hongrois for (solo) *cimbalom; Etudes de concert: in A; A min. (Tempest); C; D; D min.; B flat; F (Chorale); Pizzicato and glissando;* (i) *Hungarian rhapsody for cimbalom and string quintet.* arr. of LISZT: *Le Dieu des Hongrois;* arrangements for flute and cimbalom: (ii) SCHUBERT: *Ave Maria.* FIELD: *Nocturne.*
(B) *** HM Dig. HMA 1903075 [id.]. Viktória Herrencsár; (i) Zsolnai, Tóth, Papp, Nagy, Tibay; (ii) Béla Drahos.

A fascinating collection. Géza Allaga founded a school for what has come to be regarded as Hungary's national instrument, the cimbalom (though it was in use in various forms for thousands of years and originated in Asia). He left a complete course of study for beginners and experts: many of these pieces obviously demand much bravura. Allaga's invention is always agreeable and his use of folk-tunes in the two extended works, the one solo and the other with an agreeably warm string backing, is also very pleasing. The soloist here is both a virtuoso and a sensitive musician. Here there is much subtlety, both of colour and of dynamic range, while Béla Drahos produces an elegant flute line in the Schubert and Field arrangements. The recording is excellent.

Allegri, Gregorio (1582–1652)

Miserere.

(M) *** Decca 421 147-2 [id.]. King's College Ch., Willcocks – PALESTRINA: *Collection.* ***

(M) **(*) EMI Dig. CD-EMX 2180 [(M) id. import]. St John's College, Cambridge, Ch., Guest – LASSUS: *Missa super bella* **(*); PALESTRINA: *Veni sponsa Christi.* ***

Mozart was so impressed with Allegri's *Miserere* when he heard it in the Sistine Chapel (which originally claimed exclusive rights to its performance) that he wrote the music out from memory so that it could be performed elsewhere. The famous King's performance, with its arresting treble solo so beautifully and securely sung by Roy Goodman, is now coupled with Palestrina at mid-price.

The new digital recording from St John's is finely sung, and the three-dimensional balance is very realistic. Guest offers more verses (with subtly varied dynamics) and his performance runs to nearly 14 minutes. His unnamed treble soloist sings less ethereally than Roy Goodman, with a strong upward leap in his famous repeated phrase. The performance is otherwise impressive but has less magic than the King's version.

Almeida, Francisco António de (*c.* 1702–55)

Motets: *Beatus vir; O quam suavis.*

(M) *** DG Codex 453 182-2. Jennifer Smith, Magali, Schwartz, Fernando Serafim, Gulbenkian Chamber Ch. & O, Michel Corboz – CARVALHO: *Te Deum;* SEIXAS: *Adebat Vincentius* etc.; TEIXEIRA: *Gaudate, astra.* ***

These two beautiful (and beautifully sung) motets establish the Portuguese baroque composer, Francisco António de Almeida, as a composer of individuality. *O quam suavis* opens with richly expressive writing for soprano, contralto and chorus, and turns to exuberance in *Esurientes reples bonis*. *Beatus vir* is lighter in style and makes considerable florid demands on both soprano and tenor soloists, ending with an expansive *Amen* from the chorus. The recording is in every way excellent, fresh and clear within a warm acoustic.

Anderson, Leroy (1908–75)

Belle of the ball; Blue tango; Chicken reel; China doll; Fiddle-faddle; The first day of spring; The girl in satin; Horse and buggy; Jazz legato; Jazz pizzicato; The phantom regiment; Plink, plank, plunk!; Promenade; Saraband; Scottish suite: The bluebells of Scotland. Serenata; Sleigh ride; Song of the bells; Summer skies; The syncopated clock; The typewriter; The waltzing cat. Arr. of HANDEL: *Song of Jupiter.*

(M) *** Mercury 432 013-2 [id.]. Eastman-Rochester Pops O, or O, Frederick Fennell.

The reissue of Fennell's Mercury performances is most welcome; although certain key numbers such as *Bugler's holiday*, *Forgotten dreams* and *A Trumpeter's lullaby* are missing from this record, they do arrive on a later issue (see below). His performances have a witty precision which is most attractive. The sound throughout is truthful, if not opulent.

(i) *Carol suite:* excerpts. *A Christmas festival. Goldilocks: Pirate dance.* (ii) *Irish suite. Bugler's holiday; Forgotten dreams; Penny-whistle song; Sandpaper ballet; Trumpeter's lullaby.*

(M) *** Mercury 434 376-2 [id.]. (i) London Pops O; (ii) Eastman-Rochester Pops O, Frederick Fennell – COATES: *Four ways; London suites.* **(*)

Here Mercury complete their reissues of the vintage Fennell recordings of Leroy Anderson, including the *Irish suite*. Commissioned by the Boston Eire Society in 1947, this is one of Anderson's more ambitious enterprises. Some very familiar Irish tunes are used and the composer's orchestral treatment impresses his personality firmly on the music without spoiling the freshness of the melodic ideas. '*The wearing of the green*' with its alternating pizzicato and brass sonorities is very effective, but the highlight is a clever arrangement of *The Minstrel boy* in the form of a haunting little funeral march, advancing and retreating. The half-dozen orchestral lollipops include several favourites, notably *Bugler's holiday* and *Forgotten dreams*. Fennell also includes some arrangements of notable Christmas carols, and the vintage, rather dry and studio-ish recording suits the bright precision of the playing.

Arensky, Anton (1861–1906)

Symphonies Nos. 1 in B min., Op. 4; 2 in A, Op. 22; Dream on the Volga: Overture. Intermezzo in G min., Op. 13; Nal and Damayanty: Introduction. Suites Nos. 1 in G min., Op.7; 2 (Silhouettes), Op. 23; 3 in C (Variations), Op. 33.

(B) **(*) BMG/Melodiya Twofer Dig. 74321 53462-2 [id.]. USSR SO, Svetlanov.

Arensky's *First Symphony*, composed shortly after his graduation in 1882, is a work of great fluency and charm. It is beautifully put together and has considerable melodic freshness. The *Second* is the more individual of the two and is full of highly attractive ideas: its four movements are linked together, the finale returning to the material of the opening movement; however, there is little serious attempt at organic cohesion. The *Overture* to the opera *Dream on the Volga* (1888) opens bombastically but also has its attractive moments, though its inspiration is less consistent than either. The *Second suite* (*Silhouettes*), which also comes on the first disc, also has considerable charm, particularly the fourth movement, *Le Rêveur*, which is almost the Russian equivalent of Elgar's *Dream children*. The work derives from a set of pieces for two pianos dating from 1892, and it is scored with great skill and, in the case of *La coquette* and *Polichinelle*, delicacy. The performances here are spirited and the analogue recordings, dating from 1983, are fully acceptable, although the brass are at times raw in climaxes.

The second CD offers the other two *Suites* and was recorded in 1987 and 1990. The *First Suite* (1885) opens with a characteristic miniature set of variations on a Russian folksong ('*She swings the small broom*') and includes an appealingly lyrical balletic *Dance*; but it is more famous for its *Basso ostinato* slow march (a classical 'pop' on Russian radio) with a very simple melody, most winningly scored. The whole of the *Third Suite* (1894) is in itself a set of variations on a gracious theme and, like the *Second*, originates in music conceived for the piano. Its ten movements include an enticingly fragile *Waltz*, an exotic pastiche *Minuet* (which sounds a bit like Liadov), an equally engaging *Gavotte* and *Scherzo* and a *Nocturne* complete with piano solo, and it ends with a buoyant *Polonaise*. This work is every bit as inventive as the *Variations on a theme of Tchaikovsky* and deserves to be better known. The *Intermezzo in G minor* is slight, but the *Introduction to Nal and Damayanty*, in spite of another momentary burst of bombast at its centre, is melodically appealing and pleasingly atmospheric. All this music is very vividly played and recorded and, if climaxes are just a little overwhelming at times, they are not really coarse. A thoroughly worthwhile set which greatly increases our knowledge of this composer, so admired by Tchaikovsky, who was his lifelong friend.

Variations on a theme of Tchaikovsky, Op. 35a.

(B) *** EMI forte CZS5 69361 (2) [CDFP 69361]. LSO, Barbirolli – RIMSKY-KORSAKOV: *Scheherazade* **; GLAZUNOV: *The Seasons; Concert waltzes.* ***

(B) *(*) Mercury Double 434 391-2 (2) [id.]. Philharmonia Hungarica, Dorati – TCHAIKOVSKY: *Symphonies Nos. 1–3.* ***

Rimsky-Korsakov, whose pupil he was, may have been unduly harsh in dismissing Arensky, whose talent he had seen dissipated in drink and gambling. These delightful variations, arguably his best-known work, originally formed the slow movement of the *Second String quartet in A minor*, composed in 1894, a year after Tchaikovsky's death, and subsequently arranged for full strings. The theme itself comes from the *Sixteen Songs for children*, Op. 54 (1883), and is entitled 'When Jesus Christ was but a child'. (Tchaikovksy himself made an orchestral transcription of it in 1884.) Sir John Barbirolli's recording, made in the Kingsway Hall in 1965 and first published in harness with the Tchaikovsky *Serenade for strings*, is warm and spacious. There is affection too, of course, and a splendid flexibility of phrasing and dynamic. Thus the slow variation, which obviously is modelled on the famous *Andante cantabile* from Tchaikovsky's *D major String quartet*, is wonderfully gentle. The playing of the LSO under this endearing conductor is suitably affectionate. It comes as part of a quite attractive two-CD Russian music package, let down a little by Svetlanov's rather idiosyncratic *Scheherazade*.

Dorati's performance is polished and elegantly turned, yet it is not easy to decide whether the fact that this recorded account conveys so little of the naïve charm of the music is altogether the conductor's fault or that of the engineers. The recording was made in the Grosse Saal of the Vienna Konzerthaus in 1958. The effect is curiously dry, and the string players are made to seem too close to the listener.

Piano trios Nos. 1 in D min., Op. 32; 2 in F min., Op. 73.
(M) *(*) Chandos Enchant Dig. CHAN 7048 [id.]. Borodin Trio.

The Chandos performances of the two Arensky *Piano trios* were recorded four years apart, in 1986 and 1990 respectively, and their coupling represents a sad mis-match. The delightful *D minor Trio* was composed a year after Tchaikovsky's death and a decade after Tchaikovsky's own contribution to the genre. As their endearing opening shows, the Borodins give a first-class account of it, warm, full-blooded and full of delicate touches. The Scherzo comes off with a delightful lift and the Borodins' genial playing does full justice to the whole. Excellent recording too. The *F minor Trio* is a bigger work than its better-known predecessor and it has considerable eloquence and charm – as well as dignity. Alas, the Borodins rarely permit the music to speak for itself. They tend to overproject and sweeten the piece, particularly in the *Romance* and the trio section of the exuberant Scherzo. Here the violinist is not quite impeccable and, although the Scherzo itself comes off well, the playing here is horribly sugary. The recording is vivid – but this is not a coupling to recommend with any confidence.

Arnell, Richard (born 1917)

Punch and the child (ballet), *Op. 49*.
(B) (***) Sony mono SBK 62748; *SBT 62748*. RPO, Beecham – BERNERS: *Triumph of Neptune;* DELIUS: *Paris*. (***)

Richard Arnell enjoyed something of a vogue immediately after the war. His *Fourth Symphony* scored some success at the Cheltenham Festival in the late 1940s and his imaginative and inventive ballet, *Punch and the child*, was mounted by the New York City Ballet. Yet his present representation in the catalogue is meagre in the extreme and by no means commensurate with his gifts. Sir Thomas Beecham recorded the *Punch and the child suite* on five 78-r.p.m. sides in 1950. Its musical inspiration is as fresh, individual and memorable as its neglect is unaccountable. We have relished this score over the years, and its attractions remain as strong as ever in this well-transferred set. The sound is amazingly good for 1950 – but then it was pretty much state-of-the-art at that time – and this is very attractive indeed at bargain price.

Arnold, Malcolm (born 1921)

(i) *Clarinet concerto No. 1, Op. 20;* (ii) *Flute concertos Nos. 1, Op. 45; 2, Op. 111;* (iii) *Horn concerto No. 2, Op. 58;* (iv) *Oboe concerto, Op. 39;* (v) *Trumpet concerto, Op. 125*.
(B) *** EMI Eminence (SIS) Dig./analogue CD-EMX 2271 [(M) id. import]. (i) Hilton; (ii) Adeney; (iii) Civil; (iv) Hunt; (v) Wallace; Bournemouth Sinf.; (i; iii–v) Del Mar; (ii) Thomas.

This is a compilation of superb concerto performances, made towards the end of the LP era, with the two *Flute concertos* added to the original LP package, here superbly played by the dedicatee. All of them demonstrate Arnold's mastery in writing both for woodwind and for brass instruments, each crisply conceived within a compact frame, with each bringing out Arnold's gifts of surprise and ready lyricism.

Having been a trumpeter himself, he writes with uncommon skill for the instrument, and the same brilliance characterizes John Wallace's dazzling playing. Like so much of his music, it has a broad appeal but touches a richer vein of imagination in the slow movement. The *Oboe concerto*, written for Leon Goossens, is played with quite superb panache and virtuosity by Gordon Hunt, who is surely second to none among the later generation of players; Janet Hilton in the *First Clarinet concerto* and Alan Civil in the *Second Horn concerto* are hardly less brilliant. It is appropriate to have included here the *First Flute concerto* in a winningly light-hearted performance by its dedicatee, Richard Adeney, alongside the second, written two decades later. This is a deeper, subtler and more melancholy work, which Adeney plays with complete understanding, especially the wistfully memorable *Andante grazioso*. All this music is well crafted and readily tuneful in Arnold's most spontaneous manner, and the composer's admirers will find much to delight them in these performances, which are very well recorded. All but the *Flute concertos* are digital and were recorded in the composer's presence in 1984; the two concertos for flute are analogue and date from five years earlier.

(i) *Flute concerto, Op. 45;* (ii) *Oboe concerto, Op. 39. Sinfoniettas Nos. 1, Op. 48; 2, Op. 65; 3, Op. 81.*
(BB) *** Arte Nova/BMG Dig. 74321 46503-2 [id.]. (i) Anna Pyne; (ii) Malcolm Messiter; L. Festival O, Ross Pople.

This is the identical programme of three *Sinfoniettas* plus concertos which Ross Pople recorded earlier for Hyperion with his London Festival Orchestra. In between he has radically rethought his interpretations, often choosing quite different speeds, sometimes faster (as in the *Sinfonietta No. 1*), sometimes much slower (as in the first movements of the other two *Sinfoniettas*). The changes in whichever direction generally bring lighter textures and manner, with Anna Pyne a more warmly expressive flute soloist than her predecessor, and the oboist, Malcolm Messiter, lighter than before. Very well recorded, at super-bargain price it makes an excellent issue, bringing together charming, beautifully crafted works that are far too little heard in the concert hall.

Guitar concerto, Op. 67.
(M) *** RCA 09026 61598-2. Julian Bream, Melos Ens., composer – Richard Rodney BENNETT: *Concerto;* RODRIGO: *Concierto de Aranjuez.* ***

There are few guitar concertos to match the effectiveness of this jazz-inflected piece, written in 1957 for Julian Bream, whose first recording, made two years later with the composer directing the Melos Ensemble, is surely definitive. It was recorded by Decca engineers, so the balance is exemplary and the sound has plenty of atmosphere and the most vivid colouring.

4 Cornish dances, Op. 91; 8 English dances, Set 1, Op. 27; Set 2, Op. 33; 4 Irish dances, Op. 126; 4 Scottish dances, Op. 59; 4 Welsh dances, Op. 138.
(B) *** Naxos Dig. 8.553526 [id.]. Queensland SO, Andrew Penny.

The advantage this Naxos disc has over its competitors – to say nothing of its price – is the inclusion of the four *Welsh dances*, the last to be written and closer in mood to the *Cornish* and *Irish dances* than to the cheerful ebullience of the masterly *English dances* of 1950–51. They remain perennial favourites, and Andrew Penny and the Queensland Orchestra present them with their colours gleaming. The Scottish set goes particularly well too, notably the third dance with its glorious lyrical evocation of the Scottish lakes and mountains, while the closing Highland fling, with echoes of *Tam O'Shanter* on an inebriated Glaswegian Saturday night, are wittily and lustily caught. Then Arnold's optimism became more sporadic and he includes a sadly reflective picture of the deserted copper mines in his Cornish set, while the two central *Irish dances* are curiously disconsolate, although there is an Irish jig to liven things up. But the *Welsh dances* continue that element of Celtic melancholy which Penny captures admirably. These performances have the composer's imprimatur (he was present at the recording sessions) and can be cordially recommended. Only Arnold's own Lyrita recordings surpass them, and then only marginally. The Naxos sound might be thought a shade over-resonant, but it does not lack brilliance.

(i) *8 English dances, sets 1–2, Opp. 27 & 33; Homage to the Queen* (ballet), *Op. 42; 4 Scottish dances, Op. 59.* (ii) *The Sound Barrier* (rhapsody), *Op. 38.*
(M) (***) EMI mono/stereo CDM5 66120-2. (i) Philh. O, Robert Irving; (ii) RPO, composer.

It was a pity to sandwich *Homage to the Queen* (written for the Coronation celebrations) in between the *English* and *Scottish dances*, for their unceasing melodic fecundity serves only to emphasize the relative lack of similarly memorable ideas in the stage work. Dame Ninette de Valois is reported as describing Arnold as 'the finest ballet composer since Tchaikovsky' and what she obviously meant was that he provided a series of very danceable musical vignettes, vividly scored. For Arnold, like Tchaikovsky, worked closely to the detailed demands of his choreographer Frederick Ashton, to create appropriate music for the four sections, *Earth*, *Water*, *Fire* and *Air*. The ballet opens with a regal, fanfare-style march after the style of Walton and Bliss, but without a *nobilmente* tune. Then the evocative opening of *Earth*, with its bird-calls, develops a string line which becomes lyrically skittish (the effect rather like Hérold's *La Fille mal gardée*). But the most translucent scoring comes in *Water*, with its delicate *Pas de trois*, producing a fragile Waltz, and, for the first 'Man's variation', an aural impression of swimming through swirling waters. The *Fire* section is pungently, exuberantly aggressive, but *Air* brings aural relief and the writing here often recalls Arnold's flight simulation for *The Sound Barrier* (see below). But it is not until the final *Pas de deux* that the listener's attention is caught and held by a really striking melodic flow. Both the ballet and the *Dances* are very well played indeed by the Philharmonia under Robert Irving, but, in spite of the Kingsway Hall ambience, one sadly misses the spaciousness and warmth of stereo. In the Scottish group (which are stereo), Irving gives a particularly beautiful account of the lovely lyrical third number. The programme opens with Arnold himself conducting the orchestral rhapsody he fashioned out of his score for the David Lean film, *The Sound Barrier*, and anyone who remembers the visual imagery will find it is readily recalled by the music.

The Sound Barrier (rhapsody) after film score, *Op. 38*.
(M) *** ASV Dig. CDWHL 2058. RPO, Kenneth Alwyn – BAX: *Malta G.C.* etc. ***

Malcolm Arnold's *Rhapsody*, adapted in 1952 from his film score, shows the composer at his most characteristically inventive. It has five tiny subdivisions but makes a satisfying whole, not a note too long, and is kaleidoscopically orchestrated. Kenneth Alwyn and the RPO clearly relish the virtuosity demanded of them, and the recording is equally brilliant.

Symphonies Nos. 1, Op. 22; 2, Op. 40.
(BB) **(*) Naxos Dig. 8.553406 [id.]. Nat. SO of Ireland, Andrew Penny.

Comparison between Hickox's account and the composer's own recording of the *First Symphony* is instructive. With Hickox, the first movement is much more tautly paced. Andrew Penny in his Naxos version matches Hickox closely, but the National Orchestra of Ireland cannot command the richness of sonority of the LSO, nor are their (otherwise excellent) wind soloists quite so strong in personality. However, there is an agreeable lightness of touch in Dublin, and the presentation of the delectable melody of the *Andantino* (shared by flute and violins) brings a whimsical charm. Indeed the Dublin performances of both symphonies are fresh and spontaneous, but in the poignant *Lento* of the *Second*, with its plangent funeral march, Hickox's much more spacious tempo is profoundly moving when the LSO playing sustains such a high degree of concentration. The finale, too, is joyously exuberant, whereas the genial skittishness of the Dublin orchestra has less abandon. However, it must be said that the composer was present at these sessions and undoubtedly Penny consulted him over questions of tempo and especially that for the slow movement of the *Second Symphony*, which certainly communicates strongly in the Dublin performance. The Naxos recording is excellent, full and spacious, but the full-priced Chandos is very much in the demonstration bracket.

Symphonies Nos. (i) *2, Op. 40;* (ii) *5, Op. 74;* (i) *Peterloo overture, Op. 97.*
(M) *** EMI CDM5 66324-2. (i) Bournemouth SO, Groves; (ii) CBSO, composer.

The recoupling of two of Arnold's most impressive symphonies can be warmly welcomed. Both recordings date from the 1970s. The composer secures an outstanding response from the Birmingham orchestra; in many ways his performance has not been surpassed, particularly in the expressive power of the slow movement. Groves, too, in Bournemouth is equally dedicated, and this is one of his finest recordings. The CD transfer is outstandingly successful, and the overture makes a highly effective encore. Splendid value at mid-price.

Symphonies Nos. 3, Op. 63; 4, Op. 71.
(BB) *** Naxos Dig. 8.553739 [id.]. Nat. SO of Ireland, Andrew Penny.

Arnold's symphonies reflect his experience of life in its broader context, with disappointments, frustrations and even tragedy all mirrored. But both the *Third* and the *Fourth*, though they have moments of desolation, bring an affirmation of life and its human values. There is melody in plenty in each work. In the first movement of the *Third* the main theme brings a certain emotional austerity, while another particularly fine tune, very Arnoldian in character, dominates the first movement of the *Fourth*. The *Lento* of the *Third* is memorably poignant here, but the slow movements of both symphonies are movingly eloquent. Among the wind soloists the plaintive timbre of the principal oboe is particularly memorable. Andrew Penny and his Dublin orchestra give finely played and spontaneous performances that can readily stand alongside the full-price competition, and this Naxos record understandably has the composer's imprimatur. Penny's pacing, overall shaping and concern for detail bring readings which are very persuasive in following the composer's quixotic mood-changes, while still holding the structures together. The recording is of high quality, atmospheric and with the orchestral colours emerging vividly; the special percussion effects in the exuberantly fugal finale of the *Fourth* are also very telling.

Symphony No. 9, Op. 128.
(BB) *** Naxos Dig. 8.553540 [id.]. Nat. SO of Ireland, Andrew Penny.

Just ten years after Sir Malcolm Arnold wrote his *Ninth Symphony* this superb first recording arrived to confirm the work as a fitting culmination to his symphonic series. The baldness of the arguments, with two-part writing the general rule, and with structure built on repetition and juxtaposition rather than thematic development, might initially be thought disconcerting. What matters are the actual results, and they consistently speak in a true Arnoldian accent. With occasional echoes of Shostakovich, the ear is regularly tweaked by the terracing of sounds, at extremes of register as well as of dynamic, culminating in the long slow finale, almost as long as the other three movements together, registering a mood of tragedy and disillusion. The parallel with the final *Adagio* of Mahler's *Ninth Symphony* is clear, though without neurosis or self-pity. As Arnold explains in his interview included on the disc, the whole piece reflects 'the five years of hell' he suffered before writing this work. The symphony ends quietly on a major triad, a firm D major chord, a mere sop towards granting release. The other three movements are just as direct, bald in their arguments but pointful, not facile, built on instantly memorable material. So the first movement, *Vivace*, quickly establishes Arnold's mode of duetting, with occasional jazzy slurrings. The second movement, *Allegretto*, brings hypnotic, chaconne-like repetitions on a theme with modal overtones. The third movement starts like a typical Arnold Scherzo, weightier than the rest of the work, but then grows ever angrier. As to the performance, this is not just concentrated and consistently committed but warmly resonant, with the strings sounding glorious and the woodwind and brass consistently brilliant. The recording is rich and firmly focused.

Auber, Daniel (1782–1871)

Overtures: The Bronze horse; Fra Diavolo; Masaniello.

❁ (M) *** Mercury 434 309-2 [id.]. Detroit SO, Paray – SUPPE: *Overtures.* ***

Dazzling performances, full of verve and style, which will surely never be surpassed. The present recordings, made in the suitably resonant acoustic of Detroit's Old Orchestra Hall, shows Mercury engineering (1959 vintage) at its very finest.

Auric, Georges (1899–1983)

Overture.

(M) *** Mercury (IMS) 434 335-2 [id.]. LSO, Dorati – FETLER: *Contrasts;* FRANCAIX: *Piano concertino;* MILHAUD: *Le boeuf sur le toit;* SATIE: *Parade.* ***

Georges Auric's breezy *Overture* is irrepressibly high-spirited and its melodic freshness and Dorati's vivacious performance help to dispel the impression that it is a shade too long for its content. Vividly clear and transparent sound from near the end of the Mercury vintage era: 1965.

Avison, Charles (1709–70)

12 Concerti grossi after Scarlatti.

(B) *** Ph. Duo 438 806-2 (2) [id.]. ASMF, Marriner.

Marriner and the ASMF pioneered a complete recording of these works by the Newcastle-upon-Tyne composer, Charles Avison, which he ingeniously based on the keyboard sonatas of Domenico Scarlatti, and Marriner's fine set, with Iona Brown leading the solo group, has much grace and style. It makes a fine bargain on a Philips Duo two-discs-for-the-price-of-one.

The Bach family, including Johann Sebastian

Johann Christoph (1642–1703) **Johann Michael** (1648–94) **Johann Bernhard** (1676–1749) **Johann Sebastian** (1685–1750) **Johann Lorenz** (1695–1773) **Johann Ernst** (1722–77)

'The Bach family: Organ works': J. S. BACH: *Toccata and Fugue in D min., BWV 565; Fantasia and fugue in A min., BWV 904; Prelude and fugue in C, BWV 547; Prelude (Fantasia) and fugue in G min., BWV 542; Chorale with 6 variations on 'Wenn wir in höchsten Nöten sein', BWV Anh. 78; Capriccio in E, BWV 993.* J. L. BACH: *Prelude and fugue in D min.* J. M. BACH: Chorales: *Allein Gott in der Höh sei Ehr; Wenn wir in höchsten Nöten sein.* J. C. BACH: *Prelude and fugue in E flat;* Chorales: *Warum betrübst du dich, mein Herz; Wach auf, mein Herz, und singe; Aus meines Herzens Grunde.* J. B. BACH: *Passacaglia (Chaconne) in B flat; Partita on 'Du Friedefürst, Herr Jesu Christ'.* J. E. BACH: *Fantasia and fugue in F.*

(M) *** Teldec/Warner 4505 92176 (2). Wilhelm Krumbach (Herbst organ of the Schlosskirche, Lahm/Itzgrund, Germany).

Seven generations of Bach's family were professional or semi-professional musicians, most employed as church Kantors, which inevitably involved composing. Johann Christoph and Johann Michael Bach were distant uncles of Johann Sebastian; Johann Bernhard Bach was his first cousin once removed; Johann Lorenz was his first nephew once removed (and also his pupil); Johann Ernst was the son of Johann Bernhard. So much for the family tree, but what of the music? The whole family were – naturally enough – good at chorales, and both Johann Lorenz and Johann Christoph could write a respectable prelude and fugue. But the star here is Johann Bernhard, whose *Passacaglia in B flat* is a splendid piece, while the *Chorale partita on Du Friedefürst Herr Jesu Christ* is also very inventive. The programme ends with Johann Ernst's remarkably flamboyant *Fantasia and fugue in F*, but that is much later than the other works. Performances are first class and so is the organ. It was good to have the *Chorale variations* and *Capriccio* of Johann Sebastian as an illuminating yardstick but, had the other of his works been omitted, this programme could have fitted economically on to a single CD. Nevertheless this is a fascinating set.

Bach, Carl Philipp Emanuel (1714–88)

Cello concertos: in A min., Wq. 170, H. 432; in B flat, Wq. 171, H. 436; in A min., Wq. 172, H. 439.
(M) *** Virgin/Veritas EMI Dig. VM5 61401-2. Anner Bylsma, OAE, Leonhardt.

These concertos also have alternative versions for both keyboard and flute, but they suit the cello admirably. Bylsma's expressive intensity communicates strongly, without ever taking the music outside its boundaries of sensibility, and these artists convey their commitment to this music persuasively.

Flute concerto in D min., Wq.22.
(BB) **(*) ASV CDQS 6012. Dingfelder, ECO, Mackerras – HOFFMEISTER: *Concertos Nos. 6 & 9.* **(*)

Those who are interested in the Hoffmeister coupling will find Ingrid Dingfelder's playing both spirited and stylish.

(i) *Flute concertos: in A min., Wq.166; in B flat, Wq.167; in A, Wq.168; in G, Wq.169;* (ii; iii) *Oboe concertos: in B flat, Wq.164; in E flat, Wq.165;* (ii; iv; v) *Solo in G min., for oboe and continuo*; (v) *Solo in G for harp, Wq.139.*
(B) **(*) Ph. Duo 442 592-2 (2) [id.]. (i) Aurèle Nicolet, Netherlands CO, David Zinman; (ii) Heinz Holliger; (iii) ECO, Leppard; (iv) Rama Jucker; (v) Ursula Holliger.

Nicolet uses a modern instrument and plays very well, but the effect with a rather heavy string accompaniment (partly the result of the acoustic) makes less of the music than the rival versions on Capriccio. But those are at full price, and the Philips Duo set offers a great deal more music. Holliger's accounts of the *Oboe concertos* are masterly. In addition to the excellence of the support from the ECO under Leppard, the Philips engineering is distinguished. The bonuses for oboe and continuo (in this instance harp and cello) and Ursula Holliger's harp *Solo* also add to the attractions of this very generous set.

Double concerto for harpsichord and fortepiano in E flat.
(M) *** Teldec/Warner 0630 12326-2. Uittenbosch, Antonietti, Leonhardt Cons. – J. C. BACH: *Sinfonia concertante in F;* W. F. BACH: *Double concerto for 2 harpsichords.* **(*)

(i) *Double concerto in E flat for harpsichord & fortepiano, Wq.47;* (ii) *Double concerto in F, for 2 harpsichords, Wq.46;*(i) *Sonatina for 2 harpsichords & orchestra in D, Wq.109.*
(BB) *** DHM Baroque Esprit 05472 77410-2 [id.]. (i) Eric Lynn Kelley, Jos van Immersel (fortepiano or harpsichord); (ii) Alan Curtis, Gustav Leonhardt; Coll. Aur., Maier.

The spirited and delightful *E flat Concerto for harpsichord and fortepiano* comes from Bach's last year and ought to be far better known than it is. It has a chirpily inviting opening theme and is given a wholly persuasive account here, with the solo instruments naturally balanced and a warm acoustic assisting a lively (but painless) authentic accompaniment, although the orchestral flutes seem rather forward. The *Sonatina for two harpsichords and orchestra* is one of fifteen; it was written in 1762 and is ambitiously scored – as the lively opening tutti demonstrates – for three trumpets, two each of flutes, oboes and horns, bassoon and strings. The first movement (of two), which opens with an exuberantly brief *Presto* (to return later) and then mellows, is a free fantasia, characteristically quirky and diverse. There are surprises, too, towards the end of the second, which is a Minuet with variations. The *F major Concerto*, scored for strings with the addition of two horns, comes from a different world: it was composed much earlier (probably in 1740) for Frederick II's court, yet is still thoroughly representative of this composer, with a memorable *Largo* slow movement. It is also very well played and, at its very economical price, this is a reissue not to be missed. It completely upstages the competing Erato disc from Koopman and Mathot with the Amsterdam Baroque Orchestra (2292 45306-2) which offers only two of the three works here.

A hardly less attractive account of the *Concerto for harpsichord and fortepiano* also comes on Teldec in a higher price-range. The orchestral balance is somewhat better here and the fortepiano has a slightly bolder, more tangible image. The interplay between the two soloists is felicitous, and choice between the two performances must depend on couplings.

Oboe concertos: in B flat, Wq.164; in E flat, Wq.165; (Unaccompanied) *Oboe sonata in A min., Wq.132.*
(BB) **(*) Naxos Dig. 8.550556 [id.]. József Kiss, Ferenc Erkel CO – MARCELLO: *Concerto.* **(*)

József Kiss's account of Bach's pair of *Oboe concertos* is sensitive and musical, if without quite the individuality of Ebbinge's versions on Erato, but they are very well accompanied and beautifully recorded. The solo *Sonata* is also worth having on disc, although one might have liked more dynamic light and shade here. But with an enjoyable Marcello coupling, this is well worth its modest cost.

6 Hamburg sinfonias, Wq.182/1–6.
(BB) *** Naxos Dig. 8.553285 Capella Istropolitana, Christian Benda.

(i) *6 Hamburg Sinfonias, Wq. 182/1–6; Berlin Sinfonias: in C, Wq. 174; in D, Wq. 176;* (ii) *Quartets for flute, viola, fortepiano and* (optional) *cello: Nos. 1 in A min.; 2 in D; 3 in G, Wq. 93–5.* (iii) (Keyboard) *Fantasy in C, Wq. 59/6.*
(B) *** O-L Double 455 715-2 (2) [id.]. (i) AAM, Hogwood; (ii) McGegan, Mackintosh, Pleeth, Hogwood; (iii) Hogwood.

The sharp originality of C. P. E. Bach was never more apparent than in these symphonies. The abrasiveness of the writing comes out more sharply in the kind of authenticity favoured by Hogwood's Academy of Ancient Music in 1979. They have mellowed somewhat since then, but the music-making here is typical of their earlier style; some listeners may find that their angularity, though undoubtedly stimulating, does not make for relaxed listening. Indeed Hogwood continually has one responding as to new music, not least in the dark, bare slow movements. The two *Berlin symphonies* with wind are marginally less original, but still make refreshing listening. The three *Quartets* come from the last year of Bach's life and are all beautifully fashioned, civilized pieces with many of the expressive devices familiar from this composer. There is a highly chromatic slow movement for the D major work and some of the outer movements are characteristically unpredictable. Although the works were designated by Bach as *Quartets*, no bass part survives. In these Oiseau-Lyre performances the cello line is added judiciously where it seems useful to reinforce the texture, and the result has added weight and gravitas without losing any of the charm of the writing. Christopher Hogwood uses a fortepiano rather than harpsichord and makes a good case for doing so (with documentary support in the notes). He secures a wide dynamic range and clean, intelligent articulation. The playing overall is absolutely first rate; the recording is most naturally balanced and could hardly be bettered. Moreover the keyboard *Fantasia in C* is a most remarkable work – it is roughly contemporary with Mozart's *C minor Fantasy* and is more than just a bonus. It is splendidly played by Hogwood. Altogether this is one of the most stimulating of Hogwood's Oiseau-Lyre Doubles.

Using modern instruments at higher modern pitch, Benda directs light, well-sprung accounts of the six *Hamburg Sinfonias* for strings, written after Carl Philipp Emanuel had left the employ of the Emperor of Prussia and could at last please himself in adventurous writing. They are particularly striking in their unexpected twists of imagination and they contain some of his most inspired and original ideas. With more varied textures and tonal contrasts than in most period performances, Benda's have extra light and shade. The darkly chromatic slow movement of No. 3, for example, has a hushed mystery rarely caught. The excellent sound is full and open as well as immediate. This makes an excellent primary bargain recommendation.

4 Hamburg sinfonias, Wq.183/1–4.
(BB) **(*) Naxos Dig. 8.553289 [id.]. Salzburg CO, Yoon K. Lee – W. F. BACH: *Sinfonia in F.* **(*)

4 Hamburg sinfonias, Wq.183/1–4; String sinfonia in B min., Wq.182/5 (H661).
(M) *** Virgin Veritas/EMI Dig. VER5 61182-2 [CDM 61182]. OAE, Gustav Leonhardt.

Unlike the six *Hamburg sinfonias* which C. P. E. Bach wrote earlier for Baron von Swieten, these four later works involve wind as well as strings. The writing is just as refreshing in its unexpectedness and originality. Gustav Leonhardt's account of this second set, Wq.183, is the one to have if you want them on period instruments. They are lively and alert, and distinguished by fine musical intelligence. This set is to be preferred, albeit by a small margin, to that by Koopman (Erato 2292 45430-2) and in any case includes an extra work.

The Naxos Salzburg versions are also freshly played, the results spick and span, with polished playing from strings and woodwind alike. Obviously Yoon K. Lee knows about period-performance styles and, though modern instruments are used here, textures are clear and clean. While there is plenty of dramatic contrast, by the side of Leonhardt the expressive music seems just a shade cool. But the results are certainly stimulating, and this disc is worth its modest cost.

CHAMBER AND INSTRUMENTAL MUSIC

Duo for flute and violin in E min., Wq.140; 12 Short pieces for 2 flutes, 2 violins & continuo, Wq.81; Sonata for flute & continuo in G (Hamburg Sonata), Wq.133; Trios for flute, violin & continuo: in B min., Wq.143; in C, Wq.147; (i) Cantata: *Phyllis and Thirsis, Wq.232.*

(BB) *** DHM Baroque Esprit Analogue/Dig. 05472 77435-2 [77188-2]. Soloists, Les Adieux, Schola Cantorum Basiliensis.

A wholly engaging anthology. The dozen pieces for two flutes, two violins and continuo deftly vary textures and the result is most attractive when the authentic timbres are so fresh. The following *Hamburg Flute sonata* needs to be played separately because there is a pitch change as it begins; but it is the *Trio sonatas* which form the kernel of the concert, and they each have touchingly nostalgic *Adagios* to contrast with their bright outer movements. The programme ends with a miniature (7-minute) pastoral cantata, *Phyllis and Thirsis*, obviously selected because it includes obbligatos for two flutes. Although designed as a solo soprano work, it is even more effective in dialogue between tenor and soprano, and especially so when both soloists (Nigel Rogers and Rosmarie Hofmann) rise to the occasion as they do here. Excellent recording – a real bargain.

Flute sonatas: in C, Wq.73; in D, Wq.83; in E, Wq.84; in G, Wq.85; in G, Wq.86.

(BB) **(*) ASV Quicksilva Dig. CDQS 6205 [(M) id.]. Christopher Hyde-Smith, Jane Dodd (harpsichord).

This collection is preferable to its Naxos competitor – see below. The ASV performances have plenty of life and feeling and, though again the recording is resonant and with the flute close-miked, the effect is very spirited. The collection includes one of the least predictable of these works, Wq.73 (*in C major*), written in 1745, with its striking *Allegro di molto* opening movement, alongside Wq. 84 (*in E major*) of four years later, which has an equally remarkable central *Adagio di molto*.

Flute sonatas: in D, Wq.83; in E, Wq.84; in G, Wq.85; in G, Wq.86; in C, Wq.87.

(BB) **(*) Naxos Dig. 8.550513 [id.]. Béla Drahos, Zsuzsa Pertis (harpsichord).

These sonatas sound less exploratory in idiom and less unpredictable than is often the case with this composer in these simply stated and highly musical performances by Drahos and Pertis. They are recorded in an ecclesiastical acoustic and, although the acoustic could with advantage have been drier, the effect is natural.

Keyboard sonatas: in B flat, Wq.62/16; In G, Wq.65/22; in E min., Wq.65/30; in A, Wq.65/37; in G, Wq.65/48; in A, Wq.70/1; Rondo in E flat, Wq.61/1.

(BB) *** Naxos Dig. 8.5536450 [id.]. François Chaplin (piano).

François Chaplin plays these works freshly and confidently on the modern piano rather than on the clavichord (or harpsichord) which the composer would have expected, and he makes no attempt to imitate those instruments with clipped articulation and restricted colouring, although his style is nimble and never heavy. Even the earliest work here, Wq.65/22 (1748), with its flowing *Andante* and neatly pointed finale proves most effective on the modern instrument. The result demonstrates how foward-looking these sonatas are, especially the appealingly expressive slow movements of the later works. The A minor *Andante con tenerezza* from the Sonata Wq.70/1 (1758) surely anticipates Mozart, and the fine *Adagio e sostenuto* from the *G major Sonata*, Wq.65/48, is another highlight. This was a late work (1783), written for the 'Bogen-Clavier', an early attempt at designing a keyboard instrument on which notes could be sustained. The closing *Rondo* of 1786 is particularly successful in using the piano's fuller sonority.

Oboe sonata in G min., Wq.135.

(BB) **(*) DHM/BMG Baroque Esprit 05472 77440-2 [id.]. Michel Piguet, Colin Tilney – J. S. BACH: *Oboe sonatas* **(*); W. F. BACH: *Polonaise in E flat.* ***

C. P. E. Bach's '*Hoboe solo*', as it is described on the manuscript, was probably written around 1740. Opening with a brief *Adagio*, Bach moves on to a perky *Allegro* and concludes with a movement marked *vivace*, in effect a theme with three variations. Although always spirited, it is the expressive quality of the writing which makes this sonata so individual, especially in the finale. The performance is polished and responsive, but the resonant yet forward recording does reduce the effective dynamic range.

Quartets (Trios) for flute, viola and fortepiano Nos. 1 in A min.; 2 in D; 3 in G. Wq. 93/5; Sonata for flute and continuo (Hamburg), Wq. 133.

(BB) *** HM/BMG Baroque Esprit Dig. 05472 77464-2 [(M) id.]. Les Adieux.

These delightful (1788) *Quartet/Trios* are also offered by Hogwood (see above), where the missing bass line has been replaced. Les Adieux present the music very successfully in a trio format. Piano, flute and viola are balanced so beautifully and detail is revealed so minutely that the listener is given the impression that an added cello would be 'a fifth wheel on the wagon'. The playing matches the music in its finish, with the most engaging lightness of touch and spontaneity, which also extends to the *'Hamburg' Flute sonata*, written two years earlier. Highly recommended.

Viola da gamba sonatas (for viola da gamba and continuo): *in G min., Wq. 88; in C & D, Wq. 136/7; Harpsichord sonatas in A min. (Württemberg No. 1), Wq. 49/1; in E (Prussian No. 3), Wq.48/3.*
(B) *** HM Musique d'abord Dig. HMA 1901410 [id.]. London Baroque (Charles Medlam, William Hunt, Richard Egarr).

Carl Philipp Emanuel wrote his sonatas for viola da gamba during a period when all over Europe the instrument was being replaced by the cello. The solo line lies comparatively high and Charles Medlam achieves an impressively full singing cantilena. Of the three works the *G minor* is particularly fine and it is very beautifully played. So are the splendid keyboard sonatas, where the level of invention is more immediately striking than in the two other gamba works. They are played with eloquence and spirit by Richard Egarr. The recording throughout is most naturally balanced, and at such a modest price this is a reissue which should not be missed by admirers of this highly individual composer.

Bach, Johann Christian (1735–82)

Clavier concertos, Op. 1/1–6; Op. 7/1–6.
(B) *** Ph. Duo (IMS) 438 712-2 (2) [id.]. Ingrid Haebler (fortepiano), V. Capella Ac., Melkus.

(i) *Clavier concertos, Op. 13/1–6;* (ii) *6 Sinfonias, Op. 3.*
(B) *** Ph. Duo 456 064-2 (2) [id.]. (i) Ingrid Haebler (fortepiano), V. Capella Ac., Melkus; (ii) ASMF, Marriner.

J. C. Bach composed three sets of *Clavier concertos*, each comprising six works. All the concertos here are in major keys and are attractive, well-wrought compositions. It would be difficult to find a more suitable or persuasive advocate than Ingrid Haebler, who is excellently accompanied and most truthfully recorded. There is some delightful invention here and it is difficult to imagine it being better presented.

The *Sinfonias* are beguilingly played by the Academy of St Martin-in-the-Fields under Sir Neville Marriner, and beautifully recorded. None of this can be called great music but it has an easy-going and fluent charm. Erik Smith, who has edited them, describes them as 'in essence Italian overtures, though with an unusual wealth of singing melody'.

Sinfonia concertante in F for oboe, cello and orchestra, T.VIII/6.
(M) **(*) Teldec/Warner 0630 12326-2. Schaeftlein, Bylsma, Leonhardt Cons. – C. P. E. BACH: *Double concerto for harpsichord and fortepiano* ***; W. F. BACH: *Double concerto for 2 harpsichords*. **(*)

The *Sinfonia concertante in F* is a pleasing but not distinctive work in two movements, given a good rather than distinctive performance.

Sinfonias concertantes in A for violin, cello and orchestra, SC 3; E flat for 2 violins, 2 violas, cello and orchestra (MSC E flat 1); E flat for 2 clarinets, bassoon and orchestra (MSC E flat 4); G for 2 violins, cello and orchestra, SC 1.
(BB) *** ASV CDQS 6138 [(M) id.]. London Festival O, Ross Pople.

The performances here are eminently vital and enthusiastic, and the recording is very bright and present. This is an invigorating disc which can be recommended strongly, especially at super-bargain price.

Sinfonias, Op. 3/1–6.
(BB) ** Naxos Dig. 8.553083 [id.]. Camerata Budapest, Gmür.

Bach's Op. 3 symphonies are essentially three-part Italian overtures and are full of lyrical melody, often of considerable charm. These works break no barriers but they clearly influenced the young Mozart, and the writing is easy-going and fluent. The *cantabile* quality of the writing is well captured by these elegant and polished performances by the Camerata Budapest, and Hanspeter Gmür's pacing of allegros is well judged and lively. The recording, however, made at the Festetich Castle, is very resonant. Yet horns and oboes are nicely integrated in a slightly recessed balance which is wholly natural.

Sinfonias, Op. 6/1–6.
(BB) **(*) Naxos 8.553084 [id.]. Camerata Budapest, Hanspeter Gmür.

The music of Op. 6 shows a distinct advance on Op. 3, with allegros more dramatic and often very spirited, and slow movements touchingly expressive. Affinities with Mozart are the more striking, and a link with Haydn is also suggested, particularly in the remarkable *G minor Symphony*, the last of the set, with its stormy outer movements suggesting *Sturm und Drang* and a darkly dramatic *Andante*. This is very strongly played here, as is the striking *E flat Symphony*, Op. 6/3; the weightiness of the recordings, which is very well balanced, suits the added gravitas of the performances, which retain also the music's 'singing' qualities.

6 Sinfonias, Op. 6; 6 Sinfonias, Op. 9; 6 Sinfonias, Op. 18; Overture, La calamità de cuori.
(B) *** Ph. Duo 442 275-2 (2) [id.]. Netherlands CO, David Zinman.

David Zinman secures good, lively playing from the Netherlanders and few (except dedicated authenticists) will quarrel with the results. A case could be made for giving some of the outer movements less elegance and greater weight. But if there are times when one feels that Zinman is too brisk, any newer versions using original instruments are likely to be brisker! Certainly Zinman gives stimulation and pleasure with the vigour of his presentation of the outer movements and the charm of the slower ones.

Sinfonias, Op. 9/1–4; Sinfonia concertante in A for violin and cello; Sinfonia concertante in E flat, for 2 violins, oboe and orchestra.
(BB) **(*) Naxos 8.553085 [id.]. Camerata Budapest, Hanspeter Gmür.

This disc is of interest not so much for the symphonies as for the two *Sinfonias concertantes* which are beautifully played, with stylish and appealing contributions from the soloists, all drawn from the orchestra. The solo writing in the *A major Sinfonia concertante* is quite elaborate, and in the *Andante* of the E flat work there is a surprise when the two solo violins introduce Gluck's *Che farò senza Euridice*, which is then taken up by the oboe. The Op. 9 symphonies are not perhaps as interesting overall as Op. 6, but the second of the set of four has a real lollipop *Andante con sordini*, presented over a pizzicato accompaniment. The balance is excellent.

6 Sinfonias (Grand overtures), Op. 18.
(BB) **(*) Naxos Dig. 8.553367 [id.]. Failoni O, Hanspeter Gmür.

Continuing their Naxos series, Gmür and the Failoni Orchestra give warm and graceful accounts of Op. 18. The spirited allegros are slightly cushioned by the resonance, but slow movements are phrased very musically (particularly the lovely, almost Handelian melody of Op. 18/2, which also has a fine oboe solo from Laszló Párkányi).

Bach, Johann Sebastian (1685–1750)

Complete orchestral works

(i) *The Art of Fugue; Brandenburg concertos Nos. 1–6;* (ii) *Harpsichord concertos Nos. 1–7;* (ii–iii) *Double harpsichord concertos Nos. 1–3; Triple harpsichord concertos Nos. 1–2;* (ii–iv) *Quadruple harpsichord concerto;* (v) *Oboe concertos Nos. 1–2; Oboe d'amore concerto;* (ii; vi) *Triple concerto for flute, violin and harpsichord;* (i; vii) *Violin concertos Nos. 1–2;* (i; vii–viii) *Double violin concerto;* (i) *A Musical offering; Orchestral Suites Nos. 1–4.*
(B) **(*) Ph. 456 377-2 (9) [(M) id.]. (i) ASMF, Marriner; (ii) Leppard, ECO; (iii) with Andrew Davis, Philip Ledger; (iv) Blandine Verlet; (v) Heinz Holliger, ASMF, Iona Brown; (vi) with Richard Adeney, José Luis Garcia; (vii) Henryk Szeryng; (viii) Maurice Hanson.

With the performances here given a consistent bedrock of excellence by the fine playing of the Academy of St-Martin-in-the-Fields under Sir Neville Marriner, this bargain compilation is certainly worth considering by collectors who need such a comprehensive anthology and who enjoy Bach's orchestral music played with the full expressive warmth, colour and finesse made possible by the use of modern instruments. The recordings too, dating from a vintage Philips recording decade, 1973–82, are of the highest quality. The highlight of the collection is the set of *Brandenburg concertos*, recorded at St John's, Smith Square, in 1980. They have long been a top recommendation, both for their artistic credentials and for their communication of spontaneous enjoyment. The *Art of Fugue* and *Musical offering*, which are available separately, also show Marriner and his group in fine form. The relative disappointment is the set of *Orchestral Suites*. This was Marriner's second recording and is much less impressive, not as vibrant as his earlier, Argo set, which is still available on a single Decca disc. Szeryng's accounts of the *Violin concertos* are also less than ideal for rather similar reasons (see below). Holliger's performances of the *Oboe* and *Oboe d'amore concertos* are much more recommendable, stylishly pointed, if leaning at times towards romantic expressiveness in slow movements. However, this is understandable when the *Siciliano* of the *D minor* (better known as the central movement of the *F minor Harpsichord concerto*) is so beautiful. The one striking omission here is the *Concerto for violin and oboe*, BWV 1060; but that is included in its alternative, keyboard format. Raymond Leppard and the ECO take over for the *Harpsichord concertos*, joined by distinguished soloists, and, as can be seen from our comments concerning their separate Duo reissue, they are among the finest modern-instrument versions. In short, this set offers much to please and stimulate the listener but, like almost all compilations of its kind, its appeal is not consistent throughout.

Ton Koopman Edition

Ton Koopman Edition, Part 1: *Brandenburg Concertos; Harpsichord concertos; Violin concertos.*
(M) *(*) Erato/Warner Dig. 0630 16162-2 (6). Soloists, Amsterdam Bar. O, Koopman.

This is not a set to recommend as a whole, as the *Brandenburg Concertos* are the only Koopman performances which can claim an unqualified recommendation.

Brandenburg concertos Nos. 1–3, BWV 1046–8; (i) *Triple concerto for flute, violin and harpsichord in A min., BWV 1044.*
(M) *** Erato/Warner Dig. 0630 16163-2 [id.]. Hazelzet, Manze, Koopman, Amsterdam Bar. O, Koopman.

Brandenburg concertos Nos. 4–6, BWV 1049–51; (i) *Organ concerto in D min., BWV 1059.*
(M) *** Erato/Warner Dig. 0630 16164-2. (i) Koopman; Amsterdam Bar. O, Koopman.

Relaxed and intimate, Koopman's account makes a highly recommendable mid-price alternative to Pinnock for those who prefer expressive contrasts to be less sharply marked. Like Pinnock, Koopman is not afraid to read *Affettuoso* on the slow movement of No. 5 as genuinely expressive and warm, though without sentimentality. As with Pinnock, players are one to a part, with excellent British soloists included in the band. In the *Third Concerto*, Koopman effectively interpolates the *Toccata in G*, BWV 916, as a harpsichord link between the two movements. The sound on CD is immediate, but not aggressively so. The *Triple concerto* is quite successful as a performance but, like the keyboard concertos discussed below, the resonant recording clouds inner detail. However, the little *Organ concerto* (reconstructed from music in Bach's Cantata No. 35) sounds attractively intimate.

Harpsichord concertos Nos. 1–2, BWV 1052–3; Nos. 5–6, BWV 1056–7.
(M) ** Erato/Warner Dig. 0630 16166-2. Koopman; Amsterdam Bar. O, Koopman.

The solo *Harpsichord concertos* are more successful in Koopman's hands than the multiple works, the effect neat and intimate if short of being rhythmically buoyant. But the keyboard profile is too slight to balance satisfactorily with the full orchestral sound, and clarity is often impaired by the resonance.

Harpsichord concertos Nos. 3–4, BWV 1054–5; 7 in G min., BWV 1058; (i) *Triple harpsichord concertos No. 1 in D min.; 2 in C, BWV 1063–4.*
(M) *(*) Erato/Warner Dig. 0630 16167-2. Koopman, (i) with Mathot, Marisaldi; Amsterdam Bar. O, Koopman.

Double harpsichord concertos Nos. 1–3, BWV 1060–62; (i) *Quadruple harpsichord concerto in A min., BWV 1065.*
(M) *(*) Erato/Warner Dig. 0630 16168-2. Koopman, Mathot, (i) with Mustonen, Marisaldi; Amsterdam Bar. O, Koopman.

Koopman is a fine player, but his set of the multiple *Harpsichord concertos* cannot be recommended with any confidence, for the performances and recording are disappointing. The harpsichords are made to sound jangly, with mechanical noises intruding, while the orchestra seems too heavy, lacking the transparency of period performances and with Koopman often failing to lift rhythms.

Violin concertos Nos. 1 in E; 2 in A min.; (i) *Double violin concerto in D min., BWV 1041–3.*
(M) * Erato/Warner Dig. 0630 16165-2. Monica Huggett, (i) with Alison Bury; Amsterdam Bar. O, Koopman.

Here allegros are reasonably lively, but slow movements are uninspiring in the two solo concertos, and the justly famous solo interplay in the *Double concerto* only just falls short of dullness – a remarkable achievement when the music itself is so inspired.

Ton Koopman Edition, Part 2: Keyboard works.
(M) **(*) Erato/Warner Dig. 0630 16169-2 (8) (details below).

The Art of fugue, BWV 1080 (version for two harpsichords).
(M) *** Erato/Warner Dig. 0630 16173-2. Ton Koopman, Tini Mathot (harpsichords).

Koopman chooses a pair of instruments made by Willem Kroesbergen of Utrecht, himself leading with a copy of a Rückers, while his colleague, Tini Mathot, uses another modern copy, but of a Couchet. The partnership works well: pacing is well judged and contrapuntal detail is clear, yet within a not too dry acoustic. The approach is didactic, but by no means rigid.

Chromatic fantasia and fugue in D min., BWV 903; French suite No. 5 in G, BWV 816; Italian concerto in F, BWV 971; A Musical offering, BWV 1079: Ricercar; Toccata in G, BWV 916.
(M) *** Erato/Warner Dig. 0630 16171-2. Ton Koopman (harpsichord).

Koopman is at his liveliest here, particularly in the brilliant *Chromatic fantasia*. The *French suite*, bright and brisk except for the thoughtful *Loure*, has plenty of character, and the *Italian Concerto* comes off equally vividly, helped by the clean projection of the Dutch harpsichord, built by Willem Kroesbergen of Utrecht, which Koopman is using for his Bach series.

French suites Nos. 1–6, BWV 812–17.
(M) *** Erato/Warner Dig. 0630 16172-2. Ton Koopman (harpsichord).

Ton Koopman fits all six *French suites* on to a single 70-minute CD. He uses a copy of a Rückers to admirable effect and these performances are stimulatingly rhythmic, exciting and thoughtful by turns. The best-known *Fifth suite* is especially spontaneous. The effect of the recording – not too closely balanced – is vivid and realistic. Ornaments are nicely handled and there is not a trace of pedantry here. A first choice among harpsichord recordings of this repertoire.

Goldberg Variations, BWV 988.
(M) **(*) Erato/Warner Dig. 0630 16170-2. Ton Koopman (harpsichord).

Koopman opens by taking the *Aria* very slowly and deliberately, so that the brilliance of the first variation makes a striking contrast. His survey produces plenty of vitality, articulation is clean, ornamentation is crisp and rhythms have plenty of lift. He does not play all the repeats (the playing time is 62 minutes), but the result flows convincingly and one has a sense of ongoing spontaneity. The recording is bright and realistic and the Kroesbergen harpsichord is an instrument of real character. Not an out-and-out first choice, but distinctly enjoyable and well worth considering at mid-price.

The Well-tempered Clavier, Book I, Preludes and fugues Nos. 1–24, BWV 846–69.
(B) ** Erato/Warner Duo Dig. 0630 16174-2 (2). Ton Koopman (harpsichord).

The Well-tempered Clavier, Book II, Preludes and fugues Nos. 25–48, BWV 870–93.
(B) ** Erato/Warner Duo Dig. 0630 16175-2 (2). Ton Koopman (harpsichord).

Ton Koopman uses a fine copy of a Rückers harpsichord and plays with consistent vitality and often with obvious thoughtfulness. But his speeds are often brisk, and at times there is a feeling that the forward momentum is pursued somewhat relentlessly. This is more striking in the first book than in the second. He is well recorded, and this set is inexpensive, being offered on two Bonsai Duo issues with each of the two CDs offered for the price of one. However, the non-existent documentation and inadequate titling is characteristic of this poorly produced bargain series.

Choral works: *Mass in B min., BWV 232; St Matthew Passion, BWV 244; St John Passion, BWV 245.*
(M) **(*) Erato/Warner Dig. 0630 16176-2 (7). Schlick, Wessel, Guy de Mey, Türk, Kooy, Prégardien, Mertens, Amsterdam Bar. Ch., Netherlands Bach Soc. Ch., Breda Sacramentskoor, Amsterdam Bar. O, Ton Koopman.

Koopman's collection of the three major Bach oratorios makes a fair mid-priced recommendation for those wanting period performances; each work is also available separately at premium price. Excellent, stylish soloists contribute to all three sets. Koopman's account of the *B minor Mass* is purposeful, consistently persuasive. The keenly responsive choral singing – rather soft-grained as recorded – is warmer than with most period performances, but it lacks something in brightness and bite. The soloists are at their finest in the *St John Passion*, and here the chorus has a much more dramatic profile (see below). In the *St Matthew Passion* Koopman is comparatively relaxed, avoiding speeds as controversially fast as Gardiner's, and again the choral sound lacks bite.

Orchestral Music

The Art of fugue, BWV 1080.
(M) ** DG Dig. 447 293-2. Col. Mus. Ant., Goebel.

The Cologne performance has the advantage of being fitted on to a single, mid-priced disc. The movements are divided between strings and solo harpsichord, and the two harpsichord players are often imaginative and expressive. The rhythmic vigour of the playing of Musica Antiqua confounds the scholarly idea that this is music *not* intended for public performance. But there are snags to the authentic style, notably the bite on the string-tone and also the expressive bulges which are at times exaggerated. The recording is remarkably clean and present.

The Art of fugue, BWV 1080; A Musical offering, BWV 1079.
(B) *** Ph. Duo 442 556-2 (2) [id.]. ASMF, Marriner.

How to perform *The Art of fugue* has always presented problems, since Bach's own indications are so sparse. Sir Neville Marriner in the edition he prepared with Andrew Davis has varied the textures most intelligently, giving a fair proportion of the fugues and canons to keyboard instruments, organ as well as harpsichord. In each instance the instrumentation has been chosen as specially suitable to that particular movement. Marriner's style of performance is profoundly satisfying, with finely judged tempi, unmannered phrasing and resilient rhythms, and the 1974 recording is admirably refined. Similarly, in the *Musical offering* Marriner uses his own edition and instrumentation: strings with three solo violins, solo viola and a solo cello; flute, organ and harpsichord. The performance here is of high quality, though some of the playing is a trifle bland. It is excellently recorded and is among the most successful accounts of the work.

Brandenburg concertos Nos 1–6, BWV 1046–51.
(B) *** Hyperion Dyad Dig. CDD 22001 (2) [id.]. Brandenburg Consort, Roy Goodman.
(B) *** EMI Dig. CD-EMX 2200 (*Nos. 1, 3 & 4*); CD-EMX 2201 (*Nos. 2, 5 & 6*) [(M) id. import]. Hanover Band, Anthony Halstead.
(B) *** Carlton Dig. PCD 2006 (*Nos. 1–3*); PCD 2009 (*Nos. 4–6*) [(M) id.]. ECO, Ledger.
(B) *** EMI forte CZS5 69749-2 (2) [CDFB 69749]. Polish CO, Jerzy Maksymiuk (with CORELLI: *Concerto grosso, Op. 6/8;* MANFREDINI: *Concerto grosso, Op. 3/12;* TORELLI: *Concerto a quattro, Op. 8/6;* LOCATELLI: *Concerto grosso, Op. 1/8* ***).
(BB) **(*) EMI Seraphim CES5 68516-2 (2) [CDEB 68516]. Bath Festival CO, Sir Yehudi Menuhin.
(BB) ** Naxos Dig. 8.550047 (*Nos. 1–3*); 8.550048 (*Nos. 4–6*). Capella Istropolitana, Bohdan Warchal.
(M) ** Teldec/Warner 9031 77611-2 (2) [id.]. VCM, Harnoncourt.
(B) (*) Millennium MCD 80075 (*Nos. 1–3*); MCD 80121 (*Nos. 4–6*) [MCA MCAD2 9831]. V. State Op. O, Hermann Scherchen.

Undoubtedly Pinnock's DG set of *Brandenburgs*, played on original instruments, represents the peak of his achievement as an advocate of authentic performance with sounds that are clear and refreshing but not too abrasive. The recordings are available on three mid-priced CDs (423 492-2) coupled with the *Orchestral Suites*, but the latter are somewhat controversial, bringing a distinct loss of breadth and grandeur.

In considering the other versions, that by the Linde Consort, coupled with the *Musical offering* (see below), can be spoken of in the same breath as Pinnock's set. However, the excellent Hyperion set of the *Brandenburgs* now re-emerges on a Dyad, with the two discs offered for the price of one. Roy Goodman not only directs but also acts as a string soloist. The stylish, lively playing is another attractive example of authenticism, lacking something in polish (notably from the horns in No. 1) but not in spirit, with the last three concertos especially fresh. There is also fine trumpet-playing from Stephen Keavy in No. 2. Characterization is strong and slow movements are often appealingly expressive, especially the delicately managed *Affettuoso* of No. 5 which, like No. 4, gains from the fine flute contribution of Rachel Brown. Tempi of outer movements are very brisk, but often bring the lightest rhythmic touch. Very good sound.

Anthony Halstead and the Hanover Band make a good alternative. The playing is consistently fresh and tempi are admirably chosen to give a feeling of liveliness and a joyful alertness without pressing on too hard while, throughout, lyrical lines flow pleasingly and textures are clean and transparent. The recording was made in the Henry Wood Hall and its warm acoustic provides an admirable background ambience for the music-making.

On Carlton, Ledger also has the advantage of fresh and detailed digital recording. He directs resilient, well-paced readings of all six concertos on modern instruments, lively yet never over-forced. The slow movements in particular are most beautifully done, persuasively and without mannerism. Flutes rather than recorders are used in No. 4.

When they were first issued, the EMI Polish set of *Brandenburgs* (recorded when the orchestra was on tour in England in 1977) was welcomed as the fastest on record – especially No. 3, in which a slow movement from a G major violin sonata is interpolated between the two regular movements. But now fast tempi are more the norm and the Polish players are left at the starting gate by Siegbert Rampe's La Stravaganza in Hamburg. Yet in its own right the Polish set is a first-class example of a stylish account on modern instruments. The crisp articulation and buoyancy of the playing are exhilarating. The orchestra is augmented with English recorder soloists who are obviously enjoying themselves, as does the trumpeter, who is called to flights of virtuosity in No. 2. No. 5 has a first-class contribution from the solo harpsichord player, Wladyslaw Klosiewicz. The analogue sound is first class, full and clear and very well balanced. What makes the set doubly attractive at its very modest price is the inclusion of a 1984 collection of key *concerti grossi* by Corelli, Manfredini, Torelli and Locatelli, each with a beautiful *Pastoral* slow movement to make a Christmas connection. They are very beautifully played and recorded.

Menuhin's stylish 1959 set of *Brandenburgs* has stood the test of time. It is played by the chamber-sized Bath Festival Orchestra, which includes gambas – Dennis Nesbitt and Ambrose Gauntlett – and recorders. Rhythms are sprung lightly and joyfully, and tempi are uncontroversially apt. The excellent soloists (unnamed in the current – inadequate – documentation) include Barry Tuckwell, Janet Craxton and Michael Dobson, while Dennis Clift is the first-rate trumpeter. Throughout there is a spontaneity that is consistently refreshing. With the pair of CDs offered for the price of one mid-priced disc, this is the least expensive among the more distinguished recordings of these much-recorded works.

Very well played and recorded, the Capella Istropolitana's set of the *Brandenburgs* offers comfortably old-fashioned performances, with speeds consistently on the slow side, both in Allegros and in slow movements. With rhythms generally well sprung, the results become sluggish only occasionally, as in No. 3 – but those who favour latter-day ideas on Bach interpretation should keep clear.

Harnoncourt's 1964 analogue set (recorded in the Great Hall of the Schönberg Palace) has now been reissued as part of Teldec's Das Alte Werk series. It was originally an early adventure in authenticity; it has undoubted interest but is of uneven musical appeal. The excessive closeness of the sound-picture, which is consistent throughout, means that there is nothing like a real pianissimo, and internal balances produce variable degrees of success: Nos. 2 and 5, for instance, integrate better than does No. 4. Generally tempi are traditional, but here and there – as in the plodding speed for the first movement of No. 2 and the insensitively fast first movement of No. 6 – the direction is less convincing.

Scherchen's Viennese *Brandenburgs* (from 1959), in spite of their warmth, are a non-starter. Of curiosity value only, they are obviously under-rehearsed: there is poor ensemble in No. 1, and the solo trumpet does not sound quite comfortable in the first movement of No. 2. Scherchen's tempi are very leisurely indeed, incredibly so in the first movement of No. 3, and they are funereal in No.5.

(i) *Brandenburg concertos Nos. 1–6;* (ii) *Flute concerto in G min.* (from *BWV 1056*); *Double concerto for violin, oboe and strings in D min.* (from *BWV 1060*).

(B) *** Decca Double 443 847-2 (2) [id.]. (i) ECO, Britten; (ii) ASMF, Marriner.

Britten made his recordings in the Maltings concert-hall in 1968. The result is a fairly ample sound that in its way goes well with Britten's interpretations. There is some lack of textural delicacy in the slow movements of Nos. 1, 2, 4 and 6; but the bubbling high spirits of the outer movements are hard to resist, and the harpsichordist, Philip Ledger, follows the pattern he had set in live Britten performances, with Britten-inspired extra elaborations a continual delight. As a makeweight for the Double Decca reissue, two more of Marriner's stylish performances of reconstructions of Bach's harpsichord concertos for alternative instruments have been added. First-class (originally Argo) recording, too.

Brandenburg concertos Nos. 1–6; Double concertos: (i) *for 2 harpsichords in C min., BWV 1062;* (ii–iii) *for violin & oboe in C min., BWV 1060;* (ii; iv) *Triple violin concerto in D* (arr. Hogwood from *Triple harpsichord concerto*), *BWV 1064*.

(B) **(*) O-L Double Dig. 455 700-2 (2) [id.]. AAM, Hogwood, with (i) Christophe Rousset, Hogwood; (ii) Catherine Mackintosh; (iii) Stephen Hammer; (iv) Christopher Hirons, Monica Huggett.

Though Hogwood's set of *Brandenburgs* is notably less persuasive than Pinnock's full-priced period-instrument set, with often brisk speeds, more metrical and less well sprung, the distinctive point is that, unlike most rivals, he has chosen the original Cöthen score rather than the usual text as sent to the Margrave of Brandenburg. Besides many detailed differences, this version has no *Polonaise* in the *First Concerto*, and the harpsichord cadenza in No. 5 is much less elaborate, 'more convincingly proportioned', as Hogwood himself suggests. Some may prefer the extra directness of Hogwood's approach over Pinnock's, with charm never a part of the mixture, more abrasive string-tone and brisker, less expressive slow movements, although Hogwood has a very considerable price advantage and now offers three extra concertos, each featuring fine solo contributions. Stephen Hammer's oboe playing in the *Adagio* of BWV 1060 is most sensitive, and the combination of Rousset and Hogwood himself in the work for two harpsichords is most felicitous, while many ears will find the *Triple violin concerto* in Hogwood's arrangement aurally more pleasing than Bach's alternative scoring for three harpsichords, when the solo playing brings such an easy bravura. Throughout the transparency and the linear clarity make a good case for the use of period instruments, although at times there is a hint of rhythmic stiffness in slow movements. Excellent recorded sound, with the expected added presence on CD.

Brandenburg concertos Nos. 1–6; (i) *Oboe concertos: in A* (from *BWV 1055*); *in D min.* (from *BWV 1059*); *in F* (from *BWV 1053*).
(M) **(*) DG 445 578-2 (2). COE, (i) with Douglas Boyd.

A spirit of fun infects the COE version of the *Brandenburg concertos*. Using modern instruments, these are among the happiest performances ever, marked by easily bouncing rhythms and warmly affectionate – but never sentimental – slow movements. Some may want more severity, but the joyful exuberance of Bach's inspiration is inescapable. Unfortunately, the first movement of No. 1 – the movement which many will sample first – takes relaxation too far, becoming almost ragged; conversely, the first movement of No. 6 is uncharacteristically rigid. Otherwise these performances, well recorded, give pure joy. However, to make this mid-priced reissue more inviting, DG have added the three *Oboe concertos*, reconstructed from keyboard concertos and cantata movements. The soloist, Douglas Boyd, principal oboe of the COE from its foundation, directs his colleagues in delectable performances. His resilient and imaginative playing goes with well-sprung rhythms, matching the infectious sense of fun found in the *Brandenburgs*. First-rate sound.

Brandenburg concertos Nos. 1–6; (i) *Organ concerto in D min., BWV 1059;* (ii) *Triple concerto for flute, violin and harpsichord in A min., BWV 1044.*
(M) *** Erato/ Warner Dig. 0630 13733-2 (2). Amsterdam Bar. O, Koopman, with (i) Koopman (organ); (ii) Hazelzet, Manze, Koopman (harpsichord).

Relaxed and intimate, Koopman's account of the *Brandenburgs* makes a recommendable alternative to Pinnock, for those who prefer expressive contrasts to be less sharply marked. As with Pinnock, players are one to a part, with excellent British soloists included in the band. In the *Third Concerto*, Koopman effectively interpolates the *Toccata in G*, BWV 916, as a harpsichord link between the two movements. The sound on CD is immediate, but not aggressively so. The two additional concertos make an attractive bonus, well played and recorded. In each case the slow movement is a highlight, particularly that of the reconstructed organ concerto, heard in a revision by Koopman himself.

Brandenburg concertos Nos. 1–3; (i) *Violin concertos Nos. 1 in A min.; 2 in E, BWV l041–2.*
(M) *** Ph. 442 386-2 [id.]. ECO, Leppard; (i) with Arthur Grumiaux.

Brandenburg concertos Nos. 4–6; (i) *Triple concerto in A min. for violin, flute and harpsichord, BWV 1044.*
(M) *** Ph. 442 387-2 [id.]. ECO, Leppard; (i) with Grumiaux, Garcia & Adeney.

Brandenburg concertos Nos. 1–6, BWV 1046–51; (i) *Violin concertos Nos. 1 in A min.; 2 in E;* (i–ii) *Double violin concerto in D min., BWV 1041–3.*
(BB) *** Virgin Classics Dig. Double VBD5 61403-2 (2) [CDVB 61403]. Scottish Ens., Jonathan Rees; with (i) J. Rees; (ii) Jane Murdoch.

Brandenburg concertos Nos. 1–6, BWV 1046–51; Violin concertos Nos. (i) *1 in A min.;* (ii) *2 in E;* (i; ii) *Double violin concerto in D min., BWV 1041–3.*
(BB) **(*) CfP Silver Double CDCFPSD 4769 (2) [id.]. (i) Kenneth Sillito; (ii) Hugh Bean; Virtuosi of England, Davison.

The Jonathan Rees set is the first issue in a new series of Doubles, issued to celebrate the tenth anniversary of the Virgin Classics label, with the two discs offered in the UK at the cost of one mid-priced CD. These modern-instrument Scottish *Brandenburgs* are in every way competitive. Directed with much spirit, they are freshly played, with warm, clear recording and excellent internal balance. The tempi seem very apt when the players so convey their enjoyment and the sound has such a pleasing bloom. Rees then becomes the principal soloist in equally warm, buoyant performances of the *Violin concertos*, with Jane Murdoch matching his stylishness in the *Double concerto*. Allegros are sprung infectiously, while slow movements are allowed full expressiveness without sentimentality. In the clear, digital recording the harpsichord continuo of Sally Heath is prominent without being distracting.

Leppard's mid-1970s Philips set with the ECO is higher-powered than the Rees Scottish performances, whose relaxed manner will for many be easier to live with. But the exhilaration of the Leppard set is undeniable: there is much to enjoy here and the soloists include John Wilbraham's trumpet in No. 2 and a piquant recorder contribution from David Munrow in No.4. The remastered sound is fresh and full. Grumiaux's accounts of the two solo concertos come from 1964, but the playing from one of the most musical soloists of our time is extremely satisfying. It has a purity of line and an expressive response that communicate very positively, and Leppard's stylish accompaniments have striking buoyancy. The *Triple concerto* (recorded two decades later) has plenty of vitality, too; although the balance is a little contrived, the effect is certainly vivid.

Arthur Davison's set of *Brandenburgs* was vividly recorded (in 1972), although the microphones are close, somewhat limiting the dynamic range. The playing is polished, robust and lively; slow movements are sensitive, and the brisk, unfussy approach of the conductor is impressive; however, in the last resort these performances lack the individuality of the Menuhin set offered at the same price on Seraphim (see above). What rights the balance on this CfP Silver Double is the set of *Violin concertos* which have been added to the second disc. Kenneth Sillito and Hugh Bean, both of them distinguished orchestral leaders as well as fine virtuosi, are outstandingly successful as soloists in the *Double concerto*. This is one of the most beautiful accounts of the lovely slow movement on record, deeply felt but pure and restrained. Though the accompaniments are not always ideally resilient, all three performances can be recommended warmly. The solo concertos are shared, Kenneth Sillito playing the *A minor Concerto* and Hugh Bean the *E major*. The spacious (1975) recording was made in the Fairfield Halls, Croydon. Excellent value.

Brandenburg concertos Nos. 1–6; A Musical offering, BWV 1079.
(M) *** Virgin Veritas/EMI Dig./Analogue VED5 61154–2 (2) [CDMB 61154]. Linde Consort, Hans-Martin Linde.

The Linde Consort is one of the most stylish and responsive of authentic performing groups working in Europe, and their recording sounds very fresh and vivid on CD. It can be strongly recommended, with sprung rhythms and generally well-chosen tempi, and these CDs deserve to rank alongside Pinnock's set. But, quite apart from the considerable bonus of the *Musical offering*, many will prefer the Linde version of the *Brandenburgs*, for the 1981 EMI recording is rather fuller than the DG Archiv sound, with the strings very slightly less immediate. In *Brandenburg No. 3* there is a distinct gain in body and warmth, and No. 6 (also for strings alone) again brings a slightly more ample texture, without loss of inner definition. In the *Musical offering* (recorded a year earlier) Hans-Martin Linde draws on the thinking of the American scholar, Ursula Kirkendale, whose conclusion favours the same sequence of movements as that adopted by Spitta – not that this is necessarily a major consideration, since with a little effort the listener can exercise his or her own preferences in playing the disc. Generally speaking, Linde is as stylish and accomplished as any of his rivals, and he and his six colleagues offer the preferred version of this work using original instruments. They are again warmly as well as clearly recorded; indeed the analogue to digital transfer is particularly natural, and this set offers remarkable value.

Brandenburg concertos Nos. 1–6, BWV 1046–51; Orchestral suites Nos. 1–4, BWV 1066–9; Chorale: Jesu, joy of man's desiring.
(BB) ** RCA Navigator 74321 30364-2 (3) [(M) id. import]. Augmented Lucerne Festival Strings, Baumgartner.

Brandenburg concertos Nos. 1, 5 & 6, BWV 1046, BWV 1050–51.
(M) ** [RCA Best 100 09026 61719-2]. Augmented Lucerne Festival Strings, Baumgartner.

Brandenburg concertos Nos. 2–3, BWV 1047–8; Orchestral suite No. 2, BWV 1067.
(M) ** [RCA Best 100 09026 61559-2]. Augmented Lucerne Festival Strings, Baumgartner.

Rudolf Baumgartner's recordings were made in 1977–8 and offer full, pleasingly natural sound, not sharply defined but not clouded either. Tempi are appreciably less brisk in the *Brandenburgs* than we would expect today, but the playing remains stylish in its way and certainly alive, while Baumgartner's warm *espressivo* in slow movements is undoubtedly appealing. In the *Suites* there is less difference in pacing, but the style is still more relaxed and dance movements are elegant. Aurèle Nicolet's flute contribution to No. 2 is a highlight and the famous *Badinerie* is most winning. Some will undoubtedly find Baumgartner too leisured in his manner, but what comes over here is the breadth of Bach's music, and the glorious *Air* from the *Third Suite* is very beautiful when the violin textures are rich and the phrasing has a restrained depth of feeling.

Brandenburg concertos Nos. 1–4, BWV 1046–9.
(B) **(*) [EMI Red Line Dig. CDR5 69877]. ASMF, Marriner.

Brandenburg concertos Nos. 5–6, BWV 1050–51; Orchestral Suite No. 1, BWV 1066.
(B) **(*) [EMI Red Line Dig. CDR5 69878]. ASMF, Marriner.

Orchestral Suites Nos. 2–4, BWV 1067–9.
(B) **(*) [EMI Red Line Dig. CDR5 69879]. ASMF, Marriner.

Marriner's third recordings of the *Brandenburgs* and *Suites* are currently available only in the USA. They are unexceptionable, with fine teamwork, superb ensemble and well-judged speeds, never too hectic. However, although the playing is freshly conceived, it also has a certain urbane quality (although this does not apply to George Malcolm's harpsichord contribution). The vividness of the playing is enhanced by the excellent sound, full in texture yet transparent too. Marriner's earlier Philips set, a little more eccentric and not quite so safe, might be preferred by some, but that is available only in a nine-disc boxed set – see above.

Brandenburg concertos Nos. 1–3; Orchestral Suite No. 1 in C, BWV 1066.
(M) (*) DG (IMS) Dig. 447 287-2. Col. Mus. Ant., Goebel.

Brandenburg concertos Nos. 4–6; Orchestral Suite No. 4 in D, BWV 1069.
(M) (*) DG (IMS) Dig. 447 288-2. Col. Mus. Ant., Goebel.

Reinhard Goebel's set with Cologne Musica Antiqua is one to have you disbelieving your ears. Even in an age of period performance that favours fast speeds, his allegros are hectic to the point of recklessness, in several instances comically impossible. It is hard not to laugh out loud at the speeds for both movements of No. 3 (the second more than the first) and even more at the sketchy strumming which purports to be the first movement of No. 6, 'without tempo indication', as the booklet reminds us. At Goebel's headlong speed the semiquaver arpeggios are hardly audible and even the repeated quavers sound rushed. It is a tribute to the virtuosity of the Cologne ensemble that otherwise they cope so well, usually playing with a good rhythmic spring. Abrasive, choppy of phrasing and employing squeeze techniques on sustained notes, they use a normal baroque orchestra with four first and four second violins, and again allegros are pushed forward to the point of frenzy. Vivid recording, but these reissues (available separately) cannot be recommended with any confidence, even to the most dedicated proponents of authenticity.

Brandenburg concertos Nos. 1–6; Orchestral Suites Nos. 3–4, BWV 1067–8.
(B) *(*) Teldec/Warner Ultima Dig. 0630 18944-2. VCM, Harnoncourt.

It is a sign of the maturing art of authentic performance that Harnoncourt's digital set of *Brandenburgs*, recorded in the early 1980s, sounds so laboured. Speeds are slow and rhythms heavy. There is some expert playing, both solo and ensemble, but the artificially bright and clinically clear recording gives an aggressive projection to the music-making. The pair of *Orchestral Suites*, too, are sadly lacking in finesse. His earlier, analogue versions of all these works are preferable (see above), but even these have been upstaged by more recent versions.

Harpsichord concertos Nos. 1–7, BWV 1052–8; No. 8 in D min. (reconstructed Kipnis), *BWV 1059.*
(B) *** Sony SB2K 53243 (2) [S2K 53243]. Kipnis, L. Strings, Marriner.

Harpsichord concertos Nos. 1–7, BWV 1052–8; Double harpsichord concertos Nos. 1–3, BWV 1060–62.
(B) *** Ph. Duo Analogue/Dig. 454 268-2 (2) [id.]. Raymond Leppard, Andrew Davis, Philip Ledger, ECO, Leppard.

Harpsichord concertos Nos. 1 in D min.; 2 in E; 3 in D; 4 in A; 5 in F min.; 6 in F; 7 in G min., BWV 1052–8; (i) *Double harpsichord concertos: Nos. 1 in C min.; 2 in C; 3 in C min., BWV 1060–62;* (i; ii) *Triple harpsichord concertos Nos. 1 in D min.; 2 in C, BWV 1063–4;* (i–iii) *Quadruple harpsichord concerto in A min., BWV 1065.*
(B) *** DG Analogue/Dig. 447 709-2 (3) [(M) id. import]. Pinnock with (i) Gilbert; (ii) Mortensen; (iii) Kraemer; E. Concert.

Harpsichord concertos Nos. (i) *1–5, BWV. 1052–6;* (i–ii) *Double harpsichord concertos Nos. 1–2, BWV 1060–61;* (iii; iv) *Triple harpsichord concerto in C, BWV 1064;* (iii–v) *Quadruple harpsichord concerto in A min., BWV 1065.*
(B) *** EMI CZS5 72010-2 [CDZB 71010] (2). George Malcolm; (i) Menuhin Festival O, Y. Menuhin; (ii) with Simon Preston; (iii) Pro Arte O, Boris Ord, with (iv) Eileen Joyce, Thurston Dart; (v) Denis Vaughan.

Pinnock's performances of the Bach *Harpsichord concertos* first appeared in 1981, and they have dominated the catalogue ever since. In the solo concertos he plays with real panache, his scholarship tempered with excellent musicianship. Pacing is brisk, but to today's ears, used to period performances, the effect is convincing when the playing is so spontaneous and the analogue sound bright and clean. The *Double*, *Triple* and *Quadruple concertos* are digital, and the combination of period instruments and playing of determined vigour certainly makes a bold effect. There is a bit more edge on the strings and everything is clearly laid out and forwardly projected. Outer movements emphasize the bravura of Bach's conceptions and, if slow movements could at times be more relaxed, those ears prepared to accept a hint of aggressiveness in the energetic musical flow will find this set as stimulating now as when it first appeared.

Anyone wanting the solo and double harpsichord concertos accompanied on modern instruments will find it hard to better this Philips Duo set. Leppard, Davis and Ledger play with skill and flair; the ECO shows plenty of life and, if the performances overall are less incisive than the English Concert versions with Pinnock, they have resilience and communicate such joy in the music that criticism is disarmed. The Philips sound is very realistic, the harpsichords life-size and not too forward; one does reflect that modern strings, however refined, create a body of tone which tends slightly to outweigh the more slender keyboard timbres. However, in the works for two or more harpsichords there is a pleasing absence of jangle. Excellent value.

Between 1967 and 1970 Igor Kipnis undertook a series of sessions with the London Strings (the St Martin's Academy under a pseudonym), recording not merely the well-known keyboard concertos but also an eighth work reconstructed by Kipnis himself from a fragment of nine bars identical with the *Sinfonia* of *Cantata No. 35*. Kipnis scored that movement for concertante forces and added two other movements from the same cantata; that is typical of his eager approach to Bach. The recording was made either in EMI's No. 1 Studio at Abbey Road or at the London Olympic studios, which produce a very similar balance of sound. This is more realistic than many made by CBS records at that time and the effect on CD is full and vivid. The music-making is infectious, the accompaniments are characteristic of the vintage ASMF recordings. At budget price this can certainly be recommended.

George Malcolm's five solo and two double concertos appeared on separate LPs between 1971 and 1974, and their praises were duly sung as being just about the best versions around in the analogue stereo era. Malcolm proved consistently brilliant in execution as the principal soloist, even if at the time his registration sometimes seemed controversial. His fast speeds for allegros were also unusual then, but they do not seem so today. His individuality is splendidly matched by Menuhin's warm and energetic conducting style, and he plays the famous slow movement of the *F minor* very simply and touchingly. The orchestra sounds pleasingly robust but never heavy, and the harpsichord balance is expertly managed. In the two *Double concertos* Simon Preston makes a lively partner, and the virtuosity in such movements as the finale of the *C major Concerto*, BWV 1060, is breathtaking. The degree of expressiveness in slow movements is entirely at one with the readings overall, and the recording is warm, vivid and well balanced. The recordings of the *Triple* and *Quadruple concertos* were made much earlier, in 1958, and now appear for the first time in stereo. Here Eileen Joyce skilfully leads the solo group. She was rarely heard playing the harpsichord but proves thoroughly at home. George Malcolm is thus relegated to the second position and Thurston Dart is third, with Denis Vaughan joining them for the *Quadruple concerto*. The orchestral style under Boris Ord is heavier than with Menuhin (especially in the *Largo* of BWV 1065) but not the solo playing, which is nimble and sparkling. Moreover the keyboard instruments are life-size and there is no jangle. Indeed the finale of the *Quadruple concerto* is delightfully and joyfully infectious. The recording in no way sounds its age. A first-class set that stands up well against all the later competition.

Clavier concertos Nos. 1–5; 7, BWV 1052–6, 1058.
(M) (**) Sony mono (*No. 1*)/stereo SM2K 52591 (2) [full price S2K 52591]. Glenn Gould (piano), Columbia SO, Bernstein (*No. 1*) or Golschmann.

The quality is variable; the *D minor Concerto* was recorded in 1957 with Bernstein conducting and the remainder date from various times: the *F minor*, BWV 1056, from 1958; the *D major*, BWV 1054, and *G minor*, BWV 1058, from 1967 and the remaining two from 1969, all with Vladimir Golschmann conducting. The performances are strongly personal and, whether or not you like them, strangely compelling. The finale of the *A major* is very, very fast and there is some odd but not excessively intrusive vocalise.

Clavier concertos Nos. 1 in D min., BWV 1052; 2 in E, BWV 1053; 3 in D, BWV 1054.
(BB) *** Naxos Dig. 8.550422 [id.]. Hae-won Chang (piano), Camerata Cassovia, Robert Stankovsky.

Clavier concertos Nos. 4 in A, BWV 1055; 5 in F min., BWV 1056; 6 in F, BWV 1057; 7 in G min., BWV 1058.
(BB) *** Naxos Dig. 8.550423 [id.]. Hae-won Chang (piano), Camerata Cassovia, Robert Stankovsky.

This splendid Naxos set marks the début both of the highly gifted young Korean pianist, Hae-won Chang, and of the excellent chamber ensemble drawn from members of the CSSR State Philharmonic Orchestra, based in Košice. Miss Chang is a highly sympathetic Bach exponent, playing flexibly yet with strong rhythmic feeling, decorating nimbly and not fussily. Robert Stankovsky directs freshly resilient accompaniments; and both artists understand the need for a subtle gradation of light and shade. Slow movements are highly imaginative and give much pleasure. The *Adagio* of the *D minor Concerto* (No. 1) and the *Siciliano* of the *E major* are appealingly thoughtful, while the famous *Largo* of the *F minor Concerto* is played with great delicacy of feeling. The *Larghetto* of the *A major* brings some memorably expressive dynamic contrasts from the Camerata strings. The imitative finale of the *F major* is attractively relaxed and brings some particularly felicitous ornamentation from the soloist. The digital recording, made in the House of Arts, Košice, is first class, with the piano balanced not too far forward.

Clavier concertos Nos. 1 in D min., BWV 1052; 2 in E, BWV 1053; 3 in D, BWV 1054; 4 in A, BWV 1055; 5 in F min., BWV 1056; 6 in F, BWV 1057; 7 in G min., BWV 1058; French suite No. 5.
(M) **(*) EMI Dig. CDM5 65173/4-2 [id.]. Andrei Gavrilov (piano), ASMF, Marriner.

In terms of dexterity and clarity of articulation, Andrei Gavrilov cannot be faulted and he produces some beautiful sound when his playing is lyrical and relaxed. If at times one feels he pushes on relentlessly, and his incisive touch can be a bit unremitting in some movements, there are also a lot of memorable things. Indeed in the slow movement of the *D minor* and *F minor concertos* there is playing of real poetry and delicacy – and, for that matter, in the finale of the *A major*. The recordings are excellently balanced, with the piano well integrated into the overall picture.

Clavier concerto No. 1 in D min., BWV 1052.
(M) **(*) Decca 448 598-2 [id.]. Vladimir Ashkenazy (piano), LSO, Zinman – CHOPIN: *Piano Concerto No. 2* ***; MOZART: *Piano concerto No. 6.* **(*)

This is no imitation of a plucked string instrument but the piano on its own terms, with a wide variety of colour in the first movement and gentle half-tones in the *Adagio*. In the finale there are some surprisingly pianistic figurations. David Zinman's accompaniment is most stylish, buoyantly rhythmic in the allegros; textures are fuller than we would expect today, but the effect is never heavy. Excellent (1965) recording, but this seems a curious coupling for a fine Chopin reissue in Decca's Classic Sound series.

Oboe d'amore concertos: in D, BWV 1053; in A, BWV 1055. Oboe concertos: in G min., BWV 1056; in D min., BWV 1059; (i) *Double concerto for oboe and violin in C min., BWV 1060.*
(BB) ** Naxos Dig. 8.554169 [id.]. Christian Hommel; (i) with Lisa Steward; Cologne CO, Helmut Müller-Brühl.

These works (except BWV 1059 and 1060) are generally better known in their harpsichord versions, but Chrisian Hommel, a most sensitive soloist, makes a good case for the present formats. The problem of the slow movement in BWV 1059 is solved by the interpolation of a very beautiful *Adagio* by Alessandro Marcello. The Cologne Chamber Orchestra under Helmut Müller-Brühl provide neat, polished accompaniments, although he is not as deft as Marriner (with the ASMF) in this repertoire. The Naxos recording is fresh, well balanced and natural.

Violin concertos Nos. (i) *1–2;* (ii) *Double violin concerto, BWV 1041–3;* (iii) *Double concerto for violin & oboe in C min., BWV 1060.*
✿ (M) *** Ph. 420 700-2. Grumiaux; (ii) Krebbers, (iii) Holliger; (i–ii) Les Solistes Romandes, Arpad Gerecz; (iii) New Philh. O, Edo de Waart.
(M) *** Nimbus Dig. NI 7031 [id.]. Oscar Shumsky, Scottish CO; with (ii) John Tunnell; (iii) Robin Miller.
(M) *** Classic fM Dig. 75605 57008-2. Joji Hattori, with (i) James Clark, (ii) Robin Williams; SCO, Hattori.
(M) **(*) Sony Stern Edition I Analogue/Dig. SMK 66471 [id.]. Isaac Stern, with (i) ECO/Schneider; (ii) Perlman, NYPO, Mehta; (iii) Gomberg, NYPO, Bernstein.

Arthur Grumiaux is joined in the *Double concerto* by Hermann Krebbers. The result is an outstanding success. The way Grumiaux responds to the challenge of working with another great artist comes over equally clearly in the concerto with oboe, reconstructed from the *Double harpsichord concerto in C minor*. Grumiaux's performances of the two solo concertos are equally satisfying.

One has only to sample the simple beauty of Shumsky's playing in the *Andante* of the *A minor Violin concerto* to be won over to his dedicated Bach style, which is not quite as pure as Grumiaux's but is seductive in its simplicity of line and tonal beauty. John Tunnell makes highly musical exchanges with him in the *Double violin concerto* and Robin Miller is a no less appealing partner in the work for violin and oboe, and his line in the slow movement is beautifully echoed by Shumsky. Shumsky directs the orchestra from the bow and, although the sound is full in the way of modern-instrument performances, rhythms are resilient and there is no excess weightiness in the bass. The recording is warm to match. A most enjoyable collection for those looking for (fairly) modern (1984) digital recordings of these works at mid-price.

This Classic fM disc is outstanding in every way, not just offering performances which stand high among versions using modern instruments, but full, immediate recording and a generous measure of four concertos instead of the more usual three, with the *Violin and oboe concerto*, reconstructed from the *Double harpsichord concerto in C minor*, as well as the three great violin works. Joji Hattori, winner of the Menuhin International Competition in 1989, plays with a tone both sweet and pure, flawless in intonation and immaculate in crisply alert passage-work. As director, he draws from the orchestra playing both clear and well sprung, with the clarity enhanced by the recording, and he is well matched by both his duet partners. These performances gain over most versions using modern instruments not just in the transparency of texture but also in the choice of speeds, brisk but never breathless, with slow movements in particular flowing sweetly and easily, never stickily romantic. An ideal Bach concerto compilation.

At a time when the pursuit of authenticity has accustomed us to pinched sound in Bach and Vivaldi, it is good to have such rich performances as these by Stern, although one has to accept that orchestral accompaniments are heavier and tempos of allegros are slower under Schneider and Bernstein than we would expect today. Stern's glorious tone and richness of line is compensation enough. The solo concertos were recorded in London in 1976, the *Concerto for violin and oboe* in the Avery Fisher Hall a decade earlier; but the *Double concerto*, most inspirational of all, came from Stern's sixtieth birthday concert in the autumn of 1980. Stern nobly concedes first place to Perlman in this work. Mehta is perhaps not the ideal conductor in this music, but the feeling of a live occasion comes over strikingly and the slow movement is glorious. The applause at the close is well deserved. Bernstein takes over for the *Concerto for oboe and violin* and, with tempi relaxed, he clearly relishes the beauty of the *Adagio* in which Gomberg and Stern exchange the melody in a gentle conversation. In this work the recording is very resonant, and at times in the finale the balance between the soloists has the violin dominating at the expense of the oboe.

(i) *Violin concertos Nos. 1 in A min.; 2 in E;* (i; ii) *Double violin concerto in D min., BWV 1041–3;* (i; iii) *Double concerto for violin and oboe in C min., BWV 1060. Orchestral Suites Nos. 1 in C;* (iv) *2 in B min.* (for flute and strings); *3 in D, BWV 1066–8.*
(BB) *** EMI Seraphim (SIS) CES5 68517-2 (2) [CDEB 685172]. (i) Y. Menuhin; (ii) Christian Ferras; (iii) Leon Goossens; (iv) Elaine Schaffer; Bath Festival CO, Sir Yehudi Menuhin.

This is one of the very best bargains in the EMI/Seraphim catalogue, offering a pair of discs for the cost of one mid-priced CD. The documentation – or lack of it – is no credit to the famous old EMI trademark, but the music-making is of the highest order. The *Violin concertos* date from 1960 and, played as they are here by Menuhin (in very good form), both the solo concertos take flight, for their balance of warmth, humanity and classical sympathy is very appealing. In the *Double violin concerto* Ferras matches his timbre beautifully to that of Menuhin and the duet is a real partnership, with the slow movement especially fine. Leon Goossens makes a ravishing contribution to the *Adagio* of the *Concerto for violin and oboe*, the only slight snag being that the oboe is too backwardly balanced in the outer movements. To complete this attractive Menuhin/Bach package, we are offered three of the four *Orchestral Suites*, where Menuhin finds an admirable balance between freshness and warmth, conveying the music's spirit and breadth without inflation. The *Suites* date from 1961 and the *Concerto for violin and oboe* from 1962; and the current remastering brings sound which is quite full, yet clear.

(i) *Violin concertos Nos. 1 in A min.; 2 in E;* (ii) *Double concerto, BWV 1041–3;* (iii) *Orchestral Suite No. 4 in D, BWV 1068.*
(B) **(*) DG Classikon 449 844-2 [(M) id. import]. (i–ii) D. Oistrakh, RPO, Goossens; (ii) with I. Oistrakh; (iii) Munich Bach O, Karl Richter.

It is good to have David Oistrakh's justly renowned performances back in the catalogue on DG's bargain Classikon label, since the playing is peerless and can be ranked alongside the Grumiaux versions. In the *Double concerto* father and son are suitably contrasted in timbre and the performance of the great slow movement is Elysian. The 1961 recording hardly sounds dated. Richter's account of the *Fourth Orchestral Suite* is rhythmically unstylish in the matter of double-dotting, but is otherwise alert – less heavy than we had remembered.

(i) *Violin concertos Nos. 1 in A min.; 2 in D min., BWV 1041–2; Double violin concerto in D min., BWV 1043.* (Unaccompanied) *Violin partita No. 2 in D min., BWV 1004.*
(M) *(*) Ph. Dig./Analogue 454 128-2. Gidon Kremer; (i) with ASMF.

Kremer adopts (by electronic means) both solo roles in the *Double concerto* and thus the interplay of human personality is lost in this most human of works. Kremer also directs the accompanying ensemble, so these interpretations cannot be accused of any kind of artistic inconsistency – indeed they have the forward thrust of a determined advocate, in slow movements as well as allegros, which are extremely vigorous. The same comment might be applied to his recording of the solo *Partita*, which includes the famous *Chaconne*. There is no doubting the facility of his playing but he conveys little sense of musical enjoyment. The end effect is relentless and, despite vivid recording (the concertos are digital), these performances offer only limited rewards.

Violin concertos Nos. 1 in A min.; 2 in E; Double violin concerto in D min., BWV 1041–3; Sonata in E min., BWV 1023 (arr. Respighi for violin and strings); *Suite No. 3, BWV 1068: Air*.
(BB) **(*) Naxos Dig. 8.550194 [id.]. Nishizaki, Jablokov, Capella Istropolitana, Oliver Dohnányi.

The first thing about the Naxos recording that strikes the ear is the attractively bright, gleaming sound of the orchestral string-group, who play with fine resilience. Neither soloist is a strong personality and the espressivo in the *Adagio* of the *E major* solo *Concerto* and in the famous lyrical dialogue of the slow movement of the *Double concerto* brings rather deliberate phrasing. Yet these players are certainly musical, and there is a sense of style here and plenty of vitality in allegros. The Respighi arrangement is effective enough, and the concert ends with Bach's most famous string tune, played simply and eloquently.

Violin concertos Nos. 1 in A min.; 2 in E; (i) *Double concerto, BWV 1041–3.*
(M) *** HM/BMG GD 77006 [77006-2-RG]. Sigiswald Kuijken; (i) Lucy van Dael; La Petite Bande.

Kuijken is a fine Bach player, and these performances of the *Violin concertos* are well worth considering by those who want period performances on original instruments. The slight edge on the solo timbre is painless and La Petite Bande provide lively, resilient allegros, the playing both polished and alert. Excellent, well-balanced, 1981 digital recording. But the measure is short.

(i) *Violin concertos Nos. 1 in A min.; 2 in E;* (i–ii) *Double violin concerto in D min., BWV 1041–3. Orchestral suites Nos. 1–4, BWV 1066–9.*
(B) ** Ph. Duo 446 533-2 (2) [id.]. ASMF, Marriner; with (i) Henryk Szeryng; (ii) Maurice Hasson.

Henryk Szeryng first recorded the Bach *Violin concertos* for Philips with the Winterthur Collegium Musicum in the 1960s, and those performances were imbued with both dignity and classical feeling; the slow movements were particularly fine. Alas, his later (1976) recordings with Marriner cannot match the earlier versions in spontaneity, depth of feeling or understanding; moreover they do not displace the finest of rival accounts. The *Double concerto* (with Maurice Hasson) is particularly disappointing. Similarly, Marriner's second analogue recording of the four *Orchestral Suites*, made in 1978, is no match for his first (1970) set for Argo/Decca (see below). The movements in which he has changed his mind – for example the famous *Air* from the *Suite No. 3*, which here is dangerously slow – are almost always less convincing, and that reflects the very qualities of urgency and spontaneity which made the earlier, Argo version so enjoyable. It must be said, however, that the Philips sound is full and naturally balanced, though ears used to period instruments may find textures too ample (not the case in the remastered Decca record).

Violin concertos Nos. 1 in A min.; 2 in E, BWV 1041–2; (i) *Double concerto for violin & oboe in C min., BWV 1060.*
(B) **(*) [EMI Dig. Red Line CDR5 72559]. Zimmermann; (i) Black; ECO, Tate – MOZART: *Violin concerto No. 3.* ***

Zimmermann's silkily romantic style is very pleasing in what now sounds a rather old-fashioned way, with speeds extreme in both directions and warm vibrato colouring the slow movements. This is enjoyable enough, but the substitution of the *Violin and oboe concerto* (worthwhile in itself) for the *Double violin concerto* hardly makes it any more attractive as a grouping.

Double violin concerto in D min., BWV 1043.
(M) *(*) RCA 09026 61746-2 [id.]. Heifetz, Friedman, London New SO, Sargent – BRAHMS: *Double concerto;* MOZART: *Sinfonia concertante.* **

Heifetz and Friedman make a good if unequal partnership, although the slow movement certainly brings a distinctive interplay. The close balance of the soloists tells against the performance, and Sargent's accompaniment seems relatively unstylish to today's ears. The 1961 stereo is acceptable.

A Musical offering, BWV 1079.
(BB) **(*) Naxos Dig. 8.553286 [id.]. Capella Istropolitana, Christian Benda.
(M) ** Teldec/Warner 0630 13563-2. VCM, Harnoncourt.

Bach dedicated his *Musical offering* to Frederick the Great, and he added to the title (in Latin): *'By command of the King the theme, and the rest worked out in canonic style'*. Christian Benda uses a small chamber group. Strings alone, with a minimum of vibrato, play the framing *Ricercars*, the opening taken fairly briskly, the conclusion slowly and rather more expressively. The first group of canons add in flute, oboe, and bassoon; in the second group, the stringed instruments predominate. A harpsichord joins in the first, and the cor anglais and bassoon dolorously share the last (common) solution of the four offered alternative proposals for solving Bach's so-called 'puzzle canon'. Bach here provides one part only and leaves the performers to decide where the second part should enter. The *Trio sonata*, at the centre, is given a pleasing performance, expressive and lively, and overall this seems a thoroughly musical interpretation of a work about which Bach left little in the way of instructions, as to either the order of the 13 movements or their instrumentation. The recording is excellent, clear yet with a pleasing bloom, and the result, if understandably a little didactic at times, is undoubtedly fresh.

Harnoncourt's recording dates from 1970. It is musically sound, somewhat plain-spun and a little lacking in imaginative vitality; but it is well recorded and is offered at mid-price. Short measure at 46 minutes.

Orchestral suites Nos. 1–4, BWV 1066–9.
(M) *** Decca 430 378-2; *430 378-4* [id.]. ASMF, Marriner.
(BB) Naxos *(*) Dig. 8.554043 [id.]. Capella Istropolitana, Jaroslav Dvořák.
(B) * Decca Dig. 448 231-2 [id.]. Stuttgart CO, Karl Münchinger.

Orchestral suites Nos. 1–4; Violin concerto movement in D, BWV 1045; Sinfonias from Cantatas Nos. 29; 42; 209.
(B) *** Hyperion Dyad Dig. CDD 22002 (2) [id.]. Brandenburg Consort, Roy Goodman.

Roy Goodman directs brisk and stylish readings of the four Bach *Orchestral Suites*, which are aptly supplemented by four *Sinfonias*, each following a suite in the same key. Though in the *Suites* Goodman in his eagerness occasionally chooses too breathless a tempo for fast movements, the lightness of rhythm and the crispness of ensemble are consistently persuasive, with textures cleanly caught in excellent, full-bodied sound. These are among the finest versions on a long list, with Rachel Brown an exceptionally warm-toned flautist in No. 2. Goodman observes all repeats, making the opening overtures longer than usual.

Marriner's 1970 recording of the Bach *Suites* with the ASMF comes on a single CD (77 minutes 48 seconds) and the remastering of the fine (originally Argo) recording is fresh and vivid. The playing throughout is expressive without being romantic, and always buoyant and vigorous. A fine bargain for those not insisting on original instruments; there is nothing remotely unstylish here.

Naxos originally issued the Capella Istropolitana set of the Bach *Suites* on two CDs, which apparently makes this new transfer on to a single, 80-minute disc an exceptional bargain. The performances on modern instruments are clean and direct in their Bachian manners, with crisp ensemble and clear recording. Unfortunately, Dvořák finds it hard to give the necessary lift to rhythms, tending to drive on with first beats evenly stressed in sewing-machine style, often at fast speeds. The more measured dance movements tend to become heavy with this treatment and, though the melody of the celebrated *Air* of the *Suite No.3* is well moulded, it goes with a stodgy rhythm below. Readers would be much better advised to pay rather more for Marriner's set.

Münchinger's 1985 digital set of the four *Orchestral Suites* has, alas, been bypassed by musical history. In the days of LP he pioneered the performance of Bach on an apt scale, but the present performances, although well played and brilliantly recorded, sound unattractively heavy, with rhythms unlifted.

Orchestral suites Nos. 1–3, BWV 1066–8.
(BB) ** RCA Navigator 74321 24196-2 [(M) id. import]. Lucerne Festival Strings, Baumgartner.

Rudolf Baumgartner offers quite stylish performances, beautifully recorded in the late 1970s. This is the way we used to hear these works played before the advent of period instruments. He has excellent wind players, notably the flautist Aurèle Nicolet, the soloist in No. 2. Only three of the four *Suites* are included, but this Navigator CD is in the very lowest price-range and is certainly enjoyable.

CHAMBER MUSIC

(Unaccompanied) *Cello suites Nos. 1–6, BWV 1007–12.*
(M) *** Sony Dig. S2K 63203 (2) [id.]. Yo-Yo Ma.
(M) *** DG 449 711-2 (2) [id.]. Pierre Fournier.
(B) *** Ph. Duo 442 293-2 (2) [id.]. Maurice Gendron.
(M) (***) EMI mono CHS5 66215-2 (2) [ZDHB 66215]. Pablo Casals.
(B) ** Cal. Approche Dig. CAL 6527 (*Nos. 1-3*); CAL 6528 (*Nos. 4-6*) [(M) id.]. Evzen Rattay.

Yo-Yo Ma's recording was made in connection with a series of TV programmes in which the visual imagery (with a different producer for each of the six *Suites*) ranged from garden scenes to the ice-skating of Torvill and Dean! As all the project collaborators realized, Bach's music stands up admirably without visual aids, but one may hope that this enterprising approach found a wider audience for this remarkable and uniquely inspired music. Ma's playing has a characteristic rhythmic freedom and favours the widest range of dynamic. The improvisatory effect is seemingly spontaneous and these performances are very compelling indeed, for Ma seems right inside every bar of the music. The break betweeen the two CDs comes in the middle of the (*Fourth*) *E flat major Suite*, so the second disc opens with the *Sarabande*, played very freely and with inspired concentration, while the famous *Gavotte* of No. 6, boldly accented, is no less individual. The first-class recording is very real and natural, with the warm acoustic never blurring the focus. The set comes generously illustrated with photo images from the TV series and excellent documentation.

Fournier's richly phrased and warm-toned performances carry an impressive musical conviction. Fournier can be profound and he can lift rhythms infectiously in dance movements, but above all he conveys the feeling that this is music to be enjoyed. This recording has been remastered splendidly for reissue in DG's 'Legendary Recordings' series and now has even greater presence and realism.

No one artist holds all the secrets in this repertoire, but few succeed in producing such consistent beauty of tone as Maurice Gendron, with the digital remastering firming up the focus of what was originally an excellent and truthful analogue recording. His phrasing is unfailingly musical, and although these readings have a certain sobriety (save, perhaps, for No. 6 which has distinct flair) their restraint and fine judgement command admiration. At Philips's Duo price, they can be given a warm welcome back to the catalogue.

It was Casals who restored these pieces to the repertory after long decades of neglect. Some of the playing is far from flawless; passage-work is rushed or articulation uneven, and he is often wayward. But he brought to the *Cello suites* insights that remain unrivalled. Casals brings one closer to this music than do most of his rivals. The sound is inevitably dated but still comes over well in this transfer.

Even alongside Maurice Gendron, let alone Yo-Yo Ma, Evzen Rattay's accounts seem very literal. He is a fine player and is naturally recorded, but rhythmically there is seldom much lift-off and little of the introspective feeling one finds in Ma, with the *Sarabande* of the *E flat major Suite* thoughtful, but hardly inspirational. On the whole the later suites (on the second disc) come off better than the earlier ones (the *Sarabande* of the *C minor Suite* notably so). Rattay is content to let the music speak for itself, and that is by no means a small virtue, but there is simply not the degree of imaginative flair one expects from an artist immersed in such wonderful music.

(Unaccompanied) *Cello suites Nos. 1–6, BWV 1007–12;* (i) *Viola da gamba sonatas Nos. 1–2, BWV 1027–8.*
(M) **(*) Mercury (IMS) 432 756-2 (2) [id.]. Janos Starker, (i) with György Sebök.

The Mercury set is not to be confused with the incandescent set Janos Starker made in the early days of mono LP (issued in the UK on the old Nixa label). These later performances come from 1963 and 1965 and are of great integrity and dedication, without having quite the same electric communication of the earlier recording. The two *Viola da gamba sonatas* are not ideally balanced and favour György Sebök's piano; though there is no question of his artistry, the actual sound of his instrument is a bit shallow and wanting in colour. Recommended, but not in preference to Fournier.

Flute sonatas Nos. 1 in B min.; 2 in E flat; 3 in A; 4 in C; 5 in E min.; 6 in E, BWV 1030–35.
(BB) *** ASV Quicksilva CDQS 6108 [(M) id.]. William Bennett, George Malcolm, Michael Evans.

Flute sonatas Nos. 1 in B min., BWV 1030; (i) *4 in C* (with continuo), *BWV 1033; 6 in E, BWV 1035* (with continuo). *Sonata in G min., BWV 1020* (now attrib. C. P. E. Bach); (i) *Trio sonata in G, BWV 1039.*
(BB) ** Naxos Dig. 8.553755 [id.]. Petri Alanko, Anssi Mattila (harpsichord); (i) with Jukka Rautasalo.

(i–ii) *Flute sonatas Nos. 2 in E flat, BWV 1031; 3 in A, BWV 1032;* (i–iii) *5 in E min.* (with continuo), *BWV 1034.* (i) *Partita for solo flute in A min., BWV 1013.*
(BB) ** Naxos Dig. 8.553754 [id.]. (i) Alanko; (ii) Mattila (harpsichord); (iii) with Rautasalo.

Flute sonatas (for flute and harpsichord) *Nos. 1 in B min., BWV 1030; 3 in A, BWV 1032; 5 in E min., BWV 1034; 6 in E, BWV 1035.*
(M) *** HM Suite Dig. HMT 790065 [id.]. Marc Beaucoudray, William Christie.

William Bennett uses a modern flute, and in the first three sonatas he and George Malcolm manage without the nicety of including a viola da gamba in the continuo. In *Sonatas Nos. 4–6* the two players are joined by Michael Evans and the bass is subtly but tangibly reinforced and filled out, though the balance remains just as impressive. The playing, as might be expected of these artists, has superb character: it is strong in personality yet does not lack finesse. Moreover it is strikingly alive and spontaneous and, since the CD transfer brings the most vivid presence without the sound being in the least overblown, this can be enthusiastically recommended at super-bargain price to all but those who demand the finer points of authenticity above all else. Bennett himself has made the reconstruction of the first movement of BWV 1032.

These two Naxos CDs inexpensively cover all Bach's major *Flute sonatas*, including one now thought to be by his son, Carl Philipp Emanuel. They are played very musically and in good style. However, the

ASV Quicksilva super-bargain disc remains a more obvious choice unless the collector finds the other works essential.

Those looking for period performances will surely be delighted with the Harmonia Mundi disc. Marc Beaucoudray makes the most delightful sounds on his baroque flute (not in the least watery), and the balance with William Christie's (Dowd) harpsichord could not be improved on. They play beautifully together, with great sensitivity and a true sense of baroque style; the result is altogether captivating. The acoustic, too, is ideally judged.

Sonatas for solo guitar (trans. from *Unaccompanied Violin sonatas Nos. 1 in G min.; 2 in A min.; 3 in C, BWV 1001, 1003 & 1005*, arr. Barrueco).
(M) *** EMI CDM5 56416-2 [id.]. Manuel Barrueco.

Instead of playing the usual lute suites, Manuel Barrueco has transcribed Bach's three *Sonatas for Unaccompanied Violin*, and the results are astonishingly successful. He makes them entirely his own, and such is the magnetism of this playing that, while under his spell, one almost forgets their original provenance. His technical mastery is matched by his sense of line and colour. The thoughtful improvisational feeling in the opening *Adagio* of the *C major Sonata* or the *Grave* which begins the *A minor* is very compelling. The fugues are beautifully clear, and his crisp articulation of the closing *Allegros* of both these works shows extraordinary control and unexaggerated virtuosity, to say nothing of a remarkable use of light and shade. The famous swirling *Presto* which ends the *G minor* (No. 1) is a *tour de force*. In short, Barrueco is a true Bach player, and these performances are a joy to the ear, for the guitar is beautifully recorded.

Lute suites transcribed for guitar

Lute suites (arranged for guitar) *Nos. 1–3, BWV 995–7. Prelude in C min.; Fugue in G min., BWV 999–1000.*
(B) *** Sony SBK 62972; *SBT 62972* [id.]. John Williams (guitar).

Lute suite No. 4, BWV 1006a; Prelude, fugue and allegro in E flat, BWV 998. (Unaccompanied) *Cello suite No. 3, BWV 1009: Bourrées Nos. 1–2.* (i) arr. guitar and organ: *Cantata No. 140: Chorale: Wachet Auf!; Fugue à la gigue in G, BWV 877; Italian concerto, BWV 971: Allegro. Trio sonata No. 6 in G, BWV 530; Violin sonata No. 4, BWV 1017: Adagio.*
(B) **(*) Sony Analogue/Dig. SBK 62973; *SBT 62973* [id.]. John Williams (guitar); (i) with Peter Hurford (organ).

John Williams shows a natural response to Bach, and his performances of the four *Lute suites* are among his finest records. The first of these two discs can be recommended unreservedly: the flair of his playing, with its rhythmic vitality and sense of colour, is always telling. It includes, besides the first three *Suites*, the *Prelude in C minor*, BWV 999, followed by the *Fugue in G minor*, BWV 1000, which originates in the unaccompanied *Violin sonata*, BWV 1001. The guitar is closely balanced but, when the volume is turned down, its image has a believable presence and background noise is not a problem.

The second disc opens with a most winning account of the *Fourth Suite* which includes a famous and catchy *Gavotte en Rondeau*, beloved of all guitarists from Segovia onwards. The work overall is of course a transcription of the *Partita in E major for unaccompanied violin* (BWV 1006) and ends with the famous *Chaconne*, which sounds interesting on the guitar but is not nearly as compulsive as the original. The transcriptions of the *Bourrées* from the *Cello suite* are effective enough; but not all listeners will care for the rest of the programme of rather contrived duets for guitar and organ (an unlikely combination), in spite of the distinguished presence of Peter Hurford and skilful balancing by the Sony engineers. Indeed the slow and squelchy treatment of the chorale, *Wachet auf*, with the organ playing the cantus firmus and the guitar accompanying is unendearing, and the *Adagio* from the *Violin sonata* sounds equally awkward. However, the delightful *Fugue à la gigue* (probably not by Bach at all), played as a dialogue, works infectiously, partly because here Hurford's registration is so apt. The *Trio sonata* works quite well too, for similar reasons; but in the movement from the *Italian concerto* the guitar sounds curiously like an added-on continuo.

(i) *Lute suites Nos. 1 in E min., BWV 996; 2 in C min., BWV 997;* (ii) *Trio sonatas Nos. 1 in E flat, BWV 525; 5 in C, BWV 529* (ed. Bream).
(M) *** RCA 09026 61603-2 [id.]. Julian Bream (i) (guitar); (ii) (lute), George Malcolm.

This RCA compilation comes from records made between 1965 and 1969. The two *Lute suites* are played with great subtlety and mastery on the guitar; the *Trio sonatas* were originally written for organ; here they are heard on lute and harpsichord and are elegantly played and cleanly recorded within a convincing ambience. Perhaps the harpsichord is a little less well defined in the bass register than is ideal, but the effect is pleasingly transparent and intimate.

(i) *Oboe sonatas* (for oboe and harpsichord) *in G min., BWV 1020; in G min., BWV 1030b. Fugue on a theme of Albinoni in B min., BWV 951.*
(BB) **(*) DHM/BMG Baroque Esprit 05472 77440-2 [id.]. Michel Piguet, Colin Tilney – C. P. E. BACH: *Oboe sonata* **(*); W. F. BACH: *Polonaise in E flat.* ***

As can be seen above and below, these two sonatas are better known in their versions for violin (BWV 1020) and flute (BWV 1030). But they are certainly pleasing on the baroque oboe (especially the *Siciliana* slow movement of the latter). Michel Piguet's timbre is appealing, and it is given an expansive bloom by the resonant recording, although the close microphones (one can hear the player take a breath) mean a reduction in the effective dynamic range. The *Fugue* is used as a central interlude and seems to have been recorded at a different time, since the pitch is fractionally different; however, there are sufficiently long pauses to make this relatively unimportant.

Viola da gamba sonatas Nos. 1–3, BWV 1027–9.
(M) *** HM/BMG GD 77044 [77044-2-RG]. Wieland Kuijken, Gustav Leonhardt.

The three sonatas for viola da gamba and harpsichord come from Bach's Cöthen period, and the *G minor*, BWV 1029, is arguably the highest peak in this particular literature. Kuijken and Leonhardt are both sensitive and scholarly musicians. This is the most authentic account to have appeared on the market in recent years and is among the most rewarding.

Viola da gamba sonatas Nos. 1–3, BWV 1027–9; (i) *Trio sonata in G for 2 flutes and continuo, BWV 1039.*
(M) ** Teldec/Warner 0630 13583-2. Nikolaus Harnoncourt, Herbert Tachezi; (i) with Brüggen, Stastny.

Harnoncourt is brisk and full-blooded in the opening of the *G major* (he is twice as fast as most of his competitors). Immediate comparison betrays the age of the recording (1969) though, taken in its own right, it is eminently acceptable. This gives a bonus in the form of the *G major Sonata* (in which Harnoncourt changes over to the cello and joins the continuo).

(i) *Viola da gamba sonatas Nos. 1–3, BWV 1027–9;* (ii) *Violin sonatas* (for violin and harpsichord) *Nos. 1–6, BWV 1014–19.*
(M) **(*) Sony SM2K 52615 (2) [S2K 52615]. (i) Leonard Rose or (ii) Jaime Laredo; Glenn Gould (piano).

Leonard Rose does not project a larger-than-life instrumental personality like Rostropovich, but his tone is subtly coloured and beautifully focused, his playing shows a fine sensibility, and his slightly introvert style is admirably suited to the *Viola da gamba sonatas* of Bach. Moreover, he and Glenn Gould achieve a very close partnership indeed, although some of Gould's ornamentation is questionable. At times Glenn Gould's clean, staccato articulation in outlining the rhythm of slow movements (usually taken very slowly) seems a shade eccentric, but when both artists do it together, as in the *Andante* of BWV 1027, the effect is both individual and pleasing. In the *Violin sonatas* there is some lovely quiet lyrical playing from Laredo. Again Gould's unforced staccato style is very apparent in slow movements but the violin line floats serenely above, and again faster movements are enjoyably spirited. There is undoubtedly pleasure to be had from this pair of discs, for all the unconventionality of Gould's contribution.

(Unaccompanied) *Violin sonatas Nos. 1–3, BWV 1001, 1003 & 1005; Violin partitas Nos. 1–3, BWV 1002, 1004 & 1006.*
(M) *** DG 457 701-2 (2) [id.]. Nathan Milstein.
(B) *** Ph. Duo 438 736-2 (2) [id.]. Arthur Grumiaux.
(B) *** DG Double 453 004-2 (2) [id.]. Henryk Szeryng.
(M) (***) Sony mono MP2K 46721 (2) [id.]. Henryk Szeryng.
(M) *** HM/BMG GD 77043 (2) [77043-2-RG]. Sigiswald Kuijken.
(M) ** DG (IMS) Dig. 445 526-2 (2). Shlomo Mintz.
(B) ** Teldec/Warner Ultima Dig. 3984 21035-2 (2) [id.]. Thomas Zehetmair.
(B) ** Hyperion Dyad Dig. CDD 22009 (2) [id.]. Elizabeth Wallfisch (baroque violin).

Milstein's set from the mid-1970s remains among the most satisfying of all versions. Every phrase is beautifully shaped, there is a highly developed feeling for line, and these performances have an aristocratic poise and a classical finesse which is very satisfying. This seems an admirable choice for reissue in DG's series of Originals.

Arthur Grumiaux's fine performances were recorded in Berlin in 1960–61. The venue offers a pleasingly warm background ambience against which the violin is forward, recorded in strong profile with complete realism and with no microphonic exaggeration of the upper partials. He strikes just the right balance between expressive feeling and purity of style. Some may prefer a rhythmically freer, more charismatic approach, as with Perlman and Milstein for instance; but Grumiaux's simplicity of manner, without exaggerated temperament, lets the music unfold naturally, and his readings of all six works are the product of superlative technique and a refined musical intellect. At bargain price this set is very tempting.

When they were first issued in 1968, Henryk Szeryng's performances came under the shadow of the much-praised Grumiaux set, recorded at the beginning of the 1960s. They now emerge on CD with astonishing presence and vividness, aided by DG's 'original-image bit-processing'. Szeryng's tone has never been caught before on record with such leonine fullness and beauty. The technical mastery and polish are quite remarkable, his intonation flawless. His opening attack on the *G minor Sonata* is very compelling, as is the positive, bold style – he plays every note as if he means it! Yet these performances are rhythmically free and full of subtle touches of baroque light and shade; there is a thoughtful, improvisatory feeling too. The resilient *Preludio*, delicately expressive *Loure*, and the joyful *Gavotte en Rondeau* of the *E major Partita* are among the most persuasive on record, so full of character, while the improvisational feeling which permeates this music-making is heard at its most impressive in Szeryng's imaginative and never predictable progress through the famous *Chaconne* which climaxes BWV 1004.

We are grateful to a *Gramophone* reader for drawing our attention to Szeryng's earlier set, recorded in mono in the mid-1960s. The recording is equally real and present and the performances are just as fresh, never identical but following the same general pattern of interpretation. In the *First Sonata*, for instance, the opening *Adagio* is actually slightly faster in the earlier, Sony performance but, because Szeryng's style is slightly less deliberate, the DG version *seems* faster. The closing *Presto* of the same work again brings fascinating minor differences. One certainly would not say that generally one performance is finer than the other, both having much refreshment to offer, yet when one comes to the famous *Chaconne* of the *D minor Partita* there is no question that the earlier account is seemingly more spontaneous.

Kuijken's accounts are as little painful or scratchy as you are ever likely to get in the authentic field and are of the highest quality.

Schlomo Mintz takes all the technical difficulties in his stride and his excellently recorded accounts give much musical satisfaction. His playing has youthful vitality and power, but the famous *Chaconne* from the *D minor Partita* finds him wanting. Intonation is generally secure but goes seriously awry in the middle of the *G minor Fugue*. The recording has a remarkably vivid presence (although the ear is conscious of the microphones), and this set (originally on three full-priced CDs) is now much more economically priced on two mid-priced discs. But this would not be a first choice.

Thomas Zehetmair's style is curiously restless; his line tends to have subtle dynamic surges, a feeling almost of rocking between phrases, and the effect is at times emotionally jagged; even the famous *Chaconne* of BWV 1004 could be more positive. Yet the pieces which depend on running passage-work (the *Courant* of the *Partita in B minor*, the *Gigue* of the *D minor* or the brilliant *Presto* of the *G minor Sonata*) are played with a wonderful, lightly articulated bravura which has much imaginative light and shade, while the *Fuga* of the *A minor Sonata* has its simple polyphony well under control without being tense. But in a piece like the *Siciliana* which precedes that *Presto* of BWV 1001 the improvisational restlessness disturbs Bach's underlying serenity, and elsewhere the feeling that the music runs like a mountain stream, over pebbles certainly but essentially flowing onward, is often disturbed in these readings. The recording is close but faithful and gives a very realistic impression against an acoustic which is not too dry.

Elizabeth Wallfisch uses a baroque instrument and bow. Her playing is technically secure and extremely fluent, sometimes quite dazzling – witness the spiccato playing of the *Double* in the *B minor Partita*, taken incredibly fast. The *Tempo di borea* in the same work is strikingly characterful. The famous *Chaconne* has plenty of leonine character too, even if it is not very prepossessing. But it is difficult to warm to her angular lyrical style, and the bold-edged timbre gets tiresome after a while. Was this really the way Bach would have imagined this music? This set is for dedicated 'authenticists' only, for all its imaginative touches.

(Unaccompanied) *Violin partita No. 2 in D min.; Sonata No. 3 in C.*

(M) ** Decca Dig. 460 005-2 [id.]. Kyung Wha Chung, Chicago SO, Sir Georg Solti – BERG: *Violin concerto.* ***

Kyung Wha Chung is so commanding an artist that one hardly expects anything other than total mastery. However, the natural warmth of her approach to Bach brings a feeling here of romanticism that will not appeal to all ears. There are extremes of dynamics, touches of rubato that many will not find convincing and, for all the technical assurance, some traces of less than secure intonation, though these are rare. She is recorded very realistically, but under the circumstances this seems an inappropriate coupling for the Berg *Concerto*.

Violin sonatas (for violin and harpsichord) *Nos. 1–6, BWV 1014–19.*
(M) *** HM/BMG GD 77170 (2) [77170-2-RG]. Sigiswald Kuijken, Gustav Leonhardt.

Violin sonatas Nos. 1–6, BWV 1014–19; 1019a; Sonatas for violin and continuo, BWV 1020–24.
✿ (B) *** Ph. Duo 454 011-2 (2) [id.]. Arthur Grumiaux, Christiane Jaccottet, Philippe Mermoud (in *BWV 1021 & 1023*).

Violin sonatas (for violin and harpsichord) *Nos. 1–6, BWV 1014–19; Sonatas for violin and continuo, BWV 1021 & 1023.*
(M) **(*) Virgin Veritas/EMI Dig. VED5 61237-2 (2). John Holloway, Davitt Moroney, Susan Sheppard.

The Bach *Sonatas for violin and harpsichord* and for *violin and continuo* are marvellously played, with all the beauty of tone and line for which Grumiaux is renowned; they have great vitality too. His admirable partner is Christiane Jaccottet, and in BWV 1021 and 1023 Philippe Mermoud (cello) joins the continuo. There is endless treasure to be discovered here, particularly when the music-making is so serenely communicative.

Sigiswald Kuijken uses a baroque violin, and both he and Gustav Leonhardt give us playing of rare eloquence. This reissue is an admirable example of the claims of authenticity and musical feeling pulling together rather than apart. This is a wholly delightful set and the transparency of the sound is especially appealing.

In addition to the six *Sonatas for violin and harpsichord*, the Virgin set presents the two surviving *Sonatas for violin and continuo* (in the latter, Davitt Moroney uses a chamber organ) known to be authentic. (Grumiaux also includes them, plus two more sonatas now thought not to be by Bach.) John Holloway has long experience in the early-music field, but violin tone is as much a matter of personal taste as is the human voice. Some will find the actual sound he makes unpleasing: it is vinegary and at times downright ugly. Yet those who take a different view will find him not wanting in artistry. Both Davitt Moroney and Susan Sheppard give excellent support, and the recording cannot be faulted in its clarity and presence; for those who must have original-instrument performances, first choice remains with Kuijken who, although he omits BWV 1021 and 1023, is no less authentic.

KEYBOARD MUSIC

(i) *The Art of Fugue, BWV 1080;* (ii) *Applicato in C, BWV 994; Aria & 10 Variations in the Italian style; Chorale: Joy and peace, BWV 512; Fantasia in G min., BWV 917; Invention in C, BWV 772 & 772a* (1720 & 1723 versions); *Italian concerto, BWV 971; Marches: in D and E flat, BWV Anh. 122 & 127; Musette in D, BWV Anh. 126; 2 Minuets in G, BWV Anh. 115–16; Polonaise in F, BWV Anh. 117a; Prelude and fugue in A min., BWV 895; Suite in F, BWV 623* (incomplete). (TELEMANN): *Suite in A, BWV 824* (wrongly attributed to J. S. B).
(B) *** Sony SB2K 63231 [S2K 63231]. (i) Charles Rosen; (ii) Rosalyn Tureck (piano).

Charles Rosen's superb account of *The Art of Fugue* is one of the great achievements of Bach keyboard recording. The use of a modern piano may appear controversial, but Rosen justifies his choice by his manner of playing, neutralizing any unwanted romantic overtones. The authority of his performance is remarkable and the depth of thought that lies behind the playing creates a satisfying sense of architecture. The 1967 recording is firm and clear, just right for such an exposition, and this performance has a mastery to set alongside Rosen's outstanding recording of Beethoven's *Hammerklavier Sonata*. He recorded Bach's *Goldberg variations* and the *Musical offering* at the same time, and we hope Sony have plans to reissue these recordings also.

Miss Tureck's sound-world is firmly centred in the modern piano, and she is not inhibited from drawing on its full range of colour. Yet her crisp staccato articulation often uncannily recalls its plucked keyboard predecessor and her instinctive feeling for Bach's line and texture is consistently refreshing. Here she makes a perfect foil for Rosen in offering an essentially lightweight programme, mainly of short keyboard vignettes in which we can hear Bach relaxing and enjoying himself. The *Applicato in C*, which opens the recital delightfully, is a simply decorated upward scale whose downward course is interrupted with a smile; the *Musette in D* with its echoed main idea is equally engaging, while Tureck's sharp accents bring much character to the *D major March*. The little *F major Suite* with its thoughtful central *Sarabande* and joyous closing *Gigue* show the light and shade of this pianism at its most winning, as does its equally charming companion in A major. This was wrongly attributed, and is now thought to be by Telemann, and again it brings a delectable closing *Gigue*. One of the highlights of the recital is the slightly dolorous *Aria in the Italian style*, followed by ten crisply diverting and wonderfully fluent variations, with the tenth magically reprising the gentle mood of the opening. Tureck's playing not only shows the utmost felicity but also sensitive control of dynamic contrast. The 1981 digital recording is rather forward but not shallow;

the *Italian concerto* dates from 1979 and the sound is more clattery, less well focused. The playing too, although both vigorous and sensitive, is very slightly below par. But this set is not to be missed by anyone who enjoys hearing Bach on the piano, and it is a great bargain.

The Art of fugue, BWV 1080; Italian concerto, BWV 971; Partita in B min., BWV 831; Prelude, fugue and allegro in E flat, BWV 998.
(M) *** HM/BMG GD 77013 (2) [77013-2-RG]. Gustav Leonhardt (harpsichord).

Under the fingers of Leonhardt every strand in the texture emerges with clarity and every phrase is allowed to speak for itself. This is a very impressive and rewarding set, well recorded and produced.

Capriccio in B flat (on the departure of a beloved brother), BWV 992; Chorale preludes: Befiehl du deine Wege, BWV 727; Es ist gewisslich an der Zeit, BWV 307 & 734; Ich ruf zu dir, Herr Jesu Christ, BWV 639; In dulci jubilo, BWV 751; Jesu, joy of man's desiring, from BWV 147; Nun komm' der Heiden Heiland, BWV 659; Wachet auf, from BWV 140; Wir danken dir, Gott, BWV 29; Harpsichord concerto in F min., BWV 1056: Largo. Flute sonata in E flat, BWV 1031: Siciliano. English suite No. 3 in G, BWV 808; French suite No. 5 in G, BWV 816; Toccata in D, BWV 912; The Well-tempered Clavier, Book I, excerpts; Preludes and fugues Nos. 4, BWV 849; 9–14, BWV 854–9; Book II, excerpts: Preludes Nos. 3, BWV 872; 6–7, BWV 875–6; 15, BWV 884; 24, BWV 893.
(B) *** DG Double 439 672-2 (2) [id.]. Wilhelm Kempff (with GLUCK: *Orfeo ed Euridice: Ballet music* ***).

Played like this, Bach is a joyful and compelling master, far removed from the relentless plod favoured by some harpsichordists. Though Kempff was well into his eighties when these recordings were made, his intellectual vigour, technical command and musical feeling seem ever fresh. The sound is truthful, warm and clear, and everyone who cares about Bach and piano playing should investigate this issue. One can only lament that, although this new Double DG series (two CDs for the price of one) is generous value, the documentation is inadequate.

Chaconne in D min. (arr. Busoni from (unaccompanied) *Violin partita No. 2 in D min., BWV 1004*).
(M) *** RCA 09026 62590-2 [id.]. Artur Rubinstein – FRANCK: *Prelude, chorale and fugue* ***; LISZT: *Piano sonata in B min.* **(*)

Rubinstein recorded this performance in Rome in 1970, when he was already in his eighties, but the freshness and spirit are a delight. The transfer of the 1970 recording is just a little clangy, but not unpleasantly so.

Chorale preludes: Ich ruf' zu dir, BWV 639; Nun komm' der Heiden Heiland, BWV 659 (both arr. Busoni); *Chromatic fantasia and fugue in D min., BWV 903; Fantasia and fugue in A min., BWV 904; Italian concerto in F, BWV 971; Fantasia in A min., BWV 922.*
(M) *** Ph. 454 409-2; 442 400-2. Alfred Brendel (piano).

Brendel's fine Bach recital originally appeared in 1978; it has been digitally remastered for the CD format and now appears for the first time at mid-price. The performances are of the old school, with no attempt to strive after harpsichord effects, and with every piece creating a sound-world of its own. The *Italian concerto* is particularly imposing, with a finely sustained sense of line and beautifully articulated rhythms. The recording is in every way truthful and present, bringing the grand piano very much into the living-room before one's very eyes. Masterly. This disc is currently available on two different catalogue numbers.

Chorales: *Ich ruf' zu dir, Herr Jesu Christ, BWV 639; Jesu, joy of man's desiring,* from *BWV 147; Partita No. 1 in B flat, BWV 825; Prelude and fugue No. 8 in B flat min., BWV 853; Sicilienne* from *Flute sonata, BWV 1031; Toccata, BWV 914.*
(B) **(*) Cal. Approche CAL 6203. Inger Södergren (piano) – BERG: *Sonata.* **(*)

Södergren opens with the famous chorale, *Jesu, joy of man's desiring*, and its gentle outline sets the mood for this recital, relaxed and thoughtful pianism of deep musicality. The *Partita* might be found not crisp enough for those favouring the Bach style of Rosalyn Tureck, and the *Toccata* is not forceful either. But this is appealing in a less assertive way, with slightly muted keyboard colours. Playing which is very persuasive in its intimacy, while the piano-image is warm and glowing.

Chromatic fantasia and fugue, BWV 903; 4 Duets, BWV 802–5; English suites Nos. 1–6, BWV 806–11; Goldberg variations, BWV 988; 2- & 3-Part Inventions, BWV 772a–786; French suites Nos. 1–6, BWV 812–17; Partitas Nos. 1–6 BWV 825–30; Partita in B min., BWV 831; Well-tempered Clavier, Books I–II, Preludes and fugues Nos. 1–48, BWV 846–93.
(B) *** Decca Dig. 452 279-2 (12) [(M) id. import]. András Schiff (piano).

András Schiff recorded Bach's major keyboard works for Decca over a decade between 1982 and 1991, and it is perhaps remarkable that, during an era when original instruments are all the rage, he has made such a convincing case for recording this music on the piano. Moreover he makes no apologies for the range of dynamic and colour that the modern keyboard can command and of which Bach can have had no inkling. Yet Schiff's playing is so stylish, his expressive phrasing and rubato so natural, the presentation so spontaneous, that the critical listener is disarmed and is encouraged to sit back and simply enjoy the music. Most of these recordings are available separately; only in the *Inventions* is there a suspicion that Schiff's expressive freedom approaches the outer boundaries of what is permissible, and even here the musical flow remains convincing. The Decca recording, natural and not too resonant, is surely ideal for such repertoire.

Chromatic fantasia and fugue in D min., BWV 903; Italian concerto, BWV 971; French suites Nos. 1 in D min., BWV 812; 2 in C min., BWV 813.
(BB) ** Naxos Dig. 8.550709 [id.]. Wolfgang Rübsam (piano).

French suites Nos. 3 in B min., BWV 814; 4 in E flat, BWV 815; 5 in G, BWV 816; 6 in E, BWV 817.
(BB) ** Naxos Dig. 8.550710 [id.]. Wolfgang Rübsam (piano).

Partitas Nos. 1 in B flat, BWV 825; 2 in C min., BWV 826; Capriccio on the departure of a beloved brother, BWV 992; Prelude and fuguetta in G, BWV 902.
(BB) ** Naxos Dig. 8.550692 [id.]. Wolfgang Rübsam (piano).

Partitas Nos. 3 in A min., BWV 827; 4 in D, BWV 828.
(BB) ** Naxos Dig. 8.550693 [id.]. Wolfgang Rübsam (piano).

Partitas Nos. 5 in G, BWV 829; 6 in E min., BWV 830.
(BB) ** Naxos Dig. 8.550694 [id.]. Wolfgang Rübsam (piano).

Toccatas Nos. 1 in F sharp min.; 2 in C min.; 3 in D; 4 in D min.; 5 in E min.; 6 in G min.; 7 in G, BWV 910/916.
(BB) ** Naxos Dig. 8.550708 [id.]. Wolfgang Rübsam (piano).

Wolfgang Rübsam is embarking on a complete survey of Bach's keyboard music on the piano for Naxos. His manner is simple and thoughtful, never inflexible, always sensing the flow of the musical line. Ornamentation is unfussy, and the only cavil is that his expressive playing brings little hesitations, which are very much part of his style and to which one adjusts, although this may trouble some listeners. Nothing here is metronomic and tempi are never pushed too hard. The *Chromatic fantasia*, brilliantly articulated as it is, is not treated as a chance for virtuoso display for its own sake and some might feel that the *Toccatas* are not flamboyant enough, but Rübsam sees them as being like sinfonias, beginning with a flourish and with the music satisfyingly brought together in the closing sections. The recording is clear and truthful.

English suites Nos. 1–6, BWV 806–11.
(B) *** Sony Seon S2BK 62949 [S2K 62949]. Gustav Leonhardt (harpsichord).
(M) ** Sony SM2K 52606 (2) [S2K 52606]. Glenn Gould (piano).

Leonhardt's earlier (1973) set (originally issued in the UK on Philips in harness with the *French suites*) is by no means to be dismissed at budget price. Here he uses a Skrowroneck harpsichord, vividly recorded, and if the volume level is set back a little the effect is very convincing, for the church acoustic is pleasing. At his best, Leonhardt combines scholarship and artistry, and his learning seldom inhibits his natural musical instincts. The music flows freshly and expansively, even if he is not equally inspired in every movement. He is inconsistent in the matter of repeats, sometimes observing them throughout, sometimes not. But this is a rewarding venture, well worth its modest price.

Glenn Gould often inspires the adjective 'wilful', and certainly these performances have much that is eccentric. At the same time there is undoubtedly a strong musical personality to which the listener cannot remain indifferent. The vocalizations are tiresome and, although phrasing is often imaginative, there is some bizarre ornamentation and accentuation and the piano sound tends to be dry and unappealing, although it represents the effect intended by Gould himself.

English suites Nos. 2 in A min.; 3 in G min., BWV 807–8.
(M) *** DG Dig. 445 573-2. Ivo Pogorelich (piano) (with Domenico SCARLATTI: *Keyboard sonatas Kk. 87, 135, 380 & 450* ***).

The young Yugoslav pianist plays both *Suites* with a welcome absence of affectation. It is all beautifully articulate and fresh. Moreover, to make this reissue even more attractive, DG have added four well-chosen keyboard sonatas of Domenico Scarlatti, which also show this artist at his most perceptive. The recording is one of DG's best, with natural piano-sound and an excellent sense of presence.

English suite No. 2 in A min., BWV 807; Partita No. 2 in C min., BWV 826; Toccata in C min., BWV 911.
(M) *** DG 423 880-2. Martha Argerich (piano).

Martha Argerich's playing is alive and keenly rhythmic but also wonderfully flexible and rich in colour. She is very well recorded.

(i) *French suites Nos. 1–6, BWV 812–17;* (ii) *English suite No. 3 in G min., BWV 808; Italian concerto in F, BWV 971.*
(B) **(*) EMI forte Dig. CZS5 69479-2 (2) [CDFB 69479]. (i) Andrei Gavrilov (piano); (ii) Stanislav Bunin (piano).

Gavrilov's 1984 set of the *French suites* is full of interesting things, and there is some sophisticated, not to say masterly, pianism. The part-writing is keenly alive and the playing full of subtle touches. He draws a wide range of tone-colour from the keyboard and employs a wider dynamic range than might be expected. There is an element of the self-conscious here and a measure of exaggeration in some of the *Gigues*, but there is much that is felicitous, too. To fill up the pair of discs, Stanislav Bunin's performances of the *Third English suite* and the *Italian concerto*, recorded six years later, have been added. His style is bold and direct, less flexible than Gavrilov's approach but totally unselfconscious. The slow movement of the *Italian concerto* is pleasingly thoughtful. Both artists receive excellent recording.

French suites Nos. 1–6; Partita No. 7 in B min., BWV 831.
(M) ** Sony SM2K 52609 (2) [S2K 52609]. Glenn Gould (piano).

Brilliant though Glenn Gould's playing is, it is far too idiosyncratic to justify an unqualified recommendation. Needless to say, there are revealing touches, marvellously clear part-writing and some impressive finger dexterity. There are some odd tempi and a lot of very detached playing that inspires more admiration than conviction. The sound is clear and clean and is acceptably transferred.

French suite No. 5 in G, BWV 816; Fugue in 3 parts, BWV 953; Fughetta, BWV 961; Italian concerto; 3 Minuets, BWV 841–3; 2 Minuets, BWV anh. 114–15; Partita No. 1 in B flat, BWV 825; 6 Little Preludes, BWV 939–43 & BWV 999; 6 Preludes, BWV 924–8 & BWV 930.
(B) ** EMI Debut CDZ5 69700-2. Richard Egarr (harpsichord).

Richard Egarr is a pupil of Gustav Leonhardt and he makes his first recording on a modern Katzman copy of a 1638 Rückers. He is intimately recorded and here combines miniatures (some of these pieces come from the *Clavier-Büchlein*, intended to instruct the young Wilhelm Friedemann Bach) with one or two major works. He plays very musically, but not all will take to his little nudges of rubato which thoughtfully prevent the melodic line from being austere but which do not always sound entirely spontaneous. A promising début, nevertheless.

Goldberg variations, BWV 988.
(B) *** HM Dig. HMT 7901240 [HMC 901240]. Kenneth Gilbert (harpsichord).
(M) *** Virgin Veritas/EMI Dig. VER5 61153-2. Maggie Cole (harpsichord).
(M) *** DG 439 978-2. Wilhelm Kempff (piano).
(M) *(**) Sony Dig. SMK 52619 [id.] (1981 recording). Glenn Gould (piano).
(M) ** Teldec/Warner 3984 21351-2 [id.]. Gustav Leonhardt (harpsichord).
(BB) *(*) Naxos Dig. 8.550078 [id.]. Chen Pi-hsien (piano).

Goldberg variations; Well-tempered Clavier: Fugues in E, BWV 878; F sharp min., BWV 883.
(M) (**(*)) Sony mono SMK 52594 [id.] (1955 recording). Glenn Gould (piano).

Kenneth Gilbert gives a refreshingly natural performance of the *Goldberg*. He uses a recent copy of a Rückers–Taskin, and it makes a very pleasing sound. His is an aristocratic reading; he avoids excessive display and there is a quiet, cultured quality to his playing that is very persuasive. His is an essentially introspective account, recorded in a rather less lively acoustic than is Pinnock (at full price on Archiv), and Gilbert is a thoughtful and thought-provoking player. His approach to repeats is discussed in the accompanying notes and seems eminently sensible. This can be strongly recommended alongside Maggie Cole, but the Harmonia Mundi reissue has a distinct price advantage (in the UK only).

Maggie Cole's playing is completely straightforward and she holds the listener's interest throughout. At mid-price (in the UK only), this make a very strong recommendation for those wanting a digital harpsichord version of this work.

Kempff's version is not for purists, but it has a special magic of its own. Ornaments are ignored altogether in the outlining of the theme and the instances of anachronisms of style are too numerous to mention. Yet, for all that, the sheer musicianship exhibited by this great artist fascinates and his playing is consistently refreshing. The 1969 recording is very natural. Rosalyn Tureck's version, however, remains very special indeed – but that is at full price.

Glenn Gould's famous (1955) mono recording enjoyed cult status in its day, and its return will occasion rejoicing among his admirers. He observes no repeats and in terms of sheer keyboard wizardry commands admiration, even if you do not respond to the results. There is too much that is wilful and eccentric for this to be a straightforward recommendation, but it is a remarkable performance nevertheless.

Gould's later, stereo version was one of the last records he made. In his earlier record he made no repeats; now he repeats a section of almost half of them and also joins some pairs together (6 with 7 and 9 with 10, for example). Yet, even apart from his vocalise, he does a number of weird things – fierce staccatos, brutal accents, and so on – that inhibit one from suggesting this as a first recommendation even among piano versions. The recording is, as usual with this artist, inclined to be dry and forward, which aids clarity.

Leonhardt's set of the *Goldberg variations* is now more than 30 years old, but the sound remains undimmed. Indeed the transfer to CD freshens it and the focus is beautifully clear and immediate. It is eminently scholarly but without the vitality of some others. Leonhardt's later recording for Deutsche Harmonia Mundi is preferable, and that will no doubt reappear before too long.

Chen Pi-hsien comes from Taiwan; she has made a considerable name for herself over the last few years, both in England and on the Continent, as an artist of refined musical intelligence and taste. Her account of the *Goldberg variations* is both clean in articulation and fluent; she takes a pretty brisk, no-nonsense view of the theme but, generally speaking, her tempi are not unduly fast. At the same time, hers is not as searching or as subtle a performance as one would expect from an artist of this repute or from one who has studied with Leygraf, Kempff and Nikolayeva. The piano sound as such is not in the first flight, and at times the piano seems in less than fresh condition. She plays the 'Black Pearl' variation with poetic feeling and good taste. Some repeats are made, but most are ignored. The recording, made in the Festeburgkirche in Frankfurt, is acceptable rather than good.

Goldberg variations, BWV 988; Fantasia in C min., BWV 906; Fantasia and fugue in F min., BWV 904; Italian concerto in F, BWV 971.
(M) **(*) DG 439 465-2. Ralph Kirkpatrick (harpsichord).

Ralph Kirkpatrick is at his best in this work, providing light and subtle registration, and the music benefits both in clarity and in colour. The playing is lively when it should be, controlled and steady in the slow, stately, contrapuntal variations. He is a scholarly rather than an intuitive player and his thoughts are rarely without interest. Though not a first choice, this version includes three extra items where he uses his modern Neupert harpsichord to good effect, while sounding more pedantic, particularly in the *Italian concerto.*

15 2-Part Inventions; 15 3-Part Inventions; Fragments of Anna Magdelena's Notebook: March in D; 3 Minuets in G; Minuet in D min.; Musette in D; 2 Polonaises in G min.
(BB) ** Naxos Dig. 8.550679 [id.]. János Sebestyén (piano).

János Sebestyén is by no means inflexible, but his performances are straighter than those of Schiff. They have less individuality, but this is sensitive, well-structured Bach playing, truthfully recorded, and there is the welcome bonus of eight small-scale keyboard pieces which Bach provided for his second wife.

Partitas Nos. 1–6, BWV 825–30.
(M) *** Virgin Veritas/EMI Dig. VED5 61292-2 (2). Gustav Leonhardt (harpsichord).

Partitas Nos. 1–6, BWV 825–30; Partita in B min. (Overture in the French style), BWV 831.
(B) *** Ph. Duo 442 559-2 (2) [id.]. Blandine Verlet (harpsichord).

Blandine Verlet's Philips Duo set is not only inexpensive, it is the only set of the *Partitas* to include the later *Overture in the French style*, BWV 831, which is played with much character. Indeed the performances throughout are direct and spontaneous, thoughtful and strongly characterized. Not an out-and-out first choice, which lies with Christophe Rousset at full price on Oiseau-Lyre. But he does not give us the *B minor Partita* and, in its price range, Verlet can certainly be strongly recommended.

Gustav Leonhardt's set was recorded (in 1986) on a Dowd (modelled on an eighteenth-century German instrument by Michael Mietke) in the excellent acoustic of the Doopsgezinde Gemeente Kerk in Haarlem. In terms of sheer sound it is among the most satisfactory available versions, and in terms of style it combines elegance, spontaneity and authority. There is nothing didactic about this playing, but it is never less than thought-provoking. In many respects it is musically the most satisfying of current sets, save for the fact that Leonhardt observes no repeats. This will undoubtedly diminish its appeal – which is a great pity, since both illumination and pleasure are to be had from this set. It is offered at medium price, but the first disc plays for only 40 minutes 36 seconds and the second for 54 minutes 36 seconds.

Partitas Nos. 1–7, BWV 825–31; 4 Duets, BWV 802–5; Italian Concerto, BWV 971.
(B) ** Ph. Dig. Duo 456 068-2 (2) [id.]. Jean-Louis Steuerman (piano).

Eminently straightforward and unfussy playing from Steuerman which some collectors may prefer to the more purely 'pianistic' version like Schiff's. Steuerman has a well-developed sense of style, as one might expect from a prizewinner at the Leipzig Bach Competition, and he does not cultivate beauty of sound for its own sake. At times he is a little inhibited – as if he mistrusts spontaneity – and there are others when he is a little prosaic and literal. He is also somewhat inconsistent about repeats. Nevertheless he remains a generally sound guide to the *Partitas* and he is certainly well recorded. For this inexpensive reissue he adds some worthwhile bonuses, for his *Italian Concerto* has infectious buoyancy in the outer movements, while the *Andante*, like the serene *Sarabande* in the *B minor Partita*, BWV 831, (now added to the set) has a simple beauty which is affecting. The *Duets* (which derive from the so-called *Organ Mass* in the third volume of the *Clavierübung*) are engagingly fresh, the rhythmic articulation consistently deft. Not a first choice for the *Partitas*, but excellent value.

8 Preludes for W. F. Bach, BWV 924–31; 6 Little Preludes, BWV 933–8; 5 Preludes, BWV 939–43; Prelude, BWV 999; Prelude, fugue and allegro in E flat, BWV 998; Preludes and fughettas: in F & G, BWV 901–2; Fantasia in C min., BWV 906; Fantasia and fugue in A min., BWV 904.
(M) **(*) DG (IMS) Dig. 447 278-2. Kenneth Gilbert (harpsichord).

Splendid artistry from this scholar-player; he is predictably stylish and authoritative. He uses a harpsichord by a Flemish maker, Jan Couchet, enlarged by Blanchet in 1759 and by Taskin in 1778, overhauled by Hubert Bédard. Even played at the lowest setting, the sound seems a bit unrelieved and overbright. This really has 'presence' with a vengeance. The excellence of the playing however is not in question.

Toccatas: in F sharp min.; C min.; D; D min.; E min.; G min.; G; BWV 910–16.
(M) ** Sony SM2K 52612 (2) [S2K 52612]. Glenn Gould (piano).

The seven *Toccatas* offer some of Glenn Gould's finest Bach playing. They are often quite complex in structure, but Gould has their full measure. The recording balance is close and rather dry but truthful and with rather more bloom than in previous incarnations. The one overriding snag is the vocalise.

The Well-tempered Clavier (48 Preludes & fugues), BWV 846–93.
(B) *** HM Musique d'Abord HMA 1901285/8 [id.]. Davitt Moroney (harpsichord).
(B) **(*) Ph. Duo 446 548-2 (2) [id.]. Friedrich Gulda (piano).

The Well-tempered Clavier, Book I, Preludes and fugues Nos. 1–24, BWV 846/69.
(M) (***) BMG/RCA mono GD 86217 (2) [6217-2-RC]. Wanda Landowska (harpsichord).

The Well-tempered Clavier, Book II, Preludes and fugues Nos. 25–48, BWV 870/93.
(M) (***) BMG/RCA mono GD 87825 (3) [7825-2-RC]. Wanda Landowska (harpsichord).

Davitt Moroney uses a modern harpsichord (built in 1980) which has a full-bodied yet cleanly focused image but which is rather too closely balanced. Yet the effect is certainly tangible and realistic, the perspective convincing. His thoughtful, considered approach is satisfying in its way, stylistically impeccable, although the playing is less concentrated than with Gilbert, the result less exuberantly spontaneous than with Van Asperen (see our main volume). But it will suit those who like a thoughtful, unostentatious approach to Bach, yet one which does not lack rhythmic resilience. Moreover, with full documentation it is a very real bargain on Harmonia Mundi's Musique d'Abord budget label.

Gulda's recording of the '48' was originally made in 1973. The bold CD transfer brings out the more sharply not only the relative dryness of acoustic (although it is by no means confined) but also the pianist's commendable reluctance to use the sustaining pedal. His approach is strong and direct, sometimes severe, yet has undoubted dedication. In Book I the listener is occasionally aware of strong accenting, yet Gulda can also play lightly and thoughtfully (as in the *Preludes in C sharp minor* and *G sharp minor*) and provide keen but unexaggerated virtuosity (as in the *moto perpetuo* of the *D major*). He uses a fairly wide dynamic range with fine judgement and can build a fugue impressively to an unexaggerated climax (as in the *A flat*). In Book II the playing often seems more serene, and again the use of light and shade is always apt. Pacing is generally convincing and if at times his musical personality brings a degree of eccentricity in this respect (the organlike *C minor fugue* is very slow and deliberate and the *E major* of the same book is very strong and loud) at others his playing can be pleasingly light and unassertive, as in the flowing *G minor Prelude* and its neat, yet precise, following fugue. If not matching Schiff, these readings are sound and certainly not dull.

It is good that RCA have restored Landowska's celebrated records of the '48' to circulation, together with her original notes. They were recorded between 1949 and 1954 and are now accommodated on five well-filled CDs. They still sound marvellous and have a colour, vitality, authority and grandeur that make it difficult to stop listening to them. Styles in Bach playing may have changed over the intervening forty years – it would be strange if they had not – but this playing still carries all before it. The CD transfer has the usual advantages of the medium. Strongly recommended.

The Well-tempered Clavier, Book I, Preludes and fugues Nos. 1–24, BWV 846–59.
(BB) ** Naxos Dig. 8.553796/7 [id.]. Jenö Jandó (piano).

Nothing in this world is predictable, but we were surprised to find that after the success of Book II (see below) Jandó's Book I is disappointing. They were recorded two years apart, and the easy spontaneous flow which distinguishes the earlier recording appears only sporadically in the more recent set. The simple presentation of the familiar *First Prelude* augurs well (as indeed does *No. 13 in F sharp* which opens the second disc), but too often elsewhere the music seems to be pressed forward unrelentingly, even at times stoically, and the piano-tone hardens. Of course many of these remarkable pieces are played with an agreeable simplicity, but too often chosen tempi seem to value bravura more than poise.

The Well-tempered Clavier, Book II, Preludes and fugues Nos. 25–48, BWV 870–93.
(BB) *** Naxos Dig. 8. 550970/1 (2) [id.]. Jenö Jandó (piano).

Like András Schiff on Decca, Jandó sees the *Well-tempered Clavier* in pianistic terms; he varies his touch from boldly assertive to a light staccato or a more mellow, expressive style. He can also be thoughtful, almost improvisatory, and then commanding. He uses light and shade judiciously. His approach brings great variety to the music and, like his choice of tempi, seems apt, although some listeners may not always agree with his choices. The piano timbre is firm, clear and realistic, and this makes a thoroughly recommendable super-bargain alternative to Schiff, who remains rather special.

The Well-tempered Clavier, Book I, Preludes and fugues Nos. 1, 5–6, 8, 19–20 & 23–24. Book II, Nos. 4, 6, 12, 14 and 19.
(BB) **(*) Naxos Dig. 8.554160 [id.]. Jenö Jandó.

A well-chosen selection to show Jandó at his best in the chosen selection from both Books, although the first excerpt from Book II (*No. 4 in C sharp minor*, BWV 983) immediately demonstrates his playing at its most appealing.

ORGAN MUSIC

Complete organ music

Peter Hurford complete Decca series

Disc 1: *Preludes & fugues, BWV 531–2, 548–50; Toccatas & fugues, BWV 540, 565* (444 411-2).

Disc 2: *Fantasias & fugues, BWV 542, 561; Kleines harmonisches Labyrinth, BWV 591; Preludes & fugues, BWV 533, 551; Toccata, adagio & fugue, BWV 564; Toccata & fugue, BWV 538; Trio, BWV 585* (444 412-2).

Disc 3: *Fantasias, BWV 562, 572; Fantasia & fugue, BWV 537; Fugues, BWV 575–7, 579, 581; Passacaglia & fugue, BWV 582; Pedal-Exercitium, BWV 598; Prelude & fugue, BWV 535; Trio, BWV 583* (444 413-2).

Disc 4: *Clavier-Ubung, Part 3* (beginning): *German organ Mass (Prelude & fugue in E flat, BWV 552, & Chorale preludes, BWV 669–71, 676, 678, 680, 682, 684, 686, 688)* (444 414-2).

Disc 5: *Clavier-Ubung, Part 3* (conclusion): *Chorale preludes, BWV 672–5, 677, 679, 681, 683, 685, 687, 689; 24 Kirnberger Chorale preludes, BWV 690–713* (444 415-2).

Disc 6: *6 Trio sonatas, BWV 525–30* (444 416-2).

Disc 7: *Canonic variations: Vom Himmel hoch, BWV 769; Chorale partitas: Christ, du bist der helle Tag; O Gott, du frommer Gott; Sei gegrüsset, Jesu gütig, BWV 766–8; Chorale variations: Ach, was soll ich Sünder machen, BWV 770* (444 417-2).

Disc 8: *Chorale preludes, BWV 730–40; Schübler chorale preludes, BWV 645–50; Chorale variations: Allein Gott in der Höh' sei Ehr, BWV 771* (444 418-2).

Disc 9: *Chorale preludes, BWV 726–9; Concertos Nos. 1–6, BWV 592–7* (444 419-2).

Disc 10: *Arnstadt chorale preludes, BWV 714, 719, 742 & 1090–1117* (from Yale manuscript, copied Neumeister) (444 420-2).

Disc 11: *Arnstadt chorale preludes, BWV 957, 1118–20* (from Yale manuscript, copied Neumeister); *Leipzig chorale preludes, BWV 651–62* (444 421-2).

Disc 12: *Leipzig chorale preludes, BWV 663–8. Chorale preludes, BWV 714–25* (444 422-2).

Disc 13: *Allabreve in D, BWV 589; Fugue, BWV 580; Prelude, BWV 568; Preludes & fugues, BWV 534, 536, 539, 541; 8 Short Preludes & fugues, BWV 553–60; Trios, BWV 584 & 586* (444 423-2).

Disc 14: *Aria in F, BWV 587; Canzona in D min., BWV 588; Fantasia, BWV 571; Fugues, BWV 574 & 578; Pastorale, BWV 590; Preludes, BWV 567 & 569; Preludes & fugues, BWV 546–7* (444 424-2).

Disc 15: *Fantasia, BWV 563; A Musical offering: Ricercar, BWV 1079/5. Preludes & fugues, BWV 535a* (incomplete), *543–5; Prelude, trio & fugue, BWV 545b; Toccata & fugue in E, BWV 566; Trio, BWV 1027a* (444 425-2).

Disc 16: *Chorale preludes Nos. 1–41 (Orgelbüchlein), BWV 599–639* (444 426-2).

Disc 17: *Chorale preludes Nos. 42–6 (Orgelbüchlein), BWV 640–44. Chorale preludes, BWV 620a, BWV 741–8, BWV 751–2, BWV 754–5, BWV 757–63, BWV 765, BWV Anh. 55; Fugue in G min., BWV 131a* (444 427-2).

❀ (B) *** Decca Analogue/Dig. 444 410-2 (17) [id.]. Peter Hurford (organs of Ratzeburg Cathedral, Germany; Church of Our Lady of Sorrows, Toronto, Canada; New College Chapel, Oxford; Knox Grammar School Chapel, Sydney, Australia; Eton College, Windsor; Stiftskirche, Melk, Austria; Augustinerkirche, Vienna, Austria; All Souls Unitarian Church, Washington, DC, USA; Domkirche, St Pölten, Austria; St Catharine's College Chapel, Cambridge).

With the exception of the 35 *Arnstadt chorale preludes*, as copied by Neumeister – discovered quite recently in the Music Library of Yale University – which were added in 1986, Peter Hurford recorded his unique survey of Bach's organ music for Decca's Argo label over a period of eight years, 1974–82. One of the activities for which Bach was renowned was trying out organs, especially new ones (and he was hard to please), so it is highly appropriate that Hurford uses ten different organs, moving from Ratzeburg in Germany to Toronto in Canada, back home to New College, Oxford, then to Sydney, Australia, and so on. Each organ is caught superbly by the recording engineers, and the registration features a range of baroque colour that is almost orchestral in its diversity. The digital recording of the Vienna Bach organ chosen for the *Neumeister chorales* is particularly beautiful. Hurford here omits the three pieces which are already familiar (BWV 601 and 639 from the *Orgelbüchlein*, and BWV 637), all of which can be found within their proper sequences in the order in which they were published by the Bach Gesellschaft edition which was followed in Schmieder's catalogue. However, Hurford does include BWV 714 (which in the Neumeister manuscript is 27 bars longer than previously known versions), BWV 719 and 742 (hitherto not thought to be authentic Bach) and BWV 957 (until now not regarded as an organ work).

It was Peter Hurford's achievement to influence a complete change in approach to this repertoire, moving away from an enduring and essentially pedagogic, German tradition (shown at its best by organists like Helmut Walcha on DG Archiv). Wolfgang Rübsam on Philips (see below) had already pioneered a new look at Bach's organ music on record, and Hurford carried it forward to fruition, choosing organs which could produce a fine palette of colour, yet carefully registering textures which do not cloud the polyphonic argument, notably in the chorale preludes which can so easily become overladen. Vigour and energy are the keynotes of his approach to the large-scale works and, without losing their majesty, he never lets the fugal momentum get bogged down by the the music's weight and scale. We hear Bach's organ writing with new ears, its human vitality revealed alongside its extraordinary architecture. It can readily be seen that the new layout has been well thought out. Moreover it is supported with extensive notes by Clifford Bartlett which are both scholarly and readable; full specifications of all the organs used are included. The recordings are splendidly transferred to CD and remain among the finest ever and, with its greatly improved documentation, this set of 17 bargain-price CDs must be counted a supreme investment in this repertoire.

Wolfgang Rübsam Complete Philips series

Volume I, Disc 1: *Fantasia, BWV 572; Preludes and fugues, BWV 531–2; 535, 541, 544–5, 549–50; Toccata and fugue in D min., BWV 565* (438 172-2).

Disc 2: *Fugues, BWV 577–8; Fugue on a theme of Corelli, BWV 579; Prelude, BWV 568; Preludes and fugues, BWV 533–4; 536; 543; 546–7; Toccata and fugue in D min. (Dorian), BWV 538* (438 173-2).

Disc 3: *Canzona in D min., BWV 588; Preludes and fugues, BWV 537, 539–40, 542, 548; Prelude, Adagio-trio; Fantasia and fugue* (without BWV No.) (438 174-2).

Disc 4: *Allabreve in D, BWV 589; Fantasias: in C min.* (without BWV No.); *in C min., BWV 562; Fugues, BWV 575, 581; Passacaglia in C min., BWV 582; Pedal-Exercitium, BWV 598; Toccata, BWV 564; Toccata and fugue in E, BWV 566; Trios, BWV 583, 586, 1027a* (438 175-2).

Disc 5: *Fantasia in G, BWV 571; Trio sonatas for 2 keyboards and pedal, BWV 525–9* (438 177-2).

Disc 6: *Trio sonata No. 6, BWV 530; Chorales, BWV 691a, 717, 725; Chorale partitas, BWV 766–7; 770; Chorale preludes, 745, 747* (438 178-2).

Disc 7: *Canonic variations on 'Vom Himmel hoch', BWV 768; Chorale partita on 'Sei gegrüsset, Jesu gütig', BWV 768; Chorale variations on 'Allein Gott in der Höh' sei Ehr', BWV 771; Chorale: 'Wie schön leuch't uns der Morgenstern', BWV 739; Fugue in C min. (Theme Legrenzianum, elaboratum cum subjecto pedaliter), BWV 574; Pastorale in D, BWV 590* (438 179-2).

Disc 8: *Orgelbüchlein: Chorales, BWV 599–644* (438 180-2).

Volume II, Disc 9: *Chorales, BWV 653b; O Lamm Gottes unschuldig* (without BWV No.); *Chorale preludes, BWV 748–50, 754, 756, 759; Fuga sopra il Magnificat, BWV 733; 6 Schübler chorales, BWV 645–50; Clavier-Ubung, Part 3: German organ Mass* (beginning): *Prelude in E flat, BWV 552, & Chorale preludes, BWV 669–74* (438 182-2).

Disc 10: *Clavier-Ubung, Part 3: German organ Mass* (cont.); *Chorale preludes, BWV 675–89; Fugue in E flat, BWV 552; Duets 1–4, BWV 802–5* (438 183-2).

Disc 11: *6 Concertos after various composers, BWV 592–7; Leipzig chorales Nos. 1–3, BWV 651–3* (438 184-2).

Disc 12: *18 Leipzig chorales, Nos.4–18* (438 185-2).

Disc 13: *Chorales and Chorale preludes, BWV 690, 692–4, 700, 703, 710, 715, 719, 722, 724, 729, 732, 734, 738, 746, 751, 755, 757–8, 763; Chorale fugues and fuguettas, BWV 699, 701–2, 716; Fantasia super 'Valet will ich dir geben', BWV 735; Fantasia in C, BWV 570; Fugues, BWV 570 & BWV 576; Kleines harmonisches Labyrinth, BWV 591; Prelude in C, BWV 567; Prelude and fugue in A min., BWV 551; Trio in G min., BWV 584* (438 187-2).

Disc 14: *Chorales and Chorale preludes, BWV 691, 695, 705–9, 711–12, 714, 718, 720, 723, 726, 730, 740–44, 752, 765; Chorale fantasia, BWV 713; Chorale fuguettas, BWV 696–8, 704* (438 188-2).

Disc 15: *Aria in F, BWV 587; Chorales and Chorale preludes, BWV 721, 760–62, 727–8, 731, 736–7; Fantasia con imitazione, BWV 563; Fantasia and fugue in A min., BWV 561; Fugue in D, BWV 580; Prelude in A min., BWV 569; Trio in C min., BWV 585; The Art of Fugue, BWV 1080* (beginning): *Contrapunctus 1–5* (438 189-2).

Disc 16: *The Art of Fugue* (conclusion): *Contrapunctus 6–11; Canon all'Ottava; Fua a 3 soggetti. Chorale: 'Wenn wir in Höchsten Nöten sein', BWV 668a* (438 190-2).

(B) *** Ph. 456 080-2 (16). Wolfgang Rübsam (organs of Frauenfeld & Freiburg).

As can be seen, Wolfgang Rübsam's magnificent survey of Bach's organ music, made at the beginning of the 1970s, has been re-ordered and reissued, still on 16 CDs and with excellent documentation, but now in two boxes of 8 discs, contained within a sturdy slip-case. The bulk of the music was recorded on the fine instrument at St Nikolaus in Frauenfeld, Switzerland; for the chorale preludes and a few miscellaneous works, Rübsam turned to the Belgian Hockhois organ at Freiburg Münster. Sonically the results are highly stimulating, offering the widest range of colour, a rich overall blend without clouding of detail, and plenty of support from the pedals. The *Trio sonatas* are especially attractive and compare well with Simon Preston's set (DG 437 835-2) in both their luminous palette and their liveliness. The six solo *Concertos*, based on music of others, principally Ernst and Vivaldi, are comparably successful, although here Rübsam adopts extreme tempi, with adagios very measured against sprightly allegros.

But the key to the success of any Bach survey must lie with the way the performer approaches the large-scale concert pieces, notably the *Preludes and fugues* and *Toccatas and fugues*, and these are nearly all in the first volume. Certainly in these works Rübsam is consistently vital, and his registration often tickles the ear. The famous *Toccata, adagio and fugue*, BWV 564, is very well judged, a work that can easily become ponderous, while the *Passacaglia in C minor*, BWV 582, has a convincing forward momentum and plenty of imaginative detail.

The so-called *German organ Mass* is split between CDs, which should not have been necessary, and the *Art of Fugue* has now been placed at the end; a suitable postlude is provided with a complete version of the *Chorale*, BWV 668a. There are many special insights here and, with such a spontaneous approach,

Rübsam's distinguished and consistently enjoyable survey may readily be placed alongside that of Peter Hurford on Decca, while the newly remastered Philips analogue recording is of comparable demonstration quality – a very major achievement.

Wolfgang Rübsam Naxos series

The Art of fugue, BWV 1080; Chorale partita: Sei gegrüsset Jesu gütig, BWV 768; Passacaglia and fugue in C min., BWV 582.

(BB) ** Naxos 8.550703/4 [id.]. Wolfgang Rübsam (Flenthrop organ of Duke Chapel, Dale University, Durham, USA).

Two decades after his first integral recording of Bach's organ music for Philips, Wolfgang Rübsam has begun a second digital survey for Naxos. He has crossed the Atlantic and – based now in the Chicago area, where he is resident organist at the University – he has had an opportunity to discover the quality of modern American organs. As this splendidly recorded Naxos series demonstrates, many of them have a magnificent panoply of colour fully worthy of the baroque repertoire. Rübsam's long experience has meant that he has developed a fine ear for registration and throughout these Naxos CDs he perceptively draws on the rich palette and glowing combinations that these American organs can provide. For some of the earlier records in the series Rübsam continued to use European organs. The documentation that comes with the individual CDs cannot be faulted. The only snag is that cueing is ungenerous and individual movements of composite works are unbanded.

However, since making his Philips recordings, Rübsam's playing has become more considered, less eccentric in rubato, less exuberant. Although underlying structural insights are never in doubt, tempi are often relatively staid and at times one misses the youthful freshness that is so striking in the earlier set.

For *The Art of Fugue* he has a particularly fine organ at his disposal and, excellent Bach player that he is, he displays the work's detail admirably. He alters the order of the presentation of the Contrapunctus, but that will not matter too much to most collectors. There are two substantial bonuses, but both these works are played very slowly and deliberately indeed. The timing here for the mighty *Sei gegrüsset chorale partita* is 25 minutes. Its extraordinarily complex polyphonic detail is certainly revealed but the effect seems heavy and didactic. Although repeats and different ornamentation may come into the equation, some organists bring it off as much as ten minutes quicker. Similarly the *Passacaglia and fugue* is quite remorseless and takes 19 minutes, against Rübsam's earlier Philips version, which is 12 minutes 21 seconds!

Allabreve in D, BWV 589; Canzona in D min., BWV 588; Chorale fantasia: Valet will ich dir geben, BWV 736; Chorale prelude: Wir glauben all' an einen Gott, BWV 740; Chorale partita: O Gott, du frommer Gott, BWV 767; Preludes and fugues: in G min., BWV 535; in G, BWV 550; Trio in G min., BWV 584.

(BB) ** Naxos Dig. 8.553033 [id.]. Wolfgang Rübsam (Taylor & Boody organ of St Joseph's Memorial Chapel, Holy Cross College, Worcester, Massachusetts).

Rübsam conjures some most attractive sounds from this splendid Taylor & Boody organ, particularly in the simple and beautiful chorale, *Wir glauben all' an einen Gott, Vater*, the *Trio in G minor* and the *Prelude in G minor*, BWV 535, which shows him at his best. But in the latter work, when the fugue follows one senses some stiffness in his fingers. The fantasia on *Valet will ich dir geben* takes the cantus firmus to the pedals, with an antiphonal triple rhythm above, and the piece does not hang together too well. The opening pedal passage in the *G major Prelude* is much more successful, although the fugue is marred by a rather jerky rhythmic flow. The *Canzona* flows more evenly, but its course is again unhurried, as indeed is the massive closing *Allabreve*.

Clavier-Ubung, Part 3 (beginning): *German organ Mass: Prelude in E flat, BWV 552; Chorale preludes, BWV 669–81.*

(BB) ** Naxos Dig. 550929 [id.]. Wolfgang Rübsam (Silbermann organ of Freiburg Cathedral).

Clavier-Ubung, Part 3 (conclusion): *Chorale preludes, BWV 682–9; 4 Duets, BWV 802–5; Fugue in E flat, BWV 552.*

(BB) ** Naxos Dig. 550930 [id.]. Wolfgang Rübsam (Silbermann organ of Freiburg Cathedral).

Wolfgang Rübsam sometimes seems rather didactic in the chorales which make up the *German organ Mass*. However, he makes the very most of the reedy colours of the Freiburg organ which make it so suitable for this music. At the close he registers the four *Duets* very lightly to make a complete contrast with the massive closing five-part *E flat Fugue* which is here presented steadily and massively but not without momentum.

Chorale preludes and fantasias, BWV 714, 717–18, 720, 722, 724–5, 733–5, 737–8 & 741; Fantasia con imitatione in B min., BWV 563; Prelude in A min., BWV 569; Fugue in C min., BWV 575; Preludes and fugues: in E min., BWV 533; in A min., BWV 551.

(BB) ** Naxos Dig. 8.553629 [id.]. Wolfgang Rübsam (Brombaugh organ at Lawrence University Chapel, Appleton. Wisconsin).

The chorales register well on this fine organ, but Rübsam is his usual steady self and one would like more flair in the *Preludes and fugues* and especially in the *Fugue on the Magnificat*, BWV 733, which ends the programme rather heavily.

Concertos (for solo organ) *Nos. 1 in G,* (after Ernst), *BWV 592; 2 in A min.* (after VIVALDI: *Concerto in A min., Op. 3/8, RV 522); BWV 593; 3 in C* (after VIVALDI: *Concerto in D, Op. 7/11, RV 208), BWV 594; 4 in C* (after ERNST), *BWV 595; 5 in D min.* (after VIVALDI: *Concerto in D min., Op. 3/11, RV 565*); *BWV 596; 6 in E flat* (arr. of Concerto by an unnamed composer), *BWV 597; Trio in C min.* (after FASCH), *BWV 585; Trio in G* (after TELEMANN), *BWV 586; Aria in F* (from COUPERIN: *Les Nations*), *BWV 587.*

(BB) *** Naxos Dig. 8.550936 [id.]. Wolfgang Rübsam (Flenthrop organ of St Mark's Cathedral, Seattle, Washington).

This is a strikingly successful collection, one of the finest records in this Naxos series, and it is very comprehensive in including the rarely played 'Anonymous' Concerto transcription, BWV 597. This is a most engaging piece, particularly the jaunty closing section, and it is nicely registered, as are the other individual movements here, by Couperin, Fasch and Telemann. Rübsam readily conveys his enjoyment of the Vivaldi concertos and he contrasts the difference between tutti and concertino most effectively. He gives a very grand performance of the C major transcription of RV 208 with which he opens the recital. With cadenza interpolations he extends the work to well over 18 minutes, yet it does not outstay its welcome. The serene slow movement of the *D minor Concerto*, RV 565, is also memorable, helped by the lovely sounds which can be provided by this splendid organ, which is ideal for this repertoire. Yet Rübsam's tempi for allegros remain buoyant throughout and the playing is always seemingly spontaneous. The recording is in the demonstration class.

Leipzig organ chorales Nos. 1–8, BWV 651–8; Toccata, adagio and fugue, BWV 564.

(BB) **(*) Naxos Dig. 8.550901 [id.]. Wolfgang Rübsam (Taylor & Boody organ of St Joseph's Memorial Chapel, Holy Cross College, Worcester, Massachusetts).

Leipzig organ chorales Nos. 9–18, BWV 659–67; Canonic variations: Vom Himmel hoch, BWV 769; fugue, BWV 564.

(BB) **(*) Naxos Dig. 8.550901 [id.]. Wolfgang Rübsam (Taylor & Boody organ of St Joseph's Memorial Chapel, Holy Cross College, Worcester, Massachusetts).

Bach designates the opening *Leipzig chorale* as a fantasia on *Komm, heiliger Geist* for full organ (*in organo pieno*), with the chorale melody in the pedals. Rübsam presents it massively, and then registers Bach's second treatment of the same chorale to make the widest contrast, as he is to do throughout the series when there is more than one setting. If his tempi are at times rather restrained, he makes the very most of the colourful range of this fine organ, and in *Nun danket alle Gott* uses a trumpet stop arrestingly. He ends the first disc with a very impressive account of the mighty BWV 564. The opening *C major Toccata*, with its thundering pedals, is suitably flamboyant, the *Adagio* is tranquil, and the closing fugue, very well paced, is weighty without being weighed down. The second CD includes the *Canonic variations on Vom Himmel hoch*, a very complex piece in which Bach's continuing canonic treatment is an extraordinary example of his most ingenious polyphony. At face value it might seem an academic exercise, but the continual reappearance of the cantus firmus, whether in the upper parts or the pedals, creates a musical *tour de force*, ever intriguing the ear of the listener. Rübsam's performance, which opens very enticingly, has fine momentum, yet can relax too. Detail always remains clear and he revels in the way the chorale melody is continually popping up. The splendid recording, rich in texture but never clouding, helps both Bach and his interpreter. The programme then ends with the finale Leipzig chorale, *Thron tret ich* ('Before Thy throne I stand') and Rübsam catches its reverent atmosphere to perfection.

Kirnberger chorale preludes Nos. 1–12, BWV 690–701; Chorale partita: Christ du bist der helle Tag, BWV 766; Fugue in C min., BWV 574; Preludes and fugues: in C min., BWV 549; in E, BWV 566.

(BB) ** Naxos Dig. 8.553134 [id.]. Wolfgang Rübsam (Taylor & Boody organ of Christ Church Cathedral, Indianapolis, USA).

The first dozen of Bach's so-called Kirnberger chorales (collected for a student of that name) are framed by the two *Preludes and fugues,* and the *C minor* provides a grandiloquent end to the recital with its powerful use of the pedals and brilliantly decorated final cadence. The second piece is the set of extended chorale variations on *Christ du bist de helle Tag*, which are very relaxed but imaginatively registered. So too are the following chorales (the organ has a splendidly diverse palette), simply presented, but with those slightly eccentric touches of rubato which are Rübsam's hallmark. They even extend to the central *C minor fugue*. One cannot fault this organist's feeling for colour (witness the alternative settings of *Vom Himmel hoch*), but he is less ready to move away from his purposefully steady tempi.

Kirnberger chorale preludes Nos. 13–24, BWV 702–13; Chorale variations: Ach was soll ich Sünder machen?; Fugues: in G, BWV 576; in G min. BWV 578; Toccata and fugue in F, BWV 540.

(BB) **(*) Naxos Dig. 8.553135 [id.]. Wolfgang Rübsam (Brombaugh organs at Ackerman Auditorium, Collegedale Southern College School of Music, Lawrence University Chapel, Appleton, Wisconsin).

The expansive *Toccata in F*, BWV 540, which opens this disc has an arrestingly powerful introductory use of the pedals, but the fugue might have had more momentum (the overall playing time is 17 minutes 33 seconds). Rübsam then presents the remaining Kirnberger chorales registered in glowing colours. The two Brombaugh organs have some unusual stops; *Allein Gott in der Höh' sei Ehr* is particularly striking, as is the very brief chorale fughetta, *Gottes Sohn ist kommen*, BWV 703. This begins very slowly, although the brilliant variants which immediately follow are very clearly articulated. Equally the detail of the *Fugue in G minor*, which acts as a centrepiece, is very well projected, and again the piquant reeds are telling. The programme ends with extended variations on *Ach, was soll ich Sünder machen?* Rübsam's registration of the chorale is particularly beautiful, and the following mutations have a similarly vivid palette. Rübsam is a sound guide in this repertoire and the disc is worth exploring for the spicy sounds he conjures out of these two very characterful organs.

Orgelbüchlein: 19 Chorale preludes for Advent, Christmas, New Year and the Purification, BWV 599–617; Fantasia in C, BWV 570; Fugue on a theme of Corelli in B min., BWV 579; Preludes and fugues in C, BWV 531; in F min., BWV 534; Prelude in G, BWV 568.

(BB) *** Naxos Dig. 8.553031 [id.]. Wolfgang Rübsam (Flenthrop organ of Duke Chapel, Duke University, Durham, USA).

Orgelbüchlein: 27 Chorale preludes for Passiontide; Easter; Pentecost; and expressing Faith, BWV 618–44; Fantasia in C, BWV 570; Fugue in B min., BWV 579; Preludes and fugues: in C, BWV 531; in F min., BWV 534; Prelude in G, BWV 568.

(BB) *** Naxos Dig. 8.553032 [id.]. Wolfgang Rübsam (Flenthrop organ of Duke Chapel, Duke University, Durham, USA).

The *Orgelbüchlein* (or 'Little Organ book') includes 46 chorale preludes for the church year, written by Bach partly at Weimar and concluded later at Cöthen. Rübsam has obviously thought deeply about each chorale and its meditative character. His presentation here is very well planned, with preludes and fugues acting as introductions and postludes to the eight groupings, each of which centres on one of the key periods of the Church calendar. Rübsam introduces Advent with Bach's solemn yet expressive *B minor Fugue* based on a theme of Corelli, and *Nun komm' der Heiden Heiland* follows on naturally. He finds great variety for his presentation of each chorale: *Herr Christ, der ein'ge Gottessohn* could hardly be more jubilant. The Christmas section is preceded by the flamboyant and joyous *Prelude and fugue in C*, with its resounding pedals, and the first recital is rounded off with a characteristically spacious account of the imposing *F minor Prelude and fugue*, BWV 534.

On the second disc Passiontide is heralded by the poignantly atmospheric *C minor Fantasy*, and later the ear is struck by the beauty of Rübsam's presentation of *Christe, du Lamme gottes* and the meditative feeling of *Da Jesus an dem Kreuze stund'* and *O Mensch bewein' dein Sünde gross* ('O man, bewail your great sins'). The Easter chorales are, not surprisingly, more robust and outward-giving, while the four Pentecost chorales are touchingly contemplative. There is infinite variety of mood and colour in the last group, opening with a piece symbolizing the ten commandments and showing Bach reflecting on various aspects of the Christian faith. The introduction of the closing *Prelude and Fugue in D minor*, BWV 539, is grave and dignified, but the fugue itself is optimistic and vital, ending the concert satisfyingly. The Duke University Chapel organ is a magnificent instrument, and the recording is superb throughout.

Pastorale in F, BWV 590; Preludes and fugues: in D, BWV 532; in E min. (Wedge), BWV 548; in E flat (St Anne), BWV 552; Toccata and fugue in D min., BWV 565.

(BB) ** Naxos Dig. 8.550184 [id.]. Wolfgang Rübsam (Flenthrop organ of Oberlin College, USA).

The opening of the *St Anne's Prelude* is very grand and portentous, and the fugue itself winds along very slowly and heavily. The *Pastorale in F* brings aural balm and is delightfully registered. Then comes the famous *Toccata and fugue in D minor*, which is a shade mannered, although the *Toccata* itself is certainly not without flair. The fugue then proceeds with good momentum until its close, where Rübsam produces an overwhelming cadence, with superbly resonant pedals. The *Prelude* – and especially the *fugue* – in D shows Rübsam at his most individual, and the E minor work, BWV 548, certainly commands attention, although the florid detail of the fugue could be detailed more cleanly. The Flenthrop organ itself sounds magnificent.

Preludes and fugues: in A, BWV 536; in G, BWV 541; in G min., BWV 542; in A min., BWV 544; in C min., BWV 546.
(BB) **(*) Naxos Dig. 8.550652 [id.]. Wolfgang Rübsam (Schnitger organ, Martinkerk, Groningen, Netherlands).

These *Preludes and fugues*, like the *Trio sonatas* below, were recorded in November 1989, before Rübsam moved his project across the Atlantic. He registers very fully indeed, tempi are steady, and it is the monumental architectural effect of Bach's writing that carries each work through to its resonant conclusion, helped by the full-bodied Naxos engineering. The Dutch organ sounds superb, but in the earlier Weimar pieces (BWV 536 and BWV 542) one might ideally have expected more exuberance, less seriousness of purpose. The cueing does not help: ten cues are listed, but in the event there are only five tracks, one for each work.

6 Schübler chorales, BWV 645–50; Fantasia in G, BWV 572; Fantasia and fugue in C min., BWV 537; Prelude and fugue in C, BWV 545; Toccata and fugue in D min. (Dorian), BWV 538.
(BB) ** Naxos Dig. 8.553150 [id.]. Wolfgang Rübsam (Metzler organ of St Michael's Church, Eutin, Germany).

This is another of Rübsam's earlier recitals, recorded in Germany in 1988. He presents the six famous *Schübler chorales*, not as a group but singly or in pairs, with other more ambitious pieces in between. The best-known first chorale (*Wachet auf*) brings his characteristic little hesitations in the rhythmic flow, but otherwise the presentation is effectively serene. The brilliant *Fantasia in G*, BWV 572, makes an attractive diversion later in the recital, while the *Fantasia and fugue in C minor*, which comes second, immediately produces an extraordinary pedal effect, halfway between a 'raspberry' and a loud note on a double bassoon! As so often with this player, the fugue is very steady. The 'other' (*Dorian*) *D minor Toccata and fugue* is powerfully but very massively presented and, although the closing *C major Fugue* offers a wider variety of style, it too ends stolidly on the full organ. The recording of this little-known German instrument is of very high quality.

Trio sonatas Nos.1–6, BWV 525–30; Prelude and fugues: in A min., BWV 543; in C, BWV 547.
(BB) ** Naxos Dig. 8.550651 (Nos. 1–3 & BWV 543); 8.550653 (Nos. 4–6 & BWV 547). Wolfgang Rübsam (Schnitger organ, Martinkerk, Groningen, Netherlands).

The Groningen organ makes some luscious sounds, which bring plenty of colour to this outgoing music, especially in slow movements. Rübsam's playing has a pleasingly amiable rhythmic feeling and flow, and the slightly idiosyncratic line one notices in his Bach piano records, although present, is not too disturbing. Each disc closes with a major *Prelude and fugue*, weightily played, but with unclouded textures: the C major, BWV 547, is the more impressive of the two performances.

Chorale preludes: An Wasserflüssen Babylon, BWV 653; Herr Jesu Christ, BWV 709 & 726; Liebster Jesu, BWV 731; Wir glauben all' an einen Gott, BWV 765 (4 Neumeister chorales): Wir glauben all' an einen Gott, BWV 1098; Gott is mein Heil, BWV 1106; Herzlich lieb hab ich dich, O Herr, BWV 1115; Was Gott tut, das ist wohlgetan, BWV 1116. Concerto in F (after Vivaldi's *Concerto, Op. 3/3*); *Fantasia and fugue in C min., BWV 537; Fugue in C min.* on a theme by Legrenzi, *BWV 574; Preludes and fugues: in C, BWV 531; in B min., BWV 544; in C, BWV 547; in A min., BWV 895* (attrib.); *6 Schübler chorales, BWV 645–50; Toccata and fugue in D min. (Dorian), BWV 538; Trio sonata in G, BWV 1039/1027a.*
(B) *** Nimbus Dig. Double NI 5500/1 [id.]. Kevin Bowyer (Marcussen organ of Sct. Hans Kirke, Odense, Denmark).

Kevin Bower is another of the younger generation of organists who is embarking on a complete Bach survey, but he has chosen to produce a series of carefully planned recitals rather than grouping works together in their respective genres. Half a dozen CDs have already appeared at premium price and have been highly praised in our main (1996) *Guide*. However, we are glad to welcome the present pair of two-for-the-price-of-one Doubles, which may well tempt the collector to try the series as a whole. The advantage of Bowyer's programming in this way is that each recital can be enjoyed individually.

As with the previous single discs, the two recitals which are paired together in this first Nimbus double (Volume 8) are meant to be listened to separately. Both are highly enjoyable and bring plenty of contrast. On the first, after the vigorous *Fugue in C minor*, BWV 574, the arrangement of Vivaldi's concerto from *L'Estro armonico* for manuals only (no pedals) works extremely well, with the rich blending of colours in the *Largo* well contrasted with the framing allegros. Bowyer's choice of chorales is also intended to give maximum contrast, and sometimes he plays them in pairs to show Bach's imaginatively varied treatments of the same *cantus firmus*. One of the most beautiful is the moving five-part setting of *An Wasserflüssen Babylon*. The *Trio sonata in G* is a conjectural reconstruction, but a very successful one: it has a delightfully registered *Adagio* and finale. The *Preludes and fugues* have plenty of life and vigour: the early C major work is full of rhythmic energy. Bowyer also opens the famous first *Schübler chorale* with a bouncing rhythmic lift, and is equally enticing in his brilliant registration of the buoyant closing chorale of the set, *Kommst du nun, Jesu*, BWV 650. The recital ends with a superbly exuberant account of the *Dorian Toccata and fugue in D minor* which here proves quite as exciting as its more famous companion in the same key (BWV 565). The Nimbus recording of the magnificent Danish organ is superb in every respect, although the action sounds are also clearly picked up by the microphones.

Clavier-Ubung. Part 3: German organ Mass: Prelude in E, BWV 552; Chorale preludes, BWV 669–89; 4 Duets, BWV 802–5; Fugue in E flat (St Anne), BWV 552. Concerto in G (after VIVALDI: *Violin concerto in G*) *BWV 973; Fugue in G min., BWV 578; Passacaglia and fugue in C min., BWV 582.*
❁ (B) *** Nimbus Dig. Double NI 5561/2 [id.]. Kevin Bowyer (Marcussen organ of Sct. Hans Kirke, Odense, Denmark).

Both discs of Kevin Bowyer's second Nimbus Double (Volume 9 in his ongoing Bach series) are meant to be heard together, with the programme centring on Bach's so-called *German organ Mass*. This is music which can seem heavy and boring, but never so here; indeed, this account is unsurpassed on CD. Bowyer's approach is essentially more secular than some (notably that of Marie-Claire Alain), but that does not mean that the music is trivialized. After the powerful introductory *Prelude*, Bach presents each chorale in two contrasting versions, the first elaborate, then a simpler setting without pedals (although occasionally this order is reversed). Bowyer's imagination is inspired to use all the resources of the splendid organ to emphasize the contrapuntal and stylistic differences. The opening 'Kyrie' (*Gott Vater in Ewigkeit*) creates an initially sombre atmosphere, and Bach's second treatment of the same chorale (which does not follow on directly) is very gentle. Later on there is to be the widest variety of mood. The fughettas are always pointed with rhythmic sharpness, so that the brief second version of *Wir glauben all' an einen Gott* (BWV 681) is quite different from the majestic initial presentation, meant to convey the power of God's Ten Commandments (BWV 680). When Bowyer uses the organ's fullest resources, as in the *Aus tiefer Not schrei' ich zu dir* (BWV 686) the effect is weighty but not oppressive (as Wolfgang Rübsam can too readily be on Naxos). With the four deceptively simple *Duets*, Bach lightens the overall mood and Bowyer gives them sparkling registrations to make a foil for the weighty power of the closing *St Anne's fugue*, which holds the listener from the first bar to the last. Bowyer then continues his recital with a captivating account of Bach's transcription of one of Vivaldi's liveliest violin concertos and follows with the slightly dolorous *G minor Fugue*, registered with great clarity. He ends with a superbly eloquent performance of the great *Passacaglia and fugue in C minor*, the pacing exactly right (with some remarkable detail at the centre of the work), and with the tension held at the highest level throughout.

Other organ music

33 Arnstadt chorale preludes (from Yale manuscript).
(B) *** HM Dig. HMA 1905158 [id.]. Joseph Payne (organ of St Paul's, Brookline, Mass.).

Joseph Payne collects the complete set together on a single CD and is very economically priced. Now reissued on Harmonia Mundi's budget Musique d'Abord label, this is even more attractive.

6 Trio sonatas, BWV 525–30 (see also arrangements under Chamber Music – above).
(M) **(*) DG (IMS) Dig. 447 277-2. Ton Koopman (organ of Waalse Kerk, Amsterdam).

Ton Koopman's set comes from 1982 and is very well recorded on a highly suitable Dutch organ. The opening of the very first sonata promises well, with a buoyant rhythmic lift; the central *Adagio* is nicely coloured and the finale spirited. The *Adagio e dolce* of *No. 3 in D minor* again shows an apt choice of colouring, but the finale (marked *Vivace*) tends to jog along and the similarly indicated opening movement of No. 6 is also relaxed. Other versions of these works are that bit more spirited but not more glowing, and this is certainly enjoyable.

Organ recitals

Allabreve in D, BWV 589; Canzona in D min., BWV 588; Fantasie in G, BWV 572; Passacaglia and fugue in C min., BWV 582; Pastorale in F, BWV 590; Prelude in A min., BWV 569; Toccata and fugue in D min., BWV 565; Toccata and fugue in D min. (Dorian), BWV 538.

(M) **(*) (IMS) DG Dig. 447 292-2. Ton Koopman (organ of Maassluis Grote Kerk).

This recital comes into competition with an earlier bargain recital (see below) which duplicates four items here. Choice between the two programmes will be a matter of taste; this one has the advantage of placing the two *D minor Toccatas and fugues* side by side, although the layout is less than ideally planned, with the *Allabreve* coming immediately after the sombre *Canzona*.

Canonic variations on 'Vom Himmel hoch', BWV 769; Fantasia in G, BWV 572; Fantasia and fugue in G min., BWV 542; Passacaglia in C min., BWV 582; Preludes and fugues: in D, BWV 532; in E flat, BWV 552; 6 Schübler chorale preludes, BWV 645–50; Toccatas and fugues: in D min., BWV 536 (Dorian) & 565; in F, BWV 540; Trio sonata No. 3 in D min. BWV 527.

(B) ** DG Double 453 064-2 (2) [id.]. Helmut Walcha (organs of St-Pierre-le-Jeune, Strasbourg, St Laurenskerk, Alkmaar).

It is good to be inexpensively reminded of the German tradition of playing in this repertoire, as represented by its most distinguished exponent, Helmut Walcha. The *Canonic variations* and *Schübler chorales* (recorded in Strasbourg, and part of his complete survey, made at the beginning of the 1970s) show him at his most didactic. The playing is calm and assured and certainly authoritative. Its control is never in doubt, but the famous chorales are rather straitlaced and entirely lacking in charm. Most of the rest of the programme was recorded at St Laurenskerk in 1963–4. The remastered recordings sound extremely well, the reedy brightness supported by an underlying depth, and there is a sense of perspective too, particularly in the interplay of the famous *D minor Fugue*, which was the first piece to be recorded (in 1959) and which shows Walcha at his more extrovert. The other performances are usually registered effectively, notably the first movement of the *Trio sonata*, but Walcha's pulse remains steady. Structures are well controlled and detail is lucid, but at times there is a ponderous feeling, which one does not experience with players like Peter Hurford, Kevin Bowyer and Christopher Herrick.

Canzona in D min., BWV 588; Fantasie in G, BWV 572; Passacaglia and fugue in C min., BWV 582; 6 Schübler chorales, BWV 645–50; Toccatas and fugues in F, BWV 540; in D min., BWV 565.

(B) **(*) DG Dig. 439 477-2 [(M) id. import]. Ton Koopman (various organs).

Ton Koopman uses two different organs here, principally that of the Grote Kerk, Maassluis, but the *Schübler chorales* are recorded on that of the Waalse Kerk, Amsterdam, whose reeds are brightly and colourfully projected. The recital opens with the famous *Toccata and fugue in D minor*, BWV 565, and this performance has an engaging eccentricity in that Koopman introduces decoration into the opening flourishes. The performance has an excitingly paced fugue and is superbly recorded. Contrast is provided by the *Canzona in D minor*, a slow and rather solemn contrapuntal exercise. Overall the performances are well structured and alive, if sometimes rather considered in feeling. The recital ends with the mighty *Passacaglia and fugue in C minor*, BWV 582.

Chorale preludes: Erbarm' dich mein, O Herre Gott, BWV 721; Herzlich tut mich verlangen, BWV 727; O Mensch, bewein' dein' Sünde gross, BWV 622; Wir gläuben all an einen Gott, BWV 680; Fugue in B min. on a theme of Corelli, BWV 579; Passacaglia and fugue in C min., BWV 582; Pastorale in F, BWV 590; Toccata and fugue in D min., BWV 565.

(B) *** EMI Dig. CD-EMX 2218 [(M) id. import]. Peter Hurford (organ of Martinkerk, Groningen, Holland).

Having left his complete Decca Bach series long behind him, Peter Hurford here sets off on his travels again to record a familiar programme on a remarkably fine Groningen organ. This new recital whets the appetite for more. Perhaps the most famous *Toccata and fugue* is a fraction less flamboyant than before, and several of the chorale preludes are very relaxed and thoughtful. The *Pastorale*, too, is fairly static. But in the closing *Passacaglia and fugue* he demonstrates how he can hold and build tension when setting off at a very measured pace. What a masterpiece this is! The EMI engineers do him proud.

Chorale preludes: Herzlich tut mich verlangen, BWV 727; In dulci jubilo, BWV 729; Liebster Jesu, wir sind hier, BWV 730; Nun freut euch, lieben Christen g'mein, BWV 734; Nun komm, der Heiden Heiland, BWV 659; Wachet auf, ruft uns die Stimme, BWV 645; Wo soll ich fliehen hin, BWV 694; Fantasias: in C min., BWV 562; in G, BWV 572; Fantasia and fugues: in C min., BWV 537; in G min., BWV 542; Passacaglia and fugue in C min., BWV 582; Preludes and fugues: in A min., BWV 543; in D, BWV 532; in E flat (St Anne), BWV 552; Toccata, Adagio and fugue in C, BWV 564; Toccatas and fugues in D min. (Dorian), BWV 538; BWV 565.

(B) *** Decca Duo 443 485-2 (2) [id.]. Peter Hurford (organs of Ratzeburg Cathedral; Knox Grammar School, Sydney, Chapel; Church of Our Lady of Sorrows, Toronto; New College, Oxford, Chapel; All Souls' Unitarian Church, Washington, DC).

A generous 146-minute collection of major Bach organ works, taken from Peter Hurford's complete survey (see above), brings two separate recitals, each framed by major concert pieces, with the beautifully played chorales used in between the large-scale pieces to add contrast. The current bright transfers seem to have added an extra sharpness of outline to the sound of some of the big set pieces, but this is something which will be more noticeable on some reproducers than on others, and the various organs are caught with fine realism and plenty of depth.

Chorale preludes: Ich ruf zu dir, Herr Jesu Christ, BWV 639; Wachet auf, BWV 645; Kommst du nun, Jesu, BWV 650; Christ Fantasia and fugue in G min., BWV 542; Vom Himmel hoch, da komm ich her, BWV 606; Passacaglia and fugue in C min., BWV 582; Prelude and fugue in E min., BWV 548; Toccata and fugue in D min., BWV 565.

(M) ** Decca 455 291-2 [id.]. Karl Richter (organ of Victoria Hall, Geneva).

These were among Decca's earliest stereo recordings, and the organ of Geneva's Victoria Hall sounds magnificent, with the resonant bass full and beautifully focused. It never sounded as good as this on LP and it certainly suits this repertoire. However, the style of the playing is in the old German tradition. Richter's tempi are characteristically steady. Some will feel that the famous D minor work which opens the disc is too relaxed, but Richter's way is the very opposite of flamboyant. The first of the Schübler Chorales (*Wachet auf*) is positively stoic and, while the *Passacaglia and fugue in C minor* is impressively controlled, its forward progess is very measured.

Chorale preludes: Jesu bleibet meine Freude, BWV 147; Ich ruf' zu dir, Herr Jesu Christ, BWV 639; Fugue in G min., BWV 578; Passacaglia and fugue in C min., BWV 582; Prelude and fugue in E flat (St Anne), BWV 552; Toccata, Adagio and fugue, BWV 564; Toccata and fugue in D min., BWV 565.

(BB) *(*) Naxos Dig. 8.553859 [id.]. Wolfgang Rübsam (various organs).

This recital centres on the famous D minor *Toccata and fugue*, played with a fair degree of panache and with a very powerful ending. The *G minor Fugue*, however, does not flow as spontaneously as it might and is heavily registered, although detail remains clear. *Jesu, joy of man's desiring* might also have benefited from a lighter touch. The best thing here is the *Toccata, Adagio and fugue*, one of Rübsam's most impressive performances, but the *St Anne Fugue*, like the leaden *Passacaglia and fugue in C minor*, needs more momentum.

(i) *Concertos in D min., BWV 596; in A min., BWV 593* (after Vivaldi); (ii) *Passacaglia and fugue in C min., BWV 582; Toccata, adagio and fugue in C, BWV 564; Toccata and fugue in D min., BWV 565.*

(B) ** EMI forte (SIS) CZS5 69328-2 (2) [CDFB 69328]. Fernando Germani (organ of (i) Selby Abbey, Yorkshire; (ii) Royal Festival Hall, London) – FRANCK: *Chorales Nos. 1–3* etc. *(*); WIDOR: *Toccata.* **(*)

The Festival Hall with its dry acoustics, where BWV 564, 565 and 582 were recorded in 1959, proves a fascinatingly different way of hearing Bach. Germani plays the *Toccatas* brilliantly enough but presents the fugues in a very relaxed fashion, and especially so the *C minor Passacaglia*, and while the listener can hear every detail of the registration in crystal clarity, he lets the tension build itself slowly to its climax. Each of these performances becomes aurally quite a *tour de force* – if also a somewhat didactic experience. For the *Concertos* we are transferred to the warmer ambience of Selby Abbey. These works are much more Vivaldi than Bach, although it is surprising how much of Bach's personality is superimposed by Germani on that of the Italian composer. This is emphasized in the *D minor Concerto* by a certain heaviness of style in the playing; whereas in the *A minor* Germani finds slightly more Italianate jauntiness in the writing of the outer movements and a pealing-bell effect for the finale. He sets the mood of the *Adagio*, which he plays very slowly indeed, as a serene contrast. The recordings are superb, but the Abbey organ is not ideally chosen for the concertos, which need more sonic brilliance.

VOCAL MUSIC

Cantatas Nos. 1–14; 16–52; 54–69; 69a; 70–117; 119–140; 143–159; 161–188; 192; 194–199 (complete).

(B) *** Teldec/Warner Analogue/Dig. 4509 91765-2 (60) [id.]. Treble Soloists from V. Boys' & Regensburg Choirs, Esswood, Equiluz, Van Altena, Van Egmond, Hampson, Nimsgern, Van der Meer, Jacobs, Iconomou, Holl, Immler, King's College, Cambridge, Ch., V. Boys' Ch., Tölz Boys' Ch., Ch. Viennensis, Ghent Coll. Vocale, VCM, Harnoncourt; Leonhardt Cons., Leonhardt.

Cantatas Nos. (i) *1: Wie schön leuchtet uns der Morgenstern; 2: Ach Gott, vom Himmel; 3: Ach Gott, wie manches Herzeleid; 4: Christ lag in Todesbanden; 5: Wo soll ich fliehen hin; 6: Bleib bei uns;* (ii) *7: Christ unser Herr zum Jordan kam; 8: Liebster Gott; 9: Es ist das Heil; 10: Meine Seele erhebt den Herrn;* (i) *11: Lobet Gott in seinen Reichen;* (ii) *12: Weinen, klagen, sorgen, zagen; 13: Meine Seufzer, meine Tränen; 14: Wär Gott nicht mit uns diese Zeit; 16: Herr Gott, dich loben wir;* (i) *17: Wer Dank opfert, der preiset mich; 18: Gleichwie der Regen und Schnee vom Himmel; 19: Es erhub sich ein Streit.*

(M) *** Teldec/Warner 4509 91755-2 (6) [id.]. Esswood, Equiluz, Van Altena, Van Egmond, treble soloists; (i) V. Boys' Ch., Ch. Viennensis, VCM, Harnoncourt; (ii) Tölz Boys' Ch., King's College Ch., Leonhardt Cons., Leonhardt.

Cantatas Nos. (i) *20: O Ewigkeit, du Donnerwort; 21: Ich hatte viel Bekümmernis;* (ii) *22: Jesus nahm zu sich die Zwölfe; 23: Du wahrer Gott und Davids Sohn;* (i) *24: Ein ungefärbt Gemüte; 25: Es ist nicht Gesundes an meinem Leibe; 26: Ach wie flüchtig, ach wie nichtig; 27: Wer weiss, wie nahe mir mein Ende!; 28: Gottlob! nun geht das Jahr zu Ende; 29: Wir danken dir, Gott; 30: Freue dich, erlöste Schar; 31: Der Himmel lacht! die Erde jubilieret;* (ii) *32: Liebster Jesu, mein Verlangen; 33: Allein zu dir, Herr Jesu Christ;* (i) *34: O ewiges Feuer, O Ursprung der Liebe; 35: Geist und Seele wird verwirret; 36: Schwingt freudig euch empor.*

(M) *** Teldec/Warner 4509 91756-2 (6) [id.]. Esswood, Jacobs, Van Altena, Equiluz, Van Egmond, Van der Meer, Nimsgern, Wyatt, (i) V. Boys' Ch., Ch. Viennensis, VCM, Harnoncourt; (ii) Hanover Boys' Ch., King's College Ch., Leonhardt Cons., Leonhardt.

Cantatas Nos. (i) *37: Wer da gläubet und getauft wird; 38: Aus tiefer Not schrei ich zu dir; 39: Brich dem Hungrigen dein Brot; 40: Dazu ist erschienen der Sohn Gottes;* (i) *41: Jesu, nun sei gepreiset; 42: Am Abend aber desselbigen Sabbats; 43: Gott fähret auf mit Jauchzen; 44: Sie werden euch in die Bann tun;* (ii) *45: Es ist dir gesagt, Mensch, was gut ist; 46: Schauet doch und sehet;* (i) *47: Wer sich selbst erhöhet; 48: Ich elender Mensch, wer wird mich erlösen; 49: Ich geh' und suche mit Verlangen; 50: Nun ist das Heil und die Kraft;* (ii) *51: Jauchzet Gott in allen Landen; 52: Falsche Welt, dir trau ihr nicht; 54: Widerstehe doch der Sünde; 55: Ich armer Mensch, ich Sündenknecht; 56: Ich will den Kreuzstab gerne tragen;* (i) *57: Selig ist der Mann; 58: Ach Gott, wie manches Herzeleid; 59: Wer mich liebet, der wird mein Wort halten; 60: O Ewigkeit, du Donnerwort.*

(M) *** Teldec/Warner 4509 91757-2 (6) [id.]. Kweksilber, Jelosits, Esswood, Jacobs, Van Altena, Equiluz, Van Egmond, Van der Meer, Kunz, Schopper, (i) V. Boys' Ch., Tölz Boys' Ch., Ch. Viennensis, VCM, Harnoncourt; (ii) Hanover Boys' Ch., Leonhardt Cons., Leonhardt.

Cantatas Nos. (i) *61: Nun komm, der Heiden Heiland; 62: Nun komm, der Heiden Heiland; 63: Christen, ätzet diesen Tag; 64: Sehet, welch eine Liebe; 65: Sie werden aus Saba alle kommen;* (ii) *66: Erfreut euch, ihr Herzen; 67: Halt im Gedächtnis Jesum Christ;* (i) *68: Also hat Gott die Welt geliebt; 69 & 69a: Lobe den Herrn, meine Seele; 70: Wachet! betet! betet! wachet!; 71: Gott ist mein König; 72: Alles nur nach Gottes Willen* (ii) *73: Herr, wie du willt, so schicks mit mir; 74: Wer mich liebet, der wird mein Wort halten; 75: Die Elenden sollen essen;* (i) *76: Die Himmel erzählen die Ehre Gottes;* (ii) *77: Du sollt Gott, deinen Herren, lieben; 78: Jesu, der du meine Seele.*

(M) **(*) Teldec/Warner 4509 91758-2 (6) [id.]. Esswood, Equiluz, Kraus, Van Egmond, Van der Meer, Visser, (i) Tölz Boys' Ch., VCM, Harnoncourt; (ii) Hanover Boys' Ch., Ghent Coll. Vocale, Leonhardt Cons., Leonhardt.

Cantatas Nos. (ii) *79: Gott der Herr ist Sonn' und Schild;* (i) *80: Ein feste Burg; 81: Jesus schläft, was soll ich hoffen?; 82: Ich habe genug; 83: Erfreute Zeit im neuen Bunde; 84: Ich bin vergnügt mit meinem Glücke; 85: Ich bin ein guter Hirt; 86: Wahrlich, wahrlich, ich sage euch; 87: Bisher habt ihr nichts gebeten;* (ii) *88: Siehe, ich will viel Fischer aussenden; 89: Was soll ich aus dir machen, Ephraim?; 90: Es reisset euch ein schrecklich Ende; 91: Gelobet seist du, Jesus Christ; 92: Ich habe in Gottes Herz und Sinn;* (i) *93: Wer nur den lieben Gott lässt walten; 94: Was frag' ich nach der Welt; 95: Christus, der ist mein Leben; 96: Herr Christ, der ein'ge Gottes-Sohn; 97: In allen meinen Taten;* (ii) *98: Was Gott tut, das ist wohlgetan; 99: Was Gott tut, das ist wohlgetan.*

(M) **(*) Teldec/Warner 4509 91759-2 (6) [id.]. Esswood, Equiluz, Van Egmond, Huttenlocher, Van der

Meer, (i) Tölz Boys' Ch., V. Boys' Ch., Ch. Viennensis, VCM, Harnoncourt; (ii) Hanover Boys' Ch., Ghent Coll. Vocale, Leonhardt Cons., Leonhardt.

Cantatas Nos. (ii) *100: Was Gott tut, das ist wohlgetan;* (i) *101: Nimm von uns, Herr, du treuer Gott; 102: Herr, deine Augen sehen nach dem Glauben;* (ii) *103: Ihr werdet weinen und heulen;* (i) *104: Du Hirte Israel, höre; 105: Herr, gehe nicht ins Gericht;* (ii) *106: Gottes Zeit ist die allerbeste Zeit (Actus tragicus); 107: Wass willst du dich betrüben;* (i) *108: Es ist euch gut, dass ich hingehe; 109: Ich glaube, lieber Herr, hilf meinem Unglauben!; 110: Unser Mund sei voll Lachens; 111: Was mein Gott will, das g'scheh allzeit; 112: Der Herr ist mein getreuer Hirt;* (ii) *113: Herr Jesu Christ, du höchstes Gut; 114: Ach, lieben Christen, seid getrost;* (i) *115: Mache dich, mein Geist, bereit; 116: Du Friedefürst, Herr Jesu Christ;* (ii) *117: Sei Lob und Ehr dem höchsten Gut.*

(M) *** Teldec/Warner 4509 91760-2 (6) [id.]. Esswood, Jacobs, Van Altena, Equiluz, Van Egmond, Huttenlocher, Lorenz, Van der Meer, (i) Tölz Boys' Ch., VCM, Harnoncourt; (ii) Hanover Boys' Ch., Ghent Coll. Vocale, Leonhardt Cons., Leonhardt.

Cantatas Nos. (i) *119: Preise, Jerusalem, den Herrn; 120: Gott, mann lobet dich in der Stille; 121: Christum wir sollen loben; 122: Das neugebor'ne Kindelein; 123: Liebster Immanuel, Herzog der Frommen; 124: Meinen Jesum lass ich nicht; 125: Mit Fried und Freud ich fahr dahin; 126: Erhalt uns, Herr, bei deinem Wort;* (ii) *127: Herr Jesu Christ wahr' Mensch und Gott; 128: Auf Christi Himmelfahrt allein; 129: Gelobet sei der Herr, mein Gott;* (i) *130: Herr Gott, dich loben alle wir; 131: Aus der Tiefen rufe ich, Herr, zu dir;* (ii) *132: Bereitet die Wege, bereitet die Bahn; 133: Ich freue mich in dir; 134: Ein Herz, das seinen Jesum lebend weiss; 135: Ach Herr, mich armen Sünder;* (i) *136: Erforsche mich, Gott, und erfahre mein Herz; 137: Lobe den Herren, den mächtigen König der Ehren.*

(M) **(*) Teldec/Warner 4509 91761-2 (6) [id.]. Esswood, Jacobs, Van Altena, Equiluz, Van Egmond, Hartinger, Heldwein, Holl, Huttenlocher, Thomaschke, (i) Tölz Boys' Ch., VCM, Harnoncourt; (ii) Hanover Boys' Ch., Ghent Coll. Vocale, Leonhardt Cons., Leonhardt.

Cantatas Nos. (i) *138: Warum betrübst du dich, mein Herz?; 139: Wohl dem, der sich auf seinen Gott; 140: Wachet auf, ruft uns die Stimme;* (ii) *143: Lobe den Herrn, meine Seele; 144: Nimm, was dein ist, und gehe hin;* (i) *145: Ich lebe, mein Herze, zu deinem Ergötzen; 146: Wir müssen durch viel Trübsal; 147: Herz und Mund und Tat und Leben; 148: Bringet dem Herrn Ehre seines Namens;* (ii) *149: Man singet mit Freuden vom Sieg; 150: Nach dir, Herr, verlanget mich; 151: Süsser Trost, mein Jesus kömmt;* (i) *152: Tritt auf die Glaubensahn; 153: Schau, lieber Gott, wie meine Feind; 154: Mein liebster Jesus ist verloren; 155: Mein Gott, wie lang, ach lange; 156: Ich steh' mit einem Fuss im Grabe* (ii) *157: Ich lasse dich nicht, du segnest mich denn; 158: Der Friede sei mit dir; 159: Sehet, wir gehn hinauf gen Jerusalem;* (i) *161: Komm, du süsse Todesstunde; 162: Ach! ich sehe, jetzt, da ich zur Hochzeit gehe.*

(M) **(*) Teldec/Warner Analogue/Dig. 4509 91762-2 (6) [id.]. Esswood, Equiluz, Van Egmond, Hampson, Holl, (i) Tölz Boys' Ch., VCM, Harnoncourt; (ii) Hanover Boys' Ch., Ghent Coll. Vocale, Leonhardt Cons., Leonhardt.

Cantatas Nos. (i) *163: Nur jedem das Seine;* (ii) *164: Ihr, die ihr euch von Christo nennet; 165: O heil'ges Geist und Wasserbad; 166: Wo gehest du hin?;* (i) *167: Ihr Menschen, rühmet Gottes Liebe; 168: Tue, Rechnung! Donnerwort; 169: Gott soll allein mein Herze haben;* (ii) *170: Vergnügte Ruh', beliebte Seelenlust;* (i) *171: Gott, wie dein Name, so ist auch dein Ruhm;* (ii) *172: Erschallet, ihr Lieder;* (i) *173: Erhöhtes Fleisch und Blut; 174: Ich liebe den Höchsten von ganzem Gemüte;* (ii) *175: Er rufet seinen Schafen mit Namen; 176: Es ist ein trotzig und verzagt Ding;* (i) *177: Ich ruf zu dir, Herr Jesu Christ; 178: Wo Gott der Herr nicht bei uns hält; 179: Siehe zu, dass deine Gottesfurcht.* (ii) *180: Schmücke dich, O liebe Seele; 181: Leichtgesinnte Flattergeister;* (i) *182: Himmelskönig, sei willkommen.*

(M) **(*) Teldec/Warner Dig. 4509 91763-2 (6) [id.]. Esswood, Equiluz, Van Altena, Van Egmond, Holl, (i) Tölz Boys' Ch., VCM, Harnoncourt; (ii) Hanover Boys' Ch., Ghent Coll. Vocale, Leonhardt Cons., Leonhardt.

Cantatas Nos. (i) *183: Sie werden euch in den Bann tun;* (ii) *184: Erwünschtes Freudenlicht;* (i) *185: Barmherziges Herze der ewigen Liebe; 186: Argre dich, O Seele, nicht;* (ii) *187: Es wartet alles auf dich;* (i) *188: Ich habe meine Zuversicht; 192: Nun danket alle Gott; 194: Höchsterwünschtes Freudenfest;* (ii) *195: Dem Gerechten muss das Licht immer wieder aufgehen;* (i) *196: Der Herr denket an uns;* (ii) *197: Gott ist unsrer Zuversicht; 198: Lass, Fürstin, lass noch einen Strahl;* (i) *199: Mein Herze schwimmt im Blut.*

(M) **(*) Teldec/Warner Dig. 4509 91764-2 (6) [id.]. Bonney, Esswood, Jacobs, Elwes, Equiluz, Van Egmond, Hampson, Holl, Van der Kamp, (i) Tölz Boys' Ch., VCM, Harnoncourt; (ii) Hanover Boys' Ch., Ghent Coll. Vocale, Leonhardt Cons., Leonhardt.

The remarkable Teldec project, a recording of all Bach's church cantatas begun in the 1970s, has reached completion. These were originally offered in 45 volumes, each usually combining two CDs at upper-mid-price. Now the whole series has been repackaged and is offered in two alternative choices: as a 60-CD box (with more music on each disc) at bargain price or as a series of ten separate collections, each of six CDs, at mid-price.

The recordings got off to a very good start but, later in the project, various flaws of intonation, and sometimes a feeling that the ensemble would have benefited from more rehearsal, plus occasionally sluggish direction, slightly undermined the overall excellence. However, the authentic character of the performances is in no doubt. Boys replace women not only in the choruses but also as soloists (which brings occasional minor lapses of security), and the size of the forces is confined to what we know Bach himself would have expected. The simplicity of the approach brings its own merits, for the imperfect yet otherworldly quality of some of the treble soloists refreshingly focuses the listener's attention on the music itself. Less appealing is the quality of the violins, which eschew vibrato and, it would sometimes seem, any kind of timbre! Generally speaking, there is a certain want of rhythmic freedom and some expressive caution. Rhythmic accents are underlined with some regularity and the grandeur of Bach's inspiration is at times lost to view. Nevertheless, overall this is an astonishing achievement, and there is much glorious music here which, to do justice to Harnoncourt and Leonhardt, usually emerges freshly to give the listener much musical nourishment. The CD transfers of the earlier analogue recordings are first class. There is no background noise to speak of and the sound is clarified and refined to bring striking presence to voices and accompaniment. The acoustic is usually not too dry – and not too ecclesiastical, either – and the projection is realistic. The later digital recordings are altogether excellent, and this is an infinitely rewarding series.

Cantatas (for Easter): *Nos. 1: Wie schön leuchtet der Morgenstern; 4: Christ lag in Todesbanden; 6: Bleib bei uns, denn es will Abend werden; 12: Weinen, Klagen, Sorgen, Zagen; 23: Du wahrer Gott und Davids Sohn; 67: Halt im Gedächtnis Jesum Christ; 87: Bisher habt ihr nichts gebeten in meinem Namen; 92: Ich habe in Gottes Herz und Sinn; 104: Du Hirte Israel, höre; 108: Es ist euch gut, dass ich hingehe; 126: Erhalt uns, Herr, bei deinem Wort; 158: Der Friede sei mit dir; 182: Himmelskönig, wei willkommen.*

(B) ** DG 439 374-2 (5) [id.]. Edith Mathis, Anna Reynolds, Hertha Töpper, Peter Schreier, Ernst Haefliger, Dietrich Fischer-Dieskau, Theo Adam, Munich Bach Ch. & O, Karl Richter.

DG's Archiv label have offered a major reissue from Karl Richter's series of Bach's cantata recordings, made over the years. Thanks to Richter, we had the most comprehensive survey of Bach cantatas ever to be put on record before the ambitious Harnoncourt/Leonhardt venture got into its stride. The present reissues are grouped into five bargain boxes, the first three centring on the three key celebrations of the Church year and Volumes 4 and 5 covering the middle and later Sundays after Trinity. The set of thirteen cantatas in Volume 2 are all linked by the theme of Easter and the Passion. The performances are variable, some being impressive and spacious, others less sensitive. There is not space here to detail every performance; suffice to say that readers wanting a more vigorous and full-blooded approach to this repertoire than Harnoncourt's and Leonhardt's will find this a welcome offering, particularly as solos are reliable, as indeed is the fine obbligato playing. The digitally remastered transfers sound very good indeed, and collectors need have no worries on that score. Richter, of course, was heavy-handed at times, but he often brought a weight and dignity to this music that are sometimes missing in the more authentic versions. This appears to be the only set among these Richter reissues available in the USA.

Cantatas Nos. (i) *4: Christ lag in Todesbanden;* (ii) *51: Jauchzett Gott in allen Landen;* (i) *56: Ich will den Kreuzstab gerne tragen;* (i; iii) *140: Wachet auf, ruft uns die Stimme;* (iv) *147: Herz und Mund und Tat und Leben;* (ii) *202: Weichet nur, betrübte Schatten (Wedding cantata).*

(B) *** DG Double 453 094-2. (i) Fischer-Dieskau; (ii) Maria Stader; (iii) Edith Mathis; Peter Schreier; (iv) Ursula Buckel, Hertha Töpper, John van Kesteren, Kieth Engen, Ansbach Festival Soloists; Munich Bach Ch. & O, Karl Richter.

Richter's stereo Bach cantata series for DG, which spanned two decades beginning in the late 1950s, is shown at its finest in this well-chosen half-dozen which are all among Bach's finest works in this form. *Christ lag in Todesbanden* is early: the chorale melody is quoted in plain or varied form in each movement and dominates the proceedings. The words of the Luther hymn hail the triumph of Christ over the grave, and the cantata can all too readily sound dull and sombre, given the wrong approach. Richter seems wholly in sympathy with the music and secures some splendid choral singing and dignified playing from the orchestra. Fischer-Dieskau's solo contribution is also distinguished and the recording extremely fine. Fischer-Dieskau is also featured in the solo cantata, *Ich will den Kreuzstab gerne tragen*. Some might feel that here he is at times a little too expressive and over-sophisticated, but he pays characteristic attention to the text, and he has a sensitive obbligato oboist in Manfred Clement. Richter is at times a trifle heavy-handed, but this remains a memorable account. *Jauchzet Gott* demands an abnormally high tessitura from the solo soprano, and Maria Stader is in splendid voice here (a virtuoso performance which is also most moving) and also in the Wedding cantata, *Weichet nur*, which is one of Bach's most immediately appealing works. She is stylishly partnered by a first-class trumpeter (Willi Bauer) in the former and in the latter by the other instrumental soloists, Kurt Hausmann (oboe), Fritz Henker (bassoon) and Otto Büchner (violin). Here the harpsichord soloist, Helwig Bilgram, is less than ideal, and the discipline of the choir is not always impeccable; but these performances truly belong to Stader, and her singing is firm and clear and shows no sense of strain. *Wachet auf, ruft uns die Stimme* (which opens the programme) shows Richter's team at their most impressive throughout, with all the soloists on excellent form and the obbligato wind players, Manfred Clement (oboe) and Edgar Shann (cor anglais) making notable contributions. When the tenor solo, *Zion hört die Wächter singen*, features the chorale, Bach opens with a (famous) noble counter-melody from the strings, and the gloriously heartwarming sound from the Munich orchestra is utterly different from what one would expect from a period-instrument performance today. *Herz und Mund und Tat und Leben* is another very successful performance, with both the soprano and contralto arias beautifully sung by Ursula Buckel and the rich-timbred contralto, Hertha Töpper, respectively. The tenor, John van Kesteren, is also impressive. This cantata contains the famous chorale, *Wohl mir, dass ich Jesum habe* (better-known as 'Jesu, joy of man's desiring') and this is spaciously and warmly presented. Again the obbligato playing is of a high order. All in all, this set with its first-class CD transfers can be given the warmest welcome.

Cantatas Nos. (i) *4: Christ lag in Todesbanden;* (ii) *56: Ich will den Kreuzstab gerne tragen; 82: Ich habe genug.*

(M) (***) DG mono 449 756-2 [id.]. Dietrich Fischer-Dieskau, with (i) Helmut Krebs, Frankfurt Hochschule Ch., Lehmann; (ii) Karl Ristenpart CO, Ristenpart.

Fischer-Dieskau made these mono recordings in the early 1950s. His voice sounds remarkably fresh and youthful. It is interesting to compare his comparatively simple flowing lines in this music with his later, more sophisticated approach as shown on the DG Double above. In these earlier performances the warmth and intensity are in no doubt but there is less conspicuous dramatization. *Ich habe genug* has great lyrical beauty (especially the glorious second aria, '*Schlummert ein*'), helped by the warmth of the string-playing from Karl Ristenpart's excellent chamber orchestra. Hermann Töchter is the fine oboe soloist both here and in BWV 56, and the choral contributions are most pleasingly restrained to match the style of the soloist. The voice is closely balanced, but in all other respects the mono recording is very good indeed. A most interesting and rewarding candidate for DG's series of 'Originals'.

Cantatas (for the latter part of the Church year) *Nos. 5: Wo soll ich fliehen hin; 26: Ach wie flüchtig, ach wie nichtig; 38: Aus tiefer Not schrei ich zu dir; 55: Ich armer Mensch, ich Sündenknecht; 56: Ich will den Kreuzstab gerne tragen; 60: O Ewigkeit, du Donnerwort; 70: Wachet! betet! betet! wachet!; 80: Ein feste Burg ist unser Gott; 96: Herr Christ, der ein'ge Gottessohn; 106: Gottes Zeit ist die allerbeste Zeit (Actus tragicus); 115: Mache dich, mein Geist, bereit; 116: Du Friedefürst, Herr Jesu Christ; 130: Herr Gott, dich loben alle wir; 139: Wohl dem, der sich auf seinen Gott; 140: Wachet auf, ruft uns die Stimme; 180: Schmücke dich, O liebe Seele.*

(BB) **(*) DG 439 394-2 (5). Mathis, Buckel, Schmidt, Töpper, Schreier, Haefliger, Fischer-Dieskau, Adam, Engen, Munich Bach Ch. & O, Karl Richter.

This fifth Richter box collects cantatas that Bach composed for the last ten Sundays of Trinity, plus three others, a Reformation Festival piece (No. 80), a cantata for St Michael's Day (No. 130) and Bach's funeral cantata, *Gottes Zeit* – the so-called *Actus tragicus* (No. 106); it is given a first-rate performance, with fine solo singing and committed direction. Most of these cantatas are chorale-based and nearly all emerge with the dignity and majesty one expects from these forces. They were all recorded in the Munich Herkulessaal, for the most part in 1978, and the sound is warm and spacious. Karl Richter's heavy tread seems over the years to have moderated into a more flexible and human gait, though a certain inflexibility and lack of imagination still surface occasionally.

Cantatas (for the middle Sundays after Trinity) *Nos. 8: Liebster Gott, wann werd' ich sterben?; 9: Es ist das Heil uns kommen her; 17: Wer Dank opfert, der preiset mich; 27: Wer weiss, wie nahe mir mein Ende!; 33: Allein zu dir, Herr Jesu Christ; 45: Es ist dir gesagt, Mensch, was gut ist; 51: Jauchzet Gott in allen Landen; 78: Jesu, der du meine Seele; 100: Was Gott tut, das ist wohlgetan; 102: Herr deine Augen sehen nach dem Glauben; 105: Herr, gehe nicht ins Gericht; 137: Lobe den Herren, den mächtigen König der Ehren; 148: Bringet dem Herrn Ehre seines Namens; 178: Wo Gott der Herr nicht bei uns hält; 179: Siehe zu, dass deine Gottesfurcht nicht Heuchelei sei; 187: Es wartet alles auf dich; 199: Mein Herz schwimmt im Blut.*

(B) **(*) DG 439 387-2 (6). Buckel, Mathis, Stader, Hamari, Töpper, Schreier, Haefliger, Van Kesteren, Fischer-Dieskau, Engen, Munich Bach Ch. & O, Karl Richter.

The fourth box in Richter's series runs to six CDs and offers the cantatas composed for the sixth Sunday after Trinity through to the seventeenth. Like the others, it continues the 'unauthentic' approach of Karl Richter and forms a welcome alternative to the Harnoncourt/Leonhardt venture. Again the spacious venue is the Munich Herkulessaal. The chorus is probably larger than it should be, but the results are invariably musical, and Richter shows greater flexibility and imagination than often has been the case. Just occasionally his heavy touch is felt, but so much of this set is first rate that reservations can be all but overruled. The soloists are thoroughly dependable.

Cantatas Nos. 8: Liebster Gott, wann werd' ich sterben?; 51: Jauchzet Gott, in allen Landen; 78: Jesu, der du meine Seele; 80: Ein feste Burg ist unser Gott; 140: Wachet auf, ruft uns die Stimme; 147: Herz und Mund und Tat und Leben.
(B) *** O-L Double 455 706-2 (2) [id.]. Soloists, Bach Ens., Joshua Rifkin.

Rifkin's performances opt for the one-to-a-part principle not only in his instrumental ensemble but also as far as the choruses are concerned. He opts for female sopranos rather than boy trebles but uses adult male altos. Not all will find his solutions congenial and the use of one voice to a part in the chorales is not always convincing. But there is some good singing in this series, and the playing is lively enough. Even those for whom the avoidance of vocal vibrato seems an unnatural constraint may find themselves persuaded. One feels the need for greater weight and a more full-blooded approach at times, but this is outweighed by the sensitivity and intelligence that inform these excellently balanced recordings. Rifkin uses a later Leipzig text for *Jauchzet Gott*. Julianne Baird is an excellent singer who possesses a pleasing voice and has commendable technique. The recording is excellent. *Jesu, der du meine Seele*, another fine work, shows all the four soloists (here Julianne Baird, Allan Fast, Frank Kelley and Jan Opalach) to good advantage.

Cantatas (for Ascension Day; Whitsun; Trinity): *Nos. 10: Meine Seele erhebt den Herrn; 11: Lobet Gott in seinen Reichen; 21: Ich hatte viel Bekümmernis; 24: Ein ungefärbt Gemüte; 30: Freue dich, erlöste Schar; 34: O ewiges Feuer, O Ursprung der Liebe; 39: Brich dem Hungrigen dein Brot; 44: Sie werden euch in den Bann tun; 68: Also hat Gott die Welt geliebt; 76: Die Himmel erzählen die Ehre Gottes; 93: Wer nur den lieben Gott lässt walten; 129: Gelobet sei der Herr, mein Gott; 135: Ach, Herr, mich armen Sünder; 147: Herz und Mund und Tat und Leben; 175: Er rufet seinen Schafen mit Namen.*
(B) **(*) DG 439 380-2 (6). Edith Mathis, Ursula Buckel, Anna Reynolds, Hertha Töpper, Peter Schreier, Ernst Haefliger, John van Kesteren, Dietrich Fischer-Dieskau, Kurt Moll, Kieth Engen, Munich Bach Ch. & O, Karl Richter.

The first performance offered here (Volume 3 of the Richter series) is the glorious Ascension cantata, *Lobet Gott in seinen Reichen* (No. 11), which opens and closes joyfully with resplendent trumpets. All four soloists are first rate, and Anna Reynolds is especially memorable in her famous aria, *Ach, bleib doch, mein liebstes Leben*, warmly supported by the strings of the Munich ensemble. Richter's other performances have a breadth and sense of space that are really quite impressive. He makes heavy weather of *Ein ungefärbt Gemüte* (No. 24), but on the whole the dignity of these performances outweighs the occasional pedestrian moments. No. 147, *Herz und Mund und Tat und Leben* (which includes *Jesu, joy of man's desiring*), is among the best of Richter's series. Ursula Buckel sings beautifully, as does the tenor, John van Kesteren, and the choral singing is also very good. On the whole a successful box.

Cantata Nos. (i) *11: Lobet Gott in seinen Reichen (Ascension oratorio);* (ii) *50: Chorus: Nun ist das Heil und die Kraft.*
(M) **(*) Virgin Veritas/EMI Dig. VM5 61340-2. (i) Kirkby, Tubb, Cable, Jochens, Charlesworth; (ii) Van Evera, Cable, Crook, Grant, Tubb, Trevor, Jochens, Charlesworth; Taverner Players, Parrott – *Magnificat*. **(*)

Bach's cantata, BWV 11, is also known as the 'Ascension oratorio' as it was written for Ascension Day (19 May) 1735, with the biblical events narrated by the Evangelist. The first alto aria, *Ach, bleibe doch, mein liebstes Leben*, was later taken by its composer to form the *Agnus Dei* in the *Mass in B minor*. It is impressively sung here by Margaret Cable, and the other soloists do not disappoint either. As in the coupled *Magnificat*, the five soloists also economically provide the choruses, one voice to a part, and eight singers pit themselves antiphonally against Bach's spectacular orchestration (including three trumpets) for the chorus from the companion cantata, used as an encore. Some might feel that a larger group would have been more effective here, although the vocal detail is fairly clear. Parrott's performances are certainly refreshingly different and very well recorded.

Cantatas (for Advent and Christmas): *Nos. 13: Meine Seufzer, meine Tränen; 28: Gottlob! nun geht das Jahr zu Ende; 58: Ach Gott, wie manches Herzeleid; 61: Nun komm, der Heiden Heiland; 63: Christen ätzet diesen Tag; 64: Sehet, welch eine Liebe hat uns der Vater erzwiget; 65: Sie werden aus Saba alle kommen; 81: Jesus schläft, was soll ich hoffen?; 82: Ich habe genug; 111: Was mein Gott will, das g'scheh allzeit; 121: Christum wir sollen loben schon; 124: Meinen Jesum lass ich nicht; 132: Bereitet die Wege, bereitet die Bahn; 171: Gott, wie dein Name, so ist auch dein Ruhm.*

(B) **(*) DG 439 369-2 (4). Edith Mathis, Sheila Armstrong, Lotte Schädle, Anna Reynolds, Hertha Töpper, Peter Schreier, Ernst Haefliger, Dietrich Fischer-Dieskau, Theo Adam, Munich Bach Ch. & O, Karl Richter.

It is useful to have this anthology (Volume 1 in this Richter series), which collects the cantatas appropriate to the Christmas festival; though there are some reservations to be made, there need be nothing but admiration for the purpose of the enterprise. The instrumental playing is extremely fine throughout and much of the solo singing is of genuine distinction. There is a greater boldness about Richter's approach than, say, Harnoncourt's, but he is at times a little earthbound and not free from pedantry. However, it is good to hear full-bodied choral singing and warm orchestral textures. The acoustic is a pleasing one; it has warmth and clarity at the same time, considering the forces used. There is much noble music-making and much noble music in this set.

Cantatas Nos. 27: Wer weiss, wie nahe mir mein Ende!; 158: Der Friede sei mit dir; 198: Lass, Fürstin, lass noch einen Strahl (Trauer-Ode).

(M) *** Teldec/Warner 4509 93687-2. Rotraud Hansmann, Helen Watts, Kurt Equiluz, Max van Egmond, Hamburg Monteverdi Ch., Concerto Amsterdam, Jürgen Jürgens.

This is one of the most outstanding Bach cantata records on the market. Not only are the performances extremely sensitive yet vital, with excellent solo and choral singing as well as enthusiastic but disciplined instrumental support, but the cantatas themselves are among Bach's most inspired. The recording, from the mid-1960s, is also first rate.

Cantatas Nos. (i; ii) *32: Liebster Jesu mein Verlangen;* (i) *51: Jauchzet Gott in allen Landen;* (iii) *56: Ich will den Kreuzstab gerne tragen;* (i; ii) *57: Selig ist der Mann;* (iv–vii) *74: Wer mich liebet, der wird mein Wort halten;* (iii) *82: Ich habe genug;* (v; vi; ii) *128: Auf Christi Himmelfahrt allein;* (v–vi) *134: Ein Herz, das seinen Jesum lebend weiss;* (iv–vii) *147: Herz und Mund und Tat und Leben;* (viii) *151: Süsser Trost, mein Jesus kömmt;* (iv; v; vi; ii) *173: Erhöhtes Fleisch und Blutt;* (iv–vi) *191: Gloria in excelsis Deo;* (i) *199: Mein Herze schwimmt im Blut. Sinfonias from Cantatas Nos. 4; 29; 31 (Sonata); 49; 106 (Sonatina in B flat); 52; 142 & 146 (Concertos); 150; 169; 174; 196; 207 (March); 221; Cantata No. 65:* Chorale: *Die Kön'ge aus Saba; Cantata No. 147: Jesu, joy of man's desiring. Christmas oratorio: Sinfonia;* Chorale: *Ach, mein Herzliebes Jesuslein.* (ix) (Organ) *Chorale & Choral prelude: In dulci jubilo, BWV 729 & BWV 368; Chorale variations on 'Vom Himmel hoch', BWV 738.*

(B) ** Ph. 454 346-2 (5). (i) Ameling; (ii) Prey; (iii) Souzay; (iv) Cotrubas; (v) Hamari; (vi) Equiluz; (vii) Reimer; (viii) Giebel, Finnilä, Ellenbeck; Ch. of German Bach Soloists; or Kantorei Barmen Gemarke; or Netherlands Vocal Ens.; or Berlin Capella; German Bach Soloists & O, Helmut Winschermann; (ix) Schönstedt (organ).

The thirteen cantatas performed here by Winschermann and his German Bach Soloists, apart from being among Bach's finest, seem to have no special linking factor except that many of them were composed for feast days. They were recorded in the late 1960s and early 1970s, and the sound is very musically balanced, especially in the matter of solo voices and solo wind and brass instruments, although the chorus could be better defined. This is immediately noticeable in the first cantata offered here, *Gloria in excelsis Deo* (No. 191) written for Christmas Day in 1745. *Liebster Jesu* (No. 32), however, is a solo cantata (the chorus sings only in the final chorale). Written for the first Sunday after Epiphany, it is one of the highlights of the set and receives eloquent treatment. Elly Ameling sings most beautifully and the oboe obbligato (Saschko Gawriloff) calls for special mention too. Hermann Prey is no less impressive. Winschermann is a very sympathetic accompanist but (as elsewhere) he alternates between harpsichord and organ in the accompaniment (there should be no harpsichord) and some listeners will find this eccentric. The companion cantata for the same forces (No. 57: *Selig ist der Mann*) is another of Bach's most deeply felt sacred works, and here Winschermann is less searching than he might be. Both these works are very well recorded.

Elly Ameling follows the example of the opening trumpet (Maurice André) when she begins *Jauchzet Gott* (No. 51) and her voice has an appropriate clarion ring to it. The accompaniment is admirably done. The problem of the alternation of harpsichord and organ continuo arises again in the two solo cantatas (Nos. 56 and 82 – *Ich habe genug*) sung with great simplicity of feeling by Gérard Souzay; these are both very recommendable performances. The Netherlands Vocal Ensemble opens No. 74 strongly, and here they are well caught by the engineers. The contributions from all four soloists are dramatically managed, with the tenor (Kurt Equiluz) both commanding and lyrical in his aria, *Kommt, eilet*. Winschermann directs with spirit. No. 128 is notable for its fine opening chorus (with excellent horn-playing), its bass solo (Prey) with a splendid trumpet obbligato (Maurice André), and a fine tenor/alto duet (Equiluz and Hamari) with Helmut Winschermann himself contributing a delicate oboe d'amore obbligato; No. 134, too, is notable for another extended tenor/alto duet by the same soloists, and Kurt Equiluz's contribution also stands out in No. 173 (the cantata for Whit Monday). The instrumental playing in this cantata is most pleasing, as is the closing chorale.

The extended opening chorus of No. 147 (*Herz und Mund und Tat und Leben*) is very well sung by the Netherlands group against a vivid accompaniment, and it is a pity that the choral sound is not more cleanly focused. But all the soloists are impressive (so is the obbligato playing) and the famous final chorale (better known as *Jesu, joy of man's desiring*) is beautifully sung. Winschermann's performance is far better than Richter's old Archiv account, with the continuo here varied very effectively, using harpsichord to provide contrast with organ when appropriate. No. 151 is even more appealing with its lovely pastoral soprano aria, *Süsser Trost, mein Jesus kömmt* (Agnes Giebel intertwining with a flute obbligato), and later offering an equally beautiful contribution from the contralto (Birgit Finnilä, with oboe d'amore). Elly Ameling returns to open her solo cantata, *Mein Herze schwimmt in Blut* (No. 199), strongly and dramatically, and the intensity of her words comes over with commitment. With much sensitive playing and singing, this is very enjoyable indeed, and if Ameling does not always convey the aching depth of feeling in the way a singer like Janet Baker can, her singing has a freshness and eloquence that tells in a quite different way. The recording too is of Philips's very best, full and natural, and makes one reflect how beautiful Bach cantatas can sound using modern string instruments. The final disc looks like a miscellaneous hotch-potch but turns out to be an attractive collection of sinfonias (some in the form of 'concertos' or 'sonatas', two of them quoting from the *Brandenburg Concertos*) to demonstrate the variety of Bach's instrumentation, plus some famous vocal chorales, and with a couple of organ solos thrown in for good measure. They are very well played and sung, although the recording is at times a bit resonant.

Cantatas Nos. 51: Jauchzet Gott in allen Landen; 78: Jesu, der du meine Seele; 140: Wachet auf, ruft uns die Stimme.

(M) *** O-L Dig. 443 188-2 [id.]. Baird, Minter, Fast, Thomas, Kelley, Opalach, Bach Ens., Rifkin.

As in his other Bach records, Joshua Rifkin goes for the one-to-a-part principle in his instrumental ensemble (save for the violins), resting his case on the number of copies of the parts surviving at Leipzig. Rifkin uses a later Leipzig text for *Jauchzet Gott*. Julianne Baird is an excellent singer who possesses a pleasing voice and has commendable technique. The recording is excellent. For the reissue *Jesu, der du meine Seele* has been added, another very fine work which shows all the four soloists (here Julianne Baird, Allan Fast, Frank Kelley and Jan Opalach) to good advantage.

Cantatas Nos. (i) *51: Jauchzet Gott in allen Landen;* (ii–vi) *80: Ein feste Burg is unser Gott;* (vii–viii) *82: Ich habe genug;* (ix; iv; vi) *106: Gottes Zeit ist die allerbeste Zeit (Actus tragicus);* (ii–vi) *140: Wachet auf, ruft uns die Stimme;* (x; viii) *147: Herz und Mund und Tat und Leben.*

(B) **(*) EMI Rouge et Noir Analogue/Dig. (No. 51) CZS5 68544-2 (2) [CDZB 68544]. (i) Donath, ASMF, Marriner; (ii) Ameling; (iii) J. Baker, (iv) Altmeyer; (v) Sotin; (vi) S. German Madrigal Ch. & Consortium Musicum, Gönnenwein; (vii) Souzay; (viii) Geraint Jones O, Jones; (ix) Mathis, Michelow, Crass; (x) Sutherland, Watts, Wilfred Brown, Hemsley, Geraint Jones Singers.

Although by today's authentic standards these now sound to be rather old-fashioned Bach performances, they are certainly not unstylish. Gönnenwein is thoroughly reliable and *Eine feste Burg* achieves generally high standards. *Wachet auf* is equally attractive and Janet Baker's contribution, though small, is distinguished. The singing throughout is admirable, as it is in *Gottes Zeit*, Bach's funeral cantata, which has different soloists. Gönnenwein secures highly musical results on the whole but misses the last ounce of inspiration. For the solo cantata, *Jauchzet Gott*, Helen Donath's performance, though fresh, is slightly marred by her close vibrato. When one turns to *Ich habe genug*, it is to encounter artistry of a very high order indeed. Gérard Souzay, recorded at his peak in 1958, gives an intimate, wonderfully dedicated performance which is surely one of the finest recorded accounts of any of Bach's solo cantatas.

Joan Sutherland is not usually associated with Bach, but in the famous *Herz und Mund und Tat und Leben*, dating from the very beginning of her recording career, she displays an unfamiliar facet of her vocal facility, making of Bach's tricky lines a memorably beautiful impression, rich in ornament and variety of timbre. Helen Watts is impressive too, and the other soloists also sing with heart as well as the voice. The Geraint Jones Singers and Orchestra give firm and buoyant support and the famous chorale, *Jesu joy of man's desiring*, is beautifully sung. Good, vivid recording.

Cantatas Nos. (i) *51: Jauchzet Gott in allen Landen;* (ii) *202: Weichet nur (Wedding cantata);* (i) *209: Non sa che sia dolore.*
(M) *** Teldec/Warner 3984 21711-2. Agnes Giebel, André, Leonhardt, Concerto Amsterdam, Schroeder; or Leonhardt Consort.

Jauchzet Gott is one of the most brilliant of Bach's solo cantatas, not only because of the virtuosity of the soprano part but also for the splendour of the trumpet obbligato. Agnes Giebel gives a dazzling account – and so for that matter does the trumpeter, Maurice André. In the so-called *Wedding cantata* Giebel sings superlatively and Gustav Leonhardt's continuo support is beyond praise. *Non sa che sia dolore* is also sung excellently, and here she is most stylishly accompanied by the Leonhardt Consort.

Cantatas Nos. 51: Jauchzet Gott in allen Landen; 208: Was mir behagt, ist nur die muntre Jagd (Hunt cantata).
(BB) **(*) Naxos Dig. 8.550643 [id.]. Kertesi, Pászthy, Nemeth, Mukk, Gáti, Hungarian R. Ch., Failoni CO, Budapest, Antál.

The Naxos accounts offer excellent value artistically for those who do not insist on period instrument ensembles. The soloists are all of a high standard and, although the recorded balance is not always ideal, the sound has warmth and immediacy, and Matyás Antál gets good results from his orchestra.

Cantatas Nos. (i) *63: Christen, ätzet diesen Tag;* (ii) *65: Sie werden aus Saba alle kommen;* (iii) *Magnificat, BWV 243.*
(B) ** DG 439 489-2. (i) Mathis, Reynolds, Schreier; (ii) Adam; (ii; iii) Haefliger; (iii) Stader, Töpper; (i; iii) Fischer-Dieskau; Munich Bach Ch. & O, Karl Richter.

In Bach's *Magnificat* Richter is a bit heavy-handed at times, but there is plenty of vigour and the chorus responds well to his direction. The soloists are very good, except for Hertha Töpper who lacks refinement in some of the florid writing. Sonically this sounds its age – it dates from the early 1960s – but the remastering is quite acceptable on CD, though the opening chorus could do with greater freshness, even if its vitality is in no doubt. Both cantatas are fine works – No. 63 joyfully celebrates Christmas Day with gleaming trumpets, and the Epiphany cantata is hardly less festive. In the former, Edith Mathis's soprano aria is beautifully sung, but in the two duets these very individual voices match less comfortably; however, Ernst Haefliger and Theo Adam both make fine contributions to the following work. Again the sound is good rather than outstanding.

(i) *Cantatas Nos. 80: Ein feste Burg ist unser Gott; 140: Wachet auf, ruft uns die Stimme;* (ii) *Organ concerto No. 3 in D min.* (reconstructed Schureck from *BWV 35 & BVW 1059*).
(B) **(*) Decca Eclipse Dig. 448 706-2; *448 706-4* [(M) id. import]. (i) Fontana, Hamari, Winbergh, Krause, Stuttgart Hymnus Ch., Stuttgart CO, Münchinger; (ii) Peter Hurford, N. Sinf., Hickox.

This digital coupling of two of Bach's most popular cantatas is most welcome at bargain price. Münchinger has the advantage of excellently transparent and well-detailed Decca digital recording and a fine team of soloists and there is little of the pedantry that has at times afflicted his performances. On CD, extra pleasure is afforded by the attractive ambience and by the tangibility of the chorus, whose vigorous contribution is given striking body and presence. For the Eclipse reissue a reconstructed organ concerto has been added, with movements taken partly from the *D minor Harpsichord concerto*, BWV 1059, and partly from a sinfonia in Cantata No. 35, *Geist und Seele sind verwirret*, featuring a solo organ. Peter Hurford is the admirable soloist, and this makes an enjoyable interlude between the two cantatas.

Cantatas Nos. (i) *80: Ein feste Burg ist unser Gott; 140: Wachet auf, ruft uns die Stimme;* (ii; iii) *147: Herz und Mund und Tat und Leben;* Motet: (iii) *Jesu, meine Freude, BWV 227.*
(B) (*) EMI forte (SIS) CZS5 68670-2 (2) [CDFB 68670]. (i) Ameling, Baker, Altmeyer, Sotin, S. German Madrigal Ch. & Instrumentalists, Consortium Musicum, Gönnenwein; (ii) Sutherland, Watts, Brown, Hemsley; (iii) Geraint Jones Singers & O, Jones.

This is obviously a British replacement for the collection above from EMI France which is much more generous and far preferable. Here three cantantas are omitted (Nos. 51, 82 and 106) and Bach's most famous motet is added. But as this is sung comparatively indifferently, that is no advantage. Moreover the new transfers of the Gönnenwein performances on the second disc leave much to be desired, with the opening chorus of each poorly focused – and particularly *Ein feste Burg*, with its distorting trumpets bringing unpleasant roughness and congestion.

Cantatas Nos. 80: Ein feste Burg ist unser Gott; 147: Herz und Mund und Tat und Leben.
(BB) **(*) Naxos Dig. 8.550642 [id.]. Kertesi, Nemeth, Mukk, Gáti, Hungarian R. Ch., Failoni CO, Budapest, Antál.

Like its companion above, this Naxos disc is eminently good value. Neither performance disappoints in any significant respect; both are reasonably spirited in direction and offer satisfactory singing. Those who do not insist on period-instrument ensembles will find a great deal to enjoy here, particularly the singing of Ingrid Kertesi. The sound has real warmth and immediacy.

Cantata No. 82: Ich habe genug.

✿ (M) (***) EMI CDH7 63198-2 [id.]. Hans Hotter, Philh. O, Bernard – BRAHMS: *Lieder.* (***) ✿

One of the greatest cantata performances ever. Glorious singing from Hans Hotter and wonderfully stylish accompanying from Anthony Bernard and the Philharmonia. This 1950 mono recording was never reissued on LP, and it sounds eminently present in this fine transfer.

Cantatas Nos. (i; ii) *82: Ich habe genug;* (i; iii; iv) *159: Sehet, wir gehn hinauf gen Jerusalem;* (iii) *170: Vergnügte Ruh', beliebte Seelenlust.*

✿ (M) *** Decca 430 260-2 [id.]. (i) Shirley-Quirk; (ii) Lord; (iii) J. Baker; (iv) Tear, St Anthony Singers; ASMF, Marriner.

John Shirley-Quirk's performance of *Ich habe genug* is much to be admired, not only for the sensitive solo singing but also for the lovely oboe obbligato of Roger Lord. But this reissue is to be prized even more for the other two cantatas. Both Dame Janet Baker and Shirley-Quirk are in marvellous voice, and *Vergnügte Ruh'* makes a worthy companion. This is among the half-dozen or so cantata records that ought to be in every collection.

Cantatas Nos. (i) *131: Aus der Tiefen rufe ich;* (ii) *198: Lass Fürstin lass noch einen Strahl (Trauerode).*

(B) ** Sony SB2K 62656 (2) [S2K 62656]. (i) Driscoll, Oliver; (ii) Nixon, Bonazzi, Castel, Binder; (i–ii) American Concert Ch., Margaret Hillis, Columbia SO, Craft – MONTEVERDI: *Vespro della Beata Vergine.* **

Cool and intimate – if not distinctive – performances from Craft, but with good choral singing and excellent accompaniments from a well-balanced chamber orchestra who produce excellent wind soloists for the obbligatos. Marni Nixon was an interesting choice as soprano soloist for the *Trauerode* and she sings simply and freshly, as do her colleagues. The tenor and bass are quite effective in the companion work, and the bass aria with chorus (*So du willst . . . Erbarm dich*) works well. The early stereo is remarkably convincing.

Cantatas Nos. 140: Wachet auf, ruft uns die Stimme; 147: Herz und Mund und Tat und Leben.

(M) **(*) Teldec/Warner Dig./Analogue 4509 95987-2. Bergius, Rampf, Esswood, Equiluz, Hampson, Tölz Boys' Ch., VCM, Harnoncourt.

This separate reissue accompanies the complete Teldec cantata series, offering a coupling of two familiar cantatas, both made famous by their chorales. In No. 147, some may be a little disconcerted by the minor swelling effect in the phrasing of *Jesu, joy of man's desiring*, but otherwise the authentic approach brings much to enjoy. The production and recording are well up to the usual Telefunken standard. However, John Eliot Gardiner's highly accomplished full-price performances on DG Archiv are well worth the extra money.

Cantatas Nos. 199: Mein Herze schwimmt im Blut; 202: Weichet nur, betrübte Schatten (Wedding); 209: Non sa che sia dolore.

(BB) *** Naxos Dig. 8.550431 [id.]. Friederike Wagner, Capella Istropolitana, Christian Brembeck.

Those who adjudge the meagre string-tone of some period-instrument groups unacceptable should find the sound-world favoured by Christian Brembeck and the Capella Istropolitana much more congenial. *Mein Herze schwimmt im Blut* comes from Bach's Weimar years, and Friederike Wagner proves both sympathetic and lively; and both *Weichet nur, betrübte Schatten*, popularly known as the '*Wedding cantata*', and No. 209, *Non sa che sia dolore* (both well represented in the catalogue), are given thoroughly enjoyable performances. Not for devotees of authentic performance practice, but enjoyable for those who prefer a more traditional approach. Decent recording too.

Cantatas Nos. (i) *208: Was mir behagt, ist nur die muntre Jagd! (Hunt). 212: Mer hahn en neue Oberkeet (Peasant).*

(M) *** Teldec/Warner Dig. 4509 97501-2 [2292 46151-2]. Angela Maria Blasi, Robert Holl; (i) with Yvonne Kenny, Kurt Equiluz; Arnold Schönberg Ch., VCM, Harnoncourt.

Harnoncourt tops off the complete Teldec set of Bach's church cantatas with admirably ebullient accounts of a pair of Bach's secular cantatas, celebrating the name-days of two local dignitaries. The delightful *Hunt cantata* is rich in melodic invention of the highest quality, including the famous aria, *Schafe können sicher weiden*, with its obbligato for a pair of flutes, better known as 'Sheep may safely graze', sung here quite gloriously by Angela Maria Blasi. Indeed the solo contributions in both works are splendid, and Blasi and the robust Robert Holl both enjoy themselves hugely in the boisterous *Peasant cantata* in their alternating bursts of extravagant praise, lyrical and exuberant, for Carl Heinrich von Dieskau, Chamberlain at the Court of the Elector of Saxony and Lord of the Manor. A later lyrical eulogy from the soprano is introduced by a quotation of the famous *La Folia*, and the musical interest of this remarkably inspired cantata (considering its ragbag of a text) is Bach's use of various old melodies familiar to his audience; and indeed the Overture is a patchwork, almost a musical switch of such tunes. The exuberance of the performance carries over to Harnoncourt's accompaniments – no scholarly rectitude here – and the recording is first rate.

Cantatas Nos. 211: Schweigt stille, plaudert nicht (Coffee cantata); 212: Mer hahn en neue Oberkeet (Peasant cantata).
(BB) **(*) Naxos Dig. 8.550642 [id.]. Kertesi, Mukk, Gáti, Failoni CO, Budapest, Mátyás Antál.

Very serviceable accounts on Naxos of the *Coffee* and *Peasant cantatas*, and those who appreciated Ingrid Kertesi's *Jauchzet Gott* will find her singing gives as much pleasure here. Mátyás Antál's direction is lively and this is as enjoyable an issue as the other cantatas from this source, save only for the tenor, who falls short of distinction. The recording is warm and spacious.

Major choral works

(i) *Christmas oratorio, BWV 248;* (ii) *Easter oratorio, BWV 249;* (iii) *Magnificat, BWV 243;* (iv) *Mass in B min., BWV 232;* (v) *St John Passion, BWV 245;* (vi) *St Matthew Passion, BWV 244.*
(B) *** Decca 455 783-2 (10) [id.]. (i; vi) Pears, Lübecker Kantorei; (i–vi) Ameling; (i–iv) Watts, (i–iv; vi) Krause; (ii–iv) Krenn; (iii) Van Bork, V. Ac. Ch.; (iv) Minton, V. Singakademiechor; (v) Ellenbeck, Berry, Hamari, Hollweg, Ackerman; (v–vi) Prey, Stuttgart Hymnus Boys' Ch.; (vi) Höffgen, Wunderlich, Blankenburg, Messthaler; Stuttgart CO, Münchinger.

This Decca set, admirably recorded over a decade between 1964 and 1974, impressively celebrates Münchinger's achievement in recording all Bach's major choral works (apart from the cantatas) with consistent freshness and a remarkable degree of authenticity for the period. Although much has happened to the style of Bach performances since then, it is impossible not to respond to this alert, vigorous music-making. The soloists are consistently excellent, with Elly Ameling always sweet-toned and sensitive and Peter Pears standing out as the Evangelist in the *Christmas oratorio* and unrivalled in his insights among tenors of his generation in the *St Matthew Passion*. In the latter work, Münchinger's direction does not attain the spirtual heights of an interpretation such as Klemperer's, but it makes a remarkable impact when the choral singing is so impressive and the sound so vivid – although some may object to the deliberate closeness with which the voice of Hermann Prey as Jesus has been recorded. The *Christmas oratorio* (particularly successful) and the *Mass in B minor* (slightly less so) are already available separately as Decca Doubles. Münchinger is at his finest in both the *Easter oratorio* and the *Magnificat*, both given compellingly spacious readings. The *Magnificat* is still as fine as any in the catalogue – after the Gardiner version, which has a more authentic feel. In their day both these performances were very highly regarded. The *St John Passion* is hardly less telling. The dynamic range is strikingly wide and the sound itself (as throughout) is astonishingly bright and full. The superb line-up of soloists, all of them clear-toned and precise, is led by the young-sounding tenor, Dieter Ellenbeck, as the Evangelist. The musical balance of the score is pointed most satisfyingly without idiosyncrasy, using organ continuo with no harpsichord. Throughout the set the polished response of the Stuttgart orchestra is an added joy, not least the obbligato solo playing. In short, with the CD transfers often producing sound of demonstration realism, within an effectively expansive ambience, this set is remarkable value. Both musically and technically these are Bach performances to live with.

Christmas oratorio, BWV 248.
(B) *** EMI forte CZS5 69503-2 (2) [CDFB 69503]. Elly Ameling, Janet Baker, Robert Tear, Dietrich Fischer-Dieskau, King's College, Cambridge, Ch., ASMF, Philip Ledger.
(B) *** Decca Double 455 410-2 (2) [id.]. Peter Pears, Elly Ameling, Helen Watts, Tom Krause, Ch., Stuttgart CO, Münchinger.
(M) **(*) Teldec/Warner 9031 77610-2 (2) [id.]. Treble soloists from V. Boys' Ch., Esswood, Equiluz, Nimsgern, V. Boys' Ch., Ch. Viennensis. VCM, Harnoncourt.

With generally brisk tempi (controversially so in Dame Janet's cradle-song, *Schlafe mein Liebster*, in Part II) Philip Ledger's 1976 King's performance anticipates more recent 'authentic' practice. The result is an intensely refreshing account which grows more winning the more one hears it. It was Ledger who played the harpsichord continuo in many of Benjamin Britten's performances of this work, and some of Britten's imagination comes through here, helped by four outstanding and stylish soloists. The King's acoustic gives a warm background to the nicely styled performance of choir and orchestra and, although in the CD transfer the choral focus is not absolutely clean, the sound overall is attractively balanced – certainly the timpani at the very start sound spectacularly impressive. On EMI's two-for-the-price-of-one forte label, this makes an obvious choice for those wanting a recommendable lower-priced version.

Returning to Münchinger's admirably lively 1967 recording with its splendidly vivid Decca sound gave us much pleasure. With an excellent team of soloists and with Lübeck trebles adding to the freshness, this lively set is representative of modern Bach scholarship as determined in the era immediately preceding authenticism. There is some excellent playing from the Stuttgart orchestra (especially the trumpets) to add to the vividness. At Double Decca price this makes an excellent alternative to the EMI Ledger set, and the recording is even better focused.

Harnoncourt has rarely been more successful than here. It will not be to everyone's taste to have a boy treble and male counter-tenor instead of women soloists, but the purity of sound of these singers is most affecting. Above all, Harnoncourt in this instance never allows his pursuit of authentic sound to weigh the performance down: it has a lightness of touch which should please everyone. The recording, from 1971/2, as usual from this source is excellent.

Christmas oratorio: Arias and choruses.

(M) *** Teldec/Warner 9031 74893-2. Treble soloists from V. Boys' Ch., Esswood, Equiluz, Nimsgern, V. Boys' Ch., Ch. Viennensis, VCM, Harnoncourt.

The highlights from Harnoncourt's outstandingly spontaneous performance of the *Christmas oratorio* are attractive, particularly as the CD plays for nearly 78 minutes.

(i) *Easter oratorio, BWV 249;* (ii) *Magnificat, BWV 243.*

(B) ** Sony SBK 60261; *SBT 60261* [id.]. (i) Judith Raskin, Maureen Forrester, Richard Lewis, Herbert Beattie, Temple University Ch., Phd. O, Ormandy; (ii) Lee Venora, Jennie Tourel, Russell Oberlin, Charles Bressler, Norman Farrows, Schola Cantorum, Bernstein.

With a thrift common among eighteenth-century composers Bach reworked secular material for his attractive *Easter oratorio*. The opening Sinfonia is dramatic with its hint of 'thunders and lightenings' in the style of the *St Matthew Passion*, but generally it is a genial work – and on the whole a genial performance is called for. All this is well understood by Ormandy, who makes an impressive beginning. He has good soloists and a fine choir, but not all will like this large-scale version (lively though it certainly is) and for which the spaciously resonant recording is certainly suitable. In the *Magnificat* Bernstein attempts a more authentic approach, with the result that from time to time we can faintly hear a harpsichord. The soloists are a mixed team, with Oberlin and Bressler standing out by reason of their fine control of cantilena. The chorus sounds comparatively heavy, although they sing well together as a team. But one misses the freshness of a more authentic style. The sound is good.

Magnificat in E flat, BWV 243a (original version).

(M) *** O-L 443 199-2. Nelson, Kirkby, C. Watkinson, Elliot, D. Watkinson, Christ Church Ch., AAM, Preston – KUHNAU: *Der Gerechte kommt um;* VIVALDI: *Nisi dominus; Nulla in mundo pax sincera.* ***

The original version of the *Magnificat* is textually different in detail (quite apart from being a semitone higher) and has four interpolations for the celebration of Christmas. Preston and the Academy of Ancient Music present a characteristically alert and fresh performance, and the Christ Church Choir is in excellent form. One might quibble at the use of women soloists instead of boys, but these three specialist singers have just the right incisive timbre and provide the insight of experience. The reissue is now joined with two Vivaldi motets and an interesting piece by Kuhnau, which is much more generous than the old full-priced coupling.

Magnificat in D, BWV 243.

(BB) *** Naxos Dig. 8.554056 [id.]. Crookes, Whitaker, Trevor, Robinson, Gedge, Oxford Schola Cantorum, N. CO, Nicholas Ward – VIVALDI: *Gloria.* ***

(M) **(*) Virgin Veritas/EMI Dig. VM5 61340-2. Van Evera, Tubb, Trevor, Crook, Grant, Taverner Cons. & Players, Parrott – *Cantata No. 11* etc. **(*)

(M) ** EMI CDM7 64634-2 [id.]. Popp, Pashley, J. Baker, Tear, Hemsley, Garrard, New Philh. Ch. & O, Barenboim – FAURE: *Requiem.* ***

(M) * Teldec/Warner Dig. 0630 13573-2 [2292 42984-2]. Heichele, Gardow, Esswood, Equiluz, Holl, V. Boys' Ch., Ch. Viennensis, VCM, Harnoncourt – HANDEL: *Utrecht Te Deum.* *(*)

The fresh and lively Naxos version of the *Magnificat*, originally let down by its indifferent cantata coupling, is here attractively re-coupled with an outstanding version of Vivaldi's *Gloria*, also using modern instruments. None of the soloists from the choir, all of them stylish, is identified on the reissue; our listing of their names is retained from the original issue.

Parrott favours a chorus with one voice to each part, using women (rather than boys) to sing the soprano and alto parts, which gives the performance a lightweight, almost chamber-like character, helped by brisk tempi. The singers are impressive individually and they also make a good team, and the music-making is extremely lively – the opening chorus fizzes. Although not all will respond to Parrott's briskness, the music-making is characteristically fresh, with a fine, authentic instrumental contribution (especially the woodwind obbligati) from the Taverner group, and this well-balanced recording certainly has its place in the catalogue.

Barenboim's way with Bach in his 1968 recording of the *Magnificat* is nothing if not boisterous, and he sets a very fast tempo for the opening. But no one should miss the joyfulness of the music as presented here. The solo singing too is more imaginative than in many rival versions, and Dame Janet Baker's singing of the two mezzo arias is intensely moving. The recording – made in a fairly small south London church – was originally agreeably warm and smooth, but the CD transfer, alas, has added an artificial edge to the upper range.

Harnoncourt's 1984 version now resurfaces at mid-price. It is generously coupled with a major Handel piece, but the squareness of rhythm, with repeated quavers chugging instead of lifting, makes the result pedestrian despite some excellent solo singing. The chorus is far less imaginative, pedestrian like the playing. The sound is clear but on the dry side, not at all atmospheric.

Masses (Missae breves): in F, BWV 233; in A, BWV 234; in G min., BWV 235; in G, BWV 236. 5 Sanctuses: in C; D; D min.; G; D, BWV 237–41; Christe eleison in G min., BWV 242.

(M) ** Erato/Warner 4509 97236-2 (2) [id.]. Staempfli, Capt, Rossier-Maradan, Perret, Schaer, Elwes, Dufour, Huttenlocher, Brodard, Lausanne Vocal Ens., Michel Corboz.

Bach's *Short Masses* (sometimes described as 'Lutheran' – although they are sung in Latin) are comparatively little known. Taking their material from cantatas, they have considerable musical interest, with the *A major*, BWV 234 (which draws on *Cantata No. 67* for its *Gloria*), perhaps the most inspired. Yet all four offer many beauties and it is difficult to understand their neglect. The Corboz versions date from 1974 and their style now seems rather old-fashioned, with weighty sounds from both chorus and orchestra. The spacious tempi in the *Kyries* seem almost lethargic. Yet the *Glorias* are ebullient and the solo singing from a very good team is of high quality: indeed Wally Staempfli's *Qui tollis* in the *A major Mass* is even more lyrically beautiful than Barbara Bonney's account. In their more leisured way these performances are still enjoyable, for the recording is full-bodied and mostly pleasing, not as clear as with Schreier but better defined than with Herreweghe (both at full price), although the horns are not cleanly caught in BWV 233. What makes the Corboz set the more interesting is his inclusion of a brief *Christe eleison* (a duet, nicely sung here by Staempfli and Nicole Rossier-Maradan) and five settings of the *Sanctus*, of varying length from less than two minutes (BWV 237, 239 and 241) to the ambitious BWV 238, scored for trumpets, which Herreweghe also includes. These scores exist in Bach's own hand, so, while doubt has been cast on the authenticity of the four shorter pieces, Bach obviously admired them.

Mass in B min., BWV 232.

(B) *** EMI forte (SIS) Dig. CZS5 68640-2 (2) [CDFB 68640]. Donath, Fassbaender, Ahnsjö, Hermann, Holl, Bav. R. Ch. & O, Jochum.

(M) *** Virgin Veritas/EMI Dig. VMD5 61337-2 (2) [ZDCB 47292]. Kirkby, Van Evera, Iconomou, Immler, Kilian, Covey-Crump, David Thomas, Soloists from Tölz Boys' Ch., Taverner Cons. & Players, Parrott.

(M) **(*) Teldec/Warner 4509 95517-2 (2). Hansmann, Iiyama, Watts, Equiluz, Van Egmond, V. Boys' Ch., Ch. Viennensis, VCM, Harnoncourt.

(B) **(*) Decca Duo 440 609-2 (2) [(M) id. import]. Ameling, Minton, Watts, Krenn, Krause, V. Singakademiechor, Stuttgart O, Münchinger.

(B) ** DG Double 439 696-2 (2) [id.]. Janowitz, Ludwig, Schreier, Kerns, Ridderbusch, V. Singverein, Karajan.

(BB) ** Naxos Dig. 8.550585/6 [id.]. Wagner, Schäfer-Subrata, Koppelstetter, Schäfer, Elbert, Slovak Philharmonic Ch., Capella Istropolitana, Christian Brembreck.

Jochum's memorable, dedicated (1980) performance, marked by resilient rhythms, remains among the most completely satisfying versions even today. It makes a superb bargain on EMI's forte label, with two discs offered for the cost of a single premium-priced CD. The choral singing – by far the most important element in this work – is superb and, though the soloists are variably balanced, they make a fine, clear-voiced team. Brigitte Fassbaender's *Agnus Dei* is very beautiful; coming as it does before the final choral *Donna nobis pacem*, it helps to leave Bach's inspired music resonating in the listener's memory. The digital recording is admirably spacious and clear. Presentation is attractive; documentation is just about adequate, but with no text.

Parrott, hoping to re-create even more closely the conditions Bach would have expected in Leipzig, adds to the soloists a ripieno group of five singers from the Taverner Consort for the choruses. The instrumental group is similarly augmented with the keenest discretion. Speeds are generally fast, with rhythms sprung to reflect the inspiration of dance; however, the inner darkness of the *Crucifixus*, for example, is conveyed intensely in its hushed tones, while the *Et resurrexit* promptly erupts with a power to compensate for any lack of traditional weight. Soloists are excellent, with reduction of vibrato still allowing sweetness as well as purity. If you want a performance on a reduced scale, the recording, made in St John's, Smith Square, is both realistic and atmospheric.

Harnoncourt's version marked a breakthrough in the development of the authentic movement. It confirms that, in parallel with his account of the *Christmas oratorio*, this is one of his most effective Bach performances on a chamber scale, with the choir, including boys' voices, projecting keenly. Rhythmically he is not as imaginative as his finest authentic rivals, and the brisk *Sanctus* is disappointing, but he rises warmly to the final *Dona nobis pacem*, given a real sense of occasion. First-rate solo singing, notably from Helen Watts, aptly firm and even. Nicely balanced recording, good for its late-1960s vintage.

Münchinger's is a strong, enjoyable performance with an exceptionally fine quintet of soloists and very good recording. On balance it makes a fair recommendation; however, with fastish tempi and a generally extrovert manner it is efficient rather than inspiring. The chorus sings well but is placed rather backwardly. The recording dates from 1971 and has been successfully remastered. The chorus sounds vibrant and clear and the trumpets offer no transfer problems. Good value in Decca's Duo series, but not a first choice.

Karajan conveys intensity, even religious fervour, and the very opening brings an impressive first entry of the choir on *Kyrie*. But then, after the instrumental fugue, the contrapuntal entries are sung in a self-consciously softened tone. There is a strong sense of the work's architecture, and the highly polished surfaces do not obscure the depths of the music, but (despite a fine solo team) this is hardly a first choice, although in its two-for-the-price-of-one format it is certainly reasonably priced.

There is certainly room for a bargain digital version of the *B minor Mass*, and the Naxos set offers a chamber-scale performance on modern instruments. With generally well-chosen speeds it offers a good middle-of-the-road approach, and the orchestral playing is first rate, very well recorded, with string-playing finely detailed and with trumpets braying out superbly to bring out the joy of such numbers as the *Gloria*. The soloists are a reliable team, with the contralto, Martina Koppelstetter, outstanding in her two big solos, *Qui tollis* and *Agnus Dei*, the latter taken broadly with fine concentration. In this of all Bach's choral works the chorus is central to any performance, and sadly the backward placing of the chorus takes away bite from the singing except in the big, extrovert moments like the very opening of the *Kyrie* and the *Sanctus*, where the singers suddenly seem more confident.

Motets: *Singet dem Herrn ein Neues Lied; Der Geist hilft unser Schwachheit auf; Jesu, meine Freude; Fürchte dich nicht, ich bin bei dir; Komm, Jesu, komm!; Lobet den Herrn alle Heiden, BWV 225–30.*
(M) *** Teldec/Warner Dig. 0630 17430-2 [2292 42881-2]. Stockholm Bach Ch., VCM, Harnoncourt.
(BB) ** Naxos Dig. 8.553823 [id.]. Scholars Bar. Ens.
(B) ** Carlton Dig. 30367 02152 [(M) id.]. Yorkshire Bach Ch., Seymour, with Gray, Anderson, Farrell.

To Bach's motets, which include some of the greatest music he ever wrote for chorus, went the honour of being the first of his vocal music to be issued digitally in 1980. The recording is very successful indeed, beautifully fresh and clear, the acoustic attractively resonant without clouding detail, and the accompanying instrumental group giving discreet yet telling support. The vigour and joy of the singing come over splendidly in *Singet dem Herrn* which opens the collection, while the expressive feeling of *Jesu, meine Freude* is matched by a sense of drama. This is one of Harnoncourt's most impressive Bach records, and the conductor's timing and use of pauses are finely judged, while the Stockholm chorus show stamina as well as sympathy; the spontaneity of their performance is impressive. At mid-price this must now be the prime recommendation for these six works.

The Scholars Ensemble on Naxos offer an intimate view of these gloriously complex works, one voice per part, using period instruments for accompaniment. The result has an earthy vigour, even if flaws in ensemble and intonation are highlighted, thanks partly to the close-balanced recording.

The Yorkshire Bach Choir under Peter Seymour give a beautifully refined account of the six great motets. This is a relatively large-scale reading, accompanied by cello, violone and organ, with the chorus set at a slight distance in a warm acoustic. This could hardly provide a sharper contrast with the Naxos version, with sweetness of tone and clean ensemble the keynote, though period enthusiasts will find the performances far too smooth. Harnoncourt's Stockholm recording remains a clear first choice.

St John Passion, BWV 245.

(M) **(*) RCA GD 77041 (2) [77041-2-RG]. Prégardien, Van der Kamp, Schlick, Jacobs, Van der Meel, Van Egmond, La Petite Bande Ch. & O, Sigiswald Kuijken.

(BB) ** Naxos Dig. 8.550664/5 [id.]. Soloists, Scholars Baroque Ens.

(i) *St John Passion;* (ii) *Cantata No. 140: Wachet auf.*

(B) ** Ph. Duo 462 173-2 (2) [id.]. (i) Giebel, Höffgen, Haefliger, Young, Berry, Crass, Netherlands R. Ch., Concg. O, Jochum; (ii) Ameling, Baldin, Ramey, London Voices, ECO, Leppard.

At mid-price on BMG/Deutsche Harmonia Mundi, directed by Sigiswald Kuijken, Prégardien as the Evangelist provides a beautiful and intense performance. Harry van der Kamp as Jesus also stands out with his fresh, firm and resonant bass, while Barbara Schlick is the radiant soprano. With excellent sound, the chorus sings the brief, elaborate 'turba' choruses of comment with exemplary point, and only the big choruses fall short.

The Concertgebouw under Jochum offer a relatively conventional interpretation of the *St John Passion*. The performance has some quite outstanding contributions from the soloists, particularly from Giebel and Haefliger, and some eloquent instrumental playing. As one would expect from Jochum, there is a splendid warmth and musical spontaneity about the set, which was recorded in a spacious acoustic and has considerable breadth of tone. It is not, however, particularly concerned with authenticity; the forces are of traditional size and the continuo role is divided between harpsichord and organ. Nevertheless there is much to enjoy and admire here, for the transfer to CD has improved both the immediacy of the sound and the projection of the performance. The cantata makes an acceptable bonus, though it is not entirely successful and, even apart from the rather too measured tempo of the first of the duets, Elly Ameling's intonation is not completely true. There are good things, of course, but the sound is not up to the usual Philips high standard; the choral focus is a little rough.

With a choir of only eight singers providing the soloists too, the Scholars Ensemble takes an attractively intimate view of this masterpiece, both dramatic and meditative. With no director, the ensemble relies on understanding and team-work, which generally works well. The 'turba' choruses of crowd-comment are most effective, but eagerness does not always go with precision. One registers the soloists, not as vocal stars, but as intelligent young singers with fresh rather than beautiful voices. As the Evangelist, Roger Doveton uses his clean, light tenor with imagination, even if he is not quite flexible enough to make the longer recitatives as compelling as they should be.

St John Passion, BWV 245 (sung in English).

✿ (B) *** Decca Double 443 859-2 (2) [id.]. Peter Pears, Heather Harper, Alfreda Hodgson, Robert Tear, Gwynne Howell, John Shirley-Quirk, Wandsworth School Boys' Ch., ECO, Britten.

Benjamin Britten directed live performances of this, the more dramatic of Bach's *Passions*, at the Aldeburgh Festival and elsewhere, which culminated in this wonderfully vivid recording, made at The Maltings in April 1971. Britten characteristically refuses to follow any set tradition, whether baroque, Victorian or whatever; and, with greater extremes of tempo than is common (often strikingly fast), the result makes one listen afresh. The soloists are all excellent, Heather Harper radiant, and though the Wandsworth School Boys' Choir has its rough edges, it reinforces the freshness of the interpretation. The excellent accompaniments from the English Chamber Orchestra resonate grandly, and the ear relishes the richly resilient textures of modern string instruments giving splendidly full support to the singers, while there is also outstanding continuo playing from Philip Ledger. A superb bargain.

St Matthew Passion, BWV 244.

(M) *** EMI CMS7 63058-2 (3). Pears, Fischer-Dieskau, Schwarzkopf, Ludwig, Gedda, Berry, Hampstead Parish Church Ch., Philh. Ch. & O, Klemperer.

(BB) *** Naxos Dig. 8.550832/34 [id.]. József Mukk, István Gáti, Judit Németh, Ibolya Verebits, Péter Köves, Péter Cser, Ferenc Korpás, Rózsa Kiss, Agnes Csenki, Hungarian R. Children's Ch., Hungarian Festival Ch. & State SO, Géza Oberfrank.

While it certainly will not appeal to the authentic lobby, Klemperer's 1962 Philharmonia recording of the *St Matthew Passion* represents one of his greatest achievements on record, an act of devotion of such intensity that points of style and interpretation seem insignificant. The whole cast clearly shared Klemperer's own intense feelings, and one can only sit back and share them too, whatever one's preconceptions.

At bargain price the new version from Naxos uses modern, not period, instruments but, following authentic trends, has brisk speeds and well-sprung rhythms. Though the performance takes no less than 35 minutes less than, say, Richter's, in its alertness it never seems rushed, with the Hungarian State Symphony Orchestra and Festival Choir on excellent form, conducted by Géza Oberfrank. A refreshingly lithe and young-sounding Evangelist, József Mukk, leads a team of Hungarian soloists with fresh, clear voices. The obbligato wind-playing is also attractive (if closely balanced) and the recording is spacious and full, and kind to voices.

St Matthew Passion, BWV 244 (abridged).
(M) (**) EMI (SIS) mono CHS5 65509-2 (2). Grümmer, Höffgen, Dermota, Fischer-Dieskau, Edelmann, V. Singakademie, V. Boys' Ch., VPO, Furtwängler.

Furtwängler conducted the *St Matthew Passion* at Easter 1954, barely six months before he died, and the recording, arriving belatedly, gives a vivid reminder of a great, dedicated occasion. The sound is limited and the choral sound lacks definition; despite that, however, the power of the massive double chorus at the start comes over strongly with the chorale descant for trebles shining brightly above. Speeds are consistently slow, never more disconcertingly to the modern ear than in the chorales, made heavy and funereal, and slowness regularly begets monstrous rallentandos. In addition, 14 numbers were omitted at the performance, and two more have been cut because of technical problems with the recording. However damaging that may be, the result is neatly contained on two well-filled discs in place of the usual three. The four soloists, well caught by the recording, sing the arias as well as contributing to the narrative, with Anton Dermota light and sweet as the Evangelist and the young Fischer-Dieskau thrilling as Jesus.

St Matthew Passion: Arias and choruses.
(B) **(*) DG Classikon 439 447-2 (from complete recording with Schreier, Fischer-Dieskau, Mathis, J. Baker, Salminen, Regensburger Domspatzen, Munich Bach Ch. & O, Karl Richter).

Many collectors who have another complete set will be glad to have this 73-minute Classikon bargain selection from Richter's dedicated second (1979) stereo recording, particularly as Dame Janet Baker's *Erbarme dich* is included.

St Matthew Passion (complete; in English).
(BB) ** ASV CDQSS 324 (3) [(M) id.]. Robert Tear, John Shirley-Quirk, Felicity Lott, Alfreda Hodgson, Neil Jenkins, Stephen Roberts, Bach Ch., St Paul's Cathedral Ch. Boys, Thames CO, Willcocks.

For anyone wanting the *St Matthew Passion* in English, ASV on its super-bargain Quicksilva label offers Sir David Willcocks's traditional account, recorded in 1978 with the Bach Choir, a splendid memento for anyone who has enjoyed his annual performances at the Festival Hall in London. The outstanding soloists include Robert Tear's Evangelist and John Shirley-Quirk's Christus, with Felicity Lott as the soprano soloist and the late Alfreda Hodgson as the contralto; but Peter's denial – usually a supremely moving moment – is here less powerful than usual. The pity is that this version fails to lift quite as it ought. Willcocks, most experienced of choirmasters, draws light and rhythmic singing from the chorus, and the chorales avoid heaviness. The (originally) Argo recording is clear and well balanced.

Vocal collections

Arias: *Mass in B min.: Agnus dei; Qui sedes. St John Passion: All is fulfilled. St Matthew Passion: Grief for sin.*
(M) (***) Decca mono 433 474-2. Kathleen Ferrier, LPO, Boult – HANDEL: *Arias.* (***) ✿

On 7th and 8th October 1952, Kathleen Ferrier made her last and perhaps greatest record in London's Kingsway Hall, coupling four arias each by Bach and Handel. The combined skill of John Culshaw and Kenneth Wilkinson ensured a recording of the utmost fidelity by the standards of that time. Now it re-emerges with extraordinary naturalness and presence.

Transcriptions

Chaconne (from *Partita No. 2 in D min., BWV 1004*) (arr. Busoni).
(M) *** Nimbus Dig. NI 8810 [id.]. Ferruccio Busoni (piano) – CHOPIN: *Preludes* **; LISZT: *Etudes d'exécution transcendante* etc. ***

This is the nearest we shall ever come to hearing Busoni play and, as nearly always, the impression with a first-class modern recording taken from a piano-roll gives an uncanny feeling of the artist's presence. His famous transcription of the Bach *Chaconne* is almost as much Busoni as it is Bach, but it is none the less compelling for that. The prodigious account of it by its arranger projects powerfully in this splendid digital recording, in the Nimbus Duo-Art Grand Piano series. The recording dates from 1925, but the reproduction makes it sound as if it were made yesterday.

Arrangements: Bach–Stokowski

Chorales: Jesu, joy of man's desiring; Sheep may safely graze; We all believe in one God (Fugue on *Wir glauben all' an einen Gott), BWV 680; English suite No. 2, BWV 807: Bourrée. Komm süsser Tod, BWV 478; Chaconne* (from *Partita No. 2 in B min.* for unaccompanied violin), *BWV 1004; Well-tempered Clavier*, Book 1: *Prelude in B min., BWV 869. Easter oratorio: Chorale. Toccata and fugue in D minor, BWV 565.*
✿ (M) *** RCA mono 09026 60922 [id.]. SO, Leopold Stokowski.

The *Toccata and fugue in D minor* is a mono recording made in 1947, and absolutely no technical apologies need be made for it. The sound is clear and full and has an impressively resonant bass. The violins sound more real than many stereo recordings made in America over the next two decades. The rest of the programme dates from three years later. The sobriquet, 'Symphony Orchestra', in this case describes a pick-up group of musicians drawn from the New York Philharmonic and NBC Symphony. They play marvellously. The collector's item here is the incredibly wayward account of Bach's famous *Chaconne*, with its funereal opening tempo. Milstein's account takes 14 minutes; Stokowski stretches it out to 17 minutes 22 seconds and his indulgent *espressivo* alters its character entirely.

Chorale prelude: Wir glauben all' an einen Gott ('Giant fugue'), BWV 680; Easter cantata, BWV 4: Chorale; Geistliches Lied No. 51: Mein Jesu, BWV 487; Passacaglia and fugue in C min., BWV 582; Toccata and fugue in D min., BWV 565; Well-tempered Clavier, Book 1: Prelude No. 8 in E flat min., BWV 853 (all orch. Stokowski).
(M) *** Decca Phase Four 448 946-2 [id.]. Czech PO, Stokowski (with Concert of miscellaneous orchestral transcriptions – see under LSO ***).

Stokowski's flamboyant arrangements of Bach organ works inspired some of the Philadelphia Orchestra's ripest records in the old days of 78-r.p.m. records. Here with spectacular, closely balanced but truthful Phase Four sound to match, big, bold and reverberant, the results are massively satisfying for anyone prepared to put his purist conscience to one side for a moment. Stokowski, over ninety at the time, challenges his players in expansive tempi, but the results are passionate in concentration. The famous *D minor Toccata and fugue* (for which Disney's animators provided extraordinarily imaginative visual imagery in *Fantasia*) is perhaps a shade less vital here than in Stokowski's earlier, mono version with the Philadelphia Orchestra, but the stereo sumptuousness is ample compensation. Most remarkable of all is the mighty *Passacaglia and fugue in C minor*, highly romantic in its decorative detail, but moving steadily to an overwhelming climax.

Bach, Wilhelm Friedemann (1710–84)

Double concerto for 2 harpsichords in D, F46.
(M) **(*) Teldec/Warner 0630 12326-2. Uittenbosch, Curtis, VCM, Harnoncourt – C. P. E. BACH: *Double concerto for harpsichord and fortepiano* ***; J. C. BACH: *Sinfonia concertante in F.* **(*)

Wilhelm Friedemann's *Double concerto* is a much less remarkable piece than Carl Philipp Emanuel's concerto for harpsichord and fortepiano. It is well enough played here, though tuttis are a bit gruff and rather heavily accented.

Sinfonia in F.
(BB) **(*) Naxos Dig. 8.553289 [id.]. Salzburg CO, Yoon K. Lee – C. P. E. BACH: *Sinfonias.* **(*)

Wilhelm Friedemann Bach's *F major Sinfonia* is not really a match for those by his brother, Carl Philipp Emanuel, with which it is coupled. But it is agreeable enough and certainly not entirely conventional. It is given a lively account in Salzburg; modern instruments are used but textures are clean and fresh and the recording is faithful and well balanced.

Fantasia in C min., F2; 8 Fugues, F31; March, F30; Prelude, F29; Sonatas: in G, F7; F min., F8; Suite in G min., F24.
(B) *** HM Dig. HMA 1901305 [id.]. Christophe Rousset (harpsichord).

Here is another recital to confirm Wilhelm Friedemann's strong musical personality. The extraordinary *Fantasia in C minor* has a darkly dramatic opening, then immediately evokes memories of Johann Sebastian's *Chromatic fantasia* in its florid brilliance. The two sonatas are also impressive works. Christophe Rousset was nineteen when he recorded this recital and he plays with remarkable maturity and discernment throughout. He certainly brings out the diversity of the eight succinct miniature *Fugues* which readily demonstrate Wilhelm's contrapuntal mastery.

Polonaise in E flat, F 12/5.
(BB) *** DHM/BMG Baroque Esprit 05472 77440-2 [id.]. Colin Tilney – J. S. BACH: *Oboe sonatas;* C. P. E. BACH: *Oboe sonata*. **(*)

Wilhelm Friedmann's *Polonaise* is not a lively dance form in the modern sense, but a fairly placid piece with a constantly repeated refrain. Played here very simply, it is rather engaging.

Baird, Tadeusz (1928–81)

Colas Breugnon: suite.
(M) *** EMI CDMS5 65418-2 [id.]. Polish CO, Jerzy Maksymiuk – SZYMANOWSKI: *Violin concertos Nos. 1–2*. **(*)

Baird's delightful neo-classical suite (for flute and strings) has much in common with Warlock's *Capriol suite*. It is beautifully played and recorded.

Balakirev, Mily (1837–1910)

Symphony No. 1 in C.
❀ (M) (***) EMI mono CDM5 66595-2. Philh. O, Karajan – ROUSSEL: *Symphony No. 4*. (***) ❀

Symphony No. 1 in C; Islamey (orch. Lyapunov); *Tamara.*
(BB) **(*) Naxos Dig. 8.550792 [id.]. Russian State SO, Igor Golovschin.

Balakirev's *First Symphony* took shape over a period of 30 years. Rimsky-Korsakov speaks of the first movement having been at least one-third complete and of there being sketches for the Scherzo and finale as early as 1866, though it was not finished until 1898, 100 years ago, and it took half a century to reach the gramophone. Karajan's recording with the Philharmonia was recorded in November 1949; it is true to say that, while the recording may have been surpassed, the performance remains unequalled – even by Beecham and Svetlanov. The symphony is an endearing piece, finely wrought, melodious, brilliantly scored and memorable. The Scherzo sounds mercurial and effervescent in Karajan's hands, and the slow movement is done with great sensitivity. We have not compared it with the original 78s, but the present transfer is an improvement over its earlier LP and CD issues. Its last appearance in the catalogue was short-lived, so snap this up before it disappears, particularly in view of the equally superb coupling.

Golovschin may not quite have the uncanny grip on the rather loose-structured first movement which Karajan and indeed Beecham found, but his reading is exciting, convincing in its pacing and control of tension. Moreover it is very well played by a Russian ensemble who have this music in their bones. The two supporting works are hardly less successful. *Islamey* starts off with tremendous Slavonic bustle and again produces a subtly alluring oriental flavour in its central section, while *Tamara* is warmly atmospheric and held together very well, again with glowing woodwind contributions and the Eastern melodic influences deliciously caught. The 1993 recording was made at the Mosfilm Studio and is vivid and full; the acoustic is not confining and the stereo ambience brings plenty of bloom. Golovschin's account of the symphony may not quite match its illustrious predecessors, but it remains very good value in the budget range.

Symphonies Nos. (i) *1 in C;* (ii) *2 in D min.*
(M) *** Revelation RV 10038. (i) USSR State SO, Svetlanov; (ii) Grand SO of R. & TV, Rozhdestvensky.

Rescued from the Soviet radio archive, these performances of the early 1970s have a passion and urgency, a natural feeling for idiomatic phrasing and rhythm, which make you forget any slight shortcoming in the recorded sound. This Russian performance from Svetlanov of No. 1 is altogether tauter and more urgent than the version he recorded in London for Hyperion. Rarely if ever has there been such a radiant account on disc of the lovely slow movement, surging warmly forward, with resonant strings and with a prominent harp, superbly played, adding flair. Though as a rule the *Second Symphon*y seems rather pale after the powerful inspiration of No. 1, Rozhdestvensky convinces one that it is a worthy successor, rich and passionate in the dance rhythms of the first movement, furious and swaggering in the Scherzo, electrically alert in the slow movement and Polacca finale. An ideal coupling, strongly recommended.

Symphony No. 2 in D min.; Russia.
(BB) **(*) Naxos Dig. 8.550793 [id.]. Russian State SO, Igor Golovschin.

The *Second Symphony* is a late work. The first movement is tautly constructed; Golovschin controls its layout impressively and at the same time provides plenty of impetus. The Scherzo has Slavonic gusto but, as with the *First Symphony*, it is the *Andante* where this very Russian performance is so telling – spacious and refined, the strings swelling out spontaneously from a romantic onward flow that is beautifully shaped.

The opening of *Russia* is warmly atmospheric and its integrated folk material again brings seductive woodwind playing and highly responsive strings; after the brass livens things up in a folk dance, Golovschin sustains a raptly beautiful close. As with the *First Symphony*, this may not match its finest predecessors (Rozhdestvensky, above, among them) but this inexpensive Naxos disc remains very good value.

Au jardin; Chant du pêcheur; Gondellied; Islamey. Nocturne No. 3; Polka; Scherzo No. 3; Sonata (Esquisses); Toccata; Valse-impromptu; Valse mélancholique.
(M) * Chante du Monde Russian Season Dig. RUS 788110. Michael Kollontaï.

An unimpressive recital. Michael Kollontaï is now in his late forties, a composer as well as pianist who has taught at the Gnessin Institute and the Moscow Conservatoire, where this recording was made. He produces some beautiful tone in *Au jardin*, where he is more backwardly balanced than in *Islamey*. In the latter he takes no risks and there is none of the effortless virtuosity that great pianists like Barère, Arrau, Cziffra, Cherkassky and Berezovsky bring to it. By their side his is really rather ordinary and there is some ugly left-hand tone. Nothing to write home – or anywhere else – about.

Islamey (oriental fantasy).
(M) *** EMI CDM7 64329-2 [id.]. Andrei Gavrilov – PROKOFIEV: *Concerto No. 1;* TCHAIKOVSKY: *Piano concerto No. 1* etc. ***
(B) **(*) EMI Dig. CD-EMX 2213 [(M) id. import]. Piers Lane – MUSSORGSKY: *Pictures at an exhibition;* STRAVINSKY: *3 Movements from Petrushka.* **

Gavrilov's dazzling account of Balakirev's fantasy is outstandingly charismatic; it is well recorded, too. It comes in harness with an equally dazzling version of Prokofiev's *First Piano concerto* and a performance of the Tchaikovsky *B flat minor Concerto* which is rather less convincing.

A recommendable and exhilarating account of *Islamey* from Piers Lane, not quite the equal of Berezovsky or the legendary Simon Barere but full of spontaneity. Very well recorded.

Banchieri, Adriano (1568–1634)

Barca di Venetia per Padova.
(B) *** HM Dig. HMC 90856.58 (3) [(M) id. import]. Ens. Clément Jannequin, Dominique Visse – MARENZIO: *Madrigals* **(*) ; LASSUS; VECCHI: *Madrigal comedies.* ***

Banchieri's *Barca di Venetia per Padova* ('Boat from Venice to Padua') was published in 1605, the year following *Il Zabaione musicale* (see below). It is a similar and equally diverting kaleidoscope of short madrigals, but here linked – and at times dominated – by a robust (semi-parlando) tenor 'Argomento' which briefly but histrionically underlines the details of the voyage. With the passengers including lawyers, a student, a fisherman, a music-master and a bookseller, a drunken German and a pair of courtesans, the solos and ensembles are wildly contrasted and include a quintet in different dialects, a touching *madrigal affettuoso* ('provided' by the musician) and a no less charmingly lyrical *Madrigal cappriccioso*. The arrival at Fusina brings a light-hearted ensemble with a *Tra, la, la* refrain, before the courtesans, in a duet with the men, immodestly extol the detailed enticements of male and female bodies. The arrival of a group of Jewish brethren brings a grotesque parody of a prayer meeting, followed by a lovely pastiche of a madrigal of Marenzio. On arrival at Padua, the passengers pay the boatman and praise Banchieri's settings. When landing they are accosted by a beggar dressed as a soldier but are not taken in and, after a nostalgic closing number, tell him bluntly, 'Go and work, you swindler!' The performance here has polish, vitality and style, and it is vividly recorded, too. It makes a highly stimulating and at times touching entertainment and, with its apt Marenzio coupling, comes as part of a Harmonia Mundi Bargain CD Trio of '*Comédies madrigalesques*' which is well worth exploring.

Festino nella sera del giovedi grasso avanti cena, Op. 18; Il Zabaione musicale.
(BB) *** Naxos Dig. 8.553785 [id.]. R. Svizzara (Lugano) Ch., Sonatori de la Gioiosa Marca, Treviso, Diego Fasolis.

Adriano Banchieri, a close contemporary of Monteverdi, here presents two musical entertainments built on varied sequences of madrigals. *Il Zabaione musicale*, first published in 1604 and described as a 'sylvan invention', consists of an introduction and three Acts, made up of 17 very brief madrigals. Each Act is dramatically separate, representing – so one modern scholar suggests – the development of the madrigal as a form. The *Festino* – an 'Entertainment for the Eve of Carnival Thursday before Dinner' – is an even more relaxed entertainment. Published in Venice in 1608, it is a sequence of 21 very light-hearted madrigals, some of them involving animal and bird noises, as for example the memorable quartet for owl, cuckoo, cat and dog. Diego Fasolis draws superb singing from his Lugano choir, with incisively crisp ensemble, colourfully enhanced by brass and timpani. The intensity of the performance helps to bring out the genuine, rip-roaring humour, which in less taut performances might seem heavy or simply childish. Excellent recording made in the studios of Radio Lugano. A splendid example of Naxos enterprise, with documentation that other companies sometimes fail to match at higher prices. Full texts and an English translation are provided.

Bantock, Granville (1868–1946)

The Pierrot of the minute: overture.
(M) *** Chandos CHAN 6566 [id.]. Bournemouth Sinf., Norman Del Mar – BRIDGE: *Summer* etc.; BUTTERWORTH: *Banks of Green Willow.* ***

Bantock's overture is concerned with Pierrot's dream, in which he falls in love with a Moon Maiden who tells him their love must die at dawn, but he will not listen. He wakes to realize that his dream of love lasted a mere minute. The writing is often delicate and at times Elgarian, and the piece is well worth investigating. The 1978 recording sounds remarkably fresh.

Barber, Samuel (1910–81)

Adagio for strings, Op. 11.
(M) *** DG Dig. 427 806-2. LAPO, Bernstein – BERNSTEIN: *Overture Candide; West Side Story; On the Town* ***; GERSHWIN: *Rhapsody in blue.* **(*)
(M) *** DG Dig. 439 528-2 [431 048-2]. LAPO, Bernstein – COPLAND: *Appalachian spring* ***; GERSHWIN: *Rhapsody in blue.* **(*)

Bernstein's DG recording (variously coupled), with modern digital sound, is preferable to his Sony account, but the earlier version is just as deeply felt.

(i) *Adagio for strings, Op. 14;* (ii) *Piano concerto, Op. 38;* (iii) *Violin concerto, Op. 14;* (iv) *2nd Essay for orchestra, Op. 17; Overture: The School for Scandal, Op. 5.*
(M) **(*) Sony Theta SMK 6004 [id.]. (i) Phd. O, Ormandy; (ii) John Browning, Cleveland O, Szell; (iii) Isaac Stern, NYPO, Bernstein; (iv) NYPO, Schippers.

Barber's career has a number of parallels with that of William Walton: a vein of acid-tinged romanticism that can readily blossom, as in the *Adagio for strings*, or the *Violin concerto*; comparatively sparse output, mainly of major works; and a comparative failure to maintain full intensity in later work. His first popular success, the *School for Scandal* overture, has a Waltonesque orchestral brilliance and a most touching secondary theme. The *Piano concerto*, written for John Browning, is one of those later works and, though technically it is most impressive and the seriousness cannot be denied, it never quite adds up to the sum of its parts. The seven-in-a-bar finale is the most immediately attractive movement and will provide firm enjoyment from the start: the weighty first movement improves upon acquaintance and the intermezzo-like slow movement has a tender, lyrical vein. However, although the performance here from its dedicatee and Szell is of superlative quality, it is not helped by the forward balance of the (originally CBS) recording or the shallowness of the fortissimo piano-tone and the fierceness of the tuttis. The *Violin concerto* is a different matter and Stern's performance with Bernstein is unsurpassed (see below). The famous *Adagio* is played with great eloquence by the Philadelphia strings under Ormandy and the early (1957) stereo is impressively spacious. The *Second Essay* is a highly concentrated piece about ten minutes in length with quixotic mood-changes and, like the light-hearted Overture, it is played superbly by the New York Philharmonic Orchestra under Schippers. The recording is brightly lit but acceptable.

Adagio for strings, Op. 11; (i) *Violin concerto, Op. 14.*
(M) *** Sony SMK 63088 [id.]. (i) Stern; NYPO, Bernstein – SCHUMAN: *In praise of Shahn; To thee old cause.* ***

Barber's *Violin concerto* is a relaxed, lyrical work with plenty of touches of the characteristic neo-romanticism of this composer. This is a performance of the greatest polish and assurance: it is full of conviction and feeling, and Stern is in his element in the virtuosic finale. Bernstein secures as eloquent and expressive an orchestral accompaniment as one could wish for. This comes as part of the Sony 'Bernstein Century' series together with Bernstein's 1971 account of the *Adagio*, measured and intense. In both works the newly remastered recording sounds very good indeed, though in the concerto the soloist is fairly far forward. The latter is also available paired with Maxwell Davies, but many will count the two fine William Schuman works a more apt coupling.

(i) *Adagio for strings;* (ii) *Essay No. 2 for orchestra; Music for a scene from Shelley; Serenade for strings, Op. 1;* (ii; iii) *A Stopwatch and an ordnance map, Op. 15;* (iv) Chorus: *Let down the bars, O Death!* (ii; v) *A Hand of bridge* (chamber opera), *Op. 35*.

(M) *** Van. 08.4016.71 [OVC 4016]. (i) I Solisti di Zagreb, Antonio Janigro; (ii) Symphony of the Air, Golschmann; (iii) with Robert De Cormier Chorale; (v) with Neway, Alberts, Lewis, Maero; (iv) Washington Cathedral Ch., Callaway.

An admirable and highly rewarding anthology of works by a composer whose *Adagio for strings* has wrongly overshadowed his achievement elsewhere. Excellent singing and playing throughout.

Violin concerto, Op. 14.

❀ (M) *** Sony Stern Edition II SMK 64506 [id.]. Stern, NYPO, Bernstein – MAXWELL DAVIES: *Violin concerto*. ***

Isaac Stern gave the Barber *Violin concerto* its stereo première in 1964 and his performance, which is consistently inspired, is of superlative quality. It has warmth, freshness and humanity, and the slow movement is glorious. The CBS forward balance for the orchestra is less than ideal, but the recording is otherwise very good and has been impressively remastered. This is one of Stern's most important and most distinguished recordings: one feels that he realized that the work was a masterpiece from the very beautiful opening phrase. And yet it has taken three decades for the work to begin to find a permanent place in the concert repertoire.

Medea (ballet): suite.

(M) *** Mercury (IMS) 432 016-2 [id.]. Eastman-Rochester O, Howard Hanson – GOULD: *Fall River legend* etc. ***

Hanson's performance is both polished and dramatic, and the brilliant 1959 Mercury recording has astonishing clarity and vivid presence.

Symphony No. 1, Op. 9.

(M) (**) Bruno Walter Edition: Sony mono SMK 64466 [id.]. NYPO, Bruno Walter (with DVORAK: *Slavonic dance, Op. 46/1*) – R. STRAUSS: *Death and transfiguration* etc. (**(*))

Walter is an unexpected conductor in the music of Samuel Barber, but he recorded the *First Symphony* in 1945, two years after the composer had revised his score. It is a fresh, powerfully intense reading, let down by harsh, two-dimensional, mono sound.

PIANO MUSIC

Piano sonata, Op. 26.

(M) (***) RCA mono GD 60377 [60377-RG]. Vladimir Horowitz (with FAURE: *Nocturne No. 13;* POULENC: *Presto* ***) – KABALEVSKY; PROKOFIEV: *Sonatas* etc. (***)

(M) **(*) [RCA 60415-2-RG]. Van Cliburn (with DEBUSSY: *Estampes: Soirée dans Grenade; Jardins sous la pluie; Etude No. 5; Images, Book I: Reflets dans l'eau; Préludes, Book 2: La terrasse des audiences du clair de lune; Feux d'artifice* **; MOZART: *Piano sonata No. 10* **).

Horowitz gave the première of Barber's *Sonata* and his performance has never been surpassed. It is a remarkable work and, in Horowitz's hands, completely riveting: sample his playing in the quicksilver Scherzo or the articulation of the spirited closing *Fuga*. The 1950 sound is confined but fully acceptable. Of the encores, the scintillating Poulenc *Presto* shows the great pianist at his most dazzling, with a good (if not outstanding) supporting programme.

Van Cliburn's recording is pretty masterly and, although the sound could be more ingratiating and have a warmer ambience, it is still acceptable. This CD has been withdrawn in the UK.

VOCAL MUSIC

(i) *Andromache's farewell;* (ii) *Dover Beach;* (iii) *Hermit songs;* (iv) *Knoxville: summer of 1915*.

(M) (***) Sony mono/stereo MPK 46727 [id.]. (i) Arroyo, NYPO, Schippers; (ii) Fischer-Dieskau, Juilliard Qt; (iii) Leontyne Price, composer; (iv) Eleanor Steber, Dumbarton Oaks O, William Strickland.

This collection of vintage recordings makes a splendid mid-priced Barber compendium, representing four of his finest vocal works, all in superb performances. Excellent CD transfers. No texts are provided but words are exceptionally clear.

(i) *Hermit songs, Op. 29;* (ii) *Knoxville: Summer of 1915* (cantata); (i) Songs: *The Daisies; Nocturne; Nuvoletta; Sleep now.* (ii) *Antony and Cleopatra* (opera): scenes: *Give me some music; Give me my robe.*
(M) (***) RCA mono/stereo 09026 61983-2 [id.]. Leontyne Price, with (i) composer (piano); (ii) New Philh. O, Schippers.

The evocative cantata to words by James Agee, *Knoxville: Summer of 1915*, has never been done more hauntingly and is well coupled with the heroine's arias from the opera, *Antony and Cleopatra*. Far rarer is the private recording of the *Hermit songs*, also specially written for Price. Accompanied by the composer, she is more rugged than Studer in the collected song edition, but just as intense. The mono sound is very limited but conveys the atmosphere of a historic occasion. Otherwise good stereo sound.

Vanessa (opera): complete.
(M) *** RCA GD 87899 (2) [7899-2-RG]. Steber, Elias, Resnik, Gedda, Tozzi, Met. Op. Ch. & O, Mitropoulos.

Vanessa inhabits much the same civilized world as Strauss or Henry James. Although it has not held the stage, its melodic freshness and warmth will ensure a reversal of its fortunes some day. This, its only recording so far, was made at the time of its first performance in 1958, but no apologies are needed for its quality; it stands the test of time as well as does the opera itself.

Barraud, Henry (born 1900)

Offrande à une ombre.
(M) **(*) Mercury 434 389-2 [id.]. Detroit SO, Paul Paray – CHAUSSON: *Symphony;* LALO: *Le rois d'Ys; Namouna.* **(*)

Henry Barraud, who is now on the way to rivalling the longevity of his countryman, Paul le Flem, was a pupil of Dukas and Louis Aubert. He was active in the French resistance, and his wartime *Offrande à une ombre* was dedicated jointly to a fellow-composer, Maurice Jaubert, who fell in 1940 during the retreat from Alsace, and to Barraud's brother, Jean, who was shot by the Gestapo. After the war Barraud became head of music at French Radio and subsequently its Director General. He was a prolific composer whose style owes something to Dukas and Roussel. *Offrande à une ombre* is an effective ten-minute piece, which is eminently well played by the Detroit orchestra and Paray. The recording was made in 1957 and appears in stereo for the first time. It completes an excellent programme.

Barrios, Agustin (1885–1944)

Aconquija; Aire de Zamba; Le catedral; Cueca; Estudio; Una limosna por el amor de Dios; Madrigal (Gavota); Maxixa; Mazurka appassionata; Minuet; Preludio; Un sueño en la floresta; Valse No. 3; Vallancico de Navidad.
(M) *** Sony SBK 47669; *SBT 47669* [id.]. John Williams – PONCE: *Folia de España.* ***

In the expert hands of John Williams this collection provides a very entertaining recital, ideal for late-evening listening. The recording is excellent. The remarkable extended set of Ponce *Variations* added for the CD reissue brings the total playing time up to 77 minutes.

Bartók, Béla (1881–1945)

Concerto for orchestra.
(M) *** Decca 417 754-2 [id.]. Chicago SO, Solti – MUSSORGSKY: *Pictures.* ***
(B) **(*) EMI forte CZS5 72664-2 (2) [(M) id. import]. Chicago SO, Seiji Ozawa – JANACEK: *Sinfonietta* ***; LUTOSLAWSKI: *Concerto for orchestra* **(*); STRAVINSKY: *Firebird ballet.* **(*)

Solti gave Bartók's *Concerto for orchestra* its compact disc début. The upper range is very brightly lit indeed, which brings an aggressive feeling to the upper strings. This undoubtedly suits the reading, fierce and biting on the one hand, exuberant on the other. Superlative playing from Solti's own Chicago orchestra, and given vivid sound.

Ozawa's EMI reissue produces dazzling playing from the Chicago orchestra. The performance is full of life and energy. There are more searching and more atmospheric accounts available, but this stands alongside the Solti version for brilliance. However, as with the Lutoslawski coupling, the CD transfer brings sound which, though most vivid, is rather two-dimensional.

(i) *Concerto for orchestra;* (ii) *Piano concertos Nos. 1–3*; (i; iii) *Violin concerto No. 2 in B min.*
(B) *** Ph. Duo 438 812-2 (2) [id.]. (i) Concg. O, Haitink; (ii) Kovacevich, LSO or BBC SO (in *No. 2*), Sir Colin Davis; (iii) Szeryng.

This is as enticing a bargain Bartók collection as you could find. Not unexpectedly in Haitink's 1960 *Concerto for orchestra*, the orchestral playing is of the highest quality and the recording is both atmospheric and clear. The performance is more subtle, less tense than Solti's mid-priced version, although the element of dramatic contrast is not missing. Szeryng joins Haitink for the *B minor Violin concerto* with equally satisfying artistic results. Haitink keeps a firm grip on proceedings and there is a genuine sense of momentum and impetus about the performance that is really exciting. The 1969 recording is vivid, and firmly and realistically focused. Kovacevich's direct, concentrated readings of the three *Piano concertos* are hardly less persuasive. Sir Colin Davis accompanies sensitively and vigorously. No complaints about the bright, full recording.

(i) *Concerto for orchestra;* (ii) *Dance suite; 2 Portraits, Op. 5; Mikrokosmos* (orch. Serly): *Bourrée; From the diary of a fly.*
(M) *** Mercury (IMS) 432 017-2 [id.]. (i) LSO; (ii) Philharmonia Hungarica, Dorati.

Dorati secures outstandingly brilliant and committed playing from the LSO. The recording, made in Wembley Town Hall, shows characteristic expertise of balance. The rest of the programme was recorded in 1958 in the Grosse Saal of the Vienna Konzerthaus, which affords Dorati's fine orchestra of Hungarian émigrés plenty of body without blurring outlines.

Concerto for orchestra; (i) *The Miraculous Mandarin* (complete ballet).
(M) **(*) Virgin/EMI Dig. CUV5 61192-2 [CDZ 61106]. (i) Dumont Singers; Melbourne SO, Iwaki.

Iwaki and the Melbourne orchestra have an obvious advantage over their direct mid-priced and bargain rivals in presenting the complete *Miraculous Mandarin* ballet, not just the suite, as coupling for the *Concerto for orchestra*. The recording is excellent, spacious and full, though transferred at a rather low level. The playing is finely pointed but is often too well-mannered for Bartók, lacking something in fierceness and excitement. The ballet is generously indexed with tracks.

Concerto for orchestra; The Miraculous Mandarin: suite; 2 Pictures, Op. 10.
(B) *(**) Sony SBK 48263 [id.]. Phd. O, Ormandy.

The Philadelphia *Concerto for orchestra* is superbly played and there is plenty of panache in Ormandy's reading. The snag is that, even with careful digital remastering, the upper strings are inclined to be a bit shrill. Predictably, Ormandy also draws a brilliant, polished performance from his orchestra in *The Miraculous Mandarin*. Opus 10 combines an uninhibitedly romantic piece, fittingly labelled *In full bloom* (cue for the full Philadelphia sound), with a *Village dance*, fairly easy-going by Bartókian standards. A generous triptych (74 minutes) and it is a pity there have to be reservations about the recording, which certainly does not lack vividness.

Concerto for orchestra; Music for strings, percussion and celesta.
(M) **(*) DG 457 890-2. BPO, Karajan.
(BB) *(*) Naxos Dig. 8.550261 [id.]. Belgian R. & TV PO (Brussels), Alexander Rahbari.

Karajan's recording of the *Concerto for orchestra* comes from 1966 and that of the *Music for strings, percussion and celesta* from 1973: they have been remastered very successfully. In the *Concerto* the Berlin Philharmonic, in superb form, give a performance that is rich, romantic and smooth – for some ears perhaps excessively so. Karajan is right in treating Bartók emotionally, but comparison with Solti points the contrast between Berlin romanticism and earthy Hungarian passion. With Solti, any rubato is linked to the Hungarian folk idiom, where Karajan's moulding of phrases is essentially of the German tradition. The *Music for strings, percussion and celesta* has well-upholstered timbre, and here Karajan's essentially romantic view combines with the recording to produce a certain urbanity. He avoids undue expressiveness in the opening slow fugue (except in a big rallentando at the end) and the third movement is given a performance of great atmosphere. However, the playing of the Berlin strings is a pleasure in itself and the sound is impressive and full-bodied.

Rahbari directs the Belgian orchestra in a warm and comfortable, rather than a brilliant, performance of the *Concerto for orchestra*. Though ensemble is not perfect, the impulse gives a feeling of live performance, with the night music of the slow movement beautifully atmospheric, helped by warmly reverberant sound. There is some first-rate solo playing from the woodwind, and the brass and percussion come over with satisfying weight. The *Music for strings, percussion and celesta* makes the ideal coupling; but, even more taxing in its technical demands, it brings a rougher performance, not always biting enough, but again warmly atmospheric in the slow third movement. At super-bargain price it deserves a qualified recommendation.

Concerto for orchestra; Music for strings, percussion and celesta; Hungarian sketches.
(M) *** RCA 09026 61504-2 [id.]. Chicago SO, Fritz Reiner.

Reiner's version of the *Concerto for orchestra* was recorded in 1955 but in its latest CD format the sound approaches demonstration standard in its spacious warmth, clarity and impact. The performance is most satisfying, surprisingly straightforward from one brought up in central Europe, but with plenty of cutting edge. The *Music for strings, percussion and celesta*, recorded three years later, suffers from a forward balance which prevents a true pianissimo, yet the concentration of the playing all but overcomes this defect, and the folk-based set of five *Hungarian sketches*, which completes the programme, is utterly seductive when played and recorded with such vividness of colour and a natural understanding of the music's rhythmic impetus.

Piano concertos Nos. 1–3.
(M) *** DG 447 399-2 [id.]. Géza Anda, Berlin RSO, Ferenc Fricsay.
(M) *** Decca Dig./Analogue 448 125-2. Ashkenazy, LPO, Solti.
(BB) **(*) Naxos Dig. 8.550771 [id.]. Jenö Jandó, Budapest SO, András Ligeti.

The Géza Anda recordings with Fricsay from the beginning of the 1960s are rather special. Both artists show a feeling for the music's inner world and its colouring, which is magnetic in the slow movements. The performances are refined yet urgent, incisive but red-blooded too. They make a worthy addition to DG's series of 'Originals'. The recording, from the beginning of the 1960s, is vivid and remarkably atmospheric, yet still tangible in detail.

The partnership of Ashkenazy and Solti, combined with vintage Decca sound, makes this Ovation mid-price reissue a strong competitor. The *Second* and *Third Concertos* were recorded first in 1978–9 and both performances spark off the kind of energy and dash one would usually expect only at a live performance. With the Slavonic bite of the soloist beautifully matched by the Hungarian fire of the conductor, the readings of both works are wonderfully urgent and incisive. The tempi tend to be fast, but the focus of the playing is superbly clear. The *First Concerto* came last, recorded digitally in 1981; the performance is even tougher, urgent and biting, with the widest range of dynamics, never relaxing in the outer movements. The sound is slightly sharper but the Kingsway Hall aura remains, and the slow movements in all three works bring a hushed inner concentration, beautifully captured in warmly refined recording. With red-blooded Hungarian qualities underlined, these three works from three different periods of Bartók's career seem more closely akin than usual, with the *First* – especially the brilliant finale – marginally the most aggressive, the *Third* somewhat mellower.

With an all-Hungarian cast, Naxos offers invigorating accounts of the three Bartók *Piano concertos* with Jandó on top form, playing with exciting bravura throughout. The energy of the motoric *First Concerto* is not brutalized; and in the slow movement with its important percussion parts and the haunting 'Night music' of the *Second* the resonance of the recording ensures that there is plenty of atmosphere, even if in outer movements the violent brass interjections could be more cleanly focused. Apart from the excess of resonance, the recording is vivid and well balanced.

Piano concerto No. 2 in G.
(B) **(*) [EMI Red Line Dig. CDR5 72101]. Tzimon Barto, LPO, Eschenbach – RACHMANINOV: *Piano concerto No. 3.* *(*)
(B) *(*) EMI forte CZS5 68637-2 (2) [CDFB 68637]. Sviatoslav Richter, O de Paris, Maazel – PROKOFIEV: *Piano concerto No. 5* *(*); TCHAIKOVSKY: *Piano concertos 1–3.* **

Tzimon Barto is more at home in Bartók than he is in Rachmaninov. His playing has energy and an appropriate toughness of character and no lack of spontaneity. The piano is recorded none too flatteringly, but the orchestra is caught brilliantly and colourfully. However, the coupling is less recommendable.

Richter seldom disappoints in the recording studio, but his 1969 partnership with Maazel did not seem to strike any sparks and, although his bravura cannot be gainsaid, the musical effect has far less than his usual incisiveness and strength of projection. The recording is not special either.

Piano concerto No. 3.
(M) *** DG 447 666-2. Géza Anda, Dresden State O, Karajan – SCHUMANN: *Symphony No. 4.* ***
(BB) *** Arte Nova Dig. 74321 52248-2 [id.]. Russell Sherman, SWF SO, Gielen – BERG: *3 Pieces from the Lyric suite;* CARTER: *Piano concerto* etc. ***

A most lyrical account of the concerto from the 1972 Salzburg Festival by Géza Anda, more spacious and ruminative than his earlier version with Fricsay, and accompanied with enormous sensitivity and imagination by Karajan and the Staatskapelle, Dresden. A very special performance, and very well recorded too.

As in the Carter and Berg, Gielen directs an intense, crisply pointed account of the Bartók *Concerto*, matched by the sharply rhythmic, well-pointed playing of Russell Sherman. This makes a generous and unusual coupling of twentieth-century masterpieces, well recorded, and made the more attractive at super-budget price.

Viola concerto; Violin concerto No. 1; (i) *Rhapsodies Nos. 1–2.*
(M) *** EMI CDM7 63985-2. Yehudi Menuhin, New Philh. O, Dorati; (i) BBC SO, Boulez.

Menuhin with his strongly creative imagination plays these concertos with characteristic nobility of feeling, and he and Dorati make much of the Hungarian dance rhythms. There is a comparably earthy, peasant manner in Menuhin's playing of the two *Rhapsodies*, and it is matched by Boulez's approach, warm and passionate rather than clinical. The soloist is rather close. However, the balance responds to the controls, and this remains one of Menuhin's most worthwhile reissues.

Violin concertos Nos. (i) *1;* (ii) *2.*
(M) *** Decca Dig./Analogue 425 015-2 [id.]. Kyung Wha Chung, Chicago SO or LPO, Solti.
(M) *** Sony Stern Edition II SMK 64502 [id.]. Stern; (i) Phd. O, Ormandy; (ii) NYPO, Bernstein.

Though on Decca the soloist is rather forwardly balanced, the hushed intensity of the writing, as well as bitingly Hungarian flavours, is caught superbly, thanks to the conductor as well as to the soloist. The expressive warmth behind Bartók's writing is fully brought out, and there is no sentimental lingering. Among modern recordings, this leads the field in both works.

Stern recorded what was known then as the Bartók *Violin concerto* in 1958, and it was among the 'Late arrivals' in our very first hardback *Stereo Record Guide*. Stern brings to this mature masterpiece an enviable combination of tautness and lyricism, steely strength and melting beauty of tone. The accompaniment is sensitive and subtle; Bernstein is evidently in complete sympathy with both the music and the soloist, and the overall impression is of understanding between these two inspirational artists. The earlier concerto was written in 1907–8 for the violinist Stefi Geyer as the composer's love-token, and Stern's passionate playing suits it to perfection, his ardour readily surmounting the clash of styles in the second and final movement, with Debussy and Strauss – particularly the latter – alternating with the genuine Hungarian Bartók. The 1961 recording brings a balance which favours the soloist in a manner typical of CBS, but otherwise it sounds well in its successfully remastered format.

Violin concerto No. 2 in B min.
(M) *** EMI CDM5 66060-2. Perlman, LSO, Previn – CONUS: *Violin concerto;* SINDING: *Suite.* ***

Perlman's is a superb performance, totally committed and full of youthful urgency, with the sense of spontaneity that comes more readily when performers have already worked together on the music in the concert hall. The contrasts are fearlessly achieved by both soloist and orchestra, with everyone relishing virtuosity in the outer movements. The slow movement is deliberately understated by the soloist, with the fragmentation of the theme lightly touched in, but even there the orchestra has its passionate comments. The 1973 recording is full and gains much from the Kingsway Hall acoustics for, though Perlman is balanced characteristically forward and the CD transfer has brightened the orchestral tuttis, the sound has plenty of depth and ambient warmth. With its interesting new couplings, this is one of the most stimulating reissues taken from EMI's 'Perlman Collection'.

(i) *Violin concerto No. 2; Second Suite for orchestra* (revised, 1943 version).
(M) **(*) Mercury (IMS) 434 350-2 [id.]. (i) Sir Yehudi Menuhin; Minneapolis SO, Dorati.

Menuhin's third version of the *Second Violin concerto* dates from 1957. It is much better recorded than either of his earlier records, and (even taking into account the comments above) remains thoroughly worthwhile, with the solo playing demonstrating those special qualities of lyrical feeling and warmth for which Menuhin was justly famous. His performance is especially appealing in the haunting theme and variations of the central *Andante tranquillo* but, with Dorati accompanying animatedly, the finale has plenty of impetus and fire. The rare coupling makes this Mercury reissue doubly attractive. Anyone who enjoys the *Concerto for orchestra* will respond to the early *Second Orchestral Suite*, which was revised in the year (1943) when the former was written. It is a colourful, half-hour-long piece in four movements; the second introduces a vibrant fugue and the *Andante* opens with an unusual extended recitative from the bass clarinet. The energetic, folksy finale ends serenely (*molto quieto*). Dorati is a persuasive advocate, and the characteristically graphic Mercury recording has no lack of primary colours.

(i) *Dance suite;* (ii) *Music for strings, percussion and celesta;* (i) *The Wooden Prince* (complete), *Op. 13.*
(M) **(*) Sony SM2K 64100 (2) [S2K 64100]. (i) NYPO; (ii) BBC SO; Boulez – SCRIABIN: *Poème de l'exstase.* ***

In *The Wooden Prince* Boulez is the most compelling of advocates, maintaining his concentration throughout; the *Dance suite* brings a performance just as warm, but a degree less precise. The 1975 analogue recording, originally among CBS's best, emerges vividly on CD with plenty of atmosphere, although the upper strings could be more expansive. The *Music for strings, percussion and celesta* was made in Walthamstow two years later and was one of Boulez's finest records of that period. Unfortunately the recording suffers from the artificial balance sometimes favoured by CBS. However, for those who can overlook this there are genuine rewards in this magnetic music-making, and the Scriabin coupling is quite superb.

Divertimento for strings.
(M) *** EMI CDM5 65079-2. ECO, Daniel Barenboim – HINDEMITH: *Trauermusik;* SCHOENBERG: *Verklaerte Nacht.* ***

Barenboim's passionate earthiness makes this a very strong account of the *Divertimento* and the result is red-bloodedly involving, with a vigorous communication of high spirits in the finale. The work is, of course, in concerto grosso style and here the solo quartet is a distinguished one (José-Luis Garcia, John Tunnel, Cecil Aronowitz and Adrian Beers). The 1969 Abbey Road recording brings admirably full string textures. With excellent couplings this makes a first-rate triptych.

Divertimento for strings; Music for strings, percussion and celesta.
(M) *** Decca 448 577-2 [id.]. ASMF, Marriner – SHOSTAKOVICH: *Piano concerto No. 1.* ***
(B) *** HM HMA Dig. 190 3052 [id.]. Liszt CO, Rolla.

The *Music for strings, percussion and celesta* (1936) and the *Divertimento for strings* (1939) were both written for Paul Sacher's Basle Chamber Orchestra. The Liszt Chamber Orchestra comprises seventeen players, including Janos Rolla who directs from the first desk, though they are augmented for the *Music for strings, percussion and celesta*. These are both expert performances and distil a powerful atmosphere in the slow movements of both pieces. They command beautifully rapt *pianissimo* tone and keen intensity. The sound is less reverberant than for some rivals, but there is no lack of ambience. Readers who want accounts of these works that would not have greatly differed from Sacher's at the first performance will not be disappointed: indeed, this is the best available.

A superlative coupling from Marriner, fully worthy of Decca's Classic Sound series, even though the recording originally appeared (in 1970) on the Argo label. Marriner follows the composer's intentions, like Sacher using a chamber-sized group, and his reading (helped by the superb Argo engineering) also reveals extra detail, extra expressiveness, extra care for tonal and dynamic nuances. In the slow opening fugue Marriner meticulously observes Bartók's instructions to keep the music down to a pianissimo as far as bar 26, yet there is no sense of cold, withdrawn playing; quite the opposite. In the second movement the terracing of subtly different tempi is managed much more adeptly than usual, and all the playing reflects the working together beforehand in democratic conference which was the general procedure in preparing a St Martin's performance at that time. The *Divertimento* is given a similarly vivid performance and the recording is again outstandingly good. With a generous and attractive Shostakovich bonus, this is a reissue not to be missed.

Divertimento for strings; Romanian folk dances.
(M) **(*) DG (IMS) Dig. 445 541 [id.]. Orpheus CO – STRAVINSKY: *Dumbarton Oaks Concerto* etc. ***

The American Orpheus Chamber Orchestra give an eminently well-prepared account of the *Divertimento*. A good performance with a sense of mystery and intensity of feeling, if not entirely idiomatic. The recording is very clean and well balanced. The *Romanian folk dances* are also attractively done, and the recording is fresh and immediate.

Hungarian folk-dance suite, Op. 18; Hungarian pictures.
(M) *** Chandos Dig. CHAN 7083 [id.]. Philh. O, Järvi – ENESCU: *Romanian rhapsodies.* ***

The *Folk-dance suite* and the *Hungarian pictures* (the latter also drawn from various folk-based pieces), originally written for piano, are lightweight Bartók but are vividly colourful here and are aptly coupled with Enescu's pair of *Romanian rhapsodies*. A lightweight but attractive disc, particularly when playing and recording are suitably red-blooded.

(i) *Hungarian pictures;* (ii) *The Miraculous Mandarin* (complete ballet); *Music for strings, percussion and celesta;* (iii) *Rhapsody for piano and orchestra;* (ii) *Suite No. 1, Op. 3; 2 Pictures, Op. 10.*
(B) **(*) Decca Double 448 276-2 (2). (i) Israel PO, Mehta; (ii) Detroit SO, Dorati; (iii) Pascal Rogé, LSO, Weller.

Mehta gives a fine performance of the five *Hungarian pictures* which Bartók scored for orchestra in 1931, some 20 years after their original composition as piano pieces. They have great charm, and the glowing orchestral colours are well realized here. The Israel Philharmonic, recorded in Kingsway Hall, sounds far finer than when it faces the microphones on home ground. Pascal Rogé shows genuine feeling for the keyboard colour of Bartók's *Rhapsody*: in his hands the music is far from abrasive, with an atmospheric recording to match. The rest of the programme is in the hands of Antal Dorati. The *Suite No. 1*, regarded as revolutionary at its first Viennese performance in 1905, now strikes the ear as conservative, but it is a warm and colourful work, impressive in structural control, with the five movements in arch form. Dorati's approach is strong and vigorous to match, as it is in the much more advanced *Pictures* of 1910. The two major works here, the complete *Miraculous Mandarin* ballet and the *Music for strings and percussion*, are recorded digitally, and the range and brilliance of the sound are spectacular. This makes up for any lessening of tension in the actual performances compared with Dorati's previous recordings of both works for Mercury. Though the playing in the early ballet is polished enough, it finally lacks the flamboyance needed, the bold display of controlled barbarism. The *Music for strings, percussion and celesta* also lacks the final degree of intensity, although both make a considerable impact when the recording is so vividly projected.

Hungarian sketches; Romanian folk dances.

(M) *** Mercury (IMS) 432 005-2 [id.]. Minneapolis SO, Dorati – KODALY: *Dances; Háry János.* ***

Dorati, himself a Hungarian, provided the pioneer stereo recording of these works, yet the 1956 sound is vivid and full and wears its years very lightly indeed. The Minneapolis orchestra, on top form, provides plenty of ethnic feeling and colour.

(i) *The Miraculous Mandarin* (complete); (ii) *2 Portraits, Op. 5.*

(M) *** DG (IMS) Dig. 445 501-2 [id.]. LSO, Abbado; (i) with Amb. S.; (ii) Shlomo Minz – JANACEK: *Sinfonietta.* ***

(i) *The Miraculous Mandarin* (complete). *4 Orchestral pieces, Op. 12;* (ii) *3 Village scenes.*

(M) *** Sony SMK 45837 [id.]. (i) Schola Cantorum; (ii) Camerata Singers; NYPO, Pierre Boulez.

Abbado directs a fiercely powerful performance of Bartók's barbarically furious ballet – including the wordless chorus in the finale – but one which, thanks to the refinement of the recording, makes the aggressiveness of the writing more acceptable while losing nothing in power. The Janáček coupling is highly appropriate and equally successful; before that, however, the ear is sweetened by Minz's warmth in the *Portraits.*

Boulez also proves a strong and sympathetic advocate in all this music, and his approach is surprisingly warm. This is even more striking in *The Miraculous Mandarin.* The New York orchestra responds with deeply expressive playing and, with spacious recording, many will prefer it on that account.

The Miraculous Mandarin (ballet): suite.

(M) **(*) EMI (SIS) CDM5 65922-2. Philh. O, Irving – KABALEVSKY: *The Comedians* (suite); KHACHATURIAN: *Gayaneh; Masquerade:* suites; SHOSTAKOVICH: *Age of Gold.* **(*)

Irving had already conducted Bartók's ballet at Covent Garden before he recorded the suite in 1960, one of the first in stereo. He transmits his own confidence to the orchestra, and even if the punches are not as shattering as some later versions, with such superb playing from the Philharmonia the evocation is most compelling, especially in the sexily sinuous *Dance of the Young Girl.* The Kingsway Hall recording is remarkably full and richly coloured.

Music for strings, percussion and celesta.

(M) (***) Mercury mono 434 378-2 [id.]. Chicago SO, Rafael Kubelik – MUSSORGSKY: *Pictures at an exhibition.* (***)

This was the second LP Mercury made in Chicago in 1951, following the coupled *Pictures at an exhibition*, and if the sound is not as spectacular as the Mussorgsky/Ravel score, that is partly because in those early LP days the timbre of the upper strings still remained somewhat illusive to the available microphones. But the balance is excellent, and the warmth and intensity at the work's opening are maintained throughout, and especially in the evocation of the *Adagio*, with subtly concentrated string-playing. The rhythmic freedom and energy of the second and fourth movements combine to make Kubelik's performance highly compelling overall.

Rhapsodies for violin and orchestra: No. 1 in G min.; 2 in D min.

(B) *** [EMI Red Line Dig. CDR5 69806]. Kyung Wha Chung, CBSO, Rattle – DVORAK: *Violin concerto.* ***

(M) ** Sony Stern Edition II SMK 64503 [id.]. Stern, NYPO, Bernstein – PROKOFIEV: *Violin concertos.* **(*)

Kyung Wha Chung gives commanding, inspired performances, full of fire and imagination, helped by the inspirational accompaniment of Rattle and the Birmingham orchestra. The *Rhapsodies* are flamboyant works, each in two nicely contrasted movements.

Stern and Bernstein seem less happy with the *Rhapsodies* than with the mature *Concerto*. The first, a colourful and immediately attractive piece, is played well enough; however, the second, taut and pithily rhythmic, surely needs a drier acoustic. Neither Stern nor Bernstein seems comfortable, and the constant rhythmic thrusting becomes monotonous.

The Wooden prince (complete); *Music for strings, percussion and celesta*.
(M) **(*) Mercury (IMS) 434 357-2 [id.]. LSO, Dorati.

Dorati's performances of both works are brilliantly authentic. *The Wooden Prince* is given a fresh, dynamic reading, vivid in its detail, with the reminders of Stravinsky and the Debussian textures brilliantly caught. The *Music for strings, percussion and celesta* is comparably atmospheric, the playing full of tension, and Dorati brings out the Hungarian dance inflexions in the finale. The recordings, from 1964 and 1960 respectively, hardly sound their age except for a degree of rawness in the upper range of the strings in the more strident moments of the ballet.

CHAMBER AND INSTRUMENTAL MUSIC

(i) *Contrasts. Mikrokosmos:* excerpts.
(M) (***) Sony mono MPK 47676. Composer; (i) with Joseph Szigeti, Benny Goodman.

Contrasts was commissioned by Benny Goodman. In 1940 Bartók added a further movement, and it was in this form that the three artists made their recording. That same year Bartók recorded 31 pieces from *Mikrokosmos* and these performances are indicative of the wide range and delicacy of keyboard colour that Bartók commanded. The sound is surprisingly good, given that it is over half a century old! An indispensable issue.

(i) *Contrasts. Violin sonatas Nos. 1–2*.
(BB) *** Naxos Dig. 8.550749 [id.]. György Pauk, Jenö Jandó; (i) with Kálmán Berkes.

The appearance of both the *Violin sonatas*, together with *Contrasts* for clarinet, violin and piano, making 75 minutes of music for less than £5 (or its equivalent), will cause a stir, particularly when they are played by such an experienced artist as György Pauk and his fellow Hungarian, Jenö Jandó. Given the refinement and subtlety of Pauk's playing here, it would be churlish not to give it a three-star recommendation, the only very small qualification being the balance, which favours the piano too much in both sonatas. In the superb account of *Contrasts*, in which Kálmán Berkes joins them, the balance is better. Outstanding value.

44 Duos (for 2 violins).
(M) ** Carlton Dig. 30366 00042 [id.]. Lydia Mordkovitch (playing both parts).

(i) *44 Duos. Solo Violin sonata*.
(BB) *** Naxos Dig. 8.550868 [id.]. György Pauk, (i) with Kazuki Sawa.

György Pauk's impressive recording of the remarkable *Solo Sonata* of 1944, commissioned by Menuhin, is alone worth the price of this Naxos CD. His account is commanding, yet there is nothing about this playing that draws attention to the virtuosity of the artist rather than the artistry of the composer. Everywhere his pacing seems just right and his playing effortless. In the *44 Duos*, composed in 1931 and intended, like the *Microcosmos*, for pedagogical use, Pauk is partnered by the Japanese violinist, Kazuki Sawa, who was at one time a pupil. Pauk and Sawa offer expertly judged and splendidly characterful accounts of these pieces, and there is an impressive rapport and spontaneous give-and-take between the two musicians. The Naxos recording is very good indeed and enhances the attractions of this super-bargain issue.

Lydia Mordkovitch is an artist of quality whose achievements are widely recognized. In the *44 Duos*, however, she opts to record both parts so that the spontaneous give-and-take and sense of dialogue is less easily conveyed. She, too, is accorded excellent sound by the engineers, but the Naxos rival scores in having the *Solo Sonata* as well.

Piano quintet.
(BB) **(*) ASV Quicksilva Dig. CDQS 6217 [(M) id.]. Suzanne Bradbury, Silvestri String Qt – SCHUMANN: *Piano quintet*. **(*)

(i–ii) *Piano quintet*; (i; iii) *Andante* (for violin and piano); *Rhapsodies Nos. 1 & 2*.
(BB) *** Naxos Dig. 8.550886-2. (i) Jenö Jandó; (ii) Kodály Qt; (iii) György Pauk.

Readers who enjoyed the *Contrasts* and the two *Violin sonatas* from Naxos (see above) will need no prompting to invest in this companion disc. The *Piano quintet* dates from 1903–4 (there were two earlier attempts at the medium) and is closer to the world of Richard Strauss and Dohnányi than to the Bartók with whom we are familiar. A substantial work in the received idiom, over 40 minutes in length, it is wholly uncharacteristic. The *Andante* for violin and piano comes from 1902 and is otherwise not recorded. It is slight but charming. The two *Rhapsodies* come from 1928. They were written respectively for Joseph Szigeti and Zoltán Székely and are more popular in style than the *Fourth Quartet*, written the same year. Very good playing from György Pauk and alert playing from Jandó, whose humming is at times faintly audible. No quarrels with either recording or performances.

On ASV Quicksilva an alternative version of the early *Piano quintet*, written when the composer was engaged on such works as *Kossuth* and the Lisztian Op. 1 *Rhapsody for piano and orchestra*. These artists make a good case for this eclectic and predominantly romantic score in which traces of Brahms, Dohnányi, Liszt and Strauss mingle with Debussy. In the early years of the century, Bartók himself used to programme his quintet with the Schumann, so that the coupling is particularly apposite. The performances and recording are both recommendable – though not perhaps in preference to the Naxos coupling.

String quartets Nos. 1–6.
(M) *** DG 445 241-2 (3). Tokyo Qt.
(B) *** Teldec/Warner 0630 12334-2 (2). Eder Qt.
(M) *** Audivis Astrée V 4809 (3) [id.]. Végh Qt.
(B) **(*) Ph. Duo 442 284-2 (2) [id.]. Novák Qt.
(B) ** Hyperion Dyad Dig. CDD 22003 (2) [id.]. New Budapest Qt.

The performances by the Tokyo Quartet bring an almost ideal combination of fire and energy with detailed point and refinement. The readings are consistently satisfying, outshining even the Emersons. Though the polish is high, the sense of commitment and seeming spontaneity are greater too. So the range of expression includes in the fullest measure not only the necessary Bartókian passion but the sparkle and wit, each interpretative problem closely considered and solved with finesse and assurance. Unlike the other DG set, the layout of the Tokyo performance is on three discs, but they are offered at mid-price (in the UK only) and the splendid recording is admirably transferred to CD.

Considerable competition comes from the Eder Quartet, a much-respected Hungarian ensemble whose complete digital set now returns to the catalogue on a pair of budget-priced CDs. Their playing has great intensity and is full of insights. There is a sense of onward movement without any feeling that the music is over-projected or held on a tight rein; on the contrary, one is hardly aware of the bar-line. And what a wonderful quality of sound they produce in No. 1 at the Debussy-like episode (fig. 9) and such rapt tone and concentration of atmosphere at the *pianopianissimo* passage into which it leads. The same must be said about nearly all the playing here. The recording too approaches the demonstration bracket.

The analogue Végh recordings date from 1972, but the CD transfers are splendidly managed: there is a fine sense of presence, but also the ambient fullness one associates with the best analogue recordings, and there is bite without edginess on top. The Végh players sometimes respond with more expressive warmth than some would expect to be applied to Bartók; but others (including I.M.) will find this the very quality in their music-making which prevents the music from becoming too aggressive. On the whole they give very perceptive performances. They are not flawless technically but they understand what this music is about and, above all, they produce an effect of seeming spontaneity. They were last reviewed by us in 1988 (then at full price). Welcome back.

The Novák Quartet, a fine Czech group, bring plenty of grip to their performances and there is certainly no lack of fire and expressive intensity. If not as polished as the Tokyo versions, they have the advantage of being complete on a pair of Duo CDs, which Philips offer for the cost of one premium-price disc. So there is no question of their bargain status, as the recording is firm and well balanced.

Like the Novák Quartet, the New Budapest Quartet enjoy an advantage in accommodating all six *Quartets* on two discs (odd numbers on the first CD and even numbers on its companion). The performances are generally very good, though they are not as imaginative or as compelling as the Tokyo Quartet. Nor does the recording have the tonal richness and bloom of the Alban Berg or Tokyo Quartet on DG (the former at full price). But if you need an economically priced set of these works, the Eder or Novák are the ones to go for.

String quartets Nos. 3–4 & 6.
(M) *** Sony mono/stereo SMK 62705 [id.]. Juilliard Qt.

Perhaps the finest thing on this CD is the *Fourth Quartet*, recorded in the late 1940s, only three years after the Juilliard Quartet's formation. The sound is astonishingly fresh for the period and those who have the original LPs will find the improvement quite remarkable. Old LPs, particularly in early stereo, are often wrecked by modern transfers, but this mono disc is greatly enhanced. The playing is magnificent, as is that of the *Third Quartet*, which comes from the group's second Bartók cycle, and their first in stereo.

By this time (1963), their personnel had changed: Robert Koff had been replaced as second violin by Isidore Cohen and the cellist was Claus Adam and not Arthur Winograd. The *Sixth Quartet* comes from their last cycle, their second in stereo and first in digital sound (recorded in 1981) when the only survivor from the original quartet was the founder-leader, Robert Mann. It is a powerful performance but more 'professional' and less immediately felt than their great mono performance, and the greater use of vibrato produces a warmer, less idiomatic feel than either of their earlier accounts. All the same, this is a valuable disc, well worth the asking price.

PIANO MUSIC

Allegro barbaro; 6 Dances in Bulgarian rhythm; 3 Hungarian folksongs; 15 Hungarian peasant songs; Mikrokosmos: Vol. 2/37, 40 & 50; Vol. 3/73, 82 & 87; Vol. 4/100, 113, 115–16 & 120; Vol. 5/122, 126, 128–31, 133, 135 & 138; Vol. 6/140, 144, 146–7; 3 Rondos on Slovak folk tunes; Sonatina.
(BB) *** Naxos Dig. 8.550451-2. Balázs Szokolay.

Balázs Szokolay is a highly musical player, as befits the son of a distinguished composer (his father is the composer of the opera, *Blood Wedding*, after the Lorca play). His playing is always vitally intelligent and perceptive, and he is acceptably recorded. This is a thoroughly recommendable recital and excellent value, though Szokolay is by no means as well recorded as Kocsis (at full price) on Philips, nor does he quite have the latter's subtlety or distinction.

For Children (Books 1–4) complete; *Mikrokosmos (Books 1–6)* complete.
(M) *** Teldec/Warner 9031 76139-2 (3). Dezsö Ránki.

Dezsö Ránki here shows his musicianship and plays all 85 pieces with the utmost persuasion and with the art that conceals art, for the simplicity of some of these pieces is deceptive; darker currents lurk beneath their surface. He gives us the composer's original edition of 1908–9. Ránki also plays the *Mikrokosmos* with an effortless eloquence and a welcome straightforwardness. He is very clearly if forwardly recorded, and he is given a realistic presence.

For Children, Books I & II (revised version); *15 Hungarian peasant songs; Mikrokosmos: 6 Bulgarian dances. 10 easy pieces; 6 Rumanian popular dances; A simple air; Sonata; Sonatine.*
(B) *** EMI Rouge et Noir CZS5 68101-2 (2). Michel Béroff.

Bartók's pieces for children are a collection of Hungarian (Book I) and Slovak (Book II) folksongs which possess a beguiling simplicity and (when taken in small doses) unfailing musical interest. Choice between Michel Béroff and Dezsö Ránki is simplified by the fact that Béroff records the revised score and Ránki gives us the original edition of 1908/9. Moreover Ránki's set is coupled with *Mikrokosmos*, whereas Béroff offers a number of Bartók's other major piano works. Béroff's playing has an unaffected eloquence that is touching, and the recording is very good. Neither appears to be available in the USA.

Mikrokosmos (complete).
(B) **(*) HM HMA 190968/9 [id.]. Claude Helffer (with Haakon Austbö).

Bartók originally intended the piano pieces he began composing in 1926 as a pedagogic exercise with his young son Péter in mind, and it is naturally of great value to hear so intelligent a voice in this repertoire, though to record the complete set may be taking comprehensiveness a bit too far; music-lovers will be concentrating on the second of these CDs. Claude Helffer gives an intelligent account of all six Books, though at times he tends to invest detail with rather more expressive emphasis than this most simple of music can bear. The piano recording is realistic and naturally remastered. Even though the cueing is ungenerous (there are only twelve bands to cover 153 pieces), this is good value in the bargain range.

OPERA

Bluebeard's Castle (sung in Hungarian).
(M) *** Sony SMK 64110 [id.]. Nimsgern, Troyanos, BBC SO, Boulez.
(M) *** Decca 443 571-2 [id.]. Berry, Ludwig, LSO, Kertész.
(M) **(*) [Mercury Dig. 434 325-2]. Mihály Székely, Olga Szönyi, LSO, Dorati – BERG: *Wozzeck* (excerpts). **(*)
(B) (**) DG Double mono 445 445-2 [(M) id. import]. Dietrich Fischer-Dieskau, Hertha Töpper, Berlin RIAS O, Fricsay – STRAVINSKY: *Oedipus Rex*. (**(*))

Bartók's idea of portraying marital conflict as an opera was as unpromising as could be, but in the event *Bluebeard's Castle* is an enthralling work with its concentration on mood, atmosphere and slow development, as Bluebeard's wife finds the key to each new door. Its comparative absence of action makes it ideal for the gramophone. Boulez reveals himself as an impressively warm Bartókian, the soloists are vibrantly committed and the recording is outstandingly vivid, presenting the singers in a slightly contrasted acoustic as though on a separate stage. Boulez has rarely if ever made a finer Bartók record. A full libretto is provided.

In 1965 Kertész set new standards in his version of *Bluebeard's Castle* with Christa Ludwig and Walter Berry, not only in the playing of the LSO at its peak, in the firm sensitivity of the soloists and the brilliance of the recording, but also in the natural Hungarian inflexions inspired by the conductor. There is still a strong case for preferring the reading conducted by a Hungarian, especially as the Decca sound approaches demonstration standard, but on performance the later, Sony CD has the balance of advantage.

Antal Dorati, drawing brilliant playing from the LSO, recorded in vivid, immediate Mercury sound, finds power rather than mystery in Bartók's unique one-Acter. Székely as Bluebeard is taut and intense, using his characterful bass imaginatively. Olga Szönyi is more uneven, strong and incisive but with squally moments. Though rival versions are more atmospheric than this, Dorati relates the work more clearly to later Bartók. The CD transfer is very vivid, though tape-hiss is quite high. As a practical advantage, the disc uniquely offers an equally positive account of the three concert-excerpts from Berg's *Wozzeck*. There are adequate notes, but no libretto. This is available only in the USA.

Though seriously marred by having small but damaging cuts, Fricsay's version is worth considering for the inspired contribution of the conductor, always electrifying in Hungarian music. It is also a shortcoming that a German translation is used instead of the original Hungarian. Fischer-Dieskau is here in fresher voice than in his later version in Hungarian, but this Bluebeard does not sound at all sinister. Hertha Töpper is an expressive Judith, but the voice is not always steady.

Bax, Arnold (1883–1953)

Malta G.C. (complete); *Oliver Twist: suite* (film-scores).
(M) *** ASV Dig. CDWHL 2058. RPO, Kenneth Alwyn – ARNOLD: *The Sound Barrier*. ***

Both these film-scores are in the form of a series of miniatures; on the whole, *Oliver Twist* stands up more effectively without the visual imagery. The use of concertante piano is effective in a brief nocturnal portrayal of Oliver and later in a sequence called *Oliver and Brownlow*. *Oliver and the Artful Dodger* and *Fagin's romp* both give rise to effective and inventive scherzando writing, and the finale brings a resplendent Waltonian jubilation. In *Malta G.C.* much of the score is concerned with wartime action: it is the gentler music, the *Intermezzo* and *Reconstruction* and again the final apotheosis, that brings the most memorable writing. Kenneth Alwyn conducts the RPO with fine flair and commitment, Eric Parkin is the brief soloist and the recording is brilliantly colourful and vivid, if at times a little lacking in the richest sonority. Originally issued by Cloud Nine, this is welcome back in the catalogue at mid-price, with Arnold's *Rhapsody* as a bonus.

Symphonies 1–7.
(M) *** Chandos Dig. CHAN 8906/10 [id.]. LPO or Ulster O, Bryden Thomson.

Chandos have repackaged the cycle of seven symphonies and it makes better sense for those primarily interested in these richly imaginative symphonies to pay for five rather than seven CDs. The recordings continue to make a strong impression and are all available separately – but at full price.

Symphony No. 1; The Garden of Fand; In the faery hills.
(BB) *** Naxos Dig. 8.553525 [id.]. RSNO, David Lloyd-Jones.

This first disc in what Naxos plan to be a Bax series offers warmly idiomatic readings of two early symphonic poems as well as the *First Symphony*, dating from 1921. The refined originality of the orchestration is brought out in recording less weighty than in rival versions, such as that on Chandos at full price, but finely detailed. So the misty opening of the central slow movement of the symphony is given fine transparency, with dynamic contrasts sharply defined. After two darkly intense movements – inspired by Ireland and its troubles – the finale brushes aside any gloom in brilliant writing, brisk and lively, that in its glitter seems to echo the second movement of Rachmaninov's cantata, *The Bells*. In the two symphonic poems, more specifically inspired by Irish themes, Lloyd-Jones draws equally warm and sympathetic performances from the Scottish orchestra, bringing inner clarity to the heaviest scoring. First-rate sound, though Bryden Thomson on Chandos has even richer recording.

CHAMBER AND INSTRUMENTAL MUSIC

Nonet.
(M) (***) Dutton Lab. mono CDAX 8014 [8014 full price]. Goossens, Thurston, Slater, Watson, Korchinska, Griller Qt – MOERAN: *String trio;* FERGUSON: *Octet;* DELIUS: *Violin sonata No. 3*. (***)

The *Nonet* for flute, oboe, clarinet, string quartet, double-bass and harp is one of Bax's most magical and inventive works, and its neglect on record is quite unaccountable. (There are in it touches reminiscent of the *Third Symphony*, which was finished at about the same time.) After these 78s were made in 1937 with the same artists (save only for the clarinettist, Frederick Thurston) who had given its première in 1930, the piece remained unrecorded throughout both the mono and stereo LP eras. But this remains a beautiful and totally committed performance well worth having in its own rights, as indeed are the various couplings.

VOCAL MUSIC

I sing of a maiden; Mater ora filium; This world's joie.
(M) *** EMI Dig. CDM5 65595-2. King's College, Cambridge, Ch., Cleobury – FINZI: *Choral music;* VAUGHAN WILLIAMS: *Mass.* ***

Bax's ambitious setting of a medieval carol, *Mater ora filium*, is one of the most difficult *a cappella* pieces in the choral repertory. Here under Stephen Cleobury the King's College choir gives it a virtuoso performance, with trebles performing wonders in the taxingly high passages. Perhaps the composer anticipated, when he wrote this piece, that trebles would one day be able to cope with such writing, but the timbre of boys' voices adds to the poignancy of the piece. It is particularly apt too, when the original inspiration for the piece came from his hearing Byrd's *Mass in five voices*. The other two Bax pieces, also setting medieval texts, are also done most beautifully, with the unaccompanied voices vividly recorded against the spacious acoustic of King's Chapel. Besides the original Finzi coupling, the reissue includes a splendid analogue performance of Vaughan Williams's beautiful *Mass in G minor*.

Beethoven, Ludwig van (1770–1827)

The Complete Beethoven edition

DG Complete Beethoven Edition
(B) **(*) DG Analogue/Dig. 453 700-2 (87) [id.] (with MOZART: *Piano concerto No. 20*).

DG's Complete Beethoven Edition, issued as a 20-volume, 87-CD set to celebrate the company's centenary, is packaged in a substantial, suitcase-like cardboard box and is accompanied by its own illustrated book. It is a remarkable achievement and well documented on the whole; but, as is so often the case with huge projects of this kind, the performances, though of a fairly consistent high standard and well (often very well) recorded, are of uneven appeal. Most collectors would do better to concentrate on individual volumes, all available separately in the mid-price range.

Volume 1: *Symphonies: Nos. 1–9.*
(M) *** DG 453 701-2 (5) [id.]. BPO, Karajan (with Janowitz, Rössel-Majdan, Kmentt, Berry, V. Singverein in *No. 9*).

This was Karajan's second cycle, recorded in 1961 and 1962, and is on many counts the most successful of his four cycles. Karajan's refinement is shown in every movement of the *First Symphony* yet the result is very far from being Mozartian and small-scale. The finale is particularly exciting. The slow movement seemed controversially on the fast side at the time of the recording, but the moulding of phrase is beautiful. The approach to the *Second Symphony* is completely consistent with that of No. 1. In the *Eroica* the refinement of detail never gets in the way of the dramatic, dynamic urgency of the whole performance, and only in the *Funeral march* does Karajan give the music anything less than the weight one wants. He gives a splendid interpretation of *No. 4*, with the dynamic contrasts heavily underlined. In the slow movement there is a glow to the playing that almost makes it sound like Schubert, though Karajan's reading of the dotted rhythm is curiously unpointed. The *Fifth Symphony* suggests swaggering extroversion, the hero striding forward, with speeds in the Toscanini tradition. The *Pastoral* is the one real failure of the integral set. If he thought to imitate Toscanini, Karajan failed to note what importance Toscanini places on lyricism as well as hard driving; the impression from Karajan is hard and unyielding. The *Seventh Symphony* tingles with excitement. Again, it is hard-driven in the Toscanini manner and in the last resort it does not quite have the lift to the dance-rhythms that the Italian Toscanini managed to retain, even when driving at his hardest. In the *Eighth Symphony* there is a hint of over-driving, but the performance remains a strong recommendation. Karajan then gives one of the most completely satisfying performances of the *Ninth Symphony* available. It is strong and refined and has an urgency that carries the argument through from first to last with the vitality of a live performance. The soloists are excellent, and the Vienna Singverein, taken specially to Berlin, sing with great passion, though the balance could be better. The slow movement is the only one which might cause any serious disappointment, for there Karajan does not achieve the spiritual quality one hears in live performances, though the sheer beauty of sound, particularly in the hushed playing, is magical. This set still also appears to be available in a separate bargain-price box – see below (DG 429 036-2).

Volume 2: *Complete concertos: Piano concertos Nos.* (i; ii) *1–2;* (i; iii) *3–5;* (iv) *in E flat, WoO 4;* (v) *in D, Op. 61* (arr. composer); *Violin concertos:* (vi) *in D, Op. 61;* (vii) *in C, WoO 5;* (viii) *Triple concerto in C, Op. 56;* (ix) *Romances Nos. 1–2;* (x) *Romance cantabile for piano, flute and bassoon in E min., H. 13;* (xi) *Rondo for piano and orchestra in B flat, WoO 6.*

(M) ** DG Analogue/Dig. 453 707-2 (5) [id.]. (i) Pollini, VPO; (ii) Jochum; (iii) Boehm; (iv) Ander, Berlin CO, Gülke; (v) ECO, Barenboim (piano and cond.); (vi; viii) Mutter, BPO, Karajan; (vii) Kremer, LSO, Tchakarov; (viii) with Zeltser, Ma; (ix) Shaham, Orpheus CO; (x) Patrick Gallois, Pascal Gallois, Philh. O, Myung-Whun Chung (piano and cond.); (xi) Richter, VSO, Sanderling.

The Concerto box in DG's Beethoven Edition, with the juvenilia and completed fragments included, is a mixed bag. Even the choice of Pollini's first piano concerto cycle is controversial, though these performances are preferable to the second set under Abbado. Here the reserve in Pollini's playing is counterbalanced by the warmth of his accompanists: Karl Boehm in Nos. 3 to 5, Eugen Jochum in the first two.

If Pollini is sometimes wilful in this account of the *First Concerto* but with refreshing clarity of articulation, his is a performance, brisk rather than poetic, which vividly reflects the challenge of an unexpected partnership between pianist and conductor. The recording was taken from live performances but betrays little sign of that. The *Second Concerto* (also live) is one of the more attractive of the series, but it cannot match its finest rivals. It was an early (1982) digital issue and provides excellent presence for the piano, but the strings are curiously lacking in fullness of focus. The concentration of the playing and the single-minded clarity of Pollini's reading of the *Third Concerto* are matched by Boehm's strong, clear-minded accompaniment. The result is undoubtedly fresh, and Pollini certainly brings personal insights to bear on his reading, with the slow movement serenely dedicated. Yet overall the performance is on the sober side for a youthful concerto.

The performances of Nos. 4 and 5 are two of the most strikingly individual, with believable piano-timbre and a full, well-focused orchestral tapestry. After the poised account of the *Fourth Concerto*, the distinction of Pollini's interpretation of the *Emperor* is never in doubt, and the result sounds spontaneously expressive. If at times the solo playing sounds a little withdrawn, the strong and wise accompaniment of Boehm and the Vienna Philharmonic again provides a nice balance. The slow movement is elegant and the finale is urgent and energetic; those not seeking a grand romantic manner in the concerto will find this satisfying in a quite different way.

Anne-Sophie Mutter's early and beautiful recording of the *Violin concerto* with Karajan makes an excellent choice. The slow basic tempi for the *Violin concerto* were her own choice, she claims, and were certainly not forced on her by her superstar conductor. The first two movements have rarely, if ever, been more expansively presented on record, but the purity of the solo playing and the concentration of the whole performance make the result entirely convincing. The finale is relaxed too, but is well pointed, at a fair tempo, and presents the necessary contrast. Good atmospheric recording and attractively warm sound.

Karajan is a more domineering conductor in the *Triple concerto*. His young trio of soloists – Yo-Yo Ma and Mark Zeltser, as well as Mutter – are full of imagination but hardly the best-matched team. After Karajan's formidable crescendo, within his very positive opening tutti, these soloists seem rather small-scale. But there are benefits from the unity brought by the conductor when each of the young players has a positive contribution to make, no less effectively when the recording-balance in this work does not unduly favour the solo instruments. Yo-Yo Ma's playing is not immaculate, and he does not dominate each thematic statement, but the urgency, spontaneity and – in the slow movement – the depth of expressiveness make for an enjoyable version, well recorded.

Gil Shaham in the two *Romances* is outstanding, sweetly lyrical on an intimate scale; but the problems of the compilers are displayed in the extra works: for the *E flat Piano concerto* of 1784 (completed, like the rare *Romance cantabile*, by the Swiss musicologist, Willy Hess) comes in a recording licensed from Berlin Classics. As for the recording of the *Romance*, a curious five-minute piece with piano, flute and bassoon soloists, that has never been available in Britain before. Like the other juvenilia, the *E flat Piano concerto* of 1784 and the first movement of a *C major Violin concerto* (probably 1790–92), it is attractive and fresh but not very individual. Nevertheless, in good performances all the rarities are very welcome, particularly when the whole package has been squeezed on to only five CDs.

The arrangement of the *Violin concerto* for piano and orchestra alters the character of the music entirely, bringing down the emotional scale and substituting charm where in the original there is great spiritual depth. The work could surely not receive a more dedicated or affectionate performance than it does here; Barenboim makes the most of the limited piano part, and he is delightful in the slow movement.

Volume 3: *Orchestral works and music for the stage:* (i–ii) *12 Contredanses, WoO 14;* (iii) *12 German dances, WoO 8; Minuets: WoO 7;* (i; iv) *WoO 3; Ritterballett, WoO 1; Wellington's victory, Op. 91;* (v–vi) Overtures: *Coriolan, Op. 62; Zur Namensfeier, Op. 115;* (vii) Overture and ballet music: *The Creatures of Prometheus, Op. 43;* Overtures and incidental music: (i; vi; viii; x–xii) *The Consecration of the house, H.118 (Opp. 113–14, 124, WoO 98);* (with ix) *The Ruins of Athens, Op. 113;* (i; vi; xiii) *Egmont, Op. 84;* (xiv) *King Stephen, Op. 117;* Miscellaneous items: (xviii–xix; xxi) *Es ist vollbracht, WoO 97; Germania, WoO 94;* (i; vi; ix; xv) *Leonore Prohaska, WoO 96;* (xvi) *2 arias for The Beautiful shoemaker's wife, WoO 91; Tarpeja, WoO 2:* (xvii) *Entr'acte,* (xxi) *Triumphal march;* (xix–xxi) *Vestas feuer, H.115.*

(M) **(*) DG Analogue/Dig. 453 713-2 (5) [id.]. (i) BPO; (ii) Maazel; (iii) ASMF, Marriner; (iv) Karajan; (v) VPO; (vi) Abbado; (vii) Orpheus CO; (viii) Augér, Hirte, Crass; (ix) McNair; (x) RIAS Chamber Ch.; (xi) Berlin R. Ch.; (xii) Klee; (xiii) Studer, Ganz; (xiv) Fischer-Dieskau, Jackwerth, Rühl, Mende, Aljinovicz, Santa Cecilia Ch. & O, Myung-Whun Chung; (xv) Eichhorn; (xvi) Gedda, Rothenberger, Convivium Musicum München, Keller; (xvii) Gothenberg SO, Neeme Järvi; (xviii) BBC Singers; (xix) Finley; (xx) Kuebler, Leggate, Gritton; (xxi) BBC SO, A. Davis.

As the splendid Orpheus Chamber Orchestra recording of *The Creatures of Prometheus* demonstrates, there is much to admire in this lesser-known Beethoven score, often anticipating later, greater works in sudden flashes, with moods varying widely from tragedy to country-dance felicity. However, the other incidental music is musically more variable, even if each score has memorable items. Abbado (who also directs the overtures) is certainly a stylish and committed advocate and gives excellent accounts of the music for *The Consecration of the House* and *Egmont*; Klee is equally impressive in *The Ruins of Athens*, a recording made much earlier for DG's Beethoven Bicentenary Edition. *King Stephen*, conducted by Myung-Whun Chung, was newly recorded (in Rome) and includes spoken melodrama (Fischer-Dieskau) as well as music of varying interest. Other more striking novelties include *Germania*, Beethoven's commemoration of the Allies' entry into Paris in 1814, and an operatic trio, *Vestas Feuer*, most dramatically sung by Susan Gritton, David Kuebler and Gerald Finley. Karajan's version of Beethoven's great commercial success, *Wellington's victory*, is very well played, but there is no sense of occasion and the battle-sounds are not entirely convincing; he is obviously happier with the much lighter *Ritterballet* and presents these dance vignettes most affectionately. Marriner and his Academy are equally felicitous in the *German dances* and *Minuets*. The recording is consistently excellent throughout.

Volume 4: (i) *Fidelio* (complete); (ii) *Leonore* (complete); *Overtures:* (iii) *Fidelio, Op. 72c; Leonora Nos.* (iv) *1, Op. 138;* (v) *2, Op. 72a;* (vi) *3, Op. 72b.*

(M) *** DG Analogue/Dig. 453 719-2 (4) [id.]. (i) Janowitz, Kollo, Jungwirth, Sotin, Popp, Dallapozza, Fischer-Dieskau, V. State Op. Ch.; (ii) Martinpelto, Begley, Hawlata, Best, Oelze, Schade, Miles, Bantzer, Monteverdi Ch.; (i; iii–iv) VPO; (i; iii) Bernstein; (iv) Abbado; (ii; v) ORR, Gardiner.

Gardiner prepared for his recording of *Leonore* with a series of live performances, culminating in a brilliant semi-staging in Salzburg. More than ever before, he presents this first version of the opera *Fidelio* as a masterpiece in its own right. At white heat, with the same team as on tour he set down this recording, confirming his passionate belief in Beethoven's first thoughts as a powerful alternative, quite distinct in aim. Gardiner's argument, brilliantly expressed in a note, is that *Leonore* in 1804 is the more spontaneous and immediate work, while *Fidelio* of ten years later is retrospective and considered in its response to tyranny and injustice. As he says, 'What strikes me so forcibly about *Leonore* is its power and purity of emotion,' even though it presents a more expansive, less taut telling of the story, in three Acts instead of two. He goes on to claim with fair justice that the portraits of both hero and heroine are more poignant in the earlier version, where later they are presented as more self-assured and certain, more universal.

However, there are several dramatic moments added in *Fidelio* which one misses in *Leonore*. So, the heroine's big aria, *Komm Hoffnung*, does not have the great outburst of *Abscheulicher!* as an introduction; but the tenderly reflective recitative you have instead is moving in a different way. One also misses the great fortissimo outburst from the chorus at the start of the final scene, but the *Leonore* solution is even more evocative, with the chorus drawing closer and closer in its signalling of freedom.

Hillevi Martinpelto in the title-role conveys youthful ardour as well as power, well contrasted with the sweetly expressive Marzelline of Christiane Oelze. The tenor, Kim Begley, emerges in sharply focused, heroic strength as Florestan, with Michael Schade providing an ideal lyric contrast as Jaquino. Franz Hawlata as Rocco and Alastair Miles as Don Fernando are both first rate, and if Matthew Best as Pizarro comes too close to sing-speech, he is certainly evil-sounding.

The choice of Bernstein's reading of *Fidelio* seems apt, for it is full of dramatic flair. The recording was made in conjunction with live performances by the same cast at the Vienna State Opera. Lucia Popp as Marzelline is particularly enchanting, and though Bernstein later rises splendidly to the high drama of Act II, it remains a drama on a human scale. Gundula Janowitz sings most beautifully as Leonore. Kollo as Florestan is intelligent and musicianly but indulges in too many intrusive aitches, and the rest of the cast make strong contributions. The choice of different conductors to present the overtures works well: all are first-class performances.

Volume 5: *Piano sonatas Nos. 1–32.*
(M) *** DG 453 724-2 (8) [id.]. Wilhelm Kempff.

As in 1970, when DG issued their Beethoven Bicentenary Edition, Wilhelm Kempff's stereo cycle of the piano sonatas remains the choice (rather than the earlier, mono set), with the sound noticeably improved, not just over the original shallow-sounding LPs but also over the earlier CD issue. Kempff's Beethoven has been providing a deeply spiritual experience for record-collectors since the 1920s, and there is no doubt whatever as to the inner compulsion which holds all these performances together. More than any other pianist, Kempff has the power to make one appreciate and understand Beethoven in a new way, and that is so however many times one has heard him. His insight remains unsurpassed: his magnetism, his unfailing sense of spontaneity, his ability to clarify textures with astonishingly clean articulation and sharp dynamic contrasts and, not least, his lyrical flow, with extreme speeds generally avoided. Helpfully, the couplings – on eight discs instead of the nine for the earlier CD issue – this time follow those for the Kempff centenary issue of his mono set on DG Dokumente. Kempff may be erratic over observing exposition repeats, but the sense of live communication is what matters. He is occasionally fast (for example in the slow movements of Opp. 26 and 110) but he is invariably illuminating and has many felicitous touches. The late sonatas bring a sharp, clean attack, set against sublime lyricism which, with Kempffian logic, leads on to Schubert.

Volume 6: *Piano works:* (i) *Allegrettos in B min., WoO 61; in C min., WoO 53; H.69; Allegretto quasi andante in G min., WoO 61a; Allemande in A, WoO 81;* (ii) *Andante favori, WoO 57; Bagatelles: Opp. 33; 119;* (iii) *126;* (ii) *WoO 52; WoO 56;* (iii) *'Für Elise', WoO 59;* (i) *WoO 60;* (viii) *Canons à 2 in A flat, G, H.274/5; Ecossaises:* (vi) *WoO 83;* (i) *WoO 86; Fantasia in G min. Op. 77; Fugue in C, H.64; 12 German dances, WoO 13; 7 Ländler in D, WoO 11; 'Lustig-traurig' in C min., WoO 54; 6 Minuets, WoO* (ii) *10;* (i) *82;* (ii) *Polonaise in C, Op. 89;* (i) *Prelude in F min., WoO 55;* (ii) *Rondos in A, WoO 49; in C, Op. 51/1; WoO 48; in G, Op. 51/2;* (i) *Rondo a capriccio in G ('Rage over the lost penny'), Op. 129;* (ix) *Sonatas, WoO 47, Nos. 1 in E flat; 2 in F min.; 3 in D;* (i) *in C, WoO 51; 2 Sonata movements in F, WoO 50;* (ii) *6 Variations in F, Op. 34; Variations in C min., WoO 63; in F, WoO 64; in D, WoO 65; in C, WoO 68; in G, WoO 70;* (i) *in A, WoO 66; in C, WoO 72; in B flat, WoO 73; in F, WoO 75, 76; in G, WoO 77;* (iv) *15 Variations and fugue on a theme from Prometheus (Eroica variations), Op. 35;* (vi) *32 Variations on an original theme in C min., WoO 80;* (vii) *33 Variations on a waltz by Diabelli, Op. 120;* (v) *12 Variations on a Russian dance, WoO 71; Variations on 'God save the King', WoO 78,* and *'Rule, Britannia', WoO 79; 9 Variations on 'Quant'è più bello', WoO 69;* (i) *Waltzes, WoO 84–5.* Works for piano duet: (ix, x) *Grosse Fuge in B flat, Op. 134; 3 Marches, Op. 45; Sonata in D, Op. 6.* Solo pieces for miscellaneous instruments: (xi) *Fugue in D, WoO 31. Grenadier march, H.107; 5 Pieces, WoO 33* (both works for mechanical clock). *2 Preludes through all twelve major keys, Op. 39.*
(M) ** DG Analogue/Dig. 453 733-2 (8) [id.]. (i) Gianluca Cascioli; (ii) Mikhael Pletnev; (iii) Anatol Ugorski; (iv) Emil Gilels; (v) Olli Mustonen; (vi) Wilhelm Kempff; (vii) Daniel Barenboim; (viii) Walter Olbertz; (ix) Jörg Demus; (x) Norman Shetler; (xi) Simon Preston (organ).

This set is surely dominated by Gilels's magisterial account of the *Eroica variations* which seems to storm the heavens. Artistic wisdom is in abundant evidence. Good sound, too. However, Barenboim's is an intensely personal reading of the *Diabelli variations*, one which seems to stem from a purely spontaneous response to Beethoven's vast structure. Barenboim gives the illusion of an improvisation, with expressive exaggerations in both directions, which may initially strike the listener as mannered but which – caught by the engineer on the inspiration of the moment – has genuine magic. The sound is excellent. Outstanding among the other recordings are Pletnev's *Bagatelles*, Opp. 33 and 119, which are full of individual perceptions. By his side Ugorsky sounds relatively mundane in Op. 126. Many of the lesser-known pieces, including a good deal of trivia, are entrusted to Gianluca Cascioli and he doesn't let the side down, often making them seem more than just chips from the master's workbench, with the *Fantasia*, Op. 77, standing out. Olli Mustonen's four sets of *Variations* have been borrowed from Decca. He plays them with a sure sense of style. However, it must be said that overall these eight CDs contain a great deal of music, which, however well played and recorded, one would not want to return to very often.

Volume 7: (i) *Violin sonatas Nos. 1–10;* (ii) *6 German dances, WoO 42;* (iii) *Rondo in G, WoO 41; 12 Variations on Mozart's 'Se vuol ballare'* from *Le nozze di Figaro, WoO 40.*
(M) *** DG Analogue/Dig. 453 743-2 (4) [id.]. (i) Kremer, Argerich; (ii) Garrett, Canino; (iii) Menuhin, Kempff.

Having two such volatile artists as Kremer and Argerich in partnership for the Beethoven *Violin sonatas* makes for exciting, heart-warming results. Perlman and Ashkenazy may be more centrally recommendable for being just as communicative and less idiosyncratic, but Kremer and Argerich have one magnetized from first to last by their individuality in performances that consistently sound spontaneous and fresh. So the three early sonatas of Opus 12, taken at high speed with wonderfully clean piano articulation, have rare sparkle and wit, and the openings of both the *Spring Sonata* and the *Kreutzer*, less plain than usual, convey a thoughtfulness that looks forward to the last, most enigmatic of the sonatas, *No. 10 in G.* Later in the *Kreutzer* too, there is an improvisatory feeling, with each artist challenging the other in bravura and flair. The performance is crowned by a dashing and light account of the tarantella finale which, so far from sounding rushed, is exhilaratingly joyful. As to the *G major Sonata*, the contrasts of mood are vividly caught, with rapt mystery at the very start giving way to lightness and point in the dotted rhythms of the second theme. That is typical, and the recorded sound, well balanced, adds to one's impression of overhearing two artists simply enjoying themselves in revealing Beethoven. The *German dances*, *Rondo* and *Variations* are slight but are stylishly presented.

Volume 8: *Cello sonatas: Nos. 1–5; 7 Variations on 'Bei Männern, welche Liebe fühlen', WoO 46; 12 Variations on 'Ein Mädchen oder Weibchen', Op. 66,* both from Mozart's *Die Zauberflöte. 12 Variations on 'See the conqu'ring hero comes'* from Handel's *Judas Maccabaeus, WoO 45.*
(M) *** DG Dig. 453 748-2 (2) [id.]. Mischa Maisky, Martha Argerich.

Mischa Maisky and Martha Argerich make a strong partnership and there is enormous character about their playing here. Indeed it would be possible to feel that their readings are overcharacterized, so attentive are they to every dynamic nuance and hairpin that is marked (and plenty that aren't). All the same, the performances are exhilarating and will be relished by many collectors, particularly in such vivid recordings.

Volume 9: *Piano trios:* (i) *Nos. 1–9; 10 (14 Variations on an original theme in E flat), Op. 44; 11 (10 Variations on 'Ich bin der Schneider Kakadu'), Op. 121a;* (ii) *Allegretto in E flat, H.48; Trio in E flat* (arr. of *Septet, Op. 20), Op. 38;* (iii) *Trio in D* (arr. of *Symphony No. 2*), *Op. 36.*
(M) **(*) DG Analogue/Dig. 453 751-2 (5) [id.]. (i) Kempff, Szeryng, Fournier; (ii) Beaux Arts Trio; (iii) Besch, Brandis, Boettcher.

The Kempff–Szeryng–Fournier set of trios is, needless to say, a distinguished one, but the sound is none too convincing and the manner is more public than private. Indeed the engineers have not wholly succeeded in securing an altogether homogeneous sound; each player seems somewhat detached from the other. Nonetheless a fine set, with some superb playing in the early trios. The other items are of mixed interest, although they are well done.

Volume 10: *String trios: Nos. 1–4; Serenade in D, Op. 8.*
(M) **(*) DG Dig. 453 757-2 (2) [id.]. Anne-Sophie Mutter, Bruno Giuranna, Rostropovich.

This glamorous trio of soloists certainly produces some splendid playing, but the recording is rather forward and dry. This music ideally needs more of a sense of intimacy than it receives here.

Volume 11: The early quartets: *String quartets* (i) *Nos. 1–6, Op. 18/1–6;* (ii) *Fugue from Handel's Solomon overture, H.36; Minuet in A flat, H.33;* (iii) *Preludes and fugues in F, H.30; in C, H.31; String quartets in F,* (ii) *H.32* (*Op. 18/1* first version); (i) *H.34* (arr. of *Piano sonata, Op. 14/1*).
(M) **(*) DG Analogue/Dig. 453 760-2 (3) [id.]. (i) Amadeus Qt; (ii) Hagen Qt; (iii) Mendelssohn-Qt.

The Op 18 set is the best part of the complete Amadeus cycle. The character of the playing is intimate if rather suave. Sometimes one might ideally ask for more bite even at the expense of polish, but certainly the technical perfection of the playing here yields its own pleasures, for Beethoven's music has its own natural spontaneity. The 1961 recording still sounds well. The other items are of undoubted interest, but hardly essential listening.

Volume 12: The middle quartets: *String quartets Nos. 7 in F; 8 in E min., 9 in C (Rasumovsky), Op.59/ 1–3; 10 in E flat (Harp), Op. 74; 11 in F. min., Op. 95.*
(M) **(*) DG Dig. 453 764-2 (2) [id.]. Emerson Qt.

We are at odds over the Emerson performances of the mid-period Beethoven quartets. E. G. finds them very compelling indeed, above all for the transparency of sound – not just a question of the relatively intimate recording, but of flawless matching and balancing in the ensemble. In that matching their nearest rivals are the Italian Quartet, but the dynamic range of the Emersons is far greater, with pianissimos of breathtaking delicacy and vibrant attack of fortissimos. R. L. agrees that their playing is in a class of its own technically, but he comments that the sheer thrust of this playing is less appropriate in music composed before the discovery of electricity, let alone the jet-engine. Of course the DG recording is marvellous, but for the most part this music-making is brilliant but shallow. The Editor prefers to stand aside from the controversy, but his choice in Op. 59 remains with the Lindsays (at mid-price), with the Italians hardly less satisfying and offering marvellous value in the bargain range (see below).

Volume 13: The late quartets: *String quartets Nos. 12 in E flat, Op. 127; 13 in B flat, Op. 130; 14 in C sharp min., Op. 131; 15 in A min., Op. 132; 16 in F, Op. 135; Grosse Fuge, Op. 133.*
(M) ** DG 453 768-2 (3) [id.]. LaSalle Qt.

Technically, the LaSalle Quartet are unfailingly impressive and they bring unanimity of ensemble and fine tonal blend to these awe-inspiring scores. But there is no sense of mystery, little feeling of inwardness or depth. The recordings (made between 1972 and 1977) were of DG's best analogue quality, and they have been transferred cleanly and firmly to CD.

Volume 14: *Chamber works:* (i) *Canon in A, WoO 35;* (ii–iii) *Duets, in G for 2 flutes, WoO 26;* (i) *in A for 2 violins, WoO 34; in E flat for viola & cello, WoO 32;* (iv) *Fugue in D for string quintet, Op. 137;* (v–vi) *Horn sonata in F, Op. 17;* (i) *6 Ländler for 2 violins & bass, WoO 15; 6 Minuets for 2 violins & bass, WoO 9;* (vii) *Piano & wind quintet, Op. 16;* (viii; xii) *Piano quartets Nos. 1–3;* (ix) *Pieces for mandolin & piano: Adagio, WoO 43b; Sonatinas in C, WoO 44a; in C min., WoO 43a; Variations in D, WoO 44b;* (i) *Prelude and fugue in E min. for 2 violins & cello, H.29;* (x) *Serenade in D for flute, violin & viola, Op. 25;* (iv) *Septet in E flat, Op. 20;* (xi) *Sextet in E flat, Op. 81b;* (xii–xiii) *String quintet in C, Op. 29;* (ii; xiv) *Themes with variations for piano & flute, Opp. 105 & 107;* (xv) *Trio in B flat for piano, clarinet & cello, Op. 11;* (v; xvi) *Trio in G for piano, flute & bassoon, WoO 37.*
(M) **(*) DG Analogue/Dig. 453 772-2 (6) [id.]. (i) Hagen Qt, Posch; (ii) Gallois; (iii) Rampal; (iv) VPO Ens.; (v) Barenboim; (vi) Bloom; (vii) Levine, Vienna–Berlin Ens.; (viii) Eschenbach; (ix) Fietz, Webersinke; (x) Zoeller, Brandis, Ueberschaer; (xi) Seifert, Klier, Drolc Qt; (xii) Amadeus Qt (members); (xiii) Aronowitz; (xiv) Licad; (xv) Kempff, Leister, Fournier; (xvi) Debost, Sennedat.

The best things here are the early *Piano quartets* of 1785, written in Bonn, which come from the original Beethoven Bicentenary Edition: the *C major String quintet* with the Amadeus and Cecil Aronowitz (one of the best things they ever did) and the *Septet*. The transfers hold up well against the original LPs, and in the Bonn quartets the playing, particularly that of Christoph Eschenbach, is vital and intelligent. The early *Piano quartets* are in themselves not among Beethoven's greatest works but, played like this, they are very persuasive. For the *G major Trio*, for piano, flute and bassoon, DG offer a 1981 recording, made with the principals of the Orchestre de Paris when Barenboim was with them. It is not an important work but it is far from unattractive, and Barenboim plays with sensitivity and imagination. The recording is well balanced. Both this and the *Horn sonata* come off very well. Myron Bloom is a horn player of distinction, even if his view of the sonata does not efface memories of the Tuckwell–Ashkenazy performance on Decca (see below). The early *E flat Sextet*, Op. 81, was recorded for the 1970 Edition and sounds remarkably fresh. So does the 1970 Zoeller–Brandis–Ueberschaer set of the *Serenade*, Op. 25. The Levine Vienna–Berlin Ensemble version of the Op. 16 *E flat Quintet* for piano and wind, which was made in 1986, is less satisfactory. Despite the eminence of the artists, who include Karl Leister and Günter Högner, there is not quite the same finish that one encounters in the best of rival versions. Levine is far from unimaginative or insensitive – on the contrary, he is a very fine pianist; the playing is spirited but the balance is far too close and overbearing. The 1970s recording by Jörg Demus and members of the Berlin Philharmonic wind would have been a better choice. The Op. 11 *Trio* with Karl Leister, Pierre Fournier and Wilhelm Kempff is a delight, and so is the 1975 recording of the *Septet*, which has more space round the sound than the Op. 16 *Quintet*. The other pieces, such as the *E minor Prelude and fugue* for quartet and the other earlier works, are not great Beethoven and are unlikely to engage the listener very often. However, the high standard of presentation and handsome appearance of the booklet is a distinct plus.

Volume 15: *Wind music:* (i–ii) *Ecossaise in D, WoO 22;* (iii) *3 Equale for four trombones, WoO 30;* (i–ii) *Marches, WoO 18-20, WoO 24, WoO 29;* (i) *Octet in E flat, Op. 103;* (i–ii) *Polonaise in D, WoO 21;* (iv) *Rondino in E flat, WoO 25;* (i) *Sextet in E flat, Op. 71;* (v) *Trio in C, Op. 87; Variations on Mozart's 'Là ci darem la mano'*, both for 2 oboes and cor anglais.

(M) *** DG 453 779-2 (2) [id.]. (i) BPO (members); (ii) cond. Hans Priem-Bergrath; (iii) Philip Jones Brass Ens.; (iv) Netherlands Wind Ens.; (v) Holliger, Elhorst, Bourgue.

For Beethoven's wind music, DG draws on the Philips catalogue and, in the case of the three impressively sonorous *Equali* for trombones, the Philip Jones Brass Ensemble on Decca. Despite its late opus number, the *C major Trio*, Op. 87, for the unlikely combination of cor anglais and two oboes is an early work, dating from 1794, and its scale is larger than its neglect would lead one to expect. There are four movements which show no mean degree of organic cohesion and an awareness of formal design. The *Là ci darem variations* in a similar scoring were performed in 1797 but not published until the present century. They are also ingeniously written and are often diverting. It goes without saying that artists of the calibre of Heinz Holliger, Hans Elhorst and Maurice Bourgue make the most of the possibilities here and are accorded excellent and well balanced sound (by Philips). Neither work is major Beethoven but both are rewarding. The attractive *Rondino for wind octet* is given a crisp, clean performance by the Netherlands Wind Ensemble (also from Philips); the *Wind Sextet,* Op. 71, and *Octet in E flat*, Op. 103, are DG recordings from 1970, played by members of the Berlin Philharmonic Orchestra, who are equally alert and civilized; Hans Priem-Bergrath then directs the Berlin ensemble in the various marches and dances to lively effect.

Volume 16: *Lieder:* (i) *Abendlied unterm gestirnten Himmel;* (iv; ix) *Abschiedsgesang an Wiens Bürger;* (i) *Adelaide; Als die Geliebte sich trennen wollte; Andenken; An die ferne Geliebte, Op. 98;* (iii; ix) *An den fernen Geliebten, Op. 75/5; An die Geliebte* (ii; ix) 2nd version; (i) 3rd version; *An die Hoffnung, Op. 32* (1st version), *Op. 94* (2nd version); (iii; ix) *An einen Säugling;* (ii; ix) *An Laura; An Minna;* (i) *4 Ariettas and a duet, Op. 82; Aus Goethes Faust, Op. 75/3; Der Bardengeist; Das Blümchen Wunderhold, Op. 52/8;* (vii; x) *Der edle Mensch;* (ii; ix) *Elegie auf den Tod eines Pudels; Erhebt das Glas mit froher Hand; Feuerfarb', Op. 52/2; Der freie Mann; Gedenke mein!;* (i) *Das Geheimnis; Gesang aus der Ferne* (vi; x) 1st version; (i) 2nd version; (iii; ix) *Der Gesang der Nachtigall; Gretels Warnung, Op. 75/4;* (i) *In questa tomba oscura; Der Jüngling in der Fremde;* (iii; ix) *Kennst du das Land, Op. 75/1;* (ii; ix) *Klage;* (v; x) *Der Knabe auf dem Berge;* (ii; ix) *Des Kriegers Abschied;* (iv; ix) *Kriegslied der Österreicher;* (i) *Der Kuss; Die laute Klage; Die Liebe, Op. 52/6;* (viii; x) *Das liebe Kätzchen;* (i) *Der Liebende; Das Liedchen von der Ruhe, Op. 52/3; 6 Lieder, Op. 48; 3 Lieder, Op. 83; 2 Lieder, WoO 118; Maigesang, Op. 52/4;* (iii; ix) *Man strebt, die Flamme zu verhehlen;* (iv; ix) *Der Mann von Wort;* (i) *Marmotte, Op. 52/7; Merkenstein* (vi; x) *WoO 144* (1st version), (ii–iii; ix) *Op. 100* (2nd version); (iii; ix) *Mollys Abschied, Op. 52/5; Neue Liebe, neues Leben* (vi; x) *WoO 127* (1st version), (i) *Op. 75/2* (2nd version); (ii; ix) *Oh care selve, oh cara;* (i) *Opferlied; La partenza;* (ii; ix) *Plaisir d'aimer; Punschlied; Que le temps me dure* 1st version; (v; x) 2nd version; (i) *Resignation; Ruf vom Berge; Schilderung eines Mädchens; Sehnsucht, WoO 146;* (iii; ix) *Sehnsucht, WoO 134* (4 versions); (ii; ix) *Ein Selbstgespräch; So oder so; La tiranna;* (i) *Urians Reise um die Welt, Op. 52/1; Vita felice; Der Wachtelschlag; Zärtliche Liebe; Der Zufriedene, Op. 75/6.*

(M) **(*) DG Analogue/Dig. 453 782-2 (3) [id.]. (i) Fischer-Dieskau, Demus; (ii) Schreier; (iii) Stolte; (iv) Leib; (v) Helzel; (vi) Maus; (vii) Person; (viii) Horn; (ix) Olbertz; (x) Hilsdorf.

Fischer-Dieskau recorded the Beethoven songs in the days of mono LP, and these re-makes of 1966 show little change in his conception of them. Beethoven's songs are a neglected part of his output and they number among them many small masterpieces that should not be overlooked by the discriminating collector. Demus is a sensitive accompanist and the recording is good. For the major share of the remainder of the box DG draw on Telefunken recordings dating mainly from the 1970s, with Peter Schreier in excellent form. However, his colleague in the duets, Adele Stolte (who is also heard alone), is unworthy of him, and other artists who contribute are no great shakes either. It would have been better for DG, if they were not prepared to make new recordings, to have left these offerings aside and reissued the Fischer-Dieskau set alone.

Volume 17: *Folksong arrangements: 7 British songs, WoO 158b; 25 Irish songs, WoO 152; 20 Irish songs, WoO 153; 12 Irish songs, WoO 154; 25 Scottish songs, WoO 108; 12 Scottish songs, WoO 156; 26 Welsh songs, WoO 155; Songs of various nationalities, WoO 157, 158a, c.*

(M) *** DG Dig. 453 786-2 (7) [id.]. Lott, Watson, Wyn-Davies, Philogene, Walker, Murray, Ainsley, Robinson, Spence, Allen, Maltman; Layton, Osostowicz, Blankestijn, Smith, Martineau.

Unlike most of the other volumes in DG's Complete Beethoven Edition, this one is entirely new, an enchanting kaleidoscopic collection of folksong arrangements, mainly British, which reveals over and over again the composer's extraordinary imagination, even when he was just supposed to be doing hack-work, writing on commission from the publisher, George Thomson of Edinburgh. So Beethoven's setting of *Auld lang syne* has a vigorous Scottish snap to it, and he treats *God save the King* canonically, while *Charlie is my darling* is in 2/4 time, and *The Miller of Dee* is made the darker by a stylized accompaniment that is almost the Beethovenian equivalent of Benjamin Britten's twentieth-century free-ranging folksong accompaniments.

Altogether 168 songs are included, ending with a disc of non-British settings just as fascinating, particularly the Spanish ones. There is also one for which the words are lost. Beethoven consistently gives the lie to those commentators who have dismissed these songs as pot-boilers, always responding positively and individually, and regularly bringing surprises in his accompaniments for piano trio, with each song usually involving a postlude. And who cares if Beethoven occasionally gets the country wrong for a song, dubbing a setting of Robert Burns as Irish!

Malcolm Martineau as accompanist is the hero of the enterprise, regularly providing the sparkle needed, and almost all the singing is first rate, though the microphone occasionally brings out unevenness of production, as in the singing of the prize-winning young baritone, Christopher Maltman. An outstanding set in every way.

Volume 18: *Secular vocal works:* (i) *Abschiedsgesang;* (ii) *Ah! perfido, Op. 65;* (iii) *Bundeslied, Op. 122; Elegischer gesang, Op. 118;* (i; iv–vi) *Cantata campestre; Hochzeitslied; Lobkowitz-Kantate;* (vii) *Chor auf die verbündeten Fürsten;* (i) *Gesang der Mönche;* (viii; xi) *Mit Mädeln sich vertragen; Prüfung des Küssens;* (ix–xi) *Ne' giorni tuoi felici;* (ix; xi) *No, non turbati; Primo amore;* (iii; xii) *Opferlied, Op. 121b;* (viii–xi) *Tremate, empi, tremate, Op. 116;* (i; vi; xiii) *43 Canons and musical jokes;* (i) *18 Italian partsongs.*

(M) ** DG Analogue/Dig. 453 794-2 (2) [id.]. (i) Berlin soloists; (ii) Studer, BPO, Abbado; (iii) Amb. S., LSO, Tilson Thomas; (iv) Jehser; (v) Olbertz; (vi) Knothe; (vii) BBC Singers, BBC SO, A. Davis; (viii) Vogel; (ix) Kuhse; (x) Büchner; (xi) Berlin Staatskapelle, Apelt; (xii) Haywood; (xiii) Berlin Singakademie Ch.

This two-disc set contains much that will intrigue the dedicated Beethovenian – the 43 *Canons and musical jokes*, for instance – but whose appeal will elude the general listener. For three of the more important inclusions DG have drawn on the Sony catalogue and outstanding performances from Michael Tilson Thomas of the *Bundeslied*, *Opferlied* (with Lorna Haywood an impressive soloist) and the remarkable *Elegischer Gesang* ('Elegiac song'). Cheryl Studer's dramatic if not really memorable *Ah! perfido* is new, as is most of the rest, much of it truly ephemeral although well sung and recorded.

Volume 19: *Large choral works:* (i–iii) *Cantatas on the accession of Emperor Leopold II, WoO 88;* (iii–iv) *On the death of Emperor Joseph II, WoO 87;* (v) *Choral fantasia for piano, chorus and orchestra in C min., Op. 80;* (vi) *Christus am Oelberge, Op. 85;* (vii) *Der glorreiche Augenblick, Op. 136;* (i; viii–ix) *Mass in C, Op. 86;* (ix) *Meeresstille und glückliche Fahrt, Op. 112;* (x) *Missa solemnis in D, Op. 123.*

(M) *** DG Analogue/Dig. 453 798-2 (5) [id.]. (i) Margiono; (ii) Shimell; (iii) German Opera Ch. & O, Thielemann; (iv) Schäfer, Bieber, von Halem; (v) Kissin, RIAS Ch., BPO, Abbado; (vi) Harwood, King, Crass, V. Singverein, VSO, Klee; (vii) Orgonasova, Vermillion, Robinson, Hawlata, Ch. di voci bianche dell'Arcum, St Cecilia Ac. Ch. & O, Myung-Whun Chung; (viii) Robbin, Kendall, Miles; (ix) Monteverdi Ch., ORR, Gardiner; (x) Studer, Norman, Domingo, Moll, Leipzig R. Ch., Swedish R. Ch., VPO, Levine.

Just two years after Karajan died, the 1991 Salzburg Festival honoured its late music director in a performance of Beethoven's *Missa solemnis* conducted by James Levine. As the recording consistently demonstrates, the results have an incandescence that conveys the atmosphere of a great occasion, as this work should. This version has no rival, and the DG engineers have obtained the richest, weightiest sound yet on any recording made in the tricky Salzburg venue, not least from the massed choruses. An intense, visionary experience, this was an ideal choice for the Beethoven Edition. And it is only in relation to the vast vision of the *Missa solemnis* that the *Mass in C* unfairly tends to be regarded as less than a masterpiece. Gardiner's performance shows otherwise. With clean textures and sprung rhythms, married to an expressive warmth not regularly associated with period manners, it is ever refreshing. Aptly clear-toned soloists match the freshness of the Monteverdi Choir: Charlotte Margiono, Catherine Robbin, William Kendall and Alastair Miles.

Beethoven's oratorio, *Christus am Oelberge*, is an even more under-rated work, compellingly dramatic for much of the time. James King as a Heldentenor soloist underlines the operatic quality, and the radiance of Elizabeth Harwood's voice is powerfully caught, while Franz Crass makes a comparably intense partner.

Bernhard Klee draws lively playing from the Vienna Symphoniker, and the recording, one or two balances apart, is first rate.

The two cantatas concerned with regal death and accession are fine new recordings directed by DG's latest young lion of the rostrum, Christian Thielemann; he gives us considered and serious-minded performances which aptly combine vitality and gravitas. The Viennese celebration, *Der glorreiche Augenblick* – as is happens, recorded in Rome – heard under the baton of the equally perceptive Myung-Whun Chung, is equally telling, with its principal soloist, Luba Orgonasova, making a major contribution to its success. Excellent recording throughout ensures a warm welcome for this volume, an essential purchase unless you already have the two *Masses*.

Volume 20: Historic recordings: *Piano concertos Nos.* (i) *3 in C min., Op 37;* (ii–iii) *5 in E flat (Emperor), Op. 73;* (iv) *Violin concerto in D, Op. 61. Symphonies Nos.* (v) *3 in E flat (Eroica), Op. 55;* (vi) *5 in C min., Op. 67;* (vii) *7 in A, Op. 92;* (viii) *9 in D min. (Choral), Op. 125. Overtures:* (ix) *Coriolan, Op. 62;* (x) *Egmont, Op. 84; Leonore No. 2, Op. 72;* (ix) *Leonore No. 3, Op. 72. Violin sonatas Nos.* (xii; ii) *5 in F, 'Spring', Op. 24;* (xiii; ii) *9 in A, 'Kreutzer', Op 47;* (ii) *Rondo a capriccio in G, Op. 129.* (xiv) *An die ferne Geliebte* (song-cycle), *Op. 98.* Lieder: *Andenken, WoO 136; In questa tomba oscura, WoO 133; Der Wachtelschlag WoO 129. Zärtliche Liebe, WoO 123* (with: (xiii) MOZART: *Piano concerto No. 20 in D min., K.466* (with cadenzas by Beethoven)).

(M) (***) DG mono/stereo 453 804-2 (6) [id.]. (i) Annie Fischer, Bav. RSO, Fricsay; (ii) Wilhelm Kempff; (iii) BPO, Peter Raabe; (iv) Josef Wolfsthal, BPO, Manfred Gurlitt; (v–ix) BPO; cond. (v) Carl Schuricht; (vi) Artur Nikisch; (vii) Ferenc Fricsay; (viii) Fritz Busch, with Kerstin Lindberg-Torlind, Else Jena, Erik Sjöberg, Holger Byrding, Danish R. Ch. & O; (ix) Furtwängler; (x) Berlin Op. O, Otto Klemperer; (xii) Wolfgang Schneiderhan; (xiii) Georg Kulenkampff; (xiv) Heinrich Schlusnus, Sebastian Peschko & Franz Rupp; (xiii) Sviatoslav Richter, Warsaw PO, Wislocki.

The earliest record of the set is the famous 1913 Nikisch account of the *Fifth Symphony*, the first complete recording of any symphony. There is not very much that anyone can do to make this sound anything other than primitive. New to us was the wartime (1941) set of the *Eroica* from Carl Schuricht and the Berlin Philharmonic. Though it was listed in Clough & Cuming's *World Encyclopaedia of Recorded Music*, for obvious reasons it never enjoyed much currency outside Germany. It is most impressive in every way: totally dedicated, vibrant and alive, beautifully shaped and powerfully conceived. Ferenc Fricsay's recording of the *Seventh Symphony* was omitted from DG's 1994 ten-CD compilation (plus a bonus disc) devoted to this great conductor. At the time there were impressive *Sevenths* from Klemperer and Colin Davis which are still available, but this still has a fire, a gravitas and an integrity that make a powerful impression. The *Ninth Symphony* was made in Copenhagen in the autumn of 1950 with the legendary *Staatsradiofoniens Orkester* under Fritz Busch. There is nothing that distracts the attention away from Beethoven to the performer's art. It is a selfless and classical account, but a fine rather than a great performance.

As far as the concertos are concerned, Annie Fischer's 1957 account of the *Third* with the Bavarian Radio Orchestra under Ferenc Fricsay is the better-known and fully deserves resurrection. It is a performance of stature and was widely admired at the time. Wilhelm Kempff's fine (1936) *Emperor Concerto* is enormously impressive. Though it is not necessarily superior to either of his post-war records, with Paul van Kempen and Ferdinand Leitner, the balance is exceptionally fine. Kempff's delicate *pianopianissimo* tone in the first-movement exposition is nothing short of a marvel. Josef Wolfsthal's 1929 account of the *Violin concerto* was in fact his second recording of the piece, so he must have been regarded as a major talent during the 1920s. He was a pupil of Carl Flesch and, had he lived beyond his thirty-second year, would have become a pretty commanding figure. The playing is breathtaking; the octaves at the opening of the cadenza have to be heard to be believed.

The 1959 account by Sviatoslav Richter of Mozart's *D minor Concerto*, K.466, made in Warsaw, is included because of the Beethoven cadenzas the great Russian pianist used. Among other high-points are the 1942 Furtwängler Berlin Philharmonic *Coriolan overture* (marvellously dramatic and intense), the 1935 set of the *Kreutzer Sonata* with the legendary Georg Kulenkampff and Wilhelm Kempff, which has remarkable purity, and the famous pre-war *An die ferne Geliebte* with Heinrich Schlusnuss which is hardly less welcome. The presentation of this is set is very handsome indeed.

Other recordings

Piano concertos Nos. 1–5.

(M) ** Ph. Dig. 456 045-2 (3) [id.]. Alfred Brendel, Chicago SO, James Levine.

(i) *Piano concertos Nos. 1–5;* (ii) *Triple concerto for violin, cello and piano, Op. 56.*

(M) *** Sony SB3K 48397 (3) [S3K 48397]. (i) Fleisher, Cleveland O, Szell; (ii) Stern, Rose, Istomin, Phd. O, Ormandy.

Piano concertos Nos. 1–5; Rondos, Op. 51/1–2.
(M) (***) DG mono 435 744-2 (3) [id.]. Wilhelm Kempff, BPO, Van Kempen.

(i) *Piano concertos Nos. 1–5. 6 Bagatelles, Op. 126; Für Elise.*
(B) **(*) Decca 443 723-2 (3) [id.]. Ashkenazy, (i) Chicago SO, Solti.

(i) *Piano concertos Nos. 1–5. Piano sonata No. 32 in C min., Op. 111.*
(B) *** DG 427 237-2 (3). Kempff; (i) BPO, Leitner.

(i) *Piano concertos Nos. 1–5. Diabelli variations, Op. 120.*
(M) **(*) Decca 433 891-2 (3). Wilhelm Backhaus; (i) VPO, Schmidt-Isserstedt.

Piano concertos Nos. 1–5; (i) *Choral Fantasia, Op. 80.*
(M) *** EMI (SIS) CMS7 63360-2 (3) [Ang. ZDMC 633602]. Daniel Barenboim, New Philh. O, Klemperer, (i) with John Alldis Ch.

Piano concerto No. 1 in C, Op. 15; (i) *Choral Fantasia* (for piano, chorus and orchestra), *Op. 80.*
(B) *** EMI CfP CD-CFP 6025 [(M) id. import]. John Lill, SNO; (i) with SNO Ch., Sir Alexander Gibson.

Piano concertos Nos. 2 in B flat, Op. 19; 4 in G, Op. 58.
(B) *** EMI CfP CD-CFP 6026 [(M) id. import]. Lill, SNO, Gibson.

Piano concertos Nos. 3 in C min., Op. 37; 5 in E flat (Emperor), Op. 73.
(B) *** EMI CfP CD-CFP 6027 [(M) id. import]. Lill, SNO, Gibson.

Kempff's stereo accounts all come from the early 1960s and still sound remarkably good for their age, and the wisdom Kempff dispensed is as fresh as ever. A set to invest in, even if you have other recordings.

Fleisher made his series with Szell during 1961. Throughout, their musical partnership was at its peak and these performances are uncommonly rewarding. The remastering has greatly improved the recording, flattering the piano more than it did on LP, while the orchestra gains from the Severance Hall ambience. However, the balance in the *Triple concerto* has the soloists placed unnaturally forward.

The combination of Barenboim and Klemperer, recording together in 1967/8, is nothing if not stimulating and, for every wilfulness of a measured Klemperer, there is a youthful spark from the spontaneously combusting Barenboim. The concentration is formidable and especially compelling in the slow movements. The *Choral Fantasia* too is given an inspired performance. The remastered sound is vivid and clear and quite full.

There is a mood of carefree delight running through the earlier of Kempff's two cycles of the Beethoven *Piano concertos*. Even more than his stereo cycle, this one, recorded in mono in 1953, finds Kempff at his most individual, turning phrases and pointing ornamentation with a sparkle and sense of fun to have you smiling in response. Kempff is often idiosyncratic, as in his decision in the first four concertos to play his own cadenzas, making them sound like spontaneous improvisations. This is a classic recording guaranteed to give delight, which has been transferred to CD in full, immediate, well-detailed sound.

John Lill has never been more impressive on record than in his set of the Beethoven concertos, recorded in 1974–5 and appearing on CD for the first time only now. In each of the works he conveys a sense of spontaneity and a vein of poetry that in the studio have too often eluded him. Gibson and the Scottish National Orchestra provide strong, direct support, helped by very good analogue recording using the spacious City Hall, Glasgow, with its acoustic strikingly open at the top. As a set this makes a very impressive cycle. The *First Concerto* immediately catches the listener up: it is refreshingly direct, with a thoughtful yet lively account of the first movement and concentrated readings of the slow movement and finale. In the coupled *Choral Fantasia* Lill gives a formidable account of the opening cadenza, and the vocal contributions are effective and well balanced. In the *Second Concerto* Lill again plays with ease and imagination and he is at his finest in the *Third*, a work for which in the concert hall too he has shown a special affinity. He is crisp and direct and rather fast in the first movement, spacious and concentrated in the central *Largo*, sparkling in the finale. The *Fourth Concerto* then reveals that in this most poetic of Beethoven's works he can relax, with individual touches of imagination and a fine range of tone-colour. There is fire too in the first movement – though, in all three, Gibson is somewhat square in his accompaniment. In the *Emperor*, the first to be recorded, Lill's combination of power and poetry is again captured with striking spontaneity, making this set very competitive with other versions at whatever price.

The partnership of Ashkenazy and Solti is fascinating. Where Solti is fiery and intense, Ashkenazy provides an introspective balance. Ashkenazy brings a hushed, poetic quality to every slow movement, while Solti's urgency maintains a vivid forward impulse in outer movements. Sometimes, as in the *C minor Concerto*, one feels that the music-making is too intense. Here a more relaxed and lyrical approach in the first movement can find a warmth that Solti misses. But for the most part the listener is given an overriding impression of freshness, and the *Emperor* performance, while on the grandest scale, has a marvellous individual moment in the first movement when Ashkenazy lingers over the presentation of the second subject. The Chicago orchestral playing is characteristically brilliant, and the one real snag is the very bright recording, which on CD is made to sound uncomfortably fierce at times, while the piano timbre is not as full in sonority as Decca usually provides.

Backhaus recorded the Beethoven concertos with the highly supportive Schmidt-Isserstedt in 1958–9 when he was in his mid-seventies (the *Diabelli variations* date from 1955). His bold style, sometimes lacking in grace and wit, yet had remarkable authority, and now these early stereo recordings emerge with remarkable freshness. For every moment of wilfulness there is a balancing sense of spontaneity; if charm and subtlety of touch are not his strong points, the composer's spirit is ever present. Not surprisingly, it is the *Emperor* which shows the pianist at his most commanding. The recordings, made in the Sofiensaal, are amazingly good. In the *Diabelli variations* the moments of brusqueness are much more apparent and the close balance prevents a real pianissimo.

Brendel's Chicago version was intended to prove how much more effective live recording is than studio performance, but the results – recorded at Orchestra Hall, Chicago – belie that. Anything Brendel does has mastery and distinction but, compared with his earlier studio recordings of the concertos on Turnabout and with Haitink and the Concertgebouw, this sounds self-conscious, less rather than more spontaneous-sounding. He did after all know that the tape was running, and that in itself must have affected the performances. The recorded sound gives a good sense of presence but is badly balanced, and loud applause at the end of each concerto is most intrusive.

(i) *Piano concertos Nos. 1–5;* (ii) *Violin concerto, Op. 61.*
(BB) ** RCA Navigator Dig./Analogue 74321 30366-2 (3). (i) Ax, RPO, Previn; (ii) Ughi, LSO, Sawallisch.

Piano concertos Nos. 1 in C, Op. 15; 3 in C min., Op. 37.
(BB) ** RCA Navigator 74321 29240-2. Emanuel Ax, RPO, Previn.

(i) *Piano concerto No. 2 in B flat, Op. 19*; (ii) *Violin concerto in D, Op. 61.*
(BB) ** RCA Navigator 74321 24200-2. (i) Ax, RPO, Previn; (ii) Ughi, LSO, Sawallisch.

Piano concertos Nos. 4 in G, Op. 58; 5 in E flat (Emperor), Op. 73.
(BB) ** RCA Navigator Dig. 74321 17890-2. Ax, RPO, Previn.

Piano concerto No. 5 (Emperor); Choral Fantasia (for piano, chorus and orchestra), Op. 80.
(BB) ** [RCA Basic 100 09026 61714-2]. Ax, RPO, Previn.

This three-disc super-bargain set offers exceptionally generous measure. These are thoughtful, unassertive performances, which in the first two concertos clearly relate the music to Mozart. Previn gives his very musical soloist good support, particularly in the slow movements, which are gentle and touching. Finales are enjoyably brisk and sparkling. The *Third Concerto* is given rather more weight, without ever being forceful: here the finale is more relaxed and measured – pleasingly lyrical in feeling. The warmly lyrical account of the *Fourth Concerto* shows these artists at their best (although the central dialogue could be more dramatic), but the relaxed playing in the *Emperor* makes this a less bitingly compelling version than it can be, with the finale less weighty than usual. The *Choral Fantasia* is available (on a separate CD) only in the USA. Excellent, natural, 1985–6 digital recording, warmly resonant but clear. Ughi's 1981 account of the *Violin concerto* also has realistic and well-balanced sound. His performance is in every way recommendable, fresh and unaffected, marked by consistent purity of tone in every register. If the last degree of imagination of the kind which creates special magic is missing in all these performances, their freshness makes them well worth considering for those with limited budgets.

Piano concertos Nos. 1 in C, Op. 15; 2 in B flat, Op. 19.
(B) *** Ph. Virtuoso 422 968-2 [(M) id. import]. Stephen Kovacevich, BBC SO, Sir Colin Davis.
(M) ** EMI (SIS) CDM5 66090-2. Weissenberg, BPO, Karajan.

Piano concertos Nos. 3 in C min., Op. 37; 5 in E flat (Emperor), Op. 73.
(M) ** EMI (SIS) CDM5 66091-2. Weissenberg, BPO, Karajan.

(i) *Piano concerto No. 4 in G, Op. 58;* (ii) *Triple concerto for violin, cello and piano in C, Op. 56.*
(M) ** EMI (SIS) CDM5 66092-2. (i) Weissenberg; (ii) David Oistrakh, Rostropovich, Richter; (i–ii) BPO, Karajan.

Philips have now restored to the catalogue Stephen Kovacevich's recordings of the Beethoven concertos on their new Virtuoso logo. These first two works, ideally coupled, bring characteristically crisp and refreshing readings from Kovacevich with Sir Colin Davis; they convey their conviction with no intrusive idiosyncrasies. That these model performances and recordings come on the cheapest Philips label is something to marvel at. The current remastering of recordings from the early 1970s is very successful.

The orchestral focus in tuttis is perhaps not absolutely sharp, but the piano image is very real and the balance quite excellent.

Alexis Weissenberg's playing in the set of piano concertos, reissued as part of EMI's Karajan Edition, sounds rather run-of-the-mill, although there are individual felicities and Karajan and the Berlin Philharmonic create a strong impression in the beautifully played accompaniments. There are no complaints on sonic grounds (the recordings are full and well balanced and date from the mid- to late 1970s). The *Triple concerto* is treated with apt opulence by the star soloists, with Beethoven's priorities among them well preserved in the extra dominance of Rostropovich over his colleagues. This is warm, expansive music-making. The 1969 recording is rather too reverberant and orchestral climaxes could be smoother, but the sound is better focused here than on LP, and the balance between the soloists and the orchestra is well managed.

Piano concertos Nos. 1 in C, Op. 15; 2 in B flat, Op. 19; 3 in C min., Op. 37; 4 in G, Op. 58.
(B) *** EMI forte CZS5 69506-2 (2) [CDFB 69506]. Gilels, Cleveland O, Szell.

(i) *Piano concertos Nos. 1–4;* (ii) *Romances for violin and orchestra Nos. 1–2, Opp. 40 & 50.*
(B) *** Ph. Duo 442 577-2 (2). (i) Stephen Kovacevich, BBC SO, Sir Colin Davis; (ii) Arthur Grumiaux, Concg. O, Haitink.

Gilels is an incomparable Beethoven player. He is unfailingly illuminating and poetic and his playing is consistently a matter for marvel. It goes without saying that Szell has tremendous grip and that the playing of the Cleveland Orchestra is beyond reproach, with a rhythmical point that has an exhilarating lift. The recordings, made in Severance Hall in 1968, are dry and clear rather than expansive, but certainly do not lack atmosphere. A treasurable set.

The first four concertos bring characteristically crisp and refreshing readings from Kovacevich and Davis which convey their conviction with no intrusive idiosyncrasy, while Nos. 3 and 4 would be top recommendations even if they cost far more. These are model performances and, throughout, the playing of Kovacevich has a depth and thoughtful intensity that have rarely been matched. The recording, from the early 1970s, is refined and well balanced and has been admirably transferred to CD. Grumiaux's *Romances* date from a decade earlier, but the Concertgebouw acoustic brings a characteristic fullness, and the solo playing is peerless.

Piano concerto No. 1 in C, Op. 15; Rondo in B flat, WoO 6.
(BB) **(*) Naxos Dig. 8.550190 [id.]. Stefan Vladar, Capella Istropolitana, Wordsworth.

Stefan Vladar's performance of Beethoven's *C major Concerto* is among the finest in his Naxos super-bargain series. The first movement has striking freshness and spontaneity, and the spacious *Largo* makes an eloquent contrast with the sparkle of the joyful finale. Excellent accompaniments from Wordsworth and the Capella Istropolitana, alert and sympathetic and full of spirit. The coupling, however, is not generous, although here too the playing is strong in personality. Throughout, the digital recording is fresh, full and clean.

Piano concertos Nos. 1 in C, Op. 15; 2 in B flat, Op. 19.
(B) *** Decca Eclipse Dig. 448 982-2; *448 982-4* [(M) id. import]. Alicia de Larrocha, Berlin RSO, Chailly (with SCHUBERT: *Moment musical No. 6 in A flat, D.780* ***).
(M) *** DG Dig. 445 504-2 [id.]. Martha Argerich, Philh. O, Sinopoli.
(M) *** Virgin Veritas/EMI Dig. VER5 61296-2 [CDM 61296]. Tan (fortepiano), L. Classical Players, Norrington.
(M) *(**) Beethoven Edition DG Dig. 447 908-2 [id.]. Pollini, VPO, Jochum.

Alicia de Larrocha recorded all five of the Beethoven concertos in the early 1980s with the Berlin Radio Symphony Orchestra playing freshly under Chailly. The set was rather uneven, but the first two concertos were given delightful performances, lightly pointed, on a Mozartian scale, but with beautifully poised accounts of both slow movements. Full, vivid recording, made in Jesus-Christus-Kirche. The Schubert *Impromptu* also is played with simplicity but with much poetic feeling.

The conjunction of Martha Argerich and Giuseppe Sinopoli in Beethoven produces performances which give off electric sparks, daring and volatile. Argerich's contribution in phrase after phrase brings highly individual pointing. She is jaunty in allegros rather than lightweight – one might even ask for more pianissimo – and slow movements are songful, not solemn. Very distinctive and stimulating performances, given full, vivid – albeit not ideally balanced – sound in a rather reverberant acoustic.

Melvyn Tan's coupling of the first two concertos, using a fortepiano, brings performances of natural, unselfconscious expressiveness which will delight those looking for versions on period instruments. Even when Tan's speeds for slow movements are very fast indeed, his ease of expression makes them very persuasive, avoiding breathlessness while simultaneously conveying more gravity than you might expect.

Pollini's second (digital) Beethoven cycle with Abbado (DG 439 770-2) – recorded live in December 1992 and January 1993 – proved something of a disappointment. One problem is that the piano-sound in the latter is often shallower than that of the first set; Pollini admirers will therefore be glad to see this earlier series reappearing as part of DG's Beethoven Edition. Pollini is sometimes wilful in his earlier account of the *First Concerto* but, with refreshing clarity of articulation, his is a performance, brisk rather than poetic, which vividly reflects the challenge of an unexpected partnership between pianist and conductor, and it has a keener sense of spontaneity than his later, digital version with Abbado. The recording was taken from live performances but betrays little sign of that. The *Second Concerto* (also live) is one of the more attractive of his Beethoven concerto series, but it cannot match its finest rivals. This CD was an early (1983) digital issue and it provides excellent presence for the piano, but the strings are curiously lacking in fullness of focus; the earlier, analogue recordings with Boehm were rather warmer and more natural-sounding.

Piano concertos Nos. 1 in C, Op. 15; 3 in C min., Op. 37.
(M) *(*) DG 449 757-2. Michelangeli, VSO, Giulini.

Recorded at a live concert in 1980, the partnership of Michelangeli and Giulini in the *First Concerto* is intensely disappointing, with Michelangeli strangely metrical – a fault accentuated by the forward balance and rather thin tone of the piano. The *C minor Concerto* (also live, from the previous year) is marginally – but only marginally – more appealing. The piano timbre is fuller, and certainly Giulini prepares for the piano entry in the first movement with a well-shaped opening ritornello. But Michelangeli's clear-cut, literal approach is difficult to adjust to, particularly in the slow movement, which is very considered indeed. The finale is at its finest in the coda. This reissue in DG's series of 'Originals' is for Michelangeli addicts only. Applause included in the first issue of these recordings has now been removed.

Piano concertos Nos. 1 in C, Op. 15; 4 in G, Op. 58.
(M) **(*) [RCA Basic 100 09026 68083-2; *68083-4*]. Rubinstein, Boston SO, Leinsdorf.

Rubinstein gives sparkling, totally spontaneous-sounding performances of both concertos. In No. 1 the performance conveys the joy rather than the stress of early Beethoven. There are no half-tones, with no dynamic much below *mezzo forte*, but the sense of presence is vividly conveyed in bright sound to bring out the clarity of articulation. In the gentle opening solo of No. 4 the manner is easy and confidential; the exchanges of the slow movement are contrasted cleanly and sharply, with no inner intensity but with keen, bright persuasion. The finale is wonderfully volatile, with rhythms neatly pointed. The 1960s recordings are bright and sharply focused, with the piano given close balance.

Piano concertos Nos. 1 in C, Op. 15; 5 in E flat (Emperor).
(B) *** Tring Dig. TRP 075 [(M) id. import]. Michael Roll, RPO, Howard Shelley.

Michael Roll, the very first winner of the Leeds Competition in 1963, when he was still in his teens, has for too long been neglected by the record companies. Here he gives magnetic performances of both concertos, at once sparkling and powerful, marked by articulation of diamond clarity, with rhythms persuasively sprung. Though in both works Roll favours allegros on the fast side, generally maintained steadily, he never presses so hard that detail is lost. That is so even in the finale of the *First Concerto* – controversially fast – which yet has plenty of wit and point. In the *Emperor*, Roll adopts a daringly wide dynamic range, with pianissimos that hold the ear on a thread, as in the link into the finale, which then brings delightfully crisp snapping rhythms. Much is owed to the inspired conducting of another outstanding pianist, Howard Shelley, who draws from the RPO playing comparably incisive and just as intense, drawing an apt contrast between early and late Beethoven in the two works, so that the first-movement tuttis have the listener more than usually expectant. The full, immediate recording enhances the transparency of the textures.

Piano concertos Nos. 2 in B flat, Op. 19; 3 in C min., Op. 37.
(B) *** Tring Dig. TRP 076 [(M) id. import]. Michael Roll, RPO, Howard Shelley.

Michael Roll is again at his finest here. This excellent bargain disc, offering bright, fresh, spontaneous-sounding performances of Nos. 2 and 3, recorded in full and warm digital sound, is most welcome. There is a touch of clatter in the piano-tone at the top, but the natural expressiveness and the magnetic urgency of the playing, with beautifully even passage-work, firm left hand and the crispest of trills makes one's ears adjust very quickly, and the orchestral playing under a fine pianist-turned-conductor is equally compelling.

Piano concertos Nos. 2; 4.
(M) *** Sony SBK 48165; *SBT 48165* [id.]. Fleisher, Cleveland O, Szell.

This coupling by Leon Fleisher and George Szell brings masterly examples of their inspired artistry. No. 2

receives a powerful, intense, spontaneous-sounding performance, giving weight to early Beethoven. In No. 4 Fleisher and Szell are even more searching, with the soloist's refreshingly imaginative playing matched by glorious sounds from the Cleveland Orchestra. The bright, forward recordings, both made in Severance Hall, have been transferred with satisfying fullness and body.

Piano concertos Nos. 2; 5 (Emperor), Op. 73.
(BB) **(*) Naxos Dig. 8.550121 [id.]. Stefan Vladar, Capella Istropolitana, Barry Wordsworth.

Vladar's fine account of the *Emperor* (see below) is also available coupled with an infectiously vigorous performance of the *Second Concerto*, again very well accompanied by Wordsworth and his chamber group. The sound is full and open, though the 'twangy' Bösendorfer keyboard timbre may be a drawback for some listeners.

Piano concerto No. 3 in C min., Op. 37.
(M) ** EMI CDM7 64750-2. Sviatoslav Richter, Philh. O, Muti – MOZART: *Piano Concerto No. 22.* **

Richter's 1978 version may be controversial – like its Mozart coupling – but clearly a master is at the keyboard and Muti draws a sympathetic accompaniment from the Philharmonia players. The performance is consciously wayward, essentially lyrical, but it has undoubted authority, and the remastered recording sounds well.

Piano concertos Nos. 3 in C min., Op. 37; 4 in G, Op. 58.
(B) *** Ph. Virtuoso 426 062-2 [(M) id. import]. Stephen Kovacevich, BBC SO, Sir Colin Davis.
(M) **(*) Beethoven Edition DG 447 909-2 [id.]. Pollini, VPO, Boehm.
(BB) **(*) Naxos Dig. 8.550122 [id.]. Stefan Vladar, Capella Istropolitana, Barry Wordsworth.
(B) ** Decca Dig. 448 230-2 [(M) id. import]. Alicia de Larrocha, Berlin RSO, Chailly.

The Philips versions of Nos. 3 and 4 from Kovacevich and Sir Colin Davis would be top recommendations even if they cost far more. In both works the playing of the soloist has a depth and thoughtful intensity that have rarely been matched. The refined Philips recording has transferred admirably to CD: the balance is altogether excellent and the loss of focus is minimal.

The concentration of the playing and the single-minded clarity of Pollini's reading of the *Third Concerto* are matched by Boehm's strong, clear-minded accompaniment. The result is strikingly fresh, and Pollini brings undoubted personal insights to bear on his reading, with the slow movement serenely dedicated. Yet overall the performance is on the sober side for a youthful concerto that should perhaps sparkle more than it does here, although the result is by no means lacking in spontaneity. There is an aristocratic feeling about Pollini's account of the *Fourth,* and the clarity of his vision achieves a delicate balance between classical poise and poetic sensitivity. Boehm is a faithful accompanist who prevents the end result from being too chilly, although the 'question-and-answer' approach to the *Andante* is coolly individual. The closeness of the piano's balance is apparent in the transfer to CD, but the recordings, from the latter part of the 1970s, are of fine DG analogue quality.

Vladar's cycle of Beethoven concertos for Naxos is recorded with a Bösendorfer piano, and the bright, rather dry sound in the instrument's higher tessitura stems from the character of this particular instrument. It adds classical bite to performances which are dramatic and fresh, with the slow movement of No. 3 strongly contrasted in its expressive feeling. The brightness in the piano's upper range seems less obvious in the *G major Concerto* – in all other respects the sound is very good in both works – and its essential lyricism is well understood by soloist and conductor alike. At super-bargain price, this is certainly recommendable.

Alicia de Larrocha's set of the Beethoven concertos with the Berlin Radio Symphony Orchestra, made in the mid-1980s, proved to be very uneven, with Nos. 3 and 4 the least attractive. Here de Larrocha sounds self-conscious in her somewhat weighty manner. She receives good support from Chailly and the Decca sound is full and vivid.

Piano concertos Nos. 3 in C min., Op. 37; 5 in E flat (Emperor), Op. 73.
(M) ** Sony SMK 63080 [id.]. R. Serkin, NYPO, Bernstein.

The remastered CD of the 1964 Serkin/Bernstein account of the *Third Concerto* has improved the sound, which is now relatively spacious. Between them these artists give a super-brilliant performance of the first movement, with strong orchestral accents from Bernstein which at times almost brutalize the music. The slow movement is serene and poised, but the aggressive feeling returns in the orchestral tuttis of the finale, which are similarly fierce, partly the effect of the microphones being so close to the violins. Serkin's *Emperor* is characteristically commanding; the reading is strong and nobly sensitive in the great *Adagio*. The snag is again the rather coarse (1962) recording, which the new transfer is unable to mitigate.

Piano concerto No. 4 in G, Op. 58.
✿ (M) ** RCA/Melodiya 74321 40722-2 [id.]. Maria Grinburg, USSR SO, Neeme Järvi – R. STRAUSS: *Don Juan; Till Eulenspiegel.* (*)

Maria Grinburg's work was represented in the second volume of the 'Russian Piano School' (discussed in our 1997 *Yearbook*). Born in 1908, she made relatively little headway outside the then Soviet Union, though she did appear in the Netherlands. On the Melodiya disc from the 'Great Russian Pianists' series her Scarlatti has an astonishing elegance and subtlety, and her Brahms is quite masterly. This 1965 account of the Beethoven *G major Concerto* has unusual depth and beauty, and its slow movement in particular is as beautifully realized as any before the public; it is almost worthy of a Gilels. The sound is not absolutely first class – hence the two stars – but artistically this is remarkable. (The Strauss couplings are marvellously played, but the recordings are very coarse and unpleasant – hence the difference in star ratings.)

Piano concertos Nos. (i) *4 in G, Op. 58;* (ii) *5 in E flat (Emperor).*
(M) *** DG 447 402-2 [id.]. Wilhelm Kempff, BPO, Leitner.
(B) *** DG Classikon 439 483-2; *439 483-4* [(M) id. import]. Pollini, VPO, Boehm.
(BB) *** Belart 450 022-2. Friedrich Gulda, VPO, Horst Stein.
(M) *(*) Ph. Dig. 446 193-2. Brendel, Chicago SO, Levine.

The Kempff/Leitner performances, now reissued in DG's 'Originals' series, bring an outstanding mid-priced recommendation for this particular coupling. The digital remastering has perceptibly enhanced the sound, with the most natural balance in the *Fourth Concerto*. Here Kempff's delicacy of fingerwork and his shading of tone-colour are as effervescent as ever, and the fine control of the conductor ensures the unity of the reading. Although Kempff's version of the *Emperor* is not on an epic scale, it has power in plenty, and excitement, too. As ever, Kempff's range of tone-colour is extraordinarily wide, from the merest half-tone, as though the fingers were barely brushing the keys, to the crisp impact of a dry fortissimo. Leitner's orchestral contribution is of high quality and the Berlin orchestral playing has vigour and warmth. Here some reservations need to be made about the quality of the remastered CD. The bass is somewhat over-resonant and the orchestral tuttis are very slightly woolly; the piano timbre is natural but the slight lack of firmness in the orchestral focus is a drawback, though it does not seriously detract from the music-making.

Those wanting to sample Pollini's earlier set of the Beethoven concertos could hardly do better than invest in this bargain Classikon coupling of two of the most strikingly individual performances, of Nos. 4 and 5, excellently transferred, with believable piano-timbre and a full orchestral tapestry well focused within the warm ambience of the Grosser Saal of the Vienna Musikverein. After the poised account of the *Fourth Concerto*, the distinction of Pollini's interpretation of the *Emperor* is never in doubt and, though recorded in the studio, the performance sounds more spontaneously expressive, with a vein of poetry that is largely missing in the later, live recording. If at times the solo playing sounds a little withdrawn, the strong and wise accompaniment of Boehm and the Vienna Philharmonic again provides a nice balance. The slow movement is elegant and the finale is urgent and energetic; those not seeking a grand romantic manner in this concerto will find this satisfying in a quite different way.

Excellently recorded by Decca at the beginning of the 1970s, Gulda's fine performances are in every way recommendable. He chose to use a Bösendorfer piano – which at the time seemed idiosyncratic but which, to present-day ears, offers a sound with something of the clean profile and tang of a fortepiano, while bringing a wider range of colour to slow movements. The strings are bright and fresh, yet there is a satisfying weight. Both the performances are most enjoyable, strong and direct and with a consistent spontaneity. No. 4 with its eloquent opening is particularly fine, with a memorable central *Andante*. The *Emperor* is another marked success, with tempi maintained consistently through each movement and strength rather than inflexibility emerging through the compulsive quality of the playing from soloist and orchestra alike. At super-bargain price, the CD can be given the warmest welcome.

Brendel's digital coupling of Nos. 4 and 5 – like the live complete set from which it is taken – is a disappointment. Though Brendel's mastery and highly individual imagination are never in doubt, the performances are far less spontaneous-sounding than those he recorded earlier with Haitink in the studio. The audience noises, odd balances and intrusive applause are other disadvantages, while in the *Emperor* the relative constriction of the sound is distracting.

(i) *Piano concertos Nos. 4 in G, Op. 58; 5 in E flat (Emperor), Op. 73. Andante in F (Andante favori), WoO 57; Bagatelle in A min. (Für Elise), WoO 59; 6 Bagatelles, Op. 126; 6 Ecossaises, WoO 83; Piano sonatas Nos. 3 in C, Op. 2/3; 11 in B flat, Op. 22; 18 in E flat, Op. 31/3; 23 in F min. (Appassionata), Op. 57; 24 in F sharp, Op. 78; 29 in B flat (Hammerklavier), Op. 106; 30 in E, Op. 109; 5 Variations on 'Rule Britannia', WoO 79; 6 Variations in F, Op. 34; 15 Variations and fugue on a theme of Prometheus (Eroica), Op. 35; 33 Variations on a waltz by Diabelli, Op. 120.*
(M) **(*) Ph. Brendel Edition Analogue/Dig. 446 922-2 (5). Brendel, (i) with Chicago SO, Levine.

Brendel's coupling of the *Fourth* and *Fifth Concertos* is also available separately (see above) and its disappointments are indicated there. Brendel's command and individuality come over more powerfully in the *Emperor concerto*, but the poorly balanced sound and audience noises remain a problem. The *Sonatas* are altogether more successful, with Op. 2/3 fresh and sparkling and *No. 11 in B flat* among the very best of his analogue cycle, with first-class sound. No. 18 is marvellously responsive to the changing character of the invention: Brendel is aware of the interpretative pitfalls and how to solve them! The *Appassionata* is undeniably an impressive performance and excellent recording. Again, very truthful piano-sound. The digital *Hammerklavier* and Opus 78 both come, not from Brendel's complete sonata cycle, but from live recordings, made at the Queen Elizabeth Hall in London a decade later. Though there is greater urgency and dramatic tension in the allegro movements, the great *Adagio* of the *Hammerklavier*, intense as it is, lacks the spacious sublimity of his earlier version, taken even more slowly. The audience make their presence felt only between movements, and the recording is very believable. Brendel's *Diabelli variations* were also recorded live. The playing has energy and urgency; understandably it is not flawless, but the tensions are conveyed superbly. The sound is again excellent, though not as delicate in dynamic range as in a studio recording. The *Eroica variations*, not as flamboyant as with some, plainly point to the magnificence of their culminating development in the *Eroica* finale. Again very realistic recording. The other variations (recorded digitally) show Brendel's consistent thoughtfulness and imagination which bring out the truly Beethovenian qualities in even the most trivial pieces. It is a pity that Philips did not choose the analogue recordings of the two concertos, but for the most part this is an impressive box.

(i) *Piano concerto No. 4 in G, Op. 58;* (ii) *Triple concerto for violin, cello and piano in C, Op. 56.*
(B) *** Tring Dig. TRP 077 [(M) id.]. (i) Michael Roll; (ii) Jean-Jaques Kantorow, Raphael Wallfisch, Michael Roll; RPO, Howard Shelley.

As in his other Tring recordings of Beethoven concertos, Michael Roll is both dramatic and poetic in the *Fourth Concerto*, springing rhythms infectiously even when he adopts a speed on the fast side. This is Beethoven playing of a winning freshness, helped by the playing of the RPO under another fine pianist, Howard Shelley, and with full and brilliant sound. The *Triple concerto* makes an ideal fill-up, with Roll joined by equally inspired partners in Jean-Jacques Kantorow and Raphael Wallfisch. An outstanding bargain.

Piano concerto No. 5 in E flat (Emperor), Op. 73.
(M) *** RCA 09026 61961-2 [id.]. Van Cliburn, Chicago SO, Reiner – TCHAIKOVSKY: *Piano concerto No. 1.* ***

(i) *Piano concerto No. 5 (Emperor). Piano sonata No. 7 in D, Op. 10/3.*
(M) (***) EMI mono CDH7 61005-2 [id.]. Edwin Fischer, (i) with Philh. O, Furtwängler.

(i) *Piano concerto No. 5 in E flat (Emperor);* (ii) *Piano sonata No. 15 in D (Pastoral), Op. 28.*
(BB) **(*) Naxos Dig. 8.550290 [id.]. (i) Stefan Vladar, Capella Istropolitana, Barry Wordsworth; (ii) Jenö Jandó.

(i) *Piano concerto No. 5 (Emperor); Piano sonata No. 21 in C (Waldstein), Op. 53.*
(M) ** Carlton IMP Dig. PCD 2038 [(M) id. import]. Cristina Ortiz, City of L. Sinfonia, Hickox.

Piano concerto No. 5 (Emperor); Piano sonata No. 30 in E, Op. 109.
(B) *** Ph. Virtuoso 422 482-2 [(M) id. import]. Stephen Kovacevich, (i) LSO, Sir Colin Davis.

Piano concerto No. 5 in E flat (Emperor); Grosse Fuge in B flat, Op. 133.
❁ (B) *** EMI Eminence Dig. CD-EMX 2184 [(M) id. import]. Stephen Kovacevich, Australian CO.

Kovacevich is unsurpassed today as an interpreter of this most magnificent of concertos. His superb account for Philips, now on Virtuoso, has set a model for everyone and, with its sonata coupling, remains highly recommendable. This new Eminence version, with the soloist directing from the keyboard, is recognizably from the same inspired artist, though speeds are consistently faster and the manner is sharper and tauter. The piano-sound on the digital recording is aptly brighter and more faithful than on the Philips, making this a first choice for this much-recorded work, even with no allowance for price. The current very successful remastering of the 1969 Philips recording brings an excellent sound-balance, with the piano treble pearly and more natural than before. For coupling there is one of the most deeply perceptive performances of a late Beethoven sonata on record, and many will choose this bonus in preference to the *Grosse Fugue* on Eminence. Those who do should be well satisfied, and indeed the Rosette might apply equally well to either account of the concerto. (The Eminence disc is available in the USA only as a mid-price import.)

Van Cliburn creates much excitement and intensity in the outer movements, with powerful support from Reiner. It is an individual but satisfying reading, with the slow movement a little restrained in the phrasing but poised in its beauty, and this effectively offsets the virtuosity of the outer movements. The finale is by no means driven too hard; if anything it is slower than usual but has a fine lilt and genuine bravura. The remastered recording sounds very well indeed.

A generally sound reading of the *Emperor* from Cristina Ortiz and Hickox, with a strong feeling of forward momentum in the first movement but without sufficient relaxation for the work's lyrical contrasts. The beautiful slow movement, however, is not lacking in poise, and the finale is brightly vivacious. With excellent, modern, digital recording, this has its attractions for a newcomer to the music. Ortiz is undoubtedly articulate and strong in the first movement of the *Waldstein*. After preparing with considerable skill for the entry of the great lyrical theme of the finale, however, she then sets off buoyantly and entirely without subtlety – whereas Kempff, for instance, gives the listener the impression that the famous melody is growing spontaneously out of the music which has gone before.

Stefan Vladar's super-bargain version on Naxos is both commanding and exciting. The bold opening flourish immediately indicates the very characteristic Bösendorfer timbre. The performance, while powerfully direct, still has many individual touches to indicate the degree of imagination at work both from the soloist and in Wordsworth's strong, sympathetic accompaniment. The *Adagio*, which is persuasively shaped, may lack something in idiosyncrasy, but there is a real sensitivity here and the finale is appropriately vigorous and joyful. The sound is splendidly full, with the solo instrument dominating, yet with the orchestra well in the picture. For an encore Jenö Jandó offers an appealing performance of the *Pastoral sonata*, also well recorded. The first two movements are a trifle subdued, but the scherzo is nicely buoyant and the finale catches the spirit of the work's sobriquet engagingly.

Edwin Fischer's 1951 recording with Furtwängler and the Philharmonia Orchestra is one of the classics of the gramophone, one of the most imperious and imperial of *Emperors*. It did not receive its full due when it first came out on LP, though this was due partly to the inferior quality of the EMI pressing; but its remastered form does it much greater justice. The *D major Sonata* was recorded in 1954, Fischer's last recording session, and within a year both soloist and conductor had died.

(i) *Piano concerto No. 5 in E flat (Emperor), Op. 73. 32 Variations on an original theme in C min., WoO 80; 12 Variations on a Russian dance from 'Das Waldmädchen' (Wranitzky), WoO 71; 6 Variations on a Turkish march from 'The Ruins of Athens', Op. 76.*

(B) *** EMI forte (SIS) CZS5 69509-2 (2) [CDFB 69509]. Emil Gilels; (i) Cleveland O, Szell – DVORAK: *Symphony No. 8.* **(*)

Of the many versions of the *Emperor Concerto* available, few are more superb than Gilels's. Here strength is matched with poetry in no small measure, with Szell offering the strongest backing. The Severance Hall recording is bright in regard to violin tone but has plenty of supporting ambience. The *C minor Variations* are marvellously done, and the other two sets bring the strongest characterization and contrasting moments of poetry and charm. Gilels's playing is masterly throughout and the piano is truthfully caught; the pianism implies a wide dynamic range, even if the engineers reduce it somewhat by the close balance. Not to be missed.

(i) *Piano concerto No. 5 (Emperor). 15 Variations and fugue in E flat (Eroica variations), Op. 35.*

(M) *(**) Decca 452 302-2 [id.]. Clifford Curzon, (i) VPO, Knappertsbusch.

Curzon's is a refined and thoughtful reading of the *Emperor*. His playing in the slow movement is beautifully controlled and brings out the poetry gently and movingly. The finale is the only movement where one feels that his restraint shifts the viewpoint back almost to Mozart; there is a restraint about this essentially rumbustious movement which seems almost to be too much of a good thing. Yet the keen intelligence of the playing and the inner concentration working throughout the reading are by no means to be dismissed. The Vienna Philharmonic plays strongly and authoritatively under Knappertsbusch, but the 1957 recording seems hardly worthy of reissue in Decca's Classic Sound series, for the string tutti are fierce and there is a degree of roughness in orchestral tuttis, although the piano timbre is convincing enough. The *Eroica variations* are transferred at a higher level and the piano is much more forward, so one needs to be prepared to adjust the volume control; moreover something curious happens on the bold opening chord: it seems to fluctuate and there is a beat in the tuning. Otherwise the sound is fuller than in the concerto and Curzon's fine performance holds the variations together splendidly.

(i) *Piano concerto No. 5 (Emperor);* (ii) *Piano concerto in E flat, WoO 4* (arr. & orch. Willy Hess); (iii) *Violin concerto in D, Op. 61;* (iv) *Triple concerto for violin, cello and piano in C, Op. 56.*
(B) **(*) Ph. Duo 442 580-2 (2) [id.]. (i) Kovacevich, LSO, Sir Colin Davis; (ii) Lidia Grychtolowna, Folkwang CO, Heinz Dressel; (iii) Herman Krebbers, Concg. O, Haitink; (iv) Szeryng, Starker, Arrau, New Philh. O, Inbal.

Kovacevich's superb 1969 account of the *Emperor* is here part of an attractive Duo compilation which includes also the early *E flat Piano concerto* (WoO 4) which the composer wrote when he was only fourteen. The present performance uses a reconstruction by Willy Hess in which the dominating flute colouring of the orchestration is hardly characteristic and not helped by less than distinguished playing from the wind section of the Folkwang Chamber Orchestra. The performance is spirited, especially the finale; but the piece sounds more like a concerto in the style of the sons of Bach rather than showing much evidence of the pen of even an immature Beethoven. Krebbers' 1974 recording of the *Violin concerto* is distinguished and will disappoint no one. In his hands the slow movement has a tender simplicity which is irresistible, and it is followed by a delightfully relaxed and playful reading of the finale. In the first movement Haitink and his soloist form a partnership which brings out the symphonic strength more than almost any other reading. If the balance of the soloist is a shade too close, the recording is otherwise excellent, and it has transferred with vivid fullness to CD. The companion account of the *Triple Concerto* with Arrau, Szeryng and Starker again brings full and spacious Concertgebouw recording, but Arrau and his colleagues are less strongly projected and, by adopting very unhurried tempi, they run the risk of losing concentration. The outer movements, with the solo playing almost on a chamber scale, lack the bite and bravura of the finest rivals. However, at 'two CDs for the price of one', this set remains well worth consideration for both the *Emperor* and the *Violin concerto.*

(i) *Piano concerto No. 5 (Emperor);* (ii) *Violin concerto in D; Romances Nos. 1–2, Opp. 40 & 50.*
(BB) **(*) EMI Seraphim Dig./Analogue CES5 68520-2 (2) [CDEB 68520]. (i) Youri Egorov, Philh. O, Sawallisch; (ii) Josef Suk, New Philh. O, Boult, or ASMF, Marriner – MOZART: *Piano concerto No. 20.* **(*)

Youri Egorov in his first concerto recording, made in the early 1980s, gives a refreshingly direct but still individual account of the *Emperor*, helped by authoritative conducting from Sawallisch. The slow movement is the controversial point, taken at a very measured *Adagio* which might have flowed better had Egorov adopted a more affectionate style of phrasing. Suk also chooses a very measured tempo for the first movement of the *Violin concerto*, and some may feel that there is not enough urgency and concentration to sustain the interpretation, especially as Suk's tone, as recorded, is on the small side. But otherwise the analogue recording, from the beginning of the 1970s, is excellent, and Suk's playing is both noble and spacious. The *Romances* are very successful, too. Good value at EMI's bargain-basement price for the two discs.

(i) *Piano concerto No. 5 in E flat (Emperor);* (ii) *Triple concerto for violin, cello and piano in C, Op. 56.*
(M) *** Sony SBK 46549; *SBT 46549* [id.]. (i) Leon Fleisher, Cleveland O, Szell; (ii) Stern, Rose, Istomin, Phd. O, Ormandy.

Leon Fleisher is a pianist who worked with special understanding in the Szell regime at Cleveland, and by any count his reading of the *Emperor* is impressive for its youthful dramatic vigour. For the coupling, Stern, Rose and Istomin – three friends who invariably reveal their personal joy in making music together – make a wonderful trio of soloists. Unfortunately the CBS balance, as usual, favours the soloists so that the contrast of their soft playing is endangered; but the performance as a whole is so compelling that it would take a much more serious recording fault to undermine the concentration.

(i) *Piano concerto No. 5 (Emperor). Overtures: Coriolan, Op. 62; Creatures of Prometheus, Op. 43; Leonora No. 3.*
(M) *** Chandos Dig. CHAN 7028 [id.]. (i) John Lill; CBSO, Walter Weller.

John Lill has recorded all the Beethoven concertos for Chandos with considerable success, but the *Emperor* suits his bold, authoritative Beethoven style especially well. The breadth and majesty of the opening movement is arresting, the slow movement is coolly serene and the finale vigorously joyful. So are Walter Weller's performances of the three overtures, which come first on the disc and are splendidly alive. The CBSO is on top form throughout, and the full, resonant sound is of best Chandos vintage. A good alternative mid-priced choice for those who fancy the programme, and John Lill's admirers certainly won't be disappointed.

Piano concerto No. 5 (Emperor); (i) *Choral Fantasia, Op. 80.*
(M) **(*) Beethoven Edition DG Analogue/Dig. 447 910-2 [id.]. Pollini, VPO; (i) Boehm; (ii) Soloists, V. State Op. Ch., VPO, Abbado.

Although perhaps not the most joyful of *Emperors*, the command and individuality of Pollini's performance are compelling, helped by Boehm's warmth. The coupled *Choral Fantasia* is comparatively lightweight, with a very poised introductory cadenza, but proves enjoyably fresh. Rarely, each of its nine sections is separately cued.

Violin concerto in D, Op. 61.
✿ (M) *** DG 447 403-2 [id.]. Schneiderhan, BPO, Jochum – MOZART: *Violin concerto No. 5.* ***
✿ (B) (***) Dutton Lab. mono CDEA 5018 [(M) id. import]. Georg Kulenkampff, BPO, Hans Schmidt-Isserstedt (with MOZART: *Adagio* from *Violin concerto in A, K.219* (***)) – SCHUMANN: *Violin concerto.* ***
(B) *** DG Double 453 142-2 (2) [id.]. Pinchas Zukerman, Chicago SO, Barenboim – BRAHMS: *Concerto* **(*); MENDELSSOHN; TCHAIKOVSKY: *Concertos.* ***
(BB) *** Belart 461 355-2 [(M) id. import]. Campoli, LPO, Krips – MENDELSSOHN: *Violin concerto.* ***
(M) **(*) RCA 09026 61742-2 [id.]. Heifetz, Boston SO, Munch – BRAHMS: *Concerto.* ***
(M) ** Decca Dig. 460 014-2 [id.]. Kyung Wha Chung, VPO, Kondrashin – WALTON: *Violin concerto.* ***
(M) ** Classic fM Dig. 75605 57016-2. Maria Bachmann, RLPO, Pešek – MENDELSSOHN: *Violin concerto.* **

(i) *Violin concerto in D, Op. 61. Overtures: The Consecration of the house, Op. 124; Coriolan, Op. 62; Zur Namensfeier, Op. 115.*
(M) ** Beethoven Edition DG 447 906-2 [id.]. (i) Ferras; BPO, Karajan.

(i) *Violin concerto in D;* (ii) *Romances Nos. 1 in G, Op. 40; 2 in F, Op. 50.*
(B) *** Ph. Virtuoso 420 348-2 [(M) id. import]. Arthur Grumiaux; (i) Concg. O, Sir Colin Davis; (ii) New Philh. O, Edo de Waart.
(BB) *** Naxos Dig. 8.550149; *4550149* [id.]. Takako Nishizaki, Slovak PO (Bratislava), Kenneth Jean.
(B) **(*) [EMI Red Line Dig. CDR5 69787]. Zimmermann, ECO, Tate.
(M) **(*) Carlton Dig. 30367 00242 [(M) id. import]. Jaime Laredo, SCO.

Wolfgang Schneiderhan's stereo version of the *Violin concerto* is among the greatest recordings of this work: the serene spiritual beauty of the slow movement, and the playing of the second subject in particular, have never been surpassed on record; the orchestra under Jochum provides a background tapestry of breadth and dignity. As an added point of interest, Schneiderhan uses cadenzas that were provided for the transcription of the work for piano and orchestra. This makes an entirely justified reissue in DG's 'Legendary recordings' series, and the current transfer of the well-balanced (1962) analogue recording is fresh and realistic. Moreover the new Mozart coupling is both more appropriate and more generous.

Kulenkampff was born in 1899 and was in his mid-thirties when he recorded the Beethoven *Violin concerto* in 1936. In the days of 78-r.p.m. shellac discs it was one of the marks of the real gramophone connnoisseur to prefer the Kulenkampff Telefunken set to such popular (and easily obtained) versions as Heifetz's or Kreisler's. It was not just snobbery (scoff though some did), for even before the war Telefunken had achieved a sound-quality that in its range and immediacy sounds remarkably faithful even today. Added to that, Kulenkampff brought thoughtfulness and relaxation to a performance that in no way inhibited its spontaneity. His pianissimo tone above the stave could be fabulously pure, and this created a serenity which was to be passed on to future generations of interpreters, notably Schneiderhan and Grumiaux. Above all, this is a performance of enormous individuality, and Hans Schmidt-Isserstedt's accompaniment has great verve, with the finale scintillating in the spirit of the dance. Even with the removal of inhibition brought about by tape techniques, few violinists have approached Kulenkampff on record in sense of freedom and spaciousness, and for that alone this CD is invaluable. Once again the new Dutton transfer works its usual miraculous magic: the ear soon forgets that this is an old mono recording and revels in Kulenkampff's beautiful playing, particularly at the Elysian close of the *Larghetto*. RL chose the earlier Telefunken LP transfer as one of his eight LPs in *The Great Records* (published over 30 years ago) and spoke then of the purity of spirit and spaciousness of Kulenkampff's playing. There is a radiance that casts a strong spell, and rarely has its slow movement been given a greater sense of repose.

It seems a somewhat opportunistic idea to join up Zukerman's 1977 recording of the Beethoven *Violin concerto* on a DG Double with three key recordings by Milstein, and one wonders what the latter would have thought about it, had he still been with us. But in the event it is a highly recommendable account, with outstanding analogue sound. Barenboim's support is completely authoritative: he and Zukerman give a spacious and persuasive view of the first movement, held in complete concentration. Warmth, classical feeling and tonal richness are together in perfect balance, and the slow movement is rapt in both its simplicity and its intensity of feeling. With immaculate playing from the Chicago Symphony Orchestra, this is a reading that Milstein would surely not have been reluctant to own, and for anyone wanting these four key concertos this is an excellent recommendation.

Grumiaux's memorably beautiful account is totally classical in feeling and deeply moving. It is warmly recorded, and this bargain disc stands high in the list of recommended versions of the *Concerto*. The *Romances*, too, are very persusive. The *Concerto*, together with the *F major Romance*, is additionally available on a Duo, alongside the concertos of Brahms, Mendelssohn and Tchaikovsky (442 287-2 – see Collections, below.)

Campoli was to re-record the concerto later for HMV, but this early stereo Decca version has an appealing, freshly spontaneous lyricism, and the slow movement has depth and a simple poetry. Krips is in obvious sympathy with his soloist, and the orchestra displays a pleasingly light touch in the finale. The age of the recording hardly comes through, though it was very good in its day. But this Belart reissue is even more notable for the captivating Mendelssohn coupling, a work Campoli was born to play. A splendid bargain.

Those looking for a super-bargain, digital version will find that Nishizaki's highly spontaneous performance can measure up to many accounts by more famous names. Helped by a strongly sympathetic backing from the excellent Slovak Philharmonic under Kenneth Jean, her playing is individual yet unselfconscious and has a fresh simplicity of approach which is consistently appealing. The *Larghetto* is poised and serene, and the finale is nicely buoyant. The two *Romances* are also very well played. The digital recording, made in the Reduta Concert Hall in Bratislava, is first class, the violin well forward but with the resonantly full orchestral tapestry spaciously caught.

Zimmermann's account is restrained and classically pure in the received tradition of Kulenkampff and Schneiderhan. Tate supports him with what is essentially a chamber orchestra tapestry, using modern instruments to achieve a natural clarity of detail. The slow movement is serene but without quite the degree of intensity that his predecessors achieve; but the peformance overall has freshness and spontaneity. The finale is very spirited, and here the orchestral bassoonist shows himself adept at ornamentation. The two *Romances* are nicely judged.

Heifetz's unique coupling of the Beethoven and Brahms *Concertos* on a single disc is only possible because of his consistent refusal to linger. RCA's digital transfer of a recording originally made in the very earliest days of stereo has a fine sense of realism and presence, with the soloist only a little closer than is natural. The extra immediacy of CD reinforces the supreme mastery of a performance which may adopt fast speeds but never sounds rushed, finding time for individuality and imagination in every phrase. For some listeners, the comparative lack of serenity in the first movement (though not in the *Larghetto*) will be a drawback, but the drama of the reading is unforgettable. Heifetz's unique timbre is marvellously captured; the assured aristocracy of the playing confounds criticism.

Laredo, directing the outstanding players of the Scottish Chamber Orchestra, gives a clean-cut, satisfying reading of the *Concerto*, presented on a convincing chamber scale. Speeds are a degree faster than usual in all three movements and some of the dramatic contrasts are reduced, with the closeness of sound in the slow movement not allowing a really gentle pianissimo, but that is apt for the scale. There are more inspired readings but, with the *Romances* as coupling, well recorded in full digital sound, this is certainly worth considering.

Kyung Wha Chung's 1979 Decca performance is totally superseded by her later, full-priced, EMI version with Tennstedt (CDC7 54072-2). The earlier account, measured and thoughtful, lacks the compulsion one would have predicted, largely due to the often prosaic conducting of Kondrashin. There is poetry in individual movements – the minor-key episode of the finale, for example, which alone justifies the unusually slow tempo – but, with too little of the soloist's natural electricity conveyed and none of her volatile imagination, it must be counted a disappointment despite the first-class digital sound. The Walton coupling seems inappropriate under the circumstances.

In spite of the strong impact from the orchestra, Ferras's reading is not memorable. His tone is small, like Schneiderhan's, and he attempts a classical reading, but there the comparison ends. The first movement is cool, although gracious, and even though the second subject of the slow movement is played with very considerable tension it does not convey the quality of magic that Schneiderhan finds. The overtures come from Karajan's outstanding survey of the mid-1960s, but they are also available separately as a set.

The coupling of the Beethoven and Mendelssohn *Concertos* is surprisingly rare, and Maria Bachmann's disc on this mid-priced Classic fM label, very well recorded, is to be welcomed. It offers performances of both concertos which consistently display her exceptionally sweet, pure tone and flawless technique. Her performance of the Beethoven is meticulous as an interpretation, but, when her principal teacher was Ivan Galamian, with whom Kyung Wha Chung and Pinchas Zukerman (among others) also studied, it is surprising that its very purity and directness and its lack of idiosyncrasy make the result rather bland, too easy, hardly magnetic. So the meditative moments, whether in the first movement or the slow movement, for all their sweetness lack inner tension, and the finale, bold and fresh, lacks the excitement of a genuine performance.

(i) *Violin concerto in D, Op. 61;* (ii) *Triple concerto in C, Op. 56.*
(M) **(*) Sony Stern Edition I SM2K 66941 (2) [S2K 66941]. Isaac Stern, with (i) NYPO, Barenboim; (ii) Leonard Rose, Eugene Istomin, Phd. O, Ormandy – BRAHMS: *Concertos*. **(*)

It was a pity that Sony chose Stern's later recording of the *Violin concerto* with Barenboim, instead of his earlier version which showed so readily the intensely creative bond that had been established between Stern and Bernstein in those early years. The account with Barenboim dates from 1975. Stern gives here a characteristically romantic reading but one that is less spontaneous-sounding than his earlier version and, although the sound is fuller, the CBS highlighting gets in the way of an ideal balance. The *Triple concerto*, recorded a decade earlier in 1964, brings a recording from three friends who reveal their personal joy in making music together. Though Stern is undoubtedly the leader of the trio, the dominance over his colleagues is benevolent. Rose's cello solos are so superbly expressive in the slow movement that it acquires a depth beyond its spare proportions, and the finale brings some wonderful springy polacca rhythms that take Beethoven very close to Eastern Europe. Unfortunately the close CBS balance is unflattering to the soloists so that their soft playing is endangered, but the performance as a whole is so compelling that it would take a much more serious recording fault to undermine the listener's attention.

Triple concerto for violin, cello and piano in C, Op. 56.
(M) *** EMI CDM5 66219-2 [id.]. D. Oistrakh, Rostropovich, S. Richter, BPO, Karajan – BRAHMS: *Double concerto*. ***
(B) *** EMI forte (SIS) CZS5 69331-2 (2) [CDFB 69331]. David Oistrakh, Lev Oborin, Sviatoslav Knushevitzky, Philh. O, Sargent – BRAHMS: *Double concerto;* MOZART: *Violin concerto No. 3;* PROKOFIEV: *Violin concerto No. 2*. ***
(BB) *** CfP Silver Double Dig. CDCFPSD 4775 (2). Zimmermann, Cohen, Manz, ECO, Saraste – DVORAK: *Cello concerto;* ELGAR: *Cello concerto;* TCHAIKOVSKY: *Variations on a rococo theme*. ***
(B) *** Carlton IMP Classics Dig. 30367 0091-2 [(M) id. import]. Trio Zingara, ECO, Heath – BOCCHERINI: *Concerto No. 7*. ***

(i) *Triple concerto, Op. 56. Overtures: King Stephen, Op. 117; Leonora No. 3, Op. 72b; The Ruins of Athens, Op. 113.*
(M) **(*) Beethoven Edition DG 447 907-2 [id.]. (i) Mutter, Ma, Zeltser; BPO, Karajan.

(i) *Triple concerto, Op. 56;* (ii) *Symphony No. 10: First movement* (realized & completed Cooper).
(M) *** Chandos Dig. CHAN 6501 [id.]. (i) Kalichstein–Laredo–Robinson Trio, ECO, Gibson; (ii) CBSO, Weller.

The star-studded cast on the EMI recording makes a breathtaking line-up. This is warm, expansive music-making that confirms even more clearly than before the strength of the piece. The resonant recording suffers from loss of focus in some climaxes, but this is not too serious. The new transfer is remarkably vivid and has firmed up the orchestral tuttis most satisfactorily. Now recoupled with a similarly commanding account of the Brahms *Double concerto*, this is an irresistible mid-priced bargain.

The earlier EMI recording, also featuring distinguished Russian soloists, dates from the early days of stereo, yet the sound is excellent for its period and the balance (with Walter Legge producing) perhaps the most successful this concerto has received in the recording studio. Sargent does not direct the proceedings with Karajan's flair, but he is authoritative and musical, and his soloists make a good team as well as displaying plenty of individual personality. The slow movement is strikingly eloquent. On EMI's two-for-the-price-of-one forte label, this concertante collection is highly recommendable.

On Classics for Pleasure, with first-rate modern digital recording and with Robert Cohen leading an excellent team of prize-winning young soloists (his solo in the slow movement is superb), this makes an outstanding bargain version, keenly competitive with almost any full-priced issue, if not always as elegantly pointed as some. Jukka-Pekka Saraste and the ECO provide a lively, understanding accompaniment and the performance has splendid spontaneity throughout, with the finale sparkling in its sense of occasion. The recording is exceptionally well balanced, with most of the problems solved: the soloists forward, but not exaggeratedly so, and the orchestral backing given fine impact within the convincing acoustics of London's Henry Wood Hall. Coupled with three outstanding performances by Cohen, this is among the finest of these very economically priced Silver Doubles.

The 1984 Chandos version of the *Triple concerto* with three young American soloists is exceptionally well recorded. Sharon Robinson, the cellist, takes the lead with pure tone and fine intonation, though both her partners are by nature more forceful artists. A clean-cut, often refreshing view of the work, it is now reissued coupled with Weller's strong version of Barry Cooper's completion of the first movement of Beethoven's projected *Tenth Symphony*, also very well recorded.

On Carlton, Felix Schmidt, who is also the cello soloist in the Boccherini, plays with consistently beautiful, firm and clean tone, well matched by his two partners, creating the illusion of live performance, full of bounce and vigour. At bargain price, in full and vivid digital sound, it makes an excellent recommendation.

After the formidable crescendo within Karajan's very positive opening tutti, the soloists seem rather small-scale. But there are benefits from the unity brought by the conductor when each of the young players has a positive contribution to make, no less effectively when the recording balance for once in this work does not favour the solo instruments unduly. Yo-Yo Ma's playing is not immaculate, and he does not dominate each thematic statement, but the urgency, spontaneity and – in the slow movement – the depth of expressiveness make for an enjoyable version, well recorded. Throughout the overtures one cannot but marvel at the superlative playing of the Berlin Philharmonic Orchestra, without a suggestion of routine in pieces that must be almost over-familiar, and this applies especially to *Leonora No. 3* with its electrifying coda.

12 Contredanses, WoO 14; 12 German dances, WoO 8; 12 Minuets, WoO 7; 11 Mödlinger dances, WoO 17.
(BB) *** Naxos 8.550433 [id.]. Capella Istropolitana, Oliver Dohnányi.

It is always a delight to catch Beethoven relaxing and showing how warmly he felt towards the Viennese background in which he lived. The excellent Capella Istropolitana group used for the recording seems to be of exactly the right size, and they play the music with light rhythmic feeling, yet with plenty of spirit. Dipped into, this will give pleasure.

The Creatures of Prometheus: Overture and ballet music, Op. 43 (complete).
(BB) *** Naxos Dig. 8.553404 [id.]. Melbourne SO, Michael Halász.
(M) *** Beethoven Edition DG Dig. 447 911-2 [id.]. Orpheus CO.

The Naxos issue provides an excellent version at bargain price of Beethoven's bright and original score. The playing is neat and fresh with rhythms well pointed. Though the string sound is at times a little cloudy, such dramatic passages as the military trumpets and timpani of the *Allegro con brio* (No. 8) are very well caught, bringing out the panache of the playing. In the big *Adagio* (No. 5) the important cello solo (as well as those for wind and harp) reflects the quality of the Melbourne players.

The very talented conductorless Orpheus Chamber Orchestra plays most stylishly, helped by bright, clean recording, and this makes an equally recommendable alternative version.

OVERTURES

Overtures: The Consecration of the house, Op. 124; Coriolan, Op. 62; The Creatures of Prometheus, Op. 43; Egmont, Op. 84; Fidelio, Op. 72c; King Stephen, Op. 117; Leonora Nos. 1–3, Opp. 138; 72a; 72b; The Ruins of Athens, Op. 113; Zur Namensfeier, Op. 115.
(M) *** DG (IMS) 427 256-2 (2) [id.]. BPO, Karajan.

Karajan's set of overtures was recorded in the middle and late 1960s. They are impressive performances that have stood the test of time. They show an imposing command of structure and detail as well as the customary virtuosity one expects from this conductor and the Berlin Philharmonic. The sound is fresh and bright.

(i) Overtures: *The Consecration of the house, Op. 124; Coriolan, Op. 62; The Creatures of Prometheus, Op. 43; Egmont, Op. 84; Fidelio, Op. 72c; King Stephen, Op. 117; Leonora Nos. 1–3, Opp. 138, 72 a–b; The Ruins of Athens, Op. 113; Zur Namensfeier, Op. 115;* (ii) *12 Contredanses, WoO 14; 12 German dances, WoO 8; 12 Minuets, WoO 7.*
(B) *** Ph. Duo 438 706-2 (2) [id.]. (i) Leipzig GO, Masur; (ii) ASMF, Marriner.

Masur's performances of the *Overtures* are more direct than those of Karajan and they are wholly satisfying in their strong motivation and lack of mannerism. The Philips recording from the early 1970s is of high quality, and the remastering has enhanced its vividness and impact, although the characteristic Leipzig resonance remains. To complete the second CD, Marriner and the Academy offer a splendid foil with the dance music. Even as a composer of light music Beethoven was a master, and this collection, beautifully played and recorded (in 1978), can be equally warmly recommended though, again, the acoustic is perhaps slightly over-resonant.

Overtures: The Consecration of the house, Op. 124; Coriolan, Op. 62; The Creatures of Prometheus, Op. 43; Egmont, Op. 84; Fidelio, Op. 72c; Leonora No. 3, Op. 72b; The Ruins of Athens, Op. 113.
(BB) ** Naxos Dig. 8.550072 [id.]. Slovak PO, Stephen Gunzenhauser.

This was one of Naxos's first recordings in Bratislava, and the Philharmonic Hall is made to sound too reverberant, notably at the very start of the first overture on the disc, *Fidelio*. The other items are affected in varying degrees, but the tension of the performances is never in doubt so that, even with this reservation, such a generous collection of seven overtures in vigorous interpretations, well played, makes an attractive bargain.

Overtures: *Coriolan; Creatures of Prometheus; Egmont; Fidelio; Leonora No. 1; Leonora No. 3; The Ruins of Athens.*
(BB) *** RCA Navigator 74321 21281-2. Bamberg SO, Eugen Jochum.

Not surprisingly, Jochum provides a superb collection of overtures, naturally spontaneous and full of warmth and drama. The finest performance of all is *Leonora No. 3*, which makes a thrilling end to the programme. The Bamberg Symphony Orchestra are in excellent form and the recording has a full, spacious acoustic with a natural brilliance. A real bargain.

Overtures: *Coriolan, Op. 62; Leonore No. 2, Op. 72.*
(M) (***) EMI mono CHS5 65513-2 (3) [ZHC 65513]. BPO or VPO, Furtwängler – BRAHMS: *Symphonies Nos. 1–4* etc. (**(*))

These studio recordings of Beethoven overtures, the one from Vienna in 1947, the other from Berlin in 1954, make a good supplement to Furtwängler's Brahms cycle, with Vienna mellower-sounding than Berlin, but both less harshly recorded than on the Brahms broadcasts.

SYMPHONIES

Symphonies Nos. 1–9; 10 (realized Dr Barry Cooper): *1st movt.*
(M) *** Chandos CHAN 7042 (5) [id.]. CBSO, Weller (with Barstow, Finnie, Rendall, Tomlinson, CBSO Ch. in *No. 9*).

Symphonies Nos. 1–9.
(B) *** EMI CfP Dig. CDBOXLVB 1 (5) [(M) id.]. RLPO, Sir Charles Mackerras (with Joan Rodgers, Della Jones, Peter Bronder, Bryn Terfel, RLPO Ch. in *No. 9*).
(B) *** RCA Dig. 74321 20277-2 (5). N. German RSO, Günter Wand (with Wiens, Hartwig, Lewis, Hermann, combined Ch. from Hamburg State Op. and N. German R. in *No. 9*).
(B) *** DG 429 036-2 (5) [id.]. BPO, Karajan (with Janowitz, Rössel-Majdan, Kmentt, Berry, V. Singverein in *No. 9*).
(M) (**(*)) EMI mono CHS7 63606-2 (5) [CDHE 63606]. VPO or Stockholm PO, Furtwängler, (with soloists & Ch. in *No. 9*).
(BB) ** RCA Navigator 74321 30365-2 (5). Boston SO, Erich Leinsdorf (with Jane Marsh, Josephine Veasey, Plácido Domingo, Sherrill Milnes, Pro Musica Ch., New England Conservatory Ch. in *No. 9*).

Symphonies Nos. 1-9; Overtures: Coriolan; Egmont.
(B) **(*) O-L Dig. 452 551-2 (5) [(M) id. import]. AAM, Hogwood (with Augér, Robbin, Rolfe Johnson, Reinhardt, London Symphony Ch. in *No. 9*).

Symphonies Nos 1–9; Overtures: Coriolan; Egmont; Leonora No. 3.
(B) **(*) Decca 430 792-2 (6) [(M) id. import]. Chicago SO, Solti (with Lorengar, Minton, Burrows, Talvela, Chicago Ch. in *No. 9*).

Symphonies Nos. 1–9; Overtures: Creatures of Prometheus; Egmont; Fidelio.
(BB) *** Royal Classics HR 703732 (5) [(B) id.]. BPO, Cluytens (with Brouwenstijn, Kerstin Meyer, Nicolai Gedda, Frederick Guthrie, St Hedwig's Cathedral Ch. in *No. 9*).

Symphonies Nos. 1–9; Overtures: Egmont; Fidelio; King Stephen.
(M) **(*) Sony SB5K 48396 (5) [S5K 48396]. Cleveland O, George Szell (with Addison, Hobson, Lewis, Bell, Cleveland Ch. in *No. 9*).
(M) ** Sony SX5K 64201 (5) [S5K 64201]. NYPO, Bernstein (with Arroyo, Sarfaty, de Virgilio, Scott, Juilliard Ch. in *No. 9*).

Symphonies Nos. 1–9; Overture Leonora No. 3.
(M) (***) RCA mono GD 60324 (5) [60324-2-RG]. NBC SO, Toscanini (with Farrell, Merriman, Peerce, Scott, Shaw Chorale in *No. 9*).

Sir Charles Mackerras's Beethoven cycle is among the most recommendable of all at any price, beautifully recorded and interpretatively refreshing, in a refined way steering a satisfying mid-course between traditional and period performance. So the brass have a satisfying braying roundness and the timpani echo period practice not only in the sharp attack (presumably with hard sticks) but also in their prominent balance, as in the finale of No. 5. Unlike many other cycles, this was not completed quickly, and that may well have added to the freshness of manner, with the last of the five discs (coupling Nos. 2 and 8) as electrifying as the first to be issued, No. 9. Speeds are on the fast side, but it is a measure of Mackerras's mastery that rhythms are always beautifully sprung without any hint of breathlessness and with consistently refined detail.

Wand's digital set with the North German Radio Orchestra, recorded between 1985 and 1988, makes another first-class bargain choice, and indeed is thoroughly recommendable irrespective of cost, offering performances without idiosyncrasy yet full of character that are consistently satisfying to live with. There is a directness about Wand's approach to Beethoven, both early and mature, which is the opposite of dull or stuffy. Throughout the orchestral playing is of the highest quality and the recording is superb, both clean and atmospheric, and admirably transparent (witness the very opening of the first movement of No. 9). The *First Symphony* is strikingly fresh, with briskly vivacious allegros matched by those in the *Fourth*, which is particularly attractive and has splendid rhythmic bounce. No. 2 and the vigorous No. 8 have hardly less vitality, while slow movements have a simple eloquence and warmth that are most satisfying. Wand is generous with exposition repeats. In the *Seventh* – with the horns beautifully balanced in textures both clear and full-bodied – every single repeat is observed; yet, although tempi are relatively steady, the propulsion remains unflagging from first to last. The *Eroica* is admirably paced, a strong reading with plenty of underlying lyrical feeling, and again the horns are impressive in the Trio of the Scherzo and in the joyous finale. The *Pastoral*, taken rather steadily, does not have a very resonant bass, but the cello line is full and warm and the finale radiant. It is far preferable to the Karajan account in his 1961–2 analogue set and, while at times those performances may have a more dramatic edge, there is no lack of urgency and adrenalin flow with Wand; and the added fullness and naturalness of the RCA recording are especially telling in the even-numbered symphonies. The *Fifth* makes a powerful statement and, with its fine slow movement (bringing a neat coda to lead to the Scherzo) and compulsive finale, can be mentioned alongside Giulini's Los Angeles version – see below. The whole series is capped by a powerful account of the *Ninth* with weight and rhythmic bite in equal measure and here, like the *Eroica*, the *Adagio* is movingly intense. The finale is led by a fine team of soloists with the tenor, Keith Lewis, appealingly ardent and the soprano, Edith Wiens, notably secure in her big moment. The combined choruses of North German Radio and Hamburg State Opera, very effectively balanced, sing with fervour, and after Wand's spacious broadening at the centre of the movement the closing pages bring a thrilling culmination. You can't better this if you want a complete set of the Beethoven symphonies played on modern instruments. RCA have now made Wand's discs available separately at mid-price: *Symphonies Nos. 1* and *6* (74321 20278-2); *Symphonies Nos. 2* and *7* (74321 20279-2); *Symphonies Nos. 3* and *8* (74321 20280-2); *Symphonies Nos. 4–5* (74321 20281-2); *Symphony No. 9* (74321 20282-2).

Of Karajan's four recorded cycles, the 1961–2 set is the most consistent and in many ways the most compelling, combining high polish with a biting sense of urgency and spontaneity. There is one major disappointment, in the over-taut reading of the *Pastoral*, which in addition omits the vital repeat in the scherzo. Otherwise these are incandescent performances, superbly played. On CD the sound is still excellent, the best-balanced in any of his Beethoven series and on five CDs at bargain price, this makes outstanding value for money.

Walter Weller's Beethoven cycle for Chandos is by far his finest achievement on record. Although this is the City of Birmingham Symphony Orchestra, there is a warm, refined, Viennese quality in the playing and interpretation, to remind you that this conductor started his career as concertmaster of the Vienna Philharmonic. The Chandos sound is full and glowing to match, the best to date given to any conductor in a collected Beethoven cycle. Now reissued at medium price and still including Barry Cooper's realization of the *Tenth Symphony*, though now without the rehearsals and the overtures, this set represents even better value for money.

Recorded between 1957 and 1960, the Cluytens set offers excellent traditional readings, very well played and recorded in full, open recording which, thanks to the warm acoustic, still sounds very well indeed as transferred in Holland. Cluytens's reading of the *Pastoral* was always very highly regarded, and it fully deserves its high reputation, but the other performances in their way are comparably impressive, weighty, often at relatively broad speeds, but with resilient rhythms. At super-bargain price an excellent recommendation.

Hogwood's set with the Academy of Ancient Music now reappears in a five-disc bargain box and thus, in terms of economy, upstages Norrington, whose competing recordings have been reissued separately at mid-price. While Gardiner remains the prime recommendation for a Beethoven cycle on period instruments,

Hogwood's set makes the safest recommendation in the lower price category. It is the most vividly recorded, with the keenest sense of presence and, above all, the sound adds appropriate weight to the *Ninth*, with the London Symphony Chorus fuller and more vivid than rival choirs for Norrington and Goodman. Hogwood also has the finest quartet of soloists, though in the first movement he is too rigid. Like his rivals, Hogwood has taken note of Beethoven's metronome markings, but he applies them rather less consistently. His pointing of rhythms is not always as alert or imaginative as that of his direct rivals; as a whole, the cycle may lack something in individual moments of insight but, with clean and generally well-disciplined playing, it is consistently satisfying.

Norrington's determination to observe Beethoven's metronome markings regularly leads to refreshing results, though some of the more extreme speeds come to sound wilful, especially in the *Choral Symphony* where the slow movement becomes a sweet interlude rather than a meditation, far shorter than the other movements. The male soloists, too, leave much to be desired. Hogwood is to be preferred here, as he is in the *Pastoral*, although Norrington scores in the *Eroica*, a very convincing and powerful performance. The recording, made in Abbey Road, is faithful and well balanced, though not always as full and immediate as it might be.

Szell's compellingly strong, direct view of Beethoven brings much to stimulate. The marvellously polished and always responsive Cleveland playing never brings a suspicion of routine, but reservations must be made about the close CBS sound-balance which prevents a real pianissimo from registering, even though the ear readily senses when the orchestra is playing gently.

The *Eroica* in Bernstein's earlier, New York cycle of the Beethoven symphonies was a mould-breaking interpretation, with a fast speed for the first movement made to sound fresh and exhilarating. The other symphonies too are given high-voltage performances, strong and purposeful, if occasionally self-indulgent; but the recordings are relatively coarse and lacking in contrast. The finer performances include No. 2 (where the orchestra play as if their very lives depended upon it) and No. 8, an interpretation with considerable sweep and genuine stature. No. 4 is also impressive; though tempi are on the brisk side, the playing pulsates with highly disciplined energy. Yet there is a loss of mystery at the opening. The *Pastoral* is admirably free of undue expressive vehemence; at the same time there is not the subtlety or richness of detail that one finds in the finest readings. The *Seventh* is characteristically vital, but only in the *Eroica* does the New York version outshine Bernstein's later readings for DG. However, the *Fifth* is also one of the finest of the earlier cycle. It is a strong, dramatic reading, not quite as distinguished as the *Eroica*, but as concentrated and vital as the *Eighth*. The *Ninth* is by no means to be dismissed, with a finely shaped first movement which has genuine breadth and eloquence. However, many will find the Scherzo too frenetic: it must be one of the fastest on record. The slow movement has considerable warmth, but not quite enough inwardness and repose; but the finale is dramatic and intense, with some fine contributions from the soloists and chorus, the latter quite well caught by the CBS engineers. The CD transfers make the most of the original masters, but the quality cannot match the later, DG recordings.

Solti's epic first cycle, recorded in the mid-1970s with his own Chicago orchestra, has a firm centrality to it, following the outstandingly successful version of the *Ninth* with which he started the series. The performance of the *Eroica* has comparable qualities, with expansive, steady tempi and a dedicated, hushed account of the slow movement. Here and elsewhere Solti shows a willingness to relax, as well as to press dramatically forward, and there is plenty of sunshine in the even-numbered symphonies, though Nos. 1 and 8 are arguably too weighty in their tone of voice. For the very first time on record, every repeat was observed throughout, but this means that the *Ninth* has its first movement on the fifth disc and the rest on the sixth. The recordings were made between 1972 and 1974 in three different venues (including the Sofiensaal in Vienna for Nos. 6 and 7). The CD transfers bring an admirable consistency, with plenty of weight in the bass balancing the bright top register, and with an open acoustic allowing plenty of detail. Balance in the finale of No. 9 rather favours the orchestra, but not distractingly so. At bargain price Solti admirers should not miss this set, particularly as these performances are generally more satisfying than his later, digital series.

By unearthing a live recording of No. 2, made in the Royal Albert Hall in 1948, and borrowing a radio recording of No. 8 made in Stockholm, EMI managed to put together a complete Furtwängler cycle, and very impressive it is interpretatively. The sound of those two ad hoc recordings may be very rough indeed, with heavy background noise, but the performances – with one or two oddities – are electrifying. No. 9 comes in the dedicated performance given at Bayreuth in 1951, uniquely historic, but the others are EMI's studio versions, not always as inspired as Furtwängler's live performances but still magnetic and, with generally well-balanced mono sound, very well transferred.

Erich Leinsdorf recorded his cycle of Beethoven symphonies between 1962 and 1969. The first disc, coupling the *First* and *Seventh Symphonies*, immediately demonstrates his interpretative style. There is no doubting the polish and commitment of the Boston orchestra's playing, but the hard-driven first-movement allegros of Nos. 1, 2 and 4, though generating a high voltage, also bring fierceness and a very literal rhythmic feeling, without a compensating sense of relaxation and warmth in slow movements. Indeed, in the *Fourth* Leinsdorf gives a curiously pedantic impression in the first movement, as though he is conducting the quavers, and the stodgy accompaniment to the slow movement's great melody is unappealing. The first movement of the *Fifth* is bold but square, even if the finale erupts powerfully. The *Pastoral Symphony* is beautifully played (like the slow movement of the *Fifth*) but lacks charm, and the *Eighth* is without geniality. The *Choral Symphony* epitomizes Leinsdorf's approach to the cycle overall: the opening two movements are powerful and sharply articulated, the rhythmic drive compelling if unrelenting. The atmosphere of the *Adagio* brings repose but remains cool. The introduction of the finale then erupts very dramatically and Leinsdorf presses on forcefully. He has a well-matched and distinguished team of soloists – Jane Marsh, Josephine Veasey, Plácido Domingo and Sherrill Milnes – who blend well even under pressure. The soprano's big moment is managed confidently. The combined Pro Musica and New England Conservatory Chorus (recorded with fine clarity) respond with great vigour to the conductor's energetic drive. The close of the symphony is pressed onwards to the point of frenzy, and no one could fail to be excited by the coda. Overall, Leinsdorf's lack of poise and humanity means that his readings have one dimension missing, but the orchestra consistently plays superbly. The Boston acoustic adds weight and resonance to the sound which, in these excellent CD transfers, remains both clear and full.

The NBC Toscanini versions are faster and more tense than the earlier Beethoven readings that he committed to records, but they are far from rigid or unloving, and they are crowned by performances of breathtaking power in the *Eroica* and the *Ninth*. Listening to this Beethoven is never a relaxing experience, but it is a uniquely involving one.

Symphonies Nos. 1–4.
(B) *** Ph. Duo 454 032-2 (2) [id.]. Leipzig GO, Kurt Masur.

Symphonies Nos. 5–8.
(B) ** Ph. Duo 454 035-2 (2) [id.]. Leipzig GO, Masur.

(i) *Symphony No. 9 (Choral);* (ii) *Overtures: Consecration of the house; Fidelio; Leonora Nos. 1–3;* (iii) *Choral Fantasia, Op. 80.*
(B) *(*) Ph. Duo 454 038-2 (2) [id.]. (i) Tomowa-Sintow, Burmeister, Schreier, Adam and Ch.; (i–ii) Leipzig GO, Masur; (iii) Brendel, LPO, Haitink.

Kurt Masur's earlier, analogue Beethoven cycle has a very great deal to recommend it. In sheer naturalness of utterance, unforced expressiveness and the superlatively disciplined response of the orchestral playing, the Gewandhaus set has a good deal to offer. The first two symphonies are attractively fresh, with the slow movement of the *Second* memorable. The *Eroica* is uncommonly fine, particularly its nobly paced slow movement which is totally free of excessive emphasis in expression. In the *Fourth Symphony* Masur is particularly successful, and the Gewandhaus Orchestra respond with marvellously alert playing. In the slow movement Masur brings great imagination and poetry to his reading; the homogeneous, cultured orchestral sound of the Gewandhaus Orchestra and its rhythmic resilience and vitality are in themselves a source of pleasure. So the first of these three Duos is certainly recommendable. However, neither the *Fifth* nor the *Pastoral* matches the finest in the catalogue: the former does not have the blazing intensity of Carlos Kleiber and the latter does not eclipse Boehm, Ashkenazy or, indeed, Klemperer. Nor can one say that the *Choral Symphony* has the stature of Karajan. It is a spacious, well-proportioned and noble account, well worth hearing; but competition is stiff and other versions are more strongly characterized. Thus the last of the Duo sets is the least recommendable, despite the inclusion of Haitink's fine account with Brendel of the *Choral Fantasia*.

(i) *Symphonies Nos. 1–9. Overtures: Consecration of the house; Coriolan; Creatures of Prometheus; Egmont; Fidelio; King Stephen; Leonora No. 2; The ruins of Athens;* (ii) *Missa solemnis.*
(BB) **(*) Nimbus Dig. NI 1760 (7) [(B) id.]. Hanover Band, (i) cond. Roy Goodman or Monica Huggett; with Eiddwen Harrhy, Jean Bailey, Andrew Murgatroyd, Michael George, Oslo Cathedral Ch. in *No. 9*; (ii) Marianne Hirsti, Carolyn Watkinson, Murgatroyd, George, Oslo Cathedral Ch., cond. Terje Kvam.

Those wanting period-instrument performances of this repertoire will find these pioneering Hanover Band performances well worth considering, when the overall package is so inexpensive. Though the performances are variable, the big challenges are taken splendidly: these readings convey the fire and exuberance of live performance. In characteristic Nimbus manner, the recordings are set in a reverberant acoustic, which means that the woodwind sometimes appear a little disembodied; but the sound is warm and undistracting. Monica Huggett directs Nos. 1, 2 and 5; Roy Goodman Nos. 3, 4 and 7–9. In Nos. 1 and 2, the string-playing is scrawnier than it later became and the sound has less body. No. 5, also recorded early, is different: a strong and biting performance, full of energy and imagination. In the later recordings Goodman draws consistently fresh, individual readings from his team, with rhythms well sprung in exhilarating *allegros*. Even more remarkable is the way he can convey hushed intensity in slow movements, even when, following Beethoven's metronome markings, his speeds are much faster than we are used to. That is true also of the slow movement of the *Ninth*, in contrast to Norrington's exploratory version; but also, even more strikingly, of the *Eroica* Funeral march. In the *Allegretto* of No. 7 too, the wistful melancholy of the main theme has rarely been conveyed so touchingly. Consistently the feeling of spontaneity is most winning. The collection of overtures (also shared by the two conductors) is incomplete but is enjoyably full of character. Like the symphonies, they were recorded at different times in the 1980s in conjunction with the Hanover Band's other Beethoven recordings for Nimbus. The playing has plenty of vitality. *Leonora No. 2* is particularly successful, but the lighter works have comparable vigour and sparkle.

This *Missa solemnis*, like the symphonies, was the first ever recording of the work on period instruments and the first to be issued complete on a single CD. The conductor, Terje Kvam, is chorus-master of the Oslo Cathedral Choir and he gives a first-class performance, fresh and gripping. If this is no match for such high-powered conductors as Klemperer and Bernstein in terms of weight and power, the simple intensity of the performance, with period instruments giving extra clarity and bite, brings a scale and manner to make the work seem more liturgical than usual, although the fine chorus ensures that the drama of the writing is also vividly projected. The acoustic is reverberant, but the result is not to muffle but to add to the spaciousness and impact of an account which in its own way is spontaneously memorable. Overall this inexpensive set is both stimulating and rewarding.

Symphonies Nos. 1 in C, Op. 21; 3 in E flat (Eroica); 6 in F (Pastoral); 8 in F, Op. 93.
(B) **(*) Decca Double (IMS) 440 627-2 (2) [id.]. VPO, Pierre Monteux.

Symphonies Nos. 2 in D, Op. 36; 4 in B flat, Op. 60; 5 in C min., Op. 67; 7 in A, Op. 92; Overtures: Egmont; King Stephen.
(B) *** Decca Double (IMS) 443 479-2 (2) [id.]. LSO, Pierre Monteux.

Pierre Monteux, recording for Decca in his last years, did not include the *Choral Symphony* (the company turned to Ansermet and Stokowski instead). But he recorded all the rest, and with distinction. Listening to these performances together as a sequence, the listener discovers the continuing thread of enhancing energy that brings all Monteux's music-making to life, together with consistent imagination in his phrasing and glowing treatment of the detail of slow movements. The Double Decca reissues have been sensibly divided into the performances with the VPO and those with the LSO and thus provide an obvious first choice for those not wanting both sets.

For some reason, the 1960 VPO coupling of Nos. 1 and 8 brings a hint of discoloration in the woodwind. But the ear soon adjusts when in both works Monteux steers an ideal course, neither underestimating the weight nor making the music too heavy. The *Eroica* was the first to be recorded (in 1957) and again it is as masterly as it is individual. The first movement (without exposition repeat) is superbly dramatic – the climax of the development wonderfully built up – and only in the *Funeral march* are there any real reservations. A slower speed would have allowed a greater sense of tragedy; and his oboe soloist is on the flat side, though never beyond tolerance. The early stereo is relatively coarse and does not allow a real pianissimo. The *Pastoral* dates from only a year later, yet the recording is strikingly better, full, warm and vivid. The performance emerges as finer than we had remembered it, even if the VPO were not on the form they were for the *Eroica*.

At the beginning of the 1960s Monteux achieved a special understanding with the players of the LSO, and his 1960 coupling of Nos. 2 and 4 shows this genial rapport to rewarding effect. The performance of No. 2 is essentially light in style, but the alertness of the LSO playing makes it strong and enjoyable. No. 4 is hardly less successful. You have only to listen to the way Monteux leads into the second subject or the way he floats the high violin melody in the slow movement to realize that a master is at work. The finale is exhilaratingly hectic in the fast, flying manner that he tends to adopt in Beethoven finales: it is very exciting when played with such precision. In a hardly less memorable performance of the *Fifth*, the volatile Frenchman plays his part. Where hitherto these Beethoven performances have tended to be straight and direct, here there is not only strength and drive but an element of waywardness. It is a personal reading, but a compelling one in all four movements, with fine articulation from the LSO, unashamedly strong, even aggressive in the finale.

The series is capped by an unforgettable account of the *Seventh Symphony*. Monteux opens with a powerful slow introduction, followed by a hard-driven 6/8 *Allegro* but with the rhythms nicely pointed, and a fast *Allegretto* to recall the famous early mono LP by Erich Kleiber. Then comes a wide speed-change for the trio after the Scherzo and an absolute headlong finale, out-Toscanini-ing Toscanini in its incandescent excitement, with the horns singing out flamboyantly at the close. Throughout, the full, atmospheric recording adds just the right degree of weight, and this Monteux/LSO box offers Beethoven performances as stimulating as any available. This Double Decca is well worth having in its own right.

Symphonies Nos. 1 in C, Op. 21; 2 in D, Op. 36; 3 (Eroica); Overture Coriolan.
(BB) **(*) Carlton LSO Double 30368 001157 (2) [(B) id.]. LSO, Wyn Morris.

Symphonies Nos. (i) *1–2;* (ii) *3 (Eroica);* (i) *Overtures: Coriolan; Fidelio; The Ruins of Athens* (with *Turkish march*).
(B) ** Teldec/Warner Ultima 3984 21335-2 (2). (i) Bamberg SO; (ii) Hamburg State PO; Joseph Keilberth.

This is one of the first of a series of Carlton CD Doubles retailing at just under £10 in which the linking factor is the LSO. In this instance the conductor is also the same, and the results are undoubtedly stimulating. Wyn Morris draws a clear distinction between the two earliest symphonies: the *First*, brightly paced, resilient and strongly classical in feeling; the *Second* clearly looking forward, with a particularly eloquent account of the slow movement, not overlooking its anticipations of the *Pastoral Symphony*. Both first-movement exposition repeats are included. The recording is full-bodied, but the resonance prevents absolute sharpness of detail, and the violins could be sweeter on top. Nevertheless this is a most rewarding pairing. Wyn Morris then conducts a taut reading of the *Eroica*, dark and intense, with allegros consistently urgent, and the LSO responds with both bite and refinement. The *Coriolan overture* is also very successful, and altogether this is excellent value.

Keilberth's performances of the symphonies date from the late 1950s and early 1960s and were first noticed by us in the original (1966) *Penguin Guide to Bargain Records*. He is a sound Beethovenian and his account of the *First Symphony* is strikingly crisp and sprightly. The *Second* is no less vital and the *Eroica* is finest of all: strong, fresh and dramatic. The recordings always sounded full and weighty but suffered from a fierce upper range, which still persists with the remastering for CD, but is tameable. The *Overtures*, which are new to us, are also lively and enjoyable, and the zestful *Turkish march* from *The Ruins of Athens* makes a spirited encore. Anyone buying this inexpensive Double on impulse should not be disappointed.

Symphonies Nos. 1 in C; 2 in D; Overture Coriolan.
(M) *** Bruno Walter Edition: Sony SMK 64460 [id.]. Columbia SO, Bruno Walter.

Bruno Walter's CBS recordings of the Beethoven symphonies now reappear on a series of mid-priced discs as part of the Bruno Walter Edition. They were recorded in 1958/9 in the American Legion Hall in Hollywood, which provided an attractive ambient warmth, while the upper-string timbre remained fresh and lively. The Columbia Symphony was a pick-up orchestra of outstanding musicians whom Walter moulded into a cohesive body of players of some distinction. The most controversial point about his interpretation of the *Second Symphony* is the slow movement, which is taken very slowly indeed, with plenty of rubato. But the rich warmth of the recording makes the effect very involving. For the rest, the speeds are well chosen, with a fairly gentle allegro in the finale which allows the tick-tock accompaniment to the second subject to have a delightful lift to it. On technical grounds this reissue can stand alongside most of the more recent competition, and the remaining hiss is not disturbing.

Symphonies Nos. 1–2 (trans. Liszt).
(M) ** Teldec/Warner Dig. 4509 97952-2 [2292 43661-2]. Cyprien Katsaris (piano).

Although this is less remarkable than Katsaris's recordings of the Liszt transcriptions of the later symphonies, the clarity of the playing illuminates the detail of both works and the performances have plenty of vitality.

Symphonies Nos. 1 in C; 3 in E flat (Eroica), Op. 55.
(B) *** Carlton IMP Dig. 30367 02382 [(M) id.]. Sinfonia Varsovia, Sir Yehudi Menuhin.
(B) *** EMI CfP Dig. CD-CFP 6067 [id.]. RLPO, Mackerras.
(M) **(*) Virgin Veritas/EMI Dig. VM5 61374-2 [CDCFP 61374]. L. Classical Players, Norrington.
(M) (***) RCA mono GD 60252 [60252-2-RG]. NBC SO, Toscanini.
(M) ** Ph. Dig. 454 132-2. Concg. O, Haitink.

The one irritant to Menuhin's performances on Carlton is the welcoming applause that comes before the music begins and also at the close of No. 1, but not before the opening of No. 3. Otherwise these highly musical performances, strong but on a convincing chamber scale, are among the most satisfying available. The opening movement of the *First Symphony* is spacious, but the finale goes with the wind, with articulation often as light as thistledown. The pacing and control of the first movement of the *Eroica* are masterly and the *Funeral march* brings a noble depth of feeling. The wide dynamic range of the playing, so striking here, is equally telling at the opening of the buoyant and vigorous Scherzo. Gorgeous horn playing too. The recording is first class, full-bodied and naturally balanced with a most convincing hall ambience.

Sir Charles Mackerras, as in his other Beethoven readings on the Classics for Pleasure label, consciously seeks to reconcile the new doctrines of period performance with traditional ones; as he says himself, with the collaboration of an orchestra willing to modify tone and technique he succeeds remarkably well, with fast speeds so subtly controlled that there is no sense of haste. The *First* is fresh and alert in a Haydnesque way, while the *Eroica* has ample power, with heightened dynamic contrasts and with the flowing speed for the *Funeral march* still conveying dedication. The horns in the trio of the Scherzo are superb, helped by first-rate recording.

Norrington's Beethoven cycle now reappears on the Virgin label at mid-price, in this case with a new pairing. No. 1 lacks the lively energy of the best of the series, but the *Eroica* is one of the most successful performances. It is consistently even faster than his closest period-performance rivals, yet one quickly forgets any feeling of haste when rhythms are so crisp and supple in their spring, and the great *Funeral march* has natural gravity.

Toscanini's are performances which convey breathtaking power, notably the magnificent account of the *Eroica*, never comfortable but far from rigid or unloving.

Haitink gives strong and straightforward, if not distinctive, readings of both symphonies, beautifully played; but the digital recording, though warm and pleasing, is disconcertingly opaque by modern Concertgebouw standards.

(i) *Symphonies Nos. 1 in C, Op. 21; 3 in E flat, Op. 55; 5 in C min., Op. 67;* (ii) *Overtures: Creatures of Prometheus; Egmont; Fidelio.*
(BB) **(*) EMI Seraphim CES5 68518-2 (2) [CEDB 68518]. (i) Munich PO; (ii) BPO; Rudolf Kempe.

Kempe's performances were recorded over a relatively brief period, and this shows in their merits as well as their limitations. Plainly the Munich orchestra responded to this challenge, producing fresh, spontaneous-sounding playing, not always perfectly disciplined but natural and communicative. Kempe as a Beethovenian believes in letting the music speak for itself at sensitive and unexaggerated tempi, so that even the introduction of No. 1 is weighty. Otherwise the crisp articulation of the Munich woodwind makes for refreshing results in the allegros, with the Munich strings producing sweet tone in the slow movement. Not all the symphonies sound as intense as they might – No. 5, for example. But even here the performance is warmly enjoyable, if not electrifying. Exposition repeats are normally observed, though not in the *Eroica*. Here Kempe takes a spacious view of the first movement. Initially it may sound unexciting, but then (as with Klemperer) the structure builds up strongly and compellingly. The *Funeral march* is subdued and inward, spontaneous-sounding in its concentration up to the hushed distintegration of the main theme. The oboe solos (Kempe himself was an oboist before he became a conductor) are beautiful. Fast speeds and fine articulation in the last two movements, although here the violins lose just a little of their bloom. The overtures feature the Berlin Philharmonic and are very well played indeed. Good value.

Symphonies Nos. 1 in C; 4 in B flat, Op. 60; Egmont overture.
(M) *** DG 419 048-2. BPO, Karajan.

Symphonies Nos. 1 in C; 4 in B flat; Overture Leonora No. 1.
(B) (***) Dutton Lab. mono CDEA 5004 [(M) id.]. BBC SO, Toscanini.

Karajan's 1977 version of No. 1 is exciting, polished and elegant; in No. 4 the balance is closer, exposing every flicker of tremolando. Yet the body and ambience of the recording combine to give a realistic presence, and overall this is very impressive.

The Toscanini recordings were made in London's Queen's Hall in 1937 and 1939, and they remain among the most treasurable Beethoven performances in the Toscanini legacy. All the electricity and concentration are here, yet there is a degree of warmth not often present in his NBC records. The sound too is remarkably good, and the Dutton transfers betray the 78 shellac source only with the slight hint of wow on the woodwind, caused by the pressings not being centred absolutely perfectly; one immediately adjusts to this when the playing has such magnetism. On our copy the cueing for the individual movements of the *Fourth Symphony* was faulty.

Symphonies Nos. 1 in C, Op. 21; 5 in C min., Op. 67.
(B) (**) [EMI Red Line Dig. CDR5 69782]. Phd. O, Muti.

Muti's coupling brings characteristically taut and urgent readings of both symphonies, with early Beethoven treated just as earnestly as if it were from the middle period. The Philadelphia Orchestra plays with the brilliance instilled by Muti; sadly, however, the recording is among the harshest from this source: edgy and aggressive, without much body and with ill-defined focus.

Symphonies Nos. 1 in C; 6 in F (Pastoral), Op. 68.
(M) *** EMI CDM5 66792-2 [id.]. Philh. O, Klemperer.
(M) **(*) DG 447 901-2 [id.]. VPO, Bernstein.
(BB) **(*) Naxos Dig. 8.553474 [id.]. Nicolaus Esterházy Sinfonia, Béla Drahos.

Symphonies Nos. 1 in C; 6 in F (Pastoral), Op. 68; Overture Egmont, Op. 84.
(B) **(*) Sony SBK 46532; *SBT 46532* [id.]. Cleveland O, Szell.

With Klemperer, the slow speeds and heavyweight manner – in principle not apt for No. 1 – may get in the way of some listeners' enjoyment. That said, the compulsion of Klemperer in Beethoven remains strong, with rhythmic pointing consistently preventing stagnation. Moreover Klemperer's account of the *Pastoral* is one of the very finest of all his records and well worth the cost of this disc. The Scherzo may be eccentrically slow but, with superbly dancing rhythms, it could not be more bucolic, and it falls naturally into place within the reading as a whole. The exquisitely phrased slow movement and the final *Shepherd's hymn* bring peaks of beauty, made the more intense by the fine, digital transfer, reinforcing the clarity and fullness of the original sound, with violin-tone amazingly fresh and clean for 1958, although thinner than we would expect today. The woodwind are given an attractive bloom.

Bernstein's second stereo cycle of the Beethoven symphonies was made with the Vienna Philharmonic Orchestra and first released as a set in 1980. Highly dramatic, perceptive, rich in emotion but never sentimental, these performances have a spontaneous quality that stemmed in part from his technique of recording. As in his other records for DG, Bernstein opted to have live performances recorded and then – with some tidying of detail – edited together. Balances are not always perfect, with microphones placed in order to eliminate audience noise, but the results are generally undistracting and the projection is very immediate. In No. 1 the allegros are fast but not hectic, the slow introductions and slow movements carefully moulded but not mannered. In this work the live recording is not ideally clear but is very acceptable. The reading of the *Pastoral* has plenty of character and, with its combination of joy and serenity, is persuasive, even if the performance fails to bite in the *Storm* sequence. There are some inevitable inconsistencies in the sound-balance, which is vivid rather than refined and mellow.

In his projected Beethoven cycle on the Naxos label Drahos offers fresh, spontaneous-sounding performances, beautifully played by a chamber-sized group from Budapest, with recording outstandingly vivid. Plainer and less subtle than the finest versions, these lively, well-sprung performances make excellent bargains.

Szell's dynamic performance of the *First Symphony* makes up for any absence of charm. In the *Pastoral* Szell is subtle in his control of phrasing, for all the firmness of his style. However, it is a pity that the close-up sound robs the slow movement of much of its gentleness and delicacy of atmosphere. The finale, by contrast, is attractively relaxed.

Symphonies Nos. 1; 7 in A, Op. 92.
(BB) **(*) ASV CDQS 6066 [(M) id. import]. N. Sinfonia of England, Richard Hickox.
(BB) **(*) RCA Navigator 74321 29239-2. Boston SO, Erich Leinsdorf.

Hickox's view of both works is unaffected and direct and so gets the best of both worlds: finely detailed yet substantial; and the very lack of idiosyncrasy makes for easy listening. The CD transfer is full and agreeable but provides a rather resonant bass.

Leinsdorf's Beethoven is a bit gruff but is very compelling when the Boston orchestral playing has such polish and character. The *First Symphony* hardly ever smiles, but its vigour and strength clearly look forward to the *Eroica Symphony*. The *Seventh* brings relatively measured but rhythmically strong outer movements which, like the *Allegretto*, generate considerable tension: its conclusion is powerfully positive and really lifts off at the exciting close. The Boston acoustic adds a weighty resonance to the sound, without blurring; indeed these late-1960s recordings are very successful in their clear, full CD transfers. Excellent value.

Symphonies Nos. 2 in D; 5 in C min., Op. 67.
(M) **(*) DG 447 902-2 [id.]. VPO, Bernstein.
(M) **(*) EMI CDM5 66793-2 [id.]. Philh. O, Klemperer.
(B) **(*) Sony SBK 47651; *SBT 47651* [id.]. Cleveland O, George Szell.
(BB) **(*) Naxos 8.553476 [id.]. Nicolaus Esterházy Sinfonia, Béla Drahos.

Bernstein's performance of No. 2 has touches that obviously stemmed from the inspiration of the moment, and the tension rises superbly at the end of the finale. He seems intent on emphasizing how much bigger a symphony this is than No. 1 and, though the ensemble is not always flawless and the recording has a rather boomy bass, the liveness is captivating. For his Vienna version, Bernstein rethought his reading of the *Fifth*, giving it resonance and spaciousness as well as drama. Some of the Toscanini-like tension of his earlier, New York account has evaporated from the first movement, but the warmth and conviction of the whole performance are most persuasive, ending with a blazing account of the finale. Again the recording balance is good, if not ideal.

The new coupling, reissued as part of EMI's 'Klemperer Legacy', emphasizes the consistency of Klemperer's approach to Beethoven, with the *Second Symphony*, like the *First*, sounding the more powerful through weighty treatment. Only in the finale is the result rather too gruff. The *Fifth* is plainly less electric than his earlier, mono version but, with exposition repeats observed in both outer movements, this retains its epic quality. As with the others in this mid-priced series, the new CD transfers bring a clean and natural sound on top and plenty of weight and fullness.

There is some marvellously clean articulation from the strings in the first movement of Szell's No. 2 and the adrenalin runs free; yet here, as in the similarly brilliant account of No. 5, Szell understands the need to give full scope to the lyrical elements.

With the Esterházy Sinfonia, Béla Drahos on Naxos conducts clean-cut readings of both works, with the excellent, well-balanced recording capturing the chamber scale very effectively. In No. 2 few will complain that this is a less dramatic reading than some, easy and sweet in the slow movement, leading to a cheekily youthful account of the finale. In No. 5 the call of fate at the very opening may seem lightweight, with a limited dynamic range there and later, but in the context of a chamber series this is a very viable view, refreshing in its clarity, easily flowing in the middle movements, taut in the outer movements.

Symphonies Nos. 2 in D, Op. 36; 6 in F (Pastoral).
(B) *** Carlton IMP Dig. 30367 02292 [(M) id.]. Sinfonia Varsovia, Sir Yehudi Menuhin.

After the usual opening applause, Menuhin's *Second Symphony* is weighty, mature-sounding, the first movement lacking something in bite though not buoyancy. The *Larghetto* is nobly phrased, the finale vigorous and high-spirited, but by no means frivolous. Alongside the *Choral Symphony*, Menuhin's performance of the *Pastoral* crowns his cycle. The chamber-scale and the combination of warmth and lightness of touch bring a joyous momentum in the first movement, taken briskly but never sounding hurried. Detail is glowing and the bass-line, so important in this symphony, is always firm and full. The *Andante* flows just as a brook should, and the *Peasant merry-making* is brisk and sparkling. The storm then bursts in with great drama, and the heartfelt *Shepherds' thanksgiving* brings a glorious lyrical apotheosis. The fullness of the sound, with a natural, unexaggerated brilliance, adds to the impact of an exceptionally satisfying reading, superbly played.

Symphonies Nos. 2 in D; 7 in A, Op. 92.
(M) *** DG 419 050-2; *419 050-4* [id.]. BPO, Karajan.

In Karajan's *Second*, the firm lines give the necessary strength. The *Seventh* is tense and exciting, with the conductor emphasizing the work's dramatic rather than its dance-like qualities.

Symphonies Nos. 2; 8 in F, Op. 93.
(B) *** EMI CfP Dig. 6068 [(M) id.]. RLPO, Sir Charles Mackerras
(M) *** Virgin Veritas/EMI Dig. VM5 61375-2 [CDM 61375]. L. Classical Players, Norrington.
(BB) **(*) ASV CDQS 5067 [(M) id. import]. N. Sinfonia, Hickox.
(B) **(*) Tring TRP 039. RPO, James Lockhart.

Mackerras rounded off his outstanding Beethoven cycle with performances of these two even-numbered works which bring out the dramatic bite in performances at once refined and full of sharp contrasts. In this music Mackerras's adoption of a manner which with modern instruments takes account of period practice works exceptionally well, with exhilarating results. Recorded sound a degree fuller and more immediate than in the earlier discs of the series.

The coupling of Nos. 2 and 8 was the first of Norrington's Beethoven series and showed the London Classical Players as an authentic group with a distinctive sound, sweeter and truer in the string section than most, generally easier on non-specialist ears. In following Beethoven's own metronome markings for both symphonies the results are exhilarating, never merely breathless, bringing far more than proof of an academic theory.

Richard Hickox directs his chamber-scale orchestra in fresh, warm and relaxed readings of these two even-numbered symphonies. Playing is refined and rhythms resilient. The scale is well established by the slightly backward balance of the modest string section, with the focus rather sharper in No. 8 than in No. 2.

Well-played, sensibly paced and very well-recorded accounts from the RPO under James Lockhart. The electricity of Monteux is missing, but there is an agreeable weight, and the easygoing account of No. 8 is particularly warm and enjoyable. Exposition repeats are observed. Excellent value.

Symphony No. 3 in E flat (Eroica), Op. 55.
(M) (***) RCA mono GD 60271 [60271-2-RG]. NBC SO, Toscanini – MOZART: *Symphony No. 40.* (**)
(M) **(*) DG 447 444-2 [id.]. LAPO, Giulini (with SCHUMANN: *Manfred overture* ***).

Symphony No. 3 (Eroica); Grosse Fuge, Op. 133.
(M) *** EMI CDM5 66793-2 [id.]. Philh. O, Klemperer.

Symphony No. 3 (Eroica); Overtures: Coriolan; Fidelio.
(M) **(*) [RCA 09026 609622]. Chicago SO, Reiner.

Symphony No. 3 (Eroica); Overture Fidelio.
(B) *** Tring TRP 026 [(M) id. import]. RPO, Guenther Herbig.

Symphony No. 3 (Eroica); Overtures: Leonora Nos. 2 & 3.
(M) (***) EMI mono CDM7 63855-2 [id.]. Philh. O, Klemperer.

Symphony No. 3 (Eroica); Overture: Leonora No. 3.
(M) **(*) DG 419 049-2 [id.]. BPO, Karajan.

The digital remastering of Klemperer's spacious 1961 version of the *Eroica* weightily reinforces its magnificence, keenly concentrated to sustain speeds slower than in his earlier, mono account. That alternative, mono version by Klemperer was among the very first records he made with the Philharmonia for EMI, but the success of these first Beethoven works revealed his full strength. This *Eroica* is one of his supreme achievements. The *Grosse Fuge* sounds impressively monolithic.

Although he does not include the first-movement exposition repeat, Guenther Herbig's 1994 recording of the *Eroica* with the RPO is most compelling, strong and aptly paced, and with the concentration of the playing at a high level throughout. The climax of the *Funeral march* has real emotional intensity and, after an exhilarating Scherzo with superb horn-playing, the genial finale caps the performance with the horns again impressive in a thrilling coda. The RPO are clearly on their toes and begin the CD with a fresh and vital account of the *Fidelio overture*. With full, brilliant, digital sound, naturally balanced in a concert-hall acoustic, this is very highly recommendable in the lowest price-range.

Toscanini's version has a far keener emotional intensity than the studio recording which appeared earlier as part of his Beethoven cycle in the BMG Toscanini series. Toscanini had a special insight into this of all Beethoven's symphonies, making this disc a valuable addition to his discography.

Not everyone will identify readily with the fiery intensity of fast tempi in the outer movements of Karajan's 1977 performance, even if this version includes a more intense account of the *Funeral march* than in earlier recordings. A point to consider is the absence of the exposition repeat in the first movement; but this is among the most polished as well as the most dramatic accounts available. An exciting performance of *Leonora No. 3* makes a fairly generous bonus. The sound, though possessing ample fullness and weight, is well defined and clean.

Reiner's is undoubtedly a compulsive *Eroica*, big-boned and spectacular in its epic qualities, but the first movement does not maintain an unerring single sweep forward, and the *Funeral march* is majestic and not greatly touched by tragedy. Characteristically full, late-1950s Chicago sound.

Giulini's refined and individual reading, with its almost eccentrically measured view of the first movement, was an early product of his love affair with the Los Angeles orchestra. Even though it is by no means a general recommendation among recordings of the *Eroica*, there is some justification for its reissue in DG's series of 'Legendary' Originals, for it remains an extraordinary example of a conductor transforming an orchestra's usual character, and it can also be valued for its new revelations. The coupling, an excellent performance of Schumann's *Manfred overture*, was originally offered as a makeweight for the *Rhenish Symphony*, which is now much more generously re-coupled.

Symphony No. 3 (Eroica) (trans. Liszt); *Eroica variations, Op. 35.*
(M) ** Teldec/Warner Dig. 4509 97953-2 [2292 43661-2]. Cyprien Katsaris (piano).

This is one of the less impressive of the Katsaris series of Liszt's remarkable transcriptions. The first movement of the *Eroica* is heavily rhetorical and the *Marcia funèbre* sounds comparatively uninvolved. The rest of the work is more impressive, as are the appropriately coupled *Variations*.

Symphonies Nos. 3 (Eroica); 8 in F, Op. 93.
(M) **(*) Bruno Walter Edition: Sony SMK 64461 [id.]. Columbia SO, Bruno Walter.
(M) (***) RCA mono GD 60269 [60269-2-RG]. NBC SO, Toscanini.
(B) **(*) Sony SBK 46328; *SBT 46328* [id.]. Cleveland O, Szell.
(M) **(*) DG 447 903-2 [id.]. VPO, Bernstein.
(BB) **(*) Naxos Dig. 8.553475 [id.]. Nicolaus Esterházy Sinfonia, Béla Drahos.

It is a pleasure to turn from other accounts of the *Eroica* and hear as beautiful and sympathetic a performance as Walter's. He is not monumental in the different ways of Klemperer and, before him, Toscanini; but this interpretation has all the ripeness of the best of Walter's work with the Vienna Philharmonic Orchestra between the wars. The digitally remastered recording has all the amplitude one needs for such a reading: its expansive qualities bring rich horns as well as full-bodied strings. The coupled *Eighth* has comparatively slow speeds, especially in the inner movements. The first goes well enough, but after that the pacing hampers the sustaining of any high degree of intensity, although the reading is of course interesting and sympathetic.

Toscanini's 1939 recording of the *Eroica*, made live, brings one of the most compelling recordings he ever made. Not only does he conduct at white heat, he is far more flexible in his musical manners than he became later, both moulding melodic lines with Italianate warmth and allowing himself far freer rubato. The *Eighth* is hard-driven and on the biggest scale (Toscanini, exceptionally for the days of 78s, observes the exposition repeat in the first movement). Yet this is a performance which sustains a satisfying power, far more persuasive in rhythm and phrasing than Toscanini's later NBC version.

Szell's is a fine performance in the Toscanini tradition, hard-driven and dramatic. The digital remastering is very successful: the sound is firm, full and brilliant. The performance of the *Eighth* is also a compelling one. The first-movement repeat is taken and the performance is not over-driven.

Bernstein's 1980 Vienna Philharmonic recording of the *Eroica* brings a degree of disappointment compared with his earlier (1964) Sony record (SMK 47514), which is electrically intense. There is less incandescence in the first movement, after a very powerful emphasis for the opening chords. The first-movement exposition repeat is still observed and this is undoubtedly a strong and dramatic reading, with a dedicated account of the *Funeral march*. This emerges as more clearly a march than before, yet is very measured indeed; but its intensity is enhanced by the presence of an audience. The *Eighth* is both strong (first-movement exposition repeat again included) and genial, coming out not so much a 'little' symphony as a jovial yet commanding one, with a bouncing, neatly pointed *Allegretto*, a mellow Minuet and a vigorous though not overdriven finale with a crisp, positive coda.

Drahos's performances on Naxos with his excellent chamber orchestra from Budapest benefit greatly from the superb sound, clearer and with more vivid presence than on many other recent discs. The performances have the same qualities of freshness and spontaneity that mark the other initial disc in the series, making a good bargain, even if there are more searching readings of the *Eroica*.

Symphonies Nos. 3 (Eroica); (i) *9 in D min. (Choral).* Overtures: *Coriolan; Creatures of Prometheus; Egmont.*
(B) ** DG Double (IMS) 437 368-2 (2) [id.]. VPO, Karl Boehm, (i) with Gwyneth Jones, Troyanos, Thomas, Ridderbusch, V. State Op. Konzertvereinigung.

Except in the *Funeral march*, Boehm was not at his finest in his VPO *Eroica*, made in the early 1970s. His Berlin Philharmonic version, recorded a decade earlier, had greater spontaneity. The Vienna version has sanity and good sense, but its sobriety undermines the intensity of the playing. But the *Funeral march*, without undue moulding of phrase, is still deeply devotional. The *Ninth* is a good deal more successful, although again Boehm was to record a further, even more intense (digital) version just before he died. Yet this Vienna performance made a fine culmination to his earlier cycle. Even in this titanic work the natural, unforced quality about Boehm's interpretation commands respect. In the slow movement you may well feel that his view is too straight – that quality is underlined when he chooses slow tempi for both the *Adagio* and *Andante* themes, which are therefore given less contrast than usual. But the tone of voice is dedicated, and the work ends with a superbly dramatic yet controlled account of the finale, with excellent playing and singing all round. There is some forward balance of soloists in the finale of No. 9, but otherwise the recording of both symphonies is excellent.

(i) *Symphony No. 3 (Eroica);* (ii) *Wellington's victory (Battle symphony), Op. 91.*
(M) ** [RCA Basic 100 09026 61713-2]. (i) Boston SO, Leinsdorf; (ii) Phd. O, Ormandy.

Leinsdorf's opening movement of the *Eroica* is strong but heavy, and the performance overall, which is played superbly, has plenty of drive, even if the conductor hardly ever allows himself to relax. Ormandy certainly takes *Wellington's victory* seriously, assembling his British and French armies at either side of the audio spectrum and laying out the composer's battle-plan with enthusiasm. The special effects in the battle are impressive (and spectacularly recorded) and the culminating victory hymn has a Beethovenian grandeur. This is very enjoyable, but there are more resilient accounts of the *Eroica*.

Symphonies Nos. 4 in B flat; 5 in C min.; Egmont: Overture.
(M) **(*) Sony SMK 63079 [id.]. NYPO, Bernstein.
(B) **(*) Decca 433 600-2. VPO, Schmidt-Isserstedt.

Bernstein's earlier (1962) New York recording of the *Fourth Symphony* has genuine stature. Tempi are pressed on urgently, but the playing has both polish and concentration and the slow movement has an appealingly relaxed *espressivo*. The *Fifth* (from a year earlier) is also one of the finest of the Bernstein cycle, strong and dramatic, not quite as memorable as the *Eroica* he recorded at the same time, but concentrated and vital. The recording has been improved in the present transfers. The element of harshness remains, notably in the finale, but though the sound lacks the widest dynamic range there is a fairly convincing depth. *Egmont* is comparably dramatic and sounds really well.

Schmidt-Isserstedt's late-1960s account of the first movement of the *Fourth* has more relaxation in it than is common these days. This does not mean that the reading is too small-scale or wayward, but that he finds a different range of Beethoven qualities. The *Fifth* is strong and direct, only the Scherzo offers controversy in its slow tempo. Both recordings are vivid and full; the *Fifth* has a slightly less clean transfer than the *Fourth*, which sounds excellent.

Symphonies Nos. 4 in B flat, Op. 60; 5 in C min., Op. 67; 6 in F (Pastoral), Op. 68; Egmont: Overture, Op. 84.
(BB) **(*) Carlton LSO Double Dig. 30368 01197 (2) [(B) id.]. LSO, Wyn Morris.

In the *Fourth* and *Fifth Symphonies* Wyn Morris generally adopts speeds close to those of Karajan and, though he cannot match that master in sharpness of focus or pointed intensity, his urgency goes with fine, biting strength, helped by some first-rate playing from the LSO. These are readings which, more than many, convey the varying tensions of a live performance. The sound is bright and slightly abrasive but with enough body to sustain that. The weight of the readings is enhanced by the observance of all repeats. Morris takes a characteristically fresh and direct view of the *Pastoral*. The speed for the first movement is brisk, and he does not allow even a momentary easing for the entry of the second subject, let alone a slowing of tempo. Next to more relaxed readings, Morris sounds tense; on his own terms, however, it works well, as does his brisk treatment of the other movements. The piece becomes less atmospheric – with the entry into the *Storm* hardly suggesting raindrops – but one appreciates the structural originality the more. A similarly taut account of the *Egmont overture* follows.

Symphonies Nos. 4 in B flat; 6 in F (Pastoral), Op. 68.
✿ (M) *** Bruno Walter Edition: Sony SMK 64462 [id.]. Columbia SO, Walter.
(B) *** EMI CfP Dig. CD-CFP 6069 [id.]. RLPO, Mackerras.
(M) (***) RCA mono GD 60254 [60254-2-RG]. NBC SO, Toscanini.

For those collectors wanting a sampler of Bruno Walter's Beethoven series of the late 1950s, the coupling of the *Fourth* and *Sixth Symphonies* is the one to go for. Walter's reading of the *Fourth* is splendid, the finest achievement of his whole cycle. There is intensity and a feeling of natural vigour which makes itself felt in every bar. All aspects of this symphony – so much more varied than we have realized – are welded together here and show what depths it really contains. The recording is full, yet clear, sweet-toned with a firm bass. The pairing with the *Pastoral* is apt. The present version dates from the beginning of the 1960s and, like his recording of the *Fourth Symphony*, it represents the peak of his Indian summer in the American recording studios. It is an affectionate and completely integrated performance from a master who thought and lived the work all his life. The sound is beautifully balanced, with sweet strings and clear, glowing woodwind, and the bass response is firm and full.

Following the pattern of his other Classics for Pleasure recordings of Beethoven with the Liverpool orchestra, Sir Charles Mackerras adopts consistently fast speeds in both symphonies, except in the slow introduction to No. 4. Crisp, light articulation allows for superb definition from the strings in the outer movements of No. 4, with resilient rhythms, and Mackerras's rubato in such a passage as the opening of the *Pastoral* demonstrates how subtly he avoids any feeling of rigidity. With hard sticks used by the timpanist, the Storm has rarely sounded so thrilling, resolving on an ecstatic, slowing finale.

The *Pastoral* was one of Toscanini's favourite Beethoven symphonies and the performance has a natural, unforced freshness which allows the most delicate shading and persuasive moulding between sections. No. 4 is more characteristic of the later Toscanini, though the fast, fierce manner in the first movement conveys joyful exuberance, and the slow movement brings fine moulding.

Symphonies Nos. 4 in B flat; 7 in A, Op. 92.
(M) *** EMI CDM5 66795-2 [id.]. Philh. O, Klemperer.
(M) *** Virgin Veritas/EMI Dig. VM5 61376-2 [CDM 61376]. L. Classical Players, Norrington.
(BB) *** Naxos Dig. 8.553477 [id.]. Nicolaus Esterházy Sinfonia, Béla Drahos.
(M) *** DG 447 904-2 [id.]. VPO, Bernstein.

Symphonies Nos. 4 in B flat; 7 in A; King Stephen overture, Op. 117.
(B) *** Sony SBK 48158; *SBT 48158* [id.]. Cleveland O, Szell.

This coupling is perhaps the most impressive of the new Beethoven symphony pairings offered in EMI's 'Klemperer Legacy'. The *Fourth* brings one of the most compelling performances of all, with Klemperer's measured but consistently sprung pulse allowing for persuasive lyricism alongside power. The exposition repeat is observed in the first movement and the sound is fresh yet full. Klemperer's 1955 recording of the *Seventh* is among his very finest Beethoven interpretations on disc, and it sounds all the more vivid and present in its stereo version. Speeds are consistently faster, the tension more electric, with phrasing moulded more subtly than in the later version. The 1955 sound is remarkably full, with good inner detail.

The coupling of Nos. 4 and 7 is one of the most successful of the Drahos Naxos series so far. No. 4 has a pervading joyful vitality, while in No. 7 Drahos keeps a spring in the rhythms without forcing the pace, lifting the finale with bouncing accents, leading to a thrilling coda. The orchestral playing is first class and the recording outstanding in its combination of vivid clarity and atmospheric warmth: there is certainly no lack of weight in either symphony. This disc would be recommendable if it cost far more.

The coupling of Nos. 4 and 7 also shows Norrington at his very best. In both symphonies he adopts fast speeds and in the *Seventh* sforzandos are sharply accented and rhythms lightly sprung. He follows Beethoven's metronome markings – as in the brisk second-movement Allegretto – but finds time for detail and fine moulding of phrase. The recording is warm, but not ideally clear on detail.

Szell is at his finest in both symphonies. Along with powerful outer movements, tense and spontaneous-sounding, go exceptional accounts of the slow movements in both symphonies and in No. 7 Szell makes the second movement a genuine *Allegretto*, taking it almost as fast as a period specialist like Roger Norrington, and with magnetic concentration.

In No. 4, Bernstein's taut manner brings out the compactness of argument. The development is especially fine: in context one registers it as the message of No. 1 retold in the language of the *Fifth*. If the Beethovenian tensions in Bernstein's Vienna performance of the *Seventh* are less marked than in his earlier, New York recording, here that makes for extra spring and exhilaration in the lilting rhythms of the first movement, while the *Allegretto* is reposeful without falling into an ordinary *Andante*, and the last two movements have the adrenalin flowing with a greater sense of occasion than in most of this Bernstein series. One almost regrets the lack of applause. The recordings are among the best and brightest in the series, with No. 7 especially vivid and full-blooded. An outstanding coupling.

Symphonies Nos. 4 in B flat, Op. 60; 8 in F, Op. 93; Coriolan overture.
(B) *** Carlton IMP Dig. 30367 02392 [(M) id.]. Sinfonia Varsovia, Sir Yehudi Menuhin.

On the Carlton disc the applause precedes not only Mehuhin's warmly lyrical but not undramatic *Coriolan* but also the *Fourth Symphony*. The opening of the symphony is immediately full of tension, the allegro joyful and vigorous without being over-driven, and the rapt *Adagio* is played most beautifully. There is lyrical feeling underlying the sprightliness of the Scherzo, and the Trio blossoms. The articulate delicacy from wind and strings alike carries through into the finale with its vigorous forward impulse. The opening movement of the *Eighth* brings more joyous spirits and a most elegant second subject. This elegance also pervades the *Allegretto*, but here Menuhin's pacing is rather too relaxed and there is a lack of rhythmic uplift. However, all is forgiven when the finale erupts with buoyant energy. Again very fine playing, with the widest dynamic range, adds much to the character of the performance, and the spacious yet clear sound-picture is very satisfying.

Symphonies Nos. 4; 5 in C min. (trans. Liszt).
(M) *** Teldec/Warner Dig. 4509 98954-2 [2292 44921-2: *No. 5* only]. Cyprien Katsaris (piano).

Simply astonishing! Apart from his dazzling technique, Katsaris has enormous musicianship, a great range of colour and a real sense of scale. It is as if one is encountering this music for the first time. Readers will note that this mid-priced reissue is a recoupling.

Symphonies Nos. (i) *5 in C min.;* (ii) *6 in F (Pastoral);* (iii) *7 in A; Overtures Egmont; Leonora No. III.*
(B) ** Teldec/Warner Ultima 0630 18946-2 (2). (i) Hamburg PO; (ii) Bamberg SO; (iii) BPO; Keilberth.

These recordings date from 1960–61 when Telefunken was producing very good analogue sound, bright but full in the bass. The *Pastoral*, beautifully played in Bamberg, is easily the finest performance here, the pacing never forced (the slow movement flows beautifully), the Storm excitingly dramatic and the finale warmly lyrical but strong. However, Keilberth's leisurely approach to the first movement of the *Fifth* will not suit all tastes. At first, at this speed the music-making seems lacking in tension, yet in fact it is beautifully controlled, and the slow speed for the *Andante* also makes for some stylish playing. But the Scherzo is snail-paced and the finale, as though to compensate, is taken so quickly that it does not match the rest of the performance. The *Seventh* brings more excellent playing, this time from the Berlin

Philharmonic. However, once again some may quibble with his choice of tempo, here a rather fast allegretto for the second movement, and the performance does not quite hang together as, say, Davis's does. Keilberth seems a degree unwilling to produce a yielding, lilting beat even when the dance is at its most 'apotheotic' and there is a consequent lack of lift.

Symphonies Nos. 5 in C min.; 6 in F (Pastoral); 7 in A; 8 in F, Op.93.
(B) ** Sony Take 2 SB2K 63266 (2) [S2K 63266]. Phd. O, Eugene Ormandy.

Though he was always a most supportive conductor in Beethoven concertos, Ormandy is a variable interpreter of the symphonies. This neat package at bargain price on Sony's Essential Classics label brings much fine playing from the Philadelphia Orchestra, above all the strings, but the performances are far more effective, with keener tension, in such outward-going movements as the finale of the *Fifth*, the last three of the *Pastoral* and the last two of the *Seventh*. Only in the *Eighth* is Ormandy totally at home from first to last. The *Fifth* lacks dramatic bite at the start (with no exposition repeat, an omission very rare on record, even in the 78-r.p.m. era) and in the slow movements of Nos. 5, 6 and 7 Ormandy's relatively slow pacing makes for heaviness. Warm, full, 1960s sound.

Symphony No. 5 in C min., Op. 67.
(M) *** DG (IMS) Dig. 445 502-2 [id.]. LAPO, Giulini – SCHUMANN: *Symphony No. 3 (Rhenish)*. ***
(BB) **(*) Tring Dig. TRP 022 [(M) id. import]. RPO, Claire Gibault – SCHUBERT: *Symphony No. 8 (Unfinished)*. **
(BB) ** Naxos Dig. 8.550289 [id.]. Zagreb PO, Edlinger – SCHUBERT: *Symphony No. 8*. **

Symphony No. 5; Overture Leonora No. 3.
(M) *(*) [RCA Basic 100 09026 61551-2; *61551-4*]. Boston SO, Munch – SCHUBERT: *Symphony No. 8 (Unfinished)*. *(*)

Giulini's 1982 Los Angeles recording of Beethoven's *Fifth* is among the finest performances this symphony has ever received on record. The performance possesses majesty in abundance and conveys the power and vision of this inexhaustible work. The slow movement is glorious; the horn entry in the Scherzo is stunning and the finale almost overwhelming in its force and grandeur. Giulini also has the advantage of outstanding digital sound, clear, full and splendidly balanced, and the Schumann coupling is hardly less distinguished.

Claire Gibault's career has centred on the opera house. She was assistant conductor to John Eliot Gardiner at Lyon, where she gained wide experience, and she has conducted *Pelléas et Mélisande* at Covent Garden. But she has much concert-hall experience and, as this record suggests, she is a formidable exponent of Beethoven. The *Fifth Symphony* is not an easy work to bring off on record, but her performance with the RPO is admirably paced, direct and powerful. She has the advantage of excellent, full-bodied recording and it is a pity that in the Schubert coupling her tempo for the second movement is not entirely convincing.

Richard Edlinger directs the Zagreb orchestra in a crisp, dramatic performance, generally adopting urgent speeds in reflection of modern ideas on Beethoven's metronome markings. Slow movements flow easily and rhythms in allegros are generally well sprung. Well recorded, with horns ripely caught and lower strings warm and full, this disc is well worth its super-bargain price.

Munch's early-stereo Boston *Fifth* is a strong performance, well conceived as a whole. The playing is reasonably spontaneous-sounding and the reading overall enjoyable, if not memorable. But the Boston recording has an element of coarseness mixed in with the reverberation, and as the coupling is not very attractive this does not seem a very happy choice for RCA's Basic 100 series.

Symphonies Nos. 5 in C min.; 6 (Pastoral).
(B) **(*) DG 439 403-2 [(M) 419 051-2: *Nos. 5 & 8*]. BPO, Karajan.
(M) **(*) Virgin Veritas/EMI Dig. VM5 61377-2 [CDM 61377]. L. Classical Players, Norrington.
(M) (**(*)) Avid mono AMSC 583 [id.]. (i) LPO, Weingartner; (ii) VPO, Walter.
(BB) ** BMG Arte Nova Dig. 74321 49695-3 [id.]. Zürich Tonhalle O, David Zinman.

Symphonies Nos. 5–6; Creatures of Prometheus overture.
(M) *(*) Mercury 434 75-2 [id.]. LSO, Antal Dorati.

Karajan's 1962 *Fifth* is thoroughly recommendable, if anything more intense than his later (1977) version, more spacious in the *Andante* and with blazing horns in the finale. The *Pastoral* is a brisk, lightweight performance, very well played, and marred only by the absence of the repeat in the Scherzo. The sound has freshness and body, and this is undoubtedly good value.

No. 5 shows Norrington at his most exciting and inspired, relishing his fast speeds, while the finale has an infectious swagger. No. 6, however, fails to live up to expectations. The EMI sound leaves something to be desired in refinement and clarity, and Norrington is at times surprisingly fussy in his treatment. The *Scene by the brook*, for example, fails to flow when the phrasing is so short-winded, and there is not quite the same flow of energy that makes the *Fourth* so refreshing.

To many older collectors, Felix Weingartner's Beethoven had no rivals and few modern peers. In his hands the composer speaks to you as if without any interpretative mediator. The *Fifth Symphony*, recorded with the London Philharmonic in 1933, is Beethoven pure and true. But if it is straightforward and plain, there is no lack of character and fire. The recording sounds less dated than one might expect, though there is a curious touch of dryness, characteristic of these Avid transfers: the ambience is not quite natural. To younger collectors Weingartner is a figure from the past, whereas Bruno Walter, thanks to his Indian summer of recordings from the 1960s, is well known. His 1936 account of the *Pastoral* with the Vienna Philharmonic is tauter and brisker than one had remembered, yet it seems leisurely and expansive. This is a performance of stature, though the strings do not have quite enough sweetness above the stave. This is true of the original 78s.

With bright, immediate recording David Zinman conducts the Zurich Tonhalle Orchestra in unusually direct and incisive readings which suggest that his Beethoven sympathies were once roused by Toscanini's example. They come as part of a planned cycle which uses the recently published Barenreiter edition, newly prepared by Jonathan Del Mar. In No. 5 that brings a full repeat of the Scherzo and Trio before the usual partial and lightweight reprise of the Scherzo leading into the mysterious link to the finale. If in No. 5 Zinman's approach works extremely well in an exceptionally powerful reading, the *Pastoral* is more problematical. The opening allegro at a brisk speed is rarely allowed to relax, sounding a little breathless at times, with plenty of energy but not much warmth. The slow movement by contrast is spaciously done, and the *Storm* is biting rather than atmospheric, with the finale rather plain, strong and intense rather than warmly persuasive. Excellent playing and fresh, clean recording.

Dorati's are crisp, efficient performances. His strongly rhythmic approach works well enough in the *Fifth* (although the *Andante* lacks lyrical warmth), but the first movement of the *Pastoral* is entirely lacking in charm. Bright, forwardly balanced recording, made in Watford Town Hall in the early 1960s.

Symphonies Nos. 5; 7 in A, Op. 92.
✿ (M) *** DG 447 400-2 [id.]. VPO, Carlos Kleiber.
(B) *** Carlton IMP Dig. 30367 02402 [(M) id.]. Sinfonia Varsovia, Sir Yehudi Menuhin.
(B) *** EMI CfP Dig. CD-CFP 6070. RLPO, Sir Charles Mackerras.
(M) *** Decca Eclipse Dig. 448 222-2; *448 222-4* [(M) id. import]. Philh. O, Ashkenazy.
(M) **(*) Bruno Walter Edition: Sony SMK 64463 [id.]. Columbia SO, Bruno Walter.
(M) (***) EMI mono CDM7 63868-2 [id.]. Philh. O, Klemperer.

Symphonies Nos. 5; 8; Fidelio: overture.
(M) *** DG 419 051-2; *419 051-4* [id.]. BPO, Karajan.

If ever there was a legendary recording, it is Carlos Kleiber's version of the *Fifth* from the mid-1970s. In Kleiber's hands the first movement is electrifying but still has a hushed intensity. The slow movement is tender and delicate, with dynamic contrasts underlined but not exaggerated. In the Scherzo the horns, like the rest of the VPO, are in superb form, and the central section has enormous energy; the finale, even more than usual, releases the music into pure daylight. The latest remastering has certainly enhanced the sound: the upper range of the strings has more body than before, and there is little to complain of when this is undoubtedly one of the greatest performances of the work ever put on record. Kleiber's *Seventh* is a performance in which symphonic argument never yields to the charm of the dance. Kleiber's incisively dramatic approach is marked instead with sharp dynamic contrasts and thrustful rhythms. Another controversial point is that Kleiber, like his father, maintains the pizzicato for the strings on the final phrase of the *Allegretto*, a curious effect. The current digital remastering has again greatly improved the sound, with more resonance and weight in the middle strings – and how gloriously the horns come through in the tuttis of the outer movements.

After the inevitable opening applause, Menuhin opens the *Fifth* unselfconsciously, immediately setting a brisk tempo for the allegro, which is played comparatively lightly. The *Andante* too begins with a sense of delicate lyricism, and it is in the finale that the performance explodes into what Menuhin's note describes as the 'joyful illumination' of the fate theme. The allegro certainly dances along in the first movement of the *Seventh*, but here the pacing is relatively steady. The *Allegretto* is deeply eloquent and, as in the *Fifth*, it is the finale which carries the work to its exhilarating yet weighty conclusion. Playing and recording are well up to the high standard, although ensemble could be crisper in the first movement of the *Fifth*.

Sir Charles Mackerras and the Royal Liverpool Philharmonic also give revelatory performances of both the *Fifth* and *Seventh*. The speed for the first movement of the *Fifth* initially takes one's breath away, so fast is it. Sir Charles has learnt from period practice. Here he demonstrates that fast speeds in Beethoven can go with clarity and rhythmic spring. Tempi are on the fast side in all four movements but, thanks to the rhythmic control, they never sound hectic. The dramatic contrasts in this exhilarating performance are underlined by the superb recording, both weighty and atmospheric. The coupling is an equally refreshing account of the *Seventh Symphony*. Those two favourite symphonies are normally too long to fit on a single disc, if (as here) exposition repeats are observed: the brisker speeds make all the difference.

Karajan's 1977 version of the *Fifth* is magnificent in every way, tough and urgently incisive, with fast tempi bringing weight as well as excitement. The coupling is an electrically intense performance of the *Eighth* plus the *Fidelio overture*.

Ashkenazy's reading of the *Fifth* is urgent and vivid and is notable for its rich, Kingsway Hall recording. Well-adjusted speeds here, with joyful exuberance a fair substitute for grandeur. The reading of the *Seventh* is equally spontaneous. This CD ranks high among records of these two symphonies, especially for those for whom outstanding recording quality is a priority.

In Bruno Walter's reading of the *Fifth*, the sound-balance is richer and more satisfying than in many more modern recordings. The first movement is taken very fast, yet it lacks the kind of nervous tension that distinguishes Carlos Kleiber's famous version. The middle two movements are contrastingly slow. In the *Andante* (more like an *adagio*) there is a glowing, natural warmth, but the Scherzo at this speed is too gentle. The finale, taken at a spacious, natural pace, is joyous and sympathetic, but again fails to convey the ultimate in tension. Walter's *Seventh* has a comparatively slow first-movement allegro. The *Allegretto* also seems heavier than usual (partly because of the rich, weighty recording). It is rather mannered, with *marcato* emphases on most of the down beats, but the important point is that genuine tension is created with the illusion of an actual performance. The Scherzo is also rather wayward, but in contrast the finale goes with a splendid lift to the playing and very brilliant horns and trumpets in the exciting coda.

Klemperer never surpassed these first EMI interpretations of either symphony. Though the recording is in mono only, both works have a clarity, immediacy and fidelity of balance that enhance electrifying readings, revealing Klemperer at his peak.

Symphony No. 6 in F (Pastoral), Op. 68.
(M) *** DG 447 433-2 [id.]. VPO, Boehm – SCHUBERT: *Symphony No. 5.* ***

Symphonies No. 6 (Pastoral); Overtures: Coriolan; Creatures of Prometheus.
(BB) *** ASV CDQS 6053 [(M) id. import]. N. Sinfonia, Richard Hickox.

Symphony No. 6 (Pastoral); Overtures: Egmont; Leonora No. 3.
(B) *** Decca Eclipse Dig. 448 986-2; *448 986-4* [(M) id. import]. Philh. O, Ashkenazy.

Symphony No. 6 in F (Pastoral); Overture Leonora No. 3.
(B) **(*) [EMI Red Line Dig. CDR5 72551]. Phd. O, Muti.

Boehm's 1971 version of the *Pastoral* is as fine as any offered at full price. It is a beautiful, unforced reading, one of the best played, and in its day one of the best recorded. It still sounds fresh in its current reissue in DG's 'Originals' series with a Schubert coupling. In the first movement Boehm observes the exposition repeat (not all versions do); and though the dynamic contrasts are never underplayed and the phrasing is affectionate, there is a feeling of inevitable rightness about Boehm's approach, no sense of an interpreter forcing his will. Only the slow movement with its even stressing raises any reservation, and that very slight.

Ashkenazy's performance has a beguiling warmth and it communicates readily. With generally spacious tempi, the feeling of lyrical ease and repose is most captivating, thanks to the response of the Philharmonia players and the richness of the recording, made in the Kingsway Hall. The two overtures make a thoroughly satisfactory makeweight, and this is a clear front runner in the bargain range.

Hickox directs a persuasively paced reading, with a small orchestra used to give a performance of high contrasts, intimate in the lighter textures but expanding dramatically in the tuttis, while the finale, fresh and pure, brings a glowing climax. With warm, analogue recording giving a fine sense of presence, this is one of the best of the Hickox Beethoven series. The two *Overtures* come in vigorously dramatic readings.

With the first two movements youthfully urgent, Muti's is an exhilarating performance, fresh and direct. It is a strong, symphonic view, rather than a programmatic one. The recording is robustly rich and wide-ranging, though the high violins do not always live up to the 'Philadelphia sound'.

Symphonies Nos. 6 in F (Pastoral); 8 in F, Op. 91.
(BB) *** Belart 450 058-2 [(M) id. import]. Concg. O, Eugen Jochum.
(M) ** DG Dig. 445 542-2 [id.]. VPO, Abbado.

Jochum's Concertgebouw coupling on Belart (originally Philips) dates from the end of the 1960s. It still sounds extremely well, resonantly full-bodied, vivid and clear. Like his newer EMI recording, this is a leisurely reading, the countryside relaxing in the sunshine. In the first movement Jochum is essentially undramatic until the radiant final climax in the coda which he links with the similar burst of energy in the finale. The slow movement has an Elysian stillness and repose; the *Storm* is not over-romaticized. With beautiful playing from the Concertebouw Orchestra, the reading is sustained without a hint of lethargy and the finale has a joyful ebullience. The *Eighth* too is an outstanding performance, with plenty of energy – the second-movement *Allegretto* is particularly sprightly – again superbly played and very well recorded if with a little more edge on the violins than in the *Pastoral*. But this is not inappropriate, and this inexpensive coupling offers a splendid alternative view of two of Beethoven's friendliest symphonies.

Abbado's reading of the *Pastoral* is unexceptional, slowish and easy-going in the first movement, fresh but unmagical in the slow movement and finding full inspiration only in the finale. It is not helped by dull and rather thick (if quite agreeable) sound. However, the *Eighth* is an incandescent performance, fresh and rhythmic. The sound is full and atmospheric and, with such weight, it is instantly established as more than a little symphony. Speeds are beautifully judged, and the tensions of a live occasion are vividly conveyed.

Symphonies Nos. 6 (Pastoral); 8 in F (trans. Liszt).
(M) **(*) Teldec/Warner Dig. 4509 97955-2 [2292 42920-2: *No. 6* only]. Cyprien Katsaris (piano).

Katsaris, using an instrument with the ideal combination of weight and clarity, makes an excellent exponent of Liszt's transcription of the *Pastoral Symphony*, direct and fresh, if not especially illuminating interpretatively. The *Eighth* is much more perceptive. Good if rather resonant recording.

Symphonies Nos. (i) *6 in F (Pastoral); 8 in F, Op. 93;* (ii) *9 in D min. (Choral), Op. 125.*
(BB) **(*) EMI Seraphim CES5 68519-2 (2) [CDEB 68519]. (i) Munich PO, Rudolf Kempe; (ii) Armstrong, Reynolds, Tear, Shirley-Quirk, London Symphony Ch., LSO, Giulini.

Kempe's performance of the *Pastoral* is one of the most genially satisfying in the set. With warm, reverberant sound, few will be disappointed with either this or the comparable No. 8 (first-movement exposition repeat included). For the *Choral Symphony* EMI turned to Giulini's LSO account, also from the early 1970s. This is affected positively by the recording acoustic: close, immediate and full. Giulini's tempo in the first movement is unusually slow. He insists on precise sextuplets for the opening tremolando, with no mistiness – and he builds the architecture relentlessly, finding the resolution only in the concluding coda. The Scherzo is lithe and powerful, with shattering timpani. The slow movement is warm and Elysian rather than hushed, while the finale, not always quite perfect in ensemble, is dedicatedly intense, with excellent contributions from chorus and the solo team.

Symphonies Nos. 7 in A, Op. 92; 8 in F, Op. 93; (i) *9 in D min. (Choral), Op. 125.*
(BB) *(*) Carlton LSO Double Dig. 30368 01207 (2) [(B) id.]. (i) Hargan, Della Jones, Rendall, Howell; LSO, Wyn Morris.

Wyn Morris directs strong, spontaneous-sounding readings of the *Seventh* and *Eighth Symphonies*, not always as refined in execution as the finest, but recorded superbly. Though there are some distracting fluctuations of speed, Morris draws consistently resilient playing from the LSO, a vital quality in these two works written in parallel, both becoming apotheoses of the dance. Disappointingly, the *Ninth* displays too many signs of haste in the recording, with the orchestral ensemble often slack. There are many finer versions at all prices, which puts this Double out of court.

Symphony No. 7 in A, Op. 92.
✿ (B) *** EMI forte CZS5 69364-2 (2) [CDFB 69364]. RPO, Sir Colin Davis – SCHUBERT: *Symphony No. 9* ***; ROSSINI: *Overtures.* **(*)

Sir Colin Davis's early (1961) *Seventh* is a great performance that can be spoken of in the same breath as Carlos Kleiber's *Fifth*. Originally issued as a bargain LP on the HMV Concert Classics label, it soon established itself as a firm recommendation and dominated the catalogue in the early stereo era. It sounds marvellous in its current remastering, the horns coming through thrillingly in the codas of both outer movements. As for the performance overall: here is an ideal illustration of the difference between a studio run-through and an interpretation that genuinely takes one forward compellingly from bar to bar. Admittedly the opening of the slow introduction is a shade lacking in weight, but from then on there is scarcely a blemish. The first movement, with delicious pointing of the dotted rhythms, has both stylishness and strength. The slow movement, taken at a measured speed, is beautifully controlled, not only in the detailed phrasing but over the architectural span of the whole movement. The scherzo, with all repeats taken, is wonderfully rumbustious, with some superb woodwind playing. The finale, taken very fast indeed, barely allows one to breathe for excitement. Unforgettable!

Symphony No. 7 (trans. Liszt).
(M) *** Teldec/Warner Dig. 4509 97956-2 [2292 43065-2]. Cyprien Katsaris (with SCHUMANN: *Exercises on Beethoven's Seventh Symphony* **).

Cyprien Katsaris does wonders in translating Liszt's transcription into orchestral terms, providing an unexpectedly illuminating listening experience. The sound is excellent. Well worth having at mid-price.

Symphonies Nos. 7 in A; 8 in F.
(BB) **(*) Arte Nova Dig. 74321 56341-2 [id.]. Zürich Tonhalle O, David Zinman.
(B) **(*) [EMI Red Line Dig. CDR5 69785]. Phd. O, Muti.

Zinman's coupling of Nos. 7 and 8 has similar qualities to his earlier coupling of Nos. 5 and 6, again with echoes of Toscanini. That works very well in No. 7, with speeds on the brisk side, which yet have rhythmic resilience, notably in the *Allegretto*. In No. 8 Zinman, like Toscanini, takes a rather fierce view of this most compact of the symphonies, with a clipped manner and a fast speed in the first movement and with little or no charm in the middle movements. Even so, with clean, crisp ensemble and vivid recording with plenty of detail, the power of the piece is reinforced, making this worth considering at super-bargain price.

The vigour and drive of Muti's account of the *Seventh* are never in doubt – but, surprisingly, the ensemble of the Philadelphia Orchestra is less than immaculate. There is spontaneity, but it is paid for by a lack of precision. The *Eighth* is also lively, and it brings greater polish. The recording is a fair example of EMI's 'new Philadelphia sound'.

Symphony No. 8; Overtures: Coriolan; Leonora Nos. 1–3, Opp. 138; 72a; 72b.
(M) ** EMI CDM5 66796-2 [id.]. Philh. O, Klemperer.

Klemperer's approach to the *Eighth* is deliberately on the heavy side. He obviously feels that the business about the 'Little Symphony' has been overdone and that it is time for the weight of Beethoven's musical argument to be brought out. Weight there certainly is, but it is very doubtful whether slow speeds and a rather stiff beat will make it apparent in the right way. The Klemperer approach has its justification at the wonderful moment of the recapitulation of the first movement. Riding on the climax of the development, the main tune surges in on a towering fortissimo. But the *Allegretto* is too metronomic even for a movement intended as a playful portrayal of that useful timepiece, and the finale plods for much of its length. Klemperer's approach to the three *Leonora overtures* is strong rather than volatile, but such is his control over tension that the result here is neither dull nor heavy. Good, clear, full-bodied transfers.

Symphony No. 9 in D min. (Choral), Op. 125.
(B) *** EMI CfP Dig. CD-CFP 6071 [id.]. Joan Rodgers, Della Jones, Peter Bronder, Bryn Terfel, RLPO Ch. & O, Sir Charles Mackerras.
(M) *** DG 415 832-2 [id.]. Tomowa-Sintow, Baltsa, Schreier, Van Dam, V. Singverein, BPO, Karajan.
(M) *** DG Dig. 445 503-2 [id.]. Norman, Fassbaender, Domingo, Berry, V. State Op. Ch. Soc., VPO, Karl Boehm.
(BB) *** ASV CDQS 6069 [(M) id.]. Harper, Hodgson, Tear, Howell, Sinfonia Ch., London Symphony Ch. (members), N. Sinfonia, Hickox.
(B) *** Carlton IMP Dig. 30367 02412 [(M) id. import]. Jean Glennon, Dalia Schaechter, Algirdas Janutas, Benno Schollum, Lithuania Kaunas State Ch., Sinfonia Varsovia, Menuhin.
(B) *** Tring TRP 051 [(M) id. import]. Gillian Webster, Catherine Wyn-Rogers, Martyn Hill, Robert Hayward, Amb. S., RPO, Leppard.
(B) *** DG Classikon 439 495-2. G. Jones, Schwarz, Kollo, Moll, V. State Op. Ch., VPO, Bernstein.
(M) *** DG 447 905-2 [id.]. Gwyneth Jones, Schwarz, Kollo, Moll, V. State Op. Ch., VPO, Bernstein.
(BB) *** Naxos Dig. 8.553478 [id.]. Papian, Donose, Fink, Otelli, Nicolaus Esterházy Ch. & O, Drahos.
(M) **(*) RCA 09026 61795-2 [id.]. Curtin, Kopleff, McCollum, Gramm, Chicago SO & Ch., Fritz Reiner.
(M) **(*) Virgin Veritas/EMI Dig. VM5 61378-2 [CDM 61378]. Kenny, Walker, Power, Salomaa, Schütz Ch., L. Classical Players, Norrington.
(BB) **(*) Discover Dig. DICD 920151 [id.]. Gauci, Van Deyck, George, Rosca, Cantores Oratorio Ch., Belgian Nat. R. & TV PO, Rahbari.
(M) (**(*)) RCA mono GD 60256; [60256-2-RG]. Farrell, Merriman, Peerce, Scott, Shaw Ch., NBC O, Toscanini.
(M) (**(*)) Avid mono AMSC 591 [id.]. Helletsgruber, Anday, Maikl, Mayr, V. State Op. Ch., VPO, Weingartner.

(M) *(*) Bruno Walter Edition: Sony SMK 64464 [id.]. Cundari, Rankin, Da Costa, Wilderman, Westminster Ch., Columbia SO, Bruno Walter.

Symphony No. 9 (Choral); Overture: Coriolan.
(M) *** DG 447 401-2. Janowitz, Rössl-Majdan, Kmentt, Berry, V. Singverein, BPO, Karajan.

Symphony No. 9 (Choral); Overture: The Creatures of Prometheus, Op. 43.
(M) ** EMI CDM5 66797 [id.]. Lövberg, Ludwig, Kmentt, Hotter, Philh. Ch. & O, Klemperer.

(i) *Symphony No. 9 (Choral). Overture Egmont, Op. 84.*
(M) *** Decca Phase Four 452 487-2 [id.]. (i) Harper, Watts, Young, McIntyre, L. Symphony Ch.; LSO, Stokowski.
(M) ** Ph. Dig. 442 644-2. (i) Janet Price, Birgit Finnilä, Horst Laubenthal, Marius Rintzler, Concg. Ch.; Concg. O, Haitink.

(i) *Symphony No. 9 (Choral), Op. 125. Overture Fidelio.*
(B) **(*) Sony SBK 46533; *SBT 46533* [id.]. (i) Addison, Hobson, Lewis, Bell, Cleveland O Ch.; Cleveland O, Szell.

Sir Charles Mackerras conducts the Royal Liverpool Philharmonic in an exceptional, inspired account of the *Ninth*, one which – more than any other with a traditional symphony orchestra – has learnt from the lessons of period performance. Articulation is light and clean, vibrato is used sparingly, making textures unusually clear; and, like Roger Norrington, Sir Charles has taken careful note of Beethoven's controversial metronome markings. The recording is among the very finest ever given to this symphony, warm yet transparent and with plenty of body; and the singing in the finale is splendid, even if the tenor, Peter Bronder, is on the strenuous side. Anyone wanting a refreshingly different version of the *Ninth*, which yet brings all the dramatic power and intensity of a more conventional reading, need not hesitate.

Of the three stereo recordings Karajan has made of the *Ninth*, his 1977 account (415 832-2) is the most inspired in its insight, above all in the *Adagio*, where he conveys spiritual intensity at a slower tempo than in his earlier, 1962 version. In the finale, the concluding eruption has an animal excitement rarely heard from this highly controlled conductor. The soloists make an excellent team, with contralto, tenor and bass all finer than their predecessors. The sound has tingling projection and drama.

Stokowski's 1967 version, recorded in the Kingsway Hall, makes another very impressive mid-priced choice for the *Ninth*. The Phase Four recording has been vividly remastered and retains its fullness, both vocally and orchestrally. The soloists are closely balanced and when they combine with the chorus, who sing with great ardour, the result is sonically thrilling. Indeed there is the sort of tension about this recorded performance which one expects from a great conductor in the concert hall, and that compulsion carries one over all Stokowski's idiosyncrasies, including a fair amount of retouching in the orchestration. The first movement is strong and dramatic, taken at a Toscanini pace; the Scherzo is light and pointed, with timpani cutting through; the slow movement has great depth and *Innigkeit* – and that, perhaps more than anything, confirms the greatness of the performance, for the finale, with some strangely slow tempi, is uneven, despite fine singing, yet ends resplendently. The *Egmont Overture*, recorded just over five years later, is a strong, exciting performance without idiosyncrasy. The sound here is full but slightly fierce on top.

Karl Boehm's reading is spacious and powerful, and in its broad concept it has much in common with Klemperer's version. Yet overall there is a transcendent sense of a great occasion; the concentration is unfailing, reaching its peak in the glorious finale, where ruggedness and strength well over into inspiration. With a fine, characterful team of soloists and a freshly incisive chorus formed from singers of the Vienna State Opera, this is strongly recommendable.

Karajan's 1962 version is less hushed and serene in the slow movement than either of his two later versions, but the finale blazes even more intensely, with Janowitz's contribution radiant in its purity. This reflected the electricity of the Berlin sessions, when it rounded off a cycle recorded over two weeks. Even so, it is strange that DG chose this recording rather than the 1977 account for reissue in their 'Originals' series of legendary recordings, as the latter version is even finer. The *Coriolan* coupling is an added bonus.

Hickox's performance, using an orchestra of the size Beethoven originally had, brings some of the advantages of period performance: clarity of articulation and texture; otherwise one might not realize that the string band is any smaller than one on a regular recording of the *Ninth*. In his pacing throughout the work, Hickox is unerring and conveys from first to last the tension of a genuine performance, in a way that some of his rivals among international stars do not manage. This is the most successful issue in his Beethoven series for ASV. The performance culminates in a glowing account of the choral finale with four excellent soloists. At super-bargain price this is very competitive indeed.

Though the first movement is less biting than the rest, the *Ninth Symphony*, often a disappointment in complete cycles, in Menuhin's hands brings a fitting culmination, thanks also to the fresh, clear singing of the Lithuanian choir and a young, rather lightweight quartet of soloists. Following the Gardiner thesis, the drum-and-fife sequence in the finale is taken very fast, like a French military march. But with a deeply felt slow movement this must be counted among the very finest modern performances on bargain label.

Raymond Leppard and the RPO offer a bright, incisive performance, enhanced by sharply focused, forward and well-detailed recording. The precise triplets in the opening tremolos may lack mystery but they lead to a well-terraced reading in which the entry of the recapitulation makes a shattering impact. Speeds, on the broad side in all the fast movements, never sound too slow, thanks to rhythmic lift and crisp ensemble, while the slow movement flows smoothly and songfully rather than meditating deeply. The fresh, forward balance of voices, both chorus and soloists, adds to the impact of the finale, making this another excellent recommendation at bargain price.

Bernstein's characterful VPO account of the *Ninth* crowns his Beethoven series superbly. The very start conveys immediate electricity, reflecting the presence of an audience, and the first movement is presented at white heat from first to last, with only a slight rallentando detracting from the thrust. The Scherzo is resilient, the *Adagio* deeply convincing in its distinctive contrasting of inner meditation in a very slow first theme with lighter, more carefree interludes in a fast-flowing *Andante*. In the finale Gwyneth Jones's soprano is as well controlled as it ever has been on record, and otherwise this is a superb account, sung and played with dedication, if a fraction less intense than the earlier movements. The recording needs no apology: it is bright, full and immediate. This seems to be available both on DG's Classikon bargain label (with very limited documentation) and at mid-price.

Bela Drahos with his outstanding chamber orchestra from Budapest here rounds off a refreshingly direct Beethoven cycle, with all nine symphonies given electrically alert, spontaneous-sounding performances. At super-budget price it is a fine bonus to have recorded sound more vivid than on almost any recent Beethoven discs. The performance of the *Ninth* is typically dramatic, with a brisk, intense reading of the first movement, a well-sprung Scherzo equally biting, and an Adagio which rather follows period practice in its flowing speed, sweet and beautifully moulded rather than hushed. With a superb chorus and well-matched soloists, the finale is urgently intense, working to a superb climax.

As bitingly dramatic as Toscanini in the first movement and electrically intense all through, Szell directs a magnetic, seemingly inevitable account of the *Ninth* which demonstrates the glories of the Cleveland Orchestra. The chorus sings with similarly knife-edged ensemble, set behind the orchestra but not too distantly. The performance of the *Fidelio overture* is electrifying.

Reiner's 1961 reading conveys power rather than mystery. Ensembles have knife-edged precision, rhythms are beautifully sprung and speeds are relatively broad, not least in the slow movement which, like the first, is presented in the full light of day. In the drum-and-fife episode of the finale too, Reiner's speed is surprisingly slow, but there and throughout he sustains tension magnetically, helped by the warm Chicago ambience. This is a fine example of Reiner's mastery and well worth hearing, even if there are greater accounts of the *Ninth* on CD.

Much of the sharp intensity and exhilaration of Norrington's reading of the *Ninth* comes over on his record, with many of his contentions over observing Beethoven's fast metronome markings validated in the success of the performance. What has to remain controversial is the slow movement which, at tempi far swifter than we are used to, becomes a sweet interlude rather than a meditation, far shorter than the other movements. A more serious snag is the contribution of the male soloists. Petteri Salomaa's tremulous, aspirated singing on the command '*Nicht diese Töne*' is painful, while Patrick Power's plaintive tenor timbre goes with a very slow pace for the drum-and-fife march passage. Nevertheless the impact of the whole performance is considerable, with reverberant recording still allowing the bite of timpani and valveless horns to cut through the texture. In no sense, except in the number of performers involved, is this a small-scale performance, rather an intensely refreshing view of a supreme masterpiece.

Among versions at super-bargain price, Rahbari's Brussels version, digitally recorded, makes an excellent recommendation, consistently conveying vigour and spontaneity, as in a live, rather than a studio performance. The first movement is strong and purposeful, the Scherzo excitingly fast, with the slow movement sustaining measured speeds well, and the finale is helped by confident choral and solo singing. The recording is reverberant, but not so as to muddle an involving performance.

Toscanini's electrifying account of the *Ninth* is marred somewhat by the excessive treble emphasis, more noticeable than on the earlier, full-priced reissue.

Weingartner's 1935 account of the *Ninth Symphony* was a mainstay of the 78-r.p.m. catalogue, and it was long unchallenged. It remains impressive at every level and, like all of Weingartner's cycle, presents Beethoven truthfully without any intervening filter or interpretative veneer. Weingartner's soloists are good, too, in particular the magisterial Richard Mayr. Over sixty years old it may be, but it still ranks high among *Ninths*. The transfer is very serviceable if not outstanding.

Walter's *Ninth* has many fine moments but suffers from slow tempi and a comparatively low level of tension. The first three movements were recorded in California in January 1959 and the finale in New York City four months later. Somehow the interpretation went off the boil and the choral finale fails to rise to the sense of occasion that a really great *Ninth* should have. Those interested in discovering Walter's methods of preparation for the final performances will be glad to know that there is a separate disc including recorded excerpts from the rehearsals of *Symphonies Nos. 4*, *5*, *7* and *9* (SMK 64465).

Klemperer's 1958 sound is amazingly good for its period, with the finale fresher and better balanced than in many recent recordings. However, his weighty vision is marred by a disappointing quartet of soloists; and the slow speeds for the first two movements – the Scherzo seems to go on for ever – come to sound ponderous. Yet the flowing account of the slow movement shows Klemperer at his finest. The new CD transfer offers extra refinement, with the choral sound in the finale given astonishing presence and tangibility.

Haitink's digital *Ninth* was made at a live concert in the Concertgebouw, but one would hardly know that: there are few if any signs of an audience and – disappointingly – the performance rather fails to convey the feeling of an occasion, lacking a little in tension even in comparison with Haitink's earlier, studio version with the LPO. The reading, as in his earlier, analogue account, is satisfyingly unidiosyncratic, direct and honest, but with this work one needs more.

(i) *Symphony No. 9 (Choral);* (ii–iii) *Ah perfido* (concert aria), *Op. 65;* (iv) *Calm sea and prosperous voyage (Meerstille und glückliche Fahrt; cantata), Op. 112;* (v; iii) *Cantata on the death of Emperor Joseph II, WoO 87;* (vi) *Choral Fantasy* (for piano, chorus and orchestra), *Op. 80.*

(B) ** Sony Take 2 SB2K 63240 (2) [S2K 63240]. (i) Amara, Chookasian, Alexander, Macurdy, Mormon Tabernacle Ch., Phd. O, Ormandy; (ii) Régine Crespin; (iii) NYPO, Schippers; (iv) John Alldis Ch., New Philh. O, Boulez; (v) Martina Arroyo, Justino Diaz, Camerata Singers; (vi) Rudolph Serkin, Westminster Ch., NYPO, Bernstein.

An enterprising bargain double is here let down by Ormandy's account of the *Choral Symphony*. Fast and clear-cut, even on the opening tremolos, he makes it clear that mystery plays no part in his concept of the *Ninth*. Though the resonance of the Philadelphia players, particularly the strings, is as ever impressive, with superb articulation in the Scherzo, Beethoven's deeper qualities are smoothed over, above all in the slow movement. Among the soloists, the bass is disappointing and the recording is no more than acceptable. The *Cantata on the death of Emperor Joseph II* is a Beethoven curiosity, written in 1790 but not performed until 1884, after the composer's death. The piece is mainly of interest in including a theme he was to use again for the climax of *Fidelio*, when the hero is freed. The performance here is lively but fails to make a case for returning the work to the repertoire. *Meerstille* (*Calm sea and a prosperous voyage*) with its deeply meditative, highly original first half (raptly caught by Boulez) is a different matter, yet it is surprisingly brief at just over eight minutes. Régine Crespin's *Ah perfido!* is powerful, but its very forthright style is somewhat overwhelming, since the singing is not always well focused. The recording is good. In the *Choral Fantasia* Serkin is not flattered by the piano sound, but his opening solo cadenza is arresting. It is a forceful performance, but its drama is certainly compulsive.

Symphony No. 9 (trans. Liszt).

(M) *** Teldec/Warner Dig. 4509 97957-2 [2292 42985-2]. Cyprien Katsaris (piano).

Cyprien Katsaris's performance is nothing short of a *tour de force*: his virtuosity is altogether remarkable and there is a demonic Beethovenian vehemence and drive. The piano is closely observed in a reverberant acoustic ambience and listeners may at times be disturbed by its somewhat jangly quality. But at mid-price this should not be missed.

Wellington's victory (Battle symphony), Op. 91.

✿ (M) *** Mercury 434 360-2 [id.]. Cannon & musket fire directed Gerard C. Stowe, LSO, Dorati (with separate descriptive commentary by Deems Taylor) – TCHAIKOVSKY: *1812; Capriccio italien*. *** ✿

(M) ** DG 447 912-2 [id.]. BPO, Karajan – *Ecossaise* etc. **; *Egmont*. **(*)

This most famous of all Mercury records was one of the most successful classical LPs of all time, selling some two million copies in the analogue era. Remastered for CD, it sounds far more convincing than it ever did in its vinyl format – indeed its sense of spectacle is quite extraordinary. Until 1804 Beethoven had been a Bonapartist and dedicated the *Eroica Symphony* to Napoleon; later, much disillusioned by events, he withdrew the dedication and instead became an anti-Bonapartist. No one was more pleased than he when in 1813 the Emperor's army was defeated by the British near the Basque city of Vitoria; encouraged by an entrepreneurial inventor, Johann Nepomuk Maelzel, Beethoven wrote a very commercial piece to celebrate the occasion. It was conceived to be performed on Maelzel's panharmonicon, a huge orchestral machine incorporating flutes, trumpets and percussion; but Beethoven also made an orchestral version, indicating in the score the exact spots at which the cannon and musketry were to be fired. It was in its orchestral form that the piece was eventually performed, and it is good to know that the venture was financially successful for both parties!

As the opposing armies march in, one on each side of the stereo spectrum, Beethoven represents the French army with a popular war-ditty, '*Malbrouck s'en va t'en guerre*' which, at the moment of defeat, reappears dejectedly in the minor key. The British are allotted *Rule Britannia* and, at the moment of victory, *God save the King*. In between comes an astonishing fusillade of fire, in which no one could complain at the use of period cannon and muskets or the engaging way the firing peters out as the battle comes to an end. Gerard C. Stowe deserves his share of the Rosette for these authentic special effects, as does Wilma Cozart Fine for her expert and painstaking re-editing and, not least, Dorati and the LSO for the excellent performance of Beethoven's music. This is surely an account which is unlikely to be bettered or realistically simulated in a live performance, and it is good to hear the endearing voice of Deems Taylor (famous for his commentary in Walt Disney's *Fantasia*) explaining how it was all done. Moreover the presentation, with handsome colour reproductions of appropriate paintings (and excellent documentation), is a model of its kind.

Karajan's version of *Wellington's Victory* is elegant rather than spectacular. It is beautifully played and the digital remastering adds presence to the opening assembly to left and right; but there is no sense of occasion and the battle-sounds are not entirely convincing, with the resonant acoustics of the Berlin Jesus-Christus Kirche bringing atmosphere but not helping to focus the spectacle. This cannot compare with its Mercury competitor, although the refined bravura of the Berlin Philharmonic in the closing section is impressive.

CHAMBER MUSIC

(i) *Cello sonatas Nos. 1–5;* (ii) *7 Variations on 'Bei Männern, welche Liebe fühlen'* (from Mozart's *Die Zauberflöte), WoO 46; 12 Variations on 'Ein Mädchen oder Weibchen'* (from Mozart's *Die Zauberflöte), Op. 66; 12 Variations on 'See the conqu'ring hero comes'* (from Handel's *Judas Maccabaeus), WoO 45.*

(B) *** Ph. Duo 442 565-2 (2) [id.]. (i) Mstislav Rostropovich, Sviatoslav Richter; (ii) Maurice Gendron, Jean Françaix.

(B) *** EMI Eminence Dig. CD-EMXD 2506 (2) [(M) id. import]. Raphael Wallfisch, John York.

(M) *** EMI CMS7 63015-2 (2) [ZDMB 63015]. Jacqueline Du Pré, Daniel Barenboim.

(B) *** DG Double 453 013-2 (2) [id.]. Pierre Fournier, Wilhelm Kempff.

(M) *** DG (IMS) 437 352-2 (2) [id.]. Pierre Fournier, Friedrich Gulda.

(B) *** EMI Rouge et Noir CZS5 69422-2 (2) [(M) id. import]. Paul Tortelier, Eric Heidsieck.

(B) **(*) Hyperion Dyad Dig. CDD 22004 (2) [id.]. Anthony Pleeth, Melvyn Tan (fortepiano).

(B) **(*) Teldec/Warner Ultima 0630 17368-2 (2). Janos Starker, Rudolph Buchbinder.

Made in the early 1960s, the classic Philips performances by Mstislav Rostropovich and Sviatoslav Richter, two of the instrumental giants of the day, have withstood the test of time astonishingly well and sound remarkably fresh in this transfer. The performances of the *Variations* by Maurice Gendron and Jean Françaix have an engagingly light touch and are beautifully recorded. Indeed by their side the Rostropovich/Richter recording is noticeably drier and less vivid. But at its new price this reissue is very tempting.

Raphael Wallfisch and John York make an inspired duo in the *Cello sonatas*, giving powerful performances which hold a satisfying balance between romantic warmth and classical strength. With John York an incisive pianist, clean in attack, well matched against Wallfisch's wide tonal and expressive range, these are disciplined readings over tempo and phrasing which yet are never rigid, always sounding spontaneous. With a wide dynamic range, well caught in the excellent recording, the dramatic power as well as the lyrical warmth are enhanced. The sequence builds up to a superb climax on the last, and arguably the greatest, of the sonatas, Op. 102 No. 2, with the *Adagio* exceptionally spacious, bringing out an inner intensity to relate it to the late *Quartets*. That leads to a broad account of the fugal finale, powerful rather than urgent, bringing satisfying Bachian overtones. The three sets of variations provide a valuable makeweight with equally compelling performances, making this Eminence set a splendid bargain alternative to Rostropovich and Richter for those seeking modern, digital recording.

The set of performances by Jacqueline Du Pré with Daniel Barenboim was recorded live for the BBC during the Edinburgh Festival of 1970. The playing may not have the final polish that studio performances would no doubt have achieved, but the concentration and intensity of the playing are wonderfully caught.

Fournier and Kempff recorded their cycle of the sonatas at live festival performances, but the Paris audience is relatively unintrusive and these artists were inspired by the occasion to produce unexaggeratedly expressive playing and to give performances which are marked by their light, clear textures and rippling scale-work, even in the slow introductions which are taken relatively fast. Clearly Kempff is the leading personality here, and if some of the weight is missing such a stylish spontaneity is irresistible. Admirers of both artists will find this set a fine bargain as a DG Double, the sound enhanced by the current remastering, beautifully clear, with the cello timbre somewhat dry.

Fournier's earlier accounts, made in the Brahms-Saal of the Vienna Musikverein in 1959, though not less spontaneous have more gravitas. Gulda's contribution is strong: he is more than a passive partner. The *Variations* are slight pieces, intended to divert, but once again in Fournier's hands they assume a greater significance than one might expect. The recording of both instruments is close but full and natural, beautifully balanced against an ideal acoustic.

The Tortelier set with Eric Heidsieck dates from the early 1970s and has the advantage of more modern and perhaps slightly better sound than the Philips set. The performances are distinguished and make a useful alternative, as the style is bolder than the way of Fournier and Kempff on DG, and less chimerical, too; indeed Tortelier and Heidsieck are nearer to Rostropovich and Richter, although they have their own insights. The variations have been added and make a bonus for the reissue, which comes at two CDs for the price of one. The CD transfer is admirably natural and clean, with the variations sounding particularly fresh.

Though the cello is balanced rather forwardly in relation to the fortepiano, the Hyperion collection of Beethoven's music for cello and piano – not just the five *Sonatas* but the three sets of variations too – makes an attractive issue for anyone wanting period versions. Tan recorded these performances with Pleeth in 1987, not long before he began his Beethoven series for EMI, and his imagination is comparably keen here. Anthony Pleeth is a responsive enough partner but, although his phrasing has warmth, his tone is comparatively wan and despite the balance it is Tan who easily dominates the set and makes the allegros sparkle. The *Variations* are particularly enjoyable in this respect.

Janos Starker's warmly inspirational style is immediately apparent at the *Adagio* opening of the first *F major Sonata* and again at the beginning of the *G minor*. The slow movements of the two later sonatas, Op. 102, also show him in eloquent voice. The bolder, more direct approach of his partner, Rudolph Buchbinder, who tends to dominate, gives these readings a classical strength, perhaps at times a little unyielding but always highly musical and attentive to the music's detail. The *Variations* come off particularly well and, without making the music seem trivial, have an attractive lightness of touch. The 1980 recording is truthful, with good presence, the acoustic very slightly dry in relation to the piano. Not a first choice perhaps, but individual and rewarding, and good value.

Cello sonatas Nos. 1 in F; 2 in G min., Op. 5/1–2; 7 Variations on Mozart's 'Bei Männern', WoO 45; 12 Variations on Handel's 'See the conqu'ring hero comes', WoO 46; 12 Variations on Mozart's 'Ein Mädchen', Op. 66.
(BB) ** Naxos Dig. 8.550479 [id.]. Csaba Onczay, Jenö Jandó.

Although they do not have the personality of, say, Fournier and Gulda – let alone Rostropovich and Richter – Csaba Onczay and Jenö Jandó turn in serviceable accounts of both *Sonatas*. The cellist is a little colourless and does not have quite as much fervour or character as the pianist. Decent recording.

Cello sonatas Nos. 3 in A, Op. 69; 4 in C; 5 in D, Op. 102/1–2.
(BB) *(*) Naxos Dig. 8.550478 [id.]. Csaba Onczay, Jenö Jandó.

A rather unsatisfactory balance diminishes the attractions of the Naxos coupling. The pianist is far too dominant and, though he is a responsive and at times sensitive partner, he can also be a little perfunctory. Indeed, some of his fortissimos are a shade brutal. Csaba Onczay is a musical player but his personality is swamped here. A pity, for the acoustic environment in which they are recorded is much more congenial than many others from this source. Not quite the bargain it first appears.

Cello sonatas Nos. 3 in A, Op. 69; 5 in D, Op. 102/2.
(M) *** EMI CDM7 69179-2. Jacqueline du Pré, Kovacevich.

The Du Pré/Bishop-Kovacevich recordings of Nos. 3 and 5 come from 1966, the year after Jacqueline had made her definitive record of the Elgar *Concerto*. Du Pré's tone ranges from full-blooded fortissimo to the mere whisper of a half-tone, and these artists allow the most free range of expressive rubato. With excellent recording, these performances are most welcome on CD, sounding crisp and present in their new format.

Clarinet trio, see *Septet* (below).

Ecossaise, WoO 22; March for wind sextet, WoO 29; Military marches, WoO 18–20; 24; Polonaise, WoO 21.
(M) ** DG 447 912-2 [id.]. BPO Wind Ens., Hans Priem-Bergrath – *Egmont* **(*); *Wellington's victory*. **

The performances of Priem-Bergrath and the BPO Wind Ensemble are routine ones but vigorous and well played. The mellow piece for wind sextet (WoO 29) without percussion, the *Ecossaise* and *Polonaise* bring variety, although one or two of the military pieces are quite attractive, notably the *'Yorkshire' March in F*, WoO 19. The 1969 recording, made in the Jesus-Christus Kirche, Berlin (a curious venue), is brightly resonant and, considering the acoustic, the CD definition is surprisingly good.

(i) *Flute trio in G* (for flute, bassoon & piano), *WoO 37;* (ii–iii) *Horn sonata in F, Op. 17;* (iii; v) *Piano and wind quintet, Op. 16;* (iv) *Serenade in D for flute, violin & viola, Op. 25;* (v) *Septet, Op. 20; Sextet in E flat, Op. 81b; Wind octet in E flat, Op. 103; Wind sextet in E flat, Op. 71.*
(M) *** DG 439 852-2 (3). (i) Zöller, Thunemann, Kontarsky; (ii) Seifert; (iii) Demus; (iv) Zöller, Brandis, Ueberschaer; (v) BPO (members).

These are all beautifully alert, civilized performances and they are recorded with clarity and definition and an appealing bloom. There are some minor reservations. There are perhaps more starry accounts of the *Piano and wind quintet* (although Demus and his colleagues play freshly and spontaneously). In the *Septet*, Op. 20, the Berlin players are richly mellifluous in style, especially noticeable in the Minuet. Outside the Beethoven Edition, there is no rival compilation of this scope on the market at present and, even if there were, it is difficult to imagine it surpassing the present set (originally issued on five LPs).

Piano quartets Nos. 1 in E flat; 2 in D; 3 in C, WoO 36.
(BB) **(*) Discover Dig. DICD 920254 [id.]. Scheuerer Qt.

The enterprising Discover label does it again by giving Beethoven's three early *Piano quartets* their CD début. Written in Bonn when the composer was fifteen, they are obviously Mozart-influenced, as the charming *Rondo* finales of Nos. 1 and 3 readily demonstrate. Indeed that for the *D major* (otherwise perhaps the least interesting) is little short of a lollipop. The *Theme and variations finale* of No. 1 is attractive too, but it is the central *Adagio* of No. 3 which hints at the mature Beethoven, and the opening *Adagio assai* of No. 1 even more so – beginning like the slow movement for a piano concerto. The bold *Allegro con spirito* second movement of the *E flat Quartet* is also obviously post-Mozartian and the four sibling performers here make the very most of it. Indeed they play throughout with pleasing freshness and plenty of vitality. The excellent pianist leads strongly, but (as we have commented before) the principal violinist could have a more generous tone. Fortunately the microphones are not near enough to exaggerate this, and the overall balance is good within a fairly resonant acoustic. This is well worth its modest cost.

Piano trios Nos. 1–11.
(M) *** Ph. 438 948-2 (3). Beaux Arts Trio.

Piano trios Nos. 1–3, Op. 1; 8 in E flat, WoO 38; 10 (Variations on an original theme in E flat), Op. 44.
(M) *** Sony Stern Edition III SM2K 64510 (2) [S2K 64510]. Stern, Rose, Istomin.

Piano trios Nos. 4 in B flat, Op. 11; 5 in D (Ghost), Op. 70/1; 6 in E flat, Op. 70/2; 7 in B flat (Archduke), Op. 97; 9 in B flat, WoO 39; 11 (Variations on 'Ich bin der Schneider Kakadu'), Op. 121a.
(M) *** Sony Stern Edition III SM2K 64513 (2) [S2K 64513]. Stern, Rose, Istomin.

Piano trios Nos. 1–11 Trio in E flat (from Septet), Op. 38.
(BB) **(*) Arte Nova Dig. 74321 51621-2 (4) [id.]. Seraphim Trio.

Piano trios Nos. 1–3; 5–7; 9–10 (Variations on an original theme in E flat); 11 (Variations on 'Ich bin der Schneider Kakadu'); Allegretto in E flat, Hess 48.
(M) **(*) EMI (SIS) CMS7 63124-2 (3) [ZDMC 63124]. Daniel Barenboim, Pinchas Zukerman, Jacqueline du Pré.

The Stern/Rose/Istomin recordings were made between 1968 and 1970, though the *Archduke* is earlier and was recorded in Switzerland in 1965. The results are outstanding: the music-making is strong, polished and alive, and Istomin is always thoughtful and imaginative in slow movements, while Rose, although a less extrovert artist than Stern, holds his own by the warmth and finesse of his lyrical phrasing. One of the highlights of the set is the *Archduke*, commandingly bold and immediate, with a glorious slow movement; the *Ghost trio* also shows these artists at their most communicative, while they do not miss the charm of the early, Op. 1 works. The recording is characteristically forward, in the CBS manner of the late 1960s, but the remastering for CD has improved the sonority at the lower end of the spectrum immeasurably. The shallowness of the piano has all but disappeared: indeed it is now a very convincing image and, while Stern is obviously close to the microphones, the fierceness noticeable on the LPs has been tamed. In every sense these recordings rank highly in the discography of the Beethoven *Piano trios* and may be recommended with enthusiasm alongside the full-price Perlman/Ashkenazy/Harrell set, with which they have much in common.

The Arte Nova set is as complete as most collectors will want. It runs to four discs (averaging out at

76 minutes each) and remains the least expensive way to collect all this highly rewarding music. The Seraphim Trio have a splendid pianist in Gottfried Hefele. (Just sample his twinkling articulation in the bravura scales of the Trio of the Minuet in Op. 1/3, or indeed his nimble playing in any of the sets of variations from Op. 11, Op. 38, Op. 44 or Op. 38). He dominates the proceedings musically, without ever taking too bold a pianistic role, for, like the Beaux Arts versions, these are real chamber performances. The playing is freshly spontaneous throughout – the group readily conveys joy and exhilaration, especially in the delightful early works on the second and third discs. The recording is well balanced and the acoustic pleasing but, for whatever reason, the string timbre is somewhat dry, especially that of the violinist, Wilhelm Walz; although the tone of the fine cellist, Jörg Metzger, is not very expansive, he plays Beethoven's lyrical lines with a pleasing, simple warmth. Although the *Archduke Trio* is a rather lightweight reading, it does not lack repose, for slow movements throughout have expressive fibre, as they must in Beethoven's music. Altogether a first-rate bargain.

In their analogue set, dating from 1965, the Beaux Arts are let down a little by the ungenerous tone of their leader, Daniel Guilet; set against the refreshing spontaneity of the playing as a whole, however, this is of little moment. Tempi are admirably chosen (save for the *Ghost Trio*, which is very brisk; the work's drama and intensity, however, are projected to brilliant effect) and phrasing is marvellously alive. Ultimately the Beaux Arts score here on account of the chamber-music quality of their playing. They convey a sense of music-making in the home rather than in the concert hall, and the naturally balanced recording also has an attractive combination of warmth and intimacy.

The Barenboim/Zukerman/du Pré set (by omitting Nos. 4 and 8) is fitted economically on to three mid-priced CDs. Even more than usual, the individual takes involved long spans of music, often complete movements, sometimes even a complete work. The result is music-making of rare concentration, spontaneity and warmth. The excellent recording has been freshened on CD.

Piano trios Nos. 1 in E flat; 2 in G, Op. 1/1–2.
(B) *** HM HMA Dig. 1901361 [id.]. Patrick Cohen, Erich Höbarth, Christophe Coin.
(BB) ** Naxos Dig. 8.550946 [id.]. Stuttgart Piano Trio.

Patrick Cohen's group shows how fresh, alive and clear-textured these engaging works can be made to sound on period instruments, and how effective is the fortepiano, not only in the vivacious allegros but also in the slow movement of the *E flat major* and the *Largo con espressione* of the *G major*. The recording is first class, and this is a real bargain in its new Musique d'Abord format.

The Stuttgart Piano Trio play these early works of Beethoven with pleasing simplicity. They have not quite the individuality of the Beaux Arts, yet both slow movements are eloquently sustained and finales have sparkle, especially that of the G major which is infectious. The recording is naturally balanced in a warm acoustic which provides a clean realistic focus.

Piano trios Nos. 3 in C min., Op,. 1/3; 8 in E flat, WoO 38; 10 (Variations in E flat), Op. 44; Allegretto in E flat, Hess 48.
(BB) **(*) Naxos Dig. 8.550947 [id.]. Stuttgart Piano Trio.

Although the first movement of Op. 1/3 is on the brisk side, it springs to life spontaneously and the variations which follow are appealingly fresh. The other early *Trio in E flat* is very persuasively done and the *Variations*, Op. 44, are hardly less successful. With excellent recording, performances on this CD have obviously more sparkle than those on its earlier companion. Again the sound is fresh and naturally balanced.

Piano trios Nos. 5 in D (Ghost); 6 in E flat, Op. 70/1–2.
(BB) * Naxos Dig. 8.550948 [id.]. Stuttgart Trio.

The Stuttgart Trio take Beethoven's marking for the first movement of the *Ghost trio* ('*Allegro vivace e con brio*') very literally indeed and they dash into the opening like an express train. Their nervous intensity permeates the performance, though the arrival of the 'Ghost' is eerily effective. The *E flat Quartet* is only marginally more relaxed and the finale totally lacks geniality. The players are not helped by the dry recording, with microphones unflatteringly close in the Clara Wieck Auditorium, and this gives the impression of brisk efficiency rather than musical enjoyment.

Piano trios Nos. 5 in D (Ghost); 6 in E flat, Op. 70/1–2; 7 (Archduke); ll (Variations on 'Ich bin der Schneider Kakadu'); 12 (Allegretto in E flat).
(M) *** Carlton Double Dig. 30366 00107 (2). Solomon Trio.

Three of Beethoven's greatest trios played with fine dedication and intelligence by Yonty Solomon, Rodney Friend and Timothy Hugh in lively but not over-bright acoustics that do justice to their music-making. These artists have an excellent rapport; there is no playing to the gallery and one is left in no doubt that it is

Beethoven's muse they are trying to serve rather than any corporate ego. The only real snag is the dominance in the aural picture of the pianist – up to a point understandable, since the keyboard part is so important, although in the *Archduke* Timothy Hugh's rich cello is very much in the picture, suitably so for what is a comparatively mellow performance. The *Kakadu variations* are also done splendidly and the brief *Allegretto in E flat* makes a fresh bonus.

Piano trios Nos. 5 in D (Ghost), Op. 70/1; 7 in B flat (Archduke).
(B) **(*) Sony SBK 53514; *SBT 53514* [id.]. Eugene Istomin, Isaac Stern, Leonard Rose.
(M) ** Ph. Dig./Analogue 454 129-2. Beaux Arts Trio.

The playing from the Istomin/Stern/Rose trio is strong, polished and alive, with good teamwork and the individual personality of each player coming over forcefully. The *Archduke* is a very impressive performance indeed (preferable to the Beaux Arts), bold and traditional in approach and full of energy. One of the slight drawbacks of the transatlantic recording is the comparative shallowness of the piano tone and the touch of thinness on the violin timbre, but the ambience is convincing, the basic sound is warm and the balance not too close to rob the music-making of its dynamic range. An impressive coupling.

On Philips, the Beaux Arts Trio offer a popular coupling and they are realistically recorded. The *Archduke* was made in 1979 at La Chaux-de-Fonds in Switzerland, and the *Ghost* was recorded digitally, two years later, in London. The *Ghost Trio* comes off marvellously and sounds very fresh, but the *Archduke* is not as spontaneous as their earlier (mid-1960s) version, even if the ensemble remains excellent. The first movement, at a very slow tempo, sounds self-conscious and mannered; the Scherzo fails to maintain its spring and so does the finale. The slow variations have little sense of flow.

(i) *Piano trio No. 5 in D (Ghost), Op. 70/1;* (ii) *Violin sonata No. 9 in A (Kreutzer), Op. 47.*
(M) **(*) DG 447 917-2 [id.]. (i) Szeryng, Fournier; (ii) Y. Menuhin; (i; ii) Kempff.

This account of the *Ghost trio*, like the *Archduke*, below, comes from the complete cycle which these artists made for DG and which first appeared in 1970. The performance opens dramatically but is for the most part comparatively restrained, sweet and lyrical rather than dramatic, with Kempff very much the dominating influence. The recording has good presence and separation, but the blend of the three instruments is not altogether homogeneous. If the Menuhin/Kempff performance of the *Kreutzer sonata* is not as immaculate as other accounts, the spontaneous imagination of the playing, the challenge between great artists on the same wavelength, is consistently present.

Piano trio No. 7 in B flat (Archduke), Op. 97.
(B) *** EMI forte CZS5 69367-2 (2). David Oistrakh, Sviatoslav Knushevitzky, Lev Oborin – BRAHMS: *Violin sonatas Nos. 1–2* **(*); SCHUBERT: *Piano trio 1* *** (with: KODALY: *Three Hungarian folksongs;* SUK: *Love song;* WIENIAWSKI: *Légende;* YSAYE: *Extase* ***).

On EMI forte a well-rounded, well-groomed yet thoroughly alive performance by three eminent soloists who are nevertheless experienced enough as chamber-music players to allow the necessary blend of personalities, the give-and-take that is essential for a great performance. They are rugged and assured in the first movement, brilliant in the last, and only a shade less compelling in the intervening movements. The Abbey Road recording is equally impressive; even though it was made in 1958, it hardly sounds dated, smooth on top with a good balance, a tribute to Walter Legge's skill in the early days of stereo; and the Schubert coupling is equally impressive. The encores derive from a concurrent recital disc. Oistrakh is placed rather near the microphones, but his tone is pure and exceptionally rich, yet he is capable of bringing off astonishing changes of tone-colour – listen to the little-known but seductive Ysaÿe work and the *Hungarian folksongs* by Kodály. Yampolski provides supportive accompaniments and the balance remains very good.

(i) *Piano trio No. 7 (Archduke);* (ii) *Violin sonata No. 5 in F (Spring), Op. 24.*
(M) **(*) DG 447 916-2 [id.]. (i) Szeryng, Fournier; (ii) Menuhin; (i; ii) Kempff.

Kempff and his colleagues give a crystalline reading of the *Archduke*. It is the clarity and imagination of Kempff's playing which sets the tone of the whole performance. He it is who grips the listener's attention with his individual touches of genius, so that by comparison Szeryng and Fournier sound less than inspired. An interesting but not a definitive version. The reading of the *Spring sonata* has the magic which characterizes the whole Menuhin/Kempff cycle, and it was a pity that DG chose not to couple the violin sonatas together instead of mixing them up with the piano trios.

Piano and wind quintet in E flat, Op. 16.
(M) *** Sony Dig. SMK 42099 [id.]. Perahia, members of ECO – MOZART: *Quintet.* ***
(BB) *(*) Naxos Dig. 8.550511 [id.]. Jenö Jandó, Kiss, Kovács, Kevehazi, Vajda – MOZART: *Quintet.* *(*)

First choice for Beethoven's *Piano and wind quintet* lies with Perahia's CBS version, recorded at The Maltings. The first movement is given more weight than usual, with a satisfying culmination. In the *Andante*, Perahia's playing is wonderfully poetic and serene, and the wind soloists are admirably responsive. With the recording most realistically balanced, this issue can be recommended with all enthusiasm.

The Naxos performance, though well recorded and naturally balanced, is a disappointment. It opens rather stoically, and the first movement then proceeds robustly, without ever really taking off. Jandó leads the *Andante* effectively enough, but the wind players, though blending well, proceed in a leisured but uninspired manner. The finale has plenty of spirit, again with Jandó dominating, but overall this will give but limited satisfaction.

Septet in E flat, Op. 20.
(B) *** Decca Eclipse Dig. 448 232-2; *448 232-4* [(M) id. import]. Vienna Octet (members) – MOZART: *Clarinet quintet.* ***

Over the years the Vienna Octet have been justly famous for their recordings of Beethoven's *Septet* for Decca, and this newest version is no disappointment. Brio and good humour mark the performance, with a warmly elegant account of the slow movement to offset the high spirits of the Minuet and the Scherzo with its galumphing horn-playing. The finale is no less infectious. The recording is wonderfully warm and real; it was made as recently as 1991. The coupled Mozart *Clarinet quintet* is somewhat cooler but no less beautifully played (using a basset clarinet) and recorded.

Septet in E flat, Op. 20; Clarinet trio, Op. 11.
(BB) *** Virgin Classics Dig. Double VBD5 64109-2 (2) [CDVB 64109]. Nash Ens. – SCHUBERT: *Octet.* **

This is another example of the apparently apt pairing of CDs in a two-for-the-price-of-one format in which the result is less than successful because of the uneven quality of the coupling. There is pure magic in these Beethoven performances, with the members of the Nash Ensemble conveying their own enjoyment in the young Beethoven's exuberant inspiration. So the *Clarinet trio* finds each player, not just the fine clarinettist Michael Collins but also the pianist Ian Brown and the cellist Christopher van Kampen, pointing rhythms and phrases as a friendly challenge to be answered and capped by colleagues, the spontaneous interplay of the moment. It is a happy phenomenon, too rarely evident on record but delectably present here. An apt sense of fun also infects the *Septet*, though the allegros in the outer movements, exhilaratingly fast, would have been even more winning at speeds a shade more relaxed. But here too the performance brims with joy. Good, atmospheric sound. However, the coupled Schubert *Octet* is not technically or musically so successful.

Septet in E flat, Op. 20; (Wind) *Quintet in E flat for oboe, 3 horns and bassoon; Sextet in E flat for 2 horns and string quartet, Op. 81b.*
(BB) ** Naxos Dig. 8.553090 [id.]. Budapest Soloists.

Beethoven's charming and companionable *Septet* – in his lifetime one of his most popular works – is here coupled with two lesser-known works that equally demonstrate his mastery of mixed ensembles, both dominated by ripe horn-tone. If through the rather abrasive violin-sound of the leader, Ildiko Hegyi, balanced rather close, the *Septet* is on the fierce side, the wind playing is superb, and the horns in the other two works are magnificent. A fair bargain, but there are better versions of the Op. 20 *Septet*.

Septet in E flat, Op. 20; Wind octet in E flat, Op. 103.
(B) ** EMI forte CZS5 69755-2 (2) [CDFB 69755]. Melos Ens. of L. – MENDELSSOHN: *Octet* **; SCHUBERT: *Octet.* **(*)

With Gervase de Peyer (whether intentionally or not) very much the dominant personality in a distinguished group, the Melos Ensemble gives a reading of Op. 20 which brims with life and energy, idiomatic and spontaneous-sounding. The snag is the rather dry effect of the CD transfer, which is unflattering to the leader, whose violin-tone is robbed of bloom. Otherwise the sound is well balanced, and the *Wind octet* is a delight.

(i) *Serenade in D for flute, violin and viola, Op. 25;* (ii) *Serenade in D* (arr. of *Op. 25*) *for flute and piano, Op. 41; Flute sonata in B flat* (attrib.); *6 National airs with variations, Op. 105; 10 National airs with variations, Op. 105* (both sets for piano with flute obbligato).
(B) ** Ph. Duo 454 247-2 (2) [id.]. (i) Larrieu, Grumiaux, Janzer; (ii) Gazzelloni, Canino.

This set claims to garner Beethoven's 'complete music for flute', but the *Sonata in B flat* is of very dubious provenance: it sounds too simplistic even for very early Beethoven, although it is nimbly played. Easily the finest work here is the thoroughly engaging *Serenade in D*; but we are offered this twice, both in its original version for flute, violin and viola and in an arrangement for flute and piano, probably made by

Franz Xaver Kleinheinz, but 'improved' by the composer. The sets of *Variations on National airs* were commissioned by the Scottish publisher, George Thomson, and were based on folksong settings which Beethoven had previously supplied and which are musically far superior. The composer's instructions were to 'write the variations in a familiar and easy and perhaps rather brilliant style so that the largest number of our young ladies can play and enjoy them'. The result is quite pleasing but highly ingenuous, although performances and recording are impeccable.

String quartets

String quartets Nos. 1–16; Grosse Fuge, Op. 133.
(M) *** Valois V 4400 (8) [id.]. Végh Qt.
(B) *** Ph. 454 062-2 (10) [id.]. Italian Qt.
(M) (***) EMI mono CZS7 67236-2 (7). Hungarian Qt.

The Végh performances were recorded in the mid-1970s; they have been rightly hailed for their simplicity and depth. Intonation may not always be absolutely immaculate, but flaws are few and trivial when one considers the wisdom and experience the Végh communicate. In short they are in a different league from most of their rivals: there is no cultivation of surface polish though there is both elegance and finesse. The CD transfers are successful in producing an altogether cleaner image and a slightly firmer focus than the original analogue LPs, although the imbalance towards the cello remains. The eight discs are now available together at mid-price.

The Italian performances, which are in superb style, now return in a bargain box to offer almost unbeatable value. The Végh versions are in some ways even finer, but they are at mid-price; however, as they are on eight discs instead of ten, the difference in cost is relatively marginal. But the current Philips remastering is very impressive indeed: the sound is much smoother than hitherto, and very naturally balanced. The recordings were made in reverse order, starting with Op. 132 in 1967 and moving backwards to Op. 18, recorded between 1973 and 1975, with Op. 59/1 in the middle (1974), but the quality is remarkably consistent and the sonority they produce is beautifully blended and splendidly focused. In Op. 18 the only reservations concern Nos. 2 and 4: the latter is perhaps a little wanting in forward movement, while the conventional exchanges at the opening of No. 2 seem a shade too deliberate. But in general their superiority in terms of sheer quartet playing is still striking: purity of intonation and superb ensemble and attack. In the *Rasumovsky Quartets* in particular their tempi are perfectly judged and every phrase is sensitively shaped; in the later quartets their searching and thoughtful interpretations will ultimately prove most satisfying.

The Hungarian Quartet's first recorded cycle of the Beethoven *Quartets*, with the mono sound firm and full, is superb, with tonal beauty never an end in itself. Polished ensemble goes with a sense of spontaneity in readings fresher and more direct than those of 1966. The spacious, unhurried playing of the great slow movements here has rarely been matched. Those primarily concerned with the music as opposed to sound-quality will find little difficulty in adjusting to the recording.

String quartets Nos. 1–16 ; Grosse fuge, Op. 133; (i) *String quintet in C, Op. 29.*
(BB) ** Nimbus Dig. NI 5173 (8) [id.]. Medici Qt, (i) with Simon Rowland Jones.

The Medici Quartet recorded their Beethoven cycle between 1988 and 1990 at The Maltings, Snape, and their survey was well received generally, both in these columns and elsewhere. Theirs are natural and unfussy readings, free from any jet-set gloss or extremes of tempo. At the same time they do not always convey the impression that they are dealing with great music, and they do not make the most of the great moments that the *Rasumovsky* and the late quartets bring. The *C major String quintet* is a bonus, particularly as they do make the most of this piece and play with real eloquence. These records are remarkably inexpensive, but they offer no challenge to the 10-CD bargain set of the Quartetto Italiano on Philips (or in its various alternative packaging) or to the Lindsays on ASV.

String quartets Nos. 1–6, Op. 18/1–6.
(M) (***) Sony mono M2K 52531 (2) [id.]. Budapest Qt.
(M) **(*) Ph. 426 046-2 (3) [id.]. Italian Qt.

The celebrated set by the Budapest Quartet first appeared in the UK on the Philips label in 1956. Unlike their 1960s re-make, which was pretty rough-and-ready, the sonority is perfectly focused and the readings have weight, animation and dedication. They have command of the music's architecture and of expressive detail that is captured in sound of outstanding fidelity, given the period. The Sony engineers have effected transfers of excellent quality which can hold their own against many later versions. These finely balanced and warmly musical readings are something special and not to be missed.

The Italian performances are in superb style. The only reservations concern Nos. 2 and 4: the latter is perhaps a little wanting in forward movement, while the conventional exchanges at the opening of No. 2 seem a shade too deliberate. The balance is truthful but the digital remastering does draw the ear to a certain thinness in the treble, slightly more noticeable in the earliest recordings.

String quartets Nos. 1–6, Op. 18/1–6; 10 in E flat (Harp), Op. 74; 11 in F min., Op. 95.
(M) *** ASV CDDDCS 305 (3). Lindsay Qt.

It is good to have the Lindsay recordings now reissued at mid-price (retaining their old catalogue numbers). Their great merit in Beethoven lies in the natural expressiveness of their playing, most strikingly of all in slow movements, which brings a hushed inner quality too rarely caught on record. The sense of spontaneity necessarily brings the obverse quality: these performances are not as precise as those in the finest rival sets; but there are few Beethoven quartet recordings that so convincingly bring out the humanity of the writing, its power to communicate. The recording of Op. 18, set against a fairly reverberant acoustic, is warm and realistic; the transfers reflect the fact that the recordings are more modern and rather fuller than the remastered Philips quality for the Italian group (see above).

String quartets Nos. 1 in F; 2 in G, Op. 18/1–2.
(BB) ** Naxos Dig. 8.550558 [id.]. Kodály Qt.

At super-bargain price, the Kodály Quartet deserve favourable consideration. They do not attempt to dress things up in the manner of jet-setting quartets and their readings of both *Quartets* are decent and straightforward, and free from idiosyncrasy. Tempi are well judged and the Naxos recordings are first rate.

String quartets Nos. 1 in F, Op. 18/1; 4 in C min., Op. 18/4; 6 in B flat, Op. 18/6.
(M) **(*) DG Dig. 447 918-2 [id.]. Melos Qt.

The performances by the Melos Quartet offer a refined blend, impeccable intonation and superb ensemble. However, admiration rather than unalloyed pleasure is one's final reaction. Speeds are on the fast side, and too often this group does not convey a sufficient sense of pleasure in the courtly exchanges that take place among the four instruments, while at times their playing has an aggressive edge. There is, however, no question as to the finesse and mastery of the playing, nor the vividness of the recording.

String quartets Nos. 1 in F; 4 in C min.; 6 in B flat, Op. 18/1, 4 & 6; 9 in C (Rasumovsky), Op. 59/3; 11 in F min., Op. 95; (i) *String quintet in C, Op. 29.*
✪ (M) (***) Sony mono MH2K 62870 (2) [id.]. Budapest Qt, (i) with Milton Katims.

String quartets Nos. 12 in E flat, Op. 127; 14 in C sharp min., Op. 131; 15 in A min., Op. 132; 16 in F, Op. 135 (with *Minuet* from *Quartet No. 5 in A, Op. 18/5*).
✪ (M) (***) Sony mono MH2K 62873 (2) [id.]. Budapest Qt.

These two-CD Sony sets are of exceptional interest. Most older collectors will recall the fine Budapest mono LP survey of the Beethoven quartets which appeared on 'Columbia Records' in the United States and on the Philips label in Britain (see above). The present issue collects the 78-r.p.m. cycle on which this group embarked during the war years between 1940 and 1945. They were for the most part recorded in the agreeable and spacious acoustic of the Liederkranz Hall in New York (with the exception of Op. 18, No. 6, and the *C major Quintet*, Op. 29, which come from the 30th Street New York Studios). Even so, the sound is thoroughly agreeable, and great care has been taken over the transfers so that the quality is clean at the top and tonally full-bodied. Indeed so vivid is the sound and so silent the surfaces, one can barely believe their relatively early provenance. Such is the calibre of the playing that they even invite comparison with the legendary Busch set, and the comparison is by no means to the latter's advantage. Certainly the fugal opening of the Budapest Op. 131 is no less searching and it is technically more secure than the Busch. The beauty of the sound is enhanced by the elegance of the presentation, which reproduces facsimiles of the original 78-r.p.m. albums and their handsome labels. An altogether outstanding and highly treasurable reissue which, however, costs rather more than our usual upper-mid-price limit.

(i) *String quartets Nos. 1 in F, Op. 18/1; 9 in C, Op. 59/3; 11 in F min., Op. 95; 12 in E flat, Op. 127; 14 in C sharp min., Op. 131; 15 in A min., Op. 132; 16 in F, Op. 135;* (ii) *Violin sonata No. 3 in E flat, Op. 12/3.*
✪ (M) *** EMI mono CHS5 65308-2 (4). (i) Busch Qt; (ii) Adolf Busch, Rudolf Serkin – SCHUBERT: *String quartet No. 8.* (***)

Beethoven's greatest music, it is often rightly said, is better than any performance of it can ever be. Listening to the Busch Quartet's pre-war HMV accounts of the quartets, however, one is almost tempted to doubt this received wisdom. Certainly no group since has ever penetrated deeper into the heart of these scores. And one is also tempted to say that the (very occasional) technical imperfections (or frailties of intonation in Op. 132) are of greater musical interest than the meticulous perfection of most modern ensembles. In addition to the Beethoven quartets there is a bonus in the form of the *Violin sonata in E flat*, Op. 12, No. 3, from Busch and Serkin, playing of warmth and humanity, and a sparkling account of the early *B flat Quartet*, D.112, of Schubert. These are classics of the gramophone and not to be missed, and they are excellently remastered and transferred.

String quartets Nos. 3 in D; 4 in C min., Op. 18/3–4.
(BB) ** Naxos Dig. 8.550559 [id.]. Kodály Qt.

These are acceptable performances which are perfectly good value for money. Taken in isolation, they are satisfactory without being in any way exceptional. They are to be preferred to many glossier alternatives at full price, and the recording quality is very good indeed. The *C minor Quartet* needs greater dramatic fire and urgency of pulse, but the *D major* has much to recommend it. Decent but undistinguished must be the verdict here.

String quartets Nos. 3 in D; 4 in C min., Op. 18/3–4.
(BB) *** Arte Nova Dig. 74321 39103-2 [id.]. Alexander Qt.

String quartets Nos. 8 in E min.; 9 in C (Rasumovsky), Op. 59/2–3.
(BB) *** Arte Nova Dig. 74321 46491-2 [id.]. Alexander Qt.

Although not necessarily a first choice, no one investing in the Arte Nova accounts of the Op. 18 *Quartets* listed above will be disappointed. The San Francisco-based Alexander Quartet won the London International String Quartet Competition in 1985, since when they have enjoyed wide concert exposure but not on record. Although these are rock-bottom-priced discs, they are top-drawer performances and excellent recordings. This group play with fine musical intelligence and exemplary taste, and the recorded sound is excellently balanced. The same goes for the two *Rasumovsky Quartets* we have had the opportunity of hearing. If the Alexander continue to maintain the standard of these two issues, their survey will have strong claims on collectors, considering the small outlay involved.

String quartets Nos. 5 in A; 6 in B flat, Op. 18/5 & 6.
(BB) ** Naxos 8.550560 [id.]. Kodály Qt.

As with the earlier recordings in their series, this Naxos coupling is well played but not well enough to displace such distinguished accounts as the Quartetto Italiano or the Tokyo. The recording is eminently acceptable, but for Beethoven only the best is good enough.

String quartets Nos. 7 in F; 8 in E min.; 9 in C (Rasumovsky), Op. 59/1–3.
(M) *** ASV Dig. CDDCS 207 (2) [id.]. Lindsay Qt.

The Lindsay set contains performances of real stature; and though they are not unrivalled in some of their insights, among modern recordings they are not often surpassed. As a recording, this set is comparable with most of its competitors and superior to many; artistically, it can hold its own with the best. They are now reissued in a box, retaining the old catalogue number, but with further reduction to mid-price.

String quartets Nos. 7 in F; 8 in E min.; 9 in C, Op. 59/1–3; 10 in E flat (Harp), Op. 74.
(M) ** Berlin Classics 0091 622 BC (2) [id.]. Suske Qt.

The Suske Quartet was formed in the mid-1960s by members of the Berlin Staatskapelle, but the division of Germany at that time prevented them from making much of a reputation outside the Eastern bloc. The sleeve-notes mention that they shared second prize with the Melos Quartet of Stuttgart at the Geneva Competition in 1966. These performances were recorded in the late 1960s and, in the case of the *Harp Quartet*, leave no doubt of their credentials. Theirs are thoughtful, serious readings that would undoubtedly have been competitive at the time. The recordings are slightly forward but perfectly acceptable, but overall they do not displace any of our existing recommendations.

String quartets Nos. 7–9 (Rasumovsky Nos. 1–3), Op. 59/1–3; 10 in E flat (Harp), Op. 74; 11 in F min., Op. 95.
(M) *** Ph. 420 797-2 (3). Italian Qt.

The remastered Italian set still sounds well: there is now only a slight thinness on top to betray their age, with no lack of body and warmth in the middle range. Their superiority in terms of sheer quartet playing is still striking: purity of intonation, perfectly blended tone and superb ensemble and attack. Their tempi are perfectly judged and every phrase is sensitively shaped, and these performances remain very recommendable at mid-price.

String quartets Nos. 7 in F; 9 in C (Rasumovsky), Op. 59/1 & 3; 11 in F min., Op. 95; 15 in A min., Op. 132.
(BB) **(*) Virgin Classics Dig. Double VBD5 61406-2 (2) [CDVB 61406]. Borodin Qt.
This is another of the Virgin Doubles (two for the cost of one medium-priced CD) issued to celebrate their tenth anniversary. In the early years, when masterminded by Simon Foster, the label seemed to have scored something of a coup in signing up the Borodin Quartet for a complete Beethoven cycle. But it was never completed, so the four quartets offered here act only as a sampler of what might have been. Arguably the Borodins are currently the greatest quartet in the known world (as the saying goes) and, in terms of tonal sophistication and finesse, they have few peers. All the same, the high expectations aroused are only partially fulfilled. The recording is first class, warm and well defined, and this, curiously enough, in some ways holds good for the music-making. The playing is not superficial (there is plenty of concentration, for instance in the slow movements of both Op. 95 and Op. 132), but at the same time it is not particularly illuminating either. These are the kind of performances which would make a strong impression in the concert hall but which do not resonate in the mind afterwards. Nevertheless, at the lowest possible price, this pair of discs is well worth considering, if you want these particular Beethoven works, which are presented most faithfully and with a truly remarkable matching of timbre and dynamics.

String quartets Nos. 7 in F (Rasumovsky), Op. 59/1; 10 in E flat (Harp), Op. 74.
(M) *** DG 447 919-2 [id.]. Amadeus Qt.
The recording of Op. 59/1 is taken from the first *Rasumovsky* set to be issued in stereo, in 1960. The four instruments of the quartet are perfectly balanced and the stereo is warm yet remarkably clear. The *F major Quartet*, a tough nut to crack both technically and from the interpretative angle, comes off very successfully, not least because of the players' attention to Beethoven's dynamic and other markings. The *Adagio* brings considerable concentration and characteristically fine tonal matching. The *Harp quartet* benefits from similarly lively, sensitive and deeply musical playing, which makes it really come out of its shell; again the sound is remarkably present and well integrated. Although not all will take to Norbert Brainin's vibrato in the slow movement, the closing *Allegretto* with variations shows this ensemble playing with extraordinary unanimity and much vigour. This is one of the very finest of the Amadeus's early stereo records and can be recommended to all their admirers.

String quartet No. 7 in F (Rasumovsky), Op. 59/1; (ii) *Violin sonata No. 9 in A (Kreutzer), Op. 47.*
(B) **(*) DG Classikon 439 453-2 [(M) id. import]. (i) Amadeus Qt; (ii) Sir Yehudi Menuhin, Wilhelm Kempff.

An unusual coupling that might well appeal to impecunious collectors. There is some splendid playing from the Amadeus in the *First Rasumovsky Quartet*. Perhaps they do not uncover all its secrets, but the self-assurance and polish of the playing does not mean that the *Adagio* is unfeeling. The 1959 recording sounds well (with a touch of thinness on top), and the same comment might apply to the 1970 *Kreutzer Sonata*, although the sound is obviously more modern. Here the Kempff/Menuhin partnership is unique. In many ways it is not as immaculate as earlier accounts, but the spontaneous imagination of the playing, the challenging between great artists on the same wavelength, is consistently present.

String quartet No. 10 in E flat (Harp), Op. 74.
(BB) **(*) Discover Dig. DICD 920171 [id.]. Sharon Qt – MOZART: *Quartet No. 1;* ***; RAVEL: *Quartet.* **(*)

The Sharon Quartet give a remarkably enjoyable account of the the *Harp Quartet*, expressive and sensitive in the *Adagio* and perceptive in the closing *Allegretto con variazioni*. They are recorded in a Cologne church, which means that the sound is a shade reverberant (the Scherzo is affected most), but the blend is attractively full and it would be carping to complain when the playing is so well matched and responsive and gives the impression of a real performance.

String quartets Nos. 12–16; Grosse Fuge in B flat, Op. 133.
(M) *** ASV Dig. CDDCS 403 (4) [id.]. Lindsay Qt.
(M) (*) Bridge mono BCD 9072 [id.]. Budapest Qt.

String quartets Nos. 12 in E flat, Op. 127; 13 in B flat, Op. 130; 16 in F, Op. 135; Grosse Fuge in B flat, Op. 133.
(B) *** Ph. Duo 454 711-2 (2) [id.]. Italian Qt.

String quartets Nos. 14 in C sharp min., Op. 131; 15 in A min., Op. 132.
(B) **(*) Ph. Duo 454 712-2 (2) [id.]. Italian Qt.

String quartets Nos. 12 in E flat, Op. 127; 16 in F, Op. 135.
(B) **(*) [EMI Red Line Dig. CDR5 69791]. Alban Berg Qt.

String quartet No. 13 in B flat, Op. 130; Grosse Fuge in B flat, Op. 133.
(B) **(*) [EMI Red Line Dig. CDR5 69792]. Alban Berg Qt.

String quartets Nos. 14 in C sharp min., Op. 131; 15 in A min., Op. 132.
(B) **(*) [EMI Red Line Dig. CDR5 69793]. Alban Berg Qt.

The Lindsays get far closer to the essence of this great music than most of their rivals. They have the benefit of very well-balanced recording; the sound of the ASV set is admirably present. They seem to find tempi that somehow strike the listener as completely right and which enable them to convey so much of both the letter and the spirit of the music. They bring much rich musical characterization and musical strength. Taken overall, these are among the very finest versions to have been made in recent years. They now reappear, their catalogue number unchanged, but at mid-price – excellent value.

As we have suggested above in considering their complete set, the merits of the Italian Quartet's performances are very considerable and their separate reissue on a pair of Philips Duos is very competitive, even if the second of the two sets seems short measure at only 90 minutes. The remastered sound is very satisfying.

Some listeners may find the sheer polish of the Alban Berg Quartet gets in the way, for this can be an encumbrance: late Beethoven is beautified at its peril. Others dig deeper into the soul of this music, and this tells in movements like the *Heiliger Dankegesang* of Op. 132 or the *Cavatina* of Op. 130. The recordings do full justice to the magnificently burnished tone that the Alban Berg command and the perfection of blend they so consistently achieve. No single version of the late quartets can give us the complete truth, and no set is more magnificently played and recorded; yet, at the same time, it is difficult to suppress the feeling that others convey even more of the stature and depth of these great and profound works.

Bridge offer a less handsomely packaged but complete set of the late quartets, recorded at the Library of Congress. The set is recorded over a longer time-span: the *B flat*, Op. 130, and the *Grosse fuge* come from as late as 1960, when the quartet was a shadow of its former self, and the remainder derive from public performances given in 1941 (Op. 127), 1943 (Opp. 131 and 135) and 1945 (Op. 132) but the gain one might expect in spontaneity and the sense of occasion are more than offset by sonic limitations: the studio recordings from Sony are vastly superior artistically and there is no comparison technically. The wartime recordings suffer from coarse and unpleasing tone and peak distortion. Those who recall the CBS stereo recordings of the Budapest in the late 1950s and early 1960s will recall their vulnerable intonation and ensemble at that stage, and their public performance of Op. 130 cannot be said to enhance their reputation – to put it mildly. In every respect, performance, recording quality and presentation, the Sony win hands down. The present reissue cannot really be recommended at all.

String quartets Nos. 13 in B flat, Op. 130; 16 in F, Op. 135; Grosse Fuge in B flat, Op. 133.
(M) ** DG 447 920-2 [id.]. Amadeus Qt.

The Amadeus provide refined performances, and there is much subtle playing here of a very high technical standard. The refinement does not prevent vigour when needed, and the performance of the *Grosse Fuge* may surprise some with the strength of the Amadeus attack. But in the last analysis the performances suffer from a lack of the 'inner' quality which should make both slow movements into experiences beyond anything else in music. Not one of the *Adagios* is taken quite slowly enough, and the great *Cavatina* of Op. 130 sounds almost casual at a swinging *Andante*. The recording sounds very fresh and vivid.

String trios Nos. 1 in E flat, Op. 3; 2 in G; 3 in D; 4 in C min., Op. 9/1–3; Serenade in D, Op. 8.
(B) *** Ph. Duo 456 317-2 (2). Grumiaux Trio.

Beethoven's *String trios* are curiously neglected, and the return of the fine performances by the Grumiaux Trio (Arthur Grumiaux, George Janzer and Eva Czako) on a Philips Duo is a cause for celebration. Their playing is supremely musical and marvellously effortless; these artists are content to let the music speak for itself and they refrain from trying to score any interpretative points. In addition, the recording is fresh and full-bodied in the best Philips chamber-music tradition, with only the slightest hint of thinness on top. The *Serenade*, Op. 8 (originally coupled with the charming companion work, Op. 25 for flute, violin and viola), has been added for good measure. This performance, though polished, is perhaps not quite as persuasive as the rest of the programme. The set is strongly recommended, just the same.

VIOLIN SONATAS

Clara Haskil: The Legacy, Volume 1: Chamber music

Violin sonatas Nos. 1–10.
(M) (***) Ph. mono 442 625-2 (5). Arthur Grumiaux, Clara Haskil – MOZART: *Violin sonatas.* (***)

Arthur Grumiaux and Clara Haskil made their celebrated recordings in 1956–7 and these versions sound remarkably well for their age. The performances are wonderfully civilized and aristocratic, and no one investing in them will regret it. They accommodate all ten *Sonatas* on three CDs at mid-price, as opposed to the four of Perlman and Ashkenazy, but they come in harness with two further CDs (equally desirable) of Mozart's mature *Violin sonatas*, as part of the 'Clara Haskil Legacy'. The discs are not at present available separately.

Other recordings

Violin sonatas Nos. 1–10.
(M) *** Decca 421 453-2 (4); 436 892-2 (*Nos. 1–3*), 436 893-2 (*Nos. 4–5*), 436 894-2 (*Nos. 6–8*), 436 895-2 (*Nos. 9–10*). Itzhak Perlman, Vladimir Ashkenazy.
(M) *** Sony Stern Edition IV Dig./Analogue SM3K 64524 (3) [S3K 64524]. Isaac Stern, Eugene Istomin.
(BB) (*) Nimbus Dig. NI 5557/5560 [id.]. Benjamin Hudson, Mary Verney (fortepiano).

(i) *Violin sonatas Nos. 1 in D; 2 in A; 3 in E flat, Op. 12/1–3; 4 in A min., Op. 23; 5 in F (Spring), Op. 24;* (ii) *Romances for violin and orchestra Nos. 1–2, Opp. 40 & 50.*
(B) *** Ph. Duo 446 521-2 (2) [id.]. Henryk Szeryng; (i) Ingrid Haebler; (ii) Concg. O, Haitink.

Violin sonatas Nos. 6 in A; 7 in C min.; 8 in G, Op. 30/1–3; 9 in A (Kreutzer); 10 in G, Op. 96.
(B) *** Ph. Duo 446 524-2 (2) [id.]. Henryk Szeryng, Ingrid Haebler.

Perlman and Ashkenazy's set of the *Violin sonatas*, now reissued on four mid-priced CDs, will be difficult to surpass. These performances offer a blend of classical purity and spontaneous vitality that it is hard to resist; moreover the realism and presence of the recording in its CD format are very striking. They are also now available (in the UK only) on four separate mid-priced CDs.

Szeryng and Haebler made their recordings between January 1978 and December 1979, with the *Kreutzer* saved until the end of the cycle. Philips used a favourite venue, La Chaux-de-Fonds in Switzerland; with clear CD transfers, the effect is very realistic and the balance impressive. Szeryng's timbre is small and thin, much less ample than Perlman's, yet firmly focused, with the recording slightly more flattering in the later sonatas. There is always a poised line and a natural warmth in his phrasing of slow movements, and allegros often gain from this relative lack of opulence. For example, the delightfully whimsical playing in the first movement of the *Second Sonata* of the Opus 12 set is captivating, as is the finale, which dances with chimerical grace. Haebler's lilt again adds to one's pleasure in the delightful *Andante scherzoso* of Op. 23, while her natural pacing and nobility of line draw the listener right into the *Adagio* of the *Spring Sonata*, a performance which is every bit as fresh as its title suggests. Throughout, her superbly eloquent playing makes an artistic bedrock over which Szeryng weaves his spell, and in the earlier sonatas Beethoven's designation that they are for piano and violin is the more apparent. Yet the violin is not dwarfed and in the later works assumes increasing dominance. The *Allegretto con variazioni* finale of Op. 30/1 is another highlight, as is the glorious slow movement of the *C minor*, Op. 30/2. Perhaps the first movement of the *Kreutzer* ideally requires a richer timbre from the violin, but the central variations are most satisfying, and the dancing finale is as light as quicksilver. The final *G major Sonata*, with its gently persuasive opening, does not disappoint either; again the finesse of Szeryng's light bowing draws a magical response from the pianist; the lovely *Adagio espressivo* is truly memorable and the *Poco allegro* finale full of graceful charm. Haebler surely has never played with more obvious distinction or greater spontaneity on record, and the recording is fully worthy of her range of pianistic colour. With the two *Romances for violin and orchestra* thrown in for good measure, this pair of Duos, taken together, make a very good bargain and, while the Perlman/Ashkenazy Decca set remains a primary recommendation for these sonatas, the inspiration of the Szeryng/Haebler partnership is very cherishable.

The performances by Stern and Istomin have striking rhythmic strengths as well as lyrical appeal: how delightfully the lilting opening theme of *No. 2 in A major* dances along, and how superbly the great *Adagio* of the *C minor*, Op. 30/2, is sustained. This and the very first sonata are analogue and were recorded in 1969; the remainder are digital and date from 1982–3. The *Spring Sonata* is more intense than some versions, but in the most involving way; the *C minor*, Op. 30/2, has similar electricity and the *Kreutzer* is splendid. The recording has great presence – some might feel the balance is too close but it suits this highly projected style of music-making; Istomin has a strong artistic personality and keeps well in the picture.

The complete set from Benjamin Hudson and Mary Verney on Nimbus is most inexpensive, but it cannot be recommended with any confidence, even to collectors who must have these works played on the fortepiano. It sounds very clattery and unappealing, while Benjamin Hudson's timbre is fiercened by the close microphones apparently necessary in a very resonant, empty hall. The performances are musical enough but are unable to rise above this most unattractive acoustic. You have only to sample, say, the slow movement of the *C minor Sonata*, Op. 30/2, to sense that these artists are uncomfortable in such a venue.

Violin sonatas Nos. 1 in D; 2 in A; 3 in E flat, Op. 12/1–3.
(BB) *** Naxos Dig. 8.550284 [id.]. Takako Nishizaki, Jenö Jandó.

Violin sonatas No. 4 in A min., Op. 23; 10 in G, Op. 96; 12 variations on Mozart's 'Se vuol ballare' from 'Le nozze di Figaro', WoO 40.
(BB) *** Naxos Dig. 8.550285 [id.]. Takako Nishizaki, Jenö Jandó.

Naxos are on to a winning combination here. These performances are wonderfully fresh and alive. Takako Nishizaki isn't a 'big' player but her timbre is admirably suited to Beethoven and she is clearly in complete rapport with Jandó, who is in excellent form. The *Mozart variations*, too, are winningly done. The recording is most naturally balanced, the acoustic is spacious without in any way clouding the focus.

Violin sonatas Nos. 2 in A, Op. 12/2; 4 in A min., Op. 23; 5 in F (Spring), Op. 24; 8 in G, Op. 30/3.
(M) **(*) Ph. 442 651-2 [id.]. Arthur Grumiaux, Claudio Arrau.

This CD combines two pairs of performances recorded in the mid-1970s. *No. 2 in A* is particularly fresh; one can sense these artists enjoying their rapport; *No. 4 in A minor*, if fractionally less spontaneous, also comes off well. But in the *Spring Sonata* and the *G major*, although the readings are sensitive, understatement and lack of tension go together to undermine a feeling of live performance. The recording is fairly closely balanced but warmly refined and truthful; by the side of Perlman and Ashkenazy, however, these readings lack the last degree of character, although by any standards they are still distinguished.

Violin sonatas Nos. 5 in F (Spring), Op. 24; 7 in C min., Op. 30/2.
(M) (***) EMI CDH7 63494-2. Adolf Busch, Rudolf Serkin (with BACH: *Violin partita No. 2* (***)).

Music-making from another age, unhurried, humane and of supreme integrity. Playing of such naturalness and artistry transcends the inevitable sonic limitations.

Violin sonatas Nos. 5 in F (Spring); 8 in G, Op. 30/3; 9 in A (Kreutzer).
(M) *** EMI (SIS) CDM7 64631-2 [id.]. Pinchas Zukerman, Daniel Barenboim.
(M) ** RCA 09026 61861-2 [id.]. Henryk Szeryng, Artur Rubinstein.

The Zukerman/Barenboim 1973 coupling of the *Spring* and *Kreutzer sonatas*, long a favourite recommendation, is made even more attractive by the inclusion of the *G major Sonata*, Op. 30/3, an equally memorable work, when the playing is just as disarmingly spontaneous. The CD transfer scarcely betrays its age.

The Szeryng/Rubinstein account of *No. 8 in G* is a particularly fine one and the 1961 recording, although dry, is quite full. The *Spring* and *Kreutzer sonatas* date from 1958, and the microphones are less flattering to Szeryng's timbre, which sounds slightly wiry. The *Spring sonata* is effective enough, but the *Kreutzer* is the least penetrating of the three performances.

Violin sonatas Nos. 5 in F (Spring), Op. 24; 9 in A (Kreutzer), Op. 47.
(B) *** Tring Dig. TRP 082 [(M) id. import]. Jonathan Carney, Ronan O'Hora.
(BB) *** Naxos Dig. 8.550283; *4550283* [id.]. Takako Nishizaki, Jenö Jandó.
(B) **(*) [EMI Red Line Dig. CDR5 69789]. Yehudi & Jeremy Menuhin.

Couplings of the *Spring* and *Kreutzer Sonatas* are legion, but the stimulating partnership of Jonathan Carney (leader of, first, the RPO and currrently of the Bournemouth Symphony Orchestra) and Ronan O'Hora need not fear comparison with the finest. These highly dramatic performances have great concentration and spontaneity. After the well-sustained *Variations*, the finale of the *Kreutzer* bursts with joy. The recording is resonant, but the balance excellent: O'Hora makes the stronger contribution, with his colleague leading from the front.

Takako Nishizaki does not produce a large sound but the balance with Jandó is expertly managed, and the result is very natural and real. The performances are delightful in their fresh spontaneity. This is a bargain.

In 1986 Yehudi Menuhin re-recorded these works, this time with his son replacing his sister, Hephzibah. Jeremy plays remarkably well, if not quite matching Hephzibah in the slow movement of the *Kreutzer*. Yehudi Menuhin's timbre turns out to be less rounded than formerly and his technique less refined, but the nobility of line is still apparent, and the spontaneity and family chemistry are as potent as ever. The *Kreutzer* finale is joyfully spirited. Excellent recording in a resonant acoustic.

Violin sonatas Nos. 6 in A; 7 in C min.; 8 in G, Op. 30/1–3.
(BB) *** Naxos Dig. 8.550286; *4.550286* [id.]. Takako Nishizaki, Jenö Jandó.

All three of the Op. 30 *Sonatas* on one CD represents very good value for money, particularly as the playing is of considerable quality.

Violin sonatas Nos. 8 in G, Op. 30/3; 9 in A, Op. 47; 10 in G, Op. 96.
(B) *** Cal. Approche CAL 6251 [(M) id.]. Petr Messiereur, Stanislav Bogunia.

Strong, direct accounts of Beethoven's last three sonatas, of striking spontaneity and recorded with great presence and vividness. This playing, if not always subtle, leaps out of the speakers and certainly holds the listener. Slow movements are felt but never sentimentalized. The *Adagio* of No. 10 is appealingly serene, and the following Scherzo and *Poco allegretto* finale offer admirable contrast. This disc is well worth its modest cost. At the time of going to press, the CD is the subject of a special offer, in a slipcase at super-bargain price, with a full Calliope catalogue.

SOLO PIANO MUSIC

Piano sonatas Nos. 1–32 (complete).
❁ (B) (***) DG mono 447 966-2 (8) [(M) id. import]. Wilhelm Kempff.
(B) *** DG 429 306-2 (9) [id.]. Wilhelm Kempff.
(B) *** EMI CZS7 62863-2 (10) [CDZ 62863]. Daniel Barenboim.
(BB) *** Nimbus Dig. NI 1774 (11) [id.]. Bernard Roberts.
(B) *** Decca 443 706-2 (10) [425 590-2] (with *Andanti favori*). Vladimir Ashkenazy.
❁ (M) (***) EMI mono CHS7 63765-2 (8) [Ang. CDHH 3765]. Artur Schnabel.
(M) **(*) Decca 433 882-2 (8). Wilhelm Backhaus.

Piano sonatas Nos. 1–32; 6 Variations in F, Op. 43; Variations and fugue in E flat on a theme from Prometheus (Eroica), Op. 35; 32 Variations in C min., WoO 80.
(M) *** Ph. 432 301-2 (11). Claudio Arrau.

In celebration of the centenary in November 1995 of the birth of Wilhelm Kempff, most inspirational of Beethoven pianists, DG have issued this welcome bargain box of the earlier of his two Beethoven sonata cycles. Those who have cherished the later, stereo cycle for its magical spontaneity will find Kempff's qualities even more intensely conveyed in this mono set, recorded between 1951 and 1956. The interpretations are the more personal, the more individual, at times the more wilful; but for any listener who responds to Kempff's visionary concentration, it is a magical series of interpretations. No other set of the sonatas so clearly gives the impression of new discovery, of fresh inspiration in the composer as a pianist. Amazingly, the sound has more body and warmth than the stereo set, with Kempff's unmatched transparency and clarity of articulation even more vividly caught, both in sparkling allegros and in deeply dedicated slow movements. A ninth disc comes free, celebrating Kempff's achievement in words and music, on the organ in Bach, on the piano in Brahms, Chopin and Beethoven (a masterly pre-war recording of the *Pathétique sonata*) and accompanying Fischer-Dieskau in four of his own songs. The discs are engagingly packaged with a portrait of Kempff on each CD jacket, although the documentation is not as lavish as when these recordings last appeared on LP in 1980 to celebrate Kempff's eighty-fifth birthday. It is worth recalling what the great pianist wrote for the booklet offered with those LPs: 'No finer 85th-birthday present could have been given to me. Not only I, but thus also listeners, have the opportunity to delve into my musical biography. For undoubtedly between the mono recordings and the stereo records which I made much later there lay changes in my own artistic viewpoint. It will be fascinating to pinpoint the differences. I should however like to emphasize that to me interpretation has always centred upon a creative or, more correctly, a post-creative element. It was so then as in later years – and it is still so today.'

Kempff's stereo recordings, all dating from 1964/5, are to the 1960s what Schnabel's were to the pre-war years – performances that represent a yardstick by which all others are judged. Kempff's shading of pianistic colour is so imaginative that the ear readily accommodates any slight dryness in the upper range. The interpretations have a commanding stature, yet Kempff brings his own individuality to every bar and a clarity and sparkle that make you want to go on listening.

Barenboim's earlier set of the Beethoven *Sonatas*, recorded for EMI when he was in his late twenties, remains one of his very finest achievements on record. The readings are sometimes idiosyncratic, with unexpected tempi both fast and slow, but the spontaneous style is unfailingly compelling. At times Barenboim's way is mercurial, with an element of fantasy. But overall this is a keenly thoughtful musician living through Beethoven's great piano cycle with an individuality that puts him in the line of master pianists.

Bernard Roberts's cycle – his second for Nimbus – can be warmly recommended, the more so when it comes at super-bargain price. These are dedicated, undistracting readings which consistently reflect Roberts's mastery as a chamber-music pianist, intent on presenting the composer's arguments as clearly as possible, not drawing attention to himself. Not that these are in any way anonymous performances, for their concentration is intense. Always spontaneous-sounding, Roberts's approach to Beethoven has an element of toughness, whether in the early works or the late, a point that comes out the more clearly when the individual discs mix works of different periods. The mature sonatas are marked by rugged power, with Roberts's virtuosity given full rein, as in the finale of the *Appassionata*. The digital sound is vivid and full-bodied, with the piano set in a helpful, relatively intimate acoustic. This is the least expensive set of the Beethoven sonatas on the market and it is well worth its modest cost.

Decca have now reissued Ashkenazy's set which occupied him over a decade from 1971 until 1980, with the *Andante favori* added on as an encore in 1981. He brings to the early sonatas the concentrated, unaffected qualities which make his recordings of the *Violin sonatas* with Perlman so eminently compelling. Interpretatively the manner is strong and direct, rightly treating the young Beethoven as a fully mature composer, no imitator of Haydn and Mozart; but the important point is that, whether in fast music or slow, he conveys the feeling of new discovery and ready communication. He is also especially persuasive in the two Op. 14 sonatas (Nos. 9 and 10). Among the famous named sonatas, there is much to admire in the *Moonlight* and, if his *Pathétique* is perhaps understated for so youthfully ebullient a work, the finale, unusually gentle, conveys the underlying power. He gives a deeply satisfying reading of the *Waldstein sonata*, where the degree of restraint, the occasional hesitations, intensify his thoughtful approach, never interrupting the broader span of the argument. The Op. 31 *D minor Sonata*, nicknamed *Tempest*, and its companion in E flat, Op. 31/3, are among the best of his cycle. He brings concentration of mind, together with a spontaneity of feeling, that illumines both works. The command of keyboard colour is as always impressive and, in terms of both dramatic tension and the sense of architecture, these are thoroughly satisfying performances. His readings of the middle-period sonatas are as masterly and penetrating as anything he has given us, and he is pretty impressive in the late sonatas. There is a rapt sense of repose in the slow movement of Op. 109 (*No. 30 in E major*) and the last two sonatas are played with a depth and spontaneity which put these readings among the finest available. However, the *Hammerklavier*, one of the last to be recorded, is not quite on this level. Curiously, it is coupled with the *Andante favori* (which comes first on the CD). The performance of the sonata is fresher and more spontaneous-sounding than in his earlier Decca version, not quite so immaculate in the playing, but still strong and direct, with power and speed in the outer movements; but the total experience is less than monumental. Overall the sound is excellent, vivid and present, if not always quite as full and natural as Barenboim's alternative and highly recommendable bargain-priced EMI set.

Arrau's Beethoven cycle, recorded during the 1960s, is a survey of extreme distinction. The great Chilean pianist possessed a quite distinctive keyboard sonority, rich and aristocratic in its finesse. The late sonatas show his artistry at its most consummate: one of the very finest of these performances (and one of the very finest records he ever made) is his *Hammerklavier*, which represents his art at its most fully realized. No apologies need be made for the recordings, which belie their age.

For many music-lovers and record collectors of an older generation, Schnabel was the voice of Beethoven; returning to this pioneering set again, one realizes that his insights were deeper than those of almost anyone who followed him, though his pianism has been surpassed. This is one of the towering classics of the gramophone and, whatever other individual Beethoven sonatas you may have, this is an indispensable reference point.

Backhaus recorded his survey over a decade, from 1958 to 1969 (with the exception of the *Hammerklavier*, which came much earlier, in 1953, and is mono). As it happens, the latter represents the peak of the cycle, offering playing of great power and concentration. Backhaus's direct, sometimes brusque manner does not derive from any lack of feeling, rather from a determination to present Beethoven's thoughts adorned with no idiosyncratic excrescences. At his best, as in the *Waldstein* and *Appassionata sonatas*, the performances present a characteristic mixture of rugged spontaneity and wilfulness which can be remarkably compelling. But there are many other examples of his positive, alert and imaginative response which balance the apparently uncompromising wilfulness of manner. He was less suited to the more lightweight works, yet even here he plainly enjoyed himself in his own way, so that his own responses are conveyed to the listener. Generally – as with the *Hammerklavier* – the bigger the challenge for him, the more impressive the performance. His massive, rather gruff style naturally suits the later rather than the earlier sonatas, but even in Op. 101, where the challenge is greatest, the uningratiating manner will not suit all tastes, and the very powerful accounts of Op. 109 and Op. 111 do not always leave the music quite enough space to breathe. But overall the set is a formidable achievement and a reminder of a keyboard giant. The recording is remarkably faithful; the only real drawback is that the close balance brings a comparative lack of dynamic range.

Piano sonatas Nos. 1 in F min.; 2 in A; 3 in C, Op. 2/1–3.
(BB) **(*) Naxos Dig. 8.550150; *4550150* [id.]. Jenö Jandó.

Jenö Jandó's complete recording of the Beethoven *Piano sonatas* is also available in two flimsy slip-cases, each comprising five CDs (8.505002 and 8.505003). This first CD (actually Volume 3) establishes Jandó's credentials as a strong, unidiosyncratic Beethovenian. If there is not the individuality of a Kempff or a Barenboim, the playing is always direct and satisfying. The piano sound is real, full and bold.

Piano sonatas Nos. 1 in F min.; 2 in A, Op. 2/1–2; 19 in G min.; 20 in G, Op. 49/1–2.
(BB) **(*) ASV CDQS 6055. John Lill.

This first record of John Lill's cycle offers some of the most characteristic performances in the series. There is a directness of utterance about Lill's Beethoven which is undoubtedly compulsive, particularly as the recording has great presence and the tone is admirably secure and realistic. Lill brings a formidable technique to all these sonatas and his deliberation at the opening of the *F minor Sonata* (No. 1) gives the first movement great character. The slow movement too is eloquently played, and the *Largo appassionato* of No. 2 also makes a strong impression, though some will feel that the fortissimo outbursts are over-characterized. The closing Rondo (*Grazioso*), however, lilts appealingly. As he shows in the two Opus 49 *Sonatas*, Lill is not strong on charm, yet there is an appealing simplicity and a strong profile. Moreover, there is an integrity about this playing that the listener cannot fail to notice.

Piano sonatas Nos. 3 in C, Op. 2/3; 4 in E flat, Op. 7; 8 in C min. (Pathétique), Op. 13.
(BB) ** ASV CDQS 6056. John Lill.

The *C major Sonata*, Op. 2/3, is one of John Lill's most successful performances and one of the best recorded. The slow movement makes a strong impression, though some will feel that the fortissimo outbursts are overcharacterized. In Op. 7 Lill's articulation from fingers of steel is thrilling, but the rhythms too rarely spring, and the rather formal *Largo, con gran espressione*, is given an uncompromising quality. The sound is believably present, though it seems shallower in the *Pathétique*, where the slow movement is thoughtful; but at times in the outer movements one has the impression that the drama is overdone.

Piano sonatas Nos. 4 in E flat, Op. 7; 13 in E flat, Op. 27/1; 19 in G min., 20 in G, Op. 49/1–2; 22 in F, Op. 54.
(BB) **(*) Naxos Dig. 8.550167; *4550167* [id.]. Jenö Jandó.

The performances of both the *E flat Sonata*, Op. 7, and the *Sonata quasi una fantasia*, Op. 27/1, in which Jandó is totally responsive to Beethoven's wide expressive range, show the continuing excellence of this series, and the three shorter works are also freshly presented.

Piano sonatas Nos. 5 in C min.; 6 in F; 7 in D, Op. 10/1–3.
(BB) *(*) ASV CDQS 6057 [id.]. John Lill.

These are among the more disappointing of Lill's sonata readings, rather square and charmless. The great D major slow movement of Op. 10/3 is taken challengingly slowly, but there is little feeling of flow. Bright, realistic, well-focused recording.

Piano sonatas Nos. 5 in C min.; 6 in F; 7 in D, Op. 10/1–3; 25 in G, Op. 79.
(BB) *** Naxos Dig. 8.550161; *4.550161* [id.]. Jenö Jandó.

The three splendid Op. 10 *Sonatas* show Jandó at his most perceptive and unselfconscious.

Piano sonatas Nos. 7 in D; 23 in F min. (Appassionata), Op. 57.
(M) *** Sony Dig. SMK 39344 [id.]. Murray Perahia.

Intense, vibrant playing from Perahia in the *D major Sonata*, with great range of colour and depth of thought, and the *Appassionata* is a performance of comparable stature. These are among the few interpretations to have appeared in recent years that can be recommended alongside Gilels. The recorded sound is truthful, and this issue is made even more attractive by being offered at mid-price.

Piano sonatas Nos. 8 (Pathétique), Op. 13; 14 (Moonlight), Op. 27/2; 15 (Pastoral), Op. 28; 17 (Tempest), Op. 31/2; 21 (Waldstein), Op. 53; 23 (Appassionata), Op. 57; 26 (Les Adieux), Op. 81a.
(B) *** Ph. Duo 438 730-2 [id.]. Alfred Brendel.
(B) *** Decca Double 452 952-2 (2) [id.]. Vladimir Ashkenzay.

In offering seven of Beethoven's most popular named sonatas, this Duo set – two discs for the price of one – is in every way an outstanding bargain, well worth having even if duplication is involved. All the performances are undeniably impressive and the recording consistently excellent. The *Tempest*, Op. 31/2, is finely conceived and thoroughly compelling, and the central movements of the *Pastoral* resonate in the memory, the performance radiant and beautifully shaped, with every detail fitting in harmoniously with the artist's conception of the whole. While Brendel's earlier *Waldstein* (on Vox/Turnabout) has claims to be considered among the very finest on record, this is only marginally less impressive and is certainly much better recorded.

This well-chosen and generous collection of named sonatas was compiled (in late 1997) to celebrate Ashkenazy's sixtieth birthday and shows him consistently as a penetrating and individual Beethovenian. His *Pathétique* is perhaps slightly understated for so ebulliently youthful a work, with the finale unusually gentle; nevertheless the performance conveys an underlying power. The *Moonlight*, however, is generally very successful, poetic and unforced, and in the *Pastoral sonata*, although the first movement is questionably slow, his freshness of manner silences criticism. He brings concentration of mind together with spontaneity of feeling to the *Tempest*, where the command of keyboard colour is, as always, impressive. Taking a broadly lyrical view, the *Waldstein* is splendidly structured. The *Appassionata* is superb, although those who feel strongly about matters of tempo may well find Ashkenazy a little too free in the first movement. *Les Adieux* brings a vehement opening movement and again memorable concentration. The very good analogue recordings were made over a period of seven years between 1973 and 1980 and they are excellently transferred to CD.

Piano sonatas Nos. 8 in C min. (Pathétique), Op. 13; 14 in C sharp min. (Moonlight), Op. 27/2; 17 in C sharp min. (Tempest), Op. 31/2.
(B) **(*) Tring Dig. TRP 027 [id.]. Cristina Ortiz.

Cristina Ortiz is at her finest on this inexpensive Tring triptych. These are considerable performances, and they are beautifully recorded. The *Pathétique* is strong and fluent; the *Tempest*, with its impulsive fluctuations of tempo handled very individually but always poetically and spontaneously, is most refreshing, especially the delightfully articulated *Allegretto* finale. However, Ortiz chooses to play the opening of the *Moonlight* very quietly indeed, and in a manner that seems deliberate as well as thoughtful. The second movement is lilting and the finale swift and strong, so the necessary contrasts are present; but not all will find the opening completely convincing.

Piano sonatas Nos. 8 (Pathétique); 14 (Moonlight); 21 (Waldstein).
(BB) ** Belart 450 058-2 [London 421 031-2]. Radu Lupu.

Radu Lupu is an unfailingly sensitive artist, and he has the undoubted gift of creating spontaneity in the recording studio; but sometimes his thoughtful, improvisatory style, which can work so well in Schubert, can seem mannered, as in the rather deliberate approach to the slow movement of the *Pathétique Sonata* or the very measured opening of the *Moonlight*. But the playing carries conviction and the performances of both these works are individual and enjoyable. Lupu is less successful in holding the concentration of the *Waldstein Sonata*, after preparing for the gentle emergence of its great principal theme very beautifully. It is this that brings the withholding of a third star despite Decca's best piano-sound, clear and realistically present. Nevertheless in the budget range this CD is by no means to be dismissed.

Piano sonatas Nos. 8 in C min. (Pathétique), Op. 13; 14 in C sharp min. (Moonlight), Op. 27/2; 21 in C (Waldstein), Op. 53; 23 in F min. (Appassionata).
(M) *** DG 447 404-2 [id.]. Wilhelm Kempff.

Kempff's masterly recordings are truly legendary and make a fitting contribution to DG's series of 'Originals'. Each performance here shows so well his ability to rethink Beethoven's music within the recording studio. Everything he does has his individual stamp; above all, he never fails to convey the deep intensity of a master in communication with Beethoven. In the *Waldstein*, although the opening movement is dramatic, Kempff's preparation for the great theme of the finale is gentle, and when it appears the effect is to give the melody a less joyous quality than we are used to. But the result is magical, for there is a compensating spiritual quality and, with the suggestion of a more restrained forward momentum, the finale gains in breadth and boldness what it loses in sheer vivacity. The *Appassionata* is characteristically clear and classically straight. Although less weightily dramatic than in other readings, the concentration is irresistible. The recording has undoubtedly gained in firmness with the clean sound of the digital remastering, and there is plenty of warmth and colour at lower dynamic levels.

Piano sonatas Nos. 8 in C min. (Pathétique), Op. 13; 14 in C sharp min. (Moonlight), Op. 27/2; 23 in F min. (Appassionata), Op. 57.
(B) **(*) [EMI Red Line CDR5 69788]. Daniel Barenboim.
(BB) **(*) Naxos Dig. 8.550045; *4550045* [id.]. Jenö Jandó.
(B) ** EMI CfP CD-CFP 6028 [id.]. Daniel Chorzempa.

Barenboim's earlier performances combine impetuosity with a confident control of line. There is a rhapsodic feel to his approach which is often very convincing. The first movement of the *Pathétique*, for example, taken rather fast, has a natural wildness about it, but it is so compelling that one forgives minor blemishes. The second movement brings a tempo so slow that the result could have seemed too static, had not Barenboim's concentration been so sure. The *Appassionata* too is rather wild and rhapsodic in the first movement, and again the slow speed for the central variations brings a simple, natural intensity which contrasts well with the lightness and clarity of the finale. The sound is first class, with excellent sonority.

Jandó's clean, direct style and natural spontaneity are particularly admirable in the slow movements of the *Pathétique* and *Appassionata*, warmly lyrical in feeling, yet not a whit sentimental. Only in the coda of the finale of the *Appassionata* does one feel a loss of poise, when the closing *presto* becomes *prestissimo* and the exuberance of the music-making nearly gets out of control.

Daniel Chorzempa has the advantage of first-class sound. His reputation was made in the organ loft, but here his technical command of the piano keyboard is never in doubt. The interpretations are rather studied, the readings of a serious young man taking great care in matters both of detail and of structure. The clarity of the style is well projected, but there is also an absence of romantic charm.

Piano sonatas Nos. 8 (Pathétique); 14 (Moonlight); 23 (Appassionata); 26 (Les Adieux).
✿ (M) *** RCA 09026 61443-2 [Basic 100 09026 62561-2; *09026 62561-4*]. Artur Rubinstein.

Artur Rubinstein almost always conveys a sense of spontaneity in his recorded performances, and the sense of a live interpretation is specially vivid here. He was not a Beethoven specialist, but it is perhaps surprising that he had never recorded the *Moonlight* before this version (dating from 1962), nor even played it in public. But there is a combination of freshness and maturity in his reading which makes it stand out even among many fine recorded versions. The improvisatory feeling in the opening movement is remarkable. The *Pathétique* has a youthful urgency in the outer movements, yet the *Adagio cantabile* has a wonderful simplicity. The impulsive surge of feeling in the *Appassionata* is equally compelling, with the finale reminding one of Richter's famous record. The exhilaration and power of Rubinstein's playing, both here and in *Les Adieux*, are beyond praise. If he has forged a special link with any Beethoven work, it is with Op. 81a. The recordings, made in the Manhattan Center, New York City, sound firmer and fuller than they did on LP and reflect great credit on John Pfeiffer's remastering for CD.

Piano sonatas Nos. 8 in C min. (Pathétique); 21 in C (Waldstein); 23 in F min. (Appassionata).
✿ (M) *** DG Analogue/Dig. 447 914-2 [id.]. Emil Gilels.
(M) **(*) Ph. Dig. 454 686-2 [422 970-2]. Claudio Arrau.

Piano sonatas Nos. 8 in C min. (Pathétique); 23 in F min. (Appassionata), Op. 57; 31 in A flat, Op. 110.
(B) *** DG Classikon Dig./Analogue 439 426-2 [(M) id. import]. Gilels.

Gilels's account of the *Appassionata* has previously been hailed by us as among the finest ever made, and much the same must be said of the *Waldstein*. It has a technical perfection denied even to Schnabel and, though in the slow movement Schnabel found special depths, Gilels is hardly less searching and profound. If the *Pathétique* does not quite rank among his very best, such are the strengths of his playing that the reading still leaves a profound impression. In this sonata the 1980 digital recording, though real and present, is nevertheless balanced too close (which brings a touch of hardness on fortissimos). In the analogue recordings of the other two sonatas, the piano is much less closely observed, to great advantage.

The *Pathétique* and *Appassionata sonatas* are also available on Classikon, in a coupling with Op. 110, and this makes a formidable bargain alternative, for the *A flat Sonata*, too, is given a performance of real stature. Even when Gilels storms the greatest heights in the closing fugue, no fortissimo ever sounds percussive or strained. This was (digitally) recorded five years later than the *Pathétique* and the balance is better judged.

Arrau's performances are magnificently recorded. They were made at different times (1984–7) and in different places (Switzerland and New York), but the digital piano sonority is full and satisfying, the image bold and realistic. This helps to make Arrau's *Appassionata* very commanding indeed, with gloriously rich timbre in the central *Andante*. It is a distinguished performance, powerful and commanding in the same way as his *Emperor concerto*. The *Waldstein* is impressive too, though not as incandescent as Kempff's. The *Pathétique* (recorded in 1986 when Arrau was eighty-three) is just a little wanting in colour and vitality, and some listeners may feel that the *Adagio cantabile* is too measured. However, the playing throughout this record is impressive and, for all the individual mannerisms, the interpretations are authoritative and convincing.

Piano sonatas Nos. 9 in E; 10 in G, Op. 14/1–2; 13 in E flat; 14 in C sharp min. (Moonlight), Op. 27/2.
(BB) ** ASV CDQS 6058. John Lill.

For the two early sonatas Lill scales down the aggressiveness in his approach to Beethoven and the results are clear and refreshing, if lacking in charm. His account of No. 13 is thoughtful but not really imaginative enough, and memories of the marvellous range of colour that Schnabel produced in the first movement flood back. The opening of the *Moonlight* is simple and quite evocative, and Lill then attacks the finale with furious bravura. Bright, clear, late-1970s recording, not lacking sonority – the CD gives a good illusion of realism and presence.

Piano sonatas Nos. 9 in E; 10 in G, Op. 14/1–2; 24 in F sharp, Op. 78; 27 in E min., Op. 90; 28 in A, Op. 101.
(BB) *** Naxos Dig. 8.550162; *4550162* [id.]. Jenö Jandó.

Opp. 90 and 101 show this artist at full stretch. These are demanding works and Jandó does not fall short, particularly in the slow movements, which are very eloquent indeed. The piano sound is most believable.

Piano sonatas Nos. 11 in B flat, Op. 22; 29 in B flat (Hammerklavier), Op. 106.
(BB) **(*) Naxos Dig. 8.550234; *4550234* [id.]. Jenö Jandó.

From its very opening bars, the *Hammerklavier* is commanding; there is rapt concentration in the slow movement, and the closing fugue runs its course with a powerful inevitability. Opus 22 is comparably impressive. Again, most realistic recording.

Piano sonatas Nos. 12 in A flat, Op. 26; 16 in G; 18 in E flat, Op. 31/1 & 3.
(BB) **(*) Naxos Dig. 8.550166 [id.]. Jenö Jandó.

Volume 7 with its trio of middle-period sonatas can be recommended with few reservations. No. 18 is a considerable success, and there is much to stimulate the listener's interest here. Excellent sound.

Piano sonatas Nos. 13 in E flat; 14 in C sharp min. (Moonlight), Op. 27/1–2; 15 in D (Pastoral), Op. 28; 26 in E flat (Les Adieux), Op. 81a.
(M) *** DG Dig. 445 593-2 [id.]. Daniel Barenboim.

Spontaneity and electricity, extremes of expression in dynamic, tempo and phrasing, as well as mood, mark Barenboim's performances. The lyrical flow in the *Pastoral* is as evident as the spontaneity of the music-making. The plainness in the first movement of the *Moonlight* is the one disappointment, with little veiled tone; however, the *Andante espressivo* of *Les Adieux* is played touchingly. The recordings are firm and the acoustic spacious.

Piano sonatas Nos. 14 in C sharp min. (Moonlight), Op. 27/2; 15 in D (Pastoral), Op. 28; 17 in D min. (Tempest), Op. 31/2; 21 in C (Waldstein), Op. 53; 22 in F, Op. 54; 23 in F min. (Appassionata), Op. 57; 24 in F sharp, Op. 78; 32 in C min., Op. 111.
(B) ** Decca Double 443 012-2 (2) [id.]. Friedrich Gulda.

This series of Beethoven sonatas was recorded in the late 1950s and Gulda proves a thoroughly reliable Beethovenian. The recording quality is good, and the directness of manner characteristic of this pianist is naturally projected. Gulda's view of Op. 101 is thoughtful and unforced, and so in its way is the *Waldstein*, though some may find too little weight. His view of the *Appassionata* is purposeful and direct, lacking something in fantasy, but satisfying on its own terms. The reading of Op. 111 is penetrating, even if it rarely rises to the supreme heights of the greatest interpretations. At Double Decca price, this is acceptable value, but Brendel's pair of Duos (Philips 438 730-2 and 438 374-2) cover this repertoire and much else besides, and offer a far better investment.

Piano sonatas Nos. 14 in C sharp min. (Moonlight), Op. 27/2; 17 in D min. (Tempest), Op. 31/2; 26 in E flat (Les adieux), Op. 81a.
(M) **(*) Beethoven Edition DG Dig. 447 913-2 [id.]. Daniel Barenboim.

Spontaneity and electricity, extremes of expression in dynamic, tempo and phrasing, as well as mood, marked Barenboim's complete DG cycle. The plainness in the first movement of the *Moonlight* is disappointing, with little veiled tone; but the light, flowing finale of the *Tempest* is magically Mendelssohnian. The *Andante espressivo* of *Les Adieux* is also played touchingly. The 1984 digital recording is firm and the acoustic spacious.

Piano sonatas Nos. 14 in C sharp min. (Moonlight), Op. 27/2; 21 in C (Waldstein), Op. 53; 23 in F min. (Appassionata), Op. 57.
(M) **(*) RCA GD 60375 [60375-2-RG]. Vladimir Horowitz.

Horowitz was not thought of primarily as a Beethoven pianist, but these recordings, made in 1956 (the *Moonlight* and *Waldstein*) and 1959, show how powerful he could be in the music of this composer. His delicacy, too, is equally impressive. The sound has been improved in the remastering process; there is some hardness on top but little shallowness, and the bass sonority is telling.

Piano sonatas: No. 15 in D (Pastoral), Op. 28; (Kurfürstensonaten) in E flat, F min., D, WoO 47/1–3; in C (incomplete), *WoO 51; Sonatinas: in G, F, Anh. 5/1–2.*
(BB) ** Naxos Dig. 8.550255 [id.]. Jenö Jandó.

Jandó's playing is fresh, clean and intelligent and, if the two *Sonatinas* are not authentic, they make agreeable listening here. The *Pastoral sonata* is admirably done.

Piano sonatas Nos. 15–18; 30–32.
(M) (**) Sony mono SM3K 52642 [S3K 52642]. Glenn Gould.

Wilful yet charismatic are adjectives to which so many have recourse whenever Glenn Gould's name is mentioned. There are no doubts as to his pianism or control or the quality of his musicianship but his late Beethoven, for all its intelligence, is pretty quirky and is marred by his vocal contributions. It can be recommended to his admirers, but others will turn to the abundant rival offerings.

Piano sonatas Nos. 16 in G; 17 in D min. (Tempest); 18 in E flat, Op. 31/1–3.
(BB) **(*) ASV CDQS 6060 [id.]. John Lill.

On ASV this is one of the most impressive discs in John Lill's series and it is very well recorded. Obviously the Op. 31 *Sonatas* strike a spark in his consciousness and the first movement of No. 16 is keenly alive, while the slow movement is characteristically direct and there are some sensitive touches. There is no want of fire in *The Tempest*, and there is much to admire in the *E flat Sonata*, although Lill's tendency to aggressiveness brings some exaggerated sforzandos in the Scherzo. But the playing throughout is strong and keenly intelligent.

Piano sonata No. 17 in D min., Op. 31/2.
✿ (B) *** EMI forte CZS5 69340-2 (2). Sviatoslav Richter – HANDEL: *Suites Nos. 9–16.* *** ✿

Richter's classic 1961 account of the so-called *Tempest Sonata* returns to circulation as a fill-up to the sublime set of Handel suites he recorded with Andrei Gavrilov at the Château de Marcilly-sur-Maulne during the 1979 Tours Festival. It previously appeared coupled with the Dvořák *Piano Concerto in G minor* that Richter recorded with Carlos Kleiber and, as far as we can hear, the new transfer does not differ to any marked degree from its predecessor. Richter makes the most of possibilities of contrast. He plays the opening extremely slowly, and then when the allegro comes he takes it unusually fast. Far from being odd, this effect is actually breathtaking. Richter observes the repeats in both the first and last movements, and this last (the *Allegretto*) he plays at a perfectly controlled tempo, never giving way to nervous virtuosity. Excellent Abbey Road sound. Not to be missed.

Piano sonatas Nos. 17 in D min. (Tempest), Op. 31/2; 21 in C (Waldstein), Op. 53; 26 in E flat (Les Adieux), Op. 81a.
(BB) **(*) Naxos Dig. 8.550054 [id.]. Jenö Jandó.

Jandó offers here the other three famous named sonatas, and very enjoyable they are in their direct manner.

Piano sonatas Nos. 17 in D min. (Tempest), Op. 31/2; 29 in B flat (Hammerklavier), Op. 106.
(M) *** DG (IMS) 419 857-2. Wilhelm Kempff.

Kempff's preference for measured allegros and fastish andantes gives a different weighting to movements from the usual, but there is a profound thoughtfulness of utterance.

Piano sonatas Nos. 27 in E min., Op. 90; 28 in A, Op. 101; 29 in B flat (Hammerklavier), Op. 106; 30 in E, Op. 109; 31 in A flat, Op. 110; 32 in C min., Op. 111.
✿ (B) *** DG Double 453 010-2 (2) [id.]. Wilhelm Kempff.
✿ (M) (***) EMI mono CHS7 64708-2 (2) [ZDBH 64708]. Solomon.
(B) *** Sony SB2K 53531 (2) [S2K 53531]. Charles Rosen.
(B) *** Ph. Duo 438 374-2 (2) [id.]. Alfred Brendel.

Kempff has never been more inspirationally revealing than in these performances of the last six Beethoven sonatas. The first movement of Op. 90 is treated very like a romantic improvisation, with strength and lyricism contrasted, while the second movement, flowing fairly fast, is almost Schubertian. Op. 101 begins with a fastish, carefree account of the visionary first movement, essentially rhapsodic in feeling. The Scherzo has all the sharpness of edge that it needs. By contrast the brief slow movement is extrovert, and the final fugue is magnificent. The *Hammerklavier* brings a preference for measured allegros and fastish *Andantes*, giving a weighting to movements that is different from the usual, but there is a thoughtfulness of utterance which brings profundity. The reading of Op. 109 then sets the style for Kempff's performances of the last three sonatas, intense in its control of structure but with a feeling of rhapsodic freedom too, of new visions emerging. The second movement of Op. 110 is not as fast as it might be, but the result is the cleaner for that and, in typical Kempff style, the great *Arietta* of Op. 111 is taken at a flowing tempo, not nearly as slowly as with many a recorded rival. These are all great performances, and the remastered recordings have been enhanced to an extraordinary degree to give an uncannily realistic piano-image, helped by the immediacy of Kempff's communication.

EMI have been slow to reissue Solomon's classic performances of the late Beethoven *Sonatas*. His stroke prevented the great pianist from completing the cycle, but he did at least give us the last six. This is Beethoven pure and unadulterated; this music-making comes as near to the truth as any in the catalogue. They have something of the depth of Schnabel, the tonal beauty of Arrau, the selflessness and integrity of Kempff and the perfect pianism of Pollini on DG or the magisterial, early Brendel set. While Solomon has been ignored in the UK, his reputation in Germany has remained high, thanks to the advocacy of such authorities as Joachim Kayser. The *Hammerklavier sonata* is one of the greatest recordings of the work ever made (this is one of the few weaknesses in Schnabel's complete set) and few have matched – let alone surpassed – it. Opp. 109 and 111 were recorded in 1951, the *Hammerklavier* a year later; Opp. 90 and 110 in 1956, not long before he was struck down. The engineers have done wonders with the transfers. The sound emerges in startling freshness and fullness. Magisterial, thoughtful, deeply lyrical and commanding performances that make so many later versions sound quite shallow.

Charles Rosen is one of the most commanding interpreters of Beethoven's longest and most taxing sonatas. The first movement of the *Hammerklavier* is magnificently strong and the fast tempo – as near Beethoven's impossible metronome marking as is reasonable – makes for an absolute concentration and no sense of hastiness. The great *Adagio* (taken slower than in his first, American recording) is played with an inner depth that allows no sentimentality, and the finale has rarely if ever been played on record with such dynamic power and clarity. A performance even for those who otherwise follow Barenboim or Brendel in their Beethoven cycles. The little *E minor Sonata* begins a little gruffly, but later Rosen shows that he can encompass the softer mood of this very different work. In the visionary last two sonatas, less searingly intense than those preceding them, some may resist the uningratiating manner, but Rosen's commanding toughness compels attention, and repeated hearings are the more rewarding. The recordings, made at the EMI studios between November 1968 and July 1970, are firm and realistic, and allow a wide range of dynamic.

Reissued in Philips's Duo bargain series, this Brendel set of the late sonatas is certainly value for money. In the glorious *E minor Sonata*, Op. 90, there are some expressive rubati that may worry some listeners, but Brendel provides a thoughtful, sensitive reading of the *E major Sonata*, Op. 109. The *A major,* Op. 101, is one of the finest of his cycle, and the sheer beauty of tone in the *A flat major*, Op. 110, is most persuasive: the playing of a thoughtful dreamer. There is a tendency in the *Adagio* of Op. 111, beautifully played as it is, for the forward impulse to lose its spontaneity, and the carefully considered account of the *Hammerklavier* has not quite the fire and sense of spontaneity that marked Brendel's earlier account on Turnabout. Yet with the help of the Philips engineers the great *Adagio* has a genuinely hushed tone (which the forward balance on Turnabout prevented from registering) and this is undoubtedly a fine performance, very well recorded. Generally speaking, this is among the most distinguished Beethoven playing of the analogue era. The recordings were made in the 1970s and are most realistic and satisfying in the latest CD transfers. The documentation, too, can be commended.

Piano sonatas Nos. 27 in E min., Op. 90; 29 in B flat (Hammerklavier), Op. 106.
(BB) ** ASV CDQS 6063. John Lill.

The *E minor Sonata* shows John Lill's thoughtful musical style at its most communicative, and he is most naturally recorded; but the *Hammerklavier* is more controversial. Lill's speed in the great *Adagio* is very slow indeed, and he does not sustain the movement with the necessary concentration; though the outer movements pack tremendous virtuosic punch, this does not match the finest versions.

Piano sonatas Nos. 28 in A, Op. 101; 29 in B flat (Hammerklavier), Op. 106; 30 in E, Op. 109; 31 in A flat, Op. 110; 32 in C min., Op. 111.
(B) *** Decca Double Analogue/Dig. 452 176-2 (2) [id.]. Vladimir Ashkenazy.
(M) **(*) DG Originals 449 740-2 (2) [id.]. Maurizio Pollini.

Distinguished performances on Decca, as one would expect, and an impressive sense of repose in the slow movement of Op. 109, while the account of No. 28 is searching and masterly. This was Ashkenazy's second recording of the *Hammerklavier*, the performance fresher, more spontaneous than the earlier version, but the total experience is less than monumental. The last two sonatas, however, are played with a depth and spontaneity which put them among the finest available. In the slow movement of Op. 111 Ashkenazy matches the concentration of the slowest possible speed which marks out the reading of his friend Barenboim, but there is an extra detachment. If anything, the interpretation of Op. 110 is even more remarkable, consistently revealing. The analogue recordings date from between 1971 and 1980, and the remastering is very successful. The *Hammerklavier* is a digital recording and has a touch of hardness on top. Highly recommendable at Double Decca price.

Pollini's recordings of the late *Sonatas* (which on LP originally included No. 27) won the 1977 *Gramophone* Critics' award for instrumental music, and they contain playing of the highest order of mastery. Joan Chissell spoke of the 'noble purity' of these performances, and that telling phrase aptly sums them up, if also hinting perhaps at a missing dimension, which the CD transfer seems to emphasize. The sound has great presence, but on the first disc there is hardness to the timbre in Opus 101 which becomes almost brittle in the fortissimos of the *Hammerklavier* with an adverse effect on the music-making. Pollini's *Hammerklavier* is undoubtedly eloquent, and so is Op. 111, which has a peerless authority and power. However, the slow movement of Op. 110 may be a trifle fast for some tastes, and in the A major work Gilels has greater poetry and humanity. The second disc brings a close balance to Opp. 109 and 110 but the recordings seem fractionally mellower, although a touch of hardness comes back in Op. 111. The current remastering for reissue as a DG 'Original' seems to have afforded no marked improvement, but the two discs are now packaged like a DG Double and are offered at a special price.

Piano sonatas Nos. 30 in E, Op. 109; 31 in A flat, Op. 110; 32 in C min., Op. 111.
(M) *** DG 447 915-2 [id.]. Wilhelm Kempff.
(M) *** Cal. Dig./Analogue CAL 6648 [id.]. Inger Södergren.
(BB) *** Naxos Dig. 8.550151 [id.]. Jenö Jandó.

The reading of Op. 109 sets the style for Kempff's performances of the late sonatas, intense in its control of structure, but with a feeling of rhapsodic freedom too, of new visions emerging. The second movement of Op. 110 is not as fast as it might be, but the result is the cleaner for that and, in typical Kempff style, the great *Arietta* of Op. 111 is taken at a flowing tempo, not nearly as slowly as with many a recorded rival. These are all great performances, and the recordings are clean and firm.

Inger Södergren, little known in her native country, is a Swedish pianist who lives in France, where she enjoys a considerable reputation; indeed her performances and recordings are regarded there with as much respect as those of Brendel. Her analogue accounts of Opp. 110 and 111 come from 1979, when they earned golden opinions. They are musically most impressive; she is obviously a pianist of keen musical insights. Her recording of Op. 109 is new: it is brighter and more forward. Op. 110 reminds one a little of Myra Hess's old mono LP, but this reading is even stronger. These performances are fit to keep exalted company and the earlier, analogue recordings are most naturally balanced. A first-class mid-priced recommendation.

The last three sonatas of Beethoven, offered in Naxos's Volume 4, are very imposing indeed in Jandó's hands. There is serenity and gravitas in these readings and a powerful control of structure.

Miscellaneous piano music

Allegretto in C min., WoO 53; Andanti favori, WoO 57; 'Für Elise', WoO 59; 6 Variations on an original theme in F, Op. 34.
(M) *** Virgin Veritas/EMI Dig. VER5 61161-2 [CDM 61161]. Melvyn Tan (fortepiano) – SCHUBERT: *Moments musicaux* etc. ***

Melvyn Tan is a spirited artist and an enormously persuasive exponent of the fortepiano. The *F major Variations* come off splendidly; this is a thoroughly enjoyable recital and is recorded with great realism and presence in the Long Gallery, Doddington Hall, Lincolnshire.

7 Bagatelles, Op. 33; 11 Bagatelles, Op. 119; 6 Bagatelles, Op. 126.
(B) *** Ph. Virtuoso 426 976-2 [(M) id. import]. Stephen Kovacevich.
(BB) **(*) Naxos Dig. 8.550474 [id.]. Jenö Jandó.

Beethoven's *Bagatelles*, particularly those from Opp. 119 and 126, have often been described as chips from the master's workbench; but rarely if ever has that description seemed so apt as in these searchingly simple and completely spontaneous readings by Kovacevich.

Jandó plays the early set of *Bagatelles*, which date from 1802, with a crisply rhythmic style, almost at times as if he was thinking of a fortepiano. Then in the later works he finds more depth of tone and is thoughtful as well as flamboyant. He has an excellent, modern, digital recording.

7 Bagatelles, Op. 33; 6 Bagatelles, Op. 126; 6 Variations in F, Op. 34; 15 Variations with fugue in E flat (Eroica), Op. 35; 32 Variations on an original theme in C min., WoO 80.
(M) *(**) Sony SM2K 52646 (2) [S2K 52646]. Glenn Gould (piano).

Glenn Gould's *Bagatelles* and *Variations* are a good deal better and less quirky than his Beethoven *Piano sonatas*, which are not competitive, given the number of great cycles in the catalogue. Gould fanatics can invest in them; others who are not converted can be assured that any eccentricity is positive and thought-provoking. Not a first choice (or anywhere near it) but deserving of a place in the catalogue.

6 Variations in F, Op. 34; 6 Variations on 'Nel cor più non mi sento', WoO 70; 15 Variations and fugue on a theme from Prometheus in E flat (Eroica variations), Op. 35; 32 Variations in C min., WoO 80.
(BB) **(*) Naxos Dig. 8.550676 [id.]. Jenö Jandó.

Jandó essays the same strong, direct style in his performances of the two major sets of variations that he does in the sonatas. Occasionally his forceful manner in Op. 35 and the *C minor Variations* reaches the point of brusqueness in its forceful accenting but no one could deny the strength of this playing. His approach is appropriately lighter in Op. 34 and the very agreeable short set based on the duet by Paisiello. Excellent recording, clear and vivid, to match the other records in his Naxos series.

33 Variations on a waltz by Diabelli, Op. 120.
(B) *** Ph. Virtuoso 422 969-2 [(M) id. import]. Stephen Kovacevich.
(M) ** Carlton IMP 30367 00112 [id.]. Charles Rosen.
(BB) *(*) Arte Nova/BMG Dig. 74321 27761-2 [id.]. Alfredo Perl.

33 Variations on a waltz by Diabelli, Op. 120; 32 Variations in C min., WoO 80.
(B) *** ASV Dig. CDQS 6155 [id.]. Benjamin Frith.

Now reissued in the lowest price range and with an equally fine account of the *32 Variations on an original theme in C minor* thrown in for good measure, the ASV reissue tends to sweep the board. Benjamin Frith gives a fresh and clear reading; tense and dedicated, this conveys Beethoven's mastery without exaggeration or self-indulgence. Clear, realistic recording to match.

Kovacevich also gives one of the most deeply satisfying performances ever recorded. Avoiding the idiosyncrasies of most other interpreters, he may at times seem austere, but his concentration is magnetic from first to last, and the variety of expression within his unmannered approach has one thinking direct to Beethoven, with fearless dynamic contrasts enhanced in the CD transfer. The reading culminates in the most dedicated account of the concluding variations, hushed in meditation and with no hint of self-indulgence. On the cheapest Philips label, it is a bargain that no Beethovenian should miss, and the remastering – with separate tracks for each variation – fully matches that of other, full-price versions.

Admirers of Charles Rosen will be glad to have his recording available again. His view of this Everest of piano literature is purposeful and tough, hard to the point of being unrelenting. With clear, somewhat twangy recording to match, one misses the gentler half-tones (as for example in the great *Adagio* variation, No. 29, where Rosen ignores the *mezza-voce* marking at a trivially fast tempo); yet there is still much to satisfy in such a formidably intense reading.

Alfredo Perl collected golden opinions for his Beethoven cycle in London's Wigmore Hall at the beginning of 1997, and it is evident from this account of the *Diabelli variations* that he is a thoughtful and capable artist. All the same, what can inspire in the concert hall or the recital room may not work in the different climate of the recorded medium. Perl is often perceptive and mainly reliable, but he can produce some ugly timbre in fortissimo passages when one does not feel that he is holding any tone in reserve. Good though it is, this is not a performance that belongs to the first flight.

VOCAL MUSIC

Adelaide; Der Kuss; Resignation; Zärtliche Liebe.
(M) *** DG Originals 449 747-2 [id.]. Fritz Wunderlich, Hubert Giesen – SCHUBERT: *Lieder;* SCHUMANN: *Dichterliebe.* ***

Wunderlich was thirty-five when he recorded these songs, and the unique bloom of the lovely voice is beautifully caught. Though the accompanist is too metrical at times, we see no reason to withhold a third star, for the freshness of Wunderlich's singing makes one grieve again over his untimely death.

(i) *An die ferne Geliebte, Op. 98.* Lieder: *Abendlied unterm gestirnten Himmel;* (ii) *Adelaide;* (i) *Andenken; An die Hoffnung; Die Ehre Gottes aus der Natur; Es war einmal ein König; In questa tomba oscura; Der Jüngling in der Fremde;* (ii) *Der Kuss;* (i) *Der Liebende; Lied aus der Ferne; Maigesang; Marmotte; Mit einem gemalten Band;* (ii) *Resignation;* (i) *Sehnsucht; Seufzer eines Ungeliebten und Gegenliebe; Der Wachtelschlag; Wonne der Wehmut;* (ii) *Zärtliche Liebe.*
(M) **(*) DG 447 921-2 [id.]. (i) Fischer-Dieskau, Demus; (ii) Wunderlich, Giesen.

Recorded in 1966, Fischer-Dieskau's Beethoven selection finds him at his vocal peak, especially in the song-cycle which he has made very much his own; though Demus's accompaniments are not as imaginative as the singer has received in other versions of these songs, Fischer-Dieskau's individuality is as positive as ever, with detail touched in as with no one else. Even so, the four items (*Adelaide*, *Zärtliche Liebe*,

Resignation and *Der Kuss*) from Fritz Wunderlich, which are placed together immediately after the song-cycle, resonate in the memory.

An die ferne Geliebte (song-cycle), *Op. 98; Goethe Lieder: Aus Goethes Faust; In questa tomba oscura; Mailied; Neue Liebe, neues Leben; Wonne der Wehmut.*
(M) *** Ph. 442 741-2 (2). Gérard Souzay, Dalton Baldwin – BRAHMS: *Lieder;* SCHUMANN: *Dichterliebe; Liederkreis* etc. ***

Souzay's lightness of touch and chimerical approach, with bursts of spontaneous ardour, suit Beethoven especially well, and any criticisms of this composer's vocal style are banished. The last song, *Nimm sie hin denn, diese Lieder*, is particularly touching. Among the miscellaneous songs Souzay finds humour in the *Flea song* from *Faust* and then brings a breath of spring to *Mailied*. Almost best of all is the delightfully gay *Neue Liebe, neues Leben*, which sounds for all the world like Schubert. The recording projects the voices vividly; although Souzay was very close to the microphone, Dalton Baldwin's support comes over strongly. It is a pity that in an important set like this no translations are provided, just the German texts.

Christus am Olberge, Op. 85.
(M) **(*) Sony MPK 45878. Raskin, Lewis, Herbert Beattie, Temple University Choirs, Phd. O, Ormandy.

Ormandy is at his most purposeful and warmly understanding, and the soloists are outstandingly fine, with the pure-toned Judith Raskin very aptly cast as the Seraph and with Richard Lewis at his freshest and most expressive as Jesus.

Egmont: Overture and incidental music (abridged), *Op. 84*.
(M) **(*) DG 447 912-2 [id.]. Janowitz, Schellow, BPO, Karajan – *Ecossaise* etc.; *Wellington's victory*. **

Egmont (incidental music), *Op. 84:* complete recording, with narration based on the text by Grillparzer, and melodrama from the play by Goethe.
(M) **(*) Decca 448 593-2 [id.]. Pilar Lorengar, Wussow (narrator), VPO, Szell.

(i) *Egmont: Overture and incidental music* (complete), *Op. 84;* (ii) *Leonora overture No. 3*.
(BB) *** Discover Dig. DICD 920114. (i) Miriam Gauci, Dirk Schortemeier, Belgian R. & TV O; (ii) LPO; Rahbari.

On the bargain Discover label, Alexander Rahbari offers all ten movements of Beethoven's *Egmont* music, not just the selection made by Szell, whose 1969 version has just been reissued in Decca's Classic Sound series. Such rarities as the third and fourth entr'actes and the melodrama, *Süsse Schlaf*, with Schortemeier as the speaker, are chips from the master's workbench rather than significant pieces, but together with the well-known items they present an attractive whole. Both in *Egmont* and in the *Leonora No. 3 overture* (with the LPO) Rahbari conducts crisp, well-sprung, often exciting performances, with Miriam Gauci the warm-toned soprano. Atmospheric recording, pleasantly reverberant.

The problem with performing Beethoven's incidental music for Goethe's *Egmont* within the original dramatic context is at least partially solved on Decca by using a text by the Austrian poet, Franz Grillparzer. The music is interspersed at the appropriate points, including dramatic drum-rolls in Egmont's final peroration, this last scene being from Goethe's original. The Decca presentation, with Klaus-Jürgen Wussow the admirably committed narrator, is dramatic in the extreme. Szell's conducting is superb, the music marvellously characterized, the tension lightened in certain places with subtlety, and the whole given a flowing dramatic impact. The songs are movingly sung by Pilar Lorengar. This has, appropriately enough, been reissued in Decca's Classic Sound series, and the CD transfer is immensely vivid. The snag is that, though a full translation is included, there are no separating bands for the spoken narrative, so that it is impossible to programme the CD to listen only to the music.

Karajan's abridged recording of *Egmont* dates from 1969 and was originally part of DG's Beethoven Edition, then as now. There is no lack of drama, and Gundula Janowitz sings the two Lieder beautifully; Erich Schellow's narration is reduced to a single melodrama before the finale. The sound is clear and vivid, and the CD transfer has brought more depth and warmth of atmosphere than one remembers on the original LP. The couplings, however, are uninspiring.

Mass in C, Op. 86.
(BB) *** Belart 461 317-2 [(M) id. import]. Palmer, Watts, Tear, Keyte, St John's College, Cambridge, Ch., ASMF, Guest – BRUCKNER: *Motets*. ***

George Guest's reading is designedly intimate. Naturally, with boys' voices in the choir and a smaller band of singers, the results are less dramatic; but, with splendid recording, the scale works admirably and the result is refreshing. Excellent value at super-bargain price.

(i) *Mass in C, Op. 86;* (ii) *Missa solemnis, Op. 123.*

(B) **(*) Ph. Duo 438 362-2 (2) [id.]. (i) Eda-Pierre, Moll; (ii) Tomowa-Sintow, Lloyd; (i; ii) Payne, Tear, L. Symphony Ch., LSO, C. Davis.

(B) ** EMI Rouge et Noir CZS5 69440-2 [CDZB 62693]. (i) Ameling, J. Baker, Altmeyer, Rintzler, New Philh. Ch. & O; (ii) Harper, J. Baker, Tear, Sotin, New Philh. Ch., LPO; Giulini.

(B) *(*) Decca Double Dig./Analogue 455 014-2 (2) [id.]. (i) Dunn, Zimmermann, Beccaria, Krause, Berlin RIAS Chamber Ch. & RSO, Chailly; (ii) Popp, Minton, Mallory Walker, Howell, Chicago Ch. & SO, Solti.

The freshness of the choral singing and the clarity of the sound make Sir Colin Davis's an outstandingly dramatic version of the *Mass in C*. The cry, *'Passus'* ('suffered'), in the *Credo* has rarely been so tellingly presented on record, and the quartet of soloists is first rate. As it is in the *Missa solemnis*, and this too is a fine performance, if not consistently generating quite the same degree of intensity: this is especially noticeable when one moves to the second disc, which opens with the *Agnus Dei* of the *Missa solemnis*, where there is a fall-off in concentration. The 1977 recording, well focused, spacious and atmospheric, is given a natural, concert-hall balance and the CD transfer is first class. Good documentation.

Giulini directs the *Mass in C* without apology – after all, it is only the dazzling splendour of the *Missa solemnis* that prevents this from being acclaimed as a Beethoven masterpiece; and in a performance as inspired, polished and intense as Giulini's, with a fine quartet of soloists and a superb choir, the effect is very compelling indeed. With so splendid a team, one expected even more from his version of the *Missa solemnis*. The recording is certainly vivid, but it rarely conveys any kind of hushed tension, an essential ingredient in this of all choral works, and the ensemble of the chorus is far from perfect; the excellent soloists are all balanced very close.

The Chailly performance of the *Mass in C* is on the right expansive scale; the singing of the Berlin RIAS Chorus has vigour and exuberance, yet conveys the full range of emotions expressed in the *Kyrie* and *Sanctus*. The solo team is also very good, although the tenor, Bruno Beccaria, is too histrionically operatic in style. The recording has the widest dynamic range, and this adds drama to the fine performance of the rare cantata which is used as an encore (it is comparatively short at just over eight minutes). The balance favours the singers, but the recording overall is admirably vivid.

Solti's view of the *Missa solemnis* is essentially dramatic, hardly spiritual at all; moreover it is let down by less than crisp orchestral ensemble and poor co-ordination with the chorus. Thus the necessary bite is not always forthcoming. The solo team is balanced much too forwardly and is not well matched either: the women outweigh the men, and the contribution of the tenor, Mallory Walker, is indifferent. His colleagues all have splendid moments, but overall, given the competition, this is a non-starter, not helped by a recording with a narrow range of dynamic.

Missa solemnis in D, Op. 123.

(M) *** DG 447 922-2 (2) [id.]. Moser, Schwarz, Kollo, Moll, Hilversum R. Ch., Concg. O, Bernstein.

(B) *** DG Double 453 016-2 (2) [423 913-2]. Janowitz, Ludwig, Wunderlich, Berry, V. Singverein, BPO, Karajan – MOZART: *Coronation Mass.* **(*)

(B) *** Sony SBK 53517; *SBT 53517* [id.]. Arroyo, Forrester, Lewis, Siepi, Singing City Choirs, Phd. O, Eugene Ormandy.

(M) **(*) DG Dig. 445 543-2 (2) [id.]. Cuberli, Schmidt, Cole, Van Dam, V. Singverein, BPO, Karajan – MOZART: *Mass No. 16.* **(*)

(B) **(*) Teldec/Warner Ultima Dig. 0630 18945-2 (2) [9031 74884-2]. Eva Mei, Marjana Lipovšek, Anthony Rolfe Johnson, Robert Holl, Arnold Schönberg Ch., COE, Harnoncourt.

(M) (**(*)) RCA mono GD 60272 (2) [60272-RG-2]. Marshall, Merriman, Conley, Hines, Robert Shaw Ch., NBC SO, Toscanini – CHERUBINI: *Requiem.* (**(*))

(M) (**) DG Originals 449 737-2 (2) [id.]. Stader, Radev, Dermota, Greindl, St Hedwig's Cathedral Ch., BPO, Boehm – REGER: *Variations and fugue on a theme by Mozart.* (**)

(i) *Missa solemnis in D;* (ii) *Choral Fantasia in C, Op. 80.*

(M) **(*) EMI (SIS) CMS7 69538-2 (2) [Ang. CDMB 69538-2]. (i) Söderström, Höffgen, Kmentt, Talvela, New Philh. Ch.; (ii) Barenboim, Alldis Ch.; New Philh. O, Klemperer.

Bernstein's DG recording was edited together from tapes of two live performances, and the result has a spiritual intensity matched by few rivals. Edda Moser is not an ideal soprano soloist, but the others are outstanding, and the *Benedictus* is made angelically beautiful by the radiant playing of the Concertgebouw concertmaster, Hermann Krebbers. The recording is a little light in bass but is outstandingly clear, as well as atmospheric.

The glory of Klemperer's set is the superb choral singing of the New Philharmonia Chorus. The soloists are less happily chosen: Waldemar Kmentt seems unpleasantly hard and Elisabeth Söderström does not sound as firm as she can be. It was, however, a happy idea to include the *Choral Fantasia* as a bonus.

On Karajan's earlier (1966) analogue recording, made in the Jesus-Christus-Kirche, both the chorus and, even more strikingly, the superbly matched quartet of soloists, never surpassed as a team in this work, convey the intensity and cohesion of Beethoven's deeply personal response to the liturgy. Gundula Janowitz is even more meltingly beautiful here than in her later, EMI recording for Karajan. Christa Ludwig, as there, is a firm and characterful mezzo, while Walter Berry is a warmly expressive bass. Best of all is the ill-fated Fritz Wunderlich whose lovely, heroic but unstrained tenor adds supremely to the radiance of the performance, one of his great recordings. The balance between soloists, chorus and orchestra is far clearer and more precise than in most recent recordings, and the clarity of detail is exemplary. Now on a DG Double, coupled with Mozart's *Coronation Mass*, the attractions of this performance are undoubtedly enhanced.

On a single disc in Sony's Essential Classics series at budget price, Ormandy's 1967 Philadelphia recording makes an excellent bargain. Ormandy takes a bold and firm view of this masterpiece. It may not plumb all the spiritual depths of the work but, with four outstanding soloists and an excellent, well-focused choir, this is an account which takes you magnetically through the drama of Beethoven's personal view of the liturgy. The vintage recording gives plenty of body to the sound, both of voices and of orchestra, not least the bright-toned trumpets.

On DG 445 543-2 Karajan conducts a powerful reading marked by vivid and forward recording for orchestra and soloists, less satisfactory in rather cloudy choral sound. This was one of Karajan's recordings made in conjunction with a video film, and that brings both gains and losses. The sense of spontaneity, of a massive structure built dramatically with contrasts underlined, makes for extra magnetism, but there are flaws of ensemble and at least one serious flaw of intonation in the singing of Lella Cuberli, otherwise a full, sweet-toned soprano.

Harnoncourt's performance was recorded live at the Salzburg Festival in July 1992 and it represents the new, post-Karajan era at that grandest of music festivals. Like Harnoncourt's (full-priced) Beethoven cycle, this performance conveys the dramatic tensions of a live occasion, with finely matched forces performing with freshness and clarity. The devotional element is clear, and though the rather distanced sound makes the results marginally less involving than the Bernstein version, also recorded live, Harnoncourt admirers will find this Ultima Double well worth its modest cost.

Toscanini's tensely dramatic account of the *Missa solemnis* leaves you in no doubt as to the work's magisterial power, even if the absence of a true pianissimo makes it less meditative than usual. Fine singing from choir and soloists alike, though the typical harshness of the recording is unappealing.

Boehm's *Missa solemnis* was recorded in the Berlin Jesus-Christus-Kirche in 1955 and must have been one of the last major mono recordings to be made there. It has a fine team of soloists and the sound is vivid, full and well balanced, but both those soloists and the chorus emerge intertwined with little or no difference of dynamic. If it were an electrically charged affair, like some of the recordings made by Fricsay in this period, this would not matter very much, but it is just a strong, brightly paced account which affords musical satisfaction but could hardly be counted preferable to the best mid-priced stereo versions.

OPERA

Fidelio (complete).

(M) *** EMI CMS7 69290-2 (2) [CDMB 769290]. Dernesch, Vickers, Kélémen, Ridderbusch, German Op. Ch., BPO, Karajan.

(B) *** DG Double 453 106-2 (2) (includes *Overture Leonora No. 3*). Leonie Rysanek, Ernst Haefliger, Dietrich Fischer-Dieskau, Gottlob Frick, Irmgard Seefried, Friedrich Lenz, Kieth Engen, Bav. State Op. Ch. & O, Fricsay.

(M) (***) EMI mono CHS7 64901-2 (2). Kirsten Flagstad, Julius Patzak, Paul Schoeffler, Josef Greindl, Elisabeth Schwarzkopf, Anton Dermota, V. State Op. Ch., VPO, Furtwängler.

(M) ** Decca Dig. 455 066-2 (2) [id.]. Hildegard Behrens, Peter Hofmann, Theo Adam, Hans Sotin, Sona Ghazarian, Chicago Ch. & SO, Solti.

(M) (**) RCA mono GD 60273 (2) [62073-RG]. Bampton, Peerce, Laderoute, Steber, Belarsky, Janssen, Moscona, Ch., NBC SO, Toscanini.

(B) *(*) Decca Double 446 104-2 (2) [id.]. Nilsson, McCracken, Böhme, Krause, Sciutti, Grobe, Prey, V. State Op. Konzertvereinigung, VPO, Maazel.

(M) *(*) RCA Dig. 74321 25278-2 (2). Adam, Nimsgern, Jerusalem, Altmeyer, Meven, Nossek, Wohlers, Leipzig R. Ch. & GO, Masur.

(M) * DG 447 925-2 (2) [id.]. Jones, King, Crass, Adam, Mathis, Schreier, Talvela, Leipzig R. Ch., Dresden Op. Ch. & State O, Boehm.

Comparison between Karajan's strong and heroic reading and Klemperer's full-price version (CDS5 56211-2) is fascinating. Both have very similar merits, underlining the symphonic character of the work with their weight of utterance. Both may miss some of the sparkle of the opening scene, but it is better that seriousness should enter too early than too late. Since seriousness is the keynote, it is rather surprising to find Karajan using bass and baritone soloists lighter than usual. Both the Rocco (Ridderbusch) and the Don Fernando (Van Dam) lack something in resonance in their lower range. Yet they sing dramatically and intelligently, and there is the advantage that the Pizarro of Zoltan Kélémen sounds the more biting and powerful as a result – a fine performance. Jon Vickers as Florestan is, if anything, even finer than he was for Klemperer; and although Helga Dernesch as Leonore does not have quite the clear-focused mastery of Christa Ludwig in the Klemperer set, this is still a glorious, thrilling performance, outshining lesser rivals than Ludwig. The orchestral playing is superb.

The Fricsay set dates from 1957, yet the recording has responded superbly to the current CD remastering, with clean, warm, well-focused sound that projects the voices naturally. The result is astonishingly modern-sounding, lacking little or nothing in body. This was the first recording of this opera to offer not just Beethoven's score but also a sprinkling of dialogue between numbers, which in DG's CD transfer are banded separately. As for Fricsay's direction, from the *Overture* onwards it matches the excitement and keen tension of a Toscanini performance, though the very clarity makes it more lightweight than many rivals. The principals sing with exceptional clarity and point. Ernst Haefliger is a fine, clear-cut Florestan, lyric in timbre rather than fully heroic, and Frick and Fischer-Dieskau offer strong, intense characterizations, with Pizarro's aria chilling in its villainy. Rysanek's Leonore is also impressive, and her *Abscheulicher* is both dramatic and beautifully shaded, one of her finest performances on record. As for Irmgard Seefried, she makes an enchanting Marzelline. This makes a splendid bargain double version and while, sadly, no libretto translation is included there is an extensive cued synopsis. In its way this is as fresh and enjoyable as Fricsay's much-admired set of Mozart's *Die Zauberflöte*. The *Leonore No. 3 Overture* is included as a supplement after the opera, not before the final scene as used to be the custom; with CD, however, listeners can re-programme it if they wish.

Taken from performances at the Salzburg Festival in 1950, with Wilhelm Furtwängler conducting an incomparably starry cast, this should not be confused with the studio recording he made with some of the same cast two years later. This is an Austrian Radio recording, previously available in pirated versions, but here treated to sound which captures the voices on stage with astonishing vividness. The epic scale of Kirsten Flagstad's voice as Leonore sometimes blasts the microphone, but it is a joy to hear such forthright power and security in a role nowadays too often given to squally singers. Elisabeth Schwarzkopf is a delight as Marzelline, vivacious in the dialogue and masterfully sustaining Furtwängler's expansive speed for the Act I quartet. With dialogue included, this is even more compelling than Furtwängler's studio recording, also with Julius Patzak as a superb Florestan, but with Paul Schoeffler a powerful Pizarro and Josef Greindl as Rocco.

Solti's set was the first ever digital recording of an opera, made in 1979. The sound is full, clean and vividly atmospheric, matched by the conductor's urgent and intense direction. With fine choral singing the ensembles are excellent, but the solo singing is too flawed for comfort. Hildegard Behrens seems ungainly in the great *Abscheulicher*, and both Peter Hofmann as Florestan and Theo Adam as Pizarro too often produce harsh, unattractive tone.

Recorded in December 1944, when victory was in sight in the Second World War, this was the first of the concert performances of complete operas that Toscanini conducted in New York. There is no attempt at a dramatic presentation. This is just Beethoven's score with no dialogue whatever, not even in the great confrontation of the Act II quartet; but that makes one concentrate the more on the music, which is plainly what Toscanini wants. Typically his choice of soloists favours voices that are clean-cut and accurate rather than conventionally beautiful, and it is good to have Rose Bampton as a powerful Leonore, an American singer too little appreciated in Europe and too little recorded. Eleanor Steber is a weightier Marzelline than usual, but the clarity and precision are impressive, well matched by the Jaquino of Joseph Laderoute. Sidor Belarsky as Rocco is similarly clean of attack and, though Herbert Janssen is not as fresh-toned as he was earlier, this is a strong and characterful performance. As Florestan, Jan Peerce, Toscanini's favourite American tenor of the time, sings cleanly too if not with great imagination. The transfer follows the honest if unflattering pattern favoured in RCA's Toscanini Edition.

Maazel's Double Decca was recorded in the Sofiensaal in 1964 and the recording is characteristically clear and vivid. Although there is no libretto, the documentation is excellent, far preferable to Boehm's DG competitor in the same price-range. But Birgit Nilsson as Leonora is below her best, and none of the other principals is particularly characterful. Moreover Maazel's direction is erratic and sounds mannered or over-forced.

Masur's version (previously issued on Eurodisc) is offered in well-balanced, modern, digital sound. It is played very well by the Leipzig orchestra, but this is a surprisingly small-scale view, lacking the full dramatic bite needed in this towering masterpiece. Neither Jeannine Altmeyer nor Siegfried Jerusalem had achieved their peak when they made the recording in 1982 and, though there is fine singing from the male members of the cast, the Marzelline of Carola Nossek is thin and unsteady. The whole performance has the feeling of a well-behaved run-through.

Boehm, returning to the orchestra he directed in the 1930s, brings a mature warmth to the score; but there are too many flaws in the singing for the set to compete seriously. Gwyneth Jones produces too many squally notes to be a satisfying Leonore, and James King is an uninspired Florestan. Theo Adam as Pizarro is no more appealing to the ear.

Fidelio: highlights.
(M) *** EMI CDM7 63077-2. Dernesch, Vickers, Ridderbusch, Van Dam, Kélémen, German Op. Ch., BPO, Karajan.
(M) *** DG 445 461-2 (from complete set, with Janowitz, Kollo, Sotin, Jungirth, Fischer-Dieskau, Popp; cond. Bernstein).
(BB) *(*) Belart 450 180-2 [(M) id. import] (from above recording with Nilsson, McCracken, Krause; cond. Maazel).

Those who acquire Klemperer's classic set will welcome just under an hour of well-chosen highlights from the fine alternative Karajan recording, made in 1970.

It is also good to have a set of highlights from the Bernstein set, recorded in conjunction with live performances at the Vienna State Opera and full of dramatic flair, yet which presents the drama on a human scale, less monumental than with Klemperer. Janowitz sings most beautifully as Leonore and, although Hans Sotin is not an especially villainous Pizarro, his vocal projection is impressive, Kollo is an intelligent and musicianly Florestan and Lucia Popp is at her delightful best as Marzelline. The selection is generous (71 minutes), including the *Overture* and the final scene, and contains a cued synopsis of the narrative.

The inexpensive Belart selection is not particularly generous (59 minutes) but serves as an effective sampler for the flawed Maazel set, already available as a Double Decca (see above).

Fidelio: Abscheulicher!.
(M) (***) RCA mono GD 60280 [id.]. Rose Bampton, NBC SO, Toscanini – GLUCK: *Iphigénie en Aulide: Overture; Orfeo ed Euridice, Act II.* (***)

Rose Bampton was the soprano chosen by Toscanini to take the role of Leonora in his concert performance and recording of the complete *Fidelio*, and here, a few months later in June 1945, he invited her to repeat her performance of the climactic *Abscheulicher* in concert. Again the performance is magnificent, firm, true and clear, a degree warmer than in the complete recording but just as heroic in attack. A welcome fill-up to the Gluck recordings on the disc.

Bellini, Vincenzo (1801–35)

Oboe concerto in E flat.
(B) *** Decca Double 452 943-2 (2) [id.]. Roger Lord, ASMF, Marriner – HANDEL: *Oboe concertos* etc.; VIVALDI: *Miscellaneous concertos.* ***

Bellini's *Oboe concerto* is brief but delectable. Its operatic lyricism is well understood by Roger Lord and Marriner, and their performance is not surpassed, even by Holliger.

Beatrice di Tenda (complete).
(M) ** Sony Dig. SM3K 64539 (3). Nicolesco, Cappuccilli, Toczyska, La Scola, Prague Philharmonic Ch., Monte Carlo O, Alberto Zedda.

Beatrice di Tenda (complete); Arias: *Norma: Casta diva. I Puritani: Son vergin vezzosa; Oh rendetemi la speme. La sonnambula: Ah, non credea mirarti.*
(M) *** (IMS) Decca 433 706-2 (3) [id.]. Sutherland, Pavarotti, Opthof, Veasey, Ward, Amb. Op. Ch., LSO, Bonynge.

Beatrice di Tenda was Bellini's last opera but one, coming after *La sonnambula* and *Norma* and before *I Puritani*. It had an unfortunate birth, for the composer had to go to the law courts to wring the libretto out of his collaborator, Romani; the result is not exactly compelling dramatically. The story involves a whole string of unrequited loves. Bellini always intended to revise the score but failed to do so before his death. As it is, the piece remains essentially a vehicle for an exceptional prima donna with a big enough voice and brilliant enough coloratura. Dame Joan Sutherland has made it her own in recent years – this recording was made in 1966 – and although here she indulges in some of the 'mooning' one hoped she had left behind, there are many dazzling examples of her art. The other star of the set is Richard Bonynge, whose powers as a Bellini conductor are most impressive. The supporting cast could hardly be better, with Pavarotti highly responsive. The recording, made in Walthamstow Assembly Hall, is of Decca's best vintage and it has transferred splendidly to CD, with vivid atmosphere and colour. Four famous arias are provided as a filler: one from Sutherland's 1964 *Norma*, two from her 1963 *I Puritani* and one from the 1962 *La sonnambula*.

Originally issued on the Ricordi label, the Sony set offers a live recording made in Monte Carlo in 1986. The scholar, Alberto Zedda, conducts most sympathetically, and Mariana Nicolesco in the title-role sings with strength and character, often using exciting and distinctive tone-colours, but spoiling Bellinian legato lines with squeezing and gusting and sudden moments of edginess. Others in the cast sing stylishly; but the Sutherland/Bonynge set is far preferable, both for the fresher, more beautiful performance and for the bright Decca sound of good (1966) vintage.

I Capuleti ed i Montecchi (complete).

(M) **(*) EMI (SIS) Dig. CMS7 64846-2 (2) [CDMB 64846]. Baltsa, Gruberová, Raffanti, Gwynne Howell, Tomlinson, ROHCG Ch. & O, Muti.

Muti's set was recorded live at a series of performances at Covent Garden when the production was new, in March 1984. With the Royal Opera House a difficult venue for recording, the sound is hard and close, far less agreeable and well balanced than in the previous EMI version of this opera, recorded in the studio with Beverly Sills and Dame Janet Baker and now deleted. On the later version, Agnes Baltsa makes a passionately expressive Romeo and Edita Gruberová a Juliet who is not just brilliant in coloratura but also sweet and tender. It is an unlikely but successful matching of a Carmen with a Zerbinetta; but it is the masterful conducting of Muti that, more than anything, makes one tolerant of the indifferent sound. That mastery is especially striking at the end of Act I, when the five principals sing a hushed quintet in which Romeo and Juliet musically reveal their understanding, singing sweetly in thirds. With excellent contributions from the refined tenor Dano Raffanti (as Tebaldo), Gwynne Howell and John Tomlinson, it is a performance to blow the cobwebs off an opera that – even in the earlier recording – seemed one of Bellini's less compelling pieces.

Norma (complete).

(M) *** Decca 425 488-2 (3) [id.]. Sutherland, Horne, Alexander, Cross, Minton, Ward, London Symphony Ch., LSO, Bonynge.

(M) **(*) EMI CMS5 66428-2 (3) [CDMB 66428]. Callas, Corelli, Ludwig, Zaccharia, Ch. & O of La Scala, Milan, Serafin.

(M) ** Sony SM2K 35902 (2) [S2K 35902]. Scotto, Troyanos, Giacomini, Plishka, Amb. Op. Ch., Nat. PO, Levine.

(M) ** EMI Dig. CMS5 55471-2 (3). Eaglen, La Scola, Mei, Kavrakos, Remigio, Gavazzi, Maggio Musicale Fiorentino Ch. & O, Muti.

Norma: highlights.

(M) *** Decca 421 886-2 [id.] (from above complete recording with Sutherland, Horne; cond. Bonynge).

(M) ** EMI CDM5 66047-2 [id.] (from above complete recording with Callas, Corelli; cond. Serafin).

In her first, mid-1960s recording of *Norma*, Sutherland was joined by an Adalgisa in Marilyn Horne whose control of florid singing is just as remarkable as Sutherland's own, and who sometimes even outshines the heroine in musical imagination. The other soloists are very good indeed. Overall this is a most compelling performance, helped by the conducting of Richard Bonynge, and the Walthamstow recording is vivid but also atmospheric in its CD format.

By the time Callas came to record her 1960 stereo version, the tendency to hardness and unsteadiness in the voice above the stave, always apparent, had grown more serious, but the interpretation was as sharply illuminating as ever, a unique assumption, helped by Christa Ludwig as Adalgisa, while Corelli sings heroically. Serafin as ever is the most persuasive of Bellini conductors.

Renata Scotto as Norma has many beautiful moments but, above pianissimo in the upper register, the voice too regularly acquires a heavy beat and the sound becomes ugly. The close (1979) recording, made in the Henry Wood Hall, does not help, any more than it does with Tatiana Troyanos as Adalgisa, whose vibrato is exaggerated, Giuseppe Giacomini sings with fair style but little imagination, and Levine's conducting is far too brutal for such a piece, favouring aggressively fast tempi.

Recorded live at the Ravenna Festival in July 1994, Muti's performance is powerfully dramatic. Muti remains characteristically forceful but is also more considerate of the singers than he once was, allowing a degree more rubato. In the title-role Eaglen is a fire-eater, formidably expressing vehemence more readily than love, and the recitative before *Casta diva* is superb. For the start of that great aria she shades down her big, bright, resonant tone, but when the voice rises above the stave, particularly in coloratura, too often it acquires an unpleasant edge. The recording does not help, with voices balanced close and with little bloom allowed. This means that the first-rate Handel tenor, Vincenzo La Scola, sounds more heroic of tone than he perhaps is, but it is a clean-cut, incisive performance; and Dimitri Kavrakos is a forthright Oroveso with a distinctive flutter vibrato. Eva Mei makes an interesting choice as Adalgisa, another soprano who is much lighter and purer than the protagonist and thus easily and convincingly distinguished, even if the matching in duet is not easy. Stage and audience noises tend to be intrusive, which in so poised a work is a marked drawback.

Il Pirata (complete).

(M) ** EMI CMS7 64169-2 (2). Cappuccilli, Caballé, Martí, Raimondi, Rome R. & TV Ch. & O, Gavazzeni.

(M) (**) EMI mono CMS5 66432-2 (2) [CDMB 66432]. Callas, Ego, Miranda Ferraro, Peterson, Watson, Sarfaty, American Op. Soc. Ch. & O, Rescigno.

Gavazzeni's is the first complete recording of *Il Pirata*, the composer's third opera, written for La Scala and first produced in 1827. In the best traditions of Italian opera, in the finale the pirate-hero is killed, his rival is condemned to death, and the heroine loses her mind. With a not very promising scenario the opera is too long for its material. Caballé is well suited to the role of the heroine, though by her finest standards there is some carelessness in her singing – clumsy changes of register and less than the expected beauty of tonal contrast. Nor is the conducting and presentation sparkling enough to mask the comparative poverty of Bellini's invention at this early stage of his career. Bernabé Martí makes a fair stab at the difficult part of the pirate. The 1970 recording flatters the voices and has plenty of atmosphere but it is not as vividly projected as the best Decca offerings from this period.

Recorded live at a concert performance in New York in January 1959, the Callas version is inevitably flawed, with harsh sound and intrusive audience noises. Though Callas herself shows signs of the vocal deterioration which afflicted her all too early in her career, with top notes often raw and uneven, hers is a fire-eating performance, totally distinctive, instantly magnetic from the moment she utters her first word, '*Sorgete*', in Act I. The rest of the cast is indifferent, with Constantine Ego strenuous in the tenor role of Ernesto. The second disc offers an alternative recording of the final scene, made in Amsterdam six months later, with Rescigno conducting the Concertgebouw Orchestra and with Callas in smoother vocal form, helped by less raw recording.

I Puritani (complete).

(M) **(*) Decca 448 969-2 (2). Sutherland, Duval, Capecchi, Flagello, Elkins, De Palma, Maggio Musicale Fiorentino Ch. & O, Bonynge.

(B) **(*) Millennium MCD 80356 (3). Sills, Gedda, Van Allan, Plishka, Quilico, Cassinelli, Begg, Ambrosian Op. Ch., LPO, Rudel.

(M) **(*) EMI CMS7 69663-2 (2). Caballé, Kraus, Manuguerra, Hamari, Ferrin, Amb. Op. Ch., Philh. O, Muti.

As in the recording of *La Sonnambula*, made a year earlier, Joan Sutherland slides about too freely in *portamento*, but the beauty and freshness of the sound, as well as the phenomenal agility, are what matter above all. The final *Ah, non giunge* is dazzling. Pierre Duval generally controls his ringing tenor well, powerful at the top, though he is far less stylish than Nicola Monti, the tenor on the *Sonnambula* set. Renato Capecchi is a strong Riccardo, if not always well enough focused. Though Bonynge conducts most sympathetically, controlling ensembles well, what confirms this as less recommendable than Sutherland's later, full-priced set is that the text is far less complete, while Pavarotti in the 1973 performance is a far more characterful Riccardo.

Now issued at bargain price on the Millennium label, Beverly Sills's 1973 recording of *I Puritani* was originally made by EMI in the month after Sutherland had completed her recording with Pavarotti. That timing rather prevented the qualities of this performance from being fully appreciated, with a good cast warmly recorded. The excellent CD transfer ensures that the edge on Sills's bright coloratura is kept in check, letting one appreciate more fully her flawless technique – with wonderfully tight trills – and her expressiveness, with moods instantly established. Only occasionally is the singing a little too strenuous, with edginess at the top. Nicolai Gedda as Arturo is more effective in bold, heroic music than he is in such Bellinian cantilena as *A te o cara* in Act I, where he distorts the line too heavily. The rest of the cast is strong and characterful, though Paul Plishka as Sir Giorgio is not ideally steady.

In the EMI version of *I Puritani*, Riccardo Muti's contribution is most distinguished. As the very opening demonstrates, his attention to detail and pointing of rhythm make for refreshing results, and the warm but luminous recording is excellent. But both the principal soloists – Bellini stylists on their day, but here below form – indulge in distracting mannerisms, hardly allowing even a single bar to be presented straight in the big numbers, pulling and tugging in each direction, rarely sounding spontaneous. The big ensemble, *A te, o cara*, in its fussiness at slow speed loses the surge of exhilaration which Sutherland and Pavarotti show so strongly.

La Sonnambula (complete).

(B) **(*) Naxos Dig. 8.660042/3 [id.]. D'Artegna, Papadjiakou, Orgonasova, Giménez, Dilbèr, De Vries, Micu, Netherlands R. Ch. and CO, Zedda.

(M) **(*) Decca 448 966-2 (2) [id.]. Sutherland, Monti, Elkins, Stalman, Corena, Maggio Musicale Fiorentino Ch. & O, Bonynge.

Recorded live in 1992 in a concert performance at the Concertgebouw in Amsterdam, the Naxos issue offers an outstanding account of Bellini's most appealing opera, the finest version at any price since Joan Sutherland's. Luba Orgonasova is an expressive and characterful heroine, agile and pointed in her phrasing of coloratura, deeply affecting in the tender legato of *Ah non credea mirarti* in the final scene, with tone delicately varied. Raul Giménez is equally stylish as Elvino, the rich landowner, using his light Rossinian tenor most sensitively, with Alberto Zedda, scholar as well as conductor, pointing the accompaniment lightly. The conditions of a live performance encourage him to give full expressive freedom to the principal singers in rubato. The other principals are not quite on this level but they make an excellent team, with Francesco Ellero d'Artegna characterfully taking the same role, Count Rodolfo, as he did in Sutherland's last recording. Live recording conditions mean that balance of voices is not always ideal, and loud applause punctuates the ends of scenes. As usual with Naxos opera issues, there is a libretto in Italian but only a detailed summary of plot in English. It does not help that CD tracks have been kept to the minimum.

La Sonnambula was the first Bellini opera that Sutherland recorded complete, in 1962, and this earlier version, now reissued at mid-price in Decca's Grand Opera series, proves even more beautiful than her remake of 1980 when the voice was weightier but less even. Though her use of *portamento* is often excessive, the freshness of the voice is a constant delight, Bonynge's direction is outstanding, and the casting is first rate too, with Nicola Monti as stylish a Bellini tenor as Italy could produce at the time. Both Sylvia Stahlman as Lisa and Margareta Elkins as Teresa sing most beautifully and with keen accuracy. Even Fernando Corena's rather coarse, *buffo*-style Rodolfo has an attractive vitality. It is a pity, however, that Bonynge could not persuade Monti and Corena to decorate their reprises, as Sutherland and Stahlman do most beautifully. The recording has come up marvellously on CD, with both pin-point clarity and immediacy of atmosphere within a warm acoustic that one had come to expect from Decca in those vintage early years of analogue stereo.

Benda, Jiří Antonín (1722–1795)

(i) *Ariadne auf Naxos. Pygmalion.*

(BB) **(*) Naxos Dig. 8.553345 [id.]. Quadlbauer, Uray; (i) Schell; Prague CO, Benda.

Though neither *Ariadne auf Naxos* nor *Pygmalion* can quite match the longer and more ambitious melodrama, *Medea*, in their originality of invention, they equally demonstrate Benda's ability not only to illustrate the dramatic details of classical stories but also to reflect the psychological developments in the central characters. *Ariadne*, his first melodrama, staged at the court theatre in Gotha in January 1775, led directly to his tackling the more ambitious subject of Medea. *Pygmalion*, with libretto adapted from a French text of Jean-Jacques Rousseau, dates from four years later, a lighter, less extended piece with a happy ending. Performances under Christian Benda are as impressive as that of *Medea* on the companion disc, but again texts and translations are separated, and no internal tracks are provided. First-rate sound and good acting, though as Pygmalion Peter Uray is not as clear in his delivery as the Ariadne, Brigitte Quadlbauer.

Medea (complete).

(BB) **(*) Naxos Dig. 8.553346 [id.]. Hertha Schell & speaking cast, Prague CO, Christian Benda (with Jan Jiří BENDA: *Violin concerto in G: Grave*).

Christian Benda, born in Brazil but claiming to trace his ancestry back to his eighteenth-century namesake from Bohemia, here presents a most characterful and compelling version of what may be counted as Jiří

Benda's masterpiece, the melodrama *Medea*. Rarely have works built on speech superimposed on music remained long in the repertory, yet this CD demonstrates why they have a place and why this one initially had such success. *Medea*, a sequence of monologues for the central character interspersed with dialogue passages with Jason and others, was first heard in Leipzig in 1775, and it marks the peak of Benda's achievement in this then-fashionable genre. At 50 minutes, not only is it the longest of his melodramas, it is tautly conceived with recurrent themes of poignant intensity. Mozart expressed his admiration and for a time was intent on writing a melodrama himself, using the device in the unfinished *Zaïde* and *Thamos, King of Egypt*. Not only is the playing of the Prague Chamber Orchestra tautly committed, the performance offers an impressive team of actors, led by Hertha Schell. Though German speakers will have no problems responding, others will be disappointed that the Naxos booklet gives the German text and English translation on different pages, not side by side. It is also an inconvenience that only one track is provided for the whole work, when it would be most helpful to have the many different sections marked. The fill-up is a treasure. Christian Benda is not just a fine conductor but a superb cellist too, and here he gives a most moving performance of a deeply expressive violin concerto slow movement, as arranged for cello. Excellent sound, with good balance between speaking voices and orchestra.

Bennett, Richard Rodney (born 1936)

Guitar concerto (for guitar and chamber ensemble).

(M) *** RCA 09026 61598-2. Julian Bream, Melos Ens., Atherton – ARNOLD: *Concerto;* RODRIGO: *Concierto de Aranjuez.* ***

Bennett's concerto, written in 1970, is dedicated to Bream. It is imaginatively conceived, and its variety of texture, glittering and transparent, consistently intrigues the ear. If the work's idiom and language start out from the twelve-tone system, there is nothing difficult for the listener to assimilate. The performance, like its Arnold coupling, is definitive and the 1972 recording is first class in every way.

Benoit, Peter (1834–1901)

Hoogmis (High Mass).

(BB) *(**) Discover Dig. DICD 920178 [id.]. Donald George, Belgian R. & TV Philharmonic Ch., Koninklijk Vlaams Antwerp Music Conservatoire Ch. & Caecilia Chorale, Gemengd Ars Musica Merksem Ch., Zingende Wandelkring Saint Norbertus Ch., Belgian R. & TV PO, Rahbari.

The bargain Discover label offers a fascinating rarity, the *Hoogmis* (*High Mass*), by the Belgian composer, Peter Benoit, a contemporary of Brahms. Alexander Rahbari's account with the BRTN Philharmonic Orchestra of Brussels and massed choirs, with the tenor, Donald George, taking the solos in the *Benedictus* and *Dona nobis pacem*, has all the thrust you need for an ambitious work lasting 55 minutes. With themes square-cut rather than individual and with crisply effective choral writing, the piece echoes Beethoven's *Missa solemnis* rather than any French model. The trouble is that the live recording, though atmospheric and full of presence, brings washy sound, and starts without warning.

Berg, Alban (1885–1935)

Chamber concerto for piano, violin & 13 wind instruments, Op. 6.

(M) *** DG 447 405-2 [id.]. Barenboim, Zukerman, Ens. Intercontemporain, Boulez – STRAVINSKY: *Concerto in E flat* etc. ***

(i) *Chamber concerto;* (ii) *3 Pieces for orchestra;* (iii) *Violin concerto.*

(M) ** Sony SMK 68331 [id.]. (i) Barenboim, Gavrilov; (i–ii) BBC SO; (iii) Zukerman, LSO; (i–iii) Boulez.

(i) *Chamber concerto;* (ii) *Violin concerto.*

(M) ** Sony Stern Edition II SMK 64504 [id.]. Isaac Stern, with (i) Peter Serkin, LSO members, Abbado; (ii) NYPO, Bernstein.

On DG, Boulez sets brisk tempi in the *Chamber concerto*, seeking to give the work classical incisiveness; but the strong and expressive personalities of the pianist and violinist tend towards a more romantic view. The result is characterful and convincing, though unaccountably Boulez omits the extended repeat in the finale. The recording is attractively atmospheric, and those who regard this as a difficult work will find the music-making here not in the least intimidating.

This Sony issue conveniently couples Berg's two concertante works with violin, featuring Isaac Stern in both. The yoking, however, is uneven, when these are recordings made 26 years apart. The 1959 recording of the *Violin concerto* underlines the coarser side of the performance in which Stern takes a red-blooded, romantic view of the work, as does Bernstein, with finer points skated over. There is coarseness in the *Chamber concerto* too, when the recording balance is aggressively close, though in other respects the sound is truthful. This is undoubtedly a virtuoso performance, but the interplay of instrumentalists is much less subtle than it might be, with Stern's violin for once placed rather backwardly in relation to the wind players. The digital sound is very immediate indeed.

Boulez's personality strongly dominates the alternative Sony performances, the *Chamber concerto* and Op. 6 *Orchestral pieces*, sharply focused in 1967, with the solo passages very forward, and the *Violin concerto* with the soloist very close indeed, recorded two decades later in 1984. Zukerman's strong, urgent reading matches Boulez's toughness; his virtuoso flair makes for a robust rather than a subtle or poetic reading. The elegiac quality is missing.

Violin concerto.

(M) *** DG 447 445-2 [id.]. Itzhak Perlman, Boston SO, Ozawa – RAVEL: *Tzigane;* STRAVINSKY: *Concerto.* ***

(M) *** Decca Dig. 460 005-2 [id.]. Kyung Wha Chung, Chicago SO, Sir Georg Solti – BACH: *Violin partita No. 2 & sonata No. 3.* **

(BB) *** RCA Navigator 74321 29243-2. Hoelscher, Cologne RSO, Wakasugi – SCHOENBERG: *Verklerte Nacht;* WEBERN: *Passacaglia for orchestra.* ***

(M) *** Sup. SU 1939-2 011. Josef Suk, Czech PO, Karel Ančerl – BRUCH: *Concerto* **; MENDELSSOHN: *Concerto.* **(*)

(M) *** EMI CDM7 63989-2. Sir Yehudi Menuhin, BBC SO, Boulez – BLOCH: *Violin concerto.* ***

The Berg *Concerto* currently must outstrip most other modern concertos, if the CD catalogues are an accurate barometer of taste. There are more than twice as many versions than of the Bartók or the Walton; only the Prokofiev *D major concerto* has comparable representation. Perlman's performance is totally commanding. The Boston orchestra accompanies superbly and, though the balance favours the soloist, the recording is excellent. This is an obvious candidate for DG's series of 'Originals' and is the more welcome at mid-price with the added bonus of the Ravel *Tzigane*. The current transfer shows the Boston acoustic at its most seductive: Berg's *Concerto* has never sounded richer or texturally more opulent on disc.

Perlman may be tougher, more purposeful in his performance of the Berg *Concerto*, but he does not excel Chung in tenderness and poetry. The violin is placed well in front of the orchestra, but not aggressively so. The recording is brilliant in the Chicago manner, but more spacious than some from this source. However, the Bach coupling rather diminishes the appeal of this CD.

Ulf Hoelscher is particularly well balanced in this fine (1977) Cologne recording, and he gives a passionately dedicated account of Berg's concerto, splendidly supported by Wakasugi and the excellent Cologne Radio Orchestra. The recording, though not as smooth and rich as Perlman's on DG, has plenty of warmth and the closing *Adagio* is very moving in its haunting intensity. This comes at the lowest possible price with two other key twentieth-century works, both very well played and recorded, although the documentation is totally inadequate.

Suk's sweet, unforced style brings out the work's lyrical side without ever exaggerating the romanticism, and the result is most moving. The arrival of the chorale theme (which Berg took from a Bach cantata) is achieved most delicately and the final coda has rarely sounded more tender and hushed on record. A most beautiful performance, with the excellent (1965) recording very firmly and naturally transferred to CD.

Menuhin's is a warm and vibrant performance and, though technically this is not as dashing or immaculate a performance as several others on record, it is one that compels admiration on its own terms of greatness.

(i) *Violin concerto;* (ii) *Lyric suite: 3 Pieces; 3 Pieces for orchestra, Op. 6.*

(B) *** DG Classikon 439 435-2 [(M) id. import]. (i) Szeryng, Bav. RSO, Kubelik; (ii) BPO, Karajan.

Another outstanding version of Berg's *Violin concerto* comes from Henryk Szeryng, who gives a persuasive, perceptive and sympathetic account of this fine work and is well accompanied by the Bavarian orchestra under Kubelik. Superb playing, and a recording that has transferred well to CD. It is perhaps remarkable that, for their bargain Classikon reissue, DG have chosen to add to this two of Karajan's key recordings of Berg's orchestral music. Karajan's purification process gives wonderful clarity to these often complex pieces, with expressive confidence bringing out the romantic overtones. A beautiful, refined recording, admirably transferred to CD.

Lyric suite: 3 Pieces.

(BB) *** Arte Nova Dig. 74321 52248-2 [id.]. SWF SO, Gielen – BARTOK: *Piano concerto No. 3;* CARTER: *Piano concerto* etc. ***

Michael Gielen's passionate devotion to this Berg work comes out in his warmly expressive, finely detailed reading, very well played and recorded. This may be an unexpected coupling, but it is a refreshing one, invaluable for anyone investigating twentieth-century music.

Lyric suite: 3 Pieces; 3 Pieces for orchestra, Op. 6.

(M) *** DG 427 424-2 (3). BPO, Karajan – SCHOENBERG; WEBERN: *Orchestral pieces.* ***

Karajan's justly famous collection of music by the Second Viennese School is here available as a set of three mid-priced CDs. Beautiful, refined recording, admirably transferred to CD.

Lyric suite: 3 Pieces; (i) *5 Altenberglieder, Op. 4.*

(BB) *** Arte Nova Dig 74321 27768-2 [id.]. (i) Vlatka Orsanic; SWFSO, Gielen – ZEMLINSKY: *Lyric symphony.* ***

The three movements which Alban Berg arranged for orchestra from his *Lyric suite* for string quartet make an ideal coupling for the Zemlinsky *Lyric symphony*, the work which Berg quotes and which prompted his title. They are beautifully played and recorded here, as are the five settings of Altenberg poems, crisp and compact yet full of emotion, here sung superbly with fresh tone and clean attack by the soprano, Vlatka Orsanic. First-rate recording. Altogether this is one of the most remarkable bargains in a catalogue which is rich in fine performances, and it is a pity that the documentation does not match the musical excellence.

3 Pieces for orchestra, Op. 6; (i) *Lulu: symphonic suite.*

(M) *** Mercury (IMS) 432 006-2 [id.]. (i) Helga Pilarczyk; LSO, Dorati – SCHOENBERG; WEBERN: *Orchestral pieces.* ***

In his pioneering 1962 Mercury coupling Dorati set the pattern for later recordings of this twentieth-century orchestral triptych, none recorded more clearly or vividly. The LSO plays fluently and warmly. For the *Lulu suite*, recorded a year earlier, Helga Pilarczyk is most impressive: the murder produces the most blood-curdling scream.

3 Pieces for orchestra, Op. 6; 5 Orchestral songs, Op. 4; (i) *Lulu: symphonic suite.*

(M) *** DG 449 714-2 [id.]. (i) M. Price; LSO, Abbado.

Abbado makes it clear above all how beautiful Berg's writing is, not just in the *Lulu* excerpts but in the early Opus 4 *Songs* and the Opus 6 *Orchestral pieces*. Now remastered and reissued as part of DG's 'Legendary Recordings', this mid-priced 'Original' offers even better value.

Lyric suite for string quartet; String quartet, Op. 3.

(M) *** Teldec/Warner 3984 21967-2. Alban Berg Qt – URBANNER: *Quartet No. 3;* WEBERN: *6 Bagatelles* etc. ***

The Alban Berg at their finest, admirably recorded in the mid-1970s, provide here a generous grouping (77 minutes) of key works by Berg and Webern, with a less important *Quartet* by Urbanner thrown in for good measure. The *Lyric suite* is very accessible in its chamber-music format, while the Op. 3 *Quartet* is another of Berg's undoubted masterpieces. The performances are excellent, the recording bright but with plenty of ambience.

Piano sonata, Op. 1.

(B) **(*) Cal. Approche CAL 6203 [(M) id.]. Inger Södergren – J. S. BACH: *Keyboard collection.* **(*)

Inger Södergren's performance of Berg's *Sonata* has real character, but she certainly softens its angst. Those attracted to her enjoyably relaxed Bach coupling may well be converted to enjoying her Berg too. Others may feel that the music's profile is a little blunted. The recording is pleasingly full and unpercussive, and with plenty of keyboard colour.

Wozzeck.

(M) (***) Sony mono MH2K 62759 (2) [id.]. Harrell, Farrell, Jagel, Mordino, Herbert, Music & Arts High School Ch., Schola Cantorum Ch., NYPO, Mitropoulos – KRENEK: *Symphonic elegy* (***); SCHOENBERG: *Erwartung.* (**(*))

No finer memorial to the genius of Dimitri Mitropoulos exists on disc than this electrifying recording of *Wozzeck*, a version that has never been surpasssed for its biting intensity and clear-headed purposefulness. It was recorded live at a concert performance in Carnegie Hall, New York, in April 1951, and though the sound is only mono the result in this transfer is extraordinarily vivid, with the voices clear and immediate.

Though the orchestra is backwardly placed, the sound is clear and detailed with no blunting of impact, so that the climactic final interlude is shatteringly strong. The cast is consistently fine, pitching the notes far more cleanly than is common in this opera and resorting relatively little to vague sing-speech. In the title-role Mack Harrell not only characterizes well, but he brings out musical beauty in the writing. As for Eileen Farrell as Marie, the power and biting precision of her singing as well as the vividness of her characterization make the character central to the whole opera, not just an attendant figure. No singer since has quite matched her achievement in creating a tougher, more buxom figure than we usually get, yet one who in the Bible-reading sequence of Act III could not be more poignant. The other characters are all defined with similar clarity. The Sony transfer is excellent, and the presentation good, with Acts I and II on the first disc, leaving room for generous fill-ups on the second disc. A full libretto with translations is provided in a separate booklet. This costs slightly more than our usual upper-mid-price limit but is well worth it.

Berio, Luciano (born 1925)

Différences; 2 Pieces; (i) *Sequenza III;* (ii) *Sequenza VII;* (i) *Chamber music.*

(M) *** Ph. (IMS) 426 662-2. (i) Cathy Berberian; (ii) Heinz Holliger; Juilliard Ens. (members), composer.

The biggest work here is *Différences* for five instruments and tape; but the two virtuoso solos – *Sequenza III* for voice and *Sequenza VII* for oboe – are if anything even more striking in their extensions of technique and expressive range. First-rate sound, well transferred.

(i) *Recital I (for Cathy);* (ii) *Folk-song suite;* (iii) *3 Songs by Kurt Weill* (arr. Berio).

(M) *** RCA 09026 62540-2 [id.]. Cathy Berberian, with (i) L. Sinf.; (ii, iii) Juilliard Ens.; all cond. composer.

Recital I is the most elaborate, colourful work that Berio ever wrote for Cathy Berberian. Against fragmentary accompaniment from the instrumental band, the soloist in this semi-dramatic piece (presented in live performances as music theatre) thinks back through her repertoire as a concert-singer from Monteverdi to the present day. The end-product is a collage of musical ideas of a kind that Berio has always handled most skilfully and, with Berberian at her most intense, the result is very compelling. Excellent recording. Also included is a first-rate recording of an enchanting collection of folksongs arranged with twinkling ingenuity by Berio, again with Berberian very much in mind. The record concludes with three Kurt Weill songs, arranged by Berio, including the *Song of sexual slavery* intended for *The Threepenny Opera*. Cathy Berberian relishes every word, and she sings *Surabaya Johnny* with comparable enjoyment to Berio's effective scoring.

Berkeley, Lennox (1903–89)

Guitar concerto.

(M) *** RCA 09026 61605-2 [id.]. Julian Bream, Monteverdi O, Gardiner – BROUWER; RODRIGO: *Concertos*. ***

This is a really splendid concerto with memorable invention and elegant architecture which presents a serious as well as attractive argument and a stylish brand of guitar writing that never leans barrenly on Spanish models. The *Lento* is particularly atmospheric. Bream's performance is superb and the recording vivid. This, with the equally stimulating Brouwer, makes an attractive if out-of-the-way coupling for the most popular of all guitar concertos.

Violin concerto, Op. 59.

(M) *** EMI CDM5 66121-2. Menuhin, Menuhin Festival O, Boult – PANUFNIK: *Concerto;* WILLIAMSON: *Concerto*. ***

The Berkeley *Concerto* dates from 1961. It is scored for a small orchestra, horns, oboes and strings, and is slightly baroque in feeling. Its inspiration at times suggests something of Berkeley's keen admiration for Stravinsky, and its craftsmanship is as polished as one would expect from this composer. Although it is not one of his strongest works, it has a movingly austere slow movement and is well worth investigating. It is beautifully played by Yehudi Menuhin and the Menuhin Festival Orchestra under Sir Adrian Boult, and is excellently recorded (at Abbey Road in 1971).

Berlioz, Hector (1803–69)

Complete orchestral works

(i) *Grande Symphonie funèbre et triomphale, Op. 15;* (i–ii) *Harold in Italy, Op. 16;* (i; iii) *Lélio, Op. 14b; Overtures:* (i) *Béatrice et Bénédict;* (iv) *Benvenuto Cellini;* (i) *Le carnaval romain, Op. 9; Le Corsaire, Op. 21; Les Francs-juges, Op. 3; Le roi Lear, Op. 4; Waverley, Op. 1;* (v) *Rêverie et caprice* (for violin and orchestra), *Op. 8;* (vi–vii) *Symphonie fantastique, Op. 14;* (i; vii) *Tristia, Op. 18* (excerpt): *Marche funèbre pour la dernière scène d'Hamlet;* (i) *La Damnation de Faust, Op. 24* (excerpts): *Menuet des follets; Marche hongroise;* (i; viii) *Romeo and Juliet, Op. 17;* (i) *Les Troyens à Carthage, Part II, Prélude, Act III;* (ix) *Les Troyens, Act IV: Royal hunt and storm; Marche pour l'entrée de la reine; Ballet music.*

(B) *** Ph. 456 143-2 (6) [id.]. (i) LSO; (ii) with Nobuko Imai; (iii) with José Carreras, Thomas Allen, John Constable (piano), Roy Jowitt (clarinet), Renata Scheffel-Stein (harp); (iv) BBC SO; (v) Arthur Grumiaux, New Philh. O, Edo de Waart; (vi) Concg. O; (vii) with John Alldis Ch.; (viii) with Patricia Kern, John Shirley-Quirk, Robert Tear, L. Symphony Ch.; (ix) ROHCG O; all (except *Op. 8*) cond. Sir Colin Davis.

(i) *Harold in Italy, Op. 16. Overtures: Le Carnaval romain, Op. 9; Le Corsaire, Op. 21; Symphonie fantastique;* (ii) *Symphonie funèbre et triomphale, Op. 15.*

(B) ** Ph. Duo 442 290-2 (2) [id.]. (i) Nobuko Imai; (ii) John Alldis Ch.; LSO, Sir Colin Davis.

Sir Colin Davis's achievement in Berlioz hardly needs restating here. These Philips recordings, made over a period of a decade and a half between 1965 and 1980, consistently reveal him to be a natural Berliozian, with any minor weaknesses more than offset by the consistent strengths. The Philips recordings, too, are of a very high standard and have all been remastered splendidly to retain their ambient warmth and refinement, while increasing their impression of natural vividness. Even the overtures, which were the first works to be recorded (all but two made with the LSO in 1965), show the Philips analogue sound at its most impressively full and atmospheric. Even if they lack the brilliance that modern digital recording would bring, they have never before sounded so good on disc. Davis's Concertgebouw recording of the *Symphonie fantastique*, made a decade later, has long been a top recommendation; it has been matched but not surpassed. Its strange successor, *Lélio*, is given by Davis without the spoken dialogue, a well-sprung reading with excellent solo contributions. *Harold in Italy* (with Nobuko Imai) is also distinguished, and in *Romeo and Juliet*, also with excellent soloists, Davis brings a rare sympathy to the score and secures playing of great vitality and atmosphere from the LSO. Although his new Vienna Philharmonic account of *Roméo et Juliette* is undoubtedly the finer recording (and perhaps performance), this classic 1968 performance more than holds its own – and still offers very good sound. The *Symphonie funèbre et triomphale*, however, needs rather more persuasive handling than he achieves. Its *Apotheosis* can be made to sound grander and more effective, but the sonority of the recording remains impressive. Curiously, *Tristia* is not given complete, with only the third section included, the *Funeral march for the last scene of Hamlet*, but that is presented most evocatively, while among the other excerpts it is good to have Davis's fine choral version of the *Royal Hunt and storm*, taken from the complete set of *Les Troyens*. Sir Colin brings special insights to Berlioz – as indeed he does to Sibelius – and there is no one to touch him in this repertoire. This set offers really outstanding value for money and is in every way a bargain.

(i) *Harold in Italy, Op. 16; Symphonie fantastique, Op. 14; Damnation de Faust: Hungarian march. Roméo et Juliette, Op. 17:* orchestral excerpts: *Roméo seul . . . Grand fête chez Capulet; Scène d'amour; La reine Mab (scherzo). Les Troyens:* (ii) *Royal hunt and storm.*

(B) **(*) Decca Double Dig. 455 361-2 (2) [id.]. Montreal SO, Charles Dutoit; (i) with Pinchas Zukerman; (ii) with Montreal Ch.

Dutoit's version of *Harold in Italy* is very richly recorded. With as characterful a soloist as Zukerman, highly individual and warmly expressive, if not always at his purest, the centre of gravity of the work is shifted. Though the beauty of the writing is very satisfying, the work seems to lose some of its purpose when the soloist comes to be phased out. With the viola's contribution all but eliminated, the *Orgy* seems just a little tame, and speeds throughout tend to be on the broad side. Again in the *Symphonie fantastique*, it is the spectacular, wide-ranging recorded sound that is the first point to note. But Dutoit tends to prefer slower speeds than usual, and that sometimes makes him seem less exciting than his finest rivals. Yet by keeping the pulse steady, he adds to structural strength while never limiting expressive warmth in lyrical passages or the crisp lifting of rhythm in allegros, and the power is most impressive. The four extended orchestral excerpts from *Roméo and Juliette* then follow, with Dutoit and his orchestra at their finest, playing warmly as well as brilliantly, with the *Queen Mab scherzo* opening the second disc. The *Royal Hunt and storm* comes from the complete set of *Les Troyens* and includes the chorus.

Harold in Italy, Op. 16.

(M) *(*) RCA 09026 62582-2. William Primrose; Boston SO, Charles Munch – D'INDY: *Symphonie sur un chant montagnard français*. **(*)

(M) (*) Revelation RV 10051 [id.]. Mikhail Tolpygo, USSR SO, David Oistrakh – BRUCH: *Scottish Fantasy*. **(*)

Primrose recorded *Harold in Italy* on three occasions (and there is a fourth, off-air version with Toscanini, made in 1939). The present issue, dating from 1958 was the third. At times Munch is positively coarse and hard-driven and Primrose not on form. Of course there are good things, but for the most part this is a disappointment.

The rough sound on this 1972 Russian recording completely rules it out of court, despite an inspired account of the Bruch which comes as coupling. The performance has plenty of fire and conviction, though one feels that these musicians are not approaching *Harold* as if they are used to playing it every day of the week. It is a pity that more could not have been done to refine the recorded sound. Mikhail Tolpygo is a fine viola player, firm and true, but he is balanced far too close, with the orchestra only half heard in the background. Those who can tolerate the coarseness of the climaxes, which come close to distortion, should hear him.

(i) *Harold in Italy, Op. 16;* (ii) *La damnation de Faust, Op. 24: Hungarian march; Ballet des sylphes; Menuet des follets;* (iii) *Les Troyens: Trojan march;* (iv) *Royal Hunt & Storm*.

(B) **(*) Sony SBK 53255; *SBT 53255* [id.]. (i) Joseph de Pasquale; (i; iii) Phd. O, Ormandy; (ii) Phd. O, Munch; (iv) O de Paris, Barenboim.

(i) *Harold in Italy, Op. 16;* (ii) *Rêverie et caprice for violin and orchestra, Op. 8; Overture Les Francs-juges, Op. 3.*

(BB) ** Naxos Dig. 8.553034 [id.]. (i) Rivka Golani; (ii) Igor Gruppman; San Diego SO, Yoav Talmi.

(i) *Harold in Italy, Op. 16;* (ii) *Overtures: Benvenuto Cellini, Op. 23; Les Francs-juges, Op. 3.*

(M) *** EMI CDM7 64745-2 [id.]. (i) Donald McInnes, O Nat. de France, Bernstein; (ii) LSO, Previn.

With the understanding players of the Orchestre National, Bernstein gives a performance that is both exciting and introspective. His earlier account with his own New York Philharmonic for CBS was sharper-focused than this. But with French players Bernstein's slightly more relaxed manner is in some ways more authentic, so that the galloping rhythms of the first and third movements are more lilting, if fractionally less precise. Donald McInnes is a violist with a superbly rich and even tone. His first entry, with the phrase echoed, is a ravishing moment and he responds at all times to the conductor, yet has plenty of individuality. The 1976 recording, made in the Salle Wagram, has an opulent spread and plenty of warmth; on CD it is brighter and more firmly focused. This goes to the top of the list of available recordings of this somewhat elusive work and is certainly first choice at mid-price. It is made the more attractive by the addition of the two overtures. Under Previn, the swing-along melody of *Les Francs-juges* swaggers boldly. Again excellent transfers, with rich, deep brass.

Ormandy's 1965 recording of *Harold in Italy* with the Philadelphia Orchestra has a lot going for it. Joseph de Pasquale is a thoughtful and cultured soloist and he is truthfully and expertly balanced in relation to the orchestra. The performance is beautifully shaped, though the finale could perhaps do with a shade more abandon. Although the recording perspective is excellent, the sound is not as transparent as some rivals, thanks to the reverberant acoustic. For all that, this is an impressive *Harold*, superbly played. The three excerpts from *La damnation de Faust* were recorded in 1963, when Munch was guest conductor in Philadelphia, and they have a Beecham-like elegance. Daniel Barenboim's recording of the *Royal Hunt and Storm* from *Les Troyens* with the Orchestre de Paris comes from the mid-1970s and has the benefit of better sound; it is well enough played though it is not really in the same street as the Munch or Ormandy performances. Nevertheless this CD is eminently recommendable and very good value.

Talmi conducts a refined and warmly expressive performance of *Harold in Italy*, making this a welcome bargain at Naxos price. Sadly, the distancing of sound, set in an over-reverberant acoustic, means that the impact and bite of the performance are undermined, and that also affects the viola soloist, Rivka Golani, in one of her most warmly sympathetic performances. The San Diego Symphony is an excellent orchestra, as one can appreciate more readily in the fill-ups, where the sound has rather more body. *Les Francs-juges* is given a light and refined reading, with a chamber quality in some of the string playing, but it is the performance of the *Reverie and Caprice* with the San Diego concertmaster as soloist which proves the most magnetic on the disc.

(i) *Harold in Italy. Roméo et Juliette* (excerpts).

(M) (***) RCA mono GD 60275 [60275-2-RG]. (i) Carlton Cooley; NBC SO, Toscanini.

Toscanini's famous 1953 recording of *Harold in Italy* is of very high voltage, with Carlton Cooley an excellent soloist. The demonic fires glow with great intensity in the *Orgy of the Brigands*; perhaps the *Pilgrims' march* is just a shade hard driven. In spite of the sonic limitations, the excitement of the performance still comes across the decades.

Overtures: *Béatrice et Bénédict; Benvenuto Cellini; Le Carnaval romain; Le Corsaire. Roméo et Juliette: Queen Mab scherzo. Les Troyens: Royal hunt and storm.*
✿ (M) *** RCA 9026 61400-2 [id.]. Boston SO, Munch (with SAINT-SAENS: *Le rouet d'Omphale* ***).

Dazzlingly brilliant performances of four favourite overtures – the virtuosity of the Boston players, especially the violins in *Béatrice et Bénédict* and *Le Corsaire* – is breathtaking. But it is for the wonderfully poetic and thrilling account of the *Royal hunt and storm* from *Les Troyens* that this CD earns its Rosette. The horn solo is ravishing and the brass produce a riveting climax as the storm reaches its peak. Then the scene of a rain-drenched countryside is magically evoked as the horn steals back in the closing bars. The early stereo (1957/9) is remarkable: one really feels the hall ambience, and John Pfeiffer's remastering is expert. *Romeo and Juliet* was recorded in 1961, and again one marvels at the articulation of the Boston violins and horns. The Saint-Saëns bonus is the earliest recording of all (1957). It is beautifully played and, after a robust climax, has the most delicate, pianissimo ending.

Overtures: *Le Carnaval romain; Le Corsaire; Damnation de Faust: Hungarian march.*
(M) **(*) Decca (IMS) 448 571-2 [id.]. Paris Conservatoire O, Martinon – BIZET: *Jeux d'enfants;* IBERT: *Divertissement;* SAINT-SAENS: *Danse macabre* etc. ***

Martinon's Berlioz recordings have been added as a bonus for this reissue (in Decca's Classic Sound series) of his highly praised 1960 collection of French music. They were recorded two years earlier and, although the playing is both brilliant and exciting, it is not on the level of the later performances. There are moments of faulty intonation in both woodwind and brass, not very serious, of course, but marring the effect for the critical ear.

Rêverie et caprice, Op. 8.
(M) *** DG Dig. 445 549-2 [id.]. Perlman, O de Paris, Barenboim – LALO: *Symphonie espagnole;* SAINT-SAENS: *Concerto No. 3.* ***

Berlioz's short concertante work for violin and orchestra uses material originally intended for *Benvenuto Cellini*. Perlman's ripely romantic approach to the *Rêverie* brings out the individuality of the melody and, with a sympathetic accompaniment from Barenboim, the work as a whole is given considerable substance. First-rate digital recording.

Roméo et Juliette: Queen Mab scherzo.
(M) (**) RCA mono GD 60314 [60314-2-RG]. Phd. O, Toscanini – MENDELSSOHN: *Midsummer Night's Dream.* (***)

Toscanini's quicksilver reading of this fairy scherzo has much in common with his fine Philadelphia recording of Mendelssohn's fairy music. The 1941 recording is clear.

Symphonie fantastique, Op. 14.
(B) (***) Dutton Lab. mono CDEA 5504 [(M) id.]. Hallé O, Barbirolli – (with FAURE: *Shylock: Nocturne* (***)) – WAGNER: *Meistersinger: suite.* (***)
(B) *** [EMI Red Line Dig. CDR5 72552]. Phd. O, Muti.
(M) **(*) Virgin Veritas/EMI (SIS) VM5 61379-2 [id.]. L. Classical Players, Norrington (with *Les Francs-juges*).
(BB) *(*) Discover Dig. DICD 920421. BRTN PO, Avi Ostrowsky.
(BB) * Carlton LSO Double Dig. 30368 01217 (2) [(B) id.]. LSO, Williams – WAGNER: *Operatic orchestral excerpts.* *(*)
(B) * Millennium Universal UMD 80393. V. State Op. O, René Leibowitz (with SIBELIUS: *Valse triste;* TCHAIKOVSKY: *String serenade: Waltz;* WEBER, orch. BERLIOZ: *Invitation to the Dance* *).

(i) *Symphonie fantastique;* (ii) *La damnation de Faust: Danse des sylphes.*
(M) *** Decca Phase Four 448 955-2 [id.]. New Philh. O; (ii) LSO; Stokowski (with DVORAK: *Slavonic dance No. 10 in E min., Op. 72/2:* Czech PO ***).

(i) *Symphonie fantastique;* (ii) *Overtures: Béatrice et Bénédict; Le Carnaval romain; Le Corsaire.*
(M) **(*) EMI CDM7 64630-2 [id.]. (i) O Nat. de France, Bernstein; (ii) LSO, Previn.
(BB) **(*) RCA Navigator 74321 21283-2 [Basic 100 09026 61721-2]. Boston SO, (i) Prêtre; (ii) Munch.

(i) *Symphonie fantastique;* (ii) *Overture: Benvenuto Cellini; Les Troyens: Royal hunt and storm.*
(M) **(*) Sony SMK 60135 [id.]. (i) LSO; (ii) NYPO; Pierre Boulez.

Symphonie fantastique; Overtures: Le Carnaval romain; Le Corsaire.
(BB) **(*) ASV CDQS 6090 [(M) id.]. RPO, Bátiz.

Symphonie fantastique; Overtures: Le Carnaval romain; Le Corsaire; La damnation de Faust: Marche hongroise. Les Troyens: Trojan march.
(M) **(*) Mercury (IMS) 434 328-2 [id.]. Detroit SO, Paul Paray.

Symphonie fantastique; Overture: Le Carnaval romain; La damnation de Faust: Marche hongroise. Les Troyens: Royal hunt and storm.
(M) (**(*)) EMI mono/stereo CDM5 66598-2. Philh. O, Karajan.

Symphonie fantastique; Overture: Le Corsaire, Op. 21.
(M) *** Carlton/RPO Dig. 3036 60022-2 [id.]. RPO, Previn.

(i) *Symphonie fantastique;* (ii) *Roméo et Juliette: Love scene; Queen Mab scherzo.*
(M) *** Ph. 446 202-2. (i) Concg. O; (ii) LSO; Sir Colin Davis.

Sir Colin Davis's 1974 Concertgebouw recording – his first with that orchestra – has dominated the catalogue for two decades. Now reissued at mid-price (in the UK only), with two excerpts from Davis's *Roméo et Juliette* as a fine bonus, it still remains a primary recommendation. The performance has superb life and colour, the slow movement memorably atmospheric and the final two movements very exciting. If the sound does not quite match recent rivals in brilliance and definition, the overall balance is very satisfying and believable. However, Martinon's fine account (coupled with *Lélio* – see below) should not be forgotten.

There is no more spectacular recording than Stokowski's, made in Phase Four in the Kingsway Hall in 1968 and multi-miked so that detail can be highlighted, and the brass is given satanic impact in the *Marche au Supplice* and finale (where the bells also toll plangently). As might be expected, the performance is as idiosyncratic as it is charismatic and it is certainly thrilling, by some Stokowskian magic conveying complete, warm-hearted conviction. Stokowski's warmth of phrasing is aptly romantic, but generally the surprising thing is his meticulous concern for markings. The hairpin dynamics are even exaggerated but, unlike many less flamboyant conductors, he refuses to whip up the coda for the finale, yet it does not affect the adrenalin flow. The close of the symphony is followed by two totally contrasted encores. First an exquisite *bonne bouche*, affectionately introducing Berlioz's sylphs from *La Damnation de Faust*. They enter slowly but with exquisite, sensuous grace, the effect more Stokowski than Berlioz perhaps, but delicious in its way. Then comes a seductive account of the *E minor Slavonic dance*, just as beautifully played by the Czech Philharmonic Orchestra.

The Dutton disc in the Concert Classics series offers superb CD transfers of three recordings which Barbirolli made for EMI in his early years with the Hallé Orchestra. This version of the *Symphonie fantastique* was recorded in 1947, just when, in the immediate post-war period, Barbirolli had built the Hallé into what was widely counted the finest orchestra in the country, even outshining the London orchestras. Like his 1959 version for Pye, this offers a spacious, beautifully moulded reading (it originally stretched to seven 78-r.p.m. discs), yet the playing is a degree more refined than in the later version, tauter and more urgent, notably in the last three movements. In the Dutton transfer the sound is satisfyingly full and weighty, belying the idea of such an early recording date. The Fauré *Nocturne* makes a fine if brief bonus.

With full-ranging digital sound, well balanced with fine presence and atmosphere, André Previn conducts the RPO in a keenly dramatic reading marked by characteristically well-lifted rhythms, with dynamic contrasts powerfully underlined, which heightens the sinister side of the composer's nightmare vision. This is one of Previn's RPO recordings which matches his achievements in his vintage days with the LSO, and it makes an excellent, mid-priced, alternative recommendation.

Bernstein directs a brilliant and understanding performance which captures more than most the wild, volatile quality of Berlioz's inspiration. Sir Colin Davis may give a clearer idea of the logic of the piece, but Bernstein (unlike Davis, omitting the exposition repeat) has even more urgency, and his reading culminates in superb accounts of the *March to the scaffold* and the *Witches' sabbath*, full of rhythmic swagger and natural flair. However, the remastering of the late-1970s analogue recording gives slight over-emphasis to the brilliance with its tendency to shrillness in the upper strings. Some weight has also been lost at the bass end, but the warm resonance of the recording retains the body of the orchestral sound. The three overtures make a fine bonus.

The balance of fierceness against romantic warmth in Muti's own personality works particularly well in this symphony, so that he holds the thread of argument together firmly without ever underplaying excitement. The sound is among the best that Muti has had in Philadelphia, full in range if not always ideally clear in texture. Nevertheless this is a strong bargain recommendation for American collectors.

Boulez's account of the *Symphonie fantastique* is intensely individual, crisp and intense, with clarity the essential all through, and with atmosphere playing little or no part (although the sharp-edged recording has plenty of ambience). As he does not miss the bizarre or diabolic elements, in many ways this approach makes the music sound even more modern than usual, underlining once again the amazing fact that Berlioz's advanced score was written in the year after Beethoven's death. Boulez's accounts of the *Royal hunt and storm* and the *Benvenuto Cellini overture* are also exciting, especially the latter, but the famous descriptive piece from *Les Troyens* has little feeling of evocation.

Paray's excitingly hard-pressed reading is full of passionate, mercurial neurosis. The first movement immediately spurts away, and it is only the conductor's firm grip that prevents the movement from getting out of hand. The *Waltz*, too, is fast, though not inelegant, and the *Adagio*, even though it has moments of pastoral repose, never drags its feet. The final two movements have great verve, and there are few performances that combine such a high level of tension with a true understanding of the music's inner pulse. Fine playing, of course, and brilliant recording, with a tendency to thinness in the violins. The encores are similarly exciting and vivid, and again one marvels that a stereo recording from as early as 1958/9 should sound so impressive today.

Bátiz's ASV CD is fully competitive in the super-bargain range. It has the advantage of an excellent digital recording, which is brilliant and well balanced. As always in the recording studio, he brings the score vividly to life, and his consistent warmth and intensity are highly persuasive. Points of detail may be less subtle than with Davis, for instance, but one has the feeling here of live music-making, and the two overtures are equally strong and spontaneous. The sound balance is more convincing than in Bernstein's remastered EMI version.

Karajan's mono account of the *Symphonie fantastique* with the Philharmonia Orchestra was made in July 1954 and the remaining items in stereo in 1958. (There is some confusion about the *Royal hunt and storm*, which is dated January 1959 on the sleeve but is listed mistakenly as 1951 on the label. It does not appear in Anthony Williams's 1978 discography.) Andrew Porter, writing in *The Record Guide*, wrote of Karajan's *Symphonie fantastique* with some disappointment: 'we feel that Karajan's performance is rather more solid than the poet's fantastic dreams should be, and prefer something more volatile, something that flickers'. An understandable response, perhaps, for the performance is kept on a firm rein, but there is no lack of temperament – take the end of *Un bal* – or poetry, as in the *Scène aux champs*. The *Royal hunt and storm* is not quite the equal of Beecham or Munch, but not far off. The orchestral playing, as one would expect from the Philharmonia, is marvellous and the recording is very good for the period.

Prêtre's excitingly chimerical Boston account was recorded in 1969, and the upper range is far from full. However, the Boston ambience brings weight and the sound is otherwise resonantly spacious, with exciting projection for the brass. It is a highly volatile performance but Prêtre's sense of neurosis is convincing, and the finale combines an element of the grotesque with high adrenalin flow. An individual and involving account. Munch's famous accounts of the three *Overtures* make a thrilling bonus, but here the sound tends to shrillness.

Norrington does his utmost to observe the composer's metronome markings; but where his Beethoven is consistently fast, some of these speeds are more relaxed than we are used to – as in the *March to the scaffold* and the *Ronde du sabbat*. As usual, his lifting of rhythms prevents the music from dragging, at the same time giving new transparency; *Les Francs-juges* Overture is, however, disappointingly low-key.

Richard Williams's version is disappointingly underpowered, springing fully to life only in the closing pages of the finale. Elsewhere the playing of the LSO is polished and well detailed but lacking in adrenalin and bite, and the slightly distanced recording does not help to give the music-making an immediate impact.

The Polish-born French conductor René Leibowitz was one of the arch champions of the Second Viennese School, the author of *Schoenberg et son école* and an important treatise on *Introduction à la musique de douze sons*. Older readers may remember his exhilarating account of Offenbach's *La belle Helène* on Nixa and Bizet's *Pearl Fishers* – though, generally speaking, he did not enjoy a great recording career. In his 1957 account of the *Symphonie fantastique* he scores points for observing the first-movement exposition repeat, but the playing of the Vienna orchestra is not as tonally sumptuous as one might expect. Some of the playing is a bit scrappy and the upper strings in *Un bal* are thin. Nor is the recording-balance entirely satisfactory. In so competitive a market it is hardly a strong recommendation. By the side of such contemporary versions as Karajan, Munch, Paray – not to mention Beecham – this does not register. It is ironic to find Leibowitz (author of *Jean Sibelius, le plus mauvais compositeur du monde* (!)) conducting *Valse triste*!

Ostrowsky's version on the Discover label brings a relatively routine reading, well recorded, which also sounds a little cautious and lacking tension. With no coupling, this is not really competitive even at bargain price.

Symphonie fantastique, Op. 14; (i) *Lélio (Le retour à la vie), Op. 14b.*

(B) *** EMI Rouge et Noir CZS5 69550-2 (2). (i) Gedda, Burles, Van Gorp, Sendrez, Topart, Fr. R. Ch., ORTF Nat. O, Martinon.

Berlioz intended *Lélio* as a sequel to the *Symphonie fantastique*, and Martinon conveniently offers the works paired at bargain price. His account of the *Symphonie* shows a unique seductiveness. Martinon gives the first-movement exposition repeat and provides the often omitted extra brass parts; though the result is brilliant, he never presses on too frenetically. Most of all, however, this reading is outstanding for its warm shaping of phrase, even if the finale, with its tolling bells of doom, has a flamboyance and power to match any available. The 1973 sound remains remarkably vivid. *Lélio* quotes the *idée fixe* from the *Symphonie*, which helps the listener to feel at home. It is difficult to imagine this performance being bettered, and the 1974 sound is suitably atmospheric.

(i) *Symphonie fantastique;* (ii) *Lélio, ou Le Retour à la vie, Op. 14b;* (iii; iv) *La Mort de Cléopâtre;* (iii–v) *Les Nuits d'été, Op. 7;* (vi) *Béatrice et Bénédict: Overture & Entr'acte; Overtures: Benvenuto Cellini; Le carnaval romain, Op. 9; Les Troyens: Royal hunt and storm.*

(M) *** Sony Theta SM3K 64103 (3) [S3K 64103]. (i) LSO; (ii) with Jean-Louis Barrault (narrator), John Mitchinson, John Shirley-Quirk, L. Symphony Ch.; (iii) Yvonne Minton; (iv) BBC SO; (v) Stuart Burrows; (vi) NYPO; all cond. Boulez.

A thoroughly worthwhile Berlioz anthology, spanning a decade of Boulez recordings for CBS from 1967 (the *Symphonie* and *Lélio*) to 1976 (the two song-cycles). Though the spoken dialogue remains obtrusively long (even when spoken most beautifully by M. Barrault), the individual cueing on CD allows one access to the music itself and the six numbers make a fascinating suite. Coupled with a unique reading of the *Fantastique* (clear-headed and intense rather than atmospheric), it shows Boulez at his most searchingly convincing. Very good recording, except for the difference of levels in *Lélio* between speech (loud and forward) and music. The dramatic scena, *La Mort de Cléopâtre*, an early work which yet gives many hints of the mature Berlioz, makes a particularly suitable companion, as it offers specific quotations of material later used in the *Symphonie fantastique* (the *idée fixe*) and the *Roman carnival overture* (the melody of the introduction). Yvonne Minton's account is dramatically incisive, less varied of expression than Dame Janet Baker's famous recording, but strongly committed. When Berlioz orchestrated *Les nuits d'été* he specified the use of more than one voice in the score, and here the cycle is shared by Minton and Stuart Burrows, with Minton's passionate response showing her at her most movingly eloquent and Burrows also at his finest. The 1972 New York collection of *Overtures* is warmer, less concerned with sharpness of detail than the earlier recordings, yet they still show toughness taking priority over flexible brilliance and the sound-balance matches the readings in its brightness, although it also has weight and atmosphere. Overall this is strongly recommended to Boulez admirers, and others will find it highly stimulating.

Symphonie fantastique, Op. 14. (i) *Roméo et Juliette, Op. 17.*

(B) *** RCA Twofer 74321 34168-2 [(M) id. import]. Boston SO, Charles Munch, (i) with Rosalind Elias, Cesare Valletti, Giorgio Tozzi and Ch.

One of the most valuable of recent 'Twofers' – an ugly term perhaps for the welcome and increasingly popular format of two discs for the price of one in a single jewel-case. Not so long ago, RCA issued Munch's wonderful mono account of the *Roméo et Juliette Symphony* in harness with Victoria de los Angeles's 1955 *Les nuits d'été*, both sounding impressively fresh enough for us to give them a qualified three-star recommendation. Of course the sound is not quite as good as these stereo performances, made almost ten years later. The later *Roméo et Juliette* is a near-ideal performance and Munch's approach is sharp and dramatic. The stabbing agony of the frenzied allegro following Juliet's death has a frightening impact, and the jollity of the Capulets' party is taut and brittle. Yet the romanticism of the love music and such tiny numbers as the off-stage chorus for the departing guests show the depth of Munch's sympathy. He encapsulates the mercurial sensibility, the ardour and incandescence of both symphonies; and the virtuosity of singers and orchestra is matched by the brilliance of the early stereo. At their price, these performances should be snapped up, even if you have either of the Davis versions.

VOCAL MUSIC

La damnation de Faust, Op. 24.

(B) **(*) DG Double 453 019-2 (2) [(M) id. import]. Mathis, Burrows, McIntyre, Paul, Tanglewood Festival Ch., Boston Boys' Ch. & SO, Ozawa.

(i) *La damnation de Faust, Op. 24;* (ii) *La mort de Cléopâtre.*

(B) **(*) EMI forte CZS5 68583-2 (2) [CDFB 68583]. Janet Baker; (i) Gedda, Bacquier, Thau, Paris Opera Ch., O de Paris, Prêtre; (ii) LSO, Gibson.

The best part of the EMI *Damnation de Faust* is Dame Janet Baker's Marguerite. This affecting music is sung most beautifully and has fine focus of tone. Prêtre is not always as perceptive as he might be and, though there are many dramatic touches in his reading of this inspired score, in general the set does not compete with either Markevitch or Ozawa in this price-range. Needless to say, Berlioz's early scena on the death of a famous classical heroine, *La mort de Cléopâtre*, is beautifully performed.

Now offered, in the UK only, on a DG Double (with translation and full documentation included), Ozawa's performance provides an alternative, in a much more moulded style. The relative softness of focus is underlined by the reverberant Boston acoustics; with superb playing and generally fine singing, however, the results are seductively enjoyable. The digital remastering has improved definition without losing the effect of the hall ambience.

L'enfance du Christ, Op. 25.

(M) **(*) RCA 09026 61234-2 (2) [id.]. Valletti, Kopleff, Souzay, Tozzi, New England Conservatory Ch., Boston SO, Munch – *Nuits d'été.* *

Charles Munch's account of *L'enfance du Christ* comes from 1956 and makes a welcome return to circulation in the economically packaged two-CD sets that look like one. Needless to say, the performance is thoroughly idiomatic and the playing of the Boston Symphony has a splendour and sonority that the (obviously dated) recording still conveys. The line-up as far as the soloists are concerned is impressive: Florence Kopleff as Mary and Gérard Souzay, then at the height of his powers, as Joseph. The chorus is a weakness; they do not have the tenderness and flexibility to be found in either of Colin Davis's accounts, and even Munch himself must yield in that Berliozian fervour to the English conductor. Leontyne Price is gloriously full-toned in her 1963 recording of *Nuits d'été*, though in terms of characterization she is no match for Danco or Crespin. She produces much the same colour in each of the songs, but the performance is well worth having for the sake of the magical playing of the Chicago orchestra under Reiner. The transfers are excellently effected.

(i; ii) *L'enfance du Christ*; (ii; iii) *Méditation religieuse; La mort d'Ophélie; Sara la baigneuse*; (iii; iv) *La mort de Cléopâtre.*

(B) *** Double Decca 443 461-2 (2) [id.]. (i) Pears, Morison, Cameron, Rouleau, Frost, Fleet, Goldsbrough O; (ii) St Anthony Singers, (iii) ECO; (iv) Anne Pashley; Sir Colin Davis.

Davis's 1961 recording of *L'enfance du Christ* (originally made for L'Oiseau-Lyre) is by no means inferior to his later, Philips set. At times the earlier performance was fresher and more urgent, and Peter Pears was a sweeter-toned, more characterful narrator. Elsie Morison and John Cameron are perfectly cast as Mary and Joseph, and Joseph Rouleau makes an impressive contribution as the Ishmaelite Father. Such moments as the famous *Shepherds' chorus* and the angelic hosannas which end Part 2 are ravishingly beautiful, particularly when the recording has transferred so freshly and atmospherically to its new format. Moreover this Decca reissue offers (on a Double Decca set with two CDs for the price of one) the entire contents of a third LP, issued in 1968 and also sounding freshly minted. This is an invaluable collection of off-beat vocal works, with fine choral singing and a splendid contribution from Anne Pashley. In a wonderfully intense account of the early scena, *La mort de Cléopâtre*, she even manages to rival Dame Janet Baker's version; in this most substantial of pieces Miss Pashley is if anything the more dramatic: the closing section, where Cleopatra in her death throes can merely mutter disconnected phrases, is most affectingly done. The other three pieces are for chorus: the gentle *Méditation religieuse* is a setting of Thomas Moore in translation; *La mort d'Ophélie*, for women's chorus, brings overtones of the choruses in *Roméo et Juliette*; and *Sara la baigneuse* is a strong, flowing setting of a Victor Hugo poem.

(i) *L'enfance du Christ, Op. 25;* (ii) *Roméo et Juliette, Op. 17* (orchestral music only).

(B) *** EMI forte (SIS) CZS5 68586-2 (2) [CDFB 68586]. (i) De los Angeles, Gedda, Soyer, Blanc, Depraz, Cottret, René Duclos Ch., Paris Conservatoire O, Cluytens; (ii) Chicago SO, Giulini.

This Cluytens performance of *L'enfance du Christ* from the mid-1960s emerges on CD with remarkable freshness and, although the earlier Colin Davis set tends to trump it on a Double Decca, it remains very competitive on EMI's forte label with its generous new coupling. Gedda may not be as sensitive as Pears on that Davis version, but de los Angeles is superlative and so, of course, is Ernest Blanc as Herod. The orchestra gives sensitive support and the choral singing is agreeably fresh – the *Shepherds' farewell*, taken at a flowing pace, is particularly beautiful. The remastered recording sounds very good indeed (much smoother than the original LPs) and shows the Salle Wagram acoustic at its most spacious. This is undoubtedly a version that will give much pleasure to Berlioz lovers; moreover it is coupled with one of Giulini's best records from the same period (1969). The Chicago orchestra responds with predictably fine discipline and beauty of tone, and also with great conviction. The brass in the opening *Combats et tumulte* sequence are characteristically impressive and, whether in the gossamer-like delicacy of the *Queen Mab scherzo* or the brilliance of the Capulets' festivities, Giulini shapes each phrase with the right degree of poetic feeling. This is an incandescent performance, and *Roméo seul* and the *Scène d'amour* are beautifully done, with the most refined response from the strings. Good recording quality, though the focus is not always absolutely clean on the otherwise well-balanced CD transfer.

Les nuits d'été (song-cycle), *Op. 7*.

(M) *(*) Sony Theta Dig. SMK 60031 [id.]. Frederica von Stade, Boston SO, Ozawa – DEBUSSY: *La Damoiselle élue* *(*); RAVEL: *Shéhérazade*. **(*)

(M) * RCA 09026 61234-2 (2) [id.]. Leontyne Price, Chicago SO, Reiner – *L'enfance du Christ*. **(*)

Les nuits d'été (song-cycle); Mélodies: *La belle voyageuse; La Captive; Zaïde*.

(BB) *** Virgin Classics Dig. Double VBD5 61469-2 (2) [CDVB 61469]. Dame Janet Baker, City of L. Sinf., Hickox – BRAHMS: *Alto rhapsody* etc.; MENDELSSOHN: *Infelice* etc.; RESPIGHI: *La Sensitiva*. ***

(i) *Les nuits d'été* (song-cycle), *Op. 7;* (ii) *La mort de Cléopâtre*.

(M) *** DG Dig. 445 594-2 [id.]. O de Paris, Barenboim, with (i) Kiri Te Kanawa; (ii) Jessye Norman.

This Virgin two-for-one-at-mid-price is a treasure-chest of Dame Janet Baker's later recordings, made in the early 1990s. Dame Janet's new recording of *Les nuits d'été* also includes extra orchestral songs. Helped by full, rich recording and a warmly sympathetic accompaniment from Hickox, the interpretation, if anything, glows even more warmly than in Dame Janet's classic EMI reading with Barbirolli (now coupled on a forte double with *Roméo et Juliette* – see below).

The coupling of Jessye Norman in the scena and Dame Kiri Te Kanawa in the song-cycle makes for one of the most ravishing of Berlioz records, with each singer at her very finest. Norman has natural nobility and command as the Egyptian queen in this dramatic scena, while Te Kanawa encompasses the challenge of different moods and register in *Les nuits d'été* more completely and affectingly than any singer on record in recent years.

Frederica von Stade, always intelligent and naturally musical, yet sounds less spontaneous than usual in a disappointing version of this most magical of orchestral song-cycles, not helped by Ozawa's cool and uninvolved accompaniment. Good recording.

Leontyne Price's account suffers from rather generalized responses and little variety of colour or dynamics, though her voice is striking enough and she is well supported by Reiner and the Chicago orchestra in its heyday.

(i) *Les nuits d'été* (song-cycle); (ii) *Te Deum*.

(B) ** Sony SBK 63043; *SBT 63043* [id.]. (i) Yvonne Minton, Stuart Burrows, BBC SO, Boulez; (ii) Jean Dupouy, Ch. d'Enfants de Paris, Maîtrisse de la Resurrection, Ch. & O. de Paris, Barenboim.

In the Boulez version of *Nuits d'été* the six songs are shared between male and female voices. Yvonne Minton brings an almost operatic flair to *Le spectre de la rose*, *Sur les lagunes* and especially *L'île inconnue*, and Burrows is hardly less ardent in his heady opening *Villanelle*, while both *Absence* and *Au cimetière* are touchingly done, although his wide vibrato is sometimes intrusive. But this performance certainly does not lack variety of characterization, and Boulez provides sympathetic support. The coupling is unexpected, but Barenboim's Paris version of the *Te Deum* brings a strong and characterful performance, occasionally exaggerated but with fine choral singing and a stylish tenor soloist. The organist, Jean Guillou, who makes a notable contribution, also deserves a credit. The recording is full and makes a vivid impact in its CD transfer.

Requiem Mass (Grande messe des morts).

(B) ** EMI Rouge et Noir CZS5 69647-2 (2) [CDZB 69647]. Robert Tear, CBSO Ch., CBSO, Frémaux – FAURE: *Requiem*. **(*)

It is disappointing that, for the Frémaux Birmingham set, the EMI engineers fell into the same trap as their Philips colleagues in the Davis set, only rather more heavily. The choir and orchestra are recorded relatively close, to make the result seem too small-scale for such a work. Detail is clarified and there is bloom on the sound, but the absence of any true pianissimos is just as serious as the failure to expand in the big climaxes, making a potentially fine performance far less effective than it might have been. The chorus, too, is surprisingly variable.

(i) *Requiem Mass (Grande Messe des Morts), Op. 5*. (ii) *Symphonie fantastique*.

(B) *** EMI forte Dig./Analogue CZS5 69512-2 (2) [CDFB 69512]. (i) Robert Tear, LPO Ch., LPO; (ii) LSO; Previn.

Previn's 1980 Walthamstow recording of Berlioz's great choral work is still the most impressive so far put on disc. Spectacular digital sound allows the registration of the extremes of dynamic in this extraordinary work for massed forces. The gradations of pianissimo against total pianissimo are breathtakingly caught, making the great outbursts of the *Dies irae* and the *Tuba mirum* the more telling. The acoustic is admirably chosen and there is a fine bloom on the voices, while the separation of sound gives a feeling of reality to the massed brass and multiple timpani. No doubt one day we shall have (from Gardiner perhaps) the full expansive glory experienced in a great cathedral, but meanwhile this inexpensive forte reissue will more than suffice. Previn's view is direct and incisive (like that of Sir Colin Davis on his long-established Philips version), not underlining expressiveness but concentrating on rhythmic qualities. So the *Rex tremendae* is given superb buoyancy, and even if Previn misses some of the animal excitement captured by other conductors, such as Bernstein, the contrasts of the closing *Agnus Dei* are movingly brought off. Robert Tear is a sensitive soloist, though the voice is balanced rather close.

Fortunately the coupled performance of the *Symphonie fantastique* does not disappoint (as it did when RCA issued the marvellous old Munch *Requiem* on CD, similarly paired), for Previn's reading is not only compelling but highly individual. He manages the dash off into the first-movement allegro very spontaneously, yet he presents the work above all as a symphonic structure. The pastoral serenity of the slow movement is beautifully sustained. Some may find him not volatile enough in the last two movements, which are without the rhythmic impetus of some versions. Nevertheless the *Marche au supplice* makes a very powerful impact and the finale certainly does not lack satanic force with the brass so telling. On its own direct terms this is a highly involving reading which almost completely avoids vulgarity; moreover it is a performance which gains from repeated hearing. The 1976 recording (made partly at Abbey Road and partly in Kingsway Hall) again represents EMI's finest standards of balance and truthfulness: the violins sound particularly rich.

(i) *Requiem Mass (Grande Messe des morts)*. (ii) *Symphonie funèbre et triomphale*. (iii) Choral music: *Tantum ergo; Le temple universel; Veni creator*.

(B) ** Decca Double Analogue/Dig. 452 262-2 [id.]. (i) Kenneth Riegel, Cleveland Ch. & O, Maazel; (ii) Montreal Ch. & SO, Dutoit; (iii) Soloists, Heinrich Schütz Ch. & Chorale, Norrington.

Especially by the side of Dutoit's exhilarating 1985 digital account of the *Symphonie funèbre*, Maazel's version of the *Requiem*, with the choir set at a distance, is relatively uninvolving. The recording offers clean, truthful 1978 Decca analogue sound. The *Tuba mirum*, with its spectacular brass, is certainly physically impressive, and here the chorus is boldly focused. But overall Maazel's reading is comparatively unimaginative and no match for Previn's version. The *Symphonie funèbre* is also available at full price, coupled with Dutoit's *Roméo et Juliette*, a far better investment (417 302-2 – see our main volume). The rare choral items, however, add much to the interest of the present set, showing Berlioz in an unfamiliar and rewarding light, particularly when two out of the three works have a piquant harmonium accompaniment. The *Tantum ergo* and *Veni creator* are late works and both contrast the choir with solo voices, the latter almost like the slow movement of a vocal concerto grosso, while *Le temple universel* is for double choir. It was inspired by the visit of a huge French choir to London's Crystal Palace in 1860. At the close, 4,000 French singers sang *God save the Queen*, and the audience rose to its feet and responded with the *Marseillaise*. Berlioz intended that the two choirs should sing the same words in English and French, but here Norrington manages with rather smaller forces and has both groups singing in French. The effect is undoubtedly stirring, for there is much of the spirit of the French national anthem, and the (originally Argo) recording from the late 1960s is first rate.

Roméo et Juliette, Op. 17.

(B) *** Millennium MCD 80354 (2). Resnik, Turp, Ward, London Symphony Ch., LSO, Monteux.

(M) (***) RCA mono GD 60681 (2) [09026 60681-2]. Roggero, Chabay, Yi-Kwei-Sze, Harvard Glee Club, Radcliffe Ch. Soc., Boston SO, Munch – *Nuits d'été*. **(*)

(M) (**) RCA mono GD 60274 (2) [60274-2-RG]. Gladys Swarthout, John Garris, Nicola Moscona, NBC Ch. & SO, Toscanini (with BIZET: *L'Arlésienne & Carmen suites* **).

In June 1962, at the age of 87, Pierre Monteux conducted this glowing performance of Berlioz's great dramatic symphony, and the pity is that this recording, made in the helpful acoustic of Walthamstow Assembly Rooms, has been available only intermittently since. This CD transfer brings out its full range of beauty as never before, vivid and immediate in sound, with only a slight limitation of range. What is so striking is that Monteux's pacing seems so inevitable so that, though the party music is very fast, it conveys exuberance in its light springing. The home-going of those at the party is here still joyful and eager, not sleepy as it so often is, and rarely has the love music seemed so sensuous in its hushed intensity, luscious yet refined. The *Queen Mab Scherzo* is light and witty rather than just brilliant; and the finale, with David Ward strong and firm as Friar Lawrence and with alert choral singing, makes a warmly satisfying conclusion. The other soloists too are excellent, the velvet-toned Regina Resnik and the headily clear André Turp agile in his scherzando solo. At bargain price not to be missed, though the text is not given.

Charles Munch's version dates from 1953. The RCA remastering has done wonders for the sound and in the three orchestral movements the playing of the Boston orchestra is superb, but it also occasionally sounds in its sheer brilliance (in the *Queen Mab Scherzo*, for example) as if Munch was carried away by the sheer feats of virtuosity this great orchestra could perform. This was the first recording of the whole work and the soloists, Margaret Roggero, Leslie Chabay and Yi-Kwei-Sze, are impressive. While it would be an exaggeration to call the recording boxy, the mono sound does not convey much sense of space; this nevertheless remains a valuable historical document and a welcome supplement. Moreover, it comes with a lovely account of *Nuits d'été* from Victoria de los Angeles at her prime.

Toscanini's concert performance of February 1947 brings many electrifying moments, with the melodic lines often drawn out lovingly in a Verdian way and with the virtuoso passages delivered with panache. But the sound, recorded in the notorious Studio 8H, is dry and fizzy, far less full than the RCA recording for Charles Munch in Boston, made only two years later. The Bizet coupling offers brilliant playing, but Munch is a more idiomatic Berliozian and offers a more interesting coupling in *Les nuits d'été* with Victoria de los Angeles.

Roméo et Juliette (excerpts); *Les Troyens à Carthage: Prelude and Royal hunt and storm.*
(BB) **(*) Naxos Dig. 8.553195 [id.]. San Diego Ch. and SO, Yoav Talmi.

Talmi and the San Diego orchestra offer a far more substantial selection from Berlioz's great dramatic symphony than you have on most discs of excerpts, lasting well over an hour and including important sections with chorus, such as the atmospheric passages for the party-goers at the Capulets' Ball. Talmi secures brilliant playing from his orchestra, with admirably crisp ensemble in such show-pieces as the *Queen Mab scherzo*, and with satisfying warmth in the great Love scene. It is good too on this very well-filled disc to have the *Prelude* to *Les Troyens* and the *Royal hunt and storm* (complete with offstage chorus) as makeweights. The recording is clean and detailed, but lacks full weight.

OPERA

Complete operas

(i) *Béatrice et Bénédict;* (ii) *Benvenuto Cellini;* (iii) *Les Troyens, Parts 1 & 2.*
(B) *** Ph. 456 387-2 (9) [(M) id. import]. (i) J. Baker, Tear, Watts, Van Allan, Alldis Ch., LSO; (i–ii) Eda-Pierre, Bastin, Lloyd; (ii) Gedda, Massard, Blackwell, Herincx, Cuénod, Berbié, BBC SO; (ii–iii) Soyer, ROHCG Ch.; (iii) Veasey, Vickers, Lindholm, Glossop, Begg, Partridge, Wandsworth School Boys' Ch., ROHCG O; Sir Colin Davis.

Sir Colin Davis's recordings of the three Berlioz operas (with *Benvenuto Cellini* made first in 1969, *Béatrice et Bénédict* following in 1972 and the series crowned with *Les Troyens* in 1977) makes another superb bargain package, with consistently fine CD transfers. The one blot on the set is the omission of libretto translations, although the synopses are adequately cued. If Dame Janet Baker and Robert Tear understandably stand out in *Béatrice et Bénédict*, the rest of the cast is also first rate. Similarly, it is Nicolai Gedda in superb form who dominates *Benvenuto Cellini*, but his colleagues do not let him down. Even more than the other two operas, *Les Troyens* was an ambitious team-project, with singers, chorus and orchestra all inspired by Davis and with Josephine Veasey a superb Dido. The Philips engineers rise to the occasion in capturing the opera's spectacle with brilliance, atmosphere and refined detail.

Béatrice et Bénédict (complete).
(M) ** DG 449 577-2 (2). Minton, Domingo, Cotrubas, Fischer-Dieskau, Ch. & O de Paris, Barenboim.

(i) *Béatrice et Bénédict* (complete); (ii) *Chant de la Fête de Pâcques; Irlande (9 Mélodies), Op. 2; La Mort d'Ophélie, Op. 18/2; Le Trébuchet, Op. 13.*
(B) *** Decca Double 448 113-2 (2) [id.]. (i) Veasey, Mitchinson, Cantelo, Cameron, Watts, Shirley-Quirk, Shilling, St Anthony Singers, LSO, Sir Colin Davis; (ii) Cantelo, Watts, Tear, Salter, Monteverdi Ch., Gardiner; Tunnard (piano).

It is good to have back the early (1962) Oiseau-Lyre set sounding so fresh and vivid. Above all it is a triumph for Sir Colin Davis, who readily responds to Berlioz's quirkiness, bringing out the delicacy as well as both the humour and power. The singing is equally fresh and vigorous with April Cantelo in really top form, coping splendidly with Héro's fearsome opening aria, even if she does not always avoid some ungainliness on exposed entries. Josephine Veasey as Béatrice presents an appropriately formidable figure, singing with masterly precision and confidence. John Mitchinson as Bénédict does not attempt a conventional tenor-hero approach and his distinctive voice matches an offbeat part. The other soloists and the chorus are excellent and the recording is beautifully balanced and vividly clear in detail. The result scintillates. To make the Double Decca reissue even more tempting, Decca have added the contents of a third LP of little-known vocal Berlioz. The nine songs grouped together under the title *Irlande* were inspired by the words of Thomas Moore (set here in translation) and reflect early romantic ardour for the newly discovered ballad tradition. *Le Trébuchet* is a charming Scherzo, and it is valuable to have *La Mort d'Ophélie* in the alternative solo version. The performances are all of a high standard.

Although it opens well with an exciting account of the overture, Barenboim's 1982 version of *Béatrice et Bénédict* is seriously marred by the spoken dialogue (in French) which links the numbers of this offbeat adaptation of Shakespeare. It is done by Geneviève Page in the over-intimate manner of a French film. With the transfer to CD the cueing means that the listener can programme it out at will, but even then the musical performance lacks the last degree of freshness and style, though it is good to hear Bénédict's part sung with such ringing tone by Plácido Domingo. Yvonne Minton is less warm and less characterful than Dame Janet Baker for Davis, and Dietrich Fischer-Dieskau is miscast as Somarone (the comic role added by Berlioz to replace Dogberry and Verges). The beauty of the score is caught, rather than its point and wit. Apart from the discrepancy between the narration and the rest, the recorded quality is first rate, as is the CD transfer.

Les Troyens: Grand scenes.
(M) *** Decca Dig. 458 208-2 [id.] (from complete recording, with Lakes, Pollet, Voigt, Montreal Ch. & SO; cond. Dutoit).

To assemble a single-CD selection from an opera as expansive as *Les Troyens* is an almost impossible task. Act II has been omitted altogether, but otherwise the scenes here have been judiciously chosen and include the spectacular *Trojan march* at the end of Act I, so powerfully dominated by the foreboding of Deborah Voigt's Cassandra. The *Royal hunt and storm* sequence from Act IV is followed by the great love-scene in which Aeneas (Gary Lakes) is heard at his finest. Françoise Pollet, the soprano Dido, sings consistently, with full, even tone, but in her final monologue, '*Je vais mourir*', she does not convey the heart-aching desolation that the finest mezzos achieve. However, the lyrical section that follows, '*Adieu, fière cité*', brings a tender contrast, with the reference back to the love-duet most poignant. Then, in the final solo, Pollet portrays the distraught Dido, all purpose gone in the disjointed recitative, a closing sequence of great dramatic power that alone makes this Opera Gala CD worth considering. It is nicely packaged and a full translation is included.

Berners, Lord (1883–1950)

The Triumph of Neptune (ballet suite): excerpts.
(B) (***) Sony mono SBK 62748 [id.]. Phd. O, Beecham – ARNELL: *Punch and the child* (ballet); DELIUS: *Paris*. (***)

The Triumph of Neptune was a rare example of music by an English composer being commissioned and performed by Diaghilev's Ballets Russes. The composer has often been called the English Satie, and Satie's love of circus music was echoed by Berners's taste for the music hall.

Sir Thomas recorded the nine excerpts with the Philadelphia Orchestra in 1952. Two items (the charming *Cloudland* and the delicately haunting evocation of *The frozen forest*) were not included on his earlier (1937) recording of the suite for EMI (currently unavailable). On Sony, Robert Grooter is the intoxicated sailor who makes a brave shot at singing 'The last rose of summer'. The Philadelphia Orchestra respond to this music in a brilliant if rather bemused fashion – what must they have thought of the vocal contributions they were required to add to the *Schottische*! However, they obviously enjoy the music, and Sir Thomas ensures that there is no lack of suave polish and wit. The recording is remarkably good, and this disc is also a 'must' for the sake of the couplings.

Bernstein, Leonard (1918–90)

Bernstein Edition

Bernstein Edition (complete; as listed below).
(B) *** DG 447 950-2 (12). Various artists and orchestras, cond. composer.

DG's complete Bernstein Edition is offered at bargain price, and it would be difficult to think of a dozen CDs of twentieth-century music more varied, more approachable or more stimulating. However, according to Schwann, DG's comprehensive coverage of Bernstein's music is not generally available in the USA.

(i) *Candide overture;* (ii) *On the Waterfront* (symphonic suite); (iii) *Prelude, fugue and riffs;* (i) *West Side Story:* symphonic dances.
(M) *** DG Dig. 447 952-2. (i) LAPO; (ii) Israel PO; (iii) Peter Schmidl, VPO; composer.

In his later, DG account of the *Overture* to *Candide* the composer still directs with tremendous flair, his speed a fraction slower than in his New York studio recording for CBS. The score for *On the Waterfront* is film music pure and simple and, expertly though it may underline the film's action, it does not bear too much repetition on its own. Bernstein's Israeli recording sounds fuller than his earlier version on Sony, and the same comment applies to the *West Side Story symphonic dances*. Bernstein, recorded live, is here at his most persuasive, conducting a highly idiomatic account of the orchestral confection devised from his most successful musical. It may not be quite as crisp of ensemble as his earlier, New York version, but it has even more spirit, with the players contributing the necessary shouts in the Mambo representing a street fight. The *Prelude, fugue and riffs* was also recorded live and its vibrant, rhythmic feeling does not sound in the least Viennese, although Peter Schmidl is a comparatively reticent soloist.

(i) *Concerto for orchestra (Jubilee Games);* (ii) *Dybbuk* (ballet): *suites Nos. 1–2*.
(M) *** DG Dig. 447 956-2. (i) Chama, Israel PO; (ii) Sperry, Fifer, NYPO; composer.

The *Concerto for orchestra* shows Bernstein in audacious yet searching mood. Originally planned as a two-movement work to celebrate the Jubilee of the Israel Philharmonic, it opens with the aleatory raucousness of *Free-style events*, featuring vociferous orchestral shouts; then comes the sparely scored and haunting *Mixed doubles*, a theme with seven variations given to pairs of orchestral soloists, which was added in 1989. The third-movement *Diaspora dances* is the high-spirited rhythmic composer we know from the musicals, while the final touching *Benediction* (which was added for the re-opening of a refurbished Carnegie Hall in 1986) is eloquently sung here by José Eduardo Chama. The live recording brings music-making of striking intensity, even if the Israeli playing is shown not always to be technically immaculate, especially in the demanding second movement.

The two suites taken from *Dybbuk* are no shorter than the original ballet (one of Bernstein's toughest works on a sinister subject – see below), dividing the score broadly between passages involving vocal elements and those purely instrumental. The first suite is the longer and more dramatic, the second the more contemplative. Even the jazzy dance-sequences so typical of Bernstein (often in seven-in-a-bar rhythms) acquire a bitter quality. Bernstein directs strong, colourful performances, cleanly and atmospherically recorded, with excellent vocal contributions from Paul Sperry and Bruce Fifer. The transfer to CD of the 1975 analogue studio recording is first class.

Facsimile (choreographic essay); (i) *Fancy free* (ballet); *On the Town* (3 dance episodes).
(M) *** DG Dig./Analogue 447 951-2. (i) Ruth Mense; Bernstein (vocals); Israel PO, composer.

Facsimile, written in 1946 for Jerome Robbins, tells of two boys and a girl and their balletic flirtations; its beach scenario recalls Poulenc's *Les biches*. It is an attractively inventive and resourceful, even charming score, but with no want of atmosphere and imagination, and this live performance from 1981 shows the Israel Philharmonic at their finest. The companion ballet, *Fancy free*, one of Bernstein's early successes from 1944, is another attractive example of his freely eclectic style, here raiding Stravinsky, Copland or Gershwin and putting the result effectively together, thanks to his exuberant sense of colour and rhythm. The Israel Philharmonic does not match the New York Philharmonic Orchestra (see below) in virtuosity or in command of jazz rhythms, but it still plays with tremendous spirit and also enjoys the merit (both here and in *Facsimile*) of outstanding recorded quality. What makes this version of *Fancy free* special is Bernstein's own performance of the blues number, *Big stuff*, as the ballet's epilogue; he also provides just a snippet of this number to set the scene at the opening. The colourful and vigorous dances from *On the Town* are given vivid if close-up digital sound, obviously more modern than in the CBS/Sony versions.

Divertimento for orchestra; (i) *Halil* (Nocturne for solo flute, strings and percussion); (ii) *3 Meditations* (from *Mass*) for cello and orchestra; *A Musical toast*.
(M) *** DG Dig./Analogue 447 955-2. Israel PO, Bernstein; with (i) Rampal; (ii) Rostropovich.

The *Divertimento* (written for the Boston Symphony Orchestra), easily and cheekily moving from one idiom to another, is often jokey (it even quotes the brief oboe cadenza from Beethoven's *Fifth Symphony* as a coda for the third-movement *Mazurka*) but agreeably so. *Halil*, for flute and strings, and the *Meditation* also beautifully reflect the individual poetry of the two artists for whom they were written and who perform in masterful fashion here. The other two party-pieces were recorded live in fizzing performances, *A Musical toast* for André Kostelanetz, and *Slava* (a 'political overture, fast and flamboyant') to celebrate Rostropovich in Washington. Excellent recording throughout.

Symphonies Nos. (i) *1 (Jeremiah);* (ii) *2 (The Age of anxiety)* for piano and orchestra.
(M) *** DG 447 953-2 (2). Israel PO, composer; with (i) Christa Ludwig; (ii) Lukas Foss.

(i) *Symphony No. 3 (Kaddish);* (ii) *Chichester Psalms.*
(M) *** DG 447 954-2. (i) Caballé, Wager, V. Boys' Ch.; (ii) Soloist from V. Boys' Ch.; (i–ii) Wiener Jeunnesse Ch., Israel PO, composer.

Bernstein's three symphonies have been undervalued because of his theatre music and his willingness to draw on popular influences, but their surface facility is deceptive. The *Jeremiah Symphony* dates from the composer's early twenties and ends with a moving passage from Lamentations for the mezzo soloist – here with Christa Ludwig responding sensitively. As the title suggests, the *Second Symphony* was inspired by the poem of W. H. Auden, and the work includes a concertante piano part, admirably played by Lukas Foss. The *Third Symphony*, written in memory of John F. Kennedy, is recorded here in its revised version (with a male speaker), which concentrates the original concept of a dialogue between man and God, a challenge from earth to heaven. The performances here are not always quite as polished or as forceful as those Bernstein recorded earlier for CBS in New York, but they never fail to reflect the warmth of Bernstein's writing, and the playing of the Israel Philharmonic is extremely vivid throughout. The *Chichester Psalms* were recorded live in 1977. One might have slight reservations over the treble soloist from the Vienna Boys' Choir, but otherwise the performance is first class, with the music's warmth and vigour compellingly projected. So are the CD transfers throughout both discs of (1977/8) recordings.

(i) *Serenade after Plato's Symposium* (for solo violin, string orchestra, harp and percussion); (ii) *Songfest* (cycle of American poems).
(M) *** DG 447 957-2. (i) Gidon Kremer, Israel PO; (ii) Dale, Elias, Nancy Williams, Rosenheim, Reardon, Gramm Nat. SO of Washington; composer.

The *Serenade* must rank among Bernstein's most resourceful and inspired creations, full of ideas, often thrilling and exciting, and equally often moving. Gidon Kremer has all the nervous intensity and vibrant energy to do justice to this powerful and inventive score. *Songfest*, too, is one of the composer's most richly varied works – a sequence of poems which ingeniously uses all six singers solo and in various combinations. Characteristically, Bernstein often chooses controversial words to set, and by his personal fervour welds a very disparate group of pieces together into a warmly satisfying whole. Both recordings (from the late 1970s) are of excellent quality, atmospheric and clear.

(i) *Candide* (final, revised version); (ii) *West Side story:* complete recording.
✿ (M) *** DG Dig. 447 958-2 (3). (i) Hadley, Anderson, Green, Ludwig, Gedda, Della Jones, Ollmann, London Symphony Ch., LSO; (ii) Te Kanawa, Carreras, Troyanos, Horne, Ollmann, Ch. and O; composer.

The composer's complete recordings of *Candide* and *West Side story* have been coupled together on three mid-priced discs for the Bernstein Edition to make an irresistible bargain for those who have not already acquired one or the other of these inspired scores. The humour of *Candide*, satirically reflecting Voltaire's rubbishing of enforced establishment values, at one point draws a ready parallel between the Spanish Inquisition and Bernstein's own experience during America's darkest political era. The result is a triumph, both in the studio recording (which Bernstein made immediately after the concert performances) and in the video recording of the actual concert at the Barbican. It confirms *Candide* as a classic, bringing out not just the vigour, the wit and the tunefulness of the piece more than ever before, but also an extra emotional intensity, something beyond the cynical Voltaire original. There is no weak link in the cast. Jerry Hadley is touchingly characterful as Candide, producing heady tone, and June Anderson as Cunegonde is not only brilliant in coloratura but also warmly dramatic. The character roles are also brilliantly cast. It was an inspired choice to have Christa Ludwig as the Old Woman, and equally original to choose Adolph Green, lyric writer for Broadway musicals as well as cabaret performer, for the dual role of Dr Pangloss and Martin. Nicolai Gedda also proves a winner in his series of cameo roles, and the full, incisive singing of the London Symphony Chorus adds to the weight of the performance without inflation.

What is missing in the CD set is the witty narration, prepared by John Wells and spoken by Adolph Green and Kurt Ollmann in the Barbican performance. As included on the video of the live concert (Laser disc DG 072 423-1; VHS DG 072 423-3), those links leaven the entertainment delightfully. Even those with the CDs should investigate the video version, which also includes Bernstein's own moving speeches of introduction before each Act.

Bernstein's recording of the complete score of *West Side Story* takes a frankly operatic approach in its casting, but the result is highly successful, for the great vocal melodies are worthy of voices of the highest calibre. Tatiana Troyanos, herself brought up on the West Side, spans the stylistic dichotomy to perfection in a superb portrayal of Anita. The clever production makes the best of both musical worlds, with Bernstein's son and daughter speaking the dialogue most affectingly. Bernstein conducts a superb instrumental group of musicians 'from on and off Broadway', and they are recorded with a bite and immediacy that is captivating. The power of the music is greatly enhanced by the spectacularly wide dynamic range of the recording, with a relatively dry acoustic keeping the sound-picture within an apt scale but without losing bloom.

A Quiet place (complete).
(M) *** DG Dig. 447 962-2 (2). Wendy White, Chester Ludgin, Beverly Morgan, John Brandstetter, Peter Kazaras, Vocal Ens., Austrian RSO, composer.

In flashbacks in Act II of *A Quiet place*, Bernstein incorporates his 1951 score, *Trouble in Tahiti*, with its popular style set in relief against the more serious idiom adopted for the main body of the opera. Bernstein's score is full of thoughtful and warmly expressive music, but nothing quite matches the sharp, tongue-in-cheek jazz-influenced invention of *Trouble in Tahiti*. The recording was made in Vienna, with an excellent cast of American singers and with the Austrian Radio orchestra responding splendidly on its first visit to the Vienna State Opera.

Other recordings

Candide: overture; Facsimile (choreographic essay); *Fancy free* (ballet); *On the town (3 Dance episodes)*.
(B) *** [EMI Red Line Dig. CDR5 72091]. St Louis SO, Slatkin.

Though Slatkin cannot quite match Bernstein himself in the flair he brings to his jazzier inspirations, this is a very attractive bargain collection. Next to Bernstein, Slatkin sounds a little metrical at times, but it is a marginal shortcoming, and he directs a beautiful, refined reading of the extended choreographic essay, *Facsimile*. As a gimmick, the song '*Big stuff*', before *Fancy free*, is recorded in simulation of a juke-box, complete with 78-r.p.m. surface-hiss and a blues singer with a very heavy vibrato. The sound otherwise is full rather than brilliant, set in a helpful, believable acoustic.

Candide: Overture; Fancy free (ballet); On the Waterfront: symphonic suite. West Side story: Symphonic dances.
(M) *** Sony SMK 63085 [id.]. NYPO, Bernstein.

For many this new compilation, issued under the 'Bernstein Century' logo, will be the ideal way of acquiring this orchestral theatre and film music. The fizzing account of the *Candide overture* has never been surpassed and the sparkling *Fancy free* ballet-score is hardly less rhythmically seductive. The *Symphonic dances* from *West Side Story* confirm Bernstein as a truly great tunesmith; apart from the music's life-enhancing vitality, the closing section is infinitely touching. The recordings, made between 1960 and 1963, have never sounded better: bright and free, with plenty of ambient space.

Candide: overture; West Side Story: symphonic dances.
(M) *** Sony SMK 47529 [id.]. NYPO, composer (with GERSHWIN: *American in Paris; Rhapsody in blue* ***).

Bernstein's exhilarating early New York performances of his theatre music are now reissued separately as part of the Sony 'Royal Edition'.

(i) *Candide: overture;* (ii) *On the Town: 3 Dance episodes;* (i) *West Side Story: Symphonic dances;* (iii) *America*.
(M) *** DG Dig. 427 806-2. (i) LAPO; (ii) Israel PO; (iii) Troyanos with O; composer – BARBER: *Adagio* ***; GERSHWIN: *Rhapsody in blue*. **(*)

This alternative collection offers the same performances as those included in the Bernstein Edition, and has the added attraction of including a characteristically intense account of Barber's *Adagio*. The other coupling of *Rhapsody in Blue* is, however, less successful than Bernstein's earlier, CBS/Sony account.

Dybbuk (ballet): complete.
(M) *** Sony SMK 63090 [id.]. David Johnson, John Ostendorf, NY City Ballet O, composer.

For this 'Bernstein Century' reissue, the 1974 recording of the complete ballet, *Dybbuk*, has been sensibly separated from the *Mass* with which it was previously paired. Bernstein wrote his ghoulish ballet on lost spirits for Jerome Robbins and the New York City Ballet in 1974, when this splendidly atmospheric recording was made. The score presents much the same happy and colourful amalgam of influences as you find in other Bernstein ballets, a touch of the *Rite of spring* here and a whiff of *West Side Story* there – although, at 48 minutes, it is less concentrated than the shorter works. The vocal parts, although fairly substantial (and very well done), are merely incidental. The recording is brightly lit but spacious.

3 Meditations for cello and orchestra (from *Mass*).

(B) *** DG Double 437 952-2 (2) [id.]. Rostropovich, Israel PO, composer – BOCCHERINI: *Cello concerto No. 2;* GLAZUNOV: *Chant du Ménestrel;* SHOSTAKOVICH: *Cello concerto No. 2;* TARTINI: *Cello concerto;* TCHAIKOVSKY: *Andante cantabile* etc.; VIVALDI: *Cello concertos.* ***

Bernstein's concertante piece, *Meditations for cello and orchestra*, is fully worthy of the subtlety of Rostropovich's art, and he plays it masterfully. This is part of a remarkably generous Double DG bargain anthology.

(i) *On the Town: suite;* (ii) *7 Anniversaries.*

(M) (***) RCA mono GD 60915 [60915-2]. (i) On the Town O, Bernstein; (ii) Bernstein (piano) – COPLAND: *Billy the Kid* etc. (***)

There is always something special about first recordings. There is great vitality and swagger here, and no apologies need be made for the mono recording which, though slightly shrill, has great vividness. The stage music is followed by *Seven anniversaries*, a set of vignettes composed in 1943, dedicated to family and musical friends, opening with Aaron Copland and closing with William Schuman.

Serenade after Plato's Symposium (for solo violin, string orchestra, harp & percussion).

(M) *(**) Sony Stern Edition II SMK 64508 [id.]. Stern, Symphony of the Air, composer – DUTILLEUX: *Violin concerto.* ***

The *Serenade* is based on Plato's account of an Ancient Greek banquet in which those present take turns to soliloquize on the nature of love. Stern's temperament makes him an ideal soloist and he plays very beautifully and with intense feeling. The snag is the balance of the early 1956 stereo, with the violin right out in front and climaxes unpleasantly coarse. There is no mistaking the adrenalin flow, but the lack of any kind of refinement in the orchestral tuttis is a severe drawback.

Symphonies Nos. (i) *1 (Jeremiah);* (ii) *2 (The Age of anxiety)* for piano and orchestra; (i; iii) *3 (Kaddish): To the beloved memory of President Kennedy* (original version); (vi) *Prelude, fugue and riffs;* (iv) *Serenade after Plato's Symposium* (for solo violin, string orchestra, harp & percussion); (v) *Chichester Psalms.*

(M) **(*) Sony SM3K 47162 (3). (i) Tourel; (ii) Entremont; (iii) F. Montealegre (speaker), Camerata Singers; Columbus Boychoir; (iv) Francescatti; (v) J. Bogart, Camerata Singers; (i–iv) NYPO; (vi) Benny Goodman, Columbia Jazz Combo; all cond. composer.

All three New York recordings were made in the Manhattan Center in the early 1960s; the acoustic is agreeably spacious, the bass resonantly full and the strings have plenty of body, so that no apologies need be made for the sound-quality. The *Chichester Psalms*, also impressively transferred to CD, was written in response to a commission from the Dean of Chichester. It must rank among Bernstein's most resourceful and inspired creations. Francescatti responds naturally to the Hebrew flavour of the lyrical writing of the *Serenade* but he is very closely balanced, as is the orchestra, and Bernstein's passionate climaxes are given an aggressive fierceness.

(i–iii) *Symphony No. 1 (Jeremiah);* (iv) *Anniversaries: In memoriam Nathalie Koussevitzky;* (ii; v) *Songfest.*

(M) (***) RCA stereo/mono 09026 61581-2 [id.]. (i) Nan Merriman; (ii) St Louis SO; (iii) composer; (iv) Leonard Slatkin (piano); (v) Hohenfeld, White, Spence, Planté, Hartman, Cheek, cond. Slatkin.

Songfest, a cycle for six soloists and orchestra celebrating all things American, finds Bernstein's inspiration focused sharply within a limited frame, and the result is one of his finest works. Specially moving, and beautifully sung by John Cheek, is the setting of a long-buried Whitman poem, celebrating male love; but each poem has been perceptively chosen to illustrate the variegated strands of American society. Leonard Slatkin's new recording hardly replaces Bernstein's own on DG, but it offers another fine performance, recorded in a more mellow acoustic and with a warmer ensemble. In place of the *Serenade* on the DG issue comes Bernstein's own historic first recording of the *Jeremiah Symphony*, made for RCA in 1945, with Nan Merriman the clear-toned soloist. The mono sound is limited but conveys the high voltage of the performance. Between the two main works Slatkin plays the brief piano piece commemorating the first wife of Serge Koussevitzky, taken from the *Anniversaries suite*.

(i) *Symphony No. 2 (Age of anxiety); Overture: Candide; Fancy Free* (ballet).

(M) *** Virgin/EMI Dig. CUV5 61119-2. (i) Kahane; Bournemouth SO, Andrew Litton.

Bernstein holds nothing back, but Litton in his less thrusting way is just as compelling and often more subtly expressive, helped by a more poetic, less muscular pianist, Jeffrey Kahane. Anyone fancying Litton's popular coupling need not hesitate.

VOCAL MUSIC

Chichester Psalms.

(M) *** Carlton Dig. 30366 0009-2 [id.]. Aled Jones, London Symphony Ch., RPO, Hickox – FAURÉ: *Requiem.* ***

Bernstein's *Chichester Psalms* make an instant communication and respond to familiarity too, especially in Richard Hickox's fresh and colourful reading, with Aled Jones bringing an ethereal contribution to the setting of the 23rd Psalm. The recorded sound is firm and well focused.

Mass (for the death of President Kennedy).

(M) **(*) Sony SM2K 63089 (2) [S2K 63089]. Alan Titus (celebrant), Scribner Ch., Berkshire Boys' Ch., Rock Band & O, composer.

Outrageously eclectic in its borrowings from pop and the avant garde, Bernstein's *Mass* presents an extraordinary example of the composer's irresistible creative energy. The recording is vividly present but has a convincing ambience.

STAGE WORKS

Candide (musical: original Broadway production): *Overture and excerpts.*

(M) *** Sony SK 48017 [full price id.]. Adrian, Cook, Rounseville and original New York cast, Krachmalnick.

This exhilarating CBS record encapsulates the original 1956 Broadway production and has all the freshness of discovery inherent in a first recording, plus all the zing of the American musical theatre. The lyrics, by Richard Wilbur, give pleasure in themselves. Brilliantly lively sound.

West Side Story: Symphonic dances.

(BB) ** RCA/Navigator 74321 24218-2. RCA Victor O, Bennett – GERSHWIN: *Porgy and Bess*: highlights. **

The music included in Robert Russell Bennett's early (1959) RCA recording is basically the same as that included by Bernstein himself, but with a few minor additions. The playing is extremely brilliant and the dance sequences are rhythmically idiomatic in a uniquely American manner. The sound is very resonant, noisy at times but also attractively atmospheric.

Bertrand, Anthoine de (1540–81)

Amours de Ronsard, Book 1; *Amours de Cassandre:* excerpts.

(B) *** HM Dig. HMA 1431147 [id.]. Clément Janequin Ens.

Anthoine de Bertrand's chansons as recorded here by the Clément Janequin Ensemble show him to be, if not a great master, at least a composer of feeling and considerable resource. The performances are excellent throughout, and admirably recorded. At bargain price this is well worth trying.

Berwald, Franz (1796–1868)

(i) *Piano concerto in D;* (ii) *Violin concerto in C sharp min., Op. 2; Festival of the Bayadères; Overture: The Queen of Golconda; Serious and joyful fancies.*

(M) *** EMI CDM5 65073-2. (i) Marian Migdal; (ii) Arve Tellefsen; RPO, Björlin.

All these performances were recorded in 1976 and appeared in a four-LP set in harness with the four symphonies and the other tone-poems. This CD creams off the very best performances and makes a highly recommendable pendant to the Järvi DG set of the symphonies. The *Violin concerto* (1820) is an early work, written in the shadow of Spohr and Weber, but it has great charm and a keen melodic facility. A beautiful and elegant performance from Arve Tellefsen and the RPO under the late Ulf Björlin. The *Piano concerto* (1855) is a strange piece. The piano plays all the time without a moment's rest – indeed the score notes that the work can be performed without orchestra. There are some beautiful ideas, including the Chopinesque second group, and they are heard to splendid advantage in Marian Migdal's poetic and imaginative reading. The three shorter pieces are also delightful: the two tone-poems are vintage Berwald and come from the same period (1841–2) as the *Sinfonie sérieuse*, and it is possible that the *Queen of Golconda overture* (1862) also incorporates (either in part or in whole) a lost *Humoristisches Capriccio* written in the 1840s. Very acceptable performances of the orchestral pieces, excellent ones of the *Concertos*, and very good transfers make this a highly desirable issue, particularly at its competitive price.

Symphonies Nos. 1 in G min. (Sérieuse); 2 in D (Capricieuse); 3 in C (Singulière); 4 in E flat.
(M) *** DG Dig. 445 581-2 (2). Gothenburg SO, Järvi.

Neeme Järvi's set of the Berwald *Symphonies* appeared in the mid-1980s and is still eminently recommendable; this is music that is wholly in the life-stream of the Gothenburg orchestra. The only reservation one might make concerns the brisk opening movement to the *Sinfonie singulière*, but Järvi's most recent rival (Roy Goodman on Hyperion) is, if anything, faster. Järvi's account of the *E flat Symphony* has marginally greater sparkle and lightness of touch. The DG recording, balanced by Michael Bergek (more familiar on the BIS label), is excellent in every way, and the warmer acoustic of the Gothenburg Concert Hall may sway some readers in favour of this version, particularly in view of the much more modest outlay involved.

Symphonies Nos. 1–4; (i) *Piano concerto in D.*
(BB) ** Naxos Dig. 8.553051/2 [id.]. (i) Niklas Sivelöv; Helsingborg SO, Okko Kamu.

All four Berwald *Symphonies*, with the *Piano concerto* thrown in for good measure – and all at super-bargain price! The recordings are very good and the performances decent. The Helsingborg orchestra is impressive, though their strings are not as fine as those of the Gothenburg orchestra. Okko Kamu's performance of the *Sinfonie singulière* is impressive and is to be preferred to Goodman or Järvi, but the *E flat Symphony* needs a more mercurial touch and greater lightness. The standard is that of a very acceptable broadcast by one of the old regional BBC orchestras. Niklas Sivelöv in the 1855 *Piano concerto in D major* gives a good account of himself, though Marian Migdal on EMI is the more poetic player. Very good recorded sound.

Symphonies Nos. 1 in G min. (Sérieuse); 3 in C (Singulière); Play of the elves (Elfenspiel).
(M) **(*) EMI CDM5 65303-2 [id.]. RPO, Björlin.

Symphonies Nos. 2 (Capricieuse); 4 in E flat; Overture: Estrella de Soria; Racing; Reminiscences from the Norwegian mountains.
(M) **(*) EMI CDM5 65866-2 [id.]. RPO, Björlin.

These CDs continue EMI's reissues from a 1976 boxed set containing all Berwald's orchestral music. The performances here are thoroughly sympathetic and certainly worth considering at mid-price. They sound warm and fresh, though the orchestral playing under the late Ulf Björlin is a little deficient in vitality; the recordings were made during a heat-wave. Both Järvi and Ehrling with the LSO are more vital and alert in the *Singulière*, and the former's account of the *Sérieuse* is comparably rewarding, while Erling's account of No. 4 is also more vital and alert. By their side, Björlin does not succeed in creating the same degree of tension in shaping melodic lines. The tone-poems are wholly neglected, but their invention is often captivating. The *Reminiscences from the Norwegian mountains* is attractively atmospheric, while *Play of the elves* is a delightful piece under whose deceptively Mendelssohnian surface resides an inventive and original mind. The *Overture Estrella de Soria* is full of resourceful and finely drawn ideas. There are no current alternatives at present, so this pair of CDs is by no means to be written off, as the EMI engineers have provided excellent recording, well transferred to CD.

Symphony No. 1 in G min. (Sinfonie sérieuse); Overtures: Drottningen av Golconda; Estrella de Soria; Tone-poems: *Festival of the Bayadères; Play of the Elves; Reminiscences from the Norwegian mountains.*
(M) *** Bluebell ABCD 047. Swedish RSO, Sixten Ehrling.

The *Sinfonie sérieuse* was recorded in 1970 and issued on the Swedish Radio's own label. It is arguably the finest account of the work ever recorded (including Ehrling's later BIS version). It is classically proportioned, beautifully played and unerringly paced. The overtures and tone-poems were recorded in 1966 and appeared on Swedish EMI and then briefly on American Vox/Turnabout. Excellent performances, more vital and imaginative than the RPO versions from the 1970s by the late Ulf Björlin. Very well recorded too.

Symphonies Nos. 3 in C (Sinfonie singulière); 4 in E flat.
(M) (***) DG mono 457 705-2 [id.]. BPO, Igor Markevitch – SCHUBERT: *Symphony No. 4.* (***)

In the mid-1950s Markevitch pioneered this pair of Berwald symphonies internationally on LP and, as so often with recording premières, he gave superlative performances, with the Berlin Philharmonic proving outstandingly responsive. The DG recordings, made in the Berlin Jesus-Christus-Kirche, also come from a vintage period. When these accounts reappeared on the Heliodor label a decade later, they were reviewed by E.G. in our very first (1966) *Penguin Guide to Bargain Records*. This music was then very fresh to our ears and, as DG has again reissued the symphonies in their series of 'Legendary Originals' it seems appropriate to quote from that orginal notice: 'Berwald was born in the year before Schubert and died in 1868, well after the birth of Sibelius. So not only is this coupling appropriate, but in an extraordinary way he spans the whole of that momentous period of musical history. The *C major Sinfonie Singulière* has a lyricism comparable with Schubert's, yet there are Nordic hints that recall no one so much as Sibelius. The slow movement, for example, is punctuated by a capricious scherzo, and even the lyrical section is interrupted by wild fortissimo exclamations. Perhaps the closest link is with Berlioz. The opening of the finale here has a strong affinity, but elsewhere the likeness is more in the general character of the music – curiously modern before its time – than in the detailed idiom itself. The *Fourth E flat Symphony* is perhaps a shade less individual than its companion, but is just as enjoyable. Berwald's ''controlled oddity'', his ability like Berlioz to invent the most unlikely melodies and use them in the most unlikely ways, makes his music endlessly interesting.' It is sufficient to add now that, partly because of the warmly atmospheric mono sound, the remastering has been outstandingly successful, and these fine readings celebrate an underestimated conductor at the peak of his interpretative form. The Schubert coupling is also very fine indeed.

Grand septet in B flat.
(M) *** EMI (SIS) CDM5 65995-2. Gervase de Peyer, Melos Ens. – SPOHR: *Double quartet* **; WEBER: *Clarinet quintet.* **(*)

The *Septet* is an earlier work than any of Berwald's four symphonies. It dates from 1828, though how far it embodies material from an earlier work for the same combination is a matter for conjecture. Like the symphonies, it has a freshness and grace that should earn wide appeal, and the Melos Ensemble give an immaculately polished account of it. It is vividly recorded and well balanced.

(i) *Piano quartet in E flat;* (ii) *Septet in B flat;* (ii–iii) *Serenade.*
(BB) ** Naxos Dig. 8.553714 [id.]. (i) Joakim Kallhed, Schein Qt; (ii) Arion Wind Quintet, Schein Qt; (iii) with Thomas Annmo.

This CD offers some Berwald chamber music from the early part of his career. The *Septet* (1818) is very well played by these fine Swedish musicians, recorded in the excellent acoustic of Flatås church in Gothenburg. Although the performance is not quite as elegant as the mid-price Melos account on EMI, it is eminently serviceable and very well recorded. So, for that matter, is the *E flat quartet for piano and wind* (1819), a less interesting but still worthwhile piece. The rarity is the *Serenade in F* for the unusual combination of tenor, clarinet, horn, viola, cello, double-bass and piano (1825). It is a kind of *opera buffa* scena with a lot of charm. The singer is balanced a little distantly and there is some dubious intonation from one of the instrumentalists about nine minutes in. All the same this is a good disc and worth the money.

Biber, Heinrich (1644–1704)

Balletae à 4 violettae Nos. 1–7; Battalia in D; Peasants' churchgoing sonata in B flat à 6; Sonatas Nos. 1–2 à 8 for 2 clarini, 6 violae; 3–4 à 5 violae; Sonata à 7 for 6 trumpets, tamburin and organ (168).
(M) *** Teldec/Warner 4509 97914-2. VCM, Harnoncourt.

This is as good and varied an introduction to Biber's music as any. His *Battle* evocation is as spectacular as any of the baroque era and Harnoncourt is just the man for it. The battle sequence itself has some hair-raising instrumental effects, including barbaric pizzicati representing the cannon. The picture of '*the dissolute company*' brings a half-minute of well-organized instrumental cacophony to suggest that Biber could even anticipate Charles Ives. In the *March* there is a bizarre fife-and-drum imitation by violin and double bass. The piece closes with a *Lament of the wounded musketeers*. The *Sonatas* for strings and clarini (and notably the *Peasants' churchgoing*) show this Bohemian-born Viennese Court Kapellmeister as a resourceful and inventive musician who knew how to manage lyrical pictorial effects as well as dramatic ones. His musical ideas are certainly attractive. The performances have great character – Nikolaus Harnoncourt was always good at explosive accents – and are very well recorded.

Harmonia artificiosa-ariosa (7 Partitas), Nos. 1–3 & 5 for 2 scordatura violins & continuo; 4 for scordatura violin, viola di braccio & continuo; 6 for 2 violins & continuo; 7 for 2 violas d'amore & continuo (complete).
(M) *** Chandos Dig. 0575/6 [id.]. Purcell Quartet with Elizabeth Wallfisch.

This complete recording of Biber's masterly *Harmonia artificosa-ariosa* shows us the amazing range of these seven partitas (or suites), which were published posthumously in 1712. (The term *scordata*, incidentally, indicated a different system of tuning.) Each work consists of a very free opening *Prelude* or a more structured *Sonata* (slow–fast–slow), usually improvisational in feeling, and includes the usual dance forms of *Allemande* and *Sarabande*, plus an *Aria* with divisions, and often closes with a lighthearted *Gigue*, although the *Third* ends with a remarkable *Canon in uniso*, liberally decorated with violin cascades, which readily relates to the more famous piece by Biber's contemporary, Pachelbel. The *Fifth Sonata in G* ends with a splendid *Passacaglia*. The *Aria* in the *Sixth* has thirteen variations plus finale, and, including all repeats, the Purcell performance extends this remarkable movement to over 13 minutes, with playing of the highest order to hold the listener's attention readily throughout. This set displays the spontaneity and scholarship of the very best period-instrument performances. The Purcell Consort tend to bring a spacious espressivo to slower movements and their extra weight (with use of organ continuo) is especially telling in the passacaglias. You cannot go wrong with this recording, splendidly balanced and truthful. Chandos have been forced to use a pair of discs, playing for 43 minutes and 47 minutes respectively. But the cost has been reduced accordingly, and this set retails at upper-mid-price, probably costing slightly under £20 for the two CDs.

Rosenkranz sonatas Nos. 1–16 (complete); *Passacaglia*.
(M) *** DG Codex 453 173-2 (2). Edward Melkus, Huguette Dreyfus, Lionel Roff, Karl Scheit.
(M) **(*) DHM/BMG Dig. GD 77102 (2). Franzjosef Maier, Franz Lehrndorfer, Max Engel, Konrad Junghänel.

The *Sonatas of the Rosary* are among the finest instrumental pieces of their kind before Bach. The sequence follows the Passional narrative from the Annunciation and Nativity through to the Crucifixion and Ascension, and the Assumption and Coronation of Mary. The more one hears of them the greater they seem: the language is remarkable for its purity of style and achieves the kind of spirituality and nobility of inspiration one encounters in the greatest music of this period. Melkus ends with an impressive *Passacaglia in G minor*, intended for the feast of the Holy Guardian Angels (2nd October). He plays most beautifully, and care is taken to vary the quality and colour of the continuo instruments, with Lionel Rogg's organ contribution aptly filling out the sonority when necessary. The 1967 recording, if forwardly balanced, has impeccable clarity and a pleasing bloom, exhibiting the usual high standards of DG Archiv recordings of the analogue era.

The alternative version from Franzjosef Maier is also of high quality, displaying genuine poetic feeling and sensibility. However, the Deutsche Harmonia Mundi recording, although full and pleasing, could ideally provide better internal definition, and the DG set makes a clear first choice.

Sonata St Polycarp à 9 (for 8 trumpets and bass); In festo trium regium muttetum Natale (Epiphany cantata); Laetatus sum à 7 (cantata); Requiem in F min.
(M) *** Teldec/Warner 3984 21798-2. Soloists, V. Boys' Ch., Ch. Viennensis, VCM, Harnoncourt.

The music of Heinrich Biber is more familiar now than when this recording was made, in 1968; it is one of Harnoncourt's most distinguished pioneering Das Alte Werk collections, much admired in its day. The *Polycarp sonata*, using eight trumpets, makes a thrilling sound, and the two cantatas contain music that is both beautiful and striking. The larger-scale *Requiem* has since been recorded with greater success by Philip Pickett, but that is a premium-priced disc. Alongside it Harnoncourt's version tends to lack consistency of musical purpose. But even this has fine moments, and the authenticity of the performance, here and in the smaller pieces, adds to the record's value. The sound is excellent.

Birtwistle, Harrison (born 1934)

The Mask of Orpheus (complete).
(M) *** NMC Dig. D 050 (3). Garrison, Bronder, Rigby, Owens, Opie, Ebrahim, BBC Singers & O, Andrew Davis.

Birtwistle's *The Mask of Orpheus* is arguably on every level the most challenging opera ever written. The idiom may not be as abrasive as in some of Birtwistle's other works, often with lyrical vocal lines, but the telling and retelling of the Orpheus legend, with one version superimposed on another and with music reflecting that, makes it hard to take in for the listener who is unprepared. Even so, what immediately comes out is the magnetic intensity of Birtwistle's score, magnificently achieved here in this live recording, edited from two concert performances given at the Royal Festival Hall in London in March 1996.

The libretto is by Peter Zinovieff, himself an electronics composer, who collaborated with Birtwistle on the important electronic effects. The words are fluid, so that the printed text gives only an outline of what is presented. Birtwistle, like Zinovieff, is more interested in ritual than in telling a story, assuming that the outlines of the myth are well known to any listener.

Act I is the longest and most enigmatic of the three Acts, with dreamlike superimposition of images and text, broadly based on the death of Eurydice, poisoned by a snake. Act II, following Orpheus in his progress through the Underworld over 17 arches, is far more direct, with the text more clearly defined, with the music building up powerfully in crescendo over the longest span, and with the different arches marked each time by an electronic sigh rather like those in the Bartók opera, *Bluebeard's Castle*. Act III, with its structure echoing the movement of the tide on a beach, rounds off the epic scheme, ending in Orpheus's death at the hands of the Dionysiac women, and the final fading of the myth.

With Andrew Davis controlling his massed forces masterfully, helped by Martyn Brabbins as assistant conductor, the purposefulness of the writing, the intense originality of a score dotted with havens of sheer beauty, is never in doubt. Central to success is the thrilling performance of the American tenor, Jon Garrison, as Orpheus the man, well supported by Peter Bronder as Orpheus the myth. Jean Rigby and Anne-Marie Owens, less prominent in the story, similarly take on the divided and superimposed role of the heroine, Eurydice woman and myth. The recorded sound is superb, vivid in conveying the different musical layers, electronic as well as instrumental and vocal. The documentation is very full – though, even using it, this is not an easy piece. It is good that NMC have issued this important set as 'three discs for the price of two', making it an excellent bargain.

Bizet, Georges (1838–75)

(i) *L'Arlésienne: suites Nos. 1–2; Carmen: suites Nos. 1–2;* (ii) *Jeux d'enfants; The Fair Maid of Perth: suite; Symphony in C;* (iii) (Piano) *Variations chromatiques;* (iv) *Agnus Dei;* (v) *Chanson d'avril;* (vi) *Carmen:* excerpts; (vii) *Les Pêcheurs de perles:* Duet: *Au fond du temple saint.*

(B) ** Ph. Duo 442 272-2 (2) [id.]. (i) LOP, Dorati; (ii) LSO, Roberto Benzi; (iii) Marie Françoise Bucquet; (iv) José Carreras; (v) Gérard Souzay, Dalton Baldwin; (vi) Jane Rhodes, Albert Lance, Paris Op. Ch. & O, Benzi; (vii) Léopold Simoneau, René Biano.

Roberto Benzi has made too few records. He has the gift of bringing music fully alive in the recording studio, and his 1965 LSO version of the Bizet *Symphony* is most attractive, standing comparison with the finest versions. He is supported by first-rate LSO playing, with the oboe distinctive in the slow movement. The personality of the orchestra comes through strongly in the couplings and the performance of the surprisingly rare *Jolie fille de Perth suite* approaches Beecham in finesse. In *Petit mari, petite femme* from *Jeux d'enfants* (another successful performance) the leading string parts are played as cello and violin solos, which is not the composer's idea but which works very well. The sound is admirable. The earlier Lamoureux Orchestra recordings of the *Carmen suites* (1959) and *L'Arlésienne* (1960) are extremely lively under Dorati (especially the latter, where pacing is very alert and brisk) but the sound is a little dated. Apart from the song provided by Souzay and Baldwin, the vocal items are not really an asset, and the three popular excerpts from *Carmen* are undistinguished. The performance of the *Variations*, too, is a routine one. But the set is very nearly worth getting for the Benzi performances alone.

L'Arlésienne: suites Nos. 1–2; Symphony in C.

(B) **(*) [EMI Red Line Dig. CDR5 69881]. ASMF, Marriner.

L'Arlésienne: suites Nos. 1–2: excerpts; *Carmen: suites Nos. 1–2:* excerpts; *Symphony in C.*

(BB) *** RCA Navigator 74321 17901-2 [(M) id. import]. Bamberg SO, Georges Prêtre.

From Prêtre a most enjoyable and generous super-bargain disc, originating from the Eurodisc catalogue, very warmly and naturally recorded, most elegantly played and offering 77 minutes of music. The most important numbers are included in the two orchestral suites and, if the playing in *L'Arlésienne* is a little low-key, the *Carmen* vignettes alternate vividness with pleasing instrumental delicacy. The performance of the *Symphony*, complete with exposition repeat, is alert, yet has much refinement as well as warmth, the oboe solo in the slow movement played most engagingly. There is plenty of vigour in the outer movements and, although the ambience is resonant, it does not cloud detail.

Marriner's EMI account of Bizet's *Symphony*, which is generous with repeats in the outer movements, does not quite re-create the sparkling lightness of touch of his earlier Argo (Decca) version. In the first movement there is plenty of energy, but not the same sense of complete spontaneity. But it is still very enjoyable, and the two *L'Arlésienne suites* are beautifully played, the *Adagietto* given a gossamer delicacy. The Abbey Road recording is first class.

L'Arlésienne: suites Nos. 1–2; Symphony in C; (i) *Carmen:* highlights.

(B) **(*) Erato/Warner Ultima 0630 18947-2 (2) [(M) id. import]. Strasbourg PO, Alain Lombard; (i) with Régine Crespin, Gilbert Ply, Jeannette Pilou, José van Dam, Nadine Denize, Maria Rosa Carminati, Ch. of Opéra du Rhin.

These Strasbourg performances under Alain Lombard date from the mid-1970s. The two *L'Arlésienne suites* are nicely turned, and the *Symphony* too is alive and well, with an elegant oboe solo in the *Adagio* and an infectiously spirited finale. The analogue sound is full and pleasing, rather than especially brilliant, but is enjoyable enough. What makes this Ultima Double especially tempting is the substantial set of highlights from what is obviously a spontaneously vivid, complete recording of *Carmen*, hitherto unfamiliar to us. It brings an all-French (or rather, in the case of José Van Dam, Belgian) cast of principals. Régine Crespin is generally in excellent voice, exuding a beguiling charm with an underlying sexy sultriness, and she is well partnered by Gilbert Ply, a boldly romantic Don José who rises passionately to the occasion in the *Flower song*. Some will feel that van Dam's Escamillo isn't very Spanish-sounding, but his vigorous delivery of the *Toreador song* certainly carries the day. Lombard directs the proceedings with evident relish, helped by the enthusiasm of the Rhine Opera Chorus and warmly atmospheric recording with plenty of depth. Jeannette Pilou's Micaëla is freshly appealing. The Quintet in Act II is neatly done, and the finale combines passion with high drama to make a riveting climax for the opera's closing scene. Though the singing is not always refined, there are few more compelling sets of highlights from *Carmen* than this.

L'Arlésienne: suites Nos. 1–2; Carmen: suite No. 1.
(M) *** DG (IMS) 423 472-2. LSO, Abbado.

L'Arlésienne (incidental music): *suites Nos. 1–2; Carmen* (opera): *suites Nos. 1–2.*
(BB) **(*) Naxos Dig. 8.550061 [id.]. Slovak PO, Anthony Bramhall.
(M) ** [RCA Basic 100 09026 61722-2]. Phd. O, Ormandy.

L'Arlésienne: suites Nos. 1–2; Carmen: suite No. 1; suite No. 2: excerpts.
(BB) **(*) Carlton LSO Double Dig. 30368 01167 (2) [(B) id.]. LSO, Rafael Frühbeck de Burgos – Collection: London Symphony Ch. & O. ***

(i) *L'Arlésienne: suites Nos. 1–2; Carmen: suites Nos. 1–2;* (ii) *Jeux d'enfants.*
(M) **(*) Ph. (IMS) 446 198-2. (i) ASMF, Marriner; (ii) Concg. O, Haitink.

L'Arlésienne: suites Nos. 1–2; Carmen: suite No. 1; suite No. 2: excerpts; *Patrie overture.*
(M) **(*) Mercury 434 321-2. Detroit SO, Paray – THOMAS: *Overtures: Raymond; Mignon.* ***

Among analogue couplings of *L'Arlésienne* and *Carmen suites*, Abbado's 1981 DG recording stands out, available at medium price on CD. The orchestral playing is characteristically refined, the wind solos cultured and eloquent, especially in *L'Arlésienne*, where the pacing of the music is nicely judged.

Anthony Bramhall makes his Naxos début directing excellent performances with the Slovak Philharmonic Orchestra. The solo wind playing has an appealing delicacy of colour, the principal flute plays with finesse, and only the violin substituting for Micaëla's aria is a little below the generally high standard. There is plenty of flair in the *Danse bohémienne* and the closing *Farandole* from *L'Arlésienne*; with vivid digital sound and a nicely atmospheric ambience, this inexpensive disc is most attractive.

Raphael Frühbeck de Burgos offers three more items than Abbado, and in an even cheaper price-range; he also has the advantage of full, modern, digital recording, made in Watford Town Hall. The LSO playing is bright-eyed and polished, but Frühbeck's tempi are not always as naturally apt as those of Abbado, and the effect is rather less spontaneous. Nevertheless this remains good value for those who want an inexpensive digital recording of Bizet's colourful music and who are attracted to the new pairing with an outstanding CD of operatic choruses from Hickox – see under Vocal Recitals: L Symphony Ch., LSO, Hickox.

The Mercury *L'Arlésienne* and *Carmen suites* were recorded as early as 1956 and, apart from some background hiss, it would be impossible to guess, so full is the sound. Paray's performances are neat and polished, certainly Gallic if without quite the panache of Beecham's version, made for EMI a year later. Paray adopts a phlegmatic tempo for the famous dotted tune in *L'Arlésienne*; by the same token, his *Minuetto* in the second suite is very brisk indeed. But this music-making is attractively alive, and in the flamboyant (if slightly empty) *Patrie overture*, recorded two years later in Old Orchestral Hall, the Detroit brass enjoy themselves hugely. What makes this disc especially attractive is the inclusion of the two overtures of Thomas, which are superbly done.

Marriner's Philips collection is generous, offering 11 items from *Carmen* and both *L'Arlésienne suites*, while Haitink's *Jeux d'enfants* is delectably played and superbly recorded in the Concertgebouw. The London recording, too, is attractively rich and naturally balanced. But the musical characterization – despite fine LSO playing, notably from the flautist, Peter Lloyd – is sometimes lacking in flair and the last degree of *brio*. There are minor touches of eccentricity: Marriner's tempo suddenly quickens for the middle section of the *Menuet* from the second *L'Arlésienne suite* and, although there is much to ravish the ear, the orchestrations of the vocal numbers from *Carmen* are sometimes less than convincing.

Predictably, Ormandy's performances have zest, polish and flair, and the recording is spacious; but the forward balance means that the sound is not ideally refined in terms of subtlety of dynamic and delicacy of texture, even though the Philadelphia wind-playing is of high calibre.

Carmen: suites Nos. 1–2; Jeux d'enfants.
(B) **(*) [EMI Red Line Dig. CDR5 69861]. O Nat. de France, Ozawa – LALO: *Symphonie espagnole;* SARASATE: *Zigeunerweisen.* **(*)

Eminently good performances from the Orchestre National de France under Ozawa, and the recording is both vivid and atmospheric. If the couplings are suitable, this is worth considering, even if other accounts of this much-played repertoire have even more character.

Jeux d'enfants (Children's games), Op. 22.
(M) *** Decca (IMS) 448 571-2 [id.]. Paris Conservatoire O, Martinon – BERLIOZ: *Overtures* **(*); IBERT: *Divertissement* ***; SAINT-SAENS: *Danse macabre* etc. ***
(B) *** CfP CD-CFP 4086 [id.]. SNO, Gibson – RAVEL: *Ma Mère l'Oye;* SAINT-SAENS; *Carnival.* ***
(B) ** Tring Dig. TRP 046 [(M) id.]. RPO, Andrea Licata – PROKOFIEV: *Peter;* SAINT-SAENS: *Carnival.* **(*)
(BB) ** Carlton LSO Double Dig. 30368 01187 (2) [(B) id. import]. LSO, Wordsworth – DEBUSSY: *La Mer* etc. ***; RAVEL: *Ma Mère l'Oye* **(*); SAINT-SAENS: *Carnival of the animals.* **

Martinon's memorable account of *Jeux d'enfants* was part of a famous 1960 Decca anthology of French orchestral music, now reissued in the 'Classic Sound' series. The crisp trumpet fanfares in the opening piece set the seal on a performance notable for its vivid colour and delicacy of feeling. The sound is remarkably good.

From Classics for Pleasure a fresh approach, lively orchestral playing and excellent mid-1970s sound; with excellent couplings, this is highly recommendable.

The RPO under the Italian conductor, Andrea Licata, play sympathetically and are well recorded, and this makes a fully acceptable coupling for Gielgud's *Peter and the wolf.*

Barry Wordsworth draws crisp and sympathetic playing from the LSO, although there could be greater individuality. The recording is vivid at higher dynamic levels but seems to recede somewhat at pianissimos, and it is difficult to find a volume setting that suits both the gentle *Berceuse* and the brightly coloured opening *Marche.*

Roma suite; Symphony in C.
(BB) **(*) ASV Dig. CDQS 6135 [(M) id.]. RPO, Enrique Bátiz.

Bátiz's performances are attractive, with very good playing from the RPO. As with the full-price Plasson account of *Roma,* it is the first and last movements which come off the most effectively. Bátiz receives excellent (1990) digital recording, engineered by Brian Culverhouse. In the *Symphony* the sound is noticeably full and weighty, and this adds to the impression that the performance is less lighthearted than usual in the first movement (repeat included), though there is no lack of vitality and, with its rather serious manner, it is still both effective and enjoyable.

Symphony in C.
(B) *** Sony SBK 48264 [id.]. Nat. PO, Stokowski – SMETANA: *Vltava.* ***

Stokowski's exhilaratingly polished account of the Bizet *Symphony* was recorded at Abbey Road in May/June 1977, only three months before he died; it is a superb example of his last vintage recording period, as vital and alive as anything he recorded in his youth. In fact, not only was it Stokowski's last recording, it was the very last time he conducted a full orchestra. David Theodore's oboe solo in the *Adagio* is very elegantly done and the *moto perpetuo* finale is wonderfully light and sparkling. A fine bargain coupling, ranking alongside the top recommendations of Beecham and Marriner. The couplings, too, show Szell at his finest.

Symphony in C; Jeux d'enfants; La jolie fille de Perth: suite.
(BB) ** Naxos Dig. 8.553027 [id.] (without *Jolie fille Sérénade*). New Zealand SO, Donald Johanos.

On Naxos, Johanos secures some sprightly playing from his New Zealand group, with a nice oboe solo in the slow movement. But string textures are a little lean, and it is a distinct drawback that the *Fair maid of Perth suite* is without the famous *Serenade.*

PIANO MUSIC

2 Caprices; Les chants du Rhin (suite); La chasse fantastique; 3 Esquisses musicales; Magasin des familles (suite); Marine; Nocturnes Nos. 1 in F; 2 in D; 4 Préludes; Romance sans paroles; Thème; Variations chromatiques; Waltz in C; Grande valse de concert.
(B) *(*) HM Dig. HMA 1905223/4 [id.]. Par Setrak.

Bizet was a formidable pianist, but his output for the instrument is not extensive. Much of it is eclectic and derivative: the early pieces (and this two-disc set includes three recently discovered juvenilia) inherit the pyrotechnics of Liszt and Thalberg, while the *Nocturne in F major* and the *Romance sans paroles* (the second comes as the opening movement of the *Magasin des familles*) obviously use both Chopin and Liszt as models. By far the most interesting pieces are the *Variations chromatiques*, which Glenn Gould has recorded, and the *Trois Esquisses musicales*, which show some of the composer's charm and individuality. Par Setrak makes rather heavy going of the opening of the *Variations* and the piece takes some time to get under way. However, he is quite persuasive in the *Esquisses*. Elsewhere the playing, though unidiosyncratic and often sympathetic, lacks the extra degree of subtlety that can make second-rate music seem better than it is. The recording is a bit hard, but otherwise is quite truthful, the acoustic rather dry but not unacceptably so.

OPERA

Carmen (opera; complete).

(B) *** DG 427 440-2 (3) [(M) id.]. Horne, McCracken, Krause, Maliponte, Manhattan Op. Ch., Met. Op. O, Bernstein.

(M) *** RCA 74321 39495-2 (3) [full price 6199-2-RG]. Leontyne Price, Corelli, Merrill, Freni, Linval, V. State Op. Ch., VPO, Karajan.

(B) **(*) DG 427 885-2; *427 885-4* (3/2) [(M) id.]. Berganza, Domingo, Cotrubas, Milnes, Amb. S., LSO, Abbado.

(B) **(*) CfP CD-CFPD 4454 (2) [(M) id. import]. Grace Bumbry, Jon Vickers, Mirella Freni, Les Petites Chanteurs à la Croix de Bois, Paris Op. Ch. & O, Frühbeck de Burgos.

(M) (**) EMI (SIS) mono CMS5 65318-2 (2). Michel, Angelici, Jobin, Dens, Chellet, Notti, Vieuille, Leprin, Thirace, Smati, Arschodt, Théâtre Nat. de l'Opéra-Comique Ch. & O, Cluytens.

(M) *(*) RCA 74321 25279-2 (2). Moffo, Corelli, Donath, Cappuccilli, Augér, Schönberg Boys' Ch., German Op. Ch. & O, Berlin, Maazel.

(B) * Decca Double 443 871-2 (2) [id.]. Regina Resnik, Del Monaco, Sutherland, Krause, Geneva Grand Theatre Ch., SRO, Schippers.

(B) * Naxos Dig. 8.660005/7 [id.]. Alperyn, Lamberti, Titus, Palade, Schaechter, Liebeck, Slovak Philharmonic Ch., Bratislava Children's Ch., Slovak RSO (Bratislava), Alexander Rahbari.

Bernstein's 1973 *Carmen* was recorded at the New York Metropolitan Opera. Some of his slow tempi will be questioned, but what really matters is the authentic tingle of dramatic tension which permeates the whole entertainment. Marilyn Horne – occasionally coarse in expression – gives a most fully satisfying reading of the heroine's role, a great vivid characterization. The rest of the cast similarly works to Bernstein's consistent overall plan. It is very well transferred and comes on three bargain CDs.

With Karajan's RCA version, made in Vienna in 1964, much depends on the listener's reaction to the conductor's tempi and to Leontyne Price's smoky-toned Carmen. Corelli has moments of coarseness, but his is still a heroic performance. Robert Merrill sings with gloriously firm tone, while Mirella Freni is, as ever, enchanting as Micaëla. With spectacular recording, full of atmosphere, and attractively re-packaged at mid-price in RCA's UK Opera Treasury series, this is a very strong contender.

Superbly disciplined, Abbado's performance nails its colours to the mast at the very start with a breathtakingly fast account of the opening prelude. Conductor and orchestra can take a large share of credit for the performance's success for, though the singing is never less than enjoyable, it is on the whole less characterful than on some rival sets. Teresa Berganza is a seductive if somewhat unsmiling Carmen – not without sensuality, and producing consistently beautiful tone, but lacking some of the flair which makes for a three-dimensional portrait. Ileana Cotrubas as Micaëla is not always as sweetly steady as she can be; Milnes makes a heroic matador. The spoken dialogue is excellently produced, and the sound is vivid and immediate. This makes a possible bargain alternative to the Bernstein set with Marilyn Horne and James McCracken, and readers will note that it is now again available on cassette as well as CD.

Frühbeck's version of 1970, made before the Oeser edition appeared, was the first to use the original (1875) version of Bizet's score without the cuts that were made after experience in the theatre, and with spoken dialogue instead of the recitatives which Guiraud composed after Bizet's early death. Well recorded on two bargain-priced discs, it makes a fair recommendation, though Grace Bumbry gives a generalized portrait of the heroine, singing with firm tone but too rarely with musical or dramatic individuality. Vickers makes a strong, heroic Don José; and though, surprisingly, Frühbeck's conducting lacks sparkle, it is very well paced. Paskalis makes a gloriously rich-toned Escamillo and Freni an exquisite Micaëla.

Recorded in 1950 in close, immediate mono sound, the Cluytens set from the Opéra-Comique may seriously lack atmosphere and poetry, but it is worth hearing for its all-French cast, representatives of a well-trained, stylish generation soon to disappear. Solange Michel's mezzo in the title-role is firm and rich if hardly voluptuous in a Carmen-like way. One admires the singing, not least for its flawless diction, but not the characterization. It is much the same with the Escamillo of Michel Dens, and equally Raoul Jobin as Don José who, with Martha Angelici, seems more concerned for beauty of production than for portrayal of character. Cluytens as ever times the score beautifully.

At mid-price on only two discs, Maazel's 1979 RCA version (previously on Eurodisc), using the expanded Oeser edition, makes a doubtful bargain. The casting is starry – with such celebrated singers as Arleen Augér and Jane Berbié in the small roles of Frasquita and Mercedes – but almost totally non-French and not always apt. Anna Moffo, lacking mezzo weight, is hardly an ideal Carmen, and she makes up for that by underlining her characterization too heavily. Franco Corelli too is heavy-handed as Don José, not as effective as he was for Karajan in his earlier recording. Helen Donath makes a charming Micaëla, light and sweet, while Piero Cappuccilli as Escamillo produces a stream of strong, firm tone, even if – like others in the cast – his French is not his strong point. As in his later, Erato version (the one used in Franco Rosi's film), Maazel directs a bright and forceful performance, dramatically tense, exaggerated by the fierceness of the recorded sound in tuttis. Otherwise the recording (not digital) is reasonably atmospheric.

Even at Double Decca price and despite brilliant engineering of a 1963 recording, produced by John Culshaw, the Schippers set is not recommendable. It is very variable. Resnik has a big, fruity tone, but her aim is wild. Del Monaco sings coarsely, and vocally the main joy is having Sutherland as Micaëla, even if it sounds as though Lucia had strayed into the wrong opera. Schippers drives very hard indeed. There is no libretto and the synopsis is not related to the cueing of each separate number.

The Naxos version on three discs at budget price brings refined playing from the Czecho-Slovak Radio Symphony Orchestra but low tensions and little feeling of atmosphere. As Carmen, Graciela Alperyn sings with rich, firm tone and secure control but lacks all dramatic weight, making a colourless figure. Giorgio Lamberti is a coarse Don José and Doina Palade a fluttery Micaëla, though Alan Titus is a good, virile Escamillo.

Carmen: highlights.

(M) *** Decca 458 204-2 (from complete recording, with Tatiana Troyanos, Plácido Domingo, José van Dam, Kiri Te Kanawa, John Alldis Ch., LPO; cond. Solti).

(B) **(*) DG Classikon 439 496-2; *439 496-4* [(M) id. import] (from above set, with Berganza, Domingo; cond. Abbado).

(M) ** EMI CDM5 65566-2 [id.]. Callas, Gedda, Massard, René Duclos Ch., Children's Ch., Paris Nat. Op. O, Prêtre.

Solti's Decca performance was remarkable for its new illumination of character, Tatiana Troyanos a subtle as well as a seductive Carmen, Escamillo (José van Dam) very sympathetic, not just the flashy matador who steals the hero's girl, while Plácido Domingo portrays Don José as weak rather than just a victim. The reissued mid-priced set of highlights from this sharply characterful set is generous (75 minutes) and handsomely repackaged in a slipcase. A full translation is included, and the remastered recording sounds both brilliant, full-bodied, and atmospheric, though still somewhat over-weighted in the bass.

The bargain highlights selection on DG Classikon offers a fairly generous sampler of the Berganza/Domingo/Abbado set with some 69 minutes of well-chosen excerpts, including all the hits. The documentation relates the music to the narrative in a brief but succinct synopsis.

The selection from the Callas set is very generous, with a playing time of 71 minutes 35 seconds, but is not designed so much to highlight the heroine as to provide as many 'pops' as possible from the opera.

Carmen: highlights (sung in English).

(B) **(*) CfP CD-CFP 4596 [id. import]. Johnson, Smith, Herincx, Robson, Hunter, Greene, Stoddart, Moyle, Sadler's Wells Ch. & O, Sir Colin Davis.

Those who enjoy opera in English will find this a highly successful example, thanks both to the strongly animated conducting of Sir Colin Davis and to the rich-voiced, reliable singing of Patricia Johnson as Carmen.

Les pêcheurs de perles (complete).

(M) (***) EMI mono (SIS) CMS5 65266-2 (2). Angelici, Legay, Dens, Noguera, Théâtre Nat. de l'Opéra-Comique Ch. & O, Cluytens.

(i) *Les pêcheurs de perles* (complete); (ii) *Ivan IV:* highlights.

(M) ** EMI CMS5 66020-2 [CDMB 66020] (2). (i; ii) Micheau; (i) Gedda, Blanc; (ii) Roux, Legay, Sénéchal, Noguera, Savignol; (i) Paris Opéra-Comique O, Dervaux; (ii) French R. Ch. & O, Tzipine.

Unavailable since the early days of LP, this superb EMI Cluytens set of 1954 offers the finest, most warmly expressive performance on disc of this delectable opera. Ironically, its nearest rival is the Philips set of the previous year under Jean Fournet, also in mono, both of them outshining later stereo sets. Cluytens is an even more sensitive conductor than his Philips rival, less foursquare, getting the music to flow flexibly;

and his cast, idiomatically French, has no weak link. Martha Angelici as the heroine, Leila, is both sweet and bright, with no Gallic shrillness, and Henri Legay has a degree of heroic timbre in the rounded, lyric quality of his tenor, while Michel Dens, as in other French opera recordings of the period, proves a firm, characterful baritone. With excellent choral and orchestral work, one gets the impression of a stage experience translated to the studio. The mono transfer is a little dull on orchestral sound, but it captures voices vividly. According to Schwann, this is not available in the USA.

Paul Dervaux is a no more than efficient conductor, failing to draw out the relaxed charm of this exotic score with its soaringly lyrical set numbers. The lack of affection infects the principals, who are all stylish artists but who here sing below their best, even the dependable Nicolai Gedda. On two mid-price CDs, the set might still be worth considering, however, when it also includes selections from the opera which Bizet wrote immediately after *Pearlfishers*, *Ivan IV*. There is a fine scena for the heroine, beautifully sung by Janine Micheau; and the heady-toned tenor, Henri Legay, an outstanding artist, sings superbly in his vengeance aria. It is also good to hear the fine bass, Pierre Savignol. In the newly reissued set, full and clearly printed translations are provided for both operas. The CD transfers hardly betray the age of the recordings.

Bliss, Arthur (1891–1975)

Adam Zero (ballet; complete); *A Colour Symphony*.

(BB) *** Naxos Dig. 8.553460 [id.]. N. Philh. O, David Lloyd-Jones.

Naxos here offer the first of a planned series of Sir Arthur Bliss's music, including his best-known major work, the *Colour Symphony* of 1922. Full of striking ideas and effects to illustrate four heraldic colours, the symphony here receives a refined and idiomatic reading, marked by superb wind-playing. More valuable still is the first complete recording of the ballet, *Adam Zero*, in which the process of creating a ballet is presented as an allegory for the ongoing life-cycle. Lloyd-Jones directs a dramatically paced performance, amply confirming this as one of Bliss's most inventive, strongly co-ordinated scores, shamefully neglected. Full, well-balanced sound.

Checkmate (ballet): *5 dances*.

(M) *** Chandos CHAN 6576 [id.]. West Australian SO, Schönzeler – RUBBRA: *Symphony No. 5* ***; TIPPETT: *Little music*. **(*)

The idea of a ballet based on chess with all its opportunities for symbolism and heraldic splendour appealed to Bliss, and the score he produced remains one of his most inventive creations. The five dances on the Chandos issue are well played under Hans-Hubert Schönzeler and, with its valuable Rubbra coupling, this is very welcome.

A Colour Symphony; (i) *Cello concerto;* (ii) *The Enchantress* (scena for contralto and orchestra).

(M) *** Chandos Enchant Dig. CHAN 7073 [id.]. (i) Raphael Wallfisch; (ii) Linda Finnie; Ulster O, Vernon Handley.

Raphael Wallfisch is a powerful soloist in the *Cello concerto*, which Bliss wrote for Rostropovich in 1970, launching into the piece with a bite and attack which are instantly compelling. This is a reading which brings out the red-blooded warmth of the writing, with the soloist strongly supported by the Ulster Orchestra under Handley. They are equally persuasive accompanying Linda Finnie in the extended scena which Bliss wrote for Kathleen Ferrier nearly 20 years earlier, when he had just completed his opera, *The Olympians*. There, similarly, Bliss was inspired by the individual artistry of a great musician, even though, as he himself said, he found it hard to reconcile the goodness of Ferrier with the character of Simaetha, the central figure in the passage of Theocritus which he chose to set. For this reissue Chandos have added Vernon Handley's authoritative and enthusiastic account of the *Colour Symphony* and throughout the recording is well up to house standard.

(i) *A Colour Symphony; Introduction and allegro;* (ii) *Men of Two Worlds: Baraza;* (i) *Things to come* (film music): *suite* and excerpts: *Ballet for children; Pestilence; Attack; The world in ruins*.

(M) (***) Dutton Lab. CDLXT 2501 [id. full price]. (i) LSO, composer; (ii) Eileen Joyce, Ch. & Nat. SO, Muir Mathieson.

A Colour Symphony was the work that brought Bliss fame as an *enfant terrible*, but nowadays its flavour seems more Elgarian than modern, with the merest hint that Bliss knew his early Stravinsky. The sounds are attractive and the recording (1956 vintage) captures them well (courtesy of Mike Dutton's admirably faithful CD transfer of Decca's excellent Kingsway Hall recording). But, as with so much of this composer's output, in all honesty the thematic material is never very memorable. The *Introduction and allegro*, written for Stokowski (also in the early 1920s), is another well-constructed, completely professional but unmemorable work. For the film *Men of Two Worlds: Baraza* Eileen Joyce was recruited to the piano part of a score of which only a snippet survives, including a chorus and some touches of syncopation. It is quite vigorous, if at times somewhat coarse, but nevertheless rather endearing. Again, the 1946 recording in Dutton's vivid transfer sounds astonishingly good, like a broadcast transcription rather than an old record, only with more ambience. But Bliss's masterpiece was his incidental music for Korda's H. G. Wells film, *Things to come*. Bliss rescued his material and recorded an early set of four excerpts for Decca on 78-r.p.m. discs in 1936. This included a section called *The world in ruins*, missing from the final orchestral suite, which the composer published and recorded later in stereo in 1957. In terms of memorability of ideas, Bliss never surpassed this music, and the *March* is unforgettable in its gutsy, flamboyantly tuneful vitality.

(i) *Cello concerto. Music for strings; 2 Studies, Op. 16.*
(BB) ** Naxos Dig. 8.553383 [id.]. Tim Hugh, E. N. Philh., David Lloyd-Jones.

This second issue in the Naxos Bliss series couples one of Bliss's most successful works, the *Music for strings*, commissioned for the 1935 Salzburg Festival, with the *Cello concerto*, given in a reading far more reflective, less boldly extrovert, than the rival version on Chandos. The recording is partly responsible, not as full and forward as usual from this source, with the solo cello rather backwardly placed. Poetry rather than power is the keynote, centring on the *Larghetto* slow movement. The *Music for strings* also lacks a little in bite and definition, but this is a useful and enjoyable coupling, well supplemented by the two early *Studies*, a pastoral piece and a vigorous piece with a nautical flavour.

(i) *Introduction and allegro;* (ii) *Theme and cadenza for violin and orchestra.*
(BB) (***) Belart mono 461 353-2 [(M) id. import]. (i) LSO, composer; (ii) Alfredo Campoli, LPO, Boult – ELGAR: *Violin concerto.* (***)

The *Introduction and allegro* (for full orchestra) was written for Stokowski and is a well-constructed piece with good ideas; it sounds very impressive in this virile performance under the composer's direction. The *Theme and variations* is shorter but no less striking. It was originally written for a radio play written by the composer's wife. One could do with more short concertante pieces like this. The performance, with Campoli a first-rate soloist, is authentic and vividly alive. The excellent mid-1950s Decca recording is well transferred, to make this a very desirable coupling.

Things to come: suite; Welcome the Queen.
(BB) ** Belart 450 143-2 [(M) id. import]. LSO, composer – ELGAR: *Pomp and circumstance marches 1–5.* **

The composer's own excellent (1957) recording of his *Things to come suite* is additionally available on a super-bargain Belart reissue, offering its original couplings of *Welcome the Queen* and Elgar's five *Pomp and circumstance marches*. The former was an occasional piece, written by Bliss in the Elgar tradition of pageantry; the piece is of no particular distinction except for a very gracious middle tune. The performance could hardly be more authentic but the (originally very good) recording is not flattered by the current transfer, which is excessively bright and thin on top.

VOCAL MUSIC

Morning heroes (A choral symphony conceived as a Requiem for the victims of the First World War).
(M) **(*) EMI CDM7 63906-2. Westbrook (nar.), RLPO Ch. & O, Groves.

Inspired by the death of his younger brother in the First World War, and dedicated to all the victims of that conflict, *Morning heroes* is one of the most warmly emotional of all Bliss's works, a choral symphony with spoken narration in five movements, lasting over an hour. It may not be quite as distinctive as comparable works by Britten or Vaughan Williams, but Sir Charles Groves on EMI provides a strong performance, even if the music itself has a curious element of complacency. Fine recording and an excellent transfer.

Bloch, Ernest (1880–1959)

Violin concerto.
(M) *** EMI CDM7 63989-2. Y. Menuhin, Philh. O, Kletzki – BERG: *Violin concerto.* ***

Menuhin's deeply felt and finely recorded 1963 account is passionate and committed from the very first note, and any weaknesses in the score are quite lost when the playing is so compelling. Paul Kletzki accompanies with equal distinction. The 1964 Kingsway Hall recording sounds very well indeed.

(i) *Israel Symphony;* (ii) *Schelomo.*
(M) **(*) Van. 08 4047.71 [OVC 4047]. (i) Christensen, Basinger, Fraenkel, Politis, Heder, Watts; (ii) Nelsova; Utah SO, Abravanel.

Bloch's *Israel Symphony* is a large-scale work, but its way of anticipating the style of Hollywood film composers means that the music has something in common with the soundtracks of Hollywood's biblical epics. The performance here has the vigour and spontaneity that are characteristic of Abravanel's Utah performances, and the only snag is that the soloists, who are introduced at the end of the work, are wobbly and not especially distinguished. *Schelomo* is an appropriate coupling. The recordings were made in 1967 and are transferred to CD with great success.

Schelomo (Hebraic rhapsody) for cello and orchestra.
(M) *** Virgin Ultraviolet Dig. CUV5 61125-2. Steven Isserlis, LSO, Hickox – ELGAR: Cello concerto. **(*)
(M) *** Sony SBK 48278 [id.]. Leonard Rose, Phd. O, Ormandy – FAURE: *Elégie* ***; LALO: *Concerto* **(*); TCHAIKOVSKY: *Rococo variations.* ***

The dark intensity of Isserlis's solo playing and the sharp, dramatic focus of Hickox in the big climactic orchestral tuttis are magnetic, preventing Bloch's youthful outpouring on Solomon and the Song of Songs from sounding self-indulgent. Warm, refined recording.

A darkly passionate, rhapsodical account from Leonard Rose, with an equally strong accompaniment from Ormandy. The recording balance is close, which reduces the possible dynamic range, but the compelling power of the music-making triumphs – this very good 71-minute compilation is worthy of a fine (perhaps underrated) cellist.

Blow, John (1649–1708)

Anthems: *Cry aloud, and spare not; I was glad; O sing unto the Lord.*
(M) **(*) Decca 436 256-2. King's College, Cambridge, Ch., ASMF, Willcocks – HANDEL: *Coronation anthems.* ***

These anthems impress, both by their grandeur and by the confidence of the part-writing for individual solo voices, sung here by members of the choir. *O sing unto the Lord* is a particularly eloquent and expressive piece. *I was glad*, with its trumpet obbligato, was composed for the opening of the chancel of St Paul's Cathedral (all that was completed in 1697). The performances, if lacking something in robust flair, are agreeably secure, and the recording is spacious and full, even if the focus of the King's acoustic lacks something in sharpness.

Ode on the death of Mr Henry Purcell; Amphion Anglicus (songs): *Cloë found Amintas lying all in tears; Why weeps Asteria; Loving above himself (Poor Celadon); Shepherds, deck your crooks; Ah Heav'n! What is't I hear?; Epilogue: Sing, sing ye muses.*
(B) *** Sony Seon SBK 60097 [id.]. René Jacobs, James Bowman, soloists, Leonhardt Consort, Gustav Leonhardt.

The *Ode on the death of Mr Henry Purcell* is a most welcome addition to the catalogue, particularly as it is performed so superbly here under Gustav Leonhardt. There are some striking chromaticisms and dissonances and some inventive and noble music. James Bowman is the only native singer (he is in good voice, too) but the others – notably René Jacobs – are no less intelligent and stylish. Both the performance and recording are fine for this short but rewarding disc.

Venus and Adonis.
(B) *** HM Dig. HMA 190 1276 [id.]. Argenta, Dawson, Varcoe, Covey-Crump, L. Bar. & Ch., Medlam.
Venus and Adonis is like a Lully opera in miniature. Charles Medlam with London Baroque gives a period performance and takes care that the early instruments are well blended rather than edgy and the choral sound is full, bright and clean. The soloists too are all remarkable for sweetness and freshness of tone. This record is now offered at bargain price in the Musique d'Abord series.

Boccherini, Luigi (1743–1805)

Cello concertos Nos. 1 in E flat, G.474; 2 in A, G.475; 3 in D, G.476; 4 in C, G.477.
(BB) **(*) Arte Nova Dig. 74321 34041-2 [id.]. Emil Klein, Hamburg Soloists.

Cello concertos Nos. 5 in D, G.478; 6 in D, G.479; 7 in G, G.480; 8 in C, G.481.
(BB) *** Arte Nova Dig. 74321 51632-2 [id.]. Emil Klein, Hamburg Soloists.

The Romanian musician, Emil Klein, successfully manages the joint roles of solo cellist and conductor of the Hamburg Soloists (he is their director on a regular basis outside the studio). Klein is now in the process of recording all Boccherini's cello concertos for Arte Nova, and he proves to be an excellent player with a small, sweet, cleanly focused timbre. He is equal to the considerable technical demands of these works, his intonation secure in the instrument's upper range, as is readily shown in the demanding higher tessitura of the *Adagio* of G.479 (where he shares a luscious duet with the orchestra's principal violin), and before that in G.478. This same D major work produces some fizzing bursts of virtuosity in the closing Rondo, and there are nicely pointed rhythms in the finale of G.477. Comparable, sharply articulated bravura adds to the character of the first movement of G.480, while the famous slow movement of that same work is shaped with touching eloquence. The Hamburg Soloists are a somewhat larger chamber group than their name suggests, although their tonal spectrum is amplified by a rather too reverberant acoustic on the first disc – the only small drawback to an estimable quartet of performances. The resonance seems better contained on the second, and on both nicely alert playing from the orchestra adds to the listener's pleasure. Klein is not a larger-than-life solo personality but he is thoroughly at home in this repertoire.

Cello concertos Nos. 1 in E flat, G.474; 7 in G, G.480; 9 in B flat, G.482.
(M) **(*) Virgin Veritas/EMI Dig. VER5 61239-2. Wouter Möller, Linde Consort, Linde.

The Linde Consort, renowned for their baroque repertoire, now venture equally authentically into the *galant* world of Boccherini. Here we have the original version of the *B flat Concerto* played freshly, if without strong individuality, by the excellent Wouter Möller. The orchestral group (4.2.2.1, with 2 oboes, 2 hand horns and harpsichord) plainly seeks a chamber style, but the resonant acoustic amplifies the effect of both the forwardly placed soloist and the accompanying group. Möller plays the fine slow movement of G.482 with restrained *espressivo*, and his articulation in allegros is neatly rhythmic throughout. Linde provides polished accompaniments, and intonation (so important when there is only the merest hint of vibrato) is excellent: the finale of the *B flat Concerto* has an attractively easy pacing. The other works are hardly less successful, and the *G major* (No. 7) brings out the very best in the performers, with articulate, resilient strings in the outer movements and Möller comparatively intense in the *Adagio*.

Cello concerto No. 2 in D, G.479.
(B) *** DG Double 437 952-2 (2) [id.]. Rostropovich, Zurich Coll. Mus., Sacher – BERNSTEIN: *3 Meditations;* GLAZUNOV: *Chant du Ménestrel;* SHOSTAKOVICH: *Cello concerto No. 2;* TARTINI: *Cello concerto;* TCHAIKOVSKY: *Andante cantabile* etc; VIVALDI: *Cello concertos.* ***

Although essentially a performance in the grand manner, Rostropovich is so compelling that reservations are swept aside. He is given an alert accompaniment by Sacher, and the recording has fine body and presence. This is now part of a self-recommending Double DG bargain anthology.

Cello concertos Nos. 4 in C, G.477; 6 in D, G.479; 7 in G, G.480; 8 in C, G.481.
(M) *** Teldec/Warner 4509 97991-2 [(M) id. import]. Anner Bylsma, Concerto Amsterdam, Schröder.

These concertos were originally published as Nos. 1–4 but are numbered as above in the Gérard catalogue. They are scored for strings with the addition of simple horn parts in Nos. 4 and 8, and they are agreeable works which sit easily between the *galant* and classical styles. There are few moments of routine in the writing, and it is always elegant and pleasing. *No. 6 in D major* is a particularly fine work, while the finale of No. 8 is very jolly. Anner Bylsma is a fine player and seems eminently suited to this repertoire, while Schröder's accompaniments are most stylish and full of vitality. Charm, too, is an important element and it is not missing here, while the sombre *Adagio* of No. 7 has undoubted eloquence and is ideally paced to contrast with the sprightly and tuneful finale. The 1965 recording is first class and, like so many of Teldec's *Das alte Werk* series, the immaculate CD transfer makes the very most of the sound.

(i) *Cello concertos Nos. 6 in D, G.479; 7 in G, G.480;* (ii) *9 in B flat, G.482; 10 in D, G.483.*
(B) *** Erato/Warner Ultima 3984 201040-2 (2) [(M) id. import]. Frédéric Lodéon; (i) Lausanne CO, Jordan; (ii) Bournemouth Sinf., Guschlbauer.

This set combines two sets of performances recorded four years apart. Lodéon was in his thirties at the time and plays splendidly throughout. His playing has genuine style and real eloquence, and in the *G major concerto*, G.480, originally unearthed by Maurice Gendron, he is wonderfully fresh and fervent; in his hands the better-known *D major Concerto*, G.479 (also recorded by Bylsma and Rostropovich), has genuine tenderness and depth. He is well accompanied by both groups, but the two Lausanne performances (from 1981) have slightly superior sound and the balance of the soloist is less obviously spotlighted. The snag to this pair of records is the playing time of only 85 minutes, whereas the competing Bylsma collection manages to get four concertos (including G.479 and G.480) on a single mid-priced CD.

Cello concerto No. 7 in G, G.480.
(M) *** Carlton IMP Classics Dig. 30367 00912 [id.]. Felix Schmidt, ECO, Heath – BEETHOVEN: *Triple concerto.* ***

This is the concerto from which Grützmacher extracted the slow movement in his phoney, cobbled-together 'Boccherini Concerto', the movement everyone remembers. It makes an unusual but apt and attractive coupling for the Trio Zingara's excellent version of the Beethoven *Triple concerto.*

(i) *Cello concerto No. 9 in B flat* (original version, revised Gendron); (ii; iii) *Flute concerto in D, Op. 27* (attrib.; now thought to be by Franz Pokorny); (iv) *Symphonies Nos. 3 in C; 5 in B flat, Op. 12/3 & 5;* (v) *Guitar quintets Nos. 4 in D (Fandango); 9 in C (La Ritirata di Madrid);* (vi) *String quartet in D, Op. 6/1;* (iii) *String quintet in E, Op. 13/5: Minuet* (only).
(B) *** Ph. Duo 438 377-2 (2) [id.]. (i) Gendron, LOP, Casals; (ii) Gazzelloni; (iii) I Musici; (iv) New Philh. O, Leppard; (v) Pepe Romero, ASMF Chamber Ens.; (vi) Italian Qt.

Entitled 'The best of Boccherini including the *Minuet*', this most attractive anthology was assembled especially for the Philips Duo series. It is well documented and the famous *Minuet* could hardly be presented more winningly. It is the one digital recording here. It is good, too, that Gendron's version of the *Cello concerto* is included, for he pioneered the return of the original version (without Grützmacher's reworking), and he plays it admirably. The *Flute concerto* is a galant piece, elegantly played by Gazzelloni, and one can see why it was mistakenly attributed; Boccherini is all too readily dismissed as *la femme de Haydn*, but underneath the surface charm and elegance that one associates with him there are deeper currents and an altogether special pathos to disturb the attentive listener. Both *Symphonies* are full of vitality in these excellent performances under Raymond Leppard and are very well recorded. The Italian Quartet's performance of the *D major Quartet* is notable for its freshness and refinement. The *Guitar quintets* were arranged by Boccherini for his Spanish patron, the Marquis Benavente. The guitar part was obviously intended for the Marquis to perform, so its contribution is sometimes limited to an accompanying role; but the music has considerable charm, though it is somewhat uneven. The performances are unfailingly warm and sensitive and they are well recorded too, although there is a touch of thinness on top. The set is supported with good documentation.

Cello concerto in B flat (arr. Grützmacher).
(BB) *** Naxos Dig. 8.550059; *4550059* [id.]. Ludovít Kanta, Capella Istropolitana, Peter Breiner – HAYDN: *Cello concertos Nos. 1 & 2.* ***

Ludovít Kanta's playing is distinguished by imaginative and musicianly phrasing and a warm tone. The Slovak players under Peter Breiner give a good account of themselves, and this can hold its own against versions costing twice or three times as much.

Symphonies: in D, G.490; in D min. (La casa del diavolo), Op. 12/4; in A; in F, Op. 35/3–4.
(B) **(*) HM Dig. Musique d'Abord HMA 190121 [id.]. Ensemble 415, Chiara Banchini.

Boccherini could write sunny, three-movement symphonies with winning *Andantes*, like the attractive A major work here, Op. 35/3, in which the central movement is a serenade. The F major work, Op. 35/4, has an assertive opening movement but is most notable for its agreeable finale, which has a central Minuet. But Boccherini could also be both innovative and dramatic, as in the *D minor Symphony*, subtitled *La casa del diavolo*. Here he quotes from Gluck in the energetic finale, introduces the fast movements with a recitativo declamation, and provides an individual central *Andantino*. This moves forward in an elegant *moto perpetuo* on the violins, with comments from two solo cellos. It is presented most delicately, while allegros are alert and bustling. Indeed, these period-instrument performances by the excellent Ensemble 415, led by Chiara Banchini, are very enjoyable. The slight drawback is the resonance of the recording which tends to cloud the busier fortissimos.

Symphonies, Op. 12, Nos. 1 in D; 2 in E flat; 3 in C; 4 in D min.; 5 in B flat; 6 in A.
(B) *** Ph. Duo 456 067-2 (2) [id.]. New Philh. O, Leppard.

Boccherini's Op. 12 was published in 1776. The scoring is for the normal classical orchestra, including two flutes or oboes and horns; but the composer's individuality emerges in his writing for the strings – with divided cellos – which are always predominant in the main argument. Even so, there are many pleasing touches of woodwind colour. The *E flat Symphony* (No. 2) is a remarkably fine work, virtually a sinfonia concertante with important bravura duets, first for two violins, then for a pair of cellos (the composer's own instrument); there is even a cadenza. The other symphonies are all of comparable interest, with Boccherini's silken melancholy strongly featured in the lyrical writing. The composer's craftsmanship is as ever deft, although perhaps his attempt at cyclic construction brings a too easy solution in *No. 6 in A major* when, after the *Grave* introduction to the finale, he simply repeats the latter part of the first movement, starting at the central double bar! In short, this set of six attractive symphonies is well worth exploring, particularly as Leppard consistently secures playing from the highly alert New Philharmonia Orchestra that is polished, elegant and never superficial. The Philips 1971 recording is excellent and so is the CD transfer, losing nothing of the bloom but firming up the overall focus admirably.

CHAMBER MUSIC

Guitar quintets Nos. 1–7, G.445/51; 9 (La Ritirata di Madrid), G.453.
(B) *** Ph. Duo 438 769-2 (2) [id.]. Pepe Romero, ASMF Chamber Ens.

Boccherini wrote or arranged twelve *Guitar quintets*, but only the present eight have survived, plus another version of *No. 4 in D* (*Fandango*), G.448. Although some of the music is bland, it is nearly all agreeably tuneful in an unostentatious way, and there are some highly imaginative touches, with attractive hints of melancholy and underlying passion. These performances by Pepe Romero (often willing to take a relatively minor role) and members of the ASMF Chamber Ensemble are wholly admirable, and Philips are especially good at balancing textures of this kind in the most natural way, the guitar able to be assertive when required without overbalancing the ensemble. The recording is slightly less smooth than the original LPs, but the CD transfer has brought greater presence and a bolder outline. This is an engagingly undemanding set to dip into in the late evening.

Guitar quintets Nos. (i) *4 in D (Fandango), G. 448. 7 in E min., G. 451; 9 in C (La Ritirata di Madrid), G. 453.*
(B) *** DG Classikon 449 852-2 [(M) id. import]. Narciso Yepes, Melos Qt; (i) with Lucero Tena.

In the DG bargain compilation from 1971 the sound is very good, full yet lively, and well projected. The playing is expert and, in the boisterous *Fandango* finale of No. 4, Lucero Tena makes a glittering contribution with his castanets. '*La Ritirata di Madrid*', famous from a string quintet, Op. 30/6, is used as the finale of the C major work. This picturesque evocation is created with a set of 12 brief variations set in a long slow crescendo, followed by a similarly graduated decrescendo, a kind of Spanish patrol with the 'night watch' disappearing into the distance at the end.

Piano quintets: in A min., Op. 56/2, G.412; in E flat, Op. 56/3, G.410; in E min., Op. 57/3, G.415; in C, Op. 57/6, G.418.
(BB) *** DHM Baroque Esprit 05472 77448-2 [id.]. Les Adieux.

This a particularly attractive group of Boccherini works, and it is made the more so by its reissue on the bargain Baroque Esprit label. The lovely *E minor* (Op. 57/3) which starts the disc and the *A minor* (Op. 56/2) both have those hints of beguiling, almost sultry melancholy that makes this composer's musical language so distinctive. This accomplished period-instrument group turn in performances of great finesse and charm, though the recording-balance places the listener very much in the front row of the salon.

String quartet in E flat, Op. 58/2.
(M) *** Cal. CAL 6698. Talich Qt – HAYDN: *Quartet No. 74;* MENDELSSOHN: *Quartet No. 2;* MICA: *Quartet No. 6.* ***

Boccherini's tuneful *E flat major Quartet*, Op. 58/2, opens with a friendly *Allegro lento*, yet characteristically its *Larghetto* brings a touch of gentle melancholy. The finale is a spirited *Allegro vivo*, played here with much geniality. Indeed the Talich are on top form and are very naturally recorded, so that this well-planned collection amounts to more than the sum of its parts.

3 String quintets (with double bass), Op. 39/1–3 (G.337–9); String quartet in G (La Tiranna), Op. 44/4 (G 223).
(M) *** HM Suite Dig. HMT 7901334 [id.]. Ensemble 415.

Boccherini wrote only three (out of a total of 125) quintets using a double-bass to (lightly) carry the bottom line of the harmony. They date from 1787 and the device seems very effective, with the careful balance of Ensemble 415 ensuring that Boccherini's scheme works extremely well. All three works are very attractive and none is predictable. The first opens with an elegant and rather touching *Andante lento*, with the following two movements chimerically changing mood and tempo; the second has a gentle *Adagio* with pizzicato accompaniment, the third brings a delicate central *Pastorale*, and all three quintets have contrasting bursts of good-humoured energy in outer movements. The programme is completed with a two-movement *Quartet*, the first of which is based on a Spanish dance of the time, hence its sobriquet. The performances here are first class, refined and sensitive, and using period instruments always to bring aural pleasure. The recording is excellent too. A highly recommendable bargain reissue.

KEYBOARD MUSIC

6 Quartets, Op. 26; Fandango (from *Quintettino, Op. 40/2*) (arr. for two harpsichords).
(M) **(*) HM Suite Dig. HMT 7901233. William Christie, Christophe Rousset (harpsichords).

It is not known who made this arrangement for two harpsichords of Boccherini's six *Quartets*, published in 1781 as Op. 32, but in the hands of William Christie and Christophe Rousset – who are obviously enjoying themselves – the music is robustly jolly and communicative and made to sound as if written for the keyboard, especially the imitative opening of No. 3. Each sonata is in two movements, with the second a minuet. The *Larghetto* which begins No. 2 has its moments of quirkiness, while the *Andante appassionato* opening movement of the last sonata sounds almost like that of a transcribed Haydn *Sturm und Drang* symphony. The *Fandango* from Op. 40/2 is, not surprisingly, the most striking movement of all; but there is plenty of verve throughout, even if the close balance of the two harpsichords means that the dynamic range is limited.

Boeck, August de (1865–1937)

Symphony in G.
(BB) *** Discover Dig. DICD 920126 [id.]. Brussels BRT PO, Karl Anton Rickenbacher – GILSON: *De Zee.* ***

The *Symphony in G* of August de Boeck, like Paul Gilson's suite, *De Zee*, with which it is coupled, is a ripely exotic work, full of Russian echoes. You might describe it as the Borodin symphony that Borodin didn't write, sharply rhythmic in the fast movements and sensuous in the slow movement, brilliantly orchestrated and full of tunes that are only marginally less memorable than those of the Russian master. Well played and recorded and, at Discover International's bargain price, an ideal disc for experimenting with.

Boieldieu, François (1775–1834)

Harp concerto in 3 tempi in C.
❁ (M) *** Decca 425 723-2; *425 723-4*. Marisa Robles, ASMF, Iona Brown – DITTERSDORF; HANDEL: *Harp concertos* etc. *** ❁

Boieldieu's *Harp concerto* has been recorded elsewhere but never more attractively. The (originally Argo) recording is still in the demonstration class and very sweet on the ear. To make the reissue even more attractive, three beguiling sets of *Variations* have been added, including music by Handel and Beethoven and a *Theme, variations and Rondo pastorale* attributed to Mozart.

Boismortier, Bodin de (1689–1755)

(i) *Suites for solo flute Nos. 3, 5 & 6;* (ii) *Harpsichord suites Nos. 1–4.*
(B) *** Cal. Approche Analogue/Dig. CAL 6865 [(M) id.]. (i) Luc Urbain; (ii) Mireille Lagacé.

These four *Harpsichord suites* were Boismortier's only works for harpsichord, published as a set in Paris in 1731. They are very much in the style of the *Pièces de clavecin* of Rameau, and Boismortier follows his practice in giving each movement a colourful sobriquet. *La Cavernesque*, which begins the *First Suite*, is aptly titled. The invention is attractive, if perhaps not as individual as with Rameau, although the finale of the last suite shows Boismortier writing a very characterful set of variations. Mireille Lagacé is an excellent advocate and she uses a restored Hemsch, which is truthfully recorded and suits the repertoire admirably. Interleaved with the harpsichord works are three suites for unaccompanied flute, also made up with dance movements but each with an introductory *Prelude* which has an improvisatory feeling about it. Again the playing is highly responsive, and altogether this makes a rewarding concert and helps to bring yet another name out of the musical history books.

Première suite de clavecin.
(B) ** Cal. Approche CAL 6838 [(M) id.]. Mireille Lagacé – RAMEAU: *6 Concerts en sextuor.* **

Bodin de Boismortier was a contemporary of Rameau, and his musical career was divided between Spain and France. His harpsichord pieces (each of which have sobriquets, like those of Rameau) have a reasonable degree of individuality, particularly the gentle melancholy of the sarabande (*La Valtudinière*) and the rhythmically winning closing *Pièce en rondeau* (*La Décharnée*). They are expertly played by Mireille Lagacé, who uses a restored 1754 Hemsch, and the recording is realistic, provided you turn down the volume.

Boito, Arrigo (1842–1918)

Mefistofele (complete).
(M) **(*) Decca 440 054-2 [id.]. Siepi, Del Monaco, Tebaldi, Cavalli, Santa Cecilia Academy, Rome, Ch. & O, Serafin.
(M) (**(*)) EMI mono CMS5 65655-2 (2) [CDMB 65655] with Act IV omitted. Christoff, Prandelli, Moscucci, Rome Op. Ch. & O, Gui.
(M) ** EMI CMS5 66501-2 (2) [CDMB 66501]. Norman Treigle, Plácido Domingo, Montserrat Caballé, Amb. Op. Ch., LSO, Rudel.

On the stereo (1958) Decca Rome set, Serafin, the most persuasive Italian conductor of his day, draws glorious sounds from his performers, even from Mario del Monaco, who is here almost sensitive. Tebaldi is a rich-toned Margherita – almost too rich-toned for so frail a heroine – and Siepi makes an excellent Mefistofele. The Decca engineers came up trumps: the stereo remains remarkably spacious, particularly in the Prologue, making a good mid-priced alternative to the later Decca version.

Though it omits Act IV, the episodic scene with Helen of Troy in the Underworld, there is much to enjoy in Vittorio Gui's 1955 mono recording with Boris Christoff in the title-role. Gui is a master at building tension and, though the chorus has a backward balance, the choral close to the Prologue is hardly less incandescent than in Toscanini's classic concert performance. Giacinto Prandelli, who made several important recordings in the early days of LP, is here a lyrical Faust, stylish if lacking full heroic power, while Orietta Moscucci is a soprano not afraid to sing softly, as at the opening of her big aria, *L'altra notte*. Hers is a sweet voice, if with edge at the top under pressure. But the glory of the set is the towering impersonation of Christoff as Mefistofele, thrillingly dark-toned and intense from first to last, the more vivid for being balanced close. Orchestral sound is dim, but Gui's conducting compensates.

On the mid-1970s EMI set Caballé assumed the principal role of Margherita; though her performance lacks detail and she misses some of the dark intensity that makes Freni's full-priced Decca account with Pavarotti and Ghiaurov (410 175-2) so moving, particularly in *L'altra notte*, she is in very good voice. Norman Treigle, renowned in the role of Mefistofele at the New York City Opera, sings strongly. Though he is not as characterful as Ghiaurov, the Faust/Margherita duet is beautifully done. Plácido Domingo as Faust is stylish and confident, and Rudel conducts with warmth. The sound, however, even in its remastered form, cannot compete with either of the spectacular Decca sets, particularly in the Prologue.

Mefistofele: Prologue.
(M) (***) RCA mono GD 60276 [60276-2-RG]. Moscona, Robert Shaw Ch., Columbus Boychoir, NBC SO, Arturo Toscanini – VERDI: *I Lombardi; Rigoletto*: excerpts. (**)

The hair-raising intensity of Toscanini's performance gives Boito's multi-layered *Prologue* a cogency never matched since on record. The dryness of sound even seems to help, when offstage choruses are accurately focused, and the singing of the Robert Shaw Chorale has thrillingly dramatic bite.

Bononcini, Antonio (1677–1726)

Stabat Mater.
(B) *** Decca Double 443 868-2 (2) [id.]. Palmer, Langridge, Esswood, Keyte, St John's College,

Cambridge, Ch., Philomusica, Guest – PERGOLESI: *Magnificat in C; Stabat Mater* **(*); D. SCARLATTI: *Stabat Mater;* A. SCARLATTI: *Domine, refugium factus es nobis; O magnum mysterium;* CALDARA: *Crucifixus;* LOTTI: *Crucifixus.* ***

This fascinating Double Decca collection centres on three different settings of the *Stabat Mater dolorosa*, a medieval poem describing the anguish of Mary during her son's crucifixion, an experience with which women, especially, have readily identified down through the ages. Although its origins date from the end of the thirteenth century, it was not until 1727 that it became part of the Roman liturgy.

Antonio Bononcini is not to be confused with Handel's rival, Giovanni, his older brother. Antonio's *Stabat Mater* is a work of genuine melodic distinction and affecting tenderness; there are some striking harmonies, even moments of drama, and in general a nobility and simple expressiveness that leave a strong impression. The St John's performance is wholly admirable and is very well recorded.

Bononcini, Giovanni (1670–1755)

Griselda (highlights).

(M) *** Decca 448 977-2 (2). Elms, Sutherland, M. Sinclair, Elkins, Malas, Amb. S., LPO, Bonynge – GRAUN: *Montezuma.* ***

Bononcini is remembered well enough as Handel's rival as an opera composer, but how rarely one has the chance to study his theatrical music. All credit to Richard Bonynge for resurrecting what by all accounts is his most impressive work, and providing a sample of a score of numbers. By no stretch of the imagination does this music match Handel's in inspiration, but the numbers are nicely varied, with several lovely arias for the patient Griselda (sung by Lauris Elms), several simpler pastoral airs and a couple of jolly bass arias. Joan Sutherland's contribution in the castrato role of Ernesto is limited to four arias and a duet but, with bright, lively conducting from Richard Bonynge the whole performance is most enjoyable. Excellent (1966) Kingsway Hall recording and a full translation provided. It was perhaps a pity that this reissue had to come in harness with Graun's *Montezuma*, but that too is well worth having on CD.

Borodin, Alexander (1833–87)

'The World of Borodin': (i) *In the Steppes of Central Asia; Prince Igor:* (ii) *Overture;* (ii–iii) *Polovtsian dances;* (iv) *Symphony No. 2 in B min.;* (v) *String quartet No. 2: Nocturne;* (vi) *Scherzo in A flat;* (vii, viii) *Far from the shores of your native land;* (vii, ix) *Prince Igor: Galitzky's aria.*

(M) *** Decca Analogue/Dig. 444 389-2; *444 389-4.* (i) SRO, Ansermet; (ii) LSO, Solti; (iii) with London Symphony Ch.; (iv) LSO, Martinon; (v) Borodin Qt; (vi) Ashkenazy; (vii) Nicolai Ghiaurov; (viii) Zlatina Ghiaurov; (ix) London Symphony Ch. and LSO, Downes.

An extraordinarily successful disc that will provide for many collectors an inexpensive summation of the art of Borodin. The compilation, which was originally offered on LP, has been updated and extended, with the changes of performers all to advantage. There can be few if any other collections of this kind that sum up a composer's achievement so succinctly or that make such a rewarding and enjoyable 76-minute concert. Solti's *Prince Igor overture* is unexpectedly romantic, and very exciting too; there is no finer account in the current catalogue, and the same can be said for the *Polovtsian dances*, with splendid choral singing – even if the chorus takes a little longer to warm up than in the famous Beecham version. Both recordings date from 1966 and have vintage Decca sound. The *Nocturne* follows the *Overture* so effectively that one might have thought it the composer's own plan. Then comes *Galitzky's aria* (complete with chorus), where the sound is over-bright, but no matter, and the *Scherzo in A flat* follows – with Ashkenazy in fine form – before the choral *Polovtsian dances*. Ansermet's *In the Steppes of Central Asia* is warmer and more atmospheric than we had remembered it and, if the Suisse Romande violins fail to do its voluptuous main theme full justice, Ansermet's interpretation is spacious and vivid. After Nicolai Ghiaurov has reminded us of the melancholy side of the Russian spirit, we come finally to Martinon's unsurpassed 1960 LSO performance of the *B minor Symphony*, notable for its fast tempo for the famous opening theme. The strong rhythmic thrust suits the music admirably, the Scherzo has vibrant colouring and the slow movement, with a beautifully played horn solo, is most satisfying. The sound has remarkable presence and sparkle, and only in the massed violin tone (which is good) is there a suggestion that the recording is not modern.

'Essential Borodin': Symphonies Nos. (i) *1 in E flat;* (ii) *2 in B min.;* (iii) *3 in A min.; In the Steppes of Central Asia;* (iv) *String quartet No. 2 in B min.;* (v–vi) Song: *From the shores of your far-off native land. Prince Igor:* (vii) *Overture;* (vii–viii) *Polovtsian dances;* (v; viii–ix) *Galitzky's aria; Konchak's aria.*

(B) *** Decca Double Analogue/Dig. 455 632-2 (2) [(M) id. import]. (i) RPO, Ashkenazy; (ii) LSO, Martinon; (iii) SRO, Ansermet; (iv) Borodin Qt; (v) Nicolai Ghiaurov; (vi) Zlatina Ghiaurov; (vii) LSO, Solti; (viii) L. Symphony Ch.; (ix) LSO, Edward Downes.

Decca have now happily expanded the programme contained on '*The World of Borodin*' (see above) to fit on a Double, and in doing so they represent the composer even more comprehensively for very little extra outlay. Ashkenazy's reading of the *First Symphony* is less high-powered than Martinon's superb account of No. 2, but its many delights come over richly, thanks not only to the quality of the RPO playing but also to the warm (1992) digital recording. Ansermet's touch in the unfinished *Third* is attractively alive and spontaneous, with some delightful moments from the SRO woodwind. The early stereo (1954) shows its age with distinct thinness in the upper range of the strings, but the warm ambience remains. What makes this extended programme especially attractive is the inclusion of the whole of the *Second String quartet*, rather than just the slow movement. The performance by the eponymous Borodin Quartet is masterly in every respect, and the new transfer of their 1961 recording is admirably full and gives a natural presence to the four players. In *Prince Igor* Ghiaurov now adds a second role by singing Konchak's aria from Act II in addition to Galitzky's aria from Act I.

In the steppes of Central Asia; Prince Igor: Overture; Polovtsian march and dances; Symphony No. 2 in B min.

(B) *** Tring Dig. TRP 104 [(M) id. import]. RPO, Ole Schmidt.

Too long neglected on disc, Ole Schmidt in the Royal Philharmonic Collection with ideal couplings offers an outstanding version at bargain price of the Borodin *Second Symphony*, beautifully played and recorded in vivid, open sound, one of the very finest at any price. In the first movement of the symphony Schmidt avoids the pitfall of adopting too slow a speed, thus avoiding any ponderousness while giving the music an idiomatically earthy tang. So, the flurries at the opening have a fiercely Slavonic bite, heightened by the way that Schmidt slightly exaggerates the pauses between them; from then on, rhythms are delectably sprung. After that brisk first movement Schmidt takes a relatively relaxed view of the *Prestissimo Scherzo*, again beautifully sprung. At a nicely flowing tempo the great horn solo of the slow movement is gloriously played by the RPO's long-time principal, Jeffrey Bryant. Beautifully shaded with perfectly controlled rubato, his radiant playing matches and even outshines the finest of the past. The crisply sprung finale is then full of panache. The *Prince Igor overture* again brings masterly horn-playing, while the *Polovtsian dances* and *March* also show off the brilliance of the RPO wind soloists. With performances like these it is all the more welcome to have the full complement of RPO players individually named.

In the Steppes of Central Asia; Prince Igor: Polovtsian dances.

(BB) ** Naxos Dig. 8.550051 [id.]. Slovak PO, Nazareth – MUSSORGSKY: *Night* etc. **

The sinuous oriental flavour of *In the Steppes of Central Asia* is well caught in the Naxos performance, although the first climax is rhythmically a little ponderous. The *Polovtsian dances*, if without the last degree of refinement, have plenty of zestful exuberance. Vivid digital sound makes this coupling with Mussorgsky excellent value.

Prince Igor: Overture and Polovtsian dances.

(M) *** Virgin/EMI Dig. CUV5 61135-2. RLPO Ch. & O, Mackerras – MUSSORGSKY: *Night* etc. **

A splendid account of the *Prince Igor overture*, with the brilliant, jaggedly thrusting imitation in the allegro given plenty of bite and the lyrical secondary melody glowingly phrased by principal horn and strings alike. The *Polovtsian dances* proceed with comparable brilliance and fervour, with the Royal Liverpool Philharmonic Choir producing expansive lyrical tone and joining in the frenzy of the closing section with infectious zest. Excellent recording too, vivid and full; if only the Mussorgsky coupling had produced comparable electricity, this record would have been a world-beater.

Symphonies Nos. 1–2; 3 in A min. (completed & orch. Glazunov).

(BB) ** Naxos Dig. 8.550238 [id.]. Bratislava RSO, Stephen Gunzenhauser.

The Naxos disc is a fair bargain in offering good recordings of all three symphonies (76 minutes) at a very modest price indeed. One ideally needs a more sumptuous body of sound for this music than the Bratislava Radio Symphony Orchestra can provide, but Gunzenhauser brings plenty of buoyant vitality to the first movement of the *Second Symphony*. Altogether these are fresh, pleasing performances but not distinctive.

(i) *Symphonies Nos. 1–3; Prince Igor:* (i; ii) *Overture and Polovtsian dances;* (iii) *In the Steppes of central Asia;* (iv) *String quartet No. 2: Notturno* (arr. for orchestra).

(B) ** Sony SB2K 62406 (2) [S2K 62406]. (i) Toronto SO, Andrew Davis; (ii) with Ch.; (iii) NYPO, Bernstein; (iv) St Petersburg Camerata, Sondeckis.

At bargain price in Sony's Essential Classics series, this makes a fairly recommendable compilation, with Andrew Davis's readings of the three symphonies and of the *Prince Igor* items bluff and bouncy, supplemented by two favourite bonus items. With the extra brightness of the CD transfer the amiable qualities of Davis's readings consistently come out. There is no neurasthenia in his view of Borodin here, consistently strong, purposeful and well sprung, with the warmly lyrical folk flavour of the themes regularly brought out. The Sony (originally CBS) recording may be too upfront and may lack a genuine pianissimo, but that matches the rugged quality of the performances, which yet bring some fine playing from the Toronto wind and brass principals. The two encores are new to the present bargain reissue, and neither is outstanding. The *Nocturne* from the *Second String quartet* is described as being 'arranged for violin and string orchestra by Rimsky-Korsakov', but proves to have no soloist, and to be scored for a fuller orchestra, including woodwind. The performance is warm, but its sentience is rather too sultry and lethargic. Similarly, and more surprisingly, Bernstein's *In the Steppes of central Asia* is heavily expressive and fails to spring fully to life and be truly evocative; moreover, its first climax is rather square. Both these pieces are much better recorded than the three symphonies. Good value, if the sound quality is acceptable.

Symphony No. 2 in B min.; Prince Igor: Overture; Polovtsian dances.

(BB) ** ASV Dig. CDQS 6018 [(M) id.]. Mexico State SO, Bátiz.

Bátiz's bright, modern digital recording certainly makes a vivid impression and the performances are extremely spirited, although one is made to realize that the Mexican State Orchestra, though impressively rehearsed, cannot match the finest European orchestras in virtuosity and finesse. The *Polovtsian dances* are without a chorus, and the effect is slightly shrill; but the energy of the performance is arresting. This is issued in the super-bargain range and is very good value.

Symphony No. 2 in B min.; Nocturne (orch. Tcherepnin).

(M) *** DG (IMS) Dig. 445 568-2. Gothenburg SO, Järvi – RIMSKY-KORSAKOV: *Symphony No. 2 (Antar).* ***

In a surprisingly rare coupling, Järvi's expansive approach to both these Russian symphonies works well when the DG recording is so warm and full-bodied. His account of the Borodin *Second* is at its finest in the *Andante* in which the key melody, so beautifully introduced by the solo horn, returns on the full strings in a flood of romanticism; but even in the first movement, which lacks the exhilaration of Martinon's much faster basic tempo, the return of the dominating idea on the brass in the coda is very powerful. Tcherepnin's added orchestral colour in the *Nocturne* remains controversial, but this too is very well played and recorded.

String quartets Nos. 1 in A; 2 in D.

(BB) *** BMG/Arte Nova Dig. 74321 51633-2 [id.]. Russian Qt.

(BB) ** Naxos Dig. 8.550850 [id.]. Haydn Qt of Budapest.

The popularity of Borodin's *Second Quartet*, using themes later made popular in the musical, *Kismet*, has tended to get in the way of appreciation of the equally delightful *First Quartet*, making this a very welcome coupling at bargain price. The Russian Quartet, a group of women players with exceptionally warm, fruity tone, make persuasive advocates of both works, with charm and tender lyricism brought out in the *First Quartet*, and with the sweetness and warmth in the *Second Quartet*. Warm, immediate sound to match.

The Haydn Quartet of Budapest play both works with a passionate display of Slavonic temperament. Their playing does not lack light and shade but the Unitarian Church acoustic makes their agreeably sumptuous textures seem forwardly orchestral, and the close microphones restrict the dynamic range. Perhaps that will not be a drawback for some listeners, and such opulence of tone suits the music, even if it robs the performances of subtlety.

String quartet No. 2 in D.

(BB) *** CfP Silver Double CD-CFPSD 4772 (2) [(B) id.]. Gabrieli String Qt – BRAHMS: *Clarinet quintet* **(*); DVORAK: *String quartet No. 12* ***; SCHUBERT: *String quartet No. 14.* ***

(M) *** Classic fM Dig. 75605 57027-2. Chilingirian Qt – DVORAK: *Quartet in F, Op. 96;* SHOSTAKOVICH: *Quartet No. 8.* ***

(M) **(*) Cal. CAL 6202 [id.]. Talich Qt – TCHAIKOVSKY: *Quartet No. 1.* ***

(M) **(*) Decca 425 541-2; *425 541-4*. Borodin Qt – SHOSTAKOVICH; TCHAIKOVSKY: *Quartets*. **(*)
(M) *(*) DG (IMS) Dig. 445 551-2 [id.]. Emerson Qt – DVORAK: *Quartet No. 12* **; TCHAIKOVSKY: *Quartet No. 1*. *(*)

As part of an outstanding Classics for Pleasure Silver Double compilation of Romantic string quartets, the Gabrielis offer a finely wrought, sensitive and thoroughly polished performance of the Borodin, warm in feeling. At less than the price of its main competitor, this is excellent value, for the recording is first class and beautifully transferred to CD.

On the Classic fM label the Chilingirian Quartet offer powerful, incisive performances of an apt and generous coupling, bringing together three of the most popular of Slavonic string quartets. With Levon Chilingirian an exceptionally alert leader whose violin-tone is given a slight edge by the full, immediate recording, rhythms in the Borodin are consistently well sprung, with no sentimentality in a warmly expressive account of the celebrated slow movement.

The Talich performance is characteristically refined and beautifully played; although there is no lack of warmth and the leader shapes the famous theme of the *Notturno* with ravishing purity of timbre and line, the performance lacks something in Slavonic voluptuousness compared with the Borodin Quartet. The digital recording is however first class, full and naturally balanced, and this is easily preferable to the Borodins' Decca alternative. Moreover the Tchaikovsky coupling is outstanding in every way.

The Borodins' version of the *Second Quartet* on Decca is very fine. However, the forward recording, though rich-textured, approaches fierceness in the CD transfer, and most will prefer a softer-grained effect.

The Emerson Quartet are unrivalled in terms of technical expertise. It seems curmudgeonly not to respond to their superlative playing, but it is all very chromium-plated. Good, if very present, DG recording.

Songs: *Arabian melody; Arrogance; The beauty no longer loves me; The false note; The fisher-maiden; From my tears; From the shores of thy far native land; Listen to my song little friend; The magic garden; The queen of the sea; The sea; The sleeping princess; Song of the dark forest; There is poison in my songs; Those people; Why art thou so early, dawn?*.
(M) *** EMI CMS7 63386-2 (3). Christoff, Tcherepnin, Reiss, Lamoureux O, Tzipine – *Prince Igor*. **(*)

Accompanied at the piano in all but three of the songs by the composer Alexander Tcherepnin, Christoff gives glorious performances of these rare items, sung, of course, in Russian.

Prince Igor (opera) complete.
(M) **(*) EMI CMS7 63386-2 (3). Chekerliiski, Christoff, Todorov, Sofia Nat. Theatre Op. Ch. & O, Jerzy Semkow – *Songs*. ***
(M) ** BMG/Melodiya 74321 29346-2 (3) [id.]. Petrov, Tugarinova, Eisen, Atlantov, Vedernikov, Obraztsova, Bolshoi Theatre, Moscow, Ch. & O, Mark Ermler.

In the colourful EMI recording of *Prince Igor*, Act III is completely omitted, on the grounds that it was almost entirely the work of Rimsky-Korsakov and Glazunov. Boris Christoff as both Galitzky and Konchak easily outshines all rivals. Jerzy Semkow with his Sofia Opera forces is most sympathetic, but the other soloists are almost all disappointing, with the women sour-toned and the men often strained and unsteady. The sound is limited but agreeably atmospheric.

Recorded in Moscow in 1969, the BMG/Melodiya set offers at mid-price a lusty, red-blooded performance of the traditional text, presented in close, vivid sound. The male cast could hardly be bettered, with Ivan Petrov most impressive as Igor and Artur Eisen as Galitsky equally firm and dark, and with Alexander Vedernikov a resonant, powerful Konchak. Vladimir Atlantov was unmatched at the time among Russian tenors, clear and unstrained, while Yelena Obraztsova as Konchakova was also in her prime with her firm, ripe chest-register. Though Tatyana Tugarinova has some squally moments as Yaroslavna, it is a firm voice, aptly Slavonic in timbre. The snag is the relative coarseness of the sound, underlining the hard-driven quality in Ermler's powerful treatment of the score. In the big set-numbers like the *Polovtsian dances*, one needs more subtlety, warmly committed as the results are.

Prince Igor: overture.
(M) ** Mercury 434 373-2 [id.]. LSO, Dorati – TCHAIKOVSKY: *Symphony No. 4*. **

Prince Igor: Overture and Polovtsian dances.
(BB) *** Belart 450 017-2 [(M) London 417 689-2]. LSO, Solti – GLINKA: *Ruslan and Ludmilla: overture* *** ✿; MUSSORGSKY: *Khovanshchina Prelude; Night*. ***

Solti's performances are among the finest ever recorded, with very good choral singing – even if the chorus takes a little while to warm up, the closing dance generates much adrenalin. The *Overture*, too, cuts a fine dash but is also warmly romantic, with a gloriously played horn solo.

Dorati's account of the *Prince Igor Overture* is bold and dramatic, its excitement very Slavonic in feeling. The recording is bright and vivid to match but is not out of Mercury's top drawer.

Prince Igor: Polovtsian dances.
(M) *** DG 419 063-2 [id.]. BPO, Karajan – RIMSKY-KORSAKOV: *Scheherazade.* ***
(M) *** Decca Phase Four 443 896-2 [id.]. Welsh Nat. Op. Ch., RPO Ch., RPO, Stokowski – MUSSORGSKY: *Night on the bare mountain* etc. **; TCHAIKOVSKY: *1812 overture* etc. **(*)
(M) **(*) Mercury (IMS) 434 308-2 [id.]. London Symphony Ch., LSO, Dorati – RIMSKY-KORSAKOV: *Capriccio espagnol* etc. ***

Karajan's Berlin Philharmonic version of the *Polovtsian dances* has great flair and excitement, though it lacks a chorus.

Stokowski misses out the percussion-led opening dance, but there is no question about the excitement he creates at the climax, with the chorus singing their hearts out. The recording is sumptuous and spectacular.

Dorati's Mercury recording is not among the most refined from this source, but no one could say that effect lacks vividness or boisterous vitality, and the climax is exhilarating.

Bortkiewicz, Sergei (1877–1952)

Piano concerto No. 1 in B flat, Op. 16.
(B) ** Millennium MCD 80116. Marjorie Mitchell, N. German RSO, Strickland – BUSONI: *Indian fantasy;* BRITTEN: *Piano concerto.* **

Sergei Bortkiewicz was born in St Petersburg, where he studied law as well as the piano. He studied and taught in Berlin before the First World War, when he settled in Turkey. While he was not a good enough pianist to make an international career, he was respected as a composer for the instrument. In the first of his three piano concertos, Russian and Lisztian influences mingle and there are some attractive ideas. Stephen Coombs's fine Hyperion recording, with the Arensky *F minor Concerto* as coupling, is the only current alternative and can be strongly recommended; it is uncut (CDA 66624 – see our main volume). The present recording was first published in the UK in 1964, though the sleeve gives no indication of its provenance. It attributes the orchestral contribution to the Nord Deutscher Rundfunk Orchestra, whereas the original Brunswick issue spoke of the Vienna State Opera Orchestra. It brings as coupling the only current account of Busoni's *Indian fantasy*.

Bottesini, Giovanni (1821–89)

Grand duo concertante for violin, double bass and orchestra.
(B) ** Ph. Duo 456 330-2 (2) [id.]. I Musici – MENDELSSOHN: *Octet* **(*); ROSSINI: *String sonatas* **; WOLF: *Italian serenade.* **(*)

Fun music for virtuosi, the Bottesini *Grand duo* needs panache above all, and I Musici do not play with quite enough of the magic that is essential if the work is not to outstay its welcome. But as a fill-up for the sure-fire Rossini *String sonatas* the performance is acceptable.

Boulanger, Lili (1893–1918)

(i) *Cortège; D'un matin de printemps; Nocturne* (3 pieces for violin & piano); (ii) *Du fond de l'abîme;* (iii) *Pié Jesu;* (iv) *Psaume 24;* (v) *Psaume 129;* (vi) *Vieille prière bouddhique.*
(M) *(**) EMI mono/stereo CDM7 64281-2 [id.]. (i) Menuhin, Curzon; (ii) Dominguez, Amade; (iii) Fauqueur; (iii; iv) Grunenwald; (iv) Sénéchal; (v) Mollet; (ii; iv–vi) Chorale Elizabeth Brasseur; (ii–vi) LOP, Markevitch.

Du fond de l'abîme is a haunting piece that quite transcends its very dated, dryish 1958 mono recording by Oralia Dominguez and the Lamoureux Orchestra of Paris under Igor Markevitch. The opening of the *Psaume 24* almost looks forward to the Honegger of *Le roi David*, and the *Vieille prière bouddhique* to Holst. The three pieces for violin and piano, *Cortège*, *D'un matin de printemps* and *Nocturne*, are more Ravel-like, and are beautifully played by Yehudi Menuhin and Clifford Curzon. An altogether fascinating disc: the music deserves three stars, the recordings only one.

Boulez, Pierre (born 1925)

(i) *Livre pour cordes;* (ii) *Pli selon pli.*
(M) *** Sony SMK 68335 [id.]. (i) Strings of New Philh. O; (ii) Halina Lukomska, Maria Bergman (piano), Paul Stingle (guitar), Hugo d'Alton (mandolin), BBC SO; composer.

Pli selon pli is a grandly conceived work to refute the idea that serialists and their progeny are necessarily cramped in their inspiration. The title (literally 'fold upon fold') comes from the poet Mallarmé, and Boulez's layers of invention are used to illuminate as centrepieces three Mallarmé sonnets. Neither these craggy vocalizations nor the purely instrumental passages are at all easy to understand in a conventional sense, but the luminous texture of Boulez's writing is endlessly fascinating and, for the listener with an open mind, this is a rewarding way of widening experience of the avant-garde. *Livre pour cordes*, adapted from an early string quartet, is a less demanding piece, but one equally worth studying. Definitive performances and excellent (late-1960s) recording under the composer's sharp-eared and electrifying direction.

Piano sonatas Nos. 1–3.
(BB) *** Naxos Dig. 8.553353 [id.]. Idil Biret.

The Boulez sonatas are well served by the gramophone – particularly No. 2, which Pollini has recorded for DG (see Instrumental Recitals below). Those with an interest in this repertoire will be well rewarded by Idil Biret on Naxos; she is more than equal to their technical demands and is given good sound.

Bouzignac, Guillaume (*c.* 1590–*c.* 1640)

Te Deum. Motets: *Alleluia, venite amici; Ave Maria; Clamant clavi; Dum silentium; Ecce Aurora; Ecce festivitas; Ecce homo; Flos in flores; Ha! Plange; In pace, in idipsum; Jubilate Deo; Salve Jesu Piissime; Tota pulchra es; Unus ex vobis; Vulnerasti cor meum.*
✿ (B) *** HM Dig. HMX 290850.52 (3) [(M) id. import]. Les Pages de la Chapelle, Les Arts Florissants, William Christie – Marc-Antoine CHARPENTIER: *Missa Assumpta est Maria* etc. *** ✿; DELALANDE: *Confitebor tibi Domine* etc. ***

You might call Bouzignac the Charles Ives of the sixteenth century. His music was almost totally forgotten for 250 years until rediscovered by a scholar at the beginning of this century. On record he has continued to be neglected, and this pioneering disc brings a revelation. The most refreshing quality of Bouzignac for the modern ear is that consistently he responds vividly and unpredictably to the texts of each of these motets. Often his response is so wildly individual that you would be unlikely to deduce which century the music came from, let alone which country. Vigour is the essence, as in the exuberantly light-hearted setting of *Jubilate Deo*, yet such a motet as *In pace, in idipsum* in its sustained lines has a rare meditative beauty, and the dialogue of *Unus ex vobis* even brings echoes of Russian Orthodox music. The response of William Christie, always a vivid interpreter of early music, brings out the colour in all its variety, for once with boy trebles (Les Pages de la Chapelle) added to the finely disciplined forces, vocal and instrumental, of Les Arts Florissants. This will be a thrilling discovery for many, helped by vividly immediate sound. While the separate issue (HMC 901471) remains available at full price, this now comes in a very highly recommendable Harmonia Mundi Bargain CD Trio, linked to a pair of other splendid discs, including the *Te Deums* by Charpentier and Delalande and much other fine music besides.

Boyce, William (1710–79)

Overtures Nos. 1–9.
(M) *** Chandos CHAN 6531 [id.]. Cantilena, Adrian Shepherd.

Overtures Nos. 10–12; Concerti grossi: in B flat; in B min.; in E min.
(M) *** Chandos CHAN 6541 [id.]. Cantilena, Adrian Shepherd.

This reissue offers Cantilena's complete set of the Boyce *Overtures* and includes the three *Concerti grossi*. Though these works do not quite have the consistent originality which makes the Boyce *Symphonies* so refreshing, the energy of the writing – splendidly conveyed in these performances – is recognizably the same, with fugal passages that turn in unexpected directions. Cantilena's performances readily convey the freshness of Boyce's inspiration. The recording is oddly balanced but is both atmospheric and vivid and provides a refreshing musical experience.

Symphonies Nos. 1–8, Op. 2.
(BB) ** Arte Nova Dig. 74321 34032-2. L. Festival O, Ross Pople.
(M) ** Carlton Dig. 30367 01722. Serenata of London, Barry Wilde.

Pleasing performances on Arte Nova of Boyce's eight symphonies written in either the three-part French or Italian overture styles and neatly scored, using flutes and oboes for added colour. They are nicely turned, and this is music that is easy to enjoy on modern instruments. The recording is truthful, well balanced if a little studio bound and somewhat less characterful than Pople's companion CD of Handel's *Water music*. Good value.

At the very opening of the Carlton digital disc, the ear notices that the sound is slightly abrasive: Barry Wilde, although using modern instruments, is clearly seeking a 'period-instrument' manner. The performances are lively and clean, enjoyably fresh, if not distinctive.

(i) Anthems: *By the waters of Babylon; I have surely built Thee a house; O where shall wisdom be found; Turn unto me, O Lord. Organ voluntaries Nos. 1, 2, 4 & 10.*
(M) *** Saga EC 3379-2. Arthur Wills, (i) Ely Cathedral Ch., Gerald Clifford.

The music of Boyce is most compelling, especially when sung with such warmth. The organ voluntaries have plenty of character. This makes a most stimulating introduction to valuable and rare repertoire, and the CD transfer catches the cathedral ambience to perfection.

Brade, William (1560–1630)

Hamburger Ratsmusik: Allemandes, Canzonas, Courantes, Galliards, Intradas (1609, 1614 & 1617 collections).
(M) *** HM/BMG Dig. GD 77168 (2) [77168-2-RG]. Hespèrion XX, Jordi Savall.

This collection of dances is absolutely delightful, varied in both content and instrumental colour, and excellently played by Hespèrion XX under Jordi Savall, while the recording, from 1981, is very good indeed.

Brahms, Johannes (1833–97)

CENTENARY COLLECTIONS

DG Complete Brahms Edition: Volume 1: Orchestral works: (i; ii) *Symphonies Nos. 1–4;* (i; iii) *Academic festival overture;* (iii; iv) *Hungarian dances Nos. 1–21;* (i; iii) *Serenades Nos. 1–2;* (i; ii) *Tragic overture; Variations on a theme of Haydn.*
(M) ** DG Dig./Analogue 449 601-2 (5). (i) BPO; (ii) Karajan; (iii) Abbado; (iv) VPO.

Sampler: *Hungarian dances Nos. 1–21.*
(B) *** DG Dig. 449 655. VPO, Abbado.

With variably focused recording, Karajan's last digital cycle (1986–8) of the Brahms *Symphonies* is not his finest, but he remained a natural Brahmsian to the last. The sound is full and weighty but tends to be thick and generalized in tuttis. Characteristically Karajan does not observe the first-movement exposition repeats. He draws a typically powerful and dramatic performance of the *First Symphony*, but his reading does not have the grip of his earlier account, made in the 1960s. The *Second Symphony* is far more impressive, suffering less from the thick, undifferentiated recording, when textures in this later work tend to be lighter. As a performance, it is the highlight of the cycle, a highly satisfying reading, at times warmer and more glowing than his previous versions, with consistently fine playing from the orchestra. The opening of the *Third Symphony* makes a massively bold impression, but again the ill-defined textures are a drawback, and here the omission of the exposition repeat may be counted much more serious. The *Fourth Symphony* sounds fresher, with the slow movement expansively lyrical, but the very purposeful finale is again heavily weighted. Overall this series lacks the spontaneous inspiration of Karajan's earlier recordings.

Abbado's performance of the *First Serenade* is vital, imaginative and sensitive, but the digital recording (1981) is rather dry and lacking in bloom, though clear enough. The *Second Serenade* was recorded much earlier (1967) and the sound is greatly to be preferred, with plenty of analogue bloom; the performance is very persuasive and marvellously held together, with dynamic nuances nicely observed. Again the Berlin Philharmonic play superbly both here and in the *Academic festival overture*, made at the same time. Karajan's *Tragic overture* is impressively done and, though one may criticize the recording balance, the result is powerful and immediate; he also gives an appealing performance of the *Haydn variations*. Abbado's account of the *Hungarian dances* has great sparkle and lightness, and this CD is additionally offered as a bargain sampler for the whole edition.

Volume 2: Concertos: *Piano concertos Nos.* (i; ii) *1 in D min., Op. 15;* (i; iii) *2 in B flat, Op. 83;* (iv) *Violin concerto in D, Op. 77;* (iv–v) *Double concerto for violin, cello and orchestra in A min., Op. 102.*
(M) **(*) DG Analogue/Dig. 449 607-2 (3). (i) Pollini, VPO; (ii) Boehm; (iii) Abbado; (iv) Mutter, BPO, Karajan; (v) with Meneses.

Although Pollini and the Vienna Philharmonic under Karl Boehm are given finely detailed recording, in the *First Piano concerto* other versions (notably Gilels) provide greater wisdom and humanity. Not that Pollini is wanting in keyboard command, but he is a little short on tenderness and poetry. All too often here he seems to have switched on the automatic pilot and, although the *B flat Concerto* under Abbado is much fresher and offers some masterly pianism, there are warmer and more spontaneous accounts to be had. (Admirers of Pollini will note that his accounts of the two piano concertos are also available – less expensively – on a DG Double.) Anne-Sophie Mutter's strikingly fresh version of the *Violin concerto* (available separately, coupled with the Mendelssohn *Concerto* – DG 445 515-2; *445 515-4*) can hold its own with the best, and the *Double concerto*, too, is particularly successful. With two young soloists Karajan conducts an outstandingly spacious and strong performance. Mutter conveys a natural authority comparable to Karajan's own, and the precision and clarity of Meneses's cello as recorded make an excellent match. The central slow movement in its spacious way has a wonderfully Brahmsian glow.

Volume 3: Chamber music: (i) *Cello sonatas Nos. 1–2;* (ii; iii) *Clarinet quintet, Op. 115;* (ii; iv) *Clarinet sonatas Nos. 1–2;* (ii; v; vi) *Clarinet trio, Op. 114;* (v; vii; viii) *Horn trio, Op. 40;* (v; vi; viii; ix) *Piano quartets Nos. 1–3;* (x) *Piano quintet, Op. 34;* (v; vi; viii) *Piano trios Nos. 1–3;* (xi) *String quartets Nos. 1–3;* (iii; xii) *String quintets Nos. 1–2;* (iii; xii; xiii) *String sextets Nos. 1–2;* (xiv) *Violin sonatas Nos. 1–3; F.A.E. Sonata: Scherzo.*
(M) **(*) DG Dig./Analogue 449 611-2 (11). (i) Rostropovich, Rudolf Serkin; (ii) Leister; (iii) Amadeus Qt; (iv) Demus; (v) Vásáry; (vi) Borwitzky; (vii) Hauptmann; (viii) Brandis; (ix) Christ; (x) Pollini, Italian Qt; (xi) LaSalle Qt; (xii) with Aronowitz; (xiii) Pleeth; (xiv) Zukerman, Barenboim.

The Rostropovich/Serkin partnership in the *Cello sonatas* proved an outstanding success and these performances, recorded digitally in 1982, are self-recommending. The *Piano quintet* also brings some very commanding playing from Pollini, and the Italian Quartet is eloquent too. The balance, however, is very much in the pianist's favour; he dominates the texture rather more than is desirable and occasionally masks the lower strings. There are also minor agogic exaggerations. However, neither these nor the other reservations need necessarily put off the prospective listener, even if at fortissimo levels the piano and strings in the 1979 recording could ideally be better separated. Karl Leister is a fine soloist in the *Clarinet sonatas* and his 1968 analogue recording is more convincingly balanced. The *Clarinet* and *Horn trios* date from much later (1981) and, like the *Piano quartets*, are digital. The *Clarinet trio* again brings excellent playing, although Leister's individuality comes over less strongly here than in the *Clarinet quintet* and the forward balance is less flattering. Norbert Hauptmann shines in the *Horn trio*, an enjoyably lively and warmly persuasive performance which is convincingly projected. The *Piano trios* also date from 1981 and, like the *Piano quartets* from 1982, are undoubtedly commanding. Tamás Vásáry is very impressive throughout, and the string playing from the three principals of the Berlin Philharmonic is hardly less magnificent. The *Piano quartets* are particularly successful. These artists have a thorough grasp of these unfailingly rich and inventive scores and penetrate their character completely; but again there is a problem with the recording balance, made in the Berlin Jesus-Christus-Kirche. The microphones have been placed very close and the effect is artificial: the players are very forward and it is as if one were listening to them in the confines of an enclosed space, without room for the sound to expand. The bright, forward timbre of the strings is achieved at the expense of a natural tonal bloom. The LaSalle Quartet give efficient, streamlined accounts of the *String quartets*, but their expressive style lacks tenderness. There is no question as to the polish and expertise of their ensemble, but these are not performances that bring one closer to the music. The 1978–9 analogue recording is bright and immediate. The Amadeus performances of the *String quintets* and *Sextets* were recorded a decade earlier in 1967–8, yet the sound is remarkably full and pleasingly balanced, while the music-making has plenty of life and warmth. Here the element of suaveness which at times enters the Amadeus ethos seems minimized by the immediacy. The playing is consistently polished, and tempi are well chosen. Karl Leister plays with considerable sensitivity in the *Clarinet quintet*, and there is much to enjoy here. Zukerman and Barenboim take an expansive view of the *Violin sonatas*, producing songful, spontaneous-sounding performances that catch the inspiration of the moment. Their 1974 recording is basically ripe and warm, but the CD transfer does not entirely flatter the upper partials of the violin timbre.

Volume 4: Keyboard works: Piano duet: (i) *Hungarian dances Nos. 1–21; Sonata in F min., Op. 34b; Souvenir de la Russie; Variations on a theme of Haydn, Op. 56b; Variations on a theme of Schumann, Op. 23; 16 Waltzes, Op. 39;* (ii) *4 Ballades, Op. 10; Fantasias, Op. 116; 3 Intermezzi, Op. 117;* (iii) *Pieces, Op. 76;* (ii) *Pieces, Op. 118–19; 2 Rhapsodies, Op. 79; Scherzo, Op. 4;* (iv) *Sonatas Nos. 1–3;* (v) *Theme and variations in D min.* (from 2nd movement of *String sextet, Op. 18*); (iii) *Variations on an original theme, Op. 21/1; Variations on a Hungarian song, Op. 21/2;* (v) *Variations and fugue on a theme of Handel, Op. 24;* (iii) *Variations on a theme of Paganini, Op. 35;* (v) *Variations on a theme of Schumann, Op. 9;* (iv) Arr. of BACH: *Chaconne from Partita, BWV 1004* (for left hand). Organ: (vi) *11 Chorale preludes, Op. 122; Chorale prelude and fugue in A min.; Fugue in A flat min.; Preludes and fugues in A min., G min.*

(M) *(*) DG Analogue/Dig. 449 623-2 (9). (i) Alfons and Aloys Kontarsky; (ii) Wilhelm Kempff; (iii) Tamás Vásáry; (iv) Anatol Ugorski; (v) Daniel Barenboim; (vi) Peter Planyavsky.

The Kontarskys' four-handed set of the *Hungarian dances* is vivacious and recommendable, but the *Schumann variations* and the *Waltzes* are a little short on charm. The *Double piano sonata* began as a string quintet before migrating to the keyboard and then ending life as the *Piano quintet*. The Kontarskys make heavy weather of much of it and are too prone to point-making and to interrupting the rhythmic flow of the music to be wholly recommendable. The opening theme is treated in an extremely mannered fashion and, generally speaking, one feels the lack of a true inner tension. Much the same applies to the *Haydn variations*. The *Souvenir de la Russie* is very lightweight and Brahms did not publish it under his own name. In Kempff's hands the four *Ballades* emerge very much as a young man's music and, like Opp. 116–19, these are highly individual performances with the Kempff magic most striking in the *Intermezzi*, Op. 117, and the *Pieces* of Op. 119. The Op. 79 *Rhapsodies* perhaps suit his temperament less obviously, but he plays them with conviction. He is more than acceptably recorded. Barenboim is allotted the *Theme and variations in D minor*, transcribed from the *Sextet*, Op. 18, plus the *Schumann variations*, Op. 9, and the *Variations and fugue on a theme of Handel*, Op. 24, and he shows himself in inspirational form. Both the latter sets have received more cohesive performances on record, but Barenboim has a magical way of making the listener's attention perk up at the start of each variation, and he shares his own sense of discovery with you. He is afforded first-class sound. To Vásáry, alongside the eight *Pieces*, Op. 76, go the *Variations on an original theme*, the *Variations on a Hungarian song* and the *Paganini variations*, Op. 35, which sound marvellously fresh and sparkling. His virtuosity is effortless and unostentatious and, generally speaking, he is well recorded too. The three *Sonatas* are brand-new recordings and one wonders why DG did not choose to use Zimerman's highly concentrated accounts. Ugorsky is infinitely more wayward, impulsive and self-aware, and in the first two *Sonatas* he fails to hold the architecture together convincingly. The first movement of the *F minor Sonata* is then pulled about unmercifully, and this performance is so eccentrically wilful that it cannot be taken seriously. Ugorsky is also very free in his handling of Brahms's transcription of Bach's *D minor Chaconne* for the left hand, which is more austere than the familiar Busoni arrangement, but it does not sound so here. The recording is excellent. Overall, this set is too flawed for a general recommendation.

Volume 5: Lieder: *Gesäng, Opp. 3; 6; 7; 43; 69–72;* (i) *91; Gedich, Op. 19; Lieder. Opp. 46–9; 85–6; 94–7; 105–7; WoO post. 23; Lieder und Gesänge, Opp. 32; 57–9; 63; Lieder und Romanzen, Op. 14; Ophelia-Lieder, WoO post. 23; Romanzen und Lieder. Op. 84; Die schöne Magelone (Romanzen), Op. 33; Vier ernste Gesänge (4 Serious songs), Op. 121; Zigeunerlieder, Op. 103.*

(M) *** DG Analogue/Dig. 449 633-2 (7). Jessye Norman, Dietrich Fischer-Dieskau, Daniel Barenboim; (i) with Wolfgang Christ.

Song-writing for Brahms was as natural as breathing, and this glorious collection, spanning the fullest breadth of his career, consistently bears witness to his unique genius, more as an exuberant songsmith than as a practitioner of the German Lied. For him melody lay at the very heart of song-writing and, even more than Schubert, his songs go straight to the heart of the German folksong. Through most of his career he was more concerned with the immediate musical challenge of a poem rather than its literary merit, but this magnificent collection, recorded with love and understanding and with not a suspicion of routine, effectively establishes that the Brahmsian approach to the world of Lieder provides a valid and important addition to that of ostensibly subtler Lieder-composers such as his friend, Schumann, or Hugo Wolf. Fischer-Dieskau's 1972 recording of the culminating *Four Serious songs* provides a superb conclusion, but the rest of the recordings were made between 1978 and 1982. Jessye Norman, full and golden of tone, consistently reveals her art at its most persuasive, in most ways matching even the imagination of Fischer-Dieskau, who is in equally ravishing voice. Not the least important element is the playing of Barenboim who, in accompanying Lieder, gives an impression almost of improvisation, of natural fluidity and pianistic sparkle to match every turn of the singer's expression. Beautiful, faithful recording, admirable transfers and first-class documentation.

Volume 6: Vocal ensembles: *Ballads and Romances, Op. 75; 14 Children's folksongs; 49 Deutsche Volkslieder; Duets, Opp. 20; 28; 61; 66; Liebeslieder, Op. 52; Neue Liebeslieder, Op. 65; Quartets, Opp. 31; 64; 92; 112; Zigeunerlieder, Op. 103.*

(M) *** DG Dig./Analogue 449 641-2 (4). Edith Mathis, Brigitte Fassbaender, Peter Schreier, Dietrich Fischer-Dieskau; Karl Engel, Wolfgang Sawallisch, Gernot Kahl; N. German R. Ch., Günter Jena.

This box includes all Brahms's vocal ensembles for solo voices with piano, and they receive fresh, brightly affectionate performances from an almost ideally chosen quartet of distinguished singers, accompanied by excellent, imaginative pianists. The writing here represents Brahms at his most engagingly domestic, though – as in the famous set of *Liebeslieder waltzes* – his imagination quickly took him beyond the normal capabilities of an amateur musical household. The result is seductive but surprisingly difficult. On the other hand, you find an essentially domestic delight in the lovely folksong settings of the *Deutsche Volkslieder* and *Volks-Kinderlieder*, originally devised for the family of Robert and Clara Schumann. There is treasure to be found throughout these four discs, recorded with a nice balance between intimacy and immediacy.

Volume 7: Choral works: Female chorus: *Ave Maria, Op. 12; 13 Canons, Op. 113; Psalm 13, Op. 27; 3 Geistliche Chöre, Op. 37; 4 Songs, Op. 17; 12 Songs and Romances, Op. 44.* Male chorus: *7 Canons; Little wedding cantata; Songs, Op. 41; 23 German folksongs.* Mixed chorus: *Begräbnisgesang, Op.13; 3 Fest- und Gedenksprüche, Op. 109; Marienlieder, Op. 22; Motets, Opp. 29; 74; 110; Geistliches Lied, Op. 30; Songs, Opp. 42; 62; 104; Songs and Romances, Op. 93a; Tafellied Dank der Damen, Op. 93b.*

(M) *** DG Dig. 449 646-2 (4). Mathis, Murray, Julia Raines Hahn, Gerhard Dickel, Gernot Kahl, Martin-Albrecht Rohde, Jan Schroeder, Hans-Ulrich Winkler; N. German R. Ch., Günter Jena.

This four-disc collection of Brahms's unaccompanied choral music ranges wide, representing all periods of his career in intimate, warmly characterful writing, whether in motets, part-songs, canons or folksong settings. Even more than other boxes in the DG Brahms Edition, it contains much buried treasure, not least the fine *Motets for double chorus*, Opp. 109 and 110, which open the second disc. These settings, particularly the *Fest- und Gedenksprüche*, Op. 109, using biblical texts, find Brahms using that elaborate medium in joyful complexity and understanding. The same CD includes the *Songs*, Op. 17, for women's voices, two horns and harp, ravishing pieces. The Hamburg choir gives radiant performances, beautifully recorded with no hint of routine: the recording is both clear and pleasingly atmospheric. Highly recommended.

Volume 8: Choral works with orchestra: (i; ii) *Alto rhapsody, Op. 53;* (iii) *German requiem, Op. 45; Nänie, Op. 82;* (ii; iv) *Rinaldo, Op. 50;* (ii) *Song of destiny (Schicksalslied), Op. 54; Song of the Fates, Op. 89;* (ii; v) *Song of triumph, Op. 55.*

(M) **(*) DG Dig. 449 651-2 (3). (i) Fassbaender; (ii) Prague Philharmonic Ch., Czech PO, Sinopoli; (iii) Bonney, Schmidt, V. Op. Ch., VPO, Giulini; (iv) Kollo; (v) W. Brendel.

When this box was originally issued on LP, all the music was conducted by Sinopoli; now Giulini's performance of the *German Requiem* has been substituted for Sinopoli's version, not altogether an advantage. Giulini's account is deeply dedicated but one which at spacious speeds lacks rhythmic bite. Meditation is a necessary part of Brahms's scheme, but here, with phrasing smoothed over and the choral sound rather opaque, there is too little contrast. With Sinopoli the effect was more consistently positive. The rest of the programme brings performances both challenging and controversial which – particularly in the rarer works – are a revelation. Fassbaender makes a strong, noble soloist in the *Alto rhapsody*, but it is the other works which command first attention in such a collection, not least the one generally dismissed as mere occasional music, the *Triumphlied* of 1870 which, Elgar-like, had Brahms doing his patriotic bit. Sinopoli, helped by incandescent singing from the Czech choir, gives it Handelian exhilaration. There is freshness and excitement too in the other rare works, with Sinopoli lightening the rhythms and textures. In *Rinaldo*, for example – the nearest that Brahms came to writing an opera – Sinopoli moulds the sequence of numbers very dramatically. René Kollo is the near-operatic soloist. The recordings, made in Prague, bring sound which is warm and sympathetic, with the orchestra incisively close and the chorus atmospherically behind, if sometimes a little confusingly so.

Decca '*Masterworks*'

(B) **(*) Decca Analogue/Dig. 452 328-2 (12) [(M) id. import].

Decca have celebrated the Brahms centenary more modestly than DG with a bargain set of 12 CDs in a slipcase, but also issued separately in pairs – as Decca Doubles at bargain price – and, while there is comparatively little to disappoint here, many collectors will prefer to make their own choice within this comprehensive anthology.

Volume I: *Symphonies Nos. 1–2; Academic festival overture; Variations on a theme of Haydn, Op. 56a; Tragic overture.*
(B) **(*) Decca Double 452 329-2 (2). Chicago SO, Solti.

Volume II: (i) *Symphonies Nos. 3–4;* (ii) *Hungarian dances Nos. 1–21.*
(B) *** Decca Double Analogue/Dig. 452 332-2 (2). (i) Chicago SO, Solti; (ii) RPO, Weller.

Sir Georg Solti came to the Brahms symphonies at the end of the 1970s, after a quarter-century of experience in the recording studio, having deliberately left them aside over the years. His study was intensely serious, and that is reflected in his often measured but always forceful renderings. Those who think of Solti as a conductor who always whips up excitement may be surprised at the sobriety of the approach, but in a way his Brahms performances are the counterparts of those he recorded of the Beethoven symphonies: important and thoughtful statements, lacking only a degree of the fantasy and idiosyncrasy which make fine performances great. The *Variations* are also very successful, and there is a splendidly committed account of the *Tragic overture*. However, it is the second of the two Doubles which offers the two finest performances: Solti's big-scale view of the *Third Symphony* is most compelling, and the *Fourth* shows him at his most vibrantly individual, with the *Andante moderato* second movement treated more like an Adagio, unfailingly pure and eloquent. This second box also includes Walter Weller's splendid, complete, digital set of the *Hungarian dances*. Here the RPO play with wonderful spirit as if they were enjoying every moment – and, indeed, as if their very lives depended on it. Weller secures excellent playing from every department of the orchestra. The recording is lively and bright, eminently truthful in timbre and with good, natural perspective.

Volume III: *Piano concertos Nos.* (i) *1;* (ii) *2;* (iii) *Violin concerto.*
(B) **(*) Decca Double Analogue/Dig. 452 335-2 (2). (i) Lupu, LPO, de Waart; (ii) Ashkenazy, LSO, Mehta; (iii) Belkin, LSO, Fischer.

Radu Lupu's approach to the *First Piano concerto* is that of the time when the piano was not the leonine monster it was to become later on in the century. His is a deeply reflective and intelligent performance, full of masterly touches and an affecting poetry which falls short of the thrusting combative power of a Serkin or Curzon. De Waart provides sensitive support and matches Lupu's approach admirably. Decca produce a particularly truthful sound-picture. This could be recommended enthusiastically to those who want a second, alternative view. However, Ashkenazy's account of the *Second Piano concerto* is less successful, its chief shortcoming being a lack of tension. With much beautiful detail and some wonderfully poetic playing, the performance still fails to come alive as it should. Naturally Ashkenazy is most successful in the lighter moments, but one is continually left uninvolved. On the other hand, Boris Belkin's performance of the *Violin concerto* is direct and spontaneous, a spaciously warm reading that makes a strong impression. No complaints about the recorded sound.

Volume IV: *4 Ballades, Op. 10; Intermezzo, Op. 117/2; 6 Piano pieces, Op. 118; Piano sonata No. 3, Op. 5; 2 Rhapsodies, Op. 79; Variations and fugue on a theme by Handel, Op. 24; Variations on a theme by Paganini, Op. 35.*
(B) **(*) Decca Double 452 338-2 (2). Julius Katchen.

Julius Katchen's style in Brahms is distinctive; it sometimes has a slightly unyielding quality that suits some works better than others. In general the bigger, tougher pieces come off better than, for example, the gentle *Intermezzo*. But such pieces as the two *Rhapsodies* are splendidly done, and so are the *Ballades*. The *Sonata* receives a commanding performance. However, the two sets of *Variations*, for all their sheer pyrotechnical display, are rather less compelling.

Volume V: (i; ii) *Cello sonata No. 2 in F, Op. 99;* (iii) *Clarinet quintet in B min., Op. 115;* (iv) *Horn trio in E flat, Op. 40;* (i; ii; v) *Piano trio No. 1 in B, Op. 8;* (ii; v) *Violin sonata No. 3 in D min., Op. 108.*
(B) *** Decca Double 452 341-2 (2). (i) Starker; (ii) Katchen; (iii) Brymer & Allegri Qt; (iv) Tuckwell, Perlman, Ashkenazy; (v) Suk.

The recordings of the *Piano trio* and the *Cello sonata* represent the results of Julius Katchen's last recording sessions before his untimely death. They were held at The Maltings, and the results have much warmth. Katchen and his team judge the tempi of the Op. 8 *Piano trio* admirably and they resist the temptation to dwell too lovingly on detail. The *Cello sonata* is given a strong and characterful performance, while Jack Brymer gives a masterly and finely poised account of the *Clarinet quintet*, which in terms of polish and finesse can hold its own with the very best. Apart from Brymer's well-characterized playing, the Allegri Quartet are also in excellent shape, and they are given the benefit of eminently truthful recording; but it must be conceded that something of the nostalgia and the melancholy of this score eludes them. The highlight of this set is the superbly passionate performance of Brahms's marvellous *Horn trio* from Tuckwell, Perlman and Ashkenazy. By contrast, Josef Suk's personal blend of romanticism and the classical tradition in the *Violin sonata* is warmly attractive but small in scale. An intimate performance, then, but most enjoyable and well recorded. All in all, this Double Decca is well worth investigating.

Volume VI: (i; ii) *Alto rhapsody, Op. 53;* (iii) *German Requiem, Op. 45;* (iv) *Song of destiny (Schicksalslied), Op. 54;* (v) *Geistliches Lied, Op. 30;* (vi) *Vier ernste Gesänge (4 Serious songs), Op. 121;* (i; vii) *2 songs with viola, Op. 91.*
(B) **(*) Decca Double Analogue/Dig. 452 344-2 (2). (i) Watts; (ii) SRO, Ansermet; (iii) Te Kanawa, Weikl, Chicago Ch. & SO, Solti; (iv) Amb. Ch., New Philh. O, Abbado; (v) King's College, Cambridge, Ch., Cleobury; (vi) Holl, Schiff; (vii) Parsons, Aronowitz.

Even more strikingly than in his set of the Brahms *Symphonies*, Solti favours very expansive tempi, smooth lines and refined textures in the *Requiem*. There is much that is beautiful, even if the result overall is not as involving as it might be. Dame Kiri Te Kanawa sings radiantly, but Bernd Weikl with his rather gritty baritone is not ideal. Fine recording, glowing and clear. Helen Watts gives a sensitive account of the *Alto Rhapsody*, while the *Song of destiny* brings a refined contribution from the Ambrosian Chorus with Abbado directing strongly. Helen Watts, too, is in good form in her sensitive performances of the two songs with viola as well as piano accompaniment. Cecil Aronowitz plays his obbligato with great finesse, and the combination of voice, viola and piano is particularly effective in *Gestillte Sehnsucht*, where the poet Rückert is in his most elegantly Petrarchan mood, telling of the soft evening sunlight on the woods, and the desire and longing of the solitary lover. The contributions of Robert Holl, accompanied by András Schiff, are slightly marred by the slow tempi chosen but are well sung, with due note taken of the texts.

ORCHESTRAL MUSIC

Piano concertos Nos. (i) *1 in D min., Op. 15;* (ii) *2 in B flat, Op. 83.*
(BB) *** Virgin Classics Dig. Double VBD5 61412-2 [CDVB 61412]. Stephen Hough, BBC SO, Andrew Davis.
(B) ** Teldec/Warner Ultima Dig. 0630 18948-2 (2) [(M) id. import]. Leonskaya; (i) Philh. O, Inbal; (ii) Leipzig GO, Masur.

(i) *Piano concertos Nos. 1–2.* (ii) *Academic festival overture; Tragic overture; Variations on a theme of Haydn, Op. 56a.*
(B) *** EMI forte CZS5 72649-2 (2). (i) Barenboim, Philh. O; (ii) VPO; Barbirolli.
(B) **(*) Ph. Duo 438 320-2 (2) [id.]. (i) Claudio Arrau; Concg. O, Haitink.

(i) *Piano concertos Nos. 1–2;* (ii) *Academic festival overture, Op. 80; Variations on a theme of Haydn, Op. 56a.*
(BB) *** CfP Silver Double CDCFPSD 4766 (2) [(B) id.]. (i) Tirimo, LPO, Sanderling or Yoel Levi; (ii) Hallé O, Loughran.

Piano concertos Nos. 1–2; Tragic overture, Op. 81; Variations on a theme of Haydn, Op. 56a.
(B) ** DG Double 453 067 (2) [id.]. Pollini, VPO, Boehm (*No. 1*) or Abbado (*No. 2*).

(i) *Piano concertos Nos. 1–2; Tragic overture; Variations on a theme of Haydn.*
(B) *(*) EMI CZS5 72013-2 (2) [CDZB 72013]. Arrau, Philh. O, Carlo Maria Giulini.

(i) *Piano concertos Nos. 1–2. Variations and fugue on a theme of Handel, Op. 24; Waltzes, Op. 39.*
(M) *** Sony Heritage MH2K 63225 (2) [id.]. Leon Fleisher; (i) Cleveland O, Szell.

(i) *Piano concertos Nos. 1–2. 4 Ballades, Op. 10; 8 Pieces, Op. 76.*
(B) ** RCA Dig. Twofer 74321 49183-2 (2) [id.]. Gerhard Oppitz; (i) Bav. RSO, Sir Colin Davis.

(i) *Piano concertos Nos. 1–2. 4 Ballades, Op. 10; 8 Pieces, Op. 76; Scherzo in E flat, Op. 4.*
(B) *** Ph. Duo 442 109-2 (2). Stephen Kovacevich; (i) LSO, Sir Colin Davis.

(i) *Piano concertos Nos. 1–2. 4 Ballades, Op. 10; Theme and variations in D min.* (from *String sextet, Op. 18*).
(M) *** Ph. Brendel Edition Dig. 446 925-2 (5). Alfred Brendel, (i) BPO, Abbado – SCHUMANN: *Collection.* ***

(i) *Piano concertos Nos. 1–2. Capriccio in B min., Op. 76/2; Intermezzi: in E, Op. 116/6; in E flat, Op. 117/1; in E min.; in C, Op. 119/2–3; Rhapsody in B min., Op. 79/1; 6 Pieces, Op. 118.*
(M) **(*) Decca 433 895-2 (2) [id.]. Wilhelm Backhaus; (i) VPO, Boehm.

Piano concerto No. 2 in B flat, Op. 83.
(M) *** Decca 448 600-2 (2). Backhaus, VPO, Boehm – MOZART: *Piano concerto No. 27.* **(*)

(i) *Piano concertos Nos. 1–2. Fantasias, Op. 116.*
(M) *** DG 447 446-2 (2) [id.]. Gilels; (i) BPO, Jochum.

Piano concertos Nos. (i) *1 in D min.;* (ii) *2 in B flat. Fantasias, Op. 116/1 & 4; Hungarian dances Nos. 6–7; Intermezzi, Op. 117/1–2; Pieces, Op. 76/2, 7–8; Op. 118/1–6; Op. 119/1–3; 2 Rhapsodies, Op. 79.*
(M) (**) EMI Rouge et Noir (SIS) mono CHS5 66418-2 (2) [CDHB 66418]. Wilhelm Backhaus, (i) BBC SO, Sir Adrian Boult; (ii) Saxon State O, Karl Boehm.

The Gilels performances were an obvious candidate for DG's 'Originals' series and can still hold their own against virtually all the competition, but the two concertos are also available separately – see below. However, the present set is offered at a reduced price and the remastered recording is quite outstanding: for these 'Legendary Recordings' DG have improved the sound well beyond previous incarnations of these works.

Barenboim's performance of the *First Piano concerto* with Barbirolli is among the most inspired ever committed to disc. The playing is heroic and marvellously spacious, and the performance is sustained by the intensity of concentration, especially in the pianissimo passages of the slow movement; the joyous finale uplifts the spirit and communicates a life-enhancing confidence. In the *Second Concerto* the first two movements remain grandly heroic and the slow movement has something of the awed intensity you find in the middle movement of the *First*, while the finale erupts gracefully into rib-tickling humour. This is a performance to love in its glowing spontaneity. Of the fill-ups, the *Tragic overture* is a performance of considerable distinction, the measured account of the *Academic festival overture* could do with more sparkle, while the *Haydn variations* again show the conductor at his finest. The late-1960s recordings have transferred splendidly to CD.

Stephen Hough, always an intense and imaginative recording artist, here gives keenly distinctive and deeply thoughtful readings of both Brahms *Concertos*. Clarity is regularly the keynote, so that with refined recording the transparency of textures may be disconcerting for those who insist on a fat Brahms sound. Far more than most in these works, however, Hough balances the contrasting claims of introspection and bravura in a refreshing and illuminating way. He adopts the widest range of tone and dynamic, with the recording beautifully capturing the hushed pianissimos in both works, not least in both slow movements. Equally, the incisive power of his bravura playing is thrilling, exceptionally clean in articulation with no fudging of detail even in the heaviest passages, with epic scale sustained in both of the first movements and with the finale of No. 2 sparkling delectably. Both recordings were made in 1989, but inexplicably No. 1 has been held back until this outstanding double-disc set, which in this format works out at super-bargain price.

Though Leon Fleisher's concert career was cruelly cut short when he lost the full use of his right hand, he made some superb recordings in the late 1950s and 1960s, most strikingly those with George Szell and the Cleveland Orchestra, then at its peak. The two concerto recordings are both masterly examples of their joint inspiration, bringing out the point that these are in many ways symphonies with piano, when Szell's direction is so powerful and incisive, as well as warmly expressive. Not that Fleisher in any way lacks individuality, for the crisp confidence of his virtuosity has a sureness in its musical and emotional thrust that carries one magnetically on, not just in the bravura writing but also in the poetic moments, hushed and concentrated. The sound is among the best offered by CBS at that period, with the piano forwardly balanced but not aggressively so. Generously, this Heritage issue also includes solo recordings by Fleisher of the *Handel variations* and *Waltzes*, similarly crisp and concentrated, though the 1956 mono sound here is rather clattery. Nevertheless this is an outstanding set; if you already have Gilels playing the concertos, these Cleveland readings offer a stimulating and compelling alternative view. However, it costs rather more than the usual upper-mid-price.

The *Second concerto* was Tirimo's début recording, made in 1974. He gives a commanding if measured account of the first movement, not always quite tidy in its occasional impulsiveness (but then neither is Richter). The second and fourth movements too have slow basic tempi, but the clarity of articulation gives a sharpness of focus to conceal that, and both are made exuberant and joyful. Similarly in the *First concerto*, made six years later, Sanderling and Tirimo amply justify their straight and measured manner in the thoughtful concentration of the whole reading. One has no feeling of the performance dragging, for the crisp, lifted rhythms prevent that in the outer movements, and the slow movement has a rapt quality, holding one's attention as a live performance would. With such excellent sound, this is one of the very best of Classics for Pleasure's Silver Doubles, and the set is made the more competitive by the addition of Loughran's accounts of the *Variations* and the *Academic festival overture*, fine performances both, although the latter has a rather subdued start.

Brendel's digital recordings of the two Brahms *Concertos* with Claudio Abbado and the Berlin Philharmonic as understanding partners also show him at his finest. In the *D minor Concerto* the result is both strong and spontaneous. His control of Brahmsian rubato is masterly, easily flexible but totally unexaggerated, and the basic tempi are set well and steadily. The balance is not too forward and the effect is warmly satisfying. The account of the *B flat Concerto* is hardly less striking. It has the advantage of impressive and weighty recorded sound, and the Berlin Philharmonic under Abbado produce an equally splendid warmth. The account of the Op. 10 *Ballades* is also a performance of distinction. There is some highlighting of subsidiary part-writing that may strike some as just a little self-conscious, but much else will delight the listener. The digital recording is first class.

Arrau's readings undoubtedly have vision and power, and the *D minor Concerto* is majestic and eloquent. There is some characteristic agogic distortion that will not convince all listeners, and, by the side of Gilels, Arrau seems idiosyncratic. In the *Second Concerto* his playing has a splendid combination of aristocratic finesse and warmth of feeling, and in both concertos Haitink and the Royal Concertgebouw Orchestra give excellent support. Excellent value, and the set is well documented. Arrau, when he re-recorded the two concertos for Philips, found a more suitable partner in Haitink and these later readings undoubtedly have both vision and power.

Leonskaya is an impressively direct and powerful Brahmsian, inclined to be stoic, but also thoughtful in her lyrical moments. Eliahu Inbal proves a more successful partner for her than Masur, and the Philharmonia provide a passionate opening for the *D minor Concerto*, although the secondary material is much more considered. Overall this is a spacious rather than a fiery reading and it lacks the electricity of the finest versions. The *B flat Concerto*, very broadly conceived, gives an impression of massiveness and is even less spontaneous in feeling, although the finale brings a lighter touch. These artists are given excellent, modern, digital recording, but their performances are no match for those of Gilels.

Wilhelm Backhaus was one of the most admired pre-war pianists, and he also enjoyed enormous *renommé* after the war as an interpreter of Beethoven and Brahms. His magisterial account of the *First Piano concerto* with the pre-war BBC Symphony Orchestra and Sir Adrian Boult on EMI offers a commanding view of the work's structure, though in terms of poetic feeling it is less convincing. Neither here nor in the *B flat Concerto* with Karl Boehm and the Sächsisches Staatskapelle does he exhibit the warmth of the later versions. The sound he produces has a marmoreal grandeur, but his approach is cerebral and there is a monochrome quality with little in the way of tenderness or spontaneity in either concerto. Admirers of this artist can be assured that the transfers are excellent.

Backhaus re-recorded the *First Concerto* for Decca in 1953 and no apologies need be made for the mono recording. The acoustics of the Musikverein ensure a fine spread of sound and the performance has great impetus and authority. The *Second Concerto* was made in the Sofiensaal in 1967 when Backhaus was in his eighties, and the rugged strength of his conception is matched by playing of remarkable power. His is a broad, magisterial account. The recording wears its years remarkably lightly: it sounds fresh, full-bodied and is finely detailed. (As can be seen above, this is also available separately in Decca's Classic Sound series, coupled with Mozart's *Piano concerto No. 27*.) The solo pieces date from 1956. Backhaus is again in excellent form, though the *Intermezzi*, which are played sensitively, come in for rather more subtle treatment than the *Capriccio* and *Rhapsody*.

Arrau's first stereo versions of the two Brahms concertos for EMI, made at the beginning of the 1960s, suffer from the feeling of a lack of affinity with the recording studio that has often afflicted him in the past. Nor is Giulini the ideal conductor for him, polished and weighty, without being really inspired. With the first piano entry in the *D minor Concerto* one knows exactly what sort of performance it is going to be, the notes detached with exquisite clarity. The slow movement builds to a big, authoritative climax, and the finale provides clear, muscular, unrushed playing. Arrau provides some delicious moments in the more graceful passages of the work but is never fiery in the way Curzon, for instance, is with Szell. The *Second Concerto* has a certain massive strength, helped by the full-bodied sound, but though the thought and sensitivity are there overall it hardly adds up to a very convincing performance.

Pollini's recordings with Karl Boehm and Abbado are discussed above, where they are additionally available at medium price in Volume II of DG's Complete Brahms Edition.

Gerhard Oppitz is much admired in Germany and he has the technique and dramatic power to cope with the formidable demands these concertos make. All the same, an imaginative and poetic dimension is missing and, despite good playing from the wonderful Bavarian Radio Symphony Orchestra under Sir Colin Davis and a warm acoustic, it offers no challenge to the even better-recorded Gilels–Jochum at mid-price or the many other versions with which the catalogue is endowed.

Piano concerto No. 1 in D min., Op. 15.

(M) *** Decca 425 082-2 [id.]. Clifford Curzon, LSO, Szell – FRANCK: *Symphonic variations;* LITOLFF: *Scherzo.* ***

(M) **(*) Sony SBK 48166; *SBT 48166* [id.]. Rudolf Serkin, Cleveland O, Szell – MENDELSSOHN: *Capriccio brillant* **; SCHUMANN: *Intro. and allegro appassionata.* **(*)
(BB) **(*) ASV CDQS 6083 [(M) id. import]. John Lill, Hallé O, Loughran.

(i) *Piano concerto No. 1. Variations and fugue on a theme of Handel, Op. 24.*
(M) (**) DG (IMS) mono 447 978-2 [id.]. Kempff, (i) Dresden State O, Konwitschny.

(i) *Piano concerto No. 1. 4 Ballades, Op. 10.*
(M) *** DG 439 979-2 [431 595-2]. Gilels; (i) BPO, Jochum.

(i) *Piano concerto No. 1. 4 Ballades, Op. 10; Scherzo in E flat min., Op. 4.*
(B) *** Ph. Virtuoso 442 110-2 [(M) id. import]. Stephen Kovacevich; (i) LSO, Sir Colin Davis.

(i) *Piano concerto No. 1. Capriccio in B min., Op. 76/2; Intermezzo in E flat min., Op. 118/6; Rhapsody in B min., Op. 79/1.*
(M) **(*) RCA 09026 61263-2 [id.]. Artur Rubinstein; (i) Chicago SO, Reiner.

Gilels's reading of the *D minor Concerto* has a magisterial strength blended with a warmth, humanity and depth that are altogether inspiring. Jochum is a superb accompanist and the remastered 1972 recording has a better focus on CD. The *Ballades* have never been played so marvellously on record, and the recording is very believable.

Clifford Curzon's 1962 recording, produced by John Culshaw in Kingsway Hall, returns to the catalogue, carefully remastered by the Decca engineers. The fierceness of attack in the upper strings, especially in the powerful opening tutti, sounds naturally focused on CD, adding a leonine power to Szell's orchestral contribution, and the piano tone is admirably natural. Curzon has the full measure of Brahms's keyboard style and penetrates both the reflective inner world of the slow movement and the abundantly vital and massive opening movement. The piano balance is most satisfying. For this generous reissue in Decca's Classic Sound series, the Franck *Symphonic variations* and Litolff *Scherzo* have been added.

Serkin's 1968 account with Szell, his third on LP, brought tremendous command and grandeur. This is undoubtedly a memorable performance and the support from Szell and the Cleveland Orchestra has great power. The Schumann coupling is very fine too. The CBS/Sony recording has been considerably improved in the current remastering and is fuller than before, but the balance still lacks a natural perspective and the sound ideally needs more opulence and depth. However, the hall's ambience prevents brashness, and admirers of Serkin will still want this CD.

Kovacevich's earlier Philips account of the *D minor Concerto* is also available on a Duo, which pairs it with the *Second Concerto* and also includes the solo piano music (see above). Those who want the *First Concerto* alone should be well satisfied with this separate issue on the Philips Virtuoso bargain label.

Rubinstein's Chicago recording was made in stereo as early as 1954 and the sound remains remarkably good, thanks to the sympathetic Chicago acoustics. This is a poetic and essentially lyrical reading, impulsive and intent on avoiding Brahmsian stodginess, for Reiner's control of the orchestra, volatile and imaginative, has a spacious strength. The three solo piano pieces, now added as a bonus, are characteristically chimerical. This is a fine memento of a great artist, not the most profound version but a consistently enjoyable one.

John Lill has the measure of the work's fire and drama, yet his playing is fundamentally classical; indeed, it is unfailingly impressive and scrupulous in its observance of every dynamic marking and expressive nuance. He is given warm and spirited support from Loughran and the Hallé – natural Brahmsians – even though woodwind intonation in one or two places is not wholly above reproach. Masterly and commanding playing, although at times there is a slightly reserved quality that inhibits unqualified recommendation. Nevertheless, with very good (1978) recording, this is well worth considering in the lowest price range.

Kempff's Brahms disc, issued to celebrate his centenary in 1995, offers 1957 recordings with harsh, even clangy sound in the concerto. Kempff, though as rapt and spontaneous-sounding as ever, playing with fine, individual imagination, seems however less concentrated than usual over the whole span. This reading is also available coupled (at bargain price on a DG Double) with stereo versions of the *F minor Sonata* and other major solo works, played by Kempff with great warmth and sympathy – see below. The *Handel variations* are much more characteristic, again transparent, with the crispest possible ornamentation, purposefully conveying pure joy. This calls for a separate issue.

Piano concerto No. 2 in B flat, Op. 83.
(BB) **(*) ASV CDQS 6088 [(M) id. import]. John Lill, Hallé O, Loughran.
(M) **(*) RCA 09026 64820-2 [id.]. Van Cliburn, Chicago SO, Reiner – MACDOWELL: *Piano concerto No. 2.* **(*)
(B) **(*) Sony SBK 53262; *SBT 53262* [id.]. Rudolf Serkin, Cleveland SO, Szell – R. STRAUSS: *Burleske.* *(**)

(M) ** Ph. 456 659-2. Alfred Brendel, Concg. O, Haitink.

(i) *Piano concerto No. 2 in B flat, Op. 83. Variations on a theme of Haydn, Op. 56a.*
(M) * EMI (SIS) CDM5 66093-2 [id.]. BPO, Karajan, (i) with Hans Richter-Haaser.

(i) *Piano concerto No. 2; 4 Ballades, Op. 10.*
(M) *** DG 439 466-2; *439 466-4* [435 588-2 (with *Fantasias*, Op. 116, instead of *Ballades*)]. Gilels; (i) BPO, Jochum.

(i) *Piano concerto No. 2. Intermezzi: in E min., Op. 116/5; in B flat min., Op. 117/2; Rhapsody in G min., Op. 79/2.*
(M) *** RCA 09026 61442-2 [id.]. Rubinstein, (i) RCA Victor SO, Krips.

The partnership of Gilels and Jochum produces music-making of rare magic and the digital remastering has improved definition: the sound is full in an appropriately Brahmsian way. Readers will note that this reissue is now recoupled with the *4 Ballades*, Op. 10 (instead of the *Fantasias*, Op. 116), which seems perverse when the Gilels version of the *First Concerto* has the same coupling.

Rubinstein was at his peak in 1958, and his technical mastery brings a charismatic response to the changing moods of the first movement, while the finale is a delight with its deftness of articulation and rippling lyricism. Rubinstein was lucky to have Josef Krips as his collaborator, for he brings a Viennese touch to the orchestra and matches Rubinstein's spontaneity. This is a reading which emphasizes the bright and luminous aspects of the work and is all the more refreshing for that, even if other accounts have more gravitas and weight. The three substantial encores are well chosen to make a miniature (15-minute) solo recital after the concerto; once again, the sound is realistic and the playing distinguished.

John Lill's 1982 version with the Hallé Orchestra under James Loughran is in many ways a strong account, well thought out, finely paced and without the slightest trace of self-indulgence, and it is the space and power of Brahms's conception that are given priority, rather than his poetry. Not that the performance is wanting in feeling or imagination. There is a stronger sense of the philosopher musing than of the poet dreaming. The recorded sound is eminently well balanced, and in the budget range this is competitive.

Van Cliburn, for all his youthful confidence and bravura, misses some of the finer shading. Even so, this remains an impressive performance. It is hardly an accident that Van Cliburn, like Gilels (who recorded the work in Chicago around the same time), had a really great Brahms conductor to accompany him, and it is interesting to go back to that other version conducted by Reiner, for there, with Gilels as soloist, a straighter performance is more impressive on the whole. To hear Van Cliburn at his finest, go to the finale, where the gypsy themes have an infectious gaiety such as only Rubinstein otherwise conveys. The Chicago acoustics ensure a full-bodied, Brahmsian sound, sounding better than ever in the current remastering.

Serkin achieves an ideal balance between straightforwardness and expressiveness, while the slow movement has a genuine 'inner' intensity, with some wonderfully expressive playing by the Cleveland principal cellist. Serkin chooses a comparatively slow speed for the finale, but the flow and energy of the music are not impaired and the Hungarian motifs of the second subject sparkle with point and wit. Unfortunately the piano tone is not as full as one would ideally like, but the remastering produces a firm orchestral image and the hall ambience contributes to a Brahmsian sonority.

Brendel's earlier rending is finely recorded, but the performance falls a little below expectations. He seems too judicious and adopts a deliberately restrained approach, so keen is he to eschew the grand manner. The results, though always commanding respect, are not wholly convincing; but the engineers produce excellent analogue sound.

Whether you like the Karajan/Richter-Haaser (Karajan's name is advisedly put first) interpretation as a whole depends on whether you respond to Karajan's super-subjective way of handling the tempo as if it were a rubber band. A romantic score it may be, and deserving of a warm and human touch; but the liberties taken with the speed of the first movement alone would be enough to put one off rubato for the rest of one's life. Richter-Haaser was a capable and artistic player, but he is here so obviously a pawn of the conductor that nothing can be done. Even though the recording of both piano and orchestra is of good, late-1950s vintage and it has been impressively remastered as part of EMI's Karajan Edition, it would be a risk to buy this version and try to live with it. There are no complaints about the performance of the *Variations*; it is very well played indeed.

Violin concerto in D, Op. 77.
(B) *** EMI Dig. CD-EMX 2203 [(M) id. import]. Tasmin Little, RLPO, Handley – SIBELIUS: *Violin concerto.* ***
(M) *** RCA 09026 61742-2. Heifetz, Chicago SO, Reiner – BEETHOVEN: *Concerto.* ***

(B) *** Decca Eclipse Dig. 448 988-2; *448 988-4* [(M) id. import]. Boris Belkin, LSO, Ivan Fischer – R. STRAUSS: *Violin concerto*. **(*)

(M) (***) EMI mono CDH7 61011-2. Ginette Neveu, Philh. O, Issay Dobrowen – SIBELIUS: *Concerto*. (***)

(M) **(*) EMI CDM7 64632-2 [id.]. David Oistrakh, Fr. Nat. RSO, Klemperer – MOZART: *Sinfonia concertante*. **

(BB) **(*) RCA/Navigator Dig. 74321 29245-2 [60479-2-TV]. Ughi, Philh. O, Sawallisch – BRUCH: *Violin concerto*. **(*)

(B) **(*) DG Double 453 142-2 (2) [id.]. Nathan Milstein, VPO, Jochum – BEETHOVEN; MENDELSSOHN; TCHAIKOVSKY: *Concertos*. ***

(B) *(*) EMI forte (SIS) CZS5 69334-2 (2) [CDFB 69334]. Gidon Kremer, BPO, Karajan – SCHUMANN: *Concerto* **(*); SIBELIUS: *Concerto* ** (with Andrei Gavrilov: HINDEMITH: *Sonata;* SCHNITTKE: *Quasi una sonata;* WEBER: *Grand duo concertant* **(*)).

(M) *(*) EMI CDM5 66101-2 [id.]. Gidon Kremer, BPO, Karajan (with MOZART: *Sinfonia concertante, K.297b* **).

(M) *(*) Mercury (IMS) 434 318-2 [id.]. Szeryng, LSO, Dorati – KHACHATURIAN: *Violin concerto*. **

(BB) * Naxos Dig. 8.550195 [id.]. Nishizaki, Slovak PO, Gunzenhauser – BRUCH: *Concerto No. 1*. *(*)

(i) *Violin concerto in D; Tragic overture, Op. 81*.

(B) *** Ph. Virtuoso 422 972-2 [(M) id. import]. (i) Hermann Krebbers; Concg. O, Haitink.

Tasmin Little gives a warmly satisfying account of the Brahms, at once brilliant and deeply felt. The rapt poetry she finds in the first two movements has rarely been matched, with powerful bravura set against yearning pianissimos. She also brings an element of fun to the Hungarian dance finale, rarely caught so winningly. Even more than in her earlier recordings, there is a dramatic thrust and intensity that mirrors live communication, strongly matched by the RLPO under Handley. At mid-price the disc is even more recommendable when it also contains an equally searching and exuberant account of the Sibelius *Violin concerto*.

Hermann Krebbers, concertmaster of the Concertgebouw Orchestra, here gives one of the most deeply satisfying readings of the Brahms *Violin concerto* ever recorded: strong and urgent yet at the same time tenderly poetic, and always full of spontaneous imagination. The total commitment behind the performance is not just the achievement of the soloist but also that of his colleagues and their conductor, who perform as at a live concert. The vintage (1973) recording has been successfully remastered: the effect, with the violin slightly forward but not too obtrusively so, is full and immediate. However, the range of dynamic here is less wide than in Tasmin Little's magnetic version and, instead of offering another major concerto as coupling, the Philips bargain reissue continues to offer just the *Tragic overture* as an appropriate encore.

Like the Beethoven with which it is coupled, the CD transfer of Heifetz's dazzling performance makes vivid and fresh what on LP was originally a rather harsh Chicago recording, more aggressive than the Boston sound in the Beethoven. With the CD, the excellent qualities of RCA's Chicago balance for Reiner come out in full, giving a fine three-dimensional focus. The speeds for all three movements may be fast, but Heifetz's ease and detailed imagination make them more than just dazzling, while the central *Andante*, at a flowing speed, is delectably songful.

Those looking for a bargain digital recording should be well pleased with Boris Belkin's 1983 Decca Eclipse reissue, particularly as it is now generously recoupled with the engaging Mendelssohnian violin concerto of Richard Strauss. The performance is deeply felt, direct and spontaneous and makes a strong impression. The tempo of the first movement is measured and spacious, but this is far more than a routine performance and, with excellent sound and a good balance, it is very competitive.

Ginette Neveu's is a magnificent performance, urgently electric, remarkable not just for sweetness of tone and her pinpoint intonation but also for the precision and clarity of even the most formidable passages of double stopping. The transfer from the original 78s brings satisfyingly full-bodied sound, surprisingly good on detail.

The conjunction of two such positive artists as Oistrakh and Klemperer makes for a reading characterful to the point of idiosyncrasy, monumental and strong rather than sweetly lyrical. Oistrakh sounds superbly poised and confident, and in the finale, if the tempo is a shade deliberate, the total effect is one of clear gain. The 1961 recording seems smoother than in its most recent incarnation.

Uto Ughi's account has the advantage of a strong and passionate orchestral backing from Sawallisch and first-rate (1983) digital sound, with a good balance. As with the Bruch coupling, this is a fresh and direct reading, not as charismatic as some, but with moments of considerable lyrical intensity and by no means unimaginative in the control of light and shade. In the bargain basement it is well worth considering – and even at mid-price, as issued in the USA.

To praise Milstein's version for the refinement and beauty of the accompaniment may sound like a backhanded compliment, and so perhaps it is when, for all the beauty and brilliance of the playing, this is not quite the flawless Milstein reading of the Brahms that he had previously put on record for other companies. Jochum secures playing of great warmth and distinction from the Vienna Philharmonic, and the hint of unease in the soloist is only relative. Those who want to hear Milstein in fine (1974) analogue sound can be safely directed here, for there are no such reservations about the other three performances on this DG Double.

Gidon Kremer came well recommended as a pupil of David Oistrakh, and the Brahms *Concerto* was one of his first major recordings, made in 1976. He proved an impressive violinist and he phrases very lyrically, but he established his artistic personality in a reading which at times is a little too inward-looking, with moments of self-indulgence, particularly in the first movement. From the opening bars Karajan provides an imposing accompaniment, and the recording, which is well balanced, opens out spaciously, but is not out of the ordinary. The forte set, for all its diversity and economy, does not constitute a challenge to the premier recommendations for the three major concertos. Although the sonata recital with Gavrilov is much more successful, this hardly alters the basic appeal of this collection.

It was with the LSO that Szeryng made his earlier version of the Brahms *Violin concerto* for RCA in the early days of stereo, but the conductor then was Monteux. That fact alone may help to explain the comparative disappointment of this 1962 Mercury account. Szeryng is rarely a forthcoming artist: he seems to require encouragement in order to give a warm performance, and here Dorati (unlike Monteux) fails to provide the right support. Tempi are relaxed and the result is generally unconvincing and often cold, even though inevitably the detail is admirably managed. The recording is not one of Mercury's most impressive efforts and is not kind to Szeryng's distinctive tone-colour, making the violin-timbre sound thin.

Takako Nishizaki seems somehow not quite comfortable in this concerto, as if straining to make a bigger, more ardent reading than is natural to her. Some of the upper tessitura, so pressured, is not very sweet, and she makes Kreisler's first-movement cadenza sound laboured. The coupled Bruch suits her better, but this is not one of her recommendable records.

(i) *Violin concerto in D, Op. 77;* (ii) *Double concerto for violin, cello and orchestra in A min., Op. 102.*
(B) **(*) Sony SBK 46335; *SBT 46335* [id.]. Stern, (ii) with Rose; Phd. O, Ormandy.
(M) **(*) Sony Stern Edition I SM2K 66941 (2) [id.]. Isaac Stern, with (i) NYPO, Mehta; (ii) Rose, Phd. O, Ormandy – BEETHOVEN: *Concertos.* **(*)
(M) ** Ph. 446 194-2 [id.]. Henryk Szeryng, (ii) with János Starker; Concg. O, Haitink.
(M) ** DG Dig. 445 595-2 [431 031-2]. Gidon Kremer, (ii) with Mischa Maisky; VPO, Bernstein.

Stern's glorious 1959 account of the *Violin concerto* with Ormandy is now given a coupling that is both generous and suitable, the mid-1960s' collaboration with Leonard Rose in the *Double concerto*. The two soloists unfailingly match each other's playing, with Ormandy always an understanding accompanist.

Once again a wrong choice has been made for the Sony Stern Edition: instead of the above 1959 account of the *Violin concerto* with Ormandy, the later (1978) version has been selected. Here Stern certainly has the measure of the *Violin concerto*'s lyricism and also its rhetoric. There are many thoughtful touches, but the orchestral playing under Mehta is not particularly distinguished; it is a little undercharacterized, and the recording is not first class either. The mid-1960s recording of the *Double concerto* is another matter. Here, each soloist has a creative ear in pointing a comment so that the response is made to sound like an unfolding conversation. The forward balance brings glorious tone, even if this means that there are no pianissimos (although one can tell when they are playing quietly from the tone-colour). The CD transfer is well managed; the sound overall is full and clear.

Szeryng recorded the Brahms *Concerto* three times in stereo. The first (with Monteux on RCA) was the most mercurial. Here he has the advantage of much richer (early-1970s) recording and a superb accompaniment from Haitink, who holds the whole structure spaciously together so that the comparatively slow tempi for the outer movements remain convincing. Szeryng's playing is lyrically passionate and assured, and it communicates strongly: the reading has impressive breadth. However, when Starker joins Szeryng for the *Double concerto*, the result remains obstinately unmemorable and ultimately disappointing. Although it is not easy to fault any individual detail, the overall impact is not strong. The recording balances both soloists very closely, though the engineers produce truthful results in other respects.

Kremer's version of the *Violin concerto* is powerful in attack, but he favours consistently fast speeds: his second movement is hardly a true *Adagio*. Bernstein, who accompanies him with the VPO, is much broader than the soloist, who tries to move things on; ultimately Kremer is too narcissistic and idiosyncratic to carry a firm recommendation. The *Double concerto* was recorded at concerts in the Vienna Musikvereinsaal in 1981–2. Mischa Maisky is a superb player with wonderful tonal finesse, but some of the dynamic extremes are self-conscious, while Kremer's playing is often posturing and, again, narcissistic. The playing of the VPO for Bernstein is marvellous and the reading is expansive and warm. The excellence of the recording is not in question: there is plenty of concert-hall ambience and a wide dynamic range with real body and presence. There is an admirable breadth about much of it, but this is outweighed in the first two movements by a want of real momentum.

(i) *Violin concerto in D;* (ii) *Hungarian dances Nos. 1 & 3* (orch. Brahms); *5–6* (orch. Schmedling); (iii; iv) *Symphony No. 4 in E min., Op. 98;* (v; iv) *Variations on a theme of Haydn (St Anthony chorale), Op. 56a.*

(BB) *** EMI Seraphim CES5 68526-2 (2) [CDEB 68526]. (i) Sir Yehudi Menuhin, BPO, Kempe; (ii) RPO, Kubelik; (iii) New Philh. O; (iv) Giulini; (v) Philh. O.

Reissued in EMI's Seraphim series (two CDs for the cost of one mid-priced disc), Menuhin's recording from the end of the 1950s can be given the strongest recommendation. He was in superb form, producing tone of great beauty, while the reading is memorable for its warmth and nobility. He was splendidly accompanied by Kempe, and the sound remains satisfyingly well balanced, and now compares very favourably indeed with any of the top recommendations for this work. Giulini's account of the *Fourth Symphony* shows him as a typically thoughtful and direct Brahmsian, using measured tempi: the very opening of the work has a coaxing warmth which is persuasive. The slow movement is beautifully played too, the finale is strong, and the only snag is the relative absence of bloom on the violins, although the recording itself is full and expansive. The *St Anthony variations* date from 1962 and show Giulini and the Philharmonia on their very finest form. The recording still sounds well, and this pair of discs is more than worth its modest cost.

(i) *Violin concerto in D, Op. 77;* (ii) *Symphony No. 2 in D, Op. 73.*

(B) *** Millennium Universal UMD 80394. (i) Erica Morini, RPO, Rodzinski; (ii) Pittsburgh SO, Steinberg.

This coupling is a treasurable discovery – two very early Brahms stereo recordings, the *Violin concerto* made in London in September 1956. Erica Morini gives an inspirational performance. Her initial presentation of the main lyrical theme in the first movement is ravishingly gentle and when it reappears on the half-tone after the cadenza the effect is of total magic, drawing a parallel with a similar sequence in the Beethoven concerto. Her playing in the *Adagio* is exquisite, again using lower dynamic levels to bewitching effect, while the buoyant Hungarian finale dances away with vigour and strength, yet never becoming merely lightweight. Artur Rodzinsky proves an ideal partner, strong in ritornello yet warmly flexible in phrasing and rubato, following the lead of his soloist and always taking care with detail, and with the RPO continually responsive. The recording is bright, the soloist rather too forward – her timbre is relatively slender – but there is plenty of contrasting weight in the orchestra. Steinberg then takes over for a splendidly shaped *Second Symphony*, warmly and passionately spontaneous and gripping. The Pittsburgh strings produce a rich body of tone in the slow movement (and indeed for the second subject of the finale). The *Allegretto* is taken a fraction faster than usual, but its grazioso feeling is not lost, and the finale has splendid impetus, with a thrilling coda. The recording is brightly lit, but the Pittsburgh Hall gives plenty of ambient weight. A most rewarding coupling, well worth its modest cost.

(i) *Violin concerto in D, Op. 77;* (ii) *Violin sonata No. 3 in D min., Op. 108;* (iii) *Variations on a theme of Paganini, Op. 35.*

(M) (***) EMI (SIS) mono CDH5 66421-2. (i–ii) Joseph Szigeti; (i) Hallé O, Sir Hamilton Harty; (ii–iii) Egon Petri.

In the immediate post-war years Szigeti recorded the Brahms concerto with Bruno Walter and the New York Philharmonic and again in Philadelphia with Ormandy. As part of the Brahms centenary celebrations, EMI have restored to circulation Szigeti's 1928 recordings with the Hallé Orchestra and Sir Hamilton Harty. Szigeti somehow blends serenity with a nervous intensity that is quite distinctive, and the transfer engineers have managed to bring colour to the faded sound. He forged a strong bond with Harty, having given the première of the latter's *Violin concerto* in 1908. The *D minor Sonata*, which he recorded with Egon Petri in 1937, is a reminder of their distinguished partnership, while Petri himself is represented by his celebrated account of both books of the *Paganini variations*. Exemplary transfers by Andrew Walter and Simon Gibson.

Double concerto for violin, cello and orchestra in A min., Op. 102.

(B) *** EMI forte (SIS) CZS5 69331-2 (2) [CDFB 69331]. David Oistrakh, Pierre Fournier, Philh. O, Galliera – BEETHOVEN: *Triple concerto;* MOZART: *Violin concerto No. 3;* PROKOFIEV: *Violin concerto No. 2.* ***

(M) *** EMI CDM5 66219-2 [id.]. D. Oistrakh, Rostropovich, Cleveland O, Szell – BEETHOVEN: *Triple concerto.* ***

(BB) *** Naxos 8.550938 [id.]. Ilya Kaler, Maria Kliegel, Nat. SO of Ireland, Andrew Constantine – SCHUMANN: *Cello concerto.* ***

(M) (***) RCA mono 09026 61485-2 [id.]. Milstein, Piatigorsky, Robin Hood Dell O of Philadelphia, Reiner – R. STRAUSS: *Don Quixote*. (***)

(M) ** RCA 09026 61746-2 [id.]. Heifetz, Piatigorsky, RCA Victor SO, Wallenstein – BACH: *Double concerto* *(*); MOZART: *Sinfonia concertante*. **

(M) **(*) Bruno Walter Edition Sony SMK 64479. Francescatti, Fournier, Columbia SO, Walter (with BEETHOVEN: (mono) *Triple concerto for piano, violin and cello in C, Op. 56* – Walter Hendl, John Corigliano, Leonard Rose, NYPO, Walter *(*)).

David Oistrakh's first stereo account with Fournier dates from 1959, but the recording was balanced by Walter Legge and the sound is remarkably satisfying. The performance is distinguished, strong and lyrical – the slow movement particularly fine – and, with Galliera and the Philharmonia providing excellent support, this version, coupled with three other outstanding concerto recordings, makes an ideal choice for bargain-hunters.

This (1969) EMI recording of the *Double concerto* has claims to be regarded with equal esteem as one of the finest of all versions. The remastered sound is full and vivid and has great presence. If it places the soloists too far forward, few will grumble when the playing is so ripely, compellingly Brahmsian and the solo timbres so richly projected. The *Andante* is glorious. Szell's powerful tutti and warmly sympathetic backing keep the Cleveland Orchestra well in the picture. Coupled with an equally arresting version of Beethoven's *Triple concerto*, this reissue is a superb bargain of the first order.

The Brahms and Schumann concertos make an excellent and apt coupling, here presented on the Naxos super-budget label in warmly spontaneous-sounding recordings, very well recorded. There are not many versions of the Brahms more warmly appealing than this, for the violinist, Ilya Kaler, is as clean in attack and intonation as is Maria Kliegel, who earlier impressed with her Naxos coupling of the Dvořák and Elgar *Cello concertos*. The difficult double-stopped chords for them both together in the finale are exceptionally true and clear. After freely expressive opening cadenzas, the main allegro is clean and fresh in attack, helped by full-bodied sound. Kaler and Kliegel make the second subject tenderly expressive without having to use exaggerated rubato. Similarly there is no self-indulgence in the soaring main melody of the central *Andante*. The finale is then unhurried but with dance-rhythms so beautifully sprung, and with such delicate pointing of phrase, that any lack of animal excitement is amply replaced by wit and a sense of fun.

The Milstein–Piatigorsky–Reiner account also ranks with the great performances of the *Double concerto*. It has warmth, vitality, nobility and power; Reiner gets some fabulous playing from his Philadelphia Orchestra. It comes with a no less remarkable *Don Quixote* from Piatigorsky which should not be missed. A very good transfer.

The partnership between Heifetz and Piatigorsky is a real symbiosis and they play very beautifully in the slow movement. Wallenstein's accompaniment is sympathetic, if not outstanding, but the close balance tells against the complete success of the performance, even though it has warm, expressive feeling.

Bruno Walter's recording with Francescatti and Fournier is welcome back to the catalogue. Fournier is magnificent, and if one adjusts to Francescatti's rather intense vibrato there is much to relish here, not least the playing of the Columbia Symphony Orchestra. The remastering is clear and immediate, and the real snag for most listeners will be the mono sound of the coupling. Walter's soloists make a fine team, but John Corigliano's violin is very near the microphones and is wiry in timbre; although the performance has plenty of vitality, its warmth is minimized by the top-heavy sound-balance.

(i) *Double concerto in A min. for violin, cello and orchestra;* (ii) *Symphony No. 4 in E min.*

(B) (**(*)) Dutton Lab. mono CDEA 5006 [(M) id.]. (i) Jacques Thibaud, Pablo Casals, Pau Casals O, Barcelona, Alfred Cortot; (ii) Dresden State O, Karl Boehm.

The Thibaud/Casals/Cortot recording of the *Double concerto* is a gramophone classic, with superb contributions from all concerned; and Mike Dutton's transfer (from 78 shellac pressings) is worthy of it. Sadly the sound-balance in Boehm's suberb 1939 account of the *Fourth Symphony* with the Dresden Staatskapelle sounds less convincing. The focus is admirably clear, but the strings lack body and there is not enough middle and bass (so essential in a Brahms symphony) to balance the clean, bright upper range. Both IM and RL grew up on this performance and still hold it in great esteem, but the results here are comparatively disappointing.

Hungarian dances Nos. 1–21 (complete).

❁ (BB) *** Naxos Dig. 8.550110; *4550110* (*Nos. 1–2; 4–21*). Budapest SO, István Bogár.

(B) *** Decca Eclipse Dig. 448 240-2 [(M) id. import]. RPO, Walter Weller (with DVORAK: *Slavonic dances, Op. 46/1–3 & 6–8*; cond. Dorati **(*)).

(M) **(*) Chandos Enchant Dig. CHAN 7072 [id.]. LSO, Neeme Järvi.

The Budapest recording of the Brahms *Hungarian dances* is sheer delight from beginning to end. The playing has warmth and sparkle, and the natural way the music unfolds brings a refreshing feeling of rhythmic freedom. Bogár's rubato is wholly spontaneous. The recording is warm and full, yet transparent, with just the right brilliance on top. This is an outright winner among the available versions.

The RPO also play with wonderful spirit, as if they were enjoying every moment, and Walter Weller secures excellent playing from every department of the orchestra. The Kingsway Hall recording is lively and bright, eminently truthful in timbre and with good natural perspective. Moreover the Decca Eclipse reissue offers six *Slavonic dances* from Dvořák's Op. 46 as a considerable bonus. Dorati's performances have comparable *brio*, and the recording (in the same venue) is just as vivid, if not quite so sweet on top.

The Chandos recording is characteristically sumptuous and Järvi is warmly affectionate, attractively coaxing the rubato of a dance like No. 7 in F major. There is plenty of spirit and flexibility elsewhere, and this set is certainly warmly enjoyable. Yet both Weller and (especially) Bogár are even more spontaneously Hungarian in spirit.

Hungarian dances Nos. 1, 3, 5–6, 17–20.
(M) *** DG 447 434-2 [id.]. BPO, Karajan – DVORAK: *Scherzo capriccioso; 5 Slavonic dances.* **(*)

Karajan's performances have great panache and brilliance while the brightly lit (1959) recording, reissued in DG's 'Originals' series, is given added fullness in the current remastering, and the superlative orchestral playing is by turns warmly affectionate and dazzling. The coupling offers comparably virtuoso performances of Dvořák's *Slavonic dances* and the *Scherzo capriccioso*.

Serenades Nos. 1 in D, Op. 11; 2 in A, Op. 16.
(M) *** Sony Theta Dig. SMK 60134 [id.]. LSO, Michael Tilson Thomas.

Serenades Nos. 1–2; Hungarian dances Nos. 1, 3 & 10.
(BB) *** ASV Quicksilva Dig. CDQS 6216 [(M) id.]. Philh. O, Francesco D'Avalos.

The reissue of Michael Tilson Thomas's digital recordings of the two *Serenades* (originally issued separately) on Sony's new Theta label tends to sweep the board, irrespective of price. His account of the glorious D major work has a sunny geniality and a youthful radiance that are most persuasive, and the A major is equally fresh. He gets admirable results from the LSO, and these readings have both vitality and sensitivity. The Sony recordings are natural and well detailed.

D'Avalos, too, gets some splendid playing from the Philharmonia, who readily respond to music with which they cannot be familiar. He opens the *First Serenade* beguilingly with svelte horns, and the gently chortling woodwind in the fourth movement is beguiling, as is the bouncing finale. The winningly genial account of the *Second Serenade* is no less persuasive, with rustic overtones brought out and rhythms sprung delectably. The recording is open and fresh with the lithe string-playing pleasingly caught. The full Brahms orchestral flavour is here, and at times one is reminded of the *St Anthony variations*. The three *Hungarian dances* (all orchestrated by Brahms himself) make an infectious bonus, with the orchestra conveying their enjoyment. A fine, inexpensive alternative to the Sony coupling, which remains first choice.

(i) *Serenades Nos. 1 in D, Op. 11; 2 in A, Op. 16; Academic festival overture;* (ii) *Tragic overture, Op. 81;* (i) *Variations on a theme of Haydn, Op. 56a;* (i, iii) *Alto rhapsody, Op. 53.*
(B) **(*) EMI forte (SIS) CZS5 68655-2 (2) [CDFB 68655]. (i) LPO; (ii) LSO; (iii) with J. Baker, John Alldis Ch.; all cond. Boult.

Sir Adrian Boult's warmly lyrical approach to the two *Serenades* is less ebullient and sparkling than that of Tilson Thomas or D'Avalos, yet he gives pleasure in a different way. The mellow opening of No. 2 is particularly appealing and with excellent orchestral playing he produces ripe performances, glowing and fresh. His spacious tempi are not always conventional, but Boult's way with these delightful scores is engaging enough to blunt any criticism, when the late-1970s Abbey Road recording is suitably full. What makes this inexpensive forte reissue even more attractive is the inclusion of Dame Janet Baker's devoted account of the *Alto rhapsody*, the performance essentially meditative, even though Boult's style is unlingering and the manner totally unindulgent, supported by warm, Abbey Road sound. The *Academic festival overture* opens the programme in a rather more extrovert fashion, and the *Variations* are also vividly presented and strongly characterized, the sound here rather more lively. The eloquent *Tragic overture* also shows Boult as a true Brahmsian. In playing time (just under two hours), however, this is rather less generous than some forte doubles.

Tragic Overture, Op. 81.
(M) *** EMI (SIS) CMS5 66109-2 (2) [id.]. BPO, Karajan – BRUCKNER: *Symphony No. 8;* HINDEMITH: *Mathis der Maler* (symphony). ***

A strong and impulsive, yet highly sympathetic performance from Karajan, showing him at his most charismatic. It is very well played and excellently recorded in the Berlin Jesus-Christus-Kirche in 1970. This set is a highlight of EMI's Karajan Edition, for the couplings are equally fine.

SYMPHONIES

Symphonies Nos. 1–4.
(B) *** DG Double 453 097-2 (2) [(M) id. import]. BPO, Karajan.
(B) *** RCA Dig. 74321 20283-2 (2) [60085-2-RG (3)]. N. German RSO, Günter Wand.
(M) **(*) Mercury 434 380-2 (2) [id.]. LSO, or (*No. 2*) Minneapolis SO, Antal Dorati.
(M) (**(*)) DG mono 449 715-2 (2) [id.]. BPO, Eugen Jochum.

Symphonies Nos 1–4, Hungarian dances Nos. 1, 3 & 10; Variations on a theme of Haydn.
(M) (**(*)) EMI CHS5 65513-2 (3) [ZHC 65513]. BPO or VPO, Furtwängler – BEETHOVEN: *Overtures.* (***)

Symphonies Nos. 1–4; Academic festival overture, Op. 80; Tragic overture, Op. 81.
(B) ** Decca 430 799-2 (4) [id.]. Chicago SO, Solti.

Symphony No. 1 in C min., Op. 68; Tragic overture; Variations on a theme of Haydn, Op. 56a.
(B) *(*) [EMI Red Line Dig. CDR5 69855]. LPO, Sawallisch.

Symphonies Nos. 2 in D, Op. 73; 3 in F, Op. 90.
(B) *(*) [EMI Red Line Dig. CDR5 69856]. LPO, Sawallisch.

Symphony No. 4 in E min., Op. 98; Academic festival overture; Song of Destiny (Schicksalslied), Op. 54.
(B) **(*) [EMI Red Line Dig. CDR5 69857]. Amb. S., LPO, Sawallisch.

Symphonies Nos. 1–4; Academic festival overture; Tragic overture; Variations on a theme of Haydn; (i) *Hungarian dances Nos. 17–21.*
(M) **(*) Sony SB3K 48398 (3) [S3K 48398]. Cleveland O, George Szell; (i) Phd. O, Ormandy.

Symphonies Nos. 1–4; Academic festival overture; Tragic overture; Variations on a theme of Haydn; (i) *Alto rhapsody. Op. 54.*
(M) *(*) Virgin/EMI Dig. VBQ5 61360-2 (4) [ZDMB 61360]. Houston SO, Christoph Eschenbach; (i) with Dunja Vejzovic & Houston Symphony Male Ch.

Symphonies Nos. 1–4; Tragic overture; Variations on a theme by Haydn.
(BB) *** RCA Navigator 74321 30367-2 (3) [(M) id. import]. Dresden State O, Kurt Sanderling.

Symphonies Nos. 1–4; Tragic overture, Op. 81; Variations on a theme by Haydn, Op. 56a; (i) *Alto rhapsody, Op. 51;* (ii) *Nänie, Op. 82.*
(M) **(*) Ph. Dig. 456 030-2 (4). (i) Jard van Nes; (i–ii) Tanglewood Festival Ch.; Boston SO, Haitink.

Anyone wanting Karajan's readings of the four Brahms symphonies should be well satisfied with this DG Double, which offers his recordings made in the late 1970s. The current remastering makes the most of the analogue sound: while textures remain fresh and clear there is now more weight in the middle and lower frequencies. The playing of the Berlin Philharmonic remains uniquely cultivated: the ensemble is finely polished yet can produce tremendous bravura at times, and there is no lack of warmth. Karajan's interpretations, with lyrical and dramatic elements finely balanced, changed little over the years. A very real bargain, hard to beat, but available in the USA only as an import.

Sanderling's 1971–2 Dresden recordings of the four Brahms symphonies make a clear first choice in the super-budget range. They originally appeared on the Eurodisc label and enjoyed a brief life in the LP catalogues. They have a warmth and humanity that stand out from the general run of Brahms cycles, with the Dresden orchestra responding to Sanderling's direction with playing of an unaffected and natural eloquence, so that the performances can stand comparison with any in the catalogue at any price. The magnificence of the Dresden orchestra is immediately displayed in the *First Symphony*, and Sanderling's reading has such a natural warmth and is so strongly characterized that it has the keenest claims on the collector. Everyone plays as if they meant every note and this sense of conviction gives the performance a rare eloquence. The Dresden performance of No. 3 is marvellously rich: the slow movement is particularly warm-hearted and generous in feeling, as is the autumnal *Poco allegretto*, and here the horn soloist has a slight vibrato to show that this is an East German orchestra. This is a deeply experienced reading and yet spontaneous. The *Fourth* balances fire with lyrical feeling; the symphony is beautifully played and fluently shaped. It has a sense of enjoyment that makes it very rewarding indeed, and the *Variations* are also very successful. In the passages we sampled alongside the LPs, the present transfers have remained faithful to the original without brightening the upper strings or adding the kind of glare one encounters in so many modern digital recordings. These were for RL the touchstone of Brahms symphony records for many years during the 1970s and early 1980s, and their return to circulation is a cause for celebration; with the three discs offered at about the same cost as that of a premium-priced CD, this is a bargain *par excellence*. Strongly recommended.

One must not forget, however, that on two bargain discs from RCA one can get a set of spontaneously compelling readings from Günter Wand which are also very well played. Wand's is a consistently direct view of Brahms, yet the reading of each symphony has its own individuality. In the *First* the unity is clear, even though Wand does not observe the exposition repeat. If No. 2 is the pick of the series, a sunny, characteristically glowing reading, the *Third* (this time with exposition repeat included) just as readily shows Wand's wise way with Brahms, strong and easy and steadily paced, bringing out the autumnal moods. If the *Fourth* at first seems a shade understated, with the first movement, taken at a fastish speed, sounding melancholy rather than tragic, it is still a strong reading and provides a generally satisfying conclusion. The early (1982–3) digital recording, however, although giving plenty of bloom to the *Second Symphony*, brings a degree of fierceness on string-tone elsewhere, which verges on shrillness in No. 3. However, for EG these readings are even more inspired than Sanderling's, and the sound does not lack weight and body.

While not an obvious first choice, Dorati's Mercury set of the Brahms symphonies, made between 1957 and 1963, is also a competitive proposition at mid-price, always vital and interesting. From the very opening bar of the *First Symphony* he presses onward with no lingering whatsoever and, if anything, the first movement of the *Third* (which overall is a splendid version, for the music suits his Hungarian spirit especially well) thrusts forward even more vehemently. Yet inner movements have plenty of warmth (if not quite as much as Jochum on DG) as well as lyrical ardour, while the *Andante* of the *Fourth* opens as a gentle idyll. Finales are consistently gripping: the great horn tune in the finale of the *First*, for instance, has seldom been played with greater breadth and power, and the closing movements of both the *Second* and *Third Symphonies* have exhilarating impetus and weight. The playing of the LSO is extremely brilliant and they back Dorati's wilful surging with enormous conviction. The Minneapolis orchestra also plays very well in the *Second Symphony*, where Dorati warms to Brahms's pastoral feeling at the opening of the first movement, yet takes hold of the onward flow as soon as the allegro gets under way, while the *Adagio* expands passionately. The recording throughout is brightly lit in the Mercury manner, a bit fierce at times, but there is supporting body (Watford Town Hall was the venue). No listener could fail to be stimulated by this musicianly, strongly involved and involving music-making.

Szell's powerful view of Brahms is consistently revealed in this masterful series of performances, recorded in the 1960s when he had made the Cleveland Orchestra America's finest. His approach is generally plain and direct, crisp and detached rather than smooth and moulded. Speeds are broad, and in the manner of the time no exposition repeats are observed, not even in No. 3. Though the sound, as transferred, is not as full as on the original LPs, it is clear and bright, with superb detail.

Furtwängler's EMI compilation brings together the live recording of the *First Symphony* that he made with the Vienna Philharmonic in 1952 and live recordings of the remaining three symphonies made with the Berlin Philharmonic in 1948 and 1952, presumably taken from radio sources. The performance of the *First* is perhaps the best and it has the best sound, which otherwise is disappointingly thin, lacking in body and with some harshness; but the electricity of Furtwängler in Brahms is vividly captured. His freedom of expression, with speeds varied far more extremely than by any latterday conductor, is essentially a spontaneous style, however carefully planned. Far from making the symphonies seem rhapsodic, with structure undermined, the results are totally cohesive, thanks also to Furtwängler's magnetic concentration. Though his moulding of phrase is affectionate, with rubato freely used (rather more than tenuto), these are not performances that set Brahmsian lyricism above drama. Despite the limitations of the sound, lacking in body but with plenty of detail, and despite the bronchial audiences in Nos. 2, 3 and 4, this is an inspirational set, with the makeweights an added attraction.

Jochum's mono DG recordings of the Brahms *Symphonies* are characteristically wayward and could hardly be regarded as a primary recommendation, even though the concentration of the playing generally holds the readings together. The *First Symphony* opens strongly and, for all the flexibility of tempi, there is underlying tension which creates a sense of ongoing momentum. Although the opening seems recessed (only partly the fault of the recording), the *Second* soon springs vividly to life. It is a characteristically warm, romantic performance in the German tradition, the contrasts between lyrical and dramatic in the first movement brought out confidently with no shame about speed-changes, and this applies consistently throughout, helped by the remarkably wide dynamic range of the recording. The finale has great vitality and moves to a thrilling close. The *Third Symphony* opens massively rather than exuberantly, and Jochum's spacious approach reminds one of the *First Piano concerto*. The effect overall is warm but mannered, although the central movements have a simple lyricism, and the close of the finale is tenderly elegiac. Again in the *Fourth*, which opens simply and delicately, there are wilful speed-changes which some listeners will resist, yet they follow the lyrical flow. The second movement is for the most part gently idyllic and lacks something in momentum. On balance, Jochum is more sympathetic and exciting in the last two movements, especially the finale, which (as with the *Second Symphony*) moves strongly to a zestful close. The Berlin Philharmonic playing is splendid throughout, and the mono recordings, made between 1951 and 1956, are amazingly good, full and clear, far more detailed and vivid than the original LPs. Jochum aficionados will certainly want this set, which is priced comparably to a Polygram Double.

Haitink's set comprises the four original, full-price CDs simply accommodated in a slipcase and sold at a discount (four CDs for the price of three) – so whether this represents a competitive proposition is a moot point; they get into this volume by the skin of their teeth. That apart, they are well-judged and cultured performances which receive the benefit of excellent and very natural recorded sound. Eminently recommendable and reliable performances though probably not a first choice, given the competition from Karajan, Sanderling and others.

Sir Georg Solti's Chicago cycle was recorded in the less-than-ideal acoustics of the Medinah Temple in 1978–9. The remastered sound here is not flattering: full-bodied, but with the upper strings rather grainy (especially in No. 1) and overlit. The bass is inclined to be rather weighty, and the whole effect is less than ideally refined. The layout on four discs is extravagant, even at bargain price. These are all spacious rather than impetuous readings, marked by poised playing from the Chicago orchestra. Solti's interpretations are soundly conceived; he is a true Brahmsian. They are discussed more fully as a pair of Doubles, above, among Decca's 'Masterworks' Brahms Edition.

With their extravagant layout on four discs (partly caused by the inclusion of the first-movement exposition repeats in the first three symphonies) Eschenbach's set could compete only if the Houston performances were truly outstanding, which they are not. They are beautifully played and very well balanced and recorded. But Eschenbach, highly musical Brahmsian as he is, has not yet entirely mastered the art of bringing a performance fully to life in the recording studio. No. 1 is singularly lacking in a strong profile, for here the conductor's easy, lyrical style works least well: the effect is more like a final rehearsal than a vivid consummation. In spite of a fine introductory horn solo, the finale hangs fire and really comes together only in the coda. The conductor's recessive manner may in theory be more suitable for the pastoral No. 2, but again there is simply not enough tension to hold each movement together, until the performance suddenly springs to life in the finale. No. 3 is much more impressive: the first movement immediately generates a stronger electrical charge. It sails off heftily, and there is plenty of momentum in the finale too, with impressive brass playing and the closing pages movingly autumnal. The inner movements, however, tend to sag just a little before the end, although the playing is affectionate and warm. Easily the finest Houston performance is of the *Fourth Symphony*, where the tension is consistently maintained and Eschenbach's steady lyrical flow, often impassioned, reminds one of Karl Boehm – and there can be no higher compliment. The *Academic festival overture* and *Haydn variations* are comparatively subdued, while the *Tragic overture*, which is coupled with the *Fourth Symphony*, is equally impressive. One of the highlights of the set is the moving account of the *Alto rhapsody*. Dunja Vejzovic is in glorious voice and the choral entry is a moment of serene magic, with the Houston Chorus beautifully balanced with the solo voice. But as a general recommendation this Virgin set is a non-starter.

As a Brahmsian, Sawallisch's great strength lies in his lyrical warmth. In his EMI set (reissued only in the USA on three separate, bargain Red Line CDs), Nos. 2 and 4 are markedly more successful than Nos. 1 and 3, thanks in part to the variable sound. No. 1, for instance, lacks dramatic bite in the outer movements, not helped by the rather edgy LPO violins, but with the slow movement raptly simple and direct. No. 3 is the least appealing performance of the four, with the first two movements low on tension. The finale expands warmly, helped by fuller sound. The playing of the LPO is not consistently polished but is warmly responsive. The layout means that, apart from the disc containing No. 4, which stands out, neither of the other two reissues really competes, although the extra items are done well enough, particularly the *Schicksalslied* (with No. 4).

Symphonies Nos. 1–4; Academic festival overture; (i) *Double concerto in A min., Op. 102. Hungarian dances Nos. 1, 17, 20 & 21; Tragic overture; Variations on a theme of Haydn;* (ii) *Liebeslieder-Walzer, Op. 52;* (iii) *Song of the Fates (Gesang der Parzen). Op. 89.*

(M) (*(**)) RCA mono GD 60325; *GK 60325* (4) [60325-2-RG; *60325-4-RG*]. NBC SO, Toscanini, with (i) Mischakoff, Miller; (ii) Ch., Artur Balsam, Joseph Kahn; (iii) (without O) Robert Shaw Ch.

The *First Symphony* starts very fast and intensely; but often speeds are surprisingly broad, and the *Fourth Symphony*, Toscanini's favourite, brings a magnificent performance. The soloists in the *Double concerto* were principals in the NBC orchestra, even though Toscanini allowed them less expressive freedom than they really needed. The CD transfers do everything possible for the dry and limited original sound.

Symphonies Nos. 1–3; Academic festival overture; Tragic overture.
❁ (B) *** EMI forte (SIS) CZS5 69515-2 (2) [CDFB 69515]. LPO, Eugen Jochum.

Jochum's EMI stereo versions of the Brahms symphonies were made in the Kingsway Hall in 1976; the analogue recordings, produced by Christopher Bishop, are outstandingly full and vivid, with a rich Brahmsian ambience which means that the strings are brilliant, without edge, the bass is ample yet clean, and the overall balance is very convincing indeed. These remastered discs indeed sound better than almost any of their mid- or bargain-priced competitors (they are smoother on top than Wand's RCA set, and the violin timbre is much more distinguished than with Sanderling). The DG engineers secured a remarkably fine mono balance with Jochum's earlier, DG set (which is admired by RL) and the playing of the BPO is rather more polished and sleekly integrated than the LPO. But the LPO playing is excellent too, the greater spontaneity of its performances carrying the listener along on a wave of inspiration, and this also applies to the exuberant *Academic festival overture* and the hardly less vibrant *Tragic overture*. Moreover the first-movement exposition repeats are included in the first three symphonies and in every case are made to seem essential to the structure. The high drama of the *First Symphony* immediately shows Jochum at his most persuasive, giving the feeling of live communication in the ebb and flow of tension and natural flexibility. He is not as free as Furtwängler was – a specially revered master with him – but the warmth and lyricism go with comparable inner fire. Equally, No. 2 is a warmly lyrical reading, expansive in the first movement – helped by the richness of the recording of the middle and lower strings, allowing extremes of expression – fast and exciting in the finale. The inner movements are beautifully played and the natural fervour of the orchestral response is most compelling, justifying the natural flexibility. The *Third Symphony* represents the peak of Jochum's cycle, and this is among the most rewarding versions of this work, irrespective of price. He conveys the full weight and warmth of the work with generally spacious speeds, finely moulded. The first movement is magnificent, leading to a passionate coda, and in the central movements there is an engaging autumnal feeling, while in the finale, starting from hushed expectancy in the opening pianissimo, he builds powerfully and exuberantly and then creates a feeling of elegy in the closing pages. For IM these performances are unsurpassed; at its very reasonable price, this forte reissue is an almost obligatory purchase for any dedicated Brahmsian.

Symphony No. 1 in C min., Op. 68.
(M) *** DG 447 408-2 [id.]. BPO, Karajan – SCHUMANN: *Symphony No. 1.* ***
(BB) **(*) ASV Dig. CDQS 6101 [(B) id.]. RLPO, Marek Janowski.
(M) ** DG (IMS) Dig. 445 505-2 [id.]. VPO, Bernstein (with BEETHOVEN: *Overtures: Coriolan; Egmont* **).

Symphony No. 1; Academic festival overture, Op. 80.
(M) *** Carlton Dig. PCD 2014 [id.]. Hallé O, Skrowaczewski.

Symphony No. 1; Academic festival overture; Tragic overture.
(M) *** EMI CDM7 69651-2 [id.]. Philh. O, Klemperer.

Symphony No. 1; Academic festival overture; Variations on a theme of Haydn, Op. 56a.
(M) **(*) Bruno Walter Edition Sony SMK 64470 [id.]. Columbia SO, Walter.

Symphony No. 1; Tragic overture; Variations on a theme of Haydn, Op. 56a.
(M) **(*) Ph. 454 133-2. Concg. O, Haitink.

Symphony No. 1; Serenade No. 2 in A, Op. 16.
(M) (**) RCA mono GD 60277 [60277-2-RG]. NBC SO, Toscanini.

Symphony No. 1; Variations on a theme of Haydn, Op. 56a.
(BB) **(*) Naxos Dig. 8.550278 [id.]. Belgian R. PO, Brussels, Alexander Rahbari.

(i) *Symphony No. 1; Variations on a theme of Haydn;* (ii) *Hungarian dances Nos. 17–21.*
(B) **(*) Sony SBK 46534; *SBT 46534* [id.]. (i) Cleveland O, Szell; (ii) Phd. O, Ormandy.

Karajan's 1964 recording of Brahms's *First Symphony* (the conductor's third version of five – DG 447 408-2) seems by general consensus to be regarded as his finest. The control of tension in the first movement is masterly, the orchestral playing is of superlative quality and the result is very powerful, with the finale a fitting culmination. The remastering has restored the original full, well-balanced, analogue sound, with plenty of weight in the bass (as is obvious at the timpani-dominated opening), yet detail is firmer. The coupling with Schumann's *First Symphony* makes this a very desirable record indeed – an obvious candidate for inclusion in DG's set of legendary 'Originals'.

Klemperer's spacious opening with its thundering, relentless timpani strokes is as compelling as ever and the close of the work has a comparable majesty; and the reading remains unique for its feeling of authority and power, supported by consistently fine Philharmonia playing. The remastered sound has gained in clarity while retaining its fullness.

Walter's set of the Brahms symphonies now returns to the catalogue in the second box of Sony's 'Bruno Walter Edition' (see below), but each disc is available separately. The recordings have been carefully remastered to emerge clearer than before but with very slight loss of bloom on the high violins; otherwise the sound is full and well balanced. Walter's first two movements of the *First Symphony* have a white-hot intensity that shows this conductor at his very finest: he conveys the architecture of the first movement strongly; the second movement too is most impressive, warm and with natural, unforced phrasing. The third movement begins with a less than ravishing clarinet solo and, though the 6/8 section is lively enough, the playing is not as crisp as in the first two movements. In the finale the performance reasserts itself, although some might find the big string tune too slow. The performance of the *Variations* is relaxed and smiling, and the genial account of the *Academic festival overture* gains from the extra brightness on top.

Skrowaczewski conducts the Hallé in a powerful performance of No. 1, both warmly sympathetic and refined, with sound which is fresh, bright and clear and with a good, open atmosphere. The first movement is ideally paced, but without the exposition repeat. His view of the finale is big and bold, but with a rather old-fashioned slowing for the final appearance of the chorale theme in the coda. Nevertheless it makes an excellent bargain-price digital choice.

Szell's account of No. 1 is one of the most impressive of his set. His bold, direct thrust gives the outer movements plenty of power and impetus, and the inner movements bring relaxation and a fair degree of warmth.

Opening powerfully with thundering timpani in the manner of Klemperer, though with generally more relaxed tempi, Alexander Rahbari gives an account of Brahms's *First* that is certainly recommendable. It is a strong, direct reading, spacious yet with plenty of impetus. The inner movements are well contrasted, with soaring eloquence in the *Andante*, and though there are one or two minor idiosyncrasies in the finale the reading holds together convincingly, even the broadening at the end. The sound is full and rich, yet detail is clear. The *Variations* bring a lighter, more lyrical Brahms style but are no less spontaneously successful. A very good choice for those with limited budgets.

Janowski's plain yet sympathetic reading is greatly enhanced on a CD which is full-bodied, clearly detailed and well balanced. The added fullness is much more flattering to the orchestral timbres and makes a very satisfying sound overall. Janowski, unlike most, does observe the exposition repeat in the first movement. At super-bargain price, this is excellent value.

As an interpretation, Haitink's performance with the Concertegebouw Orchestra from the early 1970s stands up well. It is a strong, well-argued reading of considerable power, supported by first-class orchestral playing. Haitink does not observe the first-movement exposition repeat, but not everyone will object to that. The lively and well-shaped *Variations* and the excitingly volatile *Tragic overture* are an asset, and the recording is spacious and well balanced, if now somewhat sounding its age. This would have been more competitive on a bargain label.

The finale in Bernstein's version brings a highly idiosyncratic reading, with the great melody of the main theme presented at a speed very much slower than the main part of the movement. On reprise it never comes back to the slow tempo, until the coda brings the most extreme slowing for the chorale motif. These two points are exaggerations of accepted tradition and, though Bernstein's electricity makes the results compelling, this is hardly a version for constant repetition. The remastered sound is fully acceptable.

The *First Symphony* is the performance Toscanini recorded in Carnegie Hall during 1941. It differs from the version he made ten years later with the same orchestra in the greater breadth of the first movement allegro, and in the tenderness he shows in the *Andante*, which at the same time remains completely unsentimental. The sound is not at all bad for the period. There is however little one can do with the 1942 broadcast – made in Studio 8-H – of the *Serenade*. The performance, too, is held together on a tight rein and sounds unrelaxed.

(i) *Symphonies Nos. 1 in C min.; 2 in D; Academic festival overture;* (ii) *Tragic overture;* (i) *Variations on a theme of Haydn; Variations and fugue on a theme by Handel* (arr. Rubbra).
(B) ** Sony Take 2 SB2K 63287 (2) [id.]. (i) Phd. O, Ormandy; (ii) Nat. PO, Stokowski.

Ormandy's insight as a Brahms interpreter in the concertos was always recognized, but not his understanding in this purely orchestral repertory. As in the concertos, his manner is direct and warmly purposeful, with speeds (on the broad side) which are generally kept steady, even in exciting codas. The glories of Philadelphia sound are resonantly exploited with close but not aggressive focus in these 1960s recordings. Only in the *Allegretto* third movement of No. 2 does Ormandy's slow tempo bring some stodginess, though many will prefer more athletic readings of both symphonies. The rarity is the arrangement of the *Handel variations* by Edmund Rubbra, which – in a rather un-Brahmsian way – gives the principal soloists of the Philadelphia Orchestra marvellous opportunities to shine, over the highly polished ensemble. The one item conducted by Stokowski brings a complete contrast, a 1977 recording which demonstrates what fire and energy the nonagenarian conductor had only six months before he died, with fast speeds and electric tension. This is very much a three-star performance and needs to be re-coupled.

Symphony No. 2 in D; Academic festival overture.
(M) ** DG (IMS) Dig. 445 506-2 [id.]. VPO, Bernstein.

Symphony No. 2; Tragic overture.
(M) *** Carlton Dig. 30367 00982-2 [id.]. Hallé O, Skrowaczewski.
(BB) **(*) ASV Dig. CDQS 6102 [(M) id.]. RLPO, Marek Janowski.

Symphony No. 2; Tragic overture, Op. 81; Variations an a theme of Haydn, Op. 56a.
(B) *** DG Classikon 439 478-2 [(M) id. import]. BPO, Karajan.

Symphony No. 2; Serenade No. 2 in A, Op. 16.
(BB) * Naxos Dig. 8.550279 [id.]. Belgian R. & TV PO (Brussels), Alexander Rahbari.

Symphony No. 2; (i) *Alto rhapsody, Op. 53.*
(M) *** EMI CDM7 69650-2 [id.]. (i) Ludwig, Philh. Ch.; Philh. O, Klemperer.

Karajan's 1964 reading of the *Second* is also available coupled with the *Third Symphony* – see below. But anyone preferring his account of the *Haydn variations* from the same period and of the splendid *Tragic overture* from a decade later will that find the present Classikon alternative has been very well transferred.

Klemperer's is undoubtedly a great performance, the product of a strong and vital intelligence. He may seem a trifle severe and uncompromising, but he was at his peak in his Brahms cycle and he underlines the power of the *Symphony* without diminishing its eloquence in any way. The *Alto rhapsody*, with Klemperer at his most masterful and Ludwig on fine form, is a beautifully expressive performance. Ludwig sings gloriously in the opening section, and later her voice blends naturally with the male chorus.

This completes the Carlton reissue of Skrowaczewski's Hallé performances of the four Brahms symphonies, undoubtedly his finest recording achievement during his not altogether successful Manchester era. With beautifully open and transparent sound, Skrowaczewski and the Hallé Orchestra give a measured and restrained reading of the *Second Symphony*, unsensational, fresh and thoughtful. The opening may seem sleepy, but Skrowaczewski's broad speeds and patient manner build up increasingly as the work progresses. With exposition repeat observed and a generous fill-up, plus excellent digital recording, luminous to match the performance, it is a good bargain-priced recommendation.

Janowski's plain style is least convincing in this most lyrical of symphonies, with rhythms tending to sound too rigid, whether in his metrical view of the slow movement or the rather charmless account of the third. The overture is much more successful, and the digital recording is excellently balanced: this is certainly worth considering at its super-bargain price.

Bernstein in his live recording directs a warm and expansive account, notably less free and idiosyncratic than the *C minor Symphony*, yet comparably rhythmic and spontaneous-sounding. Considering the limitations of a live concert, the recording sounds well. But this is by no means a first choice, even at mid-price.

Rahbari's reading of No. 2 is warm and persuasive, but the recording is almost impossibly cavernous, distantly placed with the reverberation totally obscuring detail in tuttis. The *Serenade No. 2 in A* for wind and lower strings fares better, though even there the focus should be sharper if the freshness of this early work is to be fully appreciated.

Symphonies Nos. 2–3.
(M) *** Bruno Walter Edition Sony SMK 64471 [id.]. Columbia SO, Walter.
(B) *** DG Classikon 429 153-2 [(M) id. import]. BPO, Karajan.
(B) *** Sony SBK 47652; *SBT 47652* [id.]. Cleveland O, George Szell.
(M) **(*) Ph. 426 632-2. Concg. O, Haitink.
(M) *(*) RCA/Melodiya 74321 40719-2 [id.]. Moscow PO, Neeme Järvi.

The new Bruno Walter coupling of the *Second and Third Symphonies* is very recommendable indeed. Walter's performance of the *Second* is wonderfully sympathetic, with an inevitability, a rightness which makes it hard to concentrate on the interpretation as such, so cogent is the musical argument. As though to balance the romanticism of his approach on detail, Walter keeps his basic speeds surprisingly constant, yet little of the passion is lost in consequence. It is a masterly conception overall and one very easy to live with. Walter's pacing of the *Third* is admirable and the vigour and sense of joy which imbues the opening of the first movement (exposition repeat included) dominates throughout, with the second subject eased in with wonderful naturalness. The central movements provide contrast, though with an intense middle section in II. There is beautifully phrased string and horn playing in the *Poco Allegretto*. The finale goes splendidly, the secondary theme given characteristic breadth and dignity, and the softening of mood for the coda sounding structurally inevitable. The upper strings are brighter than before, and at times (most noticeably in the opening movement of the *Third*) they sound thinner on top than in previous incarnations; on the other hand there is an added bite, and the ambient warmth and glowing woodwind remain, while there is plenty of supporting weight.

Karajan's 1964 reading of the *Second* is among the sunniest and most lyrical accounts, and its sound is competitive even now. The companion performance of the *Third* is marginally less compelling, but still very fine. He takes the opening expansively and omits the exposition repeat. But clearly he sees the work as a whole: the third movement is also slow and perhaps slightly indulgent, but the closing pages of the finale have a memorable autumnal serenity. A bargain.

With the Cleveland Orchestra at its peak and on its toes throughout, this is an inexpensive reissue that should be in every comprehensive Brahms collection. The Severance recordings have been improved immeasurably in the remastering for CD and, although the *Second* (1967) is smoother than the *Third* (1964), that works well, for the latter is well served by the brighter lighting. When the *Second* first appeared we were unimpressed by 'the characteristic Cleveland recording quality' and found that its unexpansiveness helped to give the feeling 'that Brahms's heart is being encased in a precision-made casket'. That impression all but disappears now. The orchestral virtuosity remains and at times Szell's care for detail does become predominant, but the underlying ardour and warmth are in no doubt, especially in the *Adagio*, while the *Allegretto grazioso* has an appealing simplicity. The *Third* is a magnificent performance. Szell had recorded it in mono previously for Decca with the Concertgebouw Orchestra, and the extra polish of the Cleveland players in no way detracted from a sense of committedness in the new interpretation. Szell is dashing and heroic at the opening, then slows very unselfconsciously for the lyrical second subject, neatly dovetailing speed-changes so that the casual listener will hardly notice them. The slow movement is very much on the slow side, warmly lyrical and full of expressive emotion. So is the lovely third movement – no reserve here, rather heartbreaking romantic nostalgia. The finale brings the expected return to the dashing, dramatic approach, and overall this is a reading to set alongside that of Bruno Walter, even if (as in the *Second Symphony*), the exposition repeat is omitted.

Haitink's account of No. 2 opens soberly. The sunshine quickly breaks through, however, so that the gentle high entry of the violins is magically sweet. This is a thoughtful reading, marked by beautifully refined string playing, but in a way it is too controlled. The *Third* is much more impressive, and Haitink's firmness of grip and lyrical eloquence make this a very satisfying account. The sound is fresh yet full in the Philips manner.

This coupling of the *Second* and *Third Symphonies* emanates from a six-CD set issued in honour of Neeme Järvi's sixtieth birthday and offering performances he made in the USSR at the beginning of his career. These Brahms symphonies date from 1966, when Järvi was twenty-nine, and are recordings made with the Moscow Philharmonic. They are straightforward and unmannered readings and are decently recorded. But even at mid-price they are not competitive in the face of Bruno Walter, either of Eugen Jochum's recordings or the Sanderling.

Symphony No. 3 in F, Op. 90.
(M) *** RCA 09026 61793-2 [id.]. Chicago SO, Fritz Reiner – SCHUBERT: *Symphony No. 5*. ***

Symphony No. 3; Serenade No. 1 in D, Op. 11.
(BB) *(*) Naxos Dig. 8.550280 [id.]. Belgian R. & TV PO (Brussels), Alexander Rahbari.

Symphony No. 3; Variations on a theme of Haydn, Op. 56a.
(B) *** Carlton IMP Dig. PCD 2039 [(M) id.]. Hallé O, Scrowaczewski.
(BB) *** ASV Dig. CDQS 6103 [(M) id.]. RLPO, Marek Janowski.

Reiner's magnificent performance dates from 1956. It is a glowing, marvellously proportioned account, exposition repeat included, and prepared in masterly fashion, and with the close of the work given a touchingly gentle, valedictory feeling. Yet there is no want of momentum in the outer movements and the lyrical intensity and warmth in the slow movement are equally memorable. Here the Chicago ambience adds to the atmosphere and it is a pity that in tuttis there is some loss of refinement in the upper strings. This has been improved in the CD transfer and this is a reading of stature. Besides the estimable Schubert coupling there is an exciting account of Mendelssohn's *Fingal's Cave overture*.

Skrowaczewski chooses consistently slow tempi for the central movements, yet with refined playing there is no hint of dragging. In the third movement he underlines the tender wistfulness, with a gorgeous horn solo in the reprise, full and spacious. The hush at the start of the finale then leads to a powerfully rhythmic performance, ending with a most refined account of the gentle coda. An excellent digital lower mid-price version, well coupled with a fresh reading of the *Haydn variations*.

The *Third* is the finest of Janowski's Brahms cycle, with surging outer movements (exposition repeat included) and the central *Andante* and *Poco allegretto* given an appealing, unforced Brahmsian lyricism. An exciting and satisfying performance, given bright, full, digital sound, not absolutely refined on top. The *Variations* also have plenty of impetus and are strongly characterized. In its price-range this is very recommendable.

Though the sound is not as reverberant in Rahbari's account of No. 3 as in the Naxos version of No. 2 from the same series, the recording is thinner, with less body. The first movement is strikingly slow, but well sustained, with exposition repeat omitted. The other movements are unexceptionably paced, and the pastoral quality of the *Serenade No. 1* is well brought out, offering some first-rate wind playing.

Symphonies Nos. (i) *3 in F, Op. 90;* (ii) *4 in E min., Op. 98.*
(M) *** EMI CDM7 69649-2 [id.]. Philh. O, Klemperer.
(M) *** DG 437 645-2 [id.]. BPO, Karajan.

In No. 3, there is a severity about Klemperer's approach which may at first seem unappealing but which comes to underline the strength of the architecture. Similarly in No. 4, Klemperer's granite strength and his feeling for Brahmsian lyricism make his version one of the most satisfying ever recorded. The finale may lack something in sheer excitement, but the gravity of Klemperer's tone of voice, natural and unforced in this movement as in the others, makes for a compelling result.

In his 1978 recording Karajan gives superb grandeur to the opening of the *Third Symphony* but then characteristically refuses to observe the exposition repeat. Comparing this reading with Karajan's earlier, 1964 version (coupled with No. 2), one finds him more direct and strikingly more dynamic and compelling. In the *Fourth Symphony* Karajan refuses to overstate the first movement, starting with deceptive reticence. His easy, lyrical style, less moulded in this 1978 reading than in his 1964 account, is fresh and unaffected and highly persuasive. The scherzo, fierce and strong, leads to a clean, weighty account of the finale.

Symphony No. 4 in E min., Op. 98.
(BB) (*) Naxos Dig. 8.550281 [id.]. Belgian R. PO, Brussels, Alexander Rahbari.

Symphony No. 4; Hungarian dances Nos. 1, 3 & 10.
(M) *** Carlton Dig. 30367 00272 [id.]. Hallé O, Skrowaczewski.

Symphony No. 4; Academic festival overture.
(BB) **(*) ASV Dig. CDQS 6104 [id.]. RLPO, Marek Janowski.

Symphony No 4; Tragic overture, Op. 81.
(M) *** DG Dig. 445 508-2 [id.]. VPO, Bernstein.

Symphony No. 4; Tragic overture; (i) *Song of Destiny (Schicksalslied), Op. 54.*
(M) *** Bruno Walter Edition Sony SMK 64472 [id.]. Columbia SO, Walter, (i) with Occidental College Concert Ch.

Symphony No. 4; Variations on a theme by Haydn, Op. 56a.
(BB) **(*) RCA/Navigator 74321 24206-2. Dresden State O, Kurt Sanderling.

Walter's opening is simple, even gentle, and the pervading lyricism is immediately apparent; yet power and authority are underlying. The conductor's refusal to linger by a wayside always painted in gently glowing colours adds strength and impetus, building up to an exciting coda, the unanimity and cutting edge of the strings bringing a cumulative effect. A beautifully moulded slow movement, intense at its central climax, is balanced by a vivacious, exhilarating Scherzo. The finale has an underlying impetus so that Walter is able to relax for the slow middle section. The new transfer is very successful: the recording has never sounded fresher or warmer and there is plenty of necessary weight in the bass. The *Tragic overture* has characteristic breadth and vigour, while the *Song of destiny*, both warm and dramatic, displays the capability of the chorus to good effect. The recording is excellent.

Bernstein's 1981 Vienna version of Brahms's *Fourth*, recorded live, is exhilaratingly dramatic in fast music, while the slow movement brings richly resonant playing from the Vienna strings, not least in the great cello melody at bar 41, which with its moulded rubato comes to sound surprisingly like Elgar. This is easily the finest of Bernstein's Vienna cycle and, with generally good sound, is well worth considering.

The refinement of the very opening in Skrowaczewski's Carlton version leads to an exceptionally satisfying reading, outstanding in the lower mid-price range and finer than many full-price versions. The phrasing is affectionate without ever sounding self-conscious, and the alertness as well as the refinement of the Hallé playing confirms the excellence; if the coupling of only three *Hungarian dances* is hardly generous, they are certainly attractively presented.

Sanderling's super-bargain Dresden version has genuine fire and eloquence. It is finely recorded (in

1971), beautifully played and splendidly shaped, with some of the classical strength that distinguished this orchestra's account of the work under Karl Boehm in the days of 78s. However, it has a warmth and sense of enjoyment that make it a very rewarding performance indeed, and the *Variations* are also very successful. The warmth of the Dresden acoustic means that the quality remains pleasingly full, although the violins sound a little thin on top.

Following the success of the *Third*, Janowski gives a refreshingly direct reading of the *Fourth*. Speeds are unexceptionable, with the second-movement *Andante*, introduced very gently, slower than usual, but certainly expressive. The recording sounds vivid and full on CD and the weight of the final *Passacaglia* is well established. The coda of the symphony, like the overture which follows, brings real excitement.

After the success of his recording of Brahms's *First*, Rahbari's account of the *Fourth* is a great disappointment. His weighty approach to the outer movements brings a serious lack of momentum and the reading entirely fails to take off.

(i) *Symphony No. 4;* (ii) *German Requiem, Op. 45;* (iii) *Schicksalslied, Op. 54.*
(B) **(*) EMI forte (SIS) Analogue/Dig. CZS5 69518-2 (2) [CDFB 69518]. (i) LPO, Jochum; (ii) Jessye Norman, Jorma Hynninen; (ii–iii) BBC Symphony Ch., LPO Ch., LPO, Tennstedt.

In the *Fourth Symphony*, Jochum's very opening phrase establishes the reading as warmly affectionate and, as in Bruckner, he combines a high degree of expressive flexibility with a rapt concentration, which holds the symphonic structure strongly together. Though the orchestra is British and the LPO is in fine form, this represents the German tradition at its most communicative; more than that, however, it demonstrates Jochum's passionate feeling for Brahms, with its spirit of soaring lyricism and – in the finale especially – a strong, even irresistible forward momentum. Although the performance has its idiosyncrasies of tempo, it is highly compelling in every bar, and it is a great pity that the appeal of this inexpensive reissue is somewhat diluted by the performance of the coupling, which may not be to all tastes.

Tennstedt's is an unusually spacious view of the *Requiem*, with speeds slower than on any rival version. His dedication generally sustains them well, with a reverential manner always alert, never becoming merely monumental, though the choir's ensemble is not always perfect. Jorma Hynninen proves an excellent soloist. What does sound monumental rather than moving is Jessye Norman's solo, *Ihr habt nun Traurigkeit*, though the golden tone is glorious. The *Schicksalslied* is also given a spacious, strong performance, with the London Philharmonic Choir singing dedicatedly, and the 1984–5 digital recording is spacious to match.

Variations on a theme of Haydn (St Anthony chorale), Op. 56a.
(M) *** Decca 452 893-2 [id.]. LSO, Pierre Monteux – HAYDN: *Symphonies Nos. 94 & 101.* ***

Monteux's performance of a work that can readily seem too easy-going is quite riveting. The orchestral playing is excellent and the vigorous style gives the music a splendid forward impulse: the listener is gripped from first bar to last. The bright (1958) Kingsway Hall recording reveals the depth of sonority of Brahms's scoring at the very opening, but is otherwise slightly less glowing than in the Haydn couplings.

CHAMBER MUSIC

Complete chamber music

(i; ii) *Cello sonatas Nos. 1–2;* (iii; iv) *Clarinet quintet in B min., Op. 115;* (v; vi) *Clarinet sonatas Nos. 1–2;* (v; vii) *Clarinet trio in A min., Op. 114;* (ii; viii; ix) *Horn trio in E flat, Op. 40;* (x; xi) *Piano quartets Nos. 1–3;* (iv; xii) *Piano quintet in F min., Op. 34;* (x) *Piano trios Nos. 1–4;* (xiii) *String quartets Nos. 1–3;* (iv) *String quintets Nos. 1–2; String sextets Nos. 1–2;* (ii; ix) *Violin sonatas Nos. 1–3.*
(B) *** Ph. 454 073-2 (11) [(M) id. import]. (i) Starker; (ii) Sebók; (iii) Stähr; (iv) BPO Octet (members); (v) Pieterson; (vi) H. Menuhin; (vii) Pressler, Greenhouse; (viii) Orval; (ix) Grumiaux; (x) Beaux Arts Trio; (xi) Trampler (viola); (xii) Haas; (xiii) Quartetto Italiano.

This Philips bargain box of Brahms's chamber music happily combines a series of warmly appealing recordings made in Germany with other distinguished contributions from the Beaux Arts Trio and the Quartetto Italiano. Grumiaux and Starker lead the instrumental duos with slightly less success, but Starker and Sebók compensate by their passionate and subtle response to the *Cello sonatas* (this is a Mercury recording and is discussed separately below). The Berlin performance of the *Clarinet quintet* (led by Herbert Stähr) is exceptionally beautiful, and it is faithful to Brahms's intentions, an outstanding version in every way. It is an autumnal reading, and is recorded with comparable refinement. In the *Clarinet trio* George Pieterson is the soloist, another first-rate artist, and this account with members of the Beaux Arts group offers masterly playing from all three participants, and a very well-integrated recording. The balance in the *Horn trio* is managed even more adroitly, among the most successful on record. The fine horn player, Francis Orval, seeks not to dominate but to be one of the group, and he achieves this without any loss of personality in his playing (note the richness of his contribution to the Trio of the Scherzo). The performance is warmly lyrical and completely spontaneous, with a racy finale to round off a particularly satisfying reading, never forced but deeply felt. Arthur Grumiaux's contribution is a constant pleasure, and the pianist, György Sebók, is hardly less admirable. The Beaux Arts set of *Piano trios* includes the *A major Trio*, which may or may not be authentic but which is certainly rewarding. The performances are splendid, with strongly paced, dramatic allegros, consistently alert, and with thoughtful, sensitive playing in slow movements. Characterization is positive (yet not over-forceful), and structural considerations are well judged: each reading has its own special individuality. The sound is first class. Their recording of the *Piano quartets* is bold and full-bloodedly Brahmsian in outer movements, which have splendid impetus. Thoughtful, sensitive playing in slow movements, lively tempi in allegros, characteristic musicianship plus spontaneity combine to make this set highly recommendable throughout. Not surprisingly, the *String quartets* are marvellously played by the Italian Quartet, with detail sensitively observed. The two Op. 51 *Quartets* are especially fine, with a searching and penetrating reading of the first revealing depths that elude many other performers. The Berlin Philharmonic group return for the *String quintets* and their playing is searching and artistically satisfying, combining freshness with polish, warmth with well-integrated detail. The sound, though not entirely transparent, is full, warm and well balanced. In the *Piano quintet* they are joined by the excellent Werner Haas, and this is another performance which is strongly felt, with the *Andante* combining warmth with an imaginative use of colour and dynamic contrast. They then respond readily to the glories of the *Second Sextet*, playing with warmth and eloquence. The *First* is slightly less committed but still shows a great degree of feeling. The sound has a touch of shrillness. The *Violin sonatas* bring highly musical if rather mellifluous playing from Arthur Grumiaux, expertly partnered by György Sebók, and the overall effect is perhaps a shade bland. But this is still enjoyable, and the recording is eminently acceptable.

Cello sonatas Nos. 1 in E min., Op. 38; 2 in F, Op. 99.
(M) *** Mercury 434 377-2 [id.]. Starker, Sebók – MENDELSSOHN: *Cello sonata No. 2.* ***
(M) ** Erato/Warner 4509 96950-2. Janos Starker, György Sebók.

Starker was on his finest form when he made his Mercury recordings, and he had a splendid and understanding partner in György Sebók. These highly spontaneous performances rank alongside those by Rostropovich and Serkin: they have ardour and subtlety and an impressive sense of line. The 1964 recording is very well balanced, the acoustic is warm, yet the focus is admirably clear. With an equally fine account of the Mendelssohn *D major Sonata*, the measure is greater than with most competitors, and this CD comes at mid-price.

Starker and Sebók re-recorded the sonatas in 1979. The performances are less obviously bold, more reflective, and some listeners will like the improvisatory feeling about the playing. They are well recorded, but neither the playing nor the resonant sound provides the sharpness of focus of the earlier, Mercury set; moreover this has the advantage of an extra work.

(i) *Cello sonatas Nos. 1–2. Intermezzi: in C sharp min., Op. 117/3; in A; in E flat min., Op. 118/2 & 6; in E min.; in C, Op. 119/2–3.*
(M) ** BMG/RCA 09026 62592-2 [id.]. (i) Gregor Piatigorsky; Artur Rubinstein.

Piatigorsky and Rubinstein recorded the Brahms sonatas in 1966, though they did not appear in the UK for over a decade. They are eminently straightforward and aristocratic performances with little trace of the expressive self-indulgence that affects some partnerships in this repertoire. The balance at times gives Rubinstein greater prominence than his distinguished partner, and the recording could do with greater bloom.

(i) *Cello sonatas Nos. 1 in E min., Op. 38; 2 in F, Op. 99;* (ii) *Violin sonatas Nos. 1 in G, Op. 78; 2 in A, Op. 100; 3 in D min., Op. 108; F.A.E. Sonata: Scherzo.*
(B) **(*) Virgin Classics Dig. Double VBD5 61415-2 (2) [CDVB 61415]. (i) Leonard Rose; (ii) Jaime Laredo; Jean-Bernard Pommier.

The special interest of this Virgin Double is that it includes the last recordings made by Leonard Rose – at the Château de Malesherbes, France, in the summer of 1982. The original full-priced issue was well documented and included a warm tribute from colleague Isaac Stern. The present reissue makes no mention of this; in fact the documentation is sparse and inadequate. However, Rose achieved a fine partnership with Pommier, with whom he is ideally balanced, and though the recording is a trifle too close, it is very truthful. Not surprisingly these are strong, searching performances, especially the passionate *F major Sonata*. These artists are at their finest in the *Adagio* of this work, which is breathtaking in its concentration; they catch the special mood of the *Allegretto* central movement of the companion *E minor Sonata* less well (they are a trifle too measured). The coupled *Violin sonatas* used the same venue the previous year, but here Laredo is not flattered by the close microphones, and this makes his ardent Brahmsian response seem a bit fierce at times. Once that is said, these too are impressively committed performances. The CD opens with a vibrant account of the *F.A.E. Scherzo*, and that sets the mood for the overall approach, direct and spontaneous, but robbed of a degree of inherent warmth by the forward balance.

Clarinet quintet in B min., Op. 115.
(M) *** Carlton Dig. 30367 0097-2 [id.]. Keith Puddy, Delmé Qt – DVORAK: *Quartet No. 12.* ***
(BB) **(*) CfP Silver Double CDCFPSD 4772 (2) [(B) id.]. Keith Puddy, Gabrieli String Qt – BORODIN: *String quartet No. 2;* DVORAK: *String quartet No. 12;* SCHUBERT: *String quartet No. 14.* ***
(B) (**) Millennium mono MCD 80093 [id.]. Leopold Wlach, V. Konserthaus Qt – MOZART: *Clarinet quintet.* (**)

(i) *Clarinet quintet;* (ii) *Clarinet sonata No. 2 in E flat, Op. 120/2.*
(M) *** Chandos CHAN 6522 [id.]. Janet Hilton, (i) Lindsay Qt; (ii) Peter Frankl.

(i) *Clarinet quintet;* (ii) *Clarinet trio in A min., Op. 114.*
(BB) **(*) Naxos Dig. 8.550391. József Balogh, with (i) Danubius Qt; (ii) Jenö Jandó, Csaba Onczay.

Keith Puddy's warm tone is well suited to Brahms and, with spacious speeds in all four movements, this is a consistently sympathetic reading; the Carlton digital recording is equally fine, vivid and full. Excellent value.

Janet Hilton's essentially mellow performance of the *Clarinet quintet*, with the Lindsay Quartet playing with pleasing warmth and refinement, has a distinct individuality. Her lilting syncopations in the third movement are delightful. Hilton's partnership with Peter Frankl in the *E flat Clarinet sonata* is rather less idiosyncratic and individual; nevertheless this performance offers considerable artistic rewards, even if the resonance means that the aural focus is a little diffuse.

Although the CD transfer of the 1970 recording brings a certain thinness in the violin timbre, Keith Puddy's earlier, CfP account with the Gabrielis of this elusive work rises to fine, intense poetry in the slow movement and in the visionary closing pages of the finale. There is a spontaneity in the playing here which is a vital quality in this work, far more important than mechanical precision. Moreover all three couplings on this Silver Double are highly recommendable.

József Balogh, principal clarinet with both the Hungarian State Opera and Radio Orchestras, is a highly sensitive player with a lovely tone. He is well supported by the Danubius Quartet and their account of the *Clarinet quintet* is a rewarding one, with warmth and atmosphere, and rising to considerable heights of intensity in the *Adagio*. The *Clarinet trio* is an enjoyably fresh account, though not quite so memorable, except in the *Andantino grazioso* which is delightfully done. Nevertheless Balogh, Jandó and Onczay are thoroughly sympathetic and, with excellent recording, this is still a worthwhile disc and inexpensive to boot.

The Millennium Brahms recording dates from 1952 and its coupling from the previous year. It really sounds very good for its age, and the playing of Leopold Wlach is often out of this world. The Vienna Konserthaus Quartet are less satisfying: they can sound less than sumptuous and do not begin to match Wlach in terms of artistry and refinement. He is quite special.

(i) *Clarinet quintet in B min., Op. 115;* (ii) *Piano quintet in F min., Op. 34; String quintets Nos. 1 in F, Op. 88; 2 in G, Op. 111.*
(B) *** Ph. Duo 446 172-2 (2) [id.]. (i) Herbert Stähr; (ii) Werner Haas; Berlin Philharmonic Octet (members).

The Berlin performance of the *Clarinet quintet* is both beautiful and faithful to Brahms's instructions, an outstanding version in every way. The delicacy with which the 'Hungarian' middle section of the great *Adagio* is interpreted gives some idea of the insight of these players. It is an autumnal reading, never overforced, and is recorded with comparable refinement. The two *String quintets* are also admirably served by these same players (with Dietrich Gerhard, viola, replacing the clarinettist, Herbert Stähr). The performances are searching and artistically satisfying, combining freshness and polish, warmth with well-integrated detail. For the *Piano quintet* Werner Haas joins the group, and they give a strongly motivated, spontaneous account of this splendid work that is in every way satisfying. The piano is most convincingly balanced. The recordings come from the early 1970s and the sound is remarkably full and warm, the richness of texture suiting the *String quintets* especially well. This is among the finest bargains in the Philips Duo list.

(i) *Clarinet quintet in B min., Op. 115; String quartet No. 1 in C min., Op. 51/1.*
(M) (**(*)) EMI mono CDH7 64932-2 [id.]. (i) Reginald Kell; Busch Qt.

Reginald Kell's beauty of tone was legendary and his 1937 account of the *Clarinet quintet* with the Busch

Quartet is among the greatest recordings of the piece. Kell's vibrato was not to all tastes, but his playing here is heard at its most refined and the Busch produce a splendidly autumnal feeling in the slow movement. The *C minor Quartet*, recorded in 1932, may not be as polished as in some more recent accounts (and certainly sounds its age), but the playing is full of imagination and vitality.

Clarinet sonatas Nos. 1 in F min.; 2 in E flat, Op. 120/1–2.
(BB) *** Naxos Dig. 8.553121 [id.]. Kálmán Berkes, Jenö Jandó.

No one buying the Naxos CD coupling the two late *Clarinet sonatas* is likely to have any regrets. They are beautifully played and freshly recorded by this distinguished Hungarian duo, and they would be recommendable even in a higher price-bracket.

(i; ii) *Clarinet trio in A min., Op. 114;* (iii) *Horn trio in E flat, Op. 40;* (ii) *Piano trios Nos. 1 in B, Op. 8; 2 in C, Op. 87; 3 in C min., Op. 101.*
(B) *** Ph. Duo 438 365-2 (2) [(M) id. import]. (i) George Pieterson; (ii) Beaux Arts Trio; (iii) Francis Orval, Arthur Grumiaux, György Sebók.

The splendid Beaux Arts recording of three of the four *Piano trios* comes on a pair of joined CDs at bargain price, with two other outstanding performances thrown in for good measure. George Pieterson is a first-rate artist and his account of the *Clarinet trio* with members of the Beaux Arts group offers masterly playing from all three participants and a very well-integrated recording. The balance in the *Horn trio* is even more adroitly managed, perhaps the most successful on record. The fine horn player, Francis Orval, seeks not to dominate but to be one of the group, and he achieves this without any loss of personality in his playing (note the richness of his contribution to the Trio of the Scherzo). The performance is warmly lyrical and completely spontaneous, with a racy finale to round off a particularly satisfying reading, never forced but deeply felt. Arthur Grumiaux's playing is a constant pleasure, and the pianist, György Sebók, is hardly less admirable.

As for the *Piano trios*, the performances are splendid, with strongly paced, dramatic allegros, consistently alert and thoughtful, and with sensitive playing in slow movements. The sound is first class and the resonance of Bernard Greenhouse's cello is warmly caught without any clouding of focus. The CD transfer has brightened the top a little, but not excessively. Excellent notes, too.

(i) *Clarinet sonatas Nos. 1 in F min.; 2 in E flat, Op. 120/1–2;* (ii) *String quartets Nos. 1 in C min.; 2 in A min., Op. 51/1-2; 3 in B flat, Op. 67.*
(B) *** Ph. Duo 456 320-2 (2) [(M) id. import]. (i) George Pieterson, Hephzibah Menuhin; (ii) Italian Qt.

The three *String quartets* are marvellously played by the Quartetto Italiano, with detail sensitively observed. The two quartets of Op. 51 are especially fine, with a searching reading of the *C minor* revealing depths that elude some other performers, while the *A minor* is hardly less penetrating. As always with the Philips remastering of analogue recordings (here from 1967, 1970 and 1971 respectively), the CD transfers are admirably truthful in timbre and balance. The *Clarinet sonatas* are very well played by George Pieterson and Hephzibah Menuhin. The autumnal twilight of the lovely *Andante un poco adagio* of the *F minor* is appealingly caught, and the following *Allegretto grazioso* flows engagingly. The *E flat Sonata* is more direct, less coaxing but strongly characterized, with plenty of light and shade. Vivid recording from 1980 adds to the feeling of boldness.

Horn trio in E flat, Op. 40 (see also above).
(M) **(*) Decca 452 887-2 [id.]. Barry Tuckwell, Itzhak Perlman, Vladimir Ashkenazy – FRANCK: *Violin sonata.* ***
(BB) ** Naxos Dig. 8.550441 [id.]. Jenö Keveházi, Jenö Jandó, Ildikó Hegyi (with Heinrich HERZOGENBERG: *Trio for horn, oboe & piano, Op. 61* (with Józef Kiss); Frédéric DUVERNOY: *Horn trio* **).

A superb performance of Brahms's marvellous *Horn trio* from Tuckwell, Perlman and Ashkenazy. They realize to the full the music's passionate impulse, and the performance moves forward from the gentle opening, through the sparkling Scherzo and the more introspective but still outgiving *Adagio*, to the gay and spirited finale. The 1968 recording has been remastered for reissue in Decca's Classic Sound series, but the attempt to provide a more sharply defined sound-picture has brought a curious loss of focus at times, verging on distortion at climaxes.

The Naxos version has plenty of vitality and romantic ardour, but rather less in the way of refinement. The excellent horn player, Jenö Keveházi, has a touch of vibrato but the ear soon adjusts, and he makes a strong, full-blooded contribution. The players are somewhat backwardly placed in the fairly resonant Unitarian Church, Budapest, but the result is convincing with a good relationship between the three instruments. The other two *Horn trios* are enjoyable but not distinctive. The oboe makes an effective substitute for the violin in the Herzogenberg piece, which cribs from the Brahms finale in its second-movement *Presto*. The Duvernoy *Trio* has two movements only, slow–fast, with the second rather jolly. They are both well played and recorded.

(i) *Horn trio in E flat;* (ii) *String sextet No. 2 in G, Op. 36.*
✿ (B) *** Sony SBK 63209; *SBT 63209* [id.]. (i) Bloom, Tree, Serkin; (ii) Carmirelli, Toth, Naegele, Caroline Levine, Arico, Reichenberger.

The performance of the *Horn trio*, recorded at the Marlboro Festival in 1960, is quite splendid. Myron Bloom's horn playing is superb, and Michael Tree matches his lyrical feeling, while Rudolf Serkin holds the performance together so that, when the fervour of the music-making brings a few slips in rhythmic precision, the listener is carried along by the exhilaration of the moment. The *Trio* comes paired with another Marlboro performance, of the *G major String sextet*, by a string group led by Pina Carmirelli. Recorded in 1967, this has been very effectively remastered and the players given a striking presence. There is a degree of thinness on the violin timbre but no lack of body, and the performance is both warm and refined: it seems to gather tension as it proceeds. The finale is particularly successful.

(i) *Piano quartets Nos. 1–3;* (ii) *Piano trios Nos. 1 in B, Op. 8; 2 in C, Op. 87; 3 in C min., Op. 101.*
(M) *** Sony Stern Edition III Dig./Analogue SM3K 64520 (3) [S3K 64520]. Isaac Stern, with (i) Laredo, Yo-Yo Ma, Ax; (ii) Rose, Istomin.

The Stern–Laredo–Ma–Ax partnership produces some pretty high-voltage playing and a real sense of give-and-take. There is little sense of four stars just coming together for a recording session but more of a genuine musical rapport. The listener is placed rather closer to the artists than some readers might like. All the same, no one investing in the Sony set is likely to be in the least disappointed.

This set is still available separately on two premium-priced CDs, but the three-disc set (taken from Volume III of Sony's celebration of Stern's 'Life in Music') is the one to go for. This includes equally fine versions of the *Piano trios*, recorded in New York two decades earlier, in 1964 and 1966. Here Stern joins with Rose and Istomin to give committed, romantic performances of comparable magnetism. Allegros are relaxed but alive and there are many individual touches in the phrasing to give pleasure. The *Adagio* of the *B major*, taken very slowly, has rapt concentration; that for Op. 101 is by comparison a nicely flowing *Andante grazioso*. As with the Beethoven *Piano trios* from the same source, the remastering has improved the original recording almost out of recognition, especially in relation to the piano sonority. The balance is close, but one relishes the presence of these fine artists.

(i) *Piano quartets Nos. 1 in G min., Op. 25; 2 in A, Op. 26; 3 in C min., Op. 60. Piano trio in A, Op. posth.*
(B) *** Ph. Duo 454 017-2 (2) [(M) id. import]. Beaux Arts Trio, (i) with Walter Trampler.

The Beaux Arts set of *Piano quartets* is self-recommending at Duo price, with the *A major Piano trio* thrown in as a bonus. The recording is bold and full-bloodedly Brahmsian in outer movements, which have splendid impetus. Thoughtful, sensitive playing in slow movements, lively tempi in allegros, characteristic musicianship plus spontaneity combine to make these recordings highly recommendable throughout, alongside the Stern Sony set (see above), which is in a higher price bracket.

(i) *Piano quartet No. 1 in G min., Op. 25. 4 Ballades, Op. 10.*
(M) **(*) DG 447 407-2 [id.]. Gilels, (i) with Amadeus Qt.

As might be expected, Gilels' account of the *G minor Quartet* with members of the Amadeus has much to recommend it. The great Russian pianist is in impressive form, and most listeners will respond to the withdrawn delicacy of the Scherzo and the gypsy fire of the finale. The slow movement is perhaps somewhat wanting in ardour and the Amadeus do not sound as committed or as fresh as their keyboard partner. At medium price, however, this version enjoys an advantage, and the 1971 DG recording is well balanced and sounds very natural in its new transfer. Moreover in the *Ballades* Gilels offers artistry of an order that silences criticism. In terms of imaginative vitality and musical insight it would be difficult to surpass these readings, and the 1976 recording is also first class. This certainly is a recording worthy of inclusion in DG's Legendary series of 'Originals'.

Piano quartet No. 3 in C min., Op. 60.
(BB) *** ASV Dig. Quicksilva CDQS 6198 [(M) id.]. Schubert Ens. of London – MENDELSSOHN: *Piano quartet No. 3.****

The *C minor Piano quartet*, though well served on CD, is represented less than generously at the bargain end of the spectrum. The Schubert Ensemble of London, which includes the pianist, William Howard, give a commendable account of it, though they do not perhaps penetrate all its depths. The Beaux Arts plus Walter Trampler remain a first recommendation, but readers attracted by the coupling can be assured that the ASV version is well worth the modest outlay required.

Piano quintet in F min., Op. 34.
(BB) *** Naxos Dig. 8.550406; *4550406* [id.]. Jenö Jandó, Kodály Qt – SCHUMANN: *Piano quintet.* ***

This fine Naxos account has a great deal going for it, even though it does not include the first-movement exposition repeat. The playing is boldly spontaneous and has plenty of fire and expressive feeling. The opening of the finale has mystery too, and overall, with full-bodied recording and plenty of presence, this makes a strong impression. It is certainly a bargain.

(i) *Piano quintet in F min., Op. 34; String sextet No 1 in B flat, Op. 18.*
(B) **(*) DG Classikon 439 490-2 [(M) id. import]. (i) Eschenbach, Amadeus Qt (augmented).

Christoph Eschenbach gives a powerful – sometimes overprojected – account of his part in the *Quintet*, yet this is undoubtedly a moving performance with plenty of vitality. Good piano quality and, although the piano dominates, the Amadeus players remain well in the picture. The performance of the *Sextet* lacks something in purity of style, but the obvious tonal warmth and the undoubted merits of the ensemble, coupled with very good late-1960s recording, make this a pretty good recommendation for those with limited budgets.

Piano trios Nos. 1 in B, Op. 8 (original, 1854 version); 1 in B, Op. 8 (1889 version); 2 in C, Op. 87; 3 in C min., Op. 101.
(BB) *** Arte Nova Dig. 74321 51641-2 (2) [id.]. Trio Opus 8.

The prize-winning Trio Opus 8 is so-named because the ensemble was formed (in 1985) while the players were studying Brahms's *First Piano trio*. Their interest in it is such that they have recorded not only Brahms's final, revised version of 1889 but also the twenty-year-old composer's original (1854) score, his first major chamber work for strings (apart from the *F. A. E. Scherzo* for violin and piano). They make a very good case for it, sustaining tension powerfully in resonant, well-matched playing through even the long first movement. It certainly does not sound immature, even if both outer movements are considerably more expansive than the revised version (the opening movement has 200 more bars of music). Throughout all three works speeds are on the broad side, but that helps to give even the most compressed of these *Trios*, Op. 101 *in C minor*, heroic power in the outer movements. All three *Trios* are played with great verve and commitment and excellently crisp ensemble (especially in the sparkling Scherzos), while slow movements have fine concentration and lyrical warmth. The account of the *C major Trio*, Op. 87, is particularly fine, the outer movements boldly assertive and the inner movements persuasively contrasted. The pianist, Michael Hauber, leads the ensemble vibrantly, yet the balance places him well within the group. The cellist, Mario de Secondi, is a strikingly songful player, and his warm tone helps to offset the digital brightness on the violin timbre. This may need taming on some reproducers, the only real reservation here; but the recording is otherwise vivid and full, and the ambience is pleasing. A first-class and stimulating bargain.

Piano trios Nos. 1 in B, Op. 8; 2 in C, Op. 87; 3 in C min., Op. 101; 4 in A, Op. posth.
(BB) ** Naxos Dig. 8.550746 (*Nos. 1 & 2*); 8.550747 (*Nos. 3 & 4*). Vienna Piano Trio.

The accounts by the Vienna Piano Trio on Naxos are warm and unidiosyncratic and have no lack of vitality. Slow movements are shaped and phrased very musically, and the stronger allegros are well paced. These are not distinctive performances but they are fresh and worth their modest cost. The recording in a resonant acoustic (a hall in a castle in Budapest) has brought fairly close microphones, but the presence given to the group does not sound too noticeably artificial.

Piano trio No. 1 in B, Op. 8.
(M) (***) RCA mono 09026 61763-2 [id.]. Heifetz, Feuermann, Rubinstein – DOHNANYI: *Serenade in C;* R. STRAUSS: *Violin sonata.* (***)

A commanding performance of the *B major Trio* comes from the legendary partnership of Heifetz, Feuermann and Rubinstein. Recorded in 1941, the sound calls for considerable tolerance on the part of the listener but this is well worth extending, given the quality of the playing.

Piano trios Nos. 1 in B, Op. 8; 2 in C, Op. 87.
(M) *** Decca (IMS) 421 152-2 [id.]. Julius Katchen, Josef Suk, János Starker.

(i-ii) *Piano trios Nos. 1 in B; 2 in G; 3 in C min.;* (i) *Cello sonata No. 2 in F;* (ii) *F.A.E. Sonata: Scherzo.*
(B) *** Decca Double 448 092-2 (2) [(M) id. import]. Julius Katchen, with (i) János Starker; (ii) Josef Suk.

The Katchen/Suk/Starker recordings of the *Piano trios* and *Cello sonata* were made in The Maltings in July 1968; the *Scherzo* from the *F.A.E. Sonata* comes from the previous year and was recorded in the Kingsway Hall. The performances of the first two *Piano trios* are warm, strong and characterful, while the tough *C minor Trio* and the epic, thrustful *Cello sonata* bring a comparably spontaneous response. The *Scherzo* from the composite *F.A.E. Sonata* (written in conjunction with Schumann and Albert Dietrich as a tribute to Joachim) makes a lively end to the programme. The richness of the acoustics adds to the Brahmsian glow, and the results have a warmth that did not always characterize Katchen's recordings of Brahms. If the sound of the CD transfers is a little limited in the upper range, the ear is grateful that no artificial brightening has been applied, for it provides a real Brahmsian amplitude which is very satisfying. Highly recommended in either format.

String quartets Nos. 1–2, Op. 51/1–2; 3 in B flat, Op. 67.
(B) *** Teldec/Warner 4509 95503-2 (2) [id.]. Alban Berg Qt – DVORAK: *String quartet No. 13.* ***

We have commented on the Alban Berg performances in earlier editions. They were made in the mid-1970s when the quartet was on peak form, highly polished yet completely fresh in their musical responses. The recording is very good: the sound of the *B flat*, Op. 67, made in a Swiss church, is superior but not overwhelmingly so; the *A minor* was recorded in Palais Yusopov in St Petersburg. The Teldec performances have the inestimable advantage of being economical in price and also space; they are accommodated in the now-popular two-in-one jewel-case. This set is strongly recommended and can stand alongside the best in the catalogue.

String quartets Nos. 1 in C min.; 2 in A min., Op. 51/1–2; 3 in B flat, Op. 67; (i) *Clarinet quintet in B min., Op. 115.*
(M) (***) EMI Rouge et Noir (SIS) mono CHS5 66422-2 (2) [CDHB 66422]. Léner Qt, (i) with Charles Draper.

The Léner ensemble offer music-making from another age: civilized, free from expressive exaggeration and with nothing overprojected or forced. Three of the quartet members were pupils of Hubay, who made a virtue of his portamento. The earliest of the recordings here, the *Clarinet quintet*, comes from 1928; the three quartets were made between 1929 (Op. 67) and 1933 (Op. 51/1). The quartets unfold in a totally natural way – well, not quite wholly natural, for Léner's portamenti, very much of its period, tend to date them. Those who find it difficult to come to terms with this stylistic idiosyncrasy should perhaps look elsewhere. Portamenti apart, there is much to savour here. Connoisseurs of the clarinet will find Charles Draper's account of the *B minor Quintet* of particular interest. Draper had heard Richard Mühlfeld, the dedicatee and first performer of the work, and his slow tempo at the very opening had Brahms's own imprimatur. The transfers and annotations are excellent.

String quartets Nos. 1–3; (i) *Piano quintet in F min., Op. 34.*
(M) *** Hyperion Dyad Dig. CDD 22018 (2) [id.]. (i) Piers Lane; New Budapest Qt.

The New Budapest Quartet bring warmth and spontaneity to all three scores, responding to their dramatic fervour and lyrical flow in equal measure. Their intonation is altogether impeccable and they are scrupulously attentive to Brahms's dynamic markings, with pleasing results in terms of clarity and transparency. Both the *C minor* and *A minor Quartets* can so often sound opaque, and in this respect the New Budapest produce as clean and open a sonority as any. They also have plenty of character and rhythmic vitality. They enjoy two further advantages over some earlier rivals in that, first, they also offer an excellently shaped and musicianly account of the *F minor Piano quintet* with responsive playing from Piers Lane and, secondly, they are among the best and most naturally recorded to have appeared in recent years. At mid-price on a Hyperion Dyad Double, this admirable set tends to sweep the board for those wanting all three quartets, plus the *Piano quintet*.

String quartet No. 2 in A min., Op. 51/2.
(BB) **(*) ASV Quicksilva CDQS 6173 [(M) id.]. Lindsay Qt – MENDELSSOHN: *String quartet No. 6.* **

The Lindsays are in fine fettle here and, besides generating spontaneous excitement, the playing has much imagination and subtlety, notably in the *Andante* but especially in the *Quasi minuetto – Allegro vivace* third movement, which is articulated with superb precision. This was a live recording and the microphones are too close, but the ear adjusts to the fierceness given to the players' attack when the performance has such spontaneous thrust.

String quintets Nos. 1 in F, Op. 88; 2 in G, Op. 111.
(BB) **(*) Naxos Dig. 8.553635 [id.]. Ludwig Quartet, Bruno Pasquier.

The Naxos coupling of the two Brahms quintets is a useful addition to the lists and has a lot going for it. The performances lack the last word in polish (there is some vulnerable intonation in the first movement of the *G major*, Op. 111), and in that respect the members of the BPO Octet are preferable (see above). But the Ludwigs have plenty of enthusiasm and warmth, and the recorded sound is very good. This is worth the money, and some may prefer it to the Philips disc for its fuller recording.

String sextet No. 1 in B flat, Op. 18.
(B) ** EMI CfP CD-CFP 6039. Principals of LPO – SCHUBERT: *Piano quintet in A (Trout).* **

A strong and – for the most part – sympathetic account of the *First String sextet* from principals of the LPO, led by Rodney Friend. The first movement sets off warmly and purposefully, the interplay between the instruments lyrically sympathetic. However, although the background ambience of Conway Hall is agreeable, as the performance gathers ardour it loses something in refinement, the upper string fortissimos are not flattered by the recording, and are made rather thin and grainy by the close microphones. The *Andante* is rhythmically rather emphatic, but the vigorous Scherzo is agreeably light-footed, and the *grazioso* character of the Rondo finale is nicely caught, although the tendency to fierceness in the violin timbre remains.

Viola sonatas Nos. 1 in F min.; 2 in E flat, Op. 120/1–2; Violin sonatas Nos. 1 in G, Op. 78; 2 in A, Op. 100; 3 in D min., Op. 108. F.A.E; Sonata: Scherzo.
(B) *** DG Double 453 121-2 (2) [id.]. Pinchas Zukerman, Daniel Barenboim.

It seems a very sensible idea to join up the Zukerman/Barenboim performances of the *Violin* and *Viola sonatas* economically on a DG Double since they were recorded at the same time (1974), and both sets sound first rate in the new transfers. The *Viola sonatas* may be a little sweet for some tastes, but they are easy to enjoy, spontaneous-sounding, with the expressiveness never sounding contrived, always buoyant. The *Violin sonatas*, strong and purposeful, bring no such reservations. Here Zukerman and Barenboim are inspired to take an expansive view of Brahms, producing songful, spontaneous-sounding performances that catch the inspiration of the moment. The manner is warmer, less self-conscious than some – if at times less refined. The sound itself is very natural with good presence. The lively *Scherzo in C minor* from the *F.A.E. Sonata*, a work composed jointly with Schumann and Albert Dietrich, is thrown in for good measure.

Violin sonatas Nos. 1 in G, Op. 78; 2 in A, Op. 100.
(B) **(*) EMI forte CZS5 69367-2 (2) [CDFB 69367]. Igor Oistrakh, Ginzburg – BEETHOVEN: *Archduke trio;* SCHUBERT: *Piano trio No. 1.* ***

Violin sonatas Nos. 1 in G, Op. 78; 2 in A, Op. 100; 3 in D min., Op. 108.
(M) **(*) Ph. 446 570-2. Arthur Grumiaux, György Sebók.
(BB) ** ASV Quicksilva Dig. CDQS 6227 [(M) id.]. Krzystof Smietana, Caroline Palmer.

When they were issued on LP, we found these Grumiaux performances from the mid-1970s slightly disappointing, mellifluous rather than vital, with even an element of blandness. Returning to them in this superb CD transfer, we must revise our response, however. The very opening of the *G major Sonata* is gently appealing in a typically unassertive, Grumiaux way, and the first movement soon generates a full head of steam. The opening of the *Adagio* is restrained but tender, and the finale has an appealing lyrical flow. Moreover these artists exactly capture the nostalgic mood of the first movement of the *A major* (marked 'Allegro amabile') to perfection. If the opening of the *D minor* is reticent, again the *Adagio* is very lovely and the *Un poco presto e con sentimento* brings the lightest touch. In short, while other versions of these works may be more volatile and passionate, Grumiaux, expertly partnered by Sebók, is very persuasive, and never short of Brahmsian warmth. The recording too is beautifully balanced and natural.

Igor Oistrakh finds a rich tone and a fine lyrical line for two essentially lyrical works, and he is accompanied sympathetically by Anton Ginzburg. The recording of both instruments is beautiful, but the piano is backwardly balanced in a resonant acoustic and the violin is well forward. This is not disastrous, but it may irritate those who rightly consider that these are works for violin *and* piano.

Musical performances on ASV, albeit not of outsize personality. Krzystof Smietana and Caroline Palmer make a good partnership and the playing is free from idiosyncratic and ego-centred touches – indeed, if anything, it errs on the side of reticence. Not to be preferred to the Grumiaux–Sebök set in terms of authority and polish or, in sheer spontaneous enjoyment, to Zukerman and Barenboim on their DG Double; but these artists give pleasure and are decently recorded.

Violin sonata No. 1 in G, Op. 78.
(B) **(*) Tring Dig. TRP 081 [(M) id. import]. Jonathan Carney, Ronan O'Hora – FRANCK: *Violin sonata.* ***

As we have discovered from their Beethoven, Jonathan Carney and Ronan O'Hora have formed a finely integrated musical partnership. Some might feel that their reading of the Brahms *G major Sonata* is too ruminative, not bold enough, and this effect is heightened by the resonant, somewhat diffuse sound-picture. But there is no lack of warmth or poetic feeling, and the reading, seemingly spontaneous, certainly communicates readily.

PIANO MUSIC

Piano music, 4 hands

Hungarian dances Nos. 1–21; 18 Liebeslieder waltzes, Op. 52a.
(BB) *** Naxos Dig. 8.553140 [id.]. Silke-Thora Matthies, Christian Köhn.

Though this second volume of the Naxos edition of Brahms piano duets was recorded simultaneously with the first, it brings much livelier and more winning performances. It makes a generous and very attractive coupling to have all 21 *Hungarian dances* in their original form, coupled with the piano-duet version of the first and more popular set of *Liebeslieder waltzes*. With Brahms's extra elaborations, the vocal parts are missed less than usual. The *Hungarian dances* find the players at their most relaxed, pointing rhythms jauntily, allowing expressive tenutos in a way they are reluctant to adopt in the waltzes. Crisp, clean ensemble, matched by well-focused sound. An excellent bargain.

Hungarian dances Nos. 1, 2, 5 & 17; Liebeslieder waltzes, Op. 52a; Neue Liebeslieder waltzes, Op. 65a; 16 Waltzes, Op. 39.
(B) ** Cal. Approche Dig. CAL 6219 [(M) id.]. Inger Södergren, Fernanda Soares.

A generous bargain selection of Brahms's four-handed piano music, including the *Liebeslieder waltzes*, which are often coaxed quite seductively. The *Hungarian dances* and *Waltzes* also go well and certainly are not without sparkle, even if they are not perhaps really distinctive. The digital recording is bright and faithful.

Piano music, four hands: *15 Neue Liebeslieder waltzes, Op. 65a; Souvenir de la Russie; Variations on a theme by Schumann, Op. 23; 16 Waltzes, Op. 39.*
(BB) *(*) Naxos Dig. 8.553139 [id.]. Silke-Thora Matthies, Christian Köhn.

This first volume in the Naxos series of Brahms's four-handed piano music begins unpromisingly with the *Schumann variations* played squarely, without charm or animation. The other works on the very well-filled disc – all four of roughly 20 minutes each – are more persuasive, particularly in vigorous music. The *Souvenir de la Russie*, Brahms's first published work, a set of six fantasies on Russian and Bohemian gypsy songs, is given an apt freshness, but the slower waltzes in both Op. 39 and Op. 65a still lack charm. Silke-Thora Matthies and Christian Köhn are an effective partnership and mainly show both expertise and rapport; however, they do occasionally lapse into rather routine responses, and they lack refinement in dealing with Brahms's pianissimo writing. First-rate sound.

Solo piano music

Solo piano music.
(M) ** Astrée Audivis Dig. E 8750 (5) [id.]. Andrea Bonatta.

Ballades, Op. 10; Variations on an original theme, Op. 21/1; Variations and fugue on a theme of Handel, Op. 24 (E 8753) [id.].

Fantasies, Op. 116; 3 Intermezzi, Op. 117; Pieces, Opp. 118 & 119 (E 8599) [id.].

8 Pieces, Op. 76; 2 Rhapsodies, Op. 79; Variations on a theme of Paganini, Op. 35 (E 8754) [id.].

Piano sonatas Nos. 1 in C, Op. 1; 2 in F sharp min., Op. 2; Scherzo, Op. 4 (E 8751) [id.].

Piano sonata No. 3 in F min., Op. 5; Variations on a Hungarian song, Op. 21/2; Variations on a theme of Schumann, Op. 9 (E 8752) [id.].

Andrea Bonatta's set comprises five CDs which are housed in a slipcase and are available as five for the price of three. They do not include the Op. 39 *Waltzes* and the *Hungarian dances*, which account for Katchen's sixth CD. Bonatta uses a Steinway in four of the five CDs, and a Vienna 1923 Bösendorfer from Paul Badura-Skoda's collection in the *Paganini variations* and Opp. 76 and 79. This was recorded in Vienna in 1990 and the remainder in 1991, 1992, 1995 and 1996 respectively. Bonatta is a pianist of quality and many of his performances, such as the four *Ballades*, give pleasure. Not so the *Variations and fugue on a theme of Handel*, which is mannered and self-aware. The digital recordings are variable and not really superior to the Decca analogue sound. These discs are available separately but without the generous discount which warrants their listing as a mid-priced set here.

4 Ballades, Op. 10; 7 Fantasias, Op. 116; Hungarian dances Nos. 1–10; (i) *Nos. 11–21. 3 Intermezzi, Op. 117; 8 Piano pieces, Op. 76; 6 Piano pieces, Op. 118; 4 Piano pieces, Op. 119; Piano sonatas Nos. 1 in C, Op. 1; 2 in F sharp min., Op. 2; 3 in F min., Op. 5; 2 Rhapsodies, Op. 79; Variations on a Hungarian song, Op. 21/2; Variations on a theme by Paganini, Op. 35; Variations and fugue on a theme by Handel, Op. 24; Variations on a theme by Schumann, Op. 9; Variations on an original theme, Op. 21/1; Waltzes, Op. 39.*

(B) *** Decca stereo/mono 455 247-2 (6) [id.]. Julius Katchen, (i) with J.-P. Marty.

Katchen's magisterial survey of Brahms's keyboard music was made for Decca between 1962 and 1965, save for the last three *Ballades*, which come from the 1950s and are in mono. Although we would rank the Gilels *Ballades* and some of the Kempff recordings of the later pieces as being special (not to mention Solomon's mono account of the *F minor Sonata* (Testament) and, indeed, some of the other recordings of this work listed separately below), those wanting a comprehensive survey need look no further. Katchen is an eminently faithful and sound interpreter who brings refined musicianship and a natural authority to this repertoire; and he is given the benefit of Decca recording which was excellent for its period, and remains so. There are six CDs at a very low price and, although they are not available separately, they still make a tremendous bargain. In addition to the three *Ballades*, the following are mono recordings: the *Schumann variations*, Nos. 1, 5 and 7 of the *Fantasias* and Nos. 11–21 of the *Hungarian dances*.

4 Ballades, Op. 10; Scherzo in E flat, Op. 4; Piano sonatas Nos. 2 in F sharp min., Op. 2; 3 in F min., Op. 5; Variations and fugue on a theme by Handel, Op. 24; Variations on a theme by Paganini, Op. 35.

(M) **(*) Ph. 432 302-2 (3). Claudio Arrau.

As part of Arrau's eightieth-birthday celebrations, Philips issued a five-LP set of his Brahms recordings made in the 1970s. Two of the LPs were of the concertos (now on a Philips Duo – see above) and the remainder were accommodated on this three-CD set. The 1970s sound does justice to the wonderful sonority this great pianist produced, although he is at times characteristically 'personal', notably so in the *F minor Sonata*, where he does indulge in some generous rubato. Yet his playing is always stamped by a kind of wisdom that holds the listener, and there is no want of virtuosity in the *Handel* and *Paganini variations*.

4 Ballades, Op. 10; Piano sonata No. 3 in F min., Op. 5.

(BB) **(*) Naxos Dig. 8.550352 [id.]. Idil Biret.

As a pupil of Kempff, Idil Biret has a fine understanding of this repertoire, although her approach is more muscular than Kempff's. Thus the first of the *Four Ballades* opens with enticing lyrical feeling but has the most powerfully dramatic climax, to match the feeling of the Scottish ballad, *Edward*, on which it is based. The *Fourth Ballade* is gravely beautiful and shows her at her finest. Although it is not a first choice, Idil Biret's is a fine, often perceptive and rewarding account of the *F minor Sonata* which, both artistically and as a recording, can hold its own with all but the most exalted rivals. These performances are full of character. Good recording, made in the Heidelberg studio.

4 Ballades, Op. 10; Variations and fugue on a theme by Handel, Op. 24; Variations and fugue on a theme by Schumann, Op. 9.

(BB) *** ASV Dig. CDQS 6161 [(M) id.]. Jorge Federico Osorio.

The young Mexican pianist, Jorge Federico Osorio, has been winning golden opinions in recent years and his account of the *Variations and fugue on a theme by Handel* is tremendously impressive. There is no want of clarity, but the texture has plenty of warmth and colour and he balances the sonorities in a most musical way. He possesses an unfailing sense of the Brahms style, giving us playing that is selfless and with no hint of the idiosyncratic. This is undoubtedly his best record to date, for the Schumann set is hardly less impressive and the four *Ballades* are also played with fine sensitivity and character. On top of all this, ASV provide excellent, well-focused sound, with plenty of depth, and this now comes in the super-bargain category.

Fantasias, Op. 116.

(M) **(*) DG Dig. 445 562-2 [id.]. Yevgeny Kissin – LISZT: *Concert paraphrases of Schubert Lieder* etc. ***; SCHUBERT: *Wanderer fantasia.* **(*)

This recording comes from 1991 and finds the young virtuoso in masterful form. There is perhaps more to these extraordinary pieces than he uncovers but his pianism is glorious, and he is beautifully recorded too.

7 Fantasias, Op. 116; 3 Intermezzi, Op. 117; 8 Piano pieces, Op. 76; 6 Piano pieces, Op. 118; 4 Piano pieces, Op. 119.

(B) *** EMI forte (SIS) CZS5 69521-2 (2) [CDFB 69521]. Alexeev – SCHUMANN: *Etudes symphoniques.* ***

Fantasias, Op. 116; 3 Intermezzi, Op. 117; 6 Pieces, Op. 118; 4 Pieces, Op. 119.

(M) **(*) DG 437 249-2 [id.]. Wilhelm Kempff.

Dmitri Alexeev enjoys the advantage of really first-class piano-sound, full-bodied and totally natural and truthful. The piano timbre is rich, slightly bass-orientated, but eminently suitable for Brahms. Alexeev's playing has authority and he produces an ideally weighted sonority with the correct blend of colour. He brings the right kind of tenderness and insight to the quieter pieces. His mastery of rubato is consummate, and these performances generally hold their own with any now before the public. With its excellent Schumann coupling this is very highly recommendable.

Kempff's style in Brahms is characteristically individual: poetry emphasized rather than brilliance, subtle timbres rather than virtuosity. It follows that Kempff shines in the gentle fancies of Brahms's last period, with his magic utterly beguiling in the *Intermezzi in A minor*, *E major* and *E minor* from Op. 116 and especially in the lovely *E flat major Andante* of Op. 117. Don't be put off by the opening *Capriccio in D minor* of Op. 116 which sounds rather hard, the piano timbre lacking sonority; at lower dynamic levels the piano colouring is exquisite.

(i) *Fantasias, Op. 116; Intermezzi, Op. 117;* (ii) *Pieces, Op. 76;* (i) *Pieces, Opp. 118/119;* (ii) *Rhapsodies Nos. 1 in B min.; 2 in G min., Op. 79/1–2;* (i) *Variations and fugue on a theme by Handel, Op. 24;* (iii) *Variations on a theme by Paganini, Op. 35.*

(B) *(**) Ph. Duo Analogue/Dig. 442 589-2 (2) [id.]. (i) Stephen Kovacevich; (ii) Dinorah Varsi; (iii) Adam Harasiewicz.

The performances by Stephen Kovacevich can receive the strongest recommendation. He finds the fullest range of emotional contrast in the Op. 116 *Fantasias*, but is at his finest in the Op. 117 *Intermezzi* and the four *Klavierstücke*, Op. 119, which contain some of Brahms's most beautiful lyrical inspirations for the keyboard, while the *Allegro risoluto* of the final *Rhapsodie* of Op. 119 has splendid flair and presence. On the second CD the *Handel variations* are also impressive and it seems perverse that Philips then turned to recordings by Dinorah Varsi of the two *Rhapsodies* and eight *Klavierstücke*, Op. 76, when Kovacevich has also recorded them. However, these are already available, coupled with the two piano concertos, on another Duo. Varsi's playing is at times very impulsive (as in the Op. 79 *Rhapsody*) and her performances of the *Klavierstücke* also lack the necessary degree of poise. Adam Harasiewicz, however, plays the *Paganini variations* with some flair and towards the end produces some exciting bravura. Generally the recordings are very good; Kovacevich's Op. 116 and Op. 118 are digital.

7 Fantasias, Op. 116; 8 Pieces, Op. 76; 2 Rhapsodies, Op. 79.

(BB) **(*) Naxos Dig. 8.550353 [id.]. Idil Biret.

Biret opens her programme strongly with the agitato *Capriccio in F sharp minor* (the first of the Op. 76 group), and then articulates the second lightly and engagingly. She readily captures the graceful intimacy of the *A flat* and *B flat Intermezzi*. Of the two *Rhapsodies*, the first is very impulsive indeed, but the second is particularly fine, boldly spontaneous, its dark colouring caught well. The *Fantasias*, Op. 116, bring some beautifully reflective playing, notably in the three *Intermezzi* grouped together (in E major and E minor), while the framing *G minor* and *D minor Capriccios* are passionately felt, the latter ending the recital strongly. This is all impressively characterized Brahms playing, and the recording does not lack sonority.

3 Intermezzi, Op. 117; 6 Pieces, Op. 118; 4 Pieces, Op. 119; Scherzo, Op. 4.

(BB) * Naxos Dig. 8.550354 [id.]. Idil Biret.

In the Op. 117 *Intermezzi* Idil Biret plays with taste and an appropriate inwardness, and her playing is always the product of thought. But the close balance, together with the unventilated, claustrophobic acoustic of the Tonstudio van Geest, makes for aural fatigue. One longs for more space round the instrument.

3 Intermezzi, Op. 117; 6 Pieces, Op. 118; 2 Rhapsodies, Op. 79.

(B) **(*) Cal. Approche CAL 6679 [(M) id.]. Inger Södergren.

Inger Södergren's Brahms is imaginative and poetic: her performances of the three *Intermezzi* are enticingly intimate, while there is a commanding volatility and passion in the *Rhapsodies*. She brings out all the colour of the Op. 118 *Pieces* and captures their variety of mood and atmosphere. The analogue recording is truthful but with a touch of hardness at fortissimo levels.

8 Pieces, Op. 76; 2 Rhapsodies, Op. 79; 7 Fantasias, Op. 116.
(BB) * Naxos Dig. 8.550353 [id.]. Idil Biret.

The Naxos accounts of this repertoire are attractively priced but, as with other issues in this series, are let down by unsatisfactory recorded sound.

Piano sonatas Nos. 1 in C, Op. 1; 2 in F sharp min., Op. 2.
(BB) * Naxos Dig. 8.550351 [id.]. Idil Biret.

The Turkish-born Idil Biret gives a commanding and intelligent account of the *C major Sonata*, and her fine sense of architecture serves as a reminder that she was a pupil of Kempff. However, the studio environment in which these recordings were made is very unsympathetic: the close balance and brittle timbre of the instrument are unpleasing.

Piano sonata No. 3; 4 Ballades; Intermezzo in E, Op. 116/6; Romance in F, Op. 118/5.
(M) ** RCA 09026 61862-2 [id.]. Artur Rubinstein.

Piano sonata No. 3; Intermezzi: in E flat, Op. 117/1; in C, Op. 119/3.
(M) *** Decca 448 578-2 [id.]. Clifford Curzon – SCHUBERT: *Piano sonata No. 21.* ***

Piano sonata No. 3 in F min., Op. 5; Theme and variations in D min. (from *String sextet, Op. 18*).
(M) *** Decca 448 129-2. Radu Lupu – SCHUBERT: *Sonata No. 5* etc. ***

Curzon's account of the *F minor Sonata* is special. His approach is both perceptive and humane, and his playing has great intensity and freshness. Curzon was at his peak, powerful and sensitive and, above all, spontaneous-sounding, both in the *Sonata* and in the two *Intermezzi* which act as encores. The 1962 recording was among the finest of its day and is worthy to be reissued in Decca's 'Classic Sound' series. The generous coupling with Schubert (an equally fine performance) makes this CD very desirable indeed.

Noble, dignified and spacious are the adjectives that spring to mind when listening to Lupu's Op. 5. If he does not have the youthful ardour of a Kocsis, there is a reflective feeling that more than makes up for this, especially in the memorable account of the *Andante*. Lupu's view is inward, ruminative and always beautifully rounded. The arrangement of the slow-movement theme and variations from the *B flat major String sextet* was made by the composer and presented to Clara Schumann as a forty-first birthday present in 1860. In Lupu's hands the transcription seems tailor-made for the piano. The 1981 digital recording is most realistic, the piano set slightly back, the timbre fully coloured and the focus natural.

Rubinstein's impulsive way with Brahms, though arresting at the opening of the *Sonata*, is not always convincing. His comparatively fast pacing of the second and fourth movements means that he does not entirely catch the feeling of reverie in the *Andante*. The rather hard, unexpansive (1959) recording does not help the *Sonata*; but the two shorter pieces seem to have slightly more bloom, and the *Ballades*, too, recorded in Rome in 1970, are fuller although the balance remains close and the acoustic cool. They are given a totally unsentimental approach and there are times when one feels the playing is somewhat shorn of mystery: one misses the extremes of both tension and repose.

Variations on a theme by Paganini, Op. 35.
(BB) *** Koch Discovery Dig. DICD 920423 [id.]. Evelyne Brancart – LISZT: *Paganini études.* ***

Evelyne Brancart is a Belgian pianist who studied with Eduardo del Pueyo; she scored a number of competition successes and was a finalist at the Queen Elisabeth Competition in Brussels in 1975. In recent years she has taught at the Eastman School of Music at Rochester (New York), where these recordings were made. She has superb technique, fine musicianship and sensitivity; the recording is rather bright and forward but yields pleasing results. An enjoyable recital – though, even at super-bargain price, rather short measure at 47 minutes 40 seconds.

VOCAL MUSIC

3 Gesänge, Op. 42; 5 Gesänge, Op. 104; 7 Lieder, Op. 62; Lieder & Romanzen, Op. 93a; 4 ernste Gesänge, Op. 121.
(BB) ** Arte Nova/BMG Dig. 74321 46504-2 [id.]. Harvestehude Ch., Bantzer.

These secular songs for mixed choir find Brahms at his most amiable, music he wrote out of sheer delight. Bantzer directs finely controlled readings, from his talented Hamburg choir, which above all bring out the beauty of the writing, in places at the expense of vitality. The performances are not helped by the microphone balance, with voices defined not quite sharply enough.

Lieder: *Alte Liebe; Auf dem Kirchhofe; Auf dem See; Es liebt sich so lieblich; Geheimnis; Die Mainacht; O liebliche Wangen; Sapphische Ode; Sonntag; Verzagen.*

(M) *** Ph. 442 741-2 (2). Gérard Souzay, Dalton Baldwin – BEETHOVEN: *An die ferne Geliebte* etc.; SCHUMANN: *Dichterliebe; Liederkreis* etc. ***

Not even Souzay's lightness (at its finest in *Geheimnis* and the flowingly passionate *O liebliche Wangen*) can prevent some of these songs sounding heavy in texture. Yet his gently grave account of *Die Mainacht* is very touching, and all this singing is persuasive. Comparison with the coupled Beethoven – who comes off better as a song writer than his successor on this showing – is fascinating. Recording is close but otherwise excellent. Alas, no translations are provided.

Lieder: *An die Nachtigall; Bottschaft; Dein blaues Auge hält so still; Feldeinsamkeit; Der Gang zum Liebchen; Geheimnis; Im Waldeseinsamkeit; Komm bald; Die Kränze; Die Mainacht; Meine Liebe ist grün; Minnelied; Nachtigall; O wüsst ich doch den Weg zurück; Sah dem edlen Bildnis; Salamander; Die Schale der Vergessenheit; Serenade; Sonntag; Ständchen; Von ewiger Liebe; Von waldbekränzter Höhe; Wie bist du, Meine Königin; Wiegenlied; Wir Wandelten.*

(BB) *** Virgin Classics Dig. Double VBD5 61418-2 (2) [CVBD 61418]. Thomas Allen, Geoffrey Parsons – WOLF: *Lieder.* ***

Thomas Allen, in one of his most successful Lieder records yet, gives fresh, virile performances of a particularly attractive collection of Brahms songs. There is less underlining of words than in Brahms sung by Fischer-Dieskau or Bär but still a keen and detailed feeling for meaning as well as mood. If one generally associates the great song, *Von ewiger Liebe*, with a woman's voice, Allen triumphantly shows what benefits there are from having a baritone, hushed and intimately confidential at the start and bitingly powerful at the climax in heightened contrast. There are many such felicities here, with Geoffrey Parsons an ever-sympathetic accompanist and with sound more cleanly focused than in earlier Lieder issues from this source. Now coupled with an equally desirable recital of Wolf songs, with the two CDs offered for the cost of one mid-priced disc, this is a set not to be missed by any lover of German Lied, even though no translations are provided.

Alto rhapsody; 4 Gesänge, Op. 17.

(BB) *** Virgin Classics Dig. Double VBD5 61469-2 (2) [CDVB 61469]. Dame Janet Baker, London Symphony Ch., City of L. Sinf., Hickox – BERLIOZ: *Les Nuits d'été* etc.; MENDELSSOHN: *Infelice* etc.; RESPIGHI: *La Sensitiva.* ***

Though the Virgin recording of the *Alto rhapsody* was recorded after Dame Janet's retirement from the concert platform, the voice is in glorious condition, superbly controlled. This is a more openly expressive and spacious reading than her earlier, EMI one with Boult, matching her performances in the two Mendelssohn items. The four early Brahms songs, Opus 17, for women's chorus with two horns and harp accompaniment, are delightfully done.

(i–ii) *Alto rhapsody, Op. 53;* (ii) *Begrabnisgesang, Op. 13; Gesang der Parzen, Op. 89;* (iii) *Geistlicheslied, Op. 30;* (iv) *2 Motets, Op. 29;* (iii) *2 Motets, Op. 74; 3 Motets, Op. 110;* (ii) *Nänie, Op. 82;* (v) *Rinaldo, Op. 50;* (ii) *Song of Destiny (Schicksalslied), Op. 54.*

(B) *** Decca Double Dig./Analogue 452 582-2 (2) [(M) id. import]. (i) Jard van Nes; (ii) San Francisco Ch. and SO, Blomstedt; (iii) New English Singers, Preston; (iv) King's College, Cambridge, Ch., Cleobury; (v) James King, Ambrosian Ch., New Philh. O, Abbado.

The recordings of the five key choral works here, the *Alto Rhapsody*, *Begrabnisgesang* (Funeral hymn), *Gesang der Parzen* (*Song of the Fates*), *Nänie* and the *Song of Destiny* (*Schicksalslied*), come from an outstanding 1989 collection using the Davis Symphony Hall, San Francisco, where the Decca team have made many outstanding records. This is no exception and, with inspired singing from the splendid San Francisco Choir, darkly intense in the rare and memorable *Funeral hymn*, exultant at the opening of *Nänie* and reaching a glorious climax. The *Song of the Fates* invites a more subtle approach, especially in the matter of light and shade, but is also very dramatically expansive, and Blomstedt and his choristers are not found wanting. The programme is capped by Jard van Nes's superbly eloquent and moving account of the *Alto rhapsody*, which can stand alongside the famous versions from Dame Janet Baker and Kathleen Ferrier, although it is different from either; again the choral contribution is splendid. Throughout, the glowing support from the orchestra, especially the lower strings, adds to the character of these performances and there is no finer collection of Brahms's shorter choral works in the catalogue. The King's College Choir under Cleobury then follows on with the two lovely *a cappella* five-part Motets of Op. 29, the second of which, *Schaffe in mir, Gott, ein rein Herz* ('Create in me a clean heart, O God'), is a partial setting of Psalm 51. Both these earlier (1860) Brahms settings pay tribute to the Bach tradition, whereas the later motets of Op. 74 (1877) and especially the three of Op. 110 (1889) look forward as well as backward in style. The first of Op. 74 with its questioning *Warum?* ('Wherefore is light given?') is the most ambitious of all, the second a set of choral variations on an Advent hymn. The final set here, Op. 110, is scored for double chorus. Here the second of the three is the most traditional; the third brings vigorous interchanges between the two groups. The *Geistliches Lied* is given a serene organ accompaniment; it is in fact a double canon, but the listener is hardly aware of its underlying structural mastery, so simply do the parts flow and interweave, with an exultant outpouring on the final 'Amen'. The final item on the second disc is the most substantial and the least satisfactory. James King's rather coarse Heldentenor approach to the 40-minute cantata *Rinaldo* is less than ideal for music that is much more easily lyrical than Wagner. However, again this is rare repertoire, and there is excellent singing from the Ambrosian Chorus, and Abbado ensures that the performance overall is fairly convincing. In any case the rest of the content of this set is more than worth its asking price.

(i) *Alto rhapsody, Op. 53; Deutsche Volkslieder:* (ii) *Ach, englische Schäferin; All mein' Gedanken; Da unten im Tale; Dort in den Weiden;* (iii) *Es war einmal ein Zimmergesell;* (ii) *Es wohnet ein Fiedler; In stiller Nacht; Maria ging aus wandern; Mein Mädel hat einen Rosenmund; Schwesterlein; Die Sonne scheint nicht mehr;* (iii) *Verstohlen geht der Mond auf.* (ii) *Wach auf, mein' Herzensschöne.* (iv) Lieder: *Am Sonntagmorgen; Botschaft; Heimweh II; Junge Lieder I; Die Mainacht; Minnelied; O liebche Wangen; Regenlied; Sonntag; Uber die Heide; Von ewiger Liebe.*

(B) *** DG Classikon 439 441-2 [(M) id. import]. (i) Christa Ludwig, V. Singverein, VPO, Boehm; (ii) Edith Mathis or Peter Schreier, Karl Engel; (iii) N. German R. Ch., Jena; Kahl; (iv) Fischer-Dieskau, Barenboim.

Although the initial attraction of this highly recommendable bargain collection may be Christa Ludwig's strong and eloquent account of the *Alto rhapsody* (recorded in 1977) or the Lieder recital from Fischer-Dieskau and Barenboim (both in superb form), taken from a comprehensive survey recorded in the early 1980s, the highlight is the well-chosen selection from Brahms's folksong arrangements. These are simple, glowing settings, published only three years before the composer's death, but the product of a lifetime's love-affair with the music. Edith Mathis and Peter Schreier capture their innocent spirit delightfully, never overplaying their hands (sample Schreier's charming *Mein Mädel hat einen Rosenmund* or Mathis's lovely *Maria ging aus wandern*). Karl Engel accompanies sympathetically and the Chorus of the North German Radio (digitally recorded) provides two of the attractive choral settings.

(i) *Alto rhapsody, Op. 53;* (ii) *German Requiem; Song of destiny (Schicksalslied), Op. 54. Academic festival overture; Tragic overture; Variations on a theme by Haydn.*

(B) **(*) Ph. Duo 438 760-2 (2) [(M) id. import]. (i) Aafjé Heynis; (ii) Wilma Lipp, Franz Crass; (i; ii) V. Singverein; VSO, Sawallisch.

In the *German Requiem* Sawallisch may not penetrate the spiritual depths as deeply as a conductor like Haitink but, with a simple, dedicated manner that lets the music flow naturally and with the help of very fine choral singing and recording to point the climaxes, it is still a deeply satisfying version, with an account of the final movements both dramatic and ethereal. Franz Crass's dark bass colouring make his solos tonally distinctive, but the singing of Wilma Lipp in *Ihr habt nun Traurigkeit* is a blot, wobbly and plaintive-sounding. However, what makes this inexpensive set worth considering, even against the competition, is Aafjé Heynis's lovely singing in the *Alto rhapsody*. It is even more dedicated and 'inner' than Kathleen Ferrier's, and the tonal shading is most beautiful. The emotionally more turbulent *Song of destiny* is also a considerable success. Not all collectors will need the overtures, but they are well enough played and recorded, although the early date (1959) of the *Variations* shows in the violin timbre. Sawallisch's performance is brisk and alive, with the slower variations not quite as convincing as the quick ones.

49 Deutsche Volkslieder; 14 Folksongs for children.

(M) *** DG (IMS) 449 087-2 (2). Edith Mathis, Peter Schreier, Karl Engel; N. German R. Ch., Günter Jena.

The writing here represents Brahms at his most engagingly domestic in these lovely folksong settings and the *Volks-Kinderlieder*, originally designed for the family of Robert and Clara Schumann. There is much to treasure here and the performances are fresh and brightly affectionate. The sound is first class and the documentation includes full translations. Recommended.

German Requiem, Op. 45.

(M) *** Teldec/Warner Dig. 9031 75862-2 [id.]. M. Price, Ramey, Amb. S., RPO, Previn.

(M) *** Ph. Dig. 462 059-2. Janowitz, Krause, V. State Op. Ch., VPO, Haitink.

(M) (***) EMI mono CDH7 64705-2. Grümmer, Fischer-Dieskau, St Hedwig's Cathedral Ch., BPO, Kempe.

(M) **(*) RCA Dig. 09026 61349-2. Battle, Hagegård, Chicago Ch. & SO, Levine.

(B) **(*) EMI Dig. CZS5 69653-2 [CDZB 69653]. Norman, Hynninen, LPO Ch., LPO, Tennstedt – SCHUMANN: *Requiems*. **(*)

(BB) * Naxos Dig. 8.550213 [id.]. Gauci, Tumagian, Slovak Philharmonic Ch., Slovak RSO, Alexander Rahbari.

It is the seeming simplicity of Previn's dedicated approach, with radiant singing from the chorus and measured speeds held steadily, that so movingly conveys an innocence in the often square writing, both in the powerful opening choruses and in the simple, songful *Wie lieblich*. The great fugatos are then powerfully presented. Both soloists are outstanding, Margaret Price golden-toned, Samuel Ramey incisively dark. The recording is warmly set against a helpful church acoustic with the chorus slightly distanced.

Haitink chooses very slow tempi, but there is a rapt quality in this glowing performance that creates an atmosphere of simple dedication; at slow speed *Denn alles Fleisch* ('All flesh is as grass') is made the more relentless when, with total concentration, textures are so sharply clarified. The digital recording offers beautiful sound and, with outstanding soloists – Gundula Janowitz notably pure and poised – this is altogether a very persuasive account, an excellent alternative to Previn. The disc is very handsomely re-packaged as part of the Philips 'Choral Collection', but no texts are provided.

Rudolf Kempe's mono recording of 1955 is incandescent, glowing with warmth, a characteristic example of his dedicated intensity in such a work. His view is flexibly expressive rather than rugged and, though the mono recording is limited on orchestral sound, the voices are caught vividly and atmospherically, with the choir the more involving for being forwardly balanced, something which modern digital recordings should heed more often. There is vintage singing too from both soloists, with the young Fischer-Dieskau darkly intense and with Elisabeth Grümmer sweetly radiant, superbly sustaining Kempe's exceptionally slow speed for *Ihr habt nun Traurigkeit*.

Levine's version features the Chicago Symphony Chorus, which is probably the finest in America, while his two soloists both prove excellent, Kathleen Battle pure and sweetly vulnerable-sounding, Hagegård clear-cut and firm. Levine is not the most illuminating conductor in this work and his pacing is not always convincing; yet the performance is alive, with power as well as impetus, and it undoubtedly gives pleasure. The recording is not ideal, with inner textures growing cloudy in tuttis.

Tennstedt's is an unusually spacious view of the *Requiem*, with speeds slower than on any rival version. His dedication generally sustains them well, with a reverential manner always alert, never becoming merely monumental, though the choir's ensemble is not always perfect. Jorma Hynninen proves an excellent soloist. What does sound monumental rather than moving is Jessye Norman's solo, *Ihr habt nun Traurigkeit*, though the golden tone is glorious. On CD, generally fine, spacious recording which matches the spaciousness of the interpretation.

On Naxos, Rahbari's reading at brisk speeds tends to be too matter-of-fact and lacking in detail, with the choral singing rather dull and inexpressive. By contrast the baritone, Eduard Tumagian, is warm and resonant, and Miriam Gauci takes a big-scale, operatic view of the soprano solo.

Liebeslieder waltzes, Op. 52; New Liebeslieder waltzes, Op. 65/15.

(M) (***) Decca mono 425 995-2. Irmgard Seefried, Kathleen Ferrier, Julius Patzak, Günter, Curzon, Gá – MAHLER: *Kindertotenlieder*. (**)

Recorded at the Edinburgh Festival in September 1952, the Decca historic performance brings a dazzling team together. Though it is not the most relaxed account, there are countless touches of imagination, not least from the very distinctive tenor, Julius Patzak, and the ever-responsive Clifford Curzon taking the upper piano part. Limited but clear sound.

(i–ii) *Liebeslieder waltzes, Op. 52* (two performances); (iii) *Waltzes, Op. 39. Waltzes for piano duet, Op. 39,* (iv) *Nos. 2, 6 & 15;* (v) *Nos. 1, 2, 5, 6, 10, 14 & 15.*

(M) (***) EMI mono CDH5 66425-2. (i) Seefried, Höngen, Meyer-Welfing, Hotter; (i, iv) Wührer; Von Nordberg; (ii) De Polignac, Kedroff, Cuénod, Conrad; (ii, v) Lipatti, Boulanger; (iii) Backhaus.

This historic tribute to Brahms in waltz-time makes a fascinating study, with early recordings of the first *Liebeslieder waltzes* – one very Viennese, one very French – set in contrast and the Opus 39 *Waltzes* offered in a variety of performances, with the popular *Waltz in A flat*, as well as two others, appearing in no fewer than three versions each, from Backhaus solo, from Wührer and Von Nordberg in Vienna and from Lipatti and Boulanger in Paris, all very different and equally winning. The vocal teams in the *Liebeslieder waltzes* are strikingly different too, with the Viennese much slower and more inclined to linger, with voices beautifully blended, where the Parisian performances are brisk and incisive, with voices – not least Hugues Cuénod's high tenor – clearly separated, despite the limited mono recording of 1937. Good, smooth transfers.

(i) *Vier ernste Gesänge, Op. 121; An die Nachtigall;* (ii) *Dein blaues Auge;* (i) *Erinnerung;* (ii) *Der Gang zum Liebchen; Geheimnis;* (i) *Die Mainacht;* (ii) *Meine Liebe ist grün; O kühler Wald;* (i) *O wüsst' ich doch den Weg zurück;* (ii) *Ruhe, Süssliebchen;* (i) *Sonntag; Ständchen; Vergebliches Ständchen; Verrat; Von ewige Liebe;* (ii) *Vor dem Fenster; Ein Wanderer; Wiegenlied; Wie Melodien zieht es mir; Wir wandelten*

(M) (***) EMI mono CDH5 66426-2. Alexander Kipnis, with (i) Gerald Moore, (ii) Ernst Victor Wolff.

This disc in EMI's historic Références series brings together the great majority of the recordings made by Alexander Kipnis for EMI's Brahms Song Society edition in 1936, with the project rounded off for RCA in New York. The performances are a revelation, with Kipnis using his firm, dark bass with its very Russian timbre to bring out word-meaning and dramatic point with an intensity rarely matched. So the *Four serious songs* are both incisively powerful and movingly poetic, with legato perfectly controlled, as it is in such a taxing song as *Von ewige Liebe*. It is fascinating to find Kipnis, very much a virile singer, tackling songs normally sung by women, such as *Vergebliches Ständchen*, *Wiegenlied* or *Sonntag*, with a point and charm rarely matched, so that at times with his head voice he sounds like a bass version of Richard Tauber. The transfers, focusing on the voice, retain some surface noise but not enough to be intrusive.

Vier ernste Gesänge, Op. 121; Lieder: *Auf dem Kirchhofe; Botschaft; Feldeinsamkeit; Im Waldeseinsamkeit; Minnelied III; Mondenschein; O wüsst ich doch den Weg zurück; Sapphische Ode; Sommerabend; Ständchen.*

✿ (M) (***) EMI (SIS) CDH7 63198-2 [id.]. Hotter, Moore – BACH: *Cantata No. 82: Ich habe genug.* (***) ✿

Glorious singing from Hans Hotter, wonderfully accompanied by Gerald Moore. An excellent transfer.

Briccialdi, Giulio (1818–81)

Wind quintet in D, Op. 124.

(BB) *** Naxos Dig. 8.553410 [id.]. Avalon Wind Quintet – CAMBINI: *Wind quintets Nos. 1–3.* ***

Giulio Briccialdi was an Italian flautist of considerable fame during his lifetime. He is remembered for his modification of Theodore Boehme's improved cylindrical flute, which he extended by a B flat, as well as further changes in the mid-1850s. In later years he was a professor at the Florence Conservatory. His *Wind quintet in D major* bears a high opus number, though the CD catalogues seem to have ignored the remaining 123 works! It is carefree, empty, lightweight – and utterly charming. It is expertly played by these young German musicians – and the recording is as delightfully natural as the playing. Well worth its three stars.

Bridge, Frank (1879–1941)

Cherry Ripe; Enter Spring (rhapsody); *Lament; The Sea* (suite); *Summer* (tone-poem).

(M) *** EMI CDM5 66855-2. RLPO, Groves.

Writing in the early years of the century, the composer confidently produced a magnificent seascape in the wake of Debussy, *The Sea*, but already by 1914 his responses were subtler, more original. *Summer*, written in that fateful year, was free of conventional pastoral moods, while in the last and greatest of Bridge's tone-poems, *Enter Spring*, he was responding to still wider musical horizons in experimentation which matches that of European contemporaries. Groves's warm advocacy adds to the impressiveness. First-rate recording, most successfully remastered.

Suite for string orchestra; Summer; There is a willow grows aslant a brook.

(M) *** Chandos CHAN 6566 [id.]. Bournemouth Sinf., Norman Del Mar – BANTOCK: *Pierrot of the minute;* BUTTERWORTH: *Banks of green willow.* ***

Summer is beautifully played by the Bournemouth Sinfonietta under Norman Del Mar. The same images of nature permeate the miniature tone-poem, *There is a willow grows aslant a brook*, an inspired piece, very sensitively managed. The *Suite for strings* is equally individual. Its third movement, a *Nocturne*, is lovely. The CD transfer is excellent and one can relish its fine definition and presence.

CHAMBER MUSIC

Cello sonata.

(M) *** Decca 443 575-2 [id.]. Rostropovich, Britten – SCHUBERT: *Arpeggione sonata.* **(*)

Bridge wrote his *Cello sonata* during the First World War. The craftsmanship is distinguished and the lines delicately traced, and the modulations are often personal. The playing on Decca is of an altogether rare order, even by the exalted standards of Rostropovich and Britten, and the recording, made at The Maltings in 1968, has immediacy, warmth and great response. The reissue features its original coupling in Decca's Classic Sound series.

Britten, Benjamin (1913–76)

An American overture; Sinfonia da Requiem, Op. 20; Peter Grimes: 4 Sea interludes and Passacaglia, Op. 33.

(BB) **(*) Naxos Dig. 8.553107 [id.]. New Zealand SO, Fredman.

Myer Fredman conducts warm and purposeful performances of this group of orchestral works from early in Britten's career. Though the New Zealand strings are not as rich or as resonant as some, the purity of sound makes up for power in spontaneous-sounding performances. Dramatic and atmospheric points are well made with the help of a warm hall acoustic and full-ranging recording. Recommendable at super-budget price.

Piano concerto in D, Op. 13.

(M) **(*) Chandos CHAN 6580 [id.]. Gillian Lin, Melbourne SO, John Hopkins – COPLAND: *Concerto.* **(*)

(B) ** Millennium MCD 80116. Marjorie Mitchell, N. German RSO, Strickland – BORTKIEWICZ: *Piano concerto No. 1;* BUSONI: *Indian fantasy.* **

(i) *Piano concerto, Op. 13;* (ii) *Violin concerto, Op. 15.*

(M) *** Decca 417 308-2. (i) Sviatoslav Richter; (ii) Lubotsky; ECO, composer.

Britten wrote his formidable *Piano concerto* for a Prom in 1938. Richter is incomparable in interpreting it, not only the thoughtful, introspective moments but the Liszt-like bravura passages. With its highly original sonorities the *Violin concerto* makes a splendid vehicle for another Soviet artist, Mark Lubotsky. Recorded in The Maltings, the playing of the ECO under the composer's direction matches the inspiration of the soloists.

Gillian Lin provides a useful alternative to Richter's classic recording. Miss Lin cannot match the Soviet master in detailed imagination but, from her sharp attack on the opening motif onwards, she gives a strong and satisfying reading, well accompanied by Hopkins and the Melbourne orchestra. The 1978 recorded sound is wide-ranging and well balanced on this lively CD, which makes a useful mid-priced alternative, with its rarer Copland coupling.

A good performance by Marjorie Mitchell of the *Piano concerto*, which must have been recorded in the late 1950s or early 1960s. The sleeve is unforthcoming as to its actual provenance. It is decently recorded but is far from a first choice, given the modestly priced account available from Richter and Britten on Decca. Some collectors may want the present disc for the Busoni; as a bonus item the Britten is perfectly acceptable.

Violin concerto, Op. 15 (original version).

(M) (**) EMI mono CDM5 66053-2. Theo Olof, Hallé O, Barbirolli – HEMING: *Threnody;* RUBBRA: *Symphony No. 5; Improvisations.* (***)

Allowances have to be made for the quality of this première recording, made by the young Dutch virtuoso, Theo Olof, and the Hallé Orchestra under Barbirolli in 1948, which makes its first appearance on CD. Perhaps knowing that he was at work on a revised version of the score, Britten never sanctioned its release, though he can surely have entertained no doubts as to the virtuosity and dedication of the soloist or of Sir John, who had championed the piece in his New York days. Certainly worth hearing, but not a prime recommendation – the quality of sound is a handicap.

Violin concerto, Op. 15.

(M) *** EMI CDM7 64202-2 [id.]. Ida Haendel, Bournemouth SO, Berglund – WALTON: *Violin concerto.* ***

Ida Haendel's ravishing playing places the work firmly in the European tradition. She brings great panache and brilliance to the music, as well as great expressive warmth. This is a reading very much in the grand manner and it finds Paavo Berglund in excellent form. His support is sensitive in matters of detail and full of atmosphere. The recording is full and realistic, with a beautifully spacious perspective that creates a positively Mediterranean feeling. The soloist is balanced a little close, but the security of her technique can stand up to such a spotlight and the performance has great conviction.

(i) *Diversions for piano (left hand) and orchestra, Op. 21;* (ii) *Sinfonia da Requiem, Op. 20;* (iii) *The Young person's guide to the orchestra, Op. 34.*
(B) **(*) Sony SBK 62746. (i) Leon Fleisher, Boston SO, Ozawa; (ii) St Louis SO, Previn; (iii) LSO, Andrew Davis.

The *Diversions* is a wartime work, highly inventive and resourceful, whose neglect over the years is puzzling. Fleisher lost the use of his right hand at the height of his career, so Britten's *Diversions* is custom-made for him. He gives a sensitive and intelligent account with great sympathy and skill. His playing has strong character and he receives more than decent support from Ozawa and the Boston orchestra, and eminently truthful recording. Previn's coupling is also worth having at bargain price. It is obviously deeply felt; if not quite a match for the composer's own, it has a well-detailed (1963) recording. To complete the disc, Andrew Davis directs an account of *The Young person's guide to the orchestra* that is bright and workmanlike rather than one with any special flair or brilliance. But it is enjoyable enough and the (1975) Abbey Road recording sounds well on CD.

Matinées musicales; Soirées musicales; Variations on a theme of Frank Bridge.
(B) *** CfP Dig. CD-CFP 4598. ECO, Gibson.

Britten wrote his *Soirées musicales* for a GPO film-score in the 1930s; the *Matinées* followed in 1941 and were intended as straight ballet music. Both are wittily if rather sparsely scored, deriving their musical content directly from Rossini. The ECO play very well indeed for Sir Alexander Gibson, and readers requiring this particular coupling need not hesitate on either artistic or technical grounds. The *Frank Bridge variations* display strong characterization and virtuosity in equal measure. The recording is full and resonant; only the bright lighting of the violin-timbre above the stave betrays the early date of the digital recording (1982).

(i) *Matinées musicales; Soirées musicales;* (ii; iv) *Young person's guide to the orchestra;* (iii; iv) *Peter Grimes: 4 Sea interludes and Passacaglia.*
(M) *** Decca 425 659-2. (i) Nat. PO, Bonynge; (ii) LSO; (iii) ROHCG O; (iv) composer.

Bonynge's versions of the *Matinées* and *Soirées musicales* are here reissued, coupled with Britten's accounts of the *Young person's guide to the orchestra* and the *Sea interludes and Passacaglia.*

Prince of the Pagodas: Pas de six. Gloriana: symphonic suite; Peter Grimes: 4 Sea interludes.
(B) *** EMI Dig. CD-EMX 2231 [(M) id. import]. RLPO, Takuo Yuasa.

Takuo Yuasa conducts these orchestral pieces, drawn from Britten's stage works, with great colour and flair, matching and even outshining any rival versions. The Liverpool orchestra is in virtuoso form, and the recording is full and rich. If the programme appeals, this is good value.

Scottish ballad, Op. 26.
(B) ** Carlton Classics Dig. 30367 01732 [(M) id.]. Joshua Pierce & Dorothy Jonas, Luxembourg R. and TV SO, Ettore Stratta – MARTINU: *Double piano concerto* etc. **

Dating from Britten's war-time stay in the United States, the *Scottish ballad* for two pianos and orchestra was written for the popular piano duo of Ethel Bartlett and Rae Robertson, and it no doubt reflects their warmly energetic style. The piano writing, often heavily chordal, is curiously untypical of Britten with little of his usual spareness. Nevertheless, with its distinctive settings of Scottish themes it does not deserve its neglect, and it here receives a strong, positive performance, not helped by rather shallow recorded sound. The Martinů coupling includes two other works written for Bartlett and Robertson.

Simple Symphony, Op. 4; Prelude and fugue for 18-part string orchestra, Op. 29.
(M) *** Decca 448 569-2. ECO, composer – Concert of *English string music.* *** ✿

(i) *Simple Symphony, Op. 4; Variations on a theme of Frank Bridge;* (ii) *Young person's guide to the orchestra; Peter Grimes: 4 Sea interludes.*
(M) **(*) Nimbus NI 7017 [id.]. (i) E. String O; (ii) E. SO, Boughton.

(i) *Simple Symphony, Op. 4;* (ii) *The Young person's guide to the orchestra (Variations and fugue on a theme of Purcell), Op. 34; Peter Grimes: 4 Sea interludes.*
(B) *** [EMI Red Line Dig. CDR5 72564]. (i) ASMF; (ii) Minnesota O; Marriner.

The composer's own recording of the *Simple Symphony* was originally contained in an outstanding anthology called 'Britten conducts English music' – see the Concerts section. The *Simple Symphony* makes a splendid foil for the *Prelude and fugue*, with its charm and high spirits, aided by the glowing resonance of The Maltings where the recording was made.

William Boughton offers an attractive and generous 75-minute Britten anthology, very well played and showing the sumptuous Nimbus recording style at its most effective. The *Simple Symphony* and *Frank Bridge variations* were recorded in the Great Hall of Birmingham University in 1985 and are most sympathetically played (the *Playful pizzicato* has a resonance to match the composer's own version). The *Young person's guide* and *Sea interludes* were recorded in Birmingham's new Symphony Hall in 1991 and, while equally rich in texture, have even better definition. The famous *Variations* are amiably colourful, but Boughton is fired with a strongly emotional response to the *Sea Interludes*, bringing out the inner tensions in *Moonlight* most involvingly, while the powerful *Storm* sequence is highly spectacular.

Marriner's Minnesota account of the *Young person's guide* is very well played, and if his direct approach seems just a little stiff, the digital sound is first rate, clean and clear. The balance is fairly close and the ambient effect of Orchestra Hall, Minneapolis, colours the music warmly, yet it is not allowed to cloud any of the textures. The *Peter Grimes interludes* too are not wanting in atmosphere, and again the orchestral playing is impressive. The youthful *Simple Symphony* is delightfully spirited and fresh.

Sinfonia da Requiem, Op. 20.
(M) *** EMI Dig. CDM7 64870-2 [id.]. CBSO, Simon Rattle – SHOSTAKOVICH: *Symphony No. 10.* **

Rattle's passionate view of the *Sinfonia da Requiem* is unashamedly extrovert, yet it finds subtle detail too. The EMI recording is admirably vivid and clear, but the Shostakovich coupling is less convincing.

(i) *Sinfonia da Requiem, Op. 20;* (ii) *Symphony for cello and orchestra, Op. 68;* (iii) *Cantata misericordium, Op. 69.*
(M) *** Decca 425 100-2 [id.]. (i) New Philh. O; (ii) Rostropovich, ECO; (iii) Pears, Fischer-Dieskau, London Symphony Ch., LSO; composer.

All the performances here are definitive, and Rostropovich's account of the *Cello symphony* in particular is everything one could ask for. The CD transfers are admirably managed.

Sinfonia da Requiem, Op. 20; The Young person's guide to the orchestra, Op. 34; Peter Grimes: 4 Sea interludes & Passacaglia, Op. 33.
(M) **(*) Virgin/EMI (SIS) Dig. CUV5 61195-2 [id.]. RLPO, Libor Pešek.

Though Pešek fails to convey the full ominous weight of the first movement of the *Sinfonia da Requiem*, he then directs a dazzling account of the central *Dies Irae Scherzo*, taken breathtakingly fast, and finds an intense repose in the calm of the final *Requiem aeternam*. The *Sea interludes* sound very literal, not ideally atmospheric. The *Young person's guide* lacks a degree of tension, with the fugue not dashing enough. The recording is comfortably reverberant.

Sinfonia da Requiem, Op. 20; Peter Grimes: 4 Sea interludes and passacaglia.
✿ (B) *** EMI forte CZS5 72658-2 (2) [(M) id.]. LSO, Previn – SHOSTAKOVICH: *Symphonies Nos. 4 & 5.* **(*)

In Previn's reading of the *Sinfonia da Requiem*, the most ambitious of Britten's early orchestral works, written after the death of his parents, there is the same passionate intensity as in his earlier, St Louis version for CBS (now deleted) but with far greater subtlety of inflexion and execution. It is a warmer reading than the composer's own, less sharply incisive but presenting a valid alternative. So too in the *Four sea interludes* presented here – unlike the composer's own recording – in their concert form with tailored endings. Previn springs the bouncing rhythms of the second interlude – the picture of *Sunday morning in the Borough* – even more infectiously than the composer himself. These superb performances are presented in wonderfully expansive recordings of demonstration quality: the *Sinfonia* was recorded in 1973 in Kingsway Hall, the *Peter Grimes* excerpts at Abbey Road a year later. They are among the finest analogue recordings ever issued (particularly striking in the *Peter Grimes interludes*), which in their CD transfers have glowing inner detail and spin a richly atmospheric web of sound. It is a pity that the Shostakovich coupling is only partly recommendable: the *Fourth Symphony* is very successful but the *Fifth* fails to take off. However, many collectors will count this forte double worth having in spite of that.

Suite on English folksongs (A time there was); Young person's guide to the orchestra, Op. 34; Peter Grimes: 4 Sea interludes and Passacaglia.
(M) **(*) Sony SMK 47541. NYPO, Leonard Bernstein.

Bernstein's charismatic account of the *Young person's guide to the orchestra* brings much exhilarating bravura from the New York soloists, notably the flutes, clarinets and trumpets. The 1961 recording, made in the New York Manhattan Center, is fuller than usual from this source. The performance of *A time there was* (its title quoting Hardy) reveals a darkness and weight of expression behind the seemingly trivial plan. For violins alone, *Hunt the squirrel* is brief, brilliant and witty. Bernstein misses a little of the wit but is warmly sympathetic, and the dramatic account of the *Grimes interludes*, with a powerful *Passacaglia*, makes a good coupling.

Symphony for cello and orchestra, Op. 68.
(M) (***) Revelation mono RV 10100 [id.]. Rostropovich, Moscow PO, Britten – ELGAR: *Cello concerto.* (***)

This Russian Revelation disc offers the radio recording of the world première performance of Britten's *Cello symphony* in March 1964. It is also available in EMI's Rostropovich Seventieth Birthday Edition, but the Revelation transfer actually holds up well in comparison with Andrew Walter's EMI refurbishment. The sound is obviously limited but atmospheric – less forward than the EMI transfer. Rostropovich's performance has even more power and intensity than that in his studio recording for Decca with the ECO, made soon after, also with Britten conducting. This music-making undoubtedly communicates a sense of occasion and the Russian orchestra, very well rehearsed, play with purposeful thrust in a thorny work, with only the brass at times a little flabby. Rostropovich's command even in a completely new work is breathtaking. The recording is in mono, though nowhere on the label or sleeve do Revelation say so. But it has a lot going for it, especially in view of the Elgar coupling which, though not so well recorded, makes an apt and attractive pairing.

Variations on a theme of Frank Bridge, Op. 10.
❀ (M) (***) EMI mono CDM5 66601-2. Philh. O, Karajan – VAUGHAN WILLIAMS: *Fantasia on a theme by Thomas Tallis* (***) ❀; STRAVINSKY: *Jeu de cartes.* (**)

If all digital CDs of the 1990s sounded like this Karajan mono recording of the early 1950s, there would be no need for a *Penguin Guide*! The sound is astonishingly fresh and vivid, and the playing of the Philharmonia strings is of the highest order of distinction. They produce beautifully blended tone, rich and full-bodied, yet marvellously delicate at the pianissimo end of the dynamic spectrum. Karajan's reading is unaffected yet impassioned, quite electrifying in the *Funeral music*. This is an issue that should never be out of the catalogue and, alongside his Balakirev/Roussel coupling, marks the peak of Karajan's achievement during his London years with EMI, between 1948 and 1960.

The Young person's guide to the orchestra (Variations and fugue on a theme of Purcell), Op. 34.
(BB) *** Naxos Dig. 8.554170 [id.]. Dame Edna Everage, Melbourne SO, John Lanchbery – POULENC: *The story of Babar* *** ❀; PROKOFIEV: *Peter and the wolf.* ***
(M) **(*) Decca Phase Four 444 104-2 [id.]. Sean Connery (nar.), RPO, Dorati – PROKOFIEV: *Peter and the wolf* etc. **(*)
(B) ** CfP CD-CFP 185 [(M) id.]. Richard Baker, New Philh. O, Leppard – PROKOFIEV: *Peter and the Wolf.* **
(BB) ** Naxos Dig. 8.550499 [id.]. Slovak RSO (Bratislava), Lenárd – PROKOFIEV: *Peter* **; SAINT-SAENS: *Carnival.* **(*)

Using her own enthusiastically expanded version of the original commentary, Dame Edna will surely draw any young possum into the world of the orchestra. Her sheer exuberance offsets any twee moments, and the Melbourne orchestra illustrate vivid instrumental descriptions with splendidly alive and colourful playing. The Naxos recording is excellent and, with its highly enjoyable couplings, this inexpensive triptych would be recommendable if it cost far more than it does.

Sean Connery's voice is very familiar and his easy style is attractive. His narration should go down well with young people, even if some of the points are made rather heavily. The orchestral playing is first rate and the vivid, forwardly balanced recording – with a Decca Phase Four source – is effective enough in this context. The performance has plenty of colour and vitality.

The rather cosy narration by Richard Baker on this Classics for Pleasure reissue tends to hold up the flow of the music. The orchestral playing is lively and the recording good, but one feels that there are too many words here. This is not a version to stand constant repetition, although it would be suitable for school use.

The Slovak Radio Orchestra play well enough; although they are not as naturally at home in the variations as British orchestras, they obviously enjoy the gusto of the fugue. Bright, digital sound, but this is not a distinctive version. Separate cues are provided for each of the orchestral sections – woodwind, strings, brass and percussion – but not for the individual instruments.

CHAMBER MUSIC

Cello sonata in C, Op. 65.

(M) *** Decca 452 895-2 [id.]. Rostropovich, composer – DEBUSSY: *Sonata;* SCHUMANN: *5 Stücke in Volkston.* ***

The current reissue in Decca's Classic Sound series restores the original (1961) couplings. The strange, five-movement *Cello sonata* was written specially for Rostropovich's appearance that year at the Aldeburgh Festival, and the recording was made soon after the first performance. It is unlike anything Britten had written previously. The idiom itself is unexpected, sometimes recalling Soviet models, as in the spiky *March*, perhaps out of tribute to the dedicatee. Although technically it demands fantastic feats from the cellist, it is hardly a display piece. Each of the five movements is poised and concentrated. It is an excellent work to wrestle with on a record, particularly when the performance is never likely to be outshone. The recording is superb in every way.

(i) *Cello sonata in C, Op. 65;* (Unaccompanied) *Cello suites Nos. 1, Op. 72; 2, Op. 80.*

(M) *** Decca 421 859-2. Rostropovich; (i) with composer.

This strange five-movement *Cello sonata* is here coupled with two of the *Suites for unaccompanied cello.* This is rough, gritty music in Britten's latterday manner, but Rostropovich gives such inspired accounts that the music reveals more and more with repetition.

Cello suites (Suites for unaccompanied cello) Nos. 1, Op. 72; 2, Op. 80; 3, Op. 87.

(BB) ** Naxos Dig. 8.553663 [id.]. Tim Hugh.

Tim Hugh earlier recorded the three Britten *Suites* for Hyperion, but since then (1987) his view of them seems to have changed radically. His Naxos version is no less than nine minutes shorter overall, with speeds faster both in allegros and andantes. The manner is also more clearly dramatic, strong and positive, though the meditative depth of the earlier account is largely missing. The result is taut and tough – as if he is keen to de-gentrify Britten's muse. At times he is in just a little bit too much of a hurry, but there is plenty of spirit and fire. However, the Hyperion sound is fuller and better focused than the slightly reverberant Naxos, which is otherwise good value.

6 Metamorphoses after Ovid (for solo oboe), *Op. 49; Phantasy quartet* (for oboe and string trio), *Op. 2; 2 Insect pieces; Temporal variations* (both for oboe and piano).

(M) *** Carlton Classics Dig. 30366 00962 [id.]. Robin Canter, Medici Qt (members) or Simon Nicholls – FINZI: *Interlude.* ***

The oboist, Robin Canter, offers this complete collection of Britten's oboe music, using a ripe, sumptuous tone which in its warmth suggests the influence of Leon Goossens, whose playing inspired the first of the three early works here, the *Phantasy quartet.* It was one of the composer's first published pieces, dating from 1931 and belying the idea of a student work. The sharply inventive and varied *Temporal variations* of 1936 and the neatly pointed *Insect pieces* of 1935 were published only after the composer's death. The *Metamorphoses* of 1951 for solo oboe were written for Joy Boughton to play at an Aldeburgh Festival open-air concert, but in their brilliance and expressive range have proved favourites with oboe players, short of solo repertory. The Finzi piece makes an apt and attractive coupling, equally well recorded

VOCAL MUSIC

The Burning fiery furnace (2nd Parable), Op. 77.

(M) *** Decca 414 663-2. Pears, Tear, Drake, Shirley-Quirk, Ch. & O of E. Op. Group, composer and Viola Tunnard.

The story of *Burning fiery furnace* is obviously dramatic in the operatic sense, with vivid scenes like the *Entrance of Nebuchadnezzar*, the *Raising of the Idol*, and the putting of the three Israelites into the furnace. The performers, both singers and players, are the same hand-picked cast that participated in the first performance at Orford Parish Church, where this record was made.

Canticles Nos. 1, My beloved is mine, Op. 40; 2, Abraham and Isaac, Op. 51; 3, Still falls the rain, Op. 55; 4, Journey of the Magi, Op. 86; 5, Death of St Narcissus, Op. 89. A birthday hansel. Arr. of PURCELL: *Sweeter than roses.*

(M) *** Decca 425 716-2. Peter Pears, Hahessy, Bowman, Shirley-Quirk, Tuckwell, Ellis, composer.

This CD brings together on a single record all five of the miniature cantatas to which Britten gave the title 'Canticle', plus the *Birthday hansel*, written in honour of the seventy-fifth birthday of Queen Elizabeth the Queen Mother, and a Purcell song-arrangement. A beautiful collection as well as a historical document, with recording that still sounds well.

(i; ii) *Ceremony of carols, Op. 28;* (i; iii) *Friday afternoons, Op. 7; Francie; King Herod and the cock; The oxen;* (i) *Sweet was the song;* (iv) Song: *The Birds;* (iv; v; iii) *3 2-part settings of Walter de la Mare: The Ride-by-nights; The Rainbow; The Ship of Rio. A Wealden trio.*

(B) *** Naxos Dig. 8.553183 [id.]. (i) New L. Children's Ch., Ronald Corp; (ii) Skaila Kanga; (iii) Alexander Wells; (iv) Catherine Hopper; (v) Emily Attree; Anna Kenyon.

Ronald Corp directs bright, refreshing performances of a delightful collection of Britten choral pieces written with children's voices in mind. The New London Children's Choir is relatively large and is recorded against a lively hall acoustic, but there is no lack of impact, and the tenderness of expression as well as the liveliness is consistently refreshing. Though the *Processional* is recorded statically, losing in atmosphere, the *Ceremony of carols* brings ensemble remarkably crisp for a biggish choir, and these performances justify the decision to have full ensemble treatment for all of the *Friday afternoons* sequence. A splendid bargain.

(i) *A Ceremony of carols, Op. 28; Hymn to St Cecilia, Op. 27;* (ii) *Jubilate Deo;* (i) *Missa brevis in D, Op. 63;* (ii) *Rejoice in the Lamb* (Festival cantata), *Op. 30; Te Deum in C.*

(M) *** EMI CDM7 64653-2. King's College, Cambridge, Ch.; (i) Osian Ellis, Willcocks; (ii) James Bowman, Ledger.

The King's trebles may still have less edge in the *Ceremony of carols* than their Cambridge rivals at St John's College, and the *Missa brevis* can certainly benefit from a throatier sound, but the results here are dramatic as well as beautiful. To make a generous reissue EMI have added Philip Ledger's 1974 version of the cantata, *Rejoice in the Lamb*, with timpani and percussion added to the original organ part. Here the biting climaxes are sung with passionate incisiveness, while James Bowman is in his element in the delightful passage which tells you that 'the mouse is a creature of great personal valour'. The *Te Deum* setting and *Jubilate* make an additional bonus and are no less well sung and recorded.

A Ceremony of carols; Hymn to St Cecilia, Op. 27; Rejoice in the Lamb, Op. 30; Sacred and profane, Op. 91.

(B) *** EMI Eminence CD-EMX 2204 [(M) id. import]. Vasari Singers, Jeremy Backhouse.

Jeremy Backhouse conducts the Vasari Singers in clean-cut and refined performances of this well-chosen group of Britten choral works, helped by first-rate recording, both atmospheric and well detailed. In the *Ceremony of Carols*, where boy-treble sound is an advantage, the refinement of the women's voices here makes for a less earthy result than Britten may ideally have wanted. Yet the compensations in precision of ensemble are many, as they are in the *Hymn to St Cecilia* and *Sacred and profane*. Finest of all is the performance of the cantata, *Rejoice in the Lamb*, colourful and vigorous with an excellent quartet of soloists and strongly rhythmic accompaniment from an unidentified organist.

(i) *A ceremony of carols;* (ii) *Shepherd's carol; A Boy was born; Jesus, as Thou art our Saviour.*

(M) *** ASV CDWHL 2097. Christ Church Cathedral Ch., Francis Grier; (i) with Frances Kelly; (ii) Harry Bicket (with Collection: *'Carols from Christ Church'* ***).

A first-class account of Britten's *Ceremony of carols*, attractively vigorous, full of the right sort of rhythmic energy. There is an earthy quality which reflects the composer's own rejection of over-refined choirboy tone, yet the two treble solos, the delicate *That yongë child* (Andrew Olleson) and *Balulalow* (Edward Harris), are both delicate, and the latter soloist is radiantly assured, as he is in *Jesus, as Thou art our Saviour*. The dialogue *Shepherd's carol* is also sung most effectively. The reissue is combined with a dozen other carols by various composers, mostly English, making for a very enticing Christmas CD.

(i) *Children's crusade;* (ii) *The Little Sweep (Let's make an opera);* (iii) *Gemini variations.*

(M) (***) Decca (IMS) stereo/mono 436 393-2. (i) Hartnett, Purcell Singers, English Op. Group Boys' Ch.; Choristers of All Saints', Margaret St, composer; (ii) Soloists, Wandsworth School Boys' Ch., Burgess; composer (piano); (iii) G. & Z. Jeney.

Britten's own mono recording of *The Little Sweep* sounds amazingly vivid, with voices in particular full and immediate. As a performance it has never been surpassed in its vigour and freshness, with David Hemmings here impressive in the title-role for treble. Others in the cast, like Jennifer Vyvyan and April Cantelo, represent the accomplished group of singers that Britten gathered for his Aldeburgh Festival performances. The choruses, usually sung by the audience, are here done by the school choir. The *Children's crusade*, written for the Save the Children Fund, is darker but equally vivid. The *Gemini variations* (interchanging flute, violin and piano) was written for the Jeney twins, who play it here.

Curlew River (1st parable for church performance).

(M) *** Decca 421 858-2. Pears, Shirley-Quirk, Blackburn, soloists, Instrumental Ens., composer and Viola Tunnard.

In Britten's own version of *Curlew River*, which has its own special character, Harold Blackburn plays the Abbot of the monastery who introduces the drama, while John Shirley-Quirk plays the ferryman who takes people over the Curlew River and Peter Pears sings the part of the madwoman who, distracted, searches fruitlessly for her abducted child. The recording is outstanding even by Decca standards.

Folksong arrangements: *The ash grove; Avenging and bright; La belle est au jardin d'amour; The bonny Earl o' Moray; The brisk young widow; Ca' the yowes; Come you not from Newcastle?; Early one morning; The foggy, foggy dew; How sweet the answer; The last rose of summer; The Lincolnshire poacher; The miller of Dee; The minstrel boy; Oft in the stilly night; O Waly, Waly; The plough boy; Le roi s'en va-t'en chasse; Sally in our alley; Sweet Polly Oliver; Tom Bowling.*
(M) *** Decca 430 063-2. Peter Pears, Benjamin Britten.

It is good to have the definitive Pears/Britten collaboration in the folksong arrangements. Excellent, faithful recording, well transferred to CD.

(i) *The Golden Vanity;* (ii) *Noye's Fludde.*
(M) *** Decca 436 397-2. (i) Wandsworth School Boys' Ch., Burgess, composer (piano); (ii) Brannigan, Rex, Anthony, East Suffolk Children's Ch. & O, E. Op. Group O, Del Mar.

Britten originally wrote his 'vaudeville', *The Golden Vanity*, for the Vienna Boys, who wanted a piece in which they would not have to take the roles of girls, and they give a performance at once superbly controlled and lusty. The Wandsworth boys are completely at home in the music and sing with pleasing freshness. The coupling was recorded during the 1961 Aldeburgh Festival, and not only the professional choristers but the children too have the time of their lives to the greater glory of God. All the effects have been captured miraculously here, most strikingly the entry into the ark, while a bugle band blares out fanfares, with the stereo readily catching the sense of occasion and particularly the sound of *Eternal Father* rising above the storm at the climax of *Noye's Fludde*.

Holy sonnets of John Donne, Op. 35; 7 Sonnets of Michelangelo, Op. 22; Winter words, Op. 52.
(M) ** Carlton Dig. 30366 00562 [id.]. Justin Lavender, Julian Milford.

The disc puts these three tenor song-cycles in chronological order, which is a pity when Justin Lavender's slightly strident, throaty-sounding voice is at its least effective in the first of the three, the *Michelangelo Sonnets*, in which the the vocal lines match the mellifluous Italian text. Lavender is much better suited to the powerful Donne cycle, producing a good ringing attack, and that equally gives Julian Milford the chance to shine in comparably powerful playing. Milford is also brilliant in evoking the necessary atmosphere in each of the Hardy settings of *Winter words*, tense and alert, though there, as in the Michelangelo cycle, Lavender's singing sounds too strenuous. Good, open sound.

(i) *Les Illuminations* (song-cycle), *Op. 18;* (ii) *Nocturne;* (iii) *Serenade for tenor, horn and strings, Op. 31.*
(M) *** Decca 436 395-2 [417 153-2]. (i–iii) Peter Pears; (i) ECO; (ii) wind soloists; (ii; iii) LSO strings, composer; (iii) with Barry Tuckwell.
(B) *** EMI Dig. CD-EMX 2247 [(M) CDM 65899]. John Mark Ainsley, David Pyatt, Britten Sinfonia, Cleobury.

With dedicated accompaniments under the composer's direction, these Pears versions of *Les Illuminations* and the *Serenade* (with its horn obbligato superbly played by Barry Tuckwell) make a perfect coupling. For the CD release Decca have added the recording of the *Nocturne* from 1960. It is a work full – as is so much of Britten's output – of memorable moments. Each song has a different obbligato instrument (with the ensemble unified for the final Shakespeare song) and each instrument gives the song it is associated with its own individual character. Pears, as always, is the ideal interpreter, the composer a most efficient conductor, and the fiendishly difficult obbligato parts are played superbly. The recording is brilliant and clear, with just the right degree of atmosphere although, for some reason, the transfer of *Les Illuminations* is brighter than the other two works.

This ideal coupling of Britten's three great orchestral song-cycles finds Ainsley echoing the example of the inspirer, Peter Pears, in the shading and moulding of each phrase, above all in the *Serenade*, where the brilliant horn-playing of David Pyatt provides an extra reason for recommending the disc. Ainsley's range of expression is wide and under pressure the voice grows a little rough, as in the final Shakespeare setting of the *Nocturne*. But that is contrasted with an exceptionally beautiful use of the head-voice, with total freedom in the upper register, as in the *Lyke-Wake dirge* from the *Serenade*. Warm, immediate recording.

(i) *Noye's Fludde;* (ii) *Serenade for tenor, horn & strings, Op. 31.*

(M) **(*) Virgin/EMI Dig. CUV5 61122-2 [id.]. (i) Maxwell, Ormiston, Pasco, Salisbury & Chester Schools Ch. & O, Coull Qt, Alley, Watson, Harwood, Endymion Ens. (members); (ii) Martyn Hill, Frank Lloyd, City of L. Sinfonia, Hickox.

On the Virgin disc the instrumental forces, including a schools' orchestra as well as professional soloists, are relatively recessed. Compare the storm sequence here with the Decca account, and the distancing undermines any feeling of threat so that the entry of the hymn, *Eternal Father*, instantly submerges the orchestral sound, instead of battling against it. Not even Donald Maxwell as Noah, strong and virile, can efface memories of the incomparable Owen Brannigan.

(i) *Our Hunting Fathers, Op. 8; Folksong arrangements: The bonny Earl o'Moray; Come you not from Newcastle?; Little Sir William; Oliver Cromwell; O Waly, Waly; The plough boy;* (ii) *Serenade for tenor, horn and strings.*

(M) **(*) EMI Dig./Analogue CDM7 69522-2 [id.]. (i) Elisabeth Söderström, Welsh Nat. Op. O, Richard Armstrong; (ii) Robert Tear, Alan Civil, N. Sinfonia, Marriner.

W. H. Auden put together the sequence of poems on an anti-bloodsport theme, *Our Hunting Fathers*, designing it to shock the Norwich audience (which it did) and providing two of the poems himself. The piece, with its obvious acerbities – like the shrieks in *Rats away* – still has the power to shock, and this performance finds Söderström a committed soloist, even if a tenor voice suits this work even more. The folksongs make an attractive bonus, and the new coupling with Robert Tear's 1970 version of the *Serenade* adds to the interest of this reissue. Tear is very much in the Aldeburgh tradition set by Pears, yet he gives a new and positive slant to each of Britten's lovely songs, with the Johnson *Hymn to Diana* given extra jollity, thanks partly to the brilliant galumphing of Alan Civil on the horn. The recording's resonance provides atmosphere without clouding.

The Prodigal Son (3rd parable), Op. 81.

(M) *** Decca 425 713-2. Pears, Tear, Shirley-Quirk, Drake, E. Op. Group Ch. & O, composer and Viola Tunnard.

The last of the parables is the sunniest and most heart-warming. Britten cleverly avoids the charge of oversweetness by introducing the Abbot, even before the play starts, in the role of Tempter, confessing he represents evil and aims to destroy contentment in the family he describes: 'See how I break it up' – a marvellous line for Peter Pears. An ideal performance is given here with a characteristically real and atmospheric Decca recording.

(i) *St Nicholas, Op. 42;* (ii) *Rejoice in the Lamb, Op. 30.*

(M) (***) Decca mono 425 714-2. (i) Hemmings, Pears, St John Leman School, Beccles, Girls' Ch., Ipswich School Boys' Ch., Aldeburgh Festival Ch. & O; R. Downes; (ii) Hartnett, Steele, Todd, Francke, Purcell Singers, G. Malcolm; composer.

With rare exceptions, Britten's first recordings of his own works have a freshness and vigour unsurpassed since. Britten's performances capture the element of vulnerability, not least in the touching setting of words by the deranged poet, Christopher Smart, *Rejoice in the Lamb*.

Serenade for tenor, horn and strings.

(B) *** DG 439 464-2. Robert Tear, Dale Clevenger, Chicago SO, Giulini – DELIUS: *On hearing the first cuckoo; Summer night on the river*; VAUGHAN WILLIAMS: *Greensleeves; Lark ascending.* ***

Robert Tear's 1977 interpretation of the *Serenade* is very much in the Aldeburgh tradition set by Pears, and Giulini has long been a persuasive advocate of Britten's music. He presents the cycle as a full-scale orchestral work and Tear is at his finest, more open than in his earlier, EMI recording. Dale Clevenger is a superb horn player, and though in places some may find him unidiomatic it is good to have a fresh view of the music, especially when inexpensively coupled with fine performances of music by Delius and Vaughan Williams.

(i) *Serenade for tenor, horn and strings, Op. 31;* (ii) *7 Sonnets of Michelangelo, Op. 22; Winter words, Op. 52.*

(M) (***) Decca mono 425 996-2. Peter Pears, (i) Dennis Brain, Boyd Neel String O, composer; (ii) composer (piano).

This compilation brings together some of Britten's historic early recordings for Decca. This first recording of the *Serenade*, though not helped by unatmospheric sound, is wonderfully intense, with Dennis Brain uniquely magnetic on the horn. The first recording of the Hardy song-cycle, *Winter words*, has never been matched by more recent recordings, an intensely evocative performance with Britten drawing magical sounds from the piano in support of Pears. This version of the *Michelangelo sonnets* is not quite as fresh-toned as the even earlier EMI one, but it still offers a searchingly intense performance. Limited but clear mono sound.

(i) *Songs from the Chinese, Op. 58;* Folksong arrangements: *I will give my love an apple; Master Kilby; Sailor boy; The shooting of his dear; The soldier and the sailor. Gloriana: Second lute song of the Earl of Essex. Nocturnal* (for solo guitar), *Op. 70*.
(M) *** RCA 09026 61601-2 [id.]. Julian Bream (guitar); (i) Peter Pears (with FRICKER: *O Mistress mine*) – SEIBER: *French folksongs;* WALTON: *Anon in love.* ***

Nearly all the music on this record was written with Julian Bream in mind, and the *Nocturnal*, based on a tune by Dowland, was dedicated to him. Characteristically Britten exploits every nuance of expression that Bream's virtuosity makes possible. The haunting lute song from *Gloriana* by contrast brings a remarkable Elizabethan feeling. The *Songs from the Chinese* are based on Arthur Waley's translations of Chinese poetry. Of the folksong arrangements, it is *I will give my love an apple* where Pears's tender vocal-line is particularly memorable, while the closing *Soldier and the sailor* has all the pay-off wit for which Britten's arrangements are famous. Peter Racine Fricker's soaring setting of *O Mistress mine* seems tailor-made for Pears, his voice at its freshest throughout. With Seiber and Walton couplings equally rewarding, this (Volume 18) is outstanding among the reissues in the Julian Bream Edition where he is joined by other artists.

Spring Symphony, Op. 44.
(M) **(*) Revelation RV 10010 [id.]. Yakovenko, Postavnicheva, Mahov, Ch. & Grand USSR State SO, Rozhdestvensky (with WALTON: *Viola concerto* *).

Rozhdestvensky's Russian version of the *Spring Symphony* comes from the long-hidden archives of Moscow Radio, and it is fascinating to hear the work in Russian in a live recording made in 1963, not long after the composer's own version, for this is an invigoratingly fresh, high-voltage performance. Soloists and choirs are presented in sharp focus with no Slavonic wobbles. The boys' choir is wonderfully earthy but, sadly, is drowned by the horns in the final *Sumer is icumen in*. Though the Walton concerto suffers badly from having the viola far too close, it makes an interesting coupling, with a superstar viola player, Yuri Bashmet.

(i) *Spring Symphony;* (ii) *Cantata academica;* (iii) *Hymn to St Cecilia.*
(M) *** Decca 436 396-2. (i; ii) Vyvyan, Pears; (i) Procter, Emanuel School, Wandsworth, Boys' Ch., ROHCG O, composer; (ii) Watts, Brannigan; (ii; iii) L. Symphony Ch.; (ii) LSO; (ii; iii) Malcolm.

(i) *Spring Symphony; Peter Grimes: 4 Sea interludes.*
(M) *** EMI CDM7 64736-2 [id.]. (i) Armstrong, J. Baker, Tear, St Clement Dane's School Boys' Ch., L. Symphony Ch.; LSO, Previn.

It is the freshness of Britten's imagination in dozens of moments that makes this work as memorable as it is joyous. Thanks to the Decca engineers, one hears more than is usually possible in a live performance. Jennifer Vyvyan and Peter Pears are both outstanding, and Britten shows that no conductor is more vital in his music than he himself. The Decca reissue couples the work to the *Cantata academica*, with its deft use of a 12-note row, written for Basel, and the *Hymn to St Cecilia*, an ambitious piece written just before the war, when Britten's technique was already prodigious. The setting exactly matches the imaginative, capricious words of Auden. Performances are first class and so is the CD transfer.

Like Britten, Previn makes this above all a work of exultation, a genuine celebration of spring; but here, more than in Britten's recording, the kernel of what the work has to say comes out in the longest of the solo settings, using Auden's poem *Out on the lawn I lie in bed*. With Dame Janet Baker as soloist it rises above the lazily atmospheric mood of the opening to evoke the threat of war and darkness. The *Four Sea interludes*, which make a generous bonus, are presented in their concert form, with tailored endings. Previn springs the bouncing rhythms of the second interlude – the picture of Sunday morning in the Borough – even more infectiously than the composer himself in his complete recording of the opera.

War Requiem.
(BB) ** Naxos Dig. 8.553558/9 [id.]. Russell, Randle, Volle, Scottish Festival Ch., St Mary's Episcopal Cathedral, Edinburgh, Ch., BBC Scottish SO, Brabbins (with Boddice).

The first glory of the Naxos version, on two bargain discs, is the sound, with spatial contrasts caught thrillingly and atmospherically, thanks to the recording venue. Surprisingly, Naxos chose the former engine-shed of the Harland & Wolff shipyard, now converted into a media centre. With the benefit of a cathedral-like acoustic, it was able to cope with very large forces better than any available church, and the boys' choir in particular is beautifully caught, clear but at a distance, exactly the effect the composer had in mind. The choral singing generally is excellent, vivid and immediate in the big climaxes of such sections as *Dies irae*. Under Martyn Brabbins for the full orchestral sections, and under Nigel Boddice for the chamber orchestra settings of Wilfred Owen poems, the BBC Scottish Symphony Orchestra plays with fine point and precision, underlining the drama of the piece.

The power of the whole is not in doubt, but the solo singing is less impressive, notably that of Thomas Randle who, as recorded, sounds strained and fluttery, failing to bring out the tragic intensity of the words. It is apt that a German baritone was chosen as the other male soloist, reflecting Britten's debt to Dietrich Fischer-Dieskau as the original inspiration for that role. Michael Volle has a firm, clear, if not specially distinctive baritone and, though one can hardly complain of slight mispronunciations (as in bugel for 'bugle'), he too fails to plumb the depths of the poems. Nor is the soprano, Lynda Russell, ideal for, though it is a dramatic performance, the fruity voice too often has an edge and unevenness to it.

Winter words (song-cycle), *Op. 52*.

(BB) *** ASV CDQS 6172 [(M) id.]. Ian Partridge, Jennifer Partridge – PURCELL: *'Sweeter than Roses'* (songs). ***

Ian Partridge's soaringly fresh timbre brings surprising reminders of Peter Pears in these highly sensitive performances of atmospheric Hardy settings dating from 1953. Ian is admirably supported by sister Jennifer Partridge, and she makes the very most of the imaginative piano-writing, whether in simulating railway noises in *Midnight on the Great Western*, the creaks of *The little old table*, or setting the melancholy mood for *The choirmaster's burial* and creating the joyful chorus of the *Proud songsters*. Excellent late-1970s recording. A worthy coupling for a warmly sympathetic collection of favourite Purcell songs.

OPERA

Peter Grimes (complete).

(M) *** Ph. 432 578-2 (2). Vickers, Harper, Summers, Bainbridge, Cahill, Robinson, Allen, ROHCG Ch. & O, C. Davis.

Sir Colin Davis takes a fundamentally darker, tougher view of *Peter Grimes* than the composer himself. Jon Vickers' heroic interpretation sheds keen new illumination on what arguably remains the greatest of Britten's operas, even if it cannot be said to supplant the composer's own version. Heather Harper as Ellen Orford is very moving, and there are fine contributions from Jonathan Summers as Captain Balstrode and Thomas Allen as Ned Keene. The recording is full and vivid, with fine balancing.

(i, ii) *Peter Grimes* (scenes); (i, iii) *The Rape of Lucretia* (abridged); (iv) French folksong arrangements: *La belle est au jardin d'amour; La fileuse; Quand j'étais chez mon père; Le roi s'en va-t'en chasse; Voici le printemps;* (v) English folksongs: *The Ash grove; The Bonny Earl o' Moray; Come you not from Newcastle?; The Foggy, foggy dew; Heigh ho, heigh hi!; The King is gone a-hunting; Little Sir William; O, Waly, Waly; Oliver Cromwell; The Plough boy; The Salley Gardens; Sweet Polly Oliver; There's none to soothe.*

(M) (***) EMI mono CMS7 64727-2 (2) [CDMB 64727]. (i) Joan Cross, Peter Pears; (ii) Nancy Evans, E. Op. Group Chamber O; (iii) BBC Theatre Ch., ROHCG O, Reginald Goodall; (iv) Sophie Wyss, composer; (v) Peter Pears, composer.

Both of these abridged recordings of Britten's earliest operas, made in the 1940s, have a freshness and energy that reflect the excitement they aroused at their first appearance, transforming the British musical scene. More specifically, they illustrate both the resilient energy of Peter Pears at this early stage, lighter and fresher of voice than later, and the urgent intensity of Reginald Goodall, conducting Britten in a way very different from his later, solidly weighty manner in Wagner. Though the recordings, transferred from 78s, are boxy in sound, the closeness adds to the bite and impact. They are particularly valuable for demonstrating the character and point of Joan Cross as Ellen Orford. It was a role written for her, as indeed was the Female Chorus part in *Lucretia*. In the latter opera it is good to have Nancy Evans in the title-role, tenderly affecting, with the contrasts between the heroine's tragic grief and the beauty of the serving maids' Flower duet superbly brought out.

The recordings of folksong settings are delightful, made not just by Peter Pears for both Decca and EMI, but by Sophie Wyss (for whom *Les illuminations* was written). The wit and point of such songs as *The foggy, foggy dew* and *Little Sir William* come out even more delightfully than in later recordings, with Britten as accompanist at his most inspired.

The Turn of the screw.

(M) (***) Decca (IMS) mono 425 672-2 (2) [id.]. Pears, Vyvyan, Hemmings, Dyer, Cross, Mandikian, E. Op. Group O, composer.

Though the recording is in mono only, the very dryness and the sharpness of focus give an extra intensity to the composer's own incomparable reading of his most compressed opera. Peter Pears as Peter Quint is superbly matched by Jennifer Vyvyan as the governess and by Joan Cross as the housekeeper, Mrs Grose. It is also fascinating to hear David Hemmings as a boy treble, already a confident actor. Excellent CD transfer.

Collection

'The world of Britten': (i; ii) *Simple Symphony;* (iii; ii) *Young person's guide to the orchestra.* (iv; v) *Folksong arrangements: Early one morning; The plough boy.* (vi) *Hymn to the Virgin.* (iv; vii; iii; ii) *Serenade for tenor, horn & strings: Nocturne.* Excerpts from: *Ceremony of carols; Noye's Fludde; Spring Symphony; Billy Budd; Peter Grimes.*

(M) *** Decca 436 990-2; *436 990-4.* (i) ECO; (ii) cond. composer; (iii) LSO; (iv) Pears; (v) composer (piano); (vi) St John's College Ch., Guest; (vii) Tuckwell; & var. artists.

The Britten sampler is well worth having for the composer's own vibrant account of the *Variations on a theme of Purcell* and the *Simple Symphony*, where the *Playful pizzicato* emerges with wonderful rhythmic spring and resonance (in the warm Maltings acoustics). The Pears contributions are very enjoyable too, notably the haunting *Nocturne* from the *Serenade*, with Barry Tuckwell in splendid form. Excellent sound throughout, although the tuttis in the *Young person's guide to the orchestra* could with advantage have had a more expansive sonority.

Brouwer, Leo (born 1939)

Concerto elegiaco (Guitar concerto No. 3).

(M) *** RCA 09026 61605-2 [id.]. Julian Bream, RCA Victor CO, composer – L. BERKELEY; RODRIGO: *Concertos.* ***

Leo Brouwer has blended earlier Afro-Cuban and Javanese influences with romantic feeling, even adopting a cyclic structure as 'a homage to César Franck or the leitmotif of the nineteenth century'. The result is a piece with a short but haunting central *Lento* and a brilliant *Toccata*-like finale which sums up the earlier lyrical ideas. Bream's performance draws the music's threads together and yet displays much bravura. He is very well recorded.

Bruch, Max (1838–1920)

Double concerto in E min., for clarinet, viola and orchestra, Op. 88.

(B) *** Hyperion Dyad Dig. CDD 22017 (2) [id.]. Thea King, Nobuko Imai, LSO, Francis (with Concert – see below ***).

Bruch's *Double concerto* is a delightful work with genuinely memorable inspiration in its first two lyrical movements and a roistering finale making a fine contrast. Clarinet and viola are blended beautifully, with the more penetrating wind instrument dominating naturally and with melting phrasing from Thea King. The recording is excellent. This is part of an excellent two-disc set including other attractive concertante works by Mendelssohn, Crusell, Spohr and other less familiar names.

Violin concertos Nos. 1 in G min.; 2 in D min., Op. 44; 3 in D min., Op. 58; Serenade for violin and orchestra, Op 75; Scottish fantasy, Op. 46.

(B) *** Ph. Duo 462 167-2 (2) [id.]. Salvatore Accardo, Leipzig GO, Masur.

This Philips Duo gathers together Bruch's three *Violin concertos*, plus two other major concertante works. Although no other piece quite matches the famous *G minor Concerto* in inventive concentration, the delightful *Scottish fantasia*, with its profusion of good tunes, comes near to doing so, and the first movement of the *Second Concerto* has two themes of soaring lyrical ardour. The *Third Concerto* brings another striking lyrical idea in the first movement and has an endearing *Adagio* and a jolly finale. The engagingly insubstantial *Serenade* was originally intended to be a fourth violin concerto. Throughout the set Accardo's playing is so persuasive in its restrained passion that even the less inspired moments bring pleasure. Because of the resonant Leipzig acoustics, the Philips engineers put their microphones rather too close to the soloist and at times there is a degree of shrillness in his upper range. This is most noticeable on the first disc, containing the *G minor Concerto*, but the ear adjusts; throughout the rest of the collection one's pleasure is hardly diminished, for the orchestral recording is full and spacious.

Violin concerto No. 1 in G min., Op. 26.

(M) *** Sony Dig. SMK 64250 [id.]. Cho-Liang Lin, Chicago SO, Slatkin – MENDELSSOHN: *Concerto;* VIEUXTEMPS: *Concerto No. 5.* ***

(B) *** CfP Dig. CD-CFP 4566 [(M) id. import]. Tasmin Little, RLPO, Handley – DVORAK: *Concerto.* ***

(B) *** [EMI Red Line CDR5 69863]. Itzhak Perlman, LSO, Previn – MENDELSSOHN: *Violin concerto.* ***

(M) *** Carlton Dig. PCD 2005 [id.]. Jaime Laredo, SCO – MENDELSSOHN: *Concerto.* ***

(M) *** DG 449 091-2. Shlomo Mintz, Chicago SO, Abbado – DVORAK: *Concerto.* ***

(M) *** EMI CDM5 66220-2 [id.]. Sir Yehudi Menuhin, Philh. O, Susskind – MENDELSSOHN: *Concerto.* ***

(BB) *** EMI Seraphim CES5 68524-2 (2) [CEDB 68524]. Sir Yehudi Menuhin, LSO, Boult – MENDELSSOHN: *Violin concerto* etc. ***

(BB) **(*) RCA/Navigator Dig. 74321 29245-2 [(M) id. import]. Uto Ughi, LSO, Prêtre – BRAHMS: *Violin concerto.* **(*)

(M) **(*) Sony Stern Edition I SMK 66830 [id.]. Stern, Phd. O, Ormandy – TCHAIKOVSKY: *Méditation; Sérénade mélancolique* ***; WIENIAWSKI: *Violin concerto No. 2.* **(*)

(M) **(*) Sony SBK 48274; *SBT 48274* [id.]. Zukerman, LAPO, Mehta – LALO: *Symphonie espagnole;* VIEUXTEMPS: *Concerto No. 5.* **(*)

(M) ** Sup. SU 1939-2 011 [id.]. Josef Suk, Czech PO, Karel Ančerl – BERG: *Concerto* ***; MENDELSSOHN: *Concerto.* **(*)

(BB) *(*) Naxos Dig. 8.550195 [id.]. Nishizaki, Slovak PO, Gunzenhauser – BRAHMS: *Concerto.* *

There have been few accounts on record of Bruch's slow movement that begin to match the raptness of Lin. He is accompanied most sensitively by Slatkin and the Chicago orchestra, and this reading is totally compelling in its combination of passion and purity, strength and dark, hushed intensity. The addition of the attractive *Fifth Concerto* of Henri Vieuxtemps makes this CD more attractive than ever. The recording is excellent.

The movement in the Bruch where Tasmin Little's individuality comes out most clearly is the central *Adagio*, raptly done with a deceptive simplicity of phrasing, totally unselfconscious, that matches the purity of her sound. Her speeds in the outer movements are broader than those of such rivals as Lin. At full price this would be a first-rate recommendation: on CfP it is an outstanding bargain.

One has perhaps the faintest reservation about Perlman's reading, a glowing, powerful account that is almost too sure of itself. With Previn and the LSO backing him up richly, this is a strong, confident interpretation, forthrightly masculine. The opulent, full recording suits the performance.

Jaime Laredo with consistently fresh and sweet tone gives a delightfully direct reading, warmly expressive but never for a moment self-indulgent. The orchestral ensemble is particularly impressive, when no conductor is involved. With first-rate modern digital recording, this is a highlight of the Carlton (formerly Pickwick) mid-price catalogue.

Shlomo Mintz certainly makes the listener hang on to every phrase, and his playing is undoubtedly compelling. The vibrato is wide, but his approach is so distinctive and interesting that few listeners will not be fired. The Chicago Symphony Orchestra plays with great brilliance and enthusiasm, and Abbado's direction is most sympathetic. The vivid recording has transferred splendidly to CD.

Menuhin's performance (with Susskind) has long held an honoured place in the catalogue. It was a work to which he made a particularly individual response, and he was in very good form when he made the disc. The performance has a fine spontaneity, the work's improvisatory quality very much part of the interpretation, and there is no doubting the poetry Menuhin finds in the slow movement or the sparkle in the finale. The bright, forward sound of the 1960 recording has transferred vividly to CD.

Menuhin's second stereo recording of the Bruch *Concerto* was made in the early 1970s. While he is obviously on familiar ground, there is no sign of over-familiarity and the lovely slow movement is given a performance of great warmth and humanity. Boult accompanies admirably, and the recording is obviously fuller and more modern than the earlier version with Susskind, even if the solo playing is technically less immaculate and the solo timbre a little spare. On EMI's bargain-basement Seraphim label, this coupling with Mendelssohn remains very attractive.

Those looking for a bargain-basement coupling with the Brahms *Concerto* (though this CD is at mid-price in the USA), and very good (1982) digital recording, might well choose Ughi on RCA Navigator. His is a fresh, direct reading. It may not have the individuality of Lin, but it is still a fine performance and excellent value.

Stern's vintage account from 1966 with Ormandy is one of the great classic recordings of the work, gloriously warm-hearted and passionate, with a very involving account of the slow movement, which sustains the greatest possible intensity. The finale, too, has wonderful fire and spirit. Ormandy's accompaniment is first class and triumphs over the hopelessly unrealistic balance, with the violin way out front.

Zukerman's reissued Sony triptych shows him at his finest, and it is a pity that the close-up balance brings inevitable reservations. His Bruch is a passionately extrovert performance, tempered by genuine tenderness in the slow movement. The brilliantly lit recording increases the sense of fiery energy in the outer sections and, with the excitement of the solo playing and the strongly committed accompaniment, the larger-than-life effect is almost overwhelming.

Josef Suk's recording from the early 1960s has been remastered effectively to sound fresh and clear. He is less suited to the Bruch than to the other concertos here; although his natural warmth and simplicity of line are appealing, his account is not as imaginative as some. The finale, taken slowly, draws on the affinity with the Brahms *Concerto*.

Takako Nishizaki plays the slow movement gently and sweetly, and the first movement goes quite well. But the finale lacks sparkle, and altogether this is not one of her recommendable couplings.

Violin concerto No. 1 in G min., Op. 26; Scottish fantasy, Op. 46.
(M) *** Decca 448 597-2 [id.]. Kyung-Wha Chung, RPO, Kempe.
(M) *** RCA 09026 61745-2 [id.]. Heifetz, New SO of L., Sargent – VIEUXTEMPS: *Concerto No. 5.* ***
(B) **(*) Tring Dig. TRP 108 [(M) id. import]. Yuzuko Horigome, RPO, Yuri Simonov.

The magic of Kyung-Wha Chung, a spontaneously inspired violinist if ever there was one, comes over beguilingly in this very desirable Bruch coupling from 1972, reissued in Decca's Classic Sound series. Chung goes straight to the heart of the famous *G minor Concerto*, finding mystery and fantasy as well as more extrovert qualities. Just as strikingly in the *Scottish fantasia* she transcends the episodic nature of the writing to give the music a genuine depth and concentration, above all in the lovely slow movement. Kempe and the RPO accompany sympathetically, well caught in a glowing recording.

Heifetz plays with supreme assurance, and the slow movement shows this fine artist in top romantic form. All lovers of great violin playing should at least hear this coupling, for Heifetz's panache and the subtlety of his bowing and colour bring a wonderful freshness to Bruch's charming Scottish whimsy. Sargent accompanies sympathetically, and it is noticeable that, though the soloist is balanced much too closely, there is never any doubt that Heifetz can still produce a true pianissimo.

Yuzuko Horigome's coupling of Bruch's two most popular concertante violin works is most welcome in Tring's RPO series and, very well played and recorded, makes an excellent recommendation at bargain price. Yuzuko Horigome was the first prize-winner in the Queen Elizabeth Competition in Belgium in 1980. She plays here with rich, pure tone, using an aptly wide dynamic range, taking a relatively expansive view of both works, not always quite impulsive enough, tending at times to sound too deliberate. Nevertheless these are warmly enjoyable performances, and the recording is full and immediate, with the important harp solo in the *Scottish fantasy* clearly focused.

Kol Nidrei, Op. 47.
(M) (***) Sony mono MHK 62876 [id.]. Gregor Piatigorsky, Phd. O, Ormandy – DVORAK: *Cello concerto* (***); SAINT-SAENS: *Cello concerto No. 1.* (***) ✿

Piatigorsky's account comes from 1947 and has a keen eloquence that is as potent today as it was when it was made, just after the war. The Dvořák *Concerto* and, more especially, the Saint-Saëns under Frederick Stock are superlative. This disc costs more than our usual upper-mid-price limit but is well worth it.

Scottish fantasy (for violin and orchestra), *Op. 46.*
(B) *** EMI Eminence Dig. CD-EMX 2277 [(M) id. import]. Tasmin Little, Royal SNO, Vernon Handley – LALO: *Symphonie espagnole.* ***
(B) **(*) Revelation RV 10051 [id.]. David Oistrakh, USSR State SO, Rozhdestvensky – BERLIOZ: *Harold in Italy.* (*)

It is an excellent idea to couple Bruch's evocation of Scotland with Lalo's of Spain, both works in unconventional, five-movement, concertante form. Tasmin Little takes a riper, more robust and passionate view of both works than her direct rival on disc, the poetic Anne Akiko Meyers on RCA (full price RD 60942), projecting them more strongly, as she would in the concert hall. Little's speeds are a degree broader than those of Meyers, which gives her more freedom to point rhythms infectiously, to play with an extra degree of individuality in her phrasing, using portamentos or agogic hesitations daringly in a way that adds to the character of the reading. In this she is greatly helped by the splendid, keenly polished playing of the Scottish orchestra under Vernon Handley, a most sympathetic partner. The recording is superb, with brass in particular vividly caught. Unlike Meyers on RCA, Little plays the Guerriero finale absolutely complete. At mid-price on the Eminence label, this is an issue to recommend to anyone wanting either work.

It is sad that as inspired a version as David Oistrakh's of the Bruch *Scottish fantasy* should be coupled on Revelation with so seriously flawed a recording of *Harold in Italy*. The irony is that where the sound for the Bruch, dating from 1960, is full-bodied and generally well balanced, if limited in range, the 1974 recording of the Berlioz is very dim. With Rozhdestvensky drawing fine playing from the orchestra, Oistrakh gives the fast movements a rare sparkle, always spontaneous in his expressiveness, and in the *Andante* he builds from heartfelt meditation to the most passionate climax.

Symphonies Nos. 1 in E flat, Op. 28; 2 in F min., Op. 36; 3 in E, Op. 51; (i) *Adagio appassionato, Op. 57; Konzertstück, Op. 84; In memoriam, Op. 65; Romanze, Op. 42* (all for violin and orchestra).
(B) *** Ph. Duo 462 164-2 (2) [id.]. (i) Salvatore Accardo; Leipzig GO, Kurt Masur.

When the first of Bruch's three symphonies is the one that is most striking in its invention and each has its weaknesses, one has to deduce that he was a symphonist more by default than by nature. Yet this collected edition contains much attractive music, beautifully played and recorded, guaranteed to delight anyone wanting undemanding symphonies as alternatives to those of Brahms and Schumann. Masur's performances with the Leipzig Gewandhaus Orchestra are characteristically warm and refined, with smooth recording to match, but sparkle is largely missing. Room has also been found for the remaining works in Accardo's complete survey of Bruch's major works for violin and orchestra. The two-movement *Konzertstück* dates from 1911 and is one of Bruch's last works. *In Memoriam* is finer still and the *Adagio appassionato* and *Romanze* are strongly characterized pieces. Accardo's advocacy is just as persuasive here as in the concertos listed above.

(i) *Piano trio in C min., Op. 5;* (ii) *8 Pieces for clarinet, viola and piano, Op. 83.*
(BB) (*) Koch Discover Dig. DICD 920194 [id.]. (i) Dana Protopopescu; (ii) Freddy Artel; Instrumental Contrasts Ens.

The two works are recorded in different acoustics: the *Eight Pieces for clarinet, viola and piano* is located in a very small acoustic, the piano starved of timbre and the overall sound shallow and unpleasant. The *C minor Piano trio* has a warmer acoustic and is better balanced, but the performance is pedestrian.

Bruckner, Anton (1824–96)

Symphonies Nos. '0'; 1–9; in F min.
(B) ** Teldec/Warner Dig. 0630 14192-2 (11) [(M) 2292 46068-2]. Frankfurt RSO, Eliahu Inbal.

Eliahu Inbal has strong Brucknerian instincts and his survey of the first versions of all the Bruckner *Symphonies*, which includes the fascinating early *Study Symphony*, is of permanent interest to Brucknerians, especially as Nos. 3, 4 and 8 had never been recorded before in their original versions. Although the Frankfurt Radio Orchestra is not thought of as being in the very first rank, it responds well to Inbal's advocacy, always producing more than acceptable results and sometimes offering playing of considerable concentration and power. The recordings too, if not in the demonstration bracket, are spacious, bold and clear. The 11 discs are offered in a slip-case at bargain price, and the set could be recommended with little reservation, had the documentation been adequate. But each CD contains only a folded insert leaflet which documents the date of the edition used and the date and location of the recording. When one considers how different some of these first versions are from what is normally presented in the concert hall, this seems an unforgivable omission and, as there is no additional covering booklet, collectors would be better advised to choose from the individual issues, which are also in the budget price range.

Symphonies Nos. '0'; 1–9.
(B) **(*) Ph. 442 040-2 (9) [(M) id. import]. Concg. O, Haitink.
(B) **(*) Decca Dig. 448 910-2 (10) [id.]. Chicago SO, Solti.

Haitink's set of Bruckner symphonies (reissued as part of the Haitink Edition) has all the classic virtues: they are well shaped and free from affectation or any kind of agogic distortion. Haitink's grasp of the architecture is strong and his feeling for beauty of detail refined. He has a less developed sense of mystery and atmosphere than Jochum, whose readings have a spiritual dimension at which Haitink only hints; however, Jochum recorded the Nowak edition. Haitink's judgements on matters of text are as sound as his approach is dedicated, and he secures consistently fine playing from the Concertgebouw Orchestra. Only the *Eighth* with its generally brisk tempi is at all controversial. The CD transfers bring much more vivid sound than on LP, yet the overall balance is always convincing. The set also has the additional advantage of economy, with only No. 1 split between CDs; the other symphonies each occupy a single CD.

Solti had previously recorded the *Eighth* with the VPO for John Culshaw in the Sofiensaal as early as

1966 (see below). With the Chicago Symphony Orchestra he began with the *Sixth* (1979), following with the *Fifth* (1980) and *Fourth* (1981). Then there was a gap of four years before the *Ninth* (1985) and *Seventh* (1986) and another before the *Eighth*, recorded in Russia (1990), the *Second* (1991) and the *Third* (1992). The two early symphonies are very impressive and the *Second*, where he follows Nowak and which is similarly successful, appeared in our main volume. Alas, the *Third* is the one failure. Despite excellent Decca engineering, the result is pretty crude and coarse, with little of the refinement of sonority which distinguishes the rest of the series. In the *Fourth*, where he again chooses Nowak, Solti can hardly be faulted, selecting admirable tempi, keeping concentration taut through the longest paragraphs and presenting the architecture of the work in total clarity. Raptness is there too, and only the relative lack of Brucknerian idiosyncrasy, especially when compared with his readings of the earliest symphonies, will disappoint those who prefer a more affectionate and personal approach. This aspect of the interpretation is not helped by the slightly artificial brightness of the early digital sound-picture. This comment might also be applied to the *Fifth*, where the clarity and brilliance of the digital sound underlines Solti's precise control of the dramatic contrasts. The slow movement finds the necessary warmth, with Solti in what might for him be counted an Elgarian mood. However, in the *Sixth* it is the slow movement which is less persuasive than usual, failing to flow quite as it might so that the expressiveness does not sound truly spontaneous. It comes within a reading that is strong and rhetorical, powerfully convincing in the outer movements. Here the analogue recording emerges vividly enough in its CD format. The *Seventh* is a disappointment. Solti takes an extraordinarily spacious view and, while the Chicago orchestra respond to his affectionate care over detail with playing of great refinement and produce climaxes of great weight and power, this very relaxed approach means that the outer movements are lacking in ultimate grip and the Scherzo is comparatively lightweight. The *Adagio* is drawn out to an inordinate length and, in spite of the great beauty of the orchestral textures, many listeners will find Solti's indulgence verging on lassitude. The *Eighth* rights the balance, with an inspired reading, opening with powerful gravitas. (Solti, as before in Vienna, uses the 1890 version edited by Nowak.) The expansive *Adagio* is magnificently sustained by the most magical response from the orchestra over its long eventful progress. Without ever seeming over-intense, Solti achieves an extraordinary grip over the movement as a whole, and notably so in the extended, quietly elegiac string cantilena in the closing pages which is tenderly moving. The ambitiously extended finale then erupts boisterously and caps the performance with a finely judged balance between glowing lyricism and weighty splendour, especially in the exultant coda. The recording, made in the Great Hall of the St Petersburg Philharmonia, is superb in every respect. The *Ninth* is a similarly spacious and large-scale reading. Again there is no question of Solti rushing the argument. He gives the music full time to breathe, but here the tension is unrelenting, making the big climaxes thrillingly powerful, as in the outbursts of the long last movement. Other performances may be more deeply meditative – Walter for one – but the power of Solti and the brilliance of the playing and the digital recording are formidable.

Symphonies Nos. (i) *'0' in D min*. (ed. Wöss): *Scherzo* (only); *1 in C min*. (ed. Schalk): *Scherzo* (only); *2 in C min*. (ed. Herbeck): *Scherzo* (only); (ii) *3 in D min*. (ed. Schalk): *Scherzo* (only); (iii) *4 in E flat* (ed. Löwe and Schalk): *Scherzo* (only); (iv) *4 in E flat* (complete; ed. Haas); *5 in B flat* (complete; ed. Haas); *7 in E* (complete; ed. Löwe).

(M) (**) EMI (SIS) mono CHS6 66206 (3) [CDHC 66206]. (i) Berlin State Op. O, Fritz Zaun; (ii) VSO, Anton Konrath; (iii) Saxon State O, Karl Boehm.

Symphonies Nos. (i) *6 in A* (ed. Haas): *Adagio, Scherzo & Finale* (only); (ii) *7 in E* (ed. Löwe); (i) *8 in C min*. (ed. Haas); (iii) *9 in D min*. (ed. Orel).

(M) (***) EMI (SIS) mono CHS5 66210 (3) [CDHC 66210]. (i) BPO, Furtwängler; (ii–iii) Munich PO; (ii) Oswald Kabasta; (iii) Siegmund von Hausegger.

These two three-CD sets of historic Bruckner symphonies cover all the material in the pre-war HMV and Electrola catalogues, together with some wartime and post-war off-air recordings. The scherzo movements of *Die Nullte* (No. 0) and Nos. 1–4 come from 1928–34, but the first time EMI Electrola recorded a complete Bruckner symphony was in 1936, though this was not the very first recording: Oscar Fried and Jascha Horenstein had recorded Bruckner symphonies in the 1920s, and Ormandy's RCA account of the *Seventh* was also earlier. By 1936 the International Anton Bruckner Gesellschaft had published its authoritative edition of the 1878–80 score of the *Fourth Symphony* by Robert Haas, which Karl Boehm used; and it was, incidentally, to the same edition that he turned in 1937 for his recording of the *Fifth*. Incredible though it may seem to the younger collector, the early LP catalogues were meagre in their Bruckner offerings, and the first Bruckner symphony recorded by a British orchestra was the *Fourth*, played by the Philharmonia with Lovro von Matačić in 1955: the first under a British conductor is yet to appear (though Sir Henry Wood had recorded the *Overture in G minor* before the war).

It is the combination of childlike vision and awesome majesty that makes the Bruckner symphonies unique in music and which, on the face of it, makes the LP with its continuity (and in particular the stereo LP with its wider dynamic range and sense of space), a more congenial medium than shellac. Yet returning to these pre-war performances serves as a reminder that they possess that freshness of discovery and atmosphere which première recordings always seem to have. Boehm's *Fifth* was superseded by Jochum's, 20 years later, in the 1950s. The *Seventh* under Furtwängler comes from a 1949 broadcast. (Furtwängler made only one commercial recording of Bruckner, the slow movement of No. 7 in 1942, though there are four different surviving accounts of the whole work from his baton.)

Brucknerians will want both of these sets, but those whose funds will not stretch to both should go for the second volume. Furtwängler conducted the *Sixth Symphony* only once, in 1943, and three movements of that performance have come down to us. The *Adagio* is particularly elevated in feeling. His *Eighth*, again from a 1949 broadcast, has the ardour and intensity he brought to all his music-making. Special interest focuses on Oswald Kabasta's passionate and full-blooded wartime account of the *Seventh Symphony* and Siegmund von Hausegger's pioneering account of the *Ninth*, both with the Munich Philharmonic. This remains one of the most atmospheric of all *Ninths* and has a wonderful sense of mystery and vision which leaves you feeling that this is how this awesome music must have sounded to Bruckner in his own mind's ears. Excellent transfers.

Symphonies Nos. 1–9.
(M) *** DG 429 648-2 (9). BPO, Karajan.
(B) *** DG 429 079-2 (9) [id.]. BPO or Bav. RSO, Jochum.
(B) *** EMI CDZ7 62935-2 (9) [CDZ 629352]. Dresden State O, Jochum.

The reappearance of Karajan's magnificent cycle, long a yardstick by which others were measured – and at mid-price (if only in the UK) – must be warmly welcomed. We have sung the praises of these recordings loud and long, and in their new format they are outstanding value.

Jochum's DG cycle was recorded between 1958 (No. 5) and 1967 (No. 2), all but four (Nos. 2, 3, 5 and 6) with the Berlin Philharmonic. It enjoys the advantage of accommodating one symphony per disc. No apology need be made for either the performances or the quality of the recorded sound, which wears its years lightly. Indeed one of the finest is the 1957 *Fifth*. Jochum brought a sense of mystery and atmosphere to Bruckner that was quite unique, and it more than compensates for the occasional freedom he permitted himself. His was the first overview of Bruckner on record – followed not long afterwards by Haitink on Philips – and he still has special claims as a guide in this terrain. He communicates a lofty inspiration to his players, and many of these readings can more than hold their own with later rivals.

Jochum's EMI set, made with the Staatskapelle Dresden between 1975 and 1980, has the advantage of more modern recorded sound (though readers will be surprised how well the 1957 stereo recording of the *Fifth Symphony* on DG actually sounds). Jochum's allegiance to the Novak editions remains unchanged and, apart from various odd details, so does his overall approach. His readings have a spirituality and nobility that remain rather special, notwithstanding the claims of his many distinguished rivals. Either the DG or the EMI set will give great satisfacton.

Symphony No. '00' in F min. (Study Symphony).
(B) *** Teldec/Warner Dig. 0630 14193-2 [(M) id. import]. Frankfurt RSO, Inbal.

Bruckner's *Study Symphony*, a student work, was written in 1863. The composer, a late starter, was just turning forty and at the very beginning of his composing career. The surprise is the way the music has distinct pre-echoes of what was to come, especially the *Andante*, a remarkable piece of writing with brief tuttis stabbing into the lyrical flow. (This is particularly well brought off here.) The Scherzo, too, is entirely typical and with a delightful, flowing trio on the woodwind. The finale, however, is Schumannesque, with lyrical influences from Wagner – but none the worse for that – and its waywardness again has Brucknerian fingerprints. Inbal and his orchestra are in excellent form and they approach the music with total freshness as if it were a mature work; at times they almost convince the listener that it is. They are very well recorded, and this is well worth considering at budget price.

Symphony No. '0' in D min.
(B) *** Teldec/Warner Dig. 0630 14194-2 [(M) id. import]. Frankfurt RSO, Inbal.

Die Nullte is a work of striking quality that at times portends the greatness to come. Although it may not be ideally proportioned, some of its ideas have all the innocence and purity of utterance that distinguishes the finest early Bruckner. Inbal and his Frankfurt orchestra are again in impressive form here, giving a performance of undoubted spontaneity. The character of the first movement is immediately caught at the atmospheric opening with its neatly delineated little march theme, and the first climax expands naturally. This is not an easy movement to hold together, but Inbal succeeds both in retaining tension and in creating a natural forward flow. The hushed opening of the *Andante* is well sustained, and with warmly responsive playing the listener is held throughout. The Scherzo, too, is nicely pointed in the strings and woodwind to offer a light-hearted counterpart to the bombast from the heavy brass, and the contrasts in the powerful and exciting finale are handled equally convincingly. All in all, this is one of the most impressive of Inbal's series and is well worth its modest price.

Symphony No. 0 in D min.; (i) *Helgoland* (for male chorus & orchestra); (i; ii) *Psalm 150* (for soprano, chorus & orchestra).
(M) **(*) DG 437 250-2. Chicago SO, Barenboim, with (i) Chicago Symphony Ch., (ii) Ruth Welting.

Bruckner's early *D minor Symphony* contains some inspired music. Barenboim shows evident affection for it but, once again donning his Furtwänglerian mantle, he is not always content to let the music speak for itself. However, he gets a generally positive response from the Chicago Symphony, and the 1979 recording is full and spacious. In *Helgoland* the islanders pray to be spared from the marauding Romans; a storm saves them in this brief but graphic piece. The Chicago forces sing and play with heart-warming resonance in both this and the Psalm setting and, although Ruth Welting is too shallow a soloist in the *Psalm*, this disc is well worth considering.

Symphony No. 1 in C min. (original, Linz version).
(B) ** Teldec/Warner Dig. 0630 14195-2 [(M) id. import]. Frankfurt RSO, Inbal.

Bruckner's *First* is a somewhat intractable symphony. Although the mood is basically amiable, the composer's restless alternations of heavy tuttis, energetic passages more lightly scored, and lyrical blossoming are less well knit together than in his mature works. Inbal's direct, comparatively brisk approach – he handles the tempo changes in the first movement convincingly enough – makes quite a good case for Bruckner's earlier (1866) Linz version of No. 1, although the lack of opulence in the recording adds to the impression that the end result is lightweight. The *Adagio* does not lack tension, and the finale is held together dramatically, even if there is not the breadth or the kind of added dimension one has with Jochum or Karajan. But, unlike some of the other early versions of Bruckner symphonies in Inbal's valuable survey, the Linz edition of No. 1 is favoured in most other recordings, notably Solti's, which makes a much stronger impression.

Symphony No. 1 in C min.; (i) *Te Deum.*
(M) **(*) DG Dig. 435 068-2. Chicago SO, Barenboim; (i) with Jessye Norman, Minton, Rendall, Ramey, Chicago Symphony Ch.

Barenboim's version of the *Symphony No. 1* comes with the *Te Deum* with its starry quartet of soloists and the magnificent Chicago Symphony Chorus. In both works he directs beautifully played, spontaneous-sounding performances that mould Brucknerian lines persuasively, but in the *Symphony* the dramatic tension is less keen, lacking something in concentration. The early digital recording is good but not ideally clear, with a brightness that needs a little taming.

Symphony No. 2 in C min. (original, 1872 score).
(BB) *** Naxos Dig. 8.554006 [id.]. Nat. SO of Ireland, Georg Tintner.
(B) ** Teldec/Warner Dig. 0630 14196-2 [id.]. Frankfurt RSO, Inbal.

In his Bruckner series for Naxos, Georg Tintner here firmly favours the composer's first thoughts, arguing that later revisions are not improvements. He therefore opts for the edition of the original (1872) score, published in 1991 by Dr William Carragan, presenting the work at its most expansive and with the middle two movements in reverse order from usual, the Scherzo coming before the slow movement. The Scherzo has an extra repeat, but more important is the expansion of both the slow movement and finale, here presented in concentrated performances that feel not a moment too long. The coda of the *Andante* brings a horn solo at the very end (substituted by Herbeck in 1876), challenging to the player, which is more strikingly beautiful than the clarinet solo with which Bruckner replaced it. Excellent, refined playing from the Irish orchestra and full, rich sound, with the brass gloriously caught.

In his Frankfurt performance, so the Teldec label tells us, Inbal offers the revised version of 1877, but what we get is something much closer to the 1872 Haas edition which, like the Naxos recording, retains the Scherzo and trio with all repeats and uses the original horn, instead of the clarinet, at the end of the slow movement. Incidentally, the closing string chords are missing here, which brings one up with a start. For the most part the playing is good without being outstanding, and the recording, made at the Frankfurt Opera, is very good. However, Tintner's account remains first choice for Brucknerians seeking the composer's first thoughts.

Symphony No. 3 in D min. (original, 1873 version).
(B) *** Teldec/Warner Dig. 0630 14197-2 [(M) 4509 91445-2]. Frankfurt RSO, Eliahu Inbal.

There are in all three versions of the *Third Symphony*: the first, completed on the last day of 1873; a second, which Bruckner undertook immediately after completion of the *Fifth Symphony* in 1877; and then, after this second version proved unsuccessful, a third which he completed in 1889. The 1873 version is by far the longest, running to nearly 66 minutes (the first movement alone lasts 24 minutes), and for those who have either of the others it will make far more than a fascinating appendix. The playing of the Frankfurt Radio Orchestra under Eliahu Inbal is very respectable indeed, with a sensitive feeling for atmosphere and refined dynamic contrasts; the recording is most acceptable without being top-drawer.

Symphony No. 3 in D min. (1877 version).
(BB) * Discovery Dig. DICD 920319 [id.]. Belgian R. & TV PO, Rahbari.

Alexander Rahbari's performance with Belgian Radio forces has the merit of economy, though it is not otherwise as competitive in terms of the distinction of the orchestral playing or the excellence of the recorded sound. Bargain versions of this symphony are relatively thin on the ground; but it would make better sense to get, say, the Boehm version – which, admittedly, is the later (1889) revision – coupled with the *Fourth* on a Double Decca (see below). Both performances have genuine stature.

Symphonies Nos. 3 in D min.; 4 in E flat (Romantic) (Nowak editions).
(B) *** Decca Double 448 098-2 (2) [(M) id. import]. VPO, Karl Boehm.

There are many who admire Boehm's Bruckner, and he certainly controls the lyrical flow of these two symphonies convincingly, helped by first-rate playing from the VPO. Both recordings offer vintage Decca sound from 1970 and 1973 respectively; each has the advantage of the spacious acoustics of the Sofiensaal, and the balance provides splendid detail and a firm sonority. The effect is certainly compelling, and Boehm's sobriety was also his strength. In every bar he gives the impression that he knows exactly where he is going and, choosing the Nowak edition, he shapes each structure compellingly. If neither of these accounts is as individually imaginative as with Jochum nor as keenly dramatic as in the hands of Karajan, both have genuine stature.

Symphonies Nos. 3 in D min.; 7 in E.
(B) *** EMI forte (SIS) CZS5 68652-2 (2) [CDFB 68652]. Dresden State O, Jochum.

As a Brucknerian, Eugen Jochum has a special magnetism. Whatever the reservations that may be made on detailed points of style – Jochum believes in a free variation of tempo within a movement – his natural affinity of temperament with the saintly, innocent Austrian gives these massive structures an easy, warm, unforced concentration which brings out their lyricism as well as their architectural grandeur. So it is in these fine performances with the Dresden orchestra, made at the beginning of the 1980s. As in his earlier cycle with the Berlin Philharmonic and Bavarian Radio orchestras, he uses the Nowak edition. Thus No. 3 is based on Bruckner's 1888–9 revision, rather than the earlier and more extended score edited by Oeser. Readers wanting this alternative version will need to turn to the noble full-priced account given by Haitink. However, Jochum's Dresden readings of both the *Third* and *Seventh Symphonies* are exceptionally fine. With somewhat fuller, 1976–7 recording (made in the Lukaskirche), the *Seventh* opens magnetically; though it may miss a little of the hushed intensity that marked Jochum's earlier Berlin recording for DG, it is very compulsive. With his understanding of Bruckner developing towards a more direct and monumental approach, the authority is never in doubt, and this is matched by splendid playing from the Dresden orchestra.

Symphonies Nos. 3 in D min.; 8 in C min.
(B) **(*) Sony SB2K 53519 (2) [S2K 53519]. Cleveland O, Szell.

In No. 3 Szell does not indulge the listener in a gentle, moulded style and the close-up Cleveland recording adds to the tangibility of his reading. But this outstanding American orchestra – here at its peak in 1966 – under the most incisive of conductors is hard to resist. Szell also uses the 1889 Nowak Edition and this reissue presents a marvellously strong interpretation which is well worth having in its own right even if, for some reason, the second part of the Scherzo is omitted when the outer section is repeated. In No. 8 Szell again uses a revised text, but here the differences between this and the Nowak edition favoured by Jochum are relatively minor. Szell's interpretation as a whole is masterly, and the Cleveland Orchestra produces glorious playing, recorded, like No. 3, in the spacious acoustics of Severance Hall (in 1969). Szell's manner is direct and tempi are generally uncontroversial, the exception being the Scherzo where, like Klemperer, Szell favours a massively measured tempo to bring out the bell-like tolling of the ostinato figures. The last two movements are held together superbly. The CD transfers are expertly done: the sound remains brightly lit but the dynamic range in No. 8 is wide, partly because Szell insists on real pianissimo playing.

Symphony No. 4 in E flat (Romantic) (original, 1874 version).
(B) **(*) Teldec/Warner 0630 14198-2 [(M) 9031 77597-2]. Frankfurt RSO, Inbal.

Like the *Third*, there are three versions of the *Romantic Symphony*, and no one has recorded the original before. The differences are most obvious in the Scherzo, a completely different and more fiery movement, but the opening of the finale is also totally different. Inbal's performance is more than adequate – indeed he has a genuine feeling for the Bruckner idiom and pays scrupulous attention to dynamic refinements. The recording is well detailed, though the climaxes almost (but not quite) reach congestion. An indispensable and fascinating issue, especially attractive at bargain price.

Symphony No. 4 in E flat (Romantic).
(M) *** DG 449 718-2 [id.]. BPO, Jochum (with SIBELIUS: *Night ride and sunrise, Op. 55* with Bav. RSO (***)).
(M) *** DG 439 522-2 [(M) id. import]. BPO, Karajan.
(B) *** Ph. Virtuoso 442 044-2 [(M) id. import]. Concg. O, Haitink.
(B) **(*) [EMI Red Line Dig. CDR5 69795]. BPO, Muti.
(M) (***) Dutton Lab. mono CDEA 5007 [(M) id.]. Dresden State O, Karl Boehm (with R. STRAUSS: *Don Juan* (***)).
(M) **(*) Sony Bruno Walter Edition SMK 64481 [id.]. Columbia SO, Bruno Walter.
(M) **(*) EMI CDM5 66094-2 [id.]. BPO, Karajan.
(BB) **(*) RCA Navigator 74321 17895-2 [(M) id. import]. Leipzig GO, Kurt Masur.
(M) **(*) Carlton IMP Dig. 30367 00282 [id.]. Hallé O, Skrowaczewski.
(BB) ** Naxos Dig. 8.550154 [id.]. Royal Flanders PO, Günther Neuhold.

Jochum is very special in this work, and Karajan also has a unique feeling for it – to say nothing of Haitink, now happily restored to the catalogue. Jochum's way with Bruckner is unique. So gentle is his hand that the opening of each movement or even the beginning of each theme emerges into the consciousness rather than starting normally. The purist may object that, in order to do this, Jochum reduces the speed far below what is marked, but Jochum is for the listener who wants above all to love Bruckner. The recording has undoubtedly been further enhanced in this reissue in DG's 'Originals' series, and a fascinating mono recording of Sibelius's *Night ride and sunrise* has been added. Jochum was not thought of as a Sibelian, but this performance is undoubtedly impressive and well worth having.

Karajan's opening (on his DG version) also has more beauty and a greater feeling of mystery than almost anyone else on CD. As in his earlier, EMI record, Karajan brings a keen sense of forward movement to this music as well as showing a firm grip on its architecture. His slow movement is magnificent. The current remastering of the 1975 analogue recording, made in the Philharmonie, is very impressive. The sound may lack the transparency and detail of the very finest of his records, but it is full and firmly focused and there is no doubt that this is a performance of considerable stature.

Haitink's performance is noble and unmannered; the opening horn solo is arresting and the orchestral playing is eloquent. The new CD transfer is excellent, and this is good value and a primary bargain choice, although Jochum on DG is worth the extra cost.

With warm, slightly distanced sound, the sensuous beauty of the Berlin Philharmonic string section has rarely been caught so beautifully. Muti as a Brucknerian has a fine feeling for climax, building over the longest span, and his flexible phrase-shaping of Brucknerian melody, very different from traditional rugged treatment, reflects a vocal style of expressiveness. With that extra warmth and high dramatic contrasts, Muti takes Bruckner further south than usual. For those fancying such treatment, this is an excellent version – but it will not suit everyone.

Karl Boehm made the very first commercial recording of the *Fourth Symphony* in 1936, and the performance has a simplicity and directness of utterance that have not since been surpassed. Moreover the *Andante quasi Allegretto* (like the early Mahler of Bruno Walter) has a seamless flow which makes it difficult to believe that it was recorded in four-minute chunks. We remember well that purchasers of the 78-r.p.m. shellac set were instructed to replay the record side containing the Scherzo, with its exuberant hunting horns (which is unchanged at its reprise), after listening to the Trio. It works excellently when the sides are edited together on Mike Dutton's CD transfer, just as it did in those days of constant side-changing which was part of the pre-LP ritual of listening to recorded music. Boehm had a special relationship with the Dresden orchestra which he felt displayed 'a certain brilliancy and splendour'. He also suggested that 'the Dresden strings had a very special sound – partly due to the old Italian instruments which are communally owned by the orchestra, but mainly . . . attributable to the proximity of Czechoslovakia, which seems to me the spiritual home of good string players'. Boehm's account of Richard Strauss's *Don Juan* is full of passion at the climax, but during the seduction scene it does not emphasize the sexuality in the way some contemporary performances manage to do. The recordings were made in the Semper Opera House in Dresden, so tuttis are not as resonantly expansive as they might be, but the glowing Dresden sound is particularly well caught in the slow movement, and the Scherzo is remarkably brilliant. The Dutton transfer, as ever, re-creates the original 78 sound with the utmost faithfulness – and, indeed, improves on it.

Although not quite as impressive as his Bruckner *Ninth*, Bruno Walter's 1960 recording is transformed by its CD remastering, with textures clearer, strings full and brass sonorous. It is not quite as rich as the Haitink Concertgebouw recording on Philips but is still pretty impressive, and the superbly played 'hunting horn' Scherzo is wonderfully vivid. Walter makes his recording orchestra sound remarkably European in style and timbre. The reading is characteristically spacious. Walter's special feeling for Bruckner means that he can relax over long musical paragraphs and retain his control of the structure, while the playing has fine atmosphere and no want of mystery.

Karajan's 1970 recording for EMI, made in the Berlin Jesus-Christus-Kirche and now reissued in the Karajan Edition, had undoubted electricity and combines simplicity and strength. The playing of the Berlin Philharmonic is very fine. The resonance means that there is a touch of harshness on the considerable fortissimos, while pianissimos are relatively diffuse. However, at mid-price this remains well worth considering.

In RCA's super-bargain Navigator series, Masur with the Leipzig orchestra is obviously a sound guide in Bruckner (no pun intended) and after opening poetically he shapes individual movements spaciously and convincingly and his conception of the overall span is impressive. The horns roister appropriately in the hunting Scherzo and the *Andante* has a gentle concentration and genuine atmosphere. The resonant Leipzig recording has brought some problems with the digital remastering: there is at times an element of minor coarseness in fortissimos, but at super-bargain price one can make allowances when the interpretation is so instinctively sympathetic.

Stanislav Skrowaczewski's reading with the Hallé Orchestra is eminently straightforward and well shaped. As one would expect from this conductor, the tempi are well judged and the concept spacious and majestic, with scrupulous attention to detail in matters of both phrasing and dynamics. The playing from the Hallé is responsive and sensitive, and there is no idiosyncrasy or self-indulgence. Overall this is a fine performance, full of perceptive touches. The recording has plenty of back-to-front perspective and no lack of atmosphere, though the acoustic does not have great warmth. There is a certain digital chill in big climaxes.

Günther Neuhold uses the Nowak edition, and his is a wayward, if often powerful account. His basic tempi are slow – he begins very slowly – but his pacing is very volatile. The Royal Flanders orchestra produces a rich sonority with spectacular brass sounds, and they are obviously responsive. The digital recording has plenty of atmosphere, though the resonance means that the most expansive fortissimos are almost overwhelming. This could be regarded as an interesting and very free alternative reading; but Jochum, who is also inspirational in approach, brings more grip to the score.

Symphony No. 4 in E flat; (i) *Psalm 150.*

(B) *(*) DG Classikon 439 448-2 [(M) id. import]. Chicago SO, Barenboim, (i) with Ruth Welting, Chicago Symphony Ch.

Although it is linked to a majestic account of *Psalm 150* with the Chicago Chorus and orchestra playing with heart-warming resonance (even if Ruth Welting's contribution is too shallow), this DG Classikon coupling must be passed over. Barenboim's 1972 performance of the symphony offers good analogue sound, and the Chicago orchestra play magnificently, but Barenboim's reading is very mannered and its insights confined to the surface.

Symphonies Nos. 4 in E flat; 7 in E.

(B) ** Teldec/Warner Ultima Dig.3984 21338-2 (2) [(M) id. import]. NYPO, Masur.
(B) ** DG Double 453 100-2 (2) [(M) id. import]. Chicago SO, Barenboim.

Kurt Masur's New York account of No. 4, recorded at the Avery Fisher Hall in 1993, has all the breadth and much of the finesse one could ask for. Those with keen memories of the Mehta years can be assured that the orchestra now produces a far more cultured and refined sound. Masur's command of the architecture of the piece is undoubtedly impressive and there is no want of feeling. The weakness lies perhaps in the slow movement, where concentration flags, certainly among the audience. The *Seventh* also comes from a live concert, but it dates from two years earlier, when his relationship with the orchestra was in the bloom of youth and he was working hard to banish the unrefined sonority that was associated with his predecessor. The sound is certainly better blended than before. His opening is very spacious and expansive, with consequent accelerandi later on. The performance is generally more characterful than his Leipzig account and has quite a lot going for it – albeit not quite enough to overcome the unpleasing acoustic of the Avery Fisher Hall, hardly a Bruckner venue. Admirers of this conductor will find the present two-for-the-price-of-one set good value, and it is certainly preferable to its DG competitor; but Chailly is a much stronger bargain recommendation for the *Seventh*, and at mid-price Jochum or Karajan more than hold their own for the *Fourth*.

Barenboim's Chicago recordings of the *Fourth* and *Seventh Symphonies* were made in 1972 and 1979 respectively and, as the readings are of uneven quality and each performance is complete on a single CD, it seems rather perverse to couple them together, even as a two-for-the-price-of-one Double. The account of the *Seventh* can be numbered among Barenboim's more successful ventures in this terrain. He gives a noble account of the first movement and, though his grip is less secure on the second, the music moves to a powerful climax, made to sound very Wagnerian, and there are some perceptive moments elsewhere. However, the performance as a whole is without the quality of inspiration or the sheer atmosphere of the very finest. The well-lit Chicago sound is full and spacious but lacks the cultured sonorities that Haitink finds in the Concertgebouw, or Chailly in the Berlin Jesus-Christus-Kirche. The Chicago orchestra play magnificently in both symphonies, but Barenboim's interpretation of the *Fourth* is mannered and the insights confined to the surface. The CD transfer too brings fiercer tuttis than in No. 7.

Symphonies Nos. 4 in E flat; 7 in E; 9 in D min.
(BB) ** RCA Navigator 74321 30368-2 (3) [(M) id. import]. Leipzig GO, Masur.

Three favourite Bruckner symphonies are here offered very inexpensively on RCA's super-budget label, very well played by the Leipzig orchestra, directed by the always reliable Kurt Masur. The recording is resonant but full-blooded. No. 4 comes off the most successfully, opening poetically and with individual movements shaped spaciously and convincingly: the *Andante* has a gentle concentration and genuine atmosphere. No. 7 again brings fine playing and the sound is spacious, but this very expansive reading lacks the grip of real concentration and (whichever edition is used) the absence of cymbals at the climax of the slow movement is a great drawback. Masur's reading of the *Ninth* is again leisured, but there is rather more tension. The Leipzig orchestra certainly understands Bruckner's expansive paragraphs, and again the recording is warm and spacious. Altogether a fair recommendation in the super-bargain range.

Symphony No. 5 in B flat (original version).
(B) *(*) Teldec/Warner Dig. 0630 14199-2 [(M) id. import]. Frankfurt RSO, Inbal.

Eliahu Inbal makes a promising start to the *Fifth Symphony* and gets reasonably good playing from the Frankfurt Radio forces. Unfortunately his slow movement is far too brisk to be remotely convincing: he gets through it in 14 minutes, as against Jochum's 19 and Karajan's 21. Rather unsatisfactory.

Symphony No. 5 in B flat.
(M) (***) EMI mono CDH5 56750-2 [id.]. VPO, Furtwängler.
(BB) ** Belart 461 326-2 [(M) id. import]. Concg. O, Eugen Jochum.
(M) *(*) Decca 448 581-2. VPO, Hans Knappertsbusch (with WAGNER: *Götterdämmerung: Dawn and Siegfried's Rhine journey* **).
(BB) ** Naxos Dig. 8.553452 [id.]. RSNO, Tintner.

Furtwängler's account of the *Fifth Symphony* comes from the invaluable Salzburg Archives and was recorded at the 1951 Salzburg Festival. (The remainder of the concert included Mendelssohn's *Fingal's Cave* and Mahler's *Lieder eines fahrenden Gesellen* with the 26-year-old Fischer-Dieskau.) Considering its age, the sound is remarkably good; the EMI engineers have done wonders in restoring its colours, and the performance has that blend of warmth, majesty and radiance which distinguishes the best Furtwängler.

Jochum's Concertgebouw version was made at a concert in the Ottobeuren Abbey, Germany, in 1964. The acoustic of the Philips recording is confined, with two-dimensional brass sonorities. The string timbre too is curiously dry and studio-ish for an ecclesiastical ambience. The performance undoubtedly has the electricity of live music-making, but most listeners will want a more expansive sound in this work.

Recorded in the earliest days of stereo (1956) Knappertsbusch's VPO version of the *Fifth* uses the Schalk edition with its truncated finale. Knappertsbusch can be a persuasive Bruckner conductor, but here the reading, though spaciously conceived, does not achieve a high level of tension, and it is not helped by the sound, which has a restricted dynamic range.

Only one other Bruckner *Fifth* is as competitively priced as this fine Naxos account by the Royal

Scottish National Orchestra under Georg Tintner. The octogenarian Tintner was a member of the Vienna Boys' Choir and studied with Weingartner, but the *Anschluss* compelled him to leave Austria and his talents have been hidden in the Antipodes. He may miss some of the grandeur of this massive symphony, but he brings out the unquenchable lyricism in a way which enhances the link with Schubert and the *Great C major Symphony* in particular. So in the outer movements the massive tuttis are not as monumental or as biting as they can be and, with the flow of the music so easy, the result is not as tensely dramatic as in the finest versions. In the slow movement too the flowing speed makes it seem more lightweight than usual, and in the finale the insistent dotted rhythms are not as sharp as they might be. Yet throughout Tintner directs with a concentration to hold the attention keenly, helped by the refined playing of the Scottish orchestra, who seem to respond warmly to him; but their efforts are to little avail, given the dry acoustic in which they are recorded. This seriously diminishes one's pleasure.

Symphonies Nos. 5 in B flat (1878 edition); *Symphony No. 6 in A* (original version).
(B) **(*) EMI forte CZS5 72661-2 (2) [(M) id. import]. Dresden State O, Jochum.

Jochum's DG account of the *Fifth Symphony* (with the Bavarian Radio Orchestra) was one of the earliest and one of the finest of his first cycle, and DG should consider issuing it as one of their 'Originals'. However, the Dresden version also has a very impressive slow movement, and the *Sixth* is similarly compelling. The CD transfers are admirably spacious, and the Dresden strings have plenty of depth. But the brass is rather too brightly lit, and, especially in the climaxes of the *Sixth Symphony*, the effect is brash.

Symphony No. 6 in A (original version).
(B) ** Teldec/Warner Dig. 0630 14200-2 [(M) id. import]. Frankfurt RSO, Inbal.

Again Inbal secures good playing from the Frankfurt Radio Orchestra, and he is well served by the engineers. The recording is full-bodied and spacious and has a dramatically wide dynamic range. Nevertheless the performance, even taking into account some fine string playing in the slow movement (the best part of the performance), is a little short on personality and is ultimately bland. After the *Fifth*, the *Sixth* is probably the least well-served of Inbal's cycle.

Symphony No. 6 in A.
(M) *** EMI CDM7 63351-2 [id.]. New Philh. O, Klemperer.
(M) **(*) DG 477 525-2. BPO, Karajan.
(BB) **(*) Arte Nova Dig. 74321 54456-2 [id.]. Saarbrücken RSO, Skrowaczewski.
(BB) **(*) Naxos Dig. 8.553453 [id.]. New Zealand SO, Georg Tintner.

Klemperer directs a characteristically strong and direct reading. It is disarmingly simple rather than expressive in the slow movement (faster than usual) but is always concentrated and strong, and the finale is particularly well held together. Splendid playing from the orchestra and clear, bright recording.

Karajan is not as commanding here as in his other Bruckner recordings, yet this is still a compelling performance, tonally very beautiful and with a glowing account of the slow movement that keeps it in proportion. The 1979 analogue recording might ideally have been more expansive.

Stanislaw Skrowaczewski has proved himself an impressive Bruckner interpreter: we were not alone in admiring his account of the *Fourth* with the Hallé Orchestra. This Arte Nova recording, made in the Saarbrücken Congress Hall in 1997, is very serviceable indeed and Skrowaczewski guides his forces with unerring purpose and nobility. Tempi are well judged throughout and phrases shaped with refinement. The string-tone needs perhaps to be weightier; they are easily swamped in this rather bright acoustic by the brass. All the same this is a very good performance, not superior to Klemperer, Jochum or Karajan, but recommendable alongside Tintner, whose account has slightly less gravitas but still has its own appealing individuality.

With no slow introduction, the *Sixth Symphony* emerges as less massive in its structure than the symphonies round it, suiting Tintner's lyrical Brucknerian style well. As in other works, he brings out the Schubertian quality in the writing. So the dark first theme is ruminative rather than ominous, enhanced by the beautiful playing of the New Zealand Symphony Orchestra, notably the strings. The *Adagio* brings an exceptionally spacious reading, relaxed in manner rather than tense or glowing, and the Scherzo is both relaxed and well sprung, joyful rather than rugged or ominous. The finale then makes light of the movement's problems, building to a joyful, exuberant close. Other readings are more powerful than this, but with its easy manners it compels attention, and the recording is warmly atmospheric.

Symphony No. 7 in E (original edition).
(B) ** Teldec/Warner Dig. 0630 14201-2 [(M) 4509 97437-2]. Frankfurt RSO, Inbal.

In terms of excellence of orchestral playing and vividness of recording, Inbal's *Seventh* is well up to the standard of his Bruckner series, using the original scores; but the performance itself, although it does not lack an overall structural grip, is without the full flow of adrenalin that can make this symphony so compulsive, and the orgasmic climax of the slow movement is much less telling without those two famous cymbal-crashes.

Symphony No. 7 in E.

(B) *** Decca Eclipse Dig. 448 710-2; *448 710-4* [(M) id. import]. Berlin RSO, Chailly (with MAHLER: *Des Knaben Wunderhorn: Des Antonius von Padua Fischpredigt; Das irdische Leben* – with Brigitte Fassbaender ***).
(M) *** Ph. 446 580-2. Concg. O, Haitink.
(M) *** EMI CDM5 66095-2 [id.]. BPO, Karajan.
(M) **(*) DG Dig. 445 553-2. VPO, Carlo Maria Giulini.
(M) ** Sony Bruno Walter Edition SMK 64482 [id.]. Columbia SO, Bruno Walter.
(BB) *(*) RCA Navigator 74321 24207-2 [(M) id. import]. Leipzig GO, Masur.
(BB) *(*) ASV Dig. CDQS 6154 [(M) id. import]. Philh. O, Francesco D'Avalos.
(M) (*) Sony mono SMK 47646 [id.]. VPO, George Szell.

Chailly's account, with its superb Decca digital recording, ranks among the best available and makes an obvious first choice. He obtains some excellent playing from the Berlin Radio Symphony Orchestra and, though he may not attain the spirituality of Karajan and Jochum, his is a committed and very moving performance, and the apparent lack of weight soon proves deceptive. He has a considerable command of the work's architecture and controls its sonorities expertly. The recording, made in the Jesus-Christus Kirche, Berlin, is outstanding in every way. Warm, full tone throughout all the departments of the orchestra, yet a clean and refined sound, which is especially impressive on CD. Reissued on Eclipse with the bonus of two delightful songs from Mahler's *Des Knaben Wunderhorn* sung by Brigitte Fassbaender, this is an unbeatable bargain.

Haitink's 1978 version offers a fine alternative at mid-price. The recording is wide in range and refined in detail, yet retains the ambient warmth of the Concertgebouw. Haitink's reading is more searching than his earlier version, made in the 1960s. The Concertgebouw Orchestra play with their accustomed breadth of tone and marvellously blended ensemble.

Karajan's outstanding EMI version (recorded in the Berlin Jesus-Christus-Kirche in 1970–71) also shows a superb feeling for the work's architecture and the playing of the Berlin Philharmonic is gorgeous. The recording has striking resonance and amplitude. This EMI reading, generally preferable to his later, digital recording for DG, has a sense of mystery that is really rather special. The new transfer for the Karajan Edition enhances the quality, and this recording has never sounded better.

Giulini secures playing of the utmost refinement from the Vienna Philharmonic and shapes each paragraph lovingly – indeed, at times some might think too lovingly: the Vienna strings are occasionally prone to a little too much sweetness. All the same, here are some wonderful things and music-making of a real and affecting eloquence. The only major reservation to be made concerns a want of a consistent forward movement. The DG recording has splendid warmth and does justice to the sumptuous sounds that the Vienna orchestra produce. The balance and perspective are natural.

Walter's reading suffers from the basic fault of concentrating on detail at the expense of structure. The outer movements bring many illuminating touches and the final climax of the first is imposingly built, but overall the tension is loosely held. In the *Adagio*, which is kept moving fairly convincingly, the climax is disappointing, and made the more so by the absence of the famous cymbal clash, as Walter uses the original text. The 1963 recording has been opened up in its remastering for CD and sounds fuller and more spacious than the original LPs. The present reissue places the work on a single CD for the first time, but this is not one of Walter's finest Bruckner records.

Masur secures fine playing from the Leipzig Gewandhaus Orchestra and the recording is spacious. But the very expansive reading lacks the fullest concentration and again we have to comment that the absence of cymbals at the climax of the slow movement is a great drawback.

Francesco D'Avalos on a super-bargain ASV issue has the advantage of the Philharmonia Orchestra in his 1988 recording, but otherwise its claims are slender. D'Avalos does not give us a reading of any real character or personality and, given the rival versions now to be had at all price levels, this is really a non-starter.

Szell's VPO account was recorded 'live' by Austrian Radio at the Salzburg Festival in 1968 and, curiously, the first two movements uncharacteristically fail to ignite. The Scherzo is lively enough, but the same rather studied approach affects the finale, although here the brass are given their head. The note with this CD tells us that Szell's exacting rehearsal methods did not find favour with the Viennese players, and there is certainly little enthusiasm evident here. The mono recording is generally very satisfactory, with only a hint of congestion at climaxes.

Symphonies Nos. 7 in E; 9 in D min.
(B) (**(*)) DG Double mono 445 418-2 (2) [(M) id. import]. BPO, Furtwängler.

These are both historic accounts, conveniently packaged as a Double; but the *Seventh Symphony*, recorded when the Berlin Philharmonic were on tour in Cairo in 1951, offers less appealing sound than the *Ninth*, which emanates from the closing months of the war, October 1944, not long before Furtwängler fled from the Nazis. The terrible times through which Europe was passing lent a special intensity to music-making, and this is a performance of real vision. The *Seventh* is not quite so special; but the set is well worth acquiring, given the price, for the sake of the *Ninth*.

Symphony No. 8 in C min. (original, 1887 version).
(B) **(*) Teldec/Warner Dig. 0630 14202-2 [(M) id. import]. Frankfurt RSO, Inbal.

Eliahu Inbal continues his stimulating series with a generally impressive and well-played first version of No. 8. There are considerable divergences here from the versions we know, and readers will undoubtedly derive much satisfaction from comparing them. The recording is very good.

Symphony No. 8 in C min. (1890 version, ed. Nowak).
(M) ** Decca 448 124-2 [430 228-2]. VPO, Solti.

Splendidly recorded in the Sofiensaal in 1966, Solti's earlier, VPO version of the *Eighth* is no match for his later, Chicago recording, at present available only within his complete cycle. Again he uses the Nowak edition, and the Vienna Philharmonic responds to his direction with great fervour and incisiveness. But the account of the long slow movement lacks the inspired spontaneous feeling of his later reading, and the result seems mannered.

Symphony No. 8 in C min.
(M) *** DG (IMS) 439 969-2 (2) [id.]. BPO, Karajan – WAGNER: *Siegfried idyll.****
(BB) *** EMI Seraphim CES5 69092 [CDEB 69092] (2). BPO, Karajan – WAGNER: *Lohengrin; Parsifal Preludes.* ***
(M) *** EMI (SIS) CMS5 66109-2 (2) [id.]. BPO, Karajan – BRAHMS: *Tragic Overture;* HINDEMITH: *Mathis der Maler* (symphony). ***
(B) **(*) DG (IMS) 431 163-2 [(M) id. import]. BPO, Jochum.
(M) *** EMI Dig. CDM7 64849-2 [id.]. LPO, Tennstedt.
(B) *** RCA Dig. 09026 68047-2 (2) [id.]. N. German RSO, Wand.

Karajan's 1975 Berlin Philharmonic recording sounds very impressive in the current CD transfer. Moreover it has the advantage, not only of a lower price, but also of a first-class coupling in Wagner's *Siegfried idyll*. The analogue recording of the symphony has fine body and refinement of texture. Sonically it does not perhaps quite match the later, Vienna Philharmonic account but there is very little in it, and no one investing in this noble account is likely to be disappointed. The reading is majestic, massive in scale, yet immaculate in detail. Excellent value.

The Seraphim transfer of Karajan's 1958 Berlin Philharmonic recording is remarkably successful. The EMI sound is spacious and, if the sonorities are not quite as sumptuous as we would expect today, the strings have substance and the brass makes a thrilling impact. The performance has much in common with Karajan's later (mid-price version) for DG and has compelling power. The slow movement is very fine indeed, conveying dark and tragic feelings, and the finale makes a fine apotheosis. While Karajan's last VPO version remains special, this is very worth while. As well as the advantage of great economy, it offers outstanding performances of the *Preludes* to Acts I and III of both *Lohengrin* and *Parsifal*. With its excellent couplings this set is also among the highlights of EMI's Karajan Edition.

Jochum uses the Nowak Edition, which involves cuts in the slow movement and finale, and in addition he often presses the music on impulsively in both the outer movements and especially in his account of the *Adagio*, where the climax has great passion and thrust. The symphony fits on to a single bargain-priced CD – which is worth any Brucknerian's money.

The plainness and honesty of Tennstedt in Bruckner is heard at its finest in this impressive account of the *Eighth*. It may not have the degree of exaltation which marked the performance which he conducted with this same orchestra at the Proms just after he made this record, but the inwardness and hushed beauty of the great *Adagio* in particular are superbly projected in unforced concentration. Though Karajan conveys more of the work's visionary power, Tennstedt in his comparative reticence carries similar conviction. Where generally in the other symphonies he prefers the Haas editions to those of Nowak, here he is firmly in favour of Nowak without the additional material in the recapitulation. Fine, well-balanced recording, with the CD clarity filled out by the fullness of ambience. EMI's No. 1 Studio is made to sound like a concert hall.

Günter Wand is as far removed from the jet-set maestro as it is possible to get, and his new recording of the *Eighth Symphony* has a patrician eloquence that is impressive. It is the product of three live concerts from December 1993, and is a straightforward, selfless reading of integrity and vision. All the same, it does not significantly add to his view of the work as exemplified in his earlier cycle. The Hamburg orchestra is a fine body, though it does not quite possess the tonal lustre of the Berlin Philharmonic or Concertgebouw. This comes on two CDs, packaged as one and costing as much. Given its artistic claims and the very truthful sound, it is certainly worth considering.

Symphonies Nos. (i) *8 in C min;* (ii) *9 in D min.*
(M) (***) DG mono 449 758-2 (2) [id.]. (i) Hamburg PO, (ii) Bav. RSO; Eugen Jochum.
(M) (***) Ph. mono 442 730-2; (IMS) 430 731-2 (available separately). Concg. O, van Beinum.

Jochum's mono recordings of the *Eighth* and *Ninth Symphonies* date from 1949 and 1954. The DG sound is technically of astonishingly fine quality, particularly in the gloriously played *Adagio* of the *Eighth* which has a remarkably wide dynamic range. The performances are also remarkable for their volatility: from the very opening of the first movement of the *Ninth* (marked *Feierlich misterioso*) Jochum gives a feeling of total spontaneity as the music ebbs and flows foward. The conductor's sense of vision and unique understanding of Bruckner's spiritual base comes over as strongly here as in his later, stereo versions, if not more so. This is surely a worthy reissue for DG's series of 'Originals'.

Although van Beinum's *Ninth* has been reissued on LP, the *Eighth* makes its first appearance since the 1950s. It is a performance of considerable stature and sounds astonishingly good. One critic, Richard Osborne, writing in *Gramophone* magazine, went so far as to say that the recording has 'a splendour, and a sense of rightness that make me wonder why anyone ever bothered to convert to stereo'! In the *Eighth Symphony* tempi are on the brisk side and the musical argument proceeds with an impressive and compelling logic. And what a glorious sound the Concertgebouw Orchestra makes! These are performances of commanding integrity, well worth adding to any collection, and they are to be preferred to many full-price versions of the 1990s.

Symphony No. 9 in D min. (1896 original version).
(B) **(*) Teldec/Warner Dig. 0630 14203-2 [(M) id. import]. Frankfurt RSO, Eliahu Inbal.

Eliahu Inbal's reading of the *Ninth* with the Frankfurt Radio Orchestra is far from negligible, even though it may not be a performance of the highest stature. The playing is often very fine, and Inbal is scrupulously attentive to detail; however, there is not the sense of scale that is to be found in the finest of his rivals. In 1934, Alfred Orel published the fragmentary sketches of the finale of the symphony without attempting to impose any sequence on them. They have fascinated many scholars: Hans Redlich and Robert Simpson prepared a keyboard edition, and the present reconstruction has been made by two Italian scholars, Nicola Samale and Giuseppe Mazzuca. It is, in the very nature of things, highly conjectural and is, of course, interesting to hear once.

Symphony No. 9 in D min.
✿ (M) *** Sony Bruno Walter Edition SMK 64483 [id.]. Columbia SO, Bruno Walter.
(M) *** DG 429 904-2 [id.]. BPO, Karajan.
(B) **(*) DG 429 514-2 [(M) id. import]. BPO, Jochum.
(BB) **(*) Belart 461 375-2 [(M) id. import]. VPO, Zubin Mehta.
(BB) ** RCA Navigator 74321 29247-2 [(M) id. import]. Leipzig GO, Masur.
(B) ** [EMI Red Line Dig. CDR5 69797]. Rotterdam PO, Tate.

Bruno Walter's 1959 account of Bruckner's *Ninth Symphony* represents the peak of his achievement during his Indian summer in the CBS recording studios just before he died. Walter's mellow, persuasive reading leads one on through the leisurely paragraphs so that the logic and coherence seem obvious where other performances can sound aimless. Perhaps the Scherzo is not vigorous enough to provide the fullest contrast – though the sound here has ample bite – yet it exactly fits the overall conception. The final slow movement has a nobility which makes one glad that Bruckner never completed the intended finale. After this, anything would have been an anticlimax.

The DG Galleria reissue offers a glorious performance of Bruckner's last and uncompleted symphony, moulded in a way that is characteristic of Karajan and displaying a simple, direct nobility that is sometimes missing in this work. Even in a competitive field, this 1966 disc stands out at mid-price, to rank alongside Bruno Walter's noble 1959 version.

Jochum's reading has greater mystery than any other and the orchestral playing reaches a degree of eloquence that disarms criticism. If at times Jochum tends to phrase too affectionately so that consequently the architecture does not emerge unscathed, he is still magnetic in everything he does. The 1966 recording sounds remarkably good. A fine bargain version.

There are moments of considerable power in Mehta's reading, which comes from his vintage Decca period in the mid-1960s. The orchestral playing has great splendour, although at the opening of the finale not everyone will respond to the somewhat febrile vibrato on the strings. In overall cogency and sense of mystery this does not match Jochum, but the Decca sound is splendid, and in the lowest price-range this is certainly well worth hearing.

As in his Leipzig recording of the *Seventh Symphony*, Masur's reading is leisured and expansive, but there is rather more tension in the *Ninth*. The Leipzig orchestra certainly understands Bruckner's expansive paragraphs, and the recording is warm and spacious. A fair recommendation in the bargain basement.

Jeffrey Tate's recording is not a strong contender. His first movement has undoubted breadth and dignity, and this fine Dutch orchestra play with dedication. Tate is expansive (at times he seems discursive) and, although the recording has admirable clarity and detail, the performance itself falls short of the distinction that would prompt a collector to return to it frequently.

VOCAL MUSIC

Masses Nos. (i) *1 in D min*. (for soloists, chorus and orchestra); *2 in E min*. (for 8-part chorus and wind ensemble); (ii) *3 in F min*. (for soloists, chorus and orchestra).

❁ (M) *** DG 447 409-2 (2) [id.]. (i) Mathis, Schiml, Ochman, Ridderbusch; (ii) Stader, Hellman, Haefliger, Borg; Bav. R. Ch. & O, Jochum.

Bruckner composed his three *Masses* between 1864 and 1868, although all three works were revised two decades later. Each contains magnificent music; Eugen Jochum is surely an ideal interpreter, finding their mystery as well as their eloquence, breadth and humanity. The *Kyrie* of the *E minor* swelling out gloriously from its gentle opening is quite breathtaking, while the fervour of the passionate *F minor* work is extraordinarily compelling, with all the intensity and drive of an inspirational live performance. But throughout all three works the scale and drama of Bruckner's inspiration are fully conveyed. In these outstanding new transfers, the analogue recordings from the early 1970s are given remarkable vividness and presence, while the warm atmosphere is fully retained. A remarkable achievement and a splendid choice for DG's 'Original' series of Legendary Recordings.

(i–ii) *Mass No. 2 in E min.;* Motets: (iii) *Afferentur regi;* (iv) *Ave Maria; Christus factus est;* (iii) *Ecce sacerdos magnus; Inveni David;* (iv) *Locus iste;* (iii) *Os justi; Pange lingua;* (iv) *Virga Jesse floruit.* (v) *Te Deum.*

(B) ** Decca Double 455 035-2 (2) [id.]. (i) Schütz Choir of L., Norrington; (ii) with Philip Jones Brass Ens.; (iii) St John's College, Cambridge, Ch., Guest; (iv) John Alldis Ch., Alldis; (v) Blegen, Lilowa, Ahnsjö, Meven, V. State Op. Ch., VPO, Mehta – Richard STRAUSS: *2 Gesänge* etc. ***

Norrington's performance of the *E minor Mass* is of high quality. It is sung with great feeling and perception and is recorded in a flattering acoustic which produces fine depth and richness of sonority. The *Motets* are divided between the excellent John Alldis Choir and St John's. They gain in simple intensity from having a comparatively small body of voices, and both groups sing them with unexaggerated eloquence, with splendid supporting brass sonorities. Unfortunately this collection is let down by the performance of the *Te Deum* – not because the Decca recording is inadequate or lacking in realism, but because the singing is not really idiomatic. Mehta is a shade too boldly expressive and he chooses a chorus that is a little too operatic in character as well as in name. However, the astonishingly complex coupled *German motet* of Richard Strauss is marvellously sung and recorded and makes this Double Decca still very well worth having.

Motets: *Afferentur regi; Ave Maria; Christus factus est; Ecce sacerdos; Iam lucis orto sidere; Inveni David; Libera me; Locus iste; Os justi; Pange lingua; Salvum fac populum tuum; Tantum ergo; Tota pulchra es; Vexilla regis; Virga Jesse.*

(BB) *** Naxos Dig. 8.550956 [id.]. St Bride's Church Ch., Robert Jones.

St Bride's Church in Fleet Street in London has since its post-war restoration in 1958 boasted a choir of 12 professional singers, providing an excellent example of the Anglican cathedral and collegiate tradition being extended to key parish churches. This Naxos disc is their first commercial recording, and very impressive it is, for with crisp, clear ensemble and fresh tone from boyish-sounding sopranos they give warmly sympathetic performances of these fine Bruckner motets, an excellent selection covering most of the best known. The recording is full and vivid, set against a helpful church acoustic which does not obscure detail

Motets: *Afferentur regi virgines; Ecce sacerdos magnus; Inveni David; Os justi; Pange lingua gloriosa.*

(BB) *** Belart 461 317-2 [(M) id. import]. St John's College, Cambridge, Ch., ASMF, Guest – BEETHOVEN: *Mass in C.* ***

The St John's performances are of the highest quality and the recording is marvellously spacious. They come in the lowest price range, coupled with a fine account of Beethoven's *C major Mass*.

Te Deum.

(B) **(*) DG Double 453 091-2 (2) [(M) id. import]. Tomowa-Sintow, Baltsa, Schreier, Van Dam, V. Singverein, VPO, Karajan – VERDI: *Requiem Mass.* **(*)

Karajan's analogue account of the *Te Deum* is spacious and strong, bringing out the score's breadth and drama. This is very satisfying and, if the Verdi coupling is acceptable, this is self-recommending.

Bunin, Revol Samuilovich (1924–76)

Violin concerto.

(M) ** Revelation RV 10058 [id.]. Kogan, USSR State Academic SO, Lazarev – BARBER: *Violin concerto* **(*); BARSUKOV: *Violin concerto No. 2.* **

Like the other concertos on this disc, Bunin's is an unashamedly romantic work, in places reflecting the idiom of his teacher, Shostakovich, but generally following a more conservative style. In a committed performance like Leonid Kogan's, it makes an attractive novelty, coupled with the Barber as well as the Barsukov. Curiously, the disc fails to insert tracks between the movements in this long, 32-minute work, and the live recording is marred by audience noise.

Burgon, Geoffrey (born 1941)

Acquainted with night; Cançiones del Alma; Lunar beauty; Nunc dimittis; This ean night; Worldës blissë.

(M) *** EMI Dig. CDM5 66527-2. James Bowman, Charles Brett, City of L. Sinf., Hickox.

This collection of Geoffrey Burgon's music for counter-tenor makes a hauntingly unusual record. Appropriately, it has at the centre his most celebrated piece, the setting of the *Nunc dimittis* used as theme-music in the television adaptation of John Le Carré's *Tinker, Tailor, Soldier, Spy*, originally for treble but well within counter-tenor range. Some of the other works are just as striking. In his three settings of St John of the Cross, *Cançiones del Alma*, Burgon was consciously seeking to get away from Anglican church-choir associations of the counter-tenor voice, and some of the bell-like effects are most beautiful. *Worldës blissë*, another religious inspiration, was prompted by a dream of a counter-tenor and oboe in duet; while in *This ean night* he dared to set the same text as Britten in the *Serenade* and Stravinsky in the *Cantata*, the *Lyke-Wake Dirge*, producing – despite obvious echoes of Britten – distinctive results in the tangy duetting of counter-tenors. The performances are strongly committed, with James Bowman taking the lion's share of solos. The recording gives an aptly ecclesiastical glow to the sound while keeping essential clarity.

Busoni, Ferruccio (1866–1924)

Berceuse élégiaque.

(M) *** EMI CDM7 65869-2. New Philh. O, Prausnitz – SCHOENBERG: *Chamber Symphony No. 2* **(*); WEILL: *Symphonies Nos. 1–2.* **

Busoni's *Berceuse élégiaque* is a moving and original piece, and it is very well played and recorded here. This is the highlight of an interesting group of works which are rather less successful as performances.

Indian fantasy for piano and orchestra, Op. 44.

(B) ** Millennium MCD 80116. Marjorie Mitchell, N. German RSO, Strickland – BORTKIEVITCH; BRITTEN: *Piano concertos.* **

There is no alternative version of Busoni's *Indian fantasy* (1913) currently available in the UK catalogue. This recording was first published in the UK in 1964, though the sleeve gives no indication of its provenance. It attributes the orchestral contribution to the Nord Deutscher Rundfunk Orchestra, whereas the original Brunswick issue spoke of the Vienna State Opera Orchestra. Nothing that Busoni composed is uninteresting, and the *Indian fantasy* is no exception; though it is uneven, its atmosphere is exploratory and forward-looking. The CD transfer is an improvement on the original, though there is a slight halo of reverberation round the excellent soloist.

OPERA

Doktor Faust (opera) complete.

(M) *** DG (IMS) 427 413-2 (3). Fischer-Dieskau, Kohn, Cochran, Hillebrecht, Bav. Op. Ch. & R. O, Leitner.

Busoni's epic *Doktor Faust* was left incomplete at the composer's death. Unfortunately, this recording is full of small cuts; however, with superb, fierily intense conducting from Leitner, it fully conveys the work's wayward mastery, the magnetic quality which establishes it as Busoni's supreme masterpiece, even though it was finished by another hand. The cast is dominated by Fischer-Dieskau, here in 1969 at his very finest; and the only weak link among the others is Hildegard Hillebrecht as the Duchess of Parma. Though this is a mid-price set, the documentation is generous.

Doktor Faust: Symphonic intermezzo.

(M) ** DG 439 488-2. Bav. RSO, Ferdinand Leitner – HINDEMITH: *Mathis Symphony* **; PFITZNER: *Palestrina: 3 Preludes* **; WEILL: *Kleine Dreigroschenmusik.* ***

The symphonic intermezzo is the *Sarabande* in the form in which it occurs in the opera between scenes one and two. Leitner's account comes from the 'complete' opera that he recorded in 1969 with Dietrich Fischer-Dieskau in the title-rôle but which was marked by numerous small cuts. Decent playing and recording.

Butterworth, George (1885–1916)

The banks of green willow.

(M) *** Chandos CHAN 6566 [id.]. Bournemouth Sinf., Norman Del Mar – BANTOCK: *The Pierrot of the minute: overture;* BRIDGE: *Summer* etc. ***

On Chandos, Del Mar gives a glowingly persuasive performance of *The banks of green willow*, which comes as part of another highly interesting programme of English music, devoted also to Butterworth's somewhat older contemporaries, Bantock and Frank Bridge. The digital transfer of a 1979 analogue recording has the benefit of even greater clarity without loss of atmosphere.

Love blows as the wind (3 songs).

(M) *** EMI CDM7 64731-2 [id.]. Robert Tear, CBSO, Vernon Handley – ELGAR; VAUGHAN WILLIAMS: *Songs.* ***

These three charming songs (*In the year that's come and gone*, *Life in her creaking shoes*, *Coming up from Richmond*), to words by W. E. Henley, provide an excellent makeweight for a mixed bag of orchestral songs based on the first recording of Vaughan Williams's *On Wenlock Edge* in its orchestral form. The sound is clear yet enjoyably warm and atmospheric.

A Shropshire lad (song-cycle).

(M) *** Decca (IMS) 430 368-2. Benjamin Luxon, David Willison – VAUGHAN WILLIAMS: *Blake songs* etc. ***

Benjamin Luxon gives powerful, dramatic performances of songs which can take such treatment, not quite the miniatures they may sometimes seem. Well-balanced recording and an admirable coupling.

A Shropshire Lad (cycle of 6 songs); *Bredon Hill* and other songs: *O fair enough are sky and plain; When the lad for longing sighs; On the idle hill of summer; With rue my heart is laden.*

(BB) *** Belart 461 491-2 [(M) id. import]. Benjamin Luxon, David Williamson – FINZI: *Earth and air and rain.* ***

While Luxon can project his tone and words with great power, his delicate half-tones are equally impressive, and this applies especially to the best-known song here, *Is my team ploughing?*, which is full of touching contrasts. Both in the six songs of the regular *Shropshire Lad* cycle and in the other Housman settings (which make an ideal companion set), Luxon underlines the aptness of the music to words that has often been set by British composers, but never more understandingly than here. David Williamson's accompaniments are wholly sympathetic and the mid-1970s Decca recording is strikingly real and vivid, and very well balanced.

Buxtehude, Diderik (*c.* 1637–1707)

Trio sonatas for violin, viola da gamba and harpsichord: in A min., Op. 1/3; in B flat, Op. 1/4; in G min., Op. 2/3; in E, Op. 2/6 (BuxWV 254–5, 261; 264).
(B) *** HM Musique d'Abord HMA 901089 [id.]. Boston Museum Trio.

The Boston Museum Trio are a highly accomplished group and display an exemplary feeling for style. The music is unfailingly inventive and, despite the obvious Italianate elements, distinctive. Not only are the playing, recording and presentation of high quality, but the cost is modest.

Canzonetta in G, BuxWV 171; Ciaconas: in C min., BuxWV 159; in E min., BuxWV 160. Chorales: *Ach, Herr, mich armen Sünder, BuxWV 178; Der Tag der ist so freudenreich, BuxWV 182; Durch Adams Fall ist ganz verderbt, BuxWV 183; In dulci jubilo, BuxWV 197; Komm, heiliger Geist, Herr Gott, BuxWV 199; Nimm von uns, BuxWV 207; Nun komm der Heiden Heiland, BuxWV 211; Wie schön leuchtet der Morgenstern, BuxWV 223. Fugue in C, BuxWV 174; Magnificat primi toni, BuxWV 203; Passacaglia in D min., BuxWV 161; Preludes: in A min., BuxWv 153; in C, BuxWV 137; in D, BuxWV 139; in D min., BuxWV 140; E min., BuxWV 142; F, BuxWV 145; F sharp min., BuxWV 146; G min., BuxWV 149. Te Deum laudamus, BuxWV 218; Toccatas: in D min., BuxWV 155; in F, BuxWV 156.*
(M) *** Erato/Warner Dig. 0630 12979-2 (2) [id.]. Marie-Claire Alain (Schnitger-Ahrend organ, Groningen).

Marie-Claire Alain's admirable mid-priced, two-disc set on Erato currently seems just about the best buy for those wanting a comprehensive survey of Buxtehude's splendid organ music. The magnificent opening *Prelude in C* shows not only how ideally the Groningen organ suits this repertoire, with its bright reeds and weighty yet never clouding sonorities, but also the full calibre of Buxtehude's music. Beginning floridly and thrillingly over massive pedals, it then produces a flowing fugue, with a following lively dance section and a final toccata. Marie-Claire Alain presents it powerfully and spontaneously, and she is equally impressive in registering the chorales, using a wide palette of colour: they are gently paced but never drag. The second disc opens with the ebullient *Fugue in C* which is so like the *Fugue à la gigue* attributed to Bach (BWV 577). Then, after the impressive chaconnes, the *Canzonetta in G* is piped quite deliciously. The complex *Magnificat primi toni* and the large-scale chorale fantasia on the *Te Deum* (in which Buxtehude and Alain always ensure that the cantus firmus emerges clearly) make one understand why Bach so admired this music. The arresting *Toccata in D minor*, with its dramatic pauses, undoubtedly influenced Bach's most famous organ work in the same key. Superb playing throughout, and demonstration-standard recording.

Chorales: *Christ unser Herr zum Jordan kam; Durch Adams Fall ist ganz verderbt; Ein feste Burg ist unser Gott; Erhalt uns, Herr, bei deinem Wort; Es ist das Heil uns kommen her; Es spricht der unweisen Mund wohl; Gelobet seist du, Jesu Christ; Gott der Vater, wohn uns bei; Magnificat primi toni; 2 Preludes and fugues in A min.; Preludes and fugues: in C; F sharp min.*
(B) *** HM Musique d'Abord HMA 190942 [id.]. René Saorgin (Schnitger organ of the Church of St Michel de Zwolle, Holland).

The Schnitger organ is sensitively and colourfully registered by Saorgin: he is particularly impressive in the serene, reflective chorales, *Durch Adams Fall* and *Es spricht der unweisen Mund wohl*, while the elaborations of the *Magnificat* are finely made. Excellent recording, vividly transferred.

Ciaconas: in C min.; E min., BuxWV 159–60; Passacaglia in D min., BuxWV 161; Preludes and fugues: in D; D min.; E; E min., BuxWV 139–42; in F; F sharp min., BuxWV 145–6; in G min., BuxWV 149.
(M) *** DG (IMS) 427 133-2. Helmut Walcha (organ of Church of SS Peter and Paul, Cappel, Germany).

Helmut Walcha has the full measure of this repertoire and these performances on the highly suitable Arp Schnitger organ in Cappel, Lower Saxony, are authoritative and spontaneous. The 1978 recording is excellent and the disc comprises generous measure: 73 minutes.

(i) *Preludes and fugues: in G min.; F.* Chorales: *Herr Christ, der einig Gottes Sohn; In dulci jubilo; Lobt Gott, ihr Christen allzugleich; Chorale fantasy: Gelobet seist du, Jesu Christ.* Cantatas: (ii) *In dulci jubilo; Jubilate Domino.*
(B) *** HM Musique d'Abord HMA 190700 [id.]. (i) René Saorgin (organ of St Laurent Church, Alkmaar); (ii) Alfred Deller, Deller Cons., Perulli, Chapuis.

A good, inexpensive sampler of Buxtehude, dating from 1971. The opening *Prelude and fugue in G minor* is fully worthy of the young J. S. Bach and, like its companion, is splendidly played by René Saorgin. The chorales are more static and less interesting than Bach's treatment of the same ideas. Of the cantatas, *In dulci jubilo* is a florid piece for four voices with instrumental accompaniment, while *Jubilate Domino* is a solo cantata accompanied by viola da gamba and organ continuo. Deller is in good form throughout.

Membra Jesu nostri, BuxWV 75.

(M) *** DG Dig. 447 298-2. Monteverdi Ch., E. Bar. Soloists, Gardiner – SCHUTZ: *O bone Jesu.* ***

(BB) *** Naxos Dig. 8.553787 [id.]. Trogu, Invernizzi, Balconi, Cecchetti, Carnovich, R. Svizzera (Lugano) Ch., Sonatori de la Gioiosa Marca, Treviso, Accademia Strumentale Italiana, Verona, Fasolis (with ROSENMULLER: *Sinfonia XI* ***).

The *Membra Jesu nostri* is a cycle of seven cantatas, each a meditation on Christ on the Cross, his feet, knees, hands, side, breast, face, etc., all of a simple, dignified, expressive power that, as always with this composer, make a strong impression. The Latin text is drawn from the *Rhythmica oratio* by either the twelfth-century Cistercian, St Bernard of Clairvaux, or Arnulf of Louvain of the same order. It was composed in 1680 and dedicated to the Swedish composer, Gustaf Düben, then director of music at the German church in Stockholm. The manuscript is now in the possession of the Uppsala University Library. John Eliot Gardiner's performance is searching and devotional. Gardiner's version has the sense of one of Buxtehude's own Abendmusik. Listen to the sixth of the cantatas, *Ad cor*, and the reverential approach and feeling of the Gardiner tell; the performance feels wonderfully spacious and unhurried. This issue can be recommended wholeheartedly; a Schütz *Geistliches Konzert, O bone Jesu*, related in spirit, comes on the Archiv recording, which is now offered at mid-price.

The performance from the Swiss-Italian Radio and ensembles from Verona and Treviso under Diego Fasolis is marginally less polished and accomplished vocally than the mid-priced versions under John Eliot Gardiner and René Jacobs but it has real feeling and depth. They are most expertly balanced and the sound is excellent in every way. Readers who are unwilling to spend more (or who are perhaps allergic to Gardiner) need not hesitate.

Byrd, William (1543–1623)

Consort, keyboard music, anthems and songs: *Fantasia for 4 viols; Fantasia No. 2 for 6 viols; Fantasia No. 3 for 6 viols; Galliard; Have mercy upon me, O God; In nomine No. 2 for 4 viols; In Nomine No. 5 for 5 viols; Pavane;* (i) (Keyboard) *John, come kiss me now; Pavan in A min.; Qui passe (for my Lady Nevell);* (Vocal) (ii) *Christ rising again; Fair Britain isle; In angel's weed; Rejoice unto the Lord; Susanna fair; Triumph with pleasant melody.*

(BB) *** Naxos Dig. 8.550604 [id.]. Rose Consort, Red Byrd; (i) Timothy Roberts (harpsichord or virginals); (ii) Tessa Bonner.

Here is a useful and inexpensive cross-section of Byrd's secular output that gives a good idea not only of its artistic riches but its sheer variety. Both the ensembles recorded here, the Rose Consort of viols and Red Byrd, are in good form and Timothy Roberts and Tessa Bonner are sensitive and expert exponents of this repertoire. The recorded sound is eminently clean and well balanced, and there is plenty of space round the aural image, which greatly enhances the undoubted attractions of an attractive anthology.

VOCAL MUSIC

Cantiones sacrae, Book I (1575): *Laudate pueri; O lux beata trinitas; Tribue Domine.* Book II (1589): *In resurrectione tua; Laetentur coeli; Ne irascaris; O quam gloriosum; Tribulationes civitatum.* Book III (1591): *Cantate Domino; Esurge Domine; Haec dies; Recordare Domine; Salve Regina.*

(BB) *** ASV Quicksilva Dig. CDQS 6211 [(M) id.]. Sarum Consort, Andrew Mackay.

Byrd published the first of his three Books of *Cantiones sacrae* in conjunction with his teacher and mentor, Thomas Tallis, contributing 17 motets to this initial collection; he went on to publish two further Books alone. Although all were written to be sung in Latin, some of the more successful were translated and sung in English. Their musical range is wide: the extended *Ne irascaris* opens sombrely and is for the most part serene, while the similarly extended *Tribulationes civitatum* generates great intensity at its central cadence; the comparatively short *O lux beata trinitas*, with its soaring treble line, has a richly eloquent closing cadence (superbly done here). *O quam gloriosam* is justly renowned and the closing *Haec Dies* (the closing motet of the Third Book) moves along swiftly to climax with an exultant string of polyphonic *Allelujas*. The Sarum Consort is a finely balanced and blended group, admirably directed by Andrew Mackay, whose pacing and control of light and shade cannot be faulted. The recording, made in the ideal acoustic of Milton Abbey, is clear, yet rich in choral ambience. Excellent documentation, with full texts and translations makes this a first-rate bargain.

Motets in paired settings: *Ave verum corpus* (with PHILIPS: *Ave verum corpus*); *Haec dies* (with PALESTRINA: *Haec Dies*); *Iustorum animae* (with LASSUS: *Iustorum animae*); *Miserere mei* (with G. GABRIELI: *Miserere mei*); *O quam gloriosum* (with VICTORIA: *O quam gloriosum*); *Tu es Petrus* (with PALESTRINA: *Tu es Petrus*).
(B) *** CfP CD-CFP 4481 [(M) id. import]. King's College, Cambridge, Ch., Sir David Willcocks.

This is an imaginatively devised programme of motets in which settings of Latin texts by Byrd are directly contrasted with settings of the same words by some of his greatest contemporaries. As was the intention, quite apart from adding variety to the programme, the juxtaposition makes one listen to the individual qualities of these polyphonic masters the more keenly, and register their individuality. The recording emerges with remarkable freshness on CD, and the beauty of the singing is never in doubt.

Mass for 3 voices; Mass for 4 voices; Mass for 5 voices.
❁ (M) *** Decca 433 675-2. King's College, Cambridge, Ch., Willcocks.
(B) **(*) HM HMA 90211[id.]. Deller Cons.

Masses for 3, 4 and 5 voices; Ave verum corpus; Magnificat; Nunc dimittis.
(B) *** Decca Double 452 170-2 (2) [(M) id. import]. King's College, Cambridge, Ch., Willcocks – TAVERNER: *Western Wynde Mass*. ***

Although later versions of the *Mass for 5 voices* have produced singing that is more dramatic and more ardent, the performances of the *Masses for 3* and *4 voices*, dating from 1963, remain classics of the gramophone. Under Willcocks there is an inevitability of phrasing and effortless control of sonority and dynamic that completely capture the music's spiritual and emotional feeling. On Double Decca the 1959 recordings of the *Ave verum*, *Magnificat* and *Nunc dimittis* have been added, representing a more reticent, less forceful style than some might expect. But the singing is still affectingly beautiful and the sound comparably spacious, and the coupled Taverner programme shows the choir on top form.

Whether or not it is historically correct for Byrd's Masses to be sung by solo voices, the great merit of these French Harmonia Mundi performances is their clarity, exposing the miracle of Byrd's polyphony, even though the tonal matching is not always flawless. The 1968 recording is clean and truthful, although it lacks something in ecclesiastical atmosphere.

Mass for 4 voices; Mass for 5 voices; Infelix ego.
(BB) *** Naxos Dig. 8.550574; *4.550574* [id.]. Oxford Camerata, Jeremy Summerly.

This new coupling from the Oxford Camerata represents one of Naxos's most enticing bargains. The full-throated singing has spontaneous ardour but no lack of repose in the music's more serene moments. Summerly offers the motet, *Infelix ego*, as a bonus. These readings are distinctive in a different way from those by the King's College Choir. They are recorded outstandingly vividly, and this super-bargain coupling gives every satisfaction.

Mass for five voices.
(M) *** EMI CDM5 65211-2. King's College, Cambridge, Ch., Ledger – TALLIS: *Mass: Puer natus est nobis;* TYE: *Mass: Euge Bone*. ***

Ledger in his last two years (1980–81) as choirmaster at King's made a series of superb recordings with what must still be counted the premier collegiate/cathedral choir. The richest and most complex of Byrd's settings of the Mass here receives a superbly poised yet deeply expressive reading, atmospherically set against a warm, reverberant acoustic. Ledger combines the contemplative intensity that his predecessor, Sir David Willcocks, instilled in this choir, with an extra rhythmic urgency, and the apt couplings with music of Tallis and Tye make this a particularly desirable and generous reissue, with first-class analogue sound impressively transferred to CD.

Masses a 5: In assumptione beauæ mariæ virginis; In tempore Paschali (Propers). Antiphons: *Ave Regina cælorum; Salve Regina*. Motet: *Regina cæli*.
(M) *** HM Suite Dig. HMT 7905182 [id.]. Chanticleer.

Byrd's three beautiful Masses in three, four and five parts – see above – were written between 1593 and 1595, but the composer later wrote more music that could be used for private Mass celebration by Roman Catholics living in Protestant England. This later music was published in two volumes of *Gradualia* in 1605 and 1607. Besides a great many motets, Byrd left sequences of Mass Propers which could be used for certain key feast days of the church year. Propers, of course, are the variable texts that relate to specific days in the Church calendar and they are used in conjunction with the Mass Ordinary. But these Propers can quite effectively be grouped and sung independently, and that is just what the dozen singers of Chanticleer do here. They have chosen two main sequences, the first connected with Easter (the Mass *In tempore Paschali*) and the second for the *Assumption of the Blessed Virgin Mary*. The later is prefaced by the motet, *Regina cœli* and followed by two Marian antiphons (*Ave Regina cœlorum* and *Salve Regina*). The settings are slightly austere but are permeated by the intensity of Byrd's belief. They are obviously intended for comparatively intimate performance, and the acoustic of the recording and the chamber style of the singing bring out the music's simple beauty. Intonation here is not always absolutely immaculate, but the singing always has expressive conviction; one finds oneself carried along by the very spontaneous flow, with very little pause between movements. Ideally there should have been separate cues – instead they are merely indexed. But this is a small drawback to a stimulating and well-documented collection, including translated texts.

Caldara, Antonio (*c.* 1670–1736)

Christmas cantata (Vaticini di Pace); Sinfonias Nos. 5 & 6.

(BB) *** Naxos 8.553772 [id.]. Mary Enid Haines, Linda Dayiantis-Straub, Jennifer Lane, David Arnot, Aradia Baroque Ens., Kevin Mallon.

Caldara, an Italian contemporary of Bach and Handel, wrote this rare and delightful cantata for the Christmas celebrations in Rome in 1712. Preceded by an overture, it is a free-running sequence of 14 arias for the allegorical characters of Peace, Human Heart and Divine Love, with Justice initially representing Old Testament values. Peace, in the longest and most beautiful of the arias, a siciliano, then woos Justice to mercy through a vision of the Infant Christ. This Canadian performance is fresh and lively, with four excellent soloists (notably Mary Enid Haines as Peace) and a good period-instrument ensemble. A rarity made doubly enticing at Naxos super-bargain price.

Crucifixus.

(B) *** Decca Double 443 868-2 (2) [id.]. Soloists, St John's College, Cambridge, Ch., Philomusica, Guest – BONONCINI: *Stabat Mater* ***; PERGOLESI: *Magnificat in C; Stabat Mater* **(*); D. SCARLATTI: *Stabat Mater;* A. SCARLATTI: *Domine, refugium factus es nobis; O magnum mysterium;* LOTTI: *Crucifixus.* ***

(B) *** Decca Double 455 017-2 [(M) id. import]. St John's College, Cambridge, Ch., L. Philomusica, Guest – LOTTI: *Crucifixus* ***; PERGOLESI: *Magnificat* etc. **(*)

Antonio Caldara settled in Vienna and established an enviable reputation as a master of opera – he composed nearly a hundred! The *Crucifixus* is an elaborate sixteen-part setting of great eloquence, texturally rich and concentrated into a few seconds short of five minutes. It follows on naturally after Bononcini's beautiful *Stabat Mater*. The treble lines have some moments of insecurity but otherwise the performance is impressive and the (originally Argo) recording first class. This fine piece also comes as a filler for Decca's alternative compilation which centres primarily on Pergolesi.

Cambini, Giuseppe Maria (1746–1825)

Wind quintets Nos. 1 in B; 2 in D min.; 3 in F.

(BB) *** Naxos Dig. 8.553410 [id.]. Avalon Wind Quintet – BRICCIALDI: *Wind quintet in D.* ***

Cambini was born in Livorno (Leghorn) and spent his youth working in Naples, where he is said to have played quartets with Nardini and Boccherini. He went to Paris in the 1770s and was enormously successful both as a composer and as a conductor, but he spent his last years in poverty. He was nothing if not prolific, composing some 19 operas, nearly 150 quartets and 60 symphonies. These *Wind quintets* are doubtless inconsequential but they are charming, particularly when played so superbly and elegantly by these fine young German musicians. The recording is expertly balanced and very natural. Slight music, but so well served that it will give much pleasure.

Campra, André (1660–1744)

Cantatas: *Arion; La dispute de l'Amour et de l'Hymen; Enée et Didon; Les femmes.*

(B) *** HM Musique d'Abord Dig. HMA 1901238 [id.]. Jill Feldman, Dominique Visse, Jean-François Gardeil, Les Arts Florissants, William Christie.

Jill Feldman is at her most spirited and eloquent in the dramatic narrative of *Arion* (which has an effective flute obbligato) and Dominique Visse's tangy alto is equally telling in the altercation of the conflicting interests of Marriage and Love which need to be resolved harmoniously. In *Les Femmes* there is disillusion from a male lover who, first dolorously and then with considerable animation, laments the vagaries of the fair sex; his final conclusions are far from optimistic. This is sung with both feeling and sparkle by Jean-François Gardeil. The most ambitious of the four works is a brilliant duet celebrating the nuptials of Aeneas and Dido, which conveniently leaves out the unhappy ending to come later in the story. With sensitive and strongly paced accompaniments from Christie and Les Arts Florissants, it is difficult to imagine that these works could be re-created more tellingly, helped by the presence and atmosphere of the excellent recording.

L'Europe galante (opera-ballet): suite.

(M) *** DHM/BMG GD 77059 (2) [77059-2-RG]. Yakar, Kweksilber, René Jacobs, La Petite Bande, Leonhardt – LULLY: *Bourgeois gentilhomme*. ***

Like Couperin's *Les Nations*, though in a very different fashion, this enchanting divertissement attempts to portray various national characteristics: French, Spanish, Italian and Turkish. The three soloists all shine and the instrumentalists, directed by Leonhardt, are both expert and spirited. The recording too is well balanced and sounds very fresh on CD.

OPERA

Idomenée: highlights.

(B) *** HM Dig. HMX 290844/46 (3) [(M) id.] (from complete recording, with Delétré, Piau, Zanetti, Fouchécourt, Les Arts Florissants; cond. Christie) – LULLY: *Atys:* highlights; RAMEAU: *Castor et Pollux:* highlights. ***

This is one of Harmonia Mundi's enterprising 'Trios', compiling three discs of operatic highlights at bargain price with full documentation, including translations. *Idomenée* is a fascinating work vividly recorded (on HMC 901396/8,) and this 70-minute selection, with items well balanced to include the Overture, a brief reminder of the Prologue and excerpts from all five Acts, if taken in harness with its companions costs but a fraction of the price of the three-disc complete set. It will be interesting to see if this marketing experiment is a success.

Canteloube, Marie-Joseph (1879–1957)

Chants d'Auvergne: Series 1–5 (complete).

(B) *** Decca Double Dig. 444 995-2 (2) [id.]; *444 995-4*. Kiri Te Kanawa, ECO, Jeffrey Tate – VILLA-LOBOS: *Bachianas brasileiras No. 5*. ***

(i) *Chants d'Auvergne: Series 1–5* (complete); (ii) Appendix: *Chants d'Auvergne et Quercy: La Mère Antoine; Lorsque le meunier; Oh! Madelon, je dois partir; Reveillez-vous, belle endormie. Chants paysans Béarn: Rossignolet qui chants. Chants du Languedoc: La fille d'un paysan; Moi j'ai un homme; Mon père m'a plasée; O up!; Quand Marion va au moulin. Chants des Pays Basques: Allons, beau rossignol; Comment donc Savoir; Dans le tombeau; J'ai une douce amie; Le premier de tous les oiseaux.*

❁ (M) *** Van. 08.8002.72 [OVC 8001/2]. Netania Davrath, O, (i) Pierre de la Roche; (ii) Gershon Kingsley.

It was Netania Davrath who in 1963 and 1966 – a decade before the de los Angeles selection – pioneered a complete recording of Canteloube's delightful song-settings from the Auvergne region of France. While her voice has a lovely, sweet purity and freedom in the upper range, she also brings a special kind of colour and life to these infinitely varied settings. All 30 songs from the five series are included, plus an important appendix of 15 more, collected by Canteloube and admirably scored by Gershon Kingsley, very much in the seductive manner of the others. They are quite as delightful as any of the more familiar chants, and some of them are unforgettable, providing a programme of two hours of enchanting music which, when dipped into, will give endless pleasure. The accompaniments are freshly idiomatic, warm but not over-upholstered, and the CD transfers retain all the sparkle and atmosphere of the original recordings. We understand there are some problems in obtaining this set in the UK at present, but we are assured that it is not deleted.

In Dame Kiri Te Kanawa's recital the warmly atmospheric Decca recording brings an often languorous opulence to the music-making. In such an atmosphere the quick songs lose a little in bite, and *Baïlèro*, the most famous, is taken extremely slowly. With the sound so sumptuous, this hardly registers and the result remains compelling, thanks in large measure to sympathetic accompaniment from the ECO under Jeffrey Tate. At Double Decca price, this now makes a formidable bargain, for Dame Kiri's voice was at its freshest and most beautiful when she made these recordings in 1983/4. This set is now also available on cassette.

Chants d'Auvergne: extended excerpts.
(B) **(*) Sony Dig. SBK 63063; *SBT 63063* [id.]. Frederica von Stade, RPO, Antonio de Almeida.

Taken from two separate CD recitals made in the early 1980s, Frederica von Stade's selection is generous, with two dozen items included. Fine as her singing is, she is stylistically and temperamentally not always completely at home in Canteloube's lovely folksong settings. However, her second collection (from which the last seven items here are drawn) has more charm and personal identification than the first, so the effect is of a recital that gives greater pleasure as it proceeds. She is well accompanied and the recording is atmospheric, if not quite as sumptuous as Decca's sound for Kiri te Kanawa.

Chants d'Auvergne: L'Aio dè rotso; L'Antouèno; Baïlèro; Brezairola; Malurous qu'o uno fenno; Passo pel prat; Pastourelle.
(M) *** RCA 09026 62600-2 [id.]. Anna Moffo, American SO, Stokowski – RACHMANINOV: *Vocalise;* VILLA-LOBOS: *Bachianas brasileiras No. 5.* ***

Moffo gives radiant performances, helped by the sumptuous accompaniment which Stokowski provides. The result is sweet, seductively so. The recording, from the early 1960s, is opulent to match.

Chants d'Auvergne: L'Antouèno; Baïlèro; 3 Bourrées; Lou Boussu; Brezairola; Lou coucut; Chut, chut; La Déläissádo; Lo Fïolairé; Jou l'pount d'o Mirabel; Malurous qu'o uno fenno; Passo pel prat; Pastourelle; Postouro, sé tu m'aymo; Tè, l'co, tè.
✿ (B) *** EMI Dig. CD-EMX 9500 [(M) id. import]. Jill Gomez, RLPO, Handley.

Jill Gomez's selection of these increasingly popular songs, attractively presented on a mid-price label, makes for a memorably characterful record which, as well as bringing out the sensuous beauty of Canteloube's arrangements, keeps reminding us, in the echoes of rustic band music, of the genuine folk base. An ideal purchase for the collector who wants just a selection.

Chants d'Auvergne: Baïlèro; 3 Bourrées; Brezairola; Lou Boussu; Lou coucut; Chut, chut; La Délaïssádo; Lo Fïolairé; Jou l'pount d'o Mirabel; Malurous qu'o uno fenno; Oï ayaï; Pastourelle; La pastrouletta; Postouro, sé tu m'aymo; Tè, l'co, tè; Uno jionto postouro.
(M) *** Virgin/EMI Dig. CUV5 61120-2 [id.]. Arleen Augér, ECO, Yan Pascal Tortelier.

Arleen Augér's lovely soprano is ravishing in the haunting, lyrical songs like the ever-popular *Baïlèro*. In the playful items she conveys plenty of fun, and in the more boisterous numbers the recording has vivid presence.

Caplet, André (1878–1925)

La Masque de la mort rouge (Conte fantastique); Divertissements for harp; (i) *Les prières*, for soprano, harp & string quartet; (ii) *2 Sonnets*, for soprano & harp; (i–iii) *Septet à cordes vocales et instrumentales.*
(B) *** HM Musique d'Abord Dig. HMA 1901417 [id.]. Laurence Cabel, Ens. Musique Oblique; with (i) Sharon Coste; (ii) Sandrine Piau; (iii) Sylvie Deguy.

André Caplet's best-known work is the *Conte fantastique* for harp and strings, based on Edgar Allan Poe's *Masque of the Red Death*, a work strong on evocative menace. This bargain-priced Harmonia Mundi reissue is highly recommendable. It offers the more intimate, chamber version of the score, and the rest of the programme is admirably chosen and serves to flesh out a portrait of Caplet himself. In the other three major works, female voices are richly integrated with the string quartet, and the composer makes a great success of this combination of voices and strings, especially in the *Septet*, using a trio of two sopranos and a mezzo. Beautiful singing, sensitive playing and warmly atmospheric sound add to the listener's aural pleasure. Two solo *Divertissements* for harp make an agreeable central interlude.

Cardoso, Frei Manuel (*c.* 1566–1650)

Lamentatio; Magnificat secundi toni.
(BB) *** Naxos Dig. 8.553310 [id.]. Ars Nova, Bo Holten – LOBO: *Motets;* MAGALHAES: *Missa O Soberana luz* etc. *** (with Concert of Portuguese polyphony ***).

Cardoso's serene, flowing polyphony with its forward-looking use of augmented chords is heard at its most striking in the *Magnificat*, while his *Lamentatio* for six voices is touchingly beautiful. Remarkably eloquent singing from this fine Danish choir and good recording in a suitably ecclesiastical acoustic. The rest of the programme is hardly less stimulating.

Missa pro defunctis.
(BB) *** Naxos Dig. 8.550682 [id.]. Oxford Schola Cantorum, Jeremy Summerly – LOBO: *Missa pro defunctis.* ***

Cardoso's *Missa pro defunctis* is not as dramatic in its contrasts as the coupled setting of Duarte Lôbo, but its polyphony is characteristically long-breathed and expressively powerful. As with the Lôbo performance, a solo treble makes a brief but effective introduction for each movement, a device which works very touchingly. Here it is the *Sanctus* that one especially remembers as being gloriously rich in expressive feeling, although the *Communio* closes the work with rapt intensity. The performance by Jeremy Summerly and his Oxford Schola Cantorun is beautifully paced and the calibre of the singing itself is very impressive indeed, as is the Naxos recording.

Carissimi, Giacomo (1605–74)

Duos & cantatas: *A piè d'un verde alloro; Bel tempo per me; Così volete, così sarà; Deh, memoria è che più chiedi; Hor che si Sirio; Il mio cor è un mar; Lungi homai deh spiega; Peregrin d'ignote sponde; Rimati in pace homai; Scrivete, occhi dolente (Lettera amorosa); Tu m'hai preso à consumare; Vaghi rai, pupille ardenti.*
(B) *** HM Musique d'Abord Dig. HMA 1901262. Concerto Vocale, René Jacobs.

Carissimi's achievement as a sacred composer has long overshadowed his secular music, whose riches are generously displayed here and whose inspiration and mastery are immediately evident. These are performances of great style and are beautifully recorded. A bargain.

Carter, Elliott (born 1908)

Piano concerto; Concerto for orchestra; 3 Occasions for orchestra.
(BB) *** Arte Nova Dig. 74321 27773-2 [id.]. Oppens, SWF SO, Gielen.

Piano concerto; 3 Occasions for orchestra.
(BB) *** Arte Nova Dig. 74321 52248-2. Oppens, SWF SO, Gielen – BARTOK: *Piano concerto No. 3;* BERG: *3 Pieces from the Lyric suite.* ***

Michael Gielen directs strong, purposeful readings, very well played, of this taxing music, clarifying the thornily complex arguments with the help of vivid, sharply focused sound. Anyone wanting to sample the work of one of the most challenging composers of our day cannot do better than experiment with this disc at super-bargain price. Even with Ursula Oppens a powerful soloist, the *Piano concerto*, dating from 1964–5, is the most formidable piece for the unprepared listener (and the notes in the booklet do little to help). That leads naturally on to the *Concerto for orchestra* of 1969, when the complex arguments are more readily appreciated, partly through Carter's striking use of instrumental colour in four contrasted orchestral groupings. More approachable than either is the third work, a collection of three pieces, written between 1986 and 1989, which display to the full the astonishing vitality and questing originality of a composer of rising eighty. There are still so many notes that the ear may at first be confused, but in performances like these, recorded live, the tension is magnetic. A splendid, inexpensive introduction to one of the most intractable of twentieth-century composers.

The alternative disc brings together two of Gielen's outstanding Carter performances but offering the generous alternative coupling of Bartók and Berg works.

Concerto for orchestra.
(M) *** Sony SMK 60203 [id.]. NYPO, Bernstein – IVES: *Central Park in the dark* etc. ***

It is apt that Elliott Carter's key avant-garde orchestral work from 1969 should follow on after Ives, for its writing seems naturally to derive from that earlier master in its complexity. However, the argument here is much more thorny, the texture densely interwoven and prismatic; its energy is unquestioned, but its linear fragmentation is daunting. Certainly it could hardly be played with more expertise or display more conviction; and the close (1970) recording-balance ensures that every detail is well defined.

Carulli, Ferdinando (1770–1841)

Guitar concerto in A.
(M) **(*) DG (IMS) 439 984-2. Siegfried Behrend, I Musici – GIULIANI: *Concerto in A* ***; VIVALDI: *Guitar concertos* **(*).

The Italian virtuoso Ferdinando Carulli made his reputation in Paris, where this innocent post-Mozartian one-movement piece was written. It is elegantly played by Behrend and I Musici and immaculately recorded. A touch more vitality would have been welcome, but this is enjoyable enough.

Carvalho, João De Sousa (1745–98)

Te Deum.

(M) *** DG Codex 453 182-2. Luisa Bosabalian, Elsa Saque, Carmen Gonzales, John Mitchinson, Alvaro Malta, Gulbenkian Chamber Ch. & O, Pierre Salzmann – ALMEIDA: *Beatus vir* etc.; SEIXAS: *Adebat Vincentius* etc.; TEIXEIRA: *Gaudate, astra.* ***

The Portuguese composer João De Sousa Carvalho was a contemporary of Mozart, and there is a Mozartian impression within the extended (nine-minute) overture for two orchestras which opens his ambitious 1792 *Te Deum* (his third setting). During the course of this splendid and powerfully expressive work there is much thrilling writing for double chorus, and the florid arias – like Mozart's – are often semi-operatic in style, making great demands on the soloists, who generally rise to the occasion here, especially the fine mezzo, Carmen Gonzales, and the tenor, John Mitchinson. The two sopranos match their voices well in duet, and the quintet, *Salvum fac populum tuum, Domine*, is one of the work's highlights. The orchestration has many imaginative touches, especially the brass and wind scoring for *Judex crederis esse venturus*, an engaging march setting that bears comparison with the similar episode in the finale of Beethoven's *Choral Symphony*. The work's closing numbers bring a lively chorus, *Fiat misericordia tua, Domine*, followed by the more serene motet, *Tantum ergo*, which here ends rather abruptly. The work is unusual in that it begins (with *O salutaris hostia*) and ends using these two motets. The performance here is eloquently moving and spaciously recorded (in 1970). Even if the double chorus at times could be more sharply defined, the weight and body of the singing project splendidly and the overall focus and balance are very good. This reissued DG Archiv Codex set is made the more attractive by the substantial couplings from three major Portuguese baroque composers, all little known. Their contributions make a real bonus.

Castelnuovo-Tedesco, Mario (1895–1968)

Guitar concerto No. 1 in D, Op. 99.

(M) *** Sony SMK 60022 [id.]. John Williams, ECO, Groves – RODRIGO: *Concierto de Aranjuez;* VILLA-LOBOS: *Guitar concerto.* ***

(BB) *** Naxos Dig. 8.550729 [id.]. Norbert Kraft, N. CO, Nicholas Ward – RODRIGO; VILLA-LOBOS: *Concertos.* ***

(M) **(*) DG (IMS) 449 098-2 [id.]. Narciso Yepes, LSO, Navarro – HALFFTER: *Concerto;* RODRIGO: *Fantasia.* **

In some ways John Williams's earlier recording of this engaging concerto with Ormandy and the Philadelphia Orchestra was fresher and had more pace; he is placed well forward here. But the overall perspective is by no means unpleasing and the result is strikingly vivid. These artists make the most of the slow movement's poetry, and the concerto has no want of charm. The couplings are first class.

On Naxos a first-class version of this slight but attractive concerto, which is well suited by the relatively intimate scale of the performance. The recording is well balanced and vivid, and this is happily coupled with enjoyable versions of two other favourite concertos. The soloist, Norbert Kraft, has plenty of personality and the accompaniment is fresh and polished. Typically excellent Naxos value.

Narciso Yepes's playing is distinguished, but he has not always been lucky in choosing his accompanists. He plays this concerto admirably, receiving attentive support from Navarro and the LSO and fresh, vivid recording from DG; for the two coupled works, however, his partner was Odón Alonso and the results are less impressive, with a dry studio acoustic not flattering the music-making. The Naxos CD is a far more attractive proposition.

Catalani, Alfredo (1854–93)

La Wally (opera): complete.

(M) *** Decca 425 417-2 (2). Tebaldi, Del Monaco, Diaz, Cappuccilli, Marimpietri, Turin Lyric Ch., Monte Carlo Op. O, Fausto Cleva.

The title-role of *La Wally* prompts Renata Tebaldi to give one of her most tenderly affecting performances on record, a glorious example of her singing late in her career. Mario del Monaco begins coarsely, but the heroic power and intensity of his singing are formidable, and it is good to have the young Cappuccilli in the baritone role of Gellner. The sound in this late-1960s recording is superbly focused and vividly real.

Cavalli, Francesco (1602–76)

La Calisto (complete version – freely arranged by Raymond Leppard).

(M) *** Decca 436 216-2 (2). Cotrubas, Trama, J. Baker, Bowman, Gottlieb, Cuénod, Hughes, Glyndebourne Festival Op. Ch., LPO, Leppard.

No more perfect Glyndebourne entertainment has been devised than Leppard's freely adapted version of an opera written for Venice in the 1650s but never heard since. It exactly relates that permissive society of the seventeenth century to our own. It is the more delectable because of the brilliant part given to the goddess, Diana, taken by Dame Janet Baker. In this version she has the dual task of portraying first the chaste goddess herself, then in the same costume switching immediately to the randy Jupiter disguised as Diana, quite a different character. The opera is splendidly cast. Parts for such singers as James Bowman draw out their finest qualities, and the result is magic. No one should miss Dame Janet's heartbreakingly intense singing of her tender aria *Amara servitù*, while a subsidiary character, Linfea, a bad-tempered, lecherous, ageing nymph, is portrayed hilariously by Hugues Cuénod. The opera has transferred admirably to a pair of CDs, with each of the two Acts offered without a break; the recording, made at Glyndebourne, is gloriously rich and atmospheric, with the Prologue in a different, more ethereal acoustic than the rest of the opera. A full libretto is provided.

L'Ormindo (complete) (ed. Raymond Leppard).

(M) *** Decca 444 529-2 (2). Wakefield, Howells, Runge, Garcisanz, Berbié, Cuénod, Van Bork, F. Davis, Alister, Van Allan, LPO, Leppard.

We owe it above all to Raymond Leppard that the name of Francesco Cavalli has become famous again. As with *La Calisto*, he subjected *L'Ormindo* to his own magical Leppardization process, to produce another enchanting Glyndebourne entertainment. The gaiety of Glyndebourne is superbly caught, for wisely Decca (or, rather, Argo) opted to record the work on the editor's home ground in Sussex, using the Organ Room for studio instead of the excessively dry acoustic of the old opera house. With modern instruments in the orchestra, the sounds are nothing short of luscious, often almost Straussian in their opulence, and Leppard's array of continuo instruments constantly charms the ear. Anne Howells makes a fine Erisbe, so pure-sounding one scarcely credits the blatant immorality of the story. Indeed the whole point is that one should not question it but accept it as a product of the permissive society of 1650. Excellent contributions from the whole team, with special mention required for the veteran Hugues Cuénod in the 'drag' part of the maid, Erice. The gloriously full recorded quality has not been lost in the CD transfer.

Certon, Pierre (died 1572)

Chansons: *Amour a tort; Ce n'est a vous; C'est grand pityé; De tout le mal; En espérant; Entre vous gentilz hommes; Heilas ne fringuerons nous; Je l'ay aymé; Je neveulx poinct; Martin s'en alla; Plus nu suys; Que n'est auprès de moy; Si ta beaulté; Ung jour que Madame dormait.* Mass: *Sur le pont d'Avignon.*

(B) *** HM Musique d'Abord HMA 190 1034 [id.]. Boston Camerata, Joel Cohen.

The Mass, *Sur le pont d'Avignon*, has genuine appeal, and the chansons also exercise a real charm over the listener. The Mass is performed *a cappella*, and the chansons enjoy instrumental support. In both sacred and secular works the Boston Camerata bring freshness, musical accomplishment and stylistic understanding to bear; the recording, made in a spacious acoustic, creates the most beautiful sounds.

Cesti, Antonio (1623–69)

Cantatas: *Amanti, io vi disfido; Pria ch'adori.*

(B) **(*) HM Musique d'Abord HMA 1901011 [id.]. Concerto Vocale – D'INDIA: *Duets, Laments & Madrigals.* **(*)

Cesti's 17-minute cantata, *Pria ch'adori*, is a serenata for two voices, after the Monteverdi style, including even a *Lamento d'Arianna* in duet form. *Amanti, io vi disfido* is a much shorter, bravura piece. The performances by Judith Nelson and René Jacobs are certainly pleasingly fresh, and the distinguished instrumental group includes William Christie providing the continuo.

Chabrier, Emmanuel (1841–94)

Bourrée fantasque; España (rhapsody); *Joyeuse marche; Suite pastorale; Gwendoline: Overture. Le Roi malgré lui: Danse slave; Fête polonaise.*
(M) *** Mercury (IMS) 434 303-2 [id.]. Detroit SO, Paray – ROUSSEL: *Suite.* **(*)

The return of the finely played and idiomatically conducted Mercury collection of Chabrier's best orchestral pieces does not disappoint. Paray's whimsically relaxed and sparkling account of *España* gives great pleasure and his rubato in the *Fête polonaise* is equally winning. The *Suite pastorale* is a wholly delightful account, given playing that is at once warm and polished, neat and perfectly in scale, with the orchestra beautifully balanced. The *Marche joyeuse* was recorded in Detroit's Old Orchestral Hall a year before the rest of the programme.

España (rhapsody).
❀ (B) *** Dutton Lab. mono CDEA 5017 [(M) id.]. LPO, Sir Thomas Beecham (with Concert: *'Beecham favourites'* *** ❀).
(M) **(*) Decca (IMS) 448 576-2 [id.]. SRO, Ansermet – DUKAS: *L'apprenti sorcier* ***; DEBUSSY: *La Mer* **(*); HONEGGER: *Pacific 231* ***; RAVEL: *Boléro; La Valse.* ***

Beecham's fizzing 1939 recording has never been surpassed and is unsurpassable. The superb Dutton transfer restores all the warmth and bloom of the original 78-r.p.m. disc, made in the Kingsway Hall, where the glowing ambience adds to the lustre of a sparkling recording often used for demonstration in its day. The rest of this concert is hardly less enticing for Beecham aficionados.

Ansermet's performance lacks something in uninhibited exuberance, but it is lively enough and is sparklingly recorded (in 1964).

España (rhapsody); *Joyeuse marche; Suite pastorale; Le Roi malgré lui: Danse slave; Fête polonaise.*
(M) *** Decca 452 890-2 [id.]. SRO, Ansermet – FRANCK: *La chasseur maudit* etc. **

Extremely brilliant recording, typical of Decca's vintage sessions in the Geneva Victoria Hall during the 1960s. There is plenty of amplitude too, and a fine condiment of percussion and bass drum. *España* perhaps lacks the uninhibited exuberance that Beecham brought to it but is by no means lacking in flair. The *Suite pastorale* has appealing delicacy, with the orchestra at their best, and plenty of atmosphere, especially in the *Idyll* and the rustling *Sous bois*. The *Joyeuse marche* certainly has its measure of high spirits; the *Danse slave* has an agreeable panache and the *Fête polonaise* goes splendidly. Excellent remastering means that this shows off the Ansermet charisma to fullest effect. A reissue worthy of Decca's Classic Sound logo.

PIANO MUSIC

Music for piano duet: *Air de ballet; Cortège burlesque; Prélude et marche française; Souvenirs de Munich; Suite des valses.* Music for 2 pianos: *España; 3 Valses romantiques.*
(BB) ** Naxos Dig. 8.550380 [id.]. Georges Rabol, Sylvie Dugas.

The works for two pianos come off with some flair on the Naxos disc, and the acoustic is more open: indeed the recording is more than satisfactory. The programme opens with *España*, which has plenty of gusto (and distinct touches of orchestral colouring) while the *Marche française* (better known as the *Joyeuse marche*) is also ebullient. The second of the *Trois valses romantiques* displays real charm, while the *Cortège burlesque* and *Souvenirs de Munich* are lively and spirited. The exaggerated parody rubato in the *Air de ballet* is a minus point, and *Suite des valses* is also rhythmically self-conscious, but not irredeemably so.

Aubade; Capriccio; Impromptu in C; Julia (valse), Op. 1; Marche des Cipayes; Ronde champêtre; Souvenir de Brunehaut (valse).
(BB) * Naxos Dig. 8. 553010 [id.]. Georges Rabol.
Ballabile; Bourrée fantasque; Caprice; Feuillet d'album; Habanera; Petite valse; 10 Pièces pittoresques.
(BB) * Naxos Dig. 8.553009 [id.]. Georges Rabol.

Georges Rabol's solo performances are just about acceptable at super-bargain price, but they lack the imaginative touches that make this music spring to life, although some of the shorter pieces are modestly effective. But the *Pièces pittoresques* are disappointing. Rabol makes comparatively little of *Sous-bois* and, although the *Danse villageoise* is cleanly articulated, he almost gabbles the closing *Scherzo-waltz*.

On the second disc, the *Marche des Cipayes* has character but the rubato in the *Julia waltz* is unspontaneous, and elsewhere the impulsive manner finds little charm in the music, with the *Ronde champêtre* hardly sparkling as its name might suggest, and the *Souvenir de Brunehaut* at times rather heavy-going. The piano-tone is clear and faithful but the acoustic is unflatteringly dry and studio-ish.

Bourrée fantasque; 5 Pièces posthumes; 10 Pièces pittoresques; Suite de valses.
(BB) **(*) ASV Dig. CDQS 6166 [(M) id.]. Alan Schiller.

For those wanting an inexpensive entry into the world of Chabrier's piano music, this ASV Quicksilva disc should serve well enough. Alan Schiller, if not quite as sympathetic as Kathleen Stott on Unicorn-Kanchana, can play tenderly (as in the *Feuillet d'album* from the *Pièces posthumes*) as well as brilliantly, and he is only occasionally percussive. He lifts rhythms nicely in the *Bourrée fantasque* and characterizes strongly, although perhaps the *Idylle* (made famous in the orchestral *Suite pastorale*) could be a shade more relaxed. On the whole tempi are well chosen and his rubato is convincing. Good, clear piano recording.

OPERA

Le roi malgré lui (complete).
(M) **(*) Erato/Warner 2292 45792-2 (2). Hendricks, Garcisanz, Quilico, Jeffes, Lafont, French R. Ch. & New PO, Dutoit.

This long-neglected opera is another Chabrier masterpiece, a modified Cinderella story, ending happily, which prompts a series of superb numbers, some *España*-like in brilliance (the well-known Waltz of Act II transformed in its choral form) and some hauntingly romantic, with even one sextet suggesting a translation of Wagner's Rhinemaiden music into waltz-time. The pity is that the linking recitatives have been completely omitted from this recording, and in addition the score has been seriously cut. But Charles Dutoit is a most persuasive advocate. Star among the singers is Barbara Hendricks as the slave-girl Cinderella figure, Minka. The recording is naturally balanced and has plenty of atmosphere.

Charpentier, Gustave (1860–1956)

Louise (gramophone version conceived and realized by the composer).
(M) (***) Nimbus mono NI 7829 [id.]. Vallin, Thill, Pernet, Lecouvreur, Gaudel, Ch. Raugel & O, Eugène Bigot.

These substantial excerpts from *Louise* were recorded in 1935 under the 75-year-old composer's supervision; they feature two ideally cast French singers as the two principals, Ninon Vallin enchanting in the title-role and the tenor, Georges Thill, heady-toned as the hero, Julien. France has produced few singers to rival them since. The original eight 78-r.p.m. records are fitted neatly on to a single CD, and – in the selection of items, made by the composer himself – just the delights and none of the *longueurs* of this nostalgically atmospheric opera are included. The voices are caught superbly in the Nimbus transfers, but their system of playing the original 78s on an acoustic horn gramophone works far less well for the orchestral sound: with an early electrical recording like this it becomes muddled. Yet even Nimbus has rarely presented voices as vividly as here.

Charpentier, Marc-Antoine (1634–1704)

9 Leçons de ténèbres, H.120–125; H.135–137.
(M) **(*) Erato/Warner Dig. 4509 96376-2 (2). Widmer, Verschaeve, Crook, Caals, De Meulenaere, Ruyl, Musica Polyphonica, Louis Devos.

The first six *Leçons de ténèbres* for solo voices included here (H.120–125) come from Volume XXIII and were probably written in 1680 for the Abbaye-aux-Bois; the remainder are for three voices and, though not unrelated to the earlier ones, are later still. Neither set duplicates the repertoire already covered by the Harmonia Mundi and Virgin issues; but the performances here, although sensitive and lyrically eloquent, lack something in vitality. In that respect the solo works are rather more positive than those for three voices. The stylish instrumental accompaniments using original instruments are suitably pastel-shaded and the recording is excellent; but one feels that a rather stronger characterization would have made these performances even more appealing.

Leçons de ténèbres for Wednesday in Holy Week.
*** Virgin/EMI VC5 45107-2 [id.]. Catherine Greuillet, Caroline Pelon, Gérard Lesne, Christopher Purves, Il Seminario Musicale.

Leçons de ténèbres for Maundy Thursday.
*** Virgin/EMI VC5 45075-2 [id.]. Sandrine Piau, Gérard Lesne, Ian Honeyman, Peter Harvey, Il Seminario Musicale.

Leçons de ténèbres for Good Friday.
*** Virgin/EMI Dig. VC7 59295-2 [id.]. Gérard Lesne, Agnès Mellon, Ian Honeyman, Jacques Bona, Il Seminario Musicale.

Leçons de ténèbres for Wednesday in Holy Week, Maundy Thursday and Good Friday.
(M) *** Virgin Veritas EMI Dig. VMT5 61483-2 (3). Gérard Lesne & soloists, Il Seminario Musicale, Lesne.

This series of Charpentier's *Leçons de ténèbres* from Il Seminario Musicale offers music of great variety and beauty, featuring soloists who are naturally attuned to this repertoire. The accompaniment is provided by a varied instrumental group, including recorders, treble and bass viols, with a continuo of theorbo, bass viol and organ, and their use is consistently imaginative and refreshing to the ear. The Psalms are sung by a small choral group. The effect is warm yet refined and the lyrical melancholy of much of this music is quite haunting. It is difficult to imagine these inspired and highly expressive settings being presented more persuasively or better balanced, and the acoustic of L'Abbaye Royale de Fontevraud is ideal for the music. The documentation is first class. Charpentier's settings were enormously admired in his own time, and rightly so. The attempt on the third disc to reconstruct a Tenebrae Office for Good Friday poses many problems: although the three on this recording were all composed for Good Friday, they were not necessarily intended for the same Good Friday. Be that as it may, as the music unfolds its effect is both powerful and elevating. In the context of this service, Charpentier's music has a quiet and affecting directness as well as spirituality. Although these three CDs are individually in the premium price-range (and well worth every penny), they are now issued as a medium-price set in a slipcase, and any collector attracted to this remarkable and inspired composer should consider them.

Méditations pour le Carême; Le reniement de St Pierre.
(B) *** HM Musique d'Abord Dig. HMC 1905151 [id.]. Les Arts Florissants, William Christie.

Le reniement de Saint Pierre is one of Charpentier's most inspired and expressive works and its text draws on the account in all four Gospels of St Peter's denial of Christ. The *Méditations pour le Carême* are a sequence of three-voice motets for Lent with continuo accompaniment (organ, theorbo and bass viol) that may not have quite the same imaginative or expressive resource but which are full of nobility and interest. The performances maintain the high standards of this ensemble, and the same compliment can be paid to the recording. Now reissued on Harmonia Mundi's bargain Musique d'Abord label, this is now doubly attractive.

(i) *Messe de minuit pour Noël (Midnight Mass for Christmas Eve);* (ii) *Te Deum.*
(M) **(*) EMI CDM7 63135-2. (i) Cantelo, Gelmar, Partridge, Bowman, Keyte, King's College Ch., ECO, Willcocks; (ii) Lott, Harrhy, Brett, Partridge, Roberts, King's College Ch., ASMF, Ledger.

There is a kinship between Charpentier's lovely *Christmas Mass* and Czech settings of the Mass that incorporate folk material, even the *Kyrie* having a jolly quality about it. The King's performance is warm and musical, but there isn't much Gallic flavour. The recording comes from the late 1960s and certainly now has more bite than it did; but reservations remain about the basic style of the singing. The coupling is the best known of the *Te Deum* settings, and this time the King's performance has a vitality and boldness to match the music and catches also its douceur and freshness.

Missa Assumpta est Maria; Litanies de la Vierge; Te Deum.
❁ (B) *** HM Dig. HMX 290850.52 (3) [(M) id. import]. Soloists, Les Arts Florissants, William Christie – BOUZIGNAC: *Te Deum* etc. *** ❁; DELALANDE: *Confitebor tibi Domine* etc. ***

Christie's superb account of what is Charpentier's best-known work, the *Te Deum*, is introduced by a spectacular *Marches des Timbales*, which is quite as ear-catching as the famous *Prélude* which follows. The performance itself is unsurpassed, with splendid solo singing matched by a glorious choral contribution. This is followed by the more restrained but no less beautiful six-part *Missa Assumpta est Maria*. Its mood is set in the delicately scored opening *Simphonie*, but there is to be contrasting vigour later in the *Gloria*. The *Credo* is exquisitely serene, while gently dancing flutes introduce the chimerical *Sanctus*. The *Litanies de la Vierge*, again for six voices, returns to a profoundly contemplative mood, although there is diversity in the contrasting sections for solo groups and the full choir, and the music is far from static. The glowing *Regina angelorum* and delicately radiant *Agnus Dei* have extraordinary expressive power. The very fine performances here are matched by recording of very high quality within an acoustic which accords warmth and atmosphere without clouding detail. This CD remains available at full price, but now comes in a very highly recommendable bargain-priced triptych, linked to the *Te Deums* of Bouzignac and Delalande.

La Reniement de Saint Pierre – histoire sacrée.

(M) **(*) Erato/Warner 4509 97409-2. Robin, Chamonin, Maurant, Richez, Lesueur, Veyron-Lacroix, Ch. Philippe Caillard – COUPERIN: *Audite omnes et expanescite* etc. **

Charpentier's *La Reniement de Saint Pierre* survives in a manuscript copy of the full score in a collection assembled by Sébastien de Brossard and presented to the king in 1724, some two decades after the composer's death. Given its Italianate style, scholarly opinion favours the view that it is an early piece. The anonymous libretto is an adaptation of scenes from the Passion drawn from all four Gospels, recounting the episode in which the apostle Peter thrice denies all knowledge of Christ. It is a deeply felt work and the performance, which presumably comes from the early 1960s, is also deeply felt. Both the singing and playing give pleasure, and the poignant dissonances of the final chorus make a strong impression. There are minor reservations about the coupling, but on the whole this is a valuable reissue.

OPERA

Actéon (complete).

(B) *** HM Musique d'Abord HMA 1901095 [id.]. Visse, Mellon, Laurens, Feldman, Paut, Les Arts Florissants Vocal & Instrumental Ens., Christie.

Actéon is particularly well portrayed by Dominique Visse; his transformation in the fourth tableau and his feelings of horror are almost as effective as anything in nineteenth-century opera! The other singers are first rate, in particular the Diane of Agnès Mellon. Alert playing and an altogether natural recording, as well as excellent presentation, make this a most desirable issue and a real bargain.

Les Arts Florissants (opéra et idyle en musique).

(B) *** HM Musique d'Abord HMA 1901083 [id.]. Les Arts Florissants Vocal & Instrumental Ens., William Christie.

Les Arts Florissants is a short entertainment in five scenes; the libretto tells of a conflict between the Arts, who flourish under the rule of Peace, and the forces of War, personified by Discord and the Furies. This and the little Interlude that completes the music include some invigorating and fresh invention, performed very pleasingly indeed by this eponymous group under the expert direction of William Christie. Period instruments are used, but intonation is always good and the sounds often charm the ear. The recording is excellent. A bargain.

David et Jonathas (complete).

(B) **(*) HM Musique d'Abord Dig. HMA 190 1289/90 [id.]. Lesne, Zanetti, Gardeil, Visse, Les Arts Florissants, Christie.

David et Jonathas confirms the impression, made by many other Charpentier records during the last few years, that in him France has one of her most inspired Baroque masters. Christie's version on Harmonia Mundi may not always be especially dramatic, but it has a notably sure sense of authentic Baroque style and scale, as well as fine choral singing. However, only one of Christie's soloists is really outstanding: the characterfully distinctive counter-tenor, Dominique Visse, who gives a vivid, highly theatrical performance. Those who relish authenticity above all else will clearly take to this version, very well recorded.

Chausson, Ernest (1855–99)

Poème for violin and orchestra.

(M) *** Decca 460 006-2 [id.]. Kyung Wha Chung, RPO, Charles Dutoit – DEBUSSY; FRANCK: *Violin sonatas*. *** ✿

(M) **(*) RCA Heifetz Collection 09026 61753-2 [id.]. Heifetz, RCA Victor SO, Izler Solomon – LALO: *Symphonie espagnole* (**(*)); SAINT-SAENS: *Havanaise* etc.; SARASATE: *Zigeunerweisen*. (***)

Chung's performance of Chausson's beautiful *Poème* is deeply emotional; some may prefer a more restrained approach but, with committed accompaniment from the RPO and excellent (1977) recording, this makes an apt bonus for superb performances of the Debussy and Franck *Violin sonatas*.

Heifetz is recorded very closely, as if in the glare of a spotlight, and the performance is robbed of much of its subtlety. Even so, the playing itself is quite remarkable.

(i) Poème, Op. 25. Symphony in B flat, Op. 20.
(M) **(*) RCA GD 60683 [0926 60683-2]. (i) David Oistrakh; Boston SO, Munch (with SAINT-SAENS: *Introduction & Rondo capriccioso* ***).

Munch's 1962 account of the *Symphony in B flat* is high-powered and splendidly played. The CD transfer has, of course, improved matters, but the orchestral texture, which is fairly thick at times, is not perhaps as transparent as it might be. Some may also find the performance just a shade overdriven. David Oistrakh's 1955 account of the *Poème* is as ethereal as one would expect, and he is given excellent support by the Boston Symphony and Munch. There is a trace of hardness which, as anyone who heard him in the flesh will testify, it is impossible to imagine being his fault. Were there nothing else on this disc, it would still be worth buying for the *Poème* alone, and the Saint-Saëns encore tops it off nicely.

Symphony in B flat, Op. 20.
(M) **(*) Mercury 434 389-2 [id.]. Detroit SO, Paul Paray – BARRAUD: *Offrande à une ombre;* LALO: *Le rois d'Ys; Namouna.* **(*)

Symphony in B flat, Op. 20; Soir de fête; Viviane, Op. 5.
(M) ** EMI CDM7 64686-2. Toulouse Capitole O, Michel Plasson.

Paul Paray's 1956 performance of the Chausson *Symphony* is first class and the recording is much better than we remembered from its mono version. Indeed its only serious rival in terms of style is the Munch. It is splendidly held together and commanding in its eloquence and authority. It can be recommended alongside the Munch and in preference to most modern accounts.

Michel Plasson gives a sensitive account of the Chausson *Symphony* and, particularly in the powerful introduction and the somewhat Tristanesque slow movement, secures playing of real feeling from the Toulouse orchestra. This is an eloquent performance and, were the recording more refined, it would be a high recommendation, particularly as the couplings are such rarities – *Soir de fête*, with its poetic middle section, and the early tone-poem, *Viviane*. The recordings were made in the somewhat reverberant acoustic of the Halle-aux-Graines, Toulouse. Detail could be better focused, and the digital remastering of the two analogue masters has emphasized an unpleasing edge on the strings, though fairly acceptable results can be secured by the manipulation of the controls.

CHAMBER MUSIC

(i) *Concert for violin, piano and string quartet;* (ii) *Pièce in C for cello and piano, Op. 39.*
(B) ** HM Solo HMP 3901135 [id.]. (i) R. Pasquier, Daugareil, Simonot, B. Pasquier; (ii) Ridoux; (i; ii) Pennetier.

The Harmonia Mundi version of the *Concert* is inexpensive, and it includes also the Op. 39 *Pièce for cello and piano*. This is good value. The French team here are by no means wanting in imagination.

Piano quartet in A, Op. 30; Piano trio in G min., Op. 3.
(B) **(*) HM Musique d'Abord HMA 1901115 [id.]. Les Musiciens.

The Op. 30 *Piano quartet* of 1896 is one of Chausson's finest works. Les Musiciens comprise the Pasquier Trio and Jean-Claude Pennetier, but they are recorded rather closely, and their performance is lacking some of the subtlety and colour one knows this ensemble can command. The effect both here and in the early *G minor Trio*, Op. 3, is somewhat monochrome. However, the playing is both warm and spontaneous, and the ambience of the acoustic is pleasing.

String quartet in C min., Op. 35 (completed Vincent d'Indy).
(BB) *** Naxos Dig. 8.553645 [id.]. Quatuor Ludwig – FRANCK: *Piano quintet.* ***

Chausson came late to music, having first completed his law studies, and left it all too early, being killed in a cycling accident. He was in many ways the most naturally gifted of the Franck circle, and the *String quartet in C minor* is among his most impressive works. The success of the first movement, *Grave*, when it was first performed at Ysaÿe's house in Brussels in 1898, encouraged Chausson to go on, and he was revising the third movement when he died. Vincent d'Indy put the finishing touches to the score after Chausson's death. It is a rarity in the concert hall and on CD, now that the Muir Quartet version with Jean-Philippe Collard (also coupled with the Franck *Quintet*) is no longer available. The music is powerfully argued and the Quatuor Ludwig play it with conviction and aplomb. The recording is excellent.

VOCAL MUSIC

(i) *La Légende de Sainte Cécile, Op. 22;* (ii) *La Tempête, Op. 18.*

(M) *** EMI Dig. CDM5 55323-2 (2). (i) Isabelle Verner, Choeur de Femmes de Radio France; (ii) Laurence Dale, Raphaëlle Farman, Marie-Ange Todorovitch, François le Roux, Jean-Philippe Lafont, Ens. O de Paris, Jean-Jacques Kantorow.

Two Chausson rarities, beautiful pieces both, expertly performed by these distinguished artists. *La Tempête* comprises a dozen or so settings and is scored for unusual forces: three strings, flute, harp and celeste (the latter instrument, which Tchaikovsky presented in *Nutcracker*, making its bow, as it predates the Tchaikovsky by four years). *La Légende de Sainte Cécile*, as its opus number indicates, comes from the same period as the *Symphony in B flat* and was first put on in 1892. The shades of Wagner and Franck are never far away but, as always with this composer, the invention is fluent, the music often imaginative and always rewarding. The performances are expert and persuasive and the recording very natural. This is something of a find.

Cherubini, Luigi (1760–1842)

Symphony in D; Overtures: Ali-Baba; Anacréon; Médée.

(M) (***) RCA mono GD 60278 [60278-2-RG]. NBC SO, Toscanini (with CIMAROSA: *Overtures: Il matrimonio per raggiro; Il matrimonio segreto* (**)).

The Cherubini *Symphony* is rightly one of Toscanini's most famous records. It was made in the Carnegie Hall, so even the sound is good. The playing has great finesse and the performance sparkles, though some ears may find its high level of underlying intensity out of place in such repertoire. The overtures are just as characterful, *Anacréon* taken from a broadcast concert, again using Carnegie Hall. The other performances, including the brilliant – some might say hard-driven – Cimarosa items, were done in the famously dry Studio 8-H. The sheer incandescent energy of *Il matrimonio per raggiro* is remarkable and *Ali-Baba*, too, is very brisk indeed. With its 'Turkish' percussion, it sounds very piquant and the end is very like the 'chase' music in a silent movie. The transfers are first class.

Requiem in C min.

(B) *** EMI forte Dig. CZS5 68613-2 (2) [CDFB 68613]. Ambrosian Ch., Philh. O, Muti – VERDI: *Requiem.* ***

(M) (**(*)) RCA mono GD 60272 (2) [60272-RG-2]. Marshall, Merriman, Conley, Hines, Robert Shaw Ch., NBC SO, Toscanini – BEETHOVEN: *Missa solemnis.* (**(*))

The *C minor Requiem*, the best known, was called by Berlioz 'the greatest of the greatest of his [Cherubini's] work', and he went on to claim that 'no other production of this great master can bear any comparison with it for abundance of ideas, fullness of form and sustained sublimity of style'. Muti directs a tough, incisive reading, underlining the drama, to remind one that this was a work also recorded by Toscanini some three decades earlier. The digital recording is excellent.

Toscanini was an admirer of Cherubini's choral music, and though the start of this live performance of 1950 lacks the full Toscanini electricity, the Shaw Chorale, superbly disciplined, quickly responds to the maestro, to produce searingly incisive singing in such movements as the *Dies irae*. Characteristically dry recording.

Requiem Mass No. 2 in D min.

(M) ** BMG/Melodiya 74321 40723-2 [id.]. Estonian State Ac. Male Ch. Estonian RSO, Neeme Järvi – SHOSTAKOVICH: *Loyalty.* **(*)

Beethoven revered Cherubini and, listening to the *D minor Requiem*, one can see why. Cherubini's inspiration is always dignified and fluent, and there is a nobility about his music that is imposing. This performance, given in Tallinn in 1967, is one of Neeme Järvi's first Melodiya recordings and has been issued to mark his sixtieth birthday. It has great eloquence and the Estonian forces give of their best. The disc is of special interest in that it brings a Shostakovich rarity, *Loyalty* (not conducted by Järvi), which is not otherwise available. Apart from a touch of rawness about the string-tone, the recording – if hardly state of the art – is very satisfactory.

OPERA

Medea (complete).

(M) ** EMI CMS5 66435-2 (2) [Ang. CDMB 66435]. Callas, Scotto, Pirazzini, Picchi, La Scala Ch. & O, Serafin (with BEETHOVEN: *Ah! perfido* **).

(B) ** Decca Double 452 611-2 (2) [(M) id. import]. Gwyneth Jones, Prevedi, Lorengar, Diaz, Cossotto, Accademia di Santa Cecilia, Rome, Ch. and O, Gardelli.

The 1957 studio recording of *Medea* is a magnificent example of the fire-eating Callas. She completely outshines any rival. A cut text is used and Italian instead of the original French, with Serafin less imaginative than he usually was; but, with a cast more than competent – including the young Renata Scotto – it is an enjoyable set. Callas's recording of the Beethoven scena, *Ah! perfido*, makes a powerful fill-up, even though in this late recording (1963/4) vocal flaws emerge the more.

Cherubini's original score of 1797 is modified on Decca – as in virtually all modern revivals – by the work of the German composer, Franz Lachner, half a century later. The result brings its stylistic clashes, for Lachner's recitatives have their post-Weberian touches and even a touch or two of Wagner. But his work certainly helps to maintain the dramatic tension of the piece and to underline the fiery character of the heroine. This version gives only an imperfect idea of the work's power. Gwyneth Jones, for all her achievements thus far, was not ready to record this taxing part, particularly not in Italian, in which she was not really fluent. There are too many uncontrolled notes and, though she throws herself into the drama and Bruno Prevedi as Jason provides some stylish tenor singing, the set is only a partial success, although it is very well recorded and certainly inexpensive.

Chopin, Frédéric (1810–49)

Idil Biret Complete Chopin Edition

Piano concerto No. 1, Op. 11; Andante spianato et Grande Polonaise brillante, Op. 22; Fantasia on Polish airs, Op. 13.
(BB) **(*) Naxos Dig. 8.550368; *4.550368* [id.] (with Slovak State PO, Stankovsky).

Piano concerto No. 2, Op. 21; Krakowiak, Op. 14; Variations on Mozart's 'Là ci darem la mano', Op. 2.
(BB) ** Naxos Dig. 8.550369; *4.550369* [id.] (with Slovak State PO, Stankovsky).

Ballades Nos. 1–4; Berceuse, Op. 57; Cantabile; Fantaisie, Op. 49; Gallop marquis; Largo; Marche funèbre; 3 Nouvelles Etudes.
(BB)** Naxos Dig. 8.550508; *4.550084* [id.].

Mazurkas, Op. posth: in D; A flat; B flat; G; C; B flat; Rondos, Op. 1, Op. 16 & Op. 73; Rondo à la Mazurka, Op. 5; Souvenir de Paganini; Variations brillantes; (i) *Variations for four hands; Variations on a German theme; Variations on themes from 'I Puritani' of Bellini.*
(BB) *** Naxos Dig. 8.550367 [id.] ((i) with Martin Sauer).

Nocturnes Nos. 1–21.
(BB) *** Naxos Dig. 8.550356/7 [id.] (available separately).

Polonaises Nos. 1–6; 7 (Polonaise fantaisie).
(BB) **(*) Naxos Dig. 8.550360 [id.].

Polonaises Nos. 8–10, Op. 71; in G min.; B flat; A flat; G sharp min.; B flat min. (Adieu); G flat, all Op. posth.; Andante spianato et Grande Polonaise in E flat, Op. 22 (solo piano version).
(BB) **(*) Naxos Dig. 8.550361 [id.].

Piano sonatas Nos. 1, Op. 4; 2 (Funeral march); 3, Op. 58.
(BB) *** Naxos Dig. 8.550363; *4.550363* [id.].

Waltzes Nos. 1–19; Contredanse in G flat; 3 Ecossaises, Op. 72; Tarantelle, Op. 43.
(BB) ** Naxos Dig. 8.550365; *4.550365* [id.].

The Turkish pianist, Idil Biret, has recorded a Complete Chopin Edition for Naxos which has been made available as a boxed set in France but in England is being issued a disc at a time. She has all the credentials for the undertaking. Among others, she studied with both Cortot and Wilhelm Kempff. She has a prodigious technique and the recordings we have heard so far suggest that overall her Chopin survey is an impressive achievement.

Her impetuous style and chimerical handling of phrasing and rubato are immediately obvious in the *First Concerto*, especially in the freely poetic account of the *Larghetto* and her very flexible rhythmic approach to the *Polacca* finale. Following Stankovsky's bold tutti, Biret makes a commanding entry in the *F minor Concerto*; in the *Larghetto*, too, the solo playing brings a gently improvisational manner, and the finale really gathers pace only at the entry of the orchestra (which is recorded rather resonantly throughout). Later there is more dash from the soloist. Of the other short concertante pieces, the opening of the *Andante spianato* is very delicate and there is some scintillating playing in the following *Grande Polonaise* and *Fantasia on Polish airs* – and a touch of heaviness, too, in the former, but here Stankovsky and the Slovak State Philharmonic Orchestra, who are generally sympathetic in the concertos and quite strong in No. 1, rather take a back seat. The introductory *Largo* of the *Mozart variations* is a bit too dreamy and diffuse but, once the famous tune arrives, the performance springs to life. Similarly, the introduction to the charming *Krakowiak Rondo* hangs fire, but again the *Rondo* sparkles, with the rhythmic rubato nicely handled, though the orchestral tuttis could ideally be firmer.

The first of the solo recordings were made in the Clara Wieck Auditorium, Heidelberg; the sound is a little studio-ish but truthful and often expands impressively in fortissimo. The *Ballades* brings impetuously romantic interpretations where the rubato at times seems mannered; the *Berceuse* is tender and tractable, the *Fantaisie in F minor* begins rather deliberately but opens up excitingly later; though the playing is rather Schumannesque, it is also imaginative; the three *Nouvelles Etudes*, too, are attractively individual.

The disc called '*Rondos and variations*' (8.550367) is worth anyone's money. Much of the music here is little known and none of it second rate. The *Rondos* are more ambitious than one would expect, and the sets of *Variations* show Biret's technique at its most prodigious and glittering. Perhaps not surprisingly, the *Nocturnes* are a great success, the rubato simple, the playing free and often thoughtful, sometimes dark in timbre, but always spontaneous. The recording venue has now changed to the Tonstudio van Geest in Heidelberg and throughout is pleasingly full in timbre. The *Polonaises* demonstrate Biret's sinewy strength: the famous *A major* is a little measured, but the *A flat* is fresh and exciting and the whole set commanding, while the *Polonaise fantaisie* shows imaginative preparation yet comes off spontaneously like the others. Nos. 8–10, published as Op. 71, are early works, written between 1825 and 1828, and Biret at her most appealing makes all three sound mature. The recital ends with a fine account of the solo piano version of the *Andante spianato* (quite lovely) and *Grande Polonaise*, which is more appealing than the concertante version.

The three *Sonatas* are fitted comfortably on to one CD (75 minutes) and, irrespective of cost, this represents one of the finest achievements in Biret's series so far. The *Waltzes* brought another change of venue, to the Tonstudio in Sandhausen. The recording is bright, somewhat more resonant. Idil Biret starts impetuously and immediately favours a fast tempo in the *Grande valse brillante*, Op. 18/1. This is charismatic playing, giving opportunities for exciting bravura, but too many of these pieces are pressed on without respite. The *Ecossaises* and *Tarantelle* are also thrown off at almost breakneck speed.

Other recordings

(i) *Piano concertos Nos. 1–2. Andante spianato et Grande polonaise brillante; Ballades Nos. 1–4; Barcarolle* (1946 & 1962 recordings); *Berceuse* (1946 & 1962 recordings); *Boléro; Fantaisie in F min.; Impromptus Nos. 1–4; 51 Mazurkas; 19 Nocturnes; 3 Nouvelles-études; 6 Polonaises; Polonaise-Fantaisie; 24 Préludes; Scherzi Nos. 1–4; Sonata No. 2* (1946 & 1961 recordings); *Sonata No. 3; Tarantelle; 14 Waltzes.*

(M) *** RCA GD 60822 [60822-2-RG] (11). Artur Rubinstein, (i) with London New SO, Scrowaczewski; or Symphony of the Air, Wallenstein.

Rubinstein's principal Chopin oeuvre is offered here on 11 CDs at mid-price. His achievement was unique in this repertoire, and for the most part the remastered recordings are almost worthy of the playing. Alternative versions are offered of several pieces, but most of the recordings listed are discussed below as individual issues, many still at full price.

(i) *Piano concertos Nos. 1–2. Nocturnes Nos. 1–19; Waltz, Op. 64/2.*

(M) (***) EMI CHS7 64491-2 (2) [ZDHB 64491]. Rubinstein, (i) with LSO, Barbirolli.

(i) *Piano concertos Nos. 1 in E min., Op. 11; 2 in F min., Op. 21. Andante spianato et Grande Polonaise brillante, Op. 22; Barcarolle, Op. 60; Berceuse, Op. 57; Mazurkas Nos. 1–51; Nocturnes Nos. 1–19; Polonaises Nos. 1–7; Scherzi Nos. 1–4 Waltz in C sharp min., Op. 64/2.*

(M) (***) EMI mono CHS7 64933-2 (5). Rubinstein, (i) with LSO, Barbirolli.

Andante spianato et Grande Polonaise brillante, Op. 22; Barcarolle, Op. 60; Berceuse, Op. 57; Mazurkas Nos. 1–51; Polonaises Nos. 1–7; Scherzi Nos. 1–4; Waltz in C sharp min., Op. 64/1.

(M) (***) EMI (SIS) mono CHS7 64697-2 (3). Artur Rubinstein.

The five-CD set listed above falls into two parts, the first consisting of the two piano concertos, recorded with Barbirolli and the LSO in 1937 (*E minor*) and 1931 (*F minor*), the *C sharp minor Waltz*, recorded in 1930, and the celebrated set of the *Nocturnes* from 1936–7. This is additionally available on a two-CD

Références set. The second set of three CDs comprises the *Mazurkas* (recorded in 1938), some of the most totally idiomatic Chopin playing ever committed to record, the 1932 *Scherzi* and the *Polonaises* (1934) and various other pieces. They can be bought in two separate packages or together. Quite simply, the best advice is to get both; each of the discs is packed to capacity and the transfers are excellent. Rubinstein was at the height of his powers when he made these recordings and he rarely equalled and never surpassed them in the post-war, LP era. The *Mazurkas* and *Nocturnes* have a poetic spontaneity and aristocratic finesse that are totally convincing.

Andante spianato & Grande Polonaise brillante (for piano and orchestra), *Op. 22.*
(M) *** RCA 09026 68886-2 [id.]. Rubinstein, Symphony of the Air, Wallenstein – FALLA: *Nights in the gardens of Spain;* RACHMANINOV: *Rhapsody on a theme of Paganini.* ***

Chopin's version of the *Grande Polonaise brillante* with orchestral accompaniment – and it is very much an accompaniment rather than a partnership – has not often been recorded. The *Andante* was added as an introduction to the more obvious showpiece when the work was published. The curious marking *spianato* underlines the steady pulse of the accompaniment over which the right hand in typical Chopin fashion weaves its florid decoration. Rubinstein gives an interpretation to the manner born, at once showy and emotional, yet sensitive. Wallenstein gives good if unostentatious support, and the recording is naturally balanced.

Piano concertos Nos. (i) *1 in E min., Op. 11;* (ii) *2 in F min., Op. 21.*
(M) *** Mercury 434 374-2 [id.]. Gina Bachauer, LSO, Dorati.
(BB) *** RCA Navigator 74321 17892-2 [Basic 100 09026 68023-2]. Emanuel Ax, Phd. O, Ormandy.
(BB) *** Naxos Dig. 8.550123; *4550123* [id.]. István Székely, Budapest SO, Gyula Németh.
(B) *** DG Classikon 429 515-2 [(M) id. import]. Tamás Vásáry, BPO, (i) Semkow; (ii) Kulka.
(M) *(*) Ph. 456 657-2 [id.]. Claudio Arrau, LPO, Inbal.

The orchestral accompaniments for the two Chopin *Concertos* can surely never have been presented with such a strong profile as under Dorati, tuttis strong and expansive and with every detail coming through – the bassoon and oboe solos really catch the ear. And how beautifully he prepares for the first piano entry in the *E minor Concerto*. Gina Bachauer obviously sees these as full-bloodedly romantic concertos and Dorati gives her every support. Yet her passage-work scintillates and her phrasing and rubato have fine sensitivity. Both slow movements bring appealing delicacy, and finales have a lilting panache, while the central episode of the *Larghetto* of the *F minor* work can seldom have sounded more dramatic. With Mercury's spaciously realistic Watford Town Hall recording of orchestra and piano alike, and an excellent balance, this is very enjoyable indeed.

Emanuel Ax offers fine performances of both concertos at super-bargain price. His account of the *F minor* has admirable taste and finesse, though not quite the sense of character of his finest full-priced rivals – Rubinstein for instance. Nevertheless this is genuinely poetic playing and the finale with its light, chimerical touch is particularly pleasing. This is a digital recording and not quite top-drawer in the matter of transparency. Yet it provides a fuller and more flattering sound for the Philadelphia Orchestra than on many of their recent records. Ormandy is a highly sensitive accompanist in both works and this Navigator reissue, with its frontispiece map to show the source of the music, is well worth its modest price.

István Székely is particularly impressive in the *E minor Concerto*, but in both works he finds atmosphere and poetry in slow movements and an engaging dance spirit for the finales, with rhythms given plenty of character. Németh accompanies sympathetically; the orchestral contribution here is quite refined. The recording is resonantly full in the Hungarian manner, not absolutely clear on detail; but the piano image is bold and realistic. A splendid bargain in every sense of the word.

Vásáry's approach is much more self-effacing: his gentle poetry is in clear contrast with the opulent orchestral sound (especially in No. 1, where the recording is more resonantly expansive than in No. 2). Yet soloist and orchestra match their styles perfectly in both slow movements, which are played most beautifully, and the finales have no lack of character and sparkle. In their way, these performances will give considerable pleasure and, with recording that retains its depth and bloom, this makes a fine bargain coupling.

The latest Philips reissue of Arrau's performances restores adequate documentation about the music; but this is not a front-runner, since the great Chilean pianist's playing, while immaculately aristocratic, is also self-conscious. His rubato will not convince everyone and his expressive hesitations do not always grow naturally out of what has gone before. The recordings, made in 1971–2, are of fine Philips quality and are admirably transferred to CD. The balance gives the soloist undue prominence, but the orchestra remains well in the picture and, like Arrau's timbre, is caught truthfully. But this is not Chopin playing to kindle universal enthusiasm.

(i) *Piano concertos Nos. 1–2;* (ii) *Impromptus Nos. 1–3; Waltzes Nos. 1–19.*
(BB) ** EMI Seraphim CES5 68528-2 [CDEB 68528] (2). (i) Garrick Ohlsson, Polish Nat. RSO, Maksymiuk; (ii) Agustin Anievas.

(i) *Piano concertos Nos.1 in E min., Op. 11; 2 in F min., Op. 21. Waltzes Nos. 1–14.*
(B) **(*) Erato/Warner Ultima Analogue/Dig. 3984 21089-2 (2) [(M) id. import]. Maria João Pires; (i) Monte-Carlo Op. O, Armin Jordan.

With her natural feeling for a limpid musical phrase and her unostentatious poetry, Maria João Pires would seem the ideal soloist for the Chopin concertos. However, she is so anxious not to give the slightest hint of barnstorming that her gently relaxed, coaxing approach to opening movements is inclined to let the ongoing tension slip, particularly in the *E minor Concerto*. The responsibility is clearly hers, for Armin Jordan gives her warm support and secures remarkably refined and polished accompaniments from the Monte Carlo players. Slow movements are another matter. Here she can afford to be poetically serene, yet remain seemingly spontaneous and delight the listener with her simplicity of mood and the ease with which she throws off the filigree decoration. The two closing Rondos, although not glittering, have a delectable lift and, with glowing analogue recording from the late 1970s (the piano timbre particularly pleasing), this Chopin playing is easy to enjoy. Pires's readings are far preferable to Arrau's self-conscious rubato. The second of this pair of CDs offers the *Waltzes*, and here, unlike many of her rivals, she does not include the posthumously published pieces, and she chooses her own sequence for the basic 14, opening with the *F major*, Op. 34/3, and leaving the *Grand valse brillante* (Op. 18) as the penultimate item and ending with another *Valse brillante in A flat*, Op. 34/1. Her rubato is again individual, but she brings a real sense of style to this generally more extrovert pianism, plus good judgement and taste, along with an impeccable technique. Only rarely does she fall short of real poetic distinction. The 1984 digital recording, somewhat brighter than the analogue sound afforded the two concertos, is well suited to this repertoire. Admirers of this artist need not hesitate.

Garrick Ohlsson won the Warsaw International Chopin prize in 1970, and his set of the two concertos is to be reckoned with. He is an impressive player with no lack of technical aplomb and finesse to commend him. But he is not as subtle and aristocratic as Zimmerman or Perahia – nor for that matter is his conductor, who is prone to making bold gestures and is distinctly earthbound in the opening tutti of the *F major Concerto*. The recording is brilliant, not exactly shallow but not ideally expansive. On the second disc of this inexpensive Seraphim set, Anievas gives us the three *Impromptus* (but not the *Fantaisie-impromptu*) and all the *Waltzes*, including the five published posthumously. The opening *Grande valse brillante* is somewhat lacking in flair by the side of Ohlsson, and generally Anievas is better in the reflective music than in providing glitter. His technique is absolutely secure and there is much to enjoy, but there is a great deal of competition in this repertoire.

Piano concerto No. 1.
(M) *** DG 449 719-2 [id.]. Martha Argerich, LSO, Abbado – LISZT: *Piano concerto No. 1.* ***
(BB) **(*) Naxos Dig. 8.550292 [id.]. Székely, Budapest SO, Németh – LISZT: *Concerto No. 1.* **(*)

(i) *Piano concerto No. 1. Ballade No. 1, Op. 23; Nocturnes Nos. 4 & 5, Op. 15/1–2; 7 & 8, Op. 27/1–2; Polonaise No. 6, Op. 53.*
(M) *** EMI CDM5 66221-2 [id.]. Pollini, (i) Philh. O, Kletzki.

(i) *Piano concerto No. 1. Barcarolle in F sharp, Op. 60; Preludes, Op. 28/1, 3, 6, 10, 15–17, 20–21 & 24; Scherzo No. 3, Op. 39.*
(B) **(*) DG Classikon 439 459-2 [(M) id. import]. Argerich; (i) LSO, Abbado.

(i) *Piano concerto No. 1. Etudes: in E, Op. 10/3; A flat, Op. 25/1; Fantaisie-impromptu in C sharp min., Op. 66; Impromptu No. 3 in G flat, Op. 51; Mazurkas: in A min., Op. 68/2; B flat, Op. 7/1; Nocturne No. 2 in E flat, Op. 9; Waltz No. 12 in F min., Op. 70/2.*
(BB) **(*) Belart 461 149-2 [(M) id. import]. Tamás Vásáry; (i) BPO, Jerzy Semkow.

Pollini's classic recording still remains among the best available of the *E minor Concerto*. This is playing of such total spontaneity, poetic feeling and refined judgement that criticism is silenced. The digital remastering has been generally successful. The additional items come from Pollini's first EMI solo recital, and the playing is equally distinguished, the recording truthful.

Martha Argerich's recording dates from 1968 and helped to establish her international reputation. The distinction of this partnership is immediately apparent in the opening orchestral ritornello with Abbado's flexible approach. Argerich follows his lead and her affectionate phrasing provides some lovely playing, especially in the slow movement. Perhaps in the passage-work she is rather too intense, but this is far preferable to the rambling style we are sometimes offered. This version is now reissued in two different formats. The first comes as one of DG's 'Originals' in a coupling with an equally individual and charismatic account of Liszt's *First Concerto*, and great trouble has been taken by the DG engineers to add lustre to a recording which was originally of very high quality and which now sounds even fresher. For the bargain Classikon alternative a miscellaneous programme of encores has been added, showing well the impulsive qualities of her solo playing; however, the offering of just a (well-chosen) selection of the *Préludes* may not suit collectors who would prefer to invest in a complete set.

Returning to Vásáry's fine mid-1960s Belart (originally DG) recording of the *E minor Concerto* gave us great pleasure. He is beautifully recorded with a good balance and fine piano-tone. The gentle poetry of the solo playing is in distinct contrast with the more extrovert orchestral contribution under Semkow; but soloist and orchestra match their styles in the slow movement, which has real magic, and the finale has no lack of vivacity and sparkle. The recital which follows is rather more uneven. The pianist's self-effacing style is at its most effective in the *E major Etude* and the justly famous *E flat Nocturne*. However, he finds plenty of brilliance for the closing *Fantaisie-impromptu*. Again good recording.

István Székely is particularly impressive in the *E minor Concerto*, but in both works he finds atmosphere and poetry in slow movements and an engaging dance spirit for the finales, with rhythms given plenty of character. Németh accompanies sympathetically, building the uncut opening ritornelli impressively, and the Budapest strings caress Chopin's lyrical melodies affectingly. The orchestral contribution here is refined. The recording is resonantly full in the Hungarian manner, not absolutely clear on detail, but the piano image is bold and realistic, and the brilliance of the pianist's articulation is crisply caught. A splendid bargain.

(i) *Piano concerto No. 2 in F min., Op. 21* (complete). *Ballade No. 1 in G min., Op. 23; Barcarolle in F sharp min., Op. 60; Berceuse in D flat, Op. 57; Fantaisie-impromptu in C sharp min., Op. 66; Mazurkas: in B flat, Op. 7/1; in D, Op. 33/2; in A min., Op. 68/2; Nocturnes: in E flat, Op. 9/2; in G min., Op. 37/1; Polonaises Nos. 3 in A (Military), Op. 40/1; 6 in A flat, Op. 53; Scherzo No. 2 in B flat min., Op. 31; Sonata No. 2 in B flat min. (Funeral march), Op. 35* (complete). *Waltzes: in A flat, Op. 34/1; in D flat (Minute), Op. 64/1; in E min., Op. posth.*

(B) *** RCA Twofer 74321 34175-2 (2) [(M) id. import]. Artur Rubinstein, (i) Symphony of the Air, Alfred Wallenstein.

Including as it does complete performances of the *F minor Piano concerto* and an unsurpassed *Funeral march Sonata*, this RCA Twofer must be counted a primary choice among all the bargain collections of Chopin's piano music. Rubinstein's playing was in a class of its own. Adjectives like 'miraculous', 'inspired', 'magical' fail to do justice to the creative imagination of this pianism. He was not always recorded flatteringly; sometimes the sound is a bit hard. But for the most part it is very good – and especially so in the *Berceuse*, *Nocturnes*, the commanding *Polonaises* and the *Sonata*. The orchestral tuttis in the *Concerto* are dry and studio-ish, but the piano timbre and colouring are unimpaired, especially in the delicate filigree of the slow movement. What a superb artist Rubinstein was, and what a marvellous bargain is this 132-minute collection from a uniquely understanding advocate of the greatest of Romantic composers for the piano!

Piano concerto No. 2 in F min., Op. 21.

(M) *** Decca 448 598-2 [id.]. Vladimir Ashkenazy, LSO, Zinman – BACH: *Clavier concerto No. 1;* MOZART: *Piano concerto No. 6.* **(*)

(BB) ** ASV CDQS 6003 [(M) id. import]. Vásáry, N. Sinfonia – SCHUMANN: *Concerto.* **

(i) *Piano concerto No. 2 in F min., Op. 21. 24 Preludes, Op. 24.*

(BB) **(*) Belart 461 055-2 [(M) id. import]. Alicia de Larrocha; (i) SRO, Sergiu Comissiona.

Ashkenazy's 1965 recording is a distinguished performance: his sophisticated use of light and shade in the opening movement and the subtlety of phrasing and rubato are a constant source of pleasure. The recitativo section in the *Larghetto*, which can often sound merely rhetorical, is here shaped with mastery, and there is a delectable lightness of touch in the finale. David Zinman and the LSO are obviously in full rapport with their soloist and the vintage recording has been remastered most satisfactorily. This is now reissued in Decca's Classic Sound series with new couplings, which are perhaps less than ideally chosen, although enjoyable enough.

Alicia de Larrocha is an artist of personality and temperament, and her performance of the concerto is highly poetic. It is supported by a strongly characterful accompaniment from Comissiona. Her *rubati* carry total conviction, whereas in the *Preludes* they sometimes seem more idiosyncratic. There is, however, much to admire here, including fine Decca engineering from the 1970s, and this budget Belart reissue is worth anyone's money.

Vásáry's recording on ASV, in which he not only plays but directs the Northern Sinfonia from the keyboard, has the advantage of fresh and well-balanced sound, but the playing, while it has much delicacy and refinement, is not so boldly characterized nor so full of ardour and flair as was his earlier account on DG.

(i) *Piano concerto No. 2. Ballades Nos. 1–4; Barcarolle, Op. 60; Berceuse, Op. 57* (2 versions); *Chants polonais, Op. 74* (trans. Liszt); *Etudes, Op. 10/1–12* (2 versions); *Op. 25/1–12* (2 versions); *Nouvelles Etudes; Impromptus, Opp. 29, 36; Nocturnes Opp. 9/2; 15/1–2; 27/1; 55/1–2; 24 Preludes, Op. 28; Prelude in C sharp min., Op. 45; Piano sonatas Nos. 2, Op. 35; 3, Op. 58; Waltzes Nos. 1–14.*
(M) (***) EMI CZS7 67359-2 (6). Alfred Cortot, (i) with O, Barbirolli.

This Cortot compilation encompasses most (but not all) of the recordings he made between 1920 and 1949, arranged in roughly chronological order. His 1933 set of the *Preludes* is omitted (perhaps logically, as they appeared separately, together with the *Fantaisie-impromptu*, also omitted, some time ago). The quality of the performances is such that they would need several pages to do them justice; Cortot's spontaneity, poetic feeling and keyboard refinement are heard to prodigal effect on these six CDs. Several alternative versions (for example, both sets of the Opp. 10 and 25 *Etudes* from 1934 and 1942 are included) offer food for thought. But in any event this is playing of a quite special quality: aristocratic yet full of fire and spontaneity. The transfers are strikingly good and bring Cortot very much before one's eyes.

(i) *Piano concerto No. 2. Mazurkas Nos. 5 & 7, Op. 7/1 & 3; 15 & 17, Op. 24/2 & 4; 20–21, Op. 30/3–4; 22–23 & 25, Op. 33/1–2 & 4; 27, Op. 41/2; 32, Op. 50/3; 41, Op. 63/3; 45, Op. 67/4; 47 & 49, Op. 68/2 & 4; Piano sonata No. 3, Op. 58; Waltzes Nos. 1–14.*
(B) **(*) EMI CZS5 68226-2 (2) [ZDMB 68226]. Witold Malcuzynski; (i) with LSO, Walter Susskind.

Malcuzynski's recordings were made between 1959 and 1961. They project his musical personality with great intensity. This is especially apparent in his brilliant and highly individual collection of the fourteen *Waltzes* (a favourite of IM's), which glitter and sparkle whenever they should – and sometimes when they should not. Yet the crisp, assured playing is undeniably attractive, especially in the more extrovert numbers, thrown off with splendid panache. But his finest EMI LP was his collection of *Mazurkas*, brilliantly successful in every way. The playing is again immensely polished, yet finds an infinite range of mood and expression in a very well-chosen programme. The performance of the *B minor Sonata* is undoubtedly commanding, mannered perhaps, sometimes glittering, and certainly not insensitive. But there is a dimension missing compared with Rubinstein. The concerto is a disappointment. Again Malcuzynski offers confident, extrovert playing which inevitably provides much excitement, but this is altogether too glittering to be an ideal account of Chopin's delicate inspiration. However, it would be wrong to suggest that Malcuzynski's *Larghetto* lacks poetic feeling, and the finale has much dash and fire. The LSO under Susskind provide good support and the recording is bold, rather loud and rather over-projected. For all one's reservations, there is nothing pallid or routine about this Chopin playing, and this inexpensive 'Profile' is a thoroughly worthwhile reissue and worth seeking out before it disappears back into the EMI vaults.

Les Sylphides (ballet; orch. Douglas).
✿ (B) *** DG 429 163-2 [id.]. BPO, Karajan – DELIBES: *Coppélia*: suite; OFFENBACH: *Gaîté parisienne*: excerpts. ***
(B) *** Sony SBK 46550; *SBT 46550* [id.]. Phd. O, Ormandy – DELIBES: *Coppélia; Sylvia: suites* ***; TCHAIKOVSKY: *Nutcracker suite*. **(*)
(B) **(*) Ph. Duo 438 763-2 (2) [id.]. Rotterdam PO, David Zinman – DELIBES: *Coppélia;* GOUNOD: *Faust: ballet music*. **(*)
(B) **(*) Decca Eclipse Dig. 448 984-2; *448 984-4* [(M) id. import]. Nat. PO, Bonynge (with MASSENET: *Thaïs: Méditation* with Nigel Kennedy) – ROSSINI/RESPIGHI: *La Boutique fantasque*. **(*)

Karajan conjures consistently beautiful playing from the Berlin Philharmonic Orchestra, and he evokes a delicacy of texture which delights the ear throughout. The woodwind solos are played gently and lovingly, and one can feel the conductor's touch on the phrasing. The upper register of the strings is bright, fresh and clearly focused, the recording is full and atmospheric, and this is one of Karajan's very finest recordings. At bargain price it is unbeatable, coupled on CD not only with *Coppélia* (although the suite is not complete) but also with Offenbach's *Gaîté parisienne*.

The Philadelphia strings are perfectly cast in this score and, although the CBS sound is less svelte than the DG quality for Karajan, it is still very good. Ormandy begins gently and persuasively. Later the lively sections are played with irrepressible brilliance.

David Zinman's approach is less suavely characterful than Karajan's, but he secures smoothly beautiful playing from his Rotterdam orchestra and there is no lack of vitality. Most enjoyable, when the 1980 recording is so natural and resonantly full (obviously more modern than the DG).

Bonynge's performance shows a strong feeling for the dance rhythms of the ballet, and the orchestral playing is polished and lively. Bonynge also has the advantage of excellent (1982) digital recording, made in the Kingsway Hall. Nigel Kennedy plays very appealingly in the Massenet lollipop which acts as an encore. Even so, Karajan remains unsurpassed in this beautiful score.

CHAMBER MUSIC

Cello sonata in G min., Op. 65.
(M) **(*) EMI CMS7 63184-2 [id.]. Du Pré, Barenboim – FRANCK: *Cello sonata.* **(*)

The easy romanticism of the *Cello sonata* is beautifully caught by Jacqueline du Pré and Daniel Barenboim. Though the cellist phrases with all her usual spontaneous-sounding imagination, this is one of her more reticent records, while still bringing an autumnal quality to the writing which is very appealing. The recording is excellently balanced.

Cello sonata in G min., Op. 65; Grand duo concertante in E on themes from Meyerbeer's 'Robert le Diable'; Nocturne in C sharp min., Op. posth (arr. Piatigorsky); *Etudes: in E min., Op. 25/7; D min., Op. 10/6* (arr. Glazunov; ed. Feuermann); *Waltz in A min., Op. 34/3* (arr. Ginsburg).
(BB) *** Naxos 8.553259 [id.]. Maria Kliegel, Bernd Glemser.

Fresh and ardent performances of the *Sonata* and the remaining two pieces that comprise Chopin's complete output for cello and piano. The Naxos collection also throws in some cello arrangements for good measure. These gifted and accomplished young artists are also very well recorded indeed and, at the price, this is a bargain.

SOLO PIANO MUSIC

Vladimir Ashkenazy Chopin Edition

Albumblatt in E; Allegro de concert in A, Op. 46; Barcarolle in F sharp, Op. 60; Berceuse in D flat, Op. 57; Boléro in A min., Op. 19; 2 Bourrées; Cantabile in B flat; Fugue in A min.; Galop marquis; Hexameron: Variation in E min.; Largo in E flat; 3 Nouvelles études; Rondo in E flat, Op. 16; Souvenir de Paganini (Variations in A); Tarantelle in A flat, Op. 43; Variations brillantes in B flat, Op. 12; Wiosna (Spring) from Op. 74/2 (443 7512). *Ballades Nos. 1–4; Scherzi Nos. 1–4* (443 740-2). *12 Etudes, Op. 10; 12 Etudes, Op. 25* (443 743-2). *Impromptus Nos. 1–3; 4 (Fantaisie-impromptu); 24 Preludes, Op. 28; Preludes: in C sharp min., Op. 45; in A flat* (443 739-2). *Mazurkas Nos. 1–29* (443 747-2); *Nos. 30–68 (including 2 versions of Op. 68/4)* (443 748-2). *Nocturnes Nos. 1–12* (443 741-2); *Nos. 13–21* (443 742-2). *Polonaises Nos. 1–6; No. 7, Polonaise-fantaisie* (443 744-2); *Nos. 8–16* (443 745-2). *Sonata No. 1; Contredanse in G flat; 3 Ecossaises; Marche funèbre in C min., Op. 72/2; Rondo in C min., Op. 1; Rondo à la Mazur in F, Op. 5; Rondo in C, Op. 73; Variations on a German national air;* (i) *Variations in D* (for piano duet – with Vovka Ashkenazy) (443 750-2). *Sonatas Nos. 2–3; Fantaisie in F min., Op. 49* (443 749-2). *Waltzes Nos. 1–19* (443 746-2).
(B) *** Decca Analogue/ Dig. 443 738-2 (13) [id.].

Ashkenazy made his Chopin recordings for Decca over a decade from 1974 to 1984, using seven different locations, yet the recorded sound is remarkably consistent, always natural in colour and balance and with a good presence, whether from an analogue or a digital source. His playing is appealingly fresh, never idiosyncratic to the point of trying to superimpose his own personality over that of the composer. Consistently persuasive, these readings combine poetry with flair and (as in the *Ballades*) often bring a highly communicated warmth. The bravura brings genuine panache, whether in the large-scale, virtuoso pieces like the *Scherzi* or in the chimerical approach to a miniature like the *Souvenir de Paganini*. At bargain price this set makes an unbeatable investment. It seems likely that many of these records will become available separately during the lifetime of this book, and the *Ballades* and *Nocturnes*, *Mazurkas*, *Polonaises* and three *Sonatas* have already appeared (see below).

Nikita Magaloff complete duet and solo piano music

Allegro de concert, Op. 46; Ballades Nos. 1–4; Barcarolle, Op. 60; Berceuse, Op. 57; Boléro, Op. 19; Cantabile in B flat; Contredanse in G flat; 3 Ecossaises, Op. 72/3–5; Etudes, Op. 10/1–12; Op. 25/1–12 Fantaisie in F min., Op. 49; Fugue in A min.; Feuille d'album in E; Impromptus Nos. 1–3, 4 (Fantaisie-impromptu); Largo in E flat; March funèbre, Op. 72/2; Mazurkas Nos. 1–57; Nocturnes Nos. 1–21; Polonaises Nos. 1–16; 24 Preludes, Op. 28; Preludes Nos. 25, Op. 45; 26, Op. posth.; Rondeaux: in C min., Op. 1; à la mazurka in E, Op. 5; in E flat, Op. 16; in C (for 2 pianos), *Op. 73; Scherzi Nos. 1–4; Sonatas Nos. 1–3; Souvenir de Paganini; Variations brillantes, Op. 12; Variations on a German*

national air; Variations on a Moorish national air (for piano duet); *Variations on the 'March of the Puritans' of Bellini; Waltzes Nos. 1–17.*
(B) ** Ph. 456 376-2 (13) [(M) id. import]. Nikita Magaloff.

Magaloff made his survey over a period of four years, between 1974 and 1978, and Philips gave him consistently natural recording, although the sound is full and rounded rather than glittering. Not absolutely everything Chopin wrote is included, but the coverage is pretty comprehensive and the set is documented with a distinguished essay ('Chopin and the piano') by Joan Chissell, which effectively summarizes the major works and mentions some of the early ephemera. Magaloff's playing is not electrifying in the manner of a Pollini, but it is highly musical and faithful to the composer. His manner avoids egocentricity, and for that he earns praise; although this repertoire calls for rather more flair, more poetic intensity than he commands, the performances here are not without insights, and the complete set is by no means an inconsiderable achievement. The *Ballades*, always a sure test, have nicely controlled rubato, a poetic touch and a feeling for atmosphere. There is delicacy when required, as at the opening of the *F major* and *F minor*, although the resonant recording is not always helpful by slightly smudging the bolder romantic flourishes. Magaloff's characterization of the *Impromptus*, which follow on the same disc, is firm without being rigid (No. 1 in particular is well done), although the brilliance of the *Fantaisie-impromptu* is again affected by the reverberation.

The performances of the *Etudes* are very assured – as the opening of the *A flat major*, Op. 25, No. 1, immediately demonstrates – offering very accomplished and certainly characterful playing, and the famous *F major* (Op. 25/3) is beautifully shaped. Moreover these studies move fluently from one to another, giving the sense of live music-making. Here the piano-tone is very well judged: firm and warm in colour, yet with a nice degree of brightness. The three *Nouvelles Etudes* make an attractive pendant. The *Préludes* are similarly distinguished by individual insights and lack only the last degree of flair. Here the ear again notices that at times detail fails to tell sharply because of the resonance.

The *Mazurkas* cover a wide variety of styles and contain some of Chopin's most characteristic music. Magaloff plays them with sensibility and often quite delightfully, with a consistent feeling for their idiomatic variety. He had recorded them previously for Decca; the present set was made in 1977 and offers first-class sound. Once again it is the gentler, lyrical pieces which seem to fire his imagination; the bolder pieces are sometimes less spontaneous-sounding. The *Nocturnes* are beautifully recorded but do not command a wholehearted recommendation; there is an undoubted delicacy of touch, but the playing is at times curiously measured and deliberate in style and lacks incandescence. However, the *Polonaises*, like the *Mazurkas*, are among the best performances in the set, strongly played and well recorded, offering fine pianism and characteristic musical intelligence. The two best-known have plenty of lift, while the remainder have genuine freshness: one senses the pianist enjoying the music.

The *Scherzi*, too, have plenty of impetus, although the somewhat middle-orientated recording does not help the playing to sound dazzling and chimerical. The *Sonatas* are generally successful; the first (the product of a seventeen-year-old student) establishes a certain Schumannesque quality in Magaloff's approach, partly the effect of the bold, full recording. The central episode in the *Funeral march* of No. 2 achieves an atmosphere of gentle repose – the tempo slow and deliberate – that brings a striking contrast with the solemn outer sections. The *Third Sonata* is the most successful of the three, with lighter textures, a fine, thoughtful *Largo* and an easy virtuosity in the finale. The *Waltzes* bring out the best in Magaloff. They are enjoyably alive and, if lacking the last degree of individuality, are well characterized and communicative. Their contrasts between intimacy and bravura are nicely made (the *Grande valse brillante* is notably successful) and, like the *Etudes* and *Preludes*, the ongoing sequence has a spontaneous flow. The recording is first class. Among the shorter works, Magaloff's simplicity of the presentation suits the *Berceuse* with its delicate filigree, as does the full recording, and the lilt of the *Barcarolle* is pleasingly caught; the *Fantaisie in F minor* is rather sober, though not without colour or feeling.

The miniatures, the *Contredanse* and *Tarantelle* are stylish if not arresting, but Magaloff finds an easy brilliance for the *Variations* and other display pieces: the *Rondeaux* are nicely presented, especially the rare C major piece for two pianos. Here, as in the closing four-handed *Variations on a Moorish air* (a very familiar tune), Magaloff appears to be engaging in a duet with himself by electronic means, as no other artist is named. It makes a delicious closing lollipop.

Ballades Nos. 1–4; Polonaises: in A flat & F sharp min. (NI 5209); *Barcarolle, Op. 60; Piano sonatas Nos. 2 (Funeral march); 3 in B min.* (NI 5038); *Berceuse, Op. 57; Fantasy in F min., Op. 49; 24 Preludes, Op. 28; Prelude in C sharp min., Op. 45* (NI 5064); *Etudes, Op. 10/1–12; Op. 25/1–12; 3 Nouvelles Etudes* (NI 5095); *Mazurkas, Op. 17/4; Op. 24/2; Op. 30/4; Op. 33/4; Op. 41/1 & 4; Op. 50/3; Op. 43; Op. 56/2–3; Op. 59/1–3; Op. 63/1–3; Op. 68/4; Scherzo No. 3, Op. 39; Tarantelle in A flat, Op. 43* (NI

5393); *Nocturnes: in B, Op. 9/3; in F; F sharp; G min., Op. 15/1–3; in C sharp min.; in D flat, Op. 27/1–2; in C min.; in F sharp min., Op. 48/1–2; in E flat, Op. 55/2; in E, Op. 62/1* (NI 5012).
(BB) *(*) Nimbus Dig. NI 1787 (6) [(B) id.]. Vlado Perlemuter.

Born in 1904, Vlado Perlemuter was a pupil of Moszkowski before studying with Cortot at the Paris Conservatoire, where he later became a professor. In his day he was a pianist and teacher of great distinction and was particularly admired for his Chopin and Ravel. He recorded most of this repertoire for the BBC in the 1960s; but these performances, recorded when he was advanced in years, do not really do his art full justice. Of course there are many insights and evidences of fine sensibility, but in terms of neither keyboard mastery nor recorded sound do these successfully compete with other Chopin anthologies currently on offer.

Ballades Nos. 1–4; Nocturnes Nos. 1–21 (complete).
(B) *** Decca Double 452 579-2 (2) [id.]. Vladimir Ashkenazy.

Ashkenazy's readings of the *Ballades* are thoughtful and essentially unflashy; the rubato arises naturally from his personal approach to the music. The intimacy of the recording allows him to share this with the listener. The openings of the *First* and *Fourth Ballades* show this quality well: the music unfolds naturally and without emphasis, yet there is no lack of drama. The recording is admirably natural and satisfying. The *Nocturnes* were recorded over a decade, from 1975 to 1984. The disparity in dates seems not to have affected the consistency of sound that the Decca engineers have achieved. The playing is splendidly imaginative and atmospheric. As always, Ashkenazy is completely attuned to Chopin's unique sound-world, and the CD transfers are impeccable.

(i) *Ballades Nos. 1–4;* (ii) *Scherzi Nos. 1–4.*
(M) ** Ph. 454 135-2. (i) Bella Davidovich; (ii) Rafael Orozco.

Bella Davidovich plays the *Ballades* with unaffected sensibility; these are considerable performances, and the digital recording is most realistic. However, in the *Scherzi* Rafael Orozco is as impetuous as Davidovich is considered. The famous *B flat minor* comes off well enough with its volatile display, but in the opening *B minor*, Orozco almost gets carried away in a headlong rush of bravura, while the *C sharp minor* and *E major* are hardly less reckless, although technically impressive. Good, clear recording.

Ballades Nos. 1–4; Piano sonata No. 2 in B flat min. (Funeral march), Op. 35.
(BB) **(*) RCA Navigator Dig. 74321 24204-2 [(M) id. import]. Ax.

Emanuel Ax, recorded in 1985, is a good deal more extrovert in Chopin than in the Beethoven concertos. Indeed the *Ballades* bring volatile, boldly romantic readings, with the *A flat major* and *F minor* particularly successful. Just occasionally – as at the opening of the *G minor* – the rubato seems a little studied, but spontaneity soon reasserts itself. The *Sonata* is also a commanding performance, but with striking contrast provided in the central section of the *Funeral march*, which is played very gently. Clear recording, with just a touch of hardness. But this is very reasonably priced and good value.

Barcarolle, Op. 60; Berceuse, Op. 57; Cantabile in B flat; Contredanse in G flat; Fantaisie in F min., Op. 49; Feuille d'album in E; Fugue in A min.; Funeral march in C min., Op. 72/2; Largo in E flat; 3 Nouvelles-Etudes, Op. posth; Polonaise-Fantaisie, Op. 61; Souvenir de Paganini in A (Variations).
(B) *** Sony Analogue/Dig. SBK 53515 [id.]. Fou Ts'ong.

Fou Ts'ong is a pianist of intelligence and sensibility and his admirers need not hesitate here. The programme is enterprising – how many readers, we wonder, have heard Chopin's succinct little *Fugue in A minor*? The smaller pieces are played with a distinction and dedication that completely win one over, and the closing *Paganini variations* are disarmingly attractive. The recording, partly analogue, partly digital, is good but not quite top-drawer: in general the analogue items sound best. But this 66-minute bargain recital is well worth exploring.

Barcarolle, Op. 60; Berceuse, Op. 57; Fantaisie, Op. 49; Nocturne No. 4 in F, Op. 15/1; Polonaise No. 4 in C min., Op. 40/2; Sonata No. 3 in B min., Op. 58.
(M) **(*) Carlton Dig. PCD 2008 [id.]. John Ogdon.

John Ogdon's collection presents fresh and thoughtful performances, not as electrifying as some he recorded earlier in his career but often bold and full of individual insights. His speeds for the slower pieces are at times daringly extreme, but he sustains them well and the delicacy of much that he does is a delight, set in contrast to his natural strength in bravura. Bright, clear, realistic recording, giving the piano a powerful presence.

Etudes, Op. 10/1–12; Op. 25/1–12.
(M) *(**) Saga EC 3351-2. Vladimir Ashkenazy.
(BB) * Naxos Dig. 8.550364 [id.]. Idil Biret.

Etudes, Op. 10/1–12; Op. 25/1–12; Ballades Nos. 1 & 3.
(B) *** [EMI Red Line Dig. CDR5 69799]. Andrei Gavrilov.

Andrei Gavrilov's performances of the *Etudes* bring an exuberant virtuosity that is impossible to resist, even if some of the tempi are breathtakingly fast, as in Op. 10/4 and 5. Yet the sustained legato of the famous *No. 3 in E major* is lovely, and his poetic feeling, both here and in *No. 6 in E flat minor*, is indisputable. The impulsive bravura is often engulfing, so that one feels the need to take a breath on the soloist's behalf after the furious account of the *Revolutionary study*; but this is prodigious playing, given a bold, forward recording to match. The *Ballades* are also impulsive but full of romantic feeling too.

Ashkenazy's set first appeared in the early 1960s on the Chant du Monde label. The playing is unfailingly rewarding and demonstrates a prodigious virtuosity completely at the service of the composer, and the poetic feeling is never in doubt. The sound is perfectly acceptable if not distinguished, and this pianist's admirers will be glad to discover Ashkenazy's potential before he was signed by Decca. It is a pity that this Saga reissue is not at bargain price, when the recommendation could have been less qualified.

As has so often proved to be the case in the Naxos recordings made in the Tonstudio van Geest in Heidelberg, the artist is let down by a less than sympathetic studio environment. The instrument is rather closely balanced and, though it may not be the case, it sounds as if echo has been added, for the timbre of the piano is not completely natural. Idil Biret plays well enough, though she is not strong on poetry. This set is not really competitive, even at super-bargain price.

Mazurkas Nos. 1–57.
(B) **(*) Sony Dig. SB2K 53246 (2) [S2K 53246]. Fou Ts'ong.

Mazurkas Nos. 1–53, Opp. 6–7; 17; 24; 30; 33; 41; 50; 56; 59; 63; 67–8 & Op. posth.; Berceuse, Op. 57; Impromptus Nos. 1–3; Fantaisie-impromptu, Op. 66.
(B) ** Ph. Duo (IMS) 442 574-2 (2) [id.]. Alexander Uninsky.

Mazurkas Nos. 1–59, Op. 6/1–4; Op. 7/1–5; Op. 17/1–4; Op. 24/1–4; Op. 30/1–4; Op. 33/1–4; Op. 41/1–4; Op. 50/1–3; Op.56/1–3; Op. 59/1–3; Op. 63/1–3; Op. 67/1–4; Op. 68/1–4; & Op. 68/4 (revised version); *Nos. 60–68, Op. posth.*
(B) *** Decca Double Dig./Analogue 448 086-2 (2) [id.]. Vladimir Ashkenazy.

As can be seen, Ashkenazy's survey of Chopin's *Mazurkas* is the most comprehensive available and as such must take pride of place over Rubinstein's set (irrespective of its extremely modest cost). Ashkenazy's recordings were made over a decade in various venues between 1976 and 1985; about two-thirds of them are digital. His are finely articulated, aristocratic accounts and the sound is amazingly fresh and consistent, considering the time-span involved. He includes the posthumously published *Mazurkas* and the recording quality is more modern and more natural than that afforded to Rubinstein, with a believable presence.

After recording the *Nocturnes*, Fou Ts'ong went on to record all the *Mazurkas*, including two early works from 1826 in G and B flat major, another two in D and B flat (the latter dedicated to Alexandrine Wolowaska in 1832), the *Mazurkas in C* (1833) and *A flat* (1834) and the two A minor works of 1840 (*Notre temps* and *à Emile Gaillard*). Fou Ts'ong's style is distinctive and rhythmically strong but not lacking poetry. Sometimes the rubato seems a shade too impulsive, but for the most part the playing is compelling. The digital recording from 1984 is bold and clear.

Alexander Uninsky offers an inexpensive complete survey of the *Mazurkas*, including the four published posthumously, plus the *Impromptus*. His playing is sympathetic but not especially individual or imaginative, and after a while his rubato and control of dynamic nuance become rather predictable. Even so, many of the performances are effective and musical, especially the later works: Op. 56/1, for instance, which opens the second CD, has a pleasing poise and intimacy of feeling, although just occasionally elsewhere he tends to rush his fences. The recordings were made in three groups, dating from 1959, 1961 and 1971, but the realistic sound remains remarkably consistent, a tribute to the Philips engineering. The programme ends with the lovely *Berceuse*, which is played persuasively.

Mazurkas Nos. 1–51 (complete); *Piano sonatas Nos. 2–3.*
(B) * EMI Rouge et Noir CZS7 67413-2 (2) [id.]. Samson François.

We have never quite understood the veneration in which Samson François is still held by the French critics and public alike, given the plethora of fine pianists that France produced in the 1970s – Jean-Philippe Collard, Pascal Rogé, Michel Béroff and many others. François is often spoken of as *Le poète du piano* and yet poetic feeling is rarely present in his Chopin. Pianissimo playing is often conspicuous by its absence and he is not averse to producing quite ugly tone in fortissimo passages. Much though one would like to, it is difficult to warm to this playing. The recordings all date from the 1960s.

Nocturnes Nos. 1–21 (see also under *Ballades*).
(BB) *** Arte Nova Dig. 74321 30494-2 (*Nos. 1–10*); 74321 54451-2 (*Nos. 11–21*) (available separately) [id.]. Ricardo Castro.
(B) *** DG Dig. 453 022-2 (2) [437 464-2]. Daniel Barenboim.
(BB) **(*) Carlton IMP Double 30367 02357 [(M) id. import]. Peter Katin.
(B) **(*) Sony SB2K 53249 (2) [S2K 53249]. Fou Ts'ong.
(B) ** Teldec/Warner Ultimo Dig. 0630 18949-2 (2) [id.]. Elisabeth Leonskaya.

Nocturnes Nos. 1–4; 7–10; 12–13; 15; 18–19.
(B) *** DG Dig. 439 497-2 [423 916-2]. Daniel Barenboim.

To have an outstanding set of the *Nocturnes*, digitally recorded and in the lowest possible price-range, seems almost too good to be true, but the Brazilian pianist, Ricardo Castro, winner of the Leeds International Piano Competition in 1993, offers a series of performances to compete with any in the catalogue. They were recorded in two groups, in 1995 and 1997 respectively, but the degree of concentration is consistent throughout both discs. His thoughtful simplicity of approach captures the listener from the very first piece, *in B flat minor*, while the famous *Nocturne in E flat major*, Op. 9/2, which follows, flows with comparable spontaneity. The gently withdrawn opening of the *C sharp minor*, Op. 27/1, is judged most sensitively, and the lovely work in *B major*, Op. 32/1, is similarly seductive. On the second disc, after opening with a touchingly poised performance of *No. 11 in G minor*, warmly coloured in its middle section, Castro's thoughtful account of the *F minor*, Op. 55/1, and the two closing posthumous works, *in C sharp minor* (exquisitely presented) and the delectably articulated *C minor*, are particularly fine. The recording, made in two quite different venues, is of the highest quality, clear and natural.

Barenboim recorded the *Nocturnes* in 1981 in DG's Berlin studio, and he was very beautifully recorded. The digital master gives the advantage of a silent background, against which his playing gives much pleasure. Phrasing is beautifully moulded, seemingly spontaneous, the nuancing of colour and control of rubato thoughtful and poetic, and becoming really impetuous only in the music's more passionate moments. There is an excellent, well-chosen, single-disc selection on DG's bargain label which offer 72 minutes of music and scores 13 out of a total of 21. But the complete set is surely worth the extra outlay.

Peter Katin's set dates from 1971. He too was beautifully recorded, and these finely transferred Carlton CDs offer a most natural piano-image. He has chosen not to present the *Nocturnes* in their usual, numbered sequence, but in their order of composition, so that the pieces which were published posthumously are placed in their natural position, a scheme which works very well. His approach is serene and civilized, essentially relaxed. Only occasionally does he not penetrate to the very heart of the music; almost always the playing is highly sensitive, with subtle rubato, delicate runs and exquisite shading in the gentle music. The *D flat Nocturne*, for instance, is most poetically managed. This set is inexpensive and admirers of this fine artist need not hesitate.

Fou Ts'ong sometimes reminds one of Solomon – and there can surely be no higher tribute. He is at his very best in the gentle, poetic pieces; in the more robust *Nocturnes* his rubato is less subtle, the style not so relaxed. But this is undoubtedly distinguished and, with good transfers of well-balanced recording from the late 1970s, this is competitive at budget price.

Leonskaya has the advantage of modern digital recording from the early 1990s. She is a fine artist and has her own insights to offer, although her thoughtful, sometimes rather deliberate manner is not always wholly idiomatic. The lovely *D flat Nocturne* makes a good point of comparison with Katin, her mood more serious, less mercurial. She is not as romantically seductive but is still appealing, and she is at her most impressive with her simplicity of style in the later works on the second disc.

Nocturnes Nos. 1–21; Impromptus Nos. 1–4 (Fantaisie-impromptu).
(B) **(*) Ph. Duo 456 336-2 [id.]. Claudio Arrau.

Arrau's approach clearly reflects his boyhood training in Germany, creating tonal warmth coupled with inner tensions of the kind one expects in Beethoven. With the *Nocturnes* it can be apt to have an element of seriousness, and this is a very compelling cycle, full of poetry, the rubato showing an individual but very communicable sensibility. The *Impromptus* have been added for the present reissue. Although Arrau's Chopin is seldom mercurial, it is never inflexible, and it has its own special insights. The *Fantasie-impromptu* with its finely contoured central melody is a highlight. As always, the Philips piano recording is of the highest standard, bright but never shallow, full in the middle and resonant in the bass. With artistry of this calibre this Duo set is well worth having, even if it is not a first choice.

Nocturnes Nos. 2 in E flat, Op. 9/2; 5 in F sharp min., Op. 15; 7 in C sharp min.; 8 in D flat, Op. 27/1–2; 9 in B; 10 in A flat, Op. 32/1–2; 12 in G, Op. 37/2; Waltzes Nos. 1 in E flat (Grande Valse brillante), Op. 18; 3 in A min.; 4 in F, Op. 34/2–3; 5 in A flat, Op. 42; 9 in A flat; 10 in E min., Op. 69/1–2; 11 in G flat; 12 in F min.; 13 in D flat Op. 70/1–3.
(M) *** Decca Dig. 430 751-2; *430 751-4* [id.]. Vladimir Ashkenazy.

Ashkenazy's selection of waltzes and nocturnes is aptly chosen and felicitously arranged to make a most satisfying programme of two groups in each genre. The *Nocturnes* are mostly reflective and poetically create a magical atmosphere in Ashkenazy's hands. The famous *E flat*, the very beautiful *D flat* and *B major* and the *Sylphides Nocturne in A flat*, Op. 32/2, are highlights. First-class digital sound ensures a welcome for this reissue.

Polonaises Nos. 1–16, Op. 26/1–2; Op. 40/1–2; Op. 44; Op. 53; Polonaise-Fantaisie, Op. 61; Op. 71/1–3; Op. Posth./1–6. Albumblatt in E; Allegro de concert, Op. 46; Barcarolle in F sharp, Op. 60; Berceuse in D flat, Op. 57; 2 Bourrées; 3 Nouvelles Etudes; Fugue in A min.; Galop marquis; Tarantelle in A flat, Op. 43; Wiosna (arr. from *Op. 74/2*).
(B) *** Decca Double Analogue/Dig. 452 167-2 (2) [id.]. Vladimir Ashkenazy.

Ashkenazy's performances of the *Polonaises* have been out of the catalogue for some time. The second CD contains some items that are quite short (the piano transcription of Chopin's song *Wiosna* lasts for barely a minute, but it is very fetching). But there are substantial works too: the *Barcarolle* and *Berceuse*, the latter meltingly done, and the *Allegro de Concert* and *Nouvelles Etudes* also show Ashkenazy at his finest. The recordings are excellent. At Double Decca price this pair of CDs is self-recommending.

(i) *Polonaises Nos. 1–6;* (ii) *Piano sonata No. 3 in B min., Op. 58.*
(M) **(*) DG 449 090-2. (i) Lazar Berman; (ii) Emil Gilels.

Gilels's account of the *B minor Sonata* is thoughtful and ruminative, seen through a powerful mind and wholly individual fingers; there are some highly personal touches, for example the gentle undulating accompaniment, like a quietly tolling bell, caressing the second subject of the first movement. There is a pensive and delicately coloured slow movement; the first movement is expansive and warmly lyrical, and there is not a bar that does not set one thinking anew about this music. An altogether haunting reading. Lazar Berman's *Polonaises* are not of this calibre. He gives bold character and colour to these works and these readings possess a certain magisterial command, while the recording is good; but Berman does not invest each phrase with the intensity of Pollini or the sheer poetry of Gilels.

24 Preludes, Op. 28; Ballades Nos. 2 in F, Op. 38; 4 in F min., Op. 53; Fantaisie in F min., Op. 49.
(B) **(*) Decca Eclipse Dig. 448 985-2; *448 985-4* [(M) id. import]. Jorge Bolet.

There is some lovely playing from Bolet in this recital, especially in the two *Ballades*. He brings keen musical insights to the *Preludes* and his characterization is never wanting in the individuality that avoids any feeling of routine. But there is a certain want of fire by the side of the youngest keyboard lions on record, and he does not quite command the effortless virtuosity that distinguished his earlier Liszt recordings: he is best in the more inward-looking *Preludes*. He enjoys the benefit of first-class recording, particularly beautiful in the *Ballades*, but does not displace Ashkenazy or indeed Argerich in Op. 28.

24 Preludes, Op. 28; Preludes Nos. 25–26; Barcarolle, Op. 60; Polonaise No. 6 in A flat, Op. 53; Scherzo No. 2 in B flat min., Op. 31.
(M) **(*) DG 415 836-2; *415 836-4* [431 584-2]. Martha Argerich.

The *Preludes* show Martha Argerich at her finest, spontaneous and inspirational, though her moments of impetuosity may not appeal to all tastes. But her instinct is sure, with many poetic, individual touches. The other pieces are splendidly played.

24 Preludes, Op. 28; Sonata No. 2 in B flat min. (Funeral march), Op. 35.
(M) ** Carlton 30367 0076-2 [id.]. Howard Shelley.

This is good value at mid-price, with very generous measure. There are no grumbles about Howard Shelley's playing – his virtuosity and sensitivity can be taken for granted. He gives eminently thoughtful and musicianly accounts both of the *Preludes* and of the *B flat minor Sonata*, but the recording is rather bottom-heavy and tubby, and ideally needs more room to expand.

Preludes, Op. 28, Nos. 1–11; 14–16; 20 & 23.
(M) ** Nimbus Dig. NI 8810 [id.]. Ferruccio Busoni (piano) – BACH: *Chaconne;* LISZT: *Etudes d'exécution transcendante* etc. ***

There is no reason to believe that Busoni's Duo-Art piano-roll recordings (from 1923) do not project his Chopin manner truthfully, and he proves no stylist in this music. Indeed much of his playing, if strong in character, is heavy going. The opening *C major Etude* is gabbled, and the famous *E minor* is quite wilful, while *No. 9 in E major*, played sombrely, hardly sounds like Chopin at all. *No. 7 in A* bounces along, and in the *D flat major* (No. 15) the control of rubato is unconvincing. *No. 20 in C minor* opens very stolidly indeed, but the closing *F major* (No. 23), recorded four years after the rest of the sequence, brings a much lighter touch. Excellent sound.

Scherzos Nos. 1–4; Polonaise-fantaisie, Op. 61.
(M) *** Ph. (IMS) Dig. 442 407-2. Claudio Arrau.

Arrau's last recording of the four *Scherzi* was made in Munich, just after the artist's eightieth birthday. There is little sign of age, even if he would have produced a greater weight of sonority at the height of his powers. However, these accounts are full of wise and thoughtful perceptions and remarkable pianism, recorded with great presence and clarity. The middle section of the *First Scherzo* may strike some collectors as unusually slow and a trifle mannered, but there are magical things elsewhere, notably in the *Fourth*. Arrau's fire may have lost some of its youthful charisma, but the gains in wisdom and delicacy of feeling are adequate compensation. The Philips engineers seem to produce piano quality of exceptional realism. However, this is short measure (55 minutes).

Piano sonatas Nos. 1 in C min., Op. 4; 2 in B flat min. (Funeral march), Op. 35; 3 in B min., Op. 58.
(M) *** Decca 448 123-2. Vladimir Ashkenazy.
(M) *(*) Revelation RV 10032 [id.]. Vera Gornosteyova.

The *C minor Sonata*, Op. 4, is a comparative rarity; it comes from 1827 and is not deeply characteristic; it is of greater interest to students of Chopin's style and budding pianists than to the wider musical public. But the distance Chopin covered between this and the *B flat minor Sonata* is very striking, as Ashkenazy's 1981 performance readily demonstrates. Indeed the first movement in particular seems more concentrated in feeling and the finale is very exciting indeed. In this repertoire one cannot speak of the finest performance, for this is terrain that has been conquered by Rubinstein (RCA RD 89812), Pollini (DG 415 346-2) and Perahia (Sony SK 76242) and others, but it would be surprising if Ashkenazy's account does not (like the finest of its rivals) enjoy classic status, and it is certainly the best recorded, with very vivid sound. The *Third (B minor) Sonata* is almost as distinguished and is certainly memorable. Some might not like the accelerando treatment of the finale, but it is undoubtedly exciting. The recording throughout is well up to the high standard set by this series.

Vera Gornosteyova studied with Heinrich Neuhaus, among whose pupils were numbered Gilels and Richter, and she is obviously an artist of quality. Her reputation did not extend beyond the borders of the old Soviet Union, as she was considered politically unreliable, but she was a widely respected teacher at the Moscow Conservatoire. The present recording comes from a recital given on 25 February 1986 and would warrant consideration as it offers all three sonatas on one disc at mid-price. However, the sound is far from distinguished (a bit close and shallow) and the performances do not achieve the distinction one had hoped to encounter. Ashkenazy provides the obvious answer at mid-price.

Piano sonatas Nos. 2 in B flat min. (Funeral march), Op. 35; 3 in B min., Op. 58.
(M) ** BMG/RCA 09026 60417 [id.]. Van Cliburn – LISZT: *Sonetto del Petrarca No. 123* etc. **

Van Cliburn's Chopin *B flat minor* and *B minor Sonatas* have not been in circulation for some years and they are performances of some quality. The 1960s sound may be wanting the freshness and bloom of modern recordings, but the performances are still to be reckoned with.

Piano sonata No. 3 in B min., Op. 58.
(B) ** EMI forte CZS5 69527-2 (2) [CDFB 68664]. Anievas – LISZT: *Sonata* ***; RACHMANINOV: *24 Preludes* etc. **(*)

Agustin Anievas gives a strong if not absolutely distinctive performance of the lesser-known *B minor Sonata*. However, the slow movement has the same thoughtfulness and sensitivity that distinguish his performance of the Liszt *Sonata*, and the bravura of the finale is striking. Good recording. If the couplings are suitable, this is worth considering.

Waltzes Nos. 1–17; Polonaises: in G min.; in B flat, Op. posth.
(BB) *** ASV Dig. CDQS 6149 [(M) id.]. Allan Schiller.

Many years have elapsed since Pye Records issued a promising recital by Allan Schiller, then still in short trousers. Like the first Leeds Prizewinner, Michael Roll, a fine musician, he has never captured the public to the extent to which his gifts entitle him. His playing of the *Waltzes* is always musical and often very sensitive, though there are one or two in which he could have allowed his imagination freer rein. Very good recording quality. Not a first recommendation when artists like Rubinstein and Lipatti are around, but well worth its modest asking price.

Waltzes Nos. 1–14; Barcarolle, Op. 60; Mazurka in C sharp min., Op. 50/3; Nocturne in D flat, Op. 27/2.
❀ (M) (***) EMI CDH5 66222-2 [id.]. Dinu Lipatti.

Lipatti's classic performances were recorded by Walter Legge in the rather dry acoustic of a Swiss Radio studio at Geneva in the last year of Lipatti's short life, and with each LP reincarnation they seem to have grown in wisdom and subtlety. The reputation of these meticulous performances is fully deserved.

RECITAL COLLECTIONS

(i–ii) *Piano concerto No. 1 in E min.: 2nd movt (Romance) only. Etudes:* (iii) *in E (Tristesse), Op. 10/3;* (iv) *in G flat, Op. 10/5;* (iii) *in C min., (Revolutionary), Op. 10/12;* (iii) *in G flat, Op. 25/9;* (v) *Fantaisie-impromptu in C sharp min., Op. 66;* (vi) *Impromptu No. 1 in A flat, Op. 29;* (vii) *Mazurka No. 5 in B flat, Op. 7/1;* (viii) *Nocturne No. 2 in E flat, Op. 9/2; Polonaises: Nos.* (i) *3 in A (Military), Op. 40/1;* (ix) *6 in A flat, Op. 53; Preludes:* (x) *in A, Op. 28/7;* (v) *in D flat (Raindrop), Op. 28/15;* (iii) *Sonata No. 2 in B flat min., Op. 35: Funeral march; Waltzes Nos.* (vii) *1 in E flat (Grand valse brillante), Op. 18;* (xi) *6 in D flat (Minute), Op. 64/1;* (vii) *7 in C sharp min., Op. 64/2.*
(B) **(*) EMI CfP CD-CFP 6020 [(M) id.]. (i) Garrick Ohlsson; (ii) Polish RSO, Maksymiuk; (iii) Andrei Gavrilov; (iv) Moura Lympany; (v) John Ogdon; (vi) Andrea Lucchesini; (vii) Witold Malcuzynski; (viii) Daniel Adni; (ix) Maurizio Pollini; (x) Rafael Orozco; (xi) Dmitri Alexeev.

A very well-planned recital (except perhaps for the isolated concerto slow movement), highlighted by some excellent performances and offering consistently good recording. Malcuzynski gets the programme off to a particularly good start with a sparkling account of the *Grande valse brillante*, and Gavrilov's contributions are all distinctive, particularly his arresting accounts of Chopin's famous *Funeral march* and the brilliant *Revolutionary Etude* which follows. John Ogdon makes rather heavy going of the *Fantasie-impromptu*, but there are no other real disappointments, except perhaps the absence of more *Nocturnes*. However, there is plenty of romantic light and shade, and the recital concludes resoundingly with Pollini's '*Heroic' Polonaise in A flat major*.

Andante spianato et Grande polonaise brillante, Op. 22; Ballades Nos. 1, Op. 23; 4, Op. 52; Barcarolle, Op. 60; Etudes: in G flat, Op. 10/5; in C sharp min., Op. 25/7; Polonaise-fantaisie, Op. 61; Waltz in A flat, Op. 69/1.
(M) *** RCA GD 87752 [7752-2-RG]. Vladimir Horowitz.

All these performances derive from live recitals. The performances are fabulous; to the end of his career Horowitz's technique was transcendental and his insights remarkable. There is much excitement – but even more that is unforgettably poetic, and not a bar is predictable. With the sound so realistic, his presence is very tangible.

Andante spianato & Grande polonaise brillante, Op. 22; Ballade No. 3 in A flat, Op. 47; Fantaisie in F min., Op. 49; Polonaise-fantaisie in A flat, Op. 81; Sonata No. 3 in B min., Op. 58.
(M) ** Decca 452 308-2 [id.]. Wilhelm Kempff.

Barcarolle in F sharp, Op. 60; Berceuse in D flat, Op. 57; Impromptus Nos. 1 in A flat, Op. 29; 2 in F sharp, Op. 26; 3 in G flat, Op. 51; Fantaisie-impromptu in C sharp min., Op. 66; Nocturne in B, Op. 9/3; Scherzo No. 3 in C sharp min., Op. 39; Sonata No. 2 in B flat min. (Funeral march), Op. 35.
(M) Decca ** 452 307-2 [id.]. Wilhelm Kempff.

Reissued in Decca's Classic Sound series, these Kempff recordings from February 1958 were among the last he made for Decca before switching back to the DG label. He was 62 at that time and was virtually unknown on the London musical scene, although already his mono DG records of the Beethoven sonatas had established his European reputation. His readings of Chopin are very personal and individual. In Chopin performances we have come to expect a technical brilliance that in all honesty Kempff could no longer provide, although his musical fluency tends to cover up the technical smudges. He is at his finest in the two sonatas, and it is a pity that Decca chose not to couple them together as on the original LP, for somehow the very scale of these works seems to inspire him to the sort of concentration that invariably marks his Beethoven performances. The first theme of the first movement of the *Funeral march Sonata*, for example, has great delicacy and clarity, but this does not make for a small, prettified effect, for underneath one can clearly feel the urgency of the playing. Then in the second subject Kempff plays with great romantic warmth but, unlike so many pianists, does not lose the pulse of the movement. In the funeral march itself his speed is rather faster than usual, but again this makes for a feeling of purpose in the insistent pulse. Only in the finale of the *Third Sonata* does he sound a little less than happy but, all told, these are wonderfully poetic readings, just such performances, one feels, as Clara Schumann might have given to her circle of intimate friends. Of the other pieces included in the first recital (452 307-2) it is the *Berceuse*, *Barcarolle* and *B major Nocturne* which stand out, where Kempff shows a natural feeling for the shading of a phrase, so that it sounds not like an 'interpretation' in inverted commas, but an inevitable part of the music. On the companion disc (the *B minor Sonata* apart), while there are some truly poetic moments – the *Andante spianato*, the opening of the *A flat Ballade* and the *F minor Fantaisie* – there are otherwise passages when the pianist seems unable to surmount the technical difficulties, and there is somehow not the sense of control which he provides in the sonatas. In the opening of the *Grande polonaise brillante* there is far too little brilliance and too much labouring, and in the *Fantaisie* the comparative absence of bravura is a drawback. But whatever Kempff does, he cannot fail to be interestingly individual: for this reason all these performances are refreshing and will provide enjoyment far longer than many a more immaculate recording.

Vanguard 'Alfred Brendel collection', Volume 2: *Andante spianato et Grande polonaise brillante, Op. 22; Polonaises Nos. 4 in C min., Op. 40/2; 5 in F sharp min., Op. 44; 6 in A flat, Op. 53; 7 (Polonaise-fantaisie), Op. 61.*
(M) ** Van. 08 9163 72. Brendel – LISZT: *Hungarian rhapsodies.* ***

Although not possessing a natural affinity for Chopin – the least effective piece here is the *Andante spianato* – nothing Brendel does is unstimulating, and these rather Schumannesque performances certainly have their interest. They were very well recorded (in 1968), and the natural piano-timbre, with a full resonant bass, has been expertly transferred to CD.

'Favourite piano works': Ballades Nos. 1 in G min., Op. 23; 3 in A flat, Op. 47; Barcarolle, Op. 60; Etudes: in E; in G flat (Black keys); in C min. (Revolutionary), Op. 10/3, 5 & 12; in A min. (Winter wind), Op. 25/11; Fantaisie-impromptu, Op. 66; Mazurkas: in B flat, Op. 7/1; in D, Op. 33/1; Nocturnes: in E flat, Op. 9/2; in F sharp min., Op. 15/2; in B, Op. 32/1; in F min., Op. 55/1; Polonaises: in A (Military), Op. 40/1; in A flat, Op. 53; Preludes: in D flat (Raindrop), Op. 28/15; in C sharp min., Op. 45; Scherzos Nos. 1 in B flat min., Op. 31; 3 in C sharp min., Op. 39; Waltzes: in E flat (Grande valse brillante), Op. 18; in A min., Op. 34/2; in D flat (Minute); in C sharp min., Op. 64/1-2; in A flat, Op. 69/1; in B min., Op. 69/2; in G flat, Op. 70/1.
(B) *** Decca Double 444 830-2 (2) [id.]. Vladimir Ashkenazy.

Most music-lovers would count themselves lucky to attend a recital offering the above programme, as effectively laid out as it is on these two discs and with a total playing time of 130 minutes. The first CD, which is an all-digital programme, opens commandingly with the *Grande valse brillante* and closes with the *Polonaise in A flat*; the second (an analogue collection, but of excellent technical quality) begins with the *A flat Ballade* and ends with the *Scherzo in C sharp minor*. Overall the recordings date from between 1972 and 1984. The two discs are offered for the price of one within a standard-width jewel case, centrally hinged.

Ballades Nos. 1 in G min., Op. 23; 3 in A flat, Op. 47; Barcarolle, Op.60; Etudes: in A flat; in F min.; in A min., Op. 25/1, 2 & 11; Nocturnes: in E flat, Op. 9/2; in F sharp, Op. 15/2; in D flat, Op. 27/2; Preludes: in A; in D flat (Raindrop), Op. 28/7 & 15; Waltzes: in D flat (Minute), Op. 64/1; in E min., Op. posth.
(B) **(*) Decca Dig. 448 244-2; *448 244-4* [(M) id. import]. Jorge Bolet.

There is some really lovely playing from Jorge Bolet in this recital, assembled from recordings made between 1985 and 1987, though there is also a certain want of youthful fire. Bolet is happiest when he is at his most reflective and contemplative, less so when in the *Ballades* the music calls for more abandon. He brings keen musical insights to this music, but he is at his best in the *Barcarolle* and the quieter *Nocturnes* and the more inward-looking *Preludes*. The recording is in every way first class, and this is surely an ideal recital to relax to in the late evening.

'The best of Chopin': Ballades Nos. (i) *1 in G min., Op. 23;* (ii) *4 in F min., Op. 52;* (iii) *Barcarolle in F sharp min.;* (iv) *Berceuse, Op. 57;* (v) *Etudes, Op. 10/3, 5 & 12; Op. 25/1 & 9; Impromptus Nos.* (vi) *1 in A min., Op. 29;* (iii) *3 in G flat, Op. 51;* (vi) *4 (Fantaisie-impromptu), Op. 66;* (v) *3 Mazurkas, Op. 59;* (iii) *3 Mazurkas, Op. 63; Nocturnes Nos.* (ii) *8 in D flat, Op. 27/2;* (iii) *17 in B; 18 in E, Op. 62/1–2;* (vii) *Polonaises Nos. 6 in A flat, Op. 53;* (iii) *7 (Polonaise-fantaisie), Op. 61.* (v) *Preludes, Op. 28/4, 7, 9 & 15;* (iv) *Scherzo No. 2 in B flat min., Op. 31; Sonata No. 2 in B flat: Funeral march* (only). (viii) *Waltzes: Nos. 5 in A flat, Op. 42; 6 in D flat; 7 in C sharp min., Op. 64/1–2.*
(B) **(*) Ph. Duo Analogue/Dig. 446 145-2 (2) [(M) id. import]. (i) Harasiewicz; (ii) Arrau; (iii) Kovacevich; (iv) Orozco; (v) Magaloff; (vi) Davidovich; (vii) Cziffra; (viii) Kocsis.

'The Best of Chopin' is a hard sobriquet to live up to, but what makes the Philips Duo compilation distinctive is that at its heart is an outstanding complete 49-minute continuing recital which Stephen Kovacevich recorded in 1972. The opening bars of his *Barcarolle in F sharp minor* immediately establish this as Chopin playing of the highest order, and the two following Opus 62 *Nocturnes*, in *B major* and *E major*, are equally poetic. Here Kovacevich shows it is possible to adopt very spacious tempi and spin magic in every bar. Then comes the *Third Impromptu in G flat* and three engagingly contrasted *Mazurkas*, Op. 63, and the recital ends with a wonderfully imaginative account of the *Polonaise-fantaisie*, Op. 61, full of exquisite touches. The other performances are all reliable, especially those from Nikita Magaloff who has his own insights to offer, though Zoltán Kocsis treats his three *Waltzes* primarily as opportunities for dazzling bravura display. Arrau contributes a characterful *Nocturne in D flat*, Op. 27, No. 2, but here, as in his *F minor Ballade*, the playing seems too considered; and Adam Harasiewicz subsequently demonstrates just how it can be done with a romantically impulsive *Ballade in G minor*. The programme ends with Cziffra in impressive form in the *A flat Polonaise*, Op. 53. Good sound throughout; although the recordings were made over a long period, between 1962 and 1982, the consistency of quality is remarkable.

Ballade No. 1 in G min., Op. 23; Barcarolle, Op. 60; Fantaisie-impromptu, Op. 66; Mazurkas: in B flat, Op. 7/1; in D, Op. 33/2; Nocturnes: in E flat, Op. 9/2; in F sharp, Op. 15/2; in D flat, Op. 27/2; in G min., Op. 37/1; Polonaises: in A (Military), Op. 40/1; in A flat, Op. 53; Waltzes: in A flat, Op. 34/1; in D flat (Minute); in C sharp min., Op. 64/1–2.
(M) *** RCA GD 87725 [Basic 100 09026 61717-2]. Artur Rubinstein.

An outstanding mid-priced recital – there is no more distinguished miscellaneous Chopin collection in the catalogue – with 14 contrasted pieces, well programmed. The recording is surprisingly consistent and Rubinstein's inimitable touch gives great pleasure. Particularly memorable is the *G minor Ballade*, coaxing and dazzling by turns.

Ballade No. 1 in G min.; Berceuse in D flat; Etudes, Op. 10/1, 5, 6, & 12 (Revolutionary); Impromptu No. 1 in A flat, Op. 29; Mazurkas: in B flat, Op. 7/1; in C, Op. 67/3; in A min., Op. 68/2; in A flat, Op. posth.; Polonaise No. 6 in A flat, Op. 53; Scherzos No. 3 in C sharp min.; 4 in E, Op. 54; Waltzes Nos. 3 in A min., Op. 34/2; 14 in E min., Op. posth.
(B) **(*) DG Classikon 439 406-2; *439 406-4* [(M) id. import]. Tamás Vásáry.

An excellent bargain recital, compiled for DG's Classikon label from Vásáry's mid-1960s recordings. The layout is attractive, opening poetically with the *G minor Ballade* and *Berceuse*, ranging through the *Waltzes*, *Etudes*, *Scherzos* (very well done) and *Mazurkas*, and ending with the *A flat Polonaise*. But why no *Nocturnes*? The sound is a fraction dry but firm and believable. The documentation – which begins on the front of the liner-leaflet – is impressive.

Ballade No. 1 in G min.; Fantasy impromptu, Op. 66; Mazurkas: in B flat, Op. 7/1; in D, Op. 33/2; Nocturnes: in B flat min.; in E flat, Op. 9/1–2; in C min., Op. 48/1; Polonaises: in A, Op. 40/1; in F sharp min., Op. 44; Waltzes: in E min; in E flat, Op. 18.
(B) ** Tring Dig. TRP 087 [(M) id. import]. Ronan O'Hora.

The most commanding performance here is the *Ballade in G minor*, its romantic impulse finely judged. The *B flat minor Nocturne*, too, is beautifully played, and the *Waltzes* and *Mazurkas* show that Ronan O'Hora has a nice feeling for Chopinesque rhythmic nuance. However, in the *C minor* and (especially) the famous *E flat Nocturnes*, his hesitant rubato seems over-thoughtful and not completely spontaneous. The *Polonaises* are played without barnstorming and could effectively be more extrovert, although the *A major* is quite strong and certainly enjoyably robust. Good recording.

'Favourites': Ballade No. 1 in G min., Op. 23; Fantaisie-impromptu, Op. 66; Mazurkas: in B flat, Op. 7/1; in D, Op. 33/2; Nocturnes: in E flat, Op. 9/2; in F sharp, Op. 15/2; in B, Op. 32/1; Polonaise in A flat, Op. 53; Scherzo in B flat min., Op. 31; Waltzes: in E flat (Grande valse brillante), Op. 18; in A min., Op. 34/2; in A flat; B min., Op. 69/1–2; in G flat, Op. 70/1.
(M) *** Decca Dig. 417 798-2; *417 798-4*. Vladimir Ashkenazy.

An exceptionally attractive recital, with many favourites, played with Ashkenazy's customary poetic flair and easy brilliance. The digital recordings were made at various times during the early 1980s but match surprisingly well: the sound has striking realism and presence.

Ballade No. 3 in A flat, Op. 47; Barcarolle in F sharp min., Op. 60; Etudes: in E (Tristesse), Op. 10/3; in G flat (Black key), Op. 10/5; in C min. (Revolutionary), Op. 10/12; in A min. (Winter wind), Op. 25/11; Nocturne in F min., Op. 55/1; Polonaise in A, Op. 40/1; Scherzo No. 3 in C sharp min., Op. 39; Preludes: in D flat (Raindrop), Op. 28/15; in C sharp min., Op. 45; Waltzes: in D flat (Minute); in C sharp min., Op. 64/1–2.
(M) ** Decca 452 623-2; *452 623-4*. Vladimir Ashkenazy.

This is an admirable collection in many ways, and the performances are self-recommending. But with only 57 minutes' playing time, readers might be better advised to choose the Double Decca set, above, which costs not much more and contains a great deal more music.

Ballade No. 3 in A flat, Op. 47; Barcarolle in F sharp, Op. 60; Fantaisie in F min., Op. 49; Fantaisie-impromptu, Op. 66; Nocturnes Nos. 2 in E flat, Op. 9/2; 5 in F sharp, Op. 15/2; Prelude in D flat, Op. 28/15; Waltzes Nos. 7 in C sharp min., Op. 64/2; 9 in A flat, Op. 69/1.
(M) *** Ph. (IMS) 420 655-2. Claudio Arrau.

A fine recital, showing both poetry and the thoughtful seriousness which distinguishes Arrau's Chopin, which is West rather than East European in spirit. The CD is admirably transferred.

'My favourite Chopin': Ballade No. 3 in A flat, Op. 47; Etudes: in E, Op. 10/3; in A min. (Winter wind), Op. 25/11. Fantaisie in F min., Op. 49; Nocturne in B, Op. 62/1; Polonaise No. 6 in A flat; Scherzo No. 3 in C sharp min., Op. 39; Waltz in C sharp min., Op. 64/2.
(M) *(*) RCA 09026 68813-2 [id.]. Van Cliburn.

Dating from 1961, this was Van Cliburn's first solo piano record. It proves to be one of his less endearing recordings. There are poetic moments of course – in the *B major Nocturne* and at the opening of the *A flat Ballade* for instance – but too often his approach to Chopin seems wilful and self-conscious, and notably so in the *Fantaisie in F minor*.

Ballade No. 4 in F min., Op. 54; Barcarolle, Op. 60; Nocturne in C min., Op. 48/1; Polonaise-fantaisie in A flat, Op. 61; Scherzo No. 4 in E, Op. 54; Piano sonata No. 3 in B min., Op. 58.
(B) *** EMI Debut CDZ5 69701-2 [id.]. Nelson Goerner.

A valuable release in the welcome EMI Debut series. Nelson Goerner, still in his twenties, comes from Argentina and is a pianist of enormous talent and flair. This is playing of strong personality and poetic feeling. In every way a distinguished recital, and very well recorded too.

Ballade No. 4 in F min., Op. 52; Fantaisie in F min., Op. 49; Mazurkas: in G; in A flat; in C sharp min., Op. 50/1–3; Nocturnes: in D flat, Op. 27/2; in E, Op. 62/2; Polonaise in A flat, Op. 53; Scherzo No. 4 in E, Op. 54; Waltz in C sharp min., Op. 64/2.
(M) *** Van. Dig. 99122 [id.]. Nikolai Lugansky.

Nikolai Lugansky, a pupil of Tatiana Nikolaieva, won first prize at the 1994 Tchaikovsky Competition and made a great impression on his recent London appearance with the Russian National Orchestra and Mikhail Pletnev. His accounts of the Rachmaninov *Third* and *Fourth Concertos* on Vanguard (see below) were selfless, full of character and unfailingly musical throughout, and indeed much the same verdict can be returned on this recital. There is nothing ostentatious or in the least sensational about him; he is a refined and natural artist whose playing gives much pleasure and at its best is touched by distinction.

'Chopin masterpieces': (i) *Etudes: Op. 10, Nos. 3 in E; 5 in G flat; 12 in C min. (Revolutionary);* (ii) *Op. 25, No. 9 in G flat;* (iii) *Fantaisie-impromptu, Op. 66; Nocturnes: Nos. 2 in E flat, Op. 9/2;* (ii) *10 in A flat, Op. 32/2;* (iv) *Polonaises: Nos. 3 in A, Op. 40/1;* (v) *6 in A flat (Heroic), Op. 53;* (vi) *Preludes, Op. 28, Nos. 7 in A; 20 in C min.*; (vii) *Waltzes Nos. 1 in E flat (Grande valse brillante), Op. 18; 6 in D flat (Minute); 7 in C sharp min., Op. 64/1–2.*
(B) *** CfP CD-CFP 4501 [(M) id. import]. (i) Anievas; (ii) Adni; (iii) Ogdon; (iv) Ohlsson; (v) Pollini; (vi) Orozco; (vii) Malcuzynski.

EMI first made this compilation available in 1974 and it is as successful today as it was then. The programme includes many favourites and the selection has been made with skill. The recital opens and closes with a polonaise (Pollini is in splendid form in the final item). But this excellent roster of pianists never disappoints and the quality is consistently good. Malcuzynski's contribution is among the highlights: his *Grande valse brillante* has a characteristic glitter, while other attractive performances include the *Sylphides Nocturne in A flat* and Daniel Adni's *'Butterfly' Study*, which takes wing with charming grace. The transfers are all well managed.

Cilea, Francesco (1866–1950)

Adriana Lecouvreur (complete).
(M) **(*) Decca (IMS) 430 256-2 (2) [id.]. Tebaldi, Simionato, Del Monaco, Fioravanti, St Cecilia, Rome, Ac. Ch. & O, Capuana.

Tebaldi's consistently rich singing misses some of the flamboyance of Adriana's personality but in her characterization both *Io son l'umile ancella* and *Poveri fiori* are lyrically very beautiful. One wishes that Del Monaco had been as reliable as Tebaldi but, alas, there are some coarse moments among the fine, plangent top notes. Simionato is a little more variable than usual but a tower of strength nevertheless. The recording is outstanding for its time (early 1960s), brilliant and atmospheric.

L'arlesiana (complete).
(M) ** EMI CMS5 66762-3 (2) [CDMB 66762]. Elena Zilio, Péter Kelen, Maria Spacagna, Barry Anderson, Hungarian State Ch. & O, Charles Rosekrans.

This recording of *L'arlesiana*, made in Budapest in 1991, fills an important gap in the catalogue, bringing out the easy lyricism of this adaptation of the original Daudet story, which earlier inspired Bizet to write his incidental music to the play, *L'arlésienne*. As an opera story the oddity is that the girl from Arles herself, who wreaks such havoc on the life of the innocent Federico, is never seen or heard. The principal female role is for Federico's mother, Rosa, warmly sung in this performance by Elena Zilio, and Barry Anderson is equally strong and firm in the role of Baldassare, the old shepherd who acts as the understanding adviser to all the others. The role of the hero, Federico, originally created by the young Caruso, is taken by Péter Kelen, a tenor inclined to overdo the histrionics, often using his tenor with restraint, as in the most celebrated aria, *E la solita storia*, but then indulging in excessively emotional outbursts. The conductor, Charles Rosekrans, brings out the warmth of the lyricism, but the dramatic thrust is not always strong enough. A useful stop-gap at mid-price.

Cimarosa, Domenico (1749–1801)

(i) *Requiem* (revised Vittorio Negri); *Concertante in G for flute, oboe and orchestra* (arr. Holliger).
(M) *** Ph. Analogue/Dig. 442 657-2. (i) Ameling, Finnilä, Van Vrooman, Widmer, Montreux Festival Ch., Lausanne CO, Negri; (ii) Nicolet, Holliger, ASMF, Sillito.

Cimarosa's *Requiem* is an impressive, even formidable work. The singing here by the Montreux Festival Choir conveys a feeling of spacious eloquence and it is a pity that the recording is rather too reverberant to produce an incisive edge to the choral sound; its warm atmosphere, however, adds to the feeling of weight and serenity. The soloists are very good, though some might find the tenor, Richard van Vrooman, a trifle histrionic in the *Preces meae*. Elly Ameling's lovely singing more than compensates, and the bass, Kurt Widmer, is impressive in the *Inter oves*. Vittorio Negri secures excellent playing from the Lausanne orchestra, and the CD transfer, as usual with Philips, greatly enhances a 1969 recording which does not sound dated. What makes this reissue especially attractive is the inclusion of Cimarosa's best-known concertante work. This engaging *Concertante* is aptly operatic in feeling. The music is not without substance, but the singing lyrical secondary theme in the first movement and the interplay of flute and oboe in the *Largo* show a distinct vocal style. With such superb playing from Nicolet and Holliger, nicely turned accompaniments and first-rate digital recording, this CD, with its attractive coupling, is most entertaining.

Il maestro di cappella (complete).
(M) *** Decca 433 036-2 (2). Fernando Corena, ROHCG O, Argeo Quadri – DONIZETTI: *Don Pasquale*. ***

Corena's classic assumption of the role of incompetent Kapellmeister has been out of the catalogue for too long. Corena shows complete mastery of the buffo bass style, and he is so little troubled by the florid passages that he can relax in the good humour. The vintage 1960 recording is clear and atmospheric, with the directional effects naturally conveyed.

Clementi, Muzio (1752–1832)

(i) *Piano concerto in C. Symphonies: in B flat & D, Op. 18; Nos. 1 in C; 2 in D; 3 (Great National) in G; 4 in D; Minuetto pastorale; Overtures in C & D.*
(M) ** ASV Dig. CDDCS 322 (3) [id.]. (i) Pietro Spada; Philh. O, Francesco D'Avalos.

Clementi, publisher as well as composer, tragically failed to put most of his symphonic output into print. Six of his 20 symphonies survive, and these are here made available thanks to the researches of Pietro Spada. The four numbered works come from the first decade of the nineteenth century. They are all scored for much larger forces than the Op. 18 set and even include trombones. Their musical content explains Clementi's high reputation in his lifetime as a composer for the orchestra, not just the piano. If the *Great National Symphony* is the most immediately striking, with *God save the King* ingeniously worked into the third movement so that its presence does not emerge until the very end, the other works are all boldly individual. The *Fourth* is a remarkably powerful symphonic statement which brings some striking modulations, and there is some unexpected chromatic writing (unexpected, that is, to those who are not familiar with the famous set of the piano sonatas that Horowitz recorded). Moreover Clementi's use of the orchestra is often very imaginative, though his indebtedness to the Haydn of the *London Symphonies* is very striking.

Symphonies Nos. 1 in C; 2 in D; 3 in G (Great National); 4 in D.
(B) *** Erato/Warner Ultima 3984 21039-2 (2) [(M) id. import]. Philh. O, Claudio Scimone.

The performances by Claudio Scimone and the Philharmonia Orchestra are strong and sympathetic, and the recording (made in London's Henry Wood Hall in 1978) is full, resonant and natural, bringing weight as well as freshness. Now that Erato have accommodated these so economically both in price and in space on the shelf, they deserve a warm recommendation.

Piano sonatas: in F min., Op. 14/3; in F sharp min., Op. 26/2; in C (quasi concerto), Op. 33/3; in G min., Op. 34/2; Rondo (from Sonata, Op. 47/2).
(M) *** RCA GD 87753 [7753-2-RC]. Vladimir Horowitz (piano).

These electrifying performances from the 1950s show a Clementi of greater substance and sterner mettle than the composer we thought we knew and, though the piano sound is shallow by the side of most up-to-date recordings, the quality is a great improvement upon either of the vinyl transfers with which we have compared it.

Piano sonatas: in B flat, Op. 24/2; in G; in F sharp min., Op. 25/2 & 5; in D, Op. 37/2; 6 Progressive sonatinas, Op. 36.
(BB) *** Naxos Dig. 8.550452 [id.]. Balázs Szokolay.

Balázs Szokolay is the son of the Hungarian composer Zoltán Szokolay whose colourful opera, *Blood Wedding*, based on Lorca, scored something of a stir in the 1970s. Balázs made a strong impression at the Leeds Piano Competition some years back and we have much admired his Naxos records of some of the Grieg *Lyric pieces* (see below). This Clementi anthology is hardly less successful and his playing inspires enthusiasm. Let us hope he will go on to record some more of this master's underrated keyboard work. Decent recording; excellent value.

Coates, Eric (1886–1958)

Ballad; By the sleepy lagoon; London suite; The Three Bears (phantasy); *The Three Elizabeths* (suite).
(M) *** ASV Dig. CDWHL 2053. East of England O, Malcolm Nabarro.

Nabarro has the full measure of Coates's leaping allegros and he plays the famous marches with crisp buoyancy. *The Three Bears* sparkles humorously, as it should; only in *By the sleepy lagoon* does one really miss a richer, more languorous string-texture. Excellent, bright recording, and the price is right.

(i) *By the sleepy lagoon;* (ii) *Calling all workers* (march); (iii) *Cinderella* (phantasy); *From meadow to Mayfair: suite; London suite; London again suite;* (i) *The Merrymakers overture;* (iii) *Music everywhere* (march); (iv) *Saxo-rhapsody;* (i) *The Three Bears* (phantasy); (ii) *The Three Elizabeths* (suite); (i) *The three men* (suite): *Man from the sea.* (iii) *Wood nymphs* (valsette).
(B) *** CfP CD-CFPD 4456 (2) [id.]. (i) LSO, Mackerras; (ii) CBSO, Kilbey; (iii) RLPO, Groves; (iv) with Jack Brymer.

This collection of the music of Eric Coates includes, besides some very lively performances from Sir Charles Mackerras, several outstanding ones from the CBSO under Reginald Kilbey, who proves the ideal Coates conductor. Although the CDs bring out the brittleness in the upper range, notably in the Groves recordings, the ambient effect helps to prevent too great an imbalance towards the treble.

By the sleepy lagoon; London suite; London again suite; London Bridge march.
(B) *** Millennium UMD 80395. Eric Johnson and his O – SULLIVAN: *The Gondoliers* etc.: excerpts. **

Eric Coates, a splendid tunesmith, was a natural provider of catchy signature-tunes, and here are two: *By the sleepy lagoon*, still in use for *Desert Island Discs,* and the composer's early success, the *Knightsbridge march*, which served to introduce the BBC's wartime interview programme, *In Town Tonight*. Eric Johnson presents all the marches here with proper panache and a nice broadening for the final reprise, and he finds plenty of life in the evocations of *Covent Garden* and *Oxford Street*. But what is the more striking is the degree of romantic expansiveness he brings to the central slow movements of the two *London suites*: *Westminster*, with its famous chimes, and the unexpectedly romantic *Langham Place*. He is helped by an ardent orchestral response and a fullness of string-sound rare in recordings of Coates's music, plus plenty of weight from the brass. Most enjoyable.

The 4 Centuries: suite; The Jester at the wedding: ballet suite; The 7 Dwarfs.
(M) **(*) ASV Dig. CDWHL 2075 [id.]. East of England O, Malcolm Nabarro.

For their second anthology of music by Eric Coates, the orchestra based in Nottinghamshire (where the composer was born) offer a particularly delectable account of *The Jester at the wedding ballet suite. The Four Centuries* is a masterly and engaging pastiche of styles from four different periods, and again it receives a performance of some subtlety, although at times one wishes for a more opulent sound from the violins, and the closing jazzy evocation of the 1930s and 1940s could be more uninhibitedly rumbustious. *The Seven Dwarfs* is an early work (1930), a ballet written for a short-lived London revue. It is nicely coaxed back into life and the recording is very good.

Four ways suite: Northwards; Eastwards. London suite.
(M) **(*) Mercury 434 376-2 [id.]. London Pops O, Frederick Fennell – Leroy ANDERSON: *Collection.* ***

Polished, spirited and sympathetic performances from Fennell of Coates's best-known suite, including what was once the most popular march of all (*Knightsbridge*), though perhaps these days it is upstaged by *The Dambusters.* The novelty is the inclusion of the two engaging excerpts from the *Four ways suite*, winningly played, with pleasing rhythmic character. The dry, close, studio-ish recording is most effective here.

The Three Elizabeths (suite).
(M) **(*) Mercury 434 330-2 [id.]. London Pops O, Fennell – GRAINGER: *Country gardens* etc. **

Fennell's performance is notable for its spirit and polish: the closing march, *The Youth of Britain*, sounds particularly fresh and alert, while the slow movement is nicely expressive. But the 1965 Mercury recording, made in Watford Town Hall, though fuller and with a more attractive ambience than the coupled Grainger items, still lacks something in expansiveness, though not clarity of detail.

Coleridge-Taylor, Samuel (1875–1912)

Scenes from The Song of Hiawatha (complete).
(B) *** Decca Dig. 458 591-2 (2) [id.]. Helen Field, Arthur Davies, Bryn Terfel, WNO Ch. & O, Kenneth Alwyn.

Coleridge-Taylor's choral trilogy based on Longfellow's epic poem had its first performance under the composer in the Royal Albert Hall in 1900. It took a while to catch on, but every year from 1924 until the outbreak of war in 1939 it was given a staged presentation at the same venue. Often nearly a thousand costumed 'Red Indian' performers came to enjoy themselves hugely, singing under the baton of their tribal chief, Sir Malcolm Sargent. Part One is still regularly performed by choral societies in the north of England, though not usually with Indian costumes! The reasons for the neglect of Parts Two and Three, *The Death of Minnehaha* and *Hiawatha's Departure*, are made only too clear by this complete recording: there is a distinct falling-off in the composer's inspiration, so fresh and spontaneously tuneful in Part One. Indeed, when the main theme of *Hiawatha's Wedding Feast* returns in Part Three with the words 'From his place rose Hiawatha', one realizes how memorable it is, compared with what surrounds it. Of course the choral writing is always pleasingly lyrical and makes enjoyable listening. Part Two has plenty of drama, and towards the end Helen Field has a memorably beautiful solo passage, which she sings radiantly, echoed by the chorus, 'Wahonomin! Wahonomin! Would that I had perished for you.' There is also an almost Wagnerian apotheosis at the actual moment of the Farewell, which is sung and played here with compelling grandiloquence. Kenneth Alwyn is completely at home in this music. (By coincidence, he attended the same school in Croydon as the composer – though not, of course, at the same time!) He directs a freshly spontaneous account and has the advantage of excellent soloists (including an early appearance on CD by Bryn Terfel as Hiawatha, now featured prominently on the front of the reissue), though the Welsh Opera Choir do not seem at home in the idiom. The recording was made in the rather intractable Brangwyn Hall, Swansea, and the engineers have put their microphones fairly close to the performers. The result, while vivid, lacks the glowing ambient effect of the Royal Albert Hall, which would have been a much better venue.

(i) *Hiawatha's wedding feast. The Bamboula* (rhapsodic dance).
(B) *** EMI Eminence Dig. CD-EMX 2276 [(M) id. import]. (i) Rolfe Johnson, Bournemouth Ch.; Bournemouth SO, Alwyn.

In its day *Hiawatha's wedding feast* blew a fresh breeze through a turgid British Victorian choral tradition; since then, the work has been kept alive in fairly frequent performances by amateur choral societies. This reissue is first class in every way, and Kenneth Alwyn secures a vigorous and committed contribution from his Bournemouth forces, with Anthony Rolfe Johnson an excellent soloist in the famous *Onaway! Awake, beloved!* The music throughout is delightfully melodious and extremely well written for the voices. *The Bamboula* makes an agreeable if inconsequential encore.

Conus, Julius (1869–1942)

Violin concerto.
(M) *** EMI CDM5 66060-2. Perlman, Pittsburgh O, Previn – BARTOK: *Violin concerto No. 2;* SINDING: *Suite.* ***

Julius Conus, of French extraction from a family of musicians, wrote his *Violin concerto* in Moscow in 1896–7, a ripely romantic piece in one continuous movement with only a few memorable ideas but with luscious violin writing, while the lyrical theme of the opening movement blossoms persuasively. It was a favourite of Heifetz's and needs a powerful, persuasive advocate to sound anything more than trivial. Here the opening is very commanding and Perlman's first entry quite magical; he shows his supreme mastery in giving the piece new intensity, helped by fine playing from Previn and the Pittsburgh orchestra. The 1979 recording is vivid and, if the violin is very close, Perlman's tone is honeyed; the Pittsburgh hall ensures orchestral weight and provides an attractive background warmth.

Copland, Aaron (1900–90)

(i) *An outdoor overture;* (ii) *Fanfare for the common man;* (ii; iii) *Lincoln portrait;* (iv) *The Red Pony* (film score): suite; (i) *Rodeo: 3 dance episodes.*
(B) ** Sony SBK 62401; *SBT 62401* [id.]. (i) Cleveland Pops O, Louis Lane; (ii) Phd. O, Ormandy; (iii) with Adlai Stevenson; (iv) St Louis SO, Previn.

An attractive if not distinctive permutation of Copland works, including the underrated *Red Pony* film-score, in which Previn is very persuasive. Louis Lane and the Cleveland Pops give ebullient accounts of *An outdoor overture* and *Rodeo*, but Adlai Stevenson is a rather laid-back narrator for the *Lincoln portrait.* The recordings are forwardly balanced and resonantly larger than life.

(i) *Appalachian spring* (ballet) *suite; Billy the Kid: ballet suite;* (ii) *Clarinet concerto;* (i) *Danzón Cubano; Fanfare for the common man; John Henry; Letter from home;* (i; iv) *Lincoln portrait;* (iii) *Music for movies;* (i) *Our Town; An Outdoor overture; Quiet city; Rodeo (4 Dance episodes);* (iii) *El Salón México;* (i) *Symphony No. 3;* (v) *Las agachadas.*
(M) *** Sony SM3K 46559 (3) [S3K 46559]. (i) LSO; (ii) Benny Goodman, Columbia Symphony Strings; (iii) New Philh. O; (iv) with Henry Fonda; (v) New England Conservatory Ch.; composer.

Sony here offer a comprehensive anthology of the major orchestral works, ballet suites and film scores dating from Copland's vintage period, 1936–48. The composer directs with unrivalled insight throughout.

The remastering for CD is done most skilfully, retaining the ambience of the originals, while achieving more refined detail.

(i) *Appalachian spring* (ballet): *suite; Fanfare for the common man; An outdoor overture;* (ii) *3 Latin-American sketches;* (i) *Rodeo (4 Dance episodes);* (ii) *El Salón México.*
(M) *** Sony Theta SMK 60133 [id.]. (i) LSO; (ii) New Philh. O; composer.

This generously filled (79 minutes) CD is drawn from the composer's more comprehensive anthology above. It is eminently recommendable. Copland's own account of *Appalachian spring* is particularly evocative and beautifully recorded.

Appalachian spring (ballet) *suite.*
(M) *** DG Dig. 439 528-2 [431 048-2]. LAPO, Bernstein – BARBER: *Adagio for strings* ***; GERSHWIN: *Rhapsody in blue.* **(*)

Bernstein's DG version of *Appalachian spring* was recorded at a live performance, and the conductor communicates his love for the score in a strong yet richly lyrical reading, and the compulsion of the music-making is obvious. The recording is close but not lacking in atmosphere, and it sounds extremely vivid. It is here recoupled with his rather less recommendable second recording of Gershwin's *Rhapsody in blue.*

Appalachian spring (concert version); *Billy the Kid: suite; El Salón México; Fanfare for the common man; Rodeo: Hoe-down.*
(B) *(*) Tring Dig. TRPO 40 [(M) id.]. RPO, Philip Ellis.

The RPO play well, if without that special transatlantic syncopated bite in the popular dance rhythms, and they are richly and atmospherically recorded. *Appalachian spring* is suitably evocative, with good detail and a touching closing section, and (apart from a tiny slip of ensemble near the opening) the *Fanfare* is arresting and spectacularly resonant. The characterization of the other music is vivid; but while Bernstein's NYPO collection is available the main attraction of this disc is its low cost.

Appalachian spring (ballet): *suite; Billy the Kid* (ballet) *suite; Fanfare for the common man; Rodeo (four dance episodes).*
(BB) **(*) Naxos Dig. 8.550282 [id.]. Slovak RSO (Bratislava), Gunzenhauser.

One does not expect a Czech orchestra, excellent as the Bratislava players are, to achieve quite the exhilarating rhythmic precision that Bernstein and the NYPO bring to this music, but they play with such spontaneous enjoyment in *Rodeo* and *Billy the Kid* that one cannot help but respond. Gunzenhauser, a fine conductor of Czech music, is equally at home in Copland's folksy, cowboy idiom and all this music has plenty of colour and atmosphere. If some of the detail in *Appalachian spring* is less sharply etched than with Dorati, the closing pages are tenderly responsive. The recording is admirably colourful and vivid with a fine hall ambience, and the spectacle of the *Fanfare for the common man* is worth anybody's money. A bargain.

(i) *Appalachian spring;* (ii) *Billy the Kid* (suite); *Rodeo* (suite).
(BB) *** RCA Navigator 74321 21297-2 [(M) id. import]. (i) Boston SO, composer; (ii) Morton Gould and his Orchestra.

Copland's first recording of *Appalachian spring* was recorded in Boston in 1959 and is alone worth the modest price of this disc. The performance has an appealing breadth and warmth of humanity, helped by the Symphony Hall resonance: the Shaker climax is wonderfully expansive. Morton Gould conducts the other two ballets with enormous zest and vitality, and 'his' orchestra play as if their very lives depended on it. The early (1957) stereo is a little dated but remains arrestingly spectacular and the quieter, evocative writing is haunting, distilling a special combination of tender warmth and underlying tension. The *Corral Nocturne* and wistful *Saturday night waltz* in *Rodeo* are especially fine, and here Gould also includes the *Honky-tonky interlude* on an appropriate piano. The closing *Hoe-down* is refreshingly folksy and has great rhythmic energy.

(i) *Appalachian spring* (ballet) *suite; Billy the Kid* (ballet) complete; (ii) *Danzón cubano; El salón México.*
(M) *** Mercury 434 301-2 [id.]. (i) LSO; (ii) Minneapolis SO, Antal Dorati.

Dorati pioneered the first stereo recording of the complete *Billy the Kid* ballet, and the 1961 Mercury LP caused a sensation on its first appearance for its precision of detail and brilliance of colour, while the generous acoustics of Watford Town Hall added ambient warmth. The gunshots (track 13) were and remain electrifying, with their clean percussive transients, while the LSO playing combines tremendous vitality and rhythmic power with genuine atmospheric tension. For the CD, earlier (1957) Minneapolis versions of the *Danzón cubano* and *El salón México* have been added. The recording is crisp and clean to suit his approach.

Appalachian spring: ballet suite; Billy the Kid: ballet suite; Rodeo: 4 dance episodes; Symphony No. 3: Fanfare for the common man.
✿ (M) *** Sony SMK 63082 [id.]. NYPO, Leonard Bernstein.

Bernstein recorded these ballet scores in the early 1960s when he was at the peak of his creative tenure with the NYPO, and we are fortunate that the recordings are so good, vivid, spacious and atmospheric. No one – not even the composer – has approached these performances for racy, rhythmic exuberance or for the tenderness and depth of nostalgia in the lyrical music, especially in the opening sequence of *Appalachian spring* and the *Corral nocturne* from *Rodeo*. The opening *Buckaroo holiday* and the final *Hoe-down* from the latter ballet, taken at a tremendous pace, have an unforgettable rhythmic bite and zest, with amazing precision of ensemble from the New York players, whose adrenalin is obviously running at unprecedented levels. The evocation of *The open prairie* in *Billy the Kid* is magical and the picture of a *Street in a frontier town* has a piquant charm, while the projection of the score's more strident moments brings a characteristic pungency. The *Fanfare for the common man* is not the original, commissioned in 1942 by Eugene Goossens for the Cincinnati Orchestra, but the composer's reworking, when he introduced it as a springboard for the finale of his *Third Symphony*. *Appalachian spring* (1961) and *Rodeo* (1960) were made at the Manhattan Center, and *Billy the Kid* in Symphony Hall, Boston, in 1959. The present remastering for the 'Bernstein Century' series has tingling presence.

(i) *Appalachian spring* (ballet) *suite;* (ii) *Ceremonial fanfare;* (iii) *Dance symphony; El salón México;* (i) *Fanfare for the common man;* (i; iv) *Lincoln portrait;* (v) *Music for movies;* (vi) *Quiet city;* (iii) *Rodeo: 4 Dance episodes;* (vii) *Old American songs* (excerpts): *Simple gifts; Ching-a-ring-chaw; Long time ago; I bought me a cat; At the river.*
(B) *** Decca Double Analogue/Dig. 448 261-2 (2) [id.]. (i) LAPO, Mehta; (ii) Philip Jones Brass Ens.; (iii) Detroit SO, Dorati; (iv) Gregory Peck; (v) L. Sinf., Elgar Howarth; (vi) ASMF, Marriner; (vii) Marilyn Horne, ECO, Carl Davis.

Mehta's performance of *Appalachian spring*, made for Decca in the late 1970s, is one of the most distinguished of several fine recordings here, which also included the spectacular *Fanfare for the common man* and the *Lincoln portrait*, with Gregory Peck a comparatively unhistrionic narrator who speaks Lincoln's prose with dignity and restraint. Dorati's performances of the *Dance symphony*, *El salón México* and *Rodeo* were digitally recorded in 1981. They are notable for their bright, extrovert brilliance, having evidently been chosen for their immediate, cheerful qualities. The playing demonstrates very clearly the degree of orchestral virtuosity available in Detroit, and the only reservation is that, somewhat surprisingly, Dorati's treatment of jazzy syncopations is rather literal, though it has undoubted idiomatic feeling. But as sound this is very impressive, and the performances have much vitality. The *Music for movies* was drawn together by the composer from his film scores for *The City*, *Of Mice and Men* (both 1939) and *Our Town* (1940). The evocative opening picture of the *New England Countryside* occupies the same musical world as *Appalachian spring*, and the jaunty third piece, *Sunday traffic*, has a marked choreographic feeling. Again fine playing from the London Sinfonietta under Elgar Howarth (though not perhaps as brightly idiomatic as with Dorati) and vivid recording. Marriner's account of *Quiet city* is second to none, but the highlight of the second CD is Marilyn Horne's delightful performances of five *Old American songs*: the rhythmic sparkle of *Ching-a-ring-chaw* and the charm of *I bought me a cat* contrasting with the moving simplicity of the closing *At the river*. Excellent value.

Appalachian spring (ballet) *suite; The Tender Land* (opera): *suite.*
(M) *** RCA 09026 61505-2 [id.]. Boston SO, composer – GOULD: *Fall River legend* etc. ***

(i) *Appalachian spring* (ballet) *suite; The Tender land* (excerpts); (ii) *Billy the Kid* (ballet) *suite;* (iii) *El salón México;* (ii) *Fanfare for the common man;* (iii) *Rodeo: Hoe-down.*
(M) *** [RCA Basic 100 09026 68020-2]. (i) Boston SO, composer; (ii) Phd. O, Ormandy; (iii) Boston Pops O, Fiedler.

The composer's first (1959) Boston recording of the *Appalachian spring suite* (also available less expensively, differently coupled – see above) has moments of special resonance, its atmospheric feeling at times quite profound, helped by splendid orchestral playing and the warm Boston acoustic. The suite from *The Tender Land* is also well worth having. We are given the *Love duet* virtually complete, the Party music from Act II and the quintet, *The promise of living* (all, of course, without voices). The 'Living Stereo' remastering by John Pfeiffer and his team creates the most vivid and full-bodied sound-picture.

As can be seen, these two recordings are also available (in the USA only) in RCA's Basic 100 series, more aptly coupled with excellent versions of more of Copland's music.

Billy the Kid: ballet suite and Waltz; Rodeo: 4 Dance episodes.

(B) *** Millennium Universal UMD 80396 [id.]. Utah SO, Maurice Abravanel – GROFE: *Grand Canyon suite*. ***

The enterprising Millennium label here brings another remarkable discovery from the earliest days of stereo, offering splendidly idiomatic performances and sound still approaching demonstration quality – helped by the glowing Utah acoustic. Abravanel's 1958 pioneering recordings of Copland's *Billy the Kid* and *Rodeo* ballet suites predate Bernstein's versions. The Utah performances are full of character and colour, with the woodwind playing often quite memorable, helped by the warmly atmospheric sound. If the *Gun Battle* in *Billy the Kid* does not quite match the famous Dorati Mercury version in sheer spectacle, and Bernstein achieves greater virtuosity with the NYPO in *Buckaroo holiday* and *Hoedown*, Abravanel's performances are still to be reckoned with and they include as a bonus the engaging *Waltz* from *Billy the Kid*, with its witty bassoon and trombone solos.

(i) *Billy the Kid* (ballet suite); (ii) *Piano sonata*.

(M) (***) RCA mono GD 60915 [60915-2]. (i) RCA Victor SO, Bernstein; (ii) Bernstein (piano) – BERNSTEIN: *On the Town: suite* etc. (***)

Bernstein got to know the music of *Billy the Kid* by sitting with the composer and playing the full score on the piano. He also learned the formidable *Sonata* as it was being written in 1941. Both performances are full of nervous energy and must be regarded as definitive.

(i; ii) *Piano concerto;* (iii) *Dance symphony;* (ii) *Music for the theatre;* (iii) *2 Pieces for string orchestra; Short symphony (Symphony No. 2); Statements; Symphonic ode;* (iv; ii) *Symphony for organ and orchestra*.

(M) *** Sony SM2K 47232 (2) [S2K 47232]. (i) Composer (piano); (ii) NYPO, Bernstein; (iii) LSO, composer; (iv) with E. Power Biggs.

This second Sony Copland collection covers early orchestral and concertante music written between 1922 and 1935 and is, if anything, more valuable than the first box. The 1923 *Rondino*, the second of his *Two Pieces for string orchestra*, is the earliest work here. The *Lento* is a totally memorable piece. The *Symphony for organ and orchestra* is a powerful and strikingly innovative work, dating from 1924. It is given an extremely idiomatic and responsive performance by Power Biggs, who is fully sensitive to its atmosphere, and Bernstein balances the overall sounds with great skill and a marvellous feeling for colour. The *Piano concerto* (1927) is both abrasive and strongly jazz-influenced. The pungently flamboyant *Symphonic ode*, commissioned by the Boston Symphony, helped the orchestra to celebrate its fiftieth anniversary: it was written between 1927 and 1929. The *Dance symphony* was completed that same year. The *Short symphony* dates from 1931–3; both works are full of originality and energy and are tautly constructed. *Statements* (1934–5), as the bald title suggests, is one of Copland's less expansive works, but its six vignettes, *Militant*, *Cryptic*, *Dogmatic*, *Subjective*, *Jingo* and *Prophetic*, reveal a compression of thought and sharpness of idea that are most refreshing. All these performances have a definitive authority combined with total spontaneity of response from the participants which makes them compelling listening, and the recordings – dating from between 1964 and 1967 – are very well engineered, extremely vivid in the excellent CD transfers.

Piano concerto.

(M) *** Van. 08.4029.71 [OVC 4029]. Earl Wild, Symphony of the Air, composer – MENOTTI: *Piano concerto*. **(*)

(M) **(*) Chandos CHAN 6580 [id.]. Gillian Lin, Melbourne SO, John Hopkins – BRITTEN: *Piano concerto*. **(*)

This Vanguard record, with a supreme piano virtuoso providing a glittering account of the piano part, is very recommendable. The 1961 recording is first rate.

Gillian Lin is undoubtedly successful in the Copland *Concerto*, bringing out the jazz element in this syncopated music. The 1978 stereo recording is well balanced and realistically transferred to CD. A thoroughly worthwhile mid-priced coupling.

(i–ii) *Piano concerto; Connotations for orchestra;* (iii) *El salón México;* (ii) *Music for the theatre* (suite).

(M) *** Sony SMK 60177 [id.]. (i) Composer (piano); (ii) NYPO; (iii) (mono) Columbia SO; Bernstein.

The present collection is drawn from the two sets listed above and below – except for *El salón México*, which was Bernstein's earlier mono recording and was made with the Columbia Symphony in 1951. It has great vitality and bite: no one coaxes that sleazy dance-hall rhythm quite like Bernstein. The programme opens with the suite of *Music for the theatre*, with its spaciously atmospheric *Prologue*, unmistakably and uniquely by Copland (few composers have such indelible harmonic fingerprints); the poignant *Interlude*, shared by cor anglais and trumpet, is very reminiscent of *Quiet city*. If you already have Bernstein's disc of the ballet scores, this would be a splendid way to continue an exploration of Copland's music: the opening of the *Piano concerto* is utterly haunting. *Connotations* (which also includes the piano within the orchestra) is less obviously popular in appeal but is undoubtedly magnetic. The present transfers are first class.

(i) *Connotations;* (ii) *Dance panels; Down a country lane;* (i) *Inscape;* (ii) *3 Latin-American sketches; Music for a great city; Orchestral variations; Preamble for a solemn occasion; The Red Pony* (film score).
(M) *(**) Sony SM2K 47236 (2) [S2K 47236]. (i) NYPO, Bernstein; (ii) LSO or New Philh. O, composer.

This third Copland box from Sony is something of a disappointment – not the music, which is even rarer than before and of great interest. *The Red Pony* is vintage Copland, and the *Orchestral variations*, though strictly an orchestral version of the *Piano variations* of 1930, make a unique and impressive contribution to Copland's oeuvre. *Connotations* and to a lesser extent *Inscape*, the major work of the composer's final period, are serially orientated. *Dance panels* is an abstract ballet without a narrative line, and *Music for a great city*, with its jazz influences and nocturnal scene, derives from another film-score (*Something Wild*). The performances are all extremely successful, but the CD transfers are over-bright and, for all their vividness of detail, tiring to the ear, particularly the thin violins and the more pungent climaxes of the later works.

Symphony No. 3; (i) *Symphony for organ and orchestra.*
(M) *** Sony SMK 63155 [id.]. (i) E. Power Biggs; NYPO, Bernstein.

Copland's *Third Symphony* is one of his most ambitious and accessible works. Though its power has slightly faded since it first appeared in the 1940s, it must still rank among the very finest and most attractive of American symphonies. It possesses enormous vitality and openness and has some of Copland's most characteristic poetry as well as some grandiloquent gestures in the more expansive moments. Bernstein's very grand manner tends to make one too aware of the limits to the symphony's greatness. He builds the music up in a manner that the material will not quite stand and the result does not always avoid a feeling of inflation. Copland marks the very opening 'with simple expression', and in the folk-like trio of the second movement he puts the request '*cantando semplice*', yet at such points the New York players sound too smooth and polished. Yet there is still much to be said for a high-powered reading like this, which is very compelling, as is the account of the work for organ and orchestra, which is discussed above. The Avery Fisher Hall recordings, from 1966 and 1967 respectively, sound suitably spacious in these fine new transfers, although the organ balance is close, and in this latter work tuttis have an element of harshness.

Corelli, Arcangelo (1653–1713)

Concerti grossi, Op. 6/1–12.
(B) *** Hyperion Dyad Dig. CDD 22011 (2) [id.]. Brandenburg Consort, Roy Goodman.
(BB) *** Naxos Dig. 8.550402/3 [id.]. Capella Istropolitana, Jaroslav Krechek.
(B) **(*) Ph. Duo 456 326-2 (2) [(M) id. import]. I Musici.
(B) **(*) Decca Double 443 862-2 [id.]. ASMF, Marriner.
(BB) ** EMI/Seraphim (SIS) CES5 69143-2 (2) [CDEB 69143]. SW German R. CO, Günter Wich.

Corelli's glorious set of *Concerti grossi*, Op. 6, is now very well represented in the catalogue in all price-ranges. In fact one cannot go wrong with either of the three-star listings here. For those who prefer period performances, Roy Goodman's Hyperion set is now available as a two-for-the-price-of-one Dyad. Goodman and the Brandenburg Consort use small forces (17 string players) plus harpsichord continuo, archlute and organ. There is a sense of style and a freshness of approach here that is very persuasive. The recorded sound is first class.

At super-bargain price, the Naxos set by the Capella Istropolitana under Jaroslav Krechek represents very good value indeed. The players are drawn from the Slovak Philharmonic and have great vitality and, when necessary, virtuosity to commend them. The digital recording is clean and well lit, but not over-bright, and makes their version strongly competitive.

I Musici bring a full sonority and expert musicianship to these *Concertos*. They are especially good in slow movements, where the playing has an agreeable lightness of touch and often creates delicately radiant textures. In allegros, rhythms are less bouncy than with Goodman, and the effect is less exhilarating. Yet there is an appealing warmth here, and certainly the Philips recording provides beautifully rich string-sound. Good value as a Duo, but not a first choice.

The reissued ASMF version uses a performing edition by Christopher Hogwood and has been prepared with evident thought and care; if one cavils it is only at two small points: some fussy continuo playing here and there, and a certain want of breadth and nobility of feeling in some of the slow movements. These are perhaps small points when weighed alongside the liveliness and intelligence of these performances, so expertly played. Yet compared to the issues mentioned above, there is at times a hint of blandness, and those wanting a superbargain version should turn to the Naxos recording by the excellent Capella Istropolitana under Jaroslav Krechek, which is even more vital and has first-rate, modern, digital sound.

The performances from the excellent South West German Radio Chamber Orchestra are lively, well played, warmly expressive and not too heavily textured. The concertino group is impressive and the balance between this solo group and the ripieno is well managed. This set is inexpensive and collectors with limited budgets buying it on impulse should not be disappointed, for the breadth of Corelli's inspiration is well conveyed. But the Naxos set, which costs about the same, is even fresher and has the advantage of digital recording.

Concerti grossi, Op. 6/1–6.
(BB) *** DHM Baroque Esprit 05472 77432-2 [(B) id.]. La Petite Band, Sigiswald Kuijken.

La Petite Band have recorded the complete Op. 6, and the present CD offers the first half-dozen concertos at a very economical price; no doubt the rest will follow. Authentic instruments are used to excellent effect: textures are more transparent as a result and the playing is always expressive and musical. The 1977 recordings were made in a warm and highly sympathetic acoustic: besides being splendidly lifelike, they are also impressive in conveying the nobility and grandeur of Corelli.

Concerti grossi, Op. 6/1, 3, 7–9 & 11.
(BB) *(**) DHM Baroque Esprit 054472 77445-2 [(M) 7908-2-RC]. Tafelmusik, Jean Lamon.

This is one of Tafelmusik's earlier period performances, dating from 1989. They play Corelli's allegros with characteristic bright vitality. The recording is a bit up-front and there is a degree of abrasiveness, though no lack of ambient atmosphere; but it is the plangent quality of the lyrical music that will not suit all ears, and the famous *Pastorale* from the *Christmas concerto*, which ends the concert, surely needs more of a feeling of repose.

Concerti grossi, Op. 6/1, 3, 7, 8 (Christmas), 11 & 12.
(M) *** DG Dig. 447 289-2 [id.]. E. Concert, Pinnock.

At mid-price, with the *Christmas Concerto* included, this will admirably suit those collectors who want an original-instrument version and who are content with a single-disc selection.

Concerti grossi Op. 6/2, 6–7, 8 (Christmas).
(B) ** EMI forte CZS5 68625-2 (2) [CDFB 68625]. Virtuosi di Roma, Fasano (with LEO: *Cello concerto: Largo;* J. S. BACH: *Quadruple harpsichord concerto;* Alessandro MARCELLO: *Oboe concerto in C min.*) – VIVALDI: *Four seasons* etc. **

When Renato Fasano's collection of Corelli *Concerti grossi* was first published on LP in 1963, we noted the liveliness of the performances but also commented on the backward balance of the harpsichord continuo which is almost inaudible, and suggested that these very expressive performances were dedicated to tonal beauty rather than to revealing any new facets of the music. Three decades later (after experience of the meagre sounds of some period-instrument accounts) one's ears gratefully register the Italian sunshine in the string-timbres. The concertos are part of a popular baroque entertainment which includes a fine *Oboe concerto* by Alessandro Marcello (once attributed to his brother), which has a very beautiful central Largo, and another rather fine slow movement from a cello concerto by Leonardo Leo, in which the fine soloist (Benedetto Mazzacurati) is much more imaginative than his oboist colleague (Renato Zanfini). In the familiar Bach *Quadruple harpsichord concerto* (transcribed from Vivaldi's Op. 3/10) Fasano's lack of understanding of the principle of double-dotted notes and the function of double trills prevents the slow movement from sounding as the composer would have expected. Even so, there is much to enjoy here, and the coupled Vivaldi items (which open the programme) are fresh and enjoyable, if not distinctive.

Trio sonatas, Op. 1/9, 10 & 12 (Ciacona); Op. 2/4; Op. 3/5; Op. 4/1; Violin sonata, Op. 5/3; Concerto grosso in B flat, Op. 6/5.
(M) *** Virgin Veritas/EMI Dig. VER5 61210-2 [CDM 612102]. L. Baroque, Medlam.

Though not lacking vitality, the London Baroque performances here are graceful and comparatively restrained, lighter in feeling and texture than Pinnock and his English Concert (at full price), thus providing a genuine alternative approach. Reissued on Virgin Veritas, they also now have a price advantage.

Trio sonatas, Op. 5/1–6.
(B) *** HM Dig. HMX 290853.55 (3) [(M) id.]. Chiara Banchieri, Jesper Christensen, Luciano Contini, Käthi Gohl – TARTINI: *Concerti grossi*; VIVALDI: *Chamber sonatas*. ***

Corelli's Op. 5, of which the first six sonatas are offered here, were published in 1700. Like his *Concerti grossi*, they were enormously influential throughout Europe. Each is in five diverse movements, alternating slow and fast tempi, with usually at least one *fuga*, and ending, if not with a fugue, with a lively *Gigue*. Their invention is of the highest quality, and Chiara Banchieri and her colleagues present them with vitality, warmth and finesse. Their period-instrument manners are not excessive, and the acoustic resonance adds to the body of the sound without impairing clarity. In this Harmonia Mundi bargain-priced Trio presentation, Corelli's music is aptly linked with sonatas of Vivaldi and – rather less obviously – with concertos of Tartini.

Corrette, Michel (1709–95)

6 Organ concertos, Op. 26.
(B) *** HM Musique d'Abord HMA 190 5148 [id.]. René Saorgin (organ of L'Eglise de l'Escarène, Nice), Bar. Ens., Gilbert Bezzina.

These lively and amiable concertos are here given admirably spirited and buoyant performances, splendidly recorded using period instruments. The orchestral detail is well observed and René Saorgin plays vividly on an attractive organ. Michel Corrette's invention has genuine spontaneity and this makes an enjoyable collection to dip into, though not to play all at one go.

Couperin, François (1668–1733)

Concerts Royaux Nos. 1 in G; 2 in D; 3 in A; 4 in E min.
(B) ** HM Musique d'Abord HMA 190 1151 [id.]. Robert Claire, Davitt Moroney, Jaap ter Linden, Janet See.

Davitt Moroney and his colleagues opt for two flutes, bass viol and harpsichord in the *Concerts Royaux*. This was music intended for Louis XIV's diversion of a Sunday evening, and here the effect is just a shade wan. There is a certain uniformity of colour, and in addition their playing is just a little wanting in panache and vitality.

L'Art de toucher le clavecin; Harpsichord suites, Books 1–4, Ordres 1–27 (complete); (i) *L'apothéose de Lulli. La Paix du Parnasse; Le Parnasse ou l'Apothéose de Corelli; Pièces de clavecin: 9e Ordre: Allemand à deux. 14e Ordre: La Juilliet. 15e Ordere: Musète de Choisi; Musète de Taverni; 16e Ordre: La Létiville.*
(B) *** HM Dig. HMX 901442–52 (& HMC 901269) (12) [id.]. Christophe Rousset (harpsichord); (i) with William Christie; with Blandine Rannou (in Book 3); with Kaori Uemura (in Book 4).

Rousset's distinguished series of the *Pièces de clavecin* includes *L'Art de toucher le clavecin*, using appropriate instruments. Apart from his inherent sense of style and feeling for decoration, Rousset well understands terms like *gracieusement*, *gayement*, *très tendrement* and *agréable, sans lenteur*, which he realizes to perfection. The *Concerts royaux* were of course written for a small chamber group, but the composer also encouraged their performance on the keyboard alone. In Book 2, Rousset is joined in certain pieces (the *Allemande* which opens Ordre No. 9 is for two harpsichords) by the estimable William Christie. In Book 3, he is joined in a very few items by Blandine Rannou on a second harpsichord; and in *La Croûilli ou la Couperinète*, from Book 4, Ordre 20, Kaori Uemura provides a vigorous basso continuo for the closing section. One could carp here and there about choice of tempi and so on, but Couperin wanted his music to be played creatively and flexibly, and that is what Christophe Rousset does – and with total spontaneity, too. He is beautifully recorded within an open but not too resonant acoustic, and this series can be welcomed very cordially indeed. This whole set now comes as a special offer at bargain price and throws in as a bonus the extra disc in which Rousset is joined by William Christie and which includes *L'apothéose de Lulli* and *Le Parnasse ou l'apothéose de Corelli* among other pieces (see below). The four *Suites* are also still available separately at premium price, but the lover of this repertoire will surely want to opt for the whole series when this bargain offer is so tempting.

L'apothéose de Lulli; La Parnasse ou l'apothéose de Corelli; Pièces de clavecin: 9e Ordre: Allemande à deux; 14e Ordre: La Juilliet; 15e Ordre: Musète de Choisi; Musète de Taverni; 16e Ordre: La Létiville.
(B) *** HM Musique d'Abord Dig. HMA 190 1269 [id.]. William Christie, Christophe Rousset (harpsichords).

Couperin's preface explains that he himself played these works on two harpsichords with members of his family and pupils; and William Christie has chosen to follow his example. Surprisingly, they sound rather more exciting in this form than in the more familiar instrumental versions, largely perhaps because of the sheer sparkle and vitality of these performers.

Harpsichord suites, Book 1, Ordres 1–5.
(B) *** HM Musique d'Abord HMA 190351/3 [id.]. Kenneth Gilbert.

Harpsichord suites, Book 2, Ordres 6–12.
(B) *** HM Musique d'Abord HMA 190354/6 [id.]. Kenneth Gilbert.

Harpsichord suites, Book 3, Ordres 13–19.
(B) *** HM Musique d'Abord HMA 190357/8 [id.]. Kenneth Gilbert.

Harpsichord suites, Book 4, Ordres 20–27.
(B) *** HM Musique d'Abord HMA 190359/60 [id.]. Kenneth Gilbert.

Professor Gilbert's performances are scrupulous in matters of registration, following what is known of eighteenth-century practice in France. There is no want of expressive range throughout the series and Gilbert plays with authority and taste – and, more to the point, artistry. He is also well served by the engineers.

Harpsichord suites, Book 1, Ordre 1; Concerts Royaux Nos. 1–2.
(BB) *** Naxos Dig. 8.550961 [id.]. Laurence Cummings.

Laurence Cummings has already won golden opinions from us for his admirable and idiomatic earlier recital of Louis Couperin (see below), and his account of the *Premier Ordre* of François is hardly less fine. This is a compilation of pieces written over a period of time and published in 1713, while the two *Concerts Royaux* also included here were given at the court of Louis XIV in 1714–15 and publishd in 1722. Cummings plays a modern instrument by Michael Johnson modelled on a Taskin, and he produces pleasing and musical results. The disc bears the legend, Harpsichord Music Vol. 1, and if the remaining issues maintain the standard achieved here, both artistically and in terms of recorded sound, it will be a valuable addition to the catalogue.

Harpsichord suites, Book 2, Ordres 6, 8 & 11.
(BB) ** Naxos Dig. 8.550460 [id.]. Alan Cuckson (harpsichord).

Harpsichord suites, Book 3, Ordres 13, 17 & 18; Book 4, Ordre 21.
(BB) **(*) Naxos Dig. 8.550461 [id.]. Alan Cuckson (harpsichord).

Harpsichord suites, Book 4, Ordres 22–23; 25–26.
(BB) **(*) Naxos Dig. 8.550462 [id.]. Alan Cuckson (harpsichord).

The three Naxos discs are generously filled; the first, accommodating the *Sixième*, *Huitième* and *Onzième Ordres*, runs to 77 minutes, which represents outstanding value for money. (All three offer over 70 minutes' playing time.) Alan Cuckson also enjoys a competitive advantage over Kenneth Gilbert, whose magisterial survey on Harmonia Mundi cannot be acquired either so conveniently (one disc at a time) or at quite so modest an outlay (even though it is not so very much more expensive). Moreover Cuckson provides more than adequate presentation notes, though they fail to give any indication of the instrument he uses. The recording will sound thunderous played at a normal volume setting, for the transfer has been effected at a very high level. However, when the volume is reduced sharply, the results are satisfactory, even though the balance is really a bit too close. Perhaps Kenneth Gilbert scores in his greater expressive range and variety of colour, though Cuckson has no want of expertise and artistry. At the same time the latter's playing does not have the imaginative flair or the persuasive eloquence which could justify the claim that Couperin was to the eighteenth century what Chopin was to the nineteenth.

ORGAN MUSIC

Messe à l'usage ordinaire des Paroisses; Messe propre pour les Couvents de religieux et religieuses (reconstructed by Jean Saint-Arromen to include Plainchant and Motets: *Domine salvum fac Regem* (2 versions); *Quid retribuam tibi dominum*).

(M) *** Virgin Veritas/EMI Dig. VED5 61298-2 (2). Jean-Patrice Brosse (organ of Saint-Bertrand, Saint-Bertrand de Comminges), with Isabel Poulenard, Jacques des Longchamps, François Le Roux, Val-de-Grâce Gregorian Ch.

(i) *Messe à l'usage ordinaire des Paroisses;* (ii) *Messe propre pour les Couvents de religieuses* (reconstructed by Edward Higginbottom to include plainchant, taken from Nivers's *Graduale romanaomonasticum* of 1658).

(B) *** Decca Double 455 026-2 [id.]. Peter Hurford (organ of St-Pierre, Toulouse), with (i) Gentlemen of Ch. of New College, Oxford; (ii) Ladies of Oxford Chamber Ch.; Edward Higginbottom.

Couperin was only 21 when he wrote his pair of organ Masses in 1690; yet these works, far more than conventional commentaries on the theme of the Mass, are among the finest of all his instrumental compositions. The *Mass for Parishes* is the grander, but the *Mass for convents*, basically simpler, has its contrapuntal complexities and is not without moments of flamboyance. There have been a number of fine solo recordings of the organ scores in the past, but until now none has given us these pieces with the plainsong framework in which they were intended to be heard and which dictates the degree of flamboyance needed from the organ to achieve convincing performances. Jean-Patrice Brosse has the full measure of this music and the Saint-Bertrand organ brings the necessary plangent French timbre: indeed the opening *Plein chant du premier Kyrie en taille* which introduces the *Kyrie eleison* of the *Mass for Parishes* has a convincingly throaty vocal tang. In this work the plainsong interpolations are mostly brief and always simple, although the *Credo* is an obvious exception. Indeed one can imagine how the worshipping congregation of the time must have been thrilled by the organ spectacularly framing this declaration of faith with the elaborately registered *Dialogue sur les grands jeux* and the *Offertoire sur les grands jeux*. Brosse faithfully follows the composer's indicated registrations, and there are many piquant sounds throughout both works, using solo stops or combinations featuring the cromorne, voix-humaine, cornet or tierce, the striking pedal trompette and the beguiling jeux doux (soft flutes). In the *Mass for convents*, the organ versets are usually based on the cantus firmus of the plainchant (rather like Bach's chorale preludes only less elaborate). In reconstructing his conjectural performances, Jean Saint-Arromen has added short motets within the Elévation for the *Benedictus* and *Agnus Dei*, and these are sung effectively enough by Jacques des Longchamps (alto) and François Le Roux (baritone); although to have a vocal ending for each Mass does bring something of an anticlimax after the organ's final *Deo gratias, petit plein jeu*, it emphasizes the dedicated spiritual nature of Couperin's overall conception. These beautifully recorded performances give a splendid illusion of being in the cathedral and participating in an occasion which is alternately solemn and lively, evocative and vividly colourful.

Peter Hurford plays the two organ Masses on the restored organ, designed by Robert Delaunay in 1683, of Saint-Pierre des Chartreux. The Decca engineers have made an excellent job of marrying the acoustic with that of the Chapel of New College, Oxford, and they capture the atmosphere of both to splendid effect. Edward Higginbottom's reconstruction is less elaborate that that of Jean Saint-Arromen, using plainchant economically to follow on simply after the organ dialogues. Male voices of the New College, Oxford, Choir are used in the *Messe des Paroisses*, while in the *Messe des Couvents* women's voices are an obvious choice. They sing very beautifully and the effect is memorable, particularly when Hurford is such an obvious master of Couperin's organ writing, which is again superbly recorded. It cannot be denied that the French voices used in the Virgin Veritas alternative recording do bring an added feeling of vocal authenticity. But both versions have their own merits.

3 Leçons de ténèbres.

(B) *** HM Musique d'Abord HMA 190210 [id.]. Deller, Todd, Perulli, Chapuis.

The *Trois leçons de ténèbres* were written for performance on Good Friday. Deller's account is inevitably less than authentic, since this music, written for a convent, did not envisage performances by male voices. In every other respect, however, it has a wonderful authenticity of feeling and a blend of scholarship and artistry that gives it a special claim on the attention of collectors.

Motets: *Audite omnes et expanescite; Pour le jour de Pâques. 3 Leçons de ténèbres.*

(M) ** Erato/Warner 4509 97409-2. Nadine Sautereau, Janine Collard, Ens., Laurence Boulay – CHARPENTIER: *La Reniement de Saint Pierre.* **(*)

Boulay's performances come from the period 1954–69 and are none the worse for that. Nadine Sautereau will be familiar as the Child from the pioneering set of Ravel's *L'Enfant et les sortilèges*, made in 1948, while Janine Collard will be remembered, among other things, as Geneviève in André Cluytens's *Pelléas*, as the Innkeeper in Charles Bruck's 1957 set of Prokofiev's *Fiery Angel* and as the mother in Maazel's DG recording of *L'Enfant*. Both artists show themselves to be thoroughly at home in this idiom, and the instrumental ensemble under Laurence Boulay is admirably discreet. In the first of the *Leçons de ténèbres* Mme Sautereau sings occasionally on the flat side of the note, but for the most part both the singing and playing give pleasure.

Motets: *Domine salvum fac regem; Jacunda vox ecclesiae; Laetentur coeli; Lauda Sion salvatorem; Magnificat; O misterium ineffabile; Regina coeli; Tantum ergo sacramentum; Venite exultemus Domine; Victoria! Christo resurgenti.*
(B) *** HM Musique d'Abord HMA 1901150 [id.]. Feldman, Poulenard, Reinhart, Linden, Moroney.

The motets on this record cover a wider spectrum of feeling and range of expressive devices than might at first be imagined. The performances are eminently acceptable, with some particularly good singing from Jill Feldman; the recording is made in a spacious and warm acoustic.

Couperin, Louis (*c.* 1626–61)

Suites de pièces and complete harpsichord music.
(B) *** HM HMX 901124/27 (4) [(M) id. import]. Davitt Moroney (harpsichord).

Louis Couperin was a pupil of Chambonnières, and his keyboard output comprises enough individual dance pieces to make sixteen suites, as well as other pieces. This comprehensive survey makes out a strong case for this repertoire; readers expecting it to be greatly inferior in quality to the clavecin music of François-le-Grand will be pleasantly surprised – though, of course, there is less of the poetic fantasy of his nephew at his best. The recording is eminently truthful and the CD transfer wholly natural.

Harpsichord suites: in A min.; in C; in F; Pavane in F sharp min.
(M) *** HM/BMG GD 77058 [77058-2-RG]. Gustav Leonhardt (harpsichord).

Leonhardt has such subtlety and panache that he makes the most of the grandeur and refinement of this music to whose sensibility he seems wholly attuned. This is the best introduction to Louis Couperin's keyboard suites now before the public.

Harpsichord suites: in A min.; C; D; F (including *Le Tombeau de M. de Blancrocher*).
(BB) *** Naxos Dig. 8.550922 [id.]. Laurence Cummings.

Laurence Cummings was an organ scholar at Christ Church, Oxford, and he seems quite as much at home in this repertoire as Leonhardt. He plays a modern copy of a Ruckers, which is very well recorded by Naxos. His selection is rather more generous than Leonhardt's and he arranges his own groupings. His decoration is convincing and he plays with more spontaneity and flair than his illustrious colleague. The CD offers some 75 minutes of music and is one of Naxos's best bargains.

Coward, Noël (1899–1973)

After the ball: I knew that you would be my love. Bitter Sweet: I'll see you again; Zigeuner. Conversation piece: I'll follow my secret heart; Never more; Melanie's aria (sung in French); *Charming. Operette: Dearest love; Where are the songs we sung? Countess Mitzi. Pacific 1860: Bright was the day; This is a changing world.*
(BB) *** Belart 450 014-2 [(M) id. import]. Dame Joan Sutherland, Noël Coward, soloists, Ch. & O, Richard Bonynge.

It is fairly easy to criticize this disc on the grounds that a full operatic style does not always suit Noël Coward and that Joan Sutherland does not always get right inside the characters Coward created (she tries very hard with Countess Mitzi). But all this is swept aside in the sheer pleasure of hearing such a wonderful voice sing such delightful music. Dame Joan Sutherland's tonal lustre and sense of line in *I'll see you again* are incomparable, as is her display of fireworks in *Zigeuner*, and her gentle delicacy in *I knew that you would be my love*, with its ravishing final cadence. Noël Coward's own vocal contributions are quite small but they magically create atmosphere, and Richard Bonynge's affectionate and stylish conducting is a model.

Croft, William (1678–1727)

The Burial Service.
(M) *** EMI CDM5 66683-2 [id.]. Winchester Cathedral Ch., Martin Neary – PURCELL: *Funeral music for Queen Mary;* Concert: *'Solemn music'.* ***

William Croft's *Burial service* became world famous when it was used as part of the music for the funeral of Diana, Princess of Wales. It has a simple eloquence which is very touching, although the performance here does not attempt to simulate a processional effect at the opening as did the early Argo King's version directed by Sir David Willcocks. However, on this record the Croft follows effectively after Purcell's inspired *Funeral music for Queen Mary*, which does begin and end with an instrumental processional.

Crusell, Bernhard (1775–1838)

Introduction and variations on a Swedish air (for clarinet and orchestra), *Op. 12.*
(B) *** Hyperion Dyad Dig. CDD 22017 (2) [id.]. Thea King, LSO, Francis (with Concert – see below ***).

The Weberian Crusell *Variations* show Thea King's bravura at its most sparkling. It is far from being an empty piece; its twists and turns are consistently inventive. This is part of an excellent two-disc set including other attractive concertante works by Max Bruch, Mendelssohn, Spohr and other less familiar names.

Da Crema, Giovanni Maria (died *c.* 1550)

Con lagrime e sospiri (Philippe Verdelot); De vous servir (Claudin de Sermisy); Lasciar il velo (Jacques Arcadelt); O felici occhi miei (Arcadelt); Pass'e mezo ala bolognesa; Ricercars quinto, sexto, decimoquarto, decimoquinto, duodecimo, tredecimo; Saltarello ditto Bel fior; Saltarello ditto El Giorgio; Saltarello ditto El Maton.
(BB) *** Naxos Dig. 8.550778 [id.]. Christopher Wilson (lute) – DALL'AQUILA – *Lute pieces.* ***

Even less is known about Giovanni Maria Da Crema than his contemporary, Dall'Aquila. The pieces here are taken from a First Lute Book which he published in 1546. Some of the music is adapted from or offers simple variants on the music of others. The inclusion of the dance movements alongside reflective pieces like *Con lagrime e sospiri* gives variety to an attractive programme, and the *Pass'e mezo ala bolognesa* is rather catchy. The performances are of the highest order, and Christopher Wilson is recorded most naturally. Well worth exploring, especially at such a modest cost.

Dall'Aquila, Marco (*c.* 1480–1538)

Amy souffrez (Pierre Moulu); La cara cosa; Priambolo; Ricercars Nos. 15, 16, 18, 19, 22, 24, 28, 33, 70, 101; 3 Ricercar/Fantasias; La Traditora.
(BB) *** Naxos Dig. 8.550778 [id.]. Christopher Wilson (lute) – DA CREMA – *Lute pieces.* ***

Marco dall'Aquila was a much-admired lutenist in his day, but little is known of his background. Born in Aquila, he settled in Venice as musician and publisher. These are relatively simple lute pieces, rhythmically active but with chordal textures. They are often dolorous. The two pieces which are more individually identified, *Amy souffrez* and *La cara cosa*, are among the more striking, but the *Ricercars* can be haunting too, and there is considerable variety of style and mood. They are beautifully played by Christopher Wilson and the recording is admirably balanced: the lute is not too close and is heard within a pleasing ambience.

Debussy, Claude (1862–1918)

Complete orchestral music (as below).
(M) *** Chandos Dig. CHAN 7019 (4) [id.]. Soloists, Ulster O, Yan Pascal Tortelier.

La boîte à joujoux; Children's corner (orch. Caplet); *Danse (Tarantelle styrienne*, orch. Ravel); *Marche écossaise sur un thème populaire; Petite suite* (orch. Büsser).
(M) *** Chandos Dig. CHAN 7017 [id.]. Ulster O, Y. P. Tortelier.

(i) *Fantaisie for piano and orchestra;* (ii) *Danse sacrée et danse profane for harp and strings; L'Isle joyeuse* (orch. Molinari); (iii) *La plus que lente;* (iv) *Première rapsodie for clarinet and orchestra;* (v) *Rapsodie for alto saxophone and orchestra* (orch. Roger-Ducasse); *Sarabande* (orch. Ravel); *Suite bergamasque: Clair de lune* (orch. Caplet).

(M) *** Chandos Dig. CHAN 7018 [id.]. Ulster O, Y. P. Tortelier, with (i) Anne Queffélec; (ii) Rachel Masters; (iii) Derek Bell (cimbalom); (iv) Christopher King; (v) Gerard McChrystal.

Images; Jeux; Khamma.

(M) **(*) Chandos Dig. CHAN 7016 [id.]. Ulster O, Y. P. Tortelier.

La Mer; Nocturnes; Printemps; Prélude à l'après-midi d'un faune.

(M) ** Chandos Dig. CHAN 7015 [id.]. Ulster O, Y. P. Tortelier.

As can be seen, Chandos have now assembled Debussy's orchestral music (previously coupled with Ravel) in an upper-mid-priced box in recordings which generally represent the state of the art. There are excellent soloists in the concertante works. The subtlety and atmosphere of *La boîte à joujoux* are captured splendidly, and the concertante works are equally sensitive. Not all the performances are a first choice; *Jeux*, *La Mer* and *Printemps* spring to mind: Tortelier's *La Mer* is taut and well held together, though his generally brisk tempi do not enhance the atmosphere; and *Printemps*, though intelligently shaped, is not as evocative and relaxed as the finest versions on disc. The shorter works come off particularly well. Debussy himself orchestrated *La plus que lente* and he explained to his publisher, tongue in cheek, that the opening cimbalom solo was added because 'It's impossible to begin the same way in a brasserie as in a salon: you absolutely need a few bars' preparation!' It is a charmingly inconsequential performance with the cimbalom lacing the texture like a continuo. Now that these CDs are available separately, CHAN 7017 and 7018 are very desirable indeed.

(i) *Berceuse héroïque;* (ii; iii) *Danses sacrée et profane* (for harp and strings); (ii) *Images; Jeux; Marche écossaise; La Mer;* (ii; iv) *Nocturnes;* (ii) *Prélude à l'après-midi d'un faune;* (ii; v) *Première rapsodie for clarinet and orchestra.*

❀ (B) *** Ph. Duo 438 742-2 (2) [id.]. Concg. O, (i) Eduard van Beinum; (ii) Bernard Haitink; with (iii) Vera Badings; (iv) women's Ch. of Coll. Mus.; (v) George Pieterson.

This must now rank as the finest Debussy collection in the CD catalogue and one of the greatest bargains that the gramophone has to offer at present – all for the cost of a single premium-priced CD. Although the programme as a whole is directed by Haitink, it is good that his distinguished predecessor, Eduard van Beinum, is remembered by the opening *Berceuse héroïque*, played with great delicacy and a real sense of mystery, with the early stereo (1957) highly effective. For the *Danses sacrée et profane* Haitink takes over, with elegant playing from the harpist, Vera Badings, who is excellently balanced. Haitink's reading of *Images* is second to none and is beautifully played by the wonderful Dutch orchestra; the sonorities are delicate and the dynamic shadings sensitively observed. The superlative quality of the playing is matched by analogue recording of the very highest order. This applies equally to *Jeux*, where Haitink's reading is wonderfully expansive and sensitive to atmosphere and easily matches any recent rivals. Competition is even stiffer in the *Nocturnes*, but this great orchestra and conductor hold their own. The cruel vocal writing in *Sirènes* taxes the women of the Collegium Musicum Amstelodamense, but the choral balance is perfectly judged and few versions are quite as beguiling and seductive as Haitink's. His pacing of *La Mer* is comparable with Karajan's tempo in his 1964 recording. Both conductors pay close attention to dynamic gradations and both secure playing of great sensitivity and virtuosity from their respective orchestras; the *Dialogue du vent et de la mer* is both fast and exciting. An interesting point is that the brief fanfares that Debussy removed, eight bars before fig. 60, are here restored (as they were by Ansermet), but Haitink gives them to horns. The hazily sensuous *Prélude à l'après-midi d'un faune* and the undervalued *Clarinet rhapsody* are also played atmospherically, although the former is more overtly languorous in Karajan's hands. Again the Philips recording is truthful and natural, with beautiful perspectives and realistic colour, a marvellously refined sound.

Berceuse héroïque; Images; Jeux; Marche écossaise; La Mer; Musiques pour le Roi Lear; Nocturnes; Prélude à l'après-midi d'un faune; Printemps.

(B) *** EMI forte CZS5 72667-2 (2) [(M) id. import]. Fr. R. & TV Ch. & O, Martinon.

Martinon's is a very good *Images*, beautifully played, with the orchestral detail vivid and glowing. Climaxes expand well, but there is a touch of shrillness on the brass. *Jeux* is also very fine, with the sound attractively spacious. Martinon's account of *La Mer* first appeared in the mid-1970s. It still has plenty of atmosphere and enjoys the idiomatic advantage of fine French orchestral playing, even if it does not quite match Karajan or Haitink. The *Musiques pour le Roi Lear* is a real rarity; the colourful *Fanfare* remains impressive, and *Le sommeil de Lear* is highly evocative. The *Nocturnes* are not quite the equal of the finest versions but are still beautifully played, as indeed is *Printemps*, with Martinon penetrating its charm. At bargain price these are competitive recommendations, and the current transfers are warmly atmospheric; even if the upper end of the range is rather brightly lit, there is plenty of depth in the sound.

Berceuse héroïque; Images; Marche écossaise sur un thème populaire; Le martyre de Saint Sébastien: symphonic fragments.
(BB) ** Naxos Dig. 8.550505 [id.]. Belgian R. & TV PO, Brussels, Rahbari.

Rahbari gets good results from his Belgian Radio forces and is very capably recorded. However, when there are such distinguished performances as the Haitink *Images* or Reiner's immaculate *Ibéria* – or, better still, Monteux who offers the *Images* and *Le martyre* together, the claims of this present offering look slender.

La boîte à joujoux; Children's corner (orch. Caplet); *Danse* (orch. Ravel); (i) *Danses sacrée et profane*. (ii) *Fantaisie for piano and orchestra. La plus que lente; Khamma; Petite suite* (orch. Büsser); (iii) *Première rhapsodie for clarinet and orchestra*. (iv) *Rhapsodie for saxophone*.
(B) *** EMI forte CZS5 72673-2 (2). Fr. R. & TV O, Martinon; with (i) Marie-Claire Jamet; (ii) Aldo Ciccolini; (iii) Guy Dangain; (iv) Londe.

Caplet's orchestration of *Children's corner* and *La boîte à joujoux*, both of them containing much to enchant the ear, and Henri Büsser's orchestration of the tuneful *Petite suite* are welcome together. The rarity here is *Khamma*, which Ansermet recorded in the 1960s, a ballet whose scoring Debussy entrusted to Charles Koechlin. The two *Rhapsodies* are underrated and, although there are alternative versions of all these pieces, none is more economically priced. The performances are sympathetic and authoritative, and the recordings have been remastered successfully. The sound is full and spacious with an attractive ambient glow.

Danse (Tarantelle styrienne); Sarabande (orch. Ravel).
(M) *** Virgin/EMI Dig. CUV5 61206-2 [id.]. Lausanne CO, Zedda – MILHAUD: *Création du monde;* PROKOFIEV: *Sinfonietta*. ***

Zedda's performances with the Lausanne Chamber Orchestra are neat and polished, full of character and well recorded. But it is the couplings that make this disc especially attractive.

(i) *Danses sacrée et profane; Images. Jeux; La Mer;* (ii) *Nocturnes; Printemps;* (iii) *Première rapsodie for clarinet and orchestra*.
(M) **(*) Sony SM2K 68327 (2) [S2K 68327]. New Philh. O or (i) Cleveland O; Boulez; with (i) Alice Chalifoux; (ii) John Alldis Ch.; (iii) Gervase de Peyer.

These (originally CBS) Boulez recordings come from between 1966 and 1968 and won considerable critical acclaim when they first appeared. He secures consistently first-class playing from the New Philharmonia Orchestra, but in terms of atmosphere and poetry the results are uneven. *Jeux*, a work of seminal importance in Boulez's development, is given persuasively, and the *Images* are carefully shaped and balanced. This work, like the coolly distinctive *Danses sacrée et profane*, was recorded in Cleveland and it gains from the ambience of Severance Hall, even if the balance is close (the harp assumes an importance equal to the strings). *La Mer* and the *Prélude à l'après-midi d'un faune* (which certainly does not lack passionate feeling) are a good deal better than some accounts, but *La Mer* cannot compare with the Karajan version from the same era in subtly conveying the briny marine atmosphere. Needless to say, Gervase de Peyer gives a distinguished account of the lovely *Clarinet rhapsody*, and the contribution of the John Alldis Choir to *Sirènes*, the third of the *Nocturnes*, is poised, even if the effect overall is cool rather than ethereal. But those who respond to Boulez's clarity of vision in this repertoire will find that the Sony engineers have made a marvellous job of these transfers to CD, maximizing the ambient effect and retaining the sharply defined detail – at Barking and Abbey Road as well as at Cleveland.

(i) *Fantaisie for piano and orchestra. 2 Arabesques; Ballade; Berceuse héroïque; Children's corner; Danse; Danse bohémienne; D'un cahier d'esquisses; Estampes; 12 Etudes; Hommage à Haydn; Images 1–2; L'isle joyeuse; Masques; Mazurka; Nocturne; Le petit nègre; La plus que lente; Pour le piano; Préludes, Books 1–2; Rêverie; Suite bergamasque; Valse romantique*.
(M) (***) EMI mono CHS5 65855-2 (4) [CDHD 65855]. Walter Gieseking; (i) with Hessischen R. O, Schröder.

Gieseking's Debussy enjoyed legendary status in the 1930s and '40s, and EMI are to be congratulated for not only restoring to circulation the famous recordings he then made but also, in the case of the *Fantaisie*, even adding to them. The two sets of *Préludes* date from 1953 and 1954, as indeed do most of the recordings collected here. The earliest is *Children's corner* from 1951 when Walter Legge was producer. He and Geraint Jones between them were responsible for most of these records. The 1951 Frankfurt recording of the *Fantaisie* calls for some (albeit not great) tolerance, but the remaining performances sound better than ever. Some critics maintain that his pre-war Debussy was even finer, and some of these are to be found on Pearl and other specialist labels. Gieseking's artistry is too well known to need further exegesis or advocacy. As Bryce Morrison puts it in the accompanying notes, 'Deeply sensitive and personal, virtuosic in the truest sense, Gieseking's performances are quite without preening mannerisms or idiosyncrasy and are, from this point of view alone, instantly recognizable.' A marvellous set which all pianists should investigate.

(i) *Images;* (ii) *Jeux; Khamma;* (i) *La Mer;* (ii) *Prélude à l'après-midi d'un faune; Printemps.*
(BB) **(*) Virgin Classics Dig. Double VBD5 61424-2 (2) [CDVB 61424]. (i) Rotterdam PO; (ii) Finnish RSO; Saraste.

This collection is inexpensive and has been given good, modern, digital recording. The Rotterdam acoustic brings an evocative allure to *Images*, which is played very vividly and has both sparkle and atmosphere. *La Mer* brings similar delicacy of detail and no lack of intensity at the close of the *Dialogue du vent et de la mer*. Altogether these performances are eminently serviceable and certainly recommendable, even if there are better individual versions elsewhere. Saraste's *Jeux* is not in the same league as Haitink's. Alongside the quite impressive set of *Images*, the best thing here is his account of *Khamma*.

Images; Jeux; Le Roi Lear (incidental music).
(B) *** [EMI Red Line Dig. CDR5 72095]. CBSO, Rattle.

In *Images*, Rattle is memorably atmospheric, while in *Jeux* he is just a touch more expansive than most rivals, and also more evocative, though he does not depart from the basic metronome markings. The *King Lear* excerpts sound splendid. First-rate recording, very vivid but beautifully balanced. An outstanding disc (available only in the USA).

Images; Le Martyre de Saint Sébastien (symphonic fragments).
(M) *** Ph. 442 595-2. LSO, Monteux.

The restoration of Monteux's classic coupling to the catalogue (in the UK only) is most welcome, and it makes a splendid addition to the Debussy discography, particularly as the remastered CD has fine immediacy and detail. Indeed, one would hardly suspect that the recording dates from 1963, for the woodwind colouring is translucent and there is a fine sheen of sensuousness to the string-tone (especially in *Les parfums de la nuit*). Monteux's performance of the *Images* was notable for its freshness and impetus (although this is achieved by the electricity of the playing rather than fast tempi). There is a vivid yet refined feeling for colour which is carried through into the orchestral sections from *Le Martyre* (in its fuller form a cantata written to a text by D'Annunzio). The delicacy of texture of Debussy's exquisite scoring is marvellously balanced by Monteux and he never lets the music become static. There is very little background noise, and our only real reservation is that this might have had some more music added. The playing time is just under 58 minutes.

Images: Ibéria.
✽ (M) *** RCA GD 60179 [60179-2-RG]. Chicago SO, Fritz Reiner – RAVEL: *Alborada* etc. *** ✽

Fritz Reiner and the Chicago orchestra give a reading that is immaculate in execution and magical in atmosphere. This marvellously evocative performance, and the Ravel with which it is coupled, should not be overlooked, for the recorded sound with its natural concert-hall balance is greatly improved in terms of body and definition. It is amazingly realistic even without considering its vintage.

Images: Ibéria. La Mer; Nocturnes: Nuages; Fêtes. Prélude à l'après-midi d'un faune.
(M) (**(*)) RCA mono GD 60265 [60265-2-RG]. NBC SO, Toscanini.

By emphasizing clarity, Toscanini with his electric intensity and sense of purpose consistently compels attention. One thinks of these supreme examples of musical impressionism, not as colour pieces but as masterly structures of great originality in purely musical terms. Clean, bright transfers.

Images: Ibéria. La Mer; Prélude à l'après-midi d'un faune.
(M) *** Mercury (IMS) 434 343-2 [id.]. Detroit SO, Paray – RAVEL: *Ma Mère l'oye*. ***

Paray's collection, dating (unbelievably) from as early as 1955, gave us the first stereo recording of *La Mer* which is very exciting, balancing powerful evocation and firm overall control. The balance is slightly recessed, which provides plenty of atmosphere and a hazy warm sentience to the sound, adding luminosity to Paray's glowingly voluptuous account of *L'après-midi* with its ardently beautiful string climax. The recording was made in Detroit's Old Orchestra Hall, where the resonance adds great warmth but prevents sharply delineated detail. Yet for body, natural concert-hall balance and richness of orchestral colour there are few stereo recordings made in the mid- to late-1950s to match this.

Jeux; La Mer; Nocturnes: Nuages; Fêtes (only); *Prélude à l'après-midi d'un faune.*
(M) **(*) Sony SMK 47546 [id.]. NYPO, Bernstein.

These recordings were made in the Manhattan Center in 1960/61 and show Bernstein at his most charismatic.There is plenty to admire in the orchestral playing and Bernstein has an undoubted feeling for atmosphere which he sustains even when, as in *La Mer*, the adrenalin is running very freely. Both *Jeux* and the *Prélude à l'après-midi d'un faune* have more than a whiff of voluptuousness and the phrasing in the *Prélude* is self-conscious in places. But the feeling throughout is of live music-making, and such performances would receive a standing ovation at a concert. The remastered sound is remarkably convincing. The diffuse recording – though woodwind are picked out by the microphones – adds to the evocative feeling, and the remastered sound is remarkably convincing, although the balance is contrived.

Jeux; La Mer; Prélude à l'après-midi d'un faune.
❀ (B) *** EMI Dig. CD-EMX 9502 [(M) id. import]. LPO, Baudo.

Serge Baudo's version of *La Mer* is first class. The recording is beautifully natural and expertly balanced. The same may be said for his lovely account of *Prélude à l'après-midi d'un faune*, as atmospheric as any in the catalogue and more beautifully shaped than many. In the faster sections, *Jeux* is at times brisker than we are used to and well conveys the sense of the playfulness of the tennis match. Its competitive price makes it even more enticing.

La Mer.
(M) *** DG 447 426-2 [id.]. BPO, Karajan – MUSSORGSKY: *Pictures;* RAVEL: *Boléro.* ***
(M) *** RCA 0926 68079-2 [id.]. Chicago SO, Fritz Reiner – RESPIGHI: *Fountains & Pines of Rome.* *** ❀
(M) *** RCA 09026 60875 [id.]. Chicago SO, Reiner – RIMSKY-KORSAKOV: *Scheherazade.* ***
(M) **(*) RCA 09026 61500-2 [id.]. Boston SO, Munch – IBERT: *Escales* ***; SAINT-SAENS: *Symphony No. 3.* *** ❀
(M) **(*) Decca (IMS) 448 576-2 [id.]. SRO, Ansermet – CHABRIER: *España* **(*); DUKAS: *L'apprenti sorcier* ***; HONEGGER: *Pacific 231* ***; RAVEL: *Boléro; La Valse.* ***

La Mer; Danse (Tarantelle styrienne); (i) *Nocturnes. Prélude à l'après-midi d'un faune.*
(B) *** Sony SBK 53266; *SBT 53266* [id.]. Phd. O, Ormandy, (i) with Temple University Womens' Ch.

La Mer; (i) *Nocturnes. Prélude à l'après-midi d'un faune.*
(B) *** DG Classikon 439 407-2; *439 407-4* [(M) id. import]. O de Paris, Barenboim, (i) with Ch.
(BB) **(*) Naxos Dig. 8.550262 [id.]. Belgian Radio & TV O (Brussels), Alexander Rahbari.
(B) * Decca Eclipse Dig. 448 229-2; *448 229-4* [(M) id. import]. Cleveland O, Ashkenazy; (i) with women's chorus (with RAVEL: *Rapsodie espagnole* **).

La Mer; Nocturnes: Nuages; Fêtes (only). *Prélude à l'après-midi d'un faune. Printemps* (symphonic suite).
(BB) *** RCA Navigator 74321 21293-2 [(M) 6179-2-RG]. Boston SO, Munch.

La Mer; Images: Iberia. Nocturnes: Nuages; Fêtes (only); *Prélude à l'après-midi d'un faune.*
(M) *** [RCA Basic 100 09026 61556-2]. Boston SO, Munch.

La Mer; Prélude à l'après-midi d'un faune.
(M) *** DG 427 250-2. BPO, Karajan – RAVEL: *Boléro; Daphnis et Chloé.* ***
(M) *** EMI CDM7 64357-2 (id.]. BPO, Karajan – RAVEL: *Alborada* etc. ***

After three decades, Karajan's 1964 account of *La Mer*, now reissued in DG's Legendary Recordings series of 'Originals', is still very much in a class of its own. So strong is its evocative power that one feels one can almost see and smell the ocean. It enshrines the spirit of the work as effectively as it observes the letter, and the superb playing of the Berlin orchestra, for all its virtuosity and sound, is totally self-effacing. For CD reissue, the performance is coupled with Karajan's outstanding (1966) record of Mussorgsky's *Pictures at an exhibition* and a gripping account of Ravel's *Boléro*, but it is still also available with an equally unforgettable coupling of the *Prélude à l'après-midi d'un faune* and Ravel's *Daphnis et Chloé.*

Reiner's 1960 recording is available coupled with either Rimsky-Korsakov's *Scheherazade* or Respighi's *Fountains* and *Pines of Rome*. It has all the warmth and atmosphere that make his version of *Ibéria*, recorded at about the same time (see above), so unforgettable. The pianissimo opening has enormous evocative feeling and the *Jeux des vagues* has the same haunting sense of colour. Of course the marvellous acoustics of the Chicago Hall contribute to the appeal of this superbly played account: the effect is richer and fuller than in Karajan's remastered DG version, and Reiner's record gives no less pleasure. With Karajan, one could picture the bracing air of the northern Atlantic, whereas with Reiner, although the dialogue of the wind and waves is no less powerful, one senses a more southerly latitude. The new coupling with Respighi is surely ideal, for Reiner's magical Roman evocations are among the most unforgettably evocative recorded performances the gramophone has to offer.

The new CD transfers on the inexpensive RCA Navigator reissue have completely transformed the Munch recordings, the Boston acoustic now casting a wonderfully warm aura over the orchestra; and the sound, hitherto rather fierce in its original LP format, is gloriously expansive and translucent. The result is that the opening of *Printemps* is ravishingly sensuous and the 1956 *La Mer* (also available alternatively coupled) has plenty of atmosphere to match its undoubted excitement. There is marvellous Boston playing here, especially from the violins, and the climax of the former is driven very hard indeed (*Fêtes* is similarly pressed on with comparable emotional force). Munch's inclination to go over the top may not appeal to all listeners, but the results are very compelling when the orchestral bravura is so thrilling. The *Prélude* makes a ravishing interlude, expanding to a rapturous climax.

Ormandy is a master of French repertoire, and in his 1964 set of *Nocturnes* the orchestral playing has the superb subtlety of timbre we expect from a Philadelphia performance of a great score and it is only in the last piece, *Sirènes*, where, as so often happens, the female chorus refuses to sound quite ethereal enough. The recording is quite full and atmospheric. *La Mer* dates from the early days of stereo (1959). It is relatively closely balanced and the dynamic range is somewhat more restricted, though not impossibly so. The orchestral playing in *Jeux de vagues* has thrilling virtuosity, and subtlety too, and the sustained gentle playing at the halfway point of the *Dialogue du vent et de la mer* means that the climax in the strings which follows seems the more ecstatic. The *Prélude à l'après-midi d'un faune* (with a fine flute solo from William Kincaid) is sensuous but refined, although the early recording date is conveyed by the timbre of the violins above the stave; the *Danse* is stunningly played, yet the conductor's touch is as light as anyone could wish. Indeed, all the technical reservations notwithstanding, this is one of Ormandy's most impressive Sony reissues.

Barenboim's 1978 coupling of *La Mer* and *Nocturnes*, reissued on DG's Classikon bargain label, offers not only first-class analogue recording but performances which, although highly individual in their control of tempo, have great electricity. For some ears the effect (with the wind balanced rather forward) may lack the subtlety that distinguishes Karajan's analogue version, but there is an ardour that more than compensates. The *Prélude à l'après-midi d'un faune* has comparable languor to *Sirènes*, the last of the *Nocturnes*, if not quite the same refinement of feeling. This too is very well recorded.

Karajan's 1978 analogue re-recording of *La Mer* for EMI may not have quite the supreme refinement of his earlier DG version – partly a question of the warmer, vaguer recording – but it has a comparable concentration, with the structure persuasively and inevitably built. The *Prélude* has an appropriate languor, and there is a persuasive warmth about this performance, beautifully moulded; but again the earlier version distilled greater atmosphere and magic.

Ansermet's 1964 *La Mer*, although vibrant and vividly detailed, did not match his earlier recordings in the quality of the orchestral playing, with moments of suspect intonation. The rest of this concert, however, shows the Swiss conductor on top form.

Judging from these Naxos performances, the Flemish section of the Belgian Radio Orchestra under its Iranian-born conductor, Alexander Rahbari, is in good shape. They give eminently respectable (and certainly very well-recorded) accounts of these familiar Debussy scores and, though they would not perhaps be a first choice among a discography that includes Reiner, Giulini and Karajan (whose Salzburg assistant Rahbari was), this certainly fits the bill for young (or even not so young) collectors with limited means just starting to explore classical music. Perhaps *Fêtes* could have slightly more pace and tension (though it is far from slack), but the strength of Rahbari's *Nocturnes* is the good female choir in *Sirènes*, which are well focused and in tune. The account of *La Mer* needs just a bit more excitement, though *Jeu de vagues* comes off very well. The atmospheric and very natural recording is a major plus. You can do worse than this with a full-price disc, and no one buying this is going to feel badly let down.

Ashkenazy's Cleveland versions, although having the advantage of superb (1987) digital sound, seem unable to get inside the music; tempi are often unconvincing, and the beautiful *Prélude à l'après-midi d'un faune* lacks shape without a really strong central climax.

La Mer; (i) *Nocturnes. Prélude à l'après-midi d'un faune.*

(BB) *** Carlton LSO Double Dig. 30368 01187 (2) [(B) id. import]. LSO, Frühbeck de Burgos, (i) with L. Symphony women's chorus – BIZET: *Jeux d'enfants* **; RAVEL: *Ma Mère l'Oye* **(*); SAINT-SAENS: *Carnival of the animals.* **

Although strong in Mediterranean atmosphere, Frühbeck de Burgos's account of *La Mer* has an underlying grip, so he can concentrate on evocation at the opening and create a real pianissimo, helped by the wide dynamic range of the Walthamstow recording. Later he indulges in a moment of sultry rubato in the early part of the *Dialogue du vent et de la mer*, and yet he continues to lead the ear on spontaneously. Overall there is plenty of excitement, with the LSO's virtuosity in the finale matched by the rich-toned ardour of the strings when they rise to the emotional peak of *Jeux de vagues*. There is much subtlety of detail, both here and in the *Nocturnes*, where textures again have the sensuousness of southern climes, while the processional of *Fêtes* proceeds spectacularly, glittering with colour. The *Prélude à l'après-midi d'un faune* brings lovely, delicate flute-playing from Paul Edmund-Davies and a richly moulded string climax. If these are not conventional readings, they are full of impulse and are superbly recorded.

(i) *La Mer; Prélude à l'après-midi d'un faune;* (ii) *Prélude: La cathédrale engloutie* (orch. Stokowski).
(M) *** Decca Phase Four 455 152-2 [id.]. (i) LSO; (ii) New Philh. O; Stokowski – RAVEL: *Daphnis et Chloé: suite No. 2*. ***

Stokowski's version of *La Mer* is a Phase Four recording, using multi-microphones to most brilliant effect. Some ears will find the balance artificial, and the strings are brightly lit, but the effect is breathtaking in its vividness and impact. The performance has surprisingly slow basic tempi, even for Stokowski, and the *Prélude à l'après-midi d'un faune* is comparably languorous. But the playing has a wonderful intensity, with the sound characteristically moulded. In *La Mer*, like Ansermet and Karajan, Stokowski adds the extra brass parts in the last movement, which are authentic though excised from the printed score. Stokowski's spectacular arrangement of *La cathédrale engloutie* presents the music in wholly orchestral terms and is quite different from the piano original. Coupled with a rich version of the *Second suite* from *Daphnis and Chloé*, this is highly recommendable to all admirers of this remarkable musician.

Petite suite (orch. Büsser).
(B) *** Sony SBK 63056; *SBT 63056* [id.]. Cleveland O, Louis Lane – RAVEL: *Introduction and allegro* etc.; SATIE: *Gymnopédies Nos. 1 & 3*. ***

It is good to have a first-class performance of Debussy's *Petite suite* in Büsser's charming orchestration on bargain label. The recording dates from the late 1960s when Louis Lane was a colleague of George Szell at Cleveland and the orchestra was still at the peak of its form. The recording, made in Severance Hall, is warm and atmopheric, not as forwardly balanced as some from this source. The rest of the programme is equally recommendable.

CHAMBER MUSIC

(i) *Cello sonata;* (ii) *Danse sacrée et danse profane;* (iii) *En blanc et noir; 6 Epigraphes antiques; Lindajara; Petite suite;* (iv) *Sonata for flute, viola and harp;* (v) *Syrinx;* (vi) *String quartet in G min.;* (vii) *Violin sonata*.
(B) ** EMI Rouge et Noir CZS5 69656-2 (2) [(M) id. import]. (i) Maurice Gendron, Jacques Février; (ii) Annie Challan, Paris Conservatoire O, André Cluytens; (iii) Jean-Philippe Collard, Michel Béroff; (iv–v) Michel Debost; (iv) Yehudi Menuhin, Lily Laskine; (vi) Parrenin Qt; (vii) Christian Ferras, Pierre Barbizet.

A mixed bag, no doubt, but worth the money. The *Danses sacrée et profane for harp and strings* with Annie Challen and the underrated André Cluytens conducting the Paris Conservatoire strings is lovely, and many of the other performances are rewarding. Maurice Gendron's account of the *Cello sonata* with Jacques Février is not as well recorded as his later version for Philips (with Jean Françaix), but most of the performances here will give pleasure. Few sweep the board but none fall below a certain level of artistry. There are more magical accounts of the *Sonata for flute, viola and harp* than we have from Michel Debost, Menuhin playing the viola and Lily Laskine (this is perhaps the least successful of the performances here), but there is much musical satisfaction to be found in the Parrenins' *String quartet in G minor*, the Ferras–Barbizet account of the *Violin sonata* in the same key and the Béroff–Collard partnership's *En blanc et noir*. The recordings, mostly from the late 1960s and early 1970s, are more than adequate.

Cello sonata in D min.
(M) *** Decca 452 895-2. Rostropovich, Britten – BRITTEN: *Sonata;* SCHUMANN: *5 Stücke in Volkston*. ***
(M) ** Virgin/EMI Dig. CUV5 61198-2 [id.]. Steven Isserlis, Pascal Devoyon – FRANCK; POULENC: *Cello sonatas*. **

Like Debussy's other late chamber works, the *Cello sonata* is a concentrated piece, quirkily original. The classic version by Rostropovich and Britten has a clarity and point which suit the music perfectly. The recording is first class and, if the couplings are suitable, this holds its place as first choice. It is fully worthy of reissue in Decca's Classic Sound series

Steven Isserlis and Pascal Devoyon also make a well-matched partnership, though the latter is ill-served by the engineers. His piano entry sounds pretty thunderous, though both these fine players are exposed to rather too close a scrutiny. Isserlis brings great intensity to the middle movement, and there are many things to admire throughout this extraordinarily concentrated masterpiece; but this is not a first recommendation.

Cello sonata; Sonata for flute, viola and harp; Violin sonata; Syrinx for solo flute; Prélude à l'après-midi d'un faune (arr. Sachs for 2 violins, viola, cello, double-bass, flute, oboe, clarinet, antique cymbals, piano & harmonium).
(M) **(*) DG 449 549-2. Boston Symphony Chamber Players.

During the early years of the First World War Debussy planned to compose a set of six sonatas for various combinations of instruments, but he died before he could complete the project. However, the three that he did write are all masterpieces, particularly the exquisite *Sonata for flute, viola and harp*. It is a logical idea to assemble them on one disc and, though the performances do not wholly dislodge others from one's affections – Rostropovich's Decca account of the *Cello sonata* (417 833-2) and Kyung Wha Chung's version of the *Violin sonata* with Radu Lupu (see below) – they are very nearly as fine. As a bonus, Doriot Anthony Dwyer plays the *Syrinx* for solo flute most beautifully; but the most intriguing item, which opens the concert, is the familiar *Prélude à l'après-midi d'un faune*, heard in a very clever arrangement for chamber ensemble by Benno Sachs, a pupil of Schoenberg. Berg apparently took part at its première in 1920. Debussy's harp parts are transferred to the pianist and the harmonium gently fills in the sustained harmony. Although one misses a fuller body of violins at the central climax, the result remains remarkably transparent. The Boston musicians (who include Joseph Silverstein as violinist and Michael Tilson Thomas as an elegant pianist in the *Violin sonata*) do not disappoint in any of these pieces; but the reverberation of the Boston acoustic, although it suits the *Prélude*, very slightly clouds the textural subtleties of the *Trio*. Nevertheless this remains an attractive collection.

Cello sonata in D; Sonata for flute, viola and harp; Syrinx (for solo flute); *Violin sonata in G min.;* (i) *Chansons de Bilitis* (song-cycle).
(BB) ** Virgin Classics Double Dig. VBD5 61427-2 (2) [CDVB 61427]. Nash Ens. (members), (i) with Delphine Seyrig – RAVEL: *Chamber music*. **(*)

From the Nash Ensemble, there is a little too much of a halo of resonance round Marcia Crayford in the *Violin sonata*, and the piano looms too large both here and in the *Cello sonata*, exquisitely played by Christopher van Kampen. Nor is the *Trio sonata* ideally balanced: there is too much flute, though again there are no grumbles about the playing. The *Chansons de Bilitis* are excellently done, though the resonant acoustic serves to produce a slightly plummy sound for the ensemble which is too overpowering for Delphine Seyrig's intimate, almost whispered delivery. This is an agreeable programme, but it is not as successful sonically as it is artistically. However, this collection remains very acceptable at such a modest cost, and the Ravel coupling is apt and of comparable musical excellence.

Le petit nègre; Petite pièce; Première rapsodie; Rapsodie for cor anglais; Rapsodie for saxophone; Sonata for flute, viola and harp; (i) *Syrinx*.
(B) *** Cala Dig. CACD 1017 (2) [(M) id.]. William Bennett, Nicholas Daniel, James Campbell, Rachael Gough, (i) Simon Haram & Ens. – SAINT-SAENS: *Chamber music*. ***

Another two-CD set for the price (and shape) of one, the first volume of French chamber music for woodwind. The *Rapsodie for cor anglais* with which it opens is more familiar in its form for alto saxophone, which was originally to have been called *Rapsodie Mauresque*. Daniel plays it with great sensitivity. It is also heard in its alternative form, splendidly played by Simon Haram. The performance of the *Sonata for flute, viola and harp* is highly sensitive.

Piano trio in G.
(BB) **(*) Naxos Dig. 8.550934 [id.]. Joachim Trio – RAVEL: *Piano trio;* SCHMITT: *Piano trio: Très lent*. **(*)

The *G major Trio* is an early work, dating from about the time Debussy went to Russia as the guest of Mme Nadezhda von Meck. It came to light only in the late 1970s and is not very characteristic; it can best be described as a work more of promise than of achievement. The Joachim Trio comprise Rebecca Hirsch, Caroline Dearnley and the pianist John Lenehan, and they play with consistent sensitivity and finesse. The *Trio* has been recorded by several ensembles on a number of occasions and, though this is a thoroughly musical account and beautifully recorded, it would not necessarily be a first choice, though the attractive price-tag (and the agreeable Schmitt bonus) makes it competitive.

Sonata for flute, viola and harp.
✿ (M) *** Decca 452 891-2 [id.]. Osian Ellis, Melos Ens. (members) – RAVEL: *Introduction and allegro;* ROUSSEL: *Sérénade for flute, violin, viola, cello & harp;* ROPARTZ: *Prélude, marine et chansons*. *** ✿

The delectable *Sonata for flute, viola and harp* is ravishingly played by members of the Melos Ensemble, and it brings a hauntingly magical atmosphere to compare with its sublime Ravel coupling.

String quartet in G min.
(M) *** Ph. 420 894-2. Italian Qt – RAVEL: *Quartet.* ***
(B) *** CfP Dig. CD-CFP 4652 [(M) id. import]. Chilingirian Qt – RAVEL: *Quartet.* ***
(BB) *** Naxos Dig. 8.550249 [id.]. Kodály Qt – RAVEL: *Quartet* etc. ***
(B) **(*) Sony SBK 62413; *SBT 62413* [id.]. Tokyo Qt – RAVEL: *Quartet* **(*); FAURE: *Piano trio.* (*)
(M) ** DG (IMS) Dig. 445 509-2 [id.]. Emerson Qt – RAVEL: *Quartet.* **

The Debussy and Ravel quartets are an almost mandatory coupling these days and even Dover Scores reprint the two together! It need hardly be said that the playing of the Quartetto Italiano is outstanding. Perfectly judged ensemble, weight and tone still make this a most satisfying choice and, even if it is rather short measure, the Philips recording engineers have produced a vivid and truthful sound-picture.

At bargain price the Chilingirian coupling is also in every way competitive. They give a thoroughly committed account with well-judged tempi and very musical phrasing. The Scherzo is vital and spirited, and there is no want of poetry in the slow movement. The recording has plenty of body and presence and has the benefit of a warm acoustic: the sound is fuller than on the competing version by the Italian Quartet.

As we know from their Haydn recordings, the Kodály Quartet are an excellent ensemble and they give a thoroughly enjoyable account that can be recommended to those who do not want to spend that bit extra on the mid-priced Quartetto Italiano version. There are moments here (in the slow movement, for example) when the Kodály, too, are touched by distinction. This music-making has the feel of a live performance and is to be preferred to some of the glossier, mechanized accounts at full price: these players also have the benefit of a generous fill-up and very good recorded sound. Excellent value.

The Tokyo Quartet play with ardour and finesse. In the slow movement their blend of timbres is very beautiful. But the outer movements are very volatile indeed and, although they are of one mind, the result at times seems too restless. The 1977 recording is close but otherwise very good.

The Emersons play with amazing precision and body of sound on DG, but their performances are too high-powered to do full justice to the sensibility of Debussy's score. The playing dazzles – but then, so does strip-lighting!

(i) *String quartet in G min.;* (ii) *Cello sonata;* (iii; iv); *Sonata for flute, viola and harp;* (v) *Violin sonata in G min.;* (iii) *Syrinx.*
(M) *** Ph. 442 655-2. (i) Italian Qt; (ii) Gendron, Françaix; (iii) Bourdin; (iv) Lequien, Challan; (v) Grumiaux, Hajdu.

These excellent sonata performances from the mid-1960s do not wholly dislodge others from one's affections, for example Rostropovich's account of the *Cello sonata* or the Chung version (also on Decca) of the *Violin sonata*, but they are nearly as fine. Gendron's version of the *Cello sonata* is most eloquent and, with the estimable Italian performance of the *Quartet* added for good measure, this very naturally recorded 72-minute collection can be given a warm welcome

Violin sonata.
✿ (M) *** Decca 460 006-2 [id.]. Kyung Wha Chung, Radu Lupu – FRANCK: *Violin sonata* *** ✿; CHAUSSON: *Poème.* ***
(B) *** EMI Eminence Dig. CD-EMX 2244 [(M) id. import]. Tasmin Little, Piers Lane – POULENC: *Violin sonata;* RAVEL: *Violin sonata; Tzigane.* ***

Kyung Wha Chung plays with marvellous character and penetration, and her partnership with Radu Lupu could hardly be more fruitful. Nothing is pushed to extremes, and everything is in perfect perspective. The recording sounds admirably real.

In Debussy's elusive late *Sonata* Tasmin Little and Piers Lane also give a highly dedicated performance which tautly holds together the often fragmentary argument, making the result sound spontaneous in its total concentration. Excellent sound and a first-rate coupling.

PIANO MUSIC

Piano duet

En blanc et noir; 6 Epigraphes antiques; Lindaraja; Marche écossaise; Petite suite.
(B) *(*) HM Musique d'Abord HMA 190957 [id.]. Claude Helffer, Haakon Austbø.

(i) *En blanc et noir; Lindaraja.* (Piano): *Estampes; Images I & II; L'isle joyeuse; Masques.*
(B) *** EMI CES5 72376-2 (3) [(M) id. import]. Jean-Philippe Collard, (i) with Michel Béroff – RAVEL: *Piano music.* ***

Distinguished playing from Jean-Philippe Collard in the *Estampes* and the two sets of *Images*, and his collaboration with Michel Béroff in *En blanc et noir*, one of the most inspired of Debussy's works, is hardly less successful. Here only Werner Haas with Noël Lee, and Argerich with Stephen Kovacevich, recorded not long afterwards, were superior – and the latter is currently out of circulation. The recording, made in the early 1970s at the Salle Wagram, is less satisfactory but good enough to warrant a full 3-star recommendation on artistic grounds.

Claude Helffer and Haakon Austbø recorded their Debussy in the early 1970s, and their playing has undoubted style and a refined musicianship, though neither the instruments (in *En blanc et noir* there are some ugly unisons) nor the studio can be called ideal. The recorded sound is another matter, and the set does not present a challenge to the Collard/Béroff set on EMI or to the Werner Haas–Noël Lee partnership on Philips (see below).

Piano duet: (i) *En blanc et noir; 6 Epigraphes antiques; Lindaraja; Marche écossaise; Petite suite*. (Solo piano): *Ballade slave; Berceuse héroïque; Danse (Tarantelle styrienne); Danse bohémienne; D'un cahier d'esquisses; 12 Etudes; Hommage à Haydn; Masques; Nocturne; Le petit nègre; La plus que lente; Rêverie; Suite bergamasque; Valse romantique*.
(B) *** Ph. Duo 438 721-2 (2) [id.]. Werner Haas, (i) with Noël Lee.

2 Arabesques; Children's corner; Estampes; Images, Books 1–2; L'isle joyeuse; Mazurka; Pour le piano; Préludes, Books 1–2.
(B) **(*) Ph. Duo 438 718-2 (2) [(M) id. import]. Werner Haas.

The playing of Werner Haas is rarely routine. Book II of the *Préludes* (sample *Feux d'artifice*) and many of the pieces from Book 1 are very well worth having; the *Images* are pretty good too (*Reflets dans l'eau* sparkles iridescently), and many of the shorter pieces in the second listed volume are neatly and sensitively characterized. What makes its companion pair of CDs indispensable is the splendid collection of Debussy's music for piano duet (four hands or two pianos), recorded a decade later, in which Haas is joined by Noël Lee. The *Petite suite* is delightfully fresh, and *En blanc et noir* and the *Six épigraphes antiques* are very distinguished indeed. The (early 1960s) piano recording throughout is well up to Philips's high standard, and the CD transfers are first class. As usual with this bargain series, the documentation is very good.

Solo piano music

2 Arabesques; Ballade slave; Berceuse héroïque; Children's corner; Danse (Tarantelle styrienne); Danse bohémienne; D'un cahier d'esquisses; Elégie; Estampes; Etudes, Books I–II; Hommage à Haydn; Images, Books I–II; Images oubliées; L'isle joyeuse; Masques; Mazurka; Morceau de concours; Nocturne; Page d'album; Le petit nègre; La plus que lente; Pour le piano; Préludes, Books I–II; Suite bergamasque; Valse romantique.
✿ (BB) *** ASV Dig. CDQS 432 (4) [(B) id.]. Gordon Fergus-Thompson.

This ASV set deserves a Rosette for enterprise alone. It represents an extraordinary bargain in offering distinguished performances of Debussy's complete piano music, admirably recorded, for quite a lot less than the cost of two premium-priced CDs. Gordon Fergus-Thompson's survey maintains a consistently high standard of artistry. His set of the elusive *Etudes* is altogether excellent, and so is *Pour le piano*. He finds the full charm and character of *Children's corner*, while the shorter pieces, the *Arabesques*, the quirky *Le petit nègre* and *Rêverie* for instance, are beguilingly presented. The evocation of this unique repertoire is perceptively caught throughout, not least in the *Images*. If one places his sets of *Préludes* alongside those of Gieseking or Arrau, they are less individually distinctive, yet the characterization remains telling, especially the sequence in Book II of *General Lavine-eccentric*, *La terrasse des audiences du clair de lune*, *Ondine*, *Hommage à S. Pickwick Esq.*, *PPMPC* (with its quotation of 'God save the King' emerging boldly in the bass), *Canope*, *Les tierces alternées* and the final *Feux d'artifice*, magnetic in its luminous virtuosity. Throughout, this playing shows a genuine feeling for the Debussy palette and, with fine, modern, digital recording, the piano-image mellow and true, these records will give great satisfaction.

2 Arabesques; Children's corner; Estampes; Images, Books 1–2; L'Isle joyeuse; Pour le piano; Préludes, Book 1; Rêverie; Suite bergamasque.
(B) *** Decca Double 443 021-2 (2) [id.]. Pascal Rogé.

Pascal Rogé's playing is distinguished by a keen musical intelligence and sympathy, as well as by a subtle command of keyboard colour, and this Double Decca set must receive the warmest welcome. *Children's corner* is played with neat elegance and the characterization has both charm and perception, while the *Suite bergamasque* brings crisp, well-articulated playing in the *Passepied* and genuine poetry in the famous *Clair de lune*. *Pour le piano* is no less distinguished, and the *Images* are full of evocative imagery. In

Estampes there are occasional moments when the listener senses the need for more dramatic projection, but Rogé brings genuine poetic feeling to the first book of the *Préludes*. Here he communicates atmosphere and character in no small measure and has greater warmth than Michelangeli and Zimerman, perhaps partly the effect of the 1978 recording, which has a slightly fuller recording in the bass than the rest of the programme. The other recordings were made in 1977 and 1979 and the CD transfers are clear and firm.

2 Arabesques; Ballade; Danse; Danse bohémienne; Mazurka; Nocturne; Pour le piano; Rêverie; Suite bergamasque; Valse romantique.
(BB) * Naxos Dig. 8.553290 [id.]. François-Joël Thiollier.

La boîte à joujoux; Children's corner; Epigraphes antiques; Le petit nègre.
(BB) *(*) Naxos Dig. 8.553291 [id.]. François-Joël Thiollier.

Estampes; Images, Books I & II; Images oubliées; L'isle joyeuse; La plus que lent.
(BB) * Naxos Dig. 8.553292 [id.]. François-Joël Thiollier.

Given the quantity and quality of what is currently available on CD, François-Joël Thiollier's survey of Debussy's piano music is less than competitive. True, he captures the spirit and some of the charm of *La boîte à joujoux*, but he has neither the finesse nor the sensitivity of such rivals as Pascal Rogé (Decca), Arrau (Philips), Livia Rév (Saga), Youri Egorov (EMI) or Gordon Fergus-Thompson (ASV), all of whom are most competitively priced. The Naxos sound is decent and Thiollier is far from negligible, but readers can do far better.

2 Arabesques; Ballade; Danse bohémienne; Danse (Tarantelle styrienne); Images (1894); *Nocturne; Pour le piano; Rêverie; Suite bergamasque; Valse romantique.*
(B) *(**) Carlton Dig. 30367 01012 [(M) id.]. Martino Tirimo.

Tirimo's playing is distinguished and there is never any doubt as to his Debussian credentials. He plays only the two outer movements of the 1894 *Images*, arguing quite reasonably that the differences between the two versions of the *Sarabande* are very slight. But the balance is very close and the microphone even picks up the pedal mechanism (try the opening of the *Danse* on track 8) to an almost unacceptable extent. The acoustic of Rosslyn Hill Chapel, Hampstead, does permit the sound to expand – but some slight background noise from the environs (probably what was posing problems for the engineer) would be better than putting the listener virtually on the piano stool.

2 Arabesques; Ballade; Danse bohémienne; Images, Books 1–2; Images (1894); Mazurka; Nocturne.
(M) *** Saga EC 3376-2 [id.]. Lívia Rév.

For a long time Lívia Rév was underrated as a pianist; it was these Debussy recordings which established her reputation, receiving just acclaim when they first appeared on CD. This compilation (77 minutes 38 seconds) can hold its own with any in the catalogue. Lívia Rév has sensibility, a finely developed sense of colour, a keen awareness of atmosphere and fleet fingers. She is moreover decently recorded in a spacious acoustic, and the CD transfers are extremely successful.

2 Arabesques; Ballade; Images, Book 1: Reflets dans l'eau; Mouvement. Book 2: Poissons d'or. L'isle joyeuse; Préludes, Book 2: Feux d'artifice. Suite bergamasque.
(B) *** EMI CD-EMX 2055 [(M) id.]. Daniel Adni.

This collection dates from 1972 and is outstanding in every way: this young Israeli pianist proves himself a Debussian of no mean order. His recital is well planned and offers playing that is as poetic in feeling as it is accomplished in technique.

2 Arabesques; Berceuse héroïque; Etudes Nos. 7–8, 10–12; Images (1905; 1907); L'Isle joyeuse; Masques; La plus que lente; Préludes, Books 1–2; Rêverie.
(B) ** EMI Rouge et Noir CZS5 68988-2 (2) [(M) id. import]. Samson François.

There is some spirited playing from Samson François and the piano is well enough recorded (between 1968 and 1970), but François is not consistently sensitive nor does he always observe the dynamic nuances so important in this repertoire. Robust rather than refined, and no match for Rogé.

2 Arabesques; Children's corner; Estampes; Images, Book 1; L'Isle joyeuse; Page d'album: Pièce pour le vêtement du blessé; La plus que lente; Pour le piano; Préludes, Book 1.
(BB) ** Virgin Classics Dig. Double VBD5 61421-2 (2) [CDVB 61421]. Jean-Bernard Pommier.

Accomplished playing comes from Jean-Bernard Pommier, an intelligent artist with a good feeling for Debussy and excellent technical address. He is often perceptive; but there is strong competition here and, notably in the *Préludes* (where Pommier's bold articulation brings some hardness), the good must yield to the better. The recording is basically truthful, a little bottom-heavy at times.

2 Arabesques; Children's corner; Etudes: Pour les cinq doigts d'après M. Czerny; Pour les arpèges composés. Images: Poissons d'or. L'Isle joyeuse; Le petit nègre; La plus que lente; Préludes, Book 1: Des pas sur la neige; Book 2: Ondine; La terrasse des audiences du clair de lune; Feux d'artifice. Suite bergamasque: Prélude.
(B) *** CfP Dig. CD-CFP 4653 [(M) id. import]. Moura Lympany.

Dame Moura Lympany's choice cannot be faulted and this is among the finest recitals of its kind in the catalogue. The subtle colouring of *La plus que lente* is as impressive as the power and glowing ardour of the closing *L'Isle joyeuse*. The *Arabesques* are played rhapsodically with distinct individuality and there are few finer or more imaginative performances of *Children's corner*, here presented as children's imagery seen through adult eyes. Among the *Préludes* the remarkably compelling *La terrasse des audiences du clair de lune* comes over as truly impressionistic in feeling rather than in any way pictorial. *Feux d'artifice* flashes with brilliance. The whole recital emerges as a spontaneous experience, and it is worth noting that the pianist was 76 years young when she went into EMI's Abbey Road Studio to make this record, which is very realistically recorded indeed. The notes by Peter Avis are a model of what documentation for a miscellaneous recital should be.

(i) *2 Arabesques; Danse; L'isle joyeuse; Masque; La plus que lente; Pour le piano;* (ii) *Préludes, Books I–II* (complete); (i) *Suite bergamasque*.
(B) *** DG Double 453 070-2 (2) [(M) id. import]. (i) Tamás Vásáry; (ii) Dino Ciani.

Vásáry is at his finest in the *Suite bergamasque*, and *Clair de lune* is beautifully played, as are the *Arabesques*. Dino Ciani has a fine technique (witness *Feux d'artifice*) and plays both Books of *Préludes* with intelligence and taste. Both artists are very well recorded indeed. There is a good deal of Debussy's best-known piano music here, offered inexpensively, and this is a very satisfying pair of discs in its own right.

Arabesques 1–2; Images I and II; Préludes, Book 1: *Des pas sur la neige; La fille aux cheveux de lin; La danse de Puck;* Book 2: *Général Lavine: dans le style et le mouvement d'un cake-walk; Les terrasses des audiences du clair de lune; Feux d'artifice. Suite bergamasque.*
(BB) *(*) Naxos Dig. 8.550253 [id.]. Klára Körmendi.

The Hungarian pianist Klára Körmendi is a sympathetic advocate of Messiaen, Boulez, Berio and other contemporary composers and, judging from this recital, an idiomatic interpreter of Debussy, too. Moreover the recording, made at the Italian Institute in Budapest, at first seems more acceptable than some others Naxos have made at this venue. But when the level rises above *forte*, the sound dries out and hammers are all too evident: try *La plus que lente* (Track 5) and this will become clear.

Berceuse héroïque; D'un cahier d'esquisses; Etudes, Books 1–2; Morceau de concours; Suite bergamasque.
(M) *** Saga EC 3383-2 [id.]. Lívia Rév.

Lívia Rév is consistently imaginative and her playing has considerable poetic feeling, as well as great technical accomplishment. The *Suite bergamasque* is also highly sensitive. The 1980 recording is excellent and the disc offers 75 minutes of music.

Children's corner; Elégie; Hommage à Haydn; Page d'album; Préludes, Book 1; La plus que lente; Danse (Tarantelle styrienne).
(M) *** Saga EC 3377-2 [id.]. Lívia Rév.

Lívia Rév plays *Children's corner* very well, and her performance of the *Préludes* holds its own in terms of sensitivity and atmosphere. Her keyboard mastery is beyond question (just sample *La cathédrale engloutie*) and she is a fine colourist. The recording, too, is first class.

Children's corner; Estampes; La fille aux cheveux de lin; L'Isle joyeuse; La plus que lente; Suite bergamasque.
(M) DG 445 547-2 [id.]. Alexis Weissenberg.

Why DG should have chosen to reissue this in the Masters series is inexplicable. The recording is one of the most insensitive – indeed brutal – accounts of Debussy to have been committed to disc. Dynamic nuances are totally ignored and such subtleties as pianissimo unknown. Totally unacceptable artistically, though well enough recorded. Not recommended.

Children's corner suite; La plus que lente; Préludes, Book 1: La fille aux cheveux de lin. Suite bergamasque: Clair de lune.
(BB) (*) RCA Navigator 74321 24214-2 [(M) id. import]. Weissenberg – SATIE: *Piano music.* ***

Alas, Alexis Weissenberg is an insensitive Debussian. He begins *Children's corner* much too fast and adds unnecessary rubato to *Clair de lune*, while similarly *La fille aux cheveux de lin* lacks the simplicity which conveys innocence.

Estampes; Images, Books 1–2; Préludes, Books 1–2.
(M) *** Ph. (IMS) 432 304-2 (2). Claudio Arrau.

Claudio Arrau's versions of these solo piano works by Debussy are very distinguished. The piano timbre in these 1978/9 analogue recordings has a consistent body and realism typical of this company's finest work.

Estampes; Préludes, Books 1–2 (complete); *Images: Reflets dans l'eau.*
(BB) *** CfP Dig. Silver Double CDCFPSD 4805 (2) [id.]. Youri Egorov.

The Classics for Pleasure Silver Double has the advantage of considerable economy since it brings us the *Estampes* and the first of the *Images*, *Reflets dans l'eau*, as well as the two Books of *Préludes*, at the cost of a single medium-priced CD. Youri Egorov is a very fine player indeed; he gives performances of commanding keyboard technique, exquisite refinement and atmosphere. The recording is very good, a shade too reverberant perhaps and not quite as clear as Arrau (Philips) or Rogé (Decca). However, the hazy atmosphere in evocations like *Voiles*, *La cathédrale engloutie* and indeed in *Reflets dans l'eau* is very telling, and this must rank high in current CD sets of the complete *Préludes*.

12 Etudes; Estampes; L'isle joyeuse.
(B) **(*) Carlton Dig. 30367 0018-2 [(M) id.]. Martino Tirimo.

Martino Tirimo offers not only the *Etudes*, played with imagination and much subtlety of colour, but also a set of *Estampes* and *L'isle joyeuse*, neither quite as impressive but still worth having. He is very well recorded.

Images: Poissons d'or. Préludes: La fille aux cheveux de lin; Général Lavine – eccentric; Feux d'artifice. La Plus que lente; Rêverie.
(M) (***) EMI (SIS) mono CDM5 66067-2 [id.]. Rudolf Firkušny – SMETANA: *Polkas & dances.* (***)

This record is of special interest for the sparkling Smetana items which are Firkušny's special province. But his Debussy is also distinguished and, if the sound is limited, it is perfectly acceptable.

Préludes, Books 1–2 (complete).
✿ (M) *** EMI mono CDH7 61004-2 [id.]. Walter Gieseking.
(B) *** Carlton IMP Classics Dig. 30367 0079-2 [(M) id.]. Martino Tirimo.
(B) **(*) RCA Dig. Twofer 74321 49185-2 (2) [id.]. Catherine Collard.
(B) **(*) Nonesuch/Warner Ultima 7559 79474-2 (2) [(M) id. import]. Paul Jacobs.

Gieseking penetrates the atmosphere of the *Préludes* more deeply than almost any other artist. This is playing of rare distinction and great evocative quality. However, the documentation is concerned solely with the artist and gives no information about the music save the titles and the cues.

No grumbles about value for money or about quality from Martino Tirimo on Carlton; he accommodates both Books on the same disc. His playing is very fine indeed and can withstand comparison with most of his rivals – and, apart from the sensitivity of the playing, the recording is most realistic and natural. This is probably a first choice for those wanting a modern digital record offering the complete set, although Egorov's CfP Silver Double (see above) offers more music.

Catherine Collard's RCA set brings the problem that the reflective qualities of her playing mean that her total timing is 85 minutes – too long for a single CD. But this is a very distinguished set, and many will count the cost and layout value for money. Her playing has superb technical command and flair, matched by her evocative imagination. She brings a penetrating understanding to this many-faceted music. Book 2 is particularly fine, with *Brouillards* and *Feuilles mortes* beautifully evoked and *Ondine* glitteringly chimerical. *Canope* and *Les tierces alternées* also show her at her most sensitive, and *Feux d'artifice* is dazzling. The recording is first class, cleanly focused and fully coloured, the ambience virtually ideal.

Paul Jacobs's choice of occasionally slower tempi than his competitors also means that his complete set of *Préludes* stretches uneconomically over a pair of CDs. So, although offered as an Ultima Double, in effect they cost more. His playing is highly evocative, helped by the atmospheric analogue recording, so effective in a piece like *Brouillards*. And he can be quirky too, as in the engagingly lighthearted account of *La danse de Puck*. There is much to appeal here, but in the last resort this Nonesuch set cannot be a top recommendation.

Préludes, Book 1; Images oubliées (1894).
(M) **(*) Channel Classics Dig. CCS 4892 [id.]. Jos van Immerseel.

The special interest of Jos van Immerseel's recording of the first book of *Préludes* lies in his instrument, an Erard of 1897, of the kind which Debussy would have known and played. The sonority is gentle and veiled and curiously seductive except in *forte* passages; the timbre, particularly in the upper register of the instrument, is monochrome and dry, and this tells in a piece such as *La sérénade interrompue*. There is a real turn-of-the-century feel to the shadowy sound-world of *Des pas sur la neige* and the first of the *Images oubliées*. An interesting appendix for a Debussy discography, but essentially this is an issue for specialist collections.

Préludes, Book 2.
(M) **(*) Saga EC 3347-2 [id.]. Lívia Rév.

Lívia Rév's Saga recording of the second book of *Préludes* comes from the 1970s. We thought quite highly of it at the time, giving it a full three-star grading. The playing has great polish and finesse, and it gives pleasure. However, at 39 minutes it is no bargain. Book 2 is less well represented in the catalogue than its companion, but there is no shortage of excellent packages that offer both books in distinguished performances which are worth the extra outlay (Gieseking etc).

VOCAL MUSIC

Mélodies: (i) *Aimons-nous et dormons;* (ii) *Les Angélus;* (iii) *Ariettes oubliées;* (iv) *3 Ballades de François Villon; Beau soir;* (ii) *La Belle au Bois dormant;* (i) *Calmes dans le demi-jour;* (ii) *3 Chansons de Bilitis;* (iv) *Chanson de France;* (i) *4 Chansons de jeunesse;* (ii) *Les cloches;* (v) *Danse de jardin; L'échelonnement des haies; Fêtes galantes* (1st group); (iv) *Fêtes galantes* (2nd group); (v) *Fleur de blés;* (i) *Jane;* (iv) *Mandoline; La mer est plus belle;* (v) *Noël des enfants qui n'ont plus de maison; Nuit d'étoiles;* (i) *Paysage sentimental;* (ii) *5 Poèmes de Charles Baudelaire;* (v) *3 Poèmes de Stéphane Mallarmé;* (iv) *Le promenoir des deux amants;* (v) *4 Proses lyriques;* (i) *Romance; Rondeau; Rondel chinois;* (iv) *Le son du cor s'afflige;* (i) *Voici que le printemps; Zéphyr.*
(M) *** EMI CMS7 64095-2 (3) [ZDMC 64095]. (i) Mady Mesplé; (ii) Michèle Command; (iii) Frederica von Stade; (iv) Gérard Souzay; (v) Elly Ameling; all with Dalton Baldwin.

These three generously filled discs at mid-price offer no fewer than 55 of Debussy's songs out of a total of just over 80. Drawn from recordings made between 1971 and 1979, they were all done in the Salle Wagram in Paris with Dalton Baldwin accompanying. Arranged in the order of publication, they give an illuminating idea of the composer's development, from his earliest Fauré-like songs, through his vital discovery of the poet Verlaine as his most consistent source of inspiration, and on to the rarefied atmosphere of the late songs such as the Villon and Mallarmé settings. Charmingly, he followed those last two groups with a little simple song to words he had composed himself, *Noël des enfants qui n'ont plus de maison*, written in 1915 as a heartfelt response to the First World War. Though Mady Mesplé's bright soprano has a flutter in it as recorded, hers is the smallest contribution, and all the others are in splendid voice, with Michèle Command characterfully French and Gérard Souzay at his freshest. The most ravishing singing of all comes from Elly Ameling and Frederica von Stade. The latter sings ecstatically in Debussy's evocative setting of Verlaine's most famous poem, *Il pleure dans mon coeur* (from the *Ariettes oubliées*), with Baldwin bringing out the subtlety of the pattering accompaniment. Well-balanced, clear sound. The booklet provides an essay in English and French, with full texts in French only.

3 Ballades de François Villon; 3 Chansons de France; Fêtes galantes (2nd series); Noël des enfants qui n'ont plus de maison; 3 Poèmes de Stéphane Mallarmé; Le promenoir des deux amants.
(M) **(*) Auvidis Valois V 4803. Bernard Kruysen, Noël Lee.

Bernard Kruysen was perhaps the most distinguished Dutch baritone of his day and arguably the finest exponent of French song after Souzay. Although he was an admired broadcasting artist, he made relatively few records, though older collectors will remember the recitals issued by Valois on LP during the late 1960s. The present recital comprises the contents of one 1971 LP which, at just under 40 minutes, is distinctly poor value even at mid-price. Artistically these are strong performances, aristocratic in demeanour and well characterized. Kruysen is sensitively and perceptively accompanied by Noël Lee, and well recorded too, and though it offers short measure this disc is worth its asking price.

La damoiselle élue.
(M) *(*) Sony Theta Dig. SMK 60031 [id.]. Frederica von Stade, Susanne Mentzer, Tanglewood Festival Ch., Boston SO, Ozawa – BERLIOZ: *Nuits d'été* *(*); RAVEL: *Shéhérazade*. **(*)

Debussy's early cantata, *La damoiselle élue*, has been seriously neglected on record. It is a highly evocative setting of Rossetti in translation, using women's chorus and mezzo-soprano solo for the central role of the Blessed Damozel. Coupled with a disappointing version of Berlioz's *Nuits d'été*, von Stade's reading of Debussy's early cantata is only marginally more recommendable, failing to create the necessary atmosphere. This is due less to von Stade's singing than to the unidiomatic narrator and the chorus. Good recording.

OPERA

Pelléas et Mélisande (complete).
(B) *** Naxos 8.660047-9 (3) [id.]. Mireille Delusch, Gérard Theruel, Armand Arapian, Gabriel Bacquier, Hélène Jessoud, Ch. Regional Nord/Pas de Calais, O Nat. de Lille, Jean-Claude Casadesus.
(M) **(*) Sony SM3K 47265 (3) [S3K 47265]. Shirley, Söderström, McIntyre, Ward, Minton, ROHCG Ch. & O, Boulez.

Enterprisingly, Naxos went to Lille to record stage performances by the excellent opera company there, and though the spaciousness of Casadesus's sensitive and poetic reading means that the set stretches to three discs rather than two the result is most compelling, with fresh, young voices helping to make the drama more involving. Mireille Delusch is a bright and girlish Mélisande, well matched against the high baritone of Gérard Theruel as a boyish Pelléas. Their dreamy wonder at meeting each other is touchingly conveyed, and it provides a convincing slant on the story that the young and virile Golaud of Armand Arapian is a more credible lover-figure than is usually presented, not just a jealous villain but a puzzled and frustrated elder brother. The others are first rate too, including the veteran, Gabriel Bacquier, aptly sounding old as Arkel. The voices are to the fore in the recording, with every word made clear, though the staging occasionally brings a discrepancy of balance. The orchestra, with a modest band of strings, adds to the chamber-scale intimacy. The libretto comes in French only, but with good notes and a synopsis in English – though it would have made it easier for the non-French speaker to follow, had there been more than a minimal number of cue-points provided. An outstanding bargain nevertheless.

Boulez's sharply dramatic view of Debussy's atmospheric score is a performance which will probably not please the dedicated Francophile – for one thing there is not a single French-born singer in the cast – but it rescues Debussy from the languid half-tone approach which for too long has been accepted as authentic. He is supported by a strong cast; the singing is not always very idiomatic but it has the musical and dramatic momentum which stems from sustained experience on the stage. In almost every way this has the tension of a live performance.

De la Rue, Pierre (*c*. 1460–1518)

Missa l'homme armé; Missa pro defunctis (Requiem).
(M) *** HM Suite Dig. HMT 7901296 [id.]. Clement Janequin Ens., Dominique Visse.

Pierre de la Rue was a Flemish composer who entered into the service of Margaret of Austria, Governess of the Netherlands, whose favourite he was – and no wonder. His music is extraordinarily expressive, his flowing polyphony procures the richest harmonies and vivid colouring. His *Mass*, based on the chanson *L'homme armé*, exploits that famous tune with great resourcefulness: the music is outgoing and affirmative in spirit and full of imagination. He composed his *Requiem* before its liturgical sequence was fixed, and its format is: *Introitus* (*Requiem*); a brief *Kyrie*; *Psalmus* (No. 41); *Offertorium*; *Sanctus et Benedictus*; *Agnus Dei* and *Communio*. The lyrical melancholy of its lines is most affecting, with the harmony often resting sonorously on its firm bass. The *Sanctus and Benedictus* is simple yet remarkably diverse and powerful, the *Qui tollis* haunting. The closing *Communio* is compressed (*Lux aeterna . . . Cum sanctis . . . Requiem aeternam . . . Et lux perpetua luceat eis*) but none the less telling for that. Marvellous music, beautifully sung and recorded. A real find.

Delalande, Michel-Richard (1657–1726)

Symphonie pour les soupers du roy No. 5.
(BB) *** HM Solo Dig. HMS 926009 [id.]. Ens. La Simphonie du Marais, Hugo Reyne.

No. 5 of the twelve *Symphonies* which Delalande wrote to accompany the evening meals of Louis XIV proves to be one of the most attractive, including as it does a winningly diverse 9½-minute *Capriccio, que le Roy demandoit souvent* ('which the King demanded often'). The other movements also offer an *Air* (with tambourine) and a quick *Chaconne* (with castanets). Well worth exploring in the very lowest price-range.

Confitebor tibi Domine; Super flumina Babilonis; Te Deum.
(B) *** HM Dig. HMX 290850.52 (3) [(M) id. import]. Gens, Piau, Steyer, Fouchécourt, Piolino, Corréas, Les Arts Florissants, William Christie – BOUZIGNAC: *Te Deum* etc.; Marc-Antoine CHARPENTIER: *Missa Assumpta est Maria* etc. *** ❀

Confitebor tibi Domine (1699) and *Super flumina Babilonis* (1687) have much expressive writing, and the performances under William Christie are light and airy but not wanting in expressive feeling. The more familiar *Te Deum* is given as good a performance as any that has appeared in recent years. The sound is airy and spacious, and the performances combine lightness and breadth. While this CD remains available at premium price, it also comes in a slip-case as part of a highly recommendable bargain triptych, linked with the *Te Deum* settings of Bouzignac and Charpentier. This is a superb set in every way.

Delibes, Léo (1836–91)

Coppélia (ballet): complete.
(B) *** Decca Double 444 836-2 [id.]. SRO, Bonynge – MASSENET: *Le Carillon*. ***
(B) **(*) Ph. Duo 438 763-2 [id.]. Rotterdam PO, David Zinman – CHOPIN: *Les Sylphides;* GOUNOD: *Faust: ballet music*. **(*)

On the Double Decca reissue of his earlier (1969) analogue set, Bonynge secures a high degree of polish from the Suisse Romande Orchestra, with sparkling string and wind textures, and with sonority and bite from the brass. The Decca recording sounds freshly minted and, with its generous Massenet bonus, little-known music of great charm, this set remains very competitive.

David Zinman's performance of *Coppélia* is beautifully played and most naturally recorded. The warm acoustic of the Rotterdam concert hall certainly suits Delibes's colourful scoring and the gracefully delicate string-playing is nicely flattered. The performance has no want of vigour or refinement and, if it is without the sheer character of Bonynge's performance, it is still very enjoyable in its own right. The Chopin and Gounod couplings are similarly smooth and elegant, and all are offered at the cost of one premium-priced CD.

Coppélia (ballet; complete); *La Source: suites Nos. 2 & 3; Intermezzo: Pas de fleurs.*
(BB) *** Naxos Dig. 8.553356/7 [id.]. Slovak RSO (Bratislava), Mogrelia.

Mogrelia's complete Naxos set of *Coppélia* is very attractive indeed. The Bratislava orchestra plays with characteristic finesse and grace and with glowing lyrical feeling. There is both drama and vitality. The recording is warm and spacious, with the orchestra set slightly back. Other versions may have more surface brilliance (the *Musique des automates* in Act II could glitter more brightly), but most lovers of ballet music will enjoy the naturalness of perspective and the attractively smooth string-quality. *La Source* comes off equally well. The *Pas de fleurs Grande valse* is a real lollipop and in the two suites the music (selected rather arbitrarily) has plenty of colour and rhythmic life.

(i) *Coppélia* (ballet): complete; *Sylvia* (ballet): complete.
(M) *** Mercury (IMS) 434 313-2 (3) [id.]. (i) Minneapolis SO, Dorati; (ii) LSO, Fistoulari.

Both Mercury recordings are very early stereo (*Coppélia* 1957, *Sylvia* 1958), but neither sounds its age and *Sylvia*, using the expansive acoustics of Watford Town Hall, approaches the demonstration bracket. Fistoulari was among the very greatest of ballet interpreters and this shows him at his most inspired. The conductor displays his deep affection for the ballet in every bar; his sense of delicacy and grace and his feeling for the specially French elegance of the woodwind writing are demonstrated throughout. The LSO play superbly for him, the woodwind ensemble is outstanding and the solo playing most beautiful.

Dorati's recording of *Coppélia* makes a lively contrast. This Minneapolis recording has never sounded better than it does here. The acoustic is rather more confined at the bottom end, but the conductor's vivid combination of energy and grace is appealing in a score that teems with bright melodies and piquant orchestral effects.

Coppélia: extended excerpts; *Sylvia:* extended excerpts.
(B) *** EMI Rouge et Noir (SIS) CZS5 69659-2 (2) [CDZB 69659]. Paris Op. O, Mari.

Jean-Baptiste Mari's pair of CDs are offered for the price of one in the French Rouge et Noir series. The sound is fresh and the extra brightness of focus brings no attendant edginess. Mari uses ballet tempi throughout, yet there is never any loss of momentum, and the long-breathed string-phrasing and the felicitous wind solos are a continual source of delight. Mari's natural sympathy and warmth make the very most of the less memorable parts of the score for *Sylvia* (and they are only slightly less memorable). Seventy-five minutes are offered from each ballet.

Coppélia (ballet): suite.
(B) *** DG 429 163-2 [id.]. BPO, Karajan – CHOPIN: *Les Sylphides* *** ❀; OFFENBACH: *Gaîté parisienne:* excerpts. ***

Karajan secures some wonderfully elegant playing from the Berlin Philharmonic Orchestra, and generally his lightness of touch is sure. The *Csárdás*, however, is played very slowly and heavily, and its curiously studied tempo may spoil the performance for some. The recording is very impressive; but it is a pity that in assembling the CD the suite had to be truncated (with only 71 minutes' playing time, at least one more number could have been included). As it is, the *Scène et valse de la poupée*, *Ballade de l'épi* and the *Thème slav varié*, all present on the original analogue LP, are omitted here.

(i) *Coppélia* (ballet) suite; (ii) *Sylvia* (ballet) suite.
(B) *** Sony SBK 46550; *SBT 46550* [id.]. Phd. O, Ormandy – CHOPIN: *Les Sylphides* ***; TCHAIKOVSKY: *Nutcracker suite*. **(*)

Ormandy and the Philadelphia Orchestra are on top form here. The playing sparkles and has a fine sense of style. Both suites are done in a continuous presentation but are, unfortunately, not banded. The recording is notably full and brilliant in the CBS manner.

Coppélia; Sylvia; Naïla (ballet suites): *excerpts*.
(B) ** Millennium MCD 80402 [id.]. V. State Op. O, Abravanel – TCHAIKOVSKY: *Nutcracker:* excerpts. **

Lively, decent performances of some numbers from the Delibes ballets, but nothing to write home about either artistically or as a recording. The date is not given but we would guess that it is late 1950s.

Coppélia: suite; *Kassya: Trepak; Le roi s'amuse:* suite; *La Source:* suite; *Sylvia:* suite.
(BB) **(*) Naxos Dig. 8.550080; *4550080* [id.]. Slovak RSO (Bratislava), Ondrej Lenárd.

An attractive hour of Delibes, with five key items from *Coppélia*, including the *Music for the Automatons* and *Waltz*, four from *Sylvia*, not forgetting the *Pizzicato*, and four from *La Source*. Perhaps most enjoyable of all are the six pastiche ancient *airs de danse*, provided for a ballroom scene in Victor Hugo's play, *Le roi s'amuse*. (The second of these, a haunting *Pavane*, is also used by Respighi in his collection of *Ancient airs and dances*.) They are played most gracefully here, and the excerpts from the major ballets are spirited and nicely turned. The overall effect is not as sumptuous or individual as Bonynge's Decca recordings, but the brightly lit digital sound has body too, and the acoustics of the Bratislava Concert Hall are not unflattering to Delibes's vivid palette. The tasteful solo horn-playing brings a vibrato (most strikingly in the melody which dominates the *Andante* of *La Source*), but this is to be expected in an East European orchestra; it would be unfortunate if such a feature was considered a deterrent. Excellent value, especially for those who have not already discovered Sir Thomas Beecham's recording of *Le roi s'amuse*.

Coppélia: highlights; *Sylvia:* suite.
(BB) **(*) Belart 461 352-2 [(M) id. import]. SRO, Ansermet.

Ansermet aficionados will be glad to have this inexpensive sampler of his detailed care and the vivacity of his ballet conducting in 1960. The passage where Swanhilda pretends to be Coppélia and dances her stiff little waltz is pointed lovingly. The snag is the ungenerous playing time: 45 minutes (overall) is a bit sparse, even for a budget CD, and it is a great pity that the selection was not extended to include at least the *Dance of the Automatons*, which sparkled like a musical box on the complete recording.

Sylvia (ballet): complete.
(B) *** Decca Double 448 095-2 (2) [id.]. New Philh. O, Richard Bonynge – MASSENET: *Le Cid*. ***
(BB) *** Naxos Dig. 8.553338/9 [id.]. Razumovsky Sinfonia, Mogrelia – SAINT-SAENS: *Henry VIII ballet music*. ***

Sylvia is played by Richard Bonynge with wonderful polish and affection, and the recording is full and brilliant in Decca's best manner. The CDs offer a splendid Massenet bonus, another recording out of Decca's top drawer, and this is even more attractive as a Double Decca.

Mogrelia's performance of *Sylvia* is above all spacious, bringing out the music's pastel-shaded lyricism yet finding plenty of weight for the more vigorous music depicting the hunters. The relaxed tempo for the famous *Valse lente* is quite well sustained and the Razumovsky Sinfonia carries this slighter of Delibes's two most famous ballet scores very pleasingly, with the gentle wind solos matching the caressing warmth of the strings. The *Divertissement* of Act III (which includes some of the best numbers, including the famous '*Pizzicato*') is vividly done. However, in the performance as a whole, glowing sentience takes precedence over vitality, and some might find the atmosphere at times a little sleepy. Excellent, naturally balanced recording.

OPERA

Lakmé (complete).

(M) *** Decca 425 485-2 (2). Sutherland, Berbié, Vanzo, Bacquier, Monte Carlo Op. Ch. and O, Bonynge.

Lakmé is a strange work, not at all the piece one would expect knowing simply the famous *Bell song*. This performance seizes its opportunities with both hands. Sutherland swallows her consonants, but the beauty of her singing, with its ravishing ease and purity up to the highest register, is what matters; and she has opposite her one of the most pleasing and intelligent of French tenors, Alain Vanzo. Excellent contributions from the others too, spirited conducting and brilliant, atmospheric recording.

Delius, Frederick (1862–1934)

'World of Delius': Air and dance; Fennimore and Gerda: Intermezzo. Hassan: Intermezzo and Serenade; Koanga: La Calinda. On hearing the first cuckoo in spring; A Song before sunrise; Summer night on the river; A Village Romeo and Juliet: The Walk to the Paradise Garden. (i) *Sea drift.*

(M) *** Decca 440 323-2. ASMF, Marriner; (i) John Shirley-Quirk, L. Symphony Ch., RPO, Hickox.

This orchestral collection was admirably recorded in 1977, but the quality is not in the least dated. These are lovely performances, warm, tender and eloquent. They are played superbly and recorded in a flattering acoustic. The recording is beautifully balanced – the distant cuckoo is highly evocative – though, with a relatively small band of strings, the sound inevitably has less body than with a full orchestral group. *Sea drift* was recorded (also by Argo engineers) three years later in 1980 and is a total success. Rather than lingering, Richard Hickox is urgent in his expressiveness, but there is plenty of evocative atmosphere. This is also available as a Double Decca, coupled with music of Elgar and Holst (see below). The effect of the CD transfer is most real and tangible, the chorus set back within a warm ambience.

2 Aquarelles (arr. Fenby); *Fennimore and Gerda: Intermezzo. Hassan: Intermezzo and serenade* (all arr. Beecham); *Irmelin: Prelude. Late swallows* (arr. Fenby); *On hearing the first cuckoo in spring; A Song before sunrise; Summer night on the river.*

(M) *** Chandos CHAN 6502 [id.]. Bournemouth Sinf., Norman Del Mar.

There are few finer interpreters of Delius than the late Norman Del Mar. The 49-minute concert creates a mood of serene, atmospheric evocation – into which Eric Fenby's arrangement of *Late swallows* from the *String quartet* fits admirably – and the beauty of the 1977 analogue recording has been transferred very well to CD, with all its warmth and bloom retained.

2 Aquarelles; Fennimore and Gerda: Intermezzo. On hearing the first cuckoo in spring; Summer night on the river.

(M) *** DG 439 529-2. ECO, Barenboim – VAUGHAN WILLIAMS: *Lark ascending* etc.; WALTON: *Henry V.* ***

Barenboim's luxuriant performances have a gorgeous sensuousness and their warm, sleepy atmosphere should seduce many normally resistant to Delius's pastoralism. The couplings are no less enticing; indeed, some might feel that this music-making has a touch of decadence in its unalloyed appeal to the senses.

Brigg Fair; Dance rhapsody No. 2; On hearing the first cuckoo in spring; In a summer garden.

(B) *** Sony SBK 62645; *SBT 62645* [id.]. Phd. O, Ormandy – VAUGHAN WILLIAMS: *Fantasias* etc. ***

Ormandy and his great orchestra, on peak form in the early 1960s, give warm, stirring and highly romantic performances of these four masterpieces. *Brigg Fair* – without loss of refinement of detail – expands gloriously at the appearance of the great string-tune, echoed by the horn, while the *Dance rhapsody* is particularly successful in its spontaneous vitality. Ormandy and his engineers do not seek the fragility, the evanescence of Delius's visions; for that one can turn to Beecham. But this music responds well to a riper approach and there is no danger here of Delius sounding faded. The sound is remarkably full and expansive, far more convincing than the original LP. With its equally involving coupling, this is a true bargain.

Brigg Fair; Eventyr; In a summer garden; A Song of summer.
(B) *** CfP CD-CFP 4568 [id.]. Hallé O, Vernon Handley.

Although the tempi are sometimes controversial, Handley is an understanding and exciting Delian, and these pieces are beautifully played. The digital recording is of EMI's best quality, matching clarity of definition with ambient lustre and rich colouring. A bargain.

(i) *Brigg Fair; La Calinda* (arr. Fenby); *In a summer garden; Fennimore and Gerda: Intermezzo. Hassan: Intermezzo* and (iii) *Serenade* (arr. Beecham); (ii) *Irmelin prelude;* (i) *Late swallows* (arr. Fenby); *On hearing the first cuckoo in spring; A song before sunrise;* (ii) *A song of summer;* (i) *Summer night on the river;* (ii) *A Village Romeo and Juliet: Walk to the Paradise Garden* (arr. Beecham); (i; iv) *Appalachia* (with brief rehearsal sequence).
(M) *** EMI CMS5 65119-2 [Ang. ZDMB 65119]. (i) Hallé O; (ii) LSO; Sir John Barbirolli; (iii) with Robert Tear; (iv) Balun Jenkins, Amb. S.

Sir John shows an admirable feeling for the sense of light Delius conjures up and for the luxuriance of texture his music possesses. The languor of the string and horn tune in *Brigg Fair* is matched by the almost Mediterranean feeling of the works evoking summer, whilst the gentle evocation of *La Calinda* contrasts with the surge of passionate Italianate romanticism at the arching string-phrases of the climax of *The walk to the Paradise Garden*. Barbirolli's style is evanescent in repose and more romantic than the Beecham versions but, with lovely playing from both the Hallé and the LSO, the first-rate analogue sound from the mid- to late 1960s adds to the listener's pleasure. In *Appalachia*, perhaps Barbirolli dwells a little too lovingly on detail to suit all tastes, but for the most part he gives an admirably atmospheric reading that conveys the work's exotic and vivid colouring.

Brigg Fair; In a summer garden.
(BB) ** Naxos Dig. 8.550229 [id.]. CSR SO (Bratislava), Adrian Leaper – ELGAR: *Enigma variations* etc. **

Entitled '*English Festival*', this generous (70 minutes) Naxos collection, digitally recorded in the Concert Hall of Slovak Radio, is undoubtedly good value, for the acoustic is expansive and the playing (especially of the woodwind and the solo horn in *Brigg Fair*) is sensitive. Adrian Leaper's readings are sympathetic and well judged, although *In a summer garden* sounds rather episodic.

Brigg Fair; On hearing the first cuckoo in spring.
(BB) (**) Belart mono 461 362-2 [(M) id. import]. LSO, Anthony Collins – ELGAR: *Introduction and allegro; Serenade;* VAUGHAN WILLIAMS: *Fantasias.* (*(*))

In a summer garden; Paris (The song of a great city); A Song of summer; Summer night on the river; A Village Romeo and Juliet: Walk to the Paradise Garden.
(BB) (**) Belart mono 461 358-2 [(M) id. import]. LSO, Anthony Collins.

The straight Belart transfers of these Decca mono recordings are effective enough, but the results cannot match the quality achieved by Mike Dutton in his later, much more sophisticated transfers (from which the copyright was withdrawn in order to make way for these reissues on Polygram's own super-bargain label). The mono recordings, made in the Kingsway Hall, were much admired in their day. Collins's performance of *Paris* is spontaneously full of passionate evocation, confirming him as an inspired and individual Delian in his own right, able to create a subtle control of mood and texture reminiscent of Debussy in its atmospheric impressionism. *First cuckoo* and the other gentler evocations are luminous in their woodwind detail and *Brigg Fair* has much delicacy of feeling, for the glow of the Kingsway Hall acoustic remains. But it would have been better if this Decca reissued material had been confined to Delius alone, for the Elgar and Vaughan Williams couplings on the first of the two discs bring a pinched, thin sound to the upper strings.

(i) *Cello concerto;* (ii) *Double concerto for violin and cello. Paris (the song of a great city).*
(B) *** EMI Dig. CD-EMX 2185 [(M) id.]. (i–ii) Rafael Wallfisch; (ii) Tasmin Little; RLPO, Mackerras.

This superb new recording of the *Double concerto*, with soloists who easily outshine their predecessors on record (however distinguished), confirms the strength of a piece which establishes its own logic, with each theme developing naturally out of the preceding one. Wallfisch is just as persuasive in the *Cello concerto*, and Mackerras proves an understanding interpreter of the composer in the big tone-poem, *Paris, the song of a great city*. The recording is comparably full and atmospheric.

Piano concerto in C min.
(B) *** EMI Dig. CD-EMX 2239 [(M) id.]. Piers Lane, RLPO, Handley – VAUGHAN WILLIAMS: *Piano concerto;* FINZI: *Eclogue.* ***

Piers Lane gives a masterly performance of the Delius *Piano concerto*, weighty without pomposity, which effectively counters ideas of this merely being 'sub-Grieg', early as it is. Lane's measured, concentrated reading of the slow movement is particularly compelling. An apt and unusual coupling.

Violin concerto.

(M) **(*) EMI CDM7 64725-2. Sir Yehudi Menuhin, RPO, Meredith Davies – ELGAR: *Violin concerto.* ***

Menuhin's performance, recorded in 1976, does not show the polish of his playing in earlier years, and the timbre is not always ideally sweet; but he gives a heartfelt performance, and the semi-improvisational freedom and radiant beauty of the writing above the stave are superbly caught. Meredith Davies provides an accompaniment that is full of delicately sensitive detail, if not as richly expressive as Boult's partnership in the coupled Elgar *Concerto*. The Abbey Road recording is truthful, warmly atmospheric and well balanced, to make this an indispensable coupling for lovers of English music.

Eventyr; North country sketches; Over the hills and far away; (i) *Koanga: Closing scene.*

(B) (***) Sony SBK 62747. RPO, Beecham; (i) with RPO Ch. (members).

A particularly valuable bargain reissue offering very successful transfers of Beecham recordings which have not been available for some time and which have never seemed as firm and realistic as this. The orchestral playing is memorably fine, with some superbly romantic horn playing in *Over the hills and far away*. But it is the *North country sketches* that are especially valuable, with translucent sounds from the high violins in *Winter landscape* that are almost Sibelian in feeling. The woodwind shine in the closing *March of spring* and also in the capricious *Eventyr* (*Once upon a time*), where Beecham handles the rhapsodic changes of impetus and dynamic with characteristic passion and subtlety. The closing scene from *Koanga*, full of evocative feeling, makes a fascinating coda with its brief solo and choral sequence. No apologies need be made for the mono recordings – made in 1950–51 – for Beecham was a master of orchestral balance.

Fennimore and Gerda: Intermezzo. Irmelin: Prelude. Koanga: La Calinda (arr. Fenby). *On hearing the first cuckoo in spring; Sleigh ride; A Song before sunrise; Summer night on the river; A Village Romeo and Juliet: The Walk to the Paradise Garden.*

(B) *** CfP CD-CFP 4304 [(M) id. import]. LPO, Vernon Handley.

Those looking for a bargain collection of Delius should find this very good value; Handley's approach to *The Walk to the Paradise Garden* is strongly emotional, closer to Barbirolli than to Beecham.

On hearing the first cuckoo in spring; Summer night on the river.

(B) *** DG Classikon 439 464-2; *439 464-4* [(M) id. import]. ECO, Barenboim – BRITTEN: *Serenade*; VAUGHAN WILLIAMS: *Greensleeves; Lark ascending.* ***

Hazily sensuous in the summer sunshine, Barenboim's performances are warmly and enticingly recorded, and here offered as part of a fine bargain collection of English music.

(i) *On hearing the first cuckoo in spring; Summer night on the river;* (ii) *Appalachia;* (iii) *Hassan: Intermezzo and Serenade; Closing Scene;* (iv) *Koanga: Closing Scene;* (v) *3 Songs: Cradle song; The Nightingale; Twilight fancies.*

(M) (***) Dutton mono CDLX7011 [id. full price]. (i) Royal Philharmonic Soc. O; (ii) BBC Ch., LPO; (iii) Royal Op. Ch., LPO; (iv) Jan van der Gucht, London Select Ch., LPO; (v) Dora Labette; Sir Thomas Beecham (i–iv) cond.; (v) (piano).

Appalachia, subtitled *Variations on an old slave song*, is the product of Delius's years in the Deep South and this, its première recording, dating from 1938, is generally speaking the more atmospheric of the two that Beecham made. In fact all these performances (particularly the excerpts from *Hassan*, *On hearing the first cuckoo in spring* and *Summer night on the river*) reinforce Beecham's legendary reputation as Delius's greatest interpreter. The recordings, all pre-war, are as beautifully presented as is possible and, although their frequency-range is inevitably limited (*On hearing the first cuckoo* and *Summer night* date from 1928), they wear their years gracefully. One is unlikely ever to hear this music better played than it is here.

Paris (The song of a great city).

(B) (***) Sony mono SBK 62748. RPO, Beecham – ARNELL: *Punch and the child;* BERNERS: *Triumph of Neptune.* (***)

Many Delius connoisseurs prefer Sir Thomas's 1934 account of *Paris*, but to our ears there is nothing much wrong and a lot right about this 1955 version. There is plenty of atmosphere and the old Beecham magic still casts a strong spell. Music-making of stature, and an indispensable acquisition for admirers of both conductor and composer. The new transfer is really very good, clear and well balanced, if lacking amplitude at the climax.

CHAMBER MUSIC

Violin sonata No. 3.

(M) (***) Dutton Lab. mono CDAX 8014 [id. full price]. Sammons, Long – BAX: *Nonet;* MOERAN: *String trio;* FERGUSON: *Octet.* (***)

The *Violin sonata No. 3* was one of the pieces which Delius dictated to Eric Fenby during his last years at Grez-sur-Loing. It was written in 1930, the same year as the Bax *Nonet* (Bax, incidentally, was the pianist at its first performance the same year with May Harrison, its dedicatee). The present recording was made 14 years later, during the war, by Albert Sammons, who had championed Delius's concerto and subsequently recorded it. Both he and Kathleen Long play it *con amore* but without excess of feeling. There are modern alternatives, but this performance has something special.

VOCAL MUSIC

(i) *An Arabesque;* (ii) *Hassan* (incidental music); (iii) *Sea drift.*

(B) (**(*)) Sony mono SBK 62752. (i) Einar Nørby; (ii) Lesley Fry; (iii) Bruce Boyce; (i–iii) BBC Ch., RPO, Beecham.

It is sad that these three Delius recordings, though made between December 1954 and February 1958 (after the advent of stereo), were done in mono only. Once that is said, the results are persuasive in a way unsurpassed by any rival Delius interpreter, with the lyrical line of each passage, central to the argument, lovingly drawn out. The transfers are clear but have some roughness from the original recording.

Florida suite; Idylle de printemps; Over the hills and far away; La Quadroone; Scherzo; (i) *Koanga: closing scene.*

(BB) *** Naxos Dig. 8.553535 [id.]. E. N. Philh. O, Lloyd-Jones; (i) with Susannah Glanville, Susan Lees, Irene Evans, Sandra Francis, Sue Peerce, Shirley Thomas.

This collection of early Delius works, most of them directly inspired by his years in Florida, makes a richly enjoyable first disc in Naxos's planned new Delius series, seductively played and beautifully recorded in full and atmospheric sound. Several of the works are new to disc, including the *Idylle de printemps*, fresh and charming, leading to an ecstatic climax. *La Quadroone* and *Scherzo* were originally planned as movements in a suite, the first inspired by the sort of dances Delius came upon in Florida. Lloyd-Jones has clearly learnt from Beecham's example in his glowing and intense readings of the other three works, with the orchestra's woodwind soloists excelling themselves in delicate pointing, not least in the haunting *La Calinda*, included in the *Florida suite. Over the hills and far away*, raptly done, is richly evocative too, and the epilogue to the opera, *Koanga*, rounds off a generously filled disc with music both sensuous and passionate, featuring six female vocal soloists from Opera North, three sopranos and three mezzos.

(i) *Koanga: La Calinda;* (ii) *Late swallows;* (iii; iv) *Margot La Rouge: Prelude.* (iii; v) *A Song before sunrise;* (iii; iv) *A Village Romeo and Juliet: Walk to the Paradise Garden.* (vi) *Cynara;* (vii; iii; v) *Songs of farewell;* (viii) *To be sung of a summer night on the water;* (ix) *Wanderer's song.*

(B) *** EMI CD-EMX 2198 [(M) id. import]. (i) Philh. O, Weldon; (ii) Hallé O, Barbirolli; (iii) RPO; (iv) Meredith Davies; (v) Sargent; (vi) Shirley-Quirk, RPO, Groves; (vii) Royal Choral Soc.; (viii) Tear, King's College Ch., Ledger; (ix) Baccholian Singers of L.

A highly successful anthology, worth any Delian's money. Only George Weldon's *La Calinda* is a little stiff, and that comes at the very end. The programme opens with a ravishing account of the *Songs of farewell* under Sargent, who proves highly sympathetic in both the items he directs. This was the most ambitious work the composer attempted to write after he had become blind and paralysed. Sir Malcolm conducted the first performance in March 1932 with the Royal Choral Society, and his presentation is committed and warm-hearted in the best tradition of Delius recording, while the Abbey Road sound is full and sensuous. Barbirolli's *Late swallows* (another piece in which Eric Fenby had a hand) is hardly less evocative, and John Shirley-Quirk is equally at home in *Cynara*, a Dowson setting, while the wordless songs *To be sung of a summer night on the water* sound particularly well in their original *a cappella* vocal form. The transfers of recordings, all made in the 1960s – except the *Wanderer's song*, which is later – are managed most pleasingly.

(i) *A Mass of Life;* (ii) *An Arabesque;* (iii) *Songs of sunset.*
(M) *** EMI (SIS) CMS7 64218-2 (2) [ZDMB 642182]. (i) Harper, Watts, Tear, Luxon, LPO Ch., LPO; (ii) J. Baker, Shirley-Quirk; (ii; iii) RLPO Ch. & O; Groves.

Groves inspires his performers to a magnificent account of the *Mass of Life*, fully worthy of the work. It is good to have this music on CD in such fine, clearly focused sound – though, curiously, the very mistiness of some passages in Beecham's old mono set made the results more evocative still. The other two works are also very successful here: the *Songs of sunset* and *An Arabesque*. John Shirley-Quirk does the solo part impressively and the results fall not far short of Beecham's standard, though they lack his sense of magic. He is joined by Dame Janet Baker singing most affectingly in the *Songs of sunset*. Again very good transfers of recordings made in the Philharmonic Hall, Liverpool, in 1968.

Sea drift.
(B) *** Decca Double 443 170-2 (2) [id.]. Shirley-Quirk, L. Symphony Ch., RPO, Hickox – ELGAR: *Dream of Gerontius* **(*); HOLST: *Hymn of Jesus*. ***
(M) ** EMI CDM5 65113-2. John Noble, RLPO Ch. & O, Groves – STANFORD: *Songs of the Fleet* etc. **(*)

This dedicated performance under Richard Hickox brings John Shirley-Quirk as a characteristically sensitive soloist, and the chorus – trained by Hickox – is outstanding. The 1980 Kingsway Hall recording is both fresh and warmly atmospheric. Even though this is an inexpensive reissue, a full text is provided.This is also available as part of '*The World of Delius*' – see above.

Sir Charles Groves could be a persuasive Delian, but his 1973 recording of *Sea drift* is rather too matter-of-fact, failing to convey the surge of inspiration that so exactly matches the evocative colours of Walt Whitman's poem about the seagull, a solitary guest from Alabama. The recording is generally very good.

OPERA

Fennimore and Gerda (complete).
(M) ** EMI CDM5 66314-2. Söderström, Tear, Rayner Cook, Danish R. Ch. & SO, Meredith Davies.

Question: which opera includes in its libretto the line: 'Here is a telegram'? Not anything by Kurt Weill, or Menotti – let alone anyone more recent – but Frederick Delius who, with Philip Heseltine (Peter Warlock), wrote his own libretto for this adaptation of a novel by the Danish author, Jens Peter Jacobsen. It was Delius's last opera, full of the yearning mood-painting which is characteristic of him. It needs above all a musical persuader of the calibre of Beecham before it can really rivet the attention, and Meredith Davies falls short of that in his sympathetic but rather straight and unmagical direction. Though Elisabeth Söderström is not ideally cast, it is good to hear a singer so sensitive to the Delian vocal line. Good singing, too, from the rest of the team and excellent (1976) recording (made in Denmark), well transferred – happily on a single CD as against the original pair of LPs. Good notes, a synopsis and a full libretto are provided, so this reissue is excellent value and worth the attention of Delians.

Dering, Richard (*c.* 1580–1630)

Motets: *Ardens est cor meum; Ave Maria gratia plena: Ave verum corpus; Factum est silentium; Gaudent in coelis; O crux ave spes unica; O bone Jesu; O quam suavis; Quem vidistis, pastores?.*
(M) **(*) EMI Dig. CDM5 66788-2. King's College, Cambridge, Ch., Cleobury – PHILIPS: *Motets*. **(*)

Richard Dering and his older contemporary, Peter Philips, were Catholic expatriates who lived in the Spanish-dominated southern Netherlands. This CD contrasts and compares the two composers' settings of the same texts, drawing on Dering's *Cantiones sacrae* of 1617 and the *Cantica sacra* of 1618 and the posthumously published set of 1662. The performances are faithful, though sometimes a bit stiff; the actual sound, though good, is not ideal in focus or blend, partly perhaps but not solely due to the recording. Very recommendable all the same.

Diabelli, Anton (1781–1858)

Guitar sonata in A (ed. Bream).
(M) **(*) RCA 09026 61593-2. Julian Bream (guitar) – GIULIANI: *Grand overture* etc.; SOR: *Grand solo Sonata in C*. **(*)

Bream combined the first two movements of Diabelli's (guitar) *Sonata in F* with the two final movements of his *Sonata in A* into a single composite work with appropriate transpositions. The result makes a quite strong (if conventional) piece, which Bream brings fully to life, even if it is perhaps a shade long for its material at 18 minutes.

Dittersdorf, Carl Ditters von (1739–99)

Harp concerto in A (arr. Pilley).

✿ (M) *** Decca 425 723-2; *425 723-4*. Marisa Robles, ASMF, Iona Brown – BOIELDIEU; HANDEL: *Harp concertos* etc. *** ✿

Dittersdorf's *Harp concerto* is a transcription of an unfinished keyboard concerto with additional wind parts. It is an elegant piece, thematically not quite as memorable as the Boieldieu coupling, but captivating when played with such style.

Dohnányi, Ernst von (1877–1960)

Variations on a nursery tune (for piano and orchestra), *Op. 25*.

(M) *** Decca 448 604-2 [id.]. Julius Katchen, LPO, Boult – RACHMANINOV: *Piano concerto No. 2* etc. ***

(M) (***) Dutton mono CDLXT 2504 [id. full price]. Julius Katchen, LPO, Boult – RACHMANINOV: *Piano concerto No. 2* etc. (***)

It is surprising that the *Nursery variations*, once a regular repertory work, have fallen into relative neglect both on disc and in the concert hall. Katchen's 1954 mono recording with Boult has never been surpassed: there is a sense of new discovery, and the humour is all the more delightful for not being overplayed. So Boult conducts the grand orchestral introduction with a biting intensity worthy of Wagner, leaving Katchen to enunciate the nursery theme ('*Ah vous dirai-je maman*', or 'Twinkle twinkle little star'), not labouring the humour with any hint of archness at all. The waltz variation is given the most delectable Viennese lilt, and the final pay-off after the fugue is charmingly pointed. This vivid Dutton transfer offers full and firm piano-sound with fine presence, though there is a degree of edge on the thin, exposed high violins.

Katchen's 1959 remake of the *Nursery variations* has the advantage of Decca's finest vintage stereo and it has never sounded better than in this CD reissue, fully worthy of inclusion in Decca's Classic Sound series. The Wagnerian introduction is richly portentous, and from it grows a performance that is both perceptive and spontaneous, as full of wit as it is of lilt and flair. While the earlier account of 1954 by the same artists remains a dazzling example of Decca's mono recording at its most electrifying, collectors should not miss this more modern version which is otherwise unsurpassed and very beautifully balanced and recorded – indeed, in the demonstration bracket for its period. The generous couplings are hardly less recommendable.

Serenade in C for string trio, Op. 10.

(M) (***) RCA mono 09026 61763-2 [id.]. Heifetz, Primrose, Feuermann – BRAHMS: *Piano trio No. 1*; R. STRAUSS: *Violin sonata*. (***)

Quite sublime playing from Heifetz, Primrose and Feuermann, recorded in 1941. This performance has never been surpassed, though the recorded sound has! However, its deficiences do not diminish the artistic impact of the performance.

Donizetti, Gaetano (1797–1848)

Ballet music from: *L'assedio di Calais; Dom Sébastien; La favorita; Les martyres*.

(B) *** Ph. Duo 442 553-2 (2) [id.]. Philh. O, Antonio de Almeida – ROSSINI: *Ballet music*. **(*)

Music from the baroque period has given us dozens of records which are validly used for aural wallpaper. The ballet music from four of Donizetti's operas which were presented in Paris provides a nineteenth-century equivalent, sparkling, refreshing dances of no great originality, delivered here with great zest and resilience and fine solo playing, and excellently recorded. The Rossini coupling offers even more characterful music, and if the playing of the Monte Carlo Orchestra cannot match that of the Philharmonia, this is still very enjoyable.

String quartet in D (arr. for string orchestra).

(B) *** Decca Double 443 838-2 (2) [id.]. ASMF, Marriner – ROSSINI: *String sonatas Nos. 1–6* (with CHERUBINI: *Etude No. 2 for French horn and strings* (with Barry Tuckwell); BELLINI: *Oboe concerto in E flat* (with Roger Lord) ***).

This delightful 'prentice work has a sunny lyricism and a melodic freshness that speak of youthful genius. The composer's craftsmanship is obvious and the writing is such that (unlike Verdi's *String quartet*) it lends itself readily to performance by a string orchestra, especially when the playing is so warm-hearted and polished and the recording transferred so immaculately to CD. A fine bonus for the irresistible Rossini *String sonatas*.

Requiem.

(M) ** Decca (IMS) 425 043-2 [id.]. Cortez, Pavarotti, Bruson, Washington, Arena di Verona Lyric Ch. & O, Fackler.

There are many passages in Donizetti's *Requiem* which may well have influenced Verdi when he came to write his masterpiece. Donizetti's setting lasts for 65 minutes, but its inspiration is short-winded and it is not helped here by limited performance and recording, deriving from the Cime label. The singing and playing are generally indifferent. Pavarotti, recorded in 1979, is the obvious star, singing flamboyantly in his big solo, *Ingemisco*. Of curiosity value only.

OPERA

Anna Bolena (complete).

(B) **(*) Millennium MCD 80355 (3) [id.]. Sills, Burrowes, Verrett, Plishka, Lloyd, Kern, Tear, John Alldis Ch., LSO, Rudel.

(M) (**(*)) EMI mono CMS5 66471-2 (2) [CDMB 66471]. Callas, Simionato, Rossi-Lemeni, G. Raimondi, Carturan, La Scala, Milan, Ch. & O, Gavazzeni.

(M) ** Decca 455 069-2 (3) [id.]. Souliotis, Horne, Alexander, Ghiaurov, V. State Op. Ch. & O, Varviso.

By the light, bright character of her voice Beverly Sills is not ideally suited to the role of Donizetti's Anna Bolena, in which weight is required below, yet Sills here gives one of her finest, most characterful performances on disc, made the more effective by an excellent, full-blooded CD transfer of the original EMI recording. Anna's final scene before her execution is poignantly beautiful, prayerful, with lovely, poised singing, though the final cabaletta brings some edginess at the top. Sills is well matched by the heady tenor of Stuart Burrowes as Riccardo, with Shirley Verrett characterful as Giovanna Seymour and smaller roles excellently cast. Paul Plishka as the king sings powerfully, in firmer voice than usual. Ensembles are first rate, not least the Act I *Quintet* which finds Sills at her finest. As usual with operas on the Millennium label, no libretto is provided.

The Callas recording was made live at La Scala in 1957, with the great diva at her most searingly magnetic. This is a performance which, despite the occasional sour note, has one marvelling at the imaginative phrasing and subtlety of dynamic shading, with top notes firm and clear if characteristically edgy. Gavazzeni proves a most sympathetic conductor and, though the rest of the cast is no match for Callas, there is characterful if rather inflexible singing from Simionato as Giovanna and a fresh, clear contribution from Gianni Raimondi in the relatively small tenor role of Percy, here made the smaller by cuts. Nicola Rossi-Lemeni as Henry VIII is positive but gritty of tone in a less than convincing characterization. The radio sound is dry and limited with occasional interference, but for Callas fans this is well worth hearing.

In its day (1970) this pioneering Decca stereo recording was welcomed as being far more complete than any stage performance was likely to be, and it certainly gives an impressive idea of an opera which represents the composer in his most exuberant early flight (date 1830). Decca were later to trump their own hand by issuing Bonynge's superb digital version, outstandingly cast with Sutherland at her peak; but that remains at full price (410 096-2). In the present set Souliotis makes a formidable heroine and often produces Callas-like overtones. But with such dramatic command it is sad to report vocal carelessness that sometimes verges on the painful. The rest of the cast is more reliable, Marilyn Horne notable as Giovanna, Ghiaurov a rich-toned if rather unimaginative Henry VIII. Varviso conducts strongly and the Decca recording is characteristically vivid in its CD format.

Don Pasquale (complete).

(M) *** Decca 433 036-2 (2). Corena, Sciutti, Oncina, Krause, V. State Op. Ch. & O, Kertész – CIMAROSA: *Il maestro di cappella*. ***

(M) ** EMI (SIS) CMS5 66030-2 (2) [Angel CDMB 66030]. Sills, Kraus, Gramm, Titus, Ambrosian Op. Ch., LSO, Caldwell.

(BB) * Arte Nova/BMG Dig. 74321 49698-2 (2) [id.]. Antonucci, Sandelli, Tisi, Ruggeri, Putbus Festival Ch. & O, Keitel.

Under Kertész, Corena is an attractive *buffo*, even if his voice is not always focused well enough to sing semiquavers accurately. Juan Oncina, as often on record, sounds rather strained, but the tenor part is very small; and Krause makes an incisive Malatesta. Graziella Sciutti is charming from beginning to end, bright-toned and vivacious, and remarkably agile in the most difficult passages. The 1964 Decca recording is excellent, with plenty of atmosphere as well as sparkle.

With Beverly Sills as the heroine, the EMI set offers an impressive cast designed above all to attract the American collector. In 1978, when the recording was made, her career was winding down and when under pressure she can sound too strenuous, with the voice shrill above the stave. But just how charming she can be comes out in the final ensemble, which she treats with a delightful lightness. Opposite her Alfredo Kraus makes the most stylish Ernesto, singing with point and finesse, varying his tone beautifully. Donald Gramm is firm and dark as Pasquale, not the jolliest of *buffos* but reliable, and Alan Titus is nicely contrasted as Malatesta, equally reliable. Their patter duet in Act III is well pointed musically, but it fails to catch fire in humour, as it should, though some will welcome the omission of any comic business on the final cadence. Sarah Caldwell is similarly reliable, pointing rhythms well but rarely bringing out the full sparkle of the writing. At mid-price the Decca set remains preferable with a more idiomatic cast, and with Istvan Kertész finding much more fun in the piece. It also brings a valuable fill-up in Cimarosa's *Maestro di capella*.

The Arte Nova set, recorded at the Putbus Rossini Festival in Germany in the summer of 1997, suffers from variable balance, with the orchestra thin and distant in a dry acoustic, suggesting a recording on stage, yet without the advantage of the dramatic lift given by the presence of an audience. Not that the singing is stylish enough to win a recommendation, often too rough for Donizetti. As Norina, Paola Antonucci forces her tone on top and Patrizio Sandelli is too effortful as Ernesto. The two *buffo* roles are well enough cast, but with Wilhelm Keitel a competent yet unimaginative conductor the humour fails to take off in the final Act, with the patter duet even sounding a little cautious.

L'elisir d'amore (complete).

(M) *** Sony M2K 79210 (2) [M2K 34585]. Cotrubas, Domingo, Evans, Wixell, ROHCG Ch. & O, Pritchard.

(B) **(*) Decca Double 443 542-2 (2) [(M) id. import]. Gueden, Di Stefano, Corena, Capecchi, Mandelli, Maggio Musicale Fiorentino Ch. & O, Molinari-Pradelli.

(M) **(*) RCA Dig. 74321 25280-2 (2). Popp, Dvorský, Weikl, Nesterenko, Munich R. Ch. & O, Wallberg.

(M) **(*) EMI (SIS) CMS5 65658-2 [CDMB 65658] (2). Carteri, Alva, Panerai, Taddei, La Scala, Milan, Ch. & O, Serafin.

(B) ** Naxos Dig. 8.66045/6 [id.]. La Scola, Ruffini, Alaimo, Frontali, Hungarian State Op. Ch. & O, Pier Morandi.

On the Sony reissue delight centres very much on the delectable Adina of Ileana Cotrubas. Plácido Domingo by contrast is a more conventional hero and less the world's fool that Nemorino should be. Sir Geraint Evans gives a vivid characterization of Dr Dulcamara, though the microphone sometimes brings out roughness of tone, and Ingvar Wixell is an upstanding Belcore. The stereo staging is effective and the remastered recording bright and immediate. This set remains at full price in the USA.

With Hilde Gueden at her most seductive – an enchanting, provocative Adina, characterfully using her golden tone to bring out the minx-like qualities of the heroine – the very early (1955) Decca stereo recording offers a delightful, spontaneous-sounding performance. Not just Gueden but also the other soloists are strikingly characterful, with Giuseppe di Stefano at his most headily sweet-toned, singing with youthful ardour, Fernando Corena a strong and vehement Dulcamara and Renato Capecchi well contrasted as Sergeant Belcore, though not quite so firm of tone, but both splendidly comic. Even without a libretto it makes a good bargain, with two CDs offered for the price of one.

Wallberg conducts a lightly sprung performance of Donizetti's sparkling comic opera, well recorded and marked by a charming performance of the role of Adina from Lucia Popp, bright-eyed and with delicious detail both verbal and musical. Nesterenko makes a splendidly resonant Dr Dulcamara with more comic sparkle than you would expect from a great Russian bass. Dvorský and Weikl, both sensitive artists, sound much less idiomatic, with Dvorský's tight tenor growing harsh under pressure, not at all Italianate, and Weikl failing similarly to give necessary roundness to the role of Belcore. Like other sets recorded in association with Bavarian Radio, the 1982 sound is excellent.

Although reissued at mid- rather than bargain price (it last appeared on Classics for Pleasure), the La Scala set of *L'elisir d'amore* now comes with a full translation instead of a synopsis. It is still worth considering: it was a fine cast in its day (1959). Alva is a pleasantly light-voiced and engaging Nemorino.

Carteri's Adina ideally should be more of a minx than this, but the part is nicely sung all the same. Panerai as Belcore once again shows what a fine and musical artist he is, and Taddei is magnificent, stealing the show as any Dulcamara can and should. The drawback is Serafin's direction. The La Scala Chorus is lively enough, and it is not that the orchestral playing is slipshod, but they provide less sparkle than they should.

Naxos offers a sparkling performance of this enchanting comic opera, very well played and warmly – if reverberantly – recorded, which is sadly flawed by the choice of tenor to sing Nemorino. Vincenzo La Scola is far too strenuous in his delivery for this bel canto role, underlining too heavily. The great legato test-piece, *Una furtiva lagrima*, finds him less coarse, but this is a knowing, not an innocent, Nemorino. The others are better chosen, with Alessandra Ruffini bright-toned and vivacious as Adina, Simone Alaimo an excellent Dulcamara and Roberto Frontali agile and characterful as Belcore, both of them getting into their stride as the opera progresses.

La Favorita (complete).

(M) **(*) Decca (IMS) 430 038-2 (3). Cossotto, Pavarotti, Bacquier, Ghiaurov, Cotrubas, Teatro Comunale Bologna Ch. & O, Bonynge.

(B) ** Decca Double 452 469-2 (2). Simionato, Poggi, Bastianini, Maggio Musicale Fiorentino Ch. & O, Erede.

La Favorita has at least three outstandingly memorable numbers – *Spirito gentil*, *O mio Fernando* and *Per tanto amore* – as well as some characteristically brisk ensembles; but on the whole it falls short of the most famous Donizetti operas. The story of the young man who falls in love with his father's mistress has its dramatic point, but this was the sort of situation that Verdi was to develop much further. Fernando is strongly and imaginatively sung here by Pavarotti. The mezzo role of the heroine is taken by Fiorenza Cossotto, formidably powerful if not quite at her finest, while Ileana Cotrubas is comparably imaginative as her confidante Ines, but not quite at her peak. Bacquier and Ghiaurov make up a team which should have been even better but which will still give much satisfaction. Bright recording.

Donizetti's setting is not without its red-blooded moments, but this earlier Decca performance is not ingratiating enough to make one forget the weaknesses, for Gianni Poggi is a coarse tenor and neither Simionato nor Bastianini is in top form, for one detects the stiffness of new learning. Nor is Erede's conducting very dramatic, and the orchestra is not very vividly projected. But with very acceptable early stereo (1955) the voices and the chorus are well caught, and at Double Decca price any Donizettian could readily find this set worth while. There is, however, no translation, only an uncued synopsis.

La fille du régiment (complete).

(M) (*) Naxos mono 8.110018/9 [id.]. Pons, Jobin, Petina, Baccaloni, NY Met. Op. Ch. & O, Papi.

This recording of 1940 is one of the dimmer-sounding historic issues which Naxos have salvaged from NBC broadcast sources. Though Raoul Jobin is a superb Tonio, heady-toned and stylish, too much of the rest is flawed. Disappointingly, he omits the spectacular solo which gave Pavarotti the title 'King of the high Cs'. Lily Pons, the pocket prima donna who became a media star, is disappointing, for the light, bright, rather thin voice is not always identifiably pitched, with the topmost register, splendidly agile in coloratura, too often devolving into mere squeaks. This is the sort of performance that led to accusations of 'canary-fancying' against admirers of Donizetti. Even so, Pons makes Marie into an attractively volatile character and with her background the French text presents no problems. That is more than you can say for Salvatore Baccaloni, who as Sulpice is no more French-sounding than most Italian singers, though vocally he is strong and characterful. The conducting of Gennaro Papi is perfunctory, and the set is marred by stage and audience noises, as well as by the spoken introductions of Milton J. Cross.

Linda di Chamounix (complete).

(M) *(*) Ph. (IMS) 442 093-2 (2). Stella, Valletti, Barbieri, Capecchi, Di Palma, Teatro di San Carlo, Naples, Ch. & O, Serafin.

Despite the conducting of Serafin and fine contributions from Barbieri and Valletti, this Philips recording of 1956 is too seriously flawed to recommend except out of interest in an attractive rarity. The aria *O luce in quest'anima* has been a showpiece of the coloratura repertory, and nothing else matches it. But this opera is far from boring, and it is a pity that Antonietta Stella with her shallow, ill-controlled voice is inadequate in the title-role. The San Carlo chorus is also far too rough, and the recording is limited.

Lucia di Lammermoor (complete).

(M) *** Decca 411 622-2 (2) [id.]. Sutherland, Cioni, Merrill, Siepi, St Cecilia Ac., Rome, Ch. & O, Pritchard.

(M) (***) EMI mono CMS5 66438-2 (2) [CDMB 66438]. Callas, Di Stefano, Panerai, Zaccaria, La Scala Ch. & O, Karajan.

(M) (***) EMI mono CMS5 66441-2 (2) [CDMB 66441]. Callas, Di Stefano, Gobbi, Arie, Ch. & O of Maggio Musicale Fiorentino, Serafin.

(B) **(*) Ph. Duo 446 551-2 (2) [id.]. Caballé, Carreras, Sardinero, Ramey, Murray, Ahnsjö, Amb. S., New Philh. O, López-Cobos.

(M) ** RCA 09026 68537-2 (2). Peters, Peerce, Maero, Tozzi, Rome Op. Ch. & O, Leinsdorf.

The 1961 Sutherland version of *Lucia* remains an attractive proposition in the mid-price range. Though consonants were being smoothed over, the voice is obviously that of a young singer and dramatically the performance was close to Sutherland's famous stage appearances of that time, full of fresh innocence. Sutherland's coloratura virtuosity remains breathtaking, and the cast is a strong one, with Pritchard a most understanding conductor.

Recorded live in 1955, when Karajan took the company of La Scala to Berlin, for years this finest of Callas's recordings of *Lucia* was available only on pirate issues. Despite the limited sound, Callas's voice is caught with fine immediacy. Her singing is less steely than in the 1953 studio recording, and far firmer than in the 1959 one (now withdrawn).

Callas's earlier mono set dates from 1953. The diva is vocally better controlled than in her later stereo set (indeed some of the coloratura is excitingly brilliant in its own right), and there are memorable if not always perfectly stylish contributions from Di Stefano and Gobbi. As in the later set, the text has the usual stage cuts.

The idea behind the set with Caballé is fascinating: a return to what the conductor, Jésus López-Cobos, believes is Donizetti's original concept, an opera for a dramatic soprano, not a light coloratura. Compared with the text we know, transpositions paradoxically are for the most part upwards (made possible when no stratospheric coloratura additions are needed); but López-Cobos's direction hardly compensates for the lack of brilliance and, José Carreras apart, the singing, even that of Caballé, is not very persuasive. The recording is warm, refined in detail and atmospheric, with the choral contribution well projected; those who seek emotional histrionics in the Mad scene will find that Caballé manages much of the high coloratura remarkably effectively. Certainly this is good value as a Philips Duo reissue and, although only a synopsis of the plot is included, it is generously cued.

Recorded in 1957 using RCA's Living Stereo system, the Leinsdorf set with Roberta Peters offers a performance made in Rome featuring the favourite Met. performers of the time. Peters is a light, bright, precise soprano, amply agile in coloratura, with only a touch of shrillness on top. Next to Callas or Sutherland, this is an undercharacterized, superficial reading but easily attractive, while Jan Peerce is a heavyweight Edgardo, clear and well projected in his singing, but often over-emphatic. Giorgio Tozzi is an outstanding Raimondo, but the main snag of the set is the efficient but often rigid conducting of Leinsdorf, not really at home in this repertory, with slow music tending to sound too square. First-rate sound for the period.

Lucia di Lammermoor: highlights.

(M) *** Decca 421 885-2; *421 885-4* [id.] (from complete recording, with Sutherland, Pavarotti, Milnes, Ghiaurov, Ryland Davies, Tourangeau, ROHCG Ch. & O, Bonynge).

(M) **(*) EMI CDM7 63934-2 [id.]. Callas, Tagliavini, Cappuccilli, Ladysz, Philh. Ch. & O, Serafin.

For those who have chosen Sutherland's earlier, complete set, this 63-minute selection from her later (1971), full-price version should be ideal.

A satisfactory hour-long selection from Callas's 1959 Kingsway Hall stereo recording, with Callas not as completely in vocal control as she was in her earlier, mono sets.

Lucrezia Borgia (complete).

(M) *** Decca (IMS) 421 497-2 (2) [id.]. Sutherland, Aragall, Horne, Wixell, London Op. Voices, Nat. PO, Bonynge.

Sutherland is in her element here. Aragall sings stylishly too, and though Wixell's timbre is hardly Italianate he is a commanding Alfonso. Marilyn Horne in the breeches role of Orsini is impressive in the brilliant *Brindisi* of the last Act, but earlier she has moments of unsteadiness. The recording is characteristically full and brilliant.

Maria Stuarda (complete).

(M) *** Decca 425 410-2 (2) [id.]. Sutherland, Tourangeau, Pavarotti, Ch. & O of Teatro Comunale, Bologna, Bonynge.

In Donizetti's tellingly dramatic opera on the conflict of Elizabeth I and Mary Queen of Scots, the contrast between the full soprano Maria and the dark mezzo Elisabetta is underlined by some transpositions, with Tourangeau emerging as a powerful villainess in this slanted version of the story. Pavarotti turns Leicester into a passionate Italian lover, not at all an Elizabethan gentleman. As for Sutherland, she is at her most fully dramatic too, and the great moment when she flings the insult *Vil bastarda!* at her cousin brings a superb snarl; Richard Bonynge directs an urgent account of an unfailingly enjoyable opera. Unusually for Decca, the score is slightly cut. The recording is characteristically bright and full.

Poliuto (complete).
(M) (***) EMI mono CMS5 65448-2 (2) [Ang. CDMB 565448 2]. Callas, Corelli, Bastianini, Zaccaria, La Scala Ch. and O, Votto.

In 1960 Maria Callas returned to La Scala, having missed the two previous seasons, and had a triumph. This live recording, made at the time, demonstrates not just the scale of that triumph, but why the Milan audience were so thrilled. The signs of deterioration in the voice, which were soon to overtake her, are here barely apparent, with Callas's musical imagination and intensity of communication at their very peak. As John Steane's illuminating note makes clear, this Donizetti rarity was an odd choice for her return, when it is the tenor taking the title-role who commands centre-stage in this adaptation of Corneille's play about early Christian martyrs, *Polyeucte*. Corelli gives a heroic performance, noticeably subtler and more sensitive in scenes opposite Callas than when he is on his own. Callas herself consistently shows why this role inspired her, both in her natural gravity and poised intensity in slow music and in her biting brilliance in coloratura, marred slightly by the characteristic edge on the voice. Bastianini and Zaccaria complete the top Scala team of principals and, though the chorus is often rough, Votto heightens the dramatic impact in his conducting, right up to the improbable march at the end as hero and heroine bravely face martyrdom. Variable and limited mono sound, very dry in the orchestra, but with voices generally well caught.

Arias: *Don Pasquale: Com'è gentil. Don Sebastiano: Deserto in terra. Il Duca d'Alba: Inosservato, penetrava . . . Angelo casto e bel. La Fille du régiment: Ah! mes amis . . . Pour mon âme; Pour me rapprocher de Marie. L'elisir d'amore: Quanto è bella; Una furtiva lagrima. La Favorita: Una vergine, un' angelo di Dio; Si, che un solo accento; Favorita del re! . . . Spirto gentil. Lucia di Lammermoor: Tombe degli avi miei; Tu che a Dio spigasti l'ali. Maria Stuarda: Ah! rimiro il bel sembiante.*
(M) *** Decca 458 203-2 [id.]. Pavarotti, with various orchestras & conductors.

A cleverly chosen compilation of Pavarotti recordings of Donizetti from various sources – not just complete sets but previous recital discs. It is good to have one or two rarities along with the favourite numbers, including Tonio's celebrated 'High-C's' solo from the Act I finale of *La Fille du régiment*. Sound from different sources is well co-ordinated. In all, 13 items are included, and this makes an attractive reissue in Decca's Opera Gala series, rather handsomely presented with an additional outer slip-case. Full translations are included.

Arias: *L'elisir d'amore: Prendi, prendi per me sei libero. La Figlia del reggimento: Convien partir. Lucrezia Borgia: Tranquillo ei posa! . . . Come'è bello!.*
(M) ** EMI CDM5 66464-2 [id.]. Callas, Paris Conservatoire O, Rescigno – ROSSINI: *Arias*. **(*)

Reissued as part of EMI's Callas Edition, and very well recorded in 1963–4, this is a good example of the latter-day Callas, not always sweet-toned, and at times demonstrating less than the usual fire. If the singing rarely shows her at her most imaginative, and if there are fewer phrases that stick in the memory by their sheer individuality, that is not Donizetti's fault. Indeed there are places where one feels that in shaping her line she is being too careful, especially in the excerpt from *La Figlia del reggimento*. Yet there is still much to admire, and the remastering flatters the voice by providing a warmly atmospheric orchestral backing. If there are far better examples of her art within the Recital section below, this pairing with Rossini can certainly be recommended to Callas aficionados who want everything she recorded. Excellent documentation: full translations are provided.

Dowland, John (1563–1626)

The Collected Works (complete).
(B) *** O-L 452 563-2 (12) [(M) id. import]. Emma Kirkby, Glenda Simpson, John York Skinner, Martyn Hill, David Thomas, Consort of Musicke, Anthony Rooley.

Volume 1: *First Booke of Songes 1597* (452 564-2).

Volume 2: *Second Booke of Songs 1600* (452 565-2).

Volume 3: *Third Booke of Songs 1603* (452 566-2).

Volume 4: *A Pilgrimes Solace 1612* (beginning) *(Fourth Booke of Songs)* (452 567-2).

Volume 5: *A Pilgrimes Solace 1612* (conclusion) *(Fourth Booke of Songs)*. Keyboard transcriptions of Dowland's music: ANON.: *Can she excuse* (2 versions); *Dowland's almayne; Frogs' galliard; Pavion solus cum sola;* BYRD: *Pavana lachrymae*. FARNABY: *Lachrimae pavan*. MORLEY: *Pavana and Galiarda*. PEERSON and BULL: *Piper's Paven and Galliard*. SCHILDT: *Paduana lachrymae*. SIEFERT: *Paduana (la mia Barbara)*. WILBYE: *The Frogge* (Colin Tilney (harpsichord)) (452 568-2).

Volume 6: *Mr Henry Noell Lamentations 1597; Lachrimae 1604* (452 569-2).

Volume 7: Sacred songs: *An heart that's broken and contrite; I shame at mine unworthiness; Sorrow, come!*. Psalms: *All people that on earth do dwell* (2 versions); *Behold and have regard; Lord to thee I make my moan; My soul praise the Lord; Put me not to rebuke O Lord. A Prayer for the Queen's most excellent Majesty*. Instrumental music (mainly anon. arrangements): *Comagain (Comagain sweet love); Pavan lachrymae* (both arr. VAN EYCK); *Earl of Essex galliard; Galliard; If my complaints; Lachrimae; Lachrimae; Lachrimae Doolande; Lady Rich galliard; Lord Willoughbie's welcome home; My Lord Chamberlaine his galliard; Pipers Pavan; Solus cum sola pavan; Sorrow stay* (452 570-2).

Volume 8: Lute music: (i) *Almain; Almain; Can she excuse; Coranto; Dr Case's Pavan; A Dream; Fantasia; Fantasia; Lachrimae; Loth to depart; Melancholy galliard; Mr Dowland's midnight; Mrs Vaux galliard; Preludium; The Queen's galliard; Resolution; Sir John Smith, his almain;* (ii) *Aloe; Come away; Fancy (Fantasia); Galliard; John Dowland's galliard; Mr Giles Hobie's galliard; Pavan; The Earl of Essex, his galliard; The Lady Clifton's spirit (Galliard); The Most Sacred Queen Elizabeth, her galliard; What if a day*. (i) Anthony Bailes; (ii) Jakob Lindberg (452 571-2).

Volume 9: Lute music: (i) *Complaint; A Fancy (Fantasia); The Frog galliard; Galliard on 'Walsingham'; Galliard to Lachrimae; Jig; Lachrimae; Mignarda; Semper Dowland semper dolens;* (ii) *Captain Dogorie Piper's galliard; Dowland's first galliard; Dowland's galliard; 2 Fancies (Fantasias); 2 Galliards; Go from my window; Lady Hunsdon's puffe; Lady Laiton's almain; Lord Willoughbie's welcome home; Mr Langton's galliard; Mrs Clifton's almain; Pavan; Piper's pavan; Sir Henry Guilforde, his almain; Tarleton's jig; Walsingham*. (i) Jakob Lindberg; (ii) Nigel North (452 572-2).

Volume 10: Lute music: (i) *Pavana Johan Douland;* (ii) *Can she excuse; Farewell Fancy; Farewell (on the 'In nomine' theme); The Frog galliard; 2 Galliards; The King of Denmark's galliard; Lachrimae; La mia Barbara; Lord Strang's march; Mrs Brigide Fleetwood's pavan; Mrs Nichol's almain; Mrs Norrish's delight; Mrs Vaux's jig; Mrs White's nothing; Mrs White's thing; Mrs Winter's jump; The Shoemaker's wife, a toy; Sir Henry Umpton's funeral;* (iii) *Forlorn hope fancy; Galliard; Orlando sleepeth; Robin; Solus cum sola; The Lord Viscount Lisle, his galliard*. (i) Nigel North; (ii) Anthony Rooley; (iii) Christopher Wilson (452 573-2).

Volume 11: Lute music: *A Coy toy; Almain; Earl of Derby, his galliard; Fancy (Fantasia); Fortune my foe; Mr Knight's galliard; Sir John Langton's pavan; Sir John Souch his galliard; Tarletone's riserrectione; The Lady Rich, her galliard; The Lady Russell's pavan*. Consort music (arrangements): *Almain à 2; Can she excuse galliard; Captain Piper's pavan and galliard; Dowland's first galliard; Fortune my foe; The Frog galliard; Katherine Darcie's galliard; Lachrimae antiquae novae pavan and galliard; Lachrimae pavan; La mia Barbara pavan and galliard; Mistress Nichols alman à 2; à 5; Mr John Langton pavan and galliard; Round Battell galliard; Susanna fair; Tarleton's jigge* (452 574-2).

Volume 12: Consort music: *Lady if you so spite me; Mistress Nichols alman; Pavan à 4; Volta à 4; Were every thought an eye. A Musicall Banquet 1610: works collected by Robert Dowland* (452 575-2).

This set, recorded over half a decade in the late 1970s, is a remarkable achievement. The discs originally appeared separately, but are now available only in a bargain box, well documented and with full texts provided. However, it seems useful to make a comment about each collection individually. The contents of the *First Booke of Songes* of 1597 were recorded in the order in which they are published, varying the accompaniment between viols, lute with bass viol, voices and viols, and even voices alone. There is hardly any need to stress the beauties of the music itself, which is eminently well served by this stylish ensemble and is beautifully recorded.

The *Second Booke* contains many of Dowland's best-known songs, such as *Fine knacks for ladies*, *I saw my lady weep* and *Flow my tears*. Incidentally, the latter are performed on lute and two voices, the bass line being sung by David Thomas; this is quite authentic, though many listeners will retain an affection for its solo treatment. The solo songs are given with great restraint and good musical judgement, while the consort pieces receive expressive treatment. Emma Kirkby is at her freshest and most appealing in *Come, ye heavy states of night* and *Clear or cloudy*. Perhaps it is invidious to single her out, as the standard of performance throughout is distinguished. Refined intelligence is shown throughout by all taking part. The recording is of the highest quality.

In the *Third Booke* David Thomas gives an excellent account of himself in *What poor astronomers they are*, and Emma Kirkby's voice is again a delight. Apart from a certain reluctance to characterize, this disc also commands admiration.

A Pilgrimes Solace (1612), Dowland's *Fourth Booke of Songs*, appeared when he was fifty, and here it spreads over more than a single CD. In its Preface he dwells on the decline of his fortunes in life and love, and on the remorseless advance of age. In a collection pervaded by melancholy, variety has been achieved here by using contrasts of texture: some of the songs are performed in consort, others are given to different singers. Emma Kirkby sings with great purity and beauty of tone, though she is not always as warm or as poignant as the verse and music would warrant. However, hers is a most beautiful voice, and the disc also offers some perceptive singing from Martyn Hill. Anthony Rooley's playing is accomplished, and so is his direction of the proceedings. The eloquence of this music certainly comes over. The second of the two CDs also includes some interesting 'transcriptions', but they are less 'transcriptions for the keyboard of Dowland', rather pieces composed 'after' Dowland. The Byrd is closest to a transcription, while the Melchior Schildt is almost a recomposition. In any event, these performances are elegant and have plenty of body, and the recording, if cut at a high level, is faithful and vivid.

Volumes 6 and 7 offer a superb collection of motets and sacred songs, an invaluable counterpart to the better-known secular works, instrumental and vocal. The recording is first rate. The *Lachrimae* are most beautiful pieces and are played with splendid taste. Two baroque violins are used in the dances other than *Lachrimae*; otherwise viols are employed. The recording is worthy of these excellent and sensitive performances. The instrumental music which closes Volume 7 is an anthology of arrangements of Dowland's music, presented not as second-best (as we today think of arrangements) but as a genuine illumination, a heightening of the original inspiration. Particularly attractive are the items for two or more lutes. As ever, Rooley draws most stylish playing from the Consort, and the recording is exemplary.

Volumes 8, 9, 10 and 11 concentrate on Dowland's huge output of lute music. This impressive survey is entrusted to more than one player and contains a number of surprises. Though Dowland is best known for his melancholy – *semper dolens* etc. – he has far greater range than the popular imagination would give him credit for. Of particular note are some of the *Fantasias* from Jakob Lindberg (who uses a bandora as well as a lute); their chromatic boldness and fantasy place them among the greatest music for this instrument. Taken in large doses, some of the dances and genre pieces do not make the best effect, but, if heard in judicious musical context, their expressive power is without peer at this time. Both Christopher Wilson and Anthony Bailes play very freely and expressively (some may feel they could do with a tauter sense of rhythm), but they and their colleagues give performances that are dedicated and highly accomplished. The only reservation concerns the balance of the recordings, which is slightly too close to avoid fingerboard noises and the odd sniff and grunt. Such a tiny reservation should not deter readers from investigating a veritable treasure-trove.

The second half of Volume 11 and the first part of Volume 12 concentrate on the consort music. It is by no means certain that all of it is authentic Dowland, but this anthology does serve to remind us how widely his music was admired and arranged during his lifetime. Three of the *Pavans* and *Galliards* come from Thomas Simpson's *Opusculum* (1610) and two of the *Pavans* are direct recompositions of Dowland's *Lachrimae*. Four of the settings are from Morley's *Consort Lessons*, and there are five pieces from the Cambridge MS. which are performed most attractively here. Marvellous playing comes in the pieces from Simpson's *Taffel-consort* (1621). The recording maintains the high standard of the set, although the forward balance brings a comparatively limited dynamic range. In all other respects the sound is first class.

The final Volume concludes with '*A Musicall banquet*' (1610) which Robert Dowland, the great lutenist's son, compiled and published but which he did not compose. The composers range from his celebrated father to lesser-known masters such as Holborne and Tessier, or more familiar ones such as Caccini. The anthology is dedicated to Sir Robert Sidney and, as in many similar instances, is scarcely intended for continuous performance. Indeed the songs do not possess a particularly wide emotional range, and readers tempted by this music will find it best to take three or four songs at a time. Not all the performances are equally satisfying; problems of intonation arise in some of them and may well pose difficulties for some listeners. Overall, however, this box cannot be recommended too highly, but essentially it is meant to be dipped into rather than taken a whole CD at a time. The CD transfers are of the very highest quality. The discs are not available separately and, so far as we can determine, the set is available in the USA only as an import.

Ayres and Lute-lessons: *Prelude and Galliard; All ye whom love; Away with these self-loving lads; Come again sweet love; Come heavy sleep; Go Christal teares; If my complaints; My thoughts are winged; Rest awhile;* (Lute): *Semper Dowland, semper dolens. A shepherd in a shade; Stay sweet awhile; Tell me, true love; What if I never speede; When Phoebus first did Daphne love; Wilt thou unkind.*
(B) **(*) HM HMA 901076 [id.]. Deller Consort, Mark Deller; Robert Spencer.

Dowland's 'ayres' were designed for a consort of singers as well as for solo singer and lute, and it is good to hear them in this form. Two of the Lute Lessons are excellently played by Robert Spencer. The performances for the most part give consistent pleasure. The sound is excellent.

Consort music, lute solos and songs: *Captain Digorie Piper his galliard; The King of Denmark's galliard; M. Buctons galliard; The Earle of Essex galliard; M. George Whitehead his galliard; M. Giles Hobies galliard; M. Henry Noel his galliard; M. Nicholas Gryffith his galliard; Mistress Nichols almand; Mr John Langton's pavan; M. Thomas Collier his galliard; Semper Dowland semper dolens; Sir Henry Umpton's funerall; Sir John Such his galliard.* Lute: *A Fancy; Farewell (In nomine).* Lute and bass viol: *Dowlands adieu for Master Oliver Cromwell.* Songs: *All ye who love or fortune; Burst forth my tears; Can she excuse my wrongs; Lasso vita mia; A shepherd in a shade; Stay sweet awhile.*
(BB) *** Naxos Dig. 8.553326 [id.]. Rose Consort of Viols, with Jacob Heringman & Catherine King.

A highly enjoyably anthology to complement the companion Naxos recital, concentrating on lute songs. There is little vocal duplication here, but in any case Catherine King's fresh voice and simplicity of line are all her own and she is very touching in the melancholy songs. The Rose Consort, lively enough in the galliards, also show their sensitivity to Dowland's doleful moods, notably in the famous *Semper Dowland semper dolens*, but also in the lament for Oliver Cromwell, played sombrely on bass viol and lute. The programme ends with a moving account of *Sir John Umpton's funerall* music, darkly resonant, which would lose much of its grave poignancy without the viol colouring. The two lute solos, very well played by Jacob Heringman, offer further contrast, and the whole programme is recorded most naturally.

Can she excuse my wrongs?; Come again sweet love; Come, heavy sleep; Fine knacks for ladies; Flow my tears; His golden locks; If my complaints could passions move; In darkness let me dwell; I saw my lady weep; Lady, if you so spite me; Me, me and none but me; Now, O now I needs must part; Say love if ever thou did'st find; Sorrow stay; Stay awhile thy flying; Think'st thou then by feigning?; Time stands still; When Phoebus first did Daphne love; Wilt thou unkind thus reave me?. Lute solos: *Fortune my foe; Melancholy galliard.* (With *Galliards* by Mary, Queen of Scots. Attrib. Francis CUTTING: *Greensleeves (Divisions).* ANON.: *Bonny Sweet Robin; Callino; Kemp's Jig.*)
(BB) *** Naxos Dig. 8.553381 [id.]. Steven Rickards, Dorothy Linell (lute).

Steven Rickards has a light, precise counter-tenor voice which he uses very imaginatively in this sequence of 19 madrigals, including many of Dowland's finest. So a lively number like *Fine knacks for ladies* has a crispness and spring to bring out its lightness; even more impressively Rickards, with tone rock-steady and little or no hooting, superbly sustains the long legato lines of such great madrigals as *Flow my tears, I saw my lady weep* and *Come, heavy sleep*. Though the sequence cannot entirely avoid the monotony almost inevitable with counter-tenor tone, the songs are nicely contrasted, with well-chosen lute solos from Dorothy Linell supplementing her excellent accompaniments. She also writes a note, highlighting salient items, supplementing the general comments about Dowland by Keith Anderson. The recording, made in New York, is clear and well balanced. Full texts are provided.

Du Fay, Guillaume (*c.* 1400–1474)

Secular music (complete).
(B) *** O-L 452 557-2 (5) [id.]. Timothy Penrose, Rogers Covey-Crump, John Elwes, Paul Elliott, Paul Hillier, Michael George, Medieval Ens. of London, Peter & Timothy Davies.

Volume 1: *Belle, que vous ay ie mesfait; Ce jour de l'an voudray joye mener; Entre vous, gentils amoureux; Helas, et quant vous veray?; Invidia nimica; J'ay mis mon cueur et ma pensée; Je donne a tous les amoureux; Je requier a tous amoureux; Je veuil chanter de cuer joyeux; L'alta belleza tua, virtute, valore; Ma belle dame, je vous pri; Mon chier amy, qu'aves vous empensé; Mon cuer me fait tous dis penser; Navré je sui d'un dart penetratif; Par droit je puis bien complaindre et gemir; Passato è il tempo omaj di quei pensieri; Pour ce que veoir je ne puis; Resvellies vous et faites chiere lye; Resvelons nous, resvelons, amoureux; Se madame je puis veir* (452 558-2).

Volume 2: *Adieu ces bon vins de Lannoys; Belle plaissant et gracieuse; Belle, veullies moy retenir; Belle, vueillies vostre mercy donner; Bien veignes vous, amoureuse liesse; Bon jour, bon mois, bon an et bonne estraine; Ce moys de may soyons lies et joyeux; Dona i aredenti ray; Estrines moy, je vous estrineray; He, compaignons, resvelons nous; Helas, ma dame, par amours; J'atendray tant qu'il vous playra; J'ay grant (dolour); Je me complains piteusement; Je ne puis plus ce que y'ai peu; Je ne suy plus tel que souloye; La belle se siet au piet de la tour; La dolce uista; Ma belle dame souveraine; Portugaler; Pour l'amour de ma doulce amye* (2 versions); *Quel fronte signorille in paradiso; Vergene bella, che di sol vestita* (452 559-2).

Volume 3: *Bien doy servir de volente entiere; Ce jour le doibt, aussi fait la saison; C'est bien raison de devoir essaucier; Craindre vous vueil, doulce dame de pris; Dona gentile, bella come l'oro; Donnes l'assault a la fortresse; Entre les plus plaines danoy; Hic iocundus sumit mundus; Je prens congie de vous, amours; Las, que feray? Ne que je devenray?; Mille bonjours je vous presente; Mon bien, m'amour et ma maistresse; Pouray je avoir vostre mercy?; Qu'est devenue leaulte?; Seigneur Leon, vous soyes bienvenus; Se la face ay pale* (452 560-2).

Volume 4: *Adieu m'amour, adieu ma joye; Adieu, quitte le demeurant de ma vie; Belle, vueilles moy vangier; J'ayme bien celui qui s'en va; Je languis en piteux martire; Je n'ai doubté fors que des envieux; Juvenis qui puellam; Lamentatio sanctae matris ecclesiae constantinopolitanae; Ne je ne dors ne je ne veille; Or pleust a dieu qu'a son plaisir; Par le regart de vos beaux yeux; Puisque celle qui me tient en prison; Puisque vous estez campieur; Se la face ay pale* (2 versions); *S'il est plaisir que je vous puisse faire; Trop lonc temps ai esté en desplaisir; Va t'en, mon cuer, jour et nuitie; Vo regard et doulce maniere* (452 561-2).

Volume 5: *De ma haulte et bonne aventure; Departes vous, male bouche et envie; Dieu gard la bone sans reprise; Du tout m'estoie abandonné; En triumphant de Cruel Dueil; Franc cuer gentil, sur toutes gracieuse; Helas mon dueil, a ce cop sui ie mort; Je ne vis onques la pareille; Je vous pri, mon tres doulx ami; Les douleurs, dont me sens tel somme; Le serviteur hault guerdonné; Malheureulx cueur, que vieulx tu faire?; Ma plus mignonne de mon cueur; Mon seul plaisir, ma doulce joye; O flos florum virginum; Resistera . . .; Vostre bruit et vostre grant fame* (452 562-2).

In the fifteenth century Dufay was a famous musical personality; his output held sway over the courts and cathedrals of Europe. He is best known today for his church music, but he was also a very successful song composer and, listening to this collection, one can readily discover why. He had a spontaneous melodic flair: these chansons are essentially popular in appeal, naturally lyrical and lively, by no means 'highbrow'.

The collector with special interests in this period will naturally acquire this handsomely produced and lovingly prepared set, but the non-specialist might well be deterred by the sheer scale of the enterprise: 96 songs are quite a lot. What will surprise those who dip into these discs is the range, beauty and accessibility of this music. There is nothing really specialized about this art beyond the conventions within which the sensibility works. The texts that Peter and Timothy Davies use are those established by Heinrich Besseler, and where a song survives with only a fragmentary poem, they give the music in purely instrumental form. The documentation is thorough and the performances have great commitment and sympathy to commend them. The actual sound-quality is of the first order, and readers who investigate the contents of this box will be rewarded with much delight. The discs are not available separately, but we are glad to see that the box is available on both sides of the Atlantic

Chansons: *Adieu ces bons vins de Lannoys; Belle, que vous ay je mesfait; Bon jour, bon mois; Ce jour de l'an; Donnes l'assault à la fortress; Helas mon dueil; J'ay mis mon cuer; Mon chier amy; Par droit je puis bien complaindre; Pas le regard de vos beaux yeux; Pour l'amour de ma doulce amye; Puisque vous estez campieur; Quel fronte signorille La doce vita; Resvelliés vous et faites chiere lye; Resvelons nous; Se la face ay pale; Vergene Bella.*
(BB) ** Naxos Dig. 8.553458 [id.]. Bernhard Landauer, Unicorn Ens., Michael Posch.

This Naxos anthology with the counter-tenor Bernhard Landauer and the Ensemble Unicorn under the direction of Michael Posch offers some 17 items. They are freely interpreted, taking the text as a guideline rather than a rigid musical framework, and are given with some panache. There is an improvisatory freedom that would doubtless delight in the concert hall but is perhaps less satisfying on repetition. Well recorded by the Viennese engineers, but ultimately not as rewarding as the performances in the more authoritative Oiseau-Lyre set.

Missa L'homme armé; Motet: *Supremum est mortalibus bonum.*
(BB) *** Naxos Dig. 8.553087 [id.]. Oxford Camerata, Jeremy Summerly.

Jeremy Summerly and his Oxford Camerata give a powerfully expressive and wholly convincing account of Du Fay's masterly cyclic Mass using a Burgundian chanson as its basis. We hear this sung first in its original format as an introduction, and its message, 'The armed man should be feared', makes a dramatically appropriate contrast with the motet, *Supremum est mortalibus*, which is a peace song. The latter was written some 30 years earlier, yet shows just as readily the remarkable inventiveness and eloquence of this fifteenth-century French composer. The Mass movements are interspersed with plainchant in the same Dorian mode. With vivid yet atmospheric recording, this can be given the strongest recommendation.

Chanson and Mass: *Se la face ay pale;* Motet: *Gloria ad modum tubae.*
(M) *** Virgin Veritas/EMI VER5 61283-2 [CDM 61283]. Early Music Cons. of L., David Munrow.

David Munrow's pioneering recording of Du Fay's Mass was first issued on LP to mark the quincentenary of the composer's death in 1974 and the first-class recording, immaculately transferred to CD, sounds as fresh as on the day it first appeared. The performance of this austere yet moving work is superb in every way. The Mass itself is prefaced by the chanson on which it is based, first in its original three-part version, then in two keyboard versions from the Buxheimer Organ Book, and finally in a four-part instrumental version scored for alto cornett, alto shawm and alto and tenor sackbutts, attributed to the great Burgundian master himself. The performance is accompanied by instruments, tenor and bass viols in the solo sections of the *Gloria* and *Credo*, cornetts and sackbutts in the full sections. The soloists are all distinguished (they include James Bowman), and David Munrow himself plays the alto shawm. As a curtain-raiser before the Mass, we are offered the catchy motet, *Gloria ad modum tubae*, written in a lively canonic form, with the effect of a round. An indispensable reissue. It calls for and rewards concentrated and repeated listening.

Dukas, Paul (1865–1935)

L'apprenti sorcier (The sorcerer's apprentice).
(M) *** Decca (IMS) 448 576-2 [id.]. SRO, Ansermet – CHABRIER: *España* **(*); DEBUSSY: *La Mer* **(*); HONEGGER: *Pacific 231* ***; RAVEL: *Boléro; La Valse.* ***
(M) **(*) Chandos CHAN 6503 [id.]. SNO, Gibson (with SAINT-SAENS: *Danse macabre* **(*)) – ROSSINI/RESPIGHI: *La boutique fantasque.* **(*)

L'apprenti sorcier; La péri (with *Fanfare*); *Polyeucte: overture.*
✿ (M) *** Ph. 454 127-2. Rotterdam PO, David Zinman – D'INDY: *Symphonie sur un chant montagnard.* **

Dukas's *La péri* was written for Diaghilev in 1912. It is based on a tale from ancient Persian mythology. King Iskander discovers the Péri asleep and steals her lotus-blossom with its power of immortal youth. The Péri awakens and stimulates the King's desire with an erotic dance. The King succumbs and returns the flower, whereupon the object of his passion promptly vanishes, leaving him to reflect that he has been caught out by the oldest trick of all. Those who cherish rosy memories of the pre-war set of *La péri* by Philippe Gaubert and the Paris Conservatoire Orchestra will not be disappointed by this CD reissue of David Zinman's 1978 recording, which is every bit as haunting and atmospheric. In fact the Rotterdam Philharmonic give us here what is arguably the finest account of Dukas's colourful score ever to have been put on record. Here is a conductor acutely sensitive to the most delicate colourings and the hushed atmosphere of this evocative score, with its colours drawn as much from Rimsky-Korsakov as from Debussian impressionism. Zinman captures the fairy-tale spirit better than any of his rivals and more magically than the recently reissued Boulez version. The well-balanced recording creates a warm, misty web of sound with wide-ranging dynamics and a truthful perspective, very reminiscent of Haitink's analogue Concertgebouw recordings of Debussy's *Images*, *Jeux* and *Nocturnes*, if less sharply defined. Only in the introductory *Fanfare* could some ears crave more sonic brilliance, and that comment might also be applied to *L'apprenti sorcier*, in which the same atmospheric translucence is equally evocative at the opening before the apprentice sets off on his watery task with jaunty insouciance. Certainly no one should be disappointed with either the climax or the tale's rueful dénouement. The *Polyeucte overture* is not dissimilar in style to *La péri* but has less interesting material; it is presented equally effectively.

Ansermet's performance of *L'apprenti sorcier* is relaxed, yet it has a cumulative effect. There is plenty of atmosphere here and the detail of the recording shows the Swiss conductor at his finest. This was originally part of a very successful 1963 collection (with music by Honegger and Ravel) to which the Chabrier and Debussy works have been added for this reissue in Decca's 'Classic Sound' series.

Gibson secures excellent playing from the SNO, if without the sheer panache of some of his competitors. The recording (made in City Hall, Glasgow, in 1972) is less overtly brilliant than Ansermet's but has plenty of atmosphere. The Chandos disc, however, is ungenerous in playing time (37 minutes).

(i) *L'apprenti sorcier (The sorcerer's apprentice);* (ii) *Ariane et Barbe-bleue: Act III Prelude; La péri;* (iii) *Symphony in C.*

(M) **(*) EMI CDM7 63160-2. (i) (mono) Philh. O, Markevitch; (ii) (stereo) Paris Op. O, Dervaux; (iii) (stereo) ORTF, Martinon.

The Dukas is one of the finest of the post-Franck symphonies, more vital in argument and more independent in outlook than the Chausson or either of the d'Indy symphonies. Martinon brings real vigour and feeling to it, and the (slightly but not excessively reverberant) 1974 recording comes up well. *La péri* was recorded in 1957 and wears its years well, though the orchestral playing is not first class (the wind intonation is not always true). Markevitch's 1953 Philharmonia account of *L'apprenti sorcier* (mono, of course) is brilliantly played, but there is an ugly edit (cut-off reverberation) halfway through. Still, this is worth having.

Piano sonata in E flat min.

(M) *** EMI (SIS) CDM5 65996-2. John Ogdon – DUTILLEUX: *Sonata;* Florent SCHMITT: *Deux mirages.* ***

This performance of the Dukas *Sonata* was originally issued in the early 1970s in an enterprising five-LP box called 'Musical Philosophies', which included a number of challenging pieces. Unless our memory deceives us, none was ever reissued separately. This is one of the best performances in that set, and one of the finest – save for the Busoni *Piano concerto* – John Ogdon ever committed to disc. Some of his admirers, including the late lamented Christopher Headington, maintained that Ogdon's playing could often sound like brilliant sight-reading – that the music had not fully become part of his musical bloodstream. This is not the case here. This is a powerful, totally committed performance of a work which was much admired by Debussy and which enjoys scant exposure in the catalogue. There is an excellent account by Margaret Fingerhut on Chandos, but this EMI version is as good, is less expensive and has the advantage of even more appealing couplings than hers.

Dunstable, John (d. 1453)

Motets: *Agnus Dei; Alma redemptoris Mater; Credo super; Da gaudiorum premia; Gaude virgo salutata; Preco preheminenciae; Quam pulcra es; Salve regina misericordiae; Salve sceme sanctitatis; Veni creator; Veni sancte spiritus.*

(M) *** Virgin Veritas/EMI Dig. VER5 61342-2. Hilliard Ens., Hillier.

In the time of Henry V, John Dunstable (or Dunstaple, which is historically more correct) was not only the leading English composer of his day but also one of the most influential figures in Europe. His music has not always been well served by the gramophone, but this reissued record by the Hilliard Ensemble of nine motets and Mass movements makes a major contribution to his discography. These motets give a very good idea of his range, and they are sung with impeccable style. The Hilliard Ensemble has perfectly blended tone and impeccable intonation, and their musicianship is of the highest order. Some collectors may find the unrelieved absence of vibrato a little tiring on the ear when taken in large doses, but most readers will find this a small price to pay for music-making of such excellence, so well recorded.

Duparc, Henri (1848–1933)

Mélodies: *Au pays où se fait la guerre; Chanson triste; L'invitation au voyage; Le manoir de Rosamonde; Phidylé; Testament; La vie intérieure.*

(B) ** [EMI Red Line Dig. CDR5 69802]. Dame Kiri Te Kanawa, Belgian Nat. Op. O, Pritchard (with excerpts from: BERLIOZ: *La damnation de Faust;* CHARPENTIER: *Louise;* DEBUSSY: *L'enfant prodigue*) – RAVEL: *Shéhérazade.* **

Dame Kiri often produces a most beautiful sound and she is excellently supported by Sir John Pritchard and the Belgian Opera Orchestra; for all this, however, she is not wholly successful in terms of characterization. The EMI recording is very well balanced, and her admirers may want to sample this, but she is not at her best here.

Dupré, Marcel (1886–1971)

ORGAN MUSIC

6 Chorales, Op. 28; 2 Chorales, Op. 59; 24 Inventions, Op. 50; 4 Modal fugues, Op. 63.
(BB) *** Naxos Dig. 8.553862 [id.]. James Biery.

This is the first in what one assumes will be a comprehensive Naxos survey of Marcel Dupré's output for the organ. Apart from being a great organist and a master of the art of improvisation, Dupré was an inventive composer whose work exhibits a cultured and civilized musical mind. The 24 *Inventions*, Op. 50, which are divided to begin and end this CD, are, like Bach's *Well-Tempered Clavier*, composed in all the major and minor keys. They date from the late 1940s and early 1950s, when Dupré was in his late sixties and briefly Director of the Paris Conservatoire; they are distinguished by fastidious craftsmanship and, despite their pedagogical intent, considerable imagination. The 79 *Chorales*, Op. 28 (1930), six of which are included here, were composed in the unlikely surroundings of the beach at Biarritz and designed as stepping-stones to the Bach chorale-preludes. The *Chorales*, Op. 59, and the *Four Modal Fugues* come from the 1960s. James Biery was a pupil of Wolfgang Rübsam, who is currently also occupied in recording Bach's organ music for Naxos and who acts as producer for this disc. The recording is made on the Casavant organ of the Cathedral of Saints Peter and Paul, in Providence, Rhode Island; it is splendidly lifelike and has great clarity and definition. These pieces are mainly very short and they should be heard in groups of six or seven if they are to make their best effect rather than being heard at one fell swoop. A rewarding issue just the same.

Duruflé, Maurice (1902–86)

Requiem, Op. 9.

(B) *** Sony SBK 67182; *SBT 67182* [id.]. Kiri Te Kanawa, Siegmund Nimsgern, Amb. S., Desborough School Ch., New Philh. O, Andrew Davis – FAURE: *Requiem*. ***

(B) *** Decca Eclipse Dig. 448 711-2; *448 711-4* [(M) id. import]. Palmer, Shirley-Quirk, Boys of Westminster Cathedral Ch., L. Symphony Ch., LSO, Hickox – FAURE: *Pavane;* POULENC: *Gloria*. ***

(i; ii; iii) *Requiem. Op. 9;* (ii) *4 Motets (Ubi Caritas et Amor; Tota pulchra es; Tu es Petrus; Tantum ergo), Op. 10;* (iii) (Organ) *Prélude et fugue sur le nom d'Alain.*

(B) *** Decca Double 436 486-2 [id.]. (i) Robert King, Christopher Keyte; (ii) St John's College, Cambridge, Ch.; (iii) Stephen Cleobury (organ); George Guest – FAURE: *Requiem* etc., POULENC: *Messe* etc. ***

Those who have sometimes regretted that the lovely Fauré *Requiem* remains unique in the output of that master of delicate inspiration should investigate this comparably evocative *Requiem* of Duruflé. The composer wrote it in 1947, overtly basing its layout and even the cut of its themes on the Fauré masterpiece. The result is far more than an imitation for (as it seems in innocence) Duruflé's inspiration is passionately committed.

Andrew Davis directs a warm and atmospheric reading of Duruflé's beautiful setting, using the Desborough School Choir and the full orchestral version with its richer colourings. Kiri Te Kanawa sings radiantly in the *Pie Jesu*, and the darkness of Siegmund Nimsgern's voice is well caught. In such a performance Duruflé establishes his claims for individuality, even in the face of Fauré's setting. The recording is nicely atmospheric.

Hickox tempers the richness of the orchestral version by using boys' voices in the choir. He relishes the extra drama of orchestral accompaniment with biting brass at the few moments of high climax. Felicity Palmer and John Shirley-Quirk sing with deep feeling and fine imagination, if not always with ideally pure tone. The recording has a pleasantly ecclesiastical ambience, which adds to the ethereal purity of the trebles, and the stereo spread is wide.

The (originally Argo) St John's version also uses boy trebles instead of women singers, even in the solo of the *Pié Jesu* – exactly parallel to Fauré's setting of those words, which was indeed first sung by a treble. The alternative organ version is used here, not so warmly colourful as the orchestral version, but very beautiful nevertheless. The 1974 recording is vividly atmospheric. To this have been added the *Four Motets* on plainsong themes, each quite short but greatly varied in character, with the final *Tantum ergo* perhaps the most ambitious. They are beautifully sung here. The organ piece, another sensitive example of Duruflé's withdrawn genius, makes a further substantial bonus, especially when one realizes that this remarkably generous pair of CDs includes also the *Mass* and *Salve Regina* of Poulenc, to make an unbeatable bargain.

Dutilleux, Henri (born 1916)

Violin concerto (L'Arbre des songes).

(M) *** Sony Stern Edition II SMK 64508 [id.]. Stern, O Nat. de France, Maazel – BERNSTEIN: *Serenade.* *(**)

Dutilleux's *Violin concerto*, written for Isaac Stern, is a beautiful work. Always the perfect craftsman and consistently writing with refinement, Dutilleux shows how taut self-discipline can go with natural expressive warmth. There are passages in this tightly knit structure of seven linked sections which sound very like Walton updated; and the underlying romantic fervour finds Stern playing with warm commitment, strongly accompanied by Maazel and the Orchestre National. First-rate recording.

Le Loup (ballet): *symphonic fragments.*

(M) *** EMI CDM7 63945-2. Paris Conservatoire O, Prêtre – MILHAUD: *Création du monde*; POULENC: *Les Biches.* ***

Dutilleux's score for *Le Loup*, with its 'Beauty and the Beast' storyline bringing a tragic ending, is dominated by a haunting, bitter-sweet waltz theme of the kind that, once heard, refuses to budge from the memory. But the invention throughout has plenty of colour and variety, and Dutilleux's orchestral palette is used individually to great effect. Prêtre makes a persuasive case for the suite, and this vivid recording is part of a highly attractive triptych of French ballet scores.

(i) *Symphonies Nos. 1–2 (Le Double);* (ii) *Métaboles;* (iii) *Mystère de l'instant* (for 24 strings, cymbalum and percussion); (ii) *Timbres, espace, mouvement (La nuit étoilée);* (iv) *Ainsi la nuit (String quartet);* (v) *Les citations* (Diptych for oboe, harpsichord, double-bass & percussion); (vi) *3 Strophes sur le nom de Sacher* (for unaccompanied cello); (vii; viii) *Figures de résonances* (for 2 pianos); (vii) *Piano sonata; 3 Préludes Nos. 1–3;* (ix; viii) *2 Sonnets de Jean Cassou.*

(M) *** Erato/Warner Dig./Analogue 0630 14068-2 (3). (i) O de Paris, Barenboim; (ii) O Nat. de France, Rostropovich; (iii) Zurich Coll. Mus., Paul Sacher; (iv) Sine Nomine Qt; (v) Bourgue, Dreyfus, Cazauran, Balet; (vi) David Geringas; (vii) Geneviève Joy; (viii) composer; (ix) Gilles Cachemaille.

These three Erato CDs, issued to celebrate the composer's eightieth birthday, afford an excellent survey of Dutilleux's orchestral, chamber and instrumental music. If the exhilarating and aurally fascinating *First Symphony* is not as well served by Barenboim and the Orchestre de Paris as it is on Harmonia Mundi by their less celebrated colleagues in Lyons under Serge Baudo, it is still an involving performance, even if the Scherzo is scrambled. The *Second Symphony* is well played, and the recording of both is eminently serviceable, if neither music-making nor sound are a match for Tortelier on Chandos. *Métaboles* is otherwise the best-known orchestral work here and is now well represented in the catalogue. *Timbres, Espace, Mouvement*, inspired by Van Gogh's painting, *La nuit étoilée*, is highly imaginative, and it is good to have it under the baton of Rostropovich, who commissioned it. *Mystère de l'instant* is a set of ten miniatures, snapshots of both subtlety and ingenuity, splendidly played by the Collegium Musicum under Sacher and digitally recorded. The chamber and instrumental performances date from 1982 and are analogue. They include the *Sonata* of 1947, played by the pianist most closely associated with it over the years, Geneviève Joy – and played with great zest and panache, too! Joy is no less excellent in the *Préludes*. Dutilleux is a composer of keen imaginative awareness and consistent inventive quality, who always holds the listener – *Les Citations* is a case in point. *Ainsi la nuit* is already represented on CD, but it is very well played here. Those coming to this music fresh need not hesitate. The performances and recordings are very fine and the music stimulating and rewarding. Unlike the four separate CDs which this compilation replaces, this is quite good value in terms of playing time, with the first two CDs each timed at just under an hour, and the third playing for 75 minutes. The documentation is excellent and is illustrated with photographs of the composer and major participants.

Symphony No. 1; Timbres, espace, mouvement.

(M) *** HM Suite Dig. HMT 7905159 [id.]. O. Nat. de Lyon, Serge Baudo.

In Dutilleux's *First Symphony* there is a mercurial intelligence and a vivid imagination at work, and the orchestral textures are luminous and iridescent. What is particularly impressive is its sense of forward movement: you feel that the music is taking you somewhere. *Timbres, espace, mouvement* is a more recent work, dating from 1978. Serge Baudo is an authoritative interpreter of this composer, and the Lyon orchestra also serve him well. The engineering is superb: there is plenty of space round the various instruments and the balance is thoroughly realistic. At mid-price this reissue makes an admirable sampler for those unfamiliar with this very distinctive composer.

Piano sonata.

(M) *** EMI (SIS) CDM5 65996-2. John Ogdon – DUKAS: *Sonata;* Florent SCHMITT: *Deux mirages.* ***

An enterprising release of a totally idiomatic and thoroughly convincing account of a brilliant twentieth-century work that does not enjoy the exposure it deserves. This can take its place alongside the current recommendation by Geneviève Joy in an excellent full-priced three-CD set devoted to Dutilleux.

Dvořák, Antonín (1841–1904)

(i) *American suite in A, Op. 98b;* (ii) *Serenade for strings in E, Op. 22; Serenade for wind in D min., Op. 44.*

(B) *** Decca Eclipse Dig. 448 981-2; *448 981-4* [(M) id. import]. (i) RPO, Dorati; (ii) LPO, Hogwood.

Dvořák's *American suite*, which has clear influences from the New World, was written first as a piano version (1894) but was turned into an orchestral piece the following year. Dorati has its measure and the RPO are very responsive, while the Kingsway Hall recording-balance seems to suit the scoring rather well. It is slight but charming music and makes a good coupling for the two *Serenades*. These receive fresh, bright, spring-like accounts from Hogwood and the LPO in clean, slightly recessed sound. Textually this version of the *String serenade* is unique on record when it uses the original score, newly published, in which two sections (one of 34 bars in the Scherzo and the other of 79 bars in the finale), missing in the normal printed edition, are now included. Though these performances are not quite as winning or as rhythmically subtle as those of Schneider or Marriner (both at full price), they are still very enjoyable, and the inclusion of the extra material brings added interest.

Cello concerto in B min., Op. 104.

✿ (M) *** DG 447 413-2 [id.]. Rostropovich, BPO, Karajan – TCHAIKOVSKY: *Variations on a rococo theme.* *** ✿

(BB) *** CfP Silver Double CDCFPSD 4775 (2) [id.]. Robert Cohen, LPO, Macal – BEETHOVEN: *Triple concerto;* ELGAR: *Cello concerto;* TCHAIKOVSKY: *Variations on a rococo theme.* ***

(M) *** [RCA Basic 100 09026 68086-2; *68086-4*]. Lynn Harrell, LSO, Levine – TCHAIKOVSKY: *Rococo variations.* ***

(M) *** Sony Dig. SMK 60151 [id.]. Yo-Yo Ma, BPO, Maazel – SCHUMANN: *Cello concerto.* ***

(M) (***) EMI CDH7 63498-2 [id.]. Casals, Czech PO, Szell – ELGAR: *Concerto* (**(*)) (with BRUCH: *Kol Nidrei* (***)).

(M) **(*) RCA 09026 61498-2 [id.]. Piatigorsky, Boston SO, Munch – WALTON: *Concerto.* ***

(BB) ** Naxos Dig. 8.550503 [id.]. Maria Kliegel, RPO, Halasz – ELGAR: *Cello concerto.* **

(M) DG (IMS) Dig. 445 574-2. Maisky, Israel PO, Bernstein – SCHUMANN: *Concerto.* *

(i) *Cello concerto in B min., Op. 104;* (ii) *Symphony No. 8 in G, Op. 88.*

(B) *** DG Classikon 439 484-2; *439 484-4* [(M) id. import]. (i) Fournier; (i–ii) BPO; (i) Szell; (ii) Kubelik.

There have been a number of distinguished recordings of both the Dvořák *Concerto* and its equally seductive Tchaikovsky coupling over the two and a half decades since the Rostropovich/Karajan record was made, but none to match it for intensity of lyrical feeling and the spontaneity of the partnership. The orchestral playing is glorious. Moreover the analogue recording, made in the Jesus-Christus Kirche in September 1969, is as near perfect as any made in that vintage analogue era. The CD transfer has freshened the original, and the metaphor of 'cleaning an Old Master' readily applies to this splendid reissue.

Pierre Fournier's reading of the *Cello concerto* has a sweep of conception and a richness of tone and phrasing which carry the melodic lines along with exactly that mixture of nobility and tension the work demands. The phrasing in the slow movement is ravishing, and the interpretation as a whole balances beautifully. DG's recording, dating from 1962, is forward and vivid, with a broad, warm tone for the soloist. Kubelik's *Eighth* is appealingly direct and the polished, responsive playing of the Berlin Philharmonic adds to the joy and refinement of the performance. The 1966 sound is bright and clear, if a little dry. It has been splendidly remastered, and altogether this is a highly recommendable bargain coupling.

Robert Cohen was only twenty when he recorded the Dvořák *Cello concerto*, but his is anything but an immature reading; it is strong and forthright, very secure technically, with poetry never impaired by his preference for keeping steady speeds. The result is most satisfying, helped by a comparably incisive and understanding accompaniment from the Czech conductor, Zdenek Macal. With first-class recording, orchestrally full-bodied and with a truthful balance, this is part of an outstanding quartet of works featuring this fine cellist, which makes a very recommendable Silver Double compilation.

In Lynn Harrell's first RCA recording, made in the mid-1970s, his collaboration with James Levine in Dvořák's *Cello concerto* proved a powerful and sympathetic one. Richly satisfying accounts of the first and second movements culminate in a reading of the finale which proves the most distinctive of all. The main body of the movement is finely integrated, but it is the *Andante* epilogue which brings the most memorable playing, very expansive but not at all sentimental, with a wonderful sense of repose. The recording is bright and full and has been remastered most successfully for CD. This has been withdrawn in the UK, but in the USA it is attractively coupled with Ofra Harnoy's highly individual account of Tchaikovsky's *Rococo variations*.

The partnership of the passionately extrovert Maazel – witness his spaciously powerful orchestral introduction – and the more withdrawn artistry of Yo-Yo Ma is unexpectedly successful in Dvořák's gorgeous concerto, with the advantage of modern, digital recording, at once vivid and atmospheric. Ma's rapt concentration and refined control of colour at times bring an elegiac dimension to the reading, and Maazel accompanies with understanding and great sensitivity, fining down the orchestral textures so that he never masks his often gentle soloist, yet providing exuberant contrast in orchestral fortissimos. If Ma's playing is characteristically subtle, it is never narcissistic: sometimes there is a mere thread of tone, but it is a magical thread. The orchestra is set back within a warmly resonant concert-hall ambience which lends its bloom to the overall sound-picture – the solo cello is most skilfully balanced – and ensures that the pianissimo detail of the *Adagio* registers naturally.

Casals plays with astonishing fire and the performance seems to spring to life in a way that eludes many modern artists; the rather dry acoustic of the Deutsches Haus, Prague, and the limitations of the 1937 recording are of little consequence. This disc is one of the classics of the gramophone.

Piatigorsky's Boston recording has been improved remarkably for this CD and, although the balance is still too close and not always flattering to the soloist, with tuttis still inclined to be somewhat two-dimensional, the quality is now fully acceptable. There is no lack of orchestral colour and the acoustic of Symphony Hall is conveyed behind the music-making. The performance is the very opposite of routine, with Piatigorsky and Munch in complete rapport, producing a consistently spontaneous melodic flow; although there are also moments when intonation is less than immaculate, the inspiration of the performance carries the day.

On the Naxos bargain label it makes a generous coupling having the two greatest of all cello concertos. Maria Kliegel is a warmly expressive soloist, generally persuasive, whose tone is yet not ideally opulent, and whose expansive manner – as in the second subject of the first movement – runs to extremes. If the orchestral accompaniment was tauter, the results would be even more convincing. As it is, the reading runs the risk of self-indulgence. Yet with good, modern, digital sound and so generous a coupling, it makes a fair bargain in the lowest price range.

Maisky and Bernstein in their live recording spread the *Concerto* to an extraordinary 43 minutes. Even that might have been acceptable, had Maisky's playing been less perverse. His fluctuations of tempo and rhythm are so wilful that he sounds jerky, not persuasive. With the soloist too closely balanced and with dry orchestral sound in tuttis, this is not recommended.

(i) *Cello concerto in B min., Op. 104;* (ii) *Piano concerto in G min., Op. 33;* (iii) *Violin concerto in A min., Op. 53.*

(B) ** Decca Double Dig./Analogue 455 957-2 (2) [id.]. (i) Lynn Harrell, Philh. O, Ashkenazy; (ii) András Schiff, VPO, Dohnányi; (iii) Ruggiero Ricci, LSO, Sargent – SCHUMANN: *Introduction and Allegro appassionato*. ***

This Double Decca conveniently gathers together the three Dvořák concertos, but the performances are not among the finest available, so the set can receive only a qualified recommendation. Lynn Harrell's digital version of the *Cello concerto*, while brilliantly recorded, is relatively disappointing when compared with his fervent, earlier, analogue version with James Levine for RCA. But that is currently available only in the USA (see above). Schiff's performace of the *Piano concerto* is far more successful; indeed it is excellent. It derives from a public concert in the Musikverein, and he is given splendid support from the Vienna Philharmonic Orchestra under Dohnányi. However, the balance is unsatisfactory: the piano is very up-front and in this respect is not wholly natural. Much the same criticism applies to Ricci's ardent (1961) account of the *Violin concerto*, where the solo violin is again very forward, although the Kingsway Hall acoustic brings a warm backing ambience. Ricci does not seem temperamentally suited to the work and his performance, though not without style, has no special idiomatic character. Sargent's accompaniment, however, is in every way supportive.

(i) *Cello concerto;* (ii) *Serenade for strings, Op. 22; Serenade for wind, Op. 44;* (iii) *Symphony No. 9 in E min. (New World).*

(B) * Finlandia–Teldec/Warner Ultima 0630 18950-2 (2). (i) Arto Noras, Finnish RSO, Sakari Oramo; (ii) St Paul CO, Hugo Wolf; (iii) Philh. O, Eliahu Inbal.

Here a potentially attractive anthology, very well recorded, is let down by a series of performances which fail to be distinctive enough for the listener to want to return to them. Arto Noras is a fine young player, but in the first movement of the *Cello concerto* the volatile changes of tempo (with an abrupt slowing-down for the second subject) are unconvincing. The slow movement, too, lacks real magic: even the horn chorale sounds rather ordinary. The performances of the two *Serenades* from the St Paul Chamber Orchestra are agreeable enough but in the last resort rather bland and undercharacterized, though very well played, with the work for wind instruments much the more pleasing of the two. Inbal's *New World* is not very compelling either. He omits the first-movement exposition repeat and, like his colleague Sakari Oramo in the concerto, his slowing down for the secondary theme sounds mannered. The rest of the performance lacks real magnetism.

(i) *Cello concerto; Symphony No. 8 in G, Op.35.*

(BB) **(*) RCA Navigator 74321 21289-2 [(M) id. import]. (i) Piatigorsky; Boston SO, Munch.

Piatigorsky's 1960 recording (see above) is here also available coupled with Munch's account of the *G major Symphony*, recorded a year later. As in the *Concerto*, the improvement in the recorded sound is remarkable and the work is made to sound extremely vivid against the spacious Boston acoustic. Munch's reading is strongly characterized and, though he occasionally presses hard, the thrust comes from a natural ardour. Some might feel the finale a bit overdriven, but there is plenty of feeling in the slow movement and few would fail to respond to the passionate blossoming in the strings of the inspired lyrical theme that forms the centrepiece of the third-movement *Allegretto*.

(i) *Cello concerto;* (ii) *Symphony No.9 (New World).*

(M) *** Ph. 442 401-2 [id.]. (i) Heinrich Schiff; Concg. O; (i) Sir Colin Davis; (ii) Antal Dorati.

(B) (***) Dutton Lab. mono CDEA 5002 [(M) id.]. (i) Casals; Czech PO, Szell.

(i) *Cello concerto;* (ii) *Symphony No. 9 (New World); Carnival overture, Op. 92; Scherzo capriccioso, Op. 66.*

(BB) *** EMI Seraphim CES5 68521-2 (2) [CEDB 68521]. (i) Paul Tortelier, LSO, Previn; (ii) Philh. O, Giulini – TCHAIKOVSKY: *Variations on a Rococo theme.* ***

The two Philips performances are fascinatingly different in character. Schiff's earlier reading of the *Concerto* (from the beginning of the 1980s) brings an unexaggerated vein of poetry akin to the approach of Yo-Yo Ma – its range of emotion is on a relatively small scale, though satisfying in its intimacy. This performance sounds extremely well in its CD transfer. Dorati's *New World* is characteristically vibrant and extrovert, less subtle but compelling in its direct way; indeed the level of tension is high in the outer movements and the finale ends with a thrilling surge of adrenalin. Because of the rich Concertgebouw acoustic, the forwardly balanced recording from the late 1950s does not sound too dated; indeed the woodwind glow attractively in the *Largo*.

Tortelier's 1978 recording with Previn has a satisfying centrality, not as passionately romantic as Rostropovich's recording on DG, but with the tenderness as well as the power of the work held in perfect equilibrium. What is rather less perfect is the balance of the recording, with the microphones obviously rather too near the soloist. Giulini's recording of the *New World Symphony* was made when the Philharmonia was at its peak in 1962. The result has a refinement, coupled to an attractive directness, which for some will make it an ideal reading. The remastering gives the sound plenty of warmth and projection and, if the performance is not as physically exciting as some versions, like Reiner's Chicago account, the playing, with its beautiful moulding of phrase, is very refreshing. With two attractive bonuses (the lyrical side of the *Scherzo capriccioso* appealingly affectionate), this is a bargain on EMI's Seraphim series, offering two discs for the cost of one medium-priced CD.

When there has been such an explosion in the field of historic recordings on CD, it is specially welcome that Dutton Laboratories, responsible for some of the most vivid and truthful transfers yet, have established an attendant bargain label, the Essential Archive, with this Dvořák disc one of the first issues. In Casals's pioneering recording of the Dvořák concerto, there is little to choose between the Dutton transfer and EMI's most recent one, also using the CEDAR process, with the Dutton marginally brighter and more forward. What makes this disc fascinating is having, instead of more Casals, the recording of the *New World Symphony* made in London by Szell and the Czech Philharmonic six months after the concerto. It is a bitingly powerful performance, crisp and intense and with pinpoint articulation, all the more valuable when Szell seems not to have returned to it in later commercial recordings. And as Compton Mackenzie said at the time, it is 'trance-like' in the slow movement, to have one forgetting the limited 78 dynamic range.

Piano concerto in G min., Op. 33; Carnival overture; Slavonic rhapsody No. 2.
(B) ** Millennium MCD 80098 [id.]. Rudolf Firkušný, V. State Op. O, Somogyi.

(i) *Piano concerto in G min., Op. 33; The Water Goblin (symphonic poem), Op. 107.*
(BB) *** Naxos Dig. 8.550896 [id.]. (i) Jenö Jandó; Polish Nat. RSO, Antoni Wit.

An infectiously fresh and warmly lyrical account from Jandó and the highly supportive Polish National Radio Orchestra under Antoni Wit, which makes it difficult to understand why the piece is not a popular favourite. Jandó plays with engaging freshness and conveys his own pleasure, and Wit's accompaniment glows with colour; he then offers a splendidly vibrant and colourful portrayal of *The Water Goblin*, one of the composer's most vividly melodramatic symphonic poems. The recording is spacious and realistically balanced. The violins are a shade overbright, but otherwise the sound is first class. Very enjoyable and well worth its modest cost.

Firkušný recorded the Dvořák *Piano concerto* no fewer than three times. His final recording, made in Prague in 1992, is undoubtedly the finest, but this 1963 Westminster account which briefly appeared on HMV's Concert Classics label in this country is, like all of Firkušný's records, touched with distinction. He plays his own version of the solo part distilled from the Katz revision and Dvořák's original. The recording, though not top-drawer, has the merit of spaciousness and good detail, though the piano is rather forward. Even at its modest price it offers less than generous playing-time, and Jenö Jandó's version on Naxos is even more attractive.

Violin concerto in A min., Op. 53.
(B) *** CfP Dig. CD-CFP 4566 [id.]. Tasmin Little, RLPO, Handley – BRUCH: *Concerto No. 1.* ***
(M) *** Ph. 420 895-2. Accardo, Concg. O, C. Davis – SIBELIUS: *Violin concerto.* ***
(M) *** DG Dig. 449 091-2. Shlomo Mintz, BPO, Levine – BRUCH: *Concerto No. 1.* ***

Violin concerto in A min., Op. 53; Romance in F min., Op. 11.
(B) *** [EMI Red Line Dig. CDR5 69806]. Kyung Wha Chung, Phd. O, Muti – BARTOK: *Rhapsodies.* ***
(BB) *** Naxos Dig. 8.550758 [id.]. Ilya Kaler, Polish Nat. RSO (Katowice), Camilla Kolchinsky – GLAZUNOV: *Concerto.* ***
(M) *** Sup. SU 1928-2 011 [id.]. Josef Suk, Czech PO, Karel Ančerl – SUK: *Fantasy.* ***
(M) ** Sony Stern Edition I SMK 66827 [id.]. Stern, Phd. O, Ormandy – MENDELSSOHN: *Violin concerto.* **(*)

Tasmin Little brings to this concerto an open freshness and sweetness, very apt for this composer, that are extremely winning. The firm richness of her sound, totally secure on intonation up to the topmost register, goes with an unflustered ease of manner, and the recording brings little or no spotlighting of the soloist; she establishes her place firmly with full-ranging, well-balanced sound that co-ordinates the soloist along with the orchestra.

Kyung Wha Chung gives a heartfelt reading of a work that can sound wayward. The partnership with Muti and the Philadelphia Orchestra is a happy one, with the sound warmer and more open than it has usually been in the orchestra's recording venue. She finds similar concentration in the *Romance*.

In his Philips recording, Accardo is beautifully natural and unforced, with eloquent playing from both soloist and orchestra. The engineering is altogether excellent, and in a competitive field this must rank high, especially at mid-price.

The performance of the Russian violinist, Ilya Kaler, has great romantic warmth and natural Slavonic feeling, and he is given excellent support by Kolchinsky and the Polish orchestra. In short this is first class in every way. The very resonant acoustics of the recording, made in the Concert Hall of Polish Radio, give the soloist a somewhat larger-than-life image against a widely resonant orchestral backcloth. But the effect is easy to enjoy when the playing is so ardent; moreover these artists tend to trump the opposition by offering (besides the Glazunov) the *Romance in F minor* as a considerable (13-minute) bonus, and that is also beautifully played.

Suk's earlier performance is back in the catalogue at mid-price, effectively remastered, recoupled with the Suk *Fantasy*. Its lyrical eloquence is endearing, the work is played in the simplest possible way and Ančerl accompanies glowingly. Readers will note that, since its last appearance, the *Romance* has been restored, an equally delightful performance. This is one of Suk's very finest records.

There is dazzling playing from Shlomo Mintz, whose virtuosity is effortless and his intonation astonishingly true. There is good rapport between soloist and conductor, and the performance has the sense of joy and relaxation that this radiant score needs. The digital sound is warm and natural in its upper range.

Stern's recording is a disappointment. It is not lacking in power or eloquence, but this fine soloist seems not entirely at home in the music: his playing is less natural in feeling and not as penetrating as the finest accounts. The recording, too, has the boosted quality and false balance that mar so many records from this source made in the 1960s.

(i) *Violin concerto in A min., Op. 53; Romance in F min., Op. 11. Symphonies Nos. 7 in D min., Op. 70; 8 in G, Op. 88.*

(B) ** Teldec/Warner Ultima Dig. 3984 21036-2 (2) [(M) id. import]. (i) Thomas Zehetmair; Philh. O, Inbal.

Thomas Zehetmair plays the concerto with brilliance and precision. He is satisfyingly clean in attack and is very sympathetic in the lovely *Romance*. He is well accompanied by Inbal, and the Teldec recording is natural and well balanced. Even so, this is a performance in the central Viennese tradition, with Czech flavours played down and little feeling for the Czech idiom, even in the Slavonic dance of the finale.

The *Seventh* is marginally the finest of Inbal's performances of the last three symphonies, nicely relaxed and full of idiomatic feeling, the Scherzo gently lilting and the finale gathering force at the end. The *Eighth* is also a very attractive performance, with refined playing from the Philharmonia woodwind and strings alike. A ready comparison might be made here with Previn's account on Telarc, and this is not to Inbal's disadvantage: his reading is at times sharper in its idiomatic feeling and his finale makes a particularly satisfying conclusion. The recording is excellent throughout, and anyone wanting this particular collection of music will find this Ultima Double good value, although there are more characterful versions of all three works available elsewhere.

Czech suite.

(M) ** Ph. (IMS) 442 660-2. ECO, Mackerras – JANACEK: *Sinfonietta* etc. (*)

Mackerras gives a fresh, lively performance of a lesser-known Dvořák orchestral work, and the 1980 Philips recording is naturally balanced. Alas, the coupling is a non-starter.

Czech suite, Op. 39; A Hero's song, Op. 111; Festival march, Op. 54; Hussite overture, Op. 67.

(BB) **(*) Naxos Dig. 8.553005 [id.]. Polish Nat. RSO (Katowice), Antoni Wit.

Antoni Wit, who has already given us a memorable performance of Smetana's *Má Vlast*, is almost equally impressive in *A Hero's song*. It opens atmospherically and produces a characteristically Slavonic melodic flow, with some lovely writing for strings and horns. There is an outburst of patriotic hyperbole towards the close (with thundering trombones), which is considerably inflated by the resonant acoustics of the Concert Hall of Polish Radio, which have a similar effect on the *Hussite overture* and *Festival march*; however, no one could grumble that the result lacks spectacle, and Antoni Wit generates excitement without letting things get out of hand. The performance of the *Czech suite* is warm and relaxed, nicely rustic in feeling, but again is affected by the resonance.

Czech suite, Op. 39; Nocturne for strings, Op. 40; Prague waltzes.

(B) *** Decca Double Dig. 443 015-2 (2) [id.]. Detroit SO, Dorati – SMETANA: *Má Vlast* etc. **

The *Czech suite* can sometimes outstay its welcome, but not here; and the charming set of waltzes, written for balls in Prague – Viennese music with a Czech accent – is complemented by the lovely *Nocturne* with its subtle drone bass. The recording has an attractive warmth and bloom to balance its brightness. However, the principal Smetana coupling is less readily recommendable. Readers will note that the *Czech suite* and *Prague waltzes* are also available on Eclipse, coupled with the *New World Symphony* – see below.

Legends Nos. 1–10, Op. 59 (see also under *Stabat Mater*); *Nocturne for strings;* (i) *Romance in F min., Op. 11.*

(B) *** EMI Dig. CD-EMX 2232 [(M) id. import]. (i) Stephanie Gonley; ECO, Mackerras.

Dvořák in lighter mood inspires a charmer of a record, perfect for relaxed listening. The ten *Legends*, like the *Slavonic dances*, were originally written for piano duet and were orchestrated later, easy-going pieces given winningly pointed performances by Mackerras and the ECO, helped by glowing recorded sound. The critic Eduard Hanslick, so far from acting like Beckmesser (as Wagner portrayed him in *Meistersinger*), was delighted to receive the dedication. The ECO strings play with similar refinement in the early *Nocturne*, and Stephanie Gonley, the ECO's leader, is the characterful soloist in the longest of the pieces, the haunting *Romance* for violin and orchestra.

Overtures: *Carnival, Op. 92; Hussite, Op. 67; In nature's realm, Op. 91; My home, Op. 62; Othello, Op. 93; Scherzo capriccioso, Op. 66*. Symphonic poems: *The golden spinning wheel, Op. 109; The Noonday Witch, Op. 108; The Water Goblin, Op. 107; Symphonic variations, Op. 78.*
(B) *** Decca Double 452 946-2 (2) [id.]. LSO, István Kertész.

Kertész's collection comes into direct competition with Kubelik's DG set, which has slightly more modern recording; but the vintage Decca sound from the 1960s and 1970s stands up well, and Kertész was very much at home in this repertoire. He makes the very most of the brilliant *Carnaval overture* and also offers an outstanding version of the *Scherzo capriccioso*. *Carnaval* forms a triptych with *Othello* and *In nature's realm*, linked by a recurring main theme. Dvořák wrote them immediately before his first visit to America in 1892. The melodramatic symphonic poems are also handled most evocatively. The atmospheric *Golden spinning wheel*, the tale of the malignant *Water Goblin*, and *The Noonday Witch* (the traditional ogress threatened to erring children by distraught mothers) all have the most vivid colouring. The *Symphonic variations* is another splendid work, still played comparatively rarely. Under Kertész its Brahmsian derivations are all but submerged by the Czech composer's freshness of spirit. He is even more successful in the *Hussite overture*. This is a patriotic piece, running for nearly a quarter of an hour and including themes based on the Hussite hymn and St Wenceslas plainchant. It can easily be made to seem rhetorical, but not here, where the drama is comparably red-blooded. *My home*, a more spontaneously inspired work, is even more successful.

Overtures: *Carnival, Op. 92; Hussite, Op. 67; In nature's realm, Op. 91; My home, Op. 62; Othello, Op. 93*. Symphonic poems: *The Golden spinning wheel, Op. 109; The Noonday witch, Op. 108; The Water goblin, Op. 107; The Wood dove, Op. 110. Symphonic variations, Op. 78.*
(M) *** DG (IMS) 435 074-2 (2). Bav. RSO, Rafael Kubelik.

Kubelik's performances are among his finest on record and they are superbly played. He is splendidly dashing in *Carnival*; in the two pieces there is magic and lustre in the orchestra, and the atmospheric tension is striking. The *Symphonic variations* opens warmly and graciously, yet Kubelik is obviously determined to minimize the Brahmsian associations; his light touch and apt pacing lead on to the lively finale. The recordings, made in the Munich Hercules-Saal between 1973 and 1977, are freshly transferred to CD and generally sound excellent.

Rondo in G min. (for cello and orchestra), *Op. 94*.
(M) *** Carlton Dig. 30366 0011-2 [id.]. Tortelier, RPO, Groves – ELGAR: *Cello concerto* **(*); TCHAIKOVSKY: *Rococo variations*. ***

The Dvořák *Rondo* is one of Tortelier's party pieces, and its point and humour are beautifully caught here.

Scherzo capriccioso, Op. 66; Slavonic dances, Opp. 46/1, 3 & 7; 72/2 & 8.
(M) **(*) DG 447 434-2 [id.]. BPO, Karajan – BRAHMS: *8 Hungarian dances*. ***

These are essentially virtuoso performances from Karajan which remain stylish because of the superbly polished ensemble. The 1959 recording, originally very brightly lit, sounds better balanced in this carefully remastered reissue in DG's 'Legendary Recordings' series of 'Originals'. The *Scherzo capriccioso* is exhilarating, but, while it seems carping to criticize orchestral playing of such superlative quality, the lilt of the lyrical secondary tune does seem a trifle calculated. However, coupled with eight of the Brahms *Hungarian dances*, this reissue certainly shows the Karajan/BPO combination in dazzling form.

Scherzo capriccioso, Op. 66; Slavonic rhapsody No. 3, Op. 45/3.
(B) *** EMI forte CZS5 68649-2 (2) [CDFB 68649]. Dresden State O, Berglund – GRIEG: *Old Norwegian romance* etc.; SMETANA: *Má vlast*. ***

Berglund's *Scherzo capriccioso* is warmly engaging, not the most brilliantly exciting version on record, but with plenty of impetus and a seductively lilting second subject. The *Slavonic rhapsody* (which, with its opening harp solo, has something in common with *Vyšehrad*, the opening tone-poem in the coupled *Má vlast*) is superbly done, and the recording is pleasingly warm and full.

Serenade for strings in E, Op. 22.
(M) *** EMI CDM5 66760-2. RPO, Stokowski – VAUGHAN WILLIAMS: *Fantasia on a theme by Thomas Tallis;* PURCELL: *Dido and Aneas: Dido's lament*. ***
(M) **(*) Virgin/EMI Dig. CUV5 61144-2. LCO, Warren-Green – SUK: *Serenade*. **(*)
(BB) **(*) Naxos Dig. 8.550419 [id.]. Capella Istropolitana, Krechek – SUK: *Serenade*. ***

Serenade for strings; Romance, Op. 11.
(B) *** Carlton IMP Classics Dig. 30367 0029-2 [(M) id. import]. Laredo, SCO, Laredo – WAGNER: *Siegfried idyll*. ***

Serenade for strings; Serenade for wind in D min., Op. 44.
(M) *(*) Chandos Dig. CHAN 7060 [id.]. Philh. O, Warren-Green.

Serenade for strings; Serenade for wind; Miniatures, Op. 74a.
(BB) *** Discover Dig. DICD 920135 [id.]. Virtuosi di Praga, Oldrich Vlček.

The Stokowskian magic is very apparent in his 1975 EMI recording, not only in the ripeness of the string playing but also in the masterly control of tension. Thus the opening is slow and affectionate, without dragging or sounding too overtly expressive. There is concentration in every bar and the lyrical flow is highly engaging. In the second movement Stokowski's delicacy at a quick tempo is exhilarating, and the trio is beautifully managed, with less variation of tempo than in some versions. The lilting Scherzo is matched by the warmth of the *Larghetto*, and the finale is superbly resilient. The RPO strings are kept on their toes throughout, and the wide-ranging Abbey Road recording offers the most beautiful string-sound.

Laredo's performance of Dvořák's lovely *Serenade* is volatile, full of spontaneous lyrical feeling. The recording, made in City Hall, Glasgow, is admirably balanced to give a true concert-hall effect and add ambient lustre to the string timbre. As an encore Laredo takes the solo role in the *F minor Romance*, which he plays with appealing simplicity.

The wind players of the Virtuosi di Praga give a bright, idiomatic performance of Opus 44, using characteristically reedy tones. The *String serenade* is done with equal understanding, though the recording catches an edge on high violins. The rare *Miniatures* for string trio provide an attractive makeweight. An excellent bargain in full, bright sound.

Warren-Green and his excellent London Chamber Orchestra bring their characteristically fresh, spontaneous approach to the Dvořák *Serenade*. If without the winning individuality of the outstanding RPO version under Stokowski, this is still very enjoyable, and the Suk coupling is outstanding. Excellent sound.

Fine playing from the Capella Istropolitana on Naxos, and flexible direction from Jaroslav Krechek. His pacing is not quite as sure as in the delightful Suk coupling, and the *Adagio* could flow with a stronger current, but this is still an enjoyable and well-recorded performance.

Christopher Warren-Green's rather languorous approach in his alternative Chandos version verges dangerously near sentimentality and, despite glowing sound and fine playing from the Philharmonia strings and wind alike, neither *Serenade* is as effectively characterized as the competition.

Slavonic dances Nos. 1–16, Op. 46/1–8; Op. 72/1–8.
(M) *** DG 457 712-2 [id.]. Bav. RSO, Kubelik.
❀ (M) *** Sony SBK 48161; *SBT 48161* [id.]. Cleveland O, George Szell.
(M) *(**) Mercury 434 384-2 [id.]. Minneapolis (Minnesota) SO, Antal Dorati.
(BB) ** Naxos Dig. 8.550143 [id.]. Slovak PO, Košler.
(B) ** [EMI Red Line Dig. CDR5 69805]. BPO, Maazel.

Kubelik's set, now issued as one of DG's Originals, was given first-class DG analogue sound in its day, and it offers polished, sparkling orchestral playing. The sound has greater refinement and a rather wider range of dynamic than the competing Sony disc and for that reason many will choose it in preference to Szell, for Kubelik has a very special feeling for Dvořák and the playing of the Bavarian orchestra brings a thrilling virtuosity and a special panache of its own. But the playing of the Cleveland Orchestra has even greater flair and verve.

In Szell's exuberant, elegant and marvellously played set of the *Slavonic dances* the balance is close (which means pianissimos fail to register) but the charisma of the playing is unforgettable and, for all the racy exuberance, one senses a predominant feeling of affection and elegance. The warm acoustics of Severance Hall ensure the consistency of the orchestral sound.

Dorati's performances have splendid brio and Slavonic flair. They are also very well played, and the gentler, lyrical sections are often quite delightful. The closing number of Op. 72 is especially appealing, with its grazioso feeling affectionately caught. The snag is the curiously confined recording, full-bodied but somehow unable to expand properly. It has never sounded better than it does in this remastering for CD, but it cannot be counted one of Mercury's greatest successes.

Zdenék Košler's performances have the advantage of Slovak orchestral playing, which brings an obvious idiomatic flavour, and clean, bright, digital sound. But the performances are less exhilarating than Dorati's; in almost all cases the timings are longer. This brings a more laid-back effect, and although the vigorous dances are still lively they have less panache.

Maazel's set offers fine playing, a superb body of tone from the Berlin Philharmonic and a generally sympathetic response. But the sound is slightly opaque and, although there is no lack of vigour, the overall effect tends to undermine that final degree of spontaneity and the spirit of infectious enjoyment essential to music of the dance.

Slavonic dances, Op. 72, Nos. 9–16.
(B) *** Decca Eclipse Dig. 448 991-2; *448 991-4* [(M) id. import]. RPO, Dorati – GOLDMARK: *Rustic Wedding Symphony*. **(*)

Anyone wanting just the second set of the Dvořák *Slavonic dances* will find that Dorati's performances have characteristic brio; the RPO response is warmly lyrical when necessary, and the woodwind playing gives much pleasure. Sparkle is the keynote, and the Kingsway Hall recording adds suitable atmosphere. The 1983 recording sounds very good in this Eclipse reissue.

Symphonic poems: *The Golden spinning-wheel, Op. 109; The Noonday witch, Op. 108; The Water goblin, Op. 107; The Wood dove, Op. 110.*
(M) ** Sup. SU 3056-2 011 [id.]. Czech PO, Chalabala.

Symphonic poems: *The Golden spinning-wheel, Op. 109; The Noonday witch, Op. 108; The Wood dove, Op. 110.*
(BB) *** Naxos Dig. 8.550598 [id.]. Polish Nat. RSO (Katowice), Stephen Gunzenhauser.

The Polish orchestra seem thoroughly at home in Dvořák's sound-world and Gunzenhauser gives warm, vivid performances and is especially evocative in the masterly *Golden spinning wheel* – a favourite of Sir Thomas Beecham – with its evocative horn-calls setting the opening hunting scene and immediately creating a romantic atmosphere. There is shapely string phrasing and a fine, sonorous contribution from the brass. The concert hall of Polish Radio in Katowice has expansive acoustics – just right for the composer's colourful effects.

Originally issued on a pair of LPs, these well-played, idiomatic Supraphon performances of four favourite symphonic poems are eminently recommendable on a single, medium-priced CD for those prepared to accept somewhat emaciated violin timbre when the strings sing out above the stave, and a brass tone with slightly exaggerated brightness. Otherwise the 1961 recording, made in the Dvořák Hall in Prague, has plenty of warmth and atmosphere and is flattering to the delightful contributions of the Czech woodwind and horns. Chalabala's interpretations are thoroughly convincing.

SYMPHONIES

Symphonies Nos. 1–9.
(M) *** Chandos Dig. CHAN 9008/13 [id.]. SNO, Neeme Järvi.

Symphonies Nos. 1–9; Overtures: Carnival; In nature's realm; My home. Scherzo capriccioso.
✿ (B) *** Decca 430 046-2 (6) [(M) id. import]. LSO, István Kertész.

Järvi has the advantage of outstanding, modern, digital recording, full and naturally balanced. The set is offered at upper mid-price, six CDs for the price of four. Only the *Fourth Symphony* is split centrally between discs; all the others can be heard uninterrupted. But there are no fillers, as with Kertész on Decca.

For those not wanting to go to the expense of the digital Chandos Järvi set, Kertész's bargain box is an easy first choice among the remaining collections of Dvořák symphonies. The CD transfers are of Decca's best quality, full-bodied and vivid with a fine ambient effect. It was Kertész who first revealed the full potential of the early symphonies, and his readings gave us fresh insights into these often inspired works. To fit the symphonies and orchestral works on to six CDs some mid-work breaks have proved unavoidable; but the set remains a magnificent memorial to a conductor who died sadly young.

Symphonies Nos. 1 (Bells of Zlonice); 2 in B flat, Op. 2; 3 in E flat, Op. 10.
(B) ** Ph. Duo 446 527-2 (2) [(M) id. import]. LSO, Witold Rowicki.

Symphonies Nos. 4 in D min., Op. 13; 5 in F, Op. 76; 6 in D, Op. 60; Overtures: Hussite, Op. 67; My home, Op. 62.
(B) ** Ph. Duo 446 530-2 (2) [(M) id. import]. LSO, Witold Rowicki.

These Philips Duo reissues come into direct competition with the Decca set conducted by Kertész. Both conductors approach the music sympathetically and comparatively straightforwardly, although their tempi are not always alike, and indeed on the whole Rowicki's interpretative approach is to keep the music moving along fairly briskly. This has the advantage of freshness but in the first movement of No. 1 there is nearly three minutes' difference, and Rowicki sounds too fast. Similarly in No. 5, after Kertész's fine reading, Rowicki's initially sounds rushed and even perfunctory. He takes the outer movements very much faster, which makes for some added excitement but a less coherent argument and phrasing that inevitably sounds hurried. No. 4 is similar, although it certainly is not dull, and the Scherzo is undeniably lively. But even if there is a case for presenting the music in this way, in the middle movements, too, Rowicki's approach is a little stiffer than Kertész's. In the *Sixth* it is the *Adagio* slow movement which suffers from an over-fast tempo; it is taken as an andante, and the misjudgement is the more striking when one remembers the echo of the opening of the slow movement of Beethoven's *Ninth*. Rowicki does his best to draw flexible phrasing, despite the speed, but it would clearly have been better if he had relaxed more. The performances of the other three movements have much to be said for them, for Rowicki manages to point the phrasing engagingly – for example, in the way he leads to the oboe theme of the second subject group in the first movement, where (like Kertész) he observes the exposition repeat – very important when the fourteen bars of lead back would not otherwise be heard. In the last resort the Kertész readings of all these symphonies are more imaginative; the Philips sound (from the early 1970s) is smooth, bright and full, but the Decca is more dramatic in its incisiveness, with the orchestral colours showing rather more glow and sparkle. There is little difference in cost, and clearly the Decca complete set is the one to go for.

Symphony No. 1 in C min. (The Bells of Zlonice), Op. 3; Legends, Op. 59/1–5.
(BB) *** Naxos Dig. 8.550266 [id.]. Slovak PO, Czecho-Slovak RSO, Gunzenhauser.

Though on a super-bargain label, this Bratislava version rivals any in the catalogue both as a performance and in sound. The ensemble of the Slovak Philharmonic is rather crisper than that on the other modern rival, Järvi's Chandos disc, and the recording, full and atmospheric, has detail less obscured by reverberation. The first five of Dvořák's ten *Legends* make a generous coupling: colourful miniatures, colourfully played.

Symphony No. 2 in B flat, Op. 4; Legends, Op. 59/6–10.
(BB) *** Naxos Dig. 8.550267 [id.]. Slovak PO, Czecho-Slovak RSO, Gunzenhauser.

With speeds more expansive than those of his full-priced Chandos rival, Neeme Järvi (CHAN 8589), Gunzenhauser gives a taut, beautifully textured account, very well played and recorded, clearly preferable in every way, even making no allowance for price. The completion of the set of *Legends* makes a very generous coupling (73 minutes).

Symphonies Nos. 3 in E flat, Op. 10; 6 in D, Op. 60.
(BB) *** Naxos Dig. 8.550268; *4.550268* [id.]. Slovak PO, Stephen Gunzenhauser.

These exhilarating performances of the *Third* and *Sixth Symphonies* are well up to the standard of earlier records in this splendid Naxos series. Gunzenhauser's pacing is admirably judged through both works, and rhythms are always lifted. Excellent, vivid recording in the warm acoustics of the Bratislava Concert Hall.

Symphonies Nos. 4 in D min., Op. 13; 8 in G, Op. 33.
(BB) **(*) Naxos Dig. 8.550269; *4550269* [id.]. Slovak PO, Stephen Gunzenhauser.

Gunzenhauser's *Fourth* is very convincing. In his hands the fine lyrical theme of the first movement certainly blossoms and the relative lack of weight in the orchestral textures brings distinct benefit in the Scherzo. The slow movement, too, is lyrical without too much Wagnerian emphasis. The naturally sympathetic orchestral playing helps to make the *Eighth* a refreshing experience, even though the first two movements are rather relaxed and without the impetus of the finest versions. The digital sound is excellent, vivid and full, with a natural concert-hall ambience.

(i) *Symphony No. 5 in F, Op. 76;* (ii) *Carnival overture, Op. 92;* (iii) *The American Flag* (cantata), *Op. 102.*
(B) **(*) Sony Dig./Analogue SBK 60297; *SBT 60297* [id.]. (i) Philh. O, Andrew Davis; (ii) NYPO, Mehta; (iii) Joseph Evans, Barry McDaniel, St Hedwig's Cathedral Choir, Berlin RIAS Chamber Ch., Berlin RSO, Tilson Thomas.

Andrew Davis's account of the *Fifth Symphony*, freshly played but somewhat undercharacterized, is rather more successful than his *Sixth*, but there is nothing special about Mehta's *Carnival overture*. Yet what makes this bargain CD well worth considering is Dvořák's stirringly vigorous occasional piece. *The American Flag* was commissioned for the composer's visit to the New World in 1892, but the patriotic poem he was required to use, by Joseph Rodman Drake (1795–1820), did not reach him in time, and the work was not finally completed until 1894. In the event, Dvořák's setting has real flair. The opening sections addressing the American Eagle are spirited enough, but when the tenor (as the Foot Soldier) presents the *First address to the flag*, Dvořák produces an infectiously jigging tune which is then taken up enthusiastically by the chorus; the work continues in this vein until its effective closing apotheosis. The Berlin performance under Michael Tilson Thomas is little short of inspired; seldom has a slice of transatlantic flag-waving brought more exhilarating results. The singing of both soloists is first rate and the combined choruses are magnificent. The analogue recording could not be bettered, and this surely needs to be more aptly re-coupled with Tilson Thomas's account of the *American suite* (see below).

Symphonies Nos. 5 in F, Op. 76; 7 in D min., Op. 70.
(BB) *** Naxos Dig. 8.550270; *4550270* [id.]. Slovak PO, Stephen Gunzenhauser.

Gunzenhauser's coupling is recommendable even without the price advantage. The beguiling opening of the *Fifth*, with its engaging Slovak wind solos, has plenty of atmosphere, and the reading generates a natural lyrical impulse. The *Seventh*, spontaneous throughout, brings an eloquent *Poco adagio*, a lilting Scherzo, and a finale that combines an expansive secondary theme with plenty of excitement and impetus.

(i) *Symphony No. 6 in D, Op. 60; Scherzo capriccioso, Op. 66;* (ii) *American suite, Op. 98b.*
(B) ** Sony Dig./Analogue SBK 60295; *SBT 60295* [id.]. (i) Philh. O, Andrew Davis; (ii) Berlin RSO, Michael Tilson Thomas.

In the *Sixth Symphony* Andrew Davis gives a strong and fresh performance which lacks a little in idiomatic warmth. It is a pity that he omits the exposition repeat in the first movement. The *Scherzo capriccioso* is similarly just a little undercharacterized. But the same cannot be said for Michael Tilson Thomas's account of the *American suite*, which is most deftly handled and reveals its full charm and vigour, particularly the light-hearted, folksy finale. It is excellently recorded, the analogue sound quite as pleasing as the digital Abbey Road recording of the *Symphony*.

Symphonies Nos. 6 in D, Op. 60; 7 in D min., Op. 70; 8 in G, Op. 88; 9 (New World); Scherzo capriccioso, Op. 66.
(M) **(*) EMI CMS5 65705-2 (3). LPO, Rostropovich.

Now reissued as part of EMI's Rostropovich Edition, these performances date from 1979–80. The *Sixth Symphony* opens freshly, the first movement quite relaxed until the coda which draws everything strongly together; the performance is notable for some lovely LPO wind-playing. The slow movement is leisurely and romantic but has an imposing climax and coda. The Scherzo brings an accent on forceful vigour and is in no way lightweight, although there is more lovely pastoral woodwind playing in the Trio. The finale certainly does not lack impetus and power and its forceful close is characteristic of Rostropovich's weighty approach throughout the set. The *Seventh* is a big, thrustful reading which underplays the genial Dvořák, who now becomes biting and unrelenting. The spaciousness of the speeds is designed not for lyrical self-indugence but to underline the symphonic breadth. Even the slow movement is big and powerful, highly charged rather than warm and refined; the Scherzo, the rhythmic nudgings a trifle calculated, is emphatic rather than urgent, the most controversial point of an unconventional interpretation. The *Eighth* produces slow tempi throughout and a consciously *espressivo* manner. The slow movement sounds too studied and unspontaneous, and the performance overall disappointingly refuses to catch fire. Rostropovich's very opening chords for the *New World* suggest an epic view, and from then on, with generally expansive tempi, the reading clearly follows this weighty conception. The exposition repeat brings a slight modification of treatment the second time, and some will resist such inconsistencies as that. The conscious weight of even the *Largo* is also controversial, though in all four movements Rostropovich contrasts the big tuttis with light pointing in woodwind solos. The *Scherzo capriccioso* is incisive and energetic, lilting yet essentially symphonic in feeling; with all reservations taken into account, these readings are all full of character and only the *Eighth* lacks the fullest concentration. The Kingsway Hall recording has been very effectively remastered so that the sound is bright and fresh on top, yet remains full and expansive.

Symphonies Nos. 7 in D min., Op. 70; 8 in G, Op. 88.
(M) *** Mercury (IMS) 434 312-2 [id.]. LSO, Antal Dorati.
(B) **(*) Sony SBK 67174; *SBT 67174* [id.]. Philh. O, Andrew Davis.

Dorati's coupling brings an extraordinary successful account of No. 7, with the spontaneous feel of a live performance enhanced by the vividly realistic concert hall balance of the (1963) Mercury recording – one of their very finest. The interpretation is free, the *Poco Adagio* is impulsive and the Scherzo lifts off with a sparkle. The finale has enormous energy and bite, and an exuberant thrust, leading on to a thrilling coda. The *Eighth Symphony* was recorded four years earlier, with the acoustic of Watford Town Hall again providing a highly convincing ambience. Dorati's reading proves comparably vibrant.

Andrew Davis's coupling with the Philharmonia is reissued in Sony's 'Essential Classics' bargain series but was recorded at EMI's Abbey Road studios with Neville Boyling the balance engineer. Yet, with the violins given a bright sheen, with good detail but lacking something in warmth, and with the brass given plenty of presence and bite, the sound is more like a CBS recording than a mellower, EMI offering. Davis's comparatively lightweight account of the *Seventh* has an attractive lyrical freshness, the *Poco Adagio* simple and songful though with an eloquent climax, the Scherzo vivaciously energetic, rhythms nicely lifted. But the finale hangs fire just a little until the very end. The *Eighth* is much more compulsive and dramatically spontaneous, making the most of the music's dynamic contrasts, with high drama in the climaxes of the *Adagio*, which also has plenty of expressive feeling, and a sense of vibrant energy throughout the outer movements. The Scherzo responds least well to this approach, but the finale is thrilling (although there is some raucous tone from the brass) and there is no doubt about the individuality of the reading as a whole.

(i) *Symphonies Nos. 7 in D min., Op. 70; 8 in G, Op. 88; 9 in E min. (New World);* (ii) *10 Legends, Op. 59.*
(B) ** Ph. Duo 456 327-2 (2) [id.]. (i) LSO, Rowicki; (ii) LPO, Raymond Leppard.

Rowicki's Duo comes into direct competition with Sir Colin Davis, who remains a preferable choice unless you want the *Legends*, which are indeed a very considerable bonus, glorious music in delightful and warm-hearted performances from the LPO under Raymond Leppard. The Philips sound too is beautifully natural and fresh. Rowicki's recordings of the last three symphonies come from a complete set he recorded at the end of the 1960s and beginning of the 1970s. They are fresh, straightforward performances. No. 7 has a sprightly Scherzo, but elsewhere there is very little pointing. Cool and direct, he fails to illuminate Dvořák's individual vein of melancholy in this work, although the playing of the LSO is excellent. No. 8 lacks the extra sparkle of the Davis account, and the *New World*, too, has nothing particularly individual to offer. It rather lacks drama, especially in the first movement, and is mannered in the Scherzo. No complaints about the Philips recording, which is fresh and well balanced.

Symphonies Nos. 7 in D min., Op. 70; 8 in G, Op. 88; 9 in E min. (From the New World), Op. 95; Carnival overture, Op. 92.
(B) ** DG Double Dig. 453 124-2 (2) [id.]. VPO, Lorin Maazel.

Maazel's reluctance to relax in Dvořákian happiness and innocence in *Symphony No. 7* produces a powerful, incisive performance with the slow movement spacious and refined, though the bright recording fails to place the orchestra against any defined acoustic, making fortissimos rather aggressive. Maazel's performance of the *Eighth Symphony* is fierce, lacking the glow of warmth one associates with this work. Despite excellent, incisive playing, the hardness of the reading is underlined by the recording balance, which favours a bright treble against a rather light bass. Though the trumpet fanfare heralding the start of the finale is wonderfully vivid, the sound lacks something in body. The reading of the *New World* is similarly high-powered and is played superbly, incisive to the point of fierceness but with moments of affection, most strikingly in the poised and pure account of the slow movement. Dohnányi's Double Decca leads the field for the three last Dvořák symphonies (see below).

Symphonies Nos. (i) *7 in D min., Op. 70;* (ii) *8 in G, Op. 88; 9 (New World); Overture: Carnival, Op. 92; Scherzo capriccioso, Op. 66.*
(B) **(*) EMI forte CZS5 68628-2 (2) [CDFB 68628]. (i) LPO; (ii) Philh. O; Giulini.

Symphonies Nos. 7 in D min., Op. 70; 8 in G, Op. 88; 9 (New World); Scherzo capriccioso, Op. 66.
(B) *** Decca Double 452 182-2 (2) [id.]. Cleveland O, Christoph von Dohnányi.

Christoph von Dohnányi's Cleveland performances of the last three Dvořák symphonies from the mid-1980s are among his very finest recordings, and they make an admirable Double Decca triptych. Tempi are all aptly judged. The playing of the Cleveland Orchestra is so responsive that the overall impression is one of freshness, and the recording is in the demonstration class, using the acoustics of the Masonic Auditorium to give a convincingly natural balance. Dohnányi's *New World*, superbly played and recorded, like the companion recordings of Nos. 7 and 8, should by rights be a first recommendation, but it fails to observe the first-movement exposition repeat. That said, there is much to praise in this grippingly spontaneous performance, generally direct and unmannered but glowing with warmth. In the first movement Dohnányi, without any stiffness, allows himself relatively little easing of tempo for the second and third subjects, while the great cor anglais melody in the *Largo* and the big clarinet solo in the finale are both richly done, with the ripe and very well-balanced Decca recording adding to their opulence. The sound is spectacularly full and rich. The addition of the *Scherzo capriccioso* is apt when the performance finds an affinity with the *Eighth Symphony* in bringing out the Slavonic dance sparkle and moulding the lyrical secondary theme with comparable affectionate flair.

Giulini is at his finest in both the *Seventh* and the *New World*. In the *D minor Symphony* he and the LPO players really make the music sing, and the Dvořákian sunshine keeps breaking out. The glowing (1976) recording encourages rounded textures and rounded phrases, but it is not in any way a self-indulgent performance, and the concentration from first to last makes for buoyancy instead of the usual more biting qualities. No. 8 (like the *New World*), recorded with the Philharmonia 14 years earlier, brings a similar mellow approach, but the result is comparatively disappointing. Giulini's speeds are on the slow side, especially in the *Adagio* (though there is a spurt at the climax) and rather bland *Allegretto*, while the finale opens in a somewhat subdued fashion. Frankly this does not altogether come off. The *New World* is a different matter, refreshingly direct. It is discussed above in its alternative, Seraphim coupling with the *Cello concerto*.

(i) *Symphonies Nos. 7 in D min., Op. 70; 8 in G, Op. 88; 9 in E min. (From the New World), Op. 95;* (ii) *The Wood dove, Op. 110.*
(B) *** DG Double 439 663-2 (2) [id.]. (i) BPO; (ii) Bav. RSO; Kubelik (with SMETANA: *Má Vlast: Vltava* (with Boston SO) ***).

Symphonies Nos. 8 in G, Op. 88; 9 in E min. (From the New World), Op. 95.
(M) *** DG 447 412-2 [id.]. BPO, Kubelik.

Rafael Kubelik's performances of the last Dvořák symphonies are among the finest ever recorded. The recordings sound admirably fresh, full yet well detailed, the ambience attractive. Kubelik gives a glowing performance of the *Seventh*, one of Dvořák's richest inspirations. His approach is essentially expressive, but his romanticism never obscures the overall structural plan and there is no lack of vitality and sparkle. The account of the *Eighth* is a shade straighter, without personal idiosyncrasy, except for a minor indulgence for the phrasing of the glowingly lyrical string-theme in the trio of the Scherzo. Throughout both works the playing of the Berlin Philharmonic Orchestra is most responsive, with the polish of the playing adding refinement. The orchestral balance in the *G major Symphony* is particularly well judged. The recordings come from 1971 and 1966 respectively. Kubelik's marvellously fresh *New World*, recorded in the Jesus-Christus-Kirche and dating from 1972, also remains among the top recommendations, providing one does not mind the omission of the first movement's exposition repeat. There is a choice of formats. The best buy is surely the DG Double, which includes a comparably fine Bavarian Radio Orchestra performance of *The Wood dove*, plus Smetana's *Vltava*, recorded in Boston. However, the *Eighth* and *Ninth Symphonies* are also reissued as 'Legendary Recordings' in DG's 'Originals' series at mid-price, and the *New World* is additionally available on a DG Classikon bargain CD (439 436-2), coupled with five sparkling *Slavonic dances* (see below).

(i) *Symphonies Nos. 7 in D min., Op. 70; 8 in G, Op. 88;* (ii) *9 (New World);* (i) *Symphonic variations, Op. 78.*
(B) *** Ph. Duo 438 347-2 (2) [id.]. (i) LSO; (ii) Concg. O, Sir Colin Davis.

Sir Colin Davis's performances of Nos. 7 and 8, with their bracing rhythmic flow and natural feeling for Dvořákian lyricism, are appealingly direct yet have plenty of life and urgency. In the *New World*, however, the very directness has its drawbacks. The cor anglais solo in the slow movement brings an appealing simplicity. The reading is completely free from egotistical eccentricity and, with beautiful orchestral playing throughout, this is enjoyable in its way. The set is made the more attractive by the inclusion of the *Symphonic variations* – one of Dvořák's finest works, much underrated by the public – and here Davis's performance has striking freshness. The remastering of all the recordings is very successful.

Symphonies Nos. 7 in D min., Op. 70; 9 in E min. (New World), Op. 95.
(B) *** EMI Eminence Dig. CD-EMX 2202 [(M) id. import]. LPO, Mackerras.

At mid-price, Mackerras's coupling offers performances of both works which are among the finest ever. With Mackerras, tragedy is not uppermost in the *D minor Symphony* but rather Dvořákian openness. After a hushed, mysterious opening it is the lilting joy of the inspiration which makes the performance so winning. In the *New World* he takes a warmly expansive view, remarkable for a hushed and intense account of the slow movement and superb playing from the LPO, treated to warm, atmospheric recording.

Symphony No. 8 in G; Legends Nos. 4, 6 & 7, Op. 59; Scherzo capriccioso.
✿ (M) *** EMI (SIS) CDM7 64193-2 [id.]. Hallé O, Sir John Barbirolli.

Symphony No. 8 in G, Op. 88; Slavonic dances Nos. 3, Op. 46/3; 10, Op. 72/2.
(B) **(*) EMI forte (SIS) CZS5 69509-2 (2) [CDFB 69509]. Cleveland O, Szell – BEETHOVEN: *Piano concerto No. 5* etc. ***

Symphony No. 8 in G; Symphonic variations, Op. 78.
(B) *** EMI Dig. CD-EMX 2216 [(M) id. import]. LPO, Mackerras.

Barbirolli's account of this symphony was one of his best Pye records: the reading has immense vitality and forward impetus, the kind of spontaneous excitement that is rare in the recording studio, and yet the whole performance is imbued with a delightful, unforced lyricism. The *Scherzo capriccioso* is warm and very exciting too, and the *Legends* make a colourful bonus. This was always the finest of Barbirolli's late Dvořák symphonies technically, and the EMI documentation reveals why: it was made in 1957/8 in Manchester's recently rebuilt Free Trade Hall by the Mercury recording team, led by Wilma Cozart Fine. In remastered form it is tremendously real and vivid.

Mackerras's version of No. 8 matches in its effervescence his outstanding accounts of Nos. 7 and 9, also on Eminence. The colour and atmosphere of the piece are brought out vividly and with a lightness of touch that makes most rivals seem heavy-handed. In the *Symphonic variations* too, his relaxed treatment is consistently winning, helped by fine playing and recording. While Barbirolli's interpretation of the symphony remains very special, Mackerras has the advantage of first-rate digital recording.

Szell's reading of the *Eighth Symphony* is strong and committed, consistent from first to last, and marvellously played. In sheer adrenalin the interpretation does not quite match his earlier, Decca (mono) version in the first two movements but, with full-bodied 1970 sound, it remains both distinctive and very enjoyable. Similarly the pair of *Slavonic dances* are mellower than the earlier complete set on Sony but are still a fine example of Cleveland orchestral bravura. The transfers are first class – this is a richer sound than on many records from this source.

Symphonies Nos. 8 in G; 9 in E min. (New World).
(M) *** Sony Bruno Walter Edition SMK 64484 [id.]. Columbia SO, Bruno Walter.
(B) ** [EMI Red Line Dig. CDR5 69804]. Phd. O, Sawallisch.

Walter's account of Dvořák's *Eighth* was one of the last recordings he made (in 1962); the sound has been successfully freshened in the current remastering, but with the violas, cellos and basses remaining expansively resonant. It is a strong yet superbly lyrical reading, but the overall lyricism never takes the place of virility and Walter's mellowness is most effective in the *Adagio*. His pacing is uncontroversial until the finale, which is steadier than usual, more symphonic, though never heavy. The *New World* was recorded two years earlier and again has been effectively remastered. Once more, this is not a conventional reading, but it is one to fall in love with. Its recognizably Viennese roots lead to a more relaxed view of the outer movements than usual. Nevertheless, as so often with Walter, there is an underlying tension to knit the structure together; the *Largo* is radiant and the Scherzo lilting. The spacious finale finds dignity without pompousness and the result is more involving and satisfying than some other rivals which have greater surface excitement.

Sawallisch gives thoughtful, sympathetic readings of both symphonies, but the glow of enjoyment is not obvious, even in No. 8. Additionally, the sound presents the violins with an edge in loud tuttis which is very un-Philadelphian.

Symphony No. 9 in E min. (From the New World), Op. 95.
(M) *** Decca Phase Four 448 947-2 [id.]. New Philh. O, Dorati – KODALY: *Háry János suite*. ***
(M) *** Mercury (IMS) 434 317-2 [id.]. Detroit SO, Paray – SIBELIUS: *Symphony No. 2*. **
(M) (***) RCA mono GD 60279 [60279-2-RG]. NBC SO, Toscanini – KODALY: *Háry János suite* (***); SMETANA: *Má Vlast: Vltava*. (**)
(M) (***) Mercury mono 434 387-2 [id.]. Chicago SO, Kubelik – MOZART: *Symphony No. 38 in D (Prague)*. (**)
(M) **(*) Telarc CD 82007 [id.]. St Louis SO, Leonard Slatkin.
(M) ** Virgin/EMI Dig. CUV5 61124-2 [id.]. Houston SO, Christoph Eschenbach – TCHAIKOVSKY: *Francesca da Rimini*. **

Symphony No. 9 (New World); Carnival overture, Op. 92.
(M) *** RCA 09026 62587-2 [id.]. Chicago SO, Fritz Reiner – SMETANA: *Bartered Bride overture;* WEINBERGER: *Schwanda polka and fugue*. ***
(BB) *(*) Carlton LSO Double Dig. 30368 001177 (2) [(B) id.]. LSO, Barry Tuckwell – SIBELIUS: *Symphony No. 2* etc. **(*)

Symphony No. 9 (New World); Overtures: Carnival; Othello.
(M) *** Decca 448 583-2 [id.]. LSO, Istvan Kertész.

(i) *Symphony No. 9 (New World); Carnival overture;* (ii) *Scherzo capriccioso, Op. 66.*
(M) *** [RCA Basic 100 09026 61716-2]. Chicago SO; (i) Reiner; (ii) Levine.

Symphony No. 9 (New World); Carnival overture; Slavonic dances Nos. 1 & 3, Op. 46/1 & 3.
(M) ** Sony SMK 47547 [id.]. NYPO, Bernstein (with SMETANA: *Vltava* *(*)).

Symphony No. 9 (New World); (ii) *Czech suite; Prague waltzes.*
(B) *** Decca Eclipse Dig. 448 245-2; *448 245-4* [(M) id. import]. (i) VPO, Kondrashin; (ii) Detoit SO, Dorati.

Symphony No. 9 (New World); Scherzo capriccioso.
(BB) *(*) RCA Navigator 74321 17898-2. Phd. O, Ormandy (with SMETANA: *Vltava:* Bamberg SO, Kuhn *).

(i) *Symphony No. 9 (New World);* (ii) *Serenade for strings.*
(M) **(*) Sony SBK 46331; *SBT 46331* [id.]. (i) LSO, Ormandy; (ii) Munich PO, Kempe.

(i) *Symphony No.9 in E min. (New World);* (ii) *Slavonic dances Nos. 1, 2, 7 & 8, Op. 46/1, 2, 7 & 8; 16, Op. 72/8.*
(B) *** DG Classikon 439 436-2; *439 436-4* [(M) id. import]. (i) BPO; (ii) Bav. RSO; Rafael Kubelik.

Symphony No. 9 (New World); Slavonic dances Nos. 1, 3 and 7, Op. 46/1, 3 & 7; 10 and 15, Op. 72/2 & 7.
(M) *** DG 435 590-2. BPO, Karajan.

Symphony No. 9 (New World); Symphonic variations, Op. 78.
(B) *** CfP Dig. CD-CFP 9006 [(M) id. import]. LPO, Macal.

Kondrashin's Vienna performance of the *New World Symphony* was one of Decca's first demonstration CDs and its impact remains quite remarkable. Recorded in the Sofiensaal, the ambience of the hall prevents a clinical effect, yet every detail of Dvořák's orchestration is revealed within a highly convincing perspective. Other performances may exhibit a higher level of tension but there is a natural spontaneity here, with the first-movement exposition repeat fitting naturally into the scheme of things. The cor anglais solo in the *Largo* is easy and songful, and the finale is especially satisfying, with the wide dynamic range adding drama and the refinement and transparency of the texture noticeably effective as the composer recalls ideas from earlier movements. Previously available in a mid-priced coupling with Dorati's RPO version of the engaging *American suite* (which is still listed in Schwann [London 430 702-2]), the new budget-priced Eclipse CD is enhanced by Dorati's bright, fresh Detroit versions of the *Czech suite* and the even rarer *Prague waltzes* (Viennese music with a Czech accent).

Among earlier analogue accounts, Kertész's LSO version stands out. It remains one of the finest performances ever committed to record, with a most exciting first movement (exposition repeat included) in which the introduction of the second subject group is eased in with considerable subtlety; the *Largo* brings playing of hushed intensity to make one hear the music with new ears. Tempi in the last two movements are perfectly judged. Reissued, very successfully remastered, as part of Decca's 'Classic Sound' series, with equally fine accounts of *Othello* and the *Carnival overture*, this remains very competitive, but for most collectors the Kondrashin version is even more attractive.

Reiner's 1957 *New World* is an essentially lyrical performance without idiosyncratic disturbances. There is no first-movement exposition repeat, but how naturally the second subject is ushered in and how well the music flows, both here and in the *Largo*, with consistently lovely playing, especially in the rapt closing section. The Scherzo sparkles and its lilting rustic interlude is especially beguiling, while there is no lack of excitement in the finale. Typically warm Chicago sound. What makes this disc the more attractive are the fill-ups, not just the brilliant *Carnival overture*, which bursts with energetic orchestral bravura and yet has ravishing Slavonic feeling in the middle section. As can be seen above, Reiner's recording is available in the USA with an alternative coupling (as part of RCA's Basic 100 series): the *Scherzo capriccioso* instead of the Smetana and Weinberger items.

Macal as a Czech takes a fresh and unsentimental view of the *New World Symphony*. His inclusion of the repeat balances the structure convincingly. With idiomatic insights there is no feeling of rigidity, with the beauty of the slow movement purified, the Scherzo crisp and energetic, set against pastoral freshness in the episodes, and the finale again strong and direct, bringing a ravishing clarinet solo. The *Symphonic variations*, which acts as coupling, is less distinctive but is well characterized. A fine bargain recommendation.

Karajan's 1964 DG analogue recording is preferable to his full-price digital version. It has a powerful lyrical feeling and an exciting build-up of power in the outer movements. The *Largo* is played most beautifully, and Karajan lets the orchestra speak for itself, which it does, gloriously. The rustic qualities of the Scherzo are affectionately brought out, and altogether this is very rewarding. The recording is full, bright and open. This is now reissued, sounding as good as ever, coupled with five favourite *Slavonic dances*, given virtuoso performances.

Kubelik's *New World* (see above) remains among the top recommendations. It is brightly transferred in this Classikon reissue, where it is recoupled with five sparkling *Slavonic dances*.

Dorati's performance is immediate and direct, with bold primary colours heightening the drama throughout. Rarely have the Phase Four techniques been used to better artistic effect, and the recording is extremely vivid, without loss of warmth. Not a first choice, perhaps, but eminently recommendable if the excellent Kodály coupling is suitable.

Paray's 1960 *New World* is uncommonly fresh. In the first-movement allegro he is airy and graceful; the exposition repeat is not observed. The *Largo*, with its poised cor anglais melody, makes a gentle contrast, and the Scherzo is admirably vivacious. The finale goes furiously and its spontaneity leaves the listener with that rare feeling that the music really has been made while he or she was listening. The recording, made in Detroit's Cass Technical High School auditorium, is well balanced in a typically natural Mercury way and adds to the freshness of effect. The Sibelius coupling is generous but the interpretation, though exciting, is rather less successful.

With speeds consistently fast and the manner clipped, Toscanini's reading of the *New World* is anything but idiomatic, but it still tells us something unique about Dvořák and his perennial masterpiece, presenting a fiery, thrilling experience. The sound is fuller than most from this source and the transfer brings that out, despite the usual dryness.

Kubelik's Mercury recording of the *New World Symphony* was almost as celebrated in its day (1951) as his *Pictures from an exhibition*. The Chicago players are kept consistently on their toes. There is no first-movement exposition repeat, but how affectionately and easily Kubelik prepares for the arrival of the second subject. The *Largo* is played most beautifully, with the one proviso that the cor anglais soloist is not ripe-toned and has what comes across as a rather nervous vibrato. The sparkling Scherzo, crisply rhythmic and full of idiomatic character, then leads to a thrilling finale, where the tension is held at the highest level until the very last bar. Here the sound, hitherto remarkably good, tends to become a bit shrill.

Under Ormandy the playing of the LSO has life and spontaneity, and the rhythmic freshness of the Scherzo (achieved by unforced precision) is matched by the lyrical beauty of the *Largo* and the breadth and vigour of the finale. Perhaps the reading has not the individuality of the finest versions; but the sound is full and firm in the bass to support the upper range's brilliance. For coupling, we are offered an essentially mellow account of the *String serenade*, directed by Kempe with affectionate warmth.

The St Louis Symphony plays for Slatkin with polish and refinement; the cor anglais solo of the slow movement is so velvety it hardly sounds like a reed instrument, and the brass which introduces the *Largo* is characteristically rich in sonority. One or two mannerisms apart, the reading is both enjoyably direct and vital, and the recording, full-bodied and naturally balanced, brings out the sweetness of the strings, even in the gentlest pianissimos. This is most enjoyable but even at mid-price (with a playing-time of only 44 minutes) remains uncompetitive without a coupling.

Bernstein's *New World* begins well with a fresh, brilliant account of the first movement (exposition repeat included) and a beautifully played *Largo*. The third movement, however, is very fast and does not relax enough or beguile as it should. The finale is done not very imaginatively: it is just played through, with no magic when the earlier themes are recalled. The recording, made in New York's Manhattan Center in 1962, is good; Bernstein is back on form in the two *Slavonic dances*, while the *Carnival overture* is brilliant enough. *Vltava* makes a colourful encore, but here the recording of the violins in their famous lyrical melody is not very flattering.

Eschenbach's reading with the Houston orchestra is strong and often thoughtful, played and recorded with refinement, but it often sounds self-conscious and over-prepared, not at all idiomatic, with a very slow tempo indeed for the *Largo*. That brings out the refined beauty of the Houston string-tone, and generally ensemble is excellent. It would have been much better to have this under-appreciated orchestra in music less frequently recorded than the *New World*.

Barry Tuckwell's *New World* is well played and sensibly paced, with the elegiac *Largo* by far the most memorable movement. The Scherzo is sprightly, but otherwise this reading is seriously under-characterized and simply doesn't generate enough electricity to be competitive, in spite of first-class, modern, digital recording. The *Carnaval overture* too is lacking in exuberance.

There is nothing special about Ormandy's RCA version. He, too, omits the first-movement exposition repeat and is fairly easy-going, though he takes affectionate care over detail in the *Largo*. The remastered sound is not very refined. The *Scherzo capriccioso* is more enjoyable and much better recorded, but Kuhn's Bamberg performance of Smetana's *Vltava*, which opens the CD, is a very low-key affair.

CHAMBER AND INSTRUMENTAL MUSIC

Piano quartet No. 2 in E flat, Op. 87; Piano quintet in A, Op. 81.
(BB) *** ASV Dig. CDQS 6200 [(M) id.]. Clementi Ens.

A very enjoyable account of the *A major Piano quintet* given by an accomplished and musical group new to records. The Clementi may not be celebrated and glamorous but they are none the worse for that. The quintet is refreshingly unmannered and pleasingly musical. Of course, among bargain CDs of the *Quintet*, Curzon and the Vienna Philharmonic Quartet, coupled with the *Trout*, remains a clear first choice, but this modestly priced and well-engineered ASV disc will give a lot of pleasure in both works and can be especially recommended to those wanting modern digital sound.

Piano quintet in A, Op. 81.
(M) *** Decca 448 602-2 [id.]. Clifford Curzon, VPO Qt – SCHUBERT: *Trout quintet*. **(*)

This wonderfully warm and lyrical (1962) performance of Dvořák's *Piano quintet* by Clifford Curzon is a classic record, one by which all later versions have come to be judged, and the CD transfer retains the richness and ambient glow of the original analogue master, yet has improved definition and presence. The piano timbre remains full and real. This performance is now available coupled, most attractively, with Schubert's *Trout quintet* in Decca's Classic Sound series.

Piano quintet in A, Op. 81; Piano trio No. 4 in E min. (Dumky), Op. 90.
(M) **(*) Virgin/EMI Ultraviolet CUV5 61321-2. Nash Ens.

It is surprising that the coupling of the *A major Piano quintet* and the *Dumky Trio* has not been chosen more often. The Nash Ensemble offer good, musicianly performances that are eminently well recorded and give satisfaction, without being as memorable as such classic accounts of the quintet as that with Clifford Curzon on Decca.

(i) *Piano quintet in A, Op. 81. String quartet No. 14 in A flat, Op. 105.*
(B) (*) Millennium mono MCD 80095 [id.]. (i) Edith Farnadi; Barylli Qt.

Edith Farnadi and the Barylli Quartet give an enjoyable account of the *Piano quintet*, though some may find the Barylli's Op. 105 a shade too sweet and suave. The recordings were made in the early 1950s and originally appeared here on the Westminster label. The sound is rather dated and, while Curzon's lovely account on Decca is still in currency and so competitively priced, there is no case for preferring the Millennium reissue.

Piano trios Nos. 1 in B flat, Op. 21; 2 in G min., Op. 26; 3 in F min., Op. 65; 4 in E min. (Dumky), Op. 90.
(M) *** Carlton Dig. 30366 00247-2 (2) [id.]. Solomon Trio.
(M) *** Teldec/Warner Dig. 9031 76458-2 (2). Trio Fontenay.
(B) **(*) Ph. Duo 454 259-2 (2) [(M) id. import]. Beaux Arts Trio.

The Solomon Trio (Daniel Adni, Rodney Friend and Raphael Sommer) have the advantage of an outstandingly realistic and well-balanced recording. The resonance seems just right and one can imagine a hall extension behind one's speakers. This is a different group of players from the performers in the earlier, excellent, two-disc set of Beethoven *Piano trios* (Carlton 30366 00107), with only the violinist, Rodney Friend, common to both. But, if anything, these Dvořák performances are even more successful. It is good to welcome the pianist, Daniel Adni, back to the recording studio: it is he who holds the performances together so naturally, so that the players can relax yet bring the music fully to life. While his legato tone is warmly coloured, he can also twinkle delightfully, as in the Scherzo of Op. 21. Indeed the Czech dance movements all lilt most engagingly. The warm tone and musical phrasing of Raphael Sommer, the cellist, is a rewarding feature of the *Adagios* of Opp. 21 and 65; the latter is a performance which brings much subtlety as well as drama and brilliance. The *Dumky* is flexibly quixotic in its spontaneous mood-changes and it combines freshness with communicated affection. This set is at upper-mid-price.

First-class playing and expertly balanced modern recording combine to make the version by the Trio Fontenay very attractive indeed. Wolf Harden, the pianist, dominates – but only marginally so: his colleagues match him in lyrical ardour, and they are as sympathetic to Dvořák's warm lyricism as to the Czech dance characteristics of the livelier allegros.

The Beaux Arts versions of the *Piano trios* come from the end of the 1960s. The *F minor*, arguably the most magnificent and certainly the most concentrated of the four, is played with great eloquence and vitality, with Bernard Greenhouse's cello solo at the opening of the *Poco adagio* matched by Isidore Cohen's delicacy of feeling. And what sparkling virtuosity there is in the *Scherzo* of the *G minor*, Op. 26. The splendours of the *Dumky* are well realized in an account of great spontaneity and freshness. The pianist Menahem Pressler plays throughout with real effervescence. The recording is naturally balanced and splendidly vivid; only a degree of thinness on the violin timbre, most noticeable on the first disc but also at the first fortissimo of the *Dumky*, gives any grounds for reservation. At Duo price this is excellent value.

Piano trios No. 3 in F min., Op. 65; 4 in E min. (Dumky), Op. 90.
(B) *** HM Musique d'Abord Dig. HMA 901404 [id.]. Trio de Barcelona.
(M) **(*) Ph. (IMS) 426 095-2. Beaux Arts Trio.
(BB) ** Arte Nova Dig. 74321 51622-2 [id.]. Munich Piano Trio.

Two very enjoyable performances on Harmonia Mundi. The presentation material gives no details about the Trio de Barcelona, but they are obviously an excellent ensemble. Their accounts of both *Trios* are first rate and hold up well against the competition, including the Beaux Arts Trio – which is no mean compliment. They really have the measure of this music and portray its changing moods, dramatic fire and lyrical repose, bringing both poetic feeling and refined musicianship to both pieces. Warm, well-defined, excellent sound.

The Beaux Arts' 1969 performances of Op. 65 and the *Dumky* still sound fresh and sparkling, though the recording on CD is a little dry in violin timbre; the *F minor*, arguably the finer and certainly the more concentrated of the two, is played with great eloquence and vitality.

The Munich Piano Trio are a well-integrated group and they capture the chimerical mood changes in the *Dumky Trio* with élan and with touching sensibility in the moments of calm. They also give a perceptive and responsive account of Op. 65; but here the ear is even more struck by the close balance. In fortissimos the sound becomes rather fierce, with a lack of separation between the three instruments, and the piano rather clattery.

String quartets Nos. 1–14; Cypresses, B.152; Fragment in F, B.120; 2 Waltzes, Op. 54, B.105.
(M) *** DG 429 193-2 (9). Prague Qt.

Dvořák's *Quartets* span the whole of his creative life. The glories of the mature *Quartets* are well known, though it is only the so-called *American* which has achieved real popularity. The beauty of the present set, made in 1973–7, is that it offers more *Quartets* (not otherwise available) plus two *Quartet movements*, in *A minor* (1873) and *F major* (1881), plus two *Waltzes* and *Cypresses* for good measure, all in eminently respectable performances and decent recordings.

String quartets Nos. 8 in E., Op. 80; 11 in C, Op. 61.
(BB) *** Naxos 8.553372 [id.]. Vlach Qt.

String quartet No. 9 in D min., Op. 34; Terzetto in C (for 2 violins and viola), Op. 74.
(BB) *** Naxos 8.553373 [id.]. Vlach Qt.

String quartets Nos. 10 in E flat, Op. 51; 14 in A flat, Op. 105.
(BB) *** Naxos 8.553374 [id.]. Vlach Qt.

There is nothing 'bargain basement' about these Vlach performances except their price. The playing is cultured and has warmth and vitality, and there can be no grumbles as far as the quality of the recorded sound is concerned. The discrepancy between the numbering of the quartets is accounted for by the fact that the *E major* (No. 8) was written earlier than its companion but published later. The dark intensity on a whispered pianissimo which marks the playing of the Vlach Quartet of Prague at the hushed opening of Op. 105, one of Dvořák's masterpieces, leads on to performances of exceptional strength and refinement. The vigorous movements bring exhilaratingly sprung rhythms and slow movements that are deeply expressive. The tonal matching of the Vlach Quartet seals their claims to be an outstanding international group. Once again a discrepancy is thrown up by the numbering of the *A flat major Quartet* on the third CD as No. 14. It was written before No. *13 in G major*, Op. 106, but published afterwards. So far this has been one of Naxos's success stories, and we are inclined to think the series strongly competitive even alongside most of the full-priced alternatives. As far as the technical quality of the recordings is concerned, they fully deserve their three-star rating. The sound is natural, well focused and warm.

String quartet No. 12 in F (American), Op. 96.
(B) *** Carlton IMP Dig. 30367 0097-2 [(M) id.]. Delmé Qt – BRAHMS: *Clarinet quintet.* ***
(BB) *** CfP Silver Double CDCFPSD 4772 (2) [id.]. Gabrieli String Qt – BORODIN: *String quartet No. 2* ***; BRAHMS: *Clarinet quintet* **(*); SCHUBERT: *String quartet No. 14.* ***
(M) *** Classic fM 75605 57027-2. Chilingirian Qt – BORODIN: *Quartet No. 2;* SHOSTAKOVICH: *Quartet No. 8.* ***
(M) **(*) DG (IMS) 437 251-2. Amadeus Qt – SMETANA: *String quartet No. 1.* **(*)
(BB) ** HM Solo Dig. HMS 926010 [(B) id.]. Melos Qt.
(M) ** DG (IMS) Dig. 445 551-2 [id.]. Emerson Qt – BORODIN: *String quartet No. 2;* TCHAIKOVSKY: *Quartet No. 1.* *(*)

The Delmé Quartet on a superbly recorded Carlton IMP disc give a winningly spontaneous-sounding performance, marked by unusually sweet matching of timbre between the players, which brings out the total joyfulness of Dvořák's American inspiration.

A thoroughly satisfying account of the *American quartet* from the Gabrielis, notable for its warmth, vitality and polish, and a touching account of the slow movement. As part of a Classics for Pleasure Silver Double it makes an outstanding reissue, given first-class 1973 sound, smoothly yet vividly transferred to CD.

On Classic fM an excellent and generous coupling of three of the most popular Slavonic quartets in the repertory, with the Chilingirian Quartet giving powerful, incisive performances, though they are recorded a bit too forward. Levon Chilingirian proves an exceptionally alert leader whose violin-tone is given a slight edge by the full, immediate recording. In the Dvořák the big contrasts of mood and atmosphere are brought out, with the slow movement yearningly beautiful and the fast movements given an infectious spring. Good value at the price and, though not superior, say, to the Delmé version on Carlton, it can hold its own among the best.

Although we have some reservations about Norbert Brainin's vibrato, which at times sounds self-conscious (especially in the slow movement), admirers of the Amadeus will certainly want their 1977 coupling of Dvořák and Smetana, recorded in Finland. This is a strongly conceived performance, full of ardour. The Scherzo and exhilarating finale show their brilliance of ensemble at its most appealing and infectious. The sound is vivid, full and immediate.

On Harmonia Mundi's bargain-basement Solo label come a strong, polished account from the Melos Quartet. The work is very well played and the finale sparkles. But, though not unfeeling, one needs the players to relax more and more readily share the music's delights with us. The recording is truthful, very present.

As a quartet, the Emersons are technically in a class of their own. They can produce the sonority of a full orchestra and their virtuosity in terms of ensemble and attack is matchless. They are undoubtedly involved in the music, particularly in the lyrical secondary material of the first movement and in the *Lento*. The Scherzo and finale, too, are brilliantly played, and few could fail to respond to the genuine excitement of the bravura articulation in the last movement. This is much the most enjoyable performance among the three on this well-filled CD (78 minutes). But the vivid and present DG recording is not entirely flattering and gives a feeling of over-projection, even of slickness at times.

String quartets Nos. 12 in F (American); 14 in E flat, Op. 105.
(BB) ** Naxos 8.550251 [id.]. Moyzes Qt.

The members of the Moyzes Quartet are drawn from the ranks of the Slovak Philharmonic Orchestra and they are obviously at home in this repertoire. The slow movement of the *American quartet* is played with much warmth, and their account of Op. 105 has comparable intensity. The bright recording projects them forwardly and, although the acoustic is quite sympathetic, the effect could ideally be more intimate. However, this coupling remains very good value.

String quartet No. 13 in A, Op. 106.
(M) ** Teldec/Warner 4509 95503-2 (2) [id.]. Alban Berg Qt – BRAHMS: *String quartets Nos. 1–3.* **

An expert performance, full of sophistication in the matter of blending of timbre and control of tempo and offering immaculate ensemble. There is much to admire, although there is a degree of surface gloss which robs the music-making of its full intimacy. Even so, the panache of the finale is easy to admire. It obviously has moments of conveyed feeling but, for all its brilliance, does not sound completely spontaneous. The sound is smoother than in the Brahms couplings.

Piano duet

Slavonic dances Nos. 1–16, Op. 46/1–8; Op. 72/1–8.
(M) *** DG 449 550-2. Alfons and Aloys Kontarsky.
(BB) *** Naxos Dig. 8.553138 [id.]. Silke-Thora Matthies, Christian Köhn.

This excellently transferred DG reissue from 1980 takes its place at the top of the list of recommendations for Dvořák's *Slavonic dances* in their original version for piano, four hands, providing some of the most delectable piano duets ever written. Characteristically the excellent Kontarsky brothers offer crisp, clean performances and, more than usually, allow themselves the necessary rubato, conveying affection and joy along with their freshness (sample Nos. 4 and 5 of Op. 46, delightfully contrasted, or for sheer élan the *Furiant* of No. 8). The recording was made in the Berlin Jesus-Christus-Kirche, where the engineers put their microphones in exactly the right place: there is just the right degree of resonance, yet no feeling that they are too near.

Dvořák, like Schubert, had the gift of writing piano-duet music which is at once a joy to performers and to listeners alike. The brilliant piano duo of Matthies and Köhn are most persuasive performers, radiating their own enjoyment, bringing out inner parts, giving transparency to even the thickest textures, subtly shading their tone and, above all, consistently springing rhythms infectiously, with an idiomatic feeling for Czech dance music. The forwardly balanced recording brings out the brightness of the piano while letting warmth of tone come forward in such gentler dances as No. 3 in D. An excellent bargain.

VOCAL AND CHORAL MUSIC

(i) *Requiem, Op. 89;* (ii) *6 Biblical songs from Op. 99.*

❀ (B) *** DG Double 453 073-2 (2) [id.]. (i) Maria Stader, Sieglinde Wagner, Ernst Haefliger, Kim Borg, Czech PO & Ch., Karel Ančerl; (ii) Dietrich Fischer-Dieskau, Joerg Demus.

This superb DG set from 1959 brings an inspired performance of a work that can sound relatively conventional but which here emerges with fiery intensity, helped by a recording made in an appropriately spacious acoustic that gives an illusion of an electrifying live performance, without flaw. The passionate singing of the chorus (in the *Hostias* and *Sanctus*, for instance) is unforgettable, and the soloists not only make fine individual contributions but blend together superbly in ensembles. Ančerl controls his forces with expert precision and the Czech chorus responds to the manner born. It was a good idea to choose good German soloists rather than Czech ones, who might have sounded unrefined in comparison with chorus and orchestra. Haefliger and Borg are particularly fine. The first entry of the chorus moaning away to a gentle '*Requiem aeternam*' suggests that the balance is going to favour the orchestra, but this is all part of the deliberate control of acoustic in which the balance between soloists, chorus and orchestra is particularly well handled in DG's best analogue manner. As if that were not enough, DG have added Fischer-Dieskau's 1960 recordings of six excerpts from Op. 99. He is at his superb best in these lovely songs. Brimming over with melody and never in the least sanctimonious, they deserve to be more generally known. (The numbers included are: *Rings an den Herrn*; *Gott, erhöre meine inniges Flahen*; *Gott ist mein Hirte*; *An den Wassern zu Babylon*; *Wende dich zu mir*; and *Singet ein neues Lied*.) Joerg Demus accompanies sensitively, and the recording balance is most convincing.

(i) *Requiem, Op. 89;* (ii) *Mass in D, Op. 86.*

(B) *** Decca Double 448 089-2 (2) [id.]. (i) Lorengar, Komlóssy, Isofalvy, Krause, Amb. S., LSO, Kertész; (ii) Ritchie, Giles, Byers, Morton, Christ Church Cathedral Ch., Oxford, Cleobury (organ), Preston.

Kertész's fine (1968) account of Dvořák's *Requiem* acted as a distinguished pendant to his pioneering set of the symphonies, and it has comparable freshness. Kertész conducts with a total commitment to the score and secures from singers and orchestra an alert and sensitive response. The recording, which has the advantage of the Kingsway Hall ambience, has a lifelike balance and the CD remastering has been entirely beneficial. For this Double Decca reissue the work has been sensibly recoupled with Simon Preston's beautifully shaped Christ Church account of the *Mass in D*, recorded six years later. Again the CD remastering shows how good was the original (Argo) recording, and it is also impeccably balanced.

(i) *Stabat Mater, Op. 58;* (ii) *Legends Nos. 1–10, Op. 59.*

(B) *** DG Double 453 025-2 (2) [id.]. (i) Mathis, Reynolds, Ochman, Shirley-Quirk, Bav. R. Ch. & SO; (ii) ECO; Kubelik.

Dvořák's devout Catholicism led him to treat this tragic religious theme with an open innocence that avoids sentimentality. Kubelik is consistently responsive and this is a work which benefits from his imaginative approach. The recording, made in the Munich Herkules-Saal, is of very good quality. This set is well worth considering at this reasonable price, especially as the ten *Legends* are played so beautifully by the ECO. This music ought to be better known, with its colourful scoring and folksy inspiration of a high order. One is often reminded of the *Slavonic dances*; although the prevailing mood is more amiable, there is no lack of sparkle. Again very good recording.

OPERA

The Jacobin: highlights.

(M) **(*) Sup. 11 2250-2 [id.] (from complete recording, with Zítek, Sounová, Přibyl, Machotková, Blachut, Prusa, Tuček, Berman, Katilena Children's Ch., Kuhn Ch., Brno State PO, Pinkas).

The highlights disc is at medium price and, with 62 minutes' playing time, makes a good sampler. However, there is no libretto included, not even a synopsis, which is unhelpful in an unfamiliar work of this kind.

Rusalka: highlights.

(M) **(*) Sup. Dig. 11 2252-2 [id.] (from complete recording, with Beňačková-Cápová, Novák, Soukupová, Ochman, Drobková, Prague Ch. & Czech PO, Neumann).

This is a first-class selection, including, of course, the famous *Invocation to the moon* and offering an hour of music. But the current mid-priced reissue has neither libretto nor synopsis, merely a list of the excerpts.

Eckhard, Johann Gottfried (1735–1809)

Keyboard sonatas, Op. 1/1–3; Op. 2/1–2; in G; Menuet d'Exaudet with variations.
(BB) *** Koch Discovery Dig. DICD 920392 [id.]. Brigitte Haudebourg (fortepiano).

Born in Augsburg, Johann Gottfried Eckhard (sometimes spelt Eckhardt) was a professional copper-engraver who studied music in his spare time. He spent most of his life in Paris, where he not only composed keyboard sonatas but also painted miniatures. He soon acquired a considerable reputation as a performer, as well as a composer whose work was much influenced by C. P. E. Bach. His published sonatas included on this disc are forward-looking and embody expressive and dynamic markings characteristic of the piano. He foresaw the vogue that the piano would enjoy several years before its acceptance in Paris. His music is often inventive and, although of no great originality, is persuasively played by Brigitte Haudebourg, and decently recorded. Not an issue that will set the pulse racing but nevertheless quite rewarding in its way.

Egk, Werner (1901–83)

The Temptation of St Anthony (cantata).
(M) *** DG (IMS) 449 097-2. Dame Janet Baker, Koeckert Qt, Bav. RSO (strings), composer – ORFF: *Catulli Carmina.* ***

Egk has never made much headway in this country. His music is not unattractive, in the sense that it falls easily on the ear, though its thematic substance is often unmemorable and the composer does not have a great deal of personality. His *Temptation of St Anthony*, however, shows him at his best: it is in effect a song-cycle and Dame Janet Baker was in particularly good voice at this period of her career (the mid-1960s) and sings with great beauty. The recording, too, is good, and this can be recommended as a good sampler for those who want to investigate Egk's music for themselves.

Elgar, Edward (1857–1934)

(i) *Adieu; Beau Brummel: Minuet;* (ii) *3 Bavarian dances, Op. 27; Caractacus, Op. 35: Woodland interlude. Chanson de matin; Chanson de nuit, Op. 15/1–2; Contrasts, Op. 10/3; Dream children, Op. 43; Falstaff, Op. 68: 2 Interludes. Salut d'amour; Sérénade lyrique;* (ii; iii) *Soliloquy for oboe* (orch. Gordon Jacob); (i) *Sospiri, Op. 70; The Spanish Lady: Burlesco. The Starlight Express: Waltz. Sursum corda, Op. 11.*
(M) *** Chandos CHAN 6544 [id.]. Bournemouth Sinf., (i) George Hurst; (ii) Norman Del Mar; (iii) with Goossens.

The real treasure in this splendid collection of Elgar miniatures is the *Soliloquy* which Elgar wrote right at the end of his life for Leon Goossens. Here the dedicatee plays it with his long-recognizable tone-colour and feeling for phrase in an orchestration by Gordon Jacob. Most of the other pieces in Norman Del Mar's programme are well known but they come up with new warmth and commitment here, and the 1976 recording, made in the Guildhall, Southampton, has an appealing ambient warmth and naturalness. For the CD reissue Chandos have generously added some delightful Elgar rarities recorded by George Hurst a year earlier in Christchurch Priory. Again the recording has plenty of fullness, but the CD transfer brings more thinness to the violins than in the Del Mar recording. The disc has an overall playing time of nearly 76 minutes.

Acoustic recordings (1914–25): Abridged or excerpts: *Bavarian dances; Carillon; Carissima; Chanson de nuit; Cockaigne overture;* (i) *Cello concerto;* (ii) *Violin concerto. Enigma variations; In the South; King Olaf; Light of life; Polonia; Pomp and circumstance marches Nos. 1 & 4; Salut d'amour; The Sanguine fan; Symphony No. 2* (complete). (iii) *Fringes of the fleet;* (iv) *Sea pictures;* (iii; v) *Starlight express; Fantasia and Fugue* (Bach, arr. Elgar); *Overture* (Handel, arr. Elgar).
(M) (**(*)) Pearl GEMM mono CDS 9951/5 (5). (i) Beatrice Harrison; (ii) Marie Hall; (iii) Charles Mott; (iv) Leila Megane; (v) Agnes Nicholls; O or Royal Albert Hall O, cond. composer.

This box of five Pearl CDs gathers together all of Elgar's recordings made in the days of the acoustic gramophone. With players in limited numbers gathered round an acoustic horn, the sounds are limited but have been transferred here with astonishing fidelity. Orchestrations had to be modified to bring out the bass line, and all but the *Symphony No. 2*, among the major works, had to be cut for the medium, often drastically, as when the *Violin concerto* is reduced from 50 to 15 minutes. Speeds here are generally brisker than in his later, electrical recordings, and performances are often flawed. Marie Hall adopts an exaggeratedly portamento style in the *Violin concerto*, and Beatrice Harrison is less assured here than in her electrical recording of the full *Cello concerto*, but Leila Megane proves a formidable contralto soloist in *Sea pictures*. The sense of witnessing historic events is irresistible, with Elgar consistently hypnotic as a conductor.

'A portrait of Elgar': 3 Bavarian dances, Op. 27; Carissima; Chanson de matin; Chanson de nuit, Op. 15/1–2; Cockaigne overture, Op. 40; Dream children, Op. 43; Enigma variations, Op. 36; Froissart overture, Op. 19; Gavotte (Contrasts), Op. 10/3; Introduction and allegro for strings, Op. 47; May song; Mazurka, Op. 10/1; Nursery suite; Pomp and circumstance marches Nos. 1–5, Op. 39; Rosemary ('That's for remembrance'); Sérénade lyrique; Serenade for strings, Op. 20; Salut d'amour, Op. 12; Spanish Lady (suite); The Wand of youth suite No. 2, Op. 1b.
(B) **(*) Nimbus Dig. NI 1769 (4) [id.]. E. SO or E. String O, William Boughton.

This four-disc set is a counterpart to Nimbus's '*The spirit of England*' (see Concerts, below) and is similarly inexpensive. But there is a small drawback: it is made up of four separate Elgar collections, and Disc 3 (which at 46 minutes is not particularly generous anyway) duplicates the *Chanson de matin* and *Chanson de nuit*, already included on Disc 2 – perverse planning, especially when the first *Wand of Youth suite* is omitted. However, the latter collection (including the *Nursery suite* plus the *Dream children* and most of the miniatures) is particularly attractive, for William Boughton's performances are graceful and sympathetic and have plenty of character. The *Bavarian dances* are winningly relaxed and *The Spanish Lady suite* is well characterized. The *Introduction and allegro* has a ripely overwhelming climax, but the fugal argument is not lost. The *Enigma variations* have many pleasingly delicate touches of colour with the brass and organ making a fine effect in the finale. There is an easy swagger about the *Pomp and circumstance marches*, with the happy lyricism of the trios – not just *Land of hope and glory* – conveying Elgarian joy. The warmly reverberant acoustic of the Great Hall of Birmingham University gives the performances of these larger-scale works a spacious scale that is entirely apt. What is more questionable is the scale conveyed by the recording (in the same acoustic) for the other lighter and more intimate pieces. The manner is sparkling, the playing refined and well detailed, with rhythms nicely sprung, but the large scale implied tends to inflate the music, particularly in the *Wand of youth* excerpts. Nevertheless the relaxed geniality of each performance is likely to quieten most doubts of those attracted to the content of this inexpensive compilation.

'The lighter Elgar': (i) *Beau Brummel: Minuet;* (ii) *Carissima;* (i) *Chanson de matin, Op. 15/2;* (ii) *3 Characteristic pieces, Op. 10: Mazurka; Sérénade mauresque; Contrasts: The Gavottes AD 1700 & 1900;* (i) *Dream children, Op. 43/1–2;* (ii) *May song; Mina; Minuet, Op. 21; Rosemary (That's for remembrance);* (ii; iii) *Romance for bassoon and orchestra, Op. 62;* (i) *Salut d'amour, Op. 12;* (ii) *Sevillana, Op. 7; Sérénade lyrique;* (i; iv) *The Starlight Express, Op. 78:* Organ grinder's songs: *My old tunes; To the children.* (i) *The Wand of Youth suite No. 1:* excerpt: *Sun dance.*
❀ (M) *** EMI CDM5 65593-2. (i) RPO, Lawrance Collingwood; (ii) N. Sinfonia, Marriner; with (iii) Michael Chapman; (iv) Frederick Harvey.

The best of Elgar's lighter music has a gentle delicacy of texture and, as often as not, quite a touch of melancholy, which is irresistible to nearly all Elgarians. Its fragile nostalgia has never been better caught than on this beautifully recorded CD which combines almost all the contents of two LPs. The first (originally called '*The miniature Elgar*') was inspired by the famous Ken Russell BBC TV film of Elgar's life, and the orchestral playing under Lawrance Collingwood is especially sympathetic. Frederick Harvey joins the orchestra for two organ grinder's songs from the incidental music for *The Starlight Express*, and they have seldom been sung more winningly on record. They are splendidly alive and with as much interest in the orchestra as in the stirringly melodic vocal line. It is these items one remembers most, but the second collection under Sir Neville Marriner is hardly less successful. Not everything here is on the very highest level of invention, but all the music is pleasing and a good deal of it is delightful in its tender moods and restrained scoring, favouring flute, bassoon and the clarinet in middle or lower register. A boisterous piece like *Sevillana* may be rather conventional but it has Elgar's characteristic exuberance, which represents the other side of the coin. Very much worth having is the rhapsodic *Romance for bassoon and orchestra* with Michael Chapman the elegant soloist, but the whole programme here offers quiet enjoyment and is just the thing for the late evening. The Northern Sinfonia play with style and affection. Throughout, EMI have provided that warm, glowing sound that is their special province in recording Elgar's music, and it is remarkable that Collingwood's recordings, made at Abbey Road in 1964, and the Marriner items, using the Old Banqueting Hall, Jesmond Dene, Newcastle-upon-Tyne, in 1970, match up so well when they are juxtaposed. The CD transfers bring out all the bloom one remembers on the analogue LPs. Not to be missed.

Carissima; Chanson de matin; Chanson de nuit, Op. 15/1–2; Contrasts (Gavotte), Op. 10/3; Dream children, Op. 43; May song; Mazurka, Op. 10/1; Nursery suite; Rosemary (That's for remembrance); Salut d'amour, Op. 12; Sérénade lyrique.
(M) *** Nimbus Dig. NI 7029 [id.]. ESO, William Boughton.

The *Nursery suite* usually comes with the *Wand of Youth suites*, but those favouring the delicate *Dream children* plus a group of Elgar's orchestral miniatures will find that William Boughton's performances are graceful and sympathetic and have plenty of character. The recording too (made in Birmingham's Symphony Hall) is pleasingly full and spacious without being over-resonant, as are some offerings from this label.

Cockaigne overture, Op.40.
(BB) ** ASV Dig. CDQS 6162 [(M) id.]. Philh. O, Owain Arwel Hughes – VAUGHAN WILLIAMS: *London Symphony.* **

The playing in Owain Arwel Hughes's version of *Cockaigne* is crisper and more alert than in the coupled *London Symphony* of Vaughan Williams; but here, too, speeds are very broad indeed, at times impairing the flow, though building to a fine, ripe climax. The recording is warm and atmospheric, but the timpani is imprecisely focused.

(i) *Cockaigne overture;* (ii) *Cello concerto in E min.;* (iii) *Violin concerto;* (i) *Enigma variations, Op. 36;* (iv) *Pomp and circumstance marches Nos. 1–5, Op. 39.*
(B) *** Sony Take 2 SB2K 63247 (2) [S2K 63247]. (i) Phd. O, Ormandy; (ii) Jacqueline du Pré, Phd. O, Barenboim; (iii) Zukerman, LPO, Barenboim; (iv) Philh. O, Andrew Davis.

This stimulating juxtaposition of American and English performances of Elgar's music is distinctly rewarding and worth exploring. Jacqueline du Pré's second recording of the Elgar *Cello concerto* was taken from live performances in Philadelphia in November 1970, and this is a superb picture of an artist in full flight. Here you have the romantic view of Elgar at its most compelling. The mastery of du Pré lies not just in her total commitment from phrase to phrase but in the feeling for the whole, setting her sights on the moment in the *Epilogue* where the slow-movement theme returns, the work's inner sanctuary of repose. Zukerman's ardent account of the *Violin concerto*, recorded six years later – also with Barenboim – has comparable intensity and is discussed under its separate issue below. Andrew Davis brings plenty of imaginative flair to the five *Pomp and circumstance marches* and is sumptuously recorded (digitally in 1981, at Abbey Road). Ormandy's view of *Enigma* is characteristically forthright, lacking some Elgarian nuance – although *Nimrod* is finely shaped – but, with the help of glorious Philadelphia string-playing, urgently convincing just the same. The recording similarly is not subtle, but its ample spaciousness helps the overall sense of conviction. Ormandy paints his picture of Edwardian London with even broader strokes of the brush in vivid primary colours. The Philadelphia players rise to his exultant direction: the brass playing has superb gusto and the strings sing out their glorious romantic theme with thrilling commitment. Again the expansively resonant sound adds to the sense of spectacle.

(i) *Cockaigne overture, Op. 40;* (ii) *Cello concerto, Op. 85;* (i) *Enigma variations, Op. 36.*
(M) **(*) Ph. Analogue/Dig. 442 652-2. (i) LSO, Sir Colin Davis; (ii) Heinrich Schiff, Dresden State O, Sir Neville Marriner.

Davis's reading of the *Enigma variations* is in the main a traditional one, with each variation carefully shaped, and really first-rate playing from the LSO, contributing both intensity and warmth. In *Cockaigne*, however, Sir Colin is more wilful in his choice of tempi, and this is less evocative than it can be. The mid-1960s recording is full and naturally balanced but lacks something in brilliance. Schiff then gives a warm and thoughtful account of the *Cello concerto*, at his most successful in the lovely slow movement and the epilogue, both played with soft, sweet tone. Other readings convey more of the structural cohesion, but this lyrical, somewhat improvisational view has its place and is easy to enjoy. The digital sound is superb to match the orchestral richness, and the elegiac atmosphere at the opening of the concerto is especially persuasive.

Cockaigne overture, Op. 40; Elegy for strings, Op. 58; Enigma variations, Op. 36; Introduction and allegro for strings, Op. 47; Pomp and circumstance march No. 1; Sospiri, Op. 70.
(M) **(*) Nimbus Dig. NI 7075 [id.]. ESO, William Boughton.

Warmly affectionate performances, beautifully played and given characteristically spacious Nimbus sound, recorded in the Great Hall of Birmingham University. The resonance prevents absolute sharpness of detail, but the effect is natural. The *Introduction and allegro* has a ripely overwhelming climax, yet the fugal argument is not lost. The *Enigma variations* have many pleasingly delicate touches of colour (*Dorabella* is delightfully fey) and *Nimrod* expands spaciously from its genuine pianissimo opening to achieve a climax of dignity rather than great ardour (surely an authentic portrayal of its dedicatee, A. E. Jaeger).

There are more strongly characterized versions of the work, but this performance has undoubted spontaneity and is easy to enjoy. The brass and organ make a fine effect in the finale, which brings a noble summing up. With 75 minutes of music, this is certainly excellent value.

(i) *Cockaigne overture, Op. 40;* (ii) *Froissart overture, Op. 19; Pomp and circumstance marches, Op. 39, Nos* (i) *1 in D;* (ii) *2 in A min.; 3 in C min.;* (i) *4 in G;* (ii) *5 in C.*
(M) *** EMI CDM5 66323-2. (i) Philh. O; (ii) New Philh. O; Barbirolli.

It is good to have *Cockaigne*, Barbirolli's ripe yet wonderfully vital portrait of Edwardian London, back in the catalogue – one of the finest of all his Elgar records. *Froissart* is very compelling too (though the CD transfer is slightly less flattering here), and Barbirolli makes a fine suite of the five *Pomp and circumstance marches*. The lesser-known Nos. 2 and 5 are particularly gripping, with plenty of contrast in No. 4 to offset the swagger elsewhere. Here the sound is as expansive as you could wish.

Cello concerto in E min., Op. 85.
(M) *** Sony Dig. SMK 53333 [id.]. Yo-Yo Ma, LSO, Previn – WALTON: *Cello concerto.* ***
(BB) *** CfP Silver Double CD-CFPSD 4775 (2) [(B) id.]. Robert Cohen, LPO, Del Mar – BEETHOVEN: *Triple concerto;* DVORAK: *Cello concerto;* TCHAIKOVSKY: *Variations on a rococo theme.* ***
(M) (***) Revelation mono RV 10100 [id.]. Rostropovich, Moscow PO, Rakhlin – BRITTEN: *Cello symphony.* (***)
(M) **(*) Virgin Ultraviolet Dig. CUV5 61125-2. Steven Isserlis, LSO, Hickox – BLOCH: *Schelomo.* ***
(M) **(*) Carlton Dig. 30366 0011-2 [id.]. Tortelier, RPO, Groves – DVORAK: *Rondo;* TCHAIKOVSKY: *Rococo variations.* ***
(M) (**(*)) EMI mono CDH7 63498-2 [id.]. Casals, BBC SO, Boult – DVORAK: *Concerto* (***) (with BRUCH: *Kol Nidrei* (***)).
(BB) ** Naxos Dig. 8.550503 [id.]. Maria Kliegel, RPO, Halász – DVORAK: *Cello concerto.* **

(i) *Cello concerto in E min., Op. 85. Falstaff, Op. 68.*
(M) *(*) Chan. Dig./Analogue CHAN 6607 [id.]. (i) Ralph Kirshbaum; SNO, Gibson.

In its rapt concentration Yo-Yo Ma's recording with Previn is second to none. The first movement is lighter, a shade more urgent than the Du Pré/Barbirolli version, and in the Scherzo he finds more fun, just as he finds extra sparkle in the main theme of the finale. The key movement with Ma, as it is with du Pré, is the *Adagio*, echoed later in the raptness of the slow epilogue; there, his range of dynamic is just as daringly wide, with a thread of pianissimo at the innermost moment, poised in its intensity. Warm, fully detailed recording, finely balanced, with understanding conducting from Previn. At mid-price a splendid bargain.

Robert Cohen's performance is strong and intense, with steady tempi, the colouring more positive and less autumnal than usual, relating the work to the *Second Symphony*. Yet there is no lack of inner feeling. The ethereal half-tones at the close of the first movement are matched by the gently elegiac poignancy of the *Adagio*. Del Mar's accompaniment is wholly sympathetic, underlining the soloist's approach and his songful line. The 1978 Walthamstow recording is wide-ranging and brilliant but shows Cohen's tone as bright and well focused rather than especially resonant in the bass. Those for whom the Silver Double couplings are attractive will find this both individual and satisfying.

It is sad that Rostropovich has forsaken the Elgar concerto on the grounds that, after Jacqueline du Pré, nothing more remains to be said. Although he made records with both Sargent and Sir Adrian, he never recorded Elgar's masterpiece with either of them. (There is, however, a Russian Disc version at full price of a 1964 concert performance with Rozhdestvensky, coupled with the Respighi *Adagio con variazioni* and the Milhaud *First Concerto*.) The mid-priced Revelation disc offers an earlier account with the Moscow Philharmonic under Nathan Rakhlin, made 40 years ago, an account of considerable stature. This performance of 1958 demonstrates that Rostropovich's inspirational style, regularly sounding like a concentrated improvisation, exactly suits a work which, rejecting sonata-form until the last movement in a highly original way, is framed in recitative-like passages of double-stopping for the soloist. Both in those passages and in the main arguments of each movement Rostropovich uses the widest dynamic range, conveying a raptly reflective intensity to match even du Pré. As a whole the performance is larger than life and the slow movement is particularly impressive, full of poignancy. Rakhlin proves a most sensitive Elgarian and has great feeling for the reticence and longing that this music conveys. Compared with the later, broadcast recording, this is consistently broader in its speeds, if not as broad as du Pré. The quality of the recording calls for some tolerance but is worth it. The cello is far too forwardly balanced, making the orchestra sound dim by comparison, but the warmth of the reading is powerfully conveyed. It is in mono, though nowhere on the label or sleeve do Revelation say so.

The most distinctive point about Steven Isserlis's version on Virgin is his treatment of the slow movement, not so much elegiac as songful. Using a mere thread of tone, with vibrato unstressed, the simplicity of line and the unforced beauty are brought out. The very placing of the solo instrument goes with that, rather more distant than is usual, with the refinement of Elgar's orchestration beautifully caught by both conductor and engineers.

Tortelier's latest version of the Elgar, now reappearing on Carlton, was originally issued to celebrate the cellist's seventy-fifth birthday in March 1989. It may not be as firm and powerful as his earlier account with Boult: in the finale the septuagenarian shows signs of strain; but the performance has a spontaneity and a new tenderness which make it very compelling.

Casals recorded the Elgar *Cello concerto* in London in 1946, and the fervour of his playing caused some raised eyebrows. A powerful account, not least for Sir Adrian's contribution, even though its eloquence would have been even more telling were the emotion recollected in greater tranquillity. A landmark of the gramophone all the same, and the strongly characterized Max Bruch *Kol Nidrei* makes a fine encore.

Maria Kliegel is at her finest, deeply expressive and intense, in Elgar's miraculously compressed slow movement, and again in the comparably meditative epilogue for the finale. There she runs little risk of sounding self-indulgent within a limited span. The lyrical main theme of the first movement by contrast is pulled around in an unconvincing way, and though the virtuoso writing of the scherzo and the finale demonstrate the soloist's agility, her intonation is at times suspect. Flawed as it is – like the Dvořák with which it is coupled – it makes a fair bargain, well recorded in modern, digital sound.

Kirshbaum, a fine cellist, is disappointing here. At the very start the great double-stopped chords are anything but commanding, not helped by recessed recording, and the whole performance sounds tentative rather than expressing spontaneity. Originally issued as an analogue disc, this was displaced by a digital version, which is crisper in outline but which cannot cure the balance. The CD transfer improves detail further, but the effect is marginal: this is not a commanding version. Sir Alexander Gibson's highly spontaneous performance of *Falstaff* is another matter. It is one of the very finest of the recordings he made for Brian Couzens (who was subsequently to found Chandos) in the late 1970s. Gibson generates a strong forward momentum from the very opening bars, yet detail is consistently imaginative and the closing section is most touchingly played. The Scottish orchestra are in excellent form and play with character and commitment. The 1978 recording, made in Glasgow City Hall, has a natural perspective and has been most successfully remastered for CD. The sound has some lack of opulence but is truthful in all other respects. However, there is no internal access to *Falstaff*, which is a considerable drawback.

(i) *Cello concerto in E min., Op. 85;* (ii) *Violin concerto in B min., Op. 61.*

(M) *** Decca 440 319-2; *440 319-4*. (i) Lynn Harrell, Cleveland O, Maazel; (ii) Kyung Wha Chung, LPO, Solti.

(B) (***) Avid mono AMSC 587 [id.]. (i) Pablo Casals, BBC SO, Sir Adrian Boult; (ii) Albert Sammons, New Queen's Hall O, Sir Henry Wood.

This Decca reissue coupling Chung's heartfelt performance of the *Violin concerto* with Lynn Harrell's outstanding account of the *Cello concerto* on Decca offers a strong challenge. With eloquent support from Maazel and his fine orchestra (the woodwind play with appealing delicacy), this reading, deeply felt, balances a gentle nostalgia with extrovert brilliance. In the *Violin concerto* Chung's dreamily responsive playing in the central movement is ravishing in its beauty, not least in the ethereal writing above the stave, and so too are the lyrical pages of the outer movements. Solti responds with warmth to the expressive breadth of his soloist, and no other recording brings a wider range of dynamic or tone in the soloist's playing. Both recordings are from the late 1970s and are transferred to CD with impressive body and clarity.

Casals's recording of the Elgar *Cello concerto* with Sir Adrian Boult comes from 1946, and the Sammons set of the companion work for violin from 1929. In some ways Albert Sammons's recording has never been surpassed, though of course Menuhin's with the composer himself is also very special. Both sets are mandatory listening. The first Avid CD transfer of these recordings was singularly unsuccessful. Neither had much top, and both had a boosted, boomy bass with no transparency or detail. But as we go to press, an infinitely superior disc has arrived. The sound in both works is now excellent, the *Cello concerto* full and with the soloist firmly focused, the *Violin concerto* even more remarkable in its warmth and natural clarity, with the solo violin vividly and cleanly caught. The high level of concentration and atmospheric magnetism generated in the unsurpassed account of the finale comes over very directly to complete a remarkably compelling listening experience.

(i) Cello concerto, Op. 85; (ii) Coronation march, Op. 65; Enigma variations, Op. 36; Imperial march, Op. 32; Pomp and circumstance marches Nos. 1–5, Op. 39.

(BB) ** Carlton LSO Double Dig. 30368 01137 (2) [(B) id.]. (i) Felix Schmidt, LSO, Frühbeck de Burgos; (ii) LSO, Tuckwell – VAUGHAN WILLIAMS: *Fantasias.* **

Barry Tuckwell conducts a well-mannered reading of *Enigma*, beautifully played and recorded; but it is surprising that a musician who is so positive and individual as a soloist does not give a more sharply characterful performance in his role of conductor. The result is an *Enigma* which is a little faceless. Rhythms occasionally grow stodgy, and even *Nimrod* sounds rather too square; Tuckwell is at his best in the finale. The rest of his programme is generous, presenting not just the five *Pomp and circumstance marches* but two others just as grand. Though the broad opening of the 1911 *Coronation march* is relatively slack, the rest of the collection is splendidly taut and swaggering, with Tuckwell drawing superbly crisp ensemble from the brass. The sumptuousness of the recording adds greatly to the attractions of all the performances. Felix Schmidt, a young cellist with the widest expressive range, then follows on with a bold, emotionally intense reading of the *Cello concerto* which finds a most satisfying middle ground between the romantic freedom typified by the unique Jacqueline du Pré and the steadier way of a Paul Tortelier. Schmidt's hushed, deeply meditative account of the slow movement is among the most moving of all. With his rich, full tone opulently recorded, his account can be recommended beside the very finest versions, depending on preference as to coupling, in this instance an unconventional linking with two of Vaughan Williams's most popular works.

(i) Cello concerto in E min., Op. 85. Elegy, Op. 58. Enigma variations, Op. 36; Introduction and allegro, Op. 47.

❁ (M) *** EMI stereo/mono CDM7 63955-2 [id.]. (i) Navarra, Hallé O, Barbirolli.

This Hallé version of the *Enigma variations* was recorded in the Manchester Free Trade Hall in 1956 by the Mercury team, Wilma Cozart and Harold Lawrence. In its new CD transfer the sound is extraordinarily good, and the performance is revealed as Barbirolli's finest account ever on record. Barbirolli generates powerful fervour and an irresistible momentum: at the very end, the organ entry brings an unforgettable effect which engulfs the listener thrillingly. The *Introduction and allegro* is mono and, though not quite so impressively recorded, has comparable passion – the recapitulation of the big striding tune in the middle strings has superb thrust and warmth. The concert closes with a moving account of the *Elegy*, simple and affectionate. In between comes Navarra's strong and firm view of the *Cello concerto*. With his control of phrasing and wide range of tone-colour this 1957 performance culminates in a most moving account of the Epilogue.

(i) Cello concerto, Op. 85; (ii) Enigma variations, Op. 36.

(BB) *** Belart 450 021-2 [(M) id. import]. (i) Lynn Harrell, Cleveland O, Maazel; (ii) LAPO, Zubin Mehta.

This one of the finest discs in the whole Belart range of Polygram reissues, and one of the great Elgarian bargains. Lynn Harrell's outstanding (1980) account of the *Cello concerto* is here re-coupled with Mehta's hardly less inspired (1973) version of the *Enigma variations*. With eloquent support from Maazel and the fine Cleveland Orchestra (the woodwind play with appealing delicacy) Harrell's reading of the concerto, deeply felt, balances a gentle nostalgia with extrovert brilliance. The slow movement is tenderly spacious, the Scherzo bursts with exuberance and, after a passionate opening, the finale is memorable for the poignantly expressive reprise of the melody from the *Adagio* – one of Elgar's greatest inspirations.

Mehta, born and brought up in India, proves an equally strong and sensitive Elgarian, and the Los Angeles orchestra play Elgar's masterpiece splendidly. Instrumental detail is a constant delight; *Nimrod* is nobly built to its great climax, and the finale is full of pomp and circumstance and brings a tummy-wobbling sonic thrill with the entry of the organ at the end. With spectacular (Decca) recording quality, this can be given the very strongest recommendation.

(i) Cello concerto in E min., Op. 85; Enigma variations, Op. 36; Serenade for strings, Op. 20.

(M) *** DG (IMS) Dig. 445 511-2 [id.]. (i) Mischa Maisky; Philh. O, Sinopoli.

Maisky is highly persuasive in the *Cello concerto* and, with Sinopoli a willing partner, gives a warmly nostalgic performance, essentially valedictory in feeling. The slow movement is deeply felt, but not in an extrovert way, and the soloist's dedication is mirrored in the finale. The mood of the *Concerto* is carried over into the other works here. The lyrical variations of *Enigma* are expressively relaxed and *Nimrod* has a simple, direct nobility. Though Sinopoli avoids the usual speeding-up at the end of the finale, the thrust of that and the other vigorous climaxes is pressed home passionately. The *Serenade* is similarly expansive, and some may feel that the *Larghetto*, for all its sympathetic feeling, is too measured. The rich recording adds to the character of the readings, with the Philharmonia strings in particular playing superbly.

Violin concerto in B min., Op. 61.

(M) *** Decca 460 015-2 [id.]. Kyung Wha Chung, LPO, Solti – MENDELSSOHN: *Violin concerto in E min.* ***

(M) *** EMI CDM7 64725-2. Sir Yehudi Menuhin, New Philh. O, Boult – DELIUS: *Violin concerto.* **(*)

(BB) (***) Belart mono 461 353-2 [(M) id. import]. Alfredo Campoli, LPO, Boult – BLISS: *Introduction and allegro* etc. (***)

(M) ** DG Dig. 445 564-2 [id.]. Itzhak Perlman, Chicago SO, Barenboim – CHAUSSON: *Poème.* ***

(i) *Violin concerto in B min.; Cockaigne overture*, Op. 40.

(BB) *** Naxos Dig. 8.550489; *4.550489* [id.]. Dong-Suk Kang, Polish Nat. RSO (Katowice), Adrian Leaper.

(i) *Violin concerto; In the South (Alassio)* (concert overture).

(B) *** Sony SBK 62745; *SBT 62745* [id.]. (i) Pinchas Zukerman; LPO, Barenboim.

Nigel Kennedy's outstanding début recording (with Handley) of the Elgar *Violin concerto* has been withdrawn to make way for his full-priced version with Sir Simon Rattle. Many count the earlier performance, which is less wayward, finer even than the new one, and we hope that EMI will soon restore it to the catalogue at mid- or bargain price.

Chung's deeply felt performance is also available (see above) coupled with Lynn Harrell's similarly moving account of the *Cello concerto*, altogether a more apt coupling. However, those collectors for whom the Mendelssohn *Violin concerto* is more suitable will find Chung again on her finest form.

Menuhin's second stereo recording, in partnership with Sir Adrian Boult, is hardly less moving and inspirational than his first. Boult directs the performance with a passionate thrust in the outer movements and the warmest Elgarian understanding in the beautiful slow movement. There is an added maturity in Menuhin's contribution to compensate for any slight loss of poise or sweetness of tone, and the finale – the most difficult movement to keep together – is stronger and more confident than it was. The (1966) Kingsway Hall recording is characteristically warm and atmospheric, yet vividly focused by the CD transfer. A record indispensable for its documentary value as well as for its musical insights.

Zukerman, coming fresh to the Elgar *Violin concerto* in 1976, was inspired to give a reading which gloriously combined the virtuoso swagger of a Heifetz with the tender, heartfelt warmth of the young Menuhin, plus much individual responsiveness. Barenboim is a splendid partner, brilliant but never breathless in the main allegro and culminating in a deeply felt rendering of the long accompanied cadenza, freely expansive yet concentrated. With full but clearly defined recording, naturally balanced, at EMI's Abbey Road studios, this is a version which all Elgarians should seek out, especially at its new bargain price (with cassette equivalent). The coupling is an exciting and virile account of *In the South*, not quite as remarkable as the *Concerto* but a worthwhile bonus, even if the sound is marginally less full.

Dong-Suk Kang, immaculate in his intonation, plays the Elgar with fire and urgency. This is very different from most latterday performances, with markedly faster speeds; yet those speeds relate more closely than usual to the metronome markings in the score, and they never get in the way of Kang's ability to feel Elgarian rubato naturally, guided by the warmly understanding conducting of Adrian Leaper. Irrespective of price, this is a keenly competitive version, with excellent, wide-ranging digital sound, if with rather too forward a balance for the soloist.

Campoli gives a deeply felt but highly individual account of Elgar's great concerto. One can judge one's reaction to this performance by the control of vibrato on the opening phrase of his first entry. This is an essentially romantic approach, full of warmth, but there is no indulgence. Campoli's reading is based on an impeccable technique and he applies himself here with dedication to a work he obviously loves, and the result – with Boult securely and compellingly at the helm – is most rewarding. The 1954 Kingsway Hall recording has been impeccably transferred 'from the *ffrr* master tape' by Tony Hawkins at the Decca studios. With its equally valuable Bliss coupling, this is one of the most valuable mono reissues in Belart's 'Boult Historic Collection', although the Bliss couplings are not conducted by Boult, but by the composer.

Perlman's ease in tackling one of the most challenging violin concertos ever written brings an enjoyable performance, though he misses some of the darker, more intense elements in Elgar's inspiration. The solo instrument is forwardly balanced and the recording is bright and vivid rather than rich, lacking some of the amplitude one expects in the Elgar orchestral sound. The CD emphasizes the presence of the soloist but confirms the lack of expansiveness in the orchestra. The Chausson coupling seems a strange choice, although it is beautifully played.

Crown of India: suite, Op. 66; Enigma variations, Op. 36; Pomp and circumstance marches Nos. 1–5.

(M) **(*) Sony SBK 48265; *SBT 48265* [id.]. LPO, Barenboim.

Barenboim's view of *Enigma* is full of fantasy. Its most distinctive point is its concern for the miniature element, while the big variations have full weight, and the finale brings the fierceness of added adrenalin at a fast tempo. Tempi are surprisingly fast in the *Pomp and circumstance marches* (though Elgar's tended to be fast too) and not all Elgarians will approve of the updating of Elgarian majesty. The rumbustious approach to the *Crown of India suite* brings this patriotic celebration of the Raj vividly to life, though here the lack of opulence in the recording is a drawback. The marches, too, could do with a more expansive middle range, though *Enigma* is fully acceptable.

Elegy for strings, Op. 58; Sospiri, Op. 70; Serenade for strings in E min., Op. 58.
(M) *** EMI Dig. CDM5 66541-2. City of L. Sinfonia, Hickox – PARRY: *English suite; Lady Radnor's suite.* ***

Hickox draws beautifully refined string-playing from his City of London Sinfonia, notably in the three elegiac movements, the slow movement of the *Serenade* as well as the two separate pieces. An excellent coupling for the rare Parry items, excellently recorded.

Enigma variations (Variations on an original theme), Op. 36.
(M) *** Decca 452 303-2 [id.]. LSO, Monteux – HOLST: *Planets.* ***
(BB) *** DG Classikon 439 446-2; *439 446-4* [(M) id. import]. LSO, Jochum – HOLST: *Planets.* ***
(M) *** EMI CDM7 64748-2 [id.]. LSO, Boult – HOLST: *Planets.* ***
(B) **(*) BBC Radio Classics BBCRD 9104 [(M) id. import]. BBCSO, Sir Malcolm Sargent – HOLST: *Planets* **(*)
(M) (***) RCA mono GD 60287 [60287-2-RG]. NBC SO, Toscanini – MUSSORGSKY: *Pictures.* (**)

Monteux's *Enigma* remains among the freshest versions ever put on disc and the music is obviously deeply felt. The reading is famous for the real pianissimo which Monteux secures at the beginning of Nimrod, the playing hardly above a whisper, yet the tension electric. Slowly the great tune is built up in elegiac fashion, and the superb climax is more effective in consequence. Differences from traditional tempi elsewhere are marginal and add to one's enjoyment. The vintage Kingsway Hall stereo was outstanding in its day and it has never sounded better than in the present remastering. It is almost impossible to believe that this dates from 1958 and, with its stunning Holst coupling, this is one of the very finest (and most generous – 78 minutes) reissues in Decca's Classic Sound series.

The DG Classikon super-bargain CD couples Steinberg's exciting and brilliantly recorded complete set of the Holst *Planets* with Eugen Jochum's inspirational reading of *Enigma*. Like others – including Elgar himself – Jochum sets a very slow *Adagio* at the start of *Nimrod*, slower than the metronome marking in the score; unlike others, he maintains that measured tempo and, with the subtlest gradations, builds an even bigger, nobler climax than you find in *accelerando* readings. It is like a Bruckner slow movement in microcosm around which the other variations revolve, all of them delicately detailed, with a natural feeling for Elgarian rubato. The playing of the LSO matches the strength and refinement of the performance. The remastered recording, however, sounds brighter and more vivid than before but has lost none of its richness.

Boult's *Enigma* comes from the beginning of the 1970s, but the recording has lost some of its amplitude in its transfer to CD: the effect is fresh, but the violins sound thinner. The reading shows this conductor's long experience of the work, with each variation growing naturally and seamlessly out of the music that has gone before. Yet the livelier variations bring exciting orchestral bravura and there is an underlying intensity of feeling that carries the performance forward.

With the BBC engineers capturing the atmospheric thrill of a Prom performance in the Royal Albert Hall, Sir Malcolm Sargent's account of Elgar's *Enigma variations* gives a better idea of why he was such a Proms favourite, with the result more spontaneous than almost any of his studio recordings. The live performance may be a degree less polished, but its thrust and urgency are irresistible, building up superbly to the final variation, in which the BBC brass and the obbligato organ convey an extra frisson, even if the sound is pretty opaque and there are too many extraneous noises. But this is an inexpensive disc and, with an equally warm and expressive account of *The Planets* as the generous coupling, in some ways this makes a more persuasive case for the conductor than the mid-price EMI pairing of Sargent's studio recordings of the same works.

It is a pity that Toscanini's sharply focused but warmly expressive NBC reading of *Enigma* should come in a coupling with his severe account of the Mussorgsky. The Elgar, often expansive as well as affectionately phrased, as in the statement of the theme, gives a much more sympathetic view of the taskmaster conductor than most of his late recordings. Though traditionalist Elgarians may not always approve, it makes for an electrifying experience. The transfer is clean but not too aggressive.

Enigma variations; Coronation march, Op. 65; In the South overture, Op. 50.
(BB) *** Naxos Dig. 8.553564 [id.]. Bournemouth SO, Hurst.

George Hurst is a warmly understanding Elgarian, as his earlier recording of the *First Symphony* for Naxos powerfully demonstrates. Here with the Bournemouth orchestra he again inspires richly expressive playing, full of subtle rubato which consistently sounds natural and idiomatic, never self-conscious. Like Elgar himself, he tends to press ahead rather than linger, as in the great climactic variation in *Enigma*, *Nimrod*, as well as in the finale. Similarly in the overture, *In the South*, he reminds one that it was the Bournemouth orchestra under Silvestri which, many years ago, made a recording that brought a new assessment of what was till then an underrated work. In both *Enigma* and the overture the sound is sumptuous, with warm string-tone and ripe and weighty brass. The 'Nocturne' section of *In the South* is particularly beautiful, with outstanding solos from the viola and horn. The *Coronation march*, written for the crowning of King George V in 1911, may not be quite as memorable as Elgar's earlier ceremonial music for Queen Victoria and Edward VII, but here too Hurst inspires an opulent, red-blooded performance.

(i) *Enigma variations;* (ii) *Falstaff, Op.68.*
(M) *** EMI CDM5 66322-2. (i) Philh. O; (ii) Hallé O; Barbirolli.
(B) **(*) [EMI Red Line CDR5 72553]. LPO, Mackerras.

Ripe and expansive, Barbirolli's view of *Falstaff* is colourful and convincing; it has fine atmospheric feeling too, and the interludes are more magical here than in the Boult version. *Enigma*, too, was a work that Barbirolli, himself a cellist, made especially his own, with wonderfully expansive string-playing and much imaginative detail; the recording was made when he was at the very peak of his interpretative powers. The massed strings have lost some of their amplitude, but detail is clearer and the overall balance is convincing, with the Kingsway Hall ambience ensuring a pleasing bloom.

With recorded sound far more reverberant than is common in EMI recordings of Elgar, Mackerras's powerful readings of the composer's own favourite among his orchestral works, together with the most popular, are given a comfortable glow, while losing some inner clarity. The reading of *Falstaff* is superb, among the most electrically compelling put on disc; but *Enigma* is marred by mannered and self-conscious phrasing in the opening statement of the theme and the first variation, as well as in *Nimrod*. *Falstaff* is indexed very generously.

Enigma variations, Op. 36; Falstaff, Op. 68; Introduction and allegro for strings, Op. 47.
(M) *** Carlton Dig. 30366 00922 [(M) id.]. Nat. Youth O of Great Britain, Christopher Seaman.

This generous recoupling offers 80 minutes of music. As the recordings were made between 1989 and 1993 (*Enigma*), there must have been changes in personnel, yet the quality of the ensemble is remarkably consistent. Indeed these works have rarely been given such heartfelt performances as those by Christopher Seaman and the National Youth Orchestra. The weight of string-sound, combined with the fervour behind the playing, makes this an exceptionally satisfying reading of the *Introduction and allegro*, while *Falstaff* demonstrates even more strikingly how, working together intensively, these youngsters have learnt to keep a precise ensemble through the most complex variations of expressive rubato. The orchestra then goes on to give a wonderfully rich and ardent account of *Enigma*, yet one which opens with persuasively gentle lyricism and produces the most delicate portrayals of *Ysobel* and *Dorabella*, while the great cello variation expands gloriously and *Nimrod* explores the widest gradation of dynamic to reach its climax. The finale is engulfing in its excitement, and Seaman does not forget to add the 'tummy-wobbling' organ reinforcement to the closing pages. The recording is fully worthy of an account which has all the hallmarks of a live performance, even though it was recorded in Watford Town Hall under studio conditions.

Enigma variations; Introduction and allegro for strings, Op. 47; Pomp and circumstance march No. 1; Serenade for strings in E min., Op. 20.
(M) *(*) [RCA Basic 100 09026 68087-2; *68087-4*]. LPO, Slatkin.

Slatkin, a persuasive Elgarian in the *Symphonies* and in *The Kingdom*, is most disappointing in his reading of *Enigma*. The theme and *Nimrod* are both done sluggishly, and the whole performance fails to catch fire. The other works are much more successful, but this collection cannot be recommended with any confidence.

Enigma variations, Op. 36; Introduction and allegro for strings, Op. 47; Serenade for strings in E min., Op. 20.
(B) ** EMI Eminence Dig. CD-EMX 9503 [(M) id.]. LPO, Vernon Handley.

Vernon Handley's 1983 Eminence collection is given brilliantly wide-ranging digital sound. The readings are in the Boult tradition and very well played. But Handley's strong personal identification with the music brings a consciously moulded style that tends to rob the *Enigma variations* of its forward impulse. The

Elgarian ebb and flow of tension and dynamics are continually underlined in a highly expressive manner and, although he uncovers much imaginative detail, there is a consequent loss of spontaneity. The performances of the string works are more direct, although the *Larghetto* of the *Serenade* is also somewhat indulgent. Comparison with Boult (and, in *Enigma*, Mehta) is not in Handley's favour, although his performances are not without personal insights.

(i) *Enigma variations;* (ii) *Pomp and circumstance marches Nos. 1–5, Op. 39.*
(M) *** Chandos CHAN 6504 [id.]. SNO, Sir Alexander Gibson.
(M) *** DG 429 713-2. RPO, Norman Del Mar.
(M) *** EMI CDM7 64015-2. (i) LSO; (ii) LPO, Sir Adrian Boult.

Sir Alexander Gibson's reading of *Enigma* has stood the test of time and remains very satisfying, warm and spontaneous in feeling, with a memorable climax in *Nimrod*. The 1978 recording, made in Glasgow's City Hall, remains outstanding, with the organ sonorously filling out the bass in the finale, which has real splendour. The *Pomp and circumstance marches*, too, have fine *nobilmente* and swagger.

In the *Enigma variations* Del Mar comes closer than any other conductor to the responsive rubato style of Elgar himself, using fluctuations to point the emotional message of the work with wonderful power and spontaneity. The RPO plays superbly, both here and in the *Pomp and circumstance marches*, given Proms-style flair and urgency – although some might feel that the fast speeds miss some of the *nobilmente*. The reverberant sound here adds something of an aggressive edge to the music-making.

Boult's *Enigma* (also available coupled with Holst's *Planets* – see above) is self-recommending; it shows this conductor's long experience of the work, with each variation growing naturally and seamlessly out of the music that has gone before. Boult's approach to the *Pomp and circumstance marches* is brisk and direct, with an almost no-nonsense manner in places. There is not a hint of vulgarity and the freshness is most attractive, though it is a pity he omits the repeats in the Dvořák-like No. 2. The brightened sound brings a degree of abrasiveness to the brass.

(i) *Enigma variations;* (ii) *Pomp and circumstance marches Nos. 1–5;* (iii) *Serenade for strings.*
(B) *** Decca 433 629-2; *433 629-4* [(M) id. import]. (i) LAPO, Mehta; (ii), LSO, Bliss; (iii) ASMF, Marriner.

Mehta proves a strong and sensitive Elgarian, and this is a highly enjoyable performance. If there are no special revelations, the transition from the nobly conceived and spacious climax of *Nimrod* to a delightfully graceful *Dorabella* is particularly felicitous. The vintage Decca recording, with the organ entering spectacularly in the finale, is outstanding in its CD transfer, and this is one of Mehta's very finest records. Marriner's elegantly played yet highly sensitive account of the *String serenade* makes a fine bonus, and Sir Arthur Bliss's rumbustiously vigorous accounts of the *Pomp and circumstance marches* are worth anyone's money.

Enigma variations; Pomp and circumstance marches Nos. 1 & 4; Salut d'amour.
(BB) ** Naxos Dig. 8.550229 [id.]. CSR SO (Bratislava), Adrian Leaper – DELIUS: *Brigg Fair* etc. **

(i) *Enigma variations; Pomp and circumstance marches Nos. 1 & 4; Salut d'amour, Op. 12;* (ii) *Serenade for strings in E min., Op. 20.*
(BB) *** Naxos Dig. 8.554161 [id.]. (i) Czecho-Slovak RSO; (ii) Capella Istropolitana; Leaper.

Though Leaper's slow account of the 'Enigma' theme makes an unpromising start, his reading of the *Variations* is most beautiful, with ripely resonant string-playing and with warmly expressive rubato in *Nimrod* suggesting that the Slovak players had been won over to Elgar by Leaper's advocacy. The final variation is winningly done with weighty brass, and though the two marches sound a degree less idiomatic, the '*Land of Hope and Glory*' tune is played by them, as Elgar himself instructed, 'as though they had never heard it before'. *Salut d'amour* is not sentimentalized. Most refined of all is the Capella Istropolitana's account of the *Serenade*, with the slow movement specially beautiful, finely shaded. An excellent compilation of Elgar's most popular orchestral pieces, brilliantly recorded. There is an alternative, shorter programme coupled with Delius.

Falstaff, Op. 68; Imperial march, Op. 32; (i) *Sea pictures, Op. 37.*
(B) *** Sony SBK 63020; *SBT 63020* [id.]. LPO, Barenboim; (i) with Yvonne Minton.

Barenboim's habit of moulding the music of Elgar in flexible tempi, of underlining romantic expressiveness, has never been as convincing on record as here in *Falstaff*, where the big contrasts of texture, dynamic and mood are played for all they are worth. Rarely, even under the composer, has the story-telling element in Elgar's symphonic study been presented so captivatingly. The Gadshill episode with its ambush is so vivid one can see the picture in one's mind's eye. Yvonne Minton uses her rich tone sensitively in Elgar's orchestral song-cycle. There is perhaps less subtlety in her reading than in Janet Baker's, but she responds to this music richly and ardently. Barenboim is a persuasive Elgarian and this makes a most welcome bargain reissue, with his ripe account of the *Imperial march* thrown in for good measure. The CD transfers are excellent, with the warmly atmospheric sound in the *Sea pictures* particularly appealing.

Introduction and allegro for strings.

(M) ** RCA 09026 61424-2 [id.]. Boston SO, Munch – BARBER: *Adagio; Medea* excerpts ***; TCHAIKOVSKY: *Serenade.* **(*)

A striking performance from Munch, individual in that his tempo for the big *Sul G* unison tune must be the slowest on record. In this he shows a lack of idiomatic understanding, but otherwise the performance has plenty of vitality and the 1957 recording has filled out in the excellent remastering for CD.

Introduction and allegro for strings, Op. 47; Serenade for strings in E min., Op. 20.

(M) *** Virgin/EMI Dig. CUV5 61126-2 [id.]. LCO, Christopher Warren-Green – VAUGHAN WILLIAMS: *Tallis fantasia* etc. ***

(BB) (*(*)) Belart mono 461 362-2 [(M) id. import]. New SO of L,, Anthony Collins – DELIUS: *Brigg Fair* etc. (**); VAUGHAN WILLIAMS: *Fantasias.* (*(*))

(i; ii) *Introduction and allegro for strings, Op. 47;* (i) *Serenade for strings in E min., Op. 20;* (iii) *Elegy, Op. 58; Sospiri, Op. 70.*

(M) *(*) DG (IMS) Dig. 445 561-2. Orpheus CO (with BRITTEN: *Simple symphony* ***) – VAUGHAN WILLIAMS: *Greensleeves & Tallis fantasias.* *

Introduction and allegro for strings, Op. 47; Serenade for strings, Op. 20; Chanson de matin; Chanson de nuit, Op. 15/1–2; Elegy, Op. 58; Mot d'amour, Op. 13/1; Salut d'amour, Op. 12; The Spanish Lady, suite, Op. 49.

(BB) ** Arte Nova Dig. 74321 46494-2 [id.]. L. Festival O, Ross Pople.

Christopher Warren-Green, directing and leading his London Chamber Orchestra, directs the *Introduction and allegro* with tremendous ardour: the great striding theme on the middle strings is unforgettable, while the fugue has enormous bite and bravura. The whole work moves forward in a single sweep and the sense of a live performance, tingling with electricity and immediacy, is thrillingly tangible. It is very difficult to believe that the group contains only seventeen players (6-5-2-3-1), with the resonant but never clouding acoustics of All Saints' Church, Petersham, helping to create an engulfingly rich body of tone. Appropriately, the *Serenade* is a more relaxed reading yet has plenty of affectionate warmth, with the beauty of the *Larghetto* expressively rich but not overstated.

The London Festival Orchestra (with what seems to be a fairly small string section) give polished, committed accounts of Elgar's two major string works which have plenty of impetus (although the fugal section of the *Introduction and allegro* ideally needs sharper articulation). The lighter pieces are warmly done, but the suite from *The Spanish Lady* (five movements are included) needs a little more coaxing. The digital recording is vivid, but Barbirolli's full-priced EMI versions of the *Introduction and allegro* and *Serenade* remain unsurpassed and are well worth their premium price. The Carlton version of the *Serenade* is also very fine.

The recordings by the Orpheus Chamber Orchestra are disappointing. Though their keen articulation tells in the *Allegro* of Op. 47, the playing overall suggests a lack of experience in this repertoire; the sharply focused, vividly realistic recording of a string group that is plainly too few in number to be fully effective in this music also emphasizes the lack of ripeness in the readings. The Britten *Simple symphony* is by far the most attractive performance on this CD, fresh, sensitive and vital, missing only a degree of geniality in the *Playful pizzicato*.

Collins offers a taut and exciting performance of the *Introduction and allegro* in good style and, in suitable contrast, a mellow, poised reading of the softer and delightful *Serenade*. The recording is an early one; it is basically warm and resonant, but the upper strings are made to sound thin and pinched. Apparently when the original (LXT) LP was cut, the Decca engineers used a treble roll-off downwards from 10kc, which created a far better sound on which the reputation of the disc rested. Without it the effect is aurally tiring.

King Arthur: suite; (i) *The Starlight Express* (suite), *Op. 78.*

(M) **(*) Chandos CHAN 6582 [id.]. (i) Cynthia Glover, John Lawrenson; Bournemouth Sinf., George Hurst.

The *King Arthur suite* is full of surging, enjoyable ideas and makes an interesting novelty on record. *The Starlight Express suite* is taken from music Elgar wrote for a children's play, with a song or two included. Though the singers here are not ideal interpreters, the enthusiasm of Hurst and the Sinfonietta is conveyed well, particularly in the *King Arthur suite*. The recording is atmospheric if rather over-reverberant, but the added firmness of the CD and its refinement of detail make this an extra asset in providing a most agreeable ambience for Elgar's music.

Pomp and circumstance marches Nos. 1–5.
(BB) ** Belart 450 143-2 [(M) id. import]. LSO, Bliss – BLISS: *Things to come* etc. **

Sir Arthur Bliss was an admirable conductor for this music. He plays the marches with a rumbustious vigour, yet preserves a sense of style so that the *nobilmente* is never cheapened. The recording is bright but has less sonority than when it first appeared in 1959, and the upper range is thin.

Serenade for strings in E min., Op. 20.
(B) *** Carlton IMP Dig. 30367 02242 [(M) id.]. Serenata of London – GRIEG: *Holberg suite;* MOZART: *Eine kleine Nachtmusik* etc. ***

A particularly appealing account of Elgar's *Serenade*, with unforced tempi in the outer movements admirably catching its mood and atmosphere. The Serenata of London is led rather than conducted by Barry Wilde, and it is recorded with remarkable realism and naturalness.

Symphonies Nos. 1–2; Coronation march, Op. 65; Empire march (1924); Imperial march, Op. 32; Pomp and circumstance marches Nos. 1–5, Op. 39.
(BB) **(*) Virgin Classics Dig. Double VBD5 61430-2 (2) [CDVB 61430]. RPO, Sir Yehudi Menuhin.

Symphonies Nos. 1–2; In the South overture, Op. 50; Pomp and circumstance marches, Op. 39, Nos. 1 in D; 3 in C min.; 4 in G.
(B) **(*) Teldec/Warner Dig. 0630 18951-2 (2) [(M) id. import]. BBC SO, Andrew Davis.

Symphonies Nos. 1–2; Overtures: Cockaigne; In the South.
(B) *** Decca Double 443 856-2 (2) [id.]. LPO, Solti.

Symphonies Nos.1–2; Cockaigne overture; Pomp and circumstance marches Nos. 1–5.
(B) **(*) Ph. Duo Dig. 454 250-2 (2). RPO or LSO, André Previn.

Symphonies Nos. 1–2; Pomp and circumstance march No. 5.
(B) **(*) EMI forte CZS5 69761-2 (2) [CDFB 69761]. Philh. O, Haitink.

Solti's recordings of the two Elgar symphonies are now offered very economically together as a Double Decca. In the *First Symphony* Solti's thrusting manner will give the traditional Elgarian the occasional jolt, but his clearing away of the cobwebs stems from the composer's own 78-r.p.m. recording. The modifications of detailed markings implicit in that performance are reproduced here, not with a sense of calculation but with very much the same rich, committed qualities that mark out the Elgar performance. Again modelled closely on the composer's own surprisingly clipped and urgent reading, the *Second Symphony* benefits from virtuoso playing from the LPO and full, well-balanced sound. Fast tempi bring searing concentration, yet the *nobilmente* element is not missed and the account of the finale presents a true climax. The effect is magnificent. The CD transfers bring out the fullness satisfyingly as well as the brilliance of the excellent 1970s sound, and this applies also to the sharply dramatic account of *Cockaigne*. *In the South*, recorded in 1979, is less successful, if still exciting. But the result is nervy and tense, although the playing is excellent. Here Solti is not helped by Decca recording in which the brilliance is not quite matched by weight or body (an essential in Elgar).

Previn's Philips Duo comes into direct competition with Solti's similar Double Decca coupling, but both conductors provide interpretations which are stimulating as well as individual, Solti the more urgent, Previn the more spacious. Indeed these Previn performances find the conductor as idiomatic and understanding in Elgar as he is in Walton and Vaughan Williams. His view of the opening movement of the *First Symphony* is spacious, with moulding of phrase and lifting of rhythm beautifully judged, to bring natural flexibility within a strongly controlled structure, steadier than usual in basic tempo. Previn's espressivo style tends towards accelerando rather than tenuto, towards fractional anticipation rather than hesitation, which makes for alert allegros and a slow movement that is warm but not self-indulgent. The syncopations of the scherzo/march theme have an almost jazzy swagger, and the reading is crowned by a flowing account of the finale. There Previn confirms his ability to point Elgarian climaxes with the necessary heart-tug, above all in the lovely passage where the main theme is augmented in minims on high violins, here achingly beautiful, neither too reticent nor too heavy-handed.

The opening movement of the *Second* has a similar Elgarian ebb and flow; Previn's warmth is in no doubt, and his expressive flexibility is appealingly free; but one senses an absence of thrust and he does not display as tight a grip on the structure as Solti. Previn's *Larghetto* is deeply felt and is eloquently played by the LSO; however, although the rich *nobilmente* feeling is prevalent, he does not achieve the same degree of intense concentration which makes Solti's view so compelling. Nevertheless, many will warm to Previn's expansive approach, which is again apparent in the bold, purposeful finale. *Cockaigne* is in a similar mould, though attractively affectionate and spirited. The five *Pomp and circumstance marches* are not quite as flamboyant as some versions but are beautifully sprung. The recordings were made at Abbey Road and, if the Philips sound is more refined than the typical Elgar quality from EMI, it certainly does not lack opulence.

Menuhin, as one would expect of one who worked with the composer himself, is an urgently warm-hearted Elgarian, and his accounts of the two symphonies are well paced and sympathetic, though he stands by the letter of the score, rather than by what Elgar himself did on record. Despite delicate, refined textures in pianissimos, the playing is flawed – with some thinness on exposed violin-tone marring the *Second*, where there are also patches of rhythmic instability, notably in the finale which comes near to being perfunctory in places. In both, the sound is atmospheric and slightly distanced and diffused. The set is made the more competitive, not only by its new, low price, but also by the combination with a patriotic programme (originally released on a separate CD to coincide with the end of the Gulf War). Menuhin brings out the *nobilmente*, but there is certainly no lack of spirit. Tempi are at times extreme; thus the *First* and *Second Pomp and circumstance marches* are pressed on with such gusto that the orchestral ensemble is less crisp than it might be, while the *Coronation march* is very slow and grandiloquent, sustained by its rich sonority and expansive organ pedals. The recording of the marches, made at EMI's Abbey Road Studio, has a convincing concert-hall effect without too much resonance, and the brass are suitably resplendent.

With consistently slow tempi – far slower than Boult or Barbirolli used to adopt – Haitink's is a spacious reading of No. 1 which in its way takes a straight and thoughtful look at Elgar's score. The result is hardly idiomatic but, with superb playing from the Philharmonia under Haitink's concentrated direction, it is profound and moving, elegaically glowing with genuine Elgarian warmth. Splendid (1983) Walthamstow analogue sound to match. The *Second Symphony*, recorded a year later at Abbey Road, is more controversial, and here the CD transfer remains just a little disappointing. The ear notices more readily that the sound of the strings (middle and upper) is not as expansively opulent as expected. There is no doubt that Haitink produces some altogether wonderful playing from the Philharmonia Orchestra, and he also offers valuable and fresh insights, but the first movement in particular is very volatile, and throughout there are many wayward touches that fail to convince entirely on repeated hearing. Basically it is (like the *First*) a straight, measured view, far from idiomatically Elgarian but always illuminating and often refreshing. It is a reading which clearly relates Elgar, on the one hand, to Richard Strauss but also – and more significantly – to Bruckner. The way Haitink keeps his eye on the culminating moments of climax with his slow, steady speeds brings a very Brucknerian feeling to much of the music, and the control of transition passages has Brucknerian raptness. Elgarians will miss some of the usual spring in the 12/8 compound time of the first movement. But for many the performance will be a revelation in its strength and depth of feeling.

With sound of demonstration quality Andrew Davis conducts a broad, rather plain reading of the *First Symphony* which is yet highly idiomatic and is beautifully played. With one important reservation this is as fine as any of its bargain-price competitors. Sadly, the performance falls short at the very end, where the brassy coda fails to blaze as it should. However, Davis provides a strong and passionate account of the *Second*. It is an impetuous performance, but convincingly so, with delicacy of texture telling equally alongside the bold swagger of climaxes. The slow movement has great eloquence, and that strangely ominous warning passage in the Scherzo is conveyed powerfully. The finale has splendid impetus, and one can only lament that Davis did not insist on the organ reinforcement at the climax, which makes the Handley version unforgettable and contrasts with the valedictory feeling at the work's close. Handley remains first choice. But Davis offers an exuberant *In the South* as a bonus, catching the music's Straussian surge, yet tenderly depicting the melancholy moonlight of the central section. The recording is first class, with fine range and amplitude.

Symphony No. 1 in A flat, Op. 55.
❀ (B) *** Carlton IMP Dig. PCD 2019 [(M) id.]. Hallé O, James Judd.
(B) *** CfP CD-CFP 9018 [id.]. LPO, Vernon Handley.

(i) *Symphony No. 1 in A flat;* (ii) *Cockaigne overture.*
(M) **(*) EMI CDM7 64511-2. Philh. O, Barbirolli.
(BB) **(*) ASV CDQS 6082 [(M) id. import]. Hallé O, James Loughran; (ii) Philh. O, Owain Hughes.

(i) *Symphony No. 1 in A flat; Cockaigne overture;* (ii) *Romance for bassoon and orchestra, Op. 62.*
(B) ** Sony SBK 53510; *SBT 53510* [id.]. (i) LPO; (ii) Martin Gatt & ECO; both cond. Barenboim.

Symphony No. 1 in A flat; Chanson de matin; Chanson de nuit; Serenade for strings, Op. 20.
(M) *** EMI CDM7 64013-2 [id.]. LPO, Sir Adrian Boult.

Symphony No. 1 in A flat; Imperial march, Op. 32.
(BB) *** Naxos Dig. 8.550634 [id.]. BBC PO, George Hurst.

(i) *Symphony No. 1 in A flat;* (ii) *Introduction and allegro, Op. 47;* (iii) *Pomp and circumstance march No. 1.*
(BB) *** RCA Navigator Dig./Analogue 74321 24217-2 [(M) id. import]. (i) BBC SO, Sir Colin Davis; (ii) Boston SO, Charles Munch; (iii) Boston Pops O, Arthur Fiedler.

James Judd, more than any rival on disc, has learnt directly from Elgar's own recording of this magnificent symphony. So the reading has extra authenticity in the many complex speed-changes (sometimes indicated confusingly in the score), in the precise placing of climaxes and in the textural balances. Above all, Judd outshines others in the pacing and phrasing of the lovely slow movement which in its natural flowing rubato has melting tenderness behind the passion, a throat-catching poignancy not fully conveyed elsewhere but very much a quality of Elgar's own reading. The refinement of the strings down to the most hushed pianissimo confirms this as the Hallé's most beautiful disc in recent years, recorded with warmth and opulence.

Vernon Handley directs a beautifully paced reading which can also be counted in every way outstanding. The LPO has performed this symphony many times before but never with more poise and refinement than here. It is in the slow movement above all that Handley scores, spacious and movingly expressive. With very good sound, well transferred to CD, this is a highly recommendable alternative version.

On the bargain Naxos label comes Elgar's *First Symphony* in a warmly sympathetic version from the BBC Philharmonic under George Hurst, a conductor too long neglected on record. Masterly with Elgarian rubato, he refreshingly chooses speeds faster than have become the norm, closer to those of Elgar himself. James Judd's even warmer, more tender, more ripely recorded version on Carlton is still preferable, but no one will be disappointed with Hurst's powerful reading, well coupled with the *Imperial march*.

Boult clearly presents the *First Symphony* as a counterpart to the *Second*, with hints of reflective nostalgia amid the triumph. His EMI disc contains a radiantly beautiful performance, with no extreme tempi, richly spaced in the first movement, invigorating in the syncopated march rhythms of the Scherzo, and similarly bouncing in the Brahmsian rhythms of the finale.

The lyrical spontaneity of Sir Colin Davis's version of the *First Symphony* with the BBC Symphony Orchestra is very winning, an evocatively atmospheric live recording, made at the Royal Albert Hall during a Concertaid event in May 1985. Live recording conditions evidently relaxed Davis to give a beautifully paced performance which is warmer in its expressiveness than his usual studio performances. Though in the finale ensemble is not as crisp as earlier in the performance, and audience noises intrude in all four movements, this is persuasive in a way hard to achieve without an audience. The recording, though a little recessed, brings out the distinctive acoustic of the hall, with a real Elgarian rasp on trombones. Munch's vibrant if unidiomatic account of the *Introduction and allegro* makes a good bonus, and Fiedler is ebullient in *Pomp and circumstance*, which is also very well recorded. A fine bargain in the lowest price-range.

In Barbirolli's later (1962) Philharmonia acccount on EMI there is a hint of heaviness where, after the march introduction, the music should surge along. The slow movement, too, is very slow: it is done more affectionately in the earlier, Pye version, which we hope will reappear in due course. The present transfer of a Kingsway Hall recording has lost some of the fullness in the violins; otherwise, it sounds very well. The *Cockaigne overture* is one of Barbirolli's most notable Elgar recordings.

Loughran's performance, offered in the lowest price-range, is direct and understanding, reflecting the Hallé Orchestra's long familiarity with this symphony. There is an element of reserve here, but the performance makes a strong impression, with a memorably beautiful slow movement. The 1983 analogue recording is first class, naturally balanced but vivid. Owain Arwel Hughes's version of *Cockaigne* is crisp and alert, but speeds are very broad, at times impairing the flow, though building to a fine, ripe climax.

Barenboim, like Solti, studied Elgar's own recording before interpreting the *First Symphony*, and the results are certainly idiomatic, though in the long first movement Barenboim overdoes the fluctuations, so losing momentum. The other three movements are beautifully performed, with the *Adagio* almost as tender as in Solti's reading with the same players. The snag is the recording, which is not as opulent or well balanced as Elgar's orchestration really demands; and the same comment applies to Barenboim's colourful account of *Cockaigne*. The well-played bassoon *Romance* is placed after the symphony and before the overture.

Symphony No. 2 in E flat, Op. 63.
(B) *** CfP CD-CFP 4544 [id.]. LPO, Vernon Handley.
(BB) *** Naxos Dig. 8.550635 [id.]. BBC PO, Downes.

Symphony No. 2; Cockaigne overture, Op. 40.
(M) *** EMI CDM7 64014-2 [id.]. LPO, Sir Adrian Boult.

Symphony No. 2 in E flat; Cockaigne overture; Dream children No. 1, Op. 43/1.
(M) (**) EMI mono CDM5 66399-2. Hallé O, Sir John Barbirolli.

Symphony No. 2; The Crown of India (suite), *Op. 66.*
(M) *** Chandos CHAN 6523 [id.]. SNO, Gibson.

(i) *Symphony No. 2;* (ii) *Elegy for strings, Op. 58; Serenade for strings, Op. 20.*
(B) ** Sony SBK 67176 [id.]. (i) LPO; (ii) ECO, Daniel Barenboim.

(i) *Symphony No. 2;* (ii) *Elegy, Op. 58; Sospiri, Op. 70.*
(M) **(*) EMI CDM7 64724-2 [id.]. (i) Hallé O; New Philh. O, Barbirolli.
(BB) **(*) ASV Analogue/Dig. CDQS 6087 [(M) id. import]. (i) Hallé O, James Loughran; (ii) ASMF, Marriner.

Handley's remains the most satisfying modern version of a work which has latterly been much recorded. What Handley conveys superbly is the sense of Elgarian ebb and flow, building climaxes like a master and drawing excellent, spontaneous-sounding playing from an orchestra which, more than any other, has specialized in performing this symphony. The sound is warmly atmospheric and vividly conveys the added organ part in the bass, just at the climax of the finale, which Elgar himself suggested 'if available'. This would be a first choice at full price, but as a bargain CD there are few records to match it.

Downes uses an expansive speed in the first movement to give the writing its full emotional thrust, and the hushed tension of the slow movements leads up to towering climaxes, well controlled. The Scherzo is brilliant, delicate and witty, and the finale with its sequential writing is perfectly paced. Although it has not quite the bite and thrust of Handley's version (partly the effect of the recording-balance), its valedictory feeling at the close is very moving. Indeed the only reservation is that the sound, though warm and refined, is a degree too distanced, so that the noble opening of the work does not have its full impact. This does not displace Vernon Handley, except for those needing digital recording, but it can be recommended alongside it.

For his fifth recording of the *Second Symphony* Sir Adrian Boult, incomparable Elgarian, drew from the LPO the most richly satisfying performance of all. Over the years Sir Adrian's view of the glorious nobility of the first movement had mellowed a degree, but the pointing of climaxes is unrivalled. With Boult more than anyone else the architecture is clearly and strongly established, with tempo changes less exaggerated than usual. This is a version to convert new listeners to a love of Elgar, although, even more than in the *First Symphony*, the ear notices a loss of opulence compared with the original LP. This is also very striking in *Cockaigne*, which opens the disc.

Gibson's recording shows his partnership with the SNO at its peak, and this performance captures all the opulent nostalgia of Elgar's masterly score. The reading of the first movement is more relaxed in its grip than Handley's, but its spaciousness is appealing and, both here and in the beautifully sustained *Larghetto*, the richly resonant acoustics of Glasgow City Hall bring out the full panoply of Elgarian sound. The finale has splendid *nobilmente*. In the *Crown of India* suite Gibson is consistently imaginative in his attention to detail, and the playing of the Scottish orchestra is again warmly responsive.

Even more than in his recording of No. 1, Loughran's *Second* has an element of emotional reticence. He chooses a steady pacing for the last two movements, and the finale has less exuberance than with Handley. This is still a performance of considerable character. The 1979 sound is fresh, well balanced and spacious, though the CD transfer is a little light at the bass end. Marriner's (1983) digital recording of the *Serenade* offers well-defined and cleanly focused sound; perhaps it is just a little too 'present', but the effect is truthful and never edgy. The performance adds nothing to his earlier recording, made for Argo/Decca in the late 1960s, which generates slightly greater atmosphere. All in all, however, this bargain disc is good value.

Barbirolli's 1964 Kingsway Hall recording shows its age a little in the massed violins (especially by comparison with the richer tapestry for the two short string-pieces, beautifully played, which were recorded two years later). Barbirolli's ardour is never in doubt – witness the exuberant horn-playing in the first movement and the passion of the finale – but his interpretation is a very personal one, deeply felt but with the pace of the music often excessively varied, sometimes coarsening effects which Elgar's score specifies very precisely and weakening the structure.

Having conducted this symphony all over the world, in 1972 Barenboim made it his first exercise in Elgar recording. Following very much in the path set by Barbirolli, Barenboim underlines and exaggerates the contrasts of tempi, pulling the music out to the expansive limit. Yet this is still a red-blooded, passionate performance, capable of convincing for the moment at least, and the only snag is that the Abbey Road recording is seriously lacking in body and warmth. The string pieces sound fuller, and in the *Serenade* the *Larghetto* is touching. But in the *Elegy* Barenboim tends to dwell too affectionately on detail and the result is almost schmaltzy.

As in his stereo recording, made a decade later, Barbirolli's 1954 reading is very personal indeed. You might say that Elgar himself, when conducting, ignored many of his own markings, but there is no denying the beauty and added nobility of performances like Boult's, which maintain a more steady emotional equilibrium. In the first movement Barbirolli's speed is basically slow, then at many points he slows down the tempo still further. Undoubtedly he creates a rapt tension in the passages of pianissimo espressivo and often his own involvement almost carries the day, but inevitably the result is self-conscious and mannered. In the wayward *Larghetto* Barbirolli again varies the pacing excessively, although the climaxes are obviously deeply felt, and the structure of the finale, too, is weakened by the lack of a firm forward pulse. *Cockaigne* is, by contrast, a dramatic and sprightly performance, but the first of the *Dream children* is also invested with extra intensity and becomes almost valedictory in feeling. The mono sound is excellent throughout.

CHAMBER AND INSTRUMENTAL MUSIC

(i) *Piano quintet in A min., Op. 84. String quartet in E min., Op. 83.*
(M) *** EMI Dig. CDM5 65099-2. (i) Bernard Roberts; Chilingirian Qt.
(BB) *** Naxos Dig. 8.553737 [id.]. Maggini Qt, (i) with Peter Donohoe.
(BB) *** Discover Dig. DICD 920485. Aura Ens., (i) with Hans Joerg Fink.

(i–ii) *Piano quintet in A min.;* (i) *String quartet in E min.;* (ii–iii) *In moonlight (Canto popolare for viola and piano).*
(M) *** EMI Dig. CD-EMX 2229 [(M) id. import]. (i) Vellinger Qt; (ii) Piers Lane; (iii) James Boyd.

The Vellinger Quartet, winner of the London International Quartet Competition in 1994, is an unusually characterful group for whom contrasts of ensemble are as important as blending. In this first recording, the Vellinger approach to Elgar is impulsive, with allegros taken faster than in rival versions, to make the finale of the *Quintet* bold and thrusting and the finale of the *Quartet* light and volatile. The middle movement of the *Quartet* is light and flowing too, like an interlude rather than a meditation; but the central *Adagio* of the *Quintet* is by contrast very slow and weighty, not as thoughtful as in other versions. What crowns the disc is the little fill-up, a ravishing performance of the magical interlude which Elgar arranged for viola and piano from the central *Nocturne* passage from his *Overture In the South*. James Boyd, the Vellinger viola, plays with a richness and firmness of intonation that make one long to hear him in more solo work.

Bernard Roberts and the Chilingirian Quartet are well attuned to the Elgarian sensibility: they have dignity and restraint and they capture the all-pervading melancholy of the *Quintet*'s slow movement. In the *String quartet*, the Chilingirians are excellent too, though they do not quite match the ardour of the Medicis; indeed some people have found them too low-voltage. However, they are excellently recorded in a warm acoustic and there is plenty of space around the aural image. An impressive and rewarding issue.

The Naxos and Discover versions appeared simultaneously, both at super-bargain price, both very recommendable. The Naxos issue with the young British Maggini Quartet, joined by Peter Donohoe, promptly won an important record prize in France, stylish, nicely pointed, slightly understated readings. Yet it is the Aura Ensemble of Switzerland which, perhaps surprisingly, offers even more red-blooded, urgently expressive readings, helped by rich, forward sound. One hopes it is a sign that rare Elgar is at last communicating outside Britain.

Violin sonata in E min., Op. 82.
(BB) *** ASV Quicksilva CDQS 6191 [(M) id.]. Lorraine McAslan, John Blakely – WALTON: *Violin sonata.* ***
(M) **(*) EMI CDM5 66122-2. Yehudi Menuhin, Hephzibah Menuhin – VAUGHAN WILLIAMS: *Sonata* **(*); WALTON: *Sonata.* (**)

This was Lorraine McAslan's début recording from 1985 and, though her performance of Elgar's inspired sonata cannot quite match the virtuoso command and body of tone of Nigel Kennedy's on Chandos (CHAN 8380 – see our main volume), hers is an impressive and warm-hearted version, full of natural imagination and bringing some rapt pianissimo playing in the outer movements. She is helped by the sympathetic partnership of John Blakely, who is attractively incisive. The digital recording is faithful but rather forward, which gives the violin-tone less bloom than it might have. But this coupling with Walton is more than worth its modest cost.

The Menuhins present a large-scale view of this sonata, the least ambitious of Elgar's three late chamber works but one which still brings echoes of the *Violin concerto*. Unfortunately, though slow speeds bring their moments of insight and revelation at the hands of a Menuhin, the result overall is too heavy, and it is marred too by imperfect intonation. The recording is first rate.

Music for wind

Adagio cantabile (Mrs Winslow's soothing syrup); Andante con variazione (Evesham Andante); 5 Intermezzos; Harmony music No. 1.
(M) *** Chandos CHAN 6553 [id.]. Athena Ens.

4 Dances; Harmony music Nos. 2–4; 6 Promenades.
(M) *** Chandos CHAN 6554 [id.]. Athena Ens.

As a budding musician, playing not only the violin but also the bassoon, Elgar wrote a quantity of brief, lightweight pieces in a traditional style for himself and four other wind-players to perform. He called it 'Shed Music'; though there are few real signs of the Elgar style to come, the energy and inventiveness are very winning, particularly when (as here) the pieces – often with comic names – are treated to bright and lively performances. Excellent recording, with the CD transfers sounding as fresh as new paint.

ORGAN MUSIC

Organ sonata No. 1 in G, Op. 28.
(BB) **(*) ASV CDQS 6160 [(M) id.]. Jennifer Bate (Royal Albert Hall organ) – with Recital: *British organ music.* **(*)

The Royal Albert Hall organ is just the instrument for Elgar's early *Sonata*, a richly enjoyable piece, full of characteristic ideas, not least the grand opening. Jennifer Bate plays with all the necessary flair, with her rubato only occasionally sounding unidiomatic, bringing out the dramatic contrasts of dynamic encouraged by this vast organ in its massive setting – emphasized by its facility for causing the sound-image to recede in quieter passages. The analogue recording brings good detail, even if the very wide dynamic range means that Bate's *piano* registers as *pianissimo* because of the distancing. This is now part of a 75-minute collection of British organ music, discussed below under Recitals.

(i) *Organ sonata No. 1 in G, Op. 28;* (ii) *Vesper voluntaries, Op. 14: Introduction; Andante.*
(M) *** EMI CDM5 65594-2. (i) Herbert Sumsion (organ of Gloucester Cathedral); (ii) Christopher Robinson (organ of Worcester Cathedral) – *Choral music.* **(*)

It was a pity that Herbert Sumsion's recording of the *Organ sonata* was not made on the organ at Worcester, for which it was written, but the Gloucester instrument makes a splendidly expansive sound and the gentler pages, glowingly registered, are not as recessed as in some other versions. Sumsion opens grandly and rises to the work's closing climax. His performance is sympathetically idiomatic, though it could perhaps be more flamboyantly extrovert. He is very well recorded, as is Christopher Robinson (who does play at Worcester) in the relatively slight *Voluntaries*, used to make an interlude within the concert of choral music for which the *Sonata* acts as a pendant.

VOCAL AND CHORAL MUSIC

Choral music: *Angelus, Op. 56/1; Ave Maria, Op. 2/2; Ave maris stella, Op. 2/3; Ave verum, Op. 2/1; Give unto the Lord, Op. 74; O hearken thou, Op. 64; Te Deum and Benedictus, Op. 34.*
(M) **(*) EMI CDM5 65594-2. Worcester Cathedral Ch., Christopher Robinson; Bramma – *Organ sonata No. 1* etc. ***

Elgar was one of a handful of Roman Catholics among our major English composers (Byrd was another). Like Byrd, he wrote much of his early sacred music within a Protestant tradition, so that it was suitable for presentation at the Three Choirs Festivals (the fine *Te Deum*) and even at St Paul's Cathedral (*Give unto the Lord*). *O hearken thou* is a coronation anthem, written in the composer's official capacity for the coronation of George V. The genuinely Catholic works were written during Elgar's apprenticeship at St George's Church, Worcester. Both the *Ave verum* and the *Ave Maria* have a gentle, romantic colouring; but most memorable is the *Angelus*, with its repeated figure like an echoing bell. This was written in Italy in 1909, and it has a touch of Mediterranean sunshine in its mood. There is little in this programme to anticipate the Elgar of *Gerontius*, though much to show an emerging musical individuality. Performances are sympathetic and alive, and the cathedral ambience is highly suitable for the music. The 1969 recording has been transferred admirably to CD. The coupled organ music increases the interest of this generously full reissue (76 minutes).

The Banner of St George, Op. 33; (i) *Great is the Lord (Psalm 48), Op. 67; Te Deum and Benedictus, Op. 34.*
(M) *** EMI Dig. CDM5 65108-2. L. Symphony Ch., N. Sinfonia, Hickox; (i) with Stephen Roberts.

In telling the story of St George slaying the dragon and saving the Lady Sylene, Elgar is at his most colourful, with the battle sequence leading to beautifully tender farewell music (bringing one of Elgar's most yearningly memorable melodies) and a final rousing chorus. The three motets, written at the same period, bring 'Pomp and circumstance' into church and, like the cantata, stir the blood in Hickox's strong, unapologetic performances, richly recorded.

(i) *The Black Knight* (symphony for chorus and orchestra); Part-songs: *Fly singing bird; The snow; Spanish serenade;* (ii) *Scenes from the Saga of King Olaf, Op. 30.*
(M) *** EMI Dig. CMS5 65104-2 (2). (i) RLPO Ch. & O, Groves; (ii) Cahill, Langridge, Rayner Cook, LPO Ch., LPO, Handley.

Charles Groves conducts a strong, fresh performance of *The Black Knight*, not always perfectly polished in its ensemble but with bright, enthusiastic singing from the chorus. Neurotic tensions here are far more distant, and the happiness and confidence of the writing are what come over with winning freshness, even though Elgarians must inevitably miss the deeper, darker and more melancholy overtones. Nevertheless, the rare couplings still make this a highly desirable set.

King Olaf was the last of Elgar's works to be put on disc, and Vernon Handley, outstanding among today's Elgarians, makes it an appropriate landmark. The emotional thrust in Handley's reading confirms this as the very finest of the big works Elgar wrote before the *Enigma variations* in 1899. In its proportions it almost exactly anticipates *The Dream of Gerontius*, 90 minutes long with the first half shorter than the second, while in its big choruses its style keeps anticipating the later masterpieces, equally reflecting the influence of Wagner's *Parsifal*. The wonder is that Elgar's inspiration rises high above the doggerel of the text (Longfellow, adapted by Harry Acworth) and, though the episodic dramatic plan eventually tails off, the opposite is the case with Elgar's music, which grows even richer. Towards the end the charming 'gossip' chorus leads to the radiant pastoral duet between Olaf and Thyri, the third of his brides, followed by the exciting, dramatic chorus, *The Death of Olaf* (very Wagnerian), and finally an epilogue which transcends everything, building to a heart-tugging climax on the return of the 'Heroic Beauty' theme. Though strained at times by the high writing, Philip Langridge makes a fine, intelligent Olaf, Teresa Cahill sings with ravishing silver purity and Brian Rayner Cook brings out words with fine clarity; but it is the incandescent singing of the London Philharmonic Chorus that sets the seal on this superb set, ripely recorded, one of the finest in EMI's long Elgar history.

(i) *Coronation ode, Op. 44; The Spirit of England, Op. 80.*
(M) *** Chandos CHAN 6574 [id.]. Cahill, SNO Ch. and O, Gibson; (i) with Anne Collins, Rolfe Johnson, Howell.

Gibson's performances combine fire and panache, and the recorded sound has an ideal Elgarian expansiveness, the choral tone rich and well focused, the orchestral brass given plenty of weight, and the overall perspective highly convincing. He is helped by excellent soloists, with Anne Collins movingly eloquent in her dignified restraint when she introduces the famous words of *Land of hope and glory* in the finale; and the choral entry which follows is truly glorious in its power and amplitude. *The Spirit of England*, a wartime cantata to words of Laurence Binyon, is in some ways even finer, with the final setting of *For the fallen* rising well above the level of his occasional music.

The Dream of Gerontius, Op. 38.
(B) **(*) Decca Double 443 170-2 (2) [id.]. Pears, Minton, Shirley-Quirk, L. Symphony Ch., King's College, Cambridge Ch., LSO, Britten – DELIUS: *Sea drift;* HOLST: *Hymn of Jesus.* ***
(BB) ** Naxos Dig. 8.553885/6 [id.]. Kendall, Fryer, Best, Bournemouth Symphony Ch., Waynflete Singers, Bournemouth SO, David Hill.

(i) *The Dream of Gerontius. Organ sonata in G, Op. 28.*
(B) ** EMI Dig. CD-EMXD 2500 (2) [(M) id. import]. (i) Anthony Rolfe Johnson, Catherine Wyn-Rogers, Michael George, RLPO Ch., Huddersfield Ch. Soc.; RLPO, Handley.

(i) *The Dream of Gerontius. Sea pictures.*
(M) **(*) EMI CMS7 63185-2 (2). Dame Janet Baker, Hallé O, Barbirolli; (i) with Richard Lewis, Kim Borg, Hallé & Sheffield Philharmonic Ch., Amb. S.

Barbirolli's red-blooded reading of *Gerontius* is the most heart-warmingly dramatic ever recorded; here it is offered, in a first-rate CD transfer, in coupling with one of the greatest Elgar recordings ever made: Dame Janet Baker's rapt and heartfelt account of *Sea pictures*. No one on record can match Dame Janet in this version of *Gerontius* for the fervent intensity and glorious tonal range of her singing as the Angel, one of her supreme recorded performances; and the clarity of CD intensifies the experience. In pure dedication the emotional thrust of Barbirolli's reading conveys the deepest spiritual intensity, making most other versions seem cool by comparison. The recording may have its hints of distortion, but the sound is overwhelming. Richard Lewis gives one of his finest recorded performances, searching and intense, and, though Kim Borg is unidiomatic in the bass role, his bass tones are rich in timbre, even if his projection lacks the dramatic edge of Robert Lloyd on the full-price Boult set.

The Britten version brings searching and inspired conducting from a fellow-composer not generally associated with Elgar. Britten's approach is red-blooded, passionate and urgent, and with speeds never languishing – as in this oratorio they can. The London Symphony Chorus – supplemented by the King's Choir – is balanced backwardly in the warmly atmospheric recording made at The Maltings, but the extra projection and precision of CD brings out how bitingly dramatic the singing is, even if the actual choral sound is poorly focused. The soloists are a fine, responsive team, with Pears an involving if sometimes over-stressed Gerontius, and Yvonne Minton and John Shirley-Quirk both excellent. On CD the layout, with Delius's *Sea drift* placed first, allows the break between discs to come in the ideal place, between the oratorio's two parts. The Holst work then follows on afterwards. Full texts are provided, and there is no doubt that in Double Decca format this set is a real bargain.

On EMI Eminence at mid-price Vernon Handley's version offers a modern, digital recording which captures the sound of the chorus vividly with plenty of church atmosphere. The impact of the performance is then weakened by a relatively backward placing of soloists and orchestra. One's involvement is reduced, even with Anthony Rolfe Johnson's thoughtful portrayal of Gerontius, and Catherine Wyn-Rogers as the Angel too often sounds matter-of-fact rather than dedicated. With Handley also less intense than usual, this is disappointing next to his earlier Elgar recordings, though it is welcome to have as fill-up his 1989 account of Elgar's magnificent *Organ sonata in G*, vividly orchestrated by Gordon Jacob to create what might almost be counted Elgar's 'Symphony No. 0'.

Though it was enterprising of Naxos to promote a super-bargain recording of Elgar's great oratorio, this is a performance which, for all its many qualities, fails to take fire, giving an understated account of Elgar's passionate inspiration. The recording, made in Poole Arts Centre, is warm and refined but, with the chorus set at a slight distance, the impact is lessened. The conductor too seems more concerned with refinement than with emotional thrust, and the soloists, sensitive artists, yet make a flawed team, when the microphone brings out the unevenness of vocal production, with vibrato exaggerated. William Kendall as Gerontius is overstrained at times, and Matthew Best's baritone too often sounds gritty; though Sarah Fryer's mezzo is warm, she is not steady enough for the great meditation of her final solo. With no fill-up provided here, several mid-price versions offer better value.

(i) *The Kingdom, Op. 51;* (ii) *Coronation Ode, Op. 34.*
(M) *** EMI CMS7 64209-2. (i) Margaret Price, Yvonne Minton, Alexander Young, John Shirley-Quirk, LPO Ch., LPO, Boult; (ii) Felicity Lott, Alfreda Hodgson, Richard Morton, Cambridge University Music Soc., King's College, Cambridge, Ch., New Philh. O, Band of Royal Military School of Music, Kneller Hall, Philip Ledger.

Boult was devoted to *The Kingdom*, identifying with its comparative reticence, openly preferring it even to *Gerontius*, and his dedication emerges clearly throughout a glorious performance. It has often been suggested that it is too static, but the Pentecost scene is intensely dramatic, and the richness of musical inspiration in the rest prevents any feeling of stagnation, certainly in a performance as inspired as this. The melody which Elgar wrote to represent the Holy Spirit is one of the noblest that even he created, and the soprano aria *The sun goeth down* (beautifully sung by Margaret Price) leads to a deeply affecting climax. The other soloists also sing splendidly, and the only reservation concerns the chorus, which is not quite as disciplined as it might be and sounds a little too backward for some of the massive effects which cap the power of the work. However, there is no doubt but that the strikingly successful remastering process has brought a gain in presence while retaining the quality of the 1977 original; here the freshening brings better definition without loss of body. The coupling of the *Coronation ode* is handy and certainly welcome, rather than particularly appropriate. It is far more than a jingoistic occasional piece, though it was indeed the work which first featured *Land of hope and glory*. The most tender moment of all is reserved for the first faint flickerings of that second national anthem, introduced gently on the harp to clarinet accompaniment. All told, the work contains much Elgarian treasure, and Ledger is superb in capturing the necessary swagger and panache, flouting all thought of potential bad taste. With recording of outstanding quality – among the finest made in King's College Chapel during the analogue era – and with extra brass bands, it presents a glorious experience. Excellent singing and playing, too, although the male soloists do not quite match their female colleagues. Both works are generously cued.

The Light of Life (Lux Christi), Op. 29.
(M) *** EMI CDM7 64732-2. Marshall, Watts, Leggate, Shirley-Quirk, RLPO Ch. & O, Groves.

The Light of Life was one of the works immediately preceding the great leap forward which Elgar made with *Enigma* in 1899, and this hour-long oratorio is full of Elgarian fingerprints, not least in the choral writing and the ripe orchestration. Sir Charles Groves's understanding performance features four first-rate soloists and strongly involving, if not always flawless, playing and singing from the Liverpool orchestra and choir. The recording is vivid and full in EMI's recognizable Elgar manner and has been admirably transferred, with cleaner focus and no appreciable loss of amplitude.

The Music Makers, Op. 69; Sea pictures, Op. 37.
(M) **(*) EMI Dig. CDM5 65126-2. Felicity Palmer, L. Symphony Ch., LSO, Hickox.

Hickox's coupling of *Sea pictures* and the big cantata, *The Music makers*, brings strong, powerful performances, very individual in the song-cycle thanks to the urgent, tough and indeed characterful singing of Felicity Palmer. Hickox gives a convincing, red-blooded reading of the cantata, atmospherically recorded and with the voices well caught, but with reverberation masking some of the orchestral detail.

5 Partsongs from the Greek anthology, Op. 45: Yea, cast me from heights of the mountains; Whether I find thee; After many a dusty mile; It's oh! to be a wild wind; Feasting I watch. The Wanderer; The Reveille.
(M) *** EMI CMS5 65123-2 (2). Baccholian Singers; Jennifer Partridge (with HOWELLS: *A Dirge;* BAX: *The Boar's Head;* DELIUS: *Wanderer's song;* WARLOCK: *The Shrouding of the Duchess of Malfi; The Lady's birthday;* BRITTEN: *The ballad of Little Musgrave and Lady Barnard* ***) – HOLST: *Choral songs;* VAUGHAN WILLIAMS: *Folksong arrangements.* ***

This particularly desirable cornucopia of English songs is assembled from three different CDs, recorded at either Kingsway Hall or Abbey Road between 1969 and 1976. Elgar's *Part songs*, Op. 45, for male voices date from 1902 and are settings of Greek translations by English poets. They are all brief but vivid, and the miscellaneous group of choral songs by various other English composers brings great variety. Perhaps the most striking is Britten's extended *Ballad of Little Musgrave*, with piano accompaniment, a macabre piece presented with great drama. Here Jennifer Partridge provides a telling accompaniment, and she also contributes to the success of Peter Warlock's rollicking third 'Sociable song', *The Lady's birthday*. Excellent, truthful recording.

Songs: *Pleading; 3 Songs (Was it some golden star?; Oh, soft was the song; Twilight), Op. 59; 2 Songs (The torch; The river), Op. 60.*
(M) *** EMI CDM7 64731-2. Robert Tear, CBSO, Vernon Handley – BUTTERWORTH: *Songs;* VAUGHAN WILLIAMS: *On Wenlock Edge* etc. ***

At his most creative period in the early years of the century, Elgar planned another song-cycle to follow *Sea pictures*, but he completed only three of the songs, his Op. 59. The other three songs here are even more individual, a fine coupling for Vaughan Williams and Butterworth. Incisive and characterful, yet expressively sympathetic performances from Tear. The recording, well focused, is appropriately warm and atmospheric.

Scenes from the Bavarian Highlands, Op. 27; Ecce sacerdos magnus; O salutaris Hostia (3 settings); *Tantum ergo. The Light of Life: Doubt not thy Father's care; Light of the World.*
(M) **(*) Chandos CHAN 6601 [id.]. Worcester Cathedral Ch., Christopher Robinson; Frank Wibaut; Harry Bramma.

It is good to have a fine mid-priced performance of the original piano-accompanied version of the charmingly tuneful *Bavarian scenes*. Even without the orchestra, the music lifts up with remarkable freshness when the singing in Worcester is appropriately committed and spontaneous. The three versions of *O salutaris Hostia* are also worth having, and the strong performances of *Tantum ergo* and *Ecce sacerdos magnus* add to the interest of this reissue.

Scenes from the Bavarian Highlands, Op. 27 (orchestral version).
(M) *** EMI CDM5 65129-2. Bournemouth Ch. & SO, Del Mar – STANFORD: *Symphony No. 3.* ***

The EMI recording uses the orchestral version of the score; although the choral recording is agreeably full, balances are not always ideal, with the choral descant in the *Lullaby* outweighing the attractive orchestral detail. However, the performances are infectiously spirited, conveying warmth as well as vigour – Del Mar is a natural Elgarian. Moreover the EMI coupling of the Stanford *Third Symphony* was a happy and generous choice.

(i) *Sea pictures, Op. 37. Pomp and circumstance marches Nos. 1–5, Op. 39.*
(B) *** CfP CD-CFP 9004 [id.]. (i) Bernadette Greevy; LPO, Handley.

Bernadette Greevy – in glorious voice – gives the performance of her recording career in an inspired partnership with Vernon Handley, whose accompaniments are no less memorable, and with the LPO players finding a wonderful rapport with the voice. In the last song Handley uses a telling *ad lib.* organ part to underline the climaxes of each final stanza. The coupled *Marches* are exhilarating, and if Nos. 2 and (especially) 3 strike some ears as too vigorously paced, comparison with the composer's own tempi reveals an authentic precedent.

(i) *Sea pictures, Op. 37;* (ii; iii) *The Starlight Express: Songs: O children, open your arms to me; There's a fairy that hides; I'm everywhere; Wake up, you little night winds; O stars, shine brightly; We shall meet the morning spiders; My old tunes are rather broken; O think beauty; Dustman, Laughter, Tramp and busy Sweep.* (iii) *Dream children, Op. 43.*
(M) **(*) Decca Dig. 452 324-2. (i) Della Jones, RPO; (ii) Alison Hagley, Bryn Terfel; (iii) Welsh Nat. Op. O; all cond. Mackerras – LAMBERT: *The Rio Grande.* **(*)

These recordings from the early 1990s belong to the short-lived resuscitation of the Argo label, yet they have already reverted to Decca's mid-priced Ovation series. There has never been a more dramatic presentation of the *Sea pictures*. The opening of the *Sea slumber-song* is simple and touching but Mackerras creates a big climax for *Sabbath morning at sea*, and Della Jones brings even more histrionic feeling to the final climax of *The swimmer*. She sings richly throughout and the performance could not be more vivid; however, although *Where corals lie* is obviously deeply felt, one feels that not all the secrets of this music are fully revealed. The vocal numbers from *The Starlight Express* are well sung by Alison Hagley and Bryn Terfel, but why divorce them from the rest of the score? Mackerras is as warmly affectionate in the delicately scored *Dream children* as he is dramatic in the *Sea pictures*, and the recording throughout, made in Brangwyn Hall, Swansea, has plenty of atmosphere and presence.

The Spirit of England, Op. 80; O give unto the Lord (Psalm 29); Land of hope and glory; O hearten Thou (Offertory); *The Snow.*
(M) *** EMI Dig. CDM5 65586-2. Felicity Lott, L. Symphony Ch., N. Sinfonia, Hickox.

In his series of lesser Elgar choral works for EMI, Hickox conducts a rousing performance of *The Spirit of England*, magnificently defying the dangers of wartime bombast. He adds three short choral pieces, including a setting of Psalm 29, and ends with *Land of hope and glory* in all its splendour. The London Symphony Chorus is in radiant form and Felicity Lott is a strong soloist in the main work. First-rate EMI digital sound, made at Abbey Road in 1987.

The Starlight Express (incidental music), *Op. 78.*
(B) *** EMI CD-EMX 2267 [(M) id. import]. Masterson, Hammond-Stroud, LPO, Handley.

The Starlight Express was a children's play of 1916, adapted from a novel by Algernon Blackwood, which its promoters hoped would prove a successor to J. M. Barrie's *Peter Pan*. Though the play failed to attract a comparable following, Elgar himself recorded a whole sequence of numbers from it at the time. Even that failed to keep the music alive, and it has been left to latterday Elgarians to revive a score which reveals the composer at his most charming. On CD in this dedicated reconstruction (without the spoken dialogue) one is conscious of the element of repetition, but the ear is constantly beguiled and the key sequences suggest that this procedure would have won the composer's approval. Some of the words reflect the coy manner of the original libretto, but much of the orchestral music has that nostalgically luminous quality which Elgarians will instantly recognize. Both soloists are excellent and the LPO plays with warmth and sympathy. The 1976 recording is excellent and it matters little that, in order to fit the piece complete on to a single CD, some minor cuts have had to be made.

Enescu, Georges (1881–1955)

Roumanian rhapsody No. 1.
(M) *** Mercury 432 015-2 [id.]. LSO, Dorati – LISZT: *Hungarian rhapsodies Nos. 1–6.* **(*)
(M) **(*) Sony SMK 47572 [id.]. NYPO, Bernstein – LISZT: *Hungarian rhapsodies; Les Préludes.* **(*)

Enescu's chimerical *First Roumanian rhapsody* combines a string of glowing folk-derived melodies with glittering scoring to make it the finest genre piece of its kind in laminating Eastern gypsy influences under a bourgeois orchestral veneer. Dorati finds both flair and exhilaration in the closing pages, and the Mercury sound, from the early 1960s, is of a vintage standard. The coupling with the Liszt *Hungarian rhapsodies* is entirely appropriate.

Not surprisingly, Bernstein's charisma comes well to the fore in Enescu's chimerical *First Rhapsody*, a vividly individual performance gathering excitement as it proceeds. The recording does not match Dorati's Mercury version in richness of colour, but it has been effectively remastered. The Liszt couplings are impressive too, and the CD also includes a pair of Brahms *Hungarian dances*.

Roumanian rhapsodies Nos 1–2, Op. 11/1–2.
(M) *** Chandos Dig. CHAN 7083 [id.]. SNO, Järvi – BARTOK: *Hungarian folk-dance suite* etc. ***
(M) ** Van. 08 6151 71 [OVC 5002]. V. State Op. O, Golschmann – GOLDMARK: *Rustic wedding symphony*. ***

Järvi has a warmly idiomatic feeling for these amiable, peasant-inspired rhapsodies, moulding phrases and linking sections with spontaneity, drawing committed playing from the Royal Scottish National Orchestra, ripely recorded. Though the first of the two rhapsodies is much the more popular, the second is also lively and colourful. Together they make an apt coupling for Järvi's vividly robust accounts of similar folk-based music by Bartók.

Enescu's *First Rhapsody* is given a lively and attractive performance by Golschmann, and the Viennese players bring an idiomatic understanding to the East European lyrical temperament of the *Second*. The recording is vivid, if not as warmly lustrous as the Goldmark coupling.

Cello sonatas Nos. 1 in F min.; 2 in C, Op. 26/1–2.
(BB) *** Arte Nova Dig. 74321 54461-2 [id.]. Gerhard Zank, Donald Sulzen.

Despite the identical opus number, Enescu's two cello sonatas are separated by over three decades. The *First Sonata in F minor* comes from 1898, when he was seventeen, and the *Second in C major* is a much later piece, composed in the 1930s when Enescu was in his fifties. The *F minor Sonata* is very much in the received tradition, inventive and well constructed, muscular in character and Brahmsian in feeling. Though it is still 'conservative' in approach, the *Second Sonata* of 1935 is far more individual and searching in its musical language, a thoughtful piece with the occasional reminiscence of the *Third Violin sonata*. It deserves a firmer place in the repertory; there can be no greater praise than to say that it is worthy of its dedicatee, Casals. Gerhard Zank has impressive musical credentials (he studied with Menahem Pressler and Norbert Brainin) and he founded the Munich Piano Trio. He is a masterly and eloquent cellist, and he is well partnered by the Kansas-born Donald Sulzen. Very clean, bright (perhaps over-bright) recording with plenty of presence. We are glad to see that the sleeve-note (unusually) thanks Rainer Schmidt 'for the wonderful tuning and work he did on the Steinway Concert Grand'. It is not always that you can rely on such a beautifully conditioned and consistently true instrument on record. A rewarding disc and well worth the modest asking price.

Falla, Manuel de (1876–1946)

(i) *El amor brujo* (original version); (ii) *El corregidor y la molinara.*
(M) *** Virgin/EMI Dig. CUV5 61138-2. (i) Claire Powell; (ii) Jill Gomez; Aquarius, Cleobury.

(i) *El amor brujo* (ballet original version; complete); (ii) *El retablo de Maese Pedro (Master Peter's puppet show).*
(BB) **(*) Naxos Dig. 8.553499 [id.]. (i) Pons-Tena, Herrera; cond. Diego Dini-Ciacci; (i–ii) Natacha Valladares, I Cameristi; (ii) Jordi Galofré, cond. Maurizio Dini-Ciacci.

The Virgin issue, by omitting the dialogue, finds room for the original version of the *Three-cornered hat*, also conceived for chamber orchestra, which first appeared as a mime play with music. Much is missing from the ballet we know today. Claire Powell makes an admirable gypsy in *El amor brujo*, while Jill Gomez is equally vibrant in her contributions to the companion work. Nicholas Cleobury concentrates on atmosphere rather than drama and, helped by the transluscent textures of the outstanding Virgin Classics recording, certainly seduces the ear.

The original version of *El amor brujo*, with dialogue for two actors as well as a mezzo soloist, and using a small orchestra, is ideally coupled here with the later stage-piece drawn from Cervantes, also using chamber forces. The smaller orchestra for *El amor brujo* has extra bite, when the brass is correspondingly more prominent, as in the *Ritual fire dance*, here entitled 'Dance at the end of the day'. That brassiness compensates for a warm but rather soft-grained reading directed by Diego Dini-Ciacci. The first *Interlude* (labelled 'Pantomime' in the later orchestral suite) with its near-tango rhythms is exotically languid but dangerously slow. Under Maurizio Dini-Ciacci, *Maese Pedro*, with its neo-classical overtones, is sharper-edged, an amiable performance with first-rate soloists, including the clear-toned tenor Jordi Galofré as Maese Pedro and Natacha Valladares as a boyish narrator (Trujaman). Recordings made in Verona cope well with balance problems.

El amor brujo: complete.

(M) *** Decca 448 601-2. Nati Mistral, New Philh. O, Frühbeck de Burgos – ALBENIZ: *Suite española.* ***

(i) *El amor brujo* (complete); (ii) *Nights in the gardens of Spain.*

✿ (M) *** Decca Dig. 430 703-2; *430 703-4* [id.]. (i) Tourangeau, Montreal SO, Dutoit; (ii) De Larrocha, LPO, Frühbeck de Burgos – RODRIGO: *Concierto.* *** ✿

(B) **(*) DG Classikon 439 458-2; *439 458-4* [(M) id. import]. (i) Teresa Berganza, LSO, Navarro; (ii) Margrit Weber, Bav. RSO, Kubelik – RODRIGO: *Concierto de Aranjuez.* **

Dutoit's brilliantly played *El amor brujo* has long been praised by us. With recording in the demonstration class, the performance has characteristic flexibility over phrasing and rhythm and is hauntingly atmospheric. The sound in the coupled *Nights in the gardens of Spain* is equally superb, rich and lustrous and with vivid detail. Miss de Larrocha's lambent feeling for the work's poetic evocation is matched by her brilliance in the nocturnal dance-rhythms.

Raphael Frühbeck de Burgos provides us with another excellent mid-priced version of *El amor brujo*, attractively coupled with Albéniz. The score's evocative atmosphere is hauntingly captured and, to make the most striking contrast, the famous *Ritual fire dance* blazes brilliantly. Nati Mistral has the vibrant open-throated projection of the real flamenco artist, and the whole performance is idiomatically authentic and compelling. Brilliant Decca sound to match. Well worthy of reissue in Decca's Classic Sound series.

Navarro conducts a vibrantly atmospheric account of *El amor brujo* and Teresa Berganza is a strong, dark-throated soloist. The LSO are on top form, especially in the *Ritual fire dance*, and the recording is evocative. The performance of *Nights in the gardens of Spain* is similarly compelling. With Margrit Weber giving a brilliant account of the solo part, particularly in the latter movements, the effect is both sparkling and exhilarating. A little of the fragant nocturnal essence is lost, particularly in the opening section (where de Larrocha on Decca (430 703-2) is gentler), but the performance, with its strong sense of drama, is certainly not without its evocative qualities. A stimulating pairing; a pity the Rodrigo coupling is less recommendable.

(i; ii) *El amor brujo* (complete); (iii) *Nights in the gardens of Spain;* (ii) *The Three-cornered hat* (ballet): suite.

(M) **(*) EMI CDM7 64746-2 [id.]. (i) De los Angeles; (ii) Philh. O, Giulini; (iii) Soriano, Paris Conservatoire O, Frühbeck de Burgos.

Giulini's performances come from the early 1960s, and the disc also includes Soriano's excellent account of *Nights in the gardens of Spain.* The Philharmonia playing is polished and responsive and Giulini produces civilized, colourful performances. The recording, too, is brightly coloured and, although noticeably resonant in *The Three-cornered hat*, the present transfers offer vivid and full-bodied sound. *El amor brujo* is not as red-blooded here as it is in the hands of Dutoit, but Victoria de los Angeles's contribution is an undoubted point in its favour.

(i) *El amor brujo* (complete); (ii) *Nights in the gardens of Spain; The Three-cornered hat: Dance of the Neighbours; Dance of the Miller; Finale (Jota).*

(BB) **(*) RCA Navigator 74321 24215-2 [(M) id. import]. (i) Mistral; (ii) Achucarro; LSO, Mata.

The late Eduardo Mata made some fine recordings for RCA in Dallas during the early digital era, notably of the music of Ravel (see below), but his Falla sessions are analogue and date from the previous decade. His account of *El amor brujo* is much more exciting than Maazel's; although the famous *Ritual fire dance* is measured, it does not lack rhythmic force. Mata, too, has an uninhibited vocal soloist in Nancy Mistral and her singing is, if anything, even more earthy than Bumbry's. *Nights in the gardens of Spain* brings a highly sympathetic contribution from Joaquin Achucarro, and the performance is both evocative and exciting, if not as delicately refined as the Del Pueyo/Martinon account. The sound throughout is warmly atmospheric and vivid. The dances from the *Three-cornered hat* are more rhythmically subtle than Maazel's, although here the LSO violin timbre sounds thinner. A good super-bargain triptych, nevertheless.

(i) *El amor brujo (Love, the magician);* (ii) *The Three-cornered Hat* (ballets; both complete).

(B) *** DG Classikon 457 878-2 [(M) id. import]. Teresa Berganza, (i) LSO, García Navarro; (ii) Boston SO, Ozawa.

Teresa Berganza links this apt but surprisingly rare DG coupling. Both the recordings date from the late 1970s, and at that time Ozawa's highly colourful *Three-cornered Hat* was counted by us the best version on the market in its complete form. The Boston sound is vividly alive, even more so on CD, and has a wide dynamic range yet an admirable presence without distorting perspectives, though Berganza is not located off-stage as directed. *El amor brujo*, recorded in London's Henry Wood Hall, brings a slightly more recessed effect. The opening fanfare lacks something in glitter, but the orchestral detail is refined and the score's magical moments of evocation are beautifully done, while Berganza's contribution is vibrantly idiomatic. Here the CD transfer has brought extra projection without loss of the basic naturalness of the balance, and the impact of the famous *Ritual fire dance* is increased, yet the responsive LSO playing (wind and strings alike) ensures that the Mediterranean sultriness is equally seductive in the *Pantomime* sequence.

(i) *El amor brujo* (complete); *Three-cornered hat: Dance of the Miller's wife; Dance of the Neighbours; Dance of the Miller; Finale (Jota).*
(M) ** DG 447 414-2 [id.]. (i) Bumbry; Berlin RSO, Maazel – STRAVINSKY: *Firebird suite.* ***

The most striking thing about Maazel's *El amor brujo* is the splendid contribution of Grace Bumbry. This black singer was an unexpected choice in music by Falla, but in fact she catches the flamenco style vibrantly and her dark timbre has an idiomatic 'throaty' clang. Unfortunately the rest of the performance, though warm and often vivid, is not really memorable and the four famous dances from the *Three-cornered hat* fail to take off.

(i) *El amor brujo* (complete); *Three-cornered hat* (ballet): *3 dances. La vida breve: Interlude and dance.*
(M) *** RCA 09026 62586-2 [id.]. (i) Leontyne Price; Chicago SO, Reiner – ALBENIZ: *Iberia* etc.; GRANADOS: *Goyescas: Intermezzo.* ***

Reiner's complete *El amor brujo*, from a vintage period with the Chicago orchestra, is a fiery and colourful account, yet totally seductive in its nudging of rhythms in *The magic circle* and in the languorous *Pantomime*. Leontyne Price's contribution has all the dark, guttural fire you could ask for, flamenco singing to the manner born: the operatic voice is almost unrecognizable. The excerpts from *La vida breve* and three dances from *The Three-cornered hat* are both sultry and gripping; they have far more sparkle than many recordings made since: the final dance brings really exciting orchestral virtuosity. The recording (from 1958) still sounds amazingly good.

Nights in the gardens of Spain.
✿ (M) *** Ph. (IMS) 442 751-2 (2) [id.]. Eduardo del Pueyo, LAP, Jean Martinon – GRANADOS: *Danzas españolas* etc. ***
(M) *** RCA 09026 68886-2 [id.]. Rubinstein, San Francisco SO, Enrique Jorda – CHOPIN: *Andante spianato & Grande Polonaise;* RACHMANINOV: *Rhapsody on a theme of Paganini.* ***

(i) *Nights in the gardens of Spain. El amor brujo: Ritual fire dance.*
(M) **(*) RCA 09026 61863-2 [id.]. Rubinstein; (i) Phd. O, Ormandy – FRANCK: *Symphonic variations* ***; SAINT-SAENS: *Concerto No. 2.* **(*)

(i) *Nights in the gardens of Spain;* (ii) *The Three-cornered hat* (ballet): complete.
(B) *(*) [EMI Red Line Dig. CDR5 72097]. (i) Tzimon Barto; (ii) Ann Murray; ASMF, Marriner.

(i) *Nights in the gardens of Spain;* (ii) *The Three-cornered hat* (ballet): complete; *La vida breve: Interlude and dance.*
(M) *** Decca (IMS) 417 771-2. (i) De Larrocha, SRO, Comissiona; (ii) SRO, Ansermet.

Dating from 1955, Del Pueyo's *Nights in the gardens of Spain* was one of the very first performances to be recorded in stereo, and it has never been surpassed. Martinon's magically evocative orchestral opening is matched by the delicacy of the solo entry, and the continuing dialogue between piano and the Paris orchestra brings incandescent subtlety of colour. The thrilling climax of *En la Generalife* has a glowing, spacious rapture and the following *Danza lejana* brings an almost dream-like quality. Somehow the vibrato of the (French) horn playing is not intrusive, and the slightly diffuse orchestral tapestry presented by the early stereo suits the music admirably. After the brilliance of *En los jardines de la Sierra de Córdoba* the music sinks gently back into the repose of its closing cadence. Unforgettable.

Alicia de Larrocha's earlier (1971) recording makes an excellent alternative mid-priced recommendation, coupled with Ansermet's lively and vividly recorded complete *Three-cornered hat*; she receives admirable support from Comissiona. The Decca analogue recording entirely belies its age. The *La vida breve* excerpts make an agreeable bonus.

Rubinstein chose San Francisco for his first and finest stereo recording of Falla's masterly triptych in 1957. He and Jorda make an excellent team and they give a glittering performance, full of evocation and colour. Jorda sustains great tension in the orchestra, yet he creates a basically warm and sultry atmosphere so that the expansive *Genaralife* climax is the more riveting. In the closing section the exotic local colours and rhythms are vividly projected, and the work's gentle closing section is quite haunting. John Pfeiffer's remastering is admirable in all respects, and the disc is equally worth having for the superb account of the Rachmaninov *Rhapsody*, splendidly recorded with Reiner in Chicago a year earlier.

Rubinstein's later Philadelphia version dates from 1969. It is an aristocratic reading, treating the work as a brilliantly coloured and mercurial concert-piece rather than a misty evocation, with flamenco rhythms glittering in the finale. The two encores which follow are even more arresting.

After a ferociously fast opening fanfare for *The Three-cornered hat* (on EMI Red Line), it is as if the ASMF has run out of steam, and the ballet itself is a surprisingly low-key affair, with little to grip the listener apart from the vivid orchestration. *Nights in the gardens of Spain*, very disappointingly, is also lacking in allure, not the fault of the soloist.

Suite populaire espagnole.

(BB) * Koch Discover Dig. DICD 920407 [id.]. Laetitia Himo, Nadia Himo – MIASKOVSKY: *Cello sonata No. 2;* PROKOFIEV: *Cello sonata.* *

Readers should approach this Discover issue with some caution. Laetitia Himo and Nadia Himo are a highly accomplished French partnership, but they are recorded in a resonant, rather mushy acoustic, which diminishes pleasure.

GUITAR MUSIC

7 Spanish popular songs (*Suite populaire españolas;* arr. for guitar).

(B) *** [EMI Red Line Dig. CDR5 69850]. Manuel Barrueco – GRANADOS: *Danzas españolas.* ***

Barrueco is a magician among the new school of guitarists, and his delicate nuances of colouring in these song transcriptions are matched by his seemingly spontaneous rhythmic freedom. Excellent recording too.

PIANO MUSIC

Fantasía bética.

(BB) **(*) ASV CDQS 6079 [(M) id.]. Alma Petchersky – ALBENIZ: *Suite española.* **(*)

Falla's masterly *Fantasía bética* calls for more dramatic fire and projection than Alma Petchersky commands. But she is a musical and neat player, the recording is very acceptable and this recital (which also includes Granados's *Allegro de concierto*) is competitively priced.

Fantasia bética; Piezas españolas (Aragonesa; Cubana; Montañesa; Andaluza); El amor brujo: Danza del terror. Three-cornered hat: 2 dances. La vida breve: Danza No. 2.

(M) ** EMI CDM7 64527-2 [id.]. Alicia de Larrocha.

Another of the vibrant early recitals by the young Alicia de Larrocha, deriving from the Spanish Hispavox label, this 1958 collection is well enough recorded but offers short measure; moreover it devotes too much space to music which sounds more vivid in orchestral dress, for all the pianist's colouristic skill. The four *Piezas españolas* are another matter and are presented with great spontaneity and idiomatic feeling, with the *Montañesa* particularly haunting. The programme closes with the *Fantasia bética*, which is played with much dash and brilliance, but de Larrocha's impulsiveness nearly runs away with her.

OPERA

La vida breve (complete).

(M) *** EMI CDM7 69590-2. De los Angeles, Higueras, Rivadeneyra, Cossutta, Moreno, Orfeon Donostiarra Ch., Nat. O of Spain, Frühbeck de Burgos.

La vida breve is a kind of Spanish *Cavalleria rusticana* without the melodrama. Unquestionably the opera's story is thin, the heroine expiring with a broken heart when her lover deserts her for another; but if the music for the final scene is weakened by a fundamental lack of drama in the plot, Frühbeck de Burgos makes the most of the poignancy of the closing moments. Victoria de los Angeles deepened her interpretation over the years and her imaginative colouring of the words gives a unique authority and evocation to her performance. *Vivan les que ri'an* is most expressively done, with Frühbeck following the soloist with great skill. The flamenco singer in Act II (Gabriel Moreno) also matches the realism of the idiom with an authentic 'folk' style. The other members of the cast are good without being memorable; but when this is primarily a solo vehicle for de los Angeles, and the orchestral interludes are managed so colloquially, thisis readily recommendable. The recording remains atmospheric, as well as having increased vividness and presence. It now fits conveniently on a single CD.

Farrenc, Louise (1804–75)

Nonet for strings and wind in E flat, Op. 38; (i) *Sextet for piano and wind in C min., Op. 40; Trio for flute, cello and piano in E min., Op. 45.*
(B) ** Carlton Dig. 30366 00302 [(M) id.]. (i) Diana Ambache; Ambache Chamber Ens.

Louise Farrenc (born Jeanne-Louise Dumont) studied under Reicha at the Paris Conservatoire. Then, at the age of seventeen, she married a flute player, so it is not surprising that she shows a ready facility in writing for woodwind instruments. Her scoring in the *Sextet* anticipates Poulenc, of nearly a century later, but Farrenc's music here is not witty; indeed it looks back towards Beethoven's *Piano and wind quintet* but without that master's imaginative development of ideas. The Hummelian *Nonet* (scored for five wind instruments and four strings, with double-bass in the place of second violin) is a much more spontaneous piece. It was popular in its day; Joachim presided over its well-attended première in 1850. The *Andante con moto* is a winning set of variations on charmingly *galant* melody, and the bustling Scherzo has a swinging tune for its middle section. Similarly the *Trio* has a songful *Andante* and the Scherzo fizzes with bravura, putting both Diana Ambache and the erstwhile flautist on their mettle. But in the last resort this is well-crafted music without a highly individual voice. The recording, though well balanced, is also too resonant to provide a clear internal focus.

Fauré, Gabriel (1845–1924)

Ballade for piano and orchestra, Op. 19.
(BB) **(*) Naxos 8.550754 [id.]. Thiollier, Nat. SO of Ireland, Antonio de Almeida – FRANCK: *Symphonic variations*; D'INDY: *Symphonie sur un air montagnard français*. **(*)

Naxos offer an intelligently planned coupling: none of these works is a concerto and all were written within a relatively brief time-span. François-Joël Thiollier shows some imagination and sensitivity in Fauré's lovely *Ballade*, which is not represented as generously on CD as it should be. The orchestral playing is perfectly acceptable, without being in any way out of the ordinary; likewise the recording. All the same, it is worth the money.

(i) *Ballade for piano and orchestra, Op. 19;* (ii) *Pavane, Op. 50;* (iii) *Pelléas et Mélisande* (incidental music); (iv) *Requiem, Op. 48.*
(M) ** Ph. 446 201-2. (i) Marie-Françoise Bucquet, Monte Carlo Op. O, Paul Capolongo; (ii–iv) Rotterdam PO; (iii) with Jill Gomez, cond. Zinman; (iv) with Ameling, Kruysen, Netherlands R. Ch., cond. Fournet.

A generous (74-minute) but somewhat mixed bag, recorded between 1970 and 1980. Unassuming, reticent and charming are adjectives that come to mind on hearing Bucquet's reading of the *Ballade*. The orchestra is somewhat recessed and the piano too forward, but the sound is very acceptable. Bucquet shows traces of impetuosity at times, but this remains a sympathetic and musical performance. Moreover Fauré's incidental music for *Pelléas et Mélisande* is beautifully played by the Rotterdam orchestra under David Zinman and, to make the selection complete, Jill Gomez gives a delightful account of the song, *The three blind daughters*, not previously recorded. David Zinman's refined approach suits Fauré admirably and there is a pervasive tenderness and delicacy (the *Sicilienne* is memorable). The recording too is naturally balanced and of good quality. So far so good, but unfortunately the Fournet performance of the *Requiem* is not very competitive. The singing of the Netherlands Radio Chorus is first class, but in most other respects this is a rather cool, almost routine account, and the balance makes both soloists and the organist, Daniel Chorzempa, seem too close.

(i) *Berceuse, Op. 116. Dolly* (suite), *Op. 56; Masques et bargamasques, Op. 112; Pelléas et Mélisande* (suite), *Op. 80;* (ii) *Shylock* (suite), *Op. 57.*
(BB) *** Naxos Dig. 8.553360 [id.]. Dublin RTE Sinf., John Giorgiadis; with (i) Michael Healy; (ii) Lynda Russell.

Eminently persuasive performances in every way. Starting with an exhilarating account of the *Overture* to *Masques et bergamasques*, one of Fauré's most winning inspirations, John Georgiadis and the RTE Sinfonietta (drawn from the RTE Concert Orchestra) consistently produce polished and cultured playing and present an ideal collection of his orchestral music. This is Fauré at his most outward-going, and Georgiadis with his rhythmic flair not only brings out the colour and vigour of the fast movements but, as a fine violinist himself, persuades his Irish players to draw out the expressive warmth of such numbers as *Tendresse* in the *Dolly suite*. *Masques et bergamasques*, the *Dolly suite* and the incidental music to *Pelléas et Mélisande* are all among his best-loved works, and it is good too to have the rarer music for the Shakespeare-based play, *Shylock*, complete with two vocal movements sweetly sung by Lynda Russell. Michael Healy is the expressive violin soloist in the lovely *Berceuse*. Warm, atmospheric recording, transferred at rather a low level.

Elégie in C min. (for cello and orchestra), *Op. 24.*

(M) *** Sony SBK 48278; *SBT 48278* [id.]. Leonard Rose, Phd. O, Ormandy – BLOCH: *Schelomo* ***; LALO: *Concerto* **(*); TCHAIKOVSKY: *Rococo variations.* ***

(B) *** DG Classikon 431 166-2 [(M) id. import]. Heinrich Schiff, New Philh. O, Mackerras – LALO: *Cello concerto;* SAINT-SAENS: *Cello concerto No. 1.* ***

An ardent yet not over-pressed account from Leonard Rose of Fauré's lovely *Elégie* which admirably captures its idiom and its feeling of burgeoning yet restrained ecstasy. The recording is close, but the cello image is natural and firm. The rest of this collection is also highly recommendable.

Heinrich Schiff gives an eloquent account of the *Elégie*, and he is finely accompanied and superbly recorded.

Pavane, Op. 60.

(B) *** Decca Eclipse Dig. 448 711-2; *448 711-4* [(M) id. import]. ASMF, Marriner – DURUFLE: *Requiem;* POULENC: *Gloria.* ***

Marriner's warmly elegant account of the famous *Pavane* is used effectively on this Decca disc as an interlude between Duruflé's *Requiem* and Poulenc's *Gloria*, both fine performances.

CHAMBER MUSIC

(i) *Andante in B flat, Op. 75; Berceuse, Op. 16;* (ii) *Cello sonatas Nos. 1 in D min., Op. 109; 2 in G min., Op. 117; Elégie, Op. 24;* (iii) *Fantaisie, Op. 79; Morceau de concours;* (i) *Morceau de lecture;* (ii) *Papillon, Op. 77;* (i) *Romance, Op. 28;* (ii) *Serenade in B min., Op. 98; Sicilienne, Op. 78;* (i) *Violin sonatas Nos. 1 in A, Op. 15; 2 in E min., Op. 108;* (i–ii) *Trio in D min., Op. 120.*

(B) *** EMI Rouge et Noir CZS5 69261-2 (2) [ZDMB 62545]. Jean-Philippe Collard; (i) Augustin Dumay; (ii) Frédéric Lodéon; (iii) Michel Debost.

Piano quartets Nos. (i; ii) *1 in C min., Op. 15;* (i; iii) *2 in G min., Op. 45; Piano quintets Nos. 1 in C min., Op. 89; 2 in D min., Op. 115;* (iii) *String quartet in E min., Op. 121.*

(B) **(*) EMI Rouge et Noir CZS5 69264-2 (2) [(M) id. import]. (i) Jean-Philippe Collard; (ii) Augustin Dumay, Bruno Pasquier, Frédéric Lodéon; (iii) Parrenin Qt.

Dumay and Collard bring different and equally valuable insights, and the performances of the *Piano quartets* are masterly. In addition, there are authoritative and idiomatic readings of the two *Piano quintets*, the *Piano trio*, the two *Cello sonatas*, on the first set, above (what a fine player Lodéon is!), and the enigmatic and other-worldly *Quartet*, Fauré's last utterance, plus all the smaller pieces. This is enormously civilized music whose rewards grow with each hearing; however, one has to accept that, because the Paris Salle Wagram was employed for the recordings (made between 1975 and 1978), close microphones have been used to counteract the hall's resonance. The remastering has both increased the sense of presence and brought a certain dryness to the ambient effect, although the string timbres are fresh.

Piano quartets Nos. 1 in C min., Op. 15; 2 in G min., Op. 45.

(BB) ** Discover Dig. DIDC 920231 [id.]. Sheuerer Piano Qt.

The Sheuerers (four siblings) display a real feeling for Fauré's elusive world, and the *C minor Quartet* is certainly successful in achieving an ardent, romantic flow in the outer movements, contrasted with a nimble Scherzo and a warm yet serene *Adagio*. Gertraud Scheuerer, the pianist, firmly recorded, plays with much character and holds the music-making together, and if her brother Franz leads the strings with a somewhat meagre timbre in the upper range, both viola and cello are more generous in tone, and the resonance of the Winterthur Studio provides plenty of fullness. While the Beaux Arts recordings on a Philips Duo are in a class of their own, we hope this inexpensive Discover disc may tempt newcomers to sample these lovely works.

(i–ii) *Piano quartets Nos. 1 in C min., Op. 15; 2 in G min., Op. 45;* (i; iii) *Piano quintets Nos. 1 in D min., Op. 89; 2 in C min., Op. 115;* (i–ii) *Piano trio in D min., Op. 120;* (iii) *String quartet in E min., Op. 121.*

(M) ** Erato/Warner 4509 96953-2 [id.]. (i) Jean Hubeau; (ii) Raymond Gallois-Montbrun, Colette Lequien, André Navarra; (iii) Quatuor Via Nova.

The Erato recordings come from the late 1960s and were part of a five-LP box which also included the *Violin* and *Cello sonatas* as well as the perceptive notes by Harry Halbreich, reproduced again here. The performances are all musicianly and dedicated but workmanlike rather than subtle, intelligent but not inspired. Jean Hubeau has nowhere near the imagination or feeling for phrasing and dynamic nuance that distinguishes Collard. The digitally remastered analogue recordings are perfectly acceptable – decent but no more.

Piano trio in D min., Op. 120.
(B) (*) Sony SBK 62413; *SBT 62413* [id.]. Roth Trio – DEBUSSY; RAVEL: *Quartets.* **(*)

This performance has a certain interest in that it features André Previn playing chamber music in 1961 during his time in Hollywood. He is backwardly balanced, but his colleagues in the Roth Trio do not earn their limelight for, although they often play ardently, their intonation is not always secure.

Violin sonatas Nos. 1 in A, Op. 13; 2 in E min., Op. 108.
(M) *** Ph. 426 384-2. Arthur Grumiaux, Paul Crossley – FRANCK: *Sonata.* **(*)

Violin sonatas Nos. 1–2; Andante, Op. 75; Berceuse, Op. 16.
(BB) **(*) ASV Dig. CDQS 6170 [(M) id. import]. Fujikawa, Osorio.

Violin sonatas Nos. 1 in A, Op. 13; 2 in E min., Op. 108; Andante in B flat, Op. 75; Berceuse, Op. 16; Romance in B flat, Op. 28.
(BB) *** Naxos Dig. 8.550906 [id.]. Dong-Suk Kang, Pascal Devoyon.

From Naxos comes a version from an accomplished stylist, Dong-Suk Kang, splendidly partnered by Pascal Devoyon. Without disturbing our allegiance to other earlier issues (Grumiaux–Crossley among them, although they offer less music), this is a welcome newcomer – and very good value for money.

These *Sonatas* are beautifully played and recorded on the Philips reissue. Moreover the two artists sound as if they are in the living-room; the acoustic is warm, lively and well balanced. An excellent mid-priced recommendation.

Mayumi Fujikawa and Jorge Federico Osorio produce playing of the highest accomplishment and finesse. There is genuine passion here (particularly in the opening movement of the *E minor Sonata*) and real commitment. They are recorded in a resonant hall, and the fairly close microphones are not always flattering to the violin's upper range under stress, although not too much need be made of this: Fujikawa often makes a beautiful sound, and particularly so in the lovely *Berceuse*. For the sonatas, this would not be a first choice; but for those with limited budgets the collection is excellent value.

Violin sonata No. 2 in E min., Op. 108.
(BB) *(*) Koch Discover DICD 920306 [id.]. Josef Suk, Josef Hala – FRANCK; RAVEL: *Violin sonatas.* *(*)

The Suk–Hala account of Fauré's subtle and elusive *E minor Sonata*, Op. 108, originally appeared in the 1960s and, though the recording cannot be said to do full justice to Suk's glorious tone, the performance is a fine one. But while there are no artistic shortcomings for which allowances need be made, some tolerance is called for on sonic grounds.

PIANO MUSIC

Ballade in F sharp, Op. 19 (original solo piano version); *Barcarolles Nos. 1–13* (complete).
(BB) * Naxos Dig. 8.553634 [id.]. Pierre-Alain Volondat.

In the lowest price-range, the young French pianist Pierre-Alain Volondat couples the *Ballade* in its original solo form and the *Barcarolles*. Unfortunately it is no bargain: the playing is very ordinary and wanting in the subtleties of sonority and nuance so important in this repertoire. With pianists like Collard, Rogé and Crossley in the catalogue, to acquire this would be a false economy. Given the competition, not recommended.

Ballade in F sharp, Op. 19; Nocturnes Nos. 1–13 (complete); *9 Préludes, Op. 103; Theme and variations in C sharp min., Op. 73.*
(B) *** EMI Rouge et Noir CZS5 69437-2 (2) [ZDMB 69149]. Jean-Philippe Collard.

This is glorious music which ranges from the gently reflective to the profoundly searching. The *Nocturnes* offer a glimpse of Fauré's art at its most inward and subtle; and they take a greater hold of the listener at each hearing, the quiet-spoken reticence proving more eloquent than one would ever suspect. The *Préludes* are comparably intimate, and this is all music to which Jean-Philippe Collard is wholly attuned. His account of the *Theme and variations* is no less masterly, combining the utmost tonal refinement and sensitivity with striking keyboard authority. The recording is good, though it has not the bloom and body of the very finest piano records.

Barcarolles Nos. 1–13; (i) *Dolly. Impromptus Nos. 1–5; Mazurka, Op. 32; Pièces brèves Nos. 1–8, Op. 84; Romances sans paroles Nos. 1–3;* (i) *Souvenir de Bayreuth. Valses-caprices Nos. 1–4.*
(B) **(*) EMI Rouge et Noir CZS5 69431-2 (2) [(M) id. import]. Jean-Philippe Collard, (i) with Rigutto.

Jean-Philippe Collard has the qualities of reticence yet ardour, subtlety and poetic feeling to penetrate Fauré's intimate world but, while Collard has exceptional beauty and refinement of tone at all dynamic levels, the only regret is that full justice is not done to it by the French engineers.

Impromptus Nos. 1–6; 10 Préludes, Op. 103.
(BB) *(*) Naxos Dig. 8.553740 [id.]. Pierre-Alain Volondat.

Pierre-Alain Volondat produces a timbre suitable for Fauré, but he often seems to lose sight of any sense of pulse, flow or continuity. There is not an ugly sound anywhere, but the absence of movement in some of the *Préludes* produces an almost neurasthenic effect. He is well recorded.

Nocturnes Nos. 1–6; Theme and variations in C sharp min., Op. 73.
(BB) ** Naxos Dig. 8.550794 [id.]. Jean Martin.

Nocturnes Nos. 7–13; Préludes, Op. 103/3 & 9; 3 Romances sans paroles, Op. 17.
(BB) ** Naxos Dig. 8.550795 [id.]. Jean Martin.

Immensely civilized yet never aloof, the *Nocturnes* take a greater hold of the listener at each hearing. The French pianist Jean Martin is obviously at home here, although he does not always catch the full delicacy of feeling, the quiet-spoken reticence which is so eloquent. He is at his best in the earlier *Nocturnes*. In the later works, notably the elusive *F sharp minor* (No. 12) and *E minor* (No. 13), his approach seems too direct and positive. The three *Songs without words* come off well, but the familiar *Theme and variations*, although strongly characterized, finds more subtlety in the hands of Collard. Like Collard, Martin is fairly closely recorded in the Clara Wieck Auditorium, Heidelberg, a not unsympathetic acoustic, but greater distancing aids the effect of this music.

9 Préludes, Op. 103; Theme and variations, Op. 73; Adagietto, Op. 84/5; Capriccio, Op. 84/1; Improvisation, Op. 84/4.
(M) *** Saga EC 3397-2 [id.]. Albert Ferber.

This Saga disc is particularly valuable in making available, relatively inexpensively, the *Nine Préludes*, Op. 103, composed in 1909–10. These will repay the repeated attention the gramophone affords, for they are not immediately accessible yet are deeply rewarding. The *Theme and variations* is more extrovert and inventive in an instantly appealing way. It too is given a well-characterized and finely considered reading and there are some welcome smaller pieces. Albert Ferber is imaginative, poetic and content to let the music speak for itself. He is well recorded, too.

VOCAL MUSIC

Mélodies (complete): (i) *L'Absent;* (ii) *Accompagnement; Après un rêve; Arpège; Aubade;* (i) *Au bord de l'eau;* (ii) *Au cimetière; Aurore;* (i) *L'aurore; Automne;* (ii) *Barcarolle; Les berceaux; La bonne chanson* (songcycle), *Op. 61;* (i) *2 Cantiques (En prière; Noël); C'est la paix!; Chanson;* (ii) *Chanson d'amour;* (i) *La chanson d'Eve* (song-cycle), *Op. 95;* (ii) *Chanson du pêcheur; Chanson de Shylock; Chant d'automne; Clair de lune; Dans la forêt de septembre;* (i) *Dans les ruines d'une abbaye;* (ii) *Le Don silencieux;* (i) *2 Duos for 2 sopranos (Puisqu'ici-bas; Tarantelle); La Fée aux chansons; Fleur jetée;* (ii) *La fleur qui va sur l'eau; L'horizon chimérique* (song-cycle), *Op. 118; Hymne; Ici-bas!;* (i) *Les jardins clos* (song-cycle), *Op. 106;* (ii) *Larmes; Lydia; Madrigal de Shylock; Mai; Les matelots;* (i) *Mélisande's song; 5 Mélodies de Venise;* (ii) *Mirages* (song-cycle), *Op. 113;* (i) *Nell;* (ii) *Nocturne;* (i) *Notre amour; Le papillon et la fleur; Le parfum impérissable; Le pays des rêves;* (ii) *Pleurs d'or; Le plus doux chemin; 3 Poèmes de jour; Les présents; Prison; Le ramier; La rançon;* (i) *Rêve d'amour; La rose; Les roses d'Ispahan; Le secret;* (ii) *Sérénade du bourgeois gentilhomme; Sérénade toscane;* (i) *Seule; Soir;* (ii) *Spleen; Sylvie; Tristesse;* (i) *Vocalise-étude;* (ii) *Le voyageur.*
(M) *** EMI CMS7 64079-2 (4) [ZDMD 64079]. (i) Elly Ameling; (ii) Gérard Souzay; Dalton Baldwin.

The songs were written over the fullest span of Fauré's life, during a period of no less than 60 years, starting with a jolly waltz-song written when the composer was sixteen. The most striking melodies tend to come in the earlier songs – with the second of the four CDs offering many favourite items like *Chanson d'amour*, winningly done by Souzay, and *Les roses d'Ispahan* bringing a ravishing example of Ameling at her most radiant. Even so, the style is astonishingly consistent throughout. In the late cycles, *La chanson d'Eve*, *Les jardins clos*, *Mirages* and *L'horizon chimérique*, there is an extra subtlety in the composer's restraint; but even in that last period Fauré allowed himself one extrovert return to an earlier style, a simple, jaunty song for soprano celebrating the Armistice of 1918, *C'est la paix!*. Souzay is not quite as even in his vocal production as at the beginning of his career, but no baritone of recent years has surpassed him in this repertory, and Ameling is at her very peak throughout, fresh and even in line, with beautiful colourings. The texts of the songs are given only in French.

Mélodies: *Après un rêve; Au bord de l'eau; Aurore; Clair de lune; Dans les ruines d'une abbaye; En sourdine; Fleur; Green; Ici-bas; Mai; Mandoline; Nell; Nocturne; Notre amour; Le papillon et la fleur; Le pays des rêves; Les présents; Prison; Les roses d'Ispahan; Le secret; Soir.*

(BB) *** Virgin Classics Dig. Double VBS5 61433-2 [CDVB 61433]. Rachel Yakar, Claude Lavoix (with BIZET: *Pastorale; Rose d'amour; Sonnet;* CHABRIER: *Chanson pour Jeanne; L'île heureuse; Lied* ***) – HAHN: *Mélodies*. ***

Rachel Yakar with her warm, very French-sounding timbre is an ideal interpreter of French mélodie, bringing out the subtleties of word-meaning, though it is a pity that in this super-bargain double-disc issue no texts are provided, only a cursory survey of the genre. The selection of 22 songs could hardly be more attractive, with settings of individual poets grouped together, so that early and late settings of Verlaine can be compared and contrasted. Excellent (1991) recording from Radio France. Coupled with an equally imaginative collection of Hahn songs, plus extra cherishable items from Bizet and Chabrier, it is a delightful issue.

Requiem, Op. 48.

(B) *** Sony SBK 67182; *SBT 67182* [id.]. Lucia Popp, Siegmund Nimsgern, Amb. S., New Philh. O, Andrew Davis – DURUFLE: *Requiem*. ***

(B) **(*) EMI CZS5 69647-2 (2) [CDZB 69647]. Rayner Cook, Burrowes, CBSO Ch., CBSO, Frémaux – BERLIOZ: *Requiem*. **

Requiem; Pavane, Op. 50.

(M) *** Carlton Classics Dig. 30366 0009-2 [id.]. Aled Jones, Stephen Roberts, London Symphony Ch., RPO, Hickox – BERNSTEIN: *Chichester Psalms*. ***

(M) *** EMI CDM7 64634-2 [id.]. Sheila Armstrong, Fischer-Dieskau, Edinburgh Festival Ch., O de Paris, Barenboim – BACH: *Magnificat*. **

(B) **(*) [EMI Red Line CDR5 69858]. Chilcott, Carol Case, King's College, Cambridge, Ch., New Philh. O, Willcocks – PALESTRINA: *Missa Papae Marcelli*. **

(i) *Requiem, Op. 48. Masques et bergamasques; Pelléas et Mélisande (suite), Op. 80; Pénélope: Prélude.*

(M) *(*) Decca 452 304-2 [id.]. SRO, Ansermet; (i) with Danco, Souzay, L'Union Chorale de la Tour de Peitz.

(i) *Requiem, Op. 48;* (ii) *Cantique de Jean Racine, Op. 11;* (ii; iii) *Messe basse.*

(BB) *** Naxos Dig. 8.550765 [id.]. Beckley, Gedge, Schola Cantorum of Oxford, Oxford Camerata, Summerly (with DE SEVERAC: *Tantum ergo;* VIERNE: *Andantino;* with Colm Carey, organ ***).

(B) *** Decca Double 436 486-2 (2) [(M) id. import]. (i) Jonathon Bond, Benjamin Luxon; (ii) Stephen Cleobury; (iii) Andrew Brunt; (i–iii) St John's College, Cambridge, Ch., Guest (i) with ASMF – DURUFLE: *Requiem* etc.; POULENC: *Mass* etc. ***

(i) *Requiem, Op. 48;* (ii) *Messe basse.*

(B) **(*) EMI CfP Dig. CDCFP 6072 [id.]. (i) Arleen Augér, Benjamin Luxon; (ii) Paul Smy; King's College, Cambridge. Ch., Ledger.

The directness and clarity of Andrew Davis's reading go with a concentrated, dedicated manner and a masterly control of texture to bring out the purity and beauty of Fauré's orchestration to the full. Moreover the fresh vigour of the choral singing achieves an admirable balance between ecstasy and restraint in this most elusive of Requiem settings. The style of the phrasing is not as openly expressive as in some other versions, but that is in character with the intimacy of the reading, culminating in a wonderfully measured and intense account of the final *In Paradisum*. Lucia Popp is both rich and pure, and Siegmund Nimsgern (if less memorable) is refined in tone and detailed in his pointing. The recording, made in a church, matches the intimate manner and, with its equally fine Duruflé coupling, this is very highly recommendable.

The Naxos version makes an excellent super-bargain choice for the *Requiem* in its original orchestration.

The fresh, forward choral tone goes with a direct, unmannered interpretation from Jeremy Summerly, with soloists comparably fresh-toned and English-sounding. The recording brings out the colourings of the orchestra in sharp detail, with the organ and brass vividly caught. The performance of the *Messe basse* is comparably direct, made to sound a little square at times, but *Le cantique de Jean Racine* is most winningly done. The little meditative organ piece by Vierne and the unaccompanied motet by de Séverac are pleasing makeweights.

Richard Hickox opts for the regular full-scale text of the *Requiem*, yet at speeds rather faster than usual – no faster than those marked – he presents a fresh, easily flowing view, rather akin to John Rutter's using the original chamber scoring on his full-price Collegium issue. Aled Jones sings very sweetly in *Pie Jesu*. With its generous and equally successful coupling, this makes a strong alternative recommendation.

Barenboim's 1975 recording has been splendidly remastered. The recording was always first class, rich and full-bodied, and now the choral sound is firmer and better focused without loss of atmosphere: the moment when the trumpets enter in the *Sanctus* at the cry '*Hosanna in excelsis!*' is vibrant indeed. The Edinburgh Festival Chorus is freshly responsive so that, although the sound is beefier, the effect is never heavy and the performance is given a strong dimension of drama. Yet there is splendidly pure singing from Sheila Armstrong, and her *Pie Jesu* is even more successful here than with de los Angeles. Fischer-Dieskau is not quite as mellifluous as in his earlier account with Cluytens, but he brings a greater sense of drama. A first-rate version, including a sensitive account of the *Pavane*. It is well worth considering in the mid-price range, although the CD transfer of Bach's *Magnificat* which provides a generous coupling is less successful, with rather edgy sound.

Frémaux's alternative EMI version is attractively atmospheric, the recording comparatively recessed. Frémaux has a moulded style which does not spill over into too much expressiveness, and there is a natural warmth about this performance that is highly persuasive. Norma Burrowes sings beautifully, her innocent style most engaging. However, this is coupled with a much less recommendable set of the Berlioz *Requiem*.

The St John's account has a magic that works from the opening bars onwards. Jonathon Bond and Benjamin Luxon are highly sympathetic soloists and the 1975 (originally Argo) recording is every bit as impressive as its digital competitors, while the smaller scale of the conception is probably nearer to Fauré's original conception. The Double Decca reissue offers exceptionally generous couplings, not only the Duruflé *Requiem* but other fine music by both Duruflé and Poulenc.

The King's style is very much in the English cathedral tradition. On the earlier (1967) version, the solo soprano role is taken appealingly by a boy treble, Robert Chilcott. The recording, incidentally, was made in Trinity College Chapel and is very fine and splendidly remastered. The performance is eloquent and warmly moving, although some may feel its Anglican accents unidiomatic. The modest coupling is a melting version of the famous *Pavane*, with Gareth Morris playing the flute solo, given lovely, rich sound. As can be seen, this recording (with the *Pavane*) is available only in the USA, on EMI's budget Red Line label, including also a moderately effective account of Palestrina's most famous Mass.

In the later (1982) digital King's College recording, Ledger presents the *Requiem* on a small scale, with unusual restraint. The digital recording allows many details of scoring to register that are normally hazed over. The singing is refreshingly direct, but anyone who warms to the touch of sensuousness in the work, its Gallic quality, may well find a degree of disappointment, though the *Sanctus* conveys drama. This is less beautiful a performance than the earlier one, now also reissued, which was made with the same choir by Sir David Willcocks. On the Classics for Pleasure reissue the comparatively brief *Messe basse*, also sweetly melodic, makes a rather more apt but still not generous alternative coupling.

It was tempting for Decca to reissue this Ansermet repertoire in the Classic Sound series. The *Requiem* is very early stereo indeed (1955), but the vividly clear recording only serves to emphasize the rather thin-toned contribution of the chorus. The solo singing is good, but this CD is most notable for the orchestral items, recorded six years later: sympathetic and stylish performances, highly regarded in their day and still sounding well.

Ferguson, Howard (born 1908)

(i) *Concerto for piano and string orchestra;* (ii) *Amore langueo, Op. 18.*

(M) *** EMI Dig. CDM7 64738-2. (i) Howard Shelley; (ii) Martyn Hill, L. Symphony Ch.; City of L. Sinfonia, Hickox – FINZI: *Eclogue*. ***

Ferguson was a fine pianist in his younger days, and his concerto has something in common with the lyrical feeling of John Ireland's comparable work. As with Ireland, the finale is gay and melodically carefree. Howard Shelley's performance is admirable and Hickox secures a highly sympathetic response from the City of London Sinfonia string section. *Amore langueo* is an extended cantata, lasting just over half an hour. To the medieval mind, spiritual and secular love were not always seen as separate experiences. The setting, for tenor solo and semi-chorus, with a strong contribution from Martyn Hill, brings a powerful response in the present performance, and Ferguson's music moves with remarkable ease from the depiction of Christ's suffering on the Cross to the sometimes even playful atmosphere of lovers in the bedchamber. An unusual and rewarding piece, recorded with great vividness on CD.

Octet, Op. 4.

(M) (***) Dutton Lab. CDAX 8014 [id. full price]. Juler, James, Dennis Brain, Merrett, Griller Qt – BAX: *Nonet;* MOERAN: *String trio;* DELIUS: *Violin sonata No. 3.* (***)

Now ninety, Howard Ferguson has enjoyed something of a revival, thanks to smaller record producers such as Chandos and Hyperion. Dutton Laboratories are to be congratulated for restoring the 1943 Decca recording of his *Octet* by the Griller Quartet and the 22-year-old Dennis Brain in such fresh and present sound. This is civilized, finely crafted music in the received tradition, and none the worse for that.

Fernström, John (1897–1961)

Wind quintet, Op. 59.

(BB) ** Naxos Dig. 8.553050 [id.]. Oslo Wind Ens. – KVANDAL; NIELSEN: *Wind quintets.* **

The Swedish composer John Fernström was born in Ichang in China but spent most of his life in southern Sweden. He was active as an orchestral player and manager in Malmö, Lund and Hälsingborg. He composed no fewer than 12 symphonies and a variety of instrumental works in a generally neo-classical style. (Older readers may remember a charming *Concertino for flute, female voices and strings* that was coupled with André Gertler's LP of the Larsson *Violin concerto*.) This *Wind quintet* comes from 1943 and is pleasing and well crafted, though the thematic invention is not particularly individual. Excellent playing from the Oslo Wind Ensemble, but the recording, made in a rather small Norwegian Radio studio, is a bit bright and forward.

Fetler, Paul (born 1920)

Contrasts for orchestra.

(M) *** Mercury (IMS) 434 335-2 [id.]. Minneapolis SO, Dorati – AURIC: *Overture;* FRANCAIX: *Piano concertino;* MILHAUD: *Le boeuf sur le toit;* SATIE: *Parade.* ***

Paul Fetler's four-movement sinfonietta, *Contrasts*, is based on four notes (B flat, F, C, A flat), yet it is as impressive for its fine use of brass sonorities in the slow movement as for the neo-classical athleticism of the opening *Allegro* and the pervading energy of the finale where everything comes together. It is an eclectic work yet has distinct character. The performance is first rate, and so is the Mercury recording.

Field, John (1782–1837)

Piano concertos Nos. 1 in E flat, H.27; 3 in E flat, H.32.

(BB) *** Naxos Dig. 8.553770 [id.]. Benjamin Frith, Northern Sinfonia, David Haslam.

Benjamin Frith has already given us the Mendelssohn and Weber concertos, and the Field concertos are not a far call from them. Field performed the *First Concerto in E flat* as early as 1799, but it underwent numerous revisions before it was published in St Petersburg in 1814. The *Third*, also in E flat, was dedicated to his mentor, Muzio Clementi, who had taken him to Paris and Vienna in the early years of the century. Rival recordings from Míceál O'Rourke (Chandos) and John O'Conor (Telarc) are both at full price, so this young artist has the bargain field to himself. His playing is characteristically sensitive and fresh, and he is well supported by the Northern Sinfonia and David Haslam. Very good, warm recording, in a decent acoustic.

Finzi, Gerald (1901–56)

Eclogue for piano and string orchestra.

(M) *** EMI Dig. CDM7 64738-2. Howard Shelley, City of L. Sinfonia, Hickox – FERGUSON: *Piano concerto No. 2* etc. ***

(B) *** EMI Dig. CD-EMX 2239 [(M) id.]. Piers Lane, RLPO, Handley – DELIUS: *Piano concerto;* VAUGHAN WILLIAMS: *Piano concerto*. ***

This is the central movement of an uncompleted piano concerto which the composer decided could stand on its own. It was Howard Ferguson who edited the final manuscript and set the title, and it is appropriate that this essentially valedictory piece should be coupled with his own concerto. The mood is tranquil yet haunting, and Shelley's performance brings out all its serene lyricism. The recording is admirably realistic.

Brief as it is, this concertante piece is a haunting work, a valuable makeweight for the Eminence coupling of the Delius and Vaughan Williams *Piano concertos*. Piers Lane gives it a tenderly sympathetic reading, even if this does not quite match in magic the Howard Shelley version on EMI.

Grand Fantasia and Toccata (for piano and orchestra), *Op. 38;* (ii) *Intimations of Immortality, Op. 29.*

(M) *** EMI Dig. CDM7 64720-2 [id.]. (i) Philip Fowke; (ii) Philip Langridge, RLPO Ch.; RLPO, Hickox.

Finzi's setting of Wordsworth, which is undoubtedly Elgarian in feeling, is delightfully spontaneous. His flamboyant presentation of *Now, while the birds thus sing a joyous song* – with its exuberant syncopations – even features a xylophone solo. The rich, lyrical cantilena of this music brings constant reminders of the Elgar of *Gerontius*, while the writing remains essentially within the pastoral tradition of English song-setting. The performance here is wholly committed, with the fervour of the chorus echoing the dedication of the soloist. The choral recording is both spacious and brilliant. The coupling is another fascinatingly eclectic piece, this time for piano and orchestra. The Bachian *Grand fantasia* is followed by a genial *Toccata*, fugal in style. The piece is played compellingly by Philip Fowke, and Hickox is a fine partner. Again vividly realistic sound. Highly recommended.

Interlude in A min.

(M) *** Carlton Dig. 30366 00962 [id.]. Robin Canter, Medici Qt (members) – BRITTEN: *6 Metamorphoses after Ovid* etc. ***

Like most of the Britten oboe works on the disc, Finzi's *Interlude* for oboe quartet, ten minutes long, dates from the 1930s, a warmly evocative piece in his characteristic pastoral style, subtly different from that of his friend and mentor, Vaughan Williams. Canter and the Medici Quartet play it with the same warmth and sympathy as in the Britten *Phantasy* for the same combination.

Dies natalis.

(M) *** EMI CDM5 65588-2 [id.]. Wilfred Brown, ECO, Christopher Finzi – HOLST: *Choral fantasia; Psalm 86;* VAUGHAN WILLIAMS: *5 Mystical songs* etc. ***

Dies natalis is one of Finzi's most sensitive and deeply felt works, using meditative texts by the seventeenth-century writer, Thomas Traherne, on the theme of Christ's nativity. Finzi's profound response to the words inspires five intensely beautiful songs; only the central *Rapture*, subtitled *Danza*, provides vigorous contrast to the mood of contemplation. Finzi's setting is sung well here by Wilfred Brown. In a way, one may regard this as a preparation for Britten's later achievement in his orchestral song-cycles, and this record must be recommended to all interested in modern English song setting. The remastered recording sounds wonderfully fresh and is naturally balanced within a glowing acoustic. What a beautiful work this is!

Earth and air and rain (song-cycle to words by Thomas Hardy).

(BB) *** Belart 461 491-2 [(M) id. import]. Benjamin Luxon, David Williamson – BUTTERWORTH: *A Shropshire Lad* etc. ***

These distinctive Finzi settings of Hardy make an ideal coupling for the outstanding performances of Butterworth on the same disc. There is sometimes a flavour of Vaughan Williams and, in *When I set out for Lyonnesse*, a distinct reminder of Stanford's *Songs of the sea*. But in the touching *Waiting both* and the dramatic *Clock of the years*, Luxon demonstrates the versatility of Finzi's word-settings. Excellent accompaniments from David Williamson – his gentle postlude for the final song, *Proud songsters*, ends the cycle movingly. Fine mid-1970s (originally Argo) recording.

God is gone up; Lo, the full, final sacrifice; Magnificat.

(M) *** EMI Dig. CDM5 65595-2. King's College, Cambridge, Ch., Cleobury; Farnes – BAX: *Choral music;* VAUGHAN WILLIAMS: *Mass*. ***

The three Finzi choral pieces with organ accompaniment provide attractive contrasts to the unaccompanied Bax pieces on a beautifully planned disc which shows the King's College choir at its finest and which now includes a beautiful analogue recording of the Vaughan Williams *Mass*, recorded two decades earlier. Both the extended anthem, *Lo, the full, final sacrifice*, setting Richard Crashaw's version of an Aquinas hymn, and the *Magnificat* were commissioned works, the one for St Matthew's, Northampton, the other for Massachusetts; in their rich climaxes they bring out a dramatic side in Finzi along with his gentle beauty, splendidly conveyed by the King's choir. The recording, made in the Chapel, is so nicely balanced that part-writing is clear even against the ample acoustic.

Flotow, Friedrich (1812–83)

Martha (complete).

(M) *** RCA 74321 32231-2 (2). Popp, Soffel, Jerusalem, Nimsgern, Ridderbusch, Bav. R. Ch. and O, Wallberg.

Martha is a charming opera, and the cast of this 1978 recording (originating with Eurodisc) is as near perfect as could be imagined. Lucia Popp is a splendid Lady Harriet, the voice rich and full yet riding the ensembles with jewelled accuracy. Doris Soffel is no less characterful as Nancy, and Siegfried Jerusalem is in his element as the hero, Lionel, singing ardently throughout. Siegmund Nimsgern is an excellent Lord Tristan, and Karl Ridderbusch matches his genial gusto. Wallberg's direction is marvellously spirited and the opera gathers pace as it proceeds. The Bavarian Radio Chorus sings with joyous precision and the orchestral playing sparkles. The first-class recording has been vividly transferred, though there is a touch of edge on the voices of Lady Harriet and Nancy. The libretto promised on the back of the box is in German only, but the story of this opera is very easy to follow.

Forqueray, Antoine (1671–1745)

Harpsichord suites Nos. 1 in D min.; 3 in D; 5 in C min.

(BB) *** Naxos 8.553407 [id.]. Luc Beauséjour (harpsichord).

These suites are transcriptions of music for the viol of uncertain provenance. They were long thought to be by Forqueray's son, Jean-Baptiste, taking advantage of his father's posthumous reputation and the fact that Antoine's music remained unpublished in his lifetime. But they could possibly be the work of his second wife, who was an accomplished musician. Whatever the case may be, the music itself is of quality and originality, and it is well served by the Canadian harpsichordist, Luc Beauséjour, as recorded at the Church of St Alphonse-de-Rodriguez in Quebec. He plays with great flair and zest, and the sound is first class.

Françaix, Jean (born 1912)

Piano concertino.

(M) *** Mercury (IMS) 434 335-2 [id.]. Claude Françaix, LSO, Dorati – AURIC: *Overture;* FETLER: *Contrasts;* MILHAUD: *Le boeuf sur le toit;* SATIE: *Parade.* ***

Claude Françaix, the composer's daughter and a pupil of Nadia Boulanger, partnered by Dorati made the first recommendable stereo recording of this delectable, miniature, four-movement *Concertino* in 1965. The conductor's touch is deliciously light in the outer movements and the pianist's touch is neat and accomplished. The Scherzo is also colourful but the gentle slow movement is the final test, and this is taken a fraction too fast. However, the performance is undoubtedly successful overall, and the composer's delicate effects in the winsome finale are particularly successful when the Mercury sound-picture is so lucid.

Franck, César (1822–90)

Le chasseur maudit; (i) *Les Djinns. Les Eolides; Rédemption.*

(M) ** EMI CDM5 65153-2. (i) Aldo Ciccolini; O Nat. de Belgique, André Cluytens.

When this collection was first issued on LP in 1963, we admired the performances but commented (in Volume IV of the *Stereo Record Guide*) that the reason why the programme overall is not a success is that 'the aesthetic which inspired the music is no longer acceptable and the music itself is not of sufficient interest to overcome its outdated philosophy'. We continued: 'Indeed *Rédemption*, which was originally the orchestral centrepiece of an ambitious two-part choral work, was a failure at its first performance. *Les Eolides* has some imaginative orchestration and the closing pages of *Les Djinns* (for piano and orchestra) are effective simply because the rhetoric diminishes with the music's structural decrescendo. But the one inspiration here, our old friend *The accursed huntsman*, is worth all the rest put together.' While this dismissive statement may still be true in part (certainly there is no doubting the vitality of *Le chasseur maudit*), later recordings (by Barenboim, among others) have shown that *Rédemption* and certainly *Les Eolides* have been underrated, while Ashkenazy has made an excellent case for *Les Djinns*. Cluytens and the Belgian orchestra failed to find the *tendresse* of approach that can make much of this writing glow, and certainly here the opening of *Les Djinns* seems unnecessarily melodramatic, even though Ciccolini later finds an attractive affinity with the *Symphonic variations*. Moreover the rather dated, 1960s stereo, though not lacking fullness and atmosphere, is not kind to the Belgian violins, which sound a bit whiskery.

Symphonic poems: *La chasseur maudit; Les Eolides.*
(M) ** Decca 452 890-2 [id.]. SRO, Ansermet – CHABRIER: *España* etc. ***

Ansermet's narrative detail, not achieved at the expense of drama or momentum, means that these two symphonic poems communicate strongly, even if the string-playing in *Les Eolides* is lacking in allure. The remastering flatters these brilliantly wide-ranging recordings from 1964 and 1967, reissued in Decca's Classic Sound series.

Symphonic variations for piano and orchestra.
✿ (B) *** Decca 433 628-2 [(M) id. import]. Clifford Curzon, LPO, Sir Adrian Boult – GRIEG: *Concerto* ***; SCHUMANN: *Concerto*. **(*)
(M) *** Decca 425 082-2 [id.]. Curzon, LPO, Boult – BRAHMS: *Piano concerto No. 1;* LITOLFF: *Scherzo*. ***
(M) *** RCA 09026 61863-2 [id.]. Rubinstein; Symphony of the Air, Wallenstein (with PROKOFIEV: *Love for 3 oranges: March* ***) – FALLA: *Nights in the gardens of Spain* etc. SAINT-SAENS: *Concerto No. 2*. **(*)
(M) (**(*)) EMI mono CDM5 66597-2 [id.]. Walter Gieseking, Philh. O, Karajan – GRIEG: *Piano concerto;* SCHUMANN: *Piano concerto*. (**(*))
(BB) **(*) ASV Dig. CDQS 6092 [(M) id.]. Osorio, RPO, Bátiz – RAVEL: *Left-hand concerto* ***; SAINT-SAENS: *Wedding-cake* ***; SCHUMANN: *Concerto*. **(*)
(BB) **(*) Naxos 8.550754 [id.]. Thiollier, Nat. SO of Ireland, Antonio de Almeida – FAURE: *Ballade;* D'INDY: *Symphonie sur un chant montagnard français*. **(*)
(M) (**) Avid mono AMC 593 [id.]. Myra Hess, CBSO, Cameron – GRIEG; SCHUMANN: *Piano concertos*. (**)
(BB) *(*) EMI Seraphim CES5 68522-2 (2) [CDEB 68522]. John Ogdon, Philh. O, Barbirolli – GRIEG: *Concerto* *(*); *Peer Gynt* ***; SCHUMANN: *Concerto*. *(*)

Clifford Curzon's 1959 recording of the Franck *Variations* has stood the test of time; even after three decades and more there is no finer version. It is an engagingly fresh reading, as notable for its impulse and rhythmic felicity as for its poetry. The vintage Decca recording is naturally balanced and has been transferred to CD without loss of bloom. The Grieg *Concerto* coupling is hardly less desirable, and there is also an alternative coupling with Brahms and Litolff, reissued in Decca's Classic Sound series.

Rubinstein's recording of the *Symphonic variations* was the first to appear in stereo, and it remains one of the finest available recorded performances of it. There is refinement and charm, yet his bravura tautens the structure while his warmth and freedom prevent it from seeming hard or in any way aggressive. The 1958 recording was made in the Manhattan Center, New York City, and a warm atmosphere in this work is far preferable to crystal clarity. The two solo encores are marvellously done, particularly the Prokofiev *March*.

Gieseking's performance dates from 1951 and appears now for the first time. Artistically it belongs among the very finest accounts of the work that were made in the 1950s. Why, one wonders, was it withheld from publication, given its many beauties and the wonderful orchestral support the Philharmonia and Karajan give? Possibly the fact that once or twice the last note of a phrase does not 'speak' as Gieseking might have wished it to do – but, more likely perhaps, the piano has one or two notes that are not in perfect condition and which might be thought to prove irksome on repetition. To be truthful, it is a small price to pay for playing of such distinction and poetic feeling.

The ASV super-bargain disc offers fine performances of four concertante works including a really outstanding version of the Ravel *Left-hand concerto* and it adds up to more than the sum of its parts. It can receive a strong recommendation, for reservations about the Franck performance are minor. It has both poetry and impulse and lacks only a little in sparkle at the very end. It is very well recorded.

Naxos's coupling is intelligent enough. But it would be idle to pretend that their anthology offers playing as distinguished as, say, Curzon. François-Joël Thiollier shows some imagination, and the orchestral playing is perfectly acceptable without being in any way distinguished. All the same, many will find it tempting at this price.

Myra Hess's account of the *Symphonic variations* with the City of Birmingham orchestra under Basil Cameron was recorded during the war years and has never appeared before on CD. Nor, as far as we know, has her Schumann with Walter Goehr, with which it is coupled. As one might expect, it is a mellifluous, lyrical and beautifully proportioned reading, totally devoid of egotism. The sound is clear, but these Avid transfers bring a curious meagreness of ambience and lack of natural fullness: the effect of the remastering is not as entirely satisfying as the way in which the Dutton transfers are managed.

John Ogdon opens in improvisatory style and the result is curiously unspontaneous; the best section is the finale, where a certain rhythmic spring catches the listener's previously flagging interest. Good (1963) recording.

(i) *Symphonic variations for piano and orchestra;* (ii) *Symphony in D min.; Les Eolides;* (iii) *Violin sonata in A;* (iv) (Piano) *Prélude, choral et fugue;* (v) (Organ) *Cantabile in B; Choral No. 2; Pièce héroïque in B min.;* (vi) *Panis angelicus.*

(B) **(*) Ph. Duo 442 296-2 (2) [(M) id. import]. (i) Bucquet, Monte Carlo Op. O, Capolongo; (ii) Concg. O, Otterloo; (iii) Arthur Grumiaux, István Hajdu; (iv) Eduardo del Pueyo; (v) Pierre Cocherau (organ of Notre-Dame de Paris); (vi) José Carreras.

Although the performances are variable, this Philips Duo set is certainly worth its asking price. Its highlights are Otterloo's splendid (1964) account of the *Symphony* (plus *Les Eolides*) and the Grumiaux/Hajdu performance of the *Violin sonata*. Otterloo's reading of the *Symphony* has tremendous thrust and its romantic urgency is impossible to resist when the orchestral playing is so assured. *Les Eolides* is a welcome bonus. Grumiaux's account of the *Violin sonata* has both nobility and warmth, and if his partner is not quite his match this is still a memorable performance, most naturally recorded. Marie-Françoise Bucquet gives a perfectly satisfactory account of the *Symphonic variations*, and Carreras sings his heart out in *Panis angelicus*. But del Pueyo's piano contribution is a routine one and Cochereau's organ pieces are also unmemorable, not helped by wheezily unflattering sound.

(i) *Symphonic variations for piano and orchestra. Prélude, aria et final; Prélude, choral et fugue; Prélude, fugue et variation.*

(M) ** EMI CDM7 64561-2. Ciccolini; (i) O de Liège, Paul Strauss.

Aldo Ciccolini's set of the *Symphonic variations*, recorded with the Liège Orchestra, comes from 1974; it is good but is by no means a first choice, given the competition now on the market. He is a fine pianist and a persuasive advocate of the solo works, but the recording is not in the front rank. Serviceable, but no more.

Symphony in D min.

(M) *** DG 449 720-2 [id.]. Berlin RSO, Maazel – MENDELSSOHN: *Symphony No. 5.* ***

(M) **(*) DG (IMS) Dig. 445 512-2 [id.]. O Nat. de France, Bernstein – ROUSSEL: *Symphony No. 3.* **(*)

(M) ** Mercury 434 368-2 [id.]. Detroit SO, Paray – RACHMANINOV: *Symphony No. 2.* **

(M) ** EMI CDM5 66824-2 [id.]. New Philh. O, Klemperer – SCHUMANN: *Symphony No. 1.* **

(B) *(*) DG 439 494-2 [(M) id. import]. Chicago SO, Barenboim – SAINT-SAENS: *Symphony No. 3.* **(*)

Symphony in D min.; Le chasseur maudit.

(M) **(*) EMI Eminence Dig. CD-EMX 2236 [(M) id. import]. Phd. O, Riccardo Muti.

Symphony in D min.; Le chasseur maudit; Les Eolides.

(BB) ** Naxos Dig. 8.553631 [id.]. Arnhem PO, Roberto Benzi.

(i) *Symphony in D min.;* (ii) *Le chasseur maudit;* (iii) *Symphonic variations for piano and orchestra.*

(BB) **(*) RCA Navigator 74321 29256-2 [(M) id. import]. (i–ii) Boston SO, Munch; (iii) Leonard Pennario, Boston Pops O, Fiedler.

(M) **(*) EMI CDM7 64747-2 [id.].(i; iii) BPO, Karajan; (iii) with Alexis Weissenberg; (ii) Phd. O, Muti.

(i) *Symphony in D min.;* (ii) *Pièce héroïque* (orch. Charles O'Connell).

✿ (M) *** RCA 09026 61967-2 [id.]. (i) Chicago SO; (ii) San Francisco SO; Monteux (with (ii): D'INDY: *Istar* (***)).

Symphony in D min.; Prélude choral et fugue (orch. Pierné).
(BB) ** Naxos Dig. 8.550155 [id.]. Royal Flanders PO, Günter Neuhold.

(i) *Symphony in D min.;* (ii) *Symphonic variations for piano and orchestra*; (iii) *Pièce héroïque*.
(B) ** Sony SBK 60287; *SBT 60287* [id.]. (i) Phd. O, Ormandy; (ii) with Robert Casadesus; (iii) E. Power Biggs (Motiller organ, St George's Church, New York City).

Monteux exerts a unique grip on this highly charged Romantic symphony, and his control of the continuous ebb and flow of tempo and tension is masterly, so that any weaknesses of structure in the outer movements are disguised. The splendid playing of the Chicago orchestra is ever responsive to the changes of mood, and the sound is greatly improved. The most recent remastering by John Pfeifer for the Monteux Edition brings a further improvement; indeed, now the quality reflects the acoustics of Chicago's Orchestra Hall in the same way as the Reiner recordings, with textures full-bodied and glowing without loss of detail. Vincent d'Indy's *Istar* (mono, from 1945) is a colourful and increasingly energetic piece. Although the mono sound is boxy, the strings have plenty of middle sonority, and the vivid performance is unlikely to be bettered.

Maazel's account is beautifully shaped, both in its overall structure and in incidental details. However, though each phrase is sensitively moulded, there is no sense of self-conscious striving for beauty of effect. Maazel adopts a fairly brisk tempo in the slow movement, which, surprisingly enough, greatly enhances its poetry and dignity; his finale is also splendidly vital and succeeds in filtering out the excesses of grandiose sentiment and vulgarity which can disfigure this edifice. The work gains enormously from strong control and deliberate understatement, as well as from the refinement of tone and phrasing which mark this reading, for there is no lack of excitement. The recording, admirably well blended and balanced, is enhanced in this new CD transfer for DG's 'Legendary Recordings' series of 'Originals', and the coupling is aptly chosen, for Mendelssohn's *Reformation Symphony* was another of this conductor's finest DG recordings.

Bernstein conducts a powerful, warmly expressive performance which, thanks in part to a live recording, carries conviction in its flexible spontaneity. It has its moments of vulgarity, but that is part of the work; the reservations are of less importance next to the glowing, positive qualities of the performance. The recording is vivid and opulent, but with the brass apt to sound strident.

Munch's 1957 performance of the *Symphony in D minor* was always among the finest ever recorded, but it suffered – as it still does – from the internal balance of the orchestra, which lets the trumpets (with a nasal edge to their tone) coarsen the texture of the loud moments. Otherwise the warm Boston acoustics are heard to good effect, although in the slow movement the harp is very forward. The finale begins with tremendous élan and the quotations from previous movements are not allowed to halt the onward flow of the music; it is this similar momentum in the first movement that allows the glorious second subject to emerge so swingingly. *Le chasseur maudit* (recorded five years later) also sounds spectacular: Franck's horn-calls come over arrestingly. The *Symphonic variations* are brilliantly played by Leonard Pennario, and if Fiedler's support is strong rather than subtle this is still enjoyable. Altogether this Navigator compilation is well worth its modest cost.

Karajan's tempi are all on the slow side, but his control of rhythm prevents any feeling of sluggishness or heaviness. There is always energy underlying the performance, and by facing the obvious problems squarely Karajan avoids the perils. The impact of the recording, now sounding more brightly lit but with textures still full and bold, is considerable; there is potent atmosphere and the finale has both amplitude and plenty of bite. Weissenberg's account of the *Symphonic variations* has less distinction, but the poetry of the lyrical sections is not missed and Karajan ensures that the orchestral contribution is a strong one.

Muti's is a strongly committed but unsentimental reading of the *Symphony*. The cor anglais solo in the *Allegretto* is most beautiful and the finale is particularly refreshing in its directness. The fill-up is welcome, a vividly dramatic symphonic poem, strongly presented, but this is not especially competitive, except for those seeking a digital master. The 1983 recording, robust and vivid, is certainly improved in its CD format, generally well integrated and among EMI's better Philadelphia records made in the 1980s. Muti's *Le chasseur maudit* is vividly dramatic and strongly presented, but there is a degree of glare on the otherwise brilliant digital recording.

Paray's reading is often very exciting; he too understands the emotional ebb and flow of the music, and the tension is well held throughout. Furthermore he gives a genuine Gallic flavour to the phrasing. Mercury's 1959 sound is wide in range and impressive in sonority; if it is a bit grainy on top, that is partly the fault of Franck's unrefined scoring of tuttis.

Roberto Benzi and his Arnhem players give generally impressive accounts of these pieces. His approach to the *Symphony* has sobriety and dignity and is generally unfussy. Both *Le chasseur maudit* and *Les Eolides* come off quite well, and the Naxos recording is good. While the collector can undoubtedly do better for only a little extra outlay, this Naxos collection remains good value.

The earlier Naxos version of the *Symphony in D minor* has more than economy in its favour in that it also brings a rarity in the form of Gabriel Pierné's orchestral transcription of the *Prélude choral et fugue*. The reading of the symphony under Günter Neuhold is well shaped, free from idiosyncrasy and sensitively phrased. The conductor is Austrian and was a pupil of Swarowski, before working in various German opera houses. The orchestral playing is more than just acceptable: it is very good indeed; the only snag is the recording quality. This is pleasingly resonant but is rather opaque and suffers from glare, becoming shrill and edgy above the stave in tuttis. The performance as such gives real pleasure, and the Pierné transcription makes an interesting fill-up.

Casadesus (recorded in 1958) gives an agreeable performance of the *Symphonic variations* but is let down somewhat by the piano recording, better now than it sounded on LP, but still a bit shallow. Ormandy's account of the *Symphony*, made three years later, is bold and powerful, and the recording has impact without being glossy, but the result sounds a bit heavy-handed. Biggs then follows with an impressive account of Franck's most spectacular organ piece. All this music-making has plenty of character, without having quite the individuality or indeed the Gallic finesse of the finest performances on record.

Almost everything Klemperer recorded is interesting, and this performance has its moments, particularly in the outer movements when, by illuminating a phrase or bringing the grand manner to a sonority, the conductor shows his individuality. But in essence this reading is too heavy in style, with little trace of a French accent; although such treatment often brings a stirring feeling of cathedral architecture to the first movement, especially as it draws to its close, the *Allegretto* is too grandiose and its charm is lost. The (1966) Abbey Road recording is good, full though not very transparent.

Barenboim adopts a surprisingly plodding tempo in the first movement, the first subject lacking bite. There are also places where the reading is self-indulgent (Barenboim putting on his Furtwänglerian mantle) and, in an otherwise fine account of the slow movement, the cor anglais solo is disappointingly wooden. The 1976 sound, however, is firmer than the original and very acceptable.

CHAMBER MUSIC

Cello sonata in A (trans. of *Violin sonata*).

(M) **(*) EMI CDM7 63184-2. Du Pré, Barenboim – CHOPIN: *Sonata*. **(*)

(M) ** Virgin/EMI Dig. CUV5 61198-2 [id.]. Isserlis, Devoyon – DEBUSSY; POULENC: *Cello sonatas*. **

Du Pré and Barenboim give a fine, mature, deeply expressive reading of a richly satisfying work. They are well balanced, but the effect of the music when transferred to the cello is inevitably mellower, less vibrant.

There is some good playing from Steven Isserlis and Pascal Devoyon, but the partnership is let down somewhat by a rather overbearing recording which places both artists far too close to the microphone. Although the Franck *Sonata* really does sound better on the violin, these fine players make out as good a case as any for the transcription which the composer himself sanctioned.

Flute sonata in A (trans. of *Violin sonata*).

(M) *** RCA 09026 61615-2 [id.]. James Galway, Martha Argerich – PROKOFIEV; REINECKE: *Flute sonatas*. ***

Although the prospect of hearing the Franck *Violin sonata* arranged for flute may strike you as unappealing, the fact is that the actual experience strangely confutes expectation, thanks to the expert advocacy of these artists. Of course, in the Scherzo the flute cannot match the character and bite of the violin, but elsewhere it is surprising how well this music responds to James Galway's transcription and his sweet-toned virtuosity. Argerich is in absolutely superb form here, and the recording is truthful in quality and wide-ranging. The balance is just a trifle close but is thoroughly musical and, played at a slightly lower-level setting than usual, it yields a sound that is pleasingly fresh and well defined. An outstanding reissue.

Piano quintet in F min.

(BB) *** Naxos Dig. 8.553645 [id.]. Michaël Levinas, Quatuor Ludwig – CHAUSSON: *Quartet in C min.* ***

Like Jean-Philippe Collard and the Muir Quartet before them, Michaël Levinas and the Quatuor Ludwig couple their account of 'the king of piano quintets' (the phrase is Tournemire's) with the same Chausson rarity. Theirs is a very competitive account which is well worth the asking price. Michaël Levinas is a sensitive player, perhaps not as commanding an artist as Collard; but those who are attracted by the enterprising Chausson coupling should consider the present disc. Both the playing and the recorded sound are of a high standard.

Violin sonata in A.

❀ (M) *** Decca 460 006-2 [id.]. Kyung Wha Chung, Radu Lupu – DEBUSSY: *Violin sonata* *** ❀; CHAUSSON: *Poème*. ***

(M) *** Decca 452 887-2 [id.]. Itzhak Perlman, Vladimir Ashkenazy – BRAHMS: *Horn trio*. **(*)

(B) *** Tring Dig. TRP 081 [(M) id. import]. Jonathan Carney, Ronan O'Hora – BRAHMS: *Violin sonata No. 1*. **(*)

(M) *** DG 431 469-2. Kaja Danczowska, Krystian Zimerman – SZYMANOWSKI: *Mythes* etc. *** ❀

(M) **(*) Ph. 426 384-2. Arthur Grumiaux, György Sebok – FAURE: *Sonatas*. ***

(BB) ** Naxos Dig. 8.550417 [id.]. Takako Nishizaki, Jenö Jandó – GRIEG: *Violin sonata* etc. **

(BB) *(*) Koch Discover DICD 920306. Josef Suk, Josef Hala – FAURE: *Violin sonata No. 2;* RAVEL: *Violin sonata*. *(*)

Kyung Wha Chung and Radu Lupu give a glorious account, full of natural and not over-projected eloquence, and most beautifully recorded. The slow movement has marvellous repose and the other movements have a natural exuberance and sense of line that carry the listener with them. The 1977 recording is enhanced on CD and, with an apt Chausson coupling, this reissue remains very desirable indeed.

How beautifully and simply Perlman and Ashkenazy open the first movement and how poetically Ashkenazy responds to the melody on Perlman's bow. Yet the second movement catches the listener by the ears with the thrust of its forward impulse and the intensity of its lyrical flow. There is no lack of flexibility, and the sheer ardour of the interpretation makes it a genuine alternative to the Chung/Lupu account. The fine (1980) recording was understandably chosen for inclusion in Decca's Classic Sound series.

The delicately poised opening of the Carney/O'Hora performance sets the mood for a poetically evocative reading, which certainly does not lack impulse in the second movement or passion in the finale. The recording is truthful if rather resonant, but this serves to add romantic warmth and gives an appealing glow to the third movement, where both artists create a sense of thoughtful improvisation.

Kaja Danczowska's account of the Franck is distinguished by a fine sense of line and great sweetness of tone, and she is partnered superbly by Krystian Zimerman. Indeed, in terms of dramatic fire and strength of line, this version can hold its own alongside the finest, and it is perhaps marginally better-balanced than the Kyung Wha Chung and Radu Lupu recording.

Grumiaux's account, if less fresh than Chung's, has nobility and warmth to commend it. He is slightly let down by his partner, who is not as imaginative as Lupu in the more poetic moments, including the hushed opening bars.

Though she is an unfailingly sensitive player, Takako Nishizaki's vibrato is rather wider at the beginning of the sonata than in other of her records that we have heard, even if there is little cause for complaint elsewhere. She has both eloquence and artistry to commend her and Jenö Jandó proves an excellent partner. The recordings are made in a fairly resonant and pleasing acoustic, but the piano sounds less than freshly tuned at times.

As in the case of the coupled Fauré, the Suk–Hala account appeared in the 1960s and, though the recording cannot be said to do full justice to the great violinist's tone, the performance is a fine one. Some tolerance is called for on sonic grounds, but suitable use of the controls will yield acceptable results.

ORGAN MUSIC

Chorales Nos. 1 in E; 2 in B min., 3 in A min.; Pastorale in E, Op. 19; Pièce héroïque in B min.

(B) *(*) EMI forte (SIS) CZS5 69328-2 (2) [CDFB 69328]. Fernando Germani – BACH: *Concertos, BWV 593, 596* etc. **; WIDOR: *Toccata*. **(*)

(i) *Chorales Nos. 1–3; Pastorale, Op. 19;* (ii) *Pièce héroïque;* (i) *Prélude, fugue et variation.*

(M) *** Decca Dig. 444 568-2 [id.]. Peter Hurford (organs of (i) Basilica of Saint-Sernin, Toulouse; (ii) Royal Festival Hall).

Peter Hurford has a double advantage over Marcel Dupré on Mercury, in that he has exactly the right instrument, the Cavaillé-Coll organ at the Church of Saint-Sernin, Toulouse, and first-class 1983 Decca engineering. His are masterly performances of the three *Chorales* which Franck composed during the last years of his life: they are beautifully shaped and grandly paced. Moreover he also includes equally fine accounts of the *Pastorale* and the *Prélude, fugue et variation*, the third and fourth of the *Six Pièces*, written during the composer's early years at Sainte-Clotilde. The *Pièce héroïque* was recorded a year earlier on the organ at the Royal Festival Hall and sounds most spectacular. The organ's widely spread sound-sources add tellingly to the presentation and there is no doubt that, among modern digital recordings of this repertoire, this reissue (Volume II in Hurford's 'Organ masterpieces' series) leads the field.

The huge organ of Selby Abbey dates from 1909, although it was rebuilt in 1948. It is in three sections:

on the south side the *Great* and part of the *Pedal* face, across the chancel, the *Choir*, *Swell* and *Solo* and more of the *Pedal*. However, the largest pipes of the *Double Open Diapason* are high up in the nave triforium. Thus is offered in theory a considerably antiphonal interplay, but in effect the long reverberation period of the abbey prevents much point source, and the organ achieves (probably what it was intended to achieve in a period not devoted to clarity of texture) a large-scale – indeed overwhelming – spread of rich sound. The *Pièce héroïque* can never have sounded more massive. As for the remaining works, Germani's rather suave performances are not helped by the generally bland effect of the registration: there is not enough bite in the reeds. Hearing Franck on such a very English organ is not far removed from seeing the composer dressed in a straw hat, blazer and flannels lounging indulgently by the banks of the River Cam. No complaints about the engineering: the CD sounds far more comfortable than the original LP did. However, Peter Hurford's Decca collection of this repertoire still leads the field.

PIANO MUSIC

Prélude, choral et fugue.
(M) *** RCA 09026 62590-2 [id.]. Artur Rubinstein – BACH: *Chaconne* ***; LISZT: *Sonata*. **(*)

In music like this, strangely poised between classical form and Romantic expression, between the piano and the organ-loft, Rubinstein is also very persuasive. This performance, recorded (like the Bach) in 1970, has fire and spontaneity. The piano-tone is firm and clear: its brightness suits the music.

Frescobaldi, Girolamo (1583–1643)

Primo Libro di Toccate (1616): excerpts. *Il Secondo Libro di Toccata, Canzoni, Versi d'hinni; Magnificat; Gagliarde, Corrente*: excerpts. *Partite sopra l'aria della romanesca* (1624); *Aria di balletto* (1637).
(M) *** Virgin/Veritas EMI Dig. VM5 61398-2. Scott Ross (harpsichord).

Like Christopher Hogwood before him (whose survey stretches to a pair of full-priced CDs) Scott Ross here surveys the keyboard music of a composer whose music demands a free, improvisatory style of performance, of which he is obviously a master. Indeed he brings this repertoire unfailingly to life in a most appealing way, opening with four (very free) *Toccatas* from Book I. The excerpts from the Second Book which, alongside three more *Toccatas*, include four *Correnti*, a pair of *Canzoni* and three *Gagliarde* are framed by two highly inventive sets of variations. The first is in the form of a *Partite sopra l'aria della romanesca*, the second a rather engaging *Aria di balletto* which invites more robust treatment, not unlike Handel's variations known as *The harmonious blacksmith*. Ross's easy bravura is particularly attractive here, and his Jean-Louis Val harpsichord is very vividly recorded.

Froberger, Johann (1616–67)

Lamentation sur la mort de Ferdinand III in F, FbWV 633; Partitas (Suites) Nos. XVIII in G min.; XIX in C min., FbWV 619; XX in D, FbWV 611a; XXX in A min.; Toccatas Nos. II in D min., IX in C; XIV in G, FbWV 103; XVIII in F; Tombeau sur la mort de M. Blancheroche in C min., FbWV 632.
(M) *** HM Dig. HMT 1901372 [id.]. Christophe Rousset (harpsichord).

Froberger's music is highly exploratory in idiom, and in works such as the *Tombeau sur la mort de M. Blancheroche* he reveals great expressive poignancy. The *Partitas* and *Toccatas* too invite considerable expressive freedom. Needless to say, Christophe Rousset is impressive in this repertoire. He uses a restored (1652) Couchet double-manual harpsichord which suits all these works admirably in his hands. He is very well recorded.

Furtwängler, Wilhelm (1886–1954)

Symphony No. 2 in E min.
(M) (***) DG mono 457 722-2 (2). BPO, Furtwängler – SCHUMANN: *Symphony No. 4*. (***) ✿

Furtwängler started work on his *Second Symphony* during the war years, but he worked on it in earnest only after hostilities had ceased and while he was awaiting de-Nazification at the hands of the Allies. Furtwängler himself spoke of it as his spiritual testament, and Richard Osborne goes so far as to speak of it as equal in importance with such contemporary works as Vaughan Williams's *Sixth Symphony* and Honegger's *Symphonie liturgique*. In his note he cites in support Honegger's oft-quoted remark, 'The man who can write a score as rich as this, is not to be argued about. He is of the race of great musicians.' This is Brucknerian in its dimensions and sense of space: it runs to 82 minutes, and the finale alone is as long as most performances of Schumann's *Fourth Symphony*. It is Brucknerian, too, in its nobility. The first movement, lasting 24 minutes, is accommodated on the first CD, and the remaining three on the second. Furtwängler himself thought the present studio recording, made in the Jesus-Christus-Kirche, Berlin, in 1950 'stilted', but it sounds amazingly clear and warm in this transfer and readers should not be put off acquiring it. The Schumann coupling – one of Furtwängler's very finest mono records – makes a superb coupling.

Fux, Johann Joseph (1650–1741)

Il Concentus musico instrumentalis: Overtures (Suites) Nos. 2 in B flat; 4 in G min. Overtures (Suites) in B flat; D min.

(M) *** Van. Dig. 99705 [id.]. Il Fondamento, Paul Dombrecht.

Fux wrote a great many overtures or suites which combine the French and Italian styles, of which the present four are lively and quite colourful examples. They have a good deal in common with similar works of Telemann, even if not nearly so skilfully scored. Il Fondamento, a period-instrument group under Paul Dombrecht, who have been less successful with the music of Abel, bring these works to life quite vividly. They are agreeably recorded; though the sound could ideally be more transparent. But the thickness of texture is partly caused by the doubling up in the scoring, with the wind playing in tutti with the strings. Perhaps this was an influence from Dresden, where tutti unisons were very fashionable.

Gabrieli, Andrea (1520–86)

Aria della battaglia a 8.

(B) ** Decca Eclipse Dig. 448 993-2; *448 993-4* [(M) id. import]. Philip Jones Brass Ens., Jones – Giovanni GABRIELI: *Collection*. **(*)

The *Aria della battaglia* is a rambling piece lasting over ten minutes, rather too long to retain the listener's interest – at least in the present performance. It is very well played, without any dramatic dynamic contrasts, and tends to jog along rather than create any great degree of tension. The recording is clear and nicely resonant.

Gabrieli, Giovanni (1557–1612)

(i) *Canzon a 6; Canzon primi toni a 8; Canzon, La Spiritata, a 4; Canzon vigesimasettima a 8; Sonata a 3.* (i; ii) *Canzon per sonar a 4; Canzoni Nos. 4 a 6; 12 a 8; In ecclesiis; Jubilate Deo; O Jesu mi dulcissime; O magnum mysterium; Quem vidistis pastores?; Timor et tremor.*

(B) **(*) Decca Eclipse Dig. 448 993-2; *448 993-4* [(M) id. import]. (i) Philip Jones Brass Ens., Jones; (ii) Soloists, King's College, Cambridge, Ch., Cleobury – Andrea GABRIELI: *Aria della battaglia*. **

The first group of *Canzoni* here is played immaculately on modern brass instruments, skilfully balanced and recorded in the Kingsway Hall which gives a nicely resonant bloom, good detail and excellent antiphony. Yet the result is curiously bland. The *Sonata a 3* comes off best; otherwise there seems to be a lack of tension and not the widest range of dynamic.

When one turns to the rest of the programme, recorded four years later in 1986, the results are altogether different. The widely resonant acoustics of King's College Chapel make an admirable alternative to St Mark's for this repertoire. Particularly in the festive motet, *In ecclesiis*, with its three choirs plus organ and instrumental accompaniment, the complex layout is convincing and indeed thrilling (although here the trebles – not quite the strongest contingent this choir has ever fielded – can only just cope); but the Christmas motet, *Quem vidistis pastores?*, with its solo voices from the choir representing the shepherds, is very well managed. Other highlights include the light and joyful *Jubilate Deo* and the highly atmospheric *O magnum mysterium*; while *Timor et tremor* is richly appealing in texture. The canzoni for brass alone, which act as interludes, are undoubtedly enhanced by the King's ambience, and climaxes have real impact. At Eclipse price this is well worth having for the choral music alone.

Music for brass, Vol. 1: *Canzon à 12 in double eco; Canzon septimi toni à 8 No. 2; Canzon septimi e octavi toni à 12; Canzon noni toni à 8; Canzon noni toni à 12; Canzoni duodecimi toni à 10, Nos. 1 & 3; Canzoni VII; VIII; IX; XI; XIII; XIV; XVII; XXVIII; Sonata pian' e forte alla quarta bassa à 8.*
(BB) *** Naxos Dig. 8.553609 [id.]. LSO Brass, Eric Crees.

Starting with the *Canzon XVII* of 1615 in 12 parts, involving three choirs of instruments, Eric Crees and his brilliant players from the brass section of the LSO demonstrate at once what variety of tone they can produce, with the finest shading of timbre and texture. Even in the great *Sonata pian' e forte* of 1597 in eight parts the playing is remarkable as much for its restraint and point as for its dramatic impact. Eric Crees in his notes, at once scholarly and informative about Giovanni Gabrieli (nephew of Andrea) and his Venetian background, helpfully highlights such remarkable items as the remarkable *Double echo Canzon in 12 parts*. Beautiful sound, both clear and atmospheric, not aggressive. Naxos could not have chosen better for the first volume of what promises to be an exciting series.

Angelus ad pastores ait; Buccante in neomenia tuba; Canzon septimi toni à 8; Hodie Christus natus est; Hodie completi sunt; O Domine Jesu Christe; O magnum mysterium; Omnes gentes, plaudite manibus.
(B) **(*) EMI forte CZS5 68631-2 (2) [(M) id. import]. Cambridge University Musical Soc., Bach Ch., King's College Ch., Wilbraham Brass Soloists, Willcocks (with SCHEIDT: *In dulci jubilo* ***) – SCHUTZ: *Psalm 150* **(*); MONTEVERDI: *Vespers*. *(*)

Originally recorded in King's College Chapel, using quadraphonic sound, the CD transfer brings stereo which is notable for the opulent richness of brass and choral textures rather than inner clarity, yet is resonantly resplendent. There is an impressively wide dynamic range, as is shown by the serene motet, *O Domine Jesu Christe*. Added to the Gabrieli works is Scheidt's setting in eight parts of the famous *In dulci jubilo*, which is particularly successful. It is a pity that the principal Monteverdi coupling is not more recommendable.

Gade, Niels (1817–90)

Forårs-fantasi (Spring fantasy), Op. 23.
(M) ** EMI CDM5 66000-2. Bodil Gøbil, Minna Nyhus, Ole Jensen, Mogens Schmidt Johansen, Eyvind Møller, Danish RSO, Frandsen – NIELSEN: *Hymnus Amoris; Sleep*. **

John Frandsen's performance of Gade's charming *Spring fantasy* first appeared on the Danish Music Anthology label in the 1970s and is new to the EMI catalogue. It is a good performance, fresh, well shaped and decently recorded. Eminently worthwhile at mid-price, and attractively coupled.

Gay, John (1685–1732)

The Beggar's opera (arr. Pepusch and Austin).
✿ (BB) *** CfP Silver Double CD-CFPSD 4778 (2) [id.]. Morison, Cameron, M. Sinclair, Wallace, Brannigan, Pro Arte Ch. & O, Sargent.

The Beggar's Opera was the eighteenth-century equivalent of the modern American musical. It was first produced in 1728 and caused a sensation with audiences used to the stylized Italian opera favoured by Handel. Its impact produced a whole series of inferior ballad operas, culminating a century later in works like *Maritana* and *The Bohemian girl*, which are far removed from Gay's piece in spirit as well as in social content. This performance under Sargent is in every way first class, one of the finest things he did on record (comparable with his *Hiawatha's wedding feast* – alas, currently out of the catalogue – and the best of his Savoy operas). The soloists here could hardly be bettered, with Elsie Morison as Polly and Owen Brannigan a splendid Peachum; and the linking dialogue is spoken by actors to make the result most dramatic, with every word crystal clear. The chorus is no less effective, and the recording has a most appealing ambience. EMI chose *Let us take the road* for inclusion on their original stereo demonstration disc, and the sense of presence and atmosphere which it revealed is highly compelling throughout this highly successful 1995 remastering of a recording made at Abbey Road – astonishingly – as long ago as 1955.

Geminiani, Francesco (1687–1762)

Concerti grossi, Op. 2/1–6; Op. 3/1–4.
(BB) *** Naxos Dig. 8.553019 [id.]. Capella Istropolitana, Jaroslav Krček.

This is part of an ongoing Naxos project to record all Geminiani's concerti grossi using modern instruments but in a style which clearly reflects the freshness and vitality of period-instrument practice. The Capella Istropolitana offer excellent accounts of the whole of Op. 2 and the first four concertos of Op. 3 (with the remainder to follow). Not perhaps quite as characterful as Tafelmusik's full-price version of Op. 2 (Sony SK 48043) but invigoratingly enjoyable and very well recorded.

Concerti grossi, Op. 2/5–6; Op. 3/3; Op. 7/2; in G min. (after Corelli, *Op. 5/5*); *in D min.* (after Corelli, *Op. 5/12*); *Theme & variations (La Folia).*
(M) *** RCA Dig. GD 77010 [77010-2-RG]. La Petite Bande, Sigiswald Kuijken.

The quality of invention in the Geminiani concertos recorded here rises high above the routine. There is considerable expressive depth in some of the slow movements too. La Petite Bande is incomparably superior to many of the period-instrument ensembles. Those who are normally allergic to the vinegary offerings of some rivals will find this record a joy. It is beautifully recorded too, and makes an admirable and economical introduction to this underrated and genial composer.

Concerti grossi, Op. 3/1–6.
(B) (**) Millennium mono MCD 80079. E. Bar. Ens., Hermann Scherchen.

Recorded at the same time (September 1954) as Handel's Op. 6, Scherchen's account of Geminiani's Op. 3 is not quite as successful as the Handel (see below), although still very enjoyable for its warmth and breadth of expressive feeling. Tempi are leisured, but the graceful phrasing and the spirited articulation in allegros ensure the listener's pleasure. However, the thinness of the upper strings, as recorded, is more striking here, even if there is underlying body and ambient warmth. The other drawback is the absence of cues for individual movements.

12 Concerti grossi, Op. 5 (after Corelli).
(B) *** Ph. Duo 438 766-2 (2) [(M) id. import]. Michelucci, Gallozzi, Bennici, Centurione, I Musici.

The music on which Geminiani based his Op. 5 is drawn from the splendid *Sonatas for violin and continuo* of Corelli with the same opus number. Their skilful adaptation to *concerto grosso* form features a viola in the solo group as well as violins and cello. The basic musical material is unaltered in any harmonic or thematic sense, but textures are filled out and greater variety of colour is provided. The result is entirely successful. The music balances serenity and a noble expressive feeling in slow movements with vigorously spontaneous allegros. The performances by I Musici – at their very finest – are admirable in all respects, spirited and responsive, polished yet never bland. The recording is first class too, wide-ranging, full and clearly detailed. Highly recommended: if you enjoy Handel's Op. 6, this inexpensive reissue is not to be missed.

German, Edward (1862–1936)

Welsh rhapsody.
(B) *** CfP CD-CFP 4635 [id.]. RSNO, Gibson – HARTY: *With the wild geese;* MACCUNN: *Land of mountain and flood;* SMYTH: *Wreckers overture.* ***

This collection, appropriately entitled 'Music of four countries', offers first-class sound from the late 1960s, extremely well transferred to CD and, with its interesting and rare couplings, makes a highly recommendable bargain. Edward German is content not to interfere with the traditional melodies he uses, relying on his orchestral skill to retain the listener's interest, and in this he is very successful. The closing pages, based on *Men of Harlech*, are prepared in a Tchaikovskian manner to provide a rousing conclusion. The CD transfer is very well managed, though the ear perceives a slight limitation in the upper range.

Merrie England (complete; without dialogue).
(BB) (**) CfP Silver Double CD-CFPSD 4796 (2) [id.]. McAlpine, Bronhill, Glossop, M. Sinclair, Kern, Williams Singers, O, Michael Collins.

Although this recording dates from 1960, it cannot compare in stereo sophistication with EMI's *Beggar's Opera* of five years earlier. While all the present soloists came from Sadler's Wells, the production team was obviously drawn from EMI's popular department; the result, technically speaking, is a near disaster. All the solo voices are close-miked, usually in a most unflattering way, and too often they sound edgy, while the chorus is made artificially bright; the orchestra is lively enough, but the violins are thin. However, it must be said that Michael Collins directs the proceedings in an attractively spirited fashion. Taken as a whole, the score does not wear too well (much of it sounds like diluted Gilbert and Sullivan). But if the moments of coarseness in the libretto can be forgiven, there is much pleasing lyricism in German's music and one or two really outstanding tunes which will ensure that the score survives. Among the soloists Howell Glynne is splendid as King Neptune, and Monica Sinclair sings with her usual richness and makes *O peaceful England* more moving than usual. Patricia Kern's mezzo is firm and forward, while McAlpine as Sir Walter Raleigh sings with fine, ringing voice. The Rita Williams Singers are thoroughly professional even if just occasionally their style is suspect. However, another recording seems unlikely so this is acceptable, *faute de mieux*.

Gershwin, George (1898–1937)

An American in Paris; Catfish Row (suite from *Porgy and Bess*); *Cuban overture; Lullaby*.
(B) *** [EMI Red Line CDR5 72554]. St Louis SO, Slatkin.

Slatkin is clearly at home in *Catfish Row*, and he relishes the sophistication of Gershwin's own suite from *Porgy and Bess*, while still bringing out the special effects (bell and wind simulator in *Hurricane*). A similar sophistication in the brash *Cuban overture* does mean that some of the gutsy feeling of the piece is lost; while for *American in Paris*, although he often disguises the seams, he could at times be more extrovert. It is partly the gloriously ample acoustics of the Lovell Hall, St Louis, that makes everything seem opulent, and certainly on sonic grounds no American collector should be disappointed with this concert, especially the *Lullaby* (which derives from *Blue Monday*) in which the St Louis strings sound richly seductive.

(i) *An American in Paris;* (ii) *Cuban overture;* (ii–iii) *I got rhythm variations;* (i; iii) *Rhapsody in blue;* (ii–iii) *Second Rhapsody; Porgy and Bess:* medley.
(M) *** EMI/Angel CDM5 66086-2 [id.]. Hollywood Bowl SO; (i) Felix Slatkin; (ii) Alfred Newman; with (iii) Leonard Pennario.

This reissued programme, taken from two Capitol LPs of the early stereo era, is among the most attractive and idiomatically authentic collection of Gershwin's shorter orchestral and concertante works in the catalogue. Of course Bernstein's CBS/Sony *Rhapsody in blue* is special, but Pennario's version has hardly less rhythmic verve, and his irresistible performance of the *Second Rhapsody* has a pulsing vitality, well supported by the exuberant orchestral accompaniment, that makes the music leap out of the speakers. Alfred Newman directs this, the dazzling *I got rhythm variations* and a sparkling account of the deliciously vulgar *Cuban overture*, played with comparable Latin zest. His concertante selection from *Porgy and Bess* is equally brilliant and seductive, notably so for Pennario's bewitching introduction of '*Summertime*'. The young Felix Slatkin directs *An American in Paris* with audacious flair, not missing out the taxi horns, and the performance is made the more memorable by the panache of the violins in this remarkable orchestra of virtuosi. They are totally seductive in the great central blues tune. All the music was recorded on Stage Seven of the Samuel Goldwyn Studios, in 1956 under Slatkin and in 1961 under Newman. With close microphones, the stereo effect is both spacious and brash, and the bright sound-picture, like the somewhat shallow piano-timbre, adds to the character of the occasion – a wonderful memento of Hollywood top musicians playing music they know so well with enormous spirit and enthusiastic relish.

(i) *An American in Paris;* (ii) *Piano concerto in F;* (iii) *Rhapsody in blue*.
(BB) *** Carlton LSO Double Dig. 30368 01257 (2) [(B) id.]. (ii–iii) Gwenneth Pryor; LSO, Richard Williams – Concert: LSO, Roderick Dunk: *'That's entertainment'*. **(*)
(M) *** Ph. (IMS) 442 395-2. (ii–iii) Werner Haas; Monte Carlo Op. O, De Waart.
(BB) * Naxos Dig. 8.550295 [id.]. (ii–iii) Kathryn Selby; (i) Czech RSO (Bratislava); (ii–iii) Slovak PO; Richard Hayman.

An American in Paris; (i) *Piano concerto in F; Rhapsody in blue; Variations on 'I got rhythm'*.
(M) *** RCA 09026 68792-2 [id.]. (i) Earl Wild; Boston Pops O, Arthur Fiedler.

From the opening glissando swirl on the clarinet, the performance of the *Rhapsody in blue* by Gwenneth Pryor and the LSO under Richard Williams tingles with adrenalin, and the other performances are comparable. The *Rhapsody* has splendid rhythmic energy, yet the performers can relax to allow the big expressive blossoming at the centre really to expand. Similarly in the *Concerto*, the combination of vitality and flair and an almost voluptuous response to the lyrical melodies is very involving. *An American in Paris*, briskly paced, moves forward in an exhilarating sweep, with the big blues tune vibrant and the closing section managed to perfection. The performances are helped by superb recording, made in the

EMI No. 1 Studio; but it is the life and spontaneity of the music-making that enthral the listener throughout all three works. This was an outstanding disc in its own right, but as a Double it is joined to a series of selections of Show music which are much less repeatable than the Gershwin works.

The reissued CD on RCA's mid-price Living Stereo label is particularly generous (70 minutes) in including, besides the usual triptych, the *'I got rhythm' variations*, given plenty of rhythmic panache. Indeed these are essentially jazzy performances: Earl Wild's playing is full of energy and brio, and he inspires Arthur Fiedler to a similarly infectious response. In many ways these performances are as fine as any; if the *Rhapsody* has not the breadth of Bernstein's highly recommendable account (Sony SMK 47529), it is nearer the Paul Whiteman original and is rewarding in quite a different way. The outer movements of the *Concerto* are comparably volatile and the blues feeling of the slow movement is strong. At the end of *An American in Paris* Fiedler (like Steinberg) adds to the exuberance by bringing in a bevy of motor horns. The brightly remastered recording suits the music-making, though the resonant Boston acoustics at times prevent absolute sharpness of focus, but the current transfer gives a convincing overall sound-picture. This is also available in the USA as one of RCA's 'Basic 100' series (09026 61724-2) but, according to Schwann, this disc does not include the *Variations*.

In Monte Carlo the *Concerto* is particularly successful; its lyrical moments have a quality of nostalgia which is very attractive. Werner Haas is a volatile and sympathetic soloist, and his rhythmic verve is refreshing. Edo de Waart's *An American in Paris* is not only buoyant but glamorous too – the big blues melody is highly seductive and, as with all the best accounts of this piece, the episodic nature of the writing is hidden. There is a cultured, European flavour to this music-making that does not detract from its vitality, and the jazz inflexions are not missed, with plenty of verve in the *Rhapsody*. Very good sound.

The Naxos collection is totally unidiomatic. Everything is well played, even refined (especially the slow movement of the *Concerto*), but the rhythmic feeling of this music eludes these players: the *Rhapsody* is unmemorable and the blues tune in *An American in Paris* is square. Good, modern recording, but the jazzy element is too diluted for this music-making to be fully convincing.

(i) *An American in Paris;* (ii) *Overtures: Girl Crazy; Oh Kay!; Let 'em eat cake; Strike up the band;* (iii) *Rhapsody in blue; Second Rhapsody.*
(M) **(*) Sony Theta Analogue/Dig. SMK 60028 [id.]. (i) NYPO; (ii) Buffalo PO; Michael Tilson Thomas; (iii) Tilson Thomas (piano & cond.), LAPO.

Michael Tilson Thomas directed an earlier recording of the *Rhapsody in blue* for CBS using the composer's own piano contribution, taken from a 1924 piano roll. Here, although he is obviously an accomplished and idiomatic pianist, there is not the same hell-for-leather excitement and zest for life which that earlier version generated. Nevertheless it is still an attractively vivid performance, with very good orchestral playing. As is *An American in Paris*, in which the NYPO are thoroughly at home and the recording is both bright and warmly atmospheric, more sumptuous than the competing EMI version, which has rather more exuberance. Tilson Thomas has also taken the trouble to re-study the autographs of the *Second Rhapsody* and the result of his researches brings us closer to Gershwin's intentions. Even so, he does not make such a breathtaking impression with this piece as does Leonard Pennario in Hollywood (see above). The Broadway overtures sparkle, with the Buffalo Philharmonic clearly on their toes and enjoying themselves. These pot-pourris demand both vivacity and affectionate detail, which they receive here in good measure. All these recordings sound better than they did on their earlier CD incarnations, and altogether this is a worthwhile disc.

An American in Paris; (i) *Rhapsody in blue.*
✿ (M) *** Sony SMK 63086 [id.]. NYPO, Bernstein, (i) Bernstein (piano) – GROFE: *Grand Canyon suite.* ***

Bernstein's 1958–9 CBS (now Sony) coupling was recorded when (at the beginning of his forties) he was at the peak of his creativity, with *West Side Story* only two years behind him. This record set the standard by which all subsequent pairings of *An American in Paris* and *Rhapsody in blue* came to be judged. It still sounds astonishingly well as a recording, and the current remastering for the Bernstein Century Edition has restored all the bloom of the original. Bernstein's approach is inspirational, exceptionally flexible but completely spontaneous. The performance of *An American in Paris* is vividly characterized, brash and episodic; an unashamedly American view, with the great blues tune marvellously timed and phrased as only a great American orchestra can do it.

(i) *An American in Paris;* (ii) *Rhapsody in blue;* (iii) *Porgy and Bess* (symphonic suite; arr. Farnon).
(M) ** Decca Phase Four 448 953-2 [id.]. (i–iii) L. Festival O; (i–ii) cond. Stanley Black; (ii) S. Black (piano); (iii) cond. Robert Farnon.

Stanley Black's performances of *An American in Paris* and *Rhapsody in blue* (which he directs from the piano) are good examples of Decca's Phase Four technique, which brings an intentionally vivid forward balance and sound of striking resonance and spectacle. The performances, though obviously not transatlantic, are thoroughly idiomatic and enjoyable. Farnon's extended concert orchestral pot-pourri of all the principal tunes from *Porgy and Bess* is even larger than life, with amplified woodwind and saxophone solos, luscious violins and vibrant brass. The effect throughout is certainly sumptuous. The orchestral playing is first rate and certainly bluesy in feeling as well as vibrant.

Broadway and film music: *A Damsel in distress:* suite, arr. McGlinn. *Stiff upper lip: Funhouse sequence.* Overtures: *Girl crazy; Of thee I sing; Oh, Kay!; Primrose; Tip-Toes.*
(B) **(*) EMI forte (SIS) Dig. CZS5 68589-2 (2) [CDFB 68589]. New Princess Theatre O, McGlinn – KERN: *Overtures* **; PORTER: *Overtures and film music.* ***

This inexpensive two-disc forte set makes a pretty good collection for those who enjoy authentic re-creations of Broadway music composed by three of its greatest names. John McGlinn has recorded his selections using the original scores. The extended dance-sequence, *Stiff upper lip*, comes from a 1937 movie and has some good tunes. So has *Oh Kay!* (half a dozen) while *Girl crazy* offers the irresistible *I got rhythm*. Elsewhere the famous melodies are more thinly spread, but the marvellous playing of the New York pick-up orchestra (gorgeous saxes and brass) has splendid pep. The lively, close-miked sound gives an authentic theatre-pit brashness, with very bright violins, although the backgound ambience is warm enough.

(i) *Piano concerto in F; Rhapsody in blue. Cuban overture.*
(M) ** Mercury 434 341-2 [id.]. (i) Eugene List; Eastman-Rochester O, Howard Hanson (with SOUSA: *Stars and Stripes forever* **).

Quite highly regarded in its day, this is one Mercury reissue which sounds dated. The dry acoustics of the Eastman Theatre in Rochester are not flattering and the orchestral strings sound thin to today's ears. List and Hanson are both at home in this repertoire, but it is the scherzando element in the *Rhapsody* that one most remembers and, for the same reason, the finale of the *Concerto* is the most effective movement. The *Cuban overture* is probably the most successful piece here and *The Stars and Stripes forever* (credited to the Eastman Philharmonia) is robustly gutsy rather than particularly peppy.

Piano concerto in F; Rhapsody in blue; Second Rhapsody for piano and orchestra; Variations on 'I got rhythm'.
✿ (M) *** Classic fM Dig. 76505 57012-2 [id.]. Michael Boriskin, Eos O, Jonathan Sheffer.

This is the most seductive pairing of the *Rhapsody in blue* and the *Concerto in F* to have come our way for a long time. The performances have a superb sense of style, and are for the 1990s what Bernstein's famous versions were for the 1950s and '60s. Michael Boriskin is a native New Yorker, and he and Jonathan Sheffer immediately establish a partnership which brings an idiomatic and freshly individual approach to these two concertante masterpieces, which uniquely span the jazz world and the ethos of the concert hall. The keenly sophisticated and inventive *'I got rhythm' variations* are no less glittering and are wonderfully infectious. The Eos Orchestra is a group of first-class freelance musicians from the New York area: the individuality of their response is immediately set by Todd Levy's naughtily provocative clarinet glissando at the opening of the *Rhapsody*. The first big tutti brings a splendid jazz-band sound, and later, when the great lyrical tune arrives, a sultry saxophone colouring spices the strings. The orchestral detail throughout is a joy (especially illuminating in the less inspired *Second rhapsody*), while in the concerto the big climaxes open out to engulf the listener expansively and ardently. Boriskin's brilliant pianism is wittily skittish in the most infectious way, both in the *Rhapsody* and in the delectably played central section of the concerto's slow movement, which Neil Balm has opened so languorously with his trumpet. The finale brings dazzling yet totally unforced bravura from ever nimble fingers, matched by sparkling orchestral rhythms. The recording is first rate. This is not to be missed.

Rhapsody in blue (see also above, under *An American in Paris*).
(M) **(*) DG Dig. 439 528-2 [431 048-2]. Bernstein with LAPO – BARBER: *Adagio for strings;* COPLAND: *Appalachian spring.* ***
(M) **(*) Decca Dig. 430 726-2. Katia & Marielle Labèque, Cleveland O, Chailly – ADDINSELL: *Warsaw concerto;* GOTTSCHALK: *Grand fantasia;* LISZT: *Hungarian fantasia;* LITOLFF: *Scherzo.* ***

In his last recording of this work for DG, Bernstein rather goes over the top with his jazzing of the solos in Gershwin. Such rhythmic freedom was clearly the result of a live rather than a studio performance. This does not match Bernstein's inspired 1959 analogue coupling for CBS.

There seems no special reason for preferring the two-piano version of the *Rhapsody in blue*, and although the Labèque duo play charismatically their account is made somewhat controversial by the addition of an improvisatory element (more decorative than structural). However, the playing does not lack sparkle and the recording is first class.

Song arrangements for orchestra: *Bidin' my time; But not for me; Embraceable you; Fascinating rhythm; I got rhythm; Liza; Love is sweeping the country; Love walked in; The man I love; Oh, Lady be good; Someone to watch over me; 'S wonderful* (all arr. Ray Wright).
(M) **(*) Mercury (IMS) 434 327-2 [id.]. O, Frederick Fennell – PORTER: *Song arrangements.* **(*)

This is reputed to be Fennell's favourite record, and he directs every one of these famous tunes with affectionate style and a sparkling rhythmic lift. Unusually for this label, the smooth (1961) Mercury sound is multi-miked, yet it has plenty of ambience as well as both a silky lustre and a natural clarity. The orchestral playing is fully worthy of the sophistication of the scoring, and Gershwin's songs with their ripe tunefulness respond more easily than Cole Porter's to presentation without the lyrics.

'The authentic George Gershwin' (Piano arrangements of songs)

Volume 1 (1918–25): *Come to the moon; Drifting along with the tide; Fascinatin' rhythm; The half of it, Dearie, blues; Hang on to me; I'd rather Charleston; I was so young; Kicking the clouds away; Limehouse nights; The man I love; Nobody but you; Oh Lady be good; So am I; Swanee; Tee-Oodle-Um-Bum-Bo. Piano concerto in F: slow movt. Rhapsody in blue.*
(M) **(*) ASV Dig. CDWHL 2074 [id.]. Jack Gibbons.

Volume 2 (1925–30): *Clap yo' hands; Do, do, do; Embraceable you; He loves and she loves; I got rhythm* (2 versions); *Liza; Looking for a boy; Maybe; Meadow serenade; My one and only; Someone to watch over me; Sweet and low-down* (2 versions); *'S Wonderful; Funny face; That certain feeling; When do we dance? An American in Paris (overture); Strike up the band (overture); Irish waltz (Three-quarter blues); 3 Piano preludes.*
(M) **(*) ASV Dig. CDWHL 2077 [id.]. Jack Gibbons.

Volume 3 (1931–37): *For you, for me, for evermore; Isn't it a pity; Jilted; Let's call the whole thing off; Our love is here to stay; They can't take that away from me. Cuban overture; Second rhapsody; Porgy and Bess: suite. Good morning, Brother: excerpts. Variations on 'I got rhythm'.*
(M) **(*) ASV Dig. CDWHL 2082 [id.]. Jack Gibbons.

Volumes 1–3 (complete).
(M) **(*) ASV Dig. CDWLS 328 (3) [id.].

Jack Gibbons has transcribed Gershwin's own piano transcriptions from the records and piano rolls made by the composer himself, and in certain cases from recorded radio programmes and film sound-tracks. His playing is brightly idiomatic, fresh and spontaneous, and has received much praise for its closeness to the composer's own keyboard style. The modern digital recording adds to the appeal of this set. But the arrangements of the orchestral works (*An American in Paris*, for instance), the suite from *Porgy and Bess* and the solo piano versions of the *Rhapsody in blue*, the *Second Rhapsody* and the *'I got rhythm' variations* (drawn from the composer's four-handed versions) often sound rather prolix and are much less effective and enjoyable than the songs, although played with the same sense of style. There are also more impressive versions on disc of the three *Piano preludes*.

Gershwin Songbook (18 songs) complete; *Impromptu in two keys; Jazzbo Brown blues; Merry Andrew; 3 Preludes; Promenade; Rialto ripples; Three-quarter blues; 2 Waltzes in C* (arr. Chaplin). *Show tunes* (arr. Bennett): *Lady be good!: Little jazz bird. Oh Kay!: Someone to watch over me. Porgy and Bess: Oh Bess.*
(M) **(*) Carlton IMP 30367 00372 [id.]. Richard Rodney Bennett

A generous and useful bargain anthology including all the key piano works and a *pot-pourri* of the hits in the *Gershwin Songbook* (the composer's transcriptions of 18 of his most popular numbers). Richard Rodney Bennett's own arrangements of key show tunes are effective and he plays the whole programme with lilting warmth and a genuine rhythmic understanding. Perhaps at times one thinks of the atmosphere of a piano bar, but that is no bad thing when the concert pieces are well understood, the *Three Preludes* standing out from the rest. Good, truthful recording.

Piano arrangements of songs: *Bidin' my time; But not for me; Clap yo' hands; Do, do, do; Embraceable you; Fascinating rhythm; A foggy day; Funny face; He loves and she loves; How long has this been going on; I got rhythm; I'll build a stairway to paradise; I've got a crush on you; Let's call the whole thing off; Liza; Love is here to stay; Love is sweeping the country; Love walked in; The man I love; Maybe; Mine; Of thee I sing; Oh, Lady be good; Somebody loves me; Someone to watch over me; Soon; Strike up the*

band; Swanee!; 'S Wonderful; That certain feeling; They can't take that away from me; Who cares; Excerpts from: *An American in Paris;* Themes from *Concerto in F; Piano prelude No. 2; Rhapsody in blue*: excerpts.
(M) *** Van. 08.6002.71 [OVC 6002]. George Feyer (with Tommy Lucas, George Mell, Sy Salzberg, Edward Caccavate).

The American Hungarian émigré pianist, George Feyer, is unsurpassed in this repertory, playing all these tunes with a rhythmic lift and naturally lilting inflexions that make one almost forget that most of them also had lyrics! The rhythmic backing is first class and the 1974 recording very real. Offering some 64 minutes of marvellous melody, this CD is in a class of its own. An ideal disc to titillate the ear and senses on a late summer evening.

OPERA AND MUSICALS

Girl Crazy: suite (orch. Anderson). *Overtures* (orch. Rose): *Oh, Kay!; Funny Face; Let 'em eat cake; Of thee I sing.* Arrangements: *Of thee I sing; Wintergreen for President* (orch. Paul); *3 Preludes* (orch. Stone); (i) *Rhapsody No. 2 for piano and orchestra.*
(M) ** Decca Phase Four (IMS) 443 900-2 [id.]. (i) Votapek; Boston Pops O, Fiedler.

Arthur Fiedler's performances are played with considerable panache and obvious idiomatic understanding. There are some valuable novelties here. *Wintergreen for President* quotes glibly from a number of other sources (including *The Pirates of Penzance*), and Fiedler readily catches its circus-style roisterous ambience. The *Second Rhapsody*, one of Gershwin's near misses, is given considerable fervour in its advocacy here, with Ralph Votapek's solo contribution sparking off a good orchestral response; but even so it remains obstinately unmemorable. The three piano *Preludes* do not readily transcribe for orchestra but are effective enough. The Phase Four recording is characteristically forwardly balanced but warm and brightly vivid in its colouring.

Porgy and Bess: highlights.
(BB) ** RCA Navigator 74321 24218-2 [5234-2RG]. Price, Warfield, Bubbles, Boatwright, Henson, Webb, Burton, Alonzo Jones, Berneice Hall, Stewart, RCA Victor O, Skitch Henderson – BERNSTEIN: *West Side Story: Symphonic dances.* **

The RCA studio compilation was recorded in 1963. Both Price and Warfield sing magnificently, and the supporting group is given lively direction by Skitch Henderson. The rest of the cast comes from the opera house rather than the musical theatre, which underlined the claims of Gershwin's work to be regarded as being in the mainstream of opera, some 25 years before this was confirmed by Rattle's complete recording. (N.B.: In the USA this appears to be still available at mid-price without a coupling.)

Gesualdo, Carlo (*c.* 1561–1613)

Leçons de Ténèbres: Responsories for Maundy Thursday.
(B) *** HM Musique d'Abord HMA 190220 [id.]. Deller Cons., Deller.

The Responses for Holy Week of 1611 are as remarkable and passionately expressive as any of Gesualdo's madrigals, and in depth of feeling they should be compared only with the finest music of the age. The invention is often unpredictable and nearly always highly original. The Deller Consort bring to this music much the same approach that distinguishes their handling of the madrigal literature. The colouring of the words is a high priority, yet it never oversteps the bounds of good taste to become precious or over-expressive. The consort blends remarkably well and intonation is excellent. This is temptingly inexpensive.

Motets for 5 voices (complete): *Ave dulcissima Maria; Ave Regina coelorum; Deus refugium et virtus; Dignare me, laudare te; Domine ne despicias; Exaudit Deus deprecationem meam; Hei mihi, Domine; Illumina faciem tuam; Laboravi in gemitu meo; Maria mater gratiae; O Crux benedicta; O vos omnes; Peccanteum me quotidie; Precibus et meritus beatae Mariae; Reminiscere miserationum Tuarum; Sancti Spiritus Domine; Tribularer si nescirem; Tribulationem meam; Venit lumen tuum Jerusalem.*
(BB) **(*) Naxos Dig. 8.550742 [id.]. Oxford Camerata, Jeremy Summerly.

The dozen singers of the Oxford Camerata sing these nineteen motets with beautifully blended tone and thoughtfully moulded melodic lines. Tempi are spacious and, though not unvaried, at times perhaps rather more movement would have been advantageous. Even so, *Ave dulcissima Maria* demonstrates how well Jeremy Summerly understands Gesualdo's style, and the following, deeply felt *Domine ne despicias* is another highlight of the programme. Similarly, the flowing *Sancti Spiritus Domine* and the sustained *Hei mihi, Domine* heard together show well the expressive contrast of the writing. The recordings were made in the Chapel of Hertford College, Oxford, and the choral sound has great beauty, with a finely judged balance between atmosphere and clarity. Even without texts and translations this is a stimulating and rewarding disc, and excellent value.

Gibbons, Christopher (1615–76)

Cupid and Death (with Matthew Locke).

(B) *** DHM Baroque Esprit 0542 77428-2 [id.]. Kirkby, Tubb, Holden, Nichols, King, Cornwell, D. Thomas, Wistreich, Consort of Musicke, Rooley.

Cupid and Death, 'a masque in four entries', dates from 1653. Christopher Gibbons, the son of Orlando, seems to have been the lesser partner in the project, with Matthew Locke providing the bulk of the music for this rustic fantasy on an ancient fable. Each of the five 'entries' or Acts is formally laid out in a set sequence of items – a suite of dances, a dialogue, a song and a chorus – and Rooley's team consistently brings out the fresh charm of the music. The spoken sections have been edited out for this welcome reissue, and now the music fits neatly on to a single CD (71 minutes).

Gibbons, Orlando (1583–1625)

Almighty and everlasting God; Blessed are all they; Glorious and powerful God; Lord, grant grace; O Lord, how do my woes increase; Sing unto the Lord; This is the record of John; We praise Thee, O Father.

(B) *** Cal. Approche CAL 6621 [(M) id.]. Clerkes of Oxenford, David Wulstan – SHEPPARD: *Mass 'Cantate'; Respond: 'Spiritus Sanctus'*. ***

This collection of eight verse-anthems of Orlando Gibbons makes an admirable coupling for some lesser-known music of John Sheppard. They are written for solo groups as well as for the full choir, and often with instrumental accompaniments, and their style obviously recalls similar music by Purcell. By comparison they are not found wanting. They are splendidly sung and recorded, and this is a genuine bargain.

Gilles, Jean (1668–1705)

Messe des morts (Requiem Mass).

(M) *** DG 437 087-2. Rodde, Nirouët, Hill, U. Studer, Kooy, Ghent Coll. Voc., Col. Mus. Ant., Herreweghe (with CORRETTE: *Carillon des morts* ***).

Like his English contemporary, Purcell, the Provençal Jean Gilles died sadly young. His *Requiem*, which for many years was a favourite work in France, was rejected by the two families who originally commissioned it, so Gilles decreed that it should be used for his own funeral. So great was regional pride in eighteenth-century Provence that the work was often heard alongside the *Requiem* of Campra with alternating movements from each! Gilles's rhythmic and harmonic vigour (with plentiful false relations to add tang) is well caught in this performance on original instruments, and the singers find the music's expressive style admirably. The *Carillon* was included by Michel Corrette in his own edition of the Gilles *Requiem*, printed in 1764, and is appropriately included here as a postlude.

Gilson, Paul (1865–1942)

De Zee (suite).

(BB) *** Discover Dig. DICD 920126 [id.]. Brussels BRT PO, Karl Anton Rickenbacher – DE BOECK: *Symphony in G*. ***

Like August de Boeck, also represented on this disc, Paul Gilson was a Belgian composer, born in 1865. His suite, *De Zee*, like de Boeck's *Symphony* is full of Russian echoes. It is a series of four seascapes half-way between Wagner's *Flying Dutchman* and Debussy's *La Mer*, with Rimsky-Korsakov's *Scheherazade* mixed in. Well played and recorded and, at Discover International's bargain price, an ideal disc for experimenting with.

Giordano, Umberto (1867–1948)

Andrea Chénier (complete).

(M) *** RCA 74321 39499-2 (2) [2046-2-RG]. Domingo, Scotto, Milnes, Alldis Ch., Nat. PO, Levine.

(M) **(*) EMI CMS5 65287-2 (2) [Ang. CDMB 65287]. Corelli, Stella, Sereni, Rome Op. Ch. & O, Santini.

Andrea Chénier with its defiant poet hero provides a splendid role for Domingo at his most heroic and the former servant, later revolutionary leader, Gérard, is a character well appreciated by Milnes. Scotto gives one of her most eloquent and beautiful performances, and Levine has rarely displayed his powers as an urgent and dramatic opera conductor more potently on record, with the bright recording intensifying the dramatic thrust of playing and singing. Stylishly repackaged in RCA's mid-priced UK Opera Treasury series, this is a clear first choice for this opera on CD.

The glory of the 1964 EMI version is the Chénier of Franco Corelli, one of his most satisfying performances on record with heroic tone gloriously exploited. The other singing is less distinguished. Though Antonietta Stella was never sweeter of voice than here, she hardly matches such rivals as Scotto or Caballé. The 1960s recording is vivid, with plenty of atmosphere, and has been transferred to CD most naturally, but the RCA set in the same price range, with Domingo and Scotto, remains a clear first choice.

Fedora (complete).

(M) **(*) Decca 433 033-2 (2). Olivero, Del Monaco, Gobbi, Monte Carlo Nat. Op. Ch. & O, Gardelli – ZANDONAI: *Francesca da Rimini*. **(*)

(M) ** Sony Dig. SM2K 42181 (2) [M2K 42181]. Marton, Carreras, Hungarian R. & TV Ch. & O, Patanè.

Fedora will always be remembered for one brief aria, the hero's *Amor ti vieta*; but, as this highly enjoyable recording confirms, there is much that is memorable in the score, even if nothing else quite approaches it. Meaty stuff, which brings some splendid singing from Magda Olivero and (more intermittently) from Del Monaco, with Gobbi in a light comedy part. Fine, vintage (1969), atmospheric recording.

On Sony, Eva Marton as Fedora, the Romanov princess, is aptly cast, with José Carreras taking the role of hero. In a work that should sound sumptuous it is not a help that the voices are placed forwardly, with the orchestra distanced well behind. That balance exaggerates the vibrato in Marton's voice, but it is a strong, sympathetic performance; Carreras, too, responds warmly to the lyricism of the role of the hero, Loris, giving a satisfyingly forthright account of *Amor ti vieta*. The rest of the cast is unremarkable, and Patanè's direction lacks bite, again partly a question of orchestral balance.

Giuliani, Mauro (1781–1828)

(i; ii) *Guitar concertos Nos. 1 in A, Op. 30; 2 in A, Op. 36; 3 in F, Op. 70; Introduction, theme with variations and polonaise (for guitar and orchestra), Op. 65.* (i) *Grande ouverture, Op. 61; Gran Sonata Eroica in A; La Melanchonia; Variations on 'Ich bin a Kohlbauern Bub', Op. 49; Variations on a theme by Handel, Op. 107;* (i; iii) *Variazioni concertanti, Op. 130.*

(B) *** Ph. Duo 454 262-2 (2) [id.]. (i) Pepe Romero, (ii) with ASMF, Marriner; (iii) with Celedonio Romero.

It was a capital idea to combine Giuliani's three engaging guitar concertos on a Duo, and each disc is generously filled out with other concertante and solo music. Romero is a first-rate player, and his relaxed music-making and easy bravura bring an attractive, smiling quality. But what makes the concertos so distinctive are the splendid accompaniments provided by the Academy of St Martin-in-the-Fields under Marriner. The shaping of the naïf contours of Giuliani's orchestral ritornello for the *First Concerto* is deliciously judged, and throughout there are many delightful touches from the orchestra. The finale is irresistibly vivacious, the sparkling orchestral rhythms a constant joy. The *F major Concerto* has comparable charm. Its first movement begins with an engaging little march theme whose dotted contour reminds one of Hummel (the two composers were almost exact contemporaries), and the amiable *Siciliano* which forms the slow movement is matched by an unforceful closing Polonaise. Hummel again comes rhythmically to mind in the first movement of the *Second concerto*, which is for strings alone. The *Andantino* here is pleasingly atmospheric and the final rondo again sparkles rhythmically. The *Introduction, theme with variations and polonaise* (originally conceived for guitar and string quartet) is like a mini-concerto and, if the basic idea of the variations only just rises above the trivial, it is redeemed by a performance of vitality and charm. The Op. 49 *Variations* are agreeable but slight, but the *Sonata Eroica*, although effectively conceived and impressively presented, hardly merits its grand sobriquet as provided by Ricordi when it was published posthumously. The *Variations concertanti* for two guitars, in which Pepe is joined by Celedonio, is a more ambitious late work which exploits the duet variation form with much skill. It is played with affection and ready virtuosity. The mid-1960s recording throughout is warm and refined, very easy on the ear.

Guitar concerto in A, Op. 30.

(M) *** DG (IMS) 439 984-2. Siegfried Behrend, I Musici – CARULLI: *Concerto in A* ***; VIVALDI: *Guitar concertos.* **(*)

(B) *** Sony SBK 58168; *SBT 58168* [id.]. John Williams, ECO – RODRIGO: *Concierto de Aranjuez* etc; VIVALDI: *Concerto, RV 93.* ***

(B) **(*) Decca Eclipse 448 709-2; *448 709-4* [(M) id. import]. Eduardo Fernández, ECO, Malcolm – PAGANINI: *Sonata;* VIVALDI: *Concertos.* **(*)

Giuliani's *A major Concerto* is presented by Behrend with much elegance and finesse and is immaculately recorded. Its catchy main theme is endearing; though the music overall is slight, it is nicely crafted.

John Williams's account, too, is elegantly turned and pleasingly recorded, and choice will no doubt rest with the coupling. This reissue is excellent value.

A rather low-key, essentially chamber performance from the highly musical Fernández, who refuses to show off. He is accompanied elegantly by Malcolm and the ECO and is most naturally recorded. Some might feel the finale should be more extrovert, although it does not lack spirit; on the other hand, the intimacy of this music-making has its own appeal.

Grand overture, Op. 61; Rossiniana No. 3, Op. 121.

(M) **(*) RCA 09026 61593-2. Julian Bream (guitar) – SOR: *Grand solo sonata* etc.; DIABELLI: *Sonata in A.* **(*)

The *Grand Overture* is a rather imposing piece which Bream despatches with panache, whereas Giulini's six *Rossinianae* were, as the title suggests, based on the operas of Rossini, and one might expect the music of No. 3 to be witty and memorably tuneful, but that is not so. Bream makes cuts, but the music outstays its welcome. The playing is first class, of course, and the recording exemplary.

Variations on a theme by Handel, Op. 107.

(B) *** Sony SBK 62425; *SBT 62425* [id.]. John Williams (guitar) – PAGANINI: *Caprice 24; Grand sonata;* D. SCARLATTI: *Sonatas;* VILLA-LOBOS: *5 Preludes.* ***

The *Variations* are on Handel's famous *Harmonious blacksmith* theme. Their construction is guileless but agreeable, and they are expertly played and well recorded. This is only a small part of a well-planned and exceptionally generous collection devoted mainly to Paganini and Domenico Scarlatti.

Glass, Philip (born 1937)

Company; Façades.

(M) *** Virgin/EMI Dig. CUV5 61121-2. LCO, Warren-Green – ADAMS: *Shaker loops* *** ❁; REICH: *8 Lines* ***; HEATH: *Frontier.* ***

Company consists of four brief but sharply contrasted movements for strings; *Façades* offers a haunting cantilena for soprano saxophone, suspended over atmospherically undulating strings. The performances are full of intensity and are expertly played, and the recording is excellent.

Glazunov, Alexander (1865–1936)

Carnaval overture, Op. 45; Concert waltzes Nos. 1–2, Opp. 47 & 51; Spring, Op. 34; Salomé (incidental music), Op. 90: Introduction; Dance.

(BB) **(*) Naxos Dig. 8.553838 [id.]. Moscow SO, Igor Golovschin.

This collection of shorter pieces by Glazunov makes up a delightful disc, bringing out the composer's amiable side. The *Carnaval overture* comes from 1892, between the *Third* and *Fourth Symphonies*, and is scored for a large orchestra, including even an optional part for organ. It is a jaunty, sparkling piece with first-rate tunes. There are also some attractive ideas in *Spring* (*Vesna*), a charming work written the previous year and similarly refined and transparent in its orchestration. It is evocative in a leisurely way, playing on birdsong, building to a sensuous climax. In places Glazunov almost anticipates *The Seasons*. Some people may find the disc worth considering just for this piece. The more familiar *Concert waltzes* from the same period contain some of Glazunov's most winning tunes, the one Tchaikovskian in flavour, the other Viennese. They are played decently enough, though the last ounce of finish is missing. The novelty most likely to excite curiosity here is Glazunov's music for Oscar Wilde's *Salomé*, written in

1908, three years after Richard Strauss's celebrated opera, and apparently intended as an answer to Strauss (one of Glazunov's pet hates) but hardly achieving that, with Salome's dance leading to a Polovtsian climax. It is surprisingly conventional and tame, and Salome sheds her veils in a most unerotic fashion. But this cannot be blamed on the conductor, and generally these are warm, idiomatic performances, richly recorded.

Chant du ménestrel (for cello and orchestra), Op. 71.

(B) *** DG Double 437 952-2 (2) [id.]. Rostropovich, Boston SO, Ozawa – BERNSTEIN: *3 Meditations;* BOCCHERINI: *Cello concerto No. 2;* SHOSTAKOVICH: *Cello concerto No. 2;* TARTINI: *Cello concerto;* TCHAIKOVSKY: *Andante cantabile* etc.; VIVALDI: *Cello concertos.* ***

Glazunov's *Chant du ménestrel* shows the nostalgic appeal of 'things long ago and far away'. It is a short but appealing piece and is splendidly played by Rostropovich within a highly recommendable Double DG anthology.

Violin concerto in A min., Op. 82.

❁ (M) (***) EMI (SIS) mono CDH7 64030-2 [id.]. Heifetz, LPO, Barbirolli – SIBELIUS: *Violin concerto* (**); TCHAIKOVSKY: *Violin concerto.* (***)

(M) *** RCA 09026 61744-2 [61744-2-RG]. Heifetz, RCA Victor SO, Hendl – PROKOFIEV: *Violin concerto No. 2;* SIBELIUS: *Concerto.* ***

(BB) *** Naxos Dig. 8.550758 [id.]. Ilya Kaler, Polish Nat. RSO (Katowice), Kolchinsky – DVORAK: *Concerto* etc. ***

(B) *** Carlton Dig. 30367 0031-2 [id.]. Udagawa, LPO, Klein – Concert ***.

(M) ** Decca Phase Four 455 157-2 [id.]. Silvia Marcovici, New Philh. O, Stokowski – TCHAIKOVSKY: *Symphony No. 5.* **(*)

Heifetz's recording of the Glazunov *Violin concerto* with Barbirolli was made in 1934 when the composer was still alive. It has greater expressive breadth and spaciousness than his later record with Walter Hendl and the Chicago orchestra and there is great warmth. Intonation is incredibly sure and the tone sweet; generally speaking, this first Heifetz version of the concerto has never been surpassed. For those who want more modern, stereo sound, Heifetz is again incomparable; his account is the strongest and most passionate (as well as the most perfectly played) in the catalogue. The RCA orchestra under Hendl gives splendid support.

The Russian violinist Ilya Kaler gives a rapturously lyrical performance, and Camilla Kolchinsky's accompaniment is equally warm and supportive. The resonant acoustic of the Concert Hall of Polish Radio gives a big, spacious orchestral sound, but Ilya Kaler's tone is full to match, and the violin playing can certainly accommodate the scrutiny of the fairly close microphones. The Dvořák *Concerto* is hardly less successful, and the delightful *Romance* is thrown in for good measure.

The Glazunov also receives a heartfelt performance from Udagawa which is almost as compelling as the virtuoso stereo accounts from such master violinists as Heifetz and Perlman. In the finale she may not offer quite such bravura fireworks as they do but, with more open sound, the result is very persuasive in its lilting way.

Not all will take to Silvia Marcovici's at times slightly febrile tone-quality in Glazunov's endearing concerto. It is a high-romantic performance with a gypsy flavour, spirited but indulgent. Stokowski provides lushly sympathetic support. The recording was made live at the London Festival Hall in 1972 and, although the microphones are close, the solo playing survives their scrutiny.

Cortège solennel, Op. 50; Fantaisie, Op. 53; March on a Russian theme, Op. 76; Mazurka, Op. 18; Stenka Razin, Op. 13. Une fête slave, Op. 26.

(BB) ** Naxos Dig. 8.553538 [id.]. Moscow SO, Konstantin Krimets.

Eminently serviceable accounts of these Glazunov pieces, including the popular *Stenka Razin*. As often with recordings from this source, one is left with the suspicion that the performances would have benefited from further rehearsal. All the same, this repertoire is not generously represented at any price level and it would be curmudgeonly not to give this issue a welcome. Decent recording, too.

From the Middle Ages, Op. 79; The Kremlin, Op. 30; Poème epique, Op. posth.; Poème lyrique, Op. 12.

(BB) * Naxos Dig. 8.553537 [id.]. Moscow SO, Konstantin Krimets.

None of these is top-drawer Glazunov, and they need the most expert and sympathetic advocacy if they are to win acceptance. This is not in evidence on this disc which, despite its generous playing time and modest price, offers playing that rarely rises above the routine.

From the Middle Ages (suite), *Op. 79; The Sea, Op. 28; Spring, Op. 34; Stenka Razin, Op. 13.*
(M) *** Chandos Dig. CHAN 7049 [id.]. SNO, Järvi.

Although the music is inferior to Tchaikovsky, Glazunov's *From the Middle Ages suite* has charm, and Järvi has the knack of making you think it is better than it is. The tone-poem *Spring* was written two years after *The Sea* and is infinitely more imaginative; in fact it is as fresh and delightful as its companion is cliché-ridden. At one point Glazunov even looks forward to *The Seasons*. *Stenka Razin* has its moments of vulgarity – how otherwise with the *Song of the Volga Boatmen* a recurrent theme? – but it makes a colourful enough opening item for this collection which offers persuasive and very well-recorded performances from the Royal Scottish National Orchestra.

Raymonda (ballet; complete), *Op. 57*.
(B) *** Carlton Classics Dig. 30366 00067 (2) [(M) id.]. Kirov Op. O, Viktor Fedotov.
(BB) **(*) Naxos 8.553503/4 [id.]. Moscow SO, Alexander Anissimov.

Although Glazunov lacks the incredible fund of invention or the musical substance that Tchaikovsky commanded, his three-Act *Raymonda* (1896–8) includes much music of great charm and grace. Not only is it expertly fashioned and orchestrated (as one might expect), it offers warmth and has the capacity to delight. If the outpouring of melody is not as rich and seemingly limitless as in the great Tchaikovsky ballets, its geniality and urbanity – and some endearing numbers – make it well worth having. This new performance from the Kirov orchestra finds them in good form, even if the upper strings could be richer; the recording, too, is more than serviceable. It is good without automatically reaching the distinction of some three-star recommendations. However, on balance it would be curmudgeonly to withhold the third star, for its merits are considerable and it is unlikely that a better version will come along in the immediate future. Not that it matters, but the disc deserves a special prize for having the ugliest label.

The new Naxos version is played elegantly and affectionately, and the Moscow upper strings are fuller and warmer than those of the Kirov players as recorded. It does not lack life. But the Naxos recording, in seeking atmosphere, creates overall a rather less vibrant, less vivid effect than the Kirov version, where the colours are more brightly lit, although this is partly caused by Anissimov's tendency to more luxuriant tempi. The *Entry of the Vassal and Peasants* in Act I is a good deal more lively in Kirov than in Moscow. But that is not to say that the inexpensive Naxos version is not very enjoyable in its more sumptuously spacious manner, for the orchestral playing is very sympathetic.

Scènes de ballet.
(M) ** Revelation RV 10006 [id.]. Moscow RSO, Rozhdestvensky – PROKOFIEV: *Andante for strings* *(*); SIBELIUS: *Symphony No. 7; Rakastava.* (*)

A bizarre coupling. Will collectors of Glazunov's charming ballet music want a late Sibelius symphony, and vice versa? Whatever the thinking behind this coupling (none, we imagine), there are some appealing movements in this score, which was originally (and more appropriately) coupled with Rimsky-Korsakov's *Antar* in the mid-1970s. A decent performance and recording, but coupled with an uncompetitive Sibelius *Seventh*.

The Seasons (ballet; complete) *Op. 67*.
(M) *** EMI CDM5 65911-2. Concert Arts O, Robert Irving – SCARLATTI/TOMMASINI: *Good humoured ladies;* WALTON: *Wise virgins.* ***
(BB) **(*) Naxos Dig. 8.550079; *4550079* [id.]. Czech RSO (Bratislava), Ondrej Lenárd – TCHAIKOVSKY: *Sleeping Beauty suite.* **

The Seasons (ballet), *Op. 67; Concert waltzes Nos. 1 in D, Op. 47; 2 in F, Op. 51.*
(B) *** EMI forte CZS5 69361-2 (2) [CDFB 69361]. Philh. O, Svetlanov – ARENSKY: *Variations on a theme of Tchaikovsky* ***; RIMSKY-KORSAKOV: *Scheherazade.* **

The Seasons (complete ballet), *Op. 67; Scènes de ballet, Op. 52; Scène dansante, Op. 81.*
(BB) ** Naxos Dig. 8.553915 [id.]. Moscow SO, Anissimov.

The Seasons is an early work, first performed at St Petersburg in 1900, the choreography being by the famous Petipa. With colourful orchestration, a generous sprinkling of distinctive melody and, at the opening of *Autumn*, one of the most virile and memorable tunes Glazunov ever penned, the ballet surely deserves to return to the repertoire.

Robert Irving's recording with its happily chosen couplings serves to remind us of a first-class ballet conductor of the 1960s, working with both the Sadler's Wells and the New York City companies. His 1960 account has never been surpassed, and the recording, made at New York's Manhattan Center Ballroom, still sounds astonishingly fresh, while the resonant ambience prevents the quality from being too dated. The Concert Arts Orchestra is a pseudonym for a much better-known British combination, and they play with wit, warmth and astonishing precision. The strings are immaculate and there are consistently sensitive and charmingly delicate wind solos. Irving shapes and points the melodies with consummate balletic feeling and his reading is delightfully evocative. The stirring tune of *Autumn* is taken very fast and has strikingly more vitality than with Svetlanov.

Svetlanov's is a classic account of *The Seasons* which stands up very well to rival versions that have appeared in the almost 20 years since it was made. Svetlanov's account is played most beautifully. His approach is engagingly affectionate; he caresses the lyrical melodies persuasively so that, if the big tune of the *Bacchanale* has slightly less thrust than usual, it fits readily into the overall conception. The glowing Abbey Road recording is excellent and vividly remastered. It comes in harness with a very Russian *Scheherazade*, which he recorded with the LSO but about which we have some reservations (see below), and Barbirolli's highly persuasive version of the endearing Arensky *Variations* for strings.

Ondrej Lenárd gives a pleasing bargain account of Glazunov's delightful score, finding plenty of delicacy, while the entry of Glazunov's most famous tune at the opening of the *Autumn Bacchanale* is very virile indeed. The sound is atmospheric, yet with plenty of fullness.

The Moscow Symphony Orchestra have some fine woodwind soloists, who are often at their best here, and the strings also sing warmly enough; but the closing *Polonaise* of the attractive *Scènes de ballet* seems rather laboured, and in *The Seasons* Anissimov is inclined to let the violin melodies languish, though he is energetic enough in the famous Bacchic revelry of *Autumn*. The *Scène dansante*, a much shorter ballet score, is well worth having, again showing the composer on good melodic form. But Anissimov's account of *The Seasons* would not be a first choice.

Symphonies Nos. 1 in E (Slavyanskaya), Op. 5; 4 in E flat, Op. 48.
(BB) **(*) Naxos Dig. 8.553561 [id.]. Moscow SO, Alexander Anissimov.

What a remarkable and delightful work the Glazunov *First Symphony* is! – not only on account of the composer's youth (he was a mere sixteen at the time) but also the quality and fertility of its invention and its expert craftsmanship! Both here and in the *Fourth*, Alexander Anissimov gets an eminently sympathetic performance from the Moscow orchestra, though one can imagine livelier and lighter playing.

Symphonies Nos. 2 in F sharp min., Op. 16; 7 in F (Pastoral), Op. 77.
(BB) ** Naxos Dig. 8.553769 [id.]. Moscow SO, Alexander Anissimov.

Glazunov's *Second Symphony* dates from 1886. In spite of its Lisztian dedication, it does not have the strongest profile. However, its slow movement has a sinuous, Borodin-like melody of genuine memorability. Here Anissimov and the Moscow Symphony Orchestra respond to the music's Slavonic feeling, but overall without quite the degree of passion and drama the work demands, and the violins, as recorded, lack allure. However, the 'Pastoral' *Seventh* of 1902 (which makes a distinct melodic reference to Beethoven's work in the same key) is altogether more successful. The woodwind capture the rustic charm of the opening, and in the *Andante* the string cantilena has genuine ardour. The Scherzo (one of Glazunov's finest) is most engagingly presented, the brass as impressive as the woodwind, and the finale then bounces along vigorously. Its frequent changes of tempo and mood are held together well and Anissimov draws the music together in the coda. The recording is well balanced and full, if not top-drawer. With any reservations noted, this is fair value.

Tsar Iedesyskiy (King of the Jews).
(BB) *(*) Naxos Dig. 8.553575 [id.]. Moscow Cappella & SO, Golovschin.

Glazunov's incidental music to Konstantin Romanov's *Tsar Iedesyskiy* (*King of the Jews*), composed just before the outbreak of the First World War, is new to the catalogue and, although its invention is not always consistent in quality, the score offers considerable artistic rewards. There is an unaffected simplicity that is quite touching, and the naturalness of the musical inspiration outweighs any of its longueurs or miscalculations. Rozhdestvensky at full price (on Chandos CHAN 9467) is in every way superior to the bargain rival on Naxos, which has the merit of economy but offers a performance that is neither as well prepared nor as accomplished as the Chandos.

Glière, Reinhold (1875–1956)

Symphony No. 3 in B min. (Ilya Murometz), Op. 42.
(BB) ** Naxos Dig. 8.550858 [id.]. Slovak RSO, Johanos.

Naxos have acted sensibly in reducing the price of the Johanos version (originally on Marco Polo). While the full-price Chandos alternative is well worth the extra cost, the rougher Slovak Radio performance is perfectly acceptable and will suit those who want to explore this score at little cost.

Glinka, Mikhail (1805–57)

(i) *Andante cantabile and Rondo in D min.; Jota aragonesa (Spanish overture No. 1); Polka No. 1* (orch. Balakirev); *Prince Kholmsky* (incidental music): *Overture and Entr'actes to Acts II–V. Recollections of a summer night in Madrid (Spanish overture No. 2); Symphony on two Russian themes* (orch. Shebalin); *Waltz fantasia; A Life for the Tsar (Ivan Susanin): Overture and dances. Ruslan and Ludmilla:* (ii) *Overture; Dances; Tchernomor's march.*
(B) *** BMG/Melodiya Twofer 74321 53461-2 (2) [id.]. (i) USSR SO; (ii) Bolshoi Theatre O; Svetlanov.

An eminently recommendable survey of Glinka's orchestral output. Apart from the *Ruslan and Ludmilla* overture and the *Jota aragonesa*, little of Glinka's music is heard in the concert hall, and these recordings are most useful in filling a gap. The performances embrace a considerable time-span (1963–90) though the majoriy are from the 1970s and 1980s, and some have been available before on LP on HMV Melodiya. The playing of the USSR Symphony Orchestra is nothing if not expert and idiomatic; and the recordings, though variable in quality, are generally very good indeed.

Jota aragonaise; Kamarinskaya; Souvenir d'une nuit d'été à Madrid; Valse-fantaisie. A Life for the Tsar: 3 Dances. Ruslan and Ludmilla: Overture; March of Chernomor.
(M) *(*) Chant du Monde Russian Season Dig. RUS 788114. Tchaikovsky Russian RSO, Fedoseyev.

The present disc is pleasingly recorded but the performances under Vladimir Fedoseyev, a distinguished conductor, are surprisingly lacklustre and wanting in charm. Indeed there are times in the *Valse fantaisie* and the *Polonaise* from *A Life for the Tsar* when the effect is almost band-masterly.

Ruslan and Ludmilla: Overture.
❀ (BB) *** Belart 450 017-2 [(M) London Weekend 417 689-2]. LSO, Solti – MUSSORGSKY: *Khovanshchina Prelude; Night;* BORODIN: *Prince Igor*: excerpts. ***
(M) *** RCA GD 60176 [Basic 100 09026 68363-2]. Chicago SO, Fritz Reiner – PROKOFIEV: *Alexander Nevsky* etc. ***

Solti's electrifying account of the *Ruslan and Ludmilla* overture is probably the most exciting ever recorded (it dates from the mid-1960s) with the lyrical element providing a balancing warmth. The LSO strings are right up on their toes throughout, and it is they to whom we award a Rosette for fizzing ensemble and real sparkle. The recording is brightly lit, but not unacceptably so. The couplings are also very successful.

Reiner's performance, too, is highly infectious and the (1959) Chicago sound brings plenty of colour and warmth.

Ruslan and Ludmilla (complete).
(M) **(*) RCA/Melodiya 74321 29348 (3) [id.]. Nesterenko, Rudenko, Yaroslavtsev, Sinyavskaya, Morozov, Fomina, Bolshoi Theatre, Moscow, Ch. & O, Yuri Simonov.

The Bolshoi recording on BMG/Melodiya at mid-price brings a warm and convincing account, typical of Bolshoi standards in the late 1970s, with Yevgeni Nesterenko magnificent as Ruslan, rich, firm and heroic. Though Simonov's conducting is not as refined as Gergiev's on Philips, his thrust and purposefulness hold the piece together well and, though the recording is uneven, such a passage as the scene with the head is eerily effective. Another outstanding performance comes from Boris Morozov as the braggart, Farlaf, with his comic patter Rondo in Act II, not just brilliantly agile but resonant too and full of fun, reminding one of Chaliapin's famous recording. Alexei Maslennikov is most affecting in Finn's Ballad, and Nina Fomina is a rich, firm Gorislava. One snag is that Bela Rudenko as Ludmilla is shrill under pressure, and a few cuts are made in Act V; but it is still an enjoyable if uneven set.

Gluck, Christophe (1714–87)

Alceste (complete).
(M) (**) Naxos mono 8.110006/7 [id.]. Bampton, Maison, Warren, De Paolis, Farell, NY Met. Op. Ch. & O, Panizza.

Recorded from a broadcast in 1941, and transferred at a low level, this issue in the Naxos historic series offers scrubby and limited orchestral sound. Happily, that does not prevent one from appreciating the liveliness of the direction of Ettore Panizza (using a large orchestra) and, above all, the superb singing of Rose Bampton in the title-role. Her delivery is consistently firm as well as deeply expressive, as in her incisive account of the big aria ending Act I, *Divinités du Styx.* Her mastery makes it odd to have it emphasized in Milton Cross's spoken introduction (from the original broadcast) that she was merely deputizing for Marjorie Lawrence. Leonard Warren as the High Priest is also in superb voice, with René Maison as a forthright Admete.

Der betrogene Kadi (complete).

(M) *** CPO/EMI CPO 999 552-2. Rothenberger, Donath, Gedda, Berry, Hirte, Marheineke, Bav. State Op. Ch. & O, Suitner.

Gluck wrote this light-hearted *Singspiel*, *Die betrogene Kadi* ('The cheated Cadi'), in the year before he completed his first version of *Orfeo*, providing an astonishing contrast with that masterpiece. Taking his libretto from a French source, he amiably adopted a Turkish theme, then fashionable, so that this one-act curtain-raiser had considerable popularity in Vienna. Unlike Mozart in *Entführung*, Gluck generally avoids the exotic, preferring a gentler style. Even so, he gives the Kadi a vigorous aria which may have given Mozart the idea for some of Osmin's music. The cast is a strong one, with Helen Donath providing a sweet contrast to the ever-bright Anneliese Rothenberger, and with Walter Berry as the Kadi and Nicolai Gedda as the hero, Nuradin, characterizing well. The 1978 EMI recording still sounds full and vivid.

Le Cinesi (The Chinese women).

(M) *** HM/BMG Dig. GD 77174 [77174-2-RG]. Poulenard, Von Otter, Banditelli, De Mey, Schola Cantorum Basiliensis O, Jacobs.

Gluck's hour-long opera-serenade provides a fascinating view of the composer's lighter side and, rather like Mozart in *Entführung*, Gluck uses jangling and tinkling percussion instruments in the overture to indicate an exotic setting. Otherwise the formal attitudes in Metastasio's libretto – written some twenty years before Gluck set it – are pure eighteenth century.

Iphigénie en Aulide: highlights.

(M) *** Erato/Warner Dig. 0630 15732-2. Van Dam, Von Otter, Dawson, Aler, Monteverdi Ch., Lyon Op. O, Gardiner.

Iphigénie en Aulide was Gluck's first piece in French and it anticipated the *Tauride* opera in its speed and directness of treatment, so different from the leisurely and expansive traditions of *opera seria*. Gardiner here reconstructs the score as presented in the first revival of 1775; the recording conveys the tensions of a live performance without the distractions of intrusive stage noise. Agamemnon is here sung superbly by José van Dam. In the title-role Lynne Dawson builds up a touching portrait of the heroine. Her sweet, pure singing is well contrasted with the positive strength of Anne Sofie von Otter as Clytemnestra, and John Aler brings clear, heroic attack to the tenor role of Achille. The performance is crowned by the superb ensemble-singing of the Monteverdi Choir in the many choruses. The 74 minutes' highlights disc is well selected and the presentation admirable, with a full translation and a linking introduction provided for each excerpt. Excellent recording.

Iphigénie en Aulide (complete in German; arr. Wagner).

(M) *** RCA 74321 32236-2 (2). Moffo, Fischer-Dieskau, Schmidt, Spiess, Stewart, Augér, Bav. R Ch., Munich R. O, Eichhorn.

Look closely at the small print and you will find that this is hardly Gluck at all. Wagner's arrangement, used here is, by the standards of modern purism, a total travesty and the use of German instead of French only reinforces the stylistic conflict. But with an urgently dramatic performance, with a formidable list of soloists, excellent choral singing and fine playing, this is enjoyable entertainment in its own right. Maybe, as the scholars tell us, we shall come to regard Raymond Leppard's arrangements of Cavalli in the same light as this realization, with its enriched orchestration and harmony, its cuts and additions and its amended plot. But, compact as it is, Gluck/Wagner is every bit as effective as Cavalli/Leppard, and Wagnerians at least need not hesitate. Good stage atmosphere in the recording. The German libretto comes without a translation.

Iphigénie en Aulide: Overture. Orfeo ed Euridice, Act II.

(M) (***) BMG/RCA mono GD 60280 [id.]. Merriman, Gibson, Robert Shaw Ch., NBC SO, Toscanini – BEETHOVEN: *Fidelio: Abscheulicher!* (***)

Gluck was one of the few eighteenth-century opera composers whom Toscanini enjoyed conducting. Though the opening account of the *Iphigénie Overture* is predictably rugged and strong rather than warm or tender, there is much in the other recordings which belies the conventional view of this conductor as rigid and implacable. In Nan Merriman, strong, firm and distinctive, he chose extremely well for the title-role in *Orfeo*, and it is a pity that as a supplement to Act II – with *Che puro ciel* delicate as well as intense – she did not record *Che faro* with him too. Yet this deeply felt concert performance of Act II makes a satisfying whole, and is well supplemented by an alternative version of the *Dance of the Blessed Spirits* and the Beethoven aria. Limited sound, well transferred.

Orfeo ed Euridice (complete).

(M) *** Erato/Warner Dig. 2292 45864-2 (2). J. Baker, Speiser, Gale, Glyndebourne Ch., LPO, Leppard.
(M) **(*) RCA GD 87896 (2) [7896-2-RG]. Verrett, Moffo, Raskin, Rome Polyphonic Ch., Virtuosi di Roma, Fasano.
(M) **(*) RCA Dig. 74321 32238-2 (2). Lipovšek, Popp, Kaufmann, Bav. R. Ch., Munich R. O, Hager.
(M) ** Van. 08.4040 72 (2) [OVC 4039/40]. Forrester, Stich-Randall, Steffek, V. State Op. Ch. & O, Mackerras.
(M) ** EMI Dig. CMS5 66507-2 (2) [CDMB 66507]. Agnes Baltsa, Margaret Marshall, Edita Gruberová, Amb. Op. Ch., Philh. O, Muti.
(B) ** DG Double 453 145-2 (2). Fischer-Dieskau, Janowitz, Moser, Munich Bach Ch. and O, Richter.
(M) (**) DG (IMS) mono 439 101-2 (2). Simionato, Jurinac, Sciutti, V. State Op. Ch., VPO, Karajan.

The Erato version of *Orfeo ed Euridice*, directly based on the Glyndebourne production in which Dame Janet Baker made her very last stage appearance in opera, was recorded in 1982, immediately after the run of live performances. Often credited with being a romanticizer of the eighteenth century, Leppard in fact presents the score with freshness and power, indeed with toughness. Nowhere is that clearer than in the great scene leading up to the aria, *Che farò*, where Dame Janet commandingly conveys the genuine bitterness and anger of Orpheus at Eurydice's death. That most famous of Gluck's arias comes over fresh and clear with no sentimentality whatever, and conversely the display aria which brings Act I to a close has passion and expressiveness even in the most elaborate coloratura. Elisabeth Speiser as Eurydice and Elizabeth Gale as Amor are both disappointing but, as in the theatre, the result is a complete and moving experience centring round a great performance from Dame Janet. The complete ballet-postlude is included, delightful celebration music. The recording has been enhanced in the CD transfer, bright and vivid without edginess, with the modern orchestral strings sounding both fresh and warm. At mid-price this makes a clear first choice. Highlights (74 minutes) are available on Erato (0630 13805-9).

Clearly, if you have a mezzo as firm and sensitive as Shirley Verrett, then everything is in favour of your using the original Italian version. Fasano also uses the right-sized orchestra (of modern instruments) and adopts an appropriately classical style. Anna Moffo and Judith Raskin match Verrett in clean, strong singing, and the Rome Polyphonic Chorus is far more incisive than most Italian choirs. The recording is vivid and atmospheric but emphasizes the music's dramatic qualities rather than its tenderness. However, this makes a good alternative mid-priced recommendation.

Hager's Munich version, recorded in 1986 in full and atmospheric if slightly distanced sound, brings a good, enjoyable, middle-of-the-road performance. Marjana Lipovšek has a beautiful, rich mezzo inclined to fruitiness, which yet in this breeches role is well able to characterize Orfeo strongly and positively. So *Che farò* is warm and direct in its expressiveness, with Lipovšek avoiding distracting mannerism both here and in recitative. Lucia Popp makes a delightful Euridice and Julie Kaufman, though less distinctive, is fresh and bright as Amor. The chorus is on the heavyweight side for Gluck, but that adds to the power of the performance, which uses the 1762 Vienna version of the score, though with instrumental numbers added from the Paris version. The libretto has the full Italian text without translation.

Mackerras in his mid-1960s Vanguard recording conducts a fresh and intense performance, boldly opting for the Italian version at a time when almost all performances mixed the Vienna and Paris texts. Mackerras makes a concession in including the *Dance of the Furies* and *Dance of the Blessed Spirits* from the Paris version, and his speeds are often very slow by latterday standards. Also his Orfeo, the magnificent Canadian contralto, Maureen Forrester, for all the richness of her singing, follows the oratorio tradition. Good recording for its period.

Muti chose to record the relatively severe, 1762 version of *Orfeo ed Euridice* which eliminates some much-loved passages added later, but then he opted for a most unstylish approach, sleek and smooth but full of romantic exaggerations. The pity is that the trio of principals was quite strong. Sadly, even Agnes Baltsa cannot make *Che farò* sound stylish when the speed is so leaden. The recording is warm and rounded and the sound generally first class.

Though the singing is stylish and there is a very good chorus and much to enjoy on this Richter set, the very fact that a baritone is featured in the main role, singing a part written for alto (or tenor in the Paris version), means that this recording is not a serious contender. But Fischer-Dieskau's extra expressiveness and his response to word-meanings bring sure rewards, and the rest of the cast supports him well, so admirers of this artist will find this worth exploring at DG Double price. The 1967 recording, made in the spacious acoustics of the Munich Hercukes Saal, is excellent.

Using the usual composite text, Karajan in his 1959 Salzburg Festival performance conducts a characteristically dramatic and intense performance with a starry cast, a big-sounding orchestra and few concessions to baroque practice. Sadly, Simionato is a disappointing Orfeo, rich in the lower register but with a pronounced vibrato above.

Orfeo ed Euridice (abridged version).
(B) (***) Dutton Lab. mono CDEA 5015 [(M) id.]. Kathleen Ferrier, Ann Ayars, Zoë Vlachopoulos, Glyndebourne Festival Ch., Southern PO, Fritz Stiedry.

Recorded in 1947 after the early post-war staging of the opera at Glyndebourne, this hour-long collection of excerpts concentrates on the contribution of Kathleen Ferrier in the title-role, giving a very vivid idea of her darkly intense reading. Though this was a period when romantic treatment of eighteenth-century opera was the rule, Stiedry keeps a taut rein on the performance while letting Ferrier emerge in full expressiveness. So the climactic aria, *Che faro*, is much faster than in Ferrier's later recording in English, but no less moving in context. In their brief contributions, Ann Ayars as Euridice and Zoë Vlachopoulos as Amor sing with clean precision, though it is a pity that the booklet does not identify who is singing in which items, particularly when no text is provided. Otherwise, this is an outstanding disc, most welcome at bargain price in the Essential Archive series. The Dutton transfers are superb, offering astonishingly vivid and immediate sound, bringing to light at last an important Ferrier recording that for far too long has been buried in the vaults.

Orfeo ed Euridice: highlights.
(M) *** Decca 452 735-2 (from complete recording, with Marilyn Horne, Pilar Lorengar, Helen Donath, ROHCG Ch. & O, Solti).

Solti's recording of *Orfeo ed Euridice* was made in the Kingsway Hall in 1969. His conducting combines his characteristic brilliance and dramatic bite with warm sympathy for the eighteenth-century idiom. Where often in this opera the progress of the drama can be forgotten, here the experience is riveting when the interpretation consistently combines drama with delicacy. Marilyn Horne makes a formidably strong Orfeo, wonderfully secure, with fine control of tone. Pilar Lorengar sings sweetly and appealingly, but is not always quite steady, while Helen Donath is charming in the role of Amor. The 62-minute selection is well made, including of course *Che puro ciel* and *Che farò*, plus Solti's dramatic accounts of the *Dance of the Furies* and the winningly gracious *Dance of the Blessed Spirits*, where the ear revels in the lovely playing of the modern string instruments. The recording quality is excellent. In short, this makes an excellent sampler, although it was a pity that Decca – perhaps understandably – did not choose to include the brilliant display aria, *Addio, o miei sospiri* (taken from Bertoni's *Tancredi*) with which Horne and Solti opted to conclude Act I in the complete set. A cued synopsis is included.

Goldmark, Karl (1830–1915)

Violin concerto in A min., Op. 28.
(BB) *** Naxos Dig. 8.553579 [id.]. Vera Tsu, Razumovsky Sinfonia, Yu Long – KORNGOLD: *Violin concerto.* ***

Vera Tsu, born in Shanghai and then discovered by Isaac Stern and trained in America, is an outstanding soloist in a coupling which directly challenges an EMI disc from Itzhak Perlman. Her tone is rich to the point of fruitiness, bringing out to the full the ripe romanticism of the big Goldmark *Concerto*. Her attack is fearless in the many bravura passages, so that the dance rhythms of the dance-finale have a rare sparkle. Intonation is flawless up to stratospheric heights, and her hushed playing in the central slow movement at a very broad speed movingly demonstrates her inner concentration, helped by the equally beautiful, finely varied playing of the Razumovsky Sinfonia of Bratislava. Rich, full, open sound.

Rustic Wedding Symphony, Op. 26.
(M) *** Van. 08 6151 71 [OVC 5002]. Utah SO, Abavanel – ENESCU: *Rumanian rhapsodies Nos. 1–2.* **
(B) **(*) Decca Eclipse Dig. 448 991-2; *448 991-4* [id.]. LAPO, López-Cobos – DVORAK: *Slavonic dances Nos. 9–16.* ***

Rustic Wedding Symphony, Op. 26; Overtures: In Italy, Op. 49; In the Spring, Op. 36.
(BB) **(*) Naxos Dig. 8.550745 [id.]. Nat. SO of Ireland, Stephen Gunzenhauser.

Goldmark's *Rustic Wedding Symphony* opens with a distinctly rustic theme on the lower strings, which when taken up by the horns (with woodwind birdsong overhead) is as magical as any passage in the romantic symphonic repertory, not forgetting the beginning of Mahler's *First*. The hazily romantic evocation of a summer garden which forms the slow movement leads to a boisterous dance finale, with genial injections of fugato. The Vanguard recording from the late 1960s sounds splendid in its new CD transfer. The Utah acoustic is expansive and the music certainly blossoms here, for the playing has a pleasing freshness and spontaneity. Abravanel's approach is direct. There is plenty of warmth and the woodwind bring a Beechamesque charm to the inner movements. *In the garden* is as deeply felt as anyone could want, and altogether, with its attractive Enescu coupling (recorded not quite so glowingly), this stands high in the list of recommendations, irrespective of price.

Gunzenhauser gives a fresh, bright-eyed account of the *Rustic Wedding Symphony*. He takes both the opening movement and the Andante (*In the garden*) fast, and he loses something in poise and spacious eloquence in consequence. But the overall performance is spontaneous and enjoyable. It is well recorded and, although the violins sound thin (immediately noticeable at the opening of *In the Spring*), that is almost certainly not the fault of the engineers. Of the two jaunty overtures, *In Italy* is especially vivacious and sparkling.

López-Cobos directs a refreshing and attractive reading. In the first movement the generally fast tempi again detract from the charm of the piece, but the horns sound as magical as ever and there is sympathetic playing from the Los Angeles orchestra in the central movements. With a lively finale this is easy to enjoy when the digital recording is vivid but naturally balanced. Moreover, this inexpensive reissue offers a considerable Dvořák bonus.

Górecki, Henryk (born 1933)

Symphony No. 3 (Symphony of sorrowful songs), Op. 36.

(BB) *** Belart 450 148-2; *450 148-4* [(M) id. import]. Zofia Kilanowicz, Polish State PO (Katowice), Swoboda.

Symphony No. 3 (Symphony of sorrowful songs), Op. 36; 3 Pieces in the olden style.

(BB) *** Naxos Dig. 8.550822 [id.]. Zofia Kilanowicz, Polish Nat. RSO, Antoni Wit.

Scored for strings and piano with soprano solo in each of the three movements, all predominantly slow, Górecki's *Symphony No. 3* sets three laments taking the theme of motherhood. The first movement, nearly half an hour long, resolves on the central setting of a fifteenth-century text from a monastic collection. The second movement incongruously brings a switch to a sensuously beautiful idiom, with the soprano solo soaring radiantly. The third movement is the setting of a folksong with a two-chord ostinato as accompaniment, concluding in a passage of total peace. It is good to have two excellent super-bargain versions of this moving work. Katowice was where the symphony was written and the performance by the State Philharmonic is deeply felt, the hypnotic power of the undulating, arching climax of the first movement well caught. Zofia Kilanowicz's strong, richly timbred soprano contribution is well balanced with string textures that are satisfyingly full-bodied. There could perhaps be more variety of dynamic in the second and third movements, but the effect remains hypnotic.

The Naxos alternative has the advantage of digital recording, a wider dynamic range and, of course, background silence. The sound itself is full, but not quite as lavish as the Belart; on the other hand, detail is more refined and the focus more real. By the time she had come to re-record the work, Zofia Kilanowicz had obviously become even more immersed in the word-settings. In the work's closing section, with its hint of a gentle but remorseless tolling bell, Wit achieves a mood of simple serenity, even forgiveness. The *Three Pieces in olden style* make a fine postlude, the second with its dance figurations, the third with its fierce tremolando violins, like shafts of bright light, suddenly resolving to a very positive ending. All in all, this seems in many ways a 'best buy'.

Gottschalk, Louis (1829–69)

Grand fantasia triumfal for piano and orchestra.

(M) *** Decca Dig. 430 726-2. Ortiz, RPO, Atzmon – ADDINSELL: *Warsaw concerto* ***; GERSHWIN: *Rhapsody* **(*); LISZT: *Hungarian fantasia* ***; LITOLFF: *Scherzo*. ***

Gottschalk's *Grand fantasia* has naïvety, and a touch of vulgarity too, but the performers here give it an account which nicely combines flair and a certain elegance, and the result is a distinct success.

(i; ii) *Grande tarantelle for piano and orchestra;* (ii) *Symphony No. 1 (A Night in the tropics);* (iii) Music for one piano, four hands: *L'étincelle; La gallina; La jota aragonesa; Marche de nuit; Orfa; Printemps d'amour; Radieuse; Réponds-moi; Ses yeux; Souvenirs d'Andalousie; Tremolo.* (2 pianos): *The Union* (concert paraphrase on national airs).

(M) *** Van. 08.4051 71 [OVC 4051]. (i) Reid Nibley; (ii) Utah SO, Abravanel; (iii) Eugene List with Cary Lewis or Joseph Werner.

With nearly 77 minutes of music this well-recorded Vanguard reissue makes an ideal introduction to Gottschalk's music. The *Grande tarantelle* has a very catchy main theme which keeps returning and never wears out its welcome when the performance is so vivacious. As might be expected, the two-movement *Night in the tropics* uses its title of 'symphony' very loosely. It begins somewhat soupily, then in Abravanel's hands develops a full head of emotional steam; the second movement is a kind of samba, rhythmically very winning. The music for piano, four hands, is played with flair and scintillating upper tessitura. The opening arrangement of *La jota aragonesa* heads an ear-tickling programme, with a touch of wit in the piece called *Tremolo*. When the participants move to two pianos for *The Union* concert paraphrase, the acoustic expands and the effect is properly grand, yet the balance is not too close and the players are still able to produce delicate tonal contrasts. The orchestral recordings date from 1962, the piano pieces from 1976, and the sound is excellent throughout.

PIANO MUSIC

Bamboula; Le Bananier; Le Banjo; The Dying Poet; The Last hope; The Maiden's blush; Ojos criollos; Pasquinade; La Savane; Souvenir de Porto Rico; Suis-moi!; Tournament galop.
(M) *** Van. 08.4050.71 [OVC 4050]. Eugene List.

Eugene List made this repertoire very much his own in the USA in the late 1950s and early '60s, and his performances are second to none. The glittering roulades in *Le Bananier* and *Ojos criollos* are brought off with unaffected brilliance, and the plucking imitations at the close of *The Banjo* are equally successful. The pieces with sentimental titles are more appealing than their names might suggest. The *Souvenir de Porto Rico*, a set of variations, is given real substance, and the *Tournament galop* closes the recital at an infectious canter. The recording dates from 1956 but doesn't sound its age at all: it is very well balanced and realistic.

Gould, Morton (1913–96)

Fall River legend (ballet): *suite. Latin-American symphonette: Tango and Guaracha.*
(M) *** RCA 09026 61505-2. O, composer – COPLAND: *Appalachian spring* etc. ***

Morton Gould's own recording of the suite from *Fall River legend* is so vivid and atmospheric that at times one almost thinks this could be Copland. The two movements from the engaging *Latin-American symphonette* are also splendidly done. With astonishingly full and vivid recording (made in the New York Manhattan Center in 1960), triumphantly remastered by John Pfeiffer, the irresistibly catchy *Guaracha* is demonstration-worthy.

Fall River legend: suite; Spirituals for string choir and orchestra.
(M) *** Mercury (IMS) 432 016-2 [id.]. Eastman-Rochester SO, Howard Hanson – BARBER: *Medea: suite.* ***

The composer's orchestral suite from the ballet is brightly played by the Eastman-Rochester Orchestra under the highly sympathetic Howard Hanson, who also gives an outstandingly vibrant account of the *Spirituals*. The 1959/60 Mercury recording has remarkable clarity, range and presence.

Gounod, Charles (1818–93)

Faust: ballet music and Waltz.
(B) **(*) Ph. Duo 438 763-2 [id.]. Rotterdam PO, David Zinman – DELIBES: *Coppélia;* CHOPIN: *Les Sylphides.* **(*)

If without quite the panache of a Beecham, David Zinman's account of the *Faust ballet music* springs readily to life: it has polish and elegance. Very good (1980) recording in a warm acoustic ensures the listener's aural pleasure, making this collection a genuine bargain.

Petite symphonie in B flat (for 9 wind instruments).
(M) *** Chandos CHAN 6543 [id.]. Athena Ens. – IBERT: *3 Pièces brèves;* POULENC: *Sextet.* ***

An astonishingly fresh and youthful work, the *Petite symphonie* in fact dates from Gounod's later years; he was nearly seventy when he wrote it for one of the celebrated Parisian wind ensembles. The work has impeccable craftsmanship and is witty and civilized. It makes ideal listening at the end of the day, and its charm is irresistible in a performance as full of *joie de vivre* as that provided by the Athena group, who are particularly light-hearted in the finale. The other items are by twentieth-century French composers, and this well-recorded anthology is very successful; even if it makes short measure at 45 minutes, it is consistently enjoyable.

Symphonies Nos. 1 in D; 2 in B flat.
(M) **(*) EMI CDM7 63949-2. Toulouse Capitole O, Plasson.

Gounod's two *Symphonies* also sound youthful, though they were composed in quick succession in his mid-thirties. When listening to No. 1, the Bizet *Symphony* springs to mind. The effortless flow of first-rate ideas and the mastery, both of the orchestra, which is handled with the greatest expertise, and of symphonic form, are very striking. The *Second Symphony* is very like the *First*, and both receive decent performance from Michel Plasson. He is thoroughly in sympathy with the composer's infectious style, as is the Orchestra of the Capitole, Toulouse, although the playing is not quite as finished or as accomplished as the music deserves. The EMI engineers have produced fresh, warm sound and the CD transfer is very successful.

Faust (complete).
(M) **(*) EMI (SIS) CMS7 69983-2 (3) [Ang. CDMC 69983]. De los Angeles, Gedda, Blanc, Christoff, Paris Nat. Op. Ch. and O, Cluytens.
(M) (***) EMI (SIS) mono CMS5 65256-2 (3). De los Angeles, Gedda, Christoff, Borthayre, Angelici, Paris Opéra Ch. & O, Cluytens.

In the reissued Cluytens set, the seductiveness of de los Angeles's singing is a dream and it is a pity that the recording hardens the natural timbre slightly. Christoff is magnificently Mephistophelian. Gedda, though showing some signs of strain, sings intelligently, and among the other soloists Ernest Blanc has a pleasing, firm voice, which he uses to make Valentin into a sympathetic character. Cluytens's approach is competent but somewhat workaday. The set has been attractively repackaged and the libretto has strikingly clear print, to make a good mid-priced choice for this popular opera.

Not to be confused with the stereo remake of this opera with the same three principals (and conductor), this mono set of 1953 offers an advantage in the extra freshness of Victoria de los Angeles as Marguerite, sparkling and girlish, with Gedda also in fresher voice. Christoff is more uninhibited here, which makes his French even less idiomatic, but the result is thrilling; Jean Borthayre as Valentin and Martha Angelici as Siebel sing beautifully. The mono sound, less dry than others from this source, captures the voices well, and Cluytens proves a persuasive interpreter.

Faust (abridged version).
(M) (**(*)) Naxos mono 8.110016/7 [id.]. Jepson, Crooks, Pinza, Warren, Olheim, NY Met. Op. Ch. & O, Pelletier.

Naxos in its historic series of opera recordings from the United States here offers a performance broadcast from the Boston Opera House in April 1940 with a starry cast. Richard Crooks's ringing tenor sounds more Italianate than French, but he makes an ardent Faust, and Ezio Pinza – with French enunciation no better than one expects of Italian singers – yet gives a vividly dynamic and characterful portrait of Mephistopheles, singing superbly and offering what must be the fastest account of the *Calf of gold* aria on disc. Leonard Warren even in 1940 did not sound youthful enough for Valentin, with vibrato already obtrusive, and though Helen Jepson as Marguerite is a little shrill at times under pressure, it is a winning performance, with a brilliant account of the *Jewel song* sounding genuinely joyful. Though relatively little-known outside North America, Wilfred Pelletier, at the time in charge of the Met.'s French repertory, proves an inspired conductor. Pacing the music very well, he draws excellent ensemble from the whole company, even if the radio recording has the orchestra presented rather dimly, well behind the singers. Applause and stage noises tend to be obtrusive, with the performance preceded and punctuated by an announcer summarizing the plot.

Faust (opera): highlights.
(M) *** Teldec/Warner Dig. 0630 13806-9 (from complete recording, with Hadley, Gasdia, Ramey, Mentzer, Agache, Fassbaender, Welsh Nat. Op. Ch. & O, Rizzi).
(B) (***) EMI mono CD-EMX 2215 [(M) id.] (from above complete set, with de los Angeles, Gedda; cond. Cluytens).

The Teldec CD makes an obvious first choice for highlights from this ever-tuneful opera. The set is outstandingly cast, and the 76-minute selection is well made to include both the finale and the ballet music. Rizzi springs rhythms infectiously and draws incisive singing from the chorus. No translations are offered but there is a cued synopsis.

The one important snag in the EMI complete set was Cluytens's rather ungracious conducting. But in this generous 75-minute set of excerpts his crisp efficiency is more than acceptable. The singing gives much pleasure, particularly that of de los Angeles and Christoff, and the choral contribution is spirited. Excellent value and an ideal way of sampling a performance which has many virtues.

Faust (abridged version sung in English with ballet music; introduced by Sir Thomas Beecham).
(M) *** Dutton mono 2CDAX 2001 (2) [id. full price]. Nash, Licette, Easton, Williams, Vane, Brunskill, Carr, BBC Ch. & SO, LPO, Sir Thomas Beecham.

Beecham's 1929 recording, superbly transferred on the Dutton label, with full-bodied sound for voices and orchestra alike, gives a vivid and refreshing idea of British opera performance in the 1920s. The old Chorley translation is used, stilted and creaking but memorable – 'What rubbishy wine!' says Mephistopheles – and the team of top British singers of the day is at one in enunciating words with crystal clarity. Voices are firm and cleanly projected, with the bright-toned Miriam Licette as Marguerite delivering a splendid trill at the start of the *Jewel song*. Heddle Nash sings with heady tone as Faust, Harold Williams is a youthfully fresh Valentine and the distinctive flicker in Robert Easton's bass never gets in the way of clean focus in the role of Mephistopheles. Beecham himself is inspired, pointing rhythms and phrases infectiously, though, curiously, four of the 32 sides of the original 78s were conducted by Clarence Raybould. A supplement on the second CD includes a brief spoken introduction by Beecham, as well as the *Nubian dance* and *Adagio* from the ballet music – otherwise omitted, like the *Walpurgisnacht* scene.

Mireille (complete).
(M) (**) EMI mono CMS7 64382-2 (2) [id.]. Vivalda, Gedda, Gayraud, Dens, Ignal, Aix-en-Provence Festival Ch., Paris Conservatoire O, Cluytens.

This EMI *Mireille* is disappointing, not only thanks to limited mono sound but also to the performance, far too rigidly conducted by Cluytens to bring out the Provençal charm of this rustic opera, with even the *Farandole chorus* sounding stiff. As Mireille, Janette Vivalda sings unimaginatively with shrill, bright tone, not helped by the recording. Happily, the other soloists are more sympathetic. The young Nicolai Gedda sings most beautifully as the hero, Vincent, and the mezzo Christiane Gayraud is comparably rich as the gypsy, Taven, with Michel Dens ringingly clear, if hardly sinister, as the villain, Ourrias.

Roméo et Juliette (complete).
(B) (**(*)) Decca Double mono 443 539-2 (2) [id.]. Jobin, Micheau, Mollet, Rialland, Rehfuss, Opéra Nat. Ch. & O, Erede.
(M) ** EMI CMS5 65290-2 (2) [CDMB 65290]. Corelli, Freni, Calès, Depraz, Paris Op. Ch. & O, Lombard.

This 1953 Decca mono set is well worth considering. With a first-rate cast singing idiomatically, the result is fresh and full of fire. It is an interesting comment that in 1953 Paris could offer a far finer team of singers than latterly, with the tenor Pierre Mollet, for example, light and airy as Mercutio, not least in the *Queen Mab aria*, and Charles Cambon a fine Capulet. The only non-French singer, Heinz Rehfuss, projects with the clearest focus as Frère Laurent, while the roles of the two lovers are taken by two vintage singers of the period, not always ideally caught on record but both warmly characterful. Janine Micheau is tenderly charming as a vulnerably girlish Juliette and, as Roméo, Raoul Jobin sings stylishly and with little of the pinched tone that too often has afflicted French tenors. The transfer is more than full-bodied enough to compensate for the slightly edgy top.

On EMI, the great pity is that the casting of this great and rich opera is basically inadequate. Neither Corelli as Romeo nor Freni as Juliet is remotely in style, even though their tones are often beautiful to the ear. Why was it not possible in a French-made recording to correct the often excruciating pronunciation of the two principals? Freni with her sweet tone and natural charm comes much closer to the mark than her partner and so much revolves around the lovers' four big duets. The conducting of Alain Lombard makes up some ground with its warm, idiomatic understanding; but it could all have been so much better without difficulty. The set is well presented and documented and brightly and vividly transferred, the chorus well focused yet with plenty of atmosphere overall. The break between the two CDs comes between the first and second scenes of Act III.

Grainger, Percy (1882–1961)

Blithe bells (Free ramble on a theme by Bach: Sheep may safely graze): Country gardens; Green bushes (Passacaglia); Handel in the Strand; Mock morris; Molly on the shore; My Robin is to the greenwood gone; Shepherd's hey; Spoon River; Walking tune; Youthful rapture.
(M) *** Chandos CHAN 6542 [id.]. Bournemouth Sinf., Montgomery.

For those wanting only a single Grainger orchestral collection, this could be first choice. Among the expressive pieces, the arrangement of *My Robin is to the greenwood gone* is highly attractive, but the cello solo in *Youthful rapture* is perhaps less effective. Favourites such as *Country gardens*, *Shepherd's hey*, *Molly on the shore* and *Handel in the Strand* all sound as fresh as new paint. The 1978 recording, made in Christchurch Priory, has retained all its ambient character in its CD transfer.

Children's march; Colonial song; Country gardens; Handel in the Strand; The immovable 'Do'; Irish tune from County Derry; Mock Morris; Molly on the shore; My Robin is to the greenwood gone; Shepherd's hey; Spoon River.
(M) ** Mercury 434 330-2 [id.]. Eastman-Rochester Pops O, Fennell – COATES: *Three Elizabeths suite.* **(*)

Lively and sympathetic performances from Fennell, and good playing. But the 1959 Mercury sound here is more dated than most CDs from this source: the acoustics of the Eastman Theatre in Rochester are too dry for Grainger's more expansive string writing in the *Colonial song* and the *Irish tune from County Derry*. The pithily rhythmic pieces like *Mock Morris* come off best as the sound is always clear and clean.

Colonial song; Country gardens; Green bushes; Irish tune from County Derry; Shepherds' hey; My Robin is to the greenwood gone; Suite of Danish folksongs: The Power of love (The Power of love; Lord Peter's stable-boy; The Nightigale and the two sisters; Jutish melody: Husband and wifey); To a Nordic Princess; Ye banks and braes o' bonnie Doon.
(BB) ** Naxos Dig. 8.554263 [id.]. Slovak RSO, Keith Brion.

One rarity in this welcome Grainger collection on the Naxos label is the very first item, the *Suite of Danish folksongs: The Power of love*, with the latter the first of four very characteristic pieces, well contrasted. The other rarity, and the longest piece here, is *To a Nordic Princess*, which Grainger wrote for his own wedding, when he conducted it with an enormous orchestra in the Hollywood Bowl before an audience of over 20,000, witnesses to the ceremony. The performances of the Slovak Radio Symphony Orchestra lack something in both bite and refinement, but this is a colourful enough collection of characteristic pieces, sympathetically done and well recorded. *Country gardens* in this version is light and crisp, and *Shepherds' hey* is neat, if not quite bright or biting enough. A good bargain compilation of music by a genuine original among composers, even if it fails to convey the full intensity of Grainger's erratic genius.

Irish tune from County Derry; Lincolnshire Posy (suite); *Molly on the shore; Shepherd's hey.*
(M) *** ASV CDWHL 2067. L. Wind O, Wick – MILHAUD; POULENC: *Suite française.* ***

First-class playing and vivid recording, with the additional attraction of delightful couplings, make this very highly recommendable.

PIANO MUSIC

Complete: *'Dished up for piano', Volumes 1–5.*
(B) *** Nimbus Dig. NI 1767 (5) [id.]. Martin Jones.

'Dished up for piano', Volume 1: Andante con moto; Bridal lullaby; Children's march; Colonial song; English waltz; Handel in the Strand; Harvest hymn; The immovable 'Do'; In a Nutshell (suite) *(Arrival platform humlet; Gay but wistful; The Gum-suckers' march; Pastoral); In Dahomey; Mock morris; Peace; Sailor's song; Saxon twi-play; To a Nordic princess; Walking tune.*
*** Nimbus Dig. NI 5220 [id.]. Martin Jones.

'Dished up for piano', Volume 2: Arrangements: BACH: *Blithe bells; Fugue in A min.* BRAHMS: *Cradle song.* Chinese TRAD.: *Beautiful fresh flower.* DOWLAND: *Now, o now, I needs must part.* ELGAR: *Enigma variations: Nimrod.* Stephen FOSTER: *Lullaby; The rag-time girl.* GERSHWIN: *Love walked in; The man I love.* RACHMANINOV: *Piano concerto No. 2: Finale* (abridged). R. STRAUSS: *Der Rosenkavalier: Ramble on the last love-duet.* TCHAIKOVSKY: *Piano concerto No. 1* (opening); *Paraphrase on the Flower waltz.*
**(*) Nimbus Dig. NI 5232 [id.]. Martin Jones.

'Dished up for piano', Volume 3: Folksong arrangements: *The brisk young sailor; Bristol Town; Country gardens; Died for love; Hard-hearted Barb'ra Helen; The hunter in his career; Irish tune from County Derry; Jutish medley; Knight and shepherd's daughter; Lisbon (Dublin Bay); The merry king; Mo Ninghean Dhu; Molly on the shore; My Robin is to the greenwood gone; One more day my John* (2 versions, easy and complex); *Near Woodstock Town; The nightingale and the two sisters; O gin I were where Gowrie rins; Rimmer and goldcastle; The rival brothers; Scotch Strathspey; Shepherd's hey; Spoon River; Stalt vesselil; Sussex mummers' Christmas carol; The widow's party; Will ye gang to the Hielands, Lizzie Lindsay?.*
*** Nimbus Dig. NI 5244 [id.]. Martin Jones.

Volume 4: Arrangements: ANON.: *Angelus ad Virginem.* BACH: *Toccata and fugue in D min.* DELIUS: *Air and dance.* FAURE: *Après un rêve; Nell.* Stephen FOSTER: *Lullaby* (Easy: Grainger). GRIEG: *Piano concerto* (first movement). HANDEL: *Water music: Hornpipe.* SCHUMANN: *Piano concerto* (first movement). STANFORD: *Four Irish dances.* GRAINGER: *At twilight; The Bigelow march; Eastern intermezzo; Tiger-tiger; Klavierstücke in A min., B flat, D & E.*
*** Nimbus Dig. NI 5255 [id.]. Martin Jones.

Volume 5: Original works for up to six hands: BRAHMS: *Paganini variation No. 12.* BYRD: *The Carman's whistle.* (i) *Children's march;* DELIUS: *A Dance rhapsody.* (i–ii) *English dance.* (i) GERSHWIN: *Girl crazy: Embraceable you.* (i–ii) *Green bushes; Spoon River. Train music; Up-country song.* (i–ii) *The Warriors* (music to an imaginary ballet); *Ye banks and braes o' bonnie Doon; Zanzibar boat-song.*
*** Nimbus Dig. NI 5286 [id.]. Martin Jones; with (i) Richard McMahon; (ii) Philip Martin.

Martin Jones's splendid Nimbus survey of Grainger's piano music is available on five separate, full-priced CDs, but they now come together in a slip-case at bargain price. The playing is refreshingly alive and spontaneous. Volume 1 is particularly attractive, and that is the place to start, for there is not a dull item here. There is plenty of dash in the folksong arrangements, and charm too, and they display a much greater range than one might have expected. The transcriptions are fascinating. The opening of the Tchaikovsky *Piano concerto* – some would say the 'best bit' – is transcribed straightforwardly, with a flamboyant flourish to finish it off, and the purple patch at the end of the Rachmaninov No. 2 cannot fail to make an impact in a performance as brilliant as this. Martin Jones is equally good in the freely composed pastiche on Bach's *Sheep may safely graze* (*Blithe bells*). But he plays *Nimrod* and the *Der Rosenkavalier* excerpts too slowly; such a degree of languor might come off with the orchestra, but on the piano the effect is enervating. The fourth and fifth volumes are the most enjoyable of all. Grainger's arrangements in Volume 4 are often very free (notably the transcriptions of the first movements of the Grieg and Schumann *Concertos*, especially the former), but Jones plays them with such spontaneity that they are freshly enjoyable in their own right. The opening *Four Irish dances* of Stanford are attractively spiced, yet Grainger is careful to treat Fauré with discretion. His 'concert version' of Bach's most famous *Toccata and fugue* in based on the arrangements by Tausig and (mainly) Busoni, with whom Grainger briefly studied in 1903: Jones excitingly gives it the full bravura treatment. The *Lullaby* from *Tribute to Foster* makes a charming contrast and the *Angelus ad Virginem* with its tinkling-bell effects is delightful. But there are gentler original pieces too, and the *Eastern intermezzo* also features peals of bells. *Tiger-tiger* is simplicity itself, as is *At Twilight*, but this piece then ends with a bluesy 'added sixth' chord. The programme is rounded off with three early *Klavierstücke* (1897–8), eclectic but already full of personality.

Volume 5 offers the original works for up to six hands, and the opening *Children's march*, in which Jones is joined on one piano by Richard McMahon, could not be more rumbustiously attactive. It is in the favourite folk-treatment form of a patrol, coming gradually closer, with a strong central climax and then tapering down. *Spoon river* (where the two players move to a pair of pianos) combines dynamic range with diversity of effects. In *Ye banks and braes* (prolix but effective) and the lilting *Zanzibar boat-song* three players share a single piano. But in the intricate *Passacagalia on green bushes* (a *tour de force* which steadily increases in pace and excitement), Philip Martin joins the other two to make up the six hands, on three pianos, and this is the complex scoring of both the 'rambling' *English dance*, which is very diverting, and the closing *Warriors* ballet (which is complete). Martin Jones also has four solo pieces, including the comparatively elaborate and very pianistic *Byrd variations*, plus three miniatures: the engaging *Up-country song*, the curious fragment of *Train music* and the similarly brief and simple Brahms *Variation*. All the playing here is splendidly secure technically, and the performances not only have panache but readily convey the enjoyment of the participants. The pianos are recorded reverberantly in the Nimbus manner – but it rather suits this repertoire, and the image is absolutely truthful.

VOCAL MUSIC

Duke of Marlborough fanfare; Green bushes (Passacaglia); Irish tune from County Derry; Lisbon; Molly on the shore; My Robin is to Greenwood gone; Shepherd's hey; Piano duet: Let's dance gay in green meadow; Vocal & choral: *Bold William Taylor; Brigg Fair; I'm seventeen come Sunday; Lord Maxwell's goodnight; The lost lady found; The pretty maid milkin' her cow; Scotch strathspey and reel; Shallow Brown; Shenandoah; The sprig of thyme; There was a pig went out to dig; Willow willow.*
(M) *** Decca (IMS) 425 159-2. Pears, Shirley-Quirk, Amb. S. or Linden Singers, Wandsworth Boys' Ch., ECO, Britten or Steuart Bedford; Britten and V. Tunnard (pianos).

This is an altogether delightful anthology, beautifully played and sung by these distinguished artists. Grainger's imagination in the art of arranging folksong was prodigious. Vocal and instrumental items are felicitously interwoven, and the recording is extremely vivid, though the digital remastering has put a hint of edge on the voices.

Granados, Enrique (1867–1916)

12 Danzas españolas; Escenas poeticas, Book II (arr. for guitar and orchestra).
(BB) *** Naxos Dig. 8.855037 [id.]. Norbert Kraft, Razumovsky Sinf., Peter Breiner.

These are attractive transcriptions for guitar and orchestra of Granados's piano pieces. Both the 12 *Danzas españolas* and the second book of the *Escenas poeticas* have been effectively scored by the Slovak musician, Peter Breiner. The Canadian guitarist Norbert Kraft is a brilliant and effective player. If you want to try Granados in this orchestral garb rather than in its original keyboard form, you can invest in this with confidence.

Goyescas: Intermezzo.
(M) *** RCA 09026 62586-2 [id.]. Chicago SO, Reiner – ALBENIZ: *Iberia* etc.; FALLA: *El amor brujo* etc. ***

A totally memorable performance of the *Goyescas intermezzo* from Reiner, seductively sultry and vibrant by turns. The 1958 Chicago recording sounds amazingly rich and vivid.

GUITAR MUSIC

Cuentos para la juventud, Op. 1: Dedicatoria. Danzas españolas Nos. 4 & 5, Op. 37/4–5; Tonadillas al estilo antiguo: La maja de Goya. Valses poéticos.
❁ (BB) *** RCA Navigator Dig. 74321 17903-2 [(M) id. import]. Julian Bream (guitar) – ALBENIZ: *Collection;* RODRIGO: *3 Piezas españolas.* *** ❁

Like the Albéniz items with which these Granados pieces are coupled, these performances show Julian Bream at his most inspirational. The illusion of the guitar being in the room is especially electrifying in the middle section of the famous *Spanish dance No. 5*, when Bream achieves the most subtle pianissimo. Heard against the background silence, the effect is quite magical. But all the playing here is wonderfully spontaneous. This is one of the most impressive guitar recitals ever recorded, and for this super-bargain reissue RCA have generously added the *Tres Piezas españolas* of Rodrigo, recorded a year later and no less distinguished.

12 Danzas españolas (trans. for guitar).
(B) *** [EMI Red Line Dig. CDR5 69850]. Manuel Barrueco – FALLA: *Spanish popular songs.* ***

As in the Falla coupling, this is masterly playing, warmly coloured, subtly nuanced, and naturally idiomatic in its rhythms, so that one might think that these piano pieces had been orginally intended for the guitar.

PIANO MUSIC

12 Danzas españolas; Goyescas.
(M) *** Ph. (IMS) 442 751-2 (2). Eduardo del Pueyo – FALLA: *Nights in the gardens of Spain.* *** ❁

This set is justly described as 'the quintessence of Spanish pianism', for playing of this repertoire does not come any better than this. Eduardo del Pueyo, born in Aragon, made these recordings in 1956 (although the ear would hardly guess, so natural is the piano recording). His playing of the colourful *Spanish dances* has much flair and poetic delicacy – sample *No. 2 in C minor*, so beautifully articulated – and the magical pianissimo at the centre of No. 5 makes one wonder if Julian Bream listened to Del Pueyo before making his equally memorable account of this famous piece. But it is in the *Goyescas* that Del Pueyo's evocation so immediately captures the Spanish atmosphere, as in *Los requiebros* and *Coloquios en la reja* and especially in the haunting *Quejas o la maja y el ruiseñor*, while the idiomatic brilliance of *El pele* shows restraint as well as spontaneous virtuosity. The Falla coupling is perhaps even more remarkable.

Goyescas (complete).
❁ (B) *** Decca Double 448 191-2 (2) [id.]. Alicia de Larrocha – ALBENIZ: *Iberia* etc. ***

Goyescas (complete); *Escenas románticas; 6 Piezas sobre cantos populares españoles; Valses poéticos.*
(M) *** EMI CMS7 64524-2 (2) [CDMB 64524]. Alicia de Larrocha.

Alicia de Larrocha brings special insights and sympathy to the *Goyescas* (given top-drawer Decca sound in 1977); her playing has the crisp articulation and rhythmic vitality that these pieces call for, while she is hauntingly evocative in *Quejas o la maja y el ruiseñor*. The overall impression could hardly be more idiomatic in flavour nor more realistic as a recording. This Double Decca coupling with Albéniz's *Iberia* is very distinguished.

Alicia de Larrocha's EMI set of *Goyescas* derives from the Spanish Hispavox catalogue and was made in 1963, a decade before her first Decca set. The performance is more impulsive, at times more intensely expressive, if less subtle in feeling than the later version, and the recording, if not as fine as the Decca, is eminently realistic. The closing *Zapateado* of the *Cantos populares españoles* has a fire and sparkle characteristic of her playing at this stage of her career.

Graun, Karl Heinrich (1704–1759)

Cleopatra e Cesare (opera): 'Great arias'.
(M) *** HM Suite Dig. HMT 7901602 [id.]. Janet Williams, Iris Vermillion, Lynne Dawson, Robert Gambill, RIAS Chamber Ch., Concerto Köln, René Jacobs.

Taken from a complete three-disc set, recorded in Berlin in 1995, this generous, 77-minute selection from *Cleopatra e Cesare*, very well performed, gives a most welcome insight into the work of the Kapellmeister of Frederick the Great of Prussia. On succeeding to the throne in 1740, the new king immediately had an opera house built, and this *dramma per musica* of Graun, an *opera seria*, was the work chosen for the lavish opening. Graun may not match in imagination such contemporaries of his in Berlin as C. P. E. Bach (consigned to a very subsidiary position at Frederick's court) but this collection of overture and ten arias plus two ensembles is consistently refreshing. In this selection, fast arias predominate – no doubt a wise choice – with all the principals singing most stylishly, with clean, agile attack, not least Janet Williams and Iris Vermillion in the twin title-roles, as well as Lynne Dawson, singing most beautifully as Cornelia, widow of Pompey. Janet Williams is sweetly affecting in her big Act III aria, and Iris Vermillion with her firm, strong mezzo makes a most characterful Caesar. Under René Jacobs, a sensitive director, there is no weak link in the rest of the cast either, and recorded sound is nicely balanced to convey an apt scale for this music.

Montezuma: highlights.
(M) *** Decca 448 977-2 (2). Elms, Sutherland, M. Sinclair, Ward, Woodland, Harwood, Amb. S., LPO, Bonynge – BONONCINI: *Griselda.* ***

Karl Heinrich Graun was the court composer of Frederick the Great, and it was the Emperor himself who provided the very professional libretto for this work, based on the conquest of Mexico as portrayed in a play by Voltaire. The opera's original success had more to it than royal patronage, and its revival on CD is thoroughly deserved. One serious shortcoming of the full work is the wordiness of the recitatives between numbers (presumably Graun jibbed at cutting any of the royal text) but here the selection, while giving the flavour of recitatives, omits its longueurs. Besides Sutherland who, in the role of Princess Eupaforice, has a stunning aria to sing, Monica Sinclair in the breeches role of the Conquistador, Cortes, is especially impressive. Good singing from the others, too. Richard Bonynge conducts briskly, with a real sense of style, and this tuneful piece is every bit as attractive as the Bononcini opera with which it is coupled. The recording, too, is excellent. A full translation is provided.

Gregorian chant

'The world of Gregorian chant': Responsories; Hymns; Antiphons; Gospel tone: Vos estis sal terrae; Laudes seu Acclamationes; Gradual: Flores apparuerunt; Alleluia: Justus germinabit; Communions; Antiphon: Montes Gilboe; Ave verum corpus; Antiphonal Psalmody; Marian antiphons.
✿ (M) *** Decca 452 940-2 [425 729-2]. L. Carmelite Priory Ch., John McCarthy.

Mass Propers for Good Friday and Easter.
(M) *** DG 447 299-2. Abteikirche Münsterschwarzach, Pater Godehard Joppich.
(BB) **(*) Naxos Dig. 8.550951. Nova Schola Gregoriana, Alberto Turco.

Mass Propers for the Church Year.
(BB) *** Naxos Dig. 8.550711. Nova Schola Gregoriana, Alberto Turco.

'Gregorian chant according to the Aquitaine tradition': Mass for St John the Baptist; Mass for the Nativity of Jesus Christ.
✿ (B) *** HM Musique d'Abord HMA 190 3031 [id.]. Schola Hungarica, László Dobszay or Janka Szendrei.

'Christmas Eve' (Gregorian chant and simple polyphony from the Middle Ages): *Noel settings; Alleluia and sequence; Antiphons; Chants; Graduals; Hymns; Responses and Tropes.*

(B) *** HM Musique d'Abord Dig. HMA 190 3037 [id.]. Schola Hungarica, László Dobszay & Janka Szendrei.

The liturgy of the Catholic Church has the Mass as its central focus. The Ordinary of the Mass – those elements that are unchanging through the Church year – have been set by countless composers and include the *Kyrie* ('Lord have mercy'), the *Gloria*, *Credo* and *Sanctus* ('Holy, holy, holy') and the *Agnus Dei*, which is undoubtedly the most important of all for believers ('Lamb of God, who takes away the sins of the world, have mercy on us and grant us peace'). The Mass Propers are chants which change with the seasons of the year or the occasion of the celebration; they consist of Introit, Gradual, Alleluia, Tract, Offertory and Communion. These are amplified by Sequences (accretions to the liturgy) and Tropes (additions which amplify and heighten the meaning of the biblical text in prose or poetry). The changes brought about by the reforming Council of Trent in the sixteenth century removed many of these additions, but they are at the heart of medieval Church music.

To evaluate Gregorian Chant in a volume of this kind is hazardous and essentially subjective. Although this music does give much aesthetic pleasure in that these chants are of great antiquity and beauty, their purpose is devotional and the singers are not 'professional' in any normal sense of the word. The recent vogue for the two-CD EMI set by the monks of the Monasterio Benedictino de Santo Domingo de Silos (EMI CMS5 65217-2) is not directly related to its aesthetic merit, and it would be not entirely appropriate to compare their singing to that from other monasteries as if one were discussing various orchestras, instrumentalist or singers. Gregorian chant does induce a spirit of serenity and repose, but a study of its growth and interpretation is a highly specialized subject. However, there is one collection that stands out from all the others.

Planned by the late Alec Robertson, who also provided the fascinating detailed notes describing the music's ecclesiastical and spiritual background, the beautifully sung and excellently recorded anthology now reissued by Decca as '*The world of Gregoran chant*' is the finest possible introduction to plainsong. Extra variety of tone is provided by the use of female voices as well as male. But care is taken to see that the ladies do not introduce an unwanted romantic element, and their vibrato-less vocal line is admirably pure in character. Edgar Fleet acts as cantor and John McCarthy directs the singing with dedication and authority, using a wide dynamic range and sometimes crescendos and diminuendos to simulate a processional effect. The recording, made in Brompton Little Oratory, London, in January 1961 is absolutely natural.

DG's Archiv label offers a number of seasonal discs, such as the Gregorian chant for Good Friday and Easter from the Abteikirche Münsterschwarzach, led by Pater Godehard Joppich and recorded in 1981–2, while an inexpensive Naxos disc (with full texts provided, though no translations) by the Nova Schola Gregoriana, directed by the Italian scholar, Alberto Turco, covers this same area very effectively, and this choir is recorded in the Parish Church of Quatrelle, Mantua, which provides a suitably atmospheric setting.

However, this fine choral group are heard to even better effect in an excellently chosen 75-minute compilation of chants taken from different Sundays in the Church year. The opening *Adorate Deum*, which gives the record its title, comes from the Introit of the Third Sunday after the Epiphany, and other chants derive from the Second, Fourth, Eighth and Ninth Sundays after Epiphany, while there are also Gradualia, Versus alleluiatici, Offertoria and Communions for the Fourth, Ninth, Seventeenth, Eighteenth, Nineteenth and Twenty-third Sundays after Pentecost, the Fourth Sunday in Quadragesima (the last Friday before Passion Sunday), the Third and Fourth Sundays of Lent, and Sundays within the Octave of the Feast of the Sacred Heart, and the Sunday within the Octave of Corpus Christi. The singing has a firm profile and is well recorded, not seeking to create a purely atmospheric effect. It is a pity that texts and translations are not provided, but the back-up notes are very helpful.

The Chant of the Aquitaine tradition is quite different from anything else previously discussed, not least because it moves forward at a much faster pace, but also because the performances here use a choir which includes not only men but also both boy trebles and women's voices. While the men's voices remain dark-timbred and sonorous when singing alone, the soprano line is sweet, while the trebles are frequently plangent. For example, after they and the full choir have shared a radiant dialogue in the troped *Offertorium* of the *Mass for the Nativity*, the trebles re-enter in the *Ante communio cum tropis*, enthusiastically singing *Emitte Spiritum Sanctum tuum* and seeking the Holy Spirit with lusty fervour. The performances by the Schola Hungarica have remarkable feeling and rich, clean textures. The result is totally refreshing, and the choir is beautifully recorded within an ideal ambience: the Parish Church of Sainte Famille, Zugliget, Budapest.

Those who have enjoyed the Schola Hungarica's recording of chant according to the Aquitaine tradition will surely want to move on to their equally stimulating collection of chant and polyphony centring on

Christmas, drawing on both English and Hungarian sources. Men's and women's voices are again used to create a rich tapestry, and the opening *Noel* polyphonic settings, first for two and then three voices, are memorable. There is, of course, soaring monody, and another fine example of an early *Alleluja* and sequence (*Dominus dixit/Grates nunc*). Tempi are kept moving onwards so that the music never drags, and the recording is full and expansive. This is much more enjoyable than many more famous recordings of such repertoire.

'Liturgia defuntorum': Gregorian chant for the dead (from the Order of Burial and for All Souls' Day).
(BB) **(*) Naxos Dig. 8.553192 [id.]. Aurora Surgit, Alessio Randon.

To use a group of female voices in this repertoire (but with a male cantor) may not be completely authentic but the soaring monody gains a special character from the use of female trebles, and the added element of contrast in the responsories is also attractive. By no means all this music is solemn or dark in feeling: the closing group of chants, the *Libera me*, and especially the soaring *In paradisum – Chorus angelorum*, followed by the *Ego sum Resurrectio*, are intended to give the Christian soul an eloquent send-off. Fine singing and atmospheric yet clear recording.

Grétry, André-Ernest-Modeste (1741–1813)

Zémire et Azor: Air de ballet.
❀ (B) *** Dutton Lab. mono CDEA 5017 [(M) id.]. LPO, Sir Thomas Beecham (with Concert: *'Beecham favourites'* *** ❀).

The orchestral suite which Beecham fashioned from music from Grétry's opera produced this famous lollipop which *The Record Guide* (of Edward Sackville West and Desmond Shaw-Taylor) described as 'one of the most captivating morsels in the gramophone repertory'. It is exquisitely played here, especially the immensely delicate closing pianissimo reprise, where the Dutton transfer is wonderfully refined. This Beecham anthology, which includes also his justly renowned account of Chabrier's *España*, is an essential purchase, for every conceivable reason.

Grieg, Edvard (1843–1907)

Piano concerto in A min., Op. 16.
(B) *** Decca 433 628-2. Curzon, LPO, Fjeldstad – FRANCK: *Symphonic variations* *** ❀ ; SCHUMANN: *Concerto*. **(*)
(B) **(*) [EMI Red Line Dig. CDR5 69859]. Cécile Ousset, LSO, Marriner – SCHUMANN: *Piano concerto*. **(*)
(M) **(*) Decca 417 728-2. Radu Lupu, LSO, Previn – SCHUMANN: *Concerto*. **(*)
(M) (***) EMI mono CDH7 63497-2 [id.]. Lipatti, Philh. O, Galliera – with: CHOPIN: *Piano concerto No. 1*. (**)
(M) (**(*)) EMI mono CDM5 66597-2. Walter Gieseking, Philh. O, Karajan – FRANCK: *Symphonic variations;* SCHUMANN: *Piano concerto*. (**(*))
(BB) ** Naxos Dig. 8.550118 [id.]. Jenö Jandó, Budapest SO, Ligeti – SCHUMANN: *Concerto*. **
(M) ** [RCA Basic 100 09026 62677-2]. Rubinstein, O, Wallenstein – SCHUMANN: *Piano concerto*. **
(B) (**) Avid mono AMC 593 [id.]. Benno Moiseiwitsch, Hallé O, Leslie Heward – FRANCK: *Symphonic variations;* SCHUMANN: *Piano concerto*. (**)
(B) * Decca Eclipse Dig. 448 235-2; *448 235-4* [(M) id. import]. Jorge Bolet, Berlin RSO, Chailly (with MENDELSSOHN: *Rondo capriccioso, Op. 14* **) – SCHUMANN: *Piano concerto*. *(*)

(i) *Piano concerto in A min., Op. 16. Lyric suite, Op. 54; Peer Gynt suites Nos. 1, Op. 46; 2, Op. 55.*
(M) ** Chandos Dig. CHAN 7040 [id.]. (i) Margaret Fingerhut; Ulster O, Vernon Handley.

(i) *Piano concerto in A min.;* (ii) *Peer Gynt: extended excerpts.*
(BB) **(*) EMI Seraphim CES5 68522-2 (2) [CDEB 68522]. (i) John Ogdon, New Philh. O, Berglund; (ii) Armstrong, Amb. S., Hallé O, Barbirolli – FRANCK: *Symphonic variations;* SCHUMANN: *Piano concerto*. *(*)

(i) *Piano concerto in A min., Op. 16. Peer Gynt suites Nos. 1, Op. 46; 2, Op. 56.*
(B) *(*) Millennium Universal UMD 80397. (i) Reid Nibley; Utah SO, Abravanel.

(i) *Piano concerto in A min.;* (ii) *Peer Gynt: suites Nos. 1 and 2; Prelude; Dance of the Mountain King's Daughter.*

(M) *** Decca 448 599-2 [id.]. (i) Clifford Curzon, LPO; (ii) LSO; Fjeldstad.

(i) *Piano concerto in A min. Album Leaf, Op. 28/4; Ballade in G min., Op. 24; Lyric pieces: Op. 12/4–5; 38/1–2 & 5; 43/1 & 4; 47/6; 54/1 & 3; 68/5.*

(M) (**) RCA mono 09026 61883-2 [id.]. Rubinstein, (i) with Phd. O, Ormandy.

(i) *Piano concerto in A min. Lyric pieces: Arietta; Elves' dance; Folk melody, Op. 12/1, 4 & 5; Butterfly; Little bird; To spring, Op. 43/1, 4 & 6; Notturno, Op. 54/4; Gade, Op. 57/2; Sylph; French serenade, Op. 62/1 & 3; Salon, Op. 65/4; Summer evening, Op. 71/2.*

❀ (B) *** Tring Dig. TRPO 24 [(M) id.]. Ronan O'Hora, (i) with RPO, James Judd.

(i) *Piano concerto in A min.;* (ii) *Piano sonata in E min., Op. 7.*

(M) *** Ph. 446 192-2. (i) Kovacevich, BBC SO, Sir Colin Davis; (ii) Zoltan Kocsis – SCHUMANN: *Concerto*. ***

Whether in the clarity of virtuoso fingerwork or the shading of half-tone, Kovacevich is among the most illuminating of the many great pianists who have recorded the Grieg *Concerto*. He plays with bravura and refinement, the spontaneity of the music-making bringing a sparkle throughout, to balance the underlying poetry. The 1972 recording has been freshened most successfully and, for the mid-priced reissue, Philips have added a performance by Zoltán Kocsis of the *Piano sonata*, recorded digitally at the beginning of the 1980s. The brilliant young Hungarian pianist gives a strongly characterized reading. His style of pianism, impulsive and extrovert, is quite different from Kovacevich's. But in his own way he is very persuasive in this early and not wholly convincing piece, in which the seams are clearly audible: the *Andante* shows him at his finest. The recording is bright and immediate and suits his style. With its new addition as a supplement to the Schumann coupling, this reissue has a playing time of 78 minutes. Amazingly, this CD is not listed in Schwann.

Curzon's approach to Grieg is wonderfully poetic and this is a performance with strength and power as well as lyrical tenderness. This ranks alongside Kovacevich and Perahia (at full price) and the reading is second to none in distilling the music's special atmosphere. His performance is available coupled either with Franck and Schumann at bargain price or with more music by Grieg at mid-price. The vintage Decca recoupling is well worthy of the Classic Sound series. The performance has always been famous for its freshness, and the sound remains remarkably vivid and immediate. Similarly, in its original format Fjeldstad's *Peer Gynt* was counted to be one of the really outstanding early Decca stereo LPs. The LSO is very sensitive, and the tender string-playing in *Solveig's song* is quite lovely. Fjeldstad's persuasive direction is comparable with that of Beecham, making the listener feel he or she is experiencing this familiar music in a new way. The conductor begins *In the Hall of the Mountain King* rather slowly but builds up a blaze of excitement by the end and quite justifies his conception. The early (1958) Kingsway Hall recording retains its glowing lustre, and only when the violins are under pressure above the stave is there some loss of sweetness.

The young Manchester pianist, Ronan O'Hora, with a totally sympathetic partner in James Judd, now provides us with a recorded performance which is for the mid-1990s what Solomon and Clifford Curzon were for the later 1950s, Stephen Kovacevich for the 1970s, and Perahia for the end of the 1980s. Indeed in imagination and delicacy of feeling, combined with natural, authoritative brilliance, this new performance is unsurpassed, especially the melting arrival of the lovely second group which brings a moment of the utmost magic, matched by the gentle reverie of the *Adagio* and the tranquil, flute-led central episode of the finale. Throughout the pacing seems just right, and the interchange between soloist and orchestra brings a natural, spontaneous flow. The piano is rather forwardly balanced and some listeners may find the sound a little bright, but in the music's gentler pages the piano's timbre is beautifully coloured. The programme is completed by a wholly delightful selection of a dozen of Grieg's most cherishable *Lyric pieces*, in which the pianist's simplicity of approach is consistently disarming. As if this were not enough, this record comes in the bargain price-range and as such it is one of the great bargains of the catalogue.

Ousset's is a strong, dramatic reading, not lacking in warmth and poetry but, paradoxically, bringing out what we would generally think of as the masculine qualities of power and drive. Marriner gives persuasive support, the sound is full, firm and clear, and this reading gives a refreshingly individual slant on a much-played work.

Radu Lupu's recording dates from 1974 and is now even more brightly lit than it was originally, not entirely to advantage. But the performance is a fine one; there is both warmth and poetry in the slow movement; the hushed opening is particularly telling. The orchestral contribution under Previn is a strong one.

John Ogdon's version is disappointing. Clearly the partnership with Berglund did not work well and the end result is dull, in spite of an often bold solo contribution and fine recording from the early 1970s, most effectively remastered. Barbirolli's *Peer Gynt* selection is another matter. It dates from 1969 and was originally recorded in EMI's hi-fi-conscious Studio Two system. But the sound is ripely resonant and not very dated. If Beecham achieved greater subtlety in this music, Barbirolli (at his finest) is at least equally impressive and has memorable vocal contributions from the fresh-voiced Sheila Armstrong and the Ambrosian Singers. It is a pity that this is linked with less inspired music-making, even though the Seraphim reissue (with two discs for the cost of one medium-priced CD) is inexpensive.

The famous 1947 Lipatti performance remains eternally fresh, and its return to the catalogue is a cause for rejoicing, although the ear now notices a slightly drier quality and a marginal loss of bloom.

Rubinstein usually has something interesting to say about any major concerto; it is a great pity that his partner here, Alfred Wallenstein, shows little sensitivity or imagination in his handling of the light-textured but all-important orchestral contribution. Nevertheless Rubinstein produces some marvellously poetic and aristocratic playing towards the end of the slow movement, and the finale is both commanding and exciting, even if the orchestral response is aggressive. As can be seen, Rubinstein's performance is available (only in the USA) coupled with Schumann in RCA's Basic 100 series.

Gieseking's 1951 recording with Karajan and the Philharmonia was overshadowed at the time by Lipatti and Curzon, understandably so. It was compared unfavourably with his pre-war account; but nevertheless, although some of the passage-work is open to the charge of being cursory, there is a great deal that gives delight – not least Gieseking's beautiful and poetic tone.

Margaret Fingerhut gives a thoughtful and musicianly reading of the concerto that holds a fine balance between its virtuosic and poetic elements. Her first-movement cadenza shows tenderness as well as brilliance – as indeed does the slow movement. Only in the finale does she fall short of distinction (even so, the slow middle section has many felicitous touches). However, although Vernon Handley gets generally sympathetic and responsive playing from the Ulster Orchestra, in the last resort he proves disappointing in the other orchestral music. There are imaginative touches, but in the *Peer Gynt suites* his touch is surprisingly heavy and the music-making refuses to take off. The second suite is at times somewhat overblown. Very good recording.

Jenö Jandó's Grieg/Schumann coupling is pleasingly lyrical and direct, well accompanied and recorded. But its Philips/Kovacevich competitor is well worth the extra cost and also includes the *Sonata*.

Moiseiwitsch's classic plum-label recording with the Hallé Orchestra under Leslie Heward does not disappoint. It is every bit as fresh as one remembers and yet there is a certain classical poise which prevents its ardour getting out of hand. The recording is not so fresh; it is very much of its time, but now sounds a bit dryish and constricted, in the way of these Avid transfers. What an aristocrat of the keyboard Moiseiwitsch was! (The pianist in the Franck and Schumann couplings, incidentally, is Dame Myra Hess.)

The earlier performance by Rubinstein appeared as part of a three-CD set at the time of the 150th anniversary celebrations of Grieg's birth. His account of the *Piano concerto* with the Philadelphia Orchestra under Ormandy comes from 1942; the fill-ups, including the *Ballade in G minor*, are 1953 recordings, made in Hollywood. The *Concerto* is rather stronger on brilliance than on spontaneity, and the recording has more obtrusive background noise than many collectors would like. Both the *Ballade* and the *Lyric pieces* are well played but suffer from a shallow and claustrophobic acoustic.

Reid Nibley offers a pleasingly fresh and direct account of the concerto, but the slow movement cannot match Ronan O'Hora's Tring version in sheer poetry. The balance is excellent and the warm Utah acoustic disguises the age of the (1958) stereo, both here and in the two suites from *Peer Gynt*, which are also very well played but are not distinctive.

Bolet shows little affinity with Grieg's delightful concerto. He seeks to give a spacious reading and the result is merely lethargic and heavy; even the first-movement cadenza drags. The recording is the best part of the affair – it is of Decca's finest quality. The Mendelssohn encore hardly affects the matter.

(i) *Piano concerto in A min.;* (ii; iii) *Holberg suite, Op. 40; Lyric suite, Op. 54;* (iv; iii) *4 Symphonic dances, Op. 64;* (ii; iii) *Peer Gynt* (incidental music): *suites Nos. 1, Op. 46; 2, Op. 55.* (v) (Piano) *Lyric pieces, Op. 12: Album leaf; Arietta; Fairy dance; National song; Norwegian melody; Popular melody; Waltz; Watchman's song; Op. 43: Butterfly; Erotik; In my native country; Little bird; Solitary traveller; To Spring.*

(M) **(*) Ph. Duo 438 380-2 (2) [id.]. (i) Kovacevich, BBC SO, C. Davis; (ii) ECO; (iii) Raymond Leppard; (iv) Philh. O; (v) Zoltán Kocsis.

Including as it does the highly praised Kovacevich/Davis account of the *Piano concerto*, so imaginatively illuminating, this bargain-priced anthology does indeed include much of 'The best of Grieg', if one leaves aside the vocal music. Leppard's accounts of the two *Peer Gynt suites* are fresh, and all his performances here have an air of thoughtfulness which will appeal to many, especially as the orchestral playing is so good. However, in the slow movements of the *Holberg suite* and also occasionally in *Peer Gynt* there is just a hint of a lack of vitality. *In the hall of the Mountain King*, for instance, opens slowly then does not build up quite the head of steam one expects. The *Lyric suite*, however, is beautifully done, and the four *Symphonic dances*, recorded digitally, are also very successful, with a refined response from the Philharmonia. What makes the collection especially attractive is the inclusion of 14 of the *Lyric pieces*, played by Zoltán Kocsis with much character. Perhaps he is a bit impetuous at times (as in the *Fairy dance*), but his approach certainly suits *To Spring*, his last item.

(i) *Piano concerto in A min.;* (ii) *Peer Gynt suites Nos. 1–2.*

(B) **(*) DG Classikon 439 427-2; *439 427-4* [(M) id. import]. (i) Géza Anda, BPO, Kubelik; (ii) BPO, Karajan.

Anda's account of the *Piano concerto* is more wayward than some but is strong in personality and has plenty of life. Kubelik's accompaniment is good too, and the 1963 recording sounds well. However, Karajan's analogue *Peer Gynt suites* are in a class of their own. They were also recorded – a decade later – in the Berlin Jesus-Christus-Kirche but, for some reason, the CD transfer seems very brightly lit, although the fullness and analogue ambience are retained. They are played with much expressive feeling and demonstrate superlative orchestral skill and polish, yet at the same time sound admirably fresh: they have far more character than most of their bargain competitors.

2 Elegiac melodies, Op. 34; Erotik; 2 Melodies, Op. 53; 2 Norwegian airs, Op. 63.

(BB) **(*) Naxos Dig. 8.550330; *4550330* [id.]. Capella Istropolitana, Adrian Leaper – SIBELIUS: *Andante festivo* etc. **

Adrian Leaper secures responsive and sensitive playing from the Capella Istropolitana in this Grieg collection, and the recording is very good indeed and the balance natural.

2 Elegiac melodies; Holberg suite, Op. 40.

(BB) **(*) ASV CDQS 6094 [(M) id. import]. Swiss CO – SUK; TCHAIKOVSKY: *String serenades.* ***

The Swiss Chamber Orchestra take the first movement of the *Holberg suite* very briskly, but it is an enjoyably spick-and-span account, with good lyrical contrast; although the *Elegiac melodies* lack opulence, these brightly recorded performances make a good bonus for outstanding versions of the Suk and Tchaikovsky *Serenades*.

(i) *2 Elegiac melodies, Op. 34; Lyric suite, Op. 54: Norwegian march and Nocturne. Norwegian dance, Op. 35/2;* (i) *Peer Gynt suites Nos. 1–2* (including *Solveig's lullaby*); (i) *Sigurd Jorsalfar: Homage march, Op. 56/3.*

(B) *** Sony SBK 53257; *SBT 53257* [id.]. (i) Phd. O, Ormandy; (ii) Elisabeth Söderström, New Philh. O, Andrew Davis.

Andrew Davis offers freshly thought performances of the two *Peer Gynt suites*, beautifully played and warmly recorded at Abbey Road in 1976. A special attraction is the singing of Elisabeth Söderström, not only in *Solveig's song* but also in *Solveig's lullaby*, which has been added to the second suite. The Ormandy recordings date from a decade earlier but they make up a most attractive anthology. The orchestral playing is very good indeed and Ormandy's warmth is obvious. The transfers are well managed.

Holberg suite, Op. 40.

(B) *** Carlton Dig. IMP 30367 02242 [(M) id.]. Serenata of London – ELGAR: *Serenade;* MOZART: *Eine kleine Nachtmusik* etc. ***

The performance by the Serenata of London is first class in every way, spontaneous, naturally paced, and played with considerable eloquence. The digital recording is most realistic and very naturally balanced.

Old Norwegian romance with variations, Op. 51; 4 Symphonic dances, Op. 64.

(B) *** EMI forte Dig. CZS5 68649-2 (2) [CDFB 68649]. Bournemouth SO, Berglund – DVORAK: *Scherzo capriccioso* etc.; SMETANA: *Má vlast.* ***

Berglund has a special feeling for this composer and this was one of his finest Grieg records. The performances of the *Symphonic dances* are both fresh and volatile – as fine as any in the catalogue. They have a strong sense of drama, yet Berglund's beautifully moulded shaping of the lovely oboe solo (exquisitely delicate) in No. 2 gives a personal imprint to the music-making. The *Old Norwegian romance* is introduced persuasively, and the variations are sympathetically and imaginatively done. The digital recording, made in the Southampton Guildhall, is first class, warmly atmospheric yet with just the right degree of brilliance. On all counts this EMI forte double is highly recommendable.

CHAMBER MUSIC

Cello sonata in A min.; Intermezzo in A min.; Piano sonata, Op. 7.
(BB) *** Naxos Dig. 8.550878 [id.]. Oystein Birkeland, Håvard Gimse.

Written in 1882 when Grieg was thinking of composing a second piano concerto, the *Cello sonata* very much reflects the *A minor Concerto* in manner and material, with Grieg at his most richly distinctive. Oystein Birkeland and Håvard Gimse give the sonata an alive and sensitive account, coupled with the early and unrepresentative *Intermezzo in A minor*. They are both imaginative players and are decently recorded. Given the modest outlay involved, this competes very strongly with its rivals, but even if it were at mid- or full-price it would be highly recommendable. Håvard Gimse's performance of the early *Piano sonata*, Op. 7, is also very good indeed. Altogether a first-rate bargain.

String quartets Nos. 1 in G min., Op. 27; 2 in F (unfinished).
(BB) *** Naxos Dig. 8.550879 [id.]. Oslo String Qt – JOHANSEN: *String quartet.* ***

The Naxos account of the quartets from the Oslo String Quartet, a relatively new group, proves the best of the lot – indeed it is the best version we have had since the Budapest. They would easily sweep the board even at full price, on account of their sensitivity, tonal finesse and blend, and the keenness of their artistic responses. They (rightly) play only the first two movements of the *F major Quartet*, leaving room for a fine quartet by Grieg's biographer, David Monrad Johansen. The recording balance, made in the Norwegian Radio studios, is excellent, neither too forward nor too recessed. Three stars – and indeed verging on a Rosette.

Violin sonatas Nos. 1 in F, Op. 8; 2 in G, Op. 13; 3 in C min., Op. 45.
(BB) ** Naxos Dig. 8.553904 [id.]. Henning Kraggerud, Helge Kjekshus.

Henning Kraggerud and Helge Kjekshus are two young Norwegian artists who give enthusiastic and intelligent performances of these endearing works. They are inclined at times to rush things and do not allow phrases to breathe as they might; but for the most part they have considerable delicacy of feeling. Neither as performances nor as recordings do they displace the Dumay–Pires partnership on DG at full price (437 525-2), but they are worth the modest outlay without being three-star recommendations.

(i) *Violin sonata No. 3 in C min., Op. 45. Lyric pieces: Arietta, Op. 12/1; Berceuse, Op. 38/1; Cradle song, Op. 68/5; Little bird, Op. 43/4; Remembrances, Op. 71/7.*
(BB) ** Naxos Dig. 8.550417 [id.]. (i) Takako Nishizaki; Jenö Jandó – FRANCK: *Violin sonata.* **

Takako Nishizaki and her Hungarian partner give a very spirited and vital account of the *Sonata* that is thoroughly enjoyable and very recommendable, given the modest outlay involved. Not that the resonant acoustic is ideal, for the piano tends to sound bottom-heavy and muddy in climaxes. But Jandó proves a most sensitive player in the middle movement. In the *Lyric pieces*, which are heard in transcriptions by Vladimir Godar, the balance is quite different, placing the soloist closer to the microphone.

PIANO MUSIC

Einar Steen-Nøkleberg Complete Naxos series

Einar Steen-Nøkleberg has recorded every note of music Grieg composed for the piano so that his survey, running to 14 CDs, is the most comprehensive ever to appear either on CD or on any other medium. He has impressive musical credentials and is, among other things, the author of a book on Grieg's piano music and its interpretation. His survey displaces earlier sets in quality: he is responsive to mood and is searchingly imaginative in his approach. Of course there are other outstanding discs such as Leif Ove Andsnes's account of the Op. 7 *Sonata* as part of an outstanding full-priced recital (Virgin VC7 59300-2) and of course the Gilels anthology of *Lyric pieces*, which is listed separately below. But for most collectors this Naxos series is likely to be the first (as well as the most affordable) choice.

Volume 1: *Funeral March in memory of Rikard Nordraak; Humoresques, Op. 6; I love you (Jeg elsker dig), Op. 41/3; Melodies of Norway: The Sirens' enticement. Moods (Stimmungen), Op. 73; 4 Piano pieces, Op. 1; Sonata in E min., Op. 7.*
(BB) *** Naxos Dig. 8.550881 [id.]. Steen-Nøkleberg.

Steen-Nøkleberg does not proceed chronologically: the first disc couples early and late Grieg – the very earliest of his published pieces, written while he was still studying at Leipzig, the *Humoresques*, Op. 6, and the *E minor Piano sonata*, Op. 7, alongside the *Stimmungen* ('Moods'), Op. 73, composed in the early years of the present century (1901–5). Whether the music is early or late, Steen-Nøkleberg plays with total sympathy and dedication, and he is beautifully recorded throughout in the Lindeman Hall of the

Norwegian State Academy of Music. Only in the *Sonata* does he suffer a trace of self-consciousness.

Volume 2: *The first meeting, Op. 52/2; Improvisations on 2 Norwegian folksongs, Op. 29; Melodies of Norway: Ballad to St Olaf. 25 Norwegian folksongs and dances, Op. 17; 19 Norwegian folksongs, Op. 66.*
(BB) *** Naxos Dig. 8.550882 [id.]. Steen-Nøkleberg.

The second disc includes the remarkable *Nineteen Norwegian folksongs*, Op. 66, which are contemporaneous with what many would see as Grieg's masterpiece, the song-cycle *Haugtussa*, which the composer himself spoke of as full of 'hair-raising' chromatic harmonies. (One of the folksongs appears in Delius's *On hearing the first cuckoo in spring.*) But the earlier set, Op. 17, written not long after the first version of the *Piano concerto*, is also full of delights.

Volume 3: *4 Album Leaves, Op. 28; Ballade, Op. 24; Melodies of Norway: Iceland. Pictures from everyday life (Humoresques), Op. 19; Poetic Tone-pictures, Op. 3; Sigurd Jorsalfar: Prayer, Op. 56/1.*
(BB) *** Naxos Dig. 8.550883 [id.]. Steen-Nøkleberg.

Volume 4: *Holberg suite, Op. 40; Melodies of Norway: I went to bed so late. 6 Norwegian mountain melodies; Peer Gynt suite No. 1, Op. 46/1: Morning. Norwegian peasant dances (Slåtter) Op. 72.*
(BB) *** Naxos Dig. 8.550884 [id.]. Steen-Nøkleberg.

The third CD includes the poignant *Ballade in G min.*, Op. 24, composed by Grieg on the death of his parents, Steen-Nøkleberg is highly imaginative and, even if some may find his rubato a little extreme, the keyboard colouring is subtle and rich. He conveys a splendidly rhapsodic spontaneity and there is much feeling. This and the companion disc, with the *Seventeen Norwegian peasant dances* (*Slåtter*), Op. 72, deserve a particularly strong recommendation. These extraordinary pieces with their quasi-Bartókian clashes are most characterful in Steen-Nøkleberg's hands.

Volume 5: *Norway's melodies Nos. 1–63.*
(BB) **(*) Naxos Dig. 8.550891 [id.]. Steen-Nøkleberg.

Volume 6: *Norway's melodies Nos. 64–117.*
(BB) **(*) Naxos Dig. 8.550892 [id.]. Steen-Nøkleberg.

Volume 7: *Norway's Melodies Nos. 118–52 (EG 108).*
(BB) **(*) Naxos Dig. 8.550893 [id.]. Steen-Nøkleberg.

The next three discs are devoted to *Norges Melodier* ('Norway's Melody'), an anthology Grieg made in the mid-1870s for a Danish publisher, of 'easy to play' arrangements of tunes, some of them charming, others less so, drawn from folk melodies collected by Lindemann in his *ldre og Nyere Fjeldmelodier* ('Old and New Mountains Melodies'), from such composers as Halfdan Kjerulf and Rikard Nordraak, as well as some of his own songs. Grieg regarded it as having little to do with art, being directed primarily at amateur pianists up and down the country. Steen-Nøkleberg plays some on the house-organ or harmonium, some on the clavichord, some on a Graf piano to match those sonorities which would have been familiar in Norwegian homes in the 1870s, and some on a Steinway.

Volume 8: *Lyric pieces: Book I, Op. 12; Book II, Op. 38; Book III, Op. 43; Book IV, Op. 47.*
(BB) *** Naxos Dig. 8.553394 [id.]. Steen-Nøkleberg.

Volume 9: *Lyric pieces: Book V, Op. 54; Book VI, Op. 57; Book VII, Op. 62.*
(BB) *** Naxos Dig. 8.553395 [id.]. Steen-Nøkleberg.

Volume 10: *Lyric pieces: Book VIII, Op. 65; Book IX, Op. 68; Book X, Op. 71.*
(BB) *** Naxos Dig. 8.553396 [id.]. Steen-Nøkleberg.

Volumes 8–10 survey the delightful *Lyric pieces*. They are admirably fresh and are presented with the utmost simplicity, yet are obviously felt. One has only to sample the opening piece of Book V (included in Volume 9), *Herd boy*, Op. 54/1, or the *Nocturne*, Op. 54/4 (both part of the well-known orchestral *Lyric suite*), to discover the poetic calibre of this playing. These performances come into direct competition with Daniel Adni's not quite complete but otherwise excellent set on an EMI forte double CD. Many will like to have the coverage absolutely complete, and the three Naxos discs cost about the same. The EMI piano-sound is perhaps very slightly warmer and fuller, but the Naxos recording is wholly natural and believable. Einar Steen-Nøkleberg is totally idiomatic and authoritative, and readers wanting a complete set need not hesitate.

Volume 11: *Bergliot, Op. 42; Peer Gynt suites Nos. 1, Op. 46; 2, Op. 55; Sigurd Jorsalfar (suite), Op. 22;* (i) *Olav Trygvason, Op. 50: 2 Pieces.*
(BB) *** Naxos Dig. 8.553397 [id.]. Einar Steen-Nøkleberg; (i) Norwegian State Institute of Music Chamber Ch., Schiøll.

Volume 12: *Agitato, EG 106; Albumblad, EG 109; Norwegian dances, Op. 35;* (i) *Peer Gynt: excerpts, Op. 23* including *Dance of the Mountain King's daughter, Op. 55/5 (Op. 23/9);* 3 piano transcriptions from *Sigurd Jorsalfar. Waltz caprices, Op. 37.* arr. of HALVORSEN: *Entry of the Boyards.*
(BB) *** Naxos Dig. 8.553398 [id.]. Einar Steen-Nøkleberg; (i) Norwegian State Instute of Music Chamber Ch., Schiøll.

With the remaining four volumes we enter the realm of Grieg's transcriptions of his orchestral works and his juvenilia, as well as sketches for works that did not materialize. Volume 11 brings transcriptions of the *Sigurd Jorsalfar* music as well as the two *Peer Gynt suites*, Opp. 46 and 55, a couple of pieces from *Olav Trygvason* and *Bergliot* in which Steen-Nøkleberg is joined by the Norwegian State Institute of Music Chamber Choir. Volume 12 brings more of these transcriptions, different versions of *Sigurd Jorsalfar* and *Peer Gynt* (Op. 23 rather than the later suites), as well as the solo arrangement of the *Norwegian dances*. More valuable are the *Waltz caprices*, Op. 37, and the early *Agitato*, EG 106, and *Albumblad*, EG 109. Both these issues are recommendable but dispensable.

Volume 13: *2 Elegaic melodies, Op. 34; 2 Melodies, Op. 53; 2 Nordic melodies, Op. 63; Norwegian melodies Nos. 6 & 22; 3 Piano pieces, EG 105; 3 Piano pieces, EG 110/112;* Piano transcriptions of *Songs, Op. 41.*
(BB) *** Naxos Dig. 8.553399 [id.]. Einar Steen-Nøkleberg.

Volume 14: *At the Halfdan Kjerulf Statue, EG 167; Canon à 4 voci for organ, EG 179; Piano concerto in B min.* (fragments), *EG 120; Larsvikspola, EG 101; Mountain song, Norwegian melodies Nos. 87 & 146, EG 108; 23 Small pieces for piano, EG 104; Piano sonata Op. 7* (1st version: mvts 2 and 4); Piano transcriptions of *Songs, Op. 52.*
(BB) *** Naxos Dig. 8.553400 [id.]. Einar Steen-Nøkleberg.

The last two volumes are another matter. Volume 13 brings rarities in the shape of the *Three Piano pieces*, EG 105, and a further three, EG 110–112, all of which are otherwise available only on Love Dervinger's full-priced BIS record of the 1874 version of the *Piano concerto*. The last volume is of particular interest in that it brings – in addition to various juvenilia – the sketches for a *Second Piano concerto* – very Lisztian – and the first versions of the slow movement and finale of the Op. 7 *Sonata*. As is clear from the above, all these issues are recommendable, but those who do not want to invest in the whole package, which occupies a good deal of shelf-space, should try (in this order of urgency) Volumes 4, 3, 1, 8–10, 14 and 13.

Lyric pieces, Op. 12/1, 4 & 5; Op. 38/1–2, 5 & 7; Op. 43/1, 4 & 6; Op. 47, 1–4; Op. 54/1–4; Op. 57/6; Op. 62/3, 4 & 6; Op. 65/5–6; Op. 68/9; Op. 71/3 & 7.
(BB) *** Naxos Dig. 8.554051 [id.]. Einar Steen-Nøkleberg.

A compilation disc for those who do not want to invest in all three of this artist's discs of the *Lyric pieces*. Very distinguished playing, though not to be preferred to Gilels's anthology in the DG Originals series.

Lyric pieces: Op. 12/3, 5, 7 & 8; Op. 38/1, 3 & 6; Opp. 43, 47 & 54; Op. 57; Opp. 62, 65, 68 & 71.
(B) *** EMI forte CZS5 68634-2 (2) [CDFB 68634]. Daniel Adni.

Daniel Adni has also made a complete recording but, in order to fit the majority of the works on to two CDs (with a total playing time of 155 minutes), some of the earlier pieces from Books I and II have been omitted. Adni plays with genuine feeling for their character and a strong sense of atmosphere, and the 1973 EMI recording is very good indeed: the piano is firmly in focus and well balanced; there is plenty of presence and the Abbey Road studio has agreeable ambience. Those satisfied with a single-disc selection (costing the same as this EMI forte double) will find Gilels (DG 449 721-2) finest of all.

Lyric pieces: Op. 12/1, 6; Op. 38/5; Op. 54/1, 4 & 5; Op. 57/4, 6; Op. 62/3, 4 & 6; Op. 65/1–4; Op. 68/ 2, 4 & 5; Op. 71/1.
(BB) **(*) Naxos Dig. 8.550650 [id.]. Balázs Szokolay.

Lyric pieces: Op. 12/3, 8; Op. 38/1; Op. 43/1, 3 & 6; Op. 47/3–7; Op. 54/3, 5–6; Op. 57/1–3; Op. 62/ 1–2, 5; Op. 65/6; Op. 71/7.
(BB) **(*) Naxos Dig. 8.550557 [id.]. Balázs Szokolay.

Naxos are not always lucky with their piano recordings, but the two CDs Balázs Szokolay has recorded are very good. Szokolay's playing is not as consistently subtle in colouring or as poetic in feeling as Leif

Ove Andsnes, but it is pretty idiomatic. However, at super-bargain price it is really very good value indeed and the balance, though very slightly close, is not oppressively so. Both CDs give pleasure.

Lyric pieces: Op. 12/1; Op. 38/1; Op. 43/1–2; Op. 47/2–4; Op. 54/4–5; Op. 57/6; Op. 62/4 and 6; Op. 68/2, 3 and 5; Op. 71/1, 3 and 6–7.
❁ (M) *** DG 449 721-2 [id.]. Emil Gilels.

With Gilels we are in the presence of a great keyboard master whose characterization and control of colour and articulation are wholly remarkable. An altogether outstanding record in every way. This recording has been admirably remastered for reissue in DG's 'Originals' series and now sounds better than ever.

VOCAL MUSIC

Songs

4 Poems from Bjørnstjerne Bjørnson's Fishermaiden, Op. 21; 6 Songs, Op. 48; Peer Gynt: Solveig's song; Solveig's cradle song. Other songs: *At Rodane; A bird song; The first primrose; From Monte Pincio; Hope; I love but thee; I walked one balmy summer evening; Last spring; Margaret's cradle song; On the water; The princess; Spring showers; A Swan; To her II; Two brown eyes; Upon a grassy hillside.*
(BB) **(*) Naxos Dig. 8.553781 [id.]. Bodil Arnesen, Erling Eriken.

An inexpensive and, at 70 minutes, well-filled CD, beautifully recorded and pleasingly sung. Bodil Arnesen has a voice of great purity and radiance. She sings marvellously in tune, though some may find that in this repertoire she has something of a 'little-girl' innocent quality that does not give the whole picture. This perhaps is troubling when one is listening to all the songs straight off. Taken a group at a time, she will touch most hearts, particularly in the setting of Bjørnson's *Prinsessen* and *Det første møte*. Erling Eriksen is an excellent pianist.

Peer Gynt: extended excerpts.
(BB) *** Belart 450 018-2 [(M) id. import]. VPO, Karajan – SIBELIUS: *En Saga* etc. ***

(i) *Peer Gynt:* extended excerpts; (ii) *Old Norwegian romance with variations, Op. 51.*
(M) **(*) Ph. Dig. 454 130-2. (i) Elly Ameling, San Francisco Ch. & SO, Edo de Waart; (ii) Philh. O, Leppard.

Karajan's set of excerpts (from 1962) makes a first-class super-bargain choice on Belart, with a particularly fresh response from the VPO. It includes a beautiful account of *Solveig's song*, and the sound is warm and atmospheric. The Sibelius couplings are equally recommendable.

De Waart directs a warmly sympathetic reading of the *Peer Gynt* music, less sharply focused than some others. Ameling, a fine soloist, sings in Norwegian. The *Wedding march* is not included, but the brief unaccompanied choral piece, *Song of the church-goers*, is. Although this selection is not as complete as its two competitors, the disc does find room for the slight but engaging *Old Norwegian romance with variations*. Leppard's phrasing is subtle and he secures beautifully refined playing from the Philharmonia strings. Both recordings are warm and full, if not especially brilliant.

(i) *Peer Gynt*: excerpts. *In Autumn* (overture), *Op. 11; An Old Norwegian song with variations, Op. 51; Symphonic dance No. 2.*
(M) *** EMI (SIS) CDM7 64751-2 [id.]. (i) Ilse Hollweg, Beecham Ch. Soc.; RPO, Beecham.

Beecham showed a very special feeling for this score and to hear *Morning*, the gently textured *Anitra's dance* or the eloquent portrayal of the *Death of Aase* under his baton is a uniquely rewarding experience. Ilse Hollweg makes an excellent soloist. The recording dates from 1957 and, like most earlier Beecham reissues, has been enhanced by the remastering process. The most delectable of the *Symphonic dances*, very beautifully played, makes an ideal encore after *Solveig's lullaby*, affectingly sung by Hollweg. The *In Autumn* overture, not one of Grieg's finest works, is most enjoyable when Sir Thomas is so persuasive, not shirking the melodramatic moments. Finally for the present reissue, we are offered *An Old Norwegian folksong with variations* (not previously released in its stereo format). It is a piece of much colour and charm, which is fully realized here.

Peer Gynt (incidental music): *Overture; Suites 1–2. Lyric pieces: Evening in the mountain; Cradle song, Op. 68/5; Sigurd Jorsalfar: suite, Op. 56; Wedding day at Troldhaugen, Op. 65/6.*
(BB) **(*) Naxos Dig. 8.550140; *4550140* [id.]. CSSR State PO, Košice, Stephen Gunzenhauser.

A generous Grieg anthology on Naxos (70 minutes, all but 3 seconds) and the performances by the Slovak State Philharmonic Orchestra in Košice (in eastern Slovakia) are very fresh and lively and thoroughly enjoyable. There is wide dynamic range both in the playing and in the recording, and sensitivity in matters of phrasing.

Peer Gynt: suites Nos. 1, Op. 46; 2, Op. 55. Sigurd Jorsalfar: suite.
(B) *** DG Double 447 358-2 (2) [Galleria 419 474-2 (with *Holberg suite* but without Sibelius)]. BPO, Karajan – SIBELIUS: *The Bard* etc. ***

Karajan's earlier analogue performances from the early 1970s reappear here on a DG Double, coupled with a very generous and enticing Sibelius programme. The Grieg performances are highly expressive and superbly played. Anitra dances with allure and there is contrasting simplicity and repose in *Aase's death*. The current transfers are rather brightly lit, but there is no lack of body.

Peer Gynt: suites Nos. 1–2; Lyric pieces: Evening in the mountains; Cradle song, Op. 68/1–2; Wedding day at Troldhaugen, Op. 65/6; Sigurd Jorsalfar suite, Op. 56.
(BB) ** Naxos Dig. 8.550864 [id.]. BBC Scottish SO, Jerzy Maksymiuk.

The *Peer Gynt* music is presented with admirable simplicity by the excellent Scottish players. But although *Aase's death* brings a rapt closing pianissimo, *In the hall of the Mountain King* could use rather more impetus, and it is the second suite that has the greater character. What makes this disc worth considering is the very beautiful string-playing in the two *Lyric pieces* and the fine performance of the first two numbers from *Sigurd Jorsalfar*, *In the king's hall* engagingly presented and *Borghild's dream* full of atmosphere and drama. The famous *Homage march* is suitably regal but rather too slow and expansive. However, the jolly *Wedding dance* is very spirited.

(i) *Peer Gynt suites Nos. 1–2;* (ii) *Holberg suite;* (i) *Lyric piece: Wedding day at Troldhaugen, Op. 65/6; Sigurd Jorsalphar: suite, Op. 56.*
(BB) ** Naxos Dig. 8.554050 [id.]. (i) BBC Scottish SO, Maksymiuk; (ii) Bournemouth Sinf., Richard Studt.

Here is a further permutation from Naxos of their Grieg collection. The two *Lyric pieces*, about which we speak highly above, are replaced by a fresh if not distinctive version of the *Holberg suite*, recorded in Bournemouth. However, the slight reservations about the *Peer Gynt* characterizations remain.

(i) *Peer Gynt: suites Nos. 1–2. Lyric suite, Op. 54; Sigurd Jorsalfar: suite.*
(M) *** DG Dig. 427 807-2. (i) Soloists, Ch.; Gothenburg SO, Järvi.

Järvi's excerpts from *Peer Gynt* and *Sigurd Jorsalfar* are extracted from his complete sets, so the editing inevitably produces a less tidy effect than normal recordings of the *Suites*. However, the performances are first class and so is the recording, and this comment applies also to the *Lyric suite*, taken from an earlier, digital orchestral collection.

Grigny, Nicolas de (1672–1703)

Organ Mass.
(B) *** Cal. Approche CAL 6911 [(M) id.]. André Isoir (Cliquot organ at the Cathedral of Saint-Pierre de Poitiers).

Nicolas de Grigny was born in Reims and died there prematurely, just after his 31st birthday. He was principal organist both in Reims and at Notre Dame Cathedral, where he succeeded his father in 1698. His fame as a composer rests upon one book, including 49 pieces of music, and the present Couperin-influenced *Organ Mass* which was very influential in its own right. We know Bach had a copy which survives in his own hand. Although the *Mass* (an extensive collection of 22 movements varying considerably in length, most lasting between two and four minutes) is presented here as a solo work, when it was performed in its own time the organ undoubtedly alternated with the sung sections of the Mass. The *Dialogues* and other sections (such as *Basse de Trompette* and the spectacular *Offertoire sur les grands Jeux*, with a span of over eight minutes) were intended as solo interludes. Movements such as the tranquil *Récit de Tierce pour le Bénédictus* and the coolly beautiful *Dialogue de Flûtes pour l'Elévation* created an atmosphere of mysticism so characteristic of French cathedral music. The variety of the writing is remarkable, and certainly André Isoir's performance on the Cliquot organ at Poitiers Cathedral (with its characteristically pungent reeds but full underlying sonority) readily demonstrates the music's imaginative range. As a double encore we are offered an *Elévation en sol* and a *Symphonie* by Nicolas LeBegue, both strong pieces. The analogue recording is of fine quality and, while this reissue has specialist rather than general appeal, it is a fine example of the contrapuntal church organ music being written in France before the later domination of this field by Bach.

Grofé, Ferde (1892–1972)

Grand Canyon suite.

(M) *** Sony SMK 63086 [id.]. NYPO, Bernstein – GERSHWIN: *An American in Paris* etc. *** ✿

(B) *** Millennium Universal UMD 80396 [id.]. Utah SO, Maurice Abravanel – COPLAND: *Billy the Kid: suite and Waltz* etc. ***

(M) *(*) Decca Phase Four 448 956-2 [id.]. L. Festival O, Stanley Black – IVES: *Orchestral Set No. 2.* ***

It was Ferde Grofé who made the full orchestration for Gershwin's *Rhapsody in blue*, so this Sony coupling is particularly appropriate. In any event, although there have been more sumptuous recordings of the *Grand Canyon suite* since Bernstein made this one in 1963, his performance remains unsurpassed. He treats the music as if it was a masterpiece of orchestral impressionism (the openings of *Sunrise* and *Painted desert*, and especially the luscious strings which herald the *Cloudburst*, have compelling evocative tension) while the famous *On the trail* (John Corigliano the solo fiddler) has never sounded more infectiously witty. The closing storm has real spectacle, powerfully generated by the orchestral playing itself. The recording (made in the Avery Fisher Hall) is characteristically forward but has plenty of warmth and a spacious atmosphere: it has never sounded half as good is it does here. Congratulations to the reissue engineer, Tim Tiedmann.

If Abravanel does not quite match Bernstein's wit in *On the trail*, in all other respects his account is highly recommendable, with the Utah orchestra playing with great conviction and the resonant acoustic expansively spectacular throughout, and especially so in *Cloudburst*.

Stanley Black is thoroughly at home in Grofé's picaresque spectacular, but the exaggeratedly forward balance is unrealistic, especially with such a wide panoply of sound; in *On the trail* the bass clarinet is virtually in the listener's lap! Fortissimos are very highly modulated and, although the effect is better contained on CD than it was on LP, the biggest climaxes tend to degenerate into noise. Yet the performance is a colourful one and easy to enjoy, and the Ives coupling shows Stokowski at his most dramatically flamboyant.

Grand Canyon suite; Mississipi suite.

(M) **(*) Mercury (IMS) 434 355-2 [id.]. Eastman-Rochester O, Hanson – HERBERT: *Cello concerto No. 2.* **

It is impossible not to respond to the pictorial vividness and gusto of Hanson's performances and, even if the studio-ish acoustic of the Eastman Theater is not ideally expansive, the 1958 Mercury stereo is brilliantly detailed in the *Grand Canyon suite*. The *Mississippi suite*, a much lesser piece, is also persuasively presented, especially the exuberant portrait of *Huckleberry Finn*. But the canyon storms rage much more spectacularly on the rival versions.

Gubaidulina, Sofia (born 1931)

(i) *Bassoon concerto* (for bassoon and low strings); (ii) *Detto II* (for cello and chamber orchestra); (iii) *Misterioso* (for 7 percussion); (iv) *Rubaiyat* (cantata).

(M) *** BMG/Melodiya Analogue/Dig. 74321 49957-2 [id.]. (i) Valeri Popov, Chamber Ens., Meshchaninov; (ii) Ivan Monighetti, Chamber Ens., Nikolaevsky; (iii) Bolshoi Theatre O percussion, Grishkin; (iv) Sergei Yakovenko, Chambe Ens., Rozhdestvensky.

Sofia Gubaidulina belongs to the same generation as Alfred Schnittke and Edison Denisov, and she is now living in the West. She studied in Kazan and later with Shebalin and she received some encouragement from Shostakovich. She maintained herself for many years by composing film music, but in her serious work she has developed a bleak and distinctive voice. The *Rubaiyat*, a cantata for baritone and chamber orchestra, and the *Detto II* for cello and chamber forces were both recorded in the 1970s, as was the *Concerto for bassoon and low strings*. *Misterioso* for seven percussion instruments is later (from 1990). Her music is unlikely to enjoy wide popular appeal – no harm in that – and readers who have become interested in this composer need not hesitate.

In croce for bayan and cello; Seven last words for cello, bayan and strings; Silenzio for bayan, violin and cello.

(BB) *** Naxos Dig. 8.553557 [id.]. Elsbeth Moser, Maria Kliegel, Kathrin Rabus, Camerata Transsylvanica, György Selmeczi.

In croce is an arrangement of a work for cello and organ, composed in 1979 and arranged for bayan or push-button accordion in 1993. The *Seven last words*, composed in 1982 for cello, accordion and strings, is probably the best entry-point into Gubaidulina's strange world, mesmerizing for some, boring for others. Maria Kliegel is an intense and powerful cellist, and Elsbeth Moser is a dedicated player long associated with this repertoire. Good recorded sound.

Hahn, Reynaldo (1875–1947)

Mélodies: *L'air; Chansons grises; D'une prison; L'énamourée; Les fontaines; L'incrédule; Je me metz en vostre mercy; La nuit; Quand je fus pris au pavillon; Le rossignol des lilas; Seule; Si mes vers avient des ailes; Le souvenir d'avoir chanté.*

(BB) Virgin Classics Dig. Double VBS5 61433-2 [CDVB 61433]. Rachel Yakar, Claude Lavoix – FAURE: *Mélodies*. ***

Rachel Yakar with her warm, very French-sounding timbre is an ideal interpreter of the songs of Hahn, Bizet and Chabrier on this second disc of the set, or of Fauré on the companion disc, in this splendidly conceived Virgin bargain-priced Double. It is a pity that in this reissue no texts are given, but Yakar's way of bringing out the subtleties of word-meaning goes with beautifully clear diction. Though Hahn cannot match the other composers in depth or imagination, his facile genius in 19 songs, including the seven *Chansons grises*, setting Verlaine, and the most popular of all, a teenage inspiration, *Si mes vers avaient des ailes*, brings many delights. Excellent (1988) recording from Radio France.

Halffter, Ernesto (1905–89)

Guitar concerto.

(M) ** DG (IMS) 449 098-2. Narciso Yepes, Spanish R. & TV O, Alonso – CASTELNUOVO-TEDESCO: *Concerto* **(*); RODRIGO: *Fantasía*. **

Halffter, the favourite pupil of Manuel de Falla, echoes some of his master's later music, developing on the spareness of, for example, the Falla *Harpsichord concerto*. It is not what one thinks of as typical Spanish music, but the Spanish flavour is still there behind a gritty façade. Superb playing from Yepes and a competent accompaniment from Alonso, if not particularly glamorous recording.

Halvorsen, Johan (1864–1935)

Air norvégien, Op. 7; Danses norvégiennes.

(BB) *** Naxos Dig. 8.550329 [id.]. Dong-Suk Kang, Slovak (Bratislava) RSO, Adrian Leaper – SIBELIUS: *Violin concerto;* SINDING: *Légende;* SVENDSEN: *Romance*. ***

Dong-Suk Kang plays the attractive *Danses norvégiennes* with great panache, character and effortless virtuosity, and delivers an equally impeccable performance of the earlier *Air norvégien*.

Handel, George Frideric (1685–1759)

The Alchymist: suite; Concerti a due cori Nos. 1–3; 2 Arias for wind band; Royal Fireworks music; Water music: suites Nos. 1–3 (complete).

(B) **(*) O-L Double Analogue/Dig. 455 709-2 (2) [id.]. AAM, Hogwood.

Although it is possible to obtain the *Fireworks* and *Water music* together on a single CD, this Oiseau-Lyre Double conveniently gathers together Handel's major orchestral works, apart from the concertos and concerti grossi. The suite of 'act tunes' used for a revival of Ben Jonson's play, *The Alchymist*, at the Queen's Theatre, Haymarket, in 1710 originated from the composer's earlier Italian period and was the first orchestral music of Handel to be played in England. It consists of an Overture, a Prelude and a set of five dances with a repeated Bourée and two brief Aires. It is jolly music but, although presented here spiritedly, is much more conventional than the consistently inspired invention for the two great royal occasions. It was the *Water music* with which Hogwood's Academy of Ancient Music made its début at the Proms in the summer of 1978, and the joy of that occasion is matched by this performance, recorded earlier the same year at Walthamstow Town Hall. The timbres of the original instruments are consistently attractive, with the vibratoless string-tone not squeezed too painfully, and scholarship and imagination are convincingly joined. While it may still seem disconcerting to hear the well-known *Air* taken so fast – like a minuet – the sparkle and airiness of the invention have rarely been caught on record so endearingly. Hogwood's account of the *Fireworks music*, recorded two years later, can also be counted among the best available and has lively rhythms and keen articulation. The *Concerti a due cori*, sharing musical material taken from familiar works (including *Messiah*), are scored for two groups of wind instruments with an accompanying string orchestra plus continuo. Horns are strongly featured in the *F major Concertos* (Nos. 1 and 3). The present (1983) performances are lively enough, but the microphone-placing makes the strings sound meagre on top, and there is some less-than-perfect intonation and ensemble. Of course the resonant acoustic (Kingsway Hall) helps the aural picture, though the violins are still thin. The two *Arias for wind band* include an arrangement of an actual operatic aria (from *Teseo*) and again are rather spoilt by the inaccurate tuning of the period horns.

Amaryllis: suite; *The Faithful shepherd:* suite; *The Gods go a-begging:* suite; *The Great elopement:* suite; *The Origin of design:* suite (all arr. Beecham).
(M) (***) Dutton mono CDAX 8018 [id. full price]. LPO, Sir Thomas Beecham.

Superbly transferred by Dutton, these colourful, ever-charming transcriptions come in vintage performances from the magician himself, made in his LPO days. No one will ever quite match him in bringing out the colour and sparkle of arrangements which boldly fly in the face of all that the purists tell us. As Lyndon Jenkins's admirable note says, the first of the Handel–Beecham suites appeared in 1928: *The Gods go a-begging*, designed as ballet, with movements drawn from various operas, *Alcina*, *Rodrigo*, *Admeto* and *Teseo*, and adding the *Hornpipe* from the *Concerto grosso*, Op. 6/7. After that, Beecham's purloinings are rather harder to identify, and his modifications include a burst of *Rule Britannia* on the final cadence of the *Hornpipe* in *The Great elopement*, hilariously timed. The Dutton transfers let one appreciate the extra frequency-range of the 1945 recording of *The Great elopement*. Otherwise, rather surprisingly, the earliest recordings, dating from January 1933 – *The Origin of design* and two movements from *The Gods go a-begging* – are the most sharply focused, with astonishing body and presence.

Concerto grosso in C (Alexander's Feast); Concerti a due cori Nos. 1 in B flat; 2 in F; 3 in F; Overture in D; Solomon: Arrival of the Queen of Sheba.
(M) *** Ph. 454 131-2. ASMF, Marriner.

The *Concerti a due cori* were almost certainly written for performance with the three patriotic oratorios (No. 1 with *Joshua*, No. 2 with *Alexander Babus* and No. 3 with *Judas Maccabaeus*). They are full of good tunes (some very familiar, as they are drawn from the *Messiah*). Handel's scoring is most winning (the horn writing in both the *Second* and *Third Suites* is highly effective) and it is surprising that they are not better known and more popular. The performances here are rich-timbred and stylish, full of warmth, and one reflects how well modern instruments convey the grandeur of Handel's inspiration. This applies equally to the *Overture in D* and the better-known *Concerto grosso* associated with *Alexander's Feast*. Only perhaps in the *Arrival of the Queen of Sheba* does one feel a lighter touch would have been beneficial; Marriner's earlier, Argo recording of this piece was rather more sprightly.

Concerti grossi, Op. 3/1–6; Op. 6/1–12.
✿ (M) *** Decca 444 532-2 (3). ASMF, Marriner.

Concerti grossi, Op. 3/1–6 (including *No. 4b*); *Concerti grossi, Op. 6/1–12.*
(M) **(*) Teldec/Warner Analogue/Dig. 4509 95500-2 (4) [id.]. VCM, Harnoncourt.

This integral Decca/Argo recording of the Handel *Concerti grossi* makes a permanent memorial of the partnership formed by the inspired scholarship of Thurston Dart and the interpretative skill and musicianship of (then plain Mr) Neville Marriner and his superb ensemble, at their peak in the late 1960s. Dart planned a double continuo of both organ and harpsichord, used judiciously to vary textural colour and weight. Flutes and oboes are employed (with delightful effect) where Handel suggested in Op. 3, and in Op. 6 the optional oboe parts are used in concertos 1, 2, 5 and 6. The final concerto of Op. 3 features the organ as a solo instrument, and Christopher Hogwood's more recent researches suggest that this was not what Handel originally intended (see below); but the result here very much conjures up the composer's spirit hovering in the background. Incidentally, Thurston Dart makes the point that the warm acoustic used for the recording is different from the relatively dry theatre ambience which the composer would have expected; thus the chamber organ has been balanced with discretion, for under such circumstances there is less need to add tonal body to the ripieno. The three records come at a special lower-mid-price. But, alas, the superb CD transfer brings no separate cues for individual movements, only one band for each work.

The Teldec set is easily the most endearing of Harnoncourt's earlier authentic performances of baroque music. In Op. 3, tempi tend to be relaxed, but the performances are very enjoyable in their easy-going way, the ripe, fresh colouring of the baroque oboes, played expressively, is most attractive to the ear, and the string-sound is unaggressive. Tuttis are curiously dry, suggesting that the microphones were close to the violins; otherwise the sound is very good and the whole effect quite distinctive. So it is in Op. 6, where the recording is much more ample: indeed the digital sound is among the best Harnoncourt has ever received, with the most naturally refined string timbre, excellent detail and an ideal depth of acoustic. Here, as always, Harnoncourt is rhythmically gruff, and his is a performance bringing extremes of light and shade, and with the gentle playing of the solo group often lingeringly expressive. Some may find the almost brutal accents of the ripieno overdone and the dynamic contrasts too exaggerated, but Harnoncourt obviously values the music and in his hands its greatness and diversity are always obvious. The famous melody of No. 12 (marked *Larghetto e piano*) is played *mezzo forte* and is fast and jaunty, utterly different from our experience of it in modern-instrument performances. But vitality is the keynote of Harnoncourt's approach and the sound of his original instruments is altogether more congenial than in Pinnock's Archiv set. Altogether a stimulating experience, to make one hear Handel's greatest orchestral work afresh. Unfortunately Op. 3 (with its extra concerto) plays for 71 minutes at Harnoncourt's chosen tempi and Teldec have spread Op. 6 uneconomically over three more CDs, playing for a total of 166 minutes, an expensive way of obtaining this music, even at mid-price.

Concerti grossi, Op. 3/1–6.
(M) ** Virgin Veritas/EMI Dig. VER5 61162-2 [CDM 61162]. Linde Consort, Hans-Martin Linde.

Concerti grossi, Op. 3/1–6 & 4b.
(M) *(*) Teldec/Warner 0630 13574-2. VCM, Harnoncourt.

The Linde Consort, although they are beautifully recorded in a spacious acoustic, are much less successful with Handel's Op. 3 with its sequence of jewelled movements than with the Bach *Brandenburgs*. Indeed they do not have the vitality of their finest rivals: tempi are at times so sedate that the original full-priced issue spilled over on to a second CD (although then, as now, the alternative No. 4a is included). There is some attractively woody oboe playing and other good things, of course, and at mid-price this might have been tempting; but for the most part it is *vin ordinaire*.

Harnoncourt's Op. 3 includes No. 4b, which was in Handel's first edition instead of the present *No. 4 in F major* (HWV 315). With an oboe concerto thrown in, the set originally appeared uneconomically on a pair of CDs. For the reissue the seven concertos are fitted on to a single disc. Tempi on the whole are relaxed and the colouring of the baroque oboes is distinctly attractive. However, although the performances are enjoyable in their leisurely way, the string tuttis are pungently sharp-edged in that so familiar manner from the early days of period performance. Otherwise the sound is good. The recordings were made between December 1979 and January 1981.

(i) *Concerti grossi, Op. 3/1–6;* (ii) *Organ concertos Nos. 1–6, Op. 4/1–6.*
(B) **(*) Ph. Duo (IMS) 442 263-2 (2) [(M) id. import]. (i) ECO, Leppard; (ii) Daniel Chorzempa, Concerto Amsterdam, Schröder.

Among versions of Handel's Op. 3, Leppard's set stands high. The playing is lively and fresh, and the remastered recording sounds very good. Leppard includes oboes and bassoons and secures excellent playing all round. At times one wonders whether he isn't just a shade too elegant, but in general this reissue offers one of the best versions of Op. 3 on modern instruments. In this Duo pairing we are also offered Daniel Chorzempa's set of Handel's Op. 4 *Organ concertos*, and here we move over to period instruments. The Concerto Amsterdam, however, create a robustly substantial sound so the difference is not all that striking. They bring plenty of rhythmic buoyancy and life to the accompaniments. Chorzempa uses an appropriate Dutch organ and the balance is admirable. Regarding ornamentation, Chorzempa's approach is fairly elaborate and he interpolates a sonata movement from Op. 1 after the *Adagio* of the *Third Concerto*. The recording is again excellent, and those for whom the coupling is suitable will find this is good value.

Concerti grossi, Op. 6/1–12.
(BB) *** Belart 461 329-2 (*Nos. 1–4*); 461 330-2 (*Nos. 5–8*); 461 331-2 (*Nos. 9–12*) (available separately) [(M) id. import]. ECO, Leppard.
(B) (***) Millennium mono MCD 80078 (*Nos. 1–4*); MCD 80123 (*Nos. 5–8*); MCD 80131 (*Nos. 9–12*). E. Bar. O, Hermann Scherchen.
(M) **(*) Teldec/Warner 0630 17370-2 (3). VCM, Harnoncourt.
(BB) ** ASV Dig. CDQS 6163 (*Nos. 1–4*); **(*) CDQS 6164 (*Nos. 5–8*); ** CDQS 6165 (*Nos. 9–12*) [(M) id.]. Northern Sinfonia, George Malcolm.

Leppard's 1967 Philips set is now offered on Polygram's Belart label for little more than the cost of just one full-price CD. Moreover it sounds splendid in its newly remastered format, not in the least dated. The main group is comparatively full-bodied, which means that Leppard's soloists stand out in greater relief. There is grace and elegance here. These performances, too, have plenty of spirit and lively rhythmic feeling, while the richer orchestral texture brings added breadth in slow movements. With the sound newly minted, this is excellent value, though Leslie Pearson's harpsichord continuo is dwarfed by the tuttis. But how beautiful is Handel's famous melody from the very last concerto, marked *Larghetto e piano*, when played so smoothly and lyrically on modern instruments.

Recorded in September 1954, Scherchen's wonderfully warm and affectionate performances are sheer joy. He presents the music on the grandest scale, bringing out the full richness of the lyrical invention (the famous *Largo* from the last of the set is even more graciously beautiful than with Leppard). Indeed the playing of the English Baroque Orchestra (the ECO under a pseudonym perhaps?) is full of grace, while allegros, although leisurely paced, have a balancing rhythmic spring. At cadences Scherchen endearingly produces weighty rallentandos, just as if he were conducting the end of an oratorio aria. The recording is fresh and clear and, although the upper range of the violins is made characteristically thin by the microphones of the time (noticeable at the very opening of the first concerto), there is plenty of body of tone underneath and the ear immediately adjusts because of the attractive ambience. Above all, this highly successful presentation questions the practice of some period-instrument performances. That *Larghetto e piano* from No. 12 sounds so richly Handelian played like this. A set which is well worth considering, not as a first choice, but as a worthwhile back-up.

George Malcolm's set uses a full complement of modern string players; the playing is polished and alert but essentially expressive in style, heard at its best in the full-bodied opening of *Concerto No. 7*, with a genial fugato following. The best known, No. 5, is also strongly characterized and gives much pleasure, while throughout Malcolm conveys his own warmth for this endlessly inventive music. But although the playing is always spirited, in the faster movements rhythms are sometimes jogging rather than sprightly. The recording, made in All Saints' Church, Gosforth, is generally well balanced and agreeably realistic, although the harpsichord continuo might have been clearer. The transfer to CD creates a clean, bright focus with pleasingly natural string-timbres; moreover the set is inexpensive and has the advantage that the three discs are available separately. Those wanting a sampler could try the second (which includes Nos 5, 6 – which is hardly less successful – and 7), while the third CD includes No. 12 with its famous *Larghetto* melody which certainly sounds beautiful here, although Malcolm's tempo may seem too slow in the light of current period-instrument practice. Nevertheless the breadth of Handel's inspiration is certainly not lost in Malcolm's spacious approach.

Concerti grossi Op. 6/1–2, 4 & 6; Organ concertos Nos. 1–6, Op. 4/1–6; 7–12, Op. 7/1–6; 13–14, Second Set: Nos 1 in F (Cuckoo and the nightingale); 2 in A, HWV 296/6; 15–16, Arnold Edition: Nos. 1 in D; 2 in F, HWV 304/5; Water music: suites 1–3 (complete).
(M) ** Erato/Warner Dig. 0630 17763-2 (5). Ton Koopman (organ), Amsterdam Bar. O, Koopman.

The most impressive achievement within this box is the set of *Organ concertos*, which are unsurpassed. But as Op. 4 and Op. 7 are available separately on a bargain Duo (see below), this is obviously the way to approach them. Perhaps the disc containing the remaining four works including the *Cuckoo and the nightingale* will become available separately at mid-price (0630 17763-2). The Op. 6 *Concerti grossi* (apart from being incomplete) are disappointingly insubstantial, neat and elegant but entirely lacking in a sense of scale or grandeur. The *Water Music*, too, is essentially a small-scale performance. Again the playing is alert and polished and tempi are lively; the trumpets and horns are robust, but there is no sense that this is open-air music offering a sense of spectacle. Excellent recording, but overall this collection is a disappointment.

Concerti grossi, Op. 6/4–6; Concerto grosso, Op. 3/3.
(BB) * Naxos Dig. 8.550157 [id.]. Capella Istropolitana, Jozef Kopelman.

Concerti grossi, Op. 6/8, 10 & 12; in C (Alexander's Feast).
(BB) * Naxos Dig. 8.550158 [id.]. Capella Istropolitana, Jozef Kopelman.

As we know from their recordings of Bach, Haydn and Mozart, the Capella Istropolitana is an excellent group; their playing here is warm and polished, and the Naxos recording is flattering. But Jozef Kopelman's rhythmic manner is too easy-going – one needs more bite at the opening of Op. 6/5, and slow movements are often rather lazily expressive and almost bland.

(i) *Concerti grossi, Op. 6/5–6; Concerto grosso in C (Alexander's Feast);* (ii) *Music for the Royal Fireworks.*
(B) *(*) DG Classikon 439 408-2. (i) Munich Bach O; (ii) ECO; Karl Richter.

Richter's Munich performances of the *Concerti grossi* come from the early 1970s and reflect the older German Bach tradition in Handel in their weighty expressiveness, though the contrapuntal movements are lively enough and the playing is spirited. The ECO performance of the *Royal Fireworks music* opens grandiloquently, then features strong contrasts of light and shade. The effect is not sufficiently robust to be fully in character for open-air music, but it is enjoyable on its own terms as a concert-hall performance because of the polished ECO response. The sound is notably more modern here than in the Op. 6 *Concerti*.

(i) *Flute concerto in D* (attrib.); (ii) *Double cello concerto in G min.;* (iii) *Harp concerto in B flat, Op. 4/6;* (iv) *Oboe concertos Nos. 1–3.*
(BB) **(*) Arte Nova Dig. 74321 51634-2 [id.]. (i) Edward Beckett; (ii) Ferenc Szucs; (iii) Lucy Wakeford; (iv) Malcolm Messiter; L. Festival O, Ross Pople.

An enjoyable collection of Handelian concertos, not all of them authentic. The *Harp concerto* sounds as delectable as ever, and Malcolm Messiter is a neatly stylish soloist in the three works for oboe, although Pople's accompaniments have not quite the degree of finesse which Marriner finds for Roger Lord. The agreeable and certainly baroque *Flute concerto* is almost certainly not by Handel (the CD notes suggest that it was commissioned by an aristocratic amateur flautist in about 1737) but it is nicely played. The other real novelty is the amiable work for a pair of cellos (although only one player is credited), arranged most effectively from a *Sonata in G minor* (HWV 393). The recording is truthful and pleasingly balanced.

(i) *Harp concerto, Op. 4/6. Variations for harp.*
✿ (M) *** Decca 425 723-2. Marisa Robles, (i) ASMF, Iona Brown – BOIELDIEU; DITTERSDORF: *Harp concertos* etc. *** ✿

Handel's Op. 4/6 is well known in both organ and harp versions. Marisa Robles and Iona Brown make an unforgettable case for the latter by creating the most delightful textures, while never letting the work sound insubstantial. The ASMF accompaniment, so stylish and beautifully balanced, is a treat in itself, and the recording is well-nigh perfect.

Oboe concertos Nos. 1–3; Air and Rondo (ed. Camden); (i) *Suite in G min.* (ed. Camden); *Otho: overture.*
(BB) *** Naxos Dig. 8.553430 [id.]. Anthony Camden, (i) Julia Girdwood; City of London Sinfonia, Ward.

Oboe concertos Nos 1–3; Concerto grosso, Op. 3/3; Hornpipe in D, HWV 356; Overture in D, HWV 337/8; Sonata à 5 in B flat, HWV 288.
(M) **(*) Ph. 426 082-2 [id.]. Heinz Holliger, ECO, Raymond Leppard.

Oboe concertos Nos. 1 in B flat, HWV 301; 2 in B flat, HWV 302a; 3 in G min., HWV 287; Largo in F, HWV 302b. Solomon: Arrival of the Queen of Sheba.
(B) *** Decca Double 452 943-2 (2) [id.]. Roger Lord, ASMF, Marriner – BELLINI: *Oboe concerto in E flat;* – VIVALDI: *Miscellaneous concertos*. ***

Handel's three *Oboe concertos* have an immediate appeal, their style predominantly lyrical, and they are given sensitive, polished performances by Roger Lord and the Academy. Incidentally, the *Largo in F* uses the same musical material as the first movement of the *Second Concerto*, but with quite spectacular horn parts added to the accompaniment. Ideally the *Arrival of the Queen of Sheba* could have had a touch more wit and sparkle, but the playing is elegant enough and, with Bellini's brief but delightful concerto added for good measure, this makes a fine coupling for the Academy's generous programme of miscellaneous Vivaldi concertos, which are in every way recommendable. The vintage (originally Argo) sound is first class.

Anthony Camden, for years principal oboe of the LSO, here makes a very welcome solo appearance on disc, playing with typical point and style, using his attractively reedy tone. The regular oboe concertos are well supplemented by the *Suite in G minor* as edited by Camden, where he is joined by the prize-winning Julia Girdwood on the second oboe. The *Otho Overture* too features prominent roles for oboes in duet. Ward and the City of London Sinfonia are sympathetic accompanists using modern instruments. First-rate sound from All Saints, East Finchley. A fine alternative to Roger Lord with the ASMF for those not wanting the coupled Vivaldi programme on the Decca Double.

Holliger, a masterly interpreter, does not hesitate to embellish repeats; his ornamentation may overstep the boundaries some listeners are prepared to accept. His playing and that of the other artists in this collection is exquisite, and the recording is naturally balanced.

Organ concertos Nos. 1–6, Op. 4/1–6; 7–10, Op. 7/1–4.
(B) ** EMI forte CZS5 72676-2 (2) [(M) id. import]. Simon Preston, Festival O, Sir Yehudi Menuhin.

(i) *Organ concertos Nos. 11–12, Op. 7/5–6; 13 in F (Cuckoo and the nightingale); 14 in A, HVW 296; 15 in D min., BWV 394. Concerto a due cori in B flat;* (ii) *Violin concerto in B flat. Music for the Royal Fireworks; 3 Marches* (from *Atalanta, Joshua* and the *Occasional oratorio*).

(B) ** EMI forte CZS5 72637-2 (2) [(M) id. import]. (i) Simon Preston; (ii) Y. Menuhin; Bath Festival O, Sir Yehudi Menuhin.

In these reissues from the late 1960s, Simon Preston uses four different organs, two built comparatively recently at the Queen Elizabeth Hall and St Paul's School, Hammersmith, plus the organ in Merchant Taylors Hall, London, as well as the famous instrument at Great Packington Church which Handel himself knew and played. Preston is partnered by Sir Yehudi Menuhin and they use the Neville Boyling edition; though there are minor criticisms to be made concerning tempi and phrasing, on the whole these are enjoyable accounts. Preston is especially good in the Great Packington recordings (Op. 4/2 and 3, Op. 7/3 among them), but here the eighteenth-century organ is obviously just right for the music. He ad-libs where necessary, as Handel himself would have done. The string group gives the impression of being of a fair size, but the playing is alert as well as warm and gracious. To fill up the second disc we are offered the *Concerto a due cori No. 1 in B flat* (where Handel quotes from a *Messiah* chorus) and an agreeable arranged violin concerto in B flat (with Menuhin the soloist). Menuhin then goes on to conduct a full-scale orchestral *Fireworks music*, very slow and grand. These works are all also included and discussed under Menuhin's Seraphim issue below, which includes the *Water music*. The present concert closes with three brief marches, from *Atalanta* and *Joshua* (which includes 'See the conqu'ring hero comes' on the horns), and finally from the *Occasional Oratorio* – in all, quite a musical feast.

Organ concertos, Op. 4/1–6; Op. 7/1–6; in F (The cuckoo and the nightingale), HVW 295; in A, HWV 296; in D min., HWV 304.
(M) *** DG Dig. 435 037-2 (3) [id.]. Simon Preston, E. Concert, Pinnock.

Simon Preston's second (DG) set of the Handel *Organ concertos* comes on three discs. On the first, containing the six Op. 4 works, plus the *A major*, though the balance of the solo instrument is not perfect, the playing of both Preston and the English Concert is admirably fresh and lively. Ursula Holliger is outstanding on a baroque harp (taking the place of the organ) in Op. 4, No. 6, and she creates some delicious sounds. The second and third discs, containing the six Op. 7 works, plus the *The cuckoo and the nightingale* and the *D minor*, were recorded on the organ at St John's, Armitage, in Staffordshire, and are even more attractive for the warmth and assurance of the playing, which comes near the ideal for an 'authentic' performance. The *A major* which completes the set was recorded earlier with Op. 4. For those wanting a complete set of the *Organ concertos* this is strongly recommended.

Organ concertos, Op. 4/1–6; Op. 7/1–6.
❀ (M) *** Erato/Warner 4509 91932-2 (2) [id.]. Ton Koopman, Amsterdam Bar. O.
(B) **(*) Decca Double 452 235-2 (2) [(M) id. import]. George Malcolm (organ or harpsichord), ASMF, Marriner.

Ton Koopman's paired sets of Opp. 4 and 7 are a remarkable bargain, complete on two CDs in Erato's Duo Bonsai series. They take precedence over all the competition, both as performances and as recordings. The playing has wonderful life and warmth, tempi are always aptly judged and, although original instruments are used, this is authenticity with a kindly presence, for the warm acoustic ambience of St Bartholomew's Church, Beek-Ubbergen, Holland, gives the orchestra a glowingly vivid coloration and the string timbre is particularly attractive. So is the organ itself, which is just right for the music. Ton Koopman plays imaginatively throughout and he is obviously enjoying himself: no single movement sounds tired and the orchestral fugues emerge with genial clarity. Koopman directs the accompanying group from the keyboard, as Handel would have done, and the interplay between soloist and ripieno is a delight. The sound is first class and the balance could hardly be better.

In the matter of ornamentation and interpolations Malcolm is both imaginative and stylistically impeccable. He plays two of the concertos on the harpsichord (Op. 4/3 and Op. 7/6) and here achieves a near-perfect balance so that the harpsichord is in proper scale with the orchestra without being larger than life. Malcolm's registrations (using the organ of Merton College Chapel for Op. 4, and the instrument at St John the Evangelist, Islington, for Op. 7) are always colourful (notably in Op. 4/4). The lithe, resilient orchestral textures are vigorous in allegros, but in slow movements warmly refined and often subtly shaded, and sometimes the ear craves a more robust effect. Occasionally one feels that this element of sophistication asserts itself too readily. The vintage 1972–3 (originally Argo) recording is warm and full, and this music-making is easy to enjoy.

Organ concertos, Op. 4/2; Op. 7/3–5; in F (The cuckoo and the nightingale).
(M) *** DG Dig. 447 300-2. Simon Preston, E. Concert, Pinnock.

This is more generous than the previous (full-price) sampler from Preston's series with Pinnock. Both performances and sound are admirably fresh.

Organ concertos, Op. 4/2, 4 & 5; Op. 7/1; in F (Cuckoo and the nightingale).
(BB) ** Naxos Dig. 8.550069 [id.]. Johann Aratore, Handel Festival CO, John Tingle.

Brisk tempi and a crisply robust (unidentified) organ image, placed forwardly, ensure that these performances project with plenty of life. The orchestral support is polished, rhythmically strong and sympathetic in slow movements. The digital recording is bright and faithful; but there is a hint of relentlessness at times.

Music for the Royal Fireworks; Concerto grosso in C (Alexander's Feast); Overtures: Alceste; Belshazzar; Samson; Saul. Solomon: Arrival of the Queen of Sheba.
(M) *** DG Dig. 447 279-2 [id.]. E. Concert, Trevor Pinnock.

Pinnock's performance of the *Fireworks music* has tremendous zest; this is not only the safest but the best recommendation for those wanting a period-instrument version. The account of the *Alexander's Feast concerto* has both vitality and imagination and is no less recommendable. The vigorous and exhilarating performances of five *Overtures*, most of them hardly known at all but full of original ideas, even in the most highly structured pieces, make this a most interesting collection of works, and the Queen of Sheba's arrival is always welcome. All are freshly and cleanly recorded.

Music for the Royal Fireworks; Water music (complete).
(BB) *** Naxos Dig. 8.550109; *4550109* [id.]. Capella Istropolitana, Bohdan Warchal.
(BB) ** RCA Navigator 74321 29236-2 [(M) id. import]. Paillard CO, Jean-François Paillard.

Bohdan Warchal directs the Capella Istropolitana in bright and lively performances of the complete *Water music* as well as the *Fireworks music*, well paced and well scaled, with woodwind and brass aptly abrasive, and with such points as double-dotting faithfully observed. Textures are clean, with an attractive bloom on the full and immediate sound, to provide a strong bargain recommendation.

Re-recording this music digitally in 1990, Paillard and his chamber orchestra fail to match the vitality and sparkle of their earlier, Erato analogue coupling. This is agreeable enough and well recorded, but there is an element of routine in the playing.

(i) *Music for the Royal Fireworks;* (ii) *Water music: suites 1–3* (complete); (i) *Concerto a due cori No. 1 in B flat; Violin concerto in B flat* (arr. from *Sonata à 5*); Marches from: *Atalanta; Joshua; Occasional oratorio.*
(BB) *(*) EMI Seraphim CES5 68523-2 [CDEB 68523] [id.]. (i) Menuhin Festival O, Sir Yehudi Menuhin; (ii) Prague CO, Mackerras.

There are inexpensive couplings of the *Fireworks* and *Water music* on a single CD, which reduces the attractiveness of this Seraphim set, except to admirers of Menuhin. One wonders why EMI did not choose his version of the complete *Water music*, which is in many ways preferable to the Mackerras version. This is lively enough, but there is a heavyweight quality in the string-tone (hardly a question of recording) which at times weighs the music down despite the quality of much of the playing itself. Unfortunately Menuhin's tempi for the *Royal Fireworks music*, using a comparatively new edition by Neville Boyling, are consistently on the slow side, and the main interest of his contribution to this collection is the arrangement of the *Sonata à cinque*, presented under the title of 'Violin concerto in B flat', in which Menuhin himself is the warm-hearted if somewhat romantic soloist. The *Concerto a due cori*, with expansive strings, to present-day ears similarly sounds too ample to seem really stylish.

Music for the Royal Fireworks; Water music (complete); (i) *Oboe concerto No. 2 in B flat.*
(B) **(*) Decca Eclipse Dig. 448 227-2; *448 227-4* [(M) 417 743-2]. Stuttgart CO, Karl Münchinger, (i) with Lothar Koch.

Here is a much better way of remembering Münchinger's expertise in baroque repertoire than in the Bach *Orchestral Suites*. His style is a compromise between authenticity and the German tradition. In the complete *Water music* he uses recorders most effectively; the balance, helped by Decca's very transparent sound, is often attractively lightweight. If occasionally tempi seem a shade on the slow side, there is much to enjoy both here and in the *Fireworks music*, where the clarity reveals some shifts of perspective in the *Overture* and *Bourrée*. Some other versions of this music are more buoyant but Münchinger is consistently sympathetic and never dull. With first-class digital recording, the effect is vivid and well focused, and with an oboe concerto (well played by Lothar Koch) thrown in for good measure – and with the additional advantage of economy – this is well worth considering.

Music for the Royal Fireworks: suite; Water music: suite (arr. Harty and Szell); *The Faithful shepherd: Minuet* (ed. Beecham); *Xerxes: Largo* (arr. Reinhardt).
(BB) *** Belart 450 001-2 [(M) London 417 694-2]. LSO, Szell.

Many readers will, like us, have a nostalgic feeling for the Handel–Harty suites from which earlier generations got to know these two marvellous scores. George Szell and the LSO offer a highly recommendable coupling of them on a Belart super-bargain issue, with Handel's *Largo* and the *Minuet* from Beecham's *Faithful shepherd suite* thrown in for good measure. The orchestral playing throughout (from the early 1970s) is quite outstanding, and the strings are wonderfully expressive in the slower pieces. The horns excel, and the crisp new transfer seems to add to the sheer zest of the music-making. A splendid bargain.

Water music: Suites Nos. 1–3 (complete).
(BB) *** ASV Dig. CDQS 6152 [(M) id.]. ECO, George Malcolm.
(M) *** Vanguard/Passacaille Dig. 99713. Il Fondamento, Paul Dombrecht – TELEMANN: *Water music.* ***
(B) *** [EMI Red Line Dig. CDR5 69809]. BPO, Muti.
(M) **(*) Virgin Veritas/EMI VER5 61240-2. Linde Consort, Linde.

Water music: suites Nos. 1–3 (complete); *Concerto grosso, Op. 3/3, HWV 314.*
(BB) *** Arte Nova Dig. 74321 30498-2. L. Festival O, Ross Pople.

This super-bargain set of the complete *Water music* on the ASV Quicksilva label from George Malcolm and the English Chamber Orchestra tends to sweep the board, except for those insisting on 'authentic instruments'. Indeed in every other sense this is a completely stylish realization of Handel's intentions, with the closing dances of the *Third Suite in G* particularly elegant, while the digital recording approaches demonstration standard. The playing is first class, articulation is deft and detail admirable. There is a sense of delight in the music which makes this version especially appealing.

Il Fondamento is an excellent Belgian period-instrument group; under the lively direction of Paul Dombrecht they present Handel's *Water music* with a nice mixture of verve and elegance. The throaty reeds and robust brass ensure a vigorous response, but the more graceful numbers in the centre of the work have pleasing colour and much character. This ranks high among the 'authentic' versions and is made doubly attractive by being coupled at mid-price with Telemann's *Wassermusik*, not perhaps as inspired as Handel's but engagingly inventive and entertaining just the same.

As can be imagined, the playing of the Berlin Philharmonic under Muti is of the highest calibre, polished and elegant. In the *Overture* of the first suite, a small instrumental group is featured as a neat counterpoint to the main ripieno: throughout there is a strong emphasis on contrast, with instrumental solos often treated in a concertante manner. In the famous *Air* some might feel that the element of light and shade is over-stressed, but the playing is very responsive and the strings generally display a light touch. The horns, however, are almost aggressive in their spirited vigour in the famous fanfare tune. With a full, vivid, yet clear sound-picture, this is very easy to enjoy.

Ross Pople's account of the *Water music* is enjoyably fresh and lively, with crisp and elegant string-playing and impressive contributions from the principal oboe and the horns. The bonus from Op. 3 is well worth having. This is strikingly more characterful than Pople's companion CD of the Boyce *Symphonies*, but the recording, though truthful and well balanced, seems a little studio bound for music originally conceived for open-air performance.

Also using period instruments, the Linde Consort provides a gentler, more intimate alternative to Il Fondamento. The ensemble is not always so polished, but the easy warmth of the playing is most attractive, not least in the G major movements for flute, recorder, bassoon and strings which Linde (himself the flute- and recorder-player) turns into a separate suite after the groups in F major and D major. First-rate sound backs up bright but unabrasive performances.

CHAMBER MUSIC

Flute sonatas (for flute and continuo): *in E min., Op. 1/1a; in D, HWV 378; Halle sonatas* (for flute and continuo) *Nos. 1–3; Oboe sonatas* (for oboe and continuo): *Nos. 1 in B flat (HWV 357); in F (HWV 363a), Op. 1/5; in C min. (HWV 366), Op. 1/8; Recorder sonatas* (for recorder and continuo): *in G min. (HWV 360); in A min. (HWV 362); in C (HWV 365); in F (HWV 369), Op. 1/2, 4, 7 & 11; in B flat (HWV 377); in D min. (HWV 367a); Sinfonia in B flat for 2 violins and continuo, HWV 338; Trio sonatas: in E min. for 2 flutes and continuo, HWV 395; in F for 2 recorders and continuo, HWV 405.*
(B) *** Ph. Duo 446 563-2 (2) [(M) id. import]. ASMF Chamber Ens.

This superb Philips set assembles virtually all the important wind sonatas, plus a single *Trio sonata* for two violins and continuo, on a pair of discs offered for the price of one. William Bennett uses a modern flute very persuasively in the *Flute sonatas* and includes, besides the work from Op. 1 and the three *Halle sonatas*, a more recent discovery from a Brussels manuscript. Nicholas Kraemer and Denis Vigay provide admirable support, and the recording is most realistic and present. In the *Recorder sonatas* Michala Petri plays with her customary virtuosity and flair, and Neil Black is marvellously accomplished in the *Oboe sonatas*. Both artists share an excellent rapport with their continuo players, who include George Malcolm (harpsichord), Denis Vigay (cello) and Graham Sheen (bassoon), and again the sound is exemplary, natural and spacious. Only those seeking original instruments need look elsewhere.

Flute sonatas (for flute and continuo): *in E min., HWV 359b; in G, HWV 363b; in B min., HWV 367b* (6th movt); *in A min., HWV 374; in E min., HWV 375* (4th movt); *in B min., HWV 376; Oboe sonatas* (for oboe and continuo): *in C min., HWV 366; in B flat, HWV 357; in F, HWV 363a* (2nd movt); *Recorder sonatas* (for recorder and continuo): *in G min., HWV 360; in A min., HWV 362; in C, HWV 365; in D min., HWV 367a* (movts 1-5, 7); *in F, HWV 369; in B flat, HWV 377; Andante in D min., HWV 409.*
(B) *** Sony Seon Double SBK 60100 (2) [id.]. Frans Brüggen, Bruce Haynes, Hans Jürg Lange, Anner Bylsma, Bob van Asperen (harpsichord and organ).

These performances, on original instruments, are enormously accomplished – indeed that is an understatement: Brüggen plays with characteristic mastery and so do his companions. There are some mannerisms: he swells all too predictably on sustained notes and is generous with stress accents. However, Handelians will want to consider the set for its scholarship and expertise, even though the flute is balanced rather close, which will not be to all tastes. This makes a clear alternative to Marriner's set, although it is not so complete, including only key movements from some works; and the documentation, by leaving out the opus numbers, is less clear.

KEYBOARD MUSIC

Chaconne in G, HWV 435; The Harmonious blacksmith (Air and variations from Suite No. 5 in E, HWV 436); Suites Nos. 3 in D min., HWV 346; 4 in E min., HWV 438; 13 in B flat, HWV 434; 14 in G, HWV 441.
(M) ** DG (IMS) Dig. 447 290-2. Trevor Pinnock (harpsichord).

Although Pinnock has undoubted flair and panache, the closeness of the microphones and a fairly uniform *forte* are emphasized by the added presence of CD which, as this 1982 collection proceeds, tends to seem relentless. The result conveys expertise in plenty but rather less in the way of enjoyment; and we must register disappointment at the forward balance. *The Harmonious blacksmith* has been added from a later (1983) recital: it is brilliantly played but the problem of over-projection remains.

Suites Nos. (i) *1 in A;* (ii) *2 in F; 3 in D min.;* (i) *4 in E min.;* (ii) *5 in E;* (i) *6 in F sharp min.; 7 in G min.;* (ii) *8 in F min.*
❀ (B) *** EMI forte CZS5 69337-2 (2) [CDFB 69337]. (i) Gavrilov; (ii) Richter.

Suites (i) *Nos. 9 in G min.;* (ii) *10 in D min.; 11 in D min.;* (i) *12 in E min.;* (ii) *13 in B flat;* (i) *14 in G;* (ii) *15 in D min.;* (i) *16 in G min.*
❀ (B) *** EMI forte CZS5 69340-2 (2) [CDFB 69340]. (i) Richter; (ii) Gavrilov – BEETHOVEN: *Piano sonata No. 17.* *** ❀

Piano playing doesn't come much better than this! These recordings of the Handel *Keyboard suites* were recorded by Sviatoslav Richter and Andrei Gavrilov at the Château de Marcilly-sur-Maulne during the 1979 Tours Festival, and first appeared in 1983 in a handsome five-LP box, which was treasured by anyone fortunate enough to possess it. They were never reissued as single- or double-pack LPs in the UK and perhaps did not reach as wide a public as they might otherwise have done. They have been slow to reach CD, but EMI have made amends by issuing the set in first-class transfers, and in an economical format – two twin-CDs packaged as one, available separately, and competitively priced – and with Richter's famous 1961 account of Beethoven's *D minor Sonata*, Op. 31, No. 2, thrown in for good measure. There is no need to waste words on the playing, which is balm to the soul. The serenity and tranquillity of the slow movements and the radiance of the faster movements have never before been so fully realized. Not to be missed.

Harpsichord suites Nos. 1–8.
(B) *** HM Musique d'Abord HMA 190447/48 [id.]. Kenneth Gilbert (harpsichord).

Gilbert is a scholar as well as a distinguished player, and his version of the suites, recorded on a copy of a Taskin harpsichord by Bédard, is well worth seeking out, making a fine bargain alternative to Paul Nicholson's more comprehensive (and more expensive) set. Gilbert observes most first-half repeats but not those of the second, and he is as imaginative in the handling of decoration and ornamentation as one would expect. If one were to quibble, it would be merely that some grandeur, some larger-than-life vitality is missing (not a criticism one could apply to his full-priced competitor); but so much else is there that there is no case for qualifying the recommendation. The recording is natural and very well balanced.

Harpsichord suites Nos. 1–5.
(BB) ** Naxos Dig. 8.550415 [id.]. Alan Cuckson (harpsichord).

Harpsichord suites Nos. 6–8; 2nd Collection: *Suite No. 4. Air and variations; Sonatina in D min.; Sonata in G min.; Toccata in G min.*
(BB) ** Naxos Dig. 8.550416 [id.]. Alan Cuckson (harpsichord).

Were Alan Cuckson less closely recorded, his Naxos set would deserve a higher star rating, but after a time the effect is just a little oppressive. The performances have undoubted qualities, but the playing is at times a little too judicious to be wholly persuasive. There are some minor fluffs and fingerslips here and there (in the *Capriccio in F major*, for example) which should have been corrected, and some inelegances elsewhere.

Suite No. 5 in E (includes *The Harmonious blacksmith*).
(B) *** Decca Eclipse Dig. 448 992-2; *448 992-4* [(M) id. import]. Alicia de Larrocha, VSO, Uri Segal – MOZART: *Piano concertos Nos. 19 & 22.* ***

Alicia de Larrocha's performance was recorded in the Henry Wood Hall; she gives a robust and vital account of the best-known of Handel's *Suites*, with its famous variations, and again fully justifies the use of the piano for this repertoire. Her performance may not banish memories of Richter (his Touraine performance is now available on an EMI forte reissue) but it is thoroughly enjoyable in its own right. There is plenty of warmth, and the recording is splendidly realistic. This makes a splendid bonus for an outstanding bargain Mozart coupling.

VOCAL MUSIC

(i) *Aci, Galatea e Polifemo;* (ii) *Recorder sonatas in F; C & G* (transposed to *F*).
(B) *** HM Musique d'abord Dig. HMA 901253/4 [id.]. (i) Kirkby, Watkinson, Thomas, L. Bar., Medlam; (ii) Michel Piquet, John Toll.

Aci, Galatea e Polifemo proves to be quite a different work from the always popular English masque, *Acis and Galatea*, with only one item even partially borrowed. Charles Medlam directs London Baroque in a beautifully sprung performance with three excellent soloists, the brightly characterful Emma Kirkby as Aci, Carolyn Watkinson in the lower-pitched role of Galatea, and David Thomas coping manfully with the impossibly wide range of Polifemo's part. The three recorder sonatas are comparably delightful, a welcome makeweight. Excellent sound, full of presence. This is particularly enticing at bargain price.

Acis and Galatea (complete in English); *Il pastor fido: Hunting scene.*
(B) *** Decca Double 452 973-2 (2) [id.]. Robert Tear, Jill Gomez, Philip Langridge, Benjamin Luxon, Ch. & ASMF, Marriner – Robert Tear: *'Baroque recital'.* ***

The refinement and rhythmic lift of the Academy's playing under Marriner make for a lively and highly engaging performance of *Acis and Galatea*, marked by characterful solo singing from a strong team. The choruses are sung by a quartet drawn from a distinguished vocal sextet (Jennifer Smith, Margaret Cable, Paul Esswood, Wynford Evans, Neil Jenkins and Richard Jackson) and, with warmly atmospheric recording, the result is a sparkling entertainment. Robert Tear's tone is not always ideally mellifluous (for instance in *Love in her eyes sits playing*) but, like the others, he has a good feeling for Handelian style; the sweetness of Jill Gomez's contribution is a delight. The 1977 (originally Argo) recording is of vintage quality and this Double Decca reissue is made the more attractive by the inclusion of a further solo recital from Robert Tear of rare English baroque repertoire – music by Arne, Boyce and Hook, as well as Handel. Before this, as an interlude, comes a sprightly (orchestral) *Hunting scene* from *Il pastor fido* consisting of a *March* and a pair of *Airs pour les chasseurs.*

Acis and Galatea (complete; arr. Mozart in German).
(M) *** DG (IMS) Dig. 447 700-2 (2). MacDougall, Bonney, Schaefer, Tomlinson, E. Concert Ch. & O, Pinnock.

It may seem perverse for three English-speaking principals to choose to do *Acis and Galatea* in German, but Mozart's arrangement with added woodwind has its own interest, a parallel text to the more radical one he prepared of *Messiah*. Pinnock's performance, well recorded, is as persuasive as one could imagine, with Barbara Bonney an enchanting Galatea and John Tomlinson a characterful Polyphem, clear and precise. Jamie MacDougall as Acis sounds a little gusty at times but makes an attractively ardent hero.

(i) *Alceste: Overture and incidental music;* (ii) *Comus: vocal excerpts*.
(M) *** O-L 443 183-2. Margaret Cable, David Thomas; (i) Judith Nelson, Emma Kirkby, Christine Pound, Margaret Cable, Catherine Denley, Paul Elliott, Rogers Covey-Crump, David Thomas, Christopher Keyte; (ii) Patrizia Kwella; AAM, Hogwood.

Handel left us much to enjoy here, with the impressively dramatic *Alceste overture* in D minor and the *Grande entrée* for Admetus and Alceste and their wedding guests getting the proceedings off to a fine start. There follows a series not just of solo items but also some simple tuneful choruses, in which a small secondary vocal group participates. Hogwood draws lively performances from his usual team and, as ever, is very well recorded. The music for *Comus* was later used in the *Occasional oratorio*; the five items offered here show how refreshing was Handel's original. The performances by Patrizia Kwella, Margaret Cable and David Thomas with the Academy under Hogwood have all the freshness and vigour one associates with this conductor's earlier series of Purcell theatre music. The transfers of 1979/80 analogue recordings, made at St Jude's, London, are well up to L'Oiseau-Lyre's usual high standard.

Alexander's Feast (complete).
(M) ** Van. 08.9057.72 (2). Heather Harper, Honor Sheppard, Max Worthley, Maurice Bevan, Oriana Concert Ch. & O, Alfred Deller.

Alexander's Feast was the first and greatest of the odes by Dryden which Handel set to celebrate St Cecilia's Day. It was written in 1736 (three years before the less ambitious work he called the *Ode for St Cecilia's Day*) and was one of the composer's London successes. The invention is consistently on the highest level, without a single poor number. Not only are the vocal solos and choruses among Handel's finest, but the orchestration shows many imaginative touches. Handel holds his brass in reserve and the horns must have made something of a sensation in their colourful entry in praise of Bacchus. The trumpets, too, make a commanding entry in the opening chorus of Part 2: '*Break his bonds of sleep asunder*'. In no other work are they used with greater brilliance.

Deller's set first appeared in the UK at the end of the 1960s on the Philips label. Now it reverts to its original, Vanguard source but it has no coupling and, even at mid-price, is not a very economical purchase, as the playing time of the second CD is only 34 minutes. However, the solo singing is most distinguished, the tenor stylish rather than dramatic. Heather Harper is glorious of tone and accurate in her runs (her melisma on '*shake*' in her first aria is superb). The choral singing is very good, and one can only regret that the very resonant acoustic means that the overall sound, though rich and expansive, lacks bite and sharpness of focus.

L'allegro, il penseroso, il moderato.
(M) *** Erato/Warner 4509 99723-2 (2) [2292 45377-2]. Kwella, McLaughlin, Jennifer Smith, Ginn, Davies, Hill, Varcoe, Monteverdi Ch., E. Bar. Soloists, Gardiner.

Taking Milton as his starting point, Handel illustrated in music the contrasts of mood and character between the cheerful and the thoughtful. Then, prompted by his librettist, Charles Jennens, he added compromise in *Il moderato*, the moderate man. The sequence of brief numbers is a delight, particularly in a performance as exhilarating as this, with excellent soloists, choir and orchestra. The recording is first rate.

(i) *Apollo e Daphne* (cantata); (ii) *Oboe concerto in G min*.
(B) *** HM Musique d'Abord HMA 1905157 [id.]. (i) Judith Nelson, David Thomas; (ii) Haynes; San Francisco Bar. O; McGegan.

Apollo e Daphne is one of Handel's most delightful cantatas and tells how the determinedly chaste heroine, after an unwelcome and persistent pursuit by her godly suitor, finally escapes a fate worse than death by being transformed into a laurel bush! It has two strikingly memorable numbers, a lovely siciliano for Dafne with oboe obbligato and an aria for Apollo, *Come rosa in su la spina*, with unison violins and a solo cello. Both soloists are first rate, and Nicholas McGegan is a lively Handelian, though the playing of the orchestra could be more polished. The sound is over-resonant but has plenty of atmosphere. For the bargain-priced reissue (retaining the full documentation plus translation) a neat account of Handel's *G minor Oboe concerto* has been added.

Belshazzar (complete).
(M) **(*) Teldec/Warner 0630 10275-2 (3). Felicity Palmer, Maureen Lehane, Robert Tear, Paul Esswood, Peter van der Bilt, Stockholm Chamber Ch., VCM, Harnoncourt.

With authentic style and instruments set against a relatively intimate acoustic, Harnoncourt's opening of the fine overture to *Belshazzar* on this Teldec recording may initially seem somewhat gruff, but then Harnoncourt's concentration in number after number builds up the high drama of this oratorio. The libretto of Charles Jennens gets near to demanding stage presentation in its echoing of operatic convention, with stage directions at every turn. The drama is the more pointed when the soloists, led by Felicity Palmer and Robert Tear, keep the story-line clearly in mind with their expressive enunciation of the words. The other soloists, too, are excellent, notably Paul Esswood with his fresh counter-tenor tone, and the bass, Peter van der Bilt. In some ways most enjoyable of all is the singing of the fine Stockholm choir, delectably light and pointed in some of the end-of-scene choruses. Harnoncourt is at his best when given the chance to point a brisk number with lifted rhythms, but he is less effective in warmer music; for the unprejudiced Handelian, this account of a masterpiece should certainly prove stimulating.

Coronation anthems (1. Zadok the Priest; 2. The King shall rejoice; 3. My heart is inditing; 4. Let Thy hand be strengthened).
(M) *** Decca 436 256-2. King's College Ch., ECO, Willcocks – BLOW: *Anthems.* **(*)

(i) *Coronation anthems* (complete); (ii) *Concerti a due cori Nos. 2–3, HWV 333/4.*
(M) *** DG Dig. 447 280-2 [id.]. (i) Westminster Abbey Ch., Preston; (i–ii) E. Concert; (ii) Pinnock.

Those who like spare, 'authentic' textures will favour Preston in the *Coronation anthems* where, although the overall effect is less grand, the element of contrast is even more telling. To have the choir enter with such bite and impact underlines the freshness and immediacy. The use of original instruments gives plenty of character to the accompaniments. An exhilarating version. The new coupling of the two *Concerti a due cori* is welcome, with the performances full of rhythmic vitality.

The reissued (1961) Argo King's recording of these four anthems makes an admirable mid-priced alternative recommendation, particularly as the extra clarity and presence given to the choir improve the balance in relation to the orchestra. The Blow *Anthems* make a fine bonus.

(i) *Dixit Dominus; Laudati pueri;* (ii) *Organ concerto in F (The cuckoo and the nightingale).*
(M) ** Decca Eclipse Dig. 448 242-2; *448 242-4* [id.]. (i) Buchanan, Mackay, Chance, Kendall, Hurford, King's College, Cambridge, Ch., ECO, Cleobury; (ii) Peter Hurford, Concg. CO, Rifkin.

In his King's College Choir version of *Dixit Dominus*, Stephen Cleobury inevitably suffers, in this often elaborate music, from the heavy reverberation of the chapel. It is a fresh and direct reading, well sung but lacking the magic and urgency of the finest versions. The vocal coupling is another of Handel's early Psalm settings, written on his trip to Italy. Peter Hurford's excellent version of a favourite among Handel's organ concertos is a welcome bonus but hardly affects the appeal of the disc.

Funeral anthem for Queen Caroline: The ways of Zion do mourn.
(M) **(*) Erato/Warner 4509 96954-2 [2292 45136-2]. Norma Burrowes, Charles Brett, Martyn Hill, Stephen Varcoe, Monteverdi Ch. & O, Gardiner.

Queen Caroline – whom Handel had known earlier as a princess in Hannover – was the most cultivated of the royal family of the Georges, and when she died in 1737 he was inspired to write a superb cantata in an overture and eleven numbers including the splendid chorus, *How are the mighty fall'n*. He later used the material for the first Act of *Israel in Egypt*. Gardiner directs a stirring performance which brings out the high contrasts implicit in the music, making the piece energetic rather than elegiac. Excellent work from soloists, chorus and orchestra alike, all very well recorded in the ideal ambience of London's Henry Wood Hall, and most realistically transferred to CD. The only snag is the playing time of 44 minutes: there would have been room for another work here.

Israel in Egypt (oratorio).
(M) **(*) DG (IMS) 429 530-2 (2). Harper, Clark, Esswood, Young, Rippon, Keyte, Leeds Festival Ch., ECO, Mackerras.

(i) *Israel in Egypt*; (ii) *Chandos anthem No. 10: The Lord is my light.*
(B) *** Decca Double 443 470-2 (2) [id.]. (i) Gale, Watson, Bowman, Partridge, McDonnell, Watts, Christ Church Cathedral, Oxford, Ch., ECO, Preston; (ii) Cantelo, Partridge, King's College, Cambridge, Ch., ASMF, Willcocks.

Israel in Egypt, with *The Lamentations of the Israelites for the Death of Joseph.*
(M) **(*) Virgin Veritas/EMI (SIS) Dig. VMD5 61350-2 (2) [CDCB 54019]. Argenta, Van Evera, Wilson, Rolfe Johnson, Thomas, White, Taverner Ch. & Players, Parrott.

Simon Preston, using a small choir with boy trebles and an authentically sized orchestra, directs a performance of this great dramatic oratorio which is beautifully in scale. He starts with *The cuckoo and the nightingale organ concerto* – a procedure sanctioned by Handel himself at the first performance – and though inevitably the big plague choruses lack the weight which a larger choir gives them, the vigour and resilience are ample compensation, so that the text is illustrated with extra immediacy. Though Elizabeth Gale is not as firm a soprano as Heather Harper on Mackerras's alternative mid-priced Archiv set, the band of soloists is an impressive one and the ECO is in splendid form. The 1975 recording (originally Argo) is warmly atmospheric, more realistically balanced than the rival Archiv one, and it has been vividly transferred to CD. Moreover this Double Decca (two-for-the-price-of-one) set generously includes the tenth Chandos anthem, *The Lord is my light*, remarkable for some magnificent fugal writing and freshly performed at King's under Sir David Willcocks.

Mackerras's performance represents a dichotomy of styles, using the English Chamber Orchestra sounding crisp, stylish and lightweight and a fairly large amateur choir, impressively weighty rather than incisive. Thus the work makes its effect by breadth and grandiloquence rather than athletic vigour. The solo singing is distinguished, but its style is refined rather than earthy.

Parrott directs a clean-cut, well-paced reading which wears its period manners easily. With excellent choral and solo singing the performance is unlikely to offend anyone. Good, warm sound. Parrott follows the unique precedent of Handel's very first performance in using as the first part of the oratorio the cantata written on the death of Queen Caroline, *The Lamentations of the Israelites for the Death of Joseph*, with text duly adapted.

Jephtha (oratorio; complete).
(M) *** Van. 08 5091 73 (3). Young, Forrester, Grist, Watts, Lawrenson, Amor Artis Chorale, ECO, Somary.
(M) ** Teldec/Warner 0630 17390-2 (3) [id.]. Hollweg, Gale, Linos, Esswood, Thomaschke, Mozart Boys' Ch., Arnold Schoenberg Ch., VCM, Harnoncourt.

The Vanguard set was the first ever recording of *Jephtha*, made in 1969. It stands up surprisingly well against latterday period performances so that anyone preferring modern instruments need not hesitate. The analogue sound, full, forward and bright, is well transferred, and the freshness and liveliness of Somary's direction, with brisk speeds lightly sprung, are worlds away from the old oratorio tradition. The singers make a formidably starry team with no weak link. Alexander Young, a superb Handel singer, recorded far too little; here he sings most beautifully as Jephtha, not least in *Waft her, angels*. The Canadian mezzo, Maureen Forrester, is caught richly and firmly as Hamor, and the others are first rate too. The relatively small professional chorus is equally assured, producing bright, fresh tone, firmly and forwardly focused.

Harnoncourt's pursuit of extra authenticity, with an orchestra using original instruments, has its snags, and not just in the thin timbre of the strings. Harnoncourt takes a more operatic view of the work, but he mars the impact of that by too frequently adopting a mannered style of phrasing. The soloists too are on balance far less impressive than those on the Somary version. The recording acoustic, typically clean, is not helpful in its dryness. With a very full text this makes a long haul.

Judas Maccabaeus (complete).
(M) *** DG 447 692-2 (3). Felicity Palmer, Janet Baker, Esswood, Ryland Davies, Shirley-Quirk, Keyte, Wandsworth School Ch., ECO, Mackerras.
(M) **(*) Van. 08 4072 72 (2) [OVC 4071/2]. Harper, Watts, Young, Shirley-Quirk, Amor Artis Ch., Wandsworth School Boys' Ch., ECO, Somary.

Judas Maccabaeus may have a lopsided story, with a high proportion of the finest music given to the anonymous soprano and contralto roles, Israelitish Woman and Israelitish Man; but the sequence of Handelian gems is irresistible, the more so in a performance as sparkling as DG's reissued 1976 recording under Sir Charles Mackerras. Unlike many versions, particularly those which in scholarly fashion attempt to restore Handel's original proportions, this holds together with no let-up of intensity, and though not everyone will approve of the use of boys' voices in the choir (inevitably the tone and intonation are not flawless) it gives an extra bite of character. Hearing even so hackneyed a number as *See, the conqu'ring hero* in its true scale is a delightful surprise. The orchestral group and continuo sound splendidly crisp; when the trumpets enter in *Sound an alarm*, the impact is considerable, just as it must have been for the original Handelian audience. Though some may regret the passing of old-style fruity singing in the great tenor and bass arias, Ryland Davies and John Shirley-Quirk are most stylish, while both Felicity Palmer and Dame Janet crown the whole set with glorious singing, not least in a delectable sequence, towards the end of Act I, on the subject of liberty. The recording quality is outstanding in its CD format, fresh, vivid and clear.

On Vanguard the solo singing is excellent, with Alexander Young a ringing tenor, and Helen Watts singing the opening aria in Act III exquisitely. Very good recording – the choruses could ideally have a crisper focus, but the effect is wholly natural – and a sense of commitment throughout from all departments.

Lucrezia (cantata). Arias: *Ariodante: Oh, felice mio core . . . Con l'ali do constanza; E vivo ancore? . . . Scherza infida in grembo al drudo; Dopo notte. Atalanta: Care selve. Hercules: Where shall I fly? Joshua: O had I Jubal's lyre. Rodelinda: Pompe vane di morte! . . . Dove sei, amato bene? Serse: Frondi tenere e belle . . . Ombra mai fù (Largo).*

(M) *** Ph. 426 450-2. Dame Janet Baker, ECO, Leppard.

Even among Dame Janet's most impressive records this Handel recital marks a special contribution, ranging as it does from the pure gravity of *Ombra mai fù* to the passionate virtuosity in *Dopo notte* from *Ariodante*. Leppard gives sparkling support and the whole is recorded with natural and refined balance. An outstanding disc, with admirable documentation.

Messiah (complete).

(B) *** Ph. Duo 438 356-2 (2) [id.]. Harper, Watts, Wakefield, Shirley-Quirk, L. Symphony Ch., LSO, Sir Colin Davis.

(B) *** EMI CZS7 62748-2 (2) [Ang. CDMB 62748]. Harwood, J. Baker, Esswood, Tear, Herincx, Amb. S., ECO, Mackerras.

(M) *** Hyperion Dyad Dig. CDD 22019 (2) [id.]. Lynne Dawson, Denley, Maldwyn Davies, Michael George, The Sixteen Ch. & O, Christophers.

(B) **(*) CfP CD-CFPD 4718 (2) [id.]. Morison, Thomas, Lewis, Milligan, Huddersfield Ch. Soc., RLPO, Sargent.

(M) **(*) EMI CMS7 63784-2 (2) Trebles from King's, Bowman, Tear, Luxon, King's College, Cambridge, Ch., ASMF, Willcocks.

(BB) **(*) Naxos Dig. 8.550667/8 [id.]. Amps, Davidson, Doveton, Van Asch, Scholars Bar. Ens.

(M) **(*) Van. 08.4019 72 (2) [OVC 4018/19]. Margaret Price, Yvonne Minton, Alexander Young, Justino Diaz, Amor Artis Chorale, ECO, Somary.

(M) **(*) ASV Dig. CDDCS 230 (2). Lott, Palmer, Langridge, Lloyd, Huddersfield Ch. Soc., RPO, Mackerras.

(B) ** Decca Double 444 824-2 (2) [id.]. Ameling, Reynolds, Langridge, Howell, ASMF Ch. & O, Marriner.

(M) ** Virgin Veritas/EMI (SIS) VMD5 61330-2 (2) [CDCB 49801]. Kirkby, Emily van Evera, Cable, Bowman, Cornwell, Thomas, Taverner Ch. & Players, Parrott.

(B) * Teldec/Warner Dig. 0630 18952-2 (2) [9031 77615-2]. Elizabeth Gale, Marjana Lipovšek, Werner Hollweg, Roderick Kennedy, Stockholm Chamber Ch., VCM, Harnoncourt.

Reissued at bargain price on Philips's Duo label, the LSO recording conducted by Sir Colin Davis has not lost its impact and sounds brightly lit and fresh in its digitally remastered format. Textures are beautifully clear and, thanks to Davis, the rhythmic bounce of such choruses as *For unto us* is really infectious. Even *Hallelujah* loses little and gains much from being performed by a chorus of this size. Excellent singing from all four soloists, particularly Helen Watts who, following early precedent, is given *For He is like a refiner's fire* to sing, instead of the bass, and produces a glorious chest register. The performance is absolutely complete and is excellent value at its new price.

The choruses on EMI have not quite the same zest as on Philips, but they have a compensating breadth and body. More than Davis, Mackerras adopted Handel's alternative versions, so the soprano aria *Rejoice greatly* is given in its optional 12/8 version, with compound time adding a skip to the rhythm. A male alto is also included, Paul Esswood, and he is given some of the bass arias as well as some of the regular alto passages. Among the soloists, Dame Janet Baker is outstanding. Her intense, slow account of *He was despised* – with decorations on the reprise – is sung with profound feeling. The recording is warm and full in ambience and, with the added brightness of CD, sounds extremely vivid.

Christophers consistently adopts speeds more relaxed than those we have grown used to in modern performances, and the effect is fresh, clear and resilient. Alto lines in the chorus are taken by male singers; a counter-tenor, David James, is also used for the *Refiner's fire*, but *He was despised* is rightly given to the contralto, Catherine Denley, warm and grave at a very measured tempo. The team of five soloists is at least as fine as that on any rival set, with the soprano, Lynne Dawson, singing with silvery purity to delight traditionalists and authenticists alike. The band of 13 strings sounds as clean and fresh as the choir. Even the *Hallelujah chorus* – always a big test in a small-scale performance – works well, with Christophers in his chosen scale, through dramatic timpani and trumpets conveying necessary weight. The sound has all the bloom one associates with St John's recordings. This now seems to be a pretty clear first choice at mid-price among modern digital recordings.

It is good to have Sir Malcolm Sargent's 1959 recording now restored to the catalogue in full for, apart from the pleasure given by a performance that brings out the breadth of Handel's inspiration, it provides an important corrective to misconceptions about pre-authentic practice. Sargent unashamedly fills out the orchestration (favouring Mozart's scoring where possible). By the side of Davis, his tempi are measured, but his pacing is sure and spontaneous and, with a hundred-strong Huddersfield group, no one will be disappointed with the weight or vigour of the choruses. There is some splendid singing from all four soloists, and Marjorie Thomas's *He was despised* is memorable in its moving simplicity. The success of the CD transfer is remarkable: the old analogue LPs never sounded as clear as this.

Often though *Messiah* may have been recorded, there always seems plenty of room for alternative versions, particularly those which show a new and illuminating view of the work. Willcocks's recording, made in the Chapel at King's in 1971/2, has been described as the 'all-male *Messiah*', since a counter-tenor takes over the contralto solos, and the full complement of the trebles of King's College Choir sings the soprano solos, even the florid ones like *Rejoice greatly*; the result is enchanting, often light and airy. The bigger choruses do not lack robust qualities; however, the engineers have put their microphones fairly close and the resultant added clarity loses some of the normal King's softness of focus. The sound is thus vivid as well as atmospheric, but not quite what one would encounter sitting in the Chapel. A gimmicky version, perhaps, but one that many will find refreshing and involving.

On the bargain Naxos label comes a period performance with a difference. With fresh, immediate sound adding to the impact, the Scholars Baroque Ensemble presents the oratorio on the smallest possible scale, with individual singers from the small chorus coming forward to sing the arias. In keeping with this approach, the performance is directed by one of the basses, David van Asch, and characteristically the booklet seeks as far as possible not to highlight individual contributions like his but to emphasize teamwork. At brisk speeds, with rhythms well sprung, this will please those who fancy such an approach, though the instrumental sound is abrasive in a way one associates with the earliest period performances, and none of the singers has a voice of star quality. By their own definition, these are good choristers rather than great soloists. Given that, there is much to recommend the issue, though many more than traditionalists will prefer an approach that brings out more of Handel's grandeur.

Somary directs a crisp, small-scale performance that features sparkling orchestral playing (on modern instruments) and first-rate singing from soloists and chorus alike. His direction is not always consistent but it is never dull, and the recording is first class, warm yet bright and natural. An excellent choice for those wanting a relatively traditional approach and who have a special fondness for all or any of the soloists. The chorus is excellent, its size nicely judged.

The big disappointment of Sir Charles Mackerras's digital set with the Huddersfield Choral Society is that this great choir conveys less weight and bite than many of the small choirs on period recordings. It is largely a question of recording balance, which gives the choral ensemble too little body. The quartet of soloists is a strong and distinctive one – Felicity Lott, Felicity Palmer, Philip Langridge and Robert Lloyd – but hardly traditional-sounding. It is interesting to have Mozart's arrangement used, with its trombones and clarinets, but the traditional cuts are made here; this means that Part 1 comes complete on the first disc and the other two Parts complete on the second. Inconsistently but aptly for a British recording, the original English text is used, not the German actually set by Mozart.

Marriner's conception was to present *Messiah* as nearly as possible in the text followed at the first London performance of 1743. The losses are as great as the gains, but the result has unusual unity, thanks also to Marriner's direction. His tempi in fast choruses can scarcely be counted as authentic in any way: with a small professional chorus he has gone as far as possible towards lightening them and has thus made possible speeds that almost pass belief. Although Anna Reynolds's contralto is not ideally suited to recording, this is otherwise an excellent band of soloists – and in any case Miss Reynolds sings *He was despised* on a thread of sound. Vivid recording.

Parrott for EMI has assembled a fine team of performers, as well as his own Taverner Choir and Players. Emma Kirkby is even more responsive here than she was in her earlier recording, for Oiseau-Lyre; but, for all its great merits, the performance lacks the zest and the sense of live communication that mark out a version like Pinnock's, another period performance (at full price) which also dares to adopt slow, expressive speeds for such arias as *He was despised* and *I know that my Redeemer liveth*. Even at mid-price this is not a strong contender.

Harnoncourt's version was compiled from two public concerts in Stockholm in 1982, with ill-balanced sound that puts the choir at a distance, making it sound even duller than it is. With the exception of Elizabeth Gale, the soloists are poor, and Harnoncourt's direction lacks vigour. This cannot begin to match the Christophers version on Hyperion.

Messiah (complete; orch. Sir Eugene Goossens).
❀ (M) *** RCA 09026 61266-2 (3) [id.]. Vyvyan, Sinclair, Vickers, Tozzi, RPO Ch. & O, Sir Thomas Beecham.

Messiah (orch. Sir Eugene Goossens): highlights.
(M) *** RCA 09026 68159-2 [Basic 100 09026 61718-2]. Jennifer Vyvyan, Monica Sinclair, Jon Vickers, Giorgio Tozzi, RPO Ch. & O, Beecham.

This is a performance which at every point radiates the natural flair of the conductor, and Beecham is extraordinarily sensitive to Handel's rhetoric and pathos. The use of the cymbals to cap the choruses *For unto us a child is born* and *Glory to God* is unforgettable. Beecham's tempi are slower than we expect today, but given his expansive view of Handel, they are convincingly appropriate, with the possible exception of the *Hallelujah chorus*, which gathers speed exuberantly as it nears its end. Jennifer Vyvyan and Monica Sinclair both sing freshly. Jon Vickers brings to his tenor arias a heroic quality that is often welcome and effective. Giorgio Tozzi's English is sound and his management of the tricky bass arias (especially *Why do the nations*) compels admiration. But it is above all Beecham's set, and its sense of exultant glory in the riches of Handel's masterpiece is life-enhancing. The 1959 recording of the chorus and orchestra is full and expansive in its CD transfer and the soloists have remarkable presence and immediacy. The third disc with its 17-minute appendix of eight items – normally cut at the time this recording was made – comes as a bonus, as the set is priced as for two mid-range CDs.

Not everyone will want Beecham's complete *Messiah* with its flamboyant orchestration by Sir Eugene Goossens, but many will be intrigued enough to have a sampler; this remastered CD admirably fills the need with 19 key items offered, including the *Overture* and *Pastoral Symphony*. The soloists are excellent and so is the choral singing.

Messiah (slightly abridged).
❀ (B) (***) Dutton Lab. mono 2CDEA 5010 (2) [(M) id.]. Isobel Baillie, Gladys Ripley, James Johnson, Norman Walker, Huddersfield Ch. Soc., Liverpool PO, Malcolm Sargent.

Sargent's first recording of Handel's *Messiah* is not complete. Following his usual performance practice, three numbers are cut from Part II and four from Part III. The recording venue was Huddersfield Town Hall in 1946, when that great Choral Society was still at its peak, and Handel's masterpiece is here brought vividly to life by the most miraculous Dutton Lab. 78-r.p.m. transfer yet. What is so involving is the way this remarkably realistic and present recording (in many ways more vivid than the later stereo set), made in a series of four-minute takes, comes over as an ongoing 'live' performance, from the rich tapestry of the Overture onwards. There must be all sorts of strictures about the style of the performance, not least the slow tempi (especially in Part II) and the orchestration (Sargent uses Prout's edition, plus additions from Mozart's version) and of course its sheer weight and scale – Sargent believed there could never be too many voices. But the chorus sings throughout with enormous conviction and the four fine soloists obviously live their parts; moreover their enunciation is a model and every word is clear. Undoubtedly the star of the performance is Isobel Baillie. Her first entry in *There were shepherds* is a moment of the utmost magic, and what follows is utterly ravishing, while her gloriously beautiful *I know that my Redeemer liveth* has never been surpassed on record. Gladys Ripley sings *He was despised* with moving simplicity and restraint, and she warmly introduces *He shall feed his flock*, sharing it with Baillie, who re-enters exquisitely, like the sun suddenly shining through clouds. Her tonal purity is phenomenal, and it is caught by the current transfer with complete faithfulness. Sargent's tempi for the choruses now sound slow, notably *For unto us a Child is born*, and of course the very grand *Hallelujah*, which is very spacious indeed. But Sargent believes deeply in the music and he carries the listener with him in an ongoing inspired flow. The sound itself is truly astounding! At bargain price this is an essential investment for anyone who loves the English amateur choral tradition.

Der Messias (sung in German, arr. Mozart): complete.
(M) **(*) DG (IMS) 427 173-2 (2). Mathis, Finnilä, Schreier, Adam, Austrian R. Ch. & O, Vienna, Mackerras.

Mozart's arrangement of *Messiah* has a special fascination. It is not simply a question of trombones being added but of elaborate woodwind parts too – most engaging in a number such as *All we like sheep*, which even has a touch of humour. *The trumpet shall sound* is considerably modified and shortened. To avoid the use of a baroque instrument, Mozart shares the obbligato between trumpet and horn. Mackerras leads his fine team through a performance that is vital, not academic in the heavy sense. The remastered recording is excellent and a translation is provided.

Messiah (sung in English): highlights.
(M) *** [EMI Red Line CDR5 72431] (from above set, cond. Mackerras).
(B) **(*) CfP CD-CFP 9007 [id.] (from above stereo set, cond. Sargent).
(BB) **(*) ASV Dig. CDQS 6001 [(M) id. import]. Kwella, Cable, Kendal, Drew, Jackson, Winchester Cathedral Ch., L. Handel O, Neary.
(BB) **(*) Belart 450 045-2 [(M) id. import] (from above Philips Duo set, cond. Sir Colin Davis).
(M) **(*) Ph. 462 055-2 [(M) id. import]. Margaret Marshall, Catherine Robbins, Charles Brett, Robin Hale, Monteverdi Ch., E. Bar. Soloists, John Eliot Gardiner.

At mid-price Mackerras is first choice (available in the USA only), while the great and pleasant surprise among the bargain selections is the Classics for Pleasure CD of highlights from Sir Malcolm Sargent's 1959 recording; no one will be disappointed with *Hallelujah*, while the closing *Amen* has a powerful sense of apotheosis.

Brightly if reverberantly recorded in Winchester Cathedral, Martin Neary's collection of excerpts gives a pleasant reminder of the work of one of our finest cathedral choirs. In its authentic manner Neary's style is rather too clipped to convey deep involvement, but the freshness is attractive, with some very good solo singing.

Although it is not particularly generous, the Belart set of highlights from Sir Colin Davis's mid-1960s recording is the least expensive high-quality selection currently available. It offers a dozen key items, including most of the favourites, but not *He was despised*.

The selection from Gardiner's set centres on the choruses (which feature bright-toned sopranos). Some arias are included, notably *The trumpet shall sound*, sung with great authority by Robin Hale; but too much is missing here: any selection from *Messiah* which omits *I know that my Redeemer liveth* (sung so beautifully on the complete set by Margaret Marshall) can receive only a hesitant recommendation, even though the selection runs to 76 minutes. The presentation in Philips's 'Choral Collection' is handsome, but the notes are sparse and no texts are included.

Messiah: choruses.
(M) **(*) Ph. 446 575-2. Monteverdi Ch., E. Bar. Soloists, Gardiner.

Gardiner's complete set of choruses, using sopranos for the treble line, is fresh and pleasing enough; but this CD plays for only 51 minutes, and a selection of highlights would seem a much more sensible choice.

Ode for St Cecilia's Day.
(M) *** Teldec/Warner 0630 12319-2. Palmer, Rolfe Johnson, Stockholm Bach Ch., VCM, Harnoncourt.

Harnoncourt's Teldec version of Dryden's *Ode*, recorded in 1979, comes up well in its digital transfer to CD. It is only slightly less recommendable than Trevor Pinnock's (full-priced) Archiv version, though the non-British choir, for all its fluency, sounds less comfortable than its rival and sings rather less crisply. Anthony Rolfe Johnson is excellent on both versions, while Felicity Palmer as soprano sings most characterfully. One special point in favour of Harnoncourt is his own striking cello playing in the beautiful setting of Dryden's second stanza, *What Passion cannot Musick raise and quell!* Now reissued in Teldec's Das Alte Werk mid-priced series, it is fully competitive.

La Resurrezione.
(B) *** HM Musique d'Abord HMA 1907027/8 [id.]. Saffer, George, Nelson, Spence, Thomas, Phil. Bar. O, Nicholas McGegan.

In 1708, halfway through his four-year stay in Italy, the young Handel wrote this refreshingly dramatic oratorio. With opera as such prohibited in Rome, it served as a kind of substitute, not solemn at all, but with dramatic and moving exchanges between the central characters. There is no chorus until the close, but Handel makes up for this with a wonderful palette of orchestra colour in his accompaniments, liberally featuring trumpets, recorders and oboes. McGegan's performance is as lively as one could wish and is excellently cast. Lisa Saffer is an appealing Angel, nimble (in breathtakingly florid coloratura) and touching, especially good in her dialogues with the boldly resonant Lucifer (Michael George). But Judith Nelson is equally affecting as Mary Magdelene, whereas Patricia Spence's dark contralto (as Cleophas) and Jeffrey Thomas's fresh tenor St John bring plenty of dramatic contrast. The sounds from the period instruments of the Philharmonia Baroque Orchestra are ear-tickling, and presumably the soloists join together for the life-assertive closing chorus. Excellent recording, both atmospheric and vivid, makes for a fine bargain alternative to Hogwood (Oiseau-Lyre 421 132-2).

Samson (complete).

(M) *** Erato/Warner 2292 45994-2 (3). Tear, J. Baker, Lott, Watts, Shirley-Quirk, Luxon, L. Voices, ECO, Leppard.

(M) ** Van. 08 5084 72 (2). Peerce, Curtin, Parker, M. Smith, Utah University Symphony Chorale, Utah SO, Abravenel.

Leppard directs a highly dramatic account of Handel's most dramatic oratorio, one which translates very happily to the stage; its culmination, the exultant aria *Let the bright seraphim*, is here beautifully sung by Felicity Lott, but for long was associated with Joan Sutherland at Covent Garden. The moment when the orchestra interrupts a soloist in mid-sentence to indicate the collapse of the temple is more vividly dramatic than anything in a Handel opera, and Leppard handles that and much else with total conviction. Robert Tear as Samson produces his most heroic tones – rather too aggressively so in *Total eclipse* – and the rest of the cast could hardly be more distinguished. Dame Janet Baker – not by nature a seductress in the Dalila sense – yet sings with a lightness totally apt for such an aria as *With plaintive notes*, and the others are in excellent voice. The recording is outstanding, atmospheric and well balanced.

Cut to fit on two very well-filled discs, the Vanguard set offers a bright, vigorous performance with strong, forthright singing from Jan Peerce as a heavyweight Samson and the bright-toned soprano, Phyllis Curtin, singing not just Dalila but several incidental roles. In its own traditional terms it is enjoyable enough, with bright choral singing and brisk conducting, but for a modern-instrument version Raymond Leppard's Erato set with Robert Tear and Dame Janet Baker is far more stylish and better recorded, and it avoids disfiguring cuts.

Saul (complete).

(M) *** DG 447 696-2. Armstrong, M. Price, Bowman, Ryland Davies, English, Dean, McIntyre, Winfield, Leeds Festival Ch., ECO, Sir Charles Mackerras.

(M) ** Teldec/Warner Dig. 4509 97504-2 (2). Fischer-Dieskau, Rolfe Johnson, Esswood, Varady, Gale, V. State Op. Ch., VCM, Harnoncourt.

(M) ** Van. 08 5088 72 (2). Hemsley, Vyvyan, Watts, Handt, Sjöstedt, Copenhagen Boys' Ch., VSO, Wöldike.

With an excellent combination of soloists Mackerras steers an exhilarating course in a work that naturally needs to be presented with authenticity but equally needs to have dramatic edge, and the result is powerful on one hand, moving on yet another. The contrast of timbre between Armstrong and Price, for example, is beautifully exploited, and Donald McIntyre as Saul, Ryland Davies as Jonathan and James Bowman as a counter-tenor David are all outstanding, while the chorus willingly contributes to the drama. An outstanding set, beautifully recorded (at the Leeds Triennial Music Festival in 1972) and vividly transferred to CD.

Harnoncourt's version was recorded live at the Handel tercentenary celebrations in Vienna in 1985 and, whatever the advantages of period performance, the extraneous noises of coughs and creaks, together with the odd slip of execution, seriously reduce its merits. Dietrich Fischer-Dieskau in the name-part is most characterful, but his expressive style is very heavy for Handel, particularly in the recitatives. It is still for the most part a rich and noble performance, and Julia Varady, though not quite idiomatic, is individual too, with tone cleanly focused. The English members of the cast sing stylishly, notably Anthony Rolfe Johnson as Jonathan and Paul Esswood as David. Elizabeth Gale's bright soprano is not always sweetly caught by the microphones, but it is a sympathetic performance. Harnoncourt's direction is lively but he misses much of the grandeur of the work, and some of the cuts he makes are damaging. The Vienna State Opera Concert Choir are responsive, but they never quite sound at home coping with English words.

Dating from well before the Vanguard recordings of Handel made by Johannes Somary, Wöldike's pioneering set of *Saul* involves an earlier tradition, with a large, firmly focused orchestra set in a rather reverberant acoustic. Though recitatives are slow and laboured, Wöldike generally avoids the worst heaviness of that tradition, and there is fine singing from such soloists as Thomas Hemsley, splendid in Saul's brilliant aria *A serpent in my bosom*. Jennifer Vyvyan sings beautifully as Michal and, most moving of all, Helen Watts is superb as David, whose arias are among the highspots of the performance. The most serious snag is that the text is savagely cut, with roughly two-thirds of what you hear on such a rival period recording as John Eliot Gardiner's on Philips.

Solomon.

(M) **(*) Van. 08 5086 72 (2). Diaz, Armstrong, Tear, Rippon, Palmer, Amore Artis Chorale, ECO, Somary.

Somary in this and other recordings for Vanguard did impressive work in the 1960s and 1970s in helping to establish a new, fresher approach to Handel oratorio, well before period performance took over. With a crisp professional chorus and a formidable line-up of soloists, this offers an enjoyable, infectiously sprung performance, marred by the choice of voice for the title-role. Handel himself opted for a mezzo rather than a castrato or a tenor, but here Somary, following now-discredited tradition, has a bass, singing an octave lower than written. Admittedly Justino Diaz sings with satisfyingly dark, firm tone to make the result dramatically very convincing, and the other soloists, drawn from among the finest British singers of the time, are all excellent. For this magnificent pageant of an oratorio, John Eliot Gardiner's period performance remains a firm first premium-priced choice, but it is good to have this too, at mid-price.

Susanna: highlights.

(M) **(*) HM Suite Dig. HMT 7907168 [id.] (from complete recording, with Lorraine Hunt, Drew Minter, Jill Feldman, William Parker, Jeffrey and David Thomas, Philh. Bar. O, Nicholas McGegan).

Many collectors who might not want to stretch to the complete opera on three full-priced CDs will surely welcome this 72-minute selection of highlights from Handel's dramatic treatment of the Apocrypha story of Susanna and the Elders, particularly as it comes with full text and good documentation. The soloists are excellent and, although the dry recording acoustic is not flattering, this still makes an attractive sampler.

Theodora (complete).

(M) **(*) Van. 08.4075.72 (2) [OVC 4074/5]. Harper, Forrester, Lehane, Young, Lawrenson, Amor Artis Ch., ECO, Somary.

Theodora was a favourite with Handel himself among his oratorios; the reissued Vanguard account is traditional in style and is directed by an understanding and intelligent Handelian, Johannes Somary. With fresh and sympathetic singing from soloists who are stylistically at home in Handel, the result is most enjoyable. Maureen Forrester in particular sings superbly, but all the singing is at least reliable, and the recording has transferred warmly and vividly to CD.

Utrecht Te Deum and Jubilate.

(M) *** O-L 443 178-2. Kirkby, Nelson, Brett, Elliott, Covey-Crump, D. Thomas, Ch. of Christ Church Cathedral, Oxford, AAM, Simon Preston – VIVALDI: *Gloria.* ***

(M) *(*) Teldec/Warner Dig. 0630 13573-2 [2292 42984-2]. Palmer, Lipovšek, Langridge, Equiluz, Moser, Baumann, Arnold Schönberg Ch., VCM, Harnoncourt – BACH: *Magnificat.* *

Using authentic instruments and an all-male choir with trebles, Preston directs a performance which is not merely scholarly but characteristically alert and vigorous, particularly impressive in the superb *Gloria* with its massive eight-part chords. With a team of soloists regularly associated with the Academy of Ancient Music, this can be confidently recommended, especially as this mid-priced reissue is now coupled with a fine account of Vivaldi's best-known *Gloria* setting.

Handel's magnificent *Utrecht Te Deum* makes a generous coupling for Bach's *Magnificat*, and in a relatively intimate acoustic Harnoncourt sometimes presents allegros briskly and lightly – but, as in the *Magnificat*, that is the exception. The characterful solo singing – the murky-sounding contralto apart – marries oddly with slow, heavy speeds and leaden rhythms, and the chorus, efficient enough, lacks brightness and rhythmic spring. Dryish recording.

OPERA

Admeto, re di Tessaglia (complete).

(M) *** Virgin Veritas/EMI VMT5 61369-2 (3). René Jacobs, Rachel Yakar, Jill Gomez, James Bowman, Ulrik Cold, Rita Dams, Max van Egmont, Il Complesso Barocco, Alan Curtis.

Admeto is among the very greatest of Handel's operas, probably the most successful of all in his lifetime, and it is surprising that this recording, made in 1977 in Holland, has not appeared earlier on CD. Under Alan Curtis it was one of the first complete recordings of a Handel opera to attempt an authentic approach, and the most successful up to that time. Though recitatives are on the slow side, it certainly stands the test of time, a fine performance, very well cast, played with refinement on period instruments and excellently recorded. The original five LPs here conveniently become three CDs, one per Act. Handel wrote *Admeto* at the end of his years presenting opera at the Royal Academy (at the King's Theatre in the Haymarket), with the three greatest singers of the time in mind, the castrato, Senesino, in the title-role, and the rival prima donnas, Cuzzoni and Bordoni, as Antigona and Alceste. Here the counter-tenor René Jacobs gives an understanding and characterful performance in the title-role, but it is Jill Gomez as Antigona who steals first honours, with magnificent singing, sweet, pure and strong of tone, with ornamentation beautifully crisp. Rachel Yakar is not so sweetly caught by the microphones, but hers is a stylish performance too, and the rest of the cast has no weak link, with James Bowman outstanding as Admeto's brother, Trasimede.

(i) *Alcina* (complete); (ii) *Giulio Cesare (Julius Caesar)*: highlights.
(M) **(*) Decca (IMS) 433 723-2 (3) [id.]. Sutherland, M. Sinclair, (i) Berganza, Alva, Sciutti, Freni, Flagello, LSO; (ii) Elkins, M. Horne, Conrad, New SO; Bonynge.

The 1962 Decca *Alcina* includes some 50 minutes of highlights from *Giulio Cesare*, made a year later, which Sutherland did not undertake in a complete version. *Alcina*, however, represents the extreme point of what can be described as Sutherland's dreamy, droopy period. The fast arias are stupendous. But anything slow and reflective, whether in recitative or aria, has Sutherland mooning about the notes, with no consonants audible at all and practically every vowel reduced to 'aw'. It is all most beautiful of course, but she could have done so much better. Of the others, Teresa Berganza is completely charming in the castrato part of Ruggiero, even if she does not manage trills very well. Monica Sinclair shows everyone up with the strength and forthrightness of her singing. Both Graziella Sciutti and Mirella Freni are delicate and clear in their two smaller parts. Richard Bonynge draws crisp, vigorous playing from the LSO. The 36-year-old Walthamstow recording is vintage Decca, and the CD transfer hints at its age only in the orchestral string sound.

Not surprisingly, the *Giulio Cesare* highlights are used as a vehicle for Sutherland, and her florid elaborations of melodies turn *da capo* recitatives into things of delight and wonder. There is some marvellous singing from Marilyn Horne and Monica Sinclair too, and Bonynge conducts with a splendid sense of style. As a sample, try *V'adoro pupile* – Cleopatra's seduction aria. Full translations are provided in both works.

Alessandro (complete).
(M) **(*) HM/BMG GD 77110 (3) [77110-2-RG]. Jacobs, Boulin, Poulenard, Nirouët, Varcoe, Guy de Mey, La Petite Bande, Kuijken.

Sigiswald Kuijken directs his team of period-performance specialists in an urgently refreshing, at times sharply abrasive, reading of one of Handel's key operas. As a high counter-tenor, René Jacobs copes brilliantly with the taxing role of Alexander himself. His singing is astonishingly free and agile, if too heavily aspirated. Among the others, Isabelle Poulenard at her best sounds a little like a French Emma Kirkby, though the production is not quite so pure and at times comes over more edgily. The others make a fine, consistent team, the more effective when the recording so vividly conveys a sense of presence with sharply defined directional focus.

Almira (complete).
(M) **(*) CPO Dig. CPO 999 275-2 (3). Monoyios, Rozario, Gerrard, Thomas, Nasrawi, MacDougall, Elsner, Fiori Musicale, Andrew Lawrence-King.

Almira was Handel's first opera, written in Hamburg in 1704 and first given just before his twentieth birthday. Setting a libretto partly in German, partly in Italian and with a plot involving the loves of Almira, Queen of Castile, it is a long piece lasting almost four hours. The arias are generally more compact than in the mature Handel, with argument more constrained, less developed. Even so, one regularly detects a genuine Handelian flavour in the themes, and he himself borrowed a fair measure of the material here in later works. This recording, with three discs offered for the price of two, was made after a staging presented in both Halle and Bremen in 1994. Lawrence-King took over the direction when Thomas Albert was ill, and he secures a fresh and well-paced – if rather plain – performance, with deft playing from the German period orchestra. Ann Monoyios is a light, bright Almira, with Patricia Rozario, taxed a little by the high tessitura. equally stylish as Edilia. The two principal tenor roles are very well taken by Jamie MacDougall and Douglas Nasrawi, with the third tenor, Christian Elsner, taking the comic servant role. David Thomas sings with clean attack in the bass role of the Prince of Segovia. Good, undistracting and well scaled in an intimate acoustic.

Ariodante (complete).
(M) *** Ph. 442 096-2 (3). J. Baker, Mathis, N. Burrowes, Bowman, Rendall, Ramey, L. Voices, ECO, Leppard.

Ariodante has a story which inspired Handel to write an amazing sequence of memorable and intensely inventive arias and duets, with not a single weak link in the chain, a point superbly conveyed in this colourful, urgent performance under Raymond Leppard. The castrato role of Ariodante is a challenge for Dame Janet Baker, who responds with singing of enormous expressive range, from the dark, agonized moments of the C minor aria early in Act III to the brilliance of the most spectacular of the three display arias later in the Act. Dame Janet's duets with Edith Mathis as Princess Ginevra, destined to marry Prince

Ariodante, are enchanting too, and there is not a single weak member of the cast, though James Bowman as Duke Polinesso is not as precise as usual, with words often unclear. Though this long work is given uncut, it is among the most riveting Handel opera recordings currently available, helped by the consistently resilient playing of the English Chamber Orchestra and the refined, beautifully balanced (1978) analogue recording, transferred so successfully to CD.

Hercules (complete).

(M) *** DG Dig. 447 689-2 (2). Tomlinson, Sarah Walker, Rolfe Johnson, Jennifer Smith, Denley, Savidge, Monteverdi Ch., E. Bar. Soloists, Gardiner.

Gardiner's generally brisk performance of *Hercules* using authentic forces may at times lack Handelian grandeur in the big choruses, but it conveys superbly the vigour of the writing, its natural drama; and the fire of this performance is typified by the singing of Sarah Walker as Dejanira in her finest recording yet. John Tomlinson makes an excellent, dark-toned Hercules. Youthful voices consistently help in the clarity of the attack – Jennifer Smith as Iole, Catherine Denley as Lichas, Anthony Rolfe Johnson as Hyllus and Peter Savidge as the Priest of Jupiter. Refined playing and outstanding recording quality make this particularly welcome at mid-price.

Julius Caesar (complete; in English).

(M) *** EMI Dig. CMS7 69760-2 (3). J. Baker, Masterson, Sarah Walker, Della Jones, Bowman, Tomlinson, E. Nat. Op. Ch. & O, Mackerras.

Dame Janet Baker, in glorious voice and drawing on the widest range of expressive tone-colours, shatters the old idea that this alto-castrato role should be transposed down an octave and given to a baritone. Valerie Masterson makes a charming and seductive Cleopatra, fresh and girlish, though the voice is caught a little too brightly for caressing such radiant melodies as those for *V'adoro pupille* (*Lamenting, complaining*) and *Piangero* (*Flow my tears*). Sarah Walker sings with powerful intensity as Pompey's widow; James Bowman is a characterful counter-tenor Ptolemy and John Tomlinson a firm, resonant Achillas, the other nasty character. The ravishing accompaniments to the two big Cleopatra arias amply justify the use by the excellent ENO Orchestra of modern, not period, instruments. The full, vivid studio sound makes this one of the very finest of the invaluable series of ENO opera recordings in English.

Partenope (complete).

(M) *** HM/BMG GD 77109 (3) [77109-2-RG]. Laki, Jacobs, York, Skinner, Varcoe, Müller-Molinari, Hill, La Petite Bande, Kuijken.

With the exception of René Jacobs, rather too mannered for Handel, the roster of soloists here is outstanding, with Krisztina Laki and Helga Müller-Molinari welcome additions to the team. Though ornamentation is sparse, the direction of Sigiswald Kuijken is consistently invigorating, as is immediately apparent in the *Overture*; the 1979 recording sounds quite marvellous in its CD format.

Rinaldo (complete).

(M) *** Sony SM3K 34592 (3) [S3K 34592]. Carolyn Watkinson, Cotrubas, Scovotti, Esswood, Brett, Cold, La Grande Ecurie et la Chambre du Roy, Malgoire.

The vigour of Malgoire's direction of an opera which plainly for him is very much alive, no museum piece, makes this a very attractive set, with the one caveat that it has been reissued without a translation (the full libretto is in Italian only). However, this remains an inviting example of period-performance style. The elaborate decorations on *da capo* arias are imaginatively done, but most effectively the famous *Cara sposa* is left without ornamentation, beautifully sung by the contralto Rinaldo, Carolyn Watkinson. The finest singing comes from Ileana Cotrubas, but under Malgoire the whole team is convincing. The bright but spacious recording adds to the projection and liveliness, and the magic sounds associated with the sorceress, Armida, such as the arrival of her airborne chariot, are well conveyed, and throughout Handel's invention is a delight. Well worth having, but it is a pity about the libretto.

Rodelinda, Regina de Langobardi (complete).

(M) **(*) HM/BMG Dig. RD 77192 (3) [id.]. Schlick, Schubert, Cordier, Wessel, Prégardien, Schwarz, La Stagione, Schneider.

On this German recording from Michael Schneider and La Stagione, the celebrated *Dove sei*, inaccurately translated as 'Art thou troubl'd', is tenderly sung with plaintive tone by the British counter-tenor, David Cordier, matching the rest of the excellent, otherwise all-German cast. Barbara Schlick is pure and golden in the title-role and the tenor, Christoph Prégardien, is also outstanding as the hero, Grimoaldo. Schneider is a lively and fresh Handelian, not afraid of expressiveness but often adopting a clipped, abrasive manner. He encourages generous ornamentation in *da capo* repeats. First-rate, clean sound.

Semele (complete).

(M) *** Van. 08.5082 72 (2). Armstrong, Watts, Palmer, Tear, Diaz, Deller, Fleet, Amor Artis Chorale, ECO, Somary.

With its English words, *Semele* stands equivocally between the genres of opera and oratorio, presenting even more interpretative problems than usual. Though at times he favours slow, oratorio-like tempi, Somary still keeps in mind an operatic flavour and the Amor Artis Chorale (a pseudonym for a professional choir very familiar on record) sings splendidly, often with great vigour, and even attempts some attractive if inauthentic corporate ornamentation. Overall the performance has much charm and spirit with superb soloists. Like the rest of this Vanguard series from the 1970s, the fine recording allows excellent detail, yet is full and expansive.

Serse (*Xerxes;* complete).

(M) **(*) Sony SM3K 36941 (3) [S3K 36941]. Carolyn Watkinson, Esswood, Wenkel, Hendricks, Rodde, Cold, Bridier Vocal Ens., La Grand Ecurie et la Chambre du Roy, Malgoire.

Malgoire's vigorous, often abrasive style in baroque music makes for a lively, convincing performance of one of Handel's richest operas, helped by a fine complement of soloists. Carolyn Watkinson may not be the most characterful of singers in the high castrato role of Xerxes himself, but it is good to have the elaborate roulades so accurately sung. The celebrated *Ombra mai fù* is most beautiful. Paul Esswood is similarly reliable in the role of Arsamene (originally taken by a woman) and the counter-tenor tone is pure and true. Barbara Hendricks and Anne-Marie Rodde are both outstanding in smaller roles, and the comic episodes (most unexpected in Handel) are excellently done, Malgoire's generally heavy rhythmic pulse here paying dividends. There are detailed stylistic points one might criticize in his rendering (for instance the squeeze effects on sustained string notes) but the vitality of the performance is never in doubt, and the somewhat close recording is vivid too. As in the rest of this series of Sony reissues, the snag is the absence of an English translation.

Tamerlano (complete).

(M) *** Erato/Warner Dig. 4509 99722-2 (3). Ragin, Robson, Argenta, Chance, Findlay, Schirrer, E. Bar. Soloists, Gardiner.

(M) **(*) Sony Dig. SM3K 37893-2 (3) [S3K 37893-2]. Ledroit, Elwes, Van der Sluis, Jacobs, Poulenard, Reinhart, La Grande Ecurie et la Chambre du Roy, Malgoire.

John Eliot Gardiner's live concert performance of *Tamerlano* presents a strikingly dramatic and immediate experience. The pacing of numbers and of the recitative is beautifully thought out and the result is electrifying. Leading the cast are two outstanding counter-tenors whose encounters provide some of the most exciting moments: Michael Chance as Andronicus, firm and clear, Derek Ragin in the name-part equally agile and more distinctive of timbre, with a rich, warm tone that avoids womanliness. Nigel Robson in the tenor role of Bajazet conveys the necessary gravity, not least in the difficult, highly original G minor aria before the character's suicide; and Nancy Argenta sings with starry purity as Asteria. The only serious snag is the dryness of the sound, which makes voices and instruments sound more aggressive on CD than they usually do in Gardiner's recordings with the English Baroque Soloists.

Malgoire's performance style here is less abrasive than it has been on some other opera sets, but one looks in vain for an element of elegance or charm, despite consistently excellent contributions from a good band of soloists, with the two counter-tenors well contrasted – René Jacobs as ever a tower of strength – and with Mieke van der Sluis outstanding among the women. A warning ought to be given that this piece is slow in getting off the ground, although the continuing interchanges in Act I featuring Andronico are splendidly sung, as is his closing aria, *Chi vide mai . . . Benché mi sprezzi*. The music becomes increasingly impressive over Acts II and III, with more ensembles than Handel customarily included. Some arias have been cut, but one has been added in Act I (*Nel mondo e nell'abisso*), well sung by the bass, Gregory Reinhardt. Good, clear, but not too dry sound gives a comparatively intimate effect, and the CD transfer is first class. The snag is that, like the other reissues in this series, the full Italian libretto includes no translation.

COLLECTIONS

Arias: (i) *Agrippina: Pur ritorno a rimimiravi. Alexander's Feast: Revenge, Timotheus cries. Belshazzar: Oh, memory still bitter to my soul . . . Oppress'd with never-ceasing grief. Berenice: Si, tra i ceppi.* (ii) *Giulio Cesare: Va tacito e nascosto; Dall'ondoso periglio; Aure, deh per pietà.* (i) *Ottone: Con gelosi sospetti? . . . Dopo l'orrore. Samson: Honour and arms. Saul: To him ten thousands! . . . With rage I shall*

burst. Serse: Frondi tenere e belle? . . . Ombra mai fù. Solomon: Prais'd be the Lord . . . When the sun o'er yonder hills. Susanna: Down my old cheeks . . . Peace, crown'd with roses.
(M) **(*) 449 551-2. Dietrich Fischer-Dieskau; Munich Bach O; (i) Stadlmair; (ii) Karl Richter.

Opening with an arresting performance of *Revenge, Timotheus cries* from *Alexander's Feast*, this 1977 collection nevertheless emphasizes the lyricism of these excerpts rather than the drama. Fischer-Dieskau is at his finest in the excerpt from *Serse* with its beautifully controlled opening single-note crescendo, which is none other than our old friend, Handel's '*Largo*'. The voice is forwardly balanced and most naturally caught; although the orchestra within the resonant acoustic is quite vividly caught, the modern-instrument textures are full rather than clearly detailed, especially the two *Giulio Cesare* items now added, which were recorded much earlier (in 1969).

Arias: *Judas Maccabaeus: Father of heaven. Messiah: O Thou that tellest; He was despised. Samson: Return O God of Hosts.*
✿ (M) (***) Decca 433 474-2. Kathleen Ferrier, LPO, Boult – BACH: Arias. (***)

Kathleen Ferrier had a unique feeling for Handel; these performances are unforgettable for their communicative intensity and nobility of timbre and line. She receives highly sympathetic accompaniments from Boult, another natural Handelian.

Hanson, Howard (1896–1981)

(i) *Piano concerto, Op. 36. For the first time (suite); Merry Mount suite; Mosaics* (with composer's spoken analyses of all three orchestral works, concerning orchestral colour, pitch spectrum, musical form, and 'tone relationships').
(M) *** Mercury 434 370-2 (2) [id.]. Eastman-Rochester O or Philh. O, composer (cond. & narrator); (i) with Alfred Mouledous.

Mercury not only pioneered many of Hanson's major works on record, with the composer conducting the Eastman-Rochester Orchestra, but also invited him to talk about his music. The three orchestral works here seem ideal for the purpose and his 'guide to the instruments of the orchestra' (directly related to the scoring of the *Merry Mount suite*) is particularly instructive, the more so as the microphones have been set up to project solo instruments and groupings of woodwind, brass and strings with extraordinary realism and presence. Elsewhere Hanson discusses orchestral colour (in relation to visual colour) and musical construction in connection with his atmospheric and vividly contrasted set of variations which he calls *Mosaics* (inspired by the mosaics in Palermo Cathedral). More controversially, he expounds on 'tone relationships' as explored in his book, *The Harmonic Materials of Modern Music*. Apparently his work method was to choose a predetermined series of notes for a given composition, rather like a tone row, but which he thinks of as circular, as it is within the normal tonal system. This thesis is related to *For the first time*, in essence a dozen impressionistic vignettes, evoking a day in the life of a (somewhat precocious) child. He wakes to the sound of *Bells*, watches a pair of Irish puppies at play, explores a *Deserted house*, comes across an *Eccentric clock*, meets a group of *Clowns* on their way to the circus, enjoys his mother reading to him the tale of *Kikimora*, watches a *Fireworks* spectacle and so on, then ends his day in the world of *Dreams*. Hanson's invention is fresh and evocative, his scoring felicitous, so all this music is made to serve a double purpose. The four-movement *Piano concerto* is brilliantly played by Alfred Mouledous, especially in the Scherzo, marked *Allegro molto ritmico* (though they are not jazzy rhythms) and the *giocoso* finale, while the slow movement is eloquently expressive. The recordings here were made between 1957 and 1965 (the *Concerto*) and are characteristically vivid, though occasionally very bright on top.

Symphonies Nos. 1–7; (i) *Piano concerto in G. Elegy in memory of Koussvitzky;* (i) *Fantasy variations on a theme of Youth, Op. 40. Mosaics; Merry Mount suite, Op. 31; Pastorale for oboe, harp and strings, Op. 38; Serenade for flute, harp and strings, Op. 38;* (ii) *Lament for Beowulf, Op. 25; Song of democracy.*
(M) *** Delos Dig. DE 3150 (4) [id.]. Seattle SO, Gerard Schwarz; with (i) Carol Rosenberger; (ii) Ch.

Gerard Schwarz has proved himself a master of Hanson's Nordic idiom and a consistently convincing interpreter of his symphonies, in which he secures high commitment and playing of the highest quality from the excellent Seattle orchestra. Carol Rosenberger is an excellent soloist in the two concertante piano works; the other soloists are drawn from the orchestra, and all make admirable contributions. This is all music which is easy to enjoy, and these artists are afforded top-drawer recording from the Delos engineers within an expansive acoustic that is ideal for this repertoire. Hanson aficionados should not miss this fine set.

Symphonies Nos. 1 in E min. (Nordic), Op. 21; 2 (Romantic), Op. 30; (i) *Song of democracy.*
(M) *** Mercury 432 008-2 [id.]. Eastman-Rochester O, composer; (i) with Eastman School of Music Ch.

Hanson's own pioneering stereo recordings of his two best-known symphonies have a unique thrust and ardour. The *Song of democracy* has plenty of dramatic impact and is also very well recorded.

Symphonies Nos. 2 (Romantic), Op. 30; 4 (Requiem), Op. 34. Elegy (to the memory of my friend, Serge Koussevitsky), Op. 44.
(BB) **(*) Arte Nova Dig. 74321 43306-2 [id.]. Jena PO, David Montgomery.

David Montgomery, who studied under René Leibowitz before his career took him across the Atlantic, has the full measure of the haunting, nostaglic feeling which permeates Hanson's symphonies, and especially No. 2 – which is I.M.'s favourite American symphony. The lovely lilting central *Andante con tenerezza* is radiantly done. The Jena Philharmonic cannot quite produce the body of tone which Schwarz has at his disposal with the superb Seattle orchestra, who also find added weight in the finale (see below), but there is no lack of vigour and spontaneity in the Arte Nova account; the brass playing is excellent and the final peroration very telling. Montgomery is thoroughly at home in shaping the spacious string paragraphs which are the hallmark of this composer's writing in both works, and in No. 4 he does not miss the Sibelian influences, especially in the sombre, flowing *Requiescat* which forms the *Largo* slow movement. The touching tribute to Koussevitzky, who originally helped to put Hanson's music in front of the American public, is eloquently played; but here, as in the closing *Lux aeterna* of the *Fourth Symphony*, the strings are not as full and expansive as in Seattle. Nevertheless the Arte Nova recording is spacious and well balanced, and this inexpensive disc should tempt many collectors to become acquainted with a composer who deserves to be much better known than he is.

Symphonies Nos. (i) *2 (Romantic); 4 (Requiem); 6;* (i–ii) *7 (Sea Symphony after Walt Whitman);* (i) *Elegy in memory of Serge Koussevitzky;* (i; iii) *Fantasy variations on a theme of youth* (for piano and orchestra); (i) *Mosaics;* (iv) *Serenade for flute, harp and strings.*
(B) *** Delos Dig. Double DE 3705 (2) [id.]. (i) Seattle SO; (ii) Seattle Chorale; (iii) Carol Rosenberger; (iv) Judith Meredith, Susan Jollies, NY Chamber Ens.; all cond. Gerard Schwarz.

A warm welcome for this comprehensive introduction to the highly rewarding music of Howard Hanson, which includes his *Second Symphony*, melodically so memorable, with an indelible theme which threads through the whole work. Like this symphony, the *Fourth* has strong Nordic influences, and the *Sea Symphony* brings stirring choral writing to words of Walt Whitman. All three are superbly played in Seattle and Schwarz's powerful direction is thoroughly idiomatic and committed. The elliptical *Fantasy variations* have a fine piano soloist in Carol Rosenberger, who catches the noble serenity of the work's opening and closing sections and enters fully into the fray of the energetic central variations. *Mosaics* is another set of variations, written in 1957 for Szell and the Cleveland Orchestra and inspired by a visit to Taormina Cathedral, near Rome. The composer tells us that in the cathedral 'there is a huge mosaic of Christ looking down – the eyes seem to be looking at you and follow you wherever you go. At different times of the day, if it is bright, it looks one way, if it be sombre, it looks the other way.' The variations, after opening darkly, reflect this ambivalence, with the orchestral lighting and emotional atmosphere constantly in flux. The work's comparative shortness (12 minutes) brings a lucid compression, sustained by the composer's Nordic lyricism. The even briefer and delicately scored *Serenade* makes a delightful contrast, finely crafted. All this music is well worth getting to know, and much of it is very rewarding indeed. The recordings are in the demonstration bracket.

Symphony No. 3; Elegy in memory of my friend Serge Koussevitzky, Op. 44; (i) *Lament for Beowulf.*
(M) *** Mercury [434 302-2]. Eastman-Rochester O, composer, (i) with Eastman School of Music Ch.

For those familiar with the earlier works, the musical terrain of the *Third Symphony* is familiar: the string threnodies surge purposefully forward, there are similar rhythmic patterns and confident rhetorical gestures. This is highly accessible music. This applies also to the *Elegy*, while the cantata also makes an immediate impression and is very well sung. However, here as in the orchestral works the 1958 Mercury sound is first rate.

Harty, Hamilton (1879–1941)

A Comedy overture; (i) *Piano concerto;* (ii) *Violin concerto;* (iii) *In Ireland (Fantasy). An Irish symphony;* (ii) *Variations on a Dublin air. With the wild geese.* (iv) *The Children of Lir; Ode to a nightingale.* Arrangement: *Londonderry Air.*

(M) *** Chandos Dig. CHAN 7035 (3) [id.]. (i) Binns; (ii) Holmes; (iii) Fleming, Kelly; (iv) Harper; Ulster O, Thomson.

Bryden Thomson's box gathers together Harty's major orchestral and concertante works with great success, and each disc is also available separately – see below.

(i) *Piano concerto in B min.;* (ii) *Violin concerto in D.*

(M) *** Chandos Dig. CHAN 7032 [id.]. (i) Malcolm Binns, (ii) Ralph Holmes; Ulster O, Thomson.

Harty's *Piano concerto*, written in 1922, has strong Rachmaninovian influences, but the melodic freshness remains individual in this highly sympathetic performance. Though the *Violin concerto* has no strongly individual idiom, the invention is fresh and often touched with genuine poetry. Ralph Holmes gives a thoroughly committed account of the solo part and is well supported by an augmented Ulster Orchestra under Bryden Thomson.

An Irish symphony; A Comedy overture; (i) *In Ireland* (fantasy for flute, harp and orchestra). *With the wild geese.*

(M) *** Chandos Dig. CHAN 7034 [id.]. Ulster O, Thomson, (i) with Fleming, Kelly.

The *Irish symphony* has won great acclaim for its excellent scoring and good craftsmanship. The Scherzo is particularly engaging. It is extremely well played by the Ulster Orchestra under Bryden Thomson, while the *In Ireland fantasy* is full of delightful Irish melodic whimsy. Melodrama enters the scene in the symphonic poem, *With the wild geese*, but its Irishry asserts itself immediately in the opening theme. Again a splendid performance and a high standard of digital sound.

With the wild geese (symphonic poem).

(B) *** CfP CD-CFP 4635 [id.]. RSNO, Gibson – GERMAN: *Welsh rhapsody;* MACCUNN: *Land of Mountain and flood;* SMYTH: *Wreckers overture.* ***

With the wild geese is a melodramatic piece about the Irish soldiers fighting on the French side in the Battle of Fontenoy. The ingredients – a gay Irish theme and a call to arms among them – are effectively deployed; although the music does not reveal a strong individual personality, it is carried by a romantic sweep which is well exploited here. The 1968 recording still sounds most vivid, and this anthology makes a first-rate bargain.

VOCAL MUSIC

(i) *The Children of Lir; Ode to a nightingale.* (ii) *Variations on a Dublin air.* Arrangement: *Londonderry Air.*

(M) *** Chandos Dig. CHAN 7033 [id.]. Ulster O, Thomson, with (i) Heather Harper; (ii) Holmes.

Harty's setting of Keats's *Ode to a nightingale* is richly convincing, a piece written for his future wife, the soprano, Agnes Nicholls. The other work, directly Irish in its inspiration, evocative in an almost Sibelian way, uses the soprano in wordless melisma, here beautifully sung by Heather Harper. The performances are excellent, warmly committed and superbly recorded. The *Variations on a Dublin air*, for violin and orchestra, and Harty's arrangement of the *Londonderry Air* have been added for the reissue.

Haydn, Josef (1732–1809)

Cello concertos in C & D, Hob XVIIb/1–2.

(BB) *** Naxos Dig. 8.550059; *4550059* [id.]. Ludovít Kanta, Capella Istropolitana, Peter Breiner – BOCCHERINI: *Cello concerto.* ***

(M) *** EMI CDM7 69299-2. Tortelier, Württemberg CO, Faerber.

(M) **(*) EMI Dig. CDM7 64326-2 [id.]. Lynn Harrell, ASMF, Marriner – VIVALDI: *Concertos.* **(*)

The Capella Istropolitana is drawn from the Slovak Philharmonic at Bratislava, of which Ludovít Kanta is principal cellist. The orchestra is a very fine one and the playing very alert and fresh (try the finale of the *C major*) and Kanta is a soloist of quality. The *Concerto in C major* was discovered only in the 1960s and first recorded by Miloš Sadló and then by Mstislav Rostropovich, who introduced cadenzas by Benjamin Britten – see below. Kanta also plays contemporary cadenzas. The excellent recording is made in a bright, resonant acoustic in which every detail is clearly registered, though the players are perhaps forwardly placed. The Boccherini coupling is recorded in the (rather endearing but outdated) Grützmacher arrangement, which may put some collectors off. However, in the cadenzas the acoustic changes as noticeably as does the style.

Tortelier gives warmly expressive performances of the two *Concertos*, more relaxed than some of his rivals, but not lacking spontaneity. He is sympathetically if not always immaculately accompanied by the Württemberg Chamber Orchestra. Clear yet warm digital sound to match, very pleasingly balanced.

The attractions of Harrell's coupling are enhanced by the inclusion of two Vivaldi concertos interspersed with Haydn (although the recorded sound is strikingly different). Harrell, rather after the manner of Rostropovich, seeks to turn these elegant concertos into big, virtuoso pieces, helped by Marriner's beautifully played accompaniments. Although touches of romantic expressiveness tend to intrude, the result is enjoyable, even if cadenzas are distractingly long. The digital recording is full and vivid (the analogue Vivaldi transfers are brighter and less smooth).

(i) *Cello concerto in C, Hob VIIb/1;* (ii; iv) *Horn concertos Nos. 1–2;* (iii; iv) *Trumpet concerto in D.*
(M) *** Decca 430 633-2 [id.]. (i) Rostropovich, ECO, Britten; (ii) Tuckwell; (iii) Alan Stringer; (iv) ASMF, Marriner.

Rostropovich's earlier (1964) stereo recording of the *C major Cello concerto* for Decca is undoubtedly romantic, and some may feel he takes too many liberties in the slow movement. The coupling of first-class 1966 versions of both the *Horn concertos* by Tuckwell in peak form and Stringer's 1967 account of the *Trumpet concerto* is certainly tempting.

(i) *Cello concertos: in C, Hob VIIb/1; in D, Hob VIIb/2;* (ii) *Violin concertos: in C; in A; in G, Hob VIIa/ 1, 3 & 4;* (ii; iii) *Double concerto for violin and harpsichord in F, Hob XVIII/6.*
(B) *** Ph. Duo 438 797-2 (2) [id.]. ECO with (i) Walevska, De Waart; (ii) Accardo; (iii) Canino.

The three *Violin concertos* are all early; the *C major*, written for Tomasini, is probably the best. The other two have come into the limelight fairly recently. Accardo plays with great elegance and charm, but it would be idle to pretend that this is great music. The same goes for the *Double Concerto for violin and harpsichord*, which is of relatively slender musical interest. The soloists are perhaps a shade forward but the quality and balance are lifelike, and the 1980 recording has been well transferred. The two *Cello concertos* are, of course, much better known; Christine Walevska presents them freshly and she is well partnered by Edo de Waart and the ECO. She has a fairly small solo image and is balanced almost within the orchestra; the effect is to give a chamber-like quality to the music-making which is very agreeable, for the solo playing is not lacking in personality.

Cello concerto No. 2 in D, Hob VIIb/2.
(M) **(*) BMG/Melodiya 74321 40724 [id.]. Daniil Shafran, USSR SO, Neeme Järvi – TCHAIKOVSKY: *Andante cantabile* etc. **(*)

Daniil Shafran enjoys cult status among cellists – understandably so, you may think, on hearing this 1962 account of the Haydn *D major Concerto*, made when Järvi was twenty-five. Shafran had a wonderfully rich, singing tone and an intensity that is always held within the right limits. He obviously inspired both the USSR Symphony Orchestra and Neeme Järvi. By the side of the finest recordings of the period, the sound is a bit two-dimensional but it is more than adequate, and playing like this is very special.

(i) *Harpsichord concertos: in F, Hob XVIII/3; in G, Hob XVIII/4; in D, Hob XVIII/11;* (i; ii) *Double concerto in F for harpsichord and violin, Hob XVIII/6;* (iii) *Concertini: in C, Hob XIV/3; in C, Hob XIV/ 11; in C, Hob XIV/12; Concertino (Divertimento) in G, Hob XIV/13; Concertino in F, Hob XIV/F2; Divertimenti in C, Hob XIV/4; in C, Hob XIV/7; in C, Hob XIV/8; in F, Hob XIV/9; in C, Hob XIV/C2.*
(B) *** Ph. Duo 446 542-2 (2) [(M) id. import]. Ton Koopman; (i) Amsterdam Musica Antiqua or Amsterdam Bar. O; (ii) with Huggett; (iii) Goebel, Stuurop, Medlam.

Ton Koopman's admirable Philips Duo set covers the 14 concertante Haydn keyboard works listed in the Hoboken catalogue now thought to be authentic. (He has recorded the *Organ concertos*, Hob XVIII/1, 2, 7, 7, 8 and 10 separately, and no doubt these will reappear during the lifetime of this book.) The present coverage includes the ten small concertos from the 1760s called either *Divertimenti* or *Concertini* which are of little real substance but which still make attractive, undemanding listening. Here the accompanying group is made up of Reinhard Goebel and Alda Stuurop (violins) and Charles Medlam (cello), all playing on period instruments. The four longer concertos, including the rightly famous *D major* (scored for oboes and horns) and the *Double concerto for violin, keyboard and strings*, Hob XVIII/6, use a larger accompanying group, which Koopman directs from the keyboard, although it is not clear from the documentation which of the two orchestras is playing in which concerto. As sound, these recordings could hardly be bettered:

the balance is finely judged and the acoustic warm, with the performers not on top of the listener. Yet detail registers perfectly. The performances themselves are thoroughly alive and highly accomplished. Though occasionally Koopman might have allowed the music to unfold at a more leisurely pace, no reservations need diminish the strongest recommendation (especially bearing in mind the modest cost), save for the warning that this is not the best Haydn.

Piano concertos: in F, Hob XVIII/3; in G, Hob XVIII/4; in D, Hob XVIII/11.
(BB) *** Arte Nova Dig. 74321 51635-2 [id.]. Lisa Smirnova, Sinfonia Varsovia, Volker Schmidt-Gertenbach.

The justly popular *D major Concerto*, much the finest work here, comes, with the *F major*, from Haydn's first years at Esterháza, while the *G major*, which is somewhat later, was also written with the harpsichord in mind. But these works come off very well on the piano, especially when played with such freshness and point by Lisa Smirnova and admirably accompanied with a sure sense of style and a nice feeling for light and shade by Schmidt-Gertenbach and the excellent Sinfonia Varsovia. The recording could hardly be bettered: it is beautifully balanced.

Piano concerto in D, Hob.XVIII/11.
(B) ** Carlton Dig. 30367 01072 [(M) id.]. Dirk Joeres, Westdeutsch Sinf. – MOZART: *Piano concerto No. 12* etc. **

Dirk Joeres directs this excellent West German chamber orchestra from the keyboard and achieves a poised opening ritornello for Haydn's most personable keyboard concerto. Then as he makes his piano entry he suddenly quickens the pace to give an impression of hurry. The rest of the performance is pleasingly alive and spontaneous, although again in the Rondo there is a hint of the tempo being pressed forward. This is a pity, for both this and the Mozart coupling are potentially fine performances and they are most pleasingly recorded. Joeres plays his own cadenzas.

Violin concertos Nos. 1 in C; 4 in G, Hob VIIa/1 & 4; (i) *Sinfonia concertante in B flat for violin, cello, oboe, bassoon & orchestra, Hob I/105.*
(M) *** Virgin Veritas/EMI (SIS) Dig. VER5 61301-2. Elizabeth Wallfisch, O of Age of Enlightenment; (i) with Watkin, Robson, Warnock.

Haydn's *Violin concertos* are early works; the *C major* with its winding, serenade-like melody is probably the finer, but the *G major* too has an eloquent *Adagio* and a bustling finale. Wallfisch leads the Orchestra of the Age of Enlightenment from her bow and proves a highly sensitive soloist – these performances are if anything even more impressive than those of the Mozart concertos by the same soloist. Her serenely reflective account of the *Adagio molto* of the *C major* is memorable: the timbre is sweet yet the playing is stylish and perfectly in period. In the *Sinfonia concertante* the smiling interplay of the various wind and string soloists has never been bettered on record and the use of period instruments brings a pleasing intimacy and plenty of spirit. If you want these three works, this is the coupling to go for, and the recording is truthfully balanced and vivid.

Sinfonia concertante in B flat for violin, cello, oboe, bassoon and orchestra, Hob I/105.
(BB) **(*) ASV Dig CDQS 6140 [(M) id. import]. Frieman, Pople, Anderson, Gambold, L. Festival O, Ross Pople – STAMITZ: *Sinfonias concertantes.* **(*)

Directing the players from the solo cello, Ross Pople draws a strong and alert rather than an elegant performance from his London Festival Orchestra, well recorded in bright, firmly focused sound. Though the solo playing is not always ideally refined, there is a winning sense of musicians acting out a drama, at speeds that are comfortable, never exaggerated. The coupling of *Sinfonias concertantes* by Stamitz is very apt and attractive.

SYMPHONIES

Symphonies Nos. 1–104; Symphonies A; B. Alternative versions: *Symphony Nos. 22 in E flat (Philosopher),* 2nd version. *Symphony No. 63 in C (La Roxelane),* 1st version. *Symphony No. 53 (L'Impériale):* 3 alternative Finales: (i) *A (Capriccio)*; (ii) *C* (Paris version, attrib. Haydn); *D: Overture in D* (Milanese version). *Symphony No. 103:* Finale (alternative ending). (i) *Sinfonia concertante in B flat for oboe, bassoon, violin and cello.*
✪ (B) *** Decca 448 531-2 (33) [id.]. Philh. Hungarica, Antal Dorati; (i) with István Engl, László Baranyai, Igor Ozim, Zóltán Rácz.

Dorati was certainly ahead of his time as a Haydn interpreter when, in the early 1970s, he made this pioneering integral recording of the symphonies. Superbly transferred to CD in full, bright and immediate sound, the performances are a consistent delight, with brisk allegros and fast-flowing *Andantes*, with textures remarkably clean. The slow, rustic-sounding accounts of Minuets are more controversial, but the rhythmic bounce makes them very attractive too. The set remains the only complete survey and, indeed, is more 'complete' than one could possibly expect. It includes not only the *Symphonies A* and *B* (Hoboken Nos. 106 and 108) but also the *Sinfonia concertante in B flat*, a splendidly imaginative piece with wonderful unexpected touches. Dorati's account – not surprisingly – presents the work as a symphony with unusual scoring, rather than as a concerto. As H. C. Robbins Landon tells us in the accompanying notes, the *Symphonies A* and *B* were omitted from the list of 104 authentic symphonies by error, as the first was considered to be a quartet – wind parts were discovered later – and the second a divertimento. Dorati also includes as an appendix completely different versions of *Symphony No. 22* (*The Philosopher*), where Haydn altered the orchestration (a pair of flutes substituted for the cor anglais), entirely removed the first movement and introduced a new *Andante grazioso*; plus an earlier version of No. 63, to some extent conjectural in its orchestration, for the original score is lost. Of the three alternative finales for *L'Impériale* (No. 53), the first (A) contains a melody which Robbins Landon suggests 'sounds extraordinarily like Schubert'; the second (C) seems unlikely to be authentic; but the third (D) uses an overture which was first published in Vienna. 'In some respects,' Robbins Landon suggests, 'this is the most successful of the three concluding movements'. He feels the same about the more extended finale of the *Drum Roll Symphony*, which originally included 'a modulation to C flat, preceded by two whole bars of rests – a great Falstaffian touch'. But Haydn thought that this made the movement too long and crossed out the whole section. Robbins Landon continues: 'Perhaps, if we may be so bold as to suggest it, Haydn was for once in his life too ruthless here.'

Symphonies Nos. 1–12.
(M) * Chandos Dig. CHAN 7062 (3) [id.]. Cantilena, Adrian Sheppard.

While a collection of Haydn's first dozen symphonies may have its interest, these performances are not well enough played to command a recommendation.

Symphonies Nos. 1–20.
(M) **(*) Nimbus Dig. NI 5426/30 [id.]. Austro-Hungarian Haydn O, Adám Fischer.

The Nimbus project of recording all the Haydn symphonies on modern instruments in the Haydnsaal of the Esterházy Palace brings playing which is fresh yet warm, with the considerable reverberation adding to the weight and scale of the earlier symphonies, in a manner that some ears will relish but others will find too opulent. In the accompanying notes the conductor, Adám Fischer, comments that the chosen orchestra, which is made up of players from Vienna and Budapest, carries forward the tradition of Austro-Hungarian music-making. The playing itself is warm and elegant, and again and again in these early symphonies the ear enjoys the finesse of this music-making and its ripeness of texture, with the rich-toned Viennese horns soaring out over the strings when given an opportunity to do so. The woodwind are sprightly and offer plenty of colour, and in Nos. 6–8 the various orchestral solos are taken with distinction. The conductor's speeds are moderate. Slow movements are gracious and phrasing is cultivated; minuets are courtly and finales lively and resilient, without being rushed. The sound itself is rich in ambience and easy to enjoy, for it does not cloud.

Symphonies Nos. 82 in C (The Bear); 83 in G min. (The Hen); 84 in E flat; 85 in B flat (La Reine); 86 in D; 87 in A (Paris Symphonies).
(M) **(*) Nimbus Dig. NI 5419/20 [id.]. Austro-Hungarian Haydn O, Adám Fischer.

The expansive sound of the Austro-Hungarian Orchestra suits the *Paris Symphonies*. *La Poule* and *La Reine* (with its rhythmically powerful opening movement) both show Fischer and his players at their best, and finest of all is one of the least known, *Symphony No. 84 in E flat* with another remarkably original first movement. Slow movements are warm and poised: the *Largo* of No. 86 is particularly successful, as is the light-hearted trio of its Minuet, with a vigorous finale, lightly articulated, to cap the work off. The sound is always satisfyingly full-bodied, with the violins resonantly rich. The weighty bass is not always absolutely clean, but generally the effect is very believable.

Symphonies Nos. 88 in G; 89 in F; 90 in C; 91 in E flat; 92 in G (Oxford); Sinfonia concertante in B flat for violin, cello, oboe, bassoon and orchestra.
(M) ** Nimbus Dig. NI 5417/8 [id.]. Austro-Hungarian Haydn O, Adám Fischer.

When so much trouble has been taken to record this specially assembled orchestra in the authentic venue of the old Haydnsaal in the Esterházy Palace, it is surprising that in style Fischer's are such old-fashioned readings, apparently little influenced by the example of period performances. As with the other issues in this Nimbus series the recording is full and pleasing, but the warm resonance prevents sharpness of detail and also has the effect of blunting the string articulation. Too often one feels the need for more bite in allegros. Tempi are almost always very relaxed, so that the famous slow movement of No. 88 in G, warmly expressive as it is, very nearly drags, although Fischer brings off the *Adagio* of the *Oxford symphony* beautifully. Throughout Minuets are very stately indeed but finales dance gracefully and opening Adagios are warmly expressive; yet in the end there is an absence of conveyed exhilaration. The *Sinfonia concertante* included on the second disc is a particularly pleasing performance, with most sympathetic solo playing.

Symphonies Nos. 93–104.
(M) **(*) Nimbus Dig. NI 5200/4 [id.]. Austro-Hungarian Haydn O, Adám Fischer.

With three symphonies apiece on the first two discs of the five-disc Nimbus set, Fischer's cycle of all twelve *London symphonies* makes a neat and attractive package, with consistently fresh, resilient and refined performances. Though these works were first given in the intimate surroundings of the Hanover Square Rooms in London, they were very quickly heard in this much grander setting, and the performances reflect the fact, with broad speeds made weightier by the reverberant Nimbus recording, so that in sound the tuttis relate rather to a Karajan or Bernstein performance than to one by a regular chamber orchestra. Only in lightly scored passages does one register the true scale of the orchestra, and such a movement as the lovely *Adagio* of No. 102 with its soaring melody is given added beauty by the ambience and slow speed. The set can be warmly recommended to most who resist period performance when, even at broad speeds, rhythms are light and resilient. Never sounding breathless, Fischer's Haydn consistently brings out the happiness of the inspiration. The first-movement allegro of No. 93 gets the cycle off to a delectable start, with the three-in-a-bar rhythms given a delicious lift. Not everyone will like the reverberance of the Nimbus recording, but these are very much performances to relax with.

Other miscellaneous symphonies

Symphonies Nos. 6 in D (Le Matin); 7 in C (Le Midi); 8 in G (Le Soir).
(BB) *** Naxos Dig. 8.550722 [id.]. N. CO, Ward.
(M) **(*) Teldec/Warner Dig. 2292 46018-2. VCM, Harnoncourt.

These were almost certainly the first works that Haydn composed on taking up his appointment as Kapellmeister to the Esterházys. A splendid début in these symphonies from the Northern Chamber Orchestra under Nicholas Ward. Throughout these works the wind players obviously relish their solos, the flute chirps merrily and the bassoon immediately has a chance to shine in the Trio of the Minuet of No. 6; even the double bass has a solo in the comparable movement of No. 7. In the *Andante* of *Le Soir* the strings create a chamber-music atmosphere, and it is the intimate scale of these performances that is so attractive. Modern instruments are used, but textures are fresh and the ambience of the Concert Hall of New Broadcasting House, Manchester, adds the right degree of warmth.

Harnoncourt is nothing if not dramatic. He opens No. 6 with an impressively controlled crescendo, beginning from an almost inaudible pianissimo, while the opening of the main allegro is characteristically gruff. But this music-making bursts with vitality, and a soothing flute solo soon appears to calm the listener. How cleverly scored these works are – to seduce the players of the Esterházy orchestra with their consistently rewarding part-writing. The very opening of Harnoncourt's slow movement (of No. 6) is austere but the atmosphere lightens, and it is again a flute which gaily introduces the lively finale, only to be chased off immediately by Harnoncourt's vigorously brusque strings. So it is throughout, with tuttis edgily bold and with plenty of accents, yet with balancing passages of delicacy. It is the solo violin which begins the finale of No. 7 and, when he is peremptorily dispatched by the irate violins, the flute fortunately ventures back. No one could say that these performances lack gravitas and the poised *Andante* of No. 8, where the solo violin re-enters gracefully, is pleasingly elegant, even if the conductor rather over-characterizes the interrupting tuttis. The robust Minuet makes way for an erstwhile double-bass solo in the Trio – which must have surprised the player as much as the listening Prince. The Presto finale opens gently, but Harnoncourt is in his element when the *Tempesta* arrives. The recording is as vivid as the playing; if Harnoncourt's eccentricities prevent an unreserved period-instrument recommendation, this will certainly be welcomed by his admirers.

(i) *Symphonies Nos. 6 in D (Le Matin); 7 in C (Le Midi); 8 in G (Le Soir); 22 in E flat (Philosopher);* (ii) *26 in D min. (Lamentatione);* (i) *31 in D (Horn signal); 43 in E flat (Mercury); 44 in E min. (Trauersymphonie); 45 in F sharp min. (Farewell);* (ii) *47 in G (Palindrome);* (i) *48 in C (Maria Theresia); 49 in F min. (La Passione); 53 in D (L'Impériale); 55 in E flat (Schoolmaster); 59 in A (Fire); 60 in C (Il distratto); 63 in C (La Roxelane); 69 in C (Laudon); 73 in D (La Chasse); 82 in C (L'ours); 83 in G min. (La poule); 85 in B flat (La Reine); 92 in G (Oxford); 94 in G (Surprise); 96 in D (Miracle); 100 in G (Military); 101 in D (Clock); 103 in E flat (Drum Roll); 104 in D (London).*

(B) **(*) Ph. Analogue/Dig. 454 335-2 (10) [id.]. (i) ASMF, Marriner; (ii) ECO, Leppard (directed from harpsichord).

This fine collection, recorded between 1968 and 1981, is beautifully transferred to CD and offers Philips's most natural sound-quality. Opening with characterful accounts of the three symphonies Haydn composed not long after taking up his appointment at the Esterházy court in 1761, Marriner and Leppard between them offer consistently elegant performances of 29 'named' symphonies, not all of them by any means well known. Marriner has the lion's share; Leppard, conducting from the harpsichord, is in excellent form in the *Lamentatione* and the so-called *Palindrome*, with its set of slow-movement variations on a pair of invertible themes. Under Marriner the Academy playing is more polished and urbane than in the rival accounts under Dorati. Although ultimately there is an earthier quality in the music than Marriner perceives, these are satisfying performances that will give much pleasure, and they often have a compensating charm which Dorati misses (the *Schoolmaster*, for instance). Nos. 44 and 49 are among the highlights, and here Marriner follows Leppard by featuring a discreet harpsichord continuo. Haydn chose No. 44 for performance at his funeral (hence the title) and Marriner shapes the radiantly elegiac slow movement with much tenderness. The richly expressive string phrasing of the opening *Adagio* of the *Farewell Symphony* is superbly contrasted with the genial and buoyant rhythms of the second-movement Allegro. There is some excellent horn playing in both works. On the other hand the *Horn signal* seems curiously undercharacterized. *Il Distratto* and *La Roxelane* both have theatrical connections, and in the former Dorati's account has the greater sense of theatre, while the Academy orchestral playing is more finished. The 'named' *Paris Symphonies* are distinguished by excellent ensemble and keen articulation; they have a winning charm, yet are lively and musical, again offering a distinct alternative to Dorati. No. 94 has a particularly fine performance of the variations which form the slow movement (the 'surprise' itself most effective) and there is most delightful woodwind detail in No. 96 – the oboe solo in the trio of the Minuet is a joy. The playing in the *Clock* is very spruce and clean, and the atmosphere at the opening of the *Drum Roll* is wonderfully caught, while the first movement's second subject shows the fine pointing and lightness of touch which distinguish the music-making throughout. At bargain price the set offers excellent value, and if at times there is just a hint of blandness Marriner has set himself high standards and there is much to admire in each of these performances; if at times they fall short of real distinction, they always rise above the routine.

Symphonies Nos. 22 in E flat (Philosopher); 29 in E; 60 in C (Il Distratto).
(BB) ** Naxos Dig. 8.550724 [id.]. N. CO, Nicholas Ward.

Compared with Goodman's full-priced account, the first movement of the *Philosopher* has nothing like the same darkness of colour when presented on modern instruments by the Northern Chamber Orchestra under Nicholas Ward, and the *Adagio* (*di Lamentatione*) is also relatively easy-going. These are warm, nicely turned performances, well recorded but somewhat undercharacterized.

Symphonies Nos. 23 in G; 24 in D; 61 in D.
(BB) *** Naxos Dig. 8.550723 [id.]. N. CO, Nicholas Ward.

The fresh, stylish approach of the Northern Chamber Orchestra seems entirely suited to these three symphonies, and here Nicholas Ward makes a persuasive case for the use of modern instruments. No. 24 includes a leading semi-concertante flute part (nicely managed) and the *G major* has a wistful *Andante* for strings alone, and a vital *Presto* finale, well sprinkled with strongly accented quadruplets. The opening movement of No. 61 is obviously more mature and is presented with both character and charm. Excellent recording.

Symphonies Nos. 26 in D min. (Lamentatione); 35 in B flat; 49 in F min. (La Passione).
(BB) **(*) Naxos Dig. 8.550721 [id.]. N. CO, Ward.

Although enjoyable, the follow-up disc from Nicholas Ward and his Northern Chamber Orchestra is not quite as fresh-sounding as its predecessor. The playing remains elegant and the horns (in B flat alto) are splendid in the Minuet of No. 35. But the opening *Allegro assai con spirito* of the *Lamentatione* could do with a shade more bite, and in the *Adagio* the warm resonance makes the finely played oboe solo almost a cor anglais and the melodic line like a Handel aria. The opening slow movement of No. 49 is not as intense as it might be, though the *Allegro di molto* which follows has plenty of energy, as does the finale, while the horns shine again in the Trio of the Minuet. The resonance of the BBC's Studio 7 in Manchester brings a pleasingly mellow sound-picture, but the string detail is not sharply defined.

Symphonies Nos. 26 (Lamentatione), 35, 38–9, 41–2, 43 (Mercury), 44 (Trauer), 45 (Farewell), 46–7, 48 (Maria Theresia), 49 (La passione), 50–52, 58, 59 (Fire), 65.
(M) *** DG Dig. 435 001-2 (6). E. Concert, Trevor Pinnock.

Pinnock's forces are modest (with 6.5.2.2.1 strings), but the panache of the playing conveys any necessary grandeur. It is a new experience to have Haydn symphonies of this period recorded in relatively dry and close sound, with inner detail crystal clear (harpsichord never obscured) and made the more dramatic by the intimate sense of presence, yet with a fine bloom on the instruments. Some may find a certain lack of charm at times, and others may quarrel with the very brisk one-in-a-bar minuets and – dare one say it! – even find finales a bit rushed.

Symphonies Nos. 26 in D min. (Lamentatione); 52 in C min.; 53 in D (L'Impériale).
(M) *** Virgin Veritas/EMI Dig. VER5 61212-2. La Petite Bande, Sigiswald Kuijken.

These are fresh, vital, cleanly articulated performances which wear their authenticity lightly and even indulge in speeds for slow movements that are more expansive and affectionate than many purists would allow.

Symphonies Nos. 30 in C (Alleluja); 55 in E flat (Schoolmaster); 63 in C (La Roxelane).
(BB) *** Naxos Dig. 8.550757 [id.]. Northern CO, Nicholas Ward.

An entirely winning triptych of named Haydn symphonies, spanning a highly creative period from the three-movement *Alleluja* (1765), with its delightful woodwind contribution in the *Andante*, to *La Roxelane* (1780), where the *Allegretto* paints an engaging portrait of a flirtatious character in a play and the finale fizzes with energy. In between comes *The Schoolmaster*, whose Adagio brings a theme and variations of disarming simplicity. Alert and vivacious playing from all concerned; admirable pacing and first-class sound ensure a welcome for a disc that would be just as recommendable if it cost far more.

Symphonies Nos. 39 in G min.; 70 in D; 73 in D (La Chasse); 75 in D.
✿ (M) *** Van. 08 6152 71. Esterházy O, David Blum.

David Blum pioneered authentic chamber-orchestra performances of the mid-period Haydn symphonies (using modern instruments) in the early 1960s with his aptly named Esterhazy Orchestra, some time before Dorati began his integral Haydn cycle for Decca. There are few CDs which offer first-class accounts of four major Haydn symphonies, so this fine Vanguard reissue makes a splendid reminder of his achievement. His alert stylishness is matched by the warmth of the slow movements, which are beautifully played and are made the expressive centrepiece of each symphony. Blum's gentle pointing of the *Andante* of No. 39, with its striding forward motion, is never too heavy, while the virtuosity in the tremolos and passionate scales of the finale is exhilarating. One could make similar comments about No. 70, whose intriguing *Andante* is marked *Specie d'un Canone in contrapunto doppio*, while the finale brings a tantalizing, witty introduction, which returns at the close. No. 73 opens graciously and for its *Andante* has an engaging set of variations on Haydn's song, *Gebenliebe*. The renowned hunting finale is presented with vigour and imagination. *No. 75 in D major* brings another memorable *Poco Adagio*, its contour slightly suggestive of *God save the King* (which the composer greatly admired). David Blum's notes accompanying the recording aptly relate an entry from Haydn's diary concerning a performance of this music in March 1792. He tells how an English clergyman who was present 'fell into the most profound melancholy on hearing the slow movement because he had dreamt the previous night that this piece was a premonition of his death. He left the company at once and took to his bed.' It was a pity he did not stay to listen to the Minuet, which is contrastingly cheerful, with the flute flirting delightfully in the Trio; a month later he was reported dead! Throughout all four symphonies Blum takes the Minuets at a spirited tempo, in that way anticipating modern practice; with warm recording, full yet clear, this Vanguard CD must be placed in the pantheon of outstanding Haydn reissues.

Symphonies Nos. 42 in D; 45 in F sharp min. (Farewell); 46 in B.
(M) *** DG (IMS) 447 281-2 [id.]. E. Concert, Pinnock.

Haydn's famous *Farewell Symphony*, given a vibrant and characterful performance with a very beautiful slow movement, is here coupled with two apparently straightforward but still forward-looking works, No. 42 with its memorably solemn *Andantino e cantabile* and *No. 46 in B major*. Here the ethereal 6/8 *Poco Adagio* contrasts with an invigorating scherzando finale where the high horns (crooked in B alto) produce repeated bursts of hair-raising virtuosity. And Haydn has a characteristic trick up his sleeve for, just before the end, the Minuet returns, only to be swept away by a final rally from the horns.

Symphonies Nos. 43 in E flat (Mercury); 44 in E min. (Trauer); 49 in F min. (La Passione).
(M) ** Chandos Dig. CHAN 6590 [id.]. Cantilena, Adrian Shepherd.

Two of the symphonies (Nos. 44 and 49) offered by Adrian Shepherd's Cantilena come from the so-called *Sturm und Drang* set. This group captures their spirit effectively – particularly in the so-called *Trauer* or 'Mourning' *symphony*, in which tempi are well judged and the textures admirably clean. *La Passione* is committed enough, though the actual playing is less accomplished than in some rivals. The *E flat Symphony* (*Mercury*) is slightly less successful and is a bit matter-of-fact. Again the sound-quality is clean and pleasing and the balance generally well handled.

Symphony No. 44 in E min. (Trauer).
(B) *** Carlton Dig. 30367 02372 [(M) id.]. O of St John's, Smith Square, Lubbock – MOZART: *Symphony No. 40.* **(*)

The Orchestra of St John's are on their toes throughout their splendidly committed account of the *Trauersymphonie*. Outer movements are alert and vivacious – the finale has striking buoyancy and spring – and there is some lovely espressivo playing in the beautiful *Adagio* slow movement, which brings out the forward-looking qualities of the writing. The recording too is in the demonstration class.

Symphonies Nos. 44 in E min. (Trauer); 45 in F sharp min. (Farewell); 46 in B; 47 in G; 48 in C (Maria Theresia); 49 in F min. (Passione) (Sturm und Drang Symphonies).
(M) *** Van. 08 6166 71 (*Nos. 44–6*); 08 6167 71 (*Nos. 47–9*) (available separately) [id.]. Zagreb RSO, Antonio Janigro
(B) ** EMI forte CZS5 69767-2 (2). Polish CO, Jerzy Maksymiuk.

For the six famous *Sturm und Drang Symphonies* Vanguard turned to Antonio Janigro and the Zagreb Radio Symphony Orchestra; and these recordings, first issued in the UK on the Philips label, in their day (the early 1960s) were regarded as one of the real treasures of the bargain shelf. It was largely thanks to the gramophone and radio that most of us came to realize what sharp, vital work Haydn was producing in symphony form, long before his famous works written for Paris and London. There is an underlying frustration, even a bitterness, expressed in these middle-period works that contrasts with both earlier and later Haydn. The first two symphonies of the set are in minor keys; that in itself was an innovation for Haydn at the time, while the two unnamed symphonies in the group (Nos. 46 and 47) are quite the equals of the named ones. To write a symphony in the remote key of B major was equally daring in Haydn's time, and then to follow it with a slow movement in the tonic minor (not the usual procedure at all) was just as daring. If in the famous finale of the *Farewell Symphony* Haydn indicated to his patron, Prince Esterhazy, his and his fellows' need for a holiday, this music suggests that Haydn's frustrations were more deeply emotional than most listeners have realized, while the *Adagio* first movement of *La Passione* is one of the most striking and poignant in all Haydn symphonies. With all four movements in F minor, this work in some ways looks backwards to the classical suite rather than forward to the full-blown symphony, but the music itself is violently original. It reveals an 'inner' Haydn not normally observed in his symphonies. No. 48 provides a complete contrast, happy enough for any ceremonial occasion involving an empress (the explanation of the nickname). Janigro is fully aware of these differences and inner tensions, and his performances with a modest-sized group are exemplary, both dramatic and stylish. The recording sounds very well indeed in these excellent CD transfers, and the original notes by Christa Landon, wife of H. C. Robbins Landon, have been preserved, if in abbreviated form. It is hard to think of these as bargain reissues, so good are they.

An inexpensive EMI forte set of Haydn's key *Sturm and Drang Symphonies*, very well played and recorded, is an inviting prospect, but Maksymiuk's readings are undercharacterized and miss out on the music's passionate impulse. The playing itself is warm and polished: slow movements are gracefully serene and finales bustle with high spirits, but too often there is an emotional dimension missing. The recording is excellent.

Symphonies Nos. 44 in E min. (Trauer); 88 in G; 104 in D (London).
(BB) *** Naxos Dig. 8.550287; *4550287* [id.]. Capella Istropolitana, Barry Wordsworth.

Symphonies Nos. 45 in F sharp min. (Farewell); 48 in C (Maria Theresia); 102 in B flat.
(BB) *** Naxos Dig. 8.550382; *4550382* [id.]. Capella Istropolitana, Barry Wordsworth.

Symphonies Nos. 82 in C (The Bear); 96 in D (Miracle); 100 in G (Military).
(BB) *** Naxos Dig. 8.550139; *4550139* [id.]. Capella Istropolitana, Barry Wordsworth.

Symphonies Nos. 83 in G min. (The Hen); 94 in G (Surprise); 101 in D (The Clock).
(BB) *** Naxos Dig. 8.550114; *4550114* [id.]. Capella Istropolitana, Barry Wordsworth.

Symphonies Nos. 85 in B flat (La Reine); 92 in G (Oxford); 103 in E flat (Drum roll).
(BB) *** Naxos Dig. 8.550387 [id.]. Capella Istropolitana, Barry Wordsworth.

Like Barry Wordsworth's recordings of Mozart symphonies, also with the Capella Istropolitana on the Naxos label, this Haydn collection provides a series of outstanding bargains at the lowest budget price. The sound is not quite as clean and immediate as in the Mozart series, a little boomy at times in fact, and Wordsworth's preference for relatively relaxed speeds is a little more marked here than in Mozart, but the varied choice of works on each disc is most attractive. At their modest cost, these are well worth collecting.

Symphonies Nos. (i) *45 in F sharp min. (Farewell);* (ii) *88 in G;* (iii) *104 in D (London).*
(B) *** DG Classikon 439 428-2; *439 428-4* [id.]. (i) ECO, Barenboim; (ii) VPO, Boehm; (iii) LPO, Jochum.

A highly stimulating triptych of Haydn performances by three different conducters, all of whom have something positive to say about this repertoire. Barenboim's *Farewell Symphony* has much vitality and there is sensitive playing in the remarkable *Adagio*, one of Haydn's finest. Boehm and the VPO are at their very best in No. 88, with the slow movement gravely expansive. The playing has great polish and refinement, and Boehm's touch instantly charms in the spirited finale. Jochum's is among the most musically satisfying accounts of No. 104 in the catalogue; and all three recordings (from the 1970s) sound first class in their remastered form. A genuine bargain, playing for 77 minutes.

Symphonies Nos. 54 in G; 56 in C; 57 in D.
(BB) *** Naxos Dig. 8.554108 [id.]. Cologne CO, Müller-Brühl.

In vivid, full-ranging recordings made by German Radio, Müller-Brühl conducts lively performances with his excellent chamber orchestra of three symphonies from around 1774. Unlike the *Sturm und Drang* symphonies of the years immediately preceding, these present few problems, with winningly fresh and vigorous outer movements. The brilliant *Prestissimo* finale to No. 57 brings a main theme on stuttering repeated triplets which provides a delightful foretaste of Haydn's cackling hens in No. 83. The slow introductions to Nos. 54 and 57 and the *Adagio* movements of all three touch a deeper note of intensity, well brought out here at speeds rather broader than you find in period performances. Müller-Brühl, using modern instruments, yet reflects period practice in asking for very limited vibrato and light articulation from the strings.

Symphonies Nos. 64 in A (Tempora mutantur); 84 in E flat; 90 in C.
(BB) ** Naxos Dig. 8.550770 [id.]. Nicolaus Esterházy Sinfonia, Budapest, Béla Drahos.

Well-played but in no way distinctive performances, recorded in a pleasingly warm acoustic. The most striking performance here is of No. 90, with vigorous outer movements and a nicely paced, well-shaped *Andante*.

Symphonies Nos. 69 in C (Laudon); 89 in F; 91 in E flat.
(M) **(*) Naxos Dig. 8.550769 [id.]. Budapest Nicolaus Esterházy Sinfonia, Béla Drahos.

The resonance of the Reformed Church, Budapest, prevents the sharpest definition here. The orchestra is set back and the internal balance is natural: the strings have bloom without edginess.This is alert, thoroughly musical playing with apt tempi. The *Andante con moto* of No. 89 is elegantly done, and the variations of the *Andante* of No. 91 are neatly handled (with an elegant bassoon solo). All in all this gives pleasure, but a bit more brightness on top would have been welcome.

Symphonies Nos. 72 in D; 93 in D; 95 in C min.
(BB) *** Naxos 8.550797 [id.]. Nicolaus Esterházy Sinfonia, Béla Drahos.

These performances are polished, warm and spirited and, if the Naxos recording is again on the reverberant side, it does not cloud textures. Four horns are featured prominently in No. 72 and provide many bravura flourishes and virtuoso scales in the opening movement; the playing here is first class. The solo flute shares the stage with the principal violin in the concertante *Andante*, and he returns to grace the delightfully elegant variations which make up the finale. All in all, this engaging work is fully worthy to stand alongside its mature companions when played as seductively as this. The orchestral response is equally impressive in the fine slow movements of these later works, and throughout Béla Drahos's pacing is matched by the overall sense of spontaneity and style.

Symphonies Nos. 74 in E flat; 75 in D; 76 in E flat.
(BB) *** Naxos Dig. 8.554109 [id.]. Cologne CO, Müller-Brühl.

As in the other Haydn issues from this fine chamber orchestra, the recorded sound, engineered by German Radio, is full and vivid, both immediate and with fine bloom. The three symphonies, dating from the early 1780s, make an attractive group, characteristically lively in outer movements but each with slow movements involving the use of mysterious muted strings. Müller-Brühl, as in his other Haydn recordings, favours broad adagios and Minuets that retain the idea of a stately dance. Yet the freshness and rhythmic resilience never fail to bring the performances to life. Like its companions, an excellent recommendation.

Symphonies Nos. 80 in D min.; 81 in G; 99 in E flat.
(BB) *** Naxos Dig. 8.554110 [id.]. Cologne CO, Müller-Brühl.

Müller-Brühl, with his excellent chamber orchestra brilliantly recorded by German Radio, here couples two symphonies of 1783–4 with the first of the masterpieces which Haydn wrote for Salomon for the second of his two visits to London. No. 80 is remarkable for the dark intensity of the minor-key opening with its dramatic use of tremolo. Chromatic touches break in later too. In these later symphonies, unlike the earlier ones, Müller-Brühl does allow Minuets to acquire a hint of the Scherzo at brisker speeds. No. 99 is remarkable for Haydn's inclusion for the first time in a symphony of a pair of clarinets, so encouraging striking use of the wind section 'Harmonie' on its own. Even in this more ambitious symphony the chamber scale brings out the grandeur of the inspiration.

Symphonies Nos. 80 in D min.; 87 in A; 89 in F.
(BB) *** ASV Dig. CDQS 6156 [(M) id.]. LMP, Jane Glover.

Jane Glover conducts the London Mozart Players in strong and energetic performances of these three relatively rare symphonies. No. 87 is the least known of the *Paris symphonies*; but all three of these works show Haydn at his most inventive. *No. 80 in D minor* begins as though it were a throwback to the *Sturm und Drang* period, but then at the end of the exposition Haydn gives a winning smile, as though to say, 'I fooled you!' No. 89 ends with a dance movement which contains delectable *strascinando* (dragging) passages, where the music hesitates before launching into reprises, done with great zest by the LMP. No. 87 also has its delights, notably in the lyrical *Adagio* with lovely flute and oboe solos. Though textures are not as transparent as we are beginning to demand in an age of period performance – largely a question of the ambient recorded sound – these modern-instrument performances are as winning as they are lively, making a very real bargain.

Symphonies Nos. 82–87 (Paris); 93–104 (London Symphonies).
(B) **(*) Sony SX7K 64202 (7) [SM2K 47550 (*Nos. 82–87*); SM3K 47553 (*Nos. 93–99*); SM2K 47557 (*Nos. 100–104*)]. NYPO, Leonard Bernstein.

Bernstein's *Paris Symphonies* are impressive. He obviously enjoys the music, and the playing of the New York Philharmonic is very alive, phrasing is sensitive and dynamic nuances are carefully attended to. The rhythmic jokiness of the finale of *The Bear* is attractively managed and the witty string writing in the first movement, which led to the christening of No. 83 as *The Hen*, is very nicely pointed. The account of *No. 84 in E flat* is particularly impressive. The recordings were made in the Manhattan Center or Avery Fisher Hall between 1962 and 1967, and the CD transfers bring rather shrill violins (though there is plenty of weight), which at times make the allegros sound a bit fierce, as in the first movements of Nos. 86 and 87; but the string ensemble is excellent and, for all one's reservations about the sound, these are performances to be reckoned with: they are eminently felt.

Bernstein offers comparably large-scale performances of the *London Symphonies*, recorded between 1970 and 1975. The sound is again quite full but with a similar problem of a degree of fierceness on the violins. The performances show Bernstein's warmth and the spirited NYPO response to the conductor's often grand manner. But while there are many fine individual moments, like the *Andante* of No. 96 or the *vivace* finale of No. 99, often the phrasing is rather heavily expressive, and this especially applies to the Minuets. The last five symphonies are among the most successful, particularly the *Drum roll*, with slow movements always individual. The *Andante* of *The Clock* is particularly engaging, and the *Allegretto* of the *Military* brings spectacular percussion – no holds barred. No. 104 was the earliest to be recorded (in 1958) and sounds thinner than the others. Whatever one's reservations, this music-making is full of personality and is always committed.

Symphonies Nos. 82 in C (The Bear); 83 in G min. (The Hen); 84 in E flat; 85 in B flat (La Reine); 86 in D; 87 in A (Paris Symphonies).
(B) *** Decca Double 448 194-2 (2) [id.]. Philharmonia Hungarica, Antal Dorati.
(B) *** Ph. Duo 438 727-2 (2) [id.]. ASMF, Sir Neville Marriner.

(B) **(*) RCA Twofer 74321 34169-2 (2) [id.]. BSO, Kurt Sanderling.
(B) ** EMI forte CZS5 69383-2 (2) [ZDFB 69383]. Menuhin Festival O, Sir Yehudi Menuhin.
(M) ** DG (IMS) Dig. 445 532-2 (2) [id.]. BPO, Karajan.

Dorati's set of *Paris Symphonies* makes a fine Double Decca bargain. These performances are well up to the high standard of his integral Haydn series, freshly stylish performances with plenty of vigour. The sinewy strength of the G minor opening of No. 83 for a moment brings a hint of *Sturm und Drang*, then yields its surprise as it gives way to the clucking of its titular *Hen*, while the variations which form its slow movement are matched in charm by those based on the French folksong ('*La gentille et jeune Lisette*') which make up the *Romance: Allegretto* of No. 85. No. 84 has a first movement of the most delicate fantasy, while No. 87, after its sublime *Adagio*, ends in a mood of lithe high spirits, yet is by no means insubstantial. The only point of controversy here is Dorati's consistently slow tempi for the minuets, nicely pointed as they are.

From Marriner, spirited and well-played accounts of the *Paris Symphonies*, distinguished by excellent ensemble and keen articulation. Nos. 86 and 87 (and perhaps 84) are digital recordings, the remainder being analogue, though this is not indicated in the documentation. The playing has that touch of charm which is so essential in Haydn. It is possible to imagine performances of greater character and personality than these (in the slow movements there is a tendency to blandness) but, generally speaking, they are very lively and musical and a good alternative to the Dorati recordings. They are certainly economically priced.

Kurt Sanderling's account of the *Paris symphonies* with the Berlin orchestra are straightforward and unfussy, belonging to the big-band type which has gone out of fashion in recent years – though the orchestra in use in Paris was huge. They were recorded in 1972 and sound very good, with plenty of warmth and body to commend them. The East Berlin orchestra is first class. At times the tempi are a bit measured (in the Minuet and Trio of No. 83 for example) but everything is very musical. They can be recommended alongside, say, Marriner.

Menuhin is well served by the recording engineers, and his readings of all six *Paris Symphonies* remain unfailingly musical. The performances, on a modest scale, are well paced, elegantly phrased and have plenty of vitality. The mid-1970s recording has come up freshly. At the same time, it must be noted that these performances do not captivate or compel the listener in the way one might expect from this great musician. The discs are good value, but Dorati is a much better recommendation at the same price.

Karajan's set is big-band Haydn with a vengeance; but of course the orchestra of the *Concert de la Loge Olympique*, for which Haydn wrote these symphonies, was a large band, consisting of forty violins and no fewer than ten double-basses. It goes without saying that the quality of the orchestral playing is superb. However, these are rather heavy-handed accounts, closer to Imperial Berlin than to Paris; generally speaking, the slow movements are kept moving but the Minuets are very slow indeed, full of pomp and majesty – and, at times, too grand. In spite of the clean if slightly cool digital recordings, which have splendid presence, these performances are too charmless and wanting in grace to be wholeheartedly recommended. On CD the early-1980s digital sound has excellent presence but sounds just a little fierce in tuttis.

Symphonies Nos. 83 in G min. (The Hen); 101 in D (Clock); 104 in D (London).
(M) ** EMI (SIS) CDM5 66097-2 [id.]. BPO, Karajan.

The very resonant acoustic tells against the success of these performances. Although Karajan points the delightful second subject of the first movement of *The Hen* most delicately, and the *Andante* of the *Clock* is poised and elegant, tuttis are heavy and the very full body of strings is ill-focused. Of course there is plenty of fine playing, but the performance of No. 104 is distinctly ponderous, no match for Karajan's earlier, Vienna recording. His later set of the *London Symphonies* for DG is a much more successful example of big-band Haydn.

Symphony No. 88 in G.
✿ (M) (***) DG mono 447 439-2 [id.]. BPO, Furtwängler – SCHUBERT: *Symphony No. 9*. (***)

Even those who usually find Furtwängler's interpretations too idiosyncratic will be drawn to this glowing performance. The beauty of his shaping of the main theme of the slow movement is totally disarming, and the detail of the finale, lightly sprung and vivacious, is a constant pleasure. The Berlin Philharmonic plays marvellously well for him, and the 1951 recording, made in the attractive ambience of the Jesus-Christus Kirche in Berlin, needs no apology. In its remastered form it sounds admirably fresh, yet has plenty of body too. Here it is coupled with Schubert's *Ninth Symphony*, an ideal candidate for reissue in DG's 'Originals' series of legendary recordings.

Symphonies Nos. 88 in G; 92 in G (Oxford); 94 in G (Surprise).
(M) **(*) DG (IMS) Dig. 445 554-2. VPO, Bernstein.

All three G major symphonies emanate from concerts at the Musikvereinsaal in the mid-1980s, using the full strings of the Vienna Philharmonic and given a richly upholstered recording. For all his idiosyncrasies, Bernstein is never more winning than in Haydn, and he observes the repeat of the development and restatement in the first movement of No. 88 and gives a romantic and rather beautiful account of the *Largo*. The slow movement of the *Surprise* is also taken relaxedly, and the speed of the finale is challengingly fast. Good sound, and there is no doubt that these are 'live performances'.

Symphonies Nos. 88 in G; 92 in G (Oxford); 95 in C min.; 98 in B flat; 100 in G (Military); 101 in D (Clock); 102 in B flat; 104 in D (London).
(M) ** EMI CMS7 63667-2 (3). Philh. O or New Philh. O, Klemperer.

Klemperer, not the likeliest conductor in Haydn, in his broad, measured view yet shows his mastery in structuring and rhythmic pointing. With good analogue sound, an interesting historical document.

Symphony No. 92 in G (Oxford).
(M) (***) Dutton Lab. mono CDEA 5003 [(M) id.]. Paris Conservatoire O, Walter – SCHUBERT: *Symphony No. 9*. (***)

Only three months after the Anschluss, Bruno Walter made this Haydn recording in Paris, where he had taken refuge with the Paris Conservatoire Orchestra. These magnetic performances rather contradict the idea of Bruno Walter as the purveyor of sunshine and charm in Schubert and Haydn. One marvels at the whirlwind energy and resilience of allegros in both the Schubert and the Haydn symphonies. Even Walter's broad tempos and expressive phrasing in slow movements are firmly controlled. Despite one or two blips, Dutton's transfer, coupled with the classic account of the *Great C major Symphony* of Schubert (made in London later the same year), is infinitely superior in terms of focus, body and smoothness to the full-price VAI alternative, which is coupled with Berlioz's *Symphonie fantastique*. Those wanting this fine account of the *Oxford Symphony* should go for the Dutton.

Symphonies Nos. 92 in G (Oxford); 104 in D (London).
(B) *** Carlton IMP Classics Dig. 30367 0035-2 [(M) id.]. E. Sinfonia, Groves.
(M) (***) DG mono 457 720-2 [id.]. BPO, Hans Rosbaud – MOZART: *Violin concerto No. 4*. (***)

Sir Charles Groves's performances are robust yet elegant as well; both slow movements are beautifully shaped, with Haydn's characteristic contrasts unfolding spontaneously. In the last movement of the *Oxford*, the dancing violins are a special delight in what is one of the composer's most infectious finales.

The reputation of Hans Rosbaud was always high in Germany, and it is understandable that DG would want to feature his work in their series of 'Originals'. He is surely heard at his finest here, particularly in the beautifully played *Andante* of the *London Symphony*, which can almost be spoken of in the same breath as Furtwängler's account of the slow movement of No. 88. Throughout, the playing of the Berlin Philharmonic has remarkable finesse and polish, and they are again at their most winning in both the Minuet of the *Oxford Symphony* and its sparkling finale. Rosbaud's tempi never languish, and the recording, clear and fresh, is impressively remastered.

Symphonies Nos. 93 in D; 94 in G (Surprise); 97 in C; 99 in E flat; 100 in G (Military); 101 in D (Clock) (London Symphonies).
✿ (B) *** Ph. Duo Analogue/Dig. 442 614-2 (2). Concg. O, Sir Colin Davis.

Symphonies Nos. 95 in C min.; 96 in D (Miracle); 98 in B flat; 102 in B flat; 103 in E flat (Drum Roll); 104 in D (London) (London Symphonies).
✿ (B) *** Ph. Duo Analogue/Dig. 442 611-2 (2). Concg. O, Sir Colin Davis.

Symphonies Nos. 93 in D; 94 in G (Surprise); 97 in C; 100 in G (Military); 103 in E flat (Drum Roll); 104 in D (London).
(B) *** Decca Double 452 256-2 (2) [(M) id. import]. Philharmonia Hungarica, Antal Dorati.

Symphonies Nos. 95 in C min.; 96 in D (Miracle); 98 in B flat; 99 in E flat; 101 in D (Clock); 102 in B flat.
(B) *** Decca Double 452 259-2 (2) [(M) id. import]. Philharmonia Hungarica, Antal Dorati.

Symphonies Nos. 93–104.
(M) *** DG 437 201-2 (4). LPO, Jochum.

This Haydn series (recorded between 1975 and 1981) is one of the most distinguished sets Sir Colin Davis has given us over his long recording career, and its blend of brilliance and sensitivity, wit and humanity gives these two-for-the-price-of-one Duo reissues a special claim on the collector who has not already invested in the performances when they cost far more. There is no trace of routine in this music-making and no failure of imagination. The excellence of the playing is matched by Philips's best recording quality, whether analogue or digital. The Concertgebouw sound is resonant and at times weighty but has good definition, and the warmth and humanity of the readings are especially striking in slow movements. The *Allegretto* of the *Military Symphony* is properly grand and expansive, balanced by vital, sparkling outer movements. Excellent notes from Robin Golding. A bargain in every sense of the word.

Dorati and the Philharmonia Hungarica, working in comparative isolation in Marl in what was then West Germany (and thus in some ways reflecting Haydn's own experience which caused him to comment, 'I was forced to be original') carried through their monumental project of recording all the Haydn symphonies with consistent zeal and dedication. These final masterpieces are performed with a glowing sense of commitment; and Dorati, doubtless taking his cue from the editor, H. C. Robbins Landon, generally chooses rather relaxed tempi for the first movements – as in No. 93, which is just as deliciously lilting as in Szell's masterly version (SBK 67175 – see below). In slow movements his tempi are on the fast side, but only in No. 94, the *Surprise*, is the result really controversial. Though an extra desk of strings has been added to each section, the results are authentically in scale, with individual solos emerging unforcedly against the glowing acoustic, and with intimacy comes extra dramatic force in sforzandos. A magnificent conclusion to a magnificent project and all the more desirable, now that this series is being economically reissued in Duo format. There is adequate new documentation by Lindsay Kemp.

Jochum secures fine, stylish playing from the LPO, challenging them with often very fast tempi in outer movements. Those fast tempi sometimes prevent the music from having quite the lilt it has with Beecham or the gravitas of Sir Colin Davis; but the athletic exuberance of Jochum in Haydn, his ability to mould slow movements with tenderness that never spills over into unstylish mannerism (and to handle the sets of themes and variations to bring great diversity of atmosphere and mood), makes these wonderfully satisfying readings of Haydn's greatest symphonies. In the finale of No. 98 Jochum adds a harpsichord to the texture so that Haydn's charming little joke at the end can make its point all the better. Overall, this set will give much refreshment, and the recording is naturally balanced and clear, with its warm reverberation presenting these works on a somewhat bigger scale, yet with rather less weight than Davis brings. Many will feel this to be a perfect compromise.

Symphonies Nos. 93 in D; 95 in C min.; 97 in C; (London Symphonies).
(B) *** Sony SBK 67175; *SBT 67175* [id.]. Cleveland O, George Szell.

With superb polish in the playing and precise phrasing it would be easy for performances such as these to sound superficial, but Haydn's music obviously struck a deep chord in Szell's sensibility and there is humanity underlying the technical perfection. Indeed there are many little musical touches from Szell to show that his perfectionist approach is a dedicated and affectionate one. There is also the most delectable pointing and a fine judgement of the inner balance. Szell's minuets have a greater rhythmic spring than Bernstein's. The recordings have been splendidly remastered and the sound is fuller and firmer than it ever was on LP, with the Cleveland ambience well caught: there is still some thinness in the violins in No. 95, but it is not serious. Both Nos. 95 and 97 are strong performances; Szell brings out the maturity of first movements – the slow introduction of No. 97 immediately commands attention – and the beauty of the slow movements, among Haydn's finest (as is the *Largo cantabile* of No. 93). A highly recommendable reissue.

(i) *Symphonies Nos. 94 in G (Surprise)*; (i) *100 in G (Military)*; (ii) *String quartet No. 77 (Emperor), Op. 76/3.*
(BB) ** RCA Navigator Dig./Analogue 74321 24197-2 [(M) id. import]. (i) ECO, Jean-François Paillard; (ii) V. String Qt.

Symphonies Nos. 94 in G (Surprise); 100 in G (Military); Overture: La fedeltà premiata.
(BB) ** Tring Dig. TRP 021 [(M) id.]. RPO, Stefan Sanderling.

Symphonies Nos. 94 in G (Surprise); 100 in G (Military); 101 in D (Clock).
(M) ** [RCA Basic 100 09026 62564-2]. ECO, Paillard.

Genial, polished and well-sprung accounts of two favourite Haydn symphonies from Paillard which are enjoyable for their spirited warmth, even if the resonant acoustic slightly inflates the tuttis. The Vienna Quartet then give a lively, sympathetic account of Haydn's most famous string quartet, but here the resonant inflation is much worse, so that in the slow movement the noble melody sounds as if it is being played by a string orchestra. As can be seen, the alternative, issued in the USA as part of RCA's Basic 100 series, includes the *Clock Symphony* instead of the *Quartet*, which is surely preferable.

Vigorous performances by the RPO of two famous named G major symphonies on Tring, with no lack of finesse in the string playing and plenty of life throughout. However, although it provides agreeable bloom, the resonant acoustic prevents the kind of transparency one expects these days, and the effect is very slightly overblown. The overture is brightly done and makes a good encore.

Symphonies Nos. 94 in G (Surprise); 100 in G (Military); 101 in D (Clock).
(M) *** Ph. 442 649-2. Concg. O, Sir Colin Davis.
(B) *(*) Ph. Virtuoso 422 973-2. VSO, Sawallisch.

Sir Colin Davis's recordings from the mid-1970s are eminently recommendable. The Concertgebouw sound is resonant and at times weighty but has good definition and warmth. Those wanting these three favourite named symphonies should be well satisfied, except that all twelve of the *London Symphonies* are available, more economically priced, on a pair of bargain Duos (see above).

Although played and recorded well (between 1961 and 1963), these are not very subtle performances. Tempi are on the fast side (the finales are infectious), but Sawallisch's direct, robust style brings an element of routine, and central movements are unmemorable.

Symphonies Nos. 94 in G (Surprise); 101 in D (Clock).
(M) *** Decca 452 893-2 [id.]. VPO, Pierre Monteux – BRAHMS: *Variations on a theme of Haydn*. ***

A captivating pair of performances from Monteux. Both he and the VPO are on top form and there are no more wittily enjoyable performances of these two symphonies in the catalogue. Monteux turns a genial eye on a genial composer and secures very polished playing throughout, with many a turn of phrase to delight the ear. Highlights are the delicious *Andante* of No. 94 (with a very emphatic surprise), the swinging Minuet and the contrasting finale of the same work, bustling with vigour and high spirits. In the *Clock* the conductor sets a perky mood in the second movement and, while a pointedly droll tick-tock emphasizes Haydn's gentle humour, the violin phrasing of the elegant tune is eminently stylish. The recordings (produced by John Culshaw and Christopher Raeburn), were made in the Sophiensaal in 1959 and were considered demonstration-worthy in the early stereo era. They still sound remarkably good and are certainly worthy of inclusion in Decca's Classic Sound series. The exciting account of the Brahms coupling makes this disc doubly attractive.

Symphony No. 96 in D (Miracle).
(M) *(*) Mercury 434 396-2 [id.]. Detoit SO, Paray – MENDELSSOHN: *Symphony No. 5* etc. *(*)

Paray seldom disappoints, but this Haydn/Mendelssohn coupling is not one of his better discs. There is too much sound and fury in the wonderful *Miracle Symphony*, a performance which is hard-hitting throughout, except in the well-characterized *Andante*.

Symphonies Nos. 96 in D (Miracle); 97 in C; 98 in B flat; 99 in E flat.
(B) **(*)Teldec/Warner Ultima Dig. 3484 21337-2 (2) [(M) id. import]. Concg. O, Harnoncourt.

Harnoncourt is nothing if not wide-ranging in his Haydn interpretations; the vigorous and polished Concertgebouw playing, with hard-driven allegros and contrasting moments of great delicacy, is certainly never dull. If one accepts the gruffness of manner, the fierce accenting and the weight of the orchestral tuttis, the *Miracle* is an impressive reading, with the secondary theme of the opening movement elegant enough and with plenty of charm kept in hand for the *Andante*. The Minuet is not pressed too hard and much fizzing energy is unleashed in the finale. No. 97 is similarly compelling, with the *Adagio* beginning gracefully and the following variations very strongly characterized. The geniality of the Minuet's trio is not missed and the finale, with its vigorous downward scale, is very spirited indeed. No. 98 opens with a positive tread and the allegro is again forceful. The slow movement with its quotation of 'God save the King' is sombre and dignified, the Minuet contrastingly swift and very rhythmic. But Harnoncourt then slows down to reveal the Ländler charms of the Trio, and he obviously relishes the light-hearted finale (brusquely pointed but with much feathery delicacy from the violins). Haydn's various leg-pulling surprises are charmingly realized. No. 99 opens pontifically and the powerful thrust of the main allegro looks forward to Beethoven; yet the secondary theme is caressed disarmingly. The slow movement is measured, but Harnoncourt conveys its underlying serenity; the Minuet is fast and strongly accented, again to sound like early Beethoven. The finale is comparably vigorous and strong but also brings the most delicate articulation from the violins. Throughout the set the recording is very good indeed, and whether you take to these Haydn readings or not, their strength of character is impossible to ignore. The recording is first class throughout.

Symphonies Nos. 96 in D (Miracle); 100 in G (Military); 103 in E flat (Drum roll).
(B) *** [EMI Red Line Dig. CDR5 69810]. ECO, Tate.

Consistently Tate chooses speeds that allow the wit and sparkle of Haydn's writing to come out naturally, as in the second subject of the *Military* or in the joyful lilt of the 6/8 rhythms of the first-movement allegro in the *Drum roll*. Tate's speeds bring out Haydn's humour far more than anything faster and fiercer would do. And always, with his slow speeds, crisp articulation ensures that the music sounds light and springy, never too heavy. Warm, well-balanced sound. A most attractive triptych.

Symphony No. 97 in C.
(B) (***) Dutton Lab. mono CDLX 7019 [id. full price]. LPO, Beecham – MOZART: *Piano concerto No. 12* etc. (***)

This Haydn symphony was one of the very first recordings that Beecham made in 1944 after his wartime return from the United States. The characteristic point and elegance reflect the delight of everyone at the reunion, giving little idea of the frustrations that Beecham was beginning to feel over working with an orchestra by then self-governing. The performance is sparkling in the outer movements (the bassoon clearly audible against the strings in the finale), with a slow, moulded *Andante* and a bold Minuet marked by high contrasts. Beecham was later to record the same symphony with the RPO with the benefit of stereo, though the Dutton transfer is excellent, making this a valuable supplement to the Mozart items on the disc.

Symphonies Nos. 97 in C; 98 in B flat.
(BB) ** Naxos Dig. 8.550780 [id.]. Nicolaus Esterházy Sinfonia, Budapest, Béla Drahos.

Well played and recorded, but rather straitlaced performances of two of Haydn's last masterpieces. Fair value, but not really memorable in a competitive market.

Symphonies Nos. 99–104.
(M) *** EMI (SIS) CMS7 64066-2 (2). RPO, Sir Thomas Beecham.

The art of phrasing is one of the prime secrets of great music-making, and no detail in Beecham's performances of the *London Symphonies* goes untended. They have also great warmth, drama too, and perhaps a unique geniality. The sound throughout is full and fresh, with plenty of body, sweet violin-timbre and no edge. The first box are mono recordings; they sound admirably full-bodied and have been transferred amazingly successfully. The performances possess an inner life and vitality that put them in a class of their own.

Symphonies Nos. 101 in D (Clock); 102 in B flat; 103 in E flat (Drum Roll); 104 in D (London).
(B) *(**) Teldec/Warner Ultima Dig. 0630 18953-2 (2) [(M) id. import]. Concg. O, Harnoncourt.

As these recordings of Haydn's last four symphonies readily demonstrate, Harnoncourt can at times be an exasperatingly unpredictable conductor. These performances with the Concertebouw Orchestra, recorded in 1987–8, bring a curious stylistic mixture and bizarre eccentricities. In period-performance manner, first movements are fierce and emphatic and slow movements are clipped and short-winded (disastrously so in the glorious *Adagio* of No. 102). But there are occasional lapses into a smooth, modern manner, as in the surprisingly slack opening to the finale of the *Clock* and in the Trio of No. 102. Yet the pacing of the Minuet of No. 104 is so fast and strongly accented that this almost becomes a Scherzo. The *Drum Roll* is opened not with a roll but with a timpani fanfare, and no explanation for this is given in the notes, which are exceedingly sparse. This is all music-making of a powerful persuasion, very well played and impressively recorded, but it cannot receive a general recommendation.

CHAMBER MUSIC

Cassations (Divertimenti): in G, Hob II/1; in G, Hob II/G1; in C (Birthday), Hob II/11; in F, Hob II/20.
(M) **(*) Virgin Veritas/EMI Dig. VER5 61163-2. Linde Consort, Hans-Martin Linde.

Haydn's *Cassations* and *Divertimenti* have not the finesse of the best works of Mozart, but they have plenty of imaginative touches, particularly in their instrumentation. Two of those offered here are fairly ambitious (Hob II, Nos. G1 and 20), scored for a nonet (including a pair each of oboes and horns); the remaining two, written around 1765, are scored for a sextet (including flute and oboe), often used with charm and effectively demonstrating the special timbres of the early instruments played here. Overall the performances have plenty of character, although in the hands of, say, the ASMF they would undoubtedly be more winning still. The recording, made in a fairly reverberant acoustic, has a quite large-scale effect, but the result is not unstylish.

Divertimenti Nos. 1–12, Hob III/1–4; Hob II/6; Hob III/6–12.
(BB) *** Arte Nova Dig. 74321 31682-2 (4). Hamburg Soloists, Emil Klein.

These string *Divertimenti* (given that name by Haydn himself) are in fact his earliest string quartets (including Op. 1 and Op. 2). Legend has it that Haydn informed his publisher that he wished the term 'string quartet' to be used only from No. 19 (Op. 9) onwards, in which he finally established a four-movement format. The present works are all symmetrically structured in five movements. Each is framed by two outer *Prestos* within which there is an inner frame of two Minuets and at the centre an *Adagio*, the musical heart of each work, almost always containing the finest music. The other movements are well crafted but relatively conventional, although every so often there is something to catch the ear, for instance the hunting style of the opening movement of the very first work (which recurs in No. 6). The simplicity of the writing probably suits the quartet format (one instrument to a part) better than an expanded instrumentation. But Emil Klein and his excellent Hamburg string group make an elegant case for these chamber orchestral versions, particularly in the cantabile slow movements, which are very beautifully played, although the finales too are often quite infectious. The *Adagios* of Nos. 5 (over a pizzicato accompaniment) and 6 (similar and charmingly delicate) are particularly winning. No. 9 (which has a novel second Minuet, interchanging bowed and pizzicato passages) and No. 11 (with its skipping first movement like a nursery rhyme, fine central *Largo cantabile* and a brief *moto perpetuo* finale) are among the most attractive of the set. They were originally scored to include a pair of horns, but were rearranged into four parts by Haydn's publisher. The extended *Adagio* of No. 10 (9 minutes) is surely worthy of a place in an early Haydn symphony. Inexpensive and with excellent recording, this set is well worth considering.

Piano trios Nos. 1–46, Hob XV:1–41; Hob XIV:C1 in C; Hob XV:C1 in C; Hob XIV6/XVI6 in G; Hob XV:f1 in F min.; Hob deest in D (complete).
❀ (B) *** Ph. 454 098-2 (9) [id.]. Beaux Arts Trio.

It is not often possible to hail one set of records as a 'classic' in quite the way that Schnabel's Beethoven sonatas can be so described. Yet this set can be described in those terms, for the playing of the Beaux Arts Trio is of the very highest musical distinction. The contribution of the pianist, Menahem Pressler, is little short of inspired, and the recorded sound on CD is astonishingly lifelike. The CD transfer has enhanced detail without losing the warmth of ambience or sense of intimacy. Now offered in a bargain box of nine CDs, this is a set no Haydn lover should miss: it is desert island music.

Piano trio in E flat, Hob XV/10.
(M) ** Sony Stern Edition III SM2K 64516 (2) [id.]. Stern, Rose, Istomin – MOZART: *Piano quartet No. 2;* SCHUBERT: *Piano trios Nos. 1–2.* **

This rather over-characterized account of the *E flat Trio*, written in 1784–5, has plenty of vigour and impetus, but the close balance gives the feeling of high-powered music-making, which is not entirely sympathetic.

Piano trios, Hob XV, Nos. 24–27.
(M) *** Ph. 422 831-2. Beaux Arts Trio.

These are all splendid works. No. 25 with its *Gypsy rondos* is the most famous, but each has a character of its own, showing the mature Haydn working at full stretch. The playing here is peerless and the recording truthful and refined.

String quartets

String quartets Nos. 1–12; 19–83; String quartet fragments in D min. (Andante grazioso & Minuet), Op. 103 (includes *The Seven Last Words of Christ on the Cross, Op. 51/1–7,* with readings selected by Reginald Barrett-Ayres).
(B) *** Decca 455 261-2 (22). Aeolian Qt.

The first complete recording of the Haydn *String quartets* in stereo was Decca's project parallel to Dorati's integral recording of the symphonies, and in most ways it was equally successful. The performances were recorded over a period of four years between December 1972 and December 1976, using the critical edition by Reginald Barrett-Ayres and H. C. Robbins Landon. The recordings were made in two London churches, beginning in St George the Martyr with Opp. 71 and 74, followed by Op. 2. Though the performances of these late works are vigorously enjoyable, the engineers let the ecclesiastical acoustic provide the four players with a degree of 'helpful' reverberation which in Opp. 71 and 74 made them sound a little like a string orchestra. This is not as detrimental as a similar effect in some of the recordings by the Kodály Quartet for Naxos, for the microphone placing ensures clarity of part-writing as well as warmth. No. 69 has a magnificent slow movement, surprisingly romantic, and No. 70 is remarkably original from first to last: both are well projected here. By the time Decca came to record Op. 2, the problem was solved, and for the remaining sessions the recording team moved to St John's, Smith Square, where an excellent and realistic presence was consistently achieved, the profile of the leader (Emanuel Hurwitz) bright without being edgy.

It is not always an advantage in the early quartets of Opp. 1 and 2 that the Aeolian players are wedded to repeats. Nevertheless, on their own unpretentious level these are charming works, and Hurwitz readily takes his chances in such a *Quartet* as Op. 2/1, which includes stylish cadenzas. Though they were recorded at the time, the Op.3 *Quartets* are now claimed to be by Romanus Hofstetter, not by Haydn, and they have understandably been omitted from the present box. This is a pity for, whatever their provenance, the *Andante cantabile* of Op. 3/2 – the so-called '*Serenade*' – is understandably a popular favourite.

Though few of the quartets of Opp. 9 and 17 are consistently inspired from beginning to end (the *G major*, No. 29, is a marvellous exception), they all contain their moments of magic and every one of them has a superb finale, showing the young Haydn at full stretch. Even at this period Haydn had developed his quartet-writing beyond the stage of giving all the interesting writing to the first violin, and by now the Aeolian group, having settled into their task, play with consistent freshness and imagination.

After he had consolidated his style and technique in the fine Op. 20 set, given here in eminently well-prepared and musical accounts, Haydn sought to expand his musical boundaries. 'Written in a new and special way,' he said of his six Op. 33 *Quartets*. Tovey describes them as 'the lightest of all Haydn's mature comedies', for by the time he wrote them, in 1781, many years after the Op. 20 group, he was learning from the young Mozart. Mozart returned the compliment in the six masterpieces he dedicated to Haydn; in his turn, Haydn responded with his Op. 50 group, cogent in their monothematic form. The Aeolians came to these marvellous works fairly late on in their complete cycle, but the players' perception and energy are, if anything, keener than ever. Not all their tempi are beyond question, but the wonder is how consistently enjoyable their playing is.

The set is crowned by their admirable performances of the consistently inspired last *Quartets*, Opp. 77 and 76. The straight, unmannered approach disguises consistent imaginative thoughtfulness, and the warmth of the interplay of ideas among the instruments is engagingly spontaneous. The music's characteristic touches of humour (as in the genial bouncing opening Allegro of Op. 77/1) are not missed. The recording is in the demonstration bracket and we hope Decca may make these masterpieces available separately as a Double. *The Seven Last Words of Jesus Christ* (Nos. 50–56, Op. 51) are treated as an appendix. They were originally composed as orchestral pieces, commissioned in 1787 by the ecclesiastical authorities of Cádiz Cathedral for performance at a Good Friday service. However, it is in their string quartet format that they have become most familiar. Haydn confessed that it was 'no easy task to compose seven adagios, lasting approximately ten minutes each, and to succeed one another without fatiguing the listener'. But the result is profound, and the magnificent performances here avoid any risk of monotony by inserting poetry readings between movements. The texts (from John Donne, George Herbert, Robert Herrick and Edith Sitwell, among others) are aptly chosen and beautifully read by Sir Peter Pears. All told, this is a remarkable achievement: many of these performances are unsurpassed. The documentation consists of an excellent essay by Lindsay Kemp, but analysis is confined to Opus number groupings.

String quartets Nos. 1 in B flat; 2 in E flat; 3 in D; 4 in G, Op. 1/1–4.
(BB) **(*) Naxos Dig. 8.550398 [id.]. Kodály Qt.

String quartets Nos. 5 in E flat; 6 in C, Op. 1/5–6; 7 in A; 8 in E, Op. 2/1–2.
(BB) **(*) Naxos Dig. 8.550399 [id.]. Kodály Qt.

Haydn is credited with 'inventing' the string quartet, but he claimed that he had come across the form by accident. The Op. 1 and Op. 2 quartets are in essence five-movement divertimenti scored for four string players. The first four were published in Paris in 1764, together with two other works, under the collective title, '*Six Simphonies ou Quatuors dialogués*'. These earliest works have not quite the unquenchable flow of original ideas that the early symphonies have but, in such fresh performances as these, they make easy and enjoyable listening even if, with the performances generous in observing repeats, some movements outstay their welcome. The resonant ambience of the Unitarian Church in Budapest seems not unsuitable for works which lie midway between divertimenti and quartets, and the focus seems brighter and sharper on the second CD, recorded in June 1991, two months after the first.

String quartets Nos. 1 in B flat, Op. 1/1; 67 in D (Lark), Op. 64/5; 77 in C, Op. 76/3.
(B) ** Tring Dig. TRP 028 [(M) id.]. RPO Chamber Ens., Jonathan Carney.

In spite of the Tring listing, these are not chamber orchestra performances, although the resonant acoustic does create an almost string-orchestral texture from the four players, led by Jonathan Carey. The performances are warm and polished: they do not find enough variety of dynamic in the repetitions of the famous tune in the slow movement of the *Emperor*, but the *Lark* soars up nicely and the *Vivace* finale is infectious. But the highlight here is the very early, Op. 1 *Quartet*, which is strikingly fresh. In the *Adagio* the leader's extended solo is played most beautifully and creates a memorable level of tension.

String quartets Nos. 9 in F; 10 in B flat, Op. 2/4 & 6; 43 in D min., Op. 42.
(BB) **(*) Naxos Dig. 8.550732 [id.]. Kodály Qt.

The Unitarian Church, Budapest, continues to provide a warm, flattering tonal blend of much aural beauty, but a texture that is a little too ample for early Haydn, while the fairly close microphones reduce the dynamic range. However, the Kodály's friendly style and elegant finish suit early Haydn. (Both Op. 2 quartets are simple five-movement works, each with a pair of minuets.) These performers find exactly the right degree of expressiveness for the *Adagio* of Op. 2/4 and are equally at home in the engaging *Andante ed innocentemente* which opens the first movement of Op. 42, a splendid work, written a quarter of a century later.

String quartets Nos. 17 in F (Serenade), Op. 3/5; 38 in E flat (Joke), Op. 33/2; 76 in D min. (Fifths), Op. 76/2.
(BB) **(*) Discover Dig. DIDCD 920172 [id.]. Sharon Qt.

The Sharon Quartet are an excellent group and they give warm and spirited accounts of these three favourite quartets. They are recorded in the resonant acoustics of St John's Church in Cologne and, like some of the recordings made for Naxos by the Kodály Quartet, the resonance expands the texture, although not seriously enough to prevent enjoyment, for they make a bright, clean sound. They find charm in Hofstetter's famous '*Serenade*' of Op. 3 and are equally good in the *Variations* which form the slow movement of the *Fifths*; at the same time, they find the right approach to the '*Joke*' in the finale of Op. 33/2.

String quartets Nos. 17 in F (Serenade), Op. 3/5; 63 in D (Lark), Op. 64/5; 76 in D min. (Fifths), Op. 76/2.
(M) *** Ph. 426 097-2. Italian Qt.

First-class playing here; although the first movement of the *Lark* is a bit measured in feeling, the *Serenade quartet* is made to sound inspired, its famous slow movement played with exquisite gentleness. The *D minor Quartet* is admirably poised and classical in feeling.

String quartets Nos. 19 in C; 21 in G; 22 in D min., Op. 9/1, 3 & 4.
(BB) *** Naxos Dig. 8.550786 [id.]. Kodály Qt.

String quartets Nos. 20 in E flat; 23 in B flat; 24 in A, Op. 9/2, 5 & 6.
(BB) *** Naxos Dig. 8.550787 [id.]. Kodály Qt.

The Kodály Quartet are in excellent form throughout Opus 9. Their simple eloquence in all three slow movements on the first disc serves Haydn well: the *Largo* of Op. 9/3 is ideally paced and beautifully poised. The players then go on to give a captivating account of the finale. Indeed, all the finales here are superb, showing Haydn at full stretch. The last of the set in A major opens with a very attractive *Presto* in 6/8, which is delightfully buoyant here. It has a beautiful *Adagio*, dominated by a favourite Haydn triplet rhythm and giving much scope to the solo violin, who soars above the texture in a long cantilena and is even given space for a brief cadenza just before the movement ends. Fortunately the Naxos recording team (in December 1992 and January 1993) have mastered the acoustics of the Unitarian Church in Budapest. The microphones are in the right place, the sound is not inflated: in fact the balance brings a vividly realistic impression.

String quartets Nos. 31 in E flat; 32 in C; 33 in G min., Op. 20/1–3.
(BB) ** Naxos Dig. 8.550701 [id.]. Kodály Qt.

String quartets Nos. 34 in D; 35 in F min.; 36 in A (Sun quartets), Op. 20/4–6.
(BB) ** Naxos Dig. 8.550702 [id.]. Kodály Qt.

The Naxos Kodály series continues to bring polished, sympathetic playing of considerable warmth. Allegros are lively, but the acoustics of the Unitarian Church, Budapest, though providing beautifully rich string-textures, here make the effect almost orchestral and bring an element of blandness to the fine *Adagio* slow movements; throughout, the dynamic range of the playing is reduced by the microphone positioning. The *Adagio* of Op. 20/2 brings some fine playing, and the theme and variations of the *Poco adagio e affettuoso* of the *D major Quartet*, Op. 20/4, are attractively characterized but badly need a wider dynamic contrast. This is even more striking in the *Fuga a quattro soggetti* which forms the finale of Op. 20/2.

String quartets Nos. 32 in C; 34 in D, Op. 20/2 & 4.
(B) * Sony/Seon SBK 62954 [id.]. Amsterdam Esterházy Qt.

A comparatively early and unenticing example (1973) of Haydn quartet playing on original instruments. The ensemble is immaculate, the recorded sound admirably transparent, but the playing by this Dutch group expresses no joy in the music and the effect is at times little short of dismal. Finales come off best, but the fine set of variations which forms the slow movement of the G major work is particularly disappointing.

String quartets Nos. 32 in C, Op. 20/2; 44 in B flat, Op. 50/1; 76 in D min. (Fifths), Op. 76/2.
(BB) *** ASV Dig. CDQS 6144 [(M) id.]. Lindsay Qt.

Obviously, since these are public performances, one has to accept music-making reflecting the heat of the occasion, the odd sense of roughness (the finale of Op. 76, No. 2), for these artists take risks – and this is perhaps a shade faster than it would be in a studio. There is splendid character in these performances and plenty of musical imagination. These readings have a spontaneity which is refreshing in these days of retakes! The recordings are eminently truthful and audience noise is minimal. An excellent bargain.

String quartets Nos. 35 in F min., Op. 20/5; 40 in B flat, Op. 33/4; 70 in D, Op. 71/2.
(BB) *** ASV Dig. CDQS 6146 [(M) id.]. Lindsay Qt.

The immediacy of the Lindsays' playing here is just as striking as before, yet at the rather serious opening of the *F minor*, Op. 20/5, the approach is appropriately sober and considered as well as spontaneous. This quartet also has a tender *Siciliano* slow movement which is played with affecting simplicity and grace. The account of the *B flat Quartet*, Op. 33/4, brings a burst of applause at the end, as well it might, with its deeply thoughtful *Largo* and engaging finale. Three marvellous works, recorded with striking presence.

String quartets Nos. 37–42, Op. 33/1–6; 43 in D min., Op. 42.
(B) *** HM Musique d'Abord Dig. HMA 1903002/3 [(M) id. import]. Festetics Qt.

String quartets Nos. 37–38 & 41, Op. 33/1–2 & 5.
(BB) **(*) Naxos 8.550788 [id.]. Kodály Qt.

String quartets Nos. 39–40 & 42, Op. 33/3–4 & 6.
(BB) **(*) Naxos 8.550789 [id.]. Kodály Qt.

Although Haydn had written some fine quartets before these were published in 1782, this Op. 33 set proved a watermark. Here he finally established himself as complete master of a new medium with such skill, musical fecundity and wit that he never surpassed them in terms of cultivated musical pleasure, even if later works, Op. 76 for instance, embrace a somewhat wider range of mood and feeling.

Those wanting Op. 33 on period instruments will surely be delighted with this Musique d'Abord set from the Quatuor Festetics. These Hungarians play with great spirit (the finale of the *Joke* has the requisite sense of fun), and their overall lightness of touch and the transparency of texture are very appealing. Slow movements have freshness and just the right combination of gravitas and expressive feeling: the phrasing is smoothly linear without those unattractive bulges that seem to haunt performances on original instruments. Almost every movement has the kind of sparkle and spontaneity that make one want to return to it, and the recording is most naturally balanced in the much-used Unitarian Church of Budapest. For most listeners this will be a clear first choice, for Op. 42 is also excellently played.

The Kodály Quartet play Op. 33 with an easy relaxed warmth. Their style is low-key so that the 'Joke' finale of Op. 33/2 is rather gentle and muted; on the other hand, the reason for the sobriquet of the *Bird Quartet* is affectionately conveyed and the finale is delightfully light-hearted. Slow movements are serene and quietly musical. Minuets are generally full of character, with the trios nicely realized, and this applies especially to the charming middle section of the Scherzo in the *Joke Quartet*. In short these are performances which convey the players' affection for this wonderful music with no possible desire to put their own personalities between composer and listener, and some listeners may feel the approach brings at times just a hint of blandness, unusual in this series. The Naxos recording is wholly natural with the acoustics of the Budapest Unitarian Church beautifully caught without any textural inflation.

String quartets Nos. 43 in D min., Op. 42; 67 in D (Lark), Op. 64/5; 79 in D, Op. 76/5.
(BB) *** ASV Dig. CDQS 6145 [(M) id.]. Lindsay Qt.

The Lindsays are given a striking presence here and the spontaneity of their playing is gripping. The presto finales (particularly the moto perpetuo of *The Lark*, which overall is most strikingly done) offer fizzing bravura and the beautiful slow movement of Op. 76/5 is rapt in its quiet intensity. There are remarkably few moments of roughness of ensemble arising from the impetuosity of the playing.

String quartets Nos. 50–56 (The Seven Last Words of our Saviour on the Cross), Op. 51; 83 in B flat, Op. 103.
(BB) *** Naxos Dig. 8.550346 [id.]. Kodály Qt.

No work for string quartet, not even late Beethoven, presents more taxing interpretative problems than Haydn's *Seven Last Words of our Saviour on the Cross*. The Kodály Quartet give a memorable performance, strongly characterized and beautifully played, with subtle contrasts of expressive tension between the seven inner slow movements. They also offer an appropriate bonus in Haydn's last, unfinished, two-movement *Quartet*. The recording is first rate, vividly present yet naturally balanced, like the other issues in this attractive Naxos series.

String quartets Nos. 57 in G; 58 in C; 59 in E, Op. 54/1–3.
(BB) *** Naxos Dig. 8.550395; *4550395* [id.]. Kodály Qt.

The Kodály players enter animatedly into the spirit of the music; the leader, Attila Falvay, shows himself fully equal to Haydn's bravura embellishments in the demanding first violin writing. The Naxos sound is fresh and truthful.

String quartets Nos. 57 in G; 58 in C; 59 in E, Op. 54/1–3; 71 in C; 73 in F; 74 in G min., Op. 74/1–3.
(BB) *** Virgin Classics Dig. Double VBD5 61436-2 (2) [CDVB 61436]. Endellion Qt.

The Endellion Quartet were recorded in The Maltings, Snape (in 1988 and 1990 respectively), which provides an ideal acoustic environment. The playing is bright-eyed, fresh and vital, and in both sets they prove a sound guide to this repertoire. The overall sound is strikingly immediate but is beautifully integrated, and there are many moments of musical insight. With the two discs offered for the cost of a single mid-priced CD, this set is very competitive.

String quartets Nos. 60 in A; 61 in F min. (Razor); 62 in B flat, Op. 55/1–3 (Tost Quartets).
(BB) **(*) Naxos Dig. 8.550397. Kodály Qt.

Opus 55 brings playing from the Kodály Quartet which is undoubtedly spirited and generally polished, but the music-making at times seems plainer than usual in the Naxos series. The recording is bright and clear, with a realistic presence.

String quartets Nos. 63–8, Op. 64/1–6.
(B) *** HM Musique d'Abord Dig. HMA 1903040/1 [id.]. Festetics Qt.

String quartets Nos. 63 in C; 64 in B min.; 65 in B flat, Op. 64/1–3.
(BB) *** Naxos Dig. 8.550673 [id.]. Kodály Qt.

String quartets Nos. 66 in G; 67 in D (Lark); 68 in E flat, Op. 64/4–6.
(BB) *** Naxos Dig. 8.550674 [id.]. Kodály Qt.

The excellent Hungarian Festetics Quartet follow their esteemed recording of Haydn's Op. 33 with an equally perceptive and animated set of Op. 64. Again their readings are very positive, yet the lightness of touch is balanced by buoyant rhythmic feeling and spontaneous impetus. Slow movements are played with a restrained vibrato and nicely judged espressivo, the line not spoilt by exaggerated bulges. Minuets are infectious and finales sparkle; the first movement of Op. 64/3 for example swings along spiritedly and, after the solemn *Adagio*, the rustic charm of the Minuet is appealingly caught. The brio of the first movement of Op. 64/4 gains much from the lightness of texture, while the leader's delicate, soaring line as the *Lark* is exquisite. The exposition repeat is observed, so the listener revels in the theme's many reappearances. The glowing *Adagio – cantabile e sostenuto* is also beautifully played. Indeed the last three quartets of the set continually demonstrate not only the high quality of this music-making, but how much these works can gain from performance on period instruments when the authentic style is unexaggerated and the ensemble and tonal matching are so precise. The recording, made in the Budapest Unitarian Church, is fairly close but could hardly be more beautifully balanced.

These Kodály performances are all enjoyable, but the set seems to get better and better as it progresses. Op. 64/1–3 were recorded on 25–29 April 1992; the last to be done, the *B flat major*, is remarkably successful, with a vigorous opening *Vivace assai* and a rapt *Adagio*. The other three works date from 1–3 May, and clearly the group had found its top form. The *Adagio – cantabile e sostenuto* of No. 4 finds them at their most concentrated: the *Lark* has never soared aloft more spontaneously and the Minuet and finale of No. 6 close the set in a winningly spirited fashion. The warm acoustics of the Budapest Unitarian Church provide a mellow and expansive sound-image, but not an orchestral one, and detail remains clear. A most enjoyable set.

String quartets Nos. 67 in D (Lark), Op. 64/5; 74 in G min. (Rider), Op. 74/3; 77 in C (Emperor), Op. 76/3.
(B) *** DG Classikon 439 479-2; *439 479-4* [(M) id. import]. Amadeus Qt.

Here is a worthwhile triptych of named quartets for those seeking to sample the Amadeus Quartet in Haydn. Their superb ensemble is immediately noticeable at the opening of the *Lark Quartet*, as is Norbert Brainin's vibrato, giving the Amadeus sound its special stamp. The finale brings spiccato precision that dazzles the ear. The *Largo* of the *Rider Quartet* sounds just a little deliberate but its intensity is in no doubt, and the gutsy vibrancy of the playing in the finale is equally remarkable. These date from the 1970s; the *Emperor* was made a decade earlier and the recording is a trifle thinner, though the body of tone the group commands projects impressively. The performance shows these fine musicians in the best possible light. The CD transfers are expertly done, and this Classikon reissue is excellent value.

String quartets Nos. 69 in B flat; 70 in D; 71 in E flat (Apponyi Quartets), Op. 71/1–3.
(BB) *** Naxos Dig. 8.550394 [id.]. Kodály Qt.

The *Apponyi Quartets* are among the composer's finest. The Naxos recordings by the Kodály Quartet are outstanding in every way and would be highly recommendable even without their considerable price advantage. The digital recording has vivid presence and just the right amount of ambience: the effect is entirely natural.

String quartets Nos. 69–71 (Apponyi Quartets), Op. 71/1–3; 72 in C; 73 in F; 74 in G min. (Rider), Op. 74/1–3.
(M) *** Arcana Dig. A 918 (2). Festetics Qt.

The Festetics Quartet continue their period-instrument Haydn series with – on the whole – beautifully judged performances of Opp. 71 and 74. The playing has the customary animation and finish, with detail perceptively observed, and well-blended yet beautifully transparent textures. As before, there is nothing vinegary here, and phrasing and line are impeccably musical. Minuets are pleasing, without heaviness (sample the Trio of Op. 71/3 for delectable articulation) and finales sparkle. These are three-star performances without a doubt, and the recording could hardly be better judged. One's only reservation concerns slow movements, sometimes a little solemn. The *Largo assai* of Op. 74/3 is just a shade deliberate, and elsewhere one senses that the players are anxious to convey the depth of Haydn's writing. They do, and their thoughtfulness is appreciated – but perhaps this is achieved at the expense of a smidgen of spontaneity. However, one does not want to make too much of this: these CDs give much satisfaction, and certainly the performances have lift-off as well as gravitas.

String quartets Nos. 72 in C; 73 in F; 74 in G min. (Rider), Op. 74/1–3.
(BB) *** Naxos Dig. 8.550396 [id.]. Kodály Qt.

The Kodály Quartet are on top form here and give refreshing accounts of these three splendid quartets. Their simplicity of approach to the slow movement of the F major is particularly appealing, and the finale is sheer delight. The *Rider* is another of their most striking performances, including another memorable slow movement and a closing movement combining grace and refined ensemble with plentiful energy. The recording could hardly be bettered, completely natural and with the acoustic perfectly handled.

String quartet No. 74 in G min., Op. 74/3.
(M) *** Cal. CAL 6698. Talich Qt – BOCCHERINI: *Quartet, Op. 58/2;* MENDELSSOHN: *Quartet No. 2;* MICA: *Quartet No. 6.* ***

The *Quartet in G minor*, Opus 74, No. 3 (dedicated to Count Apponyi), is one of Haydn's greatest quartets. It brings a very beautiful, serenely introspective *Largo assai* in which, in this searching Talich performance, one has the feeling of eavesdropping on private music-making. After the blithe Minuet, the finale is engagingly light and spirited. Superb playing and most natural recording, and the rest of the performances on this generously filled mid-priced CD (76 minutes) are equally distinguished.

String quartets Nos. 74 in G min. (Rider), Op. 74/3; 77 in C (Emperor), Op. 76/3.
(B) *** Teldec/Warner 3984 21849-2 [(M) id. import]. Alban Berg Qt.

A quite superb disc in every way. Back in the early 1970s, the Alban Berg Quartet displayed admirable polish, but the end-result was without that hint of glossy perfection which poses a problem with some of their more recent, digital recordings. The playing here has wonderful resilience and sparkle. The famous slow movement of the *Emperor Quartet* has seldom been put on record with such warmth and eloquence, and the slow movement of No. 74 is even more beautiful. Indeed the performance of this *Quartet* is masterly, with the rhythmic figure in the first movement which gives the work its title admirably managed. The recording too is first class, full and clear, and this is one of the most rewarding of all Haydn quartet couplings. The playing time is only 45 minutes, but every one of them is treasurable and this disc is inexpensive.

String quartets Nos. 75 in G; 76 in D min. (Fifths); 77 in C (Emperor); 78 in B flat (Sunrise); 79 in D; 80 in E flat, Op. 76/1–6 (Erdödy Quartets).
❀ (BB) *** Naxos Dig. 8.550314; *4550314 (Nos. 75–77)*; 8.550315; *4550315 (Nos. 78–80)*. Kodály Qt.
(B) **(*) Sony SB2K 53522 (2) [S2K 53522]. Tokyo Qt.

String quartets Nos. 76 in D min. (Fifths); 77 in C (Emperor); 78 in B flat (Sunrise), Op. 76/2–4.
❀ (BB) *** Naxos Dig. 8.550129; *4550129* [id.]. Kodály Qt.

Haydn's six *Erdödy Quartets*, Op. 76, contain some of his very greatest music, and these performances by the Kodály Quartet are fully worthy of the composer's inexhaustible invention. Their playing brings a joyful pleasure in Haydn's inspiration and there is not the slightest suspicion of over-rehearsal or of routine: every bar of the music springs to life spontaneously, and these musicians' insights bring an ideal combination of authority and warmth, emotional balance and structural awareness.

The Tokyo Quartet offer superb playing and an immaculate tonal blend, and they are unfailingly intelligent. Yet it is a pity that they do not relax a little more and allow the music to unfold at greater leisure, as do the Kodály players, for they do not convey the humanity and charm that distinguish the Naxos set. The recording is faithful, but they are not as well served by the engineers as they were by DG for their prize-winning Bartók cycle; the sound, though fresh, is a little lacking in bloom at upper dynamic levels.

String quartet No. 77 in C (Emperor), Op. 76/3.
(M) * DG Dig. 445 598-2. Emerson Qt – MOZART: *String quartets Nos. 17 & 19.* *

The Emerson group produce quartet-playing of remarkable virtuosity and stunning ensemble. One can only wonder in amazement at their brilliance, definition and clarity. However, it is all very thrustful and over-projected, and quite uncongenial as Haydn playing. The Mozart with which it is coupled is even worse. In terms of skill, this deserves more than three stars – but as a musical experience one is at a loss to rate it!

String quartets Nos. 77 in C (Emperor); 78 in B flat (Sunrise), Op. 76/3–4.
(M) *** DG 449 092-2. Amadeus Qt – MOZART: *String quartet No. 17.* ***

The Amadeus's 1963 version of the *Emperor*, coupled with Mozart's *Hunt quartet*, was always one of their very best records: it has breadth and warmth, to say nothing of immaculate ensemble. The famous slow movement is particularly successful. The *Sunrise*, which was recorded seven years later, is another finely blended performance, somewhat suaver but still with plenty of vitality in outer movements. Both recordings were truthfully balanced and emerge very successfully on CD.

String quartets Nos. 81 in G; 82 in F, Op. 77/1–2; 83 in D min., Op. 103.
(B) **(*) HM Musique d'Abord Dig. HMA 1903001 [id.]. Festetics Qt.

String quartets Nos. 81 in G; 82 in F, Op. 77/1–2.
(BB) ** Naxos Dig. 8.553146 [id.]. Kodály Qt.

Although the opening of Op. 77/1 has a pleasing rhythmic character, there is a coolness about the playing of the Festetics Quartet that lends itself less well to Haydn's expressive slow movement. They are at their best in the last quartet; and the transparency of texture from the use of original instruments brings some refreshing textures elsewhere, but in the last resort the effect is too austere.

The Kodály Quartet give comparatively robust performances of both works, made to seem even more robust by the close balance which reduces the dynamic range – not that the playing is notable for pianissimo contrast. This is warm, friendly music-making and in that respect (and in that respect only) preferable to the Festetics; but the latter's playing has considerably more subtlety, and they offer an extra work.

KEYBOARD MUSIC

Piano sonatas Nos. 1–16; 17–19 (Hob Deest) 20; 28, Hob XIV/5; 29–62, Hob XVI/1–52 & G1; XVII/D1; The Seven last words on the Cross; Adagio in F; Capriccio in G on the song 'Acht Sauschneider müssen sein'; Fantasia in C; 7 Minuets from 'Kleine Tänz für die Jugend'; Variations in F min.; 5 Variations in D; 6 Variations in C; 12 Variations in E flat; 20 Variations in A.
(B) *** Decca 443 785-2 (12) [id.]. John McCabe.

John McCabe made the first successful complete survey of the Haydn *Sonatas* for Argo between 1974 and 1977, including also *The Seven last words on the Cross*, an arrangement not made by the composer but approved by him. It is remarkably successful here. Indeed two things shine through John McCabe's performances: their complete musicianship and their fine imagination. In presenting them as he does on a modern piano, McCabe makes the most of the colour and subtlety of the music, and in that respect his style is more expressive, less overtly classical than Jandó's (see below) while the recording is made to sound somewhat softer-grained by the acoustic of All Saints' Church, Petersham. Given phrasing so clearly articulated and alertly phrased, and such varied, intelligently thought-out and wholly responsive presentation, this set can be recommended very enthusiastically. The recordings are of the very highest quality, truthful in timbre and firmly refined in detail, and they must be numbered among the most successful of this repertoire ever to be put on disc, for the piano is notoriously difficult to balance in eighteenth-century music. The set is most reasonably priced and the pianist provides his own extensive and illuminating notes. To sample the calibre of this enterprise, begin with *The Seven last words* – playing of unexaggerated expressive feeling that almost makes one believe this was a work conceived in pianistic terms.

Andante with variations in F min., Hob. XVII/6; Piano sonatas Nos. 59 in E flat, Hob. XVI/49; 60 in C, Hob. XVI/50; 62 in E flat, Hob. XVI/52.
(M) *** Ph. Brendel Edition Dig./Analogue 446 921-2. Alfred Brendel – MOZART: *Piano concertos and sonatas.* **(*)

This disc acts as a mere sampler of Brendel's outstanding Haydn recordings. In Hob. XVI/49 (analogue), the first to be recorded, he observes all the repeats and the sound is first class. The rest of the programme is digital. His playing throughout is of real distinction, aristocratic without being aloof, concentrated without being too intense. Everything is cleanly articulated and finely characterized. He is accorded lifelike and vivid recording.

Piano sonatas Nos. 20 in B flat, Hob XVI/18; 30 in D, Hob XVI/19; 31 in A flat, Hob XVI/46; 32 in G min., Hob XVI/44.
(B) **(*) Naxos Dig. 8.553364 [id.]. Jenö Jandó.

Jandó continues his Haydn sonata series in his clean, direct style. The first movement of the *G minor Sonata* is particularly appealing, with its neat articulation and tight little runs, and the same might be said of the opening movement of the *A flat major* (No. 31), while its finale is similarly bright and sparkling. But first prize goes to the closing movement of the *D major*, which skips along delightfully and brings quite dazzling dexterity. The thoughtful *Adagio* of the *B flat major*, however, is just a little too studied; but this is not enough of a disadvantage to prevent a recommendation. The piano recording is very realistic.

Piano sonatas Nos. 29 in E flat, Hob. XVI/45; 33 in C min., Hob. XVI/20; 34 in D, Hob. XVI/33; 35 in A flat, Hob. XVI/43.
(BB) *** Naxos Dig. 8.553800 [id.]. Jenö Jandó.

Jandó is on very good form here. His style is a little plain and classical but never insensitive, and he is well recorded. A useful addition to a fine series.

Piano sonatas Nos. 36 in C, Hob XVI/21; 37 in E, Hob XVI/22; 38 in F, Hob XVI/23; 39 in D, Hob XVI/24; 40 in E flat, Hob XVI/25; 41 in A, Hob XVI/26.
(BB) **(*) Naxos Dig. 8.553127 [id.]. Jenö Jandó.

Piano sonatas Nos. 48 in C, Hob XVI/35; 49 in C sharp min., Hob XVI/36; 50 in D, Hob XVI/37; 51 in E flat, Hob XVI/38; 52 in G, Hob XVI/39.
(BB) *** Naxos Dig. 8.553128 [id.]. Jenö Jandó.

Jandó seems to have been very slightly below par when he recorded Volume 4 (8.553127) of his ongoing set of Haydn sonatas in May 1993. The playing is as bright and clear as before and the interpretations are well thought out, but just occasionally there is a hint of stiffness and overall there is not always the degree of spontaneity we expect from this artist.

A month later, in June of the same year, he was back on form with all the freshness that marked his earlier records in the series, as the opening of *No. 36 in C* immediately shows. The finale of *No. 37 in E major* is beautifully played, and the following two sonatas with their fine slow movements will not disappoint his admirers. Excellent piano sound, crisp but not too dry.

Piano sonatas Nos. 42 in G, Hob XVI/27; 43 in E flat, Hob XVI/28; 44 in F, Hob XVI/29; 45 in A, Hob XVI/30; 46 in E, Hob XVI/31; 47 in B min., Hob XVI/32.
(BB) *** Naxos Dig. 8.550844 [id.]. Jenö Jandó (piano).

The six sonatas offered here (in what is Volume II of Jenö Jandó's ongoing series) were written between 1774 and 1776 and were later grouped together and published by Hummel as Haydn's Op. 14. Although they are all comparatively straightforward three-movement classical sonatas, such a comment is deceptive for Haydn consistently has something individual to contribute. *No. 44 in F*, supposedly influenced by C. P. E. Bach, has a somewhat quirky first movement and a characteristically imaginative final Minuet which goes unexpectedly into the minor and has much of the format of a theme and variations. The last work of the set in B minor opens with perhaps the most striking idea of all and, after the gracious central Minuet, ends in a flurry of precocious virtuosity, with Jandó clearly in his element. He shows himself a complete master of this repertoire, and the recording, crisp and clean but not too dry, is first class.

Piano sonatas Nos. 48 in C, Hob XVI/35; 49 in C sharp min., Hob XVI/36; 50 in D, Hob XVI/37; 51 in E flat, Hob XVI/38; 52 in G, Hob XVI/39.
(M) ** Ph. 442 659-2 [id.]. Ingrid Haebler (fortepiano).

Ingrid Haebler's clean, crisp articulation and bold, somewhat unbending approach seek to project a very classical view of Haydn. Her opening *C major* (Hob XVI/35) has a rhythmic preciseness (with a momentary hint of Dresden china) to remind one a little of Mozart's most famous sonata in the same key, but the opening of the *C sharp minor* is appropriately stronger and darker, and the *Largo e sostenuto* of the *D major* is made to seem quite portentous. She finds a simple lyricism in the *E flat Sonata*, although the closing *Minuet* is again bold and firm. It will be seen that these performances have plenty of character though they are rather unsmiling. The recording is excellent and the fortepiano timbre has body and unexaggerated colour.

Piano sonatas Nos. 53 in E min., Hob XVI/34; 54 in G, Hob XVI/40; 55 in B flat, Hob XVI/41; 56 in D, Hob XVI/42; 58 in C, Hob XVI/48; Variations in F min. (Sonata, un piccolo divertimento), Hob XVII/6.
(BB) *** Naxos Dig. 8.550845 [id.]. Jenö Jandó (piano).

These are distinctly appealing performances of the three *Sonatas*, Hob XVI/40–42, dedicated to Princess Marie Esterházy, who had married the grandson of Haydn's princely patron. They are each in two movements, and in the case of the *G major* the first is marked *Allegretto e innocente*, an obvious tribute to feminine charm. But all three are fine works and not as simple as they at first appear. Jandó also gives a splendid account of the more ambitious three-movement *Sonata in E minor*, Hob XVI/34. He is a true Haydn player and this (Volume III of his projected series) is in every way recommendable, particularly as the recording is so vivid and clean: just right for the repertoire.

Piano sonatas Nos. 56 in D, Hob XVI/42; 58 in C; 59 in E flat; 60 in C; 61 in D; 62 in E flat, Hob XVI/48–52.
(M) *(**) Sony Dig. SM2K 52623 [S2K 52623]. Glenn Gould.

Gould's clean, classical style in Haydn is often refreshing, but after a while the squeaky-clean articulation, although quite remarkably crisp, becomes a little wearing and the ear craves a less staccato, less percussive approach to allegros. This is not a fortepiano imitation but a pianoforte played with the most sparing sonority. Gould undoubtedly makes a sensitively expressive response to slow movements, but an air of eccentricity remains in the overall shaping of phrases. The digital recording is clear, to match the playing.

Piano sonatas Nos. 59 in E flat; 60 in C; 61 in D; 62 in E flat, Hob XVI/49–52.
(BB) *** Naxos Dig. 8.550657 [id.]. Jenö Jandó.

Jenö Jandó here shows himself as strong and sympathetic in Haydn as in Beethoven. Although the performances are straighter, Nos. 60 and 62 compare remarkably favourably with Pletnev's masterly accounts. Without allowing himself stylistic idiosyncrasies, Jandó shows himself a thoughtfully imaginative player as well as a bold one, and the finale of the great *E flat Sonata* has splendid, unforced bravura. The recording, made in the Unitarian Church, Budapest, provides an attractive ambience without an excess of ecclesiastical resonance.

VOCAL MUSIC

The Creation (*Die Schöpfung;* in German).
(M) *** DG 449 761-2 (2) [id.]. Janowitz, Ludwig, Wunderlich, Krenn, Fischer-Dieskau, Berry, V. Singverein, BPO, Karajan.
(B) *** DG Double 453 031-2 [(M) id. import]. Blegen, Popp, Moser, Ollman, Moll, Bav. R. Ch. & SO, Bernstein.
(M) **(*) DG (IMS) Dig. 445 584-2 (2) [427 629-2]. Battle, Winbergh, Moll, Stockholm R. Ch. and Chamber Ch., BPO, Levine.
(B) **(*) EMI forte (SIS) CZS5 69343-2 (2) [CDFB 69343]. Donath, Tear, Van Dam, Philh. Ch. & O, Frühbeck de Burgos.

(i) *The Creation (Die Schöpfung):* complete (in German); (ii) *Salve regina*.

(B) *** Double Decca 443 027-2 (2) [id.]. (i) Lucia Popp, Werner Hollweg, Kurt Moll, Helena Döse, Benjamin Luxon, Brighton Festival Ch., RPO, Dorati; (ii) Arleen Augér, Alfreda Hodgson, Anthony Rolfe Johnson, Gwynne Howell, L. Chamber Ch., Argo CO, László Heltay.

Among versions of *The Creation* sung in German, Karajan's 1969 set remains unsurpassed and, now reissued as one of DG's 'Originals' at mid-price, is a clear first choice despite two small cuts (in Nos. 30 and 32). The combination of the Berlin Philharmonic at its most intense and the great Viennese choir makes for a performance that is not only polished but warm and dramatically strong too. The soloists are an extraordinarily fine team, more consistent in quality than those on almost any rival version.

Dorati, as one would expect, directs a lively and well-sprung account. The very opening is magnetic and its imaginative touches and joyfulness of spirit more than compensate for any minor lapses in crispness of ensemble. The soloists are a splendid team. The chorus is as gutsy as you like in *Die Himmel erzählen*, with the soloists nicely balanced. While Karajan is not superseded, Dorati's enjoyably spontaneous 1976 account is certainly well worth considering, especially as it is offered for the cost of a single premium-priced CD. The set opens gloriously with Heltay's lovely 1979 recording of the *Salve regina*, an early work dating from 1771, comparable in its depth of feeling with his finest vocal music. The recording is most realistic and the CD transfer of *The Creation* is strikingly vivid and immediate.

Bernstein's DG version, recorded at a live performance in Munich, uses a relatively large chorus, encouraging him to adopt rather slow speeds at times. What matters is the joy conveyed in the story-telling, with the finely disciplined chorus and orchestra producing incandescent tone, blazing away in the big set-numbers, and the performance is compulsive from the very opening bars. Five soloists are used instead of three, with the parts of Adam and Eve sung by nicely contrasted singers, confirming this as an unusually persuasive version, well recorded in atmospheric sound. This appears not to be available in the USA but is preferable to his earlier, New York version (see below).

Though James Levine with his weighty forces is occasionally heavy-handed over both dynamics and rhythm, lacking rather in elegance, he conveys the joy of inspiration in this work with characteristic boldness. He is helped not just by the highly polished playing of the orchestra but by characterful singing from all three soloists and fresh, finely disciplined choral singing. The recording, made not in the Philharmonie but in the Jesus-Christus Kirche, is weighty and satisfyingly full, with ample bloom.

Rafael Frühbeck de Burgos directs a genial performance, recorded with richness and immediacy. The soloists are all excellent and, though Helen Donath has a hint of flutter in her voice, she is wonderfully agile in ornamentation, as in the bird-like quality she gives to the aria, *On mighty pens*. The chorus might gain from a more forward balance but their singing is impressive. An enjoyable set.

(i) *The Creation (Die Schöpfung):* oratorio (complete; in German); (ii) *Mass No. 6 in G (Missa Sancti Nicholai), Hob XXII/6;* (iii) *Mass No. 7 in B flat: Missa brevis Sancti Joannis de Deo (Little organ mass), Hob XXII/7*.

(B) *(*) Ph. Duo 446 175-2 (2) [id.]. (i) Giebel, Kmentt, Frick, Bav. R. Ch. & O, Jochum; (ii) Resch, Buchbauer, Ch. Viennensis; (iii) Boehm (organ); (ii–iii) Soloists from V. Boys' Ch.; V. Boys' Ch., Wiener Dom-Orchester; cond. (ii) Furthmoser; (iii) Grossman.

Jochum, almost invariably inspired in romantic music, and certainly so in Bruckner, is less consistent in the music of the classical period, and here he fails to bring out either Haydn's sharp-edged drama or sparkling humour. It is a pity, too, that Gottlob Frick, normally the most consistently interesting of German basses, is well below form. The comparative dullness of the performance is not cancelled out by the remastering of the recording, which has enhanced the vividness of the sound compared with the original LPs. Two early Masses are used to frame the main work, both given respectable performances, with Grossman's account of the *Little Organ Mass* rather the more characterful (although his treble soloist from the Vienna Boys' Choir, who sings sweetly enough, is none too secure in pitch).

The Creation: highlights.

(B) *** DG Classikon 439 454-2 [(M) id. import] (from above recording; cond. Karajan).

(B) ** HM/BMG Baroque Esprit 05472 77465-2 [id.]. Augér, Sima, Schreier, Berry, Hermann, V. Arnold Schönberg Ch., Coll. Aur., Kuhn.

Anyone whose budget will not stretch to a complete version of Haydn's masterpiece will find that this 70-minute bargain Classikon highlights disc includes the key solos and choruses.

Kuhn's version was recorded live in 1982. Using the excellent Collegium Aureum, it is a performance on an intimate scale with original instruments. Speeds are often brisk and textures clear, but rhythms are sometimes stiff or unrelenting. Kuhn has a fortepiano in the recitatives. Outstanding among the soloists is the soprano in the first two parts, Arleen Augér (as Gabriel); however, although this selection spans nearly 80 minutes, very little of her contribution is included. Peter Schrier makes an excellent Uriel, with Walter

Berry a characterful bass as Raphael. The recording is very good, but Karajan's DG selection is a far preferable choice.

(i) *The Creation;* (ii) *Mass No. 14 in B flat (Harmoniemesse), Hob XXII/14.*

(M) ** Sony SM2K 47560 (2) [S2K 47560]. (i) Raskin, Young, Reardon, Camerata Singers: (ii) Blegen, Von Stade, Riegel, Estes, Westminster Ch.; NYPO, Bernstein.

Bernstein's first recording of *The Creation* was made in the Avery Fisher Hall in 1966. It is a fine, spontaneous account with bouncy choruses and an excellent team of soloists. The sound is not ideally refined in the upper range but it is reasonably spacious, and the warmth and vigour of the performance carry the day. The *Harmoniemesse* was done in the Manhattan Center in 1973 and the recording is obviously more modern and rather more spacious, though closely balanced. The performance has characteristic energy and pace. Good value, though Bernstein's digital DG set of *The Creation* is preferable on almost all counts, including recording quality (see above).

Masses

Masses Nos. (i–iii) *1 in F (Missa brevis), Hob XXII/1;* (i; iii–vi) *1a in G (Rorate coeli desuper), Hob XXII/3; 3 in C: Missa Cellensis in honorem Beatissimae Virginis Mariae (Missa Santae Caecilae), Hob XXII/5;* (i; iii; v–viii) *4 in E flat: Missa in honorem Beatissimae Virginis Mariae (Great organ Mass), Hob XXII/4;* (i; iii; vi; ix; x) *6 in G (Missa Sancti Nicolai), Hob XXII/6;* (xi–xv) *7 in B flat: Missa brevis Sancti Joannis de Deo (Little organ Mass);* (xi; xiii–xviii) *8 in C: Mariazeller Messe, Hob XXII/8;* (xiii–xvii; xix; xx) *9 in B flat: Missa Sancti Bernardi de Offida (Heligmesse), Hob XXII/10;* (ix; xiii–xv; xix; xxi; xxii) *10 in C: Missa in tempore belli (Paukenmesse), Hob XXII/9;* (xvi; xxiii–xxvi) *11 in D min.: Missa in augustiis (Nelson Mass), Hob XXII/11;* (xiii–xv; xxv; xxvii–xxviii) *12 in B flat: Theresienmesse, Hob XXII/12;* (xiii–xvii; xix; xxix) *13 in B flat: Schöpfungmesse (Creation Mass), Hob XXII/13;* (xiii–xvi; xxvii; xxx) *14 in B flat (Harmoniemesse), Hob XXII/14.*

(B) *** Decca 448 518-2 (7) [id.]. (i) Nelson; (ii) Kirkby; (iii) Christ Church Cathedral Ch., AAM, Preston; (iv) Cable; (v) Hill; (vi) Thomas; (vii) Watkinson; (viii); Hogwood (organ); (ix) Minty; (x) Covey-Crump; (xi) Jennifer Smith; (xii) Scott (organ); (xiii) St John's College, Cambridge, Ch.; (xiv) ASMF; (xv) George Guest; (xvi) Watts; (xvii) Tear; (xviii) Luxon; (xix) Cantelo; (xx) McDaniel; (xxi) Partridge; (xxii) Keyte; (xxiii) Stahlman; (xxiv) Wilfred Brown; (xxv) Krause; (xxvi) King's College, Cambridge, Ch., LSO, Willcocks; (xxvii) Spoorenberg; (xxviii) Greevy; Mitchinson; (xxix) Forbes Robinson; (xxx) Young, Rouleau.

Decca's survey of the complete Masses of Haydn, which appeared originally on the Argo and Oiseau-Lyre labels, omits only the newly discovered fragmentary *Missa Sunt bona mixta malis*, Hob XXII/2, of 1768 (available on Sony SK 53368). Overall this achievement stands alongside Dorati's complete recording of the symphonies (and the Beaux Arts' *Piano trios*) as one of the landmarks of the gramophone during the analogue LP era for, until the original LPs appeared, most of this music was virtually unknown by the ordinary music-lover.

Starting in 1962 with Sir David Willcocks's King's version of the *Nelson Mass*, the production team then moved down the road to St John's for the five remaining magnificent Mass settings which Haydn wrote between 1796 and 1802 for his patron, Prince Esterházy, after his return from London. With changing soloists, of generally consistent quality, George Guest directed a series of performances notable for their fresh directness and vigour, with his St John's Choir showing itself a ready match for the more famous choir at King's College and the sound even more vivid. The recordings were made between 1965 and 1969, with the *Little organ Mass* and *Mariazellermesse* following in 1977. The project was completed over the next two years with the early Masses. But the 'authentic' era had arrived and the orchestra changed from the Academy of St Martin-in-the-Fields to the Academy of Ancient Music. Simon Preston took over, and he directed his Christ Church Cathedral Choir with a comparable freshness and spontaneity to that established at St John's. The engineering team excelled themselves throughout, to produce a well-balanced and spacious yet clearly detailed sound, boldly projected against a nicely resonant acoustic. As with the companion Decca box of the symphonies, H. C. Robbins Landon has provided the notes with his usual spirited scholarship.

Masses Nos. (i) *1 in F (Missa brevis), Hob XXII/1;* (ii) *3 in C: Missa Cellensis in honorem Beatissimae Virginis Mariae (Missa Sanctae Caecilia), Hob XXII/5;* (iii) *4 in E flat: Missa in honorem Beatissimae Virginis Mariae (Great organ mass), Hob XXII/4;* (iv) *6 in G (Missa Sanctae Nicolai), Hob XXII/6.*

(B) *** O-L Double 455 712-2 (2) [id.]. (i) Emma Kirkby; (i–iv) Judith Nelson; (ii) Margaret Cable; (ii–iii) Martyn Hill, (ii–iv) David Thomas; (iii) Carolyn Watkinson; (iv) Shirley Minty, Rogers Covey-Crump; Christ Church, Oxford, Cathedral Ch., AAM, Simon Preston.

Haydn wrote the early *Missa brevis* when he was seventeen. The setting is engagingly unpretentious, some of its sections last for under two minutes and only the *Credo* takes slightly more than three and a half. The two soprano soloists, Judith Nelson and Emma Kirkby, match their voices admirably and the effect is delightful. By contrast the *Missa Cellensis* (which is split between the two discs, after the *Gloria*), at 68 minutes, is Haydn's longest setting of the liturgy. Preston directs an excellent performance with fine contributions from choir and soloists, set against a warm acoustic. In the early *E flat Mass* Haydn followed the rococo conventions of his time, generally adopting a style featuring Italianate melody which to modern ears inevitably sounds operatic. The *Missa Sanctae Nicolai* has a comparable freshness of inspiration and the performance is first rate in every way, even finer than that of the earlier *Great organ mass*, beautifully sung, with spontaneity in every bar and a highly characterized accompaniment. Both are admirably recorded, and the CD transfers are first class.

Masses Nos. (i) *3 in C (Missa Cellensis): Missa Sanctae Caeciliae, Hob XXII/5;* (ii) *7 in B flat (Little organ mass): Missa Sancti Joannis de Deo, Hob XXII/7;* (iii) *10 in C (Paukenmesse): Missa in tempore belli, Hob XXII/9.*

(B) ** DG Double 453 127-2 (2). (i) Maria Stader, Marga Höffgen, Richard Holm, Josef Greindl, Bav. R. Ch. and O, Jochum; (ii) Ursula Buckel, Regensburg Cathedral Ch., T. Schrems; (iii) Elsie Morison, Marjorie Thomas, Peter Witsch, Karl Christian Kohn, Bav. R. Ch. and O, Kubelik.

Jochum's *St Cecilia Mass* is very early stereo (1958), but the other two recordings here date from the beginning of the 1960s. Jochum clearly knows what he wants, and he gets it from his entire assembly, conveying to the listener a vivid impression of a concert, as opposed to a church performance. Among the soloists Maria Stader stands out. There are a few moments of strain but generally her singing is very fine by any standard. Richard Holm, the tenor, is very nearly a match for her, and his sense of phrasing and subtlety of timbre are impressive. Greindl and Höffgen are good in their way, but less well suited to Haydn's melodic vein in this particular work. The Kubelik version of the *Mass in time of war* is not as fine as that under Guest, but the mixed English and German team of soloists works well, and Kubelik's dramatic yet lyrical approach brings direct and forthright music-making, while not missing the colour and atmosphere in which this score abounds. The spacious recording is of good quality. In the *Little organ Mass* Ursula Buckel, on whom much depends, sings pleasingly and eloquently. The use of a prominent obbligato part for the organ is not typical of eighteenth-century liturgical music but, as played here by Franz Lehandorfer, it produces a charming effect.

Masses Nos. (i) *7 in B flat (Little organ mass): Missa brevis Sancti Joannis de Deo, Hob XXII/7;* (ii) *8 in C (Mariazellermesse): Missa Cellensis, Hob XXII/8;* (iii) *Organ concerto No. 1 in C, Hob XVIII/1.*

(M) *** Decca 430 160-2. (i) J. Smith; Scott; (ii) J. Smith, Watts, Tear, Luxon; (i; ii) St John's College, Cambridge, Ch., Guest; (i–iii) ASMF; (iii) Preston, Marriner.

With excellent singing and fine orchestral playing, this is a very desirable issue in the splendid Guest series. The CD transfers are admirably fresh and well focused, and for a bonus we are given Simon Preston's persuasive account of an early organ concerto. Preston's vivid registration and Marriner's spirited accompaniment ensure the listener's pleasure.

Masses Nos. (i) *7 in B flat (Little organ mass): Missa brevis Sancti Joannis de Deo;* (ii) *10 in C (Paukenmesse): Missa in tempore belli;* (iii) *11 in D min. (Nelson);* (iv) *14 in B flat (Harmoniemesse).*

(B) *** Decca Double 455 020-2 (2) [id.]. (i) Jennifer Smith, John Scott (organ); (ii) April Cantelo, Helen Watts, Robert Tear, Barry McDaniel; (iii) Sylvia Stahlman, Watts, Wilfred Brown, Tom Krause; (iv) Erna Spoorenberg, Watts, Alexander Young, Joseph Rouleau. (i–ii; iv) St John's College, Cambridge, Ch., ASMF, George Guest; (iii) King's College Ch., LSO, Sir David Willcocks.

Three major Masses and one shorter work are combined here to make a very tempting Decca Double for those not wanting the complete set listed above.

Masses Nos. (i) *7 in B flat: Missa brevis Sancti Joannis de Deo (Little organ mass), Hob XXII/7;* (ii) *9 in B flat (Heiligmesse): Missa Sancti Bernardi von Offida, XXII/10;* (iii) *11 in D min. (Nelson); Missa in angustiis, Hob XXII/11;* (ii) *12 in B flat (Theresienmesse), Hob XXII/12.*

(B) ** EMI forte Dig. CZS5 68592-2 (2) [CDFB 68592]. (i) Hendricks, Murray, Blochwitz, Hölle; (ii) Vaness, Soffel, Lewis, Salomaa; (iii) Marshall, Watkinson, Lewis, Holl; Leipzig R. Ch., Dresden State O, Marriner.

Although digitally recorded and presented here economically on an EMI forte double, these Marriner performances cannot compare with George Guest's series on Decca. In the *Missa brevis* Marriner favours brisk speeds, defying the weight of his forces, which is increased by the bass-heavy Dresden recording. Though the Leipzig Radio Chorus is sometimes stressed, as are the soloists, this is an enjoyably vigorous reading. The *Heiligmesse* and the *Theresienmesse* were recorded together and bring more vigorous and responsive singing from the Leipzig Chorus. Here these wonderfully disciplined singers are on top form and rise superbly to Marriner's often challengingly fast speeds; their ensemble in slow sections is sweeter than that of the soloists or even that of the orchestra. The solo singers are close-balanced so that the vibrato of the two women is exaggerated and the full quartet makes an ill-matched ensemble. Heard like this, these are voices not well suited to Haydn, and the reverberation in the recordings inflates what by latterday standards is too hefty an orchestral sound. The *Nelson mass* brings a perfectly acceptable performance, with good soloists and the Leipzig Choir still on excellent form. The ample Dresden acoustic does not prevent internal clarity, and this account brings moments which match the companion Masses in vigour; yet overall the effect is essentially cultured, weighty and just a shade bland.

Masses Nos. 9 in B flat (Heiligmesse); 11 in D min. (Nelson); 12 in B flat (Theresienmesse).

(M) ** EMI Dig. CMS5 66332-2 (2). Vaness, Soffel, Keith Lewis, Salomaa, Marshall, Watkinson, Holl, Leipzig R. Ch., Dresden State O, Marriner – MOZART: *Ave verum corpus; Vesperae solennes de confessore.* *(*)

Marriner's is a perfectly acceptable performance of the *Nelson Mass*, with good soloists and fine singing from the Leipzig Radio Choir. The Dresden acoustic is fairly ample, but it does not prevent internal clarity. There are moments of considerable vigour, but overall the effect is essentially cultured, weighty and just a shade bland. In the *Heiligmesse* and *Theresienmesse* there is also much to commend, but again it is the vigorous and responsive singing of the Leipzig Radio Choir that stands out. These wonderfully disciplined singers rise superbly to Marriner's often challengingly fast speeds, and their ensemble in slow sections is sweeter than that of the soloists – or even of the orchestra. Who but Haydn could write such joyful settings of *Dona nobis pacem*? Happily, with their irresistible message of optimism these are both works which need above all the sort of vigour that Marriner's conducting inspires. Yet the solo singers are balanced close so that the vibrato of the two women is exaggerated, and the full quartet makes an ill-matched ensemble. Heard like this, these are voices not well suited to Haydn, and the reverberation in the recording inflates what by latter-day standards is too hefty an orchestral sound.

Mass No. 10 in C (Paukenmesse): Missa in tempore belli, Hob XXII/9.

(M) *** Decca 430 157-2. Cantelo, Watts, Tear, McDaniel, St John's College, Cambridge, Ch., ASMF, Guest – MOZART: *Vesperae sollennes.* ***

Guest provides a clean, brightly recorded account with good soloists. The Argo performance sounds very fresh in its remastered format.

Mass No. 11 in D min. (Nelson): Missa in angustiis.

(M) *** Decca 421 146-2 [id.]. Stahlman, Watts, Wilfred Brown, Krause, King's College, Cambridge, Ch., LSO, Willcocks – VIVALDI: *Gloria.* ***

(i) *Mass No. 11 in D min. (Nelson): Missa in augustiis, Hob XXII/11;* (ii) *Arianna a Naxos* (orchestral version), *Hob XXVIb/2; Scena di Berenice (Berenice che fai?), Hob XXIVa/10.*

(M) *** Decca Eclipse Dig. 448 983-2; *448 983-4* [(M) id. import]. (i) Bonney, Howells, Rolfe Johnson, Roberts, L. Symphony Ch., Hickox; (ii) Arleen Augér, Handel & Haydn Society, Hogwood.

The CD of the famous Willcocks account of the *Nelson Mass* (*Missa in angustiis*: 'Mass in times of War') is admirably full-bodied and vivid; those not wanting to stretch to Pinnock's full-priced digital CD will find this a satisfactory alternative with its very generous Vivaldi coupling.

Hickox conducts a lively, well-sung reading of the most celebrated of Haydn's late Masses, most impressive in the vigorous, outward-going music which – with Haydn – makes up the greater part of the service; here the choral singing is little short of glorious. In serene moments the choral sound is slightly recessed, with inner parts less well defined than they might be. The soloists are very good, and Barbara Bonney's purity of line is impressive, although tonally she is a little thin. While in some ways the Willcocks version of 20 years earlier is even finer, in the work's more resplendent moments the London Symphony's choral focus is given greater impact by the more modern digital sound.

What makes the Eclipse reissue almost indispensable is the inclusion of Haydn's two major solo cantatas (a full half-hour of wonderful music) which he wrote for his two London visits in the 1790s. The first was written with fortepiano accompaniment (which Haydn himself played in London), and the effective string arrangement had been made by an anonymous hand. Arleen Augér was never more impressive in the recording studio than here. She is superbly dramatic in the cantata which tells of Ariadne abandoned by Theseus on Naxos, and – in melting voice – infinitely touching in the *Scena di Berenice*. Hogwood accompanies most sympathetically and the recording is perfectly balanced. Not to be missed.

Mass No. 14 in B flat (Harmoniemesse), Hob XXII/14.

(M) *** Decca 430 162-2. Spoorenberg, Watts, Young, Rouleau, St John's College, Cambridge, Ch., Guest – MOZART: *Vesperae de Dominica.* ***

Haydn was over seventy when he started writing this Mass, but his freshness and originality are as striking as in any of the earlier works. The fine performance caps the others in this outstanding series. The quartet of soloists is strong, with Helen Watts in particular singing magnificently. The brilliant and well-balanced 1966 recording has been transferred splendidly to CD, which now offers a substantial bonus in the Mozart *Vespers*, recorded at St John's over a decade later.

The Seasons (*Die Jahreszeiten;* complete; in German).

(B) *** Ph. Dig. 438 715-2 (2) [id.]. Edith Mathis, Siegfried Jerusalem, Dietrich Fischer-Dieskau, Ch. & ASMF, Marriner.

(M) *** DG 457 713-2 (2) [id.]. Janowitz, Schreier, Talvela, V. Singverein, VSO, Karl Boehm.

(B) *** Decca Double 448 101-2 (2) [id.]. Cotrubas, Krenn, Sotin, Brighton Festival Ch., RPO, Dorati.

(M) **(*) EMI CMS7 69224-2 (2). Janowitz, Hollweg, Berry, Ch. of German Op., BPO, Karajan.

Sir Neville Marriner directs a superbly joyful performance of Haydn's last oratorio, effervescent with the optimism of old age. Edith Mathis and Dietrich Fischer-Dieskau are as stylish and characterful as one would expect, pointing the words as narrative. The tenor too is magnificent: Siegfried Jerusalem is both heroic of timbre and yet delicate enough for Haydn's most elegant and genial passages. The chorus and orchestra, of authentic size, add to the freshness. The recording, made in St John's, Smith Square, is warmly reverberant without losing detail. The CD virtually transforms the sound, with added definition for both chorus and soloists, with cues for every individual item, and a total playing time of nearly two hours and a quarter. Highly recommended – a remarkable bargain by any standards.

Boehm's performance enters totally into the spirit of the music and is fully worthy of its reissue as one of DG's 'Originals'. The soloists are excellent and characterize the music fully; the chorus sing enthusiastically and are well recorded. But it is Boehm's set. He secures fine orchestral playing throughout, an excellent overall musical balance and real spontaneity in music that needs this above all else. The CD transfer of the 1967 recording is admirably managed; the sound overall is warmly expansive, the chorus have plenty of body, if not the sharpest focus, and there is an excellent sense of presence.

Dorati brings to the work an innocent dedication, at times pointing to the folk-like inspiration, which is most compelling. This is not as polished an account as Boehm's in the same price-range but, with excellent solo singing and bright chorus work, is enjoyable in its own right. The choruses of peasants in Part 3, for instance, are boisterously robust. Textually there is an important difference in that Dorati has returned to the original version and restored the cuts in the introductions to *Autumn* and *Winter*, the latter with some wonderfully adventurous harmonies. The performance as a whole is highly animated. With Dorati, this is above all a happy work, a point made all the more telling by the immediacy of the new transfer. This is all the more welcome at Double Decca price and competes strongly with the Boehm set now at mid-price.

Karajan's 1973 recording of *The Seasons* offers a fine, polished performance which is often very dramatic too. The characterization is strong, and in Karajan's hands the exciting Hunting chorus of Autumn (*Hört! Hört! Hört das laute Getön*) with its lusty horns anticipates *Der Freischütz*. The remastered sound is drier than the original but is vividly wide in dynamic range. Choruses are still a little opaque, but the soloists are all caught well and are on good form; and the overall balance is satisfactory. Those drawn to Karajan might try the fairly generous (53 minutes) highlights CD (CDM7 69010-2).

Te Deum in C, Hob XXIIIc/2.

(BB) *** RCA Navigator 74321 29238-2 [(M) 6535-2-RG]. V. Boys' Ch., Ch. Viennensis, VCO, Gillesberger – MOZART: *Requiem mass.* ***

A fine, vigorous account of the *Te Deum* by these Viennese forces, very vividly recorded, coupled to a not inconsiderable account of Mozart's *Requiem*. At super-bargain price it makes excellent value.

OPERA

L'infedeltà delusa (complete).

(M) **(*) HM/BMG 05472 77316-2 (2) [id.]. Argenta, Lootens, Prégardien, M. Schäfer, Varcoe, La Petite Bande, Sigiswald Kuijken.

L'infedeltà delusa may not be dramatically the most imaginative of stage works, but by the standards of the time it is a compact piece, punctuated by some sharply noteworthy ideas. The opera brings many memorable numbers, such as a laughing song for Nencio and a song of ailments for the spirited and resourceful heroine, Vespina. The plot of the opera is unusual for the time in giving the role of the heavy father to the tenor (well taken on RCA by Christoph Prégardien), reflecting the fact that it was expressly designed for Karl Friberth, literary adviser to Prince Esterházy as well as a singer. This version on period instruments nicely captures the flavour of a semi-domestic performance in the prince's country palace. Both the RCA sopranos, Nancy Argenta and Lena Lootens, are agile and precise, if a little edgy. Both tenors, Markus Schäfer as well as Prégardien, are stressed by the range demanded but, like the bass, Stephen Varcoe, they have clean voices, suitable for Haydn on a small scale. The scale of the whole work, much shorter than was common in the late eighteenth century, makes it the more apt for revival today. *L'infedeltà delusa* may be no *Così fan tutte* but this is a most enjoyable set, worth considering at mid-price.

Heath, Dave (born 1956)

The Frontier.

(M) *** Virgin/EMI CUV5 61121-2 [id.]. LCO, Warren-Green – ADAMS: *Shaker loops* *** ❀; GLASS: *Company* etc. ***; REICH: *8 Lines.* ***

Most minimalist composers are American and, although Dave Heath was born in Manchester, the influences on his music are transatlantic. In *The Frontier* the incisive rhythmic astringency is tempered by an attractive, winding lyrical theme which finally asserts itself just before the spiky close. The work was written for members of the LCO, and their performance, full of vitality and feeling, is admirably recorded.

Hely-Hutchinson, Victor (1901–47)

Carol Symphony.

(M) ** EMI CDM7 64131-2. Guildford Cathedral Ch., Pro Arte O, Barry Rose – QUILTER: *Children's overture;* VAUGHAN WILLIAMS: *Fantasia on Christmas carols.* **

Hely-Hutchinson's *Carol Symphony* dates from the late 1920s. It was essentially a happy idea to construct a work of this kind, but the snag is that carols, if they are good ones, don't admit improvement by 'symphonic' treatment. All you can do with them is to alter their orchestral dress, their harmony (which is seldom an improvement) or – as Constant Lambert observed about the use of folksongs – play them again, louder. Hely-Hutchinson does all these things. His first movement could do with a little judicious pruning, the Scherzo is quite effective and in the finale he gathers all the threads together and ends with a triumphal presentation of *O come, all ye faithful.* But it is the *Andante* which remains in the memory with its deliciously imaginative gossamer texture against which the solo harp embroiders *Nowell.* The performance here is lively and sensitive if not distinctive, but the close-miked recording is curiously dry and unexpansive, bearing in mind that the 1966 venue was Guildford Cathedral.

Heming, Michael (1920–42)

Threnody for a soldier killed in action.

(M) (***) EMI mono CDM5 66053-2 [id.]. Hallé O, Barbirolli – BRITTEN: *Violin concerto* (**); RUBBRA: *Symphony No. 5* etc. (***)

Michael Heming was a kind of Second World War Butterworth, though his gifts did not have time to flower into the fullest blossom. His father, the baritone Percy Heming, and Barbirolli were close friends and, when Michael was killed at El Alamein, Anthony Collins concocted (to use Michael Kennedy's word) the *Threnody for a soldier killed in action* from sketches that the young man had made. Barbirolli and the Hallé Orchestra recorded it in 1945 but it never made inroads into the repertory and, as far as we know, has never been reissued until now. A moving piece in the English pastoral tradition and a welcome fill-up to this interesting disc.

Henze, Hans Werner (born 1926)

The DG Henze Collection

(M) *** DG stereo/mono 449 860-2 (14). Various artists.

To mark the occasion of Hans Werner Henze's seventieth birthday, DG have issued (in the UK, but apparently not in the USA) a handsomely presented 14-CD set of the repertoire that the composer himself recorded in the heyday of his relationship with the company, plus a handful of other items. DG are wise to make the discs available separately as there are few who would necessarily want or could afford the whole package, even though it is very competitive at mid-price. It is important to note that none of the music Henze has composed in his fifties and sixties is represented in the collection. The most recent work is *Tristan*, a set of preludes for piano, orchestra and electronic tapes, which comes from the mid-1970s. The *Seventh Symphony* is available at full price on EMI (CDC7 54762-2), powerfully presented by Rattle and the CBSO, and presumably the *Eighth* will soon find its way on to disc.

For most collectors the best starting-point, perhaps, would be the symphonies, which come on a two-CD set. Henze recorded the first five with the Berlin Philharmonic in the mid-1960s and followed with the *Sixth*, written in 1968, a few years later. For RL the *Third* and *Fourth* remain the most haunting of the set, with the latter casting a particularly powerful spell. It is the product of a refined musical imagination and its expressionist anguish is punctuated by moments of an all-pervasive melancholy which must spring from a deep personal experience. The *First Symphony* is also a delight, springing as it does from an Appolonian neo-classicism reminiscent of Stravinsky and the pale, luminous textures of Frank Martin. The *First Violin concerto* (1947), recorded here with Schneiderhan as soloist, is one of the most rewarding of Henze's early scores, even if his debt to Hindemith is not fully discharged.

The other CDs which would make an excellent introduction to the set include the beautiful *Double Concerto for oboe and harp* (albeit not with Henze himself conducting), played by its dedicatees, Heinz and Ursula Holliger, coupled with one of his most haunting and affecting scores, the *Fantasia for strings*. This was refashioned from a score Henze composed for a film version of Musil's *Der junge Törless* in which, incidentally, they were played on viols. Likewise the beautiful *Five Neapolitan songs* with the young Fischer-Dieskau or the *Cantata della fiaba estrema*, expertly sung by Edda Moser, are wonderful pieces. If you possess the LP originals you will find the transfers, generally speaking, have an admirable clarity, but this is achieved at a certain cost: the LPs have greater openness and depth, with greater space round the aural image and a more subtle placing of instrumental detail.

(i) *2 Ballet variations;* (ii) *Piano concerto No. 2;* (iii) *Tristan* (preludes for piano, tapes and orchestra); (iv) *3 Tientos for guitar*.

(M) **(*) DG mono/stereo 449 866-2 (2). (i) RIAS SO, Ferenc Fricsay; (ii) Christoph Eschenbach, LPO; (iii) Homero Francesch, Cologne RSO; (ii; iii) cond. composer; (iv) Siegfried Behrend.

The *Piano concerto* has a deep and brooding lyricism, alternating with considerable violence and tension; but repeated hearing uncovers a vision of great originality and poetry. Eschenbach, for whom the concerto was written in 1967, is the magnificent soloist. The work, almost 50 minutes in length, was inspired by the words of Shakespeare's sonnet: 'The expense of spirit in a waste of shame is lust in action . . . None knows well to shun the heaven that leads men to this hell.' It is an interesting, often moving work, full of a sad eloquence that bursts into occasional bitter outcries of some violence. The beauty of the recording captures all the refinement and delicacy of Henze's textures. The brief *Ballet variations* come from a suite of six written early in the composer's career (1949) as music for a ballet without a narrative, composed while Henze was strongly under the influence of the Stravinsky of the *Danses concertantes*. The three *Tientos* for guitar were originally interludes in *Kammermusik*, a vocal work of a decade later, and, though again brief, are very imaginatively conceived.

Tristan, the other extended work here, is an extraordinary montage which began life as a piano prelude. This the composer sketched in 1972 and he felt the writing had a kinship with Wagner's opera. Later, during a London visit, he had nightmares in which Wagner's hero appeared to inspire further musical associations, and what followed proved itself very much like a musical nightmare. First came an extraordinary mélange of extra-musical sounds, mixed together on tape in a studio in Putney, London, including throwing glass marbles at prepared piano strings and bombarding the strings of a double-bass with tennis balls. A distorted piano performance of Chopin's *Funeral march* was thrown in for good measure, plus a 'computer-analysis' of the first four bars of Wagner's opera. Henze composed the piano preludes and orchestral interludes to go with the taped episodes, and finally he decided to re-make the lunatic tape mélange to fit the composed music more accurately. The resulting work is a six-part structure lasting just over 43 minutes. It opens with a solo piano *Prologue* with woodwind interjections, a *Lament* follows, then the *Preludes* and *Variations*, which feature the orchestra and splice in a quotation from the opening of Brahms's *First Symphony*. Next comes *Tristan's folly*, which draws on the synthesized Chopin excerpts and more distorted Brahms. A bizarre sequence of what the composer calls 'Burlesque dance movements' comes next, ending with a scream of death, with the tape supposedly reproducing the scream of a famous Wagnerian soprano. The closing *Epilogue* leads to rather more distinct distillations of Wagner, a child's heartbeat, bells chiming and so on. It is difficult to take seriously, but it certainly represents a new experience.

(i) *Ode to the west wind* (for cello and orchestra); (ii) *Concerto for double-bass;* (iii) *Violin concerto No. 1.*

(M) *** DG 449 865-2. (i) Siegfried Palm; (ii) Gary Karr; (iii) Wolfgang Schneiderhan; (i; iii) Bav. RSO; (ii) ECO; all cond. composer.

The *Violin concerto* dates from the late 1940s and shows the influence of Hindemith still exerted at this time, while the *Ode to the west wind*, inspired by Shelley's poem, was written only a few years later, in 1953. Both works contain pages of some beauty, though the later piece employs a more fragmented and complex style than the predominantly serial *Concerto*. The *Violin concerto* is the more immediately appealing work and has an eloquent slow movement, but both pieces explore a fascinating world of sound; and the performances, apart from having the composer's authority to commend them, are expertly recorded. The *Double-bass concerto* was composed in 1966 for Gary Karr. It is not among the composer's most impressive pieces, though it fascinates by its resourceful treatment of an unpromising solo instrument. The performance is exemplary.

(i) *Double concerto for oboe, harp and strings. Fantasia for strings; Sonata for strings.*

(M) *** DG 449 864-2. Zurich Coll. Mus., Paul Sacher, with (i) Heinz and Ursula Holliger.

The language of the *Fantasia*, based on incidental music for a film, is more disciplined and diatonic than is often Henze's wont. It is a moving score with a vein of melancholy that is direct in utterance. The *Double concerto* was inspired by the astonishing artistry and virtuosity of Heinz Holliger on the oboe, who performs it here with his wife, Ursula, on the harp. Highly inventive and resourceful, this performance is authoritative and is given an exemplary recording.

Symphonies Nos. (i) *1–5;* (ii) *6.*

(M) *** DG 449 861-2 (2). (i) BPO; (ii) LSO; cond. composer.

These works are the product of a highly sophisticated imagination with a most refined and sensitive awareness of atmosphere and feeling for sonority. There is much nourishment and stimulus to be found here. The *First*, with its cool, Stravinskian slow movement, is a remarkable achievement for a 21-year-old, though we hear it in a revision Henze made early in 1963. There is a dance-like feel to the *Third* (1950), written while Henze was attached to the Wiesbaden Ballet. The *Fourth* was originally intended for the opera *König Hirsch* and was meant to connote 'an evocation of the living, breathing forest and the passing of the seasons'. It is among the most concentrated and atmospheric of his works; there is at times an overwhelming sense of melancholy and a strongly Mediterranean atmosphere to its invention. The *Fifth* embraces the most violent angularity, with passages of exquisite poignancy and tranquillity. It comes from the period of *The Elegy for young lovers* and quotes from one of its arias; the language is strongly post-expressionist. One wonders, however, what its first audience, 'soldiers of the Cuban revolutionary army, sons of workers and students', must have made of the *Sixth Symphony*, composed while Henze was living in Havana! The performances are brilliant and the vivid recordings do not sound their age, those of the first five symphonies being over 35 years old.

VOCAL MUSIC

(i) *Being beauteous;* (ii) *Five Neapolitan songs;* (iii) *Versuch über Schweine (Essay on pigs);* (iv) *Whispers from heavenly death.*

(M) *** DG mono/stereo 449 869-2. (i; iv) Edda Moser; (i) RIAS Ch., BPO soloists; (ii) Dietrich Fischer-Dieskau, BPO soloists, Richard Kraus; (iii) Roy Hart, Philip Jones Brass Ens., ECO; (iv) BPO soloists; (i; iii–iv) cond. composer.

The *Versuch über Schweine* ('Essay on pigs') is a work in which Henze gives voice to his political interests. It contains a voice-part that traverses an amazing range and which certainly encompasses an extraordinary variety of timbre. *Being beauteous* is exquisite and quite moving, and *Whispers from heavenly death* is one of the composer's most fascinating works. The singing of Edda Moser is quite phenomenal both in purity of tone and in accuracy of intonation. The performances of all this repertoire could hardly be bettered, and the recording reproduces a wide dynamic range with admirable truthfulness of balance and quality of tone.

(i) *Cantata della fiaba estrema (Cantata of the ultimate fable);* (ii) *Moralitäten (Moralities);* (iii) *Musen Siziliens (Muses of Sicily).*

(M) *** DG 449 870-2. (i) Edda Moser, RIAS Ch., Berlin Philh. CO; (ii) Cornelius Schwarz, Dieter Leffler, Andreas Scheibner, Friedemann Jäckel, Titus Paspirgilis, Frieder Lang, Dresden Ch., Leipzig GO; (iii) Dresden Ch., Joseph Rollino, Paul Sheftel, Dresden State O soloists; all cond. composer.

The *Cantata*, a setting of a Roman love-poem, contains moving and often disarmingly simple music with great imaginative resource and subtlety. With Edda Moser the soloist, it cannot fail to communicate vividly. *Moralities* is a setting of 'three scenic plays' which W. H. Auden devised from three of Aesop's fables. Henze scored the work for small orchestra with a narrator, soloists and chorus interchanging the dialogue. Its manner is not in the least intimidating and the result is potently ironic rather than lightly humorous in spirit. The Latin text of the *Muses of Sicily* is taken from the *Eclogues* of Virgil. It opens with a *Pastorale* dialogue between Lycidas and Moeris and ends with the *Song of Silenus*, recounting the creation of the world from the elements of earth, air, sea and liquid. The work is entirely choral (Henze describes it as a concerto) with a vivid accompaniment for two pianos, wind instruments and timpani. The pianos are used very rhythmically, and the combination with timpani inevitably reminds the listener of Bartók, but Henze himself used a term which links the music more readily to Hindemith: he called it *Gebrauchsmusik* ('utility music'). Even if one does not take readily to all this music, Henze could never be less than stimulating. Superb singing and very good recording.

El Cimarrón (autobiography of the runaway slave Esteban Montejo) (recital for four musicians).

(M) *** DG 449 872-2. William Pearson, Karlheinz Zoeller, Leo Brouwer, Stomu Yamash'ta, cond. composer.

El Cimarrón, first heard at The Maltings in the Aldeburgh Festival of 1970, represented for Henze a new musical departure, presented at its simplest and most direct. It uses the words of a former slave, born in Cuba over 100 years ago. It is a simple but moving story with a number of left-wing propaganda slants, which fortunately do not get in the way of musical and dramatic expression. The live performance was impressive for the antics of the Japanese percussionist, Stomu Yamash'ta; but on disc the impact of the work is even more intense, because the improvisatory passages have been considerably tightened up, and the story is after all best imagined in the mind's eye – the poetic passage where the runaway lives in the forest, the biting account of the Revolution, the scene of the swaggering Yankees where a four-letter word is inserted (in English) in an otherwise German text. The performance is as near definitive as one could expect, beautifully recorded.

Das Floss der Medusa (The Raft of the Medusa) (oratorio).

(M) *** DG 449 871-2. Edda Moser, Dietrich Fischer-Dieskau, Charles Regnier, RIAS Chamber Ch., Members of the St Nikolai Hamburg Youth Ch., N. German R. Ch. & O, cond. composer.

This is a vividly imaginative work, far more approachable than the music Henze was composing before he entered into his latest 'political' period with its extreme left-wing commitment. The scheduled first performance in December 1968 in Hamburg was broken up in a political riot, but a recording had been made earlier and this is now re-released on this disc. Whatever the political bias, the message is both dramatic and moving as told in the tragic story of the crew of a shipwrecked frigate cast adrift and left to die by their officers. Henze has conceived the simple but effective idea of having the members of the crew as represented by the chorus move from one side of the stage to the other, one by one called from the land of the living, over to the side of Death (soprano soloist). A vivid experience, superbly realized.

Der langwierige Weg in die Wohnung der Natascha Ungeheuer (The Tedious way to Natascha Ungeheuer's apartment).

(M) **(*) DG 449 873-2. William Pearson, Fires of London, Philip Jones Brass Quintet, Gunter Hampel Free Jazz Ens., Giuseppe Agostini, Stomu Yamash'ta, cond. composer.

Expertly performed though it is, *Der langwierige Weg in die Wohnung der Natascha Ungeheuer* is perhaps the least satisfying or musically substantial of the works in this collection. It was unfortunate that the composer used the word 'tedious' in his title, for the writing has the air of a political tract and comes from the period when the composer was rejecting opera. The work is entitled 'Show for 17 performers', and is an allegory: Natasha Ungeheuer is 'the siren of a false Utopia who constantly lures the leftist intellectual into the cosy situation of so many middle-class socialists, who preach revolution while meanwhile living more or less the same old comfortable life'.

OPERA

Elegie für junge Liebende (Elegy for young lovers) (scenes).

(M) *** DG 449 874-2. Fischer-Dieskau, Driscoll, Dubin, Mödl, Berlin RSO & German Op. O, Berlin (members), cond. composer.

Elegie für junge Liebende was completed in 1961, being the composer's fourth extended operatic work. The libretto by W. H. Auden and Chester Kallman is set in a mountain inn, from which the hero and heroine eventually go to their deaths in a storm; but the underlying psychology of the characters, their destinies dominated by the poet, Mittenhoffer, is most complex. So is the construction of the music, both in the variety of forms for the set pieces, and in the way each character is given his or her own musical personality by the individual use of specific instrumentation and note-groupings (intervals, rather than leitmotives). The composer shows his brilliant feeling for orchestral colour and, with Fischer-Dieskau as Mittenhoffer, Martha Mödl as a strong-voiced Carolina (the poet's patron) and Liane Dubin an appealing Elisabeth, the vocal writing is fully characterized. An excellent and enterprising issue.

Der junge Lord (The Young Lord; complete).
(M) *** DG 449 875-2id.]. Mathis, Grobe, McDaniel, Johnson, Driscoll, German Op., Berlin, Ch. & O, Dohnányi.

As a reaction against his earlier, generally very serious operas, Henze in 1965 completed this piece designed as an *opera buffa*. This is Henze at his most amiable, and it results for much of the time in his Stravinskian side dominating, though he also allows himself a warmer vein of lyricism than usual. The plot in its comedy is consciously cynical, involving a snobbish community duped by a titled Englishman. He introduces an alleged English lord who finally turns out to be an ape. There is an underlying seriousness to the piece, and in this excellent performance, recorded with the composer's approval, the full range of moods and emotions is conveyed. Very good (1967) sound; in this mid-price reissue a full libretto and translation are provided.

Herbert, Victor (1859–1924)

Cello concerto No. 2 in E min., Op. 30.
(M) ** Mercury 434 355-2 [id.]. Miquelle, Eastman-Rochester O, Hanson – GROFE: *Grand Canyon suite; Mississippi suite.* **(*)

Georges Miquelle is a very musical soloist, but his tonal image is modest and he is dynamically upstaged by the orchestra everywhere but in the slow movement. He plays the work sympathetically, but Ma's newest version is much more persuasive. However, that is at full price.

Hérold, Ferdinand (1791–1833)

La Fille mal gardée (ballet, arr. Lanchbery): complete.
(M) *** Decca Dig. 430 849-2 (2) [id.]. ROHCG O, Lanchbery – LECOCQ: *Mam'zelle Angot.* ***

Lanchbery himself concocted the score for this fizzingly comic and totally delightful ballet, drawing primarily on Hérold's music, but interpolating the famous comic *Clog dance* from Hertel's alternative score, which must be one of the most famous of all ballet numbers outside Tchaikovsky. There is much else of comparable delight. Here, with sound of spectacular Decca digital fidelity, Lanchbery conducts a highly seductive account of the complete ballet with an orchestra long familiar with playing it in the theatre, now reissued coupled with Gordon Jacob's equally delicious confection, based on the music of Lecocq.

La Fille mal gardée: extended excerpts.
❀ (B) *** EMI Dig. CD-EMX 2268 [(M) id. import]. RLPO, Wordsworth.
(M) *** Decca 430 196-2. ROHCG O, Lanchbery.

Hérold's score also included tunes from Rossini's *Barber of Seville* and *Cenerentola*, together with a Donizetti selection (mainly from *L'elisir d'amore*). That the music is therefore a complete hotch-potch does not prevent it from being marvellously entertaining. The extended selection here is wonderfully persuasive and brilliantly played, displaying both affection and sparkle in ample quantity. The Kingsway Hall recording quality (produced by Ray Minshull and engineered by Arthur Lillie) is of vintage Decca excellence. One cannot believe that it dates from 1962, for the combination of ambient bloom and the most realistic detail still places it in the demonstration bracket. Lanchbery later recorded the complete ballet (see above) and that is also an outstanding set, but it involves two CDs (and includes Lecocq's *Mam'zelle Angot* ballet music as a fill-up).

However, Barry Wordsworth's scintillating account of a generous extended selection from the ballet includes all the important sequences, and the EMI CD offers some eight minutes more music than the Decca. With playing from the Royal Liverpool Philharmonic Orchestra that combines refinement and delicacy with wit and humour, this is even more highly recommendable, especially for those preferring modern, digital sound.

Hildegard of Bingen (1098–1179)

Ordo virtutum (The Play of the Virtues).
(M) *** HM/BMG Dig. 05472 77395-2 (2) [id.]. Köper, Mockridge, Thornton, Laurens, Feldman, Monahan, Lister, Trevor, Sanford, Smith, Sequentia.

The more one learns about Abbess Hildegard of Bingen, the more astonishing her achievement appears. *Ordo virtutum* is a mystery play, and this 90-minute piece includes strikingly dramatic passages, with the Devil himself intervening. This recording, made in collaboration with West German Radio of Cologne, is outstandingly fine.

Hindemith, Paul (1895–1963)

(i) *Viola concerto, 'Der Schwanendreher'*; (ii) *Violin concerto; Kammermusik No. 4 (Violin concerto), Op. 36/3.*
(BB) **(*) RCA Navigator 74321 24219-2 [(M) id. import]. (i) Igor Boguslavsky; (ii) David Oistrakh; USSR RSO, Rozhdestvensky.

David Oistrakh made his Russian recording of the *Violin concerto* the same year as his Decca version with the composer (see below). It is hardly less dazzling, and even if the sound cannot match its London counterpart it is fully acceptable; it is good to have in addition his hardly less charismatic account of the concerto which Hindemith placed fourth in his *Kammermusik*. The violist, Igor Boguslavsky, also makes an impressive solo contribution to another fine performance, of *Der Schwanendreher*, the central movement wonderfully warm. This has somewhat more refined sound, since in the two works for violin the soloist is balanced very forwardly. Rozhdestvensky provides vivid accompaniments and, although the Russian brass coarsens tuttis, this disc is more than worth its modest cost, even though the documentation is totally inadequate.

Violin concerto.
(M) *** Sony Stern Edition II SMK 64507 [id.]. Stern, NYPO, Bernstein – PENDERECKI: *Violin concerto.* ***

When it first appeared, Stern's 1964 recording tended somewhat to be eclipsed by the composer's own Decca record with David Oistrakh. Naturally the performance under Hindemith has an authority that no competitor can match. But this American account is very fine indeed: Stern plays with eloquence, and Bernstein's accompaniment is always sympathetic and at times has something special to offer. In places it scores over the composer's own (towards the end of the slow movement, for example) but the recording is less analytical than the Decca and detail is less in evidence. The new coupling is admirably chosen, and this makes another key record in Box II of Sony's Stern Edition.

(i) *Violin concerto;* (ii) *Mathis der Maler (Symphony);* (iii) *Symphonic metamorphoses on themes of Weber.*
✿ (M) *** Decca 433 081-2 [id.]. (i) David Oistrakh, LSO, composer; (ii) SRO, Kletzki; (iii) LSO, Abbado.

Oistrakh's performance of the Hindemith *Violin concerto* is a revelation. The composer, clearly inspired by the marvellous contribution of his soloist, provides an overwhelmingly passionate accompaniment and the 1962 recording still sounds extraordinarily vivid and spacious. The Rosette is for the concerto but the couplings are well chosen, both also offering vintage late 1960s Decca sound. Abbado's *Symphonic metamorphoses on themes of Weber* is second to none. Kletzki's account of *Mathis der Maler* is also impressive, very well prepared and with a similar attention to detail. He, too has the advantage of finely balanced and truthful recording, and the Suisse Romande Orchestra still plays very well for him. With 77 minutes of music offered, this is an indispensable disc for all Hindemithians, even if some duplication is involved.

Mathis der Maler (symphony).
(M) *** EMI CMS5 66109-2 (2) [id.]. BPO, Karajan – BRAHMS: *Tragic Overture;* BRUCKNER: *Symphony No. 8.* ***
(M) **(*) EMI CDM5 65868-2. Pittsburgh SO, Steinberg – MARTIN: *Petite symphonie concertante* **(*); TOCH: *Symphony No. 3.* ***
(M) ** DG 439 488-2. Boston SO, Steinberg – BUSONI: *Doktor Faust:* excerpt **; PFITZNER: *Palestrina: 3 Preludes* **; WEILL: *Kleine Dreigroschenmusik.* ***

It is good to have Karajan's recording back in the catalogue. It dates from 1957, but it was made in the

Berlin Jesus-Christus-Kirche and the sound is impressively spacious, the strings gloriously full. The warm, full-blooded performance is remarkably dramatic and convincing, the central movement very touching. Though Hindemith's markings may occasionally be ignored, Karajan is convincing in everything he does.

Steinberg's pioneering stereo recording shows the Pittsburgh orchestra at their finest, with a performance that is tense and well disciplined, yet which never allows the underlying emotion to be obscured. The final movement with its brilliant and exciting fugue comes out as a magnificent culmination. While this cannot perhaps be considered a first choice, the early (1957) stereo is remarkably full and atmospheric to match the brilliance and warmth of the performance. The Toch coupling, too, is especially worth investigating.

The Boston Symphony Orchestra under William Steinberg give a very good account of the *Mathis symphony*, even if it does not quite match in humanity or spontaneity the best of the (now many) current rivals. The 1971 recording sounds eminently acceptable and the interesting couplings undoubtedly enhance the value of this CD.

Mathis der Maler (symphony); *Nobilissima visione; Symphonic metamorphoses on themes by Carl Maria von Weber.*
(BB) ** Naxos Dig. 8.553078 [id.]. New Zealand SO, Franz-Paul Decker.

The Naxos disc is certainly not to be dismissed. It is well played under a conductor who is clearly at home in this repertoire without being inspired by it, with *Nobilissima visione* the most attractive performance. Those with limited budgets will find this well-recorded super-bargain offering value for money.

Symphonic metamorphoses on themes by Weber.
(M) *** Decca 448 579-2. LSO, Abbado – JANACEK: *Sinfonietta;* PROKOFIEV: *Symphony No. 3.* ***
(M) **(*) EMI CDM5 65175-2 [id.]. Phd. O, Ormandy – BARTOK: *Miraculous Mandarin* etc. **(*)

It is a relief to find a conductor like Abbado who is content to follow the composer's own dynamic markings and who does not give way to the temptation to score interpretative points at the music's expense. The stopped notes on the horns at the beginning of the finale, for example, are marked *piano*, and they are played here so that they add a barely perceptible touch of colour to the texture. The Decca engineers balance this so musically that the effect is preserved. This admittedly unimportant touch is symptomatic of the subtlety of Abbado's approach in a performance that in every respect is of the highest quality, while the vintage (1968) recording is surely worthy to be included in Decca's 'Classic Sound' series. Readers will note that this performance is also available coupled with the *Violin concerto* – see above.

The Philadelphia Orchestra play with splendid panache and brilliance, the humour of the second movement perhaps realized less effectively in their hands than with, say, Blomstedt. In every other respect this is first class, and the recording is full-bodied and does justice to the Philadelphia sound.

Trauermusik (for viola and string orchestra).
(M) *** EMI CDM5 65079-2 [id.]. ECO, Daniel Barenboim – BARTOK: *Divertimento for strings*; SCHOENBERG: *Verklaerte Nacht* ***.

This piece of *Gebrauchsmusik* ('utility music') was written in 24 hours in January 1936 when the composer was informed of the death of King George V. Its gentle, elegiac quality was highly suitable for the occasion, and the piece – in four sections – is not too long and is enjoyable for its simple, restrained eloquence. It is excellently performed and recorded here, and the couplings are equally successful in a quite different way.

CHAMBER MUSIC

(i) *Alto horn sonata in E flat;* (ii) *Bass tuba sonata;* (i) *Horn sonata;* (iii) *Trombone sonata;* (iv) *Trumpet sonata.*
(M) ** Sony SM2K 52671 (2) [S2K 52671]. (i) Mason Jones; (ii) Abe Torchinsky; (iii) Henry Charles Smith; (iv) Gilbert Johnson; Glenn Gould.

The *Alto saxophone sonata* and the *Alto horn sonata* are one and the same work. The Sony recordings are all from 1976. Glenn Gould has great feeling for Hindemith and plays with strong personality and commitment throughout, even though the tiresome vocalise is a strain.

Hoffmeister, Franz (1754–1812)

Flute concertos: in D; in G.
(BB) **(*) ASV CDQS 6012 [(M) id. import]. Dingfelder, ECO, Mackerras; Leonard – C. P. E. BACH: *Concerto.* **(*)

Franz Hoffmeister's two *Flute concertos* are elegantly inventive, if not distinctive. They are well recorded and make pleasant late-evening listening. The performances are sprightly and polished, and the accompaniments have plenty of spirit. The sound is brightly lit, but not excessively so.

Hofmann, Leopold (1738–93)

Sinfonias: in B flat; in C; in D; in F; in F.
(BB) *** Naxos Dig. 8.553866 [id.]. Northern CO, Ward.

Haydn's dismissive remark ('the braggart thinks that he alone has ascended the heights of Mount Parnassus') has rather coloured posterity's view of Leopold Hofmann. A pupil of Wagenseil, he was one of the leading Viennese symphonists of his day. He became Kapellmeister at St Stephen's Cathedral in 1773 and, to judge from the wide distribution of his manuscripts in Europe, he enjoyed considerable celebrity in his lifetime. In *The Age of Enlightenment* (Vol. VII of *The New Oxford History of Music*) Egon Wellesz wrote that Hofmann 'leaps into prominence in the development of the symphony because he was one of the earliest composers who consistently wrote four-movement symphonies with both slow introduction and minuets'. He preceded Haydn in this respect. Incidentally, for a brief period in 1791 Mozart acted as an assistant to him, doubtless in the hope of receiving preferment when Hofmann died.

The five symphonies recorded here show him to be lively and fresh, though no one could pretend that his music plumbs great depths – or indeed is consistently interesting. The performances are very alert and sprightly but the recording, though distinguished by clarity and presence, is handicapped by a rather dry acoustic.

Holst, Gustav (1874–1934)

'*The essential Holst*': (i) *Egdon Heath, Op. 47;* (ii) *A Moorside suite;* (iii) *The Perfect Fool, Op. 39;* (iv) *The Planets, Op. 32;* (v) *St Paul's suite, Op. 29/2;* (vi) *Ave Maria, Op. 9b; Choral hymns from the Rig Veda* (Group 3), *Op. 26/3; The Evening watch, Op. 43/1;* (vii) *The Hymn of Jesus, Op. 37;* (vi) *This have I done for my true love, Op. 34/1.*
(B) *** Decca Double Analogue/Dig. 444 549-2 (2) [(M) id. import]. (i; iii) LPO, Boult; (ii) Grimethorpe Colliery Band, Howarth; (iv) LPO, Solti; (v) St Paul CO, Hogwood; (vi) Purcell Singers, I. Holst; (vii) BBC Ch. & SO, Boult.

The brilliant Decca recording of Solti's Chicago version of the *Planets* combined with Boult's vintage accounts of *Egdon Heath* and *The Perfect Fool* ballet music is discussed below in its single-disc format. Boult's distinguished performance of the *Hymn of Jesus* is also available on another Double Decca, joined with music by Delius and Elgar. But if the present compilation is suitable, it could make a splendid basis for a Holst collection. The jolly, folksy *St Paul's suite* for strings, with its delicately etched second-movement '*Ostinato*' and characteristically haunting *Intermezzo*, could hardly be done better. Newcomers to this work will be pleased to welcome the unexpected entry of *Greensleeves* in the *Dargason* finale. *A Moorside suite* sounds splendid in its original, brass-band form (it was written for the National Championship contest at Crystal Palace in 1928) and it is superbly played by the Grimethorpe Colliery Band under Elgar Howarth, with recording approaching demonstration standard. Aptly, the first of the *Rig-Veda Choral hymns* (taken from a Sanskrit source), the *Hymn to the dawn*, brings echoes of *Neptune* from *The Planets*, while the fast and rhythmically fascinating *Hymn to the waters* is even more attractive. The vocal music serves to balance the picture of Holst as a composer, to show the more mystical side of his musical character. Beautifully atmospheric recording to match intense and sensitive performances.

Beni Mora (oriental suite); Egdon Heath; Fugal overture; Hammersmith; (i) *Invocation for cello and orchestra. Somerset rhapsody.*
(BB) *** Naxos Dig. 8.553696 [id.]. RSNO, David Lloyd-Jones; (i) with Tim Hugh.

This first disc in a Holst series from Naxos could not be more welcome, offering as it does a generous selection of music markedly more characteristic of him than the all-dominant *Planets suite*. The six works are neatly balanced, three dating from before the climactic period of *The Planets*, and three after. So the generously lyrical *Somerset rhapsody*, *Beni Mora* and the long-neglected *Invocation for cello and orchestra* (with Timothy Hugh a moving soloist) lead on to the tauter and more astringent post-war works: the Hardy-inspired *Egdon Heath*, the darkly intense prelude and fugue, *Hammersmith* and the *Fugal overture*. Fresh and idiomatic performances, superbly recorded in full and brilliant sound.

Brook Green suite; (i–ii) *Fugal concerto for flute, oboe and strings, Op. 40/2;* (ii) *In the bleak midwinter* (arr. Messiter); (iii) *Lyric movement for viola and small orchestra. 6 Morris dance tunes;* (iv) *7 Scottish airs for piano and strings. St Paul's suite, Op. 29/2.*

(BB) ** Arte Nova Dig. 74321 34022-2 [id.]. L. Festival O, Ross Pople, with (i) Edward Beckett; (ii) Malcolm Messiter; (iii) Rachel Bolt; (iv) Michael Frayson.

This repertoire is much recorded and many will look for a rather larger body of strings than Ross Pople fields here. The small chamber group works very well in the *Brook Green suite*, where ensemble is particularly fresh, rather less so in the *St Paul's suite*, where the *Dargason* finale could be crisper. There is some fine solo playing from both participants in the *Fugal concerto*, and in Holst's set of *Scottish airs*, using a concertante piano; the *Morris dance tunes* (based on the harmonizations of Cecil Sharp) are amiably enjoyable in their innocent simplicity, even if they are without the wit of a Percy Grainger. The most valuable inclusion here is the poignantly intense *Lyric movement for viola and small orchestra*, which Holst wrote in the last months of his life, obviously in a mood of melancholy bordering on despair. Rachel Bolt is a very sensitive soloist and this work makes a strong impression. Malcolm Messiter then offers a closing lollipop in his seductive arrangement of *In the bleak midwinter*, where the warmth of the playing entirely counters the carol's bleakness.

Brook Green suite for string orchestra; (i) *Fugal concerto for flute and oboe. The Perfect Fool* (ballet suite), *Op. 39; St Paul's suite for string orchestra, Op. 26/2; A Somerset rhapsody, Op. 21/2.*

(B) *** EMI CD-EMX 2227 [(M) id. import]. ECO, Sir Yehudi Menuhin.

There are a number of collections of Holst's shorter orchestral works currently available on CD, but none better played or recorded than this and none less expensive. It includes warmly characterized performances of both the works Holst wrote for St Paul's Girls' School, not just the *St Paul's suite* but also the *Brook Green suite*, both sounding fresh, while the rarer *Somerset rhapsody* is also very atmospherically presented. There is some delightful solo playing from Jonathan Snowden and David Theodore in the *Fugal concerto*, and many will welcome Menuhin's vivid account of *The Perfect Fool*, Holst's most familiar orchestral suite after *The Planets*. If the programme suits, you need look no further.

Military band suites Nos. 1–2. Hammersmith: Prelude and scherzo, Op. 52.

(BB) *** ASV CDQS 6021 [(M) id.]. L. Wind O, Denis Wick – VAUGHAN WILLIAMS: *English folksong suite* etc. ***

The London performances have great spontaneity, even if they are essentially lightweight, especially when compared with the Fennell versions on Telarc at full price. The sound is first class.

The Planets (suite), *Op. 32.*

(M) *** Decca 452 303-2 [id.]. VPO, Karajan – ELGAR: *Enigma variations.* ***

(M) *** EMI CDM7 64748-2 [id.]. LPO, Boult (with G. Mitchell Ch.) – ELGAR: *Enigma variations.* ***

(B) *** DG Classikon 439 446-2; *439 446-4* [id.]. Boston SO, Steinberg – ELGAR: *Enigma variations.* ***

(B) **(*) BBC Radio Classics BBCRD 9104 [(M) id. import]. BBC SO, Sargent – ELGAR: *Enigma Variations.* **(*)

(M) **(*) EMI CDM5 65423-2 [id.]. R. Wagner Chorale women's voices, LAPO, Stokowski – RAVEL: *Alborada* **(*); STRAVINSKY: *Petrushka.* **

(M) **(*) EMI (SIS) Dig. CDM7 64740-2. Philh. O, Rattle – JANACEK: *Sinfonietta.* ***

(B) **(*) EMI Dig. Eminence CD-EMX 9513 [(M) id.]. Amb. S., Philh. O, Rattle.

(M) **(*) Chandos Dig. CHAN 7082 [id.]. SNO & Ch., Gibson.

(BB) **(*) Carlton LSO Double Dig. 30368 01107 (2) [(B) id.]. LSO & Ch., Hickox – ORFF: *Carmina burana.* ***

(M) **(*) Ph. Dig. 442 408-2. Berlin R. Ch., BPO, Sir Colin Davis.

(BB) (***) RCA Navigator 74321 17905-2 [(B) Basic 100 09026 61724-2]. Phd. Ch. & O, Ormandy – VAUGHAN WILLIAMS: *Fantasias.* ***

(M) ** Teldec/Warner Dig. 4509 97443-2 [2292 46316-2]. New York Choral Artists, NYPO, Mehta.

(M) ** Sony SMK 63087 [id.]. NYPO, Camerata Singers, Bernstein (with ELGAR: *Pomp and circumstance march No. 1* **).

(B) * Millennium MCD 80099. V. State Op. O with Ch., Sir Adrian Boult – VAUGHAN WILLIAMS: *Tallis & Greensleeves fantasias.* *(*)

(i) *'World of Holst': The Planets;* (ii) *Egdon Heath, Op. 47;* (iii) *The Perfect Fool* (suite), *Op. 39.*

(M) *** Decca 440 318-2. LPO, cond. (i) Solti, with LPO Ch.; (ii; iii) Boult.

(i) *The Planets;* (ii) *The Perfect Fool* (suite).
(B) *** Decca 433 620-2 [(M) id. import]. (i) LAPO, Mehta; (ii) LPO, Boult.
(M) **(*) Virgin/EMI Dig. CUV5 61257-2 [id.]. RLPO, Mackerras.

(i) *The Planets* (suite); *St Paul's suite* (for strings), *Op. 29.*
(M) *** Carlton Dig. 30366 0432 [id.]. (i) Ladies of New Queen's Hall Ch.; New Queen's Hall O, Roy Goodman.
(B) *** Tring Dig. TRP 007 [(M) id. import]. RPO, Vernon Handley, (i) with Ladies of Ambrosian Ch.

Under Roy Goodman, a conductor more often associated with baroque and classical repertory, the New Queen's Hall Orchestra crowns its achievement so far in a performance favouring instruments of the kind in general use in the first quarter of the twentieth century, the result subtly different from the effect using modern instruments. These players are drawn from among top professional musicians dedicated to the idea of what an orchestra used to sound like, before the latterday emphasis on volume at all costs. They plainly love their art. The result is less aggressive, less brash than usual. Goodman is a persuasive interpreter, generally making a good case for faster speeds than are usual (maybe reflecting Holst's own recording of 1926), even if with less panache in *Jupiter* and *Uranus* than with the finest versions. Interestingly, although the wooden flutes come from a London manufacturer (Rudall, Carte), all the reed woodwind instruments (and most notably the bassoons) are French. The piston horns (French or British), trumpets (American) and trombones (Boosey & Hawkes) are narrow bore: they do not in any way lack sonority but are without that overwhelming 'fatness' of timbre one associates with wider-bore instruments. The drums will not please environmentalists as they are all covered in animal skins; but the ear registers the difference, and the gut strings bring vividly detailed textures. The immediate impact with *Mars* is in no doubt. If there is initially less menace than usual, Goodman is tremendously urgent in his pacing, developing great ferocity at the close. One recalls Alan Leo's symbol of the 'destroying angel' in the book on astrology which was the original inspiration for Holst's work. *Venus* with its delicate horn solo and translucent flutes is truly the bringer of peace, and the woodwind colouring and transparency of the strings tickle the ear in *Mercury*. The opening of *Jupiter* is light and clean, with crisp string articulation characteristic of the lighter sounds of instruments using gut strings. Brass is less forward too, partly a question of recording balance, but also reflecting the use of authentic instruments. Here the bold narrow-bore horns really come into their own, not only in the Holstian rhythmic striding themes but in the support they provide for the great central string tune. The ear continually notices the natural clarity of the sound-picture, not least in *Saturn*, which opens gently and poignantly, with the timpani coming through thrillingly at the climax and the deep bass pedal subtle in its underlining. At the beginning of *Uranus* the chortling bassoons readily recall Dukas's apprentice; the horns are ebullient, the brass – and notably the tuba – making the sharpest, fullest impact. The delicate flutes establish a gentle, lonely mysticism as *Neptune* steals in, the chorus ethereal and perfectly placed in relation to the woodwind. The refreshingly athletic account of the *St Paul's suite* which acts as an encore is a good demonstration of the bright, clean quality of gut strings; only in Holst's combination of *Greensleeves* with the *Dargason* in the finale, does the ear crave a riper sonority. John Boydon's Abbey Road recording does the orchestra full justice, and the back-up notes are well detailed.

After a sinister opening, Handley on Tring builds the climax of *Mars* impressively and the well-separated closing chords have malignant impact. The noble tune of *Jupiter* develops a similar build-up of intensity, well maintained in the spirited reprise of the opening section which has a rumbustious coda. *Saturn*, too, brings a well-graduated, melancholy climax, and the choral diminuendo to silence in *Neptune* is beautifully managed by the Ambrosians. *Venus* is warm and beautiful rather than sensuous or withdrawn, and the resonance provides a lustrous *Mercury*, undoubtedly chimerical if less sharply etched than in some versions. But the sound overall is attractively rich, giving glowing orchestral colour, the horns expansively opulent. What also makes this bargain disc especially worth considering is the bracingly fresh account of the *St Paul's suite*, offered as a bonus. The recording of the string body is also very realistic.

With Karajan at his peak, plus the challenge to an orchestra discovering this music for the first time, this extraordinarily magnetic and powerful 1961 account of *The Planets* is uniquely individual, bringing a rare tension, an extra magnetism, the playing combining polish and freshness. The superb Decca recording – produced by John Culshaw in the Sofiensaal – is fully worthy of reissue in Decca's Classic Sound series. It remains of demonstration quality, with thrilling weight, clarity of focus and sense of presence, and it has never sounded more vivid and more richly atmospheric than in its present transfer. *Mars* is remorselessly paced and, with its whining Wagnerian tubas, is unforgettable, while the ravishingly gentle portrayal of *Venus* brings ardent associations with the goddess of love, rather than seeking a peaceful purity. The gossamer textures of *Mercury* and the bold geniality of *Jupiter* contrast with the solemn, deep melancholy expressed by the VPO strings at the opening of *Saturn*. *Uranus* brings splendid playing from the Vienna brass, given splendid bite.

The Decca recording for Solti's Chicago version is extremely brilliant, with *Mars* given a vivid cutting edge at the fastest possible tempo. Solti's directness in *Jupiter* (with the trumpets coming through splendidly) is certainly riveting, the big tune red-blooded and with plenty of character. In *Saturn* the spareness of texture is finely sustained and the tempo is slow, the detail precise; while in *Neptune* the coolness is even more striking when the pianissimos are achieved with such a high degree of tension. The CD gives the orchestra great presence, and the addition of Boult's classic versions of *Egdon Heath* and *The Perfect Fool* ballet music makes this reissue very competitive and marginally preferable to the EMI alternative of the same three works.

Sir Adrian Boult gives a performance at once intense and beautifully played, spacious and dramatic, rapt and pointed. The great melody of *Jupiter* is calculatedly less resonant and more flowing than previously but is still affecting, and *Uranus* as well as *Jupiter* has its measure of jollity. The spacious slow movements are finely poised and the recording still stands up well, with added presence and definition.

Mehta's set of *Planets* set a new standard for sonic splendour when it was first issued in 1971. The new ADD transfer still provides outstanding sound, but there is a touch more edge on the strings and the quality has lost just a little of its richness and amplitude; though definition is sharper, the background hiss is fractionally more noticeable. Even so, this is a superb disc and a clear first bargain choice. As on the Solti *Planets*, Boult's splendid account of the ballet suite from *The Perfect Fool* has now been added. This was recorded a decade earlier, but the vintage Decca sound remains spectacular, with the LPO brass hardly less resplendent than their colleagues in Los Angeles.

On this Classikon super-bargain reissue, recorded in 1971, Steinberg's Boston set of *Planets* was another outstanding version from a vintage analogue period. It remains one of the most exciting and involving versions and now sounds brighter and sharper in outline, though with some loss of opulence. *Mars* in particular is intensely exciting. At his fast tempo, Steinberg may get to his fortissimos a little early, but rarely has the piece sounded so menacing on record. The testing point for most will no doubt be *Jupiter*, and here Steinberg the excellent Elgarian comes to the fore, giving a wonderful *nobilmente* swagger.

Though the label, incorrectly, suggests the Royal Festival Hall as the venue, Sargent's BBC Radio Classics account of *The Planets* was recorded, like the Elgar, in the Royal Albert Hall. One marvels that no one in the reissuing record company noticed the three-second reverberation confirming the point. Though this was a February performance, not one given at the Proms, the atmosphere is similarly electric, with the sequence of movements building warmly and atmospherically. As in the Elgar, the playing may be a degree less polished than in Sargent's studio recording, but the excitement and tension are markedly greater, and for most that is what will matter. Good, full-bodied if rather opaque sound.

Stokowski's approach to *The Planets* is both brisk and sensuous (*Venus* very much the Goddess of Love rather than the 'bringer of peace'), with every movement except *Mercury* faster than usual. Yet such is Stokowski's magnetism that at a flowing speed *Saturn* conveys rapt stillness and the fast movements have tremendous swagger. This is very early stereo (1956) and the Capitol recording of the Los Angeles Philharmonic was made in so-called 'full-dimensional sound'. It is bright and clear but lacks the allure of RCA's 'Living Stereo' of the same period.

For Simon Rattle, EMI's digital recording provides wonderfully atmospheric sound, and the quality in *Venus* and *Mercury* is also beautiful, clear and translucent. Otherwise it is not as distinctive a version as one might have expected from this leading conductor; it is sensibly paced but neither so polished nor so bitingly committed as Karajan or Boult, and *Jupiter* is disappointing, lacking in thrust and warmth. As can be seen, Rattle's set of *Planets* is also available in the UK only on the Eminence bargain label without a coupling.

Gibson's reading is characteristically direct and certainly well played. Other versions have greater individuality and are more involving, but there is no doubt that the Chandos recording has fine bite and presence, although there are moments when one would have expected a greater degree of transparency. With sound this vivid, the impact of such a colourful score is enhanced, and at mid-price this is much more competitive, a fine traditional account with plenty of character.

Richard Hickox's *Mars* is given an unremittingly fast pace and is angrily aggressive, the climax topped by ferocious percussion. The emphasized dissonance makes *Venus*, with its translucent serenity, the more striking, the playing cool and withdrawn. *Mercury* is attractively fleet, with a proper element of fantasy, and *Saturn* has an elegiac gravity of mood. The disappointments are *Jupiter* and *Uranus*: the former lacking in real jubilation, with the central melody rather square – though there is no lack of energy – and *Uranus* has a forcefulness of accentuation which precludes any geniality. *Neptune*'s mystic chorus disappears into infinity very convincingly. The recording, with its wide dynamic range, is certainly spectacular; it has excellent transparency and detail but rather misses out on expansive warmth. The overall impression is certainly powerful but lacks the feeling of human involvement. However, the Orff coupling included with this inexpensive LSO Double is thoroughly recommendable and many will count this reissue very good value.

Sir Colin Davis's *Mars* is menacingly fast, with weighty Berlin brass and barbaric accents adding to the forcefulness. The resonant recording brings sumptuous textures to *Venus*, while even *Saturn* has a degree of opulence. *Mercury*, however, is infectiously spirited, and *Jupiter*, with a grand central tune, is bucolic in its amplitude. *Uranus* brings galumphing brass, and the closing *Neptune* is both ethereal and sensuous, an unusual combination, brought about partly by the warm reverberation. There are more subtle versions than this, but it is easy to enjoy. However, this reissue offers no coupling.

Mackerras's usual zestful approach communicates readily and the Liverpool orchestra bring a lively response, but the over-reverberant recording tends to cloud the otherwise pungently vigorous *Mars*, and both *Venus* and *Saturn* seem a little straightforward and marginally undercharacterized, while again in the powerful climax of *Uranus* there is some blurring from the resonance. *The Perfect Fool*, with its vivid colouring and irregular rhythms, has much in common with *The Planets* and makes a fine coupling, especially when played with such flair.

Ormandy's 1975 RCA recording now reappears on RCA's super-bargain Navigator label and in the USA as part of the 'Basic 100' collection, generously coupled with Vaughan Williams string works. It was one of the finest records he made as principal conductor of the Philadelphia Orchestra in the last few years before he retired. The playing has great electricity, and it is a pity that RCA's balancing engineers apparently sought brilliance above all else and endeavoured to make a quite artificial sonic impact. The CD transfer brings a fierce edginess in the treble (caused by placing the microphones much too close). The orchestra does not sound like this in the flesh. Even so, this is a highly compelling reading. Ormandy paces the central tune of *Jupiter* slowly and deliberately. The performance is at its finest in *Uranus* (with crisply vigorous brass articulation) and the restrained melancholy of *Saturn*, deeply felt and somehow personal in its communication. *Neptune* too is beautifully tapered off at the close.

At the beginning of his career in the early 1970s Mehta recorded an outstanding set of *Planets* for Decca with the Los Angeles Philharmonic Orchestra (see above), and that performance (and its superb recording – still demonstration-worthy) remains a top bargain recommendation. His later, Teldec version cannot compare with it for either characterization or recording, which is resonantly unrefined. The performance sounds curiously unspontaneous: there is infinitely greater life and subtlety and more vivid colouring from the orchestral playing in Los Angeles.

Bernstein's account is brilliantly played, but although the recording is clear it lacks richness in the bass to balance the bright treble. The performance is never less than interesting, sometimes charismatic, with moments of individuality. The choral singing in *Neptune* is most refined and the closing diminuendo very beautiful. But the sound counts against this as a general recommendation.

Younger readers may not remember that Boult, after making his first mono LP of *The Planets* for Pye (subsequently PRT) with the so-called Philharmonic Promenade Orchestra, in 1959 went to Vienna to make his first stereo version. Boult's trips to Europe have often produced some unexpectedly good records – but not in this instance. The Viennese playing is barely acceptable. The orchestra sounds under-rehearsed: there are fluffs in the strings and a very clumsy principal horn solo at the beginning of *Venus*. In the big, bold tunes the players miss the breadth of the music and sound phlegmatic. Only in *Mars* does the Viennese brass add a characterful hint of Wagner, which was to be amplified in Karajan's inspired later version for Decca with the VPO. The recording is bright and fully acceptable, but this well-transferred CD can be regarded as no more than a curiosity, for the Vaughan Williams couplings are little better.

The Planets (suite), *Op. 32; Suite de ballet in E flat, Op. 10.*

(BB) ** Naxos Dig. 8.550193 [id.]. Slovak RSO, Bratislava, Adrian Leaper.

On Naxos, the Slovak Radio Orchestra under an English conductor give a direct, straightforward reading, without much subtlety of detail, but strong in effect, helped by excellent, full-bodied, digital recording. The big tune in *Jupiter*, taken spaciously, is sonorously eloquent. The novelty is the inclusion of Holst's early four-movement *Suite de ballet*, written in 1899 and revised in 1912. The invention is attractively robust, apart from the winningly fragile *Valse*, and the work is presented enthusiastically. Good orchestral playing throughout.

VOCAL MUSIC

(i) *A Choral Fantasia, Op. 51;* (ii) *Psalm 86.*

(M) *** EMI CDM5 65588-2. (i) Janet Baker; (ii) Ian Partridge, Purcell Singers, ECO, Imogen Holst – FINZI: *Dies natalis;* VAUGHAN WILLIAMS: *5 Mystical songs* etc. ***

Holst's *Choral Fantasia* – a setting of words written by Robert Bridges in commemoration of Purcell – was one of his later works, and probably the unusual combination of performers has prevented more frequent performances. It is not an easy work to grasp, and Holst's extremes of dynamic tend to hinder rather than help. But it is well worth getting to know. Dame Janet Baker once again shows her supreme quality as a recording artist. The recording, though not lacking ambient warmth, is admirably clear (indeed the organ pedals are only too clear). The sound could perhaps be more open, but there is no lack of projection and vividness, and the bloom of the analogue original remains untarnished. The setting of *Psalm 86*, with its expressive tenor part sung beautifully by Ian Partridge, is also included in this generous compilation. The recording here is outstanding, and the success of both these performances owes much to the inspired direction of the composer's daughter.

(i) *Choral Symphony, Op. 41;* (ii) *The Hymn of Jesus, Op. 37.*
(M) *** EMI CDM5 65128-2. (i) Felicity Palmer, LPO Ch., LPO, Boult; (ii) St Paul's Cathedral Ch., London Symphony Ch., LPO, Groves.

In the *Choral Symphony*, though the Keats poems give a faded aura to this ambitious work, Boult and his performers demonstrate the beauty and imagination of the writing. Holst even manages to set the *Ode on a Grecian Urn* without aesthetic problems and, until the finale, the writing is always taut and intensely individual. The finale is altogether looser-limbed, but Boult in this totally unsentimental performance manages to draw it together. As samplers, try the strange *Prelude* with its monotone mutterings or the seven-in-a-bar energy of the *Bacchanal*. A fine and unjustly neglected work, superbly performed. The 1974 recording remains richly atmospheric in its CD format, with the opening pianissimos of the *Prelude* and second movement enhanced by the background quiet. Many will feel that the mistiness of the sound suits the music, although the Scherzo could ideally be more sharply focused. The Groves recording of *The Hymn of Jesus* is on the whole finer than Boult's older, Decca account which has served collectors well over the years. Sir Charles Groves brings great sympathy and conviction to this beautiful and moving score whose visionary quality has never paled, and the recording has transferred very well to CD to make a highly desirable Holst coupling.

OPERA

(i) *At the Boar's Head, Op. 42* (complete); (ii) *The wandering scholar, Op. 50* (complete).
(M) *** EMI Dig./Analogue CDM5 65127-2 [id.]. (i) Langridge, Palmer, Ross, Tomlinson, Wilson-Johnson, Hall, Suart, George, RLPO, Groves; (ii) Burrowes, Tear, Rippon, Langdon, E. Op. Group, ECO, Bedford.

Holst's formula for his Falstaff opera, *At the Boar's Head*, is an attractive one. Finding that Shakespeare's lines went naturally to dances and tunes from Playford's collection, he used that material on a libretto drawn entirely from the revelant scenes of *Henry IV, Parts I* and *II*. The result is busy-sounding in its emphasis on chattering comedy, and dramatically it is questionable. But on record the charm, colour and originality of the piece come over well, starting with an improbable drunken opening, when Bardolph begins, without accompaniment, in what for a moment sounds like sing-speech. Plainly a piece which has never been successful on stage, yet which deserved a recording. With some fine singing and first-rate playing, it is admirably served here by excellent, early digital sound.

The wandering scholar, by contrast, works delightfully on stage, but on record its galumphing humour is less than sparkling. It is a very late work which the composer himself never saw produced, and the score required an amount of intelligent editing before it was given modern performances. Whatever one's response to the comedy, the musical inspiration has the sharp originality and economy one associates with Holst's last period, a fascinating score. The recording comes from the mid-1970s and was of very high quality, but the CD is something of a revelation in opening up the choral sound while still retaining the atmosphere and bloom of the analogue originals. The words of the soloists in *The wandering scholar* are also clear. An outstanding reissue in every way.

Honegger, Arthur (1892–1955)

Pacific 231.
(M) *** Decca (IMS) 448 576-2 [id.]. SRO, Ansermet – CHABRIER: *España* **(*); DEBUSSY: *La Mer* **(*); DUKAS: *L'apprenti sorcier* ***; RAVEL: *Boléro; La Valse.* ***

Pacific 231; Rugby.
(M) ** Sony MHK 62352 [id.]. NYPO, Bernstein – MILHAUD: *Les Choéphores* ***; ROUSSEL: *Symphony No. 3.* **(*)

Ansermet conveys all the grinding power of Honegger's railway evocation, and its surging lyricism too, but some of the detail is clouded by the resonance at the climax. An impressive performance just the same.

Leonard Bernstein's 1962 performances sounded pretty strident in their original LP incarnation, though the playing has tremendous character and virtuosity. The engineers have succeeded in taming much of the ferocity and the present transfer produces more acceptable results. However, this is not inexpensive.

Pacific 231; Pastorale d'été; Rugby; (i) *Christmas cantata (Cantata de Noël).*
(M) **(*) EMI CDM7 63944-2. O Nat. de l'ORTF, Martinon; (i) with Camille Maurane & Ch. d'Oratorio Maîtrise de l'ORTF.

These recordings all date from 1971; although in *Pacific 231* the quality is not quite as impressive as the very best modern sound, it is still very good indeed. The Orchestre National de l'ORTF (which after the reorganization of French Radio in the 1970s became the Orchestre National de France) plays well for Jean Martinon, though we have heard more atmospheric accounts of *Pastorale d'été* (Martinon is not always responsive to pianissimo indications here). The *Cantata de Noël* is given a strong performance, though not even the expert French Radio choir manages the highly exacting demands of Honegger's difficult (and not always effective) choral writing. Generally these are good performances – although the programme offers short measure at 46 minutes.

Symphonies Nos. 1–3.
(M) ** EMI CDM7 64274-2 [id.]. O de Capitole de Toulouse, Michel Plasson.

Symphonies Nos. 4–5; Pacific 231.
(M) *** EMI CDM7 64275-2 [id.]. O de Capitole de Toulouse, Michel Plasson.

Symphonies Nos. 1; 2 for strings with trumpet obbligato; 3 (Symphonie liturgique); 4 (Deliciae Basilienses); 5 (Di tre re); 3 Symphonic movements: Nos. 1, Pacific 231; 2, Rugby.
(B) *** Erato/Warner Ultima 3984 21340-2 (2) [(M) id. import]. Bav. RSO, Charles Dutoit.

Symphonies Nos. 1; 2 for strings with trumpet obbligato; 3 (Symphonie liturgique); 4 (Deliciae Basilienses); 5 (Di tre re); 3 Symphonic movements: Nos. 1, Pacific 231; 3. The Tempest: Prelude.
(M) *** Sup. 11 1566-2 (2) [id.]. Czech PO, Baudo.

Honegger's symphonies are currently much underrated and their scant representation in the concert hall scarcely reflects their artistic standing. The *First* was commissioned by Koussevitzky for the fiftieth anniversary of the Boston Symphony; the *Second* is a probing, intense wartime composition that reflects something of the anguish Honegger felt during the German occupation. The *Third* (*Liturgique*) dates from the end of the war, while the *Fourth*, composed for Paul Sacher, makes use of Swiss folk material. It is perhaps the most underrated of them all, for its delights grow fresher with every hearing and its melodic charm is irresistible. Beneath its smiling surface there is a gentle vein of nostalgia and melancholy, particularly in the slow movement. The finale is sparkling and full of high spirits, though even this ends on a bitter-sweet note. The *Fifth* is a powerful work, inventive, concentrated and vital.

Although the performances are slightly uneven, Dutoit's Ultima Double is an appealingly economical way of acquiring excellent, modern, digital recordings (dating from the early 1980s). The *First* is a highly stimulating and rewarding piece: its level of energy is characteristic of the later symphonies, and in Dutoit's hands the phrasing of the Bavarian orchestra in the beautiful slow movement has both dignity and eloquence. He again produces very cultured string-playing in the dark, introspective *Symphony for strings*, and his performance is thoroughly meticulous in the observance of detail; but here it is just a shade deficient in vitality and drive. The *Deliciae Basiliensis* also has rather measured tempi; however, this beautifully recorded performance serves to rekindle enthusiam for a much-underrated work whose sunny countenance and keen nostalgia bring unfailing delight. Dutoit then gives thoroughly idiomatic accounts of both the *Symphonie liturgique* and *Di tre re Symphonies*. In the *Fifth* he does not galvanize his orchestra into playing of the same volcanic fire and vitality that Serge Baudo secures from the Czech Philharmonic on Supraphon, but the Erato recording is fresher and more detailed. Room has been found for only two of the *Three Symphonic movements* (although Dutoit recorded all of them). *Pacific 231*, with its robust and vigorous portrait of a railway engine, is by far the best known. Both this and *Rugby* are well done; although the latter may be found a little genteel by comparison with Bernstein's (CBS/Sony) version, the playing and recording are more than adequate compensation.

These Supraphon performances come from the 1960s, but they are more than merely serviceable. The sound comes up very well indeed and the playing of the Czech Philharmonic for Baudo is totally committed. The performance of the *Fifth Symphony* has never been surpassed (except possibly by the pioneering Munch recording) and has amazing presence and detail for its period.

Michel Plasson has the advantage of fine recording from the late 1970s, and the spacious acoustics of the Toulouse Halle-aux-Grains seem right for the music. The CD transfers are natural in balance and enhance the sound, which has plenty of ambience. However, the performances do not have the panache and virtuosity that make Karajan's coupling of Nos. 2 and 3 so memorable, and at times in the most searing music one feels a lack of grip and emotional intensity. Nevertheless there are some fine moments here and Plasson finds much of the charm of No. 4, even if the Scherzo of the *Fifth Symphony* sounds rather tame. One other point: in the *Symphony for strings* (the *Second*) the trumpet for which Honegger called to strengthen the chorale, but which he did not regard as mandatory, is omitted.

Symphonies Nos. 2 for strings with trumpet obbligato; 3 (Symphonie liturgique).
✿ (M) *** DG 447 435-2. BPO, Karajan – STRAVINSKY: *Concerto in D.* ***

Karajan's accounts of these magnificent symphonies come from 1973 and still remain in a class of their own. Not even Munch's pioneering recording of the *Symphony No. 2* or its successors comes near to it for sheer poetic intensity, and the *Symphonie liturgique* has likewise never been surpassed. It is luminous, incandescent and moving. The only rival is the Jansons version with the Oslo Philharmonic on EMI, but this is at full price. The Karajan is one of his greatest records and cannot be recommended too strongly, particularly in view of its competitive price and the additional coupling. It certainly deserves its place as one of DG's 'Legendary Recordings', reissued in their Originals series.

Symphonies Nos. 3 (Symphonie liturgique); 5 (Di tre re); Chant du joie; Pacific 231; Pastorale d'été.
(M) *** Sup. 11 0667-2. Czech PO, Serge Baudo.

Symphonies Nos. 3 (Symphonie liturgique); 5 (Di tre re); Nocturne for orchestra.
(BB) ** Koch Discover DICD 920371 [id.]. Belgian Nat. Radio & TV PO, Alexander Rahbari.

Honegger's *Pacific 231* has thundered along the tracks to more striking effect than it does here under Baudo (Honegger himself steered it more briskly into the station in the days of steam), but the two symphonies are splendidly played and recorded. Serge Baudo's 1960s recording of the *Fifth* still remains among the very best versions of the work. The *Liturgique* is very good indeed, as are the remaining pieces on offer. Given the modest price of this disc plus the generous playing time, this deserves a very strong recommendation.

The Belgian Radio forces give acceptable accounts of both symphonies, though the recorded sound is a bit top-heavy and strident. They do not begin to challenge existing recommendations (Karajan in the *Liturgique* and Munch or Baudo in the *Fifth Symphony*). The rarity here is the *Nocturne for orchestra*, an imaginative piece which comes from 1936 and was composed just after *Jeanne d'Arc au bûcher*. All the same, this hardly tips the balance in this issue's favour.

Symphony No. 5 ('Di tre re').
(M) (**) DG Originals mono 449 748-2 [id.]. Lamoureux O, Igor Markevitch – MILHAUD: *Les Choéphores* (**); ROUSSEL: *Bacchus et Ariane: suite No. 2.* **

Markevitch's account of the *Fifth Symphony* with the Orchestre Lamoureux was recorded in the Salle Wagram in 1957 – in mono. The sound has plenty of depth and good perspective; it is a little set back, though there is no lack of impact in tuttis and there is plenty of space round the instruments elsewhere. Markevitch generates plenty of atmosphere; his approach, which is lyrical, is strongly characterized but not a first choice.

Christmas cantata (*Cantate de Noël*).
(B) *** EMI Eminence (SIS) Dig. CD-EMX 2275 [(M) id. import]. Sweeney, Wayneflete Singers, Winchester Cathedral Ch., ECO, Neary – POULENC: *Mass; Motets.* ***

A recording of Honegger's charming *Cantate de Noël* to do it full justice. It was the composer's last completed work and deserves to be more popular at the festive season outside France. The recording is impressively wide-ranging and well defined.

Le Roi David (complete).
(M) *** Erato/Warner 2292 45800-2. Eda Pierre, Collard, Tappy, Petel, Valere, De Dailly, Philippe Caillard Ch., Ens. Instrumental, Dutoit.
(M) *** Van. 08.4038.71 [OVC 4038]. Davrath, Sorensen, Preston, Singher, Madeleine Milhaud, Utah University Ch., Utah SO, Abravanel.

Charles Dutoit's *Le Roi David* uses the original instrumental forces and not the full orchestra favoured by most of his rivals. The recording comes from 1970, not that anyone coming to it afresh would guess that. It is a compelling performance of strong dramatic coherence.

The Vanguard version was made in 1961. It is remarkably vivid, well detailed and present, and the playing of the Utah Symphony under Maurice Abravanel is very fine. The recording also stands up well. Netania Davrath is excellent too, and so is Madeleine Milhaud, the composer's wife, as the Witch of Endor. Thoroughly recommendable.

Hotteterre, Jacques (1674–1763)

Pièces pour la flûte, Oeuvre II: *Echoes for solo flute; Suite in B flat for recorder and continuo; Suite in E min. for transverse flute and continuo.* Oeuvre III: *Trio sonatas: in C for 2 oboes and continuo; in D min. for 2 recorders and continuo; Suite in D for transverse flute and continuo.* Oeuvre V: *Suite in E min. for recorder and continuo. Suite-Sonata in C for oboe and continuo.* Oeuvre VI: *Suite in G for 2 transverse flutes.* Oeuvre VII: *L'Art de Préluder: Préludes: for recorder; for transverse flute; for oboe; for treble viola da gamba. Airs et brunettes:* Arrangements of music by Mr Lambert, Lully, de Bousset etc.: *Fanfare et les Dieux for 3 transverse flutes.* (i) *Brunette: L'autre jour ma Cloris;* (i–ii) *Air de Mr Lambert: Goûtons un doux repos.* (iii) *Méthode pour La Musette;* Oeuvre X: *(Bourrée d'Achille; Contredanses: La pharaonne; La petite janeton. Marche des dragons (Air); Musette de Mr. Clerambault; Menuet: La Badaut; Prélude et la Régence; Tes beaux yeux ma Nicole; Rigaudons).*

(B) *** Seon/Sony SB2K 62942 (2) [S2K 62942]. Frans Brüggen, Walter van Hauwe, Barthold Kuijken, Oswald van Olmen, Bruce Haynes, Wieland Kuijken, Gustav Leonhardt, Shelley Gruskin; with (i) Marjanne Kweksilber; (ii) Toyohiko Satoh (lute); (iii) Shelley Gruskin (musette).

Jacques Hotteterre, born into a family of French instrument-makers, not only played and taught the recorder and flute but he also became a member of the chamber orchestra at the court of Louis XIV. As a composer he wrote some of the earliest music for the transverse flute and encouraged its use. He also perfected the musette, a kind of miniature bagpipe which looks a bit like a large embroidered sock with a mouthpiece. (Most of the instruments used are pictured in the accompanying booklet.) The present pair of discs gathers together Hotteterre's complete wind music (written between 1708 and 1738). An original oboe and a musette, both made by the composer, are featured in their performance. The programme includes well over two hours of music and it should be approached with some caution. Some of it, intended for the composer's pupils among the nobility, is not too demanding: the *Suite in G* for two transverse flutes is relatively simplistic if not without charm. One can also imagine an amateur showing off his expertise on the transverse flute with the little piece called *Echoes*. However, Hotteterre's invention is often resourceful, and the series of short dance-movements which make up the trio sonatas are certainly characterful. In his slow movements he languishes plaintively and with some individuality. The dolorous *Sarabandes* of the two *Suites for transverse flute and continuo* are quite affecting, and the following *Gavotte*, *Minuet* and *Gigue* of the D major work are all very personable. The *Trio sonatas* for a pair of oboes (with a bassoon featured in the continuo) and for two transverse flutes are texturally most diverting, and the latter also has some fine, expressive writing. The *Suite-Sonata* for oboe consists of five vignettes, none of which outlasts its welcome, and the similarly brief *Préludes* for various instruments have an attractive, improvisatory feeling. The closing surprise number for soprano (the sensitive Marjanne Kweksilber) and viola da gamba is quite haunting. Of the *Airs et Brunettes*, *L'autre jour ma Cloris* and the *Air de Mr Lambert* also feature the soprano voice, the latter with lute. They are both marked *Tendrement* and are genuinely touching. It is a pity the documentation does not include the words! The pieces for musette (which sounds like mini-bagpipes) are all piquant: they are offered as a series of interludes between the major works. The performances by a group of very distinguished soloists are of the highest calibre, and the recording is first class. Hotteterre proves to be a considerable musician and, if dipped into, this set offers much to reward the collector interested in offbeat baroque repertoire. It is very well, if rather closely, recorded.

Howells, Herbert (1892–1983)

(i) *Fantasia for cello and orchestra;* (ii) *Hymnus paradisi; Psalm 23.*

(B) **(*) BBC Radio Classics 15656 91982 [(M) id.]. (i) Alexander Baillie; (ii) April Cantelo, David Johnston, Three Choirs Festival Ch.; RPO, Hunt.

This radio recording of Howells's choral masterpiece, made in Gloucester Cathedral in 1982, may lack something in sharpness of focus, but it gains enormously from the cathedral acoustic, giving not just atmosphere but extra weight of choral sound compared with studio recordings. With Donald Hunt a most sympathetic interpreter, one who has made a speciality of conducting Howells's music, the passionate intensity of the writing, as in the beautiful setting of *Psalm 23*, is brought out all the more. The reflective *Fantasia for cello and orchestra*, like many of Howells's works, was ignored in his lifetime. It here makes a substantial fill-up, with Alexander Baillie a most sensitive soloist, though the dry studio recording is not helpful to the cello.

Hume, Tobias (*c.* 1575–1645)

Captain Humes Poeticall Musick (1607) (music for viols, lute and voice).
(BB) *** Naxos Dig. 8.55416/7 (available separately) [id.]. Les Voix Humains.

Tobias Hume was a mercenary who served in both the Swedish and Russian armies. Relatively little is known about him. The dedications of his two collections, the *First Part of Ayres* (1605) and the *Poeticall Musick* (1607), were designed to court favour, the first from the Earl of Pembroke and the second from Queen Anne. The Preface to the former fills in the picture: 'I Doe not study Eloquence, or professe Musicke, although I doe love Sence, and affect Harmony; My Profession being, as my Education hath been Armes, the onely effeminate part of me hath been Musicke: which in me hath been alwayes Generous because Mercenarie. To prayse Musicke, were to say the Sunne is bright.' His own life seems to have been anything but bright and he spent most of his years in penurious circumstances. He was admitted to the Charterhouse almshouse in 1629, which has drawn some experts in the field (including the authors of the *Grove* entry) to place his birth date at around 1569, as the minimum age for entry there was sixty. He was a champion of the viol as opposed to the lute, and the pieces recorded here vindicate him. It is obvious that he was an accomplished composer and this excellently recorded Canadian ensemble prove persuasive advocates. A most enjoyable and welcome addition to the catalogue.

Hummel, Johann (1778–1837)

Piano concertos: in A min., Op. 85; B min., Op. 89.
(BB) *** Discover Dig. DICD 920117 [id.]. Dana Protopopescu, Slovak R. New PO, Rahbari.

The *A minor* is Hummel's most often-heard piano concerto and, at bargain price, Discover offers an outstanding coupling. Well accompanied by the Slovak Radio New Philharmonic, Dana Protopopescu, always sounding fresh and spontaneous, plays with lightness, point and poetry. On her smaller scale, she even rivals Stephen Hough in his prize-winning recording of the same two concertos for Chandos at full price, though Hough is more impulsive.

Clarinet quartet in E flat.
(M) *** O-L 444 167-2. Alan Hacker, The Music Party – WEBER: *Clarinet quintet.* ***

A delectable work, played as beautifully as the Weber coupling. Alan Hacker uses a Goulding clarinet *circa* 1880, and this would be the sound Hummel himself would have recognized. Hacker plays allegros with plenty of character and spirit and, at times, a winning bite on the timbre, yet there is plenty of warmth in the lyrical music. The Music Party also use original instruments and their positive approach brings a matching touch of abrasiveness but no lack of feeling. Lovers of the authentic style will find this very stimulating.

Piano quintet in E flat, Op.87.
(B) **(*) Hyperion Dyad Dig. CDD 22008 (2) [id.]. Schubert Ens. of L. – SCHUBERT: *Trout quintet;* SCHUMANN: *Piano quintet; Piano quartet.* **(*)

A strong account of an impressive work from the Schubert Ensemble of London, who approach the piece as one in the classical mainstream rather than a *galant* entertainment. There is plenty of energy and commitment, and the brief *Largo* is made a touching interlude; only the finale (admittedly marked *Allegro agitato*) might seem too strongly driven and with not enough balancing elegance. The recording has fine immediacy.

Humperdinck, Engelbert (1854–1921)

The Bluebird: Prelude; Star dance. Hänsel und Gretel: Overture. Königskinder: Overture; Preludes to Acts II & III. The Sleeping Beauty: suite.
(M) **(*) Virgin/EMI Dig. CUV5 61128-2. Bamberg SO, Karl Anton Rickenbacher.

By far the most memorable piece here is the *Hänsel und Gretel Overture*, although the Introduction to Act III of *Königskinder* is also very touching, characteristically using horns to evoke the Minstrel's last song. The *Overture* to the same opera is significant in demonstrating Humperdinck's characteristic failing – a prolixity of ideas, none of which is quite memorable enough to emerge from the ongoing energy of the writing. His post-Wagnerian orchestration can be too thick and this inhibits his festive pieces, but the lightly scored items have charm, for instance the *Star dance* from *The Bluebird* or the *Ballade* from *The*

Sleeping Beauty. Rickenbacher secures warm, cultured playing from his Bambergers, and the Virgin sound is full and pleasing if lacking just a little in sparkle. Worth trying at mid-price.

Hänsel und Gretel (complete).
(M) (***) EMI mono CMS7 69293-2 (2) [Ang. CDMB 69293]. Schwarzkopf, Grümmer, Metternich, Ilsovay, Schürhoff, Felbermayer, Children's Ch., Philh. O, Karajan.
(M) **(*) RCA 74321 25281-2 (2). Moffo, Donath, Fischer-Dieskau, Berthold, Ludwig, Augér, Popp, Bav. R. Ch. & RSO, Eichhorn.
(M) **(*) Decca 455 063-2 (2). Brigitte Fassbaender, Lucia Popp, Julia Hamari, Walter Berry, Norma Burrowes, Edita Gruberová, Anny Schlemm, V. Boys' Ch., VPO, Solti.

Karajan's classic 1950s set of Humperdinck's children's opera, with Schwarzkopf and Grümmer peerless in the name-parts, is enchanting; this was an instance where everything in the recording went right. The original mono LP set was already extremely atmospheric. In most respects the sound has as much clarity and warmth as rival recordings made in the 1970s. There is much to delight here; the smaller parts are beautifully done and Else Schürhoff's Witch is memorable. The snag is that the digital remastering has brought a curious orchestral bass emphasis, noticeable in the overture and elsewhere, but notably in the *Witch's ride*.

There are some fine solo performances on the mid-priced 1971 RCA set, notably from Helen Donath as Gretel and Christa Ludwig as the Witch; and Kurt Eichhorn's direction is vigorous, with excellent orchestral playing and full, atmospheric recording. It is a pity that a more boyish-sounding singer than Anna Moffo could not have been chosen for the role of Hänsel but, all told, this is a colourful and enjoyable account of a unique, eternally fresh opera, well worth considering.

Solti with the Vienna Philharmonic directs a strong, spectacular version, emphasizing the Wagnerian associations of the score. Solti does the *Witch's ride* very excitingly, and the VPO are encouraged to play with consistent fervour throughout. The result, though rather lacking in charm, is well sung, with the two children both engagingly characterized. Edita Gruberová is an excellent Dew Fairy and Walter Berry is first rate as Peter. Anny Schlemm's Witch is memorable if vocally unsteady, and there are some imaginative touches of stereo production associated with *Hocus pocus* and her other moments of magic. The recording is even more vivid in its CD transfer.

Königskinder (complete).
(M) *** EMI (SIS) CMS5 66360-2 (3). Donath, Prey, Dallapozza, Schwarz, Unger, Ridderbusch, Bav. R. Ch., Tolz Boys' Ch., Munich R. O, Wallberg.

The success of *Hänsel und Gretel* has completely overshadowed this second fairy-tale opera of Humperdinck, which contains much fine music. Humperdinck had expanded his incidental music for a play to make this opera, which was given its première in New York in 1910. In a recording as fine as this it is a piece well worth investigation. Both the conducting and the singing of the principals are most persuasive.

Ibert, Jacques (1890–1962)

Bacchanale; Bostoniana; Divertissement; Louisville concerto; Symphonie marine.
(B) ** EMI CD-EMX 2269 [(M) id. import]. CBSO, Frémaux.

Frémaux's account of the *Divertissement* is warm-hearted and vigorous, with genuine exuberance in the 'police-whistle' finale, but the Birmingham recording is somewhat over-reverberant. It suits the *Bacchanale* rather more readily, although this is an empty piece to which Frémaux applies an appropriate degree of frenzy. The three other works are very well played, but the music itself is hardly more distinguished and scarcely does justice to the inventive powers of this often charming composer.

Divertissement.
(M) *** RCA 09026 61429-2 [id.]. Boston Pops O, Arthur Fiedler – OFFENBACH: *Collection*. **
(M) *** Decca (IMS) 448 571-2 [id.]. Paris Conservatoire O, Martinon – BIZET: *Jeux d'enfants* ***; BERLIOZ: *Overtures* **(*); SAINT-SAENS: *Danse macabre* etc. ***

Fiedler's racy account of Ibert's *Divertissement* is as sparkling as you could wish, with genuine Gallic insouciance. The *Valse*, *Parade* and exuberant *Finale* have tremendous élan. The recording too is splendidly lively and atmospheric. It is a pity that the Offenbach collection which acts as coupling is recorded less successfully.

Martinon's 1960 account has never been surpassed for its sheer fizzing energy and wit, and it is a pity that, as remastered for this reissue in Decca's 'Classic Sound' series, the *Introduction* sounds rather thin and shrill. But after that the sound fills out and the performance has marvellous aplomb. The galloping finale, complete with its uninhibited police-whistle, sounds for all the world like the accompaniment to a farcical police chase from the days of the Keystone Kops.

Escales (Ports of call).

(M) *** RCA 09026 61500-2 [id.]. Boston SO, Munch – DEBUSSY: *La Mer* **(*); SAINT-SAENS: *Symphony No. 3.* *** ✿

(M) **(*) Mercury (IMS) 432 003-2 [id.]. Detroit SO, Paray – RAVEL: *Alborada* etc. ***

Short though it is, this is a first-rate work. The opening of *Palermo* offers some ravishing textures from the Boston violins (French impressionism at its most seductive); the second evocation has a piquantly oriental favour and the finale, *Valencia*, has gay dance rhythms. Munch's performances are splendid and the 1956 recording, if balanced rather closely, has brilliance and transparency; although it does not sound as rich and sumptuous as the outstanding Saint-Saëns symphony with which it is coupled, the effect is slightly preferable to Paray's fine Mercury version.

Paray's recording catches the Mediterranean exoticism of *Escales* admirably, and the 1962 Mercury recording has plenty of atmosphere as well as glittering detail. The Ravel couplings are very impressive too.

Escales; Ouverture de fête; Tropisms pour des amours imaginaires.

(M) *** EMI CDM7 64276-2. Fr. Nat. R. O, Jean Martinon.

The well-known *Escales* have genuine atmosphere in Martinon's exemplary performance, and the 1974 recording is spacious, at times sensuously so, and pleasingly natural. The strings here have more allure than in Paray's Mercury version. *Tropisms* has moments of real imagination and is a piece of greater substance than the *Ouverture de fête* which, though it has a striking principal theme, is rather inflated. All three performances are expert and the CD transfer is most impressive.

3 Pièces brèves.

(M) *** Chandos CHAN 6543 [id.]. Athena Ens. – GOUNOD: *Petite symphonie in B flat;* POULENC: *Sextet.* ***

Ibert's *Trois Pièces brèves* could hardly be played with more polish, wit and affection than in this brilliantly realized performance by the Athena group. Each of the three movements is given complete individuality of style and mood, and together they add up to a most delectable whole, especially when recorded as well as they are here.

India, Sigismondo d' (*c.* 1582–*c.* 1630)

Duets, Laments and Madrigals: *Amico, hai vinto; Ancidetemi pur, dogliosi affanti; Che nudrisce tua speme; Giunto a la tomba; Langue al vostro languir; Occhi della mia vita; O leggiadr' occhi; Quella vermiglia rosa; Son gli accenti che ascolto; Torna il sereno Zefiro.*

(B) **(*) HM Musique d'Abord HMA 901011 [(M) id. import]. Concerto Vocale – CESTI: *Cantatas.* **(*)

Sigismondo d'India was among the vanguard of the new movement founded by Monteverdi at the beginning of the seventeenth century, and his laments show him to be a considerable master of expressive resource. The performances are authoritative, though there are moments of slightly self-conscious rubato that hold up the flow. The recording is fully acceptable and the coupling is also of considerable interest; this is worth exploring.

Il primo Libro de Madrigali (1606): *Interdette speranz'e van desio. Ottavo Libro de Madrigali: Il pastor fido,* Act IV, Scene 9: *Se tu, Silvio crudel, mi saetti* (five madrigal cycle).

✿ (M) *** Virgin Veritas/EMI Dig. VER5 61165-2 [CDM 61165-2]. Chiaroscuro, L. Baroque, Nigel Rogers – MONTEVERDI: *Madrigals.* *** ✿

The opening piece, d'India's *Interdette speranz'e van desio* ('Forbidden hopes and vain desire'), is freely set, and is stimulating as well as beautiful, but it is in the cycle from his Eighth Book of Madrigals, *Se tu, Silvio crudel, mi saetti*, that one experiences not only the composer's lyrical originality to the full but also his affinity with the operatic writing of his greater contemporary, Monteverdi. The vocal dialogue (which alternates, often subtly, solo and ensemble singing) expresses disdain and anger, love, pain and fear of death; and d'India's setting is touching and dramatic by turns, and also requires effortless vocal virtuosity. The quality of the performances is superlative, refined without a hint of preciosity, and always alive. The accompaniments on theorbo and harpsichord are delicately balanced, while the recording is immaculately realistic. An outstanding collection in every way.

Il terzo Libro de Madrigali.
(B) **(*) DHM Dig. 05472 77437-2 [id.]. The Consort of Musicke, Anthony Rooley.

Sigismondo d'India's *Third Book of Madrigals* dates from 1615, and their style often echoes the composer's contemporary, Monteverdi. Rooley's Consort blend admirably and sing *a cappella* with remarkable freshness in the early works, if perhaps a little coolly. Rooley feels that the later numbers, from No. 13 onwards, need the support of a discreet continuo, and certainly the singing of these last eight settings seems freer and richer. It was a pity that the bargain reissue did not run to translations, which surely would have been in the proper Baroque Esprit. But this remains an attractive disc.

Indy, Vincent d' (1851–1931)

Diptyque méditerranéan; Poème des rivages (symphonic suite).
(M) **(*) EMI Dig. CDM7 63954-2. Monte Carlo PO, Prêtre.

Neither work represents d'Indy at his most consistently inspired, but there are still good things. As Martin Cooper put it in his study of French music, 'in the *Poème des rivages* [d'Indy] distilled the last drops of that honey he had gathered so assiduously in the garden of Franck'. The comparison often made between the *Diptyque* and the glorious *Jour d'été à la montagne* is not flattering. But the *Soleil matinal* of the *Diptyque* has a blend of the Wagner of *Parsifal* and that quality of conservative impressionism which d'Indy made so much his own after the turn of the century. There are considerable beauties in this piece and in the *Poème* and, though the recording is not top-drawer, string textures are transparent, even diaphanous at gentler moments, and the sound does not lack allure. This is well worth investigating for, despite some unevenness of inspiration, Prêtre holds the music together impressively.

Jour d'été à la montagne, Op. 61; Tableaux de voyage, Op. 36.
(M) **(*) EMI CDM7 64364-2. Loire PO, Pierre Dervaux.

Jour d'été à la montagne was inspired by the beauties of the Vivarais region of central France where d'Indy was born. *Tableaux de voyage* is a delightful suite, written originally for piano. This is a most enjoyable coupling that reveals d'Indy as a far richer and more rewarding composer than most people give him credit for, and the performances are in no sense second-rate, even though the Orchestre Philharmonique des Pays de Loire is scarcely of international standing. The recording is very good and well transferred to CD, but the measure is short (47 minutes): the original LP included also *La forêt enchantée*.

Symphonie sur un chant montagnard français (Symphonie cévenole).
(M) **(*) RCA 09026 62582-2 [id.]. Henriot-Schweitzer, Boston SO, Charles Munch – BERLIOZ: *Harold in Italy*. *(*)
(BB) **(*) Naxos 8.550754 [id.]. Thiollier, Nat. SO of Ireland, Antonio de Almeida – FAURE: *Ballade;* FRANCK: *Symphonic variations*. **(*)
(M) ** Ph. 454 127-2. Bucquet, Monte Carlo Opera O, Capolongo – DUKAS: *L'apprenti sorcier* etc. *** ✿

Nicole Henriot-Schweitzer plays the piano part most sympathetically and Munch presents a fresh and crisp performance. The early (1958) stereo recording comes up well.

On Naxos the French-born but American-trained François-Joël Thiollier gives an intelligent performance of the *Symphonie sur un chant montagnard*. Perfectly acceptable, perfectly well accompanied and decently recorded (though the soloist is rather forwardly placed by the engineers) and with an interesting coupling. It is worth the money, but there are finer accounts to be had, some (like Jean-Yves Thibaudet) at full-price.

Marie-Françoise Bucquet is a strong and personable soloist, bringing out the affinities this concertante work has with Franck's *Symphonic variations*. The playing of the Monte Carlo orchestra under Capolongo is supportive, if unrefined, and the performance is at its best in the animated finale. But this is acceptable enough when the Dukas couplings are outstandingly successful.

(i) *Symphonie sur un chant montagnard français;* (ii) *Symphony No. 2 in B flat, Op. 57.*
(M) *** EMI CDM7 63952-2. (i) Ciccolini, O de Paris, Baudo; (ii) Toulouse Capitole O, Plasson.

Aldo Ciccolini gives a good account of himself in the demanding solo part of the *Symphonie*, and the Orchestre de Paris under Serge Baudo give sympathetic support. The recording is pleasing and with a convincing piano image. In the *Second Symphony* Michel Plasson proves a sympathetic and committed advocate, and his orchestra responds with enthusiasm and sensitivity to his direction. The recording too is spacious, full and well focused.

Ippolitov-Ivanov, Mikhail (1859–1935)

Caucasian sketches (suites): *Nos. 1, Op. 10; 2 (Iveria), Op. 42; Turkish fragments, Op. 62; Turkish march, Op. 55.*
(BB) ** Naxos Dig. 8.553405 [id.]. Nat. SO of Ukraine, Arthur Fagen.

Ippolitov-Ivanov's *Caucasian sketches*, once a popular favourite, particularly the *Procession of the Sardar*, have become neglected on disc, and a super-bargain version is welcome. The other pieces are imaginatively scored but less striking. The National Symphony Orchestra of the Ukraine respond well for Arthur Fagen and there is some felicitous wind playing. At its competitive price this would be eminently recommendable were the recording better balanced and defined.

Ireland, John (1879–1962)

Piano concerto in E flat.
(M) (***) Dutton Laboratories mono CDAX 8001 [id. full price]. Eileen Joyce, Hallé O, Leslie Heward – MOERAN: *Symphony*. *** ✿

(i) *Piano concerto in E flat;* (ii; iv) *A London overture;* (iii; iv) *Mai-Dun* (symphonic rhapsody); (v) *Comedy overture;* (vi) *Greater love hath no man;* (vii) *The Sally Gardens;* (viii) *Sea fever*.
(M) (***) EMI (SIS) stereo/mono CDM7 64716-2. (i) Colin Horsley, RPO, Basil Cameron; (ii) LSO; (iii) Hallé O; (iv) Barbirolli; (v) GUS, Kettering, Band, Geoffrey Brand; (vi) Chichester Cathedral Ch., John Birch; (vii) Dame Janet Baker, Gerald Moore; (viii) Robert Lloyd, Nina Walker.

Eileen Joyce's 1942 recording of this delightful concerto readily demonstrates the flamboyant romanticism for which she was famous and even a moment or two of fantasy, plus the freshness of discovery. Leslie Heward accompanies with flair, and the orchestral playing is impressive. The superb transfers of the original 78s show the work of Dutton Laboratories at its finest, offering sound that in its body and sense of presence sets new standards in re-creating what it felt like listening to the original 78s, with the one snag that, as the original shellac pressings were the source, there is noticeable wow on the piano tone, especially striking in the central *Lento*. No complaints about the orchestra: the strings are full and warm.

However, many listeners will prefer the later, stereo recording by Colin Horsley with Basil Cameron which retains that initial freshness and has excellent sound. In this performance the slow movement has a serene poise and beauty which are ravishingly memorable. In the finale Eileen Joyce has marginally greater dash, but Colin Horsley still offers plenty of sparkle and Basil Cameron proves a fine partner. The rest of the programme includes both the *London overture* and the brass band piece on which it was based. *Mai-Dun* receives persuasive advocacy from Barbirolli, but this is not Ireland at his finest. The composer's two most famous songs are also very welcome.

A London overture.
(M) *** EMI CDM5 65109-2 [id.]. LSO, Barbirolli – VAUGHAN WILLIAMS: *London symphony*. **(*)

One of Ireland's most immediately attractive works, and Barbirolli's performance of it is a great success, as is the remastering of an outstanding recording: the effect is tangible and real in its crisply vivid focus. The main theme (rhythmically conjuring up the bus conductor's call of 'Piccadilly!') is made obstinately memorable, and the ripe romanticism of the middle section is warmly expansive in Barbirolli's hands. The freshness of the sound makes the performance sound newly minted.

A London overture; Epic march; The Holy Boy; (i–ii) *Greater love hath no man; These things shall be;* (i–iii) *Vexilla Regis*.
(M) *** Chandos Enchant Dig. CHAN 7074 [id.]. LSO, Richard Hickox, with (i) London Symphony Ch.; (ii) Bryn Terfel; (iii) Paula Bott, Teresa Shaw, James Oxley.

This CD forms as good an introduction as any to John Ireland's music, which has not enjoyed the same revival of interest as his contemporary, Arnold Bax (although, of course, Ireland's splendid *Piano concerto* should be part of any representative collection). Richard Hickox is a sympathetic interpreter of the composer and obtains sensitive results (and good singing) in *The Holy Boy* and *These things shall be* (surprisingly, the latter is not otherwise available on silver disc). He does make heavy weather of the opening of *A London overture* but more than compensates for that in his sensitive phrasing of the second group. The disc is of particular interest in that it brings a rarity, *Vexilla Regis*, for chorus, brass and organ, composed when Ireland was nineteen and still a student of Stanford. First-class recorded sound.

PIANO MUSIC

April; The darkened valley; Green Ways (The cherry tree; Cypress; The palm and May); In those days (Daydream; Meridian); London pieces (Chelsea Reach; Ragamuffin; Soho forenoons); 3 Pastels (A Grecian lad; The boy bishop; Puck's birthday); Preludes (The undertone; Obsession; The holy boy; Fire of spring); A Sea idyll; Summer evening; The towing path.
(B) **(*) CfP Dig. CD-CFP 4674 [id.]. Desmond Wright.

Though Eric Parkin has over the years recorded a far wider range of Ireland's piano music, this selection on CfP brings together most of the favourites, like *Ragamuffin* from the *London pieces* and *The holy boy*, hauntingly lyrical, the third of the four *Preludes. The darkened valley* and *The towing path*, too, show Ireland at his most tenderly expressive. Though Desmond Wright is not always gentle enough in his treatment, these are fresh, responsive performances which gather together some of the most appealing English piano music written this century, too long neglected.

Ballade; Columbine; In those days; London pieces; Prelude in E flat; Sarnia.
(BB) *** Naxos Dig. 8.553700 [id.]. John Lenehan.

Few British composers match John Ireland in the felicity of his piano writing, which is both original and subtle and which deserves wider popularity than it currently enjoys with its distinctive added-note harmonies and tender melodies, and with vigorous pieces like *Ragamuffin* (second of the four *London pieces*) adding a salty tang. As a pianist himself, he wrote music which seems to fit under the fingers, and John Lenehan proves the most persuasive advocate, warmly expressive, using rubato in a totally idiomatic way. This first selection of pieces ranges from two which Ireland wrote when he was only sixteen, already hinting at his mature style – *Daydream and meridian*, published in his old age under the composite title, 'In those days' – and his very last piece, *Columbine*, open and fresh, not at all reflecting the illness from which he was suffering. The four *London pieces* are among his most colourful, not just *Ragamuffin*, played here with quicksilver lightness, but also the barcarolle-like *Chelsea Reach*, tenderly emotional. The most ambitious work is the three-movement suite, inspired by Guernsey, *Sarnia*, far more than a set of atmospheric colour pieces, written in 1940–41 just after Ireland had escaped from the island before the Nazi invasion. This music shows Ireland's poetic imagination to particular advantage and its last movement has echoes of the *Piano concerto in E flat*. John Lenehan is not always as well recorded (the sound hardens a little in loud passages) as Eric Parkin on Chandos at full price. However, this Naxos programme is very good indeed and bargain-hunters wanting this repertoire need not hesitate. This is a disc to recommend to more than just the specialist listener.

Five songs to poems by Thomas Hardy; The Advent; Friendship in misfortune; Great things; The Heart's desire; Hymn for a child; I have twelve oxen; Love and friendship; The Merry month of May; My fair; The Sacred flame; The Sally gardens; Santa Chiara; The Scapegoat; The Soldier's return; Spring sorrow.
(M) (**(*)) Saga mono EC 3338-2. John Shirley-Quirk, Eric Parkin.

John Shirley-Quirk's performances are as fine as those on his earlier disc of Vaughan Williams and others. Eric Parkin makes a splendidly convincing accompanist, and it is the piano part which constantly impresses with its felicity rather than the vocal line. For all the attractiveness of the idiom, Ireland rarely seems to let himself go with a real tune. The melodic lines are beautiful to look at on paper but, largely through the constant wandering of key, they do not quite add up. One recalls Anna Russell's famous phrase about the modern British 'folksong' that constantly sounds as if it is going to develop into a tune but never quite does. Despite the disappointment, these are finely wrought songs, certain to be interesting to Lieder specialists, and the performances here add to that interest. The recording is more than acceptably clear.

Ives, Charles (1874–1954)

(i) *Central Park in the dark;* (ii–iii) *Holidays Symphony;* (ii) *The unanswered question.*
(M) *** Sony SMK 60203 [id.]. NYPO, (i) Seiji Ozawa & Maurice Peress (under the supervision of Bernstein); (ii) Bernstein; (iii) with Seymour Lipkin (assistant conductor), Camerata Singers, Abraham Kaplan – CARTER: *Concerto for orchestra.* ***

Central Park in the dark, as the title implies, provides a brilliant collection of evening sounds, evocative yet bewildering, Its musical complexity ideally demands two separate conductors and that is why Ozawa and Peress here directed the piece (magnetically) under Bernstein's supervision. The so-called *Holidays Symphony* (also known as *New England holidays*) consists of four fine Ives pieces, often heard separately. The first three, *George Washington's birthday*, *Decoration Day* and *The Fourth of July*, with their still-startling clashes of impressionistic imagery, are well enough known. The fourth – full title: *Thanksgiving* and/or *Forefathers Day* – is more of a rarity, bringing in a full chorus to sing a single verse of a hymn at the close. The performance is red-bloodedly convincing yet has remarkably clear detail, an extraordinary phantasmagoria of ideas, jostling and overlaying one another, with the serene central section of that final movement wonderfully touching. *The unanswered question* is probably the most purely beautiful music Ives ever wrote, with muted strings (curiously representing silence) set against a trumpet representing the problem of existence. No need to worry about Ives's philosophy when the results are so naturally moving. Superb playing (the trumpeter is William Vacchiano) and vivid recording, but the forward balance means the lack of a true pianissimo, especially noticeable in *The unanswered question*.

(i) *Central Park in the dark;* (ii) *Three places in New England;* (iii) *Piano sonata No. 2 (Concord, Mass., 1840–1860).*

(B) *** DG Classikon 439 480-2 [(M) id. import]. (i) Boston SO, Ozawa; or (ii) Tilson Thomas; (iii) Roberto Szidon (with Dieter Sonntag, flute).

An outstanding and highly recommendable bargain anthology. The Boston Symphony Orchestra plays quite magnificently in the two orchestral works, so full of evocative atmosphere, and the DG engineers produce a most musical balance. Michael Tilson Thomas gives an eloquent and poetic acccount of Ives's pioneering *Three places in New England*, completed in 1914, but which still has the power to surprise the unsuspecting listener. Most remarkable of all is Roberto Szidon's unsurpassed account of the *Concord Sonata*. It is a very demanding work, not easy to get to grips with, but the concentration of the performance here gives the reading enormous authority. Szidon is admirably recorded, whereas his most important predecessor, John Kirkpatrick, was given less than first-class sound in his CBS version. In the last movement a brief melody is given to the flute. When questioned about this, Ives replied nonchalantly that the flute was right for that particular moment in the music and, as no one was likely to play the sonata anyway, there would be no performance difficulties!

Orchestral set No. 2.

(M) *** Decca Phase Four 448 956-2 [id.]. LSO Ch., LSO, Stokowski – GROFE: *Grand Canyon suite.* *(*)

The *Second Orchestral set* consists of three highly evocative pieces crammed with the sort of wild devices that make Ives's music so distinctive. Most memorable is the third of the pieces called (extravagantly) *From Hanover Square North, at the End of a Tragic Day (1915), the Voices of the People Again Rose*. It depicts an incident on the elevated railway on the day when the *Lusitania* was sunk, when the crowd spontaneously started to sing *In the sweet bye and bye*. In such atmospheric music Stokowski's wonderful sense of dramatic development is perfectly exploited. The multi-channel Phase Four recording, made in 1970, is well suited to the music, and the LSO obviously enjoys the experience, not least in the ragtime of the second piece, and the Kingsway Hall ambience ensures plenty of atmosphere, especially in the spectacular choral finale.

Symphony No. 1 in D min.; Orchestral set No. 2. Robert Browning overture; The unanswered question.

(BB) **(*) RCA Navigator 74321 29246-2 [(M) id. import]. Chicago SO, Morton Gould.

This very first recording of the *First Symphony*, an immediately attractive work, was made in 1965; it has that special quality of freshness almost always found in recording premières, with the mercurial spirit of Ives emerging every so often, so that the result is very enjoyable indeed. The *Robert Browning overture* (at 20 minutes) has some good ideas but rather outstays its welcome, and the three pieces of the *Orchestral set* are attractive without here achieving quite the degree of sharp memorability which marks *The unanswered question*, one of the composer's most beautiful and imaginative pieces. Gould's performances are sympathetic and very well played, but they just lack the intensity that Bernstein and others brought to them, although they are still pretty magnetic. Indeed this bargain-basement CD is worth having for the symphony alone, and the mid-1960s recordings are basically warm and atmospheric, even if the violins are very brightly lit, and even fierce at times. But if you are a newcomer to Ives, this is a good (and inexpensive) place to start.

Symphonies Nos. 1 in D min.; 2.

(M) ** Van. 08 6153 71. New Philh. O, Harold Faberman.

Ives's *First Symphony* is a naïve piece written while he was still studying at Harvard. Two of the four movements were designed as composition exercises for his very conservative professor, Horatio Parker. The music is agreeable enough, but with little of the originality or bite that one associates with later Ives. Faberman conducts a warmly lyrical rather than a thrusting performance and secures some fine playing (especially from the cor anglais) in the genuinely touching *Adagio*. The *Second Symphony*, which Ives began before he had finished the *First*, marks a complete change of voice, for in this later, five-sectioned work (the outer movements are sub-divided) he uninhibitedly adopts the strange montage techniques which became his trademark. Tracking down all the quotations is a game in itself – from Beethoven and Brahms as well as the regular Ives field of such songs as *Turkey in the straw*, *Camptown races* and *Columbia the gem of the ocean*. It is not as fiercely dissonant as later works, especially in this comparatively tame – again very lyrical – performance, although the closing section makes quite a strong impact. The warmly spacious recording suits Faberman's unaggressive manner.

Symphony No. 2; Symphony No. 3 (The camp meeting).
(M) *** Sony SMK 60202 [id.]. NYPO, Bernsein (with talk: 'Leonard Bernstein discusses Charles Ives').

Bernstein re-recorded this music more recently for DG, but these earlier CBS/Sony recordings (from 1958 and 1965 respectively) have characteristic conviction and freshness. The remastered sound is amazingly improved over the old LPs, full and atmospheric, with glowing sounds from the NYPO woodwind and a satisfying depth and resonance from the strings. The balance is too close, but the dynamics of the playing convey the fullest range of emotion. The readings are in a class of their own and by their side the Faberman performances seem lukewarm. This reissue includes Bernstein's illustrated lecture on Ives (recorded in 1966). 'Suddenly Charles Ives is on the verge of being canonized,' he says. It is some tribute to Bernstein's advocacy that one welcomes the development.

Symphony No. 3; 3 Places in New England.
(M) *** Mercury 432 755-2 [id.]. Eastman-Rochester O, Howard Hanson – SCHUMAN: *New England triptych* ***; MENNIN: *Symphony No. 5*. **(*)

Ives's quixotic genius is at its most individual in the *Three places in New England*. Both works are most understandingly presented on Mercury under Howard Hanson, who is equally at home in the folksy imagery of the *Third Symphony*. The acoustics of the Eastman Theatre are less than ideally expansive, but the 1957 recording is remarkably full-bodied and vivid.

Symphonies Nos. 3 (The camp meeting); 4. 3 Outdoor scenes: Hallowe'en.
(M) ** Van. 08 6154 71. New Philh. O, Harold Faberman.

Ives confected his *Third Symphony* from music he had already written for other forces, the first and third movements from organ works and the middle movement from a piece for organ and string quartet. By Ives standards it is a mild work, but one which certainly has the stamp of his individuality, and Haberman's performance is quite persuasive, when the orchestral playing is so warm and polished. The *Fourth Symphony* is far more ambitious and was hailed in America after Ives's death as a supreme example of American music. It is hardly that, though in a dedicated performance like Stokowski's (currently unavailable in the UK) it has plenty of electricity. Faberman is more careful. He copes very ably with the composer's impossible demands in controlling conflicting rhythmic patterns, using the version for single conductor. It is not as exciting as it should be, but the slow movement is warmly played, if it is not passionately intense, and the recording (late-1960s vintage) is very good if not sharply defined. The fill-up, *Hallowe'en*, was described by the composer as 'a kind of April Fool piece for a Hallowe'en party', and with its bass-drum bangs certainly reveals the composer as having fun, even if the playing lacks the dynamic energy one seeks in so wild a composer. Nevetheless this pair of Vanguard discs is by no means to be written off, for Faberman consistently finds an underlying expansive warmth in Ives's music that is much less apparent in more aggressively spectacular performances.

Janáček, Leoš (1854–1928)

(i) *Capriccio for piano and wind; Concertino for piano and chamber ensemble;* (ii) *Lachian dances;* (iii) *Sinfonietta;* (iv) *Suite for string orchestra;* (iii) *Taras Bulba;* (v) *Mládí* (suite for wind).
(B) *** Decca Double Analogue/Dig. 448 255-2 (2) [(M) id. import]. (i) Paul Crossley, L. Sinf., David Atherton; (ii) LPO, Huybrechts; (iii) VPO, Mackerras; (iv) LAPO, Marriner; (v) Bell, Craxton, Pay, Harris, Gatt, Eastop.

This Double Decca offers much essential Janáček in absolutely first-class performances and recordings. Paul Crossley is the impressive soloist in the *Capriccio* and the *Concertino*, performances that can be put alongside those of Firkušný – and no praise can be higher. This account of *Mládí* is among the finest available; the work's youthful sparkle comes across to excellent effect here, while the late-1970s analogue sound is very truthful and well balanced. Mackerras's VPO coupling of the *Sinfonietta* and *Taras Bulba* is digital (1980). The massed brass of the *Sinfonietta* has tremendous bite and brilliance as well as characteristic Viennese ripeness. *Taras Bulba* is also given more weight and body than usual, the often savage dance-rhythms presented with great energy. The music of the *Lachian dances*, while vividly scored, is on a rather lower level of inspiration, but the performance here under the Belgian conductor, François Huybrechts, is highly idiomatic and effective, and he is helped by fine playing from the LPO and more high-quality Decca sound – using the Kingsway Hall to good effect. The *Suite for string orchestra* was Marriner's first recording with the Los Angeles Chamber Orchestra, made in England during the orchestra's 1974 tour. The recording site was St John's, Smith Square, and the sound is characteristically ripe. The *Suite* is an early and not entirely mature piece but, when played as committedly as it is here, its attractions are readily perceived, and it certainly does not want character.

(i) *Concertino for piano and seven instruments;* (ii) *Sinfonietta; Taras Bulba.*
(B) *** DG Classikon 439 437-2 [id.]. (i) Rudolf Firkušný (Bav. RSO (members)); (ii) Bav. RSO; Kubelik.

A quite outstanding bargain triptych that would make a worthwhile addition to any collection, large or small. Kubelik has a special feeling for this repertoire and he partners Firkušný in a thoroughly idiomatic account of the *Concertino*, with the dialogue between keyboard and sparsely scored accompaniment both plangent and witty. *Taras Bulba* with its unpleasant scenario of death and torture is powerfully evoked, with a discerning balance between passion and subtlety. The organ part is integrated into the texture most delicately in the first section, yet adds grandiloquence to the work's triumphant apotheosis, with its vision of a triumphant Cossack future. Virtuoso playing from the Bavarian orchestra throughout, with much excitement generated in the last two sections. The orchestra is hardly less impressive in the *Sinfonietta* (and particularly so in the central movements), while at the opening and close of the work the spacious acoustic of the Munich Herculessaal is especially suited to the massed brass effects. The vintage (1970) recording has been superbly remastered and sounds amazingly fresh.

(i) *Violin concerto. Sinfonietta; The cunning little vixen* (suite).
(BB) ** Arte Nova Dig. 74321 30481-2. (i) Christiane Edinger; SüdWestFunk SO, Neumann.

These Arte Nova performances come from the studios of SüdWestFunk in Baden-Baden and an orchestra whose conductors have included such eminent figures as Hans Rosbaud and Ernest Bour. The recording of the *Sinfonietta* dates from 1990, as does that of the *Concerto*; *The cunning little vixen* suite (presumably in Talich's version, though this is not credited) was recorded in 1986. These are perfectly serviceable and well-recorded accounts, though they are not superior to the mid-price or bargain versions of the *Sinfonietta* by Kubelik (DG) or Mackerras (Double Decca). The SüdWestFunk is a good orchestra, but its strings are not as good as those of the Vienna Philharmonic for Mackerras or the magnificent Bavarian Radio Orchestra for Kubelik. Christiane Edinger is an excellent soloist in the 1988 reconstruction of the *Violin concerto* on which Janáček was working in his last months. Acceptable though it is, this Arte Nova disc is not a front-line recommendation.

Sinfonietta.
(M) *** DG (IMS) Dig. 445 501-2 [id.]. BPO, Abbado – BARTOK: *The Miraculous Mandarin* etc. ***
(M) *** Decca 448 579-2. LSO, Abbado – HINDEMITH: *Symphonic metamorphoses;* PROKOFIEV: *Symphony No. 3.* ***
(B) *** EMI forte CZS5 72664-2 (2) [(M) id. import]. Chicago SO, Seiji Ozawa – BARTOK: *Concerto for orchestra;* LUTOSLAWSKI: *Concerto for orchestra;* STRAVINSKY: *Firebird ballet.* **(*)
(M) *** EMI Dig. CDM7 64740-2 [id.]. Philh. O, Rattle – HOLST: *Planets.* **(*)

Sinfonietta; Lachian dances; Taras Bulba.
(BB) *** Naxos Dig. 8.550411 [id.]. Slovak RSO (Bratislava), Ondrej Lenárd.

Sinfonietta; Taras Bulba.
(M) (*) Ph. (IMS) 442 660-2. Rotterdam PO, Zinman – DVORAK: *Czech suite.* **

(i) *Sinfonietta;* (ii) *Taras Bulba;* (iii) *The cunning little vixen:* suite.
(BB) **(*) RCA Navigator 74321 29251-2 [(M) id. import]. (i) USSR RSO, Bolshoi Theatre Brass O; (ii) USSR MoC SO; (iiii) Leningrad PO; Rozhdestvensky.
(B) ** Sony SBK 62404; *SBT 62404* [id.]. (i) Cleveland O, Szell; (ii) Toronto SO, A. Davis – KODALY: *Dances of Galánta; Dances of Marosszék.* **(*)

Abbado's DG recording was made in 1987, some two decades after his admirable Decca version with the LSO. Now he has the advantage of digital recording and the Berlin Philharmonic Orchestra on splendid form. The Jesus-Christus Kirche provides a superbly spacious sonority for the brass. The opening of the Berlin performance brings a tautening of the pace, but the interpretation is not greatly changed and the subtleties of colour are not diminished by the more robust body of the newer version.

In his earlier, Decca recording Abbado gives a splendid account of the *Sinfonietta* and evokes a highly sympathetic response from the LSO. His acute sensitivity to dynamic nuances and his care for detail are felt in every bar. The recording balance, too, allows the subtlest of colours to register while still having plenty of impact.

Ozawa's account too is brilliantly played and very well recorded (in 1969). The CD transfer is also very successful, full-bodied if not opulent. A useful alternative to Abbado, if the three coupings are suitable.

Rattle gets an altogether first-class response from the orchestra and truthful recorded sound from the EMI engineers; however, this CD has a less successful Holst coupling.

On Naxos we have the normal LP coupling of the *Sinfonietta* and *Taras Bulba*, but with the *Lachian dances* thrown in for good measure, all played by musicians steeped in the Janáček tradition – and all at a very modest cost. These are excellent performances and well worth the money involved; the recording, made in a fairly resonant studio, is natural and free from any artificially spotlit balance.

The very modestly priced Navigator triptych draws on three different Russian orchestras, all of which are thoroughly at home in Janáček's special sound-world. In the *Sinfonietta* the Bolshoi brass (with Slavonic vibrato) are suitably pungent, and especially arresting at the close. The inner movements are strongly characterized by Rozhdestvensky, and he is equally impressive in the vibrantly atmospheric account of *Taras Bulba*. This is a live, digital recording from 1985; the others are from 1965 and 1976 respectively, and all offer sound which is both vivid and atmospheric. The suite from *The cunning little vixen* consists of two 'interludes', each about nine minutes in length. They are beautifully played at another live concert, but the audience indicates its presence only at the beginning and end. Excellent value.

Szell's 1965 recording of the *Sinfonietta* has long been admired for its orchestral virtuosity and control. It is a very spirited and colourful account, and the new transfer brings out the ambient effect of the Severance Hall recording, even if the dynamic range remains less expansive than it should be. But the real snag here is that Andrew Davis's *Taras Bulba* has an altogether lower voltage. What a pity that was included instead of Ormandy's *Háry János suite*.

It is the mark of a complete lack of impact in a performance of Janáček's *Sinfonietta* when the most memorable movements are the second (*Andante*) and the fourth (*Allegretto*). The refined orchestral playing by the Rotterdam orchestra under Zinman and the distanced, warmly atmospheric sound-picture take all the abrasive edge from the music, and *Taras Bulba* also projects little sense of villainy in a piece in which the hero is nailed to a tree and set on fire!

Suite for string orchestra.
(B) *** Discover Dig. DICD 920234 [id.]. Virtuosi di Praga, Vlček – SUK: *Serenade for strings* etc. **(*)

The expanded Virtuosi di Praga give an appropriately ardent and certainly a bravura account of Janáček's six-movement *Suite for string orchestra*, an early work (1893) yet one full of melodic diversity and individuality. The recording shows this group of seventeen players (including the leader/director, Oldřich Vlček) as possessing a vividly full sonority, yet they do not miss the work's more subtle touches, and this inexpensive disc is a welcome addition to the catalogue.

CHAMBER MUSIC

(i) *Capriccio for piano and 7 instruments; Concertino for piano and 6 instruments. (Piano) Sonata (1.X.1905); In the mist; On an overgrown path I and II; Reminiscences; Zdenka variations.*
(M) *** DG 449 764-2 (2) [id.]. Rudolf Firkušný; (i) Bav. RSO (members), Kubelik.

Now reissued in DG's series of 'Originals', this is an eminently recommendable set. Firkušný played to Janáček as a small boy and has long been regarded as the most authoritative exponent of the piano music. Firkušný recorded the piano pieces in the early 1970s and he produces seamless legato lines, hammerless tone and rapt atmosphere. Kubelik then partners Firkušný in discerningly sympathetic accounts of the *Concertino* and *Capriccio*. The recordings, from the same period, are of high quality.

(i; ii) *Concertino;* (ii) *Mládi;* (i) *In the mists.*
(M) **(*) EMI CDM5 65304-2 [id.]. (i) Lamar Crowson; (ii) Melos Ens. – NIELSEN: *Wind quintet.* ***

The Melos Ensemble give a very characterful account of *Mládi*, a remarkable evocation of youth. The analogue recording, made in the late 1960s, is very good indeed, as it is in the *Concertino*. Lamar Crowson is completely inside the idiom here and in sensitivity and imagination is second to none. Likewise *In the mists* is poetic and unfailingly perceptive and withstands comparison with both Firkušný, Andsnes and others, save for one reservation concerning the recording: the piano is not in ideal condition and there could be more space round the sound. This does not apply in the *Concertino*, which sounds suitably vibrant.

Pohádka.

(BB) *** ASV Quicksilva Dig. CDQS 6218 [id.]. Bernard Gregor-Smith, Yolande Wrigley – PROKOFIEV; SHOSTAKOVICH: *Cello sonatas;* MARTINU: *Variations.* ***

The husband-and-wife team of Bernard Gregor-Smith and Yolande Wrigley gives a lively and sympathetic account of the three-movement *Pohádka,* which Janáček composed in 1910. It makes an admirable makeweight for the Prokofiev and Shostakovich sonatas.

(i) *String quartets Nos. 1–2;* (ii) *Pohádka for cello and piano;* (iii) *Violin sonata.*

(BB) *** Naxos Dig. 8.553895 [id.]. (i) Vlach Qt, Prague; (ii) Mikael Ericsson; (ii–iii) František Maly; (iii) Jana Vlachová.

There are doubtless finer performances of the two *Quartets* in the CD catalogue, but the Vlach Quartet, Prague (presumably so named so as to avoid confusion with the Vlach Quartet of the 1960s) give very acceptable, impassioned accounts of both and are warmly recorded. Moreoever the account of the *Violin sonata* by Jana Vlachová and František Maly is very fine, and the *Pohádka for cello and piano* is given as touching and imaginative a performance by Mikael Ericsson as any in the catalogue. Good recordings and good value for money.

PIANO MUSIC

Along an overgrown path, Books I–II; Piano sonata (1 X 1905).

(BB) *(*) Naxos Dig. 8.553586 [id.]. Thomas Hlawatsch.

Thomas Hlawatsch is Austrian born and generally has a good feeling for Janáček. The first movement of *Along an overgrown path* is curiously pedestrian, but as we proceed there are glimpses of greater feeling. The acoustic of the Festetics Castle in Keszthely is reverberant and results in some clangorous tone in climaxes, and *They chattered like swallows* is very muddied. Hlawatsch is curiously off-hand in this movement but sensitive at the opening of *Good night!*. This is acceptable enough, but readers would be better to choose the Firkušný DG collection.

Concerto for piano, two violins, viola, clarinet and horn; In the mist (including original version of fourth movt); *3 Moravian Dances; Music for Exercise gymnastique; A Recollection; Variations for Zdenka, Op. 1.*

(BB) ** Naxos Dig. 8.553587 [id.]. Thomas Hlawatsch.

In the second Naxos collection the balance is better and Hlawatsch proves a sensitive interpreter of *In the mist.* His disc is of special interest in that it includes the first version of the last movement; and there are other rarities, including the *Zdenka variations*. Firkušný studied with the composer as a child and he brings special authority to this repertoire which this present issue does not challenge.

VOCAL MUSIC

Mass in E flat; (i) *Otčenáš (The Lord's Prayer).*

(M) *** EMI Dig. CDM5 65587-2. King's College, Cambridge, Ch., Cleobury; Stephen Lane; (i) with Arthur Davies, Osian Ellis – KODALY: *Missa brevis.* **(*)

The *Mass* comes from 1907–8 and was never completely finished. It is possible that Janáček used some of it twenty years later in the *Glagolitic Mass*. Janáček's pupil, Vilém Petrželka, discovered the *Kyrie* and *Agnus Dei* and a part of the *Credo*, which he completed. It is a beautiful piece. *Otčenáš* (*The Lord's Prayer*) is earlier (1901), written originally for tenor, chorus and harmonium (or piano); accompaniment was replaced in 1906 by organ and harp. The singing is generally good, though the sound is (not unnaturally) English rather than Slavonic. There is no alternative version of either work, and they are both valuable additions to the Janáček discography.

OPERA

Jenůfa (complete).

(M) **(*) EMI CMS5 64576-2 (2). Domanínská, Kniplová, Přibyl, Zídek, Prague Nat. Theatre Ch. & O, Bohumil Gregor.

The 1969 Prague version of *Jenůfa* was originally issued on the Supraphon label, in a co-production with EMI. Its main strength lies in the fine characterization of the mother, the Kostelnička, the most complex and dominant figure in the action. Though none of the singers may be absolutely first class, and they are not free from Slav vibrato, the company has fine teamwork and Bohumil Gregor directs the performance with genuine imaginative vitality and succeeds in conveying the compelling atmosphere of the score.

However, the acoustic of this recording is rather reverberant and, though the CD transfer has improved the focus considerably, detail is inevitably smudged when compared with the later, full-priced Decca set. Even so, it remains vibrantly enjoyable and is well documented, with a clearly printed libretto.

Janiewicz, Feliks (1762–1848)

Divertimento for strings.

(B) *** EMI forte (SIS) CZS5 69524-2 (2) [CDFB 69524]. Polish CO, Maksymiuk – MENDELSSOHN: *String symphonies;* ROSSINI: *String sonatas;* JARZEBSKI: *Tamburetta; Chromatica.* ***

Feliks Janiewicz, born in Poland, travelled widely in Europe before settling in England, where he played in Haydn's London concerts. He then moved to Liverpool (where he married a Miss Eliza Breeze) and ran a music-publishing business, finally ending up in Edinburgh. He was an almost exact contemporary of Rossini, and this delightful work (one of six, written in London around 1805) might well have been another of Rossini's string sonatas, for the writing shares their brilliance and wit. The finale is a *tour de force* of bravura, relished here by this excellent Polish string band. A real find.

Jarzebski, Adam (*c.* 1590–*c.* 1649)

Tamburetta; Chromatica.

(B) *** EMI forte (SIS) CZS5 69524-2 (2) [CDFB 69524]. Polish CO, Maksymiuk – MENDELSSOHN: *String symphonies;* ROSSINI: *String sonatas;* JANIEWICZ: *Divertimento.* ***

Adam Jarzebski spent most of his career in the orchestra of the Warsaw Royal Chapel. These two delightful lollipops show him to be a composer of real personality, the *Tamburetta* bouncing along joyously, with staccato bowing from the Polish strings adding to the rhythmic life, the second changing its mood from dance-like vivacity to stately yet slightly doleful elegance. Marvellous bravura playing from the Polish strings and vividly bright recording add to the music's projection.

Jessel, Léon (1871–1942)

Schwarzwaldmädel (The Black Forest Maiden).

(M) ** EMI CDM5 66380-2. Lindner, Fack, Koller, Kusche, Dallapozza, Finke, Mitglieder des Stuttgart Liederkranz, Stuttgart PO, Willy Mattes.

Schwarzwaldmädel ('The Black Forest Maiden') is the best known of the many operettas of Leon Jessel, a jolly piece full of amiable echoes of German folk-music. First heard in Berlin in 1917, it provided at the time an obvious antidote to wartime gloom, with its undemanding story of lovers' tiffs, and has since remained in the German repertory. This Stuttgart recording, made in 1976, winningly brings out the colour and vigour of the piece, using soloists very much in tune with the operetta style. The tenor, Adolf Dallapozza, makes a ringing hero, though Dagmar Koller as the coquettish heroine, Malwine von Hainau, with her shrill soprano is far less persuasive. With no spoken dialogue between numbers, the 14 numbers in three Acts fit easily on a single CD, but the recording, made in the Stuttgart Philharmonie, is rather too reverberant for a comic operetta. The booklet provides only a synopsis and no text or information on the work or its composer.

Joachim, Joseph (1831–1907)

(i) *Violin concerto in Hungarian style, Op. 11. Overtures: Hamlet, Op. 4; Henry IV, Op. 7.*

(B) *** Carlton Dig. 30367 02092 [id.(M)]. (i) Elmar Oliveira; LPO, Leon Botstein.

Joseph Joachim's fame rests as a legendary performer and the dedicatee of the Brahms *Violin concerto*, rather than as a composer. Nevertheless his concerto is one of the most demanding works written for the instrument in the nineteenth century. Conservative in outlook and indebted to Mendelssohn and Beethoven, it is a very considerable achievement – as, for that matter, is the playing of Elmar Oliveira in this truthful, present and well-balanced recording. The conductor Leon Botstein also gives committed accounts of the splendid *Henry IV* and *Hamlet Overtures*. An enterprising and rewarding release.

Johansen, David Monrad (1888–1974)

String quartet, Op. 36.
(BB) *** Naxos Dig. 8.550879 [id.]. Oslo String Qt – GRIEG: *String quartets.* ***

David Monrad Johansen was an important figure in Norwegian musical life during the 1930s. His *String quartet*, composed in 1969 when in his early eighties, is persuasively played by the Oslo String Quartet and is impeccably recorded. It is a well-crafted piece but not as distinctively personal as *Pan* or the best of his mature works.

Joplin, Scott (1868–1917)

Bethena; Bink's waltz; Cascades; The Chrysanthemum (Afro-America intermezzo); Easy winners; The Entertainer; Gladiolus rag; Maple leaf rag; Original rags; Pine apple rag; Pleasant moments (ragtime waltz); Searchlight rag; Solace (Mexican serenade); Sunflower slow-drag (ragtime two-step); Swipesy cakewalk.
(B) ** Sony Dig. SBK 62833; *SBT 62833* [id.]. Roy Eaton.

Roy Eaton's relaxed, very personalized rhythmic style is much less deadpan than with some presenters of these famous rags. He certainly charms in his easy account of the *Swipesy cakewalk*, but in *The Chrysanthemum*, *Easy winners* and particularly *The Entertainer* some might find his little touches of hesitant rubato too personalized, although this works better in the *Bethena* concert waltz. Eaton certainly feels the music's basic pulse and his echoing of phrases is often effective, especially so in the *The Cascades*. But this is not for those who like their Joplin rags straight. Good, clear, digital sound.

Rags: *Bethena (concert waltz); Cascades rag; Country club (ragtime two-step); Elite syncopations; The Entertainer; Euphonic sounds (A syncopated novelty); Fig leaf rag; Gladiolus rag; Magnetic rag (syncopations classiques); Maple leaf rag; Paragon rag; Pine apple rag; Ragtime dance; Scott Joplin's new rag; Solace (Mexican serenade); Stoptime rag; Weeping willow (ragtime two-step).*
(M) *** Nonesuch Elektra/Warner 7559 79449-2; *7559 79449-4* [id.]. Joshua Rifkin.

Joshua Rifkin is the pianist whose name has been indelibly associated with the Scott Joplin revival, originally stimulated by the soundtrack music of the very successful film, *The Sting*. His relaxed, cool rhythmic style is at times more subtle than that of other interpreters and, although the piano timbre is full, there is a touch of monochrome in the tone-colour. The current remastering gives the piano a natural presence.

Josquin Desprez (died 1521)

Absalom fili mi; Ave Maria; Missa l'homme armé sexti toni.
✿ (BB) *** Naxos Dig. 8.553428 [id.]. Oxford Camerata, Jeremy Summerly (with VINDERS: *Lament on the death of Josquin* ***).

Continuing his exploration of the various early Masses based on the medieval chanson, *L'homme armé*, Jeremy Summerly arrives at Josquin Desprez, whose date of birth now appears to be later than previously thought – some time in the late 1450s. The *Missa l'homme armé sexti toni* is so called to make a distinction between this and Josquin's other Mass using the same cantus firmus, the *Missa L'homme armé super voces musicales*, where the last note of the cantus is different, F instead of G, as favoured by most other composers, including Dufay (see above). The character of the melody is made more positive here. Another interesting feature of the Josquin setting is his interpolation of a trope (*Laeta Dies*) following the *Credo* and before the *Sanctus*. This uses a non-liturgical text ('The happy day of our great leader bringing gifts of new light today is reborn') and returns to a bold re-presentation of the cantus firmus, only very slightly altered. The effect is undoubtedly dramatic at the centre of a work where the flowing lines of the polyphony have such a rich harmonic implication, especially noticeable in the *Kyrie* and again in the *Agnus Dei*, which moves with such serene confidence. The long *Credo* breaks free, with the polyphony becoming more animated, and so becomes the central focus of the whole Mass – and what a beautiful Mass it is; very beautifully sung and recorded here. The *Ave Maria* is used to create a tranquil mood before the Mass itself begins, and the very touching motet, *Absalon, fili mi*, makes a poignant coda. This is followed by the radiant elegy of Josquin's contemporary, Jheronimus Vinders, with its soaring treble line, surely a fitting tribute. With full texts provided, this CD is one of the very finest of this distinguished Naxos series.

Motets: *Absolom, fili mi; Ave Maria, gratia plena; De profundis clamavi; In te Domine speravi per trovar pietà; Veni, Sanctus Spiritus*. Chansons: *La déploration de la mort de Johannes Ockeghem; El grillo; En l'ombre d'ung buissonet au matinet; Je me complains; Je ne me puis tenir d'aimer; Mille regretz; Petite camusette; Scaramella va alla guerra; Scaramella va la galla.*
(M) *** Virgin Veritas/EMI (SIS) Dig. VER5 61302-2 [CDC 54659 full price]. Hilliard Ensemble.

Josquin spent much of his life in Italy, first as a singer in the choir of Milan Cathedral and subsequently in the service of the Sforza family. Although Josquin research has become something of a light industry, little of his vast output has reached the wider musical public and still less has been recorded. As Paul Hillier points out in his notes, 'in the carnival songs and frottole we encounter a native Italian style which composers such as Isaac and Josquin may have ennobled but which in turn had its own influence on this music. This fusion of learned polyphony and tuneful rhythmic gaiety laid the foundations of the Italian madrigal.' The chansons recorded here have both variety of colour and lightness of touch, while the motets are sung with dignity and feeling by the Hilliard Ensemble. Indeed, these performances will kindle the enthusiasm of the uninitiated as will few others. The 1983 recording, made in London's Temple Church, is expertly balanced and eminently truthful.

Kabalevsky, Dmitri (1904–87)

Colas Breugnon: Overture and suite. The Comedians (suite); Romeo and Juliet (suite).
(BB) *** Naxos Dig. 8.553411 [id.]. Moscow SO, Vasily Jelvakov.

Three of Kabalevsky's best-known scores coupled together at super-bargain price in very acceptable performances and in decent sound. Kabalevsky speaks a patois akin to the language of Shostakovich and Prokofiev but without a scintilla of their depth and genius. The opera *Colas Breugnon* is based on Romain Rolland's novel *Le maître de Clamécy* and dates from 1938, though it was revised twice after the war. The suite from *The Comedians*, a play called the *Inventor and the Comedian*, composed two years later, is cheap and cheerful, quite attractive and very well laid out for the orchestra – though, as in the score for *Romeo and Juliet* (which derives from 1956), some of its faster movements are tiresomely scatty. Still, there are others which are inventive and atmospheric.

The Comedians (suite), *Op. 26: Galop; Gavotte; Epilogue.*
(M) **(*) EMI (SIS) CDM5 65922-2 [id.]. Hollywood Bowl SO, Alfred Newman – BARTOK: *Miraculous Mandarin;* KHACHATURIAN: *Gayaneh; Masquerade;* SHOSTAKOVICH: *Age of Gold.* **(*)

The brash immediacy of the vibrant playing of the Hollywood orchestra under Newman is emphasized by the close balance and vivid sound. The audacious *Galop* has seldom produced this degree of projection and energy, yet the *Gavotte* has a proper elegance, and the closing movement is as busy as a bee.

(i) *Cello concertos Nos. 1 in G min., Op. 49; 2 in C min., Op. 77. Spring* (symphonic poem), *Op. 65.*
(BB) **(*) Naxos Dig. 8.553788 [id.]. (i) Alexander Rudin; Moscow SO, Igor Golovschin.

The sleeve-note and the label refer to the *Second Cello concerto* as being in G major, which does not inspire confidence. It was written in 1963 for the late Daniil Shafran, who recorded it for Melodiya, and its sombre C minor first movement is among the most impressive pieces Kabalevsky ever wrote. The enchanting *First Concerto in G minor* was written in 1949 for Knushevitzky and it wears well. Alexander Rudin is a first-rate soloist who yields nothing to the majority of his full-priced rivals. The orchestral playing is decent and acceptable but falls short of distinction. Good recording; though Marina Tarasova, who couples the two concertos on Olympia (at slightly below full price), is even better, this Naxos disc is generally worth the money. The short, slight and charming symphonic poem is not otherwise available.

Piano sonata No. 3, Op. 46.
(M) (***) RCA mono GD 60377 [60377-2-RG]. Vladimir Horowitz – BARBER; PROKOFIEV: *Sonatas* etc. (***)

Horowitz cannot give Kabalevsky's music the calibre of the Barber or Prokofiev sonatas with which it is coupled, and the 1947 recording is a bit subfusc. But the power of the playing certainly comes through, especially in the brilliant finale.

Kalinnikov, Vasily (1866–1901)

Overtures: The Cedar and the palm; Tsar Boris.
(M) *** Chandos Enchant Dig. CHAN 7093 [id.]. SNO, Järvi – RIMSKY-KORSAKOV: *Scheherazade* etc. ***

Kalinnikov's *Cedar and the palm overture*, his final work for orchestra, is an atmospheric piece (based on a Heine poem). It has eminently nostalgic Slavonic invention and, like its companion, *Tsar Boris*, vividly colourful scoring. Kalinnikov's portrayal of the *Tsar*, however, has none of the sombre desolation of Mussorgsky's opera and ends joyously with a resplendent fanfare. Järvi's performances with his responsive Scottish players are very sympathetic and the Chandos recording is in the demonstration class.

Symphonies Nos. 1 in G min.; 2 in A.

(BB) *(*) Naxos Dig. 8.553417 [id.]. Ukraine Nat. SO, Kuchar.

The Kalinnikov symphonies have something of the fluent sense of purpose that distinguishes Borodin or Glazunov, while the poetic slow movement of the *First* has an atmosphere almost akin to early Rachmaninov. Theodore Kuchar's versions with the Ukraine National Symphony Orchestra on Naxos are agreeable but not much more than that. The orchestral playing is not very polished and, although the recording is perfectly acceptable, this is a case where collectors wanting to explore this repertoire would do better to consider the splendidly spirited and idiomatic versions from Järvi and the Royal Scottish National Orchestra on Chandos at full price (CHAN 8614).

Kern, Jerome (1885–1945)

Overtures: (i) *The Cat and the fiddle; The Girl from Utah; Have a heart; Leave it to Jane; O, Lady! Lady!;* (ii) *Show Boat;* (i) *Sitting pretty; Sweet Adeline; Very warm for May;* (i, iii) Film music: *Swing Time* (suite).

(B) ** EMI forte (SIS) Dig. CZS5 68589-2 (2) [CDFB 68589]. (i) Nat. PO; (ii) L. Sinf.; (iii) Ambrosian Ch.; McGlinn – GERSHWIN: *Broadway and film music* **(*); PORTER: *Overtures.* ***

These Jerome Kern overtures, recorded from the original band-parts of musicals dating from between 1914 (*The Girl from Utah*) and 1939 (*Very warm for May*), are musically unimpressive. They are all played with an infectious sense of style, but really memorable tunes are thin on the ground. In *Sweet Adeline*, instead of his own material, Kern uses a pot-pourri of period songs from the 1890s, including *Daisy, Daisy* and *The Band played on*. By far the most attractive music comes in the film score from *Swing Time*, which includes *The way you look tonight*. For this reissue, the *Overture* from McGlinn's complete recording of *Showboat* has been added, but that is not much more than a pot-pourri.

Ketèlbey, Albert (1875–1959)

'Appy 'Ampstead; Bells across the meadows; In a Chinese temple garden; In a monastery garden; In a Persian market; In the mystic land of Egypt; The Phantom melody; Sanctuary of the heart; Wedgwood blue.

(M) *** Decca 444 786-2 [id.]. RPO & chorus, Eric Rogers – *Concert of gypsy violin encores:* Josef Sakonov, L. Festival O. ***

Eric Rogers and his orchestra present the more famous pieces with both warmth and a natural feeling for their flamboyant style, while *Wedgwood blue* is so much the epitome of a salon piece that it becomes a caricature of itself. But in its way it is fetching enough; and the tunes throughout come tumbling out, vulgar but irresistible when played so committedly. The birds twittering in the monastery garden make perfect 'camp' but the playing is straight and committed, and the larger-than-life Phase Four recording suits the music admirably. Moreover it was a happy idea to couple this programme with a collection of Hungarian gypsy fireworks and other favourite lollipops, played with great panache by Josef Sakonov – see Concerts section, below.

Bells across the meadow; Chal Romano (Gypsy lad); The Clock and the Dresden figures; In a Chinese temple garden; In a monastery garden; In a Persian market; In the moonlight; In the mystic land of Egypt; Sanctuary of the heart.

(B) *** CfP CD-CFP 4637 [id.]. Vernon Midgley, Jean Temperley, Leslie Pearson (piano), Amb. S., Philh. O, Lanchbery – LUIGINI: *Ballet Egyptien.* ***

A splendid collection in every way. John Lanchbery uses every possible resource to ensure that, when the composer demands spectacle, he gets it. *In the mystic land of Egypt*, for instance, uses soloist and chorus in canon in the principal tune (and very fetchingly too). In the *Monastery garden* the distant monks are realistically distant, in *Sanctuary of the heart* there is no mistaking that the heart is worn firmly on the sleeve. The orchestral playing throughout is not only polished but warm-hearted – the middle section of *Bells across the meadow*, which has a delightful melodic contour, is played most tenderly and loses any hint of vulgarity. Yet when vulgarity is called for, it is not shirked – only it's a stylish kind of vulgarity! The recording is excellent, full and brilliant.

Khachaturian, Aram (1903–78)

Piano concerto in D flat.

❁ (M) (**(*)) RCA mono 09026 60921. William Kapell, Boston SO, Koussevitzky – LISZT: *Mephisto waltz* (**(*)); PROKOFIEV: *Piano concerto No. 3.* (**(*)) ❁

It is difficult to imagine a better-played account of the *Piano concerto* than that by William Kapell and the Boston Symphony under Koussevitzky (though not so hard to imagine better recorded sound). This incandescent performance, which Kapell recorded in his early twenties, should persuade even those who normally find the Khachaturian concerto irredeemably cheap and tawdry. Koussevitzky gets stunning results from the orchestra and Kapell's virtuosity and delicacy are remarkable. Even if the sound calls for lots of tolerance (the recording dates from 1946), the performance soon has a mesmeric effect. One is reminded of Stravinsky's response on hearing Leonard Bernstein's *Rite of Spring*: 'Wow!'

Piano concerto; Concerto rhapsody for piano and orchestra.

(BB) ** Naxos Dig. 8.550799 [id.]. Oxana Yablonskaya, Moscow SO, Dmitri Yablonsky.

Oxana Yablonskaya is a prodigious player, but she and Yablonsky are prone to over-accentuation and the opening of the work is heavy-going, as is much of the finale. There is no lack of energy and much brilliant pianism, while the music's lyrical side is well understood, with the flexotone not too obtrusive in the slow movement, but the composer's brashness is always very much to the fore. The *Concerto rhapsody for piano and orchestra* is an early work (1955) revised (and no doubt inflated) in 1968 for Nikolai Petrov for whom the prolix bravura of the opening cadenza and the motoric coda of the finale were obviously intended. Its lyrical centrepiece, which again features the flexotone, is endearing in its exotic orientalism, and the glittering – if repetitive and over-extended – finale demands and receives here torrential energy, even if the overall effect of the work is hopelessly garrulous. If only the composer knew when to stop, this could have been a more effective piece. The first modern performance of the *Piano concerto* is provided by the stimulating partnership of Dora Serviarian-Kuhn and Tjeknavorian (on ASV CDDCA 964 – see our main volume).

(i) *Piano concerto in D flat;* (ii) *Violin concerto in D min.;* (iii) *Masquerade suite;* (iv) *Symphony No. 2.*

(B) **(*) Decca Double 448 252-2 (2) [id.]. (i) De Larrocha, LPO, Frühbeck de Burgos; (ii) Ricci, LPO, Fistoulari; (iii) LSO, Stanley Black; (iv) VPO, composer.

The key performance here is the composer's own – of the *Second Symphony*. His advocacy is passionate and the recording is spectacular (although the CD remastering does not help its garish qualities). The slow movement of the *Piano concerto* as interpreted by a Spanish pianist and a Spanish conductor sounds evocatively like Falla, and the finale is also infectiously jaunty. Not so the first movement, which is disappointingly slack in rhythm at a dangerously slow tempo. Ricci is a good deal more consistent in the *Violin concerto*. He does not supply quite the demonic energy which the outer movements ideally call for, but his lyrical approach has its own attractions, and the closing pages of the slow movement are wonderfully atmospheric. The late-1950s recording does not have the projection we would expect today, but Ricci's fine playing is well focused. The *Masquerade suite* is consistently alive and colourful and is vividly if forwardly recorded.

Violin concerto in D min.

(M) ** Mercury 434 318-2 [id.]. Szeryng, LSO, Dorati – BRAHMS: *Violin concerto.* *(*)

Although more successful than the coupled Brahms concerto, Szeryng's 1964 recording of the Khachaturian does not measure up to the finest versions of the past, notably those of Leonid Kogan and David Oistrakh and, more recently, Perlman. It is a lightweight account, at its most convincing in the folksy lyricism of the *Andante* and in the sparkle of the finale, where the soloist is on top technical form. The recording is good but does not flatter the solo violin timbre.

Gayaneh (ballet): extended suite.

(M) **(*) Mercury (IMS) 434 323-2 [id.]. LSO, Dorati – SHOSTAKOVICH: *Symphony No. 5.* **(*)

Dorati understands this music as well as anyone, and his *Sabre dance* has plenty of energy; and the other dances admirably celebrate Khachaturian's local colour. The 1960 Mercury recording is brilliant, with a tendency to fierceness in the strings, which suits the music well enough. There are eight items here; Dorati omits *Gayaneh's Adagio*.

Gayaneh (ballet): extended suite. *Masquerade* (ballet): suite.

(M) **(*) EMI (SIS) CDM5 65922-2. Hollywood Bowl SO, Alfred Newman – BARTOK: *Miraculous Mandarin;* KABALEVSKY: *The Comedians* (suite); SHOSTAKOVICH: *Age of Gold.* **(*)

Alfred Newman, with brilliant playing from the Hollywood Bowl Orchestra, gives brash, highly energetic accounts of an extended suite of seven numbers from *Gayaneh*, with the *Sabre dance* and *Dance of the Kurds* leaping forward with great zest and the *Russian dance*, which opens with a piquant tic-toc, soon catching up as it noisily gathers pace. The *Galop* from *Masquerade* has similar uninhibited exuberance, but the *Romance*, like the sinuous lyrical numbers in *Gayaneh*, brings a sultry contrasting allure. Both suites generate much excitement and colour, helped by playing which is polished as well as vividly extrovert. The 1959 recording is very brightly lit but gives the strongest projection to this extremely spirited music-making.

Gayaneh: suite; Spartacus: suite.

(M) **(*) Decca 417 737-2. VPO, composer – PROKOFIEV: *Romeo and Juliet.* ***

The composer's own first selection on Decca was recorded in 1962 and offers five items from *Gayaneh* and four from *Spartacus*. Khachaturian achieves a brilliant response from the VPO and everything is most vivid, notably the famous *Adagio* from *Spartacus*, which is both expansive and passionate. It is a pity that the Decca remastering process has brought everything into such strong focus; the massed violins now have an added edge and boldness of attack, at the expense of their richness of timbre.

Gayaneh (ballet): *suites 1–3.*

(BB) * Naxos Dig. 8. 550800 [id.]. St Petersburg State SO, Anichanov.

These three suites come from Khachaturian's later revisions of his score, and little of what is offered here is of real musical interest. *Gayaneh's solo* from suite No. 1, the *Lullaby* and *Sabre dance* from suite No. 2 and *Gayaneh's Adagio* from suite No. 3 remind us of the quality of the composer's original ideas, and the *Dance of the girls* also has charm. The dozen other items are routine numbers, overscored and containing little music to which one would wish to return. They are played idiomatically and with more conviction than they deserve, and the resonant recording is acceptable.

Gayaneh (ballet): highlights; *Spartacus* (ballet): highlights.

(B) *** CfP CD-CFP 4634 [(M) id. import]. LSO, composer (with GLAZUNOV: *The Seasons: Autumn:* Philh. O, Svetlanov ***).

The composer's 1977 pairing for EMI of selections from his two famous ballets offers one more item from *Gayaneh* than on his earlier (1962) Decca coupling. The EMI sound, obviously more modern than the Decca, is a shade reverberant for the more vigorous numbers, but the present remastering presents a firmer focus than on LP. The effect is realistically spectacular with full, rich strings so that the famous *Adagio of Spartacus and Phrygia* expands opulently as well as ardently. The LSO play excitingly throughout. There is a gorgeous response from the violins in the extra item, called *Invention*, from *Gayaneh*. The inclusion of *Autumn*, the most memorable section of Glazunov's *Seasons* – its vigorously thrusting string theme stirringly conducted by Svetlanov – increases the appeal of this CD. At bargain price it is now a best buy for those wanting a suite from the two Khachaturian ballets.

Clarinet trio.

(B) *** HM Dig.HMA 1901419 [id.]. Walter Boeykens Ens. – PROKOFIEV: *Overture on Jewish themes* etc. ***

Khachaturian's *Clarinet trio* is a slight but pleasing work, full of sinuous, Armenian melodic lines. With a *Moderato* finale (in some ways the most striking movement, with the central dance section rather soberly framed), it is without the hyperbole which often distinguishes this composer's orchestral writing. It is very well played and recorded.

Klami, Uuno (1900–1961)

Kalavela suite, Op. 23; Lemminkäinen's adventures on the Island of Saari; Sea pictures; Suomenlinna overture.

(BB) ** Naxos Dig. 8.553757 [id.]. Turku PO, Jorma Panula.

While most Finnish composers of his generation were heavily indebted to Sibelius, Uuno Klami – like his somewhat older contemporary, Leevi Madetoja – was drawn towards French models. He is relatively little known and rarely if ever features in concert programmes outside his native Finland. The *Kalevala Suite* (1929–33) is his best-known work; the present issue also includes *Lemminkäinen's adventures on the Island of Saari*, which was originally intended for it but which he published separately in 1934. It is an attractive piece, as are the *Sea pictures*. The *Suomenlinna overture* is a wartime work, first performed in Stockholm under Tor Mann, but it was then lost and was subsequently rewritten. If Klami's music is derivative (Ravel, Florent Schmitt, Falla, a dash of Sibelius and a bit of early Stravinsky), it has the merit of being imaginative and, as far as orchestration is concerned, quite masterly. The Turku or Abo orchestra is not as refined or as well blended an ensemble as the best in the Nordic countries (the intonation in the wind and brass is not always perfect) but Panula gets more than serviceable results.

Kodály, Zoltán (1882–1967)

Concerto for orchestra; Dances of Galánta; Dances of Marosszék; Háry János: suite; Symphony in C; Summer evening; Theatre overture; Variations on a Hungarian folksong (The Peacock).
(B) *** Double Decca 443 006-2 (2) [id.]. Philh. Hungarica, Antal Dorati.

This is all music which, though it is always beautifully written and often colourful, is not always as cogent as it might be. The more ambitious pieces like the *Concerto for orchestra* and the three-movement *Symphony in C* are certainly enjoyable, but they lack the sharpness of inspiration that pervades the music of Kodály's friend Bartók. The *Symphony* comes from the composer's last years and lacks real concentration and cohesion. Even so, in Dorati's hands the passionate *Andante* is strong in gypsy feeling and the jolly, folk-dance finale, if repetitive, is colourful and full of vitality. *Summer evening*, too, is warmly evocative, but in the *Theatre overture*, brightly and effectively scored, the invention is thin. The 1973 sound remains of vintage quality and the CD transfers are first rate.

Dances of Galánta; Dances of Marosszék.
(B) **(*) Sony SBK 62404; *SBT 62404* [id.]. Phd. O, Ormandy – JANACEK: *Sinfonietta; Taras Bulba.* **

(i) *Dances of Galánta; Dances of Marosszék;* (ii) *Háry János: suite.*
(B) *** EMI CfP CD-CFP 6029 [(M) id. import]. LPO, Walter Susskind.
(M) *** Mercury (IMS) 432 005-2 [id.]. (i) Philharmonia Hungarica; (ii) Minneapolis SO; Dorati – BARTOK: *Hungarian sketches* etc. ***

Dances of Galánta; Dances of Marosszék; Variations on a Hungarian folksong (The Peacock).
(BB) ** Naxos Dig. 8.550520 [id.]. Slovak RSO (Bratislava), Adrian Leaper.

Susskind's triptych is one of the very best CDs in the Classics for Pleasure catalogue. It was recorded (with Brian Culverhouse the producer and Kenneth Williamson the engineer) in Kingsway Hall in 1977. A famous bargain LP in its day, it has only recently appeared in this modern format. The transfer is in every way first class, and Susskind's attractive performances of Kodály's three most popular orchestral works are treated to sound of superb demonstration quality. In depth of focus and fidelity this not only compares with the best recordings from the 1970s but can upstage many modern, digital discs. Susskind's direction could be more resilient, yet he evokes a true Hungarian flavour (the cimbalom is most effectively balanced) and the playing of the LPO is excellent. Susskind's overriding attention to detail made him a more successful exponent of short rather than large-scale works in the studio, and this record, one of several he made for CfP not long before he died, is a fitting memento of his musicianship.

From sneeze to finale, the Minneapolis orchestral playing in the *Háry János suite* is crisp and vigorous; given the excellent 1956 Mercury stereo, Dorati went on to record the other two sets of dances with the Philharmonia Hungarica in 1958. The playing of the woodwind soloists in the slow dances is intoxicatingly seductive, and the power and punch of the climaxes come over with real Mercury fidelity. An outstanding disc, since the Bartók couplings are equally successful.

Ormandy and the Philadelphia Orchestra play these well-known sets of dances brilliantly and with characteristic panache. The 1962 recording too has been immeasurably improved and it is pity that the reissue is let down by the omission of the *Háry János suite*, recorded around the same time. Moreover there is no internal cueing.

The Bratislava players know just what this music is about and they play beautifully, but Adrian Leaper's direction seems a little lacking in temperament; this music should ideally sound more volatile. The recording is very good.

(i–iii; vi) *Háry János* (play with music): complete recording of music, with narration by Peter Ustinov; (iv) *The Peacock* (folksong for unaccompanied chorus); (ii; v–vi) *Psalmus Hungaricus;* (vi) *Variations on a Hungarian folksong (The Peacock).*
(M) **(*) Decca Double (IMS) 443 488-2 (2) [id.]. (i) Olga Szönyi, Márgit László, Erszébet Komlössy, György Melis, Zsolt Bende, Lásló Palócz; (ii) Wandsworth School Boys' Ch.; (iii) Edinburgh Festival

Ch.; (iv) London Symphony Ch.; (v) Lajos Kozma, Brighton Festival Ch.; (vi) LSO; all cond. Kertész.

All of Kodály's music for *Háry János* is included here, and the links are provided by Peter Ustinov in many guises. Whether the comedy stands the test of repetition is another matter, but it is good to have Kodály's full score, including a number of pieces as attractive as those in the well-known suite, and vocal versions of some that we know already. Superb recording. This Double Decca reissue also includes a much-valued performance of the *Psalmus Hungaricus*, Kodály's most vital choral work. The light tenor tone of Lajos Kozma is not ideal for the solo part, but again the authentic Hungarian touch helps. The *Peacock variations* make a marvellous display piece, and it was a happy idea to include the folksong itself, stirringly sung by the London Symphony Chorus. No attempt in the variations to build an intellectual structure: orchestral resource provides the mainspring, and the LSO revels in the virtuoso challenge. The CD transfers are first class throughout.

Háry János suite.

(B) *** Sony SBK 48162; *SBT 48162* [id.]. Cleveland O, Szell – MUSSORGSKY: *Pictures at an exhibition*; PROKOFIEV: *Lieutenant Kijé: suite.* ***

(BB) *** Naxos Dig. 8.550142; *4550142* [id.]. Hungarian State O, Mátyás Antal (with Concert: *'Hungarian festival'* ***).

(M) *** Decca Phase Four 448 947-2 [id.]. Netherlands R. O, Dorati – DVORAK: *Symphony No. 9.* ***

(M) (***) RCA mono GD 60279 [60279-2-RG]. NBC SO, Toscanini – DVORAK: *Symphony No. 9* (***); SMETANA: *Má Vlast: Vltava.* (**)

Szell – Budapest born – was in his element in *Háry János*. Superb Cleveland polish matches the vitality of the playing, with a humorous sparkle in Kodály's first two movements and the mock pomposity of the Napoleon episode wittily dramatized. The full romantic sweep of the *Song* and *Intermezzo* comes over too, with deliciously pointed woodwind in the trio of the latter. The 1969 recording was one of the very finest from this source, bold with a too-forward cimbalom, but the engineers certainly capture the exhilaration of the playing in this way. The couplings are equally fine, and this is one of the very best of all the Szell/Cleveland reissues on the Sony Essential Classics logo.

The Hungarian performance of the *Háry János suite* is also wonderfully vivid, with the cimbalom – here perfectly balanced within the orchestra – particularly telling. The grotesque elements of *The Battle and defeat of Napoleon* are pungently and wittily characterized and the *Entrance of the Emperor and his Court* also has an ironical sense of spectacle. The brilliant digital sound adds to the vitality and projection of the music-making, yet the lyrical music is played most tenderly.

The Decca recording too is exceptionally vivid and Dorati's direct manner produces the strongest musical characterization. The Phase Four techniques are not exaggerated and they do no harm to Kodály's bright orchestral colours.

There is nothing relaxed about Toscanini's view of *Háry János*. He seems not to realize that a joke is involved; but the intensity of the performance gives the music a new and bigger scale, whether appropriate or not.

(Unaccompanied) *Cello sonata, Op. 8; Cello sonata* (for cello and piano), *Op. 4*.

(B) *** HM Dig. HMA 1901325 [id.]. Lluís Claret, (i) with Rose-Marie Cabestany.

(Unaccompanied) *Cello sonata, Op. 8;* (i) *Cello sonata* (for cello & piano), *Op. 4; 3 Chorale preludes* (arr. from Bach, BWV 743, 747 & 762).

(BB) *** Naxos Dig. 8.553160 [id.]. Maria Kliegel; (i) with Jenö Jandó.

On the evidence of this record, the Andorran cellist, Lluís Claret, has a larger-than-life musical personality, and one is sorely tempted to use the word 'vintage' to describe his inspired performance of Op. 8, which has extraordinary power and intensity, while its improvisatory feeling brings the immediacy of 'live' music-making. This is a memorably compulsive account of a work which, until now, Starker has made his own. Moreover the recording is real and tangible within a suitably open acoustic. Rose-Marie Cabestany joins Claret persuasively for the less ambitious but still impressive two-movement *Sonata for cello and piano*, Op. 4, and proves an excellent partner, so that this piece is by no means an anticlimax after the major work.

Maria Kliegel in Kodaly's magnificent solo *Cello sonata* offers a warm and fanciful performance not quite as incisive as Claret's or Schiefen's on Arte Nova (see below) but just as powerful at speeds rather more flowing. So in the long central slow movement Kliegel is not so daringly expansive or darkly tragic, but she is more easily lyrical. Jenö Jandó is an outstandingly sympathetic partner in the two-movement Op. 4 *Sonata*, a performance deeply introspective in the slow first movement and full of fantasy in the *Allegro con spirito* of the finale. The three *Chorale preludes* are romantic arrangements – with the cello generally underlining the chorale melodies – of organ pieces attributed to Bach but now thought spurious.

(Unaccompanied) *Cello sonata, Op.8;* (i) *Duo for violin and cello, Op. 7.*
(BB) *** Arte Nova Dig. 74321 51623-2 [id.]. Guido Schiefen, (i) with Axel Strauss.

Arguably the greatest work for solo cello since Bach, Kodaly's solo *Sonata* in some ways provides a counterpart to Bartók's great solo *Violin sonata*. Yet where Bartók's work was one of his last, this challenging piece by Kodály in three massive movements dates from his earliest period, 1915. Guido Schiefen gives a powerful, intense performance, fearless in attacking the bravura writing, with double-stopping clean and precise and with his full cello-tone made the more dramatic by the close recorded sound. Powerful and passionate as the outer movements are, the central *Adagio* at an exceptionally broad speed is particularly impressive in its hushed concentration. The *Duo*, written the previous year, receives an equally compelling performance, making the ideal coupling. It is astonishing what full and rich sounds Kodály draws from just two instruments. Another outstanding bargain.

Missa brevis.
(M) **(*) EMI Dig. CDM5 65587-2. King's College, Cambridge, Ch., Cleobury; Stephen Lane – JANACEK: *Mass* etc. ***

The *Missa brevis*, as its subtitle, *In tempore belli*, suggests, was composed at the height of the Second World War; it was first conceived as an organ Mass; but in 1945, when the Russians were laying siege to Budapest, Kodály transcribed it for voices and organ, subsequently orchestrating it. It is one of Kodály's strongest and most deeply felt works, every bit as powerful as the *Psalmus Hungaricus*. Ferencsik's recording was of the orchestral version, whereas Stephen Cleobury gives it in its earlier form, as did László Heltay in the 1970s. Some of the treble lines could be more secure, but for the most part this is a good performance, even if it lacks the bite and intensity that Hungarian singers would bring to it.

Koechlin, Charles (1867–1961)

(i) *Ballade for piano and orchestra, Op. 50. 7 Stars Symphony (suite), Op. 13.*
(M) *** EMI Dig. CDM7 64369-2. (i) Bruno Rigutto; Monte Carlo PO, Myrat.

The 'stars' of the *Symphony* are terrestrial rather than galactic: Fairbanks and Marlene Dietrich, not Betelgeuse and Sirius. Koechlin is an interesting figure who has been spoken of as a French Charles Ives, though so glib a comparison does not do justice to his individuality of mind. The *Seven Stars Symphony* is not, strictly speaking, a symphony, rather a series of sketches evoking the great personalities of the cinema in the 1920s and '30s, and it is coupled here with an earlier work written for the pianist Henriette Fauré. Koechlin is a stimulating figure and, given the keen advocacy of these artists and the excellence of the CD sound, this enterprising reissue well rewards investigation.

Kokkonen, Joonas (born 1921)

(i) *Cello concerto;* (ii) *Symphony No. 3;* (iii) *Cello sonata.*
(M) *** Finlandia FACD 027. (i; iii) Noras; (i) Helsinki PO, Freeman; (ii) Finnish RSO, Berglund; (iii) Heinonen.

There is precious little to choose between Arto Noras's version of the *Cello concerto* and that of the young Swedish cellist, Torleif Thedéen; both play with aristocratic finesse and convey the composer's intentions with admirable fidelity; both were recorded in close collaboration with the composer, though Thedéen on full-price BIS has the advantage of digital recording. Paavo Berglund's excellent recording of the *Third Symphony* was made in the early 1970s and briefly appeared on Decca in the UK. This Finlandia record has the advantage of economy.

Korngold, Erich (1897–1957)

Violin concerto in D, Op. 35.
(BB) *** Naxos Dig. 8.553579 [id.]. Vera Tsu, Razumovsky Sinfonia, Yu Long – GOLDMARK: *Violin concerto.* ***

Vera Tsu, born in Shanghai and then discovered by Isaac Stern and trained in America, is an outstanding soloist in a coupling which directly challenges an EMI disc from Itzhak Perlman. In every way this ripely romantic version of the Korngold is a match for that and other full-price rivals, thanks to Tsu's rich, ample tone and her flawless intonation, as well as her fearless attack in bravura writing. In the quality of sound the recording outshines most other versions, rich and free, both immediate and atmospheric, with fine dynamic range and with the Chinese conductor, Yu Long, drawing beautiful, refined playing from the Bratislava orchestra.

OPERA

Die tote Stadt (complete).

(M) *** RCA GD 87767 (2) [7767-2-RG]. Neblett, Kollo, Luxon, Prey, Bav. R. Ch., Tölz Ch., Munich R. O, Leinsdorf.

(BB) ** Naxos Dig. 8.660060/1 [id.]. Sunnegardh, Dalayman, Bergström, Tobiasson, Wahlgren, Leidland, Tomson, Jonsson, Qvale, Tomtberga Children's Ch., Royal Swedish Op. Ch. & O, Segerstam.

At the age of twenty-three Korngold had his opera, *Die tote Stadt*, presented in simultaneous world premières in Hamburg and Cologne! The score includes many echoes of Puccini and Richard Strauss, but its youthful exuberance carries the day. Here René Kollo is powerful, if occasionally coarse of tone, Carol Neblett sings sweetly in the equivocal roles of the wife's apparition and the newcomer, and Hermann Prey, Benjamin Luxon and Rose Wagemann make up an impressive cast. Leinsdorf is at his finest.

Erich Korngold's bizarre opera, colourful and melodramatic, makes an adventurous choice for the Naxos label, with Leif Segerstam conducting a sympathetic performance, recorded live, with a Royal Swedish Opera cast. Katarina Dalayman, as the heroine, sings with moving tenderness in her first lyrical solo, *Glück, das mir verblieb*, but Thomas Sunnegardh with his basically pleasing tenor is overstrained by the heroic demands of the central role of Paul. Enjoyable as the performance is, this version cannot compare with the RCA set conducted by Erich Leinsdorf, which at mid-price offers a far finer performance, starrily cast with René Kollo as Paul, with vivid and more immediate sound, and with a complete text, avoiding the cuts which disfigure this live performance. It also provides a libretto and translation, where Naxos offer only the original German text plus a detailed synopsis in English.

Kraus, Joseph Martin (1756–92)

Symphonies in C; C min.; E flat; Olympie overture.

(BB) *** Naxos Dig. 8.553734 [id.]. Swedish CO, Petter Sundquist.

Born in the same year as Mozart, Kraus was similarly short-lived, dying in the year after him. That has led to his being dubbed the 'Swedish Mozart', but these lively symphonies, freshly performed by the Swedish Chamber Orchestra, suggest that his music has more in common with that of Haydn, above all the *Sturm und Drang* period. Haydn, who met Kraus in both Vienna and Esterházy, praised his music highly. Unlike Mozart, Kraus was drawn to minor keys, not just in the *C minor Symphony*, and the tough streak in the writing is emphasized by the sharpness of syncopated rhythms. The symphonies – three from the total of 12 that have survived – were written in the 1780s, but the overture, in three sections, slow–fast–slow following the French pattern, dates from the year of Kraus's death, written for a stage production of Voltaire's play of that name. Full, warm sound and excellent performances, involving a substantial string section with first-rate wind and brass playing, notably from the horns. Well worth exploring.

Kreisler, Fritz (1875–1962)

Allegretto in the style of Boccherini; Caprice viennois; Chanson Louis XIII and Pavane; Liebesleid; Liebesfreud; Minuet; The old refrain; Praeludium and allegro; Recitativo and Scherzo; Rondino on a theme of Beethoven; Schön Rosmarin; Tambourin chinois; Tempo di minuetto.

(M) *** Mercury (IMS) 434 351-2 [id.]. Henryk Szeryng, Charles Reiner (with LECLAIR: *Violin sonata No. 3 in D;* GLUCK, arr. Kreisler: *Mélodie*; LOCATELLI: *The Labyrinth* **).

It is good to have a reminder of the artistry of Henryk Szeryng, who made many of his best concerto recordings in the earliest days of stereo. His playing of these occasional pieces of Kreisler – not all of them by any means trifles – is superb. The invention of the music is always made to sound spontaneous. How stylishly and lightly he throws off a piece like '*Schön Rosmarin*' and what gentle charm he finds for the *Chanson Louis XIII*. The 1963 recording is firmly focused and truthful. The remaining items are played as virtuoso encores rather than showing any natural sympathy for the baroque style, although no one could fail to be impressed by the bravura of Locatelli's *Labyrinth*. However, in these pieces the Mercury sound brings rather more edge to the violin timbre.

Allegretto in the style of Boccherini; Allegretto in the style of Porpora; Caprice viennois; Cavatina; La Chasse in the style of Cartier; La Gitana; Grave in the style of W. F. Bach; Gypsy caprice; Liebesfreud; Liebesleid; Praeludium and allegro in the style of Pugnani; Recitative and scherzo; Schön Rosmarin; Shepherd's madrigal; Sicilienne et rigaudon in the style of Francoeur; Toy soldiers' march; Viennese rhapsodic fantasia; arr. of *Austrian National Hymn*.
(BB) **(*) ASV CDQS 6039 [(M) id. import]. Oscar Shumsky, Milton Kaye.

Oscar Shumsky's combination of technical mastery and musical flair is ideal for this music; and it is a pity that the rather dry recording and forward balance – well in front of the piano – makes the violin sound almost too close.

'Favourites': Allegretto in the style of Boccherini; Caprice viennois, Op. 2; Liebesfreud; Liebesleid; Praeludium and Allegro in the style of Pugnani; La Précieuse in the style of Couperin; Schön Rosmarin; Sicilienne and Rigaudon in the style of Francoeur; Variations on a theme by Corelli in the style of Tartini; Tambourin chinoise, Op. 3 (with Arrangements: FALLA: *La vida breve: Danse espagnole*. GLUCK: *Orfeo: Mélodie* – arr. from *Dance of the Blessed Spirits*. TCHAIKOVSKY: *Chant sans paroles, Op. 2/3*. LISZT: *La clochette* – arr. from *La campanella*).
(B) ** EMI CfP CD-CFP 6030 [(M) id. import]. Rodney Friend, Michael Isador.

Rodney Friend, at that time leader of the LPO, recorded this collection of Kreisler '*Favourites*' in 1975. The chosen venue was London's Conway Hall, but the microphones were closely placed, little of the hall ambience is felt, and the violin image is made to seem unnaturally forward and present. The piano isn't flattered either, notably in the arrangement of Liszt's *La campanella*, where the accompaniment has a life of its own. It is only fair to say that, at the time the LP first appeared, *Gramophone* found that the recital had 'all that one could wish for in terms of virtuosity, sentiment and charm'. It is charm that we find lacking, especially in *Liebesfreud*, *Liebesleid* and *Schön Rosmarin*, although *Caprice viennoise* is thrown off with some dash. Otherwise it is the classical pastiches that come off best here, played crisply and stylishly, and Gluck's famous *Mélodie*, unsentimentalized, is similarly appealing. But the dry, studio-ish presentation remains a drawback.

Aucassin et Nicolette; Caprice viennois; La Gitana; Marche miniature viennoise; 3 Old Viennese dances (Liebesfreud; Liebesleid; Schön Rosmarin); Praeludium and allegro in the style of Pugnani; Preghiera in the style of Martini; Sicilienne et rigaudon in the style of Francoeur; Slavonic fantasie on themes by Dvořák; Tambourin chinois. Arrangements of: CHAMINADE: *Sérénade espagnole*. DVORAK: *Slavonic dance, Op. 72/2*. SCOTT: *Lotus land*. TCHAIKOVSKY: *Chant sans paroles, Op. 2/3*. MENDELSSOHN: *Songs without words: Andante espressivo in G, Op. 62/1*. RACHMANINOV: *Rhapsody on a theme of Paganini: Variation*. LEHAR: *Frasquita: Serenade*. ANON.: *Londonderry Air*. ALBENIZ: *España: Tango, Op. 165/2*. HEUBERGER: *Midnight bells*.
(M) *** Classic fM Dig. 75605 57020-2. Joji Hattori, Joseph Seiger.

Joji Hattori, winner of the Menuhin International Violin Competition in 1989, brings to these Kreisler trifles not only a brilliant technique and rich, firm violin-tone, but the rhythmic flair and naughty pointing of phrase which makes them sparkle. Here is an artist who plainly loves the instrument, as Kreisler himself did. The 22 encores include not only original pieces by Kreisler, but his inspired violin arrangements of favourite pieces by such composers as Dvořák, Tchaikovsky, Rachmaninov, Lehár and others. Also a sequence of the pieces he wrote, originally attributing them to then-neglected eighteenth-century composers like Pugnani, Francoeur and Martini. The gently lyrical *Preghiera* after Martini inspires Hattori to hushed, meditative playing just as intense as his bravura fireworks in such pieces as *Tambourin chinois*. Joseph Seiger is a comparably inspired accompanist, relishing the glissando display in such a piece as *La Gitana*. Warm, full recording. A best buy among mid-priced recordings of this repertoire.

Caprice viennoise; Chanson Louis XIII & Pavane in the style of Couperin; La Gitana; Liebesleid; Liebesfreud; Polichinelle; La Précieuse in the style of Couperin; Rondino on a theme by Beethoven; Scherzo alla Dittersdorf; Tambourin chinois; Schön Rosmarin. Arrangements: BACH: *Partita No. 3 in E, BWV 1006: Gavotte*. BRANDL: *The old refrain*. DVORAK: *Humoresque*. FALLA: *La vida breve: Danza española*. GLAZUNOV: *Sérénade espagnole*. HEUBERGER: *Midnight bells (Im chambre séparée)*. POLDINI: *Poupée valsante*. RIMSKY-KORSAKOV: *Sadko: Chanson hindoue*. SCHUBERT: *Rosamunde: Ballet music No. 2*. SCOTT: *Lotus Land*. TCHAIKOVSKY: *Andante cantabile from Op. 11*. WEBER: *Violin sonata No. 1 in F, Op. 10: Larghetto*. TRAD.: *Londonderry air*.
(M) (***) EMI mono CDH7 64701-2 [id.]. Fritz Kreisler, Franz Rupp or Michael Rachelsein; or (in *Scherzo*) Kreisler String Qt.

Impeccable and characterful performances by Fritz Kreisler of his own lollipops, including those 'in the style of' pieces with which – until he owned up – he fooled his audiences into believing they were actually written by the composers in question. Most of the recordings were made with Franz Rupp in 1936 or 1938, and the transfers offer a convincingly realistic if studio-ish balance and are of excellent technical quality; a few (the *Polichinelle*, the pieces in the style of Couperin, the Schubert *Rosamunde ballet music*, the Glazunov and Weber arrangements, *The old refrain* (especially) and an indulgent performance of Heuberger's *Im chambre séparée*) date from 1930 and here the piano balance is poor, the piano badly defined. However, these were recorded before Kreisler's accident and the violin timbre is noticeably more opulent. A valuable document.

Caprice viennoise, Op. 2; La Gitana; Liebesfreud; Liebesleid; Polichinelle; La Précieuse; Recitativo and scherzo caprice, Op. 6; Rondo on a theme of Beethoven; Syncopation; Tambourin chinois; Zigeuner (Capriccio). Arrangements: ALBENIZ: *Tango, Op. 165/2.* WEBER: *Larghetto.* WIENIAWSKI: *Caprice in E flat.* DVORAK: *Slavonic dance No. 10 in E min.* GLAZUNOV: *Sérénade espagnole.* GRANADOS: *Danse espagnole.*
(M) *** DG 423 876-2. Shlomo Mintz, Clifford Benson.

Shlomo Mintz plays with a disarmingly easy style and absolute technical command, to bring out the music's warmth as well as its sparkle. A very attractive programme, given first-class recording and splendid presence without added edge on CD.

Krenek, Ernst (1900–1951)

Symphonic elegy for string orchestra.
(M) (***) Sony mono MH2K 62759 (2) [id.]. NYPO, Dimitri Mitropoulos – BERG: *Wozzeck* (***); SCHOENBERG: *Erwartung*.(**(*))

Krenek wrote this powerful piece for strings as a direct response to hearing the news of the tragic death of his friend, Anton Webern. In homage he adopts full serial technique, but the result has little of the spareness of Webern; in its overtly emotional approach and lyrical warmth it comes nearer to Berg in style. Recorded in 1951, like *Wozzeck* and *Erwartung*, it makes an unexpected but valuable fill-up, very well played. (This set costs rather more than our usual upper-mid-price limitation.)

Kreutzer, Conradin (1780–1849)

Septet (for clarinet, horn, bassoon, violin, viola, cello & double-bass), *Op. 62;* (i) *Trio in E flat* (for piano, clarinet & bassoon), *Op. 43.*
❀ (BB) *** Arte Nova Dig. 74321 54462-2 [id.]. Mithras Octet (members), (i) with Paul Rivinius (piano).

In the early days of mono LP one of the plums of the Decca catalogue was a recording of a then unfamiliar *Septet*, by Conradin Kreutzer, winningly played by members of the Vienna Octet. Since then the work seems to have been neglected; but now comes yet another delightful performance to suggest that it is almost more infectiously enjoyable than the Beethoven *Septet* on which it was modelled (in 1824). After its warmly welcoming introduction, elegantly persuasive here, the first movement sets off with a rollicking main theme which is quite unforgettable. Following Beethoven, Kreutzer's work is in six movements, with a charmingly ingenuous *Adagio* in which the clarinet (Peter Pzybylla), immediately sets the right mood. A Minuet and a spirited Scherzo (with a seductively suave Trio) frame a mock-solemn *Andante*; then the finale dances as gaily as the opening movement. The members of the Mithras Octet have the full measure of the music, playing with grace and elegance and an infectious charm, while the recording is excellent in every respect. The *Trio* is a similarly amiable and inventive work, if less distinctive. It has a doleful *Andante grazioso* and is capped by another memorably light-hearted finale. It is very well played here, but unfortunately the piano, recorded too resonantly, outbalances the pair of woodwind instruments, and this reduces the listener's enjoyment. The Rosette is for the *Septet*, which is not to be missed.

Krommer, Franz (1759–1831)

Clarinet concerto in E flat, Op. 36; (i) *Double clarinet concertos in A flat, Opp. 35 & 91.*
(BB) ** Naxos Dig. 8.553178 [id.]. Kálmán Berkes; (i) Kaori Tsutsui; Nicolaus Esterházy Sinfonia.

Both the soloists here are good players and they blend very well together; but slow movements are rather deadpan and not all the music's sense of fun comes over. Neither clarinettists nor orchestra are helped by the reverberant recording which means a forward balance for the soloists and tends to coarsen the tuttis by spreading the sound. Even so, the *Double concerto*, Op. 91, a winner if ever there was one, is very enjoyable, with the first movement swinging along merrily and the *Polacca* finale, with its jaunty duet theme introduced against orchestral pizzicatos, equally fluent.

Partitas: in F, Op. 57; E flat, Op. 71; B flat, Op. 78. Marches, Op. 31/3–5.
(BB) *** Naxos Dig. 8.553498 [id.]. Budapest Wind Ens.

The Budapest Wind, led by their exuberant clarinettist, Kálmán Berkes, are a first-rate ensemble, full of spirit and personality. These qualities inform their characterful and lively accounts of these three partitas by Krommer or Krommer-Kramář as he is sometimes known (using both the German and Czech forms of his name). The Budapest team yields nothing in terms of artistic excellence to their full-priced rival, the Sabine Meyer Wind Ensemble, and not a great deal in terms of recording quality. True, the distinguished German team offer the Op. 76 *Partita* as well, and readers who have acquired that disc (reviewed in our 1992 edition) will not have regretted doing so. But this newcomer has the merit of being every bit as accomplished, arguably more characterful, and certainly less expensive. Recommended.

Kuhnau, Johann (1660–1722)

Der Gerechte kommt um (motet).
(M) *** O-L 443 199-2. Christ Church Ch., AAM, Preston – BACH: *Magnificat;* VIVALDI: *Nisi dominus* etc. ***

Kuhnau was Bach's predecessor in Leipzig. He wrote this charming motet with a Latin text; it was later arranged in a German version, and there are signs of Bach's hand in it. The piece makes an excellent makeweight coupling for the original version of Bach's *Magnificat*.

Kvandal, Johan (born 1919)

Wind quintet, Op. 34; 3 Hymn tunes, Op. 23.
(BB) ** Naxos Dig. 8.553050 [id.]. Oslo Wind Ens. – FERNSTROM; NIELSEN: *Wind quintets.* **

The Norwegian composer Johan Kvandal is the son of the composer and Grieg scholar, David Monrad Johansen. He studied in Vienna with Joseph Marx and in Paris with Nadia Boulanger. He has a number of highly imaginative scores to his credit, including *Antagonia*, a memorable, rather Honeggerish concerto for two string orchestras and percussion which was recorded in the 1970s and is well worth tracking down. The *Wind quintet* dates from much the same period as *Antagonia* and was finished in 1971. It was written for the Oslo Wind Quintet for a payment of 25 bottles of red wine. It is well crafted but unmemorable. Excellent playing from the Oslo Wind Ensemble; but the recording, made in a rather small Norwegian Radio studio, is overlit and rather too forward.

Lalo, Edouard (1823–92)

Cello concerto No. 1 in D min., Op. 33.
(B) *** Decca Eclipse Dig. 448 712-2; *448 712-4* [(M) id. import]. Lynn Harrell, Berlin RSO, Chailly – SAINT-SAENS; SCHUMANN: *Concertos.* ***
(B) *** DG Classikon 431 166-2 [(M) id. import]. Heinrich Schiff, New Philh. O, Mackerras – FAURE: *Elégie;* SAINT-SAENS: *Cello concerto No. 1.* ***
(M) **(*) Mercury 432 010-2 [id.]. Janos Starker, LSO, Skrowaczewski – SAINT-SAENS; SCHUMANN: *Concertos.* ***
(M) **(*) Sony SBK 48278; *SBT 48278* [id.]. Leonard Rose, Phd. O, Ormandy – BLOCH: *Schelomo;* FAURE: *Elégie;* TCHAIKOVSKY: *Rococo variations.* ***

Lynn Harrell's account is highly recommendable. There is a yearning intensity in the *Intermezzo*, while the outer movements combine spontaneity and vigour. Chailly's accompaniment is attractively bold and the recording, made in the Berlin Jesus-Christus Kirche, has an attractively warm ambience, while the cello image is very tangible and the orchestra is given plenty of colour and presence. Harrell's couplings are generous in including concertos by both Saint-Saëns and Schumann.

This was Heinrich Schiff's début recording in 1977, made when he was still very young. His account of the Lalo *Concerto* is fresh and enthusiastic and very well recorded for its period. With its excellent coupling it makes a real bargain.

Janos Starker's 1962 recording with the LSO under Stanislaw Skrowaczewski sounds remarkably good for its age. Though the tutti chords are brutal and clipped, Starker plays splendidly, and the famous

Mercury recording technique lays out the orchestral texture quite beautifully and with remarkable transparency.

Leonard Rose gives a strong, spontaneous account of this sometimes intractable concerto, bringing out its melodic character as well as its vitality of invention. Ormandy's accompaniment is wonderfully supportive and it is a pity that the orchestral sound has a hint of edginess in the violins and is a bit two-dimensional.

Overture: Le roi d'Ys; Namouna – Suite No. 1.

(M) **(*) Mercury 434 389-2 [id.]. Detroit SO, Paul Paray – BARRAUD: *Offrande;* CHAUSSON: *Symphony.* **(*)

These 1958 recordings come up very well indeed, and the performances have sparkle and great lightness of touch. What delightful music it is, particularly in such authoritative hands.

Symphonie espagnole (for violin and orchestra), *Op. 21.*

(B) *** EMI Eminence Dig. CD-EMX 2277 [(M) id. import]. Tasmin Little, Royal SNO, Vernon Handley – BRUCH: *Scottish fantasy.* ***

(M) *** DG Dig. 445 549-2 [id.]. Perlman, O de Paris, Barenboim – SAINT-SAENS: *Concerto No. 3;* BERLIOZ: *Rêverie et caprice.* ***

(M) *** DG Dig. 457 896-2 [id.]. Mintz, Israel PO, Mehta – SAINT-SAENS: *Introduction & Rondo capriccioso;* VIEUXTEMPS: *Violin concerto No. 5.* ***

(M) *** Decca Dig. 460 007-2 [id.]. Kyung Wha Chung, Montreal SO, Dutoit – RAVEL: *Tzigane;* VIEUXTEMPS: *Violin concerto No. 5.* ***

(M) **(*) Sony SBK 48274; *SBT 48274* [id.]. Zukerman, LAPO, Mehta – VIEUXTEMPS: *Concerto No. 5.* **(*)

(B) **(*) [EMI Red Line Dig. CDR5 69861]. Mutter, O Nat. de France, Ozawa – BIZET: *Carmen: suites* etc.; SARASATE: *Zigeunerweisen.* **(*)

(BB) ** Naxos Dig. 8.550494 [id.]. Marat Bisengaliev, Polish Nat. RSO, Wildner (with: SARASATE: *Zigeunerweisen* ***; SAINT-SAENS: *Havanaise;* RAVEL: *Tzigane* **(*)).

(M) *(*) Decca 452 309-2 [id.]. Ruggiero Ricci, SRO, Ansermet – SAINT-SAENS: *Havanaise* etc.; SARASATE: *Carmen (fantasy)* etc. **

(M) *(*) [RCA Basic 100 09026 68338-2; *68338-4*]. Perlman, LSO, Previn – SIBELIUS: *Violin concerto.* *(*)

Symphonie espagnole, Op. 21 (omitting *Intermezzo*).

(M) (**(*)) RCA Heifetz Collection mono 09026 61753-2 [id.]. Heifetz, RCA Victor SO, Steinberg – CHAUSSON: *Poème* **(*); SAINT-SAENS: *Havanaise* etc.; SARASATE: *Zigeunerweisen.* (***)

Tasmin Little has the gift of sounding totally spontaneous on disc, with no feeling of strict studio manners, here giving a bold and characterful reading of the Lalo, warmly projected and well coupled with Bruch's comparable evocation of Scotland. She is greatly helped by the splendid, keenly polished playing of the Scottish orchestra under Vernon Handley, a most sympathetic partner. Handley is excellent in pointing the rhythms of the fast movements of the Lalo, matching his soloist, and the recording is superb, with brass in particular vividly caught.

The 1980 DG recording of Lalo's five-movement distillation of Spanish sunshine regularly pops in and out of the catalogue and, although the lively digital sound remains a trifle dry, Perlman's performance easily maintains its place near the top of the list. Barenboim combines rhythmic buoyancy with expressive flair and the richness and colour of Perlman's tone are never more telling than in the slow movement, which opens tenderly but develops a compelling expressive ripeness. The brilliance of the Scherzo is matched by the dancing sparkle of the finale. For the reissue in the Masters series, the Berlioz *Rêverie et caprice* makes an attractive if brief bonus.

Mintz, too, plays with much panache; he is highly seductive in the lilting secondary theme of the first movement and he brings a comparable touch of restrained voluptuousness to the habañera rhythms of the *Intermezzo*, while the Scherzo is light as thistledown. Mehta opens a bit heavily, but he provides a satisfactory accompaniment, while the recording, made live in the Mann Auditorium, in Israel, is acceptably full, if not ideally transparent.

Kyung Wha Chung has the advantage of a first-class Decca digital recording, fuller than the DG alternative, and with a highly effective, natural balance. Hers is an athletic, incisive account, at its most individual in the captivatingly light-weight finale, with an element almost of fantasy. Miss Chung does not have quite the panache of Perlman, but Charles Dutoit's accompaniment is first class and the orchestral characterization is strong throughout.

Heifetz's 1951 account has superb panache and there are no complaints about the mono recording.

Alas, he omitted the *Intermezzo* (a practice curiously common in his time), which is our loss, but the performance of the rest, like all the music on this CD, is dazzling.

Zukerman's performance is outstandingly successful. He plays with great dash and fire yet brings a balancing warmth. The rhythmic zest of the Scherzo, with its subtle control of dynamic shading, is contrasted with a richly expressive *Andantino*, to be followed by a dazzling display of fireworks in the finale. Mehta accompanies with sympathetic gusto, and the reverberant, larger-than-life recording suits the style of the music-making, the soloist balanced very forwardly indeed. Zukerman's couplings are more generous than Perlman's, but the effect of the DG recording is to give Perlman's account slightly more romantic finesse.

Anne-Sophie Mutter's account is second to none, with its dazzling display of bravura, the first movement immediately commanding. The Scherzo has an engaging element of fantasy; the finale is scintillating. Many will find the delicacy of her phrasing in the second subject of the first movement refreshing, with its absence of schmaltz. Similarly, the opening of the slow movement is especially imaginative, with Ozawa's strong orchestral statement answered by the soloist with gentle, touching serenity. However, there is a slight technical drawback: while the orchestral detail is good, the balance projects the violin well to the front and the slightly-too-close microphones add a touch of shrillness to the upper range. A degree of digital edge affects the orchestra, too; the orchestral violins sound thin above the stave.

Marat Bisengaliev is an accomplished player with a rich tone and secure technique, and his Slavonic temperament means that Lalo's Spanish ideas are presented with sultry flair. Jonathan Wildner is lively enough in the first movement and manages to make Lalo's quiet woodwind detail register in spite of the resonance. But he takes the *Andante* rather steadily, and the finale again could have used more sheer sparkle from the orchestra. The three encores are very successful. *Zigeunerweisen*, the highlight, has glowing gypsy panache and the luscious lyrical tune sounds properly beguiling, Saint-Saëns's *Havanaise* is stylishly sympathetic, and Ravel's *Tzigane* has real temperament and fire. The reverberant recording acoustic suits these pieces much better than the Lalo.

Ricci's is a scintillating performance with as much depth of feeling as the work may reasonably be expected to take, and Ansermet wields his usual expert baton as accompanist. But the recording (as so often with this work) suffers from an unsatisfactory placing of the soloist in relation to the orchestra. The violin is far too close and the orchestral solo voices are pushed into the background. What is more, the violin tone is harder than in the couplings, at times approaching shrillness, and this seems a curious choice for inclusion in Decca's Classic Sound series.

in his earlier, RCA, account Perlman too plays the work brilliantly, sparkling in the bravura and relishing the expressive melodies without over-indulging them. He is ably supported by Previn; but again the snag lies in the recording balance, which places the violin much too far forward. Accompanying detail is sometimes all but masked, and the harshness on the violin-tone also causes the orchestral sound to lack bloom.

Lambert, Constant (1905–51)

The Rio Grande.

(M) **(*) Decca Dig. 452 324-2. Della Jones, Kathleen Stott, BBC Singers, BBC Concert O, Barry Wordsworth – ELGAR: *Sea pictures* etc. **(*)

With bright, forward recording, this account of *The Rio Grande* is rather aggressive. Wordsworth is also literal, less than idiomatic in the interpretations of jazzy syncopations. The performance is not warmly expressive, but the power and the colour of the writing come across with fine bite and clarity.

Lambert, Michel (*c*. 1610–96)

Airs de cour: *Admirons notre jeune et charmante Déesse; Ah! qui voudra desormais s'engager; C'en est fait, belle Iris; D'un feu secret je me sens consumer; Il faut mourir plutost que le changer; Iris n'est plus, mon Iris m'est ravie; Je suis aymé de celle que j'adore; Ma bergere est tendre et fidelle; Ombre de mon amant; Par mes chants tristes et touchants; Pour vos beaux yeux, Iris; Le repos, l'ombre, le silence; Tout l'univers obéit à l'amour; Trouver sur l'herbette.*

(B) *** HM Musique d'Abord HMA 1901123 [id.]. Les Arts Florissants, William Christie.

Grove speaks of Michel Lambert's airs as models of elegance and grace, in which careful attention was paid to direct declamation. The 300 or so that survive show his artistry in characterization and dialogue to have been of the highest order. They are beautifully performed and expertly recorded by members of Les Arts Florissants and William Christie and are altogether delightful. Unlike some bargain issues, there is excellent documentation with the original texts and translation.

Leçons de Ténèbres.

(M) * Virgin Veritas/EMI Dig. VED5 61213-2 (2). Noéme Rime, Nathalie Stutzmann, Charles Brett, Howard Crook, with continuo (Philippe Foulon, Mauricio Buraglia, Ivète Piveteau).

Lambert's *Leçons de ténèbres* (three each for Holy Wednesday, Holy Thursday and Good Friday) date from 1689. The settings are austere, with a solo line (here varied among four different artists) plus continuo. While it is very enterprising of Virgin to record this offbeat repertoire, its florid lines and ornamentation mean that any performer has to be very flexible indeed and, above all, the singing has to be perfectly tuned. Here it is not. Indeed the very first *Leçon de Mercredi Saint* (Charles Brett) gets the performance off on to the wrong foot with insecure intonation. Although, later, things improve, this is not a set to recommend with any enthusiasm, for Brett is not the only soloist to be faulted in this way.

Lanchbery, John (born 1923)

Tales of Beatrix Potter (ballet arranged from popular tunes of the Victorian era).

(B) **(*) CfP CD-CFP 6074. ROHCG O, John Lanchbery.

Here is a companion score to John Lanchbery's arrangement of *La Fille mal gardée*. The music is not as distinguished melodically as the compilation of Hérold tunes, but the colourful and witty orchestration is a source of delight. This was top-drawer analogue Abbey Road sound from the beginning of the 1970s, although the resonance has brought some loss of focus in the CD transfer, as the opening bars readily show. But there is a fine ambient glow on wind and strings alike, and this still makes an attractive aural entertainment. The composer-arranger used Victorian tunes (including some by Sullivan) of the period of the Beatrix Potter stories, and they are linked so skilfully that one would think the score had been composed as original music. The ballet itself has a strong visual appeal for children but can prove boring for adults, though the music itself is very listenable.

Lassus, Orlandus (*c.* 1532–94)

Chansons and Moresche: *Allala, pia Calia; Canta Giorgia Cathalina; Chi chilichi?; Elle s'en va; En un chasteau; Fuyons tous d'amour le jeu; Hai Lucia; Je l'ayme bien; Las! me faut-il; Lucescit jam o socii; Lucia, celu; O foible esprit; O Lucia; Mais qui pourroit estre celuy; La nuict froid et sombre; Quand mon mary vient de dehors; Si du malheur; Une puce j'ay dedans l'oreille; Un triste coeur; Un jeune moine est sorti du couvent; Vignon, vignon, vignette.* Lute solos: *J'ay un mary; Quand mon mary; Le tems peult bien.*

(B) *** HM Dig. HMC 90856.58 (3) [(M) id. import]. Ens. Clément Jannequin, Dominique Visse – BANCHIERI: *Barca di Venetia per Padova* ***; MARENZIO: *Madrigals* **(*); VECCHI: *Madrigal comedies.* ***

One tends to think of the madrigals of Lassus as of a predominantly dolorous nature, and indeed the opening number here, *Las! me faut il* ('Alas must I needs bear so much woe'), and other settings like *Si du malheur* and *La nuit froide and sombre* carry their full weight of expressive melancholy. They are sung simply and beautifully here. But this excellently varied collection shows another side to this remarkable composer: his sense of fun and the grotesque, and a ready response to the most ribald goings-on. *Quand mon mary* tells of a young woman married to an older man who beats her; *Une puce j'ay dedans l'oreille, helas!* is a brilliant vignette which says: 'I have a flea in my ear, alas, that tickles and bites me day and night.' In the robust extended-narrative group of madrigals which begins with *Lucia celau*, the disenchanted Lucia complains that her lover sweats, stinks and boozes, and in *Chi chilichi?* ('Who's crowing cock-a-doodle-do?') she tells him in no uncertain terms: 'You slept all night, never once did you give me a kiss, get away from here, go squeeze your bagpipe, go and sing your song to someone else.' Her aggrieved lover, Giorgio, inelegantly tries to bring her round by singing a serenade and, when unsuccessful, points out reasonably enough, 'We are both boozers.' A welcome and pleasing central lute interlude follows from Eric Belloq. But there is more ribaldry to come, notably *Un jeune moine est sorti du couvent*, in which the novice monk successfully persuades a young and comely nun to 'jiggle', while *En un chasteau*, my lady complains that a marble statue of Hercules is inadequately endowed. *Cathalina* is another robust ensemble number, in which Giorgio's serenade to his new paramour successfully leads to night-long embraces. The singers here enter fully into the boisterous spirit of this lively music and, led by their counter-tenor director, Dominique Visse, project the Rabelaisian texts with a characterful aplomb, remarkable precision and, at times, a slightly nasal tonal edge which is very fitting. Excellent recording, with fine presence. The disc comes as part of a Harmonia Mundi CD Trio of *'Comédies madrigalesques'*, which is well worth exploring if you have a taste for such repertoire. Good documentation.

Chansons: *Bon jour mon coeur* (ensemble and solo versions); *Fleur de quinz ans; J'ayme la pierre précieuse; Margot labourez les vignes; La nuict froide et sombre; Pour courir en poste a la ville; Susanne ung jour* (with ANON.: Intablature for lute from the Wickhambrook Lute Manuscript); Motets: *Cum natus esset Jesus; In monte Oliveti; Stabat Mater*.
(M) *** Virgin Veritas/EMI Dig. VER5 61166-2. Hilliard Ens., Paul Hillier.

One half is devoted to motets, the other to chansons; both are sung one voice to a part. The tonal blend is as perfect as is usual with this ensemble, intonation is extraordinarily accurate, and there is no vibrato. The sacred pieces, and in particular the setting of the *Stabat Mater* which opens the first half, are most impressive. In some of the chansons there is a discreet lute accompaniment to lend variety. Of the chansons, *La nuict froide et sombre* is quite magical and given with great feeling and colour. One of the other songs tells of an unscrupulous friar, in which all suggestions of virtuous behaviour bring the refrain: 'Brother Lubin can't do it'; others include a simple expression of delight in a loved one, a tale of attempted seduction based on the story of Susanna and the Elders, and a hopeful offer to a fifteen-year-old girl to '*vous faire apprendre*' (teach you how it is done!). For all these racier poems, Lassus provides the most refined setting. A useful addition to the Lassus discography and beautifully recorded.

Le Lagrime di San Pietro a 7.
(BB) *** Naxos Dig. 8.553311 [id.]. Ars Nova, Bo Holten.

Le Lagrime de San Pietro ('The Tears of St Peter') is a late work, a setting of 20 verses of the poet, Luigi Transillo (1510–68), a Neapolitan best known for his lyrical love-sonnets. Like much Renaissance music, it can be performed by a vocal consort or a choir, with or without instruments. The music is rich in variety of expressive means: Howard Mayer Brown calls it a work of 'almost Baroque religious fervour'. The Naxos performance by a first-class Danish choir (6 sopranos, 2 altos, 2 counter-tenors, 4 tenors and 3 basses) is comparatively robust yet offers singing of great sensitivity and a wide range of dynamic. Word meanings are eloquently conveyed (Naxos provides a full text and translation), and Bo Holton shapes the performance to move onwards with gathering intensity towards its climax. The final and twenty-first madrigal, *Vide homo*, for which Lassus himself possibly provided the text, becomes a moving cry of shame and despair as St Peter confronts Christ on the cross, yet the music uplifts the listener on its wave of expressive feeling. The recording, made at the Copenhagen Grundtvigskirken, has a properly spacious ambience, yet is admirably clear.

(i) *9 Lamentationes Hieremiae*. (ii) *Missa pro defunctis (Requiem)* for 4 voices. (i) *Aurora lucis rutilat* (hymn for Lauds); *Magnificat on Aurora lucis rutilat*. Motets: *Christus resurgens; Regina coeli laetare; Surgens Jesus*.
(B) *** Hyperion Dyad Dig. CDD 22012 (2) [id.]. Pro Cantione Antiqua, (i) Bruno Turner; (ii) Mark Brown.

The competing Harmonia Mundi set of the *Lamentations* is available on a single, premium-priced disc (HMC 901299), whereas for approximately the same cost this Hyperion Dyad offers much more music. Within this set, Bruno Turner's 1981 digital recording of the *Lamentations* is also now accommodated on a single CD, while the second includes a selection of music for Easter Sunday, including the glorious *Aurora lucis rutilat* for two five-part choirs and the *Magnificat* based on the motet, plus Mark Brown's fine performance of the four-part *Requiem*. The performances under Bruno Turner are no less persuasive, expressive and vital. The recording too is spacious and warm. So for that matter is the Harmonia Mundi recording for the Chapelle Royale and Philippe Herreweghe, whose performances of the *Lamentations* are hardly less admirable.

Missa Bell'Amfitrit'alterna.
(BB) *** Naxos Dig. 8.550836 [id.]. Oxford Schola Cantorum, Jeremy Summerly – PALESTRINA: *Missa Hodie Christus natus est* etc. ***
(M) **(*) EMI Dig. CD-EMX 2180 [(M) id. import]. St John's College, Cambridge, Ch., Guest – ALLEGRI: *Miserere* **(*); PALESTRINA: *Veni sponsa Christi*. ***

This magnificent Mass of Palestrina's great Flemish contemporary, Lassus, makes a superb coupling for the outstanding performances of Palestrina masterpieces on the Naxos disc. This is the full Schola Cantorum of Oxford, not just the smaller Camerata group, and arguably it is too large for the dedicated, intimate polyphony of Lassus; but the singing is superb and the recording is warm and atmospheric. Yet another outstanding Naxos issue of early music.

Amphitrite was not only the mythological goddess of the sea but also a nickname for Venice, and this Mass is almost certainly connected with the city rather than with Poseidon's wife. It is a complex and varied piece of remarkable textural diversity, and it is also finely sung by the St John's Choir under Guest, although perhaps a little more Latin fervour would have been in order. The digital recording is first class.

Lawes, William (1602–45)

Collections

Consort sets a 5: in A min. & C ; Divisions on a Pavan in G min. for 2 bass viols & organ; Royal consorts Nos. 1 in D min.; 6 in D; Set a 4 in G min. (with 2 theorbos); *Lute duets: Alman; 2 Corants.*
(BB) **(*) Naxos Dig. 8. 550601 [id.]. Rose Consort of viols; Jacob Herigan, David Miller (lutes), Timothy Roberts (organ).

Naxos provide an attractive cross-section of Lawes's instrumental music, using an all-viol texture for the string parts in the *Consorts* (with organ where appropriate). The performances make a livelier and more convincing impression than those by Fretwork, although in the *Royal consorts* the well-blended interaction of inner parts is less sharply individual than with the Purcell Consort. Thus the engaging *Echo* movement of the *D minor Consort* is brought off less tellingly here, with a more measured tempo. However, the closing *Aire-Morris* of the *D major Consort* (which ends the programme) is attractively vigorous. The group also include a fascinatingly bravura set of *Divisions for viols and organ* on the same *Pavane* which opens the four-part *Set in G minor*. The pieces for two lutes could have been given more lively projection, although they are well enough played. The excellent balance helps to make this inexpensive sampler recommendable, which readers might well try.

Lecocq, Alexandre (1832–1918)

Mam'zelle Angot (ballet, arr. Gordon Jacob).
(M) *** Decca 430 849-2 (2). Nat. PO, Bonynge – HEROLD: *La Fille mal gardée*. ***

Mam'zelle Angot is a gay, vivacious score with plenty of engaging tunes, prettily orchestrated in the modern French style. Bonynge offers the first recording of the complete score, and its 39 minutes are consistently entertaining when the orchestral playing has such polish and wit. The Kingsway Hall recording is closely observed: the CD brings sharp detail and tangibility, especially at lower dynamic levels.

Lehár, Franz (1870–1948)

Friederike (complete).
(M) *** EMI CMS5 65369-2 (2). Donath, Dallapozza, Fuchs, Finke, Grabenhorst, Bav. R. Ch., Munich R. O, Wallberg.

The idea of Richard Tauber inspiring Lehár to write an operetta with the poet Goethe as the main character may sound far-fetched, but that is just what *Friederike* is, more ambitious than a genuine operetta and bringing the obvious snag for non-German speakers that there is a great deal of spoken dialogue, the more disruptive because there is no libretto, let alone an English translation. However, there is a track-by-track synopsis of each number, and in every other respect this is a delightful reissue, with Helen Donath charming and sensitive in the name-part. Dallapozza has a light, heady tenor, at times stressed by the weight of the part of Goethe but rising above all to the great Tauber number, *O Mädchen, mein Mädchen!*, based (like other numbers) on a Goethe poem, *Mailied*. Heinz Wallberg is a lively and persuasive director, and the 1980 recording has the bloom one associates with German EMI productions.

Giuditta (complete).
(M) ** EMI Dig. CMS5 65378-2 (2). Edda Moser, Hirte, Gedda, Baumann, Munich Concert Ch. & R. O, Boskovsky.

Again written as a vehicle for Richard Tauber in 1934, *Giuditta* was Lehár's own favourite among his works. It may not have the easy tunefulness of *The Merry Widow* of a quarter of a century earlier, and the Balkan flavours may be plastered on rather thick; but with its poignant, disillusioned dénouement in place of the usual happy ending it is both charming and distinctive. As a young man, Willi Boskovsky played in the orchestra at its first performance; here he proves a persuasive advocate, though the ensemble could be more polished. Gedda hardly shows his years in the Tauber role, with half-tones as honeyed as ever. But Edda Moser is disappointing in the name-part. She may be glamorous to look at, but the voice is consistently too hard to sound seductive, even in the song, *Mein Lippen, sie küssen so heiss*, made so ecstatic by Schwarzkopf on her operetta record, and by Hilde Gueden on the previous Decca set of *Giuditta*. Good 1983–4 digital recording, except that the spoken dialogue brings the performers suddenly much closer than the singing. A track synopsis takes the place of the more desirable libretto with translation.

Das Land des Lächelns (The Land of smiles) (complete).

(M) **(*) EMI (SIS) CMS5 65372-2 (2). Rothenberger, Gedda, Holm, Friedauer, Moeller, Bav. R. Ch., Graunke SO, Willy Mattes.

This 1967 recording has on the whole transferred well to CD. Don't be put off by the sound of the overture, which seems thin because of the relatively small orchestra for the opening scene, but then has plenty of theatrical presence. The recording is atmospheric and real, not only in conveying the songs but also in the spoken dialogue, which is well produced. The cast is strong. Gedda is in excellent form and, besides Anneliese Rothenberger, Renate Holm makes a charming contribution as Mi. The famous tunes, including '*You are my heart's delight*', are splendidly done. Yet again there is no libretto, especially desirable in this operetta; but we are offered a track-by-track synopsis of each number.

The Merry Widow (Die lustige Witwe; complete, in German).

(M) (***) EMI (SIS) mono CDH7 69520-2 [ZDH 69520]. Schwarzkopf, Gedda, Kunz, Loose, Kraus, Philh. Ch. & O, Ackermann.

It was the mono set, of the early 1950s, which established a new pattern in recording operetta. Ten years later in stereo Schwarzkopf was to record the role again, if anything with even greater point and perception, but here she has extra youthful vivacity, and the *Viljalied* – ecstatically drawn out – is unique. Some may be troubled that Kunz as Danilo sounds older than the Baron, but it is still a superbly characterful cast, and the transfer to a single CD is bright and clear.

The Merry Widow (Die lustige Witwe): highlights.

(B) *(*) DG Classikon 457 877-2 [(M) id. import] (from complete recording, with Elizabeth Harwood, Teresa Stratas, René Kollo, Werner Hollweg, Zoltan Kélémen, Donald Grobe, Werner Krenn, German Op. Ch., BPO, Karajan).

'Brahms's *Requiem* performed to the tunes of Lehár' was how one wit described Karajan's 1972 version of *The Merry Widow*, with its carefully measured tempi and absence of sparkle. The reverberant recording (made in the Jesus-Christus-Kirche) has been dried out a little, but this means that the choral focus is not always quite clean, although the solo voices have plenty of presence. These highlights run to 69 minutes and include all the key numbers, with an adequate synopsis. But despite some fine contributions from a starry cast, this is of curiosity value only.

Leoncavallo, Ruggiero (1858–1919)

I Pagliacci (complete).

(M) *** DG 449 727-2 [id.]. Carlyle, Bergonzi, Taddei, Panerai, La Scala, Milan, Ch. & O, Karajan.

(M) *** EMI CMS7 63967-2 (2). Amara, Corelli, Gobbi, La Scala, Milan, Ch. & O, Von Matačić – MASCAGNI: *Cavalleria rusticana*. **(*)

(M) *** RCA 74321 50168-2 (2) [09026 60865-2]. Caballé, Domingo, Milnes, John Alldis Ch., LSO, Santi – PUCCINI: *Il Tabarro*. **(*)

(B) **(*) Naxos Dig. 8.660021 [id.]. Gauci, Martinucci, Tumagian, Dvorsky, Skovhus, Slovak Philh. Ch., Czech RSO, Rahbari.

(M) **(*) EMI CMS7 63650-2 (2). Scotto, Carreras, Nurmela, Amb. Op. Ch., Philh. O, Muti – MASCAGNI: *Cavalleria rusticana*. **(*)

(M) (**(*)) Nimbus mono NI 7843/4 [id.]. Gigli, Pacetti, Basiola, Nessi, Paci, La Scala Ch. & O, Ghione – MASCAGNI: *Cavalleria rusticana*. (**)

(B) ** Decca Double 452 179-2 (2) [(M) id. import]. McCracken, Lorengar, Merrill, Benelli, Krause, St Cecilia, Rome, Ac. Ch. & O, Gardelli – MASCAGNI: *Cavalleria rusticana*. **

(B) *(*) Ph. Duo 454 265-2 (2) [id.]. Stratas, Domingo, Pons, Rinaldi, La Scala, Milan, Ch. & O, Prêtre – MASCAGNI: *Cavalleria rusticana*. *(*)

Karajan's *Pagliacci* has dominated the catalogue for three decades alongside its natural operatic partner, *Cavalleria rusticana*, so it is apt that DG have chosen it for separate reissue in their series of 'Originals', freshly remastered. Karajan does nothing less than refine Leoncavallo's melodrama, with long-breathed, expansive tempi and the minimum of exaggeration. Karajan's choice of soloists was clearly aimed to help that – but the passions are still there; and rarely if ever on record has the La Scala Orchestra played with such beautiful feeling for tone-colour. Bergonzi is among the most sensitive of Italian tenors of heroic quality, and it is good to have Joan Carlyle as Nedda, touching if often rather cool. Taddei is magnificently strong, and Benelli and Panerai could hardly be bettered in the roles of Beppe and Silvio. The combined set remains available (and unsurpassed) but on three records at premium price – although, as well as *Cav.*,

DG provide a splendid set of performances of operatic intermezzi as a filler. However, the separate *Pagliacci* is something of a bargain.

The EMI (originally Columbia) recording under Von Matačić dates from the early 1960s and is especially notable for the contribution of the tenor, Franco Corelli, as Canio, which calls for some superlatives. He is not nearly as imaginative as some of the great tenors of the past, yet he shows a natural feeling for the phrases. It is not just a question of making a big, glorious noise – though of course he does that too – but of interpreting the music; and a performance like this puts several others, by more obviously starry names, in the shade. Gobbi is a predictably magnificent Tonio; true, there are some threadbare patches towards the top of the voice, but at that time it was still a most varied instrument and Gobbi used it to the greatest dramatic effect. Lucine Amara gives a thoroughly sound performance as Nedda, both vocally and dramatically, and the recording has a vivid sense of atmosphere and movement. The coupled *Cav.* is dramatically not quite so striking, but this still makes a clear first choice in the mid-priced range for those who want the pairing with Mascagni.

For those who do not want that obvious coupling, the alternative RCA set is a first-rate recommendation, with fine singing from all three principals, vivid playing and recording, and one or two extra passages not normally included – as in the Nedda–Silvio duet. Milnes is superb in the Prologue. As with the separate Karajan reissue, this RCA set is handsomely repackaged with libretto in the Opera Treasury series.

Alexander Rahbari conducts his Slovak forces in a vigorous, red-blooded reading which with first-rate solo singing makes an excellent bargain recommendation, very well recorded, if with the chorus a little distant. Miriam Gauci is a warmly vibrant Nedda, with plenty of temperament, and Eduard Tumagian is an outstanding Tonio, not only firm and dark of tone but phrasing imaginatively. As Canio, Nicola Martinucci has an agreeable tenor that he uses with more finesse and a better line than many more celebrated rivals, even though his histrionics at the beginning and end of *Vesti la giubba* are unconvincing.

Under Muti's urgent direction both *Cav.* and *Pag.* represent the music of violence. In both he has sought to use the original text, which in *Pag.* is often surprisingly different, with many top notes eliminated and Tonio instead of Canio delivering (singing, not speaking) the final *La commedia è finita*. Muti's approach represents the antithesis of smoothness, and the coarse rendering of the *Prologue* in *Pag.* by the rich-toned Kari Nurmela is disappointing. Scotto's Nedda goes raw above the stave, but the edge is in keeping with Muti's approach, with its generally brisk speeds. Carreras seems happier here than in *Cav.*, but it is the conductor and the fresh look he brings which will prompt a choice here. The sound is extremely vivid.

The Nimbus transfer of the classic 1934 recording with Gigli focuses the voices effectively enough, giving them a mellow bloom – though the orchestra, often rather recessed, is relatively muffled. Gigli is very much the centre of attention, with Iva Pacetti as Nedda clear and powerful rather than characterful.

The Decca set conducted by Varviso centres round the Canio of James McCracken, intentionally a big-scale, heroic performance with Otello-like overtones. *Vesti la giubba* and the scene which follows open the opera promisingly, helped by vivid Decca stereo, but later on the voice is made to crack too often, with resulting crudeness. The rest of the cast is good – Merrill at his finest, Benelli sweet-toned as ever and Lorengar tenderly expressive, if fluttery in vibrato. However, the vintage (1967) Decca recording is compellingly atmospheric and histrionic in its projection: with McCracken's uncouth characterization of the central role, this is *verismo* opera with a vengeance.

The Prêtre version is taken from the soundtrack of Zeffirelli's film of the opera, and is principally remarkable for the large-scale heroic performance, superbly sung, of Plácido Domingo as Canio. Much of the rest is less recommendable. Juan Pons sings the *Prologue* impressively and exploits his fine baritone as Tonio; but Teresa Stratas and Alberto Rinaldi (Silvio) both suffer from uneven vocal production, with Stratas's earthy timbres going raw under pressure. Even at Duo price this is not very recommendable, and the extra clarity and presence of CD serve only to underline the vocal flaws. A synopsis is offered in lieu of a libretto.

I Pagliacci: highlights.
(M) **(*) EMI (SIS) CDM5 66048-2. Scotto, Carreras, Nurmela, Allen, Amb. Op. Ch., Philh. O, Muti – MASCAGNI: *Cavalleria rusticana:* highlights. **(*)

Muti uses the original text, which is often surprisingly different, with Tonio instead of Canio delivering (singing not speaking) the final *La commedia è finita*. It is an urgent performance and very involving, but the rendering of the Prologue by Kari Nurmela brings a coarse start to the proceedings.

Liadov, Anatol (1855–1914)

Baba-Yaga, Op. 56; The Enchanted lake, Op. 62; Kikimora, Op. 63; A musical snuff-box, Op. 32; 8 Russian folksongs, Op. 58.

(M) *(*) Virgin/EMI Ultraviolet Dig. CUV5 61322-2. Bergen PO, Kitaienko – STRAVINSKY: *Firebird suite* etc. *(*)

(i) *Baba Yaga, Op. 56; The Enchanted lake, Op. 62; Kikimora, Op. 63;* (ii) *8 Russian folksongs.*

(BB) **(*) Naxos Dig. 8.550328 [id.]. Slovak PO, (i) Gunzenhauser; (ii) Kenneth Jean – Concert: *'Russian Fireworks'.*

It is good to have inexpensive recordings of these key Liadov works, particularly the *Russian folksongs*, eight orchestral vignettes of great charm, displaying a winning sense of orchestral colour. The performances are persuasive, and the digital recording is vivid and well balanced.

Although the *Musical snuff-box* has charm, and Kitaienko's performances are not without atmosphere, they lack sparkle, and the Naxos Slovak collection of these same miniatures is not only preferable, it is also cheaper.

Ligeti, György (born 1923)

Chamber concerto.

(B) *** DG Classikon Dig. 439 452-2 [(M) id. import]. Ens. InterContemporain, Boulez – LUTOSLAWSKI: *Chain 3* etc.; SCHNITTKE: *Concerto grosso No. 1.* ***

This bargain DG CD presents a performance of the *Chamber concerto* that is a useful offering which admirers of this composer's cloudy sound-textures can safely investigate. In this work the specific notes matter less than the washes of colour. Excellent performance and recording.

Lindberg, Magnus (born 1958)

'Meet the composer': (i) *Action – Situation; Signification;* (ii–iii) *Kinetics;* (i–ii; iv) *Kraft;* (v; iii) *Rittrato;* (vi–vii; iii) *Zona;* (Instrumental) (viii–ix) *Ablauf;* (x) . . . *De Tartuffe, je crois* (for piano quintet); (viii; xi) *Linea d'ombra;* (vi) *Stroke;* (Piano) (xii) *Twine.*

(B) *** Finlandia/Warner Dig. Double 0630 19756-2 (2) [(M) id. import]. (i) Toimili Ens.; (ii) Finnish RSO; (iii) Salonen; (iv) Swedish RSO; (v) Avanti! CO; (vi) Anssi Karttunen; (vii) L. Sinf.; (viii) Krikku; (ix) Aaltonen, Ohenoja; (x) Endymion Ens., John Witfield; (xi) Ferchen, Pohjola, Virtanen; (xii) Tuija Hakkila.

Magnus Lindberg belongs to the younger generation of Finnish composers now moving into their middle years. He studied with Paavo Heininen in Helsinki and with Bryan Ferneyhough at the Darmstadt summer courses in the early 1980s. He also studied with Franco Donati in Siena and with Vinko Globokar in Paris. His breakthrough as a composer came with *Kraft* (the second item on the first CD), which had its première in 1984 and brought him to international attention. This Finlandia '*Meet the Composer*' set of two CDs gives a good cross-section of his work during the 1980s, when he was still in his late twenties and early thirties. If you do not respond to avant-garde music, you may still find something to reward you here, for Lindberg is a composer of imagination and intelligence.

Linkola, Jukka (born 1955)

'Meet the composer': (i) *Boogie Woogie waltz;* (ii–iii) *Crossings;* (iv) *Trumpet concerto;* (i) *Malaria;* (v; iii) *Ronia, the Robber's daughter (5 movements);* (vi; iii) *The Snow Queen* (film incidental music); (vii) *Evoe!.*

(B) *** Finlandia/Warner Dig. Double 0630 19808-2 (2) [(M) id. import]. (i) Jukka Linkola Octet; (ii) Juhani Aaltonen, Helsinki PO; (iii) cond. composer; (iv) Jouko Harjanne, Finnish RSO, Segerstam; (v) Finnish Nat. Op. O; (vi) O; (vii) Helsinki University Ch., Matti Hyökki, with Kristian & Laura Attila.

Jukka Linkola began life as a jazz musician, and it was an encounter with the music of Lutoslawski which turned him in the direction of serious contemporary music. Although his is not a voice of great individuality, he is obviously a composer of both sophistication and imagination. *Crossings* for tenor saxophone and orchestra from 1983 reveals traces of Messiaen and French music, as well as his past in the world of jazz. Kimmo Korhonen's note speaks of it as 'an exceptionally seamless and functional synthesis of the worlds of jazz and serious music'. The excerpts from the ballet, *Ronia, the Robber's daughter*, have more than the occasional reminder of Stravinsky and Prokofiev and the average Hollywood score. Even so, Linkola has the capability of taking the listener by surprise. Though not a major figure, he is far from negligible, and he is resourceful, rarely less than an entertaining aural companion and always intelligent. These two CDs are issued in Finlandia's '*Meet the Composer*' series, and for the most part his is an acquaintance worth making. Good performances and recording.

Liszt, Franz (1811–86)

(i) *Piano concertos Nos. 1 in E flat; 2 in A; 3 in E flat, Op. posth.* (arr. Rosenblatt); *Fantasia on Hungarian folksongs;* (ii) *Malédiction; Rhapsodie espagnole* (arr. Busoni); (iii) *Totentanz;* (ii) SCHUBERT/LISZT: *Wanderer fantasia.*

(BB) ** Carlton Classics Dig. 30367 02147 (2) [(B) id.]. Joshua Pierce, (i) State SO of Russia, (ii) Moscow State PO, (iii) R. & TV SO of Slovenia; all cond. Paul Freeman.

Joshua Pierce possesses a formidable technique and despatches both the concertos and the Rosenblatt reconstruction with considerable flair. He is not as poetic as such Lisztians as Richter or Brendel, and this programme comes into direct competition with the Berezovsky/Leonskaya Ultima Double, which is far superior. But the Carlton collection is enterprising and recommendable, even if it is not quite worth a three-star grading.

Piano concertos Nos. 1–2; Fantasia on Hungarian folksongs; Fantasia on themes from Beethoven's 'Ruins of Athens'; Grande fantaisie symphonique on themes from Berlioz's 'Lélio'; Malédiction; Polonaise brillante on Weber's Polonaise brillante in E (L'Hilarité); Totentanz (paraphrase on the *Dies Irae*); SCHUBERT/LISZT: *Wanderer fantasia.*

(B) *** EMI Rouge et Noir (SIS) CZS5 69662-2 (2) [CDZB 69662]. Michel Béroff, Leipzig GO, Kurt Masur.

Béroff's account of the two concertos can hold its own with the best of the competition: here there is nothing routine or slapdash, but instead excitement, warmth and spontaneity, along with his remarkable technical prowess. The Leipzig recording, too, sounds first rate in its remastered form, and the distinguished orchestral playing under Masur is given plenty of body and weight. This is especially satisfying in the Schubert *Wanderer* arrangement, while the opening of the Beethoven and Berlioz *Fantasias* are full of atmosphere. The piano timbre has plenty of body and colour, as well as sparkle. This is an exhilarating and rewarding set which can be given the strongest recommendation on all counts.

(i) *Piano concertos 1–2; Totentanz* (paraphrase on the '*Dies irae*'). *Années de pèlerinage: Book 1: 1st year: Switzerland; Book 2: 2nd year (Italy); Book 3: 3rd Year (Italy) excerpts: Aux cyprès de la Villa d'Este; Sunt lachrimae rerum; Sursum corda* (only). *Sonata in B min.; Concert paraphrase of 'Isolde's Liebestod' from Wagner's 'Tristan'. Csárdás macabre; En rêve (Nocturne); Harmonies poétiques et religieuses (Invocations; Bénédiction de Dieu dans la solitude; Pensée des morts); Funérailles. Klavierstück in F sharp; Légendes Nos.1–2; La lugubre gondola Nos. 1–2; Mosonyis Grabgeleit; Nuages gris; Prelude and fugue on the name, 'BACH'; RW (Venezia); Schlaflos! Frage und Antwort; Unstern (Sinistre); Valse oubliée No. 1; Vexilla regis Prodeunt; Weinachtsbaum (Christmas tree) suite (excerpts); Variations on 'Weinen, Klagen, Sorgen Zagen'.*

(M) **(*) Ph. Brendel Edition Analogue/Dig. 446 924-2 (5). Alfred Brendel, (i) LPO, Haitink.

Brendel's 1972 recordings of the *Concertos* and *Totentanz* have long been among the key versions of these volatile works and Haitink is a persuasive accompanist. Brendel's set of the *Second year* of the *Années de pèlerinage* was recorded that same year and proved no less outstanding. The performances are of superlative quality, the playing highly poetic and brilliant, while the analogue recording offers Philips's most realistic quality. The *First year* (*Switzerland*) came 14 years later and was recorded digitally. It has many impressive moments but also some ugly fortissimi that are not wholly the responsibility of the engineers. Brendel plays the pieces *segue*, without pauses and, although there is some atmospheric playing in the set, the moments of magic are relatively few. The four excerpts from the *Third year* were recorded as part of an outstanding (1979) analogue recital, which included the extraordinary late pieces, many of whose names are unfamiliar. The music is often surprisingly stark and bitter and Brendel's presentation of them is distinguished by a concentration and subtlety of nuance that are wholly convincing, helped by extremely lifelike recording. The *Prelude and fugue on the name 'BACH'* and the *Variations* on *'Weinen, Klagen, Sorgen, Zagen'* are better known as organ pieces but sound no less impressive on the piano when played so masterfully, and the *Harmonies poétiques et religieuses* are hardly less distinguished. However, the *Sonata* is something of a disappointment. Brendel has recorded this work three times and Philips have chosen the most recent version, made in 1991. It was a great pity that his second recording (also digital) was not chosen (voted by the *Gramophone* as 'Piano Record of the Year' in 1983). The newest account brings a similarly wide range of colour, yet there is not the same spontaneity nor a comparable firmness of grip. There is much brilliant pianism, but the overall purpose of the reading seems much less clear and even the recording, though bright and clean, is less impressive than either the 1983 version or even the analogue record, made in the 1960s. But overall this box shows Brendel as a superbly understanding Lisztian.

(i) *Piano concertos Nos. 1 in E flat; 2 in A; Totentanz for piano and orchestra;* (ii) *Piano sonata in B min.; Années de pèlerinage, 2nd Year: Après une lecture du Dante (Dante sonata); Sonetti de Petrarca Nos. 104 & 123.*

(B) *** Teldec/Warner Ultima 3984 21092-2 (2) [(M) id. import]. (i) Boris Berezovsky, Philh. O, Hugo Wolf; (ii) Elisabeth Leonskaya.

Too often when a Double features different performers on each of the two paired CDs, one or another lets the side down. Not in this case, however. Berezovsky's thrillingly extrovert yet highly musical accounts of the two concertos and the rumbustious *Totentanz* are ideally balanced by Elisabeth Leonskaya's imaginative recital of solo piano music. Berezovsky plays throughout with enormous panache and bravura, yet with melting poetic feeling too. Hugo Wolf proves a splendid partner, and the Philharmonia Orchestra – obviously enjoying themselves hugely – play with great gusto (especially the trombones) in the big tuttis. Yet each slow movement is beguilingly romantic and presented with an appealingly refined sensibility. The Scherzos scintillate (Berezovsky's fingerwork glitters), and the finales have barnstorming excitement, especially that of the *E flat concerto*, where there is a spontaneous accelerando in the closing pages. The opening of the *Totentanz* is immediately arresting: the performance has thrilling momentum, with the sometimes bizarre orchestral effects and audacious bravura from the soloist combining to maximum impact. The *Dies irae* thunders out demonically and the coda is cataclysmic. This is surely the way Liszt himself must have played, and the performances of all three works are tinglingly spontaneous. The full-blooded, resonantly spacious recording, made at Aldeburgh in 1994, increases the sense of spectacle.

Leonskaya then takes over for the *Sonata*, and she gives a very impressive reading indeed. She has a firm grip on this wayward piece, especially in the more reflective writing, where she displays much poetic feeling. The central *Allegro energico* is played superbly. Liszt's bolder romantic flourishes undoubtedly have a tendency to rhetoric, which is not minimized here, but Leonskaya clearly believes deeply in the work and is an ardent advocate. The closing pages have a powerful sense of apotheosis. She is given very good recording, much better than either Watts or Jandó (see below). The *Dante sonata* is no less authoritative, a performance as imaginative as it is compelling. The two *Petrarch sonnets* are played very freely, with flexible rubato which suits No. 123 particularly well. Even if you already have some of the music on record, this set is well worth investigating.

(i) *Piano concertos Nos. 1–2;* (ii) *Hungarian rhapsody No. 2.*

(M) *** [RCA Basic 100 09026 62679-2]. (i) Barry Douglas, LSO, Hirokami; (ii) Boston Pops, Fiedler.

(i) *Piano concertos Nos. 1–2;* (ii) *Hungarian rhapsody No. 2; Liebestraum; Les Préludes.*

(BB) **(*) RCA Navigator 74321 29244-2 [(M) id. import]. (i) Leonard Pennario, RPO, Leibowitz; (ii) Boston Pops O, Arthur Fiedler.

Piano concertos Nos. 1–2; Totentanz.

(M) *** Ph. 426 637-2. Alfred Brendel, LPO, Haitink.

Piano concertos Nos. (i) *1 in E flat;* (ii) *2 in A. Années de pèlerinage: Sonetto 104 del Petrarca. Hungarian rhapsody No. 6; Valse oubliée.*

(M) *** Mercury (IMS) 432 002-2 [id.]. Byron Janis, (i) Moscow PO, Kondrashin; (ii) Moscow RSO, Rozhdestvensky (also with SCHUMANN: *Romance in F sharp; Novellette in F.* FALLA: *Miller's dance.* GUION: *The harmonica player* ***).

Piano concertos Nos. (i) *1 in E flat;* (ii) *2 in A. Piano sonata in B min.*

(M) *** Ph. 446 200-2 [id.]. Sviatoslav Richter, (i–ii) with LSO, Kirill Kondrashin.

Sviatoslav Richter's 1961 performances on Philips are very distinguished indeed, and the recent remastering by Wilma Cozart Fine makes the very most of the recording, originally engineered by the Mercury team. It is good that both Wilma and Robert Fine receive a credit in the insert notes for the excellence of the original sound-balance. Richter's playing is unforgettable and so is his rapport with Kondrashin and the LSO, whose playing throughout is of the very highest order. For the current reissue, Richter's electrifying and highly poetic new recording of the *Sonata* has been added; Philips are, however, reluctant to suggest a recording date. The sound is vivid and present but the acoustic is rather dry for full comfort. However, given playing of this calibre, one soon adjusts.

Around the time they were recording Richter's Liszt *Concertos* for Philips in London (1962), the Mercury engineers paid a visit to Moscow to record Byron Janis in the same repertoire, and his is a comparably distinguished coupling. Janis's glittering articulation is matched by his sense of poetry and drama, and there is plenty of dash in these very compelling performances, which are afforded characteristically brilliant Mercury sound, although the piano is too close. The encores which follow the two *Concertos* are also very enjoyable.

Brendel's Philips recordings from the early 1970s hold their place at or near the top of the list. There is a valuable extra work offered here and the recording is of Philips's best. The performances are as poetic as they are brilliant, and those who doubt the musical substance of No. 2 will find their reservations melt away.

Barry Douglas's performances are very fine: he commands a wide variety of keyboard colour and keeps the flamboyant showmanship in hand, while displaying a good deal of poetic feeling. Moreover his readings are well thought out and never unimaginative. He gets highly musical support from Hirokami, and the recording is excellent. Fiedler provides the encore, a vivid account of the most famous of Liszt's orchestral rhapsodies. This is one of the very best of RCA's Basic 100 series.

Pennario's performances are assured and brilliant, yet the slow movement of No. 1 is touchingly wistful. Leibowitz provides excellent support and the opening of the *A major Concerto* is enticingly atmospheric. The recording, though forward, is full and vivid, and the result is sensitive, sparkling and spontaneous, with a thrilling lack of inhibition at the close of the *Second Concerto*. There is nothing much wrong with Fiedler's exciting Boston Pops accounts of the two orchestral works, which are also vividly recorded. It was a pity that the famous *Liebestraum* could not have been provided in its original piano format, though the orchestral version is undoubtedly luscious. This bargain-basement collection is first-class value.

Piano concerto No. 1 in E flat.

(M) *** DG 449 719-2 [id.]. Argerich, LSO, Abbado – CHOPIN: *Piano concerto No. 1.* ***

(BB) **(*) Naxos Dig. 8.550292 [id.]. Joseph Banowetz, Czech RSO, Bratislava, Oliver Dohnányi – CHOPIN: *Concerto No. 1.* **(*)

(i; ii) *Piano concerto No. 1 in E flat;* (i) *Piano sonata in B min.; Hungarian rhapsody No. 6;* (iii) *Années de pèlerinage: Valleé d'Obermann; Les jeux d'eau à la Villa D'Este.*

(B) **(*) DG Classikon 439 409-2 [(M) id. import]. (i) Martha Argerich; (ii) LSO, Abbado; (iii) Lazar Berman.

(i) *Piano concerto No. 1 in E flat; Fantasia in E min. on Hungarian folksongs; Hungarian rhapsodies Nos. 8–11, 13.*

(M) (***) Sony mono MHK 62338 Claudio Arrau, (i) with Phd. O, Ormandy.

For some reason Martha Argerich (in 1968) recorded only Liszt's *First Concerto* and not the *Second*. However, in the *E flat Concerto* there is an excellent partnership between the pianist and Abbado, and this is a performance of flair and high voltage which never becomes vulgar. It is very well recorded and, in this reissue coupled with Chopin for DG's 'Legendary Recordings' series of 'Originals', it sounds better than ever. The performance is also available on DG's bargain Classikon label, coupled with the *Sonata*, which Argerich recorded three years later. Her account has tremendous assurance and vigour and there is no lack of spontaneity. But the work's lyrical feeling and indeed its breadth are sacrificed to some extent to the insistent forward pulse of the playing. The *Rhapsody* gives no cause for complaint and the recording is clear (if not especially rich), but Lazar Berman's performances of the two excerpts from the *Années de pèlerinage* which complete the CD show how Liszt playing can be controlled as well as seemingly impulsive and poetic.

The Arrau recordings come from 1952 and have not been in circulation here for many years. The *E flat Concerto* was done in one take and prompted Ormandy to say after the playback, 'Well, what is there to say? We're done. It can't be better than this!' The rest of the programme has just as much electricity. Arrau had an aristocratic poise and a refined musicianship which were unique in this repertoire. The sound is amazingly good. This disc costs rather more than upper-mid-price.

A splendid, energetic account of the *First Concerto* from Banowetz, well coupled with Chopin, has the full measure of the work's flamboyance and its poetry. The only snag is that the delicacy of texture in the engaging scherzo means that the triangle solo is only just audible. Otherwise the wide-ranging sound is excellent.

(i) *Piano concerto No. 1 in E flat. Mephisto waltz No. 1.*
(M) **(*) BMG/Melodiya 74321 33219-2 [id.]. John Ogdon, (i) USSR State SO, Victor Dubrovsky – TCHAIKOVSKY: *Piano concerto No. 1* etc. ***

John Ogdon's Russian recording was made in 1962, immediately after he had been awarded the joint prize in the Tchaikovsky competition with Ashkenazy, whom we also hear giving a strikingly fresh account of the Tchaikovsky *Concerto*. Odgon is not quite so lucky in his accompaniment, as the playing of the Russian orchestra in the first movement brings more red-blooded gusto than refinement. However, Ogdon shows his artistry in his poetic account of the *Quasi adagio* and the performance certainly does not lack glitter or panache. Nor does his account of the *Mephisto waltz*, although the recording of the piano here is relatively unflattering. A very worthwhile coupling, just the same.

Fantasia on Hungarian folk tunes for piano and orchestra.
(M) *** Decca Dig. 430 726-2. Bolet, LSO, Ivan Fischer – ADDINSELL: *Warsaw concerto* ***; GERSHWIN: *Rhapsody* **(*); GOTTSCHALK: *Grand fantasia* ***; LITOLFF: *Scherzo*. ***

Bolet is a masterful soloist and he plays here with characteristic bravura. Like the pianist, the Hungarian conductor is an understanding Lisztian, and the accompaniment from the LSO is first rate, with a recording balance of demonstration quality.

(i) *Fantasia on Hungarian folk tunes. Hungarian rhapsodies Nos. 2, 4–5; Mazeppa; Mephisto waltz No. 2; Les Préludes; Tasso, lamento e trionfo.*
(B) *** DG Double 453 130-2 (2) [id.]. BPO, Karajan; (i) with Cherkassky.

This DG Double generally shows Karajan at his finest. Shura Cherkassky's glittering 1961 recording of the *Hungarian fantasia* is an affectionate performance with some engaging touches from the orchestra, though the pianist is dominant and his playing is superbly assured. The rest of the programme is comparably charismatic. Here as elsewhere the remastering for CD has brought out the range and body of the sound impressively, with firm detail throughout the orchestra. The cellos and basses sound marvellous in the *Fifth rhapsody* and *Tasso*, and even the brashness of *Les Préludes* is a little tempered. *Mazeppa* is a great performance, superbly thrilling and atmospheric, with a riveting coda – worthy of a Rosette. A set showing Karajan and his Berlin orchestra at their finest.

A Faust symphony.
(M) *** DG 447 449-2. Kenneth Riegel, Tanglewood Festival Ch., Boston SO, Bernstein.
(M) ** Ph. (IMS) Dig. 442 642-2. Lajos Kozma, Concg. Ch. & O, Dorati.

Bernstein on DG seems to possess the ideal temperament for holding together grippingly the melodrama of the first movement, while the lovely *Gretchen* centrepiece is played most beautifully. Kenneth Riegel is an impressive tenor soloist in the finale, there is an excellent, well-balanced choral contribution, and the Boston Symphony Orchestra produce playing which is both exciting and atmospheric. Overall, this Bernstein account (reissued as one of DG's 'Originals') makes a fine, mid-priced recommendation.

The excellence of the playing of the Royal Concertgebouw Orchestra is not in question in the Philips version, recorded at public performances in 1982, but the effect in the outer movements is inclined to be melodramatic and Dorati shows little of the firmness of grip one associates with him. The slow movement is very slow indeed. The choral entry at the end makes an impressive effect within the Concertgebouw ambience, but overall this does not offer real competition to Bernstein.

Hungarian rhapsodies Nos. 1–6.
(M) **(*) Mercury 432 015-2 [id.]. LSO, Dorati – ENESCU: *Roumanian rhapsody No. 1*. ***

Hungarian rhapsodies Nos. 1–6; Hungarian battle march; Rákóczy march.
(M) **(*) EMI CDM7 64627-2. Philh. Hungarica or LPO, Boskovsky.

Dorati's is undoubtedly the finest set of orchestral *Hungarian rhapsodies*. He brings out the gypsy flavour and, with lively playing from the LSO, there is both polish and sparkle. The Mercury recording is characteristically vivid, if not in the demonstration bracket.

Boskovsky does not fully catch the mercurial element, the sudden changes of mood which is the gypsy heritage of these pieces, but the Philharmonia Hungarica (who play in Nos. 1, 4 and 6 – *Carnival in Pest*) are obviously at home; and the LPO clearly enjoy the famous No. 2, while the *Third* with its effective use of the cimbalom, has plenty of colour. The *Rákóczy march* (No. 15 for piano) is done spiritedly by the Hungarian group, but the little-known *Hungarian battle march* does not emerge here as a lost masterpiece. The freshly remastered recordings (from 1977/8) sound well and, though Dorati on Mercury takes pride of place in this repertoire, this EMI disc certainly gives pleasure.

Hungarian rhapsodies Nos. 1 in F min.; 4 in D min.; Les Préludes.
(M) **(*) Sony SMK 47572 [id.]. NYPO, Bernstein – ENESCU: *Roumanian Rhapsody No. 1* (with BRAHMS: *Hungarian dances Nos. 5–6* **(*)).

Notable for the vivid coupled performance of the Enescu *Rhapsody*, this collection shows characteristic Bernstein brilliance, with first-rate orchestral playing throughout. The sound is a bit glossy in the violins, but has weight too, especially for the heavy brass in the final peroration of *Les Préludes*, which is wonderfully pontifical. Indeed Bernstein is very much at home in this melodramatic piece, not missing its noble lyricism alongside its excitement. The two Brahms *Hungarian dances* are played with plenty of dash.

Hungarian rhapsodies Nos. 2, 6, 9, 12, 14 & 15 (arr. Peter Wolf).
(B) *** HM Musique d'Abord Dig. HMA 1903046 [id.]. Franz Liszt CO, János Rolla.

These transcriptions for strings are most enjoyable, giving the rhapsodies a chimerical lightness of texture. They are very well played indeed by this excellent orchestra, and Rolla's performances have nicely calculated rubato and plenty of spirit. Excellent, fresh recording. Not an alternative to the usual full-orchestra versions but a worthwhile bargain supplement.

Mephisto waltz.
(M) *** RCA 09026 61246-2 [id.]. Chicago SO, Reiner – TCHAIKOVSKY: *Symphony No. 6* etc. **(*)

Reiner's account of the *Mephisto waltz* is the star item on this CD, unsurpassed on disc. The Chicago playing is superb, exciting and seductive by turns, and the hall ambience gives added lustre throughout, but especially to the woodwind detail in the score's gentler moments.

SYMPHONIC POEMS

Ce qu'on entend sur la montagne; Festklänge; Mazeppa; Orpheus; Les Préludes; Prometheus; Tasso, lamento e trionfo.
(B) **(*) Ph. Duo 438 751-2 (2) [id.]. LPO, Bernard Haitink.

Hamlet; Héroïde funèbre; Hungaria; Hunnenschlacht; Die Ideale; Mephisto waltz No. 1; Von der Wiege bis zum Grabe.
(B) **(*) Ph. Duo 438 754-2 (2) [id.]. LPO, Bernard Haitink.

Apart from *Les Préludes*, the splendid *Mazeppa* and, to a lesser extent, *Tasso*, Liszt's symphonic poems enjoy fairly limited favour. The relatively popular pieces have by no means the monopoly of Liszt's inspiration; some of his earlier efforts, such as *Ce qu'on entend sur la montagne* and *Festklänge*, suffer not only from formal weakness but also from a lack of interesting melodic invention, and many of their pages are let down by rhetorical bursts and by the repetition of melodramatic flourishes. But the final work, *From the cradle to the grave*, has a visionary quality which shows Liszt thinking far ahead of his time. In *Hamlet*, for instance, there is a lot to admire; the *Héroïde funèbre* is nobly conceived, and Haitink's restrained yet powerful performance does it full justice. *Prometheus* is also successful and *Hungaria* has an agreeable gypsy violin sequence to offset its patriotic fervour and brass chorales. *Hamlet* brings great dramatic intensity and plenty of atmosphere; *Festklänge* mixes polonaise dance-rhythms with more romantic sections. *Die Ideale* is based on Schiller's poem and has a pleasing rhapsodical feeling imbued with melancholy until the self-assurance of its closing pages. It is not an easy work to bring off, and Haitink's direct, dedicated manner does not always catch its changing moods. The performance of *Festklänge* is more successful but, like *Hunnenschlacht* ('The battle of the Huns'), it lacks extrovert bravura, although no one could complain about the impressive organ effects at the close of the latter piece. *Les Préludes* and *Mazeppa* (which sounds marvellous in Karajan's hands), though structurally well conceived, lack that strain of histrionic vulgarity which makes them more ear-catching, and in the familiar *Mephisto waltz* there is a hint of reserve not entirely in the spirit of a Bacchanalian dance. Nevertheless the orchestral playing is first rate throughout these four discs and the recording has never sounded better – far more vivid than on the original LPs. Liszt invented the symphonic poem; here is an inexpensive and, for the most part, rewarding way to sample his achievement overall. There is good documentation.

Symphonic poems: *Ce qu'on entend sur la montagne (Bergsinfonie); Festklänge; Hunnenschlacht; Die Ideale; Von der Wiege bis zum Grabe;* (i) *Dante symphony.*
(B) *** EMI forte (SIS) CZS5 68598-2 (2) [CDFB 68598]. Leipzig GO, Masur; with (i) Arndt, Leipzig Thomaskirche Ch.

On the whole Masur's survey of Liszt's symphonic poems is the finest we have had so far. The performances have a dramatic vitality that eludes Haitink, and the Leipzig orchestra's playing is even finer than that of the LPO on Philips. Some of the earlier pieces, such as *Ce qu'on entend sur la montagne* and *Festklänge*, suffer not only from formal weakness but also from a lack of interesting melodic invention. However, these performances – and, whatever one may think of it, this music – cast a strong spell, and with rare exceptions Masur proves a most persuasive advocate. It is the rich sonority of the lower strings, the dark, perfectly blended woodwind-tone and the fine internal balance of the Leipzig Gewandhaus Orchestra that hold the listener throughout. In the *Dante Symphony* Barenboim's BPO account takes pride of place, but that is on a single full-priced disc. Masur is by no means completely upstaged. He does not shirk the robust diabolism, and the closing section brings a radiantly ecstatic contribution from the Leipzig choir, led by the excellent treble, Volker Arndt. The recordings are well balanced and refined, and the CD transfers are vivid: strings and brass alike have fine presence and sonority. Liszt's influence was enormous in his lifetime – on Wagner, the Russians, the French – and listening to these performances one realizes that his personality has lost none of its magnetism, even in a field that he was slow to conquer.

Symphonic poems: *Hamlet; Die Ideale; Orpheus; Von der Wiege bis zum Grabe (From the cradle to the grave).*
(BB) *(*) Naxos Dig. 8.553355 [id.]. New Zealand SO, Michael Halász.

Michael Halász gets a vital and often sensitive response from his fine New Zealand orchestra in these tone-poems, but pleasure is diminished by the quality of the recorded sound. All is well in *piano* and *pianissimo* passages, but the close balance proves uncomfortable in *tutti* where there is some trace of glare and congestion. But artistically this is very good and, had there been more space round climaxes, it would have come close to three stars. Haitink's complete set on Philips or Masur on EMI offer a more refined balance.

Symphonic poems: *Mazeppa; Orpheus; Les Préludes; Tasso, lamento e trionfo. Mephisto waltz No. 2.*
(M) ** EMI CDM7 64850-2 [id.]. Leipzig GO, Kurt Masur.

Masur is not altogether at home in the melodrama of *Les Préludes* and *Mazeppa* – although the latter is excitingly done, if without the panache of Karajan. He breezes through *Orpheus* at record speed and misses the endearing gentleness that Beecham brought to it in the early 1960s. Nevertheless these performances are all strongly characterized and extremely well played and, although the digital remastering has robbed the sound of some of its rich sonority in the lower strings, the brightness of the new sound-balance has a different kind of appeal.

Mazeppa; Les Préludes; Prometheus; Tasso, lamento e trionfo (symphonic poems).
(BB) *** Naxos Dig. 8.550487 [id.]. Polish Nat. RSO (Katowice), Michael Halász.

Michael Halász has the full measure of this repertoire and this is one of the most successful collections of Liszt's symphonic poems to have emerged in recent years. He draws some remarkably fine playing from the Katowice Radio Orchestra. The brass playing is very impressive throughout, especially the trombones and tuba, who have the epic main theme of *Mazeppa*, but its grandiloquence is no less powerful in *Les Préludes*, weighty and never brash. The recording is spacious, with full natural string textures, but it is the resounding brass one remembers most.

Totentanz (for piano and orchestra).
(M) *** RCA 09026 61250-2 [id.]. Byron Janis, Chicago SO, Reiner – Concert: *'The Reiner sound'*. ***

Recorded in 1959, this is still one of the most exciting accounts of Liszt's *Dance of death* in the catalogue. It opens in thrillingly dramatic fashion, but the scherzando element later is no less successful. A powerful partnership between Janis and Reiner ensures that the tension is well held throughout, and the Chicago ambience makes its own evocative contribution. Though the close balance is not as natural as some of the earlier Chicago recordings, the sound here is fuller and more realistic than on the original LP.

PIANO MUSIC

Complete piano music, Vol. 1: *Concert paraphrases: Fantasia on themes from Meyerbeer's 'Les Huguenots'; Réminiscences de Saint-Saëns. Impromptu in F sharp; La lugubre gondola I & II; Nuages gris; Totentanz; Unstern: sinistre; disastro.*
(BB) ** Naxos Dig. 8.553852 [id.]. Arnaldo Cohen.

Arnaldo Cohen's recital is the first of what is planned to be a complete survey of the piano music; however, it is to be undertaken by various artists rather than just one, as is the case with the mammoth full-priced Hyperion set. It ranges from comparative rarities, such as the transcriptions of *Danse macabre* and the fantasia on themes from Meyerbeer's *Les huguenots*, to the searching and introspective later pieces like *La lugubre gondola* and the forward-looking *Nuages gris*. Arnaldo Cohen is not wanting in virtuosity or sensitivity, though he does not give us the artistry of a Brendel, Arrau or Bolet. He produces some lovely sounds, but one is aware of hammers and there is some less than beautiful tone in fortissimos.

Complete piano music, Volume 2: *12 Etudes d'exécution transcendante, G 139*.
(BB) *(*) Naxos Dig. 8.553119 [id.]. Jenö Jandó.

After Jandó's fine set of the *Années de pèlerinages* this is a disappointment. The playing is brilliant enough, but the very resonant acoustic of the Budapest studio is unflattering to say the least. *Mazeppa* in particular is ugly, and fortissimos are made to sound hard and clangorous.

Complete piano music, Vol. 3: *Harmonies poétiques et réligieuses, Nos. 1–6; Les morts; Resignazione; Ungarns Gott* (two-hand).
(BB) *** Naxos Dig. 8.553073 [id.]. Philip Thomson.

Complete piano music, Vol. 4: *Ave Marias in D flat; G; E; d'Arcadelt; 6 Consolations; Harmonies poétiques et réligieuses, Nos. 7–10; Ungarns Gott* (left-hand).
(BB) *** Naxos Dig. 8.553516 [id.]. Philip Thomson.

Philip Thomson is a Canadian pianist who has specialized in Liszt. He exhibits considerable artistry in the two discs listed above and commands not only the virtuosity which this repertoire calls for in abundance but also great poetic feeling. (He seems to be a remarkable all-rounder, having occupied teaching posts in both China and the United States, being an accomplished violinist, champion table-tennis player, and even parachute jumper.) He commands a wide range of keyboard colour and refinement of pianissimo tone and has the benefit of very good recorded sound as well. Both his Liszt recitals are touched by distinction and are a real bargain.

Complete piano music, Vol. 5: *Schubert song transcriptions* (Vol. 1): *Auf dem Wasser zu singen; Du bist die Ruh; Frühlingsglaube; Gretchen am Spinnrade; Horch, horch, die Lerch; Der Müller und der Bach; Schwanengesang: Aufenthalt; Der Doppelgänger; Ihr Bild; Ständchen; Sei mir gegrüsst; Trockne Blumen; Der Wanderer; Winterreise: Wasserflut.*
(BB) ** Naxos Dig. 8.553062 [id.]. Oxana Yablonskaya.

Oxana Yablonskaya is a much-respected artist with a powerful technique and leonine tone, perhaps more at home in the bigger Rachmaninov and Tchaikovsky repertoire than in these lyrical transcriptions of Schubert. She is occasionally short on poetry and quite often on pianissimo!

Complete piano music, Volume 6: *Piano sonata in B min.; 2 Legends (St Francis of Assisi preaching to the birds; St Francis of Paola walking on the water); Faust Symphony: Gretchen* (2nd movt).
(BB) ** Naxos Dig. 8.553594 [id.]. Jenö Jandó.

Jandó gives a forceful, often impulsive, but impressively contoured account of the *Sonata*, with a bold range of expressive and dynamic range to bring out the work's structural originality and its satisfying resolution. He is impressive, too, in the pair of *Legends* and builds a compelling climax in the second. But Kempff is even more imaginative in these evocative pieces, and he has the advantage of a more real and more comfortable piano-sound. The Clara Wieck Auditorium favoured by Naxos is less flattering: too often the piano timbre is made to sound hard and the acoustic sometimes over-balances the bass, even though Jandó's right hand is brilliantly dominant. Liszt's transcription of the *Gretchen* movement from *Faust* is sensitively played, but it has its longueurs without the glowing orchestral colours.

Complete piano music, Volume 7: Concert paraphrases of Rossini: *Soirées musicales; Overture William Tell.*
✿ (BB) *** Naxos Dig. 8.553961 [id.]. Kemal Gekić.

Liszt made his Rossini transcriptions in 1836, and they are rarely heard in the recital room or on record. The only rival is Leslie Howard's set on Hyperion, and this performance by the Yugoslav-born Kemal Gekić at super-bargain price has infinitely more wit, lightness of touch and subtlety of articulation. Were the price-tags reversed, this would still be the preferred recommendation. In fact this is dazzling playing that sparkles when required and has an effortless brilliance that is quite captivating. Gekić has real flair and is very well recorded too, with natural, lifelike quality. One looks forward to returning to this disc.

Complete piano music, Volume 9: Concert paraphrase of sacred music: *Alleluja; Ave maris stella; 11 Chorales; Hungarian Coronatiom Mass: Benedictus; Offertorium. L'Hymne du pape; In festo transfigurationis; O Roma noblis; Sancta Dorothea; Stabat Mater; Urbi et orbi; Weihnachtslied; Zum Haus des Herrn ziehen wir*.
(BB) *** Naxos Dig. 8.553659 [id.]. Philip Thomson.

This Canadian-born pianist made a strong impression earlier in this Liszt survey, and he does so again now. These transcriptions from the 1860s and '70s are rarely heard in recital and, apart from Leslie Howard's survey, are seldom encountered on disc. Philip Thomson brings a wide dynamic range and a fund of keyboard colour to this repertoire. As in the earlier discs, the recording is eminently acceptable without being outstanding.

Années de pèlerinage (complete): *Book 1, 1st Year: Switzerland; Book 2, 2nd Year: Italy; Supplément: Venezia e Napoli; Book 3, 3rd Year: Italy.*
(B) *** DG 437 206-2 (3). Lazar Berman.

The *Années de pèlerinage* contain some of Liszt's very finest inspiration, and Lazar Berman's 1977 complete recording is fully worthy of it. Berman's technique is fabulous, more than equal to the demands made by these 26 pieces. The playing is enormously authoritative and quite free of empty display and virtuoso flamboyance, even though its brilliance is never in question. Indeed Berman brings searching qualities to this music: much of the time he is thoughtful and inward-looking in pieces like *Angelus* and *Sunt lachrymae rerum*. The imaginative colour and flair he displays in *Les cloches de Genève* and the simple freshness of *Eglogue* are matched by the felicity of the watery evocations, *Au lac de Wallenstadt* and *Les jeux d'eaux à la Villa d'Este*, while the power of the *Dante sonata* is equalled by the coruscating glitter of his articulation of the *Tarantella* from the *Supplément, Venezia e Napoli*. The recording, made in the Munich Alter Herkulessaal, is excellent. It is firmly and faithfully transferred to CD and does full justice to Berman's range of colour and dynamics. Moreover this box is remarkably inexpensive.

Années de pèlerinage: 1st Year (Switzerland); 2nd (with supplement) & 3rd Years (Italy): complete. *Hungarian rhapsodies Nos. 1–19* (complete).
(M) **(*) EMI CMS7 64882-2 (4). György Cziffra.

Cziffra's accounts of the complete *Années de pèlerinage* show the same prodigious virtuosity and keyboard command that make his set of *Hungarian rhapsodies* unforgettable. His account of the *Dante sonata* is enormously dramatic and produces the same fabulous digital dexterity that makes the *Tarantella* from the Italian Supplement, *Venezia e Napoli*, so breathtaking. In the more poetic pieces from Book 1, *Au lac de Wallenstadt* and *Au bord d'une source*, he finds more restrained romantic feeling, and in the Third Year *Les jeux d'eau à la Villa d'Este* brings some most delicate articulation. But at times the music's passion takes him over the top (as with *Aux cyprès de la Villa d'Este*) and he is not helped by a degree of hardness on piano timbre that is already somewhat dry. Remarkable pianism just the same. As can be seen below, the *Hungarian rhapsodies* (in which he is in his element) are available separately.

Années de pèlerinage, 1st Year (Switzerland).
(BB) *** Naxos Dig. 8.550548 [id.]. Jenö Jandó.

Even remembering his excellent Beethoven and Haydn recordings, Jandó's performances of the Liszt *Années de pèlerinage* represent his most impressive achievement on record to date. The solemn opening of *La chapelle de Guillaume Tell* immediately shows the atmospheric feeling he can generate in this remarkable music, and its later, more grandiose rhetoric is handled with powerful conviction. The recording is first class, and the feeling throughout is very much of the spontaneity of live music-making.

Années de pèlerinage, 2nd year (Italy); Supplement: Venezia e Napoli.
✿ (BB) *** Naxos Dig. 8.550549 [id.]. Jenö Jandó.

Jandó offers Lisztian playing of the highest order, confirming the *Années de pèlerinage* as being among the supreme masterpieces of the piano. *Sposalizio* is superbly evoked, and the three contrasted *Petrarch Sonnets* bring the most imaginatively varied characterization, with No. 123 especially chimerical. But clearly Jandó sees the *Dante sonata* as the climactic point of the whole series. His performance has tremendous dynamism and power. One has the sense of Liszt himself hovering over the keyboard. Again first-class recording and the feeling of a continuous live recital. This is the disc to try first, and we have awarded it a token Rosette.

Recital I: *Années de pèlerinage, 3rd Year: Tarantella. Harmonies poétiques et religieuses: Pensées des morts; Bénédiction de Dieu dans le solitude; Legend: St Francis of Assisi preaching to the birds. Mephisto waltz No. 1; Rhapsodie espagnole.* Recital II: *Années de pèlerinage, 2nd Year: Aux cyprès de la Villa d'Este; Après une lecture du Dante (Dante Sonata). 3rd Year: Aux cyprès de la Villa d'Este; Les jeux d'eaux à la Villa d'Este. Ave Maria; Ave Maria (Die Glöcken von Rom); La lugbre gondola* (2 versions); *Recueillement.*
✿ (BB) *** Virgin Classics Dig. Double VBD5 61439-2 [CDVB 61439]. Stephen Hough.

Few pianists of the younger generation have quite such a magic touch as Stephen Hough, and this budget-priced Virgin Double rescues two of his finest recitals. The first, from 1987, has been reissued before, but the second, published four years later, appeared and disappeared very quickly. The performances are all magnetic. On the first disc, he brings sparkle and wit to the fireworks of the *Mephisto waltz* and the *Tarantella* from the third year of the *Années de pèlerinage* with phenomenal articulation, and he plays the extended slow movement of the *Bénédiction* with velvety warmth. The delicate tracery of the birdsong sounds in *St Francis's sermon to the birds* equally displays Hough's love of keyboard sound, beautifully caught in vivid recording. The second collection is mainly of rarer music and is imaginatively chosen to include two different versions of both *Aux cyprès de la Villa d'Este* and the darkly original *La lugubre gondola*, in each case with the second version longer and more elaborate than the first. The cascades of *Les jeux d'eaux à la Villa d'Este* make a glittering centrepiece, but this follow-up programme includes also the calming *Recueillement*, and is above all thoughtful; the extravagance of the powerful *Dante sonata* makes way for the closing *Ave Maria*, evocatively picturing *Die Glöcken von Rom*. The recording is excellent, but the documentation is abysmal, and even the frontispiece (a detail from Giordano's *L'archange Michel écrasant les anges rebelles*) seems far less appropriate than the pictures of the actual fountains and cypresses at the Villa d'Este which illustrated the second recital when it first appeared at full price. Nevertheless the concentration of the playing here is unforgettable.

Années de pèlerinage, 2nd Year: Sonetto del Petrarca No. 123; Etude de concert: Un sospiro; Mephisto waltz.
(M) ** BMG/RCA GD 60417 [id.]. Van Cliburn – CHOPIN: *Piano sonatas Nos. 2–3.* **

Van Cliburn is as at home in the world of Liszt as he is sympathetic to Chopin. These pieces are encores for the two sonatas, and the performances are distinctive. The recording, however, is not ideally flattering.

Années de pèlerinage, 3rd Year (Italy) (complete).
(BB) *** Naxos Dig. 8.550550 [id.]. Jenö Jandó.

The opening *Angelus* shows Jandó at his most imaginatively expansive and commanding, while *Les jeux d'eaux à la Villa d'Este* sparkles and glitters: this is playing of great appeal. The dark power of *Sunt lacrymae rerum* and the *Marche funèbre* bring resounding sonority from the piano's lower octaves, and then Jandó provides more expansive rhetoric for the composer's flamboyant and not entirely convincing spiritual apotheosis, *Sursum corda*. A splendid and satisfying culmination to a set of performances that can be compared with the finest from the past. The secret of Jandó's playing is that he is deeply involved in every note of Liszt's music.

Années de pèlerinage, 2nd year: 3 Sonetti di Petrarca (Nos. 47, 104 & 123). Concert paraphrase on the *Quartet* from Verdi's *Rigoletto; Consolations Nos. 1–5; Liebesträume Nos. 1–3.*
(M) *** DG 435 591-2. Daniel Barenboim.

Daniel Barenboim proves an ideal advocate for the *Consolations* and *Liebestraume*, and he is highly poetic in the *Petrarch sonnets*. His playing has an unaffected simplicity that is impressive and throughout there is a welcome understatement and naturalness, until he arrives at the *Rigoletto paraphrase* which is played with plenty of flair and glitter. The quality of the recorded sound is excellent.

Années de pèlerinage, 2nd Year (Italy): Sposalizio; Il penseroso; Canzonetta del Salvator Rosa; Sonetto del Petrarca Nos. 47, 104 & 123; Supplement: Venezia e Napoli: Gondoliera. 2 Legends: St Francis of Assisi preaching to the birds; St Francis of Paola walking on the water.
(M) *** DG 449 093-2. Wilhelm Kempff.

In the early days of mono LP, Kempff made a famous record of Liszt piano music for Decca. He plays much of the same programme here, adding *Sposalizio*, and he had lost none of his magic and sense of poetry in the intervening years. Few listeners will fail to respond to these evocative and masterly performances, and one wonders why DG chose not to reissue this outstanding recital as a 'Legendary Recording' rather than putting it on their mid-priced Galleria label. The recording is excellent.

Concert paraphrases: BEETHOVEN: *Symphony No. 5 in C min.; Symphony No. 6 (Pastoral):* 1st movt.
(M) *(*) Sony SMK 52636 [id.]. Glenn Gould.

It is not easy to comment on Glenn Gould's Liszt–Beethoven transcriptions – or, for that matter, on anything by this artist. For his admirers he can do nothing wrong, while his detractors find him perverse. However, no one can deny his remarkable keyboard prowess and mastery – and even the most sceptical are often bowled over by the quality of his insights. These performances come from the 1960s and are handicapped by shallow recorded sound. Nor – even at mid-price – are they particularly generous on playing-time.

Concert paraphrase: BEETHOVEN: *Symphony No. 6 (Pastoral).*
(M) * Sony SMK 52637 [id.]. Glenn Gould.

Gould certainly holds your attention – but this is distinctly short measure. The sound is shallow and coarse, very unsuitable for such lyrical music.

Concert paraphrases of Schubert Lieder: *Auf dem Wasser zu singen; Gretchen am Spinnrade; Der Müller und der Bach; Ständchen. Hungarian rhapsody No. 12.*
(M) *** DG Dig. 445 562-2 [id.]. Yevgeny Kissin – BRAHMS: *Fantasias;* SCHUBERT: *Wanderer fantasia.* **(*)

There is – as always – much to admire in Kissin's playing, and he is in good form in these Liszt–Schubert transcriptions. Both *Der Müller und der Bach* and *Ständchen* are beautifully done. The Brahms and the *Wanderer fantasia* find him in good rather than outstanding form.

Concert paraphrases: (i) BELLINI: *Réminiscences de 'Norma'.* GOUNOD: *Faust: Waltz.* MEYERBEER: *Le Prophète: The Skaters (Illustration No. 2).* (ii) SCHUMANN: *Widmung.* (i) TCHAIKOVSKY: *Eugene Onegin: Polonaise.* (iii) VERDI: *Aida: Danza sacra e duetto final. Don Carlo: Coro di festa e marcia funèbre. Ernani. I Lombardi: Salve Maria de Jérusalem. Rigoletto. Miserere du Trovatore.* WAGNER: (iv) *Der fliegende Holländer: Spinning chorus;* (v) *Lohengrin: Elsa's bridal procession. Parsifal: Feierlicher marsch.*
(B) **(*) Ph. Duo 456 052-2 (2) [(M) id. import]. (i) Michele Campanella; (ii) Misha Dichter; (iii) Claudio Arrau; (iv) Alexander Uninsky; (v) Zoltán Kocsis.

Michele Campanella offers dextrous accounts of the Bellini, Gounod, Meyerbeer and Tchaikovsky items; even if he is rhythmically a touch heavy-handed, his glittering upper tessitura is compensation. When Kocsis takes over, his eloquence is remarkable, and the solemn march from *Parsifal* (which Liszt totally rewrote in his transcription) is the highlight of the collection. In his Verdi selection Arrau characteristically refuses to indulge in display for its own sake, even in these deliberate showpieces. His technique (in 1972) is effortlessly superb and, if there is inevitably a lack of sheer excitement, he shows what inner intensity some of this music contains in deeply expressive playing. The recording throughout is very good, outstanding for Arrau and Kocsis.

Concert paraphrases: BELLINI: *Réminiscences de 'Norma'.* VERDI: *Rigoletto; Miserere du Trovatore.* WAGNER: *Tannhäuser overture; Am stillen Herd* from *Die Meistersinger; Liebestod* from *Tristan und Isolde. Années de pèlerinage, 2nd Year: Sonnetti del Petrarca Nos. 123 & 124; Consolation No. 3; Hungarian rhapsody No. 12 in C sharp min.*
(BB) **(*) CfP Silver Double CDCFPSD 4745 (2) [id.]. Craig Sheppard – *Sonata* etc. ***

Craig Sheppard was the second prizewinner in the Leeds Piano Competition of 1972, a formidable challenger to the eventual winner, Murray Perahia. Though he lacks Perahia's individuality, Sheppard's playing of Liszt on this record is a fine tribute to his musicianship and technique, especially in the *Concert paraphrases*. He does not manage to disguise the awkwardness of the *Pilgrim's chorus* section of *Tannhäuser* where the pianist is expected to play the big tune and the swirling (string) accompaniment simultaneously with only two hands. But the *Trovatore* scene has fine, red-blooded melodrama, and the passion of the *Liebestod* is excitingly projected. The *Réminiscences de 'Norma'*, too, are stylishly done. The other items come from his début recital in 1973 and are almost equally compelling. The piano tone is bold and clear. It was a happy idea on this Silver Double reissue to couple these performances with a memorable account of the *Sonata* by another celebrated prizewinner, Bernard d'Ascoli – see below.

Concert paraphrases: SCHUBERT: *Der Müller und der Bach;* VERDI: *Rigoletto paraphrase. Etudes d'éxécution transcendante: Mazeppa. Fantasia and fugue on the theme B-A-C-H; Hungarian rhapsody No. 12 in C sharp min.; Mephisto waltz No. 1.*
(BB) *(*) Koch/Discover Dig. DICD 920499 [id.]. Lambis Vassiliadis.

The Greek-born pianist Lambis Vassiliadis is a gifted artist who possesses a formidable technique and no mean flair. He makes light of all the technical obstacles in this repertoire, though we can imagine some may find him a trifle wilful in the way he inserts small rubati or accellerandi here and there. If there is much to admire, there are few grounds for real pleasure or for preferring his disc to others in this highly competitive field. He is recorded forwardly in a smallish studio in Ohio, and the uninviting sound does him no favours.

Concert paraphrases: Faust waltzes; Réminiscences de 'Don Juan' (Mozart); Réminiscences de 'Robert le Diable': Valse infernale (Meyerbeer); Concert study: Gnomenreigen; Mephisto polka; Mephisto waltz No. 1.
(M) **(*) Van. 08.4035.71 [OVC 4035]. Earl Wild.

The title of this recital is '*The demonic Liszt*', and as a display of brilliant piano playing it could hardly be bettered. Earl Wild's technique is prodigious. The articulation in *Gnomenreigen* has a fairy lightness and the *Mephisto polka* has a similar blithe delicacy of touch, while the more sinister waltz which follows is played with formidable energy and power. There is glittering upper tessitura in the *Don Juan fantasy.*

But one ideally needs a programme designed to give more contrast, and the 1968 piano recording is on the dry side.

(i) *12 Etudes d'exécution transcendante, G. 139;* (ii) *6 Etudes d'exécution transcendante d'après Paganini, G. 140;* (i) *3 Etudes de concert (Il lamento; La leggierezza; Un sospiro), G. 144; 2 Etudes de concert (Waldesrauschen; Gnomenreigen), G. 145.*
(B) **(*) Ph. Duo 456 339-2 (2) [id.]. (i) Claudio Arrau; (ii) Nikita Magaloff.

Arrau made his recording of the twelve *Etudes d'exécution transcendante* in 1974, and it was a formidable achievement for an artist in his seventies. Arrau always played with great panache and musical insight, which more than compensates for the occasional smudginess in the recorded sound. He always produced a wonderfully distinctive tone, and his enormous range of keyboard colour was splendidly captured by the Philips engineers of the day. Younger players, Cziffra for one, have brought more obvious virtuosity to these pieces, but Arrau's playing is most masterly and poetic, and the recording, if too reverberant, is admirably truthful and rich in timbre. The three *Etudes de concert*, too, are strongly characterized; indeed some might find Arrau's richly textured romanticism in *Un sospiro* a little overwhelming. However, his bravura in *Gnomenreigen* is riveting. So too is Nikita Magaloff's virtuosity in the *Paganini studies*, and here the bright, less sumptuous piano-tone projects his digital dexterity with fine glitter. He gives scintillating accounts of *La campanella* and *Arpeggio* and tickles the ear with a delectably sparkling *La chasse*. The set, of course, ends with variations on the famous theme used also by Brahms and Rachmaninov, also played with fine dash. Overall this is most impressive and can be recommended enthusiastically.

Etudes d'exécution transcendante No. 10; Hungarian rhapsody No. 12; La leggierezza; Liebestraüme No. 3; Waldesrauschen.
(M) * Revelation Dig. RV 10031 [id.] Evgeni Kissin – SCHUMANN: *Etudes symphoniques* etc. *

These performances come from recitals this charismatic young Russian gave in 1984 and 1989, when he was thirteen and eighteen respectively. The playing is dazzling, but the recorded sound is close and crude and does not begin to do justice to the sound we know he produces.

Etudes d'exécution transcendante d'après Paganini: Nos. 3 (La Campanella); 5 (La Chasse). Etudes d'exécution transcendante: Feux follets; Polonaise No. 2 in E.
(M) *** Nimbus Dig. NI 8810 [id.]. Ferruccio Busoni (piano) – BACH: *Chaconne;* CHOPIN: *Preludes.* **

Very convincingly reproduced from a 1915 Duo-Art piano-roll, in first-class digital sound, this gives a stunning impression of Busoni's transcendental technique in music which calls for the kind of scintillating virtuosity this remarkable artist could so readily provide. Occasionally in *Feux follets* he seems somewhat wilful, but the bravura is prodigious, and the two *Paganini studies* are superb, while there is some glittering upper tessitura in the central section of the characterful *Polonaise*. Fascinating.

Fantasia & fugue on 'B-A-C-H'; Variations on Bach's 'Weinen, Klagen, Sorgen, Zagen'.
(BB) *(*) Naxos Dig. 8.550408 [id.]. Michael Ponti – BRAHMS: *Handel variations.* *(*)

Michael Ponti is fully equal to the considerable artistic and physical demands these pieces pose and generates genuine atmosphere and excitement. The recording, made in a rather small studio, does not open out in climaxes and, though the artist and the engineer cope as well as they can with this handicap, there is no pretending that the piano sound equals that of, say, the best Philips or EMI recordings.

Grandes Etudes de Paganini Nos. 1–8.
(BB) *** Koch Discover Dig. DICD 920423 [id.]. Evelyne Brancart – BRAHMS: *Paganini variations.* ***

Evelyne Brancart displays a glittering technique, fine musicianship and a Lisztian sensibility. The recording is rather bright and forward but this is not ineffective in such repertoire. An enjoyable disc – though, even at super-bargain price, it is rather short measure at under 48 minutes.

Hungarian rhapsodies Nos. 1–19.
(B) ** Ph. Duo 438 371-2 (2) [id.]. Michele Campanella.

Hungarian rhapsodies Nos. 1–19; Rhapsodie espagnole.
(B) *** DG Double 453 034-2 (2) [id.]. Roberto Szidon.

Hungarian rhapsodies Nos. 1–15; Rhapsodie espagnole.
(B) *** EMI Rouge et Noir CZS5 69003-2 (2). György Cziffra.

Cziffra's performances are dazzling. They are full of those excitingly chimerical spurts of energy and languorous rubato that immediately evoke the unreasonably fierce passions of gypsy music. Yet the control is absolute (try the delectably free opening of *No. 12 in C sharp minor*, or the *D minor* (No. 7)). There is plenty of power in reserve and poetry too (the introduction to *No. 5 in E minor* is made to seem very like

Chopin). For sheer glitter, sample *No. 10 in E major*. The high degree of temperament in the playing, with hardly two consecutive phrases at an even tempo, makes even Szidon (who has the full measure of the music) seem almost staid. Cziffra with coruscating brilliance sets every bar of the music on fire. Some might find him too impulsive for comfort (and they should turn to the DG alternative), but this is surely the way Liszt would have played them: the *Rákóczy march* (No. 15) is a *tour de force*. The recording, made in the Salle Wagram, Paris, in 1957/8 (or, in the case of Nos. 2, 6, 12 and 15, in the Hungaraton Budapest Studio a year earlier), is a little dry and close but otherwise truthful, and it does not lack sonority. The *Rouge et Noir* reissue offers two discs for the price of one.

Roberto Szidon offers Liszt playing of the highest order. He has flair and panache, genuine keyboard command and, when required, great delicacy of tone. He is well recorded too, and this DG Double is not only inexpensive but also provides (as does Cziffra on EMI) an excellent version of the *Rhapsodie espagnole*. Cziffra's performances are from an artist of an even more volatile personality, but Szidon is by no means upstaged: his style is equally valid and his approach is always imaginatively illuminating.

Michele Campanella's bargain survey of the Liszt *Hungarian rhapsodies* has no want of technical command or finesse, and there are moments when the bravura provides excitement, as in the closing pages of the famous *No. 2 in C sharp minor*. But for the most part these performances lack the flair and spontaneity of Roberto Szidon's set, where the playing is not only more gripping but also much more imaginatively illuminating. The Philips set is provided with adequate documentation and has characteristically fine recording.

Vanguard 'Alfred Brendel collection': *Hungarian rhapsodies Nos. 2–3, 8, 13, 15 (Rákóczy march); Csárdás obstinée*.
(M) *** Van. 08 4024 71 [OVC 4024]. Brendel (also on 08 9163 72, with CHOPIN: *Andante spianato; Polonaises* **).

This is one of Brendel's finest records from the 1960s. It remains available singly, but now also comes (as part of Vanguard's 'Alfred Brendel collection') in a slip-case with a Chopin recital recorded at around the same time. However, this is rather less enticing and the separate Liszt issue is the one to go for.

Mephisto waltz.
(M) (**(*)) RCA mono GD 60921. William Kapell – KHACHATURIAN: *Piano concerto;* PROKOFIEV: *Piano concerto No. 3*. (**(*)) ✿

William Kapell's *Mephisto waltz*, recorded in 1945, must be one of the most dazzling ever, and it ranks alongside the likes of Horowitz, Cziffra, Richter and Pletnev. Moreover it comes with incandescent accounts of the Khachaturian *Piano concerto* (with Koussevitzky, no less), and the Prokofiev *Third Piano concerto*.

Piano sonata in B min.
(M) *** RCA 09026 61614-2 [id.]. Emil Gilels – SCHUBERT: *Sonata No. 17*.
(B) *** EMI forte CZS5 69527-2 (2) [(M) id. import]. Anievas – CHOPIN: *Sonata No. 3* **; RACHMANINOV: *Preludes Nos. 1–24* etc. **(*)
(M) **(*) RCA 09026 62590-2 [id.]. Artur Rubinstein – BACH: *Chaconne;* FRANCK: *Prelude, chorale and fugue*. ***

Piano sonata; Concert study No. 2 (La Leggierezza).
(BB) *** CfP Silver Double Dig. CDCFPSD 4745 (2) [id.]. Bernard d'Ascoli – *Concert paraphrases* etc. **(*)

(i) *Piano sonata in B min.;* (ii) *Concert paraphrase: Réminiscences de 'Don Juan';* (i) *Grande Etudes de Paganini Nos. 1–6* (1851 version); (ii) *Hungarian rhapsody No. 10*.
(B) ** Sony SBK 62644; *SBT 62644* [id.]. (i) André Watts; (ii) Charles Rosen.

Gilels's version of the Liszt *Sonata* is masterly. It has something in common with Curzon's stunning account (recently restored to the catalogue – see below) and can be spoken of alongside Pletnev. It is as penetrating in its way as Horowitz's famous pre-war record was virtuosic, and the playing here is equally astonishing technically. The 1964 recording leaves little cause for complaint on CD. It is vividly transferred and is not without body.

Anievas gives a fine and memorable performance, notable for its thoughtfulness and its subtlety in the control of tension. The lyrical impulse is finely balanced to bring out the music's poetry as well as its fire and strength. There may be more flamboyant interpretations available which more readily project the music's bravura, but few other recorded performances are as satisfying or are more successful in revealing the work's stature. The recording too is generally very good and, although the reverberation prevents absolute clarity in the bass in florid passages, the effect is firmer in the excellent CD transfer.

Bernard d'Ascoli displays classical qualities in his refreshing and intense reading of this most romantic of sonatas. It is the sort of interpretation that one might have expected Wilhelm Kempff to have given, with articulation of pearly clarity, wonderful singing legato in the big melodies and an emphasis on control and concentration rather than thrusting urgency. Yet there is no lack of power, and the result is most satisfying. The delicate account of *La Leggierezza* makes a fine encore. The early (1982) digital recording is dry but faithful, and the coupled recital from Craig Sheppard, another prizewinner, makes this a very recommendable Silver Double.

Rubinstein's performance of the *Sonata* was recorded in 1965, and there is some hardness of timbre in fortissimos. But at *piano* and *mezzo forte* levels (and there is a wider range of dynamic here than on some Rubinstein records) the tone is subtly coloured, and Rubinstein's mercurial approach to the music is wonderfully spontaneous, bringing an astonishing fire and brilliance for a pianist of his age, and considerable poetry to the more thoughtful moments.

Opening the *Sonata* with arrestingly impetuous bravura, André Watts gives a strong, direct interpretation, not one that rides roughshod over the work's lyrical inspiration, but an ongoing account which finds light and shade as well as tempestuous excitement in the closing *Allegro energico*, with its sombre change of mood in the coda beautifully managed. He then plays Liszt's revised 1851 set of the *Paganini studies*, and here the often scintillating dexterity is always matched by a sense of style. Charles Rosen takes over to give Liszt's Mozartian concert paraphrase with panache, and he follows it with a dashing account of the *Tenth Hungarian rhapsody*. This is all remarkable pianism and it is a pity that the hard and close – although certainly clear – piano-image is less than sympathetic.

Piano sonata in B min.; Berceuse; Concert study: Gnomenreigen. Liebestraum No. 3 in A flat; Valse oubliée No. 1.

(M) *** Decca 452 306-2 [id.]. Clifford Curzon (with SCHUBERT: *Impromptu in A flat, D.935/2*).

Curzon shows an innate understanding of the *Sonata*'s cyclic form, so that the significance of the principal theme is brought out subtly in relation to the music's structural development. There are only a few performances to compare with this and none superior, and Decca's recording matches the playing in its excellence. The shorter pieces too are imaginatively played. The excellent recording was made in the Sofiensaal in 1963, but the fairly close microphones create something of a studio effect. For the reissue in Decca's Classic Sound series, Curzon's warm and beautiful account of Schubert's *A flat Impromptu* has been added. This was recorded at The Maltings, and here the sound is noticeably richer and has a fuller sonority.

Miscellaneous Recitals

Piano sonata; Années de pèlerinage, 1st Year: Au bord d'une source; 2nd Year: Sonetto 104 del Petrarca; 3rd Year: Les jeux d'eau à la Ville d'Este; Concert paraphrases: Die Forelle; Erlkönig (Schubert); *Réminiscences de 'Don Juan'* (Mozart); *Rigoletto* (Verdi). *Consolation No. 3; Etudes d'exécution transcendante d'après Paganini: La campanella. Etudes de concert: Gnomenreigen; Un sospiro. Harmonies poétiques et religieuses: Funérailles. Hungarian rhapsody No. 12 in C sharp min.; Liebesträume No. 3 in A flat; Mephisto waltz No. 1.*

(B) *** Decca Double Dig. 444 851-2 (2). Jorge Bolet.

The full range of the late Jorge Bolet's achievement for Decca in the music of Liszt is admirably surveyed here, ending with his commanding account of the *Sonata*. He can be romantic without sentimentality, as in the *Consolation*, *Un sospiro* or the most famous *Liebesträume*, yet can dazzle the ear with bravura or beguile the listener with his delicacy of colouring, as in the *Années de pèlerinage*. All the recordings here save the Mozart *Concert paraphrase* are digital and are as clear and present as one could wish.

ORGAN MUSIC

Fantasia and fugue on 'Ad nos, ad salutarem undam'; Prelude and fugue on B-A-C-H; Variations on 'Weinen, Klagen, Sorgen, Zagen'.

(BB) *** ASV CDQS 6127 [(M) id. import]. Jennifer Bate (Royal Albert Hall organ) – SCHUMANN: *4 Sketches.* ***

Jennifer Bate gives superb performances of the three major Liszt warhorses. The clarity and incisiveness of her playing go with a fine sense of line and structure, and there is plenty of exuberance in the *'Ad nos' Fantasia and fugue*. Even making no allowance for the Royal Albert Hall's acoustic problems, the analogue recording captures an admirable combination of definition and atmosphere, well conveyed on CD. This makes a fine super-bargain alternative to the competing digital versions, which are only marginally more sharply defined.

VOCAL MUSIC

Missa choralis; Via crucis.

(M) ** Saga EC 3399-2. BBC N. Singers, Gordon Thorne; Francis Jackson.

It was Saga (now a mid-price rather than a bargain label) who pioneered the coupling of Liszt's *Missa choralis* and *Via crucis*, and the performances – especially of the latter – are committed and effective, with Francis Jackson's powerful organ-playing very impressively dramatic. The Saga recording is, however, comparatively studio-ish, with the organ very forward.

Litolff, Henri (1818–91)

Concerto symphonique No. 4: Scherzo.

(M) *** Decca 425 082-2 [id.]. Clifford Curzon, LPO, Sir Adrian Boult – BRAHMS: *Piano concerto;* FRANCK: *Symphonic variations.* ***

(M) *** Decca Dig. 430 726-2. Ortiz, RPO, Atzmon – ADDINSELL: *Warsaw concerto* ***; GERSHWIN: *Rhapsody* **(*); GOTTSCHALK: *Grand fantasia* ***; LISZT: *Hungarian fantasia.* ***

(B) *** EMI CfP CD-CFP 6045. Peter Katin, LPO, Sir John Pritchard – TCHAIKOVSKY: *Piano concerto No. 1.* *(*)

Curzon provides all the sparkle Litolff's infectious *Scherzo* requires, and the 1958 Walthamstow Town Hall recording makes a delightful encore for the Brahms *Concerto* and the Franck *Symphonic variations* in this reissue in Decca's Classic Sound series. The fine qualities of the original sound, freshness and clarity, remain impressive.

Cristina Ortiz's version may lack extrovert brilliance but it has an agreeable elegance. The intimacy of this version is emphasized by the balance, which places the piano within the orchestral group, making the gentle central section especially effective. The Decca couplings are all appealing and the CD is impressively natural.

From Katin a scintillating performance of a charming miniature, brilliantly recorded. What a pity the Tchaikovsky coupling does not have this kind of panache.

Lôbo, Duarte (c. 1565–1646)

Missa pro defunctis.

(BB) *** Naxos Dig. 8.550682 [id.]. Oxford Schola Cantorum, Jeremy Summerly – CARDOSO: *Missa pro defunctis.* ***

Here is another new name from the great age of Renaissance polyphony to conjure with – the Portuguese composer, Duarte Lôbo, Mestre de Capela at Lisbon Cathedral. He was an almost exact contemporary of Manuel Cardoso, whose music we have already discovered and who provides an eloquent coupling for this splendid Naxos CD. As performed here, Lôbo's *Missa pro defunctis* for double choir is a work of beautiful flowing lines (following directly on from Palestrina), bold dramatic contrasts and ardent depth of feeling. The *Agnus Dei* is particularly beautiful. A solo treble briefly introduces each section except the *Kyrie*, which adds to the effect of the presentation. This is another triumph from Jeremy Summerly and his excellent Oxford group (38 singers), who catch both the Latin fervour and the underlying serenity of a work which has a memorably individual voice.

Motets: *Audivi vocem de caelo; Pater peccavi.*

(BB) *** Naxos Dig. 8.553310 [id.]. Ars Nova, Bo Holten (with Concert of Portuguese polyphony ***) – CARDOSO: *Motets;* MAGALHAES: *Missa O Soberana luz* etc. ***

Lôbo's two beautiful motets, *Audivi vocem de caelo* ('I heard a voice from heaven') and *Pater peccavi* ('Father, I have sinned') confirm the individuality of his writing. They are part of an outstandingly sung collection which is among the most desirable records of its kind in the catalogue.

Locatelli, Pietro (1695–1764)

Concerti grossi, Op. 1/1–12.
(BB) *** Naxos Dig. 8.553445/6 [id.]. Capella Istropolitana, Jaroslav Kreček.

Locatelli's Op. 1 first appeared in 1721 but was revised in 1729 when their composer settled in Amsterdam. Though indebted to Corelli (with the eighth of the set ending with a Christmas *Pastorale* which is beautiful in its own right), they have a style and personality of their own. Their invention is vigorous, their expressive range appealing. If you enjoy *concerti grossi* you won't be disappointed here. The Capella Istropolitana play with crisp attack, plenty of sparkle and resilient rhythms; the style of the slow movements reveals a keen identity with the lessons of period performances, even though modern instruments are used and phrasing is unexaggerated by bulges. The recording is admirable, with textures clear and with attractive, light sonorities. Most enjoyable and highly recommended.

12 Flute concertos, Op. 2.
(M) ** Van. Dig. 99099 (2). Jed Wentz, Musica ad Rhenum.

The Vanguard set is fluent and highly musical, and the continuo group (including organ in Nos. 2, 4, 6, 9 and 11) is very effective, although Jed Wentz's period flute sounds a little pale. Even so, this is offered at mid-price and is very well recorded. Readers will note that the cueing goes wrong for the final double sonata (in which, presumably, Wentz plays a duet with himself), which starts at track 19 (not 18), since the previous sonata has four sub-divisions, not the indicated three.

6 Trio sonatas, Op. 5.
(M) **(*) Van. Dig. 99087. Musica ad Rhenum.

Locatelli's Op. 5 *Trio sonatas* are full of agreeable, singing melody and have plenty of lively invention too. It is optional to use a pair of flutes or two violins in their performance, and it might have been a good idea to vary the instrumentation, as two flutes used continually can prove too much of a good thing. However, Jed Wentz and Marion Moonen play with style and they blend nicely together; the continuo group includes a bassoon for added colour. Good performances, without any of the acerbities one associates with period performance, nicely recorded.

Loewe, Carl (1796–1869)

Ballads and Lieder: *Archibald Douglas; Canzonette; Die drei Lieder; Edward; Elvershöh; Erlkönig; Freibeuter; Frühzeitiger Frühling; Der getreue Eckart; Gottes ist der Orient!; Die Gruft der Liebenden; Gutmann und Gutweib; Der heilige Franziskus; Heinrich der Vogler; Herr Oluf; Hinkende Jamben; Hochzeitlied; Ich denke dein; Im Vorübergehen; Kleiner Haushalt; Lynkeus, der Türmer, auf Fausts Sternwarte singend; Meeresleuchten; Der Mohrenfürst auf der Messe; Der Nöck; Odins Meeresritt; Prinz Eugen; Der Schatzgräber; Süsses Begräbnis; Tom der Reimer; Der Totentanz; Trommelständchen; Turmwächter Lynkeus zu den Füssen der Helena; Die Uhr; Die wandelnde Glocke; Wandrers Nachtlied; Wenn der Blüten Frühlingsregen; Der Zauberlehrling.*
(M) *** DG 449 516-2 (2). Fischer-Dieskau, Demus.

For the most part this set was recorded in 1968–9, with a second group of songs added a decade later. With the great German baritone consistently in fine voice, it makes an ideal selection of some of Loewe's most memorable songs and ballads. Fischer-Dieskau, admirably accompanied by Jörg Demus, gives performances which have the commitment and intensity of spontaneous expression while remaining flawlessly controlled and strongly thought through. This alternative setting of the *Erlkönig*, preferred by many in the nineteenth century, is in its way as dramatic as Schubert's, if musically less subtle. The following *Edward* is also extraordinarily dramatic, while the magnificent *Die Uhr* ('The timepiece') opens lightly but develops an unexpected depth of feeling. The story-telling in other songs is also so graphic that it might be thought that even a non-German speaker would have little need to refer to the translations. However, it is an excellent feature of the set that these are provided in full. Splendidly vivid recording: if you enjoy Schubert, you can hardly fail to relish the best of Loewe.

Frauenliebe (song-cycle) *Op. 60*. Goethe, Heine and Rückert Lieder: *Der du von dem Himmel bist; Erste Liebe; Hinkende Jamben; Ich hab in Traume geweinet; Im Traume sah ich die Geliebte; Irrlichter; Die Lotusblume; Mädchenwünsche; Meine Ruh ist hin; O süsse Mutter; Die Pfarrjüngferchen; Sehnsucht; Süsses Begräbnis; Szene aus Faust; Uber allen Gipfeln ist Ruh.*
(M) *** DG Dig. 445 575-2. Brigitte Fassbaender, Cord Garben.

Carl Loewe's songs are much more imaginative than their status as 'interesting historical documents' suggests, and they are full of easy melody. Records of them are so rare that, despite occasional shortcomings, this collection should be snapped up before it succumbs to the deletions axe. *Frauenliebe*, Loewe's cycle of nine songs set to poems of Adelbert von Chamisso, inevitably invites comparison with Schumann, and if it has less depth than *Frauenliebe und Leben* Loewe's sequence remains infinitely touching; Brigitte Fassbaender sings it tenderly and with much charm. There are nine songs in all, although the composer published only seven of them as his Op. 60. Loewe's heroine is impulsive and soon falls deeply in love, and we follow her progress to a Schubertian dream of happiness, the wedding ring and revelling in marital bliss, her lover's sudden death and the poignant epilogue addressed to her daughter who, by the nature of things, will follow in her mother's footsteps. The final words of blessing are not sung but gently spoken. Not all the other songs here suit Fassbaender so well; she is best in the gentler settings. Goethe's *Scene with Faust* is lovely, as is *Uber allen Gipfeln ist Ruh*, while Rückert's *Irrlichter* ('Will-o'-the-wisps'), sung precociously fast, is captivating. But it is a pity that the recital opens with Goethe's *Meine Ruh ist hin*, which brings some repeated ugly upward scoops. Nevertheless this rare CD is not to be missed.

Lortzing, Albert (1801–51)

Die Opernprobe.

(M) *** CPO/EMI CPO 999 557-2. Marheineke, Gedda, Hirte, Litz, Lövaas, Berry, Bav. State Op. Ch. & O, Suitner.

Best known for his opera, *Der Wildschütz*, still popular in Germany today, Lortzing wrote this light-hearted satire in 1851, his very last piece, given its first performance on the day before he died. As a singer and actor himself, writing his own librettos, he had the gift of composing operas which, helped by his easy tunefulness, work well. *Die Opernprobe* ('The opera rehearsal') involves disguises and confusions of identity in the household of a music-loving Count who encourages his servants to perform. In a sparkling overture and ten numbers, mostly brief, it tells a simple story of true love triumphant, ending with a substantial finale in Mozartian style. Otmar Suitner directs a lively performance, very well sung and well produced in its dialogue, with first-rate (1974) EMI sound.

Lotti, Antonio (*c.* 1667–1740)

Crucifixus.

(B) *** Decca Double 443 868-2 (2) [id.]. St John's College, Cambridge, Ch., Philomusica, Guest – BONONCINI: *Stabat Mater* ***; PERGOLESI: *Magnificat in C; Stabat Mater* **(*); D. SCARLATTI: *Stabat Mater;* A. SCARLATTI: *Domine, refugium factus es nobis; O magnum mysterium;* CALDARA: *Crucifixus*. ***

(B) *** Decca Double 455 017-2 [(M) id. import]. St John's College, Cambridge, Ch., L. Philomusica, Guest – CALDARA: *Crucifixus* ***; PERGOLESI: *Magnificat* etc. **(*)

This short *Crucifixus*, which takes less than four minutes, may well have inspired the noble Caldara setting with which it frames Bononcini's beautiful *Stabat Mater* in this highly desirable collection of choral music. The Lotti setting is less elaborate in texture than Caldara's but it is hardly less noble or affecting. Performance and recording are excellent. Alongside the Caldara setting, this fine piece also comes as a filler for Decca's alternative compilation which centres on Pergolesi.

Lovenskjold, Herman (1815–70)

La Sylphide (ballet) complete.

(M) *** Chandos Dig. CHAN 6546; *MBTD 6546* [id.]. Royal Danish O, David Garforth.

La Sylphide (1834) predates Adam's *Giselle* by seven years. It is less distinctive than Adam's score, but it is full of grace and the invention has genuine romantic vitality – indeed the horn writing in the finale anticipates Delibes. The wholly sympathetic playing is warm, elegant, lively and felicitous in its detailed delicacy, yet robust when necessary and always spontaneous. A most enjoyable disc, superbly recorded.

Ludford, Nicholas (1485–1557)

Masses; Magnificat benedicta & Motets (as listed below).
❁ (M) *** ASV/Gaudeamus CDGAX 426 (4) [id.]. The Cardinall's Musick, Andrew Carwood.

Nicholas Ludford is one of the least familiar of the Tudor masters; he never enjoyed the fame of his older contemporary, Fayrfax, or the much younger Tallis. Ludford has remained outside the repertoire of most cathedral choirs, little more than a name to those with an interest in early music. According to Dr John Bergsagel's *Grove* article, Ludford composed 11 complete Masses and three incomplete, thus making him 'the most prolific of English composers of masses'. This four-CD box gathers together the four splendid discs of Ludford's music performed by Carwood and his excellent group of singers, who are individually as impressive as in the blended whole. This is music of remarkably passionate feeling, and it brings to life a composer who spent much of his working life in St Stephen's Chapel at St Margaret's, Westminster. He was an ardent Catholic and was very happily married – he paid for his wife to have her own pew and gave her an elaborate ceremonial burial. He then married again, and his second wife was instructed to prepare something more modest for his interment alongside his beloved first spouse. His music is little short of extraordinary, and we hope our Rosette will tempt collectors to explore it, either through this comprehensive box or by trying one of the individual premium-priced issues (CDGAU 131, CDGAU 132, CDGAU 133 and CDGAU 140).

Luigini, Alexandre (1850–1906)

Ballet Egyptien, Op. 12 (suite).
(B) *** CfP CD-CFP 4637 [id.]. RPO, Fistoulari – KETELBEY: *Collection*. ***

Because of its bandstand popularity, Luigini's amiable and tuneful *Ballet Egyptien* has never been taken very seriously and there is some sparkling doggerel by Richard Murdoch which snappily fits bizarre words about 'Dame Ella Wheeler Wilcox' neatly to the famous opening rhythm. However, the four-movement suite is highly engaging (both the two central sections have good tunes), especially when played as affectionately and stylishly as here under that master conductor of ballet, Anatole Fistoulari. The 1958 recording has come up remarkably freshly, and this makes an excellent bonus for an outstanding Ketèlbey concert.

Lully, Jean-Baptiste (1632–87)

Dies irae; (i) *Te Deum*.
(M) **(*) Erato/Warner 0630 11226-2. Jennifer Smith, Devos; (i) Bessac, Vandersteene, Huttenlocher; Valence Vocal Ens., Paillard CO, Paillard.

Both these works are for double choir, but Paillard makes no attempt to divide his forces, relying mainly on contrast between soloists, singly and in a group, chorus and orchestra. The *Dies irae* is a noble piece encapsulating a mood of dark melancholy, and it makes a strong impression here, with a notably dedicated contribution from the two soloists. The effect has a striking, elegiac beauty. The sudden choral interjections at a faster pace are convincingly managed. Here the choral focus in the CD transfer could be cleaner, but the sound has plenty of body and a most attractive ambience. The better-known *Te Deum* dates from 1677. It opens regally with brilliant high trumpets and is a work of contrasting splendour and breadth rather than the general-purpose pomp often favoured by Lully and his followers. Paillard and his forces give a thoroughly committed and eloquent account of the piece, and the recording is richly expansive, with the choral sound cleaner. Incidentally, it was while conducting this work that Lully vigorously brought down the heavy stick that served to mark the beat on to his right foot; gangrene eventually set in, and a couple of months later he died!

Le bourgeois gentilhomme (comédie-ballet; complete).
(M) *** HM/BMG GD 77059 (2) [77059-2-RG]. Nimsgern, Jungmann, Schortemeier, René Jacobs, Tölz Ch., La Petite Bande, Leonhardt – CAMPRA: *L'Europe galante*. ***

Lully's score is unmemorable and harmonies are neither original nor interesting; but the performance puts Lully's music into the correct stage perspective and, with such sprightly and spirited performers as well as good 1973 recording, this can hardly fail to give pleasure. The orchestral contribution under the direction of Gustav Leonhardt is distinguished by a splendid sense of the French style.

Atys: highlights.

(B) *** HM Dig. HMT 7901249 [(M) id. import] (from complete recording, with Guy de Mey, Agnès Mellon, Les Arts Florissants, cond. Christie).

(B) *** HM Dig. HMX 290844/46 (3) [id.] (from complete recording, cond. Christie) – CAMPRA: *Idomenée:* highlights; RAMEAU: *Castor et Pollux:* highlights. ***

Atys remains one of Christie's greatest successes on record; it is full of good things, and many of them are also included on the single-disc highlights selection (notably the delightful Sleep scene of Act III). With consistently fine singing and superb recording, this disc contains about a third of the opera (68 minutes).

This CD is offered as part of one of Harmonia Mundi's enterprising 'Trios', in this case offering three discs of operatic highlights together in a slip-case at bargain price. But unlike its companions, *Idomenée* and *Castor et Pollux*, no translation is included for *Atys*. Christie's full-price performance is highly recommended by us (on HMC 901257/9), with Guy de Mey memorable in the principal role. Taken as a package with its two companions, this collection of highlights costs only a fraction of the price of the three-disc complete set.

Lutoslawski, Witold (1916–94)

(i) *Chain II. Chain III; Novelette;* (i; ii) *Partita.*

(M) *** DG Dig. 445 576-2. (i) Mutter, (ii) Philip Moll; (i; ii) BBC SO, composer.

Chain III; Novelette.

(B) *** DG Classikon Dig. 439 452-2 [(M) id. import]. BBC SO, composer – LIGETI: *Chamber concerto;* SCHNITTKE: *Concerto grosso No. 1.* ***

Chain II, a 'dialogue for violin and orchestra', follows up the technique of *Chain I* (of which at present there is no really satisfactory recording), contrasting fully written sections with *ad libitum* movements, where chance plays its part within fixed parameters. *Chain III* then makes a sustained contrast with its ear-catching orchestral colours. The *Partita* is a development of a piece for violin and piano which Lutoslawski originally wrote for Pinchas Zukerman, with the first, third and fifth movements now scored for violin and orchestra. With Mutter and the composer the most persuasive advocates, both concertante pieces establish themselves as among the finest examples of Lutoslawski's latterday work. *Novelette*, an attractive, scherzo-like piece, full of incandescent energy, is common to both the main, mid-priced programme and the Classikon reissue, coupled with other stimulating works by Ligeti and Schnittke. DG here are obviously treading water to see if they can sell this kind of *avant-garde* music in a wider marketplace at budget price.

(i) *Chain II; Interlude; Partita. Musique funèbre; Symphony No. 4.*

(BB) *** Naxos Dig. 8.553202 [id.]. (i) Bakowski; Polish Nat. RSO, Wit.

This is the most approachable of the first issues in Naxos's adventurous Lutoslawski series. The *Symphony No. 4* is his culminating masterpiece which, in its concentration over two linked movements, seems to echo Sibelius's *Seventh.* The darkly intense *Funeral music* in memory of Bartók is another beautiful and concentrated work, while the two violin concertante works, *Chain II* and *Partita*, here come with the separating *Interlude*, similarly thoughtful, which Lutoslawski wrote as a link. In almost every way, not least in the playing of the violinist, Krzysztow Bakowski, these Polish performances match and even outshine earlier recordings conducted by the composer, helped by full, brilliant sound.

Concerto for orchestra.

(B) **(*) EMI forte CZS5 72664-2 (2) [(M) id. import]. Chicago SO, Seiji Ozawa – BARTOK: *Concerto for orchestra* **(*); JANACEK: *Sinfonietta* ***; STRAVINSKY: *Firebird ballet.* **(*)

Lutoslawski's *Concerto for orchestra* is a brilliant and inventively scored work with great potential appeal. Its idiom is accessible and its ideas have character. It plumbs no great depths, it is true, but then neither do the composer's later and less accessible works. The Swiss orchestra on Decca – see below – play impressively for Kletzki and are very well recorded. But they are no match for Ozawa's virtuoso players, and this EMI forte set is similarly priced and offers attractive couplings. The snag is that the acoustics of Chicago's Medinah Temple offered the engineers problems of microphone placing; this, coupled with the CD transfer, has led to a rather dry, somewhat two-dimensional sound-picture.

(i) *Concerto for orchestra;* (ii) *Paganini variations* (for piano and orchestra); (iii) *Musique funèbre;* (iv) *Paroles tissées.*

(B) **(*) Decca Double Analogue/Dig. 448 258-2 (2) [id.]. (i) SRO, Kletzki; (ii) Jablonski, RPO, Ashkenazy; (iii) Cleveland O, Dohnányi; (iv) Peter Pears, LSO, composer – SZYMANOWSKI: *Violin concerto No. 2; Symphonies Nos. 2–3.* **(*)

Kletzki directs a brilliant account of the *Concerto for orchestra*, and the Swiss orchestra play very well for him; moreover they are given vintage Decca sound from 1968. The slight snag is that Kletzki makes a small cut in the second movement, though with the composer's permission. However, this is an exciting performance and only the most dedicated admirer of the composer will cavil at being short-changed, if that is indeed the case. *Musique funèbre* (not perhaps one of the composer's most inspired pieces) is very well played and recorded, but it does not generate the last degree of tension. The *Paganini variations* for two pianos is very successful indeed, however: it is one of Lutoslawski's earliest and most readily appealing works. Peter Jablonski plays it in the much later transcription for piano and orchestra, and his pleasure and delight will surely be shared by the listener. The digital recording is first class. The *Paroles tissées* were written for Peter Pears, who sings the cycle here, and Lutoslawski's writing shows extraordinary understanding of that singer's special qualities and the colour of his voice. The texts are from poems of Jean-François Chabrun, with haunting imagery recurring in a manner mirrored exactly by the composer's finely textured, sharply conceived writing. Performances and recording are ideal.

(i) *Piano concerto. Little suite; Symphonic variations; Symphony No. 2.*

(BB) *** Naxos Dig. 8.553169 [id.]. (i) Piotr Paleczny; Polish Nat. RSO (Katowice), Antoni Wit.

The Naxos survey of Lutoslawski's output, though not as impeccably recorded as full-priced rivals, is still more than merely competitive. Antoni Wit gets good results from the Polish National Radio Orchestra at Katowice, and those curious about this composer but unwilling to pay a high price to satisfy their curiosity will be well rewarded. The delightful *Symphonic variations* (1939) are very much in the received tradition, with folk elements mingled with Szymanowskian textures, and the *Little suite* is also folkloric. The two major works are very well served: Piotr Paleczny is an excellent soloist in the *Piano concerto*, which Lutoslawski composed in 1988 for Krystian Zimerman, and the *Second Symphony*, written 20 years earlier, is imaginative. The sound is clean and well focused but could do with a little more space round the aural image.

(i) *Postlude No. 1;* (ii) *Preludes and fugues for 13 solo strings;* (iii) *Paroles tissées;* (iv) *3 Poèmes d'Henri Michaux.*

(M) *** EMI CDM5 65865-2. (i) Polish Nat. RSO; (ii) Polish CO; (iii) Louis Devos; (iv) Krakow R, Ch.; all cond. composer.

The searching *Preludes and fugues for thirteen solo strings* (1970–72) shows the mature Lutoslawski; the choral *Poèmes* were written a decade earlier. With their variety of effects, including whispering and syllabic monotones, the writing readily contrasts with the atmospheric *Paroles tissées* ('woven words') with its mystical feeling and remarkable word-imagery. Together with the elliptical *Postlude* this programme offers a well-planned demonstration of the composer's breadth of achievement. Performances and recordings are of a high standard, as is the recording from the late 1970s.

Symphonies Nos. 1–2; Symphonic variations.

(M) *** EMI CDM5 65076-2. Polish R. Nat. SO, composer.

The wholly beguiling *Symphonic variations*, with its Szymanowskian palette and luminosity, is an early work (1938); the symphonies date from 1947 and 1966/8, respectively. The latter consolidates the new language the composer formed after his change of style in the mid-1950s; the *First* is written against a musical background influenced by Hindemith, Bartók and Prokofiev and perhaps by Stravinsky too. But the work has its own individuality and is well worth hearing. The composer is an eloquent advocate, and the 1976/7 recordings are spacious and full-bodied with bright detail.

Symphony No. 3; (i) *Variations on a theme of Paganini;* (ii) *Les espaces du sommeil;* (iii) *Paroles tissées.*

(BB) *** Naxos Dig. 8.553423 [id.]. (i) Bernd Glemser; (ii) Adam Kruszewski; (iii) Piotr Kusiewicz; Polish Nat. RSO (Katowice), Antoni Wit.

The earliest piece here, the *Paganini variations* for two pianos, comes from 1941; during this period Lutoslawski played as a duo with a fellow composer, Andrzej Panufnik, in occupied Warsaw. But in 1978 the composer rearranged the piece for piano and orchestra. This and the *Third Symphony* from 1982 – arguably one of his finest works – are well played and recorded. Less persuasive, perhaps, is *Les espaces du sommeil* (the soloist is a bit forward, though he sings well). In the *Paroles tissées* the singer is less at ease both with the musical idiom and with the French language. All the same, this well-filled CD is recommendable in every other respect.

MacCunn, Hamish (1868–1916)

The Land of the mountain and the flood (concert overture).

(B) *** CfP CD-CFP 4635 [id.]. RSNO, Gibson – GERMAN: *Welsh rhapsody;* HARTY: *With the wild geese;* SMYTH: *Wreckers overture.* ***

MacCunn's descriptive overture is no masterpiece, but it has a memorable tune, is attractively atmospheric and is constructed effectively. Sir Alexander Gibson's performance is quite outstanding in its combination of warmth, colour and drama, and the recording is excellent. So is the CD transfer, and this enterprising collection is a real bargain.

MacDowell, Edward (1861–1908)

Piano concerto No. 2 in D min., Op. 23.

(M) **(*) RCA 09026 64820-2 [id.]. Van Cliburn, Chicago SO, Walter Hendl – BRAHMS: *Piano concerto No. 2.* **(*)

(i) *Piano concerto No. 2 in D min., Op. 23. Woodland sketches: To a wild rose, Op. 51/1.*

(M) **(*) [RCA 60420-2-RG]. Van Cliburn, (i) Chicago SO, Hendl – SCHUMANN: *Concerto.* ***

Van Cliburn is not helped by a recording balance which consistently makes him sound rather too loud; but the performance otherwise has the advantage of warm Chicago acoustics, and Walter Hendl's vigorous and sympathetic support, with its fire and spontaneity, triumph over the technical problems. The Scherzo is superb. The new coupling with Brahms is certainly worth considering, especially by admirers of this fine pianist.

On the alternative coupling MacDowell's most famous solo piano piece makes a pleasing encore, though the performance is a trifle cool. (This record is currently available in the USA only.)

Machaut, Guillaume de (*c.* 1300–1377)

Ballades, motets, rondeaux & virelais: *Amours me fait desirer; Dame se vous m'estés lointeinne; De Bon Espoir – Puis que la douce rousee; De toutes flours; Douce dame jolie; Hareu! hareu! le feu; Ma fin est mon commencement; Mes esperis se combat; Phyton le mervilleus serpent; Quant j'ay l'espart; Quant je suis mis au retour; Quant Theseus – Ne quier veoir; Se ma dame m'a guerpy; Se je souspir; Trop plus est belle – Biauté paree – Je ne sui mie certeins.*

(M) *** Virgin Veritas/EMI VED5 61284-2 (2). Early Music Cons. of L., David Munrow (within Recital: '*The art of courtly love*' ***).

This collection is within 'Guillaume de Machaut and his age', which is itself part of David Munrow's wide-ranging collection, 'The art of courtly love' – see below under Vocal Recitals. Treasures here include cantatas with James Bowman and Charles Brett beautifully matched as soloists. Everything reveals both the remarkable individuality of Guillaume de Machaut as a highly influential composer who spanned the first three-quarters of the fourteenth century, and the life and energy which Munrow consistently brought to early music, even if in some items he arguably goes too far in pepping it up, as in presenting *Dame se vous m'estés* as a bagpipe solo! Excellent CD transfers.

Messe de Nostre Dame. Le Livre dou Voir dit (excerpts): *Plourez dames; Nes qu'on porroit* (ballades); *Sans cuer dolens* (rondeau); *Le lay de bonne esperance; Puis qu'en oubli* (rondeau); *Dix et sept cinq* (rondeau).

(BB) **(*) Naxos Dig. 8.553833 [id.]. Oxford Camerata, Jeremy Summerly.

With his *Messe de Nostre Dame* (dedicated to the Virgin Mary), Guillaume de Machaut wrote the first known complete setting of the Ordinary of the Mass: *Kyrie*, *Gloria*, *Credo*, *Sanctus* and *Agnus Dei*. He chose to finish with his own simple interpolation: *Ite missa est*, which very briefly tells us, 'The mass is ended; thanks be to God.' Machaut's writing is full of extraordinary, dissonant clashes and sudden harmonic twists which are immediately resolved, so the music is both serene and plangently stimulating: here is an epoch-making work of great originality. The Oxford Camerata present the Mass as it stands (and therefore has room for extra items). Jeremy Summerly's account is undoubtedly eloquently serene; it is beautifully controlled and modulated, rather after the fashion of the famous Willcocks/King's College accounts of the Byrd Masses. The harmonic pungencies are cleanly presented but unexaggerated and the music's lines, although by no means bland, flow in relative tranquillity. Obviously much care went into the preparation of the recording, made in conjunction with BBC Radio 3 and France Musique. Reims Cathedral was chosen for the recording location because that was where the work was first performed, and even the choice of the actual recording site – in front of the organ, immediately east of the choir step – sought to produce a similar acoustic effect to what Summerly feels the composer would have experienced; and the effect is affectingly beautiful. The singers apparently experimented freely with plicas – notational signs indicating some kind of ornament – the meaning of which is uncertain but which appear frequently.

The coupled chansons were recorded, equally effectively, at the BBC's Maida Vale studio; they celebrate Machaut as poet/lover as well as composer and, at its modest price, the disc is worth having for these alone. Indeed *Le Livre dou voir dit* is one of the most remarkable cycles of poems of the Middle Ages. Its 9,094 lines of verse, arranged in octosyllabic rhyming couplets, were inspired by the passionate love between the elderly composer (Machaut was in his sixties when he wrote all the music here) and his adolescent student admirer, Péronne d'Armetières. It draws on their correspondence, which frequently shared poems, some set to music by Machaut and intended for his beloved to sing. The music itself is lighter in lyrical feeling than the Mass and its melodic and harmonic style, while recognizably similar, is far less plangent.

In the first two ballades here (*Plourez dames*, written in 1362, and *Nes qu'on porroit* of a year later) the lyrics are pervaded with melancholy and longing, and the settings share the same flowing melodic idea. *Sans cuer doleur* is still dolorous, but the lovers have now spent some time together and Machaut is lamenting their separation. (Its rondeau setting, with a haunting refrain, was apparently written earlier but was chosen by the composer to send back to Péronne because of its appropriate lyrics.) *Puis qu'en oubli sui de vous dous amis* ('Since I am forgotten by you, sweet friend') is particularly touching, given a darkness by its low-pitched line, but its languishing is not to be taken too seriously, for in the final rondeau included here, *Dix et sept*, Machaut encodes the name of his beloved in the figures.

Their relationship lasted about four years and fired the composer to what was his richest and most fruitful period of composition. His feelings are admirably detailed in the ambitious 20-minute *Lay de bonne esperance* ('Lay of good hope') with 12 stanzas telling how his new-found love aroused him from despairing lethargy when 'shot through the heart by a pair of eyes, grey-green, piercing, charming, striking, smiling and gay . . . my lady, through her sweet smiling look, made a dart of burning desire and of hope'. Machaut continues in praise of her beauty and his joy in loving and, finally, his refreshment and reward 'that I was a true lover'. It is a poem of extraordinary passion and eloquence, and it is a pity that the solo performance here, though well enough sung by Matthew Brook, does not have sufficient vocal charisma or charm to carry such an extended monologue. Never mind, the rest of the programme is very well managed, and this is certainly one of Naxos's real bargains.

Madetoja, Leevi (1887–1947)

Symphonies Nos. (i–ii) *1 in F, Op. 29;* (iii) *2 in E flat, Op. 35;* (i; iv) *3 in A, Op. 55.* (v) *Comedy Overture, Op. 53;* (i–ii) *Kullervo, Op. 15*; (i; vi) *Okon Fuoko, Op. 58; Pohjolaisia Suite, Op. 52.*
(B) *** Finlandia/Warner Double 4509 99967-2 (2) [(M) id. import]. (i) Finnish RSO; (ii) Segerstam; (iii) Tampere PO, Rautio; (iv) Saraste; (v) Helsinki PO, Panula; (vi) Kamu.

Symphonies Nos. 1 in F, Op. 29; 2 in E flat, Op. 35; 3 in A, Op. 55; Comedy overture, Op. 53; Okon Fuoko (suite), Op. 58; The Ostrobothnians (suite), Op. 52.
(M) *** Chandos Dig. CHAN 7097 (2) [id.]. Iceland SO, Petri Sakari.

Apart from Erkki Melartin, Madetoja was the leading Finnish symphonist to appear in the immediate wake of Sibelius, and this Finlandia Double is an admirably inexpensive way of getting to know his music. Aside from Sibelius himself, with whom Madetoja briefly studied, there are many influences to be discerned in the *First Symphony* (1915–26): figures like Strauss, the Russian post-nationalists, Reger and, above all, the French for whom Madetoja had a lifelong admiration. The *Second Symphony* (1917–18), composed at about the same time as Sibelius was working on the definitive version of his *Fifth*, is expertly fashioned and (despite the obvious derivations) there is some individuality too. The *Third* was written in the mid-1920s while Madetoja was living in Houilles, just outside Paris. Gallic elements surface most strongly in this piece (he had hoped to study with Vincent d'Indy, and as a conductor he championed both d'Indy and Debussy, as well as such contemporaries as Szymanowski and Janáček). The French critic Henri-Claude Fantapié mentioned Madetoja's affinities with that 'little known but important branch of French music which evolved in the shadow of impressionism' and which was represented by Roussel, Magnard and Paul Le Flem. The *Comedy Overture* (1923) is an absolute delight, and both the suite from the opera

Pohjalaisia (*The Ostrobothnians*) and the ballet-pantomime, *Okon Fuoko*, show an exemplary feeling for colour and atmosphere. The performances and recording are eminently satisfactory, though neither achieves the level of the mid-priced alternatives on Chandos with the Iceland orchestra under Sakari. The latter draws more imaginative and sensitive performances from his Reykjavik forces, but the Finlandia Double is well worth the money and will give pleasure.

Petri Sakari on Chandos offers much the same programme as his competitor on Finlandia, but he includes *The Ostrobothnians suite* instead of *Kullervo* and the *Pohjolaisia suite*. The pair of Chandos records cost rather more than the Finlandia Double, but they are worth the extra. Sakari is a first-rate exponent of these pieces and he secures an excellent response from his Icelandic players, who give dedicated accounts of the symphonies and are equally persuasive in the delightfully high-spirited *Comedy overture* and the suites. The Chandos digital recording is very naturally balanced and difficult to flaw.

'Meet the composer': Complete songs for male voice choir (52 songs).
(B) *** Finlandia/Warner Double Dig. 0630 19807-2 (2) [(M) id. import]. Helsinki University Ch., Matti Hyökki.

The present Finlandia Double assembles the contents of three previous issues, recorded in 1990–91, devoted to Madetoja's output for male voice choir, and offers no fewer than 52 partsongs, many of them of signal quality. The male voice choir is a popular medium in both Finland and Sweden, and both countries have produced a rich repertory of songs and expert groups to sing them. The Helsinki University Choir is among the very finest, and they certainly sing these pieces with wonderful ensemble and fervour. The notes (by the conductor, Matti Hyökki) provide exemplary background information as well as the texts themselves. Many of the songs have something of the modal quality of Sibelius's output in this genre; and the later songs, which Madetoja composed in the 1940s when ill-health inhibited him from finishing a fourth symphony and a violin concerto, are striking. A rewarding set.

Magalhães, Filipe de (1571–1652)

Missa O Soberana luz; Motets: *Commissa mea pavesco; Vidi aquam.*
(BB) *** Naxos Dig. 8.553310 [id.]. Ars Nova, Bo Holten – CARDOSO; LOBO *Motets.* ***

Filipe de Magalhães was the youngest of the three great Portuguese composers who all became pupils of Manuel Mendes (*c.* 1547–1605) at Evora in eastern Portugal. The others, Cardoso and Lôbo, are also represented in this outstanding concert, but Magalhães was reputedly the favourite pupil. One can see why, listening to his highly individual writing in both the Mass *O Soberana luz* and the two hardly less memorable motets, *Vidi aquam* ('I beheld the water') and *Commissa mea pavesco* ('I tremble at my sins') with its instantly poignant opening. The flowing perfection of the linear writing and the imaginative contrasts of tempo between sections of the Mass are striking enough, but the ravishing beauty of the chorale-like, 'harmonized' passages is even more remarkable. In the Mass the *Sanctus* soars radiantly and the lovely *Benedictus* is equally affecting, only to be capped by the *Agnus Dei*. The Danish performances are wonderfully eloquent and the recording, made at Kasterskirken, Copenhagen, has an ideal ambience and is beautifully clear.

Mahler, Gustav (1860–1911)

Symphonies Nos. 1–9.
(B) *** Decca Dig./Analogue 430 804-2 (10) [(M) id. import]. Buchanan, Zakai, Chicago Ch. (in No. 2); Dernesch, Ellyn Children's Ch., Chicago Ch. (in No. 3); Te Kanawa (in No. 4); Harper, Popp, Augér, Minton, Watts, Kollo, Shirley-Quirk, Talvela, V. Boys' Ch., V. State Op. Ch. & Singverein (in No. 8); Chicago SO, Solti.

Symphonies Nos. 1–9; 10 (Adagio).
(B) **(*) Ph. 442 050-2 (10). Concg. O, Haitink (with Ameling, Heynis & Netherlands R. Ch. in No. 2; Forrester, Netherlands R. Ch. & St Willibrord Boys' Ch. in No. 3; Ameling in No. 4; Cotrubas, Harper, Van Bork, Finnila, Dieleman, Cochran, Prey, Sotin, Amsterdam Choirs in No. 8).

Symphonies Nos. 1–10.
(B) **(*) DG 435 162-2 (13) [id.]. Hendricks, Ludwig, Wittek, M. Price, Blegen, Zeumer, Baltsa, Schmidt, Reigel, Prey, Van Dam, Brooklyn Boys' Ch., Westminster Ch., NY Choral Artists, V. Boys' Ch., V. Singverein, V. State Op. Ch., Concg. O, NYPO, or VPO, Bernstein.

Symphonies Nos. 1–10; (i) *Kindertotenlieder.*
(B) ** Sony Dig. S14K 48198 (14) [id.]. Marton, Norman, Battle, Sweet, Coburn, Quivar, Fassbaender, Leech, Nimsgern, Estes, V. Boys' Ch., V. State Op. Konzertvereinigung, Schönberg Ch.; (i) Baltsa; VPO, Maazel.

Solti's achievement in Mahler has been consistent and impressive, and this reissue is a formidable bargain that will be hard to beat. Nos. 1–4 and 9 are digital recordings, Nos. 5–8 are digitally remastered analogue. Solti draws stunning playing from the Chicago Symphony Orchestra, often pressed to great virtuosity, which adds to the electricity of the music-making; if his rather extrovert approach to Mahler means that deeper emotions are sometimes understated, there is no lack of involvement; and his fiery energy and commitment often carry shock-waves in their trail. All in all, an impressive achievement.

It is a measure of Bernstein's greatness as a Mahler interpreter and the electricity he consistently conveys in these edited live recordings that, despite obvious shortcomings, they so readily add up to more than the sum of their parts. The wilfulness of some of the readings, the heaviness of underlining, the exaggeratedly slow speeds, notably in Nos. 3 and 9, even seem to enrich the total experience. This is a personal statement by one great musician on another, and represents a monumental achievement.

Haitink's set of Mahler *Symphonies* comes at bargain price and offers characteristically refined and well-balanced Philips recording. The performances bring consistently fine playing from the Concertgebouw Orchestra, but Haitink is not by nature an extrovert Mahlerian. While he is always sensitive and thoughtful – and this works well enough in Nos. 1 (his earlier recording is included) and 4 (with Elly Ameling a freshly appealing soloist) and they have an attractive simplicity of approach – Nos. 2 and 8 lack the necessary sense of occasion, and No. 8 also needs greater overall grip and a more expansive recording. No. 5 is fresh and direct (the *Adagietto* a little cool) but No. 6 has more refinement than fire. The finest of the set are the deeply satisfying accounts of No. 3 (with fine contributions from both Maureen Forrester and the choristers) and the finely wrought and intensely convincing performance of No. 7. However, the series is capped by an outstanding performance of No. 9. Here Haitink is at his most inspirational and the last movement has a unique concentration, with its slow tempo maintained to create the greatest intensity of feeling. As usual from Philips, the original recordings are consistently enhanced by the CD transfers, and only No. 8 is technically disappointing.

Maazel's cycle of the Mahler symphonies with the Vienna Philharmonic brings generally broad, spacious readings, digitally recorded and generally well played. Yet these studio performances tend not to convey the full dramatic impact of these massive works, as they might have done with an audience in the concert-hall. When they are considered as a cycle, that reservation becomes all the more noticeable. On 14 discs, even at bargain price it is not an inexpensive package, even though the recorded sound is generally very impressive. The pick of the set is the *Fourth* and that shows Maazel at his most inspirational. Apart from Nos. 5 and 8 these recordings are not now available separately.

Symphonies Nos. 1–4.
(M) **(*) EMI CMS7 64471-2 (4) [ZDMC 64471]. Mathis, Soffel (in *No. 2*); LPO Ch. (in *Nos. 2 & 3*); Wenkel, Southend Boys' Ch. (*in No. 3*); Lucia Popp (*in No. 4*), LPO, Klaus Tennstedt.

Tennstedt's complete Mahler cycle is offered, spread over three separate mid-priced boxes, and will be a perfect antidote for those who find Solti's view of Mahler over-intense to the point of neurosis and the Chicago sound too massively voluptuous and brightly lit. No. 1 – the first to be recorded, in Abbey Road in 1977 – sets the style of Tennstedt's approach, with textures fresh and neat, the opening evocation of spring comparatively gentle and the style of phrasing less moulded than we have come to expect. The precision and directness, however, do not preclude coaxing use of rubato in the slow movement, while the big string melody in the finale (which comes after a powerfully dramatic opening) is both spacious and passionate at its climax. The analogue recording is first class, warm and vividly coloured and transferred admirably. In the *Resurrection Symphony*, however, most Mahlerians will prefer a more tinglingly dramatic performance than this, though Tennstedt's account is consistently dedicated, and especially so in the finale, conveying Mahlerian certainties in the light of day, underplaying neurotic tensions. The digital recording is excellent. No. 3, with its arrestingly powerful introduction, is one of the finest of the cycle. Tennstedt gives an eloquent reading, spaciousness underlined, with measured tempi. With Ortrud Wenkel a fine soloist and the Southend Boys adding lusty freshness to the bell music in the fifth movement, this performance with its movingly noble finale is very impressive, again splendidly recorded, digitally. No. 4 is hardly less successful. Again the reading conveys spaciousness and strength, yet Tennstedt's agreeably light touch in the outer movements brings an innocence entirely in keeping with this most endearing of the Mahler symphonies. He makes the argument seamless in his easy transitions of speed, yet here he never deliberately adopts a coaxing, overtly charming manner, and in that he is followed most beautifully by Lucia Popp, the pure-toned soloist in the finale. The peak of the work as Tennstedt presents it lies in the long slow movement, here taken very slowly and intensely. The 1982 digital recording, made in the Kingsway Hall, is among EMI's finest, full and well balanced.

Symphony No. 1 in D (Titan).
(M) ** Ph. 456 658-2 [id.]. Concg. O, Haitink.
(B) *(*) Tring Dig. TRP 029 [(M) id.]. RPO, Yuri Simonov.

(i) *Symphony No. 1 in D (Titan);* (ii) *Symphony No. 10: Adagio.*
(M) ** DG Dig. 445 565-2 [431 769-2 (without *No. 10: Adagio*)]. (i) Chicago SO; (ii) VPO; Abbado.

Symphony No. 1 in D min.; (i) *Lieder eines fahrenden Gesellen.*
(M) **(*) DG 449 735-2 [id.]. Bav. RSO, Kubelik, (i) with Dietrich Fischer-Dieskau.

Kubelik gives an intensely poetic reading. He is here at his finest in Mahler and though, as in later symphonies, he is sometimes tempted to choose a tempo on the fast side, the result could hardly be more glowing. The rubato in the slow funeral march is most subtly handled. In its CD reissue the quality is a little dry in the bass and the violins have lost some of their warmth, but there is no lack of body. In the *Lieder eines fahrenden Gesellen* the sound is fuller, with more atmospheric bloom. No one quite rivals Fischer-Dieskau in these songs, and this is a very considerable bonus, especially at 'Originals' price.

Abbado's Chicago reading of the *First Symphony* is consistently well paced and recorded in impressive digital sound in 1981. By rights it should be an easy first choice – yet he misses some of the natural tension which should communicate naturally from such music-making. In the *Wunderhorn* inspirations of the first two movements, too rarely does the music smile. The funeral march of the slow movement is wonderfully hushed, more spontaneous-sounding than the rest, with superb playing from the Chicago orchestra. The *Adagio* from the *Tenth*, recorded four years later, was taken from a live concert. However, Abbado is not a conductor who seems to benefit greatly from such a choice. The microphones are comparatively close, the sound is refined, but there is surprisingly little feeling of a live occasion, although the beauty of the Vienna string-playing is never in doubt.

Haitink's 1962 version did not stay in the catalogue very long, and he re-recorded the work a decade later. That later version is generally preferable; the earlier performance had a lower level of tension. However, everything is beautifully laid out in front of the listener and, in its thoughtful way, with refined Concertgebouw playing, this could be quite appealing for those who enjoy Haitink's laid-back Mahler style.

Simonov's performance is nothing if not impulsive, and its ethos is Slavic rather than German, especially in the slow movement. The peasant dance of the second movement is forcefully unidiomatic. In the outer movements there are enormously dramatic contrasts. In the first, Simonov holds back until the coda, then unleashes an explosive fortissimo, and he does the same thing twice in the finale. The free-running adrenalin cannot be doubted and there is a thrilling contribution from the RPO brass, but the result is too idiosyncratic for general recommendation despite the fine playing and spectacular digital sound.

Symphony No. 1 in D (Titan) (with *Blumine*).
(B) **(*) [EMI Red Line Dig. CDR5 69816]. Israel PO, Mehta.

Mehta's version with the Israel Philharmonic brings a hybrid – the regular four-movement version in its revised instrumentation, into which is inserted the lyrical *Blumine* movement from the original version, which Mahler later excised. Mehta's reading of the whole work, though not the most individual or illuminating, is satisfyingly warm and direct, helped by very full, forward recording, among the best in the difficult acoustic of the Mann Auditorium. A worthwhile reissue (available only in the USA).

Symphonies Nos. (i) *1;* (ii) *2 (Resurrection).*
(B) **(*) Decca Double 448 921-2 (2) [id.]. (ii) Harper, Watts, London Symphony Ch.; LSO, Solti.

Symphonies Nos. (i) *1 (Titan);* (ii) *2 (Resurrection);* (iii) *Lieder eines fahrenden Gesellen.*
(M) *** Sony SM2K 64447 (2) [S2K 64447]. (i) Columbia SO; (ii) Emilia Cundari, Maureen Forrester, Westminster Ch., NYPO; (iii) Mildred Miller, Columbia SO; Bruno Walter.

As part of the initial volume of Sony's Bruno Walter Edition, his stereo recordings of the *First* and *Second Symphonies* are now economically coupled on a pair of discs together with the *Lieder eines fahrenden Gesellen*. The *First Symphony* was recorded in Hollywood in 1961 with a specially assembled orchestra of first-class musicians; in its newly remastered form the recording sounds better than ever, richer and fuller at the bottom end of the spectrum, and the dynamic range seemingly extended. The ambient warmth emphasizes the Viennese character of the reading, with glowing detail – especially during the evocative opening section – and with the final apotheosis drawn out spaciously and given added breadth and impact. Even more than the *First Symphony*, the 1958 set of the *Resurrection Symphony* is among the gramophone's indispensable classics. In the first movement there is a restraint and in the second a gracefulness which provide a strong contrast with a conductor like Solti. The recording was one of the last Walter made in New York – in Carnegie Hall – before his series with the Columbia Symphony Orchestra; it was remarkably good for its period and the dynamic range is surprisingly wide. In the newest remastering, detail registers more clearly; while the sound is not sumptuous, in the finale the balance with the voices still gives the music an ethereal resonance, with the closing section thrillingly expansive. In the 1960 recording of the *Lieder eines fahrenden Gesellen* the superb orchestral detail glows as never before. Mildred Miller is perhaps not an inspirational soloist, but she sings well enough, and Walter ensures that the performance is dramatically alive. The tangibility of both voice and orchestra is striking and the balance is first class.

Solti's 1966 account of No. 2 remains a demonstration of the outstanding results Decca were securing with analogue techniques at that time, although the brilliance of the fortissimos may not suit all ears. Helen Watts is wonderfully expressive, while the chorus has a rapt intensity that is the more telling when the recording perspectives are so clearly delineated. The London Symphony Orchestra play Mahler's *First* like no other orchestra. They catch the magical opening with a singular, evocative quality, at least partly related to the peculiarly characteristic blend of wind timbres, and throughout there is wonderfully warm string-tone. Solti's tendency to drive hard is felt only in the second movement, which is pressed a little too much, although he relaxes beautifully in the central section. Especially memorable are the poignancy of the introduction of the *Frère Jacques* theme in the slow movement and the exultant brilliance of the closing pages. Excellent value, although Solti's individual mid-priced record of the *First Symphony* was still more tempting. However, it has been withdrawn in favour of the present set.

Symphonies Nos. (i) *1 in D;* (ii) *9 in D min.*

(BB) ** Virgin Classics Double Dig. VBD5 61475-2 [CDVB 61475]. (i) RPO, Andrew Litton; (ii) RLPO, Libor Pešek.

Andrew Litton's way with Mahler's *First Symphony* is generally fresh and direct, with well-chosen speeds, but the playing of the RPO strings is not always quite polished or taut enough. Libor Pešek, however, draws excellent playing from the Liverpool orchestra, very well recorded, in the *Ninth*, with the middle two movements exceptionally light and pointed. The hushed pianissimos are particularly beautiful, but Pešek's reading lacks a little in weight and emotional intensity. While each performance here makes an enjoyable listening experience, both fall short of the finest alternative versions.

Symphonies Nos. 1 in D; 9 in D min.; (i) *Lieder eines fahrenden Gesellen.*

(B) **(*) Teldec/Warner Ultima Dig. 3984 21339-2 (2) [(M) id. import]. NYPO, Kurt Masur; (i) with Håkan Hagegård.

In a two-disc package Masur's live Mahler recordings with the NYPO from the early 1990s are certainly worth considering. On the first disc the *Symphony No.1* and the related *Wayfaring Lad* song-cycle are given attractively fresh, unsentimental readings, even if ironic undertones are muted, with Hagegård a clear, firm, baritone soloist. The *Symphony No. 9*, complete on the second disc, is more variable. If the first movement establishes the directness of Masur's approach, powerful but lacking in mystery, and the second and third movements follow a similar pattern, clean and precise, the long, slow finale crowns the performance in a reading strong and purposeful rather than tenderly elegiac. The recording, made in Avery Fisher Hall (like that of the companion disc), yet has less air round it.

Symphonies Nos. (i) *1 in D (Titan);* (ii) *10: Adagio* (arr. Krenet, ed. Jokl).

(B) **(*) Sony Dig./Analogue SBK 53259 [id.]. (i) NYPO, Mehta; (ii) Cleveland O, Szell.

Mehta's Sony/CBS digital version of the *First Symphony*, successfully recorded in the Avery Fisher Hall in 1980, is far preferable to his later, Israeli, Decca CD. It has no less urgency and drama, but here Mehta's Viennese training comes out in the lilt of the Ländler second movement while his freely expressive rubato in the third, after the dark opening, is very appealing. While the strings lack a genuine pianissimo in the slow introduction, detail is attractively colourful and the reading overall has undoubted spontaneity. Many will also welcome the reissue of Szell's 1958 recording of the *Adagio* from the *Tenth Symphony* in Jokl's edition. Although today we are used to hearing the whole work in Deryck Cooke's completion, the Cleveland orchestral playing is stylish as well as eloquent. The sound, too, is very good.

Symphony No. 2 in C min. (Resurrection).

(M) *** EMI CDM7 69662-2 [id.]. Schwarzkopf, Rössl-Majdan, Philh. Ch. & O, Klemperer.

(M) *** Chandos CHAN 6595/6 [id.]. Lott, Hamari, Latvian State Ac. Ch., Oslo Philharmonic Ch., Oslo PO, Jansons.

(B) *** Double Decca 440 615-2 (2) [id.]. Ileana Cotrubas, Christa Ludwig, V. State Op. Ch., Mehta – SCHMIDT: *Symphony No. 4.* ***

(M) **(*) Van. 08 6155 71 [OVC 4004]. Beverly Sills, Florence Klopleff, Utah University Civic Ch., Utah SO, Abravanel.

(BB) * Naxos Dig. 8.550523 (2) [id.]. Hanna Lisowska, Jadwiga Rappé, Polish Nat. RSO (Katowice), Antoni Wit.

(i) *Symphony No. 2 in C min. (Resurrection)*; (ii) *Lieder eines fahrenden Gesellen;* (iii) *Lieder und Gesang aus der Jugendzeit:* excerpts.

(M) *** DG Dig. 445 587-2 (2). (i) Fassbaender, Plowright, Philh. Ch.; (ii) Fassbaender; (iii) Weikl; Philh. O, Sinopoli.

Sinopoli's version of the *Resurrection* has the additional advantage that the two CDs also include two Mahler song-cycles: the *Lieder eines fahrenden Gesellen*, beautifully sung by Brigitte Fassbaender, and the *Songs of Youth* '*aus der Jugendzeit*', skilfully orchestrated by Harold Byrns and well sung by Bernd Weikl, bringing extra anticipations of the mature *Des Knaben Wunderhorn* songs. In the symphony Sinopoli has meticulous concern for detail, yet he still conveys consistently the irresistible purposefulness of Mahler's writing, fierce at high dramatic moments and intense too, rarely relaxed, in moments of meditation, with *Urlicht* beautifully sung with warmth and purity by Fassbaender. The recorded sound, though not quite as full and vivid as that for Jansons, is among the most brilliant of any in this work. Rosalind Plowright is a pure and fresh soprano soloist, contrasting well with the equally firm, earthier-toned mezzo of Fassbaender.

Klemperer's performance – one of his most compelling on record – comes on a single CD, and the remastered sound is impressively full and clear, with the fullest sense of spectacle in the closing pages. The first movement, taken at a fairly fast tempo, is intense and earth-shaking, and though in the last movement some of Klemperer's speeds are designedly slow, he conveys supremely well the mood of transcendent heavenly happiness in the culminating passage, with chorus and soloists themselves singing like angels.

The crisp attack at the start of the opening funeral march sets the pattern for an exceptionally refined and alert reading of the *Resurrection Symphony* from Jansons and his Oslo orchestra. During the first four movements, this may seem a lightweight reading, but the extra resilience and point of rhythm bring out the dance element in Mahler's *Knaben Wunderhorn* inspirations rather than ruggedness or rusticity, while at the finale the whole performance erupts in an overwhelming outburst for the vision of Resurrection. That transformation is intensified by the breathtakingly rapt and intense account of the song, *Urlicht*, which precedes it. In the finale, power goes with precision and meticulous observance of markings, when even Mahler's surprising diminuendo on the final choral cadence is observed. With the Oslo Choir joined by singers from Jansons's native Latvia, the choral singing is heartfelt, to crown a version which finds a special place even among the many distinguished readings on a long list.

Zubin Mehta sounds a different conductor, not at all like his NYPO self, when he is drawing as sympathetic a Mahler performance as this from the Vienna Philharmonic. The refinement of the playing, recorded with vivid clarity and warmth, puts this among the finest versions of the symphony. The second movement has *grazioso* delicacy and, though the third movement begins with the sharpest possible timpani strokes, there is no hint of brutality, and the *Wunderhorn* rhythms have a delightful lilt. After that comes *Urlicht*, pianissimo in D flat after the Scherzo's final cadence in C minor, and Christa Ludwig is in superb form. The enormous span of the finale brings clarity as well as magnificence, with fine placing of soloists and chorus and glorious atmosphere in such moments as the evocation of birdsong over distant horns, as heavenly a moment as Mahler ever conceived. The CD transfer has brightened the analogue sound somewhat, but there is still plenty of ambient warmth.

Do not be put off by the opening of Abravanel's account which has not the degree of dramatic tension that a Klemperer or a Solti brings, for Abravanel sustains the argument without exaggeration. His freshness and straightforwardness in a work that can easily sound neurotic or be sentimentalized is beautifully managed and, though the result may not be as titanic as many will want, it is deeply satisfying. The choir and soloists as well as the orchestra are most impressive, obviously feeling the music deeply, and the Utah recording is spaciously excellent with a pleasing overall bloom. Well worth considering in the mid-price range.

Antoni Wit conducts a clean-cut, alert and well-pointed reading in full if slightly distanced sound. Yet, for all its fine qualities, it fails to bring out to the full the epic side of this work with its vision of Judgement Day. The impression of a relatively small-scale account is enhanced by the recorded sound, with the chorus and soloists – all first rate – set backwardly in a washy acoustic. Though the recording is refined and well detailed, other balances present problems too, for the first offstage clarion call is barely audible.

Symphonies Nos. (i) *2 (Resurrection);* (ii) *4 in G.*

(B) ** DG Double 453 037-2 (2) [id.]. (i) Neblett, Horne, Chicago Ch. & SO; (ii) Von Stade, VPO, Abbado.

Abbado's version of the *Resurrection Symphony* proves a performance of extremes, with variations of tempo more confidently marked than is common but with concentration so intense that there is no hint of self-indulgence. The delicacy of the Chicago orchestra in the second and third movements is as remarkable as its precision, while the great contrasts of the later movements prove a challenge not only to the performers but also to the DG engineers, who produce sound of the finest analogue quality. Generally the singing is as splendid as the playing but, if there is even a minor disappointment, it lies in the closing pages which are just a little contained. However, the later recording of the *Fourth* is disappointing, above all in the self-consciously expressive reading of the slow movement. There is much beauty of detail, but the Vienna Philharmonic has played and been recorded better than this.

Symphonies Nos. (i) *2 (Resurrection); 5: Adagietto* (only); (ii) *8: Part One* (only): *Veni, creator spiritus.*

(M) ** Sony SM2K 63159 (2) [S2K 63159]. NYPO, Bernstein; with (i) Venora, Tourel, Collegiate Ch.; (ii) Addison, Amara, Chookaskian, Tourel, Tucker, Flagello, London, NY Schola Cantorum Ch., Juilliard Ch., Columbus Boys' Ch.

Bernstein's (1962) interpretation of the *Resurrection Symphony* cannot compare with, say, Klemperer's or Walter's. In any other company one would count it expert, exciting, even moving; but any detailed comparison shows up the difference of quality, and Bernstein is made to seem comparatively shallow with his carefully contrived moulding of each phrase. The two excerpts were recorded live. The famous *Adagietto* from the *Fifth Symphony* was part of the music heard at the burial service for Robert Kennedy in 1968: it is played elegiacally and with comparative restraint, but the underlying depth of feeling still comes through. The exultant *Veni, creator spiritus* was used to celebrate the opening of the Avery Fisher Hall at New York's Lincoln Center, six years earlier. Both are very well recorded.

Symphony No. 3 in D min.

(B) (**) HM Musique d'Abord mono HMA 90501/2. Rössl-Majdan, V. Boys' Ch., V. Konzertverein O, Charles Adler.

(i) *Symphony No. 3;* (ii) *Kindertotenlieder; Des Knaben Wunderhorn: Das irdische Leben. 3 Ruckert Lieder: Ich atmet' einem linden Duft; Ich bin der Welt abhanden gekommen; Um Mitternacht.*

(M) *** Sony SM2K 47576 (2) [S2K 47576]. (i) Martha Lipton, Schola Cantorum Ch., Boys' Ch. of Church of Transfiguration; (ii) Jennie Tourel; NYPO, Bernstein.

Symphony No. 3; 5 Rückert Lieder.

(M) *** Sony M2K 44553 (2) [id.]. Janet Baker, London Symphony Ch., LSO, Tilson Thomas.

Michael Tilson Thomas inspires the orchestra to play with bite and panache in the bold, dramatic passages and to bring out the sparkle and freshness of the *Knaben Wunderhorn* ideas; but what crowns the performance is the raptness of his reading of the noble, hymn-like finale, hushed and intense, beautifully sustained. There is a formidable bonus in Dame Janet Baker's searching performances of the five *Rückert Lieder*. Excellent CBS sound, both warm and brilliant.

Bernstein's 1961 account of Mahler's *Third Symphony*, strong and passionate, has few of the stylistic exaggerations that sometimes overlaid his interpretations. Here his style in the slow movement is heavily expressive, but many will respond to his extrovert involvement. The remastered recording, made in New York's Manhattan Center, the venue of so many of the best of his early records, has added spaciousness and body in this very successful remastering for CD; it is rather less refined than the Unicorn sound but is better balanced. The vocal contributions from Martha Lipton and the two choirs contribute to the success of this venture and the generous Lieder coupling is well worth having, and Jennie Tourel is in excellent voice.

Harmonia Mundi on the Musique d'Abord label at budget price offers the very first recording of No. 3, made as recently as 1952. Charles Adler was one of the last surviving disciples of Mahler himself and, though ensemble is sometimes rough, as if the players were feeling their way, and the outer movements are spread very luxuriantly, dramatic tension is rarely absent. Though in this series documentation is limited, it is a pity that so little is made of the historic nature of the recording, with 1961 implied as the recording date.

(i) *Symphonies Nos.* (i) *3. 6; 10* (ed. Krenek): *Adagio; Purgatorio.*

(M) (**) Conifer mono 75605 51279-2 (3). VSO, Adler; (i) with Rössl-Majdan, V. Boys' Ch., V. State Op. Ch.

Recorded in 1951–2 by Charles Adler for his own label, SPA, these were pioneering efforts that pointed to the future – the first commercial recordings of each work. Though the ensemble is rough at times and the mono sound limited (if well doctored by the CEDAR process), Adler's bluff intensity demonstrates the power of each symphony in consistently concentrated performances. Speeds tend to be broad and steady, as in the first movement of No. 6, yet there is no dragging, and one readily forgives the rather seedy string-sound. No. 3 fares rather better, with good singing from the Vienna choirs and with the slow finale building up powerfully. The corrupt Krenek edition of the two completed movements from the *Symphony No. 10* is less valuable, but still makes a compelling and useful makeweight.

(i) *Symphony No. 3. Symphony No. 10: Adagio.*
(BB) ** Naxos Dig. 8.550525/6 (2) [id.]. (i) Ewa Podlés, Cracow Boys' Ch. & Philharmonic Ch.; Polish Nat. RSO, Wit.

Antoni Wit's reading for Naxos is well played and recorded but, until the final movements, lacks the power and thrust needed in this epic work. If the result is too often lightweight, fair amends are made when Ewa Podlés is a warmly characterful contralto soloist in the fourth movement and the Polish choruses sing brilliantly in the brief fifth movement, making the bell effects sound like a Christmas carol.

Symphony No. 4 in G.
(B) *** EMI Dig. CD-EMX 2139 [(M) id. import]. Felicity Lott, LPO, Welser-Möst.
(M) *** DG 419 863-2. Edith Mathis, BPO, Karajan.
(BB) *** Naxos Dig. 8.550527 [id.]. Lynda Russell, Polish Nat. RSO, Antoni Wit.
(BB) *** Arte Nova/BMG Dig. 74321 46506-2 [id.]. Hellen Kwan, Gran Canaria PO, Adrian Leaper.
(BB) **(*) RCA Navigator 74321 21286-2 [(M) id. import]. Lisa Della Casa, Chicago SO, Reiner – R. STRAUSS: *Burleske*. **(*)
(M) **(*) Van. 08 6164 71 [OVC 4007]. Netania Davrath, Utah SO, Abravanel.
(M) ** Ph. (IMS) 442 394-2 [id.]. Elly Ameling, Concg. O, Haitink.
(BB) * Koch/Discover Dig. DICD 920404 [id.]. Lena Lootens, BRTN PO, Brussels, Avi Ostrowsky.

Symphonies Nos. 4 in G; 5 (Adagietto).
(B) *** [EMI Red Line Dig. CDR5 69817]. Popp, LPO, Tennstedt.

(i) *Symphony No. 4 in G;* (ii) *Lieder eines fahrenden Gesellen.*
❀ (M) *** Sony SBK 46535; *SBT 46535* [id.]. (i) Judith Raskin, Cleveland O, Szell; (ii) Frederica von Stade, LPO, Andrew Davis.

(i) *Symphony No. 4 in G;* (ii) *Lieder und Gesang aus der Jugendzeit.*
(M) (***) Sony mono SMK 64450 [id.]. Desi Halban; (i) NYPO, Bruno Walter; (ii) Walter (piano).

George Szell's 1966 record of Mahler's *Fourth* represented his partnership with the Cleveland Orchestra at its highest peak and the digital remastering for CD brings out the very best of the original recording. The performance remains uniquely satisfying: the music blossoms, partly because of the marvellous attention to detail (and the immaculate ensemble), but more positively because of the committed and radiantly luminous orchestral response to the music itself. In the finale Szell found the ideal soprano to match his conception. An outstanding choice, generously coupled. In contrast with most other recorded performances, Frederica von Stade insinuates a hint of youthful ardour into her highly enjoyable account of the *Wayfaring Lad* cycle.

Karajan's refined and poised, yet undoubtedly affectionate account remains among the finest versions of this lovely symphony, and Edith Mathis's sensitively composed contribution to the finale matches the conductor's meditative feeling. With glowing sound, this makes another outstanding mid-priced recommendation alongside Szell's renowned Cleveland CD.

Tennstedt's reading of the *Fourth Symphony* conveys spaciousness and strength, yet his agreeably light touch in the outer movements brings an innocence entirely in keeping with this most endearing of the Mahler symphonies. He makes the argument seamless in his easy transitions of speed, yet here he never deliberately adopts a coaxing, overtly charming manner; and in that he is followed most beautifully by Lucia Popp, the pure-toned soloist in the finale. The peak of the work as Tennstedt presents it lies in the long slow movement, here taken very slowly and intensely. The 1982 digital recording, made in the Kingsway Hall, is among EMI's finest, full and well balanced. Tennstedt's account of the *Adagietto* lacks the full tenderness of Barbirolli's (starting with a slightly intrusive balance for the harp) but still makes a worthwhile bonus.

Antoni Wit conducts a fresh, spontaneous-sounding reading, beautifully played and recorded, that can be warmly recommended at Naxos's bargain price. This is more enjoyable than many full-priced issues, with easy manners at well-chosen speeds, so that the rustic *Wunderhorn* element is sharply brought out. The flowing speed for the slow movement means that there is no suspicion of self-consciousness in the warm expressiveness. Lynda Russell is a pure-toned soprano soloist in the finale, both fresh and warm, with Wit giving a good lilt to the rhythm. Excellent sound, which gives a good bite and focus to the woodwind, so important in Mahler, though the Katowice horn favours a touch of East European tone.

Spaciously recorded, the Arte Nova version offers a fresh, crisply paced reading from Adrian Leaper, demonstrating what polished ensemble the Gran Canaria Philharmonic can achieve. Woodwind soloists are most imaginative, and most striking of all is the refinement of the strings. with the opening of the slow movement bringing the gentlest pianissimo, ravishingly sustained. The finale is then beautifully sprung, with the Korean soprano, Hellen Kwan, a golden-toned soloist, aptly young-sounding. Without being in the same class as the famous Szell version, this is thoroughly recommendable in the budget range.

Walter's glowingly radiant reading suffers from the fairly limited mono sound (especially at the climax of the slow movement). But the remastering of the 1945 recording has worked wonders, and orchestral textures are clear and yet warm. Desi Halban's contribution is refreshingly individual, dramatic as well as touching, and she is comparably impressive in the songs, which Walter accompanies discreetly at the piano. Her account of *Ich ging mit Lust durch einen grünen Wald* is enchanting.

Reiner's version was made – like most of his famous recordings – in Orchestra Hall, Chicago (in 1958). The recording has been digitally remastered, with great improvement to the sound, which remains brightly lit but has attractively vivid detail, naturally glowing within the acoustic bloom of the hall. The performance is wayward, but lovingly so; and everything Reiner does sounds spontaneous. There is a mercurial quality in the first movement and plenty of drama, too; the second is engagingly pointed but with a balancing warmth, the Viennese influence strong. The slow movement has striking intensity, with its rapt closing pages leading on gently to the finale in which Lisa della Casa, in ravishing voice, matches Reiner's mood.

The *Fourth Symphony*, relatively lightweight, suits the Utah orchestra better than the weightier Mahler symphonies, and Abravanel directs a characteristically fresh and crisp reading, marked by some fine solo playing. The strings in the slow movement may not be quite as refined as in the finest rival versions, but the hushed intensity is most convincing, and the finale with Netania Davrath a firm, boyish soloist is light and urgent, bringing out the joy of the inspiration. Fair sound, fuller than in others in the Vanguard series. As with the other issues, no recording date is given.

Haitink's earlier, late-1960s Concertgebouw version is predictably well played and the recording has come up very well indeed on the mid-priced CD reissue. The performance is sober, but it has an attractive simplicity, and Elly Ameling matches Haitink's approach in her serene contribution to the finale. Although it lacks drama, this is an easy version to live with; but the later, digital, Concertgebouw account with Roberta Alexander is preferable, a most winning performance, but it is currently withdrawn. In his latest version (Philips 434 123-2) Haitink conducts the Berlin Philharmonic in a warm, highly polished reading that can hardly be faulted, except that it rather misses the innocent freshness lying behind this of all Mahler's symphonies. The child-heaven finale too is smoother than usual, with Sylvia McNair the light and boyish soloist. Full, well-balanced sound.

The Discover version from the BRTN Philharmonic offers an amiable performance with speeds consistently on the slow side, even sluggish at times, with ensemble markedly less crisp than in other studio performances such as that on the Arte Nova issue in the same price category. Lena Lootens has a warm, fruity mezzo, but she is neither as fresh nor as boyish-sounding as one looks for in the innocent *Wunderhorn* finale.

Symphony No. 5 in C sharp min.
(B) *** EMI Dig. CD-EMX 2164 [(M) id. import]. RLPO, Mackerras.
✿ (M) *** EMI CDM7 64749-2 [id.]. New Philh. O, Barbirolli.
(M) *** DG 447 450-2 [id.]. BPO, Karajan.
(BB) **(*) RCA Navigator 74321 29249-2 [Basic 100 09026 68365-2]. Boston SO, Erich Leinsdorf.
(B) (**(*)) Millennium mono MCD 80081 [id.] V. State Op. O, Hermann Scherchen.
(M) ** Van. 08 6156 71 [SVC 25]. Utah SO, Abravanel.
(M) ** Sony SMK 63084 [id.]. NYPO, Bernstein.
(B) ** Carlton 30367 02102 [(M) id.]. Symphonica of L., Wyn Morris.
(B) ** Belart 450 135-2 [(M) id. import]. LAPO, Zubin Mehta.
(M) ** Sony Theta Dig. SMK 60024 [id.]. VPO, Lorin Maazel.

(B) HM Musique d'Abord HMA 905179 [id.]. ORTF, Hermann Scherchen.

Mackerras in his well-paced reading sees the work as a whole, building each movement with total concentration. There is a thrilling culmination on the great brass chorale at the end, with polish allied to purposefulness. Barbirolli in his classic reading may find more of a tear-laden quality in the great *Adagietto*; but Mackerras, with fewer controversial points of interpretation and superb modern sound, makes an excellent first choice.

Barbirolli's famous 1969 version on any count is one of the greatest, most warmly affecting performances ever committed to disc, expansive, yet concentrated in feeling: the *Adagietto* is very moving. The recording was made in Watford Town Hall and has been remastered most successfully. A classic version, and still a fine bargain.

Karajan's 1973 recording (previously available on DG's bargain label) now reverts to mid-price as a 'Legendary Performance' in DG's series of 'Originals'. Karajan's characteristic emphasis on polish and refinement goes with sharpness of focus. His is at once one of the most beautiful and one of the most intense versions available, starting with an account of the first movement which brings more biting funeral-march rhythms than any rival. Radiant playing from the Berlin Philharmonic and full, atmospheric recording, made in the Berlin Jesus-Christus-Kirche. However, the CD transfer is very brightly lit and some softening of the brilliance on top is needed for complete comfort.

Leinsdorf is predictably less gentle than some in the famous *Adagietto* – indeed he brings out its underlying neurosis – but elsewhere his directness makes for an unexpectedly strong and convincing result. The relentlessness adds to the strength and not to any sense of the music's byways being trampled over. The recording from 1963 has the advantage of warm Boston acoustics, and this characterful performance with first-class playing from the great Boston orchestra is the least expensive recommendable version of the Mahler *Fifth* in the catalogue, though it is by no means a first choice.

Dating from 1953, Scherchen's version with the Vienna State Opera Orchestra offers a powerful, rugged performance with mono sound astonishingly full and vivid for the period. The opening *Funeral march* has ample power and thrust, and the second movement is fast and furious, while the celebrated *Adagietto* is tender, sweet and flowing rather than elegiac. The finale brings a ripely joyful conclusion, attractively wild in the coda.

Abravanel and the Utah orchestra give a neat and precise but relatively lightweight reading, not helped by the rather thin sound of the CD transfer. What is interesting is that in the great *Adagietto* Abravanel follows the original model of Bruno Walter in adopting an easily flowing speed which never sounds rushed – not elegiac, just tender. The finale, well sprung, has quicksilver energy. No recording date is given.

The *Adagietto* is the highlight of Bernstein's earlier performances, reissued on Sony. It brings a heady beauty so delicate that one holds one's breath. Elsewhere Bernstein's care for detail means that he never seems quite to plumb the depths of Mahler's inspiration. The first movement, for example, seems too careful, for all the virtuosity of the playing. The recording, too, made in the Avery Fisher Hall in 1963, is not entirely flattering. Fortunately he re-recorded the work digitally with the VPO for DG and this record (currently withdrawn) is one of the very finest of his last series of records and includes an equally elegiac account of the *Adagietto* – the music he conducted at the funeral of President Kennedy.

Wyn Morris starts with a strikingly commanding account of the *Funeral march*, but then the second movement is more cautious with the ensemble less crisp than elsewhere. In the third movement Morris captures the Viennese lilt very winningly; he takes the *Adagietto* at a flowing tempo and the finale in a broad, expansive sweep, not quite as sharply focused as it might be. In many ways it is a sympathetic reading, but not consistent in its success. The recording is both atmospheric and brightly lit, not absolutely refined in its definition at climaxes.

Brilliant as the 1977 recording is of Mehta's Los Angeles version, and the playing too, yet it misses the natural warmth of expression that the same conductor found in his reading of No. 2 with the Vienna Philharmonic (see above). Most impressive is the virtuoso Scherzo, but in their different ways the opening Funeral march and the beautiful *Adagietto* both lack the inner quality which is essential if the faster movements are to be aptly framed. The animation of the finale is exaggerated by Mehta's very fast tempo, missing the *Wunderhorn* overtones of this most optimistic of Mahler's conclusions.

Maazel's Vienna version, recorded at the beginning of the 1980s, like the others in his CBS/Sony cycle is marked by fine playing and a warmly sympathetic recording. But its fluctuations of speed begin to sound wayward, particularly in the first two movements. Though he takes a flowing view of the *Adagietto*, this is a performance which, for all its qualities, fails to hang together.

It is salutary to be reminded how bad Mahler performances could be as recently as 1965 in the live recording from Harmonia Mundi in the Musique d'Abord series. Hermann Scherchen was a great conductor but this is in every way a travesty of Mahler. Not only is the playing perfunctory in the allegros with Scherchen adopting impossibly fast speeds, but in the celebrated *Adagietto* he goes in the other direction with one of the slowest, most maudlin performances ever recorded. Worse still, there are savage cuts in both the third movement and the finale, so that the Scherzo, despite a sentimentally slow account of the second section, lasts a mere 5 minutes 35 seconds, where normally the timing is at least three times as long. The finale too, where the playing is scrappiest of all, brings another long cut in the middle. The sound is limited and dry, though the CD transfer gives it plenty of body.

Symphonies Nos. 5; 9; 10 (Adagio).
(M) *** EMI CMS7 64481-2 (3) [ZDMC 64481]. LPO, Klaus Tennstedt.

Rather like Barbirolli, Tennstedt takes a ripe and measured view of the *Fifth* and, though his account of the lovely *Adagietto* lacks the full tenderness of Barbirolli's (starting with a slightly intrusive balance for the harp), this is an outstanding performance, on the one hand thoughtful, on the other warm and expressive. The *Ninth* brings another performance of warmth and distinction, characteristically underlining nobility rather than any neurotic tension, so that the outer movements, spaciously drawn, have architectural grandeur. The second movement is gently done, and the third, crisp and alert, lacks just a little in adrenalin. The playing is excellent both here and in the *Adagio* of the *Tenth*, and the CD transfers are exemplary. These 1978/9 analogue recordings were made at Abbey Road and the effect is full and spacious. A highly recommendable set.

Symphony No. 6 in A min.
(M) *** Sony SBK 47654 [id.]. Cleveland O, Szell.
(M) **(*) Sony SMK 60208 [id.]. NYPO, Bernstein.
(B) *** Naxos Dig. 8.550529 (2) [id.]. Polish Nat. RSO (Katowice), Antoni Wit.
(B) *** Decca Double 444 871-2 (2) [id.]. Concg. O, Chailly – ZEMLINSKY: *Maeterlinck Lieder*. ***
(M) **(*) Decca 425 040-2. Chicago SO, Solti.
(B) **(*) EMI forte CZS5 69349-2 (2) [CDFB 69349]. New Philh. O, Barbirolli – R. STRAUSS: *Ein Heldenleben*. ***
(B) **(*) EMI CZS5 69252-2 (2). New Philh. O, Barbirolli – R. STRAUSS: *Metamorphosen*. **(*)
(M) ** Van. 08 6157 71 [SVC 26]. Utah SO, Abravanel.

Szell's powerful outer movements are masterfully shaped and unerringly paced, with the second-movement scherzo beautifully sprung to bring out the grotesquerie. The *Andante moderato* then brings a uniquely delicate and moving account, hauntingly wistful, tender without a hint of sentimentality. The CD transfer gives a fuller, more atmospheric impression of what the orchestra sounded like in Severance Hall, Cleveland, than most of the studio recordings of the time. At budget price, squeezed on to a single disc, this is buried treasure and a fine counterpart to Szell's classic reading of Mahler's *Fourth*.

It is good that Sony have now separated Bernstein's enormously gripping NYPO account of the *Sixth* from the *Eighth* (see below). Now on a single, mid-priced disc it is highly competitive. The remastering has further improved the sound; although the close balance remains a drawback, the actual sounds are impressive, and the performance itself is very compelling indeed.

The excellent quality of the Katowice Orchestra of Polish Radio is impressively demonstrated in all four movements of this difficult symphony. The ensemble can hardly be faulted, hardly less polished than that of Dohnányi's Cleveland Orchestra, and the full, atmospheric recording enhances that quality with string-sound that is fresh, radiant and full of bloom, thanks in part to the helpful acoustic. Wit conducts a spacious performance, clean and well sprung, with the varying moods sharply contrasted. Above all, he conveys the tensions behind the notes, with the beauty of the slow movement warmly conveyed with easy, unexaggerated rubato and with the strings coping confidently with the occasional controlled portamento. On two full discs it becomes less of a super-bargain than some Naxos issues, but it stands comparison with any rival.

Chailly's version with the Concertgebouw offers brilliant playing and spectacular sound in a reading remarkable for the broad, rugged approach in the outer movements. There is relentlessness in the slow speed for the first movement, with expressive warmth giving way to a square purposefulness, tense and effective. The third movement brings a comparably simple, direct approach at a genuine flowing *Andante*. In its open songfulness it rouses Wunderhorn echoes. Anyone fancying the unexpected but attractive Zemlinsky coupling need not hesitate.

Solti draws stunning playing from the Chicago orchestra. The sessions were in March and April 1970, and this was the first recording he made with them after he took up his post as principal conductor; as he himself said, it represented a love-affair at first sight. The electric excitement of the playing confirms this, with brilliant, immediate but atmospheric sound. Solti's rather extrovert approach is here at its most impressive. His fast tempi may mean that he misses some of the deeper emotions, and the added brightness of the CD transfer perhaps emphasizes this, but it is still a very convincing and involving performance.

Barbirolli gives a characteristically expansive account of Mahler's *Sixth Symphony*, and there are many of the same fine qualities as in his version of the *Fifth*, recorded with the same orchestra a year later. But, particularly in the first movement, the slow tempo is allowed to drag a little, so that tension falls. Such wavering of concentration will not trouble everyone, but the 1967 Kingsway Hall recording has now lost some of its bloom. Moreover there is nothing like the same illusion of a live Barbirolli performance as there is with the *Fifth*. There is a choice of couplings, and the pairing with *Ein Heldenleben* is to be preferred as it has a superior CD transfer. The alternative brings one of the most beautiful performances of Strauss's *Metamorphosen* ever recorded; but again the sound is less full than on the original LPs.

Though Abravanel, in a slightly underpowered reading, fails to bring out the darker, more ominous qualities, as in the finale, his is a fresh, spontaneous-sounding response to this enigmatic work. The Scherzo is well sprung and the slow-movement *Andante* sweetly lyrical at a flowing speed, though the recorded sound (undated), as transferred, is rather thin.

Symphonies Nos. 6, 7 & 8.

(M) *** EMI Dig. CMS7 64476-2 (4) [ZDMD 64476]. LPO, Klaus Tennstedt (with, in *No. 8*, Connell, Wiens, Lott, Schmidt, Denize, Versalle, Hynninen, Sotin, Tiffin School Boys' Ch., LPO Ch.).

While the *Eighth* marks a superb culmination, the finest of Tennstedt's cycle, and is magnificently recorded, Nos. 6 and 7 are also a very considerable achievement, and this four-CD digital box is a real bargain. Tennstedt's reading of the *Sixth* is characteristically strong, finding more warmth than usual, even in this dark symphony. So the third-movement *Andante* is warmly beautiful, open and song-like, almost Schubertian in its sweetness, though there is never any question of Tennstedt taking a sentimental view of Mahler. His expressiveness tends towards conveying joy rather than Mahlerian neurosis, and for some that may make this too comfortable a reading. Karajan has more power and bite; his scale is bigger and bolder and the Berlin playing is more brilliant. Yet the EMI digital recording brings extra range and impact in the famous hammer-blows of fate in the finale and the result overall is most satisfying. The *Seventh* is even finer. Tennstedt is predictably spacious, and the first movement's architectural span is given the kind of expansive structural unity that one associates with Klemperer; but the concentration of the LPO playing under Tennstedt brings much greater success here than Klemperer found in his disappointing New Philharmonia version. In the central movements Tennstedt is not as imaginative as Solti, who is more mercurial in the second *Nachtmusik*, but the former is again at his most impressive in the finale, showing his directness and strength, and with vigorous support from the LSO players, who are on top form throughout the symphony. The digital recording is full, yet beautifully clear in detail. As for the *Eighth*, Tennstedt's broader, grander view makes at least as powerful an impact as Solti's Decca set; even though the playing does not always have the searing intensity of the Chicago orchestra, the singing of the LPO Choir combined with the Tiffin School Boys' Choir is unforgettable, with concentrated pianissimos matched by the expansive climaxes, where the opulent sound of the Westminster Cathedral organ adds to the feeling of weight and power.

Symphonies Nos. (i) *6 in A min.;* (ii) *8 in E flat (Symphony of 1000).*

(M) *(**) Sony SM3K 47581 [S3K 47581]. (i) NYPO; (ii) Spoorenberg, Gwyneth Jones, Annear, Reynolds, Procter, Mitchinson, Ruzdjak, McIntyre, Leeds Festival Ch., London Symphony Ch., Orpington Junior Singers, Highgate School Boys' Ch., Finchley Children's Music Group, LSO; Bernstein.

Bernstein's first CBS recording of the *Sixth* was made in the Avery Fisher Hall in 1967. Like the *Third*, it stood out from the others in the set, but the bright, close-up sound remains a drawback. Like the later, digital version with the VPO, one can argue that his tempi are inclined to be too fast (particularly in the first movement, which no longer sounds like a funeral march) but the searing intensity of the performance – like a live concert – comes over readily. The later version brings more refinement of expression, but not more concentration, and involves two full-priced CDs (DG 427 697-2). The New York recording is reissued on three mid-priced CDs but includes also the *Eighth Symphony*, recorded at Walthamstow in 1966. The Leeds Festival Chorus is strongly stiffened by professional choristers, and the result is splendidly incisive. The unfortunate point, undermining much of the superb achievement in the performance, is the closeness of sound and the resultant lack of atmosphere in the recording quality.

Symphony No. 7 in E min.
(M) *** Decca 425 041-2. Chicago SO, Solti.
(M) *** DG Dig. 445 513-2; *445 513-4* [id.]. Chicago SO, Abbado.
(BB) **(*) Naxos Dig. 8.550531 [id.]. Polish Nat. RSO, Michael Halász.
(B) (**(*)) Millennium mono MCD 80082 [id.] V. State Op. O, Hermann Scherchen.
(M) ** Van. 08 6158 71 [SVC 27]. Utah SO, Abravanel

Symphony No. 7 in E min.; (i) *Kindertotenlieder*.
(B) *** DG Double Dig. 453 133-2 (2) [id.]. (i) Bryn Terfel; Philh. O, Sinopoli.

Sinopoli, always a very positive Mahlerian, is here at his most personal in presenting a colourful, sharply characterized reading. Even more than usual with Sinopoli it is a performance of extremes, controversial but powerful to a degree that makes the whole experience disturbing. In each section Sinopoli immediately establishes an individual approach, usually far slower than usual, sometimes much faster. The first *Nachtmusik*, shimmering and atmospheric, is as evocative as the lyrical second, in which Sinopoli at very slow speed uses extreme rubato in his careful moulding of phrase. In between, the third-movement Scherzo at high speed becomes a nightmare fantasy, while the vast finale is delivered with fine panache, at the end pushed to the verge of hysteria. The vivid recording (which marks the whole series) is here at its most involving, with the brass gloriously rich. Bryn Terfel's magnificent interpretation of the *Kindertotenlieder*, heartfelt and intense, crowns the issue.

In interpretation, Solti's version is as successful as his fine account of the *Sixth Symphony*, extrovert in display but full of dark implications. The tempi tend to be challengingly fast – at the very opening, for example, and in the Scherzo (where Solti is mercurial) and in the finale (where his energy carries shock-waves in its trail). The second *Nachtmusik* is enchantingly seductive, and throughout the orchestra plays superlatively. This is one of Solti's finest Mahler records and the recording is brilliant and full – the CD transfer increases the brightness.

Abbado's command of Mahlerian characterization has never been more tellingly displayed than in this most problematic of the symphonies; even in the loosely bound finale Abbado unerringly draws the threads together. The contrasts in all its movements are superbly brought out, with the central interludes made ideally atmospheric, as in the eeriness of the Scherzo and the haunting tenderness of the second *Nachtmusik*. The precision and polish of the Chicago orchestra go with total commitment, and the recording is one of the finest DG has made with this orchestra.

Very well played and treated to refined and well-balanced digital recording, the Naxos version offers excellent value on a single disc at super-bargain price. With well-chosen speeds, often brisk but unhurried, with crisp ensemble and good rhythmic point, the only snag is that, by the standards of the finest versions, it is undercharacterized, lacking both flamboyance and tragic weight. Even there one has an advantage in the haunting melody of the second *Nachtmusik*, which is the more moving for being treated in a restrained way.

Recording this symphony in 1953, Scherchen was as much a Mahler pioneer as Charles Adler in the two preceding years, yet the mono sound, very well transferred, is far finer than in Adler's recordings of Nos. 3 and 6. Here too there are moments of roughness, but what is remarkable is the thrust and power of the reading, with each of the five movements strongly characterized, with the haunting second *Nachtmusik* opening with a schmaltzy glissando from the concertmaster. Only in the finale, taken at a relatively broad tempo, does the performance lose a little of its bite at times.

As in their other Mahler symphony recordings, Abravanel and the Utah orchestra take a relatively lightweight view of this often dark work. Clean and fresh, with good forward movement in the opening *Adagio*, the first *Nachtmusik* opens on a glorious horn-call, and the second *Nachtmusik* is pure and sweet in its easy flow. Lightweight or not, the rhythmic crispness of the finale makes for a buoyant conclusion, even if – as in some of the other Vanguard issues – the sound is not as full as it might be.

Symphonies Nos. 7; 9; 10 (Adagio).
(M) **(*) Sony SM3K 47585 (3) [S3K 47585]. NYPO, Bernstein.

In 1965 Bernstein drew a performance of the *Seventh* of characteristic intensity and beauty from the New York Philharmonic; his love of the music is evident in every bar. The playing is fabulous, yet there are also reservations. His warmth of phrasing in the second subject makes Bernstein's pointing sound self-conscious and tense, and in the *Night music* of the second and fourth movements, where the New York orchestra produces playing of heavenly refinement, the same feeling is present. Even in the finale, where Bernstein's thrusting dynamism holds the disparate structure together, there is the feeling that he is unable to relax into simplicity. The recording, made in the Avery Fisher Hall, is vivid and forward, not as full-bodied or refined as the later, DG version, which on two full-priced discs costs far more but is worth the extra outlay. The New York *Ninth* – a lucky symphony on records – is undoubtedly a great performance. Here Bernstein's sense of urgency has its maximum impact, though in the finale he does not quite achieve the visionary intensity of his later recording for DG with the Berlin Philharmonic. In the *Adagio* from the *Tenth*, recorded a decade after the others in 1975, Bernstein uses the old, fallible edition, but again the passionate commitment of his performance is hard to resist, with contrasts underlined between the sharpness of the *Andante* passages and the free expressiveness of the main *Adagio*. The recording is characteristically close but quite full, and for Bernstein admirers with limited budgets this box is certainly good value.

Symphony No. 8 (Symphony of 1000).

(B) *** Sony SBK 48281; *SBT 48281* [id.]. Robinson, Marshall, Heichele, Wenkel, Laurich, Walker, Stilwell, Estes, Frankfurt Kantorei, Singakademie, Limburger Boys' Ch., Op. & Museum O, Gielen.
(M) ** Ph. 446 195-2 [id.]. Cotrubas, Harper, Van Borkh, Finnila, Dieleman, Cochran, Prey, Sotin, Amsterdam Choirs, Conc. O, Haitink.

Recorded live at the opening of the Alte Oper in Frankfurt in August 1981, Gielen's version offers a direct, fresh reading, full of atmosphere, in which brisk speeds allow ample weight. Far more than the Abbado Berlin version, it vividly conveys the atmosphere of a great event. The analogue recording is less full than some, but it is naturally balanced with plenty of presence, if with brass a little distant. The chorus sings with heartfelt intensity, and the soloists make a distinguished team, except that the ringing Heldentenor, Mallory Walker, develops a beat in the voice under stress as Dr Marianus. On a single disc at budget price in Sony's Essential Classics series, it makes an outstanding bargain.

Haitink's 1971 analogue version, characteristically thoughtful and direct, lacks the biting intensity needed to convey the work's epic purpose to the full. The solo singing has its blemishes, but on CD the recording, originally rather dull and limited, has come up very freshly, with balances cleanly registered.

Symphony No. 9 in D min.

(M) *** EMI CDM7 63115-2 [id.]. BPO, Barbirolli.
(M) *** EMI CMS7 63277-2 (2). New Philh. O, Klemperer – WAGNER: *Siegfried idyll.* **(*)
(B) (***) Dutton Lab. mono CDEA 5005 [(M) id.]. VPO, Bruno Walter.
(M) *** Sony SMK 64452 (2) [id.]. Columbia SO, Bruno Walter (with rehearsal & conversation between Bruno Walter and Arnold Michaelis).
(B) ** DG Double 437 467-2 (2) [id.]. Chicago SO, Giulini.
(BB) ** Naxos Dig. 8.550535-6 (2) [id.]. Polish Nat. RSO (Katowice), Michael Halász.

Symphony No. 9; (i) *Kindertotenlieder; 5 Rückert Lieder.*

(B) *** DG Double 453 040-2 (2) [(M) id. import]. BPO, Karajan; (i) with Christa Ludwig.

Fine as Karajan's other Mahler recordings have been, his two accounts of the *Ninth* transcend them. In the earlier, analogue version it is the combination of richness and concentration in the outer movements that makes for a reading of the deepest intensity, while in the middle two movements there is point and humour as well as refinement and polish. Helped by full, spacious recording, the sudden pianissimos which mark both movements have an ear-pricking realism such as one rarely experiences on record, and the unusually broad tempi are superbly controlled. In the finale Karajan is not just noble and stoic; he finds the bite of passion as well, sharply set against stillness and repose. This earlier (1980) analogue performance makes a remarkable bargain, reissued as a DG Double and costing half as much as the later, digital recording. Moreover the performances of the *Kindertotenlieder* and *Rückert Lieder* have a distinction and refinement of playing which stand out above all. Ludwig's singing is characterful too, with the poise and stillness of the songs beautifully caught. Even if the microphone conveys some unevenness in the voice, the recording is rich and mellow to match the performances.

Walter's Sony (originally CBS) performance was recorded in late January and early February 1961, and the producer, John McClure, took the opportunity to record a working portrait of the occasion. That is supplemented here by a 16-minute conversation between the conductor and Arnold Michaelis, dating from five years earlier. Walter's performance lacks mystery at the very start, but through the long first movement he unerringly builds up a consistent structure, controlling tempo more closely than most rivals, preferring a steady approach. The middle two movements similarly are sharply focused rather than genial, and the finale, lacking hushed pianissimos, is tough and stoically strong. A fine performance, quite different from his famous (1934) VPO account which (courtesy of Mike Dutton) is now available in a really first-class transfer.

Barbirolli greatly impressed the Berliners with his Mahler performances live, and this recording reflects the players' warmth of response. He opted to record the slow and intense finale before the rest, and the beauty of the playing makes it a fitting culmination. The other movements are strong and alert too, and the sound remains full and atmospheric, though now more clearly defined. An unquestionable bargain.

Klemperer's performance was recorded in 1967 after a serious illness. His refusal to languish pays tribute to his spiritual defiance, and the physical power is underlined when the sound is full-bodied and firmly focused. The sublimity of the finale comes out the more intensely, with overt expressiveness held in check and deep emotion implied rather than made explicit.

Bruno Walter's 1938 version with the Vienna Philharmonic was the first recording of this symphony ever issued. The opening is not promising, with coughing very obtrusive; but then, with the atmosphere of the Musikvereinsaal caught more vividly than in most modern recordings, the magnetism of Walter becomes irresistible in music which he was the first ever to perform. Ensemble is often scrappy in the first movement, but intensity is unaffected; even at its flowing speed, the finale brings warmth and repose with no feeling of haste. The new Dutton transfer (transferred direct from 78-r.p.m. shellac discs) can do little about the audience noises, but the sound-balance is further enhanced over the EMI transfer (CDH7 63029-2), and the last movement in particular offers amazingly natural and believable string-sound.

Giulini's 1977 version lacks the very quality one expects of him: dedication. He sets tempi that are a shade too measured for a sense of impetus to assert itself. The orchestral playing is of the highest quality and the Chicago recording is impressive too, though its element of glamour does not help in conveying hushed concentration. This reappears as a DG Double, but Barbirolli manages to get the work on a single CD at mid-price, so Giulini also costs more.

Under Michael Halász the Polish Radio Orchestra of Katowice plays with the polish and finesse that also mark its Mahler recordings with Antoni Wit. But only in the long, slow finale does the performance convey the tensions of live communication, thanks largely to the heartfelt yet poised playing from the rich-toned strings. In the first movement the wind soloists are the most successful, with the chill of the flute solo in the coda beautifully set against the ripe tone of the oboe. Both there and in the middle movements Halász's rhythmic control is a little staid so that, for all the precision of the virtuoso Scherzo, it lacks excitement. Whatever the reservations, with full if slightly distanced sound, this might be considered in the lower price-range, although Karajan's mid-priced DG Double set offers a generous bonus of Lieder and is an altogether better proposition for bargain-hunters.

Symphony No. 10 in F sharp (Unfinished) (revised performing edition by Deryck Cooke).

(B) **(*) Decca Double Dig. 444 872-2 (2) [(M) id. import]. Berlin RSO, Chailly – SCHOENBERG: *Verklärte Nacht*. **

Reissued at bargain price on this Double Decca, Chailly's Decca version is superbly recorded and his grasp of the musical structure is keen. The Berlin Radio Orchestra is highly responsive, although the internal tension of the music-making is not as high as in Rattle's version (at full price).

LIEDER AND SONG-CYCLES

Kindertotenlieder.

(M) (**) Decca (IMS) mono 425 995-2. Kathleen Ferrier, Concg. O, Klemperer – BRAHMS: *Liebeslieder Waltzes*. (***)

(i–ii) *Kindertotenlieder;* (iii) *Des knaben Wunderhorn,* excerpts: (*Revelge; Wer hat dies Liedlein erdacht?; Der Tamboursg'sell; Des Antonius von Padua Fishpredigt; Wo die schönen Trompeten blasen*); (i–ii) *Lieder eines fahrenden Gesellen;* (iv) *Das Lied von der Erde;* (i; v) *5 Rückert Lieder*.

(B) **(*) EMI Rouge et Noir Analogue/Dig. CZS5 69665-2 (2) [CDZB 69665]. (i) Dame Janet Baker; (ii) Hallé O, Barbirolli; (iii) Lucia Popp, Bernd Weikl, LPO, Tennstedt; (iv) Murray Dickie, Dietrich Fischer-Dieskau, Philh. O, Kletzki; (v) New Philh. O, Barbirolli.

(i) *Kindertotenlieder;* (ii) *Lieder eines fahrenden Gesellen*.

(BB) *(*) Belart 461 341-2 [(M) id. import]. Marilyn Horne, (i) RPO, Henry Lewis; (ii) LAPO, Zubin Mehta – WAGNER: *Wesendonk Lieder*. *(*)

(i) *Kindertotenlieder; Lieder eines fahrenden Gesellen;* (ii) *5 Rückert Lieder*.

(BB) *** Naxos Dig. 8.554156 [id.]. Bernadette Greevy, Nat. SO of Ireland, (i) James Fürst; (ii) Franz-Paul Decker.

Bernadette Greevy uses her opulent mezzo, firm and even, to bring out the lyrical beauty of Mahler's writing in all three of these orchestral song-cycles. She may lack a degree of vitality in such a song as the second of the *Wayfaring Lad* cycle, the song that gave Mahler his first theme in his *First Symphony*, but her poise in such a great song as the Rückert setting, *Ich bin der Welt abhanden gekommen*, is most satisfying, readily compensating for any lack of emotional weight compared with the finest interpretations. On the disc that song is placed third in the series of five and not – as is more usual – at the end. The Irish National Symphony Orchestra play with rich, velvety tone in every section, not least the strings, matching the soloist, helped by the warmly atmospheric recording, made in the National Concert Hall in Dublin.

With recordings made over a period of more than two decades, this EMI Rouge et Noir set makes a fascinating if uneven anthology. At its centre (divided between the two discs) are the three indispensable contributions from Dame Janet Baker and Barbirolli, recorded in the late 1960s: the *Kindertotenlieder*, *Lieder eines fahrenden Gesellen* and the five *Rückert Lieder*. Their collaboration represents the affectionate approach to Mahler at its warmest, singing and playing intensely beautiful with breathtaking moments. The spontaneous feeling of both soloist and conductor comes over as at a live performance and brings out the tenderness to a unique degree. *Das Lied von der Erde* (1959), which opens the collection, is chiefly valuable for the singing of Fischer-Dieskau, a thoughtful and imaginative interpretation to justify this alternative use of the male voice. His partner, Murray Dickie, does not have the Heldentenor quality required, but the recording-balance helps him, and Kletzki's reading, with the Philharmonia at its peak, has colour and imagination in plenty. Vintage recording, with plenty of ambience to match the vintage playing. However, the excerpts from Tennstedt's (1986) digital *Wunderhorn* are even more uneven. Weikl makes the major contribution in these five excerpts. But Popp, more aptly characterful, sings *Wer hat dies Liedlein erdacht?* charmingly and is very touching indeed in *Wo die schönen Trompeten blasen*.

The Ferrier version with Klemperer is a live recording taken from a broadcast in July 1951, some two years after her EMI recording with Bruno Walter. Though the voice is caught vividly and the richness of her interpretation has, if anything, intensified, the surface-hiss is daunting. Unusually coupled with the Brahms in which Ferrier's role is only incidental.

Marilyn Horne's singing of the *Kindertotenlieder* (in 1969) has a statuesque quality that does not suit Mahler's intensely personal inspiration. There is much to admire: the recording-balance is good and the voice is always beautiful, but tenderness is completely missing. The *Lieder eines fahrenden Gesellen*, recorded a decade later, are equally disappointing. Here the unevenness of Horne's vocal production is exaggerated by the close balance, and that balance undermines any refinement in the orchestral accompaniment, notably so in the third song, *Ich hab' ein glühend Messer*.

Kindertotenlieder; 3 Rückert Lieder (Ich atmet einen linden Duft; Ich bin der Welt abhanden gekommen; Um Mitternacht).

(B) *** Sony SBK 63039 [id.]. Jennie Tourel, NYPO, Bernstein – WALTON: *Belshazzar's Feast*. ***

Jennie Tourel was in excellent voice when she recorded these Mahler songs at the beginning of the 1960s. The three Rückert songs are particularly beautiful and, with Bernstein providing warmly affectionate accompaniments, this is one of her finest recordings. It is a pity that the new coupling is inappropriate, although it is most enjoyable.

Das klagende Lied: complete *(Part 1, Waldmärchen; Part 2: Der Spielmann; Part 3, Hochzeitsstücke).*

(M) **(*) Sony SMK 45841 [id.]. Hoffman, Söderström, Haefliger, Nienstedt, Lear, Burrows, LSO, Boulez.

Boulez is a distinctive Mahlerian. His clear ear concentrates on precision of texture, but the atmospheric ambience adds warmth despite the forward balance, which also ensures very little difference in sound between the two recordings. Certainly the chill at the heart of this gruesome story of the days of chivalry and knights in armour is the more sharply conveyed. *Waldmärchen* is less effective than the rest. Good singing from the chorus, less good from the soloists.

(i) *Des Knaben Wunderhorn;* (ii) *Lieder eines fahrenden Gesellen.*

(B) **(*) Carlton IMP PCD 2020 [(M) id.]. (i) Dame Janet Baker, Sir Geraint Evans, LPO; (ii) Roland Hermann, Symphonica of L.; (i; ii) Wyn Morris.

(B) *(*) [EMI Red Line CDR5 69862]. (i) Popp, Weikl, LPO, Tennstedt; (ii) Thomas Allen, ECO, Tate.

Dame Janet and Sir Geraint recorded Mahler's cycle in 1966 for Delysé, long before they both received the royal accolade. This was also Wyn Morris's first major essay in the recording studio; though he secures crisp playing from the LPO, the orchestral phrasing could ideally show more affection and be less metrical in charming songs that need some coaxing. Dame Janet in particular turns her phrases with characteristic imagination, and her flexibility is not always matched by the orchestra. Baker could hardly be more ideally cast, but Sir Geraint is more variable. However, it is good to have this recording available again at mid-price. Roland Hermann's performance of the *Lieder eines fahrenden Gesellen* is fresh, committed and intelligent, though his baritone is not always flattered by the otherwise atmospheric stereo.

Tennstedt's version of *Des Knaben Wunderhorn*, very forwardly recorded, is disappointing, too unrelenting as a performance and with flawed singing. Bernd Weikl's gruff baritone, never sweet on record, is here used at times in a forced, almost cabaret style more fitting for Kurt Weill. Popp, pointing the Ländler rhythms of the lighter songs charmingly, is not helped either by the close balance. Thomas Allen is much more successful in the *Lieder eines fahrenden Gesellen*, but this is not a disc to recommend with any enthusiasm.

Das Lied von der Erde.
(M) *** Ph. 432 279-2. Dame Janet Baker, James King, Concg. O, Haitink.
(M) *** DG 419 058-2. Christa Ludwig, René Kollo, BPO, Karajan.
(M) **(*) Sony SMK 64455 [id.]. Mildred Miller, Ernst Haefliger, NYPO, Bruno Walter.
(B) **(*) DG 439 471-2. Nan Merriman, Ernst Haefliger, Concg. O, Jochum.
(M) ** Decca 452 301-2 [417 783-2]. Fischer-Dieskau, King, VPO, Bernstein.
(B) ** EMI CfP CD-CFP 6031. Alfreda Hodgson, John Mitchinson, SNO, Gibson.
(BB) ** Naxos Dig. 8.550933 [id.]. Ruxandra Donose, Thomas Harper, Nat. SO of Ireland, Michael Halász.

(i) *Das Lied von der Erde;* (ii) *Des Knaben Wunderhorn;* (iii) *Kindertotenlieder; Lieder eines fahrenden Gesellen.*
(B) *** Ph. Duo 454 014-2 (2) [(M) id. import]. (i) Baker, King; (ii) Jessye Norman, John Shirley-Quirk; (iii) Hermann Prey; Concg. O, Haitink.

The combination of this most deeply committed of Mahler singers with Haitink, the most thoughtfully dedicated of Mahler conductors, also produces radiantly beautiful and moving results, helped by refined and atmospheric recording. James King cannot match his solo partner, often failing to create fantasy, but his singing is intelligent and sympathetic. However, this version – vividly re-transferred – is now additionally offered on a Philips Duo set, coupled with Mahler's three other key song-cycles, and as such is very tempting. In *Des Knaben Wunderhorn* the singing of both Jessye Norman and John Shirley-Quirk brings out the purely musical imagination of Mahler at his finest, while Haitink's accompaniments are refined and satisfying, especially when the 1976 analogue sound is vividly atmospheric. Hermann Prey's performances of *Kindertotenlieder* and the *Lieder eines fahrenden Gesellen* are fresh and intelligent, and the colour of the baritone voice brings a darkness of timbre which is especially poignant, as in the third song of the *Wayfaring lad* cycle. Haitink's accompaniments are again understanding, yet they create urgency through the briskness of the chosen tempi. If in the last instance Prey cannot quite match Fischer-Dieskau or indeed Dame Janet Baker (see above) in intensity of expression, these performances are still estimable, and the Philips recording (from 1970) is of very high quality – the effect is most beautiful.

Though Bruno Walter's 1960 New York version does not have the tear-laden quality in the final *Abschied* that made his earlier Vienna account (in mono) with Kathleen Ferrier unique, that is the only serious shortcoming. Haefliger sparkles with imagination and Miller is a warm and appealing mezzo soloist, lacking only the last depth of feeling you find in a Ferrier or Janet Baker; and the maestro himself has rarely sounded so happy on record, even in Mahler. The remastered recording has been freshly remastered for the Bruno Walter Edition and now has even more vivid detail.

Generally Jochum avoided conducting Mahler – as a Brucknerian, underlining the point that these massive masters of symphony are totally contrasted. His reading of *Das Lied*, beautiful and compelling as it is, helps to explain why, for it speaks of the radiant calm of the Bruckner temperament rather than of Mahlerian tensions. Excellent solo singing and fine, clean recording, vivid and kind to the voices: worth considering at bargain price.

Bernstein's 1966 recording brings tempi which, although personal, are only occasionally wilful, nearly always suiting the music naturally, so that the tenor songs sparkle as they should and, though the final *Abschied*, taken at a very slow tempo indeed, puts extra strain on everybody, Bernstein's intensity carries the performance through. Doubts do arise over the soloists. James King is a strong-voiced tenor, but his phrasing and word-pointing at times sound comparatively stiff. Fischer-Dieskau is as sensitive as ever, but it is doubtful whether even he can match the finest contralto in the role, for one needs a lightening of tone in the even-numbered songs rather than – as here – a darkening. Nor can a baritone voice give quite such precision to the notes which Mahler's rounded melodies clearly need. John Culshaw produced and the Decca engineers gave Bernstein a ravishing recording aura in the Sofiensaal in which the sound of the Vienna Philharmonic was ravishingly beautiful. However, for once the remastering for Decca's Classic Sound series is not entirely flattering: there is no lack of body and warmth, but the resonant focus is not always absolutely refined.

With good, modern, digital recording, Sir Alexander Gibson's low-key but dedicated performance has certain advantages; though the playing of the SNO is not always as refined as in rival versions, the soloists are both impressive. John Mitchinson more clearly has the measure of the outward-going tenor songs and, though Alfreda Hodgson does not convey the last degree of heartfelt tenderness in the contralto songs, hers is a beautiful voice, finely controlled.

Michael Halász conducts the excellent Irish orchestra in a fresh and crisp account of *Das Lied*, helped by two clear-toned soloists and vivid recording. The American tenor, Thomas Harper, has ample power and a free-ranging top with no Heldentenor bark, while the Romanian mezzo, Ruxandra Donose, is firm, fresh and young-sounding, equally clear in her sensitive moulding of phrase. The first five songs are admirably done, even if the word-pointing could at times be more characterful. Only in the long final *Abschied* does one feel that the performance lacks the dark intensity needed. Beautiful as it is, with polished ensemble, it remains a lightweight reading, too easy in its emotions. Nevertheless, at Naxos price it remains a fair bargain recommendation.

(i) *Das Lied von der Erde;* (ii) *5 Rückert Lieder*.

(B) **(*) Sony SBK 53518; *SBT 53518* [id.]. (i) Lilli Chookasian, Richard Lewis, Philadelphia O, Ormandy; (ii) Frederika von Stade, LPO, Andrew Davis.

A coupling for *Das Lied* is rare enough, but so generous a one as the *Rückert Lieder* on a bargain-label issue is worth investigating. Ormandy conducts a purposeful, superbly played reading, dating from 1966, that may lack something in Mahlerian magic but which, with fine solo singing, carries you magnetically through to the final climax. Richard Lewis is by his standards sometimes a little rough in tone, but his perception is unfailing, and Lilli Chookasian's warm, weighty mezzo, with vibrato well controlled, brings poise and gravity to her songs, not least the final *Abschied*. Frederika von Stade makes a characterful soloist in the *Rückert Lieder*, sometimes colouring the voice too heavily; but, with fine bloom on the 1976 sound, she brings out ravishing tonal contrasts, helped by Andrew Davis's sympathetic accompaniment.

(i) *Das Lied von der Erde. 2 Rückert Lieder:* (ii) *Ich atmet' einen linden Duft;* (iii) *Ich bin der Welt abhanden gekommen*. (iv) *Symphony No. 5: Adagietto*.

(B) (***) Dutton Lab. mono CDEA 5014 [(M) id.]. (i; iii) Thorborg; (i–ii) Kullman; (i; iii–iv) VPO, Walter; (ii) O, Sargent.

This is the first of the two great pioneering recordings of Mahler, made in the mid-1930s by Bruno Walter with the Vienna Philharmonic. As with the *Ninth Symphony* two years later, it was a live recording, made in the Musikverein. Here, as in the symphony, the intensity and concentration of the performance are heightened, making this one of the supreme accounts of this now much-recorded score. It is arguably even finer than Walter's later recording for Decca with Kathleen Ferrier, though ensemble is not always crisp, and audience noises intrude. The soloists here are excellent, both with clear, firm voices that convey full expressiveness without strain. The recording is drier than the later one of the *Ninth Symphony*, but voices are very well caught, and the Dutton transfer does wonders in improving the orchestral sound. The generous fill-ups are also welcome. *Ich bin der Welt abhanden gekommen* with Thorborg was recorded from the same concert as the main work, while the other Rückert setting – using an English translation – was recorded by Kullmann in 1938 with Sargent conducting for the twentieth-century volume of the Columbia History of Music. Walter's 1938 studio recording of the *Adagietto* from the *Fifth Symphony* is fascinating for being so much faster than latter-day readings, while still conveying total repose.

Marais, Marin (1656–1728)

L'Arabesque; Le Badinage; Le Labyrinthe; Prélude in G; La Rêveuse; Sonnerie de Sainte Geneviève du Mont de Paris; Suite in G; Tombeau pour Monsieur de Sainte-Colombe.

(BB) *** Naxos Dig. 8.550750 [id.]. Spectre de la Rose – SAINTE-COLOMBE: *Le Retour* etc. ***

Naxos have stepped in enterprisingly and chosen a programme that is not only most attractive in its own right, but which also includes the key items used in the fascinating conjectural film about the relationship between Marin Marais and his reclusive mentor, Sainte-Columbe (*Tous les matins du monde*). Spectre de la Rose consists of a first-rate group of young players using original instruments (not that a viola da gamba could be anything else), led by Alison Crum, who plays in a dignified but austere style which at first seems cool but which is very effective in this repertoire. *Le Badinage* is perhaps a little stiff and unsmiling, but the key item, Marais's eloquent lament for his teacher, *Tombeau pour Monsieur de Sainte-Colombe*, is restrained and touching. Good, bright, forward recording, vividly declaiming the plangent viola da gamba timbre. But be careful not to play this record at too high a volume setting.

La Gamme en forme de petit opéra; Sonata à la marésienne.
(B) *** HM Musique d'Abord Dig. HMX 2901105 [id.]. L. Baroque, Charles Medlam.

This bargain reissue (which at the time of going to press is packaged in a slipcase and includes a Musique d'Abord complete catalogue) is a thoroughly entertaining way of entering the world of Marin Marais. *La Gamme* is a string of short character-pieces for violin, viola de gamba and harpsichord that takes its inspiration from the ascending and descending figures of the scale. Although it is '*en forme de petit opéra*', its layout is totally instrumental and the varied pieces and dramatic shifts of character doubtless inspire the title. The *Sonata à la marésienne* also has variety and character. The London Baroque is an excellent group, and they are well recorded too.

Pièces en trio: Les Contrefaiseurs (for descant recorder, violin, viola da gamba & continuo). *6 Suites* – edited into *10 Suites: in B flat* (for oboe, viola da gamba & continuo); *in B flat* (for treble recorder, oboe, viola da gamba & continuo); *in C* (for treble recorder, violin, oboe, viola da gamba & continuo); *in C* (for treble recorder, oboe, viola da gamba & continuo); *in C min.* (for treble recorder, violin, viola da gamba & continuo); *in D* (for voice flute, descant recorder, violin, oboe, viola da gamba & continuo); *in D min.* (for oboe, viola da gamba & continuo); *in E min.* (for voice flute, violin, oboe, viola da gamba & continuo); *in G min.* (for recorder, violin, oboe, viola da gamba & continuo); *in G min.* (for treble recorder, violin, viola da gamba and continuo).
(M) **(*) Virgin/EMI Veritas Dig. VMD5 61365-2 (2). Musica Pacifica.

Marin Marais is a sophisticated and subtle composer whose music deserves more than just specialist attention. He was a great master of the gamba, in which his innate melancholy found a natural outlet. Indeed the *Suite in C minor* here ends with a slow *Passacaglia* which he entitled *La désolée*. These ten suites are arranged by the performers here from the composer's collection of six *Pièces en trio pour le flute, violon et dessus de viole avec b. c.* (basso continuo) which were published in Paris in 1692. For instance, some of the movements in the *E minor Suite* have been transposed down to make a *D minor Suite* and suit the chosen instrumentation. In addition, extra movements have been added elsewhere, taken from a manuscript collection of chamber trios by Lully and Marais (*Trios pour le coucher du Roy*) which almost certainly belong to Marais. Regarding instrumentation, the performances (as can be seen from the listings above) are sometimes presented '*en symphonie*', with multiple doublings of the treble line, as was sometimes the practice at the time. The title-page of Marais's original manuscript is decorated not only with recorders and string instruments but also with flutes and oboes, and the choice of instrumentation for the present recording endeavours to bring as much colour and variety to the music as possible, with the opening *Préludes* and closing *Passacaglias* or *Chaconnes* given a 'tutti' treatment. The continuo, too, is varied, using gamba, archlute and harpsichord. The music is often doleful in its expressive feeling, but it needs all the advocacy it can get: it would be idle to pretend that it always commands attention. Unlike some of Marais's gamba writing, these suites are of limited musical interest and belong among that repertoire which it is more rewarding to play than to hear. Some might feel that to stretch out the available music to fill a pair of CDs (136 minutes) was too much of a good thing! However, this Virgin Veritas set arrives opportunely to replace a recently deleted Teldec single-CD recording of the original six suites by the Quadro Hotteterre, and aficionados can be assured of the refinement and expertise of both playing and recording.

Marcello, Alessandro (1669–1747)

6 Oboe concertos (La Cetra).
(M) *** DG (IMS) 427 137-2. Heinz Holliger, Louise Pellerin, Camerata Bern, Füri.

The six concertos of *La Cetra* reveal a pleasing mixture of originality and convention; often one is surprised by a genuinely alive and refreshing individuality. These performances are vital and keen, full of style and character, and the recording is faithful and well projected.

Oboe concerto in D min.

(BB) **(*) Naxos Dig. 8.550556 [id.]. József Kiss, Ferenc Erkel CO – C. P. E. BACH: *Concertos*. **(*)

This enjoyable concerto, once attributed (in a different key) to Benedetto Marcello, is given a good performance here by József Kiss and is very well recorded. One might have preferred more dynamic contrast from the soloist, but his timbre is right for baroque music and he plays with plenty of spirit. This disc is well worth its modest cost for the C. P. E. Bach couplings.

Marenzio, Luca (1553–99)

Madrigals: Book VI: *Se quel dolor* (madrigal-cycle in 6 voices); Book VII: *Care mie selve; Cruda Amarilli; Questa vaghi concenti.*

(B) **(*) HM Dig. HMC 90856.58 [(M) id. import]. Ens. Clément Jannequin, Dominique Visse – BANCHIERI: *Barca di Venetia per Padova;* LASSUS; VECCHI: *Madrigal comedies*. ***

It is appropriate that Banchieri's comic dramatized account of a trip on *A boat from Venice to Padua* should be coupled with a group of these much more serious madrigals by Marenzio, for an affectionate pastiche of a work by his older contemporary is featured by Banchieri as an elegant centrepiece of the journey. Marenzio's *Cruda Amarilli* is justly celebrated, but the other settings here also carry the aristocratic lines and eloquent pathos which are the hallmark of Marenzio's writing. Indeed one might feel that the 23-minute ten-part cycle, *Se quel dolor*, an unrelieved expression of dolour over hopelessly unrequited love, is too much of a good thing. The singing here is given added colour and warmth by a judicious instrumental accompaniment, but more subtlety in the matter of light and shade within the continually flowing lines would have been welcome. However, this Banchieri/Marenzio programme comes as part of a Harmonia Mundi CD Trio of *'Comédies madrigalesques'* which is well worth exploring. Good documentation with full translations.

Madrigals: *Come inanti de l'alba; Crudele acerba; Del cibo onde il signor; Giunto a la tomba; Rimanti inpace; Sola angioletta* (sestina); *Strider faceva; Tirsi morir volea; Venuta era; Vezzosi augelli.*

(B) *** HM Musique d'Abord HMA 1901065 [id.]. Concerto Vocale, René Jacobs.

Luca Marenzio enjoyed an enormous reputation during his lifetime, particularly in England, and this record gives an altogether admirable picture of his breadth and range. There are poignant and expressive pieces such as *Crudele, acerba*, from the last year of his life, which is harmonically daring, and lighter pastoral madrigals such as *Strider faceva* and the more ambitious sestina, *Sola angioletta*, which this excellent group of singers, occasionally supported by theorbo and lute, project to striking effect. Fine singing and recording and a modest price serve to make this a most desirable issue.

Martin, Frank (1890–1974)

Concerto for 7 wind instruments, percussion and strings; Passacaglia; Petite symphonie concertante for harp, harpsichord, piano & double string orchestra.

(M) **(*) Dinemic Dig. DCCD 012 [id.]. Geneva CO, Thierry Fischer.

This Geneva account of the *Petite symphonie concertante* is more atmospheric and spacious than the performance directed by the composer himself. In fact this is the best reading (as opposed to performance) now before the public. The balance is not ideal (the piano looms far too large in the aural picture *vis-à-vis* the other soloists) and the strings sound under-strength. Thierry Fischer has recorded the *Concerto for seven wind instruments* before with the Chamber Orchestra of Europe on DG and, although this is not quite as distinguished, it is very good indeed – and a good deal cheaper. The soloists and orchestra are better balanced than in the *Petite symphonie concertante*. In the gravely eloquent *Passacaglia* one also feels the need for a greater body of string-tone. Make no mistake, however: these are all perceptive performances and are well recorded. Excellent value.

(i) *Cello concerto. The Four elements.*

(M) *** Preludio PRL 2147 [id.]. (i) Jean Decroos; Concg. O, Haitink.

Jean Decroos, from the first desk of the Concertgebouw, gives an impressive account of the *Cello concerto* and Haitink secures excellent playing from the Concertgebouw Orchestra. *The Four elements* is another Martin rarity, rich in invention and imaginative resource: its neglect is little short of scandalous. Both performances were recorded at public concerts in 1965 and 1970 respectively, but audience noise is minimal and the quality first rate.

(i; ii) *Violin concerto;* (ii) *Concerto for 7 wind instruments, timpani, percussion & strings; Etudes for strings;* (iii) *Passacaglia for strings;* (ii; iv) *Petite symphonie concertante for harp, harpsichord, piano & double string orchestra;* (ii; v) *In terra pax* (oratorio).

(B) (***) Decca Double mono/stereo 448 264-2 (2) [(M) id. import]. (i) Schneiderhan; (ii) SRO, Ansermet; (iii) Stuttgart CO, Münchinger; (iv) Jamet, Vaucher-Clerc, Rossiaud; (v) Buckel, Höffgen, Haefliger, Mollet, Stämpfli, Union Ch. & Lausanne Women's Ch.

This set contains not only the pioneering record of the *Petite symphonie concertante* but also Schneiderhan's superb (1955) performance of the *Violin concerto*, often ethereal in its beauty. Both performances have a concentration and atmosphere that have rarely been matched since. The 1951 recording of the *Petite symphonie concertante* brings a thin edge to the upper string timbre, which seems to be emphasized by the CD transfer; the *Violin concerto*, however, sounds much better, with Schneiderhan's gloriously pure timbre captured very naturally. The other orchestral recordings are vivid enough, and Münchinger's shaping of the powerful, 12-minute *Passacaglia* shows him at his most concentrated and the Stuttgart strings in excellent form. *In terra pax* is a 1963 stereo recording. The oratorio was commissioned by the Swiss Radio in preparation for the end of the 1939–45 war and it was first performed by Ansermet. Martin's music has an appropriate eloquence and spirituality, and he is admirably served by his fine soloists. The score falls into four short sections, all with biblical texts, and its sincerity and sense of compassion leave a strong impression. No complaints about the sound here.

Petite symphonie concertante.

(M) **(*) EMI CDM5 65868-2 [id.]. SO, Stokowski – HINDEMITH: *Mathis der Maler* **(*); TOCH: *Symphony No. 3.* ***

Stokowski's preoccupation with sonorities pays good dividends here as this work contains an attractive diversity of themes and, although the early stereo lacks something in opulence, he still manages to spin a full texture in the slow movement, whereas elsewhere detail is very clear. The sound is spacious too, and there is no lack of intensity. But the main interest of this CD is the splendid Toch *Symphony*.

Martinů, Bohuslav (1890–1959)

Violin concertos Nos. 1–2; Rhapsody concerto for viola and orchestra.

(M) **(*) Sup. 11 1969-2 [id.] Josef Suk, Czech PO, Václav Neumann.

The *Second Violin concerto* was written for Mischa Elman, who had heard and liked the *First Symphony* and immediately commissioned a concerto. It is an appealing and inventive score and of greater substance than its predecessor from the 1930s, which came to light only in the early 1970s; it finds Martinů very much in concerto-grosso mode. It is resourceful nevertheless, and Josef Suk is the only violinist so far to record it. By far the most poignant and eloquent of these three works is the *Rhapsody-concerto* for viola and orchestra, in which Suk is also the soloist and which dates from the period of the *Fantaisies symphoniques*. Suk is a masterly player, of course, and the Czech Philharmonic play with obvious pleasure. The recordings are analogue and inner detail is not quite as sharply focused as in the very best discs from the 1970s; at mid-price, however, this is quite competitive.

(i) *Concerto for 2 pianos and orchestra. 3 Czech dances; Fantasie.*

(B) ** Carlton Classics Dig. 30367 01732 [(M) id.]. Joshua Pierce & Dorothy Jonas, with (i) Luxembourg R. and TV SO, Stratta – BRITTEN: *Scottish Ballad.* **

Like Britten's *Scottish ballad*, with which it is coupled, Martinů's *Concerto for two pianos*, formidably difficult technically, was written for the popular piano duo of Ethel Bartlett and Rae Robertson. It is a brightly energetic piece with a dark central *Adagio* which in its neo-classical sharpness keeps echoing Stravinsky, and with an exuberant finale full of cross-rhythms. In a well-played performance here it is most welcome, though it is not helped by the shallow recorded sound. The other two pieces, for two pianos alone, come from different periods in Martinů's career. The *Fantasie* of 1929, like the concerto, brings Stravinskian echoes in its neo-classical motor-rhythms, while the *Czech dances* from 1949 are more openly lyrical, though with touches of Poulenc's *Scaramouche*.

Symphonies Nos. 1–6 (Fantaisies symphoniques).
(M) *** Sup. 11 0382-2 (3) [id.]. Czech PO, Václav Neumann.
(BB) * Naxos Dig. 8.553348 [id.]. Ukraine Nat. SO, Fagen.

Martinů always draws a highly individual sound from his orchestra and secures great clarity, even when the score abounds in octave doublings. Neumann's set was recorded in the Dvořák Hall of the House of Artists, Prague, between January 1976 (No. 6) and 1978 (No. 5). The transfers to CD are excellently done: the sound is full, spacious and bright; it has greater presence and better definition than the original LPs, yet with no edginess in the strings. Václav Neumann's performances have an impressive breadth and, though there could be more urgency and fire in places, the readings have life, colour and impetus, and are thoroughly compelling when the Czech orchestra play so vividly.

Carefully prepared but not wholly idiomatic accounts of these marvellous symphonies. One senses that the players are not really familiar with this music, though Arthur Fagen certainly guides them through the terrain with skill. The *Fantaisies symphoniques* calls for orchestral playing of effortless virtuosity (it was written for Charles Munch and the Boston Symphony) which this ensemble does not really command. The recordings are decently balanced and made in a good, resonant (but not over-resonant) studio. Not really recommendable.

Symphonies Nos. 3–4.
(M) **(*) Sup. 11 1967-2 011. Czech PO, Václav Neumann.

The Supraphon recordings were made in the 1970s and are analogue. No harm in that, of course, though the sound is a little diffuse and wanting in detail. The performances are good. Those not wanting to pay more will find these (as one would expect) thoroughly idiomatic accounts.

Oboe quartet (for oboe, violin, cello & piano); *Piano quartet; String quintet; Viola sonata.*
(BB) *** Naxos 8.553916 [id.]. Artists of 1994 Australian Festival of Chamber Music.

The best thing here is the captivating *Oboe quartet*, which is quite a discovery. Like the fine *Viola sonata* and the early *String quintet* whose slow movement is crossed by the shadow of Martinů's master, Roussel, it is not otherwise represented. Its appearance at budget price is doubly welcome in that the performances are lively and spirited and the recording eminently natural. The wartime *Piano quartet No. 1* is in the catalogue, coupled with the Suk *Piano quartet*, but that CD is currently at full price. The *Oboe quartet* is a must, not only for special admirers of the composer but for the wider musical public too.

Variations on a Slovak folksong.
(BB) *** ASV Quicksilva Dig. CDQS 6218 [id.]. Bernard Gregor-Smith, Yolande Wrigley – PROKOFIEV; SHOSTAKOVICH: *Cello sonatas;* JANACEK: *Pohádka.* ***

The *Variations on a Slovak folksong* are not top-drawer Martinů, considering that they come from his last year, in many ways a vintage period. The husband-and-wife team of Bernard Gregor-Smith and Yolande Wrigley gives a lively and persuasive account of it and, even if the piano is slightly too prominent, the recording is lively and fresh.

Mascagni, Pietro (1863–1945)

Cavalleria rusticana (complete).
(M) *** RCA 74321 39500-2. Scotto, Domingo, Elvira, Amb. Op. Ch., Nat. PO, Levine.
(M) **(*) EMI CMS7 63967-2 (2). De los Angeles, Corelli, Sereni, Rome Op. Ch. & O, Santini – LEONCAVALLO: *Pagliacci.* ***
(M) **(*) Decca 425 985-2 [id.]. Tebaldi, Bjoerling, Bastianini, Maggio Musicale Fiorentino Ch. & O, Erede.
(M) **(*) EMI CMS7 63650-2 (2). Caballé, Carreras, Hamari, Manuguerra, Varnay, Amb. Op. Ch., Southend Boys' Ch., Philh. O, Muti – LEONCAVALLO: *I Pagliacci.* **(*)
(M) (***) RCA mono GD 86510 [RCA 6510-2-RG]. Milanov, Bjoerling, Merrill, Robert Shaw Chorale, RCA O, Cellini.
(B) **(*) Naxos Dig. 8.660022 [id.]. Evstatieva, Aragall, Tumagian, Di Mauro, Michalková, Slovak Philh. Ch., Czech RSO, Rahbari – LEONCAVALLO: *I Pagliacci.* **(*)
(B) ** Decca Double 452 179-2 (2) [(M) id. import]. Souliotis, Del Monaco, Gobbi, Malagù, Rome Opera Ch. & O, Varviso – LEONCAVALLO: *I Pagliacci.* **
(M) (**) Nimbus mono NI 7843/4 [id.]. Gigli, Bruna Rasa, Marcucci, Bechi, Simionato, La Scala Ch. & O, composer – LEONCAVALLO: *I Pagliacci.* (**(*))

(B) *(*) Ph. Duo 454 265-2 (2) [id.]. Obraztsova, Domingo, Barbieri, Bruson, Gall, La Scala, Milan, Ch. & O, Prêtre – LEONCAVALLO: *I Pagliacci*. *(*)

Now reissued at mid-price (pleasingly presented in a slip-case with libretto) in RCA's Opera Treasury series, this now stands as a clear first recommendation for Mascagni's red-blooded opera, with Domingo giving a heroic account of the role of Turiddù, full of defiance. Scotto is strongly characterful too, and James Levine directs with a splendid sense of pacing, by no means faster than his rivals (except the leisurely Karajan) and drawing red-blooded playing from the National Philharmonic. The recording is vivid and strikingly present in its CD transfer. At the time of going to press, this recording is not listed in the American *Schwann Catalogue*.

Though not as vibrant as Von Matačić's *Pagliacci* coupling, this beautifully sung, essentially lyrical Santini performance could give considerable satisfaction, provided the bitterness of Mascagni's drama is not a first consideration. Like the coupling, it shows Corelli in good form; both he and de los Angeles are given scope by Santini to produce soaring, Italianate singing of Mascagni's richly memorable melodies. The recording is suitably atmospheric.

The early (1957) Decca recording with Tebaldi offers a forthright, lusty account of Mascagni's piece of blood and thunder and has the distinction of three excellent soloists. Tebaldi is most moving in *Voi lo sapete*, and the firm richness of Bastianini's baritone is beautifully caught. As always, Bjoerling shows himself the most intelligent of tenors, and it is only the chorus that gives serious cause for disappointment; they are very undisciplined. The CD sound is strikingly bright and lively.

There are fewer unexpected textual points in Muti's EMI *Cav.* than in *Pag.*, but his approach is comparably biting and violent, brushing away the idea that this is a sentimental score, though running the risk of making it sound vulgar. The result is certainly refreshing, with Caballé – pushed faster than usual, even in her big moments – collaborating warmly. So *Voi lo sapete* is geared from the start to the final cry of *Io son dannata*, and she manages a fine snarl on *A te la mala Pasqua*. Carreras does not sound quite so much at home, though the rest of the cast is memorable, including the resonant Manuguerra as Alfio and the veteran Astrid Varnay as Mamma Lucia, wobble as she does. The recording is forward and vivid.

Admirers of Milanov will not want to miss her beautiful singing of *Voi lo sapete*, and in the duet Merrill's dark, firm timbre is thrilling. Bjoerling brings a good measure of musical and tonal subtlety to the role of Turiddù, normally belted out, while Cellini's conducting minimizes the vulgarity of the piece.

As in his parallel recording of *Pag.*, Alexander Rahbari conducts a red-blooded reading of *Cav.*, making it a first-rate budget choice. Stefka Evstatieva is a warmly vibrant Santuzza, well controlled, no Slavonic wobbler, and Giacomo Aragall as Turiddù, not quite as fresh-sounding as he once was, yet gives a strong, characterful performance, with Eduard Tumagian excellent as Alfio, firm and dark. Well-focused digital recording. This set is a real bargain.

As with the coupling centring on James McCracken's lusty portrayal of Canio, it is plain enough that Decca saw this Rome version as primarily a vehicle for Souliotis. Hers can be an exciting voice and she gives a very dramatic performance, but in many details it seems unfinished and, though the voice is characterful, it is not always under complete control. If Souliotis was caught rather too early for Santuzza, Gobbi was caught just in time as Alfio, and for that many thanks. He turns the conventional figure of the carter into a real, three-dimensional character. Mario del Monaco is not at his best, but neither is he at his coarsest – a fair enough big-voiced performance. Nor does Varviso's conducting emerge with any special individuality, though it is not slack; but with magificent vintage (1966) sound from the Decca engineers, the result is undeniably dramatic.

EMI's vintage (1940) version of *Cav.*, conducted by the composer with Gigli as Turiddù, came out on CD in an ungenerous two-disc package from EMI, and we await its reissue. It is good to have it again available on CD from Nimbus, along with the curious little speech of introduction that Mascagni himself recorded. Yet the composer's sluggish speeds mean that this opera has to start awkwardly at the end of the *Pag.* disc. Nimbus's transfer captures the voices well, giving them a mellow bloom, though the focus is not nearly as sharp as on the old EMI transfer, and the orchestral sound becomes muzzy.

Taken from the soundtrack of a Unitel television film (like the companion version of *Pag.*), the Prêtre set can be recommended to those who want a reminder of the film, and maybe also to those who want to hear Domingo in ringing voice; but otherwise the flaws rule it out as a serious contender. Obraztsova's massive and distinctive mezzo is certainly characterful but sounds edgy and uneven, hardly apt for the role. One or two moments are memorable – for example, the agonized utterance of the curse *A te la mala Pasqua*, not fire-eating at all – but she, like some of the others, equally unsteady, looked better than they sound. Fedora Barbieri, a veteran of veterans among mezzos, makes a token appearance as Mamma Lucia. The recording is full and atmospheric with the sound effects needed for television. Even at Duo price this is not very tempting, for the coupled *Pagliacci* is hardly more impressive. A brief synopsis is offered in lieu of a libretto.

Cavalleria rusticana: highlights.

(M) **(*) EMI CDM5 66048-2 [CDH 63933-2]. Caballé, Carreras, Varnay, Manuguerra, Hamari, Amb. Op. Ch., Philh. O, Muti – LEONCAVALLO: *I Pagliacci:* highlights. **(*)

Caballé is in good form here and receives good support from the rest of the cast. With Muti conducting strongly, this a recommendable sampler of a highly dramatic performance, vividly recorded.

Cavalleria rusticana (complete; in English).

(M) **(*) Chandos Dig. CHAN 3004 (2) [id.]. Miricioiu, O'Neill, Joll, Montague, Bainbridge, Geoffrey Mitchell Ch., LPO, David Parry.

As in other recordings sponsored by Peter Moores, notably those for Opera Rara, David Parry proves a deeply sympathetic conductor of Italian opera, with a natural feeling for expressive rubato. This is a warmly atmospheric reading of the Mascagni score which, as well as bringing out its atmospheric beauty, helped by opulent Chandos recording with fine bloom on the LPO strings, brings home the high drama, as in the big duet between Turiddu and Santuzza and at the very end. Nelly Miricioiu is an inspired choice to take the role of the heroine, her rich, vibrant voice firmly under control, with fine legato and passionately declaimed climaxes. Dennis O'Neill with his clear Italianate tone is also excellent as Turiddu, passionate and intense whether in the big emotional outbursts or in the playful *brindisi* at the end. It is good to hear the fruity and characterful Elizabeth Bainbridge as Mamma Lucia, and Diana Montague sings with creamy beauty in Lola's Song. The serious blot comes with the Alfio of Phillip Joll, most damagingly in the Carter's song, in which the voice is pitched so vaguely it is half-way to talking, with notes spreading under pressure. A pity, when the rest is so convincing.

Massenet, Jules (1842–1912)

Le Carillon (ballet): complete.

(B) *** Decca Double Dig. 444 836-2 (2) [id.]. SRO, Richard Bonynge – DELIBES: *Coppélia.* ***

Le Carillon was written in the same year as *Werther*. The villains of the story who try to destroy the bells of the title are punished by being miraculously transformed into bronze jaquemarts, fated to continue striking them for ever! The music of this one-act ballet makes a delightful offering – not always as lightweight as one would expect. With his keen rhythmic sense and feeling for colour, Bonynge is outstanding in this repertory, and the (1984) Decca recording is strikingly brilliant and colourful. A fine bonus (37 minutes) for a desirable version of Delibes' *Coppélia*, at the cheapest possible price.

Le Cid: ballet suite.

(B) *** Decca Double 448 095-2 (2) [(M) id. import]. New Philh. O, Richard Bonynge – DELIBES: *Sylvia* (complete). ***

(M) *** Decca 444 110-2. Nat. PO, Bonynge – MEYERBEER: *Les Patineurs* (with DELIBES: *Naïla*, LSO, Bonynge; THOMAS: *Hamlet: ballet music* ***).

Over the years, Decca have made a house speciality of recording the ballet music from *Le Cid* and coupling it with Constant Lambert's arrangement of Meyerbeer (*Les Patineurs*). Bonynge's version is the finest yet, with the most seductive orchestral playing, superbly recorded, with the remastering for CD adding to the glitter and colour of Massenet's often witty scoring, and made the more attractive at Double Decca price. For the single-disc reissue in Decca's Ballet Gala series, Delibes' charming *Naïla Intermezzo* (a dainty little valse) and the lively, easily melodic – if less distinctive – ballet from Act IV of Thomas's *Hamlet* have been added, played with characteristic flair.

(i) *Piano concerto in E flat. Papillons noirs, Papillons blancs; Devant la Madone; 10 Pièces de genre, Op. 10; Eau dormante; Eau courante; Musique pour 'bercer les petits enfants'; Toccata; Valse folle; Valse triste.*

(M) ** EMI CDM7 64277-2. Aldo Ciccolini, (i) Monte Carlo Nat. Op. O, Cambreling.

Massenet's *Piano concerto in E flat* has perhaps the manners of the Saint-Saëns but none of the flair, and though some of the genre pieces and certainly the two impromptus, *Eau dormante* and *Eau courante*, have a certain charm, this has greater curiosity than musical value. Aldo Ciccolini plays with conviction and is well supported in the concerto by Sylvain Cambreling and the Monte Carlo Opera Orchestra. The sound is a bit shallow, and the piano pieces are recorded rather closely in the Salle Wagram.

Hérodiade (ballet) *suite; Orchestral suites Nos. 1; 2 (Scènes hongroises); 3 (Scènes dramatiques).*
(BB) ** Naxos Dig. 8.553124 [id.]. New Zealand SO, Jean-Yves Ossonce.

The ballet suite from *Hérodiade* comes in the final scene of the opera and the five movements are nicely scored, including flutes and harp, delicate dancing strings, a luscious tune in the middle strings, decorated by chirpy woodwind, and a vigorous dance finale. The other orchestral suites are also well worth hearing, offering a further series of sharply memorable vignettes, demonstrating Massenet's ready store of tunes and his charmingly French orchestral palette. In the *Scènes hongroises* the charming *leggiero* second movement is followed by characteristic *risoluto* brass writing. The more histrionic *Scènes dramatiques* (with a Shakespearean inspiration) brings a touching and very balletic central *Mélodrame*, originally entitled *Le sommeil de Desdémone*. The playing of the New Zealand orchestra is first class, polished and vivid, and it is a pity that the microphones are somewhat close. The wind have plenty of colour, but the string tuttis are made to sound a bit tight and fierce.

Orchestral suites: *Scènes alsaciennes; Scènes de féerie; Scènes napolitaines; Scènes pittoresques.*
(BB) *** Naxos Dig. 8.553125 [id.]. New Zealand Symphony O, Jean-Yves Ossonce.

Massenet's orchestral suites are in essence picture-postcard music, but they include plenty of tunes (perhaps not always first-rate ones) and the scoring has characteristic Gallic charm and colour. Best known are the somewhat ingenuous *Scènes pittoresques* and the *Scènes alsaciennes*, evoking everything from Sunday morning to a hunting party – with ripe horn-calls – and even the military beating a retreat. But the most touching movement is the beautiful *Sous les tilleuls* ('Under the lime trees'), with its wilting dialogue between cello and clarinet, played here with an affectionate finesse worthy of a Beecham. The second of the *Scènes napolitaines* (*La procession*) opens with a solemn church bell (nicely managed) but has colourful secular interludes, before the bell returns and a lively galop takes over for the closing *Fête*. The *Scènes de féerie* introduce a *Ballet* sequence, again scored in the best French manner, and a mysterious *Apparition*, complete with romantic horn solo. Elsewhere, wind and string playing has striking polish. With full, sparkling, yet warmly atmospheric recording, this is a first-class disc in every way. Why pay more?

OPERA

(i) *Don Quixote* (complete); (ii) *Scènes alsaciennes.*
(M) *** Decca 430 636-2 (2) [id.]. (i) Ghiaurov, Bacquier, Crespin, SRO Ch. & O, Kord; (ii) Nat. PO, Bonynge.

Massenet's operatic adaptation of Cervantes' classic novel gave him his last big success. There is genuine nobility as well as comedy in the portrait of the knight, and that is well caught here by Ghiaurov, who refuses to exaggerate the characterization. Bacquier makes a delightful Sancho Panza, but it is Régine Crespin as a comically mature Dulcinée, who provides the most characterful singing, flawed vocally but commandingly positive. Kazimierz Kord directs the Suisse Romande Orchestra in a performance that is zestful and electrifying, and the recording is outstandingly clear and atmospheric. At mid-price the Decca set also comes with an attractive fill-up, the *Scènes alsaciennes*, brightly and colourfully presented by Bonynge and the National Philharmonic Orchestra.

Esclarmonde (complete).
(M) *** Decca 425 651-2 (3). Sutherland, Aragall, Tourangeau, Davies, Grant, Alldis Ch., Nat. PO, Bonynge.

Joan Sutherland is the obvious diva to encompass the demands of great range, great power and brilliant coloratura of the central role of *Esclarmonde*, and her performance is in its way as powerful as it is in Puccini's last opera. Aragall proves an excellent tenor, sweet of tone and intelligent, and the other parts are well taken too. Richard Bonynge draws passionate singing and playing from chorus and orchestra, and the recording has both atmosphere and spectacle to match the story, based on a medieval romance involving song-contests and necromancy.

La Navarraise (complete).
(M) *** RCA 74321 50167-2. Horne, Domingo, Milnes, Zaccaria, Bacquier, Ryland Davies, Amb. Op. Ch., LSO, Henry Lewis.

La Navarraise, a compact 'lyric episode' lasting barely 50 minutes, finds Massenet challenging the *verismo* school and succeeding convincingly. The flavour is a cross between *Carmen* and *Cavalleria rusticana*, with a touch of *Il tabarro*. To earn her dowry before marrying her beloved, the intrepid heroine penetrates the enemy lines in the Carlist wars and for money assassinates the royalist general's direct adversary. Following a misunderstanding, the hero follows her and is mortally wounded. In despair she promptly goes mad – a great deal of story for so short a piece. It says much for Massenet's dramatic powers that he makes the result as convincing as he does, and the score is full of splendid, atmospheric effects. It was produced in the same year as *Thaïs* (1894) with a première at Covent Garden. Massenet originally had a heavyweight, 'Carmen' voice in mind, and Marilyn Horne seems an apter choice for the role of heroine than her competitor on the CBS/Sony set (which is currently out of the catalogue). Even if her upper register is not as firm as it was, it remains an appealing performance, and Domingo is characteristically rich-toned. Henry Lewis conducts with a sense of the work's atmosphere and grandeur, and this is an opera ideally suited to the gramophone. The recording, made at Walthamstow in 1975, is appropriately spacious, if not always absolutely refined. The documentation for this reissue in the RCA Opera Treasury series is excellent, with a full libretto. This is not currently available in the USA.

Le Roi de Lahore (complete).

✿ (M) *** Decca (IMS) Dig. 433 851-2 (2) [id.]. Sutherland, Lima, Milnes, Ghiaurov, Morris, Tourangeau, L. Voices, Nat. PO, Bonynge.

Le Roi de Lahore was Massenet's first opera for the big stage of L'Opéra in Paris and marked a turning point in his career, even introducing the supernatural, with one Act set in the Paradise of Indra. The characters may be stock figures out of a mystic fairytale, but in the vigour of his treatment Massenet makes the result red-blooded in an Italianate way. This vivid performance under Bonynge includes passages added for Italy, notably a superb set-piece aria which challenges Sutherland to some of her finest singing. Sutherland may not be a natural for the role of the innocent young priestess, but she makes it a magnificent vehicle with its lyric, dramatic and coloratura demands. Luis Lima as the King is somewhat strained by the high tessitura, but his is a ringing tenor, clean of attack. Sherrill Milnes as the heroine's wicked uncle sounds even more Italianate, rolling his 'r's ferociously; but high melodrama is apt, and with digital recording of demonstration splendour and fine perspective this shameless example of operatic hokum could not be presented more persuasively on CD.

Thaïs (complete).

(M) ** EMI CMS5 65479-2 (2) [CDMB 654792]. Sills, Milnes, Gedda, Van Allan, John Alldis Ch., New Philh. O, Maazel.

Thaïs is an exotic period-piece, set in Egypt in the early Christian era, the story of a monk who seeks to save a beautiful courtesan and is himself destroyed. Sentimental as the plot is, it inspired Massenet to some of his characteristically mellifluous writing, with atmospheric choruses and sumptuous orchestration. Maazel's conducting is crisply dramatic (and he plays the violin solo himself most tastefully in the famous *Meditation*). The casting is good, except for the heroine. Beverly Sills has a bright, almost brittle voice, and here it sounds neither seductive nor idiomatic, for the unevenness of the production, already noticeable in earlier recordings, has grown more obtrusive. She is at her best as the reformed *Thaïs* in the later scenes. Sherrill Milnes is a powerful but conventional Athanaël and, though Nicolai Gedda as Nicias sings with his usual intelligence, it is not a young enough voice for the role. A good, warm recording, well transferred on to CD, and with a complete text and translation.

Werther (complete).

(M) **(*) EMI CMS7 63973-2 (2) [Ang. CDMB 63973]. Gedda, De los Angeles, Mesplé, Soyer, Voix d'Enfants de la Maîtrise de l'ORTF, O de Paris, Prêtre.

(M) ** EMI CMS5 66516-2 (2) [CDMB 665162]. Alfredo Kraus, Tatiana Troyanos, Matteo Manuguerra, Christine Barbaux, Ch. & LPO, Plasson.

Victoria de los Angeles's golden tones, which convey pathos so beautifully, are ideally suited to Massenet's gentle melodies and, though she is recorded too closely (closer than the other soloists), she makes an intensely appealing heroine. Gedda makes an intelligent romantic hero, though Prêtre's direction could be subtler.

It is sad that Alfredo Kraus, as a rule one of the most stylish of tenors, came to record *Werther* so late in his career. His account of *Pourquoi me réveiller?* brings effortful underlining, making him almost unrecognizable. Elsewhere the strained tone is less distracting, and his feeling for words is generally most illuminating. Troyanos makes a volatile Charlotte, but the voice as recorded is grainy. Manuguerra produces rich tone as the Bailiff, but the engineers have not been kind to the LPO strings, which sound thin. Plasson is a stylish conductor but here fails to convey the full power of the piece.

Werther: highlights.

(M) ** EMI CDM7 63936-2 (from above complete recording; cond. Plasson).

With just under an hour of music included, this EMI highlights disc, pleasingly atmospheric – although the LPO strings could have more body – makes a good sampler of Plasson's set. Alfredo Kraus generally sings stylishly, though his tone is strained in *Pouquoi me réveiller?*, and Troyanos and Manuguerra both make quite impressive contributions.

Maunder, John (1858–1920)

Olivet to Calvary (cantata).

(B) **(*) CfP CD-CFP 4619 [id.]. John Mitchinson, Frederick Harvey, Guildford Cathedral Ch., Barry Rose; P. Morse (organ).

It is easy to be patronizing about music like this but, provided one accepts the conventions of style in which it is composed, the music is effective and often moving. The performance has an attractive simplicity and genuine eloquence. Frederick Harvey is particularly moving at the actual moment of Christ's death; in a passage that, insensitively handled, could be positively embarrassing, he creates a magical, hushed intensity. The choir sing beautifully, and in the gentler, lyrical writing (the semi-chorus *O Thou whose sweet compassion*, for example) sentimentality is skilfully avoided. The 1964 recording is first class in every way, and it has been admirably transferred to CD.

Maxwell Davies, Peter (born 1934)

Violin concerto.

(M) *** Sony Stern Edition II Dig. SMK 64506 [id.]. Stern, RPO, Previn – BARBER: *Violin concerto*. *** ❀

Maxwell Davies wrote this massive *Violin concerto* (over half an hour long) specifically with Isaac Stern in mind, to a commission from the RPO to celebrate its fortieth anniversary. There are parallels here with the Walton *Violin concerto* of over 40 years earlier. The composer was inspired to draw on a more warmly lyrical side that he has displayed rarely. Davies claims to have been influenced by his favourite violin concerto, Mendelssohn's, but there is little of Mendelssohnian lightness and fantasy here; for all its beauties, this is a work which has a tendency to middle-aged spread, not nearly as taut in expression as the Walton. Stern, understandably, seems less completely involved here than in the inspired Barber coupling.

Mayerl, Billy (1902–59)

All-of-a-twist; Autumn crocus; Bats in the belfry; The harp of the winds; Insect oddities: Praying mantis; Wedding of an ant. Jazzaristrix; The Jazz master; Jill all alone; Look lively; Loose elbows; Marigold; Railroad rhythm; Shallow waters; Sweet William. Arrangements: *Body and soul; Limehouse blues; Peg o' my heart; Phil the Fluter's ball; Smoke gets in your eyes*.

(M) *** Virgin/EMI Ultraviolet Dig. CUV5 61323-2. Susan Tomes.

Billy Mayerl believed he had achieved a specially English style of jazz. During the 1920s and 1930s his name was a household word, and 20,000 students enrolled in his mail-order School of Music to learn syncopated piano. He left an indelible legacy of light pieces of high quality, with writing that is often much more complex and sophisticated than the rags of Joplin and his contemporaries. His most famous lyrical numbers, such as *Marigold* and *Autumn crocus* (to quote Susan Tomes) combine 'a blend of elegance, wistfulness, nonchalance and high spirits – qualities which stamped his whole output'. The best of his pieces sound surprisingly undated, and in the hands of this stunning pianist they emerge with a refreshing spontaneity. The flashing cross-syncopations of *Bats in the belfry* and *All-of-a-twist* emerge with dazzling rhythmic freedom, for indeed this brilliant and talented artist has those 'Loose elbows' (readily demonstrable in the infectious piece of that name), which are an essential part of the Mayerl style. The gentle numbers, like *Jill all alone* and *Shallow waters*, are as winning as the picaresque *Insect oddities*. The transcriptions all emerge magnetically, and the easy, flowing flexibility of the playing is as remarkable as the dash and verve of the bravura, so well displayed in the closing *tour de force* of *Railroad rhythm*. The recording is splendidly real.

Medtner, Nikolai (1880–1951)

(i) *Piano concerto No. 2 in C min., Op. 50;* (ii) *Piano quintet in C*.

(BB) *** Naxos Dig. 8.553390 [id.]. Konstantin Scherbakov, with (i) Moscow SO, Golovschin; (ii) Danel, Tedla, Bourová, Pudhoransk.

On Naxos a very good performance of the Medtner *Second Piano concerto* with virtuosic and brilliant playing from Konstantin Scherbakov, who generates plenty of excitement. Perhaps there is a higher voltage in Demidenko's full-price, prize-winning (but not ideally recorded) Hyperion version, coupled with the *Third Piano concerto*, but Scherbakov is highly sympathetic and offers very musical playing, less narcissistic than his full-price rival. The Moscow Symphony Orchestra play well for Igor Golovschin, though they sound as if they could do with more rehearsal. There is plenty of space round the sound. Scherbakov communicates a more sympathetic musical personality than Demidenko and many will prefer him. There is an appealing makeweight in the form of the finely wrought *Piano quintet* of 1946.

(i) *Piano quintet in C. Sonata triad, Op. 11;* (iii) *Two pieces for 2 pianos, Op. 58/1–2.*
(M) *** Carlton Classics Dig. 30366 00582 [id.]. Veniamin Korobov, with (i) State Prokofiev Qt; (ii) Lyudmila Kuznetsova.

The *Sonata triad* is made up of three relatively short sonata movements: *No. 1 in A*, a *Sonata elegy in D minor* and a third in *C major*; they come from the first decade of the century and feature Medtner's personal blend of Brahms, Schumann and Rachmaninov. The two Op. 58 pieces, the *Khovorod* and *Knight Errant*, with Lyudmila Kuznetsova playing the first piano part, come off well and are better than the full-price alternative on Hyperion. There is nothing to choose between the present account of the *Piano quintet* and its Naxos rival. Korobov is a fine pianist, and though at the end of the *A major sonata* and in the *Second* there is very occasionally some less-than-refined fortissimo tone, the recording may contribute to that effect. In any event this is well worth the money.

Mendelssohn, Felix (1809–47)

Capriccio brillant for piano and orchestra, Op. 22.
(B) ** Sony SBK 48166; *SBT 48166* [id.]. Rudolf Serkin, Phd. O, Ormandy – BRAHMS: *Concerto No. 1;* SCHUMANN: *Intro. and allegro appassionato.* **(*)

Serkin is on good form here. This is a brilliant performance, not without panache, if not especially strong on charm. The recording is a little shallow, but otherwise good.

(i; ii) *Capriccio brillant in B min. for piano and orchestra, Op. 22;* (iii) *Piano concerto in A min.* (for piano and strings); (i; iv) *Piano concertos Nos. 1 in G min., Op. 25; 2 in D min., Op. 40;* (iii; v) *Double piano concerto in E* (for two pianos and strings); (i; ii) *Rondo brillant in E flat for piano and orchestra, Op. 29;* (vi) *Rondo capriccioso in E, Op. 14.*
(B) *** Decca Double 452 410-2; *452 410-4* (2) [(M) id. import]. (i) Peter Katin; (ii) LPO, Martinon; (iii) John Ogdon, ASMF, Marriner; (iv) LSO, Anthony Collins; (v) with Brenda Lucas; (vi) Jorge Bolet.

This well-filled Double Decca conveniently gathers together all Mendelssohn's major concertante works for the piano except the *Double concerto in A flat*. However, the present compilation is tempting in its own right, as Katin's early (1956) performances of the two best-known solo concertos have come up very freshly on CD; the ambient warmth of the recording disguises its age and the piano recording is excellent. Katin has the full measure of these remarkably similar works. His crisp passage-work prevents the outer movements from becoming either lifeless or brittle, and he offers a pleasingly light touch in the finales (indeed the last movement of Op. 25 scintillates). In both slow movements his style is sensitive without sentimentality, a feature mirrored in the excellent accompaniments. The two concertante occasional pieces were recorded earlier (1954) and Katin is in sparkling form. Here a mono master is used; but this is an amazing example of the way Arthur Haddy's Decca recording team could use the Kingsway Hall ambience to give an impression of stereo. So warmly convincing is the ambient effect that the ear is readily fooled unless one listens carefully, for the piano-sound and the balance are both excellent. The ambitious and successful *A minor Concerto* was written when the composer was thirteen and the *Double concerto* comes from approximately two years later. These delightful concertante rarities both have engaging ideas and are played with great verve and spirit by John Ogdon and his wife. The orchestral playing is equally lively and fresh throughout, and the vivid (originally Argo) 1969 Kingsway Hall recording has hardly dated. Jorge Bolet (recorded digitally in 1985) offers the solo *Rondo capriccioso* as a closing encore and immediately establishes his credentials of easy bravura applied with the lightest of touch.

Capriccio brillant in B min., Op. 22; Piano concertos Nos. 1 in G min., Op. 25; 2 in D min., Op. 40; Rondo brillant in E flat min., Op. 29; Serenade and allegro giocoso in B min., Op. 43.
(M) ** Ph. Dig. 454 685-2. Jean-Louis Steuerman, Moscow CO, Orbelian.

Jean-Louis Steuerman is a first-rate pianist and he is given brilliant support by the Moscow Chamber Orchestra under Constantine Orbelian. The recording, too, is most vivid. The snag is the barnstorming,

Lisztian style of the performances, which are involving but emotionally too inflated for the lyrical flow of Mendelssohn's two simple concertos. Even so, Steuerman's bravura is very impressive, though the forceful accompaniments lack charm, and at times become almost aggressive. Most successful is the ambitiously romantic slow movement of the *D minor Concerto* and the three shorter encores, especially the *Capriccio brillant*.

2 Concert pieces for clarinet and basset horn: in F min., Op. 113; in D min., Op. 114.
(B) *** Hyperion Dyad Dig. CDD 22017 (2) [id.]. Thea King, Georgina Dobrée, LSO, Francis (with Concert – see below ***).

These Mendelssohn duets for clarinet and basset horn are most diverting, with their jocular finales; and they are played with a nice blend of expressive spontaneity and high spirits. Georgina Dobrée proves a nimble partner for the ever-sensitive Thea King. This is part of an excellent two-disc set, including other attractive concertante works by Max Bruch, Crusell, Spohr and other less familar names.

(i–ii) *Piano concertos Nos. 1–2;* (iii–iv) *Violin concerto, Op. 64; Overtures:* (iv) *Calm sea and prosperous voyage;* (ii) *The Hebrides (Fingal's Cave);* (v) *String symphonies Nos. 1–12* (complete); *Symphonies Nos.* (ii) *3 (Scottish);* (iv) *4 (Italian).* (ii) *A Midsummer Night's Dream: Overture; Incidental music: Scherzo; Intermezzo; Nocturne; Wedding march; Bergomask dance.*
(BB) **(*) Nimbus NI 1765 (6) [id.]. (i) Joseph Kalichstein; (ii) SCO, Jaime Laredo; (iii) Benjamin Hudson; (iv) Hanover Band, Goodman; (v) E. String O, Boughton.

This inexpensive collection from Nimbus centres on William Boughton's complete set of the 12 *String symphonies*, written for family performance by one of the most brilliant boy-geniuses in the history of music; they contain delectable inspirations by the dozen. With the English String Orchestra on good form, Boughton provides winningly energetic readings of these delightful works, not as polished in ensemble as some rivals, but with warmly atmospheric recording helping to make them very persuasive.

Joseph Kalichstein's barnstorming accounts of the two *Piano concertos* are made to sound the more flamboyant by similarly reverberant recording and a bright piano-image. One would have liked more poise at times, yet he is sensitive to the gentler, lyrical pages. Both slow movements are beautifully played (the *Adagio* of No. 2 is tenderly affectionate) and it is impossible not to be caught up in the sheer energy and glitter of the solo bravura in the finale of the *First Concerto* and the first movement of the *Second*. Excellent support from Laredo and the Scottish Chamber Orchestra; the two concertos are separated by a strong and sensitive account of *Fingal's Cave*. Laredo's account of the *Midsummer Night's Dream overture* is similarly strong and direct, but the fairy music in the violins is neat and dainty rather than magically evocative. The *Scherzo*, however, is enjoyably jaunty, and the *Intermezzo* swirls along briskly to make a good contrast for the *Nocturne*, with its fine horn solo. The *Wedding march* does not dally either and it is followed by the *Bergomask* music which we have already sampled in the *Overture*. Here the tuba (originally ophicleide) comes through boldly to remind us of Bottom's presence.

Laredo then directs a likeably fresh and energetic account of the *Scottish Symphony*, first-movement exposition repeat included. The chamber scale adds to the freshness and transparency in the Scherzo, very much a highlight with its exuberant, trumpeting horns – which come through again splendidly in the finale. The slow movement gains too, and it is well shaped and admirably paced.

Roy Goodman and the period-instrument Hanover Band take over for the *Italian Symphony*, with string ensemble surprisingly large, an even more sympathetic performance than Sir Charles Mackerras's pioneering period recording for Virgin Classics, when here both speeds and manner are more relaxed, notably in the first two movements. In the *Violin concerto* the relative closeness of the violin – played by the leader, Benjamin Hudson – emphasizes the smallness of the instrumental image. With little or no vibrato used, portamenti, however authentic, may seem obtrusive to some ears. Yet with well-chosen speeds – a sweetly flowing *Andante* in the second movement – there is still much to enjoy. Goodman ends his contribution with a characterful version of the *Calm sea and prosperous voyage Overture*, with the period instruments bringing out the originality of the composer's orchestration, if not matching Flor (on RCA) in evocative magic.

Piano concertos Nos. 1–2; Capriccio brillant, Op. 22; Rondo brillant in E flat, Op. 29.
(BB) *** Naxos Dig. 8.550681-2 [id.]. Benjamin Frith, Slovak State PO (Košice), Robert Stanovsky.

Howard Frith on Naxos is a personable and nimble soloist: he is sensitively touching in the slow movements and makes much of the fine *Adagio* of No. 2. The Slovak orchestra accompany with vigour and enthusiasm, and if the effect is at times less sharply rhythmic this is partly the effect of a somewhat more reverberant acoustic. The piano balance here is bolder, more forward, although the orchestra certainly makes a strong impression. What gives the Naxos disc an extra edge (apart from its price) is the inclusion of the *Rondo brillant*, which Frith despatches with admirable vigour and sparkle. This disc is enjoyable in every way and is undoubtedly very good value indeed.

(i) *Piano concertos Nos. 1–2. Prelude and fugue, Op. 35/1; Rondo capriccioso, Op. 14; Variations sérieuses, Op. 54.*
(M) *** Sony SMK 42401 [id.]. Murray Perahia; (i) ASMF, Marriner.

Perahia's playing catches the Mendelssohnian spirit with admirable perception. There is sensibility and sparkle, the slow movements are shaped most beautifully and the partnership with Marriner is very successful, for the Academy give a most sensitive backing. The recording could be more transparent but it does not lack body, and the piano timbre is fully acceptable. At mid-price, a very recommendable issue.

Double piano concertos: in A flat; in E.
(BB) *** Naxos Dig. 8.553416 [id.]. Benjamin Frith, Hugh Tinney, Dublin RTE Sinf., O Duinn.

This Naxos disc challenges comparison with the outstanding Hyperion issue coupling these same two charming double concertos (CDA 66567). Mendelssohn wrote them in his early teens for his sister Fanny and himself to play, and the wonder is that the earlier of the two, written when he was fourteen, a very expansive structure of over 40 minutes, is the more identifiably Mendelssohnian, with a slow movement and finale based on material that might have been written many years later. If the Irish players are not quite as persuasive as their Scottish counterparts on Hyperion, their playing is just as refined, and Frith and Tinney are a fair match for Coombs and Munro, less powerful but just as magnetic and even more poetic. The transparent recording helps, very appropriate for such youthful music.

Violin concerto in E min., Op. 64.
(M) *** Sony Dig. SMK 64250 [id.]. Cho-Liang Lin, Philh. O, Tilson Thomas – BRUCH: *Concerto;* VIEUXTEMPS: *Concerto No. 5.* ***
(M) *** Decca Dig. 460 015-2 [id.]. Kyung Wha Chung, Montreal SO, Charles Dutoit – ELGAR: *Violin concerto.* ***
(M) *** RCA 09026 61743-2 [id.]. Heifetz, Boston SO, Munch – TCHAIKOVSKY: *Concerto* etc. **(*)
(BB) *** Belart 461 355-2. Campoli, LPO, Boult – BEETHOVEN: *Violin concerto.* ***
(B) *** [EMI Red Line CDR5 69863]. Itzhak Perlman, LSO, Previn – BRUCH: *Violin concerto.* ***
(BB) *** Naxos Dig. 8.550153 [id.]. Nishizaki, Slovak PO, Jean – TCHAIKOVSKY: *Concerto.* ***
(M) *** DG Dig. 445 515-2; *445 515-4* [id.]. Anne-Sophie Mutter, BPO, Karajan (with BRAHMS: *Violin concerto* ***).
(M) *** Carlton IMP Dig. PCD 2005 [id.]. Jaime Laredo, SCO – BRUCH: *Concerto No. 1.* ***
(M) *** EMI CDM5 66220-2 [id.]. Menuhin, Philh. O, Kurtz – BRUCH: *Concerto No. 1.* ***
(B) *** DG Double 453 142-2 (2) [id.]. Nathan Milstein, VPO, Abbado – BEETHOVEN: *Concerto* ***; BRAHMS: *Concerto* **(*); TCHAIKOVSKY: *Concerto.* ***
(M) (***) EMI mono CDH7 69799-2 [id.]. Yehudi Menuhin, BPO, Furtwängler – BEETHOVEN: *Concerto.* (***)
(M) **(*) Sony Stern Edition I SMK 66827 [id.]. Stern, Phd. O, Ormandy – DVORAK: *Violin concerto; Romance.* **
(BB) **(*) Discover Dig. DICD 920122 [id.]. Evgeny Bushkov, Slovak New PO, Rahbari – TCHAIKOVSKY: *Concerto.* **
(M) **(*) Sup. SU 1939-2 011. Josef Suk, Czech PO, Karel Ančerl – BERG: *Concerto* ***; BRUCH: *Concerto.* **
(M) (**(*)) EMI mono CDH5 65191-2. Heifetz, RPO, Beecham – MOZART: *Concerto No. 5;* VIEUXTEMPS: *Concerto No. 5.* (***)
(M) ** Classic fM Dig. 75605 57016-2. Maria Bachmann, RLPO, Pešek – BEETHOVEN: *Violin concerto.* **

Cho-Liang Lin's vibrantly lyrical account now reappears with the Bruch *G minor* plus the Vieuxtemps No. 5, to make an unbeatable mid-priced triptych. They are all three immensely rewarding and poetic performances, given excellent, modern, digital sound, and Michael Tilson Thomas proves a highly sympathetic partner in the Mendelssohn *Concerto*.

Chung favours speeds faster than usual in all three movements, and the result is sparkling and happy, with the lovely slow movement fresh and songful, not at all sentimental. With warmly sympathetic accompaniment from Dutoit and the Montreal orchestra, amply recorded, the result is one of Chung's happiest records. The unusual Elgar coupling works well enough when the performance is equally inspirational.

As one might expect, Heifetz gives a fabulous performance. His speeds are consistently fast, yet in the slow movement his flexible phrasing sounds so inevitable and easy that it is hard not to be convinced.

The finale is a *tour de force*, light and sparkling, with every note in place. The recording has been digitally remastered with success, and the sound is smoother than before.

It is good to have Campoli's delightful performance back in the catalogue. His perfectly formed tone and polished, secure playing are just right for the Mendelssohn *Concerto*, and this is a delightful performance, notable for its charm and disarming simplicity. The 1958 (originally Decca) recording is brightly lit in the CD transfer, and the vividness is marred by a degree of roughness in the orchestral focus; but no matter, this very inexpensive record gives much pleasure and is a fine reminder of a superb violinist.

Perlman gives a performance of the Mendelssohn that is full of flair, superbly matched by the LSO under Previn, always an illuminating interpreter of this composer. Ripe recording quality.

Takako Nishizaki gives an inspired reading of the *Concerto*, warm, spontaneous and full of temperament. The central *Andante* is on the slow side, but well shaped, not sentimental, while the outer movements are exhilarating, with excellent playing from the Slovak Philharmonic. Though the forwardly placed violin sounds over-bright, the recording is full and warm. A splendid coupling at super-bargain price.

In the Mendelssohn E minor, even more than in her Brahms coupling, the freshness of Anne-Sophie Mutter's approach communicates vividly to the listener, creating the feeling of hearing the work anew. Her gentleness and radiant simplicity in the *Andante* are very appealing, and the light, sparkling finale is a delight. Mutter is given a small-scale image, projected forward from the orchestral backcloth; the sound is both full and refined.

Laredo's version on a mid-price CD brings an attractively direct reading, fresh and alert but avoiding mannerism, marked by consistently sweet and true tone from the soloist. The orchestral ensemble is amazingly good when you remember that the soloist himself is directing. The recording is vivid and clean.

The restrained nobility of Menuhin's phrasing of the famous principal melody of the slow movement has long been a hallmark of his reading with Efrem Kurtz, who provides polished and sympathetic support. The sound of the CD transfer is bright, with the soloist dominating but the orchestral texture well detailed.

Milstein's DG version comes from the early 1970s. His is a highly distinguished performance, very well accompanied. His account of the slow movement is more patrician than Menuhin's, and his slight reserve is projected by DG sound which is bright, clean and clear in its CD remastering. This now comes as part of a DG Double, offering four key concerto recordings.

Menuhin's unique gift for lyrical sweetness has never been presented on record more seductively than in his classic, earlier version of the Mendelssohn *Concerto* with Furtwängler. The digital transfer is not ideally clear, yet one hardly registers that this is a mono recording from the early 1950s.

Another totally memorable performance by Stern from the late 1950s. It has great bravura, culminating in a marvellously surging account of the finale. The slow movement too is played with great eloquence and feeling but, when pianissimos are non-existent – partly, but not entirely, the fault of the close recording-balance – the poetic element is diminished, even though there is a full flood of romanticism.

The latest bargain digital recording from Discover introduces a brilliant young Russian soloist, Evgeny Bushkov, a pupil of Leonid Kogan. His silvery timbre suits the Mendelssohn concerto admirably, and he prepares and plays the secondary theme of the opening movement with appealing tenderness. The *Andante*, too, has a matching simplicity and the finale no lack of bravura and fire. He is well accompanied, and the recording, made in the Concert Hall of Slovak Radio, Bratislava, is full and well balanced. Not a first choice, however, for the coupled Tchaikovsky *Concerto* sounds less spontaneous.

Suk's small, sweet timbre is particularly suited to the Mendelssohn concerto and his intonation is immaculate. This is a highly congenial performance, not as individual as some, with a straightforwardly lyrical slow movement and a finale which gains from not being rushed off its feet. An excellent CD transfer, firm and full.

Anything that Heifetz does is pretty well without compare, and his dazzling virtuosity is well in evidence in this 1948 performance of the Mendelssohn with the RPO and Beecham. However, there would seem to be less warmth and rapport between Heifetz and Sir Thomas than there was between him and Barbirolli in the coupled Mozart concerto.

The generous and attractive coupling of the Mendelssohn and Beethoven *Concertos* is surprisingly rare, and Maria Bachmann offers direct, reliable performances of both works, very well recorded, in which she displays her pure, sweet tone and flawless technique. Nevertheless, as in the Beethoven, a lack of idiosyncrasy makes for a rather flavourless performance, beautiful but not as involving as it should be, until the finale – at a very fast tempo – brings an exciting coda.

(i) *Violin concerto in E min., Op. 64;* (ii) *Symphonies Nos. 3 (Scottish); 4 (Italian);* (iii) *A Midsummer Night's Dream: Overture and incidental music: Scherzo; Intermezzo; Nocturne; Wedding march.*

(B) *** Teldec/Erato/Warner Analogue/Dig. Ultima 0630 18954-2 (2) [(M) id. import]. (i) Olivier Charlier, Monte Carlo Op. O, Lawrence Foster; (ii) Leizig GO, Kurt Masur; (iii) LPO, Raymond Leppard.

For this Ultima reissue Warner Classics have drawn on both the Erato and Teldec back-catalogues to make another very attractive Mendelssohnian compilation. At its centre is Masur's highly recommendable coupling of Mendelssohn's two best-loved symphonies. He observes exposition repeats in both, and his choice of speeds brings out the freshness of inspiration judiciously, avoiding any suspicion of sentimentality in slow movements, which are taken at flowing tempi. Conversely, the allegros are never hectic to the point of breathlessness. The one snag is that the reverberant Leipzig recording tends to obscure detail in tuttis; the Scherzo of the *Scottish*, for example, becomes a blur, losing some of its point and charm. Otherwise, the sound of the orchestra has all the characteristic Leipzig bloom and beauty. Indeed the orchestral sound is glorious and the cultured playing always a joy to listen to, while at the climax of the first movement, by bringing out the timpani strongly, Masur finds a storm sequence almost to match *Fingal's Cave*. Olivier Charlier's account of the *Violin concerto* is warm, lyrically fresh, and nicely paced. Lawrence Foster accompanies persuasively and this is enjoyably spontaneous. Leppard's suite from *A Midsummer Night's Dream* is also very sensitively played and well recorded.

(i) *Violin concerto in E min.*; (ii) *Symphony No. 4 (Italian); Overtures: The Hebrides (Fingal's Cave); A Midsummer Night's Dream; Ruy Blas.*

(BB) *** EMI Seraphim CES5 68524-2 (2) [CEDB 68524]. LSO, with (i) Sir Yehudi Menuhin, cond. Rafael Frühbeck de Burgos; (ii) Previn – BRUCH: *Violin concerto No. 1*. ***

Menuhin's second stereo recording, with Rafael Frühbeck de Burgos, has its moments of roughness, but it has magic too: at the appearance of the first movement's second subject and in the slow movement, even if the timbre itself is a little spare. The recording sounds fuller than the earlier account with Kurtz, and this makes a good bargain on EMI's new Seraphim label, coupled with the Bruch *Concerto* and Previn's highly recommendable 1979 version of the *Italian Symphony*, plus the three most popular overtures. Previn, always an inspired Mendelssohnian, gives exuberant performances. In the symphony the outer movements are urgent, without sounding at all breathless, and are finely sprung; the essential first-movement exposition repeat is included. Recording balance has the strings a little less forward than usual, but the overall effect is agreeably full.

(i) *Violin concerto in E min.;* (ii) *A Midsummer Night's Dream: Overture, Op. 21; Scherzo; Intermezzo; Nocturne; Wedding march, Op. 61.*

(B) *** Erato/Warner Bonsai 4509 94578-2. (i) Pierre Amoyal, Bamberg SO, Guschlbauer; (ii) LPO, Leppard.

Leppard's *Overture* and suite from *A Midsummer Night's Dream* is drawn from a highly praised complete recording made in 1978 and very well recorded. Two soloists are here credited on the insert leaflet, although no vocal items have been included, which was a pity for they were well sung and there would have been plenty of room for them, as the playing time of this disc is only fractionally over an hour. Leppard gives the music sparkle and resilience, taking the *Nocturne* with its horn solo persuasively at a flowing tempo, though the *Wedding march* is here relatively heavy. Not surprisingly, Pierre Amoyal gives a fresh, sympathetic account of the *Violin concerto*, with a tenderly simple account of the slow movement and a scintillating finale. Guschlbauer provides good support, and the 1973 recording is good, so even as it stands this makes quite a good bargain recommendation.

Overtures: Athalia; Calm sea and prosperous voyage; Fingal's Cave (The Hebrides); Ruy Blas. Symphonies Nos. 3 (Scottish); 4 (Italian); (i) *A Midsummer Night's Dream: Overture and incidental music* (complete).

(B) *** RCA Twofer Dig. 74321 34177-2 (2) [(M) id. import]. Bamberg SO, Claus Peter Flor; (i) with Lucia Popp, Marjana Lipovšek, Bamberg SO Ch.

Claus Peter Flor has a wonderfully warm affinity with Mendelssohn's music, and this RCA Twofer cannot be too highly recommended, even if some duplication is involved. His collection of overtures (which received a Rosette from us in its original format, when it also included *The Marriage of Camacho*) remains the most desirable the catalogue has ever offered. The magically evocative opening of *Calm sea and prosperous voyage*, followed by an allegro of great vitality, is a demonstrable example of the spontaneous imagination of these performances, and there is no finer or more atmospheric version of *Fingal's Cave*, with its lyrical secondary theme phrased with memorable delicacy of feeling. The bold *Ruy Blas* and the nobly contoured *Athalia* are also greatly enjoyable, especially when played with such freshness and polish. The recording, made in the Dominikanerbau, Bamberg, has splendid bloom, for the hall ambience is just right for this repertoire.

The *Midsummer Night's Dream* incidental music is recorded equally beautifully, glowing and radiant. The little melodramas are omitted, but the performance is otherwise complete. Flor's stylish yet relaxed control brings the kind of intimacy one expects from a chamber group. The very opening of the fairy *Overture*, with its soft flute timbre and diaphanous violins, is quite lovely; and later the *Wedding march*, played with much vigour and élan, expands splendidly. The lightly rhythmic *Scherzo*, taken not too fast, is another highlight, and Lucia Popp's vocal contribution is delightful, especially when she blends her voice so naturally with that of Marjana Lipovšek in *You spotted snakes*. The two symphonies are essentially mellow readings, with sunnily romantic slow movements. Flor does not observe the exposition repeat in the *Scottish* (neither does Karajan), but includes the twenty-bar lead-back in the *Italian*. Even here his pacing never sounds rushed, and there is an engaging lightness of touch. The elfin horns in the Minuet are a highlight, while in the coda of the *Scottish* the horns ring out regally. Again the Bamberg acoustic adds to the character of these performances, unforced and beaming.

Symphonies for string orchestra Nos. 1 in C; 2 in D; 3 in E min.; 4 in C min.; 5 in B flat; 6 in E flat.
(BB) *** Naxos Dig. 8.553161 [id.]. N. CO, Nicholas Ward.

Symphonies for string orchestra Nos. 7 in D min.; 8 in D; 9 in C.
(BB) *** Naxos Dig. 8.553162 [id.]. N. CO, Nicholas Ward.

Symphonies for string orchestra Nos. 10 in B min.; 11 in F; 12 in G min.; 13 in C min. (Sinfoniesatz).
(BB) *** Naxos Dig. 8.553163 [id.]. N. CO, Nicholas Ward.

Nicholas Ward and the Northern Chamber Orchestra follow up the success of their Haydn recordings for Naxos with an outstanding series of the boy Mendelssohn's string symphonies, matching and even outshining rivals at whatever price. The freshness and incisiveness of the performances are enhanced by bright, clean recording, made in the Concert Hall of Broadcasting House in Manchester. Not only does Ward bring out the exhilarating sparkle and vigour of the fast movements – with Mendelssohn, even at the age of eleven, giving clear anticipations of his mature style – but he also gives apt emotional weight to such beautiful lyrical movements as the *Andante* of No. 2 or the darkly slow introduction to the one-movement *No. 10 in B minor*. All three discs can be warmly recommended to everyone, not just to those who already know these amazing inspirations of a boy genius.

Symphonies for string orchestra Nos. 2 in D; 3 in E min.; 5 in B flat; 6 in E flat.
(B) *** EMI forte (SIS) Dig. CZS5 69524-2 (2) [(M) id. import]. Polish CO, Maksymiuk – JANIEWICZ: *Divertimento;* JARZEBSKI: *Chromatica; Tamburetta;* ROSSINI: *String sonatas.* ***

This collection of the boy Mendelssohn's early *String symphonies* (written when he was only twelve) is most invigorating. These earlier symphonies from the series of 12 may look to various models from Bach to Beethoven, but the young composer keeps showing his individuality and, however imitative the style, the vitality of the invention still bursts through. The slow movement of *Symphony No. 2*, for example, is a Bachian meditation that in its simple beauty matches later Mendelssohn. The Polish strings are set in a lively acoustic, giving exceptionally rich sound, but the playing also has plenty of dash.

Symphonies Nos. 1–5.
(M) *** DG 429 664-2 (3). Mathis, Rebman, Hollweg, German Op. Ch., BPO, Karajan.
(B) **(*) RCA 74321 20286-2 (3) [(M) id. import]. Casapietra, Stolte, Schreier, Leipzig R. Ch. (in *No. 2*); Leipzig GO, Masur.

Symphonies Nos. 3 (Scottish); 4 (Italian), Op. 90.
(BB) ** RCA Navigator 74321 17891-2. Leipzig GO, Masur.

Symphonies Nos. 1–5; Overtures: *Athalia* (also *War march of the priests*); *Calm sea and a prosperous voyage, Op. 27; The Hebrides (Fingal's Cave), Op. 26.*
(B) *** Decca Analogue/Dig. 448 514-2 (3) [(M) id. import]. Ghazarian, Gruberová, Krenn, V. State Op. Ch. (in *No. 2* (*Hymn of Praise*)); VPO, Dohnányi.

Symphonies Nos. 1–5; Overture: The Hebrides (Fingal's Cave).
(M) *** Chandos Enchant Dig. CHAN 7090 (3) [id.]. Philh. O, Walter Weller (with Cynthia Haymon, Alison Hagley, Peter Straka, Philh. Ch. in *Symphony No. 2*).

Weller's set of the Mendelssohn symphonies comes up against considerable competition but can stand comparison with the finest alternatives, including Karajan and Abbado. Certainly it is the most beautifully recorded, the Chandos sound richly full-bodied, though not sharply defined. He plays the *First Symphony* as if it were a mature work, not the inspiration of a fifteen-year-old, making the strongest contrast between fast outer movements and a spaciously moulded Andante. The *Scottish* and *Italian Symphonies* follow, refreshingly spontaneous-sounding, with the sense of live performances caught on the wing here and throughout the series, compensating for the occasional lack of crispness in ensemble. Once again expansive speeds are adopted for the slow movements, as well as for the introduction to the *Scottish*, but Weller sustains them well, and these are warm, affectionate readings which include exposition repeats and build excitingly to climaxes. In the *Reformation Symphony* and in *Fingal's Cave*, which follows, there is an emotional thrust that is very involving, leading to a joyfully exultant conclusion in the finale. Again in the *Hymn of Praise* (No. 2) from the opening trombone solo onwards it is the warmth and weight of the recorded sound that tells, with a large chorus set against full-bodied, satisfyingly string-based orchestral sound. Though again speeds are often dangerously slow, as in the lovely duet for the two sopranos, *Ich harrete des Herrn*, the sense of spontaneity in the performance makes it compelling throughout. And how sympathetically Weller sustains the lilting second-movement *Allegretto*. In the finale, Cynthia Haymon and Alison Hagley are warm-toned soloists, with Peter Straka an expressive if slightly fluttery tenor, but with a timbre which suits Mendelssohn. A considerable achievement.

Dohnányi's Decca set (which includes also two key overtures, plus the lesser-known *Athalia* and the *War march of the priests*) brings performances which are fresh and direct, often relying on faster and more flowing speeds than in Abbado's full-price set, more clearly rebutting any idea that this music might be sentimental. The most striking contrast comes in the *Hymn of praise*, where Dohnányi's speeds are often so much faster than Abbado's that the whole character of the music is changed, as in the second-movement Scherzo, sharp in one, gently persuasive in the other. Many will prefer Dohnányi in that, particularly when the choral sound is brighter and more immediate too. The vintage recordings were made in the Sofiensaal between 1976 and 1978, and the two overtures and the *Italian Symphony* are digital, the Decca engineers producing sound which was among the finest of its period and which sounds excellent on CD. The snag of the set is that Dohnányi, unlike Abbado, omits exposition repeats, which in the *Italian Symphony* means the loss of the substantial lead-back passage in the first movement. However, attractively packaged in a bargain box, this is still rather enticing. The *Reformation Symphony* comes off particularly well.

Karajan's distinguished set of the Mendelssohn *Symphonies* was recorded in 1971/2 in the Berlin Jesus Christus Kirche. The early C minor work sounds particularly fresh, and the *Hymn of praise* brings the fullest sound of all; the very fine choral singing is vividly caught. The soloists make a good team, rather than showing any memorable individuality; but overall Karajan's performance is most satisfying. The *Scottish Symphony* is a particularly remarkable account and the *Italian* shows the Berlin Philharmonic in sparkling form: the only drawback is Karajan's characteristic omission of both first-movement exposition repeats. There are few reservations to be made about the *Reformation Symphony*, and the sound has been effectively clarified without too much loss of weight.

Recorded by Eurodisc in 1971/2, the earlier of Masur's two Mendelssohn *Symphony* cycles, reissued in RCA's Symphony Edition, makes an excellent bargain-priced alternative to the strongly characterized later set for Teldec. The recording is warmer and more immediate, and Masur's preference for flowing speeds in slow movements is not so marked, often with more affectionate moulding of phrase. The performances are often more vivid and more spontaneous-sounding, notably that of No. 2, the *Hymn of Praise*, where the forward focus of the voices adds to the impact of a most refreshing reading. Sadly, the two most popular symphonies, the *Scottish* and *Italian*, are the least successful, with generally slow speeds and slacker ensemble than in the rest. Masur here observes the exposition repeat in the *Italian* but not in the *Scottish*. These are also available separately on RCA's super-bargain Navigator label, but this is a case where Masur's mid-priced Teldec alternative coupling of these two key works is clearly preferable. The symphonies in the RCA set have also been issued separately at mid-price: *Symphonies Nos. 1* and *3* (74321 20287-2); *Symphony No. 2* (74321 20288-2); *Symphonies Nos. 4* and *5* (74321 20289-2).

(i) *Symphonies Nos. 1 in C min., Op. 11;* (ii) *2 in B flat (Hymn of Praise), Op. 52;* (i) *3 in A min. (Scottish), Op. 56; Overture The Hebrides (Fingal's Cave), Op. 26.*
(B) *** Ph. Duo 456 071-2 (2) [id.]. LPO; (i) Haitink; (ii) M. Price, Burgess, Jerusalem, LPO Ch., Chailly.

(i) *Symphonies Nos. 4 in A (Italian), Op. 90; 5 in D min. (Reformation), Op. 107; Calm sea and prosperous voyage overture, Op. 27;* (ii–iii) *Violin concerto in E min.;* (iii–iv) *A Midsummer Night's Dream: Overture, Op. 21; Incidental music, Op. 61.*
(B) *** Ph. Duo 456 074-2 (2) [id.]. (i) LPO; (ii) Grumiaux; (iii) Concg. O; (iv) with Woodland, Watts, Women of Netherlands R. Ch.; all cond. Haitink.

When Bernard Haitink in 1980 was prevented from rounding off his planned Mendelssohn symphony cycle with the Symphony No. 2 (*Lobgesang – Hymn of Praise*), Riccardo Chailly stepped in to record it in his place. This compilation brings together what, despite the change of conductor, is an outstanding cycle, fresh and energetic, with a geniality that regularly puts a smile on Mendelssohn's face. If one compares this with rival cycles at mid-price, this one is more warmly expressive, more lightly pointed than either Sawallisch's (the previous Philips cycle) or Dohnányi's on Decca, both of which seem plainer, even at times fierce, next to this. Only in the first movement of the *Italian Symphony* does Haitink press too hard, and even then he has time to spring rhythms. Broadly, Chailly follows a similar pattern in *Lobgesang*, another excellent performance with an outstanding trio of soloists, helped by full and vivid sound, though the fine chorus is backwardly balanced. The fourth disc contains Haitink's brilliant

Concertgebouw version of the *Midsummer Night's Dream* incidental music – ten movements, including a dazzling account of the Overture – as well as the excellent Grumiaux version of the *Violin concerto*, also with Haitink and the Concertgebouw, with 1960s sound still fresh and clear.

Symphonies Nos. 1 in C min., Op. 11; (i) *2 in B flat (Hymn of Praise), Op. 52. 5 in D (Reformation), Op. 107.*
(B) **(*) Teldec/Warner Ultima Dig. 3984 21341-2 (2) [(M) id. import]. Leipzig GO, Kurt Masur; (i) with Barbara Bonney, Michael Schönheit, Leipzig R. Ch.

Masur's mastery in Mendelssohn is due in good measure to his ability to adopt relatively fast speeds and make them sound easy and relaxed, not hurried and breathless. Mendelssohn himself, conductor of this same Leipzig orchestra, was renowned for adopting fast speeds, and in all three symphonies here Masur is faster than his principal rivals on disc, not just in allegros but in slower movements too. In Nos. 1 and 5 that works very well indeed, bringing an alert freshness with no hint of sentimentality; but the fast speeds in the big choral symphony will for many be too extreme. Where Abbado on DG, no sentimentalist, takes 29 minutes over the three instrumental movements which open the work, Masur takes only 21 minutes, an astonishing discrepancy. Nevertheless, as ever, Masur avoids breathlessness, and with excellent soloists and choir, freshly recorded with plenty of detail, the two-disc package is still competitive in bringing together Mendelssohn's three less popular symphonies.

Symphonies Nos. 1 in C min., Op. 11; 5 in D (Reformation), Op. 107; Octet, Op. 20: Scherzo.
(M) *** DG Dig. 445 596-2. LSO, Abbado.

The *First* and *Fifth* are Mendelssohn's least-played and least-recorded symphonies, so Abbado's coupling is very welcome. The youthful *First* has plenty of C minor bite. The toughness of the piece makes one wonder that Mendelssohn ever substituted the *Scherzo* from the *Octet* for the third movement (as he did in London), but Abbado helpfully includes a sparkling version of that extra Scherzo so that on CD, with a programming device, you can readily make the substitution yourself. His direct manner suits the *Reformation Symphony* equally well. Brightly lit, early-digital recording (1984), but with the warm ambience of St John's, Smith Square, adding overall bloom.

Symphony No. 2 in B flat (Hymn of praise), Op. 52.
(M) *** DG 431 471-2. Mathis, Rebmann, Hollweg, German Op. Ch., BPO, Karajan.

Symphony No. 2 (Hymn of Praise); Psalm No. 42: Wie der Hirsch schein, Op. 42.
(BB) * Arte Nova/BMG Dig. 74321 37639-2 (2) [id.]. Ulewicz, Kuhrau, Silla, Seidel, Munich Oratorio Ch., Pilsen RSO, Hantke.

We have already praised the 1972 Karajan recording of the *Hymn of praise* within the context of his complete set of Mendelssohn symphonies above. The chorus, well focused, is particularly impressive.

Recorded live in the Herkulessaal in Munich on Arte Nova, Mendelssohn's choral symphony comes in a warm but flawed performance, not helped by the poor focus of the chorus, backwardly placed. By contrast, the orchestra is prominently recorded with full, brass tone, including East European-sounding horns. Ensemble is not crisp enough to make this satisfying for repeated listening, and the tenor soloist sounds tentative. However, the first soprano, Eva-Maria Kuhrau, is superb: silver-toned, not just in the major work but also in the refreshingly direct Psalm-setting, where lighter orchestration allows the chorus to focus better. At less than 25 minutes in length, that work takes up the whole of the second disc, making this much less of a bargain than it seems.

Symphony No. 3 in A min. (Scottish), Op. 56; A Midsummer Night's Dream: Overture, Op. 21 and excerpts, Op 61; Overture: The Hebrides (Fingal's Cave).
(M) **(*) Decca 443 578-2 [id.]. LSO, Peter Maag.

Under Maag, the *Scottish Symphony* is played most beautifully, and its pastoral character, occasioned by Mendelssohn's considerable use of strings throughout, is amplified by a Kingsway Hall recording of great warmth. The response of the LSO has quite remarkable freshness in this highly spontaneous performance. The opening string cantilena is poised and very gracious and thus sets the mood for what is to follow. Unfortunately the first-movement exposition repeat is not observed, but to do so was not unusual in those days. One other small complaint: Maag is too ponderous in the final *Maestoso*, but there is a compensating breadth and the effect is almost Klempererian. The remastered sound is first class, with a natural balance and glowing woodwind detail. Only a degree of thinness of timbre in the violins when playing above the stave betrays the age of the original. *Fingal's Cave* is no less successful. Maag's *Overture* and excerpts from a *A Midsummer Night's Dream* derive from a more extended LP selection, dating from the earliest days of stereo (1957). The fairy string music is beautifully translucent, and if Maag's treatment of the *Overture*'s forthright second subject strikes the ear as rhythmically mannered, the recording includes a strong contribution from a fruity bass wind instrument which might possibly be Mendelssohn's ophicleide but which is probably a well-played tuba. The recording is clean and well projected; in the remastering, the luminous quality one remembers in the original has been retained. These vintage recordings play for 76 minutes.

Symphony No. 3 in A min. (Scottish), Op. 56; Overtures; Calm sea and a prosperous voyage; The Hebrides (Fingal's Cave); Ruy Blas.
(BB) **(*) Naxos Dig. 8.550222; *4.550222* [id.]. Slovak PO, Oliver Dohnányi.

Oliver Dohnányi conducts a joyful account of the *Scottish Symphony* on Naxos, given the more impact by forward recording. Mendelssohn's lilting rhythms in all the fast movements are delightfully bouncy, and though the slow movement brings few hushed pianissimos, its full warmth is brought out without sentimentality. The three overtures, also very well done, not least the under-appreciated *Ruy Blas*, make an excellent coupling.

Symphonies Nos. 3 in A min. (Scottish); 4 in A (Italian), Op. 90.
(BB) *** Belart 450 099-2 [(M) id. import]. LSO, Abbado.
(BB) *** ASV CDQS 6004 [(M) id. import]. O of St John's, Lubbock.
(M) **(*) DG 439 980-2. Israel PO, Bernstein.
(BB) ** Naxos Dig. 8.553200 [id.]. Nat. SO of Ireland, Reinhard Seifried.

(i) *Symphonies Nos. 3 in A min. (Scottish), Op. 56;* (ii) *4 in A (Italian), Op. 90;* (i) *Hebrides overture (Fingal's cave), Op. 26.*
(M) *** DG Originals 449 743-2 [id.]. BPO, Karajan.
(M) *** Classic fM Dig. 75605 57013-2. Ulster O, Sitkovetsky
(M) ** Mercury (IMS) 434 363-2 [id.]. (i) LSO, Dorati; (ii) Minneapolis SO, Skrowaczewski.

Karajan's 1971 account of the *Scottish* is justly included among DG's 'Originals', as it is one of his finest recordings. The performance contains some slight eccentricities of tempo: the opening is rather measured, but affectionately so, while the closing pages of the finale are taken with exuberant brilliance. The orchestral playing is superb – the pianissimo articulation of the strings is a pleasure in itself – and the conductor's warmth and direct eloquence, with no fussiness, are irresistible. The Scherzo is marvellously done and becomes a highlight, while there is no doubt that Karajan's coda has splendid buoyancy. The coupling was originally just this very characterful and evocative account of *Fingal's Cave*, but now the *Italian Symphony* has been added, recorded two years later. This is also played very beautifully and brilliantly but, good though the performance is, it does not quite match that of the *Scottish* and it is just a shade wanting in spontaneity and sparkle.

Dmitry Sitkovetsky, forsaking his violin, has since 1996 been principal conductor of the Ulster Orchestra, in succession to another violinist-turned-conductor, Yan-Pascal Tortelier. Here he draws superb performances from the orchestra of both symphonies as well as the overture, helped by outstandingly full and rich recording, made in the Ulster Hall. Consistently Sitkovetsky conveys the feeling of live performances caught on the wing. With speeds beautifully chosen and with rhythms crisp and well sprung, his readings are full of light and shade, warmly dramatic, demonstrating an expressive freedom – notably in pressing ahead – which always sounds natural, never self-conscious. With refined playing from every section, at once tense and polished, textures are exceptionally clear and transparent, so that inner details are brought out that are often obscured. The strings in particular produce some magical pianissimos, reflecting Sitkovetsky's own mastery as an instrumentalist. A very generous and apt coupling, with the exposition repeat observed in the *Italian Symphony* (important because of the long lead-back) but not in the *Scottish*.

Abbado's outstanding Decca recording of the *Scottish Symphony* (now reissued on Belart) is beautifully played and the LSO responds to his direction with the greatest delicacy of feeling, while the *Italian Symphony* has a comparable lightness of touch, matched with lyrical warmth. The vintage (1968) Kingsway Hall recording is first class; however, the absence of the first-movement exposition repeat in the *Scottish Symphony* (though not in the *Italian*) is a drawback.

Lubbock's coupling of the *Scottish* and *Italian Symphonies* makes an outstanding super-bargain issue, offering performances of delightful lightness and point, warmly and cleanly recorded. The string section may be of chamber size but, amplified by a warm acoustic, the result sparkles, with rhythms exhilaratingly lifted. The slow movements are both on the slow side but flow easily with no suspicion of sentimentality, while the *Saltarello* finale of No. 4, with the flute part delectably pointed, comes close to Mendelssohnian fairy music.

Bernstein and the Israel orchestra, recorded live in Munich in 1979, give a loving performance of the *Scottish Symphony* but their expansive tempi run the risk of overloading Mendelssohn's fresh inspiration, with the heavy expressiveness making the slow introduction and slow movement sound almost Mahlerian, as if especially for the German audience. The rhythmic lift of the Scherzo and finale makes amends; but it is a performance to bring out for an interesting change, rather than a version to recommend for repeated listening. The recording is well balanced and full. The sparkling account of the *Italian* was made a year earlier in the Mann Auditorium, Tel Aviv, but remains convincingly atmospheric if not ideally clear. It is also available at bargain price, coupled with the *Midsummer Night's Dream* incidental music – see below.

The first movement of Dorati's (1956) *Scottish*, though exciting, is hard driven, and the reading never quite recovers, although – more surprisingly – the swinging tune at the end of the finale is presented quite steadily and the coda does not take off. Skrowaczewski's *Italian* is briskly paced but extremely well played, with the Minneapolis strings on their toes in lightly articulating the outer movements. Neither conductor observes the first-movement exposition repeat. Easily the finest performance here is Dorati's *Fingal's Cave*, warmly romantic (the LSO lower strings playing beautifully in the expansive opening), exciting without being forced. The recordings are acceptable but not among the finest on this label.

Though Seifried draws refined playing from the Irish orchestra in readings with few idiosyncrasies, built on unexceptionable speeds, the impact of the performances is seriously diminished by the recording, with the orchestra set distantly in a reverberant acoustic and transferred at a very low level so that details often disappear, with tuttis growing opaque. Even in the super-bargain category there is a much more recommendable version in Lubbock's account with the Orchestra of St John's, warm and clear.

Symphony No. 4 in A (Italian), Op. 90.
(M) *** DG Dig. 445 514-2 [id.]. Philh. O, Sinopoli – SCHUBERT: *Symphony No. 8*. *** ✿

Sinopoli's great gift is to illuminate almost every phrase afresh. His speeds tend to be extreme – fast in the first movement but with diamond-bright detail, and on the slow side in the remaining three. Only in the heavily inflected account of the third movement is the result at all mannered but, with superb playing from the Philharmonia and excellent Kingsway Hall recording, this rapt performance is most compelling. For refinement of detail, especially at lower dynamic levels, the CD is among the most impressive digital recordings to have come from DG.

(i) *Symphony No. 4 in A (Italian), Op. 90; Overture The Hebrides (Fingal's Cave);* (ii) *A Midsummer Night's Dream: Overture, Op. 21; Scherzo; Nocturne; Wedding march, Op. 61*.
(B) *** DG Classikon 439 411-2; *439 411-4* [(M) id. import]. (i) Israel PO, Bernstein; (ii) Bav. RSO, Kubelik.
(M) **(*) Virgin/EMI CUV5 61131-2. LSO, Barry Wordsworth.

(i) *Symphony No. 4 in A (Italian); Overtures: The Hebrides (Fingal's Cave);* (ii) *Ruy Blas; A Midsummer Night's Dream: Overture; Scherzo; Intermezzo; Nocturne; Wedding march*.
(B) **(*) Decca Eclipse Dig. 448 237-2; *448 237-4* [430 722-2]. (i) VPO, Dohnányi; (ii) Montreal SO, Dutoit.

Bernstein's performance of the *Italian Symphony* (exposition repeat included) is sparkling and persuasive. The 1978 recording was made at a public concert and, though speeds are often challengingly fast in outer movements, they never fail to convey the exhilaration of the occasion. *Fingal's Cave* is also a live recording, made a year later, and while it has plenty of romantic warmth and Bernstein is slightly more indulgent, it too sounds spontaneously alive. In the items from *A Midsummer Night's Dream* the Bavarian orchestra are on top form, especially in the *Overture* which is beautifully played. The *Scherzo*, too, has the lightest touch from the woodwind, the *Nocturne* brings a fine horn solo and the *Wedding march* is suitably vigorous. The 1964 recording, made in the Herkules-Saal, Munich, still sounds excellent, and this bargain Classikon CD would grace any collection.

Wordsworth combines a sparkling version of the *Italian Symphony* (with attractively light articulation in the bracing outer movements and the essential first-movement exposition repeat included), with the four most important items from *A Midsummer Night's Dream* and a very lively performance of *Fingal's Cave*. If the programme is suitable, this is certainly enjoyable and the recording is first class.

Dohnányi's is a refreshing account of the *Italian*, never pushed too hard, although the *Saltarello* is taken exhilaratingly fast. It is a pity that the first-movement exposition repeat is omitted so that one misses the extended lead-back passage. However, the CD is generously full for, besides Dohnányi's slow and romantic account of the *Hebrides overture*, there is Dutoit's splendidly vital *Ruy Blas* with its commanding brass opening ringing out superbly and the scurrying violins very vivid and tangible. Indeed both this and the 32-minute selection from the *Midsummer Night's Dream* incidental music are marvellously recorded. The acoustics of Saint-Eustache in Montreal are ideal, giving a wonderful bloom to the dancing strings and a very convincing, concert-hall illusion to the whole programme. However, the playing in the incidental music is altogether more routine: the very brisk *Scherzo* conveys little charm, although the *Wedding march* is grand without being pompous.

Symphony No. 4 in A (Italian); A Midsummer Night's Dream: Overture, Op. 21; Incidental music, Op. 61: Scherzo; Intermezzo; Nocturne; Wedding march.
(BB) ** Naxos Dig. 8.550055 [id.]. Slovak PO, Anthony Bramhall.

(i) *Symphony No. 4 (Italian);* (ii) *A Midsummer Night's Dream: Overture, Op. 21; Incidental music, Op. 61: Scherzo; Intermezzo; Nocturne; Wedding march; Fanfare & funeral march; Dance of the rustics.*
(BB) *** LaserLight Dig. 15 526 [id.]. (i) Philh. O, János Sándor; (ii) Budapest PO, Kovacs.

A first-class coupling in the super-bargain range from LaserLight. Sándor gives a fresh and exhilarating account of the *Italian Symphony*, with particularly elegant Philharmonia playing, and the digital sound is excellent. The performance of a generous selection from the *Midsummer Night's Dream incidental music* also shows the Budapest orchestra on top form: this is most beguiling and is recorded in a pleasingly warm acoustic which does not cloud detail.

Though the first movement of the *Italian Symphony* is less tense than the rest – clean and neat rather than exhilarating as it should be – this Naxos performance is an attractive, alert one, well recorded and aptly, if not very generously, coupled. A fair super-bargain alternative.

Symphony No. 4 (Italian); Overtures: Fair Melusina, Op. 32; The Hebrides (Fingal's Cave), Op. 26; Son and stranger (Die Heimkehr aus der Fremde), Op. 89.
(M) *** Carlton IMP Dig. PCD 2003 [id.]. Berne SO, Peter Maag.

Peter Maag, making a welcome return to the recording studio with his Berne orchestra, here offers a winningly relaxed performance of the *Italian Symphony* (including exposition repeat), plus an attractive group of overtures, which once more confirms him as a supreme Mendelssohnian. *The Hebrides* receives a spacious reading and the two rarer overtures are a delight too, particularly *Son and stranger*, which in Maag's hands conveys radiant happiness. At bargain price, with full and brilliant recording, it is first rate.

(i) *Symphonies Nos. 4 in A (Italian), Op. 90; 5 in D min. (Reformation), Op. 107;* (ii) *Overture The Hebrides (Fingal's Cave), Op. 26.*
(M) *(*) [RCA Basic 100 09026 68090-2; *68090-4*]. (i) Boston SO, Munch; (ii) Chicago SO, Reiner.

A disappointing pair of performances from Munch, over-driven and charmless, and not helped by an unrefined recording with too much glare on the upper range. Reiner's *Fingal's Cave* occupies an altogether different sound-world.

Symphony No. 5 in D min. (Reformation), Op. 107.
(M) *** DG 449 720-2 [id.]. BPO, Maazel – FRANCK: *Symphony in D min.* ***

The *Reformation Symphony* springs grippingly to life in Maazel's hands. The Berlin Philharmonic brass make an immediate impact in the commanding introduction and the orchestral playing throughout continues on this level of high tension. The finale is splendidly vigorous, the chorale, *Ein' feste Burg is unser Gott*, ringing out resplendently. If ever one were choosing a 'best buy' for this individual symphony, Maazel's interpretation would rank very high on the list. It was aptly chosen for reissue in DG's series of 'Legendary Recordings', and the Franck coupling is hardly less impressive. The recording is spacious and has been vividly enhanced by the DG CD transfer.

Symphony No. 5 (Reformation); A Midsummer Night's Dream: Overture; (incidental music): *Scherzo; Nocturne; Wedding march.*
(M) *(*) Mercury 434 396-2 [id.]. Detoit SO, Paray – HAYDN: *Symphony No. 96.* *(*)

This is not one of Paray's more successful records. The *Midsummer Night's Dream* incidental music comes off well enough (the *Scherzo* crisply and lightly articulated, although the sound has a curious, exaggerated bass resonance). But in the *Symphony* the string-balance is close and unflattering; the brass are more telling, although they sound fierce rather than sonorous in the finale's chorale. The performance is certainly vigorous, but in no way endearing.

CHAMBER AND INSTRUMENTAL MUSIC

Cello sonata No. 2 in D, Op. 58.

(M) *** Mercury 434 377-2 [id.]. Starker, Sebók – BRAHMS: *Cello sonatas.* ***

Starker and Sebók give an outstanding account of Mendelssohn's finest *Cello sonata*, spontaneously full of ardour, yet with plenty of light and shade in the central movements, and topped by a sparkling finale, which yet retains the lyrical feeling. The 1962 recording is truthful and admirably balanced within a warm acoustic with a clear focus.

Octet in E flat, Op. 20.

(B) **(*) Ph. Duó 456 330-2 (2) [id.]. I Musici – BOTTESINI: *Grand duo concertante* **; ROSSINI: *String sonatas* **; WOLF: *Italian serenade.* **(*)

(B) ** EMI forte CZS5 69755-2 (2). Melos Ens. of L. – BEETHOVEN: *Septet; Wind octet* **; SCHUBERT: *Octet.* **(*)

I Musici give a most satisfying account of Mendelssohn's youthful string work, smooth in contour but with a fine balance between vitality and warmth. There is, however, a degree of edge to the CD remastering of an otherwise excellent (1966) recording.

The Melos performance, too, has plenty of life and impetus, and the Scherzo is played splendidly, following Mendelssohn's instructions to the letter *sempre pp e staccato*. Again the snag is the 1969 recording, which gives a rather hard, bright edge to the leader's tone. The stereo is remarkably clear, and the layout of the participating instruments is well detailed without too much loss of ambience; but the ear tires of the brightness on top.

Octet in E flat, Op. 20; String quintet No. 2 in B flat, Op. 87.

(BB) *(*) ASV Dig. CDQS 6168 [(M) id.]. Primavera Chamber Ens.

With athletic opening movements, these performances by the Primavera Chamber Ensemble are efficient and well played, but fail to charm. They are acceptably recorded.

Piano quartets Nos. 1 in C min.; 2 in F min.; 3 in B min., Op. 1–3.

(M) *** Virgin/EMI Dig. CUV5 61203-2. Domus.

Piano quartet No. 1 in C min., Op. 1; Piano sextet in D, Op. 110.

(BB) **(*) Naxos Dig. 8.550966 [id.]. Bartholdy Piano Qt (augmented).

Piano quartets Nos. 2 in F min., Op. 2; 3 in B min., Op. 3.

(BB) **(*) Naxos Dig. 8.550967 [id.]. Bartholdy Piano Qt.

The *Piano quartet No. 1 in C minor* was the composer's first published composition and was succeeded the following year by another, dedicated to '*Monsieur le Professeur Zelter par son élève Felix Mendelssohn-Bartholdy*', equally fluent and accomplished. However, none of the ideas of this *F minor* work is as remarkable as those of its successor in *B minor* of 1825. All three pieces have charm, vitality and musicianship, particularly in the hands of Domus, who play with the taste and discernment we have come to expect from them. Excellent recording.

The Bartholdy Quartet have an excellent pianist in Pier Narciso Masi, and his mercurial style is just right for these early works. The string players are always fluent and show a light-hearted vivacity in Mendelelssohn's scherzos (especially in the very winning *Allegro molto* of No. 3) and finales, and they play the simple slow movements gracefully. The *Piano sextet* also comes from the composer's youth and, like the other works, it has an engaging immediacy. The recording was made in the fairly resonant Clara Wieck Auditorium in Heidelberg, which means that the microphones are fairly close to the strings and the balance is slightly contrived. Nevertheless the sound is good and the piano well caught.

Piano quartet No. 3 in B min., Op. 3.

(BB) *** ASV Dig. Quicksilva CDQS 6198 [(M) id.]. Schubert Ens. of London – BRAHMS: *Piano quartet No. 3.* ***

Mendelssohn's *Piano quartet No. 3 in B minor* comes from 1824–5, at roughly the same time as the *C minor Symphony*, when the composer was about fifteen or sixteen. In his *Master Musician* survey, Philip Radcliffe speaks of 'the breadth of the material and the Weberian exuberance of the piano writing . . . the slow movement recalls Spohr in its luxuriant chromaticism'. This B minor work (which Mendelssohn dedicated to Goethe) has undoubted charm and, even if there are garrulous moments, they evince an astonishing precociousness. William Howard plays with great expertise and the instrumentalists are well balanced. If the coupling is suitable, this is worth its modest outlay.

Piano trios Nos. 1 in D min., Op. 49; 2 in C min., Op. 66.
(M) *** HM Suite Dig. HMT 7901335 [id.]. Trio de Barcelona.
(M) ** Sony Stern Edition III SMK 64519 [id.]. Stern, Rose, Istomin.

Lovely music, and lovely performances of both works from the excellent Trio de Barcelona, as warm-hearted as they are fresh. Each *Andante* is beautifully played – and how sprightly they are in the two Scherzos. The pianist, Albert Attenelle, clearly holds the performances together, but the balance is admirable and he never dwarfs his fine string colleagues, Gérard and Lluis Claret. The one drawback is the acoustic, which is a bit too reverberant. It does not cloud detail, however; the players are given a realistic presence, and the ear soon adjusts when the music-making is so spontaneously enjoyable.

The Sony coupling is not one of the highlights of the third box in Sony's Stern Edition. The playing is of course expert, and Eugene Istomin's pianism is pleasingly light-fingered and fluent. The Scherzo of the *C minor Trio* brings great brilliance from all three artists. But the studio acoustic is relatively dry and unflattering; the ear craves a softer ambience and more charm of the kind that comes intermittently in the *Andante con moto tranquillo* of the *D minor Trio*. Outer-movement allegros are extremely lively but a bit hard-pressed; the players don't readily convey the fact that they are enjoying themselves.

Song without words (for cello and piano), *Op. 109; Variations concertantes, Op. 17.*
(B) ** Sony SBK 48171; *SBT 48171* [id.]. Friedrich-Jürgen & Eckart Sellheim – SCHUBERT: *Arpeggione sonata*; SCHUMANN: *Adagio & allegro* etc.**

These Sony performances by Friedrich-Jürgen and Eckart Sellheim come from the 1970s. They were then known as the Sellheim Duo, and the cellist in particular brings great sensitivity and warmth to his phrasing. The piano tone is inclined to be a mite shallow and synthetic, but there is no cause to cavil. A decent two-star recommendation.

String quartet No. 2 in A min., Op. 13.
(M) *** Cal. CAL 6698. Talich Qt – BOCCHERINI: *Quartet, Op. 58/2;* HAYDN: *Quartet No. 74;* MICA: *Quartet No. 6.* ***

Mendelssohn's *Quartet in A minor*, Op. 13, has a serene and remarkably searching slow movement, before its charmingly memorable 'Intermezzo' which is linked to the lively but lyrical *Presto* finale, which has something of the character of a Mendelssohn Scherzo. A most enjoyable work, played with spirit, warmth and cultivated elegance by this superb group, who are most naturally recorded. The couplings are all equally recommendable.

String quartet No. 6 in F min., Op. 51/2.
(BB) ** ASV Quicksilva CDQS 6173 [(M) id.]. Lindsay Qt – BRAHMS: *String quartet No. 2.* **(*)

Mendelssohn wrote his *F minor Quartet* during the summer of 1847 as a tribute to his beloved sister, Fanny, who had died in May of that year. The music is full of agitation and anguish, and even the *Adagio* loses its serenity before the close. The Lindsays, recorded live at the Blackheath Concert Halls in 1988, give a fierily impassioned account of the piece which hardly ever lets up in its intensity, and the frenzied feeling which characterizes this music-making is emphasized by the close microphones, which are not flattering to the violins. While the impression is tremendously 'live', there is also an unattractively aggressive element and the feeling that the players are carried into over-characterization.

String quintets Nos. 1 in A, Op. 18; 2 in B flat, Op. 87.
(M) *** Sony/CBS MPK 45883. Laredo, Kavafian, Ohyama, Kashkashian, Robinson.

Laredo and his ensemble achieve good matching of timbre, and they give lively accounts of both these neglected works, lacking neither warmth nor finesse. The 1978 recording has responded well to remastering, and has body and presence.

PIANO MUSIC

Preludes and fugues Nos. 1–6, Op. 35; 3 Caprices, Op. 33; Perpetuum mobile in C, Op. 33.
(BB) *** Naxos Dig. 8.550939 [id.]. Benjamin Frith.

In the first of what is obviously going to be a distinguished series, Benjamin Frith offers a highly imaginative set of the Op. 35 *Preludes and fugues*, full of diversity, from the flamboyant opening *Prelude in E minor* to the expansive *Prelude No. 6 in B flat*. The *Fugues* are sometimes bold, sometimes thoughtful, sometimes quite light-hearted, yet they are never made to sound trivial. The three *Caprices* are equally varied in mood and colour and are most sensitively presented, with the last one opening solemnly and then providing characteristically light-hearted Mendelssohnian dash. The *Perpetuum mobile* makes a scintillating encore.

Acceptably full if not remarkable piano sound, recorded in St Martin's Church, East Woodhay. But the playing promises well for what is to follow.

Piano works, Vol. 3: *Piano sonata in B flat, Op. 106; Albumblatt, Op. 117; Andante cantabile e presto agitato in B; 3 Fantasies et caprices, Op. 16; Rondo capriccioso in E, Op. 14; Variations in E flat, Op. 82.*
(BB) *** Naxos Dig. 8.553186 [id.]. Benjamin Frith.

Given its quality, Mendelssohn's piano music is not generously represented in the catalogues, and Benjamin Frith's inexpensive survey is timely. The *B flat Sonata*, Op. 106, comes from 1827 when Mendelssohn was eighteen and much in awe of the Beethoven *Hammerklavier*. (Ironically, when the piece was published posthumously it was allotted the same opus number, Op. 106.) The sonata has been called 'a comfortable and domestic' version of the Beethoven and 'disappointingly pedestrian'. However, Benjamin Frith is so persuasive that he almost dispels this impression. His playing is nothing less than a delight, and in the celebrated *Rondo capriccioso* and the less inventive and more conventional *Variations in E flat* of 1841 he is as light of touch as one could possibly wish.

Piano works, Vol. 4: *Piano sonata in G min., Op. 105; Capriccio in E, Op. 118; Etude in F min.; Fantasia on 'The last rose of summer', Op. 15; 2 Pieces: Andante cantabile; presto agitato. Scherzo a capriccio in F sharp min.; Variations in B flat, Op. 83.*
(BB) *** Naxos Dig. 8.553358 [id.]. Benjamin Frith.

The *G minor sonata*, Op. 105, is the earliest of Mendelssohn's published works and was completed in 1821 when the twelve-year-old youngster was already an accomplished and assured composer. It is distinctly Haydnesque, and there is perhaps more charm than individuality. (It was this piece that the boy played when his teacher, Zelter, took him to Weimar to see Goethe, who, he said, liked it very much.) In his *Master Musicians* study of Mendelssohn, Philip Radcliffe called the *Fantasia on 'The last rose of summer'* 'a flimsy composition in which Mendelssohn appears to become less and less interested in the Irish tune'. In such imaginative fingers, however, it sounds delightful and marvellously fresh. Naxos provide quite excellent recording and the series so far is touched with distinction.

Songs without words, Books 1–8 (complete); *No. 49 in G min., Op. posth.*
(B) **(*) Hyperion Dyad Dig. CDD 22020 (2) [id.]. Lívia Rév.

Songs without words, Books 1–8 (complete); *Albumblatt, Op. 117; Gondellied; Kinderstücke, Op. 72; 2 Klavierstücke.*
(B) *** DG Double 453 061-2 (2) [id.]. Daniel Barenboim.

Songs without words (complete); *Andante and variations in E flat, Op. 82; Andante cantabile e presto agitato in B; Variations in B flat, Op. 83.*
(B) *** Ph. Duo 438 709-2 (2) [id.]. Ilse von Alpenheim.

This 1974 set of Mendelssohn's complete *Songs without words*, which Barenboim plays with such affectionate finesse, has dominated the catalogue for nearly two decades. For this reissue the six *Kinderstücke* (sometimes known as 'Christmas pieces') have been added, plus other music, so that the second of the two CDs plays for 73 minutes. The sound is first class. At DG Double price this sweeps the board in this repertoire, and it is good to see that the back-up documentation has now been restored.

Ilse von Alpenheim's set of *Songs without words* may not have quite the distinctive character of Barenboim, but she plays this music with an appealing spontaneous simplicity. Her sensibility is at times a little solemn, and just occasionally in the faster pieces she has a slight tendency to rush her fences. But these are performances which show individuality without self-conscious idiosyncrasy: the famous *Spring song*, for instance, brings an attractively light chimerical touch, and elsewhere there are many agreeable moments of poetic tranquillity. Of the encores, the *Andante and variations in E flat* is particularly appealing in this respect. The (1980) recording of the piano is first class, well up to Philips's usual high standard. Not a first choice, perhaps, but an undoubted bargain.

Lívia Rév is a thoughtful, sensitive and aristocratic artist. Her survey of the *Songs without words* has charm and warmth, and she includes a hitherto unpublished piece. The set is handsomely presented and the recording is warm and pleasing; it is, however, somewhat bottom-heavy. Yet the slightly diffuse effect suits the style of the playing. This might well now be seriously considered at its new price, especially by those who enjoy intimate music-making and want digital sound with its silent background.

Songs without words Nos. 5, Op. 19/5; 7–9, Op. 30/1–3; 15–16, Op. 38/3–4; 19–22, Op. 53/1–4; 25–

6, Op. 62/1–2; 31–3; 35–6, Op. 67/1–3 & 5–6; 37–8, Op. 85/1–2; 40, Op. 85/4; 47–8, Op. 102/5–6.
(BB) *(*) Naxos Dig. 8.550316 [id.]. Péter Nagy.

Péter Nagy is a young Hungarian pianist who was in his late twenties when he made this recording. He is a gifted player who shows considerable artistry in his handling of these charming miniatures. Unfortunately he is handicapped, as so often in solo piano recordings on this label, by the quality of the recording, made in the Italian Institute at Budapest. It says much for his sensitivity to keyboard colour that, despite the unventilated acoustic, he succeeds in holding the listener for as long as he does.

Songs without words, Op. 19/1–2; Huntsman's song, Op. 19/3; Op. 19/4; Venetian gondola song, Op. 19/6; Op. 30/4–5; Venetian gondola song, Op. 30/6; Op. 38/1–2, 5 & 6; Op. 53/5–6; Op. 62/3–4; Venetian gondola song, Op. 62/5; Op. 62/6; Spinning song, Op. 67/4; Op. 85/3, 5 & 6; Op. 102/1–2 & 4; 49 in D min. (Horseman's song).
(BB) *(*) Naxos Dig. 8.550453 [id.]. Péter Nagy.

Péter Nagy's second CD of Mendelssohn's *Songs without words* was made (a year after the first) with the same producer but, for part of the time, with a different engineer. There is, however, no significant difference; if anything, he is more closely balanced, at least in some of the pieces. As before, he plays with great poetic feeling and musical insight, and those who can adjust to the piano sound will find much to admire here.

ORGAN MUSIC

Organ sonatas Nos. 1–6, Op. 65/1–6; Preludes and fugues Nos. 1–3, Op. 37/1–3; Andantes in D & F; Allegro in B flat; Allegro, chorale and fugue in D; Allegro maestoso in C; Fugues: (Allegro) in E min.; (Lento) in F min.
(B) *(*) Hyperion Dyad Dig. CDD 22029 (2) [id.]. John Scott (organ of St Paul's Cathedral).

John Scott's survey of Mendelssohn's organ music is pretty comprehensive, but the choice of the St Paul's Cathedral organ was a mistake. The ample sounds and blurring resonance prevent any kind of bite – particularly striking in the *Allegro con brio* which opens the *Fourth Sonata* at the beginning of the second disc. The *Preludes and fugues* on the first tend to trundle on remorselessly, and even in the more lively shorter pieces the organ sound itself blunts John Scott's vigour. He is undoubtedly a master of this repertoire technically speaking (witness the closing *Allegro, choral and fugue in D*, which pays direct homage to Bach) but alongside Peter Hurford his style seems embedded in an outdated Victorian tradition of organ playing.

VOCAL MUSIC

Lieder: *Allnächtlich im Traume; Altdeutsches Liede; And'res Maienlied; An die Entfernte; Auf der Wanderschaft; Auf Flügeln des Gesanges ('On wings of song'); Bei deder Wiege; Der Blumenkranz; Da lieg' ich unter den Bäumen; Entelied; Erster Verlust; Das erste Veilchen; Es lauschte das Lamb; Frühlingslied* (3 versions: Lenau, Lichtenstein and Klingemann settings); *Grüss; Hirtenlied; Jagdlied; Minnelied* (Deutsches Volkslied); *Minnelied* (Tieck); *Der Mond; Morgengruss; Nachtlied; Neue Liebe; O Jugend; Pagenlied; Reiselied* (2 versions: Heine and Ebert); *Scheindend; Schiflied; Schlafloser Augen Leuchte; Tröstung; Venetianisches Gondellied; Volkslied (Feuchtersleben); Das Waldschloss; Wanderlied; Warnung vor dem Rhein; Wenn sich zwei Herzen scheiden; Winterlied.*
(M) **(*) EMI CMS7 64827-2 (2) Fischer-Dieskau, Sawallisch.

Though Mendelssohn generally reserved his finest song-like inspirations for the *Songs without words*, the lyrical directness of these settings of Heine, Eichendorff, Lenau and others assures him of a niche of his own among contemporary composers of Lieder. Fischer-Dieskau conveys the joy of fresh discovery but in some of the well-known songs – *Grüss* or *On wings of song* – he tends to overlay his singing with heavy expressiveness. Lightness should be the keynote, and that happily is wonderfully represented in the superb accompaniments of Sawallisch. Excellent, natural recording.

Elijah (oratorio), *Op. 70.*
(B) *** EMI forte CZS5 68601-2 (2) [CDFB 686012]. Gwyneth Jones, Janet Baker, Gedda, Fischer-Dieskau, Woolf, Wandsworth School Boys' Ch., New Philh. Ch. & O, Frühbeck de Burgos.

Frühbeck proves an excellent Mendelssohnian, neither a callous driver nor a romantic meanderer. The choice of Fischer-Dieskau to take the part of the prophet is more controversial. His pointing of English words is not always idiomatic, but his sense of drama is infallible and goes well with this Mendelssohnian new look. Gwyneth Jones and Nicolai Gedda similarly provide mixed enjoyment, but the splendid work of the chorus and, above all, the gorgeous singing of Dame Janet Baker, dominant whether in hushed intensity or commanding fortissimo, make this a memorable and enjoyable set, very well recorded (in the late 1960s) and spaciously and realistically transferred to CD. Offered in EMI's forte double series it makes a remarkable bargain.

Infelice; Psalm 47 (As pants the hart), Op. 42.

(BB) *** Virgin Classics Dig. Double VBD5 61469-2 (2) [CDVB 61469]. Dame Janet Baker, City of L. Sinf., Hickox – BERLIOZ: *Les Nuits d'été* etc.; BRAHMS: *Alto rhapsody* etc.; RESPIGHI: *La Sensitiva*. ***

The scena, *Infelice* – a piece which harks back to an earlier tradition – and the Psalm-setting both have the solos prescribed for soprano, but they suit Dame Janet well, here making a welcome foray out of official retirement for a recording. The voice is in superb condition, with the weight of expressiveness as compelling as ever. The Psalm sounds very like an extra item from *Elijah*.

A Midsummer Night's Dream: Overture, Op. 21; Incidental music, Op. 61 (complete).

(B) *** CfP Dig. CD-CFP 4593 [(M) id. import]. Wiens, Walker, LPO Ch. & O, Litton.

(M) (***) RCA mono GD 60314. Eustis, Kirk, University of Pennsylvania Women's Glee Club, Phd. O., Toscanini – BERLIOZ: *Romeo and Juliet: Queen Mab scherzo*. (**)

(i) *A Midsummer Night's Dream: Overture, Op. 21; Incidental music, Op. 61* (complete). (ii) *Overtures: The Hebrides (Fingal's Cave); Ruy Blas.*

(BB) **(*) Belart 461 354-2 [(M) id. import]. (i) Hannecke van Bork, Alfreda Hodgson, Amb. S., New Philh. O, Frühbeck de Burgos; (ii) SRO, Ansermet.

Andrew Litton includes the melodramas and uses them most effectively as links, making them seem an essential part of the structure. He has very good soloists; in the *Overture* and *Scherzo* he displays an engagingly light touch, securing very fine wind and string playing from the LPO. The wide dynamic range of the recording brings an element of drama to offset the fairy music. Both the *Nocturne*, with a fine horn solo, and the temperamental *Intermezzo* are good examples of the spontaneity of feeling that permeates this performance throughout and makes this disc a bargain.

Toscanini's Philadelphia recording offers the seven most popular numbers from the *Midsummer Night's Dream* music, including the song with chorus, *You spotted snakes*, and the final melodrama. In sparkling performances it offers a fine example of his more relaxed manners in his one Philadelphia season.

Frühbeck de Burgos's 1969 recording is absolutely complete; what's more, he makes a very strong case for the inclusion of even the shorter melodramas by bringing them vividly to life. The orchestral playing is very fine throughout – and notably so in the *Nocturne* and *Scherzo*. The performance of the *Overture*, although the fairies dance in the violins with exquisite daintiness, is not quite as magical as Flor's account (see above) and the Decca recording, though full-bodied and with plenty of bloom, is not as clear-cut and transparent as it might be. The choral focus is not ideally sharp, although the singing is enjoyable. But this remains very good value at super-bargain price, for Ansermet's accounts of the two overtures are full of vitality and drama, while the romantic element in *Fingal's Cave* is not missed. The mid-1960s sound is excellent.

OPERA

Die beiden Pädagogen (complete).

(M) *** CPO/EMI CPO 999 550-2. Fuchs, Laki, Dallapozza, Fischer-Dieskau, Wewel, Hirte, Bav, Op. Ch. & O, Wallberg.

Mendelssohn wrote this jolly piece, *Die beiden Pädagogen* ('The two pedagogues'), when he was only twelve, attacking the pedantry of schoolmasters, and with a side-swipe at ambitious fathers. It is a charming work that lay dormant from 1821 until 1960, when by chance the dialogue for this little *Singspiel* was discovered in Oxford. Starting with a brilliant overture, remarkable for deft woodwind writing, the musical ideas are charming, the manner light and sparkling in a way astonishing from a boy, even one as talented as Mendelssohn. In a piece lasting under an hour there are 11 vocal numbers, mainly brief duets and trios, culminating in a quartet with chorus much longer and more complex than the rest. In this denouement, solos are often superimposed on the choral writing with almost Mozartian skill. Under Heinz Wallberg, this CPO disc, very well recorded, offers a reissue of an EMI/Electrola recording made in 1978 with a first-rate cast. Fischer-Dieskau with great zest and style takes the *buffo* role of the schoolmaster, Kinderschreck (unnecessarily translated even in the cast-list as 'Bogy'), with Adolf Dallapozza clear and fresh in the principal tenor role of Carl, and with Krisztina Laki and Gabriele Fuchs well contrasted in the two soprano roles. A charming rarity. There is no libretto, only a detailed note and synopsis.

Die Heimkehr aus der Fremde (complete).

(M) CPO/EMI CPO 999 555-2. Donath, Schreier, Schwarz, Fischer-Dieskau, Kusche, Bav. Op. Ch. & O, Wallberg.

It was at the time of his first visit to England in 1829 at the age of twenty that Mendelssohn wrote this lighthearted little one-act *Singspiel*. *Die Heimkehr aus der Fremde* ('The return from abroad') involves the return to his home village of Hermann, who for six years has served in the Foreign Legion. The plot is complicated by an impostor, but everything works out well in the end. Lasting just over an hour, the 14 numbers plus overture skilfully and briskly take one through the plot. After the opening *Romanza* for the mother, a mezzo role, and a duet, the heroine Lisbeth is given a hauntingly beautiful aria in G minor, very sweetly sung here by Helen Donath. Hermann, the returning hero, also has a tender aria, more extended than the rest, with the young Peter Schreier perfectly cast. By that time the impostor, Kauz, has already made his mark in a jolly *buffo* aria referring to the *Dudelsack* (bagpipes), brilliantly sung by Fischer-Dieskau. The plot leads to a confrontation between the rivals which brings an echo of Beethoven's *Fidelio*. A resolution is crisply achieved, leading to a mellifluous final ensemble very characteristic of the composer. Like *Die beiden Pädagogen*, this is a rarity well worth investigating in this first-rate performance, vividly recorded.

Menotti, Gian-Carlo (born 1911)

Piano concerto in F.

(M) **(*) Van. 08.4029.71 [OVC 4071]. Earl Wild, Symphony of the Air, Jorge Mester – COPLAND: *Concerto*. ***

Menotti's *Piano concerto*, like most of his music, is easy and fluent, never hard on the ear. Its eclectic style brings a pungent whiff of Shostakovich at the opening, and there are hints of Khachaturian elsewhere. Even if it is unlikely to bear repeated listening, the charisma and bravura of Earl Wild's playing make the music sound more substantial than it is.

Merikanto, Aarre (1893–1958)

'Meet the composer': (i) *Violin concertos Nos. 2 & 4;* (ii) *Fantasy for orchestra;* (iii) *Konzertstück for cello and orchestra;* (ii) *Largo misterioso;* (iv) *Notturno;* (ii) *Pan;* (iv) *10 Pieces for Orchestra;* (ii) *Symphonic study;* (v) *Genesis* (for soprano, chorus & orchestra).

(B) *** Finlandia/Warner Double 4509-99970-2 (2) [(M) id. import]. (i) Kaija Saarikettu, Helsinki PO, James DePreist; (ii) Finnish RSO, Segerstam; (iii) Anssi Karttunen, London Sinf., Esa-Pekka Salonen; (iv) Avanti CO, Ari Angervo; (iv) Finnish RSO, Jukka-Pekka Saraste; (v) Karita Mattila, Savonlinna Op. Ch., Lahti SO, Söderblom.

As with previous issues in their '*Meet the composer*' series, Finlandia have assembled the bulk of previous LP and CD issues to give a good cross-section of Merikanto's output. In some ways he is the most rewarding of the Finnish composers after Sibelius, and this is undoubtedly a set of exceptional musical interest. His father, Oskar Merikanto (1868–1924), was also a composer and his songs enjoyed great popularity in Finland in the early years of the century. After studying with Reger in the years before the First World War, Aarre went on to Moscow, where he came into contact with the music of Scriabin among others, thus laying the foundations of the radical style he developed in the inter-war years. Works like the *Fantasy for orchestra* (1923) and *Pan* (1924) are searching in idiom and set great store by refinement of colour. The *Ten Pieces* date from 1930, the orchestra the composer had in mind being the newly founded 23-man Helsinki Radio Orchestra. The *Pieces* are highly atmospheric; the first, *Largo misterioso*, is also included with fuller orchestral forces. This is a haunting example of expressionism, highly original and powerful in its atmosphere. There are many reminders of Szymanowski in the *Second Violin concerto*, never played during the composer's lifetime, for the received wisdom was that after the Second World War Merikanto's inspiration declined in quality. To quote Seppo Heikinheimo's note in a previous issue of the concertos, 'In 1945 . . . Merikanto managed to break his morphine addiction, but his music never fully returned to what it once had been'. The collector can here judge for him or herself. The *Fourth Violin concerto* (1954) is more 'conventional in outlay': it opens with a Prokofiev-like ostinato figure and there is some lush and imaginative writing in the slow movement which again comes close to Szymanowski. Kaija Saarikettu is a commanding and brilliant soloist, and she is well accompanied by the Helsinki Philharmonic and James DePreist. *Genesis* (1956), too, is powerful and inspired music of high quality that enhances the claims of this composer on a wider public. This two-disc survey is very strongly recommended.

Merulo, Claudio (1533–1604)

(i) *Magnificat dell'ottavo tono; Missa Virginis Mariae;* (ii) *Toccata decima del 10o tono.*
(BB) ** Naxos Dig. 8.553335/6 (2) [id.]. (i) Schola of Benedictine Abbey of Santa Cruz, Valle de los Caïdos, Madrid, Laurentino Sáenz de Buruaga; (ii) Frédéric Muñoz (organ).

Claudio Merulo is also known as Claudio da Correggio (Correggio being his birthplace) though, to make matters more confusing, his real name was Merlotti. He was appointed organist of Brescia in 1556, before moving a year later to St Mark's in Venice as second organist. It is a measure of his repute that when he was promoted some years later, the new second organist was Andrea Gabrieli, a dozen or so years his senior. After leaving Venice in 1584, Merulo went to Mantua, finally becoming the organist of the ducal chapel at Parma. Though his reputation rests primarily on his keyboard music, he wrote Masses, motets and Sacrae cantiones. The *Missa Virginis Mariae* comes from four years after his promotion to first organist at St Mark's. This is primarily an organ Mass in the style of Cavazzoni, in which instrumental meditations are interspersed with short scraps of monody. The chant is musically phrased, though the Madrid choir's pitch does not always coincide with the organ. The *Missa Virginis Mariae*, like the *Missa Apostolorum* listed below, was published in the *Libro IV* of his *Messa d'intavolatura* of 1568, and listening to these pieces tempts one to endorse Willi Apel's view (in *The Age of Humanism*, Vol. IV of the *New Oxford History of Music*) that Merulo was not 'a contrapuntist of the first order'. The recording places plenty of space round the organ and the choir, though the discrepancies in response confirm that they were recorded separately, the choir in Madrid and the organ in the Church of Piedicroce, Corsica. Frédéric Muñoz is a rather stiff and not wholly persuasive interpreter.

(i) *Magnificat del secondo tono; Missa Apostolorum;* (ii) *Toccata seconda del 1o tono.*
(BB) *(*) Naxos Dig. 8.553420/1 (2) [id.]. (i) Grupo Vocal Grégor, Dante Andreo; (ii) Frédéric Muñoz (organ).

The *Missa Apostolorum* comes from Merulo's *Messa d'intavolatura* of 1568 but is a less successful recording than that of the *Missa Virginis Mariae* listed above. There is not enough space round the organ (that of the Church of Saorge in France) or the Grupo Vocal Grégor under Dante Andreo. In the opening *Toccata on the second tone* there is an unrelieved glare that tires the ear. Frédéric Muñoz is not the most interesting of organists, and by the end of the first CD he may persuade you that Merulo is not one of the most interesting composers.

Messiaen, Olivier (1908–92)

(i) *Hymne au Saint-sacrement; Les offrandes oubliées;* (ii) *Visions de l'amen.*
(M) **(*) Erato/Warner 4509 91707-2. (i) O de l'ORTF, Marius Constant; (ii) Katia and Marielle Labèque.

Constant gives atmospheric yet passionate accounts of these two early works, catching also their rich vein of mysticism. The recordings, from the beginning of the 1970s, have a pleasingly warm ambience and do not sound too dated. The Labèque duo play the *Visions de l'amen* brilliantly, their performance bolder in profile and less withdrawn in atmosphere than rival versions, but compelling nevertheless.

Turangalîla Symphony.
(B) *** EMI forte CZS5 69752-2 (2) [CDFP 69752]. Michel Béroff, Leanne Loriod, LSO, Previn – POULENC: *Concert champêtre; Organ concerto.* ***

Messiaen's *Turangalîla Symphony* was written at a time (1946–8) when – Shostakovich notwithstanding – the symphonic tradition seemed at its lowest ebb. Messiaen's conception is on an epic scale, seeking to embrace almost the totality of human experience. This is immediately implied in the Sanscrit title, a complex word suggesting the interplay of life forces, creation and dissolution, but which is also divisible: *Turanga* is Time and also implies rhythmic movement; *Lîla* is love, and with a strong inspiration from the Tristan and Isolde legend Messiaen's love-music dominates his conception of human existence. The actual love-sequences feature the ondes martenot with its 'velvety glissandi'. The piano obbligato is also a strong feature of the score. Previn's vividly direct approach, helped by spectacular recording, creates tingling electricity from first bar to last. He is at his best in the work's more robust moments, for instance the jazzy fifth movement, and he catches the wit at the beginning of the *Chant d'amour 2*. The idyllic *Garden of the sleep of love* is both serene and poetically sensuous, and the apotheosis of the love theme in the closing pages is jubilant and life-enhancing. Chailly's full-priced Decca account may have the advantage of even finer, digital recording, and it costs about the same; being (just) fitted on to a single CD, however, it is without Previn's considerable bonus: outstanding versions of two of Poulenc's finest concertos.

(i) *Couleurs de la Cité céleste;* (ii) *Et exspecto resurrectionem mortuorum.*
(M) ** Sony SMK 68332 [id.]. Groupe Instrumental à percussion de Strasbourg, with (i) Yvonne Loriod; (ii) O du Domaine Musical; Boulez (with STRAVINSKY: *Symphonies of wind instruments;* with NYPO **).

In Messiaen's own words, his *Couleurs de la Cité céleste* 'turns on itself like a rose-window', bringing together, with astonishing assurance, elements from plainsong, Greek and Hindu music, not to mention the persistent birdsong which runs through so much of this composer's writing. Boulez's account, helped by close microphones, centres on sharpness of detail rather than atmosphere; the result seems literal and fails to be seductive. Similarly, in the larger scale of *Et exspecto resurrectionem* the concentration of a series of clearly differentiated sounds and sonorities brings a negative effect. One cannot help feeling here that the musical content is spread rather thin, with too meandering a tempo predominating – pregnant pauses repeated overmuch lose their pregnancy. The Stravinsky encore makes a rather more positive impression, but this is essentially a reissue for Boulez aficionados rather than for the general collector.

Quatuor pour la fin du temps.
(M) ** HM Suite Dig. HMT 7901348 [id.]. Ens. Walter Boeykens.

(i) *Quatuor pour la fin du temps (Quartet for the end of time);* (ii) *Le merle noir.*
(M) *** EMI CDM7 63947-2. (i) Gruenberg, De Peyer, Pleeth, Béroff; (ii) Zöller, Kontarsky.

Messiaen's visionary and often inspired piece was composed during his days in a Silesian prison camp. Among his fellow-prisoners were a violinist, a clarinettist and a cellist who, with the composer at the piano, made its creation possible. The 1968 EMI account, led by Erich Gruenberg and with Gervase de Peyer the inspirational clarinettist, is in the very highest class, the players meeting every demand the composer makes upon them, and the fine, clear Abbey Road recording gives the group striking presence while affording proper background ambience. The bonus, *Le merle noir*, exploits the composer's love of birdsong even more overtly and is splendidly played and recorded here.

Walter Boeykens is the (excellent) solo clarinettist in the Harmonia Mundi performance, and his bold, plangent timbre rather dominates the proceedings – which is not quite what the composer intended. The others are good players, of course, but their balance of personality seems unequal, and it is not just the recording which suggests this, although it is rather dry and unflattering. There is also too little sense of mystery here.

(i) *Quatuor pour la fin du temps;* (ii) *Cinq rechants* (for 12 voices).
(M) *** Erato/Warner 4509 91708. Fernandez, Deplus, Neilz, Petit; (ii) Solistes des Choeurs de l'ORTF, Marcel Couraud.

The French Ensemble on Erato give a strong, powerfully integrated performance, well held together by the pianist, Marie-Madeleine Petit. Among her colleagues, Jacques Neilz, the cellist, is raptly inspirational in the fifth movement (*Louange à l'Eternité de Jésus*) and is all but matched by the playing of his violinist colleague, Huguette Fernandez; the clarinettist, Guy Deplus, does not quite manage to achieve an opening crescendo out of nothingness but still makes a sensitive contribution. The recording is very good, clear and well balanced. The coupling is the extraordinary vocal work, *Cinq rechants*, written for a choir of twelve soloists. The composer's inspiration of human passion brings both lyrical intensity and extraordinary irregular rhythmic effects (some of which have an Indian source) and the various bursts and cascades of vocal tone give the work a stimulatingly original vitality. The performance is remarkably assured and full of ardent spontaneity, and the group are vividly recorded. Excellent notes are provided by the composer.

PIANO MUSIC

Catalogue d'oiseaux (complete); *Petites esquisses d'oiseaux.*
(BB) *** Naxos Dig. 8.553532/4 (3) [id.]. Håkan Austbø.

The Norwegian pianist, Håkan Austbø, has already distinguished himself in composers such as Scriabin and Messiaen. We felt his earlier Naxos account of the *Vingt regards sur l'enfant Jésus* (see below) can hold its own with any full-price version in the catalogue. The same goes for these dedicated readings. The seven books of the *Catalogue d'oiseaux* occupied Messiaen between 1956 and 1958, and they include 13 ornithological portraits. (It was this work which prompted one French critic to write that if the birds really sang like this, '*la chasse doit devenir un devoir social*'.) The *Petites esquisses d'oiseaux* are much later. Whatever one's reactions to Messiaen's music, he creates a world entirely his own, and one must echo Harry Halbreich's verdict, 'If the general public has always followed Messiaen even in his boldest innovations, is it not because his music rejects sheer abstraction, preferring instead to reflect a living experience; fruit of the most refined ear, it is the most recognizable music possible?' Håkan Austbø is completely attuned to this sensibility, and the recording is exemplary. Aficionados of Messiaen need not hesitate.

8 Préludes pour piano; Vingt regards sur l'enfant Jésus.
(B) **(*) EMI Rouge et Noir CZS5 69668-2 [CDZB 69668]. Michel Béroff.

The *Préludes* are early works but, like *Vingt regards*, they show Béroff at his most inspired, generating the illusion of spontaneous creation. Clean, well-focused sound – but, even though the venue was the Salle Wagram, the close balance brings a lack of rich sonority, although the effect is not untruthful.

Vingt regards sur l'enfant Jésus.
(M) *** Erato/Warner 4509 91705-2 (2) [id.]. Yvonne Loriod.
(BB) *** Naxos Dig. 8.550829/30 [id.]. Håkon Austbø.

The 1973 recording by Yvonne Loriod – the composer's second wife – of *Vingt regards* has long been considered very special in its understanding and feeling for the composer's mystical sound-world. The piano recording is full but is otherwise acceptable rather than outstanding – yet the magnetism of the playing overcomes the lack of the sharpest focus.

Håkon Austbø as one-time prize-winner of the Olivier Messiaen Competition for Contemporary Music in Royan has excellent credentials for performing this repertoire, and his is an individual view, with a wider range of tempi and dynamic than Loriod. His account of the opening *Regard du Père* and the later *Regard du Fils sur le Fils* is paced much more slowly, but his playing has great concentration and evocative feeling so that he readily carries the slower tempo, and in *Par lui tout a été fait* articulation is bolder, giving the music a stronger profile, helped by the clearer, Naxos digital focus. This is undoubtedly a performance that grips the listener and can be strongly recommended as an alternative view.

ORGAN MUSIC

Complete works for organ: *Apparition de l'Eglise éternelle; L'Ascension (4 Méditations); Le banquet céleste; Le corps glorieux (7 Visions de la vie des ressuscités); Diptyque (Essai sur la vie terrestre et l'éternité religieuse); Livre d'Orgue (Reprises par interversion; Première pièce en trio; Les mains de l'abîme; Chants oiseaux; Deuxième pièce en trio; Les yeux dans les roues; Soixante-quatre durées). Messe de la Pentecôte; La Nativité du Seigneur (9 Méditations).*
(M) *** EMI mono CZS7 67400-2 (4) [CDZD 674002]. Composer (Cavaillé-Coll organ de L'Eglise de la Sainte-Trinité, Paris).

In an intensive series of sessions which began at the end of May and continued through June and July 1956, Olivier Messiaen returned to the organ in Sainte-Trinité, with which all his music is associated, and recorded everything he had written and published before that date. These performances not only carry the imprint of the composer's authority, but also the inspiration of the occasion. The large-scale works have a concentration and compelling atmosphere that are unforgettable. No apologies at all need be made for the range, breadth and faithfulness of the recording, although some must be made for the organ itself, which is not always perfectly tuned. There is minor background hiss, which is not troublesome, and technically the CD transfers are a remarkable achievement.

VOCAL MUSIC

Chants de terre et de ciel; Harawi (Chants d'amour et de mort). 3 Mélodies (Pourquoi; Le sourire; La fiancée); Poèmes pour Mi.
(M) *** EMI CMS7 64092-2 (2). Michèle Command, Marie-Madeleine Petit.

Michèle Command is here most characterful and firmly focused, with her accompanist just as warmly idiomatic. The three early songs of 1930 lead naturally to the two cycles from the late 1930s, more complex in their melodic lines. It is then that the ambitious Harawi cycle of 1945 reveals the full scope of the mature Messiaen's style, with its echoes of birdsong. This hour-long cycle belongs to what the composer regarded as his 'Tristan and Isolde' trilogy, along with the *Turangalîla Symphony* and the choral cycle, *Cinq Rechants*. Clear, undistracting sound.

Meyerbeer, Giacomo (1791–1864)

Les Patineurs (ballet suite, arr. & orch. Lambert).
(B) *** Decca Dig. 444 110-2 [(M) id. import]. Nat. PO, Richard Bonynge – MASSENET: *Le Cid* etc. ***
(M) *** Decca (IMS) 425 468-2 (3). Nat. PO, Bonynge – TCHAIKOVSKY: *Sleeping Beauty*. **(*)

Les Patineurs was arranged by Constant Lambert using excerpts from two of Meyerbeer's operas, *Le*

Prophète and *L'Etoile du Nord*. Bonynge's approach is warm and comparatively easy-going but, with such polished orchestral playing, this version is extremely beguiling. The sound too is first rate. There are alternative couplings.

Les Huguenots (complete).
(M) *** Decca (IMS) 430 549-2 (4) [id.]. Sutherland, Vrenios, Bacquier, Arroyo, Tourangeau, Ghiuselev, New Philh. O, Bonynge.

Sutherland is predictably impressive, though once or twice there are signs of a 'beat' in the voice, previously unheard on Sutherland records. The rest of the cast is uneven, and in an unusually episodic opera, with passages that are musically less than inspired, that brings disappointments. Gabriel Bacquier and Nicola Ghiuselev are fine in their roles and, though Martina Arroyo is below her best as Valentine, the star quality is unmistakable. The tenor, Anastasios Vrenios, copes with the extraordinarily high tessitura and florid diversions. Vrenios sings the notes, which is more than almost any rival could. Fine recording to match this ambitious project, well worth investigating by lovers of French opera. The work sounds newly minted on CD.

Miaskovsky, Nikolay (1881–1950)

Cello concerto in C min., Op. 66.
❀ (M) *** EMI CDM5 65419-2 [id.]. Rostropovich, Philh. O, Sargent – TANEYEV: *Suite de concert.* ***

Rostropovich's pioneering account with Sir Malcolm Sargent is still in a class of its own. It could not be played with greater eloquence and restraint, and the (1956) Abbey Road recording is amazingly full and fresh – one would never guess its age.

Symphonies Nos. (i) *2 in C sharp min.;* (ii) *22 in B min.*
(M) (*) Revelation RV 10068 [id.]. (i) USSR MoC SO, Gennady Rozhdestvensky; (ii) USSR SO, Yevgeni Svetlanov.

As anyone acquainted with his elegiac *Cello concerto* will know, Miaskovsky has an almost Elgarian melancholy and eloquence. He is perhaps 'born out of his time' and would be more at home in the last century than in ours. His music is impeccably crafted and has both nobility and an affecting warmth. The *Symphony No. 2 in C sharp minor* is pre-First World War and owes a lot to his teacher, Glière, and to Scriabin. The *Symphony No. 22 in B minor*, composed during the last war, has appeared before, but the *Second* is new to the catalogue. It is a rewarding score, but Miaskovsky enthusiasts should not get too carried away. Although Gennady Rozhdestvensky and the USSR Ministry of Culture Symphony Orchestra give an exemplary performance, the recording is unpleasantly shallow and reverberant, with shrill, acidulated strings and distortion in climaxes. Comparison of the powerful *Symphony No. 22*, which Svetlanov and the USSR orchestra released on an HMV LP in the mid-1970s, is not to the advantage of the newcomer. The beginning of the finale is particularly bad. The HMV Melodiya transfer engineers obviously took greater trouble with the tape than have Revelation. There was some measure of distortion at climaxes on the old LP but, if anything, it is worse here. The sleeve design looks cheap and shoddy. Alas, there are no alternative versions of either symphony.

Cello sonata No. 2, Op. 81.
(BB) * Koch Discover Dig. DICD 920407 [id.]. Laetitia Himo, Nadia Himo – FALLA: *Suite populaire espagnole;* PROKOFIEV: *Cello sonata.* *

At one time the neglect of Miaskovsky's musicianly and finely crafted sonatas was total, but in recent years they have served as fill-ups to Prokofiev, Shostakovich and Rachmaninov. The most obvious recommendation is the (nearly full-price) Olympia disc by Marina Tarassova, coupling both the sonatas and the wonderful *Cello concerto* (OCD 530). Readers who do not need the concerto should approach the present issue with some caution. Laetitia Himo and Nadia Himo are a highly accomplished French partnership but are recorded in a resonant and rather mushy acoustic.

Mica, Jan Adam Franisek (1746–1811)

String quartet No. 6 in C.
(M) *** Cal. CAL 6698. Talich Qt – BOCCHERINI: *Quartet, Op. 58/2;* HAYDN: *Quartet No. 74;* MENDELSSOHN: *Quartet No. 2.* ***

The Bohemian composer, Jan Mica (1746–1811), writes elegantly in the *galant* style, and this *C major Quartet* (his sixth) brings an enticing opening theme, then continues in a cultivated and courtly style. Yet the *Rondo* finale produces a quite touching central interlude and one is reminded of Boccherini. Throughout, the warmth and finesse of the Talich playing ensure our enjoyment of what is a slight but well-crafted little work.

Milán, Luis de (*c.* 1500–*c.* 1561)

El Maestro: Fantasias Nos. 7, 8, 9 & 16; Pavanas Nos. 1, 4, 5 & 6; Tento No. 1.

(M) *** RCA 09026 61606-2 [id.]. Julian Bream (lute) (with MUDARRA: *Fantasia*) – NARVAEZ: *Collection.* ***

This music was originally written for the vihuela, a hybrid instrument popular in sixteenth-century Spain, looking like a guitar but tuned like a lute. It was Milán who produced the first published book of this music in 1535, calling it *El Maestro* and including also instruction. Julian Bream seeks and achieves nobility of feeling in this repertoire and often chooses slow, dignified tempi. It all sounds splendid here on a proper lute, especially when so beautifully recorded.

Milano, Francesco Canova da (1497–1543)

(i) Lute duets: *Canon; Fantasia quarta; Fantasia quinta; Fantasia sexta; Ricercar prima; Ricercar seconda; Ricercar terza; La spagna*. Pieces for solo lute: *Fantasias Nos. 30; 55–6; 63–7; 81–3; Ricercars Nos. 2; 10; 13; 69–70; 73; 76 & 79.*

(BB) *** Naxos Dig. 8.550774 [id.]. Christopher Wilson, (i) with Shirley Rumsey.

During his lifetime Francesco Canova da Milano was known as 'Il Divino' and was, by all accounts, 'a miraculous lute player'. By the time he was twenty-two he was already in the employ of the Pope. He served the Gonzaga Court at Mantua and Cardinal Ippolito de' Medici, though he spent most of his years in the papal court working for Leo X, Adrian VI, Clement VII and Paul III. In 1538 he accompanied Paul III to Nice for his meeting with Charles V and François I, and possibly visited Paris, since two of his compositions are attributed to 'Francesco da Parigi'. He published four collections of works in Venice, Milan and Naples during his lifetime, but his music is widely encountered – in no fewer than 40 printed tablatures. He was the most prolific lute composer of his day, even more so than his close contemporary, the Spanish vilhuelist and composer, Luis de Milán.

Christopher Wilson plays this collection of pieces, including duets with Shirley Rumsey, with a natural and unforced authority. Cultured playing of highly civilized music – recorded with admirable clarity, though it is advisable to reduce the level setting to get the most lifelike and natural result.

Milhaud, Darius (1892–1974)

(i) *Ballade, Op. 61; Le carnaval d'Aix, Op. 83b* (both for piano and orchestra); *Piano concertos Nos. 1, Op. 127; 4, Op. 295; 5 Etudes for piano and orchestra, Op. 61;* (ii) *Le boeuf sur le toit, Op. 58;* (ii–iii) *Harp concerto, Op. 323;* (ii) *La création du monde, Op. 81.*

(B) *** Erato/Warner Ultima Double Dig. 3984 21347-2 (2) [(M) id. import]. (i) Claude Helffer, O. Nat. de France, David Robertson; (ii) Lyon Op. O, Nagano; (iii) with Frédérick Cambreling.

This admirable Erato Ultima Double combines two highly recommendable collections from the early 1990s and includes a great deal of Milhaud's most attractive music, very well recorded. Claude Helffer's account of Milhaud's delightful *Le carnaval d'Aix* with the Orchestre National must rank high in terms of easy-going charm and Mediterranean-like atmosphere, an altogether delightful performance. All the pieces on this disc, incidentally, are for piano and orchestra. The *Ballade* was composed for Roussel, and Milhaud made his piano début at its première in New York: its languorous opening seems to hark back to his days in Brazil. The first of the *Cinq Etudes* shows Milhaud in window-breaking, polytonal mode, as does the third, *Fugues*, while the fourth, *Sombre*, also has a high norm of dissonance; on the other hand, the second, *Doucement*, has a beguiling charm. The *First Piano concerto* is a relaxed, charming work not dissimilar to, though more complex in texture than, Jean Françaix's well-known *Concertino*. The *Fourth Piano concerto*, Op. 295 (1949), is an inventive piece of some substance with a particularly imaginative, dream-like slow movement.

Kent Nagano and the Orchestra of the Opéra de Lyon give a splendid account of themselves in both the ballets. In *La création* the playing is full of character (the jazz fugue comes off marvellously) and the opening has splendid atmosphere; and much the same may be said of Nagano's exhilarating account of the Cocteau-inspired *Le boeuf sur le toit*: the playing is first rate and so, too, is the digital recording. The

1953 *Harp concerto* was written in America for Nicanor Zabaleta. It is not top-drawer Milhaud; there is more activity than substance for much of the time, but the slow movement has many beautiful things and Cambreling makes out a very good case for the high-spirited finale.

Le boeuf sur le toit.
(M) *** Mercury (IMS) 434 335-2 [id.]. LSO, Dorati – AURIC: *Overture;* FETLER: *Contrasts;* FRANCAIX: *Piano concertino;* SATIE: *Parade.* ***

Dorati's reading, effervescent and light-hearted, catches the idiom splendidly and the music's lilt is infectiously conveyed. The LSO are obviously enjoying themselves and their playing, subtle as well as vivid, catches the audacious mood of a piece which is a trifle long for its content but which still entertains. The (1965) Mercury recording is perfectly judged, giving the music both transparency, vibrant colour and its proper edge.

La création du monde.
(M) *** EMI CDM7 63945-2 [id.]. Paris Conservatoire O, Prêtre – DUTILLEUX: *Le Loup;* POULENC: *Les Biches.* ***
(M) *** Virgin/EMI Dig. CUV5 61206-2 [id.]. Lausanne CO, Zedda – DEBUSSY: *Danse; Sarabande;* PROKOFIEV: *Sinfonietta.* ***

Prêtre's recording of *La création du monde* is unsurpassed in catching both the bitter-sweet sensuousness of the creation scene and the jazzy pastiche of the mating dance – the rhythmic touch is very much in the authentic spirit of 1920s' French jazz. The 1961 sound has been transformed in the CD remastering: it is fresh and vivid, yet admirably atmospheric. The couplings are no less attractive.

Milhaud's ballet, with its mixture of yearning melancholy and jazzy high spirits, comes off splendidly in Alberto Zedda's highly spontaneous account, its witty syncopations and brassy exuberance bringing an unbridled effervescence to offset the restrained blues feeling of the main lyrical theme. The performance doesn't miss the Gershwin affinities, and the very vivid recording makes a bold dynamic contrast between the work's tender and abrasive moments.

Suite française.
(M) *** CDWHL 2067. L. Wind O, Wick – GRAINGER: *Irish tune from County Derry* etc.; POULENC: *Suite française.* ***

Milhaud's *Suite française* for wind is an enchanting piece, full of Mediterranean colour and vitality. It would be difficult to imagine a more idiomatic or spirited performance than this one, which has excellent blend and balance. Vivid recording.

CHAMBER MUSIC

Music for wind: *La Cheminée du Roi René, Op. 105; Divertissement en trois parties, Op. 399b; Pastorale, Op. 47; 2 Sketches, Op. 227b; Suite d'après Corrette, Op. 161b.*
(M) **(*) Chandos CHAN 6536 [id.]. Athena Ens., McNichol.

Though none of this is first-class Milhaud, it is still full of pleasing and attractive ideas, and the general air of easy-going, life-loving enjoyment is well conveyed by the alert playing of the Athena Ensemble. One's only quarrel with this issue is the somewhat close balance. However, this can be remedied a little by a lower-level setting; even if the overall playing time is not very generous, this is an excellent entertainment.

String quartets Nos. 1, Op. 5; 2, Op. 16.
(B) *** Koch Discover Dig. DICD 920290 [id.]. Arriaga Qt.

The *First Quartet* comes from 1912 and is dedicated to the memory of Milhaud's fellow-Provencal, Cézanne; it is among the most diatonic of all his works. It is unusual in having two slow movements, both of which find him at his most serene. There are occasional hints of the Debussy *Quartet* and even a faint shadow of Franck in the *Grave* movement. The *Second* was composed during the first of the war years (1914–15) at about the time Milhaud was embarking on that key work in his development, *Les choéphores*, and there are signs of an emergent fascination with polytonality. The Arriaga Quartet are very persuasive. They produce some real *pianopianissimo* tone when required and communicate their feeling for the music. Try the middle movement (there are five movements in all), whose silky textures (much of it is *con sord*) come over beautifully.

PIANO MUSIC

Complete piano music

Accueil amical, Op. 326; L'Album de Mme Bovary, Op. 128; 4 Romances sans paroles, Op. 129; Une journée, Op. 269; Suadades do Brasil, Op. 67; 3 Valses extraits du film, 'Madame Bovary', Op. 128.
(BB) *(*) Koch Discovery Dig. DICD 920425 [id.]. Françoise Choveaux.

L'Automne, Op. 115; Choral, Op. 111; 4 Esquisses, Op. 227; Jeu, Op. 302; Mazurka; La Muse Ménagère, Op. 245; Printemps Cahier Nos 1–2, Opp. 25 & 66; 3 Rag-caprices, Op. 78; Le Tando des Fratellini, Op. 58c; Touches blanches; Touches noires, Op. 222/1–2.
(BB) *(*) Koch Discovery Dig. DICD 920426 [id.]. Françoise Choveaux.

Hymne de glorification; Sonatas Nos. 1, Op. 33; 2, Op. 293; Sonatine, Op. 354; Suite, Op. 8.
(BB) *(*) Koch Discovery Dig. DICD 920427 [id.]. Françoise Choveaux.

As a pianist, Milhaud was capable rather than distinguished. In earlier years he was a string player – and indeed took part in the first performance of Debussy's ethereal *Sonata for flute, viola and harp* in 1916. As the listings above show, he wrote a considerable quantity of piano music – though, taken in proportion to his output as a whole, his contribution was minuscule. While there are charming miniatures scattered here and there, the level of inspiration runs at a low ebb elsewhere. Probably the most rewarding piece is *La Muse Ménagère* ('The Household muse'), dedicated to his wife Madeleine and portraying various domestic duties as well as the household cat. Milhaud himself recorded this suite, among other things, for Columbia Records in the early 1950s. All these pieces deserve more persuasive advocacy and more charm than Françoise Choveaux brings to them, and more pleasing recorded sound.

Piano sonata No. 1; L'automne; Printemps, Books 1 & 2; 4 Sketches (Esquisses); Sonatine.
(B) ** Koch Discover Dig. DICD 920167 [id.]. Billi Eidi.

Milhaud was a capable pianist. Here is a good cross-section of his output for solo piano covering four decades from the *Première Sonate* to the *Sonatine*. Some of the music, such as the first book of *Printemps* or the *Quatre Esquisses*, is charming; none of it makes great demands on either the pianist or the listener, and some of it is pretty inconsequential. All the same, taken in small doses, there is much that gives pleasure – and would give more if the recording were not quite so bottom-heavy or wanting in transparency. Billi Eidi's playing is fluent, sensitive and totally committed.

VOCAL MUSIC

Les Choéphores, Op. 24.
(M) *** Sony MHK 62352 [id.]. Vera Zorina (narr.), McHenry Boatwright, Irene Jordan, Virginia Babikian, NY Schola Cantorum, NYPO, Bernstein – HONEGGER: *Rugby, Pacific 231* **; ROUSSEL: *Symphony No. 3.* **(*)
(M) (**) DG Originals mono 449 748-2 [id.]. Geneviève Moizan, Hélène Bouvier, Heinz Rehfuss, Claude Nollier, Chorale de L'Université, Lamoureux O, Igor Markevitch – HONEGGER: *Symphony No. 5* (**); ROUSSEL: *Bacchus et Ariane: Suite No. 2.* **

Les Choéphores is the second part of Milhaud's setting of Paul Claudel's translation of the *Oresteia* of Aeschylus. It was composed in 1915 at the height of the First World War and comprises seven scenes which cover the same events as are depicted in Strauss's *Elektra*. Milhaud scores the work for large forces, including a spoken role – effectively declaimed on Sony by Vera Zorina – plus soloists, chorus and orchestra. It marked a bold and radical departure in Milhaud's style, making use of polytonality, choral speech and arresting dramatic effects. It is a work of stark intensity, and the sleeve quotes the critic Alfred Frankenstein as hailing it as 'absolutely sensational'. Bernstein's 1961 performance never appeared on this side of the Atlantic on LP, though the Honegger and Roussel items (from much the same period) did. The performance is thrilling and the recording sounds excellent for the period. This is an important issue, much enhanced by the interest of the Roussel coupling and the excellence of the presentation.

Markevitch's 1957 recording has a lot going for it. The performance is strongly characterized, though less virtuosic than Leonard Bernstein's vivid stereo account, made in New York four years later. The mono recording is well balanced with plenty of front-to-back depth and good perspective, though it has the inevitable tonal frailty one might expect after 40 years. The soloists are generally good, but Bernstein scores with the superiority of the orchestral playing and the choral singing.

Moeran, Ernest J. (1894–1950)

(i) *Cello concerto;* (ii–iii) *Violin concerto;* (iii) *2 Pieces for small orchestra: Lonely waters; Whythorne's shadow.*

(M) *** Chandos Enchant Dig. CHAN 7078 [id.]. (i) Raphael Wallfisch, Bournemouth Sinf., Del Mar; (ii) Lydia Mordkovitch; (iii) Ulster O, Handley.

The *Cello concerto* (1945) is a pastoral work with elegiac overtones, save in its rather folksy finale. Raphael Wallfisch brings an eloquence of tone and a masterly technical address to this neglected piece, and he receives very responsive orchestral support from Norman Del Mar and the Bournemouth players. The *Violin concerto* is also strongly lyrical in feeling. The first movement is thoughtful and rhapsodic, its inspiration drawn from Moeran's love of the west coast of Ireland; the middle movement makes use of folk music; while the finale, a ruminative elegy of great beauty, is the most haunting of the three. Lydia Mordkovitch plays with great natural feeling for this music and, quite apart from his sensitive support in the *Concerto*, Vernon Handley gives an outstanding (and affecting) account of *Lonely waters*. Superb recording. This is one of the most attractive and generous (78 minutes) reissues on Chandos's new mid-priced label, Enchant, with the sobriquet here entirely appropriate.

Symphony in G min.

✿ (M) *** Dutton Laboratories mono CDAX 8001 [id. full price]. Hallé O, Leslie Heward – IRELAND: *Piano concerto.* (***)

There is always something special about first recordings, but this is remarkable in more than one respect. First, it is a wonderful performance of a great British symphony. Secondly, it celebrates a great British conductor, working at white-hot intensity, who died (so prematurely) just over a year after the original 78s appeared. Walter Legge produced the sessions in Manchester's Houldsworth Hall, and his mono sound-balance was completely natural, using the slightly dry hall acoustics to maximum advantage. Finally, no praise can be too great for Michael Dutton's CD transfer, made direct from the 78-r.p.m. shellac pressings, using the Cedar system to suppress the surface noise, yet providing sound for which no apologies whatsoever need be made, with no edginess to ruin the strings: the violins sound particularly fresh. The composer was present at the sessions and gave his imprimatur. This CD is fully worthy of it. The Ireland coupling is hardly less indispensable.

String quartets Nos. 1 in E flat; 2 in A min.; String trio.

(BB) *** Naxos 8.554079 [id.]. Maggini Qt.

Moeran's chamber music has been seriously neglected on disc, and this delightful issue could not be more welcome. The *String quartet in A minor* (1921) has a certain pastoral quality, with Irish echoes in the dance rhythms and ending on a flamboyant Rondo. It is most persuasively played here. The *String trio* of 1931, beautifully written with no feeling of thinness, is even subtler, with the pastoral idiom more equivocal in its tonal shiftings. The CD also offers something of a discovery in the form of an earlier *Quartet in E flat* that the cellist Peer Coetmore (Moeran's widow) found among the composer's papers after his death. Moeran apparently lost faith in the piece and suppressed it. Although it is not a masterpiece, there are some quite inspired things in it and the Maggini play it with great dedication and commitment. The recording is very life-like and present. A first-class bargain.

String trio in G.

(M) (***) Dutton Lab. CDAX 8014 [id. full price]. Pougnet, Riddle, Pini – BAX: *Nonet;* FERGUSON: *Octet;* DELIUS: *Violin sonata No. 3.* (***)

This is an only recording of the work, and it would be hard to imagine a better performance of this lyrical and resourceful piece, which is full of imagination. The recording sounds remarkably fresh in this fine transfer.

Mompou, Federico (1893–1987)

Suite compostellana (for guitar).

(M) *** RCA Dig. 09026 61596-2 [id.]. Julian Bream – RECITAL: *'Twentieth-century guitar'.* ***

Mompou's *Suite compostellana* is his only work for guitar – and very fine it is, beautifully written for the instrument and with a prevailing mood of wistful melancholy. Bream's performance is wonderfully sympathetic and spontaneous and the digital recording is first class.

8 Canciones i danzas; Escenas de niños; Fiestas lejanas; Paisajes; Pessebres; Suburbis.
(M) *** EMI CDM7 64470-2 [id.]. Gonzalo Soriano or Carmen Bravo.

Gonzalo Soriano plays these reflective miniatures simply and with the right degree of restrained eloquence. Mompou is the very antithesis of a gaudy impressionist; his musical pictures are restrained and delicately delineated. Carmen Bravo also finds poetry in the rest of the programme and is charmingly perceptive in his portrayal – in *Suburbis* – of *L'home de l'aristo* (the *aristo* was a cross between a hand-held miniature barrel-organ and a hurdy-gurdy). The *Escenas de niños* are gentle children's pictures, while the *Fiestas lejanas* are a series of brief vignettes, echoes and memories of past festivities. The two closing *Paisajes* with evocations of fountain, bell and lake are delightful, and the playing here catches well their delicately picaresque understatement. A rewarding and generous recital, given remarkably good recording, even though it dates from the early days of stereo.

Mondonville, Jean-Joseph Cassanea de (1711–72)

Pièces de clavecin avec voix ou violon, Op. 5/1-8
(B) *** HM Musique d'abord HMA 1901045 [id.]. Judith Nelson, Stanley Ritchie, William Christie.

Mondonville is credited with developing the harpsichord sonata with obbligato violin, which he called *Pièces de clavecin en sonates* (Opus 3). But Mondonville experimented too with the voice as a chamber-music instrument alongside a stringed instrument. In his *Pièces de clavecin avec voix ou violon* the music was composed independently of any text. The composer then fitted religious Latin texts to the musical line. What is striking is how naturally vocal the music sounds. The fine balance and expert playing of Stanley Ritchie and William Christie's sensitive harpsichord contribution add much to this presentation. But the greater part of the credit must go to the lovely singing of Judith Nelson, whose many shakes and turns are a pleasure in themselves. The sequential lines of Mondonville's writing are followed most sensitively. No. 3, *Benefac, Domine*, is particularly beautiful. The closely woven instrumental ritornello which opens No. 4, *Laudate Dominum*, includes an unnamed gamba player as part of the continuo and leads to a soaring, imitative vocal line. No. 5, *Paratum cor meum*, and No. 6, *In Domino laudabitur*, are ravishing, but No. 7, *Quare tristis es?* ('Why art thou cast down?'), is even more affecting, and it is difficult to believe that the music did not originally stem directly from the text. The final setting here, *Protector meus*, has an extended instrumental introduction. The vocal writing then becomes remarkably florid, even anticipating Mozart, and as usual building sequential phrases with plenty of decoration. The effect is very operatic, with the violin acting like an obbligato when taking over from the voice. Altogether an outstanding disc, and very well recorded.

Montemezzi, Italo (1875–1952)

L'amore dei tre re (complete).
(M) **(*) RCA 74321 50166-2 (2). Moffo, Domingo, Elvira, Siepi, Ryland Davies, Amb. Op. Ch., LSO, Nello Santi.

In 1913 at La Scala, Milan, Italo Montemezzi, one of Puccini's young successors, delivered this lurid melodrama based on a play by Sem Benelli. Set in a medieval palace ruled over by a blind king, Archibaldo, the obvious dramatic echoes of *Tristan* and *Pelleas*, combined with a red-blooded, lyrical score, brought it success not just in Italy, but more significantly in the United States, where Toscanini conducted the opera at the Met. in 1914. What it lacks, compared to Puccini – let alone to Wagner or Debussy – are memorable ideas, with melodic fragments rarely adding up to a genuine tune, and with no sustained set numbers to punctuate the free-flowing progress of the music. Nevertheless, with colourful scoring and an economical structure it makes easy listening. Even by operatic standards the plot is absurd: the heroine, Fiora, on refusing to disclose the name of her lover to the blind king, is promptly strangled by him. After that, in the final Act Archibaldo smears Fiora's lips with deadly poison, catching in turn not only the returning lover, Avito, but his own son, the heroine's husband, Manfredo, who consciously sacrifices himself by pressing his lips to those of the corpse.

This 1977 recording with Nello Santi a thrustful conductor makes as good a case for the piece as one is likely to get. Anna Moffo is an old-sounding if dramatic Fiora, but Plácido Domingo is in glowing form as Avito, and Cesare Siepi vividly heightens the melodrama as Archibaldo. As Manfredo, the baritone, Pablo Elvira, sings with firm, clean attack, as does Ryland Davies in the role of the castle guard, Flaminio. Full, warm, well-balanced sound. Synopsis and libretto with translation are provided but no background information on the work or the composer.

Monteverdi, Claudio (1567–1643)

Madrigals and motets (collection)

Disc 1: Madrigals: *Addio Florida bella; Ahi com'a un vago sol; E così a poco a poco torno farfalla; Era l'anima mia; Luci serene e chiare; Mentre vaga Angioletta ogn'anima; Ninfa che scalza il piede; O mio bene, a mia vita; O Mirtillo, Mirtill'anima mia; Se pur destina; Taci, Armelin deh taci; T'amo mia vita; Troppo ben può questo tiranno amore.*

Disc 2: Madrigals: *Bel pastor dal cui bel guardo; Lamento d'Arianna; Non è gentil cor; O come sei gentile; Ohimé, dov'é il mio ben; Zefiro torna* (with Benedetto FERRARI: *Queste pungenti spine* (cantata); (attrib. FERRARI): Final duet for MONTEVERDI: *L'Incoronazione di Poppea: Pur ti miro, pur ti godo*).

Disc 3: Motets for 1, 2 & 3 voices: *Confitebor tibi Domine* (solo); *Duo seraphim* (a 3); *Ego flos campi* (solo); *Fugge, anima mea* (a 2); *Jubilet; Laudate Dominum; Nigra sum* (all three solos); *O beata viae* (a 2); *O quam pulchra es* (solo); *Pulchra es, amica mea* (a 2); *Salve, O Regina* (solo).
(B) **(*) HM Analogue Dig. HMX 290841/3 [(M) id.]. Concerto Vocale, René Jacobs.

One of Harmonia Mundi's bargain 'trios', this Monteverdi programme is presented by the Concerto Vocale directed by the distinguished counter-tenor, René Jacobs, whose vocal artistry and virtuosity dominate many of the performances. It offers an admirable, inexpensive survey of Monteverdi's music, both his madrigals and his church music. The disc called *'Un concert spirituel'* is the highlight of the set and might have received a Rosette as an independent issue. It opens with the remarkable and beautiful *Duo seraphim* which juxtaposes overlapping long notes and rapid virtuoso diminutions, suggesting angels' wings as well as a celestial chorale. The music becomes quite sublime when on the words '*tres sunt*' a third voice enters to symbolize the Trinity. The two-part *O beata viae* begins lightly, with the vocal parts in imitation before its character becomes more reflective; the moods then alternate; and these contrasts of serenity with bravura outbursts are even more striking in the *Salve, O Regina*. Both the solo *Confitebor tibi Domine* and the duet *Fugge, anima mea* are in essence miniature cantatas, with complex duets followed by solos which additionally bring a violin obbligato. This was originally played by the soloist, who was expected to be an instrumentalist as well as a singer. *Pulchra es* is the first of Monteverdi's chamber duets, with the second voice entering unexpectedly to fill out the texture richly. The dramatically expressive *Nigra sum* soon becomes lyrically quite sensuous, especially at the decorated closing section, and *O quam pulchra es* is very like one of the composer's operatic laments, and very touching. Both are set to words from the Song of Songs. Their dolorous feeling is well caught by Jacobs, whose decoration is very assured. *Laudate Dominum* and *Jubilet* both have joyful dancing rhythms, but are again interrupted by passages of virtuoso recitative; the latter ends with jubilant '*Allelujas*'. Both are sung delightfully by Judith Nelson, and altogether this makes an outstanding concert, with imaginatively varied continuo accompaniments (including organ as well as harpsichord). They are recorded in an atmospheric acoustic, adding bloom to voices and instruments alike, without clouding detail.

The first madrigal collection is also available separately on a bargain Musique d'Abord CD (HMA 190184). It is a highly attractive collection of generally neglected items, briskly and stylishly performed, and, with continuo accompaniment, the contrasting of vocal timbres is achieved superbly. Again excellent recording.

The third programme offers repertoire that is more familiar, including the famous *Lamento d'Arianna*. However, here Jacobs allots the lead vocal role to Helga Müller-Molinari, whose general approach is too redolent of grand opera always to carry conviction, while her opulent voice does not blend readily with the instrumental support. The interest of this disc is greatly increased by the inclusion of music by Benedetto Ferrari, a Venetian composer of the generation following Monteverdi, and also a playwright and theorbo player. He is best remembered for a handful of operas and his three books of *Musiche varie*. His *Queste pungenti spine* is a spiritual cantata which comes from the 1637 book and is accompanied on the CD by the final duet from *L'Incoronazione di Poppea*, which has been attributed to him by some scholars. Listening to the one, it is very difficult to believe he really did compose the other, for the Monteverdi madrigals are on a much higher level of inspiration.

Madrigals, Books 4–5 (complete). *Book 7: Con che soavità, labbra odorate; Tempro la cetra. Book 8: (Madrigali guerrieri et amorosi): Mentre vaga; Ogni amante è guerrier.*
(B) *** O-L Dig. Double 455 718-2 (2). Consort of Musicke, Anthony Rooley.

This Oiseau-Lyre Double offers exceptional value in including the whole of the contents of Book 4 (dating from 1603) and Book 5 (1605), plus four substantial accompanied madrigals which come from the composer's later, Venetian years. Under Anthony Rooley, the well-integrated singers of the Consort of Musicke, led by the fresh-voiced Emma Kirkby, give masterly performances of the dazzling collection of madrigals comprising the fourth book, which suits their vocal style especially well. One has only to sample the moving and beautifully sung opening piece, *Ah dolente partita!*, to note the tonal beauty, flexibility and control of dramatic contrast, conveying consistent commitment, which make this one of this group's finest records, helped by the atmospheric but aptly intimate recording. Book 5 marked a turning point in Monteverdi's madrigal output, for the last six works bring an obligatory continuo and are much freer in style than their predecessors, even semi-operatic in their use of freely individual vocal solos, contrasted with more sustained, concerted passages. It might be said that the change of style in the singing here is less marked than in the competing (full-priced) collection of these works by the Concerto Italiano directed by Rinaldo Alessandro (Opus 111 Op 30–81), whose singing is distinctly Italianate and more extrovert. Nevertheless the comparatively restrained approach of Rooley's group brings its own rewards, and their refinement is reflected in the delicate lute continuo in the later numbers. The performance of the closing *Questi vaghi concerti* ('These charming songs that the birds all around are singing as day breaks') is particularly successful in combining impressive sonorities with firmly woven inner parts, heard against a comparatively expansive accompaniment. The later madrigals are even more successful, their quixotic mood-changes superbly caught. All four are among Monteverdi's most imaginative dialogue settings, displaying much operatic feeling. *Tempro la cetra* ('I tune the lute') has a noble introductory instrumental ritornello, but the most ambitious, *Ogni amante è guerrier*, crowns the programme at the end of the second CD. This is a 14-minute scena in which Rinuccini's text is given first to a tenor solo and tenor/bass duet, which frame a long, bravura bass declamation dramatically soliloquizing in the mood of the title, *Every lover is a warrior*. This is superbly sung here, and it is a pity that the soloists are not named. The recording is excellent throughout and full translations are provided.

Madrigals: *Addio Florida bella; Ahi com'a un vago sol; E così a poco a poco torno farfalla; Era l'anima mia; Luci serene e chiare; Mentre vaga Angioletta ogn'anima; Ninfa che scalza il piede; O mio bene, a mia vita; O Mirtillo, Mirtill'anima mia; Se pur destina; Taci, Armelin deh taci; T'amo mia vita; Troppo ben può questo tiranno amore.*

(B) *** HM Musique d'Abord HMA 1901084 [id.]. Concerto Vocale.

A highly attractive collection of generally neglected items, briskly and stylishly performed. The most celebrated of the singers is the male alto, René Jacobs, a fine director as well as soloist. With continuo accompaniment, the contrasting of vocal timbres is achieved superbly. Excellent recording and very good value.

Madrigals: *'Batto', qui pianse Ergasto; Gira, il nemico insidioso amore; Hor che'l ciel e la terra; O come sei gentile; Ogni amante è guerrir; Zefiro torna.*

❁ (M) *** Virgin Veritas/EMI Dig. VER5 61165-2 [CDM 61165-2]. Chiaroscuro, L. Baroque, Nigel Rogers – D'INDIA: *Madrigals*. *** ❁

A hand-picked half-dozen of Monteverdi's finest madrigals, superlatively sung, consistently bringing out the expressive originality and the extraordinary variety of the settings, to say nothing of their inherent vocal bravura. *Zefiro torna* is justly famous, but *'Batto', qui pianse Ergasto* is hardly less remarkable, and the two *Madrigali guerrieri et amorosi* are very telling indeed. The engagingly lyrical *O come sei gentile* follows immediately after the d'India dramatized cycle from *Il pastor Fido* and makes a fascinating comparison. Accompaniments are nicely balanced and the recording has an exceptionally real and vivid presence.

Madrigals (Duets and solos): *Chiome d'oro, bel thesoro; Il son pur vezzosetta pastorella; Non è di gentil core; O come sei gentile, caro augellino; Ohimè dov'è il mio ben?; Se pur destina e vole il cielo, partenza amorosa*. Sacred music: *Cantate Domino; Exulta, filia Sion; Iste confessoe II; Laudate Dominum in sanctis eius; O bone Jesu, o piissime Jesu; Sancta Maria, succurre miseris; Venite, siccientes ad aquas Domini*. (Opera) *Il Ritorno d'Ulisse in patria: Di misera regina (Penelope's lament)*.

(M) *** Carlton Dig. 30366 00442 [id.]. Emma Kirkby, Evelyn Tubb, Consort of Musicke, Rooley.

Those who have enjoyed the delightful artistry of Emma Kirkby will surely revel in this collection, mostly of duets in which she is joined by Evelyn Tubb. The two voices are admirably matched and both artists ornament their lines attractively and without overdoing it. Evelyn Tubb is given a solo opportunity in Penelope's lament from *Il ritorno d'Ulisse*, which she sings dramatically and touchingly. Anthony Rooley's simple accompaniments with members of the Consort of Musicke are also imaginatively stylish. We are pleased to report that the current reissue has been properly documented with notes and full translations.

Vespro della Beata Vergine (Vespers).

(M) *** Virgin Veritas/EMI Dig. VMD5 61347-2 (2). Kirkby, Nigel Rogers, Davis Thomas, Taverner Ch., Cons. & Players, Parrott.

(BB) *** Hyperion Dyad Dig. CDD 22028 (2) [id.]. The Sixteen, Harry Christophers.

(B) **(*) Teldec/Warner Ultima Dig. 0630 18955-2 (2) [2292 42671-2]. Margaret Marshall, Felicity Palmer, Philip Langridge, Kurt Equiluz, Thomas Hampson, Arthur Korn, Tölz Boys' Ch., Soloists from V. Hofbur Ch., Arnold Schönberg Ch., VCM, Harnoncourt.

(B) *(*) EMI forte (SIS) CZS5 68631-2 (2) [CDFB 68631]. Ameling, Burrowes, Brett, Tear, Rolfe Johnson, Hill, Knapp, Noble, King's College Ch., Early Music Cons. of L., Ledger – SCHUTZ: *Psalm 150;* G. GABRIELI: *Motets*. **(*)

Vespro della Beata Vergine (with *Magnificat*).

(B) ** Sony SB2K 62656 (2) [S2K 62656]. Prosper, Albert, Levitt, Melvin Brown, Drake, Gregg Smith Singers, Gregg Smith, Texas Boys' Ch., George Bragg, Columbia Bar. Ens., Craft – J. S. BACH: *Cantatas Nos. 131 and 198*. **

Though Andrew Parrott uses minimal forces, with generally one instrument and one voice per part, so putting the work on a chamber scale in a small church setting, its grandeur comes out superbly through its very intensity. Brilliant singing here by the virtuoso soloists, above all by Nigel Rogers, whose distinctive timbre may not suit every ear but who has an airy precision and flexibility to give expressive meaning to even the most taxing passages. Fine contributions too from Parrott's chosen groups of players and singers, and warm, atmospheric recording. At mid-price this is very competitive.

The Sixteen's version of Monteverdi's 1610 *Vespers* on Hyperion, beautifully scaled, presents a liturgical performance of what the scholar, Graham Dixon, suggests as Monteverdi's original conception. Dixon noted that this was one of the texts used in the Gonzaga family's traditional celebrations for their patron saint, St Barbara. He infers from this that Monteverdi's first idea was to be a work in her honour. In practice the occasional changes of text are minimal; the booklet accompanying the set even includes an order of tracks if anyone wishes to hear the *Vespers* in traditional form. As it is, with a liturgical approach, the performance includes not only relevant Gregorian chant but antiphon substitutes, including a magnificent motet of Palestrina, obviously relevant, *Gaude Barbara*. The scale of the performance is very satisfying, with The Sixteen augmented to 22 singers (7.4.6.5) and with members of the group taking the eight solo roles. Christophers provides a mean between John Eliot Gardiner's unashamedly grand view, with modern instruments and pitch, and Andrew Parrott's vital, scholarly re-creation of an intimate, princely devotion. This makes a clear first choice in the lower-priced category for those wanting a modern, digital recording, although Schneidt's fine DG Archiv set should certainly be considered (see below).

Harnoncourt's admirers may well be attracted to his 1986 recording, particularly as it is now available as an Ultima bargain Double. It was recorded live and gives a keen sense of occasion, with the grandeur of the piece linked to a consciously authentic approach. There is an entirely apt ruggedness in the interpretation, which is lightened by the characterful refinement of the solo singing from an exceptionally strong team of soloists, not to mention the fine singing from all three choirs. Ample, atmospheric recording.

Craft's version of the *Vespers* dates from 1967. It is very well recorded for its period, and there are some impressive sonorities here. Modern instruments are used and Craft's sense of style is not lacking; his tempi are usually well judged. Although the end effect is of a chamber performance, the refined choral singing gives pleasure, the playing of the trumpets is not lacking in splendour, and the close of the *Magnificat* is impressively spacious. The fresh-voiced Gloria Prosper stands out among the soloists, who are all good. At bargain price this might well be considered if the coupled Bach cantatas are acceptable.

On paper it may seem that the King's performance under Ledger presents an excellent midway course between Gardiner's full-priced, larger-scale dramatic performance using original instruments and Schneidt's reflective, intimate one, but in practice there are disappointments. In the first instance the CD transfer brings distortion with the full panoply of brass in the opening chorus and, although the sound improves later, Ledger's tempi are often disturbingly fast yet lacking in the rhythmic exuberance which makes the rival versions so compelling. The solo singing is good, but there is a perfunctory element which prevents this glorious music from flowering as it should.

Vespro della Beata Vergine (with *Magnificat II*); *Missa in illo tempore*.

(B) *** DG 447 719-2 (2) [(M) id. import]. Paul Esswood, Kevin Smith, Ian Partridge, John Elwes, David Thomas, Christopher Keyte, Instrumental soloists, Regensburg Cathedral Ch., Schneidt.

When Schneidt's DG Archiv set was issued on LP in 1975, we gave it a Rosette as the most dedicated and beautiful performance of Monteverdi's choral masterpiece yet put on record, finer than Gardiner's first Decca set, which was also a landmark in its day. In its excellent transfer to CD it comes up as freshly as ever. With male voices alone – soloists as well as choir – and a small, authentic band of instrumentalists (the cornetti squeaking delightfully), its intimacy is set against a gloriously free church acoustic which yet allows clarity. The Regensburg Choir uses young voices, and the tenor and bass singing is not always as incisive as it might be, but the rest is superbly sensitive, not just the bright-sounding trebles but also the superb team of soloists, all of them from Britain. In live performance it may not be possible for two male altos to take the solo parts in *Pulchra es*, but here Paul Esswood and Kevin Smith sing radiantly, while Ian Partridge in *Nigra sum* excels even his standards of expressiveness and beautiful tone-colour. Not the least attraction of this inexpensive reissued set is that, besides including (like Gardiner in his latest version) the alternative and scarcely less elaborate setting of the *Magnificat*, Schneidt adds the superb *Missa in illo tempore*.

(i) *Vespro della Beata Vergine (Vespers);* (ii) Motet: *Exultent coeli.*

(B) *** Decca Double 443 482-2 (2) [id.]. (i) Gomez, Palmer, Bowman, Tear, Langridge, Shirley-Quirk, Rippon, Monteverdi Ch. & O, Salisbury Cathedral Boys' Ch., Philip Jones Brass Ens., Munrow Recorder Consort; (ii) Monteverdi Ch., Philip Jones Brass & Wind Ens.; Gardiner (with (ii) Christmas motets: G. GABRIELI: *Angelus ad pastores; Audite principes; O magnum mysterium; Quem vidistis pastores?; Salvator noster.* BASSANO: *Hodie Christus natus est* ***).

Gardiner's earlier Decca recording was made before he had been won over entirely to the claims of the authentic school. Modern instruments are used and women's voices, but Gardiner's rhythms are so resilient that the result is exhilarating as well as grand. Singing and playing are exemplary, and the recording is one of Decca's most vividly atmospheric, with relatively large forces presented and placed against a helpful, reverberant acoustic. Now issued as a Double Decca (two CDs for the price of one), this set is well worth considering, with the addition to the *Vespers* of a collection of Christmas motets, mostly by Giovanni Gabrieli, first issued in 1972. The rich, sonorous dignity of Gabrieli's *Sonata pian'e forte* sounds resplendent, and in the choral numbers the vocal and instrumental blend is expert. The most impressive work here is Gabrieli's glorious *Quem vidistis pastores?*. Monteverdi's *Exultent caeli* is shorter, but one is again amazed by the range of expressive contrast. Then there is Gabrieli's fine *Salvator noster*, a motet for three five-part choirs, jubilantly rejoicing at the birth of Christ. The CD transfer is admirable.

OPERA AND OPERA-BALLET

Alfred Deller Edition: (i) *Il ballo delle ingrate;* (ii) *Lamento d'Arianna.*

(M) **(*) Van. 08.5063.71 [id.]. (i) Alfred Deller, McLoughlin, Ward, Cantelo, Amb. S., L. Chamber Players, Denis Stevens; (ii) Sheppard, Le Sage, Worthley, Todd, Deller, Bevan, Deller Consort, Deller.

Denis Stevens's pioneering stereo version of Monteverdi's *Il ballo delle ingrate* dates from 1956 and has an impressive cast, well backed up by the Ambrosian Singers and London Chamber Players. Although the orchestral sound seems rather ample to ears used to original instruments, this account rings true and there is much that is authentic, not least the decoration of the vocal line, especially by Deller himself who is most moving as Venus. Eileen McLoughlin makes a delightful Amor, and David Ward is suitably stentorian as Pluto. Readers will remember that Monteverdi wrote his early opera-ballet for performance at the wedding celebrations of Duke Francesco Gonzaga of Mantua. The Duke was to marry the young Infanta Margherita of Savoy, and the message of the opera is that she should be passionately generous in the arms of her husband-to-be. In *Il ballo* the ungrateful ladies have been confined to Hades for refusing their lovers' advances and at the end of the opera they sing a touching chorus of penitence for their unfortunate lack of ardour, followed by a plea from their leader (the sweet-voiced April Cantelo) that the noble ladies of the court should learn from their experience! It is all emotively communicated here and the recording is vivid, if rather close. In addition Deller directs a performance of the famous *Lamento d'Arianna*, sung by a vocal sextet comprising Honor Sheppard, Sally le Sage, Max Worthley, Philip Todd, Maurice Bevan and Deller himself. Here the individual voices, while having plenty of character, do not always match ideally in consort. Nevertheless a thoroughly worthwhile reissue in the Alfred Deller Edition.

Il ballo delle ingrate; Sestina: Lagrime d'amante al sepolcro dell'amata.

(M) *** HM Dig. HMT 1901108. Mellon, Laurens, Reinhardt, Feldman, Les Arts Florissants, Christie.

William Christie directs refreshingly dramatic accounts of both *Il ballo delle ingrate* and the complex but very beautiful *Sestina*. His performers have been chosen for character and bite, but all sing impressively. Some may find the lovely final lament of *Il ballo* too plaintive, but it is certainly touching and in keeping with the rest of the performance. In the glorious *Sestina* the richness of Christie's interpretation makes for compelling listening, and both performances are beautifully and vividly recorded. With full translations included, this is a fine bargain.

Il combattimento di Tancredi e Clorinda.

(BB) *** HM Solo Dig. HM 926015 [id.]. Françoise Semeliaz, Adrian Brand, Nicolas Rovenq, Les Arts Florissants, Christie.

Like his companion CD of *Il ballo delle ingrate*, Christie's account of *Il combattimento* is very dramatic, with the storytelling vividly projected and with Françoise Semeliaz a touching Clorinda in the tragic closing scene. The recording is admirably vivid too, and this makes an ideal candidate for Harmonia Mundi's bargain-basement Solo series. The libretto is in Italian and French only, but the narrative is easy enough to follow.

(i) *Il combattimento di Tancredi e Clorinda. Lamento della Ninfa; Mentre vaga Angioletta; Ogni amante e guerrier.*

(M) *** Teldec/Warner Dig. 4509 92181-2 [id.]. (i) Equiluz, Schmidt, Hollweg, Murray, Langridge, Hartman, Perry, Palmer, Mühle, Franzden; VCM, Harnoncourt.

Harnoncourt directs sharply characterized readings of substantial items from Monteverdi's eighth Book of Madrigals plus two *Canti amorosi*. The substantial scena telling of the conflict of Tancredi and Clorinda is made sharply dramatic in a bald way. *Ogni amante e guerrier*, almost as extended, is treated with similar abrasiveness, made attractively fresh but lacking subtlety. The two *Canti amorosi* are treated quite differently, in a much warmer style, with the four sopranos of *Mentre vaga Angioletta* producing sensuous sounds. *Lamento della Ninfa*, perhaps the most celebrated of all Monteverdi's madrigals, brings a luscious performance with the solo voice (Ann Murray) set evocatively at a slight distance behind the two tenors and a bass. On CD the recording is extremely vivid, with voices and instruments firmly and realistically placed. The documentation is first class in every way, with full translations and the composer's own fascinatingly detailed instructions as to how *Il combattimento* should be staged.

L'Incoronazione di Poppea.

(M) **(*) Teldec/Warner 2292 42547-2 (4) [id.]. Donath, Söderström, Berberian, Esswood, VCM, Harnoncourt.

(M) **(*) Teldec/Warner 0630 10027-2 (2). Yakar, Esswood, T. Schmidt, Tappy, Salminen, Perry, Zurich Opera House Monteverdi Ens., Harnoncourt.

(M) (*(*)) DG mono 457 674-2 (2). Jurinac, Lilowa, Stolze, Wiener, Cava, Rössel-Majdan, Janowitz, V. State Op. Ch. & O, Karajan.

Nikolaus Harnoncourt's well-paced and dramatic version makes a welcome reappearance at mid-price in Teldec's Harnoncourt series. First issued in 1974, it offers a starry cast, with Elisabeth Söderström as Nero (imaginative but not always ideally steady), Helen Donath pure-toned as Poppea and Cathy Berberian as the most characterful and moving Ottavia on disc. Others include Paul Esswood and Philip Langridge, and Harnoncourt's bold and brassy instrumentation adds to the bite. The snag is that, unnecessarily, the set stretches to four discs instead of three, which cancels out the price advantage over the excellent rival set from Richard Hickox.

Recorded in June 1978, only four years after his Vienna version with its very full text, Harnoncourt's Zurich recording is very different, done as it was in connection with a staged production and recorded here – not in the opera house – with stage noises and movement, presumably part of a video version. The text is cut by over an hour, which allows the whole opera to be fitted on two CDs instead of four, and the non-specialist will be little worried. The extra sensuousness of the approach is instantly established in the harp flourishes of the introduction, guaranteed to seduce the listener's ear, and the aim at a wide audience is confirmed in the choice of a tenor for the role of Nero instead of a soprano. Eric Tappy is a most stylish singer but his voice, as recorded, is rather edgy, which means that the rejoicing duet with Lucano after Seneca's death is bluff and hearty rather than pointed, and the final duet with Poppea loses some of its heavenly beauty. Rachel Yakar sings most beautifully as Poppea, while the role of Seneca is taken by the resonant, black-voiced Matti Salminen. The recording is vivid but suffers from high tape-hiss.

Karajan's mono recording of 1963, taken from an Austrian Radio broadcast, is a period piece that in every way defies the modern idea of period performance. It is 'freely adapted' for a stage production at the Vienna State Opera in 1960 with the score reduced to under three hours – so allowing the present format on two discs. The manner is grand and spacious, with speeds generally broad and recitative slow rather than crisp. At about the same period, Raymond Leppard adapted this work for Glyndebourne, but his version with its sumptuous string-writing was far more in scale than this. Sena Jurinac makes a radiant Poppea, and Gerhard Stolze's tenor is sinister enough to convey the traditional idea of Nero as a wicked Emperor; Margarita Lilowa is a fruity Ottavia and Carlo Cava a cavernous Seneca, with smaller roles taken by such singers as the young Gundula Janowitz. The comic duet between Nero and Lucano after Seneca's death is rough and boisterous rather than witty, and the finale duet between Nero and Poppea slow and sensuous. Recommended for Karajan devotees only.

Orfeo (opera): complete.

(M) *** EMI (SIS) Dig. CMS7 64947-2 (2) [CDMB 649472]. Rogers, Kwella, Kirkby, J. Smith, Chiaroscuro, L. Bar. Ens., L. Cornett & Sackbutt Ens., Charles Medlam.

(M) **(*) DG 447 703-2. Rogers, Petrescu, Reynolds, Partridge, Bowman, Hamburg Monteverdi Ch., Hamburg Instrumental Ens., Jürgens.

(M) ** Teldec/Warner 2292 42494-2 (2) [id.]. Kozma, Hansmann, Berberian, Katanosaka, Villisech, Van Egmond, Munich Cappela Antiqua, VCM, Harnoncourt.

(BB) ** Naxos Dig. 8.554094-2 (2) [id.]. Carmignani, Pennichi, Frisani, Pantasuglia, Capella Musicale di San Petronio di Bologna, Vartolo.

(M) (**) DG Codex mono 453 176-2 (2). Krebs, Guillaume, Wunderlich, Mack-Cosack, Günter, Feroubaix, Hamburg State Music School Ch., 1955 Summer Festival O, Wenzinger.

Nigel Rogers – who recorded the role of Orfeo ten years earlier for DG Archiv – in the EMI version has the double function of singing the main part and acting as co-director. Rogers has modified his extraordinarily elaborate ornamentation in the hero's brilliant pleading aria before Charon and makes the result all the freer and more wide-ranging in expression, with his distinctive fluttering timbre adding character. With the central singer directing the others, the concentration of the whole performance is all the greater, telling the story simply and graphically; and Euridice's plaint, beautifully sung by Patrizia Kwella, is the more affecting for being accompanied very simply on the lute. The other soloists make a good team, though Jennifer Smith as Proserpina, recorded close, is made to sound breathy. The brightness of the cornetti is a special delight, when otherwise the instrumentation used – largely left optional in the score – is modest. Excellent, immediate recording, making for a fine mid-priced alternative to Gardiner.

The earlier Archiv version with Nigel Rogers as Orfeo still has its place in the catalogue, especially within a lively, atmospheric performance like Jürgens's. Even in this first performance of the massive aria in which Orfeo pleads with Charon, Rogers treats the florid writing not as a technical obstacle race but as a test of expressiveness, giving the character extra depth. His fine virtuoso performance is matched by the singing of such artists as James Bowman and Ian Partridge. Alexander Malta as Charon and Stafford Dean as Pluto are wonderfully dark and firm in bass tone, while Emilia Petrescu as Euridice and Anna Reynolds as Sylvia equally combine stylishness and expressive strength. The chorus and orchestra are outstanding. The 1973 recording has an ample acoustic, simulating a performance in a nobleman's hall; but it is well focused in the CD transfer and the amplitude is agreeably rich. The sound of the plucked instruments is especially beguiling.

In Harnoncourt's version, the ritornello of the Prologue might almost be by Stravinsky, so sharply do the sounds cut. He is an altogether more severe Monteverdian than John Eliot Gardiner. In compensation, the simple and straightforward dedication of this performance is most affecting, and the solo singing, if not generally very characterful, is clean and stylish. One exception to the general rule on characterfulness comes in the singing of Cathy Berberian as the Messenger. She is strikingly successful and, though slightly differing in style from the others, she sings as part of the team. Excellent recording. The extra clarity and sharpness of focus – even in large-scale ensembles – add to the abrasiveness from the opening *Toccata* onwards, and the 1968 recording certainly sounds immediate, with voices very realistic. A highlights disc might be the best choice, and this is available (75 minutes) on Teldec 0630 13807-9.

With some first-rate solo singing and a restrained, scholarly approach, there is much to enjoy in the Naxos version. The problem is that Sergio Vartolo's speeds are consistently slow. Alessandro Carmignani is a fine, clear Orfeo, coping splendidly with all the technical problems, and his singing in the big solos has a dedicated intensity, but at such slow speeds there is a sleepwalking quality in the results, however beautiful. More seriously, the exchanges between characters never have the dramatic intensity needed. One would never recognize this conductor and his Bologna forces as the performers who present Vecchi's *L'amfiparnasso* with such brightness and vigour (also on Naxos). In the instrumental numbers the strings are often uncomfortably edgy. It is as well that full text and translation are provided, when the CD tracks on the disc are radically different from those indicated in the booklet. For once the discs provide too many separate tracks, with even ritornelli of five or six seconds separately indexed. Clear, well-balanced sound, recorded in the Theatre of Puy-en-Velay in France.

August Wenzinger's 1955 recording in mono marked a breakthrough in Monteverdi appreciation when it first appeared, with excellent solo singing, consistently clean and clear in focus. It still offers much to enjoy despite what now seems in many ways a dated approach. Though the light, delicate continuo accompaniments for the solo numbers remain very acceptable, the ritornelli involving a surprisingly large and resonant body of strings seem very out of style, particularly when in those items Wenzinger chooses such relaxed speeds. Choruses too are often too heavy and sluggish, using a full body of singers. Outstanding among the soloists is the tenor, Helmut Krebs, in his time a leading exponent of the Evangelist roles in Bach Passions and here a clear, precise and agile Orfeo, making light of the technical demands of such a solo as *Possente spirto* with elaborate decorations delicately pointed. Margaret Guillaume is warm and firm as La Musica in the opening Prologue, and it is good to hear the young Fritz Wunderlich in multiple roles, clear and stylish. Full text and translations are provided.

Il ritorno d'Ulisse in patria (complete).
(M) **(*) Teldec/Warner 2292 42496-2 (3) [id.]. Eliasson, Lerer, Hansen, Baker-Genovesi, Hansmann, Equiluz, Esswood, Wyatt, Walters, Van Egmond, Mühle, Junge Kantorei, VCM, Harnoncourt.

Harnoncourt's 1971 recording of *Il ritorno d'Ulisse* brings a sympathetic performance, generally not quite as brisk as Jacobs in his full-priced recording from the Montpellier Festival, and rather more square in rhythm, but bringing a keener sense of repose, important in Monteverdi. The solo singing is not as characterful as that on Harnoncourt's *Poppea*, though Norma Lerer makes a touching Penelope, with Sven Olaf Eliasson a stylish Ulisse, not ideally pure of timbre.

Morley, Thomas (1557–1603)

The First Booke of Ayres: A painted tale; Thyrsis and Milla; She straight he light greensilken coats; With my love; I saw my lady weeping; It was a lover; Who is it that this dark night?; Mistress mine; Can I forget; Love winged my hopes; What is my mistress; Come, sorrow, stay; Fair in a morn; Absence, hear thou; Will you buy a fine dog?; Sleep slumb'ring eyes.
(M) ** Teldec/Warner 3984 21334-2. Nigel Rogers, Nikolaus Harnoncourt, Eugen Dombois.

This integral recording of Morley's *First Booke of Songs* first appeared at the beginning of the 1970s and remains unique in a catalogue not notably generous to Morley's music. The settings heard together show the scope of the composer's imagination in his sensitivity to the words themselves, in the variety of style and metre, and in the diversity of manner of the accompaniments. The performances are fresh and direct and scholarly in the use of decoration. Nigel Rogers's vocal personality is slight but pleasant. The recording is excellent.

Mozart, Wolfgang Amadeus (1756–91)

Adagio and fugue in C minor: see also below, in VOCAL MUSIC, under Complete Mozart Edition, Volume 22.

Complete Mozart Edition, Volume 3: *Cassations Nos. 1 in G, K.63; 2 in B flat, K.99; Divertimento No. 2 in D, K.131; Galimathias musicum, K.32; Serenades Nos. 1 in D, K.100* (with *March in D, K.62); 3 in D, K.185* (with *March in D, K.189); 4 in D (Colloredo), K.203* (with *March in D, K.237); 5 in D, K.204* (with *March in D, K.215); 6 in D (Serenata notturna), K.239; 7 in D (Haffner), K.250* (with *March in D, K.249); 8 in D (Notturno for 4 orchestras), K.286; 9 in D (Posthorn), K.320* (with *Marches in D, K.335/1–2); 13 in G (Eine kleine Nachtmusik), K.525.*
(M) *** Ph. Dig. 422 503-2 (7) [id.]. ASMF, Sir Neville Marriner.

Marriner and his Academy are at their very finest here and make a very persuasive case for giving these works on modern instruments. The playing has much finesse, yet its cultivated polish never brings a hint of blandness or lethargy; it is smiling, yet full of energy and sparkle. In the concertante violin roles Iona Brown is surely an ideal soloist, her playing full of grace. Throughout this set the digital recording brings an almost ideal combination of bloom and vividness.

Cassations Nos. 1 in G, K.63; 2 in B flat, K.99; 3 (Serenade) in D, K.100.
(BB) *** Naxos Dig. 8.550609 [id.]. Salzburg CO, Harald Nerat.

The super-budget Naxos label issues a great many recorded performances that are inexpensive but are otherwise of only moderate appeal; every now and then, however, a winner appears – and this is one of them. For all their charms, these early *Cassations* (otherwise miniature serenades or divertimenti) are not likely to be a top priority for many collectors but, played with style and excellently recorded, they are very attractive at Naxos price, and they would still be so if they cost more. They were probably written in Salzburg in 1769, when Mozart was in his early teens, but in many ways they are forward-looking. Nos. 1 and 2 each have seven movements, No. 3 extends to eight. The *First* has two delightful slow movements: a delicate *Andante* and the second introduces a cantilena for solo violin (well played here by Georg Hölscher). K.99 is just as engaging and follows the pattern with a further pair of *Andantes*, and so does the *Third* (which Mozart described as a Serenade), but it is scored more ambitiously, using trumpets as well as horns. All three make enjoyable listening, and all three are here given lively, nicely turned performances, very well – if resonantly – recorded. This admirable disc is certainly worth its modest cost and nicely fills a gap in the catalogue.

CONCERTOS

Complete Mozart Edition, Volume 9: (i) *Bassoon concerto;* (ii) *Clarinet concerto;* (iii) *Flute concertos Nos. 1–2; Andante in C for flute & orchestra;* (iii; iv) *Flute and harp concerto;* (v) *Horn concertos Nos. 1–4; Concert rondo in E flat for horn and orchestra;* (vi) *Oboe concerto. Sinfonia concertante in E flat, K.297b; Sinfonia concertante in E flat, K.297b* (reconstructed R. Levin).
(M) **(*) Ph. Dig. 422 509-2 (5) [id.]. (i) Thunemann; (ii) Leister; (iii) Grafenauer; (iv) Graf; (v) Damm; (vi) Holliger; ASMF, Marriner (except (vi) Holliger).

The principal wind concertos here are recent digital versions. They are all well played and recorded. However, there is a slightly impersonal air about the accounts of the *Bassoon* and *Clarinet concertos*, well played though they are; and there are more individual sets of the works for horn. The *Sinfonia concertante* is offered both in the version we usually hear (recorded in 1972, with the performance attractively songful and elegant) and in a more modern recording of a conjectural reconstruction by Robert Levin, based on the material in the four wind parts.

(i) *Bassoon concerto in B flat, K.191;* (ii) *Clarinet concerto in A, K.622;* (iii) *Flute concerto No.1 in G, K.313; Andante in C, K.315;* (iii; iv) *Flute and harp concerto in C, K.299;* (v) *Horn concertos Nos. 1–4;* (vi) *Oboe concerto in C, K.314; Sinfonia concertante in E flat, K.297b.*
(M) *** DG Dig. 431 665-2 (3) [id.]. (i) Morelli; (ii) Neidlich; (iii) Palma; (iv) Allen; (v) Jolley or Purvis; (vi) Wolfgang; Orpheus CO.

Randall Wolfgang's plaintive, slightly reedy timbre is especially telling in the *Adagio* of the *Oboe concerto* and he plays the finale with the lightest possible touch, as does Susan Palma the charming Minuet which closes the *Flute concerto*. The *Sinfonia concertante* for wind is pleasingly fresh. All the works are given excellent modern recordings and this is a very persuasive collection, probably a 'best buy' for those wanting all the music in a digital format.

(i) *Bassoon concerto;* (ii) *Clarinet concerto;* (iii) *Oboe concerto, K.314.*
(BB) **(*) Naxos Dig. 8.550345 [id.]. (i) Turnovský; (ii) Ottensamer; (iii) Gabriel; V. Mozart Academy, Wildner.
(M) ** EMI CDM7 64355-2 [id.]. (i) Günter Piesk; (ii) Karl Leister; (iii) Lothar Koch; BPO, Karajan.

In the *Oboe concerto* the soloist on Naxos, Martin Gabriel, is excellent. The clarinettist, Ernst Ottensamer, is also a sensitive player, his slow movement is full of feeling; and there is an accomplished performance of the *Bassoon concerto* from Stepan Turnovský, who has the measure of the work's character and wit. Recommendable, particularly at the price.

The three performances on this EMI reissue come from a series of recordings of Mozart's concertante wind works that Karajan made in 1971. Günter Piesk gives a predictably fine account of the *Bassoon concerto*, but the *Clarinet concerto* is a little bland and, while Koch is also an estimable soloist in the work for oboe, the richly homogeneous orchestral accompaniments without much analytical detail, although pleasingly warm and elegantly phrased, tend to rob the music of vitality. No complaints about the CD transfers.

(i) *Bassoon concerto in B flat, K.191;* (ii) *Clarinet concerto in A, K.622;* (iii) *Violin concerto No. 3 in G, K.216.*
(M) *** EMI stereo/mono CDM7 63408-2 [id.]. (i) Brooke; (ii) Brymer; (iii) De Vito; RPO, Beecham.

Beecham's romantically expansive reading of the Mozart *Clarinet concerto* with Jack Brymer the glowing soloist is a 1958 classic recording, totally individual in every phrase, with conductor and soloist inspiring each other. The account of the *Bassoon concerto* has equal magic, thanks to the comparable partnership between Beecham and Gwydion Brooke. But the surprise here is the equally inspired and highly personal 1949 mono account of the *G major Violin concerto*, with Gioconda de Vito as soloist. She too conveys magic comparable to Beecham's own, with the slow movement again luxuriantly expansive.

(i) *Bassoon concerto in B flat, K.191. Divertimento No. 15 in B flat, K.287; Symphony No. 35 in D (Haffner), K.385; Overture: Le nozze di Figaro.*
(M) (**) BMG/RCA mono GD 60286. (i) Leonard Sharrow; NBC SO, Toscanini.

Leonard Sharrow, principal bassoon of Toscanini's NBC orchestra, gives a brilliant account of the solo part in the *Bassoon concerto*, undaunted by any rigidity in the conducting, bringing out the youthful exuberance of the writing. The coupled account of the *Haffner Symphony* is less extreme, if a degree less sparkling, than the classic 1929 version that Toscanini recorded with the New York Philharmonic, with the middle movements flowing more easily, while the *Divertimento* makes an attractive filler, despite the omission of the second Minuet, with the first violins together taking the solo violin role. Dry, limited sound.

(i) *Clarinet concerto in A, K.622;* (ii–iii) *Andante, K.315;* (ii; iv) *Flute and harp concerto in C, K.299.*
(M) *** [RCA Basic 100 09026 68024-2; *68024-4*]. (i) Stolzman, ECO, Schneider; (ii) James Galway; (iii) Lucerne Festival O, Baumgartner; (iv) Marisa Robles, LSO, Mata.

Richard Stolzman's distinguished account of the *Clarinet concerto* makes a thoroughly recommendable coupling, in RCA's Basic 100 series, for the two works with James Galway (see below).

(i) *Clarinet concerto in A, K.622;* (ii) *Flute concerto No. 1 in G, K.313;* (iii) *Oboe concerto in C, K.314.*
(M) *** Classic fM Dig. 75605 57001-2. (i) Joy Farrall; (ii) Kate Hill; (iii) Nicholas Daniel; Britten Sinfonia, Nicholas Cleobury.
(M) ** Sony Theta SMK 60129 [id.]. (i) Anthony Gigliotti; (ii) William Kincaid; (iii) John de Lancie; Phd. O, Ormandy.
(B) ** DG Classikon 439 508-2; *439 508-4* [(M) id. import]. (i) Leister, BPO, Kubelik; (ii) Linde, Munich CO, Stadlmair; (iii) Turetschek, VPO, Boehm.

No composer ever bettered Mozart's natural facility in writing for wind. His music seems to go right to the heart of the instrument for which he is writing and reveals, in glowing fashion, every facet of its personality. All three soloists on the Classic fM disc are distinguished British orchestral players, and each plays with much individuality of character. In the *Clarinet concerto* Joy Farrall's solo style lies somewhere between the freely spontaneous manner of Emma Johnson and the flexible, classical directness of Thea King. Nicholas Cleobury's gracefully poised opening ritornello sets the scene engagingly and Farrall's luminous timbre immediately seduces the ear, as does the subtlety of her gentle nuancing. She uses a basset clarinet and relishes the added duskiness of its lower register. Her glowing line is heard at its most ravishing in the *Adagio*, radiantly echoed by the strings of the Britten Sinfonia; the delicacy of the reprise is particularly magical. It is followed by a liltingly high-spirited finale. Nicholas Daniel is equally appealing in the stylishly infectious account of the *Oboe concerto* bringing another fine slow movement. Kate Hill's *Flute concerto* is hardly less delectable, especially the touching *Adagio*. The neatly pointed minuet finale is delightful. Excellent balancing and fine recording make this mid-priced triptych from Classic fM hard to beat.

The Sony collection dates from the mid-1960s and offers three soloists from the Philadelphia Orchestra. The most impressive is William Kincaid, who plays a nimble flute. His performance is always poised, and the slow movement is particularly pleasing. Provided one accepts a fairly rich orchestral tapestry, Ormandy's accompaniment is excellent, with some delightfully pointed string-playing to match the soloist in the finale. The Philadelphia strings also tell in the *Clarinet concerto*, particularly the slow movement. However, neither the clarinettist, Anthony Gigliotti, nor the oboist, John de Lancie (who has a rather small tone), is a particularly individual personality. De Lancie is better in the quick movements than the slow ones. His phrasing in the *Adagio* is on the stiff side. Gigliotti's approach to his slow movement is also rather plain; the finale is much more engaging. The recording is well balanced and very good for its period.

Karl Leister gives a thoughtfully sensitive and musical performance of the *Clarinet concerto*, but with his gentle, introvert style and lack of a forceful personality the effect is rather too self-effacing. However, Kubelik's attention to detail and gracious phrasing mean that the orchestral contribution gives great pleasure. Impeccably played and neatly phrased, Linde's performance of the *Flute concerto* has a hint of rhythmic stiffness in the outer movements. The highlight is the slow movement, where the playing is beautifully poised and the melody breathes in exactly the right way. In both works the mid-1960s recording is of good quality but shows its age a little in the string timbre. The recording of the *Oboe concerto* is from a decade later, though the sonic difference is minimal. Gerhard Turetschek proves an appealingly delicate and sweet-timbred soloist and this is very civilized music-making.

(i) *Clarinet concerto;* (ii) *Flute and harp concerto in C, K.299.*
(B) *** Carlton IMP Dig. PCD 2011 [(M) id.]. (i) Campbell; (ii) Davies, Masters; City of L. Sinfonia, Hickox.

David Campbell's agile and pointed performance of the clarinet work brings fastish speeds and a fresh, unmannered style in all three movements. His tonal shading is very beautiful. The earlier flute and harp work is just as freshly and sympathetically done, with a direct, unmannered style sounding entirely spontaneous.

(i) *Clarinet concerto in A, K.622;* (ii) *Flute and harp concerto in C, K.299;* (iii) *Serenade No. 13 in G (Eine kleine Nachtmusik), K.525.*
(BB) **(*) Belart 450 035-2 [(M) id. import]. (i) Harold Wright, Boston SO, Ozawa; (ii) Karl-Heinz Zöller, Nicanor Zabaleta, BPO, Märzendorfer; (iii) VPO, Karl Boehm.

Harold Wright's Boston performance of the *Clarinet concerto* is thoroughly musical and well recorded. The warm tone of the clarinet is especially appealing and the soloist enterprisingly plays his own cadenza in the slow movement. However, Ozawa's accompaniments, though well fashioned and neatly laid out, are rather matter-of-fact, and the overall orchestral effect is accomplished rather than inspired. There are no strictures about the Zöller/Zabaleta account of the *Flute and harp concerto*. The flautist is a most sensitive player and his phrasing is a constant source of pleasure, while Zabaleta's sense of line knits the overall texture of this solo-duet most convincingly. Märzendorfer conducts with both warmth and lightness; the outer movements have an attractive rhythmic buoyancy. The early-1960s recording is clear and clean, if not as rich as we would expect today. Of the many excellent versions of Mozart's famous *Night music* in the catalogue, Karl Boehm's 1976 performance is among the finest: polished and spacious, with a graceful *Andante* and a neat, lightly pointed finale. The sound is warm and pleasing, though at the very opening the ear picks up a slight lack of cleanness in the bass focus. But it is of little moment and soon dissipates. Excellent value.

(i) *Clarinet concerto;* (ii) *Clarinet quintet in A, K.581.*
(M) **(*) Ph. 442 390-2. Jack Brymer, with (i) LSO, Sir Colin Davis; (ii) Allegri Qt.

Jack Brymer's (1964) Philips account of the *Clarinet concerto* with Sir Colin Davis has an eloquent autumnal serenity and the reading a soft lyricism that is very appealing. However, the leisurely (1970) interpretation of the *Quintet* is more controversial. Generally the very slow tempi throughout are well sustained, although in the finale the forward flow of the music is reduced to a near-crawl. Good transfers.

(i) *Flute concertos Nos. 1–2; Andante in C, K.315;* (ii) *Flute and harp concerto, K.299;* (iii) *Sinfonia concertante for flute, oboe, horn & bassoon, K.297b* (reconstructed R. Levin); (iv) *4 Flute quartets, K.285, K.285a, K.285b; K.298.*
(B) **(*) Ph. Duo 442 299-2 [id.]. (i) Aurèle Nicolet, Cong. O, Zinman; (ii) Hubert Barwahser, Osian Ellis, LSO, C. Davis; (iii) Nicolet, Holliger, Baumann, Thunemann, ASMF, Marriner; (iv) William Bennett, Grumiaux Trio.

Aurèle Nicolet's performances of the *Flute concertos* and *Andante for flute and orchestra* are very positive, and the solo playing throughout is expert and elegantly phrased. Barwahser and Ellis give a sparkling account of the *Flute and harp concerto* and Sir Colin Davis accompanies them with the greatest sprightliness and sympathy. If these are not a top choice in this repertoire, the William Bennett accounts of the four *Flute quartets* with the Grumiaux Trio certainly are. They are, to put it in a nutshell, exquisitely played and very well recorded. The wind *Sinfonia concertante* in which the oboe and clarinet parts are replaced by flute and oboe respectively, is an interesting conjectural experiment rather than an essential part of a Mozart collection. The recordings throughout are smoothly remastered and sound fine.

Flute concertos Nos. (i) *1 in G, K.313;* (ii) *2 in D, K.314.*
(B) *** Carlton IMP PCD 2036 [(M) id.]. Judith Hall, Philh. O, Peter Thomas.

Flute concertos Nos. 1 in G, K.313; 2 in D, K.314; Andante in C, K.315.
(BB) **(*) Naxos Dig. 8.550074; *4550074* [id.]. Herbert Weissberg, Capella Istropolitana, Sieghart.
(M) *(*) Virgin Veritas/EMI (SIS) Dig. VER5 61176-2. Hans-Martin Linde, Linde Consort.

Judith Hall produces a radiantly full timbre. Moreover she is a first-class Mozartian, as she demonstrates in her cadenzas as well as in the line of the slow movements, phrased with a simple eloquence that is disarming. There is plenty of vitality in the allegros, and Peter Thomas provides polished, infectious accompaniments to match the solo playing. The balance is good and the 1987 sound is bright and clear. However, at 45 minutes 30 seconds, the offering is not particularly generous.

The Naxos record by Herbert Weissberg and the Capella Istropolitana under Martin Sieghart can hold its head quite high alongside the competition. Weissberg does not have the outsize personality of some of his rivals but he is a cultured player, and the quality of the recording is excellent. In short, good value for money and very pleasant sound.

Hans-Martin Linde conducts, as well as playing the flute. The ensemble of little more than a dozen players is expert and the textures eminently well ventilated. Listening to period flutes, one understands something of Mozart's aversion to the instrument, for the sound though at first appealing is slightly watery. Ultimately this account is let down by a want of flair and exuberance; the general approach is just a little too inhibited to be a strong recommendation. Good recorded sound and well-judged balance.

(i) *Flute concerto No. 1 in G, K.313; Andante in C, K.315;* (ii) *Flute and harp concerto in C, K.299.*
(M) *** RCA GD 86723 [6723-2-RG]. James Galway; (i) Lucerne Festival O, Baumgartner; (ii) with Marisa Robles, LSO, Mata.
(M) *** Erato/Warner 2292 45832-2 [id.]. Rampal, (i) VSO, Guschlbauer; (ii) Lily Laskine, Paillard CO, Paillard.

James Galway's silvery timbre seems as unlike an original instrument as could possibly be imagined.

Galway is well supported by the Lucerne orchestra, rather reverberantly recorded, with the solo flute placed well forward. The coupled *Flute and harp concerto* has seldom sounded more lively than it does here, with an engaging element of fantasy in the music-making, a radiant slow movement and a very spirited finale. Marisa Robles makes a characterful match for Galway and they are well accompanied.

Rampal and Lily Laskine also create a genuine symbiosis in the *Flute and harp concerto*: their interplay has great charm and delicacy, and the slow movement is a delight. The solo concerto and *Andante* find Rampal in equally good form and he is well accompanied in both instances. With well-transferred recordings from the mid-1960s, this CD is well worth its mid-price.

(i) *Flute concertos Nos. 1–2, K.313/4;* (ii) *Flute and harp concerto in C, K.299.*
(M) *** Decca 440 080-2. (i) William Bennett, ECO, Malcolm; (ii) Werner Tripp, Hubert Jellinek, VPO, Münchinger.

William Bennett gives a beautiful account of the concertos, among the finest in the catalogue. Every phrase is shaped with both taste and affection, and the playing of the ECO under George Malcolm is fresh and vital. The earlier Vienna recording of the *Flute and harp concerto* has also stood the test of time, and again the recording is smooth, full, nicely reverberant and with good detail. Refinement and beauty of tone and phrase are a hallmark throughout, and Münchinger provides most sensitive accompaniments. A first-rate (75 minutes) compilation.

(i) *Flute concerto No. 1 in G, K.313;* (ii) *Flute and harp concerto in C, K.299;* (iii) *Oboe concerto in C, K.314;* (iv) *Sinfonia concertante in E flat, K.297b.*
(BB) **(*) CfP Silver Double Dig. CDCFPSD 4808 (2) [(M) id. import]. (i; ii) Snowden; (ii) Thomas; (iii) Hunt; (iv) Theodore, Hill, Price, Busch; LPO, (i; iv) Mackerras; (ii–iii) Litton.

Jonathan Snowden's account of the *Flute concerto* is attractive, sprightly, stylish and polished (though some might not take to his comparatively elaborate cadenzas). The performance of the *Flute and harp concerto* is even more winning. Where Gordon Hunt in the *Oboe concerto* seems a less natural concerto soloist, Snowden, in collaboration with Caryl Thomas on the harp, is both sparkling and sensitive, regularly imaginative in his individual phrasing. In the first movement of the *Sinfonia concertante* for wind, Mackerras is characteristically brisk, and his performance has plenty of life throughout, and charm too, in the closing variations. The solo playing here (by a different group) is of high quality; the *Adagio* is persuasive, if with no striking individuality. With excellent digital recording, this makes an enjoyable if not a distinctive collection.

(i) *Flute and harp concerto in C, K.299; Sinfonia concertante in E flat, K.297b.*
(BB) *** Naxos Dig. 8.550159; *4550159* [id.]. (i) Jiri Válek, Hana Müllerová; Capella Istropolitana, Richard Edlinger.

Richard Edlinger's account of the *Flute and harp concerto* is thoroughly fresh and stylish, and the two soloists are excellent. Although the *Sinfonia concertante in E flat*, K.297b, is not quite so successful, it is still very impressive, and it gives much pleasure. Both performances are very decently recorded; in the lowest price-range they are a real bargain.

Horn concertos Nos. 1 in D, K.412; 2–4 in E flat, K.417, 447 & 495.
(M) **(*) Teldec/Warner 0630 17429-2 [2292 42767-2]. Hermann Baumann, VCM, Harnoncourt.
(B) *** DG Classikon 449 856-2 [(M) id. import]. Gerd Seifert, BPO, Karajan.
(M) **(*) Carlton Dig. 30366 00972 [id.]. William Ver Meulen, Houston SO, Eschenbach

Horn concertos Nos. 1–4; Concert rondo in E flat, K.371 (ed. Civil or E. Smith).
(M) *** Ph. 442 397-2. Alan Civil, ASMF, Marriner.
(BB) *** Naxos Dig. 8.550148; *4.550148* [id.]. Miloš Stevove, Capella Istropolitana, Josef Kopelman.
(B) **(*) Carlton IMP Dig. PCD 2013 [(M) id.]. Richard Watkins, City of L. Sinfonia, Hickox.

Horn concertos Nos. 1–4; Concert rondo in E flat, K.371 (arr. Tuckwell).
(M) *** EMI Dig. CDM7 64851-2. Radovan Vlatkovič, ECO, Tate – R. STRAUSS: *Horn concerto No. 1.* ***

Horn concertos Nos. 1–4; Concert rondo, K.371 (ed. Tuckwell); *Fragment, K.494a.*
(M) *** EMI CDM7 69569-2. Barry Tuckwell, ASMF, Marriner.

Horn concertos Nos. 1–4; Concert rondos: in E flat, K.371 (completed John Humphries); *in D, K.514* (completed Süssmayr); *Fragment for horn and orchestra in E flat, K.370b* (reconstructed Humphries).
(BB) *** Naxos Dig. 8.553592 [id.]. Michael Thompson, Bournemouth Sinf.

As well as offering superb performances of the four regular concertos using revised texts prepared by John

Humphries, this outstanding Naxos issue includes reconstructions of two movements designed for a horn concerto dating from soon after Mozart arrived in Vienna. The *Rondo* completed by Süssmayr is the version generally used as the second movement of K.412, which, according to the latest scholarship, was the last of the concertos to be written, not the first. The *Rondo* played here as the second movement of K.412 is Humphries's reconstruction from sources recently discovered, much more imaginative than the Süssmayr version. It is fascinating too to have extra passages in No. 4, again adding Mozartian inventiveness. Thompson plays with delectable lightness and point, bringing out the wit in finales, as well as the tenderness in slow movements. He also draws sparkling and refined playing from the Bournemouth Sinfonietta, very well recorded in clear, atmospheric sound.

Radovan Vlatkovič's tone is very full, with the lower harmonics telling more resonantly than is characteristic of a British soloist; there is also at times the slightest hint of vibrato, but it is applied with great discretion and used mostly in the cadenzas. His performances are full of imaginative touches and he has the perfect partner in Jeffrey Tate, who produces sparkling accompaniments. All in all, another outstanding set, most winningly different from the playing of the British generation. Moreover Vlatkovič includes both the *Concert rondo*, K.371, and, very appropriately, a quite outstanding account of the *First Horn concerto* of Richard Strauss which, although more romantic, has so much in common with the spirit of the Mozart concertos.

Tuckwell's first (1960) stereo recording of the *Horn concertos* on Decca is currently withdrawn. However, EMI have effectively remastered Tuckwell's second set with Marriner, and the 1972 recording sounds fuller, with slightly more body to the violins. This CD has the advantage of including not only the *Concert rondo* but also the *Fragment in E*.

Alan Civil's Philips set was made in 1973. The recording is obviously modern and the performances are highly enjoyable, with Sir Neville Marriner's polished and lively accompaniments giving pleasure in themselves. The balance has the effect of making the horn sound slightly larger than life.

Miloš Stevove is principal horn with the Slovak Philharmonic Orchestra, and with his Bohemian background he is naturally at home in this genial music. He uses the slightest trace of vibrato but it is never obtrusive, and one has only to listen to the *Larghetto* of K.447 or the *Andante cantabile* of K.495 to discover his naturally warm feeling for a Mozartian phrase. Allegros are lively and the Rondos have agreeable lift. In short, with excellent, stylish accompaniments from the Capella Istropolitana this is enjoyably spontaneous. The recording is very good too; though not quite as beautiful as the digital EMI disc, it has a compensating freshness.

Gerd Seifert has been principal horn of the Berlin Philharmonic since 1964, and his velvety, warm tone is familiar on many records. His articulation is light and neat here, and his nimbleness brings an effective lightness to the gay Rondos. Karajan almost matches his earlier accompaniments for Dennis Brain, and the orchestral playing is strong in character, although he never overwhelms his soloist. The 1969 recording now brings just a hint of over-brightness on the *forte* violins, but this adds to the sense of vitality without spoiling the elegance. This is now offered on DG's bargain Classikon label but, unlike some of its competitors, there are no added items.

Richard Watkins has the advantage of first-class modern digital recording on a bargain-priced label. He is an expert player and shows a genuine Mozartian sensibility. But this easy lyrical flow does mean that slow movements are very limpid and relaxed, and even the Rondos, articulated lightly, take wing more gently than usual. Hickox's accompaniments, on the other hand, are efficient and positive. But generally there is a somewhat self-effacing quality to the solo performances which detracts from the music's projection, and Michael Thompson's set has an altogether stronger profile.

Hermann Baumann successfully uses the original hand-horn, without valves, for which the concertos were written, and the result is not achieved at the expense of musical literacy or expressive content. Baumann lets the listener hear the stopped effect only when he decides that the tonal change can be put to good artistic effect. In his cadenzas he also uses horn chords (where several notes are produced simultaneously by resonating the instrument's harmonics), but as a complement to the music rather than as a gimmick. Unfortunately the remastering has not been entirely successful: the original recording was mellow and reverberant; now it is noticeably drier. The solo horn is given a bold – indeed, rather too tangible – presence, yet its outline is not absolutely sharp, while there is also some roughness of focus in the strings. However, this remains a fascinating demonstration of how these concertos would have sounded in Mozart's own time.

William Ver Meulen, principal horn of the Houston Symphony, is a fine expondent of what European horn-players tend to describe as the supercharged American style of playing. His performances are both strong and sensitive, with a wide expressive and tonal range. Eschenbach is a sympathetic accompanist and the recording is full and immediate. The only snag is that at mid-price with no coupling this is hardly competitive with such outstanding issues as the Naxos disc.

Piano concertos

Complete Mozart Edition, Volume 7: (i) *Piano concertos, K.107/1–3;* (ii) *Nos. 1–4;* (iii) *5, 6, 8, 9, 11–27; Concert rondos 1–2;* (iii; iv) *Double piano concertos, K.242 & K.365;* (v) *Triple concerto in F, K.242.*
(M) **(*) Ph. Analogue/Dig. 422 507-2 (12) [id.]. (i) Ton Koopman, Amsterdam Bar. O; (ii) Haebler, Vienna Capella Academica, Melkus; (iii) Brendel, ASMF, Marriner; (iv) Imogen Cooper; (v) Katia and Marielle Labèque, Bychkov, BPO, Bychkov.

Piano concertos Nos. (i) *1–4;* (ii) *5;* (iii) *6;* (ii) *8–9;* (iv) *11;* (iii) *12;* (iv) *13–16;* (iii) *17;* (iv) *18;* (iii) *19;* (ii) *20;* (iii) *21;* (iv) *22;* (iii) *23;* (iv) *24;* (ii) *25;* (iii) *26;* (ii) *27; Concert rondos for piano and orchestra: in D, K.382; in A, K.386;* (ii; v) *Double piano concerto in E flat, K.365;* (ii; v; vi) *Triple concerto in F (Lodron), K.242.*
(B) **(*) Ph. 454 352-2 (10) [(M) id. import]. Ingrid Haebler ((i) fortepiano or (ii–iv) piano), with (i) V. Capella Academica, Edward Melkus; (ii–vi) LSO; (ii) Galliera; (iii) Rowicki; (iv) Sir Colin Davis; (v) Ludwig Hofmann; (vi) Sas Bunge.

Piano concertos No. 20 in D min., K.466; 21 in C, K.467.
(BB) **(*) Belart 450 055-2 (from above) [(M) id. import]. Ingrid Haebler, LSO; (i) Galliera; (ii) Rowicki.

Piano concertos Nos. 1–6; 8–9; 11–27; Rondo in D, K.382.
(M) *** EMI CZS7 62825-2 (10) [ZDZJ 628252]. Daniel Barenboim, ECO.

Piano concertos Nos. 1–6; 8–9; 11–27; Rondos Nos. 1–2, K.382 & 386.
❀ (M) *** Sony Analogue/Dig. SX12K 46441 (12) [SXK 46441]. Murray Perahia, ECO.

(i) *Piano concertos Nos. 1–6; 8–9, 11–27; Concert rondos Nos. 1 in D, K.382;* (ii) *2 in A, K.386;* (iii) *Double piano concerto in E flat, K.365;* (iii; iv) *Triple piano concerto in F, K.242.*
(B) *** Decca Analogue/Dig. 443 727-2 (10) [id.]. Ashkenazy, (i) with Philh. O; (ii) LSO, Kertész; (iii) Barenboim, ECO; (iv) Fou Ts'ong.

By omitting the four early concertos after J. C. Bach, Sony have been able to reissue the Perahia set on twelve mid-priced CDs. The cycle is a remarkable achievement; in terms of poetic insight and musical spontaneity, the performances are in a class of their own. There is a wonderful singing line and at the same time a sensuousness that is always tempered by spirituality. About half the recordings are digital and of excellent quality and, we are glad to report, the earlier, analogue recordings have been skilfully remastered with first-class results, both in this complete set and in the separate issues below. The strings now sound smooth and full (the previously noticed edginess has disappeared) and the balance gives no cause for complaint. This is an indispensable set in every respect.

Those wanting a modern digital set of the Mozart concertos and for whom the flatteringly resonant sound of the Schiff/Végh series offers problems (see below) can readily turn to Ashkenazy, where the Decca recording is more crisply focused, with bright, athletic strings against a warm backgound ambience. Ashkenazy's set with the Philharmonia appeared over more than a decade: the early *Concertos* are the most recent (1987), while the *G major*, K.453, and the *C major*, K.467, come from 1977. The account of the *E flat Concerto*, K.365, with Barenboim and the ECO and the *Triple concerto* with Fou Ts'ong to complete the trio, is earlier still (1972). These performances have won golden opinions over the years, and the clarity of both the performances and the recordings is refreshing: indeed the fine Decca sound is one of their strongest features. With their latest remastering Decca have been able to squeeze the recordings on to ten generously full, bargain-priced CDs, which make a very attractive proposition. If their insights do not always seem to strike quite as deeply as Perahia's, the latter's complete box on Sony suffers from less than congenial remastering of the earlier, analogue recordings. No such complaint can be made about the Decca transfers, which are remarkably fresh and natural. Many of these performances are among the finest available, combining refreshing spontaneity with an overall sense of proportion and balance. *Nos. 12 in A* and *13 in C* are particularly striking; with their natural, expressive feeling and sparkle, they convey real enjoyment, and the slow movement of the *A major*, K.414, is given memorable depth. These are digitally recorded and the sound is well defined and transparent, the ambience very attractive. Nos. 15 and 16 again show characteristic sensibility: both slow movements are played very beautifully yet without a trace of narcissism, and the finales sparkle. In *No. 17 in G* there is a fine sense of movement, yet nothing is hurried; *No. 19 in F* is hardly less successful, both subtle and sparkling. *No. 23 in A* – again with fine digital recording – is beautifully judged, alive, fresh and warm, while in *No. 24 in C minor* Ashkenazy has the full measure of the music's breadth and emotional power; and his playing, while showing all the elegance and poise one could desire, never detracts from the coherence of the whole. The first movement of No. 25 is on the grandest scale, and the opening movement of the *Coronation* (No. 26) is also appropriately magisterial, yet brings some exquisitely shaded playing in the *Larghetto*, while No. 27 caps the cycle impressively. The recording of these last three concertos is again digital and very lifelike: no orchestral detail is masked and the woodwind glow, while the piano timbre is most beautiful.

The sense of spontaneity in Barenboim's performances of the Mozart concertos, his message that this is music hot off the inspiration line, is hard to resist, even though it occasionally leads to over-exuberance and idiosyncrasies. These are as nearly live performances as one could hope for on record, and the playing of the English Chamber Orchestra is splendidly geared to the approach of an artist with whom the players have worked regularly. They are recorded with fullness, and the sound is generally freshened very successfully in the remastering.

The Philips Mozart Edition *Piano concertos* box is based on Brendel's set with the ASMF under Marriner. Throughout, his thoughts are never less than penetrating. The transfers are consistently of the very highest quality, as is the playing of the Academy of St Martin-in-the-Fields under Sir Neville Marriner. To make the set complete, Ingrid Haebler gives eminently stylish accounts of the first four *Concertos* on the fortepiano, accompanied by Melkus and his excellent Vienna Capella Academica; the sound is admirably fresh. However, on disc two the ear gets rather a shock when Ton Koopman presents the three works after J. C. Bach. Convincing though these performances are, it seems a strange idea to offer an authentic approach to these three concertos alone, particularly as at the end of the disc we return to a delightfully cultured performance on modern instruments of the alternative version for three pianos of the so-called *Lodron Concerto*, K.242, provided by the Labèque duo.

Ingrid Haebler recorded the Mozart concertos with the LSO for Philips between 1965 and 1968, alternating among three different conductors, then completing the set in 1973 with eminently stylish accounts of the first four concertos played appropriately on the fortepiano, accompanied by Melkus and his excellent Vienna Capella Academica. Her readings of the remainder are distinguished by a singular poise, meticulous finger-control and great delicacy of touch. She is less concerned with dramatic intensity; but with her carefully delineated boundaries she undoubtedly gives considerable pleasure by her restrained sensibility and musicianship. She is helped throughout by finely judged recordings, warm and spacious yet crystal clear, and the orchestral response is most sympathetic, particularly in the concertos conducted by Rowicki and Davis. She is at her most characteristic in the early masterpiece, No. *9 in E flat*, K.371, with a clean, classical approach; her account of K.413 (No. 11) is also beautifully alert and the slow movement immediately impresses with its poetry; but eventually the lack of forward movement becomes more obvious. It would be difficult to imagine a more poised account of No. *17 in G major*; the playing may lack the ultimate in forward drive, but Haebler plays lovingly and with great poetry, even if one regrets a certain want of temperament. Both the *B flat Concerto* (No. 18) and the great *E flat Concerto* (No. 22) show her at her finest: she is unfailingly musical and, though she is meticulous in her attention to detail, this does not detract from the scale of the music; the fine accompaniments from Davis contribute to the success of these performances. Haebler's tempi in the *D minor concerto* (No. 20) are warmly relaxed and on the leisurely side. She displays much delicate colouring, but more forward movement throughout, and greater tautness in the finale would have been welcome. She is just a bit *too* relaxed, and matters are not helped by Galliera, who keeps his players on too slack a rein. The first movement of K.467 (No. 21) is a little straitlaced, without the breadth and dignity that some artists have brought to it or the urgency that one has from others. Haebler plays her own cadenzas – and very good they are – but in the heavenly slow movement she is not as imaginative as either Kovacevich or Casadesus, to name but two fine alternative versions, although Rowicki's direction is again excellent. Rowicki also directs the *A major Concerto* (No. 23), and this is undoubtedly a most enjoyable performance, although there are preferred versions available. In the *C minor Concerto* (No. 24) she plays with the clarity of articulation and sense of poise that one has come to take for granted from her, but she tends to scale down the dark sense of passion in this work, though Davis's strong and virile accompaniment prevents any real loss of gravitas. Galliera is at the helm in No. 25, but Haebler's rather self-conscious contribution does not encompass sufficient depth to excite enthusiasm. The first movement of the *Coronation Concerto* (No. 26) is straightforward and dignified, but in the main theme of the slow movement she exaggerates staccato markings and even plays the top A of the theme staccato. The *Double* and *Triple concertos* are given fresh, unaffected readings, and Haebler and Hofmann and, in the latter, Sas Bunge play splendidly; but other versions have more personality and inner life. To sum up: as a complete survey this cannot measure up to Perahia, who remains first choice on 12 mid-priced discs (SX12K 46441), even if Sony's recordings do not consistently match the Philips sound-quality. But Haebler has her own insights to offer, she is a highly individual Mozartian and there is much here to give pleasure when the recorded sound is so good.

For those wanting a characteristic sample of the series, Belart have made available a super-bargain coupling of the two top favourite concertos, *Nos. 20 in D minor* and *21 in C major*, the latter with its 'Elvira Madigan' associations – although Haebler's exquisitely dispassionate view of the famous *Andante* would hardly have been suitable for the sound-track. The recordings are beautifully transferred.

Piano concertos Nos. 1 in F, K.37; 2 in B flat, K.39; 3 in D, K.40; 4 in G, K.41.
(BB) ** Naxos Dig. 8.550212. Jenö Jandó, Concentus Hungaricus, Idikó Helgi.

These early concertos are given crisp, direct performances by Jandó, well accompanied. But the resonance of the Italian Institute in Budapest does not provide as sharp a focus as with the best of his other recordings of this repertoire.

Piano concertos Nos. 5–6, 8–9, 11–27.
(M) *** Decca Dig. 448 140-2 (9). András Schiff, Salzburg Mozarteum Camerata Academica, Végh.

András Schiff's cycle with the Salzburg Mozarteum Camerata Academica under Sándor Végh proves to be one of the most satisfying of recent years and – along with the new Shelley series on Chandos – arguably the finest since Murray Perahia's cycle of the late 1970s. Not all these records have been discussed by us individually, so we have gained pleasure in encountering the performances together as a set. Schiff plays a Bösendorfer piano and its relatively gentle, cleanly focused timbre has something of the precision of a fortepiano without any loss of the colour which comes with a more modern instrument. The recording is consistently more beautiful than in Perahia's Sony set, with sweet strings and glowing woodwind and the piano usually balanced naturally and integrated with the orchestra. For some listeners in certain works the warm resonance may offer a problem. This is immediately apparent in the orchestral tutti of the first concerto included here, No. 5 in D major, K.175. The rather diffuse opening of the *Coronation concerto*, K.537, is another example, yet the slighty misty focus certainly adds an air of mystery to the opening of the *D minor*, K.466. There is a comparably evocative anticipation of drama at the beginning of the *C minor*, K.491, while in the famous string passage which gently ushers in the slow movement of No. 21 in C, K.467, the effect is both warm and ethereal. The lovely A major, K.488, also gains much from the glowing ambience, particularly the beautifully played *Adagio*. The recordings were made in a variety of Viennese venues between 1984 and 1990, including the Mozarteum, the Grosser Saal of the Konzerthaus, the Viersen Festhalle, and the Millstatt Kirche, although the balance and warm ambience seem fairly consistent. This is agreeably relaxed music-making, though not in the least lacking in intensity or weight. Just occasionally Schiff dots his 'i's and crosses his 't's a little too precisely, but for the most part he is so musicianly and perceptive that this seems unimportant. In short, these are lovely performances, enhanced by the quality of the accompaniment under Végh, who is unfailingly supportive. For the most part Schiff plays his own cadenzas, but in the first movement of K.466 he uses a cadenza by Beethoven, and the finale of K.488 brings one by George Malcolm. There is an accompanying booklet which includes two essays: 'A performer's approach' by Schiff himself, and a general survey by Jeremy Siepmann called 'Mozart's Utopian visions'. All these records are also available separately in their original couplings.

Piano concertos Nos. 5–6, 8–9, 11–27; (i) *Double piano concerto, K.365;* (i; ii) *Triple piano concerto, K.242. Concert Rondos 1–2.*
(M) *** DG Dig. 431 211-2 (9) [id.]. Malcolm Bilson (fortepiano), E. Bar. Soloists, Gardiner, (i) with Robert Levin; (ii) Melvyn Tan.

Malcolm Bilson's complete set of the Mozart *Piano concertos* appears on nine mid-price CDs. Bilson is an artist of excellent musical judgement and good taste, and his survey is the only one at present available on the fortepiano, though we gather that one is under way from Melvyn Tan, who features here in the *Triple concerto*. For the most part, there is little to quarrel with here and much to enjoy.

Piano concertos Nos. 5 in D, K.175; 16 in D (Coronation), K.537; Rondo in D, K.382.
(BB) ** Naxos Dig. 8.550209 [id.]. Jenö Jandó, Concentus Hungaricus, Mátyás Antal.

Volume 9 of Jandó's Mozart series offers music-making which is fresh and direct yet somewhat lacking in individuality. There are stronger versions of K.537 available, although there are no complaints here about the digital sound, which is vivid and well balanced.

Piano concerto No. 6 in B flat, K.238.
(M) **(*) Decca 448 598-2 [id.]. Vladimir Ashkenazy, LSO, Schmidt-Isserstedt – BACH: *Clavier concerto No. 1* **(*); CHOPIN: *Piano concerto No. 2.* ***

This is an eloquent performance of a charming work, beautifully accompanied. The 1968 recording is excellent for its period, though perhaps an unexpected choice for reissue in Decca's Classic Sound series. The coupled Chopin concerto is the highlight of this reissue.

Piano concertos Nos. 6 in B flat, K.238; 8 in C, K.246; 19 in F, K.459.
(BB) *** Naxos Dig. 8.550208; *4550208* [id.]. Jenö Jandó, Concentus Hungaricus, Mátyás Antal.

No. 19 in F is a delightful concerto and it receives a most attractive performance, aptly paced, with fine woodwind playing, the finale crisply sparkling. No. 6 is hardly less successful; if No. 8 seems plainer, it is still admirably fresh. With excellently balanced recording this is a genuine bargain.

Piano concertos Nos. 6 in B flat, K.238; 17 in G, K.453; 21 in C, K.467.
(M) *** DG 447 436-2 [id.]. Géza Anda, Salzburg Mozarteum Camerata Academica.

It is proper that Géza Anda's Mozart concerto series from the 1960s should find a place in DG's 'Originals' series. His poetic account of the *C major Concerto*, K.467, is one of the most impressive from his cycle, notably for a beautifully poised orchestral introduction to the famous slow movement (a picture of 'Elvira Madigan' appears on the front of the CD). In the *G major*, K.453, Anda, who is soloist and conductor throughout the disc, errs a little on the side of heaviness of style, but again there is both strength and poetry, while the DG recording is excellent in both balance and clarity. The *B flat Concerto*, K.238, which also has a most beautiful slow movement, is played simply and eloquently, although perhaps the finale could have had a lighter touch in the orchestra (and this applies too to K.467). The recording is not quite so cleanly transferred in the early work. It comes last on the CD and is by no means of lesser appeal, and this remains a most enjoyable triptych.

Piano concertos Nos. 8 in C (Lützow), K.246; 9 in E flat (Jeunehomme), K.271; Concert rondo No. 2 in A, K.386.
✿ (M) *** Decca 443 576-2 [id.]. Ashkenazy, LSO, Kertész.
(BB) *** Koch/Discover DICD 920517 [id.]. Susan Kagan, Suk CO, Petr Macecek.

Ashkenazy's earlier, 1966 coupling with Kertész, which includes also the *A major Concert rondo*, has now been appropriately reissued in Decca's Classic Sound series and the recorded quality remains beautifully fresh and realistic. The magnificent performances originally earned the LP a Rosette and we see no reason not to carry it forward. Ashkenazy has the requisite sparkle, humanity and command of keyboard tone, and his readings can only be called inspired. He is very well supported by the LSO under Kertész, and they make an excellent case for a partnership with a sympathetic conductor, rather than having the soloist direct the proceedings from the keyboard.

These performances by the American performer and scholar, Susan Kagan are notable for an appealingly direct simplicity of approach. She is given an admirably scaled accompaniment. The Suk orchestra has a complement of 13 string players, which here seems just right. Slow movements flow naturally, with unexaggerated warmth; and there is plenty of vitality elsewhere, with ensemble pleasingly crisp. These are not self-conscious interpretations, but Mozart played freshly and spontaneously. The finale of K.271 sparkles delightfully. The *Rondo* which acts as an encore is most elegantly presented. The recording, in an intimate, slightly dry acoustic, is real and immediate. Though without the experienced insights of a Perahia, of its kind this is first class.

Piano concertos Nos. 8 in C, K.246; 13 in C, K.415; 25 in C, K.503.
(B) **(*) HM Musique d'Abord HMA 1903022. Kocsis, Franz Liszt CO, János Rolla.

Robust and thoroughly lively and musical accounts of Mozart's three C major concertos, a unique (75-minute) coupling. The slow movement of K.503 comes off especially well and the finale is infectious. Fine, modern, digital recording and a good balance ensure the appeal and value of the disc; even if the sound is a shade resonant, everything is clearly focused.

Vanguard 'Alfred Brendel Collection': *Piano concertos Nos. 9 in E flat, K.271; 14 in E flat, K.449.*
(M) *** Van. 8.4015.71 [OVC 4015]. Alfred Brendel; (i) I Solisti di Zagreb, Janigro.

Brendel's 1968 performance of No. 9 is quite outstanding, elegant and beautifully precise. The classical-sized orchestra is just right and the neat, stylish string-playing matches the soloist. Both pianist and conductor are sensitive to the gentle melancholy of the slow movement, and in the contrasting middle section of the finale Brendel's tonal nuance is beautifully shaded. The performance of K.449 is also first rate, with a memorably vivacious finale. Altogether this is an outstanding reissue with natural sound which hardly shows its age in the clean remastering.

Piano sonata No. 8 in A min., K.310; Fantasia in C min., K.396; Rondo in A min., K.511; 9 Variations on a Minuet by Duport, K.573.
(M) *** Van. 08.4025.71 [OVC 4025]. Alfred Brendel.

Vanguard '*Alfred Brendel Collection*', Vol. 1: Mozart.
(M) *** Van. 08.9161.72 (2) [OVC 9172]. Brendel.

Brendel's strikingly fresh 1968 Mozart performances, which are among his finest on record, are now gathered together in a slip-case as part of Vanguard's '*Alfred Brendel collection*'. There is no financial advantage in buying the discs together, but admirers of this artist will undoubtedly want both. On the solo disc the *Fantasia* is predictably imaginative, but so is the set of *Variations*, in which the care with shaping and detail raises the interest of the listener and the stature of the music. The analogue recording is firm and full, drier than in the concertos.

Piano concertos Nos. 9 in E flat, K.271; 15 in B flat, K.450; 22 in E flat, K.482; 25 in C, K.503; 27 in B flat, K.595.
(B) *** Ph. Duo 442 571-2 (2) [id.]. Alfred Brendel, ASMF, Marriner.

A first-class follow-up to Brendel's first Duo collection of Mozart piano concertos (see below). The account of the opening *Jeunehomme* is finely proportioned and cleanly articulated, with a ravishing account of the slow movement. The finale has great sparkle and finesse and the recording has exemplary clarity. Brendel is hardly less fine in K.450, and the *E flat Concerto* has both vitality and depth. Brendel's first movement has breadth and grandeur as well as sensitivity, while the *Andante* has great poetry. No. 25 (there is well-deserved applause at the close) was recorded at a live performance and has life and concentration, and a real sense of scale. Here as elsewhere the playing of the ASMF under Marriner is alert and supportive. K.595 is also among Brendel's best Mozart performances, with a beautifully poised *Larghetto* and a graceful, spirited finale. The recordings were made between 1974 and 1981 (No. 15 is digital) and offer characteristically fresh and natural sound. Highly recommended.

Piano concertos Nos. 9 in E flat, K.271; 17 in G, K.453.
(M) *** Chandos Dig. CHAN 9068 [id.]. Howard Shelley, LMP.

Piano concertos Nos. 9 in E flat (Jeunehomme), K.271; 17 in G, K.453; Rondo in D, K.382.
(M) *** DG (IMS) Dig. 447 291-2 [id.]. Malcolm Bilson (fortepiano), E. Bar. Soloists, Gardiner.

Howard Shelley is the latest to embrace the challenge of directing Mozart concertos from the keyboard. Shelley's playing is a delight and is possessed of a refreshing naturalness which should win many friends. There is spontaneity and elegance, a strong vein of poetic feeling and extrovert high spirits. His *G major concerto* belongs in the most exalted company and can withstand comparison with almost any rival. But both performances are touched by distinction, and they are beautifully recorded too.

This is a recoupling on DG. *Piano concerto No. 9*, K.271, was the first to be recorded (in 1983) in Malcolm Bilson's cycle; No. 17 came three years later. Bilson shows himself a lively and imaginative artist, well matched by the ever-effervescent Gardiner. The CD catches the lightness and clarity of the textures, with the fortepiano sound not too twangy and with wind balances often revelatory. The darkness of the C minor slow movement of K.271 is eerily caught; K.453, as ever, is a delight, with Bilson allowing himself a natural degree of expressiveness, within the limits of classical taste. The lightness of the keyboard action encourages the choice of fast allegros, but never at the expense of Mozart. The *Rondo*, K.382, makes a pert encore.

Piano concertos Nos. 9 in E flat (Jeunehomme), K.271; 20 in D min., K.466; 21 in C, K.467; 23 in A, K.488; 27 in B flat, K.595.
(B) **(*) EMI Rouge et Noir CZS5 69991-2 (2) [(M) id. import]. Daniel Barenboim, ECO.

The youthful *Jeunehomme concerto*, K.271, sets the style of these highly enjoyable performances, full of spirit and demonstrating masterly pianism, with an alert and musical direction of the orchestra. It also demonstrates Barenboim's willingness at times to display too great an awareness of refinements of tone and dynamics that are, strictly speaking, anachronistic. In K.271 the most serious reservation concerns the minuet at the centre of the final rondo which is far too measured. Barenboim's performances of *No. 20 in D minor* and No. 23, K.488, have all the sparkle and sensitivity one could ask for. The orchestral accompaniment is admirably alive, and one's only serious reservation concerns the somewhat fast tempo he adopts in the finale of K.466. The account of No. 23 is enchanting. There are moments when his delicacy of fingerwork comes close to preciosity, but it never quite goes over the edge. (The only snag is that this concerto is split between the two CDs.) There need be no reservations about the performance of No. 21 either; it is accomplished in every way. His version of K.595 is, however, more controversial. He again indulges in great refinement of touch and his reading of the slow movement is overtly romantic. The recordings (from the late 1960s) are fresh and naturally balanced; they are admirably transferred to CD.

Piano concertos Nos. 9 in E flat (Jeunehomme), K.271; 21 in C, K.467.
(B) **(*) Erato/Warner 0630 12814-2 [id.]. Maria-João Pires, Gulbenkian Foundation, Lisbon, CO, Guschlbauer.

These were among Pires' earlier series of Mozart recordings, made in the 1970s, and they are both stylish and sensitive. There is an element of reserve in the performance of the *Jeunehomme* – that is until the buoyant finale, which has plenty of youthful high spirits. Her seriousness of approach suits K.467 much better, and in both concertos she is well served both by Guschlbauer's warm yet alertly supportive accompaniments and by the Erato engineers. However, even at bargain price, this is not distinctive.

Piano concertos Nos. 9 in E flat (Jeunehomme), K.271; 27 in B flat, K.595.
(BB) **(*) Naxos Dig. 8.550203 [id.]. Jenö Jandó, Concentus Hungaricus, András Ligeti.

In Volume 3 of Jandó's ongoing series, the earlier concerto is the more consistently successful, refreshing in its alert vigour in outer movements, with the simple *Andantino* contrasting nicely with the exhilarating finale. K.595 does not lack strength, but this performance is without the individuality of the finest versions. Excellent sound, the piano forward but with a realistic overall balance.

Piano concertos Nos. 11 in F, K.413; 12 in A, K.414; 13 in C, K.415.
(B) *** EMI Debut CDZ5 72525-2 [id.]. Patrick Dechorgnat, Henschel Qt.

There is a special kind of intimate pleasure in hearing these three simple but masterly concertos of 1782 with just a string quartet accompaniment. The additional oboes and bassoons and the occasional flare of horns from the full orchestra are not absolutely esssential for full appreciation of this engaging music. Here the interplay between the stylish Patrick Dechorgnat and the polished and sympathetic Henschel Quartet is heard at its most appealing in the *Larghetto* of the *F major Concerto*, K.413, yet the touching *Andante* of K.414 is hardly less appealing, and the recording throughout is so expertly balanced that all three works are a great success. The opening ritornello of the *C major* is by no means underweighted, while the finale is pleasingly skittish. A first-rate début for soloist and string quartet alike.

Piano concertos Nos. 11 in F, K.413; 22 in E flat, K.482.
(BB) **(*) Naxos Dig. 8.550206 [id.]. Jenö Jandó, Concentus Hungaricus, Mátyás Antal.

Jenö Jandó is a highly musical Mozartian and his accounts of both concertos have a good deal to offer, even if in K.482 he plays the Hummel cadenza rather heavily. In this work there are moments of poetry as well as some of prose; however, there is a liveliness and enthusiasm about the whole performance that is likeable. This is well worth considering if you are on a tight budget. The recording uses the Italian Institute in Vienna (the piano is a bit too close) and produces very acceptable results.

(i) *Piano concerto No. 12 in A, K.414. Serenade No. 13 in G (Eine kleine Nachtmusik), K.525; Overtures: La clemenza di Tito; Die Entführung aus dem Serail.*
(M) (***) Dutton Lab. mono CDLX 7019 [id. full price]. (i) Louis Kentner; LPO, Beecham – HAYDN: *Symphony No. 97.* (***)

Entitled 'Beecham Classics', this disc brings together the Mozart recordings Beecham made with the LPO in 1945 after his return from the United States during the war when, to his irritation, the orchestra he had founded in 1932 had become self-governing. There is no sign of the conductor's frustration, especially not in the very last recording he made with the LPO, a magnificently strong and purposeful account of the *Clemenza di Tito overture*, recorded on 27 December 1945. The *Entführung overture* is equally characteristic in its sparkle and energy, though *Eine kleine Nachtmusik* – brighter in sound than the rest – brings one of Beecham's most notoriously perverse readings, when he treats the finale as an *Allegretto* rather than an *Allegro*, none the less beautifully sprung. The *A major Concerto*, with Louis Kentner, was recorded earlier in 1940, before Beecham left for America, and the sound is thinner and more limited, though the performance is superb from both pianist and conductor; in its point and wit it belies any idea that Kentner, specialist in romantic music, was too heavyweight a pianist for Mozart. The coupled Haydn symphony recording, dating from 1944, makes up a generously filled disc. Excellent transfers, with the Dutton engineering pointing out a slight increase in surface noise in the section of the concerto which had to be dubbed from shellac. First-rate notes from Lyndon Jenkins.

Piano concerto No. 12 in A, K.414. Rondo in A, K.386.
(B) ** Carlton Dig. 30367 01072 [(M) id. import]. Dirk Joeres, Westdeutsch Sinf. – HAYDN: *Piano concerto in D.* **

Mozart's earlier *A major Concerto* is notably successful on record, and this Carlton disc is no exception. Dirk Joeres directs the orchestra from the keyboard and achieves a performance which has poise and style as well as warmth and spontaneity. Only at the beginning of the closing *Rondo* is there a hint of the tendency to hurry which is more striking in the coupled Haydn concerto. The separate *A major Rondo* brings no such strictures. The recording is excellent, well balanced and natural.

Piano concertos Nos. 12 in A, K.414; 14 in E flat, K.449; 21 in C, K.467.
(BB) *** Naxos Dig. 8.550202; *4550202* [id.]. Jenö Jandó, Concentus Hungaricus, András Ligeti.

In Jandó's hands the first movement of K.449 sounds properly forward-looking; the brightly vivacious K.414 also sounds very fresh here, and its *Andante* is beautifully shaped. The excellent orchestral response distinguishes the first movement of K.467: both grace and weight are here, and some fine wind playing. An added interest in this work is provided by Jandó's use of cadenzas provided by Robert Casadesus. Jandó is at his most spontaneous throughout these performances and this is altogether an excellent disc, well recorded.

Piano concertos Nos. 12 in A, K.414; 19 in F, K.459.
(M) *** Chandos Dig. CHAN 9256 [id.]. Howard Shelley, LMP.

Another fine disc in Howard Shelley's musically rewarding and beautifully recorded series. Admirers of this artist need not hesitate in investing here, with the music's expressive range fully encompassed without mannerism, slow movements eloquently shaped and outer movements aptly paced and alive with vitality.

Piano concertos Nos. 12 in A, K.414; 21 in C, K.467.
(M) (***) Dutton Lab mono CDCLP 4000 [id. full price]. Moura Lympany, Philh. O, Menges – TURINA: *Rapsodia sinfonica.* (***)

These performances originally appeared on a plum-label HMV LP in 1955. (Even Moura Lympany's dazzling account of the Prokofiev and Rachmaninov *Concertos* was assigned to this less prestigious label.) Not that Dame Moura's playing is in any way lacking in distinction – indeed, these are readings of the highest finesse and subtlety. Herbert Menges gets very good playing from the Philharmonia and the sound, beautifully refurbished by Michael Dutton, sounds very fresh. Strongly recommended.

Piano concertos Nos. 13 in A, K.415; 20 in D min., K.466.
(BB) **(*) Naxos Dig. 8.550201 [id.]. Jenö Jandó, Concentus Hungaricus, András Ligeti.

This is Volume 1 in the planned complete recording of the Mozart piano concertos by Naxos with Jenö Jandó and the excellent Concentus Hungaricus, a polished chamber group using modern instruments, here directed to stylish effect by András Ligeti. These performances set a high standard in their communicative immediacy, and if they have not quite the individuality of Perahia or Ashkenazy, they are worth a place in any collection and are very modestly priced. Here the early *A major Concerto* comes up with enticing freshness, allegros are crisp and alert and the slow movement has a disarming simplicity. Ligeti creates a sense of anticipatory tension at the opening of the coupled *D minor Concerto* and this performance has plenty of drama, with the *Romance* very appealingly shaped. Jandó uses Beethoven's cadenzas with impressive authority. The balance and recording are most believable and there is good documentation throughout this series.

Piano concertos Nos. 13 in C, K.415; 24 in C min., K.491.
(M) *** Chandos Dig. CHAN 9326 [id.]. Howard Shelley, LMP.

Like Perahia before him, Howard Shelley directs from the keyboard and this, the fifth in his ongoing series, is as distinguished as its predecessors. He has immaculate keyboard manners and his strong, natural musicianship is always in evidence. An instinctive yet thoughtful Mozartian whose consummate artistry places his cycle among the very finest now on the market.

(i) *Piano concertos Nos. 14 in E flat, K.449; 15 in B flat K.450; 19 in F, K.459; 21 in C, K.467; 26 in D (Coronation), K.537; 27 in B flat, K.595;* (i; ii) *Double piano concerto in E flat, K.365. Adagio in B min., K.540; Piano sonatas Nos. 8 in A min., K.310; 11 in A, K.331; 13 in B flat, K.333; 14 in C min., K.457; Fantasia in C min., K.475; Rondo in A min., K.511.*
(M) **(*) Ph. Brendel Edition Analogue/Dig. 446 921-2 (5). Alfred Brendel, with (i) ASMF, Marriner; (ii) Imogen Cooper – HAYDN: *Andante & variations in F min.; Piano sonatas.* ***

Among Brendel's many fine recordings of the Mozart concertos, the *E flat major*, K.449, ranks highly, distinguished by beautifully clean and alive passage-work, while there is superb control and poise. The main ideas are well shaped without being overcharacterized. Tempi are wisely chosen and perfectly related. He is hardly less impressive in K.450. In K.467 the outer movements are brisk, but tempo is not in itself a problem. Each detail of a phrase is meticulously articulated, every staccato and slur carefully observed in an almost didactic fashion. But it is curmudgeonly to dwell on reservations when there is so much to delight in these performances. The playing is very impressive indeed, and so, too, is the recording. In the *Coronation concerto*, as always, Brendel's articulation and intelligence excite admiration. Only in the slow movement does one feel a trace of didacticism. There are no such reservations about No. 27, which is in every way distinguished and is beautifully recorded. The playing is immaculate: everything is deeply thought out but retains its spontaneity. Similarly the *Double concerto* (with Imogen Cooper) is elegant and poised, combining vigour with tonal refinement, and here as elsewhere Marriner's accompaniments are comparably polished. The *Sonatas*, however, bring a few reservations. The pianism is masterly, as one would expect from this great artist, but the performances of Nos. 8 and 14 strike one as the product of excessive ratiocination. There is no want of inner life, the texture is wonderfully clean and finely balanced, but the listener is all too aware of the mental preparation that has gone into the interpretations. The staccato markings in the slow movement of K.310 are exaggerated and the movement as a whole is unsmiling and strangely wanting in repose. Self-conscious playing, immaculately recorded. Both Nos. 11 and 13, however, are a joy, and beautifully recorded too. Very distinguished playing indeed.

Piano concertos Nos. 14 in E flat, K.449; 23 in A, K.488; 24 in C min., K.491.
(M) *** DG Dig. 447 295-2. Malcolm Bilson (fortepiano), E. Bar. Soloists, Gardiner.

Here are three key Mozart concertos in a generous triptych, with the tough *E flat Concerto* coming last. The much-loved *A Major*, K.488, is as fresh as you could wish for, with plenty of zing in outer movements – the horns ringing through the texture – the *Adagio* very poised. Here the ear notices the comparative lack of the darker sonority of a modern instrument, but this is still most sensitive playing, not over-elaborated. Gardiner and the English Baroque Soloists provide vigorous, large-scale orchestral tuttis, matching Bilson's expressiveness on the one hand, while on the other relishing the fast speeds he prefers in the finales and bringing wit to the last movement of K.488. The *Larghetto* of the *C minor* brings no reservations and this is a performance which combines drama with poetry; here the tempo of the finale is a moderate *Allegretto*, allowing the detail to register admirably. Excellent recording, fresh and full-bodied, yet clear.

Piano concertos Nos. 14 in E flat, K.449; 27 in B flat, K.595.
(M) *** Chandos Dig. CHAN 9137 [id.]. Howard Shelley, LMP.

Admirable performances, stylish and with a fine Mozartian sensibility. This is altogether most refreshing, and the recording is very good indeed.

Piano concerto No. 15 in B flat, K.450; (i) *Double piano concertos: in F (Lodron), K.242; in E flat, K.365.*
(BB) **(*) Naxos Dig. 8.550210 [id.]. Jenö Jandó, (i) with Dénes Várjon; Concentus Hungaricus, Antal.

Jandó is at his most spontaneous in K.450, embellishing the theme of the *Andante* most stylishly, and he is as bright and witty as one could wish in the brilliantly good-humoured finale. In the pair of *Double concertos* he is joined by Dénes Várjon in an effective partnership, and these performances are agreeably fresh and alive; compared with Brendel and Klien, however, the interchanges between the two soloists are much more plainspun. The modern Naxos sound is a considerable advance on the earlier record, with the violins sounding much better-nourished, and this is certainly good value. But Brendel and Klien bring a magic to their performance which makes one forget any inadequacies in the orchestral backing.

Piano concertos Nos. 16 in D, K.451; 20 in D min., K.466.
(M) *(*) DG Dig. 445 597-2. Rudolf Serkin, LSO, Abbado.

Serkin's digital recordings of the Mozart piano concertos for DG in the early 1980s showed a sad decline in his pianism. Those who are prepared to bear with the prosaic playing for the sake of the musical insights that do emerge will have no quarrels with this issue technically, recorded when the pianist was about eighty years of age.

Piano concertos Nos. 16 in D, K.451; 25 in C, K.503; Rondo in A, K.386.
(BB) *** Naxos Dig. 8.550207; *4550207* [id.]. Jenö Jandó, Concentus Hungaricus, Mátyás Antal.

Jenö Jandó gives a very spirited and intelligent account of the relatively neglected *D major Concerto*, K.451, in which he receives sensitive and attentive support from the excellent Concentus Hungaricus under Mátyás Antal. The performance has warmth. The players sound as if they are enjoying themselves and, although there are greater performances of the *C major Concerto*, K.503, on record, they are not at this extraordinarily competitive price.

Piano concertos Nos. 17 in G, K.453; 18 in B flat, K.456.
(BB) *** Naxos Dig. 8.550205; *4550205* [id.]. Jenö Jandó, Concentus Hungaricus, Mátyás Antal.

This is one of the finest in Jandó's excellent super-bargain series. Tempi are admirably judged and both slow movements are most sensitively played. The variations which form the *Andante* of K.456 are particularly appealing in their perceptive use of light and shade, while the very lively *Allegro vivace* finale of the same work is infectiously spirited. Jandó uses Mozart's original cadenzas for the first two movements of K.453 and the composer's alternative cadenzas for K.546. Excellent sound.

Piano concertos Nos. 17 in G, K.453; 19 in F, K.459; 21 in C, K.467; 25 in C, K.503. Adagio in B min., K.540; Fantasia in D min., K.397.
(BB) **(*) Virgin Classics Dig. Double VBD5 61445-2 (2) [CDVB 61445]. Diana Ambache, Ambache CO.

This is an attractive package, made the more so by individual performances of the supplemenary solo items, the lovely *B minor Adagio* and the great *Fantasy in D minor*. Diana Ambache is a stylish Mozartian, imaginative and spontaneous-sounding, consistently playing with clean attack and crisp, light articulation. Her control of colour is particularly pleasing. There is genuine charm without sentimentality, and pacing can hardly be faulted. The orchestra is warmly supportive but is balanced somewhat backwardly – not entirely a drawback, for string ensemble is not always flawless and the violin focus could be cleaner; yet such a movement as the finale of K.503 comes over with wit and point. The wind playing throughout is delightful, notably so in the *Allegretto* of the *F major*, K.459. Both early concertos sound particularly fresh and, if the two later works do not quite match the comparable coupling by Stephen Kovacevich, they are still very enjoyable, and the Virgin digital sound is obviously more modern.

Piano concertos Nos. 19, K.459; 20, K.466; 21, K.467; 23, K.488; 24, K.491; Concert rondos Nos. 1–2, K.382 & 386.

❀ (B) *** Ph. Duo 442 269-2 [(M) id. import]. Alfred Brendel, ASMF, Marriner.

This Philips Duo offers five key piano concertos and two concert rondos – all for the cost of one premium-price CD. A Rosette then for generosity, to say nothing of the distinction of the performances. Indeed, throughout, the playing exhibits a sensibility that is at one with the composer's world. With Brendel, K.459 sparkles all the way through and the playing of the ASMF could hardly be improved on. The slow movement is quite magical and the finale again has great zest and brilliance. The two minor-key concertos (*20 in D minor*, *24 in C minor*) are also superbly played and recorded, though perhaps they miss the last ounce of tragic intensity. There are minor qualms about K.467. The finale sounds over-rehearsed, and some of the joy and high spirits are sacrificed in the sense of momentum. Yet there remains much to delight. There are no reservations whatsoever about Brendel's account of K.488, which is among the best in the catalogue. The decoration of the solo part in the slow movement is never obtrusive, always in style. The two *Concert rondos* – the first (K.382) is the Viennese alternative to the *Salzburg concerto* (K.175) – are no less elegantly performed, and throughout the set the Philips sound-balance is impeccable.

Piano concertos Nos. 19 in F, K.459; 22 in E flat, K.482.

(B) *** Decca Eclipse Dig. 448 992-2; *448 992-4* [(M) id. import]. Alicia de Larrocha, VSO, Uri Segal – HANDEL: *Keyboard suite No. 5*. ***

Alicia de Larrocha can hold her own against most of her rivals in terms of both scale and sensitivity, though her K.482 is perhaps not as completely integrated or as touching as the Perahia, which has particularly eloquent playing from the ECO wind. She is also on good form in the *F major*; the Decca recording is beautifully transparent and clear, as well as being warmly resonant, which increases the tinge of romantic feeling in these performances. The sound is particularly natural, with the upper range smooth yet well defined. Although the ear is drawn slightly to the forward balance of the woodwind, the piano-image is most believable, the treble pellucid with no edge. At Eclipse price this is very competitive indeed, especially with the attractive Handelian bonus.

Piano concertos Nos. (i) *19 in F, K.459;* (ii) *27 in B flat, K.595. Piano sonata No. 2 in F, K.280.*

(M) **(*) DG mono/stereo 449 722-2 [id.]. Clara Haskil; (i) BPO, (ii) Bav. State O; (i–ii) Ferenc Fricsay.

Clara Haskil was at her finest in the music of Mozart, as this CD readily demonstrates, and K.595 is an outstanding performance, with an exquisitely played *Larghetto* and wonderfully fluent passage-work from the pianist in the first movement, with every bar alive. On the whole Fricsay accompanies impressively here, but at the opening of K.459 the orchestral articulation is rhythmically flabby, especially compared with the clean solo entry, and this cannot match De Larrocha and Segal on Decca. However, the central *Allegretto* redeems the performance, and both finales sparkle. So too does Haskil's buoyant finale for the *F major Sonata*, full of joy, following a predictably thoughtful *Adagio*. The piano recording is good throughout, but the orchestra could do with a stronger profile in both works, although the 1957 mono sound is perfectly acceptable. The sonata (1961) is stereo.

Piano concerto No. 20 in D min., K.466 (cadenzas Beethoven).

(M) (***) DG 453 804-2 (6) [id.]. Richter, Warsaw PO, Wislocki (with Beethoven Edition).

A great virtuoso proves his virtuosity by restraint, and this is the quality running right through Richter's extremely fine performance. Richter lets Mozart's music speak for itself but, whether in the choice of tempo, a touch of *rubato*, or some finely moulded phrase, his mastery is always apparent. Wislocki and the Warsaw orchestra provide an accompaniment of character and, although the recording sounds dated in the matter of string-tone, the piano image remains realistic.

Piano concerto No. 20 in D min., K.466.

(BB) **(*) EMI Seraphim Dig. CES5 68520-2 (2) [CDEB 68520]. Youri Egorov, Philh. O, Sawallisch – BEETHOVEN: *Piano concerto No. 5; Violin concerto*. **(*)

A generous coupling for an imaginative if slightly controversial account of the *Emperor* and *Violin concerto* in EMI's bargain-basement, two-disc series. The Mozart performance, though well played, is less distinctive, even though Egorov is stylish and Sawallisch finds plenty of drama in the outer movements and begins the finale, the most striking of the three, with great energy and bustle. The slow movement, too, is elegantly shaped. Good, bright (1985) EMI digital recording, made at Abbey Road.

Piano concertos Nos. 20 in D min., K.466; 21 in C, K.467.

(M) *** RCA GD 87967 [7967-2-RG]. Rubinstein, RCA Victor SO, Wallenstein (with HAYDN: *Andante & variations in F min.* ***).

(BB) **(*) Naxos Dig. 8.550434 [id.]. Jenö Jandó, Concentus Hungaricus, András Ligeti.

(i) *Piano concertos Nos. 20 in D min., K.466; 21 in C, K.467.* (ii) *Serenade No. 13 in G (Eine kleine Nachtmusik), K.525.*

(BB) *** RCA Navigator 74321 17888-2 [(M) id. import]. (i) Géza Anda, VSO; (ii) Bamberg SO, Jochum.

(i) *Piano concertos Nos. 20–21;* (ii) *Fantasia in D min., K.397.*

(B) **(*) DG Classikon 439 491-2; *439 491-4* [(M) id. import]. (i) Géza Anda, Salzburg Camerata Academica; (ii) Kempff.

Rubinstein has seldom been caught so sympathetically by the microphones, and the remastered 1961 recording has the orchestral sound admirably freshened. In each concerto the slow movement is the kernel of the interpretation. Rubinstein's playing is melting. Altogether Wallenstein is an excellent accompanist, for finales have plenty of sparkle. The Haydn *Andante and variations*, a substantial bonus recorded a year earlier, again demonstrates Rubinstein's aristocratic feeling for a classical melodic line: it is played most beautifully.

Both RCA performances by Anda have an attractive simplicity and are admirably spontaneous, with slow movements sensitive and graciously phrased. The delicacy of the solo playing entirely avoids any suggestions of Dresden china, while the orchestral introduction to the *D minor* has plenty of atmosphere. For a bonus, Jochum provides an agreeable account of Mozart's most famous serenade. Here the full-bodied string-sound brings robustness rather than transparency, but the finale has an appropriate rhythmic lightness. Excellent value.

On DG the *D minor* is one of Géza Anda's strongest performances, with solo playing that is both stylish and spontaneous. No. 21 is notable for its poised introduction to the famous slow movement. One notices a certain rhythmic rigidity, and a lighter touch in the finale would have been acceptable, but on the whole this is satisfying, and the remastered DG recording (from the 1960s) sounds particularly fresh. The *Fantasia* is a real bonus: Wilhelm Kempff's disarming simplicity of style hides great art. This playing is in a class of its own. Some might argue with justice that the DG versions have slightly more character, but the alternative RCA disc is both stylish and enjoyable, and it is now in the very lowest price-range and includes Jochum's account of *Eine kleine Nachtmusik*.

At super-bargain price Jenö Jandó's disc with the Concentus Hungaricus and András Ligeti can be recommended, if with certain reservations. The depth in the slow movement of the *D minor*, K.466, eludes him and he rushes the finale – but then, so did Barenboim. In the *C major Concerto*, K.467, he is eminently vital and spirited. This is a straightforward and unfussy performance, though it would be a mistake to stake too strong a claim for it (he is not as searching or poetic a player as, say, Casadesus). This will certainly reward the modest outlay involved and provide a good deal of pleasure. The recording is excellent, well detailed, warm and fresh, and the orchestral playing first class. Not an unqualified three-star recommendation but an enjoyable disc.

(i) *Piano concertos Nos. 20 in D min., K.466; 21 in C, K.467;* (ii) *22 in E flat, K.482; 23 in A, K.488.*

(BB) *** EMI Seraphim (SIS) CES5 68529-2 (2) [CEDB 68529]. Annie Fischer, Philh. O; (i) Sawallisch; (ii) Boult.

(B) ** Teldec/Warner Ultima Dig. 0630 18956-2 (2) [(M) id. import]. Daniel Barenboim. BPO.

This is one of the real bargains on EMI's Seraphim (two-for-the-price-of-one-medium-price-CD) label and well worth having, even if duplication is involved. Annie Fischer's coupling of Nos. 21–22 was very highly regarded when it first appeared in 1959 (mono only) on Columbia CX 1630. Fischer's gentle, limpid touch, with its frequent use of half-tones, gives a great deal of pleasure. The slow movements of both these concertos are beautifully done, and the pianist's intimate manner is often shared by the Philharmonia's wind soloists, who offer playing of polish and delicacy. In the *C major Concerto* she uses cadenzas by Busoni and in the *E flat Concerto* the first-movement cadenza is by Hummel, which adds another point of interest to this coupling. Her coupling of the *D minor* and *A major* followed, a year later. In the *D minor Concerto* Boult's tempi are sensible and the orchestral playing is again felicitous, particularly from the wind. The reading perhaps misses the ultimate in breadth and dramatic fire, but it is a very good performance all the same. In K.488, Fischer plays with liveliness of feeling and refinement of touch, and the passage-work is deft, and in any event this is a thoroughly enjoyable and often perceptive performance. Beethoven's cadenzas are used in the *D minor Concerto*.

Barenboim has turned to the Berlin Philharmonic Orchestra for his digital re-recordings of the key Mozart concertos. He directs them from the keyboard and they play most expressively for him; but the result is weighty in a way which sometimes makes the music look forward to Beethoven. This would not matter were the effect seemingly spontaneous, but in that respect these performances do not match his earlier, EMI series with the ECO, and the portentous opening of the *D minor Concerto* seems overdramatized. The famous slow movement of K.467 generates a languor that misses the simplicity of Mozart's ethereal inspiration, and similarly the lovely *Adagio* of the *A major*, K.488, again very leisured, is self-conscious. Of course there is much fine pianism throughout the series, even if at times Barenboim's articulation seem very precise, and the very fast tempo he chooses for the finale of K.466 loses much of the music's poise. On the whole, the *Concerto in E flat*, K.482, is the most rewarding performance, the Andante obviously deeply felt, and the finale, in which Barenboim chooses to play an abridged version of a cadenza by Edwin Fischer, is agreeably lighthearted. The recordings are very well balanced.

(i) *Piano concertos Nos. 20 in D min., K.466; 21 in C, K.467; 23 in A, K.488; 24 in C min., K.491; 25 in C, K.503.*
(B) *** Decca Double Dig./Analogue 452 958-2 (2) [id.]. Ashkenazy, Philh. O.

This Double Decca set, reissued for Ashkenazy's sixtieth birthday, now includes both the D minor and C minor masterpieces, but not K.595 (No. 27), which, however, remains available on a slightly different permutation at a similar cost – see below. K.491 and K.503 are among the finest in his series, so the present grouping is particularly attractive. The Kingsway Hall recordings cannot be faulted. They were made between 1977 and 1983; Nos. 20, 23 and 25 are digital.

(i) *Piano concertos Nos. 20 in D min., K.466; 21 in C, K.467; 23 in A, K.488; 27 in B flat, K.595. Piano sonata No. 17 in D, K.576; Rondo in A min., K.511.*
(B) *** Decca Double Analogue/Dig. 436 383-2 (2). Vladimir Ashkenazy, Philh. O.

This alternative set, with slightly different contents, is also highly recommendable on all counts, with the three favourite Mozart piano concertos included, plus a splendid *Sonata* and a charming *Rondo*. Ashkenazy's performance of the *B flat Concerto* is as finely characterized as one would expect. The *Sonata* and *Rondo* were recorded earlier (in 1967); the playing is equally fine.

Piano concertos Nos. 20 in D min., K.466; 21 in C, K.467; 25 in C, K.503; 27 in B flat, K.595.
(B) **(*) DG Double 453 079-2 (2). Friedrich Gulda, VPO, Abbado.

Abbado had much greater luck in his Mozartian partnership with Gulda than he was to experience with Serkin a decade or so later, but even so it was a pity that these two discs (from the mid-1970s) had to be reissued in tandem, for the first is much more successful than the second. Gulda uses a Bösendorfer and in Nos. 20 and 21 his tone is crisp and clear with just a hint of a fortepiano about it, admirably suited to these readings, which have an element of classical restraint; yet at the same time they are committed and do not lack warmth. Abbado's accompaniment is first class, and the orchestral wind-playing is delightful. In Nos. 25 and 27, however, Gulda is strangely cool, though he disciplines his responses impressively and there is no basic want of feeling or finesse, as for instance in the second group of the first movement of K.503, although overall there is a lack of charm. There are felicitous moments elsewhere, but the account of K.595 does not compare with the finest available, despite very good playing from the Vienna Philharmonic. The digital transfer is bright and clear, but there is also a certain shallowness of sonority.

Piano concertos Nos. 20 in D min., K.466; 23 in A, K.488.
(M) *** Chandos Dig. CHAN 8992 [id.]. Howard Shelley, LMP.

Those wanting this coupling with modern instruments will find Howard Shelley's performances no less rewarding. Characterization is strong, yet the slow movement of K.488 is very beautiful and touching. Splendid Chandos recording.

Piano concertos Nos. 20 in D min., K.466; 23 in A, K.488; Rondo in A min., K.511.
(M) *** [RCA Basic 100 09026 68337-2; *68337-4*]. Rubinstein, RCA Victor SO, Wallenstein.

These works are also available differently coupled – the present pairing is equally recommendable.

Piano concertos Nos. 20 in D min., K.466; 24 in C min., K.491.
(B) **(*) [EMI Red Line CDR5 72583]. Barenboim, ECO.

Barenboim's performance of No. 20 is discussed above. K.491 brings a more controversial performance; the very first entry of the piano shows how much Barenboim wants to make it a romantic work, and some may find the first two movements too heavily dramatized for their taste, while the finale is compensatingly fast and hectic. The sound is vividly bright.

Piano concertos Nos. 20 in D min., K.466; 25 in C, K.503; Rondo in D, K.382.
(M) * Sony Dig. SMK 64251 [id.]. Vladar, ASMF, Marriner.

Given the abundance of competition, there is little that need detain us here. Stefan Vladar is a more than capable guide in this repertoire but not as poetic or compelling as his leading rivals. The orchestral support under Marriner is musicianly but nothing out of the ordinary. In fact nothing about these performances is out of the ordinary: the recording is bottom-heavy and opaque.

Piano concertos Nos. 20 in D min., K.466; 27 in B flat, K.595.
✿ (M) *** Decca (IMS) 417 288-2. Clifford Curzon, ECO, Britten.

In September 1970 Clifford Curzon went to The Maltings at Snape, and there with Benjamin Britten and the ECO he recorded these two concertos. K.595, the last concerto of all, was always the Mozart work with which he was specially associated and, not surprisingly – when he was the most painfully self-critical and mistrusting of recording artists – he wanted to do it again. Just before he died, in September 1982, sessions had been organized to make such a recording (as they had on several previous occasions). But it was not to be, and anyone hearing this magical record, full of the glow and natural expressiveness which always went with Britten's conducting of Mozart, will recognize both performances as uniquely individual and illuminating, with Curzon at his very finest. The record was kept from issue on LP until after Sir Clifford's death, when it received its Rosette from us. It now arrives on CD still sounding full and beautiful.

Piano concertos Nos. 21 in C, K.467; 23 in A, K.488.
(M) *** Virgin/EMI Dig. CUV5 61123-2. Jean-Bernard Pommier, Sinfonia Varsovia.

A surprisingly rare coupling of what are now arguably the two favourite Mozart piano concertos here works very well indeed. Both performances have plenty of sparkle in outer movements – the first movement of K.467 is particularly arresting – and both slow movements are played simply and beautifully. Jean-Bernard Pommier's *Adagio* in K.488 compares favourably with Brendel's, and the string playing at the famous opening of the *Andante* of K.467 is ravishing in its transparent delicacy and gentle warmth. The finale of the same work is brisk but never sounds rushed. The sound is first class.

Piano concertos Nos. 21 in C, K.467; 24 in C min., K.491.
(M) *** Carlton IMP Dig. PCD 2007 [id.]. Howard Shelley, City of L. Sinfonia.

Howard Shelley gives delightfully fresh and characterful readings of both the popular *C major* and the great *C minor* concertos, bringing out their strength and purposefulness as well as their poetry, never overblown or sentimental. His Carlton (formerly Pickwick) disc makes an outstanding digital bargain, with accompaniment very well played and recorded.

Piano concertos Nos. 21 in C, K.467; 25 in C, K.503.
(B) *** Ph. Virtuoso 426 077-2; *426 077-4* [(M) id. import]. Stephen Kovacevich, LSO, Sir Colin Davis.

The partnership of Kovacevich and Davis almost invariably produces inspired music-making. Their balancing of strength and charm, drama and tenderness, makes for performances which retain their sense of spontaneity but which plainly result from deep thought, and the weight of both these great C major works is formidably conveyed. The 1972 recording is well balanced. However, the present CD transfer has thinned out the sound of the violins somewhat when they play forcefully above the stave, most noticeably at the opening of the first movement of K.467.

Piano concertos Nos. 21 in C, K.467; 26 in D (Coronation), K.537.
(M) *** Ph. 456 661-2. Alfred Brendel, ASMF, Marriner.

Brendel's account of No. 21 is already available on a generous Philips Duo (see above). Here it is coupled at mid-price with the *Coronation concerto*, which is also available in a Brendel Edition box of five discs (see above). Both are recommendable performances, but neither is perhaps among the very finest of his Mozart concerto recordings. However, coupled together, with good sound, they are attractive enough.

(i) *Piano concertos Nos. 21 in C, K.467; 26 in D (Coronation), K.537;* (ii) *12 Variations on 'Ah, vous dirai-je, Maman', K.265.*
✿ (B) *** Sony SBK 67178; *SBT 67178* [id.]. (i) Robert Casadesus, Columbia SO or Cleveland O, Szell; (ii) André Previn (piano).

The ravishing slow movement of K.467 has never sounded more magical than here, and Casadesus then takes the finale at a tremendous speed; but, for the most part, this is exquisite Mozart playing, beautifully paced and articulated. Although the orchestra tends to dwarf the pianist in tuttis, the subtleties of the solo playing are well caught. For the *Coronation concerto* the balance tends to favour the soloist, but the smaller orchestral scale is telling and the accompaniment could hardly be more stylish. Casadesus and Szell are again inspired to a totally memorable performance, and again the slow movement is captivating: Casadesus's Mozart may at first seem understated, but the imagination behind his readings is apparent in every phrase. And as if this were not enough for a bargain reissue, Sony have added a superb account of the *'Ah, vous dirai-je' variations* ('Twinkle, twinkle, little star') from the young André Previn, recorded in Hollywood in 1962. The crisp articulation and stylish overview are a joy, and the end result is wonderfully spontaneous.

Piano concertos Nos. 21 in C, K.467; 27 in B flat, K.595.
(B) **(*) [EMI Red Line CDR5 69821]. Barenboim, ECO.
(M) *(*) DG Dig. 445 516-2 [id.]. Rudolf Serkin, LSO, Abbado.

Barenboim's accounts of K.467 and K.595 are discussed above under the Rouge et Noir recording of *Piano concerto No. 9* etc. (CZS5 69991-2).

Rudolf Serkin was an artist of keen musical intellect and a fine Mozartian, as his older, CBS/Sony recordings demonstrate. But he left it rather too late in his career to begin, in his eighties, a cycle of the Mozart concertos with Abbado and the LSO. Though his thoughtfulness as an artist is often clear, his playing is at times distressingly prosaic – neither slow movement here is distinguished (the theme of the *Larghetto* of K.595 is a little sluggish, too) – with no dynamics less than mezzo forte, scrappy passage-work and uneven scales. The opening of the *B flat Concerto* is also very measured and spacious, and Serkin's contribution is wanting the grace he once commanded. There are moments of inelegance and little real sparkle in the quicker movements. Refined accompaniments from Abbado, but at times the styles clash. There are stronger and more sensitive accounts of both concertos, though few that are better recorded.

(i) *Piano concerto No. 21 in C, K.467;* (ii) *Symphony No. 41 in C (Jupiter), K.551.*
(M) ** [RCA Basic 100 09026 61708-2; *61708-4*]. (i) Rubinstein, RCA Victor SO, Wallenstein; (ii) Chicago SO, Levine.

It seems an attractive idea to pair Mozart's most popular piano concerto with the *Jupiter Symphony*, but cross-couplings of this kind are too often flawed, and so it is here. Rubinstein's account of the *C major Piano concerto*, K.467, with its beautiful slow movement is in every way a premium choice, but Levine's account of the symphony, while more than routine, is less than distinguished, given the reputation of the orchestra and the musicianship and insight of this conductor. The recording has no want of clarity and presence, but its claims cannot be pressed over rival performances.

Piano concerto No. 22 in E flat, K.482.
(M) ** EMI CDM7 64750-2. Sviatoslav Richter, Philh. O, Muti – BEETHOVEN: *Concerto No. 3.* **

Richter's 1983 recording is clearly looking forward towards Beethoven, particularly in the slow movement. He plays with all the poise and authority one would expect, and there are numerous felicities. He uses cadenzas by Benjamin Britten. Muti draws lively and sympathetic support from the Philharmonia – though, following Richter's example, the finale is weighty, if not without rhythmic bounce. Good remastered sound.

Piano concertos Nos. 22 in E flat, K.482; 23 in A, K.488.
(B) **(*) [EMI Red Line CDR5 69822]. Barenboim, ECO.

Barenboim gives a persuasive, at times even wilful account of K.482, relishing its expansiveness with dozens of spontaneous-sounding inflexions. The account of K.488 is discussed above. The orchestral accompaniment is admirably alive. Good remastered sound, firm, full and clear.

Piano concertos Nos. 22 in E flat, K.482; 26 in D (Coronation), K.537.
(M) *** DG (IMS) Dig. 447 283-2 [id.]. Malcolm Bilson (fortepiano), E. Bar. Soloists, Gardiner.

The *Coronation concerto* is presented strongly as well as elegantly, with the authentic timpani cutting dramatically through the textures in the first movement. Full and spacious recording in a helpful acoustic. The earlier concerto is hardly less vibrant and lyrically convincing, with the contrasts of the finale particularly effective.

Piano concertos Nos. 22 in E flat, K.482; 27 in B flat, K.595.
(B) ** Sony SBK 63038 [id.]. R. Casadesus, Columbia SO, Szell.

Casadesus seldom completely disappoints, but the net result of the performance of the *Piano concerto No. 27* is a feeling of coolness and reserve, despite the accomplished solo playing. K.482 is much more successful, although Szell's accompaniments are on the heavy side (partly the result of the resonant recording). Still, there is some fine solo playing, especially in the light-hearted finale, although the central section of the slow movement is a bit heavy-handed.

Piano concertos Nos. 23 in A, K.488; 24 in C min., K.491.
(M) *** DG 423 885-2. Kempff, Bamberg SO, Leitner.
(M) **(*) Decca 452 888-2 [id.]. Clifford Curzon, LSO, Kertész.
(M) **(*) Ph. Dig. 442 648-2. Mitsuko Uchida, ECO, Tate.
(BB) **(*) Naxos Dig. 8.550204 [id.]. Jenö Jandó, Concentus Hungaricus, Mátyás Antal.

(i) *Piano concertos Nos. 23 in A, K.488;* (ii) *24 in C min., K.491; Rondo in A, K.511.*
(M) *** RCA GD 87968 [7968-2-RG]. Rubinstein, RCA Victor SO, (i) Alfred Wallenstein; (ii) Josef Krips.

Kempff's outstanding performances of these concertos are uniquely poetic and inspired, and Leitner's accompaniments are comparably distinguished. The 1960 recording still sounds well, and this is strongly recommended at mid-price.

Rubinstein brings characteristic finesse and beauty of phrasing to his coupling; K.488 is especially beautiful. In K.491 the crystal-clear articulation is allied to the aristocratic feeling characteristic of vintage Rubinstein: the slow movement is memorable in its poise. Krips's accompaniment acts as a foil to the tragic tone of this great and wonderfully balanced work. The recordings, from 1958 and 1961 respectively, sound fresh, and the *Rondo*, recorded in 1959, is equally distinguished.

Curzon's vintage Kingsway Hall recording from 1968 was produced by Ray Minshull and engineered by Gordon Parry. It still sounds first class, full, warm and naturally balanced. It is certainly worthy of Decca's Classic Sound series. Curzon's account of these two concertos is immaculate and no connoisseur of the piano will fail to derive pleasure from them. Curzon has the advantage of sensitive support from Kertész and the LSO, and only an absence of the last ounce of sparkle and spontaneity prevents this from being strongly recommended. Kempff's DG record of the same coupling remains preferable. Ashkenazy, too, is in particularly fine form in these works – see above – and his Double Decca offers six concertos for comparatively little more than the present mid-priced CD.

It a pity that for this Uchida reissue Philips abandoned the original coupling (K.482 and K.488) which made a fascinating match, presenting illuminating contrasts rather than similarities. In No. 23, Uchida's thoughtful manner, at times a little understated, is ideally set against outstanding playing from the ECO with its excellent wind soloists. In No. 24, in spite of a dramatic opening from Jeffrey Tate, her tonal refinement and delicacy are sometimes in stronger evidence than her sense of scale, and that applies especially to the reticent slow movement and finale.

On Naxos, Antal's tempo in the first movement of the well-loved *A major Concerto* is bracingly brisk. The effect is undoubtedly fresh, but some ears may find the music could do with a touch more relaxation. This certainly comes in the *Adagio*, which has a simple melancholic nostalgia, and the energy returns appropriately in the vivacious closing *Allegro assai*. The operatic drama inherent in the first movement in the *C minor Concerto* is brought out well, and Jandó imaginatively and effectively chooses a cadenza by Hummel for this movement. Then, after the refined sensibility of the *Larghetto*, the finale is quite admirably paced. Recording is well up to the standard of the series.

Piano concertos Nos. (i–ii) *23 in A, K.488;* (iii; ii) *24 in C min., K.491;* (iv) *Double piano concerto in E flat, K.365.*
(B) **(*) Sony SBK 63037; *SBT 63037* [id.]. Robert Casadesus; with (i) Columbia SO; (ii) Szell; (iii) Cleveland O; (iv) Gaby Casadesus, Phd. O, Ormandy.

Casadesus's pre-war account of K.491 with Eugene Bigot was one of the glories of the Columbia catalogue, and his post-war LP was no less fine. Perhaps memory deceives, for the present account does not seem to scale quite those heights, but it is still pretty marvellous, especially the *Larghetto*, and the slightly overdriven precision of Szell hardly detracts from its merits. K.488 is certainly impressive too, and here the Columbia Symphony Orchestra is a more modest-sized group. The finale is taken very fast indeed, but the orchestra manage to stay with their brilliant soloist; however, a little more poise would have been advantageous. The remastering is very successful: the sound has more refinement than on LP and is certainly vivid. Alas, the *Double concerto* is a non-starter. In the outer movements the closely balanced pianos are made to sound aggressively hard and Ormandy's string section is fierce and inflated. The performance is lively enough, but unbeguiling. But the disc is well worth having for the two solo works.

Piano concertos Nos. 23 in A, K.488; 27 in B flat, K.595.
(M) *** Ph. 442 391-2. Alfred Brendel, ASMF, Marriner.

On Philips, two of the best of Brendel's Mozart concertos. However, these performances are included in

Brendel's two Duo sets of Mozart concertos (one in each) and these represent marvellous value; the present disc remains of interest to those requiring only this particular coupling.

Piano concertos Nos. 24 in C min., K.491; 25 in C, K.503; 26 in D (Coronation), K.537; 27 in B flat, K.595.

(B) ** Teldec/Warner Ultima Dig. 3984 21027-2 (2) [(M) id. import]. Daniel Barenboim, BPO.

The second of Barenboim's two Ultima collections of late Mozart concertos opens disappointingly. The 1988 performances of the *C minor* and *C major Concertos* refuse to take off until the light-hearted finale of K.503 displays a lightness of touch that is missing elsewhere. Both opening movements are over-weighted and the actual orchestral sound is curiously unrefined. The two final concertos were recorded the following year and they show Barenboim approaching his old form. Although the orchestral tuttis remain very fully textured, the BPO playing is elegant and both performances are agreeably spontaneous. Slow movements are appealing (though there are idiosyncratic touches in the *Andante* of K.503 that some might find self-conscious). But finales sparkle and the sound too is good. We hope this enjoyable disc can be reissued separately, for it is well recorded, provided one accepts the resonance.

Piano concertos Nos. 25 in C, K.503; 27 in B flat, K.595.

(BB) ** Belart 461 346-2 [(M) id. import]. Alicia de Larrocha, LPO, Solti.

Neither concerto finds Alicia de Larrocha in her best form. At the opening of the *C major*, Sir Georg Solti sets an impressive stage in the orchestral ritornello, but her entry lacks a matching gravitas and the reading is distinctly wanting in grandeur. The *B flat Concerto* is rather more successful. There is just a slight lack of range and character in the solo playing here, although she avoids the temptation to sentimentalize. The recorded sound, from the late 1970s, is in the best Decca tradition, but this is not really a distinguished reissue.

Piano concertos Nos. 26 in D (Coronation), K.537; 27 in B flat, K.595.

(B) ** EMI CfP CD-CFP 6033. Rafael Orozco, ECO, Charles Dutoit.

Rafael Orozco is an accomplished and intelligent artist, but there is a certain pallor about these readings. One feels the need for greater characterization and vitality, though Orozco is never insensitive. Given the excellence of the orchestral support and the good quality of the recording (made in the Henry Wood Hall in 1981), this seems good value at the asking price, yet artistically it must yield to its competitors. Barenboim, above, may be more idiosyncratic but he has more individuality, and in K.595 Gilels is unsurpassed.

(i) *Piano concerto No. 27 in B flat, K.595.*

(M) **(*) Decca 448 600-2 [id.]. Backhaus, VPO, Boehm – BRAHMS: *Piano concerto No. 2.*

Backhaus is magisterial and, if he is rhythmically rather uneven and the performance of the concerto does not always flow smoothly, the performance, very well accompanied by Boehm, has great character. The manner is a little unsmiling in its directness, but the classicism is appealing in its total lack of romantic overlay. There is something very compelling about this music-making, for Backhaus's personality projects strongly in every bar. The early (1955) stereo is remarkably truthful – worthy of Decca's Classic Sound series.

Piano concerto No. 27 in B flat, K.595; (i) *Double piano concerto in E flat, K.365.*

✿ (M) *** DG 419 059-2. Emil Gilels, VPO, Boehm, (i) with Elena Gilels.

Gilels's is supremely lyrical playing that evinces all the classical virtues. No detail is allowed to detract from the picture as a whole; the pace is totally unhurried and superbly controlled. All the points are made by means of articulation and tone, and each phrase is marvellously alive, while Boehm and the Vienna Philharmonic provide excellent support. The performance of the marvellous *Double concerto* is no less enjoyable. Its mood is comparatively serious, but this is not to suggest that the music's sunny qualities are not brought out. The quality on CD is first class, refining detail yet not losing ambient warmth.

Violin concertos

Complete Mozart Edition, Volume 8: (i) *Violin concertos Nos 1–5; 7 in D, K.271; Adagio in E, K.261; Rondo in B flat, K.269; Rondo in C, K.373.* (i; ii) *Concertone, K.190;* (iii; iv) *Double Concerto in D for violin, piano and orchestra, K.315f;* (iii; v; vi) *Sinfonia concertante in A, for violin, viola, cello and orchestra, K.320e.* (iii; v) *Sinfonia concertante in E flat, K.364.*

(M) **(*) Ph. Analogue/Dig. 422 508-2 (4). (i) Szeryng, (ii) with Poulet, Morgan, Jones; New Philh. O, Gibson; (iii) Iona Brown, with (iv) Shelley; (v) Imai; (vi) Orton; ASMF, Marriner.

Philip Wilby has here not only completed the first movement of an early *Sinfonia concertante for violin, viola and cello* (Mozart's only music with concertante cello) but also, through shrewd detective work, has reconstructed a full three-movement *Double concerto* from what Mozart left as 'a magnificent torso', to use Alfred Einstein's description; it is for violin, piano and orchestra. The result here is a delight, a full-scale 25-minute work which ends with an effervescent double-variation finale, alternately in duple and compound time. That is superbly done with Iona Brown and Howard Shelley as soloists; and the other ASMF items are very good too, with Iona Brown joined by Nobuko Imai most characterfully on the viola in the great *Sinfonia concertante*, K.364. What is a shade disappointing is to have Henryk Szeryng's readings of the main violin concertos from the 1960s instead of the Grumiaux set. Szeryng is sympathetic but a trifle reserved and not as refreshing as Grumiaux.

Violin concertos Nos. 1–7; Adagio in E, K.261; Rondos: in B flat, K.269; in C, K.273.
(BB) ** Arte Nova Dig. 74321 49710-2 (3) [id.]. Christiane Edinger, Europa SO, Wolfgang Gröhs.

Christiane Edlinger is a fine player, but her readings, though thoroughly musical, are rather plain-spun. Suk's phrasing (to name but one competitor) has altogether more individuality and his peformances convey deeper feeling. Gröhs and the Europa orchestra accompany attentively, but they too have nothing very individual to communicate about these much-recorded works. Moreover, although this set is in in the lowest price-range, the inclusion of the spurious, so-called *Concertos Nos. 6* and *7*, which are musically inferior, necessitates the inclusion of a third disc, which further reduces the attractions of this Arte Nova set.

Violin concertos Nos. (i) *1 in B flat, K.207;* (ii) *2 in D, K.211;* (iii) *3 in G, K.216;* (ii) *4 in D, K.218;* (i) *5 in A (Turkish), K.219;* (ii) *Adagio in E, K.261; Rondo in C, K.373.* (iv) *Concertone for 2 violins and orchestra in C, K.190; Sinfonia concertante in E flat for violin, viola and orchestra, K.364.*
(M) **(*) Sony Stern Edition I SM3K 66475 (3) [S3K 66475]. Isaac Stern, with (i) Columbia SO, Szell; (ii) ECO, Schneider; (iii) Cleveland O, Szell; (iv) Zukerman, ECO, Barenboim.

It goes without saying that Stern's solo playing is always splendid; it is simply that he is not always as sensitive on detail as his rivals, and this especially applies to No. 1 and rather less so to No. 5 where the accompaniment is provided by the Columbia Symphony Orchestra under Szell. The interpretation of No. 3, however, displays Stern's qualities of sparkling stylishness at their most intense in a very satisfying reading, with a beautifully poised and pointed accompaniment from the same conductor but now with the splendid Cleveland Orchestra. In Nos. 2 and 4, Stern has the benefit of rather fuller recording and his playing, as always, is full of personality. The great *Sinfonia concertante* stands among the finest available and is certainly the jewel in this set, presenting as it does two soloists of equally strong musical personality, and listening to the solo concertos again, so impressively remastered, is to relish the sheer beauty of Stern's tone and phrasing. The *Concertone* is attractive enough, if not one of Mozart's most inspired pieces, and here the dryness of the acoustic rather detracts from the charm of a work which on any count goes on too long for its material. Stern, Zukerman and Barenboim pay the central *Andantino grazioso* the compliment of a really slow tempo, and though this makes a very long movement the concentration is superb. Whatever the shortcomings of the recording, the artistry of the soloists shines out through every bar.

Violin concertos Nos. 1–5; Adagio in E, K.261; Rondo in C, K.373; Rondo concertante in B flat, K.269.
(B) *** O-L Double Dig. 455 721-2 (2) [id.]. Simon Standage, AAM, Hogwood.
(B) *** Decca Double (IMS) 440 621-2 (2) [(M) id. import]. Mayumi Fujikawa, RPO, Weller.
(M) *** Virgin/EMI VCD5 45214-2 (2). Christian Tetzlaff, Deutsche Kammerphilharmonie.
(B) **(*) EMI forte Dig. CZS5 69355-2 (2) [CDFB 69355]. Zimmermann, Württemberg CO, Faerber.
(M) **(*) DG Dig. 445 535-2 (2) [id.]. Itzhak Perlman, VPO, Levine.
(BB) **(*) RCA Navigator 74321 21277-2 (*Nos. 1–3 & Rondo, K.373*); 74321 21278-2 (*Nos. 4–5; Adagio, K.261 & Rondo K.269*) [(M) id. import]. Josef Suk, Prague CO, Libor Hlaváček.

Violin concertos Nos. 1–5; Adagio in E, K.261; Rondo in C, K.373.
(B) **(*) Sony SBK 46539/40; *SBT 46539/40* [id.]. Zukerman, St Paul CO.
(B) **(*) RCA Twofer 74321 34170-2 (2). Josef Suk, Prague CO, Libor Hlaváček.

(i) *Violin concertos Nos. 1–5;* (ii) *Adagio in E, K.261; Rondo in C, K.373;* (i; iii) *Sinfonia concertante in E flat, K.364.*
(B) *** Ph. Duo 438 323-2 (2) [id.]. Arthur Grumiaux, (i) LSO, C. Davis; (ii) New Philh. O, Leppard; (iii) with Arrigo Pellicia.

Violin concertos Nos. 1–5; (i) *Sinfonia concertante in E flat for violin, viola and orchestra, K.364.*
(BB) **(*) EMI Seraphim (SIS) CES5 68530-2 (2) [CDEB 68530]. Sir Yehudi Menuhin, Bath Festival O; (i) with Rudolph Barshai.

(B) ** DG Dig. 453 043-2 (2) [id.]. Gidon Kremer, (i) Kim Kashkashian; VPO, Harnoncourt.

Anyone seeking period-instrument performances of Mozart's concertante music for violin and orchestra need look no further than this superb Oiseau-Lyre set, which, for stylishness and spontaneity, can be ranked alongside the finest versions on modern instruments. The first two concertos are particularly felicitous. Hogwood's accompaniments are beautifully sprung, with no lack of warmth, the orchestral violins articulating neatly and gracefully to match the soloist, and the transparent textures revealing every detail of the orchestral scoring. Standage's beautifully focused, silvery tone is a constant joy. His nimble articulation in finales is coupled with an infectious rhythmic bounce to make the music sound freshly minted, and the simplicity of line in slow movements is equally refreshing, with the *Adagio* of the *G major* (K.216) serenely poised and a subtly added warmth in the *Andante cantabile* of the following *D major* (K.218). Here Hogwood caresses the lovely melody in his accompaniment in a way one might not always expect with a period-instrument performance. The following Rondeau is truly *grazioso*. The series is capped by a subtle expansion of scale for the *A major*. Hogwood's jaunty flair in the introduction keeps the music smiling, the *Adagio* is exquisitely tranquil without being over-romaticized, and the Turkish episode in the finale sparkles briskly, to make a perfect contrast with its elegant surrounding minuet. Standage plays his own cadenzas and they never outstay their welcome. The shorter pieces are also given fine performances and are never just treated as encores: the *E major Adagio* has a touchingly wistful air and the *C major Rondo* closes the programme amiably. The 1990 Abbey Road recording is first rate throughout, beautifully balanced and with not a trace of edginess anywhere.

Grumiaux's accounts of the Mozart *Violin concertos* come from the early 1960s and are among the most beautifully played in the catalogue at any price. The orchestral accompaniments have sparkle and vitality, and Grumiaux's contribution has splendid poise and purity of tone. For this generous reissue on their bargain Duo label, Philips have added the *Adagio*, K.261, and *Rondo*, K.373, recorded later in 1967, and also a fine performance of the great *Sinfonia concertante*, K.364, with Arrigo Pellicia proving a sensitive partner for Grumiaux, especially in the *Andante*. The new CD transfers are brightly lit but still faithful.

Mayumi Fujikawa has the advantage of admirably stylish and sympathetic accompaniments from Walter Weller, who secures consistently warm and polished playing from the RPO. Throughout there is much evidence of the soloist's musicianship and imagination, and every one of these performances comes sparklingly to life. Of course this set comes into direct competition with Grumiaux, also at bargain price, which must still remain a first choice. Yet the 1979/80 Decca recording is much warmer than the Philips, the violin is caught with complete naturalness and the orchestra is recorded so beautifully that this Double Decca set certainly holds its place.

Christian Tetzlaff is a first-class player and an equally first-class Mozartian. He plays all five concertos with great freshness and he simultaneously directs the Deutsche Kammerphilharmonie in polished and sympathetic accompaniments. His pacing of allegros is brisk, but exhilaratingly so, and his expressive phrasing in slow movements matches the clean, positive style of his contribution to faster movements. The performances seem to get better as he works his way through the set, and the recording balance is excellent. However, he enters a very competitive field. For a somewhat lower cost on a Philips Duo one can get Grumiaux, who is unsurpassed; and that set includes also the *Sinfonia concertante in E flat*. We also have a very soft spot for the Double Decca, similarly priced, in which the excellent Mayumi Fujikawa offers all the repertoire above and she is given a vintage Decca analogue sound of striking warmth and naturalness.

Zukerman's set has the advantage of excellent digital recording and a good balance, the violin forward but not distractingly so. The playing of outer movements is agreeably simple and fresh, and in slow movements Zukerman's sweetness of tone will appeal to many, although his tendency to languish a little in his expressiveness, particularly in the *G major*, K.216, rather less so in the *A major*, K.219, may be counted a less attractive feature, and he is not always subtle in his expression of feeling. Nevertheless this is still enjoyably spontaneous music-making and his admirers will certainly not be disappointed with K.219. The shorter pieces are played with some flair, the *Adagio* most appealingly. The St Paul Chamber Orchestra accompanies with stylish warmth. This set is excellent value and the two discs (and cassettes) are available separately, with concertos 1–3 together on the first.

However, the alternative set (available as a 'Twofer' or on two separate CDs) on RCA's super-bargain Navigator label is by no means upstaged. Josef Suk's recordings date from 1972. The solo playing has character, warmth and humanity, and its unaffected manner is especially suited to the first two concertos. The last three concertos have an agreeable simplicity and a freedom from histrionic gestures that is most welcome, and the recording, though not as vividly detailed as the DG, is agreeably smooth and natural. Hlaváček does not always make enough of the dynamic contrasts and, throughout, this music-making is dominated by Suk. This is partly a matter of the recording balance. But with any reservations noted, these are delightful performances and very good value.

Frank Peter Zimmermann is a highly talented German whose account of these concertos is also most impressive. His interpretations do not quite match those of Grumiaux (with whom, at the price, he comes into direct competition), Stern, Perlman, or even the sparkling Fujikawa on a Double Decca; but they are distinguished by fine musicianship and an effortless technical command. Zimmermann uses cadenzas by Zukerman and Oistrakh in No. 2 and Joachim in No. 4. The digital recordings have agreeable warmth and freshness and are very well balanced. Jörg Faerber is an excellent partner and gets extremely alive playing from the Württemberg orchestra. Not a first recommendation then, but certainly worth considering,

Perlman gives characteristically assured, virtuoso readings of these concertos of Mozart's youth, which, with Levine as a fresh and undistracting Mozartian, bring exceptionally satisfying co-ordination of forces. The virtuoso approach sometimes involves a tendency to hurry, and the power is emphasized by the weight and immediacy of the recording. Warmth is here rather than charm; but Perlman's individual magic makes for magnetic results all through, not least in the intimate intensity of slow movements. Those of the first two concertos are particularly graceful, but at times (and notably in the two most popular concertos, Nos. 3 and 5) he treats the works rather more as bravura showpieces than is common. However, Perlman's virtuosity is effortless and charismatic, and the orchestral playing is first class. The DG recording is well balanced, with the soloist close but not too excessively so, and the perspective is on the whole well judged.

Menuhin's recordings date from the early 1960s, a fruitful period for this fine artist, when he was closely associated with the Bath Festival. Most violinists use cadenzas by Joachim, but in all but No. 3 (where he chooses those by Franco) Menuhin uses cadenzas of his own, and many may feel that they are not Mozartian. Otherwise the style is sensibly exploited, and these performances give an engaging sense of musicians making intimate music together for the joy of it. There is plenty of warmth and colour. First movements are sufficiently ebullient, without loss of dignity and grace, due to a nice choice of tempi. The solo playing is not always immaculate, and compared, say, with Grumiaux it is romantic, yet in slow movements Mozart's melodies are floated gracefully and effortlessly. One is always conscious that this is the phrasing of a master musician who can also provide the lightest touch in finales, which are alert and extrovert. In the *Sinfonia concertante* Menuhin and Barshai comprise a splendid team with happily similar views. Throughout, the stereo has a bright sheen and, with the remastering, the orchestral violins are made to sound glassy above the stave, but the ear adjusts when the music-making is so distinctive and the acoustic is basically warm.

However expert the playing, the Gidon Kremer performances are not especially individual. The *B flat Concerto* (No. 1) is curiously uninvolving. Harnoncourt is nothing if not eccentric in his approach to Mozart. His opening movement for instance of No. 2, for instance, is brisk and clean, then the slow movement is purposefully moulded. No. 3 is discussed below. Finales are attractively spirited, with some fine wind solos from the Viennese players. However, there are much more rewarding accounts of the *Sinfonia concertante* available. The recordings are pleasingly warm.

Violin concertos Nos. 1 in B flat, K.207; 2 in D, K.211; Rondo in B flat, K.269; Andante in F (arr. Saint-Saëns from *Piano concerto No. 21, K.467*).
(BB) **(*) Naxos Dig. 8.550414 [id.]. Takako Nishizaki, Capella Istropolitana, Johannes Wildner.

This was the last disc to be recorded (in 1990) of Takako Nishizaki's fine survey of the violin concertos. The opening movement of K.207 is brisk and fresh, although this is the least individual of Nishizaki's readings. The *Second Concerto*, K.211, has rather more flair, the *Andante* touchingly phrased, and the finale has a winning lightness of touch. The *Rondo* is also an attractively spontaneous performance, and as an encore we are offered Saint-Saëns's arrangement of the famous *'Elvira Madigan'* theme from the *C major Concerto*, K.467.

(i) *Violin concertos Nos. 2 in D, K.211; 4 in D, K.218;* (ii) *Divertimento for strings No. 1, K.136.*
(B) *** [EMI Red Line Dig. CDR5 69865]. (i) Anne-Sophie Mutter, Philh. O; (ii) BPO; Muti.

Anne-Sophie Mutter made her Mozartian début with Karajan on DG with a famous youthful coupling of the *G major*, K.216, and *A major*, K.219. She went on to record the two *D major Concertos* for EMI with a different orchestra and conductor. The results are hardly less successful. She is given very sensitive support from the Philharmonia under Muti. Her playing combines purity and classical feeling, delicacy and incisiveness, and is admirably expressive. Its freshness is also most appealing. The early digital recording is very good, the images sharply defined, but the balance satisfactory. The finest of Mozart's three string divertimenti makes a good bonus.

Violin concerto No. 3 in G, K.216.

(B) *** EMI forte CZS5 69331-2 (2) [CDFB 693312]. David Oistrakh, Philh. O – BEETHOVEN: *Triple concerto;* BRAHMS: *Double concerto;* PROKOFIEV: *Violin concerto No. 2.* ***

(B) *** [EMI Dig. Red Line CDR5 72559]. Zimmermann, Württemberg CO, Faerber – BACH: *Violin concertos.* **(*)

David Oistrakh was at his finest in this beautiful 1958 performance of Mozart's *G major Concerto*. His supple, richly toned yet essentially classical style suits the melodic line of this youthful work and gives it the stature of maturity. The orchestral contribution is directed by the soloist himself and is surprisingly polished. EMI provide admirably smooth yet vivid sound, and this is just one of four marvellous performances which make up this forte compilation, one of the finest concertante bargains in the catalogue.

Zimmermann's account of the *G major Concerto* comes from his complete set (see above) and is in every way recommendable. Here it is coupled with the Bach solo concertos, but unfortunately not the *Double violin concerto*.

(i) *Violin concertos Nos. 3 in G, K.216; 4 in D, K.218;* (ii) *Duo for violin and viola in G, K.423.*

(M) **(*) DG (IMS) Dig. 439 525-2. Gidon Kremer; (i) VPO, Harnoncourt; (ii) Kim Kashkashian.

Kremer and Harnoncourt make a characterful partnership in these Mozart violin concertos. In the *G major*, K.216, the first movement flows at just the right pace, and then in the *Andante* a comma is placed to romanticize the climbing opening phrase of the main theme slightly. But with Kremer playing sweetly throughout, such individual touches may be found very acceptable (including a long cadenza in the first movement of No. 3) when there is plenty of vitality. The *Duo* (quite substantial at 17 minutes) makes an interesting bonus, with skilful playing and a good balance between Kremer and Kashkashian. But there is more to this music than these players find.

(i) *Violin concertos Nos. 3 in G, K.216; 4 in D, K.218. Serenade: Eine kleine Nachtmusik, K.525.*

(M) **(*) Sony stereo/mono SMK 64468 [id.]. (i) Zino Francescatti; Columbia SO, Walter.

Francescatti's coupling of the *Third* and *Fourth* Mozart *Concertos* is probably his best record, and in their remastered CD format these fine performances from 1958, recorded in California, are given a new lease of life. The playing is at times a little wayward, but Bruno Walter accompanies throughout with his usual warmth and insight and falls into line sympathetically with his soloist. Both slow movements are beautifully played, albeit with an intensity that barely stops short of romanticism. In some ways the *D major* suits Francescatti's opulent style of playing best. The whole atmosphere of this music-making represents the pre-authentic approach to Mozart at its most rewarding. The 1954 New York recording of the *Night music* is no great asset. The playing is acceptable but the string recording is harsh and ill-focused.

Violin concertos Nos. 3 in G, K.216; 4 in D, K.218; 5 in A, K.219.

(B) **(*) DG Classikon 449 850-2 [(M) id. import]. Wolfgang Schneiderhan, BPO.

This reissue is drawn from Schneiderhan's complete set of the violin concertos, made in the late 1960s. He plays with effortless mastery and a strong sense of classical proportion. The Berlin orchestra plays well for him, although there is a slightly unsmiling quality at times. The *A major Concerto* was perhaps the finest of the set and makes a suitable coupling for his famous record of the Beethoven, made six years earlier (see below). The sound is realistically balanced.

Violin concertos Nos. 3 in G, K.216; 5 in A (Turkish), K.219.

(BB) *** Naxos Dig. 8.550063 [id.]. Takako Nishizaki, Capella Istropolitana, Stephen Gunzenhauser.

Violin concertos Nos. 3 in G, K.216; 5 in A (Turkish), K.219; Adagio in E, K.261.

(B) **(*) Tring Dig. TRP 060 [(M) id. import]. Jonathan Carney, RPO.

This is the finest of Nishizaki's three discs of the Mozart violin concertos on Naxos. The readings are individual and possess the most engaging lyrical feeling and the natural response of the soloist to Mozartian line and phrase. A good balance, the soloist forward, but convincingly so, and the orchestral backcloth in natural perspective. A real bargain.

Jonathan Carney successfully directs the RPO from the bow, but he favours brisk tempi in outer movements, and the finale of K.216 is dangerously fast. Even so, these lively and expressive performances are very enjoyable, and well recorded too. But even though Carney offers a bonus, Takako Nishizaki takes precedence in this coupling.

Violin concerto No. 4 in D, K.218.

(M) (***) DG mono 457 720-2 [id.]. Wolfgang Schneiderhan, BPO, Rosbaud – HAYDN: *Symphonies Nos. 92 & 104.* (***)

We share DG's enthusiasm for the eminently stylish classical playing of Wolfgang Schneiderhan in

Mozart's *D major Violin concerto*. He plays it very beautifully indeed, and there may be more points of detail in the orchestra which Rosbaud presents to the listener rather more clearly than in Schneiderhan's later, stereo version, where he directed the Berlin Philharmonic himself. Nevetherless the (well-balanced) 1956 mono recording is marginally less flattering to his timbre than the stereo, and for most collectors that later version will probably be the preferred choice, unless the present Haydn coupling is thought essential, and it is certainly impressive.

Violin concerto No. 4 in D, K.218; (i) *Sinfonia concertante in E flat, for violin, viola and orchestra, K.364.*
(BB) **(*) Naxos Dig. 8.550332 [id.]. Takako Nishizaki, (i) Ladislav Kyselak; Capella Istropolitana, Stephen Gunzenhauser.

A fine account of No. 4, with Takako Nishizaki's solo playing well up to the high standard of this series and with Stephen Gunzenhauser's perceptive pacing adding to our pleasure. The *Sinfonia concertante* is very enjoyable too, if perhaps slightly less distinctive. The finale is infectious in its liveliness, its rhythms buoyantly pointed. Again, a good balance and excellent sound.

Violin concertos Nos. 4 in D, K.218; 5 in A (Turkish), K.219; Adagio in E, K.261; Rondos Nos. 1 in B flat, K.269; 2 in C, K.373.
(M) **(*) EMI CDM7 64868-2. David Oistrakh, BPO.

David Oistrakh's performances come from his complete set, recorded in 1970/71. The slow movement of K.219 is particularly fine, and so too is the finale. The three shorter concertante works also show the soloist at his finest; though the accompaniment for the *Adagio*, K.261, remains richly upholstered, this is played very beautifully. With 77 minutes of music this is excellent value, for the soloist is truthfully caught and the balance is convincing.

Violin concerto No. 5 in A (Turkish), K.219.
(M) *** RCA 09026 61757-2 [61757-2-RG]. Heifetz with CO – *String quintet, K.516* etc. ***
(M) *** DG 447 403-2 [id.]. Wolfgang Schneiderhan, BPO, Jochum – BEETHOVEN: *Violin concerto.* *** ✿
(M) (***) EMI mono CDH5 65191-2. Heifetz, LPO, Barbirolli – MENDELSSOHN: *Concerto* (**(*)); VIEUXTEMPS: *Concerto No. 5.* (***)

Marvellously exhilarating Mozart from Heifetz, though his actual entry in the first movement is quite ethereal. He directs the accompanying group himself, the only time he did so on record. The early (1954) stereo is fully acceptable and the performance memorable, with the crystalline clarity of articulation matched by warmth of timbre and aristocratic phrasing.

This was perhaps the finest of the complete set of Mozart's violin concertos which Schneiderhan recorded with the Berlin Philharmonic in the late 1960s. The recording is realistically balanced, and this makes a generous coupling for his famous record of the Beethoven, made six years earlier.

Heifetz's EMI recording first appeared in 1934 and it is evident that there was a good rapport between him and the young John Barbirolli, whom Fred Gaisberg had chosen as partner. The playing has a commendable warmth and spontaneity which is less striking in the Mendelssohn coupling, where Beecham is at the helm.

(i) *Violin concerto No. 5 (Turkish), K.219. Divertimento for strings in D, K.136; Serenade No. 13 (Eine kleine Nachtmusik); Symphony No. 29 in A, K.201.*
(M) *(*) Virgin Dig. CUV5 61132-2. (i) Warren-Green; LCO.

This was one of Christopher Warren-Green's rare disappointing records, made during his all-too-brief tenure leading the LCO. The playing is as polished as ever, but tempi are so brisk that the effect is at times almost perfunctory, particularly in the *Violin concerto*, which is undoubtedly played brilliantly.

Dances and Marches

Complete Mozart Edition, Volume 6: *La Chasse, KA.103/K.299d; Contredanses, K.101; K.123; K.267; K.269b; K.462; (Das Donnerwetter) K.534; (La Bataille) K.535; 535a; (Der Sieg vom Helden Koburg) K.587; K.603; (Il trionfo delle donne) K.607; (Non più andrai) K.609; K.610; Gavotte, K.300; German dances, K.509; K.536; K.567; K.571; K.586; K.600; K.602; K.605; Ländler, K.606; Marches, K.214; K.363; K.408; K.461; Minuets, K.61b; K.61g/2; K.61h; K.94, 103, 104, 105; K.122; K.164; K.176; K.315g; K.568; K.585; K.599; K.601; K.604; Minuets with Contredanses, K.463; Overture & 3 Contredanses, K.106.*

❁ (M) *** Ph. 422 506-2 (6) [id.]. V. Mozart Ens., Willi Boskovsky.

Much of the credit for this remarkable undertaking should go to its expert producer, Erik Smith, who, besides providing highly stylish orchestrations for numbers without Mozart's own scoring, illuminates the music with some of the most informative and economically written notes that ever graced a record. The CD transfers preserve the excellence of the mid-1960s sound. The collector might feel that he or she is faced here with an *embarras de richesses* with more than 120 *Minuets*, nearly 50 *German dances* and some three dozen *Contredanses*, but Mozart's invention is seemingly inexhaustible, and the instrumentation is full of imaginative touches.

12 German dances, K.586; 6 German dances, K.600; 4 German dances, K.602; 3 German dances, K.605.
(BB) *** Naxos Dig. 8.550412 [id.]. Capella Istropolitana, Johannes Wildner.

Fresh, bright, unmannered performances of some of the dance music Mozart wrote right at the end of his life. The playing is excellent and the recording is bright and full. An excellent super-bargain alternative to the Boskovsky Decca CD.

Complete Mozart Edition, Volume 45: *'Rarities and curiosities': Contredanses in B flat & D* (completed Smith); *The London Sketchbook:* (i) *3 Contredanses in F; 2 Contredanses in G; 6 Divertimenti.* (ii) *Wind divertimenti* arr. from operas: *Don Giovanni* (arr. Triebensee); *Die Entführung aus dem Serail* (arr. Wendt) & (i) *March, K 384.* (i; iii) *Rondo in E flat for horn and orchestra, K 371* (completed Smith); (iv) *Larghetto for piano and wind quintet, K 452a;* (v) *Modulating prelude in F/E min.* (vi) *Tantum ergo in B flat, K 142; in D, K 197;* (vii) *Idomeneo: Scene & rondo.* (viii) *Musical dice game, K.516.*
(M) *** Ph. 422 545-2 (3) [id.]. (i) ASMF, Marriner; (ii) Netherlands Wind Ens.; (iii) Timothy Brown; cond. Sillito; (iv) Uchida, Black, King, Farrell, O'Neil; (v) Erik Smith (harpsichord); (vi) Frimmer, Leipzig R. Ch. & SO, Schreier; (vii) Mentzler, Hendricks, Bav. RSO, C. Davis; (viii) Marriner & Smith.

The first CD includes the innocent little piano pieces from the child Mozart's 'London Notebook'. Erik Smith has orchestrated them and, if the results may not be important, they charm the ear at least as much as Mozart's early symphonies, with many unexpected touches. Marriner and the Academy are ideal performers and the 1971 recording is warm and refined. Then come the arrangements for wind of selections from two key operas, elegantly played by the Netherlands Wind Ensemble. Finally come the rarities and curiosities, the *Rondo for horn and orchestra* with the missing 60 bars (discovered only in 1989) now added, and the other music made good by Erik Smith. There is a curious finale in which Erik Smith and Sir Neville Marriner participate (with spoken comments) in a *Musical dice game* to decide the order of interchangeable phrases in a very simple musical composition. The result, alas, is something of a damp squib.

Wind divertimenti and Serenades

Adagios: in F, K,410; in B flat, K.411; Divertimenti for wind Nos. 3 in E flat, K.166; 4 in B flat, K.186; 8 in F, K.213; 9 in B flat, K.240; 12 in E flat, K.252; 13 in F, K.253; 14 in B flat, K.270; 16 in E flat, K.289; in E flat, K.Anh. 226; in B flat, K.Anh. 227. Serenades Nos. 10 in B flat, for 13 wind instruments, K.361; 11 in E flat, K.375; 12 in C min., K.488.
(B) **(*) Decca 455 794-2 (3) [id.]. L. Wind Soloists, Jack Brymer.

The coverage is remarkably comprehensive and the playing here of the highest order, and the only drawback is the too-close balance for the large-scale *B flat major Serenade*. All the recordings were made in Decca's West Hampstead studio and in this work the effect is rather dry; the digital remastering has taken much of the ambient bloom from the sound. However, Brymer's group gives a strong, stylish performance with plenty of imagination in matters of phrasing. Elsewhere there is presence and bloom in equal measure. These artists do not miss the sombre quality of the *C minor Serenade*, but they are not intimidated by it; and the *Andante* has a winningly gentle poignancy. The other *Divertimenti* are virtually all minor masterpieces, and even the slighter works are as diverting as their titles imply. Throughout, the ear delights in the captivating oboe-playing of Terence MacDonagh (his colleague is James Brown; Brymer and Walter Lear are the clarinettists, Roger Birnstingle and Ronald Waller the bassoonists, and the horn players are Alan Civil and Ian Beers). There are countless felicities: all the finales have a wonderfully light touch, but one remembers especially the engaging three-movement *Divertimento in F*, K.253, with its charming first-movement theme and variations and its slow Minuet with its playful Trio.

Divertimenti for wind Nos. 3 in E flat, K.166; 4 in B flat, K.186; 8 in F, K.213; 9 in B flat, K.240; 12 in E flat, K.252; 13 in F, K.253; 14 in B flat, K.270; Serenades Nos. 10 in B flat, for 13 wind instruments, K.361; 11 in E flat, K.375; 12 in C min., K.488.
(M) *** Audivis Astrée Dig. E 8627. Zefiro Ens.

Astrée Audivis offer a new digital set at mid-price (three records for the cost of two), offering the same three major *Serenades* as Jack Brymer, plus seven of the *Divertimenti*, played on period instruments by a highly sensitive Italian group called Ensemble Zefiro – they take their name very appropriately from the Greek mythological God of the Western Wind. There would have been room here for the other *Divertimenti*, but those offered are the major masterpieces and the performances are very recommendable on all counts. The sounds of the period instruments are delightfully fresh and the blending of timbres most felicitous. Moreover the ambient effect of the recording has just the right degree of resonance, affording an agreeable overall bloom, without any kind of clouding. The playing itself brings a characteristic Italianate sunny quality to Mozart yet is remarkably subtle in detail. The *Gran Partita* is particularly seductive, with only one tiny flaw. At the opening of its eloquent *Adagio* the initial oboe entry begins a little below the note: some ears might find this disturbing on repetition. Otherwise intonation is impeccable and the brilliant playing on natural horns by Raul Diaz and Dileno Baldin is most infectious. In the *C minor Serenade* with its darker sonorities, the Italians miss the sombre touch which the English players manage so adroitly, but overall the Zefiro group play with such glowing finesse and spontaneity that this Audivis set must marginally take pride of place.

Divertimenti and Serenades

Divertimenti for strings Nos. 1–3, K.136–8; Divertimento No. 7 in D, K.205.
(BB) ** Naxos Dig. 8.550108 [id.]. Capella Istropolitana, Richard Edlinger.

Pleasing performances in a welcoming and warm acoustic. The Capella Istropolitana, which is drawn from the Slovak Philharmonic, play well for Richard Edlinger. They are not quite as characterful or spirited as the ASMF under Marriner (see below), but they are well recorded.

Divertimenti for strings Nos. 1–3, K.136–8; Serenades Nos. 6 in D (Serenata notturna), K.239; 13 in G (Eine kleine Nachtmusik), K.525.
(M) **(*) Classic fM Dig. 75605 57024-2. City of L. Sinfonia, Andrew Watkinson.

These are delightful performances: fresh, warm and polished. *Eine kleine Nachtmusik* is elegant, graceful and nicely paced, and the same can be said of the three engaging *String divertimenti*. The *Serenata notturna* features the leaders of each section (two violins, viola and double-bass) as a solo concertino group, and with the timpani not over-dominant. The snag is the resonance of the recording which is rather excessive. If you don't mind that, this Classic fM programme is very recommendable.

Divertimenti Nos. 2 in D, K.131; 15 in B flat, K.287.
(BB) *** Naxos Dig. 8.550996 [id.]. Capella Istropolitana, Harald Nerat.

If this is the start of a new Naxos series of Mozart *Divertimenti* from the Capella Istropolitana under Harald Nerat, then we are in for a treat. The playing is beautifully turned and polished. The string group seems just the right size, and they phrase elegantly; the sound is full and transparent, bringing the sweetest modern violin timbre, yet the effect is as refreshing as any period performance. The *D major Divertimento* is charmingly scored for flute, oboe, bassoon, four horns and strings, with woodwind adding frequent touches of colour, but it has a gracious second-movement *Adagio* cantilena of disarming simplicity for strings alone. The *B flat Divertimento* was written five years later, in Salzburg, and is scored more simply for two horns and strings. The lovely E flat major *Adagio* has that touch of gentle pathos that is Mozart's very own, and the finale brings a recitativo from the principal violin before its light-hearted conclusion, with a feather-light response from the violins.

Complete Mozart Edition, Volume 4: *Divertimenti for strings Nos. 1–3, K.136/8; Divertimenti for small orchestra Nos. 1 in E flat, K.113; 7 in D, K.205* (with *March in D, K.290*)*; 10 in F, K.247* (with *March in F, K.248*)*; 11 in D, K.251; 15 in B flat, K.287; 17 in D, K.334* (with *March in D, K.445*)*; A Musical joke, K.622; Serenade (Eine kleine Nachtmusik), K.525.*
(M) *** Ph. Dig. 422 504-2 (5) [id.]. ASMF CO.

This is one of the most attractive of all the boxes in the Philips Mozart Edition. The music itself is a delight, the performances are stylish, elegant and polished, while the digital recording has admirable warmth and realistic presence and definition.

Complete Mozart Edition, Volume 5: *Divertimentos for wind Nos. 3 in E flat, K.166; 4 in B flat, K.186; 6 in C, K.188; 8 in F, K.213; 9 in B flat K.240; 12 in E flat, K.252; 13 in F, K.253; 14 in B flat, K.270; 16 in E flat, K.289; in E flat, K.Anh. 226; in B flat, K.Anh. 227; Divertimentos for 3 basset horns, K.439b/1–5; Duos for 2 horns, K.487/1–12; Serenades for wind No. 10 in B flat, K.361; 11 in E flat, K.375; 12 in C min., K.388; Adagios: in F; B flat, K.410–11.*
(M) *** Ph. Analogue/Dig. 422 505-2 (6) [id.]. Holliger Wind Ens. (or members of); Netherlands Wind Ens., De Waart (or members of); ASMF, Marriner or Laird.

Mozart's wind music, whether in the ambitious *Serenades* or the simpler *Divertimenti*, brings a naturally felicitous blending of timbre and colour unmatched by any other composer. It seems that even when writing for the simplest combination of wind instruments, Mozart is incapable of being dull. The playing of the more ambitious works is admirably polished and fresh, and it is interesting to note that Holliger's group provides a stylishly light touch and texture with the principal oboe dominating, while the blending of the Netherlanders is somewhat more homogeneous, though the effect is still very pleasing.

Divertimenti Nos. 10 in F, K.247; 11 in D, K.251; 15 in B flat, K.287; 17 in D, K.334.
(M) ** DG 449 094-2 (2). BPO, Karajan.

Needless to say, these are beautifully played performances (especially the slow movement and finale of K.287) and as such they prompt the liveliest admiration. At the same time there is a predictably suave elegance that seems to militate against spontaneity. Each phrase is exquisitely moulded, perfumed and powdered, and the result, although beguiling in its way, is just too much of a good thing. Cultured and effortless readings, smoothly recorded and well balanced, they somehow leave one untouched. There is too much legato and too little sparkle.

Complete Mozart Edition, Volume 25: (i) *Idomeneo* (ballet music), *K.367;* (ii) *Les petits riens* (ballet), *K.299b; Music for a pantomime (Pantalon und Colombine), K.446* (completed and orch. Beyer); *Sketches for a ballet intermezzo, K.299c* (completed and orch. Erik Smith); (iii) *Thamos, King of Egypt* (incidental music), *K.345.*
(M) *** Ph. 422 525-2 (2) [id.]. (i) Netherlands CO, David Zinman; (ii) ASMF, Marriner; (iii) Eickstädt, Pohl, Büchner, Polster, Adam, Berlin R. Ch. & State O, Klee.

This volume collects together Mozart's theatre music and makes a particularly enticing package. Zinman and his Netherlanders give a neatly turned account of the ballet from *Idomeneo*, musical and spirited. Marriner takes over with modern digital sound for *Les petits riens* and the two novelties, and the ASMF playing has characteristic elegance and finesse. The *Sketches for a ballet intermezzo* survive only in a single-line autograph, but Erik Smith's completion and scoring provide a series of eight charming vignettes, most with descriptive titles, ending with a piquant *Tambourin*. The music for *Pantalon and Columbine* (more mime than ballet) survives in the form of a first violin part, and Franz Beyer has skilfully orchestrated it for wind and strings, using the first movement of the *Symphony*, K.84, as the overture and the last movement of *Symphony*, K.120, as the finale. Beautifully played as it is here, full of grace and colour, this is a real find and the digital recording is first rate. *Thamos, King of Egypt* is marvellous music which it is good to have on record, particularly in such persuasive hands as these. The choral singing is impressive and the orchestral playing is excellent.

Masonic funeral music: see below, in VOCAL MUSIC, under Complete Mozart Edition, Volume 22.

Overtures: *Apollo et Hyacinthus; Bastien und Bastienne; La clemenza di Tito; Così fan tutte; Don Giovanni; Die Entführung aus dem Serail; La finta giardiniera; Idomeneo; Lucio Silla; Mitridate, rè di Ponto; Le nozze di Figaro; Il rè pastore; Der Schauspieldirektor; Die Zauberflöte.*
(BB) *** Naxos Dig. 8.550185; *4550185* [id.]. Capella Istropolitana, Barry Wordsworth.

Wordsworth follows up his excellent series of Mozart symphonies for Naxos with this generous collection of overtures, no fewer than 14 of them, arranged in chronological order and given vigorous, stylish performances. In Italian overture form, *Mitridate* and *Lucio Silla*, like miniature symphonies, have separate tracks for each of their three contrasted sections. Very well recorded, the disc is highly recommendable at super-bargain price.

Serenades Nos. 1 in D, K.100; 7 in D (Haffner), K.250; 9 in D (Posthorn), K.320; 13 in G (Eine kleine Nachtmusik), K.525; Serenata notturna, K.239.
(B) **(*) Decca Double 443 458-2 (2) [id.]. Vienna Mozart Ens., Willi Boskovsky.

Boskovsky and the Vienna Mozart Ensemble play with elegance and sparkle, and these performances still sound outstandingly bracing and vivid. The recordings were made in the Sofiensaal over a decade between 1968 and 1978. The account of *Eine kleine Nachtmusik*, one of the freshest and most attractive on disc and dating from 1968, now has a somewhat astringent treble, while Boskovsky's 1973 *Posthorn Serenade*, which has a natural musicality and is very well balanced, seems rather dry in the matter of string-timbre, though the bloom remains on the wind and the posthorn is tangible in its presence. Like the *Haffner serenade*, it is marvellously alive, full of the sparkle and elegance we associate with this group, with admirable phrasing and feeling for detail, yet the *Haffner* (dating from 1972) has a distinctly warmer ambience. The very engaging earliest *Serenade in D*, K.100, has the greatest glow of all, although it was recorded in 1970. Nevertheless many will count this excellent value for money in Decca's two-for-the-price-of-one series, offering 159 minutes of music on the pair of CDs.

Serenades Nos. 3 in D, K.185; 4 in D (Colloredo), K.203.
(BB) *** Naxos Dig. 8.550413; *4550413* [id.]. Salzburg CO, Harald Nerat.

Well-played, nicely phrased and musical accounts on Naxos, recorded in a warm, reverberant acoustic, but one in which detail clearly registers. The Salzburg Chamber Orchestra has real vitality, and most readers will find these accounts musically satisfying and very enjoyable.

Serenades Nos. 6 in D (Serenata notturna), K.239; 7 in D (Haffner), K.250.
(M) **(*) Erato/Warner Dig. 0630 13737-2. Pavlo Beznosiuk, Amsterdam Bar. O, Koopman.

Koopman's account is bold and his accents robust, especially in Minuets; indeed the energetic timpani are little short of explosive. But he has an excellent violin soloist in Pavlo Beznosiuk, and he ensures that the delectable *moto perpetuo* sparkles daintily. The extra transparency means that detail registers throughout. The timpani come through strongly and cleanly in the *Serenata notturna* and tend to dominate aurally, but the string playing remains elegantly turned.

Serenades Nos. (i) *6 (Serenata Notturna), K.239; 7 in D (Haffner), K.250; 9 in D (Posthorn), K.320;* (ii) *13 in G, K.525.*
(B) ** DG Double 453 076-2 (2) [id.]. (i) BPO; (ii) VPO; Karl Boehm.

These are characteristic Boehm performances from the early 1970s. A large orchestra is used and, as it is the Berlin Philharmonic, one can take it for granted that they will play with polish and refinement. The effect is warm and civilized (including the posthorn solos). There is a degree of suavity, although there is spirit in the allegros. The *Posthorn Serenade* also brings a certain dourness on the part of Boehm. He doesn't find much fun and sparkle in the music, although this is somewhat offset by Thomas Brandis's stylish solo violin contribution. The real snag is the sheer weight of sound, and on the first disc the string focus is not absolutely clean, not even in the opening *Eine kleine Nachtmusik*, which lacks textural refinement, even though Boehm's reading is polished and spacious, with a neat, lightly pointed finale.

Serenades Nos. 6 in D (Serenata Notturna), K.239; 13 in G (Eine kleine Nachtmusik), K.525.
(B) *** Carlton IMP 30367 02242 [(M) id.]. Serenata of London, Barry Wilde – ELGAR: *Serenade for strings;* GRIEG: *Holberg suite.* ***

These performances by the Serenata of London under Barry Wilde are first class in every way and, with truthful, modern recording, they are very recommendable indeed. In the *Serenata Notturna* the timpani are not too resonantly dominant, yet they add much character to the opening *Marcia-maestoso*. Wilde's pacing of the *Night music* is admirable and the playing is consistently fresh and stylish.

Serenades Nos. 6 in D (Serenata notturna), K.239; 13 (Eine kleine Nachtmusik), K.525; Serenade for wind No. 12 in C min., K.388.
(M) **(*) DG (IMS) Dig. 439 524-2. Orpheus CO.

The *Serenata notturna*, which can easily sound bland, has a fine sparkle here. The famous *Night music*, however, is rather lacking in charm with a very brisk opening movement, alert enough and very polished, but somewhat unbending. The *Wind serenade* restores the balance of excellence, alert and sympathetic and full of character. The digital recording is first class throughout.

Serenade No. 7 in D (Haffner); March, K.249.
(BB) **(*) Naxos Dig. 8.550333 [id.]. Takako Nishizaki, Capella Istropolitana, Johannes Wildner.

The K.249 *March* is given twice, as both prelude and postlude to the main *Serenade* in the authentic manner. Wildner brings out the vigour rather than the charm of the fast movements, with the Minuets on the heavy side, but with the big final allegro superbly articulated and erupting in rustic jollity. The important violin solos in earlier movements are played superbly by Takako Nishizaki. Bright, full recording. Even with the above reservations, this is an excellent bargain.

Serenade No. 9 in D (Posthorn), K.320; 2 Marches, K.320a.
(B) ** EMI CfP CD-CFP 6032 [(M) id.]. LPO, Hans-Hubert Schönzler.

Framed by two lively associated *Marches*, intended as entry and exit music, Schönzler's account of the

Posthorn Serenade is spirited, with clean string phrasing and stylish wind solos, notably from oboe and flute. The 1975 recording is bright and clear, but the microphones are close to counter the resonance of Watford Town Hall, and the treble is rather dry with the violins made to sound a bit thin. Authenticists shouldn't mind this too much, but there is also a lack of charm, although everything is alert and vivid.

Serenade No. 9 in D (Posthorn); Notturno for 4 orchestras in D, K.286.
(BB) ** Naxos Dig. 8.550092 [id.]. Capella Istropolitana, Martin Turnovsky.

Very well played, Turnovsky's account of the *Posthorn Serenade* is lively if not quite as elegant as the finest versions. At a slow speed the lovely minor-key *Andantino*, which is the fifth of the seven movements, is a degree too heavy-handed, for example; but at bargain price, with a generous fill-up and well recorded, it is a fair recommendation. The *Notturno* for four orchestras, with its antiphonal effects, also has its charms.

(i) *Serenades Nos. 9 in D (Posthorn), K.320; 13 in G (Eine kleine Nachtmusik), K.525;* (ii) *6 German dances, K.509; Minuet in C, K.409.*
(M) **(*) Sony SBK 48266; *SBT 48266* [id.]. (i) Cleveland O, George Szell; (ii) LSO, Leinsdorf.

Serenades Nos. 9 in D (Posthorn); 13 in G (Eine kleine Nachtmusik); Symphony No. 32 in G, K.318.
(M) ** DG (IMS) Dig. 445 555-2 [id.]. VPO, Levine.

Marvellously vivacious playing from the Clevelanders in the *Posthorn Serenade*, especially in the exhilarating *presto* finale, yet there is no lack of tenderness in the *concertante* third movement marked *Andante grazioso*. *Eine kleine Nachtmusik* is similarly polished and vital, and in both works the Severance Hall acoustic provides a full ambience, but it is a pity that the close balance means a reduced dynamic range. Even so, this is music-making of great character. Leinsdorf's *German dances* make a lively bonus, if not as distinctive as the Szell performances.

In the *Posthorn Serenade* Levine's tempi are well judged and the Vienna Philharmonic play with distinction. This performance is certainly among the best now available, and the coupling is no less persuasive. The recording is clean and well balanced, if lacking something in warmth. Indeed, there is a sharpness of outlines on the DG compact disc which suggests that the microphones were placed a shade too close to the musicians. For the reissue a spirited account of the Italian overture, *Symphony No. 32*, has been added.

Serenade No. 10 in B flat for 13 wind instruments, K.361.
(BB) ** Naxos Dig. 8.550060 [id.]. German Wind Soloists.

Very well drilled but not always blending as well as some rival groups, the German Wind Soloists give a fresh and attractive account of the great *Serenade for 13 instruments*, often dubbed the '*Gran partita*'. The finest versions are rather more elegant than this, and the lovely third-movement *Adagio* – the most famous, thanks to its use in the film *Amadeus* – is rather too heavy at a slow speed, though beautifully pointed with warmly expressive solos. Clean, full-bodied recording.

Serenade No. 10 in B flat for 13 wind instruments, K.361; Divertimento in F (for 2 oboes, 2 horns & 2 bassoons), K.213.
(M) **(*) Chandos Dig. CHAN 6575. SNO Wind Ens., Paavo Järvi.

The SNO Wind Ensemble's version under Paavo Järvi (son of a famous father) is enjoyably spontaneous-sounding, though ensemble is not quite as polished as in the finest versions. Speeds are well chosen, and the recording is warm, though the detail is sometimes masked by the lively acoustic. The little *Divertimento* makes an attractive bonus. Not a first choice but, at mid-price and with digital recording, worth considering.

Serenades Nos. 10 in B flat, K.361; 12 in C min., K.388.
(B) *** HM Musique d'Abord Dig. HMA 1903051. Budapest Wind Ens., Zoltán Kocsis.

The Budapest wind players blend beautifully in slow movements and phrase with pleasingly simple, expressive warmth; allegros are infectiously buoyant, especially the Rondo finale of the so-called *Grand Partita in B flat*, which also has a satisfyingly full sonority. Both works contain a notable set of variations: in K.361 it is the penultimate movement, in K.388 the finale, and the colour and diversity of the playing make a high point in each work. Kocsis himself composes a brief oboe cadenza for the latter and a clarinet cadenza for the lovely *Romance* in K.361.

Sinfonia concertante for violin, viola and orchestra in E flat, K.364.
(M) ** RCA 09026 61746-2 [id.]. Heifetz, Friedman, RCA Victor SO, Izler Solomon – BRAHMS: *Double concerto for violin and cello* **; BACH: *Double violin concerto.* *(*)
(M) ** EMI CDM7 64632-2. David & Igor Oistrakh, BPO, D. Oistrakh – BRAHMS: *Violin concerto.* **(*)

There is much to relish in the partnership of Heifetz and Primrose, and they make an eloquent dialogue in the slow movement. The soloists are very closely balanced but, in spite of that, the performance makes a strong impression, with a lively finale.

Although the solo playing from David and Igor Oistrakh is rich-timbred and beautifully matched, the orchestral accompaniment polished and the recording full and pleasing, there is a curiously literal approach to the music-making here, and the imaginative spark which can bring this glorious work fully to life is missing.

(i) *Sinfonia concertante in E flat for violin, viola and orchestra, K.364;* (ii) *Sinfonia concertante in E flat for oboe, clarinet, horn, bassoon and orchestra, K.297b.*

(B) *** Virgin/EMI Dig. CUV5 61205-2. (i) Warren-Green, Chase; (ii) Hunt, Collins, Thompson, Alexander; LCO, Warren-Green.

(BB) **(*) ASV Dig. CDQS 6139 [(M) id.]. (i) McAslan, Inque; (ii) Anderson, Hacker, Gambold, Taylor; L. Festival O, Ross Pople.

(i) *Sinfonia concertante for violin, viola and orchestra in E flat, K.364;* (ii) *Sinfonia concertante for oboe, clarinet, horn, bassoon and orchestra in E flat, K.297b;* (iii) *Rondo in B flat for violin and orchestra, K.269.*

(B) ** Sony SBK 67177; *SBT 67177* [id.]. (i) Druian, Skernick, Cleveland O (members), Szell; (ii) De Lancie, Gigliotti, Jones, Garfield, Phd. O, Ormandy; (iii) Zukerman, ECO, Barenboim.

In the ideal coupling of Mozart's paired *Sinfonias concertantes*, Christopher Warren-Green is joined by Roger Chase to provide a characteristically vital account of Mozart's inspired work for violin and viola. The *Andante* is slow and warmly expressive, yet without a trace of sentimentality. This is very satisfying, with its full-timbred sound from soloists and orchestra alike. The coupling, K.297b, is even more delectable and it would be hard to imagine a more persuasive team of wind players than those here. The full-bodied recording has plenty of space and atmosphere and the soloists in both works remain real and tangible.

The outer movements of K.364 have a fine rhythmic spring on ASV, and the *Andante* with a warm response from both soloists is touchingly expressive in a pleasingly restrained manner. Lorraine McAslan is rather near the microphone, which is not entirely flattering to her upper range in the first movement, but the viola is not too backward, and the recording projects vividly. The account of the work with wind soloists also brings a lively, alert performance with speeds relaxed enough to allow a winning lift to rhythms, making it a genial, affectionate reading which yet never falls into sentimentality. Only in the finale is the result a little heavy, but the 6/8 coda becomes all the more playful. Alan Hacker's distinctive reedy clarinet provides an extra tang, and the way the soloists appear in turn as protagonists in the variations finale is delightfully done. The sound is bright, firm and realistic. Good value.

Szell's 1963 account of K.364 was a serious contender in its day, with fine playing from Rafael Druian and Abraham Skernick, tender in the slow movement, and with a vivacious finale to round off the performance. The recording is too closely balanced but otherwise good. Ormandy's wind soloists in K.297b blend well together but display less individuality than usual in the *Adagio*; their playing has more diversity of character in the finale. Zukerman and Barenboim then provide a sprightly encore.

(i) *Sinfonia concertante for violin, viola and orchestra in E flat, K.364. Duos for violin and viola Nos. 1–2, K.423–4.*

(B) ** Cal. Approche Dig. CAL 6230 [(M) id. import]. Jan Talich Jr & Sr, (i) Talich CO, Kurt Redel.

The Calliope Approche version for the Talich duo, *père et fils*, with their eponymous Chamber Orchestra is very fresh, and it has a nice feeling of intimacy, although orchestral tuttis have a very strong profile. The snag is that the violin timbre of Jan Talich Junior is very thin and seems to catch the microphone. Also many collectors will want something more substantial than the *Duos* for a coupling, delightful though they are. As it happens, in some ways they come off more successfully than the major work.

Complete Mozart Edition, Volume 21: (i) *Sonatas for organ and orchestra (Epistle sonatas) Nos. 1–17* (complete). *Adagio & allegro in F min., K.594; Andante in F, K.616; Fantasia in F min., K.608.*

(M) **(*) Ph. 422 521-2 (2). Daniel Barenboim (organs at Stift Wilhering, Linz, Austria; Schlosspfarrkirche, Obermarchtal, Germany – K.594; K.608); (i) German Bach Soloists, Helmut Winschermann.

The *Epistle sonatas* derive their name from the fact that they were intended to be heard between the Epistle and Gospel in the Mass. Admittedly they are not great music or even first-class Mozart; however, played with relish they make a strong impression. The final *Sonata*, K.263, becomes a fully fledged concerto. The set is completed with the other works by Mozart which are usually heard on the organ, and here Barenboim's registration is particularly appealing.

Sonatas Nos. 1–17 (Epistle sonatas) for organ and chamber orchestra.
(BB) **(*) Naxos Dig. 8.550512 [id.]. János Sebestyén, Budapest Ferenc Erkel CO.

While it is understood that, apart from No. 16 in C, K.329, which has a specific solo part, the organ is not intended as a solo instrument in these *Chiesa sonatas*, it seems perverse to balance the instrument so that it blends in completely with the orchestral texture, as the Naxos engineers have done. Otherwise these alert, polished and nicely scaled performances could hardly be improved on and, apart from the controversial matter of the relationship of the organ to the orchestra, the recording is first class.

SYMPHONIES

Symphonies Nos. 1–47 (including alternative versions); in C, K.35; in D, K.38; in F, K.42a; in B flat, K.45b; in D, K.46a (K.51); in D, K.62a (K.100); in B flat, K.74g (K.216); in F, K.75; in G, K.75b (K.110); in D, K.111a; in D, K.203, 204 & 196 (121); in G, K.425a (K.444); in A min. (Odense); in G (New Lambacher).
(B) *** O-L Analogue/Dig. 452 496-2 (19) [id.]. AAM, Schröder, Hogwood.

The monumental complete recording of the Mozart symphonies, using authentic manners and original instruments, made between 1978 and 1985, now returns as a complete set on 19 bargain-priced CDs. With Jaap Schröder leading the admirably proportioned string group (9,8,4,3,2) and Christopher Hogwood at the keyboard, this was a remarkably successful joint enterprise. The playing has great style, warmth and polish and, if intonation is not always absolutely refined, that is only to be expected with old instruments. The survey is complete enough to include No. 37 – in fact the work of Michael Haydn but with a slow introduction by Mozart. The *Lambacher* and *Odense Symphonies* are also here, plus alternative versions, with different scoring, of No. 40; while the *Paris Symphony* is given two complete performances with alternative slow movements. Although Pinnock's more recent (full-price) recording remains first choice, it is much less comprehensive, and Hogwood's overall achievement is remarkable. The recording is well balanced and has plenty of ambience, the CD transfers are very successful, and the accompanying documentation is very good.

Symphonies Nos. 1–41.
(B) **(*) DG 453 231-2 (10) [(M) id. import]. BPO, Karl Boehm.

Boehm's Mozart symphony recordings with the Berlin Philharmonic, made between 1959 and 1968, were in fact just as much a pioneering project, setting the pattern for Antal Dorati's Haydn series for Decca, completed five years later. All the earlier symphonies were recorded in intensive sessions in March and November 1968, a real voyage of discovery, with performances warm and genial, with bold contrasts of dynamic and well-sprung rhythms. On matters of scholarship these performances may have been supplanted by a whole series of recordings since, but as a welcoming way to investigate Mozart early and late they certainly hold their place, with hardly a hint of routine in the playing. As with Dorati in Haydn, Minuets are slow by today's standards, but it is interesting to find some of the Minuets in the early symphonies taken more briskly, almost as fast Laendlers. This latest CD reissue, on ten discs instead of twelve, also brings the advantage of fuller and more forward transfers, with good body and presence. The new bargain box, unlike the previous one, has essays on Boehm as Mozartian by Peter Cosse and Mozart as symphonist by Heinz Becker. An excellent bargain, and not just for the historical specialist, but for all Mozartians.

Symphonies Nos. 1 in E flat, K.16; 4 in D, K.19; in F, K.19a; 5 in B flat, K.22; in G, K.45a; 6–36; 38–41.
(M) **(*) DG 435 360-2 (11). VPO, Levine.

James Levine was the players' own surprising choice of conductor when the Vienna Philharmonic agreed to record the complete Mozart symphonies for the bicentenary year, and though the performances may sometimes be heavy-handed and may lack charm, there is no lack of energy, and no risk of Mozart being sentimentalized. The string forces used are modest, even though slow movements such as that of the *Jupiter* have a Viennese smoothness. The recording is full-bodied but in places bright to the point of edginess, particularly on string-tone in allegros. Mackerras on Telarc may offer a complete Mozart cycle with more finesse and exhilaration, but all these Levine performances are enjoyable and never boring. The set comes out somewhere between mid- and bargain-price.

Symphonies Nos. (i) *1 in E flat, K.16; 4 in D, K.19; in F, K.19a; 5 in B flat, K.22; 6 in F, K.43; 7 in D, K.45; in G (Neue Lambacher); in G (Alte Lambacher), K.45a; in B flat, K.45b; 8 in D, K.48; 9 in C, K.73; 10 in G, K.74; in F, K.75; in F, K.76; in D, K.81; 11 in D, K.84; in D, K.95; in C, K.96; in D, K.97; 12 in G, K.110; 13 in F, K.112; 14 in A, K.114; 15 in G, K.124; 16 in C, K.128; 17 in G, K.129; 18 in F, K.130; 19 in E flat, K.132* (with alternative slow movement); *20 in D, K.133; in D, K.161 & 163; in D, K.111 & 120; in D, K.196 & 121; in C, K.208 & 102. Minuet in A, K.61g/1.* (ii) *21 in A, K.134; 22 in C, K.162; 23 in D, K.181; 24 in B flat, K.182; 25 in G min., K.183; 26 in E flat, K.184; 27 in G, K.199; 28 in C, K.200; 29 in A, K.201; 30 in D, K.202; 31 in D (Paris), K.297* (with alternative slow movement); *32 in G, K.318; 33 in B flat, K.319; 34 in C, K.338; 35 in D (Haffner), K.385; 36 in C (Linz), K.425; 38 in D (Prague), K.504; 39 in E flat, K.543; 40 in G min., K.550; 41 in C (Jupiter), K.551.*
(B) **(*) Ph. 454 085-2 (12) [id.]. (i) ASMF, Marriner; (ii) Concg. O, Krips.

Complete Mozart Edition, Volume 1: *Symphonies Nos. 1 in E flat, K.16; 4 in D, K.19; in F, K.19a; 5 in B flat, K.22; 6 in F, K.43; 7 in D, K.45; in G (Neue Lambacher), G.16; in G (Alte Lambacher), K.45a; in B flat, K.45b; 8 in D, K.48; 9 in C, K.73; 10 in G, K.74; in F, K.75; in F, K.76; in D, K.81; 11 in D, K.84; in D, K.95; in C, K.96; in D, K.97; 12 in G, K.110; 13 in F, K.112; 14 in A, K.114; 15 in G, K.124; 16 in C, K.128; 17 in G, K.129; 18 in F, K.130; 19 in E flat, K.132* (with alternative slow movement); *20 in D, K.133; in D, K.161 & 163; in D, K.111 & 120; in D, K.196 & 121; in C, K.208 & 102. Minuet in A, K.61g/1.*
(M) *** Ph. 422 501-2 (6) [id.]. ASMF, Marriner.

The first half of this 12-CD box is a reissue of Volume 1 of the Philips Complete Mozart Edition. Marriner's recordings confirm the Mozartian vitality of the performances and their sense of style and spontaneity. The Philips engineers respond with alive and vivid recording. Except perhaps for those who insist on original instruments, the finesse and warmth of the playing here is a constant joy. The Dutch players for Krips also bring warmth, as well as proving characteristically stylish in phrasing and execution. Quick movements can be bracingly vigorous. Both the previously underrated *No. 28 in C* and the first great masterpiece in A major, both aptly paced, are very persuasively done, with an almost ethereal delicacy from the strings in the beautiful *Andante* of No. 29 and the horns thrusting exuberantly in the coda of the finale. Although Krips's Mozartian sensibility never deserts him, the readings of some of the later symphonies are somewhat wanting in character, however, and do not do full honour to the fine Mozartian that Krips was. No. 39 goes well enough and the first movement of the *G minor* is not pressed too hard, but in the *Jupiter* Krips holds the tension much more slackly. The ample Concertgebouw sound, with its resonant bass, emphasizes the breadth of scale of the music-making, yet the digital remastering gives an attractive freshness to the violins, although the Minuets sound well upholstered. Throughout, the orchestral playing is a pleasure in itself, especially nimble in finales, which are never raced.

Symphonies Nos. 1 in E flat, K.16; 2 in B flat, K.17 (attrib. Leopold MOZART); *3 in E flat, K.18* (written by Carl ABEL); *4 in D, K.19; 5 in B flat, K.22.*
(BB) ** Naxos Dig. 8.550871 [id.]. Northern CO, Nicholas Ward.

Symphonies Nos. 6 in F, K.43; 7 in D, K.45; 8 in D, K.48; 9 in C, K.73; 10 in G, K.74.
(BB) ** Naxos Dig. 8.550872 [id.]. Northern CO, Nicholas Ward.

Naxos are here starting another complete series – of the Mozart symphonies. These first two discs cover the juvenile works, including K.17, now attributed to the composer's father, and K.18, which was Wolfgang's own copy of a work written by Carl Abel. The performances are well played, spirited and warmly recorded. On the second disc the playing of *Molto allegro* finales is very energetic and Nicholas Ward accents strongly, to give the music as much rhythmic character as possible. The recording, made in the BBC's Manchester studio Concert Hall, is attractively warm and naturally balanced, and this is enjoyable if not distinctive music-making.

Symphonies Nos. 1 in E flat, K.16; 4 in D, K.19; in F, K.19a; 5 in K.22; in G, K.45a; 6–36; 38–41.
(M) *** Telarc Dig. CD 80300 (10) [id.]. Prague CO, Mackerras.

Mackerras's is an outstanding series, with electrifying performances of the early as well as the later symphonies. Even in the trivial boyhood works there is not a suspicion of routine, with the playing full of dramatic contrasts in rhythm, texture or dynamic. Mackerras has a keen feeling for Mozart style, not least in the slow movements and minuets, which he regularly takes faster than usual. His flowing andantes are consistently stylish too, with performances on modern instruments regularly related to period practice. An outstanding instance comes in the G minor *Andante* of *No. 5 in B flat*, K.22, where Mackerras, fastish and light, makes others seem heavy-handed in this anticipation of romanticism, underlining the harmonic surprises clearly and elegantly. Consistently Mackerras finds light and shade in Mozart's inspirations, both early and late, though some may feel that, with warm reverberation characteristic of this Prague orchestra's recording venue, the scale is too large, particularly in the early symphonies. Harpsichord continuo, where used, is usually well balanced.

Symphonies Nos. 11 in D, K.84; 12 in G, K.110; 13 in F, K.112; 14 in A, K.114.
(BB) ** Naxos Dig. 8.550873 [id.]. Northern CO, Nicholas Ward.

The performances here are warm and polished and, although in the earlier works one would have liked a bit more bite in the allegros (original instruments are an advantage in this respect), Nicholas Ward rises to the occasion in the A major work, which receives a strong and (in the slow movement) expressive response from his excellent players. Well-balanced, natural sound, except that in the finale of the A major work the horns don't pierce the texture as brightly as they might.

Symphonies Nos. 15 in G, K.124; 16 in C, K.128; 17 in G, K.129; 18 in F, K.129.
(BB) **(*) Naxos Dig. 8.550874 [id.]. Northern CO, Nicholas Ward.

Symphonies Nos. 19 in E flat, K.132; 20 in D, K.133; 37 in G Introduction only (with remainder of the symphony by Michael Haydn).
(BB) *** Naxos Dig. 8.550875 [id.]. Northern CO, Nicholas Ward.

Nicholas Ward continues his stylish Mozart series even more successfully, with his fourth and fifth Naxos discs offering six symphonies written in 1772. The orchestral string-phasing is particularly elegant in slow movements (notably the wistful *Andante* of *No. 15 in G* and the charming melody which forms the centre-piece of No. 17), while the lively first movement of *No. 18 in F* effervesces neatly. Elsewhere allegros are alert and strong. Excellent, full and well-balanced recording, though not ideally sharply detailed.

No. 19 is scored for four horns, two in E flat *alt*, and they give added weight and character to the orchestral texture in outer movements but are sensibly reduced to just a pair in the *Andante*. The Minuet with its skipping five-note figure is very catchy. No. 20 is given extra brightness by a pair of trumpets. But it is the delectable *Andante* that catches the ear, dominated by a charming flute solo, with the first violins muted. The lightly rhythmic finale with its neatly articulated string-scales completes a particularly striking work, very well played here. Mozart contributed just the rather grand opening *Adagio maestoso* to the symphony once mistakenly regarded as his No. 37. Here it lasts just 1 minute 22 seconds before Michael Haydn's amiable allegro sets off with fine impetus. The regal contour of the *Andante sostenuto* is soon decorated by a flute, then comes a droll bassoon solo, and the oboe takes over galantly. There is no Minuet, but the sparkling finale completes a particularly attractive work, but one that (being wise after the event) will be recognized by most listeners as not being truly Mozartian. It is played most persuasively, and this disc is well worth having on all counts.

Complete Mozart Edition, Volume 2: *Symphonies Nos. 21–36; 37: Adagio maestoso in G, K.44* (Introduction to a symphony by M. Haydn); *38–41; Minuet for a Symphony in C, K.409.*
(M) **(*) Ph. 422 502-2 (6) [id.]. ASMF, Marriner.

As with the early works, the later symphonies in the Marriner performances, as reissued in the Philips Mozart Edition, are conveniently laid out on six mid-priced CDs, offered in numerical sequence, without a single symphony having to be divided between discs. However, the over-resonant bass remains in the recording of No. 40 and the *Haffner* (both of which date from 1970, nearly a decade before the rest of the cycle was recorded). Otherwise the transfers are of Philips's best quality, and the performances generally give every satisfaction, even if their style does not show an awareness of the discoveries made – in terms of texture and balance – by the authentic school.

Symphonies Nos. 21 in A, K.134; 22 in C, K.162; 23 in D, K.181; 24 in B flat, K.182; 26 in E flat, K.184.
(BB) ** Naxos Dig. 8.550876 [id.]. Northern CO, Nicholas Ward.

The three *Salzburg Symphonies*, K.181–2 and K.184, all written in 1773 with the young Mozart felicitously using woodwind solos within their *grazioso Andantes*, are most successful in Ward's elegant and sprightly performances, and the recording is lively to match. However, the sound is duller and less transparent in K.134 and K.162, and the playing too seems to have less zest, though it is still nicely turned.

Symphonies Nos. 24 in B flat, K.182; 25 in G min., K.183; 26 in E flat, K.184; 27 in G, K.199; 32 in G, K.318.
(B) *** [EMI Red Line Dig. CDR5 69818]. ASMF, Marriner.

Symphonies Nos. 31 in D (Paris), K.297; 33 in B flat, K.319; 34 in C, K.338.
(B) *** [EMI Red Line Dig. CDR5 69819]. ASMF, Marriner.

Symphonies Nos. 40 in G min., K.550; 41 in C (Jupiter), K.551.
(B) **(*) [EMI Red Line Dig. CDR5 69820]. ASMF, Marriner.

Marriner's third set of Mozart symphony recordings, made for EMI, is the most beautifully recorded of all. The playing, too, is graceful and elegant. With bracing rhythms and brisker pacing than in his earlier, Philips set, these readings are positive yet unidiosyncratic. Phrasing is supple and the Mozartian spirit is always alive here. There is a degree of disappointment in the *Jupiter Symphony*, which is slightly undercharacterized. For the most part, however, this music-making will give a great deal of pleasure.

Symphonies Nos. 24–36; 38–41.
(M) *** EMI Dig. [CDMF 638562] (4). ASMF, Marriner.

Symphonies Nos. 28 in C, K.200; 29 in A, K.201; 30 in D, K.202; 40 in G min., K.550; 41 in C (Jupiter), K.551.
(B) **(*) EMI Dig. CZS7 67564-2 (2) [id.]. ASMF, Marriner.

In his continuing series for EMI, Marriner secures warm and gracious playing from the Academy in the three early symphonies but, with articulation that brings neat rather than sharp rhythmic incisiveness. Slow movements are very persuasive, in both their delicacy of touch and elegant contours. In No. 29 Marriner observes more repeats than before and the performance has an affectionate breadth, with plenty of energy reserved for the last movement. Marriner is at his very best in No. 40, a work he always did very sympathetically. In the last two movements he is strikingly dramatic, with crisper articulation and faster speeds than in his earlier recording for Philips, and this time in the slow movement he observes the first-half repeat. The *Jupiter* is also very well done, but the effect is less charismatic – though, as in the others in this digital series, the recording is first rate.

Symphonies Nos. 25 in G min., K.183; 32 in G, K.318; 41 in C (Jupiter), K.551.
(BB) *** Naxos Dig. 8.550113; *4550113* [id.]. Capella Istropolitana, Barry Wordsworth.

Symphonies Nos. 27 in G, K.199/161b; 33 in B flat, K.319; 36 in C (Linz), K.425.
(BB) *** Naxos Dig. 8.550264; *4550264* [id.]. Capella Istropolitana, Barry Wordsworth.

Symphonies Nos. 28 in C, K.200; 31 in D (Paris), K.297; 40 in G min., K.550.
(BB) *** Naxos Dig. 8.550164; *4550164* [id.]. Capella Istropolitana, Barry Wordsworth.

Symphonies Nos. 29 in A, K.201; 30 in D, K.202; 38 in D (Prague), K.504.
(BB) *** Naxos Dig. 8.550119; *4550119* [id.]. Capella Istropolitana, Barry Wordsworth.

Symphonies Nos. 34 in C, K.338; 35 in D (Haffner), K.385; 39 in E flat, K.543.
(BB) *** Naxos Dig. 8.550186; *4550186* [id.]. Capella Istropolitana, Barry Wordsworth.

Symphonies Nos. 40 in G min., K.550; 41 in C (Jupiter), K.551.
(BB) *** Naxos Dig. 8.550299 [id.]. Capella Istropolitana, Barry Wordsworth.

Barry Wordsworth's series of 15 symphonies on the Naxos super-bargain-priced label brings consistently refreshing and enjoyable performances. The Capella Istropolitana consists of leading members of the Slovak Philharmonic Orchestra of Bratislava; though their string-tone is thinnish, it is very much in scale with the clarity of a period performance but tonally far sweeter. The recording is outstandingly good, with a far keener sense of presence than in most rival versions and with less reverberation to obscure detail in tuttis. Wordsworth observes exposition repeats in first movements, but in the finales only in such symphonies as Nos. 38 and 41, where the movement particularly needs extra scale. In slow movements, as is usual, he omits repeats. He often adopts speeds that are marginally slower than we expect nowadays in chamber-scale performances; but, with exceptionally clean articulation and infectiously sprung rhythms, the results never drag, even if No. 29 is made to sound more sober than usual. In every way these are worthy rivals to the best full-priced versions, and they can be recommended with few if any reservations. Anyone wanting to sample might try the coupling of Nos. 34, 35 and 39 – with the hard-stick timpani sound at the start of No. 39 very dramatic. The *Linz* too is outstanding. For some, the option of having the last two symphonies coupled together will be useful.

Bruno Walter Edition

(i) *Symphonies Nos. 25 in G min., K.183; 28 in C, K.200; 29 in A, K.201;* (ii) *35 in D (Haffner), K.385.*
(M) (***) Sony mono SMK 64473 [id.]. (i) Columbia SO; (ii) NYPO, Bruno Walter.

'The birth of a performance' (recorded rehearsals of *Symphony No. 36*); (i) *Symphonies Nos. 36 in C (Linz) K.425;* (ii) *38 in D (Prague), K.504.*
(M) (***) Sony mono SM2K 64474 (2) [S2K 64474]. (i) Columbia SO; (ii) NYPO, Bruno Walter.

Symphonies Nos. 39 in E flat, K.543; 40 in G min., K.550; 41 in C (Jupiter), K.551.
(M) (**) Sony mono SMK 64477 [id.]. NYPO, Bruno Walter.

Walter's recordings were made in the 1950s and have been impressively transferred. The early symphonies on the first CD show his touch at its lightest (especially in K.201) and there is some lovely playing, both graceful and delicate, from the New York violins in slow movements. The *Haffner* sparkles with vitality; this and the *Linz* (offered together with its justly famous rehearsal sequence) and the *Prague* all show Walter at his finest – stylish and vital yet always making the music sing. *No. 39 in E flat* is a strong performance, but the *G minor*, K.550, is curiously heavy and unspontaneous, while the *Jupiter*, more appropriately weighty, lacks incandescence.

Symphonies Nos. 25 in G min., K.183; 29 in A, K.201; 31 in D (Paris), K.297.
(M) **(*) DG 449 552-2. BPO, Karl Boehm.

These three symphonies come from the complete box (see above) that Boehm recorded in the 1960s. The playing of the Berlin Philharmonic is quite superlative, but here enjoyment is occasionally marred by the want of spontaneity that sometimes distinguished Boehm's direction. Marriner, for instance, is far more spirited in No. 25, though the orchestral playing is less cultured. The easy-going tempi are acceptable until the finale, which is very slow. The finales of Nos. 29 and 31 are more lively, but the weighty opening of the *Paris* will not appeal to everyone, although the violins articulate gracefully, and the Berlin wind phrase exquisitely throughout the disc. The mid-1960s recording is full-bodied (perhaps too much so for today's ears) and does not sound too dated.

Symphonies Nos. 29–36; 38–41; Divertimento No. 7 in D, K.205; 2 Marches, K.335.
(M) **(*) EMI CZS7 67301-2 (4) [CDZD 673012]. ECO, Barenboim.

Barenboim's recordings were made at Abbey Road over a five-year span, between 1966 and 1971. With fine rhythmic pointing and consistently imaginative phrasing, these performances certainly have a place in the catalogue. Nos. 29 and 34 are particularly successful, and the *Paris* (No. 31) is also given an outstanding performance, the contrasts of mood in the first movement underlined and the finale taken at a hectic tempo that would have sounded breathless with players any less brilliant than the ECO. The box also includes the *D major Serenade*, K.205, which responds well to Barenboim's affectionate treatment, while the two *Marches* are attractively jaunty and colourful.

Symphonies Nos. 29 in A, K.201; 31 in D (Paris), K.297; 34 in C, K.338.
(B) (***) Dutton Lab. mono CDEA 5008 [(M) id.]. LPO, Sir Thomas Beecham.

In Dutton's budget-priced Essential Classics series it is good to welcome these incomparable performances, which date from between 1937 and 1940. Although Beecham re-recorded many Mozart symphonies with the RPO after the war, he never returned to Nos. 29 or 34. Beecham's are elegant and cultivated accounts which in many ways are unique, though No. 29 brings one of his most controversial readings. One can readily accept the absence of exposition repeats and can adjust to Beecham's expansiveness and affectionate manner in all the slow movements, but in No. 29 the pace of the opening movement is eccentrically slow, even if Beecham is very persuasive in his pointing. In his note Lyndon Jenkins points out that Beecham had conducted No. 29 four times in the month before he recorded it, which must mean that the speeds were well calculated. In the finales by contrast Beecham prefers really fast speeds, exhilarating in all three here. The superb new transfers are fuller and have much finer presence, transparency and, above all, body than the earlier, EMI versions that appeared some years ago.

Symphonies Nos. 29 in A, K.201; 32 in G, K.318; 33 in B flat, K.319; 35 (Haffner); 36 (Linz); 38 (Prague); 39 in E flat, K.543; 40 in G min., K.550; 41 (Jupiter).
(M) **(*) DG 429 668-2 (3) [id.]. BPO, Karajan.

With Nos. 29, 32 and 33 added to the original LP box, these are beautifully played and vitally alert readings; and the recordings, made between 1966 and 1979, are well balanced and given full, lively transfers to CD. There are details about which some may have reservations, and the opening of the *G minor*, which is a shade faster than in Karajan's earlier, Vienna performance for Decca, may not be quite dark enough for some tastes. But the *Jupiter*, although short on repeats, has weight and power as well as surface elegance.

Symphonies Nos. 29 in A, K.201; 35 in D (Haffner), K.385; 36 in C (Linz), K.425.
(M) ** EMI (SIS) CDM5 66098-2 [id.]. BPO, Karajan.

Symphonies Nos. 38 in D (Prague), K.504; 39 in E flat, K.543 (with rehearsal extracts).
(M) ** EMI (SIS) CDM5 66099-2 [id.]. BPO, Karajan.

Symphonies Nos. 40 in G min., K.550; 41 in C (Jupiter), K.551 (with rehearsal extracts).
(M) ** EMI (SIS) CDM5 66100-2 [id.]. BPO, Karajan.

Reissued as part of EMI's Karajan Edition, Karajan's set has the rehearsal sequences for the last three symphonies thrown in for good measure – and they are certainly of interest (they are included on the individual issues as well as in the collection). Moreover, the different microphone placing means that the sound-balance is brighter, leaner-textured than in the actual recording sessions. However, as the conductor's comments are spoken in German, the non-linguist will be able to follow his intentions only with some difficulty, fascinating as is his attention to detail. This is large-orchestra Mozart, the reverberant acoustic of the Jesus-Christus-Kirche (which the EMI recording team never handled as well in eighteenth-century scores as their DG counterparts did later) giving considerable breadth and impact, but also a cushioned thickness of texture to the orchestral sound. The interpretations too have plenty of weight, although Karajan also shows poise and grace: the opening of No. 36 is especially fine. Undoubtedly the best of the set is *No. 39 in E flat*, in which the playing has superb polish and refinement of tone, and few readers will find much to quarrel with in Karajan's interpretation. The same might be said, if perhaps to a somewhat lesser extent, of *No. 40 in G minor* and certainly of the *Jupiter*. Again the playing of the orchestra is a joy in itself and the interpretations are purposeful and considered, even if they do not have the sparkle and naturalness of the very finest recorded performances of these works. No. 29, however, was not part of the original LP set: it was made in the Grünewaldkirche in 1960, and here the sound is fresher. It is a warm, polished performance, realized with much finesse, and it has plenty of life. Yet in the last analysis this music-making is wanting in the final touch of spontaneity and fire; for all the magnificent orchestral playing, the listener is sometimes left vaguely dissatisfied, and not only by the lack of transparency in the orchestral textures.

Symphonies Nos. 29 in A, K.201; 35 in D (Haffner), 39 in E flat, K.543.
(BB) ** Belart 461 347-2 [(M) id. import]. VPO, István Kertész.

It is good to have more of István Kertész's recordings returning to the catalogue. His account of *No. 29 in A* is first class in every way, with the VPO vivaciously on their toes. The *Haffner* is vibrant too, the first movement full of energy and the *Andante* neatly pointed. Both these performances come from the early 1970s. However the great *E flat Symphony No. 39*, recorded a decade earlier, does not display its full character, and here the Decca recording is somewhat less open and fresh.

(i) *Symphonies Nos. 31 in D (Paris), K.297; 36 in C (Linz), K.425;* (ii) *Overture: Le nozze di Figaro.*
(BB) *** ASV CDQS 6033. (i) LSO; (ii) RPO, Bátiz.

After a sprightly account of the *Figaro overture* from the RPO, the LSO under Bátiz provide two spirited and polished accounts of favourite named symphonies. Tempi in outer movements are brisk, but the *Presto* finale of the *Linz* (for instance) produces some sparkling playing from the strings; and in both slow movements the phrasing is warm and gracious. With excellent digital recording, this makes an enjoyable super-bargain pairing.

Symphonies Nos. 32 in G, K.318; 35 in D (Haffner), K.385; 36 in C (Linz), K.425; 39 in E flat, K.543; 41 in C (Jupiter), K.551.
(BB) *** Virgin Classics Double Dig. VBD5 61451-2 (2) [CDVB 61451]. SCO, Jukka-Pekka Saraste.

This Virgin Classics Double brings together an exceptionally successful grouping of performances. More than most other versions on modern instruments, Saraste's vividly alive accounts of the three earlier symphonies reflect the new lessons of period performance. These are more detached, less sostenuto than many modern-instrument chamber-orchestra versions and, with all repeats observed, are highly stimulating in their resilience. The recording, helpfully reverberant, yet gives lightness and transparency to textures, conveying an apt chamber scale. Saraste then offers two of the finest accounts of the two late symphonies available on any disc: fresh, again light and resilient in allegros, elegant in slow movements and with clean, transparent recording. Wordsworth and the Capella Istropolitana may have more weight in these works, but Saraste has extra polish and refinement, with generally brisker speeds, notably in slow movements and Minuets. These two CDs, offered for the cost of one mid-priced disc, make a remarkably inexpensive way of collecting four of Mozart's greatest symphonies, plus a vivacious account of the *G major Italian overture.*

Symphonies Nos. 32 in G, K.318; 35 in D (Haffner), K.385; 38 in D (Prague), K.504.
(B) **(*) Tring Dig. TRP 059 [(M) id. import]. RPO, Howard Shelley.

With the RPO strings reduced (11.9.7.6.4), Howard Shelley conducts relaxed and amiable readings of three symphonies, very well recorded. In the *Haffner* and *Prague* some may want a higher-powered, more dramatic view, notably in the latter, where Shelley does not bring out the *Don Giovanni* overtones, but these are consistently refreshing performances, clear and transparent and very well played. No. 32, in Italian overture form, is a delight, with Jeffrey Bryant leading the RPO horn section in glorious playing.

Symphonies Nos. 32 in G, K.318; 35 in D (Haffner), K.385; 39 in E flat, K.543.
(BB) *** ASV Dig. CDQS 6071 [(M) id. import]. ECO, Mackerras.

Mackerras's ASV version was recorded digitally, in 1985, before he moved on to make his integral set for Telarc. Mackerras here anticipates the urgent style of the later recordings, especially in the Minuets and, with generally brisk speeds, the ASV readings are attractively fresh and full of momentum. Mackerras rarely seeks to charm, but unfussily presents each movement with undistractingly direct manners. The strong character of the music-making is in no doubt, and the sound is appealingly bright and vivid; at super-bargain price this undoubtedly remains competitive.

Symphonies Nos. 32 in G, K.318; 33 in B flat, K.319; 35 in D (Haffner), K.385; 36 in C (Linz), K.425.
(M) *** DG (IMS) 435 070-2. BPO, Karajan.

Symphonies Nos. 35 in D (Haffner), K.385; 36 in C (Linz), K.425; 38 in D (Prague), K.504; 39 in E flat, K.543; 40 in G min., K.550; 41 in C (Jupiter), K.551.
(B) *** DG Double 453 046-2 (2) [id.]. BPO, Karajan.
(M) **(*) DG 447 416-2 (2) [id.]. BPO, Boehm.

Here on DG is Karajan's big-band Mozart at its finest. Although there may be slight reservations about the Minuet and Trio of the *Linz*, which is rather slow (and the other minuets are also somewhat stately), overall there is plenty of life here, and slow movements show the BPO at their most graciously expressive. The opening of the *G minor* may not be quite dark enough for some tastes. The *Jupiter*, although short on repeats, has power as well as surface elegance. The remastered sound is clear and lively, full but not over-weighted. The separate issue makes a good sampler.

Karl Boehm's way with Mozart in the early 1960s was broader and heavier in texture than we are used to nowadays, and the exposition repeats are the exception rather than the rule; but these Berlin Philharmonic performances are warm and magnetic, with refined and strongly rhythmic playing, and there is an attractive honesty and strength about them. The *Linz*, for instance, is an example of Boehm at his finest, with an agreeable, fresh vitality; but overall there is a comfortable quality of inevitability here, perpetuating a long Mozart tradition. The recordings sound full, vivid and well balanced in the new transfers.

Symphonies Nos. 33 in B flat, K.319; 40 in G min., K.550; Serenade No. 13 in G (Eine kleine Nachtmusik), K.525.
(B) ** ASV Quicksilva Dig. CDQS 6184 [(M) id.]. Ac. of L., Stamp.

This was the first recording of the Academy of London, a performing group with a nucleus of young American players, using modern instruments. Certainly their sparkling account of *Symphony No. 33* makes an auspicious début, with its polished precision of articulation in outer movements and the gracious *Andante* which, together with the bright, rhythmically resilient Minuet, gives the performance a sunny, almost Beechamesque atmosphere. The pacing here is so finely judged that it is a disappointment to turn to the *G minor symphony*, where the opening movement is so determinedly brisk that its underlying minor-key expressive qualities all but evaporate, although the rest of the work is attractive in a direct way. The recordings of the symphonies are naturally balanced. *Eine kleine Nachtmusik* is enjoyable, if not really distinctive. It is quite direct and well paced, and the playing does not lack vitality.

(i) *Symphonies Nos. 35 in D (Haffner), K.385; 36 in C (Linz), K.425;* (ii) *Divertimento No. 1 for strings, K.136; Serenade No. 6 (Serenata notturna).*
(M) *** Virgin/EMI Dig. CUV5 61204-2. (i) Sinfonia Varsovia; (ii) Lausanne CO, Sir Yehudi Menuhin.

As in Menuhin's winning versions of the last four Mozart symphonies, Mozart is again presented with a smile on his face. Though modern instruments are used, the scale is intimate, with textures beautifully clear. There is elegance and charm as well as energy in outer movements, and in the slow movements Menuhin moulds the phrasing with Beechamesque magic, yet never adopts excessively slow speeds or over-romantic manners. The *Serenata notturna* and the *Divertimento* make a generous coupling. Performances are similarly fresh and elegant, though, as recorded, the strings of the Lausanne Chamber Orchestra are a degree less sweet, and the acoustic is bigger and more reverberant.

Symphonies Nos. 35 in D (Haffner), K.385; 36 in C (Linz); 38 in D (Prague).
(BB) *** RCA Navigator 74321 24198-2 [Basic 100 09026 68364-2; *68364-4*]. ECO, Jean-François Paillard.
(B) (***) Dutton Lab. mono CDEA 5001 [(M) id.]. LPO, Sir Thomas Beecham.

Stylish, excellently paced performances from Paillard and the ECO, with warmly expressive slow movements – that for the *Linz* is particularly fine – and sparkling finales. Those enjoying these works in lively, traditional performances will find there is both polish and warmth here, and plenty of vitality. The recording is resonant but not so much as to obscure detail. An excellent bargain-basement triptych.

It was Beecham's advocacy in the early years of the century which led to the late Mozart symphonies finally achieving their rightful position among the greatest masterpieces of the symphonic repertoire. These recordings, which were to dominate the catalogue until the arrival of LP, were made in 1939–40, either at Abbey Road or Kingsway Hall. The *Haffner* used both venues, and the ear can detect the change of acoustic 4½ minutes into the first movement. Beecham's dictum was to present Mozart with 'the maximum of virility coupled with the maximum of delicacy', coupled also with loving care with phrasing and subtle attention to dynamic nuance. The first movement of the *Linz* is endearingly characteristic of his boldness of style, steadily paced, without any loss of vitality. Beecham's way with Minuets, however, was to present them with genial stateliness to contrast with the brilliant articulation of the dancing finales. (He even includes the exposition repeat in the finale of No. 36, as there was room for it on the 78 side.) These Dutton transfers come into direct competition with those of EMI. The contrasts are not quite consistent. In the *Haffner* and *Prague*, the Dutton sound is marginally warmer and more rounded, with the boxiness gone, where the EMI sound is brighter and more immediate, with a hint of harshness. In the slow movement of the *Haffner* it is astonishing how different the woodwind solos sound, with the balance somehow altered. Curiously, in the *Linz* the contrasts between Dutton and EMI are rather the other way about. As to the subtly pointed magic of Beecham in Mozart, that hardly needs commendation, readily defying this purist age. Highly recommended at bargain price.

Symphonies Nos. 35 in D (Haffner), K.385; 40 in G min., K.550; 41 in C (Jupiter), K.551.
(M) *** Sony SBK 46333; *SBT 46333* [id.]. Cleveland O, Szell.

As in his companion triptych of late Haydn symphonies, Szell and his Clevelanders are shown at their finest here. The sparkling account of the *Haffner* is exhilarating, and the performances of the last two symphonies are equally polished and strong. Yet there is a tranquil feeling to both *Andantes* that shows Szell as a Mozartian of striking sensibility and finesse. He is at his best in the *Jupiter*, which has great vigour in the outer movements and a proper weight to balance the rhythmic incisiveness; in spite of the lack of repeats, the work's scale is not diminished. Here the sound is remarkable considering the early date (late 1950s), and the remastering throughout is impressively full-bodied and clean.

Symphonies Nos. 36 in C (Linz), K.425; 38 in D (Prague), K.504.
(M) ** DG (IMS) Dig. 445 566-2. VPO, James Levine.

One tends to produce a double-take when reading Levine's timing for this pairing of two favourite symphonies: 77 minutes, all but ten seconds. The reason is that he plays every repeat in sight, in *Minuets*, slow movements and finales alike, so that the slow movement of the *Linz* runs to 13 minutes! The performances are characteristically lively and are marked by superb VPO playing. But listeners will surely feel, however much they may love Mozart, that this is too much of a good thing.

Symphonies Nos. 36 in C (Linz); 38 in D (Prague); 39 in E flat, K.543; 40 in G min., K.550; 41 in C (Jupiter).
(B) *** Ph. Duo 438 332-2 (2) [(M) id. import]. ASMF, Marriner.

This is an inexpensive way of acquiring first-class performances of Mozart's last five symphonies. The recordings are of high quality, all being made in 1978 or 1980, except for No. 40, which dates from a decade earlier (1970). Here the bass is a shade over-resonant, but the present transfer has made it seem firmer than previously. In terms of finesse and elegance of phrasing, the orchestral playing is of very high quality and Marriner's readings are satisfyingly paced, full of vitality and warmth. There is not a whiff of original-instrument style here, but those who enjoy the sound of Mozart in a modern orchestra of a reasonable size should be well satisfied.

Symphony No. 38 in D (Prague), K.504.
(M) (**) Mercury mono 434 387-2 [id.]. Chicago SO, Kubelik – DVORAK: *Symphony No. 9 (New World).* (***)

Kubelik's 1953 account of the *Prague* is splendid: the outer movements are alert and sparkling, the *Andante* is ideally paced, gracefully phrased and beautifully played. The effect is undoubtedly refreshing;

the ambience of Chicago's Orchestral Hall adds warmth, and the only snag is the consistent edge imparted by the single Telefunken microphone to the violin timbre.

Symphonies Nos. (i) *38 in D (Prague), K.504; 39 in E flat, K.543;* (ii) *40 in G min., K.550; 41 in C (Jupiter), K.551.*
(B) ** Decca Double Dig. 448 924-2 (2) [(M) id. import]. (i) Chicago SO; (ii) COE; Sir Georg Solti.
(B) ** Teldec/Warner Ultima Dig. 0630 18957-2 (2) [id.]. COE, Harnoncourt.

It would be easy to underestimate Solti's Chicago performances of Mozart, for the Decca sound brings a very bright sheen to the upper strings. Solti's approach is in no way glossy; indeed, there is a sense of serious purpose here, notably in the first movement of No. 39, while both slow movements are beautifully played, the phrasing supple and sensitive. The vigour of the opening of the *Prague* is undoubtedly exhilarating, and the finales of both works are alert and sparkling. On the whole, No. 39 is the more memorable: even if the Minuet sounds a bit heavy, the *Andante* shows Solti and his orchestra at their finest. For the two final symphonies Solti turned to the talented young players of the Chamber Orchestra of Europe, recorded at the Alte Oper in Frankfurt, and they respond acutely to his direction with finely disciplined ensemble, paradoxically producing an interpretation which in many places is uncharacteristic of the conductor, unforced and intimate rather than fiery. The middle movements of No. 40 are disappointing for opposite reasons, the *Andante* too self-consciously pointed, and the Minuet too heavy. The *Jupiter* is plainer and much more successful, brightly detailed and crisply articulated. The recording has plenty of bloom on the sound as well as good detail.

It is possible to admire Harnoncourt's readings but less easy to warm to them. He also conveys his admiration and his concern for their structural strength, but too little love, especially in the first two movements of the *G minor*. The *Andante* of the *Prague*, pressed forward fairly briskly, nevertheless brings refined and responsive string-playing. Harnoncourt is obviously personally involved here and in the slow movement of the *Jupiter* (although accents can be intrusive). The Minuet also goes with a swing, and the finale is pressed foward with powerful momentum. The orchestral playing throughout is of a bravura standard, but the gruff fortissimos and bold accents, with exaggerated fortissimos, too often produce a feeling of aggressiveness, and the timpani enter very forcefully at times, notably at the introduction to the *E flat Symphony*, which is certainly commanding and forward-looking. The following allegro is then comparatively measured, but the bold rhythmic outlines make it seem to flow faster than it does. There are other eccentrities later, notably the slightly mannered phrasing of the *Andante*, and the very brisk speed for the Minuet, with the tempo suddenly pulled right back for the lyrical Trio, so engagingly dominated by the clarinets. The recordings (from the early 1990s) are attractively resonant, conveying a big orchestral sound, but balance is good and detail is clear. As usual with this conductor, all major repeats are observed and, while this is especially welcome in the *Jupiter Symphony*, the opening movement of the *Prague* runs to 19 minutes 15 seconds, which many will think is too much of a good thing. Overall this can be recommended only to convinced Harnoncourt aficionados.

Symphonies Nos. 39 in E flat, K.543; 40 in G min., K.550; 41 in C (Jupiter), K.551.
(B) (***) Dutton Lab. mono CDEA 5012 [(M) id.]. LPO, Beecham.
(M) (**) BMG/RCA mono GD 60285 [id.]. NBC SO, Toscanini.

It is good to have the continuing Dutton series of reissues of Beecham's pre-war Mozart with the LPO rounded off with this generous coupling of the last three symphonies – a coupling made possible when exposition repeats are omitted in Nos. 39 and 41. As ever, the rhythmic point of the playing, not least from the LPO woodwind, is delectable so that, with brisk allegros set against expressive slow movements, these readings seem as fresh as ever, whatever changes in performance practice we have come to accept in Mozart. These always were among the best EMI recordings of the 1930s, and the Dutton transfers are excellent. Curiously, the fullest-bodied of the three recordings is the earliest recorded, that of the *Jupiter*, dating from 1934. At bargain price in the Essential Classics series, this is an exceptionally attractive issue that no Beecham admirer should miss.

There is an astonishing discrepancy between the three Mozart performances from Toscanini. Where in No. 39 the great Italian conductor's thrustful approach seems very brutal, with rhythms and phrasing so unyielding and speeds so fast that all charm is eliminated, even in the Minuet, the great *G minor Symphony* – recorded in conjunction with Toscanini's very first concert with the NBC orchestra in 1938 – is treated more sympathetically, even if the middle movements again are plain and charmless. The *Jupiter*, bigger and more challenging, inspires Toscanini to quite a different degree. The performance is searingly powerful in the outer movements, even exuberant in the finale, and the slow movement and Minuet given a rhythmic lift missing in the earlier symphonies. Limited sound with fizzy strings in No. 39.

Symphony No. 40 in G min., K.550.
(B) **(*) Carlton Dig. 30367 02372 [(M) id.]. O of St John's, Smith Square, Lubbock – HAYDN: *Symphony No. 44.* ***
(M) (**) RCA mono GD 60271 [60271-2-RG]. NBC SO, Toscanini – BEETHOVEN: *Symphony No. 3.* (***)

Lubbock's is a pleasingly relaxed account of Mozart's *G minor Symphony*, well played – the Minuet particularly deft – and nicely proportioned. The last ounce of character is missing from the slow movement, but the orchestra is responsive throughout, and the recording is in the demonstration class.

Dating from March 1950, Toscanini's version was recorded in the notoriously dry Studio 8-H in Radio City, New York; though the sound is uncomfortable, the high voltage of the interpretation makes considerable amends, with expressive warmth tempering the conductor's characteristic urgency. The slow movement is elegantly done, and even though the finale brings a measure of fierceness, Toscanini eases lovingly into the second subject.

Symphonies Nos. 40 in G min., K.550; 41 in C (Jupiter), K.551.
✿ (M) *** DG Dig. 445 548-2 [431 040-2]. VPO, Bernstein.
(M) *** Virgin/EMI Dig. CUV5 61133-2 [id.]. Sinfonia Varsovia, Sir Yehudi Menuhin.
(M) ** Decca 452 889-2 [id.]. New Philh. O, Giulini.

(i) *Symphonies Nos. 40–41;* (ii) *Serenade: Eine kleine Nachtmusik, K.525.*
(B) **(*) DG 439 472-2 [id.]. (i) BPO; (ii) VPO; Boehm.

Symphonies Nos. 40–41; Overture: The Marriage of Figaro.
(B) *** RPO TRP 004 [(M) id. import]. RPO, Glover.

Bernstein's electrifying account of No. 40 is keenly dramatic, individual and stylish, with the finale delightfully airy and fresh. If anything, the *Jupiter* is even finer: it is exhilarating in its tensions and observes the repeats in both halves of the finale, making it almost as long as the massive first movement. Bernstein's electricity sustains that length, and one welcomes it for establishing the supreme power of the argument, the true crown in the whole of Mozart's symphonic output. Pacing cannot be faulted in any of the four movements and, considering the problems of making live recordings, the 1984 sound is first rate, lacking only the last degree of transparency in tuttis. This mid-price reissue on DG's Masters label now takes its place again at the top of the list of recommendations for this coupling.

Recorded in exceptionally vivid, immediate sound, Menuhin's versions of both symphonies with the Sinfonia Varsovia find a distinctive place in an overcrowded field, with playing of precision, clarity and bite which is consistently refreshing, giving a feeling of live music-making. Menuhin reveals himself again as very much a classicist, preferring speeds on the fast side, rarely indulging in romantic tricks. He is generous with repeats – observing exposition repeats in both first movement and finale of the *Jupiter*, for example.

At bargain price in the Royal Philharmonic Collection, Jane Glover conducts fresh, urgent performances, stylishly moulded, which include exposition repeats that generally outshine her own earlier, smaller-scale readings with the London Mozart Players on ASV. With rhythms crisply sprung in fast movements and with slow movements warmly lyrical and relaxed without becoming over-romantic, these performances, brightly recorded, stand comparison with almost any version, and the *Figaro overture* provides a welcome makeweight.

Boehm sounds mellow and cultivated but still magnetic and strong. Of course, he is much less generous than some others in the matter of repeats, but the Berlin Philharmonic play very beautifully and the recording is agreeably warm and full, the reissue inexpensive. *Eine kleine Nachtmusik* was recorded a decade and a half later, and the VPO playing is polished and fresh, with a neat, lightly pointed finale.

Giulini's 1965 coupling was his first recording for Decca with the New Philharmonia Orchestra. They play well for him, and the Kingsway Hall recording is warm and detailed, of Decca's vintage quality, if perhaps not an obvious candidate for reissue in Decca's Classic Sound series. Its aural sleekness, however, matches the performances which, though they offer beautifully polished playing, are curiously lacking in vitality, neither classically poised nor romantically charged.

CHAMBER MUSIC

(i) *Adagio and fugue in C min., K.546;* (ii) *Adagio and rondo in C for glass harmonica, flute, oboe, viola & cello;* (iii) *Clarinet quintet in A, K.581;* (iv) *String quintets Nos. 4 in G min., K.516; 5 in D, K.593; 6 in E flat, K.614.*

(B) **(*) Ph. Duo 456 058-2 [(M) id. import]. (i) Italian Qt; (ii) Hoffmann, Nicolet, Holliger, Schouten, Decroos; (iii) Jack Brymer, Allegri Qt; (iv) Grumiaux Trio, Gérecz, Lesueur.

(i) *Horn quintet in E flat, K.407;* (ii) *Piano and wind quintet in E flat, K.452;* (iii) *String quintets Nos. 1 in B flat, K.174; 2 in C min., K.406; 3 in C, K.515; Adagio in B flat for 2 clarinets & 3 bassett horns.*

(B) **(*) Ph. Duo 456 055-2 (2) [(M) id. import]. (i) Timothy Brown, ASMF Chamber Ens.; (ii) Ingrid Haebler, Bamberg Wind Qt (members); (iii) Grumiaux Trio, Gérecz, Lesueur; (iv) Netherlands Wind Ens.

The six Mozart *String quintets* are available in a mid-priced box, together with a radiant account of the *Clarinet quintet* (with Bohuslav Zahradnik the sensitive soloist), on three Calliope discs which cost approximately the same as the pair of Duos above (see below). The Calliope set has been awarded a Rosette and will prove a far better investment in the long run. Moreover, bargain hunters preferring the Grumiaux ensemble's immensely civilized (1973) survey of just the *String quintets* will find them also available on three mid-priced discs, as Volume 11 of the Philips Mozart Edition (422 511-2 – see below).

Of the additional music above, the *Adagio and fugue* is not strictly a quintet at all, or the Quartetto Italiano would not have been able to present it so effectively without assistance. The *Adagio and rondo* for glass harmonica, however, proves a welcome bonus, with Bruno Hoffmann playing that rare instrument, so titillating to the ear if heard in fairly brief spans. The *Adagio in B flat* for clarinets and basset horns is also a charmer for similar reasons when performed so delectably by the Netherlands group. Of the other major works, Brymer's reading of the *Clarinet quintet* is warm and relaxed and very agreeable, if not distinctive. Timothy Brown is a personable soloist and the *Horn quintet* is given a well-projected and lively account. However, in spite of Ingrid Haebler's characteristically stylish contribution to the *Piano and wind quintet*, the Bamberg performance does not take flight, a straightforward rather than an imaginative account. Throughout all four CDs the recordings are admirably balanced and given high-quality analogue sound.

Complete Mozart Edition, Volume 14: (i) *Adagio in C for glass harmonica, K.356;* (i; ii) *Adagio in C min. & Rondo in C for glass harmonica, flute, oboe, viola & cello;* (iii) *Clarinet trio in E flat (Kegelstatt), K.498;* (iv; v) *Piano quartets Nos. 1–2;* (iv) *Piano trios Nos. 1–6; Piano trio in D min., K.442;* (vi) *Piano and wind quintet in E flat, K.452.*

(M) *** Ph. Dig./Analogue 422 514-2 (5) [id.]. (i) Bruno Hoffmann; (ii) with Nicolet, Holliger, Schouten, Decroos; (iii) Brymer, Kovacevich, Ireland; (iv) Beaux Arts Trio, (v) with Giuranna; (vi) Brendel, Holliger, Brunner, Baumann, Thunemann.

This compilation of Mozart's chamber music with piano has no weak link. The last three discs contain the complete set of the Mozart *Piano trios* recorded by the Beaux Arts Trio in 1987, a first-rate cycle which includes not only the six completed trios but also the composite work, put together by Mozart's friend, the priest Maximilian Stadler, and listed by Köchel as K.442. The Beaux Arts' teamwork – with the pianist Menahem Pressler leading the way – brings consistently fresh and winning performances, as it also does in the two great *Piano quartets* where, in recordings made in 1983, they are joined by the viola-player, Bruno Giuranna. The *Piano and wind quintet*, K.452, recorded in 1986, subtly contrasts the artistry of Alfred Brendel at the piano with that of the oboist, Heinz Holliger, leading a distinguished team of wind-players. The only non-digital recordings are those of the *Kegelstatt trio*, characterfully done by Stephen Bishop-Kovacevich with the clarinettist Jack Brymer and the viola-player Patrick Ireland, and of the two shorter works involving glass harmonica. Those last are conveniently included here as an extra, both with Bruno Hoffmann playing that rare instrument, so titillating to the ear if heard in fairly brief spans.

Adagio and rondo for flute, oboe, viola, cello and piano, K.617; (i) *Clarinet trio in E flat (Kegelstatt), K.498;* (ii) *Flute quartets Nos. 1–4, K.285, K.285a, K.285b & K.298;* (iii) *Horn quintet in E flat, K.407;* (iv) *Oboe quartet in F, K.370.*

(BB) *** Virgin Classics Dig. Double VBD5 61448-2 (2) [CVBD 61448]. Nash Ens., with (i) Michael Collins; (ii) Philippa Davies; (iii) Frank Lloyd; (iv) Gareth Hulse.

This inexpensive Virgin Double offers two CDs which pair naturally together. In the *Adagio and rondo*, originally written for glass harmonica, the wind instruments blend together most felicitously, especially in the closing Rondo, where the balance with the pianist (the very musical Ian Brown) is expertly managed. Michael Collins then proves a winningly personable soloist in the *Clarinet trio*, a work much rarer on record than the *Quintet*. He is followed by Gareth Hulse in the *Oboe quartet*, who plays exquisitely in the *Andante* and most engagingly in the neat closing Rondo. The Nash string group blend in most sensitively, and they give excellent support to Frank Lloyd's warmly lyrical account of the *Horn quartet*, where the finale rounds off the concert infectiously. The second disc contains the four *Flute quartets*, with Philippa Davies both a nimble and a highly musical flautist who has a natural feeling for Mozartian line. She is very well balanced with her Nash colleagues and these are pleasingly warm, intimate performances, nicely turned, if perhaps not distinctive. But the two discs together add up to a very pleasing concert.

Canons for strings; Canons for woodwind: see below, under VOCAL MUSIC: Complete Mozart Edition, Volume 23

Complete Mozart Edition, Volume 10: (i; vi) *Clarinet quintet;* (ii) *Flute quartets Nos. 1–4;* (iii; vi) *Horn quintet;* (iv; vi) *Oboe quartet;* (v) *Sonata for bassoon and cello, K.292.* (vi) Fragments: *Allegro in F, K.App. 90/580b for clarinet, basset horn, & string trio; Allegro in B flat. K.App. 91/K.516c for a clarinet quintet; Allegro in F, K.288 for a divertimento for 2 horns & strings; String quartet movements: Allegro in B flat, K.App. 72/464a; Allegro in B flat, K.App. 80/514a; Minuet in B flat, K.68/589a; Minuet in F, K.168a; Movement in A, K.App. 72/464a. String quintet No. 1 in B flat, K.174:2 Original movements: Trio & Finale. Allegro in A min., K.App. 79 for a string quintet. Allegro in G, K.App. 66/562e for a string trio* (completed, where necessary, by Erik Smith).

(M) *** Ph. Analogue/Dig. 422 510-2 (3) [id.]. (i) Pay; (ii) Bennett, Grumiaux Trio; (iii) Brown; (iv) Black; (v) Thunemann; Orton; (vi) ASMF Chamber Ens.

These are highly praised performances of the major chamber works featuring modern wind instruments (Antony Pay uses a normal clarinet). The rest of the items are by no means inconsequential offcuts but provide music of high quality, notably the *String quartet movement*, K.514a. The *Minuet in B flat*, K.589a, in the rhythm of a polonaise and possibly the first draft for the finale of the *Hunt quartet*, is a real charmer which, had it received more exposure, might well have become a Mozartian lollipop like the famous and not dissimilar Minuet in the *D major Divertimento*, K.334. The two pieces with solo clarinet are also very winning. The performances here are all polished and spontaneous and beautifully recorded.

(i) *Clarinet quartet in E flat, K.347a; Clarinet quintet in A, K.581;* (ii) *Quintet for clarinet, basset horn and string trio.*

(BB) ** Naxos Dig. 8.550390 [id.]. József Balogh; (i) Béla Kovács; Danubius Qt (members).

(i) *Clarinet quartets: in B flat, K.317d; in F, K.496;* (ii) *Clarinet trio (Kegelstatt) for clarinet, viola and piano, K.498.*

(BB) **(*) Naxos Dig. 8.550439 [id.]. József Balogh; (i) Danubius Qt (members); (ii) Jenö Jandó, György Konrád.

Mozart's *Clarinet quartets* are arrangements, with the first two based on violin sonatas (K.378 and K.380) while the third is a version of the piano trio, K.496. They were published posthumously in 1799 and it seems unlikely that Mozart made the arrangements himself. Never mind, they are most enjoyable in this form and suit the clarinet very well. They are most persuasively presented here, and very well recorded. Unfortunately József Balogh, who plays so sympathetically in the *Quartets*, is less memorable in the *Quintet*, where he paces the famous *Larghetto* a shade too fast. However, he makes up a good team with Jandó and Konrád for the fine *Kegelstatt trio*. Here the performance is relaxed but enjoyable (it could have used a shade more momentum in the first movement).

Clarinet quintet in A, K.581.

(B) *** Decca Eclipse Dig. 448 232-2; *448 232-4* [(M) id. import]. Peter Schmidl, Vienna Octet (members) – BEETHOVEN: *Septet in E flat, Op. 20.* ***

(BB) **(*) Belart 450 056-2 [(M) id. import]. Jack Brymer, Allegri Qt – SCHUBERT: *Trout quintet.* ***

(B) (**) Millennium mono MCD 80093 [id.]. Leopold Wlach, V. Konserthaus Qt – BRAHMS: *Clarinet quintet.* (**)

Peter Schmidl, using a basset clarinet, is sometimes just a little cool, but his intimate approach has its own appeal. He phrases gently and beautifully, with imagination in his nuancing and much delicacy in matters of light and shade. Of course these Viennese players use modern instruments, and the sound they make is consistently full and smooth. The closing section of the finale is sheer joy, with some delicious chortling articulation from the soloist. The 1989 Decca recording is state-of-the-art, and while this would not necessarily be a clear first choice for the *Quintet*, it is very distinguished, and the splendid Beethoven coupling makes this Eclipse reissue an outstanding bargain.

Brymer's interpretation of the *Clarinet quintet* is warm and leisurely, and he chooses slow tempi throughout. With his tone so succulent, and with velvety support from the Allegri Quartet, he is almost entirely successful in sustaining them although, as the finale proceeds, the forward flow of the music is reduced to a near crawl before the quickening at the coda. The recorded sound is warm and flattering, and this is still very beguiling.

The Wlach–Vienna Konserthaus recording dates from 1951 and its coupling from the following year. It sounds very good for its age and the playing of Leopold Wlach is very beautiful indeed. The Vienna Konserthaus Quartet do not equal him in tonal distinction or sensitivity, but his artistry is quite special.

(i) *Clarinet quintet in A, K.581;* (ii) *Clarinet trio in E flat, K.498;* (iii) *Flute quartets: in D, K.285; in G, K.285a; in C, K.285b; in A, K.298;* (iv) *Horn quintet in E flat, K.407;* (v) *Oboe quartet in F, K.370;* (vi) *Quintet in E flat, for piano and wind, K.452.*

(B) *(*) EMI Rouge et Noir CZS5 69998-2 (2). (i–ii) Druart, Lepauw; (i) Manzone, Ponticelli, Tetard; (ii) Ciccolini; (iii) Debost; (iii; v) Jarry, Collot, Tournus; (iv) Schneider, Vienna Sextet (members); (v) Bourgue; (vi) Genult, Consortium Classicum.

There are good things here, of course, but the *Clarinet quintet* and *Clarinet trio*, both recorded in 1971, diminish the attractions of the set. The blend and intonation of these fine players is far from impeccable and the performances are pretty lacklustre. Considering the distinction and character of French wind-playing, this is a disappointment. The companion performances are better: Maurice Bourgue recorded the *Oboe quartet* in 1973 and the *Flute quartets* come from 1968. The *Horn quintet* and the *Quintet for piano and wind* are later (1978 and 1988 respectively) and fare better but, taken all round, this is not a particularly appealing set.

(i) *Clarinet quintet in A, K.581; Divertimento No. 1 for strings in D, K.136* (quartet version).

(M) *** Saga EC 3387-2 [id.]. (i) Thea King; Aeolian Qt.

With great refinement in matters of tonal shading, and consistently beautiful phrasing, this Saga recording remains among the most attractive versions of the *Quintet*. Miss King's articulation in the third-movement solos and in the delightfully pointed finale is a joy. The closing pages of the work are especially beautiful. This is all helped by excellent support from the Aeolian Quartet and a most realistically balanced recording from Saga. The ungenerous filler is bright and breezy, with very fast tempi for the outer movements and a graceful, if matter-of-fact account of the *Andante*.

(i) *Clarinet quintet in A, K.581;* (ii) *Flute quartet No. 1 in D, K.285;* (iii) *Oboe quartet in F, K.370.*

(B) **(*) EMI Dig. CDZ5 69702-2 [id.]. (i) Nicholas Carpenter; (ii) Jaime Martin; (iii) Jonathan Kelly; Brindisi Qt (members).

The three soloists introduced here in EMI's Debut series are all principals with various British orchestras. Each is a first-rate artist and all three performances here are fresh and enjoyable, with the *Flute quartet* the most successful of the three, perhaps because its charming, serenade-like *Adagio*, with the soloist poised over a pizzicato accompaniment, cannot fail to beguile the listener. In both the other works the slow movements, although played persuasively, are just a little plain; to make up for it, all three finales are sprightly, with that of the *Clarinet quintet* being particularly successful. The members of the Brindisi Quartet provide admirable support, and the recording is excellent, vivid and transparent.

(i) *Clarinet quintet in A, K.581;* (ii) *Horn quintet in E flat, K.407;* (iii) *Oboe quartet in F, K.370.*

(M) *** Ph. 422 833-2. (i) Antony Pay; (ii) Timothy Brown; (iii) Neil Black; ASMF Chamber Ens.

It is a delightful idea to have the *Clarinet quintet*, *Oboe quartet* and *Horn quintet* on a single CD. Here, Antony Pay's earlier account of the *Clarinet quintet*, played on a modern instrument, with the Academy of St Martin-in-the-Fields players must be numbered among the strongest now on the market for those not insisting on an authentic basset clarinet. Neil Black's playing in the *Oboe quartet* is distinguished, and again the whole performance radiates pleasure, while the *Horn quintet* comes in a well-projected and lively account with Timothy Brown. The recording, originally issued in 1981, is of Philips's best.

(i) *Clarinet quintet;* (ii) *Oboe quartet in F, K.370.*

(B) *** CfP CD-CFP 4377 [(M) id. import]. (i) Andrew Marriner; (ii) Gordon Hunt, Chilingirian Qt.

(B) *** Carlton Dig. 30367 02332 [(M) id. import]. (i) Keith Puddy; (ii) Douglas Boyd; Gabrieli Qt.

On the bargain-priced CfP version, recorded in 1981, the young Andrew Marriner's persuasive account occupies the front rank, quite irrespective of price. Marriner's playing in the *Quintet* is wonderfully flexible; it reaches its apex in the radiantly beautiful reading of the slow movement, although the finale is also engagingly characterized. The *Oboe quartet* is delectable too, with Gordon Hunt a highly musical and technically accomplished soloist. The CfP issue was recorded in the Wigmore Hall and the sound-balance is most believable.

The alternative bargain-priced Carlton CD brings a reading of the *Clarinet quintet* which is clean and well paced and, if lacking the last degree of delicacy in the slow movement, is never less than stylish. The young oboist, Douglas Boyd, then gives an outstanding performance in the shorter, less demanding work, with the lilting finale delectably full of fun. The digital recording is vividly immediate and full of presence, with even the keys of the wind instruments often audible.

(i) *Clarinet quintet in A, K.581; String quartet No. 20 in D (Hoffmeister), K.499.*
(M) **(*) Whitehall Associates Dig. MQCD 6001 [id.]. (i) Jack Brymer; Medici Qt.

The Medici String Quartet have set up their own label. Jack Brymer joins them for their first Mozart CD and has a benign influence in a fine, mellifluous performance of the *Clarinet quintet*. He plays the *Adagio* as a sustained half-tone and conjures from the strings comparably soft playing. Perhaps a little more dynamic variety would have been an advantage, but the concentration is sustained right through. The finale is delightful; there is an attractive improvisational feeling in the lyrical variation before the main theme makes its joyful return. The recording is truthful, but the close balance is more noticeable in the coupled *Hoffmeister quartet*, which is a lively, well-integrated performance, if without the individuality of the *Quintet*. However, at mid-price this coupling is certainly worth considering.

(i) *Clarinet quintet in A, K.581; String quintet No. 4 in G min., K.516.*
(B) ** DG Classikon 439 460-2; *439 460-4* [(M) id. import]. Amadeus Qt, with (i) Gervase de Peyer; (ii) Cecil Aronowitz.

It was a happy idea to pair what are perhaps Mozart's two greatest *Quintets* on this bargain Classikon reissue. Gervase de Peyer gives a warm, smiling lead in the *Clarinet quintet*, with a sunny opening movement, a gentle, expressive *Larghetto* and a delightfully genial finale. The Amadeus accompany with sensibility, and the 1975 recording is flawless. The recording of the *String quintet* (with its Elysian slow movement) was made six years earlier but the CD transfer shows its age by a degree of edginess on top which is emphasized by the accented playing at higher dynamic levels. This performance has also been admired, and there is no question about the refinement and polish of the playing, although the effect is not as fresh and pleasing as with K.581 because of the sound-quality.

(i) *Clarinet quintet in A, K.581;* (ii) *Violin sonatas in F, K.376; E flat, K.481.*
(B) *** Cal. Approche CAL 6628 [(M) id.]. (i) Bohuslav Zahradnik, Talich Qt; (ii) Peter Messiereur, Stanislav Bogunia.

The *Clarinet quintet* is exquisitely done. Bohuslav Zahradnik's contribution has much delicacy of feeling and colour; he is highly seductive in the slow movement, and even in the finale the effect is gentle in the most appealing way without any loss of vitality. The recording balance is exemplary. The two *Violin sonatas* are also beautifully played in a simple, direct style that is wholly persuasive. The recording is clearly detailed and well balanced, if slightly more shallow.

Clarinet trio in E flat (Kegelstatt), K.498.
(BB) ** HM HMS 926017 [id.]. Michel Portal, Bruno Pasquier, Jean-Claude Pennetier.

Mozart's *Clarinet trio* with its almost certainly spurious 'skittle alley' association is not encountered on record nearly as often as the better-known *Quintet*. So this fluent, very musical, if not distinctive French performance on Harmonia Mundi's bargain-basement Solo label might acceptably fill a gap in any collection where economy is of prime importance. It is very well if forwardly recorded.

Complete Mozart Edition, Volume 13: (i) *Divertimento in E flat for string trio, K.563;* (ii) *Duos for violin and viola Nos. 1–2, K.423/4;* (i) *6 Preludes and fugues for string trio, K.404a;* (iii) *Sonata (String trio) in B flat, K.266.*
(M) *** Ph. 422 513-2 (2) [id.]. (i) Grumiaux, Janzer, Szabo; (ii) Grumiaux, Pelliccia; (iii) ASMF Chamber Ens.
(B) *** Ph. Duo 454 023-2 (2). As above.

Grumiaux's 1967 recorded performance of the *Divertimento in E flat* remains unsurpassed; he is here joined by two players with a similarly refined and classical style. The recording has been remastered again: the balance still favours Grumiaux but he also dominates the performance artistically (as he does also in the *Duos*) and the result is now fully acceptable. In the *Duos*, which are ravishingly played, the balance is excellent, and Arrigo Pelliccia proves a natural partner in these inspired and rewarding works. The *Sonata for string trio* is well played by the ASMF Chamber Ensemble and it has a modern, digital recording. Of the six *Preludes and fugues*, the first three derive from Bach's *Well-tempered clavier*, the fourth combines an *Adagio* from the *Organ sonata*, BWV 527, with *Contrapunctus 8* from the *Art of fugue*, the fifth is a transcription of two movements from the *Organ sonata*, BWV 526, and the sixth uses music of W. F. Bach. The performances here are sympathetic and direct, the recorded sound bold, clear and bright. As can be seen, this set has now been issued on a Duo, with a resulting saving in cost.

Flute quartets Nos. 1 in D, K.285; 2 in G, K.285a; 3 in C, K.285b; 4 in A, K.298.
(M) *** Van. 08.4001.71 [OVC 4001]. Paula Robinson, Tokyo Qt (members).
(BB) ** ASV CDQS 6099 [(M) id. import]. Richard Adeney, Melos Ens. (members).
(BB) ** Naxos Dig. 8.550438 [id.]. Jean Claude Gérard, Villa Musica Ens.

(i) *Flute quartets Nos. 1 in D, K.285; 2 in G, K.285a; 3 in C, K.285b; 4 in A, K.298*; (ii) *Andante for flute and orchestra in C, K.315.*
(B) *** DHM 05472 77442-2 [id.]. Barthold Kuijken; (i) Members of Coll. Aur.; (ii) La Petite Band.

The Collegium Aureum set is the only bargain version using period instruments. Kuijken plays a beguilingly soft instrument from Dresden, made by August Grenser in 1789, and the effect has great charm, even to ears not much enamoured of period instruments. The playing of the three string instruments is also very smooth and accomplished, and the ensemble is beautifully recorded in a warm acoustic. The pitch is lower by a semitone, but few listeners will mind this. The *Andante for flute and orchestra* makes an engaging encore.

The Vanguard recording of the *Flute quartets* (presumably from the 1960s – no date is given) is most winning. Paula Robinson displays a captivating lightness of touch and her silvery timbre seems eminently suited to Mozart. Needless to say, the Tokyo Quartet provide polished accompaniments which combine warmth with much finesse, and the recording is most naturally balanced.

The performances by Richard Adeney with distinguished members of the Melos Ensemble (Hugh Maguire, Cecil Aronowitz, Terence Weill) date from 1978. The balance treats the flute very much in a solo capacity and is vividly close, although the characterful playing of Adeney's colleagues is not masked. The effect is undoubtedly lively and spontaneous but has not the imaginative insight or persuasive charm of the best versions. However, this excellently transferred CD is in the lowest price-range and represents good value.

On Naxos, rather upfront recording with insufficient room round the cello. Good playing from all concerned and, if the level is reduced, the results are acceptable, though lengthy exposure to the sound induces a certain acoustic claustrophobia. There is nothing wrong with the performances, which all give pleasure. Excellent value in the lowest price-range.

(i) *Flute quartets Nos. 1–4;* (ii) *Oboe quartet in F, K.370.*
(M) *** DG 453 287-2. (i) Andreas Blau; (ii) Lothar Koch; Amadeus Qt (members).

The flute was not Mozart's favourite wind instrument, yet he wrote some delightful music for it, none more so than these delectably elegant quartets. On DG, although the flute dominates, the other instruments are not over-weighted. The phrasing throughout breathes naturally. The enchanting slow movement of K.285, in which the flute cantilena is floated over a pizzicato accompaniment, is beautifully done, and the ear is caught by the gracious shaping of the *galant* themes used as the basis for variations in the second movement of K.285c or the no less charming opening movement of K.298. Blau is a fine artist and the Amadeus accompany him with subtlety and distinction. These performances are matched by the refinement of Koch in the *Oboe quartet*. With creamy tone, nice embellishments (especially in the finale) and very stylish phrasing, he is splendid. The Amadeus accompany with sensibility and here the string part-writing has rather more interest and the balance is flawless. The excellent analogue recordings date from the late 1970s. Most other recommended versions of the flute works have no extra work, so this superior, mid-priced DG disc is very competitive indeed.

(ii) *Horn quintet in E flat, K.407;* (ii) *Oboe quartet in F, K.370; A Musical Joke, K.522.*
(BB) **(*) Naxos Dig. 8.550437 [id.]. (i) József Kiss; (ii) Jenö Keveházi; Kodály Qt.

Highly musical if not especially individual performances of the *Horn quintet* and *Oboe quartet*; in the latter the oboe is balanced forwardly and seems a bit larger than life; but no matter, the recordings have a pleasingly resonant bloom. The *Musical Joke* really comes off well: the horn players have a great time with their wrong notes.

(i) *Piano quartets Nos. 1–2;* (i) *Horn quintet in E flat, K.407.*
✿ (M) *** Decca mono 425 960-2. (i) Clifford Curzon, Amadeus Qt; (ii) Dennis Brain, Griller Qt.

All versions of the Mozart *Piano quartets* rest in the shadow of the recordings by Clifford Curzon and members of the Amadeus Quartet. No apologies need be made for the 1952 mono recorded sound. The performances have a unique sparkle, slow movements are elysian. One's only criticism is that the *Andante* of K.478 opens at a much lower dynamic level than the first movement, and some adjustment of the controls needs to be made. The *Horn quintet* coupling was recorded in 1944 and the transfer to CD is even more miraculous. The slight surface rustle of the 78-r.p.m. source is in no way distracting and Dennis

Brain's performance combines warmth and elegance with a spirited spontaneity, and the subtleties of the horn contribution are a continuous delight. A wonderful disc that should be in every Mozartian's library.

Piano quartet No. 2 in E flat, K.493.

(M) ** Sony Stern Edition III SM2K 64516 (2) [S2K 64516]. Stern, Katims, Schneider, Istomin – HAYDN: *Piano trio;* SCHUBERT: *Piano trios.* **

A perfectly respectable account from Stern and his colleagues, not very flatteringly recorded (Stern's violin sounds wiry) during the 1957 Casals Festival in Puerto Rico. There is plenty of life here, but a lack of charm until the finale, which goes well.

Piano trios Nos. 1 in B flat, K.254; 2 in G, K.496; 3 in B flat, K.502; 4 in E, K.542; 5 in C, K.548; 6 in G, K.564.

(M) *** Teldec/Warner Dig. 0630 12336-2 (2) [2292 46439-2]. Trio Fontenay.

(i) *Piano trios Nos. 1 in B flat, K.254; 2 in G, K.496; 3 in B flat, K.502; 4 in E, K.542; 5 in C, K.548; 6 in G, K.564;* (ii) *Clarinet trio (Kegelstatt) in E flat, K.498.*

(B) *(**) Ph. Duo 446 154-2 (2) [id.]. (i) Beaux Arts Trio; (ii) Brymer, Kovacevich, Ireland.

The Trio Fontenay have already given us excellent accounts of the Brahms and Dvořák *Piano trios* and they are equally happy in the music of Mozart. As before, the splendid pianist, Wolf Harden, dominates the music-making by strength of personality, although the others are well in the picture, and the playing of the cellist, Niklas Schmidt, is notable. The playing of this group is consistently fresh and spontaneous: the *Allegretto* finale of the *G major*, K.496, has a seemingly improvisational freedom and the *E major*, K.542, which opens the second disc, is particularly memorable, the opening *Allegro* light and sparkling, with a delightful *Andante grazioso* to follow and a very spirited finale. Indeed these musicians are completely at one with Mozart and the recording is truthful and well balanced. Although the Beaux Arts set remains very tempting on a Philips Duo (and it throws in the *Clarinet trio* for good measure, this Teldec set has the advantage of modern digital recording and carries the strongest recommendation at mid-price. The only snag is the absence of accompanying musical notes.

The Beaux Arts Trio's earlier performances, made in the late 1960s, still sound vivid and fresh. As music-making, this has almost equal artistic claims on the listener and, though the timbre of Daniel Guilet's violin is noticeably much thinner than the ear would expect in a more modern recording, if pinched it is well focused. Different ears and different reproducers will react to this with varying degrees of dissatisfaction; but Menahem Pressler's piano playing is most naturally caught. In the *Clarinet trio* the balance is such that Jack Brymer's clarinet dominates and Stephen Kovacevich's piano is slightly recessed, but the overall effect is beautiful, warmer than in the *Piano trios*. But the later, digital set of the *Piano trios* is well worth the extra cost.

Piano and wind quintet in E flat, K.452.

(M) *** Sony Dig. SMK 42099 [id.]. Perahia, members of ECO – BEETHOVEN: *Quintet.* ***

Piano and wind quintet in E flat, K.452; Adagio & rondo for glass harmonica, flute, oboe, violin & viola, K.617.

(BB) *(*) Naxos Dig. 8.550511 [id.]. Jandó, Kiss, Kovács, Keveházi, Vajda, Kovács, Konrád, Koó – BEETHOVEN: *Quintet.* *(*)

An outstanding account (now at mid-price) of Mozart's delectable *Piano and wind quintet* on CBS, with Perahia's playing wonderfully refreshing in the *Andante* and a superb response from the four wind soloists, notably Neil Black's oboe contribution. Clearly all the players are enjoying this rewarding music, and they are well balanced, with the piano against the warm but never blurring acoustics of The Maltings at Snape.

Like its Beethoven coupling the Naxos performance, although excellently recorded, finds little magic in Mozart's delightful *Quintet*. The first movement is brisk and alive but has no added imaginative touches, and the *Larghetto* proceeds on its leisurely course uneventfully. The finale, however, is quite sprightly. The coupling, in which Jandó changes over to the celeste, is charming in its delicate textures but hardly affects one's response to the main work.

String quartets

Complete Mozart Edition, Volume 12: *String quartets Nos. 1–23.*

(M) *** Ph. 422 512-2 (8) [id.]. Italian Qt.

The earliest recordings by the Italians now begin to show their age (notably the six *Haydn Quartets*, which date from 1966): the violin timbre is thinner than we would expect in more modern versions. But the quality is generally very satisfactory, for the Philips sound-balance is admirably judged. As a set, the performances have seen off all challengers for two decades or more; one is unlikely to assemble a more consistently satisfying overview of these works, or one so beautifully played. They hold a very special place in the Mozartian discography.

String quartets Nos. 1 in G, K.80; 2 in D, K.155; 4 in C, K.157.
(BB) ** Naxos Dig. 8.550541 [id.]. Eder Qt.

String quartets Nos. 3 in G, K.156; 5 in F, K.158; 6 in B flat, K.159; 17 in B flat (Hunt), K.458.
(BB) ** Naxos Dig. 8.550542 [id.]. Eder Qt.

String quartets Nos. 7 in E flat, K.160; 8 in F, K.168; 9 in A, K.169; 22 in B flat (Prussian No. 2), K.589.
(BB) **(*) Naxos Dig. 8.550544 [id.]. Eder Qt.

String quartets Nos. 10 in C, K.170; 11 in E flat, K.171; 15 in D min., K.421.
(BB) **(*) Naxos Dig. 8.550546 [id.]. Eder Qt.

String quartets Nos. 12 in B flat, K.172; 13 in D min., K.173; 21 in D (Prussian No. 1), K.575.
(BB) **(*) Naxos Dig. 8.550545 [id.]. Eder Quartet.

String quartets Nos. 16 in E flat, K.428; 18 in A, K.464.
(BB) ** Naxos Dig. 8.550540 [id.]. Eder Qt.

String quartet No. 19 in C (Dissonance), K.465; Divertimenti: in D, K.136; in B flat, K.137; in F, K.138.
(BB) ** Naxos Dig. 8.550543 [id.]. Eder Qt.

String quartets Nos. 20 in D (Hoffmeister), K.499; 23 in F (Prussian No. 3), K.590; Adagio and fugue in C min., K.546.
(BB) **(*) Naxos Dig. 8.550547 [id.]. Eder Qt.

There is nothing cheap about the Naxos recordings except the asking price. The Eder Quartet are an extremely fine ensemble with an admirable sense of style and exemplary musicianship. The snag is the venue, the Sashalom Reformed Church in Budapest, which affords the group the most beautiful sound, but the effect overall is almost orchestral and too often loses the intimacy of the medium. However, it seems to affect some performances more than others, and the three early quartets (K.160 and K.168–9) on the third disc, which in their first-movement allegros keep reminding us of the Salzburg *Divertimenti* (K.136–8), are not affected too adversely. The slow movement of the F major, K.168, is very touching, and it is beautifully played. The *Second Prussian Quartet* is also elegantly done, although once again the resonant acoustic gives an unwanted expansion of tone and takes some of the edge off the playing. The fourth and fifth discs include five of the amazingly mature Viennese quartets of 1773, with their portents of the later Mozart, notably the touching *Un poco Adagio* of K.170 and the remarkable opening movement of the *D minor*, K.173, which also has an engagingly courtly *Andantino grazioso*. They are played most sympathetically and the warmth of the sound is undoubtedly agreeable. The *Dissonance* opens with the Eder group creating considerable atmospheric tension; then the Allegro sets off rather determinedly. The fairly close balance prevents a real pianissimo, but the effect is real if inflated. The three Salzburg *Divertimenti* (which we also often hear in chamber-orchestra presentation), which are better suited by the acoustic, are given sympathetic, lively performances, if lacking the last ounce of sparkle. The later *Hoffmeister* and the two *Prussian Quartets* show the composer at full stretch, and the Eder performances will not disappoint. The players bring a potent intensity to the climax of the *Adagio and fugue* and, although they could perhaps have achieved more attack at the opening of the fugue, this effect is partly caused by the warm resonance. For those with limited budgets, this series is worth considering.

String quartet No. 1 in G, K.80.
(B) *** Koch Discover Dig. DICD 920171 [id.]. Sharon Qt – BEETHOVEN: *Harp quartet;* RAVEL: *Quartet in F.* **(*)

The Sharon Quartet give an excellent account of Mozart's *First* divertimento-like *Quartet*, which he wrote in Italy at the age of fifteen. The playing has life and finesse and, although the recording (made in a Cologne Church) is reverberant, detail is clear; indeed the acoustic rather suits the music.

String quartets Nos. 14 in G, K.387; 15 in D min., K.421; 16 in E flat, K.428; 17 in B flat (Hunt), K.458; 18 in A, K.464; 19 in C (Dissonance), K.465 (Haydn Quartets); 20 in D (Hoffmeister), K.499; 21 in D, K.575; 22 in B flat, K.589; 23 in F, K.590 (Prussian Quartets Nos. 1–3).
(M) *** Teldec/Warner 4509 95495-2 (4) [9031 72460-2]. Alban Berg Qt.

The Teldec recordings were made by the Alban Berg in the latter half of the 1970s; the performances have not since been surpassed, and now they make one of the most distinguished sets of Mozart's late quartets currently available, with the additional advantage of economy. The playing is thoroughly stylish and deeply musical; it is entirely free from surface gloss and there are none of the expressive exaggerations of dynamics and phrasing that marred this group's later records of Beethoven's *Rasumovsky Quartets* for EMI. The *Haydn Quartets* are consistently successful; the *Hunt* (1979) is still possibly the finest on the market and the *Dissonance* too is first class, with a wonderfully expressive account of the slow movement. Although dynamic gradations are steep, there is no sense of exaggeration – on the contrary these are wholly excellent performances, which are recommended with enthusiasm. The account of the *First Prussian Quartet* has much style and character, and the group are at their very best in Mozart's last two quartets. Their readings have an honesty and a directness that are enhanced by polish and finesse. Ensemble cannot be faulted and, though competition is strong, their claims still rank very high. The recordings have been transferred impeccably. The sound is rather more brightly astringent in the treble than the Franz Schubert Quartet on Nimbus and is obviously less modern but does not lack underlying warmth. The disc coupling K.464 and K.465 offers slightly more expansive sound than the earlier recordings.

String quartets Nos. 14–19 (Haydn quartets); 20 in D (Hoffmeister), K.499; 21–22 (Prussian Nos. 1–3).
(B) *** Nimbus Dig. NI 1778 (5) [id.]. Franz Schubert Qt of Vienna.

This is an outstanding set in every way, and for those wanting Mozart's last ten and – by general consensus – greatest quartets, this Nimbus bargain box rather sweeps the board. The Franz Schubert Quartet play with a refreshing lack of affectation, natural warmth, and great sweetness of tone. There is nothing narcissistic about their playing, and the listener is held from start to finish. In the six *Haydn Quartets* comparison with the Talich and the Franz Schubert Quartet of Vienna is in no way disadvantageous to the Viennese group, who have the advantage of first-class, modern, digital recording (made between 1992 and 1994), most naturally balanced in a pleasing acoustic.

Slow movements bring plenty of warmth; that of the *Dissonance Quartet* is genuinely searching, to reflect the evocative character of the opening. The players' lighter touch in their lively account of the *Hunt Quartet* gives equal pleasure. The *Hoffmeister Quartet* also brings pleasing bonhomie, and the three final quartets, all with memorable slow movements, cap the series impressively. They were written for the Prussian king but, because of the composer's death, he never received them; they offer plenty of opportunities for the cello (of which the king was a keen amateur player), which are vividly though not exaggeratedly realized here.

String quartets Nos. 14 in G, K.387; 15 in D min., K.421; 16 in E flat, K.428; 17 in B flat (Hunt), K.458; 18 in A, K.464; 19 in C (Dissonance), K.465 (Haydn Quartets).
✿ (M) *** Astrée Audivis Dig. E 8596 (3) [id.] (*K.387 & K.421:* E 8746; *K.428 & K.458:* E 8747; *K.464 & K.465:* E 8748). Mosaïques Qt.

(i) *String quartets Nos. 14–19 (Haydn Quartets)*; also *String quartet No. 3 in G, K.156;* (ii) *Violin sonata No. 18 in G, K.301.*
(M) *** Cal. CAL 3241/3 [id.]. (i) Talich Qt; (ii) Peter Messiereur, Stanislav Bogunia (with HAYDN: *String quartet No. 74 in G min., Op. 74/3* **(*)).

String quartets Nos. 14 in G, K.387; 15 in D min., K.421.
(M) **(*) Whitehall Associates Dig. MQCD 6004 [id.]. Medici Qt.

String quartets Nos. 16 in E flat, K.428; 19 in C (Dissonance), K.465.
(M) **(*) Whitehall Associates Dig. MQCD 6002 [id.]. Medici Qt.

String quartets Nos. 17 in B flat (Hunt), K.458; 18 in A, K.464.
(M) **(*) Whitehall Associates Dig. MQCD 6003 [id.]. Medici Qt.

The set of six quartets dedicated to Haydn contains a high proportion of Mozart's finest works in the genre and, although we have long had a special liking for the full-price Chilingirian performances on CRD, this new set by the Mosaïques Quartet must take pride of place, the more particularly as it is offered at mid-price. As with their previous award-winning performances of Haydn, this is playing of great distinction which offers new insights in every one of the six quartets. Phrasing is wonderfully musical, textures are elegantly blended, there is great transparency yet a full sonority, and this music-making unfolds freshly and naturally with absolutely none of the disadvantages one usually associates with period performances. Slow movements have great concentration and often rapt intensity, yet allegros are alert and vital and finales are a joy. None more so than the closing movement of K.387, which opens delicately but develops a striking impetus, and then the secondary theme dances liltingly. The *Hunt* brings a comparable rhythmic lightness in outer movements and a gently sustained *Adagio*. The first movement of K.428 is thoughtful, yet strong and penetrating, the *Andante* has a powerful atmosphere, while the genial touch in the finale wittily reminds us of Haydn. The underlying tautness at the opening of the *Dissonance Quartet* and the plangent textures possible with original instruments are the more telling when the mood suddenly lightens at the allegro, and this performance again makes the strongest contrast between the profound slow movement and the vigorously extrovert yet engagingly neat closing *Allegro molto*. The recording is first class, real and present, while allowing the widest range of dynamic. The three CDs are separately packaged but come in a slip-case so we assume that later they will be available separately.

The performances by the Talich Quartet are immaculate in ensemble and the performances have a special kind of shared intimacy which is yet immediately communicative. There is complete understanding of what Mozart is trying to say and a warmth and elegance of phrasing which is totally appealing. The analogue recordings are beautiful, very smooth on top, the balance slightly middle- and bass-orientated. The set has now been issued complete on three mid-priced discs with a pair of bonuses. The *Violin sonata* follows after the *Dissonance Quartet*; after the finale of the *Hunt*, K.458, and a pause of about 12 seconds, the Haydn quartet, Op. 74/3, begins, with a level disconcertingly higher and the transfer more immediate. This too is a fine performance – but be prepared! Perhaps the *Dissonance* could have a stronger profile but it, too, is beautifully played and recorded.

The Medici provide a polished, well-integrated set of 'Haydn' quartets, fresh and alert, if without always the touch of extra individuality that appears in their account of the *Clarinet quintet*. The studio recordings are rather closely balanced (although they are not airless) and the leader is obviously near the microphone. These records are competitively priced and certainly give pleasure.

String quartet No. 17 (Hunt), K.458.
(M) *** DG 449 092-2. Amadeus Qt – HAYDN: *String quartets Nos. 77–78.* ***

The Amadeus, recorded in 1963, give a strikingly fine account of the *Hunt*, famous in its day. The reading is well characterized and, though there are some touches that will not have universal appeal (in the slow movement, for example, these artists do not always allow the music to speak for itself), this is, generally speaking, a most satisfying version, notable for a finely blended and naturally balanced recording, which has been transferred beautifully to CD.

String quartets Nos. 17 in B flat (Hunt), K.458; 19 in C (Dissonance), K.465.
(B) *** EMI CfP CD-CFP 6034 [(M) id. import]. Lindsay Qt.
(BB) **(*) Naxos Dig. 8.550105 [id.]. Moyzes Qt.
(M) * DG Dig. 445 598-2. Emerson Qt – HAYDN: *String quartet No. 77.* *

A highly competitive issue at CfP price. This same coupling is available on a premium-priced CD from the Alban Berg Quartet, to which we awarded a Rosette in our 1996 main *Guide* (Teldec/Warner 2292 43037-2) and if this should be reissued at mid-price it would sweep the board. There is also a justly famous Amadeus version of the *Hunt* on DG (see above) and the Lindsay Quartet can well withstand the comparison. They play most beautifully, with unforced expressiveness and an alert and vital sensitivity. In the slow movement some readers may even prefer them to their rivals, for they are without the slightest affectation. Their recording too is more modern (1975) and wider in range. In the *Dissonance Quartet*, so called because of its bold opening, there is again much sensitivity. Recommended on all counts.

The Moyzes Quartet come from Bratislava and are an accomplished ensemble, distinguished by a generally sweet and light tone and decently recorded in the clean acoustic of the Concert Hall of Slovak Radio. The performances are very well prepared and neatly played, phrasing is musical and often sensitive. Greater diversity of colour would be welcome, and the players do not command quite a wide enough range of dynamics, so that the overall effect is just a little bland. But the performances still have a lot going for them and can be recommended.

The Emersons are stunningly articulate performers; they are meticulous too: every 't' is crossed and every 'i' dotted. In terms of sonority and ensemble the listener is bowled over by their virtuosity. But this is eminently self-aware, over-projected playing that might possibly be appropriate in William Schuman or Elliott Carter but is totally out of place in Mozart. They are not helped by a rather unspacious (though not unacceptable) recorded sound.

String quintets

Complete Mozart Edition, Volume 11: *String quintets Nos. 1–6.*
(M) *** Ph. 422 511-2 (3). Grumiaux Trio, with Gerecz, Lesueur.

(i) *String quintets Nos. 1–6;* (ii) *Clarinet quintet in A, K.581.*
❁ (M) *** Cal. CAL 9231/3 [id.]. Talich Qt, with (i) Bohuslav Zahradnik; (ii) Karel Rehak.

Glorious performances from the augmented Talich Quartet, with both the *C major* and *G minor* (together on the first disc), unforgettable in their expressive warmth, matching of timbre and easy, unforced spontaneity. The *Adagio* of the *G minor* is raptly beautiful. The second disc contains performances of the highest quality: just sample the delicacy of the playing in the lovely *Adagio* of K.174 or the energy of the simple yet spirited finale. The *C minor Quintet* is of course the composer's transcription of the *Serenade for wind*, K.388, and the players make the very most of the splendid variations which form the finale. The *Clarinet quintet* is exquisitely done. Bohuslav Zahradnik's contribution has much delicacy of feeling and colour; he is highly seductive in the slow movement, and even in the finale the effect is gentle in the most appealing way without any loss of vitality. The recording balance is exemplary in all three works and the acoustic admirably chosen. A rewarding triptych in every way – and a playing time of 80 minutes 17 seconds! The third disc, containing K.593 and K.614, is equally rewarding. The playing time is only 49 minutes 26 seconds, but this is still a disc to treasure. The recording balance is exemplary throughout and the acoustic admirably chosen. Everything is clear and naturally projected without any digital exaggeration. The three discs are currently offered for the price of two. The set has already been awarded a Diapason d'Or.

The Grumiaux ensemble's survey of the *String quintets* offers immensely civilized and admirably conceived readings. Throughout the set the vitality and sensitivity of this team are striking, and in general this eclipses all other recent accounts. The remastering of the 1973 recordings for CD is very successful indeed.

String quintets (Nos. 1) in B flat, K.174 (with original version of *Trio of the Minuet* and *Finale*); *(2) in C, K.515.*
(BB) **(*) Naxos Dig. 8.553103 [id.]. Eder Qt, with János Fehérvári.

String quintets (Nos. 4) in C min., K.406; (3) in G min., K.516.
(BB) *(*) Naxos Dig. 8.553104 [id.]. Eder Qt, with János Fehérvári.

String quintets Nos. (5) in D, K.593; (6) in E flat, K.614.
(BB) *** Naxos Dig. 8.553105 [id.]. Eder Qt, János Fehérvári.

The augmented Eder Quartet move on to offer a complete set of the *String quintets*, and the first disc again displays their unexaggerated Mozartian style, a fine blend of tone and musicianship. The *Andante* of the *C major Quintet* is particularly eloquent, the finale as lively as it is graceful. The recording (again using the Budapest Unitarian Church) is full and natural, with the resonance adding ambient bloom without too much inflation. While not a match for the Talich, these performances are eminently recommendable to those with limited budgets. But after the success of the first disc, the second is disappointing. The playing is still thoughtful and ensemble is clean, but there is an element of routine, and neither performance really takes off. It is not until the opening *Adagio* of the finale of the *G minor Quartet* that the Eder account achieves real concentration. The last two quartets come off very well indeed. The opening *Larghetto* of the *D major* is warmly intense, and the allegro immediately lifts off. The *Adagio* is beautifully played, the finale delightfully light-hearted. The *E flat major Quintet* is similarly well judged, with a poised *Andante* and another infectious closing movement. The recording is close but very realistic.

String quintets (Nos. 2) in C, K.515; (3) in G min., K.516.
(M) **(*) HM Suite Dig. HMT 7901512 [id.]. Ensemble 415.

String quintets (Nos. 2) in C, K.515; (3) in G min., K.516; 5 in D, K.593; 6 in E flat, K.614.
(B) **(*) Hyperion Dyad Dig. CDD 22005 [id.]. Salomon Qt, Simon Whistler.

The Salomon Quartet use period instruments, and this Dyad reissue comes into direct competition with the full-price Virgin Veritas collection of the same four quintets by Hausmusik. The Salomon group, understandably, are at their very best in the *G minor Quintet*, with the beauty of the *Adagio* sensitively caught. The final work is also splendidly played, but the *C major* and *D major Quintets* are cooler. The Hyperion recording is excellent, and this Dyad costs the same as a single premium-priced CD; but on almost all counts Hausmusik, who are also most realistically recorded, find greater depth in this music and in particular bring out a hauntingly dark yet gentle melancholy in slow movements, while finales bounce along joyfully.

Ensemble 415 (leader Chiara Banchini) couple the two favourite Mozart *String quintets* and play them with warmth and the delicacy of texture possible from period instruments. Although one has to adjust to some linear swelling, this music-making is certainly enjoyable. Opening movements have plenty of rhythmic lift and slow movements are refined in feeling, although without quite the degree of rapt concentration found by Hausmusik. However, the finale of the *G minor* (which opens with a hushed *Adagio* and then finds its release in the following allegro) is very succesful. The recording is excellent.

Violin sonatas

Complete Mozart Edition, Volume 15: *Violin sonatas Nos. 1–34; Sonatinas in C & F, K.46d & 46e; Sonatina in F (for beginners), K.547; Sonata in C, K.403* (completed Stadler); *Adagio in C min., K.396; Allegro in B flat, K.372; Andante & allegretto in C, K.404; Andante in A & Fugue in A min., K.402* (completed Stadler); *12 Variations on 'La bergère Célimène', K.359; 6 Variations on 'Hélas, j'ai perdu mon amant', K.360.*

(M) **(*) Ph. Analogue/Dig. 422 515-2 (7). Gérard Poulet, Blandine Verlet; Arthur Grumiaux, Walter Klien; Isabelle van Keulen, Ronald Brautigan.

The early sonatas, from K.6 through to K.31, were recorded in the mid-1970s by Gérard Poulet with Blandine Verlet on harpsichord. The various fragments, sonatinas, sonatas (K.46d, K.46e, K.403 and K.547) and variations were recorded in 1990 by Isabelle van Keulen and Ronald Brautigan. For the remaining four CDs, Philips have turned to the set by Arthur Grumiaux and Walter Klien, recorded digitally in the early 1980s. There is a great deal of sparkle and some refined musicianship in these performances, and pleasure remains undisturbed by the balance which, in the 1981 recordings, favours the violin. The later recordings, from 1982 and 1983, are much better in this respect.

Violin sonatas Nos. 1–16, K.6–15 & 26–31.

(B) *** Ph. Duo (IMS) 438 803-2 (2) [id.]. Gérard Poulet, Blandine Verlet.

These early *Violin sonatas* include the young Mozart's first works to appear in print. It seems impossible to determine how much there is of Mozart's father, Leopold, in their composition; certainly he masterminded the project (and the music of J. C. Bach was also a probable influence), but the precociously sprightly invention is consistently ear-catching and, even if the keyboard dominates the musical argument, the violinist is always making attractive comments. The performances here are most persuasive in their vitality and freshness, and they are very well balanced and recorded (in 1975). This set derives from Volume 15 of Philips's Complete Mozart Edition and is well worth having as a separate issue. There is much to delight and fascinate the ear, although these are records to dip into rather than to play all through!

Violin sonatas: in E flat, K.58 (attrib.); Nos. 21 in E min., K.304; 33 in E flat, K.481.

(B) * Sony Seon SBK 62953 [id.]. Sigiswald Kuijken, Gustav Leonhardt (fortepiano).

An apparently illustrious partnership, recorded in 1977, proves disappointing. From the opening of the early *E flat Sonata* (probably not by Mozart) Gustav Leonhardt's fortepiano contribution is rhythmically didactic and his precise articulation in the *Adagio* of K.481 is unappealing, although it better suits the closing *Theme and variations*. However, Sigiswald's baroque violin is given a thin, buzzy timbre by its forward placing, and altogether this is not very congenial.

Violin sonatas Nos. 17 in C, K.296; 18 in G, K.301; 19 in E flat, K.302; 20 in C, K.303; 21 in E min., K.304; 22 in A, K.305; 23 in D, K.306; 24 in F, K.376; 25 in F, K.377; 26 in B flat, K.378; 27 in G, K.379; 28 in E flat, K.380; 32 in B flat, K.454; 33 in E flat, K.481; 34 in A, K.526; Violin sonatina in F, K.547.

(B) *** Decca 448 526-2 (4) [(M) id. import]. Szymon Goldberg, Radu Lupu.

This was one of Radu Lupu's first recordings for Decca and he plays with uncommon freshness and insight, while Szymon Goldberg brings a wisdom, born of long experience, to these sonatas which is almost unfailingly revealing. Lupu gives instinctive musical support to his partner and both artists bring humanity and imagination to their performances. In short this is very distinguished and admirably fills an important gap in the catalogue. There is no better sampler than the third of the four discs, in which the delightful closing *Theme and variations* of the *A major Sonata*, K.305, shows the complete rapport shared by these artists, to be followed memorably by the ambitious opening *Adagio* of the *G major*, K.379, which sounds so like Beethoven. Another set of variations which completes this work is presented with disarming simplicity. The poised beauty of the *Andante* of the *E flat Sonata*, K.380, then leads to a winningly sparkling closing Rondo. The recordings were made in the Kingsway Hall in 1974 and were expertly balanced by Christopher Raeburn. They have been most naturally transferred to CD, and this Decca bargain box can be given the strongest recommendation.

Violin sonatas Nos. 17 in C, K.296; 18 in G, K.301; 19 in E flat, K.302; 20 in C, K.303; 21 in E min., K.304; 22 in A, K.305; 23 in D, K.306; 24 in F, K.376; 25 in F, K.377; 12 Variations in G on 'La bergère Célimène', K.359.

(B) *** Ph. Duo 462 185-2 (2) [id.]. Henryk Szering, Ingrid Haebler.

This is the first of two Duos (the second should arrive during the lifetime of this book) covering the major sonatas. Ingrid Haebler brings an admirable vitality and robustness to her part. Her playing has sparkle and great spontaneity. Szeryng's contribution is altogether masterly, and all these performances find both partners in complete rapport. The analogue recordings from the mid-1970s provide striking realism and truthfulness, and they have been transferred immaculately to CD. The *Variations* included in the set are managed with charm. The intimate atmosphere of these performances is particularly appealing.

Violin sonatas Nos. 17 in C, K.296; 24 in F, K.376; 26 in B flat, K.378.
(BB) ** Naxos Dig. 8.550065 [id.]. Takako Nishizaki, Wolf Harden.

Takako Nishizaki does not produce a big (or always a particularly beautiful) tone and at times she is covered by Wolf Harden's crisp accompaniment, which the engineer favours. All the same, she is a far from insensitive artist and her playing is always tasteful. However, this is not as good as some of her other records on this label. Wolf Harden is an excellent pianist and always supportive.

Clara Haskil: The Legacy, Volume 1: Chamber music

Violin sonatas Nos. 18; 21; 24; 26; 32; 34.
(M) (***) Ph. mono 442 625-2 (5) [id.]. Arthur Grumiaux, Clara Haskil – BEETHOVEN: *Violin sonatas Nos. 1-10.* (***)

Violin sonatas Nos. 18 in C, K.301; 21 in E min., K.304; 24 in F, K.376; 26 in B flat, K.378.
(M) (***) Ph. mono 442 629-2. Arthur Grumiaux, Clara Haskil.

Violin sonatas Nos. 32 in B flat, K.454; 34 in A, K.526.
(M) (***) Ph. mono 442 630-2. Arthur Grumiaux, Clara Haskil.

These six sonatas come – coupled with the complete *Violin sonatas* of Beethoven – as Volume One of Philips's so-called 'Clara Haskil Legacy'. This was a celebrated partnership and these classic accounts, which have excited much admiration over the years (and which doubtless will continue to do so), have been excellently transferred. The original mono recordings come from the late 1950s, yet the sound is remarkably vivid and true, and background noise has been virtually vanquished. The performances represent the musical yardstick by which all later versions were judged and are highly recommendable. The discs currently are not available separately.

ORGAN MUSIC

Andante in F, K.616; Adagio and allegro in F min., K.594; Fantasia in F min. (Adagio and Allegro), K.608 (all for musical clock); *Allegro in G (Veronese), K.72a; Gigue in G, K.574;* (i) *Epistle Sonatas: in F, K.244; in C, K.328.*
(M) ** Teldec/Warner 0630 17371-2. Herbert Tachezi (organ of Basilika Maria Treu, Vienna); (i) with Alice and Nicholas Harnoncourt and Walter Pfeiffer.

Mozart is never really thought of as a composer for the organ, but he loved its challenge and, whenever he travelled, always made a point of seeking out a local instrument. The problem for us was that he liked best of all to improvise and seldom wrote anything down. Until now, the only 'organ works' we have had on record have been the three pieces he wrote for Count Deym's mechanical organ attached to a clock. Mozart had no opinion of the mechanism for which his music was commissioned and is known to have wished the pieces were intended for a large instrument. To these Herbert Tachezi adds a brief *Allegro* and an attractive *Gigue*, plus two of the *Epistle sonatas*, in which he is joined by the Harnoncourt Trio. The performances overall are acceptable and well registered, but there is nothing distinctive about this record, although the sound is excellent. Readers interested in exploring Mozart's organ music will find a much fuller recital available on a splendid Decca full-priced CD (443 451-2), admirably played by Thomas Trotter on a Dutch organ and given demonstration sound-quality.

PIANO MUSIC

Complete works for piano

Piano duet:(i–ii) *Andante and variations, K.501; Sonatas, K.19d; K.381; K.357–8; K.497; K.521;* 2 Pianos: *Fugue, K.426; Sonata, K.448;* (iii) *Larghetto & Allegro in E flat* (reconstruction). Solo piano music: (i) *Sonatas Nos. 1–18;* (iv) *8 Variations in G, K.24; 7 Variations in D, K.25; 12 Variations in C, K.179; 6 Variations in G, K.180; 9 Variations in C, K.264; 12 Variations in C, K.265; 8 Variations in F, K.352; 12 Variations in E flat, K.353; 12 Variations in E flat, K.354; 6 Variations in F, K.398; 10 Variations in G, K.455; 12 Variations in B flat, K.500; 9 Variations in D, K.573; 8 Variations in F, K.613; Adagio in B min., K.540; Eine kleine Gigue in G, K.574; Fantasia in D min., K.397; Minuet in D, K.355; Rondos: in D, K.485; in A min., K.511; 21 Pieces for keyboard, K.1, K.1a–1d;1f; K.2–5; K.5a; K.33b; K.94; K.312; K.394–5; K.399–401; K.408/1; K.453a; K.460.*

(B) **(*) Ph. 456 132-2 (10) [(M) id. import]. (i) Ingrid Haebler; (ii) Ludwig Hoffmann; (iii) Jörg Demus and Paul Badura-Skoda; (iv) Ingrid Haebler (piano) or Ton Koopman (harpsichord).

Ingrid Haebler with the help of several other artists gives us a complete ten-disc survey of Mozart's keyboard music for two and four hands. She has the solo sonatas to herself and, above all, she gets the scale right. In this repertoire it is quite wrong, on the one hand, to inflate or romanticize; on the other, it is equally unfair to miniaturize them. Haebler's classical approach avoids both these pitfalls. There is sparkle and lightness in the allegros, but also real thoughtfulness – without rhythmic exaggerations in slow movements. The early sonatas are very successful. The intensity with which, for instance, she plays the opening *Adagio* of *No. 4 in E flat*, K.282, varying the tension with the mood of the material, is magical. The well-known later works in *D major*, K.311, *C major*, K.330, and *A major*, K 331, show a similar feeling for colour and atmosphere. The shorter pieces, too, bring some fine performances, notably the great *Fantasy in F minor* and the delightfully played *Rondo in A minor*. In the various sets of *Variations* Haebler again proves an intelligent and perceptive artist who characterizes with some subtlety. Ton Koopman then offers 21 short pieces, including some juvenilia which he despatches with some degree of brusqueness. However, he is not helped by the close balance of his harpsichord. The quality of the piano-sound, however, is very good indeed, beautiful and true in Philips's best analogue manner. The piano duet music is also available separately on a Philips Duo and is discussed below.

Piano duet

(i) *Andante with 5 variations, K.501; Fugue in C min., K.426; Sonatas for piano duet: in C, K.19d; D, K.381; G, K.357; B flat, K.358; F, K.497; C, K.521; Sonata in D for two pianos, K.448;* (ii) *Larghetto and Allegro in E flat* (reconstructed Badura-Skoda).
(M) ** Ph. 422 516-2 (2). (i) Haebler, Hoffman; (ii) Demus, Badura-Skoda.
(B) **(*) Ph. Duo 454 026-2 (2) [(M) id. import]. (i) Haebler, Hoffman; (ii) Demus, Badura-Skoda.

This two-CD set includes all the music Mozart composed for piano duet or two pianos, in elegant (if at times a little too dainty) performances by Ingrid Haebler and Ludwig Hoffman in recordings dating from the mid-1970s. Also included is a Mozart fragment, the *Larghetto and Allegro in E flat*, probably written in 1782–3 and completed by Paul Badura-Skoda, who recorded it in 1971 for the Amadeo label with Jörg Demus. Despite the occasional distant clink of Dresden china, all these performances give pleasure and are very decently recorded.

Sonatas for piano duet: in C, K.19d; in B flat, K.358; in G, K.357; in D, K.381; in D, K.448 (for 2 pianos); in F, K.497; in C, K.521.
(M) *** Teldec/Warner Dig. 0630 12335 (2). Güher and Süher Pekinel.

This excellent duo are in their element in Mozart. Their playing is full of life and spirit, yet their vigour never rides roughshod over Mozart. The *Andante* of K.381 is beautifully poised, while the *molto allegro* finale of its *D major* companion (for two pianos) is memorably bold, rhythmic and infectious. Excellent, modern, digital recording makes this a first recommendation for this repertoire, even if the documentation is totally inadequate.

Solo piano music

Piano sonatas Nos. 1–18 (complete).
(M) *** EMI CZS7 67294-2 (5). Daniel Barenboim.

Piano sonatas Nos. 1–18; Fantasia in C min., K.475.
❀ (M) *** Ph. Dig. 422 517-2 (5). Mitsuko Uchida.
(B) *** Decca 443 717-2 (5) [id.]. András Schiff (piano).
(M) ** Nimbus NI 1775 (6) [id.]. Marta Deyanova.

Piano sonatas Nos. 1–18; Sonatas in C, K.46d; in F, K.46e.
(B) *** DG 419 445-2 (5) [(M) id. import]. Christoph Eschenbach.

On Philips, Mitsuko Uchida's collection, with beautiful and naturally balanced digital recording made in the Henry Wood Hall, London, has now been reissued on 5 mid-priced CDs by omitting the shorter pieces, except for the *C minor Fantasia*. Miss Uchida's set of the Mozart *Sonatas* brings playing of consistently fine sense and sound musicianship. There is every indication that this will come to be regarded as a classic series to set alongside those of Gieseking and Walter Klien. Every phrase is beautifully placed, every detail registers, and the early *Sonatas* are as revealing as the late ones. The piano recording is completely realistic, slightly distanced in a believable ambience. This series is available in the USA on separate CDs.

Barenboim's distinguished set of the Mozart *Piano sonatas* is reissued not only at mid-price but now on five CDs instead of the original six. Barenboim, while keeping his playing well within scale in its crisp articulation, refuses to adopt the Dresden china approach to Mozart's *Sonatas*. Even the little *C major*, K.545, designed for a young player, has its element of toughness, minimizing its 'eighteenth-century drawing-room' associations. Though – with the exception of the two minor-key sonatas – these are relatively unambitious works, Barenboim's voyage of discovery brings out their consistent freshness, with the orchestral implications of some of the allegros strongly established. The recording, with a pleasant ambience round the piano sound, confirms the apt scale.

András Schiff's earlier, Decca recordings now also reappear, in a bargain box. Schiff, without exceeding the essential Mozartian sensibility, takes a somewhat more romantic and forward-looking view of the music. His fingerwork is precise yet mellow, and his sense of colour consistently excites admiration. He is slightly prone to self-indulgence in the handling of some phrases, but such is the inherent freshness and spontaneity of his playing that one accepts the idiosyncrasies as a natural product of live performance. The piano is set just a little further back than in the Philips/Uchida recordings, and the acoustic is marginally more open, which suits his slightly more expansive manner.

Christoph Eschenbach gives consistently well-turned, cool and elegant performances without affectation or mannerism. Those looking for an unidiosyncratic, direct approach to Mozart should find this poised, immaculate pianism to their taste. The famous *Andante grazioso* variations which form the first movement of the *Sonata in A*, K.331, are entirely characteristic, played very simply and directly. Other pianists are gentler, more romantic, but Eschenbach's taste cannot be faulted and the clean precision of the *Rondo alla Turca* finale is very impressive.

Marta Deyanova is an excellent Mozartian and she has her own distinct insights to offer in these sonatas: her style is crisp and clean, without artifice. There is an attractive sense of poise, as at the opening of the *F major*, K.289, while the *Adagio* of the same work is a fine demonstration of her thoughtful lyricism in slow movements, full of imaginative touches of light and shade, yet never precocious or out of style. But while we enjoyed these performances a great deal, the characteristically resonant recording which Nimbus seem to favour for their piano records slightly blurs the outlines of the playing, and the empty hall effect will not be to all tastes.

Piano sonatas Nos. 1 in C, K.279; 4 in E flat, K.282; 5 in G, K.283; 6 in D, K.284.
(BB) ** Naxos Dig. 8.550447 [id.]. Jenö Jandó.

Piano sonatas Nos. 3 in B flat, K.281; 7 in C, K.309; 11 in A, K.331; 17 in D, K.576.
(BB) ** Naxos Dig. 8.550448 [id.]. Jenö Jandó.

Piano sonatas Nos. 8 in A min., K.310; 10 in C, K.330; Allegro & Andante, K.533; Rondo, K.494.
(BB) ** Naxos Dig. 8.550445 [id.]. Jenö Jandó.

Piano sonatas Nos. 9 in D, K.311; 12 in F, K.332; 15 in C, K.545; 16 in B flat, K.570.
(BB) ** Naxos Dig. 8.550446 [id.]. Jenö Jandó.

Piano sonatas Nos. 11 in A, K.331; 14 in C min., K.457; Fantasia in C min., K.475; Variations on 'Ah, vous dirai-je, maman', K.265.
(BB) ** Naxos Dig. 8.550258 [id.]. Jenö Jandó.

Jenö Jandó again here proves himself a thoughtful and intelligent Mozartian and seeks a crisp, classical profile for the Mozart *Sonatas*. They are presented very directly, with brisk, strong allegros and slow movements played simply rather than invested with any deeper feelings. The recordings, made in Budapest Unitarian church, use close microphones to create a clean, bright piano image against the background resonance; however, this results in some ugliness in loud passages. Compared with artists like Ashkenazy and Brendel, these readings offer no added illumination, even if they are often delicate and always alert and sensitive.

Piano sonatas Nos. 2 in F, K.280; 4 in E flat, K.282; 14 in C min., K.457; Fantasia in C min., K.475.
(BB) ** Koch Discover Dig. DICD 920144 [id.]. Aldo Ciccolini.

Piano sonatas Nos. 3 in B flat, K.281; 12 in F, K.332; 13 in B flat, K.333.
(BB) ** Koch Discover Dig. DICD 920148 [id.]. Aldo Ciccolini.

Piano sonatas Nos. 7 in C, K.309; 10 in C, K.330; 16 in C, K.545.
(BB) ** Koch Discover Dig. DICD 920145 [id.]. Aldo Ciccolini.

Aldo Ciccolini's new digital survey of the Mozart *Sonatas* is strikingly well recorded: the presence of the piano is very tangible. However, the forwardness emphasizes the playing style, which is very strong, even percussive, in its directness of articulation. That is not to suggest a lack of sensibility, only that (for some ears) the effect may seem too forceful for this repertoire. When Ciccolini relaxes and plays lightly, he can readily charm the ear, but the fortissimos are very strongly accented indeed.

Piano sonatas Nos. 3 in B flat, K.281; 10 in C, K.330; 13 in B flat, K.333; Adagio in B min., K.540; Rondo in D, K.485.
(M) *** DG Dig. 445 517-2; *445 517-4* [431 274-2]. Vladimir Horowitz.

Playing of such strong personality from so great an artist is self-recommending. With Horowitz there were astonishingly few reminders of the passage of time and the artistry and magnetism remain undiminished. The recordings were made in the pianist's last vintage period, between 1985 and 1989, in either a New York studio, the pianist's home, or an Italian studio in Milan (K.333). As usual, the piano is tightly tuned and the sound is slightly shallow, though very suitable for Mozart. Remarkable playing, not always completely free from affectation; but for variety of articulation just sample the *Allegretto grazioso* finale of K.333 and, for simply expressed depth of feeling, the *Adagio*, K.540.

Piano sonatas Nos. 8 in A min., K.310; 11 in A, K.331; 13 in B flat, K.333; 14 in C min., K.457; Adagio in B min., K.540; Fantasia in C min., K.475; Rondo in A min., K.511; 9 Variations in D on a minuet by Dupont, K.573.
(B) **(*) Ph. Duo Analogue/Dig. 454 244-2 (2) [(M) id. import]. Alfred Brendel.

The recordings of the *A major Sonata*, K.331, and the *B flat*, K.333, come from 1971 and 1975 respectively and they show Brendel at his very finest, while (not to be forgotten) the *B minor Adagio* is also memorable. So thoughtful and illuminating are Brendel's insights in these works that, even if you possess other versions of them, this will uncover new areas of feeling. K.331, with its engaging opening theme and variations and justly famous *Alla turca* finale, is a joy. The analogue recording, too, is most realistic. However, the *A minor*, K.310, and the *C minor*, recorded digitally in the following decade, are more controversial. The pianism is masterly, as one would expect from this great artist, but both performances strike one as the product of excessive ratiocination. There is no want of inner life, the texture is wonderfully clean and finely balanced, but the listener is too aware of the mental preparation that has gone into it. The first movement of the *A minor* has immaculate control but is more than a little schoolmasterly, particularly in the development. The staccato markings in the slow movement are exaggerated and the movement as a whole is unsmiling and strangely wanting in repose. Brendel seems unwilling to seduce us by beauty of sound, and the result is self-conscious playing, immaculately recorded. Fortunately he is back on form in the *Fantasia in C minor*, the *Rondo* and the *Variations*.

Complete Mozart Edition, Volume 18: *8 Variations in G, K.24; 7 Variations in D, K.25; 12 Variations in C, K.179; 6 Variations in G, K.180; 9 Variations in C, K.264; 12 Variations in C, K.265; 8 Variations in F, K.352; 12 Variations in E flat, K.353; 12 Variations in E flat, K.354; 6 Variations in F, K.398; 10 Variations in G, K.455; 12 Variations in B flat, K.500; 9 Variations in D, K.573; 8 Variations in F, K.613; Adagio in B min., K.540; Eine kleine Gigue in G, K.574; Fantasia in D min., K.397; Minuet in D, K.355; Rondos: in D, K.485; in A min., K.511; 21 Pieces for keyboard, K.1, K.1a–1d;1f; K.2–5; K.5a; K.33b; K.94; K.312; K.394–5; K.399–401; K.408/1; K.453a; K.460.*
(M) ** Ph. Analogue/Dig. 422 518-2 (5) [id.]. Ingrid Haebler or Mitsuko Uchida (both piano), Ton Koopman (harpsichord).

Although the gentle clink of Dresden china can occasionally be heard, Ingrid Haebler is an intelligent and perceptive artist who characterizes these variations with some subtlety. The quality of the sound is very good indeed: there is both warmth and presence. Mitsuko Uchida gives us various short pieces, such as the *A minor Rondo*, K.511, and the *B minor Adagio*, K.540, which she plays beautifully – though at less than 40 minutes her disc offers rather short measure. However, Haebler and Koopman make up for that, the latter offering 21 short pieces, including some juvenilia, which he despatches with some degree of brusqueness. He is very brightly recorded.

VOCAL MUSIC

Complete Mozart Edition, Volume 20: (i) *Alma Dei creatoris, K.277;* (ii) *Ave verum corpus, K.618;* (i) *Benedictus sit Deus Pater, K.117; Cibavit eos ex adipe frumenti, K.44;* (iii) *Dixit et Magnificat, K.193;* (i) *Ergo interest, an quis, K.143;* (ii) *Exsultate, jubilate, K.165;* (i) *God is our refuge* (motet), *K.20; Inter natos Mulierum, K.72;* (iii) *Litaniae de BMV (Lauretanae), K.109 & K.195;* (i) *Kyries, K.33; K.90–91; K.322–3;* (ii) *Kyrie, K.341;* (iii) *Litaniae de venerabili altaris sacramento, K.125 & K.243;* (i) *Miserere mei, Deus, K.85; Misercordias Domini, K.222; Quaerite primum regnum Dei, K.86; Regina coeli, laetare, K.108; K.127; K.276; Sancta Maria, mater Dei, K.273; Scande coeli limina, K.34; Sub tuum praesidium,*

K.198; Te Deum laudamus, K.141; Veni, Sancte Spiritus, K.47; Venite, populi, venite, K.260; (ii) *Vesperae solennes de confessore, K.339;* (iii) *Vesperae solennes de Domenica, K.321.*

(M) *** Ph. 422 520-2 (5) [id.]. (i) Nawe, Reinhardt-Kiss, Schellenberger-Ernst, Selbig, Burmeister, Lang, Büchner, Eschrig, Ribbe, Pape, Polster; (ii) Te Kanawa, Bainbridge, Ryland Davies, Howell, London Symphony Ch. & LSO, Sir Colin Davis; (iii) Frank-Reinecke, Shirai, Burmeister, Riess, Büchner, Polster, (i; iii) Leipzig R. Ch. & SO, Kegel.

It is fascinating to find that the boy Mozart's very first religious piece is an unaccompanied motet, written in London to an English text, *God is our refuge* – which here the Leipzig singers very forgivably pronounce 'reefuge'. Herbert Kegel with the Dresden Staatskapelle and his Leipzig Radio Choir are responsible for the great majority of the pieces here, fresh and alert if on occasion rhythmically too rigid. The big exception is the great setting of the *Solemn vespers*, K.339, for which Sir Colin Davis's 1971 version has understandably been preferred, when the young Kiri Te Kanawa sings the heavenly soprano setting of *Laudate Dominum* so ravishingly. She is also the soloist in the early cantata *Exsultate, jubilate* with its brilliant *Alleluia*. Those 1971 recordings, made in London, are bass-heavy, but the rest brings very fresh and clean recording, with the choir generally more forwardly placed than in the recordings of Mozart's Masses, made by the same forces.

Complete Mozart Edition, Volume 22: (i) *Adagio and fugue in C min., K.546; Maurerische Trauermusik, K.477.* (ii) *La Betulia liberata* (oratorio), *K.118.* (iii) *Davidde penitente* (cantata), *K.469.* (iv) *Grabmusik (Funeral music), K.42.* (v; i) Masonic music: *Dir, Seele des Weltalls, K.429; Ihr unsre neuen Leiter, K.484; Die ihr unermesslichen Weltalls Schöpfer, ehrt, K.619; Lasst uns mit geschlung'gnen Händen, K.623; Laut verkünde unsre Freude, K.623; Lied zur Gesellenreise, K.468; Lobgesang auf die feierliche Johannisloge, K.148; Die Maurerfreude, K.471; Zerfliesset heut, geliebte Brüder, K.483.* (vi) *Passionslied: Kommet her, ihr frechen Sünder, K.146.* (vii) *Die Schuldigkeit des ersten Gebots* (Singspiel), K.35.

(M) **(*) Ph. Analogue/Dig. 422 522-2 (6) [id.]. (i) Dresden State O, Schreier; (ii) Schreier, Cotrubas, Berry, Fuchs, Zimmermann, Salzburg Chamber Ch. & Mozarteum O, Hagen; (iii) M. Marshall, Vermillion, Blochwitz; (iv) Murray, Varcoe; (v) Schreier, Blochwitz, Schmidt, Leipzig R. Ch.; (vi) Murray; (vii) M. Marshall, Murray, Nielsen, Blochwitz, Baldin; (iii; iv; vi; vii) Stuttgart RSO, Marriner.

The two big oratorios are both early works, *La Betulia liberata* and (even earlier, dating from his twelfth year) *Die Schuldigkeit des ersten Gebots* ('The Duty of the First Commandment'). *Davidde penitente* is the cantata largely derived from the torso of the *C minor Mass*, while the sixth disc, in many ways the most inspired of all, contains the Masonic music, vividly done in Dresden under the direction of Peter Schreier. For convenience that disc also includes the purely instrumental Masonic music, the *Maurerische Trauermusik* and the *Adagio and fugue in C minor*. Directed by Leopold Hager, *La Betulia liberata* is a plain, well-sung performance that does not quite disguise the piece's excessive length. Sir Neville Marriner is the conductor both of *Die Schuldigkeit* and of *Davidde penitente*, giving sparkle to the early oratorio and vigour to the cantata, a fine piece. Full texts are given, and informative notes on individual works.

Complete Mozart Edition, Volume 23: (i) *2 Canons for strings; 14 Canons for woodwind; 10 Interval canons for woodwind;* (ii) *6 Canons for female voices; 3 Canons for mixed voices; 13 Canons for male voices; 4 puzzle canons for mixed voices.* (iii) *53 Concert arias. Aria* (with ornamentation by Mozart) for: J. C. BACH: *Adriano in Siria.* (iv) *8 Vocal Duets, Trios and Quartets.* (v) Alternative arias and duets for: *Così fan tutte; Don Giovanni; Die Entführung aus dem Serail; La finta semplice; Idomeneo; Lucio Silla; Mitridate; Le nozze di Figaro.*

(M) *** Ph. 422 523-2 (8) [id.]. (i) Bav. RSO (members); (ii) Ch. Viennensis, Mancusi or Harrer; (iii) Moser, Schwarz, Popp, Mathis, Gruberová, Sukis, Araiza, Ahnsjö, Lloyd, Berry, Kaufmann, Blochwitz, Lind, Burrows, Eda-Pierre; (iv) Blochwitz, Schariner, Pape, Kaufmann, Lind, Jansen, Schreier; (v) Blochwitz, Szmytka, Wiens, Gudbjörnson, Vermillion, Schreier, Mathis, Burrows, Tear, Terfel, Kaufmann, Lind, Scharinger.

This Philips set offers not just a collection of a dozen or so ensembles and a whole disc of 35 canons (some of them instrumental) but also some fascinating alternative versions and substitute arias for different Mozart operas, from *La finta semplice* and *Mitridate* through to the three Da Ponte masterpieces. It is fascinating to have Bryn Terfel, for example, as Figaro in a varied recitative and slightly extended version of the Act I aria, *Non piu' andrai*. Eva Lind is vocally a less happy choice for the items involving Susanna and Zerlina, and generally the sopranos chosen for this collection, stylish Mozartians as they are, have less sumptuous voices than those on the Decca set.

Complete Mozart Edition, Volume 24: (i) Lieder: *Abendempfindung; Als Luise die Briefe ihres ungetreuen Liebhabers; Die Alte; An Chloë; An die Freude; An die Freundschaft; Die betrogene Welt; Dans un bois solitaire; Geheime Liebe; Der Frühling; Gessellenreise; Die grossmütige Gelassenheit; Ich würd' auf meinem Pfad; Das Kinderspiel; 2 Kirchenlieder (O Gottes Lamm; Als aus Agypten); Des kleinen Friedrichs Geburtstag; Die kleine Spinnerin; Komm, liebe Zither, komm; Lied der Freiheit; Das Lied der Trennung; Un moto di gioia; Oiseaux, si tous les ans; Ridente la calma; Sehnsucht nach dem Frühling; Sei du mein Trost; Das Traumbild; Das Veilchen; Verdankt sei es dem Glanz der Grossen; Die Verschweigung; Warnung; Wie unglücklich bin ich nit; Der Zauberer; Die Zufriedenheit (2): (Was frag' ich viel nach Geld und Gut; Wie sanft, wie ruhig fühl' ich hier); Die Zufriedenheit im niedrigen Stande.* (ii) *6 Notturni for voices and woodwind, K.346; K.436/9 & K.549.*

(M) *** Ph. 422 524-2 (2) [id.]. Elly Ameling, (i) with Dalton Baldwin (piano or organ) or Benny Ludemann (mandolin); (ii) with Elisabeth Cooymans, Peter van der Bilt, Netherlands Wind Ens. (members).

Elly Ameling is the ideal soprano for such fresh and generally innocent inspirations, with her voice at its purest and sweetest when she made the recordings in 1977. In the 1973 recordings of the *Notturni* (setting Italian texts by Metastasio) she is well matched by her soprano and baritone partners, though these are mostly plainer, less distinctive miniatures. Included are two hymns with organ and two tiny songs with mandolin, while aptly the very last of the series, K.598, is one of the lightest of all, *Children's games*, sparklingly done. The recordings come up with fine freshness and presence.

51 Concert arias.

(B) *** Decca 455 241-2 (5) [id.]. Kiri Te Kanawa, Edita Gruberová, Teresa Berganza, Krisztina Laki, Elfrieda Hobarth, Gösta Winbergh; VCO, György Fischer; or LSO, John Pritchard; Dietrich Fischer-Dieskau, V. Haydn O, Reinhard Peters; Fernando Corena, ROHCG, Argeo Quadri.

This very comprehensive coverage is based on a five-LP Decca set of the complete concert arias for female voice, published in 1981, to which those for male voice have subsequently been added. The use of the Kingsway Hall or Vienna Sofiensaal has ensured full, spacious recording. Originally each of five female artists was given a record apiece, which means that the order of items is arbitrary. Berganza's collection includes the most demanding soprano aria of all, *Ch'io me scordi di te*, recorded (with Pritchard and the LSO) a decade earlier than the rest. Te Kanawa opens the programme, and her items range from one of the very earliest arias, *Oh temerario Arbace!*, already memorably lyrical, to the late *Vado ma dove?*. Gruberová's contribution is hardly less brilliant and charming, her singing full of sparkle and character, and superbly articulated. The others, Elfrieda Hobarth and Krisztina Laki, are less individual personalities but do not disappoint vocally. Laki immediately displays a delightfully fresh voice with a true, clear upper range and impressive coloratura in her opening aria, the little-known *Fra cento affanni*, K.88, and she is equally impressive in the lyrical flow of *Non curo l'affetto*, which again demands comparable bravura. Elfrieda Hobarth's style is more operatic and she becomes a veritable Queen of the Night in tackling the fearsome upper tessitura of *Ma che vi fece, o stelle*, K.368, and *Mia speranza adorata!*, K.416, both of which are accomplished with confident bravado. If she displays less in the way of seductive charm, this is still remarkably well-focused singing.

The digital recordings by Gösta Winbergh, an exceptionally stylish Mozart tenor, were added later; he rises splendidly to the challenges of such splendid arias as *Per pietà non ricercate*, K.420, and *Aura che intorno spiri*, K.431, using his clean, heady tenor very effectively if without the final degree of personal charisma. Throughout the series György Fischer's conducting is lively and responsive but is sometimes lacking in detail. Fischer-Dieskau's contribution was a separate undertaking, recorded in 1969, and it includes a beautiful aria from 1787, *Mentre ti lascio*, which reveals Mozart's inspiration at its keenest. The other items too bring their delights. Fischer-Dieskau sings most intelligently, if with some pointing of word and phrase that is not quite in character with the music. Fernando Corena's three contributions were among the first of any Mozart arias to be recorded in stereo, in 1960. In *Alcandro, lo confesso . . . Non so d'onde viene*, K.512, and *Per questa bella mano*, K.612 (which includes a virtuoso double bass solo in the orchestra), he is less than ideally stylish and in the latter not always absolutely secure in intonation. Admittedly, some of the florid passages are fiendishly difficult for a bass to cope with but, when strained, Corena has a tendency to slide between the notes to ungainly effect. Yet he is at his very finest in the *buffo* aria, *Rivolcete a lui lo sguardo*, K.584, originally written for *Così fan tutte* and later cut because of its length. It is a superb piece which Alfred Einstein called 'the most remarkable *buffo* aria ever written', and it suits Corena's voice well, so that the full power is brought out magnificently. The CD transfers throughout are of high quality, and full translations are included, but the accompanying essay by Kenneth Chalmers documents the music only sketchily, because of limited space.

Concert arias: *Ah! lo previdi . . . Ah, t'invola, K.272; Alma grande e nobil core, K.578; A questo seno . . . Or che il cielo, K.374; Bella mia fiamma . . . Resta, o cara, K.528; Betracht dies Herz und frage mich, K.42; Misera, dove son! . . . Ah! non son io che parlo, K.369; Vado, ma dove? o Dei!, K.583.*
(M) *** DG 449 723-2 [id.]. Gundula Janowitz, VSO, Wilfried Boettcher.

In 1966 when this recording was made (in the Grosser Saal of the Vienna Musikverein) Gundula Janowitz's voice combined a glorious tonal beauty with a surprising degree of flexibility so that Mozart's cruelly difficult divisions – usually written deliberately to tax the original ladies involved – present no apparent difficulty. Janowitz is helped by a flattering, reverberant acoustic, but there is no mistaking the singer's ability to shade and refine the tone at will. An excellent collection of delightful concert arias that are too often neglected nowadays, thanks to the vagaries of modern concert-planning.

Concert arias: *Ah! lo previdi . . . Ah t'invola, K.272; Bella mia fiamma . . . Resta oh cara, K.528; Chi sa, K.582; Nehmt meinen Dank, ihr holden Gönner, K.383; Non più, tutto ascolta . . . Non temer, amato bene, K.490; Oh temerario Arbace! . . . Per quel paterno amplesso, K.79/K.73d; Vado, ma dove?, K.583.* Opera arias: (ii) *Le nozze di Figaro: Porgi amor; E Susanna non vien! . . . Dove sono.* (iii) *Der Schauspieldirektor: Bester Jüngling!*
(M) *** Decca 440 401-2 [id.]. Kiri Te Kanawa: (i) VCO, György Fischer; (ii) LPO, Solti; (iii) VPO, Pritchard.

Kiri Te Kanawa's Decca set of Mozart's concert arias for soprano, recorded in 1982, makes a beautiful and often brilliant recital. Items range from one of the very earliest arias, *Oh temerario Arbace*, already memorably lyrical, to the late *Vado, ma dove*, here sung for its beauty rather than for its drama. Atmospheric, wide-ranging recording, which has transferred well to CD. The arias from *Figaro* and *Schauspieldirektor* come from the complete Decca sets and show the singer at her finest.

Concert arias: *Alma grande e nobil core, K.578; Ch'io mi scordi di te?, K.505; Nehmt meinen Dank, K.383; Vado, ma dove?, K.583.* Lieder: *Abendempfindung; Als Luise die Briefe; Die Alte; An Chloë; Dans un bois solitaire; Im Frühlingsanfang; Das Kinderspiel; Die kleine Spinnerin; Das Lied der Trennung; Oiseaux, si tous les ans; Ridente la calma; Sehnsucht nach dem Frühling; Das Trumbild; Das Veilchen; Der Zauberer; Die Zuhfriedenheit.*
(M) *** EMI mono/stereo CDH7 63702-2 [id.]. Schwarzkopf, Gieseking; Brendel; LSO, Szell.

Schwarzkopf's classic series of the Mozart songs with Gieseking makes a splendid reissue at mid-price; it includes the most famous one, *Das Veilchen*. As a generous coupling, the disc also includes Schwarzkopf's much later recordings, with Szell conducting four concert arias – including the most taxing of all, *Ch'io mi scordi di te?*, with Brendel playing the piano obbligato. Though the voice is not quite so fresh in the concert arias, the artistry and imagination are supreme, and stereo recording helps to add bloom.

Arias: *Artaserse: Per pietà, bell'idol mio. Il barbiere di Siviglia: Schon lacht der holde Frühling* (arr. BEYER). *Demofoonte: Se tutti i mali miei. Didone abbandonata: Basta, vincesti . . . Ah, non lasciarmi. I due baroni di Rocca Azzura: Alma grande e nobil core. A questo seno deh vieni . . . Or che il cielo a me ti rende. Ezio: Misera, dove son? . . . Ah! non son io che parlo. Le nozze di Dorina: Voi avete un cor fedele. Le nozze di Figaro: Un moto di gioia.* Arias from: *Der Schauspieldirektor; Die Entführung aus dem Serail.*
(M) *** Decca Analogue/Dig. 448 249-2 [id.]. Edita Gruberová, VCO, Fischer.

This collection comes from a box, covering all the Mozart arias and concert arias for soprano, which first appeared at the beginning of the 1980s (see above). It brings brilliant and charming performances from Gruberová. Among the other rare items it includes an alternative aria for Susanna in *Figaro*, *Un moto di gioia*. The excerpts from *Der Schauspieldirektor* and *Die Entführung* come from much later but are also impressively sung.

Concert arias: *Bella mia fiamma . . . Resta, o cara!, K.528; Ch'io mi scordi di te?, K.505.* Arias: *Don Giovanni: Or sai chi l'onore; Crudele! Ah, no, mio bene; Non mi dir. Idomeneo: Se il padre perdei; O smania! . . . D'Oreste e d'Ajace. Le nozze di Figaro: Porgi, amor; Deh vieni non tardar; E Susanna non vien! . . . Dove sono. Il rè pastore: L'amerò, sarò costante. Die Zauberflöte: Ach, ich fühl's.*
(M) *** RCA 09026 61357-2 [id.]. Leontyne Price, New Philh. O, Adler or Santi; RCA Italiana Op. O, Molinari-Pradelli; LSO, Downes.

This record is an adjunct to Leontyne Price's four-disc miscellaneous 'Prima donna' collection (see Recitals, below) and the items here make an equally outstanding representation of her art. One does not think of her primarily as a Mozartian, yet the very opening concert aria, *Ch'io mi scordi*, shows the extra dimension of drama in her vocal personality, never at the expense of the vocal line. She is thrilling as Electra and *Or sai chi l'onore* (*Don Giovanni*) is scarcely less vehement. The glorious legato line is heard at its most ravishing in the major *Figaro* arias, whether as Susanna (*Deh vieni*) or the Countess (*Dove sono*), and the excerpt from *Il rè pastore, L'amerò, sarò costante*, with its weaving violin obbligato, is radiant. Nearly all these recordings were made in the late 1960s, when the voice was at its freshest. Accompaniments are highly sympathetic and the vocal quality is most natural and vivid, and with lovely orchestral sound.

Concert arias: *Il burbero di buon cuore: Chi sà. Vado, ma dove, K.583. Exsultate, jubilate, K.165.* Arias: *La clemenza di Tito: Parto, parto. Idomeneo: Ch'io mi scordi . . . Non temer, amato bene. Le nozze di Figaro: Al desio di chi t'adore; Un moto di gioia mi sento.*
(M) *** Erato/Warner Dig. 4509 98497-2 [id.]. Dame Janet Baker, Scottish CO, Leppard.

In a Mozart programme, recorded in 1984, which extends well beyond the normal mezzo-soprano repertoire, Dame Janet sings with all her usual warmth, intensity and stylishness, hardly if at all stretched by often high tessitura. The biggest challenge is the most taxing of all Mozart's concert arias, *Ch'io mi scordi di te?*, with Leppard a brilliant exponent of the difficult obbligato part. There Baker, so far from being daunted by the technical problems, uses them to intensify her detailed rendering of words. The two *Figaro* items are alternative arias for Susanna, both of them delightful. Sesto's aria from *Clemenza di Tito* presents another challenge, magnificently taken, as does the early cantata, *Exsultate, jubilate*, with its famous *Alleluia*. The other two arias were written for Louise Villeneuve – Dorabella to be – as an enrichment of her part in an opera by Soler, more delightful rarities. Excellent sound with wonderful presence, and warmly sympathetic accompaniment.

(i–ii) *Ave verum corpus, K.618;* (iii–iv) *Exsultate, jubilate, K.165; Masses Nos.* (i–iii; v) *10 in C (Missa brevis): Spatzenmesse, K.220;* (ii–iii; vi) *16 in C (Coronation), K.317.*
(M) *** DG 419 060-2 [429 820-2]. (i) Regensburg Cathedral Ch.; (ii) Bav. RSO, Kubelik; (iii) Edith Mathis; (iv) Dresden State O, Klee; (v) Troyanos, Laubenthal, Engen; (vi) Procter, Grobe, Shirley-Quirk, Bav. R. Ch.

Kubelik draws a fine, vivid performance of the *Coronation Mass* from his Bavarian forces and is no less impressive in the earlier *Missa brevis*, with excellent soloists in both works. Then Edith Mathis gives a first-class account of the *Exsultate, jubilate* as an encore. The concert ends with Bernard Klee directing a serenely gentle account of the *Ave verum corpus* (recorded in 1979).

(i) *Ave verum corpus, K.618;* (ii) *Exsultate, jubilate, K.165;* (i–iii) *Masses Nos. 10 in C (Spatzenmesse; 'Sparrow Mass');* (iv) *16 in C (Coronation), K.317;* (i) *Offertorium de tempore (Misericordias Domine), K.222;* (iv) *Vesperae de Domenica, K.321;* (i–iii) *Vesperae solennes de confessore, K.339.*
(B) **(*) Erato/Warner Duo 4509 95362-2 (2). (i) Philippe Caillard Chorale; (ii) Rotraud Hansmann; (iii) Annie Bartelloni, Michel Sénéchal, Roger Soyer; V. Bar. Ens.; (iv) Patricia Wise, Monika Bürgener, Michael Cousins, Heinz Ecker, Lisbon Gulbenkian Foundation Ch. & O; all cond. Guschlbauer.

A splendid Erato Bonsai Duo collection of Mozart church music that is much more than the sum of its parts. Throughout, Theodor Guschlbauer knows just where he is going and his pacing always feels right. The choral contributions, whether of the Lisbon Chorus or the smaller, Philippe Caillard group, have both discipline and commitment: these singers really rise to the occasion. The performance of the *Spatzenmesse* is particularly attractive. It is full of high spirits and is a remarkably concise piece (the *Kyrie* lasts only 1 minute 44 seconds and the *Sanctus* is a burst of joy merely 57 seconds long). The *Benedictus* provides a fine ensemble for the solo team. Before that, we have heard the excellent soprano soloist, Rotraud Hansmann, showing her mettle in the *Exsultate, jubilate*, where the famous *Alleluia* sparkles, and she is no less impressive in the more demanding and equally well-known *Laudate Dominum* of the *Solemn Vespers*, which she sings with serene radiance. In the *Laudate Dominum* of the *Vesperae de Domenica*, Patricia Wise is not her match. This is a more florid piece, much more difficult technically; it is well enough managed, but one feels that the singer is under pressure. But she leads the solo team confidently in the *Bendictus* of the *Coronation Mass*, another very lively performance, and seems altogether more at ease in the final *Agnus Dei*, where she is joined at the end by her colleagues; then the chorus closes the work vigorously in a glorious culmination, very operatic in feeling. These reservations are of minor account: all this music is greatly enjoyable, and the analogue recordings, all from the late 1960s (except K.317 and K.321, which are a decade later), are of good quality and excellently transferred. This is well worth exploring – but be warned: no documentation is provided about the music except for the cued list of tracks.

(i) *Ave verum corpus, K.618;* (ii) *Vesperae solennes de confessore, K.339.*
(M) *(*) EMI Dig./Analogue CMS5 66332-2 (2). (i) Swedish R. Ch., Stockholm Chamber Ch., BPO, Muti; (ii) Moser, Hamari, Gedda, Fischer-Dieskau, Bav. R. Ch., Bav. RSO, Jochum – HAYDN: *Heiligmesse; Nelson Mass; Theresienmesse.* **

Muti's account of the *Ave verum corpus* with the combined Swedish choirs, digitally recorded, is very acceptable; but the lack of clarity of choral focus in Jochum's 1977 analogue recording of the *Vespers* puts it out of court. Moreover the fruity-toned Edda Moser is hardly the right choice for the heavenly *Laudate Dominum*. Gedda too is below form. The coupled Haydn Masses are more successful, but overall this is not a set to recommend with any confidence.

(i) *Exsultate, jubilate, K.165;* (ii) *Litaniae Lauretanae in D, K.195; Mass No. 16 (Coronation), K.317;* (iii) *Requiem mass (No. 19) in D min., K.626.*

(B) **(*) Double Decca 443 009-2 (2) [id.]. (i) Erna Spoorenberg; (ii; iii) Cotrubas, Watts, Tear, Shirley-Quirk; (ii) Oxford Schola Cantorum; (iii) ASMF Ch; (i–iii), ASMF, Marriner.

It is good to have Marriner's 1971 (Argo) recordings of two of Mozart's most appealing early choral works, the *Litaniae Lauretanae* and the *Coronation Mass*, back in the catalogue on this Double Decca set. The solo work is particularly good (notably Ileana Cotrubas in the two lovely *Agnus Dei* versions) and the Academy Choir is on its best form. Erna Spoorenberg's impressive *Exsultate, jubilate* was recorded earlier (1966). However, Marriner generates less electricity than usual in the coupled (1977) *Requiem Mass*. It is interesting to have a version which uses the Beyer Edition and a text which aims at removing the faults of Süssmeyer's completion. Solo singing is good, and some of the choruses (the *Dies irae*, for instance) are vibrant, but at other times they are less alert and the tension slackens. The sound is excellent, well balanced and vivid.

Masonic music (see also above, in Complete Mozart Edition, Volume 22)

Masonic music: *Masonic funeral music (Maurerische Trauermusik), K.477; Die ihr des unermesslichen Weltals Schöpfer ehrt* (cantata), *K.619; Die ihr einen neuen Grade, K.468; Dir, Seele des Weltalls* (cantata), *K.429; Ihr unsre neuen Leiter* (song), *K.484; Lasst uns mit geschlungnen Händen, K.623a; Laut verkünde unsre Freude, K.623; O heiliges Band* (song), *K.148; Sehen, wie dem starren Forscherange, K.471; Zerfliesset heut', geliebte Brüder, K.483.*

(M) *** Decca 425 722-2. Werner Krenn, Tom Krause, Edinburgh Festival Ch., LSO, Kertész.

This Decca reissue contains the more important of Mozart's Masonic music in first-class performances, admirably recorded. Most striking of all is Kertész's strongly dramatic account of the *Masonic funeral music*; the two lively songs for chorus, *Zerfliesset heut'* and *Ihr unsre neuen Leiter*, are sung with warm humanity and are also memorable. Indeed the choral contribution is most distinguished throughout, and Werner Krenn's light tenor is most appealing in the other items which he usually dominates.

Complete Mozart Edition, Volume 19: *Masses Nos. 1 in G (Missa brevis), K.49; 2 in D min. (Missa brevis), K.65; 3 in C ('Dominicus'), K.66; 4 in C min. (Weisenhaus), K.139; 5 in G (Pastoral), K.140; 6 in F (Missa brevis), K.192; 7 in C (Missa in honorem Ssmae Trinitatis), K.167; 9 in D (Missa brevis), K.194; 10 in C (Spatzenmesse; 'Sparrow Mass'), K.220; 11 in C ('Credo'), K.257; 12 in C (Spaur-Messe), K.258; 13 in C ('Organ solo'), K.259; 14 in C (Missa longa), K.262; 15 in B flat (Missa brevis), K.275; 16 in C ('Coronation'), K.317; 17 in C (Missa solemnis), K.337; 18 in C min. (Great), K.427; 19 in D min. (Requiem), K.626.*

(M) **(*) Ph. Analogue/Dig. 422 519-2 (9) [id.]. Mathis, Donath, M. Price, McNair, Montague, Shirai, Casapietra, Trudeliese Schmidt, Lang, Schiml, Markert, Burmeister, Knight, Schreier, Araiza, Heilmann, Baldin, Ryland Davies, Rolfe Johnson, Ude, Jelosits, Adam, Polster, Andreas Schmidt, Hauptmann, Rootering, Grant, Eder; Leipzig R. Ch.; Monteverdi Ch.; V. Boys' Ch.; John Alldis Ch.; Ch. Viennensis; Leipzig RSO; E. Bar. Soloists; Dresden State O; LSO; VSO; Dresden PO; Kegel; C. Davis; Gardiner; Schreier; Harrer.

Only the *C minor Mass* has period performers. John Eliot Gardiner's inspired reading, with superb soloists as well as his Monteverdi Choir and English Baroque Soloists, has rightly been chosen, and the *Requiem* comes in another outstanding modern version, with the Dresden Staatskapelle and Leipzig Radio Choir conducted by Peter Schreier, as imaginative a conductor as he is a tenor. That same choir and orchestra under the choir's regular conductor, Herbert Kegel, is responsible for the great bulk of the rest of the Masses. With the chorus tending to be placed a little backwardly, it does not always sound its freshest, but performances – with consistently clean-toned soloists, including latterly Mitsuko Shirai – are bright and well sprung. Sir Colin Davis and the LSO in the earliest recording here, dating from 1971, take a weightier view than any in the *Credo Mass*, K.257, with sound bass-heavy, but again his vigour and freshness are very compelling. Two favourite Masses, the *Coronation Mass* and the *Spatzenmesse* (Sparrow Mass), come in performances conducted by Uwe Christian Harrer with the Vienna Symphony Orchestra and the Vienna Boys' Choir; boys also distinctively take the soprano and alto solos. Though Harrer's speeds tend to be slow, the rhythmic buoyancy is most compelling, with choral sound full and forward.

Mass No. 4 in C min. (Weisenhausmesse), K.139.
(M) *** DG (IMS) 427 255-2. Janowitz, Von Stade, Moll, Ochman, V. State Op. Ch., VPO, Abbado.

By any standards this is a remarkably sustained example of the thirteen-year-old composer's powers, with bustling allegros in the *Kyrie*, *Gloria* and *Credo*, as well as at the end of the *Agnus Dei*, while the *Gloria* and *Credo* end with full-scale fugues. This far from negligible piece sounds at its very best in Abbado's persuasive hands.

Masses Nos: (i–ii) *4 in C min. (Weisenhaus), K.139;* (iii) *7 in C (Missa in honorem Ssmae Trinitas), K.167;* (i–ii) *11 in C (Credo), K.257; 257;* (ii; iv) *16 in C (Coronation), K.317; 17 in C (Missa solemnis), K.337.*
(B) **(*) Decca Double 455 032-2 (2) [(M) id. import]. (i) Susanne Mentzer, Bernadette Manca di Nissa, Neil Mackie, Stephen Roberts; (ii) King's College, Cambridge, Ch., ECO, Cleobury; (iii) V. State Op. Ch., VPO, Münchinger; (iv) with Margaret Marshall, Ann Murray, Rogers Covey-Crump, David Wilson-Johnson.

Mozart's early *C minor Mass* was composed for the dedication of a new orphanage church, the Waiserhausekirche am Rennweg, in 1768, and it is notable both for its rich choral writing and for the fine *Benedictus*, a dialogue between soprano and chorus. The tenor's *Agnus Dei* is then sonorously introduced by a trombone chorale, and all the soloists then join the chorus, with the trumpets entering resplendently for the *Amen*. It is presented here most effectively by Cleobury and his team. The *Missa Trinitas*, written in Salzburg five years later, is even more ambitious, using a big orchestra with copious brass (four trumpets and three trombones) as well as oboe, strings and organ. Münchinger offers a strong, direct account, but the disappointment of this 1974 recording, made in the Sofiensaal, is how little is made of the trumpets which, even in the *Credo*, are backwardly balanced. However, one does not want to make too much of this, for the choral singing is admirably fresh and beautifully recorded, and the overall balance with the orchestra is well judged. The other recordings are digital and were made a decade later. Stephen Cleobury, inheritor of the King's choral tradition in the 1980s, is perhaps at his finest in the *Credo Mass* and, with the help of his excellent soloists, gives a vividly exuberant performance of a work that shows its composer at his most sunnily high-spirited throughout. The *Missa solemnis in C major*, K.337, was the very last of the 15 settings that Mozart wrote for Salzburg, another work that is just as inspired as the better-known *Coronation Mass* (they were written for the Easter celebrations of 1779 and 1780), and with a similar anticipation of the Countess's music for *Figaro* in the *Agnes Dei* (reminding us of *Dove sono* in K.317, of *Porgi amor* in K.337). Though Cleobury's direction here could be rhythmically more lively, both performances are of high quality, with excellent soloists and fresh choral singing.

Mass No. 16 in C (Coronation), K.317.
(M) **(*) DG Dig. 445 543-2 (2) [id.]. Battle, Schmidt, Winbergh, Furlanetto, V. Singverein, VPO, Karajan – BEETHOVEN: *Missa solemnis*.**(*)
(B) **(*) DG Double 453 016-2 (2) Tomowa-Sintow, Baltsa, Krenn, Van Dam, V. Singverein, BPO, Karajan – BEETHOVEN: *Missa solemnis*. ***

Karajan's 1985 recording of Mozart's *Coronation Mass* is certainly vibrant, with fine choral singing and good soloists. Kathleen Battle sings beautifully in the *Agnus Dei*, and the recording is bright, if not ideally expansive.

Karajan's earlier, 1976 recording of the *Coronation Mass* is a dramatic reading, lacking something in rhythmic resilience perhaps; but, with excellent solo singing as well as an incisive contribution from the chorus, there is no lack of strength and the score's lyrical elements are sensitively managed. The current remastering has further improved the sound.

Masses Nos. (i; ii) *16 in C (Coronation), K.317;* (i; iii) *18 in C min. (Great), K.427;* (i; iv) *Requiem Mass, K.626.*
(B) **(*) Ph. Duo 438 800-2 (2) [id.]. (i) Helen Donath, Ryland Davies; (ii) Gillian Knight, Stafford Dean; John Alldis Ch., LSO; (iii) Heather Harper, Stafford Dean, L. Symphony Ch., LSO; (iv) Yvonne Minton, Gerd Nienstedt, Alldis Ch., BBC SO; Sir Colin Davis.

These very successful CD transfers demonstrate the best features of the original recordings, which date from between 1967 and 1971. Sir Colin Davis's vital account of the *Coronation Mass* is given with a fine team of soloists; and in the so-called *'Great' Mass in C minor* the use of the Robbins Landon edition – which rejects the accretions formerly used to turn this incomplete torso of a work into a full setting of the liturgy – prompts him to a strong and intense performance which brings out the darkness behind Mozart's use of the C minor key. Again he is helped by fine soprano singing from Helen Donath, and from Heather Harper too. The *Requiem*, with a smaller choir, is more intimate and the soloists are more variable, yet with his natural sense of style Davis finds much beauty of detail. While the scale is authentic and the BBC orchestra is in good form, this reading, enjoyable as it is, does not provide the sort of bite with which a performance on this scale should compensate for sheer massiveness of tone. These recordings are also available separately: Nos. 16 and 19 (462 056-2); No. 18 plus the *Exsultate, jubilate* (462 058-2).

Masses Nos. 16 in C (Coronation), K.317; 17 in C (Missa solemnis), K.337; (i) *Epistle sonatas Nos. 16, K.329; 17, K.336.*

(M) **(*) Virgin Veritas/EMI Dig. VER5 61244-2. Patrizia Kwella, Ulla Groenwold, Christoph Prégardien, Franz-Josef Selig, Cologne Chamber Ch., Coll. Cartusianum, Peter Neumann.

Peter Neumann directs a most enjoyably spirited account of the *Coronation Mass* and couples it with the much rarer *Missa solemnis*, K.336, which is on a similar scale and which is also very well sung. The singers, a well-blended team, are balanced somewhat backwardly within an ecclesiastical acoustic, which takes off a little of the bite from the chorus too, but the effect remains vivid. Hogwood's version of the *Coronation Mass* (paired with the *Vespers*) is even finer, and he has Emma Kirkby as a radiant soprano soloist (O-L 436 585-2). But that is at full price, and Patrizia Kwella makes fine solo contributions to both the Virgin performances.

(i) *Mass No. 18 in C min., K.427;* (ii) *Vesperae solennes de confessore, K.339.*

(M) ** Ph. 446 197-2. (i) Marshall, Palmer, Rolfe Johnson, Howell, ASMF & Ch., Marriner; (ii) Burmeister, Büchner, Polster, Leipzig R. Ch. & SO, Kegel.

In the *C minor Mass* Marriner secures a good response from his artists in a well-thought-out and conscientious reading, and there is some fine singing. But this performance falls short of being really inspired and does not quite communicate the sense of stature that this music calls for. Similarly the Leipzig Radio Chorus sings impressively under Kegel and the soloists are good, but in the last resort this performance lacks the kind of compulsive individuality to make it memorable.

Requiem Mass (No. 19) in D min., K.626.

(M) *** Virgin/EMI Dig. CUV5 61260-2 [id.]. Yvonne Kenny, Alfreda Hodgson, Arthur Davies, Gwynne Howell, N. Sinfonia Ch., London Symphony Ch., N. Sinfonia, Richard Hickox.

(BB) *** RCA Navigator 74321 29238-2 [RCA Papillon 6535-2-RG]. Equiluz, Eder, Vienna Boys' Ch., V. State Op. Ch. & O, Gillesberger – HAYDN: *Te Deum.* ***

(B) **(*) [EMI Red Line CDR5 69867]. Donath, Ludwig, Tear, Lloyd, Philh. Ch. & O, Giulini.

(B) **(*) Ph. Virtuoso 420 353-2 [id.]. Donath, Minton, Ryland Davies, Nienstedt, John Alldis Ch., BBC SO, Sir Colin Davis.

(BB) *(*) Naxos Dig. 8.550235 [id.]. Hajóssyova, Horská, Kundlák, Mikuláš, Slovak PO & Ch., Košler.

Richard Hickox's excellent version of the *Requiem Mass* on the Virgin Ultraviolet label matches any in the catalogue. With generally brisk speeds and light, resilient rhythms, it combines gravity with authentically clean, transparent textures in which the dark colourings of the orchestration, as with the basset horns, come out vividly. All four soloists are outstandingly fine, and the choral singing is fresh and incisive, with crisp attack. The voices, solo and choral, are placed rather backwardly; otherwise the recording is excellent.

The surprise version is Gillesberger's. Using treble and alto soloists from the Vienna Boys' Choir, who sing with confidence and no little eloquence, this performance also has the advantage of a dedicated contribution from Kurt Equiluz. Gillesberger's pacing is well judged and the effect is as fresh as it is strong and direct. The 1982 recording is excellent, vivid yet full, and the result is powerful but not too heavy. This is very well sung indeed, as is the rare Haydn coupling. This is a real bargain.

Giulini directs a large-scale performance which brings out both Mozartian lyricism and Mozartian drama, and anyone who fancies what by today's standards is an inauthentic approach may consider this version. The choir is in excellent, incisive form, and the soloists are a first-rate quartet. As one would expect, what Giulini's insight conveys is the rapt quality of such passages as the end of the *Tuba mirum* and the *Benedictus*. The recording is warm rather than brilliant.

Davis gives a comparatively small-scale performance which in principle should have given the sort of 'new look' to the Mozart *Requiem* that was such a striking success in Handel's *Messiah*. But somehow that does not happen, for the choral sound itself is weighty and thick, and, while this account is enjoyable, in the last resort it is not memorable. Readers will note that this performance is also available on a Philips Duo, above, combined with the *Coronation* and *Great C minor Masses*, and overall that seems to be a rather more enticing proposition.

Though the chorus and soloists are first rate on the Naxos issue, recorded in Bratislava, the style of the performance is on the heavy side, with generally slow speeds and rhythms that are often square and plodding. The four soloists are all firm and fresh-toned, though their tuning together is not always impeccable.

(i) *Requiem Mass (No. 19) in D min., K.626;* (ii) *Le nozze di Figaro: Bravo signor . . . Se vuol ballare; Non più andrai. Così fan tutte: Rivolgete a lui lo sguardo; Donne mie, la fate a tanti.*
(M) *(*) Sony Theta Dig. SMK 60025 [id.]. (i) Lynn Dawson, Jard van Nes, Keith Lewis, Simon Estes, Philh. Ch. & O, Giulini; (ii) Ferruccio Furlanetto, VSO, Marin.

Despite fine singing from soloists and chorus, Giulini's Sony version is a disappointment. His earlier, EMI recording was far finer, with speeds already on the slow side but not dragging as they tend to do in this later one. The heavyweight recording does not help. The coupling seems curiously innappropriate: four *buffo* baritone arias, given lively performances by Furlanetto but offering little musical variety.

Vesperae de domenica, K.321.
(M) *** Decca 430 162-2. Marshall, Cable, Evans, Roberts, St John's College, Cambridge, Ch., Wren O, Guest – HAYDN: *Harmoniemesse.* ***

Aptly coupled with Haydn's *Harmoniemesse*, Mozart's vibrant *Vesperae de domenica* opens with a series of brilliant choral settings (with contrasting solo quartet), accompanied by trumpets and strings. Margaret Marshall is appropriately agile in the lively soprano solo of the *Laudate Dominum*, and the work closes with an ambitious *Magnificat* in which all the participants are joined satisfyingly together. The St John's performance is full of vigour and the 1980 recording is full and vivid.

Vesperae solennes de confessore, K.339.
(M) *** Decca 430 157-2. Palmer, Cable, Langridge, Roberts, St John's College, Cambridge, Ch., Wren O, Guest – HAYDN: *Paukenmesse.* ***

Although Guest's version of Mozart's masterpiece does not always match the full-price recording by Sir Colin Davis for Philips (see above under *Ave verum corpus*) – with Felicity Palmer a less poised soloist than Kiri Te Kanawa – the Decca account has the advantage of authenticity in the use of boys in the chorus. Moreover the CD transfer of the 1979 Argo recording is preferable to the less well-defined Philips sound.

OPERA

Complete Mozart Edition, Volume 26: *Apollo et Hyacinthus* (complete).
(M) *** Ph. 422 526-2 (2) [id.]. Augér, Mathis, Wulkopf, Schwarz, Rolfe Johnson, Salzburg Chamber Ch. & Mozarteum O, Hager.

The opera was written when Mozart was eleven, with all but two of the parts taken by schoolchildren. The style of the writing and vocalization is rather simpler than in other dramatic works of the boy Mozart, but the inspiration is still remarkable, astonishingly mature. The orchestration is assured and full of imaginative touches. The performance here is stylish and very well sung. Excellent, clear and well-balanced recording, admirably transferred to CD.

Complete Mozart Edition, Volume 30: *Ascanio in Alba* (complete).
(M) **(*) Ph. 422 530-2 (3) [id.]. Sukis, Baltsa, Mathis, Augér, Schreier, Salzburg Chamber Ch., Salzburg Mozarteum O, Hager.
Ascanio in Alba (complete).
(B) *** Naxos Dig. 8.660040-2 (2). Windsor, Chance, Feldman, Milner, Mannion, Paris Sorbonne University Ch., Budapest Concerto Armonico, Jacques Grimbert.

Mozart at the age of fifteen wrote this charming, ever-inventive 'festa teatrale' for the coronation of the Archduke Ferdinand to an Italian princess in Milan in 1771. A court entertainment rather than an opera proper, it designedly identifies characters in a classical story, with the bride and bridegroom taking part in a delightful and original closing trio. The Naxos version, squeezing the dozens of arias and choruses on to two 79-minute discs, easily outshines previous recordings with a lightly sprung, stylishly conducted performance featuring an outstanding cast. The counter-tenor, Michael Chance, sings flawlessly in the castrato role of Ascanio, son of Venus, even-toned and brilliantly flexible. The others are fresh-toned too. Lorna Windsor, bright and clear as Venus, is nicely contrasted with the girlish-sounding Silvia of Jill Feldman, who sings with fine assurance in one of the two extended arias. The other, even more extended and demanding, is given to Fauno, with Rosa Mannion arguably the most accomplished soloist of all. The excellent tenor taking the role of Aceste is Howard Milner. Well recorded with transparent textures, if with chorus backwardly balanced, this makes an outstanding bargain in every way, rare Mozart that for most will be a delightful discovery.

Hager makes an excellent start with an exceptionally lively account of the delightful overture, but then the choruses seem relatively square, thanks to the pedestrian, if generally efficient singing of the Salzburg choir. Hager's speeds are sometimes on the slow side, but the singing is excellent, with no weak link in the characterful cast, though not everyone will like the distinctive vibrato of Lilian Sukis as Venus. The 1976 analogue recording is full and vivid. But this set is now completely upstaged by the new Naxos version.

Complete Mozart Edition, Volume 27: *Bastien und Bastienne* (complete); Lieder: *Komm, liebe Zither, komm; Die Zufriedenheit.*
(M) *** Ph. Dig. 422 527-2 [id.]. Dominik Orieschnig, Georg Nigl, David Busch, V. Boys' Ch., VSO, Harrer.

On Philips, the opera is performed by boy trebles instead of the soprano, tenor and bass originally intended. Members of the Vienna Boys' Choir give a refreshingly direct performance under Uwe Christian Harrer, missing little of the piece's charm. The two songs with mandolin accompaniment, also sung by one of the trebles, make an attractive fill-up. First-rate 1986 digital sound.

Complete Mozart Edition, Volume 44: *La clemenza di Tito* (complete).
(M) *** Ph. 422 544-2 (2) [id.]. Dame Janet Baker, Minton, Burrows, Von Stade, Popp, Lloyd, ROHCG Ch. & O, Sir Colin Davis.

La clemenza di Tito (complete).
(M) *** DG 429 878-2 (2). Berganza, Varady, Mathis, Schreier, Schiml, Adam, Leipzig R. Ch., Dresden State O, Boehm.

Sir Colin Davis's superb set is among the finest of his many Mozart recordings. Not only is the singing of Dame Janet Baker in the key role of Vitellia formidably brilliant; she actually makes one believe in the emotional development of an impossible character, one who progresses from villainy to virtue with the scantiest preparation. The two other mezzo-sopranos, Minton as Sesto and Von Stade in the small role of Annio, are superb too, while Stuart Burrows has rarely if ever sung so stylishly on a recording as here. Davis's swaggering manner transforms what used to be dismissed as a dry *opera seria*. Excellent recording.

Boehm gave the work warmth and charm, presenting the piece more genially than we have grown used to. The atmospheric recording helps in that, and the cast is first rate, with no weak link, matching at every point that of Sir Colin Davis on his Philips set. Yet, ultimately, even Julia Varady for Boehm can hardly rival Dame Janet Baker for Davis, crisper and lighter in her coloratura. Davis's incisiveness, too, has points of advantage; but, to summarize, any Mozartian can safely leave the preference to his feelings about the two conductors, the one more genial and glowing, the other more urgently dramatic.

(i) *Così fan tutte;* (ii) *Don Giovanni;* (iii) *Le nozze di Figaro.*
(B) *** Ph. 456 375-2 (9) [(M) id. import]. (i–iii) Ganzarolli; (i) Caballé, J. Baker, Cotrubas, Gedda; (i–ii) Van Allan, ROCG Ch. & O; (ii) Arroyo, Te Kanawa, Burrows, Roni; (ii–iii) Wixell, Freni; (iii) Norman, Minton, Casula, Grant, Tear, BBC Ch., BBC SO; all cond. Sir Colin Davis.

Philips wisely decided to omit Sir Colin Davis's recording of *Die Zauberflöte* from this very tempting bargain box; it was the least successful of his Mozart opera series and in any case is available separately and inexpensively on a Duo (see below). The other three performances are sheer delight. The sparkling *Così fan tutte* brings a superb female trio in Caballé, Janet Baker and Cotrubas, and the men fall only slightly short of this very high standard. In *Don Giovanni* the very consistency of the whole cast is its major asset, led by Kiri Te Kanawa as Donna Elvira and Mirella Freni's engaging Zerlina, while Ingvar Wixell and Wladimiro Ganzarolli strike sparks off each other as the Don and Leporello; and the same comment applies to *Nozze di Figaro*, where those same two male singers are equally successful in the comparable master and servant roles. Throughout all three operas Davis's lively pacing brings a flowing spontaneity as at live performances. The Philips sound, from clean CD transfers of recordings made between 1971 and 1974, is always fresh and immediate.

Complete Mozart Edition, Volume 42: *Così fan tutte* (complete).
(M) *** Ph. 422 542-2; *422 542-4* (3/2) [id.]. Caballé, Dame Janet Baker, Cotrubas, Gedda, Ganzarolli, Van Allan, ROHCG Ch. & O, Sir Colin Davis.

Così fan tutte (complete).
✿ (M) *** EMI CMS7 69330-2 (3) [Ang. CDMC 69330]. Schwarzkopf, Ludwig, Steffek, Kraus, Taddei, Berry, Philh. Ch. & O, Boehm.
✿ (M) (***) EMI mono CHS7 69635-2 (3) [Ang. CDHC 69635]. Schwarzkopf, Otto, Merriman, Simoneau, Panerai, Bruscantini, Philh. Ch. & O, Karajan.
(M) (***) EMI mono CHS7 63864-2 (2). Souez, Helletsgruber, Nash, Domgraf-Fassbaender, Brownlee, Eisinger, Glyndebourne Festival Ch. & O, Fritz Busch.

(M) **(*) EMI CMS7 63845-2 (3). M. Price, Minton, Popp, Alva, Evans, Sotin, Alldis Ch., New Philh. O, Klemperer.

(B) ** Naxos Dig. 8.660008/10 [id.]. Borowska, Yachmi, John Dickie, Martin, Coles, Mikulas, Slovak Philharmonic Ch., Capella Istropolitana, Johannes Wildner.

Boehm's classic set has been handsomely repackaged and remains a clear mid-price choice. Its glorious solo singing is headed by the incomparable Fiordiligi of Schwarzkopf and the equally moving Dorabella of Christa Ludwig; it remains a superb memento of Walter Legge's recording genius and still bears comparison with any other recordings made before or since.

Commanding as Schwarzkopf is as Fiordiligi in the 1962 Boehm set, the extra ease and freshness of her singing in the earlier (1954) version under Karajan makes it even more compelling. Nan Merriman is a distinctive and characterful Dorabella, and the role of Ferrando has never been sung more mellifluously on record than by Leopold Simoneau. The young Rolando Panerai is an ideal Guglielmo, and Lisa Otto a pert Despina; while Sesto Bruscantini in his prime brings to the role of Don Alfonso the wisdom and artistry which made him so compelling at Glyndebourne. Karajan has never sparkled more naturally in Mozart than here, for the high polish has nothing self-conscious about it. Though the mono recording is not as clear as some others of this period, the subtleties of the music-making are very well caught.

The energy and sparkle of Sir Colin Davis are set against inspired and characterful singing from the three women soloists, with Montserrat Caballé and Janet Baker proving a winning partnership, each challenging and abetting the other all the time. Cotrubas equally is a vivid Despina, never merely arch. Though Gedda has moments of rough tone and Ganzarolli falls short in one of his prominent arias, they are both spirited, while Richard van Allan sings with flair and imagination. Sparkling recitative, and recording which has you riveted by the play of the action.

The legendary Glyndebourne performance, the first ever recording of *Così fan tutte*, is the finest of the three pioneering sets recorded on 78s in the mid-1930s with the newly founded Glyndebourne company. The sound in the CD transfer, though limited, is amazingly vivid, with voices very well focused and with a keener sense of presence than on many recordings of the 1990s. Busch at the time was a progressive Mozartian, preferring athletic treatment, and nowadays even the use of a piano for the recitatives instead of a harpsichord seems less outlandish with the emergence of the fortepiano. John Brownlee as Don Alfonso is very much the English aristocrat, with 'fruffly-fruffly' English vowels instead of Italianate ones, but he is a fine, stylish singer. Ina Souez and Luise Helletsgruber are technically superb; and Heddle Nash and Willi Domgraf-Fassbaender as their lovers are at once stylish and characterful, with Irene Eisinger as a delightfully soubrettish Despina. Cuts are made in the recitatives according to the custom of the time and, more seriously, four numbers disappear – including, amazingly, Ferrando's *Tradito, schernito* and Dorabella's *E amore un ladroncello*. The bonus is that, with those cuts, the opera fits on to only two mid-price CDs.

Klemperer's last opera set was predictably idiosyncratic. When the record company jibbed at his suggestion of recording this sparkling comedy, he is alleged to have protested (aged eighty-six at the time), 'What do you want? A posthumous interpretation?' The result proved by no means as funereal as had been predicted, with fine rhythmic pointing to lighten the slow tempi. There is fine singing too from the whole cast (Alva alone at times disappointing) to make the whole a satisfying entertainment, a different view of Mozart to be heard at least once. It is a pity the recitatives are not more imaginatively done. An excellent transfer to CD.

On three budget-price CDs (each costing slightly more than this super-bargain label's orchestral and instrumental repertory) the Naxos version comes out at a price comparable to the Glyndebourne two-disc set, yet provides a text without the omissions of the latter, and the modern digital recording is fresh and bright. But with the exception of Joanna Borowska as a strong, stylish Fiordiligi, the Czech cast is in a different league. After Borowska, Peter Mikulas is the most successful of the soloists, a forthright, clean-toned Don Alfonso. John Dickie, as recorded, sounds rather too throaty as Ferrando and Rohangiz Yachmi as Dorabella has too fruity a vibrato for Mozart. After a gabbled overture, Wildner directs a well-played, generally well-paced performance. It is worth remembering that for the price of these discs one would be well pleased to come across such a performance in the opera house, be it in Bratislava or elsewhere.

Così fan tutte: highlights.

(B) (***) EMI Eminence mono CD-EMX 2211 [(M) id. import] (from above complete recording, with Schwarzkopf, Merriman, Otto, Panerai, Simoneau, Bruscantini; cond. Karajan).

(BB) **(*) Belart 450 114-2 [(M) id. import] (from complete recording, with Janowitz, Fassbaender, Prey, Schreier, Grist, VPO, cond. Boehm).

(M) **(*) Teldec/Warner Dig. 0630 15801-9 [9031 76455-2] (from complete recording, with Margiono,

Delores Ziegler, Anna Steiger, Van der Walt, Cachemaille, Hampson, Netherlands Op. Ch., Concg. O, Harnoncourt).

For those without the complete set (given a Rosette – see above), the highlights CD from the 1954 Karajan mono set, with Schwarzkopf at her very finest, is surely indispensable, even if the documentation is inadequate and there is no proper cued synopsis.

These Belart highlights come from Karl Boehm's third (DG) recording of the opera and, with 72 minutes of music included, it makes an attractive memento. It was recorded live during the Salzburg Festival performance on the conductor's eightieth birthday. It has a splendid cast, and the zest and sparkle of the occasion come over delightfully. Even if at times ensemble leaves a good deal to be desired, at super-budget price it makes a genuine bargain.

Harnoncourt, the period-instrument specialist, as in his other Mozart opera recordings here favours an orchestra of modern instruments while adopting speeds of period style. He gives a quirkily magnetic reading and many will be glad of a fairly comprehensive sampler (74 minutes), especially when – as usual with the Warner Classics Opera Collection series – it is documented with a full translation and linking narrative. Though *O soave sia il vento* is raced along, Fiordiligi's great Act II aria, *Per pietà*, is taken very slowly indeed. Even so, Charlotte Margiono sustains the line immaculately, and she is similarly accommodating over another of Harnoncourt's eccentricities, making the emphatic opening of Fiordiligi's other big aria, *Come scoglio*, into a hushed meditation. There is no real weak link in the cast, but Harnoncourt's perverse tempi prevent a full recommendation for the complete set.

Complete Mozart Edition, Volume 41: *Don Giovanni* (complete).

(M) *** Ph. 422 541-2; *422 541-4* (3/2) [id.]. Wixell, Arroyo, Te Kanawa, Freni, Burrows, Ganzarolli, ROHCG Ch. & O, Sir Colin Davis.

Don Giovanni (complete).

(M) *** Decca 411 626-2 (3). Siepi, Danco, Della Casa, Corena, Dermota, V. State Op. Ch., VPO, Krips.

(M) *** EMI (SIS) CMS7 63841-2 (3) [Ang. CDMC 63841]. Ghiaurov, Claire Watson, Ludwig, Freni, Gedda, Berry, Montarsolo, Crass, New Philh. Ch. & O, Klemperer.

(M) (***) EMI mono CHS7 63860-2 (3) [Ang. CDHB 63860]. Siepi, Schwarzkopf, Berger, Grümmer, Dermota, Edelmann, Berry, Ernster, V. State Op. Ch., VPO, Furtwängler.

(M) (***) EMI mono CHS7 61030-2 (3). Brownlee, Souez, Von Pataky, Helletsgruber, Baccaloni, Henderson, Mildmay, Glyndebourne Fest. Ch. & O, Fritz Busch.

(M) (***) EMI mono CHS5 66657-2 (3). Gobbi, Schwarzkopf, Welitsch, Seefried, Kunz, Dermota, Poell, Greindl, V. State Op. Ch., VPO, Furtwängler.

(M) **(*) Decca 448 973-2 (3) [id.]. Bacquier, Sutherland, Lorengar, Horne, Krenn, Gramm, Monreale, Grant, Amb. S., ECO, Bonynge.

(M) **(*) DG (IMS) 437 341-2 (3). Fischer-Dieskau, Jurinac, Stader, Seefried, Haefliger, Kohn, Sardi, Kreppel, Berlin RIAS Chamber Ch. & R.O, Fricsay.

(M) (**(*)) Naxos mono 8.110013/14 [id.]. Pinza, Novotna, Bampton. Sayão, Kipnis, Harell, Cordon, NY Met. Op. Ch. & O, Walter.

(M) ** Decca (IMS) 444 594-2 (3) [id.]. Siepi, Corena, Nilsson, L. Price, Ratti, Valletti, Blankenburg, Van Mill, V. State Op. Ch., VPO, Leinsdorf.

Sir Colin Davis has the advantage of a singing cast that has fewer shortcomings than almost any other on disc and much positive strength. Martina Arroyo controls her massive dramatic voice more completely than one would think possible, and she is strongly and imaginatively contrasted with the sweetly expressive Elvira of Kiri Te Kanawa and the sparkling Zerlina of Mirella Freni. As in the Davis *Figaro*, Ingvar Wixell and Wladimiro Ganzarolli make a formidable master/servant team with excellent vocal acting, while Stuart Burrows sings gloriously as Don Ottavio, and Richard Van Allan is a characterful Masetto. Davis draws a fresh and immediate performance from his team, riveting from beginning to end, and the recording is now better defined and more vivid than before.

Krips's recording of this most challenging opera has kept its place as a mid-priced version that is consistently satisfying, with a cast of all-round quality headed by the dark-toned Don of Cesare Siepi. The women are not ideal, but they form an excellent team, never overfaced by the music, generally characterful, and with timbres well contrasted. To balance Siepi's darkness, the Leporello of Corena is even more saturnine, and their dramatic teamwork is brought to a superb climax in the final scene – quite the finest and most spine-tingling performance of that scene ever recorded. The 1955 recording – genuine stereo – still sounds remarkably well.

The lumbering tempo of Leporello's opening music will alert the listener to the predictable Klemperer approach and at that point some may dismiss his performance as 'too heavy' – but the issue is far more complex than that. Most of the slow tempi which Klemperer regularly adopts, far from flagging, add a welcome breadth to the music, for they must be set against the unusually brisk and dramatic interpretation of the recitatives between numbers. Added to that, Ghiaurov as the Don and Berry as Leporello make a marvellously characterful pair. In this version the male members of the cast are dominant and, with Klemperer's help, they make the dramatic experience a strongly masculine one. Nor is the ironic humour forgotten with Berry and Ghiaurov about, and the Klemperer spaciousness allows them extra time for pointing. Among the women, Ludwig is a strong and convincing Elvira, Freni a sweet-toned but rather unsmiling Zerlina; only Claire Watson seriously disappoints, with obvious nervousness marring the big climax of *Non mi dir*. It is a serious blemish but, with the usual reservations, for those not allergic to the Klemperer approach, this stands as a good recommendation – at the very least a commanding experience. The set now reappears at mid-price, its catalogue number unchanged, but the presentation more stylish.

The historic Furtwängler performance was recorded live by Austrian Radio at the 1954 Salzburg Festival, barely three months before the conductor's death. Though speeds are often slow by today's standards, his springing of rhythm never lets them sag. Even the very slow speed for Leporello's catalogue aria is made to seem charmingly individual. With the exception of a wobbly Commendatore, this is a classic Salzburg cast, with Cesare Siepi a fine, incisive Don, dark in tone, Elisabeth Schwarzkopf a dominant Elvira, Elisabeth Grümmer a vulnerable Anna, Anton Dermota a heady-toned Ottavio and Otto Edelmann a clear and direct Leporello. Stage noises often suggest herds of stampeding animals, but both voices and orchestra are satisfyingly full-bodied in the CD transfer, and the sense of presence is astonishing.

The early Glyndebourne set shows Fritz Busch an inspired Mozartian, pointing the music with a freshness and absence of nineteenth-century heaviness rare at the time. A piano is used for the *secco* recitatives; but the interplay of characters in those exchanges has never been caught more infectiously on disc. John Brownlee as Giovanni may have a rather British-stiff-upper-lip Italian accent but his is a noble performance, beautifully sung, and he is brilliantly set against the lively, idiomatically Italian Leporello of Salvatore Baccaloni. Audrey Mildmay as Zerlina makes a delightful foil for the excellent, if otherwise little-known Ina Souez and Luise Helletsgruber. Koloman von Pataky uses his light, heady tenor well as Ottavio, and David Franklin and Roy Henderson are first rate as the Commendatore and Masetto respectively. Keith Hardwick's digital transfers are astonishingly vivid, with very little background noise.

The 1950 EMI set with Tito Gobbi in the title-role should not be confused with the later Furtwängler recording, also made at the Salzburg Festival and issued by EMI, with Schwarzkopf as Elvira. The speeds, spacious by most standards, are here a degree faster than they became four years later. Gobbi, not usually a Mozartian, yet gives a commanding, keenly characterful portrayal of the Don, very much the centre of the drama, swaggering and snarling, a menacingly dangerous seducer. Schwarzkopf as ever is a comparably commanding and characterful Elvira, no wilting flower, and Ljuba Welitsch in 1950 was at her peak, a radiant Anna, with Irmgard Seefried a magical Zerlina and Anton Dermota a honeyed Ottavio. Erich Kunz is the vintage Leporello, and if neither Alfred Poell as Masetto nor Josef Greindl as the Commendatore can match the others vocally, the team could otherwise hardly be stronger. The sound is rough on the orchestra but improves after the overture, while voices are very well caught, though stage balances vary.

Richard Bonynge's reading of *Don Giovanni*, recorded in 1968 and originally dismissed as too lightweight, was in many ways ahead of its time, using a chamber orchestra, with plentiful appoggiaturas in the vocal lines, even if some *Andantes* are on the slow side. The Kingsway Hall recording vividly captures an ideal scale. Though the overture is rather underpowered, tension never lapses after that, and the cast is exceptionally strong, finer than in most modern versions. Sutherland is commanding as Donna Anna, even finer than for Giulini on EMI. Gabriel Bacquier, at his peak as the Don, makes a vigorous hero, with Donald Gramm a firm if sober-sided Leporello and Werner Krenn an outstanding, heady-toned Ottavio, while Clifford Grant sings with thrillingly black tone as the Commendatore. Pilar Lorengar, with a hint of flutter in the voice, is a vulnerable rather than a biting Elvira, while the choice of Marilyn Horne as a full mezzo Zerlina, strange by latterday standards, follows historic precedent, with the singer scaling her powerful voice down. A mid-priced set for more than Sutherland devotees.

As he has shown in his recording of *Die Zauberflöte*, Fricsay is a forceful, dramatic Mozart conductor, but here the absence of charm is serious. This is mainly felt in some ridiculously fast speeds. Zerlina, Masetto and their rustic friends are hustled unmercifully along in 6/8, and poor Zerlina has an even worse time when it comes to her aria, *Batti batti*. Seefried being the superb artist she is, her charm comes through. The cast is generally strong, but unfortunately there is a serious blot in the Donna Elvira of Maria Stader; she is made to sound shrill and some of her attempts to get round the trickier florid passages leave a good deal to be desired. Yet most of the singing is very stylish. Haefliger shows himself as one of the finest Mozart tenors of the time, Karl Kohn is a fine, incisive Leporello, Ivan Sardi an exceptionally rich-voiced Masetto, and Seefried a truly enchanting Zerlina. As so often on records, Sena Jurinac is not quite as thrilling here as one remembers her in the flesh. Fischer-Dieskau is a particularly interesting choice of Don; his characterization proves powerful and forwardly projected. Yet with all these plus points, the set does not quite add up to the sum of its parts, even though there is much to enjoy. The 1958 recording was made in the Berlin Jesus-Christus Kirche, so the stereo is remarkably atmospheric.

The vintage Bruno Walter recording, made live at the Met. in New York in March 1942, is one of the most desirable of the Naxos historic issues. To get such a performance, so starrily cast, at bargain price on only two discs makes it an obvious recommendation. Bruno Walter's brisk speeds may not allow the sort of detailed expressiveness one finds in either of the Furtwängler versions, but the bite of the drama is irresistible. Ezio Pinza is an engagingly characterful Don, even if he is not the most natural Mozartian, and he takes the *Champagne aria* at an impossibly fast speed. Even so, his is a commanding performance vocally, matched by the rest of the cast. Few Annas equal Rose Bampton for her combination of purity and power, with every note cleanly in place; though Jarmila Novotna as Elvira is less polished, it is a strong performance, and Bidu Sayão makes a charming Zerlina. Charles Kullman – earlier Walter's tenor soloist in his 1936 *Das Lied von der Erde* – is a clear-toned Ottavio, and though Alexander Kipnis as Leporello is not at his best in Act I, the biting clarity of his performance is magnetic. The 1942 sound, one of the better recordings from this source, has voices forwardly balanced. Whether to fit the opera on to two discs, or simply following the original Prague score, Elvira's aria, *Mi tradi*, is omitted.

The Leinsdorf set from the early 1960s was uncut and very well recorded. It originally appeared on RCA but now reverts to its home label. The excellent Don of Cesare Siepi, already established in the Krips version, is if anything even more impressive here. Leontyne Price is a fine Elvira, but Birgit Nilsson is rather miscast as Anna: she makes very gusty noises in trying to get round some of the more difficult passages. Valletti and Corena are both very good, but in the last resort it is the conducting of Leinsdorf which makes one qualify a recommendation. This is far preferable to his *Marriage of Figaro* (see below), but there is something of the same inflexibility.

Don Giovanni: highlights.

(M) *** EMI CDM5 65567-2 (from complete recording, with Sutherland, Schwarzkopf, Waechter, Philh. Ch. & O, Giulini).

(B) **(*) [EMI Red Line Dig. CDR5 69824] (from complete recording, with Shimell, Ramey, Studer, VPO, Muti).

(B) ** EMI CfP CD-CFP 6015 [(M) id. import] (from complete recording, with Roger Soyer, Antigone Sgourda, Heather Harper, Helen Donath, Luigi Alva, Sir Geraint Evans, Alberto Rinaldi, Scottish Op. Ch., ECO, Barenboim).

(B) ** Sony SBK 62663; *SBT 62663* [id.] (from complete set, with Raimondi, Moser, Te Kanawa, Berganza, Riegel, Van Dam, King, Paris Op. Ch. & O, Maazel).

(BB) ** CfP Silver Double CDCFPSD 4739 (2) [(M) id.]. Shirley-Quirk, Armstrong, Tear, Mathes, Dean, Garrard, Murray, Jackson, SCO, Gibson – R. STRAUSS: *Der Rosenkavalier*. ***

Not surprisingly, the Giulini EMI selection concentrates on Sutherland as Donna Anna and Schwarzkopf as Donna Elvira, so that the Don and Leporello get rather short measure, but Sciutti's charming Zerlina is also given fair due. The complete set is at full price, as is Muti's.

Muti's *Don Giovanni* is on a big scale but is nevertheless refreshingly alert (using a fortepiano continuo). It is perhaps a set to sample rather than to have complete. Shimell makes a rather gruff Don, not as insinuatingly persuasive as he might be; like the others, he is not helped by the distancing of the voices. With Samuel Ramey convincingly translated here to the role of Leporello and Cheryl Studer an outstanding Donna Anna, the rest of the casting is strong and satisfying. The selection of highlights is not particularly generous but does include most of the key numbers.

Barenboim's EMI set from the early 1970s is by no means a front-runner, but Roger Soyer is a personable Don and admirers of Sir Geraint Evans will surely welcome his Leporello. Among the ladies, Heather Harper (Donna Elvira) and Helen Donath as Zerlina both shine (*Là ci darem la mano* is very pleasing). The selection is generous (77 minutes) and is provided with a good cued synopsis.

This bargain Sony set of highlights generously (79 minutes) represents the performance which Lorin Maazel directed so strongly and urgently for the Losey film of the opera. An obvious strength is the line-up of three unusually firm basses: José van Dam a saturnine Leporello, Malcolm King a darkly intense Masetto, and Ruggero Raimondi a heroic Giovanni. With Kiri Te Kanawa a radiant Elvira, the dramatic scale is certainly impressive, although neither Teresa Berganza as a mezzo Zerlina nor Edda Moser as Donna Anna matches her. Unfortunately the recording, made in a Paris church, has the voices close against background reverberation. However, the presentation is very good for a bargain CD with an excellent cued synopsis, and this is well worth its modest cost.

This collection of highlights from the Scottish Opera's 1975 production is welcome enough on a bargain Silver Double with some enjoyable singing. John Shirley-Quirk is an intelligent rather than a flamboyant Don, singing his serenade in delightful half-tones and almost coping with Gibson's impossibly fast tempo for the *Champagne aria*. Rachel Mathes as Donna Anna brings a powerful recording voice, but none of the others is presented at peak form. This may be the fault of the conductor, who misses some of the bite of dramatic tension. The selection, which includes the *Overture*, is not particularly generous, and the recording could be more refined and atmospheric.

Die Entführung aus dem Serail (complete).

(BB) *** Arte Nova/BMG Dig. 74321 49701-2 (2) [id.]. Habermann, Ellen, Bezcala, Kalchmair, Ringelhahn, Linz Landestheatre Ch., Linz Bruckner O, Sieghart.

(M) *** DG 429 868-2 (2). Augér, Grist, Schreier, Neukirch, Moll, Leipzig R. Ch., Dresden State O, Boehm.

(B) ** DG Double 439 708-2 (2). Köth, Schädle, Wunderlich, Lenz, Böhme, Bav. State Op. Ch. & O, Jochum.

(i) *Die Entführung aus dem Serail* (complete); (ii) Overtures: *Così fan tutte; Don Giovanni; Le nozze di Figaro; Der Schauspieldirektor; Die Zauberflöte*.

(B) (*) Decca Double mono 443 530-2 (2). Lipp, Loose, Ludwig, Klein, Koreh, Woester, V. State Op. Ch., VPO; (ii) LSO; Josef Krips.

With an excellent cast of young singers, the Arte Nova set offers an outstanding version of *Entführung* to rival almost any in the catalogue. With Martin Sieghart a crisp and urgent conductor, stylistically impeccable, drawing fine playing from the Linz Bruckner Orchestra, the performance gains from having been recorded in conjunction with live performances on stage, a point consistently reflected in the interplay between the soloists. Ingrid Habermann is a formidable Konstanze, fresh and clear, bright in coloratura yet creamy of tone in lower registers, undaunted by the demands of *Martern aller Arten*. The American, Donna Ellen, is a lively Blonde with a clear, unstrained top register. The Polish tenor, Piotr Bezcala, is a stylish, honey-toned Belmonte, with power as well as lyric beauty, only occasionally lachrymose in attack, while Oliver Ringelhahn is a well-contrasted Pedrillo, though pushed to the limit in his big Act II aria, *Frisch zum Kampfe*. Best of all is the Osmin of Franz Kalchmair, whose firm, dark bass copes masterfully with every demand of the role, cleanly focused from top to bottom. Still youthful-sounding, he yet conveys a compelling portrait of this prickly character. Good sound, though the spoken dialogue (well edited) is not consistent. At super-bargain price, the set comes with full libretto, including English translation.

Boehm's is a delectable account, superbly cast and warmly recorded. Arleen Augér proves the most accomplished singer on record in the role of Constanze, girlish and fresh, yet rich, tender and dramatic by turns, with brilliant, almost flawless coloratura. The others are also outstandingly good, notably Kurt Moll whose powerful, finely focused bass makes him a superb Osmin, one who relishes the comedy too. The warm recording is beautifully transferred, to make this one of the most sympathetic versions of the opera on CD, with the added attraction of being at mid-price.

It is the greatest pity that the role of Constanze in Jochum's performance is taken by the shrill and shallow-sounding Erika Köth. Otherwise it would be an admirable DG Double recommendation, well recorded, with lively direction from Jochum and a wonderful contribution from the late-lamented Fritz Wunderlich.

The Double Decca alternative was not just the first complete recording of *Entführung* but the first complete opera to appear on Decca LP. Under Krips's sparkling direction, with a cast drawn from the vintage post-war team at the Vienna State Opera, it is a fine if flawed performance, and it is sad that the Decca transfer deals so shabbily with a historic recording. The orchestral sound on CD completely lacks the body of the original LPs, emerging very thinly and with an impossibly fizzy top, quite different from the far fuller sound given to the overtures, recorded in London the following year. Voices are somewhat better treated. Finest among the soloists are the two tenors: both Walther Ludwig and Peter Klein sing with clear, heady tone. But Emmy Loose as Konstanze and Wilma Lipp as Blondchen are caught brightly to the point of shrillness, which tires the ear, with Loose slightly fluttery. Endre Koreh is a powerful, characterful Osmin, again with a slight flutter in the voice. Decca engineers need to listen more closely to the results they achieve from some of these early master tapes. Something obviously went wrong after the original LP issues; and this is by no means the only example of an early recording on this label which offers unacceptably 'toppy' sound in its CD transfer.

Die Entführung aus dem Serail: highlights.

(B) *(*) EMI CfP CD-CFP 6035 [(M) id. import]. Dame Margaret Price, Danièle Perriers, Ryland Davies, Kimmo Lappalainen, Noel Mangin, LPO, Pritchard.

Dame Margaret Price, so accomplished a Constanze, is rather diappointing in this 1972 collection of highlights, with her hooting tone too often catching the microphone, while the rest of the cast also fails to capture the light-hearted sparkle of the Glyndebourne production on which the recording is based.

Complete Mozart Edition, Volume 33: *La finta giardiniera* (complete).
(M) *** Ph. 422 533-2 (3) [id.]. Conwell, Sukis, Di Cesare, Thomas Moser, Fassbaender, Ihloff, McDaniel, Salzburg Mozarteum O, Hager.

Leopold Hager has a strong vocal team, with three impressive newcomers taking the women's roles – Jutta-Renate Ihloff, Julia Conwell (in the central role of Sandrina, the marquise who disguises herself as a garden-girl) and Lilian Sukis (the arrogant niece). Brigitte Fassbaender sings the castrato role of Ramiro, and the others are comparably stylish. It is a charming – if lengthy – comedy, which here, with crisply performed recitatives, is presented with vigour, charm and persuasiveness. The recording, made with the help of Austrian Radio, is excellent.

Complete Mozart Edition, Volume 28: *La finta semplice* (complete).
(M) *** Ph. Dig. 422 528-2 (2). Hendricks, Lorenz, Johnson, Murray, Lind, Blochwitz, Schmidt, C. P. E. Bach CO, Schreier.

Schreier's version replaces the earlier, Orfeo full-priced set from Leopold Hager, particularly when it comes at mid-price on two discs instead of three. The digital recording is wonderfully clear, with a fine sense of presence, capturing the fun of the comedy. Ann Murray has never sung more seductively in Mozart than here as Giacinta, and the characterful Barbara Hendricks is a delight in the central role of Rosina.

Idomeneo (complete).
(M) *** DG 429 864-2 (3). Ochman, Mathis, Schreier, Varady, Winkler, Leipzig R. Ch., Dresden State O, Boehm.
(M) ** Ph. 422 537-2 (3). Francisco Araiza, Susanne Mentzer, Barbara Hendricks, Roberta Alexander, Uwe Heilmann, Werner Hollweg, Harry Peeters, Bav. R. Ch. & RSO, Sir Colin Davis.
(B) (**) DG mono 447 662-2 (3) [id.]. Kmentt, Haefliger, Grümmer, Lorengar, Capecchi, V. State Op. Ch., VPO, Fricsay.

Boehm's conducting is a delight, often spacious but never heavy in the wrong way, with lightened textures and sprung rhythms which have one relishing Mozartian felicities as never before. As Idomeneo, Wieslaw Ochman, with tenor tone often too tight, is a comparatively dull dog, but the other principals are generally excellent. Peter Schreier as Idamante also might have sounded more consistently sweet, but the imagination is irresistible. Edith Mathis is at her most beguiling as Ilia, but it is Julia Varady as Elettra who gives the most compelling performance of all, sharply incisive in her dramatic outbursts, but at the same time precise and pure-toned, a Mozartian stylist through and through.

To have a major new opera-set like this, issued from the start on a mid-priced label, is generous, but Sir Colin Davis's second version of Mozart's great *opera seria* was designed as part of the Philips Complete Mozart Edition and is priced accordingly. It comes with the fine qualities of presentation associated with the series; the text aims at completeness, with an appendix on the third disc containing major numbers like Arbace's two arias, omitted in the main text, as well as the ballet music designed to be performed after the drama is over. It also has the advantage over Davis's previous recording that the role of Idamante is given to a mezzo instead of a tenor, following Mozart's original Munich text. Such a number as the great Quartet of Act III benefits much by that – but unfortunately, as in Davis's previous version, there are flaws in the casting; his reading has also grown smoother and less incisive, less fresh than before, if now at times grander. Francisco Araiza's efforts to produce the heroic tone needed often sound strained, and he is not clean enough in his attack; while Barbara Hendricks as Ilia adopts an even less apt Mozartian style, with too much sliding and under-the-note attack, missing the purity needed for this character. Uwe Heilmann as Arbace is also disappointing, and it is as well that his arias are left to the appendix. Others in the cast are far finer, but the total result is less than completely satisfactory, particularly arriving so soon after John Eliot Gardiner's brilliant and dramatic full-priced version for DG Archiv using period instruments. The Philips recording is full and warm, but the Gardiner set is well worth its extra cost.

Fricsay's live recording from the 1961 Salzburg Festival is intensely dramatic and offers some fine singing from such soloists as Elisabeth Grümmer as Elettra and Pilar Lorengar as Ilia. Sadly, Waldemar Kmentt is a strained Idomeneo and, worst of all, the Paumgartner text used by Fricsay is impossibly corrupt, with numbers cut, rearranged and altered. Having Idamante as a tenor remains a drawback too, even with Ernst Haefliger, and live recording involves varying balances and intrusive audience noises.

Idomeneo: highlights.
(M) **(*) Teldec/Warner 0630 15802-9 (from complete recording, with Hollweg, Trudeliese Schmidt, Yakar, Palmer, Equiluz, Tear, Estes, Zurich Opera Ch. & Mozart O, Harnoncourt).

Using a text very close to that of the Munich première of Mozart's great *opera seria*, and with the role of Idamante given to a soprano instead of being transposed down to tenor register, Harnoncourt presents a distinct view, one which in principle is preferable to general modern practice, and it is well worth sampling. This is hardly a performance to warm to, but it is refreshing and alive. The vocal cast is good, with Werner Hollweg a clear-toned, strong Idomeneo and Felicity Palmer finding the necessary contrasts of expression as Elettra. However, it is surprising that in an account which aims at authenticity, appoggiature are so rarely used. The selection runs to 72 minutes and the excellent documentation includes a translation.

Complete Mozart Edition, Volume 32: *Lucio Silla* (complete).
(M) *** Ph. 422 532-2 (3) [id.]. Schreier, Augér, Varady, Mathis, Donath, Krenn, Salzburg R. Ch. & Mozarteum Ch. & O, Hager.

The sixteen-year-old Mozart wrote his fifth opera, on the subject of the Roman dictator Sulla (Silla), in double quick time. There are many pre-echoes of later Mozart operas, not just of the great *opera seria*, *Idomeneo*, but of *Entführung* and even of *Don Giovanni*. On Philips the castrato roles are splendidly taken by Julia Varady and Edith Mathis, and the whole team could hardly be bettered. The direction of Hager is fresh and lively, and the only snag is the length of the *secco* recitatives. However, with CD one can use these judiciously.

Complete Mozart Edition, Volume 29: *Mitridate, rè di Ponto* (complete).
(M) **(*) Ph. 422 529-2 (3) [id.]. Augér, Hollweg, Gruberová, Baltsa, Cotrubas, Salzburg Mozarteum O, Hager.

Hager's fresh and generally lively performance (the rather heavy recitatives excepted) brings splendid illumination to the long-hidden area of the boy Mozart's achievement. Two of the most striking arias (including an urgent G minor piece for the heroine, Aspasia, with Arleen Augér the ravishing soprano) exploit minor keys most effectively. Ileana Cotrubas is outstanding as Ismene, and the soloists of the Salzburg orchestra cope well with the often important obbligato parts. The CD transfer is vivid and forward and a little lacking in atmosphere.

Complete Mozart Edition, Volume 40: *Le nozze di Figaro* (complete).
(M) *** Ph. 422 540-2 (3) [id.]. Freni, Norman, Minton, Ganzarolli, Wixell, Grant, Tear, BBC Ch. & SO, Sir Colin Davis.

Le nozze di Figaro (complete).
(M) *** EMI CMS7 63266-2 (2) [Ang. CDMB 63266]. Schwarzkopf, Moffo, Cossotto, Taddei, Waechter, Vinco, Philh. Ch. & O, Giulini.
✿ (B) *** CfP CD-CFPD 4724 (2) [(M) id. import]. Sciutti, Jurinac, Stevens, Bruscantini, Calabrese, Cuénod, Wallace, Sinclair, Glyndebourne Ch. & Festival O, Gui.
(M) **(*) Decca 417 315-2 (3). Gueden, Danco, Della Casa, Dickie, Poell, Corena, Siepi, V. State Op. Ch., VPO, Erich Kleiber.
(M) *** DG 449 728-2 (3) [id.]. Janowitz, Mathis, Troyanos, Fischer-Dieskau, Prey, Lagger, German Op. Ch. & O, Boehm.
(M) **(*) EMI CMS7 63849-2 (3). Grist, Söderström, Berganza, Evans, Bacquier, Hollweg, Alldis Ch., New Philh. O, Klemperer.
(M) (**(*)) EMI mono CMS7 69639-2 (2) [Ang. CDMB 69639]. Schwarzkopf, Seefried, Jurinac, Kunz, Majkut, London, V. State Op. Ch., VPO, Karajan.
(M) (**(*)) EMI mono CHS5 66080-2 (3) [CDHC 66080]. Kunz, Seefried, Schwarzkopf, Schöffler, Gueden, V. State Op. Ch., VPO, Furtwängler.
(M) ** Decca 455 059-2 (3). José Van Dam, Ileana Cotrubas, Tom Krause, Anna Tomowa-Sintow, Frederica von Stade, Jane Berbié, Jules Bastin, Heinz Zednik, V. State Op. Ch., VPO, Karajan.
(M) *(*) Decca 444 602-2. Tozzi, Peters, Della Casa, London, Elias, Corena, V. State Op. Ch., VPO, Leinsdorf.

Like others in EMI's series of Mozart operas, Giulini's set has been pleasingly re-packaged and has a cleanly printed, easy-to-read libretto, giving an advantage over the competing CfP set. It remains a classic, with a cast assembled by Walter Legge that has rarely been matched, let alone surpassed. Taddei with his dark bass-baritone makes a provocative Figaro; opposite him, Anna Moffo is at her freshest and sweetest as Susanna. Schwarzkopf as ever is the noblest of Countesses, and it is good to hear the young Fiorenza Cossotto as a full-toned Cherubino. Eberhard Waechter is a strong and stylish Count. On only two mid-priced discs it makes a superb bargain, though – as in the other EMI two-disc version, the Gui on CfP – Marcellina's and Basilio's arias are omitted from Act IV.

The effervescent 1955 stereo Glyndebourne recording makes a bargain without equal on only two CDs from CfP. The transfer on CD brings sound warmer, more naturally vivid and with more body than on many modern recordings. Just as Sesto Bruscantini is the archetypal Glyndebourne Figaro, Sena Jurinac is the perfect Countess, with Graziella Sciutti a delectable Susanna and Risë Stevens a well-contrasted

Cherubino, vivacious in their scenes together. Franco Calabrese as the Count is firm and virile, if occasionally stressed on top; and the three character roles have never been cast more vividly, with Ian Wallace as Bartolo, Monica Sinclair as Marcellina and the incomparable Hugues Cuénod as Basilio. The only regret is that Cuénod's brilliant performance of Basilio's aria in Act IV has had to be omitted (as it so often is on stage) to keep the two discs each within the 80-minute limit. There is no libretto; instead a detailed synopsis is provided, with cueing points conveniently indicated. But this set costs little more than a third the price of the Decca/Solti version.

The pacing of Sir Colin Davis has a sparkle in recitative that directly reflects experience in the opera house, and his tempi generally are beautifully chosen to make their dramatic points. Vocally the cast is exceptionally consistent. Mirella Freni (Susanna) is perhaps the least satisfying, yet there is no lack of character and charm. It is good to have so ravishingly beautiful a voice as Jessye Norman's for the Countess. The Figaro of Wladimiro Ganzarolli and the Count of Ingvar Wixell project with exceptional clarity and vigour, and there is fine singing too from Yvonne Minton as Cherubino, Clifford Grant as Bartolo and Robert Tear as Basilio. The 1971 recording has more reverberation than usual, but the effect is commendably atmospheric and on CD the voices have plenty of presence.

Kleiber's famous set was one of Decca's Mozart bicentenary recordings of the mid-1950s. It remains an attractively strong performance with much fine singing. Few sets since have matched its constant stylishness. Gueden's Susanna might be criticized but her golden tones are certainly characterful and her voice blends with Della Casa's enchantingly. Danco and Della Casa are both at their finest. A dark-toned Figaro in Siepi brings added contrast and, if the pace of the recitatives is rather slow, this is not inconsistent within the context of Kleiber's overall approach. It is a pity that the Decca remastering, in brightening the sound, has brought a hint of edginess to the voices, though the basic atmosphere remains. Also, the layout brings a less than felicitous break in Act II. In this respect the cassettes were superior – and they had smoother sound, too.

Boehm's version of *Figaro*, reissued by DG as a 'Legendary Recording', is also among the most consistently assured performances available. The women all sing most beautifully, with Janowitz's Countess, Mathis's Susanna and Troyanos's Cherubino all ravishing the ear in contrasted ways. Prey is an intelligent if not very jolly-sounding Figaro, and Fischer-Dieskau gives his dark, sharply defined reading of the Count's role. All told, a great success, with fine playing and recording, here impressively remastered. This and Abbado's version of Verdi's *Macbeth* are the first two opera recordings – and the first multi-CD sets – to be included in DG's 'Originals' series.

Klemperer may seem to have been the most solemn of conductors but he had a great sense of humour. Here he shows very clearly how his humour fits in with the sterling characteristics we all recognize. Though the tempi are often slow, the pointing and shading are most delicate and the result, though hardly sparkling, is full of high spirits. A clue to the Klemperer approach comes near the beginning with Figaro's aria *Se vuol ballare*, which is not merely a servant's complaint about an individual master but a revolutionary call, with horns and pizzicato strings strongly defined, to apply to the whole world: 'I'll play the tune, sir!' Sir Geraint Evans is masterly in matching Klemperer; though his normal interpretation of the role of Figaro is more effervescent than this, he is superb here, singing and acting with great power. Reri Grist makes a charming Susanna and Teresa Berganza is a rich-toned Cherubino. Gabriel Bacquier's Count is darker-toned and more formidable than usual, while Elisabeth Söderström's Countess, though it has its moments of strain, gives ample evidence of this artist's thoughtful intensity. Though this is not a version one would regularly laugh over, it represents a unique experience. The recording has transferred very well to CD.

Recorded in 1950, Karajan's first recording of *Figaro* offers one of the most distinguished casts ever assembled; but, curiously at that period, they decided to record the opera without the secco recitatives. That is a most regrettable omission when all these singers are not just vocally immaculate but vividly characterful – as for example Sena Jurinac, later the greatest of Glyndebourne Countesses, here a vivacious Cherubino. The firmness of focus in Erich Kunz's singing of Figaro goes with a delightful twinkle in the word-pointing, and Irmgard Seefried makes a bewitching Susanna. Schwarzkopf's noble portrait of the Countess – not always helped by a slight backward balance in the placing of the microphone for her – culminates in the most poignant account of her second aria, *Dove sono*. The sound, though obviously limited, presents the voices very vividly.

Furtwängler's vintage recording of *Figaro* from the Salzburg Festival was made by Austrian Radio in 1953, the only year when he conducted it there. Fascinatingly, at the conductor's insistence the performance is in German, reverting to the pre-war custom in Salzburg. It is a revelation to compare his reading of *Figaro* with Karajan's in the EMI studio recording made only a year earlier with the same orchestra, the Vienna Philharmonic, and with three of the same principals: Elisabeth Schwarzkopf as the Countess, Irmgard Seefried as Susanna and Erich Kunz as Figaro. Next to Furtwängler, Karajan – who recorded the opera without the secco recitatives – sounds stiff and plain, surprisingly lacking in humour. By contrast, many of Furtwängler's speeds are very broad though, even at their most extreme, there is always a lift to the rhythm to give Mozartian sparkle. The result is an exceptionally warm and relaxed reading, in which all the principals joyfully bring out the comedy, Kunz and Seefried above all. Schwarzkopf is in superb voice, rich and full, more creamy-toned than with Karajan, though her later performance on Giulini's 1959 recording is finest of all. Hilde Gueden as Cherubino and Paul Schoeffler as the Count are also most characterful, even if Schoeffler no longer sounds young. The snag is that, even with Basilio's and Marcellina's arias cut in the last act – as habitually they were in those days – the performance stretches to three CDs. Also, as with other EMI historic issues, no libretto is provided, just a detailed synopsis.

With Karajan on Decca, the speed and smoothness of the *Overture* establish the character of the whole performance. Too much is passed over with a deftness which quickly makes the result bland, despite superb singing and playing. Only Frederica von Stade as Cherubino establishes the sort of individuality of expression that is the very stuff of operatic drama; she alone emerges as a rounded character. With a bloom on the sound and added presence in the CD transfer, the performance is a joy to the ear but is likely to leave any Mozartian unsatisfied.

Vocally the 1960 Leinsdorf set is impressive. Giorgio Tozzi makes a fine Figaro, with a rich, dark voice (weaker admittedly at either end of the register) which is flexible enough to cope with all the vocal acting that a really comic and convincing Figaro should display. The Susanna of Roberta Peters is attractive if not always quite as stylish as one would ideally ask. There is much sparkle in her singing and, if anything, her tone-colour is too rich, for when she comes up against the Countess of Lisa della Casa there is a risk of confusion, even if in the 'Letter duet' the result is most beautiful. Della Casa displays genuinely patrician qualities with some lovely mezza voce in *Dove sono*. The Cherubino of Rosalind Elias is not quite ideal but is still impressive, and Fernando Corena is a magnificent Dr Bartolo. One could continue with the list of vocal felicities, but the snag is the ham-fisted conducting of Leinsdorf. The ridiculously fast speed in the Overture results in some scrambled playing even from the Vienna Philharmonic, and then in number after number he chooses speeds that are much too fast, and – even more serious – manages to eliminate all the charm from Mozart's score in an interpretation notable for its graceless qualities. We need a highlights disc from this set to rescue some of the more successful numbers from an excellent cast.

Le nozze di Figaro: highlights.

(M) *** EMI CDM5 66049-2 [id.] (from above complete recording, with Schwarzkopf, Moffo, Cossotto, Taddei, Waechter; cond. Giulini).

(B) *** DG Classikon 439 449-2; *439 449-4* [429 822-2] (from above set, with Janowitz, Mathis, Prey, Fischer-Dieskau; cond. Boehm).

(M) **(*) Decca 452 732-2 (from above recording, with Siepi, Gueden, della Casa, Danco, Poell; cond. Erich Kleiber).

(M) ** O-L Dig. 443 191-2 (from complete recording, with Salomaa, Bonney, Hagegård, Augér, Drottningholm Theatre Ch. & O, Ostman).

The Giulini CD makes a clear first choice for a highlights CD from *Nozze di Figaro*. The selection may play for only 62 minutes but every item is treasurable, not least *Non più andrai*, the Countess's two arias, and the long excerpt from the Act II finale. The new transfer is extremely vivid, and the synopsis relates the excerpts to the narrative.

Boehm's selection includes many of the key numbers, but with a little over an hour of music it is less than generous and inadequately documented; but the singing is first class and the sound vivid.

It is good to have a reminder of Erich Kleiber's classic 1956 set. It is a pity that the selection, though not really ungenerous (66 minutes), did not find room for an extended excerpt at the close of Act II (where Kleiber's overall control was revelatory); but the disc ends with the final ten minutes of Act IV, which is some compensation and, of course, includes the key arias. Gueden's enchanting, golden-toned Susanna both blends and contrasts beautifully with Della Casa's Countess (their Letter duet in Act III is delightful); and Danco, too, is at her finest as Cherubino. A dark-toned Figaro in Siepi brings striking contrast, and altogether this is a disc to treasure. The new transfer is vivid, smoother than before, and the cued synopsis is well managed. An essential purchase for all lovers of this wonderful opera who do not already have the complete set.

Ostman's was the first period-instrument performance of *Figaro*, and his ruthlessly metrical pressing forward undermines the opera's fun and dramatic point. The opera is impressively cast, with Barbara Bonney a charming Susanna and Augér singing beautifully as the Countess (in spite of the conductor's fast speeds). Håkan Hagegård is a splendid Count. The excerpts play for 66 minutes.

Complete Mozart Edition, Volume 39: *L'Oca del Cairo* (complete).

(M) *** Ph. Dig. 422 539-2 [id.]. Nielsen, Wiens, Coburn, Schreier, Johnson, Fischer-Dieskau, Scharinger, Berlin R. Ch. (members), C. P. E. Bach CO, Schreier – *Lo sposo deluso*. ***

We owe it to the Mozart scholar and Philips recording producer, Erik Smith, that these two sets of Mozartian fragments, *L'Oca del Cairo* and *Lo sposo deluso*, have been prepared for performance and recorded. *L'Oca del Cairo* ('The Cairo goose'), containing roughly twice as much music as *Lo sposo deluso*, involves six substantial numbers, most of them ensembles, including an amazing finale to the projected Act I, with contrasted sections following briskly one after the other. It is very well conducted by Peter Schreier, who also takes part as one of the soloists. Dietrich Fischer-Dieskau takes the *buffo* old-man role of Don Pippo, and Anton Scharinger is brilliant in the patter aria in tarantella rhythm for the major-domo, Chichibio, bringing a foretaste of Donizetti. Fresh, bright digital recording.

Complete Mozart Edition, Volume 35: *Il rè pastore* (complete).
(M) **(*) Ph. Dig. 422 535-2 (2) [id.]. Blasi, McNair, Vermillion, Hadley, Ahnsjö, ASMF, Marriner.

Il rè pastore (complete).
(M) **(*) RCA 74321 50165-2 (2). Grist, Popp, Saunders, Alva, Monti, O of Naples, Vaughan.

'There is nothing for Mozart to do but write beautiful music,' says Alfred Einstein of this early piece, written in 1775 for a state occasion in Salzburg. It is a pastoral story of shepherds and shepherdesses, and not a single character is anything but utterly, boringly good. Not exactly a music drama, then, but still a splendid example of Mozart's youthful genius at work, the more enchanting for being performed here with real style and verve. Denis Vaughan – once a Beecham protégé – is a lively advocate and, when first issued in 1967, this recording reinforced his then blossoming reputation. Among the singers, Lucia Popp is wonderfully sweet-toned and her high legato phrases never concede even a momentary blemish. Reri Grist's voice is harder, less smooth, but in a way that is fitting enough in the castrato role of Aminta, and her singing of the most famous number, *L'Améro*, is expressively beautiful. Arlene Saunders is a graceful Tamiri, and Nicola Monti and Luiga Alva make a quite stylish pair of tenors, even if their florid singing is not always quite immaculate. Not the least important quality of Denis Vaughan's direction is his editing, very scholarly for the late 1960s, with a plentiful sprinkling of appoggiature smoothing the blunt phrase-endings. He also plays the continuo in the recitatives most effectively. The one slight snag is the CD transfer, which has brightened what was a pleasingly full and lively analogue sound: the voices now have a degree of added edge and the orchestral tuttis bring some rough moments. However, this remains a vivid musical experience, and a full libretto is provided.

The alternative version by Marriner and the Academy, with a first-rate cast and with plenty of light and shade, and superbly played, does not efface memories of the 1979 DG version conducted by Leopold Hager, which offered even purer singing. Here Angela Maria Blasi, despite a beautiful voice, attacks notes from below, even in *L'amero*. Excellent sound.

Complete Mozart Edition, Volume 36: *Der Schauspieldirektor* (complete).
(M) **(*) Ph. 422 536-2 (2) [id.]. Welting, Cotrubas, Grant, Rolfe Johnson, LSO, Sir Colin Davis – *Zaïde*. ***

(i–v; viii) *Der Schauspieldirektor*. Concert arias: (ii; vii; ix) *Misera, dove son!, K.369; Un moto di gioia, K.579; Schon lacht der holde Frühling, K.580*. (i; vii; ix) *Vado, ma dove? oh Dei!, K.583; Bella mia fiamma, addio, K.529; Nehmt meinen Dank, ihr holden Gonner!* (iv; vi; x) *Die Entführung: Ha! Wie will ich triumpheren*. (v; viii) *Le nozze di Figaro: Overture*.
(M) *** Decca Dig. 452 624-2 [id.]. (i) Te Kanawa, (ii) Gruberová, (iii) Heilmann, (iv) Jungwirth; (v) VPO; (vi) V. Haydn O; (vii) VCO; (viii) Pritchard; (ix) Fischer; (x) Kertész.

This Decca recording of the four musical numbers from *Der Schauspieldirektor* (presented 'dry' with no German dialogue) was made only six months before Sir John Pritchard died, an apt last offering from him, a great Mozartian. Having two such well-contrasted star sopranos adds point to the contest, and the performances are a delight, though the recorded sound is not as well focused as usual from this source. The *Figaro overture*, also conducted by Pritchard, is another completely new item. The rest is reissue material, with three concert arias each from Gruberová and Dame Kiri, taken from Decca's 1981 boxed set of the collected arias. Manfred Jungwirth's bitingly dark account of Osmin's aria from *Entführung* dates from ten years before that, a welcome extra. The single mid-priced disc comes with full translations and note and the reissue is something of a bargain.

There is no contest whatsoever between the two rival prima donnas presented in the Philips recording. *Ich bin die erste Sängerin* ('I am the leading prima donna'), they yell at each other; but here Ileana Cotrubas is in a world apart from the thin-sounding and shallow Ruth Welting. Davis directs with fire and electricity a performance which is otherwise (despite the lack of spoken dialogue) most refreshing and beautifully recorded (in 1975) in a sympathetic acoustic.

Complete Mozart Edition, Volume 31: *Il sogno di Scipione* (complete).

(M) *** Ph. 422 531-2 (2) [id.]. Popp, Gruberová, Mathis, Schreier, Ahnsjö, Thomas Moser, Salzburg Chamber Ch. & Mozarteum O, Hager.

Il sogno di Scipione presents an allegorical plot with Scipio set to choose between Fortune and Constancy. Given the choice of present-day singers, this cast could hardly be finer, with Edita Gruberová, Lucia Popp and Edith Mathis superbly contrasted in the women's roles (the latter taking part in the epilogue merely), and Peter Schreier is joined by two of his most accomplished younger colleagues. Hager sometimes does not press the music on as he might, but his direction is always alive. With fine recording, vividly and atmospherically transferred to CD, the set is not likely to be surpassed in the immediate future.

Complete Mozart Edition, Volume 39: *Lo sposo deluso*.

(M) *** Ph. 422 539-2 [id.]. Palmer, Cotrubas, Rolfe Johnson, Tear, Grant, LSO, Sir Colin Davis – *L'Oca del Cairo*. ***

The music presented here from *Lo sposo deluso* is the surviving music from an unfinished opera written in the years before *Figaro*, and it contains much that is memorable. The *Overture*, with its trumpet calls, its lovely slow middle section and recapitulation with voices, is a charmer, while the two arias, reconstructed by the recording producer and scholar, Erik Smith, are also delightful: the one a trial run for Fiordiligi's *Come scoglio* in *Così*, the other (sung by Robert Tear) giving a foretaste of Papageno's music in *The Magic Flute*.

Complete Mozart Edition, Volume 36: *Zaïde*.

(M) *** Ph. 422 536-2 (2) [id.]. Mathis, Schreier, Wixell, Hollweg, Süss, Berlin State O, Klee – *Der Schauspieldirektor*. **(*)

Zaïde, written between 1779 and 1780 and never quite completed, was a trial run for *Entführung*. Much of the music is superb, and melodramas at the beginning of each Act are strikingly effective and original, with the speaking voice of the tenor in the first heard over darkly dramatic writing in D minor. Zaïde's arias in both Acts are magnificent: the radiantly lyrical *Ruhe sanft* is hauntingly memorable, and the dramatic *Tiger aria* is like Constanze's *Martern aller Arten* but briefer and more passionate. Bernhard Klee directs a crisp and lively performance, with excellent contributions from singers and orchestra alike – a first-rate team, as consistently stylish as one could want.

Die Zauberflöte (complete).

✿ (M) (***) DG mono 435 741-2 (2). Stader, Streich, Fischer-Dieskau, Greindl, Haefliger, Berlin RIAS Ch. & SO, Fricsay.

(M) (***) EMI (SIS) mono CHS7 69631-2 (2) [Ang. CDHB 69631]. Seefried, Lipp, Loose, Dermota, Kunz, Weber, V. State Op. Ch., VPO, Karajan.

(B) *** Naxos Dig. 8 660030/31 (2) [id.]. Norberg-Schulz, Kwon, Lippert, Leitner, Tichy, Rydl, Hungarian Festival Ch., Failoni O, Budapest, Halász.

(M) **(*) DG Originals 449 749-2 (2) [id.]. Lear, Peters, Wunderlich, Fischer-Dieskau, Crass, Hotter, BPO, Boehm.

(M) **(*) RCA 74321 32240-2. Donath, Geszty, Schreier, Adam, Hoff, Leib, Vogel, Leipzig R. Ch., Dresden State O, Suitner.

(B) (***) Dutton mono 2CDEA 5011 (2) [(M) id.]. Lemnitz, Roswaenge, Berger, Hüsch, Strienz, BPO, Beecham.

(M) (**(*)) Pearl mono GEMMCDS 9371 (2). Lemnitz, Roswaenge, Berger, Hüsch, Strienz, Ch. & BPO, Beecham.

(B) ** Ph. Duo Dig. 442 568-2 (2) [id.]. Margaret Price, Serra, Schreier, Moll, Melbye, Venuti, Tear, Dresden Kreuzchor, Leipzig R. Ch., Dresden State O, Sir Colin Davis.

(B) ** Decca Double 448 734-2 (2) [414 362-2]. Gueden, Lipp, Simoneau, Berry, Böhme, V. State Op. Ch., VPO, Karl Boehm.

From the early LP era Fricsay's is an outstandingly fresh and alert *Die Zauberflöte*, marked by generally clear, pure singing and well-sprung orchestral playing at generally rather fast speeds. In some ways Fricsay anticipates the Mozart tastes of a later generation, even if his approach to ornamentation is hardly in authentic-period style. Maria Stader and Dietrich Fischer-Dieskau phrase most beautifully, but the most spectacular singing comes from Rita Streich as a dazzling Queen of the Night – the finest on record – and the relatively close balance of the voice gives it the necessary power such as Streich generally failed to convey in the opera house. It is this unique contribution which nudges us towards a Rosette; but Ernst Haefliger, too, is at his most honeyed in tone as Tamino, and only the rather gritty Sarastro of Josef Greindl falls short – and even he sings with a satisfyingly dark resonance. This was the first version to spice the musical numbers with brief sprinklings of dialogue, just enough to prevent the work from sounding like an oratorio. Even including that, DG has managed to put each of the Acts complete on a single disc. The transfer of the original 1954 mono recording (made in the Berlin Jesus-Christus-Kirche) is remarkably full-bodied, with a pleasant ambience and sense of presence.

Apart from the Fricsay set with Rita Streich which includes some spoken dialogue, there has never been a more seductive recording of *Zauberflöte* than Karajan's mono version of 1950. The Vienna State Opera cast here has not since been matched on record: Irmgard Seefried and Anton Dermota both sing with radiant beauty and great character, Wilma Lipp is a dazzling Queen of the Night, Erich Kunz as Papageno sings with an infectious smile in the voice, and Ludwig Weber is a commanding Sarastro. There is no spoken dialogue; but on two mid-priced CDs instead of three LPs, it is a Mozart treat not to be missed, with mono sound still amazingly vivid and full of presence.

Though Kurt Rydl is the only established recording artist among the soloists, the Naxos set offers a very satisfying performance, well conducted and well recorded, with some very stylish solo singing. At budget price with a fair measure of German dialogue included (but on separate tracks to allow it to be programmed out if preferred), this makes a first-rate recommendation, competitive with some of the classic sets. As Tamino, Herbert Lippert is a good, clean-cut Germanic tenor, hardly ever strained, with fine legato in *Dies Bildnis*. The young Norwegian, Elisabeth Norberg-Schulz, is a bright, girlish Pamina, who sustains a slow speed for *Ach, ich fühl's* very effectively, tenderly making it an emotional high point. Rydl is a powerful Sarastro, if not always perfectly steady, and Tichy is a delightful Papageno, defying Halász's uncharacteristically stodgy tempo for his first aria, and from there consistently conveying characterful humour without vocal exaggeration. Perhaps the most exciting newcomer is Hellen Kwon, an outstanding Queen of the Night, using full, firm tone with bright attack in her two big arias. The recording is clear and well balanced, with the Queen's thunder vividly caught.

One of the glories of Boehm's DG set is the singing of Fritz Wunderlich as Tamino, a wonderful memorial to a singer much missed. Fischer-Dieskau, with characteristic word-pointing, makes a sparkling Papageno on record and Franz Crass is a satisfyingly straightforward Sarastro. The team of women is well below this standard – Lear taxed cruelly in *Ach, ich fühl's*, Peters shrill in the upper register (although the effect is exciting), and the Three Ladies do not blend well – but Boehm's direction is superb, light and lyrical, but weighty where necessary to make a glowing, compelling experience. Fine recording, enhanced in this new transfer for reissue as one of DG's 'Originals'. It is now divested of its previous coupling of *Der Schauspieldiretor* and fitted on to two instead of three CDs.

The RCA (originally Eurodisc) set is well cast, directed with breadth and spirit, and vividly recorded. Indeed, considering that the recording was made at the beginning of the 1970s, it sounds remarkably well, although with a forward balance there is not the subtlety of perspective one finds in more modern sets. There are no real flaws here. The finest performances come from Peter Schreier, an outstanding Tamino, ardent and stylish; Sylvia Geszty's Queen of the Night is fierce to the point of shrillness, but it is a forceful projection and balances with Donath's somewhat ingenuous portrayal of Pamina, prettily sung. Theo Adam is a commanding Sarastro and Renata Hoff and Günther Leib make an attractive team as Papagena and Papageno; while the orchestral playing is first rate, the contribution of the Leipzig Radio Choir is less impressive. There is a minimum of dialogue and it is separately cued. Not a top choice, but enjoyable just the same. The accompanying libretto is in German with no translation.

Beecham's magical pre-war set of *Zauberflöte* has had three earlier CD transfers, all of them seriously flawed, which makes it specially welcome that Mike Dutton comes up with a transfer which at last does justice to the original sound, full and vivid; and the two discs are offered at bargain price. There is glorious singing from Tiana Lemnitz as Pamina, brilliant coloratura from Erna Berger as Queen of the Night, and sharp characterization from Gerhard Hüsch as Papageno. Helge Roswaenge is a Germanic Tamino and Wilhelm Strienz a firm but lugubrious Sarastro. No spoken dialogue, but much warmth and sparkle. Recorded in Berlin between November 1937 and March 1939, Beecham's recording of *Zauberflöte* was also the first opera set produced by Walter Legge. It brings a classic performance. Beecham was at his peak, pacing each number superbly, and the vocal delights are many, not least from Tiana Lemnitz as a radiant Pamina, Erna Berger as a dazzling Queen of the Night, and Gerhard Hüsch as a delicately comic Papageno, bringing the detailed art of the Lieder-singer to the role. Of the currently available transfers of this Beecham recording to CD, the Pearl is the one which captures the original 78 recording most naturally, with the keenest sense of presence for the voices, even if it leaves it with plentiful surface hiss.

The last of Sir Colin Davis's recordings of Mozart's major operas, and the only one made outside Britain, is also the least successful. With speeds often slower than usual and the manner heavier, it is a performance of little sparkle or charm, one which seems intent on bringing out serious, symbolic meanings. Thus, although Margaret Price produces a glorious flow of rich, creamy tone, she conveys little of the necessary vulnerability of Pamina in her plight. Luciana Serra sings capably but at times with shrill tone and not always with complete security; while Peter Schreier is in uncharacteristically gritty voice as Tamino, and Mikael Melbye as Papageno is ill-suited to recording, when the microphone exaggerates the throatiness and unevenness of his production. The greatest vocal glory of the set is the magnificent, firm and rich singing of Kurt Moll as Sarastro. The recording is excellent. Although this Duo reissue is inexpensive, it is upstaged by the competing Halász Naxos set from Budapest.

The principal attraction of this Decca reissue from the earliest days of stereo, apart from its modest cost, is the conducting of Karl Boehm. With surprisingly good recording quality (vintage 1955), vivid, warm and full in the bass, that might well be counted recommendation enough, in spite of the absence of dialogue, particularly when the Tamino of Léopold Simoneau and the Papageno of Walter Berry are strongly and sensitively sung. But the rest of the singing is variable, with Hilde Gueden a pert, characterful Pamina, unhappy in the florid divisions, and Wilma Lipp an impressive Queen of the Night, but Kurt Böhme a gritty and ungracious Sarastro. For its age the sound is remarkably atmospheric. No libretto/translation is provided, but there is a good synopsis, and it is a pity that it is not cued.

Die Zauberflöte: highlights.

(M) *** EMI CDM5 65568-2 (from complete recording, with Janowitz, Putz, Popp, Gedda, Berry, Frick, Schwarzkopf, Ludwig, Hoffgen (3 ladies), Philh. Ch. & O, Klemperer).

(B) *** [EMI Red Line Dig. CDR5 72098] (from complete recording, with Popp, Gruberová, Lindner, Jerusalem, Brendel, Bav. RSO & Ch., Haitink).

(B) (***) EMI mono CD-EMX 2220 [(M) id. import] (from above recording with Seefried, Lipp; cond. Karajan).

(B) **(*) DG Classikon 449 845-2; *449 845-4* [(M) id. import] (from above recording, with Lear, Peters, Wunderlich, Fischer-Dieskau, Crass; cond. Boehm).

(M) **(*) Decca 458 213-2 [id.] (from complete recording, with Lorengar, Deutekom, Burrows, Talvela, Prey, Stoltze, V. State Op. Ch., VPO, Solti).

Those looking for a first-rate set of highlights from *Die Zauberflöte* will find the mid-priced Klemperer disc hard to beat. It makes a good sampler of a performance which, while ambitious in scale, manages to find sparkle and humour too. A synopsis details each individual excerpt, and in this case the inclusion of the *Overture* is especially welcome. The remastered sound has plenty of presence, but atmosphere and warmth too.

This selection from the full-priced Haitink set is well made to include many favourites, with the Papageno/Papagena music well represented to make a contrast with the lyrical arias and the drama of the Queen of the Night. Gruberová has never sounded more spontaneous in her brilliance than here; in that role she is both agile and powerful. Popp makes the most tenderly affecting of Paminas. The gravitas of Haitink's approach does not miss the work's elements of drama and charm, though nothing is trivialized. Superb recording in spectacularly wide-ranging, digital sound.

The Karajan Vienna State Opera selection on Eminence will be a good way for many to sample a highly enticing mono set with a superb cast, all on the top of their form. The selection lasts 68 minutes, but seven of these are taken up by the Overture, a less than sensible idea, even if it is superbly played. It is disgraceful, though, that the front of this CD – aimed at a popular market – does not make it absolutely clear that the sound is mono.

The hour of excerpts from Boehm's recording is not obviously directed towards bringing out its special qualities, although there would have been room on the CD (which includes the *Overture*) for at least another quarter of an hour of music, to measure up with the companion selection from *Don Giovanni*. One would have liked more of Wunderlich's Tamino, one of the great glories of the set. However, the key arias are all included and the sound is fresh and full. This is now on DG's bargain Classikon label, which means that the synopsis is not cued.

Solti's highlights, which come from his earlier (1970) analogue set, are certainly worth sampling. On the male side the cast is very strong indeed, with Stuart Burrows a stylish, rich-toned Tamino. Martti Talvela is a bold Sarastro and Hermann Prey rounds out the character of Papageno with intelligent pointing of words. Pilar Lorengar's Pamina is sweetly attractive as long as your ear is not worried by her intrusive vibrato, while Cristina Deutekom's Queen of the Night is technically impressive, though the coloratura has a curious colouristic flaw. Solti's reading is tough and brilliant, but it is aguable that in highlights this is less worrying than in a complete set, even if the almost total absence of charm is disconcerting. The selection is generous (73 minutes) and the disc is handsomely packaged in Decca's Opera Gala series, with a full translation included.

Recitals

Arias from: *La clemenza di Tito; Così fan tutte; Don Giovanni; Die Entführung aus dem Serail; Idomeneo; Le nozze di Figaro; Die Zauberflöte.*

(M) *** Ph. (IMS) Dig. 442 410-2. Cheryl Studer, ASMF, Marriner.

This is a very impressive recital indeed. Only the aria from *Idomeneo* could be considered a little under-characterized – and that is a marginal criticism; the Queen of the Night's arias from *Die Zauberflöte* are superbly done, as is the opening *Martern aller Arten* (from *Die Entführung*) and the excerpts from *Così* and *Don Giovanni* are hardly less memorable in a quite different way. Excellent accompaniments and recording, but the measure is fairly short (55 minutes).

Arias: *Don Giovanni; Die Entführung aus dem Serail; Idomeneo; Le nozze di Figaro; Die Zauberflöte.*

(M) (***) EMI (SIS) mono CDH7 63708-2. Elisabeth Schwarzkopf (with various orchestras & conductors, including John Pritchard).

Just how fine a Mozartian Schwarzkopf already was early in her career comes out in these 12 items, recorded between 1946 and 1952. The earliest are Konstanze's two arias from *Entführung*, and one of the curiosities is a lovely account of Pamina's *Ach ich fühl's*, recorded in English in 1948. The majority, including those from *Figaro* – Susanna's and Cherubino's arias as well as the Countess's – are taken from a long-unavailable recital disc conducted by John Pritchard. Excellent transfers.

ANTHOLOGIES

'Fifty Years of Mozart singing on record': (i) *Concert arias;* Excerpts from: (ii) *Mass in C min., K.427;* (iii) *La clemenza di Tito;* (iv) *Così fan tutte;* (v) *Don Giovanni;* (vi) *Die Entführung aus dem Serail;* (vii) *La finta giardiniera;* (viii) *Idomeneo;* (ix) *Le nozze di Figaro;* (x) *Il rè pastore;* (xi) *Zaïde;* (xii) *Die Zauberflöte.*

(M) (***) EMI mono CMS7 63750-2 (4). (i) Rethberg, Ginster, Francillo-Kaufmann; (ii) Berger; (iii) Kirkby-Lunn; (iv) V. Schwarz, Noni, Grümmer, Hahn, Kiurina, Hüsch, Souez, H. Nash; (v) Vanni-Marcoux, Scotti, Farrar, Battistini, Corsi, Leider, Roswaenge, D'Andrade, Pinza, Patti, Maurel, Renaud, Pernet, McCormack, Gadski, Kemp, Callas; (vi) Slezak, L. Weber, Tauber, Lehmann, Nemeth, Perras, Ivogün, Von Pataky, Hesch; (vii) Dux; (viii) Jurinac, Jadlowker; (ix) Stabile, Helletsgruber, Santley, Gobbi, Lemnitz, Feraldy, Schumann, Seinemeyer, Vallin, Rautawaara, Mildmay, Jokl, Ritter-Ciampi; (x) Gerhart; (xi) Seefried; (xii) Fugère; Wittrisch; Schiøtz, Gedda, Kurz, Erb, Kipnis, Galvany, Hempel, Sibiriakov, Frick, Destinn, Norena, Schöne, Kunz.

This is an astonishing treasury of singing, recorded over the first half of the twentieth century. It begins with Mariano Stabile's resonant 1928 account of Figaro's *Se vuol ballare*, snail-like by today's standards, while Sir Charles Santley in *Non piu andrai* a few tracks later is both old-sounding and slow. The stylistic balance is then corrected in Tito Gobbi's magnificently characterful 1950 recording of that same aria. Astonishment lies less in early stylistic enormities than in the wonderful and consistent purity of vocal production, with wobbles – so prevalent today – virtually non-existent. That is partly the result of the shrewd and obviously loving choice of items, which includes not only celebrated marvels like John McCormack's 1916 account of Don Ottavio's *Il mio tesoro* (breaking all records for breath control, and stylistically surprising for including an appoggiatura), but many rarities. The short-lived Meta Seinemeyer, glorious in the Countess's first aria, Germaine Feraldy, virtually unknown, a charming Cherubino, Johanna Gadski formidably incisive in Donna Anna's *Mi tradi*, Frieda Hempel incomparable in the Queen of the Night's second aria – all these and many dozens of others make for compulsive listening, with transfers generally excellent. There are far more women singers represented than men, and a high proportion of early recordings are done in languages other than the original; but no lover of fine singing should miss this feast. The arias are gathered together under each opera, with items from non-operatic sources grouped at the end of each disc. Helpfully, duplicate versions of the same aria are put together irrespective of date of recording, and highly informative notes are provided on all the singers.

Muldowney, Dominic (born 1952)

(i) *Piano concerto;* (ii) *Saxophone concerto.*

(M) *** EMI CDM5 66528-2. (i) Peter Donohoe, BBC SO, Mark Elder; (ii) John Harle, L. Sinf., Diego Masson.

Dominic Muldowney, born in 1952 and music director at the National Theatre since 1976, has latterly become a composer laudably concerned with direct communication to a wide range of listeners. These two colourful and dramatic concertos are excellent examples of his more recent style, far more approachable than his earlier work. His *Piano concerto* is a formidable work in a continuous half-hour span of many different sections. It uses Bachian forms, along with tough Bachian piano figuration, to move kaleidoscopically in a kind of musical collage of references to different genres, including jazz and the popular waltz. With Peter Donohoe giving one of his finest performances on record, and with colourful playing from the BBC Symphony Orchestra under Mark Elder, the piece emerges powerfully, with occasional gruff echoes of Hindemith. The *Saxophone concerto* (written for the outstanding virtuoso of the instrument, John Harle, who plays it on the record) is a more compact, strongly characterized work in three movements, each throwing up a grateful number of warm, easy tunes without any sense of compromise or incongruity. Warm, well-balanced recording.

Mussorgsky, Modest (1839–81)

The Capture of Kars (Triumphal march); St John's night on the bare mountain (original score); *Scherzo in B flat. Khovanshchina: Prelude to Act I;* (i) *Introduction to Act IV. The Destruction of Sennacherib.* (i; ii) *Joshua.* (i) *Oedipus in Athens: Temple chorus. Salammbô: Priestesses' chorus* (operatic excerpts all orch. Rimsky-Korsakov).

❀ (M) *** RCA 09026 61354-2 [id.]. (i) London Symphony Ch.; (ii) Zehava Gal; LSO, Abbado.

To commemorate the centenary of Mussorgsky's death, in 1981 Abbado and the LSO came up with this very attractive and revealing anthology of shorter pieces. The *Khovanshchina Prelude*, very beautifully played indeed, is well enough known, but it is good to have so vital and pungent an account of the original version of *Night on the bare mountain*, different in all but its basic material from the Rimsky-Korsakov arrangement. Rimsky was right to prune it: at 12 minutes, without the slow end-piece, it is a shade over-long, but Mussorgsky's scoring is so original and imaginative that the ear is readily held. Best of all are the four choral pieces; even when they are early and untypical (*Oedipus in Athens*, for example), they are immediately attractive and very Russian in feeling, and they include such evocative pieces as the *Chorus of Priestesses* (intoning over a pedal bass) from a projected opera on Flaubert's novel. The recording is first rate and the CD transfer enhances the original considerably, giving the chorus greater presence without loss of atmosphere or perspective. This is one of the most attractive Mussorgsky records in the catalogue and is not to be missed: the performers are on their toes throughout.

Night on the bare mountain (orch. Rimsky-Korsakov).

(M) *** EMI CDM5 65715-2 [id.]. O de Paris, Rostropovich – RIMSKY-KORSAKOV: *Scheherazade; Capriccio espagnol.* **(*)

(M) *** Mercury (IMS) 432 004-2 [id.]. LSO, Dorati – PROKOFIEV: *Romeo and Juliet suites.* ***

A bold, exciting account from Rostropovich, emphasizing the richness of Rimsky-Korsakov's orchestration rather than the starkness of Mussorgsky's original conception – but not necessarily the worse for that, when the recording is full-blooded to match.

Dorati's fine 1960 account of *Night on the bare mountain* comes as an encore for Skrowaczewski's outstanding Prokofiev, and it is interesting at the end of *Romeo and Juliet* to note the subtle shift of acoustic from the Minneapolis auditorium to Wembley Town Hall.

Night on the bare mountain; Khovanshchina: Prelude (both arr. Rimsky-Korsakov).

(BB) *** Belart 450 017-2 [(M) id. import]. LSO, Solti – GLINKA: *Ruslan and Ludmilla: overture* *** ❀; BORODIN: *Prince Igor:* excerpts. ***

Solti's *Night on the bare mountain* can stand up to all the competition in its vintage (1967) recording with its fine amplitude and great brilliance. This remains one of Solti's finest analogue recordings, offering also the highly atmospheric *Khovanshchina Prelude*, which is beautifully played.

(i) *Night on the bare mountain* (arr. Rimsky-Korsakov); (ii) *Pictures at an exhibition* (orch. Ravel).

(M) *** RCA [id.]. 09026 61958-2 [id.]. Chicago SO, Reiner – *Concert of Russian showpieces.* ***

(B) **(*) Decca Eclipse Dig. 448 233-2; *448 233-4* [(M) id. import]. Montreal SO, Dutoit – RIMSKY-KORSAKOV: *Capriccio espagnol* etc. **(*)

(BB) ** Naxos 8.550051 [id.]. Slovak PO, Nazareth – BORODIN: *In the Steppes of Central Asia* etc. **

(M) ** Virgin/EMI Dig. CUV5 61135-2. RLPO Ch. & O, Mackerras – BORODIN: *Prince Igor: Overture and Polovtsian dances.* ***

Reiner's RCA *Pictures* (recorded in 1957) is another demonstration of vintage stereo using simple microphone techniques to achieve a natural concert-hall balance.The sound-balance is full and atmospheric and Reiner's approach is evocative to match – the sombre picture of *The old castle*, the lumbering

Ox-wagon, the unctuous picture of *Samuel Goldenberg* (powerfully drawn in the strings) and the superb brass playing in the *Catacombs* sequence are all memorable. The final climax of *The Great Gate of Kiev* is massively effective. The Chicago brass is again very telling in *Night on the bare mountain*, made two years later, a performance just as strongly characterized. The current CD transfers are very impressive indeed.

Dutoit's *Night on the bare mountain* is strong and biting, but the adrenalin does not flow as grippingly as in, say, Solti's version. Dutoit's *Pictures* have each movement strongly characterized and there is a sense of fun in the scherzando movements. But overall this is less involving than with Reiner, and the brilliant recording is not as sumptuous as some other versions, although it has the bloom characteristic of the Montreal sound.

The super-bargain Naxos coupling is vividly played and recorded and is well worth its modest price. *Night on the bare mountain* is played flexibly, yet does not lack excitement. The *Pictures*, too, have plenty of character. The climax of *Bydlo* is dramatically enhanced by a fortissimo contribution from the timpanist, and the detail throughout is well observed, from the bleating Schmuyle to the chirping chicks. *Tuileries* and *Limoges* bring lightly etched orchestral bravura, while the closing picture of the Kiev Gate has architectural grandeur and a sense of majesty. Enjoyable, if lacking the last touch of individuality.

Mackerras surprisingly comes over at a lower voltage than usual. Although his opening *Promenade* is fairly brisk, the first few pictures, though well played, are almost bland and, while *Bydlo* reaches a fairly massive climax, it is not until *Limoges* that the performance springs fully to life; then *The hut on fowl's legs* is powerfully rhythmic, with an impressive tuba solo. *The Great Gate of Kiev* is not as consistently taut as in some versions, but it is properly expansive at the close, with the recording, always full-bodied, producing an impressive breadth of sound. Perhaps the tam-tam might ideally have been placed a fraction nearer. *Night on the bare mountain*, although vivid enough, lacks Satanic bite, and the closing pages fail to wring the heartstrings.

(i) *Night on the bare mountain* (arr. and orch. Stokowski); (ii) *Boris Godunov: symphonic synthesis* (arr. Stokowski).

(M) ** Decca Phase Four 443 896-2 [id.]. (i) LSO; (ii) SRO; Stokowski – BORODIN: *Polovtsian dances* ***; TCHAIKOVSKY: *1812 overture* etc. **(*)

Pictures at an exhibition. (arr. and orch. Stokowski).

(M) ** Decca Phase 4 443 898-2 [id.]. New Phil. O, Stokowski – SCRIABIN: *Poème de l'extase;* STRAVINSKY: *Firebird suite* etc. **(*)

Stokowski's *Night on the bare mountain* begins with a grotesque balance at the opening, with the heavy brass to the fore. This is Stokowski's own orchestration, so gauche emphasis is fair enough. Few records have more noise on them at climaxes, but the bizarre orchestral effects are telling in a crude way, and the gentle coda is beautifully done in Stokowski's romantically drenched, ecstatic manner. Stokowski's arrangement omits the familiar brass fanfare motif which Rimsky added in his more sophisticated version.

The extended symphonic synthesis from *Boris Godunov* has a technicolor hue; yet, for all the hyperbole of the presentation, Stokowski's magnetism ensures that the music's power communicates, even if the stark austerity of Mussorgsky's original is missing.

Similarly Stokowski's arrangement of *Pictures at an exhibition* is not notable for its subtlety. The pictures are blown up with Phase Four immediacy, so that the orchestra sounds right on top of the listener. With a restricted dynamic range, the sound is very coarse and the inner tension is stretched to breaking point. The closing climax is harsh. Even so, the sheer personality of this music-making makes its impact.

Pictures at an exhibition (orch. Ravel).

(M) *** DG 447 426-2 [id.]. BPO, Karajan – DEBUSSY: *La Mer;* RAVEL: *Boléro*. ***

(B) *** Sony SBK 48162; *SBT 48162* [id.]. Cleveland O, Szell – KODALY: *Háry János suite;* PROKOFIEV: *Lieutenant Kijé suite*. ***

(M) *** DG (IMS) Dig. 445 556-2. LSO, Abbado – RAVEL: *Une barque sur l'océan* etc. ***

(M) *** DG (IMS) 415 844-2. Chicago SO, Giulini – RAVEL: *Ma mère l'Oye; Rapsodie espagnole*. ***

(M) *** EMI Dig. CDM7 64516-2 [id.]. Phd. O, Muti – STRAVINSKY: *Rite of spring*. ***

(M) *** Decca Dig. 417 754-2 [id.]. Chicago SO, Solti – BARTOK: *Concerto for orchestra*. ***

(M) (***) Mercury mono 434 378-2 [id.]. Chicago SO, Rafael Kubelik – BARTOK: *Music for strings, percussion and celesta*. (***)

(B) **(*) Belart 450 081-2 [(M) id. import]. New Philh. O, Lorin Maazel – PROKOFIEV: *Piano concerto No. 3*. **(*)

(M) (**) RCA mono GD 60287 [60287-2-RG]. NBC SO, Toscanini – ELGAR: *Enigma variations*. (***)

Among the many fine versions of Mussorgsky's *Pictures* on CD, Karajan's 1966 record stands out. It is undoubtedly a great performance, tingling with electricity from the opening Promenade to the spaciously conceived finale, *The Great Gate of Kiev*, which has real splendour. Other high points are the ominously powerful climax of *Bydlo* as the Polish ox-wagon lumbers into view very weightily, and the venomously pungent bite of the brass – expansively recorded – in the sinister *Catacombs* sequence, which is given a bizarre majesty. Detail is consistently pointed with the greatest imagination, not only in the lighter moments but, for instance, in *The hut on fowl's legs*, where the tuba articulation is sharp and rhythmically buoyant. Throughout, the glorious orchestral playing, and especially the brass sonorities, ensnare the ear; even when Karajan is relatively restrained, as in the nostalgic melancholy of *The old castle*, the underlying tension remains. The remastered analogue recording still sounds marvellous, and this reissue, in DG's 'Originals' series of legendary recordings, includes a uniquely evocative performance of Debussy's *La Mer* as well as a very exciting account of Ravel's *Boléro*.

Szell's 1963 Cleveland performance also remains among the greatest of all recordings of Ravel's vividly inspired orchestration and is recommendable alongside Karajan. Even if the recording has a somewhat less expansive dynamic-range, the character of each portrait is firmly drawn with vivid strokes of orchestral colour, helped by the feeling that the orchestral players are enjoying their own effortless virtuosity. The portrayal of *Goldenberg and Schmuyle* brings superbly full articulation from the lower strings and *Baba-Yaga* makes the most incisive impact. Indeed it is the precision with which Ravel's instrumentation is conveyed that makes each thumbnail sketch so indelible. Whether in the cheeping and chattering of the unhatched chicks, the bravura swirl of the *Limoges Market*, or the dignified grandiloquence of that final great gateway of Kiev, the controlled brilliance of the recording projects everything with extraordinary vividness.

Abbado takes a straighter, more direct view of Mussorgsky's fanciful series of pictures than usual. He is helped by the translucent and naturally balanced digital recording; indeed, the sound is first class, making great impact at climaxes yet also extremely refined, as in the delicate portrayal of the unhatched chicks. Abbado's speeds tend to be extreme, with both this and *Tuileries* taken very fast and light, while *Bydlo* and *The Great Gate of Kiev* are slow and weighty. This now reappears at mid-price, coupled with Ravel.

Giulini's 1976 Chicago recording has always been among the front runners. He is generally more relaxed and often more wayward than Karajan, but this is still a splendid performance and the finale generates more tension than Karajan's most recent, digital version, though it is not as overpowering as the earlier, analogue recording.

Muti's reading, given the excellence of its recorded sound, more than holds its own, although the balance is forward and perhaps not all listeners will respond to the brass timbres at the opening. The lower strings in *Samuel Goldenberg and Schmuyle* have extraordinary body and presence, and *Baba-Yaga* has an unsurpassed virtuosity and attack, as well as being of a high standard as a recording. The coupling is no less thrilling. This can be recommended even to those readers who have not always responded to later records from this conductor.

Solti's performance is fiercely brilliant rather than atmospheric or evocative. He treats Ravel's orchestration as a virtuoso challenge, and with larger-than-life digital recording it undoubtedly has demonstration qualities, and the transparency of texture, given the forward balance, provides quite startling clarity.

Kubelik's famous (1951) mono version of Ravel's masterly scoring was the Mercury recording which coined the term (and subsequent trademark) 'Living presence', taken from Howard Taubman's review in *The New York Times*. The realism of the recording (in spite of some thinness in the top range of the strings) still has the power to astonish. It is most naturally balanced and, although without the additional illumination of stereo, still conveys much of the splendid acoustic of Chicago's Orchestral Hall. The success of the record is not just technical, but musical too. The performance has great freshness with not a hint of routine anywhere; there are many subtleties, particularly as one picture or promenade is dovetailed into another. The melancholy of *The old castle* is touchingly caught and the tuba solo of *Bydlo* is similarly dolorous, even if the playing here is slightly below par technically, while the musical portrayal of Samuel Goldenberg is made to seem peculiarly Hebraic. The orchestral virtuosity in *Tuileries*, *Limoges* and the *Chicks' ballet* is not overt but has a Ravelian delicacy; similarly, the central section of *Baba-Yaga* has a gently sinister quality that is very telling. The brass at the climax of *The Great Gate of Kiev* is splendid; if the tam-tam does not come through in the way it does on the equally famous Telarc stereo record, the majesty of the dénouement is very tangible.

Maazel's Belart account from 1972 offers an immensely vivid reading, brilliantly recorded, with only a touch of brashness at the end. Moreover, this bargain CD has an unexpected and attractive coupling.

Toscanini was no colourist, and his regimented view of the exotic Mussorgsky–Ravel score is at its least sympathetic in the opening statement of the opening *Promenade*, not just rigidly metrical but made the coarser by the cornet-like trumpet tone. Many of the individual movements are done with greater understanding – for example, the *Ballet of the unhatched chicks* – but too often Toscanini's lack of sympathy undermines the character of this rich score. Clean, bright transfer.

(i) *Pictures at an exhibition* (orch. Ravel); (ii) *Pictures at an exhibition* (original piano version).
(M) **(*) Ph Dig. 442 650-2. (i) VPO, Previn; (ii) Brendel.

Previn's Philips version was recorded during live performances in Vienna. Obviously the Philips engineers had problems with the acoustics of the Musikvereinsaal, as the bass is noticeably resonant and inner definition is far from sharp. Otherwise the balance is truthful; but the performance, though not lacking spontaneity, is not distinctive, and there is a lack of the kind of grip which makes Karajan's version so unforgettable.

Brendel's performance of the original piano score has its own imaginative touches and some fine moments: the *Ballet of the Unhatched Chicks* is delightfully articulated, and both the *Bydlo* and *Baba-Yaga* are powerful, the latter coming after a darkly evocative *Catacombs/Cum mortuis* sequence. Brendel keeps the music moving but effectively varies the style of the Promenades. The closing pages, however, need to sound more unbuttoned: Brendel is weighty, but fails to enthral the listener. The recording is faithful.

(i) *Pictures at an exhibition* (orch. Ravel); (ii) *Boris Godunov* (original version): highlights (including *Death scene*).
(M) *** Sony Theta Dig. SMK 60008 [id.]. (i) BPO, Giulini; (ii) Nicolai Ghiaurov, Nicola Ghiuselev, Dimiter Petrov, Josef Frank, Sofia Nat. Op. Ch., Bodra Smyana Children's Ch., Sofia Festival O, Tchakarov.

It was a splendid idea to reissue Giulini's newest (1989) Sony account of Mussorgsky's *Pictures*, which can be counted among the finest recent versions, with highlights from Tchakarov's Sofia *Boris Godunov*. The *Pictures* were recorded in the Jesus-Christus-Kirche, Berlin, the sound is rich and spacious, the orchestral playing superb. The reading has a pervading sense of nostalgia which haunts the delicate portrayal of *The old castle* and even makes the wheedling interchange between the two Polish Jews more sympathetic than usual. A powerful and weighty *Baba-Yaga*, yet with the bizarre element retained in the subtle rhythmic pointing of the middle section, leads naturally to a majestic finale, with the Berlin brass full-bloodedly resplendent, and the tam-tam flashing vividly at the climax. Ghiaurov gives a magnificent performance as Boris and Tchakarov brings out the reflective side of the score well. But the complete set is flawed. It is partly a question of backward balance, partly a lack of bite in the performance. But the opening chorus of wandering minstrels from the *Prologue* makes a fine impact and the intensity of Boris's monologue, *I have achieved power*, and above all the death scene (both included here), with Ghiaurov singing beautifully, rarely snarling in sing-speech, make this set of excerpts particularly valuable. Nicola Ghiuselev is magnificent as Pimen in his Act I aria, *Just one last story*, and if Dimiter Petrov is at times an unsteady Varlaam, he is not ineffective in his contribution to the second scene of Act I, and this is the only drawback in a thoroughly worthwhile and unusual coupling.

PIANO MUSIC

Pictures at an exhibition.
(M) ** EMI Dig. CD-EMX 2213 [(M) id. import]. Piers Lane – BALAKIREV: *Islamey* **(*); STRAVINSKY: *3 Movements from Petrushka.* **
(BB) *(*) HM Solo Dig. HMS 926016 [id.]. Brigitte Engerer.

Pictures at an exhibition; Une larme; On the southern shore of the Crimea: Gurzuf; Capriccio; Sorochintsy Fair: Hopak.
(BB) * Naxos Dig. 8.550044 [id.]. Jenö Jandó – BALAKIREV: *Islamey.* (*)

Pictures at an exhibition (piano version, ed. Horowitz).
(M) (***) RCA mono GD 60321 [09026 60321]. Vladimir Horowitz – TCHAIKOVSKY: *Piano concerto No. 1.* (***) ❀

Pictures at an exhibition (piano version, ed. Horowitz); *Sunless: On the river* (arr. Horowitz).
(M) (***) RCA mono GD 60449 [60449-2-RG]. Horowitz – TCHAIKOVSKY: *Piano concerto No. 1.* (***)

Horowitz's famous 1951 recording (GD 60321), made at a live performance at Carnegie Hall, is as thrilling as it is perceptive. Mussorgsky's darker colours are admirably caught and the lighter, scherzando evocations are dazzlingly articulated. But it is the closing pictures which are especially powerful, the pungent *Baba-Yaga*, and the spectacular *Great Gate of Kiev*, where Horowitz has embroidered the final climax to add to its pianistic resplendency. This has now been reissued as Volume 44 in the Toscanini Edition, admirably paired with his equally devastating account of Tchaikovsky's *First Piano concerto*, recorded at a live concert in 1943. This is an indispensable coupling and no admirer of great pianism should be without this record. RCA have also reissued this version of the *Pictures*, plus Horowitz's arrangement of *On the river* from Mussorgsky's song-cycle, *Sunless*, coupled with the 1941 *studio* recording of the Tchaikovsky concerto, a performance which we find less satisfying.

A very good set of the *Pictures* from Piers Lane, well characterized and straightforward. Not a performance of commanding stature, perhaps, and not outstanding enough to be a first recommendation. It is accorded excellent sound by the EMI team and Andrew Keener. In this repertoire one needs transcendental virtuosity and keyboard colour in abundance, as well as imagination; with Horowitz around, this must take second place.

Brigitte Engerer has a sound technique and her *Great Gate of Kiev* expands to an impressive climax. Elsewhere she characterizes musically. But there is some lack of vividness and sparkle in the lighter evocations and the last degree of spontaneity is missing. With truthful recording, this seems good value, but one needs more charisma in this music.

Jandó's *Pictures* are not strong on colour or imagination, nor are the other rarities played with the distinction he has brought to other repertoire. Despite the modest outlay required, this is not money well spent, given the quality of the competition. Apart from Béroff's now deleted recordings, the shorter Mussorgsky pieces are not well served on disc; they are well worth the attention of pianists, and it is a pity that these accounts are relatively pedestrian.

The Complete Songs.

❀ (M) (***) EMI (SIS) mono CHS7 63025-2 (3) [ZDHC 63025]. Boris Christoff, Alexandre Labinsky, Gerald Moore, French R. & TV O, Georges Tzipine.

Boris Christoff originally recorded these songs in 1958; they then appeared in a four-LP mono set with a handsome book, generously illustrated with plates and music examples, giving the texts in Russian, French, Italian and English, and with copious notes on each of the 63 songs. Naturally the documentation cannot be so extensive in the CD format – but, on the other hand, one has the infinitely greater ease of access that the new technology offers. The Mussorgsky songs constitute a complete world in themselves, and they cast a strong spell: their range is enormous and their insight into the human condition deep. Christoff was at the height of his vocal powers when he made the set with Alexandre Labinsky, his accompanist in most of the songs; and its return to circulation cannot be too warmly welcomed. This was the first complete survey, and it still remains the only really recommendable set.

Boris Godunov (original, 1869 version): excerpts: *Coronation Scene; Varlaam's song; Apartment scene; St Basil scene; Death scene.*

❀ (M) *** Chandos CHAN 3007. Tomlinson, Kale, Bayley, Rodgers, Best, Opera North Ch., E. N. Philh. O, Paul Daniel.

This generous, 75-minute selection of excerpts from *Boris Godunov* is an important addition to the excellent series of operatic recordings in English, sponsored by Peter Moores, and is highly recommendable even when compared with current Russian versions of Mussorgsky's masterpiece. John Tomlinson has never been in finer voice on disc than here, with his dark bass-baritone perfectly focused. This is an exceptionally lyrical view of the self-tortured tsar, both dramatically powerful and warmly expressive, letting one appreciate the beauty of Mussorgsky's melodies. Tomlinson is helped by Paul Daniel's inspired direction and opulent recorded sound, with excellent support from singers in the vintage Opera North production, including Stuart Kale as Prince Shuisky, Clive Bayley as Varlaam, Joan Rodgers as Xenia and Matthew Best as Pimen. Anyone who supports the ideas of opera sung in English should not miss this highly compelling disc.

Boris Godunov: highlights.

(M) ** Erato/Warner Dig. 0630 13812-9 (from complete recording, with Raimondi, Polozov, Vishnevskaya, Plishka, Tesarowicz, Riegel, Gedda, Washington Ch. Arts Soc. & Ontario Soc. Nat. SO, Rostropovich).

Recorded live in Washington, Rostropovich's recording, using Mussorgsky's original score unadulterated by Rimsky-Korsakov, sounds very much like what it is: a well-drilled concert performance with some fine choral singing. This perhaps matters less on a highlights CD, and Raimondi's warmly Italianate voice in the name-part brings out the lyricism of the lines more often barked or grunted. But although Boris's death scene is wonderfully controlled in hushed intensity, the Tsar's inner agony is missing. The Coronation scene, too, lacks something in weight. The documentation includes a translation without the original Russian, a sensible enough decision.

Mysliveček, Josef (1737–81)

Violin concerto in C.
(B) *** Discover Dig. DICD 920265 [id.]. Ivan Zenaty, Virtuosi di Praga, Oldrich Vlček (with DVORAK: *Romance; Mazurka* ***) – VANHAL: *Violin concerto.* ***

Born in Bohemia almost a generation before Mozart, Mysliveček wrote fresh, vigorous music, of which this violin concerto is a fine example, its central slow movement a brief, gentle interlude. The Vanhal coupling is a comparable work, equally attractive. On this well-recorded bargain issue Ivan Zenaty with his clean, full tone proves an outstanding advocate, with the Virtuosi di Praga providing lively support on modern instruments. In the two shorter concertante works of a century later, Zenaty and the orchestra readily adapt their style to the romanticism of Dvořák, tender in the *Romance*, flamboyant in the *Mazurka*.

Narváez, Luys de (1500–c. 1555)

El Delphin de Musica, Book 1: *Fantasia No. 5.* Book 2: *Fantasias Nos. 5–6;* Book 3: *La canción del Emperor.* Book 4: *O gloriosa domina (Seys differencias).* Book 5: *Arde coracón, arde; Ye se asiente el Rey Raminor.* Book 6: *Conde claros; Guárdame las vacas; Tre diferencias por otra parte; Baxa de contrapunto.*
(M) *** RCA 09026 61606-2. Julian Bream (lute) – MILAN: *Collection.* ***

The collection Bream plays here is more diverse than the coupled Milán pieces and he includes some arrangements of the popular songs of the time and some of the earliest-known *differencias* (variations). Bream is in his element in this repertoire and each piece is eloquently felt and strongly characterized; the music's nobility is readily conveyed. The recording is first class.

Nicolai, Carl Otto (1810–49)

The merry wives of Windsor (Die lustigen Weiber von Windsor): complete.
(M) *** Decca (IMS) 443 669-2 (2). Ridderbusch, W. Brendel, Malta, Ahnsjö, Sramek, Donath, T. Schmidt, Sukis, Bav. R. Ch. & SO, Kubelik.
(M) **(*) EMI CMS7 69348-2 (2). Frick, Gutstein, Engel, Wunderlich, Lenz, Hoppe, Putz, Litz, Mathis, Ch. & O of Bav. State Op., Heger.

Kubelik's performance may be slightly lacking in dramatic ebullience, but its extra subtlety has perceptive results – as in the entry of Falstaff in Act I, where Kubelik conveys the tongue-in-cheek quality of Nicolai's *pomposo* writing. Ridderbusch portrays a straight and noble Falstaff. Although as an opera this may not have the brilliant insight of Verdi or all the atmosphere of Vaughan Williams, it has its own brand of effervescence which is equally endearing and is well caught here. The dialogue is crisply edited, and the recording, while fairly reverberant, is vividly atmospheric. *Faute de mieux*, it should receive a strong recommendation.

The great glory of the fine EMI set is the darkly menacing Falstaff of Gottlob Frick in magnificent voice, even if he sounds baleful rather than comic. It is good too to have the young Fritz Wunderlich as Fenton opposite the Anna Reich of Edith Mathis. Though the others hardly match this standard – Ruth-Margret Putz is rather shrill as Frau Fluth – they all give enjoyable performances, helped by the production, which conveys the feeling of artists who have experienced performing the piece on stage. The effectiveness of the comic timing is owed in great measure to the conducting of the veteran, Robert Heger. From the CD transfer one could hardly tell the age of the recording, with the voices particularly well caught.

Nielsen, Carl (1865–1931)

(i) *Clarinet concerto, Op. 57;* (ii) *Flute concerto;* (iii) *Helios overture, Op. 17; An imaginary journey to the Faeroe Islands; Pan and Syrinx.*
(B) ** Sony SBK 63041 [id.]. (i) Stanley Drucker; (ii) Julius Baker; (i–ii) NYPO, Bernstein; (iii) Phd. O, Ormandy.

Both soloists here are sensitive, and Julius Baker gives a fine account of the *Flute concerto*, even if Bernstein backs him with a rather emphatic and heavyweight reading of the accompaniment and the orchestral violins are thin and unflatteringly recorded. Neither version is as satisfying or as perceptive as the mono recording by Ib Erikson and the *Flute concerto*'s dedicatee, Gilbert Jesperson, who bring greater humanity and imagination to the music. They are better recorded, too. The balance in the Sony recording gives excessive prominence in the *Clarinet concerto* to the side-drum. The Ormandy coupling offers two works which were recording premières when they first appeared in 1967. *An imaginary journey to the Faeroe Islands* is well played and quite atmospherically recorded, although the more boisterous closing section is made to seem a bit noisy. The finer of the two works is *Pan and Syrinx*, a programmatic piece that tells of a nymph who, pestered by the boy-god Pan, flees in desperation until the other gods take pity on her and turn her into a reed. The ending of the work is particularly atmospheric and poetic, but the level of inspiration throughout is high and her impassioned pleadings are most poignantly realized. Ormandy's account is eloquent enough, though a trifle driven. However, both this and the *Helios overture*, which traces the golden arc of the sun until it sinks into the sea, are effectively realized.

(i) *Clarinet concerto, Op. 57;* (ii) *Flute concerto;* (iii) *Maskarade:* excerpts.
(M) (***) Dutton Lab. mono CDLXT 2505 [id. full price]. (i) Ib Erikson; (ii) Holger Gilbert-Jespersen; Danish State RSO; (i) Wöldike; (ii–iii) Jensen.

Like the Jensen account of the symphonies (see below), this excellent transfer from Dutton Laboratories offers us a link with Nielsen's own times. Holger Gilbert-Jespersen gave the first performance of the *Flute concerto* in Paris in 1926 and was its dedicatee. This 1954 recording gives as good an indication of Nielsen's intentions as we will ever have. The *Clarinet concerto* with Ib Erikson is no less masterly – and what good sound!

(i) *Clarinet concerto, Op. 57. Overture: Amor og digteren (Love & the poet), Op. 54; Little suite for strings, Op. 1; Pan and Syrinx, Op. 49.*
(M) *** HM Suite Dig. HMT 7901489 [id.]. (i) Walter Boeykens; Beethoven Academie, Jan Caeyers.

Walter Boeykens was for many years first clarinet of the Orchestre Philharmonique de la Radio Télévision Belge, and the players in the Beethoven Academie, which Jan Caeyers founded in 1993, come from the Belgian Chamber Ensemble. The orchestra is the same size as the forces involved in the first performance of the *Eroica Symphony* – hence their title. Walter Boeykens gives a remarkably perceptive account of the *Clarinet concerto*, one which gets to the heart of this often elusive and other-worldly score. This artist blends taste and grace on the one hand with the vociferous and awkward outbursts which Nielsen perceived in the personality of its dedicatee, Aage Oxenvad. There is always an undercurrent of tenderness and poetic feeling, as well as a scrupulous concern for the letter and spirit of the score. The makeweights include a rarity in the late overture, *Amor og digteren* (1930), and the rarely heard *Pan and Syrinx*. Jan Caeyers has as genuine a feeling for Nielsen as has Boeykens in the concerto, and *Pan and Syrinx* comes off very well indeed. Both these versions are as good as any in the catalogue. At the price, this disc makes strong claims on the collector, even if at 54 minutes it is comparatively short in playing time.

(i) *Clarinet concerto, Op. 57;* (ii) *Flute concerto;* (iii) *Violin concerto, Op. 33. An imaginary journey to the Faroe Islands (Rhapsodic overture); Helios overture, Op. 17; Pan and Syrinx, Op. 49; Saga-drøm, Op. 39; Symphonic rhapsody.*
(B) *** EMI forte CZS5 69758-2 (2) [CDFB 69758]. (i) Stevennson; (ii) Lemmser; (iii) Tellefsen; Danish RSO, Blomstedt.

These recordings come from a 1975 EMI boxed set of eight LPs which also included the symphonies, which Blomsted was to go on to record even more successfully for Decca. The remaining performances are very competitive in this forte reissue. The *Violin concerto* is wonderfully fresh and has strong lyrical appeal. Arve Tellefsen is a first-class soloist and his recording is distinguished and stands up well alongside more recent, full-priced versions. Kjell-Inge Stevennson is pretty stunning in the remarkable and other-worldly *Clarinet concerto*. If ever there was music from another planet, this is surely it! Its sonorities are sparse and monochrome; its air rarefied and bracing. The charm and subtleties of the *Flute concerto* are hardly less well realized by Frantz Lemmser's nimble and sensitive account. Moreover, since the orchestra is Danish, the other works (such as the marvellous *Pan and Syrinx* and the atmospheric *Helios overture*) are played with authentic accents. The collection also includes a novelty in the *Symphonic rhapsody* (1889), composed before the *First Symphony*. Throughout the EMI engineers secure a natural sound-balance. The recordings were originally made in quadraphony and the warm ambience reflects that, as does a certain lack of brilliance. But the CD transfers are faithful, and altogether this is a very satisfying way to get to know Nielsen's shorter orchestral scores as well as the concertos. In its economical new format this is a most attractive proposition, and the recordings still sound very warm and fresh.

Symphonies Nos. 1 in G min., Op. 7; 2 (Four temperaments), Op. 16; 3 (Sinfonia espansiva), Op. 27; 4 (Inextinguishable), Op. 29; 5, Op. 50; 6 (Sinfonia semplice).

(B) *** RCA Dig. 74321 20290-2 (3) [id.]. Royal Danish O, Paavo Berglund (with soloists in *No. 3*).

(M) ** Chandos Dig. CHAN 7094 (3) [id.]. Royal Stockholm PO, Rozhdestvensky (with Kringelborn and Frederiksson in *No. 3*).

Berglund's set with the Royal Danish Orchestra, in which Nielsen once served, was recorded between 1987 and 1989. The ever-fresh *First Symphony* is given a thoroughly straightforward account and Berglund holds the architecture of the work together in a most convincing way. Berglund's account of the *Sinfonia espansiva* (No. 3) is perhaps the finest of his cycle. The playing of the Royal Danish Orchestra is beautifully prepared and full of vitality. His two soloists, though unnamed, are very good and the general architecture of the work is well conveyed. The *Fourth* (*Inextinguishable*) is more problematic. Generally speaking, Berglund stays close to the tempo markings but, in his desire to convey the sense of drama and urgency, he tends to be impatient to move things on, particularly in the closing paragraphs. The playing is spirited enough, but even the Royal Danish Orchestra sounds a little out of breath at the end! The *Fifth* opens with a strong sense of atmosphere. The second movement's complex structure is well controlled and satisfyingly resolved. Apart from some loss of focus at the climax of the first movement, the recording encompasses the wide dynamic range with impressive sonority and colour. In the *Sinfonia semplice* (No. 6) Berglund again proves a perceptive guide. His performance matches Blomstedt's in integrity and insight and is obviously the product of much thought. Here as elsewhere, the RCA engineers produce a recording of splendid body and presence. In the event, Berglund's set can be strongly recommended alongside (though not in preference to) Blomstedt, and it also has a distinct price advantage. Three CDs have been reissued separately at mid-price: *Symphonies Nos. 1–2* (74321 20291-2); *Symphonies Nos. 3–4* (74321 20292-2); *Symphonies Nos. 5–6* (74321 20293-2).

Excellent playing from the Royal Stockholm Philharmonic and exemplary recording from the Chandos team do not prevent Rozhdestvensky's cycle from being a disappointment. This music is in these Swedish players' blood, but Rozhdestvensky does not have his finger on its pulse. He does not give us the whole picture, even if he comes close to it at times. He carefully displays details of the terrain without actually bringing the whole landscape before our eyes; its mystery eludes him. There is always a cultured response from the orchestra and musically shaped phrasing, and the Russian conductor shows obvious affection for Nielsen's scores, but something essential is missing: the urgent level of energy and that vital current which carries the listener forward. There are many felicitous moments, but the end result is too urbane, and tempi overall are just that little bit too leisurely and expansive.

Symphonies Nos. (i) *1 in G min. Op. 7; 2 in B min., Op. 16;* (i & ii) *3 (Espansiva), Op. 27;* (iii) *4 (Inextinguishable), Op. 29;* (i) *5, Op. 50;* (iii) *6 (Sinfonia semplice);* (i; iv) *Clarinet concerto, Op. 57;* (i; v) *Flute concerto;* (i; vi) *Violin concerto, Op. 33.*

(M) *** BIS Dig. CD 614/6 (4) [id.]. Gothenburg SO, (i) Myung-Whun Chung; (ii) with Raanoja, Skram; (iii) Neeme Järvi; (iv) with Olle Schill; (v) Patrick Gallois; (vi) Dong-Suk Kang.

Myung-Whun Chung's accounts of the *First* and *Second Symphonies* can hold their own against the very best, and his version of the *Sinfonia espansiva* is one of the very best. It has the inestimable advantage of the Gothenburg Hall acoustic and warm, splendidly present recording. The concertos are all excellent – some may prefer them to the rival collection on EMI (above). Dong-Suk Kang's reading of the *Violin concerto* is eloquent in every respect and a worthy alternative to Cho-Liang Lin on Sony; and both Patrick Gallois and Olle Schill are magnificent soloists. The package as a whole with four records for the price of three is eminently competitive.

Symphonies Nos. 1 in G min., Op. 7; 2 (The Four Temperaments), Op. 16; Bøhmisk-danske folkteone.

(M) **(*) EMI CDM5 65306-2 [id.]. Danish RSO, Blomstedt.

The EMI recordings are very good indeed and have a warmth and clarity that challenge comparison with Blomstedt's more recent, full-priced Decca set with the San Francisco Symphony Orchestra.

Symphonies Nos. (i) *1 in G min., Op. 7;* (ii) *4 (Inextinguishable), Op. 29;* (i) *Saul and David: Prelude to Act II;* (iii) *The fog is lifting.*

(BB) ** RCA Navigator 74321 21296-2 [(M) id. import]. (i) LSO, Previn; (ii) Chicago SO, Martinon; (iii) James Galway, Sioned Williams.

Nielsen's enchanting *First Symphony* is a spontaneous, lyrical work, astonishingly fresh in impact and remarkably individual, for all its debt to Brahms and Dvořák. André Previn's account with the LSO is highly sympathetic: the playing is affectionate, fresh and alive, and he is agreeably free from mannerisms. Some may feel that he takes too relaxed and lyrical a view of the slow movement; he dwells too affectionately on the oboe idea at 4 bars after A; and the third movement could undoubtedly be tauter and have a greater sense of pulse. The outer movements prompt no reservations and Previn observes repeats, which is an essential in this work. The *Prelude* is a fine piece and also well worth having. Previn is well recorded in a spacious acoustic, although the 1967 recording shows its age a little in the upper string timbre. Martinon's account of No. 4 is altogether less beguiling, the outer movements full of explosive brilliance and lacking in spontaneity. Despite superior orchestral playing, the reading is really too hard-driven to be really acceptable. The encore from James Galway with harp accompaniment is pleasing enough but hardly affects one's reservations about this uneven coupling.

(i) *Symphonies Nos. 1 in G min., Op. 7; 5, Op. 50;* (ii) *Helios overture, Op. 17.*
✿ (M) *** Dutton Lab. mono CDLXT 2502 [id. full price]. Danish State RSO; (i) Thomas Jensen; (ii) Erik Tuxen.

These are exemplary transfers of the première recording of the *First Symphony* and the first LP recordings of the *Fifth* (the very first was on 78s under Tuxen) and the *Helios Overture*. Jensen and Tuxen both played under Nielsen, and their performances have a special authenticity. The quality of these Decca recordings is captured with absolute fidelity in these stunning transfers; the engineers of the day, working in the pleasingly warm yet crisp acoustic of the Danish Radio concert hall produced remarkably truthful results. An indispensable issue that belongs in every Nielsen collection.

Symphonies Nos. 1 in G min., Op. 7; 6 (Sinfonia semplice).
(BB) **(*) Naxos Dig. 8.550826 [id.] Nat. SO of Ireland, Leaper.

Symphonies Nos. 1 in G min, Op. 7; 6 (Sinfonia semplice); Maskarade: Overture; Prelude to Act II.
(B) ** Sony SBK 63040 [id.]. Phd. O, Ormandy.

Very good performances indeed of Nielsen's first and last symphonies from Adrian Leaper and the National Symphony Orchestra of Ireland. The sound is exceptionally well balanced, with exemplary detail and good perspective. The playing is well prepared, full of vitality, and phrasing is always intelligent. Blomstedt on EMI and Berglund with the Danish Orchestra on RCA are finer still (these players have the music in their blood), but the Naxos disc remains very good value for money.

Ormandy's phrasing seems at times a bit prosaic in the *First Symphony*. He omits the repeats, and his virtues take some time to impinge on one's consciousness. He holds the middle movements together very well, but the sound has too much added brilliance, and the treble range is not altogether comfortable. His account of the *Sixth* is direct and sensible rather than inspired, but the orchestral playing (as one would expect from Philadelphia) is extremely fine, especially the strings in the *Adagio*, and the recording is much smoother. The fill-ups are nicely done and the *Prelude* to the Second Act of *Maskarade* is an exquisite piece, played most warmly.

Symphonies Nos. 2 (The 4 Temperaments), Op. 16; 3 (Sinfonia espansiva), Op. 27.
(BB) *** Naxos Dig. 8.550825-2. Nat. SO of Ireland, Adrian Leaper.

Adrian Leaper gets vibrant and involving playing from the Dublin orchestra in *The Four Temperaments*; it has that higher voltage and vital current which eluded them in the *Fourth Symphony*. This *Second* is as good as any in the catalogue (save for the Jensen), and the *Espansiva* is well paced, with tempi well judged throughout. The orchestra sounds better rehearsed and more accustomed to the Nielsen idiom than they did in their earlier disc, and they are certainly well enough recorded. Not necessarily a first choice but highly competitive. You can do far worse and pay more! Good value.

Symphonies Nos. 3 (Sinfonia espansiva); 4 (Inextinguishable), Op. 29.
(M) **(*) EMI CDM5 65415-2. Danish RSO, Blomstedt.

This continuation of Blomstedt's earlier EMI series from the mid-1970s is thoroughly recommendable: these performances have much of the grip and eloquence of his later, Decca set. No. 4 is excellent, with some fine woodwind playing from the Danish orchestra. The CD transfers are full and present.

(i) *Symphonies Nos. 3 (Sinfonia espansiva), Op. 27;* (ii) *5, Op. 50.*
(M) **(*) Sony SMK 47598-2. (i) Ruth Guldbaeck, Niels Moller, Royal Danish O; (ii) NYPO, Bernstein.

The genial *Espansiva* with the Royal Danish Orchestra has a lot going for it. And yet, for all the excellence of the orchestral playing, this performance misses something of the music's innocence. Bernstein is at his finest in the *Fifth*, giving an immensely powerful reading, and the passion of the string cantilena and the following movement through into the finale are indicative of the spontaneous feeling which pervades the whole symphony. The well-detailed, resonant recording adds to the impact of the performance.

Symphony No. 4 (Inextinguishable), Op. 29.
(M) *** DG (IMS) Dig. 445 518-2 [id.]. BPO, Karajan – SIBELIUS: *Tapiola.* ***

One of the very finest performances of Nielsen's *Fourth* comes from Karajan. The orchestral playing is altogether incomparable; there is both vision and majesty in the reading and a thrilling sense of commitment throughout. The wind playing sounds a little over-civilized – but what exquisitely blended, subtle playing this is. It is also excellently recorded, although there is an editing error in the finale.

Symphony No. 4 (Inextinguishable); Pan and Syrinx.
(M) *** EMI CDM7 64737-2. CBSO, Rattle – SIBELIUS: *Symphony No. 5.* ***

Simon Rattle's version of the *Inextinguishable* dates from the late 1970s and is also very fine indeed, though it is perhaps a shade judicious when put alongside his live broadcast (with the Philharmonia) dating from the same period. All the same, it deserves a strong recommendation, particularly given the fact that it is at mid-price and comes with an altogether outstanding account of *Pan and Syrinx* (the best ever on record) and his classic account of Sibelius's *Fifth Symphony*. Excellent sound.

Symphonies Nos. 4 (Inextinguishable); 5, Op. 50.
(BB) ** Naxos Dig. 8.550743 [id.]. Nat. SO of Ireland, Adrian Leaper.

There is nothing to grumble at in the Naxos coupling of these two symphonies – but nothing to get excited about either, though Leaper is a fine musician with a good feel for this repertoire. The *Fourth* is well prepared but neither highly charged nor tautly held together. Similarly, the *Fifth Symphony* is decently played but does not cast as strong a spell as the classic accounts from Jensen or Blomstedt. The recorded sound is more than acceptable.

Symphonies Nos. 5, Op. 50; 6 (Sinfonia semplice).
(M) **(*) EMI CDM5 65867-2 [id.]. Danish RSO, Blomstedt.

Blomstedt's recordings with the Danish Radio Orchestra were much respected in the 1970s and they stand up well to the test of time. His later, full-priced, San Francisco performances are perhaps superior and deeper in some respects, though the Copenhagen acoustic is warmer. In any event no one investing in them will find cause for disappointment.

CHAMBER MUSIC

Wind quintet, Op. 43.
(M) *** EMI CDM5 65304-2 [id.]. Melos Ens. – JANACEK: *Concertino* etc. **(*)
(BB) ** Naxos Dig. 8.553050 [id.]. Oslo Wind Ens. – FERNSTROM; KVANDAL: *Wind quintets.* **

The Melos account of the *Wind quintet* was made in the 1960s but still sounds fresh and vibrant. In its day it was a first recommendation and it still ranks among the very best. It comes, too, with a valuable Janáček coupling that includes *Mládi* and the *Concertino*.

A very good account of the *Wind quintet* from the Oslo players, recorded in a rather small Norwegian Radio studio. The sound is bright and forward. It does not displace either the full-priced Sony digital version by the Vienna/Berlin Ensemble (SK 45996) or the mid-priced Melos performance but is worth the asking price. Neither of the couplings is of comparable stature, but those with a taste for music off the beaten track will doubtless welcome them.

Complete piano music, Vol. 1: *Chaconne, Op. 32; The Dream of a merry Christmas; Humoresque-Bagatelles, Op. 11; 5 Piano pieces, Op. 3; Symphonic suite, Op. 8; Theme with variations, Op. 14.*
(BB) * Naxos Dig. 8.553574 [id.]. Peter Seivewright.

Peter Seivewright's survey of Nielsen's piano music, of which this is the first instalment, is very well recorded and comes with excellent notes from Jack Lawson. It has the advantage of economy, but little else. It costs about a third as much as Leif Ove Andsnes on Virgin, though the two programmes are not entirely identical; in terms of artistry, Seivewright does not begin to challenge the Norwegian player. Seivewright irons out dynamic contrasts and is unimaginative in matters of phrasing or characterization. In the *Five Pieces*, Op. 3, he is heavy-handed, and he is not much better elsewhere. The Virgin full-priced disc, which was given a Rosette in our main volume, is the one to go for (VC5 45129-2).

VOCAL MUSIC

Hymnus Amoris, Op. 12 (1896–7); Sleep, Op. 18 (1903–4).
(M) ** EMI (SIS) CDM5 66000-2. Kirsten Schulz, Bodil Gøbil, Tonny Landy, Bent Norup, Mogens Schmidt Johansen, Hans Christian Andersen, Copenhagen Boys' Ch., Danish RSO, Mogens Wöldike – GADE: *Forårs-fantasi.* **

Neither of these lovely cantatas is otherwise available at mid-price and both are eminently worth acquiring. These finely shaped performances were recorded by these artists and Mogens Wöldike in 1977 when he was in his eighties, but they still have an appealing freshness. Neither is superior to the Chandos accounts listed in our main edition, which also offer *Springtime on Fünen* and the late *Motets*, Op. 55; but for readers who have neither of those, this would make a perfectly acceptable buy.

Nono, Luigi (1924–90)

Fragmente; Stille, an Diotima (Silence for Diotima).

(M) ** DG (IMS) Dig. 437 720-2. LaSalle Qt.

If anyone can convert the listener to the music of Luigi Nono, it is the LaSalle Quartet, for whom he wrote this taxing, endlessly pauseful work in two substantial movements of nearly 20 minutes each. The economy-conscious collector might well complain not only of the short overall playing time (38 minutes) but of the high proportion of silence on the disc. But the intensity of the playing will help the uncommitted listener to concentrate on intentionally weighty expression in which late Beethoven was an inspiration – not that one would readily recognize it. Full, immediate recording.

Novák, Vítězslav (1870–1949)

(i) Symphonic poems: *About the Eternal longing, Op. 33; In the Tatras, Op. 26;* (ii) *Moravian-Slovak suite, Op. 32.*

(M) **(*) Sup. 11 0682-2 [d. 111922]. (i) Czech PO; (ii) Brno State PO, Karel Sejna.

In the Tatras (1902), an opulent Straussian tone-poem, and *About the Eternal longing* (1903/4) were inspired by unrequited love for a beautiful young pupil, Ruženа. The *Slovak suite* is a heavenly score. *Two in love*, its third movement, could well become as widely popular as any piece of music you care to think of. *In the church*, the opening movement, has something in common with Mozart's *Ave verum corpus*, though more obviously romantic, and the closing *At night* is beguilingly atmospheric. All three works here are persuasively played. The recording of the two symphonic poems is atmospheric and clear but a bit pale in the more expansive tuttis; the suite has slightly more body and colour.

The Storm, Op. 42.

(M) *** Sup. SU 3088-2 211. Soloists, Czech PO Ch. & O, Košler.

The Storm is arguably Novák's finest composition, and this was its first stereo recording, made in 1978. It is a work of great beauty and imagination, scored with consummate mastery and showing a lyrical gift of a high order. It has warmth and genuine individuality; the idiom owes something to Richard Strauss as well as to the Czech tradition, and there is an impressive command of both melody and structure. This is noble, moving and powerful music – very different from, say, Janáček but recognizably from the same part of the world, and equally fresh. The performance is fully worthy and has splendid dramatic feeling, helped by good soloists and a fine chorus. The recording, too, is admirably balanced, and there is considerably more depth on this vivid CD transfer than on LP, and plenty of weight, even if the soloists are rather too forward. This is one of the best Supraphon reissues for some time.

Nyman, Michael (born 1948)

(i) *Piano concerto;* (ii) *On the Fiddle; Prospero's Books.*

(B) *** Tring Dig. TRP 097 [(M) id.]. (i) Peter Lawson; (ii) Jonathan Carney; RPO, Carney.

Michael Nyman's brand of minimalism has been most effective in illustrating a whole sequence of films, including the Oscar-winning *The Piano*, in which this concerto was evocatively used. This Tring version of that work, with Peter Lawson a fine, muscular soloist, costs only a third as much as the Argo issue with the composer conducting (443 382-2) and is just as powerful as that original, helped by fuller and more immediate sound. (However, for R.L. the sound-picture is too forward and over-resonant: minimalist music needs the widest range of dynamic to make its fullest effect.) The most attractive of the three pieces (and the shortest) is the trilogy, *On the fiddle*, drawn from Nyman's music for three films directed by Peter Greenaway (*Full fathom five* comes from *The Tempest*, *Angelfish decay* uses a sequence from *A Zed and Two Noughts* and *Miserere paraphrase* derives from *The Cook, The Thief, His Wife and Her Lover*). Here, with the solo violin taking a central role, Nyman reverts to warmly melodic writing, and the RPO leader, Jonathan Carney, is a most persuasive advocate, both as soloist and as conductor. The music for the

Shakespeare-based film with John Gielgud, *Prospero's Books*, is more conventionally minimalist, with nagging repetitions at generally fast speeds. This too is magnetic in its way, using a smaller ensemble. An excellent bargain for anyone who has responded to Nyman's film music.

Strong on Oaks, strong on the causes of Oaks.
(M) ** Carlton Dig. 30366 01092 [id.]. E. Sinfonia, Bramwell Tovey – TAVENER: *The protecting veil.* **

Inspired to write this five-movement piece through a commission from the new town of Stevenage, Michael Nyman based his title on the meaning of the original Saxon name for that place, 'Strong Oak', adding a modern touch in echoing Tony Blair's election slogan, 'Tough on crime, tough on the causes of crime'. Using his undemanding brand of minimalism with its open intervals and high contrasts, Nyman presents an attractive 16-minute suite, well performed by the orchestra for which it was intended, helped by full-ranging sound.

Obrecht, Jacob (1457–1505)

Missa Caput; Salve Regina: in 4 parts; in 6 parts. Venit ad Petrum.
(BB) *** Naxos Dig. 8.553210 [id.]. Oxford Camerata, Jeremy Summerly.

This late-fifteenth-century Flemish musician was one of the most remarkable composers of the period, writing polyphonic church music of rare purity that ranges over a wider emotional range than was common at the time. Obrecht's music has an austere beauty that is quite affecting, particularly in these performances by the Oxford Camerata and Jeremy Summerly. The *Missa Caput* survives in a manuscript at the court of Ferrara but could possibly have been compiled in Bruges. Both of the *Salve Regina* settings are based on plainchant melody and are *alternatim* settings, the music alternating between a polyphonic treatment of the chant and the unadorned chant itself. Jeremy Summerly and his Oxford Camerata, recorded in the Chapel of Hertford College, Oxford, give expert and committed accounts of this music and they are accorded first-class sound. To adapt the comment of the author of the accompanying notes, listening to this music persuades one of the fifteenth-century view that 'music was capable of lifting one's soul to a contemplation of heavenly things'.

Ockeghem, Johannes (*c.* 1410–97)

Alma Redemptoris Mater; Ave Maria; Missa L'homme armé.
✿ (BB) *** Naxos Dig. 8.554297 [id.]. Oxford Camerata, Jeremy Summerly (with Josquin DESPREZ: *Memor esto veri tui* ***).

The soaring opening *Ave Maria*, gloriously sung, immediately sets the seal on the inspirational power of Ockeghem's music. It is followed by the plainchant, *Alma Redemptoris Mater*, and then its polyphonic setting, simple and flowing and harmonically rich. The more we discover of this remarkable composer, who was to become Director of the French Chapel Royal, the more he emerges as the key musical figure of the fifteenth century. The robust ballad, *L'homme armé*, follows ('The armed man must be feared'), sounding vigorously jolly, like a carol. It must have been hugely popular in its day since so many composers used it as a basis for a Mass. Josquin's opening *Kyrie* is both serene and a little austere, yet he cannot help writing lines which bring underlying harmonic richness, and the polyphony in the *Gloria* and *Credo* moves onward inventively, while the work's dramatic and emotional peak is readily found in the extended *Sanctus* (by far the longest section of the Mass) and resolved in the sublime melancholy of the *Agnus Dei*. In short, this is a work of striking individuality and beauty, and it is sung superbly here, and marvellously paced. Josquin's setting of sixteen verses from Psalm 119, *Memor esto verbi tui*, with its expressively fertile imitative devices, makes an eloquent postlude and looks to the future – it dates from the first decade of the sixteenth century. The recording, made in the Chapel of Hertford College, Oxford, could hardly be bettered. It dates from February 1997, thus aptly celebrating the 500th anniversary of Ockeghem's death. Summerly and his illustrious group have never made a better record than this.

Requiem (Missa pro defunctis); Missa Mi-Mi (Missa quarti toni).
(M) *** Virgin Veritas/EMI Dig. VER5 61219-2. Hilliard Ens., Hillier.

Ockeghem's *Missa pro defunctis* is the first surviving polyphonic *Requiem*. The *Missa Mi-Mi* is his most widely performed Mass and survives in three different sources in the Vatican Library; in one it is called *Missa Quarti Toni* and in another *My-My*, which is assumed to derive from the short motif that appears in the bass section at the beginning of each main section and consists of a descending fifth. These performances, reissued on Virgin Veritas, have the expertise, secure intonation, blend and ensemble that one expects from these singers, and the music itself has an austere and affecting simplicity. Although it has had a qualified welcome from specialists in this field and despite a certain blandness, it would be curmudgeonly not to welcome such generally persuasive accounts of both works. At mid-price these make an eminently serviceable introduction to the sacred music of this composer and they are very well recorded, too.

Offenbach, Jacques (1819–80)

Gaîté parisienne (ballet, arr. Rosenthal): complete.

❀ (M) *** RCA 09026 61847-2 [id.]. Boston Pops O, Arthur Fiedler – ROSSINI/RESPIGHI: *Boutique fantasque*. ***

(M) ** EMI CDM7 63136-2. Monte Carlo Op. O, Rosenthal – WALDTEUFEL: *Waltzes*. ***

(M) * Mercury 434 365-2 (2) [id.]. Minneapolis SO, Dorati – ADAM: *Giselle* **(*); Johann STRAUSS: *Graduation ball*. *

Gaîté parisienne (ballet, arr. Rosenthal): complete; Overtures: *La Belle Hélène; Orpheus in the Underworld. Contes d'Hoffmann: Intermezzo*.

(M) *** [RCA Basic 100 09026 68366-2; *68366-4*]. Boston Pops O, Fiedler.

Fiedler's *Gaîté parisienne* is irresistible – one of his very finest records. The orchestra are kept exhilaratingly on their toes throughout and are obviously enjoying themselves, not least in the elegantly tuneful waltzes and in the closing *Barcarolle*, which Fiedler prepares beautifully and to which the generous acoustic of Symphony Hall affords a pleasing warmth without in any way blunting or coarsening the brilliance. The percussion, including bass drum in the exuberant *Can-Can*, adds an appropriate condiment and John Pfeiffer's superb new transfer makes the recording sound remarkably fresh and full. Unbelievably it dates from 1954, one of the very first of RCA's 'Living Stereo' records and still one of the finest. Fiedler's recording comes additionally (in the USA) in RCA's Basic 100 series, coupled with more Offenbach – zestful accounts of familiar overtures, plus the famous *Barcarolle*. We are inclined to choose *La boutique fantasque*, but those preferring the overtures should still be well satisfied, although here the sound is less brilliant.

Maurice Rosenthal's absolutely complete version from the mid-1970s has now been restored to the catalogue, together with the documentation giving the sources for all the music in the score, the snag being that the identification is not always accurate. The performance, though often idiomatically persuasive, has not the verve and glamour of that by Fiedler and Karajan. The sound, however, has been greatly improved, with the original excess resonance considerably tempered.

Dorati conducts with plenty of spirit but is let down by a close, impossibly dry recording with lustreless violins. The orchestra sounds as if it is in a studio cushioned in cotton wool.

(i) *Gaîté parisienne* (ballet, arr. Rosenthal; complete); (ii) *Overtures and suites* from: *Orpheus in the Underworld* (1874 version, with *Pastoral ballet*); *Le voyage dans la lune* (with *Snowflakes ballet*).

(M) *** Ph. 442 403-2 [id.]. (i) Pittsburgh SO, Previn; (ii) Philh. O, Almeida.

An outstanding coupling. In *Gaîté parisienne* Previn realizes that tempi can remain relaxed and the music's natural high spirits will still bubble to the surface. The orchestral playing is both spirited and elegant, with Previn obviously relishing the score's delightful detail. This is mirrored by the Philips digital sound-balance, which has substance as well as atmosphere and brilliance. Perhaps the tuba thumping away in the bass is a shade too present, but it increases one's desire to smile through this engagingly happy music. The *Snowflakes ballet* from *Le voyage dans la lune* is a charmer, and the ballet from *Orpheus in the Underworld* is hardly less delectable. The other surprise is the *Orpheus overture*, not the one we know – which, it must be admitted, is a better-crafted piece – but a more extended work in pot-pourri style, with some good tunes. Almeida is no less high-spirited than Previn, and the Philharmonia's response is both polished and elegant. Excellent recording too.

Gaîté parisienne (ballet, arr. Rosenthal): extended excerpts.

(B) *** DG 429 163-2 [id.]. BPO, Karajan – CHOPIN: *Les Sylphides* *** ❀; DELIBES: *Coppélia:* suite. ***

Karajan's selection is generous. On the DG disc, only Nos. 3–5, 7 and 19–21 are omitted. The remastering of the 1972 recording is highly successful; textures have been lightened to advantage, and the effect is to increase the raciness of the music-making, while its polish and sparkle are even more striking.

(i) *Musette (Air de ballet)*. Overtures: *La Belle Hélène; La Grande-Duchesse de Gérolstein; Orpheus in the Underworld. Les belles Américaines: Waltz* (orch. Robert Russell Bennett). *Contes d'Hoffmann: Intermezzo; Introduction; Minuet; Barcarolle. Geneviève de Brabant: Galop. La Périchole:* Pot-pourri.
(M) ** RCA 09026 61429-2 [id.]. Boston Pops O, Arthur Fiedler – IBERT: *Divertissement*. ***

For once the CD transfer of this RCA 'Living Stereo' recording from 1956 is disappointing. The Boston resonance intrudes on the music-making and tends to blunt the effect of the playing, so that one has the impression that Fiedler is fielding a second team. But the selection is interesting and generous, and Samuel Mayes is a sympathetic cello soloist in the *'Air de ballet from the 17th Century'*. Curiously, the Ibert *Divertissement*, which acts as coupling and which was recorded a month later, is as racy as you could wish, and the recorded sound is comparably lively.

Le Papillon (ballet; complete).
(B) *** Decca Double 444 827-2 (2) [id.]. Nat. PO, Bonynge – TCHAIKOVSKY: *Nutcracker*. ***

Le Papillon is Offenbach's only full-length ballet and it dates from 1860. The quality of invention is high and the music sparkles from beginning to end. In such a sympathetic performance, vividly recorded (in 1972 in the Kingsway Hall), it cannot fail to give pleasure.

Cello duos, Op. 54: Suites Nos. 1–2.
(B) *** HM Musique d'Abord 1901043. Roland Pidoux and Etienne Péclard.

Offenbach was himself a very accomplished cellist, and these two works are tuneful and imaginatively laid out to exploit the tonal possibilities of such a duo. Offenbach's natural wit is especially apparent in the *First Suite in E major*. The performances are excellent and so is the recording.

OPERA

Les Contes d'Hoffmann (The Tales of Hoffmann): complete.
(M) ** EMI (SIS) CMS7 63222-2 (2) [Ang. CDMB 63222]. Gedda, D'Angelo, Schwarzkopf, De los Angeles, Benoit, Faure, Ghiuselev, London, Sénéchal, Blanc, Choeurs René Duclos, Paris Conservatoire O, Cluytens.
(M) (**) Naxos mono 8.110011/2 [id.]. Bovy, Maison, Tibbett, Bada, NY Met. Op. Ch. & O, Abravanel.
(M) (*(*)) EMI Classics (mono) CMS5 65260-2 (2). Jobin, Doria, Bovy, Boué, Musy, Pernet, Soix, Bourdin, Revoil, Bourvi, Opéra Comique O, Cluytens.

Several bad mistakes in casting prevent the mid-1960s EMI set from being the rare delight it should have been. It has some marvellous moments, and the whole of the *Barcarolle* scene with Schwarzkopf is a delight, but the very distinction of the cast-list makes one annoyed that the result is not better. André Cluytens surprisingly proved quite the wrong conductor for this sparkling music, for he has little idea of caressing the music and rarely fails to push on regardless. Gianna d'Angelo's Olympia is pretty but shallow, George London's Coppelius and Dr Miracle unpleasantly gruff-toned and, most disappointing of all, Victoria de los Angeles is sadly out of voice, with the upper register regularly turning sour on her. But with such artists even below their best there are characterful moments which take the listener along well enough. Cluytens in his ruthlessness has a certain demonic energy which has its dramatic side. The recording is atmospheric and the CD transfer has given it added liveliness.

Recorded from an NBC broadcast in January 1937, the Naxos historic version has very limited sound with intrusive surface hiss, but the atmosphere of a live performance at the Met. is well caught. It is fascinating to have such a masterly singer as Lawrence Tibbett in the four villainous roles, dark and incisive in each. Neither René Maison as Hoffmann (slightly pinched in his tone-colours, though singing out well) nor Vina Bovy in the four heroine roles (bright to the point of shrillness) can match that, but it is good to hear the veteran, Angelo Bada, in the four small servant roles. With Maurice Abravanel directing a warmly idiomatic performance, crisper in the orchestral playing than in the choral singing, there is much to enjoy. A reasonable recommendation at the price.

The EMI mono version, recorded in the studio in 1948, offers a characteristic Opéra Comique cast of the period, with Vina Bovy taking the heroine roles as at the Met., but with no greater success, for the dryness of the studio acoustic is no help to such a light, bright voice. With André Cluytens less incisive than usual in his direction, the star of the performance is Raoul Jobin in the title-role, clear and stylish, combining lyric beauty with some heroic strength. Unlike the Met. performance, this one divides the other roles, idiomatically sung by the Opéra Comique team, though the closeness of balance for the voices makes the results totally unatmospheric, a severe disadvantage in such numbers as the *Barcarolle*.

Les Contes d'Hoffmann: highlights.

(M) *** Decca 421 866-2 (from complete set, with Sutherland, Domingo, Tourangeau, Bacquier, R. Suisse Romande & Lausanne Pro Arte Ch., SRO, Bonynge).

(M) ** Erato/Warner Dig. 0630 17355-2 [id.] (from complete recording, with Alagna, Van Dam, Dessay, Vaduva, Jo, Lascarro, Dubosc, Ragon, Bacquier, Lamprecht, Lyon Op. Ch. & O, Nagano).

Bonynge's recorded performance of *Contes d'Hoffmann* has never been surpassed, either on record or in the opera house. The edition chosen (based on a production originally pioneered by the Carl Rosa Opera Company under Arthur Hammond) is far more effective than any other in current use. Joan Sutherland is superb, not only in all four soprano roles, but also as Stella in the Epilogue. Both Domingo and Gabriel Bacquier also give outstanding performances, and the splendid Decca recording sparkles even more vividly in its CD transfer. While we would remind readers that the full-priced set (on a pair of CDs) is worth every penny of its cost (Decca 417 363-2), the highlights disc is one of the best of its kind from any opera. Offering just over an hour of music, it offers a superbly managed distillation of nearly all the finest items and is edited most skilfully. Indeed, were not the complete opera itself indispensable, we would carry over its justly deserved Rosette to this selection.

The selection from Kent Nagano's Erato set is certainly generous and, while the Decca highlights easily takes pride of place, this is worth trying if only to sample Sumi Jo's contribution as Giulietta, Natalie Dessay as Olympia (the two roles might effectively have been reversed), and Leontina Vaduva as Antonia, although none of these characterizations are distinctive. José van Dam is much more impressive in the three villainous roles, but the rather edgy recording is not flattering to Roberto Alagna's Hoffmann.

La Périchole (complete).

(M) *** Erato/Warner 2292 45686-2 (2). Crespin, Vanzo, Bastin, Lombard, Friedmann, Trigeau, Rhine Op. Ch., Strasbourg PO, Lombard.

La Périchole: highlights.

(M) *** Erato/Warner 0630 15735-9 [id.]. as above.

Though both Régine Crespin in the title-role and Alain Vanzo as her partner, Piquillo, were past their peak at that time, their vocal control is a model in this music, with character strongly portrayed but without any hint of vulgar underlining. Crespin is fresh and Vanzo produces heady tone in his varied arias, some of them brilliant. Jules Bastin is characterful too in the subsidiary role of Don Andres, Viceroy of Peru. Lombard secures excellent precision of ensemble from his Strasbourg forces, only occasionally pressing too hard. The recorded sound is vivid and immediate, and the libretto provides a detailed synopsis of the action between the texts and translations of numbers. While the complete set is very much worth having, the 67-minute selection can be strongly recommended too, as the documentation includes the essential translation.

'The world of Offenbach': Overtures: (i–ii) *La Belle Hélène;* (iii–iv) *La Fille du tambour-major;* (i–ii) *Orpheus in the Underworld;* (iii–iv) *Le Papillon: Pas de deux* (excerpt); *Valse des rayons. Les Contes d'Hoffmann:* (v; i; iv) *Ballad of Kleinzach; O Dieu! De quelle ivresse* (vi; i; iv) *Doll song* (vi–vii; i; iv) *Barcarolle* (2 versions). *La Grande Duchess de Gérolstein:* (viii–x) *Portez armes . . . J'aime les militaires. La Périchole:* (viii; i; x) *O mon cher amant (Air de lettre); Ah! quel dîner.* (vi; i; iv) *Robinson Crusoé: Conduisez-moi vers celui que j'adore (Waltz song).* (xi; iv) *Valse tyrolienne.*

✿ (M) *** Decca Analogue/Dig. 452 942-2. (i) SRO; (ii) Ansermet; (iii) LSO; (iv) Bonynge; (v) Domingo; (vi) Sutherland; (vii) Tourangeau; (viii) Crespin; (ix) V. Volksopernorchester; (x) Lombard; (xi) Sumi Jo, ECO.

This 'lucky-bag' of Offenbachian goodies which Decca have expanded for CD from the original LP selection is bursting with lollipops to make a marvellously entertaining 74 minutes. The programme now opens and closes with the *Barcarolle*, first heard in an orchestral version and later as a duet shared by Sutherland and Tourangeau. Ansermet and Bonynge offer much character in the overtures; even if the former takes the famous can-can which closes the *Orpheus* overture more slowly than usual, he invests it with much rhythmic vigour. Bonynge has another scintillating can-can to offer in *La Fille du tambour-major*, which opens with an arresting side-drum, and he now also includes two items from Offenbach's only ballet, *Le Papillon*. The various excerpts from Bonynge's complete *Contes d'Hoffmann* are matched by Régine Crespin's delightful contribution as *La Périchole*, and Sutherland returns to sing the *Waltz song* from *Robinson Crusoé*. The other additional item is Sumi Jo's sparkling *Valse tyrolienne*. With splendidly vivid recording this is an unmissable sampler, to match and even surpass 'The world of Borodin'.

Orff, Carl (1895–1982)

Carmina Burana.

(M) *** Ph. Dig. 462 063-2 [id.]. Gruberová, Aler, Hampson, Shinyukai Ch., Knaben des Staats & Berlin Cathedral Ch., BPO, Ozawa.

✿ (M) *** Sony SBK 47668 [id.]. Harsanyi, Petrak, Presnell, Rutgers University Ch., Phd. O, Ormandy.

(BB) *** Carlton LSO Double Dig. 30368 01107 (2) [(B) id.]. Walmsley-Clark, Graham-Hall, Maxwell, Southend Boys' Ch., London Symphony Ch., LSO, Hickox – HOLST: *The Planets*. **(*)

(B) **(*) [EMI Red Line CDR5 69868]. Augér, van Kesteren, Summers, Southend Boys' Ch., Philh. Ch. & O, Muti.

(BB) *** RCA Navigator Dig. 74321 17908-2 [(M) Basic 100 09026 68085-2; *68085-4*]. Hendricks, Aler, Hagegård, St Paul's Cathedral Boys' Ch., L. Symphony Ch., LSO, Mata.

(M) *** DG 447 437 [id.]. Janowitz, Stolze, Fischer-Dieskau, Schöneberger Boys' Ch., Berlin German Op. Ch. & O, Jochum.

(BB) ** Naxos Dig. 8.550196 [id.]. Jenisová, Dolezal, Kusnjer, Slovak Philharmonic Ch., Czech RSO (Bratislava), Gunzenhauser.

(M) ** Decca Phase Four 444 105-2 [id.]. Burrowes, Devos, Shirley-Quirk, Brighton Festival Ch., RPO, Dorati.

(M) * Sony SMK 60128 [id.]. Blegen, Riegel, Binder, Cleveland Ch. & O, Tilson Thomas (with: SCHOENBERG: *Gurre-Lieder: Lied der Waldtaube* (Jessye Norman) ***).

Ozawa's digital recording of Orff's justly popular cantata carries all the freshness and spontaneity of his earlier successful Boston version. The *Cours d'amours* sequence is the highlight of his reading, with the soprano, Edita Gruberová, highly seductive; Thomas Hampson's contribution is also impressive. Ozawa's infectious rubato in *Oh, oh, oh, I am bursting out all over*, interchanged between male and treble chorus towards the end of the work, is wonderfully bright and zestful, with the contrast of the big *Ave formosissima* climax which follows made to sound spaciously grand. Taken overall, this Philips version readily goes to the top of the list alongside Ormandy, and it has the additional advantage of spectacular, demonstration-worthy, digital recording. It comes handsomely repackaged as part of the Philips 'Choral Edition', but it is a pity that a translation could not have been included.

Ormandy and his Philadelphians have just the right panache to bring off this wildly exuberant picture of the Middle Ages by the anonymous poets of former days, and there is no more enjoyable analogue version. It has tremendous vigour, warmth and colour and a genial, spontaneous enthusiasm from the Rutgers University choristers, men and boys alike, that is irresistible. The soloists are excellent, but it is the chorus and orchestra who steal the show; the richness and eloquence of the choral tone is a joy in itself. This is quite splendid, one of Ormandy's most inspired recordings and, even if you already have the work in your collection, this exhilarating version will bring additional delights.

Richard Hickox, on his brilliantly recorded Carlton CD, uses the combined London Symphony forces, but adds the Southend Boys' Choir, who make sure we know they understand all about sexual abandon – their *Oh, oh, oh, I am bursting out all over* is a joy. Penelope Walmsley-Clark, too, makes a rapturous contribution: her account of the girl in the red dress is equally delectable. The other soloists are good but less individual, and the chorus rises marvellously to climaxes, while the sharp articulation of consonants when the singers hiss out the words of *O Fortuna* in the closing section is a highlight. The documentation provides a vernacular narrative for each band but no translation. Coupled with Hickox's brilliant account of Holst's *Planets*, this is one of the most successful of Carlton's LSO Doubles.

Muti's is a reading which underlines the dramatic contrasts, both of dynamic and of tempo, so the nagging ostinatos as a rule are pressed on at breakneck speed; the result, if at times a little breathless, is always exhilarating. The soloists are first rate; the Philharmonia Chorus is not quite at its most polished, but the Southend Boys are outstandingly fine. However, the digital remastering of the 1980 analogue recording is disappointing. The chorus and soloists seem to have lost a degree of immediacy.

Mata's splendid 1980 digital recording now comes at super-bargain price and is highly recommendable on all counts. It is a joyously alive and volatile reading, not as metrical in its rhythms as most; this means that at times the London Symphony Chorus is not as clean in ensemble as it is for Hickox. The choristers of St Paul's Cathedral sing with purity and enthusiasm but are perhaps not boyish enough, though the soloists are first rate (with John Aler coping splendidly, in high, refined tones, with the Roast Swan episode). There is fine warmth of atmosphere and no lack in the lower range; indeed in almost every respect the sound is superb. This is unbeatable value for those wanting a bargain-priced version.

Jochum's 1968 recording of *Carmina Burana* has never sounded better than it does in this reissue in DG's 'Originals' series. The choral pianissimos lack the very last degree of immediacy, but the underlying tension of the quiet singing is very apparent. The recording has a wide dynamic range and when the music blazes it has real splendour and excitement. Fischer-Dieskau's singing is refined but not too much so, and his first solo, *Omnia Sol temperat*, and later *Dies, nox et omnia* are both very beautiful, with the kind of tonal shading that a great Lieder singer can bring; he is suitably gruff in the Abbot's song – so much so that for the moment the voice is unrecognizable. Gerhard Stolze too is very stylish in his falsetto *Song of the roasted swan*. The soprano, Gundula Janowitz, finds a quiet dignity for her contribution and this is finely done. The closing scene is moulded by Jochum with wonderful control, most compelling in its restrained power.

The Slovak Chorus sing Orff's hedonistic cantata with lusty, Slavonic enthusiasm, and it is a pity that some of the score's quieter passages are somewhat lacking in bite because of the resonance. But the Tavern scene comes across especially vividly and the culminating *Ave formosissima* and *O Fortuna* are splendidly expansive. The soprano, Eva Jenisová, is the most impressive of the three soloists, who generally do not match their Western rivals. This is an enjoyable performance, with exciting moments, but the Ormandy and Ozawa versions are worth the extra outlay.

Dorati's version was recorded in the Kingsway Hall in 1976 in Decca's Phase Four system. The result is a beefy, vibrant account with good singing and playing. Despite some eccentric speeds, Dorati shows a fine rhythmic sense, but the performance cannot match the best available. The remastered recording brings a bold impact in fortissimos, but the quieter, more atmospheric passages are less cleanly defined.

Tilson Thomas's version in its original form was described as a surround-sound spectacular, but in fact the recording quality is disappointingly coarse. The singing and playing are as impressive as one would expect, but the conductor's wilful idiosyncrasies prevent any sort of recommendation. Tilson Thomas frequently indulges in vulgar accelerandi in an attempt to heighten climaxes, with results that are mannered rather than pointed. The inclusion of Schoenberg's *Song of the Woodbird*, beautifully sung by Jessye Norman, offers small compensation.

Catulli Carmina.

(M) *** DG (IMS) 449 097-2. Arleen Augér, Wieslaw Ochman, Berlin Op. Ch., 4 pianos & percussion, Jochum – EGK: *The Temptation of St Anthony*. ***

Though in sheer memorability it cannot match *Carmina burana*, Orff's sequel (using much the same formula) has its nagging attractions. For anyone hypnotized by the earlier and more popular work, *Catulli Carmina* is the Orff piece to recommend next. Jochum's version has never been surpassed. His chorus sings with sharp, rhythmic point and, if imagination is called for in such music, Jochum matches flexibility with a spark of humour in his control of mechanistic rhythms. His soloists are individual and sweet-toned. The recording is very fine, although even on CD evocative pianissimos sound a little recessed.

(i) *Die Kluge;* (ii) *Der Mond.*

(M) *** EMI CMS7 63712-2 (2) [Ang. CDMB 63712]. (i) Cordes, Frick, Schwarzkopf, Wieter, Christ, Kusche; (ii) Christ, Schmitt-Walker, Graml, Kuen, Lagger, Hotter; Philh. Ch. & O, Sawallisch.

Sawallisch's pioneering Orff recordings of the mid-1950s are vivid and immediate on CD, with such effects as the thunderbolt in *Der Mond* impressive still. Elisabeth Schwarzkopf is characterful and dominant as the clever young woman of the title in *Die Kluge*. It is good too to hear such vintage singers as Gottlob Frick and Hans Hotter in unexpected roles. Musically, these may not be at all searching works, but both short operas provide easy, colourful entertainment, with Sawallisch drawing superb playing from the Philharmonia. No texts are provided, but the discs are very generously banded.

Pachelbel, Johann (1653–1706)

Canon and Gigue in D.

(M) *** Sony Theta SMK 60161. ECO, Leppard – Concert: *'Music of the Baroque'*. ***

A finely graduated and attractively decorated account of Pachelbel's simple but highly effective *Canon* from Raymond Leppard and the ECO, with a restrained opening leading to an impressive but nicely judged central climax. The sound is both full and bright, and this comes as part of a particularly generous collection of Baroque lollipops, all presented with comparable elegance and finish.

Pacius, Fredrik (1809–91)

Kung Karls Jakt (King Charles's Hunt) (opera): complete.

(M) *** Finlandia Dig. FACD 107. Törnqvist, Lindroos, Krause, Grönroos, Jubilate Ch., Finnish Nat. Op. O, Söderblom.

Fredrik Pacius became known as 'the father of Finnish music', for he brought the Finnish capital, then a provincial backwater, into contact with the mainstream of European music. His opera *King Charles's Hunt* brings pretty simple musical ideas. Some are pleasant but there is little evidence of much individuality. There is some fine singing from Pirkko Törnqvist as the fisherman's daughter, Leonora, Peter Lindroos as her fiancé, and from Walton Grönroos as the coup leader, Gustaf Gyllenstjerna. The young King is a speaking role. Much care has been lavished on the production and Ulf Söderblom holds things together admirably. No masterpiece is uncovered but it will be of interest to collectors with a specialist interest in the beginnings of opera in the northern countries.

Paganini, Niccolò (1782–1840)

Andante amaroso; Balletto campestre (Variations on a comic theme; orch. Tamponi); *Larghetto con passione; Moto perpetuo in C, Op. 11; Polacca with variations in A; Sonata for grand viola; Sonata Maria Luisa in E; Sonata Varsavia; Variations on The Carnival of Venice; Variations on a theme from Rossini's Mosè.*
(B) *** EMI CZS7 67567-2 (2) [(M) id. import]. Salvatore Accardo, COE, Tamponi.

Salvatore Accardo here explores the by-ways of Paganini's concertante music for violin and orchestra (with one piece for viola), and much of the virtuosity is stunning – sample the *Moto perpetuo*. As can be seen from the listing, Paganini's favourite device was a set of variations on a simple, often ingenuous theme, alternating *galant* lyricism with fiendish bravura. Accardo is equally at home in both. The orchestral accompaniments are of minimal interest but they are warmly supportive; the flattering ambience of the recording and the good balance ensure that the sounds reaching the listener are pleasingly believable: the CD transfers are admirably faithful. The two discs are offered for the price of one. There are, however, no notes about the music.

Violin concertos Nos. 1–6.
(M) *** DG 437 210-2 (3). Accardo, LPO, Dutoit.

Paganini's concertos can too often seem trivial and long-winded; it is a tribute to the virtuosity and artistry of Salvatore Accardo that they reveal so much musical interest in his hands. But – as we have observed before – Accardo's technique is formidable and his intonation marvellously true; these qualities, blended with good taste, make this series of performances distinctive. Apart from No. 5 (which, like No. 6, was orchestrated by Federico Mompellio), these are all genre works written to a formula in which the composer produced a series of contrasting lyrical operatic melodies to offset the fireworks of the outer movements. Having said this, Paganini's invention holds up well throughout these works. Tuttis are stereotyped but have plenty of impulse, the lyrical tunes are all very engaging, and the violinistic display is consistently ear-tickling when presented with such panache. Accardo is beautifully accompanied by Dutoit who always keeps even the most conventional passage-work alive. The recordings were made in Barking Town Hall in 1974/5 and the remastering preserves the hall ambience, yet has a cleaner orchestral bass than the LPs.

Violin concerto No. 1 in D, Op. 6.
(B) ** BMG/Melodiya 74321 40720-2 [id.]. Victor Tretyakov, Moscow PO, Neeme Järvi – TCHAIKOVSKY: *Violin concerto.* **

(i) *Violin concerto No. 1 in D, Op. 6. Caprices for solo violin Nos. 1, 3–4, 9–11, 14, 16–17, 24.*
(B) *** DG Classikon 439 473-2; *439 473-4* [(M) id. import]. Salvatore Accardo; (i) LPO, Charles Dutoit.

Violin concerto No. 1 in D, Op. 6; I Palpiti; Perpetuela; Sonata napoleone.
(M) *** DG 439 981-2 [id.]. Accardo, LPO, Dutoit.

Accardo's account of No. 1 is offered on an inexpensive Classikon disc but is also available recoupled at mid-price with attractive, shorter concertante pieces, of which the *Perpetuela* is quite dazzling and *I Palpiti* is like an operatic air with variations.

On Melodiya, both the Paganini concerto and its coupling were recorded in 1966 when the nineteen-year-old Viktor Tretyakov had just won the Tchaikovsky Competition, and these performances presumably come from the final concert. Tretyakov, who has had relatively little exposure in the West, plays with staggering brilliance and virtuosity. The sound is not particularly good even for its period, and the recording engineers place the young soloist far too forward.

Violin concertos Nos. 1 in D, Op. 6; 2 in B min. (La Campanella), Op. 7.
(BB) *** Naxos Dig. 8.550649 [id.]. Ilya Kaler, Polish Nat. RSO, Gunzenhauser.
(B) *** DG 429 524-2 [id.]. Shmuel Ashkenasi, VSO, Esser.

The young Russian virtuoso, Ilya Kaler, was a pupil of Leonid Kogan and is fully equal to Paganini's once devilish technical demands and the phrasing of warm Italianate melody. His bouncing staccato in the sparkling spiccato finales of both concertos is managed adeptly and in every respect his technique is commandingly secure. Stephen Gunzenhauser is a sympathetic accompanist throughout, and the Polish Radio Orchestra play with suppleness and bring a sense of elegance and style to this music. There is no lack of dazzle in the fireworks, and no damp squibs here. With very good notes, this is an excellent example of a Naxos super-bargain at its best, an easy first choice for this coupling.

At bargain price on CD, Ashkenasi's coupling of the two favourite Paganini *Concertos* is also good value. He surmounts all the many technical difficulties in an easy, confident style and, especially in the infectious *La Campanella* finale of No. 2, shows how completely he is in control. The microphone is close, but his timbre is sweet and the high tessitura and harmonics are always cleanly focused.

Cantabile and valse; 6 Sonatas for violin and guitar, Op. 2; Sonata for gran viola and guitar; Variations di bravura on Caprice No. 24.
(B) **(*) Naxos Dig. 8.550759 [id.]. Scott St John, Simon Wynberg.

Cantabile in D; 6 Sonatas for violin and guitar, Op. 3; Sonata concertata in A; Variations on Barucabà, Op. 14.
(B) **(*) Naxos Dig. 8.550690 [id.]. Scott St John, Simon Wynberg.

As can be seen, Naxos are planning a complete edition of Paganini's music for violin and guitar. Scott St John plays with flair and considerable virtuosity: his approach has extrovert dazzle but rather less charm , and he dominates the performances strongly. The recording venue is resonant, which means close microphones, but the violin timbre is bright without being edgy.

Centone di sonate for violin and guitar, Nos. 1–12.
(BB) **(*) Naxos Dig. 8.553141 (Nos. 1–6); 8.553142 (Nos. 7–12) (available separately). Moshe Hammer, Norbert Kraft.

Moshe Hammer plays with plenty of character and an agreeable cantabile line. He is truthfully recorded in a resonant ecclesiastical acoustic, and the effect is slightly smoother in Volume II (*Sonatas Nos. 7–12*), made three months after Volume I. But both records reproduce realistically and offer enjoyable music-making.

24 Caprices, Op. 1.
(M) *** DG 429 714-2; *429 714-4* [id.]. Salvatore Accardo.
(BB) *** Naxos Dig. 8.550717 [id.]. Ilya Kaler.
(M) *** Decca (IMS) 440 034-2 [id.]. Ruggiero Ricci.
(M) *(**) EMI CDM7 64560-2 [id.]. Michael Rabin.

Accardo succeeds in making Paganini's most routine phrases sound like the noblest of utterances and he invests these *Caprices* with an eloquence far beyond the sheer display they offer. There are no technical obstacles and, both in breadth of tone and in grandeur of conception, he is peerless. He observes all the repeats and has an excellent CD transfer.

Those looking for a bargain will surely not be disappointed with the Russian fiddler, Ilya Kaler, on Naxos. He studied under Kogan and in 1981 won the Grand Prize at the Genoa Paganini competition. His playing is technically very assured, the lyrical bowing vibrant in a Slavic way, and, like Ricci, he projects a strong profile. The 1992 Naxos recording, truthful and real, is very well balanced: the violin is present but the engineers also convey the acoustic of Orum Hall, Valparaiso, Indiana. How attractively this colours the opening of the famous *No. 9 in E major*, which has superb variety of bowing!

Ricci's Decca recording dates from 1959 but it is remarkably real, with a vivid presence. Ricci's playing often offers a breathtaking display of bravura and, oddly enough, his very occasional imperfections (usually minor slips of intonation) come at points where they are least expected – in the easier rather than the more difficult parts. The playing has great personality and the quicksilver articulation is often dazzlingly precise, conveying enormous dash, for instance in *No. 5 in A minor*. A most enjoyable and stimulating set, and the violin sounds life-size. However, Kaler and Accardo are even more polished.

Michael Rabin was a prodigiously gifted virtuoso whose career was cut short in its prime by a freak accident in 1972 when he was only 36. His playing here is consistently mesmerizing, hardly less astonishing in its fizzing bravura (compare No. 5) than Ricci. The snag is that he was given a closely miked recording (in 1958) in the Capitol studios in New York and, although his technique stands up brilliantly to the immediacy of the aural scrutiny, the effect of the CD transfer is to add a degree of shrillness to the violin timbre above the stave, and at times the upper tessitura is made to sound scratchy.

Caprice No. 24, Op. 1/24; Grand sonata in A.

(B) *** Sony SBK 62425; *SBT 62425* [id.]. John Williams (guitar) – GIULIANI: *Variations on a theme by Handel;* D. SCARLATTI: *Sonatas;* VILLA-LOBOS: *5 Preludes*. ***

Grand sonata in A.

(B) **(*) Decca Eclipse 448 709-2; *448 709-4* [(M) id. import]. Eduardo Fernández – GIULIANI; VIVALDI: *Concertos*. **(*)

John Williams is in excellent form in the *Grand sonata*, with its charming central *Romanza* and ingenuous closing *Andantino variato* (originally a duo for guitar and violin), and the famous *Caprice*, for violin solo, both arranged by Williams. The recording is only marginally balanced too forwardly and is otherwise truthful. Most enjoyable.

Fernández's playing is rightly much admired by fellow guitarists. His technique is immaculate and his somewhat self-effacing approach always puts the composer first. He is beautifully recorded and the effect is engagingly intimate to suit the gentle, improvisatory nature of his playing, especially the pensive central *Romanza*. Some might feel that the finale needs more extrovert feeling, but there is certainly no lack of dash or bravura.

Palestrina, Giovanni Pierluigi da (1525–94)

(i) *Good Friday Liturgy: Improperia (Reproaches). Lamentations of Jeremiah: No. 9, Incipit oratorio Jeremiae prophetae:* (iii) original and (ii) revised versions. (i) *Mass and Motet: Dum complerentur; Mass and motet: Tu es Petrus;* (iv) *Missa Papae Marcelli*. Motets: (ii) *Illumina oculos meos; Jubilate Deo; Laudate dominum omnes gentes; Pueri Hebraeorum.*

(M) ** DG (IMS) Analogue/Dig. 439 961-2 (2). (i) Regensburger Domchor, Hans Schrems; (ii) cond. Theobald Schrems; (iii) Pro Cantione Antiqua, Bruno Turner; (iv) Westminster Abbey Ch., Simon Preston.

An interesting and well-planned Palestrina collection, if not one to laud to the skies, except for the Westminster Abbey performance of the *Missa Papae Marcelli*. The Regensburg Choristers sing wonderfully well in the works of Mozart and Haydn, but they have not quite the same fluency in music of the sixteenth century. Although the music flows well, the Mass singing is inclined to be square and here, as in the motets, the singers are not always careful to give the music plenty of light and shade. On the first CD *Incipit oratio Jeremiae prophetae* is heard from the Regensburgers, richly textured, in its shorter, revised version – although it is not absolutely sure that Palestrina himself made the revision. Then on the second disc Bruno Turner and his excellent Pro Cantione Antiqua give the original version containing a longer ending for the section, *Aquam nostram*, with a full repetition of the final phrase '*Lassis non dabatur*'. Performance tempi are very similar, but the latter takes over three minutes longer. Moreover Bruno Turner performs the work with a small vocal consort, with no more than two or three voices to each part. Its more limited sonority undoubtedly suits the *Lamentation*, which is beautifully sung. All this music is given good analogue recording from the early 1960s, although the definition of the words is misty. The second of the CDs opens with Simon Preston's digital recording of Palestrina's most famous work, the *Missa Papae Marcelli*. The account by the Westminster Abbey choristers transcends any such stylistic limitations. The digital recording is first class. All Saints', Tooting, was used rather than the Abbey, and the acoustics are both intimate and expansive, while detail is beautifully caught – a model of how to manage this repertoire on CD.

Canticum canticorum; Madrigals for 5 voices, Book I: 8 Madrigali spirituali.

(M) *** Virgin Veritas/EMI Dig. VED5 61168-2 (2) [ZDMB 61168]. Hilliard Ens., Paul Hilliard.

The Hilliard Ensemble provide beautifully shaped performances, with refined tonal blend and perfect intonation, but they are more remote and ultimately rather cool in emotional temperature. The second CD includes eight Petrarch settings from the First Book of Madrigals. Excellent recording.

Masses

'The Palestrina 400 collection': Missa Assumpta est Maria (with Plainchant: *Assumpta est Maria*); Motet: *Assumpta est Maria. Missa Benedicta es* (with Plainchant: *Benedicta es.* JOSQUIN: *Benedicta es*). *Missa brevis; Missa Nasce la gioja mia* (with PRIMAVERA: *Madrigal: Nasce la gioja mia*). *Missa Nigra sum* (with Plainchant: *Nigra sum.* LHERITIER: *Nigra sum*). *Missa Papae Marcelli. Missa Sicut lilium inter spinas;* Motet: *Sicut lilium inter spinas I.*

(M) *** Gimell/Ph. Analogue/Dig. 454 890-2 (4). Tallis Scholars, Peter Phillips.

This highly recommendable and well-documented box gathers together four CDs recorded by the Tallis Scholars between 1981 and 1989. As is their practice, this group records the Masses together with the motets on which they are based, even if they are by other composers. Their performance of the most famous of Palestrina's works, the *Missa Papae Marcelli*, brings a characteristically eloquent performance. The singing has ardour, purity of tone and a simplicity of line which is consistently well controlled. The *Missa Assumpta est Maria* is also one of Palestrina's most sublime works. It is sung with the group's customary beauty of sound and well-blended tone. The *Missa Benedicta es* is recorded with Josquin's motet on which it is based, together with the plainchant sequence on which both drew. It would seem that the Mass was the immediate predecessor of the *Missa Papae Marcelli* and was composed while the music of *Benedicta es* was still at the forefront of the composer's mind. The *Missa Nasce la gioja mia* is a parody Mass, modelled on the madrigal of the same name by Giovan Leonardo Primavera, and the *Missa Nigra sum* is another parody Mass, based on a motet by Jean Lhéritier, and it follows its model quite closely; its text comes from the Song of Solomon. The *Missa Sicut lilium inter spinas* ('like a lily among thorns') is based on the motet of the same name. All this is magnificent music, beautifully sung and recorded, while the chosen acoustics of Merton College, Oxford (or, in the case of *Assumpta est Maria* and *Sicut lilium*, the Church of Saint Peter and Saint Paul, Salle, Norfolk), seem ideal for the music.

Lamentations of Jeremiah the Prophet I–III (Fourth Book for 4 & 5 voices).
(M) *** Carlton Dig. 30366 00762 [(M) id.]. Pro Cantione Antiqua, Bruno Turner.

Many composers have set the Lamentation Lessons for the Tenebrae services on Maundy Thursday, Good Friday and Holy Saturday but, remarkably, Palestrina did so on five different occasions. The present (fourth) setting was discovered only at the beginning of the nineteenth century, and it is recorded here complete for the first time. The music has a serene but poignant simplicity, which Bruno Turner captures admirably with spacious tempi. The concentration is obvious and the quality of the singing from a group of eight (including several famous names) is of a high order. So is the recording, which is very well balanced in the warm acoustic of St Alban's Church, Brook Street, London.

Missa Aeterna Christi munera (with *Hymn*); *Missa l'homme armé*.
(M) **(*) Carlton Dig. 30366 00772 [(M) id.]. Pro Cantione Antiqua, Mark Brown.

This 1992 Carlton coupling of two fine Palestrina masses from the Pro Cantione Antiqua under Mark Brown could hardly be bettered in terms of ensemble and accomplishment. This is an all-male ensemble (there are 12 singers in all, counter-tenors, tenors and basses) and the forces are modest – one to a part for much of the time – with resultant textural clarity, though the vocal colour is inevitably dark and there is no lack of weight. This suits *L'homme armé* particularly well, and this is the more memorable of the two performances. The balance could with advantage have been more distant, as it is in the chants with which the Mass movements are interspersed; more air round the voices would have given greater aural variety and relief, though a somewhat lower-than-usual level setting helps matters. The singing itself is superb. The group includes such distinguished singers as Michael Chance, Ian Partridge and Stephen Roberts, and the impact of the performances is enhanced by the closeness of the sound, set in the warm but intimate acoustic of St Jude's, Hampstead. Many will also appreciate the inclusion of apt plainsong passages between the sections of the liturgy.

Missa Aeterna Christi munera; Missa Papae Marcelli.
(BB) **(*) Naxos Dig. 8.550573 [id.]. Oxford Camerata, Jeremy Summerly.

Summerly's are bold, flowing performances, lacking something in mysticism and ethereal dynamics, but sung very confidently, with textures clear and the performances alive and compelling. The Oxford Camerata consists of twelve singers, of whom a third are female, and the blend is impressive. The account of the lesser-known *Missa Aeterna Christi munera* is particularly compelling. The recording was made in Dorchester Abbey, so the ambience is flattering, although the balance is fairly close.

Mass & Motet: *Assumpta est Maria*. Motets: *Ave Maria; Beata es, Virgo Maria; Hodie gloriosa semper Virgo Maria; Regina coeli; Magnificat septimi toni*.
(B) **(*) EMI Dig. CDZ5 69703-2 [(M) id. import]. Clare College, Cambridge, Ch., Timothy Brown.

This is an exceptionally well-chosen collection, mainly of shorter works, but also including the splendid *Missa Assumpta est Maria* which was not published in the composer's lifetime but survives in the music library of the Sistine Chapel. The programme ends with an equally fine *Magnificat* setting. We are familiar with the excellent Clare College Choir and their rich sound, partly achieved by using women's voices, from earlier recordings under their previous director, John Rutter. This EMI Debut CD introduces their new conductor, Timothy Brown, and the choir responds expressively to his melismatic direction, immediately arresting in the beautiful opening motet with which the Mass is associated. The choir is beautifully recorded, and the only minor criticism is the relatively restricted dynamic range, which may partly be caused by the microphone placing, but which certainly reduces the dramatic contrast of the singing. But this remains a thoroughly worthwhile bargain disc, although it is a pity that the documentation has so little to say about the music.

Hodie Beata Virgo; Litaniae de Beata Virgine Maria in 8 parts; Magnificat in 8 parts (Primi Toni); Senex puerum portabat; Stabat Mater.
(M) *** Decca 421 147-2. King's College Ch., Willcocks – ALLEGRI: *Miserere.* ***

The flowing melodic lines and serene beauty which are the unique features of Palestrina's music are apparent throughout this programme, and there is no question about the dedication and accomplishment of the performance. Argo's recording is no less successful, sounding radiantly fresh and clear.

Masses: *Ecce ego Joannes; Sine nomine.*
(BB) *** Belart 461 018-2 [(M) id. import]. Mary Thomas, Jean Allister, Edgar Fleet, Christopher Keyte, Carmelite Priory Ch., London, John McCartney – VICTORIA: Mass & Motet: *O quam gloriosum.* ***

The reissue of these distinguished (originally Oiseau-Lyre) recordings by the London Carmelite Priory Choir under John McCartney, made in the early 1960s, is very welcome indeed on Polygram's super-budget label, Belart. The two works offered here make a good foil for each other, for they are contrasted in style and texture. The Mass 'without name' is a small-scale work, whereas *Ecce ego Johannes* is more ambitious and dramatic. Both are beautifully sung and very well recorded. With the availability of this record so inexpensively and with extra works by Victoria (not on the original LP) included for good measure, one hopes that more music-lovers will be tempted to sample this wonderfully expressive and rewarding music.

Missa Hodie Christus natus est; Motet: Hodie Christus natus est; Stabat Mater.
(BB) *** Naxos Dig. 8.550836 [id.]. Oxford Schola Cantorum, Jeremy Summerly – LASSUS: *Missa Bell'Amfitrit'alterna.* ***

Where in their account of Palestrina's *Missa aeterna Christi munera*, also on Naxos, Summerly's group are restrained in their devotional manner, this celebrated Mass for Christmas has them joyful and exuberant. The choir, over 30 strong, brings out both the beauty and the drama of the writing, and equally so in the brief motet setting the Christmas words. The magnificent *Stabat Mater* is wisely given to a smaller group of 16 singers, two to a part, with added clarity in the complex polyphony. Well coupled with one of Lassus's best-loved Masses, representing the work of Palestrina's close contemporary from Flanders, the two supreme polyphonic masters who died in the same year.

Missa Papae Marcelli.
(B) ** [EMI Red Line CDR5 69858]. King's College, Cambridge, Ch., Willcocks – FAURE: *Requiem; Pavane.* **(*)

From King's College a smooth, limpid performance, well recorded. The singing style is direct and unmannered. However, although the control of dynamic is impressive, the inner mystery of the music is not readily conveyed.

Missa Papae Marcelli; Alma Redemptoris Mater (antiphon); *Peccantem me quotidie* (motet); *Stabat Mater.*
(BB) **(*) ASV CDQS 6086 [(M) id. import]. L. Pro Cantione Antiqua, Bruno Turner.

Bruno Turner uses small forces throughout his well-conceived programme (the concert opens with the Mass), and these are most beautiful performances of all four pieces, offering both intelligence and sensitivity in the handling of each line. Partly because of the recording balance, which is rather forward, one can hear the inner parts with uncommon clarity and, although this is not achieved at the expense of the overall sonority, some might feel that the clear and precise acoustic robs the music of some of its mystic atmosphere. This is not the only way of performing and recording Palestrina, but it is none the less impressive, and it makes one listen to the linear detail with fresh ears.

Missa Papae Marcelli; Stabat Mater.
(M) *** Carlton Dig. 30366 0070-2 [(M) id.]. Pro Cantione Antiqua, Mark Brown.

Mark Brown and the Pro Cantione Antiqua give an account of these celebrated pieces that aspires to total authenticity in that the forces used are those Palestrina himself would have known: no boys' voices, no women and just one-to-a-part, with the Mass sections interspersed with plainchant. The Pro Cantione Antiqua sing with eloquence and power against the background of a resonant acoustic. The 1986 recording is splendidly balanced. Whatever other versions you may have of either work, this has special claims, and its outward severity does not preclude depth of feeling – rather the reverse.

Veni sponsa Christi.

(M) *** EMI Dig. CD-EMX 2180 [(M) id. import]. St John's College, Cambridge, Ch., Guest – ALLEGRI: *Miserere;* LASSUS: *Missa super bella.* **(*)

Veni sponsa Christi is a parody Mass – which implies no suggestion of satirical mimicry, but simply means that it uses pre-existing music, here an earlier Palestrina motet based on Gregorian chant. Every section of the Mass is introduced by the same idea with much subtle variation, and this impressive work ends with two *Agnus Dei* settings, the second with an additional tenor part. It receives an eloquent, imaginatively detailed and finely shaped performance here, and the relative restraint of the Anglican choral tradition suits Palestrina's flowing counterpoint better than it does the Lassus Venetian coupling.

Palmgren, Selim (1878–1951)

'Meet the composer': Piano concertos Nos. (i–ii) *1, Op. 13;* (iii; ii) *2 (The River), Op. 33;* (iv; ii) *3 (Metamorphoses), Op. 41;* (iii; ii) *4 (April), Op. 85;* (v; ii) *5, Op. 99;* (ii) *Pictures from Finland, Op. 24;* (vi) *Piano sonata in D min., Op. 11;* Piano pieces: *Raindrops, Op. 54/1; Preludes Nos. 12 (The Sea); 24 (The War), Op. 17/12 & 24; Spring: Dragonfly; May night, Op. 27/3–4; Dusk, Op. 47/1.*

(B) *** Finlandia/Warner Double Dig. 0630 19810-2 (2) [(M) id. import]. (i) Eero Heinonen; (ii) Turku PO, Jacques Mercier; (iii) Juhani Lagerspetz; (iv) Matti Raekallio; (v) Raija Kerppo; (vi) Izumi Tateno.

Palmgren is familiar to piano students, particularly of the older generation, through pieces like *May night* and *Moonlight.* At one time in Finland itself he was even thought to threaten Sibelius's pre-eminence. During the First World War the public found it easier to assimilate Palmgren's *Second* and *Fourth Piano concertos* and his piano miniatures than the more severe and challenging *Fourth* and *Fifth Symphonies* of Sibelius. Palmgren was spoken of as 'the Chopin of the north' for he wrote more idiomatically for the piano than his countryman; but his music is limited both in its emotional range and in its repertory of pianistic devices. He was a fine pianist and accompanied his wife, Maikki Järnefelt, who by her first marriage had been Sibelius's sister-in-law and a noted interpreter of his songs. Palmgren taught briefly in America at the Eastman School of Music when Howard Hanson had become its first director.

This valuable Double in Finlandia's '*Meet the Composer*' series collects the five *Piano concertos*, which range in the composer's career from 1903 to 1941, and some of his piano miniatures, as well as the early *Sonata in D minor*, Op. 11, of 1900. There is poetic feeling here, tinged at times by a certain gentility. Palmgren was influenced by impressionism, though his melancholic sensibility is undoubtedly Nordic. All the soloists are persuasive in the concertos and are well supported by the Turku orchestra under Jacques Mercier. The orchestra gives an eminently acceptable account of the *Pictures from Finland*, Op. 24, from 1908. In the *Sonata* and the solo miniatures the pianist is the Japanese-born Izumi Tateno, who has lived in Finland since his student days. He plays these pieces with great sympathy and is very well recorded. A useful survey of Palmgren's music, recorded in very decent sound.

Panufnik, Andrzej (1914–91)

(i) *Arbor Cosmica;* (ii) *Symphony No. 3 (Sinfonia sacra).*

(M) *** Elektra Nonesuch/Warner Dig. 7559 79228-2 [id.]. (i) NY Chamber Symphony; (ii) Concg. O; composer.

The *Sinfonia sacra* is one of Panufnik's most warmly and immediately communicative works, and it here receives a magnificent performance from the Concertgebouw under the composer. As the title implies, *Arbor Cosmica* directly reflects a visual concept, this time the branches of a tree. The 12 'evocations' are all generated from a single three-note chord, each with the structure mapped out like a tree. The composer draws dedicated performances both from the Concertgebouw and from the New York Chamber Symphony, with the former inevitably sounding richer and fuller. It is good that this has been reissued at mid-price, for this music is well worth getting to know.

Violin concerto.

(M) *** EMI CDM5 66121-2. Menuhin, Menuhin Festival O, composer – L. BERKELEY: *Concerto;* WILLIAMSON: *Concerto.* ***

The *Violin concerto* presents an interesting structure in three movements, the meatiest in argument being the finale, the only quick movement. It requires the imagination and commitment of a Menuhin to sustain the first two movements, starting with a quasi-cadenza *senza misura*. After that the central *Adagio* is sweeter, more obviously lyrical before the toughness of the finale. A valuable work, outstandingly performed and very well recorded (at Abbey Road in 1975).

Paray, Paul (1886–1979)

Mass for the 500th anniversary of the death of Joan of Arc.

(M) **(*) Mercury (IMS) 432 719-2 [id.]. Yeend, Bible, Lloyd, Yi-Kwei-Sze, Rackham Ch., Detroit SO, Paul Paray – SAINT-SAENS: *Symphony No. 3.* ***

Paray's *Mass*, much admired by the composer, Florent Schmitt, could hardly have a more eloquent performance. The soloists are good and the choir are inspired to real fervour by their conductor, who at the close (in a brief recorded speech) expresses his special satisfaction with the singing of the closing, very romantic *Agnus Dei*. Excellent (1957) Mercury stereo, using the Ford Auditorium in Detroit.

Parry, Hubert (1848–1918)

An English suite; Lady Radnor's suite.

(M) *** EMI Dig. CDM5 66541-2. City of L. Sinfonia, Hickox – ELGAR: *Elegy for strings* etc. **(*)

On EMI, Parry's two elegant and beautifully crafted suites make an unusual and very apt coupling for the Elgar string music. The combination of straightforward, warm expression with hints of melancholy below the surface is very Elgarian. Both suites were written later than the Elgar *Serenade*, with *An English suite* published only after the composer's death. The Bach tributes in *Lady Radnor's suite* are surface-deep; the slow minuet for muted strings is particularly beautiful. Refined playing and first-rate recording.

Symphony No. 2 in F min. (Cambridge); Overture to an unwritten tragedy; Symphonic variations in E.

(BB) **(*) Naxos Dig. 8.553469 [id.]. RSNO, Andrew Penny.

Challenging the outstanding full-priced Parry series from Chandos conducted by Matthias Bamert, Naxos here offers a very acceptable alternative to the *Symphony No. 2*, similarly coupled with the *Symphonic variations* and with an extra item in the *Overture*. The playing of the Royal Scottish National Orchestra is just as polished as that of the LPO on Chandos, but Penny's manner is less warmly expressive at speeds generally a little faster, and the recorded sound is rather less opulent.

Symphony No. 5 in B min.; Symphonic variations; Elegy to Johannes Brahms; (i) *Blest pair of Sirens.*

(M) *** EMI CDM5 65107-2. LPO, Boult, (i) with LPO Ch.

The *Fifth* and last of Parry's symphonies is in four linked movements, terser in argument than the previous two in the series and often tougher, though still with Brahmsian echoes. After the minor-key rigours of the first movement, *Stress*, the other three movements are comparably subtitled *Love*, *Play* and *Now*, with the Scherzo bringing echoes of Berlioz and the optimistic finale opening with a Wagnerian horn-call. The *Elegy for Brahms* conveys grief, but its vigour rises above passive mourning into an expression of what might almost be anger. This was the last record made by Sir Adrian Boult, whose recording of the slow movement of the symphony is particularly beautiful here. Equally impressive is the *Elegy*, not merely an occasional piece but a full-scale symphonic movement which builds to a powerful climax. The sharply inventive *Symphonic variations* fills out the Parry portrait. Recording and performances are exemplary, a fitting coda to Sir Adrian's recording career. To make the CD even more representative, it is good to welcome so enjoyably professional a motet as Parry's *Blest pair of Sirens*. The performance by the London Philharmonic Choir should be more incisive, but it still conveys much of the right atmosphere. Throughout, the digital remastering has been wholly beneficial.

English lyrics: *And yet I love her till I die; Blow, blow, thou winter wind; Bright star; From a city window; Looking backward; Love is a bable; Marian; No longer mourn for me; O mistress mine; On a time the amorous Silvy; Take, O take those lips away; There; There be none of beauty's daughters; Thine eyes still shine for me; Welsh lullaby; When comes my Gwen; When lovers meet again; Weep you no more; When icicles hang by the wall; When we two parted.*

(BB) **(*) Belart 461 493-2 [(M) id. import]. Robert Tear, Philip Ledger – VAUGHAN WILLIAMS: *Songs of travel; Linden Lea.* ***

Between the 1880s and 1920 Parry published a dozen sets of what he called 'English lyrics', 74 in all. He was perhaps not among the greatest of English song composers but his melodic line is always fresh, and these songs are all appealing for their easy lyricism. Opening with *Bright star*, which is a little like one of Stanford's sea songs, the disc includes a number of items to cherish, notably the lovely *Welsh lullaby* (Philip Ledger's gentle accompaniment setting the mood admirably), the touching if slightly sentimental *Thine eyes still shine for me* and the charming *Weep you no more*. The light-hearted *On a time the amorous Silvy* and the sparkling *Love is a bable* show Parry at his most spontaneous and *When icicles hang by the wall*, with its owl calls, is an effective novelty number. Many, like *When lovers meet again, Looking backward* and *Take, O take those lips away* and the engaging *And yet I love her till I die* are in the direct tradition of English ballads. Robert Tear sings them with conviction and the right lightness of touch; his voice here has developed a beat since he recorded the coupled Vaughan Williams songs, seven years earlier in 1972, but this is still an enjoyable recital, not least because of Ledger's sympathetic and stylish accompaniments.

Pärt, Arvo (born 1935)

(i) *Cantus in memory of Benjamin Britten; Festina lente; Summa;* (i; ii) *Tabula rasa;* (ii) *Fratres; Spiegel im Spiegel.*

(B) *** EMI Dig. CD-EMX 2221 [(M) id. import]. (i) Bournemouth Sinf., Richard Studt; (ii) Tasmin Little, Martin Roscoe.

An admirable and enterprising compilation from EMI Eminence to tempt those who have not yet sampled this composer's highly individual sound-world with its tintinnabulation (ringing bells). *Summa* is another version of the vocal *Creed* and is certainly effective, if not superior in its new costume. In the two chamber works Tasmin Little holds the listener's attention by the intensity of her commitment and the powerful projection of her playing. But most striking of all is the ambitious *Tabula rasa* with strong contrasts between the erupting energy of the opening *Ludus* and the aptly named second-movement *Silentium* which, of course, isn't silent but spins a compulsive atmospheric web. Fine performances and evocative sound, spread within an ecclesiastical acoustic, and first-rate recording combine to give this programme persuasive advocacy, if not to convince the listener that Pärt is one of the greatest composers of our time.

Fratres for cello and piano.

(B) ** Carlton Dig. 30367 02362 [(M) id.]. Ulrich Boeckheler, Susan Starr – PROKOFIEV; SHOSTAKOVICH: *Sonatas.* **

A rather haunting fill-up, composed originally for an early music group in 1977. Like so much of Pärt's music, it uses the simplest of musical elements but to often striking effect. Even those who find the fashionable minimalist unstimulating may enjoy this piece. Ulrich Boeckheler and Susan Starr play it with sympathy and are excellently recorded.

Patterson, Paul (born 1947)

Concerto for orchestra, Op. 45; Europhony, Op. 55; (i) *Missa brevis, Op. 54.*

(M) *** EMI Dig. CDM5 66529-2. LPO, Owain Arwel Hughes; (i) with LPO Ch.

This disc offers representative examples of Patterson's recent work, much more approachable in idiom than his earlier music. The gem of the collection is the *Missa brevis*, using a seemingly simple style boldly and freshly. It must be as grateful for the singers as it is for the listener, with moments of pure poetry as in the *Benedictus*. The two orchestral pieces, though less individual, are colourful and immediately attractive. Their openness of idiom conceals the ingenuity of their construction, with *Europhony* clearly developing on variation form. Vigorous performances and wide-ranging recording.

Penderecki, Kryszstof (born 1933)

(i) *Anaklasis;* (ii; iii) *Capriccio for violin and orchestra;* (iii) *De natura sonoris I & II; The dream of Jacob; Fonogrammi; Threnody for the victims of Hiroshima;* (iv) *Canticum canticorum Salomonis.*

(M) *** EMI CDM5 65077-2 [id.]. (i) LSO; (ii) Wanda Wilkomirska; (iii) Polish Nat. RSO; (iv) Krakow Philharmonic Ch.; composer.

A splendid anthology and an admirable introduction to Penderecki's music. The longest work is the setting of a text from the *Song of Solomon* for large orchestra and sixteen solo voices. The other, shorter pieces will probably have a more lasting impact. The beautiful and touching *Threnody* for 53 strings (1959–61) is the best-known piece and originally made the composer's name internationally; it is here given a magnificent performance. So is the ambitious *Capriccio* in which Wilkomirska proves a superb soloist. *Anaklasis*, an inventive piece for strings and percussion, and *De natura sonoris* are more obviously brilliant in their use of contrasts, while *The dream of Jacob* of 1974 is as inventive as the rest but sparer and more cogent. Performances are definitive and the recordings, a co-production between EMI and Polish Radio, are of a very high standard.

(i; iii) *Cello concerto;* (iii) *Emanationen for 2 string orchestras;* (ii–iii) *Partita for harpsichord and orchestra;* (iv) *Symphony.*

(M) *** EMI CDM5 65416-2 [id.]. (i) Siegfried Palm; (ii) Felicja Blumenthal; (iii) Polish RSO; (iv) LSO; composer.

For those who admire such athematic music, these 1972–3 recordings of Penderecki's works in authentic performances under the composer's own direction will have much to commend them. Blumenthal makes a fine contribution to the *Partita* and Palm is a superb player in the *Cello concerto*. Penderecki's music relies for its appeal on its resourceful use of sonorities, and his sound-world is undoubtedly imaginative, albeit limited. The *Symphony*, the composer's most ambitious orchestral work so far, was commissioned by a British engineering firm and first heard in Peterborough Cathedral. That setting has influenced the range of sumptuous orchestral colours devised by the composer. You may regard this as merely a sequence of brilliant effects rather than a logically argued symphony, but in this committed performance it is certainly striking and memorable. Fine recording enhances the value of this disc, and the CD transfers combine fullness with admirable presence.

Violin concerto.

(M) *** Sony Stern Edition II SMK 64507 [id.]. Stern, Minnesota O, Skrowaczewski – HINDEMITH: *Violin concerto.* ***

This concerto, written for Isaac Stern in 1977, marked Penderecki's return to a more conservative idiom. Even so, his fingerprints are clearly identifiable and the compression of thematic material, combined with spare, clean textures, makes for memorable results. The single movement, which lasts nearly 40 minutes, contains within it the traces of a funeral march, a Scherzo and a meditative adagio. The performance here is passionately committed, with Stern at his most inspired, and the recording is splendidly detailed. With its hardly less valuable Hindemith coupling, this is a key reissue in the second box of Sony's Stern Edition.

Pergolesi, Giovanni (1710–36)

(i) *Magnificat in C;* (ii) *Miserere II in C min.;* (iii) *Salve Regina in C min.;* (iv) *Stabat Mater* (revision and organ part by M. Zanon).

(B) **(*) Decca Double 455 017-2 (2) [(M) id. import]. (i) Vaughan, J. Baker, Partridge, Keyte, King's College Ch., ASMF, Marriner; (ii) Wolff, James, Covey-Crump, Suart, Magdalen Coll., Oxford, Ch., Wren O, Bernard Rose; (iii) Kirkby, AAM, Hogwood; (iv) Raskin, Lehane, O. Rossini di Napoli, Caracciolo – CALDARA: *Crucifixus.* LOTTI: *Crucifixus.* ***

This more ambitious if slightly uneven collection of Pergolesi's choral music (although only the *Salve Regina* and the *Stabat Mater* are almost certainly authentic) makes a useful alternative to the Double Decca set below, with the Willcocks performance of the *C major Magnificat* common to both. The *Stabat Mater* is modest in its demands, requiring originally two castrati plus strings and continuo. In this Napoli performance, the voices of the two soloists blend nicely, yet have enough difference in timbre (without the contralto sounding plummy) for the listener to separate them. The delightful opening tonal suspensions, which are eloquently sung, make this immediately apparent. The orchestral accompaniment is spirited and the warm acoustic of the Naples Conservatorio adds richness to a fairly small body of strings. There is a discreet organ continuo and the overall effect is fresh and enjoyable, making a good if perhaps not distinctive alternative to Guest's St John's version. The *Miserere*, whether authentic or not, is undoubtedly moving. The singers here are all of quality, particularly Richard Suart; Bernard Rose secures expressive and persuasive results from the Magdalen College choir and the Wren Orchestra. The (originally Argo) recording sounds magnificently real and vivid. Last but not least comes Emma Kirkby's radiantly expressive and spirited *Salve Regina*, the finest solo contibution to this collection. Here period instruments enter the sound-picture, and the accompaniment from Hogwood's Academy matches Kirkby's depth of feeling, particularly in the touching closing '*O clemens*'.

(i) *Magnificat in C;* (ii) *Stabat Mater.*

(B) **(*) Decca Double 443 868-2 (2) [id.]. (i) Vaughan, J. Baker, Partridge, Keyte, King's College Ch., ASMF, Willcocks; (ii) Palmer, Hodgson, St John's College, Cambridge, Ch., Argo CO, Guest –

BONONCINI: *Stabat Mater;* D. SCARLATTI: *Stabat Mater;* A. SCARLATTI: *Domine, refugium factus es nobis; O magnum mysterium;* CALDARA: *Crucifixus;* LOTTI: *Crucifixus.* ***

This well-planned Double Decca collection centres on three different settings of the *Stabat Mater dolorosa*. Pergolesi's version dates from 1735 and, subsequently, settings were made by many other composers, including Vivaldi and Haydn. Pergolesi conceived a work which has secular and even theatrical overtones, and its devotional nature is unexaggerated. George Guest directs a sensible, unaffected performance, simple and expressive, with relaxed tempi, not overladen with romantic sentiment. He has very good soloists, Felicity Palmer and Alfreda Hodgson blending very well together. It is a performance that does not emphasize the music's dramatic variety, and the choral singing, though felt, is not particularly vibrant. The *Magnificat* – doubtfully attributed, like so much that goes under this composer's name – is a comparatively lightweight piece, notable for its rhythmic vitality. The King's College Choir under Willcocks gives a sensitive and vital performance, and the recording matches it in intensity of atmosphere.

Stabat mater (revised Alberto Soresina).
(M) **(*) Ph. 462 054-2 [id.]. Lear, Ludwig, RIAS Ch., Berlin RSO, Maazel – VIVALDI: *Stabat mater.* **(*)

This is an unashamedly romantic performance of Pergolesi's most famous choral work. Evelyn Lear and Christa Ludwig could hardly be bettered when it comes to expressive musicianship and beauty of tone, but those who have concern for authenticity of style may be disturbed by the weight of emotion the performers find in what is fundamentally simple music. In this Maazel must take most of the blame. It is music that can so easily sound sentimental, something he narrowly skirts. But the singing itself is glorious, and it is easy to be swayed by the rich opulence of the sounds here, with the chorus joining in vigorously at the close. The reissue comes as part of the Philips Choral Collection, which means handsome packaging, but a limited 'sleeve-note' and no texts.

(i) *Stabat Mater;* (ii) *Orfeo* (cantata).
(BB) ** Naxos Dig. 8.550766 [id.]. (i–ii) Julia Faulkner; (ii) Anna Gonda; Budapest Camerata, Michael Halász.

On Naxos, Michael Halász chooses the version of the *Stabat Mater* using just the two soloists without chorus, and the resonant ambience of the hall of Festetich Castle, Budapest, adds a spacious effect to the voices, so that the result is convincing, with the vibratos of the two singers matching quite closely. The pacing here is lively and the style of the soloists at times operatically expressive. The contribution of the soprano, Julia Faulkner, is slightly more impressive than that of the contralto, Anna Gonda, and it is the former who provides a fine performance of the *Orfeo* cantata. This encapsulates the famous story in two recitatives, each followed by an expressive aria-soliloquy from Orfeo about his predicament and his resolve to secure the return of his beloved Euridice. The Budapest Camerata accompany throughout with plenty of life and finesse. They are warmly recorded and the balance is most satisfactory.

Pfitzner, Hans (1869–1949)

Palestrina (opera) complete.
(M) *** DG 427 417-2 (3). Gedda, Fischer-Dieskau, Weikl, Ridderbusch, Donath, Fassbaender, Prey, Tölz Boys' Ch., Bav. R. Ch. & SO, Kubelik.

Though Pfitzner's melodic invention hardly matches that of his contemporary, Richard Strauss, his control of structure and drawing of character through music make an unforgettable impact. It is the central Act, a massive and colourful tableau representing the Council of Trent, which lets one witness the crucial discussion on the role of music in the church. The outer Acts – more personal and more immediately compelling – show the dilemma of Palestrina himself and the inspiration which led him to write the *Missa Papae Marcelli*, so resolving the crisis, both personal and public. At every point Pfitzner's response to this situation is illuminating, and this glorious performance with a near-ideal cast, consistent all through, could hardly be bettered in conveying the intensity of an admittedly offbeat inspiration. This CD reissue captures the glow of the Munich recording superbly and, though this is a mid-price set, DG has not skimped on the accompanying booklet.

Palestrina: 3 Preludes.
(M) ** DG 439 488-2. Bav. RSO, Leitner – BUSONI: *Dr Faust* **; HINDEMITH: *Mathis Symphony* **; WEILL: *Kleine Dreigroschenmusik.* ***

Ferdinand Leitner's version of the three *Preludes* was recorded in 1958 and originally appeared in harness with the *Symphony in C*, Op. 46. It is well enough played, though Kubelik in the complete recording and

Christian Thielemann with the Orchestra of the Deutsches Oper, Berlin, make a stronger impression.

Philips, Peter (*c.* 1561–1640)

Motets: *Ave verum corpus; Ave Maria gratia plena; Ecce vicit Leo; Factum est silentium; Gaudent in coelis; Hodie nobis de coelo; O bone Jesu; O crux ave spes unica; O quam suavis.*

**(*) EMI Dig. CDM5 66788-2. King's College, Cambridge, Ch., Cleobury – DERING: *Motets.* **(*)

Both Peter Philips and his younger contemporary, Richard Dering, were Catholics and spent much of their lives on the Continent. This CD contrasts and compares the two composers' beautiful and expressive settings of the same texts. The performances are faithful, but the actual sound is not always perfect in either focus or blend, partly but not solely due to the recording.

Pizzetti, Ildebrando (1880–1968)

Murder in the Cathedral (Mord in der Kathedral) (complete).

(M) (**(*)) DG mono 457 671-2 (2). Hotter, Equiluz, Dermota, Stolze, Schöffler, Berry, Ludwig, V. State Op. Ch. & O, Karajan.

In 1960, during his controversial reign as music director of the Vienna State Opera, Karajan conducted Pizzetti's thoughtful adaptation of T. S. Eliot's play about Thomas à Becket, *Murder in the Cathedral.* This important première on disc offers an Austrian Radio recording in mono of a live performance using the German translation. The sound is limited, with the orchestra sounding rather thin, but the result is convincingly atmospheric, with the formalistic structure which Pizzetti took from Eliot compellingly conveyed. In an economically planned adaptation of the play, nicely tailored, the idiom is easily lyrical without using memorable melodic material, giving the impression of a pageant rather than an opera. The all-star cast helps to intensify Karajan's powerful, concentrated reading, with such fine singers as Christa Ludwig, Anton Dermota and Walter Berry in incidental roles, and with Hans Hotter outstanding in the title-role, strong and characterful, more smoothly lyrical than in Wagner.

Pleyel, Ignaz (1757–1831)

(i) *Sinfonia concertante for violin, cello and strings in D. Symphony in A; Flute quartet in B.*

(BB) ** Discover Dig. DICD 920130 [id.]. (i) Bushkov, Kozodov; Moscow Concertino (members), Bushkov.

The name of Ignaz Pleyel is famous as a French manufacturer of pianos but, around the time that Haydn was visiting London for the Salomon concerts, Pleyel was far better known as a composer and his easily tuneful, facile music was enormously popular. His writing is a bit like Boccherini without the pathos. Here the *Flute quartet* (for flute, violin, viola and cello) has surface charm and the *Symphony* is fluent, if rather too long. It has a catchy theme for its closing *Rondo*, and the *Sinfonia concertante* – easily the best work here, and half as long as the *Symphony* – is full of similarly neat invention and again brings an engaging finale. The whole programme is given persuasive advocacy by this excellent Russian group who are thoroughly within the style of the music and play with expert precision and much vitality. The snag is that they are forwardly balanced and rather dryly recorded, and the dynamic contrast of their playing is reduced by the close microphones. Even so, this inexpensive disc gives a fascinating glimpse of an interesting and distinctly talented musician.

Ponce, Manuel (1882–1948)

Folia de España (Theme and variations with fugue).

(M) *** Sony SBK 47669; *SBT 47669* [id.]. John Williams (guitar) – BARRIOS: *Collection.* ***

Ponce's *Variations on 'Folia de España'* are subtle and haunting, and their surface charm often conceals a vein of richer, darker feeling. The performance is first rate and the sound admirably clean and finely detailed, yet at the same time warm.

Ponchielli, Amilcare (1834–86)

La Gioconda (complete).
(M) ** Decca 444 598-2 (3). Milanov, Elias, Di Stefano, Warren, Santa Cecilia Ac., Rome, Ch. & O, Previtali.

The Previtali set is worth hearing for a vintage performance from Zinka Milanov, rather past her best, with raw tone both above and below, but she floats a glorious top B flat on *Come t'amo*. Leonard Warren was another favourite singer at the Met., but his somewhat woolly baritone did not always record well. Di Stefano, however, produces much heroic tone, and the recording is fair for its late-1950s vintage.

Porter, Cole (1891–1964)

Overtures: *Anything goes; Can-Can; Gay divorce; Kiss me, Kate. Night and day* (from *Gay divorce*).
(B) *** EMI forte (SIS) Dig. CZS5 68589-2 (2) [CDFB 68589]. L. Sinf., McGlinn – GERSHWIN: *Broadway and film music* **(*); KERN: *Overtures*. **

These overtures were not put together or scored by the composer but by the professionals of the day. As *Gay divorce* does not include the most famous number from the show, a separate arrangement of *Night and day* has been included, richly scored. The performances here are definitive and the bright recording fits the music like a glove.

Song arrangements for orchestra: *Anything goes; Begin the beguine; Blow, Gabriel blow; In the still of the night; It's de-lovely; I've got you under my skin; My heart belongs to Daddy; Night and day; It's all right with me; Ridin' high; So in love; You'd be so nice to come home too* (all orch. Ray Wright).
(M) **(*) Mercury (IMS) 434 327-2 [id.]. O, Frederick Fennell – GERSHWIN: *Song arrangements*. **(*)

The lyrics are missed more than most with orchestral arrangements of Cole Porter songs and, though Ray Wright's scoring is imaginative and admirably sophisticated, this is essentially a CD to use as a pleasing background for a dinner party, rather than for concentrated listening. Unusually for this label, the recording is multi-miked, so the stereo effects are unashamedly directional. But the sound is silky-smooth as well as being clearly defined and, of its kind, this is very good indeed.

Poulenc, Francis (1899–1963)

(i) *Les animaux modèles;* (ii; iii) *Les biches* (complete ballet); (ii) *Bucolique;* (i; iv) *Concert champêtre (for harpsichord & orchestra);* (i; v) *Double piano concerto in D min.;* (vi) *2 Marches et un intermède (for chamber orchestra); Les mariés de la Tour Eiffel (La baigneuse de Trouville; Discourse du Général).* (ii) *Matelote provençale; Pastourelle;* (vi) *Sinfonietta; Suite française.*
(B) *** EMI Rouge et Noir Analogue/Dig. CZS5 69446-2 (2) [(M) id. import]. (i) Paris Conservatoire O; or (ii) Philh. O; (iii) with Amb. S.; (iv) with Van de Wiele, or (v) composer and Février; (vi) O de Paris; all cond. Prêtre.

Les biches comes here in its complete form, with the choral additions that Poulenc made optional when he came to rework the score. The music is a delight, and so too is the group of captivating short pieces, digitally recorded at the same time (1980): *Bucolique*, *Pastourelle* and *Matelote provençale*. High-spirited, fresh, elegant playing and sumptuous recorded sound enhance the claims of all this music. The *Suite française* is another highlight. It is well played and recorded in a pleasing, open acoustic. Poulenc himself was a pianist of limited accomplishment, but his interpretation (with partner) of his own skittish *Double concerto* is infectiously jolly. In the imitation pastoral concerto for harpsichord, Aimée van de Wiele is a nimble soloist, but here Prêtre's inflexibility as a conductor comes out the more, even though the finale has plenty of high spirits. The *Sinfonietta*, too, could have a lighter touch, yet has personality too. *Les animaux modèles* is based on the fables of La Fontaine, with a prelude and a postlude, but here the recording is rather lacking in bloom, and the *Deux Marches* are also a trifle overbright. With nearly 156 minutes' playing time, these CDs are well worth exploring.

(i) *Aubade (Concerto choréographique);* (ii) *Concert champêtre for harpsichord and orchestra;* (iii) *Organ concerto in G min.;* (i) *Piano concerto in C sharp min.;* (i; iv) *Double piano concerto in D min.*
(B) *** Erato/Warner Ultima 3984 21342-2 (2) [(M) id. import]. Rotterdam PO, James Conlon; with (i) Duchable; (ii) Koopman; (iii) Alain; (iv) Collard.

The Erato Ultima Double is one of the most attractive of all Poulenc issues. The *Aubade* is an exhilarating work of great charm. It dates from the late 1920s and is a send-up of Mozart, Stravinsky etc. The *Piano concerto* has a most beguiling opening theme and evokes the faded charms of Paris in the 1930s. The skittish *Double concerto* is infectiously jolly. One could never mistake the tone of voice intended. The performances of two of the solo works by François-René Duchable and the Rotterdam orchestra have a certain panache and flair that are most winning. The *Double concerto* too captures all the wit and charm of the Poulenc score, with the 'mock Mozart' slow movement particularly elegant. Perhaps in these two solo works Duchable is a shade too prominent, but not sufficiently so to disturb a strong recommendation, for the sound is otherwise full and pleasing. The *Organ concerto*, too, has never come off better on record than in Marie-Claire Alain's performance using the excellent Flenthrop organ in Rotterdam's concert hall, the Doelen. The *Concert champêtre* always offers problems of balance as it is scored for a full orchestra, but the exaggerated contrast was clearly intended by the composer. The performance is most perceptive, with a particularly elegant and sparkling finale. James Conlon provides admirable accompaniments throughout a highly recommendable pair of discs.

Aubade (Concerto choréographique); Piano concerto in C sharp min.; (i) *Double piano concerto in D min.*

(M) ** EMI CDM7 64714-2 [id.]. Tacchino, (i) Paris Conservatoire O; (ii) Ringeissen, Monte Carlo PO; Prêtre.

On EMI the performance of the *Aubade* is nicely pointed, and the *Concerto* too receives a finely poised and brilliantly executed performance. However, the *Double concerto*, where Gabriel Tacchino is joined by Bernard Ringeissen, is disappointing, with the result brash and hard-driven. It was a great pity that EMI didn't choose the composer's own version of this work with Jacques Février. Poulenc may have been only an amateur pianist, but his interpretation (with partner) had an agreeable lightness of touch, bringing out all the humour.

Les Biches (ballet suite).

(M) *** EMI CDM7 63945-2 [id.]. Paris Conservatoire O, Prêtre – DUTILLEUX: *Le Loup;* MILHAUD: *Création du Monde.* ***

Prêtre has re-recorded *Les Biches* digitally in its complete format (see above). This 1961 recording of the suite, omitting the chorus, is well worth having in its own right: the racy style of the orchestral playing is instantly infectious in the opening *Rondeau* with its catchy trumpet solo. The remastered sound-picture is much better focused than in its old LP format; and this is one example where the bright vividness of CD is entirely advantageous, for there is just the right degree of ambient atmosphere. With excellent couplings this is a most desirable triptych.

Concert champêtre (for harpsichord); *Concerto in G min. for organ, strings and timpani.*

(B) *** EMI forte CZS5 69752-2 (2) [CDFB 69752]. Simon Preston, LSO, Previn – MESSIAEN: *Turangalîla Symphony.* ***

On EMI forte each of the recordings is realistically balanced, and Simon Preston, who plays the solo parts in both concertos (the first artist to have done so in the recording studio), produces readings of great fluency and authority, to say nothing of wit in the work for harpsichord. Previn too has a genuine feeling for the music: the orchestral playing is always musical, often sparkling, and the recording is first class. It set new standards in its day (1977).

(i) *Concert champêtre; Concerto in G min. for organ, strings and timpani;* (ii) *Piano concerto in C sharp min.;* (iii; iv) *Double piano concerto;* (v) *Sextet for piano, flute, oboe, clarinet, bassoon & horn;* (iii) *Sonata for 2 pianos;* (vi) *Gloria.*

(B) *** Decca Double Analogue/Dig. 448 270-2 (2) [(M) id. import]. (i) Malcolm (harpsichord or organ), ASMF, Iona Brown; (ii) Rogé, Philh. O, Dutoit; (iii) Eden & Tamir; (iv) SRO, Comissiona; (v) Rogé, Gallois, Bourgue, Portal, Wallez, Cazalet; (vi) Greenberg, Lausanne Pro Arte Ch., SRO, López-Cobos.

George Malcolm pairs an excellent account of the *Organ concerto* with the *Concert champêtre*; in the latter he changes over to the harpsichord with equal felicity. In this work the engineers did not succumb to the temptation to make the solo instrument sound larger than life. Some might feel that in the finale Malcolm rushes things a bit, but the music effervesces and in every other respect this is an exemplary account. Pascal Rogé is completely attuned to the spirit and sensibility of this still-underrated master and there is much tenderness in his account of the *Piano concerto* as well as a gamin-like *joie de vivre* that is also shared by Eden and Tamir in their twinklingly light-hearted account of the *D minor Double piano concerto*. They are less successful in the *Sonata for two pianos*. This relatively late work (1953) should not be confused with the more popular two-piano sonata which they have also recorded. Here again they bring their formidable technique to bear on tricky music, but the result lacks the lighter, more sparkling qualities they found so readily in the *Concerto*. Pascal Rogé takes over at the keyboard again for the

Sextet, a disarmingly fresh performance, its only slight drawback being the reverberance of the Salle Pleyel. A generous and inexpensive anthology, mainly of the highest calibre. López-Cobos's excellent account of the *Gloria* is discussed below.

Double piano concerto in D min.

(M) *** Teldec/Warner Dig. 4509 97445-2 [id.]. Güher and Süher Pekinel, French R. PO, Janowski – SAINT-SAENS: *Carnival of the animals*. ***

The Pekinel Duo come from mixed Spanish/Turkish parentage and their account of Poulenc's *Double concerto* is second to none. They play with great dash and sparkle, relishing the Mozartian pastiche of the *Larghetto* and the sensuous Ravelian/Satiesque nostalgia of the other lyrical ideas. Janowski provides a lively and thoroughly supportive accompaniment, and the recording balance is excellent. The only drawback is the brief time-span of this coupling (38 minutes overall), but the Saint-Saens zoological fantasy is equally enticing, so this is still a very attractive disc.

The story of Babar the elephant (orch. Jean Françaix).

❀ (BB) *** Naxos Dig. 8.554170 [id.]. Barry Humphries, Melbourne SO, John Lanchbery – BRITTEN: *Young person's guide to the orchestra*; PROKOFIEV: *Peter and the wolf*. ***

Barry Humphries adopts an engagingly cultivated male persona to tell *The story of Babar* with an elegance and a sense of innocence which make the narrative seem completely believable, within a children's world where elephants can assume human vanities and aspirations. He is genial, gently touching and animated by turns, but always stylish; and so is Lanchbery's matching orchestral accompaniment, which catches the moments of nostalgia and joy with equal sensitivity and flair. The dance after the wedding (in Jean Françaix's uninhibited scoring) momentarily recalls *Les Biches*. The effect here is infinitely more involving than the composer's rather bald, original piano version, and Jean de Brunhoff's tale has never been presented more effectively on record, or better recorded. A delight and very highly recommended, as the couplings are first rate too.

Suite française.

(M) *** ASV CDWHL 2067. L. Wind O, Wick – GRAINGER: *Irish tune from County Derry* etc.; MILHAUD: *Suite française*. ***

This engaging suite is based on themes by the sixteenth-century composer, Claude Gervaise. Poulenc scored them for a small ensemble of wind instruments and they come up very freshly in these artists' hands. Excellent recording and couplings. Thoroughly recommended.

CHAMBER MUSIC

Cello sonata in A.

(M) ** Virgin/EMI Dig. CUV5 61198-2 [id.]. Steven Isserlis, Pascal Devoyon – DEBUSSY; FRANCK: *Cello sonatas*. **

Steven Isserlis and Pascal Devoyon play most sensitively and are inside this idiom, but the close scrutiny to which the microphone subjects them does them some disservice. Both artists show subtlety and intelligence, and their performance deserves a recommendation.

Cello sonata; Clarinet sonata; Duo sonata for 2 clarinets; Sonata for clarinet and bassoon; Elégie for horn & piano; Flute sonata; Oboe sonata; Sextet for piano, flute, oboe, clarinet, bassoon and horn; Sonata for horn, trombone and trumpet; Trio for piano, oboe and bassoon; Violin sonata.

(B) ** EMI Rouge et Noir CZS5 69267-2 (2) [(M) id. import]. Fournier, Février, Portal, Gabai, Wallez, Civil, Bourgue, Debost, Casier, Boutard, Faisandier, Bergès, Wilbraham, Iveson, Y. Menuhin.

This is another generous EMI Poulenc collection of some 145 minutes of music on two CDs (offered for the price of one) and much of it (the chattering *Duo for two clarinets*, for instance) has an appeal and charm that deserve to reach a wider audience. Not all the performances are equally distinguished, and Jacques Février's pianism does not always have the finish such repertoire ideally demands. It is good to have Fournier's elegant account of the *Cello sonata* restored to the catalogue, though in the *Violin sonata* Menuhin gives less pleasure. Bourgue's account of the *Oboe sonata* is enjoyable, though he has since recorded it again (at full price) for Decca with Pascal Rogé, to even greater effect. Both the *Trio for piano, oboe and bassoon* and the *Sextet* are rather dryly recorded (and the CD transfer doesn't improve matters); however, although the playing could be more elegant, there is a high-spirited, knockabout quality that is eminently likeable. The brass trio is one of the disc's highlights, most entertainingly played and given better sound, too. The recordings were made betwen 1964 and 1974 and are acceptable, if often forwardly balanced and without a great deal of bloom. But with the reservations noted, this is a serviceable and modestly priced introduction to some delightful music.

(i) *L'invitation au château (for clarinet, violin & piano);* (ii) *Mouvements perpétuels for flute, oboe, clarinet, bassoon, horn, violin, viola, cello & bass;* (iii) *Rapsodie nègre for flute, clarinet, string quartet, baritone & piano;* (iv) *Sextet for flute, oboe, clarinet, bassoon, horn & piano;* (v) *Sonata for clarinet; Sonata for clarinet & bassoon;* (vi) *Sonata for 2 clarinets;* (vii) *Sonata for flute and piano;* (viii) *Oboe sonata;* (ix) *Trio for oboe, bassoon & piano;* (x) *Villanelle for piccolo & piano.*

(B) *** Cala Dig. CACD 1018 (2) [id.]. (i–vi) James Campbell; (i–ii) Peter Carter; (i) John York; (ii–iv; vii; x) William Bennett; (ii; iv; viii; ix) Nicholas Daniel; (ii; iv–v; ix) Rachel Gough; (ii; iv) Richard Watkins; (ii) Roger Tapping, Bruno Schrecker, Chris West; (iii) Allegri Qt (Peter Carter, David Roth, Roger Tapping, Bruno Schrecker), Peter Sidhom; (iii; viii–ix) Julius Drake; (iv; vii; x) Clifford Benson; (vi) David Campbell – RAVEL: *Introduction and allegro* etc. ***

These Cala discs are a terrific bargain. The Poulenc accounts for the bulk of the two CDs (two hours' music in fact), all of it full of sparkle and freshness of invention. The discs comprise the complete chamber music for woodwind by Ravel and Poulenc, with the exception of works written primarily for the voice. The performances have great elegance and finesse. There are rarities, such as the *Rapsodie nègre* and *L'invitation au château* for clarinet, violin and piano which Cala claim as a first recording. Poulenc has this rare gift of being able to move from the most flippant high spirits to the deepest poignancy, as in the *Oboe sonata*, expressively played by Nicholas Daniel. His pianist, Julius Drake, is highly sensitive, though the piano is not always ideally focused in the excessively resonant acoustic. Elsewhere, in the captivating incidental music to a play by Jean Cocteau and Raymond Radiguet, *L'invitation au château*, the playing is expert, tasteful and stylish. The *Mouvements perpétuels*, the *Sextet* and the various wind sonatas are beautifully played with great relish and spirit. This is a most attractive set, which deserves the widest dissemination. Had the piano been as well balanced as it is played, this would have earned a Rosette.

Sextet (for piano and wind).

(M) *** Chandos CHAN 6543 [id.]. Ian Brown, Athena Ens. – GOUNOD: *Petite symphonie in B flat;* IBERT: *3 Pièces brèves.* ***

From Ian Brown and the Athena Ensemble a bravura and responsive performance of Poulenc's many-faceted *Sextet*, catching its high spirits as well as its wit, and the gentle melancholy which intervenes at the close of the boisterous finale. The recording is excellent, slightly dry, yet with a nice ambience. Even though the programme is short measure, every minute is enjoyable.

Violin sonata.

(B) *** EMI Eminence CD-EMX 2244 [(M) id. import]. Tasmin Little, Piers Lane – DEBUSSY: *Violin sonata*; RAVEL: *Violin sonata; Tzigane.* ***

In this well-designed collection of violin-and-piano music, Tasmin Little and Piers Lane give outstanding performances, very well recorded, aptly and subtly changing style for each composer, as here in Poulenc's *Sonata*, longer but generally lighter in tone than the other works included. In the slow movement Little produces her sweetest, warmest tone, and she relishes the virtuoso demands of the *Moto perpetuo* finale.

PIANO MUSIC

Sonata for piano (4 hands); *Sonata for 2 pianos. Badinage; Capriccio; Elégie; L'Embarquement pour Cythère; 3 Feuillets d'album; 5 Impromptus; Promenades.*

(M) ** EMI CDM7 63946-2. Jacques Février, Gabriel Tacchino.

Jacques Février was a close collaborator of the composer and recorded the *Concerto for two pianos* with him only a year before Poulenc's death. His authority notwithstanding, there are more accomplished versions of this repertoire now on the market at full price from Rogé, Crossley and others.

L'Album des six: Valse in C. L'Eventail de Jeanne: Pastourelle française d'après Claude Gervaise; 15 Improvisations; 3 Intermezzi; Mélancholie; 3 Mouvements perpétuels; Napoli; 8 Nocturnes; 3 Novelettes; Pièce brève sur le nom d'Albert Roussel; 3 Pièces (Pastorale; Hymne; Toccata); Presto in B min.; Les soirées de Nazelles; Suite in C; Suite française d'après Claude Gervaise; Thème varié; Valse improvisation sur le nom de Bach; Villageoises.

(B) ** EMI Rouge et Noir Analogue/Dig. CZS5 69671-2 [CDZB 69671] (2). Gabriel Tacchino.

This set is based on two different recitals recorded in the Salle Wagram, the first in 1966 and the second digitally in 1983. However, the *Pièce brève*, *Valse improvisation* and *15 Improvisations* have been taken over to the first disc. Not that it matters much, for the analogue recording has been hardened by the CD transfer and sounds little different from the brightly edged digital sound. The *Suite française* is the piano transcription of dances by the sixteenth-century French composer, Claude Gervaise, which have been recorded in their orchestral form by Georges Prêtre. They are delightful and are crisply played by Tacchino.

He does, however, tend to favour brisk tempi. The first of the *Mouvements perpétuels* seems a fraction fast, and he tends to rush the third. *Les soirées de Nazelles* was written between 1930 and 1936. Each piece is given a sobriquet, and the descriptive mood is slightly more serious here than in the *Thème varié*, with its 11 brief miniatures – also titled – alternately lyrical and droll. The six *Villageoises* (1933) are witty and brittle, with a general feeling of pastiche. The *Polka* even includes a whiff of Handel's *Harmonious blacksmith*. The three *Intermezzi* are agreeably romantic, while the *Pièce brève* and *Valse improvisation* are obviously intended as encores. The latter was written for Horowitz and features a continuous accelerando, which Tacchino brings off with only moderate flair. Slight though much of the other music is, some of it is curiously haunting, and one finds pieces like the *C minor Nocturne* (No. 4 of the set of eight), illustrating a passage from a novel by Julian Green, obstinately memorable. Many of the pieces have a delicately observed period flavour as well as Poulenc's sophisticated harmonic sense. A pity about the shallowness of the sound. Sometimes Tacchino characterizes a shade too strongly, but the piano timbre does not help. The set is worth exploring, just the same.

CHORAL MUSIC

Ave verum corpus; Exsultate Deo; Laudes de Saint-Antoine de Padoue; (i) *Litanies à la Vierge Noire; 4 Motets pour le temps de Noël; 4 Motets pour le temps de pénitence; Salve Regina.*

(M) *** EMI CDM5 65165-2 [id.]. Groupe Vocale de France, John Alldis; (i) with Marie-Claire Alain.

An outstanding collection. This is music that ideally needs French voices, and John Alldis has trained his French group splendidly so that they combine precision and fervour with a natural feeling for the words. The soaring *Ave verum* is matched by the exhilaration of the *Exsultate Deo* and the originality of the *Litanies* with its stabbing bursts of organ tone. The *Salve Regina* is very fine too, and the four *Christmas motets* have the right extrovert joyfulness and sense of wonder. The recording is made within an ecclesiastical ambience, yet definition is admirable.

Gloria.

(B) *** Decca Eclipse 448 711-2; *448 711-4* [(M) id. import]. Greenberg, SRO Ch., Lausanne Pro Arte Ch., SRO, López-Cobos – DURUFLE: *Requiem;* FAURE: Pavane. ***

The *Gloria* is one of Poulenc's last compositions and is among his most successful. López-Cobos gives a fine account, expansive yet underlining the Stravinskian elements in the score. The recording is first class, full-bodied and with clean definition.

(i) *Mass in G. Exultate Deo;* (ii) *Litanies à la Vierge Noire. Salve Regina.*

(B) *** Double Decca 436 486-2 (2) [(M) id. import]. St John's College, Cambridge, Ch., Guest; (i) with Jonathon Bond; (ii) Stephen Cleobury – FAURE; DURUFLE: *Requiems.* ***

As an extraordinarily generous bonus for the two great *Requiems* of Fauré and Duruflé, this Double Decca set offers the Poulenc *Mass in G* together with two motets, *Exultate Deo* and *Salve Regina*, finely wrought pieces in performances of great finish. Then, together with Stephen Cleobury, they give us the cool, gently dissonant *Litanies à la Vierge Noire*, a dialogue between voices and organ in which the voices eventually take dominance. It is beautifully done and the St John's College forces cope with the delicacy and sweetness of Poulenc's chromatic harmony throughout. The (originally Argo) recording is eminently realistic and truthful.

Mass in G; 4 Motets pour le temps de Noël.

(B) *** EMI Eminence Dig. CD-EMX 2275 [(M) id. import]. Mark Harris, Winchester Cathedral Ch., Neary – HONEGGER: *Christmas cantata.* ***

The shadow of Stravinsky hovers over the *G major Mass*, and it is rather more self-conscious than his later choral pieces, certainly more so than the delightful *Quatre Motets pour le temps de Noël*. Martin Neary gets excellent results from the Winchester Cathedral Choir and his fine treble, Mark Harris. The EMI recording is also first rate, with well-defined detail and firm definition. The reissue offers only 58 minutes but is recommendable in every other respect.

Power, Leonel (d. 1445)

Missa, Alma redemptoris mater. Motets: *Agnus Dei; Ave Regina; Beata viscera; Credo; Gloria; Ibo michi ad montem; Quam pulchra es; Salve Regina; Sanctus.*

(M) *** Virgin Veritas/EMI Dig. VER5 61345-2. Hilliard Ens., Hillier.

Power was a contemporary of Dunstable and was born probably in the mid-1370s. One of the leading composers represented in the Old Hall MS. (some 20 pieces are attributed to him), Power spent the last years of his life at Canterbury, but the music on this disc is earlier, coming from the period before 1413. The *Missa, Alma redemptoris mater* is probably the earliest, in which all the Mass sections are linked by a common cantus firmus and there is also a complex mathematical design. The music is of an austere beauty that is quite striking, as indeed is the remarkable singing of the Hilliard Ensemble. The digitally remastered recording comes from the early 1980s and is vivid and present. Strongly recommended.

Praetorius, Michael (1571–1621)

Dances from Terpsichore (Suite de ballets; Suite de voltes). (i) Motets: *Eulogodia Sionia: Resonet in laudibus; Musae Sionae: Allein Gott in der Höh sei Ehr; Aus tiefer Not schrei ich zu dir; Christus der uns selig macht; Gott der Vater wohn uns bei; Polyhymnia Caduceatrix: Erhalt uns, Herr, bei deinem Wort.*

(M) **(*) Virgin Veritas/EMI VER5 61289-2 [CDM 61289]. Early Music Cons. of L., Munrow; (i) with boys of the Cathedral and Abbey Church of St Alban.

Terpsichore is a huge collection of some 300 dance tunes used by the French Court dance bands of Henri IV. They were enthusiastically assembled by the German composer, Michael Praetorius, who also harmonized them and arranged them in four to six parts; however, any selection is conjectural in the matter of orchestration. One of the great pioneers of the 'authentic' re-creation of early music, David Munrow's main purpose was to bring the music fully to life and, at the same time, imaginatively to stimulate the ear of the listener. This record, made in 1973, is one of his most successful achievements. Munrow's instrumentation is imaginatively done: the third item, a *Bourrée* played by four racketts (a cross between a shawm and comb-and-paper in sound), is fascinating. The collection is a delightful one. After this stimulating aural feast, Munrow offers six of the composer's eloquent motets, the finest of which is *Erhalt uns, Herr, bei deinem Wort* for four choirs, each with its own accompanying instrumental group, although the shorter *Gott der Vater wohn uns bei* for double choir is hardly less resplendent, and the joyful *Allein Gott in der Höh sei Ehr* (for counter-tenor and triple choir) is also most stimulating, with crumhorns added to the third accompanying group. The only snag is the lack of a really clean focus in the CD transfer, especially in the exultant closing *Christus der uns selig macht*. The Abbey Road acoustic is reverberant, creating a wide amplitude, and the remastering has not altogether been a success in trying to sharpen up the focus. But the result remains rich in amplitude, and this inspired music, which often reminds the listener of Giovanni Gabrieli, is sung superbly by the choir.

Christmas music: *Polyhymnia caduceatrix et panegyrica Nos. 10, Wie schön leuchtet der Morgenstern; 12, Puer natus in Bethlehem; 21, Wachet auf, ruft uns die Stimme; 34, In dulci jubilo.*

(M) *** Virgin Veritas/EMI VM5 61353-2. Taverner Cons. Ch. & Players, Parrott – SCHUTZ: *Christmas oratorio.* ***

This is the finest collection of Praetorius's vocal music in the current catalogue. The closing setting of *In dulci jubilo*, richly scored for five choirs and with the brass providing thrilling contrast and support for the voices, has great splendour. Before that comes the lovely, if less ambitious *Wie schön leuchtet der Morgenstern*. Both *Wachet auf* and *Puer natus in Bethlehem* are on a comparatively large scale, their combination of block sonorities and florid decorative effects the very essence of Renaissance style. The recording is splendidly balanced, with voices and brass blending and intertwining within an ample acoustic, and all the more welcome in this mid-priced Veritas reissue.

Prokofiev, Serge (1891–1953)

Andante for strings, Op. 50 bis.

(M) *(*) Revelation RV 10006 [id.]. Moscow RSO, Rozhdestvensky – GLAZUNOV: *Scènes de ballet* **; SIBELIUS: *Symphony No. 7; Rakastava.* (*)

The *Andante for strings* is a transcription Prokofiev made of the slow movement of his *First String quartet*, Op. 50, which was written in 1930. It is a beautiful piece and Rozhdestvensky shapes it with real eloquence. (It was previously coupled with his 1970s' account of the *Third Symphony*.) The sound is perfectly acceptable but not distinguished – and it is difficult to detect any improvement on the original LP. What a weird coupling though!

(i; ii) *Autumn, Op. 8;* (i; iii) *Chout* (ballet): *suite;* (iv) *Lieutenant Kijé* (suite); (v; vi) *The Prodigal Son: suite; Scythian suite;* (v; vii) *The Stone flower: suite.*

(B) ** Decca Double 448 273-2 (2) [id.]. (i) LSO; (ii) Ashkenazy; (iii) Abbado; (iv) Netherlands R. PO, Dorati; (v) SRO; (vi) Ansermet; (vii) Varviso.

Autumn is the earliest work here, an atmospheric orchestral sketch written in 1910 and well worth having when Ashkenazy's performance is so sympathetic. Abbado's version of the suite from *Chout*, again with the LSO, offers a generous part of the score and reveals a characteristically sensitive ear for balance of texture. The analogue recording, made in the Kingsway Hall in 1966, was a model of its kind. Dorati's *Lieutenant Kijé* brings a complete contrast. The up-front recording was made in Decca's hi-fi-conscious Phase 4 system (ensuring that every detail is clear, yet with a reasonably wide dynamic range and plenty of ambience). The result is not subtly refined, indeed it is very boldly characterized. But Dorati secures excellent playing from the Netherlands orchestra. Ansermet then takes over for *The Prodigal Son* and the *Scythian suite*, and he is undoubtedly sympathetic, though the Suisse Romande Orchestra has neither the polish nor the opulence of tone to do either score real justice. The mid-1960s Decca recording, however, is well up to standard and captures with admirable clarity the detail of Prokofiev's scoring, especially the brutal complexities of the *Scythian suite*. If only the playing had more panache (the third movement seriously lacks sensuousness), this would have been more strongly recommendable. As it happens, Silvio Varviso has rather greater success in this respect. The Swiss orchestra seems to respond enthusiastically to some guest conductors and here they are at their best, while the recording remains faithful and vivid. Any confirmed Prokofievian will enjoy this.

Chout, Op. 21; The Prodigal Son, Op. 46 (both complete).
(M) ** Koch/Consonance 81-5004. Moscow R. & TV SO, Rozhdestvensky.

The reissuing at mid-price of the old HMV/Melodiya LPs of the complete scores of Prokofiev's ballets, *Chout* and *The Prodigal Son*, makes better sense than his symphonies. Neither are as well represented in the catalogue as are the symphonies, and neither is otherwise coupled together. Of course there are better full-priced (and three-star) versions (Järvi on Chandos, for one) but, despite some raw-sounding brass and less-than-opulent sound, this is a useful reissue.

Cinderella (ballet; complete), *Op. 87; Symphony No. 1 in D (Classical), Op. 25.*
(B) *** EMI Dig./analogue. forte CZS5 68604-2 (2) [CDFB 68604]. LSO, Previn.

Artistic honours are very evenly divided between the (full-price) Ashkenazy and Previn recordings of Prokofiev's *Cinderella*. Some dances come off better in Previn's EMI version and there is an element of swings and roundabouts in comparing them. Detail is more closely scrutinized by the Decca engineers; Ashkenazy gets excellent results from the Cleveland Orchestra. There are many imaginative touches in this score – as magical indeed as the story itself – and the level of invention is astonishingly high. On CD, the recording's fine definition is enhanced, yet not at the expense of atmosphere, and the bright, vivid image is given striking projection. However, the EMI engineers have a more spacious acoustic within which to work and yet lose no detail. Moreover this now comes on EMI's very economical two-for-the-price-of-one forte series, and the CD reissue adds a splendid account of the *Classical Symphony*, sunlit and vivacious and hardly less well recorded five years previously.

(i) *Cinderella:* excerpts; (ii) *Romeo and Juliet:* excerpts.
(B) *** EMI CD-EMX 2194 [(M) id. import]. (i) RPO, Irving; (ii) Philh. O, Kurtz.

Kurtz's *Romeo and Juliet* comes from the mid-1960s, but Irving's performances are from 1958, yet it would be difficult to guess the dates of either from the sound here, which is admirable in its definition and body. Irving secures very fine playing from the RPO, crisply rhythmic and sympathetic. In *Romeo and Juliet* Kurtz's performances are slightly lacking in dramatic tension in the longer movements, but the shorter dances come off superbly. But what beautifully shaped phrasing the Philharmonia give us and what full timbre!

Cinderella (ballet): *suites Nos. 1–3, Opp. 107–109; On the Dnieper (suite), Op. 51 bis; Scythian suite, Op. 20.*
(BB) * Naxos Dig. 8.550968/9 [id.]. Ukraine State SO, Theodor Kuchar.

This music demands playing of sparkle, lightness of touch and virtuosity (and, in the case of the remarkable *Scythian suite*, imagination and high voltage). On Naxos neither the playing nor the recording are at all bad, but nor are they outstanding enough to warrant recommendation. André Previn and the LSO offer the complete *Cinderella* ballet (EMI); his account offers infinitely greater pleasure, and neither the *Cinderella* suites nor any of the other music on Naxos is given with anything approaching the same sense of style. The makeweights – if one can call the *Scythian suite* a makeweight – are not played with the virtuosity and brilliance they call for. This is not really a bargain but more of a false economy.

Cinderella: suite No. 1, Op. 107; Lieutenant Kijé (suite); The Love for 3 Oranges: March; Scherzo; The Prince and Princess. Romeo and Juliet: Madrigal; Dance of the girls with lilies.
(BB) *** Naxos Dig. 8.550381 [id.]. Slovak State PO, (Košice), Andrew Mogrelia.

The calibre of this excellent Slovak orchestra is well demonstrated here, and its perceptive conductor, Andrew Mogrelia, is at his finest in his gently humorous portrait of *Lieutenant Kijé*, the three 'best bits' from *The Love for Three Oranges* and the charming items from *Romeo and Juliet*. Excellent recording.

Cinderella: ballet suite; 2 Pushkin waltzes, Op. 120; The Stone flower (ballet), Op. 118: 2 Waltzes; Waltz suite, Op. 110.
(M) *** Chandos Enchant Dig. CHAN 7076 [id.]. RSNO, Järvi.

The Chandos full-price catalogue is rich in Prokofieviana, always giving stimulation and pleasure in the hands of Neeme Järvi. This mid-priced collection, entitled '*Waltz suite*', is lightweight but very winning. From the full score of *Cinderella* Prokofiev chose three suites, and the selection here draws on the First and Third, opening with the ballet's yearning Introduction, moving on to the *Quarrel* between the Ugly Sisters and including the Courtiers' elegant *Pavane* and the *Adagio* danced by Cinderella and the Prince. The *Waltz suite*, Op. 110, is drawn from various works, including *Cinderella* and the opera, *War and Peace*, while the final *Mephisto waltz* comes from incidental music for the film, *Lermontov*. The pair of excerpts from *The Stone flower* come from the fourth scene and include the *Waltz of the Diamonds*, and the two equally engaging *Pushkin waltzes*, one passionate, the other more delicate, are part of the music Prokofiev wrote for a production of *Eugene Onegin*. The variety of the composer's invention and his often piquant scoring negate any suggestion that a succession of pieces in triple time could be too much of a good thing. The orchestral playing throughout is very persuasive, with the sensuousness of much of the writing brought out, especially in *Cinderella*, the highlight of the programme. The recording is first class.

Concertino in G min. for cello and orchestra, Op. 132; Symphony-concerto in E min. for cello and orchestra, Op. 125; 2 Pushkin waltzes, Op. 120.
(BB) *** Naxos Dig. 8.553624 [id.]. Rudin, Ukraine Nat. SO, Kuchar.

The Russian cellist, Alexander Rudin, proves a powerful interpreter of these two concertante works of Prokofiev, consistently incisive in attack and with clean intonation, not just breasting the technical problems but playing with natural warmth. Though in the thorny arguments of the *Symphony-concerto* Rostropovich, the dedicatee, is even more purposeful, often at faster speeds, Rudin can match and even outshine most other rivals, not least in the beauty of his half-tones, as in the slow movements of both concertante works. He and the conductor, Theodore Kuchar, inspire the Ukraine orchestra to play with similar incisiveness, helped by vivid, immediate sound. Here more than usual, the *Concertino* – completed after Prokofiev's death by Kabalevsky and Rostropovich – with its warm lyricism emerges as fully representative of the composer. The two charming Pushkin-based *Waltzes* make an attractive fill-up, winningly pointed.

Piano concertos Nos. 1–5.
(B) *** Decca Double 452 588-2 (2) [id.]. Ashkenazy, LSO, Previn.
(B) **(*) Teldec/Warner Ultima Dig. 3984 21038-2 (2) [id.]. Vladimir Krainev, Frankfurt RSO, Dmitri Kitaenko.
(B) *(*) BMG/Melodiya Twofer 74321 30645 (2) [(M) id. import]. Victoria Postnikova, USSR MoC SO, Gennady Rozhdestvensky.

Piano concertos Nos. 1 in D flat, Op. 10; 3 in C, Op. 26; 4 in B flat, Op. 53.
(BB) *** Naxos Dig. 8.550566 [id.]. Kun Woo Paik, Polish Nat. RSO (Katowice), Antoni Witt.

Piano concertos Nos. 2 in G min., Op. 16; 5 in G, Op. 55.
(BB) *** Naxos Dig. 8.550565 [id.]. Kun Woo Paik, Polish Nat. RSO (Katowice), Antoni Witt.

(i) *Piano concertos Nos. 1–5;* (ii) *Autumnal, Op. 8;* (iii) *Overture on Hebrew themes, Op. 34.*
(M) *** Decca 448 126-2 (*Nos. 1, 2 & 4*); 448 127-2 (*Nos. 3 & 5; Autumnal; Overture*) [id.]. (i) Ashkenazy, LSO, Previn; (ii) LSO, Ashkenazy; (iii) Puddy, Ashkenazy & Gabrieli Qt.

(i) *Piano concertos Nos. 1–5;* (ii) *Overture on Hebrew themes. Visions fugitives, Op. 22.*
(B) **(*) EMI Rouge et Noir CZS5 69452-2 (2) [CDZB 62542]. Michel Béroff; (i) with Leipzig GO, Masur; (ii) with Portal, Parrenin Qt.

Ashkenazy is a commanding soloist in both the *First* and *Second Concertos*, and his virtuosity in the *First* is quite dazzling. If he is curiously wayward in the opening of the *Second*, there is no question that this too is a masterly performance. The best-known, the *Third Concerto*, is keen-edged and crisply articulated, and the only reservation here concerns the slow movement, in which the piano entry immediately after the theme is uncharacteristically mannered. However, Ashkenazy is undoubtedly authoritative in No. 4

and he gives an admirable account of No. 5: every detail of phrasing and articulation is well thought out, and yet there is no want of spontaneity or any hint of calculation. Throughout, Previn and the LSO accompany sympathetically, and the recently remastered recording makes the most of the vintage mid-1970s Kingsway Hall sound. The orchestral quality is full-bodied, but in the CD transfer the resonance means that the focus is less than ideal, as is shown in in the very first tutti of the *D flat major Concerto*. However, the piano quality is admirable. The criticisms are minor and should not inhibit readers from acquiring these most distinguished performances, for Ashkenazy has great panache. The early *In Autumn* is eminently worth having, as is the chamber performance of the *Overture on Hebrew themes*. As can be seen, the five concertos are also available, slightly differently laid out even more economically on a Double Decca set, without the additional items. The transfers appear to be identical.

Kun Woo Paik's playing throughout these five concertos has exhilarating bravura. Tempi are dangerously fast at times and occasionally he has the orchestra almost scampering to keep up with him, but they do, and the result is often electrifying. The famous theme and variations central movement of the *Third concerto* is played with great diversity of mood and style and the darkly expressive *Larghetto* of No. 5 is very finely done. The *First concerto*, which comes last on the first CD has great freshness and compares well with almost any version on disc. In short, with vivid recording in the Concert Hall of Polish Radio, which has plenty of ambience, this set is enormously stimulating and a remarkable bargain. It has far better sound than the remastered Decca recording for Ashkenazy.

Vladimir Krainev and the Frankfurt Radio Orchestra under Dmitri Kitaenko are also formidable contenders in their Ultima Double format. The recordings were made in 1992 and offer sound of considerable warmth and naturalness. Krainev is a virtuoso of the first order and, apart from the *Third*, which has greater brilliance than poetic feeling, his accounts of these concertos have much to recommend them. Though not quite the equal of Ashkenazy, these are eminently worthwhile accounts that will give pleasure.

A satisfying Rouge et Noir set from Michel Béroff, who plays masterfully and is a pianist of genuine insight where Prokofiev is concerned; Masur gives him excellent support. Béroff is free from some of the agogic mannerisms that distinguish Ashkenazy in the slow movement of the *Third*, and he has great poetry. The balance is good; although the overall sound-picture is not wholly natural, it is certainly vivid, and the timbre of the piano is captured sympathetically. However, in the transfer to CD, a degree of hardness and opaqueness has crept in.

The Melodiya recordings come from 1983–7. Given the poetic fantasy and formidable technical address Postnikova commands, one might have had high expectations of this cycle, yet it is curiously disappointing and at times even pedestrian. Of course there are good things but, without beating about the bush, the fact remains that there are better versions of all five individual concertos available, and the same applies should you want them as a complete set. The recordings are serviceable.

(i) *Piano concerto No. 1 in D flat. Suggestion diabolique, Op. 4/4.*

(M) *** EMI CDM7 64329-2 [id.]. Gavrilov, (i) LSO, Rattle – BALAKIREV: *Islamey;* TCHAIKOVSKY: *Piano concerto No. 1.* ***

A dazzling account of the *First Piano concerto* from Andrei Gavrilov. This version is second to none for virtuosity and sensitivity. Apart from its brilliance, this performance scores on other fronts too; Simon Rattle provides excellent orchestral support and the EMI engineers offer most vivid recording, while the *Suggestion diabolique* makes a hardly less dazzling encore after the concerto.

Piano concerto No. 3 in C, Op. 26.

(M) *** DG 447 438-2 [id.]. Martha Argerich, BPO, Abbado – RAVEL: *Piano concerto in G* etc. ***

(M) *** Mercury (IMS) 434 333-2 [id.]. Byron Janis, Moscow PO, Kondrashin (with PROKOFIEV: *Toccata;* SCHUMANN: *Sonata No. 3;* MENDELSSOHN: *Songs without words, Op. 61/1;* PINTO: *3 Scenes from childhood* ***) – RACHMANINOV: *Piano concerto No. 3.* ***

(M) **(*) [RCA 09026 62691-2]. Van Cliburn, Chicago SO, Reiner – SCHUMANN: *Piano concerto.* ***

(BB) **(*) Belart 450 081-2 [(M) id. import]. Israela Margalit, New Philh. O, Maazel – MUSSORGSKY: *Pictures.* **(*)

❀ (M) (**(*)) RCA mono 09026 60921 [id.]. William Kapell, Dallas SO, Dorati – KHACHATURIAN: *Piano concerto* (**(*)) ❀; LISZT: *Mephisto waltz.* (**(*))

This is another ideal choice for reissue in DG's 'Originals' series of 'Legendary Recordings'. Martha Argerich made her outstanding record of the Prokofiev *Third Concerto* in 1968, while still in her twenties, and this record helped to establish her international reputation as one of the most vital and positive of women pianists. There is nothing ladylike about the playing, but it displays countless indications of feminine perception and subtlety. The *C major Concerto* was once regarded as tough music but here receives a sensuous performance, and Abbado's direction underlines that from the very first, with a warmly romantic account of the ethereal opening phrases on the high violins. When it comes to the second subject, the lightness of Argerich's pointing has a delightfully infectious quality, and surprisingly a likeness emerges with the Ravel *G major Concerto*, which was written more than a decade later. This is a much more individual performance of the Prokofiev than almost any other available and brings its own special insights. The 1967 recording, made in the Berlin Jesus-Christus Kirche, always excellent, sounds even more present in this new transfer.

Byron Janis's record with Kondrashin has a certain historical éclat in containing the first recordings made in the Soviet Union (in 1962) by non-Russian recording engineers. The result was a triumphant success, artistically and technically. Janis's account of the Prokofiev *Third Concerto* is outstanding in every way, soloist and orchestra plainly challenging each other in a performance full of wit (particularly in the delightfully managed slow-movement variations), drama and warmth. Even though it was made three decades ago, the Mercury recording sounds amazingly clean and faithful. The recital (recorded in Russia the following year – except for the Schumann, which was made in the USA) is comparatively low-key, except perhaps for the captivating *Scenes from childhood* of Octavio Pinto, which combine charm with glittering yet unostentatious bravura.

Van Cliburn plays with both sympathy and astonishing digital brilliance. However, the 1960 recording is closely balanced, as if the producer, Richard Mohr, decided to counteract the richness of the Chicago ambience with his microphone placing. With a very forward (indeed at times too forward) piano-image and a relatively sharp focus for the violins, he has certainly made his point, and there is no doubting the strong projection of the music-making. We wonder whether he realized that this concerto had its first performance in this very hall (with the composer as pianist) in December 1921, and that the work makes its greatest effect in an expansive acoustic, as is shown by alternative recordings. Nevertheless this remains a distinctive and immensely stimulating account, and the background resonance still adds its warmth.

The performance by Israela Margalit and Maazel is not the most poised available but it has a splendid feeling of spontaneity and enjoyment, and there is no lack of wit in the central theme and variations. The recording balance is somewhat contrived, the resonance of the acoustic competing with the microphone spotlighting, but the end-result is unfailingly vivid and the piano image is tangible. It is not unlikely that those who buy this disc for the Mussorgsky may find themselves turning just as readily to the concerto, for the personality and colour of the score emerge strongly here.

William Kapell's account of the *Third Piano concerto* is dazzlingly brilliant, and the Dallas orchestra under Antal Dorati rise to the occasion too. Indeed this is arguably the most incandescent and vital performance of this concerto ever committed to disc. It comes with an equally remarkable performance of the Khachaturian with the Boston Symphony under Koussevitzky, a powerhouse of vitality. Playing like this silences any criticism one might voice about the recorded sound, which admittedly is pretty grim.

(i) *Piano concerto No. 3 in C, Op. 26;* (ii; iii) *Violin concerto No. 1 in D, Op. 19;* (iii) *Lieutenant Kijé (suite), Op. 60.*

(B) *** DG Classikon Analogue/Dig. 439 413-2 [(M) id. import]. (i) Martha Argerich, BPO; (ii) Shlomo Mintz; (iii) Chicago SO; all cond. Abbado.

Martha Argerich's highly individual performance of Prokofiev's *C major Concerto* (see above) is here coupled with the *First Violin concerto*, which also has a magical opening, and once again Abbado's accompaniment is peerless, while Mintz phrases with imagination and individuality. *Lieutenant Kijé* is hardly less successful and also sounds splendid; Abbado gets both warm and wonderfully clean playing from the Chicago orchestra. This compilation is one of the very finest reissues on DG's bargain Classikon label.

Piano concerto No. 5 in G, Op. 55.

(B) *(*) EMI forte CZS5 68637-2 (2) [CDFB 68637]. Sviatoslav Richter, LSO, Maazel – BARTOK: *Piano concerto No. 2* *(*); TCHAIKOVSKY: *Piano concertos Nos. 1–3.* **

(i) *Piano concerto No. 5. Piano sonata No. 8 in B flat, Op. 84; Visions fugitives, Op. 22/3, 6 & 9.*

(M) *** DG Originals 449 744-2 [id.]. Richter, (i) with Warsaw PO, Rowicki.

Richter's Warsaw account of the *Fifth Piano concerto* is a classic. It was recorded in 1959, yet the sound of this excellent CD transfer belies the age of the original in its clarity, detail and vividness of colour. In any event it cannot be recommended too strongly to all admirers of Richter, Prokofiev and great piano-playing. Richter then plays the *Eighth Sonata* and the excerpts from the *Visions fugitives* with comparable mastery, the latter deriving from a live recital. In both cases the recording is surprisingly good.

In the 1970 EMI recording of this last of the Prokofiev concertos, Richter is presented in far sharper focus – not just a question of recording acoustic (here the Kingsway Hall).

(i) *Violin concertos Nos. 1 in D, Op. 19; 2 in G min., Op. 63;* (ii) *5 Melodies* (for violin and piano). *Solo violin sonata, Op. 115.*
(BB) *(*) Arte Nova/BMG Dig. 74321 49687-2 [id.]. Rouben Aharonian, with (i) Russian PO, Samuel Friedmann; (ii) Irina Kandinskaya.

Accomplished performances from all concerned on the Arte Nova disc. Rouben Aharonian is a rather commanding, at times thrustful player. However, he is forwardly balanced in the *D major Concerto* and his tone suffers from an unpleasant glare in fortissimo passages. For this the recording is probably to blame, for the effect is rather synthetic with little front-to-back perspective. There are times when the sound is close to discoloration. The *Cinq Mélodies* are very well played and beautifully accompanied by Irina Kandinskaya.

Violin concertos Nos. (i) *1;* (ii) *2. Solo Violin sonata in D, Op. 115; Sonata for 2 Violins in C, Op. 56.* (iii) *Violin sonatas Nos. 1–2; 5 Melodies, Op. 35b; Love for 3 Oranges: March* (arr. Heifetz).
(M) **(*) EMI Dig. CMS5 66605-2 [CDMB 66605]. Frank Peter Zimmermann; (i) BPO, Maazel; (ii) Philh. O, Janssons; (iii) Alexander Longquich.

EMI on two mid-priced discs have here compiled a complete collection of Prokofiev's violin works in thoughtful, refined readings from Frank Peter Zimmermann. If he does not quite compete with the finest rivals in the two concertos, it is useful to have them together, when they originally appeared with different couplings. The solo and duo sonatas, never issued in Britain before, were recorded at different times in Holland, with Zimmermann taking both parts in the curious *Two-violin Sonata*. These are outstanding performances, with Zimmermann bringing tense concentration to the often gritty arguments of the *Duo Sonata* and finding pure delight in the *Solo Sonata*, written in the simplest diatonic manner, totally transcending any limitations imposed by Soviet bureaucrats. Otherwise Zimmermann offers finely crafted performances, marked by poetry in the lyrical movements and quicksilver lightness in such a movement as the central *Scherzo* of the *First Concerto*, which is taken exceptionally fast. Zimmermann's is a relatively relaxed style, with a degree of restraint and consistently sweet, pure tone. Though that means there is a lack of bite and spikiness in the concertos and the violin-and-piano sonatas, it works very well in the *Cinq mélodies*, transcribed from the *Songs without words*, written in 1920 as vocalises for the soprano, Nina Koshetz. In the *Sonatas* Zimmermann is not helped by the slightly distant recording-balance, and the pianist is sometimes rhythmically a little square, not as responsive as his partner. Nevertheless the set is well worth considering.

Violin concertos Nos. 1 in D, Op. 19; 2 in G min., Op. 63.
(M) *** Decca 425 003-2 [id.]. Kyung Wha Chung, LSO, André Previn – STRAVINSKY: *Violin concerto.* ***
(M) **(*) Sony Stern Edition II Dig. SMK 64503 [id.]. Isaac Stern, NYPO, Mehta – BARTOK: *Rhapsodies.* **

Chung on mid-price Decca offers compelling Prokofievian readings in excellent analogue sound, more overtly emotional if not quite so commanding. Her performances emphasize the lyrical quality of these *Concertos*, with playing that is both warm and strong, tender and full of fantasy. Previn's accompaniments are deeply understanding, while the Decca sound has lost only a little of its fullness in the digital remastering, and the soloist is now made very present. The Stravinsky coupling is equally stimulating.

In his digital recordings, made in the Avery Fisher Hall in 1982, Stern's are warmly and boldly extrovert readings, a degree freer in expression and more spontaneous-sounding than his 1965 versions, recorded in Philadelphia, even if Ormandy offered riper accompaniments than Mehta does here. Stern may here lack the depth of poetry of Chung and the fearless brilliance of Perlman, but his accounts are full of character and not without distinction in their own right.

(i) *Violin concertos Nos. 1 in D, Op. 19; 2 in G min., Op. 63. Solo violin sonata, Op. 115.*
(BB) ** Naxos Dig. 8.553494 [id.]. Tedi Papavrami, (i) Polish Nat. RSO, Antoni Wit.

Papavrami, Albanian-born but Paris-based, has a pure, silvery tone coupled with immaculate intonation, here offering fresh, direct readings of Prokofiev's two masterly concertos and making light of any technical difficulties. In a way the playing seems too effortless when the overall impression is rather lightweight, lacking a little both in bite and in the emotional thrust implied by these deeply intense works. Nevertheless his poised, hushed intensity at the restrained start of the central *Andante* of No. 2 is most beautiful. The *Solo Violin sonata* that Prokofiev wrote right at the end of his life, deceptively simple in its tonal idiom, finds Papavrami at his finest, providing an attractive makeweight.

Violin concerto No. 2 in G min., Op. 63.

(M) *** RCA 09026 61744-2 [61744-2-RG]. Heifetz, Boston SO, Munch – GLAZUNOV; SIBELIUS: *Concertos*. ***

(B) *** EMI forte CZS5 69331-2 (2) [CDFB 69331]. David Oistrakh, Philh. O, Galliera – BEETHOVEN: *Triple concerto;* BRAHMS: *Double concerto;* MOZART: *Violin concerto No. 3*. ***

In the *arioso*-like slow movement, Heifetz chooses a faster speed than is usual, but there is nothing unresponsive about his playing, for his expressive rubato has an unfailing inevitability. In the spiky finale he is superb, and indeed his playing is glorious throughout. The recording is serviceable merely, though it has been made firmer in the current remastering. But no one is going to be prevented from enjoying this ethereal performance because the technical quality is dated.

David Oistrakh's account of Prokofiev's *G minor Concerto*, made in 1958, occupies a place of honour in the catalogue. In some respects it has never been surpassed, though Heifetz's recordings with Koussevitzky and Munch fall into a special category. Oistrakh's is a beautifully balanced reading which lays stress on the lyricism of the concerto, and the orchestral support he receives could hardly be improved upon. The 1958 recording is admirably spacious and atmospheric, with finely focused detail and great warmth. The CD transfer is immaculate. An altogether marvellous performance, and this forte compilation of four very distinguished concertante recordings is extraordinary value for money.

Lieutenant Kijé (incidental music): *suite, Op. 60.*

(B) *** Sony SBK 48162; *SBT 48162* [id.]. Cleveland O, Szell – KODALY: *Háry János suite*; MUSSORGSKY: *Pictures at an exhibition*. ***

(B) *** EMI Dig. CD-EMX 2214 [(M) id. import]. LPO, Takuo Yuasa – RIMSKY-KORSAKOV: *Scheherazade*. ***

Szell, even more than in the *Háry János* coupling, is on his highest form. Seldom on record has the *Lieutenant Kijé* music been projected with such drama and substance, and Szell is wonderfully warm in the *Romance* without a suggestion of sentimentality. The recording, like the couplings, is balanced too closely, but the orchestral playing is so stunning one hardly minds, for the opening and closing trumpet-calls are properly distanced.

There are many fine accounts of Prokofiev's *Lieutenant Kijé* currently available, but Yuasa's also ranks among the best, the performance beguiling in its affectionate geniality and sense of nostalgia, yet with the *Troika* strongly rhythmic but without heaviness. The full, warm recording helps in this impression, slightly softer in focus than in the vivid coupling.

(i) *Lieutenant Kijé* (suite); *Love for 3 Oranges:* suite; (ii) *Peter and the wolf;* (iii) *Romeo and Juliet* (ballet): excerpts; (iv) *Scythian suite, Op. 20;* (i) *Symphony No. 1 (Classical).*

(B) ** Ph. Duo 442 278-2 (2) [(M) id. import]. (i) LSO, Marriner; (ii) Alec McCowen, Concg. O, Haitink; (iii) Rotterdam PO, Edo de Waart; (iv) LAPO, Previn.

Marriner's LSO accounts of the *Lieutenant Kijé* and *Love for Three Oranges suites* and the *Classical Symphony* are all lively, well played and naturally recorded; but one only has to compare the symphony with his earlier, Decca/Argo version (currently withdrawn) to discover an extra dimension in that performance. In *Peter and the wolf* Alec McCowen uses a new text by Erik Smith which is intelligently prepared to give a fresh look at the story. However, the addition of bird imitations, including the duck quacking 'Let me out!' inside the wolf's stomach at the end, is rather twee and seems designed to appeal to the youngest of listeners. Yet taken as a whole the presentation is vivid, and undoubtedly children will enjoy its liveliness. Perhaps the finest performance comes from the Rotterdam Philharmonic, who play (and very well too) 11 well-chosen numbers from Prokofiev's great Shakespearean ballet score. The recording is full and atmospheric. But the most vivid sound of all comes in Previn's *Scythian suite*, which approaches the demonstration bracket. However, the performance does not quite match this degree of drama: for some reason Previn was not on his best form on this occasion.

The Love for 3 Oranges: suite.

(B) ** Sony SBK 53621; *SBT 53621* [id.]. Phd. O, Ormandy – SHOSTAKOVICH: *Symphony No. 5* etc. **(*)

(i) *Love for 3 Oranges* (suite); (ii) *La pas d'acier:* suite, *Op. 41 bis;* (i) *Scythian suite, Op. 20.*

(B) (**) EMI Rouge et Noir mono CZS5 69674-2 (2). (i) French Nat. R. O; (ii) Philh. O, Markevitch – STRAVINSKY: *Le baiser de la fée* etc. (***)

(i) *Love for 3 Oranges* (suite), *Op. 33a; Scythian suite, Op. 20;* (ii) *Symphony No. 5, Op. 100.*

(M) **(*) (IMS) Mercury 432 753-2 [id.]. (i) LSO; (ii) Minneapolis SO, Antal Dorati.

Dorati's account of Prokofiev's powerful and atmospheric *Scythian suite* was recorded at Watford Town

Hall in 1957; the remastering confirms the excellence of the original engineering. The suite from the *Love for Three Oranges* is similarly striking in its characterization and vivid primary colours, with the resonance not blunting the rhythms. The CD is worth considering for these two performances; but the *Fifth Symphony*, recorded in Minneapolis two years later, is less successful. Dorati's reading is similarly forceful but the effect is hard and often unsympathetic.

Superb orchestral playing of course, but Ormandy's view of the score is larger than life, spectacle seemingly more important than subtlety, which the close recording tends to emphasize. The excitement is undeniable, but the famous *March* seems rather inflated and heavy.

Sharply characterized performances from Markevitch, brilliantly played. No apologies need be made for the mono sound, which is both brilliant and atmospheric and is transferred to CD without added edge or thinness. However, it is the Stravinsky coupling which makes this reissue distinctive. The pair of CDs are now offered in EMI's French 'two for the price of one' series.

Peter and the wolf, Op. 67.

❀ (M) *** Virgin/EMI Dig. CU5 61137-2 [id.]. Gielgud, Ac. of L., Richard Stamp – SAINT-SAENS: *Carnival*. ***

(BB) *** Naxos Dig. 8.554170 [id.]. Dame Edna Everage, Melbourne SO, John Lanchbery – BRITTEN: *Young person's guide to the orchestra* ***; POULENC: *The story of Babar*. *** ❀

(BB) *** ASV CDQS 6017 [(M) id. import]. Angela Rippon, RPO, Hughes – SAINT-SAENS: *Carnival*. ***

(B) **(*) Tring Dig. TRP 046 [(M) id.]. Sir John Gielgud, RPO, Andrea Licata – BIZET: *Jeux d'enfants;* ** SAINT-SAENS: *Carnival*. **(*)

(B) ** CfP CD-CFP 185 [(M) id.]. Richard Baker, New Philh. O, Leppard – BRITTEN: *Young person's guide*. **

(BB) ** Naxos Dig. 8.550499 [id.]. Jeremy Nicholas, Slovak RSO (Bratislava), Lenárd – BRITTEN: *Young person's guide* **; SAINT-SAENS: *Carnival*. **(*)

(i) *Peter and the wolf;* (ii) *Lieutenant Kijé* (suite).

(M) **(*) Decca Phase Four 444 104-2 [id.]. (i) Sean Connery (nar.), RPO; (ii) Netherlands R. PO; Dorati – BRITTEN: *Young person's guide*. **(*)

(i; ii) *Peter and the wolf;* (iii) *Lieutenant Kijé: suite;* (iv) *Love for 3 Oranges: suite;* (ii) *Symphony No. 1 in D (Classical).*

❀ (B) *** Decca 433 612-2 [(M) id. import]. (i) Sir Ralph Richardson, (ii) LSO, Sargent; (iii) Paris Conservatoire O, Boult; (iv) LPO, Weller.

Sir John Gielgud's highly individual presentation of Prokofiev's masterly narrative with orchestra brings a worthy successor to our previous favourite version, by Sir Ralph Richardson for Decca; moreover Richard Stamp and the Academy of London have the advantage of a superb, modern, digital recording, warmly atmospheric but with a strikingly wide dynamic range. At the end, Sir John, who has presided over these events with a wonderfully benign involvement, becomes Grandfather himself with his restrained moral questioning of Peter's youthful bravado. Throughout, his obvious relish for the colour as well as the narrative flow of the text has been splendidly matched by the detail and impetus of Richard Stamp's accompaniment.

Sir Ralph Richardson brings a great actor's feeling for words to the narrative; he dwells lovingly on their sound as well as their meaning, and this genial preoccupation with the manner in which the story is told matches Sargent's feeling exactly. Sir Malcolm Sargent's direction of the accompaniment shows his professionalism at its very best. The original coupling, Sargent's amiable, polished account of the *Classical Symphony*, has now been restored. All the tempi, except the finale, are slow but Sir Malcolm's assured elegance carries its own spontaneity. The sound is vivid. Boult's Paris recording of *Lieutenant Kijé* offers more gusto than finesse, but the result is exhilaratingly robust and the very early (1955) stereo comes up remarkably well. Weller's *Love for three oranges* is a first-class performance, given top-drawer 1977 recording. But our Rosette is for *Peter and the wolf*.

If you react adversely to Dame Edna Everage's exuberantly eccentric persona, the Naxos version cannot be recommended. But for those willing to be included among her possums it is a highly entertaining and very dramatic narrative, with the orchestral accompaniment splendidly paced to match the gripping onward flow of the story. The wolf-horns positively snarl, the flute-bird chirps merrily and the cat-clarinet has a certain elegant insouciance, while the hunter's guns are like thunder. There are twee moments, but children will readily respond to Dame Edna's very positive involvement with her characters, and so will most parents. At the close she throws away the humour of Grandfather's grumble but not the childish delight on discovering that the duck is still alive after all, inside the wolf. The couplings are equally splendid.

Angela Rippon narrates with charm yet is never in the least coy; indeed she is thoroughly involved in the tale and thus also involves the listener. The accompaniment is equally spirited, with excellent orchestral playing, and the recording is splendidly clear, yet not lacking atmosphere. This makes an excellent super-bargain recommendation.

Sean Connery uses a modern script by Gabrielle Hilton which brings a certain colloquial friendliness to the narrative and invites a relaxed style, to which the actor readily responds. If you can accept such extensions as 'dumb duck' and a pussy cat who is 'smooth, but greedy and vain', you will not be disappointed with Connery's participation in the climax of the tale, where Dorati supports him admirably. Both *Peter and the wolf* and *The Young person's guide to the orchestra* start with the orchestra tuning up, to create an anticipatory atmosphere, and the introductory matter is entirely fresh and informal. In *Lieutenant Kijé* Dorati is characteristically direct, with everything boldly characterized, and he secures excellent playing from the Netherlands orchestra. As with *Peter and the wolf*, the extremely vivid Decca Phase Four recording (not unnaturally balanced but ensuring every detail is clear) gives the performance a strong projection.

Sir John Gielgud made his second recording of *Peter and the wolf* six years after the first, which is orchestrally superior. In this new version the narrative may be more mature but the manner is just as friendly and avuncular; Gielgud becomes increasingly caught up in the story as it progresses, and so do we. The moment when the wolf catches its prey is vividly exciting (and the oboe soloist here responds poignantly) and at the end of the story Gielgud's pleasure in discovering that the duck is still alive bubbles over with merriment. The Italian conductor directs competently and there is some good solo playing from the RPO, but it is the enthusiastic participation of Gielgud and his wonderfully varied vocal inflexions that make this performance so enjoyable. Voice and orchestra are recorded in different acoustics but are quite well edited together.

Richard Baker, balanced well forward in a different acoustic from the orchestra, provides an introductory paragraph which might become tedious on repetition. But he enters into the spirit of the story well enough and is only occasionally coy. Leppard gives an excellent account of the orchestra score, and the recording is vivid. But in the last resort, one's reaction to this record depends on how one takes to the narration, and there will be mixed views on that.

On Naxos, Jeremy Nicholas is recorded in a separate acoustic from the orchestra and his contribution was obviously laminated on afterwards, since the players do not always take over the narrative flow very spontaneously. The narration is gentle, mellow, even cosy, and young children will almost certainly respond to it. The orchestral sound is colourful, the drum shots especially dramatic. This is fair value, but there are far more distinctive versions available. However, with some 20 (descriptive) cues provided, young listeners can re-enter the story at any point.

Romeo and Juliet (ballet), *Op. 64* (complete).
(M) *** Decca Double 452 970-2 (2) [id.]. Cleveland O, Lorin Maazel.
(B) *** EMI forte CZS5 68607-2 (2) [CDFB 68607]. LSO, Previn.
(BB) ** Naxos Dig. 8.553184/5 [id.]. Ukraine Nat. SO, Mogrelia.

Almost simultaneously in 1973 two outstanding versions of Prokofiev's complete *Romeo and Juliet* ballet appeared, strongly contrasted to provide a clear choice on grounds of interpretation and recording. Previn and the LSO made their recording in conjunction with live performances at the Royal Festival Hall, and the result reflects the humour and warmth which went with those live occasions. Previn's pointing of rhythm is consciously seductive, whether in fast, jaunty numbers or in the soaring lyricism of the love music. The Kingsway Hall recording quality is full and immediate, yet atmospheric too.

Maazel by contrast will please those who believe that this score should above all be bitingly incisive. The rhythms are more consciously metrical, the tempi generally faster, and the precision of ensemble of the Cleveland Orchestra is little short of miraculous. The recording is one of Decca's most spectacular, searingly detailed, but atmospheric too. With the reissue of the Maazel set as a Double Decca, honours are even between both sets: if you want the finest sound and a gripping sense of drama, choose Maazel; if you prefer a more genial manner, Previn is your man.

The Ukraine orchestra on Naxos sounds in better shape than it did in the Prokofiev symphonies under Theodor Kuchar, even though in *Romeo and Juliet* it is not in the same league as the LSO for Previn or the Cleveland Orchestra for Maazel. Some years ago a superbargain release of Prokofiev's marvellous score would have been a most welcome addition to the catalogue – and highly competitive too. But with Maazel and Previn now leading the field, this is a less attractive proposition. The playing is admirable and so, too, is the sound; and there is no lack of a feeling of theatre. But the better is the enemy of the good! The other snag is that the synopsis is not related to the 52 separate cues, which are unidentified with titles.

Romeo and Juliet (ballet), *Op. 64:* extended excerpts.
(BB) **(*) Naxos Dig. 8.550380 [id.]. Slovak State PO (Košice), Andrew Mogrelia.

The Naxos selection draws on the three suites, offering 55 minutes of music, and is very vividly recorded. The Slovak orchestral playing has plenty of character and there is no lack of emotional bite, even if the strings do not have the weight of their colleagues in Minneapolis or Cleveland. Prokofiev's colours are given a strikingly individual tang by these excellent East European musicians, and this is both rewarding and excellent value for money.

Romeo and Juliet (ballet): *suites Nos. 1 & 2, Op. 64.*
(M) *** Mercury (IMS) 432 004-2 [id.]. Minneapolis SO, Skrowaczewski – MUSSORGSKY: *Night.* ***
(B) **(*) Decca Double 440 630-2 (2) [id.]. SRO, Ansermet – TCHAIKOVSKY: *Swan Lake.* **(*)
(B) *(*) [EMI Red Line Dig. CDR5 69826]. Phd. O, Muti – RESPIGHI: *The Pines of Rome.* ***

Skrowaczewski's recording of the two ballet suites was made in 1962. The playing of the Minneapolis orchestra is on a virtuoso level. The crystal-clear acoustic of the hall in Edison High School, with its backing ambience, seems ideally suited to the angular melodic lines and pungent lyricism of this powerful score, to underline the sense of tragedy without losing the music's romantic sweep. The fidelity and spectacle of the Mercury engineering reach a zenith in the powerful closing sequence of *Romeo at Juliet's tomb*. At mid-price this is highly recommendable.

Ansermet's performances have both atmosphere and passion (notably *Romeo with Juliet before his departure*). After the ominous introduction, the playing is rhythmically a bit sluggish. But *Juliet as a young girl* and the *Madrigal* are charming, and the love scene of *Romeo and Juliet* is genuinely touching; the *Death of Tybalt* bursts with energy, and *Masks* is nicely pointed. If the Suisse Romande Orchestra in 1961 was not one of the world's greatest ensembles, Ansermet was very persuasive and he brings everything vividly to life. The dramatically vibrant recording is well up to Decca's vintage standard of the early 1960s.

Muti gives us the first suite as published, then in the second he omits the *Dance* that forms the fourth number and the penultimate *Dance of the girls with lilies*. There is very impressive virtuoso playing from the Philadelphia Orchestra and a full-blooded if over-brilliant digital recording. There are some magical moments, such as the opening of the *Romeo and Juliet* movement of the first suite, but for the most part the performance is over-driven. Had Muti relaxed a little, the gain in atmosphere and charm would have been enormous. Other versions bring one closer to the heart of this wonderful score. Muti leaves us admiring but unmoved. Moreover the sharpness of detail and the 'digital' edge on the upper strings in fortissimo increase the feeling of aggressiveness.

Romeo and Juliet: suite No. 1.
(M) ** DG (IMS) Dig. 445 577-2. Nat. SO of Washington, Rostropovich – SHOSTAKOVICH: *Symphony No. 5.* **

Rostropovich gives a carefully prepared account, thoroughly attentive to details of dynamic markings and phrasing, but symphonic rather than balletic in approach. At no time does the listener feel tempted to spring into dance. Nevertheless the effect is atmospheric in a non-theatrical way, and to some ears the feeling of listening almost to an extended tone-poem is most rewarding, though to others the effect of Rostropovich's approach is ponderous at times. To be fair, some movements give no cause for complaint, and the sound, with sharply focused detail undoubtedly makes a vivid impact.

Romeo and Juliet: suites Nos. 1 & 2: excerpts.
(M) **(*) Sony SBK 48169; *SBT 48169* [id.]. NYPO, Mitropoulos – STRAVINSKY: *Rite of spring.* *

Under Mitropoulos, the New York Philharmonic played with tremendous conviction and dramatic flair. His *Romeo*, though not in every respect representative of the great conductor, should be investigated by all who admire this score. It is handicapped by its coupling, a very ordinary *Rite* under Mehta.

Romeo and Juliet (ballet): *suite.*
(M) *** Decca 417 737-2. Cleveland O, Maazel – KHACHATURIAN: *Gayaneh; Spartacus.* **(*)

An intelligently chosen selection of six pieces (including *Juliet as a young girl*, the *Balcony scene* and *The last farewell*) makes a generous coupling for Decca's Khachaturian ballet scores.

Sinfonietta in A, Op. 48.
(M) *** Virgin/EMI Dig. CUV5 61206-2 [id.]. Lausanne CO, Zedda – DEBUSSY: *Danse* etc.; MILHAUD: *Création du monde.* ***

Prokofiev could not understand why the early *Sinfonietta* failed to make an impression on the wider musical public, and neither can we. Alongside the *Classical Symphony* the *giocoso* outer movements have a more fragile geniality but they are highly delectable, as are the somewhat angular *Andante*, the brief *Intermezzo* and the witty Scherzo. The use of the orchestral palette is as subtle as it is engaging and, with Alberto Zedda's affectionately light touch and fine Lausanne playing, the piece emerges here with all colours flying. The fairly resonant sound, with the orchestra slightly recessed, adds to the feeling of warmth without blunting the orchestral articulation.

SYMPHONIES

Symphonies Nos. 1–7; Overture russe, Op. 72; Scythian suite, Op. 20.
(B) **(*) Decca 430 782-2 (4) [(M) id. import]. LSO or LPO, Walter Weller.

Weller began his 1970s Kingsway Hall recordings with the LSO (Nos. 1, 5 and 7) then turned to the LPO. The performances are polished and very well played, though at times they are emotionally a little earthbound. Transfers are well managed, though there is some loss of naturalness in the upper range. The finest of the set is No. 2. Elsewhere, the bitter tang of Prokofiev's language is again toned down and the hard-etched lines smoothed over. The *Seventh* suits Weller's approach readily and he catches the atmosphere of its somewhat balletic second movement particularly well. The *Russian overture* has plenty of energy but the *Scythian suite*, too, needs more abrasiveness. However, those who normally find Prokofiev's orchestral writing too pungent could well be won over by these performances.

Symphonies Nos. 1 in D, Op. 25 (Classical); 2 in D min., Op. 40; Autumn, Op. 8; Dreams, Op. 6.
(BB) * Naxos Dig. 8.553053 [id.]. Ukraine Nat. SO, Theodore Kuchar.

Symphonies Nos. 3 in C min., Op. 44; 7 in C sharp min., Op. 131.
(BB) (*) Naxos Dig. 8.553054 [id.]. Ukraine Nat. SO, Theodore Kuchar.

Symphony No. 5 in B flat, Op. 100; The Year 1941, Op. 90.
(BB) (*) Naxos Dig. 8.553056 [id.]. Ukraine Nat. SO, Theodore Kuchar.

Symphony No. 6 in E flat min., Op. 111; Waltz suite, Op. 110.
(BB) * Naxos Dig. 8.553069 [id.]. Ukraine Nat. SO, Theodore Kuchar.

The Naxos cycle has had an indifferent press but, at its competitive price, it perhaps deserves better than to be dismissed out of hand. Even so, it is not so much of a bargain as all that! The *Fourth Symphony* has not yet appeared, and when it does the set will run to five CDs – or even six if Naxos decide to issue the original (1930) version and the post-war revision separately. The first disc brings two early rarities, *Autumn* and *Dreams*, as well as the *First* and *Second Symphonies*. It soon becomes evident that the Ukraine National Orchestra is not in the first rank. Interpretatively things are less impressive: the *Classical Symphony* is heavy-handed and ponderous in Kuchar's hands. Each movement (with the exception of the finale) is too slow. The latter has some sparkle, but the rest is hard work. In the first movement of the *Second Symphony* the strings, which are not the weightiest, are rather swamped by the brass, and the imaginative set of variations which comprise the second movement are distinctly lacklustre in this performance.

The *Third*, related as it is to the opera, *The Fiery Angel*, is undoubtedly one of Prokofiev's most extraordinary creations, and the *Seventh* with its touch of bitter-sweetness is consistently underrated. To anyone traversing the complete cycle, the weaknesses of the orchestra will now become all too apparent, and the playing has far too little punch and the conducting too little imagination. Neither score deserves such routine phrasing. The *Fifth* is so generously represented on CD, even at mid-price, that any newcomer has to be very good indeed to pose an effective challenge. This cannot even be classified as *vin ordinaire*; it is very ordinary indeed, and not even the presence of a rarity, *The Year 1941*, lifts this to a really recommendable category. The *Sixth Symphony* fares better, not so much in matters of orchestral finesse as in interpretative intention. However, intentions and deeds are two different things and, even though the playing has more character and conviction than the *Fifth*, it never rises to anything like distinction. Nor does the recording.

(i) *Symphony No. 1 in D (Classical);* (ii) *Romeo and Juliet* (ballet): highlights.
(B) *** DG Classikon Dig. 439 492-2 [(M) id. import]. (i) Orpheus CO; (ii) Boston SO, Ozawa.

An outstanding coupling in every way. The Orpheus performance of the *Classical Symphony* has freshness and wit – the droll bassoon solo in the first movement against sparkling string-figurations is delightful. In the cantilena of the *Larghetto* some ears might crave a greater body of string-tone, but the playing has fine poise, and the minuet and finale have equal flair. Moreover, *Romeo and Juliet* was one of Ozawa's finest recordings. The playing has elegance and an attractive rhythmic lightness and point. There is no lack of drama or feeling, but it is the stylishness and beauty of the playing one remembers, together with the conductor's obvious affection for the score. The sound throughout is of DG's best, warm yet transparent and with a most attractive ambience.

Symphonies Nos. 1 in D (Classical), Op. 25; 5 in B flat, Op. 100.
(M) *** DG 437 253-2 [id.]. BPO, Karajan.
(M) *** Ph. (IMS) Dig. 442 399-2. LAPO, André Previn.
(M) *** [RCA Dig. 09026 61350-2]. LPO or St Louis SO, Slatkin.
(M) **(*) Sony SBK 53260; *SBT 53260* [id.]. Phd. O, Ormandy.
(BB) **(*) Naxos Dig. 8.550237 [id.]. Slovak PO, Stephen Gunzenhauser.
(M) ** BMG/Melodiya Dig. 74321 32042-2 [id.]. Moscow Philh. O, Dmitri Kitaienko.

Symphonies Nos. 1 in D (Classical), Op. 25; 5 in B flat, Op. 100; Russian overture, Op. 72.
(BB) ** Belart 461 320-2 [(M) id. import]. LSO or LPO, Walter Weller.

Karajan's 1979 recording of the *Fifth* is in a class of its own. The playing has wonderful tonal sophistication and Karajan judges tempi to perfection so that proportions seem quite ideal. The recording has an excellent perspective and allows all the subtleties of orchestral detail to register; however, the digital remastering has overtly brightened the upper range, while the bass response is drier. Nevertheless this remains among the most distinguished *Fifths* ever recorded, and it is coupled with Karajan's 1982 digital recording of the *Classical Symphony*, in which his performance is predictably brilliant and the playing beautifully polished, with grace and eloquence distinguishing the slow movement.

In the first movement of the *Fifth*, Previn's pacing seems exactly right: everything flows so naturally and speaks effectively. The Scherzo is not as high-voltage as some rivals, but Previn still brings it off well; and in the slow movement he gets playing of genuine eloquence from the Los Angeles orchestra. He also gives an excellent account of the perennially fresh *Classical Symphony*. The recording is beautifully natural, with impressive detail, range and body. Although Karajan reigns supreme in this coupling, his analogue recording does not match this Philips competitor, and those wanting modern, digital sound will find Previn an ideal mid-priced alternative.

Ultimately the same holds for Slatkin's St Louis performance on RCA at mid-price. It is eminently well shaped, spacious and characterful, and there is no want of virtuosity or lyricism. Thoroughly recommendable, without being a first choice.

The Philadelphia Orchestra play superbly and with much wit in the *Classical Symphony*. Ormandy's expansive warmth in the *Adagio* and the easy brilliance of the orchestral articulation in the second and fourth movements make for splendid results in the *Fifth*. Although the early stereo recording could be more opulent and less brightly lit, it still conveys impressively the ample body of tone this great orchestra was creating in the late 1950s.

The Naxos recording coupling the most popular of the Prokofiev symphonies, Nos. 1 and 5, on the face of it is very good value indeed. The recording is altogether first class: there is splendid detail and definition, and the balance is extremely well judged. Moreover the American conductor, Stephen Gunzenhauser, gets very good playing from the excellent Slovak Philharmonic and the performances have the merit of being straightforward and unaffected. Gunzenhauser is not a high-voltage conductor, and artistically neither symphony is as well served as it is by Karajan's mid-1960s recording, currently out of circulation but due back before long. All the same, tempi are generally well judged in No. 5. The first movement of the *'Classical' Symphony* is a bit sedate and wanting in sparkle; the finale comes off best.

Weller's performance of the *Classical Symphony* is excellent, perhaps lacking the last degree of imagination, but with first-class playing from the LSO. The *Fifth Symphony* also has undoubted merits, and again the LSO are in top form; but Weller's reading is let down by a slow movement which lacks real bite and forward impetus (it is much slower than the metronome marking). Weller also makes too much of the *l'istesso tempo* in the Scherzo. The *Russian overture* (played by the LPO) has plenty of vitality. What makes this disc worth considering for super-bargain hunters is the Decca recording, which is strikingly vivid and well balanced too.

Given the current competition, Dmitri Kitaienko's accounts of the *First* and *Fifth Symphonies* with the Moscow Philharmonic are little more than also-rans. With Karajan, Previn, Ormandy and Koussevitzky in the catalogue, all at modest prices, these performances are unlikely to prompt the pulse to beat faster.

Symphonies Nos. 1 in D (Classical), Op. 25; 5 in B flat, Op. 100; Romeo and Juliet: excerpts; Chout: final dance.
✿ (M) (***) RCA mono 09026 61657-2 [id.]. Boston SO, Koussevitzky.

Koussevitzky's *Fifth Symphony* and the four movements from *Romeo and Juliet* are quite simply breathtaking and have never been equalled, except perhaps by Karajan's 1969 record with the Berlin Philharmonic. Yet this has even more fire, zest and virtuosity, and the recordings, made in 1945–6, are remarkably good.

The *Classical Symphony* is not to be confused with Koussevitzky's sparkling account on 78-r.p.m. records. Both the *Classical Symphony* and the *Danse finale* from *Chout* come from 1947 and were recorded when the orchestra were on a visit to Carnegie Hall, New York. Likewise these are thrilling performances on which it would be very difficult to improve and, again, few allowances have to be made for the sound-quality. An outstanding issue in every way.

Symphonies Nos. 1 in D (Classical), Op. 25; 7 in C sharp min., Op. 131.
(M) *(*) Koch/Consonance 81-5006 [id.]. Moscow RSO, Rozhdestvensky.

Symphonies Nos. 1 (Classical); 7; Love for 3 Oranges (opera): *suite.*
(B) *** CfP CD-CFP 4523 [id.]. Philh. O, Malko.

All the performances CfP are quite excellent, and the *Seventh Symphony*, of which Malko conducted the UK première, is freshly conceived and finely shaped. What is so striking is the range and refinement of the 1955 stereo recording: the excellence of the balance and the body of the sound are remarkable.

These performances from Rozhdestvensky appeared on the HMV/Melodiya label in the early 1970s and they did admirable service at the time, even if the Moscow Radio Orchestra was not the last word in finesse. Their reappearance, while welcome, finds them in a far more competitive climate and, although they are good, they would no longer be the first recommendation they once were. It is possible to imagine better transfers; an A/B sample of the *Seventh Symphony* against the HMV LP is not to the advantage of the newcomer.

Symphonies Nos. 2 in D min., Op. 40; 3 in C min., Op. 44.
(M) * Koch/Consonance 81-5007 [id.]. Moscow RSO, Rozhdestvensky.

The sound here does not wear its years well, though the performance – particularly in the second movement of No. 2 – is very immediate and convincing. No. 3 sounds earlier than the 1971 LP and is much rougher and more constricted. Sonically, it is only marginally better than the Revelation disc listed below. The *Second Symphony* is probably worth considering at mid-price, but the *Third* rates only half a star!

Symphony No. 3 in C min., Op. 44.
(M) *** Decca 448 579-2. LSO, Abbado – HINDEMITH: *Symphonic metamorphoses on themes of Weber.* JANACEK: *Sinfonietta.* ***
(M) * Revelation RV 10025 [id.]. USSR State SO, Gennady Rozhdestvensky – SHOSTAKOVICH: *Symphony No. 5.* *

In the *Third Symphony* Abbado penetrates the atmosphere and mystery of the highly imaginative inner movements most successfully. These movements exert quite a powerful spell, and their impact is all the greater for Abbado's total lack of exaggeration. The outer movements are slightly less successful, needing a shade more bite and momentum. But the Decca recording has fine body and presence, and if the couplings are suitable this is still very recommendable.

Rozhdestvensky's account of the *Third Symphony* comes from 1961 and is in its way quite electrifying. It is full of character and has a hell-for-leather quality which is communicative. The *Third Symphony* was a great rarity at this time and was probably new to the players too. The grim sound-quality is such as to rule it out as more than a one-star recommendation. But readers should try to hear it for themselves as it has tremendous fire, and this may for some collectors outweigh the abysmal sound.

(i) *Symphony No. 5;* (ii) *Lieutenant Kijé* (suite).
(M) **(*) Sony SMK 66933 [id.]. (i) Israel PO, Bernstein. (ii) Nat. O of France, Maazel.
(B) **(*) EMI Eminence (SIS) Dig. CD-EMX 2273 [(M) id. import]. RPO, Vernon Handley.

It would be easy to underestimate Bernstein's version of the *Fifth Symphony*. Edited from live performances, it is a consistently powerful reading, but with the romantic expressiveness underlined. Bernstein is superb at building climaxes, and the playing has great concentration, but for some ears there is too much emotional weight. The recording is bold and full (made in 1979) with a strong, firm bass line.

Maazel, too, gives an exceptionally dramatic and strongly characterized account of Prokofiev's colourful suite, recorded two years later. Though he does not miss the nostalgia of *Lieutenant Kijé*, it is the pungency of the rhythms and the sharp pointing of detail that register most strongly, helped by the resonant acoustic, which adds an effective degree of edge to Prokofiev's bolder scoring. Inner detail registers vividly at all dynamic levels; while Maazel is clearly seeking a strong projection rather than refinement, the committed orchestral response is exhilarating.

Having the full five-movement *Lieutenant Kijé suite* as well as the *Fifth Symphony* makes a stimulating coupling on Vernon Handley's EMI disc with the RPO. The amiability of the *Kijé* performance, colourful in its illustration of the different situations, spreads over into the *Symphony*. This is a more easy-going reading than most, beautifully played but putting an emphasis on expressiveness rather than on dramatic bite. The Scherzo is jolly in an easily jazzy way rather than sharp; and, for all its seductive beauty, the slow movement is rather too soft-grained for Prokofiev, partly a question of the recording acoustic in St Augustine's Church, Kilburn. In the relaxed account of the finale, the marking *giocoso* is characteristically what Handley emphasizes. An agreeable version for those who fancy the coupling, even if this account of the *Symphony* misses some of its darker side.

CHAMBER AND INSTRUMENTAL MUSIC

Cello sonata in C, Op. 119.

(BB) *** ASV Quicksilva Dig. CDQS 6218 [(M) id. import]. Bernard Gregor-Smith, Yolande Wrigley – MARTINU: *Variations;* JANACEK: *Pohádka;* SHOSTAKOVICH: *Cello sonata.* ***

(BB) **(*) Arte Nova Dig. 74321 27805-2 [id.]. Emil Klein, Cristian Beldi – SHOSTAKOVICH: *Cello sonata.* **(*)

(BB) ** Carlton Dig. 30367 02362 [(M) id.]. Ulrich Boeckheler, Susan Starr – PART: *Fratres*; SHOSTAKOVICH: *Cello sonata.* **

(BB) * Koch Discover Dig. DICD 920407 [id.]. Laetitia Himo, Nadia Himo – FALLA: *Suite populaire espagnole;* MIASKOVSKY: *Cello sonata.* *

Once shunned by the gramophone, the *Cello Sonata* now enjoys abundant representation on CD. There are over 20 current listings. Both these ASV and Arte Nova performances are very serviceable and are unlikely to disappoint. Bernard Gregor-Smith and Yolande Wrigley have the benefit of the better recording: there is greater bloom and a more lively acoustic, though the piano is sometimes more dominant in the aural picture than is ideal. They are more relaxed and thoughtful in approach than the Romanian partnership.

However, Emil Klein and Cristian Beldi give a very well-characterized account of the *Sonata*, tautly held together and vital in feeling, though the sound is a bit drier than the ASV listed above. The balance between cello and piano is better-judged, even if the timbre of the latter is less realistic. Artistically there is not a great deal to choose between these performances, though, if choose one must, the ASV would be the one to have on account of the fresher sound and the additional Martinů and Janáček items.

Ulrich Boeckheler and Susan Starr on Carlton are given excellent recording quality and are accorded a most musically balanced sound. Boeckheler was a pupil of Navarra, and his partner teaches at the Curtis Institute. Their Prokofiev is broad and lyrical, imaginative and well held together, with the wit of the middle movement well projected.

Readers should approach the Discover issue with some caution. Laetitia Himo and Nadia Himo are a highly accomplished French partnership, but they are recorded in a resonant, rather mushy acoustic, which diminishes pleasure.

Flute sonata in D, Op. 94.

(M) *** RCA 09026 61615-2 [id.]. James Galway, Martha Argerich – FRANCK; REINECKE: *Sonatas.* ***

Prokofiev's *Flute sonata* (1943) is one of his sunniest and most serene wartime compositions. It is difficult to imagine a more delightful performance than this one, with its combination of effortless virtuosity and spontaneity of feeling; every detail falls naturally into place. The recording is most sympathetic.

Overture on Hebrew themes (for clarinet, piano & string quartet), *Op. 34; Quintet* (for oboe, clarinet, violin, viola & cello), *Op. 39.*

(B) *** HM Musique d'Abord Dig. HMA 1901419 [id.]. Walter Boeykens Ens. (with KOKAI: *Clarinet quartettino* ***) – KHACHATURIAN: *Clarinet trio.* ***

Prokofiev composed his *Overture on Jewish themes* in 1919 at the request of a Jewish commission from a small ensemble of musical refugees in New York (hence the instrumentation). He warmed to a pair of melodies taken from a collection provided by the commission, and the result is a delightful work, at first nostalgic, then energetic and jocular. The *Quintet* was written to accompany a ballet commissioned by a Russian dancer whom the composer had met while working with Diaghilev. It has a wide range of moods: gentle, sardonic, burlesque; while highly characteristic of its composer, it also brings clear rhythmic influences from Stravinsky. Both works are performed here with vigour, affection and wit; indeed they are beautifully played and recorded. The *Quartetettino* (for clarinet and string trio) by Rezsö Kókai (1906–62) provided as a bonus is deliciously flimsy in texture (suggesting Françaix with Hungarian inflexions) but with a touching folk-tune-like *Canzonetta* for its slow movement.

(i) *String quartets Nos. 1 in B min., Op. 50; 2 in F, Op. 92;* (ii) *Cello sonata, Op. 119.*

(BB) *** Naxos Dig. 8.553136 [id.]. (i) Aurora Qt; (ii) Grebanier, Guggenheim.

The Prokofiev *Quartets* are better served nowadays than used to be the case, if not at the bargain end of the CD catalogue. These Naxos performances are therefore welcome, particularly as the coupling is generous and the performances more than adequate. The members of the Aurora Quartet all come from the San Francisco Symphony and give thoroughly straightforward, unaffected accounts of both *Quartets*. They are recorded in a warm, resonant acoustic. (Indeed, criticism we have seen from a respected source that its resonance is excessive strikes us as quite unfounded.) The performance of the *Second Quartet* may not have the character of the pioneering Hollywood set (reissued on Testament; see our 1996 main edition) but then what other account has! The *Cello sonata* makes a substantial bonus. Michael Grebanier is a principal cellist of the San Francisco Symphony and Janet Goodman Guggenheim is a pupil of Rosina Lhevinne, who teaches at the University of California at Berkeley. Theirs is a thoroughly musical account, not perhaps as strongly characterized as some, but eminently satisfying, and well recorded. A more than acceptable makeweight to the two *Quartets*, and this CD is well worth the money.

Violin sonatas Nos. 1 in F min., Op. 80; 2 in D, Op. 94a.
(M) *** DG (IMS) Dig. 445 557-2. Shlomo Mintz, Yefim Bronfman – RAVEL: *Violin sonata in G.* ***

(i) *Violin sonatas Nos. 1–2;* (ii) *Violin concerto No. 2 in G min., Op. 63.*
(M) *** RCA 09026 61454-2 [id.]. Itzhak Perlman; (i) Vladimir Ashkenazy; (ii) Boston SO, Leinsdorf.

Both the *Violin sonatas* date from the years immediately after Prokofiev returned to the Soviet Union. The *F minor Sonata* is one of his very finest works, and the *D major*, originally written for the flute and sometimes heard in that form, has a winning charm and melodiousness. Both works are masterly and rewarding. Shlomo Mintz made a great impression with his coupling of the two *Concertos*, and his recording of the *Sonatas* is hardly less successful. Mintz has a wonderful purity of line and immaculate intonation, and his partner, Yefim Bronfman, is both vital and sensitive. These are commanding performances, imaginative in phrasing and refined in approach. The DG recording is excellent. This is a clear first choice.

Perlman and Ashkenazy also play both works superbly, and the 1969 recording is well balanced, slightly dry in timbre but otherwise truthful. Their coupling is the *Second Violin concerto*, recorded three years earlier. It is an enjoyably fresh and spontaneous account and, even if Leinsdorf provides an accomplished rather than a highly individual accompaniment, the finale comes off particularly vividly. Good recording, with the soloist balanced well forward.

PIANO MUSIC

Piano sonata Nos. 2 in D min., Op. 14; 7 in B flat, Op. 83; 8 in B flat, Op. 84.
(BB) ** Naxos Dig. 8.553021 [id.]. Bernd Glemser.

Bernd Glemser is a highly accomplished and far from unimaginative artist who copes well with the formidable demands made by Prokofiev's piano writing. Taken in isolation, all three performances make a good impression, and the sound, too, is perfectly decent. But it is no use pretending that, on artistic merits, this artist can challenge Pollini, Horowitz and Richter (all at mid-price) in the *Seventh Sonata* or Gilels and Richter in the *Eighth*.

Piano sonata No. 7 in B flat, Op. 83.
(M) *** DG 447 431-2 [id.]. Maurizio Pollini – *Recital.* ***

This is a great performance by Pollini, well in the Horowitz or Richter category. It is part of a generous CD of twentieth-century music, now reissued in the 'Originals' series.

Piano sonata No. 7; Toccata in C, Op. 11.
(M) (***) RCA mono GD 60377 [60377-2-RG]. Vladimir Horowitz – BARBER; KABALEVSKY: *Sonatas* etc. (***)

Horowitz's account of the *Seventh Sonata* is justly legendary. When he had recorded it in 1945 he sent a copy of the disc to the composer, who returned an autographed score to express his admiration. The better-known *Toccata* is hardly less electrifying, and the somewhat confined mono sound is never distracting with playing of this degree of magnetism.

VOCAL MUSIC

Alexander Nevsky (cantata), Op. 78.
(M) *** EMI CDM7 63114-2. Anna Reynolds, London Symphony Ch., LSO, Previn – RACHMANINOV: *The Bells.* ***

(M) ** Decca Dig. 430 738-2. Arkhipova, Cleveland Ch. & O, Chailly – TCHAIKOVSKY: *Francesca da Rimini.* *(*)

(i) *Alexander Nevsky, Op. 78. Lieutenant Kijé (suite), Op. 60.*
(M) *** RCA GD 60176 [60176-2-RG]. (i) Rosalind Elias, Chicago SO Ch.; Chicago SO, Reiner – GLINKA: *Ruslan Overture.* ***

(i) *Alexander Nevsky, Op. 78;* (ii) *Lieutenant Kijé, Op. 60; Scythian suite, Op. 20.*
(M) *** DG 447 419-2 [id.]. (i) Elena Obraztsova; London Symphony Ch., LSO; (ii) Chicago SO; Claudio Abbado.

Abbado's performance of *Alexander Nevsky* culminates in a deeply moving account of the tragic lament after the battle (here very beautifully sung by Obraztsova), made the more telling when the battle itself is so fine an example of orchestral virtuosity. The chorus is as incisive as the orchestra. The digital remastering of the 1980 recording has been all gain, and the sound is very impressive indeed. A fine account of *Lieutenant Kijé* and what is probably the best version of the *Scythian suite* to appear in many years make this a desirable reissue in DG's Legendary Recordings series. Abbado gets both warm and wonderfully clean playing from the Chicago orchestra and he is accorded excellent engineering. The *Scythian suite* has drive and fire: in the finale – and even in the second movement – Abbado could bring greater savagery and brilliance than he does but, given the power that the Chicago orchestra do bring to this score and the refined colouring that Abbado achieves in the atmospheric *Night* movement, there need be no real reservation in recommending this strongly.

All the weight, bite and colour of the score are captured by Previn, and though the timbre of the singers' voices may not suggest Russians, they cope very confidently with the Russian text; Previn's direct and dynamic manner ensures that the great *Battle on the ice* scene is powerfully effective. Anna Reynolds sings the lovely *Lament for the dead* most affectingly. The sound is sharply defined, with plenty of bite; just a little of the old analogue ambient fullness has gone.

Reiner's version, recorded in 1959, was another of the astonishingly vivid early achievements of the RCA stereo catalogue. The performance is gripping from the first bar to the last, with choral singing of great fervour and a movingly eloquent contribution from Rosalind Elias in the great *Lament*. The *Lieutenant Kijé suite*, recorded two years earlier, is another colourful example of the Chicago orchestra at their peak, the sound again full and atmospheric.

Chailly has the advantage of full-blooded Decca digital sound, and its richness adds to the emotional weight of the opening sections. The *Battle on the ice* is characteristically impulsive and, with Irina Arkhipova touchingly expressive in her elegiac aria, Chailly finds an effective exuberance in the work's closing pages. The recording is not always ideally clear on detail, although it is not short on spectacle, and the chorus projects well; but this is not strongly competitive, for the Tchaikovsky coupling is disappointing.

Ivan the Terrible, Op. 116 (film music, arr. in oratorio form by Stasevich).
(M) *** EMI CDM7 69584-2. Arkhipova, Mokrenko, Morgunov (narrator), Ambrosian Ch., Philh. O, Muti.

This oratorio was put together long after Prokofiev's death by the scholar Abram Stasevich, and the result is diffuse; the device of adding a spoken narration (in Russian) could well prove irritating on repetition. Nevertheless, with fine playing and choral singing, there are many imaginative ideas here to relish, not least those using broad, folk-like melodies. The Kingsway Hall recording is admirably spacious, and though the histrionic style of the narrator, Boris Morgunov, is unappealing, the two other soloists are excellent in their limited roles. The remastering has been highly successful and the effect is often thrillingly vivid, with the chorus especially telling.

OPERA

War and Peace (complete).
(M) ** BMG/Melodiya 74321 29350-2 (3) [id.]. Kibkalo, Vishnevskaya, Petrov, Arkhipova, Maslennikov, Krivchenya, Bolshoi Theatre, Moscow, Ch. & O, Melik-Pashayev.

The Melodiya issue, recorded in 1961, is based directly on the Bolshoi production of two years earlier, using the theatre's star singers of the period. The CD transfer is full and immediate, with sound of satisfying weight, yet the voices are so far forward that any subtlety in the singing is minimized. Too often the style of the time seems to have been to sing as loud as possible, so that both Yevgeny Kibkalo as Andrei and Vladimir Petrov as Pierre fail to bring out the tender elements in those key characters. Yet it is good to have Galina Vishnevskaya in her prime singing the role of Natasha, far fresher and firmer than she is in the much later Rostropovich Erato recording, made in Paris, which is currently withdrawn. Irina Arkhipova is also excellent as Helene. Alexei Krivchenya sings nobly as General Kutuzov, though again the recording renders the singing crude to a degree, with too little air round any of the voices. The most serious flaw is that, unlike later recordings, this première version makes damaging cuts in the score. At mid-price, with Melik-Pashayev bringing out the epic power as well as the lyrical warmth of Prokofiev's writing, it is well worth hearing, although it can be regarded only as a stop-gap until the Rostropovich set reappears, which will surely be in the lifetime of this book.

Puccini, Giacomo (1858–1924)

Capriccio sinfonico; Crisantemi; Minuets Nos. 1–3; Preludio sinfonico; Edgar: Preludes, Acts I & III. Manon Lescaut: Intermezzo, Act III. Le Villi: Prelude; La Tregenda (Act II).
(M) *** Decca Dig. 444 154-2. Berlin RSO, Ricardo Chailly.

In a highly attractive collection of Puccinian juvenilia and rarities, Chailly draws opulent and atmospheric playing from the Berlin Radio Symphony Orchestra, helped by outstandingly rich and full recording. The CD is of demonstration quality. The *Capriccio sinfonico* of 1876 brings the first characteristically Puccinian idea in what later became the opening Bohemian motif of *La Bohème*. There are other identifiable fingerprints here, even if the big melodies suggest Mascagni rather than full-blown Puccini. *Crisantemi* (with the original string quartet scoring expanded for full string orchestra) provided material for *Manon Lescaut*, as did the three little *Minuets*, pastiche eighteenth-century music.

Messa di gloria.
(M) *** Erato/Warner Dig. 4509 96367-2 [id.]. Carreras, Prey, Amb. S., Philh. O, Scimone.
(M) *** Ph. 434 170-2. Lövaas, Hollweg, McDaniel, West German R. Ch., Frankfurt RSO, Inbal (with MOZART: *Vesperae solennes, K.339: Laudate Dominum:* Te Kanawa, LSO, C. Davis ***).

(i) *Messa di gloria;* (ii) *Capriccio sinfonico; Preludio sinfonico*.
(B) **(*) Erato/Warner 0630 12818-2 [(M) id. import]. (i) Johns, Huttenlocher, Ch. & O of Gulbenkian Foundation, Lisbon, Corboz; (ii) Monte-Carlo Op. O, Scimone.

Puccini's *Messa di Gloria*, completed when he was twenty, rebuts any idea that this composer was a late developer. Very much under the influence of Verdi (hearing *Aida* was a profound formative experience), Puccini still showed his positive character as a composer, writing bold melodies with just a hint here and there of individual fingerprints and using the orchestra with astonishing maturity. The various parts were written at different times and even for different purposes; but with the exception of an over-sweet setting of *Agnus Dei* (later used in *Manon Lescaut*) the work stands well together. Best of all is the ambitious and strong setting of the *Gloria*, the longest section and the earliest written. It has a cheeky recurring march theme which may be doubtfully apt for church but which is richly enjoyable. The section ends with a formidable fugue, echoing Beethoven's *Missa solemnis*, no less.

The return of Scimone's second (1983) digital recording of the Puccini *Messa di gloria* at mid-price makes this version much more competitive, even though it has no fill-up. He and a fine team are brisker and lighter than their predecessors on record, yet effectively bring out the red-bloodedness of the writing. José Carreras turns the big solo in the *Gratias* into the first genuine Puccini aria. His sweetness and imagination are not quite matched by the baritone, Hermann Prey, who is given less to do than usual, when the choral baritones take on the yearning melody of *Crucifixus*. Excellent, atmospheric sound.

This 1975 Philips version, available as a limited edition, is excellent value at mid-price. It has stylish soloists, a fine choral contribution and clean, well-balanced recording. Kiri Te Kanawa's ravishing account of the *Laudate Dominum* from Mozart's *Solemn Vespers* is thrown in as an enticing encore.

The Lisbon performance from Corboz is more affectionate than Scimone's mid-priced digital version, also on Erato, but that has a stronger profile and remains a preferable choice. Nevertheless there is splendid choral singing in Lisbon, and the reverberant recording has been made to sound firmer and cleaner on CD, while the sound is impressively full. The present reissue has a price advantage, and the coupling includes two fascinating early orchestral works, with the *Capriccio sinfonico* suddenly producing out of a hat the famous theme that was to become the Bohemian motif of *La Bohème*. The playing of the Monte Carlo orchestra is committed, if not very polished.

OPERA

La Bohème (complete).
(B) *** Decca Double 448 725-2 (2) [(M) 425 534-2]. Tebaldi, Bergonzi, Bastianini, Siepi, Corena, D'Angelo, St Cecilia Ac. Ch. & O, Serafin.
(B) (***) Decca Double mono 440 233-2 (2) [id.]. Tebaldi, Prandelli, Gueden, Inghilleri, Corena, Arié, Luise, Santa Cecilia Ac., Rome, Ch. & O, Erede.

(M) **(*) RCA 74321 39496-2 (2) [RCD2-0371 full price]. Caballé, Domingo, Milnes, Raimondi, Alldis Ch., Wandsworth School Boys' Ch., LPO, Solti.
(M) **(*) EMI CMS7 69657-2 (2) [Ang. CDMB 69657]. Freni, Gedda, Adani, Sereni, Mazzoli, La Scala, Milan, Ch. & O, Schippers.
(B) ** Naxos Dig. 8.660003/4 [id.]. Orgonasova, Welch, Gonzales, Previati, Senator, Slovak Philharmonic Ch., Slovak RSO (Bratislava), Will Humburg.
(B) ** DG Double Dig. 453 109-2 [(M) id. import]. Angelina Réaux, Jerry Hadley, Barbara Daniels, Thomas Hampson, James Busterud, Paul Plishka, St Cecilia Ac., Rome, Ch. & O, Bernstein.
(B) ** Ph. Duo 442 260-2 (2) [id.]. Ricciarelli, Carreras, Putnam, Wixell, Lloyd, ROHCG Ch. & O, Sir Colin Davis.
(M) (**) Nimbus mono NI 7862/3 [id.]. Albanese, Gigli, Oili, Menotti, Baracchi, Baronti, La Scala, Milan, Ch. & O, Berrettoni.
(M) (**) Sony mono MH2K 62762 (2) [id.]. Sayão, Tucker, Valentino, Benzell, Moscona, Met. Ch. & 0, Antonicelli.

Tebaldi's second Decca set with Bergonzi dominated the catalogue in the early days of stereo; technically it was an outstanding recording in its day, and it still sounds astonishingly vivid, with a very convincing theatrical atmosphere. At Double Decca price, it is one of the great operatic bargains in the current catalogue. Vocally the performance achieves a consistently high standard, with Tebaldi as Mimì the most affecting. Carlo Bergonzi is a fine Rodolfo; Bastianini and Siepi are both superb as Marcello and Colline, and even the small parts of Benoit and Alcindoro (as usual taken by a single artist) have the benefit of Corena's magnificent voice. The veteran Serafin was more vital here than on some of his records. The recording, not far off 40 years old, has its vividness and sense of stage perspective enhanced on CD. The set comes with a perfectly adequate cued synopsis, for *La Bohème* is an exceptionally easy opera to follow.

The very early Decca set was one of the very first complete operas to appear on LP. Recorded in 1951, it immediately won glowing praise, above all for Tebaldi's radiant and rich-voiced portrayal of Mimì. The effect is still extraordinarily atmospheric in its sense of stage perspective, with sound effects mostly adding to the realism and not overdone. Like the companion early Decca *Die Fledermaus*, the one drawback was the whistly sound of the violins (something to do with the microphones in use at Decca at that time). The CD transfer has improved the violin focus, but the effect is still emaciated above the stave. Yet one soon adjusts to this, for the acoustic is basically warm and evocative. It is still a lovely performance, and there are no appreciable weaknesses in the cast: Gueden (if not always completely Italianate in style) an exceptionally characterful Musetta (a part that fitted her like a glove), Pradelli a most likeable Rodolfo, engagingly light-voiced yet stirring at climaxes, Inghilleri rather old-sounding but still interesting as Marcello. Erede keeps the music flowing: he is not a great conductor but he controls the great love duet of Act I spaciously. The atmospheric opening of Act III at the Paris toll-gate is remarkably evocative, with the kind of production values that were to lead on to the vintage Decca opera recordings of the stereo era already apparent. Indeed, at times here one could almost think stereo had already arrived.

The glory of Solti's set of *Bohème* is the singing of Montserrat Caballé as Mimì, an intensely characterful and imaginative reading which makes you listen with new intensity to every phrase, the voice at its most radiant. Domingo is unfortunately not at his most inspired. *Che gelida manina* is relatively coarse, though here as elsewhere he produces glorious heroic tone, and he never falls into vulgarity. The rest of the team is strong, but Solti's tense interpretation of a work he had never conducted in the opera house does not quite let either the full flexibility of the music or the full warmth of romanticism have their place. The recording, however, is both vivid and atmospheric, and this recording is welcome back to the catalogue, pleasingly packaged in RCA's mid-priced Opera Treasury series. At the moment it remains at full price in the USA.

The engineers placed Freni rather close to the microphone, which makes it hard for her to sound tentative in her first scene, but the beauty of the voice is what one remembers, and from there to the end her performance is conceived as a whole, leading to a supremely moving account of the Death scene. Nicolai Gedda's Rodolfo is not rounded in the traditional Italian way, but there is never any doubt about his ability to project a really grand manner of his own. Thomas Schippers' conducting starts as though this is going to be a hard-driven, unrelenting performance, but after the horseplay he quickly shows his genuinely Italianate sense of pause, giving the singers plenty of time to breathe and allowing the music to expand. The resonant, 1964 recording has transferred vividly to CD and the set has been attractively re-packaged with an excellently printed libretto.

Well played and atmospherically recorded, the Naxos version of *La Bohème* offers an outstanding performance by Luba Orgonosova as Mimi. The creamy quality of the voice, coupled with her warm expressiveness and her vocal poise, brings out the tenderness of the character to the full; and it is a pity that none of the others matches her. Jonathan Welch as Rodolfo and Fabio Previati as Marcello are both strained and unsteady at times, while Carmen Gonzales tries too hard as Musetta. Yet with Will Humburg pacing the opera effectively, and with the well-disciplined Slovak Philharmonic Chorus adding to the atmospheric beauty, this is a fair bargain.

Bernstein's is a very distinctive but flawed version of *La Bohème*. He decided to work with a team of young singers, mainly American, of whom two, Jerry Hadley and Thomas Hampson, were later to become stars. Live performances in Rome were edited together, following the recording pattern Bernstein preferred latterly, and that seems to have encouraged him to draw out Puccini's sparkling score as expansively as possible, with rallentandos so extreme they tax even the longest-breathed of his young soloists. Bernstein's characteristic rhythmic flair keeps the music from stagnating, but it means that many expressive points are underlined too heavily, and flow is impaired. Unfortunately, the Mimi of Angelina Réaux and the Musetta of Barbara Daniels are less impressive than they might be, when the microphone exaggerates the pronounced vibrato in their voices. Réaux at least does sound Italianate. Jerry Hadley (not surprisingly) sings freshly, only occasionally straining, but is quite un-Italian-sounding, and James Busterud makes a disagreeably gritty Schaunard. It is Thomas Hampson as Colline who shines out from the team in the one performance of real quality; but it is the conductor's personality above all which dominates everything. Set in an ample acoustic, the recording of voices and orchestra has an agreeable bloom and spaciousness, with generally good balance. The synopsis is exceptionally well documented, and this is a DG Double which will surely have great interest for American collectors, even if it cannot be a general recommendation.

As in *Tosca*, Sir Colin Davis here takes a direct view of Puccini, presenting the score very straight, with no exaggerations. The result is refreshing but rather lacking in wit and sparkle; pauses and hesitations are curtailed. Ricciarelli's is the finest performance vocally. Carreras gives a good generalized performance, wanting in detail and in intensity, and rather failing to rise to the big moments. Wixell makes an unidiomatic Marcello, rather lacking in fun, and Robert Lloyd's bass sounds lightweight as Colline. Ashley Putnam makes a charming Musetta. However, in this Duo reissue, with two CDs offered for the price of one, many will feel this is good value, although it includes a synopsis rather than a libretto.

It is good to have the classic recording with Gigli restored to the catalogue in Nimbus's Prima Voce series, when EMI's own CD transfer, drier and less atmospheric, has been deleted. The Nimbus transfer process (recording an acoustic-horn gramophone in a large room) works well here, with plenty of body in the sound, without too much masking of reverberation, and with a bloom on the voices. The glory of the set is Gigli's Rodolfo, with a chuckle in the voice bringing out the fun, while Gigli uses his pouting manner charmingly, with the occasional sob adding to the charm. He adds little touches, as when he murmurs '*Prego*' when ushering Mimì out, before she discovers she has lost her key. He dwarfs the others, with even Albanese a little shrill as Mimì.

As Lord Harewood says in his introduction, the 1947 Sony recording provides a snapshot of the Metropolitan Opera in the post-war period, relying on good teamwork rather than starry casting. Outstanding in the cast is Richard Tucker as Rodolfo, at the beginning of his career, having taken on the role only a month earlier. Clear and ringing of tone, he gives a finely detailed reading, without the lachrymose manners he later adopted. Bidu Sayão was for years a favourite Mimi at the Met., and though there is a hardness in the voice on top, not helped by the very dry, close-balanced recording acoustic, one can appreciate her fresh charm on stage. Francesco Valentino is an uncharacterful Marcello and Mimi Benzell a thin-toned, bright Musetta. The mono recording, limited in range, could hardly be less atmospheric, a serious snag in this opera, making Antonicelli's conducting seem heavier-handed than it is. The set is not inexpensive.

La Bohème: highlights.

(B) ** EMI CfP CD-CFP 6016 [(M) id. import] (from above complete recording, with Freni, Gedda, Adani, Sereni; cond. Schippers).

(B) ** [EMI Red Line CDR5 72561] (from complete set, with Scotto, Kraus, Milnes, Neblett, Plishka, Manuguerra, Amb. Op. Ch., Trinity Boys' Ch., Nat. PO, Levine).

(M) ** Erato/Warner Dig. 0630 17353-2 [id.] (from complete recording, with Te Kanawa, Leech, Titus, Gustafson, Quilico, Amb. S., LSO, cond. Nagano).

The Schippers set of highlights, recorded in Rome, is worth having for Freni's moving portrayal of Mimi and Gedda's individual and strong characterization of Rodolfo. But the selection is not particularly generous (59 minutes) and the cued synopsis is very brief.

With the complete set not currently available, American collectors might consider this highlights alternative with Scotto as Mimi on EMI Red Line, even though the singing is flawed.

Cast from strength, the Erato *Bohème* is marred primarily by Nagano's less than sympathetic conducting, although Richard Leech could be more romantic in his great Act I love scene. Moreover Kiri Te Kanawa's portrayal of Mimì, well sung though it is, fails to convey a young enough heroine. However, the lack of theatrical atmosphere so noticeable in the complete set is less troubling in a set of highlights.

La Fanciulla del West (The Girl of the Golden West) complete.

❀ (M) *** Decca (IMS) 421 595-2 (2) [id.]. Tebaldi, Del Monaco, MacNeil, Tozzi, St Cecilia Ac., Rome, Ch. & O, Capuana.

The Decca set of *La Fanciulla del West* has been remastered for CD with spectacular success. Tebaldi gives one of her most warm-hearted and understanding performances on record, and Mario del Monaco displays the wonderfully heroic quality of his voice to great – if sometimes tiring – effect. Cornell MacNeil as the villain, Sheriff Rance, sings with great precision and attack, but unfortunately has not a villainous-sounding voice to convey the character fully. Jake Wallace's entry and the song *Che faranno i viecchi miei* is one of the high spots of the recording, with Tozzi singing beautifully. Capuana's expansive reading is matched by the imagination of the production, with the closing scene wonderfully effective.

Gianni Schicchi (complete).

(M) *** RCA Dig. 74321 25285-2. Panerai, Donath, Seiffert, Bavarian R. Ch., Munich R. O, Patanè.

The RCA (formerly Eurodisc) recording of *Gianni Schicchi* brings a co-production with Bavarian Radio, and the recording is vivid and well balanced. Central to the performance's success is the vintage Schicchi of Rolando Panerai, still rich and firm. He confidently characterizes the Florentine trickster in every phrase, building a superb portrait, finely timed. Peter Seiffert as Rinuccio gives a dashing performance, consistently clean and firm of tone, making light of the high tessitura and rising splendidly to the challenge of the big central aria. Helen Donath would have sounded even sweeter a few years earlier, but she gives a tender, appealing portrait of Lauretta, pretty and demure in *O mio babbino caro*. Though Italian voices are in the minority, it is a confident team. In its reissued form, access to the disc has been greatly improved and there are now seven cues.

Madama Butterfly (complete).

(B) *** Decca Double 452 594-2 (2) [(M) 425 531-2]. Tebaldi, Bergonzi, Cossotto, Sordello, St Cecilia, Rome, Ac. Ch. & O, Serafin.

(M) *** RCA GD 84145 (2) [60202-2-RG]. Moffo, Elias, Valletti, Cesari, Catalani, Rome Op. Ch. & O, Leinsdorf.

(M) *** EMI CMS7 69654-2 (2) [Ang. CDMB 69654]. Scotto, Bergonzi, Di Stasio, Panerai, De Palma, Rome Op. Ch. & O, Barbirolli.

(M) **(*) EMI CMS7 63634-2 (2) [Ang. CDMB 63634]. De los Angeles, Bjoerling, Pirazzini, Sereni, Rome Op. Ch. & O, Santini.

(B) (**(*)) Decca Double mono 440 230-2 (2). Tebaldi, Campora, Inghilleri, Rankin, Santa Cecilia Academy, Rome, Ch. & O, Alberto Erede.

(M) ** RCA 09026 68884-2. Leontyne Price, Richard Tucker, Rosalind Elias, Philip Maero, RCA Italiana Op. Ch. & O, Leinsdorf.

(M) ** RCA 74321 32242-2 (2). Chiara, King, Prey, Schmidt, Bav. R. Ch., Munich R. O, Patanè.

(B) ** Naxos Dig. 8.660015/6 (2). Gauci, Ramiro, Tichy, Ch. & Slovak RSO (Bratislava), Rahbari.

Serafin's sensitive and beautifully paced reading finds Tebaldi at her most radiant. Though she was never the most deft of Butterflies dramatically (she never actually sang the role on stage before recording it), her singing is consistently rich and beautiful, breathtakingly so in passages such as the one in Act I when she tells Pinkerton she has changed her religion. The excellence of the Decca engineering in 1958 is amply proved in the CD transfer, the current remastering now providing full, atmospheric sound from the very beginning, opening out further as the orchestration grows fuller, with voices very precisely and realistically placed. At Double Decca price this is a pretty formidable bargain.

Anna Moffo's Butterfly proves delightful, fresh and young-sounding, and the *Flower duet* with Rosalind Elias is enchanting. Valletti's Pinkerton has a clear-voiced, almost Gigli-like charm – preferable to most rivals – and with Corena as the Bonze the only blot on the set vocally is the unimaginative Sharpless of Renato Cesari. Leinsdorf is efficient and undistracting and, with vivid recording (balanced in favour of the voices), this makes a first-class mid-priced recommendation, costing less than half the price of the full-price Decca Karajan set with Freni, Ludwig and Pavarotti.

Under Sir John Barbirolli, players and singers perform consistently with a dedication and intensity rare in opera recordings made in Italy, and the whole score glows more freshly than ever. There is hardly a weak link in the cast. Bergonzi's Pinkerton and Panerai's Sharpless are both sensitively and beautifully sung; Anna di Stasio's Suzuki is more than adequate, and Renata Scotto's Butterfly has a subtlety and perceptiveness in its characterization that more than make up for any shortcoming in the basic beauty of tone-colour.

Victoria de los Angeles' 1960 recording displays her art at its most endearing, her range of golden tone-colour lovingly exploited. Opposite her, Jussi Bjoerling produces a flow of rich tone to compare with that of the heroine. Mario Sereni is a full-voiced Sharpless, but Miriam Pirazzini is a disappointingly wobbly Suzuki; Santini is a reliable, generally rather square and unimaginative conductor who rarely gets in the way. With recording quality freshened, this fine set is most welcome either on a pair of mid-priced CDs or in its CfP cassette format.

Astonishingly, this Decca mono set was made (in 1951) before Tebaldi ever sang the part in the opera house. In the last resort she lacks temperament but there is much magnificent singing. Campora is a fine Pinkerton and the fresh young voices of the two lovers are particularly convincing in Act I. Erede's conducting is strong and dramatic, and there is much to relish, not least the amazingly atmospheric Decca recording, which is very kind to the voices. The orchestra sounds thinner, but the violins have more body here than on those old Ace of Clubs LP pressings. The two CDs come in a single jewel-case with an independent plot summary unrelated to the 40 cues.

Leontyne Price was in glorious voice when, in July 1962, she recorded this opera under Erich Leinsdorf. This is a weighty portrait of Butterfly, with Price's gloriously rich, creamy tone seamlessly controlled, even if occasionally she indulges in unwanted portamenti. The obvious snag is that some of the vocal acting sounds too crude for Puccini's little woman, and Tucker is at times similarly coarse as Pinkerton. Leinsdorf's conducting creates plenty of tension but is metrical and unresilient, and with that rigidity comes a straitjacketing of emotion. The CD transfer, though atmospheric and vivid, giving the voices plenty of presence (and a touch of edge), makes the violins sound fierce when under pressure. However, the set is worth considering for Price's contribution alone.

The Patanè version is chiefly valuable for the performance of Maria Chiara in the title-role. Here is a soprano who, on the strength of her early recital discs for Decca, promised much but who since then has tended to be ignored by the record companies. This co-production between BMG and Bavarian Radio, recorded in 1972, confirms what beauty and intensity of expression she could bring to a role such as Butterfly, consistently creamy of tone and imaginative in phrasing. It is astonishing what a transformation her arrival in Act I brings to a performance which until then has been square and uninspired. Neither James King as Pinkerton (referred to as 'B.F. Linkerton', German-style, in this Munich performance, despite the Italian text) nor Hermann Prey as Sharpless is at all ingratiating in the opening scene, with Patanè tending to rush the music, giving little rhythmic lift. King's voice is reliable but has no honey in it – apt, you might say, for an unsympathetic American hero – and Prey is surprisingly gritty of tone. Trudeliese Schmidt is a firm, strong Suzuki, backing up Chiara superbly, who is most moving in Act II. By her example she consistently inspires Patanè to mould the music persuasively. Voices are well caught by the recording, but the orchestral sound is thin.

Rahbari conducts a warm, well-paced reading of *Butterfly* with an excellent young Maltese soprano in the name-part, Miriam Gauci. She sings with a warm vibrato, yet this does not disturb her attractively girlish portrait. The light-toned Yordy Ramiro is here more successful in Puccini as Pinkerton than he is in his Verdi recordings for Naxos. Though Gabriel Tichy makes a colourless Sharpless and the final Suicide scene is lacking in orchestral bite, this makes an enjoyable, atmospherically recorded version. As with other Naxos operas, there is a full text but no translation. The tracking is exceptionally generous, neatly linked with a detailed synopsis.

Madama Butterfly: highlights.

(M) *** EMI CDM5 65580-2 [ZDM 64311] (from above complete set, with Scotto, Bergonzi, Di Stasio; cond. Barbirolli).

(M) (*(*)) Decca mono 452 729-2 [id.] (from above set, with Tebaldi, Campora, Rankin, Ighilleri; cond. Erde).

The EMI selection (54 minutes) offers only slightly more music than the Tebaldi selection, but it does include the essential *Humming chorus*. For those owning another complete set, it offers a fine sampler of Barbirolli's deeply felt performance with its admirably consistent cast. Scotto's Butterfly was one of her finest recorded performances. The transfer does reveal the age of the 1966 recording in the orchestral sound, but the voices are full and vividly projected.

This highlights disc from Erede's 1951 mono set offers only 55 minutes of excerpts. Collectors would do far better to spend a little more and invest in the excellent new transfer of the complete recording on a Decca Double (see above).

Madame Butterfly: highlights (sung in English).

(B) **(*) CfP CD-CFP 4600. Collier, Craig, Robson, Griffiths, Sadler's Wells O, Brian Balkwill.

This 1960 recording was the first of a series of Sadler's Wells highlights discs of opera in English. There are few better examples, for the clear recording lets the listener hear almost every word, and this is achieved without balancing things excessively in favour of the voices. Marie Collier got inside the part very well; she has a big, full voice and she sings most movingly. Charles Craig is a splendid Pinkerton: his singing achieves international standards and he was in particularly fresh voice when this record was made. As to the choice of extracts, the one omission which is at all serious is the entry of Butterfly. As it is, the duet of Pinkerton and Sharpless cuts off just as she is about to come in. The recording wears its years lightly; just occasionally the bright CD transfer brings a touch of peakiness in the vocal climaxes, but the performance remains very involving.

Manon Lescaut (complete).
(B) *** Naxos Dig. 8.660019/20 (2) [id.]. Gauci, Sardinero, Kaludov, BRT Philh. Ch. & O, Rahbari.
(M) (***) RCA mono GD 60573 (2) [60573-2-RG]. Albanese, Bjoerling, Merrill, Rome Op. Ch. & O, Perlea.
(M) **(*) EMI CMS7 64852-2 (2) [Ang. CDMB 64852]. Caballé, Domingo, Amb. Op. Ch., New Philh. O, Bartoletti.

On the bargain Naxos issue, Miriam Gauci gives one of the most sensitive performances of this role on any set. Her Act II aria, *In quelle trine morbide*, is beautifully poised and her monologue in the death scene, *Sola, perduta, abbandonata*, is the more moving for being restrained at the start, building from there in intensity without sacrificing musical values. The young Bulgarian, Kaludi Kaludov, is a clean-cut, virile Des Grieux, opening up impressively in his big moments. Vincente Sardinero makes a powerful Lescaut, and Rahbari, as in his Bratislava recordings of *Cav.* and *Pag.*, is a red-blooded interpreter of Italian opera, generally pacing well, even if at the very start he is disconcertingly hectic. Though the Brussels orchestra plays with refinement – the strings in particular – the sound is thinner than in the Slovakian recordings, with the orchestra set slightly back. This is the least expensive *Manon Lescaut* in the catalogue but, even if it cost more, it would still be very recommendable.

In Perlea's 1954 recording, the mono sound may be limited, but no Puccinian should miss it, when Jussi Bjoerling gives the finest ever interpretation on record of the role of Des Grieux. Robert Merrill too is superb as Manon's brother, giving delightful irony to the closing scene of Act I, which has rarely sounded so effervescent. The Manon of Licia Albanese is sensitively sung, but the voice is not at all girlish.

The EMI version, conducted by Bartoletti, is chiefly valuable for the performance of Montserrat Caballé as the heroine, one of her most affecting, with the voice alluringly beautiful. Otherwise the set is disappointing, with Plácido Domingo unflattered by the close acoustic, not nearly as perceptive as in his much later, DG performance under Sinopoli. Bartoletti's conducting is also relatively coarse, with the very opening forced and breathless. The new transfer to CD, however, has improved the sound, which is now much more vivid and atmospheric; and the presentation, with a clearly printed libretto, is also attractive.

Manon Lescaut: highlights.
(M) *** DG Dig. 445 466-2 (from complete recording, with Freni, Domingo, Bruson, ROHCG Ch., Philh. O, Sinopoli).

Most of the key items are included in this well-chosen mid-price selection of highlights from the brilliant Sinopoli set which is a strong alternative full-priced recommendation for this opera. An adequate synopsis with track cues is provided in lieu of a libretto. The playing time is 66 minutes.

Suor Angelica (complete).
(M) **(*) RCA 74321 40575-2. Popp, Lipovšek, Schiml, Jennings, Bav. R. Ch., Munich R. O, Patanè.

Suor Angelica (complete); *Tosca: Vissi d'arte*.
(M) *** Decca 458 218-2 [id.]. Sutherland, Ludwig, Collings, London Op. Ch., Finchley Children's Music Group, Nat. PO, Bonynge.

Puccini's atmospheric picture of a convent is superbly captured in the Decca version, with sound of spectacular depth. Bonynge's direction is most persuasive, and Sutherland rises superbly to the big dramatic demands of the final scenes. With Sutherland, Angelica is in no sense a 'little woman' or even an inexperienced girl, but a formidable match for the implacable Zia Principessa, here superbly taken by Christa Ludwig, detailed and unexaggerated in her characterization. The supporting cast is outstanding, and the pity is that Sutherland did not record the piece rather earlier, before the beat developed in her voice. The first offstage entry and opening scene catch it rather distractingly. The recording is attractively re-packaged in Decca's Opera Gala series, with full translation included, plus an encore, *Vissi d'arte* from *Tosca*, recorded six years earlier in 1972.

Patanè's performance is idiomatic and consistently well placed. Neither Lucia Popp as Angelica nor Marjana Lipovšek as the vindictive Zia Principessa is ideally cast – the one overstressed, the other sounding too young – but these are both fine artists who sing with consistent imagination, and the recording is pleasingly atmospheric. There is a libretto/translation provided, and the only snag is the lack of cueing: only two tracks are indicated, one 28 minutes into the opera and the second 12 minutes later.

Il Tabarro (complete).

(M) *** RCA 74321 45081-2. Nimsgern, Tokody, Lamberti, Pane, Bav. R. Ch., Munich R. O, Patanè.

(M) **(*) RCA 74321 50168-2 (2) [09026 60865-2]. Leontyne Price, Domingo, Milnes, John Alldis Ch., New Philh. O, Leinsdorf – LEONCAVALLO: *I Pagliacci*. ***

Patanè in his larger-than-life direction may at times run the risk of exaggerating the melodrama, but the result is richly enjoyable. Ilona Tokody, already well known from Hungaroton opera sets, makes a powerful, strongly projected Giorgetta, somewhat showing up the relative weakness of the tenor, Giorgio Lamberti, as her lover, Luigi. His over-emphatic underlining mars his legato, but the main love-duet comes over with gutsy strength. Siegmund Nimsgern makes a powerful Michele, a shade too explosive in the climactic final aria, but generally firm and clean in his projection, making the character more sinister. The full and brilliant recording has voices set convincingly on a believable stage, well balanced against the orchestra, the effect appealingly atmospheric. There is a libretto/translation and the reissue is much more generously cued than before, providing ten tracks in all.

Leontyne Price may not be ideally cast as the bargemaster's wife, but she is fully in character. Sherrill Milnes is rather young-sounding for the bargemaster, but he sings memorably in the climactic aria. Plácido Domingo makes a fresh-voiced and well-characterized young bargee, while Leinsdorf is at his most sympathetic. This RCA set is handsomely repackaged with libretto in the Opera Treasury series.

Tosca (complete).

(B) *** Decca Double 452 620-2 (2) [(M) 421 670-2]. Leontyne Price, Di Stefano, Taddei, V. State Op. Ch., VPO, Karajan.

(M) *** RCA 74321 39503-2 (2). Leontyne Price, Domingo, Milnes, Plishka, Alldis Ch., Wandsworth School Boys' Ch., New Philh. O, Mehta.

(M) **(*) EMI Dig. CMS5 66504-2 (2) [CDMB 66504]. Scotto, Domingo, Bruson, Amb. Op. Ch., St Clement Danes School Boys' Ch., Philh. O, Levine.

(B) (***) Decca Double (IMS) mono 440 236-2 (2) [id.]. Tebaldi, Campora, Mascherini, Santa Cecilia Academy, Rome, Ch. & O, Alberto Erede.

(M) ** EMI CMS5 66444-2 (2) [CDMB 66444]. Callas, Bergonzi, Gobbi, Paris Op. Ch., Paris Conservatoire O, Prêtre.

(BB) ** Koch/Discover Dig. DICD 920360-1 (2) [id.]. Gauci, Aragall, Sardinero, Coral Carmina, Coral Polifonica de Puig Reig, Coral Infantil Escola Pia Balmes, Rahbari.

(B) *(*) Naxos Dig. 8. 660001/2 [id.]. Miricioiu, Lamberti, Carroli, Slovak Philharmonic Ch., Slovak R. SO (Bratislava), Alexander Rahbari.

Now reissued on a Double Decca, Karajan's Vienna set is unbeatable value. Karajan deserves equal credit with the principal singers for the vital, imaginative performance, recorded in Vienna. Taddei himself has a marvellously wide range of tone-colour, and though he cannot quite match the Gobbi snarl he has almost every other weapon in his armoury. Leontyne Price is at the peak of her form and Di Stefano sings most sensitively. The sound of the Vienna orchestra is enthralling – both more refined and richer than usual in a Puccini opera – and it sounds quite marvellous in its digitally remastered format, combining presence with atmosphere and making a superb bargain.

Price made her second complete recording of *Tosca* (for RCA) ten years after the first under Karajan, and the interpretation remained remarkably consistent, a shade tougher in the chest register – the great entry in Act III a magnificent moment – and a little more clipped of phrase. That last modification may reflect the relative manners of the two conductors – Karajan more individual in his refined expansiveness, Mehta more thrustful. On balance, taking Price alone, the preference is for the earlier set, but Mehta's version also boasts a fine cast, with the team of Domingo and Milnes at its most impressive. The recording, too, is admirable, even if it yields to the Decca in atmosphere and richness. The current reissue in RCA's Opera Treasury series (at the moment for the UK only) is very agreeably packaged. The set remains at premium price in the USA.

With extreme speeds, both fast and slow, and with fine playing from the Philharmonia Orchestra, Levine directs a red-blooded performance which underlines the melodrama. Domingo here reinforces his claim to be the finest Cavaradossi today, while the clean-cut, incisive singing of Renato Bruson presents a powerful if rather young-sounding Scarpia. Renata Scotto's voice is in many ways ideally suited to the role of Tosca, certainly in its timbre and colouring; as caught on record, however, the upper register is often squally. The digital recording is full and forward.

Tosca was one of Tebaldi's finest parts, and her earlier Decca mono set showed her at her most moving. In addition, Campora and Ezo Mascherini gave far more satisfying support as Cavaradossi and Scarpia respectively than did del Monaco and George London in the later Decca stereo set. The 1951 recording too stands the test of time remarkably well, the orchestra a little distant but the whole effect satisfyingly atmospheric. The choral climax with Scarpia in the *Te Deum* at the end of Act I is remarkably effective, even without the advantage of stereo. Erede's conducting is fittingly full-blooded, and Tebaldi admirers should not hesitate at the very reasonable price, even if there is no libretto/translation, only a synopsis.

The Callas stereo *Tosca* is exciting and disappointing in roughly predictable proportions. There are few points of improvement over the old mono set, with Callas in the title-role and De Sabata conducting far more imaginatively than Prêtre here. When it comes to vocal reliability, the comparison is just as damaging. Gobbi is magnificent still, but no more effective than he was before, and Bergonzi's Cavaradossi, intelligent and attractive, is not helped by an unfavourable recording balance. Callas's mono set remains the one to have, and is well worth its premium price (CDS5 56304-2 [CDCB 471742]). Those who want to sample the 1964 stereo set could do so with the set of highlights, also at medium price (CDM5 66504-2 [ZDM 630672]).

With a powerful team of principals, the Discover issue offers a recording made in Barcelona that is enjoyably red-blooded, but one that is seriously marred by the oddity of balances. The principals are well forward in what sounds like a different acoustic. Miriam Gauci is a forthright, vibrant Tosca, and Giacomo Aragall – who earlier sang this same role for Solti on Decca – a ringing Cavaradossi who yet hardly ever sings quietly, both of them more convincing vocally than dramatically. In character Vicente Sardinero is splendidly sinister, more effective than either. However, as on his Naxos issue of this opera with Nelly Miricioiu – better recorded but variably cast – Alexander Rahbari is a waywardly idiosyncratic Puccinian.

The Naxos version at budget price is worth hearing for the vibrant and strong performance of Nelly Miricioiu as Tosca, a soprano who deserves to be recorded far more. She is not helped by the principals around her and least of all by the conductor, Alexander Rahbari, whose preference for slow speeds undermines any tension the soprano builds up. Yet she both brings echoes of Maria Callas in her dramatic moments and gives a beautifully thoughtful and inward account of *Vissi d'arte*, finely controlled at a spacious speed. Giorgio Lamberti is a coarse-grained Cavaradossi, hammy in his underlining, and Silvano Carroli, despite a fine, weighty voice, is a rough-edged Scarpia, too often shouting rather than vocalizing. Good digital sound and refined playing.

Tosca: highlights.

(M) *** Decca 452 728-2 [425 728-2] (from above set, with Leontyne Price, di Stefano, Taddei; cond. Karajan).

(B) ** EMI CfP Dig. CD-CFP 6017 [EMI Red Line CDR5 69827] (from above complete recording, with Scotto, Domingo, Bruson; cond. Levine).

(B) *** DG Classikon 439 461-2; *439 461-4* [(M) id. import] (from complete recording, with Ricciarelli, Carreras, Raimondi, Corena, German Op. Ch., BPO, Karajan).

The highlights disc from Karajan's superb Decca version, produced by John Culshaw and splendidly recorded in the Sofiensaal in 1962, is attractive enough in itself, but offers only 59 minutes of the opera. Collectors will find the complete set an infinitely better investment and it does not cost very much more than this in its Decca Double reissue (see above).

Scotto, in generally good voice, makes a highly convincing Tosca, and Domingo is among the very finest Cavaradossis of our time. Bruson is a powerful if rather youthful-sounding Scarpia, and Levine's direction is suitably red-blooded. With 65 minutes offered and a rather more extended cued synopsis than is usual with the Classics for Pleasure/[Red Line] highlights series, this is certainly good value, and the digital recording provides excellent presence for the singers.

The new bargain Classikon 70-minute selection from Karajan's powerful, closely recorded Berlin version is welcome. The breadth of Karajan's direction is well represented in the longer excerpts; there is also Tosca's *Vissi d'arte* and Carreras's two famous arias from the outer Acts. Now Scarpia's music in Act II is much better represented, essential when Raimondi is such a distinctive Scarpia with his dark, bass timbre.

Tosca (complete; sung in English).

(M) *** Chandos Dig. CHAN 3000 (2) [id.]. Eaglen, O'Neill, Yurisich, Rose, Shore, Daszak, Geoffrey Mitchell Ch., Peter Kay Children's Ch., Philh. O, Parry.

Opera in English on disc is a neglected cause, and the Peter Moores Foundation here sponsors the most persuasive example yet on CD of opera in translation. Above all, it offers the first recording to demonstrate the powers of Jane Eaglen at full stretch in one of the most formidable, vocally satisfying portrayals of the role of Tosca in years. The thrilling security with which she attacks one top note after another is a delight, vehement in presenting Tosca's jealousy. She is well matched by Dennis O'Neill as Cavaradossi, aptly Italianate in every register, with only occasional unevenness. Gregory Yurisich makes a powerful Scarpia, younger-sounding than most, and a plausible lover, with David Parry pacing the score masterfully to heighten tensions, helped by opulent recording.

Il Trittico: (i) *Il Tabarro;* (ii) *Suor Angelica;* (iii) *Gianni Schicchi.*

(M) *** EMI (SIS) mono/stereo CMS7 64165-2 (3). (i; iii) Gobbi; (i) Pradelli, Mas; (ii–iii) De los Angeles; (ii) Barbieri; (iii) Canali, Del Monte, Montarsolo; Rome Op. Ch. & O; (i) Bellezza; (ii) Serafin; (iii) Santini.

The classic EMI set of *Il Trittico* has dominated the catalogue since the earliest days of LP, with Tito Gobbi giving two of his ripest characterizations. The central role of the cuckolded bargemaster, Michele, in *Il Tabarro* inspires him to one of his very finest performances on record. Though this version of Puccini's *grand guignol* opera, set on a barge on the Seine in Paris, is a mono recording, not stereo, it conveys the sense of horror far more keenly than any, with Gobbi's voice vividly caught on CD. The central leaf of the triptych, *Suor Angelica*, brings a glowing performance from Victoria de los Angeles, giving a most affecting portrayal of Angelica, the nun ill-treated by her noble family, with Fedora Barbieri formidable as her unfeeling aunt, the Zia Principessa. De los Angeles reappears, charmingly girlish as Lauretta, in *Gianni Schicchi*, where the high comedy has never fizzed so deliciously outside the opera house. She and Gobbi come together just as characterfully in this final opera. Though Gobbi's incomparable baritone is not by nature comic-sounding, he is unequalled as Schicchi, sardonically manipulating the mourning relatives of Buoso Donati, as he frames a new will for them. Puccini, the master of tragedy, here emerges a supreme master of comic timing too. Only *Gianni Schicchi*, recorded last in 1958, is in genuine and excellent stereo; *Il Tabarro* (1955) and *Suor Angelica* (1957) are mono, but all the transfers are expert, clear and convincingly balanced.

Turandot (complete).

(M) *** EMI (SIS) CMS7 69327-2 (2) [Ang. CDMB 69327]. Nilsson, Corelli, Scotto, Mercuriali, Giaiotti, Rome Op. Ch. & O, Molinari-Pradelli.

(M) **(*) EMI CMS5 65293-2 (2) [Ang. CDMB 65293]. Caballé, Carreras, Freni, Plishka, Sénéchal, Maîtrise de la Cathédrale, Ch. of L'Opéra du Rhin, Strasbourg PO, Lombard.

(M) ** [RCA 09026 62687-2] [id.]. Nilsson, Bjoerling, Tebaldi, Tozzi, Rome Op. Ch. & O, Leinsdorf.

(B) *(*) Decca Double 452 964-2 (2) [433 761-2]. Inge Borkh, Mario del Monaco, Renata Tebaldi, Santa Cecilia, Rome, Ch. & O, Erede.

The EMI set brings Nilsson's second assumption on record of the role of Puccini's formidable princess. As an interpretation it is very similar to the earlier, RCA performance, but its impact is far more immediate, thanks to the conducting of Molinari-Pradelli. Corelli may not be the most sensitive prince in the world, but the voice is in glorious condition. Scotto's Liù is very beautiful and characterful too. With vividly remastered sound, this makes an excellent mid-priced recommendation, though the documentation, as yet, does not include an English translation.

Having earlier sung Liù opposite Joan Sutherland for Decca, Caballé went on to assume the more taxing role of Turandot. With Mirella Freni as Liù there is again a powerful confrontation, not between black and white but between subtler, less fixed characters. So from the very start Caballé conveys an element of mystery while Freni underlines the dramatic rather than the lyrical side of Liù's role. The pity is that the recording is unflattering to the voices – allowing Caballé less warmth and body of tone than usual, while setting Freni so close that a flutter keeps intruding. Lombard, so alert and imaginative in French music, proves a stiff and unsympathetic Puccinian so that the tenor, José Carreras, for example, is prevented from expanding as he should in the big arias. Nor is the Strasbourg Philharmonic a match for the LPO on Decca. A good CD transfer and excellent back-up documentation.

On RCA, Birgit Nilsson is certainly an icy princess. She has power and attack, even if some of her top notes are too hard to be acceptable even from the Princess Turandot. Tebaldi, in fine voice as Liù, is warm and sympathetic, and Bjoerling is a splendid Calaf. This was one of his last recordings (in 1959), but he was as clear-voiced and youthful-sounding as ever. The rest of the cast matches this standard, but Leinsdorf's conducting is chilly, and the recording, not too cleanly focused in its CD format, like the performance lacks ripeness and warmth.

Inge Borkh is not the most biting of princesses, and the early (1955) Decca recording is a little unkind to her upper register, bringing out the unevenness there. Tebaldi sings beautifully as Liù, but the characterization is rather too hefty. And Mario del Monaco is his own loud-voiced self as the stranger prince. What a wonderfully heroic voice this is, yet how consistently del Monaco seeks to use it with blundering lack of restraint. The Ping (Fernando Corena), Pang (Mario Carlin) and Pong (Renato Ercolani) are excellent. There are undoubtedly enjoyable things here, but the performance overall lacks atmosphere and sheer vitality; nor does the singing match that on the other sets.

Turandot: excerpts.

(M) (***) EMI mono CDH7 61074-2. Dame Eva Turner, Martinelli, Albanese, Favero, Tomei, Dua, ROHCG Ch., LPO, Barbirolli.

The excerpts were recorded at two separate 1937 performances and fascinatingly duplicate most of the items, with the second performance in each pair marginally more spacious and helpful in sound, and generally warmer and more relaxed as a performance. Martinelli's heroic timbre may be an acquired taste, but he is stirringly convincing, and Dame Eva Turner gloriously confirms all the legends, even more commanding than in her earlier studio accounts of the big aria, *In questa reggia*. Keith Hardwick's excellent transfers, for all the obvious limitations of recording on stage at Covent Garden, give a superb sense of presence.

Turandot: highlights.

(M) *** Decca 458 202-2 [id.] (from complete recording, with Sutherland, Pavarotti, Caballé, Ghiaurov, John Alldis Ch., Wandsworth School Boys' Ch., LPO, cond. Mehta).

(M) *** DG Dig. 435 409-2 [id.] (from complete set, with Ricciarelli, Domingo, Hendricks, Raimondi, V. State Op. Ch., V. Boys' Ch., VPO, Karajan).

(B) ** EMI CfP CD-CFP 6018 (from above complete recording, with Caballé, Carreras, Freni; cond. Lombard).

A generous and shrewdly chosen 70-minute collection of excerpts from the glorious full-priced Decca set of *Turandot. Nessun dorma*, with Pavarotti at his finest, is here given a closing cadence for neatness. The vintage Decca sound is outstandingly full and vivid. The reissue in Decca's Opera Gala series is neatly packaged in a slipcase and includes a full translation.

Domingo is at his very finest on the DG alternative CD, and he is exceptionally well represented in this 70-minute selection of highlights, as indeed is the chorus.

It is difficult to enthuse about a highlights CD that plays for only 53 minutes, even at bargain price, and if key items are included and put in narrative perspective by a very brief synopsis. So this will mainly be of interest to Caballé admirers (although the recording does not particularly flatter her).

COLLECTIONS

'The Essential Puccini': Preludio sinfonico; Famous arias, duets and choruses from: *La Bohème; La Fanciulla del West; Gianni Schicchi; Madama Butterfly; Manon Lescaut; La Rondine; Suor Angelica; Tosca; Turandot.*

(B) **(*) Decca Double Analogue/Dig. 444 555-2 (2) [(M) id. import]. Caballé, Chiara, Freni, Te Kanawa, Sutherland, Tebaldi, Bergonzi, Bjoerling, Carreras, Pavarotti, Corena, Ghiaurov, Krause, Milnes, Siepi (with various orchestras & conductors).

Many collectors will welcome a sampler of the vintage set of *La Bohème* with Tebaldi and Bergonzi at the height of their powers. Five items are included here, including the love scene from Act I. Tebaldi is also at her most seductive in *Madama Butterfly*, which is generously represented with well over half an hour of excerpts, including the whole of the Act I Love duet. She also provides the key arias from *Gianni Schicchi* and *La Rondine*, while Suor Angelica's ravishing *Senza mamma, o bimbo, tu sei morto* comes from Maria Chiara's glorious 1971 début recital, which Decca should urgently restore to the catalogue. Dame Kiri gives a movingly passionate if comparatively unsubtle characterization of *Manon Lescaut*; with three numbers included, her partner, Carreras, recorded just before his illness, sounds a little strained. It was a pity that Rescigno's recording was chosen for the 30 minutes or so of *Tosca* excerpts, especially as a highlights disc from that set is already available. Freni as Tosca is below her best form and, though Sherrill Milnes does not disappoint as Scarpia, Pavarotti's *E lucevan le stelle* is the high point. Joan Sutherland's assumption of the role of the formidable *Turandot* is justly esteemed, as is Caballé's melting Liù, while Pavarotti delivers a splendid *Nessun dorma*. With Bjoerling on hand to provide a superb *Ch'ella mi creda* from *Fanciulla del West*, this is something of a (143-minute) Puccini feast, with the ripely expansive Decca sound fairly consistent throughout (although the early Tebaldi recordings give some indication of their age in the violin tone). The snag is that the documentation is totally inadequate.

'Favourite Puccini': (i) *La Bohème: Mi chiamano Mimì; Donde lieta uscì;* (ii) *Musetta's waltz song. Gianni Schicchi: O mio babbino caro. Madama Butterfly: Un bel dì;* (iii; iv) *Spira sul mare; Flower duet; Con onor muore . . . Tu, tu.* (ii) *Manon Lescaut: In quelle trine morbide;* (iii) *Sola, perduta, abbandonata.* (ii) *La Rondine: Chi il bel sogno di Doretta.* (iii) *Suor Angelica: Senza mamma, O bimbo, tu sei morto.* (i) *Tosca: Vissi d'arte. Turandot: Tu, che di gel sei cinta;* (i; v) *In questa reggia. Le Villi: Se come voi.*

(M) *** Sony analogue/Dig. SMK 48094 [id.]. (i) Eva Marton; (ii) Kiri Te Kanawa; (iii) Renata Scotto; (iv) with Wixell and Knight; (v) with Carreras.

Kiri Te Kanawa's six ravishing contributions are the highlight of this collection – there is currently no more luscious Puccini singing than this – but the others are very characterful too, even if Eva Marton's Mimì is a shade forceful; she is better suited to the role of Turandot. However, *In questa reggia*, which ends the disc excitingly, delivers a damp squib by fading out. Before that there is much to enjoy, not least Scotto's beautiful *Senza mamma* from *Suor Angelica* and the two moving excerpts (Butterfly's entrance and the opera's climax) from Maazel's complete set of *Madama Butterfly*. The sound is excellent throughout, although sometimes the vocal balance is very forward. There is no back-up documentation, apart from a list of titles and performers.

Arias: *La Bohème: Si, mi chiamano Mimì; Donde lieta uscì. Gianni Schicchi: O mio babino caro. Madama Butterfly: Un bel dì; Con onor muore. Manon Lescaut: In quelle trine morbide; Sola, perduta. Suor Angelica: Senza mamma. Turandot: Signore acolta!; In questa reggia; Tu che di gel sei cinta.*
(M) (***) EMI mono CDM5 66463-2 [id.]. Maria Callas, Philh. O, Serafin.

This collection of Puccini arias was Callas's first EMI recital, recorded in mono in Watford Town Hall in September 1954. Now reissued as part of EMI's Callas Edition, it brings a classic example of her art. She was vocally at her peak. Even when her concept of a Puccinian 'little woman' has eyes controversially flashing and fierce, the results are unforgettable, never for a moment relaxing on the easy course, always finding new revelation, whether as Turandot or Liù, as Manon, Mimì or Butterfly. Well-balanced recording, with the voice vividly projected by the transfer and with plenty of depth and detail in the orchestra.

Arias: *Madama Butterfly: Un bel dì; Tu? tu? piccolo Iddio!* (Death of Butterfly). *La Rondine: Che il bel sogno di Doretta. Tosca: Vissi d'arte. Turandot: Signore ascolta; Tu che di gel sei cinta.*
(M) **(*) RCA 09026 68883-2 [id.]. Leontyne Price, Rome Opera O, Oliviero de Fabritiis or Artur Basile – VERDI: *Arias*. ***

There is some glorious singing in this recital from the beginning of the 1960s. Perhaps Leontyne Price does not always get right inside each heroine at this stage in her career, but *Un bel dì* is thrilling, with a sharp contrast of tone between the incisiveness of the opening and the delicacy of *Chi sarà, Chi sarà*. In *Vissi d'arte* she forces a little too hard so that her vibrato becomes a wobble, but the two *Turandot* arias are very beautiful. Most welcome of all is Magda's aria from *La Rondine*, sweet, charming and lyrical. The recording was always very good indeed, and it sounds even more vivid in this CD transfer, without any loss of bloom.

Purcell, Henry (1659–95)

Gardiner Purcell Collection

'Gardiner Purcell Collection'.
(M) *** Erato/Warner 4509 99773-2 (8). Soloists, Monteverdi Ch. & O, Equale Brass Ens., E. Bar. Soloists, Gardiner.

To commemorate the tercentenary of Purcell's death, the following reissued Erato recordings, all directed with distinction by John Eliot Gardiner, are also available together in a slip-case (at a slightly reduced price); they would make a splendid basis for any Purcell collection. Not all are now available separately.

Come, ye sons of art away; Funeral music for Queen Mary (1695).
(M) *** Erato/Warner 4509 99775-2 [96553]. Lott, Brett, Williams, Allen, Monteverdi Ch. & O, Equale Brass Ens., Gardiner.

Come, ye sons of art, the most celebrated of Purcell's birthday odes for Queen Mary, is splendidly coupled here with the unforgettable funeral music he wrote on the death of the same monarch. With the Monteverdi Choir at its most incisive and understanding the performances are exemplary, and the recording, though balanced in favour of the instruments, is clear and refined. Among the soloists Thomas Allen is outstanding, while the two counter-tenors give a charming performance of the duet, *Sound the trumpet*. The *Funeral music* includes the well-known *Solemn march* for trumpets and drums, a *Canzona* and simple anthem given at the funeral, and two of Purcell's most magnificent anthems setting the *Funeral sentences*. Recording made in 1976 in Rosslyn Hill Chapel, London.

Ode on St Cecilia's day (Hail! bright Cecilia).
(M) *** Erato/Warner Dig. 4509 99776-2. Jennifer Smith, Stafford, Gordon, Elliott, Varcoe, David Thomas, Monteverdi Ch., E. Bar. Soloists, Gardiner.

Gardiner's characteristic vigour and alertness in Purcell come out superbly in this delightful record of the 1692 *St Cecilia Ode* – not as well known as some of the other odes he wrote, but a masterpiece. Soloists and chorus are outstanding even by Gardiner's high standards, and the recording excellent. Recording made in 1982 in the Barbican Concert Hall, London.

Dioclesian; Timon of Athens.
(M) *** Erato/Warner Dig. 4509 99777-2 (2). Dawson, Fisher, Covey-Crump, Elliott, George, Varcoe, Monteverdi Ch., E. Bar. Soloists, Gardiner.

The martial music, shining with trumpets, is what stands out in *Dioclesian*, adapted from a Jacobean play first given in 1622. Gardiner is such a lively conductor, regularly drawing out the effervescence in Purcell's inspiration, that the result is delightfully refreshing, helped by an outstanding team of soloists. The incidental music for *Timon of Athens* offers more buried treasure, including such enchanting inventions as *Hark! how the songsters of the grove*, with its 'Symphony of pipes imitating the chirping of birds', and a fine *Masque for Cupid and Bacchus*, beautifully sung by Lynne Dawson, Gillian Fisher and Stephen Varcoe. Excellent Erato sound. Recordings made in Rosslyn Hill Chapel, London, in 1987. This is not now available separately.

The Indian Queen (incidental music; complete).
(M) *** Erato/Warner 4509 99778-2 [96551]. Hardy, Fisher, Harris, Smith, Stafford, Hill, Elwes, Varcoe, Thomas, Monteverdi Ch., E. Bar. Soloists, Gardiner.

The reissued Erato version is fully cast and uses an authentic accompanying baroque instrumental group. The choral singing is especially fine, with the close of the work movingly expressive. John Eliot Gardiner's choice of tempi is apt and the soloists are all good, although the men are more strongly characterful than the ladies; nevertheless the lyrical music comes off well. The recording is spacious and well balanced. Recording made in 1979 in Henry Wood Hall, London.

King Arthur (complete).
(M) *** Erato/Warner Dig. 4509 99774-2 (2) [96552]. Jennifer Smith, Gillian Fischer, Priday, Ross, Stafford, Elliot, Varcoe, Monteverdi Ch., E. Bar. Soloists, Gardiner.

Gardiner's solutions to the textual problems carry complete conviction, as for example his placing of the superb *Chaconne in F* at the end instead of the start. Solo singing for the most part is excellent, with Stephen Varcoe outstanding among the men. *Fairest isle* is treated very gently, with Gill Ross, boyish of tone, reserved just for that number. Throughout, the chorus is characteristically fresh and vigorous, and the instrumentalists beautifully marry authentic technique to pure, unabrasive sounds. Digital recording, made in 1983 in St Giles, Cripplegate, London.

The Tempest (incidental music).
(M) *** Erato/Warner 4509 99779-2 [96555]. Jennifer Smith, Hardy, Hall, Elwes, Varcoe, David Thomas, Earle, Monteverdi Ch. & O, Gardiner.

Whether or not Purcell himself wrote this music for Shakespeare's last play (the scholarly arguments are still unresolved), Gardiner demonstrates how delightful it is, a masterly collection, in performances both polished and stylish and with excellent solo and choral singing. At least the overture is clearly Purcell's, and that sets a pattern for a very varied collection of numbers, including three *da capo* arias and a full-length masque celebrating Neptune for Act V. The 1979 recording, made in London's Henry Wood Hall, is full and atmospheric; the words are beautifully clear, and the transfer to CD is admirably natural.

INSTRUMENTAL MUSIC

(i) *3 Fantasias for 3 Viols; 9 Fantasias for 4 Viols; Fantasia on one note for 5 viols; In nomine for 6 viols; In nomine for 7 viols;* (ii) *Chacony in G min.*
(M) **(*) DG 447 153-2 [id.]. (i) VCM, Alice Harnoncourt; (ii) E. Concert, Pinnock.

The Purcell *Fantasias* and *In nomines* are among the most searching and profound works in all music, and the 1963 Vienna Concentus, led by Alice Harnoncourt (with Nikolaus at the time playing 'second fiddle'), provide a set of performances of these wonderful pieces, darkly sombre in colour, using original instruments with a minimum of vibrato. Then at track 16 there is a splash of cold water in the face as Trevor Pinnock and his English Concert (recorded two decades later) demonstrate modern ideas of authenticity of style and pitch with a brightly astringent and strikingly vital account of the famous *Chacony in G minor*. This transition is not entirely comfortable, and it is better to listen to this piece as a separate item.

Sonatas in 3 parts: Nos. 1–12 (complete).
(M) *** HM Suite Dig. HMT 7901439 [id.]. London Baroque.

Purcell's set of 12 *Sonatas in 3 Parts* was published in 1683. The Italian influence is undeniable but they remain very much Purcell's own in their contrapuntal interest, their deeply expressive harmonic richness and their English seriousness of purpose. The period performances from London Baroque are full of vitality and warmth; indeed the rich blending of the violons of Ingried Seifert and Richard Gwilt in partnership with the viola da gamba of Charles Medlam gives the music plenty of warmth. The full resonance of the recording is helpful, but that in itself brings the one drawback: the effective dynamic range is reduced, although there is no lack of light and shade in the playing itself; and the continuo, featuring both harpsichord and organ (as was the practice at the time), comes through as it should, beautifully. So this fine set must receive the strongest advocacy, for the music itself is very rewarding indeed.

Sonatas in 3 parts: Nos. 1 in G min.; 2 in B flat; 3 in D min. Sonatas in 4 parts: Nos. 2 in E flat; 3 in A min.; 5 in G min.; 6 in G min.: Chacony; 9 in F (Golden).
(BB) *(*) Discover Dig. DICD 920251 [id.]. Slovak Radio Qt.

The Slovak Radio Quartet is an excellent ensemble using modern instruments, and this is a well-chosen programme of marvellous music. The recording is close but truthful; the snag is the almost total absence of dynamic contrast in the playing.

VOCAL MUSIC

Anthems: *Man that is born of woman; O God, thou has cast us out; Lord, how long wilt thou be angry?; O God, thou art my God; O Lord God of hosts; Remember not, Lord, our offences; Thou knowest, Lord, the secrets of our hearts.* Verse anthems: *My beloved spake; My heart is inditing; O sing unto the Lord; Praise the Lord, O Jerusalem; They that go down to the sea in ships. Morning Service in B flat: Benedicte omnia opera; Cantate Domino; Deus miscreatur; Magnificat; Nunc dimittis. Evening service in G min.: Magnificat; Nunc dimittis. Latin Psalm: Jehovah, quam multi sunt hostes mei. Te Deum and Jubilate in D.*
(M) *** DG (IMS) 447 150-2 (2) [id.]. David Thomas, Christ Church Cathedral, Oxford, Ch., E. Concert, Simon Preston.

The admirable Christ Church two-disc collection of anthems, verse-anthems and excerpts from service settings was recorded in the London Henry Wood Hall in 1980 and lies at the very kernel of the DG-Archiv Purcell Collection. With some of the music not otherwise available, it is self-recommending. Apart from David Thomas's fine contribution (in the verse-anthems) the soloists come from the choir – and very good they are too, especially the trebles. The performances are full of character, vigorous yet with the widest range of colour and feeling, well projected in a recording which simulates a cathedral ambience yet is naturally focused and well detailed – analogue sound at its best.

Anthems: *O sing unto the Lord; Praise the Lord, O Jerusalem; They that go down to the sea in ships.* Ode: *My heart is inditing; Te Deum and Jubilate Deo in D.*
(M) *** DG 427 124-2. Ch. of Christ Church Cathedral, Oxford, E. Concert, Preston.

The well-chosen selection on this mid-priced collection is taken from the above set. The recording, made in London's Henry Wood Hall, is both spacious and well detailed.

Ayres, Theatre music and Sacred songs: *Awake awake, ye dead (Hymn for the Day of Judgement); Birthday ode for Queen Mary: Strike the viol. Dioclesian: O how happy's he; Chaconne. The earth trembled (A hymn on our Saviour's Passion). The Fairy Queen: One charming night. How plaisant is this flow'ry plain and grove* (ode). *The Indian Queen: Ye twice ten hundred deities; Wake Quivera. Ode for St Cecilia: Raise, raise the voice; Oedipus: Hear, ye sullen pow'rs below; Come away, do not stay. The Old Bachelor: Thus to a ripe consenting maid. Olinda: There ne'er was so wretched a lover as I* (duet). *Timon of Athens: Hark how the songsters. Pavane and Trio.*
(B) **(*) HM Musique d'Abord HMA 190214 [id.]. Deller Cons. & Ens., Deller.

Deller has put together what one might regard as a sampler of Purcell's vocal music, a varied collection which includes some of his finest inspirations. Always fresh and often lovely performances, given good if not outstanding recording.

Alfred Deller Edition: (i) *Come ye sons of art (Ode on the birthday of Queen Mary, 1694);* Anthems: (ii) *My beloved spake;* (iii) *Rejoice in the Lord alway (Bell anthem);* (iv) *Welcome to all the pleasures (Ode on St Cecilia's Day, 1683).*
(M) **(*) Van. 08.5060 71 [id.]. Alfred Deller, Deller Consort; (i) Mark Deller, Mary Thomas, Bevan, Oriana Concert Ch. & O; (ii) Cantelo, English, Bevan; (iii; iv) Kalmar O; (iii) Thomas, Sheppard, Tear, Worthley; Oriana Concert O; (iv) Cantelo, McLoughlin, English, Grundy, Bevan.

An enjoyable anthology, now reissued as part of the Alfred Deller Edition, showing Deller at his finest. The other soloists are good too, especially the tenor, Gerald English. The two anthems make a fine centrepiece, responding to the demand of Charles II for composers 'not to be too solemn' and to 'add symphonies, etc., with instruments' to their sacred vocal music. The *Bell anthem* is so called because of the repeated descending scales in the introduction. The warm, expressively played accompaniments are rather different from the effect one would achieve today with original instruments. The recording is closely balanced; although made at either Walthamstow or Cricklewood Church, the effect is not quite as spacious as one would expect, though pleasingly full.

Come, ye sons of art, away (Ode on the birthday of Queen Mary); Ode for St Cecilia's Day: Welcome to all the pleasures. Of old when heroes thought it base (The Yorkshire Feast song).

(B) *** DG Classikon Dig. 449 853-2 [(M) id. import]. Jennifer Smith, Michael Chance, Timothy Wilson, Stephen Richardson, John Mark Ainsley, Michael George, E. Concert Ch., E. Concert, Pinnock.

Pinnock directs exuberant performances of all three works. The weight and brightness of the choral sound go with infectiously lifted rhythms, making the music dance, as in the first chorus of *Welcome to all pleasures*, the best-known of the Queen Mary *Odes*, the one for 1694. There the line, 'to celebrate this triumphant day', could not come over more catchingly. The soloists are all outstanding, with the counter-tenor duetting of Michael Chance and Timothy Wilson for *Sound the trumpet* delectably pointed. The neglected *Yorkshire Feast song* (composed in 1690 for 'an otherwise obscure gathering of York nobility') is full of wonderful inspirations, like the tenor and counter-tenor duet, *And now when the renown'd Nassau* – a reference to the new king, William III.

Funeral music for Queen Mary (with (i) *Queen's epicedium*); *March and canzona on the death of Queen Mary*. Funeral sentences: *Man that is born of a woman; In the midst of life are we in death; Thou knowest, Lord, the secrets of our hearts*. Anthems: *Hear my prayer; Jehova quam multi sunt*. (ii) *3 (Organ) Voluntaries: in D min.; in G; in C*.

(BB) *** Naxos Dig. 8.553129 [id.]. Oxford Camerata, Summerly; with (i) Carys-Ann Lane; (ii) Laurence Cummings.

The glorious, darkly intense funeral music which Purcell wrote on the death of Queen Mary, including processional instrumental numbers – tragically used for the composer's own funeral soon after – is here given an outstandingly fresh and clear rendering, vividly recorded, matching even the finest rival versions. The sharpness of focus in the sound means that Purcell's adventurous harmonies with their clashing intervals are given extra dramatic bite in these dedicated performances, marked by fresh, clear soprano tone in place of boy trebles. The choice of extra items – full anthems with their inspired counterpoint rather than verse anthems – is first rate, including as it does the magnificent *Jehova, quam multi sunt* and the wonderfully compressed *Hear my prayer*, both beautifully done. Aptly, the extended solo song for soprano (with simple organ accompaniment), *The Queen's epicedium*, is also included with the funeral music, sung with boyish tone by Carys-Ann Lane.

Funeral music for Queen Mary: March and canzona; Funeral sentences: Man that is born of woman; In the midst of life: Thou knowest, Lord. Jehova, quam multi sunt hostes.

(M) *** EMI CDM5 66683-2 [id.]. Winchester Cathedral Ch., Martin Neary – CROFT: *Burial Service;* Concert: *'Solemn music'*. ***

Martin Neary's version of the unforgettable Purcell *Funeral music*, with Baroque Brass of London as well as the Winchester Cathedral Choir, is most welcome. The simple but magnificent *March* for drums and brass comes with a *Canzona* and four motets which, for all their brevity, find Purcell at his deepest. The choral ensemble is not ideally crisp, but the coupling of more valedictory music is very appropriate, most of it unjustly neglected. The recording is pleasantly warm and atmospheric.

In guilty night (Saul and the Witch of Endor); Man that is born of woman (Funeral sentences); Te Deum and Jubilate Deo in D.

(B) **(*) HM Musique d'Abord HMA 190207 [id.]. Deller Cons., Stour Music Festival Ch. & O, Deller.

In guilty night is a remarkable dramatic scene depicting Saul's meeting with the Witch of Endor. The florid writing is admirably and often excitingly sung by Alfred Deller himself as the King and Honor Sheppard as the Witch. The *Te Deum and Jubilate* are among Purcell's last and most ambitious choral works; the *Funeral sentences* from early in his career are in some ways even finer in their polyphonic richness. The chorus here is not the most refined on record but, with sensitive direction, this attractive collection is well worth hearing. The recording is good.

Jubilate Deo in D; The noise of foreign wars; Ode for St Cecilia's Day; Raise, raise the voice; Te Deum; (i) *Trumpet sonata*.

(BB) *** Naxos Dig. 8.553444 [id.]. Bern, Bisatt, Robson, Purefoy, Honeyman, Guthrie, The Golden Age Ch. & O, Robert Glenton; (i) with David Staff.

These superb examples of Purcell's choral music, both church music and secular cantatas, as well as a brief, joyful trumpet sonata, make an attractive collection, well recorded. The singing is excellent from a group which includes such distinguished singers as the counter-tenor, Christopher Robson, though the instrumental group is lacking in bite in the string section, hardly matching the wind. But this is not enough to detract from the pleasure of the music-making overall. David Staff on the trumpet is outstanding, in both the sonata and the choral works too. Specially fascinating is the première recording of the *Noise of foreign wars*, a substantial fragment of a cantata only recently identified as being by Purcell.

(i) *Odes for Queen Mary's birthday: Come ye sons of art; Love's Goddess sure.* (ii) *Funeral music for Queen Mary (March; Canzone;* Funeral sentences: *Man that is born of woman; In the midst of life; Thou knowest, Lord; March;* Anthems: *Hear my prayer, O Lord; Remember not, Lord, our offences).* Anthems: *Blessed are they that fear the Lord; My beloved spake; Rejoice in the Lord alway.* (iii) (Organ) *The Queen's doleur; Trumpet minuet in C* (including *March* from *The Married Beau); Trumpet tunes in C & D; Voluntary in A.*

(B) *** EMI Rouge et Noir (SIS) CZS5 69270-2 (2) [(M) id. import]. (i) Burrowes, Bowman, Lloyd, Brett; Ch.; York Skinner, Hill, Shaw, Lloyd; L. Early Music Cons., Munrow; (ii) Cockerhan, King, Hayes, Chilcott, Morell, Castle, Byram-Wigfield, Robarts, Grier, King's College Ch., ASMF, Philip Jones Brass Ens., Ledger; (iii) Jean-Patrice Brosse (organ of Cathedral of Sainte Marie de Saint Bertrand de Comminges).

Purcell wrote a series of ceremonial odes for the birthdays of Queen Mary, and rarely has a courtier writing occasional pieces been so deeply and genuinely inspired. *Come ye sons of art* is the richest of the sequence, with its magnificent overture or symphony (no doubt intended to outdo those French at Versailles), and such memorable pieces as the duet, *Sound the trumpet. Love's goddess sure*, though not quite so grand, brings more Purcellian delights. The late David Munrow inspires fine playing and singing from his excellent forces and gives sensitive, intelligent performances of both works, which deliberately opt for an intimate scale, using old instruments and an authentic style of string playing; the results are entirely congenial to the ear. The intimacy clearly detracts from the sense of grandeur and panoply which are apt for this music but, with refined yet full sound to match, this alternative approach is equally satisfying. The coupling, made around the same time (1976/7), at King's is hardly less stimulating. As can be seen from the listing above, *Queen Mary's funeral music* consists of far more than the unforgettable *March* for lugubrious trombones (sackbuts) with punctuating timpani (later repeated without timpani), which still sounds so modern to our ears. Philip Ledger has the advantage of spacious sound (the original LP was issued in quadraphony) and his account of the *March* is darkly memorable. The anthems are well sung too, if slightly less alertly. The organ pieces, very well played, are particularly characterful heard on a comparatively pungent French organ. They are used as a postlude for the two birthday odes, while the voluntary (on disc 2) becomes an overture to introduce the three great verse anthems. The trumpet ayres are jolly, with a hurdy-gurdy effect in the Minuet framing a march from *The Married Beau*; the *Voluntary in C* is dark in timbre to match the dolorous piece specifically dedicated to the Queen.

Other Collections

Songs: *Ah! How sweet it is to love; The earth trembled; An evening hymn; If music be the food of love; I'll sail upon the dog star; I see she flies me ev'rywhere; Let the night perish; Lord, what is man; Morning hymn; A new ground.* Arias: *Birthday ode for Queen Mary: Crown the altar. Bonduca: Oh! Lead me to some peaceful gloom. History of Dioclesian: Since from my dear Astrea's sight. The Indian Queen: I attempt from love's sickness to fly. The Mock marriage: Man that is for woman made. Oedipus: Music for a while. Pausanias: Sweeter than roses. The Rival sisters: Take not a woman's anger ill.*

(BB) *** ASV CDQS 6172 [(M) id.]. Ian Partridge, Jennifer Partridge – BRITTEN: *Winter words.* ***

Appropriately entitled 'Sweeter than Roses', this is a warmly sympathetic collection of favourite Purcell songs from a tenor whose honeyed tones are ideally suited to recording. The style smoother than we have come to expect latterly – this is a reissue of an earlier Enigma issue – but with ever-sensitive accompaniment from George Malcolm, who also contributes one brief solo, this is an excellent recommendation for those who resist the style of authenticity. Atmospheric recording, with the voice well forward. The CD transfer is very faithful, with the voice caught in its presence and natural bloom and the harpsichord image believable and nicely focused.

Anthems: *Blow up the trumpet in Zion; Hear my prayer, O Lord; I will sing unto the Lord as long as I live; Lord, how long wilt thou be angry?; O God, the King of glory; O God, thou art my God; O God, thou hast cast me out; Remember not, Lord, our offences. Funeral music for Queen Mary (March; Canzone; Funeral sentences: Man that is born of woman; In the midst of life; Thou knowest Lord; March; Queen's Epicedium; Thou Knowest, Lord, the secrets of our hearts; March). Organ voluntaries: in C; D min.; G.*
(BB) ** Naxos Dig. 8.553129 [id.]. Oxford Camerata, Jeremy Summerly; Laurence Cummings.

A worthy attempt to provide a single, budget-priced CD for the tercentenary, celebrating Purcell's church music but also including his *Funeral music for Queen Mary*. In the latter work, a modest brass group appears for the *Marches*, but otherwise the vocal music is organ-accompanied by Laurence Cummings, who also provides acceptable accounts of three solo voluntaries. Although the anthems are sung with warmth and eloquence, the most impressive performance here is the Latin motet, *Jehova, quam multi sunt hostes mei*, with excellent solo contributions from Andrew Carwood and Michael McCarthy. Similarly, it is a soloist who stands out at the centre of the *Funeral music*, with the girl treble Carys-Anne Lane's touching account of *Incassum Lesbia* (the *Queen's Epicedium*). Translations are provided for both works. Pleasing, spacious recording in the Chapel of Hertford College, Oxford. Good value, but this is not in the same class as the two-disc Christ Church collection, above.

STAGE WORKS AND THEATRE MUSIC

Dido and Aeneas (complete).
❀ (M) *** Decca 425 720-2. Dame Janet Baker, Herincx, Clark, Sinclair, St Anthony Singers, ECO, Anthony Lewis.
(M) (***) EMI mono CDH7 61006-2. Flagstad, Schwarzkopf, Hemsley, Mermaid Theatre Singers & O, Geraint Jones.
(BB) **(*) Naxos Dig. 8.553108 [id.]. Scholars Bar. Ens.
(M) ** EMI (SIS) CDM5 65664-2 [id.]. De los Angeles, Glossop, Harper, Johnson, Amb. S., ECO, Barbirolli.

Janet Baker's 1962 recording of *Dido* is a truly great performance. The radiant beauty of the voice is obvious enough, but the emotion is implied, as it should be in this music, not injected in great uncontrolled gusts. Listen to the contrast between the opening phrase of *When I am laid in earth* and its repeat a few bars later: it is a model of graduated mezza voce. Then with the words *Remember me!*, delivered in a monotone, she subdues the natural vibrato to produce a white tone of hushed, aching intensity. Anthony Lewis and the ECO (Thurston Dart a model continuo player) produce the crispest and lightest of playing, which never sounds rushed. The other soloists and chorus give very good support. Herincx is a rather gruff Aeneas, but the only serious blemish is Monica Sinclair's Sorceress. She overcharacterizes in a way that is quite out of keeping with the rest of the production. Like most vintage Oiseau-Lyre recordings, this was beautifully engineered.

Though Flagstad's magnificent voice may in principle be too weighty for this music, she scales it down superbly in her noble reading, which brings beautiful shading and masterly control of breath and tone. Schwarzkopf is brightly characterful as Belinda, and though Thomas Hemsley is not ideally sweet-toned as Aeneas, he sings very intelligently; even in this age of period performance, this traditional account under Geraint Jones sounds fresh and lively still, not at all heavy. The mono sound, obviously limited, yet captures the voices vividly, and this above all is Flagstad's set.

Using minimum forces, with one-to-a-part strings, the Scholars Baroque Ensemble offer an intimate view of Purcell's compressed epic, taking their cue from the first documented performance in Josias Priest's girls' school in Chelsea. Though the instrumental sections are rather rough in ensemble, the performance is vigorous and compelling, with choral ensemble excellent. Speeds are well chosen, often on the brisk side, yet with Dido's two great ground-bass arias – not just *Dido's lament* at the end but *Ah Belinda!* at the beginning – both given necessary emotional weight. Kym Amps is a warmly expressive heroine, singing with moving restraint in the *Lament*, while Anna Crookes as Belinda sings with fresh, clear tone, and Sarah Connolly with her rich mezzo makes an impressive Sorceress. Though David van Asch, leader of the group, is a dry-toned Aeneas, he compensates by his expressiveness. Two improvised guitar dances and an interlude for two violins are added to the surviving musical text where the libretto suggests. Clear, immediate recording. Well worth having at its modest cost, though Dame Janet reigns supreme in this opera.

Barbirolli – not the most likely conductor in this opera – takes some trouble with his text, using the Neville Boyling Edition that Mackerras, on DG Archiv, also prefers. But on questions of authenticity most other versions have considerable advantages, and Barbirolli finds fewer moments of high emotional intensity, such as would justify a 'personality' reading, than one would expect. The tempi are generally perverse, with slow speeds predominating – sometimes grotesquely slow – but with Dido's '*When I am laid in earth*' taken equivalently fast. Victoria de los Angeles makes an appealing Dido, but she does not have the dramatic weight of Janet Baker and the tone sometimes loses its bloom on top. The other singers are good, and the 1965 recording is fresh and immediate, but with keen competition this version commands only a very qualified recommendation.

Dido and Aneas: Dido's lament (arr. Stokowski).
(M) *** EMI CDM5 66760-2. RPO, Stokowski – DVORAK: *String serenade;* VAUGHAN WILLIAMS: *Fantasia on a theme by Thomas Tallis*. ***

Stokowski's indulgent arrangement of Purcell's famous *Lament* is certainly not for purists. But Stokowski feels this music deeply: it is beautifully played and recorded, and the lovely melody is genuinely touching.

The Fairy Queen (complete).
(B) *** Naxos Dig. 8.550660-1 (2) [id.]. Diane Atherton, Kym Amps, Angus Davidson & Soloists, The Scholars Bar. Ens., led by David van Asch.
(BB) **(*) HM HMP 390257/8 [id.]. Sheppard, Knibbs, Bevan, Platt, Alfred Deller, Jenkins, Mark Deller, Buttrey, Clarke, Stour Music Ch. & O, A. Deller.

Purcell's setting of Shakespeare's *Midsummer Night's Dream*, written in 1692, followed in the wake of the great success of *Dido and Aeneas*. The music takes the form of five masques, each symbolizing one aspect of the play. For Naxos at bargain price the Scholars Baroque Ensemble offer an outstanding version of Purcell's semi-opera, not always quite as beautifully sung as the finest rivals, but stylishly presented with a refreshing vigour in its scholarly approach. The recording too is exceptionally bright and immediate, regularly giving the illusion of a dramatic entertainment on stage. Logically this version, unlike previous ones, presents the purely instrumental numbers designed as interludes for *A Midsummer Night's Dream* as an appendix, rather than including them during the course of the musical entertainment of five separate masques. So the performance starts with the very brief Overture instead of the First Musick Prelude, and the variety of expression throughout is well caught and contrasted. The humour of the Scene of the Drunken Poet is touched in delightfully without exaggeration, thanks to David van Asch, as is the Dialogue between Corydon and Mopsa, though the counter-tenor, Angus Davidson, has a flutter in the voice that the recording exaggerates. One or two of the others are not always quite steady either. Outstanding among the sopranos are Diane Atherton, singing most beautifully in the Night solo of Act II, and Kym Amps, not only bright and agile in *Hark! The echoing air* but making the plaint, *O ever let me weep*, of Act V into the emotional high-point of the whole performance. In the edition specially prepared for the Ensemble it is made the more affecting with lamenting oboe obbligato. Instrumental playing on period instruments is first rate, and the chorus sings consistently with bright, incisive attack.

Deller's set was recorded – very well too – at the Stour Music Festival in 1972 and, although the balance is rather forward, the acoustic is pleasingly warm and the voices and orchestra combine effectively. All the solo singing is of a high standard, with Honor Sheppard particularly memorable as Night in Act II, well matched by Jean Knibbs's Mystery in some of Purcell's most evocative writing. Norman Platt is a suitably bucolic Drunken Poet in Act I and becomes one of a pair of West Country haymakers (Alfred Deller obviously enjoying himself as his companion, Mopsa) in Act III. The many ensembles are eloquently sung and, although this has not quite the sophistication of Gardiner's full-price set, its robust warmth and Deller's considerable concern for detail make for an enjoyable entertainment, well worth its modest price when so smoothly and vividly transferred to CD.

King Arthur: highlights.
(M) *** Erato/Warner Dig. 0630 15736-9 (from complete recording, with Jennifer Smith, Fischer, Priday, Ross, Stafford, Elliott, Varcoe, Monteverdi Ch., E. Bar. Soloists, Gardiner).

A well-chosen, 64-minute selection from John Eliot Gardiner's complete version (see Gardiner Purcell collection, above), this is a novelty, but as the selection includes all the key items (including Philadel's chorus with the spirits and the Frost scene) some collectors could be attracted to it. Gardiner's soloists are all good, although the men are more strongly characterful than the ladies and it is the choral singing which one remembers. The recording is spacious and the documentation is very full indeed.

The Indian Queen (complete; with Daniel PURCELL (*c.* 1661–1717): *The Masque of Hymen*).
(BB) **(*) Naxos Dig. 8.553752 [id.]. Soloists, Ch., Scholars Baroque Ens.

The music which Purcell wrote in 1694, the year before he died, to turn the play *The Indian Queen* (Dryden one of the two authors) into a semi-opera with a sequence of masques works well on disc. In this Naxos version it comes with the added bonus of the concluding *Masque of Hymen*, which Daniel Purcell added after his brother's death, making a celebratory instead of a tragic conclusion. Though Daniel Purcell hardly matches his brother in originality, that generous supplement is welcome, though arguably the finest music of all comes at the very end of the main work in the tragic slow fugal sinfonia and chorus – all dismal sounds.

The work overall suits the lively style of the Scholars Baroque Ensemble admirably, on a scale rather more intimate than you find on most rival versions, with one instrument per part. Bright, clear recording to match, with dances and trumpet-tunes well sprung. The choral work is first rate; but when the singers come to their solos, the voices (mostly unidentified as to who sings what) are uneven, often with delivery rather unsteady. The fresh-toned soprano, Anna Crookes, makes an honourable exception. Yet solos are usually short, and what matters is the overall freshness, vigour and intensity.

Theatre music (collection).

Disc 1: *Abdelazar: Overture and suite. Distressed Innocence: Overture and suite. The Gordian Knot Untied: Overture and suite; The Married Beau: Overture and suite. Sir Anthony Love: Overture and suite.*

Disc 2: *Bonduca: Overture and suite. Circe: suite. The Old Bachelor: Overture and suite. The Virtuous Wife: Overture and suite.*

Disc 3: *Amphitrion: Overture and suite; Overture in G min.; Don Quixote: suite.*

Disc 4: *Overture in G min. The Double Dealer: Overture and suite. Henry II, King of England: In vain, 'gainst love, in vain I strove. The Richmond Heiress: Behold the man. The Rival Sisters: Overture; 3 songs. Tyrannic Love: Hark my Damilcar!* (duet); *Ah! how sweet it is to love. Theodosius:* excerpts. *The Wives' Excuse:* excerpts.

Disc 5: *Overture in D min.; Cleomenes, the Spartan Hero: No, no, poor suff'ring heart. A Dialogue between Thirsis and Daphne: Why, my Daphne, why complaining?. The English Lawyer: My wife has a tongue:* excerpts. *A Fool's Preferment:* excerpts. *The History of King Richard II: Retir'd from any mortal's sight. The Indian Emperor: I look'd and saw within. The Knight of Malta: At the close of the ev'ning. The Libertine:* excerpts. *The Marriage-hater Match'd: As soon as the chaos . . . How vile are the sordid intregues. The Massacre of Paris: The genius lo* (2 settings). *Oedipus:* excerpts. *Regulus: Ah me! to many deaths. Sir Barnaby Whigg: Blow, blow, Boreas, blow. Sophonisba: Beneath the poplar's shadow. The Wives' Excuse:* excerpts.

Disc 6: *Chacony; Pavans Nos. 1–5; Trio sonata for violin, viola de gamba & organ. Aureng-Zebe: I see, she flies me. The Canterbury Guests: Good neighbours why?. Epsom Wells: Leave these useless arts. The Fatal Marriage: 2 songs. The Female Virtuosos: Love, thou art best. Love Triumphant: How happy's the husband. The Maid's Last Prayer:* excerpts. *The Mock Marriage: Oh! how you protest; Man is for the woman made. Oroonoko: Celemene, pray tell me. Pausanius: Song (Sweeter than roses) and duet. Rule a Wife and Have a Wife: There's not a swain. The Spanish Friar: Whilst I with grief.*

(M) *** O-L (IMS) 425 893-2 (6) [id.]. Kirkby, Nelson, Lane, Roberts, Lloyd, Bowman, Hill, Covey-Crump, Elliott, Byers, Bamber, Pike, David Thomas, Keyte, Shaw, George, Taverner Ch., AAM, Hogwood.

Most of the music Purcell wrote for the theatre is relatively little heard and much of the music comes up with striking freshness in these performances using authentic instruments. As well as the charming dances and more ambitious overtures, as the series proceeds we are offered more extended scenas with soloists and chorus, of which the nine excerpts from *Theodosius*, an early score (1680), are a particularly entertaining example. Before that, on Disc 3 we have already had the highly inventive *Overture and incidental music* for *Don Quixote*, with much enchanting singing from both the soprano soloists, Emma Kirkby and Judith Nelson. Disc 4 also includes a delightful duet from *The Richmond Heiress*, representing a flirtation in music. There are other attractive duets elsewhere, for instance the nautical *Blow, blow, Boreas, blow* from *Sir Barnaby Whigg*, which could fit admirably into *HMS Pinafore* (Rogers Covey-Crump and David Thomas) and the jovial *As soon as the chaos* from *The Marriage-hater Match'd*. In *Ah me! to many deaths* from *Regulus*, Judith Nelson is at her most eloquent while, earlier on Disc 5, she sings charmingly the familiar *Nymphs and shepherds*, which comes from *The Libertine*, a particularly fine score with imaginative use of the brass. The equally famous *Music for a while*, beautifully sung by James Bowman, derives from *Oedipus*. The last disc also includes a splendidly boisterous *Quartet* from *The Canterbury Guests*. The collection is appropriately rounded off by members of the Academy giving first-class performances of some of Purcell's instrumental music, ending with the famous *Chacony*. The discs are comprehensively documented and with full texts included.

Quilter, Roger (1877–1953)

A Children's overture.

(M) ** EMI CDM7 64131-2. Light Music Society O, Sir Vivian Dunn (with TOMLINSON: *Suite of English folk dances*) – HELY-HUTCHINSON: *Carol Symphony;* VAUGHAN WILLIAMS: *Fantasia on Christmas carols*. **

This charming overture, skilfully constructed from familiar nursery rhymes, hitherto has not been available on CD except for a full-priced Marco Polo version. Its neglect is inexplicable. Sir Vivian Dunn gives a good if not remarkable performance and the recording too is pleasing rather than outstanding. But the music itself is a delight. Ernest Tomlinson's suite of six folk-tunes, simply presented and tastefully scored, makes an attractive bonus. Again the sound is acceptable but could be richer.

Rachmaninov, Sergei (1873–1943)

Piano concertos Nos. (i) *1;* (ii) *2* (2 versions); (i) *3–4;* (ii) *Rhapsody on a theme of Paganini;* (iii) *The Isle of the Dead; Symphony No. 3; Vocalise*. (piano, 4 hands): (iv) *Polka italienne*. (Solo piano): *Barcarolle, Op. 10/3; Daisies* (song transcription); *Etudes-tableaux, Op. 33/2 & 7 & Op. 39/6; Humoresque, Op. 10/5; Lilacs* (song transcription; 2 versions); *Mélodie, Op. 3/3; Moment musical, Op. 16/2; Oriental sketch; Polichinelle, Op. 3/4; Polka de W. R.* (3 versions). *Preludes: in C sharp min., Op. 3/2* (3 versions); *in G min.; in G flat, Op. 23/5 & 10; in E, G, F min., F, G sharp, Op. 32/3, 5–7, 12; Serenade, Op. 3/5* (2 versions); (v) BEETHOVEN: *Violin sonata No. 8 in G, Op. 30/3*. SCHUBERT: *Violin sonata in A, D.574.* GRIEG: *Violin sonata in C min., Op. 45*. BACH: *Partita No. 4, BWV 828: Sarabande*. HANDEL: *Suite No. 5: Air and variations (The Harmonious blacksmith)*. MOZART: *Piano sonata in A, K.331: Theme and variations; Rondo alla Turca*. BEETHOVEN: *32 Variations in C min. WoO 80*. LISZT: *Concert paraphrase of Chopin: Polish songs (Return home; The maiden's wish). Concert paraphrases of Schubert: Das Wandern; Serenade. Polonaise No. 2; Concert study: Gnomenreigen; Hungarian rhapsody No. 2.* MENDELSSOHN: *Song without words: Spinning song, Op. 67* (2 versions). *Etudes, Op. 104b/2–3*. SCHUBERT: *Impromptu in A flat, Op. 90/4*. GLUCK: *Orfeo ed Euridice: Mélodie*. SCHUMANN: *Der Kontrabandiste* (arr. Tausig); *Carnaval, Op. 9*. PADEREWSKI: *Minuet, Op. 14/1*. CHOPIN: *Sonata No. 2 (Funeral march); Nocturnes, Op. 9/2; Op. 15/2; Waltzes: Op. 18 (Grand valse brillante), Op. 34/3; Op. 42; Op. 64/1* (2 versions); *Op. 64/2; Op. 64/3* (2 versions); *Op. 69/2; Op. 70/1; in E min., Op. posth.; Ballade No. 3; Mazurkas, Op. 63/3, Op. 68/2; Scherzo No. 3*. BORODIN: *Scherzo in A flat*. TCHAIKOVSKY: *The Seasons: November (Troika;* 2 versions). *Humoresque, Op. 10/2; Waltz, Op. 40/8*. SCRIABIN: *Prelude, Op. 11/8.* Johann STRAUSS Jr: *Man lebt nur einmal (One lives but once;* arr. Tausig). DAQUIN: *Le coucou.* SAINT-SAENS: *Le Cygne* (arr. Siloti). GRIEG: *Lyric pieces: Waltz; Elfin dance*. DOHNANYI: *Etude, Op. 28/6*. HELSELT: *Etude, Op. 2/6 (Si oiseau j'étais)*. MOSZKOWSKI: *Etude, Op. 52/4 (La jongleuse)*. DEBUSSY: *Children's corner: Dr Gradus ad Parnassum; Golliwog's cakewalk*. Domenico SCARLATTI: *Pastorale* (arr. Tausig). Transcriptions: KREISLER: *Liebesfreud* (3 versions). BACH: (Unaccompanied) *Violin Partita No. 3, BWV 1003: Preludio; Gavotte & Gigue*. MENDELSSOHN: *A Midsummer Night's Dream: Scherzo.* SCHUBERT: *Wohin?*. MUSSORGSKY: *Gopak*. TCHAIKOVSKY: *Lullaby, Op. 16/1*. RIMSKY-KORSAKOV: *Flight of the bumble bee*. BEETHOVEN: *Ruins of Athens: Turkish march*. BIZET: *L'Arlésienne: Minuet.* TRAD.: (vi) *Powder and Paint*.

❁ (M) (***) RCA mono 09026 61265-2 (10) [id.]. Sergei Rachmaninov (piano); with Phd. O, (i) Ormandy; (ii) Stokowski; (iii) cond. composer; (iv) with Natalie Rachmaninov; (v) Fritz Kreisler; (vi) Nadejda Plevitskaya.

(i) *Piano concerto No. 2; Rhapsody on a theme of Paganini;* (ii) *Vocalise*.

(M) (***) Carlton mono GLRS 104. Rachmaninov, Phd. O, Stokowski; (ii) composer, Phd. O.

Spurred by the 50th anniversary of Rachmaninov's death, RCA has issued a ten-disc box at mid-price collecting all the recordings the composer made from 1919, the time he arrived in America, until 1942, the year before his death. These include all four of his *Piano concertos* (No. 3 irritatingly cut) as well as the *Paganini rhapsody*, the *Third Symphony* and the tone-poem, *The Isle of the Dead* (also with cuts). Among Rachmaninov's many solo piano recordings it is fascinating to compare his different readings of the most celebrated piece of all, the *Prelude in C sharp minor*. The stiff performance of 1919 (made for Edison) leads to a much freer and subtler reading in 1921, while the 1928 version, using the new electrical process, remains free and subtle but is emotionally less charged. The acoustic recordings, made between 1920 and 1925, are on balance the most cherishable of all, with the sound astonishingly full and the readings sparkling and spontaneous. That is true even of his 1924 recording of the *Piano Concerto No. 2*, now for the very first time issued complete. As in his classic electrical recording of five years later, he is partnered by Stokowski and the Philadelphia Orchestra, but the earlier one has a more volatile quality, with the fingerwork even clearer. Interpreting Chopin, Rachmaninov was also at his freshest and most imaginative in the early recordings, yet dozens of items here bear witness to the claim often made that he was the greatest golden-age pianist of all, bar none. The delicacy of his playing in Daquin's little piece, *Le coucou*, shows how he was able to scale down his block-busting virtuosity and, though in Beethoven's *32 Variations in C minor* he omitted half-a-dozen variations so as to fit the piece on two 78 sides, it is full of flair. There is magic too in his collaborations with Fritz Kreisler, not just in Beethoven but also in the Grieg and Schubert sonatas, and in the private recordings, when he accompanies a gypsy singer in a traditional Russian song or plays a piano duet, the *Polka italienne*, with his wife, Natalie. Transfers are commendably clean but with high background hiss. The ten discs come in a box at mid-price.

For those who want just the two electrical concertante recordings made with Stokowski, the Pickwick CD serves admirably. The transfers are slightly less sharp in detail but agreeably full. Both here and in the RCA version of the second recording of the *C minor Concerto* the woodwind triplets which accompany the reprise of the main theme of the slow movement come out vividly as in no other recording. Even in a live performance these very effective decorations tend to become buried.

Piano concertos Nos. 1–4.
(B) *** Decca Double 444 839-2 (2) [id.]. Vladimir Ashkenazy, LSO, Previn.
(B) *** EMI CZS7 67419-2 (2) [(M) id. import]. Collard, Capitole Toulouse O, Plasson.
(B) ** DG Double 453 136-2 (2) [id.]. Vásáry, LSO, Ahronovitch.

Piano concertos Nos. 1; 4; Rhapsody on a theme of Paganini, Op. 43.
(M) ** Ph. 446 582-2 (2). Zoltán Kocsis, San Francisco SO, Edo de Waart.

(i) *Piano concertos Nos. 2–3. Vocalise, Op. 34/14.*
(M) ** Ph. 446 199-2 (2). (i) Zoltán Kocsis; San Francisco SO, Edo de Waart.

(i) *Piano concertos Nos 1–4;* (ii) *Rhapsody on a theme of Paganini.*
(B) *** BMG/Melodiya Twofer Dig. 74321 40068-2 (2) [(M) id. import]. Victor Eresko; (i) USSR SO, Gennady Provotorov; (ii) Leningrad PO, Vladimir Ponkin.

Piano concertos Nos. (i) *1 in F sharp min;* (ii) *2 in C min;* (iii) *3 in D min.;* (i) *4 in G min.;* (ii) *Rhapsody on a theme of Paganini, Op. 43.*
(B) **(*) EMI forte (SIS) CZS5 68619-2 (2) [CDFB 68619]. Anievas, New Philh. O; (i) Frühbeck de Burgos; (ii) Atzmon; (iii) Ceccato.

Piano concertos Nos. 1 in F sharp min., Op. 1.; 4 in G min., Op. 40; Rhapsody on a theme of Paganini, Op. 43.
(M) *** Chandos CHAN 6605 [id.]. Earl Wild, RPO, Horenstein.

Piano concertos Nos. 2 in C min., Op. 18; 3 in D min., Op. 30.
(M) *** Chandos CHAN 6507 [id.]. Earl Wild, RPO, Horenstein.

The new Double Decca set of the four Rachmaninov concertos now tends to sweep the board. The current transfers (unlike the previous, mid-priced incarnation) are admirable, fully capturing the Kingsway Hall ambient warmth yet not lacking brilliance and clarity, and with the *Third Concerto* better focused than when it first appeared on LP. The vintage 1972 performances, with their understanding partnership between Ashkenazy and Previn, have achieved classic status. The *Second Concerto*'s slow movement is particularly beautiful; it is almost matched by the close of the first movement of the *Third* and the restrained passion of the opening of the following *Adagio*. The individuality and imagination of the solo playing throughout, combined with the poetic feeling of Previn's accompaniments and the ever-persuasive response of the LSO, provide special rewards. An outstanding bargain in every way.

Issued as a 'Twofer', two discs for the price of one, the Melodiya digital versions of the four Rachmaninov *Piano concertos* (1984) plus the *Paganini rhapsody* (1983) make an excellent bargain in performances full of flair. The notes give no information about the pianist, Victor Eresko, but he proves a formidable virtuoso who in No. 3 opts for the weightier and more difficult of Rachmaninov's two cadenzas: even in that he betrays no strain whatever, not just technically brilliant but spontaneously expressive through thickets of notes. In his articulation Eresko plays with the crispest definition, not just in bravura passage-work, but magically in the light, quicksilver skeins of notes so characteristic of Rachmaninov, and in such movements as the finales of Nos. 3 and 4 he points rhythms with a sparkle of wit, making most others seem a little plain. He also brings off the virtuoso codas to each of these works with splendid panache, to set this up as a most attractive set, well recorded and a first-rate bargain.

Jean-Philippe Collard's recordings of the four Rachmaninov concertos date from the late 1970s. Collard is completely at home in this repertoire; his account of the *First* has splendid fire and can hold its own with all comers (even Pletnev and Ashkenazy, though the former is incomparable in the slow movement); and much the same goes for its companions. Perhaps the *Third Piano concerto* is the least incandescent in his hands, but readers wanting an alternative, inexpensive set (all four concertos for the price of one CD) need look no further, for this is playing of quality, and the recording, though not outstanding, is fully acceptable.

The Earl Wild set with Horenstein originally derived from RCA. It was produced by Charles Gerhardt and was recorded at the Kingsway Hall in 1965. They worked marvellously together, with Horenstein producing an unexpected degree of romantic ardour from the orchestra and both artists finding the natural feeling for the ebb and flow of phrases, so readily demonstrated in the composer's own performances, and which has now become a hallmark of Rachmaninovian interpretation. Earl Wild's technique is prodigious and sometimes (as in the first movement of the *Fourth Concerto*) he almost lets it run away with him. What is surprising is how closely the interpretations here seem to be modelled on the composer's own versions – not slavishly, but in broad conception. This applies strikingly to the *First Concerto* and the *Rhapsody*. The first movement of the *C minor Concerto* is faster than usual, but the expressive fervour is in no doubt; the *Adagio*, too, blossoms readily. In terms of bravura, the *Third Concerto* is in the Horowitz class. The digital remastering is a great success, the overall balance is truthful and the hall ambience brings a rich orchestral image and plenty of brilliance. However, unfortunately there are three cuts in the *Third Concerto*, one in the second movement and two in the third, a total of 55 bars. Horenstein does not quite match Stokowski's flair, although his rather straighter approach is still idiomatically sensitive and is helped by the rich body given to the strings by the Kingsway ambience. All in all, this is a first-class and very rewarding set, and the sumptuousness of the sound belies the age of the recording.

Anievas cannot match Ashkenazy as a searching and individual interpreter of Rachmaninov, but his youthful freshness makes all these concerto performances highly enjoyable. With three Mediterranean conductors to help him, and with bright, vivid EMI recording, not as atmospheric as the quality Decca provide for Ashkenazy, the result brings a combination of brilliance and romanticism which never lets go, even if it rarely produces the moments of magical illumination that mark the most inspired interpretations. Like Ashkenazy, Anievas gives the *Third Concerto* absolutely uncut and uses the longer, more difficult version of the first-movement cadenza. It is a strong, direct interpretation, though at the very end of the finale the presentation of the big melody nearly goes over the top.

Kocsis has fleet fingers and he dashes through the first two concertos with remarkable panache and striking brilliance. But in No. 2 he gives the listener all too little time to savour incidental beauties or to surrender to the melancholy of the slow movement. He takes the first movement of the *Third Concerto* at express speed; undoubtedly there is some exciting playing here and he earns at least one listener's thanks for opting for the shorter cadenza in the first movement, which he plays with electrifying bravura. The *Fourth Concerto* is a good deal less rushed, though it is full of excitement and virtuosity when this is required, and the *Rhapsody* brings more thrilling playing. But there are moments, both here and in the concertos, when Kocsis should perhaps rein in his fiery high spirits. He is carried away just a little too far by his own virtuosity and, although this can be very exciting, it is not the whole story. The Philips recording places him rather forward but there is no lack of orchestral detail, and there is plenty of range. Readers should note that the two discs are available separately, one coupling the *First* and *Fourth Concertos* with the *Paganini variations*, the other the *Second* and *Third Concertos* with the orchestral *Vocalise*.

Vásáry's set has its merits, but it is far from a primary recommendation. Ahronovitch's direction is nothing if not impetuous, and this account of the *First Concerto* is full of vigour, with bursts of vivid romanticism. Vásáry's more introvert manner seems to fit well within this dashing framework, and there is no doubt about the freshness of this performance. Moreover the memorable theme of the finale is affectionately shaped, yet not indulged. The *Second Concerto* is also effective, with a fine climax in the first movement. But after that the tension is allowed to drop, and the languorous *Adagio* does not distil the degree of poetry which makes the Ashkenazy/Previn performance so beautiful. The recording is bold and colourful. Vásáry uses the longer version of the first-movement cadenza in the *Third Concerto*. The slow movement is indulgent and lacks momentum. Vásáry's playing itself is clean, often gentle in style, but the conductor's extremes of tempi are less appropriate here than in the *First Concerto*. The first movement of the *Fourth Concerto* has a strong forward impulse, with relaxation of tempo for the lyrical music. There is poetry in the slow movement, even if the brilliance of the finale carries also a lack of poise. Good recordings.

(i–ii) *Piano concertos Nos. 1–4; Rhapsody on a theme of Paganini, Op. 43;* (ii) *Symphonies Nos. 1–3; Etudes-tableaux, Op. 39* (orch. Respighi); *The Isle of the dead, Op. 44; Vocalise, Op. 34/14*. (i) *Piano sonata No. 2 in B flat min., Op. 30; Variations on a theme of Corelli, Op. 42.*
(BB) **(*) Nimbus Dig. NI 1761 (6) [(B) id.]. (i) John Lill; (ii) BBC Nat. O of Wales, Tadaaki Otaka.

The Nimbus box is singularly inexpensive, and it offers a great deal of music. It has many merits, but there are drawbacks too. Tadaaki Otaka gives characterful and excellently shaped readings of all three symphonies. Each unfolds with complete naturalness and unfailing musical instinct that reflects great credit on the gifted Japanese conductor. There is not the degree of Slavonic temperament that distinguishes Ashkenazy's readings but, even if Otaka does not wear his heart on his sleeve, there is no lack of intensity of feeling or indeed of panache, while there is no trace of unwelcome showmanship either. Tempi are eminently well judged and phrases are well shaped. In the beautiful slow movement of the *Second Symphony* the clarinet solo (Martin Ronchetti) is particularly sensitive. Apart from the excellent orchestral playing, there is a natural concert-hall perspective with plenty of warmth from the acoustic. *The Isle of the dead* is no less well served, while Respighi's masterly transcriptions of the four *Etudes-tableaux* make an appealing bonus. In the *Concertos* John Lill's extrovert bravura in Nos. 1 and 4 brings much exciting pianism, but his powerful fingers can at times produce tone which seems too hard. In the finale of No. 1 the lyrical secondary theme of the finale blossoms affectingly in Otaka's hands. But overall one feels that Lill's approach to these works is too Lisztian and, though his brilliant playing in the formidable *Third Concerto* is bold and strong (he uses the second, more big-boned and powerful of the two cadenzas), the work's romantic fires do not burn fiercely enough. He takes a spacious, almost severe view of the score which some might feel undercharacterized. The *Second Concerto* opens broadly but rather heavily, and neither Lill nor the conductor find the poetry at the reprise of the slow movement which is so moving in the Decca Ashkenazy/Previn account. The energetic finale brings a contrastingly spacious tempo for the 'big tune', justified by the powerful reprise. The *Paganini Rhapsody* is carried along by the sheer brilliance and impetus of the solo playing, and here Otaka touches in the orchestral detail affectingly and vividly, while no one should be disappointed with the *18th Variation*. Lill plays the original version of the *B flat minor Sonata* and, needless to say, his playing commands admiration, both here and in the *Corelli variations*, although towards the end of that work his tone again hardens.

(i) *Piano concertos Nos. 1–4; Rhapsody on a theme of Paganini, Op. 43*. (ii) (2 Pianos): *Suites Nos. 1–2, Opp. 5 & 17; Russian rhapsody; Symphonic dances, Op. 45*. (Piano) *Etudes-tableaux, Opp. 33 & 39; 24 Preludes* (complete); *Piano sonata No. 2 in B flat min., Op. 36; Variations on a theme by Corelli, Op. 42*.

✿ (B) *** Decca 455 234-2 (6) [id.]. Ashkenazy; (i) LSO, Previn; (ii) with André Previn (piano).

This bargain box was perhaps the finest of Decca's special reissues made to celebrate Ashkenazy's sixtieth birthday. All these performances are very distinguished indeed. The vintage Decca recordings (made over a decade and a half between 1971 and 1986, mostly in the Kingsway Hall, but also at Walthamstow and All Saints', Petersham) are fully worthy of the quality of the music-making. Ashkenazy's readings, with Previn an admirable partner (whether conducting or at the keyboard), are unsurpassed on CD, except by the composer's own historic versions; while they are also available on a series of Double Deccas, any collector not involved in too much duplication will find this bargain box will make an ideal linchpin for a Rachmaninov collection.

Piano concerto No. 1 in F sharp min., Op. 1.

(M) *** Mercury (IMS) 434 333-2 [id.]. Byron Janis, Moscow PO, Kondrashin – PROKOFIEV: *Piano concerto No. 3*. ***

As in the Prokofiev coupling, on the occasion of the first Western-engineered recordings made in the USSR, soloist and orchestra plainly challenged each other to the limit, and the American technical team brilliantly captured the warmly romantic and chimerical interpretation which resulted. The solo playing stands alongside that of Horowitz in this repertoire, scintillating in the finale, yet never offering virtuosity simply for its own sake. Even now the recording is impressive for its clarity of texture and subtle detail within a warm acoustic. The CD represents one of Wilma Cozart Fine's most successful transfers.

Piano concertos Nos. (i) *1 in F sharp min., Op. 1;* (ii) *2 in C min., Op. 18. Etudes-tableaux Opp. 33 & 39:* excerpts.

(M) (*) Revelation mono RV 10064 [id.]. Sviatoslav Richter; (i) Leningrad PO; (ii) Moscow RSO; Kurt Sanderling.

Sviatoslav Richter's performances of the Rachmaninov *First* and *Second Piano concertos*, recorded with the Moscow Radio and Leningrad Philharmonic Orchestras respectively, both under Kurt Sanderling, date from the 1950s. The *First* originally appeared on a mono Parlophone LP, which in some respects was a slight improvement on this transfer. There is, incidentally, no indication on the Revelation disc that it is mono. Stereo techniques were in use by the mid-1950s, and the prospective buyer should be told. The *Second* offers rather better sound and of course some pretty dazzling playing. The quality is nowhere near as good as it is for Sanderling's account of the *Second Symphony* made at much the same time. Four of the *Etudes-tableaux* are thrown in for good measure – but why buy this when you can get Richter playing the same concerto in superior recorded sound and very handsomely presented in DG's Originals series?

Piano concertos Nos. (i) *1 in F sharp min., Op. 1;* (ii) *3 in D min., Op. 30.*

(M) *** RCA 09026 68762-2 [id.]. Byron Janis; (i) Chicago SO, Fritz Reiner; (ii) Boston SO, Munch.

(BB) ** Belart 461 348-2 [(M) id. import]. (i) Peter Katin, LPO, Boult; (ii) Alicia de Larrocha, LSO, Previn.

Byron Janis in his late twenties (in March 1957) gives a dashing account of the *F sharp minor Concerto*, freshly charismatic. With Reiner at the helm the performance cannot help but be commanding: how beguilingly warm and relaxed is the phrasing of the lyrical string-melody in the finale! Then in December of the same year Janis went to Boston to record the greater *D major* work, with Munch an equally perceptive partner; here it is the acoustics of Boston's Symphony Hall which cast a glow over the proceedings and the piano balance is very well judged. Janis's reading is basically lyrical, not unlike Ashkenazy's, but more impetuous and with a particularly exciting finale. Janis's tempo for the main theme of the first movement is brisk (he tells us the reason for his choice in the accompanying notes); but the contrast with the second subject is nicely made and Munch's orchestral backcloth reveals much subtlety of colour-shading. He is an excellent partner and contributes a strong surge of romanticism to the *Adagio*. Both recordings sound greatly improved in the present transfers (by Jon Samuels and Harold Hagopian respectively), so that the piano timbre, originally rather brittle, is now really quite impressive. Janis was to go on to re-record both works for Mercury, but the present coupling has a youthful spontaneity which is hard to resist. The disc is almost worth having for the excellent documentation alone: it includes a fascinating essay from the soloist, paying tribute to Reiner as 'one of the greatest conductors of our era' and comparing him with Munch ('a highly inspired and spontaneous musician' who didn't like rehearsing but 'believed in saving the "magic" for the performance'). The conducting technique of both musicians is described in detail, and Janis also talks about the difficulties of recording in the diffused acoustics of an empty hall.

Boult brings a sympathetic freshness to the *First Concerto* and his conducting is matched by Katin's spirited and mercurial playing. The pianist does not attempt a conventional bravura style, and some may be disappointed on this account, but in this, the shortest of Rachmaninov's concertos, the added clarity and point given to so many passages more than make amends (if indeed amends need be made). The orchestra responds well but does not always play with perfect precision. However, the early-1970s Decca stereo is excellent: bright, with good definition and balance. The 1975 recording of the *Third Concerto* is even finer, warm and glowing. Alicia de Larrocha is a cultured player whom we do not associate with barn-storming bravura; she gives an individual performance, full of imaginative detail, but not one which holds together very cohesively, despite Previn's understanding accompaniment.

Piano concertos Nos. 1 in F sharp min.; 4 in G min.; Rhapsody on a theme of Paganini, Op. 43.

(BB) *** Naxos Dig. 8.550809 [id.]. Bernd Glemser, Polish Nat. RSO, Wit.

This exceptionally generous Naxos disc is worth anyone's money. Bernd Glemser has a boldly impetuous way with Rachmaninov and, with excellent support from the Polish National Radio Orchestra under Antoni Wit, he generates plenty of excitement and expressive fervour in all three works here. If Janis and Reiner are that bit more characterful in the *F sharp minor Concerto*, and Rubinstein is even more charismatic in the *Rhapsody*, Glemser is by no means unimaginative or wanting in poetic feeling, and he gives a very enjoyable account of the more elusive *Fourth Concerto*, dynamic and spirited in the outer movements and in the *Largo*, presenting the 'Three blind mice' theme with appealing warmth but also a touch of gravity, which negates any suggestion of triviality.

Piano concerto No. 2 in C min., Op. 18.

(M) *** RCA 09026 61961-2 [id.]. Van Cliburn, Chicago SO, Reiner – BEETHOVEN: *Concerto No. 5.* ***

(M) *** DG 447 420-2 [id.]. Sviatoslav Richter, Warsaw PO, Stanislaw Wislocki – TCHAIKOVSKY: *Piano concerto No. 1.* (**)

(B) *** Decca Eclipse Dig. 448 221-2; *448 221-4* [(M) id. import]. Cristina Ortiz, RPO, Moshe Atzmon – TCHAIKOVSKY: *Piano concerto No. 1.* *(*)

With Reiner making a splendid partner, Van Cliburn's 1958 account of the Rachmaninov *C minor Concerto* is second to none. The pacing of the first movement is comparatively measured, but the climax is unerringly placed, remaining relaxed yet enormously telling. The finale too does not seek to demonstrate runaway bravura but has sparkle and excitement, with the lyrical element heart-warming to match the very beautiful account of the central *Adagio*, full of poetry and romantic feeling. The recording is wonderfully rich, with the Chicago acoustic adding a glorious ambient glow, while the piano, though forwardly placed, has an unexpected body and fullness of timbre. In the finale the cymbals demonstrate an excellent upper range, and the enhancement of the digital remastering almost makes this seem as if it were made yesterday.

The coupling with Beethoven's *Emperor* is unusual but stimulating, with Reiner again participating impressively.

With Richter the long opening melody of the first movement is taken abnormally slowly, and it is only the sense of mastery that he conveys in every note which prevents one from complaining. The slow movement too is spacious – with complete justification this time – and the opening of the finale lets the floodgates open the other way, for Richter chooses a hair-raisingly fast allegro. He does not, however, let himself be rushed in the great secondary melody, so this is a reading of vivid contrasts. The sound is very good. It's a great pity that the performance chosen as the new coupling for DG's series of Legendary Recording performances should be Tchaikovsky's *First Concerto*, with Karajan and the Berlin Philharmonic. The Rachmaninov readily fits this description, but the Tchaikovsky certainly does not, except as an example of a performance where two great artists pull simultaneously in different directions.

Cristina Ortiz's account has the advantage of rich Decca digital sound. The performance is warmly romantic, the first-movement climax satisfyingly expansive and the *Adagio* glowingly poetic, while the finale brings sparklingly nimble articulation from Ortiz and a fine expressive breadth from the strings in the famous lyrical melody. However, the Postnikova version of the Tchaikovsky *B flat minor Concerto* which acts as coupling is too eccentric to be recommendable.

Piano concertos Nos. (i) *2 in C min., Op. 18;* (ii) *3 in D min., Op. 30.*

(M) **(*) Decca 425 047-2. Ashkenazy, (i) Moscow PO, Kondrashin; (ii) LSO, Fistoulari.

(B) ** Sony SBK 63032; *SBT 63032* [id.]. (i) Gary Grafman; (ii) André Watts; (i–ii) NYPO; (i) Bernstein; (ii) Ozawa.

Piano concertos Nos. (i) *2 in C min, Op. 18;* (ii) *3 in D min., Op. 30. Preludes: in C sharp min., Op. 3/2; in E flat, Op. 23/6.*

(M) *** Mercury 432 759-2 [id.]. Byron Janis; (i) Minneapolis SO; (ii) LSO, Antal Dorati.

Byron Janis has the full measure of this music: his shapely lyrical phrasing and natural response to the ebb and flow of the melodic lines is a constant source of pleasure. In the finale there is all the sparkling bravura one could ask for, but the great lyrical tune is made beguilingly poetic. Although the 1960 recording has plenty of ambience, the Minneapolis violins lack the richness of the LSO strings, recorded at Watford in 1961. The simple opening of the *Third Concerto* benefits from the extra warmth, and Janis lets the theme unwind with appealing spontaneity, and in the great closing climax of the finale the passion is built up – not too hurriedly – to the greatest possible tension. Janis makes two cuts (following the composer's own practice), one of about ten bars in the second movement and a rather longer one in the finale. Two favourite *Preludes*, with the *E flat* coming first, most persuasively played, make some compensation.

Ashkenazy's first (1963) recording of the *C minor Concerto* is more successful than his much later, digital account with Haitink, but less compelling than his second version with Previn, which remains uniquely beautiful. But the performance with Kondrashin offers superb Walthamstow sound and, though Kondrashin does not hold the first movement at a consistent level of tension and its climax is almost over-stated in its accented emphasis, the close of the *Andante* is ravishing (if not quite as fine as with Previn) and no one should be disappointed with the passionate climax of the finale. The *Third Concerto* is another matter. Anatole Fistoulari proved a splendid partner, and this reading is the freshest and most spontaneous of his four recordings of this elusive work. Both CD transfers are outstandingly successful and the vintage (again Walthamstow) sound-balance is very satisfying, present, full-bodied and vivid.

Another disc, cashing in on the success of the film *Shine* and tackily entitled 'Rachmaninov goes to the cinema', couples the *D minor* in André Watts's very good account with the New York Philharmonic under Ozawa, made in 1969, with the 1964 Gary Grafman/Bernstein version. They also throw in the *Eighteenth Variation* from the *Paganini variations*, which has frequently been plundered for soundtracks. It is perfectly good value for money, accepting that it is at bargain price, but there are much better things around.

(i) *Piano concerto No. 2;* (ii) *Rhapsody on a theme of Paganini.*

(M) *** Decca 417 702-2 [id.]. Ashkenazy, LSO, Previn.

(BB) *** Naxos Dig. 8.550117; *4550117* [id.]. Jandó, Budapest SO, Lehel.

(B) *** CfP Dig. CD-CFP 9017. Tirimo, Philh. O, Levi.

(M) *** Decca 448 604-2 [id.]. Julius Katchen; (i) LSO, Solti; (ii) LPO, Boult – DOHNANYI: *Variations on a nursery tune.* ***

(M) (***) Dutton mono CDLXT 2504 [id. full price]. Julius Katchen; (i) New SO of L., Fistoulari; (ii) LPO, Boult – DOHNANYI: *Variations on a nursery theme.* (***)

(B) ** [EMI Red Line Dig. CDR5 69829]. Andrei Gavrilov, Phd. O, Muti.

(B) ** EMI Eminence Dig. CD-EMX 9509 [(M) id.]. Philip Fowke, RPO, Yuri Temirkanov.

(i) *Piano concerto No. 2 in C min., Op. 18; Rhapsody on a theme of Paganini, Op. 43;* (ii) *Preludes: Op. 3/2; Op. 23/4; Op. 32/10.*
(B) ** DG Classikon 449 843-2; *449 843-4.* (i) Vásáry, LSO, Ahronovitch; (ii) Lazar Berman.

For those not investing in the Double Decca, which includes all four concertos played by the same artists, Decca's recoupling of Ashkenazy's earlier recordings with Previn is a very desirable CD indeed. At mid-price it makes a first choice. In the *Concerto*, the gentle, introspective mood of the *Adagio* is among the most beautiful on record. The finale is broad and spacious rather than electrically exciting, but the scintillating, unforced bravura provides all the sparkle necessary. The *Rhapsody* too is outstandingly successful. The Kingsway Hall sound is rich and full-bodied in the best analogue sense. Detail is somewhat sharper in the *Rhapsody*; in the *Concerto*, however, atmosphere rather than clarity is the predominating factor.

Katchen re-recorded the *C minor Concerto* with Solti in stereo in 1958, seven years after his mono recording with Fistoulari, and the *Paganini variations* with Boult the following year. Even today the Kingsway Hall stereo is impressively rich and full, especially in the famous *Eighteenth Variation*. If there remains something very special about Katchen's earlier mono versions (see below), most listeners will revel in the vintage sound of this remake, fully worthy of reissue in Decca's Classic Sound series. Katchen's performances of both works offer drama and excitement in plenty – the outer movements of the *Concerto* reach the highest peak of excitement, with bravura very much to the fore. Solti makes a splendid partner here; Boult sees that the *Rhapsody* is superbly shaped and has diversity and wit as well as romantic flair. With three works offered, this reissue can be recommended very highly.

Jenö Jandó's performances of both works are strongly recommendable. Jandó has the full measure of the ebb and flow of the Rachmaninovian phraseology, and the slow movement is romantically expansive, the reprise particularly beautiful, while the finale has plenty of dash and ripe, lyrical feeling. The *Rhapsody* is played brilliantly, as fine as any performance in the catalogue. The digital recording is satisfyingly balanced, with a bold piano image and a full, resonant orchestral tapestry.

Concentrated and thoughtful, deeply expressive yet never self-indulgent, Tirimo is outstanding in both the *Concerto* and the *Rhapsody*, making this another of the most desirable bargain versions of this favourite coupling, irrespective of price. Speeds for the outer movements of the *Concerto* are on the fast side, yet Tirimo's feeling for natural rubato makes them sound natural, never breathless, while the sweetness and repose of the middle movement are exemplary. The digital recording is full, clear and well balanced.

This vivid Dutton transfer helps to explain why Julius Katchen's coupling of the Rachmaninov and Dohnányi *Variations* was a classic of the mono LP catalogue, surviving well into the stereo era. The very opening (both musically and sonically) is enormously commanding: Katchen and Boult together capture a sense of new discovery that keeps one riveted from one variation to the next, each one sharply characterized. Katchen's muscular purposefulness in Rachmaninov's virtuoso variations gives way to a most poetic account of the great eighteenth variation, with the entry of the melody magically prepared in the subdued seventeenth. Katchen's rubato is extreme but tenderly spontaneous-sounding. The piano sound is full and firm with fine presence, yet (as in so many early Decca transfers) there is a degree of thinness on exposed high violins, and that shortcoming is more noticeable in the transfer of the *Concerto*, a recording dating from three years earlier, in 1951, with shallower piano tone but with compensating warmth of atmosphere. Katchen's is again a fine reading and, if it is not quite as magnetic or individual as that of the *Rhapsody*, for IM (who wrote the notes accompanying the CD, but not the preceding comments) it was the performance from which he came to discover and love the work, and it remains special, most notably for the fine contribution of the conductor, Anatole Fistoulari.

The partnership of the impetuous Ahronovitch and the more introvert pianist works well enough in the *Concerto*. The first movement has a fine climax, but after that the tension is lower and the languorous *Adagio* does not distil the degree of poetry achieved elsewhere. The conductor's chimerical style is better suited to the *Rhapsody*, with its opening faster than usual and with strong contrasts of tempo and mood between brilliant and lyrical variations. The sound of the recordings is very good. The *Preludes* provide a useful bonus, but this reissue is hardly a front runner.

Gavrilov's playing here is distinguished by flamboyant virtuosity and a self-regarding brilliance that are not wholly pleasing. In both performances there is finely shaped and responsive orchestral support, but neither in the concerto nor in the *Rhapsody on a theme of Paganini* does the pianist bring the aristocratic distinction or naturalness of utterance that he commanded in his earlier recordings.

Philip Fowke gives tasteful, well-mannered performances, ultimately lacking the fire and bravura needed in both these display works. The modern, digital recording can hardly be faulted, but there are far preferable CDs of this coupling.

(i) *Piano concerto No. 2; Rhapsody on a theme of Paganini;* (ii) *Symphony No. 2 in E min., Op. 27.*
(BB) *(*) Carlton LSO Double Dig. 30368 01117 (2) [(B) id.]. LSO, with (i) David Golub, cond. Wyn Morris; (ii) cond. Rozhdestvensky.

This is an unfortunate example of mismatching of performances for a double-CD reissue. David Golub is a brilliant pianist and is thoroughly in sympathy with Rachmaninov, but Wyn Morris provides sometimes listless accompaniments, and occasionally in the *Paganini variations* he almost gets left behind by his soloist. The recording is very good, but these concertante works are not recommendable. Rozhdestvensky's performance is another matter; he gives a very Tchaikovskian reading of Rachmaninov's *E minor Symphony*. There is plenty of vitality but, with the big string melodies blossoming voluptuously, the slow movement, after a beguiling opening clarinet solo, has a climax of spacious intensity, its power almost overwhelming. The finale is flamboyantly broadened at the end, and the feeling of apotheosis is very much in the Tchaikovsky mould. With the LSO responding superbly, this is a most satisfying account, and the richness, brilliance and weight of the recording add to the compulsion of the music-making. We hope that Carlton will later decide to reissue this recording on a separate CD.

(i) *Piano concerto No. 2 in C min.; Rhapsody on a theme of Paganini, Op. 43;* (ii) *Vocalise.*
(M) *** [RCA Basic 100 09026 61851-2; *09026 61851-4*]. (i) Rubinstein, Chicago SO, Reiner; (ii) Anna Moffo, American SO, Stokowski.

As far as we can trace, Rubinstein's coupling from the 1950s has never been issued in the UK; it is still not available here, although his superb account of the *Paganini Rhapsody* is offered, coupled with Chopin and Falla, and is discussed below. Rubinstein was in his seventies when he recorded both works and he could still show the muscular virtuosi a thing or two. Unlike Katchen, he refuses to take the first and last movements of the concerto any faster than he wants. He shows that a more measured speed can be just as exciting and in the long run gives a warmer, more sympathetic result. Rubinstein has the uncanny knack in almost any recording of creating the tension of a live performance, and here the result is most compelling in both works. The Chicago acoustics add much to the attractions of this disc, which has a highly seductive encore, the *Vocalise*, sung as a wordless melisma by Anna Moffo, warmly accompanied by Stokowski.

(i) *Piano concertos Nos. 2–3; Rhapsody on a theme of Paganini. Preludes: in C sharp min., Op. 3/2; in B flat & G min., Op. 23/2 & 5; in B min. & D flat, Op. 32/10 & 13; Etudes-tableaux, Op. 39/1, 2 & 5.*
(B) *** Double Decca 436 386-2 (2) [id.]. Ashkenazy, (i) LSO, Previn.

This pair of Decca CDs – offered for the cost of a single premium-price disc – includes outstanding performances of Rachmaninov's three greatest concertante works for piano and orchestra, plus five favourite *Preludes* and three of the Op. 39 *Etudes-tableaux*. The digital remastering offers first-class transfers, full and well-balanced, with the Kingsway Hall ambience casting a pleasing glow over the proceedings. This is very highly recommendable, including as it does Ashkenazy's outstanding version of the *C minor Piano concerto*, where the slow movement is memorably beautiful.

Piano concerto No. 3 in D min., Op. 30.
(B) *(*) [EMI Red Line Dig. CDR5 72101]. Tzimon Barto, LPO, Eschenbach – BARTOK: *Piano concerto No. 2.* **(*)

Barto has all the technique neccessary for this remarkable romantic concerto, and he plays the longer, more challenging cadenza. Although Eschenbach follows him capably, and there are some moments of high tension, Barto's approach to the music's emotional ebb and flow is too idiosyncratic and self-aware to carry complete conviction, and even the work's close is unconvincing.

Piano concertos Nos. 3 in D min, Op. 30; 4 in G min., Op. 40.
(M) **(*) Van. Classics Dig. 99091. Nikolai Lugansky, Russian State Ac. SO, Ivan Shpiller.

It is odd to look back at the 5th edition of *Grove's Dictionary of Music and Musicians* to see in what low esteem Rachmaninov was held in the 1950s. Eric Blom, no less, wrote of his 'artificial and gushing tunes' and more or less wrote off the *Fourth Concerto* altogether, 'as a failure from the start'. Nikolai Lugansky is a young Russian pianist of quality, born in 1972 (which makes him a year or so younger than Evgeni Kissin and Leif Ove Andsnes). These performances do not have the slightest trace of ostentation. He produces a wonderful sound, allows phrases to breathe naturally and the music to unfold freely. In short he is content to serve Rachmaninov rather than his own ego. He plays the cadenza that Rachmaninov himself recorded rather than the overblown alternative favoured by the majority of pianists these days, and in the *Fourth Concerto* his playing is wonderfully fluid. There is ample virtuosity, but it takes second place to poetic fantasy. To put it in a nutshell, Lugansky is a real artist whose thoughts about the music carry more weight for this listener than many barnstorming virtuosi. There are drawbacks, however, for the orchestral playing is not of comparable distinction. The strings of the Russian Academic Symphony Orchestra do not produce as sumptuous or opulent a tone as they did in the days of Svetlanov, and the horn vibrato may worry some collectors; moreover the recording is not in the very first flight, though it is far from inadequate. Both these shortcomings should produce a two-star rating, but the artistic merits of Lugansky's unfailingly musical and aristocratic playing just carry it across into a three-star bracket.

The Isle of the dead, Op. 29.
(M) *** RCA 09026 61250-2. Chicago SO, Reiner – Concert: *'The Reiner sound'*. ***
(M) *** DG Dig. 445 558-2. BPO, Maazel – RIMSKY-KORSAKOV: *Scheherazade*. **

Reiner builds the arch-like span of the music to an impassioned climax and manages the return to the sombre opening mood with equal distinction. The recording, made in 1957, is fairly closely balanced and, although the Chicago ambience remains, the upper strings lose some of their tonal weight at the climax and the range of dynamic is slightly reduced. Nevertheless this shows Reiner at his finest and there are other good things in this compilation.

At a fast speed Maazel's powerful reading of *The Isle of the dead* is less sombre and brooding than usual; but the climaxes have real fervour, and the result is intensely compelling. The 1981 recording is strikingly vivid and full, and it is a pity that the Rimsky-Korsakov coupling is far less recommendable.

The Isle of the dead, Op. 29; Symphonic dances, Op. 45.
(M) *** Decca Dig. 430 733-2. Concg. O, Ashkenazy.
(BB) **(*) Naxos Dig. 8.550583 [id.]. RPO, Enrique Bátiz.

Ashkenazy's is a superb coupling, rich and powerful in playing and interpretation, *The Isle of the dead* relentless in its ominous build-up, while the *Symphonic dances* have extra darkness and intensity too. The splendid digital recording highlights both the passion and the fine precision of the playing.

Bátiz gives the *Symphonic dances* an attractively spontaneous performance, full of lyrical intensity, with some splendid playing from the RPO strings. The vivid recording helps give the feeling that Bátiz almost goes over the top in his extremely passionate climax for *The Isle of the dead*. The performance certainly emanates darker feelings, and at super-bargain price this remains well worth considering.

Rhapsody on a theme of Paganini, Op. 43.
(M) *** RCA 09026 68886-2 [id.]. Rubinstein, Chicago SO, Reiner – CHOPIN: *Andante spianato & Grande Polonaise;* FALLA: *Nights in the gardens of Spain*. ***

Rubinstein's early stereo (1956) account of Rachmaninov's romantic showpiece is new to the British catalogue. There is no finer version. Rubinstein's playing is dazzling and it continually delights with its poetic sensibility and flair. Reiner is with him in every bar, orchestral detail persuasively delineated, and the warm Chicago acoustic ensures a glorious blossoming of string-tone at the *Eighteenth*. Both pianist and conductor relish the *Dies irae* each time it appears, and the closing pages reach a high pitch of excitement. The recording, with the piano forward but not unattractively so, sounds little short of ideal in Richard Mohr's splendid new remastering.

(i) *Rhapsody on a theme of Paganini, Op. 43. Etudes-tableaux, Opp. 33 & 39; Piano sonata No. 2, Op. 36; Moment musical, Op. 16/3; Preludes: Op. 3/2; Op. 23/1, 2 & 4; Op. 32/12; Variations on a theme of Corelli, Op. 42.*
(B) *** EMI Rouge et Noir CZS5 69677-2 (2) [CDZB 69677]. Collard; (i) Capitole Toulouse O, Plasson.

These are impressive and competitive performances, recorded in the 1970s when this artist was beginning to make a name for himself. In the *Rhapsody on a theme of Paganini* he can hold his own with the finest, though he is not as well recorded as Ashkenazy. His account of the *Variations on a theme of Corelli* is exemplary and the *Second Sonata* is no less powerful. Collard plays the 1913 version but, like Horowitz, incorporates elements of the revision. Nowadays we tend to think of Collard primarily as an interpreter of French music, and this compilation serves as a salutary reminder of his credentials as a virtuoso of the old school; moreover the set is priced very competitively.

Symphonic dances, Op. 45; (i) *The Bells, Op. 35.*
(M) **(*) BMG/Melodiya 74321 32046-2 [id.]. (i) Shumskaya, Dovenman, Bolshakov, Russian State Chamber Ch. Moscow PO, Kyrill Kondrashin.

Kondrashin's classic 1969 performance with the Moscow Philharmonic returns in a less than distinguished transfer. One wonders whether the impression, that our LPs sounded better, is deceptive – until you hear them side by side. All the same, this is an electrifying performance and, like *The Bells*, which comes from 1966, shines through all sonic limitations.

Symphonic dances, Op. 45; (i) *Vocalise, Op. 34/14.*
(M) *** Sony SMK 57660 [id.]. Novosibirsk PO, Arnold Kaz; (i) with Nelly Lee – STRAVINSKY: *Jeu de cartes.* **(*)

Arnold Kaz is not a household name and Novosibirsk is not on the common tourist trail, but there is nothing offbeat about this performance. Indeed the *Symphonic dances* get a more than respectable performance; the playing of the Novosibirsk Philharmonic is warm and musical, and Arnold Kaz draws imaginative and sensitive phrasing from his players. A far more enjoyable performance than many from better-known orchestras and glossier maestros – and very well recorded. Without disrespect to Nelly Lee, who trained (and now teaches) at St Petersburg, it would have been better to have had the purely instrumental version of *Vocalise.*

SYMPHONIES

Symphonies Nos. 1–3.
(B) *** Decca Double Dig. 448 116-2 (2) [id.]. Concg. O, Ashkenazy.

Symphonies Nos. 1–3; The Isle of the dead, Op. 29; Symphonic dances, Op. 45; Vocalise, Op. 34/14; Aleko: Intermezzo & Women's dance.
(M) *** EMI CMS7 64530-2 (3) [ZDMC 64530]. LSO, André Previn.

Symphonies Nos. 1–3; The Isle of the dead, Op. 29; Symphonic dances; (i) *The Bells, Op. 35.*
(B) *** Decca 455 798-2 (3) [id.]. Concg. O, Ashkenazy; (i) with Natalia Troitskaya, Ryszard Karczykowski & Concg. Ch.

Symphonies Nos. 1–3; The Rock, Op. 7.
(M) **(*) DG (IMS) Dig. 445 590-2 (2). BPO, Maazel.

Symphonies Nos 1–3; Vocalise, Op. 34/14.
✿ (B) *** Sony SB2K 63257 (2) [full price – id.]. Phd. O, Ormandy.
(B) ** BMG/Melodiya Twofer 74321 40064-2 (2) [id.]. USSR SO (No. 1); Bolshoi Theatre O (No. 2); USSR R. & TV Large SO (No. 3); Svetlanov.

Ormandy pioneered the recording of the three Rachmaninov symphonies in stereo, and in many ways his performances remain unsurpassed. Certainly they have never sounded as good as they do in these splendid new transfers. The *Second Symphony* came first in 1959 and has perhaps the most naturally balanced sound. The performance has great intensity of feeling and the passion of the string-playing in the work's closing pages is quite overwhelming. Even if there are minor cuts, other early stereo versions by Boult and Kletzki pale into insignificance alongside this remarkable account. The *First Symphony* had to wait until 1966 and yet was still the work's first stereo version, an exceptionally strong performance of a work that is notoriously difficult to hold together. Ormandy's thrustful view of the outer movements is supported by superbly committed Philadelphia playing, with the orchestra on top form. The conductor's own commitment is obvious in every bar. The balance has woodwind solos spotlighted, but the spacious acoustic of Philadelphia Town Hall provides the necessary ambient warmth. In some ways the *Third Symphony* is even more distinguished and now that the artificial brilliance of the old LP has been tamed one can at last appreciate the body of tone this great orchestra could command in its heyday. The performance has memorable dedication and fervour, and the orchestral response achieves an irresistible balance between subtlety of detail, tenderness and romantic passion. The playing itself is marvellous, and this warmth of feeling carries over into the touchingly shaped *Vocalise* which acts as a final encore. A bargain set not to be missed, even if you have more modern versions of these splendid works.

The Ashkenazy digital set of the three symphonies, made between 1980 and 1982, now comes either as a Double Decca or in a bargain box of three discs, one symphony to each CD and coupled respectively with *The Isle of the dead*, *Symphonic dances* and the dramatic cantata, *The Bells*, which is outstanding in every way. The two orchestral works are equally rich and powerful in playing and interpretation, *The Isle of the dead* relentless in its ominous build-up, while the *Symphonic dances* have extra darkness and intensity too. The performances of the symphonies, passionate and volatile, are intensely Russian; the only possible reservation concerns the slow movement of the *Second*, where the clarinet solo is less ripe than in some versions. Elsewhere there is drama, energy and drive, balanced by much delicacy of feeling, while the Concertgebouw strings produce great ardour for Rachmaninov's long-breathed melodies. The vivid Decca sound within the glowing Concertgebouw ambience is ideal for the music.

While Ashkenazy's digital Double Decca set of the three Rachmaninov symphonies with the Concertgebouw Orchestra will probably remain first choice for many collectors, Previn's LSO set at mid-price offers some alternative couplings. His 1973 account of the *Second Symphony* – a passionately committed performance, with a glorious response from the LSO strings – has been remastered for CD a second time, with improvement in the body of the string timbre. This remains a classic account, unlikely to be surpassed. No. 1 is a forthright, clean-cut performance, beautifully played and very well recorded. It may lack some of the vitality that one recognizes in Russian performances (Ashkenazy is more volatile and remains first choice in this work) but is still very enjoyable. Previn's account of the *Third*, however, is outstanding and the LSO's playing again has enormous bravura and ardour. This, like *The Isle of the dead* and *Symphonic dances*, has been remastered very successfully and the performances of the two shorter works have plenty of atmosphere and grip. With the *Aleko* excerpts and the *Vocalise* also included, this EMI box remains very competitive.

Maazel's set is also very impressive and offers superb playing from the Berlin Philharmonic. However, the DG engineers secured a less sumptuous sound in the Berlin Philharmonie than their Decca colleagues, and this emphasizes Maazel's fiercer way with Rachmaninov's passionate impulse. The climaxes of the *Second Symphony* in particular would have been enhanced by a warmer middle and lower range. Maazel's readings are not to be dismissed: the *First Symphony* is particularly fine, with Rachmaninov's often thick orchestration beautifully transparent. The *Third* too is distinctive, unusually fierce and intense. The result is sharper and tougher than one expects, less obviously romantic, and the finale is made to sound rather like a Walton comedy overture at the start, brilliant and exciting; but at the end it lacks joyful exuberance. Exhilaration is the keynote throughout and there is an abundance of adrenalin, yet the lack of expansive romantic warmth is undoubtedly a drawback. Moreover (although it also includes *The Rock*) this is at mid-price, while the Ashkenazy recordings are on a Double Decca – two discs for the cost of one premium-priced CD.

Though recorded in the 1960s, Svetlanov's readings of the Rachmaninov symphonies, at one time available from EMI on LP, come in full-bodied, atmospheric sound. This version of No. 1 stands among the very finest ever, warm and concentrated and full of panache, not least in the celebrated theme at the start of the finale. No. 3 is first rate too, persuasively done with resonant strings. In No. 2 Svetlanov is rather heavier-handed, and he is not helped by an acid clarinet in the slow movement. Though the finale is exhilarating, it brings the fatal snag that the recapitulation is drastically cut. Otherwise this economically priced reissue would be very competitive.

Symphony No. 1 in D min.; The Rock (fantasy), *Op. 7; Vocalise, Op. 34/14; Aleko: Intermezzo.*
(B) *** DG Classikon Dig. 449 854-2 [(M) id. import]. BPO, Maazel.

Maazel's is a superb performance, beautifully transparent and consistently clarifying detail. He may lack something in Slavonic passion but, with generous fill-ups, the positive strength of the reading stands well against any rival. The 1984 recording is drier than Ashkenazy's Decca.

Symphony No. 2 in E min., Op. 27.
✿ (M) (***) DG mono 449 767-2 [id.]. Leningrad PO, Kurt Sanderling.
(BB) *** ASV CDQS 6107 [(M) id.]. Philh. O, Ling Tung.
(M) **(*) Chandos Dig. CHAN 6606 [id.]. SNO, Sir Alexander Gibson.
(B) ** EMI forte CZS5 69776-2 (2) [CDFB 69776]. RPO, Temirkanov – TCHAIKOVSKY: *Manfred* etc. **
(M) ** Mercury 434 368-2 [id.]. Detroit SO, Paray – FRANCK: *Symphony*. **
(B) ** [EMI Red Line Dig. CDR5 69828]. LAPO, Rattle.

Symphony No. 2 in E min.; The Rock, Op. 7.
(BB) **(*) Naxos Dig. 8.550272 [id.]. Slovak RSO (Bratislava), Stephen Gunzenhauser.
(M) ** Sony SMK 57650 [id.]. St Petersburg Philharmonic Ac. SO, Dmitriev.

Sanderling's famous mono recording dates from 1956, but one would never guess, so voluptuously full is the sound of this current DG re-transfer and so remarkably refined the detail. Here is a great Russian orchestra at their very peak, obviously inspired by their conductor, Kurt Sanderling, and carried away on a tide of passion, underpinned by the very Russian melancholy of the slow movement, and especially at its close. (There is a haunting clarinet solo and some lovely oboe playing too.) The string playing throughout is glorious, reaching its apotheosis in the great climaxes of the finale, where Rachmaninov bares his very soul in a flood of yearning romantic feeling. From the first note to the last this is the kind of live performance one would only dream of experiencing – yet amazingly it was made in the studio. Of other recorded versions only Ormandy's (see above) reaches this intensity of feeling, and even he cannot quite match the Russian fervour of the Leningrad violins as they are caught up in that tremendous final climax. A great performance and, astonishingly, the mono sound is fully worthy of it.

Ling Tung's reading is refined but he knows just how to mould the sweeping lines necessary to bring out the rapture inherent in this lovely symphony, notably at the climax of the slow movement and at the very satisfying close. This is a case where the CD transfer brings a striking improvement in the vividness of a 1978 recording which is backwardly balanced. One needs to play back at a fairly high level, then the Philharmonia strings emerge with a warmly natural, radiant sheen of tone. At super-bargain price this is well worth considering.

Gibson and the Scottish National Orchestra have the advantage of an excellent digital recording, made in the Henry Wood Hall in Glasgow. The brass sounds are thrilling, but the slightly recessed balance of the strings is a drawback and there is not the body of tone demonstrated by the best version recommended above. But this is a freshly spontaneous performance and overall the sound is admirably natural, even if it includes some strangely unrhythmic thuds at climaxes (apparently the conductor in his excitement stamping on the podium).

Gunzenhauser directs the Slovak Radio Symphony Orchestra – on this showing not quite so refined a band as the Slovak Philharmonic, also from Bratislava – in a warmly expressive reading of the Rachmaninov *Second*, with rubato consistently persuasive and idiomatic-sounding. The playing at times lacks bite, and the great clarinet solo in the slow movement is balanced too far back, but the red-bloodedness of Rachmaninov's inspiration is never in doubt. The slow movement brings sumptuous climaxes, and the finale is given attractively bouncy treatment at a more measured speed than usual. Highly recommendable at super-bargain price, with very good sound.

Alexander Dmitriev's players have the cumbersome name of the St Petersburg Philharmonic Academic Symphony Orchestra (though it used to be known as the Leningrad Radio or the Leningrad Symphony) and they produce excellent results. Dmitriev does not wear his heart on his sleeve; he is concerned about the overall shape of a paragraph rather than dwelling on individual beauty of incident. The rather recessed sound diminishes the appeal of the disc, but it still has much to recommend it.

Temirkanov regularly adopts a free rubato style which in the outer movements gives his reading an attractive expressive warmth. He carries that style a fraction too far in the big melody of the Scherzo's first episode, making the result soupy; but by contrast the slow movement – at a relatively fast tempo which tends to get faster – runs the risk of sounding perfunctory. The 1977 Kingsway Hall recording is splendidly rich and full, and the playing generally brilliant, though the ensemble cannot match that of Previn and the LSO on the same label.

Paul Paray's Rachmaninov *Second* was one of the first in stereo (1957). The performance is a vivid one, the Detroit orchestra play very well for him, and there is no lack of passion; yet something is missing. The conductor does not always display a natural feeling for Rachmaninov's yearning, winding string cantilena. Sometimes he seems to break the long melodic line into little phrases in order to increase the intensity, but with the opposite effect. This is enjoyable, but it is not among the finest early versions.

Rattle's first recording with the Los Angeles Philharmonic proved to be a disappointment. The problems of recording in the orchestra's home, the Chandler Pavilion, have brought sound that is clear but lacks body in the string section, with violins made to sound emaciated. Rattle's performance also lacks urgency, with spacious speeds often lacking the necessary tension, particularly in the finale which is unexciting compared with the finest rivals.

Symphony No. 3 in A min., Op. 44; Isle of the dead, Op. 29; Vocalise, Op. 34/14.
❀ (M) (***) RCA mono 09026 62532-2 [id.]. Phd. O, Sergei Rachmaninov.

RCA deserve congratulations for making these wonderful recordings available on a separate CD, an immense boon for those who cannot afford the ten-CD Complete Rachmaninov Edition. Rachmaninov's own recording of the *Third Symphony*, *Isle of the dead* and *Vocalise*, made in 1939 and 1929 respectively, are an indispensable part of any serious collector's library. They also sound magnificent – and not simply for their age. Only one conductor has ever matched these: Koussevitzky, whose Boston performances from the 1940s (never issued commercially and not currently available) are electrifying. The rest (even by such idiomatic interpreters as Ashkenazy and Previn) pale by comparison.

Symphony No. 3 in A min., Op. 44; Mélodie in E, Op. 3/3; Polichinelle, Op. 3/4.
(BB) ** Naxos Dig. 8.550808 [id.]. Nat. SO of Ireland, Alexander Anissimov.

The Russian conductor, Alexander Anissimov, conducts the Irish orchestra in a spacious, warmly expressive reading of the *Symphony No. 3*, offering in addition (as a none-too-generous coupling) orchestral versions – arranger unidentified – of two early piano works. In the symphony, speeds are on the slow side and the manner is relaxed, which means that, for all the refinement of the playing, until the finale the result lacks a little in tension and bite compared with the finest versions. The finale, bright and alert, then rounds the performance off with splendid flair, helped by very vivid recorded sound. A fair recommendation at super-budget price.

Symphony No. 3 in A min., Op. 44; Vocalise, Op. 34/14.
(M) *** EMI CDM5 66759-2. Nat. PO, Stokowski.

It was Stokowski who in 1936 in Philadelphia conducted the first performances of Rachmaninov's last symphony. Nearly 40 years later he re-recorded it with Sydney Sax's fine group of selected orchestral players, and the result is rewarding and exciting. There are idiosyncrasies aplenty, not least a tempo for the finale that whirls one along in exhilarating danger; but this is a splendid example of Stokowski's energy in old age, his ability to inspire players to a totally individual and riveting performance, full of romantic warmth and fervour, not directly comparable with others. The recording, made at West Ham Central Mission, has a wide dynamic range and good definition and it produces the richest patina of string-tone.

PIANO MUSIC

Piano duet

Suites Nos. 1–2, Opp. 5 & 17; 6 Duets, Op. 11; Symphonic dances, Op. 45.
(BB) **(*) Arte Nova Dig. 74321 51638-2 (2) [id.]. Irina Tchernoussova, Elisabeth Romanovskaya. – STRAVINSKY: *Rite of spring.***(*)

These two Russian pianists make a splendid duo, crisp and incisive, giving fresh and clear performances not only of Rachmaninov's two delightful *Suites* (the first of them here listed under its alternative title, *Fantaisie tableau*), but also of Rachmaninov's own two-piano version of his last major work, the *Symphonic dances*. Though this duo cannot quite match the inspired performances by Vladimir Ashkenazy and André Previn on a Decca Double issue either in rhythmic imagination or mystery, these are fresh and agile performances, consistently well pointed and with brisk speeds never sounding breathless. The clear, well-balanced sound helps, and it is good also to have the six little piano duets as supplement as well as Stravinsky's piano-duet version of the *Rite of spring*.

(i) *Suites Nos. 1–2, Opp. 5 & 17; Symphonic dances, Op. 45; Russian rhapsody;* (Solo piano) *Etudes-tableaux, Op. 33; Variations on a theme by Corelli, Op. 42.*
(B) *** Decca Double 444 845-2 (2) [id.]. Vladimir Ashkenazy, (i) with André Previn.

The colour and flair of Rachmaninov's writing in the two *Suites* (as inspired and tuneful as his concertos) are captured with wonderful imagination – reflective of a live performance by Ashkenazy and Previn in the summer of 1974. The two-piano version of the *Symphonic dances* was written not as an arrangement of the orchestral score but as a preparation for it. The ingenuity of Rachmaninov's handling of a difficult medium produced a work which in pianistic detail as well as sharpness of argument is masterly. Ashkenazy and Previn are challenged to a dazzling performance, and they are hardly less persuasive in the coupled *Russian rhapsody*, an early piece, musically rather naïve but well worth hearing in a performance as fine as this. Ashkenazy's superb solo performances of the *Etudes-tableaux* and the *Corelli variations* (a rarity and a very fine work) cap the appeal of this bargain Double. The recording throughout is superb, with a natural presence and a most attractive ambience.

Solo piano music

Barcarolle in G min., Op. 10/3; Etudes-tableaux, Op. 39/4 & 6; Humoresque in G, Op. 10/5; Lilacs, Op. 21/5; 5 Morceaux de fantaisie, Op. 3: (Elégie in E flat min.; Prelude in C sharp min.; Mélodie in E; Polichinelle in F sharp min.; Sérénade in B flat min.); Polka de W. R.; Prelude in G min., Op. 23/5. Transcriptions: MUSSORGSKY: *Hopak.* SCHUBERT: *Wohin?.* RIMSKY-KORSAKOV: *Flight of the bumble-bee.* KREISLER: *Liebeslied; Liebesfreud. The Star-spangled banner.*
(M) *** Decca 425 964-2 [id.]. Sergei Rachmaninov (Ampico Roll recordings, 1919–29).

Daisies, Op. 38/3; Etudes-tableaux, Op. 33/2 & 7; Op. 39/6; Humoresque, Op. 10/5; Lilacs, Op. 21/5; Mélodie, Op. 3/5; Moment musical, Op. 16/2; Oriental sketch; Polka de W. R.; Preludes: in C sharp min., Op. 3/2; in G flat, Op. 23/10; in E, F min. & F, Op. 32/3, 6 & 7; Serenade, Op. 3/5. Transcriptions: BACH: *Violin partita No. 2: Prelude; Gavotte; Rondo; Gigue.* MENDELSSOHN: *Midsummer Night's Dream: Scherzo.* KREISLER: *Liebesfreud.* SCHUBERT: *Wohin?.* MUSSORGSKY: *Gopak.* TCHAIKOVSKY: *Lullaby, Op. 16/11.* RIMSKY-KORSAKOV: *The Flight of the bumble-bee.*
(M) (***) RCA mono GD 87766 [7766-2-RG]. Sergei Rachmaninov.

These two records make a fascinating comparison. The RCA collection includes virtually all Rachmaninov's solo electric 78-r.p.m. recordings, made between 1925 and 1942, with most dating from 1940. The second offers the composer's Ampico piano-roll recordings, made during a shorter time-span, between 1919 and 1929, when Rachmaninov was at his technical peak. The Ampico recordings were reproduced on a specially adapted Estonia concert grand in the Kingsway Hall and recorded in stereo in 1978/9. On CD the sound is outstandingly real and the impression on the listener is quite uncanny when the recital opens with the *Elégie in E flat minor*, which was put on roll in October 1928 yet has all the spontaneity and presence of live music-making. A number of items are common to both discs, so it is possible to make direct comparisons. The Ampico system at that time could accurately reflect what was played, including note duration and pedalling, but the *strength* at which the notes were struck had to be edited on to the roll afterwards by a skilled musician/technician. It can only be said that listening to these Ampico recordings never brings a feeling of any mechanical tone graduation, and in pieces like the *Humoresque in G major* or the *Polka de W. R.* not only does Rachmaninov's scintillating bravura sound absolutely natural, but also his chimerical use of rubato is more convincing on the earlier recordings. *The Flight of the bumble-bee*, a *tour de force* of exuberant articulation, brings only one second's difference in playing time between the two versions.

Etudes-tableaux, Opp. 33 & 39 (complete).
(BB) *(*) Naxos Dig. 8.550347 [id.]. Idil Biret.

On the face of it, Idil Biret's disc of both the Opp. 33 and 39 sets of the *Etudes-tableaux* represents good value for money; after all, it costs less than half as much as Vladimir Ovchinnikov's full-price EMI set. However, it would represent a false economy: the Naxos piano recordings, made in this venue, do not constitute a real challenge to existing recommendations.

Etudes-tableaux, Opp. 33 & 39; Fragments; Fughetta in F; Mélodie in E; Moments musicaux; Morceaux de fantaisie; Morceaux de salon; 3 Nocturnes; Oriental sketch; 4 Pieces; Piece in D min.; 25 Preludes (complete); *Sonatas 1–3* (including original & revised versions of *No. 2*); *Song without words; Transcriptions* (complete); *Variations: on a theme of Chopin ; on a theme of Corelli*.
(M) *** Hyperion Dig. CDS 44041/8 (8). Howard Shelley.

Hyperion have collected Howard Shelley's exemplary survey of Rachmaninov into a mid-price, eight-CD set, and very good it is, too. Shelley can hold his own against most rivals not only in terms of poetic feeling (as you would expect from a distant descendant of the great poet) but in keyboard authority and virtuosity. The recordings are variable in quality but are mostly excellent.

Elégie, Op. 3/1; Etudes-tableaux, Op. 39/3 & 5; Moments musicaux, Op. 16/3–6; Preludes, Op. 23/1, 2, 5 & 6; Op. 32/12.
(B) *** EMI CD-EMX 2237 [EMI Red Line CDR5 69869 (with RAVEL: *Gaspard de la nuit*)]. Andrei Gavrilov – SCRIABIN: *Preludes.* ***

There is some pretty remarkable playing here, especially in the stormy *B flat major Prelude*, while the *G sharp minor* from Op. 32 has a proper sense of fantasy. More prodigious bravura provides real excitement in the *F sharp minor Etude-tableau*, Op. 39/3, and in the *E minor Moment musical*, while Gavrilov relaxes winningly in the *Andante cantabile* of Op. 16/3 and the *Elégie*. Sometimes his impetuosity almost carries him away, and the piano is placed rather near the listener so that we are nearly taken with him, but there is no doubt about the quality of this recital.

24 Preludes (complete).
(B) ** Carlton IMP Dig. PCD 2052 [id.]. Peter Katin.

24 Preludes (complete); *3 Nocturnes; Polka de WR.*
(B) **(*) EMI forte CZS5 69527-2 (2) [CDFB 68664]. Agustin Anievas – CHOPIN: *Sonata No. 3* **; LISZT: *Sonata.* ***

24 Preludes (complete); Piano sonata No. 2 in B flat min., Op. 36.
(BB) *** Decca Double 443 841-2 (2) [id.]. Vladimir Ashkenazy.

There is superb flair and panache about Ashkenazy's playing. Perhaps the stormy *B flat major Prelude*, Op. 23/2, is even more hair-raising in Sviatoslav Richter's hands but, as the *G minor Prelude* demonstrates, Ashkenazy's poetic feeling is second to none. At Double Decca price this sweeps the board. As a bonus, the compact discs offer the *Second Piano sonata*, with Ashkenazy generally following the 1913 original score but with some variants. He plays with great virtuosity and feeling, and the result is a *tour de force*.

Anievas recorded the Rachmaninov *Preludes* in the early 1970s, but they were soon withdrawn and, later, Ashkenazy's set dominated the catalogue. Anievas certainly has the measure of all this music, although in the lyrical *Preludes* he returns to the coaxing style of the *Nocturnes* and, though he is gently persuasive and undoubtedly poetic, the effect is Chopinesque. His bravura is never barnstorming (Richter creates an altogether more hair-raising effect in the *B flat Prelude*, Op. 23/2) but Anievas finds plenty of colour and much variety of character in these so varied pieces, and he is well recorded.

Peter Katin's performances are neatly fitted on to a single CD, just seconds short of 80 minutes. The recording was made in 1972 but the bold, clear image itself lends a certain romantic splendour to these performances. Katin has the measure of lyrical music, and it is only in the pieces which make their full effect by sheer bravura that he is at times less than completely convincing.

10 Preludes, Op. 23; 5 Morceaux de fantaisie, Op. 3.
(BB) (**) Naxos Dig. 8.550348 [id.]. Idil Biret.

No major quarrels with Idil Biret here. She sounds at home in this repertoire – but, as with so many of the piano records she has made for Naxos in the Heidelberg studios, the quality of the sound is in every respect unsatisfactory.

13 Preludes, Op. 32; arr. of KREISLER: *Liebesleid; Liebesfreud.*
(BB) (**) Naxos Dig. 8.550466 [id.]. Idil Biret.

It is impossible to recommend Idil Biret's account of the Op. 32 set of *Preludes*. Her playing sounds thoroughly idiomatic, but the claustrophobic, clatttery sound is distinctly unpleasant.

Piano transcriptions: J. S. BACH: *Partita in E min., for unaccompanied violin* (*Preludio; Gavotte; Gigue*). BIZET: *Minuet from l'Arlésienne.* KREISLER: *Liebesleid; Liebesfreud.* MENDELSSOHN: *Midsummer Night's Dream: Scherzo.* MUSSORGSKY: *Sorochinsky Fair: Gopak.* RACHMANINOV: *Lilacs, Op. 21/5; Daisies, Op. 38/3.* RIMSKY-KORSAKOV: *Flight of the bumble-bee.* SCHUBERT: *Wohin?.* SMITH: *The Star-Spangled Banner.* TCHAIKOVSKY: *Lullaby.*
(BB) ** CfP Silver Double CD CFPSD 4748 (2) [(B) id.]. Ian Hobson – CHOPIN: *Etudes, Opp. 10 & 25.* **

Ian Hobson's formidable virtuosity is heard to remarkable effect here, but even so one feels he should learn to relax more. His clean articulation suits the Bach transcriptions and Bizet's *Minuet* and is suitably brilliant, if at times less precise, in the famous Mendelssohn display piece. He plays Mussorgsky's *Gopak* boldly with wilful rubato, the coda not entirely convincing, but the *Flight of the bumble-bee* dazzles. The two famous Rachmaninov songs are affectionate, but Schubert's *Wohin?* brings a too insistent staccato; not all will respond to his forcefulness in the Kreisler pieces, and *Liebesfreud*, for all its chimerical bravura, would have benefited from more poise.

Piano transcriptions: J. S. BACH: *Prelude, Gavotte & Gigue.* FRANZ BEHR: *Polka W. R.* BIZET: *Minuet from l'Arlésienne.* KREISLER: *Liebesleid; Liebesfreud.* LISZT: *Hungarian rhapsody No. 2.* MENDELSSOHN: *Midsummer Night's Dream: Scherzo.* MUSSORGSKY: *Gopak.* RACHMANINOV: *Aleko: Dance of the young gypsy maidens. Daisies, Op. 38/3; Lilacs, Op. 21/5.* RIMSKY-KORSAKOV: *Flight of the bumble-bee.* SCHUBERT: *Wohin?.* SMITH: *The Star-spangled banner.* TCHAIKOVSKY: *Lullaby.*
(BB) ** Naxos Dig. 8.550978 [id.]. Idil Biret.

Idil Biret plays with considerable panache and demonstrates her impressive technical command in the *Midsummer Night's Dream Scherzo* and Rimsky's *Bumble-bee*. However, at times her rubato is not entirely convincing and seems rather mannered. She is well recorded.

Piano sonata No. 2 in B flat min., Op. 36; Moments musicaux, Op. 16; Variations on a theme of Corelli, Op. 42.
(BB) (*) Naxos Dig. 8.550349 [id.]. Idil Biret.

Idil Biret plays with a good deal of authority, but the small acoustic is quite unsuited to this kind of repertoire and cannot accommodate powerful fortissimo passages with any degree of comfort.

VOCAL MUSIC

The Bells, Op. 35.
(M) *** EMI (SIS) CDM7 63114-2. Sheila Armstrong, Robert Tear, John Shirley-Quirk, London Symphony Ch., LSO, Previn – PROKOFIEV: *Alexander Nevsky.* ***

In *The Bells*, as in Previn's equally fresh and direct account of the other Russian choral work included on his CD, Prokofiev's *Alexander Nevsky*, the London Symphony Chorus sings convincingly in the original language. Previn's concentration on purely musical values as much as on evocation of atmosphere produces powerful results, even when the recording as transferred to CD has lost just a little of its ambient warmth in favour of added presence and choral brilliance.

Liturgy of St John Chrysostom, Op. 31.
❀ (B) *** EMI forte CZS5 68664-2 (2) [CDFB 68664]. Maximova, Zorova, Vidov, Stoytsov, Petrov, Bulgarian R. Ch., Milkov.

Rachmaninov's *Liturgy of St John Chrysostom*, written in 1910, is an even fuller setting than Tchaikovsky's (of 1878), on which to some extent it was modelled, and it had no more success than its predecessor in convincing the church dignitaries that the powerful emotional feeling so readily projected by its music was not too secular in feeling for use within the context of a religious service. (One must remember that Rachmaninov – like Tchaikovsky – was somewhat equivocal in his allegiance to the Christian faith.) Yet listening to this glorious performance by the Chorus of Bulgarian Radio, recorded in the spacious acoustics of the Alexander Nevsky Memorial Cathedral in Sofia, one can be in no doubt that the work's powerful expressive feeling has an underlying deep spirituality, while the performance itself conveys great religious fervour. Apart from the continuing dialogue between cantor (Ivan Petrov) and chorus (in which the soloists also participate), there are moments of overwhelming simple beauty, as in the sublime, sustained *Cheroubikon* ('Cherubic hymn') which comes immediately before the *Litany of supplication* and is wonderfully celestial here. This makes a complete contrast with the powerful declamation of the *Credo* and the affirmation of the *Mercy of peace*. The setting of *Our Father*, with its almost minimalist simplicity, is hardly less moving. Indeed it would be difficult to imagine this superbly recorded performance being bettered and, although the spacious tempi (which are sustained with continuing concentration) mean that the performnance, which takes 97 minutes, stretches to a pair of CDs, the set is offered in EMI's forte series so that the two discs are offered for the price of one. It is a pity that a full text with translation is not included, but the presentation is otherwise fully acceptable.

6 Songs, Op. 4; 6 Songs, Op. 8; 12 Songs, Op. 14; 12 Songs, Op. 21; 15 Songs, Op. 26 (including (i) *Two partings*); *14 Songs, Op. 34; 6 Songs, Op. 38; Again you leapt, my heart; April! A festive spring day; By the gates of the holy dwelling; Did you hiccup?; Do you remember that evening?; A flower fell; From St John's Gospel; I shall tell you nothing; Letter to Konstantin Stanislavsky; Night; Powdered paint* (folksong); *Song of disappointment; Twilight has fallen.* (Piano solo): *Daisies; Lilacs.*
(M) *** Decca 436 920-2 (3). Elisabeth Söderström, Vladimir Ashkenazy, (i) with John Shirley-Quirk.

Recorded between 1974 and 1979, Elisabeth Söderström's set of the major Rachmaninov songs is a glittering jewel in the Decca catalogue. She is a fluent and radiant soloist, often inspired by her accompanist to performances of pure poetry, ranging over the wide span of Rachmaninov's career as well as his whole emotional range, so that you find, for instance, the highly characteristic *Brooding*, or the richly intense *O do not grieve*, alongside a comic skit on a drinking song, *Did you hiccup, Natasha?*. Sonia's final speech in Chekhov's *Uncle Vanya* becomes a song which nicely skirts sentimentality, and there is also a letter in music sent to Stanislavsky on the tenth anniversary of the Moscow Arts Theatre. John Shirley-Quirk joins the team for the wry dialogue, *Two partings*, and Ashkenazy allows himself two solo items in the composer's transcriptions of *Daisies* and *Lilacs*. The recording is vivid in its immediacy and presence. Full translations are provided.

Vocalise, Op. 34/14 (arr. Dubensky).
(M) *** RCA 09026 62600-2. Anna Moffo, American SO, Stokowski – CANTELOUBE: *Songs of the Auvergne;* VILLA-LOBOS: *Bachianas Brasileiras No. 5.* ***

Rachmaninov's *Vocalise* was a favourite showpiece of Stokowski, usually in a purely orchestral arrangement; but here with Moffo at her warmest it is good to have the vocal version so persuasively matching the accompaniment.

Rameau, Jean Philippe (1683–1764)

6 Concerts en sextuor (for strings).
(M) ** Cal. CAL 6838 [id.]. Caen CO, Dautel – BOISMORTIER: *Première suite de clavecin.* **

The anonymous arrangement of Rameau's five suites of *Pièces de clavecin en concert* for string sextet is a novelty and a pleasing one. The arranger used Rameau's instrumental version for harpsichord and two violins: the two violin parts are retained, the upper voice of the harpsichord is given to the third violin, its middle voice to the viola, and the cello follows the bass line. However, these two instruments are not always divided, and the music becomes a true sextet only when the bass has a separate part. The additional *Sixth Suite* is a further transcription of four pieces taken from the third book for the harpsichord, published in 1728, and is very effective, including the famous *La Poule* (clucking realistically on violins to anticipate Saint-Saëns). The music is played spiritedly on modern instruments by the Caen Chamber Orchestra under Jean-Pierre Dautel; if, as recorded, the violins seem a shade pallid, this approaches the sound (if not always the degree of polish) we expect from a period group.

Dardanus: suite; *Les Indes galantes:* suite.
(BB) *** DHM Baroque Esprit 05472 77420-2. Coll. Aur.

This early example of authentic performance dates from the 1960s. Any abrasiveness deriving from the use of original instruments is countered by the generous acoustics of the Cedernsaal in the Schloss Kirchheim. But the playing has both life and elegance and the sound, though warm and full, is by no means bland: the flutes and oboes (and trumpets in *Les Indes galantes*) bring plenty of added colour. The selection from *Les Indes galantes* is shorter than that provided by Herreweghe, but many will welcome the coupling with *Dardanus*, and the overall playing time is quite generous: 69 minutes. At super-bargain price this is very recommendable.

Hippolyte et Aricie: orchestral suite.
(M) *** HM/BMG GD 77009 [77009-2-RG]. La Petite Bande, Kuijken.

This record collects virtually all the orchestral music from *Hippolyte et Aricie*; the melodic invention is fresh and its orchestral presentation ingenious. Sigiswald Kuijken gets delightful results from his ensemble. In every way an outstanding release – and not least in the quality of the sound.

Les Indes galantes: suites for orchestra.
(B) *** HM Musique d'Abord HMA 1901130 [id.]. Chappelle Royale O, Philippe Herreweghe.

Besides the harpsichord arrangements listed below, Rameau also arranged his four 'concerts' of music from *Les Indes galantes* for orchestra. The result makes nearly three-quarters of an hour of agreeable listening, especially when played so elegantly – and painlessly – on original instruments, and very well recorded (in 1984) by Harmonia Mundi.

Pièces de clavecin en concert Nos. 1–5.
(M) *** Teldec/Warner 3984 21767-2. Brüggen, Sigiswald and Wieland Kuijken, Leonhardt.
(B) *** HM Dig. HMX 2901418 [(M) id.]. Christophe Rousset, Ryo Terakado, Kaori Uemura.

The *Cinq pièces de clavecin en concert* are for harpsichord but are more familiar in ensemble versions: in addition to the harpsichord parts, Rameau included additional parts for violin or flute, second violin and bass viol. These pieces, published in 1741, are played on Teldec with a sure sense of style and a real understanding of the niceties of the period. They are recorded on period instruments – but, rest assured, this is no dull, pedantic performance full of musicological rectitude and little musical life. On the contrary, it is scholarly but has genuine liveliness and authenticity of feeling. The music, of course, is delightful, and very much helped by the admirably fresh, transparent recording. This disc has recently been reissued as part of the Leonhardt Edition.

The instrumental *Pièces de clavecin* usually include a flute, but they are equally valid in this alternative format with baroque violin and viola da gamba. The Harmonia Mundi team are attractively spirited and rhythmically buoyant; the effect with period instruments brings a slightly abrasive edge at times, but not disagreeably so. The star here is Christophe Rousset, whose very imaginative contribution lights up this music-making. The recording is realistic, the balance excellent. At bargain price this is well worth considering.

Pièces de clavecin en concerts: 1st Concert: *La coulican; La livri; La vézinet;* 2nd Concert: *La laborde; La boucon; L'agaçante; Menuets 1–2;* 3rd Concert: *La poplinière; La timide, Rondeaux 1–2; Tambourines 1–2 en rondeau;* 4th Concert: *La pantomime; L'indiscrète; La Rameau;* 5th Concert: *La Forqueray; La Cupis; La Marais*.
(BB) *(*) Naxos Dig. 8.550464 [id.]. Alan Cuckson, Elisabeth Parry, Kenneth Mitchell, Alison Crum.

As with Alan Cuckson's companion records of Rameau on Naxos, the close balance does the artists a disservice. Not that these performances are strong on elegance (there are some tentative moments and the intonation of the flautist is momentarily vulnerable) and, though Alan Cuckson himself plays with spirit, the performances overall communicate more rectitude than pleasure.

KEYBOARD MUSIC

Pièces de clavecin, Book 1 (1706); *Nouvelles suites* (*c.* 1728).
(BB) ** Naxos Dig. 8.550463 [id.]. Alan Cuckston (harpsichord).

Pièces de clavecin (1724, revised 1731); *5 Pièces* (1741); *La Dauphine* (1747).
(BB) ** Naxos Dig. 8.550465 [id.]. Alan Cuckston (harpsichord).

Alan Cuckston's survey of Rameau's keyboard music is doubly welcome in the lowest price-range. Each disc is generously filled and the first, comprising the *Premier Livre* of 1706 and the *Nouvelles suites*, runs to 75 minutes. But first a word of warning: both discs sound thunderous if played at a normal playback level. Even when the volume is drastically cut, the balance remains too close to be ideal. At a time when presentation material is minimal or non-existent on many budget CDs, it is a pleasure to record that Alan Cuckson's notes are informative and, relatively speaking, extensive. All the same, this set does not offer a serious challenge to Kenneth Gilbert's survey on two full-priced Archiv CDs; the latter has far greater elegance and finish.

Suite de clavecin in E min. (1724).
(BB) *** HM Solo HMS 926018 [id.]. William Christie (harpsichord).

Rameau's *E minor Suite* is one of his most inventive, from the bursting birdsong of *Le Rappel des oiseaux* to the charming portrait of *La villageoise*, while the penultimate movement, a tender *Musette en rondeau*, is splendidly contrasted with the rumbustious closing *Tambourin*. William Christie plays the whole suite with infectious spontaneity and in fine style, and his Goujon-Swanen harpsichord is vividly recorded. This makes a splendid and inexpensive sampler for those unwilling to venture into a full-length programme of this attractive keyboard repertoire.

Grand motets: *In convertendo; Quam dilecta. Laboravi.*
(B) *** HM HMT 7901078 [(M) id. import]. Gari, Monnaliu, Ledroit, De Mey, Varcoe, Chapelle Royale Ch., Ghent Coll. Voc., Herreweghe.

These two motets are among Rameau's finest works. The Ghent Collegium Vocale is stiffened by forces from La Chapelle Royale in Paris. They produce excellent results, and the soloists are also very fine indeed. The instrumental ensemble includes several members of La Petite Bande, so its excellence can almost be taken for granted. The brief *Laboravi* makes an appealing little encore. This CD is even more attractive at bargain price.

OPERA-BALLET AND OPERA

Anacréon (complete).
(B) *** HM Musique d'Abord HMA 190190 [id.]. Schirrer, Mellon, Feldman, Visse, Laplénie, Les Arts Florissants, Christie.

The music here has charm; the performance is as authoritative and stylish as one would expect from William Christie's group. It is not essential Rameau, but it has moments of great appeal. The recording is admirable and this reissue is a genuine bargain.

Les Boréades (complete).
(M) *** Erato/Warner 4509 99763-2 (3). Jennifer Smith, Rodde, Langridge, Aler, Lafont, Monteverdi Ch., E. Bar. Soloists, Gardiner.

It was John Eliot Gardiner who in April 1975 conducted the first-ever public performance of this last opera of Rameau, written after he had reached his eighties. The composer died during the rehearsal at the Paris Opéra, and the piece was never staged, until in 1982 Gardiner presented it with enormous success at the Aix-en-Provence Festival with the same cast as here. Though the story – involving the followers of Boreas, the storm god – is highly artificial in a classical way, the music, involving many crisp and brief dances and arias, is as vital and alive as anything Rameau ever wrote, completely contradicting any idea of classical opera as static or boring. Gardiner here directs an electrifying performance with generally first-rate singing, except that Jennifer Smith's upper register, in the central role of Alphise, Queen of Baltria, is not sweet. Chorus and orchestra are outstanding and the recording excellent. Bizarre copyright problems prevented a libretto from being included, which makes it hard to follow the plot because the synopsis is not cued. However, the set is very welcome on CD as part of the Gardiner 'French Baroque Edition'.

Dardanus (complete).
(M) **(*) Erato/Warner 4509 95313-2 (2) [id.]. Gautier, Eda-Pierre, Von Stade, Devlin, Teucer, Soyer, Van Dam, Paris Op. Ch. & O, Raymond Leppard.

Though the French chorus and orchestra (using modern instruments) here fail to perform with quite the rhythmic resilience that Leppard usually achieves on record, the results are refreshing and illuminating, helped by generally fine solo singing and naturally balanced (if not brilliant) 1980 analogue recording, smoothly transferred to CD, with the choral sound quite vivid. José van Dam as Ismenor copes superbly with the high tessitura, and Christiane Eda-Pierre is a radiant Venus. The story may be improbable (as usual), but Rameau was here inspired to some of his most compelling and imaginative writing. Well documented and well worth exploring.

Les Fêtes d'Hébé: 3rd Entrée: *La Danse.*

(M) *** Erato/Warner 4509 99765-2. Jill Gomez, Anne-Marie Rodde, Jean-Claude Orliac, Monteverdi Ch. & O, Gardiner.

Les Fêtes d'Hébé was first staged in 1739 in Paris; it was the fourth major work Rameau had composed for the lyric stage and his second in the opera-ballet genre, *Les Indes galantes* being the first. In its complete form *Les Fêtes d'Hébé* consists of a prologue and three Acts dedicated to poetry, music and, finally, the dance. This last is a pastoral interspersed with dances in which Mercury courts the shepherdess Eglé.

Few people have done more in recent years for Rameau's music than John Eliot Gardiner, and this performance is distinguished by his great feeling for this composer and an alive sensitivity. He secures excellent playing and singing from his forces, and the music itself is inventive and delightful. In short, this is a record not to be missed, particularly if you are a newcomer to Rameau. It is beautifully recorded and the CD transfer is smooth, with lovely textures, choral and orchestral, both warm and transparent, with the soloists most naturally balanced.

Hippolyte et Aricie (complete).

(M) ** Decca 444 526-2 (2). Tear, Hickey, J. Baker, Shirley-Quirk, Rhys-Thomas, St Anthony Singers, ECO, Anthony Lewis.

This early-1965 Decca (originally Argo) set still sounds well. Lewis, as usual, secures playing of liveliness and feeling and the St Anthony Singers do not disappoint. Of the soloists, both Dame Janet Baker and John Shirley-Quirk give pleasure, though the rest of the cast is uneven and their French is not uniformly good. The snag is that Angela Hickey as Aricie does not always seem to be secure, and her very opening aria, after the Overture, *Temple sacré séjour tranquille*, brings fluttery vibrato. The recording has admirable clarity and detail.

Les Indes galantes (complete).

(M) *** Erato/Warner 4509 95310-2 (3) [id.]. Jennifer Smith, Hartman, Elwes, Devos, Huttenlocher, Ens. Vocale à Coeur Joie de Valence, Paillard O, Valence, Paillard.

The plot of *Les Indes galantes* is complicated but brings opportunities for a splendid tempest and sailors' chorus in Act I, which is set in Turkey. Act II moves to Peru, with a Sun Festival and a volcano erupting (admittedly not as spectacular as the tempest), and Act III with its floral festival is appropriately pastoral and picturesque. Finally we are taken to an Amazonian forest, where the two principal European characters are courting an Indian girl, Zima. She chooses one of her own tribe instead, but a pipe of peace ensures a final reconciliation; there are spectacular trumpets and a triumphant aria from the heroine before the closing ballet. The work is full of lyrical inspiration, and Jennifer Smith sings ravishingly in the roles of Phani, Fatime and Zima, while John Elwes as Tacmas and Adario brings a headily beautiful light-tenor response. Gerda Hartman as Hébé, Emilie and Zaire is charmingly lightweight, if not always quite as secure as Smith, and Philippe Huttenlocher sings all his roles with distinction. The duets and ensembles are often inspired, and the quartet, *Tendre amour*, in Scene 7, which comes before the ballet divertissement of Act III, is fully worthy of Mozart. Paillard directs the proceedings with much flair and warmth, and the 1974 recording is vividly atmospheric. With first-class documentation and a full translation, this is a set to cherish.

Naïs (complete).

(M) *** Erato/Warner 4509 98532-2 (2). Russell, Caley, Caddy, Tomlinson, Jackson, Parsons, Ransome, E. Bach Festival Ch. and Bar. O, McGegan.

Rameau's opera *Naïs* tells of Neptune's courtship of the water-nymph Naïs and is full of bold invention. The overture has some astonishing dissonances and syncopations, and the opening battle scenes in which the Heavens are stormed by the Titans and Giants are quite striking. The performance, based on the 1980 English Bach Festival production, is full of spirit and uses authentic period instruments to good effect. The work is not long, and the rewards of the music are such as to counterbalance any reservations one might have as to imperfections in ensemble or the like. Admirers of Rameau will need no prompting to acquire this attractive reissue. The unconverted should sample the opening, which will surely delight and surprise. The sound of this 1980 recording is strikingly well balanced, vivid and present. Highly recommended.

La Princesse de Navarre (complete).

(M) *** Erato/Warner 0630 12986-2 (3) [id.]. Hill-Smith, Harrhy, Chambers, Rees, Goldthorpe, Caddy, Wigmore, Savidge, E. Bach Festival Singers and Bar. O, McGegan.

La Princesse de Navarre is a collection of dance movements which Rameau used in other works, as well as interludes for the Voltaire comédie. The finest is a chaconne of some magnificence, in which dancers and singers participate. This edition is the first to incorporate all the music Rameau composed for the work. He made substantial revisions, probably more than once and possibly as late as 1763 when Voltaire added a new Prologue for a performance at Bordeaux. There is some altogether delightful music here and those older readers who saw the Covent Garden staging in 1976 will not need reminding as to its quality. Of course, listening to 55 minutes of dances (even though some of them are choral) in close proximity is not the ideal way of enjoying Rameau, but a cued CD recording gives one the opportunity to pick and choose. Very good performances, and excellent recording too.

Pygmalion (complete).
(M) **(*) HM/BMG GD 77143. Elwes, Van der Sluis, Vanhecke, Yakar, Paris Chapelle Royal Ch., La Petite Bande, Leonhardt.

Leonhardt's 1980 account with John Elwes as Pygmalion and Mieke van der Sluis as Céphise is rather leisurely, but his soloists make a good team, while the use of period instruments brings attractive transparency of texture. The documentation (including full translation) is first class.

Zoroastre (complete).
(M) **(*) HM/BMG GD 77144 (3). Elwes, De Reyghere, Van der Sluis, Nellon, Reinhart, Bona, Ghent Coll. Vocale, La Petite Bande, Kuijken.

Though Kuijken's characteristically gentle style with his excellent authentic group, La Petite Bande, fails to give the piece all the bite and urgency it needs, this is nevertheless a fine presentation of a long-neglected masterpiece, with crisp and stylish singing from the soloists, notably John Elwes in the name-part and Gregory Reinhart as Abramane. The Ghent Collegium Vocale, placed rather close, sing with vigour in the choruses, but the individual voices fail to blend. The excellent documentation (144 pages, including translations) puts the mid-priced issues of many of the large international companies to shame.

Ravel, Maurice (1875–1937)

Alborada del gracioso.
(M) **(*) EMI CDM5 65423-2 [id.]. French Nat. R. O, Stokowski – HOLST: *The Planets* **(*); STRAVINSKY: *Petrushka.* **

Stokowski's idiomatic account from the French National Orchestra dances infectiously and the 1958 recording sounds fuller than the coupled *Planets*; but the fortissimos remain rather harsh, if extremely vivid.

(i) *Alborada del gracioso;* (ii) *Une barque sur l'océan; Boléro;* (i; iii) *Piano concerto for the left hand;* (ii; iv) *Daphnis et Chloé* (complete ballet); (ii) *Fanfare pour L'Eventail de Jeanne; Menuet antique; Ma Mère l'Oye* (complete ballet); (i) *Pavane pour une infante défunte; Rapsodie espagnole;* (ii) *Shéhérazade: Ouverture de féerie. Le tombeau de Couperin; La valse; Valses nobles et sentimentales.*
(M) **(*) Sony SM3K 45842 (3) [S3K 45842]. (i) Cleveland O; (ii) NYPO; Boulez; (iii) with Entremont; (iv) Camerata Singers.

Boulez's distinguished Sony set offers a glitteringly iridescent account of the *Ouverture de féerie*, which is omitted by Dutoit. Entremont's account of the *Left-hand concerto* is strong and characterful and not lacking in poetic colour; but the CBS sound is a little fierce and does not altogether flatter the piano timbre. On the whole, however, the remastering makes the most of recordings which were originally among the best of their period (1972–5). The *Alborada* is quite brilliant and, throughout, Boulez allows all the music ample time to breathe; gentler textures have the translucence for which this conductor is admired. *Une barque sur l'océan* has a genuine magic, while the complete *Daphnis et Chloé* has a sense of ecstasy. Boulez is also at his very best in *Ma Mère l'Oye* with its luminous textures, and his *Rapsodie espagnole* is equally distinctive: it is beautifully shaped and atmospheric in an entirely different way from Karajan's; Boulez's Spain is brilliant, dry and well lit. Both *Boléro* and *La valse* generate considerable tension and have powerful climaxes. There is no doubt that this music-making with its cleanly etched sound is immensely strong in character, and many listeners will respond to it very positively.

Alborada del gracioso; Une barque sur l'océan; Boléro; Ma Mère l'Oye (complete); *Menuet antique; Ouverture de féerie; Pavane pour une Infante défunte; Rapsodie espagnole; Le tombeau de Couperin; La valse; Valses nobles et sentimentales.*
(B) *** EMI forte (SIS) CZS5 68610-2 (2) [CDFB 686102]. O de Paris, Martinon.

Like his version of *Daphnis et Chloé*, Martinon's *Ma Mère l'Oye* is exquisite, among the finest ever put on record (and one does not forget Dutoit and Previn). Although the *Valses nobles et sentimentales* and

La valse do not eclipse the 1961 Cluytens versions (see below) and the present *La valse* has a rather harsh climax, there is much ravishing delicacy of orchestral playing, notably in *Le tombeau de Couperin* and the rare *Ouverture de féerie* (*Shéhérazade*) with its Rimskian associations – a major 14-minute piece which is not included in most other comparable collections. The CD transfers of mid-1970s analogue recordings, originally made quadraphonically and which were remarkably lifelike and natural on LP, bring a degree of glare on fortissimos, but otherwise the sound is warm and luminously coloured and, throughout, the refined virtuosity of the Orchestre de Paris is a constant source of delight. Excellent value.

Alborada del gracioso; Une barque sur l'océan; Boléro; Ma Mère l'Oye (complete ballet); *Menuet antique; Pavane pour une infante défunte; Rapsodie espagnole; Le tombeau de Couperin; La valse; Valses nobles et sentimentales.*
(M) *** EMI Rouge et Noir (SIS) CZS7 67897-2 (2). Paris Conservatoire O, Cluytens.

These 1961 performances, made in the Salle Wagram, Paris, are as good as any in the catalogue. They have a strongly idiomatic and atmospheric feel; the *Rapsodie espagnole*, *La valse* and the *Valses nobles* are exceptionally good, and so too is the complete *Ma Mère l'Oye*. The only snag is the wide vibrato of the horn in *Pavane pour une infante défunte*. The recordings still sound remarkably realistic, and not just for the period: they are very good by present-day standards. The two-disc set makes a genuine bargain.

Alborada del gracioso; Boléro; Daphnis et Chloé (ballet): *suite No. 2; Menuet antique; Ma Mère l'Oye* (complete ballet); *Pavane pour une infante défunte; Rapsodie espagnole; Le tombeau de Couperin; La valse; Valses nobles et sentimentales.*
(B) **(*) Ph. Duo 438 745-2 (2) [(M) id. import]. Concg. O, Bernard Haitink.

Although Haitink's Ravel collection, recorded in the early 1970s, is not as magnetic as the superb companion Debussy set on Philips Duo, these are still fine performances, distinguished by instinctive good judgement and taste. The playing of the Amsterdam orchestra is eminently polished and civilized, even if the heady, intoxicating qualities of the music are missed. The *Rapsodie espagnole* lacks the last ounce of dash in the *Feria*, but the *Habañera* is lazily appealing when the orchestral playing is so sleek and refined. There is perhaps not quite enough atmosphere in *Le tombeau de Couperin*, and Haitink's *La valse* fails to captivate or excite the listener as do the finest versions of this piece. Yet the orchestral playing seduces the ear with its refinement and finish, and the engineers produce a sound to match: the perspective is truthful and the overall effect on CD most pleasing, with the remastered recordings improved in firmness of outline without loss of atmosphere or bloom.

(i) *Alborada del gracioso; Boléro; Daphnis et Chloé: suite No. 2; La valse;* (ii) *Ma Mère l'Oye* (complete ballet); *Pavane pour une infante défunte; Le tombeau de Couperin*. DEBUSSY, orch. RAVEL: *Danse (Tarantelle syrienne); Sarabande.*
(B) ** Teldec/Warner Ultima Dig. 0630 18959-2 (2) [(M) id. import]. (i) Cleveland O (with Ch.), Dohnányi; (ii) St Paul CO, Hugh Wolf.

As so often with paired CDs using different performers, the results here are uneven. On the first CD, the Teldec recording for Dohnányi is in the demonstration bracket and the playing of the Cleveland Orchestra is virtuosity itself. But there is no magic here, no sense of mystery or atmosphere in *Daphnis*, and little sense of the intoxication one encounters in Karajan, Ormandy or in such Ravel conductors as Reiner or Munch. Nor does *La valse* fare better, and the *Alborada del gracioso* emerges as just a display piece. As sound, this is worth a three-star rating, but as a musical experience Ravel-lovers will not want it. The performances from the St Paul Chamber Orchestra under Hugh Wolf are a different matter. They too are very well recorded, only the concert-hall effect is more natural. The playing is polished and musical, and *Le tombeau de Couperin* is both elegant and stylish. The two orchestrations of Debussy are pleasing and the *Tarantelle danse* is spirited and has delicacy of feeling, with a neatly rhythmic horn solo. The horn playing in the *Pavane* is quite beautiful.

(i) *Alborada del gracioso;* (ii) *Boléro; Pavane pour une infante défunte; Rapsodie espagnole;* (iii) *Tzigane;* (ii) *La valse.*
(M) **(*) [RCA Basic 100 09026 61712-2; *61712-4*]. (i) Chicago SO, Reiner; (ii) Boston SO, Munch; (iii) Perlman, LSO, Previn.

We have a special affection for these Munch performances as they were originally discussed (in 1960) in our very first hardback *Stereo Record Guide*. In spite of effective remastering, neither *Boléro* nor *La valse* is in the first class now – in the former the dynamic range is relatively restricted and the opening side-drum, though clear enough, is too loud in relation to the final climax. In those heady early days of stereo we were taken by the Boston sound, which we found full-blooded yet well separated; we were impressed, for instance, by the balance of the harp in the opening section. We also noted that the Boston trombone soloist does not slur his production with glissandi, which Ravel must have intended, as he permits it in his own Polydor recording (made in the early 1930s – which he supervised but apparently didn't conduct). In the *Pavane*, the Boston principal horn, James Stagliano, plays warmly and elegantly. Munch then uses the glittering *Rapsodie espagnole* to demonstrate his orchestra's virtuosity, with the percussion department well captured, and the string glissandi too. The playing is highly polished, but Munch's reading could perhaps be more sensitive and sensuous, particularly in the outer movements. *La valse* is exciting, but with the closing pages hard-driven and rather frenetic. Reiner's *Alborada* comes from the same period, and his reading misses nothing in colour or atmosphere, with the Chicago acoustic adding to the vividness and sense of space. The programme concludes with Perlman's earliest stereo recording of the *Tzigane*. His performance is brilliantly involving, and Previn accompanies imaginatively; but, as too often with this artist, the violin is given an exaggeratedly close balance which is not flattering.

Alborada del graciso; Boléro; Rapsodie espagnole; (i) *Daphnis et Chloé* (complete ballet). *Le tombeau de Couperin; La valse; Valses nobles et sentimentales.*
(B) *** RCA Twofer Dig. 74321 34171-2 (2) [id.]. Dallas SO; (i) with Ch.; Eduardo Mata.

In the late 1970s Eduardo Mata helped to build the Dallas orchestra into a splendid band, and here he directs a warmly atmospheric and magnetic reading of *Daphnis et Chloé* for which RCA (in 1979) produced one of the finest of their early digital recordings. Two decades later it remains near the demonstration bracket for its clarity and allure (helped by the splendid acoustics of the Dallas auditorium). The closing pages with chorus are particularly impressive.

Mata's *Le tombeau de Couperin* has elegance and finesse, while the expansive climaxes of *Boléro* and *La valse* are very compelling. The recording has the most spectacular dynamic range, while the Dallas hall provides plenty of atmosphere. The *Alborada* flashes, the *Rapsodie* shimmers and there is a balmy underlying patina of sensuous colour. At bargain price this is highly recommendable. The climax of the *Valses nobles et sentimentales* again impresses for its dynamic range and fine orchestral playing, and altogether this makes an outstanding compilation.

(i) *Alborado del gracioso; Boléro; Rapsodie espagnole; Le tombeau de Couperin;* (ii) *Valses nobles et sentimentales.*
(B) **(*) Sony SBK 48163; *MBK 48163* [id.]. Phd. O, (i) Ormandy; (ii) Munch.

Ormandy was a first-class Ravel conductor, as those who can recall his wartime *Daphnis et Chloé* (and, for that matter, its successors) can testify. These performances are eminently well worth the money at bargain price, even if the recording is not three-star by 1990s standards.

(i) *Alborada del gracioso;* (ii) *Boléro;* (i) *La valse.*
(M) *** EMI CDM7 64357-2. (i) O de Paris; (ii) BPO; Karajan – DEBUSSY: *La Mer.* ***

Karajan's digitally remastered 1978 EMI Berlin Philharmonic *Boléro* has fine presence and a splendid forward impetus. The Paris *Alborada* and *La valse* have been tacked on for this reissue. They were recorded in 1974 as part of an outstanding French concert of Ravel's orchestral music (now withdrawn).

Alborada del gracioso; Pavane pour une infante défunte; Rapsodie espagnole; Le tombeau de Couperin; La valse.
(M) *** Mercury (IMS) 432 003-2 [id.]. Detroit SO, Paray – IBERT: *Escales.* **(*)

Paray's Ravel performances enjoyed a high reputation in the 1960s. His *Rapsodie espagnole* can be spoken of in the same breath as the Reiner/RCA and Karajan/EMI versions, with its languorous, shimmering textures and sparkling *Feria*. His *Alborada* glitters and the *Pavane* is glowingly elegiac. *La valse*, too, is impressively shaped and subtly controlled. *Le tombeau de Couperin* has great refinement and elegance: the solo oboist plays beautifully. All have been excellently remastered.

Alborada del gracioso; Pavane pour une infante défunte; Rapsodie espagnole; Valses nobles et sentimentales.
✿ (M) *** RCA GD 60179 [60179-2-RG]. Chicago SO, Reiner – DEBUSSY: *Ibéria.* *** ✿

These performances are in an altogether special class. In the *Rapsodie espagnole*, the *Prélude à la nuit* is heavy with fragrance and atmosphere; never have the colours in the *Feria* glowed more luminously, while the *Malagueña* glitters with iridescence. In the three and a half decades since it first appeared, this is the recording we have turned to whenever we wanted to hear this work for pleasure. No one captures its sensuous atmosphere as completely as did Reiner, and the recorded sound with its natural concert-hall balance is greatly improved in terms of clarity and definition.

Une barque sur l'océan; Rapsodie espagnole; La valse.
(M) *** DG (IMS) Dig. 445 556-2. LSO, Abbado – MUSSORGSKY: *Pictures at an exhibition.* ***

Abbado has impeccable taste in this repertoire, and it goes without saying that the LSO plays superbly throughout. No complaints about the 1986 digital recording either.

Boléro.
(M) *** DG 447 426-2 [id.]. BPO, Karajan – DEBUSSY: *La Mer;* MUSSORGSKY: *Pictures.* ***

Boléro; Daphnis et Chloé: suite No. 2.
(M) *** DG 427 250-2. BPO, Karajan – DEBUSSY: *La mer; Prélude.* ***

Karajan's 1964 *Boléro* is a marvellously controlled, hypnotically gripping performance, with the Berlin Philharmonic at the top of its form. It is available either with a superb suite from *Daphnis et Chloé*, or among DG's Legendary Recordings series of 'Originals'; the couplings on both discs show Karajan at his very finest.

Boléro; (i) *Daphnis et Chloé: suite No. 2; Ma Mère l'Oye (suite); Valses nobles et sentimentales.*
(BB) *** Naxos Dig. 8.550173; *4550173* [id.]. (i) Slovak Philharmonic Ch.; Slovak RSO (Bratislava), Kenneth Jean.

The Slovak Radio Orchestra, which is a fine body and is superbly recorded, respond warmly to Kenneth Jean. At the price, this is very good value indeed; the *Ma Mère l'Oye* can hold its own alongside all but the most distinguished competition: indeed *Les entretiens de la belle et de la bête* is as keenly characterized as Dutoit at full price, and *Le jardin féerique* is enchanting. For those wanting these pieces this is a real bargain.

Boléro; (i) *Daphnis et Chloé: suite No. 2; Pavane pour une infante défunte; La valse.*
(M) *** Decca Dig. *430 714-4.* Montreal SO, Dutoit; (i) with chorus.

A sampler of Dutoit's beautifully made Montreal recordings, still available at mid-price, on cassette only.

Boléro; Ma Mère l'Oye (complete); *Pavane pour une infante défunte; Rapsodie espagnole; La valse.*
(M) *** Ph. (IMS) 442 542-2 [id.]. LSO, Pierre Monteux.

For this Philips reissue Polygram have taken the opportunity to combine recordings from two separate sources. Monteux's 1964 version of the complete *Ma Mère l'Oye* is a poetic, unforced reading, given naturally balanced sound. *La valse* is impressive too, and *Boléro* has well-sustained concentration, even though some will raise an eyebrow at the slight quickening of pace in the closing pages. These three recordings are taken from a Philips original which has responded well to its digital remastering, retaining its warmth while obtaining a clearer profile. The *Pavane* and *Rapsodie espagnole*, however, come from a Decca source and date from two years earlier, yet the sound has strikingly more range and an added lustre. The *Pavane* is warm and poised; the *Rapsodie espagnole* can be spoken of in the same breath as Reiner's version. Monteux moves naturally and spontaneously from the exotic nocturnal atmosphere of the opening *Prélude à la nuit* to the flashing brilliance of the closing *Feria*.

Boléro; Le tombeau de Couperin; (i) *Tzigane;* (ii) *Shéhérazade* (song-cycle).
(B) *** DG Classikon Dig. 439 414-2 [(M) id. import]. (i) Salvatore Accardo; (ii) Margaret Price; LSO, Abbado.

Abbado is on excellent form and brings out all the subtle colourings of Ravel's orchestration, in which he is greatly helped by the excellent DG recording. There is some lovely oboe playing in *Le tombeau de Couperin* and Accardo is superb in *Tzigane*. Margaret Price's singing is ravishingly ecstatic in both *Asie* and *La flûte enchantée*, even if she does not always seem to be quite inside the sensibility of the music. Only in *Boléro* is there any idiosyncrasy: near the climax Abbado makes a perceptible gear-change, pressing the tempo forward somewhat; his involvement is also conveyed in his vocal contributions to the closing pages. The recording here is spectacular. A genuine bargain.

Boléro; La valse.
(M) *** Decca (IMS) 448 576-2 [id.]. SRO, Ansermet – CHABRIER: *España* **(*); DUKAS: *L'apprenti sorcier* ***; DEBUSSY: *La Mer* **(*); HONEGGER: *Pacific 231.* ***

Outstanding 1963 performances from Ansermet, very well recorded. Nearly all the music included here shows the Swiss conductor at his best.

(i–ii) *Piano concerto in G; Piano concerto for the left hand;* (ii) *La valse;* (i) (Piano) *Valses nobles et sentimentales.*
(B) *** CfP CD-CFP 4667 [(M) id.]. (i) Philip Fowke; (ii) LPO, Baudo.

(i) *Piano concerto in G; Gaspard de la nuit.*
(M) *** DG 447 438-2 [id.]. Martha Argerich, (i) BPO, Abbado – PROKOFIEV: *Piano concerto No. 3.* ***

Argerich's half-tones and clear fingerwork give the *G major Concerto* unusual delicacy, but its urgent virility – with jazz an important element – comes over the more forcefully by contrast. Other performances may have caught the uninhibited brilliance in the finale more fearlessly, but in the first movement few other versions can match Argerich's playing. The compromise between coolness and expressiveness in the slow minuet of the middle movement is tantalizingly sensual. Her *Gaspard de la nuit* abounds in character and colour, even if certain touches may disturb the perspective. The remastered recordings (the concerto comes from 1967, *Gaspard* from 1975) sound first class; the concerto balance is very successful and there is crisp detail, while the solo piano has fine presence and no want of colour. The reissue is rightly part of DG's 'Originals' series of 'Legendary Recordings'.

The performances of the *Concertos* by Philip Fowke with Baudo and the LPO are particularly attractive in the way they bring out the jazzy side of Ravel's inspiration, treating the misplaced accents and syncopations less strictly than some, but with winning results. In the slow movement of the *G major Concerto* the Spanish overtones also come out strongly, and Fowke's solo playing in the *Valses nobles et sentimentales* is clean, bright and rhythmic in a muscular way, without ever becoming brutal or unfeeling; nor does he lack poetry. Baudo and the orchestra also give a strongly characterized reading of *La valse*, brisker than some, with waltz rhythms powerfully inflected. Excellent 1988 recording, made in St Augustine's, Kilburn, vivid and attractively atmospheric; this disc and tape are irresistible at bargain price.

(i) *Piano concerto in G; Piano concerto for the left hand in D. A la manière de Borodine; A la manière de Chabrier; Gaspard de la nuit; Jeux d'eau; Menuet antique; Menuet sur le nom de Haydn; Miroirs; Pavane pour une infante défunte; Prélude; Sonatine; Le tombeau de Couperin; Valses nobles et sentimentales.*
(B) **(*) Ph. Duo 438 353-2 (2) [id.]. Werner Haas; (i) Monte-Carlo Opéra O, Galliera.

This well-recorded pair of CDs offers virtually all Ravel's piano music at a bargain price. Werner Haas has a genuine Ravel sensibility and he plays with delicacy and a fine feeling for the music's colour and its moments of gentle rapture. His tempi are consistently apt and he is fully equal to the technical demands of *Gaspard de la nuit*. His crisp articulation in the *Toccata* of *Le tombeau de Couperin* and the *Alborada* from *Miroirs* shows how a ready technical facility is always placed at the service of the composer. Faster passages are very slightly blurred by the resonant acoustic, but otherwise the recording is lifelike and very pleasing. The performances of the two *Concertos* match the rest, refined and satisfying. Perhaps the playing here is a little strait-laced (elsewhere Haas is often pleasingly flexible) but Galliera's fine accompaniments add to the authority of these performances, and the 1968 recording is well balanced. These are performances one could live with, and this set is excellent value.

Piano concerto for the left hand in D.
(BB) *** ASV Dig. CDQS 6092 [(M) id.]. Osorio, RPO, Bátiz – FRANCK: *Symphonic variations* **(*); SAINT-SAENS: *Wedding-cake* ***; SCHUMANN: *Concerto.* ***

Jorge Federico Osorio's account of the *Left-hand concerto* can hold its own with the best and it is very well recorded. With its tempting bargain couplings, about which there are only minor reservations, this disc is a genuine bargain. He also gives a crisp and colourful performance of the *Alborada* in an alternative, full-price coupling with Prokofiev.

Daphnis et Chloé (ballet; complete).
✿ (M) *** RCA 09026 61846-2 [Basic 100 09026 68081-2; *68081-4*]. New England Conservatory & Alumni Ch., Boston SO, Munch.
(M) * Ph. Dig. 454 684-2. Tanglewood Ch., Boston SO, Haitink.

(i) *Daphnis et Chloé* (complete); *Alborada del gracioso; Boléro.*
(M) **(*) DG Dig. 445 519-2 [id.]. LSO, Abbado; (i) with L. Symphony Ch.

Daphnis et Chloé (complete); *Boléro.*
(B) *** [EMI Red Line Dig. CDR5 69830]. CBSO & Ch., Rattle.

Daphnis et Chloé (complete); *Pavane pour une infante défunte; Rapsodie espagnole.*
(M) *** Decca 448 603-2 [id.]. ROHCG Ch., LSO, Pierre Monteux.

(i) *Daphnis et Chloé* (complete); (ii) *Shéhérazade*.
(M) **(*) Sony SMK 47604 (i) Schola Cant., NYPO; (ii) Horne, Fr. Nat. R. O; Bernstein.

Charles Munch's Boston account is one of the great glories of the 1950s, superior in every way to his later version from the 1960s. The playing in all departments of the Boston orchestra is simply electrifying. The sound here may not be as sumptuous as the Monteux on Decca, but the richness of colour lies in the playing, and there is a heady sense of intoxication that at times sweeps you off your feet, and the integration of the chorus is impressively managed. Try the *Danse de supplication de Chloé* (track 15) and the ensuing scene in which the pirates are put to flight, and you will get a good idea of how dazzling this is, with the ballet ending in tumultuous orchestral virtuosity.

Monteux conducted the first performance of *Daphnis et Chloé* in 1912; Decca's 1959 recording, a demonstration disc in its day, captured his poetic and subtly shaded reading in vivid colours in the most agreeably warm ambience. The performance was one of the finest things Monteux did for the gramophone. Decca have added his 1962 recording of the *Pavane*, wonderfully poised and played most beautifully, and the highly spontaneous *Rapsodie espagnole*. A worthy addition to the Classic Sound series.

Simon Rattle conducts the CBSO in a most warmly expressive reading of Ravel's great ballet score. The moulding of phrase and subtle flexibility of rubato bear tribute not only to his feeling for Ravel but to the responsiveness of the Birmingham orchestra as well as its fine chorus, trained by Simon Halsey. The sensuous beauty of the slow sequences is enhanced by the mistily evocative recording, though the dynamic range is so extreme that it is hard to set the controls at a convenient level to give clarity to pianissimos without making the climaxes too aggressively loud. Such showpiece numbers as the *Danse guerrière* and the final *Danse générale* have a winning resilience and energy, and interestingly Rattle translates his affectionate manner in Ravel to his performance of *Boléro*, relatively slow and easily expressive, not as hard-edged as it can be.

Bernstein's *Daphnis et Chloé* dates from 1964 and comes with an altogether seductive *Shéhérazade* with Marilyn Horne, one of the most sensuous accounts committed to disc. Bernstein is at his very best here and each movement is characterized to perfection. The sound, too, is very good. Horne's *Shéhérazade* weaves the most erotic tales, and while one is under its spell the claims of the incomparable Suzanne Danco and Régine Crespin are almost (though not quite) forgotten. By comparison, Bernstein's 1961 *Daphnis* is less successful; there are good things, of course – most notably the last part, which comprises the second suite, but there are moments of less-than-perfect intonation which diminish its appeal. The sound is a vast improvement on the CBS original – but then it needed to be. In spite of the *Daphnis*, this record is a must.

The brilliant playing of the LSO under Abbado is helped by an exceptionally analytical DG recording which has the widest possible dynamic range – so much so that the pianissimo at the very opening is barely audible for almost thirty seconds. For all its refinement and virtuosity, this is a performance to admire rather than love, lacking the atmospheric warmth that marks, say, the Monteux version.

Haitink's version brings a powerful performance, marked by extremes of tempo and dynamic. Its directness is matched by the superb playing of the Boston orchestra, but sadly this is one of the relative failures by the Philips engineers working in Boston. The sound, at rather a low level, lacks body and is curiously misty, giving the Boston strings an acid edge which scarcely reflects their beauty.

(i; ii) *Daphnis et Chloé* (ballet): *suites Nos. 1–2*; (iii) *Ma Mère l'Oye (Mother Goose) suite;* (i; iv) *La valse;* (i; iv; v) *Shéhérazade* (song-cycle).
❁ (M) *** Dutton Lab. CDK 1201 [id. full price]. (i) Paris Conservatoire O; (ii) Munch; (iii) Nat. SO, Sidney Beer; (iv) Ansermet; (v) with Suzanne Danco.

Despite an apology about the opening – 'Noise at start of Track 1 as original master' – the detail and depth of focus of the early *ffrr* 78 recording for *Daphnis* are remarkable, with *Daybreak* matching later Munch readings in warmth – indeed its sense of ecstasy has never been surpassed on disc – and with the final *Danse générale* given tremendous thrust. The recording was made at Walthamstow in October 1946, and *La valse* under Ansermet at Kingsway Hall followed a year later. The sound is fuller in bass with even greater clarity, but under Ansermet the ensemble is rougher in a work that cries out for virtuoso treatment. Ansermet is far stronger in *Shéhérazade*, recorded with the same orchestra in Paris in May 1948. With the bright-toned, very French-sounding Danco enunciating the text to bring out every word, it is a taut and purposeful rather than an atmospheric reading, but it still has a flavour all its own. The conductor in *Ma Mere l'Oye* is Sidney Beer, with the orchestra he himself assembled from among London's leading players of the time, many still in the armed forces. Though he sounds rather matter-of-fact at the start after Munch or Ansermet, there is plenty of charm later, with excellent solo work and with the final

Le jardin féerique rapt in concentration. This Kingsway Hall recording is so luminous that one can hardly believe it is mono, or that the uncannily present and vivid transfers are made direct from 78 shellac discs dating from 1945. The Rosette, however, is for Munch's *Daphnis et Chloé*.

Daphnis et Chloé: suite No. 2.

(M) *** Decca Phase Four 455 152-2 [id.]. L. Symphony Ch., LSO, Stokowski – DEBUSSY: *La Mer* etc. ***

Stokowski's Phase Four version comes from 1969 and was recorded in the Kingsway Hall to impressive effect. He secures a glowing performance with sumptuous playing, and the multi-channel technique is used to produce exactly the right disembodied, ethereal effect for the off-stage chorus. It is true that the close balance highlights some of the woodwind bird-noises excessively, but with the chorus the pervading presence is richly satisfying. Stokowski takes the choral parts from the complete ballet rather than the usual *Suite No. 2*. He adds a fortissimo chord at the very end, but after such an involving performance few will begrudge him that.

(i) *Introduction and allegro for harp, flute, clarinet and strings* (orchestral version); (ii) *Ma Mère l'Oye* (ballet suite); (iii) *Pavane pour une infante défunte;* (iv) *La valse*.

(B) *** Sony SBK 63056; *SBT 63056* [id.]. (i) Cleveland O, Louis Lane; (ii) Philh. O, Tilson Thomas; (iii) Cleveland O, Szell; (iv) Phd. O, Ormandy – DEBUSSY: *Petite suite;* SATIE: *Gymnopédies Nos. 1 & 3*. ***

This is a first-class anthology which gives great satisfaction. The orchestral version of Ravel's haunting *Introduction and allegro* is less delicately textured than the chamber version, but as played by the splendid Cleveland Orchestra under Louis Lane it does not lose its magic or its refinement of feeling. The warm ambience of Severance Hall is another asset, as is the delicate harp playing of Alice Chalifoux. The 1969 recording is not too forwardly balanced. Similarly Michael Tilson Thomas is wholly attuned to the sensibility of Ravel's ravishing *Ma Mère l'Oye* ballet suite and this is a highly seductive performance, glowingly played and lustrously recorded (digitally in 1988). Szell takes over the Cleveland podium for the *Pavane*, which brings more first-class playing, particularly from the orchestra's principal horn. Finally Ormandy and the Philadelphia Orchestra give a sensuous, exciting, bravura account of *La valse*, with the 1963 sound suitably spacious and with plenty of atmosphere.

Ma Mère l'Oye (complete ballet).

(M) *** Mercury (IMS) 434 343-2 [id.]. Detroit SO, Paray – DEBUSSY: *Ibéria* etc. ***

(BB) **(*) Carlton LSO Double Dig. 30368 01187 (2) [(B) id. import]. LSO, Wordsworth – BIZET: *Jeux d'enfants* **; DEBUSSY: *La Mer* etc. ***; SAINT-SAENS: *Carnival of the animals*. **

Ma Mère l'Oye (complete); *Rapsodie espagnole*.

(M) *** DG (IMS) 415 844-2. LAPO, Giulini – MUSSORGSKY: *Pictures*. ***

Paray's gently evocative *Ma Mère l'Oye* is most beautifully played and recorded. The score's calm innocence with its undercurrent of quiet ecstasy is caught perfectly and the translucence of the sound, recorded in Detroit's Ford Auditorium, offers rather more transparency than with the hardly less fine Debussy couplings. *Laideronette, Empress of the Pagodas* with its impressive stroke on the tam-tam is thoroughly exotic, and the closing portrayal of the *Fairy garden* is exquisite. So lustrous is the sound that it is almost impossible to believe the early recording date: 1957.

The Giulini Los Angeles performance conveys much of the sultry atmosphere of the *Rapsodie espagnole*. Indeed some details, such as the sensuous string responses to the cor anglais tune in the *Feria*, have not been so tenderly caressed since the intoxicating Reiner version. The *Ma Mère l'Oye* suite is also sensitively done; though it is cooler, it is still beautiful.

Barry Wordsworth finds the balletic grace in Ravel's beautiful score and creates some lovely diaphanous textures. There is plenty of vitality too, and the LSO's response is consistently sympathetic. A fine performance, if not perhaps an especially individual one. The recording is very good, the wide dynamic range suiting this music rather better than some of the couplings.

Ma Mère l'Oye (ballet): *suite*.

(B) *** CfP CD-CFP 4086 [(M) id.]. SNO, Gibson – BIZET: *Jeux d'enfants;* SAINT-SAENS; *Carnival*. ***

Gibson is highly persuasive, shaping the music with obvious affection and a feeling for both the innocent spirit and the radiant textures of Ravel's beautiful score. The orchestral playing is excellent and, with excellent couplings, this is very recommendable.

Tzigane (for violin and orchestra).

(M) *** EMI CDM5 66058-2. Itzhak Perlman, O de Paris, Barenboim – SAINT-SAENS: *Havanaise;* VIEUXTEMPS: *Violin concertos Nos. 4 & 5.* ***

(M) *** DG Dig. 447 445-2 [id.]. Itzhak Perlman, NYPO, Mehta – BERG; STRAVINSKY: *Concertos.* ***

(M) *** Decca Dig. 460 007-2 [id.]. Kyung Wha Chung, RPO, Dutoit – LALO: *Symphonie espagnole;* VIEUXTEMPS: *Violin concerto No. 5.* ***

Perlman's classic (1974) account of Ravel's *Tzigane* for EMI is marvellously played; the added projection of the CD puts the soloist believably at the end of the living-room. The opulence of his tone is undiminished by the remastering process and the orchestral sound retains its atmosphere, while gaining in clarity.

Perlman's later digital version is very fine and the recording is obviously modern. But the earlier, EMI performance has just that bit more charisma.

With its seemingly improvisatory solo introduction, *Tzigane* is a work which demands an inspirational artist, and Kyung Wha Chung is ideally cast, catching the atmosphere of this elusive piece with natural affinity.

CHAMBER MUSIC

Introduction and allegro for harp, flute, clarinet and string quartet.

❁ (M) *** Decca 452 891-2 [id.]. Osian Ellis, Melos Ens. – DEBUSSY: *Sonata for flute, viola and harp;* ROUSSEL: *Sérénade for flute, violin, viola, cello & harp;* ROPARTZ: *Prélude, marine et chansons.* *** ❁

The beauty and subtlety of Ravel's sublime sextet are marvellously realized by this rightly famous Melos account from 1961. The interpretation has great delicacy of feeling and the recording is miraculously perfect, with a natural presence against a warm ambience – that of Walthamstow Town Hall, although one would never guess, so intimate is the effect. (It was achieved by grouping the musicians under the balcony in a corner at the back of the hall.) Coupled with Debussy's magical *Sonata*, Roussel's almost equally enchanting *Sérénade* and delightful music by Guy Ropartz, this is a reissue to treasure and is truly worthy of Decca's Classic Sound series, although the collection originally appeared on the Oiseau-Lyre logo. It was conceived by Mrs Hanson-Dyer who originally owned that label. However, the recording team was from Decca: Ray Minshull, producer, and Kenneth Wilkinson, engineer. Well over three decades later they can surely be proud of the results.

(i) *Introduction and allegro;* (ii–iv) *Piano trio;* (v) *Pièce en forme de habanera;* (iii; iv) *Sonata for violin and cello;* (vi) *String quartet in F;* (vii; viii) *Tzigane;* (iii; ii) *Violin sonata;* (ix; viii) *Ma Mère l'Oye* (for piano, 4 hands); (x–xi) *3 Chansons madécasses;* (x; xii) *3 Poèmes de Stéphane Mallarmé.*

(B) ** EMI CZS5 69279-2 (2) [(M) id. import]. (i) Challen & Ens.; (ii) Pludermacher, (iii) Jarry, (iv) Tournus; (v) Paul Tortelier, Iwaski; (vi) Parrenin Qt; (vii) Ferras, (viii) Barbizet; (ix) François; (x) Benoit, (xi) & Ens.; (xii) O de Paris Soloists, Jacquillat.

These recordings emanate from the French catalogues of the 1970s and, even if few of the performances would be a first choice, in only one instance do they fall below a certain level of accomplishment. Indeed at nearly 80 minutes on each CD (and two CDs for the price of one) they represent very good value for money. The Parrenin's account of the *String quartet* is the best known of the performances and among the finest things here. But the performances of the *Piano trio* by Gérard Jarry, Georges Pludermacher and Michel Turnus and the Jarry–Pludermacher *Violin sonata* are also thoroughly enjoyable. The *Mallarmé Songs* are really far better suited to a soprano and Jean-Christophe Benoit does not convince here or in the *Chansons madécasses*, though he has undoubted taste. The 1965 *Introduction and allegro* is more than acceptable, though it is not superior to the famous (and slightly earlier) Melos set on Decca. The only failure is an insensitive and unimaginative *Ma Mère l'Oye* by Samson François and Pierre Barbizet. There are enough good things here to make it recommendable, particularly at the price.

(i) *Introduction and allegro;* (ii) *Pièce en forme de habañera.*

(B) *** Cala Dig. CACD 1018 (2) [id.]. James Campbell; (i) William Bennett, Ieuan Jones, Allegri Qt; (ii) John York – POULENC: *L'invitation au château* etc. ***

These Cala performances are recommendable in their own right, but they come in a particularly valuable two-CD set for the price of one, which includes over two hours of music for wind instruments by Poulenc. It is sheer delight from start to finish and cannot be too strongly recommended.

Piano trio in A min.

(BB) **(*) Naxos Dig. 8.550934 [id.]. Joachim Trio – DEBUSSY: *Piano trio in G;* SCHMITT: *Piano trio: Très lent.* **(*)

There is no shortage of fine premium-priced recordings of Ravel's sublime *Piano trio*, arguably the greatest example of the genre written in this century; and any bargain contender has to have special claims to dislodge the best of them. However, this Naxos version by the Joachim Trio who comprise Rebecca Hirsch, Caroline Dearnley and the pianist John Lenehan is worth any collector's notice. They play with sensitive musicianship and finesse. Their performance is imaginative and beautifully recorded, and it is far from uncompetitive.

(i) *Piano trio in A min.;* (ii) *String quartet in F;* (iii) *Violin sonata in G.*
(M) **(*) Ph. 454 134-2. (i) Beaux Arts Trio; (ii) Italian Qt; (iii) Grumiaux, Hajdu.

Ravel's *String quartet* usually comes in harness with the Debussy *Quartet*; here it is offered as part of a triptych of Ravel's key chamber-works. The performance by the Quartetto Italiano has long been praised by us. The Beaux Arts give a predictably fine account of the *Trio*, and the only slight criticism would be an occasional want of charm by the violinist, Daniel Guilet, but that is a small reservation. In the *Violin sonata* Grumiaux's playing has great finesse and beauty of sound. The recordings date from 1966 and are very naturally balanced, but the CD transfer demonstrates their age by a degree of shrillness of the fortissimo string-timbre.

Piano trio in A min.; Sonata for violin and cello; (i) *Chansons madécasses; 3 Poèmes de Stéphane Mallarmé* (song-cycle).
(BB) **(*) Virgin Classics Double Dig. VBD5 61427-2 (2) [CDVB 61427]. Nash Ens. (members), (i) with Sarah Walker – DEBUSSY: *Chamber music.* **

The Virgin anthology offers a very good introduction to the less familiar Ravel, if you exclude the *Piano trio*. The *Sonata for violin and cello* is expertly played by Marcia Crayford and Christopher van Kampen – as good an account as any – and in the *Piano trio* Ian Brown joins them in a performance of real stature and eloquence. In the *Chansons madécasses* and the exquisite *Trois poèmes de Stéphane Mallarmé* Sarah Walker is *primus inter pares* rather than a soloist, though she is not balanced as reticently by Andrew Keener's team as is Delphine Seyrig in the Debussy *Chansons de Bilitis*. This is a pity, but it is not an insuperable obstacle to an apt and inexpensive Ravel coupling.

String quartet in F.
(M) *** Ph. 420 894-2. Italian Qt – DEBUSSY: *Quartet.* ***
(B) *** CfP Dig. CD-CFP 4652 [(M) id. import]. Chilingirian Qt – DEBUSSY: *Quartet.* ***
(BB) **(*) Discover Dig. DICD 920171 [id.]. Sharon Qt – BEETHOVEN: *Harp quartet* **(*); MOZART: *Quartet No. 1.* ***
(B) **(*) Sony SBK 62413; *SBT 62413* [id.]. Tokyo Qt – DEBUSSY: *Quartet* **(*); FAURE: *Piano trio.* (*)

String quartet in F; (i) *Introduction & allegro for harp, flute, clarinet and string quartet.*
(BB) *** Naxos Dig. 8.550249 [id.]. Kodály Qt, (i) with Maros, Gyöngyössy, Kovács – DEBUSSY: *Quartet.* **(*)

For many years the Italian Quartet held pride of place in this coupling. Their playing is perfect in ensemble, attack and beauty of tone, and their performance remains highly recommendable, one of the most satisfying chamber-music records in the catalogue.

The Chilingirian recording has plenty of body and presence, and also has the benefit of a warm acoustic. The players give a thoroughly committed account, with well-judged tempi and very musical phrasing. The Scherzo is vital and spirited, and there is no want of poetry in the slow movement. At mid-price this is fully competitive and the sound is preferable to that of the Italian Quartet on Philips.

The Naxos version can more than hold its own. Artistically and technically this is a satisfying performance which has the feel of real live music-making. The *Introduction and allegro* is not as magical or as atmospheric as that of the Melos Ensemble from the 1960s, nor is it as well balanced (the players, save for the harp, are a bit forward), but it is still thoroughly enjoyable.

The Sharon Quartet are completely at home in this music and play with ardour and sensitivity. The resonant acoustic (a Cologne church) suits the work better than the Beethoven coupling. It certainly does not cloud the Scherzo or the energetic account of the finale (which also has much delicacy of feeling) and adds warmth and atmosphere to the *très lent*. Very good playing: if the couplings are suitable, this is a bargain.

The Tokyo Quartet play with great finesse and tonal beauty, especially in the warm yet refined account of the *très lent*. They certainly observe the marking of the finale, *vif et agité* and perhaps elsewhere there could be a touch more poise. But their music-making is thoroughly alive. The sound is very good.

Violin sonata in G.
(M) *** DG (IMS) Dig. 445 557-2. Shlomo Mintz, Yefim Bronfman – PROKOFIEV: *Violin sonatas*. ***
(BB) *(*) Koch Discover Dig. DICD 920306 [id.]. Josef Suk, Josef Hala – FAURE: *Violin sonata No. 2;* FRANCK: *Violin sonata*. *(*)

The Ravel *Violin sonata* has come into its own in recent years. Shlomo Mintz and Yefim Bronfman's account offers highly polished playing, even if it is not so completely inside Ravel's world in the slow movement. The glorious sounds both artists produce are a source of unfailing delight and they are beautifully recorded too. At mid-price, coupled with outstanding versions of the two Prokofiev *Sonatas*, this is very recommendable.

A fine performance from Suk and Hala, attractively coupled, is let down by somewhat indifferent sound.

Violin sonata; Tzigane.
(B) *** EMI Eminence Dig. CD-EMX 2244 [(M) id. import]. Tasmin Little, Piers Lane – DEBUSSY; POULENC: *Violin sonatas*. ***

In this well-designed collection of violin-and-piano music, Tasmin Little and Piers Lane give outstanding performances, very well recorded, aptly and subtly changing style for each composer, equally bringing out the contrast of tone in the two Ravel works here, the *Sonata* fleeting and elusive, the *Tzigane* more rhetorical and extrovert. Pointing of rhythm could hardly be more persuasive, with Little relishing the colour-changes in the central Blues movement of the *Sonata*. Excellent sound.

PIANO MUSIC

Solo piano music

Complete solo piano works: *A la manière de Borodine; A la manière de Chabrier; Gaspard de la nuit; Jeux d'eau; Menuet antique; Menuet sur le nom de Haydn; Miroirs; Pavane pour une enfante défunte; Prélude; Sérénade grotesque; Sonatine; Le tombeau de Couperin; La valse; Valses nobles et sentimentales.* (i) *Sites auriculaires; Ma mère l'Oye* (i–ii) *Frontispièce.*
(B) *** EMI CES5 72376-2 (3). Jean-Philippe Collard, with (i) Michel Béroff; (ii) Katia Labèque – DEBUSSY: *En blanc et noir* etc. ***

Jean-Philippe Collard is arguably the greatest French pianist of his generation and his Ravel playing never falls below distinction. The recordings were made between 1977 and 1980. There are so many beautiful things here that it would be curmudgeonly to complain. What a beautiful sense of line he achieves in *Ondine*, the first of the *Gaspard de la nuit*, though it must be admitted that the right-hand ostinato is far from the *pianopianissimo* which Ravel marks. For the most part, however, his playing silences criticism. *Le gibet* is wonderfully atmospheric, as is so much else, particularly the superb *Noctuelles*. The recording, made in the Salle Wagram, is not wholly sympathetic; there is a glassy, shallow quality, particularly in the upper part of the spectrum.

A la manière de Borodine; A la manière de Chabrier; Gaspard de la nuit; Habanera; Jeux d'eau; Menuet antique; Menuet sur le nom de Haydn; Miroirs; Pavane pour une infante défunte; Prélude; Sonatine; Le tombeau de Couperin; Valses nobles et sentimentales; (i) *Ma Mère l'Oye.*
(B) ** Sony SB2K 53528 (2) [S2K 53528]. Philippe Entremont, (i) with Dennis Lee.

Entremont is not insensitive but he sets greater store by clarity of detail than atmosphere. The recording is closely balanced and at times shallow, but it sounds much better on CD than on its original LP issue. There are some good things here, but also some less effective moments: at the opening of the second CD *Ondine* seems prosaic by the side of the finest performances.

A la manière de Borodine; A la manière de Chabrier; Gaspard de la nuit; Jeux d'eau; Menuet antique; Menuet sur le nom de Haydn; Miroirs; Pavane pour une infante défunte; Prélude; Sérénade grotesque; Sonatine; Le tombeau de Couperin; Valses nobles et sentimentales.
(M) *** Chandos Dig. CHAN 7004/5 [id.]. Louis Lortie.

Chandos have now put Louis Lortie's two Ravel discs together. The first, including *Le tombeau de Couperin*, *Jeux d'eau*, *La valse* and the *Valses nobles et sentimentales*, was warmly welcomed in our 1992 edition and we found his *Gaspard de la nuit* with its chilling and atmospheric account of *Le gibet* particularly impressive. Now that these are repackaged at mid-price, let us hope that they will gain the wider dissemination to which their merits entitle them. The Chandos sound, which emanates from The Maltings, Snape, is very realistic and truthful.

A la manière de Borodine; A la manière de Chabrier; Gaspard de la nuit; Jeux d'eau; Menuet antique; Menuet sur le nom d'Haydn; Miroirs; Pavane pour une infante défunte; Prélude; Sonatine; Le tombeau de Couperin; Valses nobles et sentimentales; (i) *Ma mère l'Oye.*
(B) ** Decca Double 440 836-2 (2) [(M) id. import]. Pascal Rogé, (i) with Denise Françoise.

Pascal Rogé made these recordings in 1973/4 at the beginning of his Decca contract. He is well recorded (though the effect is a little cool) and his playing is sensitive. His performances of the *Sonatine*, *Le tombeau* and the *Valses nobles et sentimentales* were widely praised on their first appearance, but we have heard more imaginative accounts of *Le tombeau*: the *Forlane* is not keenly delineated and characterized. He produces some finely coloured tone in *Miroirs*, but overall it is a shade pallid and under-characterized, and he does not match either Ashkenazy or Argerich – and certainly not Pogorelich – in *Gaspard de la nuit* in terms of authority or panache. Yet there is much that is good here, and the set certainly indicated his natural gifts in this repertoire, which were to be realized more fully in later records.

A la manière de Borodine; A la manière de Chabrier; Gaspard de la nuit; Jeux d'eau; Menuet antique; Menuet sur le nom de Haydn; Miroirs; Pavane pour une infante défunte; Prélude; Sonatine; Valses nobles et sentimentales.
(B) *(*) EMI Rouge et Noir CZS5 68997-2 (2). Samson François.

Samson François enjoyed cult status in the France of the 1960s. This was, of course, before the arrival on the scene of such artists as Michel Béroff, Jean-Philippe Collard and Pascal Rogé. It is difficult to understand why François was singled out for such admiration as his Ravel is often downright insensitive. He was at his best in the *Concerto for the left hand*, not represented in this collection; but elsewhere he is distinctly cavalier about dynamic markings and tends to confuse *pianissimo* with *mezzo-forte*. The transfers are decent and can be recommended to his admirers.

A la manière de Borodine; A la manière de Chabrier; Jeux d'eau; Menuet antique; Menuet sur le nom de Haydn; Miroirs; La parade; Pavane pour une infante défunte; Prélude; Sérénade grotesque; Sonatine.
(BB) ** Naxos Dig. 8.550683 [id.]. François-Joël Thiollier.

Whatever, you may ask, is *La parade*? The sleeve-note suggests that this sequence of dances, some in fragmentary form, derives from the improvisations Ravel made in 1898 for Isadora Duncan's classes, which would date alongside the *Pavane pour une infante défunte*. It certainly does not have the elegance or finish of the *Pavane* or any of the other pieces on this record, and its presence should not sway the collector in its favour. The Franco-American pianist, François-Joël Thiollier, has excellent credentials: he is a pupil of Casadesus and Sascha Gorodnitzki. His playing here is not insensitive, yet it falls short of real distinction: he is no match for Collard or Rogé, and nor is the recorded sound.

Gaspard de la nuit; Menuet antique; Pavane pour une infante défunte; Sonatine; Le tombeau de Couperin.
(BB) *(*) Naxos Dig. 8.550254 [id.]. Klára Körmendi.

Klára Körmendi belongs to the middle generation of Hungarian pianists and has specialized in contemporary music. She is a very capable player but, as so often in recordings from this source, is handicapped by a less than flattering recording acoustic. Although not as dry as in some of the Naxos recordings made in Heidelberg, the rather close balance robs this music of much of its magic and atmosphere. The sound is more three-dimensional than for Casadesus, recorded in the early 1950s; but we are well served in this repertoire and this disc does not pose a strong challenge.

Gaspard de la nuit; Le tombeau de Couperin; La valse; Valses nobles et sentimentales.
(BB) **(*) Naxos Dig. 8.553008 [id.]. François-Joël Thiollier.

Having damned Thiollier's companion disc (above) with faint praise, it is good to be able to welcome the present collection with more enthusiasm. Indeed there is much to admire here. He has a refined tonal palette and a good command of pianissimo tone. His rubati are not entirely (and in some cases not at all) convincing in the *Valses nobles et sentimentales*, and the *Prélude* from *Le tombeau de Couperin* is unacceptably fast, almost gabbled. Nor is his playing free from mannerism. The ritardandi in the *Rigaudon* are intolerable. However, he always produces beautiful sound and he is well recorded. At under a fiver, this is worth considering.

VOCAL MUSIC

(i) *Chansons madécasses;* (ii) *Don Quichotte à Dulcinée; 5 mélodies populaires grêcques;* (iii) *3 poèmes de Stéphane Mallarmé.*
(M) *** Sony SMK 64107 [id.]. (i) Norman, Ens. InterContemporain; (ii) José van Dam; (iii) Jill Gomez; BBC SO, Boulez – ROUSSEL: *Symphony No. 3.* **(*)

With three characterful and strongly contrasted soloists, Boulez's collection of Ravel songs with orchestra (including arrangements) makes a delightful mid-priced collection and is especially valuable as the *Don Quichotte* and the *Greek popular songs* are rarely heard in this orchestral form. Van Dam may not be as relaxed here as he was with piano accompaniment (on the HMV recording with Dalton Baldwin which is currently withdrawn), but the dark, firm voice is just as impressive. Excellent sound, full and atmospheric, with translations provided; the addition of Boulez's impressive (1975) version of Roussel's *Third Symphony* makes this reissue all the more desirable.

Mélodies: *Ballade de la Reine; Morte d'Aimer; Canzone italiana; Chanson du rouet; Chanson espagnole; Chanson française; Chanson hébraïque; Chansons madécasses; 5 mélodies populaires grecques; 2 Epigrammes de Clément Marot; 2 Mélodies hébraïques; Don Quichotte à Dulcinée; Un grand sommeil nuit; Les grands vents venus d'outremer; Histoires naturelles; Manteau de fleurs; Noël des jouets; Rêves; Ronsard à son âme; Sainte; Scottish song; Shéhérazade* (complete); *Si morne!; Sur l'herbe; Tripatos; 3 Poèmes de Stéphane Mallarmé; Vocalise en forme de Habanera.*

(B) *** EMI (SIS) Dig. CZS5 69299-2 (2) [(M) id. import]. Norman, Mesplé, Lott, Berganza, Van Dam, Bacquier, Capitole Toulouse O or Paris CO, Plasson; Dalton Baldwin (piano).

With a composer whose expressive range in song-form (or mélodie) might have seemed limited, it is an excellent idea in the EMI set to have six strongly contrasted singers, each given an apt area to cover. So Teresa Berganza as well as singing *Shéhérazade* has two songs inspired by Spain, the *Vocalise in the form of an Habanera* and the *Chanson espagnole* from the set of five *Chants populaires*, each of which is allotted to a different singer. Felicity Lott's *Chanson écossaise* is a rarity, *Ye banks and braes* sung in a convincing Scots accent. For all the shallowness of Mady Mesplé's voice, it works well in the *Mélodies populaires grecques*, while Jessye Norman, rich-toned if not quite as characterful as usual, has the *Chansons madécasses* as well as lesser-known songs. It is the contribution of the two men that provides the sharpest illumination: José van Dam magnificently dark-toned in the *Don Quichotte* songs and the *Mélodies hébraïques* (making *Kaddish* thrillingly powerful in its agony of mourning), while Gabriel Bacquier twinkles in Figaro tones in the point songs. Excellent sound, and the pair of CDs particularly generous (136 minutes) in offering the contents of three LPs and now being offered as an inexpensive Rouge et Noir reissue.

Shéhérazade (song-cycle).

(M) **(*) Sony Theta Dig. SMK 60031 [id.]. Frederica von Stade, Boston SO, Ozawa – BERLIOZ: *Nuits d'été*; DEBUSSY: *La Damoiselle élue.* *(*)

(B) ** [EMI Red Line Dig. CDR5 69802]. Dame Kiri Te Kanawa, Belgian Nat. Op. O, Pritchard – DUPARC: *7 Mélodies.* **

Ozawa is an experienced and sympathetic advocate of Ravel, and he and the Boston orchestra provide a seductive web of sound for von Stade's beguiling account of this most sensuous of French song-cycles. The centrepiece, *La flûte enchantée*, is particularly ravishing; as the recording is warm and atmospheric, it is a pity that the Berlioz and Debussy couplings are so much less successful.

Dame Kiri is somewhat bland here in comparison with some of her rivals and, despite good orchestral playing and good recording, this is not among the most memorable recorded versions of the cycle.

OPERA

(i) *L'heure espagnole;* (ii) *L'enfant et les sortilèges* (both complete).

(M) *** DG 449 769-2 (2) [id.]. (i) Berbié, Sénéchal, Giraudeau, Bacquier, Van Dam, Paris Opera O; (ii) Ogéas, Collard, Berbié, Sénéchal, Gilma, Herzog, Rehfuss, Maurane, RTF Ch. & Boys' Ch., RTF Nat. O; Maazel – RIMSKY-KORSAKOV: *Capriccio espagnol;* STRAVINSKY: *Le chant du rossignol.* *** ❁

Maazel's recordings of Ravel's two one-Act operas were made in the early 1960s and, though the solo voices in *L'enfant* are balanced rather closely, the remastered sound in both operas is wonderfully vivid and atmospheric and each performance is splendidly stylish. The singing is delightful: neo-classical crispness of articulation goes with refined textures that convey the ripe humour of one piece, the tender poetry of the other. The inclusion of Maazel's superb early stereo accounts of Rimsky's *Capriccio* (with the Berlin Philharmonic), and *Le chant du rossignol* glitteringly played by the Berlin Radio Orchestra, two classics of the gramophone, ensures this set a place at the top of the list of DG's illustrious 'Originals'.

L'enfant et les sortilèges (complete).

(B) *** EMI Dig. CD-EMX 2241 [(M) id.]. Wyner, Augér, Berbié, Langridge, Bastin, Amb. S., LSO, Previn.

Previn's dramatic and highly spontaneous reading of *L'Enfant* certainly brings out the refreshing charm of this still neglected masterpiece. Helped by a strong and stylish team of soloists, this makes superb entertainment. On CD, the precision and sense of presence of the digital recordings come out the more vividly, with subtle textures clarified and voices – including the odd shout – precisely placed. That precision goes well with Previn's performance, crisply rhythmic rather than atmospherically poetic. Those wanting a modern, digital recording should be well satisfied with this at mid-price, for a full libretto with translation is included.

L'heure espagnole (complete).

(M) (***) EMI mono CDM5 65269-2. Duval, Giraudeau, Vieuille, Herent, Clavensy, O. du Théâtre Nat. de l'Opéra-Comique, André Cluytens.

This recording, with Denise Duval as Concepcion and Jean Giraudeau as Gonzalve, was recorded at the Théâtre des Champs-Elysées in 1952 and makes its first appearance in Britain. Denise Duval is altogether superb, as is the rest of the cast for that matter. Apart from the quality of the singing, the artists of this period understood the importance of diction and acting. The sound comes up very well indeed, and the set should give much pleasure.

Rawsthorne, Alan (1905–71)

Violin concertos (i) *No. 1;* (ii) *No. 2;* (iii) *Improvisations on a theme by Constant Lambert;* (iv) *Divertimento*.

(B) *** BBC Radio Classics 15656 91952 [(M) id.]. (i) Theo Olof, New Philh. O, Sir Adrian Boult; (ii) Manoug Parikian, BBC SO, Rudolf Schwarz; (iii) BBC Concert O, Frank Shipway; (iv) BBC N. SO, Bryden Thomson.

(i) *Violin concertos No. 1–2. Fantasy overture: Cortèges*.

(BB) *** Naxos Dig. 8.554240 [id.]. (i) Rebecca Hirsch; BBC Scottish SO, Lionel Friend.

This is the kind of issue that more than justifies the BBC label, and it is one of a small number that have been retained for distribution by Carlton, while the rest have been deleted just as we go to press. The *Divertimento* apart, it brings repertoire to the catalogue that has never been commercially available in admirable broadcast performances. Rawsthorne's *First Violin concerto* was started in 1940, but some of his manuscripts were lost when his house was bombed, and the concerto was not completed until 1947 – after, as the composer put it, he had been successively 'blown up and called up'. Dedicated to William Walton, it blends the apparently rhapsodic with the close concentration of Rawsthorne at his best. Theo Olof gave its first performance in 1948 with Sir John Barbirolli and spoke of 'its manifold, beautiful singing phrases'. His eloquent performance with Sir Adrian Boult and the New Philharmonia comes from 1972. The *Second concerto*, composed in 1956, is a more enigmatic, less openly lyrical piece from 1956. Parikian's performance comes from a 1968 broadcast in the BBC Maida Vale studios. The *Improvisations on a theme by Constant Lambert* is another rarity. The two composers were exact contemporaries and close friends; indeed, some years after Lambert's death, Rawsthorne married his widow. The theme comes from Lambert's ballet, *Tiresias*, and, as always with Rawsthorne, the ideas are beautifully laid out.

Choosing between the BBC version and the newcomer from Naxos is not easy. Of course the newer recording has the advantage of cleaner and more present sound. The Naxos recording brings the accomplished Rebecca Hirsch as soloist, with excellent orchestral support from the BBC Scottish Symphony under Lionel Friend. Apart from her championship of Poul Ruders's music (his *Second Concerto* is dedicated to her), she has established herself also as a fine chamber musician and is a member of the Joachim Trio. Her performances hold their own with their distinguished rivals, and the value of the disc is enhanced by another première recording of Rawsthorne's *Cortèges*, commissioned by the BBC and first performed at the 1945 Prom season. It is an imaginative and at times haunting piece, very well played and recorded here. Artistically, both these recordings deserve a three-star rating, but perhaps the excellently balanced (and slightly cheaper) Naxos recording should have priority for those for whom modern recording is of the essence. Both issues enrich the discography of an unjustly neglected and important figure in British music.

Reger, Max (1873–1916)

Variations and fugue on a theme by Mozart, Op. 132.

(M) (**) DG Originals 449 737-2 (2) [id.]. BPO, Boehm – BEETHOVEN: *Missa solemnis*. (**)

Recorded in 1956, this Boehm version must have just missed being in stereo. The sound is good and the orchestral playing is first class, but the performance is curiously uninvolving. Boehm gets off on the wrong foot by taking Mozart's theme (from the *A major Piano sonata*, K.331) remarkably slowly.

PIANO MUSIC

Variations and fugue on a theme of Bach, Op. 81.

(BB) **(*) Naxos Dig. 8.550469 [id.]. Wolf Harden – SCHUMANN: *Humoreske*. **(*)

Wolf Harden's account of the Reger *Variations and fugue on a theme of Bach*, Op. 81, is very fine. Unfortunately there is far less air or sense of space round the piano here and the instrument sounds much drier than in the Schumann coupling. Yet such is the compelling quality of his playing that it would be curmudgeonly to withhold a recommendation on this count.

Reich, Steve (born 1936)

8 Lines.

(M) *** Virgin/EMI Dig. CUV5 61121-2 [id.]. LCO, Warren-Green – ADAMS: *Shaker loops* *** ✽; GLASS: *Company* etc. ***; HEATH: *Frontier*. ***

Steve Reich's *8 Lines* is minimalism in its most basic form, and, although the writing is full of good-humoured vitality, the listener without a score could be forgiven for sometimes thinking that the music was on an endless loop. The performance is expert.

(i) *Six Pianos;* (ii) *Music for mallet instruments;* (iii) *Variations for winds, strings and keyboards.*

(B) *** DG Analogue/Dig. 439 431-2. (i–ii) Chambers, Preiss, Hartenberger, Becker, Velez, composer; (ii) Ferchen, Harms, Jarrett, LaBarbara, Clayton; (iii) San Francisco SO, De Waart.

This collection – which might be entitled 'Stuck in a groove' – admirably charts the progress of Reich's minimalism. Both the first two pieces exploit the composer's technique of endlessly repeating a very brief fragment which gradually becomes transformed, almost imperceptibly, by different emphases being given to it. The *Variations* mark a new departure, using a large orchestra. The recording throughout is of high quality and the San Francisco (digital) sound is easy to wallow in.

Reicha, Antonín (1770–1836)

Wind quintets: in F (1811); in E flat; in B flat, Op. 88/2 & 5; in D; in A, Op. 91/3 & 5.

(B) *** Hyperion Dyad Dig. CDD 22006 (2) [id.]. Academia Wind Quintet of Prague.

This Dyad combines two separate collections, recorded in 1987 and 1989 respectively. The second disc, which includes the rather more ambitious *A major* and *B flat major Quintets* (the latter has a highly unusual opening movement, continually alternating allegros and adagios), is, if anything, even more rewarding than the first. Czech wind-playing in Czech wind music has a deservedly high entertainment rating, and the present performances are no exception. The music itself has great charm and geniality; it is ingenuous yet cultivated, with some delightful, smiling writing for the bassoon. The players are clearly enjoying themselves, yet they play and blend expertly. The sound too is admirable.

Reinecke, Carl (1824–1910)

Flute sonata (Undine), Op. 167.

(M) *** RCA 09026 61615-2 [id.]. James Galway, Martha Argerich – FRANCK; PROKOFIEV: *Sonatas*. ***

Carl Reinecke was a prolific composer (in all genres); he was also pianist, fiddler and teacher, and at one time conductor of the Leipzig Gewandhaus Orchestra. He has undoubted facility, and some of the invention here is quite striking (as in the sonata's first movement). His writing, which has sudden florid bursts, makes an engaging vehicle for an artist of Galway's calibre, and this makes a fine bonus for the coupling of two masterly works by Prokofiev and Franck.

Respighi, Ottorino (1879–1936)

Ancient airs and dances: suites Nos. 1–3.

(BB) ** Naxos Dig. 8.553564 [id.]. Nat SO of Ireland, Rico Saccani.

On Naxos a clear, direct, well-played account, somewhat lacking in atmosphere. This is partly caused by the effect of the closely balanced, bright, clean recording. The Orpheus Chamber Orchestra account on

DG is far more satisfying and, although it costs much more, it also includes *The Birds suite* and the *Three Botticelli pictures*, which are equally impressive (see our main volume).

(i) *Ancient airs and dances: suites Nos. 1–3;* (ii) *Belfagor:* overture; (iii) *The Birds* (suite); (ii) *The Fountains of Rome; The Pines of Rome;* (iii) *3 Botticelli pictures (Trittico Botticelliano).*
(B) **(*) EMI forte Dig. CZS5 69358-2 (2) [CDFB 693582]. (i) LA CO, or (iii) ASMF; Marriner; (ii) LSO, Gardelli.

Sir Neville Marriner's account of the suites of dances is attractively light and gracious, offering an almost French elegance, with pleasingly transparent textures. *The Birds* and *Trittico Botticelliano* are no less delightful, and they are beautifully recorded. So far so good; but Lamberto Gardelli's performances of *The Pines* and *Fountains of Rome*, though warmly sympathetic and finely played, bring less of a feeling of drama. There are some lustrous sounds here, but these accounts generate neither the atmospheric magic nor electricity experienced in the competing versions from Reiner or Karajan. The *Belfagor overture* is an acceptable bonus, a dramatic and lively piece, strongly characterized and vivid.

(i) *Ancient airs and dances: suites Nos. 1–3; The Birds (Gli uccelli); 3 Botticelli pictures (Trittico botticelliano);* (ii) *Feste romane; the Fountains of Rome; The Pines of Rome.*
(B) *** Teldec/Warner Ultima Dig. 0630 18970-2 (2) [(M) id. import]. (i) St Paul CO, Hugo Wolff; (ii) LPO, Carlo Rizzi.

This outstanding Teldec Ultima Double gathers together first-class performances of the key Respighi orchestral works, offered on two discs for the cost of a single premium-priced CD. The playing of the St Paul Chamber Orchestra in the first group is excellent: they are responsive equally to dynamic contrasts and to changes of colour. Hugo Wolff gets a sympathetic and spirited response throughout and the *Ancient airs and dances* are beautifully played; the recording is bright but spacious. Carlo Rizzi's vivid acount of the Roman triptych is hardly less impressive. The recording is immensely spectacular and its moments of hyperbole are thrilling in a very physical way, as at the huge, overwhelming climax of *The pines of the via Appia* and, in *Feste romane*, the crude spectacle of *Circuses* with its distant brass effects or the dazzlingly vulgar closing picture of *La Befana* with its reminders of the Shrovetide Fair in *Petrushka*. The *Fountains* too are brilliantly pictorial, from the turning of the *Triton* to the imagined processional of Neptune evoked by the *Trevi*. Yet Respighi's gently luminous evocation of *The Pines of the Janiculum* and the heady, sensuous nostalgia of *Villa Medici at sunset* are drawn with subtle colours. The LPO respond with superb virtuosity and dash, balanced by warm sensitivity.

(i) *Ancient airs and dances: suite No. 3 for strings;* (ii) *The Birds; The Fountains of Rome; The Pines of Rome.*
(M) ** Ph. (IMS) Analogue/Dig. 446 573-2. (i) I Musici; (ii) San Francisco SO, Edo de Waart.

Ancient airs and dances: suite No. 3 for strings; The Fountains of Rome; The Pines of Rome.
(M) *** DG 449 724-2 [id.]. BPO, Karajan (with BOCCHERINI: *Quintettino*; ALBINONI: *Adagio in G min.* (arr. Giazotto) ***).

Karajan's highly polished, totally committed performances of the two most popular Roman pieces are well supplemented by the *Third suite* of *Ancient airs and dances*, brilliantly played and just as beautifully transferred, more impressive in sound than many more recent Karajan recordings. In the symphonic poems Karajan is in his element, and the playing of the Berlin Philharmonic is wonderfully refined. The opening of the *Ancient airs* brings ravishing tone from the Berlin Philharmonic strings, and they sound even more lavish in Giazotto's famous arrangement of Albinoni's *Adagio*. That has been added as a bonus for this remastered reissue in DG's 'Legendary Recordings' series of 'Originals', while Boccherini's *Quintettino* makes an engaging additional lollipop.

De Waart conducts brilliant and sympathetic performances of the two symphonic poems, but an unnatural balance in the early (1983) digital recording, with unrealistic placing of instruments, is underlined on the finest reproducers. Conversely, I Musici's set of *Ancient airs and dances*, recorded two decades earlier, is pleasant but rather characterless. It is no match for Karajan's version in elegance.

(i) *The Birds* (suite); *Brazilian impressions;* (ii) *The Fountains of Rome; The Pines of Rome.*
(M) **(*) Mercury (IMS) 432 007-2 [id.]. (i) LSO; (ii) Minneapolis SO, Antal Dorati.

The Minneapolis Northrop Auditorium – for all the skill of the Mercury engineers – never produced a web of sound with quite the magical glow which Orchestral Hall, Chicago, could provide in the late 1950s. Nevertheless, in Dorati's hands the opening and closing evocations of the *Fountains of Rome* have a unique, shimmering brightness which certainly suggests a sun-drenched landscape, although the turning-on of the Triton fountain brings a shrill burst of sound that almost assaults the ears. The tingling detail in the companion *Pines of Rome* is again matched by Dorati's powerful sense of atmosphere, while the finale has an overwhelming juggernaut forcefulness. The coupling of *The Birds* and *Brazilian impressions* was made in the smoother, warmer acoustics of Watford Town Hall in 1957, and here the vividness of detail particularly suits Dorati's spirited account of *The Birds*, bringing pictorial piquancy of great charm and strongly projected dance-rhythms. *Brazilian impressions* recalls Debussy's *Ibéria*, though it is much less subtle. The finale, *Canzone e danza*, certainly glitters in Dorati's hands even if overall this work does not represent Respighi at his finest.

The Birds (Gli uccelli); Church windows (Vetrate di chiesa).
(B) **(*) Sony SBK 60311; *SBT 60311* [id.]. Phd., Ormandy – SCARLATTI: *The Good-humoured ladies.* **(*)

This pairing offers a suitable contrast of simplicity and flamboyance. The four-movement suite, *Church windows*, is not a masterpiece of the first order of the Roman *Pines* or *Fountains*, but it shows the same brilliant feeling for orchestral colour. The picture of the baby Jesus in *The flight into Egypt* has a Latin intensity of feeling which suits Ormandy and the rich-textured Philadelphia sound, and in the second movement the conception of St Michael, sword in hand, is spectacularly painted with broad strokes of the orchestral brush. The finale, a papal blessing scene, is on the largest scale. Ormandy rises to the occasion and the spectacular recording is a match for the Philadelphia big guns – although subtlety is not the keynote here and the listener is all but overwhelmed. *The Birds* is slighter, but the playing is full of charm, especially the delicate tracery of the final cuckoo evocation.

La boutique fantasque (arr. of Rossini) – see under ROSSINI.

Piano concerto in A min.; Fantasia slava for piano and orchestra; Toccata for piano and orchestra.
(BB) *** Naxos Dig. 8.553207 [id.]. Konstantin Scherbakov, Slovak RSO (Bratislava), Howard Griffiths.

An enterprising Naxos CD offers three concertante piano works of Respighi, missing out the *Concerto in modo misolidio* and including instead the more rhetorical *Toccata*, written in 1928, three years after the former piece. At 22 minutes it is too long for its content but has some attractive lyrical writing. The much more concise and rather engaging *Fantasia slava* suddenly surprises the listener by quoting a tune familiar from a Dvorák *Slavonic dance*. The Russian pianist, Konstantin Scherbakov, is a persuasive and at times dazzlingly brilliant soloist and he is accompanied persuasively by the Slovak Radio Symphony Orchestra (Bratislava) under Howard Griffiths. The recording is excellent and this disc, if not preferable to Tozer's full-priced Chandos coupling, is well worth its modest cost.

Feste romane; The Fountains of Rome; The Pines of Rome (symphonic poems).
(BB) *** Naxos Dig. 8.550539 [id.]. RPO, Bátiz.
(M) *** Decca Dig. 430 729-2. Montreal SO, Dutoit.
(B) **(*) Sony SBK 48267; *SBT 48267* [id.]. Phd. O, Ormandy.
(BB) **(*) RCA Navigator 74321 24208-2 [09026 61401-2]. Phd. O, Eugene Ormandy.
(M) (**(*)) RCA mono GD 60262; *GK 60262* [60262-2-RG]. NBC SO, Toscanini.

The Fountains of Rome.
(B) *** [EMI Red Line Dig. CDR5 69831]. Phd. O, Muti – RIMSKY-KORSAKOV: *Scheherazade.* **(*)
The Pines of Rome.
(B) *** [EMI Red Line Dig. CDR5 69826]. Phd. O, Muti – PROKOFIEV: *Romeo and Juliet.* *(*)

The Fountains of Rome; The Pines of Rome.
✿ (M) *** RCA 09026 68079-2 [id.]. Chicago SO, Fritz Reiner – DEBUSSY: *La Mer.* ***

(i) *The of Fountains Rome; The Pines of Rome;* (ii) *Rossiniana* (suite after Rossini).
(M) ** Decca Phase Four 444 106-2 [id.]. (i) New Philh. O, Charles Munch; (ii) RPO, Dorati.

Reiner's legendary recordings of *The Pines* and *Fountains of Rome* were made in Symphony Hall, Chicago, on 24 October 1959, and the extraordinarily atmospheric performances have never been surpassed since. The opening of the *Fountain of Valle Giulia at dawn* captures a sultry Italian warmth, and the slightly recessed orchestral image in the glowing hall acoustics adds to the magic, both here and in *The pines of the Janiculum*, where there is exquisitely rapturous response from the strings. The turning on of the Triton fountain brings an unforced cascade of orchestral brilliance, while the triumphal procession of Neptune's chariot across the heavens which forms the powerful centrepiece of the Trevi portrait has an overwhelmingly spacious grandeur. Similarly the climax of *The pines of the Appian Way* is prepared with subtle control, and when the big moment comes it is electrifying. The marvellous orchestral playing is matched by the skill of RCA's technical team, led by Dick Mohr, and indeed by the new generation of transfer engineers, who have put it all on CD with complete fidelity.

The Naxos recording, engineered by Brian Culverhouse in St Barnabas, Mitcham, is also in the demonstration bracket. The climax of *The Fountain of Trevi at mid-day*, when Neptune parades across the heavens, is enormously spectacular, and here a computer organ was used to provide the underlying sustained pedal (the church organ was out of pitch), and effectively clean and weighty it is. The *Pines* and *Fountains* bring extremely fine playing with much warmth and finesse from the RPO, while the cascading waters of the *Triton fountain* become a positive torrent. The focus of the Naxos recording is sharp, and this brings an extra degree of brazen splendour to the tumultuous popular crowd sequences in the *Circus* and *Jubilee* scenes of the *Feste romane*, while at the close of the *October festival* the mandolin serenade emerges more tangibly.

Dutoit, as in other brilliant and colourful pieces, draws committed playing from his fine Montreal orchestra. Where many interpreters concentrate entirely on brilliance, Dutoit finds a vein of expressiveness too, which – for example in the opening sequence of *The Pines of Rome* – conveys the fun of children playing at the Villa Borghese. The recorded sound is superlative on CD, where the organ pedal sound is stunning. At mid-price, this is now very competitive, especially for those who enjoy the Montreal ambience.

It seems a curious idea to split Muti's recordings of Respighi's Roman triptych, as they were originally issued together. But the performances are warmly red-blooded and captivatingly Italianate in their inflexions. With brilliant playing from the Philadelphia Orchestra and warmly atmospheric recording, far better than the EMI engineers have generally been producing in their Philadelphia series, these are exceptional for their strength of characterization. Each scene is vividly dramatized and, with the recording so spectacular, these performances make a very considerable impact on the listener.

Ormandy's Sony/CBS *Feste romane* dates from the early days of stereo. The performance has great electricity and enormous surface excitement, and it is a pity that the sound-quality is fiercely brilliant. In the other two works the effect is more opulent, and the Philadelphia playing is fabulous, while the recording has come up astonishingly well. The atmospheric central movements of the *Pines* are ravishing (as is the *Villa Medici Fountain*) and the final evocation of the Roman troops on the Appian Way is overtly sinister. It is a pity that such electrifying performances need some technical indulgence because of the microphone balance, but this is still a very exciting example of the Ormandy/Philadelphia regime at its most spectacularly compelling.

On RCA Navigator, Ormandy again plays all three works with enormous gusto and panache, and the orchestral virtuosity is thrilling, with the robust vulgarity of *Feste romane* breathtaking in its unbuttoned zest. The cascade at the turning on of the Triton fountain is like a dam bursting, and all the pictorial effects spring vividly to life. The 1973–4 recording is immensely spectacular. It is atmospheric too, but brightly lit to the point of garishness, and not all ears will respond to the tingling brilliance. But the performances make an unforgettable impact.

Toscanini's recordings of the Roman trilogy are in a class of their own; they (and Reiner in the *Pines* and the *Fountains*) are the yardstick by which all others are measured. This is electrifying playing, which comes over well in this transfer – though, to be fair, the old LPs had a rounder, fuller (less acidulated) tone on the strings above the stave.

Munch's Phase Four coupling is made artificially spectacular by the microphone placing. The instrumental spotlighting is done with some panache; the treble glitters, though the effect is unrefined, and the 1966 Kingsway Hall recording adds ambient warmth. The sense of spectacle is tangible and to some extent redeems the comparative lack of subtlety in the presentation. Those who regard these scores as 'picture-postcard music' will find that this is what the Decca sound-balance conveys. Respighi's *Rossiniana suite*, arranged from piano pieces taken from Rossini's *Quelques riens pour album*, is not as inspired a score as *La Boutique fantasque*, but it is beautifully played and Dorati's affection is persuasive. The recording, made a decade later, is smoother too.

PIANO MUSIC

Ancient airs and dances; 6 Pieces; 3 Preludi sopra melodie gregoriane; Sonata in F min.

(BB) *** Naxos Dig. 8.553704 [id.]. Konstantin Scherbakov.

Although Respighi was a string player (he was for a time principal violist at the Imperial Opera in St Petersburg), he writes idiomatically and effectively for the piano. He followed his famous set of *Antiche Danze ed Arie*, transcriptions from lute tablature of ancients airs and dances for orchestra, with some for the piano. He also transcribed others for the piano: the first by the Genovese, Simone Molinaro, *Balletto detto Il Conte Orlando* bears a strong resemblance to the first movement of *The Birds*, as does the *Gagliarda* by Vincenzo Galileo (father of the famous scientist). The anonymous *Italiana* is familiar from the orchestral suites, though its treatment is very different. Of the other pieces, the *Notturno* from the *Six Pieces* has a distinctly Rachmaninovian feel. The *F minor Sonata* (1897–8) is a rarity and was not published until the 1980s. Apart from a version on Nuovo Era label, there is no alternative account, and it is difficult to imagine one that is more persuasive than this – at any price level. Anyone who has heard

Konstantin Scherbakov's record of the Medtner *Second Piano concerto* on Naxos will know that he is a pianist of quality, combining the highest musicianship with sensitivity and refinement. He is excellently recorded too.

VOCAL MUSIC

(i) *Deità silvane;* (i; ii) *Lauda per la Natività del Signore. 3 Botticelli pictures (Trittico botticelliano).*
(B) *** Decca Double 444 842-2 (2) [id.]. (i) Robert Tear; (ii) Jill Gomez, Meriel Dickinson; L. Chamber Ch.; Argo CO, Heltay – ROSSINI: *Petite messe solennelle.* **

The two rarities here are most appealing. The *Lauda per la Natività del Signore* is a setting of words attributed to Jacapone da Todi, a Franciscan of the thirteenth century, and is ingeniously scored for two flutes, piccolo, oboe, cor anglais, two bassoons, piano (four hands) and triangle, while the voices are wonderfully handled. The *Deità silvane* was originally for soprano and piano, but the composer scored it in 1926 for single wind, horn, percussion, harp and strings – to great effect. All this music, including the much better-known *Botticelli pictures*, shows great skill in the handling of pastel colourings, and the performances reflect credit on all concerned, including the recording team. It is a pity that the coupling is less readily recommendable.

La Sensitiva.
(BB) *** Virgin Classics Dig. Double VBD5 61469-2 (2) [CDVB 61469]. Dame Janet Baker, City of L. Sinf., Hickox – BERLIOZ: *Les Nuits d'été* etc.; BRAHMS: *Alto rhapsody* etc.; MENDELSSOHN: *Infelice* etc. ***

Tautly structured over its span of more than half an hour, Respighi's setting of Shelley's poem, *The sensitive plant* (in Italian translation), is a most beautiful piece which Dame Janet and Richard Hickox treat to a glowing first recording. The vocal line, mainly declamatory, is sweetly sympathetic and the orchestration is both rich and subtle. Altogether this makes a quite outstanding anthology.

Rimsky-Korsakov, Nikolay (1844–1908)

Capriccio espagnol, Op. 34.
(M) *** DG 449 769-2 (2) [id.]. BPO, Lorin Maazel – RAVEL: *L'heure espagnole; L'enfant et les sortiléges* ***; STRAVINSKY: *Le chant du rossignol.* *** ❁

Maazel's 1960 recording of the *Capriccio espagnol* has never been surpassed and remains one of his finest recorded performances. With gorgeous string and horn playing and a debonair, relaxed virtuosity in the *Scene e canto gitano*, leading to remarkable bravura in the closing sequence, every note in place, this is unforgettable. The remastering has restored the recording's analogue allure and, although the fortissimo violins are a little thin above the stave, the ear readily adjusts when the playing is so exciting. A true candidate for DG's 'Originals'.

(i) *Capriccio espagnol;* (ii) *Le coq d'or: suite; Dubinushka;* (iii) *May night overture;* (iv) *Russian Easter festival overture; Scheherazade;* (ii) *Snow Maiden: suite;* (v) *Tsar Sultan:suite;* (i) *Flight of the bumble-bee.*
(B) **(*) EMI Rouge et Noir CZS5 69680-2 (2) [(M) id. import]. Philh. O, with (i) André Cluytens; (ii) Efrem Kurtz; (iii) Constantin Silvestri; (iv) Lovro von Matačić; (v) Paul Kletzki.

A generous anthology reissued as one of French EMI's Rouge et Noir Doubles, although the provenance is English, and Walter Legge and Peter Andry were among the producers. The recordings were made at Abbey Road between 1956 and 1963, and they were highly regarded in their day. Some of the allure in the treble has been lost with the CD remastering but the bright colouring remains, and the Philharmonia are on top form, as they immediately demonstrate in an exciting *Scheherazade*. Matačić's direction has plenty of drive in the opening movement, and the silky strings in the slow movement are matched by the lustre of the woodwind solos. The finale is really exciting. The *Russian Easter festival overture* is also very successful. Broad and lyrically conceived, it wrings every ounce of colour from the music; the slower string subject of the allegro is glowing in its reprise, and the famous trombone solo is played with great dignity. The rest of the programme brings more of Rimsky's marvellous orchestral ideas. Efrem Kurtz is thoroughly at home in *Le coq d'or* and *The Snow Maiden* (where the charming *Danse des oiseaux* matches the other more lively lollipop, the *Dance of the tumblers*, in character) and Kletzki is vibrant in *Tsar Sultan*. Cluytens closes the first disc and opens the second with virtuoso accounts of the *Capricio espagnol* and *Flight of the bumble-bee* respectively; in the former the sound is brilliant but lacking in voluptuousness.

Capriccio espagnol; Le coq d'or: suite; May night overture; Russian Easter festival overture; Sadko (musical picture), *Op. 5; Symphony No. 2 (Antar), Op. 9;* (i) *The Snow Maiden: suite; The Tale of Tsar Saltan: suite.*
(B) ** Ph. Duo 442 605-2 (2) [id.]. Rotterdam PO, David Zinman; (i) with Roberta Alexander & Women's Ch.

This is an exceptionally generous and attractive compilation, including most of Rimsky's short orchestral works, plus *Antar*. The Rotterdam orchestra plays with appealing freshness and the recording is pleasingly rich and atmospheric. Zinman secures quite lustrous playing in the *Capriccio*, and he finds plenty of atmosphere and colour in *Sadko* and the *May night overture*, with its languorous opening horn solo. *Antar* again brings beauty and warmth in the orchestral playing, with the central movements appealingly done. But here, as in the *Russian Easter festival overture*, more zest would have been welcome, and in the famous Spanish caprice the adrenalin begins to run only at the end. In the *Snow Maiden suite* the *Dance des oiseaux* brings an effective vocal contribution, but the *Tumblers* are not very boisterous fellows. The sinuously sentient qualities of *Le Coq d'or* are somewhat over-refined, and in *Tsar Saltan* the bumble-bee buzzes gently. Generally there is a lack of charisma here, not helped by recording which, though full and rich, lacks sparkle.

Capriccio espagnol, Op. 34; Le coq d'or: suite; Russian Easter festival overture, Op. 36.
(M) *** Mercury (IMS) 434 308-2 [id.]. LSO, Antal Dorati – BORODIN: *Prince Igor: Polovstian dances.* **(*)

Dorati's 1959 *Capriccio espagnol* brings glittering bravura and excitement from the LSO players, and the *Russian Easter festival overture*, recorded at Walthamstow at the same sessions, is equally dynamic and colourful. Even more remarkably, the rich-hued and vibrant *Le coq d'or* dates from as early as 1956, yet hardly sounds dated. The playing has plenty of allure in its evocation of Queen Shemakha, yet has drama and well defined detail.

Capriccio espagnol; Russian Easter festival overture.
(B) **(*) Decca Eclipse Dig. 448 233-2; *448 233-4* [(M) id. import]. Montreal SO, Dutoit – MUSSORGSKY: *Night on the bare mountain* etc. **(*)

Dutoit's *Capriccio espagnol* is comparatively genial and relaxed; the *Russian Easter festival overture* is strong, with a fine climax. In both works the Montreal recording is full, with iridescent detail.

Christmas Eve (suite); Dubinushka, Op. 62; May night overture; Russian Easter festival overture, Op. 36; Sadko (musical picture), Op. 5; (i) *Scheherazade, Op. 35; The Snow Maiden (suite). Tsar Saltan (suite), Op. 57; Tsar Saltan* (opera): *The Flight of the bumble-bee.*
(B) **(*) Decca Double 443 464-2 (2) [id.]. SRO, Ansermet, (i) with Geneva Motet Ch.

This is all repertoire for which Ansermet was famous in the early stereo era, and *Scheherazade* must be counted a historic recording. It dates from 1960, and the sound is very impressive for its period, the sonorous rasp of the brass at the start and the weighty spectacle of the shipwreck sequence in the finale, with its splashing tam-tam, offers quality regarded as of demonstration standard in its day and not very far short of it now in this newly remastered CD transfer which has a greatly improved focus. Ansermet's skill as a ballet conductor comes out persuasively. The outer movements with their undoubted sparkle are the finest: the first is dramatic and the last is built steadily to a climax of considerable impact. The music's sinuous qualities are not missed and every bar of the score is alive. *May night* was recorded a year earlier and the strings have far less lustre; but the *Tsar Saltan suite*, also made in 1959, shows Ansermet and the Decca engineers in glittering form, especially in the recording of brass and woodwind and, if again the upper strings are rather thin, the third movement is certainly vibrant in its colourful detail. The *Flight of the bumble-bee* is rather leisurely, but perhaps we are too used to this piece being used as a virtuoso show-off.

The second disc opens with a characteristic (1959) account of the *Russian Easter festival overture*. The whole performance is warmly coloured rather than specially vital, although it is by no means dull. Ansermet is at his finest in the *Christmas Eve suite*; Rimsky's scenario is particularly delightful. This is most enjoyable music and it is played with much affection and that mixture of spontaneity and remarkably graphic orchestral palette which made Ansermet's performances special. It is a great pity that the separate movements of this 24-minute suite are not separately cued. *Dubinushka* is an engaging if repetitive arrangement of the radical song, *The little oak stick*, treated in polonaise style, and it has some typical brass fanfare writing. Ansermet is (again in 1958) well served here by the engineers, as he is in *Sadko*, an exotic fairy-tale handled with characteristic aplomb. The earliest recording offered is *The Snow Maiden suite* (1957) and if the best item turns out to be our old friend, the *Dance of the tumblers*, the choral *Dance of the birds* is also an attractive trifle (although the choral singing could be more refined). Once again the sound is remarkably warm and richly coloured, and once again Decca omit to provide cues for individual movements. Yet even allowing for such reservations, this set can certainly be recommended at Double Decca price: the performances and recordings have far more character than David Zinman's Rotterdam compilation on Philips discussed above.

Christmas Eve: Overture and suite. Greeting (to Glazunov). Mlada, Act III: Night on Mount Triglav (orchestral suite). On the Tomb: Prelude, Op. 61. Tsar's Bride: Overture and Intermezzo.
(BB) * Naxos Dig. 8.553789 [id.]. Moscow SO, Igor Golvschin.

A fascinating programme, including several novelties, is let down by a continuing lack of tension (in spite of good orchestral playing) and dull recording. It is difficult to believe that Rimsky's charming *Christmas Eve suite* could sound so lustreless, and the composer's 1901 re-drafting of the third Act of *Mlada* in purely orchestral form is equally uncompelling. The dreamlike scenario has a great deal in common with Mussorgsky's *Night on a bare mountain*, but the *Ronde fantastique*, depicting the dance of the ghosts of the dead and the later witches' sabbatha (*Ronde infernale*), is here blunted by the lack of bite and venom in playing and recording which is atmospheric but lacks glitter. The piece that comes off best is the *Tsar's Bride overture*. *On the Tomb* was dedicated to Mitrovan Belyayev, a Russian music sponsor and publisher based in Leipzig. He ensured an international copyright for music written in Russia, where there was no such protection. The *Greeting* to Glazunov makes a brief encore in a 75-minute concert which has unexpected longueurs.

Le coq d'or: suite. Mlada: suite. The Snow Maiden: suite.
(BB) ** Naxos Dig. 8.550486 [id.]. Slovak RSO (Bratislava), Donald Johanos.

Donald Johanos finds a light touch for Rimsky's more piquant orchestral effects, and the *Dance of the birds* in the *Snow Maiden suite* sparkles engagingly. If the famous *Dance of the tumblers* lacks the last degree of unbuttoned zest, the Suite from *Le coq d'or* has attractively picaresque detail, although here the music for Queen Shemakha is lacking in sensuous allure. However, the famous *Cortège* from *Mlada* ends the programme with boisterous exuberance. The recording is vividly detailed and atmospheric, but not sumptuous.

Scheherazade (symphonic suite), *Op. 35.*
(B) *** EMI CD-EMX 2214 [(M) id.]. LPO, Takuo Yuasa – PROKOFIEV: *Lieutenant Kijé*. ***
(M) *** RCA GD 60875 [09026 60875-2]. Chicago SO, Fritz Reiner – DEBUSSY: *La Mer*. ***
(M) *** RCA 09026 68168-2 [id.]. Chicago SO, Fritz Reiner – STRAVINSKY: *Chant du rossignol*. ***
(B) **(*) [EMI Red Line Dig. CDR5 69831]. Phd. O, Muti – RESPIGHI: *The Fountains of Rome*. ***
(M) *** DG 419 063-2; *419 063-4* [id.]. BPO, Karajan – BORODIN: *Polovtsian dances*. ***
(BB) **(*) Carlton LSO Double Dig. 30368 01247 (2) [(B) [id.]. LSO, John Mauceri – Concert: LSO, Ahronovitch: *'Russian Spectacular'*. **(*)
(M) ** DG (IMS) Dig. 445 558-2 [id.]. BPO, Maazel – RACHMANINOV: *Isle of the dead*. ***
(B) ** EMI forte CZS5 69361-2 (2) [CDFB 693612]. LSO, Svetlanov – ARENSKY: *Variations on a theme by Tchaikovsky;* GLAZUNOV: *The Seasons; Concert waltzes*. ***

(i) *Scheherazade;* (ii) *Capriccio espagnol, Op. 34.*
(B) **(*) DG Classikon Analogue/Dig. 439 443-2 [(M) id. import]. (i) Boston SO, Ozawa; (ii) Gothenburg SO, Neeme Järvi.
(B) **(*) Tring Dig. TRP 003 [(M) id. import]. RPO, Barry Wordsworth.
(M) **(*) EMI CDM5 65715-2 [id.]. O de Paris, Rostropovich – MUSSORGSKY: *Night on the bare mountain*. ***

(BB) ** RCA Navigator 74321 17899-2. (i) Phd. O, Ormandy; (ii) RCA Victor SO, Kondrashin.

(i–ii) *Scheherazade;* (iii–iv) *Capriccio espagnol;* (i; iv) *Russian Easter festival overture, Op. 36.*
(M) *** Ph. 442 643-2. (i) Concg. O; (ii) Kondrashin; (iii) LSO; (iv) Markevitch.

Scheherazade; Le coq d'or: Introduction & Cortège; Sadko, Op. 5.
(BB) ** Naxos Dig. 8.550098 [id.]. Czech RSO (Bratislava), Ondrej Lenárd.

Scheherazade (symphonic suite), *Op. 35; Dubinushka, Op. 62; Tale of Tsar Saltan: Flight of the bumble-bee.*
(M) *** Chandos Enchant Dig. CHAN 7093 [id.]. RSNO, Järvi – KALINNIKOV: *Overtures*. ***

(i) *Scheherazade;* (ii) *May night overture; Sadko* (musical picture), *Op. 5.*
(BB) **(*) Belart 450 132-2 [(M) id. import]. (i) LSO, Monteux; (ii) SRO, Ansermet.

Scheherazade; Russian Easter festival overture; The Maid of Pskov: Hunt and storm.
(M) (***) Biddulph mono WHL 010 [id.]. Phd. O, Stokowski.

(i–ii) *Scheherazade;* (i; iii) *Russian Easter festival overture, Op. 36;* (iv) *Tsar Saltan* (opera): *Flight of the bumble-bee; March.*
(M) *** [RCA Basic 100 09026 68335-2; *68335-4*]. (i) Chicago SO; (ii) Reiner; (iii) Stokowski; (iv) LSO, Previn.

Scheherazade; Tsar Saltan: orchestral suite.
(BB) *** Naxos Dig. 8.550726. Philh. O, Bátiz.

Kondrashin's version of *Scheherazade* with the Concertgebouw Orchestra has the advantage of splendid (1980) analogue recorded sound, combining richness and sparkle within exactly the right degree of resonance. Hermann Krebbers' gently seductive portrayal of Scheherazade's narrative creates a strong influence on the overall interpretation. His exquisite playing, especially at the opening and close of the work, is cleverly used by Kondrashin to provide a foil for the expansively vibrant contribution of the orchestra as a whole. Kondrashin creates an irresistible forward impulse, leading to a huge climax at the moment of the shipwreck. On CD one notices that inner detail is marginally less sharp than it would be with a digital recording, but the analogue glow and naturalness more than compensate, and the richness of texture is just right for the music. The couplings are generous, giving an overall playing time of 74 minutes. Markevitch gives an excellent account of the *Russian Easter festival overture* with the same orchestra, with fine orchestral playing to bring out the score's glowing colours in the Amsterdam acoustic. The *Capriccio espagnol*, too, is brilliantly played by the LSO, and here the sound also has considerable allure, with the present CD transfer much more vivid than the original LP. Alas, this seems not to be available in the USA.

On EMI's mid-priced label, Eminence, comes another romantically compulsive account, with the sinuously supple contribution of the orchestral leader, Stephen Bryant, in the role of the heroine believably placed in the orchestral texture. Takuo Yuasa's reading is more spacious, less urgent than Kondrashin's, but the central movements are full of colour and warmth, and the finale brings grippingly animated orchestral virtuosity and a powerful climax, with the tam-tam flashing out at the moment of the shipwreck. The poetic close has a lustrous rapture. At mid-price, with a splendid Prokofiev coupling, no one will be disappointed with this, for the sound is full-bodied and brilliant, with an attractive ambient glow.

Reiner's first movement opens richly and dramatically and has a strong forward impulse. Sidney Harth, the orchestral leader, naturally balanced, plays most seductively. Reiner's affectionate individual touches have much in common with Beecham's (full-price) version and sound almost as spontaneous; the finale, brilliant and very exciting, has a climax of resounding power and amplitude. The Chicago Hall acoustics provide the orchestra with plenty of body (the brass-laden introduction is weightily arresting), yet in John Pfeiffer's newest transfer detail is more clearly focused and immediate, while the strings retain all their bloom in the third movement. Above all, Reiner's is a virtuoso reading with phenomenally crisp ensemble, to have one relishing not just the brilliance but the individual finesse of the Chicago orchestra and its principals. The new coupling also shows Reiner and his orchestra at their finest, and it is particularly appropriate, for Stravinsky's glittering orchestral palette in *Le chant du rossignol* owes much to Rimsky. Reiner's recording also comes, differently coupled, in RCA's Basic 100 collection (available only in the USA). Most notable is Stokowski's superb *Russian Easter festival overture* (also recorded in Chicago), but the two colourful excerpts from *Tsar Saltan* show Previn and the LSO in top form, and they too are vividly recorded.

Järvi's version of *Scheherazade* with the RSNO may not be the most high-powered or weighty, nor is it idiosyncratic in the way of Beecham or Reiner, but it is given one of Chandos's most sumptuous and spectacular digital recordings and, as with Kondrashin, Järvi's reading generates a vivid narrative feeling. The playing is no less fine than in versions from the most distinguished international orchestras. For those looking for a modern, digital version, this is well worth considering, and it offers a smiliarly brilliant account of the colourful *Dubinushka*, plus a buzzing, convincingly scaled *Bumble-bee*. The coupled overtures by Kalinnikov are also well worth having.

Muti's reading is colourful and dramatic in a larger-than-life way that sweeps one along. The great string theme of the slow movement has all the voluptuousness one expects of the Philadelphia strings, more spacious than usual, in one of the best of EMI's latter-day Philadelphia recordings, even if not ideally balanced. There is a glare in the upper range to which not all ears will respond, even if the racy finale, with its exciting climax, carries all before it.

Bátiz's reputation for spontaneity in the recording studio is demonstrated at its most telling. His performance is impulsive, full of momentum and seductively volatile. David Nolan's picture of Scheherazade is rhapsodically evanescent and in the key second movement the lilting Philharmonia wind solos are a constant pleasure. The slow movement combines refinement with its sensuous patina, and the finale has fine zest and excitement. The colourful *Tsar Saltan suite* is comparably dramatic and vivid. In short, with first-class recording, both clear in detail and full-bodied, at super-bargain price this is hard to beat.

Karajan's 1967 recording is greatly enhanced in its CD format. The added presence increases the feeling of ardour from the glorious Berlin strings in the *Andante*. The outer movements have great vitality and thrust, and the bright percussion transients add to the feeling of zest. Yet Michel Schwalbé's sinuously luxuriant violin solos are still allowed to participate in the narrative. The fill-up is a sizzling account of the Borodin *Polovtsian dances*, with no chorus, but managing perfectly well without.

John Mauceri conducts a powerful, dramatic reading marked by incisive, crisply disciplined playing from the LSO, just as impressive in the warmly expressive rubato of the great lyrical passages. To match this, the recording is brilliant rather than sensuously beautiful, clear and well balanced and with fine presence. Michael Davis is a persuasive violin soloist, and in Mauceri's hands the melodic line of the third movement is appealingly supple, while there is no lack of excitement in the finale.

The recordings from Monteux and Ansermet on the Belart reissue come from the earliest days of stereo. Monteux's version of *Scheherazade* is, if anything, more vivid than Kondrashin's, the performance vital, sensuous, exciting and full of charisma. In the finale Monteux holds back the climax until the very last minute and then unleashes his forces to devastating effect. The orchestral playing is not as polished as the Concertgebouw's but it has tremendous zest and plenty of voluptuous feeling in the central movements. The snag is that the remastered recording, although brilliant, lacks the opulence that makes the Philips disc so luxuriantly enjoyable. Ansermet finds all the colour in the *May night overture* and *Sadko*, an exotic Rimskian fairy-tale with another storm for its climax; here the Decca engineers, working in Geneva, provide a glittering orchestral palette.

Ozawa's earlier (1977) Boston *Scheherazade* is an attractive performance, richly recorded. The first movement is strikingly spacious, building to a fine climax; if the last degree of vitality is missing from the central movements, the orchestral playing is warmly vivid. The finale is lively enough, if not earth-shaking in its excitement; the reading as a whole has plenty of colour and atmosphere, however, and is certainly enjoyable. Moreover Järvi's digital *Capriccio espagnol* is a distinctive and worthwhile bonus, brilliantly recorded.

Barry Wordsworth's RPO version is offered in the bargain price-range and is certainly recommendable. As the dramatic opening shows, the digital recording is spectacularly full and wide-ranging and, while the solo violin (Jonathan Carney) is rather forwardly balanced, it means that 'Scheherazade' immediately takes a dominating role. The first movement has a fine, spacious sweep and, if the wind solos in the second movement are made to seem rather less spontaneous, the slow movement has an agreeable allure at the opening, and the finale brings plenty of orchestral bravura and excitement. What makes this disc particularly attractive is the outstanding coupling. *Capriccio espagnol* is an elusive work on disc but here vitality is the keynote. The variations are sumptuous but provide plenty of glitter. Then with stabbing brass the *Scena e canto gitano* prepares the way for a vibrant close. The Tring recording was made in All Saints' Church, Petersham, and to counter the resonance the microphones are fairly close, which adds to the brilliance and produces a vivid orchestral presence.

Rostropovich's 1974 account with the Orchestre de Paris (now reissued as part of the Rostropovich Edition) offers glowingly rich sound. The performance of the first movement, spacious and opulent, is very convincing, but in the second the conductor's flexibility in the matter of rubato is not entirely matched by precision in the orchestral playing. This is perhaps a small matter when there is so much lambent allure in the central movements and in the performance as a whole; there is much infectious rhythmic pointing, while the finale is splendidly exciting. The *Capriccio espagnol*, recorded four years later, is similarly sumptuous and appealing.

This collection of Leopold Stokowski's recordings of Rimsky-Korsakov centres on the first of his five versions of *Scheherazade*. Made in 1927, it is wilder and more passionate than later ones; fascinatingly, an alternative version of the first movement, never issued before, is included as a supplement. At a slightly broader speed, spreading to an extra 78-r.p.m. side, it is even more persuasive, and Stokowski's Philadelphia Orchestra, unlike British groups of the time, plays with high polish as well as passion. Equally impressive is Stokowski's intense, volatile account of the *Russian Easter festival overture*, dating from 1929, while the *Hunt and storm* sequence from the *The Maid of Pskov* comes from ten years later, with the sound drier and marginally less full. The Biddulph transfers are excellent, with plenty of body.

There is nothing to detain the collector in the performance by Maazel. The playing of the Berlin Philharmonic Orchestra is, of course, peerless, and in the slow movement they make some gorgeous sounds (though the acoustics of the Philharmonie are not entirely flattering on CD). But Maazel's reading is essentially spacious and the outer movements are wanting in electricity. The main attraction here is the compelling Rachmaninov performance of the coupling.

Ormandy's version dates from 1973 and offers some characteristically brilliant playing from the Philadelphia Orchestra: the wind solos in the central movements are superb, especially the principal bassoon and clarinet. The leader, too, is a suitably sinuous storyteller. Ormandy's is a spacious reading, lacking the last degree of drive in the finale, in spite of the bravura orchestral response. But the close-miked recording, though clean and clear, is simply not sumptuous enough to add the necessary glamour to this score, although it must be admitted that at the opening of *The young prince and the young princess* the voluptuous body of Philadelphia string-tone is quite overwhelming and triumphs over the unflattering acoustic. When one turns to the coupled *Capriccio espagnol* one enters a different sound-world; even though that recording was made in 1958 – 14 years before the main work – its natural resonance ensures bloom on the orchestra and it is still impressive on all counts. As for the performance, it remains among the finest ever put on disc. Kondrashin generates great flair and excitement, with glittering colour and detail in the variations and the *Scene e canto gitano*. In the closing section the ensemble occasionally slips momentarily with Kondrashin's breathless onward thrust, but the excitement is very tangible.

Svetlanov's version of this perennial favourite with the LSO was made in 1978. But it is disappointing, despite John Georgiadis's subtly seductive image of Scheherazade herself. The broad, powerful opening movement, taken very spaciously indeed, is balanced by a finale which is almost aggressively brilliant. The inner movements are extremely volatile, with much ebb and flow of tempo, not always convincing, so that they are less contrasted than usual. The LSO wind solo playing is impressive, but the strings sometimes have an almost febrile timbre which is less than glamorous. Svetlanov's conception undoubtedly brings out the Russianness of the score, and it is certainly vivid; but in such a competitive field this could hardly be a strong contender, which is a pity when the Arensky and Glazunov couplings are so seductive.

The alternative Naxos *Scheherazade* directed by Ondrej Lenárd is well played and offers warm, vivid sound. It has glamour but is without the finesse or body of string tone of the finest Western versions. On the other hand, wind solos are excellent and there is plenty of excitement in the finale. Of the couplings, while it is a pity that the whole of the *Coq d'or* suite was not chosen, the performance of *Sadko* has plenty of atmosphere and a really spectacular climax.

Symphonies Nos. 1 in E min., Op. 1; 2 (Antar), Op. 9; 3 in C, Op. 32; Capriccio espagnol, Op. 36; (i) *Piano concerto in C sharp min., Op. 30. Russian Easter festival overture, Op. 36; Sadko, Op. 5.*
(M) **(*) Chandos Dig. CHAN 7029 (3) [id.]. (i) Geoffrey Tozer; Bergen PO, Kitaienko.

Kitaienko makes the most of Rimsky's *First Symphony*, as he does of *Antar*, its exoticism well conveyed. Indeed he draws very good playing from the Bergen Philharmonic throughout. In the *Third Symphony* he is comparably successful in the opening movement, and the lustrous colours of the secondary material glow appealingly, but the Scherzo lacks sparkle. Similarly, while he gets very lively results in the *Capriccio espagnol*, *Sadko* takes a while to warm up, although it has a spectacular close. With Tozer at the keyboard he shares a warmly lyrical view of the *Piano concerto* but, partly because of the resonant sound, the finale lacks something in sparkle.

Symphonies Nos 1–3; Scheherazade, Op. 35.
(B) ** BMG/Melodiya Twofer 74321 40065-2 (2) [id.]. USSR SO, Svetlanov.

In the Rimsky-Korsakov symphonies, Svetlanov is a most persuasive interpreter, pointing rhythms and phrasing more subtly than such a rival as Kitaienko on Chandos. Unfortunately the recorded sound is less full and immediate than many from this source, though not seriously enough to mar enjoyment. Ironically, it is the earliest recording, that of *Scheherazade*, made in 1969, that has the most body, with impressive weight and dynamic range. The performance is superb, warmly expressive and spontaneous-sounding, with an excellent, warm reading of the love scene of the third movement. The one reservation is that the ensemble is less crisp than in the finest latterday versions.

Symphony No. 2 (Antar), Op. 9.
(M) *** DG (IMS) Dig. 445 568-2. Gothenburg SO, Järvi – BORODIN: *Symphony No. 2* etc. ***

As with the Borodin coupling, Järvi's account is essentially spacious. Glorious playing from the Gothenburg strings and warm, lustrous DG recording combine to make the most of Rimsky's languor, and the central movements are by no means lacking in vitality.

Symphony No. 3 in C, Op. 32.
(M) * Revelation RV100083 [id.]. Moscow RSO, Gennady Rozhdestvensky (with ARENSKY: *Suvorov march;* TANEYEV: *Oresteya Overture*).

Rimsky-Korsakov's *Symphony No. 3 in C* is not a work that is likely to set the Thames on fire – or the Neva for that matter. Revelation offer it in a 1962 recording by the Moscow Radio Orchestra, identified on the label by its somewhat grandiloquent title 'Grand Symphony Orchestra of All-Union Radio and TV', conducted by Gennady Rozhdestvensky. Though it does not offer a serious challenge to either of Svetlanov's RCA recordings, the sound is open and pleasing. It is far more acceptable than in the fill-up, Taneyev's *Oresteya Overture*, made ten years later. This is raucous in climaxes and coarse, as is also the Arensky *Suvorov march* – not a particularly interesting piece. No stars (or separate listings) for them. Given the extravagant claims Revelation make about their recordings, it is worth noting that little trouble has been taken over the transfers, and at 53 minutes this is distinctly short measure. Not worth the money.

Rochberg, George (born 1918)

Violin concerto.
(M) *(**) Sony Stern Edition II SMK 64505 [id.]. Stern, Pittsburgh SO, Previn – STRAVINSKY: *Violin concerto.* (***)

For many years George Rochberg wrote in the twelve-note idiom, then he subsequently rediscovered tonality. His *Violin concerto* instantly proclaims that it is earnest and modern, opening with a suitably astringent gesture from the soloist before relapsing into a neo-romanticism redolent of Bartók and Szymanowski. This is therefore a work which fails to be structurally convincing and which also mixes rather hollow avant-garde dissonance with real music. Nevertheless it has some appealing moments, but it is rather like the rhyme about the little girl with 'a little curl right in the middle of her forehead'. It is beautifully played by Isaac Stern and the Pittsburgh orchestra under Previn, who approach it as if it were a concerto of the very first order. Every now and again they almost manage to convince us that it is better than in fact it is! No complaints about the 1977 recording, which has fine detail and a good balance.

Rodgers, Richard (born 1902)

Slaughter on 10th Avenue (ballet from the musical, *On Your Toes*).
(M) *** RCA 09026 68550-2 [id.]. Boston Pops O, Arthur Fiedler – Concert. **(*)

Rodger's brief (nine-minute) ballet score, written for the musical *On Your Toes* and choreographed by Balanchine, has three splendid tunes, two of them quite unforgettable, the one gloriously lyrical, the other bouncingly rooty-tooty. Fiedler makes the very most of them and integrates the score splendidly in a frisson-creating performance that has never been surpassed. The orchestra plays superbly, and the early stereo recording also has an amplitude and bite which fit the music exactly. This comes as part of one of the earliest Boston Pops 'Living Stereo' reissues – the RCA equivalent of Decca's 'Classic Sound'.

Rodrigo, Joaquín (born 1902)

A la busca del más allá; (i) *Concierto Andaluz* (for 4 guitars); (ii) *Concierto de Aranjuez* (for guitar); (iii) *Concierto de estío* (for violin); (iv) *Concierto en modo galante* (for cello); (v) *Concierto heroico* (for piano); (vi) *Concierto madrigal* (for 2 guitars); (vii) *Concierto pastoral* (for flute); (viii) *Concierto serenata* (for harp). (ii) *Fantasia para un gentilhombre. Música para un jardín; Per la flor del Iliri blau; 5 Piezas infantiles; Soleriana; Zarabanda lejana y villancico.*
(M) *** EMI Dig. CDZ7 67435-2 (4) [CDZD 674352]. (i) Moreno, Garibay, López, Ruiz; (ii) Alfonso Moreno; (iii) Augustín Léo Ara; (iv) Robert Cohen; (v) Jorge Osorio; (vi) Moreno, Mariotti; (vii) Lisa Hansen; (viii) Nancy Allen; LSO; Mexico State PO; RPO, Enrique Bátiz.

The only missing concertos are the second *Guitar concerto* (*Concierto para una Fiesta*) and the later *Cello concerto* (*Concierto como un divertimento*) commissioned by Julian Lloyd Webber. The present

EMI recordings were made between 1980 and 1985, many of them in Watford Town Hall, and are of excellent quality, although the early digital technique often brings an overlit sound to the treble, perhaps appropriate for music drenched in Spanish sunshine. The *Summer concerto* for violin ('conceived in the manner of Vivaldi') is the composer's own favourite, and Augustin Léo Ara catches its neo-classical vitality admirably. The *Cello concerto* is given a masterly performance by Robert Cohen; he combines elegance of phrasing with warm beauty of timbre. The *Concierto serenata* for harp, a favourite of ours, has an unforgettable piquancy and charm. Nancy Allen consistently beguiles the ear with her gentleness. The *Concierto pastoral* is a spikier piece than usual from this composer and its brilliant introduction is far from pastoral in feeling, but Rodrigo's fragmented melodies soon insinuate themselves into the consciousness. Rodrigo's *Piano concerto* has a programmatic content, with the four movements written 'under the sign of the Sword, the Spur, the Cross and the Laurel'. The performers give a strong, extrovert account of the piece.

The *Concierto Andaluz* has its weaknesses but remains engaging if a trifle inflated. A similar comment might be made about the effect of the duo *Concierto madrigal*, with its set of twelve delightful vignettes, many with a medieval flavour, but the four guitar soloists here do not achieve the strongest profile, and this is also one reason why Alfonso Moreno's account of the famous *Concierto de Aranjuez*, though bright and sympathetic, is in no way outstanding. The symphonic poem, *A la busca del más allá*, is evocative and powerfully scored; *Música para un jardín* is a quartet of cradle songs, originally conceived for the piano and scored with all the piquancy at the composer's command. The *Five Children's pieces* are delightful, while the two neo-classical evocations of eighteenth-century Spain (*Soleriana*) are also unostentatiously appealing. *Per la flor del Iliri blau* is based on a Valencian legend, and Rodrigo is more impressive in moments of gently atmospheric detail than in the melodrama. The *Zarabanda lejana* was Rodrigo's first work for guitar. He later orchestrated it and added the *Villancico* to make a binary structure, the first part nobly elegiac, the second a gay dance movement.

(i) *Concierto Andaluz* (for 4 guitars); (ii) *Concierto de Aranjuez;* (ii; iii) *Concierto madrigal* (for 2 guitars); (ii) *Concierto para una fiesta; Fantasia para un gentilhombre*. Solo guitar pieces: *Bajando de la Meseta; En los trigales; Fandango; Junto al Generalife; 3 Little Pieces; Romance de Durandarte; Sonata a la española; Tiento antiquo*.
(M) *** Ph. 432 581-2 (3). (i) Los Romeros; (ii) Pepe Romero; (iii) Angel Romero; ASMF, Marriner.

This distinguished set gathers together all Rodrigo's major concertante guitar works in first-class performances and adds a rewarding recital of solo works as a postlude, all played with natural spontaneity and complete authority by an artist who feels this music from his innermost being. The *Sonata* is no less strongly Spanish in character and the genre pieces are comparably picturesque in evoking Mediterranean atmosphere and local dance-rhythms. If the *Concierto para una fiesta* does not quite repeat the success of the *Concierto de Aranjuez*, it still has plenty of Andalusian colour, and Pepe Romero's performance has all the freshness of new discovery. He is equally magnetic in the solo items. Throughout, Marriner and the Academy provide accompaniments which are thoroughly polished and have much warmth, and the Philips sound is most natural and beautifully balanced.

Concierto de Aranjuez (for guitar and orchestra).
✿ (M) *** Decca Dig. 430 703-2; *430 703-4* [id.]. Carlos Bonell, Montreal SO, Dutoit – FALLA: *El amor brujo* etc. *** ✿
(M) *** Sony SMK 60022 [id.]. John Williams, ECO, Barenboim – CASTELNUOVO-TEDESCO; VILLA-LOBOS: *Guitar concerto*. ***
(BB) *** Naxos Dig. 8.550729 [id.]. Norbert Kraft, N. CO, Nicholas Ward – CASTELNUOVO-TEDESCO: *Concerto* ***; VILLA-LOBOS: *Concerto*. **(*)
(BB) ** Arte Nova Dig. 74321 51624-2 [id.]. Orlandini, Gran Canaria PO, Leaper – TURINA: *Canto a Sevilla*. ***
(B) ** DG Classikon 439 458-2; *439 458-4* [(M) id. import]. Narciso Yepes, Spanish R. & TV O, Alonso – FALLA: *El amor brujo; Nights in the gardens of Spain*. **(*)

Concierto de Aranjuez; (i) *Concierto madrigal* (for 2 guitars); *Fantasia para un gentilhombre*.
(M) *** Ph. 432 828-2 [id.]. Pepe Romero; (i) Angel Romero; ASMF, Marriner.

(i) *Concierto de Aranjuez;* (ii) *Fantasia para un gentilhombre*.
(B) *** Decca Eclipse Dig. 448 243-2; *448 243-4* [(M) id. import]. Carlos Bonell, Montreal SO, Dutoit – ALBENIZ: *Rapsodia española*; TURINA: *Rapsodica sinfónica*. ***
(M) *** Decca Dig. 417 748-2. Carlos Bonell, Montreal SO, Dutoit (with FALLA: *Three-cornered hat* ***).

(B) *** Sony SBK 58168; *SBT 58168* [id.]. John Williams, (i) Phd. O (members), Ormandy; (ii) ECO, Sir Charles Groves – GIULIANI: *Concerto, Op. 30;* VIVALDI: *Concerto, RV 93*. ***

(i) *Concierto de Aranjuez; Fantasia para un gentilhombre. En los trigales; Pastoral; Sonata a la española.*
(B) *** CfP Dig. CD-CFP 4614 [EMI Red Line CDR5 69832]. Ernesto Bitetti, (i) Philh. O, Antoni Ros-Marba.

(i) *Concierto de Aranjuez; Fantasia para un gentilhombre. En los trigales; Pequeña Sevillana; Sonata a la española.*
(B) ** Tring Dig. TRP 0050. Carlos Bonell; (i) RPO, Kaspszyk.

The Bonell/Dutoit *Concierto* was originally paired with the *Fantasia para un gentilhombre*. Decca made this issue even more attractive by adding a bonus of three dances from Falla's *Three-cornered hat* (taken from Dutoit's complete set). In the *Fantasia*, the balance between warmly gracious lyricism and sprightly rhythmic resilience is no less engaging. There is now a third, even more generous coupling on Decca's Eclipse bargain label which is well worth considering, as the Albéniz and Turina concertante works for piano are given dazzling, sultry performances by De Larrocha and Frühbeck de Burgos.

Decca then reissued the much-praised Bonell/Dutoit recording of the *Concierto* a second time, now re-coupled with Alicia de Larrocha's splendid digital recording of Falla's *Nights in the gardens of Spain* plus Dutoit's outstanding complete *El amor brujo*. This is a very attractive pairing and the reasons for the success of the Rodrigo performance remain unaltered: an exceptionally clear, atmospheric and well-balanced digital recording plus Bonell's imaginative account of the solo part, and the strong characterization of the orchestral accompaniments by Charles Dutoit and his excellent Montreal orchestra.

John Williams's 1974 recording of the *Concierto de Aranjuez* with Barenboim is superior to his earlier version with Ormandy (see below). The playing has marvellous point and spontaneity, and the famous *Adagio* has rarely been played with this degree of poetic spontaneity. This performance can challenge the best of its competitors. The balance is characteristically forward, but the result is extremely vivid and clearly focused.

Pepe Romero's performance of the *Concierto de Aranjuez* has plenty of Spanish colour, the musing poetry of the slow movement beautifully caught. The account of the *Fantasia* is warm and gracious, with the Academy contributing quite as much as the soloist to the appeal of the performance. Angel joins Pepe for the Renaissance-inspired duet, *Concierto madrigal*, which is very attractive indeed, making this a very viable alternative to the Decca couplings.

Norbert Kraft is a soloist of personality and he receives spirited, sensitive accompaniments from the Northern Chamber Orchestra under Nicholas Ward. Indeed the work sounds remarkably fresh using a smaller-sized orchestral group, which can bring a degree of intimacy yet produce sufficient body of violin-tone for the rapturous tutti near the end of the *Adagio*. This Naxos CD deserves a place near the very top of the list. The recording is very well balanced, with the guitar given a most convincing relationship with the orchestra and the sound itself vividly realistic.

An excellent bargain anthology from CfP, vividly recorded. Rodrigo's two favourite concertante guitar works are combined with some worthwhile solo items which are very well played by Ernesto Bitetti; indeed the *Sonata a la española*, which ends the programme, is dedicated to him. He gives a rather introspective performance of it, but the *Concierto* is bright-eyed while still finding a languorous intimacy in the slow movement. The performance of the *Fantasia*, too, is especially successful, with Ros-Marba and the Philharmonia providing a brilliantly coloured orchestral backing, full of bracing rhythmic vitality. They are helped by the lively yet atmospheric digital sound.

John Williams made his first stereo recording of the *Concierto de Aranjuez* in 1965 with the estimable Eugene Ormandy, and followed with the *Fantasia* two years later, when Sir Charles Groves was hardly less sympathetic, especially in the expressive music. The performance of the *Concierto* has an agreeably ruminative, improvisatory quality, especially in the slow movement, and Ormandy provides a chamber-scaled background tapesty which nevertheless has a vivid palette; only in the finale does one feel that the relaxed mood loses some of the music's sparkle. The balance is near ideal, with the guitar nicely placed in relation to the orchestra in a pleasingly atmospheric ambience (in fact a pair of town halls, one in Philadelphia, the other in Barking!). Williams was to record the *Concierto* again with greater charisma, but this early, more intimate account remains very appealing, and the couplings are good, too.

Neatly played and very well recorded, the Arte Nova version of this favourite Rodrigo concerto yet lacks a little in lift and sparkle in the outer movements, though the haunting beauty of the central slow movement is brought out persuasively. A fair coupling for the rare 40-minute cantata by Turina, which is well worth seeking out.

Carlos Bonell's new recording of the *Concierto* for Tring does not begin to match his earlier, Decca account with Dutoit. Kaspszyk's accompaniments are comparatively limp and, although there is a pleasing intimacy in the scale of the music-making, it fails to spring vividly to life. Of the solo pieces easily the finest performance is of the *Sonata a la española*.

Yepes' late-1960s version of the *Concierto* is not very imaginatively conducted by Alonso, who is rhythmically rather stiff in the finale. Yepes is at his finest in the *Adagio*, but the studio recording is dry and unflattering.

The Julian Bream Edition

Concierto de Aranjuez.

(M) *** RCA 09026 61598-2. Julian Bream, Melos Ens., Sir Colin Davis – ARNOLD: *Concerto;* BENNETT: *Concerto* ***.

(M) *** RCA Dig. 09026 61605-2 [id.]. Julian Bream, COE, Gardiner – BERKELEY; BROUWER: *Concertos.* ***

(i) *Concierto de Aranjuez;* (ii) *Fantasia para un gentilhombre. Invocation and dance (Hommage à Manuel de Falla); 3 Piezas españolas.*

(M) *** RCA Dig. 09026 61611-2. Julian Bream, (i) COE, Gardiner; (ii) RCA Victor CO, Leo Brouwer.

The differences between Bream's two earlier RCA readings of the *Concierto*, the first (analogue) with Colin Davis in 1963, the second (digital) with Gardiner in 1982, are almost too subtle to analyse and perhaps depend as much on the personalities of the two conductors as on that of the soloist. Certainly neither account is upstaged by the most recent, full-priced version with Rattle. Sir Colin Davis's direction is at its best in the opening movement, as crisply rhythmic as you could like, and in the slow movement Bream is raptly inspirational. Maybe the Gardiner version has a little extra dash and, for those who prefer an all-Rodrigo programme, this could be a good choice and the famous *Adagio* is played in a very free, improvisatory way, with some highly atmospheric wind solos in the orchestra. The *Fantasia para un gentilhombre* is mellower at its noble opening, but Leo Brouwer, himself a guitarist, brings plenty of orchestral vitality to the later sections of the score. The *Tres Piezas españolas* add to the value of the disc: the second piece, a Passacaglia, is one of Rodrigo's finest shorter works, and both this and the *Homage to Falla* show Bream at his most inspirationally spontaneous. The alternative coupling is with concertos by Berkeley and Brouwer.

(i) *Concierto pastoral* (for flute and orchestra); *Fantasia para un gentilhombre* (arr. Galway for flute and orchestra); (ii) *Concierto de Aranjuez* (for guitar and orchestra).

(M) *** RCA Analogue/Dig. 09026 68248-2 [id.]. (i) James Galway, Philh. O, Mata; (ii) Kazuhito Yamashita, Paillard CO, Paillard.

The *Concierto pastoral* was composed for James Galway in 1978. Its spikily brilliant introduction is far from pastoral in feeling, but the mood of the work soon settles down. At first hearing, the material seems thinner than usual, but Rodrigo's fragmented melodies and rhythmic ostinatos soon insinuate themselves into the listener's memory. The slow movement is especially effective, with a witty scherzando centrepiece framed by the *Adagio* outer sections. Galway's performance is truly superlative, showing the utmost bravura and matching refinement. He is beautifully recorded, and the small accompanying chamber orchestra is well balanced. The arrangement of the *Fantasia* is a very free one, necessitating re-orchestration, exchanging clarinet and horn instrumentation for the original scoring for trumpet and piccolo. The solo part too has been rewritten and even extended, apparently with the composer's blessing. The result is, to be honest, not an improvement on the original. But Galway is very persuasive, even if there is a persistent feeling of inflation. The brilliant Japanese guitar player, Kazuhito Yamashita, is not mentioned at all on the front of the CD, yet he contributes a memorable solo contribution to the famous *Concierto de Aranjuez*, especially in the slow movement, where he adds a cadenza. The finale too has plenty of adrenalin. Paillard and his orchestra support him well enough, although the orchestral playing at times lacks refinement. But this digitally recorded performance is full of life and may be regarded as a bonus.

Fantasia para un gentilhombre.

(M) ** DG (IMS) 449 098-2. Narciso Yepes, Spanish R. & TV O, Alonso – CASTELNUOVO-TEDESCO: *Concerto* **(*); HALFFTER: *Concerto.* **

Yepes plays impressively, as usual, but Alonso's accompaniment is merely serviceable. These artists have been recorded in a studio with a dry acoustic, which hardly adds glamour to Rodrigo's colourful orchestral palette.

(i) *Fantasia para un gentilhombre* (arr. Galway). (ii) *Pavana real* (ballet; complete). *3 viejos aires de danza.*

(B) **(*) EMI Eminence Dig. CD-EMX 2248 [(M) id.]. (i) Lisa Hansen; Mexico State SO, Bátiz, (ii) with Rafael Jiménez, Luis A. Cansino.

The arrangement for flute and orchestra of the *Fantasia para un gentilhombre* we already know in James Galway's own recording, but it is winningly presented here by Lisa Hansen, and Bátiz's accompaniment is felicitous, with some splendid wind solos from the excellent principals of the Mexican orchestra. The other works are new to CD. The ballet *Pavana real* ('Royal pavan') dates from the same year as the *Fantasia* (with which it has much musically in common) and is set in the Royal Court of Valencia in the early sixteenth century. Each Act opens arrestingly with a regal fanfare, and the music thereafter is vividly neo-classical. The third-movement *Zarabanda* is charming, and the following Interlude (*Cantiga del pastor*) brings a delicious solo interplay between cor anglais and guitar (Rafael Jiménez). The narrative draws on the writings of Luis de Milán and includes both a sung ballad (Luis Cansino) and, as the key to the resolution of the plot, one of Milán's own noble pavanes. Like the other engaging court dances in the last Act (*May Fiesta*), this is scored most winningly. The *Tres viejos aires de danza* also look back in time in their inspiration and atmosphere, with a graceful opening *Pastoral* leading to a perky *Minuet* and a lively closing *Jiga*. Throughout, the orchestral ensemble is pleasingly crisp. The Mexican strings are not opulent but their phrasing is brightly responsive. Bátiz has a tendency to be rhythmically a little too forceful, but his performances are warm-hearted and certainly do justice to these attractive scores. Rodrigo remains an underrated composer: this is music that deserves to be aired in the concert hall. The recording is rather forwardly balanced, but the focus is clean and the basic acoustic quite pleasing, with no lack of bloom on the woodwind.

Juglares (Esayo sinfónico); Palillos y panderetas; 2 piezas caballerescas; Soleriana (ballet suite). (i) *Sones en la Giralda (Fantasia sevillana for harp and orchestra).*
(B) **(*) EMI Eminence Dig. CD-EMX 2249 [(M) id.]. (i) Ieuan Jones; Mexico State SO, Bátiz.

At least two of the five works on Bátiz's second collection are new to the gramophone, and the programme includes both Rodrigo's first (*Juglares*, 1923) and last (*Palillos y panderetas*, 1982) orchestral piece. *Juglares* ('Minstrels') is comparatively brief. It has a delectably folksy opening, with squeeze-box effects, and even a reminder of *Petrushka*, but the slow middle section brings the composer's familiar penchant for looking back in time, here by using a plainchant theme. The two *Piezas caballerescas* (1945) similarly contrast a solemnly archaic *Madrigal* (ingeniously scored for four solo cellos) with a catchy *Danza de cortesia*. *Soleriana* (1953) is another neo-classical ballet score, which in this instance turns directly to the keyboard music of Antonio Soler and, to a lesser extent, Domenico Scarlatti. In its stylish yet vivid use of the orchestral palette, the suite has much in common with Respighi's *Ancient airs and dances*, and it brings a memorable central *Pastoral*. *Palillos y panderetas* ('Drumsticks and tambourines'), is characteristically picaresque and was inspired by the city of Madrid which was the composer's home for the greater part of his life. Another charming central *Pastoral* brings a quaint little slow march with woodwind interchanges over a tapping side-drum. The concertante *Fantasia sevillana*, for harp and orchestra, dates from the previous year. It opens with haunting delicacy of atmosphere, and with its popular dance rhythms (and even an unintended (?) whiff of Chabrier's *España*) is also an evocation of a more modern Spain, yet still remembering the past. (La Giralda is the imposing Moorish tower which stands beside Seville Cathedral.) Bátiz is thoroughly in sympathy with all this music, and the Mexico State Symphony Orchestra, obviously very well rehearsed, play with crisp, vibrant rhythms and clean ensemble. Wind solos have plenty of lustre and character. But, as on the companion disc, the lack of opulence in the string timbres is emphasized by the close balance, especially in *Soleriana*; although the basic ambience is pleasing, a more recessed effect would have greatly increased the appeal of the music-making. Nevetherless this remains a valuable issue.

SOLO GUITAR MUSIC

Tres Piezas españolas.
❁ (BB) *** RCA Navigator Dig. 74321 17903-2. Julian Bream (guitar) – ALBENIZ: *Collection;* GRANADOS: *Collection.* *** ❁

Rodrigo's *Three Spanish pieces* are characteristically inventive, the central *Passacaglia* quite masterly and the closing *Zapateado* attractively chimerical in Julian Bream's nimble figers. This 1983 recording has been added to what was already one of the finest of all recorded guitar recitals of Spanish music. An outstanding bargain in every way.

Roman, Johan Helmich (1694–1758)

Drottningholm music; Little Drottningholm music.
(BB) *** Naxos Dig. 8.553733 [id.]. Uppsala CO, Halstead.

Johan Helmich Roman, a younger contemporary of Bach and Handel, is often described as the father of

Swedish music. Studying in London in his early twenties, he met and was influenced by Handel, and on his return to Sweden he became Court Kapellmeister in 1727, having been deputy for six years. In 1744, the year before he resigned his court position, he wrote 24 pieces for the very grand four-day ceremonies celebrating the marriage of the future King of Sweden to a daughter of Frederick the Great of Prussia. From first to last they are full of delightful invention, starting with a swaggering *Allegro* which, like other movements, owes something to the example of Handel's *Water music*, and ending with a bouncy *vivace Jig*. Unlike the previous recording on Musica Sueciae, Halstead's Naxos version – just as exhilarating, often at brisker speeds – uses period instruments to bring out the great variety of instrumental colour. Halstead also includes eight extra pieces, written to be used in reserve at the wedding, under the title *Little Drottningholm music*. Fresh, lively performances and excellent sound.

Ropartz, Joseph Guy (1864–1955)

Symphony No. 3 (for soloists, chorus and orchestra).
(M) *** EMI Dig. CDM7 64689-2. Pollet, Stutzman, Dran, Vassar, Orféon Donostiarra Ch., Toulouse Capitole O, Plasson.

Like the Magnard symphonies, the *Third Symphony* of Ropartz has much nobility and there is a sense of scale and grandeur. There is much in the pantheistic vision of its opening pages that one cannot fail to respond to, and some felicitous harmonic invention. There is a certain unrelieved thickness of texture, particularly in the finale. However, there is a personality here, and all lovers of French music will find it rewarding. Even if the recording (and some of the solo singing) is not of the very highest order, the orchestral playing under Michel Plasson is thoroughly committed.

Prélude, marine et chansons for flute, violin, viola, cello and harp.
❁ (M) *** Decca 452 891-2 [id.]. Osian Ellis, Melos Ens. – DEBUSSY: *Sonata for flute, viola and harp;* RAVEL: *Introduction and allegro;* ROUSSEL: *Sérénade for flute, violin, viola, cello and harp.* *** ❁

Guy Ropartz is the least familiar name on this delectable collection of twentieth-century chamber music. Born in Brittany, he studied under Massenet and, later, Franck. His *Prélude, marine et chansons* has a comparable intimacy of feeling with the works by his more famous contemporaries. It abounds in Gallic delights to charm the listener's ear, especially the wistful central movement, which is exquisitely played, as is the charmingly perky finale. The recording could hardly be more enticing in its delicacy of atmosphere.

Rossini, Gioachino (1792–1868)

Ballet music from: *Mosè; Otello; Le siège de Corinthe; William Tell.*
(B) **(*) Ph. Duo (IMS) 442 553-2 (2) [id.]. Monte Carlo Op. O, Antonio de Almeida – DONIZETTI: *Ballet music*. ***

Not all these items are lightweight, and Almeida draws positive and vigorous performances from the Monte Carlo orchestra. The strings often play with finesse, notably in the famous *William Tell ballet*, but the orchestra cannot quite provide the colour and degree of zestful brilliance which makes the Philharmonia Donizetti coupling so attractive. The sound in Monte Carlo, although agreeable, is less vivid than in London. Even so, this is very enjoyable.

La boutique fantasque (ballet, arr. Respighi) complete.
(B) **(*) Decca Eclipse Dig. 448 984-2; *448 984-4* [(M) id. import]. Nat. PO, Bonynge – CHOPIN: *Les Sylphides*. **(*)

Bonynge goes for sparkle and momentum above all in Respighi's brilliant and sumptuous rescoring of Rossini, a magical ballet if ever there was one. The Decca compact disc has great brilliance and the orchestral colours glitter and glow within the attractive resonance of Kingsway Hall, although there is a degree of digital edge on the treble. Bonynge's exuberance is certainly exhilarating when the sound is so spectacular.

La boutique fantasque: extended suite.
(M) *** RCA 09026 61847-2 [id.]. Boston Pops O, Arthur Fiedler – OFFENBACH: *Gaîté parisienne*. *** ❁

Fiedler offers nearly half an hour of the ballet, not missing out much of importance. The performance sparkles, the playing has warmth and finesse and the Boston acoustics add the necessary atmosphere at the magically evocative opening. John Pfeiffer's remastering of this 1956 recording leaves little to be desired and the coupling is indispensable.

La boutique fantasque: suite.

(M) **(*) Chandos CHAN 6503 [id.]. SNO, Gibson (with SAINT-SAENS: *Danse macabre* **(*)) – DUKAS: *L'apprenti sorcier*. **(*)

(M) **(*) Sony SBK 46340 [id.]. Phd. O, Ormandy – TCHAIKOVSKY: *Sleeping Beauty:* highlights. **

Gibson's version of the suite is strikingly atmospheric. Helped by the glowing acoustics of Glasgow's City Hall, the opening has much evocation. The orchestra is on its toes and plays with warmth and zest, and the 1973 recording has transferred vividly to CD.

Ormandy presents Respighi's glittering orchestration with much brilliance and dash, and the Philadelphia Orchestra has all the sumptuousness one could ask for. This is more extrovert music-making than Gibson's and it is undoubtedly exhilarating, even if the effect of the recording is less refined.

String sonatas Nos. 1–6 (complete).

(BB) *** Decca Double 443 838-2 (2) [id.]. ASMF, Marriner (with CHERUBINI: *Etude No. 2 for French horn and strings* (with Barry Tuckwell); BELLINI: *Oboe concerto in E flat* (with Roger Lord) ***) – DONIZETTI: *String quartet*. ***

(B) *** EMI forte (SIS) Analogue/Dig. CZS5 69524-2 (2) [CDFB 69524]. Polish CO, Maksymiuk – MENDELSSOHN: *String symphonies;* JANIEWICZ: *Divertimento;* JARZEBSKI: *Chromatica; Tamburetta.* ***

(B) ** Ph. Duo (IMS) 456 330-2 (2) [id.]. I Musici – BOTTESINI: *Grand duo concertante* **; MENDELSSOHN: *Octet* **(*); WOLF: *Italian serenade*. **(*)

We have a very soft spot for the sparkle, elegance and wit of these ASMF performances of the Rossini *String sonatas*, amazingly accomplished products for a twelve-year-old. The parts were only discovered in the Library of Congress just after the Second World War. The music corresponds with previously known works for wind quartet and early string quartets, but there is no doubt that the original scoring was for two violins, cello and double-bass which takes a genuine solo role in the *Third Sonata*. Marriner offers them on full orchestral strings but with such finesse and precision of ensemble that the result is all gain. The 1966 recording still sounds remarkably full and natural, and the current CD transfer adds to the feeling of presence. The overall playing time of just over 80 minutes means that the six sonatas will not comfortably fit on a single CD, so the new Double Decca two-for-the-price-of-one format is ideal, with other music added. Apart from the Donizetti *Quartet*, which has an appropriately Rossinian flavour, the two minor concertante works are well worth having, with both Barry Tuckwell (in what is in essence a three-movement horn concertino) and Roger Lord in excellent form.

Jerzy Maksymiuk with the Polish Chamber Orchestra consistently chooses challengingly fast speeds, and the playing is bracingly brilliant. Though some of the fun is lost, the wit remains, and these virtuoso performances are still most enjoyable for their exhilarating dash. Nos. 2, 3, 4 and 5 were recorded in analogue sound, earlier than the rest, but the difference is minimal and no one will complain at the quality, which is excellent. A fine alternative to the Marriner versions, and made the more attractive by the couplings, notably the Janiewicz *Divertimento*, so like Rossini in style, and also the two Jarzebski lollipops which stand out for their strength of personality.

The performances by I Musici are enjoyable too, though they hardly achieve the delectable wit and point which make the Decca set so enchanting. The playing is both refined and alert, and the 1971 recording is good (if not as fine as the Argo/Decca engineering).

VOCAL MUSIC

Petite messe solennelle.

(M) **(*) Decca Dig. 444 134-2 (2) [id.]. Dessì, Scalchi, Sabbatini, Pertusi, Bologna Teatro Comunale Ch. & O, Chailly.

(B) ** Double Decca 444 842-2 (2) [id.]. Marshall, Hodgson, Tear, King, Holford & Constable (pianos), Birch (harmonium), L Chamber Ch., Heltay – RESPIGHI: *Botticelli pictures* etc. ***

(i) *Petite messe solennelle;* (ii) *Stabat Mater.*

(B) **(*) EMI forte Dig. CZS5 68658-2 (2) [CDFB 68658]. (i) Popp, Fassbaender, Gedda, Kavrakos, King's College Ch., Katia & Marielle Labèque, Briggs, Cleobury; (ii) Malfitano, Baltsa, Gambill, Howell, Maggio Musicale Fiorentino Ch. & O, Muti.

(B) ** Decca Double 455 023-2 (2) [id.]. Pavarotti; (i) Freni, Valentini-Terrani, Raimondi, Magiera, Rosetta, La Scala Ch., Gandolfi; (ii) Lorengar, Minton, Sotin, L. Symphony Ch., LSO, Kertész.

Rossini's *Petite messe solennelle* must be the most genial contribution to the church liturgy in the history of music. The description '*Petite*' does not refer to size, for the piece is comparable in length to Verdi's *Requiem*; rather it is the composer's modest evaluation of the work's 'significance'. But what a spontaneous and infectious piece of writing it is, bubbling over with characteristic melodic, harmonic and rhythmic invention. The composer never overreaches himself. 'I was born for *opera buffa*, as well Thou knowest,' Rossini writes touchingly on the score. 'Little skill, a little heart, and that is all. So be Thou blessed and admit me to paradise.'

Sawallisch's recording of Rossini's original score of this work – originally Ariola, later Eurodisc – would surely merit the granting of the composer's wish, but perversely it remains out of the catalogue. However, the EMI/King's version provides a different and contrasting view from Sawallisch's. Recorded, not in King's College Chapel – which would have been much too reverberant for Rossini's chamber textures – but in the Music Faculty at Cambridge, this is very enjoyable in its own right. The use of the refined trebles of King's College Choir brings a timbre very different from what Rossini would have expected from boys' voices – but, arguably, close to what he would have wanted. That sound is hard to resist when the singing itself is so movingly eloquent. The work's underlying geniality is not obscured, but here there is an added dimension of devotional intensity from the chorus which, combined with outstanding singing from a fine quartet of soloists and beautifully matched playing from the Labèque sisters, makes for very satisfying results. The recording, too, attractively combines warmth with clarity.

Rossini loses nothing of his natural jauntiness in his setting of the coupled *Stabat Mater*, but Muti's view is a dramatic one, and it is sad that he did not record it with the Philharmonia or with the Vienna Philharmonic, with whom he gave a memorable reading at the 1983 Salzburg Festival. As it is, the Florence Festival forces are sometimes rough – notably the orchestra – and the singing at times unpolished, though the solo quartet is a fine one. Warm but rather unrefined recording.

Chailly chooses Rossini's orchestral version (made in 1867), although Rossini himself preferred his original, as do we. Nevertheless, with a fine solo team, Daniella Dessì and Gloria Scalchi both singing beautifully (and ravishing in their *Qui tollis* duet), and with the bass rising to the occasion in the *Quoniam tu solus sanctus*, this is a very considerable account. The Bologna Chorus are not helped by a somewhat backward balance which, within the warmly resonant acoustic, does not provide an ideal sharpness of focus. But they sing with much ardour, especially in the *Gloria* and *Credo*, and Chailly ensures that the *Et resurrexit* caps the performance ebulliently. Apart from the choral balance (and that is not a real problem when the performers are so committed), the recording is glowing and vivid.

Heltay's 1977 Decca version is given a recording of striking realism and presence (the choral entry in the *Gloria* is arresting in its impact) but, although it does not lack drama, the reading misses the composer's whimsical geniality. Both Margaret Marshall and Alfreda Hodgson sing eloquently; there is some finely shaped and expressive choral singing and good support from the two pianists, with John Birch on the harmonium. But the music-making does not fully catch the music's spirit and can give only limited satisfaction.

Kertész was a refined and thoughtful musician, and in the *Stabat Mater* he seems intent on avoiding any charges of vulgarity. This brings out an unexpected degree of beauty, notably in the fine choral singing, and even *Cujus anima* is given extra delicacy, with Pavarotti singing most beautifully and linking back to the main theme with a subtle half-tone. Soprano, mezzo and bass may not have all the idiomatic Italian qualities, but their singing matches Kertész's interpretation. The 1971 Kingsway Hall recording is warmly atmospheric. Unfortunately, Decca did not ask Kertész to record also the *Petite Messe solennelle*. Regrettably Gandolfi takes a coarse view of a work which demands some refinement, letting his famous soloists have their head. Freni has some beautiful moments in the *Crucifixus* and *O salutaris*, but Pavarotti and Raimondi are both well below their best, and the chorus is fruity-sounding in the wrong way.

Stabat Mater.

(B) (***) DG Double mono 439 684-2 (2). Stader, Radev, Haefliger, Borg, Berlin RIAS Chamber Ch., St Edwige's Cathedral Ch., Berlin RIAS SO, Fricsay – VERDI: *Requiem*. (***)

(B) ** Sony SB2K 53252 (2) [S2K 53252]. Arroyo, Wolff, Bianco, Diaz, Camerata Singers, NYPO, Schippers – VERDI: *Requiem*. **

It is the vitality and drama that come over most strongly in Fricsay's strong and spontaneous account of a work that can easily sound lightweight. Even the tenor's *Cujus anima*, jaunty as the rhythm may be, has a warm, lyrical resilience, and the fervour of the choral singing is matched by the soloists. The effect is very much of compellingly live music-making; and this makes a worthy coupling for Fricsay's electrifying account of the Verdi *Requiem*. The mono recording from the mid-1950s has astonishing vividness and the conveyed atmosphere means that no apologies whatever need be made for the sound.

Schippers conducts a strong and enjoyable performance with fine choral singing. But the soloists are uneven. Beverly Wolff and Justino Diaz are often impressive, but Martina Arroyo, though confident, sounds too gusty when the voice is under fortissimo pressure. The remastering is excellent and the sound is pleasingly full-bodied and clear.

OPERA

Overtures: *Armida; Il barbiere di Siviglia; Bianca e Faliero; La cambiale di matrimonio; La Cenerentola; Demetrio e Poblibio; Edipo a Colono; Edoardo e Cristina;* (i) *Ermione. La gazza ladra; L'inganno felice; L'Italiana in Algeri; Maometto II; Otello.* (i) *Ricciardo e Zoraide. La scala di seta; Semiramide; Le siège de Corinthe; Il Signor Bruschino; Tancredi; Il Turco in Italia; Torvaldo e Dorliska; Il viaggio a Reims; William Tell. Sinfonia al Conventello; Sinfonia di Bologna.*
(M) *** Ph. 434 016-2 (3). ASMF, Marriner; (i) with Amb. S.

Marriner's three discs span all Rossini's overtures, but one must remember that the early Neapolitan operas, with the exception of *Ricciardo e Zoraide* and *Ermione*, make do with a simple Prelude, leading into the opening chorus. *Ricciardo e Zoraide*, however, is an extended piece (12 minutes 25 seconds), with the choral entry indicating that the introduction is at an end. *Maometto II* is on a comparable scale, while the more succinct *Armida* is an example of Rossini's picturesque evocation, almost like a miniature tone-poem. Twenty-four overtures plus two sinfonias make a delightful package in such sparkling performances, which eruditely use original orchestrations. Full, bright and atmospheric recording, spaciously reverberant, admirably transferred to CD, with no artificial brilliance.

Overtures: *Il barbiere di Siviglia; La cambiale di matrimonio; La Cenerentola; La gazza ladra; L'Italiana in Algeri; La scala di seta; Semiramide; Il Turco in Italia; William Tell.*
(M) *** Classic fM Dig. 75605 57031-2; *75605 57031-4*. Sinfonia Varsovia, Sir Yehudi Menuhin.

Mehuhin and his Polish group, the Sinfonia Varsovia, turn from their successful recordings of Mozart symphonies to present a hardly less stylish or enjoyable collection of nine favourite Rossini overtures. There is a nice balance between wit and finesse, geniality and grace. Tempi are often brisk, but when there is a surge of vivacity there is no loss of poise. The wind solos are elegantly done and the string phrasing combines neatness with graceful warmth. Above all there is spontaneity here, and even at times a Beechamesque twinkle. The recording, made in the No. 1 Studio of Polish Radio in Warsaw, is full and resonant but not excessively so.

Overtures: *Il barbiere di Siviglia; La cambiale di matrimonio; La gazza ladra; L'Italiana in Algeri; Otello; La scala di seta; Semiramide; Le siège de Corinthe; Il signor Bruschino; Tancredi; Torvaldo e Dorliska; Il Turco in Italia; Il viaggio a Reims; William Tell.*
(B) *** Decca Double 443 850-2 (2) [(M) id. import]. Nat. PO, Riccardo Chailly.

In 1981 Chailly and the National Philharmonic made the first compact disc of Rossini overtures (in the Kingsway Hall) and these performances are now combined with their further compilation, recorded at Walthamstow Assembly Hall in 1984, to make a desirable bargain double, with each collection presented on a separate disc. The balance of the recordings is truthful, with the orchestral layout very believable. At times on the first disc there is a degree of digital edge on tuttis, but the bustle from the cellos is particularly engaging. The solo playing is fully worthy of such clear presentation: the cellos at the opening of *William Tell* and the principal oboe and horn in *The Italian girl* and *Il Turco in Italia* respectively all demonstrate that this is an orchestra of London's finest musicians. Just occasionally elsewhere the ensemble slips when Chailly lets the exhilaration of the moment triumph over absolute discipline and poise. But under Chailly the spirit of the music-making conveys spontaneous enjoyment too, especially in *The thieving magpie* and the nicely paced account of *William Tell*. Incidentally, *Il viaggio a Reims* had no overture at its first performance, but one was cobbled together later, drawing on the ballet music from *Le siège de Corinthe*. The other novelties, *Otello* – played with great dash – and *Torvaldo e Dorliska*, with its witty interchanges between woodwind and strings, are among the highlights. *Semiramide* is also elegantly played and *The Barber* is nicely elegant, and overall the performances are undoubtedly as infectious as they are stylish.

Overtures: *Il barbiere di Siviglia; La cambiale di matrimonio; L'inganno felice; L'Italiana in Algeri; La scala di seta; Il Signor Bruschino; Tancredi; Il Turco in Italia.* (i) *Introduction, theme and variations for clarinet and orchestra in E flat.*
❁ (M) *** DG Dig. 445 569-2; *445 569-4* [id.]. Orpheus CO; (i) with Charles Neidlich.

This crackingly good CD by the conductorless Orpheus Chamber Orchestra has always been one of the most enjoyable collections of Rossini overtures ever put on disc; at mid-price and with Charles Neidlich's scintillating account of the concertante clarinet work also included, it is irresistible. The wit of the latter is caught with such sparkle and humour that one cannot help but smile with pleasure. In the overtures the orchestra displays astonishing unanimity of style and ensemble. Not only is the crispness of string phrasing a joy, but the many stylish wind solos have an attractive degree of freedom. These are performances that in their refinement and apt chamber scale give increasing pleasure with familiarity. The DG recording is marvellously real, with the perspective perfectly judged.

Overtures: *Il barbiere di Siviglia; La Cenerentola; La gazza ladra; L'Italiana in Algeri; La scala di seta; Semiramide; Il Signor Bruschino; Il Turco in Italia; William Tell.*
(M) *** Ph. 446 196-2. ASMF, Sir Neville Marriner.

This generous (76-minute) collection of nine overtures is drawn from two separate LPs, originally published in 1974 and 1976. All the performances are vivacious and, for the earlier record (*Il Barbiere*, *L'Italiana in Algeri*, *La scala di seta*, *Il Signor Bruschino* and *Il Turco in Italia*), Marriner resurrected the original and lighter orchestrations (*sans* heavy brass and bass-drum). They emerge the more sparkling, and *Il Signor Bruschino* brings the tapping of a triangle stick, not the usual bows (although the writer of the excellent notes for this reissue was obviously not told of this change). However, no one need fear that William Tell is minus trombones or lacks an enthusiastic closing *galop*. There is no shortage of recommendable anthologies of Rossini overtures at mid- and bargain-price, but this is certainly among them.

Overtures: *Il barbiere di Siviglia; La Cenerentola; La gazza ladra; L'Italiana in Algeri; La scala di seta; Il Signor Bruschino.*
(M) (*) Mercury 434 345-2 [id.]. Minneapolis SO, Antal Dorati – VERDI: Overtures. **

This is one of Mercury's and Dorati's rare failures. The dead acoustics of the Northrop Auditorium are entirely unsuitable for Rossini's warmth and wit and, although the orchestral playing is lively and quite polished, Dorati's deadpan performances compensate little.

Overtures: *Il barbiere di Siviglia; La Cenerentola; La gazza ladra; L'Italiana in Algeri; Le siège de Corinthe; Il Signor Bruschino.*
(M) *** DG (IMS) 419 869-2 [431 653-2]. LSO, Abbado.

Brilliant playing, with splendid discipline, vibrant rhythms and finely articulated phrasing – altogether invigorating and bracing. There is perhaps an absence of outright geniality here, but these are superb performances and this remains one of the very finest collections of Rossini overtures ever, for the wit is spiced with a touch of acerbity, and the flavour is of a vintage dry champagne which retains its bloom, yet has a subtlety all its own.

Overtures: *Il barbiere di Siviglia; La Cenerentola; La gazza ladra; La scala di seta; Il Signor Bruschino; William Tell.*
✿ (M) *** RCA GD 60387 [60387-2-RG]. Chicago SO, Fritz Reiner.

As with the others in RCA's remastered Reiner/Chicago series, the 1958 sound-quality has been improved phenomenally; they are preferable to most digital collections. The blaze of brass tone, supported by a rich orchestral backcloth and resonant bass drum, at the galop in the *William Tell overture*, is all-engulfing, a thrilling moment indeed; at the same time the scurrying violins display the utmost virtuosity. But it is the sparkle and vivacity of these performances that one remembers above all – and, in *La Cenerentola*, the wit, as well as fizzing orchestral bravura. One would have liked the opening flourish of *La scala di seta* to be neater – it is presented too lavishly here – but this is the solitary reservation over a magnificent achievement.

Overtures: *Il barbiere di Siviglia; La gazza ladra; L'Italiana in Algeri; La scala di seta; Semiramide; William Tell.*
(B) **(*) DG Classikon 439 415-2 [(M) id. import]. BPO, Karajan.

Karajan's virtuoso performances are polished like fine silver. The main allegro of *La scala di seta* abandons all decorum when played as fast as this, and elsewhere bravura often takes precedence over poise. However, with the Berlin Philharmonic on sparkling form, there is wit as well as excitement. The 1971 recording was made (like so many other vintage Karajan recordings) in the Berlin Jesus-Christus-Kirche, but the remastering casts very bright lighting on the upper range, which makes sonic brilliance approach aggressiveness in some climaxes.

Overtures: *Elisabetta, Regina d'Inghilterra; La scala di seta; Semiramide; Tancredi; Il Turco in Italia; William Tell.*
(M) *** [RCA Basic 100 09026 61554-2; *61554-4*]. LSO, Abbado (with VERDI: *Overtures: La forza del destino; I vespri siciliani* ***).

Zestful performances from Abbado, with exhilaratingly fast tempi, the LSO players kept constantly on their toes and obviously revelling in their own virtuosity. The effect is more genial than on his earlier, DG record with the same orchestra (see above). The exuberance comes to the fore especially in *Tancredi* – there is even a brief clarinet glissando – in a revised version by Philip Gosset. But some might feel that *La scala di seta* would be more effective if a fraction more relaxed and poised, something Beecham understood perfectly, and his account has never been surpassed. *William Tell* opens with elegant cellos, then offers an unashamedly vulgar storm sequence and a final galop taken at breakneck pace. *Elisabetta, Regina* is our old friend, *The barber of Seville*. It is listed as such on the CD; but there is a subtle change here which surely implies the use of the proper title – a triplet in the first theme of the allegro which is consistently repeated each time the tune appears. This overture too is brilliantly played but does not lose its essential stylishness. The two Verdi overtures which act as a bonus are well suited by Abbado's spiritedly dramatic readings. The remastered recording is vividly bright, but it matches Abbado's approach. A pity that this enjoyable collection is not available in the UK.

Overtures: *La gazza ladra; L'Italiana in Algeri; Semiramide; Il Signor Bruschino; William Tell.*
(B) **(*) EMI forte CZS5 69364-2 (2) [CDFB 69364]. RPO, Sir Colin Davis – BEETHOVEN: *Symphony No. 7* *** ✿; SCHUBERT: *Symphony No. 9.* ***

Sir Colin Davis's 1962 collection, recorded at Abbey Road, brings playing that is admirably stylish with an excellent sense of nuance. *Semiramide* is superb, reminding one of Beecham, as does the spunky opening of *The Thieving Magpie*. *William Tell* is pretty good too, the opening beautifully played. In *Il Signor Bruschino* it seems as if the bow-tapping device is done by the leader alone, which is rather effective. The CD transfer is vivid, but very brightly lit, with some loss of the body of the original; but the orchestral balance is natural.

L'assedio di Corinto (*The siege of Corinth;* complete).
(M) **(*) EMI CMS7 64335-2 (3). Sills, Verrett, Diaz, Theyard, Howell, Lloyd, Amb. Op. Ch., LSO, Schippers.

Thomas Schippers made this recording in London in 1974 in preparation for a production at the Met. in New York with virtually the same cast. The pity is that he has encouraged the coloratura prowess of the prima donna, Beverly Sills, at the expense of the composer's final thoughts, with display material from Rossini's earlier version. Some of the most striking passages are the patriotic choruses, recognizably Rossinian but not at all in the usual vein. Sills, as so often on record, is variable, brilliant in coloratura but rarely sweet of tone, and she is completely upstaged by Shirley Verrett, singing magnificently as Neocle. Some strong singing too among the others, though not all the men are very deft with ornamentation. The recording, made at All Saints', Tooting, has plenty of atmosphere and has achieved a very satisfactory CD transfer.

Il barbiere di Siviglia (complete).
(M) *** EMI (SIS) CMS7 64162-2 (2) [CDMB 641622]. De los Angeles, Alva, Cava, Wallace, Bruscantini, Glyndebourne Festival Ch., RPO, Gui.
(B) *** Naxos Dig. 8.660027/29 [id.]. Ganassi, Serville, Vargas, Romero, De Grandis, Hungaria R. Ch., Failoni CO, Budapest, Will Humburg.
(M) *** RCA 09026 68552-2 (3) [id.]. Merrill, Peters, Valletti, Tozzi, Corena, Met. Op. Ch. & O, Leinsdorf.
(M) **(*) DG 457 733-2 (2) [id.]. Teresa Berganza, Hermann Prey, Luigi Alva, Enzo Dara, Paolo Montarsolo, Amb. Ch., LSO, Abbado.
(M) ** EMI (SIS) CMS5 66040-2 (2) [Ang. CDMB 66040]. Sills, Gedda, Milnes, Capecchi, Raimondi, Barbieri, John Alldis Ch., LSO, Levine.
(B) (**) Decca Double (IMS) mono 443 536-2 (2) [(M) id. import]. Simionato, Misciano, Bastianini, Corena, Siepi, Maggio Musicale Fiorentino Ch. & O, Erede.

Victoria de los Angeles is as charming a Rosina as you will ever find: no viper this one, as she claims in *Una voce poco fa*, and that matches the gently rib-nudging humour of what is otherwise a 1962 recording of the Glyndebourne production. It does not fizz as much as other Glyndebourne Rossini on record but, with a characterful line-up of soloists, it is an endearing performance which in its line is unmatched. The recording still sounds well. The CDs have been handsomely re-packaged and the documentation is freshly printed.

Though the cast is not as starry as with most full-price rivals, the Naxos set makes a first-rate bargain. The singing is hardly less stylish, with Sonia Ganassi a rich-toned Rosina, controlling vibrato well, and with Ramon Vargas an agile and attractively youthful-sounding Almaviva. Roberto Serville as Figaro conveys the fun of the role brilliantly. The *buffo* characters are strongly cast too, with Basilio's *La calunnia* (Franco de Grandis) delightfully enlivened by comments from Bartolo (Angelo Romero), both very much involved in their roles. Will Humburg's often brisk speeds, with crisp recitative matched by dazzling ensembles, never prevent the music (and the singers) from breathing. The only reservation is that the glowing Glyndebourne version under Gui with Victoria de los Angeles as Rosina comes (on only two discs) at an even more reasonable price, though with a text not quite so complete.

When this 1958 Leinsdorf set first appeared, it was greeted with approbation for its completeness. With a playing time of 160 minutes, it was first issued on four LPs; now it comes on three mid-priced CDs. However, much material which is almost always omitted in the opera house here finds its way back. Moreover the cast is consistently impressive. Roberta Peters sparkles as Rosina, her voice always sweet and her coloratura (not always avoiding intrusive aitches) exquisitely agile and pointed. Robert Merrill could be a more genuinely comic Figaro, but his vocal acting is certainly impressive and his voice is beautifully focused. Valletti, Corena and Tozzi are all splendid. Leinsdorf manages to provide genuine lightness and so convey the proper sparkling style. Within the fairly wide reverberation the sound remains clear, and the CD transfer has not lost its original bloom. While our first choice for this opera remains with Bartoli and Nucci on Decca at full price, this RCA reissue is well worth having in its own right. Roberta Peters is a sparkling Rosina, a singer too little known in Europe, who here lives up to her high reputation at the Met., dazzling in coloratura elaborations *in alt*. Robert Merrill may not be a specially comic Figaro, but the vocal characterization is strong, with the glorious voice consistently firm and well focused. Valletti, Corena and Tozzi make up a formidable team, and Leinsdorf conducts with a lightness and relaxation rare for him on record. Good, clear sound of the period, set against a reverberant, helpful acoustic.

Abbado's recording of *Il barbiere* was a curious choice for inclusion among DG's 'Legendary Originals'. It is a clean, satisfying performance, but one which lacks the last degree of sparkle. Berganza's interpretation of the role of Rosina remains very consistent with her earlier performance on Decca, but the Figaro here, Hermann Prey, is more reliable, and the playing and recording have an extra degree of polish. The text is not absolutely complete, but the omissions are of minimal importance. With fresh recorded sound and plenty of immediacy, this remains competitive, but hardly a primary recommendation.

Recorded in 1956, the Double Decca mono set of *Il barbiere*, well transferred, is well worth hearing for the characterful portrayals of the principal characters, all from vintage Italian singers at their peak. As Rosina, Simionato may not be ideally flexible in her ornamentation, but her rich, robust mezzo could not be more firmly distinctive, and Bastianini offers a comparably strong, purposeful and clean-cut Figaro. Fernando Corena as Bartolo and Cesare Siepi as Basilio make a classic pair of *buffo* basses, even if Siepi's massive *La calunnia* is astonishingly slow. Alvinio Misciano, the least well-known of the principals, is a clear-toned *tenore di grazia*, only occasionally ungainly as Almaviva. Erede conducts a warmly idiomatic reading.

James Levine, in one of his earliest opera recordings (made in 1975), directs a fresh, alert and vigorous account of *Il barbiere* with a starry cast. Sherrill Milnes makes a strong, forthright Figaro, the central focus of the performance, with Ruggero Raimondi a sonorous Bartolo. Nicolai Gedda begins unpromisingly with an effortful account of *Ecco ridente*, and though he is more characteristically stylish later the voice sounds too heavy and strained for Rossini. Beverly Sills too is variable, so light and bright a soprano is questionably cast in the role of Rosina, originally for a mezzo. Though her self-portrait in *Una voca poco fa* is a lightweight one, her coloratura is dazzlingly brilliant, and her admirers will no doubt forgive the shrillness of tone under pressure. Warm, full recording. This is currently not available in the UK.

Il barbiere di Siviglia: highlights.

(M) *** EMI CDM5 65570-2 (from complete recording, with Gobbi, Callas, Philh. Ch. & O, Galliera).

(M) **(*) Decca 452 737-2 [id.] (from complete set, with Manuel Ausensi, Teresa Berganza, Ugo Benelli, Fernando Corena, Nicolai Ghiaurov, Rossini Ch. & O of Naples, cond. Varviso).

(M) *(*) Sony Dig. SMK 53501 [id.]. Marilyn Horne, Nucci, Ramey, Dara, Barbacini, La Scala, Milan, Ch. & O, Chailly.

On EMI, Callas remains supreme as a minx-like Rosina. The highlights disc offers most of the key solo numbers from Act I, while in Act II it concentrates on Rossini's witty ensembles, including the extended Second Act *Quintet*. The *Overture* is included and, while it is stylishly played, it would have been better to have offered more of the vocal music. The complete opera remains at full price.

Berganza proved an agile Rosina in the 1964 Decca set, and Ugo Benelli is charming as the Count. Silvio Varviso secures electrifying results in the high-spirited ensembles, Corena's fine Dr Bartolo is well known, and Ghiaurov sings with characteristic richness as Basilio. Manuel Ausensi's gruff Figaro will be counted by many a drawback, but overall this well-recorded selection (61 minutes) is worth having. It includes a cued synopsis.

Chailly's 1982 set is generally coarse and disappointing, not helped by indifferent playing by the Orchestra of La Scala. This highlights CD is mainly of interest for those wanting to hear Marilyn Horne's formidable Rosina, the voice still agile if not as cleanly focused as it once was. The others do not match her. The selection offers 74 minutes, including the Overture.

La Cenerentola (complete).

(M) (***) EMI (SIS) mono CMS7 64183-2 (2). Gabarain, Oncina, Bruscantini, Noni, Glyndebourne Festival Ch. & O, Gui.

Gui's 1953 recording of *Cenerentola* has mono sound of amazing clarity and immediacy. Sadly the text is seriously cut, but the effervescence of Gui's live performances at Glyndebourne has been infectiously caught. Juan Oncina produces the most sweet-toned singing as the Prince, with the vintage baritone, Sesto Bruscantini, a vividly characterful Dandini, almost another Figaro. The title-role is sung by the Spanish mezzo, Marina de Gabarain, a strikingly positive singer with a sensuous flicker in the voice, very much in the style of the legendary Conchita Supervia.

La Cenerentola: highlights.

(M) *** Teldec/Warner Dig. 0630 15804-9 (from complete recording, with Larmore, Giménez, Quilico, Corbelli, Scarabelli, ROHCG Ch. & O, Rizzi).

(M) ** Sony SMK 53502 [id.]. Terrani, Araiza, Trimarchi, Dara, Ravaglia, W. German R. (male) Ch., Cappella Coloniensis, Ferro.

On Carlo Rizzi's Teldec version with Covent Garden forces, Jennifer Larmore makes an enchanting heroine, both tenderly expressive in cantilena and flawlessly controlled through the most elaborate coloratura passages. The rest of the cast was chosen just as effectively and there is no weak link; throughout, Rizzi brings out the sparkle. With vivid recording and nearly 75 minutes of music included, this makes a splendid choice for a disc of highlights, especially for collectors who have the competing full-priced Decca set with Cecilia Bartoli. As usual with the Warner Opera Collection series, a full translation is included.

Ferro's *La Cenerentola* lacks that essential ingredient of Rossini: fizzing high spirits. Even the heroine's brilliant final aria hangs fire, in spite of a generally fine, stylish contribution from Lucia Valentini Terrani. The cast overall is strong and the selection here runs to 76 minutes. But overall this is disappointing.

Le Comte Ory (complete).

✿ (M) (***) EMI mono CMS7 64180-2 (2). Oncina, Roux, Jeannette and Monica Sinclair, Glyndebourne Festival Ch. & O, Gui.

Gui's classic recording of *Le Comte Ory*, with the same Glyndebourne forces who gave this sparkling opera on stage, brings pure delight. In limited but clearly focused mono sound, Gui conveys an extra sparkle and resilience, even over Gardiner's brilliant Philips version. There is a natural sense of timing here that regularly has you laughing in joy, as in the dazzling finale of Act I, one of the most infectiously witty of all recordings of a Rossini ensemble. Juan Oncina in his prime as the Count, the Hungarian Sari Barabas as the Countess Adèle and Michel Roux as the Count's friend are superbly matched by Monica Sinclair as the Countess's housekeeper and Ian Wallace as the Count's tutor. Some 10 minutes of text have been cut, but that allows the complete opera to be fitted on two CDs, each containing a complete act.

Elisabetta Regina d'Inghilterra (complete).

(M) *** Ph. 432 453-2 (2). Caballé, Carreras, Masterson, Creffield, Benelli, Jenkins, Amb. S., New Philh. O, Masini.

The first surprise in this lively operatic setting of the Elizabeth and Leicester story comes in the overture, which turns out to be the one which we know as belonging to *Il barbiere di Siviglia*. It is one of a whole sequence of self-borrowings which add zest to a generally delightful score. In a well-sprung performance like this, with beautiful playing from the LSO and some very fine singing, it is a set for any Rossinian to investigate. Of the two tenors, José Carreras proves much the more stylish as Leicester, with Ugo Benelli, in the more unusual role of a tenor-villain, singing less elegantly than he once did. Caballé produces some ravishing sounds, though she is not always electrifying. Lively conducting and splendid recording.

Ermione (complete).

(M) *** Erato/Warner Dig. 2292 45790-2 (2). Gasdia, Zimmermann, Palacio, Merritt, Matteuzzi, Alaimo, Prague Philharmonic Ch., Monte Carlo PO, Scimone.

Ermione begins very strikingly with an off-stage chorus, introduced in the slow section of the overture, singing a lament on the fall of Troy. The use of dramatic declamation, notably in the final scene of Act II, also gives due weight to the tragedy; however, not surprisingly, Rossini's natural amiability keeps bursting through, often a little incongruously. Though the three tenors in this Monte Carlo set from Erato are good by modern standards – Ernesto Palacio (Pirro), Chris Merritt (Oreste) and William Matteuzzi (Pilade) – they are uncomfortably strained by the high tessitura and the occasional stratospheric top notes. Cecilia Gasdia makes a powerful Ermione, not always even enough in her production but strong and agile; while Margarita Zimmermann makes a firm, rich Andromaca. Scimone, not always imaginative, yet directs a strong, well-paced performance. The recording is rather dry on the voices, but the hint of boxiness is generally undistracting and this set is a must for true Rossinians.

La gazza ladra: highlights.

(M) * Sony Dig. SMK 53503 [id.]. Ricciarelli, Matteuzzi, Ramey, Di Nissa, D'Intino, Furlanetto, Prague Philharmonic Ch., Turin RAI SO, Gelmetti.

Here are 74 minutes of music from a recording made at the Rossini Festival in Pesaro in 1989. Alas, the results are too rough and unstylish to give much pleasure. The cast is strong, with four excellent singers in the principal roles, but ensemble is slipshod and the recording unflatteringly dry. Of curiosity value only.

Guillaume Tell (William Tell) (sung in French).

(M) *** EMI (SIS) CMS7 69951-2 (4) [CDMD 699512]. Bacquier, Caballé, Gedda, Mesplé, Amb. Op. Ch., RPO, Gardelli.

The interest of the 1973 EMI set is that it is sung in the original French. Gardelli proves an imaginative Rossini interpreter, allying his formidable team to vigorous and sensitive performances. Bacquier makes an impressive Tell, developing the character as the story progresses; Gedda is a model of taste, and Montserrat Caballé copes ravishingly with the coloratura problems of Mathilde's role. While Chailly's full-price Decca set puts forward a strong case for using Italian with its open vowels, this remains a fully worthwhile alternative, with excellent CD sound. Indeed the current remastering is first class in every way and the choral passages, incisively sung, are among the most impressive; moreover the set now comes with full translation.

Guglielmo Tell (William Tell: slightly abridged; in Italian).

(BB) ** Arte Nova Dig. 74321 49704-2 (3) [id.]. Pons Tena, Martins, Muños, Specht, Galkin, Kapilov, Tisi, Sánchez, Putbus Festival Ch. & O, Wilhelm Keitel.

The Putbus Festival in Germany, founded in 1992 to present the operas of Rossini, here offers a sample of its work in the last and grandest of the operas. Unlike the rival versions at full price, this bargain issue offers, not the complete four-hour text, but a version of just under three hours, neatly tailored for stage presentation. The recording was made in 1996 at studio sessions linked to the staging and, with Wilhelm Keitel drawing crisp and refined playing from his chamber-sized orchestra and excellent chorus, the drama of the piece comes over well. The cast has been chosen largely from young singers, and the central role of William Tell himself is very well taken by the Spanish baritone, Ismael Pons Tena, firm and clean of delivery with a strong presence. Sadly, too many of the others have voices in which unevenness is brought out by the microphone, so that both Daniel Muños in the principal tenor role of Arnaldo and Monica Martins as the heroine, Matilde, are too unsteady to give much pleasure in Rossini's legato lines. Carmen Gonzales as Jemmy, Tell's son, and Sybille Specht as Edwige are both sweeter and truer. A useful set for anyone wanting to sample inexpensively Rossini's grandest inspiration, recorded in full, immediate sound.

L'Italiana in Algeri (complete).

(M) *** Erato/Warner 2292 45404-2 (2) [id.]. Horne, Palacio, Ramey, Trimarchi, Battle, Zaccaria, Prague Ch., Sol. Ven., Scimone.

(M) (**) EMI mono CHS7 64041-2 (2). Petri, Sciutti, Valletti, Simionato, Cortis, La Scala O & Ch., Giulini.

Scimone's highly enjoyable version is beautifully played and recorded with as stylish a team of soloists as one can expect nowadays. The text is complete and alternative versions of certain arias are given as an appendix. Marilyn Horne makes a dazzling, positive Isabella, and Samuel Ramey is splendidly firm as Mustafa. Domenico Trimarchi is a delightful Taddeo and Ernesto Palacio an agile Lindoro, not coarse, though the recording does not always catch his tenor timbre well. Nevertheless the sound is generally very good indeed.

Set in a dry, intimate acoustic, Giulini's mono version wears quite well in this CD reissue, with the rhythmic point of his conducting bringing plenty of sparkle, even if the singing is flawed. The characterful Simionato, in one of her most cherished roles as Isabella, is relatively disappointing, lacking charm. Her powerful mezzo is made to sound a little fluttery, less flatteringly caught than in her Decca recordings and with coloratura plentifully aspirated. Mario Petri produces woolly tone as the Bey, Mustafa, but the tenor, Cesare Valletti, a pupil of Tito Schipa, is excellent, and the Taddeo of Marcello Cortis is fresh and clear, while Graziella Sciutti is a delight in the role of Mustafa's wife, Elvira. The text is seriously cut, and the booklet gives only the Italian text without translation.

L'Italiana in Algeri: highlights.
(M) *** Sony SMK 53504 [id.] (from complete recording, with Valentini Terrani, Ganzarolli, Araiza, Cologne R. Ch., Capella Coloniensis, Ferro).
(M) *** Erato/Warner 0630 15738-9 (from above complete recording, with Horne, Palacio, Ramey, Trimarchi, Battle, Zaccaria, Prague Ch., Sol. Ven., Scimone).

On Sony a set of highlights (72 minutes) from a first-rate version, with Lucia Valentini Terrani seductively leading a consistently strong cast.

At mid-price Scimone's selection (73 minutes) is excellent value with its full translation. However, the comparable Sony highlights disc remains a marginal first choice although the documentation is less complete.

Mosè in Egitto (complete).
(M) *** Ph. 420 109-2 (2). Raimondi, Anderson, Nimsgern, Palacio, Gal, Fisichella, Amb. Op. Ch., Philh. O, Scimone.
(M) * Ph. (IMS) 442 100-2 (2) [id.]. Rossi-Lemeni, Lazzari, Taddei, Filippeschi, De Palma, Danieli, Mancini, Ch. & O of Teatro di San Carlo di Napoli, Serafin.

Scimone here justifies his claim that the 1819 version is dramatically more effective than both the earlier Italian one and the later Paris one. Rossini's score brings much fine music and, among the soloists, Raimondi relishes not only the solemn moments like the great invocation in Act I and the soaring prayer of Act III, but also the rage aria in Act II, almost like Handel updated if with disconcerting foretastes of Dr Malatesta in Donizetti's *Don Pasquale*. The writing for the soprano and tenor lovers (the latter the son of Pharaoh and in effect the villain of the piece) is relatively conventional, though the military flavour of their Act I cabaletta is refreshingly different. Ernesto Palacio and June Anderson make a strong pair, and the mezzo, Zehava Gal, is another welcome newcomer as Pharaoh's wife. Siegmund Nimsgern makes a fine Pharaoh, Salvatore Fisichella an adequate Arone (Aaron). The well-balanced recording emerges most vividly on CD.

This early (1956) Serafin set first appeared in highlights form on a bargain LP. The recording now sounds immensely more vivid in its CD format and Serafin's direction is undoubtedly lively. The ensembles are more impressive than the solo numbers. Rossi-Lemeni as Moses is woolly-sounding, and Filippeschi, the tenor, is coarse and unimaginative. This costs the same as Scimone's later set on the same label which is superior in every way.

L'occasione fa il ladro (complete).
(M) **(*) Claves Dig. CD 50-9208/9 [id.]. Bayo, De Carolis, Zennaro, Provvisionato, Previati, Massa, ECO, Viotti.

On two discs, this is one of the longer one-Acters in the Claves series, bringing one of the more recommendable performances, with Viotti at his most relaxed. Maria Bayo as the heroine sings warmly and sweetly, with no intrusive aspirates in the coloratura. The soubrette role of Ernestina is also charmingly done, and the *buffo* characters sing effectively, though the tenor, Iorio Zennaro, is hardly steady enough for Rossinian cantilena. The two discs come in a single hinged jewel-box at upper mid-price.

Otello (complete).
(M) *** Ph. 432 456-2 (2). Carreras, Von Stade, Condò, Pastine, Fisichella, Ramey, Amb. S., Philh. O, López-Cobos.

The libretto of Rossini's *Otello* bears remarkably little resemblance to Shakespeare – virtually none at all until the last Act. It is some tribute to this performance, superbly recorded, and brightly and stylishly conducted by López-Cobos, that the line-up of tenors is turned into an asset, with three nicely contrasted soloists. Carreras is here at his finest – most affecting in his recitative before the murder, while Fisichella copes splendidly with the high tessitura of Rodrigo's role, and Pastine has a distinct timbre to identify him as the villain. Frederica von Stade pours forth a glorious flow of beautiful tone, well-matched by Nucci Condò as Emilia. Samuel Ramey is excellent too in the bass role of Elmiro.

La pietra del paragone (complete).
(M) **(*) Van. 08 9031 73 (3) [OVC 8043/5]. Carreras, Wolff, Bonazzi, Elgar, Reardon, Foldi, Diaz, Murcell, Clarion Concerts Ch. & O, Jenkins.

This recording of the *opera buffa*, *La pietra del paragone*, made by Vanguard in New York in 1972, presents the young José Carreras in an incidental role, just one in an attractively fresh-voiced cast of soloists. It is given a vigorous, if occasionally hard-pressed performance under Newell Jenkins with what is called the Clarion Concerts Orchestra and Chorus. The plot of disguises and deceit is a throwback to artificial eighteenth-century conventions, involving a house-party with a couple of poets and a venal critic brought in. For modern performance the problem is the length, though on disc that evaporates when Rossini's invention is at its peak in number after number.

Semiramide (complete, but with traditional cuts).
(M) *** Decca (IMS) 425 481-2 (3) [id.]. Sutherland, Horne, Rouleau, Malas, Serge, Amb. Op. Ch., LSO, Bonynge.

Rossini concentrates on the love of Queen Semiramide for Prince Arsace (a mezzo-soprano), and musically the result is a series of fine duets, superbly performed here by Sutherland and Horne (in the mid-1960s when they were both at the top of their form). In Sutherland's interpretation, Semiramide is not so much a Lady Macbeth as a passionate, sympathetic woman and, with dramatic music predominating over languorous cantilena, one has her best, bright manner. Horne is well contrasted, direct and masculine in style, and Spiro Malas makes a firm, clear contribution in a minor role. Rouleau and Serge are variable but more than adequate, and Bonynge keeps the whole opera together with his alert, rhythmic control of tension and pacing. The vintage Decca recording has transferred brilliantly to CD.

Tancredi (complete).
(B) *** Naxos Dig. 8.660037/8 [id.]. Podles, Jo, Olsen, Spagnoli, Di Micco, Lendi, Capella Brugensis, Brugense Coll. Instrumentale, Alberto Zedda.

The enterprise of Naxos in recording one of the rarer operas of Rossini is triumphantly rewarded, for this set completely displaces the only rival version from Sony. That came on three full-priced discs against the two here, and the eminent Rossini scholar and conductor, Alberto Zedda, proves a far more resilient, generally brisker and lighter Rossini interpreter than his counterpart. Sumi Jo completely outshines Lella Cuberli as the heroine, Amenaide,in dazzlingly clear coloratura, as well as imaginative pointing of phrase, rhythm and words. The mezzo, Ewa Podles, is less characterful, yet the voice is firm and rich as well as flexible; but it is the tenor, Stanford Olsen, previously heard as Belmonte on John Eliot Gardiner's recording of *Entführung*, who offers some of the freshest, most stylish and sweetly tuned singing from a Rossini tenor in recent years. The recording is a little lacking in body, but that partly reflects the use of a small orchestra, and the voices come over well. Having a studio rather than a live recording (like the Sony) means that ensembles are crisper and better focused. An Italian libretto is provided but no translation. Instead, a helpful synopsis is geared to the different tracks on the discs; had there been a libretto, this could well have received a Rosette.

COLLECTIONS

Arias from *L'assedio di Corinto; Bianca e Faliero; Elisabetta, Regina d'Inghilterra; Guglielmo Tell; Otello; Semiramide; Tancredi.*
(M) **(*) Virgin/EMI CUV5 61139-2 [id.]. Katia Ricciarelli, Lyon Op. Ch. & O, Ferro.

Admirers of this artist will surely want this recital, even if Ricciarelli was past her peak when it was recorded in 1989. There is rare material here, sung with much character and at times (as the opening excerpt from *L'assedio di Corinto* and the *Romanza* from *William Tell* readily show) her line is beautifully spun. But elsewhere, when under stress, she sounds less comfortable, although her vigorous sense of dramatic style often carries the day. Ferro conducts sympathetically and the Lyon Opera Chorus gives good support. The recording is vivid, too.

Arias: *L'assedio di Corinto: L'ora fatal s'appressa . . . Giusto ciel! Avanziam . . . Non temer, d'un basso affetto . . . I destini tradir ogni speme! . . . Signor che, tutto puoi . . . Sei tu che stendi, o Dio! La Cenerentola: Nacqui all'affanno . . . Non più mesta. La donna del lago: Mura felici; Tanti affetti. L'Italiana in Algeri: Cruda sorte! Semiramide: Bel raggio lusinghier. Tancredi: Di tanti palpiti.*
✿ (M) *** Decca 458 219-2 [id.]. Marilyn Horne, SRO or ROHCG O, Henry Lewis.

For this reissue in Decca's Opera Gala series, Marilyn Horne's now famous Rossini recital disc is more generously filled than ever, making one of the most cherishable of all Rossini aria records ever issued. Moreover full translations are included, which is especially valuable in the long 25-minute scene from *L'assedio di Corinto* which (with the excerpts from *La donna del lago*) dates from 1972. The rest of the selection derives from two recitals the great mezzo also recorded with her then husband, Henry Lewis, in 1964–6 when she was at the zenith of her powers. The voice is in glorious condition, rich and firm throughout its spectacular range, and is consistently used with artistry and imagination, as well as brilliant virtuosity in coloratura. By any reckoning this is thrilling singing, the more valuable for the inclusion of the rarities – which, with Horne, make you wonder at their neglect. The sound is full and brilliant, hardly showing its age at all.

Arias from: *Il barbiere di Siviglia; La Cenerentola; La donna del lago; L'Italiana in Algeri; Maometto II; Semiramide; Tancredi.*
(BB) *** Naxos Dig. 8.553543 [id.]. Ewa Podles, Hungarian State Op. Ch. & O, Morandi.

The Hungarian mezzo, Ewa Podles, earlier the star singer in the complete set of Rossini's *Tancredi* on Naxos, is here even more impressive in one of the finest Rossini recitals in years. Hers is a rich and even voice which is not only weighty throughout its range but is also extraordinarily agile, dazzling in the elaborate divisions in all these coloratura numbers. She may find it hard to convey the fun and sparkle in Rossini, but the bright-eyed intensity provides fair compensation even with Cinderella or Rosina, and the cabaletta of Cinderella's final aria is breathtaking in its bravura at a formidably fast tempo. By contrast, this great voice is an ideal vehicle for the *opera seria* arias here, with the male characters very well characterized. First-rate accompaniment too.

Arias: *La Cenerentola: Nacqui all'affano. Guglielmo Tell: S'allontano alfin!; Selva opaca. Semiramide: Bel raggio lusinghier.*
(M) **(*) EMI CDM5 66464-2 [id.]. Callas, Paris Conservatoire O, Rescigno – DONIZETTI: *Arias.* **

These recordings from 1963–4 have been admirably remastered so that the orchestra always provides a vivid and atmospheric backing for the voice. If the performances show a degree of cautiousness that rarely marked Callas's earlier work, this only goes to show how conscious she was of all the criticisms and how she did her utmost to avoid any real blots. In general she succeeds, often producing golden tone. The Rossini excerpts rightly come first on the CD, for they offer much for aficionados to enjoy. Yet there is something less positive about the end result than in her earlier recordings of this repertory, and, more seriously, the performances do not have that refinement of detail which at her peak lit up so many phrases and made them unforgettable. Good documentation and full translations are provided.

Rousseau, Jean-Jacques (1712–78)

Le devin du village (complete).
(M) *** CPO/EMI CPO 999 559-2 [id.]. Micheau, Gedda, Roux, Ch. Raymond St-Paul, Louis de Froment CO, Froment.

It tends to be forgotten that, as well as being one of the most influential philosophers and authors of his time, forerunner of the Romantic movement, Rousseau was also a composer who devised a new form of notation and even produced a musical encyclopedia. The one-act Intermezzo, *Le devin du village* ('The village soothsayer'), is his most celebrated work, written in 1752, an unpretentious piece in what Rousseau conceived as the Italian style of the day, which he vigorously supported against the French, even though he here uses a French text. Starting with an overture in the Italian style, fast–slow–fast, it is charming in a plain and straightforward style, hardly original, and the baldness of the writing is rather underlined in this performance with continuo in bare chords. The 25 sections, mostly very short indeed, last well under an hour, offering a simple story of the soothsayer reconciling the estranged lovers, for a price. All three soloists are first rate, with Micheau at her most seductive, and the young Gedda heady-toned.

Roussel, Albert (1869–1937)

Bacchus et Ariane (complete ballet), *Op. 43; Le festin de l'araignée (The spider's feast): symphonic fragments.*
(M) *** EMI Dig. CDM7 64690-2. O Nat. de France, Prêtre.

This is a particularly valuable mid-priced reissue from 1986. *Bacchus et Ariane* teems with life and is full of rhythmic vitality and richness of detail. It has perhaps less of the poetic feeling of *Le festin* but is nevertheless an exhilarating score. The recording, made in the generous acoustic of the Salle Wagram, is a shade too reverberant at times, but no essential detail is masked. Georges Prêtre obtains an excellent response from the Orchestre National de France in both scores. This supersedes Martinon's albeit excellently balanced earlier version on Erato which contained merely the two suites (or Acts) of the ballet and had no fill-up. The CD freshens detail a little, although the resonance means that the improvement is relatively limited. However, the background silence is certainly an asset in *The spider's feast.*

Bacchus et Ariane: Suite No. 2.
(M) ** DG Originals 449 748-2 [id.]. Lamoureux O, Igor Markevitch – HONEGGER: *Symphony No. 5;* MILHAUD: *Les Choéphores.* (**)

Markevitch's spirited and atmospheric account of the second suite from *Bacchus et Ariane* comes from

1960 and, unlike its companions (Honegger's *Fifth Symphony* and Milhaud's *Les Choéphores)*, is in stereo. It is very well played and recorded with plenty of space round the aural image, but the sound naturally lacks the body and focus of a modern recording, although it is fully acceptable.

Suite in F, Op. 33.

(M) **(*) Mercury (IMS) 434 303-2 [id.]. Detroit SO, Paul Paray – CHABRIER: *Bourrée fantasque* etc. ***

The outer movements of Roussel's *Suite in F* have a compulsive drive which also infects the harmonically complex, bittersweet central *Sarabande*. The scoring is rich (some might say thick), and the resonance of the Detroit Ford Auditorium makes it congeal a little. It is well played and alive, with Paray at his best in the closing *Gigue*.

Symphonies Nos. 1 in D min. (Le poème de la forêt), Op. 7; 2 in B flat, Op. 23; 3 in G min., Op. 42; 4 in A, Op. 53.

(B) *** Erato/Warner Ultima Dig. 3984 21090-2 (2) [(M) id. import]. Fr. Nat. O, Charles Dutoit.

Roussel's *First Symphony* is subtitled '*The poem of the forest*'; its first movement, *Forêt d'hiver*, is a kind of prelude, and the closing bars have some of the balminess of a Mediterranean night. The *Second Symphony* has some of the opulence of the first two Bax symphonies, particularly in the lower wind and in some of the music's brooding, atmospheric slow sections. The *Third* is both Roussel's most concentrated and his best-known symphony. It needs rather more bite and attack than Dutoit provides, but this is still a more than serviceable account. The *Fourth* is a delightful score and has Roussel's most infectiously engaging Scherzo and a captivating finale. Here Dutoit does not match the pioneering Karajan set with the Philharmonia from 1949 (EMI) which is taut and atmospheric. Not that Dutoit is wanting in character, and he gets first-class playing from the Orchestre National, who are in excellent form, while the CD transfers do particular justice to the richness of Roussel's scoring and are particularly imposing in the definition at the bottom end of the register. For all these minor reservations, this is an excellent set in every way and splendid value for money.

Symphony No. 3 in G min., Op. 42.

(M) **(*) Sony Heritage MHK 62352 [id.]. NYPO, Leonard Bernstein – HONEGGER: *Rugby; Pacific 231* **; MILHAUD: *Les Choéphores*. ***

(M) **(*) DG (IMS) Dig. 445 512-2 [id.]. O Nat. de France, Bernstein – FRANCK: *Symphony*. **(*)

(M) **(*) Sony SMK 64107 [id.]. NYPO, Boulez – RAVEL: *Chansons*. ***

A vividly characterized and enormously vital account of Roussel's magnificent *Third Symphony*. It was Bernstein's mentor, Koussevitzky, who commissioned the work for the fiftieth anniversary of the Boston Symphony Orchestra, and Bernstein's reading is as highly charged as one could wish for. The Sony performance comes from 1961 and in the original LP format was shrill and reverberant. The present transfer has tamed some though not all of its ferocity and cleaned up some of the detail. Though the recording is not perfect, this is still the best performance of the symphony in the current catalogue, and it comes with a Milhaud rarity new to these shores. However, Sony's Heritage series is not inexpensive.

This is a much less comfortable symphony than the Franck with which it is coupled on DG, and Bernstein compulsively brings out all its energy and pungent dissonance, and yet he lightens the mood attractively for the high-spirited finale. The 'live' recording is extremely vivid but a shade harsh.

Boulez's first movement is surprisingly slow (it is still pungent but has less electricity and brilliance than Bernstein's CBS disc, just reissued). The slow movement, however, has great warmth and humanity. Unfortunately, the recording, made in the Manhattan Center in 1975, is not as first rate as the performance: the acoustic is reverberant and there is plenty of body, but the upper strings are rather shrill. Nevertheless, with the splendid Ravel couplings, this makes an alternative mid-priced recommendation.

Symphony No. 4 in A, Op. 53.

❁ (M) (***) EMI mono CDM5 66595-2. Philh. O, Karajan – BALAKIREV: *Symphony No. 1*. (***) ❁

Karajan's pioneering version of Roussel's marvellous *Fourth Symphony* was recorded in November 1949, yet it still sounds exceptionally fresh. Having treasured this in its 78-r.p.m. form and on LP and in its brief CD incarnation, it is good to have it back again. What a performance! It is vastly superior to most of its successors, Ansermet or Cluytens, and is better even than Munch. Like the Balakirev with which it is coupled, it is a performance of real stature.

CHAMBER MUSIC

Sérénade for flute, violin, viola, cello and harp, Op. 30.
❀ (M) *** Decca 452 891-2 [id.]. Osian Ellis, Melos Ens. – DEBUSSY: *Sonata for flute, viola & harp;* RAVEL: *Introduction and allegro;* ROPARTZ: *Prélude, marine et chansons.* *** ❀

Roussel's charming *Sérénade* fits naturally into this collection of greater and lesser masterpieces of twentieth-century French chamber music. Osian Ellis's musicianship is very much in evidence, his fine technique and musicality matching the degree of sensitivity of the other members of the group. This Melos version has held its place in the catalogue for more than three decades. It is an inspired account and is beautifully engineered, well worthy of inclusion in Decca's Classic Sound series.

(i) *Evocations, Op. 15;* (ii) *Résurrection (Prélude symphonique d'après Tolstoi), Op. 4.*
(M) *** EMI Dig. CDM5 65564-2. (i) Gedda, Stutzmann, Van Dam, Orféon Donostiarra, Anton Ayestaran; (ii) Toulouse Capitole O, Plasson.

It is good to see this coupling returning to the catalogue at mid-price. *Évocations* dates from 1910–11 and reflects something of the impression that Roussel's travels in the Far East and, more particularly, India made on him. It is full of exotic colours and atmosphere, which come splendidly to life in this eminently satisfactory (1986) recording. Plasson directs an excellent performance and adds *Résurrection*, the very first orchestral piece Roussel composed while still under the tutelage of Vincent d'Indy.

Royer, Pancrace (1705–55)

Pièces de clavecin, Book 1.
(B) *** HM Musique d'Abord Dig. HMA 901037 [id.]. William Christie (harpsichord).

Royer's *Pièces de clavecin* of 1746 was his only collection to appear in print. They originate as transcriptions of arias and choral movements from his highly imaginative stage works. In our main full-priced survey we accorded a Rosette to Christophe Rousset's Oiseau Lyre record (436 127-2), made with great flair and finesse on a 1751 Hemsch that had belonged to Rameau's patron, *fermier général* La Poupelinière. William Christie's Harmonia Mundi recording, made in the 1980s, is hardly less fine and at bargain price deserves an enthusiastic recommendation alongside the Rousset.

Rubbra, Edmund (1901–86)

(i) *Piano concerto in G, Op. 85;* (ii) *Soliloquy, Op. 57. Symphony No. 4, Op. 53.*
(B) *** BBC Radio Classics 15656 91932. (i) Malcolm Binns; (ii) Raphael Sommer; LSO, Vernon Handley.

All three performances were recorded at the BBC's Maida Vale Studios in 1976 in the presence of the composer, as part of the BBC's celebrations marking his 75th birthday – and that no doubt served to encourage all concerned to give of their very best. The *Fourth Symphony* is very well played indeed and has no reason to fear competition from either of its full-priced competitors (Richard Hickox on Chandos or Norman Del Mar on Lyrita), except in one respect: the acoustic of Maida Vale Studio One lends the orchestral texture a certain opaqueness. However, even if you have either of its rivals, the symphony is worth duplicating for the sake of the *Piano concerto in G major*. At the time of writing, there is no alternative in the catalogue, although Denis Matthews's pioneering account with the BBC Symphony Orchestra and Sir Malcolm Sargent may well reappear within the lifetime of this book. Perhaps inspired by the special occasion, Malcolm Binns gives a most searching reading of the solo part and, right from the word go, leaves us in no doubt that he has the full measure of this extraordinary work. Make no mistake, this is music of profound tranquillity and a strange and compelling beauty. The *Soliloquy* for cello and small orchestra was written for William Pleeth, the cellist of the Rubbra–Gruenberg–Pleeth Trio, a meditative score whose spirit is beautifully captured here. The BBC recording is eminently satisfactory, and the whole issue is one of the most worthwhile to have appeared on this label.

Symphony No. 5 in B flat, Op. 63.
(M) *** Chandos CHAN 6576 [id.]. Melbourne SO, Schönzeler – BLISS: *Checkmate* ***; TIPPETT: *Little music.* **(*)

Symphony No. 5 in B flat, Op. 63; Loth to depart (Improvisations on virginal pieces by Giles Farnaby), Op. 50/4.
(M) (***) EMI mono CDM5 66053-2. Hallé O, Barbirolli – BRITTEN: *Violin concerto* (**); HEMING: *Threnody for a soldier killed in action.* (***)

Barbirolli here provides the very first recording of any Rubbra symphony. Made in 1950, it originally appeared on seven 78-r.p.m. discs with the haunting *Loth to depart* as a fill-up. Although it has reappeared on LP both in the early 1950s and in HMV's British Music series in the late 1960s, it has never sounded as fresh and 'present' as it does in Andrew Walter's exemplary transfer. Sir Adrian Boult gave its première in 1949 but Barbirolli was quick to take it up, and his spacious and affectionate reading stands up well nearly half a century after its composition.

Rubbra's *Fifth Symphony* is a noble work which grows naturally from the symphonic soil of Elgar and Sibelius. Although the Melbourne orchestra is not in the very top division, they play this music for all they are worth, and the strings have a genuine intensity and lyrical fervour that compensate for the opaque effect of the octave doublings. Altogether, though, this is an imposing performance which reflects credit on all concerned. The recording is well balanced and lifelike; but the ear perceives that the upper range is rather restricted.

Symphony No. 10 (Sinfonia da camera), Op. 145; Improvisations on virginal pieces by Giles Farnaby, Op. 50; A tribute to Vaughan Williams on his 70th birthday (Introduction and danza alla fuga), Op. 56.
(M) *** Chandos CHAN 6599 [id.]. Bournemouth Sinf., Schönzeler.

Rubbra's *Tenth Symphony* is a short, one-movement work, whose opening has a Sibelian seriousness and a strong atmosphere that grip one immediately. Schönzeler is scrupulously attentive to dynamic nuance and internal balance, while keeping a firm grip on the architecture as a whole. The 1977 recording has been impressively remastered. It has a warm acoustic and reproduces natural, well-placed orchestral tone. The upper range is crisply defined. The *Farnaby variations* is a pre-war work whose charm Schönzeler uncovers effectively, revealing its textures to best advantage. *Loth to depart*, the best-known movement, has gentleness and vision in this performance. Strongly recommended. Even though this CD plays for only 40 minutes, it remains indispensable.

String quartets Nos. 1 in F min., Op. 35; 2 in E flat, Op. 51; 3, Op. 112; 4, Op. 150.
(M) ** Conifer Dig. 75605 51260-2 (2) [id.]. Sterling Qt.

It is a source of astonishment that only one of Edmund Rubbra's quartets, the *Second*, has so far been recorded commercially. The *First*, written in 1933 before the *First Symphony* but substantially revised in 1946, half a century ago, was inscribed to Vaughan Williams, who took a personal interest in its development, and the *Fourth* of 1977 is dedicated to Robert Simpson, another master of the quartet medium. These are impressive quartets and have been hailed as masterpieces; they deserve the most dedicated, subtle and persuasive advocacy. The Sterling Quartet have the dedication, but the sound they produce is wanting in bloom and is at times raw and unpleasant. No doubt the close balance is partly to blame. Nor, in the *First Quartet*, do they produce as wide a dynamic range as the music demands. This music is important, so the set must perforce be recommended *faute de mieux*.

Rubinstein, Anton (1829–94)

Barcarolles Nos. 2, Op. 45 bis; 3, Op. 50/3 bis; 4; 3 Caprices, Op. 21; Fantaisie in E min., Op. 77; 2 Mélodies, Op. 3; 2 Morceaux, Op. 30; 3 Sérénades, Op. 22; Theme and variations, Op. 88.
(B) ** Hyperiod Dyad CDD 22023 (2) [id.]. Leslie Howard.

Anton Rubinstein is enjoying a modest revival and his distinct if slender talent repays investigation. Leslie Howard is as always an assured and accomplished guide in this repertoire, though this music needs more charm and imagination if it is to be wholly persuasive. These performances are conspicuously short on charm. The recording successfully reproduces the illusion of a salon acoustic but there is a faint whiff of claustrophobia.

Piano sonatas Nos. 1 in E min., Op. 12; 2 in C min., Op. 20; 3 in F, Op. 41; 4 in A min., Op. 100.
(B) *** Hyperion Dyad Dig. CCD 22007 (2) [id.]. Leslie Howard.

Leslie Howard copes with the formidable technical demands of these *Sonatas* manfully. He proves highly persuasive in all four works, though the actual invention is scarcely distinguished enough to sustain interest over such ambitious time-spans. Rubinstein wrote these pieces for his own use, and doubtless his artistic powers and strong personality helped to persuade contemporary audiences. The 1981 recordings sound excellent, and this set is more enticing as a Dyad, with two discs offered for the price of one. Returning to these works, one is surprised to find how enjoyable the music is, with some good lyrical ideas, phrased romantically, to balance the arrestingly flamboyant rhetoric which Leslie Howard obviously relishes.

Sainte-Colombe (died *c.* 1700)

Le Retour; Tombeau les Regrets.

(BB) *** Naxos Dig. 8.550750 [id.]. Spectre de la Rose – MARAIS: *L'Arabesque* etc. ***

The popular success of the fascinating conjectural film (*Tous les matins du monde*) about this mysterious, reclusive composer and his relationship with his brilliantly talented young pupil, Marin Marais, led to the soundtrack album becoming a bestseller. However, this enterprising and inexpensive Naxos recital includes the 'hits' from the film. The two Sainte-Colombe works included are austerely but certainly touchingly played by a fresh-sounding 'authentic' group led by Alison Crum (viola da gamba) and Marie Knight (baroque violin). The Naxos recording is vivid, but its forward balance means that for a realistic effect a modest setting of the volume control should be chosen.

Saint-Saëns, Camille (1835–1921)

'The essential Saint-Saëns': (i) *Carnival of the animals;* (ii) *Piano concerto No. 2 in G min., Op. 22;* (iii) *Violin concerto No. 3 in B min., Op. 61;* (iv) *Danse macabre, Op. 40;* (v) *Havanaise, Op. 83; Introduction and rondo capriccioso, Op. 28;* (vi) *Symphony No. 3 in C min. (Organ), Op. 78; Samson et Dalila:* (vii) *Air et danse bacchanale;* (viii) *Mon coeur s'ouvre à ta voix.*

(B) **(*) Decca Double 444 552-2; *444 552-4* (2) [(M) id. import]. (i) Ortiz; (i; ii) Rogé; (iii) Bell; (v) Kyung Wha Chung; (vi) Priest; (viii) Horne; (i) L. Sinf.; (ii; v) RPO; (iii; vii) Montreal SO; (iv) Philh. O; (i–v; vii) cond. Dutoit; (vi) LAPO, Mehta.

Mehta's Los Angeles recording of the *Third Symphony* opens this programme spectacularly. It is among the more recommendable versions of this much-recorded work, for he draws a well-disciplined and exuberant response from all departments of the orchestra, and the recording certainly does not lack flamboyance in the finale. Joshua Bell's performance of the *Violin concerto* is very attractive indeed, with the Montreal sound casting a glow over the proceedings so that even the brass chorale sounds genial. The pianissimo opening is full of atmosphere and the *Andantino* has a pleasingly lyrical simplicity, with the work's romanticism blossoming throughout. The snag to this otherwise fairly enticing Double Decca compilation is that Dutoit's *Carnival of the animals* – in a crisp, clean, digital recording with very bright sound – is a sad disappointment, lacking genial characterization and charm. *The Swan* is played in a very matter-of-fact way. However, Charles Dutoit shows himself in a better light in his deft account of the *Danse macabre*, while Kyung Wha Chung is on top imaginative form, playing with flair in both the famous violin showpieces. Marilyn Horne's ripe characterization of Saint-Saëns's most famous aria, 'Softly awakes my heart', will not disappoint: the excerpts from *Samson et Dalila*, including the roistering *Bacchanale*, end the first disc, while Pascal Rogé's account of the favourite Saint-Saëns *Second Piano concerto*, which is second to none, closes the concert. The two discs play for 149 minutes.

Carnival of the animals (original chamber version).

(BB) ** Carlton LSO Double Dig. 30368 01187 (2) [(B) id. import]. Julian Jacobson, Nigel Hutchinson, LSO (members), Wordsworth – BIZET: *Jeux d'enfants* **; DEBUSSY: *La Mer; Nocturnes* ***; RAVEL: *Ma Mère l'Oye*. **(*)

(BB) ** HM Solo Dig. HMS 926019 [id.]. Ens. Musique Oblique.

Barry Wordsworth opts for the original, chamber version for flute, clarinet, string quintet and percussion. The two pianists make a lively contribution and the wide dynamic range of the recording means that the opening and closing sections of the work have their high spirits projected strongly. When the percussive condiment is added, the group makes a considerable impact, but in the more gentle zoological portraits the effect is a bit wan, and the imagery tends to recede. It is difficult here to achieve a volume setting which does not offer problems of changing levels within the domestic circumstances which Saint-Saëns envisaged.

Musique Oblique have a pair of lively pianists in Alice Ader and Denis Pascal, and their furiously galloping *Wild asses* are in bold contrast to the somnolent *Tortoises* and the ponderous *Elephant*. Each of the portraits is vividly drawn, and only the lacklustre *Le Cygne* brings disappointment. Otherwise there is plenty of Gallic brio and the composer's witty quotations are nicely observed. The recording is clear and vivid, and this is enjoyable enough, but there are more individual versions.

Carnival of the animals.

(M) *** Teldec/Warner Dig. 4509 97445-2 [id.]. Güher and Süher Pekinel, French R. PO, Janowski – POULENC: *Double piano concerto.* ***

(M) *** Virgin/EMI Dig. CUV7 61137-2 [id.]. Anton Nel, Keith Snell, Ac. of L., Richard Stamp – PROKOFIEV: *Peter.* *** ✿

(B) *** CfP CD-CFP 4086 [(M) id. import]. Katin, Fowke, SNO, Gibson – BIZET: *Jeux d'enfants;* RAVEL: *Ma Mère l'Oye.* ***

(BB) *** ASV CDQS 6017 [(M) id.]. Goldstone, Brown, RPO, Hughes – PROKOFIEV: *Peter.* ***

(B) **(*) Tring Dig. TRP 046 [(M) id.]. RPO, Andrea Licata – BIZET: *Jeux d'enfants;* ** PROKOFIEV: *Peter.* **(*)

(BB) **(*) Naxos Dig. 8.550499 [id.]. Lapšansky, Toperczer, Slovak RSO, Lenárd – BRITTEN: *Young person's guide;* PROKOFIEV: *Peter.* **

The piano duo, Güher and Süher Pekinel – of mixed Turkish/Spanish parentage – make a sparklingly spontaneous contribution to Saint-Saëns's zoological fantasy, readily dominating the performance with their scintillating pianism. Janowski and the French Radio Orchestra provide admirable support, and Saint-Saëns's portrait gallery comes vividly and wittily to life. The gentle dignity of Eric Levionnais's *Le Cygne* makes a touching highlight, leading on to an exhilarating finale. The performance is beautifully recorded and naturally balanced within an attractively warm ambience; although the playing time (38 minutes) is short, this mid-priced CD remains highly recommendable.

Richard Stamp directs an outstanding version of Saint-Saëns's witty zoology, full of affectionate humour. After Robert Bailey's gentle, slightly recessed image of *The Swan*, the finale bursts on the listener with infectious vigour, the two pianists producing flourishes of great bravura. Throughout, one responds to the polished overall presentation and sense of fun; although some may feel that the recording is rather resonant, it adds a genial warmth to the vitality of the proceedings.

On CfP the solo pianists, Peter Katin and Philip Fowke, enter fully into the spirit of the occasion, with Gibson directing his Scottish players with affectionate, unforced geniality. The couplings are attractive and the CD transfer confirms the vivid colourfulness and presence of the mid-1970s recording.

The two pianists on ASV also play with point and style, and the accompaniment has both spirit and spontaneity. *The Swan* is perhaps a trifle self-effacing, but otherwise this is very enjoyable, the humour appreciated without being underlined. The recording is excellent, and this makes a good super-bargain CD recommendation.

With a pair of unnamed pianists who play brilliantly and enjoy their wrong notes in the self-portrait, this is a vivid performance on Tring, with the solo orchestral instruments closely miked, with the effect of changing the balance in each portrait. The double-bass sounds lugubriously larger-than-life, but the cello plays his famous portrayal of *The Swan* in a very melancholy fashion.

The Slovak Radio performance is given very attractive sound by the ambience of the Bratislava Hall, with pianos well balanced and the individual orchestral soloists naturally projected. Although Ondrej Lenárd begins rather seriously, the performance develops plenty of life and character. The pianists are particularly good at being *Kangaroos*. This is the most enjoyable of the three performances on this Naxos disc.

(i) *Carnival of the animals;* (ii) *Le Cygne; Piano concertos Nos.* (iii) *2 in G min., Op. 22;* (iv) *4 in C min., Op. 44;* (v) *Violin concerto No. 3 in B min., Op. 61;* (vi) *Danse macabre, Op. 40;* (v) *Introduction and Rondo capriccioso, Op. 28;* (vii) *Symphony No. 3 in C min. (Organ), Op. 78.*

(B) **(*) Ph. Duo 442 608-2 (2) [(M) id. import]. (i) Villa, Jennings, Pittsburgh SO, Previn; (ii) Gendron, Gallion; (iii) Davidovich, Concg. O, Järvi; (iv) Campanella, Monte Carlo Op. O, Ceccato; (v) Szeryng, Monte Carlo Op. O, Remoortel; (vi) Concg. O, Haitink; (vii) Chorzempa, Rotterdam PO, Edo de Waart.

This inexpensive Duo collection is described as 'The Best of Saint-Saëns' and indeed it does include good and sometimes fine performances of many of the composer's most attractive orchestral and concertante works. Notable here is Previn's (1980) digital recording of the *Carnival of the animals*, as fine as almost any available. And, to please everyone, Philips have also included a second performance of *Le Cygne* by the inestimable Maurice Gendron, when this famous piece is treated to a more assertively romantic but no less elegant presentation. Bella Davidovich then gives a most sympathetic account of the *G minor Piano concerto* and she draws pleasing tone-quality from the instrument, even if she lacks the last degree of brilliance and flair, notably in the Scherzo. Yet she has the advantage of excellent orchestral support from the Concertgebouw Orchestra (who also give a lively account of the *Danse macabre* under Haitink) and again natural digital recording. In the *C minor Concerto* (which is analogue) the effect is harder, partly because Michele Campanella is a more boldly extrovert soloist; but this account has undoubted vitality and no lack of *espressivo*. Henryk Szeryng gives clean, immaculate performances of the *B minor Violin concerto* and the *Introduction and Rondo capriccioso*. His approach is aristocratic rather than seductive, though in the encore the bravura and sense of style make for impressive results. The contribution of the Monte Carlo orchestra is adequate. De Waart's 1976 recording of the famous *Organ Symphony* cannot be said to be among the most exciting versions available but, with polished orchestral playing and refined Philips sound, it is certainly enjoyable, with a warm *Poco adagio*, and the organ glories at the end of the symphony are given plenty of breadth and impact by the recording.

(i) *Carnival of the animals;* (ii) *Danse macabre, Op. 40; Suite algérienne, Op. 60: Marche militaire française. Samson et Dalila: Bacchanale.* (ii; iii) *Symphony No. 3 in C min., Op. 78.*

(M) *** Sony SBK 47655; *MBK 47655* [id.]. (i) Entremont, Gaby Casadesus, Régis Pasquier, Yan Pascal Tortelier, Caussé, Yo-Yo Ma, Lauridon, Marion, Arrignon, Cals, Cerutti; (ii) Phd. O, Ormandy; (iii) with E. Power Biggs.

It would be churlish to bracket the third star for this very generous Sony collection (75 minutes 35 seconds) because the *Carnival of the animals* – performed in its original chamber version – strikes the listener as somewhat lacking in lustre at the opening. The ear adjusts to the rather dry effect. It is a starry cast: Yo-Yo Ma personifies *The Swan* gently and gracefully, and the finale is extremely spirited. Ormandy and his splendid orchestra play the other orchestral lollipops with fine panache – the exuberance at the end of the *Samson et Dalila Bacchanale* is overwhelming, with thundering drums. The catchy *French military march* also goes with a swing. No complaint about the 1962 sound in the *Symphony*. The performance is fresh and vigorous, with the conductor's affection fully conveyed. The alert, polished Philadelphia playing brings incisive articulation to the first movement and Scherzo. E. Power Biggs has the full measure of the hall's Aeolian-Skinner organ, and he makes a spectacular contribution to the finale, which Ormandy structures most excitingly.

Cello concertos Nos. 1 in A min., Op. 33; 2 in D min., Op. 119; Allegro appassionato in B min., Op. 43; Suite in D min., Op. 16; Carnival of the animals: The swan (orch. Vidal).

(BB) **(*) Naxos Dig. 8.553039 [id.]. Kliegel, Bournemouth Sinf., Monnard.

The Naxos issue brings together Saint-Saëns's cello music in sensitive, warmly expressive performances, slightly marred by the small scale conveyed by the recording, with the strings of the Bournemouth Sinfonietta sounding unusually thin. As in other concerto recordings for Naxos, Maria Kliegel proves a most sympathetic soloist, technically immaculate, undeterred even by the relatively ungrateful writing for the cello in the *Second Concerto*, so much less striking a work than No. 1. It is good to have the early *Suite*, a colourful collection of genre pieces, and the dashing *Allegro appassionato*, both originally with piano accompaniment and here arranged by the composer himself. Saint-Saëns's most celebrated cello piece, *The Swan*, makes an attractive supplement, played in an orchestral arrangement by Paul Vidal, which adds strings to the usual harp accompaniment.

Cello concerto No. 1 in A min., Op. 33.

(B) *** Decca Dig. Eclipse 448 712-2; *448 712-4* [(M) id. import]. Lynn Harrell, Cleveland O, Marriner – LALO; SCHUMANN: *Concertos*. ***

(M) *** Mercury (IMS) 432 010-2 [id.]. Janos Starker, LSO, Dorati – LALO: *Concerto* **(*); SCHUMANN: *Concerto*. ***

(B) *** DG 431 166-2 [(M) id. import]. Heinrich Schiff, New Philh. O, Mackerras – FAURE: *Elégie;* LALO: *Cello concerto*. ***

✿ (M) (***) Sony Heritage mono MHK 62876 [id.]. Gregor Piatigorsky, Chicago SO, Stock – BRUCH: *Kol Nidrei;* DVORAK: *Cello concerto*. (***)

Harrell's reading of the Saint-Saëns, altogether more extrovert than Yo-Yo Ma's (see below), makes light of any idea that this composer always works on a small scale. The opening is positively epic, and the rest of the performance is just as compelling, with the minuet-like *Allegretto* crisply neo-classical. The addition of the Lalo *Concerto* makes this reissue very competitive.

Starker plays the Saint-Saëns *A minor* with charm and grace, and Dorati provides first-class support. The 1964 recording comes up amazingly well and is excellently (and naturally) balanced.

Schiff gives as eloquent an account of this concerto as any on record. He sparks off an enthusiastic response from Mackerras, and the recorded sound and balance are excellent. At bargain price, this deserves the strongest recommendation.

Piatigorsky's account of the Saint-Saëns *A minor Concerto* must rank among the very best ever made. While you are listening to it, you think it cannot have been surpassed since. The orchestral accompaniment under Frederick Stock shows the Chicago orchestra to have been every bit as fine when this was made as it was in its heyday under Reiner. Stock brings delicacy and virtuosity to this score, and not the least astonishing is the quality of the recorded sound, which dates from March 1940! It is superior to the post-war Philadelphia recordings with which it is coupled. The presentation, as always with this series, is distinguished and reproduces the handsome original covers of the 78-r.p.m. sets. This disc costs rather more than an ordinary mid-priced issue but is well worth it.

(i) *Cello concerto No. 1 in A min., Op. 33;* (ii) *Piano concerto No. 2 in G min., Op. 22;* (iii) *Violin concerto No. 3, Op. 61.*

❁ (M) *** Sony Dig. SMK 66935 [id.]. (i) Yo-Yo Ma, O Nat. de France, Maazel; (ii) Cécile Licad, LPO, Previn; (iii) Cho-Liang Lin, Philh. O, Tilson Thomas.

Three outstanding performances from the early 1980s are admirably linked together in this highly desirable CBS mid-price reissue. Yo-Yo Ma's performance of the *Cello concerto* is distinguished by fine sensitivity and beautiful tone, while Cécile Licad and the LPO under Previn turn in an eminently satisfactory reading of the *G minor Piano concerto* that has the requisite delicacy in the Scherzo and seriousness elsewhere. Cho-Liang Lin's account of the *B minor Violin concerto* with the Philharmonia Orchestra and Michael Tilson Thomas is exhilarating and thrilling; indeed, this is the kind of performance that prompts one to burst into applause; his version is certainly second to none and is arguably the finest yet to have appeared.

Piano concertos Nos. 1 in D, Op. 17; 2 in G min., Op. 22; 3 in E flat, Op. 29; 4 in C min., Op. 44; 5 in F, Op. 103.

(B) *** Decca Double 443 865-2 (2); *443 865-4* [id.]. Pascal Rogé, Philh. O, RPO or LPO, Dutoit.

(B) *** EMI Rouge et Noir CZS5 69258-2 (2) [ZDMB 694432]. Aldo Ciccolini, O de Paris, Serge Baudo.

(i) *Piano concertos Nos. 1 in D, Op. 17; 2 in G min., Op. 22; 3 in E flat, Op. 29; 4 in C min., Op. 44; 5 in F, ('Egyptian'), Op. 103;* (ii) *Septet in E flat, Op. 65.*

(B) (***) EMI Rouge et Noir mono CZS5 69470-2 (2) [CDZB 69470]. Jeanne-Marie Darré, with (i) French Nat. RO, Louis Fourestier; (ii) Delmotte, Logerot, Pascal Qt.

Played as they are on Decca, these concertos can exert a strong appeal: Pascal Rogé brings delicacy, virtuosity and sparkle to the piano part and he receives expert support from the various London orchestras under Dutoit. Altogether delicious playing and excellent piano-sound from Decca, who secure a most realistic balance. On CD the five *Concertos* are successfully accommodated on two discs and the digital remastering is wholly successful, retaining the bloom of the analogue originals, yet producing firmer detail and splendid piano-sound. Now reissued as a Double Decca set (two records for the price of one) the value is obvious.

Alternatively there is an immensely enjoyable collection on EMI. There may be little development of style between the *First Concerto*, written when the composer was twenty-three, and the *Fifth* (*The Egyptian*), written at Luxor when he was in his fifties; but this is first-rate gramophone material. Beethoven, Bach and Mendelssohn all receive their due in the *First Concerto*; the *Second* and *Fourth* are already well known; but No. 5 is here unexpectedly attractive, with oriental atmosphere tingeing the music rather than overwhelming it. The finale, in which Egyptian ideas are punctuated in turn by early honky-tonk and a big Tchaikovsky-style melody, is delightful. Only No. 3 falls short in its comparatively banal ideas – and even in that there is a hilarious finale which sounds like a Viennese operetta turned into a concerto. The performances from Ciccolini and his colleagues are admirably spirited and emerge freshly on CD. The vibrant, at times slightly brash, 1970 sound gives the music-making strong character and projection, with a bold and often glittering piano image, and the warm acoustics of the Salle Wagram providing plenty of ambience. This is another very welcome reissue in EMI's French 'two for the price of one' series.

Jeanne-Marie Darré is little known outside her native France, where her recordings of the Saint-Saëns *Piano concertos* enjoy classic status. The performances come from the 1950s and are wonderfully high-spirited and vivacious. She is said to have played all five concertos in the course of one concert in celebration of her twenty-first birthday! Both in the concertos and in the delightful *Septet*, in which Roger Delmotte is the trumpeter, she sparkles and glitters. Well worth considering even if you have a good modern set, for the sound is very good.

Piano concerto No. 2 in G min., Op. 22.

(M) **(*) RCA 09026 61863-2 [id.]. Rubinstein, Phd. O, Ormandy – FALLA: *Nights in the gardens of Spain* etc. **(*); FRANCK: *Symphonic variations for piano and orchestra.* ***

(B) **(*) BMG/Melodiya 74321 40721-2 [id.]. Grigori Sokolov, USSR SO, Neeme Järvi – TCHAIKOVSKY: *Piano concerto No. 1.* **(*)

Rubinstein's version was made in 1969, and he is partnered by that most understanding of accompanists, Eugene Ormandy. Rubinstein's secret is that, though he appears sometimes to be attacking the music, his phrasing is full of little fluctuations so that his playing never sounds stilted. The recording of the piano is rather dry, even hard at times, but the glitter seems just right for the centrepiece.

Grigory Sokolov was a mere sixteen when he gave his dazzling account of the Saint-Saëns *G minor Concerto*, with which he won the Tchaikovsky Piano Competition in 1966. The publicity material quotes Harold Schonberg in the New York *Times* calling it 'a startling performance' and hailing the 'truly refined lightness of the finale'. The Tchaikovsky concerto from the following year is no less remarkable, not just for virtuosic display but also for poetic depth. A remarkable response from both the young soloist and from the USSR Symphony Orchestra and Neeme Järvi. The recording may be pretty rough-and-ready but what playing!

Piano concertos Nos. 2 in G min., Op. 22; 4 in C min., Op. 44.
(BB) **(*) Naxos Dig. 8.550334 [id.]. Idil Biret, Philh. O, James Loughran.

At least on this occasion Idil Biret has the benefit of decent sound, for the recording was made at St Barnabas, London. She makes rather heavy weather of the opening of the *G minor Concerto* and her performance sounds just a little portentous and wanting in charm, though the scherzo is played with delicacy and character. The accompaniment by the Philharmonia Orchestra under James Loughran is very good and the recording is very good indeed. There are performances of greater subtlety to be had – albeit not at this price – and, generally speaking, those wanting these two engaging concertos will not be disappointed – certainly not by the very natural but vivid recording, even if the piano is a bit too closely balanced. There is much to enjoy here.

Violin concertos Nos. 1 in A, Op. 20; 2 in C, Op. 58; 3 in B min., Op. 61; Caprice andalou, Op. 122; Le Déluge, Op. 45: Prélude. Havanaise, Op. 83; Introduction and Rondo capriccioso, Op. 28; Morceau de concert, Op. 62; Romances: in D, Op. 37; in C, Op. 48; (i) *La Muse et le Poète, Op. 132.* (Also includes: YSAYE: *Caprice d'après l'Etude en forme de valse, Op. 52/6.*)
(BB) **(*) EMI Rouge et Noir (SIS) CZS5 72001-2 (2) [CDZB 72001]. Ulf Hoelscher, New Philh. O, Pierre Dervaux; (i) with Ralph Kirshbaum.

This two-CD box collects all Saint-Saëns's music for violin and orchestra (with a short bonus from Ysaÿe) in performances of excellent quality. Ulf Hoelscher is an extremely accomplished soloist who plays with artistry as well as virtuosity, and he uncovers music of genuine worth and much charm which is not as well known as the *Third Violin concerto*. The *Second*, incidentally, has a most attractive *Andante* and a catchy *Allegro scherzando* finale, while the first of the two *Romances* deserves to be much better known. The aptly named *Morceau de concert* is most engaging, and the relatively ambitious extended duo concertante piece, *La Muse et le Poète*, in which Hoelscher is admirably partnered by Ralph Kirschbaum, seems much more substantial here than usual. In this EMI set Pierre Dervaux directs excellent accompaniments, and the recording (made at Abbey Road in 1977) is basically of excellent quality. The slight snag is the forward balance of the solo violin, which means that, with the CD remastering, Hoelscher's timbre in the upper range is made to sound just a bit thin. This is also noticeable in the orchestral violins in the closing *Le Déluge Prélude*.

Violin concertos Nos. (i) *1 in A, Op. 20;* (ii) *3 in B min., Op. 61*; (iii) *Havanaise, Op. 83; Introduction and Rondo capriccioso.*
(M) *** Decca 460 008-2. Kyung Wha Chung, (i) Montreal SO, Charles Dutoit; (ii) LSO, Lawrence Foster; (iii) RPO, Dutoit.

Saint-Saëns's *First Violin concerto* is a miniature – in three sections, but playing altogether for only just over 11 minutes. Kyung Wha Chung presents it delightfully, equally at home in its persuasively simple lyricism and in the energetic bravura of the outer sections. Dutoit provides an admirable accompaniment. She then gives a characteristically passionate account of the *B minor Concerto*, the finest of Saint-Saëns's violin concertos, so intense that even a sceptical listener will find it hard not to be convinced that this is a great work. Such music needs this kind of advocacy, and Miss Chung is splendidly backed up by the LSO under Lawrence Foster. The 1975 analogue recording is slightly less flattering to her than the 1980 digital sound in Montreal, but it remains full and clear. In the famous pair of *morceaux de concert* Chung shows both rhythmic flair and a touch of the musical naughtiness that gives these pieces their full charm; again Dutoit accompanies most sympathetically.

Violin concerto No. 3 in B min., Op. 61.
(M) *** DG Dig. 445 549-2 [id.]. Perlman, O de Paris, Barenboim – LALO: *Symphonie espagnole;* BERLIOZ: *Rêverie et caprice.* ***

On DG, Perlman achieves a fine partnership with his friend, Barenboim, in a performance that is both tender and strong, while Perlman's verve and dash in the finale are dazzling. The forward balance is understandable in this work, but orchestral detail could at times be sharper. The Berlioz *Rêverie et caprice* has been added for this reissue.

Danse macabre, Op. 40; (i) *Havanaise, Op. 83; Introduction and Rondo capriccioso, Op. 28. Le jeunesse d'Hercule, Op. 50; Marche héroïque, Op. 34; Phaéton, Op. 39; Le rouet d'Omphale, Op. 31.*
(M) *** Decca 425 021-2 [id.]. (i) Kyung Wha Chung, RPO; Philh. O; Charles Dutoit.

A splendidly conceived anthology. The symphonic poems are beautifully played, and the 1979 Kingsway Hall recording lends the appropriate atmosphere. Charles Dutoit shows himself an admirably sensitive exponent, revelling in the composer's craftsmanship and revealing much delightful orchestral detail in the manner of a Beecham. Decca have now added Kyung Wha Chung's equally charismatic and individual 1977 accounts of what are perhaps the two most inspired short display-pieces for violin and orchestra in the repertoire.

Danse macabre; Le rouet d'Omphale.
(M) *** Decca (IMS) 448 571-2 [id.]. Paris Conservatoire O, Martinon – BIZET: *Jeux d'enfants* ***; BERLIOZ: *Overtures* **(*); IBERT: *Divertissement.* ***

Martinon's are delightful, Beechamesque performances, offering excellent orchestral playing and a characteristic sense of delicacy and style. The 1960 recording is excellent, and this collection of French music, reissued in Decca's 'Classic Sound' series, is well worth exploring.

Havanaise, Op. 83.
(M) *** EMI CDM5 66058-2. Itzhak Perlman, O de Paris, Barenboim – RAVEL: *Tzigane;* VIEUXTEMPS: *Violin concertos Nos. 4 & 5.* ***

Perlman plays this Saint-Saëns warhorse with splendid panache and virtuosity on EMI; his tone and control of colour in the *Havanaise* are ravishing. The digital remastering brings Perlman's gorgeous fiddling right into the room, at the expense of a touch of aggressiveness when the orchestra lets rip; but the concert-hall ambience prevents this from being a problem.

Havanaise, Op. 83; Introduction and Rondo capriccioso, Op. 28.
(M) (***) RCA Heifetz Collection mono 09026 61753-2 [id.]. Heifetz, RCA Victor SO, Steinberg – CHAUSSON: *Poème* **(*); LALO: *Symphonie espagnole* (**(*)); SARASATE: *Zigeunerweisen.* (***)
(M) (***) EMI mono CDH7 64251-2 [id.]. Heifetz, with (i) LSO; (ii) LPO; Barbirolli – SARASATE: *Zigeunerweisen;* VIEUXTEMPS: *Violin concerto No. 4;* WIENIAWSKI: *Violin concerto No. 2.* (***)
(M) ** Decca 452 309-2 [id.]. Ruggiero Ricci, LSO, Gamba – LALO: *Symphonie espagnole* *(*); SARASATE: *Carmen (fantasy)* etc. **

On RCA the Heifetz performances have quite extraordinary panache: his chimerical bowing in the coda of the *Havanaise* is utterly captivating. Indeed this dazzling playing is unsurpassed on record and the 1951 mono recording, if closely balanced, is very faithful. Even if you have these works in more modern versions, this marvellous disc should not be passed by.

Heifetz recorded the *Introduction and Rondo capriccioso* in London on the same day that he recorded the Wieniawski *Concerto*. Everything he touched at this time was pretty stunning. The *Havanaise* was made two years later, on the same day as the Sarasate *Zigeunerweisen*. Exemplary transfers and splendid sound.

Ricci is on excellent form here, and he is well supported by the LSO under Gamba. His *Introduction and Rondo* is well shaped and brilliantly interpreted, but the *Havanaise* is surely too fast for comfort. The languid feeling, suggestive of a warm relaxing atmosphere, certainly lies within the playing, but the overall effect is rather too streamlined. Better sound and balance here than in the Lalo coupling, but this is hardly a candidate for Decca's Classic Sound series.

Henry VIII: ballet music.
(BB) *** Naxos Dig. 8.553338/9 [id.]. Razumovsky Sinfonia, Mogrelia – DELIBES: *Sylvia.* ***

This ballet-divertissement, described as a '*fête populaire*', comes in Act II of the opera, and in the outer movements Saint-Saëns wittily introduces first a Scottish reel then an Irish jig with Gallic insouciance. But all six numbers, which are enjoyably tuneful, unashamedly incorporate a great many airs from both countries, and Mogrelia presents them affectionately and vividly. With excellent recording, this is a genuine bonus to a pleasing account of Delibes's *Sylvia*.

Introduction & Rondo capriccioso.
(M) *** DG Dig. 457 896-2 [id.]. Mintz, Israel PO, Mehta – LALO: *Symphonie espagnole;* VIEUXTEMPS: *Violin concerto No. 5.* ***

Mintz dazzles the ear with Saint-Saëns's fireworks, while always playing with elegance and finesse. If the couplings are suitable, this is highly recommendable.

Symphonies: in A; in F (Urbs Roma); Symphonies Nos. 1–3.
(B) *** EMI Rouge et Noir CZS5 69683-2 (2) [CDZB 69683]. French Nat. R. O, Martinon (with Bernard Gavoty, organ de l'église Saint-Louis des Invalides in *No. 3*).

The *A* and *F major* works were totally unknown and unpublished at the time of their recording and have never been dignified with numbers. Yet the *A major*, written when the composer was only fifteen, is a delight and may reasonably be compared with Bizet's youthful work in the same genre. Scored for strings with flute and oboe, the charming Scherzo is matched by the *moto perpetuo* finale, and the whole work makes delightful gramophone listening. More obviously mature, the *Urbs Roma Symphony* is perhaps a shade more self-conscious, but more ambitious too, showing striking imagination in such movements as the darkly vigorous Scherzo and the variation movement at the end.

The first of the numbered symphonies is a well-fashioned and genial piece, again much indebted to Mendelssohn, and to Schumann too, but with much delightfully fresh invention. The *Second* is full of excellent ideas. Martinon directs splendid performances of the whole set, well prepared and lively. The account of the *Third* ranks with the best: freshly spontaneous in the opening movement, and the threads knitted powerfully together at the end of the finale. Here the recording could do with rather more sumptuousness. Elsewhere the quality is bright and fresh, with no lack of body, and it suits the Saint-Saëns textures very well.

Symphony No. 3 in C min., Op. 78.
❀ (M) *** RCA 09026 61500-2 [id.]. Berj Zamkochian, Boston SO, Munch – DEBUSSY: *La Mer* **(*); IBERT: *Escales*. ***
(B) *** Carlton Dig. PCD 2010 [(M) id.]. Chorzempa, Berne SO, Maag.
(M) *** Mercury (IMS) 432 719-2 [id.]. Marcel Dupré, Detroit SO, Paray – PARAY: *Mass*. **(*)
(B) **(*) DG Classikon 439 494-2 [id.]. Gaston Litaize, Chicago SO, Barenboim – FRANCK: *Symphony*. *(*)

Symphony No. 3 in C min., Op. 78; Phaéton, Op. 39; Le rouet d'Omphale, Op. 31.
(B) *** [EMI Red Line Dig. CDR5 69833]. O de France, Ozawa.

Symphony No. 3 in C min.; Carnival of the animals; Cyprès et lauriers, Op. 156.
(M) ** Carlton Dig. 30366 00012 [id.]. Kynaston, Youngho & Jingho Kim, Philh. O, Djong Victorin Yu.

(i) *Symphony No. 3;* (ii) *Danse macabre; Le Déluge: Prélude, Op. 45; Samson et Dalila: Bacchanale.*
(M) *** DG 415 847-2 [id.]. (i) Litaize, Chicago SO, Barenboim; (ii) O de Paris, Barenboim.

Symphony No. 3; Le rouet d'Omphale; Samson et Dalila: Bacchanale.
(BB) ** Naxos Dig. 8.550138 [id.]. Slovak RSO (Bratislava), Stephen Gunzenhauser.

Munch's Boston recording dates from 1960 (three years after Paray's Detroit version), yet in its currently remastered form it sounds overwhelmingly spectacular. While the resonance enhances the blend of organ and strings in the *Poco adagio*, which has an enveloping warmth, and projects the huge and thrilling organ entry in the finale, the balance allows sparkling detail and represents one of the most successful and most believable recordings ever made in Symphony Hall. The performance is stunning, full of lyrical ardour and moving forward in a single sweep of great intensity. The couplings, showing Munch and his Bostonians at their peak, are equally valuable, if not quite so outstandingly recorded.

Barenboim's inspirational 1976 version has long dominated the catalogue. Among the reissue's three attractive bonuses is an exciting account of the *Bacchanale* from *Samson et Dalila*. The performance of the *Symphony* glows with warmth from beginning to end. A brilliant account of the Scherzo leads into a magnificently energetic conclusion, with the Chicago orchestra excelling itself with radiant playing in every section. The digital remastering is not wholly advantageous: while detail is sharper, the massed violins sound thinner and the bass is drier. In the finale, some of the bloom has gone, and the organ entry has a touch of hardness. It is now also available in a bargain Classikon disc, but here the Franck coupling is not an asset.

Ozawa's version is coupled with attractive performances of two of Saint-Saëns's most colourful symphonic poems in which the conductor is in his element. The *Symphony* too is very enjoyable, and this performance certainly wears well. Ozawa's finale makes a splendidly opulent effect. The sound is in the demonstration class.

Maag's extremely well-recorded Berne performance has a Mendelssohnian freshness and the sprightly playing in the Scherzo draws an obvious affinity with that composer. The closing pages have a convincing feeling of apotheosis and, although this is not the weightiest reading available, it is an uncommonly enjoyable one in which the sound is bright, full and suitably resonant.

The fine Paray/Mercury recording dates, astonishingly, from 1957. The early date brings just a hint of shrillness to the violins in the first movement; otherwise the sound remains bold, full and remarkably well detailed. Marcel Dupré's weighty organ entry introduces a finale which is powerfully co-ordinated, building to an impressive climax. However, not everyone may want the coupling, enjoyable as it is.

Gunzenhauser directs a fearless performance of the Saint-Saëns *Organ Symphony*, not always ideally refined and scorning the dangers of vulgarity. With big, weighty organ sound, the boldness is most convincing, even if the slow movement becomes too sugary. This super-bargain issue is made the more attractive by its apt coupling of shorter pieces, all vividly played.

Djong Victorin Yu's recording was made in the Royal Festival Hall and is notable for its refined detail – although, surprisingly, at the massive organ entry the two pianos are no clearer than in Maazel's Pittsburgh version, and the end result of the (by no means unexciting) performance is much less overwhelming. The *Carnival of the animals* is fresh but not distinctive either, and the main interest of this Carlton CD is the inclusion of Saint-Saëns's *Cyprès et lauriers*, written to celebrate the signing of the Treaty of Versailles at the end of the First World War. After a solemn *Poco adagio* its roisterous Allegro skirts vulgarity by a small margin: an infectiously rumbustious dialogue between organ and orchestra complete with trumpet fanfares which could surely become a popular 'hit' if given sufficient exposure. It is most invigorating in the splendidly committed account given here, and the recording is first class.

Wedding-cake (Caprice-valse), Op. 76.

(BB) *** ASV Dig. CDQS 6092 [(M) id.]. Osorio, RPO, Bátiz – FRANCK: *Symphonic variations* **(*); RAVEL: *Left-hand concerto* ***; SCHUMANN: *Concerto.* **(*)

A delightfully lightweight performance of Saint-Saëns's frothy but engaging *morceau de concert*, infectious and sparkling. Nicely recorded, too.

CHAMBER MUSIC

Bassoon sonata, Op. 168; Clarinet sonata, Op. 167; Caprice on Danish and Russian airs for flute, oboe, clarinet and piano, Op. 79; Feuillet d'album, Op. 81 (arr. Taffanel); *Oboe sonata, Op. 166; Odelette for flute and piano, Op. 162; Romance in D flat for flute and piano, Op. 37; Tarantelle for flute, clarinet and piano, Op. 6.*

(B) *** Cala Dig. CACD 1017 (2) [id.]. William Bennett, Nicholas Daniel, James Campbell, Rachael Gough, & Ens. – DEBUSSY: *Chamber music.* ***

The *Sonatas for clarinet*, *for oboe* and *for bassoon*, Opp. 166–168, are elegantly finished but surprising pieces, with an unaccustomed depth of feeling. The *Caprice* is a diverting kind of pot-pourri, inspired by the composer's visit to Russia in 1876, when he met Tchaikovsky and returned to Paris with the score of *Boris Godunov*, thus kindling the flame of interest in Mussorgsky that burned so brightly in later years. Paul Taffanel's arrangement of the *Feuillet d'album*, Op. 81, for flute, oboe and two each of clarinets, bassoons and horns, is a first recording and, like almost everything on this record, refreshing and elegant. That goes for the performances too, which are well recorded though the piano is occasionally overpowering. Strongly recommended – and outstanding value, considering that one gets two CDs for the price of one, economically packaged and liberally annotated.

Piano trios Nos. 1 in F, Op. 18; 2 in E min., Op. 92.

(BB) *** Naxos Dig. 8.550935 [id.]. Joachim Trio.

It is good that at long last there seems to be a revival of interest in Saint-Saëns and particularly in his chamber music. These trios are separated by almost 30 years; the *F major*, Op. 18, comes from 1863, some four years after the *A minor Symphony* (No. 2) and the *First Piano concerto*, and the five-movement *E minor* is from 1892. No quarrels with the playing of the Joachim Trio (Rebecca Hirsch, Caroline Dearnley and John Lenehan). The pianist in particular has elegance and charm. This is delightful and inventive music and is well recorded. It is well worth the money.

OPERA

Samson et Dalila (opera): complete.

(M) **(*) DG 413 297-2 (2) [id.]. Obraztsova, Domingo, Bruson, Lloyd, Thau, Ch. & O de Paris, Barenboim.

(M) (**(*)) EMI Classics mono CMS5 65263-2 (2). Luccioni, Bouvier, Cabanel, Cambon, Medus, Paris Opéra Ch. & O, Fourestier.

Barenboim proves as passionately dedicated an interpreter of Saint-Saëns here as he did in the *Third Symphony*, sweeping away any Victorian cobwebs. It is important, too, that the choral passages, so vital in this work, be sung with this sort of freshness, and Domingo has rarely sounded happier in French music, the bite as well as the heroic richness of the voice well caught. Renato Bruson and Robert Lloyd are both admirable too; sadly, however, the key role of Dalila is given an unpersuasive, unsensuous performance by Obraztsova, with her vibrato often verging on a wobble. The recording is as ripe as the music deserves.

EMI's 1946 recording from the Paris Opéra provides a formidable showcase for outstanding singers, little known outside France, who represented a singing tradition that largely fell into ruins in following decades. José Luccioni was a favourite in Paris, his voice combining lyric beauty with heroic timbre that made him an outstanding choice as Samson. His diction and command of style are as sure as his vocal production, and so it is with Hélène Bouvier, boasting a rich mezzo, rock-steady throughout its range, and again a perfect command of style. Sadly, her career was cut short by polio. Paul Cabanel as the High Priest was also at the end of his career but is impressive too. Choral singing and orchestral playing are often ragged, and the sound from 78-r.p.m. discs is very limited; but this is a performance with plenty of feeling, well worth investigating.

Samson et Dalila: highlights.
(M) ** EMI CDM7 63935-2. Gorr, Vickers, Blanc, Diakov, Ch. René Duclos, O of Paris Nat. Op., Prêtre.

Many will rest content with a set of highlights from *Samson et Dalila*, and this 53-minute EMI selection just about passes muster. Jon Vickers and Rita Gorr sing vibrantly and make an appealing duo, and the 1962 recording has plenty of atmosphere. The only drawback is the direction of Georges Prêtre. Rather than any lack of tension in his conducting, there is rather too much tautness in the score's more relaxed moments.

Salieri, Antonio (1750–1825)

(i) *Fortepiano concerto in B flat;* (ii) *Double concerto for flute and oboe in C. Sinfonia in B flat (La Tempesta di mare).*
(M) ** Erato/Warner Dig. 0630 12987-2 [id.]. (i) Badura-Skoda; (ii) Hoogendoorn & Borgonovo; Sol. Ven., Scimone.

Salieri certainly did not poison Mozart but, listening to this well-crafted but somewhat empty music, one could well imagine that he might have wanted to, out of sheer envy. For his writing skilfully goes through all the motions of the eighteenth-century concerto and sinfonia without much hint of real inspiration. The *Double concerto* is his best-known work and has been recorded before. Its chatter is pleasant enough, but here the effect is rather like a couple of old gossips meeting at a vicarage fête. The *Fortepiano concerto* is conventional: its first-movement secondary theme has a touch of charm, but the closing Minuet with variations is a routine affair. The *Sinfonia* is the freshest piece in the programme, but it is of doubtful attribution: it might as easily have been written by Salieri's elder brother, who lived in Italy. Indeed its character is different from the two companion works. The sparkling if repetitive first movement (presumably this is the supposed tempest) has a sunny Italian quality, the central *Andante* a courtly, old-fashioned elegance and the finale is really rather neat. It is played here with much vigour, and Scimone is just as persuasive in the two concertos; moreover his soloists are excellent. So is the recording.

Sallinen, Aulis (born 1935)

Chamber music Nos. I, Op. 38; (i) *II, for alto flute and strings, Op. 41;* (iii) *III, for cello and strings (The Nocturnal dances of Don Juanquixote), Op. 58. Some aspects of Peltoniemi Hintrik's funeral march* (*Quartet No. 3* arr. for strings); *Sunrise serenade for 2 trumpets, piano and strings, Op. 63.*
(BB) *** Naxos Dig. 8.553747 [id.]. Finnish CO, Kamu, with (i) Hanna Juutilainen; (ii) Mats Rondin.

Best known for his symphonies and his often atmospheric operas, *The Horseman* and *The Red Line* and *The King goes forth to France*, the Finnish composer Aulis Sallinen has composed a number of works for string orchestra which are widely admired in his home country. His music is tonal and accessible, 'audience friendly', and the present pieces are in no way forbidding. However, they strike the present writer as all too insubstantial, the invention thin and repetitive. They are given dedicated performances by the exemplary soloists and Okko Kamu and the Finnish Chamber Orchestra. Others may respond more warmly to this music, and those who do will find the playing and recording very good indeed.

Sammartini, Giovanni Battista (1700–1775)

Symphonies in D; G; String quintet in E.

(B) *** HM Musique d'Abord HMA 1901245 [id.]. Ens. 145, Banchini – Giuseppe SAMMARTINI: *Concerti grossi* etc. ***

Giovanni Battista was the younger of the two Sammartini brothers; he spent his whole life in Milan. On this record, the Ensemble 145, led by Chiara Banchini, offer two of his symphonies; although neither attains greatness, they have genuine appeal. Good recording.

Sammartini, Giuseppe (*c.* 1693–1750)

Concerti grossi Nos. 6 & 8; (i) *Recorder concerto in F.*

(B) *** HM Musique d'Abord HMA 901245 [id.]. (i) Conrad Steinmann; Ens. 145, Banchini – Giovanni SAMMARTINI: *Symphonies* etc. ***

Giuseppe settled in England in the 1720s and he was a refined and inventive composer. The Ensemble 145 is a period-instrument group; they produce a firmly focused sound, even though the textures are light and the articulation lively. Excellent playing from Conrad Steinmann in the *Recorder concerto.*

Sarasate, Pablo (1844–1908)

Carmen (fantasy), Op. 25 (arr. Zimbalist); *Zigeunerweisen, Op. 10/1.*

(M) ** Decca 452 309-2 [id.]. Ruggiero Ricci, LSO, Gamba – LALO: *Symphonie espagnole* *(*); SAINT-SAENS: *Havanaise* etc. **

Ricci plays with dazzling virtuosity an arrangement by Zimbalist that adds further embellishments to Sarasate's brilliant fantasia. *Zigeunerweisen* has plenty of gypsy fire and an opulent lyrical line. The solo violin is placed rather near to the microphones but can stand the scrutiny, even if the 1959 sound is not as flattering as the quality EMI provide for Perlman (at full price).

Zigeunerweisen, Op. 20.

(M) (***) RCA Heifetz Collection mono 09026 61753-2 [id.]. Heifetz, RCA Victor SO, Steinberg – CHAUSSON: *Poème* **(*); LALO: *Symphony espagnole* (**(*)); SAINT-SAENS: *Havanaise* etc. (***)

(M) (***) EMI mono CDH7 64251-2 [id.]. Heifetz, LPO, Barbirolli – SAINT-SAENS: *Havanaise* etc.; VIEUXTEMPS: *Concerto No. 4;* WIENIAWSKI: *Concerto No. 2.* (***)

(B) **(*) [EMI Red Line Dig. CDR5 69861]. Mutter, O Nat. de France, Ozawa – BIZET: *Carmen: suites* etc; LALO: *Symphonie espagnole.* **(*)

What can one say about the Heifetz performances except that they are unsurpassed: they are dazzling in the fireworks and with the most luscious tone and sophisticated colouring in the lyrical melody. The RCA recording is dry but faithful. This is a marvellous disc. In London Heifetz is luscious and dazzling by turns in this sumptuous gypsy display-piece.

A sparkling performance of Sarasate's gypsy pot-pourri from Anne-Sophie Mutter, given good support from Ozawa. There are some dazzling fireworks, but some may feel her playing in the famous principal lyrical melody too chaste; others will enjoy the total absence of schmaltz. The balance places the solo violin well forward, and the timbre is very brightly lit.

Sarmanto, Heikki (born 1939)

'Meet the composer': (i–ii) *Kalevala Fantasy: Return to life.* (iii) *Max and the Enchantress; Sea of balloons;* (iv–v; ii) *Suomi (A symphonic jazz poem for orchestra);* (iii; vi) *The Traveller: Northern atmosphere.* (Instrumental): (iv; vii) *Distant dreams: Tender wind. Pan fantasy: The awakening; In the night.* (Vocal) (viii) *Carrousel;* (ix) *Light of love;* (x) *New England images;* (xi; iii) *New Hope Jazz Mass: Have mercy on us.* (x) *Northern pictures.*

(B) ** Finlandia/Warner Dig. Double 0630 19809-2 (2) [id.]. (i) UMO Jazz O; (ii) dir. composer; (iii) Heikki Sarmanto Ens.; (iv) with Juhani Aaltonen; (v) with O; (vi) with Vasile Pantir, Tom Rainey; (vii) composer (keyboards); (viii) Helen Merrill, Tapiola Sinf., Torrie Zito; (ix) Karen Parks, Samuel McKelton, Opera Ebony, Kyösti Haatanen; (ix–x) Sarmanto Jazz Ens.; (x) Finnish Chamber Ch., Eric-Olof Söderström; (xi) Maija Hapuoja, Gregg Smith Vocal Qt, Long Island Symphonic Choral Assoc., Gregg Smith.

Heikki Sarmanto firmly 'eludes all attempts at categorization', writes Antti Suvanto in his notes for this set. Sarmanto was a theory pupil of Joonas Kokkonen and he went on to further studies in the United States. The main influence on the music that represents him here is Duke Ellington, though few of the pieces here rival his model. He is accomplished and inventive, though the choral pieces really do strike us as having more facility than taste. There is some good playing from the various artists involved, and Sarmanto is obviously a skilled as well as a prolific musician. On the whole, however, his music strikes us as deeply unappealing.

Satie, Erik (1866–1925)

Les aventures de Mercure (ballet); *La belle excentrique: Grand ritournelle. 5 Grimaces pour 'Un songe d'une nuit d'été'; Gymnopédies Nos. 1 & 3; Jack-in-the-box* (orch. Milhaud); *3 Morceaux en forme de poire; Parade* (ballet); *Relâche* (ballet).
(M) **(*) Van. 08.4030.71 [OVC 4030]. Utah SO, Maurice Abravanel.

A generous mid-price collection of Satie's orchestral music, well played and given full, vivid recording from the beginning of the 1970s; if Abravanel fails to throw off some of the more pointed music with a fully idiomatic lightness of touch, these are still enjoyable performances; the ballet scores have plenty of colour and rhythmic life.

(i) *Les aventures de Mercure;* (ii) *Gymnopédies 1 & 3* (orch. Debussy); (iii) *Les pantins dansent;* (iv) *Choses vues à droite et à gauche (sans lunettes);* (v; i) *Geneviève de Brabant* (orch. Desormière); (vi) *Messe des pauvres;* (v; vii; iii) *Le piège de Méduse* (comédie lyrique); (viii; i) *Socrate* (drame symphonique).
(B) *(**) EMI Rouge et Noir CZS5 69686-2 (2) [CDZB 69686]. (i) O de Paris, Dervaux; (ii) Paris Conservatoire O, Auriacombe; (iii) LOP, Ciccolini; (iv) Yan-Pascal Tortelier, Ciccolini (piano); (v) Mesplé, Benoit, Paris Op. Ch.; (v) Pierre Bertin (nar.); (vi) René Duclos Ch. (members); Gaston Litaize (organ de l'Eglise Saint François-Xavier); (vii) Deschamps, Falcucci, Laurence; (viii) Millet, Guiot, Esposito, Mesplé.

In Auriacombe's account of the familiar *Gymnopédies* the burden of expressiveness is carried by the fine Paris woodwind soloists rather than the conductor, but Dervaux (although hampered a little by the resonant acoustic) brings reasonable spirit and no lack of warmth to the engagingly scored *Les aventures de Mercure*. He finds the necessary elegance for the *Danses des grâces* in the Second Tableau and real *tendresse* for the charming *Nouvelle danse* in the Third. Later Ciccolini, taking over the conductor's baton, is suitably sprightly in the quirkily rhythmic *Les pantins dansent*. There is some fine singing in *Socrate*; the performance catches well the calm, expressive serenity of the melodic lines. But no libretto or translation is provided either here or in the two works with narrator, *Le piège de Méuse* and *Geneviève de Brabant*. This latter cantata opens with a narration lasting nearly 12 minutes before the music begins and, although Pierre Bertin is eloquent as only a Frenchman can be, the non-French-speaker will be dismayed to find that the entry of the the music is not even cued! Yet there is much that is attractive in Satie's piquant word-settings, both here and in the cabaret-styled *Le piège de Méduse* (with its reminders of Offenbach); however, without the written words or separating tracks, the listener's patience will be sorely tried. The *Messe des pauvres* is a lively Rosicrucian organ Mass, often forcefully played on a bold, grainy-sounding organ, with soprano and bass voices *ad lib.* interrupting the opening *Kyrie* and *Dixit Dominus*. The three brief *Choses vues à droite et à gauche* are scored for violin and piano. Here Yan-Pascal Tortelier joins Ciccolini (who moves over to the piano) to present them with engaging finesse and wit. The recordings were all made in the Salle Wagram between 1967 and 1974, and the transfers are of excellent quality.

Gymnopédies Nos. 1 & 3 (orch. Debussy).
(B) *** Sony SBK 63056; *SBT 63056* [id.]. (i) Cleveland O, Louis Lane – DEBUSSY: *Petite suite;* RAVEL: *Introduction and allegro* etc. ***

Satie's *Gymnopédies*, heard in Debussy's orchestration, are beautifully played by the excellent Cleveland band. Louis Lane has the full measure of the languorous melancholy of these haunting pieces, and his chosen tempi are admirably judged. The sound too is warmly atmospheric.

Parade.
(M) *** Mercury (IMS) 434 335-2 [id.]. LSO, Dorati – AURIC: *Overture;* FETLER: *Contrasts;* FRANCAIX: *Piano concertino;* MILHAUD: *Le boeuf sur le toit.* ***

Satie's *Parade* is the most audacious piece in an excellent Mercury compilation of (mostly) twentieth-century French music, its scoring including several extra-musical effects. Dorati makes it all fit together wittily and entertainingly, and the LSO make the most of the vivid scoring, with the brass obviously relishing their slightly vulgar theme which is somewhat reminiscent of Kurt Weill. The necessary atmosphere and colour are given to the more restrained sections of the score, and the Mercury recording team excel themselves in presenting Satie's kaleidoscopic circus colours with the utmost vividness.

PIANO MUSIC

(i) (Piano, four hands): *Musique d'ameublement; Parade; Socrate*. (Piano) *Fête donnée par des chevaliers normands en l'honneur d'une jeune demoiselle; Le fils des étoiles; 6 Gnossiennes; 3 Gymnopédies; Ogives; Préludes du Nazaréen Nos. 1–2; 3 Sonnneries de la Rose Croix; Uspud; Vexations*.
(M) *(*) Sony Dig. SM3K 52508 (3) [S3K 52508]. Riri Shimada, (i) with Noriko Tokuoka.

The three discs are accommodated in a slipcase and annotated separately. Presumably they will eventually become available separately. The first CD offers *Le fils des étoiles*, four *Gnossiennes* and the *Trois Sonneries de la Rose Croix* and the two *Préludes du Nazaréen* and runs to fifty long minutes. The second comprises the *Gymnopédies*, *Ogives*, the *Fifth* and *Sixth Gnossiennes* and *Uspud*, a 'Christian ballet', written in the early 1890s. The last, in which Shimada is joined by Noriko Tokuoka, has John Cage's arrangement of *Socrate*, and Hirosh Yamaguchi's of *Parade* and the *Musique d'ameublement*. Listening to her *Gymnopédies* on the second CD, it is very apparent that Riri Shimada is not strong on imagination or poetic feeling. Her approach is generally plain and at times prosaic; and she is short on charm. There are few of the tonal subtleties and delicacy of articulation in which John McCabe (Saga) or William Masselos (RCA) indulge. Things are not greatly helped by the balance, which does not flatter the piano-sound. The 1987 recordings were made at Fukushima Hall in Tokyo. They do improve, however, with the last disc, which has a wider range of colour and dynamics. Each booklet produces a large photograph of Riri Shimada without giving any career details.

Aperçus désagréables; La belle excentrique (fantaisie sérieuse) (both for 4 hands); *Croquis et agaceries d'un gros bonhomme en bois; Descriptions automatiques; Embryons desséchés; En habit de cheval* (for 4 hands); *Le fils des étoiles, wagnerie kaldéenne du Sar Peladan; 6 Gnossiennes; 3 Gymnopédies; Jack-in-the-box; 3 Mouvements en forme de poire* (for 4 hands); *3 Nocturnes; Peccadilles importunes; 3 Petites pièces montées* (for 4 hands); *Pièces froides; Préludes flasques (pour un chien); Première pensée et sonneries de la Rose Croix; 3 Sarabandes; Sonatine bureaucratique; Sports et divertissements; 3 Valses distinguées du précieux dégoûté*.
(B) **(*) EMI Rouge et Noir CZS5 68994-2 (2) [CDZB 672822]. Aldo Ciccolini.

Although Satie's achievement is sometimes overrated by his admirers, about much of this music there is a desperate melancholy and a rich poetic feeling which are altogether unique. The *Gymnopédies*, *Gnossiennes*, *Sarabandes* and *Pièces froides* show such flashes of innocence and purity of inspiration that criticism is disarmed, while the wit of the sharper vignettes is most engaging. Aldo Ciccolini is widely praised as a Satie interpreter and he plays here with unaffected sympathy. He certainly understands the *douloureux* feeling of the famous *Gymnopédies*, with which his recital opens, and he also finds the '*conviction et tristesse rigoureuse*' of the *Gnossiennes*. There is a noble, aristocratic dignity expressed in the *Première pensée et sonneries de la Rose Croix*, yet *La belle excentrique* is thrown off with great dash and élan. In the works where (by electronic means) Ciccolini provides all four hands, the percussive edge of the pianism seems somewhat accentuated by the recording (and this occasionally happens with the bolder articulation in some of the solo pieces too), but generally the piano recording is most realistic, and the CD transfer has plenty of colour and sonority. Altogether this 158-minute collection forms an excellent introduction to Satie's world.

Avant-dernières pensées; Chapitres tournés en tous sens; Le fils des étoiles; Gnossiennes Nos. 1–6; 3 Gymnopédies; Je te veux; Le piège de Méduse; Prélude de la porte héroïque du ciel.
(M) * Classic fM Dig. 75605 57022-2. John Lenehan.

No complaints about John Lenehan on artistic grounds, but the small and dryish acoustic of the Classic fM recording is a distinct handicap and diminishes pleasure. John McCabe on Saga will give far more satisfaction in this repertoire.

Avant-dernières pensées; Chapitres tournés en tous sens; Le fils des étoiles; Gnossiennes Nos. 2–3; 5 Grimaces pour 'Un songe d'une nuit d'été'; Je te veux (valse); Nocturnes Nos. 2–3 & 5; Les Pantins dansent; Pièces froides (Airs à faire fuir 1–3); Le Piège de Méduse; Première pensée rose & croix; Prélude de la porte héroïque du ciel; Rêverie du pauvre; 2 Rêveries nocturnes; 3 Valses distinguées du précieux dégoûté; Valse-ballet.
(M) *** Saga EC 3393-2 [id.]. John McCabe.

This entertaining and attractive anthology gets better and better as it proceeds. John McCabe has the full measure of Satie's understated melancholy and cool, lyrical nostalgia. The programme ranges from neglected early works like the simple, almost Chopinesque *Valse-ballet*, Satie's first published piano piece dating from 1885, to the quietly nostalgic elegy of the *Rêverie du pauvre* and the thoughtfully ambivalent *Deux Rêveries nocturnes*. The hauntingly simple *Je te veux* and the two sets of pieces, *Le Piège de Méduse* and *Le fils des étoiles*, are particularly memorable, while the *Cinq Grimaces* end the recital with quirky good humour. The intelligent planning of this 62-minute recital and the penetrating response of the pianism places this CD among the finest Satie collections, and the recording, though not vividly present, is natural within a highly suitable ambience.

(i) *Avant-dernières pensées; Embryons desséchés; Gnossiennes Nos. 1–5; Gymnopédies Nos. 1–3; Nocturne No. 1; Sarabandes Nos. 1–3; Sonatine bureaucratique; 3 Valses distinguées du précieux dégoûté;* (ii) *Croquis et agaceries d'un gros bonhomme en bois; Descriptions automatiques; Je te veux; Poudre d'or.*
(B) **(*) Sony SBK 48283 [id.]. (i) Daniel Varviso; (ii) Philippe Entremont.

Both recitals here were recorded in 1979. Daniel Varviso has the measure of these pieces and plays admirably. Perhaps the first of the *Embryons desséchés* could have greater delicacy and wit, and there could be greater melancholy in the second of the *Gymnopédies*. But there are many good things here and one's main reservation concerns the closely balanced recording of the piano and the slightly dry sound. Entremont, too, is placed forwardly, but he brings charm to the two waltzes, *Je te veux* and *Poudre d'or*, while the *Descriptions automatiques* are engagingly crisp and witty. The collection is generous (71 minutes).

Chapitres tournés en tous sens; Croquis et agaceries d'un gros bonhomme en bois; Descriptions automatiques; Embryons desséchés; Enfantillages pittoresques; 6 Gnossiennes; 3 Gymnopédies; Menus propos enfantins; Passacaille; Pas trop vif; 6 Pièces de la période; Ragtime Parade; Véritables préludes flasques.
(BB) (*) Naxos Dig. 8.550305 [id.]. Klára Körmendi.

Klára Körmendi's recital is taken from a four-disc survey (8.550696/7/8/9) which is not really recommendable. The playing is less at fault than the recording. The sound itself is very hard and unappealing, and it is very difficult to derive much pleasure from it.

Chapitres tournés en tous sens; Croquis et agaceries d'un gros bonhomme en bois; Gnossiennes Nos. 2 and 4; 3 Gymnopédies; Heures séculaires et instantanées; Nocturnes Nos. 2 and 4; Nouvelles pièces froides; Passacaille; Le Piège de Méduse; Prélude No. 2 (Le fils des étoiles); Sonatine bureaucratique.
(B) ** CfP CD-CFP 6075 [(M) id.]. Peter Lawson.

Satie's deceptively simple piano writing has to be played with great sensitivity and subtlety if justice is to be done to its special qualities of melancholy and irony. Peter Lawson's recital opens with the famous *Gymnopédies*, played coolly but not ineffectively. The highlight is a perceptive and articulate characterization of *Le Piège de Méduse*, seven epigrammatic *morceaux de concert*. Elsewhere his way is quietly tasteful and, though he catches something of Satie's gentle and wayward poetry, he is less successful in revealing the underlying sense of fantasy. Good recording.

Chapitres tournés en tous sens: 1: Celui qui parle trop. Croquis et agaceries: 3: Españaña. Embryons desséchés; Gnossiennes Nos. 1–3; Gymnopédies Nos. 1–3; Nocturne No. 3: Un peu mouvementé. Le piège de Méduse; Premier minuet; Sports et divertissements; Véritables préludes flasques; Vieux séquins et vieilles cuirasses: 2: Danse cuirassée.
(BB) *** RCA Navigator 74321 24214-2 [(M) id. import]. William Masselos – DEBUSSY: *Children's corner* etc. (*)

William Masselos made his reputation with the piano music of Charles Ives, but he proves equally at home with another musical eccentric and this is an outstanding and well-chosen selection of Satie's piano music, beautifully played and well recorded (in 1968), which makes this the least expensive recommendable Satie CD in the catalogue. Alas, the Debussy couplings are played by Alexis Weissenberg, who is altogether less sensitive.

Danses gothiques; 3 Gymnopédies; 6 Gnossiennes; 4 Ogives; Petite ouverture à danser; Pièces froides; 4 Préludes; Prélude de la porte héroïque du ciel; Prière; 3 Sarabandes; Sonneries de la Rose Croix.
(B) ** Ph. Duo 462 161-2 (2) [(M) id. import]. Reinbert de Leeuw.

Reinbert de Leeuw is a sensitive player and thoroughly attuned to Satie's sensibility. He takes the composer at his word by playing many of the pieces *très lente*; indeed, he overdoes this at times, though this impression may be caused by listening to too much slow music all at once. There is no doubt that the playing creates and maintains a mood of poetic melancholy; this is helped by the beautiful recorded quality, so very effective on CD.

Embryons desséchés; 6 Gnossiennes; 3 Gymnnopédies; Je te veux; Nocturnes Nos. 1–5.
(B) *(*) Tring Dig. TRP 069 [(M) id. import]. Ronan O'Hora.

After the success of his Grieg *Lyric pieces* Ronan O'Hora's Satie collection is a great disappointment. The melancholy half-light of this music eludes him and, instead of conveying *tristesse*, the performances are merely limp, as is demonstrated at the very beginning of the recital by the three *Gymnopédies*.

Saxton, Robert (born 1953)

(i) *Chamber symphony (Circles of light);* (ii) *Concerto for orchestra; The Ring of eternity;* (i) *The Sentinel of the rainbow.*
(M) *** EMI Dig. CDM5 66530-2. (i) L. Sinf.; (ii) BBC SO; Knussen.

Robert Saxton is one of the most immediately communicative of the younger generation of British composers, using the orchestra with a panache that plainly reflects his own pleasure in rich and colourful sound. These four works, all written between 1983 and 1986, bring fine examples, notably the *Concerto for orchestra*, first given at the Proms in 1984. Its four linked sections broadly follow a symphonic shape, as do those of the *Chamber symphony* of 1986, which uses smaller forces, with solo strings. That later work has the title *Circles of light* and was inspired by a quotation from Dante, when in the *Divine Comedy* he looks into the eyes of his beloved, Beatrice, and links what he sees to the movement of the heavens. The other two works, both lasting around 15 minutes, also have evocative titles and are linked in the composer's mind to the *Concerto for orchestra* to form a sort of trilogy. Oliver Knussen draws intense, committed playing both from the BBC Symphony Orchestra in the *Concerto for orchestra* and *The Ring of eternity*, and from the London Sinfonietta in the chamber-scale works. Full, warm recording.

Scarlatti, Alessandro (1660–1725)

Concerti grossi Nos. 1 in F min.; 2 in C min.; 3 in F; (i) *Sinfonie di concerti grossi for flute and strings Nos. 7 in G min.; 8 in G; 9 in G min.; 10 in A min.; 11 in C; 12 in C min.*
(M) *** Ph. (IMS) Dig./Analogue 434 160-2 [id.]. (i) William Bennett; I Musici.

These noble and elevated works, though not radical in style, have invention of real quality to commend them. I Musici give performances of much eloquence and warmth and great transparency; the latter is welcome in the fugal movements, especially as the 1979 analogue recording is of the very first rank. The *Sinfonie di concerti grossi* feature a flute soloist, in this instance the excellent William Bennett, who plays fluently and in fine style. The performances are lively and attractive, and eminently freshly recorded in Philips's best digital sound.

Motets: *Domine, refugium factus es nobis; O magnum mysterium.*
(B) *** Decca Double 443 868-2 (2) [id.]. Schütz Ch. of L., Roger Norrington – BONONCINI: *Stabat Mater* ***; PERGOLESI: *Magnificat in C; Stabat Mater* **(*); D. SCARLATTI: *Stabat Mater;* CALDARA: *Crucifixus;* LOTTI: *Crucifixus.* ***

These two motets are fine pieces that show how enduring the Palestrina tradition was in seventeenth-century Italy. They are noble in conception and are beautifully performed here and, given first-class sound, make a fine bonus for this enterprising Double Decca collection of Italian baroque choral music.

Scarlatti, Domenico (1685–1757)

The Good-humoured ladies (ballet suite; arr. Tommasini).
(M) *** EMI CDM5 65911-2. Concert Arts O, Robert Irving – GLAZUNOV: *The Seasons;* WALTON: *Wise virgins.* ***
(B) **(*) Sony SBK 60311; *SBT 60311* [id.]. Cleveland O, Louis Lane – RESPIGHI: *The Birds; Church windows.* **(*)

Scarlatti's music in Tommasini's witty arrangement chatters along very like a group of dear old ladies gossiping over their cups of tea. Irving points this up most beautifully and (especially in the finale) offers some very brilliant orchestral playing, while the *Andante* (from the *Sonata in B minor*, Kk 87) is touchingly tender. The recording is first class and completely belies its age (1961).

Louis Lane directs freshly an enjoyable account of this delightfully light-hearted music, so wittily scored. The Clevelanders respond with style and delicacy, and the 1970 Severance Hall recording is warm and pleasing, even if ideally it could be a little more transparent. However, the so-called '*Cats' fugue*' is neatly and clearly articulated, and Lane scores a bonus point by including the *Overture*.

Keyboard sonatas, Kk. 1, 9, 11, 87, 96, 132, 135, 141, 146, 159, 198, 208, 247, 322, 380, 435, 466, 474 & 481.
(BB) ** Naxos Dig. 8.550252 [id.]. Balázs Szokolay (piano).

Balázs Szokolay is the son of the composer of the opera, *Blood Wedding*, and he made a strong impression at the last Leeds International Competition. His Scarlatti recital suffers from the airless acoustic of the Italian Institute in Budapest, though there is no doubt that he is a good stylist. The colourless sound greatly diminishes pleasure, but the playing is often so alert and intelligent (as in the *G major*, Kk. 146 (Longo 349) or the *C major*, Kk. 159 (Longo 194)) as to make one forget the sonic limitations! The two stars are a compromise: the playing is worth three, the recording barely rates one.

Keyboard sonatas, Kk. 3, 52, 184–5, 191–3, 208–9, 227, 238–9, 252–3.
(B) *** Sony Seon SBK 60099 [id.]. Gustav Leonhardt (harpsichord).

Very distinguished playing from Gustav Leonhardt, who often plays with dash and exuberance, as in the first sonata here, Kk. 3 *in A minor*. He uses a copy of a Dulcken harpsichord, and these are consistently characterful performances which project direct to the listener in well-focused, clean sound, recorded in a pleasant acoustic.

Keyboard sonatas, Kk. 7, 33, 49, 54, 87, 96, 105–7, 159, 175, 206–7, 240–41, 347–8, 380–81, 441–4, 518–19, 524–5.
(B) *** HM HMP 90 1164/5 [(M) id.]. Rafael Puyana (harpsichord).

Rafael Puyana gives eminently red-blooded performances of these *Sonatas*, which are refreshing and invigorating. He uses a three-manual harpsichord from 1740 by Hass of Hamburg, restored by Andrea Goble, which makes a splendidly rich sound, present and lively. Authoritative playing, though he tends, with some exceptions, to concentrate on the more outgoing and brilliant rather than the inward-looking *Sonatas*.

Keyboard sonatas, Kk. 9, 27, 33, 69, 87, 96, 159, 193, 247, 427, 492, 531; Fugue in G min., K.30.
(M) *** Erato/Warner 4509 96960-2. Anne Queffélec (piano).

Anne Queffélec employs a modern Steinway with great character and aplomb. She immediately captures the listener in the dashing opening of the *D major Sonata*, Kk. 96, with its lively fanfares and, in the gentler *B minor*, Kk. 27, her rippling passage-work is Bach-like in its simplicity. She alternates reflective works with those sonatas calling for sparkling bravura and her choice is unerringly effective. The recital closes with a *Fugue* which unfolds with calm inevitability. The 1970 recording is first class; the piano is naturally focused and has plenty of space, without any resonant blurring.

Keyboard sonatas, Kk. 32, 64, 69, 87, 133, 146, 160, 198, 208, 213, 380, 429, 466, 481, 511, 517; Toccata in D min.
(B) **(*) Cal. Approche CAL 6670 [(M) id.]. Inger Södergren.

The ever sensitive Inger Södergren gives an appealing recital of 16 well-contrasted *Sonatas* plus a brilliant account of the highly individual *Toccata in D minor*. Some might feel that her gentle, almost wistful treatment of the lyrical sonatas errs towards being too romantic but her crisp articulation in the lively pieces is unimpeachable, and she is very well recorded.

Keyboard sonatas, Kk. 213–14; 318–19; 347–8; 356–7; 380–81; 454–5; 478–9; 524–7.
(B) *** DG Classikon 439 438-2 [(M) id. import]. Ralph Kirkpatrick (harpsichord).

At the beginning of the 1970s, when this recital first appeared on LP, Ralph Kirkpatrick's monumental study of Domenico Scarlatti was the standard work on the subject, and it remains an enormously readable and erudite book. These performances, paired according to his theory, have all the panache and scholarship one would expect from this artist, in addition to a welcome degree of freedom and poetry. Some of his Bach playing has seemed pedantic, so it is a pleasure to welcome this brightly recorded bargain collection back to the catalogue without reservation.

Keyboard sonatas, Kk. 159, 175, 208, 213, 322 & 380 (arr. for guitar).
(B) *** Sony SBK 62425; *SBT 62425* [id.]. John Williams (guitar) – GIULIANI: *Variations on a theme by Handel;* PAGANINI: *Caprice; Grand sonata;* VILLA-LOBOS: *5 Preludes.* ***

Guitar arrangements of Scarlatti sonatas have their charms when played by an artist as imaginative as John Williams. He manages by percussive plucking to sound at times almost like a harpsichord, while his gentle playing is always beguiling especially in the delightful *D major Sonata*, Kk. 159. The recording is faithful, somewhat close and larger than life, but never unacceptably so. This diverse and well-planned recital (76 minutes) is very enjoyable indeed.

Stabat Mater.

(B) *** Decca Double 443 868-2 (2) [id.]. Schütz Ch. of L., Roger Norrington – BONONCINI: *Stabat Mater* ***; PERGOLESI: *Magnificat in C; Stabat Mater* **(*); A. SCARLATTI: *Domine, refugium factus es nobis; O magnum mysterium;* CALDARA: *Crucifixus;* LOTTI: *Crucifixus*. ***

(B) **(*) Sony SBK 48282; *SBT 48282* [id.]. BBC Singers, John Poole – VIVALDI: *Stabat Mater; Dixit Dominus*. **(*)

Norrington's performance is admirable, though not always impeccable in matters of tonal balance; and the recording is very good. Overall this well-designed Double Decca set combines three fine *Stabat Mater* settings with other comparable baroque choral music, all well performed and impressively recorded.

A thoroughly musical, if not distinctive, performance from the BBC Singers, who blend well together and are realistically recorded. An attractive coupling for two enjoyable period performances of Vivaldi.

Schein, Johann Hermann (1586–1630)

Banchetto musicale (1617): *Nos. 2, Suite a 5 in D; 6, Suite a 5 in D; 16, Suite a 5 in A; 20, Suite a 5 in E; 26, Canzon a 5 in A (Corollarium). Venus Kräntzlein* (1609): *Nos. 17, Intrada a 5 in D; 20, Intrada a 5 in G; 22, Gagliarda a 5 in D; 23, Canzon a 5 in A*.

(M) *** Virgin Veritas/EMI Dig. VM5 61399-2. Hespèrion XX, Jordi Savall.

Johann Hermann Schein was one of Bach's predecessors as Cantor of St Thomas's Church in Leipzig. His instrumental music has much in common with that of his Italian contemporary, Giovanni Gabrieli, although the interplay between various groups, usually brass and strings (or recorder), is much less spectacular, more simplistic. The *Canzon in A major* (*Corollarium*), however, is a more ambitious piece, very much in the contrapuntal Gabrieli manner The *Banchetto musicale* is (like Telemann's *Tafelmusik*) intended as a background for meals, although the sonorous brass writing with occasional bravura roulades would suggest that the banqueting hall would have needed to be very spacious. However, the very pleasing expressive music (especially the *Padouanas*) invites lower dynamic levels. The *Intradas* open with a drum-beat, suggesting the musicians marching in to the feast. The performances here are stylish and pleasing, responding to the music's dolorousness. Perhaps they could have been more robust, but the result is very suitable for domestic listening and is very well recorded.

Schickele, Peter (born 1935)

Oboe concerto.

(M) *** Carlton Dig. 30366 0065-2 [id.]. Pamela Pecha, Moscow PO, Paul Freeman – VAUGHAN WILLIAMS: *Oboe concerto;* R. STRAUSS: *Oboe concerto*. ***

Peter Schickele (also known as P. D. Q. Bach) is a professional American musical joker, but his humour does not cross the Atlantic very comfortably, so he is not well known in the UK. He studied composition under Milhaud, so it is not surprising that his well-crafted and highly spontaneous concerto has its exotic side, especially in its central *Chant*. But Schickele's invention throughout the piece is ear-tickling and this work is in every way winning, ending with a touching *Epiloque*. It is a pity that the very sparse notes provided with this CD do not provide more information about its gestation, but they do tell us that the present performer is its dedicatee, and she gives it a performance of great character and immediate appeal. She is both well accompanied and vividly recorded.

Schmidt, Franz (1874–1939)

Symphony No. 4 in C.

(B) *** Decca 440 615-2 (2) [id.]. VPO, Zubin Mehta – MAHLER: *Symphony No. 2 (Resurrection)*. ***

This neglected symphony is in one long movement, whose material all derives from the inspired, long-breathed trumpet theme with which it opens. Schmidt's music has an elegiac feel to it and a nobility of utterance which places him almost as the natural successor to Bruckner. The orchestration is masterly and the chromaticism, though occasionally reminiscent of Reger, is never cloying. Mehta's impressive recording of it with the Vienna Philharmonic from the early 1970s, easily one of his most memorable discs, has recently been reissued by Decca as the coupling for his Mahler *Second*. Mehta finds a dignity that reminds one a little of Elgar. The brightened recording gains in vividness in its CD transfer but loses a little of its fullness, though the Vienna ambience remains very telling.

Das Buch mit sieben Siegeln (The Book with 7 seals).
(M) (***) Sony mono SM2K 68442 (2) [S2K 68442]. Gueden, Malaniuk, Dermota, Wunderlich, Berry, V. Singverein, VPO, Mitropoulos; Alois Forrer (organ).

Given the recent interest in Schmidt's symphonies, it is no surprise that attention should now shift to his oratorio, *Das Buch mit sieben Siegeln* (*The Book with 7 seals*). After he finished the *Fourth Symphony* in 1933, he devoted his remaining creative years to this setting of the *Revelation of St John the Divine*, completing it in 1937. The mid-price Sony version comes from Austrian Radio tapes of a live performance, given as part of the Salzburg Festival in August 1959, with an illustrious line-up under the legendary Dmitri Mitropoulos. The Sony is a mono recording but, given the eloquence and dedication of Mitropoulos's conducting, any sonic limitations are soon forgotten. Under his inspired direction every phrase means something. There is nothing routine and much that is inspired – certainly the singing of Anton Dermota, who took part in the first performance in 1938 and thus brings special authority to the role. It is difficult to grade this recording. Given its fervour and intensity, the Mitropoulos cannot have fewer than three stars despite the mono sound.

Schmitt, Florent (1870–1958)

Piano trio: Très lent.
(BB) **(*) Naxos Dig. 8.550934 [id.]. Joachim Trio – DEBUSSY; RAVEL: *Piano trios*. **(*)

This three-minute fragment, about which the notes are uninformative, is rather haunting and, like the rest of the programme, beautifully played and recorded.

Deux mirages.
(M) *** EMI CDM5 65996-2. John Ogdon – DUKAS; DUTILLEUX: *Sonatas*. ***

Florent Schmitt's piano music is not well served on CD, so that John Ogdon's splendid account of the *Deux mirages* is all the more welcome. The first was written in 1920 and is an elegy for Debussy. Like so much of Florent Schmitt's music, it is strong on atmosphere and makes for compelling listening. The second is a dazzling virtuoso piece, written for Cortot and inspired by the legend of Mazeppa. Ogdon takes its formidable technical hurdles in his stride. The disc also brings impressive accounts of the Dukas and Dutilleux *Sonatas* and deserves the strongest recommendation.

Schnittke, Alfred (born 1934)

Concerto grosso No. 1.
(B) *** DG Classikon Dig. 439 452-2 [(M) id. import]. Kremer, Grindenko, Smirnov, COE, Schiff – LIGETI: *Chamber concerto;* LUTOSLAWSKI: *Chain 3* etc. ***

With his semi-baroque pastiche, the *Concerto grosso No. 1*, Schnittke has provided the nearest he can get to a popular hit, so it will be interesting to see whether this budget Classikon reissue provides it with a large market; certainly the *Toccata* second movement and the *Rondo* are very striking. The soloists are balanced very forwardly in relation to the ripieno, but they can certainly stand up to the aural scrutiny, and the performance overall makes a strong impact.

Concerto grosso No. 1; Quasi una sonata; Moz-Art à la Haydn; A Paganini.
(M) *** DG (IMS) Dig. 445 520-2 [id.]. Kremer, Smirnov, Grindenko, COE, Schiff.

The *Concerto grosso* is already available at bargain price on Classikon in this very performance. If, however, you want to jump in at the deep end of the Schnittke repertoire, the present collection offers the formidable, at times even ferocious, *Quasi una sonata* with its extraordinary scratchings and abrasions, the pastiche *Moz-Art à la Haydn*, which is almost humorous, and the virtuoso solo violin piece, *A Paganini*. The performances here are expert, very committed and brilliantly recorded.

Schoenberg, Arnold (1874–1951)

'Arnold Schoenberg Exposition'.
(B) **(*) Sony SM4K 62364 (4).

This admirable four-CD survey (not available in the USA) gives the listener an opportunity to investigate Schoenberg's development and also to make an assessment of his atonal explorations. In making a powerful contribution to the influence of the Second Viennese School, Schoenberg left a trail of wreckage behind in the field of traditional writing. Other composers, less individually suited to the straitjacket of the atonal system, climbed aboard the bandwagon, often with disastrous results (for them and us), and the onward progress of tonal diatonic writing was forced into a musical backwater. Fortunately times are changing, and it will be interesting to see how much of Schoenberg's output survives to become part of the major repertoire of the twenty-first century. All four CDs are available separately in the UK (and Germany), and the boxed set offers a considerable further saving. Neither the box nor the individual CDs are available in the USA, not even '*Schoenberg in America*'!

'The Early tonal years': (i) *Chamber symphony No. 1, Op. 9;* (ii) *Verklaerte Nacht (String sextet), Op. 4;* (iii) *Friede auf Erden, Op. 13;* (iv) *Gurrelieder: Song of the wood-dove.*
(M) *** Sony SMK 62019. (i) Marlborough Festival O (members); (ii) Trampler, Ma, Juilliard String Qt; (iii) BBC Singers; (iv) Jessye Norman, Ens. InterContemporain (members), Boulez.

The first disc, not unexpectedly, opens with Schoenberg's post-Wagnerian *Verklaerte Nacht* with its erotically potent, Tristanesque chromaticism, written in 1902. The Juilliard performance of what is in effect a symphonic poem for string sextet is highly charged but rather over-characterized, especially at the opening, so that the composer's volatile but seamless, sensuous flow does not proceed as evenly as would be ideal. Nevertheless, technically it is marvellously played and richly and atmospherically recorded. Schoenberg then reacted against himself, and in 1906 took a new path with the polyphonically complex *First Chamber Symphony* for 15 instruments. In spite of the work's formal and textural compression, its diaphanous scoring for the string quintet at times almost returns to the 'transfigured' mood of the earlier work. The Marlborough performance is committed and highly spontaneous. *Friede auf Erden* ('Peace on earth') for unaccompanied chorus was written the following year, its part-writing even more thornily complex. Here its vocal difficulties, which inhibited early performances, are readily surmounted by the BBC Singers under Boulez and they make it sound almost mellifluous. In the lovely *Lied der Waldtaube* ('Song of the wood dove') from *Gurrelieder* (1911), which closes the programme, Jessye Norman is a radiant soloist, crowning her performance with a thrilling top B flat.

'The Expressionist years': (i) *String quartet No. 2 in F sharp min., Op. 10;* (ii) *6 Small pieces for piano, Op. 19;* (iii) *Pierrot lunaire, Op. 21;* (iv) *Die glückliche Hand, Op. 18.*
(M) **(*) Sony SMK 62020. (i) Valente, Juilliard String Qt; (ii) Glenn Gould; (iii) Yvonne Minton (reciter), Debost, Pay, Zukerman, Harrell, Barenboim; (iv) Nimsgern, BBC Singers and SO; (iii; iv) Boulez.

The *Second String quartet* (1907–8) is individual and powerful; its last two movements (both slow) are intensified by the contribution of a soprano, here Benita Valente, who is given settings of a prayerful Litany and its answer. The Juilliards are less sympathetic than they were in *Verklaerte Nacht*: there is no lack of intensity but there is a want of real pianissimo, not helped by the close balance. Glenn Gould displays a ready grasp of the six minuscule piano *Pieces* (1911). But the key work here is *Pierrot lunaire* (1912), a setting of 21 poems by Albert Giraud for recitalist and modest-sized instrumental ensemble, which brings many technical and interpretative problems. However, Boulez's approach places Schoenberg's score within the mainstream of vocal writing, and many listeners will relish the comparative lack of difficulty in coming to terms with its highly original language. *Die glückliche Hand* (which the composer translated as 'The hand of Fate') is much more successful, with Nimsgern an impressive bass soloist. The disc ends with a six-minute interview with Halsey Stephens, 'Schoenberg the painter', recorded in 1949.

'Dodecaphony': (i) *Variations for orchestra, Op. 31;* (ii) *Suite for piano, Op. 25;* (iii) *Moses und Aron: Act II, scene 3.*
(M) ** Sony SMK 62021. (i; iii) BBC SO, Boulez; (ii) Glenn Gould; (iii) Palmer, Knight, Manning, Watts, Cassilly, Winfield, Hermann, Orpheus Boys' Ch.

Boulez's strong, compulsive account of the orchestral *Variations*, composed between 1926 and 1928, is also available coupled with a matching orchestral version of *Verklaerte Nacht* (see below). Here it is supplemented by a recorded talk by the composer, made by Radio Frankfurt in 1931. Gould's 1964 recording of the piano *Suite*, Op. 25, has the expected concentration. But it was a curious idea to select just the third scene of the second Act of *Moses and Aron* (1932), effective though it is, when the complete recording of the opera from which it comes is readily available. It is certainly well performed and recorded.

'Schoenberg in America': (i) *Piano concerto in C, Op. 42;* (ii) *Phantasy for violin with piano accompaniment, Op. 47;* (iii) *String trio, Op. 45;* (iv) *Dreimal tausand Jahre, Op. 50a;* (v) *Kol Nidre, Op. 39;* (vi) *Psalm 130, Op. 50b;* (vii) *A survivor from Warsaw, Op. 46.*
(M) *** Sony SMK 62022. (i) Ax, Philh. O, Salonen; (ii) Menuhin, Gould; (iii) Juilliard Qt (members); (iv; vi) BBC Singers; (vii) Günther Reich; (v; vii) Shirley-Quirk, BBC Ch. & SO; (iv–vii) Boulez.

With Schoenberg's *Piano concerto* we take a jump of a decade to 1942. It is a work which consciously echoes the world of the romantic concerto in twelve-note serial terms, but the thick and (at times) glutinous textures favoured by the composer tend to obscure the focus of the argument rather than making it sweeter on the ear. The soloist, Emanuel Ax, immediately displays an engaging lyrical feeling at the opening, and his performance is warmly sympathetic (the *Giocoso* finale very attractively handled). But despite flatteringly luminous (1992) recording, made in Watford Town Hall, Salonen does not convince the listener that the work is orchestrally a complete success. Of Schoenberg's final two chamber works, the intractable *String trio* was begun in 1946 when the composer was in hospital, recovering from a heart attack; Schoenberg suggested that its restless progress reflected the course of his illness, treatment and convalescence. It is confidently played by the Juilliard group and the 1985 recording is very well balanced. The *Phantasy for violin and piano* (1949), though not opening very invitingly, is perhaps marginally more approachable. This distinguished account by Menuhin and Gould is a mono recording from 1965, made by CBC in Toronto, and it is of first-class quality. But perhaps the most striking music here, apart from *A survivor from Warsaw* with its extraordinary opening so vividly and dramatically projected, is the remaining triptych of vocal pieces from the BBC Singers. In such choral works, particularly when inspired by a Jewish theme, as in the magnificent *Kol Nidre* of 1938 for narrator, mixed chorus and orchestra, the composer's full romanticism broke out. Fine performances and excellent sound.

Other miscellaneous collections

(i) *Accompaniment to a motion picture scene, Op. 34;* (ii) *Chamber symphony No. 1, Op. 9;* (i; iii) *Die Jakobsleiter* (oratorio fragments, completed Zillig).
(M) *** Sony SMK 48462 [id.]. (i) BBC SO; (ii) Ens. InterContemporain (members); (iii) Nimsgern, Bowen, Partridge, Hudson, Shirley-Quirk, Rolfe Johnson, Wenkel, Mesplé, BBC Singers; Boulez.

It is good to see the reappearance of Boulez's first Schoenberg survey on Sony at mid-price, even if, as seems likely, he re-records the repertory. The performance of the film scene is as atmospheric as one would expect, if not as emotionally involved as the *Chamber Symphony*, given a strong, warmly enjoyable account. (The second *Chamber Symphony* is coupled with *Moses und Aron* – see below.) *Die Jakobsleiter* is an ambitious oratorio, which he left fully sketched out. It was completed and orchestrated by Winifried Zillig, revealing an exceptionally powerful piece. Strongly cast, the performance has passion and commitment and the recording projects it vividly.

(i) *Chamber Symphony No. 1 , Op. 9;* (ii) *5 Pieces for orchestra;* (i) *Variations, Op. 31; Verklaerte Nacht;* (iii) *Ewartung, Op. 17; 6 Songs, Op. 8.*
(B) **(*) Double Decca Analogue/Dig. 448 279-2 (2). (i) LAPO, Mehta; (ii) Cleveland O, or (iii) VPO, with Anja Silja, Dohnányi.

It was to Los Angeles that Schoenberg moved to live out his last years, and it would have gladdened him that his local orchestra had achieved a degree of brilliance to match that of any orchestra in America. The *First Chamber Symphony* is given a rich performance under Mehta, arguably too fast at times but full of understanding for the romantic emotions which underlie much of the writing. The Op. 31 *Variations*, among the most taxing works Schoenberg ever wrote, somehow reveal their secrets and their unmistakable greatness more clearly when the performance has such a sense of drive, while Mehta's *Verklaerte Nacht* has warmth and intensity yet is free of schmalz; it is sympathetically recorded and the Los Angeles strings play with great virtuosity and opulence of tone. The Cleveland Orchestra are comparably at home in Schoenberg's seminal *Five Pieces*. Their perfection of ensemble goes with a remarkable depth of feeling, and the digital recording, full, rich and weighty, is of demonstration standard, not as brightly lit as the quality the Decca engineers provide for Mehta. Schoenberg's searingly intense monodrama, *Ewartung*, makes an apt bonus. Silja is at her most committed. The sound under pressure may be raw, but the self-tortured questionings of the central character come over grippingly; again the digital sound is outstandingly vivid.

Chamber Symphony No. 2.
(M) **(*) EMI CDM5 65869-2 [id.]. New Philh. O, Prausnitz – BUSONI: *Berceuse élégiaque* ***; WEILL: *Symphonies Nos. 1–2.* **

The two movements of Schoenberg's *Chamber Symphony No. 2* were composed 23 years apart, the first elegiac and passionate, the second beginning vivaciously but ending in a darker mood. Prausnitz's account has plenty of character and feeling, and is well played and recorded, but it is not distinctive.

Pelleas und Melisande (symphonic poem), *Op. 5.*
(M) **(*) EMI CDM7 65078-2 [id.]. New Philh. O, Barbirolli – R. STRAUSS: *Metamorphosen.* **(*)

It was Richard Strauss who suggested to Schoenberg the subject of Maeterlinck's drama as an opera. Schoenberg opted for a Straussian symphonic poem, and this he completed before he ever knew that Debussy had turned the same subject into an opera. What Barbirolli underlines is the red-bloodedness of the emotions portrayed, and his account is full of passion. The recording is expansive to match, though the tuttis are vibrant rather than refined.

Pelleas und Melisande, Op. 5; Variations for orchestra, Op. 31; Verklaerte Nacht (orchestral version), *Op. 4.*
(M) *** DG 427 424-2 (3). BPO, Karajan – BERG: *Lyric suite; 3 Pieces;* WEBERN: *Collection.* ***

The Straussian opulence of Schoenberg's early symphonic poem has never been as ravishingly presented as by Karajan and the Berlin Philharmonic in this splendidly recorded version. The gorgeous tapestry of sound is both rich and full of refinement and detail, while the thrust of argument is powerfully conveyed. These are superb performances which present the emotional element at full power but give unequalled precision and refinement. The Op. 31 *Variations*, the most challenging of Schoenberg's orchestral works, here receives a reading which vividly conveys the ebb and flow of tension within the phrase and over the whole plan. Superb recording, excellently remastered.

(i) *Pelleas und Melisande* (symphonic poem), *Op. 5;* (ii) *Verklaerte Nacht, Op. 4.*
(M) *** DG 457 721-2 [id.]. BPO, Karajan.
(B) ** Sony SBK 63035; *SBT 63035* [id.]. (i) O de Paris, Barenboim; (ii) NYPO, Boulez.

Karajan's unsurpassed performances of these two early Schoenberg masterpieces, taken from the above set, makes an ideal candidate for separate reissue in DG's series of Originals.

Barenboim's 1977 recording of Schoenberg's extended symphonic poem is not without atmosphere or ardour, but it is distantly balanced within the blurring acoustics of Notre Dame, Paris, and lacks tangibility, besides being opaque. When one turns to *Verklaerte Nacht*, the effect is infinitely more vivid. Boulez secures highly responsive playing from the strings of the New York Philharmonic, and he has the passionate measure of the composer's sensuously poetic evocation to the full.

3 Pieces for chamber orchestra (1910); *Suite, Op. 29; Verklaerte Nacht* (string sextet version), *Op. 4.*
(M) *** Sony Analogue/Dig. SMK 48465 [id.]. Ens. InterContemporain (members), Boulez.

Boulez first recorded *Verklaerte Nacht* in the version for full strings – see below – but this beautifully played account for solo strings is even more impressive. The neo-classical *Suite* – with Boulez this time conducting a mere seven players – reveals a totally different side of the composer, a spiky piece presented at its sharpest in this reading. There is no lack of intimacy and expressive feeling, and the CBS recording is first class. The *Three Pieces for chamber orchestra* were found after Schoenberg had died and date from 1910. They are atonal and the third piece was unfinished. This is an earlier analogue recording but of good quality.

5 Pieces for orchestra, Op. 16.
(M) *** Mercury (IMS) 432 006-2 [id.]. LSO, Dorati – BERG: *3 Pieces; Lulu suite;* WEBERN: *5 Pieces.* ***

Dorati, in his pioneering coupling with other works written at the same period by Schoenberg's emergent pupils, used the version the composer made in 1949, with a slightly reduced orchestra. The performance is strong; the 1962 sound is admirably vivid and clear.

(i) *5 Pieces for orchestra, Op. 16;* (ii) *Ode to Napoleon Buonaparte, Op. 41* (for string quartet, piano & reciter); (iii) *Serenade, Op. 24* (for clarinet, bass clarinet, mandolin, guitar, violin, viola, cello & bass voice).
(M) *** Sony SMK 48463 [id.]. (i) BBC SO; (ii) David Wilson-Johnson; (iii) John Shirley-Quirk; (ii–iii) Ens. InterContemporain (members), Boulez.

With Boulez, the *Five Pieces for orchestra* emerge as colourfully expressive, hardly more elusive than Debussy when played as strongly as this. The Abbey Road recording has plenty of body and atmosphere. The *Serenade* finds Schoenberg in rather crustily neo-classical mood, and even Boulez with his team (including Shirley-Quirk) cannot bring out all the lightness the composer seems to have intended. With David Wilson-Johnson a characterfully ironic narrator, the Byron setting of the *Ode to Napoleon* is more warmly memorable. Both are very clearly recorded and, if the balance is close, there is plenty of ambient warmth.

(i) *Variations for orchestra, Op. 31;* (ii) *Verklaerte Nacht, Op. 4;* (i; iii) *Die glückliche Hande, Op. 18.*
(M) **(*) Sony SMK 48464 [id.]. (i) BBC SO; (ii) NYPO; (iii) Siegmund Nimsgern, BBC Singers; Boulez.

Boulez's account of the thornily immediate *Variations* and the coupled New York Philharmonic performance of *Verklaerte Nacht* may lack the warmth, final polish and subtlety of Karajan's celebrated versions, but Boulez's earthiness, unrelentingly forceful, is compelling in the former, while in the latter he has the full measure of Schoenberg's poetry and secures responsive playing from the New York Philharmonic. The Sony recording is vivid but not as richly beautiful as the Berlin sound. There is also a bonus here in the 'psychological pantomime', *Die glückliche Hande*, which is sharply observed, with Nimsgern a fine soloist.

Verklaerte Nacht.
(BB) *** RCA Navigator 74321 29243-2 [(M) id. import]. Georgian State CO, Liana Isakadze – BERG: *Violin concerto*; WEBERN: *Passacaglia for orchestra.* ***
(M) *** EMI CDM5 65079-2 [id.]. ECO, Daniel Barenboim – BARTOK: *Divertimento for strings*; HINDEMITH: *Trauermusik.* ***
(B) ** Decca Double Dig. 444 872-2 (2) [(M) id. import]. Berlin RSO, Chailly – MAHLER: *Symphony No. 10.* **(*)

On the evidence of this CD, the Georgian State Chamber Orchestra has a first-class string section, and they play Schoenberg's sensuous string work with a uniquely Slavonic ardour to grip the listener in the intensity of the final climax. Isakadze controls the emotional ebb and flow unerringly, and there is refinement here as well as passion. The recording is admirably full and vivid, and this comes at the lowest possible price with two other key twentieth-century works.

Barenboim is a most persuasive advocate of this score and receives a warmly immediate response from his players. He is given very good (1967) Abbey Road sound, lacking only a very little in refinement in the extreme upper range, and with plenty of body. This is highly involving, and interestingly coupled.

Chailly's version of Schoenberg's work is very well played and recorded, but it is in no way distinctive.

OTHER CHAMBER MUSIC

(i) *Verklaerte Nacht* (string sextet version), *Op. 4;* (ii) *String quartet No. 2 in F sharp min., Op. 10.*
(B) **(*) DG Classikon 439 470-2 [(M) id. import]. LaSalle Qt, with (i) McInnes and Pegis; (ii) Margaret Price – WEBERN: *6 Bagatelles* etc. ***

For those who feel that Schoenberg's *Verklaerte Nacht* is best served by the version for solo strings, the LaSalle Quartet give a virtuosic account with no lack of expressive feeling. At times they are inclined to rush things, but the digital recording, if rather bright, is faithful enough. It is good also to have on this bargain disc, not just the chamber version of the post-Wagnerian symphonic poem, but also the rather later *Second Quartet*. Its last two movements (both slow) are intensified by the contribution of a soprano, here the secure and sympathetic Dame Margaret Price. Unfortunately the back-up notes (which are otherwise adequate) omit the words of her two songs, settings of poems by Stefan George – *Litanei* and *Entrückung* ('Transport') – particularly as they are important in establishing the composer's intentions. The 1969 analogue recording, however, cannot be faulted, and the couplings are well chosen and generous.

Piano music: *3 Pieces, Op. 11; 6 Small Pieces, Op. 19; 5 Pieces, Op. 23; 3 Pieces, Op. 33a & b; Suite, Op. 25.*
(M) *** DG (IMS) 423 249-2 [id.]. Maurizio Pollini.

This CD encompasses Schoenberg's complete piano music. Pollini plays with enormous authority and refinement of dynamic nuance and colour, making one perceive this music in a totally different light from other performers. He is accorded excellent sound (very slightly on the dry side), extremely clear and well defined.

VOCAL MUSIC

Music for chorus: *2 Canons; 3 Canons, Op. 28; Dreimal Tausend Jähre, Op. 50a; Friede auf Erden, Op. 13; 3 Folksongs, Op. 49; 3 German folksongs; Kol Nidrei, Op. 39; 4 Pieces, Op. 27; 6 Pieces, Op. 35; Psalm 130, Op. 50b; Modern Psalm No. 1, Op. 50 C; A Survivor from Warsaw, Op. 46.*
(M) *** Sony SM2K 44571 (2) [S2K 44571]. John Shirley-Quirk, Günther Reich, BBC Singers, BBC SO, Pierre Boulez.

With passionately committed performances from the BBC Singers, this superb collection of choral music explodes any idea that Schoenberg was a cold composer. His adoption of an idiom far removed from abrasive atonality in most of these pieces makes this one of the most approachable of Schoenberg sets, with the use of a narrator in three of the works adding spice to the mixture. The later works, written in America, use twelve-note technique with astonishingly warm, rich results. First-rate recording. Translations are given of the full texts.

Choral works: *Dreimal Tausend Jahre, Op. 50a; 3 Folksongs, Op. 49; Friede auf Erden Op. 13; 4 Pieces, Op. 27; 6 Pieces, Op. 35; Psalm 130, Op. 50b; 3 Satires, Op. 28.*
(BB) *** Arte Nova/BMG Dig. 74321 27799-2 [id.]. South German R. Ch., Stuttgart, Huber.

Schoenberg's writing for choir was often taxing, but it drew from him some of his most warmly expressive music, whether he was employing his serial technique or relaxing in a more conventional tonal idiom – which he did on occasion, even in his last years. Though this disc does not – as is claimed on the cover – contain the complete choral works, omitting those with orchestra for example, it offers most of the finest in superlative performances, beautifully recorded. Comparing these readings with those of Pierre Boulez in his pioneering recordings for Sony with the BBC Chorus, the Stuttgart choir is consistently crisper in ensemble and more clearly confident in matching and pitching. So much so that Rupert Huber, the conductor, can readily and without serious problem adopt faster, more flowing speeds, which give the performances greater impact. It is astonishing to find the early *Friede auf Erden* ('Peace on earth'), once thought to be unperformable, sung here with an expressive ease and confidence such as you might find in a Bach performance. At super-bargain price, an issue to suggest to anyone hitherto daunted by this bogeyman composer, as well as to his regular admirers.

Erwartung, Op. 17.
(M) (**(*)) Sony Heritage mono MH2K 62759 (2) [id.]. Dow, NYPO, Mitropoulos – BERG: *Wozzeck*; KRENEK: *Symphonic elegy*. (***)

Mitropoulos recorded Schoenberg's sinister monodrama in 1951, the same year as his recordings of *Wozzeck* and the Krenek piece. Unlike the Berg opera, this was recorded in the studio and, though the performance does not crackle with quite such high-voltage electricity, it has similar clarity and purposefulness. Dorothy Dow tackles the formidable vocal line with freshness and clarity, though the timbre of her voice, firm but with a hint of flutter, does not provide quite enough variety to bring out the full emotional weight of the central character's soul-searching on finding the body of her lover. The result is not as chilling as it can be, though satisfying musically. As with the Berg, full libretto and translations are provided, but this CD is comparatively expensive.

(i) *Erwartung, Op. 17;* (ii) *Gurrelieder: Song of the Wood-dove;* (iii) *Pierrot lunaire, Op. 21.*
(M) ** Sony SMK 48466 [id.]. (i) Janis Martin, BBC SO; (ii) Jessye Norman, Ens. InterContemporain (members); (iii) Minton, Barenboim, Debost, Pay, Zukerman, Harrell; Boulez.

The monodrama *Erwartung* contrasts well with the lovely *Lied der Waldtaube* in its chamber scoring. Boulez brings passionate feeling to both, and the recording is full and immediate. As can be seen from the cast list, the performance of *Pierrot lunaire* gathers together a distinguished group of instrumentalists, but here the result lacks the expressive intensity one expects of Boulez in this music. With Yvonne Minton eschewing sing-speech, the vocal line is precisely pitched, with frequent recourse to half-tones. It is a musical result, but it hardly conveys the cabaret associations which are important in this highly coloured, melodramatic work.

(i) *Gurrelieder;* (ii) *4 Orchestral songs.*
(M) *** Sony SM2K 48459 (2) [S2K 48459]. (i) Jess Thomas, Napier, Nimsgern, Bowen, Reich, BBC Singers & Ch. Soc., Goldsmith's Ch. Union, Men's voices of LPO Ch.; (i; ii) Yvonne Minton, BBC SO; Boulez.

Boulez's warm, expressive style using slow, luxuriating tempi brings out the operatic quality behind Schoenberg's massive score. With Boulez, the Wagnerian overtones are richly expressive and, though Marita Napier and Jess Thomas are not especially sweet on the ear, they show the big, heroic qualities which this score ideally demands, while Yvonne Minton is magnificent in the *Song of the Wood-dove*. Boulez builds that beautiful section to an ominous climax and, at mid-price, remains competitive, for the CBS/Sony recording has attractively vivid and atmospheric sound, and this set also offers a generous coupling of Yvonne Minton's fine account of the *Orchestral songs*.

Pierrot lunaire, Op. 21.
(M) *** Chandos CHAN 6534 [id.]. Jane Manning, Nash Ens., Rattle – WEBERN: *Concerto*. ***

Jane Manning is outstanding among singers who have tackled this most taxing of works, steering a masterful course between the twin perils of, on the one hand, actually singing and, on the other, simply speaking; her sing-speech brings out the element of irony and darkly pointed wit that is an essential. Rattle draws strong, committed performances from the members of the Nash Ensemble and, apart from some intermittently odd balances, the sound is excellent.

OPERA

(i) *Moses und Aron* (complete); (ii) *Chamber Symphony No. 2, Op. 38.*
(M) *** Sony SM2K 48456 (2) [S2K 48456]. (i) Reich, Cassilly, Palmer, Knight, BBC Singers, Orpheus Boys' Ch., BBC SO; (ii) Ens. InterContemporain; Boulez.

Pierre Boulez is helped not just by the passionately committed singing and playing (with Günter Reich expansive in his fully rounded characterization of Moses) but also by the rich, atmospheric recording, so that the operatic qualities are allowed to blossom. It is typical of Boulez that in the final scene Moses' mounting frustration in the face of the glib, articulate Aron is superbly built up, so that the final words – *O Wort, du Wort das mir fehlt* – come with a compelling sense of tragedy. Though the composer planned a third Act, such a moment makes a telling conclusion. Richard Cassilly makes a big-scaled Aron, a worthy brother-adversary to the central tragic figure. The *Second Chamber Symphony*, given an equally committed performance, follows the end of the opera to make a good bonus on the second CD.

Schubert, Franz (1797–1828)

BICENTENARY COLLECTIONS

DG '*Schubert Masterworks*'
(B) ** DG 453 660-2 (20) [(M) id. import]. Various artists, as below.

Although, as can be seen below, there are many fine recordings included in DG's celebratory box of Schubert 'Masterworks', there are also a few which are less recommendable and, although the purchase of the complete set represents a considerable saving, collectors would do far better to pick and choose. There is no additional booklet with the slipcase, and the great drawback to the individual CDs in this set is the documentation, which, for a company of the calibre of DG, is unbelievably sparse. Each CD has an attractively illustrated booklet using various pictures of the composer and of contemporary life, from 'A Schubert evening in a Viennese town-house' to (less appropriately) 'Ball game in Atzenbrugg'. But the documentation is restricted to a single, brief, autobiographical note about the composer, which is repeated with each CD, with nothing further added about the music.

(i) *Konzertstück in D, D.345; Rondo in A for violin and strings, D.438;* (ii) *Duo in A, D.574; Fantasy in C, D.934.*
(M) *** DG analogue/Dig. 453 665-2. Gidon Kremer, with (i) LSO, Emil Tchakarov; (ii) Valery Afanassiev.

This is not only one of Kremer's most impressive records, it happily fills a gap in the catalogue in combining two of Schubert's most engaging concertante works with a pair of his finest works for violin and piano, the *Duo* from 1817 and the *Fantasy* from a decade earlier. All four have that freshness and (at times) innocence of invention which make Schubert's instrumental music so engaging, yet Kremer and Afanassiev (a splendid partnership) treat the *Duo* as a major sonata by observing the first-movement exposition repeat. They also show imaginative flair in the *Fantasy*, especially in its chimerical *Allegretto*. The concertante pieces are equally successful, the recording is excellent, and this was an excellent choice for including within DG's special bicentenary collection.

Symphonies Nos. 1 in D, D.82; 2 in B flat, D.125; Rosamunde: Overture (Die Zauberharfe), D.644.
(M) **(*) DG 453 661-2. BPO, Boehm.

Symphonies Nos. 3 in D, D.200; 4 in C min. (Tragic), D.417; Rosamunde: Ballet music Nos. 1–2, D.797.
(M) ** DG 453 662-2. BPO, Boehm.

Symphonies Nos. 5 in B flat, D.485; 6 in C, D.589.
(M) *** DG 453 663-2. BPO, Boehm.

Symphonies Nos. 8 in B min. (Unfinished), D.759; 9 in C (Great), D.944.
(M) *** DG 453 664-2. BPO, Boehm.

Boehm's cycle of the Schubert symphonies was recorded over a decade between 1963 and 1973, and the Berlin Philharmonic plays with striking warmth and finesse throughout. Boehm does not smile as often as Schubert's music demands – especially by the side of Beecham in Nos. 3 and 5, but he is always sympathetic. Certainly the Berlin wind are a joy to listen to, and it is only in the early symphonies that he does not quite capture the youthful sparkle of these delightful scores, although in its way No. 1 is brightly and elegantly done and No. 2 also is characteristically strong; both are classical in spirit. No. 4 offers splendidly disciplined playing, but this is not one of the more characterful interpretations of the set. It is good that Boehm's warmly graceful account of No. 5 and the glowing performance of No. 6, one of Schubert's most genial works, are coupled together, for both symphonies show Boehm at his best, taking an easy-going view, with relaxed tempi that never grow heavy. The remastered sound is remarkably fine, fresher and clearer and without loss of bloom, although the focus in No. 6 is not absolutely sharp.

Boehm capped his series with an outstanding account of the *Unfinished Symphony* and one of the finest of all recorded performances of the *Great C major*. The *Unfinished* combines deep sensitivity and great refinement, and the points of detail as well as the overall warmth keep this version among the very finest on record. The opening of the development – always a key point – is magically done, and, throughout, the superb recording quality gives unusual clarity while allowing the Berlin Philharmonic ensemble its natural opulence. Boehm's performance of the *Ninth*, recorded three years earlier, stands in the lyrical Furtwängler tradition rather than in the forceful Toscanini stream, but it is the balance between the conflicting interests in this symphony which distinguishes Boehm's reading. His modification of tempo in the various sections of the first movement is masterly in its finesse, often so subtle that it requires close attention to spot it. In the slow movement the rhythmic spring to the repeated quavers is delectable, with the Berlin players really on their toes. Nor is there any lack of drama in the performance, for the playing is marvellous throughout. Only in the finale, taken rather fast, is the playing slightly less gripping, and even there one has excitement in plenty. The recording is very good indeed and in its CD transfer sounds fresh, warm and full. One notes, however, that on its last appearance this coupling appeared on DG's bargain Classikon label, so now it costs more – but it's well worth it.

(i) *Arpeggione sonata, D.821;* (ii) *Piano quintet in A (Trout), D.667. Adagio in E flat ('Notturno')* (for piano trio), *D.897.*
(M) **(*) DG 453 667-2. (i) Pierre Fournier, Jean Fonda; (ii) Christoph Eschenbach, Koeckert Qt.

Pierre Fournier made one of the key modern arrangements of the *Arpeggione sonata* for cello (also used by Tortelier) and he gives this a wholly persuasive account. He is beautifully balanced and recorded. Alongside it comes an enjoyably alert performance from Christoph Eschenbach and members of the Koeckert Quartet of the *Trout*. There is a good deal of sparkle and character – the variations are given plenty of individual interest, the outer movements striking momentum – and Eschenbach himself plays with genuine elegance. The recording acoustic is clear and rather dry; some may find it a trifle unexpansive. The *Notturno* has the advantage of a warmer acoustic and is played most sympathetically.

(i) *Octet in F, D.803;* (ii) *Introduction and variations for flute and piano on 'Trock'ne Blumen'* from *Die schöne Müllerin, D.802.*
(M) *** DG 453 666-2. (i) V. Chamber Ens.; (ii) Aurèle Nicolet, Karl Engel.

The Vienna Chamber Ensemble do not overlap in personnel with the New Vienna Octet, who have recorded this work for Decca, though their performance has a similar polish and urbane Viennese warmth. This is mellifluous Schubert, and very engaging it is: fresh and elegant. This dates from 1980, and the CD transfer maintains the smoothness and realism of the LP. Very enjoyable. The innocent set of variations on a melancholy little tune makes a slight but pleasing encore.

Piano trios Nos. 1 in B flat, D.898; 2 in E flat, D.929.
(M) ** DG 453 671-2. Trio di Trieste.

The Trio di Trieste give eminently lively and sensitive accounts of these *Trios*, and they are well recorded, although the ear notices that the microphones are close at the very opening of the *B flat trio*. These performances are not distinctive, but they are thoroughly serviceable.

String quartets Nos. 12 in C min. (Quartettsatz), D.703; 15 in G, D.887.
(M) ** DG 453 670-2. Melos Qt.

There are many points of interest here, even if there are some mannered touches. The recording, however, is a little hard and close, and it inhibits a whole-hearted recommendation.

String quartets Nos. 13 in A min. (Rosamunde), D.804; 14 in D min. (Death and the Maiden), D.810.
(M) ** DG 453 669-2. Melos Qt.

It is a pity that the quality of the recorded sound is not more appealing in this coupling, though remastering has brought added presence. Generally speaking, the Melos Quartet's playing is impressive enough, but they wear their hearts a little too much on their sleeves; the slow movements are just a shade too sentimental.

String quintet in C, D.956.
(M) **(*) DG 453 668-2. Melos Qt, Mstislav Rostropovich.

Rostropovich plays as second cello in the Melos performance, and no doubt his influence from the centre of the string texture contributes to the eloquence of the famous *Adagio* which, like the performance as a whole, is strongly, even dramatically, characterized. The emphasis on the rhythmic articulation of the outer movements leaves no doubt as to the power of Schubert's writing, and there is no lack of atmosphere in the opening and closing sections of the slow movement. The recording is live and immediate. A fine version, but not a first choice.

(i) *Allegro in A min., Lebenstürme, D.947;* (ii) *Divertissement à l'hongroise in G min., D.818; Fantasia in F min., D.940;* (i) *Marche militaire in D, D.733/1; Rondo in A, D.951.*
(M) ** DG 453 675-2. (i) Paul Badura-Skoda, Jörg Demus; (ii) Alfons and Aloys Kontarsky.

The *Fantasia* is one of Schubert's greatest works for piano duet; from the Kontarskys we have a bright, aggressive performance, but one almost totally lacking in charm and poetry. The technique is formidable, as is the unanimity between two players who in twentieth-century music have few rivals; but here they make Schubert sound relatively heartless, whatever the incisive strength of the performance. The recording is bright to match. The playing of Badura-Skoda and Demus, on the other hand, has the right lightness of touch and a feeling for the delicacy and individual nuance of the phrases. The players communicate their enjoyment too as the music passes from one to the other.

Fantasy in C (Wanderer), D.760; 4 Impromptus Nos. 1–4, D.899; 5–8, D.935.
(M) **(*) DG 453 672-2. Wilhelm Kempff.

Predictably fine playing from Kempff, and many individual moments of special pleasure: the gentle opening theme of D.899/1, the curving arches of triplets in the second of the set, the lovely way Kempff floats the flowing tune of the *G flat major* over its accompaniment, and the exquisite playing at the reprise of the first section of the *A flat* (all these from D.899). But elsewhere Kempff's approach is sometimes more classical than romantic and the phrases are presented concisely, rather than allowed to unfold lovingly. Often the second presentation of a theme is marginally more relaxed. But all the pieces are characterized very individually. The recordings of the *Impromptus* are admirably faithful and beautifully transferred, if a little dry in acoustic. In the *Wanderer fantasy* high drama is missing, but the result is compelling, with a moulding of the structure which gives a complete illusion of spontaneity.

Piano sonatas Nos. 19 in C min., D.958; 20 in A, D.959.
(M) *** DG 453 673-2. Wilhelm Kempff.

Kempff is never less than illuminating in Schubert, and these highly spontaneous performances are nicely turned and well shaped, as one would expect from so authoritative a Schubertian, and there are numerous imaginative insights. The recording gives pleasingly realistic sound, even if it is not of DG's very finest.

Piano sonata No. 21 in B flat, D.960; 6 Moments musicaux, D.780.
(M) **(*) DG 453 674-2. Daniel Barenboim.

To say that Barenboim gives a Kempff-like reading of Schubert's greatest sonata, D.960, is not to deny his characteristic individuality but to point out that his is a reflective, lyrical view of the work, marked by clean semi-quaver work and sharp dynamic contrasts. Yet the slightest sense of artifice is destructive in this composer, and Barenboim's delivery of the first movement's opening statement is just a shade self-conscious. The artless grace and Blake-like innocence of this idea do not quite come across here. The second movement is slow and concentrated, the Scherzo light and sparkling with a real sense of joy. The finale is sharpened with clear-cut contrasts, yet there is curious inelegance in the second subject, an obtrusive left-hand staccato at the end of the first half of the theme. In the *Moments musicaux* Barenboim's mood is often thoughtful and intimate; at other times we are made a shade too aware of the interpreter's art, and there is an element of calculation that robs the impact of freshness. The recording is excellent.

Choruses: *Chor der Engel, D.440; Das Dörfchen, D.598; Gesang der Geister über den Wassern, D.714; Glaub, Hoffnung und Liebe, D.954; Gondelfahrer, D.809; Jägerlied, D.201; Kantate für Irene Kiesewetter, D.936; Klage um Ali Bey, D.140; Lützows wilde Jagd, D.205; Die Nacht, D.983C; Die Nachtigall, D.724; 23rd Psalm, D.706;* (i) *92nd Psalm, D.953.*
(M) **(*) DG 453 679-2. Austrian R. Ch., ORF SO (members), Gottfried Preinfalk, with (i) Rudolph Katzböck.

An enjoyable and well-planned programme of Schubert's shorter choral works, including the engaging *Song of the Spirits over the waters*, the *Jägerlied* and *Lützows wilde Jagd* (complete with horns) and a pair of fine Psalm settings. Sympathetic if not distinctive performances, flattered by the warm acoustic.

Mass No. 6 in E flat, D.950.
(M) **(*) DG Dig. 453 680-2. Mattila, Lipovšek, Hadley, Pita, Holl, V. State Op. Ch., VPO, Abbado.

Abbado takes a spacious rather than a dramatic view of Schubert's most popular setting of the Mass, making the music look forward to Bruckner. This is quite unlike the performance from Bruno Weil on Sony (see below) but is intriguing in its way. With first-rate singing from soloists and chorus it is certainly stimulating, with well-balanced digital sound, but it would not be a prime choice.

Die schöne Müllerin, D.795; An die Musik; Du bist die Ruh; Erlkönig; Heidenröslein; Der Musensohn.
✿ (M) *** DG 453 676-2. Dietrich Fischer-Dieskau, Gerald Moore.

With the transfer barely giving an indication of its analogue source back in 1972, Fischer-Dieskau's classic version of *Die schöne Müllerin* remains among the very finest ever recorded. Though he had made several earlier recordings, this is no mere repeat of previous triumphs, now combining his developed sense of drama and story-telling, his mature feeling for detail and yet spontaneity too, helped by the searching accompaniment of Gerald Moore. It is a performance with premonitions of *Winterreise*. With extra Lieder added to fill out the recital, this is now one of the most cherishable of Fischer-Dieskau's many superb Schubert CDs.

(i) *Schwanengesang, D.957;* (ii) *Ave Maria (Ellens Gesang III); Die Forelle; Gretchen am Spinnrade; Die Junge Nonne; Wiegenlied.*
(M) ** DG Analogue/Dig. 453 678-2. (i) Hermann Prey, Leonard Hokanson; (ii) Gundula Janowitz, Irwin Gage.

Prey's DG recording of *Schwanengesang* was made live at a recital at the 1978 Hohenems Festival. It gains little in intensity from that and suffers from inevitable vocal shortcomings (the early songs a little cautious) and rather humdrum accompaniment. The other favourite songs, very well sung by Janowitz, make an attractive supplement.

Winterreise (complete).
(M) *** DG 453 677-2. Dietrich Fischer-Dieskau, Daniel Barenboim.

Fischer-Dieskau's fifth recording of Schubert's greatest cycle, made in 1979, has the voice still in superb condition. Prompted by Barenboim's spontaneous-sounding, almost improvisatory accompaniments, it is highly inspirational. In expression this is freer than the earlier versions and, though some idiosyncratic details will not please everyone, the sense of concentrated development is irresistible. The recording is very natural and beautifully balanced. However, the last appearance of this version was on DG's bargain Classikon label (see below), so the present reissue brings a price increase. In any case, first choice remains with either Fischer-Dieskau's early-1970s set with Gerald Moore (DG 415 187-2) or his later collaboration with Brendel, which produced an exceptionally moving performance, full of new insights (Ph. 411 463-2). Both are premium-price CDs.

Decca '*Masterworks*'
(B) **(*) Decca Analogue/Dig. 452 389-2 (12) [(M) id. import].

As with their comparable Brahms compilation, Decca have delved into their back-catalogue to celebrate the bicentenary of Schubert's birth. For collectors understandably not willing to take the plunge into the contents of all 12 well-filled CDs, the music is all available separately in a series of Double Deccas.

Volume I: *Symphonies Nos.* (i; iii) *4 in C min. (Tragic), D.417; 5 in B flat, D.485;* (i; iv) *8 in B min. (Unfinished), D.759;* (ii; iv) *9 in C (Great), D.944;* (i; v) *Rosamunde: Overture (Die Zauberharfe); Entr'acte to Act III; Ballet music No. 2, D.797.*
(B) *** Decca Double 452 390-2 (2) [(M) id. import]. (i) VPO; (ii) LSO; (iii) Kertész; (iv) Krips; (v) Monteux.

Apart from a few extreme tempi – a fast minuet in No. 4, a fast first movement and a slow start to the second in No. 5 – the Kertész performances of the symphonies offer attractive, stylish Schubert playing. He does not always find the smile in Schubert's writing, but the playing of the Vienna Philharmonic is beyond reproach and the recordings are exemplary for their day (1970). Krips then directs an unforced, very satisfying account of the *Unfinished*, helped by excellent playing and good (1969) recording. However, this lacks some of the bite which even this symphony should have. The same conductor's reading of the *Great C major* is a different matter, one of the very finest performances of this much-recorded symphony ever put on record. It has a direct, unforced spontaneity which shows Krips's natural feeling for Schubertian lyricism at its most engaging. The playing is polished yet flexible, strong without ever sounding aggressive. The pointing of the trio in the Scherzo is delectable, and the feathery lightness of the triplets in the finale makes one positively welcome every single one of its many repetitions. As a whole, this reading represents the Viennese tradition at its very best. The early (1958) stereo sounds amazingly good, and the set is worth acquiring for this performance alone.

Volume II: (i) *Arpeggione sonata, D.821* (arr. for cello); (ii) *Fantasy in C, D.934;* (iii) *Octet, D.803;* (iii; iv) *Piano quintet in A (Trout), D.667.*
(B) **(*) Decca Double 452 393-2 (2) [(M) id. import]. (i) Rostropovich, Britten; (ii) Goldberg, Lupu; (iii) V. Octet; (iv) Curzon.

Even if Clifford Curzon's 1957 recording of the *Trout* sounds its age because of thin violin-timbre, it remains a classic performance in every respect. A similar comment might be made about the Vienna recording of the *Octet*, made in the Sofiensaal in the same year, which also has somewhat meagre violin-timbre. But the performance has the glow of the Vienna Octet at its peak under the leadership of Willi Boskovsky. The horn has a Viennese fruitiness, but that only makes the performance more authentic. The account of the *Fantasy in C* by Goldberg and Lupu has a comparable Schubertian freshness, and here the 1979 recording is first class, as it is in Rostropovich's account of the *Arpeggione sonata*, which is undoubtedly charismatic but very much more idiosyncratic.

Volume III: (i) *String quartets Nos. 12 (Quartettsatz);* (ii) *14 (Death and the Maiden);* (iii) *15 in G;* (i; iv) *String quintet in C, D.956.*
(B) **(*) Decca Double 452 396-2 (2) [(M) id. import]. (i) Weller Qt; (ii) VPO Qt; (iii) Gabrieli Qt; (iv) Gürtler.

In the *Death and the Maiden* the Vienna players' homogeneity is such that one hears one instrument rather than four, and one senses one mind rather than the four usually sympathetic minds of a great quartet. Admittedly Boskovsky, the first violinist, plays wonderfully in the variations, but he is *primus inter pares* for the greater part of the time. The tempi are generally excellent, and the slight but effective holding back of the Scherzo lends it a much more telling character. The *G major Quartet* is another of Schubert's most profound and searching utterances, and the Gabrieli players have its measure. Their performance is compelling from beginning to end, and it has genuine sensitivity and depth of feeling. The inspired *String quintet* and the remarkable *Quartettsatz* also brings fine playing by the Weller Quartet, though they are a trifle sweet and suave; other performances of the former are much more searching. The Decca engineers have achieved a natural balance and the most realistic quality of sound throughout.

Volume IV: (i) *Piano sonata No. 21, D.960;* (ii) *Fantasia in C (Wanderer), D.760;* (iii) *Impromptus Nos 1–4, D.899; 5–8, D.935; Moments musicaux 1–6, D.780.*
(B) **(*) Decca Double Analogue/Dig. 452 399-2 (2) [(M) id. import]. (i) Curzon; (ii) Ashkenazy; (iii) Schiff.

Not surprisingly, Curzon's is a memorable account of the *B flat Sonata*. Tempi are aptly judged, detail is finely drawn but never emphasized at the expense of the architecture as a whole, and the piano sounds very truthful in timbre. Ashkenazy gives a predictably fine account of the *Wanderer fantasy* but is let down somewhat by the clangorous recording. The *Impromptus* and *Moments musicaux*, however, as played most sympathetically by András Schiff, are most satisfactorily recorded and they laid the foundations for his Schubertian odyssey. The performances are idiomatic, intelligent and humane, and no one who has found satisfaction in Schiff's current survey of the sonatas will be disappointed by them.

Volume V: *Die schöne Müllerin, D.795; Winterreise, D.911; An die Laute, D.905; Der Einsame, D.800; Die Taubenpost, D.957/14.*
(B) **(*) Decca Double 452 402-2 (2) [(M) id. import]. Pears, Britten.

Schubert's darkest song-cycle, *Winterreise*, was in fact originally written for high, not low, voice; quite apart from the intensity and subtlety of the Pears/Britten version, it gains enormously from being at the right pitch throughout. When the message of these poems is so gloomy, a dark voice tends to underline the sombre aspect too oppressively, where the lightness of a tenor is even more affecting. That is particularly so in those songs in which the wandering poet in his despair observes triviality – as in the picture of the hurdy-gurdy man in the last song of all. What is so striking about the Pears performance is its intensity. One continually has the sense of a live occasion. As for Britten, he re-creates the music, sometimes with a fair freedom from Schubert's markings but always with scrupulous concern for the overall musical shaping and sense of atmosphere. The sprung rhythm of *Gefror'ne Tränen* is magical in creating the impression of frozen drops falling, and almost every song brings similar magic. Pears is imaginative too in *Die schöne Müllerin*, if for once in rather gritty voice; and Britten again brings a composer's insight to the accompaniments. Other versions provide more charm in this most sunny of song-cycles, but the Pears/Britten partnership remains uniquely valuable. The transfers of both cycles have fine presence and realism.

However, *Winterreise* is still available separately at mid-price (Decca 417 423-2) and is even more recommendable in this form.

Volume VI: (i) *Masses Nos. 4 in C, D.452;* (ii) *5 in A flat, D.678;* (iii) *6 in E flat, D.950;* (iv) Part songs: *Christ ist erstanden, D.440; Gott meine Zuversicht (Psalm 23), D.706; Nachthelle, D.892; Ständchen, D.921.*

(B) ** Decca Double 452 405-2 (2) [(M) id. import]. (i) Bryn-Julson, Jan de Gaetani, Rolfe Johnson, King, L. Sinf. Ch. & O, Atherton; (ii) Eathorne, Greevy; (ii–iii) Evans, Keyte; (iii) Palmer, Watts, Bowen; (ii–iii) St John's College Ch., ASMF, Guest; (iv) Elizabethan Singers, Louis Halsey; Viola Tunnard (piano).

David Atherton's lively account of the last of Schubert's four early Masses, the *C major*, D.452, has refreshment to offer but is not noticeably inspired by any of the detailed sentiments of the liturgy. George Guest's performances of the two later Masses are faithful but lack the distinction which marked his recordings of the Haydn Masses on the same label; neither the singing nor the playing in the *A flat Mass* is in the least routine, but the music-making lacks a really individual profile. The *E flat Mass* is more successful: the freshness of the singing here (the chorus far more important than the soloists) and the resilient playing of the Academy make their mark when the mid-1970s (originally Argo) recording is also very fine. Nevertheless the current period performances under Bruno Weil find an added dimension in these richly rewarding masterpieces, and the singing and playing on Sony are little short of inspired (see below). The part songs, recorded much earlier in 1967, are splendidly sung, even if Helen Watts, the soloist in *Ständchen*, sounds just a little matronly; and it is difficult to imagine the musical listener not responding to them with the warmth of feeling that this open-hearted music inspires.

ORCHESTRAL MUSIC

(i–ii) *Konzertstück in D, D.345; Polonaise in B flat, D.580; Rondo in A, D.438;* (i; iii) *Rondo brillant in B min., D.895;* (iv) *Notturno in E flat, D.897.*

(M) *** Teldec/Warner Dig. 0630 14538-2. (i) Zehetmair; (ii) Deutsche Kammerphilharmonie; (iii) David Levine; (iv) Haydn Trio.

This was the nearest Schubert came to writing a violin concerto. None of this music is ambitious but it all has a characteristic charm, especially when played with such a light touch. Indeed Zehetmair is the ideal soloist, sweet-toned and stylish. The engaging *Polonaise* is placed between the *Konzertstück* and *Rondo*, both with slow introductions. Zehetmair ably directs his own orchestral accompaniments; then comes the sparkling *Rondo brillant* for violin and piano in which David Levine is a fine partner. As the measure is short, Teldec have added on the *Notturno* for piano trio, most persuasively presented by the Haydn Trio of Vienna.

Symphonies Nos. 1–6; 8–9.

(BB) *** Arte Nova Dig. 74321 54458-2 (4) [id.]. Putbus Festival O, Wilhelm Keitel.

(B) **(*) Nimbus Dig. NI 5270/3 [id.]. Hanover Band, Roy Goodman.

Symphonies Nos. 1–6; 8 (Unfinished); 9 (Great); Overtures: Fierabras; In the Italian style in C; Des Teufels Lustschloss.

(B) **(*) Decca 430 773-2 (4). VPO, István Kertész.

(i) *Symphonies Nos. 1 in D, D.82; 2 in B flat, D.125; 3 in D, D.200; 4 in C min. (Tragic), D.417; Overtures in the Italian style Nos. 1 in D; 2 in C, D.590/1;* (ii) *Overtures: in B flat, D.470; in E min., D.648.*

(B) **(*) Ph. Duo 446 536-2 (2) [(M) id. import]. (i) Dresden State O, Sawallisch; (ii) LPO, Leppard.

Symphonies Nos. 5 in B flat, D.485; 6 in C, D.589; 8 in B min. (Unfinished); 9 in C (Great).

(B) **(*) Ph. Duo 446 539-2 (2) [(M) id. import]. Dresden State O, Sawallisch.

Symphonies Nos. 1 in D, D.82; 2 in B flat, D.125.

(M) **(*) EMI (SIS) CDM5 66102-2 [id.]. BPO, Karajan (with WEBER: *Der Freischütz: Overture* **(*)).

Symphonies Nos. 3 in D, D.200; 4 in C min. (Tragic), D.417; Rosamunde: Ballet music 1–2.

(M) ** EMI CDM5 (SIS) 66103-2 [id.]. BPO, Karajan.

Symphonies Nos. 5 in B flat, D.485; 6 in C, D.589; Rosamunde: Overture (Die Zauberharfe), D.644.

(M) **(*) EMI (SIS) CDM5 66104-2 [id.]. BPO, Karajan.

Symphonies Nos. 8 in B min. (Unfinished), D.759; 9 in C (Great), D.944.

(M) **(*) EMI CDM5 66105-2 [id.]. BPO, Karajan.

The Schubert symphonies are extremely well served in all price ranges, and there is a great diversity of choice as to style of performance among the boxed sets. But we are inclined to feel that, taking everything into consideration, including price and first-class, modern digital recording, the new Arte Nova cycle must head the list for bargain-hunters. Founded in 1992, the Putbus Festival in Germany was originally designed to present Rossini opera, but here the music director, Wilhelm Keitel, with his modestly sized Putbus Festival Orchestra shows what freshness and polish he can achieve in more general repertory. In full, immediate, yet open sound these performances are as fresh and direct as any you will find. Springing rhythms persuasively to avoid any sense of excessive haste, Keitel follows period practice to the extent of favouring fast speeds, whether in allegros or andantes. Light, crisp articulation also helps to bring transparent textures, with dynamic contrasts dramatically brought out and Scherzo-like Minuets given extra bite, thanks to sharp observance of accented cross-rhythms. If the earlier symphonies up to No. 6 are remarkable above all for their freshness, the *Unfinished* then brings the one idiosyncratic interpretation. The first movement is taken very slowly and steadily, with the basic tempo chosen no doubt to suit the lyrical second subject, warmly played by a modest group of cellos. The central climax in the development section then brings mystery and intensity without an accelerando in the build-up. The second movement is also rather broader than one would expect from Keitel's earlier approach. The *Great C major Symphony* – with all repeats observed, so that it has to occupy a whole disc on its own – brings steady speeds, again on the brisk side, and a fresh, direct manner. The coda of the first movement brings an exciting accelerando before a minimal slowing at the very end. In the central ostinato climax of the slow movement, crisply done, the tempo remains steady, with minimal expansion on the cello theme following. The Scherzo and finale then follow the pattern of the whole set in performances of keen intensity and polished ensemble.

The price of the Sawallisch set is also very competitive, and the late-1960s recording is of Philips's best Dresden quality, full, weighty and resonant without undue clouding, while the strings and woodwind have plenty of bloom. Where Sawallisch excels is in the way he can command attention with the gentlest pianissimo at the beginning of a movement; when all but two of the symphonies (Nos. 5 and 8) have slow introductions, and even the *Unfinished* has its introductory phrase, that is very important. It is characteristic that in the *Unfinished* Sawallisch's tempi for both movements are very slow, but they are beautifully sustained by the hushed intensity of the playing, and it is the same in the sustained tread of the first movement of the *Ninth*. Here Sawallisch's reading is both dramatic and refreshingly direct, and the range of sonority commanded by the Dresden orchestra is heard at its most impressive, particularly in the beautifully played *Andante*, while the finale has fine impetus.

What the conductor proves again and again in the mature symphonies is his mastery in pointing a Schubert phrase without seeming to do so and without blunting its essential simplicity. Because of this, the *Fifth* is a most endearing performance, warm and graceful yet with plenty of vigour in the last two movements. Where Sawallisch is rather less successful is in conveying the high spirits of the very early symphonies. His accounts of Nos. 1 and 2 could be lighter and fresher, although finales go with a swing. But by No. 3 conductor and orchestra are working very happily together and the playing is stylish and elegant, the *Allegretto* very winning. By comparison the first movement of the *Tragic* is weighty and No. 6 is by no means lightweight either, although the *Andante* is graceful and the Scherzo bursts with energy. However, comparison with Kertész in the earlier symphonies is by no means to Sawallisch's disadvantage, and in the later works the Dresden sound undoubtedly brings an added gravitas. The first of the two Philips Duos includes the pair of engaging *Overtures in the Italian style*, of which the first, in its introduction, quotes the lovely lyrical tune also used by Schubert in his *Rosamunde (Die Zauberharfe) overture*, although with its contour slightly different. Two other overtures, almost completely unknown, are admirably played by Leppard and the LPO, making a useful bonus as all four make a natural link with the spirit of one or other of the symphonies.

Kertész began with Nos. 8 and 9 and the overtures (which are well worth having), and these two symphonies are the finest performances in the cycle. The *Ninth* is fresh, dramatic and often very exciting, the *Unfinished* highly imaginative and comparably dramatic in its wide dynamic contrasts. In the two early symphonies Kertész scores with the spirited VPO playing and a light touch, and this also applies to Nos. 3 and 6, even if they are without the last ounce of character. The playing of the VPO is beyond reproach throughout, and it has a pervading freshness, helped by the transparent yet full Decca sound.

As in his Beethoven cycle, also recorded for Nimbus, Goodman draws lively, beautifully sprung performances of the Schubert symphonies from the players of the Hanover Band. For anyone wanting period performances of these works, they can be warmly recommended as a mid-priced set, with the reservation that the characteristic Nimbus balance is more damaging here than it is in Beethoven. The strings are attractively caught in a warm acoustic, but the reverberation tends to obscure detail in tuttis, with the woodwind set so far backwards that it is often barely audible, and even the rasp of the natural horns is underplayed. Nos. 1 and 4 (*Tragic*) have also been issued separately on NI 5158, and the *Unfinished* is available coupled with the *Overture and incidental music from Rosamunde* (NI 5274), both at full price.

Although they sound a little old-fashioned now, Karajan presents a most polished and beautifully played set of Schubert symphonies. Now reissued as part of EMI's Karajan Edition, they were recorded in the latter part of the 1970s in the Philharmonie. The point and elegance of the Berliners' playing in the early symphonies is most persuasive, yet the results are never mannered. Undoubtedly many ears will react adversely to the reverberant acoustic for giving the impression of too large a band, one which rather lacks the brightness and transparency one associates with Schubert's songful writing; and the *Fourth Symphony*, the *Tragic*, finds Karajan less compelling. The *Unfinished*, dating from 1975, with Berlin refinement at its most ethereal, has an other-worldly quality, rapt and concentrated. The first movement is the original first take restored. There were technical problems with it and so Karajan re-recorded the movement a month later. Those problems have now been solved by the current re-mix, with excellent results. The *Great C major* (1977) is also compelling, but here some may find that the reverberant acoustic gives the impression of too much weightiness. But this is not a superficial reading: it has plenty of impetus and power, while the *Andante* has freshness too. The finale has undoubted thrust, although tuttis bring a degree of heaviness, caused as much by the sound itself as by the playing. The disc which includes the first two symphonies opens with a weightily dramatic performance of Weber's *Der Freischütz overture*, recorded digitally in 1981.

(i) *Symphonies Nos. 1–6; 8 (Unfinished); 9 in C (Great);* (ii) *String quartets Nos. 13–15;* (iii) *String quintet in C, D. 956;* (iv) *Piano sonatas Nos. 7 in E flat, D.568; 11 in C, D.613 (Unfinished); in F min., D.625/505 (Unfinished); 13 in A, D.664; 18 in G, D.894; 21 in B flat, D.960; 21 in B flat, D.960;* (v) Song-cycles: *Die schöne Müllerin; Winterreise.*

(BB) *(*) Nimbus Dig./Analogue NI 1768 (12) [(B) id.]. (i) Hanover Band, Roy Goodman; (ii) Chilingirian Qt; (iii) Brandis Qt, Wen-Sinn Yang; (iv) Marta Deyanova; (iv) Shura Gehrman, Nina Walker.

This super-super-budget set of 12 CDs is very inexpensive indeed (working out at about £2.50 a disc). But it is seriously flawed, and the separate bargain issue of Goodman's pioneering set of the complete symphonies on period instruments is much more readily recommendable – see above.

The chamber-music performances, too, are of high quality. The Brandis account of the *String quintet* is warmly enjoyable and, if these players do not quite match the the range of dynamic in the slow movement which distinguishes the Aeolian and Cleveland versions, there is no lack of concentration. The Chilingirians too give strongly committed, characterful and spontaneous-sounding readings of the last three *Quartets* and, like the Brandis group, they are given natural sound, full of presence.

Alas, the *Piano sonatas*, played by Marta Deyanova with an at times over-insistent left hand, are not at all recommendable, especially when one considers the current competition. Her extremely measured pacing and idiosyncratic waywardness test the listener's patience in the opening movement of the *G major Sonata*, D.894 (No. 18) which lasts 29 minutes 18 seconds but seems but much longer! The *E flat major Sonata*, D.568 (No. 7) after a fresh opening movement brings similar wilfulness, which Schubert partly invites by marking his slow movement *Andante molto*. And while Deyanova's performance of the *A major Sonata*, D.664 (No. 13), is much more appealing, again her wayward response in the Andante is too obviously self-indulgent, and the final *B flat Sonata* (D.960) is even less persuasive.

The two song-cycles, however, are something of a collector's item. They were recorded in 1972–3, nearly two decades before the rest of the programme. Shura Gehrman is the performing name of the founder of Nimbus Records (Numa Libin, also known as Count Labinsky). He has a strong, full-blooded baritone voice, and he tends to over-dramatize in the livelier songs, while his delivery is uneven and at times forceful. But, for all the histrionics, the narrative experience of both cycles is strikingly well communicated – which is very necessary in this instance, as Nimbus provide no back-up translations! In each cycle he seems to take a while to settle down, but the singing is never bland, and later the melancholy songs are often touching. Nina Walker is balanced hopelessly backwardly, within a bath of reverberation, especially in *Die schöne Müllerin*, but still manages to make a supportingly poetic contribution throughout.

Symphonies Nos. 1 in D, D.82; 2 in B flat, D.125.

(BB) **(*) Naxos Dig. 8.553093 [id.]. Failoni O of Budapest, Michael Halász.

Michael Halász and the Failoni Orchestra are affectionately easy-going rather than overtly dramatic, but they play both these works most winningly, finding all the delicacy of Schubert's inspiration. The recording too is full and naturally balanced, and one's only reservation is that the resonance of the Italian Institute in Budapest makes the tuttis spread and lose some of the sharpness of focus. But this is a most enjoyable disc nevertheless and well worth its modest cost.

Symphonies Nos. 1 in D, D.82; 8 in B min. (Unfinished), D.759.

(B) ** [EMI Red Line Dig. CDR5 69834]. VPO, Muti.

Symphonies Nos. 3 in D, D.200; 5 in B flat, D.485.
(B) ** [EMI Red Line Dig. CDR5 72573]. VPO, Muti.

The pair of Muti discs cannot be recommended with any confidence. His robust approach is not endearingly Schubertian, even though he has the Vienna Philharmonic at his disposal. With the playing relatively routine, despite the conductor's natural electricity and his preference for urgent speeds, there is nothing here to set the blood tingling or charm the ear.

Symphonies Nos. 1 in D, D.82; 5 in B flat; Overture in the Italian style in D, D.590; Overture Des Teufels Lustschloss, D.84.
(M) *** Carlton Dig. 30367 01272 [id.]. E. Sinfonia, Sir Charles Groves.

This coupling of the *First* and *Fifth Symphonies* gets Groves's cycle off to an excellent start. First-movement allegros (exposition repeats included) have weight, yet rhythms are nicely sprung. Both *Andantes* are gracious and well paced, and the finale of No. 1 dances airily. The Minuet/Scherzo of No. 5 is particularly attractive; the Trio with its glowing horns flows agreeably. The two *Overtures* are a distinct asset: the piece in Italian style is relaxed and sunny, while the drama and pathos of *Des Teufels Lustschloss* ('The Devil's Pleasure Castle') are well caught with some fine, sonorous brass. It is the elegance and warmth of the orchestral playing which contribute so much to these performances, as does the first-rate Abbey Road recording, which has both body and glowing detail.

Symphonies Nos. 2 in B flat, D.125; 6 in C, D.589; Overture Die Zwillingsbrüder.
(M) ** Carlton Dig. 30367 01282 [id.]. E. Sinfonia, Sir Charles Groves.

Groves's account of the *Second Symphony* is alert and well played but a little plain. The finale (marked *Presto vivace*) is neatly articulated by the strings but is a bit too slow. The conductor readily shows his affection in No. 6, and he finds much of its charm. The Scherzo is pleasingly vigorous to offset the graceful finale but, heard alongside Boehm or Beecham, the playing here is less spontaneous in feeling. The overture brings some fine wind-playing but could be more spirited. Very good recording.

Symphonies Nos. 3 in D, D.200; 4 in C min. (Tragic), D.417.
(BB) *(*) Arte Nova Dig. 74321 37858-2 [id.]. L. Festival O, Ross Pople.

Ross Pople conducts his London Festival Orchestra in amiable performances, not nearly as taut as those on the complete Arte Nova set from Putbus, seriously let down by rather dim recording of limited dynamic range.

Symphonies Nos. 3 in D, D.200; 4 in C min. (Tragic), D.417; Overtures: Der häusliche Krieg, D.787; In the Italian style in C, D.591; Der Teufel als Hydraulicus, D.4.
(M) **(*) Carlton Dig. 30367 01292 [id.]. E. Sinfonia, Sir Charles Groves.

Groves is in good form in this extremely generous anthology. First movements are a little lacking in rhythmic point, but the *Allegretto* of No. 3 has plenty of charm and the *Andante* of the *Tragic* is gentle and gracious; both finales are vivaciously done. The two unknown overtures are a real bonus. *Der häusliche Krieg* (only rediscovered in the early 1960s) opens with an attractive horn chorale and later becomes quite jolly; *Der Teufel als Hydraulicus* is only half its length but is agreeable enough. It is the earliest of Schubert's orchestral works, written when the composer was fourteen. The *Italian overture* is also affectionately done.

Symphonies Nos. 3 in D, D.200; 5 in B flat, D.485; 6 in C, D.589.
✿ (M) *** EMI CDM7 69750-2 [id.]. RPO, Beecham.

Beecham's are magical performances in which every phrase breathes. There is no substitute for imaginative phrasing and each line is shaped with affection and spirit. The *Allegretto* of the *Third Symphony* is an absolute delight. The delicacy of the opening of the *Fifth* is matched by the simple lyrical beauty of the *Andante*, while few conductors have been as persuasive as Beecham in the *Sixth* 'little' *C major Symphony*. The sound is now just a shade drier in Nos. 3 and 6 than in their last LP incarnation but is generally faithful and spacious. This is an indispensable record for all collections and a supreme bargain in the Schubert discography.

Symphonies Nos. 3 in D, D.200; 6 in C, D.589.
(BB) *** Naxos Dig. 8.553094 [id.]. Failoni O of Budapest, Michael Halász.

These are entirely delightful performances, fully capturing the innocent charm of these youthful symphonies. The Failoni strings play with airy grace and the woodwind bring a similar delicacy of colour to their solos and gentle chording. Michael Halász is most sensitive and in the *Allegretto* second movement of No. 3 – Schubert at his most endearingly ingenuous – the conductor's style is Beechamesque in its affectionate elegance. The economy of Schubert's scoring means that the resonant acoustic affects the clarity of the tuttis only marginally and it certainly lends an attractive bloom to the proceedings.

Symphonies Nos. 3 in D, D.200; 8 in B min. (Unfinished), D.759.
(M) **(*) DG Originals 449 745-2 [id.]. VPO, Carlos Kleiber.

Carlos Kleiber's 1979 Schubert coupling has been greatly admired in some quarters, so it is not surprising that DG have chosen it for reissue in their series of 'Originals'. Kleiber is certainly a refreshingly unpredictable conductor; sometimes, however, his imagination goes too far towards quirkiness, and that is certainly so in the slow movement of No. 3, which is rattled through jauntily at breakneck speed. The effect is bizarre even for an *Allegretto*, if quite charming. The Minuet too becomes a full-blooded Scherzo, and there is little rest in the outer movements. The *Unfinished* brings a more compelling performance, but there is unease in the first movement, where first and second subjects are not fully co-ordinated, the contrasts sounding a little forced. The recording brings out the brass sharply, and is of wide range.

Symphony No. 4 in C min. (Tragic), D.417.
(M) (***) DG mono 457 705-2 [id.]. BPO, Igor Markevitch – BERWALD: *Symphonies Nos. 3 & 4.* (***)

Although it derives from a (very fine) mono LP, first issued in the mid-1950s, Markevitch's remains a hotly competitive version, perhaps not as introspective as might be – but then, despite the label 'Tragic', this is a fresh, early work. The Berlin Philharmonic plays with its characteristic warmth and brilliance, and the reverberant recording hardly sounds its age at all.

Symphony No. 4 in C min. (Tragic), D.417; Grand duo in C, D.812 (orch. Joachim).
(BB) **(*) Naxos 8.553095 [id.]. Failoni O of Budapest, Michael Halász.

Halász presents the *Tragic Symphony* – Schubert himself gave the work its title – sympathetically and, though this is not a strongly dramatic reading, the resonant acoustic adds a certain weight, and the *Andante* is warmly and expressively played. This inexpensive disc is valuable for its coupling, the orchestration of the large-scale *Grand Duo* for piano duet, written in 1824 and orchestrated by the violinist Josef Joachim. The work is convincingly played, with gravitas and freshness nicely balanced. The warm resonancy of the Budapest Italian Institute suits this work very well.

Symphonies Nos. 4 in C min. (Tragic); 5 in B flat; Rosamunde overture.
(M) **(*) DG (IMS) 449 099-2. BPO, Karl Boehm.

A good (if, in the last analyisis, not outstanding) version of the *Tragic* from Boehm, with splendid, disciplined playing from the Berlin Philharmonic, who are recorded well, if resonantly. The *Fifth* is a different matter, the first movement wonderfully light and relaxed; the slow movement, though also relaxed, never seems to outstay its welcome, and in the last two movements the Berlin playing makes for power as well as lightness. The *Rosamunde overture* tops off a generally enjoyable disc.

Symphonies Nos. 4 in C min. (Tragic), D.417; 8 in B min. (Unfinished).
(BB) ** Discovery Dig. DICD 920213 [id.]. Helsingborg SO, Avi Ostrowsky.

Ostrowsky finds drama in the outer movements of the *Tragic Symphony*, but his slower tempo for the *Andante* is not necessarily an advantage. In the *Unfinished*, he is very dramatic indeed with the wide dynamic range, emphasizing the conductor's bold contrasts. The orchestra plays sympathetically throughout and the Helsingborg Concert Hall provides a very suitable acoustic. Very good recording.

(i) *Symphonies Nos. 4 (Tragic); 8 (Unfinished);* (ii) *9 in C (Great).*
(BB) ** EMI Seraphim CES5 68534-2 (2) [CDFB 568534]. (i) VPO, Kubelik; (ii) Hallé O, Barbirolli (with BRAHMS: *Variations on a theme by Haydn:* VPO, Barbirolli ***).

Here is a case where a super-bargain two-disc set falls down seriously by the mis-matching of performances of an entirely different calibre. Barbirolli's 1966 account of the *Great C major Symphony* is a warm, lyrical reading, with its speeds perfectly chosen to solve all the notorious interpretative traps with the minimum of fuss. The Hallé playing may miss the last degree of polish but it is far more important that the Barbirollian magic is conveyed at its most intense. Barbirolli is completely consistent and although, characteristically, he may always indulge in affectionate phrasing, he is usually steady in maintaining tempi broadly throughout each movement. The second subject of the first movement, for example, brings no 'gear-change' but equally no sense of the music being forced; and again with the tempo changes at the end of the movement, Barbirolli's solution is very satisfying. The recording is full and vivid, as it is in the coupled Brahms *St Anthony variations*, where the VPO playing is first class and Barbirolli is again at his finest. Alas, the only thing to praise on the second of these paired CDs is the warm and pleasing sound. Kubelik's VPO performance of the *Tragic Symphony* opens dramatically enough and is well played, but there is an element of routine throughout until the temperature picks up in the finale. The *Unfinished* is even more run-of-the-mill, lapsing into downright dullness in the second movement.

Symphony No. 5 in B flat, D.485.
(M) *** DG 447 433-2 [id.]. VPO, Boehm – BEETHOVEN: *Symphony No. 6.* ***
(M) *** RCA 09026 61793-2 [id.]. Chicago SO, Fritz Reiner (with MENDELSSOHN: *Hebrides overture* ***) – BRAHMS: *Symphony No. 3.* ***

Boehm's recording of the *Fifth Symphony* dates from the very end of his career. In his eighties he preferred a tauter, more incisive view than he had given in his 1967 Berlin performance, weightier, but still with a light rhythmic touch, while the slow movement is not lacking grace. The finale is strong and purposeful and this is Boehm at his finest, with superbly polished and responsive VPO playing in repertoire they know and love. The 1980 recording is full and warm, taken from a live performance at the Hohenems Schubertiade, and rightly reissued now in DG's 'Legendary Recordings' series of 'Originals'.

Reiner's is a most attractive performance, brightly and clearly recorded, yet with a glowing ambience. This reading of No. 5, essentially sunny and with an easy-going *Andante*, brings a strongly vigorous finale, following a third movement where Reiner indulges the trio with an affectionate rallentando. Mendelssohn's famous Hebridean overture comes as an exciting encore: its storm has seldom sounded more dramatic, yet the lyrical warmth is not missed. Again, fresh sound.

Symphonies Nos. 5 in B flat, D.485; 8 in B min. (Unfinished).
(M) *** Sony Bruno Walter Edition SMK 64487 [id.]. Columbia SO or NYPO, Walter (with: BEETHOVEN: *Overture Leonora No. 3* ***).
(B) *** EMI CfP CD-CFP 6036 [(M) id. import]. LPO, Sir John Pritchard.

Bruno Walter brings special qualities of warmth and lyricism to the *Unfinished*. Affection, gentleness and humanity are the keynotes of this performance; while the first movement of the *Fifth* is rather measured, there is much loving attention to detail in the *Andante*. The 1961 recording emerges fresh and glowing in its CD format and, like the rest of the Walter series, completely belies its age. The sound is richly expansive as well as clear, and the CD is in every way satisfying.

Pritchard's performances are superbly refreshing. In the *Fifth Symphony* his simplicity of approach is disarming and his directness allows for nudging delicacy, for example at the very start, while the playing of the LPO is beautifully refined; the slow movement, too, is both serene and warm. The reading of the *Unfinished* is magnetic, unusually direct, establishing the first movement as a genuine symphonic allegro but with no feeling of breathlessness, even in the melting lyricism of the incomparable second subject. The high dramatic contrasts – as in the development – are fearlessly presented, with fine intensity, and the second movement, too, brings purity and freshness. This makes a genuine alternative to Walter, and the 1980 recording, very naturally balanced, is obviously more modern. A real bargain.

Symphonies Nos. 5 in B flat, D.485; 8 in B min. (Unfinished); Overtures: In the Italian style in C; Rosamunde (Die Zauberharfe).
(B) ** Decca Eclipse Dig. 448 707-2; *448 707-4* [(M) id. import]. San Francisco SO, Blomstedt.

Blomstedt seldom disappoints, but his account of the *Fifth*, played on a chamber scale with plenty of finesse, nevertheless lacks Schubertian charm. The *Unfinished*, too, is relatively uneventful until the second movement, when at last the performance begins to glow luminously. Nothing wrong with the overtures or the excellent Decca recording, but this remains a coupling that for the most part fails to be memorable, at least partly the result of the weighty sound.

Symphonies Nos. 5 in B flat, D.485; 8 in B min. (Unfinished), D.759; 9 in C (Great), D. 944.
(B) *** Decca Double Dig. 448 927-2 (2) [(M) id. import]. VPO, Solti.

This Double Decca combining three favourite Schubert symphonies is one of the most attractive of all Solti's many reissues on the Decca label. There have been more charming versions of No. 5 but few that so beautifully combine freshness with refined polish. The *Unfinished* has Solti adopting measured speeds but with his refined manner keeping total concentration. The *Great C major Symphony* is an outstanding version, among the very finest, beautifully paced and sprung in all four movements, and superbly played. It has drama as well as lyrical feeling, but above all it has a natural sense of spontaneity and freshness. The recordings all confirm the Vienna Sofiensaal as an ideal recording location, and the glowing detail, especially in No. 9, is a source of consistent pleasure.

Symphonies Nos. 5 in B flat, D.485; 8 in B min. (completed by Brian Newbold).
(M) **(*) Virgin Veritas/EMI Dig. VER5 61305-2 [CDM 61305]. OAE, Mackerras.

Though not as magnetic as his account of No. 9, Mackerras's performance of No. 5 has comparable qualities of freshness and resilience. Tempi are only marginally brisker than traditional performances, and the slow movement has grace if not quite the degree of warmth that Boehm and Walter find. The special claims of the Veritas reissue is that the *'Unfinished' Symphony* is here heard as finished by Brian Newbold. However, although he uses the composer's music, the result cannot match the first two movements in dramatic intensity, a point emphasized by Mackerras's vibrantly powerful reading. He opens in the mysterious depths with the darkest *pianopianissimo*, and the plangent period timbres bring a real sense of *Sturm und Drang*, with powerful contrasts and strong, forceful accents in the second movement. Excellent recording. A stimulating coupling but not, perhaps, a first choice.

Symphonies Nos. 5 in B flat, D.485; 9 in C, D.944 (The Great).
(M) (**) RCA mono GD 60291 [60291-2-RG]. NBC SO, Toscanini.

In his 1947 performance of No. 9, Toscanini is tauter and faster than either his earlier or later recording. A useful antidote for it serves to remind one that Schubert was still a young man when this was composed with what was a bright future ahead and that the valedictory halo which came to surround it was a nineteenth-century phenomenon.

Symphonies Nos. (i) 6 in C; (ii) 9 in C (Great).
(M) **(*) Mercury 434 354-2 [id.]. (i) LSO, Schmidt-Isserstedt; (ii) Minneapolis SO, Skrowaczewski.

A unique coupling of the two C major symphonies – each completely different in character – and two most interesting readings. One could not mistake this account of the *Sixth* as a Beecham performance – Schmidt-Isserstedt is after all a more deliberately matter-of-fact conductor. But helped by the warm, glowing ambience of Watford Town Hall, which in turn underlines the bubbling gaiety of the work, all is joy until the finale, when one does perhaps begin to feel the *Allegro moderato* to be a little too moderate. In the *Ninth* Skrowaczewski is attractively straightforward and animated. He manages to maintain a steady speed through the whole of the coda in the first movement without sounding ruthless and, after a sympathetic *Andante*, the Scherzo and finale have compelling impetus. This performance certainly fills an interpretative gap and and again reveals the strength of the conductor's personality. The 1961 Minneapolis recording is full-bodied but (as so often in the Northtrop Auditorium) the violins are made to sound fierce.

'The essential Schubert': (i) *Symphonies Nos. 8 in B min. (Unfinished), D.759; 9 in C (Great) D.944;* (ii; iii) *Piano quintet in A (Trout), D.667;* (ii) *Impromptu in G flat, D.899/3; Moment musical, D.780/3; Rosamunde:* (iv) *Jägerchor; Ballet music in G.* Lieder: (v) *An Sylvia;* (vi) *Ave Maria;* (vii) *Die Forelle;* (v) *Heidenröslein.*
(B) *** Decca Double Analogue/Dig. 444 546-2 (2) [(M) id. import]. (i) VPO, Solti; (ii) Clifford Curzon; (iii) V. Octet (members); (iv) V. State Op. Ch., VPO, Münchinger; (v) Hermann Prey, Karl Engel; (vi) Leontyne Price, VPO, Karajan; (vii) Gabriele Fontana, György Fischer.

Whatever constitutes the 'essential' Schubert (and there is a great deal more of it than can be included on a pair of CDs), the *Unfinished* and *Great C major Symphonies* are certainly indispensable, and Solti does these marvellous works full justice. Both bring superb VPO playing. The *Unfinished* has great concentration and atmosphere and there are few accounts of No. 9 that are more glowingly resilient, lyrically fresh and sunny, yet with plenty of drama. The Decca recording too is outstanding in its richness and detail. Clifford Curzon's vintage recording of the *Trout* is hardly less distinguished, a good-natured reading with an admirable rapport between the pianist and the excellent Viennese players. Again vigour and freshness go hand in hand. The recording is beautifully balanced and has a pleasingly warm ambience. Curzon's performances of the most beautiful of Schubert's *Impromptus* and a favourite *Moment musical* are hardly less winning, while Hermann Prey and Gabriele Fontana (who is delightfully innocent-sounding in *Die Forelle*) give fine accounts of three famous songs. The inclusion of the *Hunting chorus* from *Rosamunde* alongside the familiar *Ballet music* is a pleasant surprise and, if so much else is missing (notably the *String quintet* and great final *Piano sonata in B flat*), this is still a thoroughly worthwhile set in its own right, playing for 148 minutes.

Symphony No. 8 in B min. (Unfinished), D.759.
✿ (M) *** DG Dig. 445 514-2 [id.]. Philh. O, Sinopoli – MENDELSSOHN: *Symphony No. 4 (Italian).* ***
(M) *** DG (IMS) 415 848-2. BPO, Karajan – MENDELSSOHN: *Symphony No. 4.* ***
(BB) ** Naxos Dig. 8.550289 [id.]. Slovak PO, Michael Halász – BEETHOVEN: *Symphony No. 5.* **
(BB) ** Tring Dig. TRP 022 [(M) id. import].RPO, Claire Gibault – BEETHOVEN: *Symphony No. 5.* **(*)
(M) *(*) [RCA Basic 100 09026 61551-2; *61551-4*]. Boston SO, Munch – BEETHOVEN: *Symphony No. 5 etc.* *(*)

Sinopoli secures the most ravishingly refined and beautiful playing; the orchestral blend, particularly of the woodwind and horns, is magical. It is a deeply concentrated reading of the *Unfinished*, bringing out much unexpected detail, with every phrase freshly turned in seamless spontaneity. The contrast, as Sinopoli sees it, is between the dark – yet never histrionic – tragedy of the first movement, relieved only partially by the lovely second subject, and the sunlight of the closing movement, giving an unforgettable, gentle radiance. The exposition repeat is observed, adding weight and substance. This takes its place among the recorded classics. The warmly atmospheric recording, made in Kingsway Hall, is very impressive.

Karajan's 1965 DG recording of the *Unfinished* sounds fresher still in remastered form. Its merits of simplicity and directness are enhanced by the extraordinary polish of the orchestral playing, lighting up much that is often obscured. The first movement is extremely compelling in its atmosphere; the slow movement too brings tinglingly precise attack and a wonderful sense of drama.

Michael Halász's very plain reading of the *Unfinished* comes as an alternative coupling for Richard Edlinger's account of the Beethoven *Fifth*. It may lack mystery at the start, and the second subject is presented simply and with little expressive pointing, but the first movement still builds inexorably to the big crescendo at the start of the development, and the second movement has a folk-like freshness. Well recorded and aptly coupled, it has its clear place among versions in the least expensive category.

Claire Gibault is both dramatic and sensitive to the work's powerful romantic feeling. Her reading has a striking momentum, but for many listeners her tempi for the second movement will seem fractionally too fast.

Although it has a certain lyrical impulse, Munch's performance is disappointingly heavy in style. It is not helped by the Boston reverberation which in places produces an element of coarseness in the sound.

Symphonies Nos. 8 (Unfinished); 9 in C (Great).
❀ (M) *** Decca 452 892-2. (i) VPO; (ii) LSO; Josef Krips.
(B) *** DG Classikon 439 475-2; *439 475-4*. BPO, Karl Boehm.
(B) *** RCA Twofer Dig. 09026 68314-2 (2) [id.]. BPO, Günter Wand.
(M) **(*) Sony SBK 48268; *SBT 48268* [id.]. Cleveland O, Szell.
(BB) **(*) Arte Nova Dig. 74321 51627-2 [id.]. Linz Bruckner O, Martin Sieghart.
(M) **(*) Erato/Warner Dig. 4509 99611-2 (2). Lyon Op. O, Gardiner.

Krips recorded the *Unfinished* in the very early days of mono LP, a gentle, glowing performance; and here in 1969 with the LSO he directs an unforced, flowing and wonderfully satisfying account, helped by excellent playing and splendid Sofiensaal recording, produced by Christopher Raeburn. This may lack some of the dramatic bite of more histrionic accounts but the atmospheric opening of both movements is immediately gripping, and concentration is maintained consistently to the beautifully shaped final coda. This makes a splendid coupling for Krips's much earlier LSO recording of the *Ninth*, which has long been counted by us as one of his very finest records, perhaps *the* finest. The performance similarly has a direct, unforced spontaneity which shows Krips's natural feeling for Schubertian lyricism at its most engaging. The playing is polished, yet flexible, dramatically strong without ever sounding aggressive. In the final two movements Krips finds an airy exhilaration which makes one wonder how some other conductors can ever keep the music earthbound as they do. The pointing of the Trio in the Scherzo is delectable, and the feathery lightness of the triplets in the finale makes one positively welcome every one of its many repetitions. As a whole, this reading represents the Viennese tradition at its finest. It is interesting that Decca have chosen to reissue these performances on a Classic Sound disc, for it would be more suited to DG's 'Legendary performance' series of Originals. Great care has been taken with the remastering, which retains the glowing Kingsway bloom and expansiveness of the original 1948 LP. The hint of coarseness in fortissimos is minimized and this is a Schubert coupling to treasure.

Boehm's mid-1960s version of the *Unfinished Symphony* with the Berlin Philharmonic combines deep sensitivity and great refinement, and the points of detail as well as the overall warmth keep this version among the very finest on record. The opening of the development – always a key point – is magically done, and, throughout, the superb recording quality gives unusual clarity while allowing the Berlin Philharmonic ensemble its natural opulence. Boehm's performance of the *Ninth*, recorded three years earlier, stands in the lyrical Furtwängler tradition rather than in the forceful Toscanini stream, but it is the balance between the conflicting interests in this symphony which distinguishes Boehm's reading. His modification of tempo in the various sections of the first movement is masterly in its finesse, often so subtle that it requires close attention to spot it. In the slow movement, the rhythmic spring to the repeated quavers is delectable, with the Berlin players really on their toes. Nor is there any lack of drama in the performance, for the playing is marvellous throughout. Only in the finale, taken rather fast, is the playing slightly less gripping, and even there one has excitement in plenty. The recording is very good indeed and in its CD transfer sounds fresh, warm and full. An outstanding reissue – this is surely a coupling that deserved a place in DG's 'Legendary Performances' series; at Classikon price it is a real bargain.

In a two-disc format, two for the price of one, Günter Wand offers visionary performances of both works, superbly played in live Berlin performances and glowingly recorded. Wand's magnetism, the dedication he conveys, depends not on any self-consciously expressive gestures but on direct response to the music and to Schubert's detailed markings. Consistently he makes the playing sound spontaneous, even in the tricky problems of speed-changes in the *Great C major*. In the manner of his generation he does not observe exposition repeats in the outer movements or second-half repeats in the Scherzo, but this is a beautifully co-ordinated, strong and warm reading. The *Unfinished* is just as magnetic, again with no exaggeration, but with every interpretative problem solved as though it did not exist.

Szell's, too, is a splendid performance of the *Unfinished*, strong yet sensitive. Phrasing and general discipline are so immaculate, one would expect the result to seem cold but, on the contrary, Szell never lacks warmth here, and drama and beauty walk hand in hand in the second movement. Apart from the lack of a real pianissimo, the 1960 recording is very good for its time. The *Ninth* dates from the previous year. Szell's control of tempo in the first movement brings a convincing onward flow, and the performance is notable for the alertness and rhythmic energy of the playing, yet there is no lack of resilience in the *Andante*. The Scherzo has great brio and leads naturally to the brilliant finale, where few rivals can match the precision of the hectic triplet rhythms. The sound is fuller in this remastered form than it was originally on LP, although the finale is a little lacking in weight, especially in the closing pages.

Apparently making a speciality of Schubert symphonies, the Arte Nova label here offers an excellent alternative to the Putbus set in very well-played, traditional performances from the Bruckner Orchestra, recorded in full, atmospheric sound. The refinement of the string-playing is brought out above all in the *Unfinished*, while the *Great C major* – with exposition repeats omitted – observes usual performance practice in the broadening in the first-movement coda and in the cello theme of the slow movement after the climax in the *Andante*. Good value, but not really distinctive in a much-recorded coupling.

Gardiner made these recordings in 1986 and 1987, before he had espoused the cause of original instruments. In the opening movement of the *Great C major* he negotiates all the problems inherent in the tempo changes with consummate ease: indeed the coda of the first movement is particularly satisfying. The *Andante* is certainly *con moto* but is elegantly handled, and it is surprising, considering that the performance was recorded live, that the reading overall lacks the last degree of compulsive zest, although the warm acoustic does tend to blunt some of its attack and the bite of the modern string instruments. The resonance suits the *Unfinished*, which is most impressive and dramatic, yet with the second movement glowingly lyrical. But one feels that this is not Gardiner's last word on either symphony.

Symphony No. 9 in C (Great), D.944.
(M) *** Virgin Veritas/EMI Dig. VER5 61245-2 [CDM 61245]. O of Age of Enlightenment, Mackerras.
(M) (***) DG mono 447 439-2 [id.]. BPO, Furtwängler – HAYDN: *Symphony No. 88*. (***) ❀
(B) *** EMI forte (SIS) CZS5 69364-2 (2) [CDFB 69364]. Cleveland O, George Szell – BEETHOVEN: *Symphony No. 7* *** ❀; ROSSINI: *Overtures*. **(*)
(B) *** EMI CfP CD-CFP 6037. LPO, Sir John Pritchard.
(M) **(*) Ph. Dig. 442 646-2. ASMF, Marriner.
(M) ** Carlton Dig. 30367 001162 [id.]. E. Sinfonia, Sir Charles Groves.
(BB) *(*) Naxos Dig. 8.553096 [id.]. Failoni O of Budapest, Michael Halász.
(B) *(*) [EMI Red Line Dig. CDR5 69836]. VPO, Muti.

Symphony No. 9 in C (Great); Rosamunde overture (Die Zauberharfe, D.644).
(M) * Sony Theta Dig. SMK 60127 [id.]. BPO, Barenboim.

Symphony No. 9 in C (Great); Rosamunde: Overture; Ballet music; Entr'acte No. 3.
(M) **(*) Bruno Walter Edition: Sony SMK 64478 [id.]. Columbia SO, Bruno Walter.

Symphony No. 9 in C (Great); Rosamunde: Overture; Entr'acte No. 2; Ballet No. 2.
(M) **(*) DG (IMS) Dig. 445 559-2. Chicago SO, James Levine.

Symphony No. 9 in C (Great); Rosamunde: Ballet music Nos. 1–2.
(B) (***) Dutton Lab. mono CDEA 5003 [(M) id.]. LSO, Bruno Walter – HAYDN: *Symphony No. 92*. (***)

In the first recording to use period instruments, Sir Charles Mackerras and the Orchestra of the Age of Enlightenment on the Virgin Classics label give a winning performance, one that will delight both those who prefer conventional performance and devotees of the new authenticity. The characterful rasp and bite of period brass instruments and the crisp attack of timpani are much more striking than any thinness of string-tone. It is a performance of outstanding freshness and resilience. With every single repeat observed, the heavenly length is joyfully as well as powerfully sustained and the warm, atmospheric recording gives a fine sense of presence. Now at mid-price, it is even more recommendable.

Coupled with a unique version of Haydn's *Symphony No. 88*, also recorded in the Jesus-Christus-Kirche in Berlin, Furtwängler's reading makes a perfect candidate for reissue in DG's 'Legendary Performances' series. As with the Haydn, Furtwängler gives the *Great C major* a glowing performance, if a highly individual one. The first movement brings an outstanding example of his wizardry, when he takes the recapitulation at quite a different speed from the exposition and still makes it sound convincing. In the beautifully played *Andante*, his very slow tempo is yet made resilient by fine rhythmic pointing. The mono recording dates from 1951 and the sound is remarkably fresh and very well balanced, with the dynamic range in the slow movement strikingly wide.

Szell's Cleveland account was his second in stereo with that orchestra (the first is discussed above, paired with the *Unfinished*). It was made in Severance Hall by an EMI team led by Peter Andry and – although subsequently issued on the CBS Epic label – it has the hallmarks of an HMV recording from the beginning of the 1970s, with a wider dynamic range than Szell usually enjoyed and better overall balancing. It sounds remarkably good in this new CD transfer. Szell's powerful reading provides a reminder that the parallels between him and another great disciplinarian conductor, Toscanini, were sometimes significant. Szell's approach is similarly direct, but lyrical feeling underlies the surface brightness and the crisply sprung rhythms are exhilarating. With superb playing from the Cleveland Orchestra the result is certainly dramatic, and the seemingly spontaneous return of the opening horn tune in the coda of the first movement is manipulated with masterly skill. The slow movement is refreshingly unindulgent but by no means without warmth. But it is in the hectic triplets of the finale that the orchestra is unmatched in precision, with a sparkling lightness of articulation that is a joy to the ear.

As in *Symphonies Nos. 5* and *8*, Sir John Pritchard gives a superbly fresh account of the *Great C major Symphony* and one which is as vital as it is refreshing. As in the *Unfinished*, the tempi are on the fast side and the manner is direct, but the results are never breathless. It is always a significant sign when one welcomes repeats observed in this already long symphony, and at the time he made this recording (1975) Pritchard observed repeats more than anyone else on record. Only the exposition repeat in the finale is omitted – which is a pity when the repeat in the first movement adds so effectively to the scale of the argument. The very opening brings a slightly square account of the introductory horn-theme, but after that the resilience of the LPO playing is consistent, with the players often keenly challenged by the fast tempo and later able to relax into the lyricism of the beautiful slow movement.

Bruno Walter's classic account of the *Great C major*, recorded in London in September 1938, enjoyed great celebrity in the 1940s and early 1950s, and is in many respects a more vital performance than his later version for CBS/Sony, enjoyable though that is. The cosily charming Walter glows from the *G major Rosamunde ballet*, but the vitality and resilience of allegros in the *Great C major* are what really strike the listener. Walter's relaxed tempos and expressive phrasing in the slow movement seem just right, with the speed variations in the first movement far less free than with many conductors since. Excellent transfers. A fine addition to the new Dutton bargain-price series.

Bruno Walter's 1959 CBS recording has been impressively enhanced on CD; the warm ambience of the sound – yet with no lack of rasp on the trombones – seems ideal for his very relaxed reading. The performance has less grip than Furtwängler's, while Solti shows greater spontaneity; but in the gentler passages there are many indications of Walter's mastery, not least in the lovely playing at the introduction of the second subject of the *Andante*. There is much to admire, even if this never quite achieves the distinction of the conductor's earlier recordings of this symphony. Needless to say, the *Rosamunde* music makes an endearing bonus.

Taken from his collected edition of Schubert symphonies, Sir Neville Marriner's account of the *Great C major* makes up for any lack of weight with the fresh resilience of the playing, consistently well sprung. All repeats are observed, bringing the timing of the *Symphony* to over an hour; however, the fill-up offered with the full-priced issue (a two-movement fragment, D.615, written just after the *Sixth Symphony* and orchestrated by Brian Newbold) has now been omitted and, although the recording is first rate, this makes the present reissue distinctly less tempting in a competitive market-place.

Levine conducts a refined performance, beautifully played and excellently recorded, which is commendably free from mannerism yet which may on that account seem under-characterized. He omits the exposition repeats in the outer movements (just as was universally done until recently). Conversely, all the repeats in the Scherzo are observed, which unbalances the structure.

Groves gives a straightforward, direct account of Schubert's *Ninth*, negotiating the tempo changes confidently and maintaining a strong lyrical flow. The English Sinfonia play well for him but, although the finale goes well, the reading as a whole has no special insights to offer; there are more gripping versions available. Excellent recording.

The *Ninth* is the one disappointment of the Halász Naxos cycle. His control of tempo in the first movement is not always convincing, and the *Andante* does not avoid a suspicion of routine. The Scherzo goes well, but the conductor's grip on the finale is not always taut enough, and the listener is made conscious of its length.

Muti's reading with the Vienna Philharmonic is bright and polished and finely detailed, but at no point does it lift in inspiration to convey Schubertian joy. Speeds are generally well chosen, but the end of the first movement brings the sort of exaggerated series of rallentandos that one thought had been left behind years ago. The recording, while full-ranging, is not one of EMI's cleanest.

Barenboim's Berlin reading is disappointing, lacking the bite of spontaneity that always used to mark his records, at times – despite the refinement of the playing – even stodgy, notably in the slow movement. The Trio is sluggish too, while the finale is rushed breathlessly. The recording, congested in tuttis, adds to the disappointment.

CHAMBER AND INSTRUMENTAL MUSIC

Arpeggione sonata, D.821 (arr. for cello) (see also under *Trout quintet*).

(M) *** Finlandia FACD 705. Arto Novas, Tapani Valsta – SHOSTAKOVICH: *Cello sonata.* ***

(BB) *** Naxos Dig. 8.550654 [id.]. Maria Kliegel, Kristin Merscher – SCHUMANN: *Adagio and allegro* etc. ***

(M) **(*) Decca 443 575-2 [id.]. Rostropovich, Britten – BRIDGE: *Cello sonata.* ***

(B) ** Sony SBK 48171; *SBT 48171* [id.]. Friedrich-Jürgen & Eckart Sellheim – MENDELSSOHN: *Song without words* etc.; SCHUMANN: *Adagio & allegro* etc. **

From the fine partnership of Novas and Valsta comes a curious and certainly successful, if ungenerous coupling. However, both the Schubert and Shostakovich performances are very persuasive and these artists are very well recorded.

At super-bargain price, Maria Kliegel and Kristin Merscher are highly competitive. The performances are well shaped and sensitive, though perhaps lacking the last ounce of distinction and character you find in, say, the Rostropovich–Britten account. All the same, neither the Schubert nor the Schumann coupling will disappoint at this price, given the general high standard of playing and recording.

Rostropovich gives a curiously self-indulgent interpretation of Schubert's slight but amiable *Arpeggione sonata*. The playing of both artists is eloquent and it is beautifully recorded, but it will not be to all tastes. However, the 1968 recording is particularly valuable for its coupling of the Bridge *Sonata*. The reissue is part of Decca's Classic Sound series.

Unlike the Kliegel–Merscher partnership, who are recorded in digital sound, Friedrich-Jürgen and Eckart Sellheim's performances on Sony come from the 1970s – and are none the worse for that! The cellist in particular brings great sensitivity and warmth to his phrasing, more so than his partner who, though admirably vital, is less well served by the microphone. The piano-tone is inclined to be a bit shallow and synthetic. Still, there is a great deal of pleasure to be had here.

Octet in F, D.803.

(M) *** Teldec/Warner Dig. 0630 14543-2 [id.]. Berlin Soloists.

(M) *** DG 437 318-2 [id.]. V. Chamber Ens.

(B) **(*) EMI forte CZS5 69755-2 (2). Melos Ens. of L. – BEETHOVEN: *Septet; Wind octet;* MENDELSSOHN: *Octet.* **

(BB) ** Virgin Classics Dig. Double VBD5 64109-2 (2) [CDVB 64109]. Nash Ens. – BEETHOVEN: *Clarinet trio; Septet.* ***

(B) * Sony Dig. SBK 62655; *SBT 62655* [id.]. Cleveland Octet.

(i) *Octet in F, D.803;* (ii) *Minuet and Finale in F for wind octet, D.72.*

✿ (B) *** Decca Eclipse Dig. 448 715-2; *448 715-4* [(M) id. import]. (i) Vienna Octet; (ii) Vienna Wind Soloists.

As a companion disc to their equally delectable version of the Beethoven *Septet*, the Vienna Octet give a gloriously warm-hearted and sparkling account of Schubert's *Octet*. The *Andante with variations* has great charm and the high spirits of the finale are bucolic in their joy, with the coda managed superbly. This is quite irresistible, and the two charming miniatures from Schubert's youth make a delightful encore. Demonstration sound-quality and the lowest possible price take this straight to the top of the list.

The Berlin Soloists give a strong and stylish performance which, on a bigger scale than most, designedly brings out the symphonic power of a piece lasting over an hour. Every single repeat is observed, and with such distinguished playing that length is readily sustained. This is very well characterized, not just in the big, symphonic movements but in the charming *Andante variations* too.

The Vienna Chamber Ensemble do not overlap in personnel with the New Vienna Octet, who have recorded this work for Decca, though their performance has a similar polish and urbane Viennese warmth. This is mellifluous Schubert, and very engaging it is: fresh and elegant. This dates from 1980, and the CD transfer maintains the smoothness and realism of the LP. Very enjoyable.

Very highly regarded in its day (1967), the Melos account is little inferior to the competing Viennese performance, although less agreeably engineered. The playing is fresh and polished, yet spontaneous, with excellent ensemble. The recording is well detailed and truthful and, if the violin timbre could be more flattering, the sound has more ambient warmth than its Beethoven and Mendelssohn couplings.

The Nash Ensemble's version on Virgin Classics returns to the catalogue in the form of an inexpensive, two-for-one-mid-price Double. It brings a refined performance, recorded in a warm church acoustic that gives the impression of a full concert hall, on the large side for this music. There is much beautiful solo playing – not least from the clarinettist, Michael Collins – but with underlying rhythms often on the square side the result is more studied, less spontaneous than in the very finest versions.

The Sony Cleveland digital version, although polished, is a non-starter. The balance is close, which does not flatter the violins in the opening movement. The following *Adagio* is sluggish and the performance is entirely lacking in the feeling of joy and high spirits which characterize this delightful work. Even the finale fails to take off.

(i) *Octet in F, D.803;* (i–ii) *Piano quintet in A (Trout), D.667;* (iii) *Violin sonatinas Nos. 1–3, D.384/5 & D.408.*

(B) *** O-L Dig./Analogue Double 455 724-2 (2) [id.]. (i) AAM Chamber Ens.; (ii) Stephen Lubin (fortepiano); (iii) Jaap Schröder, Christopher Hogwood (fortepiano).

We have long praised the Academy's 1988 recording of the *Octet* using period instruments for bringing out the open joyfulness of Schubert's inspiration, with excellent matching and vivid recording. The reading is not at all stiff or pedantic, but personal and relaxed. Lightness is the keynote, with speeds never eccentrically fast. The vibrant account of the *Trout*, from three years later, is even more successful. At first the opening tempo may seem brisk, but the lyrical flow is impetuous rather than hurried. Stephen Lubin leads zestfully from his fortepiano and there is also a nice rhythmic spring in the *Andante*, while the famous variations bring the most engaging and sparkling pianism of all, with telling moments of drama to offset the music's more delicate pages. The recording was made in the Henry Wood Hall and the balance is just about perfect, the sound both warm and transparent, so that the ear relishes the interplay and never seeks the fuller sonority of a modern piano. Moreover every note played by the double-bass comes through clearly and often subtly, so that one realizes anew how cleverly Schubert scored for this instrument which makes a constantly telling contribution to the texture. The present pairing makes a clear choice for those wanting these favourite works, played on original instruments, and the three *Violin sonatinas*, which (with repeats included) offer a further 55 minutes of Schubertian delights. Jaap Schröder uses a Stradivarius and Christopher Hogwood a fortepiano from about 1825 by Georg Haschka. If it does not produce the range of nuance and tonal subtlety of which the modern piano is capable, its lightness of colour has its own special charm. Schröder plays with fine artistry, and both artists are truthfully recorded (in 1978). The CD transfers cannot be faulted.

Piano quintet in A (Trout), D.667.

(M) **(*) Decca 448 602-2 [id.]. Curzon, Vienna Octet (members) – DVORAK: *Piano quintet.* ***

(BB) *** Belart 450 056-2 [(M) id. import]. Ingrid Haebler, Arthur Grumiaux, Georges Janzer, Eva Czako, Bernard Cazauran – MOZART: *Clarinet quintet.* **(*)

(B) **(*) Hyperion Dyad Dig. CDD 22008 (2) [id.]. Schubert Ens. of L. – HUMMEL: *Piano quintet;* SCHUMANN: *Piano quintet; Piano quartet.* **(*)

(B) ** EMI CfP CD-CFP 6039 [(M) id. import]. Dame Moura Lympany, principals of LPO – BRAHMS: *String sextet No. 1.* **

Piano quintet in A (Trout); Adagio and rondo concertante in F, D.487.

(BB) **(*) Naxos Dig. 8.550658 [id.]. Jenö Jandó, Kodály Qt, with István Tóth.

Piano quintet in A (Trout); Notturno in E flat, D.897.

(BB) ** Naxos Dig. 8.550057 [id.]. Leonard Hokanson, Villa Musica Ens.

(i) *Piano quintet in A (Trout);* (ii) *String quartet No. 14 (Death and the Maiden).*

(M) *** Ph. 442 656-2. (i) Beaux Arts Trio with Samuel Rhodes & Georg Hörtnagel; (ii) Italian Qt.

(M) **(*) Decca 417 459-2. (i) Curzon, Vienna Octet (members); (ii) VPO Qt.

(M) **(*) DG Originals 449 746-2 [id.]. Amadeus Qt, with (i) Gilels, Zepperitz.

(M) **(*) Sony SBK 46343; *SBT 46343* [id.]. (i) Horszowski, Budapest Qt (members), Julius Levine; (ii) Juilliard Qt.

(B) ** DG Classikon 439 416-2; *439 416-4* [(M) id. import]. (i) Demus, Schubert Qt; (ii) Amadeus Qt.

Piano quintet in A (Trout); Violin sonata in A, D.574.

(M) ** Van. 8.8005.71 [OVC 8005]. Peter Serkin, Schneider Ens.

(i) *Piano quintet in A (Trout); Fantasia in C (Wanderer), D.760.*
(B) *** [EMI Red Line Dig. CDR5 72567]. Sviatoslav Richter, (i) with Borodin Qt.

(i) *Piano quintet in A (Trout);* (ii) *Der Hirt auf dem Felsen.*
(B) **(*) Carlton IMP Dig. 30367 01822 [(M) id.]. (i–ii) Ian Brown; (i) Nash Ens.; (ii) Felicity Lott, Michael Collins.

From the augmented Beaux Arts Trio comes one of the most delightful and fresh *Trouts* now available. Every phrase is splendidly alive, there is no want of vitality and sensitivity, and a finely judged balance and truthful (1976) recording make it a most desirable version. The Italian Quartet's version of the *Death and the Maiden* dates from a decade earlier, but the recording was first class in its day, and this sounds every bit as good as the *Trout*. The performance remains one of the finest available. The slow movement is particularly eloquent, showing a notable grip in the closing pages.

Clifford Curzon's 1958 recording of the *Trout* sounds its age in the thin violin timbre, although the piano tone has plenty of colour. It remains a memorable performance, with a distinguished account of the piano part and splendidly stylish support from the Vienna players. The Vienna Philharmonic performance treats *Death and the Maiden* with comparable affection; the playing is peerless, Boskovsky, the leader, showing all his skill and musicianship in the variations. Both recordings have a warm ambience and in the string quartet the upper range is full. The *Trout* is additionally available, impressively remastered, coupled to Dvořák's Op. 81 *Piano quintet* in Decca's Classic Sound series.

Richter dominates the EMI digital recording of the *Trout quintet*, not only in performance but in balance. Yet this account has marvellous detail, with many felicities drawn to the attention that might have gone unnoticed in other versions. The first movement is played very vibrantly indeed, and the second offers a complete contrast, gently lyrical. The variations have plenty of character and, taken as a whole, this is very satisfying, even though other versions are stronger on Schubertian charm. The performance of the *Wanderer fantasia* comes from as long ago as 1963 but still sounds well. It is very distinguished indeed and makes a superb bonus, even if the piano-timbre is a shade hard.

There is some admirably unassertive and deeply musical playing from Miss Haebler and from the incomparable Grumiaux. These artists do not try to make 'interpretative points' but are content to let the music speak for itself. The quality of the recorded sound is good. Philips have added a pair of *String trios*, given characteristically refined performances by Grumiaux and his companions, delightful music superbly played. This account is even more attractively coupled on Belart with Mozart's *Clarinet quintet*.

Horszowski's contribution to the *Trout* is undoubtedly distinguished and his clean, clear playing dominates the performance which, although full of imaginative detail, is a little on the cool side – though refreshingly so, for all that. The Juilliard Quartet are far from cool in the *Death and the Maiden quartet*, the unanimity of ensemble consistently impressive. In both works the sound is a little dry, but not confined.

The Jandó/Kodály *Trout* is above all bracing. The first movement is soon moving along briskly and at a concert one could well be swept along by the momentum of the performance, for there is relaxation in the *Andante* and the famous *Variations* are mellow and strongly characterized. The polish and impetus of this playing is never in doubt and the recording is excellent, but this account obviously comes from east of Vienna. The *Adagio and rondo concertante* sounds a stronger work here than usual and the rondo is spirited and jolly.

In the 1975 recording of the *Trout* there is a masterly contribution from Gilels, and the Amadeus play with considerable freshness. The approach is very positive, not as sunny and spring-like as in some versions, but rewarding in its seriousness of purpose. The recording balance is convincing and the remastering creates a firm and vivid sound-image. The Amadeus's account of the *Death and the Maiden quartet* was their first analogue recording of this work in 1959. The unanimity of ensemble is remarkable. The quartet play as one in dealing with the finer points of phrasing, for example at the very beginning of the variations. The early DG stereo, too, is commendable. But, although one cannot fault these players' sensitivity to Schubertian line and nuance, in the last resort this performance has not the depth of the very finest versions.

The account by the Nash Ensemble on Carlton also brings a fill-up in the shape of *The Shepherd on the rock*. They are rather forwardly recorded here and their account is just a little wanting in the spontaneity that distinguishes the finest of the current versions. Ian Brown is, as always, a sensitive artist.

A lively, immediate account from the Schubert Ensemble of London, strongly led by the pianist, William Howard. The first movement is brisk but committed, and the famous variations are well characterized. There are more touching accounts on record but few more vivaciously spontaneous, with a vivid recording to match.

On DG Classikon, Demus dominates, partly because the piano recording and balance are bold and forward, and the string timbre is thinner. Nevertheless the transfer brings very acceptable sound and there is – as befits the eponymous quartet – a real feeling for Schubertian lyricism here, and the performance has spontaneity. The earlier of the Amadeus's two stereo versions of the *Death and the Maiden quartet* gives a wonderful impression of unity as regards the finer points of phrasing, for example at the very beginning of the variations, even if this account has not the depth of the very finest versions. The DG transfer is well managed, although the sound is a little dated.

Dame Moura Lympany's performance sets off in a brisk manner, the playing lively and fresh. In the second movement the interpretation relaxes and the variations are attractively done. The matter-of-fact approach is enhanced by the overall spontaneity of the music-making. The balance, however, is less than ideal, favouring the piano and not ideally sympathetic to the first violin (John Brown) with less body to his tone as recorded than to the lower strings, while in his decorations of the '*Trout*' theme he is too distant. But in most respects this is a lively and enjoyable performance, if not a primary choice.

The Naxos budget recording by Leonard Hokanson and the Villa Musica Ensemble was made in the normally cramped acoustic of the Tonstudio Van Geest in Heildelberg, but this is one of the most satisfactory recordings to have emerged from that venue. Of course one would welcome a greater back-to-front perspective and more air round the piano, but fortunately the formidable sensitivity and artistry of Leonard Hokanson dominate an account which is both highly musical and spontaneous.

Peter Serkin and Schneider's group give a bold, vigorous account of the *Trout* with a well-shaped set of variations. The wistful side of Schubert is missing here, but this music-making is easy to enjoy for its spontaneity. The recording is full and forward, the double-bass nicely resonant; but the violin timbre discloses the mid-1960s recording date.

(i; ii) *Piano quintet in A (Trout);* (i; iii) *Piano trios Nos. 1 in B flat, D.898; 2 in E flat, D.929; Notturno in E flat, D.897; Sonata in B flat, D.28* (both arr. for piano trio).
(B) **(*) EMI CZS7 62742-2 (2). (i) Hephzibah Menuhin; (ii) Amadeus Qt, J. Edward Merrett; (iii) Sir Yehudi Menuhin & Maurice Gendron.

The 1958 Hephzibah Menuhin/Amadeus *Trout* has a pleasingly domestic sense of scale and considerable charm, even though the bright recording creates a balance in favour of the upper register of the piano and the upper strings. The Amadeus Quartet play with nicely judged feeling. Intimacy is also the keynote of the works for piano trio, and in the *Trios* Menuhin relaxes with his pianist sister and cellist friend to produce delightfully spontaneous-sounding performances. The atmosphere of the *Second Trio* is caught perceptively and the unassertive music-making captures the music's spirit very appealingly. These recordings are cleanly remastered; the sound lacks something in fullness but the focus is natural and the balance realistic.

(i) *Piano quintet in A (Trout), D. 667. String quartets Nos. 13 in A min., D.804; 14 in D min. (Death and the Maiden), D.810; 15 in G, D.887;* (ii) *String quintet in C, D.956.*
(M) ** EMI (SIS) CMS5 66144-2 (4). Alban Berg Qt, with (i) Leonskaja, Hörtnagel; (ii) Heinrich Schiff.

Compilations of this kind always bring the inherent danger that a single performance may be much less successful than the rest and so reduce the appeal of the set as a whole. If EMI had included just the string works here, this box would have been very attractive. But the *Trout* (in which the quartet are joined by Elisabeth Leonskaja and Georg Hörtnagel) brings the keenest disappointment. Despite the excellence of the recording and some incidental beauties, it remains a curiously uninvolving performance with routine gestures. There is little real freshness here and Leonskaja's playing is not rich in sensitivity or in variety of colour.

The *A minor Quartet*, however, is beautifully managed, though the slow movement (with the theme of the *Rosamunde Entr'acte*) is very fast indeed. The exposition repeat is omitted in the first movement of *Death and the Maiden* but otherwise this, too, is a very impressive performance. The playing is breathtaking in terms of tonal blend, ensemble and intonation throughout both these works; if at times one is not always totally involved (except perhaps in the Minuet and Trio of the *A minor*) there is much to relish and admire. In the *G major* the Alban Berg players are most dramatic. Indeed they tend to over-dramatize: pianissimos are the barest whisper and ensemble has razor-edged precision. Yet again they do not observe the exposition repeat in the first movement. They are strikingly well recorded, however, and beautifully balanced; but the sense of over-projection somehow disturbs the innocence of some passages.

In the great *C major Quintet*, where they are joined by Heinrich Schiff, they produce a timbre which is richly burnished and full-bodied. Once more there is no first-movement exposition repeat, but theirs is still a most satisfying account, strongly projected throughout. Given the sheer polish and gorgeous sound that distinguishes such playing, this account ranks high among current recommendations and the recording is admirable. But as a collection this must be approached with some caution.

Piano trios Nos. 1 in B flat, Op. 99; 2 in E flat, Op. 100.
(M) ** Sony Stern Edition III SM2K 64516 (2) [S2K 64516]. Stern, Rose, Istomin – HAYDN: *Piano trio;* MOZART: *Piano quartet No. 2.* **

The Sony performances of the two Schubert *Piano trios* (recorded in 1964 and 1969 respectively) cannot compare with the Stern/Rose/Istomin accounts of the Beethoven and Brahms *Trios*. Although there is a lively impetus, there is also an element of fierceness in the way these artists approach both first-movement allegros. Inner movements come off much better. They cannot help but respond to the beautiful *Andante* of the *E flat Trio*, with Leonard Rose's fine cello playing well in evidence; and finales do not lack sparkle. But overall this is music which calls for a more relaxed, more intimate response. The recording is clear, but the New York studio ambience is not flattering.

Piano trios Nos. 1–2; Adagio in E flat ('Notturno') (for piano trio), *D.897; Sonata in B flat* (for piano trio), *D.28.*
(M) *** Teldec/Warner Dig. 0630 12337-2 (2) [id.]. Haydn Trio of Vienna.
(BB) **(*) Arte Nova Dig. 74321 51643-2 (2) [id.]. Trio Opus 8.

(i) *Piano trios Nos. 1–2; Adagio in E flat ('Notturno')* (for piano trio), *D. 897; Sonata in B flat* (for piano trio), *D. 28;* (ii) *String trios: in B flat* (in one movement), *D. 471; in B flat, D. 581.*
(B) *** Ph. Duo 438 700-2 (2) [id.]. (i) Beaux Arts Trio; (ii) Grumiaux Trio.

The Beaux Arts set of the Schubert *Piano trios* from the late 1960s is another of the extraordinary bargains now offered on the Philips Duo label. The performances provide impeccable ensemble with the pianist, Menahem Pressler, always sharply imaginative and the cellist, Bernard Greenhouse, bringing simple dedication to such key passages as the great slow-movement melody of the *Trio No. 2 in E flat*. Written during Schubert's student days, the attractive early *Sonata in B flat* has the same kind of fluency as Beethoven's *First Piano trio*, though the lyrical flow has the unmistakable ring of Schubert. The *Notturno*, played here with great eloquence, recalls the rapt, hushed intensity of the glorious slow movement of the *String quintet*. The recording is naturally balanced, a little dry in the treble, which means that Daniel Guilet's violin timbre is sometimes a little ungenerous; but the CD transfer never makes it sound edgy. What makes the set doubly attractive is the inclusion of the two much rarer *String trios*, also early works from 1816/17. The four-movement *B flat Trio* is a sheer delight with that quality of innocence which lets Schubert's music stand apart, obviously post-Mozartian yet with a simplicity all its own. Given such persuasive advocacy, both pieces cannot fail to make a strong impression. The Grumiaux performances are deeply musical, unforced and well shaped, while the 1969 recording has vividness and presence as well as a natural, lifelike sound-quality.

The Haydn Trio of Vienna are a highly musical and well-integrated group who undoubtedly are at one with the Schubertian spirit. Their playing is full of vigour and their characterization is strong and often robust, yet with a balancing intimacy. Both slow movements are beautifully yet simply played and the cellist, Walter Schulz, is not wanting in the *Andante* of D.929, while the Scherzo which follows sparkles lightly as it should: here the excellent pianist, Heinz Medjimorec, is delectably nimble. In the *Notturno* the contrast is very marked between the hushed opening and the assertive middle section. With excellent, well-balanced, modern digital recording this stands high among current lower-priced recommendations, although one regrets that the accompanying documentation is inadequate.

The Opus 8 Trio also give sensitive and lively performances and show true Schubertian feeling. The *B flat Trio* is particularly successful, setting off with plenty of impetus and with the interplay of the slow movement both intimate and touching. The *Notturno* is also very successful. These artists have excellent ensemble, and they play with seeming spontaneity; the pianist, Michael Hauber, guides the performances very musically and the internal balance is well managed. The recording has a basically warm ambience, but at passionate moments there is a degree of fiercessness on the violin timbre which precludes an unqualified recommendation. Excellent value just the same.

Piano trio No. 1 in B flat, D.898.
(B) *** EMI forte (SIS) CZS5 69367-2 (2) [CDFB 69367]. David Oistrakh, Sviatoslav Knushevitzky, Lev Oborin – BEETHOVEN: *Archduke trio* ***; BRAHMS: *Violin sonatas Nos. 1–2.* **(*)

Schubert's music needs warmth and humanity, and this well-integrated Russian team on the bargain forte reissue give both these qualities in abundance. They strive for beauty of tone and accuracy of ensemble (both of which they achieve with apparent ease) and imbue the music with just that essence of clarity and warmth that it demands by right. The tempi are extremely sensible, and in more than one way sensitive, and the Scherzo is handled in masterly fashion by all three players. Excellent piano-tone and a good round sound from the strings. The encores are beautifully played and, if the couplings are suitable, this makes a fine bargain.

Piano trio No. 1 in B flat; Sonata movement in B flat.
(BB) **(*) Naxos Dig. 8.550131; *4550131* [id.]. Stuttgart Piano Trio.

The Stuttgart Piano Trio may be at budget price but this is not a bargain-basement performance; the playing is musicianly and intelligent and there are many sensitive touches. Although the sound is somewhat less than ideal, there is a reasonable amount of air round the three instruments.

Piano trio No. 2 in E flat; Notturno in E flat, D.897.
(BB) (**) Naxos Dig. 8.550132 [id.]. Stuttgart Piano Trio.

Coming to the Stuttgart Piano Trio's disc of the *E flat Trio* after its predecessor is something of a disappointment. The recording venue and team may be the same, but there is greater airlessness and tutti passages come close to discoloration. The playing is very good and deserves a high rating; it is even stronger in character and finesse than the *B flat Trio*, but the oppressive and unpleasant sound militates against it and it comes close to 'breaking up' at the very beginning.

String quartets

String quartets Nos. 1–15.
(M) ** DG 419 879-2 (6). Melos Qt of Stuttgart.

The early quartets have an altogether disarming grace and innocence, and some of their ideas are most touching. The Melos are an impressive body whose accounts of this repertoire are unmannered and on the whole sympathetic. They are let down by recording quality that is less than distinguished, but the remastering has brought added presence.

String quartet No. 8 in B flat, D.112.
(M) (***) EMI mono CHS5 65308-2 (4). Busch Qt (with MENDELSSOHN: *Capriccio in E min.*) – BEETHOVEN: *String quartets*. *** ❀

The excellence and lightness of spirit the Busch communicate in this quartet is exhilarating. There is an alternative transfer available on Pearl (see above).

String quartets Nos. 9 in G min., D.173; 13 in A min., D.804.
(B) *** Teldec/Warner 3984 21968-2 [(M) id. import]. Alban Berg Qt.

Here is another vintage disc from the Alban Berg Quartet to match their splendid coupling of Haydn's Op. 74/3 and Op. 76/3, and this superb playing can only add to their laurels: finely integrated ensemble matched to genuine depth of feeling. The *A minor Quartet* has its slow movement based upon Schubert's famous *Rosamunde* melody, and the eloquence of the response here is gloriously natural and unforced. Tha *Andantino* of the *G minor* is also memorably done, and the crisp articulation in the finale is a joy. The recording is admirably balanced and truthful.

String quartets Nos. 11 in E, D.353; 14 in D min. (Death and the Maiden), D.810.
(M) ** DG 447 531-2. Melos Qt.

Generally speaking, the Melos Quartet's playing is expert enough but, though the comparatively rare *E major Quartet* is welcome, their account of the *Death and the Maiden* would not be a first recommendation. The performance certainly has intensity but the players occasionally wear their hearts a little too much on their sleeves.

String quartets Nos. 12 in C min. (Quartettsatz), D.703; 13 in A min., D.804; 14 in D min. (Death and the Maiden); 15 in G, D.887.
❀ (B) *** Ph. Duo 446 163-2 (2) [(M) id. import]. Italian Qt.

The Italian Quartet's 1965 coupling of the *Quartettsatz* and the *Death and the Maiden quartet* was counted the finest available in its day, with the famous variations played with great imagination and showing a notable grip in the closing pages. Technically the playing throughout is remarkable. There is just a hint of edge on the sound at times, but the original recording was very well balanced, and the CD adds to the immediacy. These players' understanding of Schubert is equally reflected in their performance of the *A minor Quartet*, recorded a decade later. Originally the long exposition repeat was omitted to get the work on a single LP side; now it has been restored. The familiar '*Rosamunde*' slow movement is (to our ears) beautifully paced – though some may find it a bit slow – and again has an impressive command of feeling. The 1976 sound, too, is first class. The *G major Quartet* is, if anything, even finer. The conception is bold, the playing is distinguished by the highest standards of ensemble, intonation and blend, and the recording is extremely vivid, making this – even after nearly two decades – one of the most thought-provoking accounts of the *Quartet* now before the public. The 1977 recording still sounds remarkably real and present. The CD transfers throughout this set are a great credit to the Philips engineers.

String quartets Nos. 12–15; (i) *String quintet in C, D. 956.*
(M) *** Nimbus Dig. NI 1770 [id.]. Brandis Qt, (i) with W.-S. Yang.

This is a first-class set in every way and an excellent recommendation for those wanting digital recordings of the late *Quartets* plus the *Quintet* in a mid-priced box. The Brandis Quartet, a fine Central European group, have warmth and they bring a natural eloquence to all these quartets which are all the more potent for being free of interpretative point-making. In the great *C major Quintet*, with beautiful matching, they again convey spontaneous expressiveness, and they are not afraid to linger a little over the first movement's lovely second-subject melody. Their slow movement, played freely, has rapt tension but, again, also conveys warmth, rather an ethereal, withdrawn atmosphere which communicates in a quite individual way. They are very naturally recorded.

String quartets Nos. 12 in C min. (Quartettsatz), D.703; 14 in D min. (Death and the Maiden), D.810.
(BB) **(*) Naxos Dig. 8.550221; *4550221* [(M) id. import]. Mandelring Qt.

The Mandelring Quartet are very good indeed. The performances are sensitively and sensibly played and very decently recorded, and anyone tempted by this Naxos disc will not be disappointed for so modest an outlay.

String quartets Nos. 13 in A min., D.804; 14 in D min. (Death and the Maiden), D.810.
(B) *** Ph. Virtuoso 426 383-2 [(M) id. import]. Italian Qt.

This separate bargain issue, taken from the above Duo, is thoroughly worthwhile in its own right. The sound is excellent.

String quartets Nos. 13 in A min., D.804; 14 in D min. (Death and the Maiden), D.810; 15 in G, D.887; (i) *String quintet in C.*
(B) ** EMI CZS7 67422-2 (2). Hungarian Qt, (i) with Laszlo Varga.

There is some remarkably fine playing here, obviously intensely felt, and, in finales particularly, a remarkable combination of virtuosity and unanimity of ensemble. But alongside the finest versions the account of the great *C major Quintet* disappoints and, throughout, the closely observed recordings (which date from between 1958 and 1970) are not flattering to the violin timbre, which is very bright, while the lack of a Schubertian ambient glow adds to the problem. There is much to admire here, not least the ardour generated in *Death and the Maiden*, but even so Brandis and the Quartetto Italiano are altogether preferable in the three late quartets.

String quartet No. 14 in D min. (Death and the Maiden).
(BB) *** CfP Silver Double CD-CFPSD 4772 (2) [(B) id.]. Gabrieli String Qt – BORODIN: *String quartet No. 2* ***; BRAHMS: *Clarinet quintet* **(*); DVORAK: *String quartet No. 12.* ***

Like the other performances on this Classics for Pleasure Silver Double, the Gabrielis give a direct, sensitive and polished account of Schubert's great *D minor Quartet*, not wearing their hearts on their sleeves but genuinely touching in the slow movement. The recording, from the beginning of the 1970s, is first class and has been smoothly transferred to CD. For those collectors wanting all four works, this is excellent value.

String quartets Nos. 14 in D min. (Death and the Maiden); 15 in G.
(M) (***) EMI (mono) CDH7 69795-2 [id.]. Busch Qt.

The Busch Quartet's account is more than fifty years old, but it brings us closer to the heart of this music than almost any other. The slow movement of the *Death and the Maiden quartet* is a revelation, and the same must be said of the *G major*, which has enormous depth and humanity. For its age, the sound is still amazing.

String quintet in C, D.956.
(M) *** Saga EC 3368-2. Aeolian Qt, Bruno Schreker.
(B) *** EMI CfP CD-CFP 6038 [(M) id. import]. Chilingirian Qt, Jennifer Ward Clarke.
(B) (***) Millennium mono MCD 80124 [id.]. V. Konzerthaus Qt.
(M) * Carlton Classics Dig. 30366 00942 [id.]. Orford Qt, Ofra Harnoy (with BOCCHERINI: *Sonata No. 6;* CASALS: *Song of the birds* **).

String quintet in C; String trio in B flat, D.581.
(BB) *** ASV Quicksilva Dig. CDQS 6207 [(M) id.]. Locrian Ens.
(BB) *** Naxos Dig. 8.550388 [id.]. Villa Musica Ens.

(i) *String quintet in C, D.956;* (ii) *Auf der Strom, D.943;* (iii) *Gretchen am Spinnrade; Nacht und Träume; Rastlose Liebe.*

(M) *** Sony Theta Dig. SMK 60032 [id.]. (i) Cleveland Qt, Yo-Yo Ma; (ii) Benita Valente, Myron Bloom, Rudolf Serkin; (ii) Kiri Te Kanawa, Richard Amner.

The Cleveland Quartet and Yo-Yo Ma have won golden opinions for their account of the *Quintet* on Sony. They are scrupulous in observing dynamic markings (the second subject is both restrained and *pianissimo*) and they also score by observing all repeats. Their performance has feeling and eloquence, as well as a commanding intellectual grip. Moreover they are admirably recorded and thus present a strong challenge at mid-price. For the reissue, some Schubert Lieder have been added. A fine performance from Benita Valente of Schubert's extended scena evoking a lover's departure, *Auf der Strom* ('On the river'), which has both passion and charm, is made memorable by Myron Bloom's glorious horn obbligato. Of the following three songs from Kiri Te Kanawa, *Gretchen am Spinnrade* has a delightful simplicity and *Nacht and Träume* is tonally ravishing. So this vocal music makes a considerable bonus.

However, the new recording of the *Quintet* on ASV Quicksilva by members of the Locrian Ensemble must also be given the strongest recommendation. It is for the 1990s what the famous old Saga version was for the 1960s. It has polish, warmth (particularly in the lovely secondary theme of the first movement) and deep feeling. The hushed pianissimo playing in the *Adagio* is magnetic, rapt in its intensity, and the players have the advantage of a silent background and excellent, truthful recording in a pleasing acoustic. The lighter, single-movement *Trio in B flat* is also played most persuasively, its nostalgic feeling nicely caught.

The augmented Aeolian Quartet give a strong, virile performance. It might seem bald, were it not for the depth of concentration that the players convey in every bar. In the slow movement the Aeolians daringly adopt the slowest possible *Adagio*, and the result might have seemed static but for the inner tension which holds one breathless through hushed pianissimos of the most intense beauty. The analogue recording, though not of the clearest in terms of individual definition of instruments, has been transferred to CD with remarkable presence, and the body of tone has not been lost. This remains very recommendable. There are few premium-priced issues which approach – let alone match – its intensity. However, it is in some ways upstaged by the digital Quicksilva CD.

Vividly recorded (in 1980), with clear placing of instruments in a smallish but not dry acoustic (in fact a chapel), the Chilingirian version presents a most compelling account, totally unmannered and direct in style but full of concentration and spontaneity. So one has the consistent sense of live performance, and the great melody of the first movement's second subject emerges without any intrusive nudging or overexpressiveness. The slow movement too has natural intensity, though the closeness of the recording prevents one from observing a really soft pianissimo. Throughout, the string timbres and blending are most natural.

The Villa Musica players tackle the great *C major Quintet* with a freshness and concentration that are consistently compelling, even if the finale is neat and clean rather than urgently dramatic. The little *String trio* makes an attractive and generous fill-up, another assured and stylish performance. With clear, well-balanced recording this super-budget issue makes an outstanding bargain and offers another excellent alternative to the Saga version for those wanting digital sound.

The Vienna Konzerthaus Quartet are right inside this music and they give a simple, direct and refreshingly unexaggerated reading of great appeal. There is real tension here, and it is a pity that the early recording-balance prevents a real pianissimo registering in the slow movement where there is no lack of intensity; otherwise the sound is excellent and, even as it stands, this is a most rewarding version.

On Carlton, Ofra Harnoy fails to inspire the Orford players to give more than a routine performance. The first movement is very plain, even angular, and the *Adagio* is almost totally lacking in tension.

Violin sonatinas, Nos. 1–3; Fantasy in C, D.934.

(BB) *(**) Naxos Dig. 8.550420 [id.]. Dong-Suk Kang, Pascal Devoyon.

Korean-born Dong-Suk Kang plays with style and panache and is given excellent support by Pascal Devoyon. Neither is well served by the recording, however, made in a cramped studio that robs the piano-tone of some of its timbre, while the close balance does less than complete justice to the sound this fine violinist makes in the flesh. Nevertheless it still gives pleasure. Performances three star; the recording one.

Violin sonatinas Nos. 1–3; Rondo in B min. (Rondeau brillant), D.895; Duo in A (Grand duo), D.574; Fantasie in C, D.934.

(M) *** Sony Stern Edition IV Dig./Analogue SM2K 64528 (2) [S2K 64528]. Isaac Stern, Daniel Barenboim (with: HAYDN: *Violin concerto in C, Hob VIIa/1* with Chamber O **).

It is good to have these 1988 Stern recordings reissued at mid-price in time for the bicentenary. The performances have a natural warmth and plenty of character, yet there is an unaffected simplicity and directness of style which suits the three early *Sonatinas*, written in 1816 but not published until two decades later. One has only to sample the *Andante* of the *G minor*, D.408, or the sturdy opening of the *Allegro* of the *Rondo brillant* to appreciate the affinity these artists have with Schubert's muse. The *Grand duo* (the title was invented by Diabelli for the work's posthumous publication) dates from little more than a year later, but both artists provide the necessary added flair (especially in the Scherzo) for this rather more ambitious piece. The gentle, mysterious opening of the *Fantasie* is superbly caught and the lilting *Allegretto* makes a perfect foil for the songful *Andantino* (which readily takes wing on Stern's bow). The finale is a joy. The Haydn *Concerto*, excellently recorded in mono in 1947, is a very acceptable bonus. Stern directs the work himself and the highlight of the performance is his touching account of the *Adagio*, although the accompanying guitar-like orchestral pizzicatos could ideally have had a lighter touch. A superb set just the same.

PIANO MUSIC

Piano music for four hands

Allegro in A min. (Lebensstürme), D.947; Divertissement à la Française in E min., D.823; Divertissement à la Hongroise in G min., D.818; Fantasia in F min., D.940; Grand duo in C, D.812; 4 Ländler, D.814.
(B) *** EMI forte CZS5 69770-2 (2) [CDFB 69770]. Christoph Eschenbach and Justus Frantz.

German dance in G min., D.818; Grande marche funèbre, D.859; Grande marche héroïque, D.885; 6 Grandes marches et trios, D.819; Grand Rondeau (Allegretto quasi andantino), D.951; Kindermarsch in G min., D.928; 2 Ländler in E, D.618; 2 Marches caractéristiques, D.886; 2 Marches héroïques, D.602; 3 Marches militaires, D.733.
(B) *** EMI forte CZS5 69764-2 (2) [CDFB 69764]. Christoph Eschenbach and Justus Frantz.

Christoph Eschenbach and Justus Frantz made their extensive survey of Schubert's four-handed piano music in 1978 and 1979, and the Abbey Road recording was of high quality. The CD transfers occasionally bring a touch of hardness in the treble, but the underlying sound is full and well rounded and has plenty of colour. The first collection listed includes the greatest work ever written in the genre, the *F minor Fantasia*. The opening here may suggest that the performances is too reticent, but that is deceptive and this is as powerful a reading as any available with its rhythms well sprung; and the same comment applies to *Grand Duo*, while the wide range of mood in the *Lebensstürme* (a title almost certainly not Schubert's own) is encompassed impressively. The delicate interplay between the two pianists is a constant delight, whether in the simple *Ländler*, the charming central *Andantino varié* of the *Divertissement à la Française* or the cimbalom imitations in the companion Hungarian-style *Divertissement*, both extended three-movement works showing the composer at his most felicitously inventive and presented here joyfully.

The second collection includes a great many marches, but their expressive range is very much wider than might be expected. Much of it is jolly and extrovert, but there is delicacy and lyricism too, as in the fifth *Grand march and trio* of D.819 *in E flat minor*, which is quite dolorous, while the sixth has a brio to match the most famous *Marche militaire*. In the hands of Eschenbach and Frantz the third *Marche héroïque* of D.602 is quite charming, more like an impromptu. The *German dance in G minor* opens with appealing restraint and the *Kindermarsch* brings a delightful, child-like simplicity, while the two *Marches caractéristiques* sparkle with brilliance. Most remarkable of all are the *Grandes marches funèbre et héroïque*, written to mark, first, the death of Tsar Alexander I of Russia in 1825 and then the coronation of his successor, Nicholas I. The first is highly eloquent, but it is the second, in A minor, which is the more extended (17 minutes), with a characteristic lyrical strain as its centrepiece. The closing *Grand rondeau*, most touchingly played, was written in June 1828, only five months before the composer's death at the age of thirty-one. Choice in this instance will depend on how much of this repertoire you want in your collection, for the playing of Anne Queffélec and Imogen Cooper on the competing Erato set is no less eloquent than their rivals, and they are very well recorded. At times Escenbach and Frantz score in sheer freshness, but the EMI sound has a brighter edge.

Andantino varié in B min., D.823; Duo in A min., D.947; Fantasia in F min., D.940; Grand duo sonata in C, D.812; 3 Marches militaires, D.733; 6 Polonaises, D.824; Rondo in A, D.951; Variations on an original theme in A flat, D.813.
(M) *** Erato/Warner 0630 11231-2 (2). Anne Queffélec and Imogen Cooper.

It is good to have a thoroughly recommendable mid-priced set of Schubert's music for piano/four hands, including the great *F minor Fantasia*. Some of this music (including that piece) has also been recorded by Gilels and his daughter Elena for DG, and that shorter survey will no doubt resurface before too long; but the playing of Anne Queffélec and Imogen Cooper is hardly less eloquent than their rivals', and they also offer a commanding account of the *Grand duo sonata*. The slighter pieces also come off well: the *Variations* are beautifully played and have an engaging innocence, while the most famous *Marche militaire* sparkles. Its two lesser-known companions are also worth having on disc when played (like the six *Polonaises*) so brightly and spontaneously. The 1978 analogue recording is well balanced, clear and natural, the acoustic neither over-reverberant nor too confined.

Andante varié, D.823; Fantasy in F min., Op. 103; Rondo in D, D.608; 4 Marches (transcribed Liszt): *in B min.; Trauermarsche in E flat min.; Reitermarsch in C; Ungarischer Marsch in C min.*
(BB) ** Arte Nova Dig. 74321 43326-2 [id.]. Cologne Piano Duo.

The Cologne Duo (Elzbieta Kalvelage and Michael Krüker) offer musical, well-integrated performances, and their account of the *Fantasy in F minor* is by no means to be dismissed, even if they are not particularly flatteringly recorded. The Liszt transcriptions are a novelty, but one would not want to return to them too often: the *Funeral march* lasts nearly 12 minutes.

Divertissement à la hongroise, D.818; Lebensstürme, D.947; 2 Marches caractéristiques, D.886.
(BB) ** Naxos Dig. 8.550555 [id.]. Jenö Jandó, Ilona Prunyi.

No complaints about Jandó and Prunyi, and this Naxos disc makes a useful supplement to the Erato collection, although the playing is not in the same league.

(i) Piano duet: *Fantasy in F min., D.940; Introduction and variations on an original theme in B flat, D.603; 2 Marches caractéristiques in C, D.886; Rondo* (for piano duet) *in D, D.608*. (Piano) *6 German dances, D.783; Impromptus Nos. 1–4, D.899; 5–8, D.935; 6 Moments musicaux, D.780; Piano sonatas Nos. 3 in E, D.459; 4 in A min., D.537; 7 in E flat, D.568; 9 in B, D.575; 13 in A, D.664; 14 in A min., D.784; 16 in A min., D.845; 17 in D, D.850; 18 in G, D.894; 19 in C min., D.958; 20 in A, D.959; 21 in B flat, D.960.*
(B) **(*) Ph. 456 367-2 (7) [(M) id. import]. Ingrid Haebler, (i) with Ludwig Hoffmann.

It is surprising that, in a box of this kind, the notes, which cover the music more than adequately, make no mention of Ingrid Haebler. To quote Stanley Sadie in *New Grove*: 'Her piano style is essentially feminine and unassertive and she has been criticized for reticent playing. But she has qualities which make her a distinguished and faithful interpreter of Schubert.' Her *Moments musicaux* can be ranked with the finest available. She is just as beautifully recorded as Brendel (the sound fractionally sharper-focused) and, although her approach is rather more romantic, the rubato is so natural and musical that she has strong claims to be placed alongside his much-praised set.

Her stereo survey of the *Sonatas* was incomplete and somewhat uneven but she has special insights to offer, and the disarming simplicity of her Schubertian style cannot fail to give pleasure when she is so well recorded. All these performances date from the 1960s, but the CD transfers consistently present a piano-image that is always natural and truthfully balanced. She is at her finest in the early sonatas. The Scherzo of the *E major* (No. 3), D.459, sparkles engagingly, while the contrast of the finale is stylishly managed. How neatly and crisply she articulates the central *Allegretto quasi Andantino* of the *A minor* (No. 4), D.537, while the first-movement *Allegretto* of the *E flat Sonata*, D.568 (No. 7), flows along no less delightfully. The little *A major Sonata*, D.664, was written in 1819, the year of the *Trout Quintet*, and its untroubled happiness is beautifully caught. Here Haebler's clear, direct manner may leave some listeners wanting a little more pointing of rhythm, but the clarity and complete absence of sentimentality are most refreshing. The *G major Sonata*, D.894, was described by Schumann as Schubert's most perfect work, and Haebler's clarity of approach helps to display the architecture most effectively. As ever, she plays with real insight and freshness but does not quite give the rhythmic impetus that should carry one through the longest moments. Every detail is beautifully judged, but Haebler makes it a little too evident that this is a studio performance without the emotional 'lift' of a live audience. She is back on form in the *A minor Sonata*, D.784, which is really very good. It may be a small-scale performance but how characterfully she opens the first movement, her playing full of subtle light and shade, while the finale ripples engagingly. The companion *A minor Sonata*, D.845, brings another fine performance, with the *Andante* and Scherzo particularly attractively done. The later *A major Sonata*, D.959, brings a most beautifully played *Andantino*, which opens very touchingly and then becomes improvisatory in feeling, before returning to the tragic opening mood. The lightly etched Scherzo leads to an impressive finale. The *C minor Sonata*, D.958, is less successful: it wants greater power. Haebler sounds a little inhibited here. The greatest sonata of all, *No. 21 in B flat*, is another small-scale performance. Detail is sensitively outlined and meticulously observed, but there is a certain want of weight and tragic sense in her reading which detracts from the overall impression that this performance – for all its merits – conveys.

The music for piano duet was among the first to be recorded (in 1961) but one would not guess this from the excellent quality with which it reproduces. The playing is very good indeed and finds Miss

Haebler and her partner in top form. As is immediately apparent at the sensitive opening of the *F minor Fantasy*, this is relaxed and spontaneous playing that should give much pleasure – and what delightful music this is!

Solo piano music

(i) *Allegretto in C min., D.915; 12 German dances, D.790;* (ii) *Impromptus Nos. 1–4, D.899; 5–8, D.935;* (i) *3 Klavierstücke, D.946;* (iii) *6 Moments musicaux, D.780; 12 Valses nobles, D.969.*
(B) ** EMI CZS5 69561 (2) [CDZB 69561]. (i) Cyprien Katsaris; (ii) Agustin Anievas; (iii) Andor Foldès.

It is very tempting for record companies to use more than one artist when compiling a back-catalogue, two-disc recital, but the results too often are of varying calibre; so it is here in this otherwise generous and well-planned programme.

Agustin Anievas opens the collection with the first *C minor Impromptu* of D.899, playing dramatically and with poise, and his digital dexterity in the following *E flat major* is impressive; but there is no Schubertian coaxing until the glorious *G flat* work, and he makes less than he might of the striding theme which underlies the following piece in A flat. The tendency for the otherwise truthful Abbey Road 1976 recording to harden in *fortes* is not helpful. In short, this playing is fresh but not touched with real distinction, although the simplicity of presentation of the second set, D.935, is quite appealing. When one turns to Cyprien Katsaris for the *Allegretto* and three late *Klavierstücke*, the playing is much more penetrating, while the charming *German dances* bring an agreeably lighter touch. Not surprisingly, Andor Foldès's set of the six *Moments musicaux* has much Schubertian lyrical feeling, besides offering the most realistic recording (made in Berlin earlier in the decade).

Allegretto in C min., D.915; 3 Klavierstücke (Impromptus), D.946.
(M) ** Carlton IMP Classics Dig. 30367 00902 [id.]. Dirk Joeres – VORISEK: *Impromptus.* **

It was an intelligent idea to couple these Schubert *Impromptus* with the Voříšek pieces that inspired them (and indeed the whole genre). The German pianist, Dirk Joeres, is a sensitive and imaginative player, and his playing will give pleasure, though his recording is just a shade bass-heavy.

Allegretto in C min., D.915; Moments musicaux Nos. 1–6, D.780; 2 Scherzi, D.593; 12 Valse nobles, D.969.
(M) **(*) DG (IMS) 435 072-2. Daniel Barenboim.

Some of the finest playing here comes in the two *Scherzi*. The *Allegretto in C minor* is given an effective, improvisatory quality, but the twelve *Valses nobles* are played too forcefully for their full charm to be revealed. In the *Moments musicaux* there is much to admire, yet there is an element of calculation that robs the impact of freshness. The piano-tone on DG has impressive presence and weight.

Fantasia in C (Wanderer), D.760.
(M) *** Ph. 420 644-2. Alfred Brendel – *Sonata No. 21.* ***
(M) *** DG 447 451-2 [id.]. Maurizio Pollini – SCHUMANN: *Fantasia, Op. 17.* ***
(M) **(*) DG Dig. 445 562-2 [id.]. Yevgeny Kissin – BRAHMS: *Fantasias* **(*); LISZT: *Concert paraphrases of Schubert Lieder* etc. ***

Brendel's playing is of a high order, and he is truthfully recorded and coupled with what is perhaps Schubert's greatest *Sonata*, so this is excellent value at mid-price.

Pollini's account is outstanding and, though he is not ideally recorded and the piano timbre is shallow, the playing still shows remarkable insights. Moreover the Schumann coupling is equally fine.

Kissin, the amazing young Russian, gives a fine account of the *Wanderer*, though it is not quite as persuasive (perhaps he himself is not quite as persuaded by the music) as the finest rivals. Of course there is some very fine pianism, but other artists, Kempff for instance, find greater depths. Good DG recording.

Fantasia in C (Wanderer), D.760; Andante in A, D.604; Allegretto in C min., D.915; 3 Klavierstücke (Impromptus), D.946; Scherzo in B flat, D.593/1; 13 Variations on a theme by Anselm Hüttenbrenner in A min., D.576.
(M) *** DG 453 289-2. Wilhelm Kempff.

Although there is no lack of strength in the *Wanderer fantasia*, the high drama which such a pianist as Sviatoslav Richter finds is missing; but the result with Kempff is totally disarming. He then injects all his habitual magic into the other often deceptively simple pieces. His playing is utterly disarming in the second of the three *Klavierstücke*, which were written in the last year of Schubert's life, easy, happy inspirations that wear greatness easily. The *Andante* and *Allegretto* are engaging too, and the *Scherzo* hops along winningly, more like a Laendler, while the *Hüttenbrenner variations* (echoes here of the *Allegretto* of Beethoven's *Seventh Symphony*) are more decoratively insubstantial; but whatever the tone of Schubert's voice, Kempff's crystal touch and natural intensity make for pure delight. Excellent analogue recording (from 1967–71) naturally transferred.

Fantasia in C (Wanderer), D.760; Piano sonatas Nos. 4 in A min., D.537; 13 in A, D.664.
(BB) ** Naxos Dig. 8.550846 [id.]. Jenö Jandó.

Jenö Jandó gives eminently satisfactory performances of the *A major sonata*, D.664, and the *Wanderer Fantasy*. At the same time, it would be idle to pretend that he matches the artistry of a Brendel or Pollini in this repertoire. He is decently recorded.

Impromptus Nos. 1–4, D.899; 5–8, D.935; 3 Klavierstücke, D.946; Moments musicaux Nos. 1–6, D.780; Allegretto in C min., D.915; 6 German dances, D.820; Grazer Galopp, D.925; Hungarian melody in B min., D.817; 12 Ländler, D.790.
(B) *** Decca Double Dig. 458 139-2 (2) [(M) id. import]. András Schiff.

Impromptus Nos. 1–4, D.899; 5–8, D.935; 3 Klavierstücke (Impromptus), D.946; 6 Moments musicaux, D.780; 12 German dances, D.790; 16 German dances, D.783.
❀ (B) *** Ph. Duo 456 061-2 (2) [(M) id. import]. Alfred Brendel.

Brendel's analogue set of the *Impromptus* is magical, and the *Moments musicaux* are among the most poetic in the catalogue. It is difficult to imagine finer Schubert playing than this; to find more eloquence, more profound musical insights, one has to go back to Edwin Fischer – and even here comparison is not always to Brendel's disadvantage. The *Klavierstücke* are searching, with Brendel going even deeper than in his earlier recording on Turnabout, and in his hands the *German dances*, although retaining their underlying charm, sound anything but trivial. The recordings date from the early 1970s and offer Philips's very finest analogue quality; the remastering is expert and the focus is very slightly cleaner, without any loss of bloom.

It was with this pair of 1990 discs that András Schiff laid the foundations for his Schubertian odyssey. The playing is idiomatic, intelligent and humane, and the recording is more than acceptable. It is impossible to recommend his *Impromptus* in preference to those of Brendel, but no one will be disappointed with them. We had hoped the arrangement of repertoire would have been reordered by Decca so that (as with major competitors) the eight *Impromptus* would have been placed on a single CD. However, their reissue as a Double means that all this music is easily accessible, and Schiff has the advantage of very natural digital recording, the effect lighter-textured than with Brendel.

Impromptus Nos. 1–4, D. 899; 5–8, D.935.
(BB) **(*) Naxos Dig. 8.550260 [id.]. Jenö Jandó.

Though his set of the *Impromptus* is not ideally recorded (the microphones are a bit too close, with unpleasing results in fortissimo passages), Jandó has been worse served by the engineers. He is a very musical player and his unaffected (and often perceptive) readings are more than acceptable. The Schiff and (earlier) Brendel versions are unchallenged, but no one investing in the present set is likely to be greatly disappointed.

4 Impromptus, D.899/1–4.
(BB) ** HM Solo Dig. HM 926020 [id.]. Alain Planès.

Anyone wanting just the four *Impromptus* of D.899 (once offered alone on a early Decca mono LP by Clifford Curzon) will find Alain Planès at his best in the lovely, lyrical *G flat major* (No. 3). In the opening piece in C minor, his articulation seems too precise and deliberate, but in the two other works he is freshly impulsive, and here more poise might be in order. He is well recorded, but this is no match for Brendel.

4 Impromptus, D.899; Impromptu in B flat, D.935/3; Moments musicaux, D.780/1, 2 & 6.
(B) **(*) LaserLight Dig. 15609 [id.]. Jenö Jandó.

At last Jenö Jandó is heard recorded in an acoustic that does justice to his talent. The sound, at least in the opening *B flat major Impromptu* of D.935, is fresh and truthful, the ambience is warm, and the playing is very good. The balance is not as good in the three *Moments musicaux* or in the D.899 *Impromptus*: it is closer and marginally drier.

Moments musicaux Nos. 1–6, D.780; 3 Klavierstücke, D. 946.
(M) *** Virgin Veritas/EMI Dig. VER5 61161-2. Melvyn Tan (fortepiano) – BEETHOVEN: *Allegretto in C min.* etc. ***

Moments musicaux Nos. 1–6, D.780; 3 Klavierstücke, D.946; Allegretto in C min., D.915.
(BB) **(*) Naxos Dig. 8.550259 [id.]. Jenö Jandó.

These pieces sound very effective indeed on Melvyn Tan's fortepiano (a modern instrument by Derek Adlam, modelled on an 1814 Viennese instrument). Tan finds a remarkable range of colour and, though the effect is less mellow than with a modern instrument, one's ears adjust almost immediately, so strongly does his playing project. Indeed, with textures clear but by no means bare, the music's inner emotional feeling is conveyed the more readily, while the perky *No. 3 in F minor* has a most engaging character when articulated with such precison.

Though the venue is the Italian Institute in Budapest, Jandó is much better recorded here than he is in some other contexts. He proves a thoroughly sympathetic and sensitive Schubertian, but he is still too upfront (try the opening of the fifth *Moment musical*, where the hammers and the piano mechanism are distinctly audible). The opening of the *Drei Klavierstücke* is a shade too fast (Jandó does not completely convey its dark, disturbing overtones) but the middle section is beautifully judged. The little *Allegretto in C minor*, D.915, is also very nicely played. Thoughtful and intelligent music-making, acceptably recorded, and very good value for money.

Piano sonatas

Piano sonatas Nos. 1 in E, D.157; 2 in C, D.279; 3 in E, D.459; 4 in A min., D.537; 5 in A flat, D.557; 6 in E min., D.566; 7 in E flat, D.568; 9 in B, D.575; 11 in F min., D.625; 13 in A, D.664; 14 in A min., D.784; 15 in C, D.840 (Relique); 16 in A min., D.845; 17 in D, D.850; 18 in G, D.894; 19 in C min., D.958; 20 in A, D.959; 21 in B flat, D.960.
(M) *** EMI Eminence Dig. CDBOX FS1 (8) (also available separately). Martino Tirimo.
(M) *** DG 423 496-2 (7) [id.]. Wilhelm Kempff.
(M) *** Decca Dig. 448 390-2 (7). András Schiff.

It is a far cry from the geographical certainty of Beethoven's great cycle of 32 piano sonatas to the haphazard, fragmented series of sonatas which Schubert left behind on his premature death at the age of 31. Viewed as a whole, however, with the culminating works of his final years providing a sublime equivalent to the late Beethoven works, the Schubert series is just as revealing of a supreme master, here more than ever in this new recorded cycle.

Martino Tirimo, scholar and musical thinker as well as virtuoso, in these eight magnificent discs fills an important gap. As he says in his note to the last of the series, 'It is surely extraordinary that we have had to wait until 200 years after Schubert's birth for an edition to present all 21 sonatas in their complete form and in chronological order, and for a recording of them all which includes every movement of each work.' These discs superbly supplement his printed *Urtext* edition, already established as a new authority.

One has to remember how relatively recently it is that Schubert's sonatas have been appreciated at all. Even the great Artur Schnabel, as a pioneer, concentrated on a select few, and it is much more recently that pianists like Wilhelm Kempff, Alfred Brendel and András Schiff have sought to give us complete cycles. Yet even they have baulked at the works left incomplete, only occasionally – as Schiff does – including a fragment of a movement, finishing the music in mid-air.

Tirimo here uses his own completions in eight substantial movements. As he says, the evidence is that Schubert left them incomplete – generally cut off at the start of the recapitulation, with all the material already assembled – fully intending to round them off later, obviously not intending to reject them. It is a fair justification, and Tirimo's texts, imaginative as they are, prove revelatory, not intrusive.

Almost all the discs include one of the late sonatas, and most also have works previously left incomplete. All can be recommended warmly but, if a first choice has to be made, the third disc makes an excellent recommendation. In addition to the late *C minor Sonata* – the least known of the three masterpieces Schubert wrote in the year of his death – that has an amazing four-movement work in F sharp minor, previously left as a single-movement torso. The opening is astonishing, poetic and visionary, looking far beyond the early nineteenth century, with a haunting idea very close to the wonderful first theme of Schubert's *F minor Fantasy* for piano duet.

Another excellent sampler is the fifth disc, which includes as well as the late *A minor Sonata* the magnificent *C major Sonata* of the same year, 1825, sometimes nicknamed *Reliquie*, with the two usual movements here supplemented by a Minuet and Rondo most sensitively completed by Tirimo. And anyone who doubts that here is a master to bracket with the great Schubertians of our time should hear the final disc, with its searching account of the last masterpiece in B flat, in which the *Adagio* slow movement matches the finest versions of the past in its rapt, hushed intensity.

Wilhelm Kempff's cycle was recorded over a four-year period (1965–9) and elicited much admiration in our earlier editions. DG has now collected the sonatas into a seven-CD box and those wanting a comprehensive survey of this repertoire will find much refreshment here. There have been performances of comparable stature: Gilels in the *A minor*, D.784, and *D major*, D.850, Lupu (*G major*, D.894), Perahia (*A major*, D.960) and Richter, but before the arrival of the Tirimo Edition there was no individual overview of the whole cycle that was as consistently satisfying as Kempff's. The recordings are not state of the art (there is an occasional hint of shallowness) but there is a wisdom about his playing which puts it in a special category.

With the collection (like Kempff's survey) including the *First Sonata*, D.157 (written when the composer was eighteen), and also the fragment of the *Eighth* (which Kempff omits), Schiff sets the seal on his seven-CD survey for Decca which has excited golden opinions. In his note he calls them 'among the most sublime contributions written for the piano' – and he plays them as if they are, too. Schiff has some distinguished rivals and the complete set from Kempff remains very special indeed – Kempff has never been surpassed in the great *B flat Sonata*. Yet Schiff's is a survey that blends pianistic finesse with keen human insights. He has a good feeling for the architecture of these pieces and he invests detail with just the right amount of feeling. The modern, digital recordings, made in the Brahms-Saal of the Musikverein in Vienna, are eminently satisfactory. Readers considering adding a new cycle to their collections need have no serious qualms about starting here, especially with the CDs conveniently packaged in a mid-priced box. They are still available separately at full price.

Tirimo Complete Sonata Edition

Piano sonatas, Vol. 1: *Nos. 3 in E, D.459; 5 in A flat, D.557; 18 in G, D.894.*
(B) *** EMI Eminence Dig. CD-EMX 2279 [(M) id.]. Martino Tirimo.

Martino Tirimo may have made his name on disc with his Debussy and prize-winning Rachmaninov, but there are few more thoughtful pianists than he. This is the first disc in a uniquely complete recorded cycle. Though the sound is less immediate and more reverberant than on rival discs, Tirimo not only reveals new textual points but consistently matches great Schubertians like Kempff, Brendel and Schiff, in readings marked by delicate phrasing and bold choice of speeds. So in the late *G major Sonata* Tirimo is initially gentler than his rivals, both in the expansive first movement and in the lyrical *Andante*, playing with a velvet legato; but then in fast speeds for the *Allegro* Minuet and the *Allegretto* finale, he heightens the drama. Most impressive too is the natural weight and gravity he brings to the central *Adagio* in the five-movement *Sonata No. 3 in E*, a problematic work which Tirimo discusses most illuminatingly in his notes.

Piano sonatas, Vol. 2: *Nos. 2 in C, D.279; 17 in D, D.850.*
(B) *** EMI Eminence Dig. CD-EMX 2278 [M) id.]. Martino Tirimo.

This second disc in Tirimo's cycle closely follows the first, both in the authority of the playing and – rather less happily – in the reverberant recording. Here too there is a late sonata, the great *D major*, with Tirimo bringing out the dramatic contrasts, springing rhythms persuasively and illuminating new textual points, notably in the second-movement *Andante. No. 2 in C*, a striking teenage inspiration, is the more impressive when it comes in a version with the witty *Allegretto* finale completed by Tirimo. He also includes an alternative version of the Minuet, with a different Trio.

Piano sonatas, Vol. 3: *Nos. 1 in E, D.157; 9 in F sharp min., D.571* (completed Tirimo); *19 in C min., D.958.*
(B) *** EMI Eminence Dig. CD-EMX 2280 [M) id.]. Martino Tirimo.

The *Sonata in F sharp minor* (No. 9) opens hauntingly. It was written in 1817, and the unfinished first movement became separated from the *Allegro* (finale) and Scherzo, which existed independently; more musical detective work isolated the slow movement, and the work has now been put together and completed most successfully by Tirimo: it is one of the illuminating performances here. The trickling theme of its Scherzo is charmingly Schubertian. The *First (E major) Sonata* was written soon after the composer's eighteenth birthday. The opening is boldly classical, but Schubertian fingerprints appear in the lilting secondary material, and the disconsolate *Andante in E minor* is very touching in Tirimo's hands. The recording remains truthful and one soon adjusts to the resonance.

Piano sonatas, Vol. 4: *Nos. 4 in A min., D.537; 11 in C, D.613* (complete Tirimo); *20 in A, D.959.*
(B) *** EMI Eminence Dig. CD-EMX 2281 [M) id.]. Martino Tirimo.

The *Sonata in C*, D.613, dates from the year after the *F sharp minor* (on the previous disc). The *Adagio* was the only completed movement of the three and was published independently in 1869. It is one of Schubert's finest and is played very winningly here. The other two movements had to wait 28 years before being printed in the complete edition of Schubert's works. Tirimo successfully completed the first movement (which the composer left at the end of the development section) and the engaging *Allegretto* finale. There is much else to delight the listener in his playing here, especially the subtle lilt at the opening of the central movement, marked *Allegretto quasi Andantino*, while his veiled tone in the touching *Andantino* of the *A major Sonata* is matched by the sparkling, light-hearted Scherzo. Excellent if noticeably resonant sound.

Piano sonatas, Vol. 5: *Piano sonatas Nos. 15 in C (Reliquie), D.840; 16 in A min., D.845.*
(B) *** EMI Eminence CD-EMX 2282 [(M) id. import]. Martino Tirimo.

In the fifth volume of his Schubert cycle, Tirimo strikingly couples the great *A minor Sonata* (dedicated to Archduke Rudolf, Beethoven's patron, and one of only three published in the composer's lifetime) with the unfinished *Sonata in C*, to which a publisher gave the sentimental title, *Reliquie*. The first of the two completed movements is among the most powerful and ambitious that Schubert ever wrote, here masterfully interpreted, but Tirimo's completion of the last two movements – the finale presenting formidable problems – satisfyingly sets that towering movement in a full four-movement structure to match the *A minor* work in achievement.

Piano sonatas, Vol. 6: *Piano sonatas Nos. 7 in D flat, D.567; 12 in F min., D.625; 14 in A min., D.784.*
(B) *** EMI Eminence CD-EMX 2283 [(M) id. import]. Martino Tirimo.

The *Sonata in D flat* – a rare key for a sonata in Schubert's time – is an alternative version of the *E flat Sonata*, D.568, sufficiently different to justify its inclusion as a separate work. The *F minor Sonata*, unlike most of the fragmentary ones, was left with its first movement incomplete, a broodingly dark movement with some strikingly original piano writing, making its completion most welcome. The *A minor*, D.784, much more compact than the later *A minor*, is the first of what might be counted as Schubert's late sonatas, with a slow movement weightier than its length might suggest and a haunting *moto perpetuo* finale. As in the rest of the cycle, Tirimo offers dedicated performances, and the warm recording is eminently truthful.

Piano sonatas, Vol. 7: *Piano sonatas Nos. 8 in E flat, D.568; 10 in B, D.575; 13 in A, D.664.*
(B) *** EMI Eminence CD-EMX 2284 [(M) id. import]. Martino Tirimo.

The penultimate disc of Tirimo's outstanding Schubert cycle couples the one sonata which throughout a century or so of neglect remained a popular work with pianists, the *A major*, D.664, blissfully lyrical throughout. It is a measure of Tirimo's insight that he brings out searching qualities behind the happiness of inspiration. The other works on the disc are two of the seven sonatas that Schubert wrote in 1817, the *E flat* with a G minor slow movement darker than the rest (originally conceived for another work) and a leisurely Minuet like a slow polonaise. The *B major* too brings strikingly experimental writing. Performances and recording well up to standard.

Piano sonatas, Vol. 8: *Piano sonatas Nos. 6 in E min., D.566; in C sharp min.* (fragment), *D.655; in E min.* (fragment), *D.769a; 21 in B flat, D.960.*
(B) *** EMI Eminence CD-EMX 2285 [(M) id. import]. Martino Tirimo.

Martino Tirimo impressively rounds off his Schubert cycle – the most comprehensive yet recorded – with a deeply dedicated account of the last and greatest of the sonatas, that in B flat. He contrasts the spacious, visionary music of the first two movements sharply against the crisply rhythmic writing of the last two, bringing out the lilting lightness while firmly establishing their relationship with the earlier movements. The extra items make a valuable supplement, two tantalizing fragments from minor-key first movements that incomprehensibly failed to get completed, and the *E minor Sonata* of 1817, which had all four movements finally assembled as recently as 1948, with the second-movement *Allegretto* and the finale easily flowing in Schubert's most winning manner.

Other sonata recordings

Piano sonatas Nos. 1 in E, D.157; 14 in A min., D.784; 20 in A, D.959.
(M) *** Decca 425 033-2 [id.]. Radu Lupu.

Lupu is sensitive and poetic throughout. In the *A major* work he strikes the perfect balance between Schubert's classicism and the spontaneity of his musical thought, and at the same time he leaves one with the impression that the achievement is perfectly effortless, with an inner repose and depth of feeling that remain memorable long after the record has ended. Excellent vintage Decca recording, made in the Kingsway Hall in the late 1970s.

Piano sonatas Nos. 4 in A min., D.537; 13 in A, D.664; 14 in A min., D.784; 15 in C, D.840; 16 in A min. (Relique), D.845; 19 in C min., D.958; 20 in A, D.959; 21 in B flat, D.960; Allegretto in C min., D.915; 11 Ecossaises, D.781; Fantasia in C (Wanderer), D.760; 12 German dances, D.790; 16 German dances, D.783; Hungarian melody in B min., D.817; 6 Moments musicaux, D.780.
(M) *** Ph. Brendel Edition Analog/Dig. 446 923-2 (5). Alfred Brendel.

Four out of the five records here come from Brendel's earlier, analogue set of Schubert recordings, but the first, pairing Nos. 4 and 13, is digital. Here Brendel's account of the *A minor Sonata*, D.537, sounds a little didactic: the gears are changed to prepare the way for the second group, and this sounds unconvincing on the first hearing and more so on the repeat. He also broadens on the modulation to F major towards the end of the exposition, only to quicken the pulse in the development. The result is curiously inorganic. The *A major*, D.664, is also given with less simplicity and charm than one expects from this great artist. There are some disruptive and studied agogic fluctuations which are not always convincing. No complaints about the sound, which is clear, well focused and natural. The analogue recordings which Brendel made in the early 1970s are noticeably more naturally flexible, even if his approach to tempo is that of a romantic, often making accelerandi to heighten climaxes. Both in *Sonatas 14 in A minor* and *15 in C major* he manages to convey romantic feeling within a relatively taut framework; indeed in the *C major* his eloquence and poetry leave nothing to be desired. No. 16, D.845, is one of the very finest of the series, with a searching reading of the first movement, free in expression, but direct too. The variations of the slow movement are given heavenly length, while the Scherzo and finale have strength and urgency. *No. 20 in A major*, however, suffers from rather more agogic changes than is desirable, and the *C minor Sonata*, D.958, is also not free from this charge. But one does not want to make too much of this, for the result is nearly always made to seem convincing. Brendel's performance of the final *B flat major Sonata* is as impressive and full of insight as one would expect; his playing of the *Wanderer fantasia* is also of a high order, and throughout he is truthfully recorded. The *German dances* are delightful and particularly beautifully played, while the *Moments musicaux* are given wonderfully poetic performances and rank very highly indeed in Brendel's Schubert discography. The slightly soft-grained recording is exemplary.

Piano sonata No. 5 in A flat, D.557; 2 Scherzi, D.593.
(M) *** Decca 448 129-2. Radu Lupu – BRAHMS: *Piano sonata No. 3.* ***

In the little three-movement *A flat Sonata* Lupu strikes the perfect balance between Schubert's classicism and the spontaneity of his musical thought, and at the same time he leaves one with the impression that this achievement is perfectly effortless. The *Andante* unfolds with appealing delicacy and the finale combines delicacy with strength. The two *Scherzi* are hardly less successful, the first particularly light and charming, the second rather more quixotic in mood. The analogue recording from the mid-1970s is as natural and fresh as the performances themselves.

Piano sonatas Nos. 13 in A, D.664; 14 in A min., D.784; Hungarian melody, D.817; 12 Waltzes, D.145.
✿ (M) *** Decca 443 579-2. Ashkenazy.

A magnificent record in every respect. Ashkenazy is a great Schubertian who can realize the touching humanity of this giant's vision as well as his strength. There is an astonishing directness about these performances and a virility tempered by tenderness. This matches Ashkenazy's own high standards, and Decca have risen remarkably to the occasion. The 1966 analogue recording, reissued in Decca's Classic Sound series, has splendid range and fidelity. We gave the original LP a Rosette and see no reason to withhold it now.

Piano sonatas Nos. 14 in A min., D.784; 18 in G, D.894.
(BB) ** Naxos Dig. 8.550730 [id.]. Jenö Jandó.

Neither the *A minor* nor the *G major Sonata* by Jenö Jandó is strong on poetic feeling or charm, though there is a good grasp of structure and a considerable musical intelligence at work. All the same, in great music one wants great playing and Jandó does not challenge the best the catalogue has to offer.

Piano sonatas Nos. 15 in C (Unfinished), D.840; 19 in C min., D.958; 16 German Dances, D.783.
(M) *** Van. 08.4026.71 [OVC 4026]. Alfred Brendel (also on 08 9165 72 with SCHUMANN: *Etudes symphoniques; Fantasia in C* ***).

Brendel was at his finest and most spontaneous in the 1960s. The *C minor Sonata* is particularly fine, with a thoughtful, improvisatory feeling in the slow movement which is consistently illuminating. The two-movement *C major Sonata* also has a memorable *Andante*, and the *German Dances* are an endless delight. The recording is full and bold. Brendel's fine performances from the 1960s are now additionally available in a slip-case coupled with Schumann as part of Vanguard's 'Alfred Brendel collection'.

Piano sonatas Nos. 15 in C (Relique), D.840; 21 in B flat, D.960.
(M) **(*) DG (IMS) 445 716-2. Daniel Barenboim.

To say that Barenboim gives a Kempff-like reading of Schubert's greatest sonata, D.960, is not to deny his characteristic individuality but to point out that his is a reflective, lyrical view of the work, marked by clean semi-quaver work and sharp dynamic contrasts. Yet the slightest sense of artifice is destructive in this composer, and Barenboim's delivery of the first movement's opening statement is just a shade self-conscious. The artless grace and Blake-like innocence of this idea do not quite come across here. The second movement is slow and concentrated, the Scherzo light and sparkling with a real sense of joy. The finale is sharpened with clear-cut contrasts, yet there is curious inelegance in the second subject, an obtrusive left-hand staccato at the end of the first half of the theme. But this issue remains attractive for its imaginative coupling, the unfinished *C major Sonata*, a formidably large-scale argument, presented in its full stature by Barenboim. The recording is truthful, bold and clear.

Piano sonata No. 17 in D, D.850.
(M) *** RCA 09026 61614-2 [id.]. Emil Gilels – LISZT: *Sonata*. ***

Like the Liszt *Sonata* with which it is coupled, Gilels's highly perceptive account captures the music's Schubertian spirit in a somewhat similar way to Curzon's very persuasive account. If in his own way Gilels is authoritative and commanding, like Curzon he finds a special magic to engage the ear in the delightful finale.

Piano sonata No. 17 in D, D.850; Impromptus in A flat; in G flat, D.899/3–4; Moments musicaux Nos. 1–6, D. 780.
(M) *** Decca 443 570-2. Clifford Curzon.

Some who know more forceful interpretations may find this too wayward, but Schubert surely thrives on some degree of coaxing. Curzon could hardly be more convincing – the spontaneous feeling of a live performance captured better than in many earlier discs. Curzon also gives superb performances of the *Moments musicaux*. These readings are among the most poetic in the catalogue, and the recording throughout is exemplary. The *Impromptus* make an attractive bonus (the *G flat major* particularly magical) in this reissue in Decca's Classic Sound series, and they too are beautifully played. The recording remains of Decca's finest analogue quality.

Piano sonatas Nos. 17 in D, D.850; 20 in A, D.959; 21 in B flat, D.960; March in E, D.606; Moments musicaux, D.780.
(M) (***) EMI mono CHS7 64259-2 (2) [ZDHB 64259: *Sonatas Nos. 20 & 21* only]. Artur Schnabel.

It was thanks to Schnabel's championship that the *Piano sonatas* re-entered the repertory for they were rarities in the recital rooms of the 1920s and early 1930s. Both the *A major* and *B flat Sonatas* sound as well as they are ever likely to, for neither was state-of-the-art piano-sound. The *Moments musicaux* sound remarkably full-bodied. The playing is full of characteristic insights, though it must be admitted that later recordings of the *B flat* from Kempff and Curzon surpassed Schnabel technically. But as always with this artist there is imagination of a remarkable order. These recordings are now fifty years old, but some of the playing Schnabel offers – at the opening of the *B flat* and in the slow movements of all three *Sonatas* – will never be less than special.

Piano sonatas Nos. 18 in G, D.894; 21 in B flat, D.960; Impromptus Nos. 1–4, D.899.
(B) ** Erato/Warner Double Dig. 4509 91928-2 (2) [(M) id. import]. Maria-João Pires.

Maria-João Pires is a perceptive and thoughtful artist, but she is not ideally served in these sessions: her instrument is not in ideal condition – at least in the *B flat Sonata*. She is a player of strong Schubertian instinct and there is some beautiful phrasing. All the same, this is not a front-runner among current recordings.

Piano sonata No. 19 in C min., D.958; Moments musicaux Nos. 1–6, D.780.
(M) *** Decca Dig. 417 785-2. Radu Lupu.

Lupu's performance has a simple eloquence that is most moving. His *Moments musicaux* are very fine indeed. The Decca recording is very natural and, at mid-price, this is extremely competitive.

Piano sonatas Nos. 19 in C min., D. 958; 20 in A, D. 959; 21 in B flat, D. 960; 3 Impromptus (Klavierstücke), D. 946/1–3.
(B) **(*) Ph. Duo 438 703-2 [id.]. Alfred Brendel.

Brendel's analogue recordings of the Schubert late *Sonatas* were among the finest of his records made in the early 1970s and would seem an obvious recommendation on Philips's Duo bargain label. But the *A major* suffers from rather more agogic changes than is desirable. Some listeners may find these interferences with the flow of the musical argument a little too personal. The *C minor Sonata* is not free from this charge but it remains an impressive performance. Brendel's account of the *B flat Sonata* is characteristically imposing. Here his mood is both serious and introspective; moreover he is at his very finest in the *Klavierstücke*. This is eloquent and profoundly musical playing. Throughout, the recording is well up to Philips's high standard of realism and the CD transfers are impeccable, with the background hiss a problem only for eagle ears.

Piano sonatas Nos. 19 in C min., D.958; 21 in B flat, D.960.
(BB) *(*) Naxos Dig. 8.550475 [id.]. Jenö Jandó.

Jenö Jandó gives carefully thought-out but ultimately unrewarding accounts of these sonatas. It would be an exaggeration to call the first movement of the *B flat Sonata* pedestrian, but he rarely conveys its tenderness and sublimity. The listener (or at least this listener) remained untouched. The recording, made at the Reformed Church in Budapest in 1991, is very satisfactory, though the microphone picks up some vocalization, albeit not particularly disturbing, from the pianist.

Piano sonata No. 20 in A, D.959; Impromptus Nos. 1–4, D.935.
(B) *(*) Sony SBK 63042; *SBT 63042* [id.]. Rudolf Serkin.

In its day (the mid-1960s), Serkin's account of the *A major Sonata* was a much-praised performance by a much-admired pianist. But we must confess to holding a minority view, for the playing seems far less sensitive than one expects from an artist of this stature. Of course there are moments of poetry, and his command of the structure is impressive enough, but his fortissimos are brutally ugly (and that isn't only the fault of the hard, close recording). A great disappointment, and the *Impromptus*, too, are no match for those from Brendel.

Piano sonatas Nos. 20 in A, D.959; 21 in B flat, D.960.
(M) *** Virgin Veritas/EMI VER5 61272-2. Melvyn Tan (fortepiano).

Melvyn Tan uses a fortepiano that was much admired by Beethoven. He is a compelling artist of keen musical intelligence who makes you listen, even when you might not agree with every expressive or agogic hesitation. Generally speaking, tempi are well judged, though the *Andantino* of the *A major* and the slow movement of the *B flat* are far too fast. However, by the end of each movement he almost convinces you that he is right and, in the case of the *B flat*, he succeeds. His account of this sonata is very impressive: there is depth of feeling as well as many felicities of sonority. Whether or not you are completely persuaded, these performances will make you think afresh about this music. The recording is first class.

Piano sonata No. 21 in B flat, D.960.
(M) *** Decca 448 578-2 [id.]. Clifford Curzon – BRAHMS: *Piano sonata No. 3* etc. ***
(M) *** Ph. 420 644-2. Alfred Brendel – *Wanderer fantasia*. ***

Curzon's is among the finest accounts of the *B flat Sonata* in the catalogue. Tempi are aptly judged and everything is in fastidious taste. Detail is finely drawn but never emphasized at the expense of the architecture as a whole. It is beautifully recorded, and the piano sounds very truthful in timbre. For the reissue in Decca's 'Classic Sound' series, the Brahms *F minor Sonata* has been added, an equally perceptive account, plus a pair of *Intermezzi*, to make this quite outstanding value.

Brendel's earlier analogue performance is as discerning and full of insight as one would expect. He is not unduly wayward, for his recording has room for the *Wanderer fantasy* as well, and he is supported by excellent Philips sound.

Piano sonata No. 21 in B flat, D.960; Impromptus: in G flat; in E flat, D.899/2 & 3; in B flat, D.935/3; Moments musicaux: in A flat; in F min., D.780/2 & 5.
❀ (B) *** DG Classikon 439 462-2; *439 462-4* [(M) id. import]. Wilhelm Kempff.

It is a tribute to Kempff's inspirational artistry that with the most relaxed tempi he conveys such consistent, compelling intensity in Schubert's greatest sonata. Kempff's long-breathed expressiveness is hypnotic, so that here quite as much as in the *Great C major Symphony* one is bound by the spell of the heavenly length. Rightly, Kempff observes the first-movement exposition repeat with the important nine bars of lead-back and, though the overall manner is less obviously dramatic than is common, the range of tone-colour is magical, with sharp terracing of dynamics to plot the geography of each movement. This remarkable performance belongs to a tradition of pianism that has almost disappeared, and we must be eternally grateful that its expression has been so glowingly captured. After the sonata we are offered an attractively diverse mini-recital of *Moments musicaux* and *Impromptus*, opening with the treasurable *G flat Impromptu*, D.899/2. This is perhaps the very finest of all the distinguished reissues on DG's Classikon bargain label so far.

VOCAL MUSIC

Lieder on record (1898–1952): Volume 1, 1898–1939 (all with piano unless otherwise indicated): *Ave Maria* (1898) Edith Clegg; sung in English. *Ungeduld* (1901) Paul Knüpfer. *Heidenröslein* (1902) Minnie Nast. *Litanei* (1901); *Ständchen: Zögernd leise* – with Hofoper Ch. & O, Bruno Seidler (1908) both Marie Götze. *Ständchen* (sung in English): *Hark, hark! the lark* (1902) David Bispham. *Die schöne Müllerin: Der Neugierige* (1902) Franz Naval. *Rastlose Liebe* (1902); *Die Allmacht* (1910) both Edyth Walker. *Erlkönig* (1906); *Du bist die Ruh; Die Liebe* (1907) all three Lilli Lehmann. *Der Wanderer* (1902) Ernst Wachter. *Schwanengesang: Abschied* (1904); *Winterreise: Der Leiermann* (1934) both Harry Plunket-Greene; sung in English. *An die Leier* (1909) Pauline Cramer. *Die Forelle* (1902) Leopold Demuth. *Schwanengesang: Am Meer* (1904) Gustav Walter. *Die junge Nonne* (1907) Susan Strong (with orchestra). *Der Wanderer* (1906); *Schwanengesang: Aufenthalt* (1912); *Winterreise: Der Leiermann* (1910) all three Lev Sibiriakov; sung in Russian. *Frühlingsglaube* (1910) Heinrich Hensel. *Der Kreuzzug* (1905) Wilhelm Hesch. *Schwanengesang: Ständchen* (1907 with orchestra) & *Liebesbotschaft* (1909) both Leo Slezak. *An die Musik; Du bist die Ruh* (1911 – both with Arthur Nikisch, piano); *Suleika II* (1929 – with Coenraad V. Bos, piano); *Ellens Gesang* (1939 – with Gerald Moore, piano) all four Elena Gerhardt. *Die schöne Müllerin: Das Wandern* (1914); *Winterreise: Der Leiermann* (1928) both Sir George Henschel (accompanying himself on the piano). *Die schöne Müllerin: Der Müller und der Bach* (1911) Elise Elizza. *An die Musik; Gruppe aus dem Tartarus* (1910) both Ottilie Metzger. *Sei mir gegrüsset* (1921) Friedrich Brodersen. *Die schöne Müllerin: Undgeduld & Wohin?* (1922–3) both Frieda Hempel. *Gruppe aus dem Tartarus* (1924); *Erlkönig* (1936, with Gerald Moore) both Alexander Kipnis. *Du bist die Ruh* (1924); *Die Liebe hat gelogen* (1927, with Edwin Schneider) both John McCormack. *Im Abendrot; Verklärung* (1929) both Aaltje Noordewier-Reddingius. *Winterreise: Rückblick; Frühlingstraume & Mut!* (1927) all three Richard Tauber, with Mischa Spoliansky. *Gretchen am Spinnrade; Mignon II* (1928) both Meta Seinemeyer, with O, Frieder Weissmann. *Die Forelle; Lachen und Weinen* (1928); *Winterreise: Der Lindenbaum* (1931) all three Vanni Marcoux, with Piero Coppola; sung in French. *An die Musik* (1926) Ursula van Diemen, with Arpád Sándor. *Memnon* (1932) Harold Williams, with Herbert Dawson. *Das Lied im Grünen* (1930) Sigrid Onegin, with Clemens Schmalstich. *Schwanengesang: Der Doppelgänger. Der Tod und das Mädchen* (1930 with O, Eugene Goossens) both Feodor Chaliapin (sung in Russian). *Schwanengesang: Aufenthalt; Ihr Bild. Die schöne Müllerin: Pause* (1928) all three Hans Duham, with Ferdinand Foll. *Sei mir gegrüsset; Auf dem Wasser zu singen; Geheimes* (1927) all three Lotte Lehmann with O, Manfred Gurlitt. *Winterreise: Der Lindenbaum. Der Tod und das Mädchen* (1926) both Julia Culp, with Fritz Lindemann.
(M) (***) EMI mono CHS5 66150-2 (3).

The first item in this fascinating historical survey really offers a frisson to the listener, even though it is a very swoopy account of *Ave Maria* sung in English. It is what is thought to be the very first recording of a Schubert song, delivered in 1898 by Edith Clegg, a contralto known only for having sung at Covent Garden in 1909. From then on the focus grows ever clearer, both in sound and in vocal technique, with even the second item, *Ungeduld* from *Die schöne Müllerin*, recorded by the German bass, Paul Knüpfer, in 1901 with a forwardness and clarity that defy the years.

Each item brings its revelations, with the American, David Bispham, singing *Hark, hark! the lark* in 1902 in a prim D'Oyly Carte English accent; the soprano, Lilli Lehmann, in 1906 giving an intensely dramatic account of *Erlkönig*; Harry Plunket-Greene (born 1865), vivid in 1934 electrical recording, characterfully giving *Der Leiermann* from *Winterreise* in English, every word clear, but with an Irish accent, the narrative effect like a folksong; Lev Sibiriakov transforming the same song to become intensely Russian (again extraordinarily vivid recording, made in St Petersburg by Fred Gaisberg); and Sir George Henschel (born 1850) at 78 recording that same song in the original German with a firmness and point for any modern singer to envy. It is amazing to think that the tenor, Gustav Walter, who was recorded in a ringing account of *Am Meer* at the age of 70, was born in 1834, within six years of Schubert's death.

It is a set which telescopes history and tells, among much else, what store all these vintage singers set by firm, clear delivery with not a hint of a wobble among them. Quite apart from such starry names as Chaliapin, Tauber and McCormack, Alexander Kipnis (who gives another memorable account of *Erlkönig*), the brilliant Frieda Hempel and the golden-toned Meta Seinemeyer demand special mention. Anyone listening to these 65 items, lasting 3 hours, will be amazed at the riches, with freshness the keynote, stylistically flawed only occasionally in sentimental *rallentandos*. Texts are given in the booklet but, alas, none of the potted biographies from the original LP set nor (worse still) an index of songs. Unmissable just the same.

Lieder on record, 1898–1952: Volume 2, 1939–52: *Schwanengesang: Der Atlas* (1930); *Erlkönig* (orch. Berlioz); *Schwanengesang: Der Doppelgänger* (1934) all three Charles Panzéra, with O, Piero Coppola (sung in French). *Die Forelle* (1927); *Der Hirt auf dem Felsen* (1929) both Lotte Schöne, the second with Berlin State Op. O, Leo Blech); *Schwanengesang: Am Meer* (1929) Friedrich Schorr, with Robert Jäger. *Gretchen am Spinnrade* (1929) Dusolinna Giannini, with Michael Raucheisen. *Erlkönig* (1930) Georges Thill, with Henri Etcheverry (baritone), C. Pascal (treble) & O. *Der Tod und das Mädchen* (1929) Maria Oiszewska, with George Reeves. *Nachtviolen; An die Geliebte; Das Heimweh* (1938) all three Elisabeth Schumann, with Leo Rosenek. *Der Jüngling an der Quelle* (1936) Elisabeth Schumann, with Elizabeth Coleman. *An die Nachtigall* (1933); *Der Schmetterling* (1937) both Elisabeth Schumann, with George Reeves. *Der Musensohn* (1932) Therese Behr-Schnabel, with Artur Schnabel. *An die Laute; Am See* (1932); *Der Wanderer an den Mond* (1937) all three Karl Erb, with Bruno Seidler-Winkler. *Schwanengesang: Frühlingssehnsucht* (1937) Karl Erb, with Gerald Moore. *Auflösung; Schwanengesang: Liebesbotschaft* (1935); *Wiegenlied: Schlafe, schlafe; Wiegenlied: Wie sich der Auglein* (1933) all five Ria Ginster, with Gerald Moore. *Ganymed; Rosamunde: Der Vollmond strahlt. Winterreise: Das Wirthaus* (1938); *Schwanengesang: Kriegers Ahnung* (1937) all four Herbert Janssen, with Gerald Moore. *Mignon I; Nachtstücke; Die junge Nonne* (1937) all three Susan Metcalfe-Casals, with Gerald Moore. *Erlkönig* (1937) Marta Fuchs, with Michael Raucheisen. *Schwanengesang: Die Taubenpost* (1937) both Gerhard Hüsch, with Gerald Moore. *Lied eines Schiffers; Widerschein* (1939) both Gerhard Hüsch, with Hanns Udo Müller. *Auf dem Wasser zu singen* (1943) Frida Leider, with Michael Raucheisen. *Die schöne Müllerin: Halt!; Eifersucht und Stolz* (1945); *Schäfers Klagelied* (1949) all three Aksel Schiotz, with Gerald Moore. *Die Vögel; Liebhaber in allen Gestalten* (1948) both Elisabeth Schwarzkopf, with Gerald Moore; *Seligkeit* (1946) Elisabeth Schwarzkopf, with Karl Hudez. *Im Frühling; Auf der Bruck* (1950) both Peter Pears, with Benjamin Britten. *Der Hirt auf dem Felsen* (1947) Margaret Ritchie, with Reginald Kell (clarinet) & Gerald Moore. *Schwanengesang: Ihr Bild* (1947) Julius Patzak, with Hermann von Nordberg. *Auf dem Wasser zu singen* (1948) Irmgard Seefried, with Gerald Moore. *Heidenröslein* (1947) Irmgard Seefried, with Hermann von Nordberg. *Am Bach im Frühling; Gruppe aus dem Tartarus; Meerstille; Wandrers Nachtlied I–II* (1949) all five Hans Hotter, with Gerald Moore. *An die Leier* (1949) Flora Nielsen, with Gerald Moore. *Prometheus* (1949) Bernhard Sönnerstedt, with Gerald Moore. *Aus Heliopolis I* (1949) Endré Koréh, with Hermann von Nordberg. *Die schöne Müllerin: Am Feierabend; Trock'ne Blumen. Nacht und Träume. Schwanengesang: Das Fischermädchen* (1951) all four Dietrich Fischer-Dieskau, with Gerald Moore. *Die Allmacht; Frühlingsglaube; Wandrers Nachtlied II* (1952) Kirsten Flagstad, with Gerald Moore.
(M) (**(*)) EMI mono CHS5 66154-2 (3).

This second volume in EMI's historic survey of Schubert song on record brings almost comparable delight, even if there are fewer surprises when many, if not most, of the singers are already familiar from their recordings. The 64 items lead up to the two great exponents of Lieder in our time, Schwarzkopf and Fischer-Dieskau, here both vividly characterful at the start of their recording careers. In timbre the charming Lotte Schöne might almost be mistaken for the even more sparkling Elisabeth Schumann, here represented in five brief songs. Naturally German singers predominate, but some of the most cherishable items are from non-German singers: Charles Panzéra and Georges Thill from France (heard in a version of *Erlkönig*, sung very dramatically in French as a trio with Henri Etcheverry and a boy treble), Peter Pears and Margaret Ritchie from Britain, as well as transatlantic singers like Dusolina Giannini (fresh and powerful in *Gretchen am Spinnrade*), Flora Nielsen and Susan Metcalfe-Casals, whose very rare recordings, privately made for her by EMI, are a revelation. The only disappointments are the recordings of Therese Behr-Schnabel (accompanied by her husband), recorded when she was 58, and Herbert Janssen, whose rapid flutter in the voice is distracting among performances of immaculate firmness. The programme ends with three songs from Kirsten Flagstad, in 1953 past her prime but still commanding. Excellent transfers, as in the first volume, with the same reservations over documentation.

Dietrich Fischer-Dieskau: The EMI Recordings

The First Recital (1951): *Der Atlas; Ihr Bild; Fischermädchen; Die Stadt; Am Meer; Der Doppelgänger; Erlkönig; Nacht und Träume; Du bist die Ruh; Ständchen.*

Volume I (1955): *Der Wanderer an den Mond; Uber Wildemann; Der Einsame; Auflösung; Der Kreuzzug; Totengräbers Heimweh; Nachtviolen; Frühlingssehnseht; Geheimnes; Rastlose Liebe; Liebesbotschaft; Im Abendrot; Abschied.*

Volume II (1957): *Dem Unendlichen; Die Sterne; An die Musik; Wehmut; Kriegers Ahnung; Der Zwerg; Der Wanderer; Frühlingsglaube; Die Taubenpost; An Silvia; Im Frühling; Auf der Bruck.*

Volume IIIa (1958): *Ständchen; Alinde; Nähe des Geliebten; Normanns Gesang; In der Ferne.*

Volume IIIb (1958): *Aufenthalt; Lied des gefangenen Jägers; Greisengesang; Erlkönig; Nachtstück.*
(all with Gerald Moore).

Volume IV (1959): *Gruppe aus dem Tartarus; Die Götter Griechenlands; Ewartung; Sehnsucht; Der Taucher.*

Volume V (1959): *Der Sänger; Die Bürgschaft; Der Fischer; Einsamkeit.*

Volume VIa (1959): *Am Strome; Der Alpenjäger; Erlafsee; Wie Ulfru fischt; Beim Winde; Trost; Auf der Donau* (1959).

Volume VIb (1959): *Abendstern; Liedesend; Sehnsucht; Heliopolis; Zum Punsche; Der Sieg; An die Freunde.*
(Volumes IV–VIb with Karl Engel).

Volume VII (1962): *Der Atlas; Ihr Bild; Das Fischermädchen; Die Stadt; Am Meer; Der Doppelgänger; Lachen und Weinen; Dass sie hier gewesen; Sei mir gegrüsst; Du bist die Ruh; Im Walde (Waldesnacht).*

Volume VIII (1965): *Seligkeit; Heidenröslein; Ständchen; Des Fischers Liebesglück; Fischerweise; Der Jüngling an der Quelle; An die Laute; Die Forelle; Auf der Riesenkoppe.*

Volume IX (1965): *An die Entfernte; Auf dem Wasser zu singen; Der Schiffer; Der Wanderer; Nachtgesang; Das Zügenglöcklein; Der Jüngling und der Tod; Das Heimweh; Das Lied im Grünen; Der Tod und das Mädchen; Der Winterabend; Der zürnende Barde; Der Strom; Litanei auf das Fest Aller Seelen.*
(all with Gerald Moore).
(M) *** EMI mono/stereo CMS5 65670-2 (6). Dietrich Fischer-Dieskau, Gerald Moore or Karl Engel.

This HMV set makes an admirable survey of Fischer-Dieskau's Schubert recordings for EMI over a decade and a half before he moved to Deutsche Grammophon to make the extensive survey listed below. It is particularly interesting to compare the earliest recordings (the first in mono), with the voice and manner still youthfully fresh, to the second generation, again with Gerald Moore but also with Karl Engel. The contrast is fascinating, with the voice still younger than on DG. The transfers are superbly managed and full translations are provided to make this an indispensable supplement to the DG sets.

Lieder, Volume 1 (1811–17); Volume 2 (1817–28); Song cycles: *Die schöne Müllerin; Schwanengesang; Die Winterreise.*
(B) *** DG 437 214-2 (21) [(M) id. import]. Fischer-Dieskau, Gerald Moore (as below).

Fischer-Dieskau's monumental survey of all the Schubert songs suitable for a man's voice (some of the longer ones excepted) was made over a relatively brief span, with the last 300 songs concentrated on a period of only two months in 1969, yet there is not a hint of routine. The two big boxes of nine discs come at bargain price, whereas the smaller box, containing the song-cycles, comes at mid-price. Nor has the background information been skimped. Each box contains complete German texts and English translations (plus summaries in French) as well as introductory essays. The one serious omission is an alphabetical list of titles. It makes it unnecessarily hard to find a particular song – much the most likely way of using so compendious a collection.

This collection of 21 CDs is offered at bargain price, as are the two separate 9-disc collections of Lieder listed below. The three great song-cycles – also included here – cost more if purchased separately.

Lieder, Volume I (1811–17): *Ein Leichenfantasie; Der Vatermörder* (1811); *Der Jüngling am Bache* (1812); *Totengräberlied; Die Schatten; Sehnsucht; Verklärung; Pensa, che questo istante* (1813); *Der Taucher* (1813–15); *Andenken; Geisternähe; Erinnerung; Trost, An Elisa; Die Betende; Lied aus der Ferne; Der Abend; Lied der Liebe; Erinnerungen; Adelaide; An Emma; Romanze: Ein Fräulein klagt' im finstern Turm; An Laura, als sie Klopstocks Auferstehungslied sang; Der Geistertanz; Das Mädchen aus der Fremde; Nachtgesang; Trost in Tränen; Schäfers Klagelied; Sehnsucht; Am See* (1814); *Auf einen Kirchhof; Als ich sie erröten sah; Das Bild; Der Mondabend* (1815); *Lodas Gespenst* (1816); *Der Sänger* (1815); *Die Erwartung* (1816); *Am Flusse; An Mignon; Nähe des Geliebten; Sängers Morgenlied; Amphiaraos; Das war ich; Die Sterne; Vergebliche Liebe; Liebesrausch; Sehnsucht der Liebe; Die erste Liebe; Trinklied; Stimme der Liebe; Naturgenuss; An die Freude; Der Jüngling am Bache; An den Mond; Die Mainacht; An die Nachtigall; An die Apfelbäume; Seufzer; Liebeständelei; Der Liebende; Der Traum; Die Laube; Meeres Stille; Grablied; Das Finden; Wandrers Nachtlied; Der Fischer; Erster Verlust; Die*

Erscheinung; Die Täuschung; Der Abend; Geist der Liebe; Tischlied; Der Liedler; Ballade; Abends unter der Linde; Die Mondnacht; Huldigung; Alles um Liebe; Das Geheimnis; An den Frühling; Die Bürgschaft; Der Rattenfänger; Der Schatzgräber; Heidenröslein; Bundeslied; An den Mond; Wonne der Wehmut; Wer kauft Liebesgötter? (1815); *Der Goldschmiedsgesell* (1817); *Der Morgenkuss; Abendständchen: An Lina; Morgenlied: Willkommen, rotes Morgenlicht; Der Weiberfreund; An die Sonne; Tischlerlied; Totenkranz für ein Kind; Abendlied; Die Fröhlichkeit; Lob des Tokayers; Furcht der Geliebten; Das Rosenband; An Sie; Die Sommernacht; Die frühen Gräber; Dem Unendlichen; Ossians Lied nach dem Falle Nathos; Das Mädchen von Inistore; Labetrank der Liebe; An die Geliebte; Mein Gruss an den Mai; Skolie – Lasst im Morgenstrahl des Mai'n; Die Sternenwelten; Die Macht der Liebe; Das gestörte Glück; Die Sterne; Nachtgesang; An Rosa I: Warum bist du nicht hier?; An Rosa II: Rosa, denkst du an mich?; Schwanengesang; Der Zufriedene; Liane; Augenlied; Geistes-Gruss; Hoffnung; An den Mond; Rastlose Liebe; Erlkönig* (1815); *Der Schmetterling; Die Berge* (1819); *Genügsamkeit; An die Natur* (1815); *Klage; Morgenlied; Abendlied; Der Flüchtling; Laura am Klavier; Entzückung an Laura; Die vier Weltalter; Pflügerlied; Die Einsiedelei; An die Harmonie; Die Herbstnacht; Lied: Ins stille Land; Der Herbstabend; Der Entfernten; Fischerlied; Sprache der Liebe; Abschied von der Harfe; Stimme der Liebe; Entzückung; Geist der Liebe; Klage: Der Sonne steigt; Julius an Theone; Klage: Dein Silber schien durch Eichengrün; Frühlingslied; Auf den Tod einer Nachtigall; Die Knabenzeit; Winterlied; Minnelied; Die frühe Liebe; Blumenlied; Der Leidende; Seligkeit; Erntelied; Das grosse Halleluja; Die Gestirne; Die Liebesgötter; An den Schlaf; Gott im Frühling; Der gute Hirt; Die Nacht; Fragment aus dem Aeschylus* (1816); *An die untergehende Sonne* (1816/17); *An mein Klavier; Freude der Kinderjahre; Das Heimweh; An den Mond; An Chloen; Hochzeitlied; In der Mitternacht; Trauer der Liebe; Die Perle; Liedesend; Orpheus; Abschied; Rückweg; Alte Liebe rostet nie; Gesänge des Harfners aus Goethes Wilhelm Meister: Harfenspieler I: Wer sich der Einsamkeit ergibt; Harfenspieler II: An die Türen will ich schleichen; Harfenspieler III: Wer nie sein Brot mit Tränen ass. Der König in Thule; Jägers Abendlied; An Schwager Kronos; Der Sänger am Felsen; Lied: Ferne von der grossen Stadt; Der Wanderer; Der Hirt; Lied eines Schiffers an die Dioskuren; Geheimnis; Zum Punsche; Am Bach im Frühling* (1816); *An eine Quelle* (1817); *Bei dem Grabe, meines Vaters; Am Grabe Anselmos; Abendlied; Zufriedenheit; Herbstlied; Skolie: Mädchen entsiegelten; Lebenslied; Lieden der Trennung* (1816); *Alinde; An die Laute* (1827); *Frohsinn; Die Liebe; Trost; Der Schäfer und der Reiter* (1817); *Lob der Tränen* (1821); *Der Alpenjäger; Wie Ulfru fischt; Fahrt zum Hades; Schlaflied; Die Blumensprache; Die abgeblühte Linde; Der Flug der Zeit; Der Tod und das Mädchen; Das Lied vom Reifen; Täglich zu singen; Am Strome; Philoktet; Memnon; Auf dem See; Ganymed; Der Jüngling und der Tod; Trost im Liede* (1817).

(B) *** DG 437 215-2 (9) [(M) id. import]. Dietrich Fischer-Dieskau, Gerald Moore.

This remarkable project, with Volume I recorded between 1966 and 1968 and Volume II over two months of intensive sessions in 1969, is an astonishing achievement in bringing together the greatest Schubertian of our time and the finest accompanist in a wide survey of the Lieder for solo voice. Already in 1811, as a boy in his early teens, Schubert was writing with astonishing originality, as is shown in the long (19 minutes) opening Schiller setting, a *Funeral Fantasy* with its rough, clashing intervals of a second and amazing harmonic pointers to the future. Drama comes very much to the fore in the second song here, *Der Vatermörder* ('A father died by his son's hand'), while the composer's endearing, flowing lyricism makes both *Der Jüngling am Bache* and *Die Schatten* sound remarkably mature. *Totengräberlied* ('Dig, spade, dig on!') brings a characteristically light touch to a gravedigger's soliloquy as he reflects that rich and poor alike, handsome and noble, are all in the end reduced to bones. Throughout these nine well-filled CDs the diversity of Schubert's imagination holds the listener, and his melodic gift almost never disappoints, especially when the performances are so completely at home with the music. The songs are presented in broadly chronological order and the arrangement of items ensures that each disc of the nine makes a satisfying recital in its own right. The CD transfers are impeccable, adding a little in presence to what were originally very well-balanced recordings.

Lieder, Volume II (1817–28): *An die Musik; Pax vobiscum; Hänflings Liebeswerbung; Auf der Donau; Der Schiffer; Nach einem Gewitter; Fischerlied; Das Grab; Der Strom; An den Tod; Abschied; Die Forelle; Gruppe aus dem Tartarus; Elysium; Atys; Erlafsee; Der Alpenjäger; Der Kampf; Der Knabe in der Wiege* (1817); *Auf der Riesenkoppe; An den Mond in einer Herbstnacht; Grablied für die Mutter; Einsamkeit; Der Blumenbrief; Das Marienbild* (1818); *Litanei auf das Fest Allerseelen* (1816); *Blondel zu Marien; Das Abendroth; Sonett I: Apollo, lebet noch dein Hold verlangen; Sonett II: Allein, nachdenken wie gelähmt vom Krampfe; Sonett III: Nunmehr, da Himmel, Erde schweigt; Vom Mitleiden Mariä* (1818) ; *Die Gebüsche; Der Wanderer; Abendbilder; Himmelsfunken; An die Freunde; Sehnsucht; Hoffnung; Der Jüngling am Bache; Hymne I: Wenige wissen das Geheimnis der Liebe; Hymne II: Wenn ich ihn nur hab; Hymne III: Wenn alle untreu werden; Hymne IV: Ich sag es jedem; Marie; Beim Winde; Die Sternennächte; Trost; Nachtstück; Prometheus; Strophe aus Die Götter Griechenlands* (1819); *Nachthymne; Die Vögel;*

Der Knabe; Der Fluss; Abendröte; Der Schiffer; Die Sterne; Morgenlied (1820); *Frühlingsglaube* (1822); *Des Fräuleins Liebeslauschen* (1820); *Orest auf Tauris* (1817); *Der entsühnte Orest; Freiwilliges Versinken; Der Jüngling auf dem Hügel* (1820); *Sehnsucht* (1817); *Der zürnenden Diana; Im Walde* (1820); *Die gefangenen Sänger; Der Unglückliche; Versunken; Geheimnes; Grenzen der Menschheit* (1821); *Der Jüngling an der Quelle* (1815); *Der Blumen Schmerz* (1821); *Sei mir gegrüsst; Herr Josef Spaun, Assessor in Linz; Der Wachtelschlag Ihr Grab; Nachtviolen; Heliopolis I: Im kalten, rauhen Norden; Heliopolis II: Fels auf Felsen hingewälzet; Selige Welt; Schwanengesang: Wie klage'ich's aus; Du liebst mich nicht; Die Liebe hat gelogen; Todesmusik; Schatzgräbers Begehr; An die Leier; Im Haine; Der Musensohn; An die Entfernte; Am Flusse; Willkommen und Abschied* (1822); *Wandrers Nachtlied: Ein Gleiches; Der zürnende Barde* (1823); *Am See* (1822/3); *Viola; Drang in die Ferne; Der Zwerg; Wehmut; Lied: Die Mutter Erde; Auf dem Wasser zu singen; Pilgerweise; Das Geheimnis; Der Pilgrim; Dass sie hier gewesen; Du bist die Ruh; Lachen und Weinen; Greisengesang* (1823); *Dithyrambe; Der Sieg; Abendstern; Auflösung; Gondelfahrer* (1824); *Glaube, Hoffnung und Liebe* (1828); *Im Abendroth; Der Einsame* (1824); *Des Sängers Habe; Totengräbers Heimwehe; Der blinde Knabe; Nacht und Träume; Normans Gesang; Lied des gefangenen Jägers; Im Walde; Auf der Bruck; Das Heimweh; Die Allmacht; Fülle der Liebe; Wiedersehn; Abendlied für die Entfernte; Szene I aus dem Schauspiel Lacrimas; Am mein Herz; Der liebliche Stern* (1825); *Im Jänner 1817 (Tiefes Leid); Am Fenster; Sehnsucht; Im Freien; Fischerweise; Totengräberweise; Im Frühling; Lebensmut; Um Mitternacht; Uber Wildemann* (1826); *Romanze des Richard Löwenherz* (1827); *Trinklied; Ständchen; Hippolits Lied; Gesang (An Silvia); Der Wanderer an den Mond; Das Zügenglöcklein; Bei dir allein; Irdisches Glück; Wiegenlied* (1826); *Der Vater mit dem Kind; Jägers Liebeslied; Schiffers Scheidelied; L'incanto degli occhi; Il traditor deluso; Il modo di prender moglie; Das Lied im Grünen; Das Weinen; Vor meiner Wiege; Der Wallensteiner Lanznecht beim Trunk; Der Kreuzzug; Das Fischers Liebesglück* (1827); *Der Winterabend; Die Sterne; Herbst; Widerschein* (1828); *Abschied von der Erde* (1825/6).
(B) *** DG 437 225-2 (9) [(M) id. import]. Dietrich Fischer-Dieskau, Gerald Moore.

Volume II of this great project brings the mature songs; performances and recording are just as compelling as in Volume I. In their Berlin sessions Fischer-Dieskau and Moore adopted a special technique of study, rehearsal and recording most apt for the project. The sense of spontaneity and new discovery is unfailing, since each take was in fact a performance. On a later occasion, both artists might have taken a different view but, using the ease of access possible with CD, this collection is a unique way of sampling the many different aspects of Schubert's genius. The collection opens appropriately with *An die Musik* of 1817 and, as before, the songs in this volume are laid out chronologically with certain obvious exceptions – on disc 4, for instance, *Orest auf Tauris* (1817) is placed alongside the highly contrasted *Der entsühnte Orest*, 'Orestes purified' (1820) – and the closing recital on disc 9 is suitably concluded with *Abschied von der Erde* ('Farewell to the Earth'), dating from 1825/6. Once again there is much unfamiliar repertory to discover: the four *Hymnes* grouped together on the second disc are little known but show the composer's imaginative diversity in a specifically religious connotation, while the unexpected song dedicated to *Herr Josef Spaun, Assessor in Linz*, which closes the fourth CD, is strikingly operatic. Both booklets offer full translations and each includes also brief essays by Fischer-Dieskau and Walther Dürr on the composer.

Lieder, Volume III: Song-cycles: *Die schöne Müllerin; Schwanengesang; Die Winterreise*.
(M) *** DG 437 235-2 (3) [(M) id. import]. Dietrich Fischer-Dieskau, Gerald Moore.

Fischer-Dieskau and Moore had each recorded these great cycles of Schubert several times already before they embarked on this set in 1971/2 as part of DG's Schubert song series. It was no mere repeat of earlier triumphs. If anything, these performances – notably that of the darkest and greatest of the cycles, *Winterreise* – are even more searching than before, with Moore matching the hushed concentration of the singer in some of the most remarkable playing that even he has put on record. As in the extensive recitals listed above, Fischer-Dieskau is in wonderfully fresh voice, and the transfers to CD have been managed very naturally.

Lieder: *Abendbilder; Am Fenster; Auf der Bruck; Auf der Donau; Aus Heliopolis; Fischerweise; Im Frühling; Liebeslauschen; Des Sängers Habe; Der Schiffer; Die Sterne; Der Wanderer; Wehmut; Das Zügenglöcklein*.
(M) *** DG 445 717-2. Dietrich Fischer-Dieskau, Sviatoslav Richter.

Recorded live in 1977, this beautifully balanced selection of Schubert songs displays the singer's enormous range of expression, as well as the acute sensitivity of the pianist in responding. The songs have been grouped almost in a cycle, starting with a biting expression of self-torment (*Des Sängers Habe*, translated colloquially as 'Break my luck to smithereens'). This is sung perhaps too aggressively here (understandably so) but gradually the mood lightens from melancholy (*Wehmut*) to brighter thoughts (*Das Zügenglöcklein* – 'The little bell'). Not many of these songs are well known, but it is a programme to delight aficionado and newcomer alike, atmospherically recorded with remarkably little interference from audience noises.

Elly Ameling collection ('The early years'): Disc 1: *An die Laute; An die Nachtigall* (2 settings); *An Sylvia; Der Blumenbrief; Du bist die Ruh'; Du Liebst mich nicht; Das Lied im Grünen; Der Einsame; Fischerweise; Die Gebüsche; Im Abendroth; Im Freien; Im Haine; Die Liebe hat gelogen; Der liebliche Stern; Das Mädchen; Die Männer sind méchant; Minnelied; Nacht und Träume; Nachtviolen; Rosamunde: Romanze. Schlummerlied; Der Schmetterling; Seligkeit; Die Sterne; Die Vögel; Der Wachtelschlag.* Disc 2: *Ave Maria; Gretchen am Spinnrade; Gretchens Bitte; Heidenröslein; Jäger, ruhe von der Jagd; Der König in Thule; Die junge Nonne; Die Liebende schreibt; Liebhabner in allen Gestalten; 4 Mignon Lieder (Kennst du das Land; Nur wer die Sehnsucht kennt; Heiss mich nicht reden; So lass mich scheinen); Nähe des Geliebten; Raste, Krieger!; Scene aus Faust; Suleika I & II.* Disc 3: *Abendbilder; An die Musik; An den Mond; Bertas Lied in der Nacht; Die Blumensprache; Erster Verlust; Frülingssehnsucht; Der Knabe; Nachthymne; Schwestergruss; Sei mir gegrüsst; Die Sterne; Wiegenlied.* Disc 4: *Am Bach im Frühling; An den Tod; An die Entfernte; An die untergehende Sonne; Auf dem Wasser zu singen; Die Forelle; Fülle der Liebe; Ganymed; Die Götter Griechenlands; Im Abendroth; Im Frühling; Der Musensohn; Der Schiffer; Schwanengesang: Sehnsucht; Sprach der Liebe.*

(M) *** Ph. Analogue/Dig. 438 528-2 (4). Elly Ameling, Dalton Baldwin (CDs 1–3); Rudolf Jansen (CD 4).

Elly Ameling appeared on the international scene in the mid-1960s. These records cover her period of maturity from 1972 until 1984. Her lovely voice with its diamond purity is consistently appealing and she is a persuasive interpreter, whether in the engaging *Mignon* songs or in the most familiar favourites: the poised freshness of *Nacht und Träume*, the innocence of *Nachtviolen* or the more emotionally fraught *Die Liebe hat gelogen*. These, like so much else, are most affecting; the analogue recordings on the first two discs show her at the peak of her form, with Dalton Baldwin most sensitive in support. The third disc, digitally recorded in 1982, had the distinction of being the first Lieder recital to appear on compact disc and readily deserved its accolade. It is a typically characterful and enchanting collection, starting with *An die Musik* and including other favourites like the *Cradle song* as well as lesser-known songs that admirably suit the lightness and sparkle of Ameling's voice. The fourth CD offers a 1984 digital recital with Rudolf Janson accompanying. It brings more delights, even if the voice is not quite as fresh and agile as in the earlier collections, notably the 1972 recordings included on the second disc. Yet she is able to bring new depths to such a song as *An die Entfernte* and her breath control remains immaculate – as in the opening *Ganymed* – while she still brings delightful bounce to the ever-popular *Der Musensohn*. Her voice is caught naturally by the engineers and the balance is excellent. A treasurable collection, marred only by the absence of translations: only the German texts are given.

Lieder recitals

Hyperion Schubert Edition. Lieder: (i) *Die Allmacht;* (ii) *Alinde;* (iii) *Als ich sie erröten sah;* (iv) *Am Bach im Frühling;* (v) *Am See;* (vi) *Am Strome;* (vii) *An den Frühling;* (viii) *An die Sonne;* (ix) *An Emma;* (x) *An Silvia;* (xi) *Auflösung;* (xii) *Blondel zu Marien;* (xiii) *Erlkönig;* (xiv) *Jüngling an der Quelle;* (xv) *Der liebliche Stern;* (xvi) *Lied, D.284;* (xvii) *Lied eines Schiffers an die Dioskuren;* (xviii) *Lob der Tränen;* (iii) *Mein;* (xix) *Romanze;* (xx) *Rückweg;* (xxi) *Sehnsucht;* (xxii) *Seufzer;* (xiii) *Ständchen;* (xxiii) *Tost im Tränen;* (xxiv) *Unterscheidung.*

(BB) *** Hyperion Dig. HYP 200 [id.]. (i) Elizabeth Connell; (ii) Anthony Rolfe Johnson; (iii) Ian Bostridge; (iv) Stephen Varcoe; (v) Felicity Lott; (vi) Philip Langridge; (vii) Elly Ameling; (viii) Margaret Price; (ix) Thomas Allen; (x) John Mark Ainsley; (xi) Brigitte Fassbaender; (xii) Edith Mathis; (xiii) Sarah Walker; (xiv) Christoph Prégardien; (xv) Peter Schreier; (xvi) Janet Baker; (xvii) Thomas Hampson; (xviii) Matthias Görne; (xix) Arleen Augér, Thea King; (xx) Ann Murray; (xxi) Christine Schäfer; (xxii) Martyn Hill; (xxiii) Adrian Thompson; (xxiv) Marie McLaughlin; all with Graham Johnson.

This is a delightful sampler, featuring the widest range of the fine Lieder singers whom Graham Johnson has assembled for his magnificent project, which is covered in depth in our main *Guide*. Dame Janet Baker, Dame Margaret Price and Dame Felicity Lott are on the list, with Peter Schreier, Christoph Prégardien, Brigitte Fassbaender, Elly Ameling and the late Arleen Augér among the distinguished singers from outside Britain. Inspired newcomers include Christine Schäfer, Matthias Görne and, in some ways most striking of all, Ian Bostridge, who contributes three songs. Sarah Walker has the longest item, a serenade, *Ständchen*, quite different from the famous one, with male chorus as backing. What – understandably – are missing are the texts and detailed notes which Johnson provides for the individual discs, but the booklet includes full details of each of the first 27 discs.

Miscellaneous vocal recitals

Abendlied der Fürstin; An die Nachtigall; An die Sonne; Blanca (Das Mädchen); Du bist die Ruh; Ellens Gesang I, II & III; Gesang der Norna; Gretchen am Spinnrade; Im Freien; Der Hirt auf dem Felsen; Die junge Nonne; Klage der Ceres; Klaglied; Die Liebende schreibt; Lied de Anne Lyle; Lied der Mignon I, II & III; Das Mädchens Klage; Die Männer sind méchant; Mignons Gesang; Suleika I & II; Wiegenlied.
(B) *** DG Double 453 082-2 (2) [id.]. Gundula Janowitz, Irwin Gage.

This attractive DG Double is self-recommending. Many of the songs here are favourites, although there are one or two novelties. They come from a comprehensive survey of Lieder suitable for female voice, originally issued on five LPs and recorded in 1976–7. They receive persuasive handling from Janowitz and, with a voice so naturally beautiful and used with such musical intelligence, the results are consistently compelling, helped by the sympathetic, concentrated accompaniments of Irwin Gage. If *Gretchen am Spinnrade*, which comes near the beginning of the recital, is somewhat idiosyncratic in its speed variations, Janowitz makes it very much her own, and her *Die junge Nonne*, which opens the second CD, is similarly appealing. Perhaps the most ravishing singing comes in the *Wiegenlied* and *Du bist die ruh* and, most memorably of all, the first Suleika song (*Was bedeutet die Bewegung?*) with its gentle closing pianissimo as the singer reflects that the soft whisper of the wind suggests the breath of love. The recital ends with the famous *Shepherd on the rock* with its clarinet obbligato well played by Ulf Rodenhäuser, although it has been presented more seductively elsewhere. The recording is first rate and full translations are included.

'A Schubert evening': (i) *Abendstern; Am Grabe Anselmos; An die Nachtigall; An die untergehende Sonne'; Berthas Lied in der Nacht; Delphine; Ellen's Gesang* from *The Lady of the Lake (Raste Krieger; Jäger von der Jagd; Ave Maria); Epistel an Herrn Josef von Spaun; Gondelfahrer; Gretchen am Spinnrade; Hin und wieder; Iphigenia; Die junge Nonne; Kennst du das Land; Liebe schwärmt; Das Mädchen; Das Mädchens Klage; Die Männer sind méchant; Mignon Lieder I–III (Heiss mich nicht reden; So lasst mich scheinen; Nur wer die Sehnsucht kennt); Schlummerlied; Schwestergruss; Strophe von Schiller (Die Götter Griechenlands); Suleika songs I–II (Was bedeutet die Bewegung; Ach, um deine feuchten Schwingen); Wiegenlied; Wiegenlied (Schlafe, schlafe)*. 'Favourite Lieder': (ii) *An die Musik; An Sylvia; Auf dem Wasser zu singen; Du bist die Ruh'; Die Forelle; Frühlingslaube; Heidenröslein; Litanei; Der Musensohn; Nacht und Träume; Rastlose Liebe; Der Tod und das Mädchen.*
❁ (B) *** EMI forte CZS5 69389-2 (2) [CDFB 69389]. Dame Janet Baker, with (i) Gerald Moore; (ii) Geoffrey Parsons.

This astonishingly generous collection, offered on EMI's two-for-the-price-of-one forte label, combines a pair of recitals recorded by Dame Janet at two different stages in her career, in 1970 and a decade later. The first collection ranges wide in an imaginative *Liederabend* of Schubert songs that includes a number of comparative rarities. They move from the delectably comic *Epistel* to the ominous darkness of *Die junge Nonne*. The two cradle songs are irresistible, the Seidl setting even more haunting than the more famous one; and throughout Baker consistently displays the breadth of her emotional mastery and her range of tone-colour. With Gerald Moore (who returned to the studio out of retirement especially for the occasion) still at his finest, this is a really satisfying collection. Only the opening *Gretchen am Spinnrade* brings a performance which one feels Baker could have intensified on repetition. Yet it has an attractive simplicity and shows the lovely freshness of the voice to perfection. As it happens, this song was also included in the later (1980) recital with Geoffrey Parsons, and there it is sung with heartfelt expression, together with an equally moving account of *Die junge Nonne*. But these duplicate versions have both been omitted here. What remains is treasurable. Take a poll of favourite Schubert songs and a high proportion of these would be in the dozen offered in the 1980 group. With a great singer treating each with loving, detailed care, the result is a charmer of a recital. The very first item, Dame Janet's strongly characterized reading of *Die Forelle*, makes it a fun song, and similarly Parsons' naughty, springing accompaniment to *An Sylvia* (echoed later by the singer) gives a twinkle to a song that can easily be treated too seriously. One also remembers the ravishing *subito piano* for the second stanza of *An die Musik*. The later recording is of fine EMI vintage and catches the more mature voice naturally and with rather more presence than a decade earlier. It is a pity that, because the set is so economically priced, there are no translations, but this remains an unmissable reissue.

'The Songmakers' Almanac Schubertiade': I, *'Lebensmut': Die junge Nonne; Der zürnende Diana; Vom Mitleiden Mariä; Lachen und Weinen; Selige Welt; Mignon und der Harfner; Auflösung; Lebensmut; Weilkommen und Abscheid.* II, *'Nacht und Träume': An die Laute; Wiegenlied; Ellens Gesang II; Nacht und Träume; Licht und Liebe; Ständchen (Horch! horch! die Lerch); Der Tod und das Mädchen; Der Winterabend; Abschied von der Erde.* III, *'Das Lied im Grünen': Fischerweise; Das Lied im Grünen; Der Schiffer; Nähe des Geliebten; Frühlingsglaube; Wandrers Nachtlied; Im Frühling; Wehmut; Auf der*

Bruck. IV, *'An mein Klavier': An mein Klavier; Zum Punsche; Geheimnis; Viola; Der Hochzeitsbraten.*
(B) **(*) Hyperion Dyad CDD 22020 (2) [id.]. Felicity Lott, Ann Murray, Anthony Rolfe Johnson, Richard Jackson; Graham Johnson.

Recorded in 1983, this two-disc collection in Hyperion's two-for-the-price-of-one Dyad series presents over two hours of songs arranged by related groups – 'The romantic struggle', 'Serenades and lullabies', 'Nature and love', 'At home with the Schubertians'. That was the way Graham Johnson devised his immensely popular Songmakers' Almanac concerts, making this a forerunner of his brilliantly conceived recorded edition of the complete songs. Johnson's notes, including comments on individual items and full texts, observe a similar pattern to that adopted in the main edition, though a song like the Seidl *Wiegenlied* is allowed only three of its stanzas, not all five. The analogue recording, given an AAD transfer to CD, is not quite as clean as in the main edition, with a halo of sound round the voices, not quite sharply focused enough. But with such inspired performances one's ear quickly adjusts, to give a delightful impression of just such live events as the original Schubertiads. Left to the end are the two items which are by far the longest: the poignant *Viola*, a ballad telling of an abandoned flower, with Ann Murray a charming soloist, and the convivial *Hochzeitsbraten* ('Wedding dish'), featuring the other three soloists. All four singers are at their freshest, with Ann Murray in particularly fine voice, taking on many of the most challenging songs.

Secular vocal music and Part-songs: *Die Advocaten; An den Frühling; Andenken; Bardengesang; Bergknappenlied; Bootsgesang; Coronach; Die Entfernten; Dessen Fahne; Donnerstürme wallte; Das Dörfchen; Dreifach ist der Schritt der Zeit* (2 versions); *Ein jugendlicher Maienschwung; Eisiedelei; Erinnerungen; Ewige Liebe; Fischerlied; Flucht; Frisch atmet des Morgens lebendiger Hauch; Frühlingsgesang; Frühlingslied* (2 versions); *Geist der Liebe; Der Geistertanz; Gesang der Geister über den Wassern; Goldner Schein; Der Gondelfahrer; Gott in der Natur; Grab und Mond; Hier strecket; Hier unarmen sich getreue Gatten; Im Gegenwärtigen Vergangenes; Jünglingswonne; Klage um Ali Bey; Lacrimosa son io* (2 versions); *Leise, leise, lasst uns singen; Liebe; Liebe säusein die Blätter; Lied im Freien; Lutzows wilde Jagd; Mailied* (3 versions); *Majestät'sche Sonnenrose; Mirjams Siegesgesang; Mondenschein; Der Morgernstern; Die Nacht; Nachtgesang im Walde; Nachthelle; Die Nachtigall; Nachtmusik; Naturgenuss; Nur wer die Sehnsucht kennt; La Pastorella al prato; Punschlied; Räuberlied; Ruhe, schönstes Glück der Erde; Schlachtegesang; Der Schnee zerrinnt; Selig durch die Liebe; Ständchen (Zögernd leise); Das stille Lied; Thronend auf erhab'nem Sitz; Totengräberlied; Trinklied* (4 versions); *Trinklied aus dem 16 (Jahrhundert); Trinklied im Mai; Trinklied im Winter; Unendliche Freude* (2 versions); *Vorüber die stöhnende Klage; Wehmut; Wein und Liebe; Wer die steile Sternenbalm; Widerhall; Widerspruch; Wilkommen, lieber schöner Mai; Zum Rundetanz; Zur guten Nacht; Die zwei Tugendwege.*
(M) *** EMI CMS5 66139-2 (4). Hildegard Behrens, Brigitte Fassbaender, Peter Schreier, Dietrich Fischer-Dieskau, Capella Bavariae, Bav. R. Ch. & SO, Sawallisch.

Schubert's part-songs make up a sizeable proportion of his total output, and this outstanding four-disc collection, superbly performed and recorded with Sawallisch the most understanding guide, both as pianist and conductor, brings out many rare treasures. Many are jolly ballads to celebrate life's simple pleasures, like the opening 'Song in the open air'; others are more expressively eloquent, such as *Ruhe, schönstes Glück der Erde* ('Rest, greatest earthly blessing'), the joyous *Gott in der Natur*, and the evocative male-voice chorale, *Nachtmusik*. On the other hand, *Die Advocaten* is a light-hearted trio in which a pair of lawyers wonder whether their fees are going to be paid; their client, Mr Sempronius, then arrives to do so, if reluctantly, and they are all bewitched by the clink of coins. The longest item, *Miriam's Song of triumph, on a Biblical subject*, is almost a miniature oratorio. Two striking Psalm-settings and the *Hymn to the Holy Ghost* (with brass accompaniment) have been omitted from the original LP collection but are now included on Sawallisch's EMI set of Schubert's religious music. Another substantial piece to cherish here is the version of *The Song of the Spirits over the Waters* with eight-part chorus and strings, as well as the atmospheric *Nachtgesang im Walde*, with horns accompanying a male-voice ensemble. Not surprisingly, horns also provide a lively opening for the gleeful and much briefer *Lützows wilde Jagd*, which begins the fourth disc. The highly imaginative setting of *Wehmut*, which comes near the end of the collection, has a haunting tolling bell effect, achieved in the voices alone. The tiny songs designed for Schubert and his friends to sing together, many of them drinking songs, add to the delight of the collection. Highly recommended to any Schubertian eager for new discovery. The transfers to CD could hardly have been managed more naturally, and the singers are given a fine presence.

Lieder: *Alinde; Am Tage aller Seelen; An die Entfernte; An die Laute; Auf dem Wasser zu singen; Auf der Riesenkoppe; Die Bürgschaft; Du bist die Ruh'; Der Fischer; Der Fischers Liebesglück; Fischerweise; Die Forelle; Die Götter Griechenlands; Greisengesang; Heidenröslein; Das Heimweh; Im Walde; Der Jüngling an der Quelle; Der Jüngling und der Tod; Lachen und Weinen; Lied des gefangenen Jägers; Das Lied im Grünen; Nachtgesang; Nachtstück; Nähe des Geliebten; Normans Gesang; Der Schiffer; Sei mir gegrüsst; Seligkeit; Das sie hier gewesen; Ständchen; Strophe aus Die Götter; Der Strom; Der Tod und das Mädchen; Der Wanderer; Der Winterabend; Das Zügenglöcklein; Der zürnende Barde.*
(M) *** EMI CMS7 63566-2 (2). Dietrich Fischer-Dieskau, Gerald Moore; Karl Engel.

Dating from 1965, most of the items in this collection of Schubert songs superbly represent the second generation of Fischer-Dieskau recordings with Gerald Moore, deeper and more perceptive than his mono recordings, yet with voice and manner still youthfully fresh. The contrast is fascinating, if subtle, between that main collection and the last nine songs on the second disc: they were recorded six years earlier, with three of them accompanied by Karl Engel, and with the voice still younger but presented in drier sound. (Alas, this set has just been withdrawn.)

(i) *Am grabe Anselmos; An die Musik; An die Nachtigall; An Sylvia; Auf dem See; Auf dem Wasser zu singen; Dass sie hier gewesen; Die Forelle; Die junge Nonne; Du bist die Ruh'; Ganymed; Geheimes; Gretchen am Spinnrade; Heidenröslein; Lachen und Weinen; Der Musensohn; Rastlose Liebe; Sei mir gegrüsset; Seligkeit; Ständchen; Suleika I & II; Wiegenlied.* (ii) *Winterreise* (song-cycle), *D.911.*
(BB) **(*) Virgin Classics Dig. Double VBD5 61457-2 (2) [(B) CDVB 61457]. (i) Arleen Augér, Lambert Orkis (fortepiano); (ii) Thomas Allen, Roger Vignoles (piano).

This Virgin Double joins up Arleen Augér's collection of favourite Lieder with Thomas Allen's *Winterreise*, dating from 1991 and 1994 respectively. The distinctive point about Arleen Augér's collection of Schubert songs – which includes a high proportion of favourites – is that the accompaniment is played by Lambert Orkis on a fortepiano. Though Augér's voice is caught most beautifully, with the tone consistently sweet and pure, the scale of the accompaniment intensifies a lightweight feeling, with beauty of tone given higher priority than word-meaning. Though in intensity and concern for detail this cannot match Augér's fine full-priced disc in Graham Johnson's Schubert series for Hyperion (CDJ 33009), it clearly has its place.

On the second disc Thomas Allen, understandingly supported by Roger Vignoles, tackles this Everest of the Lieder repertory with a beauty of tone and line that sets his reading apart. Allen's concentration on purely musical qualities, far from watering down word-meaning, is used to intensify the tragic emotions of the wandering lover. Allen uses a wider dynamic range than most of his direct rivals, shading the voice down to a half-tone for intimate revelations, then expanding dramatically, using the art of the opera-singer. In the two final songs, *Die Nebensonnen* and *Der Leiermann*, he is very restrained, keeping them hushed instead of underlining expressiveness. The poignancy of Schubert's inspiration is allowed to speak for itself. The one serious reservation here is the lack of translations.

An die Laute; An die Musik; An Silvia; Der Einsame; Im Abendrot; Liebhaber in allen Gestalten; Lied eines Schiffers an die Dioskurern; Der Musensohn; Ständchen (Leise flehen meine Lieder).
(M) *** DG Originals 449 747-2 [id.]. Fritz Wunderlich, Hubert Giesen – BEETHOVEN: *Lieder;* SCHUMANN: *Dichterliebe.* ***

Few tenors have matched the young Wunderlich in the freshness and golden bloom of the voice. The open manner could not be more appealing here in glowing performances, well coupled with other fine examples of this sadly short-lived artist's work. Truly this disc is a candidate for inclusion in DG's series of 'Legendary performances'.

Lieder: *An die Musik; An Sylvia; Auf dem Wasser zu singen; Ave Maria; Du bist die Ruh'; Die Forelle; Ganymed; Gretchen am Spinnrade; Heidenröslein; Im Frühling; Die junge Nonne; Litanei; Mignon und der Harfner; Der Musensohn; Nacht und Träume; Sei mir gegrüsst; Seligkeit.*
(M) *** Carlton Classics Dig. PCD 2016 [id.]. Felicity Lott, Graham Johnson.

At mid-price, Felicity Lott's collection brings an ideal choice of songs for the general collector. With Graham Johnson the most imaginative accompanist, even the best-known songs emerge fresh and new, and gentle songs like *Litanei* are raptly beautiful.

Lieder: *An die Musik; An Sylvia; Auf dem Wasser zu singen; Ganymed; Gretchen am Spinnrade; Im Frühling; Die junge Nonne; Das Lied im Grünen; Der Musensohn; Nachtviolen; Nähe des Geliebten; Wehmut.*
(M) (***) EMI mono CDH7 64026-2. Elisabeth Schwarzkopf, Edwin Fischer.

Schwarzkopf at the beginning of her recording career and Fischer at the end of his make a magical partnership, with even the simplest of songs inspiring intensely subtle expression from singer and pianist alike. Though Fischer's playing is not immaculate, he left few records more endearing than this, and Schwarzkopf's colouring of word and tone is masterly.

Arte Nova Lieder collection, Volume 1: *Amalia; An Emma; Ave Maria (Ellens Gesang III: Hymne an die Jungfrau). 4 Canzonen, D.688 (Non t'accostar all'urnal Guarda, che bianca luna; Da quel sembiante appresi; Mio ben ricordati). Daphne am Bach; Jäger, ruhe von der Jagd! (Ellens Gesang II); Gretchen am Spinnrade; Klärchens Lied (Die Liebe); Lambertine; Liebe schwärmt auf allen Wegen (Arietta from Claudine von Villa Bella); Lied der Delphine; Das Mädchen; Misero pargoletto; La pastorella al prato; Rastlose Liebe; Suleika I & II; Vedi quanto adoro (Aria from Didone).*
(BB) **(*) Arte Nova Dig. 74321 47497-2 [id.]. Doreen DeFeis, Kenneth Duryea.

This is labelled as Volume 1 of the Arte Nova series of Schubert song recordings; it contains far rarer repertory than the second volume, from the Chinese soprano, Lan Rao. Only two of the songs chosen are top favourites – *Gretchen am Spinnrade* and *Ave Maria*, here labelled as the third of Ellen's songs to poems by Sir Walter Scott in German translation. Yet many of the rarities prove most refreshing and, though DeFeis's sweet, bright soprano lacks a little in weight and variety, the freshness and clarity of the voice make for sympathetic results, bringing out the charm of such a characteristic song as *Daphne am Bach* with its water-music accompaniment. It is good too to have seven Italian settings, most to words by Metastasio. Full texts are given, but no translations.

Arte Nova Lieder collection, Volume 2: *An die Musik; An die Nachtigall; Auf dem Wasser zu singen; Ave Maria; Du bist die Ruh; Frühlingsglaube; Ganymed; Heidenröslein;* (i) *Der Hirt auf dem Felsen. Die Liebende schreibt; Liebhaber in allen Gestalten; Mignon (Kennst du das Land); Nacht und Träume; Nur wer die Sehnsucht kennt (Lied der Mignon); Romanze; Seligkeit; Wiegenlied.*
(BB) ** Arte Nova Dig. 74321 51639-2 [id.]. Lan Rao, Micaela Gelius; (i) with Binwei Kiang.

Born in China, Lan Rao moved to Germany to study with Arleen Augér and Reri Grist, winning various Lieder prizes in Germany and Austria. Hers is a light, clear soprano, sweet and girlish, lacking a little in variety of tone. Her poise and precision are remarkable, and the youthful timbre is ideally suited to such a light-hearted song as *Seligkeit*, but in more searching songs the results seem rather undercharacterized, at times even anonymous, with the deeper feelings of such a great song as *Nacht und Träume* underplayed, however tender or easeful the expression. Micaela Gelius's accompaniments hardly help, with the clarinettist, Binwei Kiang, joining her in the final item, *The Shepherd on the rock*, where by contrast Lan Rao's tone is brighter and more forward. Nevertheless this is a well-chosen, well-recorded collection of songs, including many favourites.

Lieder: *An Sylvia; Auf der Bruck; Bei dir allein; Du bist die Ruh'; Der Einsame; Freiwilliges Versinken; Gondelfahrer; Die Götter Greichenlands; Gruppe aus dem Tartarus; Heidenröslein; Himmelsfunken; Im Haine; Der Jüngling an der Quelle; Lied eines Schiffers; Nachtviolen; Prometheus; Ständchen; Die Sterne; Waldesnacht; Der Wanderer an den Mond.*
(B) *** EMI Dig. CD-EMX 2224 [(M) id.]. Simon Keenlyside, Malcolm Martineau.

The velvety beauty of Keenlyside's cleanly focused baritone goes with fresh, thoughtful readings of 20 favourite songs, perfectly judged, with ever-sensitive accompaniment from Martineau. At mid-price it makes another outstanding recommendation for a Schubert disc which includes one or two unusual songs among many favourites.

Auf der Riesenkoppe; Der blinde Knabe; Du bist die Ruh'; Die Forelle; Das Geheimnis; Gretchen am Spinnrade; Heidenröslein; (i) *Der Hirt auf dem Felsen; Der König in Thule; La Pastorella; Schwanengesang; Die Wehmut.*
(B) **(*) EMI CfP CD-CFP 6040 [(M) id.]. Dame Margaret Price, James Lockhart; (i) with Brymer.

Dame Margaret Price was in fine voice when she made this record in 1971. Her singing of Schubert is full-throated in style, although she successfully fines down the tone for a song like *Du bist die Ruh'*. The opening recitative of *Auf der Riesenkoppe* takes us straight into the opera house; *La Pastorella* (a charming song) reminds us of Rossini, and in *The Shepherd on the rock* the sheer breadth of the singing tends to dwarf Jack Brymer's gentle but beguiling clarinet obbligato. In all other respects the two artists work well together and this is a lovely performance. *Die Forelle* is very attractively done, and *Der König in Thule* is serenely beautiful. *Heidenröslein* (transposed down a tone) has a simple, affecting charm and in *Gretchen am Spinnrade* the soaring line is sensitively controlled, but Price's involvement is obvious. James Lockhart accompanies musically but, whether or not it is the fault of the recording balance, like Brymer he tends to be dwarfed by the vocal richness. No translations are provided, but the notes give a synopsis of each song. The recital, however, plays for only 47 minutes.

(i; ii) Duets: *Antigone und Oedip; Cronnan; Hektors Abschied; Hermann und Thusnelda; Licht und Liebe (Nachtgesang); Mignon und der Harfner; Selma und Selmar; Sing-Ubungen;* (vi) *Szene aus Goethes Faust.* (ii; iii; iv; v) Trios: *Die Advokaten; Gütigster, Bester, Weisester; Die Hochzeitsbraten; Kantata zum Geburtstag des Sängers Johann Michael Vogl; Punschlied; Trinklied; Verschwunden sind die Schmerzen (a cappella).* (i–iv) Quartets: *An die Sonne; Gebet; Die Geselligkeit (Lebenslust); Gott der Weltschöpfer; Gott im Ungewitter; Hymne an den Undenlichen; Nun lasst uns den Leib begraben (Begräbnislied); Des Tages Weihe; Der Tanz.*

(M) *** DG (IMS) 435 596-2 (2) [id.]. (i) Dame Janet Baker; (ii) Fischer-Dieskau; (iii) Ameling; (iv) Schreier; (v) Laubenthal; Gerald Moore; (vi) with Berlin RIAS Chamber Ch.

Not all these duets are vintage Schubert – some of the narrative pieces go on too long – but the artistry of Baker and Fischer-Dieskau makes for magical results. Gerald Moore, who is at his finest throughout the set, relishes the magic too. The trios are domestic music in the best sense. Specially delightful are the two contrasted drinking songs, but *The wedding feast (Die Hochzeitsbraten*) is even more remarkable, a 10-minute scena in the style of *opera buffa*. The quartets, like the trios, were written for various domestic occasions, but the use of four voices seems to have led the composer regularly to serious or religious subjects. These are sweet and gentle rather than intense inspirations, but one could hardly ask for more polished and inspired performances than these. Fine recording from 1973/4, giving the singers a vivid presence on CD.

Lieder: *Berthas Lied in der Nacht; Fischerweise; Der Fluss; Die Forelle; Die gefangenen Sanger; Gretchen vor der Mater dolorosa; Hagars Klage; Heimliches Lieben; Im Frühling; Iphigenia; Kolmas Klage; Der König in Thule; Lambertine; Liebe schwarmt auf allen Wegen; Lilla an die Morgenrote; Des Mädchens Kläge* (2 versions); *Die Rose; Schwestergruss; Szene der Delphine; Thekla, eine Geisterstimme; Vergissmeinnicht; Vom Mitleiden Marias; Wiegenlied.*

(B) *** DG Double 453 139-2 (2) [id.]. Gundula Janowitz, Irwin Gage.

This second collection from Janowitz and Gage starts with what is probably Schubert's first vocal work, written when he was fourteen, *Hagars Klage*. Many of the earlier items are extended works, complete scenas or songs of many stanzas. They require persuasive handling, and Janowitz is enormously helped by the sympathetic, concentrated accompaniments of Irwin Gage. With a voice so naturally beautiful, and used with such easy musical intelligence, the results are consistently compelling, whether in the rarities or the popular songs such as *Die Forelle*. The recording is first rate.

Church music

6 Antiphons for the Blessings of the Branches on Psalm Sunday; Auguste jam coelestium in G, D.488; Deutsche Messe, D.872 (with Epilogue, The Lord's Prayer); Graduale in C, D.184; Hymn to the Holy Ghost, D.964; Kyries: in D min., D.31; F, D.66; Lazarus, D.689; Magnificat in C, D.486; Offertorium (Totus in corde) in C, D.136; Offertorium (Tres sunt) in A min., D.181; 2 Offertoriums (Salve Regina) in F, D.223 & A, D.676; Psalm 23, D.706; Psalm 92, D.953; Salve Reginas: in B flat, D.106; in C, D.811; Stabat Mater in G min., D.175; Tantum ergo (3 settings) *in C, D.460/1 & D.739; Tantum ergo in D, D.750.*

(M) *** EMI Dig./Analogue CMS7 64783-2 (3). Popp, Donath, Rüggerberg, Venuti, Hautermann, Falk, Fassbaender, Greindl-Rosner, Dallapozza, Araiza, Protschka, Tear, Lika, Fischer-Dieskau, Capella Bavariae, Bav. R. Ch. & SO, Sawallisch.

Volume two of Sawallisch's great and rewarding Schubertian survey has much glorious music, sung with eloquence and richly recorded in the Munich Hercules Hall. Even some of the shortest items – such as the six tiny *Antiphons*, allegedly written in half an hour – have magic and originality in them. Plainer, but still glowing with Schubertian joy, is the so-called *Deutsche Messe*. The *Magnificat*, too, is a strongly characterized setting, and even the three settings of St Thomas Aquinas's *Tantum ergo* (all in C) have their charm. There are other surprises. The lovely setting of the *Offertorium in C (Totus in corde)* is for soprano, clarinet and orchestra, with the vocal and instrumental lines intertwining delectably, while the no less appealing *Auguste jam coelestium* is a soprano–tenor duet. The *Salve Regina in C*, D.811, is written for four male voices, *a cappella*, and they again contribute to the performance of *Psalm 23*, where Sawallisch provides a piano accompaniment. The religious drama, *Lazarus*, has the third CD to itself. Schubert left it unfinished and, though no more dramatic than his operas, it contains much delightful music. With Robert Tear in the name-role, Helen Donath as Maria, Lucia Popp as Jemima, Maria Venuti as Martha, Josef Protschka as Nathanael and Fischer-Dieskau as Simon, it is very strongly cast and the performance is splendid; indeed the singing is outstanding from chorus and soloists alike throughout this set, and the warm, well-balanced recording adds to one's pleasure.

Kyries: in B flat, D.45; D min., D.49; Masses Nos. 1 in F, D.105; 2 in G, D.167; 3 in B flat, D.324; 4 in C, D.452; 5 in A flat, D.678; 6 in E flat, D.950; Offertorium in B flat, D.963; Salve Reginas: in F, D.379; in B flat, D.386; Stabat Mater in F min., D.383; Tantum ergo in E flat, D.962.
(M) *** EMI Dig./Analogue CMS7 64778-2 (4). Popp, Donath, Fassbaender, Dallapozza, Schreier, Araiza, Protschka, Fischer-Dieskau, Bav. R. Ch. & SO, Sawallisch.

Sawallisch's highly distinguished survey of Schubert's church music was recorded in the early 1980s. This first volume is centred on his major Mass settings, especially his masterpiece in this form, the *E flat Mass*. Though the chorus is not flawless here, the performances are warm and understanding. The earlier Mass settings bring superb, lively inspirations, not to mention the separate *Kyries* and *Salve Reginas*. Excellent, cleanly focused sound, for the most part digital, with the benefit of the ambience of the Munich Herkules-Saal.

(i) *Lazarus* (cantata); (ii) *Mass in G, D.167.*
(M) *** Erato/Warner 4509 98533-2 (2). (i) Armstrong, Welting; (i–ii) Chamonin, Rolfe Johnson; (i) Hill; (i–ii) Egel, Ch. and New Fr. R. PO, Guschlbauer.

About 80 minutes of *Lazarus* survive, and then the work comes to an abrupt end in the middle of a soprano solo! Some of it is as touching as the finest Schubert, and other sections are little short of inspired; there are some thoroughly characteristic harmonic colourings and some powerful writing for the trombones. Much of it is very fine indeed; though it would be idle to pretend that its inspiration is even, no Schubertian would want to be without it, for the best of it is quite lovely. The singers and the French Radio forces are thoroughly persuasive, and it would be difficult to fault Theodore Guschlbauer's direction or the warm quality of the sound achieved by the engineers. The *G major Mass*, an earlier piece written when Schubert was only eighteen, has less depth and subtlety than the best of *Lazarus*; but there are some endearing moments and the *Agnus Dei* is poignant. Again the performance and recording here are excellent.

Masses Nos. 1–6 (complete); *Kyries in B flat, D.45; D min., D.49; Offertorium in B flat, D.963; Salve Reginas: in F, D.379; in B flat, D.386; Stabat Mater in F min., D.383; Tantum ergo in E flat, D.962.*
(M) *** EMI Dig./Analogue CMS7 64778-2 (4). Popp, Donath, Fassbaender, Dallapozza, Schreier, Araiza, Protschka, Fischer-Dieskau, Bav. R. Ch. & SO, Sawallisch.

Sawallisch's highly distinguished survey of Schubert's church music was recorded in the early 1980s. This first volume is centred on his major Mass settings, especially his masterpiece in this form, the *E flat Mass*. Though the chorus is not flawless here, the performances are warm and understanding. The earlier Mass settings bring superb, lively inspirations, not to mention the separate *Kyries* and *Salve Reginas*. Excellent, cleanly focused sound, for the most part digital, with the benefit of the ambience of the Munich Herkules-Saal.

Song-cycles

Song-cycles: *Die schöne Müllerin, D.795; Schwanengesang, D.957; Winterreise, D.911.* Lieder: *Du bist die Ruh'; Erlkönig; Nacht und Träume.*
(M) (***) EMI (SIS) mono CMS7 63559-2 (3). Dietrich Fischer-Dieskau, Gerald Moore.

Fischer-Dieskau's early mono versions may not match his later recordings in depth of insight, but already the young singer was a searching interpreter of these supreme cycles. Gerald Moore was, as ever, the most sympathetic partner.

Song-cycles: (i) *Die schöne Müllerin, D.795* (with spoken *Prologue* and *Epilogue*); *Schwanengesang, D.957; Winterreise, D.911.* (ii) *Einsamkeit, D.620.*
(M) **(*) EMI (SIS) CMS5 66146-2 (3). Dietrich Fischer-Dieskau, (i) Gerald Moore; (ii) Karl Engel.

Fischer-Dieskau's EMI recordings of the three song-cycles were made in 1961–2, around the time of the great baritone's fortieth birthday, and they represent the second wave of his Schubert interpretations. He was to re-record them, again with Gerald Moore, for DG with even greater thought and refinement, but the direct power of expression here is superb, too. For *Die schöne Müllerin*, he also included spoken versions of the *Prologue* and *Epilogue* (taken from the songs in Wilhelm Müller's cycle) which Schubert did not set. The snag is that in the case of *Die schöne Müllerin* the 1985 digital remastering has caused the voice to sound edgy and peaky at climaxes, although the other cycles, transferred later, are altogether smoother.

As an added bonus, following after *Schwanengesang*, we are offered a rarity: Schubert's 1818 setting of Johann Mayrhofer's poem in twelve stanzas, *Einsamkeit* ('Solitude'). At nearly 19 minutes, this is almost a mini-cycle in itself, moving on from its thoughtful opening to consider zestful youth, full of activity, the happiness of comradeship (celebrated with a charming waltz rhythm), longing and requited ecstasy, gloom, freedom and ambition, finally returning to the solitude of old age. The setting does not, perhaps, represent Schubert at his greatest, but Fischer-Dieskau follows the poet's mood-changes dramatically and with characteristic sensitivity, and the listener is thoroughly involved. The sound is excellent, and it is a pity that for this reissue EMI did not cue the individual verses. However, full translations are included.

Song-cycles: *Die schöne Müllerin; Schwanengesang* (with also: *Im Freien; Der Wanderer an den Mond; Das Zügenglöcklein*); *Winterreise*. Lieder: *Alinde; An den Monde; An die Leier; An die Laute; An die Musik; An Silvia; Dass sie hier gewesen; Der Einsame; Die Forelle; Frühlingsglaube; Im Frühling; Der Schiffer; Schwanengesang; Sei mir gegrüsset*. Goethe Lieder: *Ganymed; Geheimes; Heidenröslein; Liebhaber in allen Gestalten; Der Musensohn; Rastlose Liebe; Wandrers Nachtlied*.
(M) *** EMI CMS5 66145-2 (4). Olaf Bär, Geoffrey Parsons.

Die schöne Müllerin was the first of the cycles which Olaf Bär recorded, in 1986 in Dresden, with the voice fresher and more velvety than later. The tone is all the better-suited to this young man's cycle, even more when contrasted with Fischer-Dieskau's in the companion box of EMI's Schubert Edition, especially when the digital recording is so flattering to Bär's warmly beautiful lyrical flow. In *Winterreise*, recorded two years later, again with Geoffrey Parsons a masterful accompanist, Bär again finds a beauty of line and tone to outshine almost everyone, and his singing is both deeply reflective and strongly dramatic, if without quite the power of Fischer-Dieskau's poetic projection or the sheer intensity of Britten and Pears (see above). Yet the darkness of the close is given the electricity of live communication and the sound is again outstanding, with the voice again seeming wonderfully natural and the balance with the piano bringing intimacy in a helpful atmosphere. The third disc, recorded in 1989, amplifies the collection of late songs, posthumously published as *Schwanengesang*, with three well-chosen extra items from the same period, notably *Der Wanderer an den Mond*, where Bär brings out the agony and weariness of the traveller addressing the moon. The singing throughout is characteristically sensitive and dramatic, with *Ständchen* strong and passionate rather than light and charming. The fourth disc offers 21 miscellaneous songs, most of them favourites, including 7 Goethe settings. Recorded in 1991–2, they show the voice grittier than earlier, but still searchingly expressive, with Geoffrey Parsons again the most understanding accompanist. Admirers of Bär, among whom we may be counted, will find this set a splendid survey of his Schubertian achievement, made the more attractive by the high quality of the recording.

Die schöne Müllerin (song-cycle), *D.795*.
(B) *** CfP CD-CFP 4672 [(M) id.]. Ian and Jennifer Partridge.

Die schöne Müllerin (complete); *Die Forelle; Frühlingsglaube; Heidenröslein*.
(M) ** DG 447 452-2 [id.]. Fritz Wunderlich, Hubert Geisen.

(i) *Die schöne Müllerin, D.795*; (ii) *Ständchen*; (i) *Der Musensohn, D.764*.
(BB) ** RCA Navigator 74321 29241-2 [(M) id. import]. Fritz Wunderlich; (i) Kurt Heinz Stolze; (ii) Rolfe Reinhardt.

Ian Partridge's is an exceptionally fresh and urgent account. Rarely if ever on record has the dynamic quality of the cycle of Schubert songs been so effectively conveyed, rising to an emotional climax at the end of the first half with the song *Mein!*, expressing the poet's ill-found joy welling up infectiously. Partridge's subtle and beautiful range of tone is a constant delight, and he is most imaginatively accompanied by his sister, Jennifer. The balance of the 1973 recording is forward and present: this is an outstanding bargain reissue and should win many new friends for Lieder.

Fritz Wunderlich's recording was made in 1966 and won both a Grand Prix des Discophiles and L'Orphée d'Or when it appeared the following year. It now reappears as one of DG's 'Legendary Originals'. Wunderlich had one of the most headily beautiful voices among German tenors and that alone makes his record cherishable. But when he recorded the cycle (and the three favourite songs which are also included here), he had still to develop as a Lieder singer, and for so subtle a cycle the performance lacks detail. Moreover he was handicapped by a rather unimaginative accompanist, and the recording is unflattering to the piano.

Recorded in 1957, the earlier of Wunderlich's two recordings of the cycle has him at his freshest and most eager, with the voice full and forward. Sadly the accompaniments are stodgily played. However, his admirers will find that this Navigator reissue is very inexpensive.

Schwanengesang, D.957; Lieder: Am Bach in Frühling; An die Musik; Geheimes; Gruppe aus dem Tartarus; Im Abendrot; Im Frühling; Meerstille; Sei mir gegrüsst; Wandrers Nachtlied I & II.
(M) (***) EMI mono CDH5 65196-2. Hans Hotter, Gerald Moore.

As in his darkly searching account of *Winterreise*, also recorded in mono with Gerald Moore in the 1950s, this Schubert collection coupling *Schwanengesang* with other favourite songs reveals Hotter at his peak. The voice as recorded may not always be beautiful, but the gravity and intensity of the singing reveal a master Lieder-singer, as commanding here as in his Wagner interpretations.

(i) *Schwanengesang* (song-cycle), *D.957;* (ii) Lieder: *An die Laute; An die Musik; An Silvia; Auflösung; Der Einsame; Fischerweise; Die Forelle; Der Schiffer; Der Wanderer an den Mond; Wandrers Nachtlied.*
(BB) *** ASV Quicksilva CDQS 6171 [(M) id.]. (i) John Shirley-Quirk, Steuart Bedford; (ii) Ian Partridge, Jennifer Partridge.

This ASV reissue happily combines Schubert interpretations from two fine British artists, recorded in the late 1970s. *Schwanengesang*, containing some of Schubert's last and most memorable songs, presents the interpreter with an insuperable problem in that no single voice is suited to every one of them. John Shirley-Quirk's special success is in creating a feeling of unity over the whole group. He does this partly by strong characterization, with the contrasts calculated so that each song seems to prepare the way for the one that follows. The flowing lyricism of *Liebesbotschaft* is thus dramatically halted by the declamation of *Kriegers Ahnung*, and at the close of the collection the gradation of mood from *Am Meer*, through the powerful account of *Der Doppelgänger* (one of Schubert's most original and forward-looking inspirations) to the welcome release of tension for *Die Taubenpost* is masterly. Steuart Bedford provides equally imaginative accompaniments and the recording gives the artists good presence and an excellent balance. Ian Partridge then takes over for a well-chosen group of ten of the composer's most popular songs, and the fresh lyrical flow of his tenor voice gives much pleasure, making a pleasing change of vocal colour, matched by a comparable feeling for the Schubertian phrase. The intelligence of the interpretations complements the tonal beauty of the voice; if there is a criticism, it is that there is not enough variety of mood; warmth and flexibility are paramount, sometimes at the expense of dramatic emphasis. Jennifer Partridge accompanies sensitively and matches her brother's vocal smoothness. The one apparent drawback to this otherwise enjoyably generous (77-minute) collection is the absence of texts with translations – but they *are* available on request and without charge by writing to ASV.

Winterreise (song cycle), *D.911.*
(M) *** DG 447 421-2 [id.]. Dietrich Fischer-Dieskau, Joerg Demus.
✿ (M) *** Decca 417 473-2. Peter Pears, Benjamin Britten.
(B) *** DG Classikon 439 432-2 [(M) id. import]. Fischer-Dieskau, Barenboim.
(M) (***) EMI mono CDH7 61002-2 [id.]. Hans Hotter, Gerald Moore.
(M) **(*) DG (IMS) Dig. 445 521-2 [id.]. Christa Ludwig, James Levine.
(M) **(*) DG Dig. 453 987-2. Andreas Schmidt, Rudolf Jansen.
(BB) ** ASV CDQS 6085 [(M) id.]. Robert Tear, Philip Ledger.
(BB) ** Belart 461 334-2 [(M) id. import]. Gérard Souzay, Dalton Baldwin.

There are those who regard Fischer-Dieskau's third recording of *Winterreise* as the finest of all, such is the peak of beauty and tonal expressiveness that the voice had achieved in the mid-1960s, and the poetic restraint of Demus's accompaniment. The recording still sounds well, and as a mid-price reissue in DG's Legendary Recordings series it certainly makes an excellent alternative recommendation.

What is so striking about the Pears performance is its intensity. One continually has the sense of a live occasion and, next to it, even Fischer-Dieskau's beautifully wrought singing sounds too easy. As for Britten, he re-creates the music, sometimes with a fair freedom from Schubert's markings, but always with scrupulous concern for the overall musical shaping and sense of atmosphere. The sprung rhythm of *Gefror'ne Tränen* is magical in creating the impression of frozen teardrops falling, and almost every song brings similar magic. The recording and the CD transfer are exceptionally successful in bringing a sense of presence and realism.

Fischer-Dieskau's fifth recording of Schubert's greatest cycle, made in 1979, has now appeared on DG's Classikon bargain label, with the voice still in superb condition. Prompted by Barenboim's spontaneous-sounding, almost improvisatory accompaniments, it is highly inspirational. In expression this is freer than the earlier versions, and though some idiosyncratic details will not please everyone the sense of concentrated development is irresistible. The recording is very natural and beautifully balanced, and full translations are included.

Hans Hotter's 1954 mono recording of *Winterreise* brings an exceptionally dark, even sepulchral performance, lightened by the imagination of Gerald Moore's accompaniment. Hotter scales down his great Wagnerian baritone so that only occasionally is the tone gritty. His concern for detail brings many moments of illumination, but the lack of animation makes this an unrelievedly depressing view.

With James Levine a concentrated and often dramatic accompanist, consistently adding to the sense of spontaneous and immediate communication, Christa Ludwig gives a warmly satisfying performance, making use of the mature richness of the voice rather than bringing any striking new insights. Though the different sections of *Frühlingstraum*, for example, are beautifully contrasted, it is the extra darkness of the piano in low keys that adds most to the tragedy. Full, natural recording.

Andreas Schmidt with Rudolf Jansen offers a beautifully sung, thoughtfully presented version of the greatest and most demanding of all song-cycles. With forwardly balanced sound on this 1990 digital recording, words are strikingly clear, enhancing Schmidt's use of dramatic contrast, with the voice, generally smooth and even, acquiring the necessary bite at climaxes. Everything is perfectly controlled, almost too much so: it means that the poignant dénouement at the end, conveying even greater tragedy than on the surface it seems, is to a degree underplayed, leaving one dry-eyed.

It is good to have a super-bargain version of *Die Winterreise*, but the account by Robert Tear and Philip Ledger is disappointing from two artists who might have been expected to follow in the inspired tradition of Pears and Britten. It is partly the dryness and lack of bloom on the voice in the studio recording – with the piano sounding too close – which underlines a degree of squareness in the slower songs. The vigorous songs go much better, and the CD transfer has undoubtedly improved the sound, but the basic reservations remain.

Souzay's 1962 Philips version of *Winterreise* was his second, more intense and firmly held together than his first. As always with Souzay, musical values are paramount, and his clear, direct style communicates readily, especially when he has fine support from Dalton Baldwin. As so often, the closing song, *Der Leiermann*, is made to sound particularly poignant. However, in the last resort he hardly outshines either Peter Pears or Fischer-Dieskau. The Philips recording is excellent, but the snag with this budget reissue is the absence of translations.

(i) *Winterreise* (complete); Lieder: (ii) *An die Musik; An Sylvia; Auf dem See; Auf dem Wasser zu singen; Der Einsame;* (iii–iv) *Ellens Gesang III (Ave Maria);* (ii) *Erster verlust;* (iii–iv) *Die Forelle;* (ii) *Frühlingsglaube;* (iii–iv) *Ganymed;* (ii) *Gretchen am Spinnrade;* (iii; v–vi) *Der Hirt auf dem Felsen;* (iii; v) *Der Jüngling und der Tod;* (ii) *Der König in Thule; Lachen und Weinen; Der Musensohn; Nähe des Geliebten; Rastlose Liebe; Seligkeit;* (iii–iv) Ständchen; (ii) *Die Sterne*.

(B) **(*) EMI Rouge et Noir CZS5 72004-2 [(M) id. import]. (i) Gérard Souzay, Dalton Baldwin; (ii) Brigitte Fassbaender, Erik Werba; (iii) Elly Ameling; (iv) Jorg Demus; (v) Irwin Gage; (vi) with George Pieterson.

There are splendid things here. Souzay's 1976 account of the *Winterreise* does not find him in such fresh voice as his earlier (1962) version on Philips. But Souzay is still Souzay, and the Fassbaender and Ameling interpretations are memorable.

OPERA

Die Verschworenen (complete).

(M) *** CPO/EMI CPO 999 554-2. Eda Moser, Fuchs, Dallapozza, Schary, Moll, Finke, Bav. R. Ch., Munich RO, Wallberg.

Die Verschworenen ('The Conspirators') originally had to have that title changed to 'Domestic Warfare' from fear of the censors; but in fact it is a harmless variant on the old theme of Aristophanes' *Lysistrata*, with the wives of returning crusaders withholding their favours from their menfolk. Though the heroine's lovely minor-key *Romance* near the beginning with clarinet obbligato points to serious emotions, and there is a Weber-like storm passage, this is predominantly light-hearted, with ensemble passages which for the Anglo-Saxon listener will recall Gilbert and Sullivan, as in the fourth number, a chorus in which men are set against women. Much the longest number is the extended finale, structured like a Mozart operatic finale and here, as in Schubert's other one-act operas, there are hints that he had studied Beethoven's *Fidelio*. In this very well-made recording it proves a delightful piece, lasting just over an hour, brilliantly done, with no weak link in the Munich cast and with the bass, Kurt Moll, outstanding as Count Heribert. As in other issues in this CPO series of recordings originally made by EMI, there is no libretto but a good synopsis linked to the CD tracks, though the booklet has far too many misprints.

Der vierjährige Posten (complete).

(M) *** CPO/EMI CPO 999 553-2. Donath, Schreier, Fischer-Dieskau, Brokmeier, Lenz, Bav. R. Ch. & O, Wallberg.

Schubert wrote this one-act piece ('The Four-year Post') in 1815 at the age of eighteen. With little more than half an hour of music, including a substantial overture, its eight numbers have many characteristically Schubertian touches, not just in the flowing tunes but in foretastes of the *Rosamunde* music. More intriguingly, in this rather slight story set in a border village threatened by war, they suggest that Schubert had already heard and studied Beethoven's *Fidelio*, first given in its final form in Vienna the previous year. The similarity of the military music is particularly striking. Apart from the overture, the only extended number (and the only real aria) is the prayer of Kätchen, the heroine, which in its calm beauty seems to anticipate Agathe's aria, *Und ob die Volke*, in Weber's *Der Freischütz* of six years later. The cast in this recording, originally made by EMI–Electrola, is an outstanding one, with star singers forming a splendid team. Highly recommended, the only reservation concerning the piece's brevity. No libretto is provided, only a synopsis.

Die Zwillingsbrüder (complete).

(M) *** CPO/EMI CPO 999 556-2. Donath, Gedda, Moll, Fischer-Dieskau, Munich State Op. Ch., Bav. RSO, Sawallisch.

Die Zwillingsbrüder ('The Twin brothers'), completed in 1819, deftly tells the story of twin brothers, strikingly contrasted, both returning from serving in the army, the one a rough-diamond of a soldier, the other – thought to be dead – the devoted lover. Inevitably this leads to confusion, resolved only at the end in a conventional but winning way. When Fischer-Dieskau takes the roles of both twins – who never appear on stage together – the result is delightful, with Schubert inspired to sparkling music, and with the brothers' contrasting characters well conveyed in their respective arias. The ten numbers plus overture last well under 50 minutes, making this a very viable piece for revival today. With Sawallisch drawing superb playing and singing from the whole team, this comes near to being an ideal performance, not just starrily cast but very well recorded.

Schuman, William (1910–92)

In praise of Shahn (Canticle for orchestra); (i) *To thee old cause (Evocation for oboe, brass, timpani, piano and strings).*

(M) *** Sony SMK 63088 [id.]. (i) Gomberg (oboe); NYPO, Bernstein – BARBER: *Adagio for strings; Violin concerto.* ***

Both of these works are commemorative. *To thee old cause* is dedicated to the memory of Dr Martin Luther King, and the score quotes from Walt Whitman ('*Thou peerless, passionate, good cause, Thou stern, remorseless, sweet idea*'). It features an oboe obbligato within its string textures which are reinforced by brass sonorities. In a single movement, its *Larghissimo* opening is intense and evocative; thereafter there are frequently shifting moods, although poignant lyrical feeling predominates, and the final gentle resolution suggests an acceptance of the human condition. *In praise of* (Ben) *Shahn* remembers the New York artist. It is in two sections, marked *Vigoroso* and *Lento*, although both (drawing on Eastern European Jewish folk material) include dynamic and expressive writing; indeed the closing section is full of rhythmic energy. This is music which in its atmosphere and use of dissonance often looks back to Charles Ives, although Schuman's own individual voice is never submerged. Bernstein is in his element and neither piece could receive more passionate advocacy. The (1970) Avery Fisher Hall recording is very immediate but has plenty of atmosphere too.

New England triptych.

(M) *** Mercury [432 755-2]. Eastman-Rochester O, Howard Hanson – IVES: *Symphony No. 3* etc. ***; MENNIN: *Symphony No. 5.* **(*)

William Schuman is not as outrageously original as Ives, but his sound-world is individual and wholly American. Each of the three pieces is an orchestral anthem, the first a thrustingly vibrant *Hallelujah*; the second is in the form of a round, and the finale features a marching song. Splendidly alive playing and excellent (1963) Mercury recording, admirably transferred to CD.

Symphonies Nos. 3; 5 (Symphony for strings); 8.

❁ (M) *** Sony SMK 63163 [id.]. NYPO, Leonard Bernstein.

William Schuman was born in the same year as Samuel Barber; in his youth he was a keen jazz musician and led his own group ('Billy Schuman and His Alamo Society Orchestra'). After leaving Columbia University, he studied with Roy Harris, whose powerful sense of line, rhythmic momentum and harmonic vocabulary were not lost on him. Schuman's classical sympathies surfaced in a series of ten symphonies. The first two were suppressed; indeed a listener to CBS wrote to him after a Boston Symphony broadcast of the *Second*, saying that his symphony made him 'lose faith in the power of aspirin tablets'. The *Third* (1941) is (to quote Bernstein) 'alive, radiant and optimistic', and it is without question a masterpiece which repays repeated listening. It has the sweep and power of Harris, the freshness of Copland and an entirely individual and compelling atmosphere. Bernstein's 1960 recording is superb – and superior to his later re-make for DG. The *Symphony for strings* comes from 1943 and was given in England at the first International Society for Contemporary Music Festival after the war. It is consistently imaginative, with a highly developed and sophisticated harmonic vocabulary – and is among his best works. The *Eighth Symphony* (1962), commissioned by the New York Philharmonic, is perhaps less inspired – but, make no mistake, its two companions on this record are among the finest symphonies of our time. First-rate performances and eminently serviceable recordings, all emanating from the 1960s and expertly restored. Let us hope that Sony will reissue the *Sixth*, which Ormandy coupled with the Piston *Fourth* in the days of LP. However, the present disc is a must.

Schumann, Robert (1810–56)

Cello concerto in A min., Op. 129.

(M) *** Mercury (IMS) 432 010-2 [id.]. Janos Starker, LSO, Skrowaczewski – LALO: *Concerto* **(*); SAINT-SAENS: *Concerto.* ***

(BB) *** Naxos Dig. 8.550938 [id.]. Kliegel, Nat. SO of Ireland, Constantine – BRAHMS: *Double concerto.* ***

(B) *** Decca Eclipse Dig. 448 712-2; *448 712-4* [(M) id. import]. Lynn Harrell, Cleveland O, Marriner – LALO; SAINT-SAENS: *Concertos.* ***

(M) *** Sony Dig. SMK 60151 [id.]. Ma, Bav. RSO, Sir Colin Davis – DVORAK: *Cello concerto.* ***

(M) * DG (IMS) Dig. 445 574-2. Maisky, VPO, Bernstein – DVORAK: *Concerto.*

The Schumann *Cello concerto* is not generously represented at the mid-price or bargain end of the catalogue; Janos Starker gives a persuasive account of it that is thoroughly sensitive to the letter and spirit of the score. Skrowaczewski accompanies with spirit and without the rather explosive, clipped tutti chords that rather disfigure the Lalo with which it is coupled. The 1962 recording is amazing for its age: people make great claims for these early Mercury recordings and, judging from this expertly engineered disc, rightly so!

In the Schumann, well coupled with the Brahms *Double concerto*, Maria Kliegel takes a spacious, lyrical view of the first movement. She then builds up the power of the performance, helped by sympathetic support from Constantine and the Irish orchestra, spontaneously expressive. The central *Langsam* brings simple, dedicated playing and, as in the Brahms coupling, Kliegel points the finale wittily, not least in the second subject. The soloist is well balanced, with good, immediate Naxos sound

Harrell's is a big-scale reading, strong and sympathetic, made the more powerful by the superb accompaniment from the Cleveland Orchestra. Its controversial point is that he expands the usual cadenza with a substantial sequence of his own. The digital recording is outstandingly fine.

As always, Yo-Yo Ma's playing is distinguished by great refinement of expression, and his account of the *Concerto* is keenly affectionate, although at times he carries tonal sophistication to excess and drops suddenly into *sotto voce* tone and near-inaudibility. Both he and Sir Colin Davis are thoroughly attuned to the sensibility of this composer. The balance, both between soloist and orchestra and within the various departments of the orchestra, blends perfectly.

Like the coupled Dvořák *Concerto*, Maisky's recording was taken from live performances. Bernstein seems reluctant to let the music speak for itself, and this affects the eloquent, generous-toned soloist, who similarly has moments of self-indulgence. This is not as perversely eccentric as the coupling, but even in its own right it can hardly be recommended for repeated listening.

(i) *Cello concerto in A min.;* (ii) *Piano concerto in A min.*

(M) **(*) DG 449 100-2. (i) Rostropovich, Leningrad PO, Rozhdestvensky; (ii) Argerich, Nat. SO of Washington, Rostropovich.

Rostropovich's DG performance of the *Cello concerto* is superbly made, introspective yet at the same time outgoing, with a peerless technique at the command of a rare artistic imagination. The sound is vivid. In the *Piano concerto* Rostropovich moves to the rostrum and Argerich takes on the role of soloist. The partnership produces a performance which is full of contrast – helped by a recording of wide dynamic range – and strong in temperament. There is an appealing delicacy in the *Andantino* and the outer movements have plenty of vivacity and colour. Yet in the last analysis the work's special romantic feeling does not fully blossom here, although the playing is not without poetry. The recording is admirably lifelike and well balanced.

(i) *Cello concerto;* (ii) *Piano concerto in A min.;* (iii) *Violin concerto in D min.;* (ii) *Introduction and allegro appassionata;* (iv) *Konzertstück in F for four horns and orchestra, Op. 86.*

(B) **(*) EMI Rouge et Noir Analogue/Dig. CZS5 69692-2 (2) [CDZB 69692]. (i) Paul Tortelier, RPO, Yan-Pascal Tortelier; (ii) Barenboim, LPO, Fischer-Dieskau; (iii) Kremer, Philh. O, Muti; (iv) Hauptmann, Klier, Kohler, Seifert, BPO, Tennstedt.

This is a useful collection of Schumann's concertante works and it is a pity that it is let down somewhat by Barenboim's rather too direct account of the works for piano (see below). Tortelier's is a characteristically inspirational performance of the *Cello concerto*, at its most concentrated in the hushed rendering of the slow movement. The soloist's son matches the warmth of his father's playing in the accompaniment, and both are suitably spirited in the finale. This is a less individual account than Jacqueline du Pré's, but the (1978) orchestral sound is a marked improvement on her version. The *Violin concerto* comes off pretty well in the hands of Gidon Kremer. Its vein of introspection seems to suit him, and he gives a generally sympathetic account of it and has very good support from the Philharmonia under Riccardo Muti. It is not Schumann at his most consistently inspired, but there are good things in it, including a memorable second subject and a characteristic slow movement which Kremer plays very touchingly. The (digital) recording was made in the Kingsway Hall in 1982 and is full-bodied, vivid and convincingly balanced. What makes this two-disc set well worth considering in EMI's Rouge et Noir series (offering two CDs for the price of one) is the inclusion of the exuberant *Konzertstück* with its brilliant horn playing. The four soloists from the Berlin Philharmonic play with superbly ripe virtuosity, and Tennstedt's direction is both urgent and expansive. The 1978 recording is admirably full-blooded.

(i) *Cello concerto in A min., Op. 129;* (ii) *Piano concerto in A min., Op. 54; Introduction and allegro appassionato, Op. 92.*

(M) ** EMI CDM7 64626-2 [id.]. (i) Jacqueline du Pré, New Philh. O, Barenboim; (ii) Barenboim, LPO, Dietrich Fischer-Dieskau.

The most attractive performance here is Jacqueline du Pré's 1968 recording of the *Cello concerto*. Her spontaneous style is strikingly suited to this most recalcitrant of concertos and the slow movement is particularly beautiful. She is ably assisted by Daniel Barenboim, and the only snag is the rather faded orchestral sound, unflattered by the present transfer, though the cello timbre is realistically focused. The coupling was recorded in the mid-1970s; the sound is somewhat firmer and the balance lets the piano dominate but, with the LPO below its best under Fischer-Dieskau (a good but not outstanding conductor), this is probably just as well. Barenboim is brisk and not particularly poetic, and these performances lack what he usually achieves on record: a sense of spontaneity, a simulation of a live performance.

Piano concerto in A min., Op. 54.

(M) *** Ph. 446 192-2. Kovacevich, BBC SO, Sir Colin Davis – GRIEG: *Concerto; Sonata.* ***

(M) (***) EMI mono CDH7 69792-2. Lipatti, Philh. O, Karajan – MOZART: *Piano concerto No. 21.* (*(**))

(M) (**(*)) EMI CDM5 66597-2. Walter Gieseking, Phil. O, Karajan – FRANCK: *Symphonic variations;* GRIEG: *Piano concerto.* (**(*))

(M) **(*) Decca 417 728-2. Radu Lupu, LSO, Previn – GRIEG: *Concerto.* **(*)

(M) *** RCA [60420-2-RG]. Van Cliburn, Chicago SO, Reiner – MACDOWELL: *Concerto No. 2.* **(*)

(M) *** RCA 09026 62691-2 [id.]. Van Cliburn, Chicago SO, Reiner – PROKOFIEV: *Piano concerto No. 3.* **(*)

(B) **(*) Decca 433 628-2. Gulda, VPO, Andrae – FRANCK: *Symphonic variations* *** ❀ ; GRIEG: *Concerto.* ***

(B) **(*) [EMI Red Line Dig. CDR5 69859]. Cécile Ousset, LPO, Masur – GRIEG: *Piano concerto.* **(*)

(BB) **(*) ASV Dig. CDQS 6092 [(M) id.]. Osorio, RPO, Bátiz – FRANCK: *Symphonic variations* **(*); RAVEL: *Left-hand concerto* ***; SAINT-SAENS: *Wedding-cake.* ***

(M) ** [RCA Basic 100 09026 68454-2; *68454-4*]. Rubinstein, Chicago SO, Giulini – TCHAIKOVSKY: *Piano concerto No. 1.* ***

(M) ** [RCA Basic 100 09026 62677-2]. Rubinstein, Chicago SO, Giulini – GRIEG: *Piano concerto.* **

(BB) ** Naxos Dig. 8.550118 [id.]. Jenö Jandó, Budapest SO, Ligeti – GRIEG: *Concerto.* **

(BB) ** ASV CDQS 6003 [(M) id. import]. Vásáry, N. Sinf. – CHOPIN: *Concerto No. 2.* **

(M) (**) Avid mono AMC 593 [id.]. Myra Hess, SO, Walter Goehr – FRANCK: *Symphonic variations;* GRIEG: *Piano concerto.* (**)

(B) *(*) Decca Eclipse Dig. 448 235-2; *448 235-4*. Jorge Bolet, Berlin RSO, Chailly – GRIEG: *Piano concerto.* *

(BB) *(*) EMI Seraphim CES5 68522-2 (2) [CDEB 68522]. John Ogdon, New Philh. O, Berglund – GRIEG: *Concerto* *(*); *Peer Gynt* ***; FRANCK: *Symphonic variations for piano and orchestra.* *(*)

Piano concerto in A min.; Introduction and allegro appassionato, Op. 92; Introduction and allegro, Op.134.

(BB) ** Naxos Dig. 8.550277 [id.]. Sequeira Costa, Gulbenkian O, Gunzenhauser.

(i; ii) *Piano concerto in A min.;* (i; iii) *Introduction and allegro appassionato, Op. 92. Novellette in F, Op. 21/1; Toccata in C, Op. 7; Waldszenen, Op. 82.*

(M) **(*) DG stereo/mono 447 440-2 [id.]. Sviatoslav Richter, with (i) Warsaw Nat. PO, (ii) Witold Rowicki, (iii) Stanislaw Wislocki.

(i) *Piano concerto in A min. Arabeske in C, Op. 18.*

(M) *** Mercury 432 011-2 [id.]. Byron Janis, Minneapolis SO, Skrowaczewski – TCHAIKOVSKY: *Piano concerto No. 1.* **(*)

(i) *Piano concerto in A min. Arabeske; Etudes symphoniques, Op. 13.*

(M) *** RCA 09026 61444-2 [id.]. Rubinstein; (i) RCA Victor SO, Krips.

(M) **(*) DG (IMS) Dig. 445 522-2 [id.]. Pollini; (i) BPO, Abbado.

(i) *Piano concerto in A min.; Carnaval; Kinderszenen (Scenes from childhood), Op. 15.*

(B) **(*) DG Classikon 439 476-2 [(M) id. import]. Wilhelm Kempff; (i) Bav. RSO, Kubelik.

Our primary recommendation for this favourite Romantic concerto remains with the successful symbiosis of Stephen Kovacevich and Sir Colin Davis, who give an interpretation which is both fresh and poetic, unexaggerated but powerful in its directness and clarity, and the spring-like element of the outer movements is finely presented by orchestra and soloist alike. The sound has been admirably freshened, and this is even more attractive at mid-price.

It is good to have Rubinstein's early (1958) New York (Manhattan Center) recording of the *A minor Piano concerto* restored to the catalogue as it is clearly preferable to his later, Chicago version, which suffered from a more restricted dynamic range, and few apologies have to be made for the sound. Rubinstein takes the allegros of these two interconnected movements (separated by the charming *Intermezzo*) at comparatively modest speeds and he achieves the ideal compromise between an impression of spontaneous poetry in quieter passages (his rubato is marked but most natural) and a firm overall control. It is interesting that the conductor here, Josef Krips, was also the conductor on Kempff's old mono recording, which was also notable for its relaxed allegros, and one wonders what influence he had in the matter. As couplings, we are offered Rubinstein's 1969 recording of the *Arabeske*, aristocratic in feeling and with nuances of rubato to remind us of his Chopin. The *Etudes symphoniques* were recorded at a live recital in Carnegie Hall in 1961, and the commanding playing is made the more gripping by the communication with the audience – witness the burst of adrenalin at the *Allegro marcato* (*Etude No. 4*) and the variations which follow.

Kempff, after a rather positive account of the opening chords of the *Piano concerto*, proceeds characteristically to produce an unending stream of poetry. The dialogue of the *Intermezzo* is like an intimate conversation overheard. Tempi are generally leisurely, notably so in the finale where, with fine support from the Bavarian Radio Orchestra under Kubelik, the main theme has an engaging lilt. Good early-1970s recording. Of the solo recordings neither is among Kempff's more compelling Schumann performances. The comparatively extrovert style of *Carnaval* does not seem to suit him too well and there is no special degree of illumination such as we expect from this artist either here or in the *Scenes from childhood*. Good rather than outstanding piano recording, made in the same period as the concerto.

Pascal Devoyon is aristocratic without being aloof, pensive without being self-conscious, and brilliant without being flashy. Natural musicianship and artistry are always in evidence, and at bargain price this is very competitive, with excellent playing from the LPO under Jerzy Maksymiuk.

Byron Janis's Schumann *Concerto* is a lovely performance, and the 1962 recording sounds amazingly improved over its previous incarnations, especially in regard to the orchestra. Janis's reading finds an almost perfect balance between the need for romantic ardour and intimacy in the *Concerto* – the exchanges between the piano and the woodwind soloists in the first movement are most engagingly done. Skrowaczewski provides admirable support throughout, and this is highly recommendable too.

Dinu Lipatti's celebrated EMI recording has acquired classic status and will more than repay study. The transfer is excellent. A splendidly aristocratic account in very acceptable sound.

Gieseking's 1953 recording with Karajan and the Philharmonia was overshadowed at the time by Lipatti's version. There is much to relish in Gieseking's refined performance – and in particular the exquisite intermezzo. It is well worth reviving, and Andrew Walter's transfer is first class.

Lupu's clean boldness of approach to the first movement is appealingly fresh, but the fusing together of the work's disparate masculine and feminine Romantic elements has not been solved entirely. The digital CD transfer is especially telling in the quieter moments, but tuttis are less transparent than with a digital recording.

Van Cliburn's performance is very persuasive, the first movement rhapsodical in feeling, certainly poetic but exciting too. The *Intermezzo* is pleasingly fresh and the finale admirably buoyant and spirited. Altogether this is most attractive, and so is the unusual MacDowell coupling. However, this also comes with an alternative coupling of Prokofiev, a brilliant performance but with a less naturally balanced recording, drawing one's attention to the well-integrated sound-picture offered in the Schumann *Concerto*, where the Chicago ambience adds characteristic warmth. This version is available only in the USA.

Gulda's account is refreshingly direct yet, with light, crisp playing, never sounds rushed. The *Intermezzo* remains delicate in feeling, with nicely pointed pianism. The finale is just right, with an enjoyable rhythmic lift, and the early stereo (1956), though a little dated, is fully acceptable.

Cécile Ousset, with sympathetic support from Masur, gives a spirited account of the Schumann *Concerto*, like the Grieg coupling rather weightier than one might have expected but not lacking sparkle, while the central dialogue with the orchestra is delightfully done.

Pollini's account of the concerto is not without tenderness and poetry (witness the slow movement), but he is at times rather business-like and wanting in freshness. He is handicapped by rather unventilated recording and an inconsistent balance. (The piano seems much further back in the slow movement by comparison with the first.) The coupled piano pieces, however, are in every way successful. His account of the *Symphonic studies* has a symphonic gravitas and concentration; it also has the benefit of excellent recorded quality. Pollini includes the five additional variations that Schumann omitted from both the editions published during his lifetime, placing them as a group between the fifth and sixth variations.

This reissue in DG's 'Originals' series does not always represent Richter at his very finest. The performance of the concerto is not as interesting as one would expect. Its opening speed is fast and the interpretation is in the main without idiosyncrasy, but only in the finale does one really feel that vibrant quality in his playing which marks Richter out among even the great virtuosos. One might hypothesize that the comparative sluggishness of the orchestra affected Richter's concentration. Not that the concerto and the *Introduction and allegro appassionato* (one of Schumann's less interesting works) lack style, but the tension could be greater, particularly in the latter. The focus of the late-1950s Polish recording has been improved in the concerto but in Opus 92 remains a little fuzzy around the edges, not quite up to the standard one expects from DG. The *Novellette* and *Toccata* are fabulous performances, full of hair-raising virtuosity, but shaped with an unerring sense of style and musical as well as technical control. The piano tone is dry but clear. The *Waldszenen* is a mono recording, taken from an earlier LP collection, recorded in 1956. It is beautifully played, Richter very much the poet of the forest, and the mono sound gives no cause for complaint.

Jorge Federico Osorio's account of the Schumann *Concerto* is boldly romantic yet in no way lacking in poetry. The central *Intermezzo* is beautifully in scale, but in the first movement, with Bátiz bringing strong support in the tuttis, he presses on impulsively, and the finale has similar urgency. Some may prefer a more relaxed romanticism, but there is no lack of spontaneity here and the result is undoubtedly fresh and involving. Excellent recording and recommendable couplings make this disc a genuine bargain.

More than most of his 1960s recordings, Rubinstein's account of the Schumann *Concerto* with Giulini suffers seriously from the absence of real pianissimos. The use of Chicago's Orchestra Hall has brought a warm orchestral sound and a pleasingly real piano image, but the forward balance means that everything, apart from the big orchestral tuttis, seems to continue at a pervading *mezzo forte*. There is much that is beautiful in Rubinstein's actual playing but, in his interchanges both with the wind soloists in the first movement and with the strings in the *Intermezzo*, there is little light and shade, and the gay little march theme across the beat, from the orchestra in the finale, is also too loud. This recording comes with two different couplings (both in RCA's Basic 100 series) of which the Tchaikovsky concerto is much to be preferred.

Despite his considerable reputation and distinction, the Portuguese pianist Sequeira Costa has made relatively few commercial records. This 1984 recording of the *A minor concerto* is unidiosyncratic and very well played, but perhaps not sufficiently special or insightful to offer much of a challenge to Byron Janis or Lipatti. This collection deserves some consideration for bringing the *Introduction and allegro appassionato*, Op. 92, to wider notice and for offering the *Introduction and allegro*, Op. 134. Good and musicianly though these performances are, they fall short of real distinction and suffer from the dryish recording in which orchestral tutti do not sufficiently expand.

Jenö Jandó and the Budapest orchestra under Ligeti give a well-prepared and keenly alive account of the Schumann, and they are decently recorded. However, the better is the enemy of the good and, with players of such stature as Kovacevich, Lupu and Lipatti all available, this can be praised rather than recommended.

Tamás Vásáry directing from the keyboard gives a characteristically refined yet strong account of the concerto, free from eccentricity and thoroughly straightforward. Poetic, likeable and decently recorded, this is quite recommendable for those wanting a super-bargain coupling. The recording is excellent.

Myra Hess's account of the *A minor concerto* dominated the scene during the war years and is a good rather than outstanding example of her pianism. She was a fine interpreter of Schumann, as she was of the Beethoven *G major*, but this is not quite as impressive as one's youthful memory suggested. Indeed listening to it came as something of a disappointment. Of course it has moments of great poetry, but the performance as a whole is not superior to Lipatti, Lupu or her pupil, Kovacevich. Perhaps the dryish orchestral sound may contribute to this impression, for these Avid transfers are curiously lacking in a natural fullness of ambience.

Jorge Bolet's Schumann is rather more successful than his Grieg, but he does not show any true feeling for this repertoire. The performance is agreeably relaxed – the short central movement comes off best – but the interplay between wind soloists and pianist in the first movement seems disappointingly matter-of-fact and the finale tends towards heaviness. The recording is admirable.

John Ogdon, as in the other works on this well-transferred CD, is unexpectedly below form in what should be one of the most poetic of piano concertos. Clearly the partnership with Berglund did not work well. The interchanges with the orchestral wind soloists in the first movement are lacklustre and the performance overall refuses to catch fire.

(i) *Piano concerto in A min., Op. 54;* (ii) *Violin concerto in D min.*
(M) *(**) Teldec/Warner Dig. 4509 90696-2 [id.]. (i) Argerich; (ii) Kremer; COE, Harnoncourt.

In her live recording of the *Piano concerto*, Martha Argerich gives a vividly compelling, characteristically volatile reading, at once poetic and full of fancy, powerful and often wildly individual. The performance, recorded in the Stefaniensaal, Graz, in July 1992 culminates in an account of the finale so daring one wants to cheer at the end, so freely does the adrenalin flow. Though the orchestra is hard-pressed to keep up with her at her fast basic speed, there is a splendid swing to the rhythm and no sense of haste. The central *Andantino grazioso* too brings fantasy and flair, a freely spontaneous reading; but, earlier, the first movement takes some time to settle down. Argerich plays with her usual concentration, but her wilfulness seems to unsettle the players, and the woodwind ensemble at the start is surprisingly rough, not at all typical of this superb orchestra. Kremer's performance of the still-neglected *Violin concerto* is disappointing in comparison with the warmth and bravura of his earlier version, recorded for EMI with Riccardo Muti and the Philharmonia Orchestra. Not only is the speed of the first movement slower, Kremer sounds heavy and over-emphatic to the point of self-consciousness. The slow movement then lacks the magic it had before, the hushed tenderness that made one listen intently, beautiful as Kremer's playing still is. When it comes to the finale, the choice of speed is wildly eccentric, a half-speed such as you would use for a rehearsal, dull and plodding despite the efforts of the orchestra. In neither concerto is the recorded sound ideally warm or full-bodied, with tuttis rather muddy in texture.

(i) *Piano concerto in A min., Op. 54;* (ii) *Abendlied, Op. 85/12; Adagio and Allegro in A flat, Op. 70; Fantasiestücke, Op. 73; 3 Romances, Op. 94; 5 Stücke im Volkston, Op. 102.* (Piano) *Etudes symphoniques, Op. 13. Fantasia in C, Op. 17; Fantasiestücke, Op. 12; Kinderszenen, Op. 15; Kreisleriana, Op. 16.*
(M) *** Ph. Brendel Edition Analogue/Dig. 446 925-2 (5). Alfred Brendel, with (i) LSO, Abbado; (ii) Heinz Holliger – BRAHMS: *Piano concertos; Ballades* etc. ***

Brendel's is a fresh, thoughtful account of the *Piano concerto*, missing something of the work's delicate romantic feeling in the slow movement; but on the whole this is a satisfying reading, not lacking in poetry. Neither the orchestral response under Abbado nor the Philips recording will seriously disappoint. It was a curious idea to include the series of pieces with oboe, beautifully though Holliger plays. They are available separately – see below. But the piano music is all well chosen. The very opening of the *Fantasiestücke*, Op. 12, demonstrates magically spontaneous playing; both this and the *Fantasia in C* are full of imaginative touches of colour, strong as well as poetic. The digital sound is rather more forward than one would encounter in the recital room, but it serves Brendel well and truthfully conveys the depth of timbre. *Kinderszenen* and *Kreisleriana* bring more thoughtful and poetically characterized playing from Brendel, and he is again very well recorded, while the *Etudes symphoniques* are ardent and yet beautifully controlled, again given first-class digital sound.

Violin concerto in D min., Op. posth.
(B) **(*) EMI forte (SIS) CZS5 69334-2 (2) [CDFB 69334]. Gidon Kremer, Philh. O, Muti – BRAHMS: *Violin concerto* *(*); SIBELIUS: *Concerto.* **

The vein of introspection in the Schumann *Violin concerto* seems to suit Gidon Kremer, who gives a generally sympathetic account of it and has very good support from the Philharmonia Orchestra under Riccardo Muti. It is not Schumann at his most consistently inspired, but there are good things in it, including a memorable second subject and a characteristic slow movement. The recording is full-bodied, vivid and convincingly balanced. However, the coupled pair of concertos are much less recommendable and, although the sonata recital with Gavrilov (for details, see under the Brahms coupling) brings much to praise, overall this forte set joins the 'curate's eggs' of which the bargain catalogue has no shortage.

Violin concerto in D (edited Schunemann and Kulenkampff).

(B) (***) Dutton Lab. mono CDEA 5018 [(M) id.]. Georg Kulenkampff, BPO, Hans Schmidt-Isserstedt (with MOZART: *Adagio* from *Violin concerto in A, K.219* (***)) – BEETHOVEN: *Violin concerto.* (***) 

This recording was made in 1937, and the score includes an extensive revision of the solo violin part made by the soloist. His version sounds completely convincing and, despite the repetitive finale, the work is redeemed by the lovely slow movement which, surprisingly, reminds the listener more than once of Elgar's concerto. Kulenkampff plays it with radiant lyricism, and the recording in this new Dutton transfer sounds astonishingly good for its age, if not quite as impressive as the Beethoven coupling. The Mozart *Adagio* makes an exquisite final encore.

Introduction and Allegro appassionato in G, Op. 92.

(B) *** Decca Double Dig./Analogue 455 957-2 (2) [id.]. András Schiff, VPO, Dohnányi – DVORAK: *Cello concerto* etc. ***

(B) **(*) Sony SBK 48166; *SBT 48166* [id.]. Rudolf Serkin, Phd. O, Ormandy – BRAHMS: *Concerto No. 1* **(*); MENDELSSOHN: *Capriccio brillant.* **

The *Introduction and Allegro appassionato in G major* brings the full flowering of Schumann's romanticism. Schiff and Dohnányi play it with dedication and commitment, and the recording, while favouring the soloist, is more realistic in balance than for the Dvořák coupling.

Serkin plays this somewhat elusive work with his accustomed panache and he is given excellent support from Ormandy. The piano-tone could be fuller in timbre but the overall effect has considerable warmth, and those looking for a recording of this relatively unfamiliar piece will find much here to arrest them. The Brahms coupling also shows Serkin at his finest.

Symphonies Nos. 1–4.

(M) *** DG 429 672-2 (2). BPO, Karajan.

(B) *** RCA 74321 20294-2 (2) [(M) id. import]. Phd. O, James Levine.

(B) **(*) DG Double Dig. 453 049-2 (2) [id.]. VPO, Bernstein.

(B) ** EMI forte Dig. CZS5 69370-2 (2). Cologne RSO, Hans Vonk.

(B) ** Decca Double Dig. 452 214-2 (2) [(M) id. import]. Cleveland O, Dohnányi.

Symphonies Nos. 1 in B flat (Spring), Op. 38; 2 in C, Op. 61.

(B) *** Sony SBK 48269; *SBT 48269* [id.]. Bav. RSO, Kubelik.

Symphonies Nos. 3 in E flat (Rhenish), Op. 97; 4 in D min., Op. 120; Overture Manfred, Op. 115.

(B) *** Sony SBK 48270; *SBT 48270* [id.]. Bav. RSO, Kubelik.

Symphonies Nos. 1–4: Manfred overture, Op. 115.

(M) **(*) Sony MH2K 62349 (2) [M2K 62349]. Cleveland O, George Szell.

Symphonies Nos. 1–4; Overture, scherzo and finale, Op. 52.

(M) *** EMI CMS7 64815-2 (2). Dresden State O, Sawallisch.

Symphonies Nos. 1–4; Overture, scherzo and finale in E, Op. 52; Overture: Hermann und Dorothea, Op. posth. 136.

(B) *(*) RCA Twofer 74321 34172-2 (2). Leipzig GO, Masur.

Karajan's interpretations of the Schumann *Symphonies* stand above all other recordings on modern instruments. No. 1 is a beautifully shaped performance, with orchestral playing of the highest distinction; No. 2 is among the most powerful ever recorded, combining poetic intensity and intellectual strength in equal proportions; and No. 3 is also among the most impressive versions ever commited to disc: its famous fourth-movement evocation of Cologne Cathedral is superbly spacious and eloquent, with quite magnificent brass playing. No. 4 can be classed alongside Furtwängler's famous record, with Karajan similarly inspirational, yet a shade more self-disciplined than his illustrious predecessor. However, the reissued complete set brings digital remastering which – as with the Brahms symphonies – has leaner textures than before, while in tuttis the violins above the stave may approach shrillness.

The Dresden CDs of the Schumann *Symphonies* under Sawallisch are as deeply musical as they are carefully considered; the orchestral playing combines superb discipline with refreshing naturalness and spontaneity. Sawallisch catches all Schumann's varying moods, and his direction has splendid vigour. These recordings have dominated the catalogue, alongside Karajan's, for some years and they are most welcome on CD. Although the reverberant acoustic brought a degree of edge to the upper strings, the sound-picture has the essential fullness which the Karajan transfers lack, and the remastering has cleaned up the upper range to a considerable extent. The set now appears in a mid-priced box and the individual

CDs have been restored: CDM7 69471-2 (*Symphonies Nos. 1 & 4; Overture, scherzo and finale*) and CDM7 69472-2 (*Symphonies Nos. 2–3*).

The RCA bargain 'Symphony Edition' brings a splendid set of Schumann to cap the series. Recorded in a glowingly warm acoustic, the Philadelphia Orchestra has seldom sounded so rich-textured over recent years. The strings expand gloriously in the *Adagio* of No. 2; the brass produce the most expansive sonorities in the *Rhenish*. The performances are as vital as they are warm, and Levine usually produces accelerandos at the ends of outer movements to increase the excitement. The series is capped with a superb version of No. 4, where the powerful link into the finale brings brass playing to remind one not only of Wagner but of the *Ring*, and the very flexible account of the finale itself is not only thrilling but in its control of tempo shows that Levine has listened to the famous Furtwängler interpretation, absorbed its detail and made it his own. The two discs are available separately at mid-price: *Symphonies Nos. 1* and *3* (74321 20295-2) and *Symphonies Nos. 2* and *4* (74321 20296-2).

Szell's set of Schumann symphonies was recorded in pairs, in 1958 (Nos. 1–2) and 1960 (Nos. 3–4). Over the years the individual works have been available only very sporadically in the UK and we cannot trace making a previous assessment of No. 2, with which Szell began his cycle in October 1958. It proves to be a thrilling performance of great power and strong forward thrust, yet the eloquent *Adagio* expands gloriously and brings the most ardent response from the Cleveland strings, matched by few other versions. Szell is at his most incisive and the orchestra are at their warmest in No. 1, truly a *Spring Symphony* in this exhilarating yet romantic reading. The account of the *Rhenish* is even finer, marvellously full of life. The playing is breathtaking, with the horns gloriously full-blooded. No. 4 is strong and dramatic, not as weighty as some, but equally convincing. The Cleveland players dig deep into the emotions of this music and Szell's flexibility of tempo in the finale, rather after the Furtwängler tradition, is made to seem spontaneous, such is the urgency of the overall performance. The *Manfred overture* is a great success, too. The remastering has quite transformed the recording, which throughout all four symphonies produces a richly opulent sound. The usual Cleveland problem of the close balance with the absence of any real pianissimos remains, but so does the ample hall ambience, and these vigorously passionate readings triumph over such a drawback. Szell proves himself an outstanding exponent of Schumann, able to stand alongside the finest interpreters of his day, and, were it not for the reduced range of dynamic, this set would have earned a Rosette. The two discs are packaged in an attractive stiff cardboard container, opening up like a book, with fine documentation.

Kubelik's fine Sony set also remains fully competitive. The recording was made in the Hercules-Saal, Munich, in 1979, and the advantages of that glowing acoustic can be felt in the great cathedral evocation of the fourth movement and the famous link to the finale of the *Fourth*, where the Bavarian brass is very impressive. The orchestral playing is generally very fine (if not quite as polished as the Berlin Philharmonic) and is especially eloquent in the spacious slow movements. These are strongly characterized readings with plenty of life and vitality which display the same bright and alert sensitivity to Schumann's style as did his earlier set for DG. But the Sony recording is obviously more modern, and the latest CD transfer brings plenty of body to the sound and a better focus to the violins than in the Sawallisch set. That more logically includes the *Overture, scherzo and finale*, but many will count the *Manfred overture* an equally desirable alternative.

Bernstein's VPO recordings from 1984–5 have the extra voltage which comes with live music-making at its most compulsive, and it is a pity that Bernstein, who displays a natural response to Schumann, seeks to impose personal idiosyncrasies on the performances that are not as convincing as Furtwängler's. Bernstein seems reluctant to let the music speak for itself, with heavily underlined expressiveness. The first movement of the *Spring Symphony* is pushed very hard, and the *Second Symphony* also brings the same larger-than-life projection. Slow movements are obviously deeply felt and have both warmth and humanity. In the *Rhenish Symphony* Bernstein's expressive indulgences are by no means as disruptive as some reviews have indicated, and the slight exaggeration at the climax of the fourth movement (said to be inspired by the sight of Cologne Cathedral) is forgivable when the brass playing is so overwhelmingly powerful. The outer movements of the *Fourth* are not allowed to move forward at a steady pace, but the *Romanze* has warmth and charm, even if the phrasing at the opening has an element of self-consciousness. The big transitional climax before the finale is massively conceived, yet lacks the spine-tingling sense of anticipation that Furtwängler generates at this point. Even so, with splendid orchestral playing and much engaging detail, there is a great deal to admire throughout these performances, and the resonant acoustic of the Grossersaal of the Musikverein gives the music-making a robust immediacy.

Hans Vonk's cycle offers fresh and direct readings, very well played and recorded, lacking a little in character and occasionally in dramatic tension, despite being taken from live performances. The refinement of the playing is consistently satisfying, the more commendable in live performance, and such a movement as the fourth of the five in the *Rhenish Symphony*, with its evocation of Cologne Cathedral, has fine concentration, even without emphasis. The recordings were made for EMI by German Radio in Cologne, with no intrusive audience noises. A good set, even though the performances hardly match those of Sawallisch on his much earlier EMI cycle, which also includes the *Overture, Scherzo and Finale*.

Dohnányi's Cleveland versions are superbly played and equally splendidly recorded. Thus the *Rhenish Symphony*, with its rich sonorities, cannot fail to make an impression. But overall these performances, although affectionately shaped, are seriously lacking in fire and impetus, so that inner movements come off much better than outer ones.

On the face of it, all the Schumann symphonies plus the *Overture, Scherzo and Finale* and the Overture to Goethe's *Hermann und Dorothea* thrown in for good measure and played by no less an orchestra than the Leipzig Gewandhaus must be good news. Many years ago Gerald Abraham published a famous essay called 'On a dull Overture by Schumann', the overture in question being *Hermann und Dorothea*; but we have to say that there is a touch of dullness about all these performances. They are musicianly, beautifully tailored but ultimately just a little wanting in real freshness and inspiration – even in the *Second Symphony*. Good recording quality – but while such inspired versions as Karajan, Sawallisch, Szell remain available there is no real need to consider this package.

Symphony No. 1 in B flat (Spring), Op. 38.
(M) *** DG 447 408-2 [id.]. BPO, Karajan – BRAHMS: *Symphony No. 1.* ***
(M) ** EMI CDM5 66824-2 [id.]. New Philh. O, Klemperer – FRANCK: *Symphony.* **

Karajan is totally attuned to Schumann's sensibility and he provides a strong yet beautifully shaped performance of the *Spring Symphony*. The very opening is electrifying with the Berlin Philharmonic giving of their finest, and this unsurpassed reading makes a highly appropriate coupling with Brahms in DG's Legendary Performances series of 'Originals'. The sound is an obvious improvement on the previous CD incarnation of this well-balanced analogue recording from the early 1970s, adding body and weight to the clear, fresh detail.

There is not much that is springlike about Klemperer's reading of No. 1. The opening is tremendously spacious and unsmiling, though the allegro itself has plenty of affectionate touches and a lightish rhythm. Needless to say, the orchestral playing is of high quality, with the woodwind particularly distinguished. The lack of geniality is a drawback, but it would be wrong to give the impression that the performance is merely heavy-handed. There are many touches that underline the strength of Schumann's thinking in a way that other conductors fail to do. It certainly emerges as a weightier document than in either the Kubelik or Levine versions, even though they both display greater fire and urgency.

Symphonies Nos. 1; 3 in E flat (Rhenish), Op. 97.
(BB) *** ASV Dig. CDQS 6073 [(M) id.]. RLPO, Janowski.
(BB) *(*) Naxos Dig. 8.553082 [id.]. Polish Nat. RSO, Antoni Wit.

Janowski's pairing of the *Spring* and *Rhenish Symphonies* is particularly successful. The pacing throughout both symphonies is most convincing, with a good deal of the inspirational pull that makes the Karajan readings so telling. In the Cologne Cathedral evocation of the *Rhenish*, the Liverpool brass rise sonorously to the occasion and the recording is altogether first class, bright, clear and full, with a concert hall ambience. At super-bargain price, this is strongly competitive.

Antoni Wit conducts the radio orchestra from Katwoice in warmly expressive readings of these two symphonies, lacking a degree of refinement both in the playing, with ensemble not always ideally crisp, and in the recorded sound, which is not always detailed enough.

Symphonies Nos. 1; 4 in D min.
(M) *** DG (IMS) 445 718-2. BPO Karajan.

As we go to press, Karajan's recording of the *Spring Symphony* is additionally available coupled with the splendid account of the *Fourth Symphony* at mid-price, in which the current transfer seems somewhat fuller than in the boxed set.

Symphonies Nos. 2 in C, Op. 61; 3 in E flat (Rhenish), Op. 97.
(B) **(*) DG Classikon 439 455-2 [(M) id. import]. Chicago SO, Barenboim.

Barenboim takes an overtly romantic view of these symphonies. His are weighty performances which yet bring out the lyrical, poetic warmth, underlining dramatic contrasts. The Chicago orchestra plays with extrovert brilliance, but the recording is variably successful in bringing that out.

Symphonies Nos. 2; 4 in D min., Op. 120.
(BB) ** ASV CDQS 6084 [(M) id.]. RLPO, Janowski.

This is a less successful coupling than Janowski's companion recordings of Nos. 1 and 3. No. 2 comes off better than No. 4, with some fine, expressive playing from the Liverpool strings in the *Adagio* and an exciting finale. There is no lack of freshness elsewhere. No. 4 is fast. Janowski does not relax enough to let the first movement's lyrical blossoming take the fullest effect. There is more poise in the *Romanze* (and some fine wind playing too), but the finale is pushed forward rather aggressively and the accelerandos at the end of both outer movements sound unspontaneous.

Symphony No. 3 in E flat (Rhenish), Op. 97.
(M) *** DG (IMS) Dig. 445 502-2 [id.]. LAPO, Giulini – BEETHOVEN: *Symphony No. 5.* ***

Giulini's *Rhenish* is completely free of interpretative exaggeration and its sheer musical vitality and nobility of spirit are beautifully conveyed. The Los Angeles players produce a very well-blended, warm and cultured sound that is a joy to listen to in itself. The 1980 recording is also extremely fine and, with its superb Beethoven coupling, this is very highly recommendable.

Symphony No. 4 in D min., Op. 120.
❀ (M) (***) DG mono 457 722-2 (2) [id.]. BPO, Furtwängler – FURTWANGLER: *Symphony No. 2.* (***)
(M) *** DG 447 666-2. Dresden State O, Karajan – BARTOK: *Piano concerto No. 3.* ***

Furtwängler's legendary account of the *Fourth Symphony* with the Berlin Philharmonic comes from 1953, the year before his death. It has long enjoyed classic status, and deservedly so. It is a really great performance and conveys the illusion that the musicians are spontaneously composing or improvising this music. The 'Wagnerian' preparation for the finale is quite electrifying, yet at the same time there is a commanding musical grip on the proceedings. The sound is remarkably warm and vivid for its period.

A most lyrical and powerful account of the *Fourth Symphony* from the 1972 Salzburg Festival with the Staatskapelle, Dresden, in tremendous form. Karajan's reading does not differ greatly from his Berlin version from the 1970s or the later account with the Vienna Philharmonic. A marvellous performance and good recording.

CHAMBER MUSIC

Abendlied, Op. 85/2; Adagio and allegro in A flat, Op. 70; Fantasiestücke, Op. 73; 3 Romances, Op. 94; 3 Pieces in Folk style, Op. 102/2–4.
(M) *** Ph. (IMS) 426 386-2. Heinz Holliger, Alfred Brendel.

The three *Romances* are specifically for oboe, but Holliger suggests that the others too are suitable for oboe, since the composer himself gave different options. One misses something by not having a horn in the *Adagio and allegro*, a cello in the folk-style pieces, or a clarinet in the *Fantasiestücke* (the oboe d'amore is used here); but Holliger has never sounded more magical on record and, with superbly real recording and deeply imaginative accompaniment, the result is an unexpected revelation.

Adagio & allegro, Op. 70; Fantasiestücke, Op. 73; 5 Stücke im Volkston, Op. 102.
(BB) *** Naxos Dig. 8.550654 [id.]. Maria Kliegel, Kristin Merscher – SCHUBERT: *Arpeggione sonata.* ***
(B) ** Sony SBK 48171; *SBT 48171* [id.]. Friedrich-Jürgen & Eckart Sellheim – MENDELSSOHN: *Song without words* etc.; SCHUBERT: *Arpeggione sonata.* **

Maria Kliegel and Kristin Merscher, like the Sellheim Duo, couple these charming Schumann miniatures with the Schubert *Arpeggione*, though Sony also throw in the Mendelssohn *Variations concertantes*, written for his amateur cellist brother, Paul, and one of the *Songs without words* for good measure. Kliegel and Merscher turn in fresh and musical performances and are recorded in very clean and well-focused sound. The Sellheim partnership give cultured readings, but the 1970s recordings are less fresh and natural than the Naxos.

Piano quartet in E flat, Op. 47; Piano quintet in E flat, Op. 44.
(B) **(*) Hyperion Dyad Dig. CDD 22008 (2) [id.]. Schubert Ens. of L. – HUMMEL: *Piano quintet;* SCHUBERT: *Trout quintet.* **(*)
(B) (*(*)) Millennium mono MCD 80125 [id.] Joerg Demus, Barylli Qt.

Lively, committed performances from the Schubert Ensemble of London. Although led by the excellent pianist, William Howard, this is playing from a balanced team which communicates directly and with both slow movements bringing a warmly expressive response and nicely observed detail. There are more individual versions of both works; however, if this inexpensive Dyad compilation seems tempting, the overall standard of musicianship is commendable and the amiable momentum of the music-making is enjoyable. Good if not outstanding recording.

Joerg Demus and the Barylli Quartet's mono account of these works was much (and rightly) admired in the mid-1950s. It still has much to recommend it but not quite enough to make it really competitive nowadays. The Baryllis will be a little too sweet for some tastes and the sound is a little wanting in bloom.

(i) *Piano quartet in E flat, Op. 47; Piano quintet in E flat, Op. 44. Piano trios Nos. 1 in D min., Op. 63; 2 in F, Op. 80; 3 in G min., Op. 110.*
(B) *** Ph. Duo 456 323-2 (2) [id.]. Beaux Arts Trio, (i) with Dolf Bettelheim and Samuel Rhodes.

Once again Philips have compiled a particularly generous measure for this Duo of Beaux Arts Schumann performances from the 1970s. This illustrious trio (with associates) give splendid readings of the *Piano quartet* and *quintet*. The vitality of inspiration is brought out consistently, and with that goes their characteristic concern for fine ensemble and refined textures. They are also probably the safest bet for the three *Piano trios*. Not that competition is exactly legion, but none that we have heard can outclass the Beaux Arts in terms of musicianship and finesse. Throughout, the set offers cultured and concentrated music-making, matched by truthful and present analogue recording.

Piano quintet in E flat, Op. 44.
(BB) *** Naxos Dig. 8.550406; *4550406* [id.]. Jenö Jandó, Kodály Qt – BRAHMS: *Piano quintet.* ***
(BB) **(*) ASV Quicksilva Dig. CDQS 6217 [(M) id.]. Suzanne Bradbury, Silvestri String Qt – BARTOK: *Piano quintet.* **(*)

A strongly characterized performance of Schumann's fine *Quintet* from Jenö Jandó and the Kodály Quartet. This is robust music-making, romantic in spirit, and its spontaneity is well projected by a vivid recording, made in an attractively resonant acoustic. With its comparable Brahms coupling, this makes an excellent bargain.

Suzanne Bradbury and the Silvestri Quartet give eminently satisfactory performances of the Schumann *Quintet* and, although they would not necessarily be a first choice, they deserve a recommendation, not least on account of the enterprising Bartók coupling.

Piano trios Nos. 1 in D min., Op. 63; 2 in F, Op. 80.
(M) **(*) Virgin/EMI (SIS) Dig. CUV5 61313-2. Grieg Trio.

These mid-price accounts of the first two Schumann *Trios* are new recordings and not reissues, as is the case of the 1992 Brahms *Trios* on the same label, also played by the Grieg Trio. Their approach to Schumann is admirably forthright and well characterized. The pianist Vebjørn Anvik is a commanding player (sometimes open to the criticism of being too assertive) but always intelligent. The playing of his two partners, Søvr Sigerland and Ellen-Margarete Flesjø, has splendid spirit and sensitivity. The recording is a shade lacking in transparency in the middle and lower register, thanks to a rather resonant acoustic, but this is not a serious hindrance to one's pleasure. The Beaux Arts offering on two CDs of all three *Piano trios* plus the *Fantasiestücke*, Op. 88, remains a first recommendation at premium price (Ph. 432 165-2), but this Ultraviolet version is to be preferred to the overbright Fontenay on Teldec; and no one investing in this coupling is likely to be disappointed in the least.

Fünf Stücke in Volkston (for cello and piano).
(M) *** Decca 452 895-2 [id.]. Rostropovich, composer – BRITTEN: *Sonata;* DEBUSSY: *Cello sonata in D min.* ***

Though simpler than either the Britten or Debussy sonatas with which it is coupled, this is a just as elusive a work. Rostropovich and Britten show that the simplicity is not as square and solid as might at first seem and that, in the hands of masters, these *Five Pieces in folk style* have a rare charm, particularly the last with its irregular rhythm. The excellent recording justifies the reissue under the Classic Sound logo.

PIANO MUSIC

Abegg variations, Op. 1; Fantasiestücke, Op. 12; March in G min., Op. 76/2; Novellette in F, Op. 21/1; Toccata in C, Op. 7; Waldszenen, Op. 82.
(M) (***) DG (IMS) mono 435 751-2. Sviatoslav Richter.

It was his 1956 DG mono LP of the *Waldszenen*, six of the *Fantasiestücken* and the *G minor March*, Op. 76, which served as Richter's visiting card in the West. Alec Robertson hailed his triumphant entry on the scene in the *Gramophone* magazine, and other great discs soon followed including the *Toccata* (1959) and the *Abegg variations* (1962). His supreme pianism shines through the years and, although the sound shows its age, it is an improvement over the original LP. The three stars are for the performances; some allowance must be made for the sound-quality.

Albumblätter, Op. 99; Arabeske, Op. 18; Etudes symphoniques, Op. 13.
(BB) *** Naxos Dig. 8.550144 [id.]. Stefan Vladar.

Stefan Vladar intersperses the additional studies that Schumann published as an appendix into the *Etudes symphoniques*. His account is quite simply superb in every respect and deserves recording of comparable excellence. His account of the *Albumblätter* is hardly less masterly. Artistically this rates three stars, with the compelling quality of the playing transcending the sonic limitations of the recording.

Arabeske in C, Op. 18; Blumenstück, Op. 19; Carnaval, Op. 9; Davidsbündlertänze, Op. 6; Fantasia in C, Op. 17; 8 Fantasiestücke, Op. 12; 3 Fantasiestücke, Op. 111; Faschingsschwank aus Wien, Op. 26; Humoresque in B flat, Op. 20; Kinderszenen, Op. 15; 4 Nachtstücke, Op. 23; Novelletten, Op. 21; Papillons, Op. 2; 3 Romances, Op. 28; Piano sonatas Nos. 1 in F sharp min., Op. 11; 2 in G min., Op. 22; Waldszenen, Op. 82.
(M) **(*) Ph. (IMS) 432 308-2 (7). Claudio Arrau.

Claudio Arrau's playing has warmth, poise and the distinctive, aristocratic finesse that graced everything this artist touched. Arrau has the measure of Schumann's impulsive temperament and is almost always perfectly attuned to his sensibility. Not all the rubati ring true and there are moments that seem a little self-conscious. But there is a very great deal to admire in this compilation, and few collectors will be greatly disappointed.

Arabeske in C, Op. 18; Faschingsschwank aus Wien, Op. 26; Kreisleriana, Op. 16.
(BB) *(*) Naxos Dig. 8.550783 [id.]. Jenö Jandó.

Carnaval, Op. 9; Kinderszenen, Op. 15; Papillons, Op. 2.
(BB) *(*) Naxos Dig. 8.550784 [id.]. Jenö Jandó.

After his successful Beethoven and Haydn recordings, Jandó's Schumann is disappointing. He is inclined to fast tempi and is too impulsive by half, and the result – not helped by the bold, bright piano-sound – often becomes aggressive. *Kinderszenen* and *Carnaval* both have moments of poetry and display considerable virtuosity, but the former hardly ever seems to inhabit the innocent world of children. The opening of *Kreisleriana* and the *Finale* of *Faschingsschwank aus Wien* bring much dash but not nearly enough poise, and *Papillons*, too, needs a less forthright approach.

Carnaval, Op. 9; Etudes symphoniques, Op. 13; Kinderszenen, Op. 15.
(B) ** Cal. Approache CAL 6650 [(M) id. import]. Inger Södergren.

Inger Södergren is surprisingly impetuous in the *Kinderszenen* and, while the gentle pieces (including *Träumerei*) are touching, in what the French on this CD call '*sur le cheval de bois*', she gallops very boisterously indeed. *Carnaval* has a similarly impulsive character and certainly does not lack vitality, but it is in the *Etudes symphoniques* that one finds her at her most penetrating. The piano sound is good but a trifle hard at higher dynamic levels.

Carnaval; Faschingsschwank aus Wien, Op. 26; Kinderszenen, Op. 15.
(B) *** DG Classikon 448 855-2 [(M) id. import]. Daniel Barenboim.

Barenboim's 1979 reading of *Carnaval* is one of his finest recording achievements in his role as pianist rather than as conductor. His lively imagination lights on the fantasy in this quirkily spontaneous sequence of pieces and makes them sparkle anew. *Carnival jest from Vienna* is more problematic, but the challenge inspires Barenboim, and here too he is at his most imaginative and persuasive, bringing out the warmth and tenderness, as well as the brilliance. The recital opens with a tender and charismatic reading of *Kinderszenen*. The 1979 recording is bold and truthful, but the CD transfer has lost a little of the fullness in the bass.

Davidsbündlertänze, Op. 6; Fantasiestücke, Op. 12.
(BB) *(*) Naxos Dig. 8.550493 [id.]. Benjamin Frith.

Benjamin Frith, who is also undertaking a Mendelssohn survey for Naxos, is an impressive if rather impulsive interpreter of Schumann. Yet he can be touchingly poetic, as in the opening *Des Abends*, *Warum?* and *Fabel* from the *Fantasiestücke*. However, Naxos had not, in 1991, solved their studio problem for recording the piano, and the results here in the Clara Wieck Auditorium, Heidelberg, fail to bring enough depth of sonority for this repertoire.

Etudes symphoniques.
(B) *** EMI forte (SIS) Dig. CZS5 69521-2 (2). Alexeev – BRAHMS: *Fantasias* etc. ***

Dimitri Alexeev combines the virtuoso technique which the work demands with supreme musicality and poetic feeling, the performance providing a structural cohesion not always in evidence. The digital recording, made several years later than that of the coupling, is excellent in bringing out the warmth of the piano-tone. This is a first-rate bargain.

Etudes symphoniques, Op. 13; Abegg variations, Op. 1; Widmung (trans. Liszt).
(M) * Revelation Dig. RV10031 [id.]. Evgeni Kissin – LISZT: *Etudes d'exécution transcendante No. 10* etc. *

If you are tempted, as we would be, to buy this version of the Schumann *Symphonic studies*, be warned: the sound is close and crude. Kissin was seventeen when he made this recording, the other items having been made when he was thirteen! The playing is amazing, worth three stars and more, but the sound does not begin to do him justice.

Etudes symphoniques, Op. 13; Fantasie in C, Op. 17.
(M) *** Van. 08 9165 72 (2). Brendel – SCHUBERT: *Piano sonatas Nos. 15 & 19* etc.
(M) (**(*)) DG (IMS) mono 447 977-2. Wilhelm Kempff.

Brendel's opening phrase of the *Symphonic studies* is immediately individual, and yet in essence these readings from the 1960s are not wayward, even though they are strongly personalized. There are other ways of approaching Schumann (Kempff's, for instance), but in Brendel's hands the music's structure emerges anew and has the emotional grip one associates with Beethoven. Excellent recording to match the playing.

Kempff's Schumann disc, issued to celebrate his centenary in 1995, offers two mono recordings dating from the mid-1950s. Kempff proves far happier in the dozen jewelled sections that make up the *Etudes symphoniques*, here given a rare clarity and sparkle, than in the broad span of the *C major Fantasie*, where he is less inspired. Whatever reservations one may make, however, the magnetically individual personality of the pianist rides triumphant.

Fantasia in C, Op. 17.
(M) *** DG 447 451-2 [id.]. Maurizio Pollini – SCHUBERT: *Wanderer fantasia.* ***

This is among the most distinguished Schumann performances in the catalogue. Pollini's playing throughout has a command and authority on the one hand and deep poetic feeling on the other that hold the listener spellbound. The recording is good but not outstanding. A welcome mid-priced reissue in DG's series of 'Originals'.

Fantasia in C, Op. 17; Faschingsschwank aus Wien (Carnival jest from Vienna), Op. 26; Papillons, Op. 2.
(M) *** EMI (SIS) CDM7 64625-2 [id.]. Sviatoslav Richter.

Richter's 1961 account of the *Fantasia in C* is a wonderfully poetic performance. Richter's phrasing, his magnificent control of dynamics, his gift for seeing a large-scale work as a whole – all these contribute towards the impression of unmatchable strength and vision. The recording is faithful, with genuine presence. The other two works included on this CD were recorded live during Richter's Italian concert tour a year later. The piano sound inevitably is somewhat less sonorous, shallower at fortissimo level, but fully acceptable. The account of *Papillons* is beguilingly subtle in control of colour.

Fantasia in C, Op. 17; Kreisleriana, Op. 16.
(M) *** RCA [09026 61264-2]. Artur Rubinstein.

Rubinstein's account of the *Fantasia in C* is also wonderfully subtle in its control of tempo and colour, and the poetry of the outer sections is quite magical. In spite of the close balance, Rubinstein achieves exquisite gradations of tone; the recording, made in 1965, is among the best he received during this period. *Kreisleriana* is hardly less compelling, with the great pianist at his most aristocratic, although the impetuous opening is recorded rather shallowly.

Fantasiestücke, Op. 12; Kinderszenen, Op. 15; Kreisleriana, Op. 16.
(M) *** Ph. Dig. 434 732-2 [id.]. Alfred Brendel.

Fantasiestücke is strong as well as poetic. The *Kinderszenen* is also one of the finest performances of the 1980s and is touched with real distinction. Brendel's *Kreisleriana* is intelligent and finely characterized. He is better recorded (in 1981/2) than most of his rivals and, though certain details may strike listeners as less spontaneous, the overall impression is highly persuasive.

Humoreske in B flat, Op. 20.
(BB) **(*) Naxos Dig. 8.550469 [id.]. Wolf Harden – REGER: *Variations.* **(*)

Wolf Harden's performance of the Schumann *Humoreske* is highly imaginative, idiomatic and full of sensitive touches. There is plenty of air round the aural image.

Kinderszenen, Op. 15; Kreisleriana, Op. 16; Novelette in F, Op. 21/1.
(M) *** DG Dig. 445 599-2. Vladimir Horowitz.

The subtle range of colour and articulation in *Kreisleriana* is remarkable, but then Horowitz plays in the studio just as if he were in front of a live audience, and the freshness and accuracy would be astonishing if we had not heard him repeating the trick. He was over eighty when he recorded the *Novelette* but the playing betrays remarkably little sign of frailty, and the recording given him by the DG engineers was among the finest he ever received. *Kinderszenen*, however, comes from a live recital, recorded in the Vienna Musikverein in 1987, a delightfully innocent performance never making pianistic points but letting the music speak for itself. The recording is good, but the audience's bronchial afflictions are inevitably a nuisance, even during the early spring of the year! An unmissable collection, just the same.

ORGAN MUSIC

4 Sketches, Op. 58 (ed. Bate).
(BB) *** ASV CDQS 6127 [(M) id.]. Jennifer Bate (Royal Albert Hall organ) – LISZT: *Organ music.* ***

The *Four Sketches* were originally written for a piano with pedal attachment and are here arranged for organ by E. Power Biggs. Each of the pieces is in 3/4 time, but the writing is attractively diverse; they are pleasant trifles. Rich, atmospheric recording with fair detail, impressively transferred to CD. Generously coupled with Liszt's three major organ warhorses, this makes a very tempting super-bargain reissue.

VOCAL MUSIC

Dichterliebe, Op. 48.
(M) *** DG Originals 449 747-2 [id.]. Fritz Wunderlich, Hubert Giesen – BEETHOVEN; SCHUBERT: *Lieder.* ***

Wunderlich, had he lived, would no doubt have surpassed this early recording of a favourite Schumann song-cycle but, even with an often unimaginative accompanist here, his freshness is most endearing, irresistible with so golden a voice.

(i) *Dichterliebe, Op. 48;* (ii) *Frauenliebe und Leben, Op. 42.*
(B) ** DG Classikon Analogue/Dig. 439 417-2 [(M) id. import]. (i) Dietrich Fischer-Dieskau, Christophe Eschenbach; (ii) Brigitte Fassbaender, Irwin Gage.

Fischer-Dieskau's earlier DG *Dichterliebe* (recorded between 1973 and 1977) is not quite as emotionally plangent as his later, full-price, digital version on Philips, but the contrasts between expressive warmth and a darker irony are still apparent. Eschenbach's accompaniment is always imaginative and the recording has fine presence. Fassbaender's account of the deeply moving female cycle is certainly strongly characterized, with a wide range of expression and fine detail, but she conveys little sense of vulnerability and there is little attempt to beautify the voice – though it is a fine and consistent instrument. If the underlying sentimentality of the poems is here concealed, so is much else. Irwin Gage is an excellent accompanist and the digital recording is very vivid.

Dichterliebe, Op. 48; Liederkreis, Op. 39; 5 Lieder, Op. 40.
(BB) *(*) Naxos Dig. 8.554219 [id.]. Sebastian Bluth, Anita Keller.

Sebastian Bluth has a soft, pleasing baritone, not quite as sharply focused or even as one would wish in Schumann's demanding song-cycles. He sings with crisp attack and clear diction – despite a recording balance which rather favours the piano – but his tonal contrasts are too limited to bring out the full word-meaning, making the results a little faceless.

Dichterliebe, Op. 48; 6 Gedichte, Op. 90; Liederkreis, Op. 39; Myrthen, Op. 25: Aus den östlichen; Widmung (only). *Requiem, Op. 90.* Lieder: *Auf den Sonnenschein; Die beiden Grenadiere; Dein Angesicht; Nichts Schöneres; Romanze; Der Schätzgräber; Des Sennen Abschied; Der Spielmann; Ständchen.*
(M) *** Ph. 442 741-2 (2). Gérard Souzay, Dalton Baldwin – BEETHOVEN: *An die ferne Geliebte* etc.; BRAHMS: *Lieder.* ***

Although this set, which includes a veritable feast of Lieder, is described as 'The Early Years', Souzay had made an earlier mono recording of the *Dichterliebe* for Decca with Jacqueline Bonneau which is now deleted. However, the later, mature version with Dalton Baldwin, made nine years later in 1962 (alongside the *Sechs Gedichte*, *Requiem* and two *Myrthen Lieder*), also shows exceptional insight and accomplishment, and the same may be said of the *Liederkreis* (and the miscellaneous songs), which date from 1966. Comparison with Fischer-Dieskau at full price in this wonderful song-cycle proves endlessly illuminating (what marvellous songs they are!). Both singers are, in their way, equally fine, bringing to each of the songs great imaginative feeling as well as their familiar vocal accomplishment. Fischer-Dieskau has recorded the cycle several times, yet in every instance there are many details in which Souzay's artistry and humanity will seem of such an order as to silence criticism, and his sympathy with Schumann's sensibility is extraordinary. For many listeners Souzay's comparative reticence – compared with the German baritone's intense expressive feeling – will carry the day, and few who hear Souzay's account of *Mondnacht* will deny the French singer's exceptional insight and accomplishment, while Dalton Baldwin provides wonderfully sensitive support. The recital ends with a group of (mostly) popular songs, beautifully sung, of which the closing *Dein Angesicht* is quite ravishing. The only drawback to this indispensable set is the absence of full translations – only the German texts are provided.

Frauenliebe und Leben (song-cycle), *Op. 42*.
✿ (M) *** Saga EC 3361-2 [id.]. Dame Janet Baker, Martin Isepp (with Lieder recital ***).

Janet Baker's range of expression in her earlier, Saga recording of the Schumann cycle runs the whole gamut from a joyful golden tone-colour in the exhilaration of *Ich kann's nicht fassen* through an ecstatic half-tone in *Süsser Freund* (the fulfilment of the line *Du geliebter Mann* wonderfully conveyed) to the dead, vibrato-less tone of agony at the bereavement in the final song. Martin Isepp proves a highly sensitive and supportive partner, and the recording balance – originally curiously artificial – has been immeasurably improved by the CD transfer.

Frauenliebe und Leben, Op. 42; Liederkreis, Op. 39; Aus den östlichen Rosen; Kennt du das Land; Meine rose; Der Nussbaum; Requiem; Die Soldatenbraut; Widmung.
(M) *** Carlton Classics Dig. 30367 02022 [id.]. Felicity Lott, Graham Johnson.

There are numerous versions of Schumann's *Frauenliebe und Leben* that command our allegiance, yet Felicity Lott and Graham Johnson are highly distinguished. Felicity Lott is a connoisseur's artist, far greater than many more illustrious and publicized rivals, and she sings here with great poise and a completely unaffected artistry. The recording comes from 1990 and is not new, but the finesse and musicianship of this partnership, as well as the intelligence which guides everything they do, make it treasurable. The sound, too, is very good indeed.

Das Paradies und die Peri.
(B) *** RCA Twofer Dig. 74321 34173-2 (2) [id.]. Büchner, Schmil, Kaufmann, Planté, Schopper, Sweet, Schmiege, Subrata, Titus, Schopper, Bamberg Ch. & SO, Kuhn.

Das Paradies und die Peri; 9 Romances and ballads for mixed choir, Opp. 59, 67, 75 & 145.
(M) *** EMI CMS7 69447-2 (2). Edda Moser, Marheineke, Fassbaender, Gedda, Tripp, Wewel, Düsseldorf State Musikverein Ch., Düsseldorf SO, Henryk Czyz.

The RCA Twofer derives from the Eurodisc catalogue and has a considerable price advantage over its EMI competitor. Gustav Kuhn offers a fine team of soloists and bright, well-balanced recording. The two most important soloists are certainly characterful, Sharon Sweet powerful if not always ideally firm as the Peri and Eberhard Büchner clear, fresh and keenly idiomatic as the first tenor.

Recorded in full, well-balanced analogue sound in the mid-1970s, Henryk Czyz's Dusseldorf performance is very well cast and offers a fresh, direct performance, not as well recorded as Kuhn's Bamberg version but always convincing. At mid-price and with a generous and unusual fill-up, it makes a good alternative recommendation.

(i) *Requiem in D flat, Op. 148;* (ii) *Requiem für Mignon, Op. 98b*.
(B) **(*) EMI CZS5 69653-2 (2) [CDZB 69653]. (i) Helen Donath, Doris Soffel, Nicolai Gedda; (i–ii) Dietrich Fischer-Dieskau; (ii) Brigitte Lindner, Andrea Andonian, Mechthild George, Monika Weichhold; Düsseldorf Musical Soc. Ch., Düsseldorf SO, Klee – BRAHMS: *German Requiem*. **(*)

Like Mozart, Schumann was unable to shake off the conviction that the *Requiem* was for himself. The opening *Requiem aeternam* is affecting and dignified, and the final *Benedictus* has a haunting eloquence. Bernhard Klee extracts a very sympathetic response from his distinguished team of soloists and the fine Düsseldorf chorus and orchestra. They also give an attentive and committed account of the 1849 *Requiem for Mignon*, Op. 98b. The EMI recording is natural and well balanced. This now comes in harness with Tennstedt's impressively spacious account of the Brahms *Requiem*.

Scenes from Goethe's Faust.

✿ (M) *** Decca 425 705-2 (2). Harwood, Pears, Shirley-Quirk, Fischer-Dieskau, Vyvyan, Palmer, Aldeburgh Festival Singers, ECO, Britten.

(M) **(*) EMI Dig. CMS7 69450-2 (2). Fischer-Dieskau, Mathis, Berry, Gedda, Daniels, Lövas, Schwarz, Sharp, Gramatzki, Stamm, Düsseldorf Music Soc. Ch., Tölz Boys' Ch., Düsseldorf SO, Klee.

Though the episodic sequence of scenes is neither opera nor cantata, the power and imagination of much of the music, not least the delightful garden scene and the energetic setting of the final part, are immensely satisfying. In 1972, soon after a live performance at the Aldeburgh Festival, Britten inspired his orchestra and his fine cast of singers to vivid performances, which are outstandingly recorded against the warm Maltings acoustic. This is magnificent music, and readers are urged to explore it – the rewards are considerable.

Klee takes a sharply dramatic view of Schumann's strange collection of Goethe portraits and with bright, atmospheric, digital recording the score is made to seem less wayward than it can. The cast of singers is strong, but Fischer-Dieskau is here not as steady as he was in Britten's recording of ten years earlier. Nor – particularly in the final scene – does Klee have the imaginative insights that gave that recording such compelling magic and earned it a Rosette.

Schütz, Heinrich (1585–1672)

Christmas story (Weihnachthistorie).

(M) *** Virgin Veritas/EMI VM5 61353-2. Kirkby, Rogers, Thomas, Taverner Cons., Taverner Ch., Taverner Players, Parrott – PRAETORIUS: *Christmas motets.* ***

Christmas story (Weihnachthistorie); 3 Cantiones sacrae (1625); Psalm 100.

(BB) *** Naxos Dig. 8.553514 [id.]. Agnew, Crookes, MacCarthy, Oxford Camerata, Summerly.

The reissued EMI version of Schütz's *Christmas story*, now on Virgin Veritas, has the advantage of three first-class soloists, all of whom are in excellent voice. One is soon gripped by the narrative and the beauty and simplicity of the line. There is no sense of austerity here, merely a sense of purity, with the atmosphere of the music beautifully captured by these forces under Andrew Parrott. Apart from a rather nasal edge on the violin tone, it is difficult to fault either this moving performance or the well-balanced and refined recording.

Summerly with his talented group of 10 singers – two of them doubling as soloists – give a compelling reading of Schütz's vivid and compact telling of the *Christmas story*. Aptly austere in its overall manner, with clear instrumental accompaniment, it yet brings out the beauty and vigour of the numbers depicting the different groups, in turn the angels, the shepherds and the wise men. The scholarly credentials are impeccable, with excellent notes provided, and the recording, made in Hertford College, Oxford, is full and vivid. The motets and the psalm-setting make a welcome fill-up.

(i) *Christmas story (Weihnachthistorie);* (ii) *Easter oratorio (Historia der Auferstehung Jesu Christ). Cantiones sacrae: Quid commisisti* (cycle of five 4-part motets). (iii) *Deutsches Magnificat.* Motets for double choir: *Ach, Herr, straf mich nicht* (Psalm 6); *Cantate Domino* (Psalm 96); *Herr unser Herrscher* (Psalm 8); *Ich freu mich des* (Psalm 122); *Unser Herr Jesus Christus.*

(B) **(*) Decca Double 452 188-2 (2) [(M) id. import]. Heinrich Schütz Ch., with (i) Partridge, Palmer, soloists, Instrumental Ens., Philip Jones Brass Ens.; (ii) Pears, Tear, Langridge, Elizabethan Consort of Viols, London Cornett & Sackbutt Ens.; (iii) Symphoniae Sacrae Chamber Ens., all cond. Norrington.

Norrington's Argo recordings of the *Christmas story* and the *Easter oratorio* were made before he espoused the cause of original instruments. The former offers some extremely fine singing from Ian Partridge as the Evangelist, while Peter Pears shows impressive authority and insight as well as singing beautifully in the same role for the companion work. The Heinrich Schütz Choir phrases with great feeling and subtlety; indeed, some may feel that their singing is a little too self-consciously beautiful for music that is so pure in style. A similar comment might be made about the double motets, although the sense of joy expressed in the *Quid commisisti* cycle (from the 1625 *Cantiones sacrae*) communicates strongly. The *Deutsches Magnificat* is given with admirable authority and is one of the best things in this very generous (146-minute) collection. Indeed this set offers much to enjoy and admire, and the vintage recordings, made between 1969 and 1975, have fine sonority, with the ambitious double motets given a proper sense of spectacle.

Italian Madrigals (complete).

(B) *** HM HMA 1901162 [id.]. Concerto Vocale, René Jacobs.

Schütz's first and only *Book of Italian Madrigals* reflects his encounter with the music of Giovanni Gabrieli and Monteverdi. The Concerto Vocale, led by the counter-tenor, René Jacobs, employ a theorbo which provides added variety of colour, and at times they offer great expressive and tonal range. They omit the very last of the madrigals, the eight-part *Vasto mar*.

Motets: *Auf dem Gebirge; Der Engel sprach; Exultavit cor meum; Fili mi Absolon; Heu mihi Domine; Hodie Christus natus est; Ich danke Dir, Herr; O quam tu pulchra es; Die Seele Christi, helige mich; Selig sind die Todten*.
(BB) *** ASV CDQS 6105 [(M) id.]. Pro Cantione Antiqua, L. Cornett & Sackbut Ens., Restoration Ac., Edgar Fleet.

An eminently useful and well-recorded super-bargain anthology of Schütz motets that offers such masterpieces as *Fili mi Absolon* (for bass voice, five sackbuts, organ and violone continuo) and the glorious *Selig sind die Todten* in well-thought-out and carefully prepared performances under Edgar Fleet. These accounts have a dignity and warmth that make them well worth considering. Moreover the CD transfer is excellently managed, the sound rich and clear.

O bone Jesu, fili Mariae.
(M) *** DG Dig. 447 298-2. Monteverdi Ch., E. Bar. Soloists, Gardiner – BUXTEHUDE: *Membra Jesu nostri*. ***

A wonderfully eloquent performance of this *Spiritual concerto* by one of the greatest of baroque masters. Schütz juxtaposes stanzas of a poem ascribed to St Bernard of Clairvaux with prose passages of Latin devotional literature, treating the latter as recitative and the former set homophonically, and ending the cantata in *concertato* style. Beautifully recorded.

The Psalms of David (complete).
(M) *(*) DG Codex 453 179-2 (2). Regensburger Domspätzen, Hamburg Wind. Ens., Ulsamer Coll., Schneidt.

The *Psalms of David* formed Schütz's first sacred work, published in 1619. There are 26 settings, using selected Psalms plus two other biblical texts, and they are written for single, double or triple choir, with *ad lib* instrumental support. In most of them the composer has indicated the required instrumentation. The performances here are adequate and quite well sung and played, although pacing tends to be brisk and the approach rather stiff. Unfortunately, the 1972 recording has not transferred well to CD: it is poorly focused, sometimes uncomfortably so.

Psalm 150.
(B) **(*) EMI forte (SIS) CZS5 68631-2 (2). Cambridge University Musical Soc., Bach Ch., King's College Ch., Wilbraham Brass Soloists, Willcocks – G. GABRIELI: *Motets* etc. **(*); MONTEVERDI: *Vespers*. *(*)

Schütz's setting of *Psalm 150* is for double choirs and soloists, each used in juxtaposition against the others, with built-in antiphony an essential part of the composer's conception. The majesty of Schütz's inspiration certainly comes over vividly here, the closing *Alleluja* having remarkable weight and richness, though the overall focus of the recording is not absolutely clean.

The Resurrection; Meine Seele erhebt den Herren.
(M) *** HM Dig. HMT 7901311 [id.]. Concerto Vocale, René Jacobs.

René Jacobs's account of Schütz's *Historia der Auferstehung Jesu Christi* with the Concerto Vocale is a performance of great accomplishment and taste, and quite beautifully recorded. This performance still gives great pleasure, as does the lively account of *Meine Seele erhebt den Herren* from the second Book of the *Symphoniae sacrae* (1647). This makes a fine mid-priced alternative to Bernius's excellent full-price Sony version, which includes also the *Christmas story* (SK 45943).

Sacred choral music (1648).
(M) **(*) HM/BMG Dig. GD 77171 (2). Knabenchor Hannover, Heinz Hennig.

The Hanover recording of the Schütz *Geistliche Chormusik* comes from the early 1980s and was made in collaboration with Westdeutsche Rundfunk. It is of particular value in that it offers not only all 29 motets of the collection but also alternative versions of seven of them, two in more than one form. The notes are scholarly and helpful, and at mid-price it remains an attractive proposition. On the whole the singing is very good, though the tone of the Knabenchor of Hanover is not always perfectly focused; the recording, while generally acceptable, is at times a little opaque. However, there is at the time of writing no alternative version, and the set is to be recommended. Readers will derive much satisfaction from it.

Der Schwanengesang (Opus ultimum; reconstructed by Steude).
(M) *** Virgin Veritas/EMI VED5 61306-2 (2). Hannover Knabenchor, Hilliard Ens., L. Bar., Heinz Hennig.

Schütz's *Opus ultimum* is a setting of Psalm 119, the longest psalm in the psalter, which he divides into 11 sections. He finishes off this 13-part motet cycle with his final setting of Psalm 100, which he had originally composed in 1662, and the *Deutsches Magnificat*. Steude's note recounts the history of the work, parts of which disappeared after Schütz's death; and his reconstruction of two of the vocal parts is obviously a labour of love. The project was undertaken in celebration of the European Music Year in 1985, and the recording a co-production with North German Radio. The performance is a completely dedicated one, with excellent singing from all concerned and good instrumental playing, and the conductor, Heinz Hennig, secures warm and responsive singing from his Hannover Knabenchor. The acoustic is spacious and warm and the recording balance well focused. The sound is firm, clear and sonorous. This rare set is welcome back to the catalogue on Virgin Veritas at mid-price.

Scriabin, Alexander (1872–1915)

(i–ii) *Piano concerto in F sharp min., Op. 20;* (i) *Piano sonata No. 1 in F min., Op. 6; 2 Pieces for the left hand, Op. 9;* (iii) *Fantasy, Op. 28.*
(BB) * Arte Nova Dig. 74321 54457-2 [id.]. (i) Arkady Sevidov; (ii) Russian PO, Konstantin Krimets; (iii) Olga Sevidova.

An unsatisfactory and unidiomatic account of the Scriabin *Concerto*. Arkady Sevidov is not particularly sensitive, although the close balance is not to his advantage. There is none of the quiet, poetic musing Scriabin calls for in the slow movement and, while Sevidov has no lack of brilliance, he is not strong on *pianopianissimo*. The string-tone is just a shade undernourished, though Konstantin Krimets produces a more idiomatic sound than his soloist.

Symphonies Nos. (i) *1 in E, Op. 26; 2 in C min., Op. 29; 3 in C min. (Le divin poème); 4 (Poème de l'extase), Op. 54;* (ii) *5 (Prometheus), Op. 60;* (iii) *Piano concerto in F sharp min., Op. 20. Rêverie.*
(B) ** RCA 74321 20297-2 (3). Frankfurt RSO, Kitaienko, with (i) Siniawskaia, Fedin; (ii) Figuralchor, Krainev; (iii) Oppitz.

The set from the Frankfurt Radio forces is in its way desirable, though it would be idle to pretend that it offers a serious challenge to Riccardo Muti's full-price set with the Philadelphia Orchestra on EMI. That however does not offer the early, Chopinesque *Piano concerto in F sharp minor* as part of the package; nor does it come at so competitive a price. Be warned, however, that Dmitri Kitaienko does not shrink from adding to the percussion and adding cymbal clashes at will. Not content with that, he goes even further and adds a chorus at the closing section of *Poème de l'extase*. One does not have to be a purist to find this unacceptable in the absence of any supporting documentary evidence as to Scriabin's own wishes. If the *Poème de l'extase* cannot be recommended, the *Prometheus* has much in its favour, including some impressive pianism from Vladimir Krainev. It is not however to be preferred to the Ashkenazy–Maazel full-price version on Decca, nor is Gerhard Oppitz's account of the concerto as subtle or imaginative as the Ashkenazy. However, the discs can be purchased separately, and the first three symphonies are certainly recommendable at the price. Not only are the performances thoroughly idiomatic but the recorded sound has much going in its favour too; it is rich in detail and has plenty of air round the aural image. For the record, the *First Symphony* is coupled with *Le poème de l'extase* on the first disc (74321 20298-2); the *Second* with the *Piano concerto* (74321 20299-2) and the *Third* with *Prometheus* and the *Rêverie* (74321 20300-2). The third disc carries the strongest recommendation. All the same, even here Muti remains far superior.

Symphonies Nos. 1 in E, Op. 26; 2 in C min., Op. 29; 3 in C min. (Le divin poème), Op. 43; 4 (Poème de l'extase), Op. 54.
(B) **(*) Ph. Duo 454 271-2 (2) [id.]. Frankfurt RSO, Eliahu Inbal.

For those wanting a modestly priced set of just the three Scriabin symphonies plus the *Poème de l'extase*, the Inbal/Frankfurt set, recorded in 1978–9, has the field to itself. This same orchestra went on later to re-record the symphonies under Kitaienko, but that set stretches to three (bargain) discs, to include also *Prometheus* and the early, Chopinesque *F sharp Piano concerto* (RCA 74321 20297-2 – see above). The Philips Frankfurt recordings are full, smooth and clear and the orchestral playing is refined and committed, albeit less intoxicatingly vivid than in Muti's full-priced EMI set, which is distinctly superior. The *Poème de l'extase* is beautifully played and has plenty of atmosphere and, if it is not as passionately voluptuous as in Muti's hands, it makes a considerable impression and is pleasingly lacking in vulgarity. Overall, this

Philips Duo remains a valuable and recommendable alternative investment for those with limited budgets.

Symphony No. 1, Op. 26; 2 Poèmes, Op. 32/1–2 (orch. Rogal-Levitzky); *Rêverie, Op. 24.*
(BB) ** Naxos Dig. 8.553580 [id.]. Lyudmila Ivanova, Mikhail Agafonov, Moscow Capella & SO, Igor Golovschin.

Igor Golovschin has plenty of energy, but the strings are less than sumptuous and wind intonation is far from ideal. Golovschin is not above adding the odd effect not in Scriabin's score. Decent recording but, generally speaking, not a really persuasive reading.

Symphony No. 2 in C min., Op. 29; Symphonic poem in D min., Op. posth.
(BB) * Naxos Dig. 8.553581 [id]. Moscow SO, Golovschin.

This Naxos version is indifferent rather than poor. There is some good playing but overall the orchestra lacks real tonal finesse. In this field the best bargain recommendation remains with Eliahu Inbal and the Frankfurt Radio Orchestra.

Le Poème de l'extase, Op. 54.
(M) *** Sony SM2K 64100 (2) [S2K 64100]. NYPO, Boulez – BARTOK: *Wooden Prince* etc. **(*)
(B) *** [EMI Red Line Dig. CDR5 69843]. Phd. O, Muti – TCHAIKOVSKY: *Symphony No. 6.* *
(M) **(*) Decca Phase Four 443 898-2 [id.]. Czech PO, Stokowski – MUSSORGSKY: *Pictures at an exhibition* **; STRAVINSKY: *Firebird suite; Pastorale.* **(*)

Boulez's electrifying account of *Le Poème de l'extase* (not previously released) is almost unsurpassed on record for its ardour and the way Boulez controls the overall shaping of its climaxes and balances the orchestra so that the all-important trumpet part emerges from within a texture that is inherently voluptuous, even if the sound-quality itself could be more alluring. The recording, made in the Avery Fisher Hall, is, however, full and atmospheric and the work's final orgasmic culmination is almost overwhelming, with superb playing from the NYPO. This needs to be recoupled more appropriately on a single CD.

Muti's Philadelphia performance is white-hot with passionate intensity, yet masterfully controlled, with each section following inevitably in one great span. It is a pity that the coupling is unrecommendable.

Stokowski's version of the *Poème de l'extase* was recorded live when the nonagenarian conductor visited Prague. The result, tactfully edited from more than one performance, has all the passionate commitment of a concert-hall performance, with the ebb and flow of tension and the flexibiity of phrasing the more compellingly captured. The Phase Four recording highlights individual instruments, but not disastrously so.

PIANO MUSIC

Etudes, Op. 8/7 & 12; Op. 42/5. Preludes, Op. 11/1, 3, 9, 10, 13, 14, 16; Op. 13/6; Op. 15/2; Op. 16/1 & 4; Op. 27/1; Op. 48/3; Op. 51/2; Op. 59/2; Op. 67/1. Sonatas Nos. 3, Op. 23; 5, Op. 53.
(M) (***) RCA mono/stereo GD 86215 [6215-2-RG]. Vladimir Horowitz.

The RCA engineers have done wonders to these recordings from the 1950s though some of the original shallowness and clatter remains. The *Preludes* and the legendary account of the *Third Sonata* come from 1956. The *Fifth* is much later, coming from the mid-1970s, and has more bloom. The performances form an essential part of any good Horowitz collection.

Preludes, Op. 11, Nos. 2, 4–6, 8–14, 16, 18, 20, 22 & 24.
(B) *** EMI CD-EMX 2237 [(M) id. import]. Andrei Gavrilov – RACHMANINOV: *Elégie* etc. ***

Gavrilov's selection from Opus 11 is arbitrary. At times his approach is impetuous, and dynamics can be exaggerated; but playing of this order is still pretty remarkable. The balance is not too close, yet the CD brings a tangible presence and the piano timbre is well caught.

Piano sonatas Nos. 1–10; Etude in C sharp min., Op. 2/1; Feuillet d'album, Op. 58; 2 Morceaux, Op. 57; 2 Poèmes, Op. 63; 4 Preludes, Op. 48; 5 Preludes, Op. 64; 2 Preludes, Op. 67; Vers la flamme, Op. 72.
(B) *** EMI forte CZS5 72652-2 (2) [id.]. John Ogdon.

Piano sonatas Nos. 1–10; Piano sonata in E flat min. (1887–9); Sonata fantaisie in G sharp min.
(M) **(*) DG 431 747-2 (3). Roberto Szidon.

Piano sonatas Nos. 1–10; 2 Danses, Op. 73; 4 Morceaux, Op. 51; 4 Morceaux, Op. 56; 2 Poèmes, Op. 32.
(B) *** Decca Double Analogue/Dig. 452 961-2 (2) [id.]. Vladimir Ashkenazy.

Scriabin is a composer whose fascination for harmonic effect rather than continuity of musical argument proves a serious flaw in his musical make-up. The sonatas are often more eventful pianistically than musically, and the most effective of his piano works are the miniatures, notably the early *Preludes*, Op. 11 (which are not included in the EMI set), and the *Preludes* at the other end of his career, Op. 74 (which are). John Ogdon's pioneering survey (like that of Ashkenazy which followed) encompasses all ten sonatas, none of them (apart from No. 3) very long, and a variety of smaller pieces. They give an excellent picture of Scriabin's art which is unfailingly atmospheric and at times almost claustrophobic. Ogdon is nothing if not persuasive, and the only reservation one need feel about his playing is an occasional tendency to be less than scrupulous in observing dynamic indications and a lack of finish at times, when the bravura runs are not as cleanly articulated as they might be. His account of the *Tenth Sonata*, however, is particularly fine, and if in the *Ninth* (*The black mass*) he does not match the demonic fury and power of Horowitz (and who, for that matter, does?) his is still a thoroughly felt and vividly realized reading. The shorter pieces are particularly appealing (the richly coloured *Etude in C sharp minor* which opens the first disc should tempt anyone to explore further). The piano is very well recorded throughout (at Abbey Road in 1971).

Ashkenazy's Scriabin set was reissued very economically on a Double Decca to celebrate his sixtieth birthday. The recordings were made over a decade between 1972 and 1984 in the Kingsway Hall, Walthamstow, or All Saints' Petersham, but the (first-class) sound is remarkable consistent. Ashkenazy is clearly attuned to this repertoire: he is as thoroughly at home in the miniatures as in the sonatas, readily finding their special atmosphere and colour. If he is at his very finest in the earlier sonatas, the last three are given with brilliance and vision, and there is no lack of awareness of the demonic side of Scriabin's personality.

Roberto Szidon's DG reissue offers the whole set. Szidon seems especially at home in the later works. His version of the *Black Mass sonata* (No. 9) conveys real excitement. At medium price this is an attractive reissue and can be considered alongside Ashkenazy's series. The DG recording is good but not ideal and the tone tends to harden at climaxes.

Piano sonatas Nos. 2 in G sharp min., Op. 19; 5 in F sharp, Op. 53; 6 in G, Op. 63; 7 in F sharp ('White Mass'), Op. 68; 9 in F ('Black Mass'); Fantaisie in B min., Op. 28.
(BB) ** Naxos Dig. 8.553537 [id.]. Bernd Glemser.

This is announced as being the first volume of the complete Scriabin *Sonatas* and for those who want merely to get to know the notes, as it were, this would make an eminently serviceable choice at its modest asking price. Bernd Glemser is a young German pianist of obvious talent who shows a natural sympathy for this repertoire. He commands a keen imagination, a wide range of keyboard colour and he possesses an impressive technical address. No one buying these sonatas will feel short-changed – but of course they will not feel as satisfied as they would by such rivals as John Ogdon (EMI), Roberto Szidon (DG) or Ashkenazy (Decca), all three-star recommendations. It goes without saying that Horowitz and Richter in No. 9 are in a class of their own in terms of their almost demonic vision and electrifying pianism. There are times (as in the recent Vlach's Dvořák *Quartets*) when Naxos produce at bargain price something which is as good as a full-price recommendation. Bernd Glemser's accounts are very recommendable at the price but cannot be a three-star recommendation.

Piano sonata No. 3 in F sharp min., Op. 23; 2 Poèmes, Op. 32.
(BB) ** ASV Quicksilva Dig. CDQS 6153 [(M) id. import]. Alma Petchersky – TCHAIKOVSKY: *Grand sonata.* **

Alma Petchersky is a fine player whose Villa-Lobos we have much admired in earlier editions of the *Guide*. She gives a commanding account of the *F sharp minor Sonata* and the two *Poèmes*, Op. 32. She is well recorded. Recommendable.

Seiber, Mátyás (1905–60)

Four French folk songs: Réveillez-vous; J'ai descendu; Le Rossignol; Marguerite, elle est malade.
(M) *** RCA 09026 61601-2. Peter Pears, Julian Bream (guitar) – BRITTEN: *Songs from the Chinese* etc; WALTON: *Anon in love.* ***

Mátyás Seiber's arrangements of four French folksongs are enchantingly simple and, as Bream says, the accompaniments 'use the guitar adroitly'. They bring ravishing tone and line from Pears. Vivid recording, made by a Decca team, but it was unconscionable of RCA not to provide translations, even if one can enjoy the songs without them.

Seixas, Carlos de (1704–42)

Motets: *Adebat Vincentius; Tantum ergo.*

(M) *** DG Codex 453 182-2. Jennifer Smith, Magali, Schwartz, Fernando Serafim, Gulbenkian Chamber Ch. & O, Michel Corboz – ALMEIDA: *Beatus vir* etc.; CARVALHO: *Te Deum;* TEIXEIRA: *Gaudate, astra.* ***

Carlos de Seixas was a Portuguese contemporary of Almeida and Teixeira, with whom he is joined in this stimulating collection of motets used to back up the Carvalho *Te Deum*. *Adebat Vincentius* brings a lively interplay within the double chorus, juxtaposed with a soprano/contralto duet, and thus makes a fine contrast with the serenely beautiful setting of *Tantum ergo*. Fine singing and first-class recording enhance the appeal of this eloquent music.

Séverac, Déodat de (1872–1921)

Piano, 4 hands: *L'Album pour les enfants petits et grands: Le Soldat de plomb (Histoire vraie en trois récits)*. (Piano) *Baigneuses au soleil (Souvenir de Banyuls-sur-mer); Cerdaña (5 Etudes pittoresques); Le Chant de la terre (poème géorgique); En Languedoc (suite); En vacances (petites pièces romantiques); Les Naïades et le faune indiscret; Pipperment-get (Valse brillante de concert); Premier Recueil (Au château et das le parc); Deuxième Recueil (inachevé); Sous les lauriers roses ou Soir de Carnaval sur la Côte Catalane; Stances à Madame de Pompadour; Valse romantique.*

(B) **(*) EMI CMS5 72372-2 (3). Aldo Ciccolini.

Déodat de Séverac came from the Pays d'Oc and always retained his roots in the region: he later wrote: 'Present-day composers create music of and for Paris. Thus they are becoming more and more remote from the local genius of the various regions in which they were born.' He first studied law at Toulouse before deciding on music and becoming a pupil, first of Magnard and d'Indy. He was a friend of Ravel, to whom his musical language is much indebted. All the music on these CDs is civilized and has great charm. The recordings were made between 1968 and 1977 and are serviceable rather than distinguished. But the set will give much pleasure.

Shankar, Ravi (born 1920)

Sitar concertos Nos. (i) *1;* (ii) *2 (A garland of ragas). Morning love* (based on the *Raga Nata Bhairav*); *Raga Purlya Kalyan.* (iii) *Prahhati* (based on the *Raga Gunkali*); *Raga Piloo. Swara-Kãkall.*

(B) **(*) EMI forte Analogue/Dig. CZS5 76255-2 [(M) id. import]. Ravi Shankar, with (i) LSO, Previn; (ii) LPO, Mehta; (iii) Sir Yehudi Menuhin.

This record is an oddity. It would be easy to dismiss this pair of concertos, particularly as they are in four movements each and seem very long (the first runs for 40 minutes, the second for nearly 52 minutes!) and, except for aficionados, will undoubtedly outstay their welcome. Fairly evidently they are neither very good Western music nor good Indian music. The idiom is sweet – arguably too sweet and unproblematic – but at least they represent a 'crossover' in the real sense – a painless tour over the geographical layout of the raga. It also prompts brilliant and atmospheric music-making from both Previn and the LSO and from Meta (himself Indian-born) and the LPO. Not to mention the composer himself, who launches into solos which he makes sound spontaneous in the authentic manner, however prepared they may actually be. He opens the first CD with a very Westernized raga, which he calls *Morning love*; and in the ragas, *Piloo* and *Prabhati*, when he is joined by Sir Yehudi Menuhin (who is on very good form), the latter's contribution draws an obvious parallel with Eastern European folk music.

Shchedrin, Rodion (born 1933)

(i) *Carmen* (ballet; arr. from Bizet): *suite; Concerto for orchestra (Naughty limericks).*

(BB) **(*) Naxos Dig. 8.553038 [id.]. Ukrainian State O, Theodor Kuchar.

Rodion Shchedrin's free adaptation of Bizet's *Carmen* music uses Bizet's tunes, complete with harmony, and reworks them into a new tapestry using only strings and percussion (including vibraphone). The whole thing is brilliantly done and wears surprisingly well. Kuchar's version is vividly played, with wit as well as high drama and atmosphere. The Naxos recording is excellent. The brief (8-minute) *Concerto for orchestra* with its curious subtitle is a kaleidoscopic scherzando, a whirlwind presentation of Russian folk-motives over a minimalist ostinato. It is played with great verve but rather outstays its welcome.

Sheppard, John (*c.* 1515–*c.* 1559)

Aeterne rex altissime; Audivi vocem de coelo; Beata nobis gaudia; Dum transisset Sabbatum (1st & 2nd settings); *In manus Tuas* (2nd & 3rd settings); *Gaude, gaude, gaude Maria; Hostis Herodes impie; Impetum fecerunt unanimes; In manus Tuas* (3rd setting); *Libera nos, salva nos* (2nd setting); *Sacris solemniis; Sancte Dei pretiose; Spiritus sanctus procedens* (2nd setting).
Second Service: *Magnificat; Nunc dimittis. Te Deum laudamus.*
Western Wynde mass.
(B) *** Hyperion Dyad Dig. CDD 22022 (2) [id.]. The Sixteen, Harry Christophers.

Ave maris stella. Cantate mass. Motets: *Deus tuorum militum* (1st setting); *Filiae Hierusalem venite; Haec dies; In manus Tuas Domine* (1st setting); *In pacem in idipsum; Jesu salvator saeculi, redemptis; Jesu salvator saeculi verbum; Justi in perpetuum vivent; Laudem dicite Deo; Libera nos, salva nos* (1st setting); *Paschal Kyrie; Regis Tharsis et insulae; Salvator mundi, Domine; Spiritus sanctus procedens* (1st setting); *Verbo caro factus est.*
❀ (B) *** Hyperion Dyad Dig. CDD 22021 (2) [id.]. The Sixteen, Harry Christophers.

All the music here is of such high quality and it is so superbly sung and recorded that it seems only sensible to consider these two Dyad reissues together. The first collection listed (CD 22022) will be especially attractive for some collectors, as the second of the two discs includes Sheppard's *Western Wynde mass*. However, this is a less elaborate setting of this famous theme than some others, notably that of John Taverner, for until the closing *Agnus Dei* Sheppard consistently places the melodic line on top, whereas Taverner moves the tune about within the lower parts. Nevertheless Sheppard's setting has an appealingly simple beauty, while the extended *Te Deum laudamus* which closes the programme is even richer in its harmonic progressions. The soaring second version of *Dum transisset Sabbatum* and the third version of the sombre *In manus Tuas* (with their characteristic momentary dissonances) which precede the Mass are also memorable. The companion disc offers ten more responsories, all of high quality and offering considerable variety, from the flowing antiphon, *Libera nos, salva nos*, and the gently serene second setting (for Palm Sunday) of *In manus Tuas Domine* and the more adventurous *Gaude, gaude, gaude Maria* on to the particularly rich upper lines of the first, Easter Day, setting of *Dum transisset Sabbatum* and the imaginatively contrasted *Sacris solemniis* with its fluent imitation in the upper voices.

However, we have given our Rosette to the companion set (CD 22021), for it includes Sheppard's glorious six-voiced *Cantate mass*, much more complex than *Western Wynde* and, with its glowingly textured polyphony, surely among his most inspired works. Before that on the first CD come eleven responsories, all showing the composer at his most concentrated in inspiration. The Sixteen consistently convey the rapturous beauty of Sheppard's writing, above all in the ethereal passages in the highest register, very characteristic of him. Even there, the Sixteen's sopranos seem quite unstressed by the tessitura. There are not many more beautiful examples of Tudor polyphony than this.

Mass 'Cantate'; Respond: 'Spiritus Sanctus'.
(B) *** Cal. Approche CAL 6621 [(M) id. import]. The Clerkes of Oxenford, Wulstan – GIBBONS: *Hymns.* ***

John Sheppard's *Cantate Mass* appears in the Hyperion Dyad collection, above; but for those looking for a less expensive way of examining his claims to musical mastery, the present Calliope Approche bargain reissue is ideal. The *Mass*, sung here a third higher than the manuscript indicates, and involving the sopranos in formidable problems of tessitura, is among the most distinctive of Sheppard's works, presenting surprises in a way uncommon in civilized polyphonic writing. The textures here are refreshingly clear, helped by the superb performances of the Clerkes of Oxenford. The five-part *Spiritus Sanctus* is less striking but makes an excellent bonus, equally well recorded.

Motets: *Gaude, gaude, gaude Maria; In manus tuas* (1st setting); *Laudem dicite Deo; In pace; Verbum caro.*
(B) **(*) CfP CD-CFP 4638 [(M) id.]. Clerkes of Oxenford, David Wulstan – TALLIS: *Motets.* **(*)

The performances by the Clerkes of Oxenford under David Wulstan are full of fervour, particularly in the inspired *Gaude, gaude, gaude Maria* and the closing *Verbum caro*. Wulstan presses on very strongly, and some might feel there is a lack of contrasting repose and not enough subtlety in the sheer thrust of his direction. But the commitment of the singing will surely convince anyone who buys this CD on impulse that this is great music and that its composer's name should be more familiar. The 1978 analogue recording has plenty of body and atmosphere.

Shostakovich, Dmitri (1906–75)

The Age of gold (suite), *Op. 22.*

(M) **(*) EMI (SIS) CDM5 65922-2. Philh. O, Irving – BARTOK: *Miraculous Mandarin:* suite. KABALEVSKY: *The Comedians* (suite); KHACHATURIAN: *Gayaneh; Masquerade:* suites. **(*)

The *Age of gold* is early Shostakovich, 1929 vintage, and the idiom is very much a cynical Russian pastiche of smart 1920s music from the West. Here the Philharmonia players are in their element, boisterously turning the barbs of satire into fun. The audacious *Polka* is given an English wit, matching Shostakovich with Lord Berners and Walton's *Façade*, while the closing dance with its boisterous accordions and piercing piccolos generates irrepressible energy. In between comes the *Adagio* where, with the most delicate solo playing from the oboe and principal violin, Irving creates an enchantingly fragile balletic atmosphere. The 1960 Kingsway Hall recording is remarkably full and clear.

Chamber symphony (arr. Barshai).

(M) ** Sony SMK 48372 [id.]. Dmitri Jakubovsky, St Petersburg Camerata, Saulius Sondeckis – HAYDN: *Symphony No. 49.* **

A curious hybrid for which it is hard to foresee long life in the catalogue. Those who want the Haydn will turn to the numerous surveys of the *Sturm und Drang* symphonies, and the Shostakovich *Chamber symphony* often serves as a fill-up to one of the symphonies at both this price level and above. All the same, these are spirited performances, if the coupling serves your needs, and they are are decently recorded.

Cello concertos Nos. 1 in E flat, Op. 107; 2 in G, Op. 126.

(BB) *** Naxos Dig. 8.550813 [id.]. Maria Kliegel, Polish Nat. RSO (Katowice), Antoni Wit.
(BB) *** Arte Nova/BMG 74321 49688-2 [id.]. Kyrill Rodin, Russian PO, Konstantin Krimets.

Maria Kliegel and the Polish National Radio Orchestra at Katowice under Antoni Wit give a very good account of both concertos that can be confidently recommended at this price. It can hold its own alongside the splendid full-priced Schiff account (Philips), as well as Torleif Thedéen (BIS) and Truls Mørk (Virgin), and on all counts is well worth considering.

Kyrill Rodin enters hotly contested terrain and is obviously a highly accomplished artist. He dispatches the *First Concerto* with effortless élan and no mean eloquence. The important solo horn part does not have quite the same virtuosity as the Philadelphia Orchestra's Mason Jones in Rostropovich's pioneering version (now on Sony, coupled with Bernstein's account of the *Second Piano concerto* and André Previn's of the *First*). In the slow movement his vibrato may possibly trouble some listeners. The searching opening to the *Second Concerto* is beautifully characterized and the orchestral playing is spirited and sensitive, though the strings are perhaps not quite weighty enough. The recordings are a trifle bright at the treble end of the spectrum but are generally very well balanced. It cannot be easy to essay these concertos, knowing that Rostropovich's own performances are widely and cheaply available, but these are impressive performances which have much going for them. Excellent value.

(i) *Cello concerto No. 1 in E flat, Op. 107;* (ii) *Symphony No. 5 in D min., Op. 47.*

(M) *** Sony Dig. [MDK 44903]. (i) Yo-Yo Ma, Phd. O, Ormandy; (ii) NYPO, Bernstein.

Yo-Yo Ma plays with an intensity that compels the listener, and the Philadelphia Orchestra give eloquent support. This has been reissued at mid-price, generously coupled with Bernstein's exciting (1979) account of the *Fifth Symphony*, recorded in Tokyo when Bernstein and the New York Philharmonic were on tour there. Unashamedly Bernstein treats the work as a Romantic symphony. The slow movement is raptly beautiful and the finale is brilliant and extrovert, with no hint of irony. On CD the bass is made to sound full and rich, and the slight distancing of the sound places the orchestra within a believable ambience.

(i) *Cello concerto No. 1 in E flat, Op. 107;* (ii) *Piano concertos Nos. 1 in C min. for piano, trumpet and strings, Op. 35; 2 in F, Op. 102.*

(BB) *** RCA Navigator 74321 29254-2 [(M) id. import]. USSR RSO, with (i) Mikhail Khomitser, cond. Rozhdestvensky; (ii) Eugene List, cond. Maxim Shostakovitch.

Eugene List plays the *First Piano concerto* with splendid dash and brilliance, underlining its brittle sonorities and brash swagger. He opens the *Second* with comparably crisp, rhythmic vigour and takes the finale very much up to speed; throughout there is plenty of character and spirit. Though the sound is vivid, the strings of the USSR Radio Symphony Orchestra are somewhat wanting in bloom. But both slow movements have plenty of atmosphere and List has the advantage of the authority of Maxim Shostakovich's direction. Rostropovich notwithstanding, his Russian colleague Mikhail Khomitser is a formidable soloist in the *Cello concerto*. The forward balance means that he dominates the performance, yet Rozhdestvensky provides a strong, concentrated backing. The first movement has very positive impetus and the *Andantino* develops a haunting, improvisational nostalgia. The orchestral recording could ideally be more refined but there is no lack of atmosphere. A real bargain,.

(i) *Cello concerto No. 1 in E flat, Op. 107; Piano concertos Nos.* (ii) *1 in C min., Op. 35;* (iii) *2 in F, Op. 102.*
(M) *** Sony MPK 44850. (i) Rostropovich, Phd. O, Ormandy; (ii) Previn; (iii) Bernstein; NYPO, Bernstein.

Rostropovich made this recording of the *Cello concerto No. 1* within a few months of the first performance in Russia. Shostakovich himself attended the recording session in Philadelphia and gave his approval to what is a uniquely authoritative reading. Sony have now shrewdly made an attractive triptych for CD by including Bernstein's radiant account of the *Second Piano concerto*, along with Previn's equally striking account of No. 1. Though these New York performances bring somewhat dated recording, both pianists have a way of turning a phrase to catch the imagination, and a fine balance is struck between Shostakovich's warmth and his rhythmic alertness.

Cello concerto No. 2, Op. 126.
(B) *** DG Double 437 952-2 (2) [id.]. Rostropovich, Boston SO, Ozawa – BERNSTEIN: *3 Meditations* etc.; BOCCHERINI: *Cello concerto No. 2;* GLAZUNOV: *Chant du Ménestrel;* TARTINI: *Cello concerto;* TCHAIKOVSKY: *Andante cantabile* etc.; VIVALDI: *Cello concertos.* ***

(i) *Cello concerto No. 2, Op. 126. Symphony No. 5 in D min., Op.47.*
(B) ** DG Classikon 439 481-2; *439 481-4* [id.]. (i) Rostropovich, Boston SO, Ozawa; (ii) Nat. SO of Washington, Rostropovich.

Rostropovich plays with beautifully controlled feeling, and Seiji Ozawa brings sympathy and fine discipline to the accompaniment, securing admirably expressive playing from the Boston orchestra. The analogue recording is first class. As can be seen, this is part of a remarkably generous DG Double anthology, showing Rostropovich's art over the widest range, and which is far more recommendable than the alternative bargain coupling offering a vibrant but highly idiosyncratic account of the *Fifth Symphony*. Although the finale is intense and exciting, there is also a hectoring quality which is distinctly unappealing.

Piano concertos Nos. (i) *1 in C min. for piano, trumpet and strings, Op. 35;* (ii) *2 in F, Op. 102.*
(M) *** SMK 47618-2. [id.]. (i) André Previn, William Vacciano; (ii) Leonard Bernstein; NYPO, Bernstein (with: POULENC: *Double piano concerto:* Arthur Gold & Robert Fizdale (pianos) ***).

(i) *Piano concertos Nos. 1–2. Age of Gold (suite), Op. 22a; Festive overture, Op. 96.*
(BB) **(*) Naxos Dig. 8.553126 [id.]. (i) Michael Houstoun; New Zealand SO, Christopher Lyndon-Gee.

Piano concertos Nos. 1–2; The Unforgettable year 1919, Op. 89; The Assault on beautiful Gorky (for piano and orchestra).
(B) *** CfP Dig. CD-CFP 4547 [(M) id. import]. Alexeev, Philip Jones, ECO, Maksymiuk.

Alexeev is a clear first choice in both *Concertos*, and his record would sweep the board even at full price. The digital recording is excellent in every way and scores over its rivals in clarity and presence. There is a fill-up in the form of a miniature one-movement *Concerto* from a film-score called *The Unforgettable year 1919*.

This Sony pairing of Bernstein's radiant account of the *Second Concerto* with Previn's equally striking reading of No. 1 makes an attractive alternative disc when coupled with a spiky yet genial version of the Poulenc *Double concerto*. The Shostakovich recordings are far from recent but sound most vivid. The Poulenc concerto, too, is both witty and abrasive, with an excellent contribution from the piano duo, Arthur Gold and Robert Fizdale. It was recorded at about the same time (1961) and the CD transfer of a not particularly smooth original is thoroughly satisfactory. This is one of the most winning discs in the Bernstein Royal Edition.

Michael Houstoun gives neat and crisp readings of both these concertos, each of them concealing deeper feelings behind seeming triviality and a modest scale. He is very well-accompanied by the New Zealand orchestra under Christopher Lyndon-Gee, helped by clear, atmospheric recording which lets one hear ample detail. Though these performances cannot quite match the outstanding ones of Dmitri Alexeev on CfP or Previn and Bernstein on Sony, the Naxos coupling is more generous than the former, not just the *Festive overture* but the youthfully exuberant *Age of Gold* music, here with vulgarity avoided in lightly pointed readings.

Piano concerto No. 1 in C min. for piano, trumpet and strings, Op. 35.
(M) *** Decca 448 577-2 [id.]. John Ogdon, John Wilbraham, ASMF, Marriner – BARTOK: *Divertimento; Music for strings, percussion and celesta.* ***

Ogdon, on top form, gives a clean, stylish performance which encompasses both the humour and the hints of romanticism in the *First Concerto*. He remains a little more detached than his accompanists in the tender slow movement, and the trumpet playing of John Wilbraham is masterly. In addition, the early 1970s recorded quality is most vivid. The comparatively backward balance of the strings gives the work a chamber quality to match that of the Bartók works, an unexpected but attractive coupling. The result is fully worthy of Decca's Classic Sound series, even if the recordings were all originally made by an Argo team!

Violin concertos Nos. 1 in A min., Op. 99; 2 in C sharp min., Op. 129.
(BB) *** Naxos Dig. 8.550814 [id.]. Kaler, Polish Nat. RSO (Katowice), Wit.

Here is another bargain issue from Naxos that vies with the best available, both in performance and in recording. Ilya Kaler, born in Moscow in 1963, a pupil of Leonid Kogan and winner of the Moscow Tchaikovsky Competition, already has some other impressive recordings for Naxos available. The technique is flawless, with playing that is not only brilliant but consistently beautiful tonally. The *Second Violin concerto* is particularly fine, the more wayward, more problematic work, in which Kaler relishes the key role given to the cadenzas. The haunting beauty of the performance may be measured by the gentle cadenza and final ghostly coda of the first movement, leading to a wonderfully rarefied account of the central *Adagio* and a mercurial, quicksilver one of the finale. If in the better-known *First concerto* Kaler's performance does not quite have the same intensity, that is partly a question of the marginally less taut orchestral accompaniment and of the recording balance.

Film scores: *Five days, five nights* (suite); *The Gadfly* (suite).
(BB) *(*) Naxos Dig. 8.553299 [id.]. Ukraine Nat. SO, Theodore Kuchar.

Though the playing of the Ukraine orchestra is at times slack, with some scrawny string-tone, this coupling of substantial suites from two of Shostakovich's more important film-scores makes a useful disc at super-bargain price. The *Romance* from *The Gadfly* was once a popular favourite, but the rest of the score – 40 minutes of it – is full of colour and variety, with the Ukraine players at their best in the folk-based dance movements. *Five days, five nights* was a wartime film with a far grimmer message, centring on the destruction of the city of Dresden, with Shostakovich inspired to some apt and dark invention. Recording fair, if lacking a little in body.

Symphonies Nos. 1–15; (i; ii) *From Jewish folk poetry;* (ii) *6 Poems of Marina Tsvetaeva.*
(B) *** Decca Dig./Analogue 444 430-2 (11) [(M) id. import]. Varady, Fischer-Dieskau, Rintzler; (i) Söderström, Karczykowski; (ii) Wenkel; Ch. of LPO or Concg. O; LPO or Concg. O, Haitink.

No one artist or set of performances holds all the insights into this remarkable symphonic canon, but what can be said of Haitink's set is that the playing of both the London Philharmonic and the Concertgebouw orchestras is of the highest calibre and is very responsive; moreover the Decca recordings, whether analogue or digital, are consistently of this company's highest standard, outstandingly brilliant and full. If without the temperament of a Mravinsky, Haitink proves a reliable guide to this repertoire, often much more than that, and sometimes inspired. All in all, a considerable achievement. The eleven discs are now offered together at bargain price, but they also remain available separately at mid-price – see below.

Symphonies Nos. 1 in F min., Op. 10; 12 in D min. (The Year 1917), Op. 112.
(M) ** BMG/Melodiya 74321 19848-2 [id.]. Moscow PO, Kondrashin.

Symphonies Nos. (i) *2 in B (October Revolution), Op. 14;* (ii) *14 in G min., Op. 135.*
(M) *** BMG/Melodiya 74321 19844-2 [id.]. (i) Russian Republic Ch.; (ii) Tselovalnik, Nestorenko; Moscow PO, Kondrashin.

Symphonies Nos. (i) *3 in E flat (The First of May), Op. 20; 5 in D min., Op. 47.*
(M) ** BMG/Melodiya 7432 119845-2 [id.]. (i) Russian Republic Ch.; Moscow PO, Kondrashin.

Symphony No. 4 in C min., Op. 43.
(M) *** BMG/Melodiya 74321 19840-2 [id.]. Moscow PO, Kondrashin.

Symphonies Nos. 6 in B min., Op. 54; 10 in E min., Op. 93.
(M) *(*) BMG/Melodiya 74321 19847-2 [id.]. Moscow PO, Kondrashin.

Symphony No. 7 in C (Leningrad), Op. 60.
(M) ** BMG/Melodiya 74321 19839-2 [id.]. Moscow PO, Kondrashin.

Symphony No. 8 in C min., Op. 65.
(M) *(*) BMG/Melodiya 74321 19841-2 [id.]. Moscow PO, Kondrashin.

Symphonies Nos. 9, Op. 70; 15 in A, Op. 103.
(M) **(*) BMG/Melodiya 74321 19846-2 [id.]. Moscow PO, Kondrashin.

Symphony No. 11 (The Year 1905), Op. 103.
(M) ** BMG/Melodiya 74321 19843-2 [id.]. Moscow PO, Kondrashin.

Symphony No. 13 in B flat min. (Babi Yar), Op. 113.
(M) *** BMG/Melodiya 74321 19842-2 [id.]. Eisen, Russian Republic Ch., Moscow PO, Kondrashin.

Kirill Kondrashin's cycle was made over a long period of time: the *Fourth Symphony* dates from 1962, not long after its first performance at the end of the previous year, while the last to appear (in the mid-1970s) were Nos. 7 (*Leningrad*), 14 and 15. The set is of importance in that Shostakovich himself expressed confidence in this conductor, and it is clear that in many instances he comes closer than most to the spirit of this music. Not all the performances strike us as *sans pareil*. In none of them is the playing of the Moscow Philharmonic as distinguished or as finely disciplined as in many rival accounts. Nor, to be fair, are Kondrashin's insights deeper than those of Mravinsky or (in the case of Nos. 5, 6, 7 and 11) Stokowski. It is rare to find one cycle that fulfils the aspirations with which it embarks and, although Haitink and the Concertgebouw have strong merits, there is no single survey that is absolutely ideal in every respect. Nos. 4, 13 and 14 make the strongest impression in Kondrashin's hands. Despite the sonic limitations inevitable over the course of over 30 years, the *Fourth* is almost indispensable. It has that sense of discovery, raw intensity and sheer eloquence which silence criticism – or should do. And the 1967 account of the *Thirteenth* has an authentic feel to it that makes its claims on the collector strong. Both the *Fourteenth*, song-cycle-cum-symphony and the enigmatic *Fifteenth Symphony* have much to recommend them.

Elsewhere the cycle is less even. The brisk tempi Kondrashin adopts for the first movement of both the *Sixth* and *Eighth* symphonies diminish their intensity of feeling and directness of effect and, though he makes out a stronger case for the *Third* than some rivals, he is no match for Mravinsky in the *Twelfth*. The Moscow Philharmonic strings are by no means as sumptuous as those of the USSR State Academic Symphony (or the 'USSR Symphony' as it was known at one time), nor as responsive as those in Pletnev's Russian National Orchestra; and they do not sound quite as warm or smooth as on the LP. It is difficult to generalize, but the bass is sometimes firmer and definition is keener. There are roughnesses on the originals that are not quite smoothed out.

(i) *Symphony No. 1 in F min., Op. 10;* (ii) *Festive overture, Op. 96.* Collection: *The Age of gold, Op. 22: Polka. Ballet suite No. 1: Galop; Music-box waltz; Dance. Ballet suite No. 2: Polka; Galop. The Gadfly, Op. 97a: Introduction; Barrel organ waltz; Nocturne; Folk festival; Galop. Moscow-Cheryomushki: Overture waltz; Galop.*
✿ (B) *** Sony SBK 62642; *SBT 62642* [id.]. (i) Phd. O, Ormandy; (ii) Columbia SO, André Kostelanetz.

Ormandy and the Philadelphia Orchestra recorded this version of the *First Symphony* in the presence of the composer in 1959, and their endeavours have never been surpassed. It is a beautifully proportioned, tense and vivid account, with everyone doing their utmost to get things right. The sound, too, is excellent. Still, after 37 years, a front-runner in spite of some excellent successors. The coupling could not have been better chosen: a suite of Shostakovichian orchestral lollipops selected by Kostelanetz, a dab hand at this kind of audacious light music. Readers who know the *Polka* from *The Age of gold* will know what to expect. Kostelanetz opens with a fizzing account of the *Festive overture*, Op. 96. Then comes the series of miniatures – mixed up to provide maximum contrast. Many of the pieces were virtually unknown when these performances first appeared in 1965, and even today few of them are familiar to the wider public. The fast numbers (like the Offenbachian *Galop* from *The Gadfly*) are redeemed from vulgarity by momentum and brilliant scoring, many of them suggesting the composer thumbing his nose at the Soviet authorities, and there is no better example than the *Moscow-Cheryomushki Overture waltz* with its trombone glissandi accompanying a very Russian dance-accelerando, followed by the equally infectious potpourri called *Folk festival*. But the gentler pieces are more memorable still: the hauntingly tender *Nocturne* from *The Gadfly* and the delicious *Barrel organ waltz* from the same source, matched by the *Music-box waltz* from the *Ballet suite No. 1*. Kostelanetz plays this music for all it's worth, and if again the recording is brash, this time it fits the music like a glove.

Symphonies Nos. 1 in F min., Op. 10; 3 (The First of May), Op. 20.
(M) *** Decca Dig. 425 063-2. LPO Ch., LPO, Haitink.
(BB) ** Naxos Dig. 8.550623 [id.]. Slovak RSO (Bratislava), Ladislav Slovák.

In this now popular coupling, Haitink still leads the field, when the Decca recording is outstandingly clear and brilliant. His account of No. 1 is strong and very well played. It may lack something in youthful high spirits but not in concentration. No. 3 is not one of Shostakovich's finest works but is worth having when played as commitedly as here.

On Naxos, Slovák conducts energetic performances of both Nos. 1 and 3, even if some of the playing is rough. In this coupling, Haitink offers more pointed and sharply focused readings, better played and recorded.

Symphonies Nos. (i) *1 in F min.;* (ii) *5 in D min.*
(B) (*) Millennium mono MCD 80112 [id.]. (i) Nat. SO of Washington, Howard Mitchell; (ii) RPO, Rodzinski.

Howard Mitchell's recording of the *First Symphony* originally appeared on Nixa/Westminster in the early 1950s and, though it is serviceable, is no match for the classic Ormandy account. Artur Rodzinski's *Fifth* appeared on Westminster/Nixa, with the RPO billed as the London Promenade Symphony Orchestra. The finale is taken at a tremendous lick but is disfigured by a cut of 29 bars (from two bars before fig. 119 to fig. 121) which rules it completely out of court.

Symphonies Nos. 2 (October Revolution), Op. 14; 10 in E min., Op. 93.
(M) **(*) Dig./Analogue 425 064-2. LPO Ch., LPO, Haitink.

Haitink's performance of No. 2 is admirable, and it is given excellently balanced sound with great presence and body. No. 10 is a masterpiece, and Haitink really has the measure of the first movement, whose climaxes he paces with an admirable sense of architecture. He secures sensitive and enthusiastic playing from the LPO, both here and in the malignant Scherzo. In the third movement he adopts a slower tempo than usual, which would be acceptable if there were greater tension or concentration of mood; but here and in the slow introduction to the finale the sense of concentration falters. The 1977 analogue recording (like the digital *Second*, made in the Kingsway Hall) is outstandingly realistic.

Symphonies Nos. 2 in B (October Revolution), Op. 14; 15 in A, Op. 141.
(BB) ** Naxos Dig. 8.550624 [id.]. Slovak RSO (Bratislava), Ladislav Slovák.

Slovák's version of No. 2 on Naxos begins disconcertingly with muffled growling, but then opens up well on the Allegro, with the choral second half fresh and dramatic. No. 15 may not match Haitink's version in tension but it is played and recorded well.

Symphony No. 4 in C min., Op. 43.
(M) **(*) Decca 425 065-2. LPO, Haitink.
(BB) ** Naxos Dig. 8.550625 [id.]. Slovak RSO (Bratislava), Ladislav Slovák.

Haitink brings out an unexpected refinement in the *Symphony*, a rare transparency of texture. He is helped by recording of Decca's finest quality, vividly remastered. Detail is caught superbly; yet the earthiness and power, the demonic quality which can make this work so compelling, are underplayed.

Despite some technical accidents, the Slovak version on Naxos can be recommended as a bargain for strong and purposeful playing of an enigmatic work, well recorded in immediate sound.

Symphonies Nos. 4 in C min., Op. 43; 5 in D min., Op. 47.
(B) ** EMI forte CZS5 72658-2 (2). Chicago SO, Previn – BRITTEN: *Sinfonia da requiem* etc. *** ✿

Previn's is an eminently straightforward, superlatively played and vividly recorded account of the problematic *Fourth Symphony*, whose publication Shostakovich withheld from 1936 to the early 1960s. Orchestral playing is also of the highest quality in the *Fifth Symphony*, but here there is little sense of freshness and urgency. The first movement is a good deal slower than usual, so much so that one feels the want of momentum. The Scherzo is movingly played, but the slow movement is without a sense of forward movement and the climax lacks real urgency. The recorded sound is extremely impressive.

Symphonies Nos. 4 in C min., Op. 43; 10 in E min., Op. 93.
(B) *** Sony SB2K 62409 (2) [S2K 62409]. Phd. O, Ormandy.

The *Fourth* was the symphony which Shostakovich withdrew on the eve of its première, to be replaced later by the *Fifth* as 'a Soviet artist's reply to just criticism'. Ormandy pioneered the work in the West. His reading of this strange and powerful symphony is less subtle than Kondrashin's Russian account, less refined than Haitink, but it is thoroughly convincing and has the Philadelphia Orchestra playing both brilliantly (witness the frenzied string passage at the climax of the first movement) and with real depth of feeling. The combination of irony, anguish and plangent lyricism, as in the central *Moderato*, is strongly characterized, while the curiously subdued atmosphere of the march which opens the finale is remarkably well caught. The 1963 recording, made in Philadelphia Town Hall, is spaciously full and vivid; it sounds excellent in the current CD transfer.

Ormandy went on to record No. 10 with equal success in the same venue in 1968, and again he makes a case for treating the work with a passion that is apt for Tchaikovsky. The result is not as refined in its effect as Karajan's DG version, but it still makes a compelling, indeed massive, impact, notably in the long first and third movements. Ormandy's control of string phrasing is again immaculate and his great orchestra is never less than convincing and is often superbly brilliant in the precision of its virtuosity. This makes a thoroughly worthwhile bargain coupling.

Symphony No. 5 in D min., Op. 47 (see also under *Cello concerto No. 1*).
(M) *** Erato/Warner 2292 45752-2 [id.]. Leningrad PO, Mravinsky.
(M) **(*) Mercury (IMS) 434 323-2 [id.]. Minneapolis SO, Skrowaczewski – KHACHATURIAN: *Gayaneh ballet suite*. **(*)
(M) **(*) DG 453 988-2 [id.]. Warsaw PO, Rowicki – TCHAIKOVSKY: *Francesca da Rimini*. ***
(M) ** DG (IMS) Dig. 445 577-2. Nat. SO of Washington, Rostropovich – PROKOFIEV: *Romeo and Juliet: suite No. 1*. **
(M) * Revelation RV 10025 [id.]. USSR State SO, Yuri Temirkanov – PROKOFIEV: *Symphony No. 3*. *

Symphony No. 5; Age of gold: Polka.
(B) **(*) Sony SBK 53261; *SBT 53261* [id.]. Phd. O, Ormandy – PROKOFIEV: *Love for 3 oranges: suite*. **

(i) *Symphony No. 5 in D min., Op. 47;* (ii) *Michurin* (film music) *suite, Op. 78;* (iii) *Age of Gold: Polka*.
(M) ** BMG/Melodiya 74321 32041-2. (i) USSR SO; (ii) Bolshoi Theatre O, Moscow; (iii) USSR R. & TV Ch. and Large SO; Maxim Shostakovich.

(i) *Symphony No. 5;* (ii) *Hamlet* (film incidental music), *suite, Op. 116*.
(BB) *** RCA Navigator 74321 24212-2 [without *Hamlet:* Basic 100 09026 68456-2]. (i) LSO, Previn; (ii) Belgian RSO, José Serebrier.

Previn's RCA version, dating from early in his recording career (1965), remains at the top of the list of bargain recommendations. This is one of the most concentrated and intense readings ever, superbly played by the LSO at its peak. In the third movement he sustains a slower speed than anyone else, making it deeply meditative in its dark intensity, while his build-up in the central development section brings playing of white heat. The bite and urgency of the second and fourth movements are also irresistible. Only in the hint of analogue tape-hiss and a slight lack of opulence in the violins does the sound fall short of the finest modern digital recordings – and it is more vividly immediate than most. The new coupling is appropriate. *Hamlet* obviously generated powerful resonances in Shostakovich's psyche and produced vivid incidental music: the opening Ball scene is highly reminiscent of *Romeo and Juliet*. The playing of the Belgian Radio Orchestra under Serebrier is eminently serviceable without being really distinguished, but with atmospheric recording this 28-minute suite makes a considerable bonus.

Mravinsky conducted the première of the *Fifth Symphony* in 1937, and so brings a special authority to this work. The present version is not free from the odd untidiness but there is still evidence of a commanding personality, and even though the recording itself is not in the luxury bracket, this CD must figure high on any list.

The Philadelphia Orchestra made the very first recording of the *Fifth Symphony* (under Stokowski), and they play it marvellously here: the strings produce the most opulent tone and generate considerable eloquence in the slow movement; the solo flute, too, makes a highly distinguished contribution. Ormandy has always shown a special feeling for Shostakovich and he is direct and straightforward, but neither here (in 1965) nor in his later, RCA disc does one sense the degree of commitment that marked his earlier recording of the *First Symphony*. *The Age of gold polka* makes a witty encore after the Prokofiev coupling.

Skrowaczewski's Minneapolis account of Shostakovich's *Fifth* was one of the first really successful stereo recordings of the work, with great concentration in the pianissimo string-playing in the *Largo* and a finale which, after an exhilarating *Allegro*, brings a trenchant, ponderous coda, anticipating much later performances, after the composer had revealed that his closing section was not intended to be an ingenuous triumphant celebration. The first movement has a fast opening speed, but the conductor understands Shostakovich's melodic line and, although this is a wilful reading, it is also an exciting one. The recording was made in the Northrop Auditorium in 1961 and is full yet astonishingly clear, but the upper strings have that curious thinness which was characteristic of Mercury's Minneapolis ventures at that time. However, the ear soon adjusts, and this performance is very compelling.

Rowicki's performance is surprisingly relaxed and spacious – even mellow – for an East European conductor, yet in consequence it offers its own kind of beauty in the lyrical pages, and the central climax of the first movement brings a spontaneous burst of intensity. The conductor then deliberately chooses to treat the second movement lightly, but he finds no lack of depth in the slow movement, and again there is a powerful climax. In the finale, most other versions find greater surface excitement, but Rowicki's reading here is clearly in line with his overall view: comparatively introspective, though not without underlying passion, and undoubtedly finding different insights in this often-played and much-recorded work. The 1959 DG recording is full and atmospheric and is especially fine in the quiet string passages. But this interpretation could hardly be more different temperamentally from Rozhdestvensky's coupled *Francesca da Rimini*.

Rostropovich's account is too idiosyncratic to be recommended without qualification. He secures a refined, cultured string-tone, capable of searing intensity and strength, and all sections of the orchestra play with excellent attack and ensemble. The opening is given with hushed *ppp* intensity (the marking is in fact *piano*) and all promises well until, as is so often the case with this great Russian musician, he disturbs the natural musical flow for the sake of expressive effect. The brakes are abruptly applied in the Scherzo (at fig. 56), just before the horn figure is repeated, and he also pulls other phrases around. He wrings the last ounce of intensity out of the finale, which is undoubtedly imposing, but there is also a hectoring quality which is distinctly unappealing. The recording is on the whole good, even if it is a multi-mike, somewhat synthetic balance.

The *Fifth Symphony* conducted by Maxim Shostakovich appeared in the mid-1970s on the HMV Melodiya label when it was among the first half-dozen recommendations, though it never challenged the Previn/LSO account. It is very well played by the USSR Symphony Orchestra, and the recording, too, is perfectly acceptable; but time has moved on and the climate is more competitive. Neither the addition of the *Michurin* suite from Shostakovich's film-score nor the *Polka* from *The Age of gold* affects matters much either way.

Temirkanov's account of the *Fifth Symphony* derives from a concert performance in 1981 and, though less prone to expressive exaggeration than some of his more recent recordings, it is still uncompetitive, even at mid-price. He wears his heart on his sleeve in the *Largo* and, though there are some good things, readers are better advised to turn elsewhere. Decent recording quality.

Symphonies Nos. 5 in D min.; 6 in B min., Op. 54.
❁ (M) (***) Dutton Lab mono CDAX 8017 [id. full price]. Phd. O, Stokowski.

Stokowski's electrifying première of the *Fifth* has never been surpassed on record, notably for the intensity and beauty of the string playing in the first and third movements. The new Dutton transfer is little short of miraculous in its vividness and presence, and the quality of the recording is astonishing. Stokowski's *Sixth* was made in 1940, only a few months after the work was premièred, and it brings one face to face not only with this symphony but also with the bleak, harsh times during which it came into being. It is powerfully atmospheric, the lines wonderfully sustained and the playing at times frighteningly intense. This performance has a special ring of authenticity.

Symphonies Nos. 5 in D min.; 9 in E flat, Op. 70.
(M) *** Decca Dig. 425 066-2. (i) Concg. O; (ii) LPO, Haitink.
(BB) *** Naxos Dig. 8.550427 [id.]. Belgian R. & TV O, Alexander Rahbari.
(M) **(*) Sony SMK 47615-2. NYPO, Bernstein.
(BB) * Naxos Dig. 8.550632 [id.]. Slovak RSO (Bratislava), Ladislav Slovák.

In No. 5 Haitink is eminently straightforward, there are no disruptive changes in tempo, and the playing of the Concertgebouw Orchestra and the contribution of the Decca engineers are beyond praise. There could perhaps be greater intensity of feeling in the slow movement but, whatever small reservations one might have, it is most impressive both artistically and sonically. The coupled No. 9 is superb. Without inflation Haitink gives it a serious purpose, both in the poignancy of the waltz-like second movement and in the equivocal emotions of the outer movements. The recording is outstanding in every way.

Both in the hushed intensity of the lyrical passages and in the vigour and bite of Shostakovich's violent allegros Rahbari's reading is most convincing, with dramatic tensions finely controlled in a spontaneous-sounding way. In No. 9 Rahbari opts for a controversially slow *Moderato* second movement but sustains it well, and the outer movements are deliciously witty in their pointing. The playing of all sections is first rate, and the sound is full and brilliant. An outstandingly generous coupling makes this a most attractive issue, even with no allowance made for the very low price.

This was Bernstein's first recording of the *Fifth*, made in 1959; he re-recorded it later digitally. His view of the work was admired by the composer, perhaps because the finale opens so ferociously. Bernstein revels in the high spirits of the *Ninth*, and he also manages the alternation of moods very successfully. The sound has been greatly improved in both symphonies.

Slovák's version of No. 5 on Naxos is not as well played as most in this series, making it a doubtful recommendation, even as a bargain. The earlier, Rahbari coupling on the same label is the one to go for in this price-range.

Symphonies Nos. 6 in B min., Op. 54; 12 in D min. (The Year 1917), Op. 112.
(M) *** Decca Dig. 425 067-2. Concg. O, Haitink.

Haitink's structural control, coupled with his calm, taut manner, is particularly impressive in the slow movement of No. 6. As a work, No. 12 is more problematic. There is much of the composer's vision and grandeur here but also his crudeness. However, the sheer quality of the sound and the superb responsiveness and body of the Concertgebouw Orchestra might well seduce many listeners. As with the *Sixth* the slow movement has a marvellous sense of atmosphere, which is well conveyed in this Decca performance; the Amsterdam orchestra play as if they believe every crotchet and, though not even their eloquence can rescue the finale, overall the performance is very successful.

Symphony No. 7 in C (Leningrad), Op. 60.
(M) **(*) Decca Dig. 425 068-2. LPO, Haitink.
(M) **(*) Sony SMK 47616-2. NYPO, Bernstein.
(M) (***) RCA mono GD60293 [60293-2-RG]. NBC SO, Toscanini.
(M) *(*) Teldec/Warner Dig. 2292 45414-2. Nat. SO, Rostropovich.
(BB) * Naxos 8.550627 [id.]. Slovak RSO (Bratislava), Ladislav Slovák.

Haitink is here eminently straightforward. There could perhaps be greater intensity of feeling in the slow movement, and the long first-movement *ostinato* is not presented histrionically; but the deep seriousness which Haitink finds in the rest of the work challenges comparisons with the other wartime symphony, the epic *Eighth*. The playing of the Concertgebouw Orchestra is beyond praise, and the splendid contribution of the Decca engineers ensures the success of this CD.

Bernstein brings a certain panache and fervour to his reading, particularly in the inspired slow movement, so that one is tempted to look indulgently at its occasional overstatements.

Toscanini and the NBC Orchestra bring an urgency and fervour that is altogether special and an intensity that shines through the primitive recorded sound. There is a special feeling of authenticity that conveys the flavour of the period and the vividness of the experience more effectively than many modern recordings. Be warned, however, the 1942 sound does call for some tolerance.

Rostropovich's account is eminently well-prepared and springs from undoubted feeling, though he is often a bit heavy-handed. He rarely lets the music speak for itself and the overall effect is studied. The engineers provide him with a recording of impressive dynamic range. However well schooled the playing may be, there is a literal feeling here (all *i*'s are dotted and *t*'s crossed).

Slovák's Naxos version is variably successful, with the massive first movement too lacking in tension to sustain it with its deliberate banality. Fast movements are far more successful, but the ominous strength of the work is missing. Recording drier than in most of the series.

Symphonies Nos. 7 in C (Leningrad), Op. 60; 8 in C min., Op. 65; King Lear (incidental music): (i) *Introduction and Cordelia's ballad;* (ii) *10 Buffoon's songs, Op. 58a.*
(B) **(*) BMG/Melodiya Twofer Dig. 74321 53457-2 (2) [id.]. USSR MoC SO, Rozhdestvensky; with (i) Natalia Burnasheva; (ii) Evgeni Nesterenko.

Rozhdestvensky's view of the *Leningrad Symphony*'s controversial first movement is unusually broad. It is undeniably powerful but runs the risk of overplaying the element of banality in the notorious *ostinato*. Many will prefer a brisker and more polished reading, but the ruggedness here is certainly authentic; the other movements also bring warmly expressive, spontaneous-sounding performances which lack only the last degree of subtlety. Rozhdestvensky then follows with a thrustful and incisive reading of the *Eighth*, with electrically intense playing that both holds the enormous structure together and brings out the element of fantasy which literal performances underplay. The spontaneity Rozhdestvensky regularly conveys in his recordings is here combined with sharpness of focus. In both symphonies the digital recording is full-bodied and wide-ranging with a full depth of string-tone, but it grows coarse in the biggest climaxes. The songs for Shakespeare's *King Lear* are an additional asset to the set. Natalia Burnasheva sings Cordelia's touching lyrical ballad eloquently and Nesterenko characterizes strongly the ten brief *Buffoon's songs* (most less than a minute in length) with their typical Shostakovian amalgam of grotesquerie and irony. No translations are offered, but there are good notes.

Symphony No. 8 in C min., Op. 65.
(B) *** Ph. Virtuoso 422 442-2 [Russian Disc RDCD 10917 full price]. Leningrad PO, Mravinsky.
(M) *** Decca Dig. 425 071-2. Concg. O, Haitink.
(BB) ** Arte Nova/BMG Dig. 74321 51628-2 [id.]. Novosibirsk PO, Arnold Kats.
(M) (**) RCA Melodiya mono 74321 29406-2. Leningrad PO, Mravinsky.
(BB) *(*) Naxos Dig. 8.550628 [id.]. Slovak RSO (Bratislava), Ladislav Slovák.
(M) * Ph. Dig. 454 683-2 [id.]. BPO, Bychkov.

Mravinsky's live recording in full, clear, analogue sound of high quality gives a superb idea of the magnetism of his reading, demonstrating the firm structural strength while plumbing the deep personal emotions in this stressed wartime inspiration. Most significantly, Mravinsky's flowing speed for the elusive *Allegretto* finale makes the close of the work less equivocal than usual. It is a great performance and, though ensemble is inevitably not always quite as polished as in the finest studio recordings, discrepancies are minimal.

Haitink characteristically presents a strongly architectural reading of this war-inspired symphony, at times direct to the point of severity. After the massive and sustained slow movement which opens the work, Haitink allows no lightness or relief in the Scherzo movements, and in his seriousness in the strangely lightweight finale (neither fast nor slow) he provides an unusually satisfying account of an equivocal, seemingly uncommitted movement.

The claims of the intensely gripping and powerful 1947 performance of the *Eighth Symphony* by Yevgeni Mravinsky are considerable; but those wanting a recommendable modern recording at rock-bottom price could well consider the Arte Nova account by the Novosibirsk Philharmonic Orchestra under Arnold Kats. It was, incidentally, at Novosibirsk that the symphony received its wartime première. It is a good rather than an outstanding performance, the strings are not as full-bodied or opulent as those of the Leningrad orchestra. Kats's first movement runs to 24 minutes 48 seconds as opposed to Mravinsky's 27 minutes 14 seconds, and there is little of the latter's intensity and feeling. The recorded sound is very good and no one coming to this work afresh need feel they are being in any way shortchanged. All the same, it falls short of being the full picture. (Reminder: the Russian Disc version (RDCD 10917), which has recently appeared, would appear to be the same as the 1982 account which has now reappeared on Philips. It is a splendidly intense performance, but it is unrealistically offered at full price.)

Slovák on Naxos takes a rugged view of this powerful work, with the opening, weighty and purposeful, setting the pattern. Though tension is not always sustained in the middle movements, the weight of the sound helps to convey the brutal strength of the big climaxes, resolving in a genial account of the gentle fifth movement. Sound on the dry side but vivid.

Bychkov's version is a non-starter. It is full of agogic point-making, especially in the outer movements; although very well played, it does not even begin to compare with Mravinsky's superb recording, which remains a clear first choice.

Symphonies Nos. (i) *9 in E flat;* (ii) *10 in E min*.
(M) (***) Sony mono MPK 45698 [id.]. NYPO, (i) Efrem Kurtz; (ii) Dmitri Mitropoulos.

Dmitri Mitropoulos's pioneering account of the *Tenth Symphony* with the New York Philharmonic penetrates more deeply into the heart of this score than any of the recent newcomers; only Karajan's mid-1960s version (currently withdrawn) can be put alongside it. It comes with Efrem Kurtz's 1949 version of the *Ninth* with the same orchestra, playing with great virtuosity. The sound is remarkably good for its period (an edit has removed one note from the opening phrase of the Scherzo), but apart from that hiccup this is a stunning performance.

Symphony No. 10 in E min., Op. 93.
(B) *** Carlton IMP Dig. PCD 2043 [(M) id.]. Hallé O, Skrowaczewski.
(B) **(*) EMI CfP CD-CFP 6041 [(M) id. import]. LPO, Andrew Davis.
(M) ** EMI Dig. CDM7 64870-2. Philh. O, Simon Rattle – BRITTEN: *Sinfonia da Requiem*. ***
(BB) ** Naxos Dig. 8.550326 [id.]. Belgian R. & TV O, Alexander Rahbari.

Symphony No. 10 in E min.; Festival overture, Op. 96.
(M) ** Virgin/EMI Dig. CUV5 61134-2. LPO, Andrew Litton.

Recorded in full, brilliant and weighty sound, Skrowaczewski's version of the *Tenth* is also a top recommendation. Above all, the spacious *moderato* of the long first movement has a natural power and concentration which put it among the finest versions, with the Hallé brass superbly focused at the climaxes.

Shostakovich's finest symphony draws from Andrew Davis a fresh, direct and concentrated performance, with the LPO in excellent form and clearly on their toes in the Scherzo. The reading lacks a little in individuality but is still most compelling, both in the long paragraphs of the first and third movements and in the pointedly rhythmic second and fourth. The 1974 recording, made in Barking Assembly Hall, is outstandingly natural and spacious, with excellent detail but plenty of warmth for the strings. Not a first choice, but at bargain price this has a great deal going for it.

Andrew Litton draws refined playing from the LPO in both the symphony and the brassy overture which precedes it, matched by refined, slightly distanced recorded sound. Unfortunately these are two Shostakovich works which demand more rugged treatment. Not only does the overture miss something in extrovert panache, a sense of daring; the great span of the first movement of the symphony fails to build to the necessary climax when tension is kept low, however beautiful the incidental detail. The Scherzo is more biting but is not demonic as it should be; and the last two movements, with such relaxed and refined treatment, become elegant, where they should convey bluff, rugged strength.

Rattle's Philharmonia version is curiously wayward in the two big slow movements, first and third in the scheme. In the first, Rattle is exceptionally slow, and though in principle such a view might yield revelatory results tension slips too readily. So too in the third movement. The Scherzo and energetic finale are much more successful. The recording does not help, with the strings sounding thin and lacking body.

Rahbari is less successful in No. 10 than he was in No. 5, with the playing a degree less polished and the recording more distanced and less involving. Even so, his natural expressiveness is most persuasive, and the ironic flavour in the third-movement *Allegretto* is beautifully caught.

Symphony No. 11 (The Year 1905), Op. 103.
(M) *** Decca Dig. 425 072-2. Concg. O, Haitink.
(BB) ** Arte Nova Dig. 74321 54452-2 [id.]. Jena PO, David Montgomery.
(BB) *(*) Naxos Dig. 8.550629 [id.]. Czech RSO (Bratislava), Ladislav Slovák.

1905 was the year of the first Russian uprising, which foreshadowed the revolution to come rather more than a decade later. The result is a programme symphony conceived on a fairly large scale and, as in the *Leningrad Symphony*, its style is sometimes repetitive. Haitink's sense of architecture is as impressive as always, even if at times he seems almost detached, lacking the last degree of tension. However, the Concertgebouw Orchestra plays superbly, and the Decca sound is as brilliant and realistic as ever.

The American conductor, David Montgomery, latterly experienced in the film world, conducts a spacious and refined account. Speeds are generally astonishingly slow – with a total timing some quarter of an hour longer than Ashkenazy's full-priced version on Decca – but are very well sustained, with recording at a low level that brings out detail well in the polished playing of the Jena Philharmonic. Expressive warmth takes priority over dramatic bite, but at bargain price this is a quite viable version, although Haitink is finer.

The Naxos account from Bratislava follows the pattern of the Naxos Shostakovich series, with a clean-cut reading from Slovák almost as expansive as Montgomery's on Arte Nova. The string-sound, as recorded, is edgier and more biting than that of that rival version, which brings an advantage at moments of dramatic climax, though generally the playing, less polished, has not quite the same concentration.

Symphony No. 12 in D min. (The Year 1917), Op. 112.
(M) *** Erato/Warner 2292 45754-2 [id.]. Leningrad PO, Mravinsky.

The *Twelfth Symphony* is one of Shostakovich's more problematic essays in the genre. However, when a conductor of Mravinsky's quality is at the helm and drawing playing of electrifying intensity from the Leningrad Philharmonic, that impression is almost dispelled. Mravinsky's first version appeared in the early 1960s and long reigned supreme, but this Erato account, taken from a concert performance in 1984, is even higher in voltage, and the recording does ample justice to their playing.

Symphony No. 13 in B flat min. (Babi-Yar), Op. 113.
(M) *** Decca Dig. 425 073-2. Marius Rintzler, Concg. Male Ch. & O, Haitink.
(M) **(*) Teldec/Warner 2292 45349-2 [id.]. Ghiuselev, Nat. SO of Washington, Rostropovich.
(BB) ** Naxos Dig. 8.550630 [id.]. Peter Mikuláš, Slovak Philharmonic Ch. and RSO (Bratislava), Ladislav Slovák.

The often brutal directness of Haitink's way with Shostakovich works well in the *Thirteenth Symphony*, particularly in the long *Adagio* first movement, whose title, *Babi-Yar*, gives its name to the whole work. That first of five Yevtushenko settings, boldly attacking anti-semitism in Russia, sets the pattern for Haitink's severe view of the whole. Rintzler with his magnificent, resonant bass is musically superb but, matching Haitink, remains objective rather than dashingly characterful. The resolution of the final movement, with its pretty flutings surrounding a wry poem about Galileo and greatness, then works beautifully. Outstandingly brilliant and full sound, remarkable even for this series.

Rostropovich, who can so often be overemphatic in the music of his great countryman and friend, is at his most persuasive here. Nicola Ghiuselev is a fine singer and produces some glorious tone, even though he has not the dramatic flair and commanding presence that Artur Eisen brought to Kondrashin's performance. A rewarding performance, with good recording to match.

Slovák's version on Naxos is marred by the roughness of the choral sound, not helped by the closeness of the voices, but once the ruggedness of the reading is accepted there is much to enjoy, with Mikuláš a firm and characterful bass soloist. Sadly, Slovák's *Allegretto* for the last movement with its gentle opening is so fast it sounds trivial. Dryish recording which yet atmospherically captures withdrawn string pianissimos.

Symphony No. 14 in G min., Op. 135.
(BB) *** Naxos Dig. 8.550631 [id.]. Hajóssyová, Mikuláš, Slovak RSO (Bratislava), Ladislav Slovák.
(M) **(*) Teldec/Warner 0630 17514-2. Vishnevskaya, Reshetin, Moscow Academic SO (members), Rostropovich.

(i) *Symphony No. 14, Op. 135;* (ii) *6 Poems of Marina Tsvetaeva, Op. 143a.*
(M) *** Decca Dig. 425 074-2. (i) Varady, Fischer-Dieskau; (ii) Wenkel; Concg. O, Haitink.

The *Fourteenth* is Shostakovich's most sombre and dark score, a setting of poems by Lorca, Apollinaire, Rilke, Brentano and Küchelbecker, all on the theme of death; Haitink's version gives each poem in its original language. It is a most powerful performance, and the outstanding recording is well up to the standard of this fine Decca series. The song-cycle, splendidly sung by Ortrun Wenkel, makes a fine bonus.

Slovák's account of No. 14 is one of the finest in his Shostakovich series for Naxos, strongly characterized in each of the eleven contrasted movements with the help of two superb soloists. Mikuláš is just as strong and individual as in No. 13, and Hajóssyová with her firm, Slavonic mezzo is equally idiomatic. Regularly, Slovák and his performers bring out the menace behind the composer's inspiration on the theme of death, with the fourth song, '*The Suicide*', particularly moving in its tenderness. The booklet gives a summary of each poem, but no texts or translations. Full, immediate sound.

Rostropovich's performance dates from 1973 and has the advantage of a very clear, analogue recording. Detail is reproduced with striking presence and definition within a good orchestral perspective. The soloists are too close and the ear senses the presence of the microphones, but the result is arrestingly vivid. The performance is dark and intense, with expressive detail sometimes underlined. Vishnevskaya may not be to all tastes (she can sing touchingly but can also sound shrill above the stave at the top of her register). Reshetin, however, is consistently impressive.

(i) *Symphony No. 15 in A, Op. 141;* (ii) *From Jewish folk poetry* (song-cycle), *Op. 79.*
✿ (M) *** Decca Analogue/Dig. 425 069-2 [id.]. (i) LPO; (ii) Söderström, Wenkel, Karczykowski, Concg. O; Haitink.

Early readings of the composer's last symphony seemed to underline the quirky unpredictability of the work, with the collage of strange quotations – above all the *William Tell* galop, which keeps recurring in the first movement – seemingly joky rather than profound. Haitink by contrast makes the first movement sound genuinely symphonic, bitingly urgent. He underlines the purity of the bare lines of the second movement; after the Wagner quotations which open the finale, his slow tempo for the main lyrical theme gives it heartaching tenderness, not the usual easy triviality. The playing of the LPO is excellent, with refined tone and superb attack, and the recording is both analytical and atmospheric. The CD includes a splendidly sung version of *From Jewish folk poetry*, settings which cover a wide range of emotions including tenderness, humour and even happiness as in the final song. Ryszard Karczykowski brings vibrant Slavonic feeling to the work which, with its wide variety of mood and colour, has a scale to match the shorter symphonies.

CHAMBER AND INSTRUMENTAL MUSIC

Cello sonata in D min., Op. 40.
(M) *** Finlandia FACD 705. Arto Noras, Tapani Valsta – SCHUBERT: *Arpeggione sonata.* ***
(BB) *** ASV Quicksilva Dig. CDQS 6218 [(M) id.]. Bernard Gregor-Smith, Yolande Wrigley – MARTINU: *Variations;* JANACEK: *Pohádka;* PROKOFIEV: *Cello sonata.* ***
(BB) **(*) Arte Nova Dig. 74321 27805-2 [id.]. Emil Klein, Cristian Beldi – PROKOFIEV: *Cello sonata.* **(*)
(B) ** Carlton Dig. 30367 02362 [(M) id.]. Ulrich Boeckheler, Susan Starr – PART: *Fratres*; PROKOFIEV: *Cello sonata.* **

Shostakovich's lyrical and witty sonata is now well represented at the bargain end of the spectrum. The distinguished Finnish cellist gives an effortlessly authoritative and totally idiomatic account of the piece, and he is well supported by his pianist. He is an aristocratic artist and never indulges in expressive overstatement. Well-balanced recording enhances the claims of what is in some respects an uncompetitive issue, given its less than generous playing time. However, the playing is equally impressive in the Schubert coupling.

Both the alternative bargain performances are very serviceable and are unlikely to disappoint. Bernard Gregor-Smith and Yolande Wrigley have the benefit of a recording with greater bloom and a more lively acoustic, though the piano is sometimes more dominant in the aural picture than is ideal.

Emil Klein and Cristian Beldi, both Romanian born, give a very well-characterized account of the *Sonata*, tautly held together and vital in feeling, though the sound is a bit drier than in the ASV listed above. The balance between cello and piano is better-judged, even if the timbre of the latter is less realistic. Artistically there is not a great deal to choose between them. On balance, ASV would be the one to have on account of the fresher sound and the additional Martinů and Janáček items.

Ulrich Boeckheler and Susan Starr on Carlton are given excellent recording quality and are accorded a sound that is balanced most musically. The first movement of the Shostakovich is broad and just a trifle too measured – even cautious. The Scherzo could also be a little more abandoned. The finale, on the other hand, is delightfully characterized.

Piano trios Nos. 1. in C min, Op. 8; 2 in E min., Op 67; (i) *Seven Romances on verses by Alexander Blok, Op. 127.*
(BB) ** Naxos Dig. 8.553747 [id.]. (i) Anita Soldh; Stockholm Arts Trio.

Although the Naxos coupling is an obvious one, there are relatively few versions that do offer the *Trios* in harness. The early (1923) *Piano trio*, with its whiff of the *First Symphony*, is far from negligible even if it does not touch the depth and pain that marks the wartime *E minor Trio*. The Stockholm Trio includes two well-established artists in the cellist Torleif Thedéen and the pianist Stefan Bojsten. They are all accomplished players and give very serviceable (rather than distinguished) accounts of both *Trios*. Anita Soldh captures the bleak atmosphere of the *Blok Romances* well, and she is given intelligent support by her partners. The recording is clean but there is touch of glare that renders it less appealing. However, it is worth the money.

(i) *Symphony No. 10 in E min., Op. 93* (arr. for piano duet); (ii) *Four Preludes from Op. 34* (arr. for violin & piano).
(M) (***) Revelation RV 70002 [id.]. Dmitri Shostakovich, with (i) Moisei Vainberg; (ii) Leonid Kogan.

The recording may be primitive but this is of great documentary interest, capturing Shostakovich and his fellow-composer Moisei Vainberg playing the *Tenth Symphony* in a piano-duet arrangement only a few months after its completion and not long before Mravinsky made the première recording. They play with great fervour and strain the instrument to the limit. The performance is surprisingly brisk (47 minutes as opposed to the usual 50) and completely involving. The transcriptions of the *Preludes* are wonderfully played by Kogan and the composer, and there are also a few bars from *The Gadfly* too.

String quartets

String quartets Nos. 1–15.
(B) *** Decca 455 776-2 (6) [id.]. Fitzwilliam Qt.

The Shostakovich *Quartets* thread through his creative life like some inner odyssey and inhabit terrain of increasing spiritual desolation. The Fitzwilliam Quartet played to Shostakovich himself and gave the UK premières of his last three *Quartets*, and they bring to the whole cycle complete and total dedication. One has only to sample the first two quartets to discover the sustained and often hushed intensity of this playing, which so consistently has the spontaneity of live music-making. They are given first-class recording too, with great presence and natural body. The recordings were made in All Saints' Church, Petersham, Surrey, between 1975 and 1977; a rather forward balance was chosen, perhaps because of the ecclesiastical acoustic, and this is slightly emphasized by the CD transfer, yet there is a natural transparency and a firm focus throughout. There are minor criticisms, but they are too trivial to weigh in the balance, for this set is by any standards a formidable achievement.

String quartets Nos. 1–15; (i) *Piano quintet in G min.* (ii) *2 Pieces for string octet, Op. 11.*
(M) *** BMG/Melodiya 74321 40711-2 (6). Borodin Qt; with (i) Sviatoslav Richter; (ii) Prokofiev Qt.

Originally issued on EMI and now reappearing on BMG/Melodiya, the Borodin Quartet's second recording of Shostakovich's complete *String quartets* is an economical investment when purchased complete. The present recordings are made in a generally drier acoustic than their predecessors, and Nos. 3 and 5 suffer noticeably in this respect. However, the ears quickly adjust and the performances can only be described as masterly. The Borodins possess enormous refinement, an altogether sumptuous tone and a perfection of technical address that is almost in a class of its own – and what wonderful intonation! These and the Bartók six are the greatest quartet cycles produced in the present century and are mandatory listening. The *Piano quintet* was recorded at a public concert at the Moscow Conservatoire, and it goes without saying that with Richter at the helm the account is a powerful one, although the quality of the sound here is noticeably dry and forward. The *Two Pieces for string octet* are now added to the second CD.

String quartets Nos. 1 in C, Op. 49; 8 in C min., Op. 110; 9 in E flat, Op. 117.
(BB) *** Naxos Dig. 8.550973 [id.]. Eder Qt.

If the Naxos disc is not necessarily a first choice, no one investing in it need fear they are getting short-changed. The Eder Quartet is a very distinguished ensemble and have a very good feeling for this repertoire. They are actually better recorded than the Borodins on EMI, and those for whom economy is a primary concern should consider this.

String quartets Nos. 2 in A, Op. 68; 12 in D flat, Op. 133.
(BB) *** Naxos Dig. 8.550975 [id.]. Eder Qt.

If anything, the Eder coupling of Nos. 2 and 12 is even more impressive than their first disc. The account of the third-movement *Adagio: Recitativo and Romance* of No. 2 with its intense, improvisatory feeling is particularly fine, and the closing *Theme and variations* is strongly characterized. Similarly the extended *Allegretto* second movement of No. 12 is powerfully argued and these performances have compelling concentration throughout. The recording too is excellent.

String quartets Nos. 4 in D, Op. 83; 6 in G, Op. 101; 7 in F sharp min., Op. 108.
(BB) *** Naxos Dig. 8.550972 [id.]. Eder Qt.

The Eder is one of the finest quartets Hungary has produced in recent years; given the excellence of both performances here, and particularly of No. 4, we can give their most recent Naxos coupling a warm welcome. Quite apart from its cost, this series is emerging as one of the most competitive of the newer versions of this powerful music. The recorded sound is superior to the Borodins and offers a serious challenge to them.

String quartet No. 8, Op. 110.
(M) *** Classic fM Dig. 75605 57027-2. Chilingirian Qt – BORODIN: *Quartet No. 2;* DVORAK: *Quartet in F, Op. 96.* ***
(M) **(*) Decca 425 541-2. Borodin Qt – BORODIN; TCHAIKOVSKY: *Quartets.* **(*)

The Shostakovich *Eighth Quartet* first achieved popularity thanks to a 1962 recording by the Borodin Quartet, in an attractive coupling on Decca with the Borodin *Second.* This is still available, but now with a Tchaikovsky bonus. On Classic fM the Chilingirians in incisive performances, both powerful and warmly sympathetic, again offer that coupling, plus the generous extra of Dvořák's most popular quartet. In the Shostakovich, the Chilingirians give a tautly controlled performance, not as flexible as some but with the power enhanced by the rich, immediate digital recording. For most collectors this will now be a preferable choice.

The Borodins' Decca performance is outstanding and the recording real and vivid, although the balance means that in the CD transfer the effect is very forward, almost too boldly immediate.

String quartets Nos. 14 in F sharp, Op. 142; 15 in E flat min., Op. 144.
(BB) *** Naxos Dig. 8.550976 [id.]. Eder Qt.

Cultured and finely shaped performances of two of Shostakovich's bleakest works. Of course the Fitzwilliam and Borodin Quartets have special claims and arguably dig deeper into the dark hollows of these scores, but for those who do not want to buy all fifteen *Quartets* at one go, these offer an excellent alternative. As quartet playing goes, the Eder are second to none, and they have the benefit of very good recording. Certainly worth the money.

24 Preludes and fugues, Op. 87.
✿ (M) *** BMG/Melodiya 74321 19849-2 (3) [id.]. Tatiana Nikolayeva.

In this repertoire, the first choice must inevitably be Tatiana Nikolayeva, 'the onlie begetter', as it were, of the *Preludes and fugues*. Her reading has enormous concentration and a natural authority that is majestic. There is wisdom and humanity here, and she finds depths in this music that have eluded most other pianists who have offered samples. Her Melodiya set, made in 1987, is clean and well focused (if a bit dry).

Loyalty (8 ballads for male choir), *Op. 136.*
(M) **(*) BMG/Melodiya 74321 40723-2. Estonian State Ac. Male Ch., Gustav Ernesaks – CHERUBINI: *Requiem in D min.* **

Loyalty is a bleak work for unaccompanied male voices and is sung by the artists and their conductor, Gustav Ernesaks, who inspired it. Shostakovich himself was present at all the rehearsals, which lends this pioneering performance of 1970 a special authority. It is a rewarding and powerful work, and the recording is eminently satisfactory.

Sibelius, Jean (1865–1957)

Andante festivo; Canzonetta, Op. 62a; Rakastava, Op. 14; Romance in C, Op. 43.

(BB) **(*) Naxos Dig. 8.550330; *4550330* [id.]. Capella Istropolitana, Adrian Leaper – GRIEG: *Elegiac melodies* etc. **(*)

Adrian Leaper has proved himself a reliable Sibelian, though at times he adopts rather brisker tempi than are ideal. Anyone sampling the composer's own version of the *Andante festivo* will discover that his broader tempo enables him to communicate greater intensity and dignity. Likewise the *Canzonetta*, which derives from the music to *Kuolema*, loses something of its allure. No such reservations apply in either the *Romance in C* or *Rakastava* – the latter is particularly eloquent and the closing paragraphs of the last movement are movingly done. Generally speaking this is a sensitively played anthology, and only a certain fierceness from the upper string-tone inhibits a three-star recommendation.

(i) *The Bard, Op. 64; En Saga, Op. 9;* (ii) *Finlandia, Op. 26; Kuolema: Valse triste, Op. 44;* (i) *4 Legends, Op. 22;* (ii) *Tapiola, Op. 112.*

(B) *** DG Double 447 358-2 (2) [id.]. (i) Helsinki R. O, Kamu; (ii) BPO, Karajan – GRIEG: *Peer Gynt suites* etc. ***

Okku Kamu offers an exceptionally fine account of *The Bard*, and *En Saga* is hardly less admirable. His set of the four *Legends* is very good indeed. He handles pictorial detail most imaginatively, and the Helsinki Radio Orchestra responds with enthusiasm and good ensemble to his lively direction. Although his account of *Lemminkäinen and the Maidens of Saari* is a trifle brisk it is certainly exciting, and the famous *Swan* glides in sombrely. The engineers produce a well-balanced and truthful sound-picture and the CD transfer is firm and clear. Karajan's performances come from the mid-1960s. *Finlandia* and *Tapiola* are still among the finest accounts available, and the rather slow *Valse triste* is certainly seductive. Good transfers.

The Bard, Op. 64; En Saga, Op. 9; King Christian II (incidental music), *Op. 27; Kuolema: Valse triste; Scene with cranes, Op. 44; Legends: The Swan of Tuonela; Lemminkaïnen's return, Op. 22/3–4;* (i) *Luonnotar, Op. 70; Pelleas and Melisande* (incidental music), *Op. 46; Pohjola's daughter, Op. 49; Spring song, Op. 16; Swanwhite* (incidental music), *Op 54.*

(B) **(*) EMI forte CZS5 69773-2 (2) [(M) id. import]. Bournemouth SO, Paavo Berglund, (i) with Taru Valjakka.

The highlight of this collection is *Luuonotar* (with which the concert opens). Taru Valjakka has a lovely voice, and Berglund rises to the occasion and provides his eloquent soloist with genuinely imaginative support. *En Saga* opens rather stoically and is straightforward and unmannered. The full, spacious recording creates a feeling of warmth in *The Oceanides* and moves its geography further south. *Pohjola's daughter* is vivid as sound but is a routine performance. *Pelleas and Melisande* is rather more successful: *At the castle gate* makes a powerful opening impression. Berglund's direct approach generally goes with moderate speeds. The catalogue is not short of more urgently exciting performances, but all those here have an honest strength and compulsion, and the recordings are generally warm and full, though some have close-up balances.

Violin concerto in D min., Op. 47.

(M) *** RCA 09026 61744-2 [id.]. Heifetz, Chicago SO, Hendl – GLAZUNOV: *Concerto;* PROKOFIEV: *Concerto No. 2.* ***

(M) *** Decca 425 080-2 [id.]. Kyung Wha Chung, LSO, Previn – TCHAIKOVSKY: *Violin concerto.* ***

(M) *** Sony Stern Edition I SMK 66829 [id.]. Stern, Phd. O, Ormandy – TCHAIKOVSKY: *Violin concerto.* ***

(M) *** Ph. 420 895-2. Accardo, LSO, C. Davis – DVORAK: *Violin concerto.* ***

(M) *** EMI Dig. CD-EMX 2203 [(M) id. import]. Little, RLPO, Handley – BRAHMS: *Violin concerto.* ***

(M) (***) EMI mono CDH7 61011-2. Ginette Neveu, Philh. O, Susskind – BRAHMS: *Concerto.* (***)

(BB) *** Naxos Dig. 8.550329; *4550329* [id.]. Dong-Suk Kang, Slovak (Bratislava) RSO, Adrian Leaper – HALVORSEN: *Air Norvégien* etc.; SINDING: *Légende;* SVENDSEN: *Romance.* ***

(B) ** EMI forte (SIS) CZS5 69334-2 (2) [CDFB 69334]. Gidon Kremer, Philh. O, Muti – BRAHMS: *Violin concerto* *(*); SCHUMANN: *Concerto.* **(*)

(M) (**) EMI mono CDH7 64030-2 [id.]. Heifetz, LPO, Beecham – GLAZUNOV: *Violin concerto* (***) ✽ ; TCHAIKOVSKY: *Violin concerto.* (***)

(M) *(*) [RCA Basic 100 09026 68338-2; *68338-4*]. Perlman, Boston SO, Leinsdorf – LALO: *Symphonie espagnole.* *(*)

(i; ii) *Violin concerto;* (ii) *En Saga, Op. 9;* (iii) *Finlandia, Op. 26; Kuolema: Valse triste, Op. 44/1;* (ii) *Legend: The swan of Tuonela, Op. 22/2.*
(M) Sony **(*) SMK 64578 [id.]. (i) Cho-Liang Lin, (ii) Philh. O; (iii) Swedish RSO; Salonen.

Heifetz's stereo performance of the Sibelius *Concerto* with the Chicago Symphony Orchestra under Walter Hendl set the standard by which all other versions have come to be judged. It is also one of his finest recordings; in remastered form the sound is vivid, with the Chicago ambience making an apt setting for the finely focused violin line.

Kyung Wha Chung has inimitable style and an astonishing technique, and her feeling for the Sibelius *Concerto* is second to none. André Previn's accompanying cannot be praised too highly: it is poetic when required, restrained, full of controlled vitality and well-defined detail. The 1970 Kingsway Hall recording is superbly balanced and produces an unforced, truthful sound. This is a most beautiful account, poetic, brilliant and thoroughly idiomatic, and must be numbered among the finest versions of the work available; the coupling with Tchaikovsky is very appropriate for reissue in Decca's Classic Sound series.

Stern's 1969 recording has in the past been rather upstaged by the superb Heifetz version. Yet his performance can match that master in technical assurance. He plays with real passion yet, as the very opening demonstrates, there is no lack of feeling for the work's special atmosphere, and poetry is never in short supply, especially towards the close of the first movement. Ormandy provides a splendid accompaniment and the Philadelphia Orchestra matches Stern's virtuosity and warmth. The violin is forwardly placed, but the balance is much more satisfactory than some recordings from this source, while the remastering has greatly improved the sound: it has plenty of body and resonance.

Of the other mid-price versions, Salvatore Accardo and Sir Colin Davis would be a strong choice alongside Chung. There is no playing to the gallery, and no schmaltz – and in the slow movement there is a sense of repose and nobility. The finale is exhilarating, and there is an aristocratic feeling to the whole which is just right.

The raptness of Tasmin Little's playing is even more striking in the Sibelius than in the Brahms with which it is generously coupled. Her hushed and mysterious account of the opening theme leads to a performance that is both poised and purposeful, magnetic in her combination of power and poetry. Kyung Wha Chung's reading with André Previn may be more overtly passionate, but Little's is just as deeply felt, with an even wider tonal range, and her virtuosity culminates in an account of the finale in which, as in the Brahms, she finds an element of wit in the pointing of insistent dance rhythms. Throughout she is splendidly matched by the colourful playing of the RLPO under Vernon Handley.

The magnetism of Neveu in this, her first concerto recording, is inescapable from her opening phrase onwards, warmly expressive and dedicated, yet with no hint of mannerism. The finale is taken at a speed which is comfortable rather than exciting, but the extra spring of the thrumming dance-rhythms, superbly lifted, is ample compensation, providing a splendid culmination.

Dong-Suk Kang chooses some popular Scandinavian repertoire pieces, such as the charming Svendsen *Romance in G*, as makeweights. Although this version of the concerto is very fine, he is perhaps a little wanting – albeit only a little – in tenderness as opposed to passion in the slow movement, but there is splendid virtuosity in the outer movements. The orchestral playing is decent rather than distinguished. In the bargain basement, this enjoys a strong competitive advantage, but even if it were at full price it would feature quite high in the current lists.

Kremer presents the *Concerto* essentially as a bravura concerto, and his is a vibrantly extrovert reading. While the recording balance places the soloist well forward, the orchestral texture has plenty of impact and good detail, and the fortissimo brass blaze out excitingly. There is undoubted poetry in the slow movement and throughout Muti gives his soloist splendid support. Other versions, however, are more searching and have more character, albeit in very different ways. The sonata recital with Gavrilov (see under the Brahms coupling) does increase the appeal of this forte collection, but none of the main concertante works is a top recommendation.

Although many first recordings have something special that stands out, the Heifetz/Beecham Sibelius *Violin concerto*, marvellous though it is, excites admiration rather than affection. And despite Sir Thomas's direction, Heifetz gave the more powerful account of it in his later, Chicago recording with Walter Hendl in the early days of stereo. (The reverse was the case with the Glazunov.) A good transfer nevertheless, and well worth having.

Perlman's RCA recording suffers from over-bright sound (the orchestral tuttis have an element of harshness) and a very close balance for the soloist. Perlman's later, EMI recording is far preferable (but that is at full price).

(i; ii) *Violin concerto in D min., Op. 47;* (iii) *En saga, Op. 9;* (ii) *Finlandia, Op. 26; Karelia suite, Op. 11;* (iii) *Symphonies Nos. 1 in E min, Op. 39; 5 in E flat, Op. 82.*
(BB) ** CfP Silver Double CDCFPSD 4763 (2) [(B) id.]. (i) Sarbu; (ii) Hallé O, Schmidt; (iii) SNO, Gibson.

Eugene Sarbu is a Romanian and was in his early thirties when he recorded the Sibelius *Concerto* in 1980. His vibrato is a little wide and intonation is not always impeccable, though he has plenty of dash and power. He makes the most of every expressive point and underlines romantic fervour rather than spirituality. His is a *zigeuner*-like approach without the purity and refinement of tone which are ideal – and which emerge in such performers as Cho-Liang Lin (full price) and Kyung Wha Chung. There is a nobility in this music that Sarbu does not always convey. But he is well supported by the Hallé, who give Ole Schmidt sensitive and responsive playing, and they are heard to excellent effect in the *Karelia* and *Finlandia* encores. The recording too is excellent. The companion disc includes Sir Alexander Gibson's recordings with the Scottish National Orchestra of the *First* and *Fifth Symphonies*, recorded in 1973–4. As always, he shows a natural feeling for the Sibelian sound world, and these performances are both straightforward and refreshingly unmannered. Both interpretations are sound; neither is inspired, although both (and especially No. 1) make enjoyable listening when the recording is agreeably spacious.

(i–iii) *Violin concerto in D min., Op. 47;* (ii–iii) *Finlandia, Op. 26*; *Karelia suite, Op. 11;* (iv–v) *Kuolema* (incidental music) *(Canzonetta; Valse romantique, Op. 62a/b; Valse triste; Scene with cranes, Op. 44/1-2);* (vi) *Tapiola, Op. 112;* (ii; iv) *Pelléas et Mélisande: suite, Op. 46.*
(B) ** Teldec/Warner Ultima Analogue/Dig. 0630 18963-2 (2) [(M) id. import]. (i) Miriam Fried; (ii) Helsinki PO; (iii) Okko Kamu; (iv) Finlandia Sinf.; (iv) Pekka Helasvuo; (vi) Finnish RSO, Berglund.

This is Miriam Fried's second recording of the *Violin concerto*. Her present reading has no want of *zigeuner* intensity, but there are more ethereal accounts of the opening bars. She brings tenderness and feeling to the slow movement, though not perhaps the purity of some accounts; but the finale lacks any real sense of exhilaration. Good playing from Okko Kamu and his fine Helsinki players; but as far as the international market is concerned, the performance here is insufficiently competitive. The Finlandia Sinfonietta are all members of the Helsinki Philharmonic – and very good they are, too. Their performances under Pekka Helasvuo are very well shaped, and the recordings are cleanly focused and well balanced. But as a set this can only receive a very qualified recommendation.

(i) *Violin concerto in D min., Op. 47;* (ii) *Finlandia, Op. 26;* (iii) *Kuolema: Valse triste, Op. 44; Karelia suite, Op. 11;* (iv) *Legend: The Swan of Tuonela, Op. 22/2; Symphony No. 1 in E min.;* (v) *Symphony No. 2 in D, Op. 43.*
(B) **(*) Sony Analogue/Dig. SB2K 63260 (2) [id.]. (i) Francescatti, NYPO, Bernstein; (ii) LSO, Hickox; (iii) Phd. O, Ormandy; (iv) Nat. PO, Stokowski; (v) NYPO, Thomas Schippers.

No one could complain about a lack of adrenalin in these Sibelius performances. Francescatti's account of the *Violin concerto* is stunning in its immediacy and impact. With Bernstein fully matching the intensity of his soloist, this is a performance impossible to forget. Francescatti's richness of tone is immediately evident in the opening theme and dominates the impassioned reading of the slow movement. The snag is the brightly lit recording, made in the Avery Fisher Hall in 1963, with the solo violin artificially balanced out in front, in a spotlight. However, orchestral detail comes through well and, as so often with these new Sony transfers, the sound itself is now very acceptable, not lacking body or ambience.

Stokowski's 1976 performance of the *First Symphony*, like his atmospherically sombre *Swan of Tuonela*, was recorded in the unlikely venue of London's West Ham Central Mission, and the sound is resonantly full and spacious. The playing is white-hot with fervour, with a terrific burst of energy at the end of the Scherzo, producing an unmarked accelerando. The melancholy of the *Andante* is poignantly caught and, if there are certain details in the reading at which a purist might cavil, Stokowski is not a conductor for purists, and the thrilling sweep of the outer movements shows him at his most spontaneously inspired. Thomas Schippers' *Second Symphony* (another 1963 Avery Fisher Hall recording) is also very impressive. If not always flowing with an uninterrupted impulse (there are some impetuous accelerandi in the first movement), this performance comes thrillingly into its own in the expansively powerful finale which is very gripping indeed. Richard Hickox's *Finlandia* also generates a thrill at its close, and it has the advantage of modern, digital sound. Ormandy's two contributions offer the usual splendid playing from the Philadelphia Orchestra (and a most sensitive cor anglais solo in the central *Ballade* of *Karelia*) but are vivid rather than highly individual performances. But with any reservations, this set is well worth its modest cost.

(i) *Violin concerto in D min., Op. 47; 6 Humoresques, Op. 87/1–2; Op. 89/3–6;* (ii) *Finlandia, Op. 26.*
(B) **(*) Erato/Warner 0630 12746-2 [(M) id. import]. (i) Amoyal, Philh. O, Dutoit; (ii) Helsinki PO, Kamu.

Amoyal's interpretation of the concerto can hold its own with most now available. He brings a splendid ardour, refined taste and great purity of tone to it, and it goes without saying that he surmounts its many technical hurdles with aplomb. He is free from that slight suggestion of the *zigeuner* which disfigures some accounts and he has greater spirituality than Kremer. The finale perhaps lacks the sheer excitement of Heifetz, whose pupil he was in the late 1960s; nevertheless it is good, and in the slow movement Amoyal has nobility and warmth. The recording is very natural, with a decent perspective and balance. For the bargain-priced reissue the surprisingly rarely recorded *Six Humoresques* have been added, improvisationally free and chimerical performances that catch the music's atmospheric delicacy, while the winningly extrovert No. 5 has plenty of verve and bravura. Okko Kamu's account of *Finlandia*, if not distinctive, generates undoubted excitement, and the recording effectively combines brilliance with sonority.

(i) *Violin concerto in D min., Op. 47;* (ii) *Symphony No. 2 in D, Op. 43.*

(B) (***) Dutton Lab. mono CDEA 5016 [(M) id.]. (i) Ginette Neveu, Philh. O, Susskind; (ii) NYPO, Sir John Barbirolli.

(BB) **(*) RCA Navigator Dig./Analogue 74321 17904-2 [(M) id. import]. (i) Dylana Jenson; Phd. O, Ormandy.

Ginette Neveu's legendary 1945 recording of the Sibelius *Violin concerto* was the fourth to be made (Heifetz's première account dates from 1936, and there were two wartime recordings, one with Guila Bustabo and Fritz Zaun, and the other with Anja Ignatius and Sibelius's brother-in-law, Armas Järnefelt conducting). The merits of the Neveu performance are far too well known to need restating and interest will centre on the quality of the Dutton transfer. The 1987 EMI transfer by Keith Hardwick, coupled with the Neveu–Dobrowen account of the Brahms, received numerous plaudits in its day, including a *Gramophone* Magazine award. The present edition represents a striking advance over its predecessor. Dutton achieves an altogether sweeter and smoother sound and succeeds in giving somewhat less prominence to the solo violin image. The *Second Symphony*, recorded in June 1940 just after the fall of France, was for British collectors merely an entry in Clough & Cuming's *World Encylopaedia of Recorded Music* (it was never issued in the UK). It dates from Barbirolli's time with the New York Philharmonic and finds Sir John and his players in good form. The first movement is one of the fastest on record, even brisker than Kajanus. Sibelius's first biographer, Erik Furuhjelm, describes a performance the composer conducted in 1916 as being faster even than Kajanus, so the present issue has illustrious antecedents. A high-voltage account, expertly transferred and well worth restoring to the catalogue. Recommended.

Dylana Jenson is a young American violinist, born in 1961, who has the full measure of this concerto. She hardly puts a foot wrong anywhere and her account has all the sense of space, nobility and warmth that one could want. The virtuosity she commands seems quite effortless and is completely at the service of the music. Her tone is fine-spun and vibrant, and she communicates the sense of atmosphere and mystery in the opening to splendid effect. The violin is forwardly placed but naturally caught and the result is most satisfying. In Ormandy's 1972 account of the *Second Symphony* the sound is undoubtedly spacious, although the violin timbre lacks something in refinement because of the close microphones. But they play marvellously and the superbly disciplined response of the whole orchestra cannot fail to hold the listener. Although Ormandy's reading rarely sheds new light on this wonderful score, there is no doubt that the rich sweep of the Philadelphia strings in the big tune of the finale – underpinned by the power and sonority of the brass – is compulsive in its intensity.

(i) *Violin concerto in D min., Op. 47. Symphony No. 5 in E flat, Op. 82.*

(BB) **(*) BMG/Arte Nova Dig. 74321 51629-2 [id.]. (i) Stephanie Gonley; Gran Canaria PO, Leaper.

At super-bargain price Arte Nova offers this unusual and generous coupling, very well recorded, with performances which compete with the finest available. Stephanie Gonley as leader of the English Chamber Orchestra has generally appeared on disc in ensembles but, as this Sibelius reading demonstrates, she is an unusually positive solo artist. Though her tonal coloration can be distracting, her playing has a rarefied intensity, an emotional impulse that reflects her outward-going strength. Others may find more inward qualities, but her ripely romantic approach in the slow movement, using a wide vibrato, and her impulsiveness in the finale are hard to resist. The symphony is given an unusually spacious reading, with speeds broader than in Leaper's earlier Naxos recording, less impulsive, more controlled than before, with cleaner ensemble. The result is a reading that is warm and at times sensuous, transparently recorded, with opulent brass and smooth strings.

(i) *En saga, Op. 9; Finlandia, Op. 26; Karelia suite, Op. 11;* (ii) *4 Legends, Op. 22;* (i; iii) *Luonnotar, Op. 70;* (ii) *Night ride and sunrise, Op. 55; Pohjola's daughter, Op. 49;* (i) *Tapiola, Op. 112.*

(B) *** Decca Double 452 576-2 (2) [(M) id. import]. (i) Philh. O, Ashkenazy; (ii) SRO, Horst Stein; (iii) with Elisabeth Söderström.

This Double Decca combines Ashkenazy's outstanding mid-priced digital collection from the 1980s as listed below with more distinguished and finely calculated performances from Horst Stein. *Night ride and sunrise* and *Pohjola's daughter* date from 1971. At the time, we commented that they offered some of the finest playing we had heard for some years from the Suisse Romande Orchestra, and the *Legends* too are impressive, with a hell-for-leather account of *Lemminkäinen's return*. The 1980 analogue sound is again first class, having fine weight and definition. Again the Suisse Romande Orchestra plays very well. Even if the body of string tone does not match that of the Philharmonia, the brooding atmosphere of *The Swan of Tuonela* is well caught, and both the first and third *Legends* are well shaped and exciting. All in all, excellent value.

(i) *En Saga; Finlandia, Op. 26; Karelia suite; Legend: The Swan of Tuonela, Op. 22/3; Pohjola's daughter, Op. 49;* (ii) *Symphonies Nos. 2 in D, Op. 43; 5 in E flat, Op. 22.*
(BB) **(*) EMI Seraphim CES5 669134-2 (2) [CDEB 69134]. (i) VPO or BBC SO, Sir Malcolm Sargent; (ii) Sinfonia of L., Tauno Hannikainen.

Sargent's collection of short orchestral works is highly successful and a fine reminder of his affinity with this repertoire. Each performance has conviction and character, and the five pieces complement one another, making a thoroughly enjoyable CD programme. The Vienna Philharmonic bring a distinctive freshness to their playing of music which must have been unfamiliar to them and Sir Malcolm Sargent imparts his usual confidence. The brass is especially full-blooded in *En Saga*, a performance full of adrenalin (as is *Pohjola's daughter*, the one item featuring the BBC Symphony Orchestra). *Finlandia* sounds unhackneyed and, with brisk tempi, *Karelia* has fine impetus and flair. The recordings, made in the Musikverein in 1961 and Kingsway Hall in 1958, are remarkably full and vivid; one would never suspect their age from these vibrant CD transfers, of EMI's best vintage.

The second disc of this inexpensive Seraphim Double offers performances of two symphonies from Tauno Hainnikainen (originally issued in the UK by the World Record Club), which made a strong impression when they first appeared. The *Second Symphony* is undoubtedly the finer of the two performances. The opening movement is extremely well knit, but it is the slow movement, with its sombre atmosphere and strength of linear feeling, that confirms Hannikainen's empathy for the Sibelian idiom, while the apotheosis of the finale is undoubtedly gripping. The interpretation of the *Fifth* is less telling. There is again a starkness of colour and atmosphere at the opening which is compelling, but the tension is not sustained evenly throughout and the very spacious finale is disappointing. Good, if slightly dry recording. An interesting reissue, especially at this modest price.

(i) *En Saga, Op. 9; Finlandia, Op. 26;* (ii) *Karelia suite, Op. 11;* (i) *Legend: The Swan of Tuonela, Op. 22/2; Tapiola, Op. 112.*
(M) **(*) EMI Analogue/Dig. EMI CDM7 64331-2 [id.]. BPO, Karajan.
(BB) *** Belart 450 018-2 (without *Tapiola*) [(M) id. import]. (i) SRO, Horst Stein; (ii) VPO, Maazel – GRIEG: *Peer Gynt*. ***

Karajan's *En Saga* is more concerned with narrative than with atmosphere at the beginning; but the climax is very exciting and the *lento assai* section and the coda are quite magical. *Tapiola* is broader and more expansive than the first DG version; at the storm section, the more spacious tempo is vindicated and again the climax is electrifying. *The Swan of Tuonela* is most persuasively done. These recordings date from 1977. The later, digital recording of *Karelia* has been added for the current reissue. Here, in the outer movements, which Karajan paces deliberately, the rather weighty bass detracts somewhat from the freshness of the presentation.

Horst Stein shows a gift for the special atmosphere of Sibelius. Moreover Decca's 1972 recording approaches the demonstration class, especially in *En Saga*. Maazel's *Karelia* is also first rate.

En Saga, Op. 9; Finlandia, Op. 26; Kuolema: Valse triste; Pohjola's daughter, Op. 49; Scene with cranes, Op. 44/1–2; Tapiola, Op. 112.
(M) * Chandos Enchant Dig. CHAN 7075 [id.]. Danish Nat. RSO, Leif Segerstam.

Although the playing of the Danish Radio Orchestra is sensitive and responsive, there is nothing really special here and, in view of the competition, this Chandos reissue fails to enchant. Leif Segerstam pays characteristic attention to detail and displays a strong sense of atmosphere, but the *Scene with cranes* is drawn out to almost twice its normal length. Things are better with *Pohjola's daughter* but *En saga* seems interminable in his hands. *Tapiola* lasts longer than most performances of the *Seventh Symphony*. All the same, this is the most impressive thing on the disc, quite powerful, though no match for Ashkenazy or Karajan. These much greater performances achieve every bit as much intensity and power without inflating the proceedings. The Chandos/Danish Radio engineering is of high quality.

En Saga, Op. 9; Karelia: Overture, Op. 10; suite, Op. 11; King Christian II suite, Op. 27; Legend: The Swan of Tuonela, Op. 22/2.
(B) **(*) Carlton IMP Dig. PCD 2026 [(M) id.]. New Finnish SO, Jan Engstrom.

Although there are finer individual performances available of all these pieces on record, none are more idiomatic, and the programme here makes for an enjoyable and generous 76-minute concert. The highlight is perhaps the *King Christian II suite*, with some particularly expressive string-playing, but *The Swan of Tuonela* glides in evocatively and both *En Saga* and *Karelia* have their share of colour and excitement. Vivid sound, only just short of the front rank.

Finlandia; Karelia suite, Op. 11. Kuolema: Valse triste. Legends: Lemminkäinen's return, Op. 22/4; Pohjola's daughter, Op. 49.
(M) **(*) EMI CDM7 69205-2. Hallé O, Barbirolli.

Finlandia, Op. 26; Karelia suite, Op. 11; Kuolema: Valse triste, Op. 44; Legends: The Swan of Tuonela; Lemminkäinen's return, Op. 22/2 & 4; Pohjola's daughter, Op. 49.
(BB) * Naxos Dig. 8.550103 [id.]. Czech RSO, Kenneth Schermerhorn.

Pohjola's daughter is extremely impressive as portrayed by Barbirolli and the Hallé Orchestra, spacious but no less exciting for all the slower tempi. *Lemminkäinen's return* is also a thrilling performance. Overall, a desirable introduction to Sibelius's smaller orchestral pieces, with admirable stereo definition.

It seems a remarkable achievement to produce a dull performance of *Finlandia*, but the Naxos version gets bogged down at the very beginning, and it is not helped by the rather opaque, bass-heavy recording. Moreover the opening of the *Intermezzo* of *Karelia* does not manage to generate much tension, and the *Alla marcia* also fails to lift off, again not helped by the sound. *Lemminkäinen* returns with a fair degree of enthusiasm and *Pohjola's daughter* builds to a quite impressive climax, although the performance is in no way distinguished. *The Swan of Tuonela* is more involving in its atmospheric evocation. But there are far finer versions of all this music on record, and this Naxos disc is a non-starter, even at budget price.

Finlandia, Op. 26; Karelia suite, Op. 11; Kuolema: Valse triste, Op. 44/1. Legends: The Swan of Tuonela, Op. 22/2. Scènes historiques: Festivo, Op. 25/3. Tapiola, Op. 112.
(M) (***) DG mono 447 453-2 [id.]. BPO, Rosbaud.

Karajan was not the only champion of Sibelius's music in post-war Germany: Hans Rosbaud, the high priest of the Second Viennese School and the 1950s avant-garde, also included it in his repertory and indeed insisted on conducting the *Fourth Symphony* when he came to the BBC Symphony Orchestra, some months before his death in 1962. These recordings come from the mid-1950s and, although some allowance must be made for the mono sound, the performances themselves have the ring of conviction. The *Tapiola* is something special, among the most terrifying evocations of that dark Nordic forest, and worthy to keep company with those of Beecham, Koussevitzky and Karajan. *The Swan of Tuonela* is a little brisk, but it is not wanting in atmosphere. The *Alla marcia* of the *Karelia suite* is a bit sedate, heavy-footed even, but Sibelians will want this disc for Rosbaud's intensely cold *Tapiola*.

Finlandia, Op. 26; Legends: The Swan of Tuonela, Op. 22/2; The Oceanides, Op. 73; Pohjola's daughter, Op. 49; Tapiola, Op. 112.
(M) **(*) Chandos CHAN 6508 [id.]. SNO, Gibson.

The Oceanides is particularly successful and, if Karajan finds even greater intensity in *Tapiola*, Gibson's account certainly captures the icy desolation of the northern forests. He is at his most persuasive in an elusive piece like *The Dryad*, although *En Saga* is also evocative, showing an impressive overall grasp. The SNO are at the peak of their form throughout these performances.

King Christian II (suite), Op. 27; Kuolema (incidental music) *(Canzonetta; Valse romantique, Op. 62a/b; Valse triste; Scene with cranes, Op. 44/1–2); Scaramouche, Op. 71; Scènes historiques: suites Nos. 1, Op. 25; 2, Op. 66. Swanwhite (suite), Op. 54; The Tempest* (incidental music): *suites Nos. 1 & 2, Op. 109/1 & 2.*
(B) ** Decca Double 448 267-2 (2) [id.]. Hungarian State SO, Jussi Jalas.

This is an attractive and inexpensive programme of lesser-known Sibelius, and it includes one real novelty in the ballet-pantomime, *Scaramouche*, composed during the First World War. As Sibelius's son-in-law, Jussi Jalas brings a special authority to this repertoire, but his Hungarian orchestra is not of the front rank. In *King Christian II* and *Swanwhite* the orchestral playing does not rise much above the routine (although in the former the *Elegy* is quite touching). The lacklustre recording does not help: the strings are a little wanting in body and richness of tone, and the wind playing is not distinguished. Jalas takes some of the *Scènes historiques* rather faster than did Barbirolli or Beecham; it must be assumed that this reflects the composer's wishes, but other versions are more convincing. The *Canzonetta* and *Valse romantique*, Op.

62, are two additional pieces that Sibelius wrote for a later production of *Kuolema*. The *Scene with cranes* from the same play (Sibelius had an almost mystical feeling for cranes) lacks the final degree of poetic intensity. Jalas's performance of the incidental music from *The Tempest* is certainly idiomatic, yet again the last ounce of poetry and mystery eludes him. The recording is acceptable, but little more; the acoustic could be more open and the string-tone have more blossom.

4 Legends, Op. 22; The Bard, Op. 64; (i) *Luonnotar, Op. 70.*
(M) *** Chandos CHAN 6586 [id.]. SNO, Gibson, (i) with Phyllis Bryn-Johnson.

Gibson offers sensitive performances of *The Bard*, which has fine atmosphere and delicate textures, and *Luonnotar*, where the soprano voice is made to seem like another orchestral instrument. The Scottish orchestra play freshly and with much commitment. *The Swan of Tuonela* has a darkly brooding primeval quality, and there is an electric degree of tension in the third piece, *Lemminkäinen in Tuonela*. The two outer *Legends* have ardent rhythmic feeling, and altogether this is highly successful. The recorded sound is excellent.

(i) *4 Legends from the Kalevela, Op. 22;* (ii) *Tapiola, Op. 112.*
(M) *** CDM5 65176-2. (i) Phd. O, Ormandy; (ii) Helsinki PO, Berglund.

A choice for the *Four Legends* is not simple. Ormandy's 1978 set is very distinguished, with the great Philadelphia Orchestra playing superbly in every department. When the violins rise above the stave, the recording (made at the Old Met.) is not as full as Gibson's on Chandos, and in the first *Legend* the wind are more closely observed than is ideal. But the remastering has added somewhat more depth to the sound-picture and Ormandy's account of this opening piece is marvellously passionate (these Maidens of Saari must have given Lemminkäinen quite a wild time!). This *Swan of Tuonola*, too, is among the very finest, darkly intense and full of atmosphere and poetry, while *Lemminkäinen in Tuonela* is brooding and menacing. In *Lemminkäinen's return* Ormandy comes close to the famous hell-for-leather excitement generated in Beecham's old 78 set. Among CD versions, Ormandy's is by far the fleetest horse. On the other hand, Berglund's *Tapiola*, recorded digitally in Helsinki a decade later, is given its impact by a spacious ruggedness. If the build-up of the storm sequence is less chillingly awesome than with Karajan, the very close of the work has a moving intensity. The recording is excellent.

Rakastava (suite), *Op. 14; Scènes historiques, Opp. 25, 66; Valse lyrique, Op. 96/1.*
(M) *** Chandos CHAN 6591 [id.]. RSNO, Gibson.

Written for a patriotic pageant, the *Scènes historiques* are vintage Sibelius. In the *Love song* Gibson strikes the right blend of depth and reticence, while elsewhere he conveys a fine sense of controlled power. Convincing and eloquent performances that have a natural feeling for the music. Gibson's *Rakastava* is beautifully unforced and natural, save for the last movement which is a shade too slow. The *Valse lyrique* is not good Sibelius, but everything else certainly is. Gibson plays this repertoire with real commitment, and the recorded sound is excellent, with the orchestral layout, slightly distanced, most believable. At mid-price this is a specially desirable collection.

SYMPHONIES

Symphonies Nos. 1–7.
(M) **(*) Chandos Dig. CHAN 6559 (3) [id.]. SNO, Sir Alexander Gibson.
(M) *(*) Finlandia Dig. 4509 99963-2 (3). Finnish RSO, Jukka-Pekka Saraste.

Symphonies Nos. 1 in E min., Op. 39; 2 in D, Op. 43; 4 in A min., Op. 63; 5 in E flat, Op. 82.
(B) *(*) Teldec/Warner Ultima Dig. 0630 18962-2 (2) [(M) id. import]. Finnish RSO, Saraste.

Symphonies Nos. 3 in C, Op. 52; 6 in D min., Op. 104; 7 in C, Op. 105; (i) *Kullervo Symphony, Op. 7*
(B) Teldec/Warner Ultima Dig. 3984 21348-2 (2) [(M) id. import]. Finnish RSO, Saraste; (i) with Monica Groop, Jorma Hynninen, Polytech Ch.

Symphonies Nos. 1 in E min., Op. 39; 4 in A min., Op. 63.
(M) ** Van. 08 6159 71 [id.]. Utah SO, Abravanel.

Symphonies Nos. 2 in D, Op. 43; 3 in C, Op. 52.
(M) ** Van. 08 6160 71 [id.]. Utah SO, Abravanel.

Symphonies Nos. 5 in E flat; 6 in D min.; 7 in C.
(M) ** Van. 08 6161 71 [id.]. Utah SO, Abravanel.

Symphonies Nos. 1, 2 & 4; Finlandia; Karelia suite.
(B) *** Decca Double Dig. 455 402-2 (2) [id.]. Philh. O, Vladimir Ashkenazy.

Symphonies Nos. 3, 5, 6 & 7; En Saga; Tapiola.
(B) *** Decca Double Dig. 455 405-2 (2) [id.] Philh. O, Vladimir Ashkenazy.

Symphonies Nos. 1 in E min., Op. 39; 4 in A min., Op. 63.
(BB) *** Belart 461 325-2 [(M) id. import]. VPO, Maazel.

Symphonies Nos. 2 in D, Op. 43; 3 in C, Op. 32.
(BB) **(*) Belart 461 321-2 [(M) id. import]. VPO, Maazel.

Symphonies Nos. 5 in E flat, Op. 82; 6 in D min., Op. 104; 7 in C, Op. 105.
(BB) *(**) Belart 461 323-2 [(M) id. import]. VPO, Maazel.

Symphonies Nos. 1–7; In Memoriam, Op. 59; The Tempest: suite No.1, Op. 109/2.
(M) *(*) Chandos Dig. CHAN 7054 (4). Danish Nat. RSO, Leif Segerstam.

(i) *Symphonies Nos. 1–7;* (ii) *Night ride and sunrise;* (i) *The Oceanides; Scene with cranes.*
(M) **(*) EMI CMS7 64118-2 (4) [ZDMD 64118]. (i) CBSO, (ii) Philh. O, Simon Rattle.

Symphonies Nos. 1–7; Nightride and sunrise, Op. 55; Pelléas et Mélisande: suite, Op. 46; Pohjola's daughter, Op. 49.
(M) (***) Beulah mono 1–4PD 8 (4) [id.]. LSO, Collins.

Symphonies Nos. 1–7; (i) *Luonnotar. Pohjola's daughter.*
(M) **(*) Sony SX4K 64207 (4) [id.]. NYPO, Leonard Bernstein; (i) with Phyllis Curtin.

Ashkenazy's Sibelius cycle has now been issued on a pair of Double Deccas, with four tone-poems added for good measure. It thus competes directly with Sir Colin Davis's series, similarly reissued on a pair of Philips Duos, and also including the *Violin concerto*. Even so, the Ashkenazy set takes precedence, partly because of the generally superior digital recording; but on performance grounds, too, these readings are very rewarding – to provide a rich and strong, consistently enjoyable cycle which is a great favourite of I. M.'s. Ashkenazy by temperament brings out the expressive warmth, colour and drama of the composer rather than his Scandinavian chill, reflecting perhaps his Slavonic background. The recordings – made between 1979 and 1984, either at Walthamstow or in the Kingsway Hall – are full and rich as well as brilliant, most of them still of demonstration quality. For those wanting a complete set, they make a most attractive first recommendation, although for R. L. the newest cycle from Sir Colin Davis and the LSO on RCA takes pride of place at premium price, and this series will almost certainly appear in a box during the lifetime of this book.

Simon Rattle's performances with the City of Birmingham Symphony Orchestra are available both as a four-CD boxed set and as individual discs. The best advice is probably to opt for the individual disc for the *Fourth* and *Sixth*, coupled together. They are both impressive, as is his *Seventh*, coupled with the *Fifth* and the highly atmospheric *Scene with cranes*. As a set the box is worth considering, but it would not be first choice.

There are those who (justly) count Anthony Collins's magnificent account of the *First Symphony* of 1952, with its haunting, other-worldly opening clarinet solo, as the finest ever put on disc, for the tension throughout the performance is held at the highest level. The closely integrated *Seventh* is also well understood by Collins, and once again the closing moments of the symphony are drawn together very impressively. The Decca recording remains remarkably vivid. Sibelians should also note that Collins's accounts of the other symphonies (with the fill-ups) have been added to this CD to make a four-disc set in a slip-case at a saving on the price of the individual records.

The finest of Lorin Maazel's performances, which originated on the Decca label in the 1960s, are the *First* and *Fourth Symphonies*. The *First* has freshness and power to commend it, along with careful attention to both the letter and the spirit of the score; the *Fourth* brings comparable concentration: the first movement is as cold and unremitting as one could wish, and throughout the work Maazel identifies with the atmosphere and mystery of this music. In both symphonies the Vienna Philharmonic responds with enthusiasm and brilliance and the Decca engineers produce splendid detail, while the overall sound has fine body. The *Second* is excellent too and is beautifully played. Maazel's reading, however, leans more to the romantic view of the work: the Tchaikovskian inheritance is stressed rather than the classical forebears, which is why it is a great favourite with I. M. The finale with ripe, vintage Decca recording is sumptuously gripping. The *Third* has a very good first movement, but the second is faster than ideal; it is not quite poetic or reflective enough. Even so, Maazel keeps a firm grip on the outer movements, and his build-up in the finale is most impressive. The *Fifth* and, more particularly, the *Sixth* do not come off so well. Maazel sounds relatively uninvolved in both works. His *Seventh Symphony*, however, proved another landmark in the Sibelius discography: it has great majesty and breadth. These three records together now cost little more than the price of a single premium-priced disc and represent the least expensive way to survey this repertoire. Certainly the first two discs are genuine bargains.

Sir Alexander Gibson's Sibelius cycle is impressive, both musically and from an engineering point of view; there are no weak spots anywhere. (Indeed, one respected critic chose Gibson's version of No. 1 as his first choice on a BBC 'Record Review' some years ago.) At the same time it must be conceded that the peaks do not dwarf, say, the Maazel *Fourth* or *Seventh*. The performances are eminently sane, sound and reliable, and no one investing in the set is likely to be at all disappointed. Taken individually, none would be an absolute first choice.

Leonard Bernstein's cycle with the New York Philharmonic was made during the 1960s when Sibelius was out of fashion; it has been in and out of the catalogue ever since. The highlights are wonderful accounts of Nos. 2, 5 and 7 (infinitely tauter and finer than his re-make with the Vienna Philharmonic) and a superb account of *Pohjola's daughter*. These would all be three-star versions, were it not for the recordings. (The *Fifth* is also available separately, see below.)

Born in Greece, Maurice Abravanel was of Portuguese-Jewish descent (one of his ancestors was chancellor to Ferdinand and Isabella of Spain) and a conductor of fine musicianship and great artistic integrity. He was a pupil of Weill and a friend of Bruno Walter and Hindemith in the 1920s and '30s. These performances are honest, straightforward and totally devoid of egocentricity. The music grips one, and in a less competitive field they would enjoy a strong recommendation. The documentation claims a copyright for the performance of 1991 though the disc is clearly marked ADD. The rather edgy upper-string-tone makes one suspect that the recording is digital. Guy Thomas's comprehensive discography of *The Symphonies of Sibelius*, published in 1990, does not mention them. If they *were* recorded in 1991, Abravanel would have been approaching eighty and these performances show no sign of any loss of grip. The playing of the Utah orchestra of which he was conductor from 1947 until 1979 is very good. These accounts really are worth hearing and, although they are not strongly individual, are far from negligible.

The three-CD Finlandia set offers all seven symphonies in performances recorded while the Finnish Radio Symphony Orchestra was in St Petersburg during the summer of 1993. No doubt fired by the white nights and the atmosphere of the occasion, Finlandia was persuaded that these were special enough to put on record. It is only three or four years since Saraste recorded a complete cycle plus a handful of other Sibelius works for RCA with the same orchestra. These included an impressive *Oceanides* and a fine *Pohjola's daughter*. None of these performances seems to mark an advance on the studio set, though there is the excitement generated by the concert hall to spice up the music-making. The opening movement of the *Third Symphony* is hopelessly rushed and though there are good things, including a fine account of the *Fourth*, there is nothing really special. The set has now additionally been made available on a pair of Ultima Doubles, the second set including Saraste's *Kullervo Symphony*, which was the finest performance of his cycle. It has a more urgent sense of movement and a greater dramatic intensity than most of its major competitors and it has excellent soloists. We hope that eventually this will become available separately at mid-price. The presence in the catalogue of such mid-price rivals as the Colin Davis Boston cycle, Maazel's Vienna set, Ashkenazy's Philharmonia and Anthony Collins's LSO recordings from the early 1950s, all performances of stature, diminishes the appeal of this Saraste cycle.

Even though it has the advantage of very good Chandos digital recording from the beginning of the 1990s, this Segerstam box, even at mid-price, is a non-starter. Segerstam pulls the *First Symphony* mercilessly out of shape. He is more intrusive than almost any rival maestro, and his posturing in the finale is simply insupportable. The account of the *Second Symphony* is more successful, broadly expansive and warm-hearted, but not a little self-indulgent, particularly in the slow movement with its exaggerated climax. In the *Third*, Segerstam sets out at exactly the right pace, but it is not long before the brakes are applied. The natural flow of the movement is impeded by similarly disruptive changes of tempo. Despite some imaginative touches in the slow movement and good orchestral playing, this is not a reading with which it would be easy to live. The first movement of the *Fifth* never really flows, nor is the slow movement allowed to speak for itself. The finale virtually grinds to a halt at letter N; *un pochettino largamente* becomes very *molto* indeed. The *Seventh* gets pulled about too, though the majestic ending comes off well, and the conductor also inflates *In Memoriam* to almost twice its normal length. The *Fourth* and the *Sixth* are Segerstam's two more successful performances; the former has many insights and in the latter he conveys a strong sense of atmosphere and is attentive to detail, although towards the end of the first movement he abruptly pulls back. However, the passage leading up to that (letter M in the score) is imaginatively done. As in the *Fourth*, the insights outweigh the moments of wilfulness, and it is good to hear the slow movement played at a really leisurely pace (even though he perhaps overdoes it). Throughout the cycle the playing of the Danish Radio Symphony Orchestra is sensitive and responsive.

Symphonies Nos. 1 in E min., Op. 39; 2 in D, Op. 43; 4 in A min., Op. 63; 5 in E flat, Op. 82.
(B) *** Ph. Duo 446 157-2 (2) [id.]. Boston SO, Sir Colin Davis.

Symphonies Nos. 3 in C, Op. 52; 6 in D min., Op. 104; 7 in C, Op. 105; (i) *Violin concerto in D min., Op. 47. Finlandia, Op. 26; Legends: The Swan of Tuonela, Op. 22/2; Tapiola, Op. 112.*
(B) *** Ph. Duo 446 160-2 (2) [id.]. (i) Salvatore Accardo; Boston SO, Sir Colin Davis.

Sir Colin Davis's set of the symphonies, recorded during the second half of the 1970s, is undoubtedly among the finest of the collected editions, and now it is not only very economical (offered for the cost of two premium-price CDs) but three tone-poems and an estimable account of the *Violin concerto* are thrown in for good measure. Indeed Accardo's performance of the latter is very high on the recommended list. *Tapiola*, too, is atmospheric and superbly played. In terms of sheer mystery and power it stands among the best. Davis's feeling for Sibelius is usually matched by the orchestral response. Nos. 1, 2, 5 and 7 were the first to be recorded, in 1975/6. The idiomatic playing Davis secures from the Boston orchestra is immediately apparent. Tempi are well judged and there is a genuine sense of commitment and power. The recording is not quite as fine as Ashkenazy's on Decca. However, the remastering has undoubtedly improved the overall depth of acoustic. Davis's accounts of the *Third*, *Fourth* and *Sixth Symphonies* are among the finest on disc and they are excellently recorded. In the *Third* Davis judges the tempi in all three movements to perfection; no conductor has captured the elusive spirit of the slow movement or the power of the finale more effectively. The *Fourth* is arguably the finest of the cycle; there is a powerful sense of mystery, and the slow movement in particular conveys the feeling of communication with nature that lies at the heart of its inspiration. The *Fifth* is a little lacking in atmosphere; it is no match for Karajan. Here Davis is idiomatic and unfussy, as in the *Seventh*. Moreover the recording of these two works is again slightly two-dimensional, although this is less noticeable now than it was on LP. The *Sixth* is altogether more impressive and much more vivid as sound.

Symphonies Nos. 1–4.
(B) *** EMI forte (SIS) Dig. CZS5 68643-2 (2) [CDFB 68643]. Helsinki PO, Berglund.

This is a very impressive set and first-class value as an EMI forte double. Berglund's rugged, sober but powerful readings bring a good feeling for the architecture of the music and no want of atmosphere. Both the playing and the interpretation of the *First* are involving in their breadth and concentration (even if in the first movement the climactic timpani echo of the main theme does not come through). In the *Second*, Berglund is scrupulously faithful to the letter of the score as well as to its spirit, and the build-up to the climax just before the restatement is magnificently handled. The slow movement also comes off well and its contrasting moods are effectively characterized. The Scherzo and finale are of a lower voltage than the finest versions. The Helsinki Philharmonic respond with no mean virtuosity and panache, but the last degree of intensity eludes them. In the *Third*, Berglund adopts sensible tempi throughout and shapes all three movements well; he evokes a haunting feeling of tranquillity in the withdrawn middle section of the slow movement, a passage where Sibelius seems to be listening to quiet voices from another planet. This was Berglund's third account of the *Fourth* and it is a performance of considerable stature: it has a stark grandeur that resonates in the mind, while the slow movement combines brooding power with poetic feeling. There are one or two other things worth noting: the first movement possesses a mystery in its development that eludes him, but the opening is marvellous in Berglund's hands. There is not a great deal of *vivace* in the second movement (Ashkenazy gets the tempo of this movement absolutely right) but Berglund's finale is superb, even if some may find the closing bars not sufficiently cold and bleak. The digital recording throughout the set is excellent.

Symphony No. 1 in E min., Op. 39.
(BB) *(*) ASV CDQS 6040. Melbourne SO, Serebrier – TCHAIKOVSKY: *Romeo and Juliet.* *(*)

With José Serebrier's Melbourne account, both the playing and recording are good (or, at any rate, decent) and Serebrier sounds as if he is enjoying the work; but the performance, it must be admitted, is not really special.

Symphony No. 1 in E min.; The Oceanides.
(M) **(*) EMI Dig. CDM7 64119-2. CBSO, Simon Rattle.

If the whole symphony was as fine as the first movement in Rattle's hands, this would be a clear first recommendation. He has a powerful grasp of both its structure and character. The slow movement is for the most part superb, but he makes too much of the commas at the end of the movement, which are so exaggerated as to be disruptive. The Scherzo has splendid character but is a good deal slower than the marking. *The Oceanides* has an atmosphere that is altogether ethereal. Simon Rattle has its measure and conveys all its mystery and poetry.

Symphonies Nos. 1 in E min.; 5 in E flat, Op. 82.
(BB) ** RCA Navigator 74321 24216-2 [(M) id. import]. Phd. O, Eugene Ormandy.

Symphonies Nos. (i) *1 in E min.;* (ii) *5 in E flat;* (iii) *Romance in C for strings, Op. 42.*
(B) **(*) Sony Classical SBK 63060; *SBT 63060* [id.]. (i) Phd. O, Ormandy; (ii) NYPO, Bernstein; (iii) Cleveland Sinfonietta, Lane.

Ormandy's Sony account of the *First Symphony* with the Philadelphia Orchestra comes from 1961 and is first rate, while Bernstein's *Fifth* from the mid-1960s is arguably the finest of his Sibelius cycle when memories of his mentor, Koussevitzky, were still vivid. There is a small bonus in the form of Louis Lane's account of the *Romance for strings.* No one attracted by this coupling need hesitate.

The sweep of the Philadelphia Orchestra is always commanding in Sibelius, but Ormandy's RCA readings are flawed. He generates considerable intensity in the *E minor Symphony*, especially in the slow movement, but then spoils the finale by pulling right back at the reintroduction of the big string theme which forms the climax. Similarly in No. 5, while the opening movement is impressive, the concentration falters in the *Andante mosso*, and the work's closing pages bring an exaggerated broadening which, despite the body of tone commanded by his fine orchestra, fails to convince. The recordings (from 1978 and 1975 respectively) are resonantly spectacular, painting the orchestral textures with broad strokes of the brush.

Symphonies Nos. 1 in E min., Op. 39; 6 in D min., Op. 104.
(BB) *** Arte Nova Dig. 74321 49705-2 [id.]. Gran Canaria PO, Adrian Leaper.
(BB) *(*) Naxos Dig. 8.550197 [id.]. Slovak PO, Adrian Leaper.

Many conductors have made more than one recording of these symphonies in a lifetime, but it is difficult to think of any precedent for a relatively young conductor making two recordings of the same coupling! The orchestra of the Gran Canaria is much finer than its Slovak counterpart in every department. The strings are more opulent and the wind too are first class. Adrian Leaper is an *echt*-Sibelian with both a command of the overall architecture and a feeling for the atmosphere. The *Sixth Symphony* is gripping, not perhaps in the same league as the Karajan, Davis and Ashkenazy but not far off. Although the *First Symphony* is very good, it does not represent the same challenge to existing recommendations. All the same, the disc is worth having, for both performances are good and the *Sixth* is magnificent. Excellent recording quality.

Symphony No. 2 in D, Op. 43.
(M) ** Mercury 434 317-2 [id.]. Detroit SO, Paray – DVORAK: *Symphony No. 9 (From the New World).* ***

Symphony No. 2 in D; Finlandia, Op. 26; Karelia suite, Op. 11.
(M) *** Decca Dig. 430 737-2 [id.]. Philh. O, Ashkenazy.

Symphony No. 2 in D; Finlandia; Kuolema: Valse triste. Legend: The Swan of Tuonela, Op. 22/3.
(M) **(*) [RCA Basic 100 09026 61856-2]. Phd. O, Ormandy.

Symphony No. 2 in D; Finlandia; Pohjola's daughter, Op. 49; The Swan of Tuonela, Op. 22/2.
(M) (**(*)) RCA mono GD 60294 [09026 60294]. NBC SO, Toscanini.

(i) *Symphony No. 2 in D;* (ii) *Karelia suite.*
(B) **(*) DG Classikon 439 499-2 [(M) id. import]. (i) BPO; (ii) Helsinki RSO; Okko Kamu.

Symphony No. 2 in D; Legend: The Swan of Tuonela, Op. 22/2.
(BB) **(*) Carlton LSO Double Dig. 30368 001177 (2) [(B) id.]. LSO, Sir Charles Mackerras – DVORAK: *Symphony No. 9* etc. *(*)

On Decca, Ashkenazy's control of tension and atmosphere makes for the illusion of live performance in the building of each climax, and the rich digital sound adds powerfully to that impression. Ashkenazy's performances of *Finlandia* and the *Karelia suite* are as fine as any and, like the symphony, are afforded first-class Decca sound.

In Ormandy's 1972 account of the *Second Symphony* the sound is undoubtedly spacious, although the violin-timbre lacks something in refinement because of the close microphones. But they play marvellously, and the superbly disciplined response of the whole orchestra cannot fail to hold the listener. Although Ormandy's reading rarely sheds new light on this wonderful score, there is no doubt that the rich sweep of the Philadelphia strings in the big tune of the finale – underpinned by the power and sonority of the brass – is compulsive in its intensity. The other pieces are played with considerable flair.

The Berlin Philharmonic give Kamu excellent support and rich sonority in his 1970 account of the *Second Symphony*, recorded not long after he won the Karajan conducting competition. One or two minor exaggerations apart, he gives a straightforward and dedicated account of the work. However, Karajan's currently withdrawn EMI version, recorded with the same orchestra a decade later, is finer in every respect and is to be preferred in spite of the addition to the DG reissue of a fill-up in the form of the *Karelia suite*, expertly played though it is by the Helsinki Radio Orchestra. Nevertheless at bargain price Kamu's disc is undoubtedly value for money.

Sir Charles Mackerras gives an eminently well-judged account of the *Second Symphony*. The tempo of the first movement is apt, a real allegretto, fast but without going to quite the same extreme as Järvi on BIS. There is no lack of tenderness and he shapes phrases with sensitivity. The fill-up, too, has no lack of atmosphere. The recording, made in the EMI Abbey Road studios, is bright and clean. Unfortunately the ill-chosen coupling, Barry Tuckwell's indifferent version of Dvořák's *New World Symphony*, precludes a recommendation.

Three recordings of the *Second Symphony* survive from Toscanini's baton: one from his BBC season in 1938, a second from 1939 and the present issue from 1940. All offer some superb playing but are a shade hard-driven. The account of *Pohjola's daughter* is arguably the most powerful and exciting ever committed to disc and in its elemental power even surpasses Kajanus and Koussevitzky.

Paray's account has plenty of tension – indeed one is immediately gripped by the excitement of the opening movement. The *Andante*, however, does not bring enough contrast and its histrionics seem episodic. The Scherzo has great energy and the finale develops a full head of steam, but overall, in spite of excellent early (1959) Mercury stereo, this reading with its impulsiveness fails to create the feeling of an organic whole.

Symphonies Nos. 2 in D; 3 in C, Op. 52.
(M) *** EMI CDM7 64120-2. CBSO, Simon Rattle.

In No. 2 the CBSO play with fervour and enthusiasm except, perhaps, in the first movement where the voltage is lower – particularly in the development, which is not easy to bring off; however, the transition to the finale is magnificent and Rattle finds the *tempo giusto* in this movement. The Birmingham strings produce a splendidly fervent unison both here and elsewhere. Rattle's account of the *Third* is vastly superior to his *First* and *Second*. The slow movement is particularly fine; few have penetrated its landscape more completely, and the movement throughout is magical. The way in which he gradually builds up the finale is masterly and sure of instinct. The recording, made in the Warwick Arts Centre, sounds very well balanced, natural in perspective and finely detailed.

Symphonies Nos. 2 in D; 5 in E flat, Op. 82.
(M) *** Chandos Dig. CHAN 6556 [id.]. SNO, Sir Alexander Gibson.

The *Second* is among the best of Gibson's cycle and scores highly, thanks to the impressive clarity, fullness and impact of the 1982 digital recording. Gibson's reading is honest and straightforward, free of bombast in the finale. Tempos are well judged: the first movement is neither too taut nor too relaxed: it is well shaped and feels right. Overall this is most satisfying, as is the *Fifth*, which has similar virtues: at no time is there any attempt to interpose the personality of the interpreter, and the finale has genuine weight and power.

Symphonies Nos. 2 in D; 7 in C, Op. 105.
(B) *** Sony SBK 53509; *SBT 53509* [id.]. Phd. O, Ormandy.
(BB) **(*) Naxos Dig. 8.550198 [id.]. Slovak PO, Adrian Leaper.

Ormandy was not so much underrated as taken for granted in an age which had the good fortune to have so many great conductors. The 1957 sound is far better than you might expect and the strings (and practically every other department) are much more sumptuous and responsive than they seem to be in Philadelphia nowadays. The *Second* gets a powerful (and, in the finale, rousing) performance, and the architecture is held together well throughout. The *Seventh*, recorded in 1960, is very impressive indeed: marvellously paced, intense and felt.

Adrian Leaper is a genuine Sibelian, but in No. 2 his first movement is a little low-key and wanting in tension. The horns, too, have a rather wider vibrato than is desirable, though this proves less obtrusive later on. There are some odd quirks of balance: the timpani sticks out at about one minute into the finale; but on the whole this is enjoyable. The *Seventh Symphony*, on the other hand, is really very impressive. This gifted conductor certainly knows how this music should move and what it is all about; he shapes phrases sensitively and with an instinctive feel for the idiom. Good recording, and excellent value at super-bargain price.

Symphonies Nos. 3 in C; 4 in A min., Op. 63.
(BB) ** Naxos Dig. 8.550199 [id.]. Slovak PO, Adrian Leaper.

Adrian Leaper has a good feel for this composer, but the tempo for the slow movement of the *Third*

Symphony is far too fast for comfort. The first movement is pretty brisk too, but he has the measure of its power and momentum. The *Fourth Symphony* is far more impressive and the Slovak orchestra, for whom this must be rare material, play with great feeling and insight. Tubular bells rather than glockenspiel are employed in the finale. Superb recording – were the *Third* as successful as the *Fourth*, this issue would rate three stars.

Symphonies Nos. 3 in C; 6 in D min.; 7 in C, Op. 105.
(M) *** Chandos CHAN 6557 [id.]. SNO, Sir Alexander Gibson.

With three symphonies offered, some 74 minutes overall, this is a fine bargain and an excellent way to experience Gibson's special feeling for this composer. The SNO is in very good form. The first movement of the *Third* has real momentum. The *Andantino* is fast, faster than the composer's marking. Such a tempo, while it gives the music-making fine thrust, means that Gibson, like Collins before him, loses some of the fantasy of this enigmatic movement. But there is more here to admire than to cavil at. The *Sixth* is impressive too, with plenty of atmosphere and some radiant playing from the Scottish violin section; the *Seventh* has a rather relaxed feeling throughout, but it does not lack warmth and, as in No. 1, Gibson draws the threads together at the close with satisfying breadth.

Symphonies Nos. 4 in A min., Op. 63; 5 in E flat, Op. 82; Finlandia, Op. 26.
(M) (***) EMI mono CDM5 66600-2 [id.]. Philh. O, Karajan

Symphonies Nos. 6 in D min., Op. 104; 7 in C, Op. 105; Tapiola, Op. 112.
(M) (***) EMI mono CDM5 66602-2 [id.]. Philh. O, Karajan.

These mono performances with Karajan and the Philharmonia Orchestra are of special interest. Erik Tawaststjerna (*Sibelius Vol. 3*) notes that when Sir Thomas Beecham telephoned in response to a number of detailed criticisms that the composer had made of his 78s of the *Fourth Symphony* in 1937, Sibelius was overwhelmed by the flood of English which he only dimly grasped. He hastily agreed the Beecham recording. Walter Legge, however, showed Sibelius's tempo and other suggestions to Karajan before he made his 1954 recording. After hearing it, Sibelius drafted a telegram speaking of Karajan's 'deep insights and great artistic grip' and went so far as to tell Legge that 'Karajan is the only one who really understands my music.' Certainly these performances are of stature and carry the composer's imprimatur. The *Fourth* was always a favourite of Karajan's, and in some ways this is even finer than the subsequent Berlin accounts – the sound is leaner and more spare and conveys the sense of desolation at the core of its bleak, wintry terrain.

The *Fifth*, recorded in 1952, has not been issued on CD before. Earlier releases have chosen Karajan's 1960 Philharmonia account, but the breadth and majesty of the earlier issue are difficult to surpass. It does not quite match the achievement of the third and greatest of his four recordings, but it is a superbly realized and impressive reading. The *Sixth* and *Seventh* are hardly less fine, even if the latter concentrates more on the seamlessness of the structure than its power. As with the *Fourth Symphony*, Karajan recorded *Tapiola* no fewer than four times – and this is a dark, chilling version to rank with the best.

Symphonies Nos. 4 in A min.; 6 in D min.
(M) *** EMI CDM7 64121-2. CBSO, Simon Rattle.

Simon Rattle's account of the *Fourth* invokes a powerful atmosphere in its opening pages: one is completely transported to its dark landscape with its seemingly limitless horizons. The string-tone is splendidly lean without being undernourished and achieves a sinisterly whispering pianissimo in the development. The slow movement is magical and the finale is hardly less masterly. Rattle's account of the *Sixth* is almost equally fine. It is still a *Sixth* to reckon with and its closing bars are memorably eloquent.

Symphonies Nos. (i) *4 in A min.;* (ii) *6 in D min., Op. 104;* (i) *The Bard, Op. 64; Lemminkäinen's return, Op. 22/4; The Tempest: Prelude.*
❀ (M) (***) EMI (SIS) mono CDM7 64027-2. (i) LPO, (ii) RPO, Sir Thomas Beecham.

In its colour Beecham's account of the *Fourth Symphony* reflects his feeling that, far from being an austere work, as is often claimed, it is ripely romantic. No performance brings one closer to the music, while the recording, made over fifty years ago, sounds astonishingly fresh and bleak in this excellent transfer, and there is a concentration, darkness and poetry that few rivalled. Beecham's 1947 account of the *Sixth Symphony* was said to be Sibelius's favourite recording of all his symphonies. Its eloquence is no less impressive. In the three shorter works on the disc Beecham's rhythmic sharpness and feeling for colour vividly convey the high voltage of Sibelius's strikingly original writing. *Lemminkäinen's homeward journey* is positively electrifying, while the *Prelude* to *The Tempest* is every bit as awesome an evocation of a storm as we had remembered. All these performances except the *Sixth Symphony* come from the late

1930s, but few allowances need be made, for they spring vividly to life in these remarkable transfers. Indispensable for all Sibelians.

Symphonies Nos. 4 in A min.; 7 in C; Kuolema: Valse triste.
✿ (M) *** DG 439 527-2. BPO, Karajan.

Karajan's celebrated 1965 account of the *Fourth Symphony* wears well. For many it remains the finest version of the *Fourth* on record, and it certainly ranks along with the Beecham as among the most insightful. The plush sonority of the Berlin Philharmonic at first deceives one into thinking that Karajan has beautified the symphony's landscape, but he comes closer to the spirit of the score than most others. (The symphony meant a great deal to him: he insisted on playing it alongside Beethoven in 1960 at his inaugural concert as the life-conductor of the orchestra at a time when Sibelius was held in the lowest esteem in Germany.) It is a performance of great concentration, deep thought and feeling. Although the new DG transfer of the recording does not have quite the body of violin-tone of the finest digital recordings, the acoustics of the Jesus-Christus-Kirche give weight and depth and a fine resonance to the bass. The performance is undoubtedly a great one. The *Seventh Symphony* is perhaps less successful though it comes off better than in Karajan's Philharmonia version, and the *Valse triste* is seductive. An indispensable record.

Symphony No. 5 in E flat, Op. 82.
(M) *** EMI CDM7 64737-2. Philh. O, Rattle – NIELSEN: *Symphony No. 4* etc. ***

Symphony No. 5 in E flat, Op. 82; Belshazzar's feast (suite), *Op. 51; En Saga, Op. 9.*
(BB) *(*) Naxos Dig. 8.550200 [id.]. Slovak PO, Adrian Leaper.

Symphony No. 5; Finlandia; Kuolema: Valse triste. Tapiola, Op. 112.
(B) *** DG Classikon 439 418-2; *439 418-4* [id.]. BPO, Karajan.

Such is the excellence of the classic Karajan DG *Fifth* that few listeners would guess its age. It is a great performance, and this 1964 version is indisputably the finest of the four he made. The fillers are familiar performances, also from the mid-1960s. *Tapiola* is a performance of great intensity and offers superlative playing; *Finlandia* is also one of the finest accounts available, but *Valse triste* is played very slowly and in a somewhat mannered fashion.

Simon Rattle's account of the *Fifth Symphony* with the Philharmonia was to the 1980s what Karajan's Berlin account was to the 1960s. It collected numerous prizes, even the *Deutscheschallplattenpreis* – and rightly! Everything about it feels right: the control of pace and texture and the balance of energy and repose. The development of the first movement has a compelling sense of mystery and the transition to the Scherzo section is beautifully judged. The Philharmonia Orchestra play splendidly and the EMI recording is very good indeed.

Adrian Leaper favours rather faster tempi than are ideal in the *Fifth Symphony* though he begins impressively. The transition to the scherzo section of the first movement is a bit precipitate and the rest of the movement goes far too fast. The exquisite music to Hjalmar Procopé's *Belshazzar's feast* has great atmosphere – but, again, would be heard to better effect if Leaper had let it take its time. We need a really poetic account of *Belshazzar's feast* and had hoped that Leaper, who has shown himself a sympathetic interpreter of Sibelius, would have brought it off. The Slovak orchestra play splendidly throughout and the recording is first class.

Symphonies Nos. 5 in E flat, Op. 82; 6 in D min., Op. 104; 7 in C, Op. 105; Finlandia, Op. 26; The Oceanides, Op. 73; Tapiola, Op. 112.
(B) **(*) EMI forte Dig. CZS5 68646-2 (2) [CDFB 68646]. Helsinki PO, Berglund.

This forte double completes Berglund's Sibelius cycle, which is now among the less expensive recommendable sets of the symphonies in the catalogue. Nos. 1–4 are on a companion forte reissue (CZS5 68643-2 – see above). Sober, straightforward, powerful readings which maintain the high standards of performance and recording that have consistently distinguished Berglund's EMI Sibelius records. There is a good feeling for the architecture of this music and no want of atmosphere. In the *Fifth Symphony*, the development section of the first movement has a mystery that eluded Berglund first time around, and there is splendid power in the closing pages of the finale. The *Sixth* is particularly fine, though the Scherzo may strike some listeners as too measured. The *Seventh* is arguably one of the finest now before the public: it has real nobility and breadth, and Berglund has the full measure of all the shifting changes of mood and colour. Moreover the Helsinki orchestra play magnificently and seem to have a total rapport with him. Berglund's account of *The Oceanides* is splendidly atmospheric and can be put alongside Rattle's, which is praise indeed! The recording is well detailed and truthful, and the perspective natural. *Tapiola* is given its impact by a spacious ruggedness, and the very close of the work has a moving intensity. All the same, despite the very good recorded sound and the economical price and packaging, these cannot be recommended in preference to or even alongside the earlier Colin Davis set with the Boston Symphony, which is similarly priced and packaged on a pair of Philips Duos.

Symphonies Nos. 5 in E flat; 7 in C; Kuolema: Scene with cranes. Night ride and sunrise.
(M) *** EMI CDM7 64122-2. CBSO, Simon Rattle.

In the *Fifth Symphony* Rattle is scrupulous in observing every dynamic nuance to the letter and, one might add, spirit. What is particularly impressive is the control of the transition between the first section and the Scherzo element of the first movement. There is a splendid sense of atmosphere in the development and a power unmatched in recent versions, save for the Karajan. The playing is superb, with recording to match. The *Seventh* is hardly less powerful and impressive: its opening is slow to unfold and has real vision. With the addition of an imaginative and poetic account of the *Scene with cranes* from the incidental music to *Kuolema*, this is the finest single disc in Rattle's Birmingham cycle.

Symphony No. 7 in C, Op. 105; Rakastava, Op. 16.
(M) (*) Revelation RV 10006 [id.]. Moscow RSO, Rozhdestvensky – GLAZUNOV: *Scènes de ballet* **; PROKOFIEV: *Andante for strings.* *(*)

Rozhdestvensky shapes the *Seventh Symphony* in noble fashion but the trombone has a ruinous and crude vibrato. *Rakastava* is beautifully played, but the sound on both recordings leaves a lot to be desired. The symphony was made in 1962 and *Rakastava* a year later. But what a weird coupling!

Tapiola, Op. 112.
(M) *** DG (IMS) Dig. 445 518-2 [id.]. BPO, Karajan – NIELSEN: *Symphony No. 4.* ***

This is Karajan's fourth and undoubtedly greatest account of *Tapiola*, for he has the full measure of its vision and power. Never has it sounded more mysterious or its dreams more savage; nor has the build-up to the storm ever struck such a chilling note of terror: an awesomely impressive musical landscape; while the wood-sprites, weaving their magic secrets, come vividly to life.

CHAMBER MUSIC

String quartets: in E flat (1885); *A min.* (1889); *B flat, Op. 4* (1890); *D min. (Voces intimae), Op. 56.*
(M) *** Finlandia/Warner Dig./Analogue 4509 95851-2 (2) [id.]. Sibelius Ac. Qt.

The *A minor Quartet* proves a delightful surprise with something of the freshness of Dvořák and Schubert. Sibelius obviously had ambivalent feelings towards the *B flat Quartet* and discouraged its performance. Its second movement bears a slight resemblance to a theme from *Rakastava*. Both are well worth resurrecting even if they do not, of course, match the mature *Voces intimae quartet* in artistry. The playing of the Sibelius Academy Quartet is exemplary and the recordings good: three are digital; *Voces intimae* dates from 1980 and is analogue.

PIANO MUSIC

The Aspen, Op. 75/3; Barcarolle, Op. 24/10; Bellis, Op. 85/1; Carnation, Op. 85/2; Couplet, Op. 34/4; Dance, Op. 94/1; Danse pastorale, Op. 34/7; Dialogue, Op. 58/6; Elegy, Op. 76/10; Fisherman's song, Op. 58/8; Impromptus, Op. 5/1–6; Op. 24; Op. 97/5; Iris, Op. 85/3; Little waltz, Op. 97/3; Moment de valse, Op. 99/7; Nocturne, Op. 24/8; Rondino, Op. 68/1; Scherzando, Op. 40/8; Serenade, Op. 58/9; Soft west wind, Op. 74/2; Song, Op. 97/2; Song without words, Op. 40/2; Study, Op. 76/2; Valse, Op. 34/1.
(M) (*) Finlandia mono FACD 808. Cyril Szalkiewicz.

Cyril Szalkiewicz enjoyed a considerable reputation in Finland during Sibelius's lifetime, but it is a moot point whether these performances are impressive enough to command an audience nowadays. They are perfectly serviceable but, now that there is a decent modern survey of this repertoire by Annette Servadei on Olympia at slightly less than premium price, the claims of this recording are less pressing.

3 Lyric pieces, Op. 41; 5 Characteristic impressions, Op. 103; 6 Impromptus, Op. 5; 5 Pieces, Op. 75; 5 Pieces, Op. 85; Finlandia (arr. composer).
(BB) *** Naxos Dig. 8. 553661 [id.]. Risto Lauriala.

Perfectly good playing and decent recording make this a useful alternative to the complete survey by Annette Servadei. Its price advantage will incline some readers to give it preference, and it also enjoys the benefit of decent recorded sound.

VOCAL MUSIC

Kullervo Symphony, Op. 7.
(BB) * Naxos Dig. 8.553756 [id.]. Rusanen, Ruutunen, Laulan Ystävät Ch., Turku PO, Panula.

The super-budget price of this Naxos version is about all there is to recommend it. The soloists are decent and the choir very good, but Jorma Panula does not succeed in inspiring really first-class orchestral playing from the Turku (Abo) orchestra. The recording is excellent but, to be frank, investing in this as a way of getting to know this remarkable work is a false economy.

Sinding, Christian (1856–1941)

Légende, Op. 46.
(BB) *** Naxos Dig. 8.550329 [id.]. Dong-Suk Kang, Slovak (Bratislava) RSO, Adrian Leaper – HALVORSEN: *Air Norvégien* etc.; SIBELIUS: *Violin concerto;* SVENDSEN: *Romance.* ***

Dong-Suk Kang plays Sinding's *Légende* with great conviction and an effortless, songful virtuosity. It is by no means as appealing as the Halvorsen and Svendsen pieces but makes a good makeweight for an excellent collection in the lowest price range.

Suite (for violin and orchestra), *Op. 10.*
(M) *** EMI CDM5 66060-2. Perlman, Pittsburgh SO, Previn – BARTOK: *Violin concerto No. 2;* CONUS: *Violin concerto.* ***

Heifetz recorded this dazzling piece in the 1950s, and it need only be said that Perlman's version is not inferior. Such is the velocity of Perlman's first movement that one wonders whether the disc is playing at the right speed.

Smetana, Bedřich (1824–84)

Má Vlast (complete).
(BB) *** Naxos Dig. 8.550931 [id.]. Polish Nat. RSO (Katowice), Antoni Wit.
(M) *** Ph. Dig. 442 641-2. Concg. O, Antal Dorati.
(B) *** EMI forte CZS5 68649-2 (2) [CDFB 68649]. Dresden State O, Berglund – DVORAK: *Scherzo capriccioso* etc.; GRIEG: *Old Norwegian romance* etc. ***
(M) *** Virgin/EMI Dig. CUV5 61223-2 [id.]. RLPO, Pešek.

Antoni Wit and his excellent Polish National Radio Orchestra give us a superbly played and consistently imaginative account of Smetana's *Má Vlast*, a work whose patriotic aspirations can so readily turn into rhetoric. Not here, however. The spacious opening of *Vyšehrad*, marginally slower than usual, glows with romantic evocation; equally the flutes, trickling down from the sources of the *Vltava*, captivate the ear and the famous stringtune is unusually gracious and relaxed. The wedding scene on the river becomes delightfully folksy rather than forcefully rhythmic, then the moonlight glitters on the waters of the lake with a phosphorescent radiance. This idyll is dramatically interrupted by the appearance of the St John's rapids, and there is a superb climax, with thundering (but not exaggerated) timpani, and the main theme gathers pace for the triumphant climax. The opening of *Šárka* brings tingling melodrama, with the neurosis then subsiding naturally for the jaunty theme which follows. *From Bohemia's woods and fields* opens with opulent expansiveness, and later the ethereal high string entry is exquisitely made. The opening horn-call of *Tábor* emerges atmospherically from the mists of the past and the music develops great weight and gravitas. *Blaník* follows on naturally, with the charming pastoral sequence offering more lovely playing from the Polish wind (and horn) soloists. Both the two final symphonic poems are full of incident, and Wit and his players are clearly involved in every bar. Each episode of the narrative is resourcefully presented, not least the charming (almost Tchaikovskian) 'marche miniature' which achieves magnificent grandiloquence, being finally joined – in a satisfyingly broad climax – by the great *Vyšehrad* theme, and the piece closes to joyous fanfares. The warm resonance of the Concert Hall of Polish Radio in Katowice seems right for this very individual reading, full of fantasy, which goes automatically to the top of the list alongside Kubelik's distinguished, and justly renowned, 1990 Czech Philharmonic version on Supraphon, which is rather special.

Dorati's is an extremely fine account of Smetana's cycle, avoiding most of the pitfalls with a reading which brings both vivid drama and orchestral playing of the finest quality. The music-making has a high adrenalin level throughout, yet points of detail are not missed. The accents of *Vyšehrad* may seem too highly stressed to ears used to a more mellow approach to this highly romantic opening piece, and *Vltava* similarly moves forward strongly. In the closing *Blaník*, Dorati finds dignity rather than bombast and the pastoral episode is delightfully relaxed, with a fine rhythmic bounce to the march theme which then leads to the final peroration. The Philips sound is splendid, with a wide amplitude and a thrilling concert-hall presence, and this reissue on the Philips Solo label makes an obvious recommendation in the mid-price range.

Whereas many recorded performances in the past have done well by *Vltava* and *From Bohemia's woods and fields* and then fallen short on the other four pieces, it is in these less well-known works that Berglund is most impressive. Indeed, if there is a criticism of this set it is that *Vltava*, although splendidly played, seems slightly undercharacterized alongside other sections of the score. The opening *Vyšehrad* is most beautifully played, full of lyrical evocation and atmosphere, as is *From Bohemia's woods and fields*, while *Sárka* is arrestingly dramatic. *Tábor* and *Blaník* are played together, and so often in previous accounts they have become engulfed in rhetoric, but not here where the national feeling that is the basis of their inspiration sounds surgingly jubilant. The closing pages of *Tábor* are beautifully managed, and the pastoral interlude in *Blaník* is engagingly lightweight so that when the closing chorale appears it has a lilting step and conjures up memories of *The Bartered Bride* rather than bombastic militarism. The end of the work has a joyous release. Berglund does not shirk the melodrama, but he never lets it get the better of him. The Dresden orchestra plays magnificently and the 1978 recording, made in the Lukaskirche, is full-blooded, with the brilliance never degenerating into fierceness. The Dvořák and Grieg couplings are also very successful, so this forte set is very competitive, if the programme is attractive.

Pešek's reading does not miss the music's epic patriotic feeling, yet never becomes bombastic. There is plenty of evocation, from the richly romantic opening of *Vyšehrad* to the more mysterious scene-setting in *Tábor*, while the climax of *Sárka*, with its potent anticipatory horn-call, is a gripping piece of melodrama. The two main sections of the work, *Vltava* and *From Bohemia's woods and fields*, are especially enjoyable for their vivid characterization, while at the very end of *Blaník* Pešek draws together the two key themes – the *Vyšehrad* motif and the Hussite chorale – very satisfyingly.

(i) *Má Vlast;* (ii) *Håkon Jarl, Op. 16;* (iii) *The Bartered Bride: Overture; Polka; Furiant.*

(B) ** Decca Double 443 015-2 (2) [id.]. (i) Israel PO, cond. Weller or (iii) Kertész; (ii) Detroit SO, Dorati – DVORAK: *Czech suite* etc. ***

Walter Weller's 1978 recording of *Má Vlast* is of Decca's vintage analogue quality, but the opening of *Vyšehrad* is curiously unevocative and, while Weller provides excellent detail in *Vltava*, the Israel Philharmonic's strings fail to captivate the ear in the glorious theme which spaciously represents the river. Weller is at his best in the later, more melodramatic pieces, and he secures generally good orchestral playing. There are no complaints about *Håkon Jarl* and under Kertész the pieces from *The Bartered Bride* are exceptionally vivid with the separate entries in the overture clearly positioned by the stereo.

Má Vlast: Vltava.

(B) *** Sony SBK 48264; *SBT 48264* [id.]. Cleveland O, Szell (with MENDELSSOHN: *Midsummer Night's Dream* ***) – BIZET: *Symphony.* ***

(M) (**) RCA GD 60279 [60279-2-RG]. NBC SO, Toscanini – DVORAK: *Symphony No. 9;* KODALY: *Háry János suite.* (***)

(M) (**) Sony mono SMK 64467 [id.]. NYPO, Bruno Walter – BRAHMS: *Hungarian dances Nos. 1, 3, 10 & 17;* J. STRAUSS: *Overtures; Waltzes.* (***)

The Clevelanders play *Vltava* superbly, from the opening trickle, through the village wedding and the moonlight sequence, to the climax at St John's rapids. The effect is both vivid and dramatic and the dynamic range not too restricted to spoil the element of contrast.

Recorded several years earlier than the other two items on Toscanini's disc, *Vltava* has painfully dry and close sound; but the intensity of Toscanini's performance still makes it a valuable document.

Although the opening has fine delicacy and the moonlight sequence is highly atmospheric, the restricted dynamic range and studio-ish sound prevent Walter's 1941 mono recording from expanding at climaxes.

(i) *Má Vlast: Vltava; Vyšehrad; From Bohemia's woods and fields;* (ii) *The Bartered Bride: 3 Dances.*

(B) ** DG Classikon 439 451-2 [(M) id. import]. (i) Boston SO, Kubelik; (ii) BPO, Karajan.

These excerpts, which offer what many would regard as the three finest of the six tone-poems making up *Má Vlast*, come from Kubelik's second (1970) stereo recording with the Boston Symphony Orchestra which, though perceptive and very well played, suffered from close microphones, thus robbing the orchestra of a good deal of the natural sumptuousness afforded by the acoustics of Symphony Hall, Boston, and in the great string-theme of *Vltava* the massed violins could ideally be richer. However, the ear adjusts and these are otherwise excellent performances. The *Polka*, *Furiant* and *Entry of the Comedians* from *The Bartered Bride* offer no such problems and are played with much panache by the Berlin Philharmonic under Karajan. But this Classikon bargain disc is not very full at 54 minutes: there would have been room for the overture, too.

String quartet No. 1 in E min. (From my life).
(M) **(*) DG (IMS) 437 251-2. Amadeus Qt – DVORAK: *String quartet No. 12.* **(*)

A strongly felt and purposeful account of Smetana's autobiographical *Quartet* from the Amadeus on top form: their ensemble, matching of timbre and unanimous of attack, is peerless. At times one feels that Norbert Brainin's lyrical vibrato is not entirely suitable for this very personal utterance: he wears his heart too openly on his sleeve; but there is no doubt that the performance overall is gripping, and the 1977 recording is vividly realistic.

(i) *String quartets Nos. 1 in E min. (From my life); 2 in D min.* (ii) *From the homeland.*
(BB) ** Naxos Dig. 8.550379 [id.]. (i) Moyzes Qt; (ii) Takako Nishizaki, Tatiana Fránova.

The Moyzes Quartet, composed of members of the Slovak Philharmonic, turn in very respectable accounts of both *Quartets*. The recording has less warmth and ambience than its top-price rivals. All the same this is to be preferred to some of the high-powered, jet-set ensembles, and is value for money.

Polkas and dances: *Bear; Furiant; Grain dance; Hop dance; Lancer; Little hen; Little onion; Neighbour's dance; Polkas Nos. 1–4; Stamping dance; Stepping dance.*
(M) (***) EMI (SIS) mono CDM5 66069-2. Rudolf Firkušný – DEBUSSY: *Recital.* (***)

Artistically this is in a class of its own. Firkušný certainly captures the spirit of his great countryman and brings zest and joy into his playing. The music, too, has great sparkle and wit. These performances originally appeared on a mono Capitol LP in the 1950s but they sound very well in the present transfer. This is really distinguished playing in the three-star category, and the inevitable sonic limitations should not inhibit collectors from investigating it.

OPERA

The Bartered Bride: overture.
(M) *** RCA 09026 62587-2 [id.]. Chicago SO, Fritz Reiner – DVORAK: *Symphony No. 9* etc.; WEINBERGER: *Schwanda: polka and fugue.* ***

The easy, bustling virtuosity of the Chicago strings makes this vivacious performance of Smetana's famous overture hard to beat when the recording, too, is full yet has clear inner detail.

The Bartered Bride: highlights.
(M) **(*) Sup. 112251-2 [id.] (from complete recording, with Beňačková, Dvorský, Novák, Kopp, Jonášová, Czech Philharmonic Ch. and O, Košler).

A well-made if not strikingly generous set of highlights from Košler's sparkling complete set. But the documentation includes only a list of excerpts unrelated to any synopsis, and there is no translation.

Smyth, Ethel (1858–1944)

The Wreckers: Overture.
(B) *** CfP CD-CFP 4635 [(M) id. import]. RSNO, Gibson – GERMAN: *Welsh rhapsody;* HARTY: *With the wild geese;* MACCUNN: *Land of the Mountain and Flood.* ***

Ethel Smyth's *Overture* for her opera, *The Wreckers* (first performed in England in 1909), is a strong, meaty piece which shows the calibre of this remarkable woman's personality for, while the material itself is not memorable, it is put together most compellingly and orchestrated with real flair. The recording is full and the CD has refined detail. This CD makes a genuine bargain.

Soler, Antonio (1729–83)

KEYBOARD WORKS

Keyboard sonatas Nos. 18 in C min.; 19 in C min.; 41 in E flat; 72 in F min.; 78 in F sharp min.; 84 in D; 85 in F sharp min.; 86 in D; 87 in G min.; 88 in D flat; 90 in F sharp; Fandango.
(M) *** Virgin Veritas/EMI VER5 61220-2. Maggie Cole (harpsichord or fortepiano).

Maggie Cole plays a dozen Soler pieces, eleven *Sonatas* and the celebrated *Fandango*, half of them on the harpsichord and the remainder on the fortepiano; she gives altogether dashing performances on both.

Good pieces to sample are *No. 87 in G minor* (track 5) and, on the harpsichord, *No. 86 in D major* (track 9) or the *Fandango* itself. The playing is all very exhilarating and inspiriting. Played at a normal level-setting, both instruments sound a bit thunderous, but played at a lower level the results are very satisfactory.

Sor, Fernando (1778–1839)

Fantasia, Op. 30; Fantasia, Op. 7; Variations on a theme of Mozart, Op. 9.
(M) **(*) RCA Dig. 09026 61607-2. Julian Bream (guitar) – AGUADO: Collection. **(*)

Both Sor *Fantasias* are ambitious and each has a central set of variations. Bream's approach is spacious and his deliberation – for all the variety and skill of the colouring – means that the listener is conscious of the music's length, although it is all agreeable enough. The more concise Mozartian *Variations* remain Sor's most famous piece, and the variety and flair of the playing demonstrate why. The studio recording, made in New York, is eminently truthful.

'Classic guitar': Grand solo (Introduction and allegro), Op. 14. Sonata in C, Op. 25.
(M) **(*) RCA 09026 61593-2. Julian Bream (guitar) – GIULIANI: *Grand overture, Op. 61* etc.; DIABELLI: *Sonata in A.* **(*)

Sor's *Grand solo* is quite an attractive piece, with an *Andante largo* introduction instead of a slow movement, and it includes the theme and variations seemingly obligatory to this composer. The *Sonata in C*, however, is extremely inconsequential and easily forgettable. But all the music is beautifully played and immaculately recorded.

Sousa, John Philip (1854–1932)

Marches: *The Ancient and Honorable Artillery Company; The Black Horse Troop; Bullets and bayonets; The Gallant Seventh; Golden jubilee; The Glory of the Yankee Navy; The Gridiron Club; High school cadets; The Invincible eagle; The Kansas Wildcats; The Liberty Bell; Manhattan Beach; The National game; New Mexico; Nobles of the mystic shrine; Our flirtation; The Piccadore; The Pride of the Wolverines; Riders for the flag; The Rifle Regiment; Sabre and spurs; Sesqui-centennial exposition; Solid men to the front; Sound off.*
(M) *** Mercury (IMS) 434 300-2 [id.]. Eastman Wind Ens., Frederick Fennell.

Fennell's collection of 24 Sousa marches (73 minutes) derives from vintage Mercury recordings of the early 1960s. The performances have characteristic American pep and natural exuberance; the zest of the playing always carries the day. One of the more striking items is *The Ancient and Honorable Artillery Company*, which incorporates *Auld lang syne* as its middle section. The sound, is, of course, first class.

Spohr, Ludwig (1784–1859)

Clarinet concerto No. 1 in C min., Op. 26.
(M) *** Classic FM Dig. 75605 57019-2. Colin Lawson, Hanover Band, Goodman – WEBER: *Clarinet concertos 1–2* etc. ***

The first of Spohr's *Clarinet concertos* may not have the memorability of the three Weber works with which it is coupled, but it provides a generous bonus on an outstanding disc. Colin Lawson, principal clarinet of the Hanover Band, plays most imaginatively with attractively reedy tone to match the period instruments of his colleagues. Full and vivid sound.

Clarinet concertos Nos. 1 in C min., Op. 26; 3 in F min.; Potpourri for clarinet and orchestra in F on Peter von Winter's opera 'Das unterbrochene Opferfest', Op. 80.
(BB) *(*) Naxos Dig. 8.550688 [id.]. Ernst Ottensamer, Slovak State PO (Košice) or RSO (Bratislava), Johannes Wildner.

Ottensamer's mellow, nicely turned performances of urbane music that can easily sound bland have not nearly enough flair and sparkle. He is best in the finales which, though low-key, are elegantly jocular; but all his chortling cannot bring the *Potpourri* back to life, for want of really indelible tunes. Warm, full recording.

Double quartet in D min., Op. 65.
(M) ** EMI (SIS) CDM5 65995-2. Gervase de Peyer, Melos Ens. – BERWALD: *Septet* ***; WEBER: *Clarinet quintet*. **(*)

The main interest of Spohr's *Double quartet* lies in its inherent antiphony, which is skilfully managed. This is what might be described as a well-wrought piece but, apart from the Scherzo which is quite catchy, the rest of the music is pleasant but unmemorable. The performance has plenty of character, but the recording, though clear and quite full, sounds a little edgy in the present transfer.

Piano trios Nos. 2 in F, Op. 123; 4 in B flat, Op. 133.
(BB) ** Naxos Dig. 8.553205 [id.]. Hartley Piano Trio.

The Naxos accounts are well played and serviceable, the *Second Trio* rather pleasing, although the Hartley Trio does not exude a very strong collective personality. The other snag is the resonant ecclesiastical acoustic, which means that the microphones have to be fairly close and in consequence the recording is less flattering and not always so cleanly focused.

Stainer, John (1840–1901)

The Crucifixion.
(B) *** CD-CFP 4519 [(M) id. import]. David Hughes, John Lawrenson, Guildford Cathedral Ch., Barry Rose; Gavin Williams.
(BB) ** ASV CDQS 6100 [(M) id. import]. James Griffet, Michael George, Peterborough Cathedral Ch., Stanley Vann; Andrew Newberry.

(i) *The Crucifixion. Come thou long-expected Jesus* (hymn); *I saw the Lord* (anthem).
(B) *** Decca 436 146-2; *436 146-4* [(M) id. import]. (i) Richard Lewis, Owen Brannigan, St John's College, Cambridge, Ch., Guest.

All five hymns in which the congregation is invited to join are included on the Decca (originally Argo) record. Owen Brannigan is splendidly dramatic and his voice makes a good foil for Richard Lewis in the duets. The choral singing is first class and the 1961 recording is of Argo's best vintage, even finer than its CfP competitor. Moreover the Decca disc includes two bonuses: a hymn set to the words of Charles Wesley and a fine eight-part anthem, *I saw the Lord*, both of which are equally well sung.

The Classics for Pleasure version (from the late 1960s) is of high quality and, although one of the congregational hymns is omitted, in every other respect this can be recommended. John Lawrenson makes a movingly eloquent solo contribution and the choral singing is excellent. The remastered recording sounds first class, but the Decca version is finer still.

A super-bargain version is welcome, and the ASV performance is sincere and eloquent in a modestly restrained way, although at times there is a lack of vitality. The two soloists make a stronger contribution, and the tenor, James Griffet, is pleasingly lyrical. However, the style of presentation does not wholly avoid hints of the sentimentality that hovers dangerously near all performances of this work. The recording is atmospheric.

Stamitz, Carl (1745–1801)

Sinfonias concertantes: (i) *in C for 2 violins and orchestra;* (ii) *in D for violin, viola and orchestra.*
(BB) **(*) ASV Dig. CDQS 6140 [(M) id.]. Richard Friedman, L. Festival O, Ross Pople; with (i) Steven Smith; (ii) Roger Best – HAYDN: *Sinfonia concertante*. **(*)

Stamitz may not match Mozart but he is a personality in his own right and such a work as the *Sinfonia concertante in C for two violins*, here projected with fine spontaneity, brings a slow movement where one of the two soloists, playing alone, presents a 'singing' cantilena almost worthy of his greater contemporary. This *Andante* is also felicitously scored, with effective writing for the horns. The first movement has some good ideas too, and it is only the *Minuet* finale that lapses into conventionality; even so, like the first movement, the writing for the two soloists is inventively conceived. The companion *Sinfonia concertante for violin and viola*, if not quite so interesting in its material, has a historic link with Mozart's work for the same combination; as such, it makes fascinating listening. However, although the two soloists here play freshly and stylishly, they lack individuality of profile and, while Ross Pople directs the orchestra strongly, with tender feeling in the central *Romance*, the earlier CBS/Sony account of this work by Stern and Zukerman (with the ECO under Barenboim) has far more personality.

Stamitz, Johann (1717–57)

Clarinet concerto No. 1 in F; (i) *Double Clarinet concerto in B flat;* (ii) *Double concerto for clarinet and bassoon in B flat.*

(BB) *** Naxos Dig. 8.553584 [id.]. Kalman Berkes, with (i) Tomoko Takashima; (ii) Koji Okazaki; Nicholas Esterhazy Sinfonia.

Stamitz wrote no fewer than 11 clarinet concertos as well as the two double concertos on this first disc of a collected edition from Naxos. The *F major* solo *Concerto* is a delightful work with a vigorous first movement leading to a lyrical minor-key Andante and a jig finale. The double concerto was a favourite form with Stamitz, with long opening tuttis in the slow movements as well as the first. Both works are linked to the sinfonia concertante format as well as to the earlier form of the concerto grosso with its strongly contrasted, lightly scored passages for the solo instruments. Both are built on attractive material, but the work for clarinet and bassoon is the more successful, with instruments sharply contrasted. As soloist as well as director, Berkes with his reedy clarinet tone is well matched by his Japanese partners, helped by full, open recording.

Stanford, Charles (1852–1924)

(i) *Concert piece for organ and orchestra;* (ii) *Clarinet concerto in A min., Op. 80. Irish rhapsodies Nos. 1 in D min., Op. 78; 2 in F min. (Lament for the Son of Ossian), Op. 84;* (iii) *3 for cello and orchestra, Op. 137. 4 in A min. (The fisherman of Loch Neagh and what he saw); 5 in G min., Op. 147;* (iv) *6 for violin and orchestra, Op. 191. Oedipus Rex prelude, Op. 29.*

(M) *** Chandos Dig. CHAN 7002/3 [id.]. (i) Gillian Weir; (ii) Janet Hilton; (iii) Raphael Wallfisch; (iv) Lydia Mordkovitch; Ulster O, Vernon Handley.

Stanford's set of *Irish rhapsodies* (two of them concertante pieces with highly responsive soloists) are the more impressive when heard as a set. They originally appeared coupled with the symphonies, but they sometimes seemed stronger and more concentrated than those more ambitious works. The rhapsodies are splendidly played and recorded. Gillian Weir makes a first-class soloist in the *Concert piece for organ and orchestra* and Janet Hilton is hardly less appealing in the work for clarinet. An essential supplement for those who have already invested in the four-CD box of the symphonies which is at full price (CHAN 9279/82).

Piano concerto No. 2 in C min., Op. 126. Concert variations on an English theme: 'Down among the dead men', Op. 21.

(M) *** Chandos Dig. CHAN 7099 [id.]. Margaret Fingerhut, Ulster O, Vernon Handley.

Stanford's *Second Piano concerto*, although in three rather than four movements, is a work on the largest scale, recalling the Brahms *B flat Concerto*. Yet Stanford asserts his own melodic individuality and provides a really memorable secondary theme for the second movement. Margaret Fingerhut is a first-rate soloist both here and and in the apt and entertaining coupling, for Stanford was a dab hand at the variations format. Handley and his Ulster Orchestra are completely at home in this repertoire, and the Chandos recording is well up to the usual high standards of the house.

Symphony No. 3 in F min. (Irish), Op. 28.

(M) *** EMI CDM5 65129-2 [id.]. Bournemouth Sinf., Norman Del Mar – ELGAR: *Scenes from the Bavarian highlands.* ***

Norman Del Mar directs a ripe performance, noting that the finale gives an attractive forward glance to Stanford's pupils, Holst and Vaughan Williams. The EMI recording is warm and well defined.

Songs of the Fleet, Op. 117; Songs of the sea, Op. 91.

(M) **(*) EMI CDM5 65113-2. Benjamin Luxon, Bournemouth SO & Ch., Del Mar – DELIUS: *Sea drift.* **

This is a very welcome coupling of Stanford at his most uninhibitedly vigorous. The four *Songs of the sea* are more immediately memorable in their boisterous way, with *The Old Superb* a real hit; but the *Songs of the Fleet* (also setting Newbolt poems, but with SATB chorus) make a pleasant sequel. Luxon's voice is quite well caught by the microphones, but the resonance takes some of the bite from the words of the chorus. Yet Del Mar's understanding of the idiom makes for lively and enjoyable results.

Stenhammar, Wilhelm (1871–1927)

(i; ii) *Piano concerto No. 2 in D min., Op. 23.* (iii) *Serenade for orchestra, Op. 31.* (iii; iv) *Florez och Blanzeflor* (ballad).
(M) *** EMI CDM5 65081-2. (i) Janos Solyom; (ii) Munich PO; (iii) Swedish RSO, Stig Westerberg; (iv) with Ingvar Wixell.

This generously filled mid-price disc could serve as an admirable introduction to this fine Swedish composer. The *Serenade for orchestra* here comes in its finished form, as opposed to Neeme Järvi's Gothenburg recording, which adds the *Reverenza* movement that Stenhammar had excised but which brings no fill-up. Westerberg's 1974 performance is glorious and very well recorded, though the Swedish Radio Orchestra's strings do not have quite the same freshness and bloom as the Järvi set. However, this remains the most recommendable account of the work to date and is to be preferred to the old Kubelik set. Similarly Janos Solyom's dazzling account of the *Second Piano concerto* remains unsurpassed and, like the *Serenade*, still sounds very good indeed. There is a Saint-Saëns-like exuberance and effervescence about this work, and the improvisatory character of the piece is beautifully captured. The early *Florez och Blanzeflor* ('Flower and Whiteflower'), a ballad by Oscar Levertin, brings a certain Wagnerian flavour but has a charm that is conveyed well by Ingvar Wixell and Westerberg.

(i) *Symphonies Nos. 1 in F; 2 in G min., Op. 34; Serenade for orchestra, Op. 31* (with *Reverenza* movement); *Excelsior Overture, Op. 13; The Song (Sången): Interlude, Op. 44; Lodolezzi sings (Lodolezzi sjunger): suite;* (ii) *Piano concertos Nos. 1 in B flat min., Op. 1;* (iii) *2 in D min., Op. 23;* (iv) *Ballad: Florez och Blanzeflor;* (v) *2 Sentimental Romances;* (vi) *Midwinter, Op. 24; Snöfrid, Op. 5.*
(M) *** BIS Dig. BIS CD 714/716 [id.]. (i) Gothenburg SO, Neeme Järvi; (ii) Love Derwinger; (iii) Cristina Ortiz; (iv) Peter Matthei; (v) Ulf Wallin; (vi) Gothenburg Ch.; (ii–v) Malmö SO, Paavo Järvi.

Järvi's performances are now repackaged at a distinctly advantageous price. Special points to note are: first, that this is the only version of the *Serenade for orchestra* to include the *Reverenza* movement which Stenhammar subsequently withdrew; secondly, that the *First Piano concerto* makes use of Atterberg's original orchestration, which came to light only recently in America; and, thirdly, this is the most comprehensive compilation of Stenhammar's orchestral music now on the market. All the performances and recordings are of high quality, and the only serious criticism to make affects the first movement of the *Second Symphony*, which Järvi takes rather too briskly. The dazzling performance of the *Second Piano concerto* by Janos Solyom has a slight edge over the Ortiz, but hers is a good account, full of sparkle. All the recordings are digital save for that of the *First Symphony*, which comes from a 1982 concert performance and has great warmth and transparency. Apart from the DG, that is its only recording, and many other works (*Midwinter*, *Lodolezzi sings* and the *Excelsior overture*) are not otherwise available. Recommended with enthusiasm.

Symphony No. 2 in G min., Op. 36; Excelsior! Overture.
(BB) **(*) Naxos Dig. 8.553888 [id.]. RSNO, Petter Sundkvist.

Petter Sundkvist's account of Stenhammar's glorious *Second Symphony* is absolutely first class interpretatively, though it is rather let down by the quality of sound, which does not match that of his Gothenburg rivals. It is the first recording of a Stenhammar symphony by a non-Swedish orchestra and the first to embody all the corrections the composer made in the autograph score. It is a meticulous, dedicated account which radiates an understanding of and love for this music. Everything is beautifully proportioned and well held together. Sundkvist also gives us an exhilarating account of the early, post-Wagnerian *Excelsior! Overture*. The Royal Scottish National Orchestra respond with enthusiasm. It is a safe recommendation at the price, but the sound is not three-star.

CHAMBER MUSIC

String quartets Nos. (i) *1 in C, Op. 2;* (ii) *2 in C min., Op. 14;* (iii) *3 in F, Op. 18; 4 in A min., Op. 25;* (i) *5 in C (Serenade), Op. 29;* (ii) *6 in D min., Op. 35.*
(M) *** Cap. CAP 21536 (3) [id.]. (i) Fresk Qt; (ii) Copenhagen Qt; (iii) Gotland Qt.

The *First Quartet* shows Stenhammar steeped in the chamber music of Beethoven and Brahms, though there is a brief reminder of the shadow of Grieg; the *Second* is far more individual. By the *Third* and *Fourth*, arguably the greatest of the six, the influence of Brahms and Dvořák is fully assimilated, and the *Fourth* reflects that gentle melancholy which lies at the heart of Stenhammar's sensibility. The *Fifth* is the shortest; the *Sixth* comes from the war years when the composer was feeling worn out and depressed, though there is little evidence of this in the music. The Copenhagen Quartet play this marvellously.

Performances are generally excellent, as indeed is the recording, and it is good to have this thoroughly worthwhile set at mid-price.

PIANO MUSIC

3 Fantasies, Op. 11; Impromptu in G flat; Late summer nights, Op. 33; 3 Small piano pieces; Sonata in G min.

(BB) *** Naxos Dig. 8.553730 [id.]. Niklas Sivelöv.

Although he was by all accounts a wonderful pianist, Stenhammar wrote relatively little piano music of real quality – with the exception of the *Sensommarnätter* (*Late summer nights*). Niklas Sivelöv, who recorded the Berwald *Piano concerto* for the Naxos label, proves a thoroughly idiomatic interpreter of the composer and is as much at home in the quasi-impressionistic third movement of the *Late summer nights* and the delicate *Poco allegretto* as he is in the virtuosic, big-boned, penultimate movement. He is very well served by the recording engineers. Well worth the money.

Stradella, Alessandro (1644–82)

Christmas cantatas: (i) *Ah, ah, troppo è ver;* (ii) *Si apra al riso* (both *per Il Santissimo natale*).

(BB) *** BMG/DHM Baroque Esprit Dig. 05472 77463 2 [id.]. (i) Mechthild Bach, Ruth Ziesak, Christoph Prégardien, (i–ii) Kai Wessel, Michael Schopper; (ii) Barbara Schlick; La Stagione Frankfurt, Michael Schneider.

With a freshness and originality one expects from the composer of *San Giovanni Battista*, Stradella's Christmas cantata, *Ah, ah, troppo è ver*, is a great deal more than a serene pastorella. Lucifer (Michael Schopper) appears at the very opening, strenuously to interrupt the good-natured *Sinfonia*, to announce his determination to thwart the influence of the Christ child. Then come three scenas, in turn depicting the Annunciation, the Nativity and the Adoration of the Magi with the Angel and Mary (Mechthild Bach), followed by the Shepherd (Ruth Ziesak), each given beautiful narrative arias, all of which are sung ravishingly here. Joseph (Christoph Prégardien) then rounds off the story-telling, and the work closes with an engagingly happy madrigal in which all participate. *Si apra al riso* is less dramatic but musically just as inspired, with two duets and a madrigal trio interspersed among the solo numbers, here with the fresh-voiced Barbara Schlick standing out from her excellent colleagues. Michael Schneider paces the music admirably and the instrumental playing is first class. Vivid recording in a pleasing acoustic completes the listener's pleasure. A real bargain.

The Strauss family

Strauss, Johann Sr (1804–49) **Strauss, Johann Jr** (1825–99)

Strauss, Josef (1827–70) **Strauss, Eduard** (1835–1916)

(all music listed is by Johann Strauss Jr unless otherwise stated)

'The Best of Johann Strauss'

Volume 1: (i) Overture: *Die Fledermaus*. Polkas: (ii) *Annen;* (iii) *Auf der Jagd;* (iv) *Unter donner und blitz;* (v) *Tick-Tack*. Waltzes: (iv) *Künstlerleben; Lagunen; Rosen aus dem Süden; Wein, Weib und Gesang.*

(BB) ** Naxos Dig. 8.550336; *4.550336*. (i) Czecho-Slovak R. O, Sieghart; (ii) Polish State PO, Dohnányi; (iii) Czecho-Slovak State PO, Alfred Walter; (v) Polish State PO, Wildner; (iv) Czecho-Slovak RSO, Lenárd.

Volume 2: (i) Overture: *Indigo und die 40 Räuber*. Polkas: (ii) *Pizzicato; Tritsch-Tratsch*. Quadrille: (i) *Die Fledermaus;* Waltzes: (ii) *An der schönen blauen Donau; Frühlingsstimmen;* (iii) *Morgenblätter;* (ii) *Tausend und eine Nacht;* (i) *Wo die Citronen blüh'n*.

(BB) ** Naxos Dig. 8.550337; *4.550337*. (i) CSSR State PO, Alfred Walter; (ii) Czecho-Slovak RSO, Lenárd; (iii) Polish State PO, Wildner.

Volume 3: (i) *Egyptischer Marsch*. Overture: (ii) *Zigeunerbaron*. Polkas: (iii) *Bitte schön;* (iv) *Im Krapfenwaldl';* (v) *Leichtes blut*. Waltzes: (i) *Accelerationen;* (i) *Du und du;* (iii) *Neu-Wien;* (i) *Wiener blut*.

(BB) ** Naxos Dig. 8.550338; *4.550338*. (i) Czecho-Slovak RSO, Lenárd; (ii) Czecho-Slovak RSO, Siegart; (iii) Czecho-Slovak State PO, Alfred Walter; (iv) Czecho-Slovak State PO, Edlinger; (v) Polish State PO, Dohnányi.

Volume 4: (i) *Perpetuum mobile*. (ii) Overture: *Karneval in Rom*. Polkas: *Eljen a Magyar!; Vergnügungszug*. Waltzes: (i) *Kaiser;* (iii) *Karnevalsbotschafter;* (ii) *Mephistos Höllenrufe; Seid Umschlungen, Millionen; Wiener bonbons*.

(BB) ** Naxos Dig. 8.550339; *4.550339*. (i) Czecho-Slovak RSO, Lenárd; (ii) CSSR State PO, Alfred Walter; (iii) Polish State PO, Dohnányi.

Volume 5: (i) *Persischer Marsch*. Overture: (ii) *Das Spitzentuch der Königin*. Polkas: *Kreuzfidel; Neue Pizzicato; Vom donaustrande*. Waltzes: *Freut euch des Lebens;* (i) *G'schichten aus dem Wienerwald;* (ii) *Liebeslieder;* (i) *Schatz*.

(BB) ** Naxos Dig. 8.550340; *4.550340*. (i) Czecho-Slovak RSO, Lenárd; (ii) CSSR State PO, Alfred Walter.

These discs make inexpensive samplers for the full-price complete Johann Strauss Edition on Marco Polo, although not quite all the repertoire is drawn from it, notably the recordings under Lenárd which are often very well done. Good value.

Boskovsky Strauss Edition

Galops: *Aufs Korn; Banditen*. Marches: *Egyptischer; Franz Joseph I Rettungs-Jubel; Napoleon; Persischer; Russischer; Spanischer. Perpetuum mobile*. Polkas: *Annen; Auf der Jagd; Bitte schön!; Champagner; Demolirer; Eljen a Magyar; Explosionen; Freikugeln; Im Krapfenwaldl; Leichtes Blut; Lob der Frauen; Ohne Sorgen; Pizzicato* (with Josef); *Neue Pizzicato; So ängst sind wir nicht; 'S gibt nur a Kaiserstadt, 's gibt nur a Wien!; Stürmisch in Lieb' und Tanz; Tik-Tak; Tritsch-Tratsch; Unter Donner und Blitz (Thunder and lightning); Vernügungszug*. Quadrilles: *Fledermaus; Orpheus; Schützen* (with Josef & Eduard). Waltzes: *Accelerationen; An der schönen Blauen Donau (Blue Danube); Bei uns z'Haus; Carnavals-Botschafter; Du und Du; Errinerung an Covent-Garden; Freuet euch des Lebens; Frühlingsstimmen (Voices of spring); Geschichten aus dem Wienerwald (Tales from the Vienna Woods); Kaiser (Emperor); Künsterleben (Artist's life); Lagunen; Liebeslieder; Mephistos Höllenrufe; Morgenblätter (Morning papers); Nordseebilder; Rosen aus dem Süden (Roses from the South); Seid umschlungen, Millionen!; Schneeglöckchen; 1001 Nacht; Wein, Weib und Gesang (Wine, women and song); Wiener Blut (Vienna blood); Wiener Bonbons; Wo die Citronen blüh'n!*. Johann STRAUSS Sr: Galops: *Sperl; Wettrennen. Radetzky march*. Polka: *Piefke und Pufka*. Waltz: *Loreley-Rhein-Klänge*. Josef STRAUSS: Polkas: *Auf Ferienreisen; Brennende Liebe; Eingesendt; Die Emancipirte; Extempore; Feuerfest; Frauenherz; Heiterer Mut; Im Fluge; Jokey; Die Libelle; Moulinet; Rudolfsheimer; Die Schwätzerin*. Waltzes: *Aquarellen; Delirien; Dorfschwalben aus Osterreich (Village swallows); Dynamiden; Mein Liebenslauf ist Lieb und Lust; Sphärenklänge (Music of the spheres); Transactionen*. Eduard STRAUSS: Polkas: *Bahn Frei!; Mit Extrapost*. Waltz: *Fesche Geister*.

(B) **(*) Decca 455 254-2 (6) [id.]. VPO, Willi Boskovsky.

These six vintage CDs (offering 86 titles) span Willi Boskovsky's long (analogue) recording career for Decca, stretching over two decades from the late 1950s onwards, when his records dominated the LP discography in the Strauss family repertoire. In 1979 he directed the first of the now famous VPO New Year Concerts (see below) and that recording tradition has continued until the present day. It has now become an annual event shared by different record companies and various conductors, capped in 1987 by Karajan, after he had set aside a period of his musical life to re-evaluate his interpretations. The result was perhaps the finest Strauss collection ever put on disc, and this premium-priced CD (DG 419 616-2) has certainly never been surpassed, including as it does a quite unforgettable account of the *Blue Danube*. Since then there have been a series of fine discs from Abbado, Carlos Kleiber, Lorin Maazel, Zubin Mehta and Riccardo Muti, all of whom have risen to the occasion and been given admirable support by the various recording teams.

Even so, Boskovsky's achievement in this repertoire remains unique, both in its range – the output of Josef, particularly his polkas, is notably well covered – and the almost unfailing sparkle of the performances. Following a sequence begun by Decca in the days of mono LPs with Clemens Kraus, he showed a unique feeling for the Straussian lilt in the waltzes and the fizzing élan and exuberance of the polkas and marches, while the playing he drew from the Vienna Philharmonic Orchestra was consistently persuasive. The Decca engineers rose to the occasion (notably so when special effects were required, as in the *Explosion* and *Thunder and lightning polkas*) and the Sofiensaal provided an ideal ambience, with plenty of warmth and bloom. The one snag is the thinness of violin-tone, especially on the earlier records – it is immediately noticeable here on *An der schönen blauen Donau*, which rightly opens the first disc. The present CD transfers are very vivid and immediate, and their brightness has also served to add a hint of coarseness to some of the lively music (for instance the engaging quadrilles on disc 6). The ear adjusts, however, when the music-making is so zestful and alive: in spite of such reservations, there is no finer or more all-embracing collection of the best of the output of the Strauss family than in this box. Appropriately, the Decca recording producer, John Parry, has provided a biographical essay, and the documentation includes Edward Hanslick's obituary, which records that Johann Jr was not only a great composer but 'an extremely charming, genuine and benevolent person'. This is surely reflected in the life-enhancing geniality of his music.

New Year's Day concert in Vienna (1979): Polkas: *Auf der Jagd* (with encore); *Bitte schön! Leichtes Blut; Pizzicato* (with Josef); *Tik-Tak*. Waltzes: *An der schönen blauen Donau; Bei uns zu Haus; Loreley-Rheine-Klänge; Wein, Weib und Gesang*. Josef STRAUSS: *Moulinet polka; Die Emanzipierte polka-mazurka; Rudolfsheimer-Polka; Sphärenklänge waltz*. Johann STRAUSS Sr: *Radetzky march*. Eduard STRAUSS: *Ohne Bremse polka* (with ZIEHRER: *Herreinspaziert! waltz;* SUPPE: *Die schöne Galathée overture*).
(B) *** Decca 448 572-2 (2). VPO, Willi Boskovsky.

Decca chose to record Boskovsky's 1979 New Year's Day concert in Vienna for their very first digital issue on LP. The clarity, immediacy and natural separation of detail are very striking throughout, and the strings of the Vienna Philharmonic are brightly lit. There is some loss of bloom and not quite the degree of sweetness one would expect now on a record made today in the Musikvereinsaal, but the ear soon adjusts. The music-making itself is another matter. It gains much from the spontaneity of the occasion, and the electricity is very apparent; it reaches its peak when the side-drum thunders out the introduction to the closing *Radetzky march*, a frisson-creating moment which, with the audience participation, is quite electrifying. The whole programme is included here (it was the 25th anniversary of the New Year Concerts and a suitable memento of Boskovsky's long Decca recording period in this repertoire with the VPO). The two discs are reissued most appropriately in Decca's 'Classic Sound' series at the cost of one premium-priced CD.

Egyptischer Marsch; Kaiser Franz Josef Marsch; Banditen-Galopp. Polkas: *Eljen a Magyar!; Furioso; Tritsch-Tratsch; Unter Donner und Blitz*. Waltzes: *An der schönen blauen Donau; Rosen aus dem Süden; 1001 Nacht; Wiener Blut; Wiener Bonbons*. Josef STRAUSS: *Die Libelle polka; Perlen der Liebe waltz*.
(M) ** Chandos Dig. CHAN 6528 [id.]. Johann Strauss O, leader Jack Rothstein (violin).

This reshuffling for Chandos's mid-priced Collect series brings fairly generous measure (69 minutes) and many will be attracted by the bright digital recording, which has plenty of bloom. The polkas go with an infectious swing and there is no lack of lilt in the waltzes, although Josef's *Perlen der Liebe* is a shade disappointing. Otherwise there is no lack of spontaneity here; good though Rothstein is, however, he does not equal Georgiadis in this repertoire.

Graduation ball (ballet; arr. Dorati)
(M) * Mercury 434 365-2 (2) [id.]. Minneapolis SO, Dorati – ADAM: *Giselle* **(*); OFFENBACH: *Gaîté parisienne*. *

Dorati conducts his own ballet arrangement with plenty of spirit, although at times his approach seems ungracious and lacking in geniality. But this is at least partly the fault of the dry recording, with the Minneapolis violins robbed of almost all their lustre.

Marches: *Egyptischer; Persischer*. Polkas: *Auf der Jagd; Pizzicato* (with Josef); *Unter Donner und Blitz; Postillon d'amour; Leichtes Blut*. Waltzes: *G'schichten aus dem Wienerwald; Morgenblätter; Wiener Blut*. Josef STRAUSS: *Sphärenklänge*.
(M) *** DG 449 768-2 [id.]. BPO, Karajan.

Karajan was almost always a persuasive conductor of Strauss waltzes and polkas, if not as consistently reliable as Boskovsky. But in making a selection for the 'Originals' series the DG producers have perceptively chosen the present collection, based on an LP originally published in 1971. A few prize items have been added, notably the engaging *Postillon d'amour polka*, which is bounced in true dance rhythm, and Josef's *Sphärenklänge*, which Karajan shapes most affectionately, particularly the lovely opening. But the original disc is most notable for the central section of the *Egyptian march* when, after opening boldly and providing some delightfully colourful detail, Karajan pulls back so that the Berlin orchestral players can make a robust vocal contribution to the middle section. The piece is then charmingly pared down, like a patrol disappearing into the distance. The *Pizzicato polka* is played very gently, as a foil to the more lively items which surround it. Of the waltzes, *Wiener Blut* lilts attractively, and *Tales from the Vienna woods* is coaxed most seductively with a particularly delicate zither solo. The sound is excellent, and altogether this is the best Karajan Johann Strauss disc in the DG catalogue, apart from his famous 1987 New Year concert in Vienna, which is unsurpassable.

Napoleon-Marsch. Polkas: *Annen; Explosionen; Tritsch-Tratsch*. Waltzes: *An der schönen blauen Donau; Morgenblätter; 1001 Nights; Wein, Weib und Gesang; Wiener Bonbons*. Josef STRAUSS: *Dorfschwalben aus Osterreich*. Johann STRAUSS Sr: *Radetzky march*.
(B) *** Decca Eclipse 433 609-2; *433 609-4* [(M) id. import]. VPO, Willi Boskovsky.

A particularly enjoyable concert of Boskovsky repertoire, chosen and ordered with skill, opening with the *Blue Danube* and closing with the rousing *Radetzky march*. The VPO are on their toes throughout. The recording dates range from 1958 to 1976; some are spikier than others in the upper range, but the warm Sofiensaal ambience is always flattering.

(i) *Overture: Die Fledermaus*. Waltzes: (ii) *An der schönen blauen Donau; Carnavals-Botschafter; Donauweibchen; Du and du; Feuilleton; Flugschriften;* (i) *Geschichten au dem Wienerwald; Kaiser;* (ii) *Die Leitartikel; Morgenblätter;* (i) *1001 Nacht;* (ii) *Wein, Weib und Gesang; Wiener Frauen*. Polkas: (i) *Im Krapfenwald'l; Leichtes Blut*. Josef STRAUSS: Waltzes: *Dynamiden; Sphärenklänge*. Johann STRAUSS Sr: *Radetzky march*.
(BB) *** EMI Seraphim Dig./Analogue CES 68535-2 (2) [CDEB 68535]. (i) VPO, Rudolf Kempe; (ii) J. Strauss O of V., Willi Boskovsky.

A fascinating juxtaposition of two quite different styles of Johann Strauss performance. From the very opening of the *Blue Danube*, the playing of Boskovsky's Johann Strauss Orchestra balances an evocative Viennese warmth with vigour and sparkle; he is at his very best exploring the novelties – *Donauweibchen* and *Wiener Frauen* are particularly winning – with a few familiar numbers like the vivacious *Morgenblätter*, *Du and du* and *Wein, Weib und Gesang* thrown in. The latter, incidentally, has an abbreviated introduction. The digital recording from the early 1980s is excellent. Kempe opens the second disc with a vivaciously volatile account of the *Die Fledermaus overture*, but in the waltzes he is unashamedly indulgent, especially in the introductions of the two Josef Strauss items, and *1001 Nacht*. With quite gorgeous playing from the VPO strings this is almost decadently voluptuous, moving to a sumptuous climax. Both polkas are infectious and *Im Krapfenwald'l*, with its cuckoo calls, brings an affectionate smile. The recordings, from 1958 and 1961, sound amazingly good. With a playing time of nearly 143 minutes, this is outstanding value.

(i) *Overtures: Die Fledermaus;* (ii) *Waldmeister*. (iii) *Perpetuum mobile*. Polkas: (iv) *Annen;* (v) *Auf der Jagd;* (vi) *Leichtes Blut;* (iv) *Pizzicato* (with Josef); (vii) *Tritsch-Tratsch;* (iv) *Vergnügungszug*. (viii) *Quadrille on themes from Verdi's 'Un ballo in maschera'*. Waltzes: (ix) *Accelerationen;* (x) *An der schönen blauen Donau;* (xi) *Du und Du;* (iv) *Frühlingsstimmen;* (vi) *G'schichten aus dem Wienerwald;* (xii) & (xiii) & (v) *Kaiser;* (iii) *Rosen aus dem Süden;* (ii) *Wein, Weib und Gesang*. Josef STRAUSS: (iv) *Dorfschwalben aus Osterreich;* (v) *Sphärenklänge*. (iv) Johann STRAUSS Sr: *Radetzky march*.
(M) *** DG (IMS) mono/stereo 435 335-2 (2). VPO, (i) Maazel; (ii) Boskovsky; (iii) Boehm; (iv) Clemens Krauss; (v) Karajan; (vi) Knappertsbusch; (vii) Mehta; (viii) Abbado; (ix) Josef Krips; (x) Szell; (xi) Erich Kleiber; (xii) Bruno Walter; (xiii) Furtwängler.

This delectable compilation for the 150th anniversary of the Vienna Philharmonic brings recordings of Strauss made between 1929 and 1990, notably from EMI, whose recordings of Erich Kleiber, Clemens Krauss and George Szell (made in the late 1920s and early 1930s) are particularly atmospheric, very well transferred. Other Clemens Krauss performances, plus more by Boskovsky and Knappertsbusch, come from the Decca label, justly famous in this repertoire. It is fascinating to compare Bruno Walter (1937), Wilhelm Furtwängler (1950) and Karajan (1987), all playing the *Emperor waltz*, and the many well-known favourites are well spiced with a few charming rarities.

Overtures: *Die Fledermaus; Waldmeister. Perpetuum mobile*. Polkas: *Eljen a Magyar!; Pizzicato* (with Josef); *Tritsch-Tratsch; Unter Donner und Blitz; Vergnügungszug*. Waltzes: *Accelerationen; An der schönen, blauen Donau; G'schichten aus dem Wienerwald; Kaiser; Morgenblätter; Rosen aus dem Süden*. Josef STRAUSS: Polkas: *Frauenherz; Die Libelle; Ohne Sorgen; Die tanzende Muse*. Waltzes: *Aquarellen; Delirien; Sphärenklänge; Transaktionen*. Johann STRAUSS Sr: *Radetzky march*.
(B) **(*) DG Double Dig. 453 052-2 (2) [id.]. VPO, Maazel.

The presence of a New Year's Day audience is most tangible in the *Pizzicato polka*, where one can sense the intercommunication as Maazel manipulates the rubato with obvious flair. He also gives a splendid account of *Transaktionen*, which has striking freshness and charm. The *Waldmeister* overture is a delightful piece and readily shows the conductor's affectionate response in its detail, while the opening of the *Aquarellen waltz* brings an even greater delicacy of approach and the orchestra responds with telling pianissimo playing. For the rest, these are well-played performances of no great memorability. The digital sound is brilliant and clear, somewhat lacking in resonant warmth.

Overtures: *Die Fledermaus; Der Zigeunerbaron. Perpetuum mobile; Persian march.* Polkas: *Annen; Champagne; Eljen a Magyar; Leichtes Blut.* Waltzes: *An der schönen blauen Donau; Kaiser; Künsterleben; Wein, Weib und Gesang.*
(B) ** EMI CfP CD-CFP 6042. LPO, Theodor Guschlbauer.

There is no real substitute on record for the VPO in this repertoire, but the LPO are obviously enjoying themselves and the playing is warmly idiomatic and stylish. The programme is drawn from two separate LPs, made in the early 1970s. Guschlbauer is clearly at home here. He is particularly good in catching the Viennese éclat in the polkas, and the shaping of the opening of each waltz is very nicely done, notably so in *Wine, women and song*, and this waltz overall is most successful. The warm acoustic of Barking Assembly Hall seems right for the music. Very enjoyable and generous (77 minutes), but not really distinctive.

Overtures: *Die Fledermaus; Der Zigeunerbaron. Perpetuum mobile;* Polkas: *Annen; Bitte schöne; Champagne; Explosionen; Neue Pizzicato; Pizzicato* (with Josef); *Unter Donner und Blitz;* Waltzes: *An der schönen Blauen Donau; Geschichten aus dem Wienerwald; Kaiser; Morgenblätter; Rosen aus dem Süden; Wein, Weib und Gesang; Wiener Blut.* Eduard STRAUSS: *Bahn Frei polka; Blüthenkranz* (waltz arr. from themes of Johann Strauss Jr). Johann STRAUSS Sr: *Radetzky march* (with ZIEHRER: *Busserl: polka* **).
(BB) ** Carlton LSO Double Dig. 30368 00127 (2) [(B) id.]. LSO, John Georgiadis.

John Georgiardis is a warmly sympathetic Strauss conductor. Although his rubato is at times a little indulgent (as in the *Die Fledermaus overture*), there is no lack of lilt in the waltzes, even if the playing is without a strong Viennese accent. However, some will count it a drawback that he substitutes strings for the the zither solo in *Tales from the Vienna woods*. There are also no traditional superimposed sound-effects in the *Explosions polka*; one waits until the very end, when there is a spectacular 'collapse' of the whole percussion department. All the polkas are spirited, and the pot-pourri waltz arranged by Eduard Strauss is one of the highlights. The sub-Straussian novelty by Ziehrer is enjoyable; although the playing throughout is of a high standard and the vivid, modern recording cannot be faulted, this is an enjoyably easy-going, rather than a distinctive, collection.

Overtures: *Die Fledermaus; Der Zigeunerbaron.* Waltzes: *An der schönen blauen Donau; Geschichten aus dem Wiener Wald; Kaiser; Wiener Blut.*
(M) (***) Bruno Walter Edition: Sony mono SMK 64467 [id.]. Columbia SO, Bruno Walter – BRAHMS: *Hungarian dances Nos. 1, 3, 10 & 17* (***); SMETANA: *Vltava.* (**)

It is good to have a reminder of Bruno Walter's way with Johann Strauss, full of vivacity, and with *Wiener Blut* obviously the conductor's favourite among the waltzes here, as he coaxes the opening beguilingly and then draws some ravishing playing from the violins. The two overtures are bright and volatile. No apologies whatsoever about the 1956 mono recording, which is warm and spacious and sounds almost like early stereo.

Perpetuum mobile. Polkas: *Annen; Auf der Jagd; Pizzicato* (with Josef); *Tritsch-Tratsch; Unter Donner und Blitz.* Waltzes: *An der schönen blauen Donau; G'schichten aus dem Wienerwald; Kaiser; Wiener Blut.* Josef STRAUSS: *Delirien waltz.*
(M) **(*) DG 437 255-2. BPO, Karajan.

Here is a selection taken from two analogue LPs which Karajan made in 1966 and 1969 respectively. The performances have characteristic flair and the playing of the Berlin Philharmonic has much ardour as well as subtlety, with the four great waltzes of Johann II all finely done (the *Emperor* has a particularly engaging closing section) and the polkas wonderfully vivacious. The current remastering is satisfactory, brightly lit, but with the Jesus-Christus Kirche providing ambient fullness.

Polkas: *Czech; Pizzicato* (with Josef). Waltzes: *Kaiser; Rosen aus dem Süden; S ängerlust; Wiener Blut; Wiener Bonbons.* J. STRAUSS Sr: *Radetzky march.* Josef STRAUSS: Polkas: *Feuerfest; Ohne Sorgen.*
(BB) **(*) ASV CDQS 6020 [(M) id. import]. LSO, leader Georgiadis (violin).

The LSO is on top form and the rhythmic feel of the playing combines lilt with polished liveliness. There is delicacy (the *Czech polka* is enchanting) and boisterousness, as in the irresistible anvil effects in the *Feuerfest polka*. The closing *Radetzky march* is as rousing as anyone could wish, while the waltzes combine vitality and charm. With good recording in a suitably resonant acoustic, which tends to emphasize the bass, this is recommendable, especially at budget price.

Polkas: *Fledermaus* (from *Die Fledermaus*); *Kreigsabenteur* (from *Der Zigeunerbaron*); *Pizzicato* (with Josef); *Unter Donner und Blitz*. Waltzes: *Accelerationen; Rosen aus dem Süden; 1001 Nacht; Wo die Zitronen blüh'n*. Eduard STRAUSS: Polka: *Bahn frei*. Waltz: *Doktrinen*. Josef STRAUSS: Waltzes: *Dynamiden; Sphärenklänge*.
❀ (M) *** RCA 09026 61688-2 [id.]. Boston Pops O, Arthur Fiedler.

Arthur Fiedler, the doyen of the Boston Pops, never made a better record than this. He shapes the introductions to these famous waltzes with captivating charm; his dancing rubato brings an authentic Viennese feel and gives the impression of total spontaneity. Obviously the waltzes by Josef and Eduard especially command his affection, and all polkas go with a swing. Eduard's *Bahn frei* sizzles with energy – an exhilarating showstopper. Strauss records don't come much better than this, and the warm Boston acoustics, superbly caught in the early days of stereo (1956–9), add a special allure to all this music-making.

Polka: *Unter Donner und Blitz;* Waltzes: *An der schönen blauen Donau; Kaiser; Morgenblätter; Rosen aus dem Süden; Schatz; Wiener Blut*. Josef STRAUSS: Waltz: *Dorfschwalben aus Osterreich*.
(M) **(*) RCA 09026 68160-2 [id.]. Chicago SO, Fritz Reiner (with: Richard STRAUSS: *Der Rosenkavalier: Waltzes;* WEBER/BERLIOZ: *Invitation to the dance* ***).

Reiner's collection was recorded in 1957 and 1960, and some of the voluptuousness of the Chicago ambience has disappeared in this fresh remastering. Although the *Thunder and lightning polka* has an unforgettable explosive exuberance, these performances are memorable for their Viennese lilt, especially the *Emperor waltz* (affectionate rather than seeking nobility of outline) and Josef's *Village swallows*. Reiner is especially persuasive in the introductory interchanges of Weber's *Invitation to the waltz* which, like the Richard Strauss *Rosenkavalier* sequence, has been added for the present reissue. The latter shows Reiner at his finest, and here the string-sound has added opulence.

Waltzes: *Accelerationen; An der schönen blauen Donau (Blue Danube); Du und Du; Frühlingstimmen (Voices of spring); Geschichten aus dem Wiener Wald (Tales from the Vienna Woods); Kaiser (Emperor); Künsterleben (Artist's life); Liebeslieder; Morgenblätter (Morning papers); Rosen aus dem Süden (Roses from the South); 1001 Nacht; Wein, Weib und Gesang (Wine, women and song); Wiener Blut (Vienna blood); Wiener Bonbons; Wo die Zitronen blühn (Where the lemon trees bloom)*. Josef STRAUSS: *Dorfschwalben aus Osterreich; Sphären-klange (Music of the spheres)*.
(B) *** Decca Double 443 473-2 (2) [id.]. VPO, Willi Boskovsky.

These recordings span Willi Boskovsky's long recording career with the VPO for Decca, stretching over two decades, when his records dominated the LP discography in the Strauss family repertoire. The first group to be recorded (*Liebeslieder*, ending disc 1, *Wiener Blut*, *Wiener Bonbons* and *Artist's life*, which open disc 2) are particularly 'live' and fresh, dating from 1958; and the last, a charmingly lilting performance of Josef Strauss's *Village swallows*, comes from 1976. One might think that such a succession of Strauss waltzes spread over two discs might produce a degree of listening fatigue, but that is never the case here, such is Johann's resource in the matter of melody and freshness of orchestration. The playing is reliably idiomatic in a coaxing, Viennese way and has striking spontaneity and life. Indeed there are some splendid performances and, if the opening item on disc 1, the *Blue Danube* (a little mannered), and the *Emperor* (lacking regality but with a beautiful coda) have been recorded elsewhere with greater memorability, *Tales from the Vienna Woods* is splendid, with a deliciously authentic zither solo; and both *Roses from the South* and *1001 Nights* are superb. *Wo die Zitronen blühn* with unashamed rubato comes off most winningly, and *Wine, women and song* with its four-and-a-half-minute introduction is another success; Josef's *Music of the spheres* is hardly less beguiling. The earliest recordings show their age a bit in the violin tone, but Decca set high technical standards from the beginning, and from the 1960s onwards the strings are tonally more expansive, while the glorious Viennese ambient glow is consistent throughout. Indeed on CD it is remarkable just how well these vintage recordings sound. With 145 minutes of music offered on a Double Decca reissue (two discs for the price of one), this is excellent value.

Waltzes: *An der schönen, blauen Donau; Frühlingsstimmen; Geschichten aus dem Wienerwald; Künstlerleben; Rosen aus dem Süden*.
(M) ** Decca Phase Four 455 154-2 [id.]. Boston Pops O, Fiedler – TCHAIKOVSKY: *Nutcracker suite*. ***

Fiedler's Phase Four Strauss programme contains characteristically lively performances, vividly recorded. There is no lack of flexibility, but no special magic either. This is enjoyable in its direct way but cannot match Fiedler's earlier Boston Pops Strauss programme for RCA, to which we have given a Rosette – see above.

Waltzes: *An der schönen blauen Donau; Geschichten aus dem Wienerwald; Kaiser; Künstlerleben; Morgenblätter; Schatz; Wiener blut; Wo die Zitronen blüh'n.*
(BB) ** RCA Navigator 74321 24205-2 [RCA Silver Seal 60490-2-RV]. Phd. O, Eugene Ormandy.

Vividly recorded between 1968 and 1971, these performances have plenty of zest and panache, with the Philadelphia string section making the very most of the sumptuous melodies. Ormandy is clearly enjoying himself and, although there are a few eccentricities of pulse and phrasing and these are obviously not Viennese performances, they are enjoyable for their ready vitality, and this Navigator selection is very modestly priced.

OPERA

Die Fledermaus (complete).
(BB) *** CfP Silver Double CDCFPSD 4793 (2) [(B) id.]. Scheyrer, Lipp, Dermota, Berry, Ludwig, Terkal, Waechter, Kunz, Philh. Ch & O, Otto Ackermann.
(M) *** EMI CMS5 66223-2 (2) [CDMB 66223]. Rothenberger, Holm, Gedda, Dallapozza, Fischer-Dieskau, Fassbaender, Berry, V. State Op. Ch., VSO, Boskovsky.
(M) (***) EMI (SIS) mono CHS7 69531-2 (2) [Ang. CDHB 69531]. Schwarzkopf, Streich, Gedda, Krebs, Kunz, Christ, Philh. Ch. & O, Karajan.
(B) *(*) Naxos Dig. 8.66017/8 [id.]. Fontana, Hopferwieser, Dickie, Karwautz, Yachmi-Caucig, Martin, Werner, Krämmer, Bratislava City Ch., Slovak RSO (Bratislava), Wildner.

On a CfP Silver Double, with a synopsis rather than a libretto, comes a vintage *Fledermaus* from 1960. It makes a superb bargain, for the singing is consistently vivacious. Gerda Scheyrer's Rosalinde brings the only relative disappointment, for the voice is not ideally steady; but Wilma Lipp is a delicious Adèle and Christa Ludwig's Orlofsky is a real surprise, second only to Brigitte Fassbaender's assumption of a breeches role that is too often disappointing. Karl Terkal's Eisenstein and Anton Dermota's Alfred give much pleasure, and Erich Kunz's inebriated Frosch in the finale comes off even without a translation. Ackermann's direction has not the subtlety of Karajan, but the final result is lively and polished, with a real Viennese flavour. The sound has come up remarkably vividly – there is a nice combination of atmosphere and clarity.

For those wanting a fairly modern, mid-priced version, EMI have just restored the mid-priced Boskovsky set to the catalogue. Though he sometimes fails to lean into the seductive rhythms as much as he might, his is a refreshing account of a magic score. Rothenberger is a sweet, domestic-sounding Rosalinde, relaxed and sparkling if edgy at times, while, among an excellent supporting cast, the Orlovsky of Brigitte Fassbaender must again be singled out as the finest on record, tough and firm. The entertainment has been excellently produced for records, with German dialogue inserted, though the ripe recording sometimes makes the voices jump between singing and speaking. The remastering is admirably vivid.

The mono recording of Karajan's 1955 version has great freshness and clarity, along with the polish which for many will make it a first favourite. Schwarzkopf makes an enchanting Rosalinde, not just in the imagination and sparkle of her singing but also in the snatches of spoken dialogue (never too long) which leaven the entertainment. As Adèle, Rita Streich produces her most dazzling coloratura; Gedda and Krebs are beautifully contrasted in their tenor tone, and Erich Kunz gives a vintage performance as Falke. The original recording, crisply focused, has been given a brighter edge but otherwise left unmolested.

A bargain version of Johann Strauss's scintillating operetta, well recorded in digital sound, complete with substantial dialogue, clearly has a place, but the singing lets this Naxos set down. After a promising account of the overture, crisp and bright if too rigid, the entry of Alfred signals the worst: lumpish, with coarse Germanic tone. When Adèle arrives, her combination of flutter in the voice and shrillness is equally impossible. Even Gabriele Fontana, who sings Rosalinde, is deeply disappointing, for the voice has plainly deteriorated since she sang the Countess in *Figaro* and Fiordiligi at Glyndebourne. Johannes Wildner is an efficient but inflexible director. The CfP Silver Double set under Ackermann costs about the same as this and is far, far preferable.

Die Fledermaus: highlights.
(B) *** [EMI Red Line Dig. CDR5 69839]. Popp, Baltsa, Lind, Domingo, Bav. R. Ch., Munich RSO, Domingo.
(M) *** EMI CDM7 69598-2 (from above recording, with Rothenberger, Holm, Gedda; cond. Boskovsky).

It was not originally intended that Plácido Domingo should sing the role of Alfred as well as conducting EMI's newest digital recording of *Fledermaus*, but the tenor who had originally been engaged cancelled at the last minute, and Domingo agreed to do the double job, singing over accompaniments that had already been recorded. The happiness of the occasion is reflected in a strong and amiable, rather than an idiomatically Viennese performance. Lucia Popp makes a delectable and provocative Rosalinde and

Seiffert a strong tenor Eisenstein, with Baltsa a superb, characterful Orlofsky. With ensembles vigorous and urgent, this is a consistently warm and sympathetic selection.

Most should be happy with the excerpts from the mid-priced Boskovsky set, which is well cast; but the complete Ackermann version on CfP costs little more and is obviously a better proposition.

Eine Nacht in Venedig (*A night in Venice;* complete).
(M) (***) EMI mono CDH7 69530-2. Elizabeth Schwarzkopf, Nicolai Gedda, Erich Kunz, Philh. Ch. & O, Otto Ackermann.
(M) (*) Naxos mono 8.110027/8 [id.]. Teirsch, Arndt-Ober, Zimmerman, Wittrisch, Schmitt-Walter, Spletter, Berlin Reichssender, Heinrich Steiner.

A Night in Venice was drastically revised by Erich Korngold many years after Strauss's death, and it is that version, further amended, which appears in this charming 'complete' recording. This single EMI mono CD is a superb example of Walter Legge's Philharmonia productions, honeyed and atmospheric. As a sampler, try the jaunty little waltz duet in Act I between Schwarzkopf as the heroine, Annina, and the baritone Erich Kunz as Caramello, normally a tenor role. Nicolai Gedda as the Duke then appropriates the most famous waltz-song of all, the *Gondola song*; but with such a frothy production purism would be out of place. The digital remastering preserves the balance of the mono original admirably.

Like the other historic issues from Naxos, this is taken from a live broadcast, though one given in Berlin in 1938. The surface noise from what presumably were acetate discs is in places too obtrusive for enjoyment, with clicks and scratches getting in the way. Nevertheless, even with very dim and limited sound, the atmosphere of what was obviously a jolly and characterful performance comes over well enough, largely thanks to the lively dialogue. A very full quota is included, helping to account for the two-hour playing-time, as against the 80 minutes of the EMI version with Gedda and Schwarzkopf. Karl Schmitt-Walter is attractively clear and incisive in the central tenor role of the Count, and the veteran *buffo*, Marcel Wittrisch, is a vigorous, flamboyant Caramello, also very much in style. Carla Spletter is a bright, clear Annina, more charming in the dialogue than in her singing. It is fascinating to hear Margarethe Arndt-Ober as Agricola, a fruity mezzo who made her debut in 1906 and sang under Toscanini at the Met. in 1914. An issue of curiosity value to recommend with caution.

Wiener Blut (complete).
(M) (***) EMI mono CDH7 69529-2 [id.]. Schwarzkopf, Gedda, Köth, Kunz, Loose, Dönch, Philh. Ch. & O, Ackermann.
(M) **(*) EMI CMS7 69943-2 (2). Rothenberger, Gedda, Holm, Hirte, Putz, Cologne Op. Ch., Philh. Hungarica, Boskovsky.

To have Schwarzkopf at her most ravishing, singing a waltz song based on the tune of *Morning Papers*, is enough enticement for this Philharmonia version of the mid-1950s, showing Walter Legge's flair as a producer at its most compelling. Schwarzkopf was matched by the regular team of Gedda and Kunz and with Emmy Loose and Erika Köth in the secondary soprano roles. The original mono recording was beautifully balanced, and the facelift given here is achieved most tactfully.

The EMI set conducted by Willi Boskovsky makes a delightful entertainment, the performance authentic and with a strong singing cast. The recording is atmospherically reverberant, but there is no lack of sparkle. However, for some there will be too much German dialogue, which also involves two CDs.

Der Zigeunerbaron (The Gipsy Baron): complete.
(M) (***) EMI mono CDH7 69526-2 (2). Schwarzkopf, Gedda, Prey, Kunz, Köth, Sinclair, Philh. Ch. & O, Ackermann.

This superb Philharmonia version of *The Gipsy Baron* from the mid-1950s, now restored to the catalogue, has never been matched in its rich stylishness and polish. Schwarzkopf as the gipsy princess sings radiantly, not least in the heavenly Bullfinch duet (to the melody made famous by MGM as *One day when we were young*). Gedda, still youthful, produces heady tone, and Erich Kunz as the rough pig-breeder gives a vintage *echt*-Viennese performance of the irresistible *Ja, das schreiben und das lesen*. The CD transcription from excellent mono originals gives fresh and truthful sound, particularly in the voices.

Strauss, Richard (1864–1949)

Symphonic poems: *An Alpine Symphony, Op. 64; Death and transfiguration, Op. 24; Don Juan, Op. 20; Ein Heldenleben, Op. 40.*
(M) *** Chandos Dig. CHAN 7009/10 [id.]. RSNO, Neeme Järvi.

Symphonic poems: *Also sprach Zarathustra, Op. 30;* (i) *Don Quixote, Op. 35. Macbeth, Op. 23; Symphonia domestica, Op. 53; Till Eulenspiegel, Op. 38.*
(M) *** Chandos Dig. CHAN 7011/12 [id.]. RSNO, Järvi; (i) with Raphael Wallfisch.

Järvi's generally distinguished survey of the Strauss symphonic poems was recorded in the sumptuous acoustics of the Caird Hall, Dundee, between 1986 and 1989. If occasionally the resonance prevents the sharpest internal clarity, the skilled Chandos engineering ensures that the orchestral layout is very believable, heard within a natural perspective. The account of *An Alpine Symphony* is ripely enjoyable, with the reverberant acoustic here very helpful. Järvi seeks to present a general scenic view within a performance that is not as electrically taut or crisp of ensemble as, say, Karajan's but which is very effective in giving a genial description of the changing landscapes. *Death and transfiguration* shows the orchestra at its finest and here detail is revealed well, within a reading which has impressive control. *Don Juan* is portrayed as a bluff philanderer and the reading seeks sentience and amplitude rather than searing brilliance. *Ein Heldenleben* is strongly characterized and warmly sympathetic from first to last, marked by powerful, thrustful playing, lacking only the last degree of refinement in ensemble.

Järvi's second box opens with the *Symphonia domestica*, a particularly successful performance, with the composer's domestic circumstances and moments of marital ardour indulged good-humouredly; it is followed by a comparably joyful portrait of *Till. Macbeth*, less than a masterpiece, is also presented very persuasively; few if any recorded performances make a better case for it. *Don Quixote* then takes a rather leisurely journey, although an amiable one. Raphael Wallfisch, the solo cellist, plays splendidly but, like the excellent violist, John Harrington, is very forwardly balanced, while inner orchestral detail is less than ideally clear. *Also sprach Zarathustra*, which closes the programme, is the least successful of the series, with the reverberant acoustic rather muddying the sound, without bringing compensating richness; moreover the organ pedal at the opening is much too dominant. But overall these two sets represent a considerable achievement, and at mid-price they are undoubtedly competitive, particularly for those collectors who enjoy Chandos's rich tapestries of sound.

An Alpine Symphony, Op. 64; Don Juan, Op. 20; Suite for 13 wind instruments, Op. 4; Symphonia domestica, Op. 53; Till Eulenspiegel, Op. 28.
(BB) **(*) Virgin Classics Double Dig. VBD 5 61460-2 [CDVB 61460]. Minnesota O, Edo de Waart.

An excellent and inexpensive anthology, very well played and recorded, over which there are only minor reservations. There is no lack of spectacle in the *Alpine Symphony*, which ends with an impressive storm and a rich-hued sunset: only the echoing horns on the way up seem rather too far away; but nothing is inflated needlessly. Similarly, anyone who feels that Strauss's domestic revelations need tempering with a little discretion will enjoy this performance, which is also very well played by the excellent Minnesota Orchestra, who do not miss the ardour of the love scene between Strauss and his wife. The *Suite in B flat* is beautifully blended and comparably refined. In *Don Juan* the orchestra may not succeed in producing quite the same sophisticated opulence of texture as is achieved by such Straussians as Reiner in Chicago or Karajan in Berlin, but they still play very well indeed and, throughout, the sound has both depth and clarity. Good value.

An Alpine Symphony; Don Juan; Salome: Salome's dance of the 7 veils.
(B) **(*) Decca Eclipse Dig. 448 714-2; *448 714-4* [(M) id. import]. Cleveland O, Ashkenazy.

An Alpine Symphony; Till Eulenspiegel.
(M) (**) DG mono 447 454-2. Dresden State O, Karl Boehm.

The Cleveland Orchestra commands as rich a sonority and as much virtuosity as any of its illustrious rivals. Ashkenazy gives a generally well-controlled and intelligently shaped reading of the *Alpine Symphony* that has much to recommend it. However, it is not quite as strong in personality as the very finest versions. That applies also to *Don Juan*, which brings comparable virtuosity from the Clevelanders. However, with recording of Decca's top quality, this is good value at bargain price.

Strauss's *Alpine Symphony* is a work that depends a great deal on its panoply of orchestral sound to make its full effect and, while Karl Boehm's 1957 mono recording is marvellously played and dramatically evocative, the recording, though clear, lacks the necessary opulence. His extremely lively portrait of *Till* comes off much better, but he recorded this again in stereo. However, the later, BPO characterization has more of the peasant about him, less of the irrepressible rogue.

An Alpine Symphony, Op. 64; Aus Italien, Op. 16; Dance suite from pieces by François Couperin; (i) *Don Quixote, Op. 35. Macbeth, Op. 23; Metamorphosen for 23 solo strings.*
(M) *** EMI CMS7 64350-2 (3) [CDZC 64350]. (i) Paul Tortelier; Dresden State O, Kempe.

This is the third of the three boxes of Richard Strauss's orchestral and concertante music, recorded during the first half of the 1970s. The Dresden orchestra is a magnificent body and the strings produce gloriously sumptuous tone, which is strikingly in evidence in *Metamorphosen*. Rudolf Kempe had recorded the *Alpine Symphony* before with the RPO, and there is little to choose between the two so far as interpretation is concerned: he brings a glowing warmth to this score. His *Aus Italien* is more convincing than any previous version: the sound with its finely judged perspective is again a decisive factor here. He gives a most musical account of the delightful *Dance suite* based on Couperin keyboard pieces, although here some might wish for more transparent textures. Perhaps one could also quarrel with the balance in *Don Quixote*, which gives Tortelier exaggerated prominence and obscures some detail. The performance, however, is another matter and must rank with the best available. *Macbeth* also is convincing, and well paced.

(i) *An Alpine Symphony, Op. 64;* (ii) *Also sprach Zarathustra, Op. 30; Don Juan, Op. 20;* (iii) *Ein Heldenleben, Op. 40;* (ii) *Till Eulenspiegel, Op. 28.*
(B) *** Double Decca 440 618-2 (2) [id.]. (i) Bav. RSO; (ii) Chicago SO; (iii) VPO; Solti.

The Bavarian Radio Orchestra recorded in the Herculessal in Munich could hardly sound more opulent in the *Alpine Symphony* and the superb quality of the 1979 analogue recording tends to counterbalance Solti's generally fast tempi. The performances of *Also sprach Zarathustra*, *Don Juan* and *Till Eulenspiegel* come from analogue originals, made in Chicago a few years earlier. Solti is ripely expansive in *Zarathustra*, and throughout all three symphonic poems there is the most glorious playing from the Chicago orchestra in peak form. For *Ein Heldenleben* Solti went (in 1977–8) to Vienna, and this is another fast-moving performance, tense to the point of fierceness in the opening tutti and elsewhere. It underlines the urgency rather than the opulence of the writing and, though many Straussians will prefer a warmer, more relaxed view, Solti finds justification in a superb account of the final coda after the fulfilment theme, where in touching simplicity he finds complete relaxation at last, helped by the exquisite playing of the Vienna Philharmonic concertmaster, Rainer Küchl. The Decca recording is formidably wide-ranging to match this high-powered performance and, as with the rest of the programme, the transfers to CD are full-bodied and vividly detailed.

Also sprach Zarathustra (1954 and 1962 recordings); *Le bourgeois gentilhomme: suite, Op. 60;* (i) *Burleske for piano and orchestra. Don Juan, Op. 20;* (ii) *Don Quixote, Op. 35. Ein Heldenleben, Op. 40; Symphonia domestica, Op. 53; Elektra:* (iii–iv) excerpts. *Der Rosenkavalier: Waltzes. Salome: Dance of the seven veils;* (iii) *Finale.*
(M) *** RCA 09026 68635-2 (5) [id.]. Chicago SO, Fritz Reiner; with (i) Byron Janis; (ii) Antonio Janigro; (iii) Inge Borge; (iv) Paul Schofield and Francis Yeend.

RCA have gathered together here their newest transfers of Reiner's famous set of Strauss recordings, dating from the earliest days of 'living stereo', using similar microphone techniques to those pioneered by the Mercury engineers in the same venue. These records are almost as famous for the ambience of Chicago's Orchestra Hall as for the magnificent playing of the orchestra, at its very peak under a conductor who was a martinet to work for, yet who achieved consistently memorable results. Straussians will find a special fascination in comparing the two versions of *Also sprach Zarathustra*: the earlier (1954) version is let down a little at the opening by the organ pedal, but the performance itself has greater and more sustained intensity; the latter version is more relaxed but has compensating warmth and spaciousness. All the discs have been remastered except that classic (early 1954) coupling of *Also sprach Zarathustra* and *Eine Heldenleben*.

Also sprach Zarathustra, Op. 30; Le bourgeois gentilhomme (suite of incidental music for Molière's play), *Op. 60;* (i) *Violin concerto in D min., Op. 8. Death and transfiguration, Op. 24; Josephslegende, Op. 63; Schlagobers* (waltz), *Op. 70; Symphonia domestica, Op. 53; Der Rosenkavalier: Waltz sequence; Salome: Dance of the 7 veils.*
(M) *** EMI CMS7 64346-2 (3) [CDZC 64346]. (i) Ulf Hoelscher; Dresden State O, Kempe.

Ulf Hoelscher's eloquent account of this attractive early *Violin concerto* is more than welcome, as is the *Symphonia domestica*. Kempe's version of this work is no less desirable than Karajan's, a little more relaxed without being in any way less masterly. His *Also sprach Zarathustra* is completely free of the sensationalism that marks so many newer performances. *Josephslegende*, however, will call for tolerance even in this committed version; Strauss's inspiration is thin here and his craftsmanship runs away with him. The rest of the programme is well worth having, particularly *Le bourgeois gentilhomme*. Recording and CD transfers are well up to standard.

Also sprach Zarathustra; (i) *Burleske for piano and orchestra. Der Rosenkavalier: waltzes.*
(M) *** 09026 68638-2 [id.]. (i) Byron Janis; Chicago SO, Fritz Reiner.

This is Reiner's second recording of *Also sprach Zarathustra*, dating from 1962. It is marginally superior technically to the earlier (1954) account, with the organ pedal better managed at the opening, and it has an impressive feeling of space. But the earlier account (which has a two-minute shorter playing time) has rather more concentration and grip, noticeable from the opening sequence onwards. Byron Janis's account of the *Burlesque* is undoubtedly distinguished. Janis plays with panache and brilliance, and the current transfer makes the very most of the recording. The *Rosenkavalier waltzes* are seductive, though the clearer sound of the new transfer has lost a little of the ample sumptuousness of the old LP.

(i) *Also sprach Zarathustra; Death and transfiguration; Don Juan; Ein Heldenleben; Till Eulenspiegel;* (ii) *Der Rosenkavalier: Waltz sequence.*
(B) *** Ph. Duo Dig./Analogue 442 281-2 (2) [(M) id. import]. Concg. O, (i) Haitink; (ii) Jochum.

Also sprach Zarathustra, Op. 30; Death and transfiguration, Op. 24; Don Juan, Op. 20; Ein Heldenleben, Op. 40; Till Eulenspiegel; Der Rosenkavalier: Waltz sequence. Salome: Salome's dance of the 7 veils.
(B) *** EMI Rouge et Noir CZS5 68110-2 (2) [(M) id. import]. Dresden State O, Rudolf Kempe.

Haitink's performances are undoubtedly distinguished, superbly played, persuasively and subtly characterized. He finds added nobility in *Death and transfiguration*, while there is no lack of swagger in the accounts of both the *Don* and *Till*. The easy brilliance of the orchestral playing is complemented by the natural spontaneity of Haitink's readings, seamless in the transition between narrative events, without loss of the music's picaresque or robust qualities. Haitink's (1974) *Also sprach Zarathustra* was often spoken of in the same breath as Karajan's analogue alternative, issued in the same year. There is no lack of ardour from the Concertgebouw players and the reading has breadth and nobility. The (1970) *Ein Heldenleben* is also one of Haitink's finest records. He gives just the sort of performance, brilliant and swaggering but utterly without bombast, which will delight those who normally resist this rich and expansive work. In the culminating fulfilment theme, a gently lyrical 6/8, Haitink finds a raptness in restraint, a hint of agony within joy, that links the passage directly to the great Trio from *Der Rosenkavalier*. The Philips sound here is admirably faithful and skilfully remastered. For good measure Jochum's *Waltz sequence* from that very opera has been added, though here the recording, though good for its age (the early 1960s), has not quite the opulence of the Haitink recordings. An indispensable set nevertheless, and one of the finest of all the Duo bargains.

Kempe's 1974 *Also sprach Zarathustra*, powerful in its emotional thrust, is admirably paced and, while the Dresden orchestra may yield in virtuosity – though not much – to the Berlin Philharmonic under Karajan, whose version was made in the same year, the EMI digital remastering retains the opulence of the Dresden acoustic and the orchestral sound has both body and bloom. Kempe's *Death and transfiguration* and *Till Eulenspiegel* are also marvellously characterized, and the Dresden Staatskapelle is hardly less refined an instrument than the Berlin Philharmonic. The rather mellow portrayal of *Till* is particularly attractive. *Don Juan* is also comparable with Karajan's reading and certainly does not come off second best. *Ein Heldenleben* glows with life under one of the most distinguished Straussians of our time and the closing pages have a special kind of rapt intensity. The richness of string-tone in *Salome's dance*, a sinuously sensuous performance, and in the *Rosenkavalier Waltz sequence* has been superbly caught in the excellent CD transfer. With two discs offered for the price of one, this is a top bargain in the Strauss discography.

Also sprach Zarathustra; Death and transfiguration; Till Eulenspiegel.
(B) *** Decca Eclipse Dig. 448 224-2; *448 224-4* [(M) id. import]. Cleveland O, Ashkenazy.

Glorious Decca Cleveland sound in this triptych and marvellously responsive playing from the orchestra. As sound, this is in the demonstration bracket; but other readings, notably those of Karajan, are just that bit more characterful.

Also sprach Zarathustra; Don Juan; Till Eulenspiegel.
(B) *(**) DG Classikon 439 419-2 [(M) id. import]. BPO, Karl Boehm.
(B) ** Tring Dig. TRP 071 [(M) id.]. RPO, Sir Charles Mackerras.

Also sprach Zarathustra; Don Juan; Till Eulenspiegel; Salome: Dance of the 7 veils.
(M) *** Decca 448 582-2 [id.]. VPO, Karajan.

Karajan's Decca version of *Also sprach Zarathustra* was a famous early stereo demonstration disc in its day (1959), with its wide dynamic range and thrilling orchestral virtuosity; all its tonal opulence is restored in the CD transfer. The other works were recorded a year later and sound freshly minted, amazingly full and sharply detailed. *Till* is irrepressibly cheeky and full of wit, and *Salome's dance* is decadently sensuous.

Don Juan brings a similar, richly voluptuous response from the Vienna strings. Again the playing is superb, as beguiling in the love music as it is exhilarating in the chase. An admirable candidate for Decca's 'Classic Sound' series.

Boehm was a fine Straussian, but *Also sprach Zarathustra* is very early stereo (1958) and, for all the ardour of the Berlin Philharmonic, the violins are made to sound thin above the stave, although the Jesus-Christus-Kirche provides plenty of ambient warmth. Boehm's *Don Juan* and *Till* were recorded five years later; the sound is fuller and the orchestral playing is marvellous. *Don Juan* brings glorious leaping strings and rich thrusting horns, and Boehm provides an attractive German-peasant-based characterization of *Till*.

Sir Charles Mackerras and the RPO turn in well-prepared and eminently serviceable performances of these celebrated scores. In quality of recorded sound the engineers serve these artists well and, although the string-tone is more opulent in the Karajan *Zarathustra* (now on DG's 'Originals') and he finds more subtlety in all three scores, this grouping is still quite good value for money.

Also sprach Zarathustra, Op. 30; (i) *Don Quixote, Op. 35.*
(M) **(*) Sony SBK 47656; *SBT 47656* [id.]. Phd. O, Ormandy; (i) with Lorne Munroe.

Ormandy's 1963 Sony *Also sprach Zarathustra*, if not as overwhelming as his later, EMI version, has much virtuoso orchestral playing to commend it and many felicities of characterization. His (1961) *Don Quixote* will also give considerable pleasure. There is some marvellous orchestral playing and the two soloists play splendidly with plenty of character but without the 'star soloist' approach favoured by so many record companies. A very competitive coupling.

Also sprach Zarathustra, Op. 30; Ein Heldenleben.
✿ (M) *** RCA 09026 61494-2 [Basic 100 09026 61709-2]. Chicago SO, Fritz Reiner.
(M) *** Ph. Dig. 442 645-2 [id.]. Boston SO, Ozawa.

These were the first stereo sessions the RCA engineers arranged with Fritz Reiner, after the company had taken over the Chicago orchestra's recording contract from Mercury. It must be said – to their enormous credit – that the RCA recording team 'got it right' from the very beginning, and the series of records they made with Reiner and his players in Orchestra Hall remain a technical peak in the history of stereo recording and the impressive feeling of space it conveyed. Later reissues have improved on its definition but none has done so with the stunning success of the present transfer. *Ein Heldenleben* shows Reiner in equally splendid form. There have been more incisive, more spectacular and more romantic performances, but Reiner achieves an admirable balance and whatever he does is convincing. If anything, the recording sounds even better than *Also sprach* and the warm acoustics of Orchestra Hall help convey Reiner's humanity in the closing pages of the work.

Ozawa's 1981 recording of *Also sprach Zarathustra* became one of the first demonstration records for compact disc, and even for today's ears the depth and unforced firmness of the organ pedal sound leading on to an extraordinary crescendo cannot fail to bring a shiver to the nape of the listener's neck. The solo strings are balanced rather close, but otherwise this is a wonderfully warm and natural sound, with both a beguiling bloom and fine inner clarity. Ozawa as a Strauss interpreter goes for seductive phrasing and warmth rather than high drama or nobility, but this remains one of his finest achievements at Boston. Ozawa's view of *Heldenleben* is similarly free-flowing, lyrical and remarkably unpompous. He consistently brings out the joy of the virtuoso writing, and though the playing of the Boston orchestra is not quite as immaculate as in the companion version of *Zarathustra* the richness and transparency are just as seductive, superbly caught by the Philips engineers. There is a remarkable sense of presence and reality. This will admirably suit those needing a recommendable digital, mid-priced disc of these two works, although Reiner's RCA analogue interpretations are even more distinctive, and the early Chicago Hall stereo is also remarkably fine.

Also sprach Zarathustra, Op. 30; Don Juan, Op. 20; Till Eulenspiegel, Op. 28; Salome: Salome's dance.
(M) *** DG 447 441-2 [id.]. BPO, Karajan.

Karajan's 1974 DG analogue version of *Also sprach Zarathustra* is coupled with his vividly characterized performance of *Till Eulenspiegel* and a thrillingly ebullient *Don Juan*, plus his powerfully voluptuous account of *Salome's dance*. The Berlin Philharmonic plays with great fervour (the timpani strokes at the very opening are quite riveting) and creates characteristic body of tone in the strings, although the digital remastering has thrown a much brighter light on the violins.

(i) *Also sprach Zarathustra, Op. 30;* (ii) *Symphonia domestica, Op. 53.*
(M) **(*) Carlton Dig. 30366 00932. Nat. Youth O of Great Britain; (i) Skrowaczewski; (ii) Christopher Seaman.

Absolutely no apologies need be made for the playing of the National Youth Orchestra in these bravura Strauss scores. The strings may not be as opulent or as finely polished as those of the Berlin Philharmonic, but they still sound pretty good, and both performances glow with life and feeling. For some reason the very opening of Skrowaczewski's *Also sprach Zarathustra* (recorded in Symphony Hall, Birmingham, in 1997) is not quite as sumptuous as usual, with the underpinning organ pedal recessed and almost self-effacing when it acts briefly as a pendant at the end of the sequence. But the strings take up the music of 'great longing' with ardour, as do the thrusting horns in their eloquent 'expression of joys and pleasures'. The violins' upper tessitura is not found wanting later, and the work's final climax generates great intensity. If anything, the *Symphonia domestica*, recorded four years earlier under Christopher Seaman, is even finer. Not surprisingly, these young players respond readily to the orgasmic passion of the 'Love scene', but the wind soloists also revel in the charming detail of the opening movement. The joyous apotheosis is splendidly managed, and overall Seaman holds the structure together with admirable cohesion. The recording, made in Watford Town Hall, approaches the demonstration bracket.

Aus Italien, Op. 16; Die Liebe der Danae (symphonic fragment); *Der Rosenkavalier: waltz sequence No. 2.*
(BB) *** Naxos Dig. 8.550342 [id.]. Slovak PO, Zdenék Košler.

On Naxos, a very well-recorded and vividly detailed account of *Aus Italien* with an excellent sense of presence. The orchestra plays very well for Zdenék Košler both here and in the ten-minute symphonic fragment Clemens Krauss made from *Die Liebe der Danae* and in the *Rosenkavalier* waltz sequence. The Slovak Philharmonic is a highly responsive body, with cultured strings and wind departments and, given the quality of the recorded sound, this represents a real bargain.

Le bourgeois gentilhomme (suite), *Op. 60; Symphonia domestica, Op. 60.*
(M) *** RCA 09026 68637-2 [id.]. Chicago SO, Fritz Reiner.

Reiner's account of *Le bourgeois gentilhomme* is superbly done – possibly the finest ever – and sounding marvellously fresh, considering its date (1956). The *Symphonia domestica* comes from two years later and is another wonderful performance, a reading of stature worthy to rank alongside the best; and the CD transfer brings splendidly vivid sound-quality.

(i) *Burleske in D min. for piano and orchestra.* (ii) *Duet-concertino for clarinet, bassoon and strings.* (iii) *Horn concertos Nos. 1–2.* (iv) *Oboe concerto in D. Don Juan, Op. 20; Ein Heldenleben, Op. 40.* (v) *Panathenäenzug for piano (left hand) and orchestra; Parergon to Symphonia domestica for piano (left hand) and orchestra. Till Eulenspiegel, Op. 28.*
(M) *** EMI CMS7 64342-2 (3) [CDZC 64342]. (i) Malcolm Frager; (ii) Manfred Weise, Wolfgang Liebscher; (iii) Peter Damm; (iv) Manfred Clement; (v) Peter Rösel; Dresden State O, Kempe.

Volume 1 of the Kempe/EMI Strauss series includes all the major concertante works except the *Violin concerto*. Most collectors will already have a *Don Juan*, which is perhaps the least electrifying of Kempe's symphonic poems, and the same surely applies to *Till Eulenspiegel*, although it is an excellent performance. The *Burleske* is well worth having (it is beautifully recorded) and there are no satisfactory alternative versions of the *Parergon* to the *Symphonia domestica* or the *Panathenäenzug*, both written for the one-armed pianist, Paul Wittgenstein, and played impressively here. Peter Damm's performances of the *Horn concertos* are first class. Similarly, while Manfred Clement's *Oboe concerto* is a sensitive reading, his creamily full timbre may not appeal to those brought up on Goossens. There can be no reservations whatsoever about the *Duet concertino*, where the sounds from bassoon and clarinet are beguilingly succulent, while the intertwining of both wind soloists with the dancing orchestral violins of the finale has an irresistible, genial finesse. Throughout, the superb playing of the Dresden orchestra under Kempe adds an extra dimension to the music-making.

Burleske for piano and orchestra.
(BB) **(*) RCA Navigator 74321 21286-2 [(M) id. import]. Byron Janis, Chicago SO, Reiner – MAHLER: *Symphony No. 4.* **(*)
(B) *(**) Sony SBK 53262; *SBT 53262* [id.]. Rudolf Serkin, Phd. O, Ormandy – BRAHMS: *Piano concerto No. 2.* **(*)

(i) *Burleske;* (ii) *Don Quixote, Op. 35.*
(M) *** RCA 09026 61796-2 [id.]. (i) Byron Janis; (ii) Janigro; Chicago SO, Fritz Reiner.

The brilliance of the *Burleske* is brought out well by Byron Janis, who does not miss the music's witty or lyrical side. Even at full price, Reiner's *Don Quixote* was a top recommendation. Reiner was a masterly Straussian and this 1959 version was one of the very finest of RCA's Chicago Hall recordings. Antonio Janigro plays stylishly and with assurance; if he brings less intensity than Fournier to the ecstatic solo cadenza in Variation V, his contribution to the close of the work is distinguished. The recording of *Burleske* is somewhat shallower than that of the tone-poem (though a considerable improvement on the original LP), but this helps to ensure that Strauss's youthful writing does not sound too sweet. On the bargain-price Navigator alternative, the recording gives a brilliantly sparkling, somewhat dry piano-image, and the orchestra too is brought forward by the comparatively close microphones (although there is no lack of ambience).

The Sony alternative is a generally excellent performance of what is still a comparative rarity on disc. Serkin plays with great brilliance, and the music's lyrical side – uncharacteristic but winning – is well understood. The current remastering is an improvement on the original, but the piano timbre is bright and somewhat clattery and the orchestral textures are made somewhat two-dimensional by the close microphones. Nevertheless this is an arresting performance.

Horn concerto No. 1 in E flat, Op. 11.

(M) *** EMI Dig. CDM7 64851-2 [id.]. Radovan Vlatkovič, ECO, Tate – MOZART: *Horn concertos Nos. 1–4* etc. ***

Radovan Vlatkovič gives a superb account of the *First Concerto* which, although ripely romantic, has so much in common with the spirit of the Mozart concertos with which it is coupled. He is particularly good in the bold central episode of the *Andante* and caps his performance with an exhilaratingly nimble account of the finale. Tate accompanies admirably and the rich, natural, Abbey Road recording could hardly be better balanced.

(i) *Horn concertos Nos. 1 in E flat, Op. 11; 2 in E flat;* (ii) *Duet concertino for clarinet and bassoon. Wind serenade in E flat, Op. 11.*

(B) *** EMI Dig. CD-EMX 2238 [(M) id.]. (i) David Pyatt; (ii) Joy Farrall, Julie Andrews; Britten Sinfonia, Nicholas Cleobury.

David Pyatt gives a ripely exuberant performance of the first of Strauss's two *Horn concertos*, which is very much in the spontaneous style of the Mozart concertos. The more elusive first movement of the *Second Concerto* is shaped – often quite subtly – in an attractively rhapsodical style; the ecstatic solo line of the *Andante*, gently introduced by the oboe, is beautifully played while the finale brings heady, lightly tongued bravura. The outer movements of the gently rapturous *Duet concertino* (a late masterpiece, written the year before the *Vier letzte Lieder*) are presented with enticing delicacy of texture, and the slow movement again brings a most touchingly doleful opening solo, this time from the bassoonist, Julie Andrews. Cleobury and the Britten Sinfonia give sensitive support throughout, and the early *Serenade* is also made the more attractive by the lightness of touch of the wind blending, its sonorities always fresh, never congealing, helped by the naturally balanced recording, made in the Henry Wood Hall, Southwark. For those who want a change from the Dennis Brain Philharmonia accounts of the *Horn concertos* from the 1950s, this would be a distinct contender.

Oboe concerto.

(M) *** Carlton Dig. 30366 0065-2 [id.]. Pamela Pecha, Moscow PO, Paul Freeman – VAUGHAN WILLIAMS: *Oboe concerto*; SCHICKELE: *Oboe concerto.* ***

Pamela Pecha was co-principal of the Cleveland Orchestra for 12 years, the first woman in the orchestra's wind section, and she gives a completely persuasive account of the Strauss *Concerto*, the opening easily flexible and the slow movement warmly songful. Paul Freeman and the Moscow Philharmonic Orchestra provide an accompaniment which does not miss the work's essential mellow dimension, and the recording has a glowing ambience which suits the music far better than the rather cool effect of the Philips sound-balance for Holliger. Moreover the Carlton couplings are particularly attractive.

Violin concerto in D min., Op. 8.

(B) **(*) Decca Eclipse Dig. 448 988-2; *448 988-4* [(M) id. import]. Boris Belkin, Berlin RSO, Ashkenazy – BRAHMS: *Violin concerto.* ***

It is good to have a thoroughly recommendable bargain version of Strauss's engaging early concerto. Though not quite a match for Xue Wei on ASV (CDDCA 780 – see our main volume), partly because just occasionally his intonation is not absolutely immaculate, Belkin finds much charm in the Mendelssohnian second group of the opening movement, and he plays the *Lento* with an appealing fragile tenderness, then following with fairy-light articulation in the dancing finale. Ashkenazy provides a gracefully supportive accompaniment and the Decca sound is excellent, although perhaps the soloist is a trifle too closely miked – perhaps because the recording was made in the Berlin Jesus-Christus Kirche.

Death and transfiguration, Op. 24.
(M) (***) RCA mono GD 60312. Phd. O, Toscanini – TCHAIKOVSKY: *Symphony No. 6.* (***)

Toscanini's characteristically taut control of tension goes with what was for him a more warmly expressive style than usual, thanks to the influence of the Philadelphia Orchestra. With the transfer giving good body to the limited sound, it is comparable with his equally intense reading of Tchaikovsky's *Pathétique* from the same period.

Death and transfiguration, Op. 24; Don Juan, Op. 20.
(M) (**(*)) Bruno Walter Edition: Sony mono SMK 64466 [id.]. NYPO, Bruno Walter (with DVORAK: *Slavonic dance, Op. 46/1*) – BARBER: *Symphony No. 1.* (**)

Death and transfiguration, Op. 24; Don Juan, Op. 20; Till Eulenspiegel, Op. 28.
(M) (***) EMI mono CDH5 65197-2. VPO, Furtwängler (with SMETANA: *Má Vlast: Vltava* ***).
(BB) ** Naxos Dig. 8.550250 [id.]. Slovak PO, Zdeněk Košler.

Death and transfiguration, Op. 24; Don Juan, Op. 20; Till Eulenspiegel, Op. 28; Salome: Dance of the 7 veils.
(M) *** EMI CDM5 66823-2 [id.]. Philh. O, Klemperer.

Furtwängler's are wonderfully rich and humane performances, with that glowing sound the great conductor made so much his own. All these recordings are mono and were produced by Walter Legge or Laurance Collingwood, with Anthony Griffith and Robert Beckett as engineers. They wear their years very lightly indeed. The performances themselves have a tremendous fall-out and resonate in the mind long after they are over. Strongly recommended.

Although it is a pity that the *Metamorphosen* could not have been included, this compilation, reissued as part of EMI's 'Klemperer Legacy', admirably reassembles the conductor's other key Richard Strauss recordings. In his hands it is *Death and transfiguration* that excites the greatest admiration, invested with a nobility too rarely heard in this work. But not everyone will respond to his teatment of the other two symphonic poems. *Don Juan* is clearly seen as 'the idealist in search of perfect womanhood' (even if his primary test is made between the sheets). Yet both here and in *Till Eulenspiegel* the all-important feeling of spontaneity is not always present. This is most noticeable at the beginning of *Till*, where the famous horn solo – beautifully played – sounds as if every note were calculated in relation to the others, instead of giving a flash of our cheeky hero popping his head round from behind a curtain and cocking a snoot at us. There is a certain solidity about most of this performance: it does not romp along with the infectious boisterousness the music suggests. The account of *Salome's dance*, however, is splendidly sensuous and, with marvellous Philharmonia playing and a superb new transfer of a recording made in the Kingsway Hall in 1960–61, this collection is certainly not lacking in strength of characterization.

Walter recorded these tone-poems in the studio in 1952; the sound, though not well balanced, is reasonably expansive for its period, a bit empty-studio-ish but much better than the coupled Barber *Symphony*. The performances are both warmly romantic and high in adrenalin; indeed the playing of the NYPO is at times quite wild in *Don Juan*. Precision of string ensemble is less impressive, but Walter finds a very special atmosphere for the opening and closing pages of *Death and transfiguration*.

Anyone impulsively picking up Košler's record of Strauss's three favourite symphonic poems may be surprised at how enjoyable it is. The Slovak Philharmonic Orchestra cannot match Abbado and the LSO in dash and brilliance, but their voluptuously relaxed, sentient feeling in *Don Juan* and the powerful atmosphere at the close of *Death and transfiguration* give the readings plenty of character, even if Košler's structural grip is rather loose. Similarly, the Bratislava solo horn opens *Till* most personably, and the work's picaresque detail is observed with pleasing geniality, but the powerful execution scene at the close is prepared rather too broadly. The digital recording makes a fine impact here, and the warm acoustic ambience of the Reduta Hall, Bratislava, gives a pleasing opulence to the Straussian textures.

Death and transfiguration; Don Juan; Till Eulenspiegel; Der Rosenkavalier: suite.
(M) ** Mercury (IMS) 434 348-2 [id.]. Minneapolis SO, Antal Dorati.

Dorati was to record these three symphonic poems again, digitally, in Detroit for Decca with greatly improved sound, but his interpretations remained much on the same lines. *Till Eulenspiegel* suits him best, and the racy impetus of the string (and horn) playing communicates excitingly despite the spiky Minneapolis sound. Detail is vividly characterized, notably the moment when Till scorns his betters and goes off whistling down the street, while the final climax is like Judgement Day itself. The suite from *Der Rosenkavalier* bursts with rhythmic vigour and displays much orchestral virtuosity at climaxes, but elsewhere the recording is a bit lean in its colouring. *Death and transfiguration*, too, needs a more sumptuous acoustic, although no one could say that Dorati is not dramatic; *Don Juan* is heroic in the pulsing energy and vigorous determination of the chase, but again the sensuality is not helped by the rather dead acoustic of the Northrop Auditorium.

Death and transfiguration, Op. 24; Don Quixote, Op. 35.
(M) (**(*)) RCA mono GD 60295 [60295-2-RG]. NBC SO, Toscanini.

By the side of Kempe (recorded five years later), Toscanini's account of *Don Quixote*, from 1953 and equally electrifying and masterly, with a superb soloist in Frank Miller, sounds a shade overdriven. It does not have quite the humanity or expressive flexibility of the Piatigorsky–Munch reading. However, his 1952 *Tod und Verklärung* is quite simply stunning.

Death and transfiguration; Metamorphosen for 23 solo strings; (i) *Vier letzte Lieder (4 Last songs).*
(M) **(*) DG 447 422-2 [id.]. BPO, Karajan, (i) with Gundula Janowitz.

(i) *Death and transfiguration;* (ii; iii) *Vier letzte Lieder;* (ii; iv) *Capriccio: closing scene.*
(B) ** DG Classikon 439 467-2; *439 467-4* [(M) id. import]. (i) Dresden State O, Boehm; (ii) Gundula Janowitz; (iii) BPO, Karajan; (iv) Bav. RSO, Boehm.

Karajan surpassed his analogue recordings of both *Death and transfiguration* and the *Metamorphosen* when he re-recorded them digitally, but the earlier versions offered here are still powerful and convincing In the *Four last songs*, Janowitz produces a beautiful flow of creamy tone while leaving the music's deeper and subtler emotions under-exposed. The transfers are very impressive, and *Death and transfiguration* can still be regarded as a showpiece among Karajan's earlier Berlin recordings.

Boehm's *Death and transfiguration* was recorded live (there is a cough near the opening to prove it) at the 1972 Salzburg Festival. It is a performance of great excitement and strong tensions, but the recording is slightly overweighted at the top. The same Janowitz coupling of the *Vier letzte Lieder* was a curious choice (as Karajan provided the accompaniment), but Boehm returns for the final scene of *Capriccio*, where Janowitz is at her best (though, as in the songs, no match for Schwarzkopf).

(i) *Death and transfiguration; Symphonia domestica, Op. 53;* (ii) *Salome's dance of the 7 veils.*
❀ (B) *** Sony SBK 53511; *SBT 53511* [id.]. (i) Cleveland O, Szell; (ii) Phd. O, Ormandy.

Szell's *Death and transfiguration* dates from 1957 and it is still unsurpassed. The opening has the most compelling atmosphere and the triumphant closing pages are the more effective for Szell's complete lack of indulgence. The recording has been vastly improved in the present transfer, with Cleveland's Masonic Temple providing a richly expansive ambience. The *Symphonia domestica*, recorded in 1964, is less naturally balanced: the engineers seem more concerned with making every detail tell, but the performance brings such powerful orchestral playing, with glorious strings especially in the passionate *Adagio*, that criticism is disarmed: there is certainly no lack of body here. The programme ends with an extraordinarily voluptuous Philadelphia performance of *Salome's dance*, which conjures up a whole frieze of naked female torsos. Ormandy directs with licentious abandon, and the orchestra responds with tremendous virtuosity and ardour, unashamedly going over the top at the climax. Here the sound is a bit glossy but, with playing like this, one can certainly adjust.

(i) *Don Juan, Op. 20;* (ii) *Ein Heldenleben, Op. 40;* (i) *Till Eulenspiegel, Op. 28.*
(M) *** Sony SBK 48272; *SBT 48272* [id.]. (i) Cleveland O, Szell; (ii) Phd. O, Ormandy.

Szell's *Don Juan*, sounding really impetuous yet never rushed, delights ear and senses by its forward surge of passionate lyricism, the whole interpretation founded on a bedrock of virtuosity from the remarkable Cleveland players. *Till* is irrepressibly cheeky (the characterization again created from the most polished orchestral response) and here the recording acoustic is almost perfect, with a warm glow on the tone of the players and every detail – and Szell makes sure one can hear every detail – crystal clear, without any loss of momentum or drama.

Ormandy's *Ein Heldenleben* is a really big conception. It is an engulfing performance, and the composite richness of tone and the fervour of the playing, from the Battle section onwards, bring the highest possible level of orchestral tension, finally relaxing most touchingly for the fulfilment sequence and closing with a sonorous brass cadence that is made to sound inevitable. The 1960 recording is more two-dimensional, less full, than the Cleveland recordings (which, surprisingly, were made as early as 1957) but is still appropriately spacious.

Don Juan; Till Eulenspiegel.
(B) ** EMI CfP CD-CFP 6043 [(M) id. import]. LPO, Sir Charles Mackerras – TCHAIKOVSKY: *Romeo and Juliet.* **
(M) (*) RCA/Melodiya 74321 40722-2 [id.]. USSR TV & R. Large SO, Neeme Järvi – BEETHOVEN: *Piano concerto No. 4.* ** ❀

From Mackerras and the LPO come good, serviceable accounts of two popular symphonic poems, recorded with fair detail and good perspective, with the orchestra slightly recessed in the warm acoustic of Barking's Assembly Hall. Now reissued in coupling with a comparable performance of Tchaikovsky's *Romeo and Juliet* directed by Sir John Pritchard, they are acceptable value, but it would be idle to pretend that there are not more distinctive versions available at a near-comparable cost.

The two Strauss tone-poems come as a fill-up to Maria Grinburg's magnificent account of the Beethoven *G major Concerto*. They were recorded in 1974 but, though both performances are exhilarating and show the virtuosity of the USSR TV and Radio Orchestra to good advantage, they are handicapped by coarse, strident and unpleasant sound. Never mind, this disc is worth having for the sake of the Beethoven alone.

Don Quixote.

(M) *** EMI (SIS) CDM5 66106-2 [id.]. Rostropovich, BPO, Karajan – WAGNER: *Die Meistersinger: Overture; Tannhäuser: Overture and Venusberg music*. ***

(i) *Don Quixote. Till Eulenspiegel*.

(B) *** EMI CZS5 68736-2 (2) [CDZB 68736]. (i) Tortelier; BPO, Kempe – Concert: *'Artist profile'*. ***

Kempe's recording of *Don Quixote* with Tortelier, unbelievably recorded as early as 1958, is one of the great classics of the gramophone. The recording has ambient warmth yet reveals every smallest detail of Strauss's magical score. The solo cello is admirably balanced, yet Tortelier's splendid contribution is still able to take a leading role in the performance. Kempe's reading is essentially traditional, yet the wit is pointed with delicious lightness of touch, which suggests complete rapport with every member of the orchestra. There is the most refreshing spontaneity throughout, and the Dulcinea passages have a sweetness and lyrical beauty that do not sound out of keeping with the humour of the work. *Till Eulenspiegel* also conveys the sparkle of the work in playing that is brilliant but never forced. Both these picaresque symphonic poems, with their frequent changes of tempo, require the right degree of flexibility, and this Kempe achieves supremely well.

The Karajan/Rostropovich account of *Don Quixote* is predictably fine. The recorded sound (1975) is impressively remastered, spectacular in its realism, with well-defined detail, superb warmth and body, and fine perspective, its only failing a tendency for Rostropovich to dominate the aural picture. He dominates artistically, too. His Don is superbly characterized, and the expressiveness and richness of tone he commands are a joy in themselves. There are moments when one wonders whether the intensity of his response does not lead to over-emphatic tone, but in general both the cello and viola soloists and the Berlin orchestra under Karajan silence criticism. Even if you already have Karajan's earlier (1969) version with Fournier for DG, which is in some ways subtler (see below – paired with *Death and transfiguration*), this EMI version is not to be missed, and the Wagner couplings are of the highest calibre.

(i) *Don Quixote, Op. 35. Don Juan, Op. 20*.

(M) *** RCA 09026 68170-2 [id.]. Chicago SO, Fritz Reiner, (i) with Antonio Janigro.

Even at full price, Reiner's *Don Quixote* was a top recommendation. Reiner was a masterly Straussian and this 1959 version was one of the very finest of RCA's Chicago Hall recordings. Antonio Janigro plays stylishly and with assurance; if he brings less intensity than Fournier to the ecstatic solo cadenza in Variation V, his contribution to the close of the work is distinguished. The recording has been freshly remastered for its new coupling with *Don Juan* and detail seems even more refined, though there is no loss of amplitude in climaxes: the ride through the air (track 10) is remarkably expansive. *Don Juan* dates from the earliest days of stereo (1959) and is most famous for its superbly thrilling climax in which the great horn-theme leaps out unforgettably, thrustfully echoed by the strings. But the lustre of the strings is hardly less remarkable, and again John Pfeiffer's new transfer is enormously improved over its first presentation on CD, with greater transparency not achieved at the expense of body of tone.

(i) *Don Quixote, Op. 35; Death and transfiguration*.

(M) *** DG 429 184-2. (i) Fournier; BPO, Karajan.

Fournier's partnership with Karajan is outstanding. He brings great subtlety and (when required) repose to the part. The finale and Don Quixote's death are very moving, while Karajan's handling of orchestral detail is quite splendid. The 1966 recording is of DG's very finest quality and (given its price) this can be strongly recommended, more particularly since the disc includes Karajan's superlative 1973 analogue version of *Death and transfiguration*.

(i) *Don Quixote, Op. 35;* (ii) *Vier letzte Lieder (4 Last Songs)*.

(BB) ** Arte Nova Dig. 74321 54466-2 [id.]. (i) Emil Klein; (ii) Hellen Kwon; O Filarmónica de Gran Canaria, Adrian Leaper.

Good performances and recordings. The Filarmónica de Gran Canaria is obviously a fine orchestra and

Emil Klein an eloquent and characterful soloist. Not a first recommendation, given the range and quality of the opposition, but far from negligible either.

Ein Heldenleben, Op. 40.

(M) *** EMI (SIS) CDM5 66108 [id.]. BPO, Karajan – WAGNER: *Der fliegende Holländer: Overture; Parsifal: Preludes.* ***

(M) *** DG 449 725-2 [id.]. BPO, Karajan – WAGNER: *Siegfried idyll.* ***

(B) *** EMI forte CZS5 69349-2 (2). LSO, Barbirolli – MAHLER: *Symphony No. 6.* **(*)

The 1974 EMI Karajan *Heldenleben* is superlatively recorded and lavishly transferred to CD. The performance shows a remarkable consistency of approach on Karajan's part and an equal virtuosity of technique and even greater sumptuousness of tone on the part of the Berlin Philharmonic than the earlier, DG performance; indeed the sound is remarkably vivid. Some have found the playing marginally less spontaneous, but it is gloriously ardent and, listening to it objectively, there seems little difference between the two readings. Couplings might dictate a choice; both discs offer the music of Wagner; the EMI is the more generous: an electrifying *Flying Dutchman overture*, and glorious playing (and recording) in the two *Parsifal Preludes*.

Although Karajan's 1959 *Heldenleben* cannot quite match his later EMI version in sumptuousness, it still sounds remarkably impressive. Its selection for reissue in DG's series of 'Originals' seems particularly apt, since this was not only the first post-war recording Karajan made for DG but also his very first in stereo. It is a superb performance. Playing of great power and distinction emanates from the Berlin Philharmonic and, in the closing section, an altogether becoming sensuousness and warmth. The remastering makes the most of the ambient atmosphere and, while not losing body and warmth, firms up the orchestral detail. The new coupling of Wagner's *Siegfried idyll*, in which Karajan was unsurpassed, could not be more appropriate.

Barbirolli recorded *Ein Heldenleben* at Abbey Road in 1969, not long before his death. By a strange coincidence, Beecham similarly devoted some of his last recording sessions to this 'hero's life'. The vigour, nobility and richness of the Beecham version seemed to sum up his achievement over the years, and here Barbirolli sets the seal on his Indian summer in the recording studio. With its ripe magic it shows the conductor at his most romantically compelling. All the tempi are slow, even by his latter-day standards. He luxuriates in every moment of this opulent score (his occasional groans of pleasure sometimes punctuating the texture) and the LSO, in superb form, follows him with warmth and ardour through every expressive rallentando. Even the battle scene is not as fast as usual. But never for a moment does the tension slip, nor is the seamless forward movement interrupted. The result is inevitably controversial but, with full-bodied Abbey Road recording and the inescapable electricity of a great occasion, this is a performance which many will relish. The CD transfer has lost some of the original opulence, but there was enough and to spare, and the sound now has greater focus and detail.

Metamorphosen for 23 solo strings.

(B) **(*) EMI Rouge et Noir CZS7 67816-2 (2) [id.]. New Philh. O, Barbirolli – MAHLER: *Symphony No. 6.* **(*)

Barbirolli's version of the *Metamorphosen* is a fine one, with a warm glow and an intense, valedictory feeling, and the playing of the NPO strings is most eloquent. The 1967 Abbey Road recording still sounds well; however, although it still has weight, the present CD transfer has lost some of its original bloom and opulence.

Symphonia domestica; (i) *Death and transfiguration.*

(M) *** EMI (SIS) CDM5 66107-2 [id.]. BPO, Karajan – WAGNER: *Lohengrin: Preludes; Tristan und Isolde: Prelude & Liebestod.* ***

Strauss's *Symphonia domestica* is quite admirably served by Karajan's mid-priced 1973 recording, which now re-emerges as part of EMI's Karajan Edition, coupled with some superb Wagner performances. The playing is stunningly good and the sumptuous Berlin strings produce tone of great magnificence. EMI provide a recording (made in the Salle Wagram, Paris, in 1973) not quite as sumptuous as the Berlin recordings mentioned above but of wide range, superbly focused detail and warm ambience.

Serenade for wind, Op. 7; Sonatine No. 1 in F for wind (From an invalid's workshop); Suite in B flat for 13 wind instruments, Op. 4; Symphony for wind (The happy workshop).

(B) *** Hyperion Dyad Dig. CDD 2015 [id.]. London Winds, Michael Collins.

(i) *Serenade for wind, Op. 7; Sonatine No. 1 in F for wind (From an invalid's workshop); Suite in B flat for 13 wind instruments, Op. 4; Symphony for wind (The happy workshop).* (ii) *Oboe concerto in D.*
(B) *** Ph. Duo 438 733-2 (2) [id.]. (i) Netherlands Wind Ens., Edo de Waart; (ii) Heinz Holliger, New Philh. O.

The *Serenade* is beautifully played by the Netherlanders, warm and mellifluous, and so is the *Sonatine*, a late work written while Strauss was recovering from an illness and appropriately subtitled. It is a richly scored piece, as thoroughly effective as one would expect from this master of complex wind-writing. Both this and the *B flat Suite*, delightful pieces, are given warmly characterized accounts by De Waart, while the performance of the *Symphony for wind instruments* is crisp and alert. Throughout this Dutch music-making the ear is struck by the Netherlanders' phrasing, which is always alive, and also by their beautifully homogeneous tone. The recordings (made between 1970 and 1972) are full, well-detailed and truthful. As if this were not bounty enough, Holliger's earlier (1970) version of the *Oboe concerto* is thrown in for good measure. The playing is masterly, an assured, styish account, and Edo de Waart accompanies persuasively. Again very good recording.

The London Winds on Hyperion are more closely observed by the microphone-balance and the effect is less suavely blended; indeed it is altogether more clearly defined and dramatic. The playing has the strongest impulse, the recording is less mellow, the autumnal feeling less apparent in the *Serenade*. But one cannot help being caught up by playing that is so vividly robust and vital, and by no means lacking in warmth and affection. Even if there is a touch of over-projection, inner detail is much clearer than on Philips, and many will like the extra bite on the sound. Both sets cost about the same, but the Philips Duo scores by throwing in Holliger's earlier (1970) account of the *Oboe concerto*. His playing is masterly and very assured. But there is a hint of efficiency at the expense of ripeness, an absence of sheer love for the music in its most absolute sense, which prevents this from being quite the ideal version.

Violin sonata in E flat, Op. 18.
(M) (***) RCA mono 09026 61763-2 [id.]. Heifetz, Brooks Smith – BRAHMS: *Piano trio No. 1;* DOHNANYI: *Serenade.* (***)

Heifetz's legendary recording of the Strauss *Sonata* with Brooks Smith, which has never been surpassed, was made in 1954 and comes with his 1941 recordings of the Brahms *B major Trio* with Rubinstein and Feuermann and a masterly account with Primrose and Feuermann of the Dohnányi *Serenade for string trio*. Self-recommending.

Piano sonata in B min., Op. 5; 5 Pieces, Op. 3; (i) *Enoch Arden, Op. 38;* (ii) *Ophelia Lieder, Op. 67.*
(M) ** Sony SM2K 52657 (2) [S2K 52657]. Glenn Gould; with (i) Claude Rains; (ii) Elisabeth Schwarzkopf.

Neither the early Op. 3 *Pieces* nor the *Piano sonata in B minor* are top-drawer Strauss, but Glenn Gould plays with such intensity that he almost convinces you that they are. Moreover the intensity is not overstated, and eccentricity surfaces only in his accompaniments of Elisabeth Schwarzkopf's *Ophelia Lieder*. Strauss's mélodrame to Tennyson's *Enoch Arden* is hardly one of the composer's success stories, but it has a certain period fascination that makes this disc worth collecting. Unfortunately, the sound is dry and the balance almost claustrophobic.

VOCAL AND CHORAL MUSIC

Choral music: *Der Abend; Hymne, Op. 34/1–2; Deutsche Motette, Op. 62.*
(B) *** Decca Double 455 035-2 (2) [(M) id. import]. Jessica Cash, Jean Temperley, Wynford Evans, Stephen Varcoe, Schütz Choir of L., Norrington – BRUCKNER: *Mass No. 2* etc. **

Strauss, usually the most business-like and practical of composers, made these unaccompanied choral pieces so difficult for any choir to sing that they have been almost totally ignored. The *German Motet*, with 16 choral lines plus soloists, has the sopranos soaring to top D flat and staying there, while the basses at one point go down to bottom B, and the shifting harmonies make one's head reel. But what matters is that in superb performances like these the music is richly poetic, quite distinct within the whole choral repertoire, with glowing reminders of Strauss's loveliest music, from the *Rosenkavalier Trio* and *Ariadne* to the *Four Last songs*. *Der Abend* might be a direct tribute to the heaven-vision of Strauss's friend, Mahler. The (originally Argo) recording is gloriously resonant and clear.

8 Lieder, Op. 10; 5 Lieder, Op. 15; 6 Lieder, Op. 17; 6 Lieder, Op. 19; Schlichte Weisen, Op. 21; Mädchenblumen, Op. 22; 2 Lieder, Op. 26; 4 Lieder, Op. 27; Lieder, Op. 29/1 & 3; 3 Lieder, Op. 31; Stiller Gang, Op. 31/4; 5 Lieder, Op. 32; Lieder, Op. 36/1–4; Lieder, Op. 37/1–3 & 5–6; 5 Lieder, Op. 39; Lieder, Op. 41/2–5; Gesänge älterer deutscher Dichter, Op. 43/1 & 3; 5 Gedichte, Op. 46; 5 Lieder, Op. 47; 5 Lieder, Op. 48; Lieder, Op. 49/1 & 2; 4–6; 6 Lieder, Op. 56; Krämerspiegel, Op. 66; Lieder, Op. 67/4–6; Lieder, Op. 68/1 & 4; 5 kleine Lieder, Op. 69; Gesänge des Orients, Op. 77; Lieder, Op. 88/ 1–2; Lieder ohne Opuszahl.
(M) *** EMI CMS7 63995-2 (6) [CDMF 63995]. Dietrich Fischer-Dieskau, Gerald Moore.

Fischer-Dieskau and Moore made these recordings of the 134 Strauss songs suitable for a man's voice between 1967 and 1970, tackling them in roughly chronological order. With both artists at their very peak, the results are endlessly imaginative, and the transfers are full and immediate, giving fine presence to the voice.

Lieder: *Ach, weh mir unglückhaftem Mann; All meine Gedanken; Breit' über mein Haupt; Freundliche Vision; Heimliche Aufforderung; Ich liebe dich; Mein Auge; Morgen; Die Nacht; Nachtgang; Nichts; Ruhe, meine Seele; Ständchen; Traume durch die Dämmerung; Wie solten wir geheim sie halten; Wozu noch, Mädchen; Zueignung.*
(M) *** Ph. (IMS) 442 744-2 (2). Gérard Souzay, Dalton Baldwin – WOLF: *Italienisches Liederbuch.* ***

In subtlety of phrasing and beauty of line Souzay is here at his finest, and songs like *Ich liebe dich* or the delightful *Serenade* sound freshly minted. There is also a superb lightness of touch when called for. The accompaniments are characteristically sensitive and perceptive, and the recording is well balanced. But why did this have to come in harness with the *Italian Lieder Book* (as part of the Philips Early Years series), rather than be available separately?

Lieder: *Allerseelen; All' mein' Gedanken; Befreit; Cäcilie; Efeu; Heimliche Aufforderung; Herr Lenz; Hochzeitlich; Junggesellenschwur; Liebeshymnus; Mein Auge; Meinem Kinde; Nachtgang; Nichts; Das Rosenband; Sehnsucht; Ständchen; Traum durch die Dämmerung; Waldseligkeit; Wasserrose; Weihnachtsgefühl; Winternacht.*
(B) *** EMI Eminence Dig. CD-EMX 2250 [(M) id. import]. Simon Keenlyside, Malcolm Martineau.

Keenlyside follows up the success of his fine Schubert recital, also for EMI Eminence (CD-EMX 2224), with this excellent collection of Strauss Lieder, beautifully sung, again with Malcolm Martineau a most sensitive accompanist. Try the highly distinctive, intimate reading of *Ständchen* ('Serenade'), with Keenlyside singing almost in a half-tone and with Martineau playing magically. The fine-spun legato of *Waldseligkeit* and the poise of *Meinem Kinde* are equally impressive. Keenlyside uses a head voice for the gentle top notes of *Allerseelen* ('All Saints' Day'), but then finds plenty of power, sharply focused, in songs like *Befreit*. The sequence is rounded off with two exhilarating songs, *Cäcilie* and *Herr Lenz* (with its pun on the name Strauss – nosegay). Though this comes at mid-price, text and translations are provided. Excellent EMI sound.

Vier letzte Lieder (4 Last Songs); *12 orchestral Lieder: Allerseelen; Befreit; Breit über; Cäcilie; Frölicher Beschluss; Ich trage meine Minne; Morgen; Das Rosenband; Traum durch die Dämmerung; Träumerei am Kamin; Waldseligkeit; Zueignung. Guntram: Prelude.*
(M) ** Classic fM Dig. 75605 57002-2. Farley, Czech State PO (Brno), Serebrier.

In full and atmospheric sound Serebrier and the Brno orchestra are warmly sympathetic accompanists to Carole Farley in a generous selection of the songs that Strauss orchestrated, as well as the sublime *Four Last Songs*. Farley sings sensitively, but this is not as sensuous a voice as this music needs. In gentler songs she shades down her tone persuasively; generally, however, the results are disappointing, for all the singer's concern for detail, with an edge to the voice and a degree of flutter that is exaggerated by the microphone. The *Guntram Prelude* makes an attractive and unusual bonus, helped by the richness of the orchestral sound.

Four Last songs; Die heiligen drei Könige. Capriccio (opera): *Moonlight music and monologue* (closing scene); *Metamorphosen for 23 solo strings.*
(M) *** DG Dig. 445 599-2. Anna Tomowa-Sintow, BPO, Karajan.

(i) *Four Last songs*. (ii) *Arabella* (opera): excerpts. (i) *Capriccio* (opera): Closing scene.
(M) (***) EMI mono CDH7 61001-2 [id.]. Elisabeth Schwarzkopf, (i) Philh. O, Ackermann; (ii) Metternich, Gedda, Philh. O, Von Matačić.

Before he made this recording of the closing scene from *Capriccio* with Anna Tomowa-Sintow, Karajan, supreme Straussian, had never previously conducted Strauss's last opera. It is a ravishing performance with one of his favourite sopranos responding warmly and sympathetically; if lacking the final touch of individual imagination that such inspired music cries out for, one senses the close rapport between conductor and singer. Similarly in the other late, great masterpiece, the *Four Last songs*, Tomowa-Sintow's lovely, creamy-toned singing tends to take second place in the attention, almost as if the voice was a solo instrument in the orchestra, and the result is undoubtedly very touching. The orchestral version of Strauss's nativity-story song makes an attractive extra item. The recording is warm, lacking a little in a sense of presence, but compensating in atmosphere. For this reissue Karajan's 1980 digital account of *Metamorphosen* has been added; it has even greater emotional urgency than his earlier, analogue version, recorded in 1971, and there is a marginally quicker pulse. Here the digital recording is rather more sumptuous.

Schwarzkopf's 1953 version of the *Four Last songs* comes with both its original coupling, the closing scene from *Capriccio*, also recorded in 1953, and the four major excerpts from *Arabella* which she recorded two years later. The *Four Last songs* are here less reflective, less sensuous, than in Schwarzkopf's later version with Szell, but the more flowing speeds and the extra tautness and freshness of voice bring equally illuminating performances. Fascinatingly, this separate account of the *Capriccio* scene is even more ravishing than the one in the complete set, and the sound is even fuller, astonishing for its period.

OPERA

Die Aegyptische Helena (complete).

(M) **(*) Decca (IMS) 430 381-2 (2). Dame Gwyneth Jones, Hendricks, Kastu, Detroit SO, Dorati.

Dorati, using the original Dresden version of the score, draws magnificent sounds from the Detroit orchestra, richly and forwardly recorded. The vocal sounds are less consistently pleasing. Gwyneth Jones has her squally moments as Helen, though it is a commanding performance. Matti Kastu manages as well as any Heldentenor today in the role of Menelaus, strained at times but with a pleasing and distinctive timbre.

Arabella (complete).

(M) **(*) Decca 430 387-2 (2) [id.]. Della Casa, Gueden, London, Edelmann, Dermota, V. State Op. Ch., VPO, Solti.

(M) (***) DG (IMS) mono 445 342-2 (3) [id.]. Reining, Hotter, Della Casa, Taubmann, VPO, Boehm.

Della Casa soars above the stave with the creamiest, most beautiful sounds and constantly charms one with her swiftly alternating moods of seriousness and gaiety. Perhaps Solti does not linger as he might over the waltz rhythms, and it may be Solti too who prevents Edelmann from making his first scene with Mandryka as genuinely humorous as it can be. Edelmann otherwise is superb, as fine a Count as he was an Ochs in the Karajan *Rosenkavalier*. Gueden, too, is ideally cast as Zdenka and, if anything, in Act I manages to steal our sympathies from Arabella, as a good Zdenka can. George London is on the ungainly side, but then Mandryka is a boorish fellow anyway. Dermota is a fine Matteo, and Mimi Coertse makes as much sense as anyone could of the ridiculously difficult part of Fiakermilli, the female yodeller. The sound is brilliant.

Recorded live in August 1947 at the Salzburg Festival, the Boehm recording was issued in 1994 to celebrate the centenary of his birth, a radiant account with an outstanding cast. Maria Reining is here in firm, true voice, conveying not just the dignity of the heroine but the depth of feeling behind her often imperious manner. Hans Hotter too in his early maturity is in splendid voice, a superb Mandryka, characterful and well focused. Lisa della Casa, destined to make the role of Arabella a speciality, is here a charming Zdenka, fresh and girlish; and the rest of the cast includes many Viennese stalwarts of the period. Despite the limitations of the orchestral sound and some very rough playing, it is a most cherishable set.

Ariadne auf Naxos (complete).

(B) **(*) DG Double Dig. 453 112-2 (2) [id.]. Anna Tomowa-Sintow, Kathleen Battle, Agnes Baltsa, Gary Lakes, Kurt Rydl, Hermann Prey, Heinz Zednik, VPO, James Levine.

(M) **(*) Decca 430 384-2 (2). Leontyne Price, Troyanos, Gruberová, Kollo, Berry, Kunz, LPO, Solti.

(M) **(*) EMI CMS7 64159-2 (2) [Ang. CDMB 61459]. Janowitz, Geszty, Zylis-Gara, King, Schreier, Prey, Dresden State Op. O, Kempe.

(M) (*(**)) DG (IMS) 445 332-2 (2) [id.]. Della Casa, Gueden, Seefried, Schock, Schöffler, VPO, Boehm.

(M) *(*) Decca 443 675-2 (2). Leonie Rysanek, Jurinac, Peters, Peerce, Berry, Dickie, Preger, VPO, Leinsdorf.

James Levine conducts a spacious, sumptuously textured reading of *Ariadne* which almost makes you forget that it uses a chamber orchestra. As Ariadne herself, Tomowa-Sintow with her rich, dramatic soprano adds to the sense of grandeur and movingly brings out the vulnerability of the character. But ultimately she fails to create as fully rounded and detailed a character as her finest rivals, and the voice, as recorded, loses its bloom and creaminess under pressure, marring the big climaxes. Both Agnes Baltsa as the Composer and Kathleen Battle as Zerbinetta are excellent: the one tougher than most rivals with her mezzo-soprano ring, little troubled by the high tessitura, the other delectably vivacious, dazzling in coloratura, but equally finding the unexpected tenderness in the character, the underlying sadness clearly implied in the Prologue duet with the Composer. She brings home just why the boy is so enamoured. The *commedia dell'arte* characters and the attendant theatrical team are strongly taken by stalwarts of the Vienna State Opera, among them Kurt Rydl, Hermann Prey and Heinz Zednik, while the Heldentenor role of Bacchus, always hard to cast, is strongly taken by Gary Lakes, clear-toned and firm, at times pinched but never strained. The very reasonable cost of this set should tempt many collectors to sample this very rewarding opera, particularly when the recording is so warmly flattering to both singers and orchestra.

Brilliance is the keynote of Solti's set of *Ariadne*. What the performance is short of is charm and warmth. Everything is so brightly lit that much of the delicacy and tenderness of the writing tends to disappear. Nevertheless the concentration of Solti in Strauss is never in doubt, and Leontyne Price makes a strong central figure, memorably characterful. Tatiana Troyanos is affecting as the composer, and Edita Gruberová establishes herself as the unrivalled Zerbinetta of her generation, though here she is less delicate than on stage. René Kollo similarly is an impressive Bacchus. The Decca CD transfer is characteristically vivid.

Kempe's relaxed, languishing performance of this most atmospheric of Strauss operas is matched by opulent recording, warmly transferred to CD. Gundula Janowitz sings with heavenly tone-colour (marred only when hard-pressed at the climax of the Lament), and Teresa Zylis-Gara makes an ardent and understanding Composer. Sylvia Geszty's voice is a little heavy for the fantastic coloratura of Zerbinetta's part, but she sings with charm and assurance. James King presents the part of Bacchus with forthright tone and more taste than do most tenors. Compared with Karajan's full-priced mono set with Schwarzkopf, this is less than ideal, but that has rather dry mono sound and here there is warmth and atmosphere in plenty, and there is a comparable price advantage over the Philips digital stero set with Jessye Norman.

Boehm had a natural affinity with this opera. It was the last one he conducted, at the Salzburg Festival in 1980, and here, 26 years earlier, his affection for this elegant, touching score similarly glows through the whole performance. Lisa della Casa is a poised, tender Ariadne, totally rapt in the final duet with Bacchus. Even though her later studio recordings of the *Lament* are more assured than this, the passion of the climax of that key solo is most involving. As in Karajan's full-priced, mono studio recording (EMI CDS5 55176-2), Irmgard Seefried as the Composer and Rudolf Schock as Bacchus have few equals; but what crowns the whole performance is the charming Zerbinetta of Hilde Gueden, not just warmly characterful but fuller-toned than almost any. The snag is the recording, fizzy in the orchestral sound, with even the voices rather thinly recorded. The Vienna State Opera recording of 1944, available on Koch, has more vivid, fuller-bodied sound.

Although one has reservations about Leinsdorf's contribution, this Decca reissue is a well-produced mid-priced version of an enchanting opera. Rysanek's rather fruity voice is not ideally cast in the part of Ariadne. Sena Jurinac, as the Composer, in the Prologue is very effective; her singing has character, and there is good support from the rest of the cast, but the performance is not strong on charm. The early (1958) recording, made in the Sofiensaal, sounds well on this new CD transfer but, with all the current competition, remains uncompetitive.

'Vienna State Opera live': Volume 23: *Ariadne auf Naxos* (complete).
(M) (***) Koch 3-1473-2 (2). Reining, Seefried, Noni, Lorenz, Schoeffler, Vienna State Op. O, Boehm (with WAGNER: *Meistersinger:* excerpts (**)).

Recorded live in June 1944, *Ariadne* is here presented in sound that is astonishingly full-bodied for the period. The sense of presence on the voices is most compelling, and it is fascinating to hear Seefried in the first of her three magnificent recorded performances, singing with, if anything, even more passion than later, in full, firm sound. Maria Reining makes a warm, touching Ariadne, and Max Lorenz as Bacchus has rarely been matched in subsequent recordings, sweeter and less strenuous than most Heldentenoren. Alda Noni makes a bright, mercurial Zerbinetta, not always note-perfect in her coloratura but with plenty of sparkle, and Paul Schoeffler is warm and wise as the Music-master. With 40 minutes of *Meistersinger* excerpts as filler, it is a historic set for non-specialists to consider.

Capriccio (complete).
(M) **(*) DG 445 347-2 (2). Janowitz, Troyanos, Schreier, Fischer-Dieskau, Prey, Ridderbusch, Bav. RSO, Karl Boehm.

In this elusive opera it is impossible to avoid comparison with Sawallisch's classic mono version with Schwarzkopf and Fischer-Dieskau (at full price). Gundula Janowitz is not as characterful and pointful a

Countess as one really needs (and no match for Schwarzkopf), but Boehm lovingly directs a most beautiful performance of a radiant score, very consistently cast, beautifully sung and very well recorded for its period (1971). There is full documentation, including translation.

Elektra (complete).

(M) ** DG (IMS) 445 329-2 (2) [id.]. Borkh, Schech, Madeira, Fischer-Dieskau, Dresden State O, Karl Boehm.

Inge Borkh is tough in the title-role with an apt touch of rawness, while Jean Madeira as Klytemnestra is firm and positive and Dietrich Fischer-Dieskau is incomparable as Orestes; their contributions are very vivid. The clarity of CD with its full body of sound brings an improvement on the original 1960 LPs, but Karl Boehm's masterly timing in this opera deserves to have a more substantial showing. The only weakness to note in the cast is the Chrysothemis of Marianna Schech, thin and unsteady and with touches of shrillness.

(i) *Elektra: Soliloquy; Recognition scene; Finale. Salome: Dance of the seven veils; Finale.*

(M) *** RCA 09026 68636-2 [id.]. Inge Borkh, Chicago SO, Fritz Reiner; (i) with Schoeffler, Yeend, Chicago Lyric Theatre Ch.

With Borkh singing superbly in the title-role alongside Paul Schoeffler and Francis Yeend, this is a real collectors' piece. Reiner provides a superbly telling accompaniment; the performance of the Recognition scene and final duet are as ripely passionate as Beecham's old 78-r.p.m. excerpts and outstrip the complete versions. The orchestral sound is thrillingly rich, the brass superbly expansive. For the reissue, Reiner's full-blooded account of *Salome's dance* has been added, and Borkh is comparably memorable in the finale scene. No Straussian should miss this disc.

Die Frau ohne Schatten.

(M) (**(*)) DG mono 457 678-2 (3). Leonie Rysanek, Grace Hoffman, Christa Ludwig, Jess Thomas, Walter Berry, Lucia Popp, Fritz Wunderlich, V. State Op. Ch. & O, Karajan.

(M) ** DG 449 584-2 (3). Fischer-Dieskau, Borkh, Bjoner, Mödl, Jess Thomas, Hotter, Bav. State Op. Ch. & O, Keilberth.

In 1964, when he was still music director of the Vienna State Opera, Karajan presented a centenary tribute to Richard Strauss in a production of his most ambitious opera, and the composer's own favourite, *Die Frau ohne Schatten*. This recording from Austrian Radio captures the intensity of the occasion, with ecstatic applause for each of the Acts. With orchestral sound in mono thin and limited (a serious shortcoming in Strauss) the voices are paramount, with words made the clearer by the closeness. The cast is an outstanding one, with Leonie Rysanek powerful as the Empress and Jess Thomas exploiting his cleanly focused Heldentenor as the Emperor. The young Walter Berry is firmly commanding as Barak, the Dyer; and best of all is Christa Ludwig as the Dyer's Wife, here early in her career singing with a freshness and intensity that she retained in her later studio recording with Solti for Decca. The mono sound is limited, with voices well caught. A good set at mid-price, though the usual stage-cuts are made in this epic score.

There are many cuts in this 1964 DG set, and that alone will deter most Straussians. Moreover Keilberth is no more vital and inspired than he was in the companion set of *Arabella*, also made during the celebration period after the opening of the new post-war Munich Opera House. It is a pity that these two factors tend to rule the set out, for the singing is mostly very good, and it is marvellous to hear the central part of Barak sung with such freshness and beauty by Fischer-Dieskau, while Jess Thomas is also in fine voice as the Emperor. Considering the circumstances of the performance, the recording too is most creditable and it has been given a first-class CD transfer.

Der Rosenkavalier (complete; remastered under direction of Schwarzkopf).

(M) (**(*)) EMI mono CMS5 56113-2 (3). Schwarzkopf, Ludwig, Stich-Randall, Edelmann, Philh. Ch. & O, Karajan.

Der Rosenkavalier (complete).

(M) **(*) Ph. (IMS) 442 086-2 (3). Lear, Von Stade, Welting, Bastin, Hammond Stroud, Netherlands Op. Ch., Rotterdam PO, Edo de Waart.

(M) (**(*)) Decca (IMS) mono 425 950-2 (3) [id.]. Reining, Weber, Jurinac, Gueden, V. State Op. Ch., VPO, Erich Kleiber.

(M) ** DG 445 338-2 (3) [id.]. Ludwig, Troyanos, Mathis, Adam, Wiener, VPO, Boehm.

It was at the urgent request of Schwarzkopf herself that this original mono version of Karajan's classic set of *Rosenkavalier* was transferred to CD in a remastering she herself approved. The main contrast with the stereo version – itself subject to several remasterings over the years – is that the voices are more sharply focused and, as it seems, more forwardly placed. One can understand Schwarzkopf's preference, but the orchestral sound in the stereo version is warmer, fuller and richer, and will certainly be preferred by the majority of collectors. But that is at premium price.

The glory of the 1976 set conducted by Edo de Waart is the singing of Frederica von Stade as Octavian, a fresh, youthful performance, full of imagination. Next to her the others are generally pleasing but rarely a match for the finest performances on other sets, though it is good to have Derek Hammond Stroud's Faninal. Evelyn Lear produces her creamiest, most beautiful tone but spreads uncomfortably in the Act III Trio. Jules Bastin gives a virile performance as Ochs; the disappointment is the Sophie of Ruth Welting, often shallow of tone. The Rotterdam orchestra plays very well for its principal conductor of the 1970s and is beautifully recorded. However, the justly celebrated full-price stereo Karajan set with Schwarzkopf, Christa Ludwig and Teresa Stich-Randall is well worth its premium price (CDS5 56242-2).

Decca's set with Erich Kleiber was the first ever complete recording of *Rosenkavalier*, and it has long enjoyed cult status. Sena Jurinac is a charming Octavian, strong and sympathetic, and Hilde Gueden a sweetly characterful Sophie, not just a wilting innocent. Ludwig Weber characterizes deliciously in a very Viennese way as Ochs; but the disappointment is the Marschallin of Maria Reining, very plain and lacking intensity. She is not helped by Kleiber's refusal to linger; with the singers recorded close, the effect of age on what was once a fine voice is very clear, even in the opening solo of the culminating trio. And ensemble is not good, with even the prelude to Act I a muddle. On the prelude more than anywhere, the CD transfer brings out a shrillness and lack of body in the orchestral sound, though voices are well caught.

Boehm's DG set, recorded live at the 1969 Salzburg Festival, is a flawed document, not just because of loud stage-noises but because the stereo recording is thin. Nevertheless it is good to hear Christa Ludwig as the Marschallin, bringing echoes of Schwarzkopf, the Marschallin with whom she sang Octavian. Tatiana Troyanos makes a warm, animated Octavian and Edith Mathis a bright, characterful Sophie, just occasionally forced into shrillness. The snag is the gritty Ochs of Theo Adam, not at all jovial even when he blusters in sing-speech. Boehm is above all a genial interpreter, relishing the waltz-rhythms, but the emotions of a live event lead him at climaxes to draw out the music exaggeratedly in a way uncharacteristic of him.

(i) *Der Rosenkavalier* (abridged version); Lieder: (ii) *All' mein Gedanken; Freundliche Vision; Die heiligen drei Könige; Heimkehr; Ich schwebe; Des Knaben Wunderhorn: Hat gesagt . . .; Morgen; Muttertändelei; Schlechtes Wetter; Ständchen* (2 versions); *Traum durch die Dämmerung;* (iii) *Mit deinen blauen Augen; Morgen; Ständchen; Traum durch die Dämmerung.*

(M) (***) EMI mono CHS7 64487-2 (2). (i) Lehmann, Schumann, Mayr, Olszewska, Madin, V. State Op. Ch., VPO, Robert Heger; (ii) Elisabeth Schumann; (iii) Lotte Lehmann (with var. accompanists).

It is good to have a fresh CD transfer, immaculate in quality, of this classic, abridged, early recording of *Der Rosenkavalier*, containing some 100 minutes of music, made in 1933 in Vienna. Lotte Lehmann as the Marschallin and Elisabeth Schumann as Sophie remain uniquely characterful and, though 78-r.p.m. side-lengths brought some hastening from Heger, notably in the great trio of Act III, the passion of the performance still conveys a sense of new discovery, a rare Straussian magic. There is no libretto, but a synopsis is cued with each excerpt. As a bonus we are offered a glorious Lieder recital, featuring both the principal sopranos, and demonstrating Lehmann's darker timbre, the richness immediately noticeable at her first song, the lovely *Mit deinen blauen Augen*. Versions of *Traume durch die Dämmerung* and the soaring *Ständchen* are sung by both artists, and two different Schumann performances are included of the latter: one (from 1927) fresh and lilting, the other (from 1930) faster and with much clearer sound. *Heimkehr* (1938) is ravishing, and *Die heiligen drei Könige*, from ten years earlier, with a remarkably well-recorded orchestral accompaniment, is also memorable. No song translations are included, but again the CD transfers are well managed.

Der Rosenkavalier: highlights.

(M) *** EMI CDM5 65571-2 [ZDM 634522]. Schwarzkopf, Ludwig, Stich-Randall, Edelmann, Waechter, Philh. Ch. & O, Karajan.

(M) *** Decca 452 730-2 [id.]. Régine Crespin, Elisabeth Söderström, Hilde Gueden, Heinz Holecek, V. State Op. Ch., VPO, Silvio Varviso.

(BB) ** CfP Silver Double CDCFPSD 4739 (2) [(B) id.]. Dernesch, Howells, Cahill, Michael Langdon, SNO, Gibson – MOZART: *Don Giovanni.* **

On EMI we are offered the Marschallin's monologue to the end of Act I (25 minutes); the Presentation of the silver rose and finale from Act II; and the Duet and Closing scene, with the Trio from Act III, flawlessly and gloriously sung and transferred most beautifully to CD. A superb disc in every way.

This Decca set of highlights, gorgeously recorded in the Sofiensaal in 1964, is a collector's item. Régine Crespin was to go on to record the complete opera very successfully with Solti, but Varviso is hardly less sympathetic here. The present 62-minute selection was a trial run – and very successful it was. Crespin's portrayal of the Marschallin may be plainer than Schwarzkopf's and the projection of character less intense, but it is gloriously sung and remains very affecting indeed: Crespin, rarely if ever made a better record. She is beautifully supported by Söderström and Gueden. The selection is admirably chosen to include the Introduction and opening scene, and the Maschallin's monologue, duet and closing scene from Act I (35 minutes in all). Then comes the Presentation of the Silver Rose from Act II (which ends without a tailoring cadence) and lastly, from Act III, the Marschallin's meeting with Sophie, the great Trio and final Duet between the two lovers. Not to be missed.

The CfP Silver Double presents a coupling with Mozart and, like that selection, this is based on a Scottish Opera production. Though the singing is flawed and the recording is less atmospheric than it might be, it makes a fair enough sampler. In particular it is good to have examples of Helga Dernesch as the Marschallin and Michael Langdon as Baron Ochs. But neither the Presentation of the Silver Rose nor the final scene of all has quite the magic one expects of a complete performance.

Salome (complete).
(M) *** RCA GD 86644 (2) [6644-2-RG]. Caballé, Richard Lewis, Resnik, Milnes, LSO, Leinsdorf.
(M) **(*) DG (IMS) 445 319-2 (2) [id.]. Gwyneth Jones, Fischer-Dieskau, Dunn, Cassilly, Hamburg State Op. O, Boehm.

Montserrat Caballé's formidable account of the role of Salome was recorded in 1968, utterly different from that of Birgit Nilsson on Decca and much closer to the personification of Behrens on the Karajan set on EMI (both at full price). For some listeners Caballé might seem too gentle, but in fact the range of her emotions is even wider than that of Nilsson. There are even one or two moments of fantasy, where for an instant one has the girlish skittishness of Salome revealed like an evil inverted picture of Sophie. As for the vocalization, it is superb, with glorious golden tone up to the highest register and never the slightest hesitation in attack. Lewis, Resnik and Milnes make a supporting team that matches the achievement of the Decca rivals, while Leinsdorf is inspired to some of his warmest and most sympathetic conducting on record.

In this violent opera Boehm conducts a powerful, purposeful performance which in its rhythmic drive and spontaneity is most compelling, not least in *Salome's dance*, which seems a necessary component rather than an inserted showpiece. Gwyneth Jones, though squally at times, is here at her most incisive, and her account of the final scene is chilling, above all when she drains her voice for the moment of pianissimo triumph, having kissed the dead lips of Jokanaan. Fischer-Dieskau characteristically gives a searchingly detailed, totally authoritative performance as John the Baptist: one believes in him as a prophet possessed. With Richard Cassilly as a powerful Herod, the rest of the cast is strong, making this a fair contender among live recordings.

Die schweigsame Frau (complete).
(M) (***) DG (IMS) mono 445 335-2 (2) [id.]. Gueden, Wunderlich, Prey, Hotter, VPO, Boehm.
(M) **(*) EMI (SIS) CMS5 66033-2 (3). Adam, Scovotti, Burmeister, Trudeliese Schmidt, Dresden State Op. Ch. & State O, Janowski.

With a cast that could hardly be bettered, Boehm masterfully relishes the high spirits as well as the classical elegance of this late Strauss opera and, though the acoustic is dry and stage noises are often fearsomely intrusive, the sense of presence on the voices makes it consistently involving. Based on Ben Jonson's *Epicene* but updated to 1780 by the librettist, Stefan Zweig, this comic opera about an old bachelor who hates noise is above all centred on lively, sharply pointed ensembles, and the starry cast is here splendidly drilled to bring out the humour. Hans Hotter in his prime makes a wonderfully bluff curmudgeon, pointing every word characterfully. Hilde Gueden – greeted with wild applause on her first entry along with Fritz Wunderlich – is a deliciously minx-ish heroine, using her distinctive golden tone, while the young Wunderlich gives a glorious performance. As the barber who aids the conspiratorial young couple against the old man, Hermann Prey has rarely sounded stronger or more beautiful on disc.

Strauss was already seventy when he tackled this exuberant comic opera, but it is evidence of Strauss's energy that he revelled in the heavy task of composing and scoring so much fast, brilliant and complex music, the ensembles pointed by touches of neo-classicism. You might count it all a lot of fuss over not very much, and this alternative EMI version is not quite as persuasive as it might be, with a church acoustic giving bloom but blurring some detail. Janowski conducts an efficient rather than a magical performance, and Theo Adam's strongly characterized rendering of the central role of Dr Morosus is marred by his unsteadiness. Jeanette Scovotti is agile but shrill as the Silent Woman, Aminta. A valuable set of mixed success. The CD transfer brings the usual advantages but underlines the oddities of the recording. The reissue (unlike the previous full-priced set) includes a libretto/booklet with full English translation.

Arias from: *Die Aegyptische Helena; Ariadne auf Naxos; Die Frau ohne Schatten; Guntram; Der Rosenkavalier; Salome.*

(M) *** RCA GD 60398 [60398-2-RG]. Leontyne Price, Boston SO or New Philh. O, Leinsdorf; LSO, Cleva.

Leontyne Price gives generous performances of an unusually rich collection of Strauss scenes and solos, strongly accompanied by Leinsdorf (or Cleva in *Ariadne*), always at his finest in Strauss. Recorded between 1965 and 1973, Price was still at her peak, even if occasionally the voice grows raw under stress in Strauss's heavier passages. It is particularly good to have rarities as well as such regular favourites as the Empress's awakening from *Die Frau ohne Schatten*, one of the finest of all the performances here.

Stravinsky, Igor (1882–1971)

The Stravinsky Edition: Volume 1, Ballets, etc.: (i) *The Firebird;* (i) *Fireworks;* (iii) *Histoire du soldat;* (i) *Petrushka;* (iv, iii) *Renard the fox;* (i) *The Rite of spring;* (i) *Scherzo à la russe;* (ii) *Scherzo fantastique;* (v) *The Wedding* (*Les Noces*) (SM3K 46291) (3).

Volume 2, Ballets etc.: (vi) *Agon;* (i) *Apollo;* (i) *Le baiser de la fée;* (i) *Bluebird (pas de deux);* (vii) *Jeu de cartes;* (viii) *Orphée;* (ix, i) *Pulcinella;* (ii) *Scènes de ballet* (SM3K 46292) (3).

Volume 3, Ballet suites: (i) *Firebird; Pétrouchka; Pulcinella* (SMK 45293) [id.].

Volume 4, Symphonies: (i) *Symphony in E;* (ii) *Symphony in C;* (i) *Symphony in 3 movements;* (x, ii) *Symphony of Psalms;* (i) Stravinsky in rehearsal: *Apollo; Piano concerto; Pulcinella; Sleeping beauty; Symphony in C; 3 Souvenirs* (SM2K 46294) [id.].

Volume 5, Concertos: (xi, i) *Capriccio for piano and orchestra* (with Robert Craft); *Concerto for piano and wind;* (xii, i) *Movements for piano and orchestra;* (xiii, i) *Violin concerto in D* (SMK 46295) [id.].

Volume 6, Miniatures: (i) *Circus polka; Concerto in D for string orchestra; Concerto for chamber orchestra, 'Dumbarton Oaks';* (ii) *4 Etudes for orchestra;* (i) *Greeting prelude;* (ii) *8 Instrumental miniatures; 4 Norwegian moods; Suites Nos. 1–2 for small orchestra* (SMK 46296) [id.].

Volume 7, Chamber music and historical recordings: (iii) *Concertino for 12 instruments;* (xiv, xv) *Concerto for 2 solo pianos;* (xv, xvi) *Duo concertante for violin and piano;* (xvii, xviii) *Ebony concerto (for clarinet and big band);* (iii) *Octet for wind;* (xix, iii) *Pastorale for violin and wind quartet;* (xv) *Piano rag music;* (xviii) *Preludium;* (xx, iii) *Ragtime* (for 11 instruments); (xv) *Serenade in A;* (iii) *Septet;* (xii) *Sonata for piano;* (xxi) *Sonata for 2 pianos;* (xviii) *Tango;* (xxii) *Wind symphonies* (SM2K 46297) [id.].

Volume 8, Operas and songs: (xxiii, iii) *Cat's cradle songs;* (xxiii, xxiv) *Elegy for J. F. K.;* (xxv, ii) *Faun and shepherdess;* (xxvi,iii) *In memoriam Dylan Thomas;* (xxvii, iii) *3 Japanese Lyrics* (with Robert Craft); (xxvii, xxix) *The owl and the pussycat;* (xxvii, iii) *2 poems by K. Bal'mont;* (xxx, i) *2 poems of Paul Verlaine;* (xxiii,i) *Pribaoutki (peasant songs);* (xxiii, i) *Recollections of my childhood;* (xxviii, xxxi) *4 Russian songs;* (xxxvii) *4 Russian peasant songs;* (xxiii, iii) *3 songs from William Shakespeare;* (xxvii, i) *Tilim-Bom (3 stories for children);* (xxxii) *Mavra;* (xxxiii) *The Nightingale* (SM2K 46298) [id.].

Volume 9: (xxxiv) *The Rake's progress* (SM2K 46299) [S2K 46299].

Volume 10, Oratorio and melodrama: (xxxv, i) *The Flood* (with Robert Craft); (i) *Monumentum pro Gesualdo di Venosa (3 madrigals recomposed for instruments);* (vii) *Ode;* (xxxvi) *Oedipus Rex;* (xxxvii, xxxviii, i) *Perséphone* (SM2K 46300) [id.].

Volume 11, Sacred works: (x) *Anthem (the dove descending breaks the air);* (x) *Ave Maria;* (xxxix, x, i) *Babel;* (xxviii, xxvi, x, iii) *Cantata;* (xl) *Canticum sacrum;* (x, ii) *Credo;* (x, iii) *Introitus (T. S. Eliot in memoriam);* (xli) *Mass;* (x, i) *Pater noster;* (xlii, i) *A Sermon, a narrative & a prayer;* (xliii, i) *Threni;* (x, i) *Chorale: Variations on: Vom Himmel hoch, da komm ich her* (arr.); *Zvezdoliki* (SM2K 46301) [id.].

Volume 12, Robert Craft conducts: (xliv, i) *Abraham and Isaac;* (iii) *Danses concertantes;* (xlv) *Double canon: Raoul Dufy in memoriam;* (xlvi) *Epitaphium;* (i) *Le chant du rossignol* (symphonic poem); (i) *Orchestral variations: Aldous Huxley in memoriam;* (xlvii) *Requiem canticles;* (i) *Song of the nightingale* (symphonic poem) (SM2K 46302) [id.].

Complete Stravinsky Edition.

(B) *** Sony SX22K 46290 (22) [SXK 46290]. (i) Columbia SO; (ii) CBC SO; (iii) Columbia CO; (iv) Shirley, Driscoll, Gramm, Koves; (v) Allen, Sarfaty, Driscoll, Samuel Barber, Aaron Copland, Lukas Foss, Roger Sessions, American Chamber Ch., Hills, Columbia Percussion Ens.; (vi) Los Angeles

Festival SO; (vii) Cleveland O; (viii) Chicago SO; (ix) Jordan, Shirley, Gramm; (x) Festival Singers of Toronto, Iseler; (xi) Philippe Entremont; (xii) Charles Rosen; (xiii) Isaac Stern; (xiv) Soulima Stravinsky; (xv) Igor Stravinsky; (xvi) Szigeti; (xvii) Benny Goodman; (xviii) Columbia Jazz Ens.; (xix) Israel Baker; (xx) Tony Koves; (xxi) Arthur Gold, Robert Fizdale; (xxii) N. W. German RSO; (xxiii) Cathy Berberian; (xxiv) Howland, Kreiselman, Russo; (xxv) Mary Simmons; (xxvi) Alexander Young; (xxvii) Evelyn Lear; (xxviii) Adrienne Albert; (xxix) Robert Craft; (xxx) Donald Gramm; (xxxi) Di Tullio, Remsen, Almeida; (xxxii) Belinck, Simmons, Rideout, Kolk; (xxxiii) Driscoll, Grist, Picassi, Smith, Beattie, Gramm, Kolk, Murphy, Kaiser, Bonazzi, Washington, D. C., Op. Society Ch. & O; (xxxiv) Young, Raskin, Reardon, Sarfaty, Miller, Manning, Garrard, Tracey, Colin Tilney, Sadler's Wells Op. Ch., John Baker, RPO; (xxxv) Laurence Harvey, Sebastian Cabot, Elsa Lanchester, John Reardon, Robert Oliver, Paul Tripp, Richard Robinson, Columbia SO Ch., Gregg Smith; (xxxvi) Westbrook (nar.), Shirley, Verrett, Gramm, Reardon, Driscoll, Chester Watson Ch., Washington, D. C., Op. Society O; (xxxvii) Gregg Smith Singers, Gregg Smith; (xxxviii) Zorina, Molese, Ithaca College Concert Ch., Fort Worth Texas Boys' Ch.; (xxxix) John Calicos (nar.); (xl) Robinson, Chitjian, Los Angeles Festival Ch. & SO; (xli) Baxter, Albert, Gregg Smith Singers, Columbia Symphony Winds & Brass; (xlii) Verrett, Driscoll, Hornton (nar.); (xliii) Beardslee, Krebs, Lewis, Wainner, Morgan, Oliver, Schola Cantorum, Ross; all cond. composer. (xliv) Richard Frisch; (xlv) Baker, Igleman, Schonbach, Neikrug; (xlvi) Anderson, Bonazzi, Bressler, Gramm, Ithaca College Concert Ch., Gregg Smith; cond. Robert Craft.

On these 22 bargain-price discs you have the unique archive of recordings which Stravinsky left of his own music. Presented in a sturdy plastic display box that enhances the desirability of the set, almost all the performances are conducted by the composer, with a few at the very end of his career – like the magnificent *Requiem canticles* – left to Robert Craft to conduct, with the composer supervising. In addition there is a handful of recordings of works otherwise not covered, mainly chamber pieces. With some recordings of Stravinsky talking and in rehearsal (included in the box devoted to the symphonies) it makes a vivid portrait.

Stravinsky may not have been a brilliant conductor, but in the recording studio he knew how to draw out alert, vigorous performances of his own music, and every one of these items illuminates facets of his inspiration which other interpreters often fail to notice. There are few if any rival versions of the *Rite of spring* – nowadays, astonishingly, his most frequently recorded work – to match his own recording of 1960 in its compelling intensity and inexorable sense of line.

Of the major ballets, *Petrushka* and *The Firebird* are valuable, but *The Rite* is required listening: it has real savagery and astonishing electricity. The link between *Jeu de cartes* from the mid-1930s and Stravinsky's post-war opera, *The Rake's progress*, is striking and Stravinsky's sharp-edged conducting style underlines it, while the curiously anonymous-sounding *Scènes de ballet* certainly have their attractive moments. *Orpheus* has a powerful atmosphere, although one of Stravinsky's most classically restrained works. A good performance, with the composer's own authority lending it special interest. However, its invention is less memorable and distinguished than *Apollo*, one of Stravinsky's most gravely beautiful scores. *Agon* is one of the most stimulating of Stravinsky's later works. The orchestra respond with tremendous alertness and enthusiasm to Stravinsky's direction. The recording of *Le baiser de la fée* is a typical CBS balance with forward woodwind. However, if the recorded quality does not inspire too much enthusiasm, the performance certainly does. Stravinsky's recording of *Pulcinella* includes the vocal numbers, which, when well sung, add to the variety and sparkle of the piece, while in the orchestra the clowning of the trombone and the humour generally is strikingly vivid and never too broad. Similarly with the chamber scoring of the suite from *The Soldier's tale*, the crisp, clear reading brings out the underlying emotion of the music with the nagging, insistent little themes given an intensity that is almost tear-laden. There is a ruthlessness in the composer's own reading of *Les Noces* which exactly matches the primitive robustness in this last flowering of Russian nationalism in Stravinsky. The earlier parts are perhaps too rigid, but as the performance goes on so one senses the added alertness and enthusiasm of the performers. *Renard* is a curious work, a sophisticated fable which here receives too unrelenting a performance. The voices are very forward and tend to drown the instrumentalists.

In the early *Symphony in E flat*, Op. 1, the young Stravinsky's material may be comparatively conventional and the treatment much too bound to the academic procedures taught him by his master, Rimsky-Korsakov, but at least in this performance the music springs to life. Each movement has its special delights to outweigh any shortcomings. The performance is obviously as near definitive as it could be. The composer's account of the *Symphony in three movements* is an object lesson for every conductor who has tried to perform this work. Stravinsky shows how, by vigorous, forthright treatment of the notes, the emotion implicit is made all the more compelling. The Columbia Symphony plays superbly and the recording is full and brilliant. Stravinsky never quite equalled the intensity of the pre-war 78-r.p.m.

performance of the *Symphony of Psalms*. That had many more technical faults than his later, stereo version, and it is only fair to say that this new account is still impressive. It is just that, with so vivid a work, it is a shade disappointing to find Stravinsky as interpreter at less than maximum voltage. Even so, the closing section of the work is very beautiful and compelling. The CD transfers of the American recordings are somewhat monochrome by modern standards but fully acceptable.

The iron-fingered touch of Philippe Entremont has something to be said for it in the *Capriccio for piano and wind*, but this performance conveys too little of the music's charm. The *Movements for piano and orchestra* with the composer conducting could hardly be more compelling. Stern's account of the *Violin concerto in D* adds a romantic perspective to the framework, and at one time, no doubt, Stravinsky would have objected. But an expressive approach to Stravinsky is permissible in a soloist, when the composer is there to provide the bedrock under the expressive cantilena. Plainly this has the forthright spontaneity of a live performance.

The *Dumbarton Oaks concerto* with its obvious echoes of Bach's *Brandenburgs* is one of the most warmly attractive of Stravinsky's neoclassical works, all beautifully played and acceptably recorded. The *Octet for wind* of 1924 comes out with surprising freshness and, throughout, the unexpected combination of neo-Bach and neo-Pop is most refreshing. The *Ragtime* could be more lighthearted, but Stravinsky gives the impression of knowing what he wants. The *Ebony concerto*, in this version conducted by the composer, may have little of 'swung' rhythm, but it is completely faithful to Stravinsky's deadpan approach to jazz.

In *Le rossignol* the singing is not always on a par with the conducting, but it is always perfectly adequate and the recording is brilliant and immediate. *Mavra* is sung in Russian and, as usual, the soloists – who are good – are too closely balanced, but the performance has punch and authority and on the whole the CD quality is fully acceptable. The songs represent a fascinating collection of trifles, chips from the master's workbench dating from the earliest years. There are many incidental delights, not least those in which the magnetic Cathy Berberian is featured.

The Rake's progress is one of the highlights of the set and has never since been surpassed. Alexander Young's assumption of the title-role is a marvellous achievement, sweet-toned, accurate and well characterized. In the choice of other principals, too, it is noticeable what store Stravinsky set by vocal precision. Judith Raskin makes an appealing Anne Trulove, sweetly sung if not particularly well projected dramatically. John Reardon too is remarkable more for vocal accuracy than for striking characterization, but Regina Sarfaty's Baba is marvellous on both counts. The Sadler's Wells Chorus sings with even greater drive under the composer than in the theatre, and the Royal Philharmonic play with warmth and a fittingly Mozartian sense of style to match Stravinsky's surprisingly lyrical approach to his score. The CDs offer excellent sound.

The *Cantata* of 1952 is a transitional piece between Stravinsky's tonal and serial periods. However, of the two soloists, Alexander Young is much more impressive than Adrienne Albert, for her voice is entirely unsuitable, with an unformed choirboy sound somehow married to wide vibrato. For the sake of Stravinsky one endures her. The *Canticum sacrum* includes music that some listeners might find tough (the strictly serial choral section). But the performance is a fine one and the tenor solo from Richard Robinson is very moving. The Bach *Chorale variations* has a synthetic modernity that recalls the espresso bar, though one which still reveals underlying mastery. The *Epitaphium* and the *Double canon* are miniatures, dating from the composer's serial period, but the *Canon* is deliberately euphonious.

The *Mass* is a work of the greatest concentration, a quality that comes out strongly if one plays this performance immediately after *The Flood*, with its inevitably slack passages. As directed in the score, trebles are used here, and it is a pity that the engineers have not brought them further forward: their sweet, clear tone is sometimes lost among the lower strands. In *The Flood*, originally written for television, it is difficult to take the bald narrations seriously, particularly when Laurence Harvey sanctimoniously keeps talking of the will of 'Gud'. The performance of *Oedipus Rex*, too, is not one of the highlights of the set. *Perséphone*, however, is full of that cool lyricism that marks much of Stravinsky's music inspired by classical myths. As with many of these vocal recordings, the balance is too close, and various orchestral solos are highlighted.

Of the items recorded by Robert Craft, the *Requiem canticles* stands out, the one incontrovertible masterpiece among the composer's very last serial works and one of the most deeply moving works ever written in the serial idiom. Even more strikingly than in the *Mass* of 1948, Stravinsky conveys his religious feelings with a searing intensity. The *Aldous Huxley variations* are more difficult to comprehend but have similar intensity. Valuable, too, is the ballad *Abraham and Isaac*.

At present, Volumes 1, 2, 7, 8, 10 and 11 are available separately *in the UK only*; *The Rake's Progress* (Volume 9) is available separately on both sides of the Atlantic.

Apollo (*Apollon musagète;* complete ballet); (i) *Capriccio for piano and orchestra. Pulcinella* (ballet): *suite.*
(M) *** Decca (IMS) 443 577-2. (i) John Ogdon; ASMF, Marriner.

This newly remastered recording in Decca's Classic Sound series remains a demonstration disc of its period (the two ballets recorded in the Kingsway Hall in 1967), particularly in the *Pulcinella* suite, where the sharp separation of instruments (for example, double-basses against trombones in the *Vivo*) makes for wonderful stereo, with the precision of the playing outshining that of almost all rival versions. The ethereal string-tones of *Apollo* make an ideal coupling, with the elegantly polished response of the Academy players comparing impressively with the outstanding Karajan version. Again, thanks both to the fine recording, made at The Maltings in 1970, and to the pointed playing of the Academy, the neo-classical quality of the *Capriccio*, a charming work, is beautifully underlined, while the soloist, John Ogdon, provides the contrasting element of sinewy toughness. An outstanding disc in every way.

(i) *Apollo (Apollon musagète)* (ballet): complete; *Circus polka;* (ii) *Petrushka* (ballet: 1911 score): complete.
(B) *** DG Classikon 439 463-2; *439 463-4* [(M) id. import]. (i) BPO, Karajan; LSO, Dutoit.

Apollo is a work in which Karajan's moulding of phrase and care for richness of string texture make for wonderful results, especially in the glorious *Pas de deux*. The recording, made in the Jesus-Christus Kirche in 1972, is of DG's highest quality and in no way sounds its age. The *Circus polka* is played with comparable panache. The coupling is Charles Dutoit's first recorded *Petrushka*, made for DG in the Henry Wood Hall in 1975/6. The result is triumphantly spontaneous in its own right, with rhythms that are incisive yet beautifully buoyant, and a degree of expressiveness in the orchestral playing that subtly underlines the dramatic atmosphere. The remastered recording is atmospheric and vivid, though not as smooth on top as the Karajan couplings. Both ballets are generously cued, and altogether this bargain Classikon coupling is very good value.

(i) *Apollo (Apollon musagète); Circus polka; 4 Norwegian moods; Suites Nos. 1–2;* (ii) *The Soldier's tale (L'histoire du soldat);* (iii) *Symphony of Psalms.*
(M) *** Ph. (IMS) 438 973-2 (2). (i) LSO; (ii) Cocteau, Ustinov, Fertey, Tonietti, Parikian & Instrumental Ens.; (iii) Russian State Ac. Ch. & O; Markevitch.

Igor Markevitch's 1963 *Apollon musagète* with the LSO is a beautifully lucid and idiomatic performance with great balletic feeling. The shorter pieces, the *Norwegian moods* and the two *Suites for small orchestra*, are done with great personality. His account of *L'histoire du soldat* was mounted in 1962 to mark his fiftieth birthday, for which he persuaded a less than youthful Jean Cocteau to appear as the narrator and Peter Ustinov as the Devil. The *Symphony of Psalms* was recorded on his visit to the USSR in the same year, and has wonderfully characterful (but not always dead-in-tune) singing. *L'histoire du soldat* is a drier recording than either its London or Moscow companions, but it says much for the skills of the engineers of the 1960s that the sound is so beautifully transparent and the string-tone silky. An altogether admirable and rewarding set.

(i) *Apollo;* (ii) *The Firebird; Petrushka* (1911 score); *The Rite of spring* (complete ballets).
❀ (B) *** Ph. Duo 438 350-2 [id.]. (i) LSO, Markevitch; (ii) LPO, Haitink.

Markevitch gives a gravely beautiful reading of *Apollon musagète*, and the slightly distanced balance is surely ideal, for the focus is excellent. No more refined account of *The Firebird* has ever been put on record than Haitink's. The sheer savagery of *Kashchei's dance* may be a little muted, but the sharpness of attack and clarity of detail make for a thrilling result, while the magic and poetry of the whole score are given a hypnotic beauty, with the LPO at its very finest. The 1973 recording has been remastered with great success, as it has in the other two Haitink ballets, made at the same time. In *Petrushka* the rhythmic feeling is strong, especially in the Second Tableau and the finale, where the fairground bustle is vivid. The LPO wind playing is especially fine; the recording's firm definition and the well-proportioned and truthful aural perspective make it a joy to listen to. The natural, unforced quality of Haitink's *Rite* also brings real compulsion. Other versions may hammer the listener more powerfully, thrust him or her along more forcefully; but the bite and precision of the playing here are most impressive. Outstanding value.

Le baiser de la fée (ballet; complete); TCHAIKOVSKY, arr. STRAVINSKY: *Sleeping Beauty: Variation d'Aurore; Entr'acte symphonique; Bluebird pas de deux.*
(M) **(*) Virgin/EMI Dig. VM5 61281-2. Hong Kong PO, David Atherton.

David Atherton has been Music Director in Hong Kong since 1989 (though he frequently returns to conduct in Europe and America). He must have regarded the Hong Kong Philharmonic as a challenge. The players are drawn from thirteen different countries and, on the evidence of this record, are a formidable ensemble. They play with considerable sophistication and finesse: the strings still do not possess quite the weight of sonority of the finest European orchestras, but they blend well together; the horns are notably good, while wind and brass rise to the occasion in producing vivid colouring for a ballet that depends so much on the orchestral palette. The performance is enjoyable too for its spontaneous feeling and, indeed, for the conductor's conveyed affection for the simple Tchaikovskian ideas which Stravinsky so cleverly welded into a convincing whole. It is good to have as encores Stravinsky's scoring of the excerpts from Tchaikovsky's *Sleeping Beauty*, not only the well-known *Bluebird pas de deux* of 1941 but also the two earlier movements, arranged for Diaghilev's 1921 London season, notably the concertante *Entr'acte symphonique* in which the orchestra's concertmaster, Mayumi Seiler, plays the violin solo. The recording is excellent and the warm acoustics of Hong Kong Town Hall add plenty of atmosphere.

Le baiser de la fée (Divertimento); Firebird (ballet) *suite* (1919 version); *Petrushka* (complete ballet; 1919 version); *Pulcinella (suite); The Rite of spring.*
(B) ** RCA Twofer Dig. 74321 34176-2 (2) [(M) id. import]. RPO, Yuri Temirkanov.

The first of these paired CDs is distinctly enjoyable. Temirkanov has a feel for balletic nuance and a fine ear for orchestral detail. *Le baiser de la fée* is particularly attractive, with the lightest touch in the Scherzo and *Pas de deux* reminding us that this delectably scored music is as much Tchaikovsky as Stravinsky. The Rimskian colours in the *Firebird* emerge vividly, yet King Kastchei and his entourage are as malignant as anyone could wish, and the finale expands gloriously. Perhaps in *Pulcinella* the warm acoustics of Watford Town Hall are a little too amiable for the dances of Pergolesi focused through Stravinsky's harmonic and rhythmic distorting lens, but they are still enjoyable. On the second CD, however, the recessive orchestral balance and atmospheric acoustic mean that *Petrushka*, and especially the *Rite of spring*, are lacking in rhythmic pungency and bite, and Temirkanov's approach to both scores seems to be primarily evocative. There is little menace when the ghost of *Petrushka* appears at the end of the ballet, and the *Rite*, blunted by the resonance, lacks rhythmic forcefulness.

(i) *Le baiser de la fée (Divertimento);* (ii) *Petrushka:* excerpts: *(Danse russe; Chez Petrushka; La fête populaire);* (i) *Pulcinella: suite;* (ii) *The Rite of spring* (complete ballet).
(B) (***) EMI Rouge et Noir mono CZS5 69674-2 (2). (i) French Nat. R. O; (ii) Philh. O, Markevitch – PROKOFIEV: *Love for three oranges* etc. (**)

Markevitch's electrifying 1959 recording of *The Rite of spring* has long been famous, even though the documentation suggests that it is mono. The Philharmonia playing is superbly exciting, and the conductor's rhythmic vitality and ruthless thrust are matched by an amazingly spectacular recording which hardly sounds dated even now. One of the highlights of the performance is the dramatic use of the tam-tam, and in Part 2 the drums are thrillingly crisp and make a powerful impact. The elegant *Divertimento*, which Stravinsky culled from his Tchaikovskian ballet *Le baiser de la fée*, was made famous by Ansermet's mono recording, but the French orchestral playing here has rather more finesse: the horns in their attractive ostinato (taken from a Tchaikovsky piano piece) articulate buoyantly, and the whole performance has flair. The three excerpts from *Petrushka* are similarly lively and colourful, and only *Pulcinella* is slightly disappointing: the trombones blow raspberries in their famous *Vivo* duet with the double basses, and elsewhere Markevitch dilutes the music's charm by his forcefulness. However, in EMI's 'two for the price of one' French series this is certainly value for money.

(i; iii) *Le baiser de la fée: Pas de deux;* (i; iv) *Firebird suite; Fireworks;* (ii; iv) *The Rite of spring.*
(M) ** [RCA Basic 100 09026 61557-2]. (i) Chicago SO; (ii) Boston SO; (iii) Reiner; (iv) Ozawa.

Ozawa gives a lightweight interpretation (in the best sense) of the *Firebird suite*, with his feeling for the balletic quality of the music coming over, sometimes at the expense of dramatic emphasis. And there are certainly more earthy accounts of the *Rite of spring* available. However, these Ozawa recordings are of high quality and Reiner's *Pas de deux* from *Le baisir de la fée* is beautifully played.

(i) *Capriccio for piano and orchestra* (1929, rev. 1949); *Concerto for piano and wind* (1924, rev. 1950); *Movements for piano and orchestra.* (Piano): *8 Easy pieces on 5 notes; 4 Etudes; 3 Movements from Petrushka; Piano rag music; Scherzo; Serenade in A; Sonata in F sharp min.* (1903/4); *Sonata* (1924); *Souvenir d'une marche bouche; Tango; Valse pour les enfants; Waltz for children.*
(B) *** EMI Rouge et Noir CZS5 67276-2 (2) [CDZB 67276]. Michel Béroff; (i) O de Paris, Seiji Ozawa.

Only the *Capriccio*, the *Concerto for piano and wind* and the *Movements* have been available before in the UK, but specialist dealers did import the solo works and no one who acquired them could have been disappointed. Michel Béroff was still in his early twenties when he made the concerto recordings in the somewhat reverberant acoustic of the Salle Wagram. They are still better than those of most rivals and certainly better than those in the Sony *Stravinsky Edition*. The *Petrushka* excerpts are wonderfully alert and vital, and splendidly characterized. There is occasionally a very slight glare about the piano sound, recorded in the 1970s, but, among bargain, mid- and full-price discs, this is a first choice for this repertoire.

Le chant du rossignol (Song of the nightingale): symphonic poem.
❀ (M) *** DG 449 769-2 (2) [id.]. Berlin RSO, Lorin Maazel – RAVEL: *L'heure espagnole; L'enfant et les sortiléges;* RIMSKY-KORSAKOV: *Capriccio espagnol.* ***
(M) *** RCA 09026 68168-2 [id.]. Chicago SO, Fritz Reiner – RIMSKY-KORSAKOV: *Scheherazade* ***

Le rossignol is an underrated Stravinsky work and its derivative opening (with its overtones of Debussy's *Nuages* and the Rimskian flavour of the opening Act) have led to its virtues being undervalued. Among them is the extraordinarily rich fantasy and vividness of colouring; this symphonic poem, which Stravinsky made from the material of his opera, deserves a much more established place in the concert repertoire.

Maazel's justly famous version dates from 1958, slightly later than Reiner's. For those who love the orchestral palette, here is feast. Maazel is nothing if not dramatic, but above all he revels in the glittering orchestral detail and the marvellous atmosphere this score commands – every bit as ear-tickling as the more famous *Firebird* ballet. The work is beautifully played; the Berlin Radio Orchestra produces a feast of chimerical glowing colours and the DG engineers of the time surpassed themselves. For today's ears the recording sounds as if it might have been made yesterday instead of 40 years ago. A legendary recording, ideally selected for DG's 'Originals', and well coupled with Ravel's two delightful neo-classical operas and Maazel's superb Berlin Philharmonic version of Rimsky-Korsakov's *Capriccio espagnol* from the same period.

Reiner's version of 1956 in its currently remastered form also brings astonishingly full and vivid sound, full of presence, an excellent coupling for his strong and dramatic reading of *Scheherazade*. Where this transitional work – composed over two separate periods – often seems to lack something in thrust, Reiner's virile, sharply focused reading relates it more clearly than usual to the *Rite of spring*. Not just in Solti's reign but in Reiner's too this was a supreme orchestra. The virtuosity of the playing and the clarity of its direction are arresting, while the refined yet glittering detail of the orchestral palette in the work's five (titled) closing sections is most evocative.

Concerto for chamber orchestra, 'Dumbarton Oaks'; 8 Instrumental miniatures; (i) *Ebony concerto.*
(M) *** DG 447 405-2 [id.]. (i) Michel Arrignon; Ens. InterContemporain, Pierre Boulez – BERG: *Chamber concerto.* ***

A highly suitable coupling for the Berg in DG's 'Originals' series. The close sound almost reminds one of the effect of some early Columbia records which Stravinsky himself made before the war: the dry, spiky, black-and-white images of the early cinema. Yet the effect on DG is never two-dimensional and lacking in ambient colour. The playing of the Ensemble InterContemporain is very brilliant indeed. There is much to enjoy in these performances, which are spiced with the right kind of wit and keenness of edge, and even those who do not normally respond to Boulez's conducting will be pleasantly surprised with the results he obtains here.

Concerto for chamber orchestra, 'Dumbarton Oaks'; Pulcinella (suite).
(M) *** DG (IMS) Dig. 445 541 [id.]. Orpheus CO – BARTOK: *Divertimento for strings* etc. **(*)

Remarkably fine playing from this conductorless group. Their ensemble in the *Pulcinella suite* is better than that of most conducted orchestras, and the overall impression they convey is one of freshness and spontaneity. Much the same must be said of *Dumbarton Oaks*, which has great zest and brilliance. The DG recording is clean and lifelike and the perspective very natural. While this disc does not eclipse memories of all rivals, it can more than hold its own with most competition, past and present.

Dumbarton Oaks concerto in E flat; Octet for wind; The Soldier's tale (L'histoire du soldat): suite.
(B) ** EMI CfP CDP 6044 [(M) id. import]. Nash Ens., Elgar Howarth.

The performance of the *Octet* is most enjoyable, witty and spontaneous. The *Dumbarton Oaks concerto* needs more bite in the outer movements, though the *Allegretto* is nicely done, with both warmth and charm. But the lack of a strongly incisive quality means that the suite from *The Soldier's tale* sounds less sharply etched than it should. There is some colourful wind-playing here, and the recording is natural with an attractively judged acoustic, but the absence of edge means that a dimension is missing.

Concerto for strings in D.
(M) *** DG 447 435-2 [id.]. BPO, Karajan – HONEGGER: *Symphonies Nos. 2 & 3* *** ❀

Karajan's version of the *Concerto in D for strings* – written within a few months of the Honegger *Symphonie Liturgique*, with which it is coupled – may strike some listeners as not quite acerbic or biting enough, but the finesse and lightness of touch of the Berlin strings and their rhythmic legerdemain are a delight. The recording is first class.

(i; ii) *Ebony Concerto;* (iii) *Violin concerto;* (iv) *Symphony in C; Symphony in three movements;* (ii) *Symphonies for wind instruments;* (v) *Symphony of Psalms.*

(B) **(*) Ph. Duo 442 583-2 (2) [(M) id. import]. (i) Pieterson; (ii) Netherlands Wind Ens., Edo de Waart; (iii) Grumiaux, Concg. O, Bour; (iv) LSO, C. Davis; (v) Russian State Ac. Ch. & SO, Markevitch.

A lithe, refined account of the *Violin concerto* from Grumiaux and the Concertgebouw Orchestra. It is enormously vital, but its energy is controlled and the tone never becomes unduly aggressive. The 1967 recording is just a little dated but preserves a good balance between soloist and orchestra. George Pieterson's version of the *Ebony concerto* with the Netherlands Wind Ensemble is not as overtly jazzy as some but it does not lack rhythmic bite, and its dry, sardonic wit and the dark sonorities of the finale make it individual. The *Symphonies for wind instruments* also show the controlled blend of colour for which this Dutch wind group are famous. Sir Colin Davis's account of the *Symphony in C* is splendidly alert, well played and stimulating. The performance of the *Symphony in three movements* is also lively, but compared with Stravinsky's own it is over-tense. Markevitch's 1964 Russian performance of the *Symphony of Psalms* is as vibrantly Slavonic as one could wish, yet the closing 'Alleluias' still bring a frisson in their raptly gentle expressive feeling. The sound is brightly vivid but not harsh.

Violin concerto in D.

(M) *** Decca 425 003-2 [id.]. Kyung Wha Chung, LSO, Previn – PROKOFIEV: *Concertos Nos. 1–2.* ***

(M) *** DG 447 445-2 [id.]. Itzhak Perlman, Boston SO, Ozawa – BERG: *Concerto;* RAVEL: *Tzigane.* ***

(M) (***) Sony mono SMK 64505 [id.]. Stern, Columbia SO, composer – ROCHBERG: *Violin concerto.* *(**)

Stern's 1951 mono recording with the composer has never been surpassed and seldom approached. The outer movements have an exhilarating combination of rhythmic bite and wit, and the two central arias bring a very special subtlety of colour and feeling. The sound is of the highest quality: no apologies whatsoever need be made for it. Listening to the record lifts the spirits, and we would have given it a Rosette were it not for the Rochberg coupling, which (as music) is very much of the second grade, even if Stern's performance is not.

Kyung Wha Chung is at her most incisive in the spikily swaggering outer movements which with Previn's help are presented here in all their distinctiveness, tough and witty at the same time. In the two movements labelled *Aria*, Chung brings fantasy as well as lyricism, less overtly expressive than Perlman (at full price) but conveying instead an inner, brooding quality. Brilliant Decca recording, the soloist diamond-bright in presence, but with plenty of orchestral atmosphere.

Perlman's precision, remarkable in both concertos on this disc, underlines the neo-classical element in the outer movements of the Stravinsky. The two *Aria* movements are more deeply felt and expressive, presenting the work as a major twentieth-century concerto. The balance favours the soloist, but no one will miss the commitment of the Boston orchestra's playing, vividly recorded. A fair candidate for DG's 'Originals' series, with the Ravel *Tzigane* now added for good measure.

Complete ballets: *The Firebird;* (i) *Les Noces; Petrushka* (original 1911 score); *The Rite of spring.*

(B) ** Decca 443 467-2 (2) [id.]. SRO, Ansermet; (i) with Retchitzka, Devallier, Cuénod, Rehfuss, Homeffer, Peter, Rossiaud, Aubert, Geneva Motet Ch.

In their day these were much-admired performances and recordings of the three major early ballets. *The Firebird* is very early stereo indeed (1955); *Petrushka* and *The Rite* come from 1957, and *Les Noces* is later (and sounds it: 1961). At this distance of time the shortcomings of the SRO, which in the late 1950s was not the fine body it had been in the immediate post-war period, are evident, and the transfers tend to exaggerate the weakness of timbre in the upper strings by making it seem thin, ill-focused and shrill. *Petrushka* suffers most, and one feels that Ansermet's lively reading could be made to sound better than this. *The Firebird* is much smoother and has plenty of ambience. Detail is exceptionally clear, filled in like vivid embroidery on fine gauze. But the massed strings still sound emaciated. On balance one is prepared to put up with the defects in the orchestra for the sake of Ansermet's view of the *Rite of spring*, which has integrity, besides generating considerable rhythmic excitement and often striking melancholy of atmosphere. Here the sound is better too. *Les Noces* is altogether disappointing. Ansermet fails to capture the essential bite of Stravinsky's sharply etched portrayal of a peasant wedding. The hammering rhythms must sound ruthless, and here they are merely tame.

The Firebird (ballet): complete (with rehearsal).

(M) *** Decca 443 572-2 [id.]. New Philh. O, Ernest Ansermet.

The Firebird (ballet: complete).

(B) **(*) EMI forte CZS5 72664-2 (2) [(M) id. import]. O de Paris, Seiji Ozawa – BARTOK: *Concerto for orchestra* **(*); JANACEK: *Sinfonietta* ***; LUTOSLAWSKI: *Concerto for orchestra.* **(*)

The Firebird (complete); *Le chant du rossignol; Fireworks; Scherzo à la russe.*
✪ (M) *** Mercury 432 012-2 [id.]. LSO, Dorati.

The Firebird (ballet; complete); *Scherzo à la Russe.*
(M) ** Ph. Dig. 454 682-2. BPO, Haitink.

The CD transfer of Dorati's electrifying, 1960 Mercury version of *The Firebird* with the LSO makes the recording sound as fresh and vivid as the day it was made; the brilliantly transparent detail and enormous impact suggest a modern digital source rather than an analogue master made over 30 years ago. The performance sounds completely spontaneous and the LSO wind playing is especially sensitive. Only the sound of the massed upper strings reveals the age of the original master, although this does not spoil the ravishing final climax; the bite of the brass and the transient edge of the percussion are thrilling. The recording of Stravinsky's glittering symphonic poem, *The song of the nightingale*, is hardly less compelling. Dorati's reading is urgent and finely pointed, yet is strong, too, on atmosphere. The other, shorter pieces also come up vividly.

Ansermet came to London in November 1968 to re-record the complete *Firebird* in the Kingsway Hall, only a few months before he died. This London version, though not immaculate in ensemble in *Kaschei's dance*, has more polished playing than that which Ansermet recorded earlier with his own Suisse Romande Orchestra, but generally the interpretations are amazingly consistent. The recording was a demonstration disc in its day and is reissued in Decca's Classic Sound series, well documented by current CD standards. The first-class transfer readily demonstrates the atmosphere and vividly dramatic detail for which this conductor's records were justly famous.

Ozawa's first (1972) recording with the Orchestre de Paris was highly praised by us in its original LP format as a *Firebird* of luxurious and exotic plumage. On CD, the sheer vividness of colour of the score strikes one with renewed force. True, in one or two pianissimo string passages there could be greater mystery and more tenderness, but for the most part this is very well played indeed. In its CD transfer the recording has even more remarkably etched detail, but the upper range now has that added digital sharpness of focus that is not quite natural. The *Infernal dance of Kashchei and his retinue* has splendid bite, but at the close the great expansive melody on the violins has a thinness at the top that is not wholly natural.

We missed Haitink's 1991 digital recording of *The Firebird* the first time around. But it proves disappointing, curiously lacking in magnetism and glitter, and although climaxes bring more adrenalin and greater sonic brilliance one is conscious of the microphones, and neither performance nor recording can compare with Dorati's electrifying Mercury version with the LSO of three decades earlier.

(i) *The Firebird* (complete); (ii) *The Rite of spring* (complete).
✪ (M) *** Sony Theta SMK 60011 [id.]. Columbia SO, composer.
(BB) *** ASV CDQS 6031 [(M) id.]. (i) RPO, Dorati; (ii) Nat. Youth O of Great Britain, Simon Rattle.
(B) *** Decca Eclipse Dig. 448 226-2; *448 226-4* [id.]. Detroit SO, Antal Dorati.

Stravinsky's own (1961) version of *Firebird* may lack the refinement of sound and the dynamic contrasts that mark the finest digital recordings, but it is of far more than documentary interest, when the composer so tellingly relates it to his later work, refusing to treat it as merely atmospheric. What he brings out more than others is the element of grotesque fantasy, the quality he was about to develop in *Petrushka*, while the tense violence with which he presents such a passage as *Kaschei's dance* clearly looks forward to *The Rite of spring*. That said, he encourages warmly expressive rubato to a surprising degree, with the line of the music always held firm. But the revelatory performance here is *The Rite of spring*, for Stravinsky's own (1960) reading has never been surpassed as an interpretation of this seminal twentieth-century score. Over and over again, one finds passages which in the balancing and pacing (generally fast) give extra thrust and resilience, as well as extra light and shade. The whole performance is magnetic, with the argument and tension held together superbly. The digital transfer may be on the bright side, but brass and percussion have thrilling impact, sharply terraced and positioned in the stereo spectrum. This is a CD that should be in every basic collection.

Dorati's tempi in the *Firebird* are comparatively fast. But this matches his dramatic approach, as does a recording balance which is rather close, although there is no serious lack of atmosphere in the score's gentler pages of evocation. Not surprisingly with Simon Rattle at the helm, the performance of the National Youth Orchestra in the once-feared showpiece coupling is not just 'good considering', but 'good absolute'; the youngsters under their young conductor (the recordings here date from 1976/7) produce warm and spontaneous playing, and the penalty of having a few imprecisions and errors is minimal. The sound here is slightly more atmospheric than in the coupling, but again there is plenty of bite and the timpani make a fine effect.

Dorati's Detroit version of *The Firebird* has the benefit of spectacular digital recording. The clarity and definition of dark, hushed passages are amazing, with the contra-bassoon finely focused, never sounding woolly or obscure, while string tremolos down to the merest whisper are uncannily precise. There is plenty of space round woodwind solos, and only the concertmaster's violin is spotlit. The performance is very precise, too; though Dorati's reading has changed little from his previous versions with London orchestras, there is just a little more caution. Individual solos are not so characterful and *Kaschei's dance* lacks just a degree in excitement; but overall this is a strong and beautiful reading, even if the Mercury LP account, an electrifying example of 1960s' analogue engineering, is not entirely superseded.

Similarly, in terms of recorded sound, Dorati's *Rite* with the Detroit orchestra scores over almost all its rivals. This has stunning clarity and presence, exceptionally lifelike and vivid sound, and the denser textures emerge more cleanly than ever before. It is a very good performance too, almost but not quite in the same league as those of Karajan and Muti, generating plenty of excitement. The only let-down is the final *Sacrificial dance*, which needs greater abandon and higher voltage. Nor are the Detroit strings as sumptuous as those of the Berlin orchestra, sounding distinctly undernourished in places. Yet too much should not be made of this. Although Dorati does not match the atmosphere of his finest rivals, the performance is so vivid that it belongs among the very best.

The Firebird: suite (1919 version).
(M) *** DG 447 414-2 [id.]. (i) Grace Bumbry; Berlin RSO, Maazel – FALLA: *El amor brujo* etc. **

There has never been a finer recorded account of the 1919 version of the *Firebird suite* than Maazel's. It was recorded in 1958 and the stereo is magically atmospheric. The orchestral playing has great éclat: its colours are wonderfully subtle. In the gentler music the effect is exquisite, with the oboe soloist in the *Dance of the Princesses* and the bassoon in the *Berceuse* playing with the utmost delicacy. The ferocity of the *Infernal dance* breaks the spell momentarily, and Maazel omits the few bars included by Stravinsky to bridge the violent change of mood. But then comes the luminous climax of the finale, with the Berlin violins quite luscious in thirds, even though here the actual sound slightly betrays the age of the recording. This is truly a Legendary Performance, fully worthy of inclusion in DG's set of 'Originals'; but it is a great pity that the equally memorable original coupling of *Le chant du rossignol* was abandoned in favour of the Falla, which by comparison is second rate. However, that is now again available, coupled with Ravel (see above).

Ballets: *The Firebird* (suite; 1919 version); *Jeu de cartes; Petrushka* (1911 version); (i) *Pulcinella* (1947 version); *The Rite of spring*.
(B) *** DG Double 453 085-2 (2) [id.]. LSO, Abbado; (i) with Teresa Berganza, Ryland Davies, John Shirley-Quirk.

An attractive compilation of essential Stravinsky at a very reasonable price. The highlight here is *Petrushka*, while both the *Firebird suite* and *Jeu de cartes* are given stunning performances. The LSO plays with superb virtuosity and spirit. The neo-classical score of *Pulcinella* is given a surprisingly high-powered reading. But if Abbado is in danger of overcolouring, the bite and flair are entirely convincingly Stravinskian, with rhythms sharply incisive. Not just the playing but the singers too are outstandingly fine. Abbado's feeling for atmosphere and colour is everywhere in evidence, heard against an excellently judged perspective. There is a degree of detachment in Abbado's reading of *The Rite of spring*, although his observance of markings is meticulous and the orchestra obviously revels in the security given by the conductor's direction. The recording here is multi-miked, and the effect is less exciting than one would have expected. Nevertheless this is a worthwhile investment if taken as a whole.

The Firebird: suite (1919 version); *Petrushka* (1947 version). *Orchestral Suites Nos. 1–2*.
(BB) * Naxos Dig. 8. 550263 [id.]. Belgian R. & TV O (Brussels), Alexander Rahbari.

Though the Belgian Radio Orchestra is a lively band, playing here with colour and expressiveness, the washy recording in the 1919 *Firebird suite* obscures far too much detail, and even *Kaschei's dance* lacks bite. The recording for *Petrushka*, though still reverberant, is better focused but, irritatingly, what would have been a complete performance is shorn off before the final section, when the ghost of Petrushka returns. Stravinsky did suggest that concert performances might end with a loud cadence in this way after the Masqueraders section, but it now seems unfortunate to record it this way. That is particularly so when there would have been plenty of room to include the hauntingly atmospheric coda for the full ballet version. As it is, the two relatively trivial *Suites* for chamber orchestra come as makeweight.

The Firebird: suite (1945 version); *The Rite of spring*.
(B) **(*) Tring Dig. TRP 109 [(M) id. import]. RPO, Simonov.

Yuri Simonov directs highly individual and certainly enjoyable performances of both ballets which are warm and idiomatic rather than bitingly brilliant, bringing out the Russian elements and echoes of Rimsky-Korsakov, Stravinsky's teacher. *The Rite of spring* is amiable rather than barbaric, even though rhythms are sprung persuasively, and though that may give only a partial view of this masterpiece, the playing is always alert, and the recording is superb, allowing one to hear inner textures. In *The Firebird* Simonov adopts daringly broad speeds for the closing sections, with the *Berceuse* made sensuous and with tension consistently well sustained. The great horn solo in the closing section is gloriously done.

Firebird (ballet): *suite; 4 Norwegian moods.*
(M) *(*) Virgin/EMI Ultraviolet Dig. CUV5 61322-2. Bergen PO, Kitaienko – LIADOV: *Baba-Yaga* etc. *(*)

Kitaienko's performances of the *Norwegian moods* bring a pleasingly folksy evocation; but the *Firebird suite*, although similarly colourful, seriously lacks dramatic profile. Both works are pleasingly recorded, but this is not in any way a distinctive record.

Firebird suite; Pastorale.
(M) **(*) Decca Phase Four 443 898-2 [id.]. Czech PO, Stokowski – MUSSORGSKY: *Pictures at an exhibition* **; SCRIABIN: *Poème de l'extase.* **(*)

Tremendously sumptuous sound from Stokowski, while some of the relatively quiet music (the dynamic range is limited by the forward balance) shows the wonderful luminosity he could uniquely command from the orchestra. Rich-textured violins dominate the beginning of the final climax, which is powerfully inflated. *The Pastorale*, a 'song without words' written in 1908, makes a pleasant and unusual bonus. It is warmly played and, again, sumptuously recorded.

Jeu de cartes.
(M) (**) EMI mono CDM5 66601-2. Philh. O, Karajan – BRITTEN: *Variations on a theme of Frank Bridge;* VAUGHAN WILLIAMS: *Fantasia on a theme by Thomas Tallis.* (***) ❀

First-class Philharmonia playing, of course, but Karajan's approach to Stravinsky's ballet rhythms is too suave to give satisfaction. This is music which, above all, needs at least a degree of bite – and that is not forthcoming here. But the Britten and Vaughan Williams couplings are a different matter; indeed, they more than justify the cost of this CD as an essential purchase.

'Stravinsky in Moscow 1962': Orpheus (ballet suite); *Petrushka* (ballet suite); *Fireworks; Ode* (elegiac chant); *Song of the Volga boatmen* (arr. for wind and percussion).
(M) ** BMG/Melodiya 74321 33220-2 [id.]. Moscow PO or USSR SO, composer (with speech of thanks).

An issue of special historic interest in that it recorded Stravinsky's return to his native country in his eightieth year for the first time after the Revolution. The visit is copiously documented in Robert Craft's various books (and his meeting with Shostakovich is also recorded in Elisabeth Wilson's brilliant *Shostakovich Remembered*). The performances have a sense of occasion. Russian orchestras in the early 1960s were unused to playing even early Stravinsky, and there was no tradition of playing much Western contemporary music at all. The *Petrushka* starts just before the *Russian dance*, omits the whole of the Third Tableau and abruptly cuts short the Fourth with the concert ending; it lasts eighteen and a half minutes. Stravinsky takes brisk (some might say headlong) tempi, and the impression is of the orchestra taking plenty of risks and playing to the very limits of their ability. The Moscow Philharmonic are pretty rough-and-ready and there is some coarse brass-tone. Nor is the *Orpheus* with the USSR Symphony Orchestra among the most idiomatic of performances. The 1917 arrangement of the *Song of the Volga boatmen* for wind and percussion is more effective. On the original Chant du Monde LPs, Robert Craft's account of *The Rite of spring* with the USSR orchestra was included, and it is rightly dropped here. There is a short word of thanks from Stravinsky, and all devotees of the composer will want to have this memento of a historic occasion, even if there are more polished accounts of these pieces (except the *Volga boatmen*) in the Sony compilation, above.

(i) *Petrushka* (complete 1911 score); (ii) *The Rite of spring.*
(M) **(*) Sony SMK 64109 [id.]. (i) NYPO; (ii) Cleveland O; Pierre Boulez.

There is a controlled intensity about Boulez's 1971 New York performance of *Petrushka* which in the original version of the score puts the ballet closer than usual to the barbaric work which followed and it is a pity that the 1971 recording, made in the Avery Fisher Hall, becomes fierce at higher dynamic levels. Similarly in *The Rite of spring*, recorded two years earlier in Severance Hall, Cleveland, tempi are generally measured. Boulez is less lyrical than the composer but compensates with relentless rhythmic urgency. After Stravinsky's own version, which is not only uniquely authoritative but also uniquely compelling, Boulez's is among the most completely recommendable accounts. The massive vividness of sound matches the monolithic quality of the interpretation.

(i) *Petrushka* (1947 score); *The Rite of spring;* (ii) *4 Etudes for orchestra*.
(M) **(*) Mercury (IMS) 434 331-2 [id.]. (i) Minneapolis SO; (ii) LSO; Dorati.

Dorati's famous (1959) Mercury recording of *Petrushka* is exceptionally clean and vivid, with the semi-clinical Minneapolis recording bringing stereoscopic detail in the two central tableaux. There is plenty of drama too, and the final scene is touchingly done. Inevitably the sound is dated, with the bright upper range as caught by the Telefunken microphones not quite natural, but this adds a sharp cutting edge and impact to Dorati's extremely violent performance of *The Rite of spring*. His speeds are fast – sometimes considerably faster than is indicated in the score – but the LSO players carry complete conviction, the tautness of the work the more clearly revealed. The orchestral *Etudes* were recorded later (1964) in Watford, and have a fuller ambience.

Petrushka: suite.
(M) ** EMI CDM5 65423-2 [id.]. BPO, Stokowski – HOLST: *The Planets;* RAVEL: *Alborada*. **(*)

The Berlin Philharmonic seems not completely happy in the *Petrushka* suite, a 16-minute selection from the complete ballet that starts with the *Russian dance*. The Berlin strings sound too saturated in tone for this music, brilliant as the wind playing is, and the 1957 recording is not particularly distinguished.

Pulcinella (ballet) complete.
(M) *** EMI CDM7 64739-2. Jennifer Smith, John Fryatt, Malcolm King, N. Sinfonia, Rattle – WEILL: *Die sieben Todsünden*. ***

Simon Rattle, within a somewhat dry recording acoustic, conveys far more than usual the links between this score and the much later neo-classical opera, *The Rake's progress*. With lively and colourful playing from the Northern Sinfonia (the solos strong and positive) and with first-rate contributions from the three soloists, the high spirits of this score come over superbly. The current CD transfer adds vividness and presence without loss of bloom, and the new coupling is very generous indeed.

(i) *Pulcinella* (complete); *Danses concertantes*.
(BB) *** Naxos Dig. 8.553181 [id.]. (i) Fiona James, Ian Bostridge, Henry Herford; Bournemouth Sinf., Stefan Sanderling.

The complete *Pulcinella ballet*, twice as long as the usual orchestral suite, comes in an outstanding version from Stefan Sanderling and the Bournemouth Sinfonietta, fresh and alert and with the impact of the crisp, clean ensemble reinforced by full and immediate sound on an apt chamber scale. This was one of the very first recordings made (in 1993) by the tenor, Ian Bostridge, and the heady beauty of his voice is superbly caught in such vocal numbers as the *Serenata*. The other soloists are also good. A full text and English translation are given, and it is good to have the far later *Danses concertantes* (1941–2) as a valuable makeweight, done with equal point and polish.

(i) *Pulcinella* (ballet; complete); *The Rite of spring*.
(B) *** DG Classikon 439 433-2 [(M) id. import]. (i) Berganza, Ryland Davies, Shirley-Quirk; LSO, Abbado.

Abbado gives a vividly high-powered reading of the neo-classical score of *Pulcinella*, with rhythms sharply incisive. Not just the playing but the singers too are outstandingly fine and Abbado's feeling for atmosphere and colour is everywhere in evidence, heard against an excellently judged perspective. There is a certain reserve in *The Rite of spring*; but on points of detail it is meticulous. There is a hypnotically atmospheric feeling at the opening of Part Two, emphasizing the contrast with the brutal music which follows. The drama is heightened by the wide dynamic range of the recording, and the effect is forceful without ever becoming ugly. An excellent Classikon bargain coupling.

The Rite of spring (complete ballet) (see also above, under *Petrushka*).
(M) *** EMI Dig. CDM7 64516-2 [id.]. Phd. O, Muti – MUSSORGSKY: *Pictures*. ***

Muti's *Rite of spring* offers a performance which is aggressively brutal yet presents the violence with red-blooded conviction. Muti generally favours speeds a shade faster than usual, and arguably the opening bassoon solo is not quite flexible enough, for metrical precision is a key element all through. The recording, not always as analytically clear as some rivals, is strikingly bold and dramatic, with brass and percussion caught exceptionally vividly. At mid-price, coupled with an equally outstanding version of Mussorgsky's *Pictures*, this is very competitive indeed.

The Soldier's tale (suite).
(M) *** Van. 08.8013.71 [OVC 8013]. Instrumental Ens., Leopold Stokowski – THOMSON: *Film scores*. ***

Stokowski works his magic upon this surprisingly neglected score, making the most of its lyrical warmth as well as the more abrasive Devil's music, which has plenty of rhythmic bite. The septet of expert instrumentalists is naturally recorded in a studio acoustic, but one which has plenty of ambience.

Symphony in C; Symphony in 3 movements.
(M) *** Chandos Dig. CHAN 6577 [id.]. Royal Scottish O, Sir Alexander Gibson.

Even when compared with the composer's own versions, these performances by the Royal Scottish Orchestra – in excellent form – stand up well. The vivid naturalness of the splendid 1982 digital recording compensates for any slight lack of bite, and the inner movements of both works are beautifully played. The cool, almost whimsical beauty of the *Andante* of the *Symphony in three movements* is most subtly conveyed, and altogether this is very enjoyable.

Symphony in C; Symphony in 3 movements; Symphonies of wind instruments.
(BB) ** Naxos Dig. 8.553403 [id.]. New Zealand SO, En Shao.

Though the recorded sound is not quite sharply focused enough to bring out the full rhythmic incisiveness needed, the Naxos performances are winningly alert, with delightfully sprung rhythms and a warmly expressive style in slow music, with fine woodwind playing. Such expressiveness may contravene the composer's idea that his music does not express emotion, but it certainly makes it more involving. The *Symphony in three movements* is more weightily presented than the *Symphony in C*, with the individual orchestration well caught, including the prominent piano, and with the jazzy syncopations of the finale infectiously played. The *Symphonies for wind* are markedly less successful, earlier and tougher in their cryptic argument, and here not rugged-sounding enough.

CHAMBER AND INSTRUMENTAL MUSIC

(i) *Divertimento* (from *Le baiser de la fée*); *Duo concertante; Suite italienne;* (ii) *Mavra: Chanson russe.*
(M) *** EMI Analogue/Dig. CDM5 66061-2. Itzhak Perlman, with (i) Bruno Canino; (ii) Samuel Sanders (with RACHMANINOV: *Vocalise, Op. 34/14;* Songs: *It's peaceful here* (arr. Heifetz); *Daisies* (arr. Kreisler) ***; TCHAIKOVSKY: *Andante cantabile* from *Op. 11; Chanson sans paroles* (arr. Kreisler); *Souvenir d'un lieu cher: Mélodie, Op. 42/2* (arr. Flesch) **).

The *Italian suite* was arranged from the Pergolesi-based ballet, *Pulcinella*, while the *Duo concertante* was written after the *Violin concerto* and for the same artist, Samuel Dushkin. The *Divertimento* is arranged from movements of the Tchaikovsky-derived ballet, *The fairy's kiss*. Stravinsky toured with Dushkin in the early 1930s, including the *Suite italienne* and the *Divertimento* in his concert programmes. (He recorded not only the *Violin concerto* but also the *Duo concertante* for Columbia with him.) Perlman plays all this music with warmth and understanding, and his achievement in the *Duo concertante*, which has often seemed a dry work, is particularly remarkable. Bruno Canino makes a sympathetic partner and the 1974 recording, originally excellent, has been clearly and cleanly transferred to CD, the sound more strongly etched than on LP. Perlman's seductively slinky account of the *Chanson russe* from *Mavra* was recorded four years later, and the two Rachmaninov songs, which are played with a delightful flowing lyricism, are digital; but in all these cases the sound is warmer and smoother. In Tchaikovsky's *Andante cantabile* Perlman seems determined to avoid any possible suggestion of sentimentality and the result is perhaps a shade cool; however, the *Chanson sans paroles* has real panache and the phrasing of the *Mélodie* from the *Souvenir d'un lieu cher* is equally appealing. Samuel Sanders gives admirable support, although he is made to sound a little self-effacing by the recording balance. But the Stravinsky collection remains one of Perlman's most rewarding achievements among his many recordings of instrumental duos.

PIANO MUSIC

Piano duet

Concerto for two pianos; Sonata for two pianos; The Rite of spring.
(BB) * Naxos Dig. 8.553386 [id.]. Benjamin Frith, Peter Hill.

Benjamin Frith and Peter Hill are both brilliant players, though their *Rite of spring* needs higher voltage and more colour. Much the same might be said of the *Concerto for two pianos*. Ultimately, though, it is not on artistic grounds that this remains a one-star recommendation, but because of the recording quality. The acoustic is badly cramped and wanting in space and ambience.

Rite of spring (arr. composer).
(BB) **(*) Arte Nova Dig. 74321 51638-2 (2) [id.]. Irina Tchernoussova, Elisabeth Romanovskaya – RACHMANINOV: *Suites Nos. 1–2* etc. **(*)

This splendid Russian duo plays Stravinsky's own piano-duet version of the *Rite of spring* with superb precision and clarity, aerating the complex textures. If the result is light and clear rather than barbaric, it certainly provides an illuminating view of this masterpiece, a generous and apt coupling for the Rachmaninov duets making up this two-disc issue.

Solo piano music

Circus polka; Piano-rag-music; Serenade in A; Sonata; 4 Studies; Tango.
(M) **(*) Saga EC 3391-2 [id.]. Thomas Rajna.

Some may feel that in Thomas Rajna's hands Stravinsky's piano music is made to sound too soft-centred and without enough rhythmic toughness – even the *Tango* and *Circus polka* have charm. But the *Sonata* is taken seriously and there is an imaginative variety of colour in the *Serenade*: its unexpectedly tranquil closing *Cadenza finala* is played with lucid imperturbability. This is always intelligent as well as sympathetic playing, and many may respond to it who would reject a more percussive approach. The recording is natural but is not projected forwardly.

3 movements from Petrushka.
(M) *** DG 447 431-2 [id.]. Maurizio Pollini – *Recital.* ***
(M) ** EMI Dig. CD-EMX 2213 [(M) id.]. Piers Lane – BALAKIREV: *Islamey* **(*); MUSSORGSKY: *Pictures at an exhibition.* **

Staggering, electrifying playing from Pollini, creating the highest degree of excitement. This is part of an outstandingly generous recital of twentieth-century piano music.

Very well recorded and played on EMI, though Piers Lane does not convey the full excitement and colour of this transcription. Faced by its formidable technical hurdles, Lane sounds just a shade cautious, and in this piece virtuosity must sound totally effortless.

VOCAL MUSIC

(i) *Mass;* (ii) *Les Noces.*
(M) *** DG (IMS) 423 251-2 [id.]. (i) Trinity Boys' Ch., E. Bach Festival O; (i, ii) E. Bach Festival Ch.; (ii) Mory, Parker, Mitchinson, Hudson; Argerich, Zimerman, Katsaris, Francesch (pianos), percussion; cond. Bernstein.

In the *Mass* the style is overtly expressive, with the boys of Trinity Choir responding freshly, but it is in *Les Noces* that Bernstein conveys an electricity and a dramatic urgency which give the work its rightful stature as one of Stravinsky's supreme masterpieces, totally original and – even today – unexpected, not least in its black-and-white instrumentation for four pianos and percussion. The star pianists here make a superb, imaginative team.

(i) *Perséphone. The Rite of spring.*
(M) *** Virgin/EMI Dig. VMD5 61249-2 (2) [ZDMD 61249]. (i) Anne Fournet, Rolfe Johnson, Tiffin Boys' School Ch., LPO Ch.; LPO, Kent Nagano.

Where Stravinsky himself – at speeds consistently more measured than Nagano's – takes a rugged, square-cut view of *Perséphone*, Nagano, much lighter as well as more fleet, makes the work a far more atmospheric evocation of spring. The playing and singing are consistently more refined, and the modern digital recording gives a warm bloom, while the sung French sounds far more idiomatic from everyone. The narration of Anne Fournet brings out all the beauty of Gide's words, with Anthony Rolfe Johnson free-toned in the taxing tenor solos. Nagano's reading of *The Rite of spring* has similar qualities. If it is less weightily barbaric than many, the springing of rhythm and the clarity and refinement of instrumental textures make it very compelling, with only the final *Danse sacrale* lacking something in dramatic bite. The two separate discs are offered in a box at the cost of a single, premium-price CD.

OPERA

Oedipus Rex.
(B) (**(*)) DG Double mono 445 445-2 [id.]. Haefliger, Töpper, Engen, Kuen, Sardi, N. German R. Ch., Berlin RIAS Chamber Ch. & O, Fricsay – BARTOK: *Bluebeard's castle.* (**)

Fricsay's bitingly dramatic version of *Oedipus Rex*, well coupled with his equally intense account of Bartók's *Bluebeard's Castle*, is musically most enjoyable. As Oedipus, Ernst Haefliger is both heroically incisive and (where needed) lyrically expressive – as in the key passage, *Invidia fortunam odit*. Hertha Töpper is a fruity Jocasta, a little fluttery and maternal-sounding, perhaps aptly. The other soloists make a strong team. The big snag is that the spoken narration is in German, very distracting when it punctuates the music so regularly. Clear, well-focused, mono recording.

Stravinsky Edition, Volume 9: *The Rake's progress* (complete).
(M) *** Sony SM2K 46299 (2) [S2K 46299]. Young, Raskin, Reardon, Sarfaty, Miller, Manning, Sadler's Wells Op. Ch., RPO, composer.

It was a splendid idea to get Stravinsky to come to London to record *The Rake's progress* in what has many elements of the original Sadler's Wells production – which incidentally the composer attended some time earlier. The casting is uniformly excellent with the Rake of Alexander Young dominating but Judith Raskin an attractive heroine. Regina Sarfaty's Baba is superbly characterized and her anger at being spurned just before the 'squelching' makes a riveting moment. The composer conducts with warmth as well as precision, both chorus and orchestra respond persuasively, and the CD transfer is excellent. A clear first choice.

Strozzi, Barbara (*c.* 1619–64)

'To the unknown goddess': Cantate, ariette e duetti, Op. 2: L'amante segreto . . . Voglio, voglio morire; Amor dormiglione . . . Amor, non dormir più; La fanciuletta semplice . . . Spesso per entro al petto; Gite o giorni dolenti; Giusta negativa . . . Non mi dite ch'io canti; La sol, fa, mi, re do . . . La mia donna perchè canta. Cantate ariete a una, due e tre voci, Op. 3: Ardo in tacito foco. Diporti di Euterpe, Op. 7: Appresso ai molli argenti; Lagrime mie . . . Lagrime mie, a che vi trattenete; Pensaci ben mio core; Tradimento.
(M) *** Carlton Dig. 30366 00412 [id.]. Catherine Bott, Paula Chateauneuf; Timothy Roberts; Frances Kelly.

Here is an opportunity to sample the extraordinarily individual seventeenth-century female Venetian composer, Barbara Strozzi (adopted daughter of Monteverdi's librettist) through her secular love songs. The very first in this recital, *Ardo in tacito foco* ('The heart forbids the tongue to pronounce the beloved's name') immediately displays her characteristic languishing musical device of a chromatically inclined downward scale, while the opening of the Lamento, *Lagrime mie, a che vi trattenete* ('My tears, why do you hold back'), with its equally luscious chromatic sighs, is just as affecting. Catherine Bott revels in its yearning line, with her embellishments adding to the languor. But there is considerable variety of mood here. *La fanciuletta semplice* ('The simple girl') and *Amor dormiglione* are both charmingly fresh and uncomplicated; the latter has a dancing, upward, vocal arpeggio, while *La sol, fa, mi, re, do* is like a sparkling folksong. *L'amante segreto*, however, is a lovely, lyrical song, soaring up high, with a sad coda. Most eloquent of all is the closing *Appresso ai molli argenti* ('Close to the soft banks of a murmuring stream') with its remarkable word-imagery set with real imaginative flair. Catherine Bott is as much a master of this repertoire as her predecessor, Maria Cristina Kiehr, was with the *Sacri musicali affetti*. She encompasses its florid upper tessitura with freshness and ease, she responds readily to moments of sensuality, and her bravura decorated runs are remarkably secure. The small accompanying group (archlute or guitar, harpsichord and double harp) is just right, and so is the recording balance. Strongly recommended, especially if you have already tried the full-price Harmonia Mundi disc.

Suk, Josef (1874–1935)

Fantasy in G min. (for violin and orchestra), *Op. 24.*
(M) *** Sup. SU 1928-2 011 [id.]. Josef Suk, Czech PO, Karel Ančerl – DVORAK: *Violin concerto* etc. ***

Suk's *Fantasy* is a brilliant piece which relates to the traditional essays in violin wizardry as well as to the Czech nationalist tradition. The work has music of characteristic fantasy, though the rhetorical brilliance is equally strong. Suk's playing is refreshing and the orchestral accompaniment under Ančerl is no less impressive. Good remastered 1960s sound.

Serenade for strings in E flat, Op. 6.
(BB) *** ASV CDQS 6094 [(M) id.]. Polish R. CO, Duczmal – TCHAIKOVSKY: *Serenade* ***; GRIEG: *Holberg suite.* **(*)
(BB) *** Naxos 8.550419 [id.]. Capella Istropolitana, Krechek – DVORAK: *String serenade.* **(*)
(M) **(*) Virgin/EMI Dig. CUV5 61144-2. LCO, Christopher Warren-Green – DVORAK: *Serenade.* **(*)

Serenade for strings in E flat, Op. 6; Meditation on an old Czech hymn (St Wenceslas), Op. 35a.
(BB) **(*) Discover Dig. DICD 920234 [id.]. Virtuosi di Praga, Oldřich Vlček – JANACEK: *Suite.* ***

Suk's *Serenade* is a gorgeous work and it receives a lovely performance from the Polish Radio Chamber

Orchestra under Agnieszka Duczmal. The opening is immediately winning, light and gracious, yet the orchestra can produce a rich body of timbre when needed. The *Adagio* is very beautifully played indeed; it follows Suk's unusual *Allegro ma non troppo e grazioso*, which is nearly a waltz but not quite. The orchestra's sparkling articulation and subtle rhythmic feeling here are most distinctive. This is altogether first rate, and the recording is full-textured and well balanced, bringing out Duczmal's many fine shadings of colour.

On Naxos another entirely delightful account of Suk's *Serenade*, which ought to be far better known. The innocent delicacy of the opening is perfectly caught and the charm of the dance movement which follows is just as winning. The *Adagio* is played most beautifully and then, with a burst of high spirits (and excellent ensemble), the finale bustles to its conclusion with exhilarating zest. The recording is first class, fresh yet full-textured, naturally balanced and transparent.

Warren-Green and his LCO also give a wonderfully persuasive account of Suk's *Serenade*, making obvious that its inspiration is every bit as vivid as in the comparable work of Dvořák. The recording, made in All Saints', Petersham, is fresh, full and natural without blurring from the ecclesiastical acoustic. However, the original CD also included the Tchaikovsky *Serenade*, which is now missing, so even at mid-price this is not such a bargain as it looks, with only 52 minutes' playing time.

Judging by the photo-insert, the Prague Virtuosi have been somewhat expanded from the eleven soloists who made up the original group, to sixteen plus the leader/conductor, Oldřich Vlček. Certainly they create a richly full-bodied sonority here and play this music idiomatically and with ardent, expressive feeling. Some might feel that the *Serenade* benefits from a slightly more subtle and less extrovert approach, but the passionately gripping account of the *Wenceslas meditation* brings an entirely appropriate emotional intensity. Splendidly vivid recording,

Sullivan, Arthur (1842–1900)

The Merchant of Venice (suite); *The Tempest* (incidental music).
(M) *** EMI CMS7 64412-2 (2) [CDMB 64412]. CBSO, Sir Vivian Dunn – *Ruddigore*. ***

The longer orchestral work, the suite of incidental music for *The Tempest*, dates from 1861, when the student composer was only nineteen. Not surprisingly it made him an overnight reputation, for it displays an astonishing flair and orchestral confidence. The shorter *Merchant of Venice* suite was composed five years later, and almost immediately the writing begins to anticipate the lively style which was so soon to find a happy marriage with Gilbert's words. The performance here is highly infectious, and the sound is first class.

(i) *Overtures: Cox and Box; Princess Ida; The Sorcerer;* (ii) *Overture in C (In Memoriam)*.
(M) **(*) EMI CMS7 764409-2 (2) [Ang. CDMB 64409]. (i) Pro Arte O, Sargent; (ii) RLPO, Groves – *The Pirates of Penzance*. ***

This collects together the overtures from the operas not recorded by Sargent in his EMI series. The performances are characteristically bright and polished. *In Memoriam* is a somewhat inflated religious piece written for the 1866 Norwich Festival.

Overture Di Ballo.
(M) ** EMI CMS7 64400-2 (2) [CDMB 64400]. BBC SO, Sargent – *Iolanthe*. ***

Sullivan's gay, Italianate overture, felicitously scored, makes a good bonus for Sargent's *Iolanthe*. However, we are indebted to a reader for pointing out that EMI have mistakenly used Sargent's recording (which is truncated) instead of the much superior Groves/RLPO version.

Pineapple Poll (ballet; arr. Mackerras).
(M) *** Decca Dig. 436 810-2 (2). Philh. O, Mackerras – *Princess Ida*. ***
(B) *** CfP CD-CFP 4618 [(M) id. import]. LPO, Mackerras – VERDI: *Lady and the fool*. ***

(i) *Pineapple Poll* (ballet; arr. Mackerras); (ii) Overtures: *Iolanthe; The Mikado; Ruddigore; The Yeomen of the Guard*.
(M) *** EMI CDM5 66538-2. (i) RPO; (ii) Philh. O; Sir Charles Mackerras.

On Decca Mackerras conducts with warmth as well as vivacity, and the elegantly polished playing of the Philharmonia Orchestra gives much pleasure. The record was made in the Kingsway Hall with its glowing ambience, and the CD transfer, though brightly vivid, has a pleasing bloom. Indeed the quality is in the demonstration bracket, with particularly natural string textures.

Mackerras re-recorded *Pineapple Poll* for Decca, but his earlier (1960) Abbey Road recording was rightly considered definitive in its day and is still striking for its sheer brio, while the playing has a real feeling of the ballet theatre. For a long while this version was leased to the American company, Arabesque, who knew a good thing when they heard it, but now it reappears from its original source, freshly remastered and sounding splendidly vivid. What makes the reissue a collector's item is the group of four overtures, recorded by the Philharmonia at their peak in 1956. They are played with marvellous vivacity and sparkle and a delightful lilting flow in the lyrical melodies. While *Iolanthe* is particularly appealing, it is *Ruddigore* that one remembers especially for the superbly polished and witty string-playing in the patter trio, 'My eyes are fully open'. The recording is excellent and does not betray its age.

Mackerras has recorded his vivacious Sullivan arrangement several times, but this LPO version of the suite on CfP, made in the London Henry Wood Hall in 1977, is striking for its brio and warmth. With an apt Verdi coupling, this is excellent value, very well transferred to CD.

Symphony in E (Irish).
(M) *** EMI CMS7 64406-2 (2) [Ang. CDMB 64406]. RLPO, Groves – *Patience*. ***

Sullivan's *Irish Symphony* is a pleasing work, lyrical, with echoes of Schumann as much as the more predictable Mendelssohn and Schubert. The jaunty *Allegretto* of the third movement with its 'Irish' tune on the oboe is nothing less than haunting. Groves and the Royal Liverpool Philharmonic give a fresh and affectionate performance, and the CD transfer of the 1968 recording is generally well managed.

The Gondoliers; The Mikado; The Pirates of Penzance: orchestral excerpts.
(B) ** Millennium UMD 80395. Eric Johnson and his O – COATES: *By the sleepy lagoon; London suites.* ***

Three orchestral selections from popular Savoy operas, nicely scored and presented with style and affection. Tempi are laid back: Eric Johnson makes no attempt to play the livelier patter songs up to vocal tempo, but instead relishes their wit in a more relaxed manner. Warm, full but not brilliant recording.

OPERAS

The major Decca and EMI sets

(i) *Cox and Box* (libretto by F. C. Burnand) complete; (ii) *Ruddigore* (complete; without dialogue).
(M) *** Decca 417 355-2 (2) [id.]. (i) Styler, Riordan, Adams; New SO of L.; (ii) Reed, Round, Sandford, Riley, Adams, Hindmarsh, Knight, Sansom, Allister, D'Oyly Carte Op. Ch., ROHCG O, Godfrey.

The Gondoliers (complete; with dialogue).
(M) *** Decca 425 177-2 (2) [id.]. Reed, Skitch, Sandford, Round, Styler, Knight, Toye, Sansom, Wright, D'Oyly Carte Op. Ch., New SO of L., Godfrey.

The Gondoliers (complete; without dialogue).
(M) **(*) EMI CMS7 64394-2 (2) [Ang. CDMB 64394]. Evans, Young, Brannigan, Lewis, Cameron, Milligan, Monica Sinclair, Graham, Morison, Thomas, Watts, Glyndebourne Festival Ch., Pro Arte O, Sargent.

HMS Pinafore (complete; with dialogue).
✿ (M) *** Decca 414 283-2; *414 283-4*. Reed, Skitch, Round, Adams, Hindmarsh, Wright, Knight, D'Oyly Carte Op. Ch., New SO of L., Godfrey.

HMS Pinafore (complete; without dialogue); *Trial by Jury*.
(M) *** EMI CMS7 64397-2 (2) [Ang. CDMB 64397]. George Baker, Cameron, Lewis, Brannigan, Milligan, Morison, Thomas, M. Sinclair, Glyndebourne Festival Ch., Pro Arte O, Sargent.

HMS Pinafore: highlights.
(B) *** Decca 436 145-2; *436 145-4* [433 881-2] (from above D'Oyly Carte Opera recording; cond. Godfrey).

Iolanthe (complete; with dialogue).
(M) *** Decca 414 145-2; *414 145-4* (2) [id.]. Sansom, Reed, Adams, Round, Sandford, Styler, Knight, Newman, D'Oyly Carte Op. Ch., Grenadier Guards Band, New SO, Godfrey.

Iolanthe (complete; without dialogue).
(M) *** EMI CMS7 64400-2 (2) [CDMB 64400]. George Baker, Wallace, Young, Brannigan, Cameron, M. Sinclair, Thomas, Cantelo, Harper, Morison, Glyndebourne Festival Ch., Pro Arte O, Sargent – *Di Ballo overture*. **

The Mikado (complete; without dialogue).
(M) *** Decca 425 190-2 (2) [id.]. Ayldon, Wright, Reed, Sandford, Masterson, Holland, D'Oyly Carte Op. Ch., RPO, Nash.
(M) **(*) EMI CMS7 644403-2 (2) [Ang. CDMB 64403]. Brannigan, Lewis, Evans, Wallace, Cameron, Morison, Thomas, J. Sinclair, M. Sinclair, Glyndebourne Festival Ch., Pro Arte O, Sargent.

Patience (complete; with dialogue).
(M) *** Decca 425 193-2 (2) [id.]. Sansom, Adams, Cartier, Potter, Reed, Sandford, Newman, Lloyd-Jones, Toye, Knight, D'Oyly Carte Op. Ch. & O, Godfrey.

Patience (complete; without dialogue).
(M) *** EMI CMS7 64406-2 (2) [Ang. CDMB 64406]. Morison, Young, George Baker, Cameron, Thomas, M. Sinclair, Harper, Harwood, Glyndebourne Festival Ch., Pro Arte O, Sargent – *Symphony*. ***

The Pirates of Penzance (complete; with dialogue).
(M) *** Decca 425 196-2; *414 286-4* [id.]. Reed, Adams, Potter, Masterson, Palmer, Brannigan, D'Oyly Carte Op. Ch., RPO, Godfrey.

The Pirates of Penzance: highlights.
(B) *** Decca 436 148-2; *436 148-4* [436 292-2]. Reed, Adams, Brannigan, Masterson, Potter, Palmer, D'Oyly Carte Op. Co. Ch., RPO, Godfrey.

The Pirates of Penzance (complete; without dialogue).
(M) *** EMI CMS7 64409-2 (2) [Ang. CDMB 64409]. George Baker, Milligan, Cameron, Lewis, Brannigan, Morison, Harper, Thomas, Sinclair, Glyndebourne Festival Ch., Pro Arte O, Sargent – *Overtures*. **(*)

(i) *Princess Ida* (complete; without dialogue); (ii) *Pineapple Poll* (ballet; arr. Mackerras)
(M) *** Decca 436 810-2 (2) [id.]. (i) Sandford, Potter, Palmer, Skitch, Reed, Adams, Raffell, Cook, Harwood, Palmer, Hood, Masterson, D'Oyly Carte Op. Ch., RPO, Sargent; (ii) Philh. O, Mackerras.

Ruddigore (complete; without dialogue).
(M) *** EMI CMS7 64412-2 (2) [CDMB 644122]. Lewis, George Baker, Brannigan, Blackburn, Morison, Bowden, M. Sinclair, Harwood, Rouleau, Glyndebourne Festival Ch., Pro Arte O, Sargent – *Merchant of Venice; Tempest:* incidental music. ***

The Yeomen of the Guard (complete; without dialogue).
(M) *** EMI CMS7 64415-2 (2) [Ang. CDMB 64415]. Dowling, Lewis, Evans, Brannigan, Morison, M. Sinclair, Glyndebourne Festival Ch., Pro Arte O, Sargent.

(i) *The Yeomen of the Guard* (complete; without dialogue); (ii) *Trial by Jury*.
(M) *** Decca 417 358-2; *417 358-4* [id.]. Hood, J. Reed, Sandford, Adams, Raffell; (i) Harwood, Knight; (ii) Round; D'Oyly Carte Op. Ch.; (i) RPO, Sargent; (ii) ROHCG O, Godfrey.

As can be seen, the two basic sets of recordings of the major Savoy Operas, nearly all from Godfrey (on Decca) and Sargent (on EMI), are now back in the catalogue at mid-price. The Decca series usually has the advantage (or disadvantage, according to taste) of including the dialogue. Certain of the operas are available only in D'Oyly Carte versions, and of these the most fascinating is *Cox and Box*. This pre-Gilbertian one-Acter is based on a play (called *Box and Cox*) with the story of two men sharing the same rooms – one is a hatter, the other works on a newspaper at night – without knowing it, so that Bouncer, the unscrupulous landlord, can collect a double rent. It was written in 1867 and thus pre-dates the first G&S success, *Trial by Jury*, by eight years. One must notice the captivating *Bacon 'Lullaby'*, so ravishingly sung by Joseph Riordan. Later on, in Box's recitative telling how he 'committed suicide', Sullivan makes one of his first and most impressive parodies of grand opera, which succeeds also in being effective in its own right. The D'Oyly Carte performance is splendid in every way. It is given a recording which, without sacrificing clarity, conveys with perfect balance the stage atmosphere.

Turning now to the major G&S successes, it seems sensible to consider the Decca and EMI alternatives together. EMI usually offer some orchestral bonuses and, in the case of *HMS Pinafore*, add *Trial by Jury* as well (as was the practice in the theatre in the heyday of the D'Oyly Carte Opera Company). Godfrey's Decca *Trial by Jury* is saved for inclusion with their outstanding *Yeomen of the Guard*. The Sargent version of *Trial by Jury* (with George Baker as the Judge) is by general consent the best there is, if only by a small margin, and the EMI version of *Pinafore* is wonderfully fresh too, beautifully sung throughout, while the whole of the final scene is musically quite ravishing.

But the 1960 Godfrey set of this opera is very special indeed, and *HMS Pinafore* is in our view the finest of all the D'Oyly Carte stereo recordings. While Owen Brannigan, on EMI, without the benefit of dialogue conveys the force of Dick Deadeye's personality remarkably strongly, Donald Adams's assumption of the role on Decca (which does have the dialogue) is little short of inspired, and his larger-than-life characterization underpins the whole piece. The rest of the cast make a splendid team: Jean Hindmarsh is a totally convincing Josephine – she sings with great charm – and John Reed's Sir Joseph Porter is a delight.

The D'Oyly Carte set of *The Gondoliers* has now been remastered and the quality brought up to Decca's usual high standard. The solo singing throughout is consistently good, the ensembles have plenty of spirit and the dialogue is for the most part well spoken. As a performance this is on the whole preferable to the Sargent account, if only because of the curiously slow tempo Sargent chooses for the *Cachucha*. However, on EMI there is still much to captivate the ear, and Owen Brannigan, a perfectly cast Don Alhambra, sings a masterly *No possible doubt whatever*. The age of the 1957 recording shows in the orchestra but the voices sound fresh and there is a pleasing overall bloom.

With *Iolanthe*, choice between the two alternatives is a case of swings and roundabouts. The 1960 Decca set was given added panache by the introduction of the Grenadier Guards Band into the *March of the Peers*. Mary Sansom is quite a convincing Phyllis, and if her singing has not the sense of style that Elsie Morison brings to the part, she is completely at home with the dialogue. Also Alan Styler makes a vivid and charming personal identification with the role of Strephon, an Arcadian shepherd, whereas John Cameron's dark timbre on EMI seems much less suitable for this role, even though he sings handsomely. However, on EMI the climax of Act I, the scene in which the Queen of the Fairies lays a curse on members of both Houses of Parliament, shows most excitingly what can be achieved with the 'full operatic treatment': this is a dramatic moment indeed. George Baker, too, is very good as the Lord Chancellor: the voice is fuller, more baritonal than John Reed's dryly whimsical delivery, yet he provides an equally individual characterization. Godfrey's conducting is lighter and more infectious than Sargent's in the Act I finale, but both performances offer much to delight the ear in the famous Trio of Act II with the Lord Chancellor and the two Earls.

The 1973 stereo remake of *The Mikado* by the D'Oyly Carte Company directed by Royston Nash is a complete success in every way and shows the Savoy tradition at its most attractive. It is a pity no dialogue is included, but the choral singing is first rate, and the glees are refreshingly done, polished and refined, yet with plenty of vitality. John Reed is a splendid Ko-Ko, Kenneth Sandford a vintage Pooh-Bah and Valerie Masterson a charming Yum-Yum. John Ayldon as the Mikado provides a laugh of terrifying bravura, and Lyndsie Holland is a formidable and commanding Katisha. The Sargent set, with its grand operatic style, brings some fine moments, especially in the finales to both Acts. Owen Brannigan is an inimitable Mikado and Richard Lewis sings most engagingly throughout as Nanki-Poo, while Elsie Morison is freshly persuasive as his young bride-to-be. All in all, there is much to enjoy here, but this remains very much a second choice.

Owen Brannigan was surely born to play the Sergeant of Police in *The Pirates of Penzance*, and he does so unforgettably in both the Decca and EMI sets. On Decca there is a considerable advantage in the inclusion of the dialogue, and here theatrical spontaneity is well maintained. Donald Adams is a splendid Pirate King. John Reed's portrayal of the Major-General is one of his strongest roles, while Valerie Masterson is an excellent Mabel. Godfrey's conducting is as affectionate as ever, and one can hear him revelling in the many added touches of colour that are made possible when he has the RPO to play for him. Sargent's version is great fun, too. Its star is George Baker, giving a new and individual portrayal of the Major-General. The opera takes a little while to warm up, but there is much to enjoy here. On balance, the Decca set is to be preferred, for Brannigan is especially vivid, and the dialogue undoubtedly adds an extra sense of the theatre.

A 62-minute selection from the vintage 1968 Decca set is self-recommending. The CD transfer is bright and lively, to the point of a degree of sibilance on the solo voices, but there is plenty of theatrical atmosphere.

Patience and *Ruddigore* were the two greatest successes of the Sargent series. Although there is no dialogue in *Patience*, there is more business than is usual in these EMI productions and a convincing theatrical atmosphere. Elsie Morison's Patience, George Baker's Bunthorne and John Cameron's Grosvenor are all admirably characterized, and the many concerted numbers beguile the ear. The extra card in the D'Oyly Carte hand is the dialogue, so important in this opera above all, with its spoken poetry; if Mary Sansom does not quite match her EMI counterpart, both Bunthorne and Grosvenor are well played, while the military numbers, led by Donald Adams in glorious voice, have an unforgettable vigour and presence. The EMI *Ruddigore* is musically superior. The whole performance is beautifully sung and Sargent's essentially lyrical approach emphasizes the associations of this delightful score with the music of Schubert. Pamela Bowden is a first-class Mad Margaret and her duet – after she has reformed – with Owen Brannigan has an irresistible gentility. The drama of the score is well managed too, and the CD transfer is first class.

There is even an interesting bonus in Sullivan's Shakespearean incidental music. But here there is competition from the That's Entertainment set, which includes the original finale – see below.

The D'Oyly Carte *Ruddigore*, too, comes up surprisingly freshly, in fact better than we had remembered it, though it is a pity the dialogue was omitted. The performance includes *The battle's roar is over*, which is (for whatever reason) traditionally omitted. There is much to enjoy here (especially Gillian Knight and Donald Adams, whose *Ghosts' high noon* song is a marvellous highlight). Isidore Godfrey is his inimitable sprightly self and the chorus and orchestra are excellent. A fine traditional D'Oyly Carte set, then, brightly recorded, even if in this instance the Sargent version is generally even finer.

Princess Ida is fake feminism with a vengeance, but it makes for a very entertaining opera. Sir Malcolm Sargent is completely at home here, and his broadly lyrical approach has much to offer in this 'grandest' of the Savoy operas. Elizabeth Harwood in the name-part sings splendidly, and John Reed's irritably gruff portrayal of the irascible King Gama is memorable; he certainly is a properly 'disagreeable man'. The rest of the cast is no less strong and, with excellent teamwork from the company as a whole and a splendid recording, spacious and immediate, this has much to offer, even if Sullivan's invention is somewhat variable in quality. The CD transfer is outstanding and the 1965 recording has splendid depth and presence. As a bonus we are offered Mackerras's 1982 digital recording of his scintillating ballet score, *Pineapple Poll*. Mackerras conducts with warmth as well as vivacity, and the elegantly polished playing of the Philharmonia Orchestra gives much pleasure.

Both recordings of *The Yeomen of the Guard*, Decca's and EMI's, are conducted by Sir Malcolm Sargent. Each has many merits. On EMI all the solo singing is very persuasive indeed, and the presence of Owen Brannigan as Wilfred is very much a plus point, while Monica Sinclair is a memorable Dame Carruthers. In both versions the trios and quartets with which this score abounds are most beautifully warm and polished. But the later Decca account has marginally the finer recording and Sir Malcolm's breadth of approach is immediately apparent in the *Overture*. Both chorus and orchestra (the RPO) are superbly expansive and there is again consistently fine singing from all the principals (and especially from Elizabeth Harwood as Elsie). This Decca *Yeomen* is unreservedly a success, with its brilliant and atmospheric recording. In any case, the trump card is the inclusion of Godfrey's immaculately stylish and affectionate *Trial by Jury* with John Reed as the Judge.

Other complete recordings

(i) *HMS Pinafore* (complete with dialogue); (ii) *The Mikado; The Pirates of Penzance:* excerpts.
(M) * Decca Phase Four 455 160-2 (2) [id.]. (i–ii) Valerie Masterson, John Reed; (i) Thomas Lawlor, Ralph Mason, John Ayldon, Christine Palmer; (ii) Donald Adams, Philip Potter, Kenneth Sandford, Soloists, D'Oyly Carte Op. Co. O, (i) James Walker; (ii) Sir Malcolm Sargent.

The Phase Four set is an artistic disaster. For a brief period after Isidore Godfrey had retired, the D'Oyly Carte company was conducted by James Walker, who was also a Decca recording producer, and it was probably he who persuaded Tony D'Amato to re-record *HMS Pinafore* at Decca's West Hampstead studio in 1971. The result is a perfect demonstration of how *not* to present Gilbert and Sullivan on record. There is no suggestion of an overall stage acoustic and the voices are often unrealistically close and dry (although the words are made crystal clear in this way). Extra background noises, including seagulls and lapping water, are added ad lib. to no artistic effect whatsoever, and there is a total lack of theatrical atmosphere. The performance is redeemed by a vintage portrayal of Sir Joseph Porter, K.C.B., by John Reed and a fresh account of Josephine's songs from Valerie Masterson (which deserve to be preserved in another form). Otherwise the whole presentation is undistinguished. James Walker directs the jaunty numbers in a curiously clipped manner and with an absence of rhythmic lightness, and there is little spontaneity anywhere; even the famous *Wedding bells* trio in Act II is dull. The dialogue is poorly directed and sounds very self-conscious. The fill-up is a set of rather curiously chosen excerpts from *The Pirates of Penzance* and *The Mikado*, recorded (also in Phase Four) six years earlier and directed somewhat more felicitously by Sir Malcolm Sargent. The sound is slightly better here, with more ambience, and the memorable items are *A wand'ring minstrel* (very nicely turned by Philip Potter) and Donald Adams's superb version of the Mikado's famous song (that laugh sounds even more horrifying than usual in Phase Four). He also sings, rather gratingly, and without geniality, the *Policeman's song* from *Pirates* after the members of his force have clumped in, apparently wearing hobnailed boots. According to the booklet, the set was planned to include also some excerpts from *Ruddigore*, recorded at the same time, but they are not listed and they are not here.

(i) *Iolanthe:* highlights; (ii) *The Mikado* (complete, without dialogue).
(B) *** CfP CD-CDPD 4730 (2) [(M) id.]. (i) Shilling, Harwood, Moyle, Dowling, Begg, Bevan, Greene, Kern; (ii) Holmes, Revill, Wakefield, Studholme, Dowling, Allister, John Heddle Nash; Sadler's Wells Op. Ch. & O, Alexander Faris.

It is a shame that only highlights are available from the 1962 Sadler's Wells *Iolanthe*, making a rather piecemeal selection; but this means they will fit handily on to a pair of CDs together with the excellent complete *Mikado* from the same year. The Sadler's Wells *Iolanthe* is stylistically superior to Sargent's earlier EMI recording and is often musically superior to the Decca/D'Oyly Carte versions. Alexander Faris often chooses untraditional tempi. *When I went to the bar* is very much faster than usual, with less dignity but with a compensating lightness of touch. Eric Shilling is excellent here, as he is also in the *Nightmare song*, which is really *sung*, much being made of the ham operatic recitative at the beginning. The lovers, Elizabeth Harwood as Phyllis and Julian Moyle as Strephon, make a charming duo, and the Peers are splendid. Their entry chorus is thrilling and their reaction to the Fairy Queen's curse is delightfully, emphatically horrified, while the whole Act I finale (the finest in any of the operas) goes with infectious stylishness. All the solo singing is of a high standard and Leon Greene sings the Sentry song well. But one has to single out special praise for Patricia Kern's really lovely singing of Iolanthe's aria at the end of the opera. The recording has splendid presence and realism.

The Sadler's Wells *Mikado* is traditional in the best sense, bringing a humorous sparkle to the proceedings, which gives great delight. Clive Revill is a splendid Ko-Ko; his performance of *Tit willow* and his verse of *The flowers that bloom in the spring* (aided by a momentary touch of stereo gimmickry) have a charming individuality. John Heddle Nash is an outstanding Pish-Tush, and it is partly because of him that the *Chippy chopper* trio is so effective. Denis Dowling is a superb Pooh-Bah, and Marion Studholme a charming Yum-Yum. Jean Allister's Katisha is first rate in every way. The part is taken very seriously and she is often very dramatic; listen to the venom she puts into the word '*bravado*' in the Act I finale. Even the chorus scores a new point by their stylized singing of *Mi-ya-sa-ma*, which sounds engagingly mock-Japanese. The one disappointment is John Holmes in the name-part. He sings well but conveys little of the mock-satanic quality. But this is a small point in an otherwise magnificent set, which has a vivacious new overture arranged by Charles Mackerras.

Collections

Highlights from: *The Gondoliers; HMS Pinafore; Iolanthe; The Mikado; The Pirates of Penzance; The Yeomen of the Guard.*
(B) **(*) CfP CD-CFP 4238 [(M) id.]. Soloists, Glyndebourne Festival Ch., Pro Arte O, Sargent.

Another attractive selection of highlights offering samples of six of Sargent's vintage EMI recordings. There is some distinguished solo singing and, if the atmosphere is sometimes a little cosy, there is a great deal to enjoy. The recordings have transferred well.

'The very best of Gilbert and Sullivan': extracts from: (i; iv) *The Gondoliers: We're called Gondolieri; In enterprise of martial kind; Take a pair of sparkling eyes; Dance a cachucha; From the sunny Spanish shore; I stole the prince; Then one of us will be a queen. HMS Pinafore: When I was a lad; I'm called little Buttercup; Never mind the why and wherefore; We sail the ocean blue; I'm called the captain of the 'Pinafore'; Oh Joy! Oh rapture unforeseen. Iolanthe: Loudly let the trumpet bray; Love unrequited; If you go in, you're sure to win; When all night long a chap remains; Said I to myself, said I; When Britain really ruled the waves.* (ii; v) *The Mikado: Three little maids from school are we; A wand'ring minstrel; On a tree by a river a little tom-tit; Behold the Lord High Executioner; As some day it may happen; The sun whose rays; Here's a how-de-do; The flowers that bloom in the spring; There is beauty in the bellow of the blast; For he's gone and married Yum-Yum.* (i; iv) *Patience: The soldiers of our queen; Am I alone and unobserved?; If you're anxious for to shine; So go to him and say to him.* (ii; iv) *The Pirates of Penzance: With cat-like tread; Poor wand'ring one; I am the very model of a modern major-general; When the foeman bares his steel; When a felon's not engaged in his employment.* (ii; vi) *Princess Ida: If you give me your attention; The woman of the wisest wit; I built upon a rock; Whene'er I spoke sarcastic joke; This helmet I suppose. Ruddigore: I know a youth who loves a little maid; When the night wind howls; My eyes are fully open to my awful situation.* (ii; iv) *The Sorcerer: My name is John Wellington Wells.* (iii–iv) *Trial by Jury: When, I good friends, was called to the bar.* (ii; vi) *The Yeomen of the Guard: When our gallant Norman foes; I have a song to sing, O!; When maiden loves, she sits and sighs; Tower warders.*
✿ (B) *** Decca Double 460 010-2 (2) [id.]. John Reed, Valerie Masterson, Gillian Knight, Thomas Round, Donald Adams, Kenneth Sandford, Joyce Wright, Owen Brannigan, Jennifer Toye, Alan Styler

and soloists, D'Oyly Carte Op. Ch., (i) New SO; (ii) RPO; (iii) ROHCG O; cond. (iv) Isidore Godfrey; (v) Royston Nash; (vi) Sir Malcolm Sargent.

If you are looking for a CD to cheer you up on a dull day, either of the pair which make up this Double Decca will serve admirably. The overall selection (jointly conceived and compiled by Dickon Stainer and Bill Holland at Polygram) earns full marks for perception and variety. *The Mikado* is (understandably) the most generously treated, including ten items (though surprisingly omitting *Brightly dawns our wedding day*), while one wishes room could have been found for *A magnet hung in a hardware shop* and *Prithee, pretty maiden* from *Patience*. But the only real miscalculation was to end the second disc with the trio, *This helmet I suppose* from *Princess Ida*, which, following immediately after John Reed's delicious *Whene'er I spoke sarcastic joke*, comes as an anticlimax. The joyous trio, *If you go in, you're sure to win*, from *Iolanthe* (which comes earlier) would have been more effective or, better still, the Act I finale, which is omitted and for which there would have just about been room. Yet this is carping. The consistent wit of Gilbert's words, the delightful Sullivan melodies and the sparkle of Godfrey's conducting are a constant joy, and the Decca recording has superb definition (every word is audible) plus admirable stage atmosphere and warmth. It is the appealing vocal personality of John Reed which dominates, shining brightly as Koko, more sardonic as Sir Joseph Porter, delectably pompous as the Major-General in *Pirates* and charmingly lyrical as the diffident hero of *Ruddigore*. Reed's virtuoso account of *My name is John Wellington Wells* is a *tour de force*, matched only by the vocal gymnastics of the patter trio, *My eyes are fully open* (*Ruddigore*). Donald Adams's *Ghost's high noon* from the same opera is unforgettable, as is Owen Brannigan's wonderfully genial *Policeman's song* from *The Pirates of Penzance*, while Valerie Masterson's *Poor wandering one* confirms her as the most charming Mabel on record. The chosen version of *The Mikado* was the 1973 re-make, conducted by Royston Nash, which was very successful, and it is Sir Malcolm Sargent who directs the excerpts from *The Yeomen of the Guard*, bringing an apt link with a previous era of recordings of the Savoy operas. This Double Decca replaces two previous Decca CDs of '*The world of Gilbert and Sullivan*', Volumes I and II (430 095-2 and 433 868-2). At the moment these discs remain available and offer a somewhat different coverage.

Suppé, Franz von (1819–95)

Overtures: *Beautiful Galathea; Boccaccio; Light cavalry; Morning, noon and night in Vienna; Pique dame; Poet and peasant.*
(M) *** Mercury 434 309-2 [id.]. Detroit SO, Paul Paray – AUBER: *Overtures.* *** ✿

Listening to Paray, one discovers a verve and exhilaration that are wholly Gallic in spirit. His chimerical approach to *Beautiful Galathea* (with a wonderfully luminous passage from the Detroit strings near the very opening) is captivating, and the bravura violin playing in *Light Cavalry* is remarkably deft. With its splendid Auber coupling this is one of Mercury's most desirable reissues.

Overtures: *Beautiful Galathea; Fatinitza; Flotte Bursche; Jolly robbers; Light cavalry; Morning, noon and night in Vienna; Pique dame; Poet and peasant. March: O du mein Osterreich.*
(BB) **(*) LaserLight Dig. 15 611 [id.]. Hungarian State Op. O, János Sándor.

Sándor's LaserLight collection is very generous and the Hungarian State Opera Orchestra know just how to play this repertoire: the *zigeuner* section in the middle of *Light cavalry* is most winning, while the cello solo in *Morning, noon and night* has an attractive, romantic simplicity. Sándor offers two extra novelties in *Flotte Bursche* (which brings an amiable quotation of *Gaudeamus igitur*) and a vivid Viennese-style march. The digital recording is basically full-bodied but has brilliance too, and this is a real bargain.

Overtures: Disc 1: *Beautiful Galathea; Jolly robbers (Banditenstreiche); Light cavalry; Morning, noon and night in Vienna; Pique dame; Poet and peasant.* Disc 2: *Fatinitza; Die Frau Meisterin; Der Gascogner; Die Irrfahrt um's Glück; Juanita; Das Modell; Wiener-Jubel.*
(B) *** RCA Twofer Dig. 74321 34174-2 [(M) id. import]. RPO, Gustav Kuhn.

By joining up Gustav Kuhn's two separate collections in a Twofer, RCA have created the most comprehensive single grouping of Suppé overtures in the catalogue. The first disc assembles the six best known, including the four popular favourites, among which *Beautiful Galathea* stands out; the second, equally distinctive, offers seven hardly less memorable novelties. Kuhn lavishes much care over detail. Tempi are spacious, generally slower than usual, but the effect is not to rob the music of vitality, rather to add to its stature. In the lyrical sections he conjures the most beautiful, expansive playing from the RPO, yet he can be racy in the galops while not rushing the music off its feet. The second programme is especially valuable in offering CD débuts for three items. Kuhn is in his element in the powerfully solemn opening of *Die Irrfahrt um's Glück* with its magical/mystical portents; yet the more volatile introduction to *Donna Juanita* is hardly less telling, and very beautifully played. Throughout, Kuhn seeks to remove any suggestion of cheapness from the music, and these are performances of real breadth. While they do not have the unbuttoned gusto of some versions, the added gravitas more than compensates. Full, resonant recording of very high quality adds to this impression.

Svendsen, Johan Severin (1840–1911)

Romance in G, Op. 26.

(BB) *** Naxos Dig. 8.550329 [id.]. Dong-Suk Kang, Slovak (Bratislava) RSO, Adrian Leaper – HALVORSEN: *Air Norvégien* etc.; SIBELIUS: *Violin concerto;* SINDING: *Légende.* ***

Dong-Suk Kang plays Svendsen's once-popular *Romance in G* without sentimentality but with full-hearted lyricism. The balance places him a little too forward, but the recording is very satisfactory.

Szymanowski, Karol (1882–1937)

(i) *Violin concerto No. 2, Op. 62;* (ii) *Symphonies Nos. 2, Op. 19;* (iii) *3 (Song of the night), Op. 7.*

(B) **(*) Decca Double Dig. 448 258-2 (2) [(M) id. import]. (i) Juillet, Montreal SO, Dutoit; (ii) Detroit SO, Dorati; (iii) with Karczykowski, Jewell Ch. – LUTOSLAWSKI: *Concerto for orchestra* etc. **(*)

Chantal Juillet is a selfless and dedicated interpreter of the *Second Violin concerto* and she is truthfully balanced. Indeed the engineers might have helped her a little, for her small tone does not always sing through Szymanowski's opulently coloured textures. But the orchestral detail emerges with great fidelity and Dutoit's conducting is unfailingly sympathetic. So is Dorati in the two symphonies, and the Decca recording is better detailed than the competing EMI version, with the richness of Szymanowski's textures fully revealed and the chorus clear and well balanced in No. 3. If the Polish performances are in some ways more penetrating, there is no doubting the superiority of the Decca sound.

(i) *Harnasie (ballet pantomime), Op. 55;* (ii) *Mandragora (pantomime), Op. 43; Etude for orchestra in B flat min., Op. 3* (orch. Fitelberg).

(BB) *** Naxos Dig. 8.553686 [id.]. Polish State PO (Katowice), Karol Stryja; (i) with Henryk Grychnik, Polish State PO Ch.; Stanislaw Meus.

Harnasie, like the Op. 50 *Mazurkas*, is the fruit of Szymanowski's encounter with the Polish folk music of the Góral mountains, and its heady exoticism is quite captivating. Stryja's recording is a good one and, though not quite as intoxicating as the full-price Satanowski on Koch, runs it pretty close. Like its rival, it is coupled with *Mandragora*, a harlequinade for chamber forces from 1920 – not Szymanowski at his most fully characteristic but a cultivated and intelligent score. Worth the money.

Symphonies Nos. 1 in F min., Op. 15; 2 in B flat, Op. 19.

(BB) *** Naxos Dig. 8.553683 [id.]. Polish State PO (Katowice), Karol Stryja.

The two-movement *First Symphony* (1906–7) was first performed in 1909 and was received coolly. Szymanowski withdrew it as a 'contrapuntal-harmonic-orchestral monster' and for long it remained unpublished. Alistair Wightman called it heavily overscored even by the standards of the period. The *Second*, which Fitelberg premièred in 1911 and recorded in the early 1950s, is heavily indebted to Reger, Scriabin and Strauss. It is overlong and overscored, but it contains original and memorable passages that perhaps justify stronger claims on the catalogue and the concert hall than it has enjoyed so far. In its previous incarnation on the Marco Polo label this had two stars but, given the modest price asked and on the principle that it justifies the modest expense involved, it deserves upgrading.

Symphonies Nos. (i) *2;* (ii) *3;* (i) *Concert overture in E, Op. 12.*

(M) *** EMI CDM5 65082-2. Polish R. Nat. SO; (i) cond. Jacek Kasprzyk; (ii) Wieslaw Ochman, Polish R. Ch. of Krakow, cond. Jerzy Semkow.

The *Second* is not as rewarding a score as the *Third*, but it is unusual in form: there are only two movements, the second being a set of variations culminating in a fugue. The influences of Strauss and Scriabin are clearly audible and not altogether assimilated. *The Song of the night* is one of the composer's most beautiful scores with its heady, intoxicated – and intoxicating – atmosphere. The Polish Radio recordings on EMI date from 1982 and the performances are the most atmospheric and sensitive currently available. The recording is expansive and has impressive atmosphere. The EMI disc also includes a gripping account of the ambitious *Concert overture*, for all the world like an undiscovered symphonic poem by Richard Strauss.

Symphonies Nos. (i) *3 (Song of the night), Op. 27;* (ii) *4 (Symphonie concertante), Op. 60. Concert overture, Op. 12.*
(BB) *** Naxos Dig. 8.553684 [id.]. (i) Wieslaw Ochmann, Polish State Philharmonic Ch.; (ii) Taduesz Zmudzinski; Polish State PO (Katowice), Karol Stryja.

Stryja's set of the *Song of the night* and the *Fourth Symphony* offers a well-filled disc that is worth its asking price. He uses a tenor in the *Third Symphony* and, although he does not produce the luxuriant and heady atmosphere of Witold Rowicki's (now deleted) version, it is well worth considering. Taduesz Zmudzinski is an effective soloist in the *Fourth Symphony* or *Sinfonia concertante* for piano and orchestra, though this is not the equal of the 1982 EMI version with Piotr Paleczny, recorded at the time of the Szymanowski centenary. The performance of the Straussian and derivative *Concert overture* is as persuasive as it can be – to be frank, the piece is really rather tedious. The sound in the *Third Symphony* is good, in the remaining pieces rather less impressive but still acceptable.

(i) *Symphony No. 4 (Symphonie concertante), Op. 60;* (ii) *Harnasie* (ballet pantomime), *Op. 55.*
(M) **(*) EMI CDM5 65307-2. (i) Piotr Paleczny, Polish Nat. RSO, Jerzy Semkow; (ii) Bachleda, Kwasny, Krakow Polish R. Ch. & SO, Antoni Wit.

Piotr Paleczny is no mean artist and he has all the finesse and imagination as well as the requisite command of colour that the *Symphonie concertante* calls for; Wit provides him with admirable support. On the whole this makes an even stronger impression than the alternative performance on Naxos, which anyway is differently coupled. *Harnasie* is also very successful: it reflects Szymanowski's discovery of the folk music of the Tatras. It calls for large forces, including a solo violinist as well as a tenor and full chorus, and poses obvious practical production problems. As always with this composer, there is the sense of rapture, the soaring, ecstatic lines and the intoxicating exoticism that distinguish the mature Szymanowski, and it comes across most tellingly here. The only snag is that the sound, though spaciously wide-ranging, is made a bit fierce on top by the CD remastering.

CHAMBER MUSIC

Mythes, Op. 30; Kurpian folk song; King Roger: Roxana's aria (both arr. Kochanski).
✿ (M) *** DG 431 469-2. Kaja Danczowska, Krystian Zimerman – FRANCK: *Violin sonata.* ***

Kaja Danczowska brings vision and poetry to the ecstatic, soaring lines of the opening movement of *Mythes, The Fountains of Arethusa*. Her intonation is impeccable, and she has the measure of these other-worldly, intoxicating scores. There is a sense of rapture here that is totally persuasive, and Krystian Zimerman plays with a virtuosity and imagination that silence criticism. An indispensable issue.

Violin sonata in D min., Op. 9; La Berceuse d'Aïtacho Enia, Op. 52; 3 Mythes, Op. 30; Notturno e Tarantella, Op. 28; Romance in D, Op. 23. arr.: *3 Paganini caprices, Op. 40.*
(BB) *** ASV Quicksilva Dig. CDQS 6215 [(M) id.]. Detlef Hahn, Mark Fielding.

Detlef Hahn and Mark Fielding survey Szymanowski's output for violin and piano in chronological order, starting with the early *D minor Sonata*, which Pawel Kochanski and Artur Rubinstein premièred in 1904, and ending with *La Berceuse d'Aïtacho Enia*, named after the villa in France in which Szymanowski spent a period of convalescence in 1925. With Hahn producing consistently rich, full tone, the warmth of the writing is brought out most persuasively, and the chronological arrangement of the pieces lets one appreciate the stylistic development of the composer from the *Sonata*, Brahmsian with Slavonic tinges, through to the highly imaginative writing of the later years from 1915 onwards. That was the watershed year which produced both the *Notturno e tarantella* and the three *Mythes*, with their highly original and imaginative use of the violin, not least in the first of the three, *The Fountain of Arethusa*. Both artists have a good feel for Szymanowski as can be heard in that evocative piece. The sound is basically full, but the upper range is rather bright. The piano is subjected to too close a scrutiny, and there is at times a hint of glare. This is not enough to inhibit a strong recommendation, for the artists respond to the music with great sympathy and their playing gives much pleasure.

PIANO MUSIC

4 Etudes, Op. 4; Mazurkas, Op. 50/1–4; Metopes, Op. 29; Piano sonata No. 2 in A, Op. 21.
(BB) *** Naxos Dig. 8.553016-2 [id.]. Martin Roscoe.

Fantasia in C, Op. 14; Masques, Op. 34; Mazurkas, Op. 50/5–12; Variations on a Polish theme, Op. 10.
(BB) *** Naxos Dig. 8.553300 [id.]. Martin Roscoe.

Martin Roscoe proves a perceptive and sensitive interpreter of Szymanowski and the first two discs augur well for this ongoing series. In the four *Mazurkas*, Op. 50, that open the first CD he shows real feeling and insight. He is equally persuasive in the early Chopinesque *Etudes*, Op. 4, and the refined impressionism of *Metopes*. The *Second Sonata*, composed for (but rarely played by) Rubinstein, is a problematic piece, full of virtuosic hurdles, romantic gestures and Regerian ingenuity. The second disc gives us the *C major Fantasy*, Op. 14, and the Op. 10 *Variations*, in which the debts to Scriabin and Chopin have yet to be fully discharged. A fine account of the *Masques*, too. This is playing of quality. As far as recording is concerned, Martin Roscoe is well served.

4 Etudes, Op. 4; 12 Etudes, Op. 33; 2 Mazurkas, Op. 62; Shéhérezade (Masques), Op. 34; Variations on a Polish theme, Op. 10.
(M) ** Channel Classics Dig. CDG 9110. Arielle Vernède.

In the repertoire that overlaps Martin Roscoe's fine Naxos anthology, Arielle Vernède offers little real challenge, though her playing is far from wanting in distinction and character. The recital does not include the Op. 10 *Variations* or the demanding but (it must be admitted) unrewarding Op. 33 *Etudes*, and this mid-price CD can be thought of as a useful supplement but not an alternative to the pair of CDs.

VOCAL MUSIC

(i) *Demeter, Op. 37b;* (ii) *Litany to the Virgin Mary;* (iii) *Penthesilea;* (iv) *Stabat Mater, Op. 53;* (v) *Veni Creator, Op. 57.*
(BB) *** Naxos Dig. 553687 [id.]. Polish State PO (Katowice), Karol Stryja, with (i) Anna Malewicz-Madej; (iii) Roma Owsinska; (iv) Jadwiga Gadulanka, Krystyna Szostek-Radkowa, Andrzej Hiolski; (v) Barbara Zogórzanka; (i–ii; iv–v) Polish State Ch., Katowice.

Szymanowski's *Stabat Mater* is not only one of his greatest achievements but one of the greatest choral works of the present century. This welcome account has the advantage of highly sensitive conducting and an excellent response from the orchestra, but some of the solo singing is less distinguished, and Jadwiga Gadulanka's intonation is less than perfect. The *Litany to the Virgin Mary* is another late work of great poignancy; but *Demeter*, composed not long after the *Violin concerto* and the *Third Symphony*, has the same exotic, almost hallucinatory textures that distinguish these works. It is all heady and intoxicating stuff, and not to be missed by those with a taste for this wonderful composer.

(i) *3 Fragments of the poems by Jan Kasprowicz, Op. 5;* (ii) *Love songs of Hafiz, Op. 24;* (iii) *Songs of the fairy-tale princess, Op. 31;* (iv) *Songs of the infatuated muezzin, Op. 42;* (v) *King Roger: Roxana's Song.*
(BB) **(*) Naxos Dig. 8.553688 [id.]. (i) Anna Malewicz-Madej; (ii & iv) Ryszard Minkiewicz; (iii) Jadwiga Gadulanka; (v) Barbara Zagórzanka; Katowice Polish State PO, Karol Stryja.

On Naxos, both the *Songs of the infatuated muezzin* and the *Love songs of Hafiz* are sung by a tenor (Ryszard Minkiewicz) with impressive insight, but the 1989 recording is more resonant and does not flatter him. Jadwiga Gadulanka is hardly less impressive than Klosinska in the extraordinary *Songs of the fairy-tale princess* and Barbara Zagórzanka sings the famous *Chant de Roxane* beautifully, and both she and Anna Malewicz-Madej in the Kasprowicz songs are very well balanced.

(i) *King Roger* (opera; complete); (ii) *Prince Potemkin: incidental music to Act V.*
(BB) *(*) Naxos Dig. 8.660062/63 [id.]. Hiolski, Ochman, Zagórzanka, Grychnik, Mróz, Malewicz-Madej, Cracow Philh. Boys' Ch., Polish State Philh. Ch. & O (Katowice), Karol Stryja; (ii) Polish Nat. RSO (Katowice), Antoni Wit.

King Roger has one of the most inspired and awe-inspiring openings in all twentieth-century opera and in Roxana's aria one of the most captivating and haunting of musical ideas. Its first Act, still composed in the exotic, heavily scented and heady atmosphere of the *First Violin concerto* and the *Song of the night*, is at variance with the sparer textures of his later folk-inflected idiom, which surfaces in the last part of the opera. There is some good singing from the Roxana of Barbara Zagórzanka and the Shepherd of Wieslaw Ochman, though it must be conceded that Andrzej Hiolski in the title-role is no longer as fresh-timbred or well-focused vocally as he was in Muza's pioneering LP version from the 1960s. But all this is academic, since the *sine qua non* of any *King Roger* is atmosphere – and this Naxos reissue of a set which first appeared on Marco Polo has all too little. It can be recommended only with the strongest reservations, the more so as the libretto comes without a translation. The incidental music from Act V of *Prince Potemkin* is only a short, ten-minute bonus.

Tallis, Thomas (*c.* 1505–85)

(i) *Audivi vocem;* (ii–iii) *Derelinquat impius;* (ii; iv) *Dum transisset sabbatum;* (ii–iii) *Ecce tempus idoneum;* (ii; iv) *Honor, virtus et potestas;* (ii–iii) *In ieiunio et fletu; In manus tuas; Lamentations of Jeremiah I and II;* (ii; iv) *Loquebantur variis linguis;* (ii–iii) *O nata lux de lumine; Salvator mundi; Sancte Deus; Spem in alium* (40-part motet); *Te lucis ante terminum* (2 settings); *Veni Redemptor gentium; Videte miraculum;* (i) *Te Deum.* (Organ) (v) *Clarifica me, pater; Fantasy; Iam lucis;* (vi) *Lesson*

(B) **(*) Decca Double Analogue/Dig. 455 029-2 (2) [id.]. (i) St John's College, Cambridge, Ch., Guest; (ii) King's College, Cambridge, Ch.; (iii) Willcocks; (iv) Cleobury; (v) Peter White; (vi) Andrew Davis.

Tallis is best known to most of us by the theme which Vaughan Williams used in his *Fantasia*. Here is a chance to get to know his music better (and relatively inexpensively) and to confirm that the curiously dark melodic colouring of the tune in the variations is typical. The performances traverse an impressive range of his output, even if they are slightly uneven in quality. The King's College Choir are in their element in music mostly written for Waltham Abbey or the Chapel Royal, whether conducted by Willcocks or Cleobury. The highlight of their programme is the magnificent 40-part motet, *Spem in alium*, in which the Cambridge University Musical Society joins forces with King's; but the simpler hymn-settings are no less impressive, with performances equally distinguished. The *Lamentations* are performed authentically, using men's voices only, and the singing, without being inexpressive, has the right element of restraint. The motets, *Sancte Deus* and *Videte miraculum*, are for full choir, and here the balance gives slight over-prominence to the trebles. The choir of St John's College under George Guest give an adequate performance of the *Te Deum* but sound happier in their motet, *Audivi vocem*. Andrew Davis is an excellent advocate of the *Organ Lesson*; the other two organ pieces are musically less interesting but are well played by Peter White. The (originally Argo) recording is full and atmospheric throughout, although the choral focus is not always sharp: the inner detail of *Spem in alium* is somewhat clouded by the King's resonance, yet its richness of sonority is very impressive indeed.

God grant we grace; Hear the voice and prayer; If ye love me; Spem in alium; In ieiunio et fletu; Lamentations, Parts I–II; Mihi autem nimis; O Lord give thy Holy Spirit; O nata lux de lumine; O sacrum convivium; Salvator mundi; Te lucis ante terminum.

(M) **(*) Carlton Classics 30366 00952 [id.]. Pro Cantione Antiqua, Mark Brown.

This well-planned and rewarding programme opens with a simple Psalm setting (more familiar as a hymn), *God grant we grace*, which is sung most beautifully. All the music is in four or (more often) five parts, intimately presented, with one voice to a part. The great 40-part motet, *Spem in alium*, which comes second, is the exception, and here the full 14-voiced group is augmented with 'friends'. It brings a spectacular contrast, but though the music reaches a rich climax Mark Brown's control of tension is uneven and there is a feeling at times that the music eddies rather than moving forward strongly. The highlight of the concert is the pair of *Lamentations*, Tallis's independent settings of the first two lessons for Maundy Thursday, which are movingly sung; and the group's refined, expressive style is heard at is best in the Latin hymns and motets, particularly the last three items, *Salvator mundi*, *O nata lux de lumine* and *Te lucis ante terminum*. The recording is natural and not too forwardly balanced, although it is surprising that at the climax of *Spem in alium* the complex polyphony is not noticeably clearer than in the more reverberant King's version under Sir David Willcocks.

Motets: *Ecce tempus idoneum; Gaude gloriosa Dei Mater; Loquebantur variis linguis; O nata lux de lumine; Spem in alium.*

(B) **(*) CfP CD-CFP 4638 [(M) id.]. Clerkes of Oxenford, David Wulstan – SHEPPARD: *Motets.* **(*)

A useful issue, since it not only juxtaposes motets by Tallis against those of his great (but less familiar) contemporary, John Sheppard, but also gives us a strongly sung bargain version of the famous 40-part motet, *Spem in alium*. Here the resonance of Merton College Chapel means that definition could be more refined, and throughout the programme David Wulstan's tempi are somewhat brisk, while at times there is also some sense of strain among the women. (Interestingly, Wulstan's timing for *Loquebantur variis linguis* is almost identical with that of Jeremy Summerly on Naxos, which yet feels slightly less tense.) Reservations notwithstanding, there are fine things on this inexpensive CD, and it can be recommended.

Alfred Deller Edition: *Lamentations of Jeremiah the Prophet*. 5 hymns: *Deus tuorum militum; Jam Christus astra ascenderat; Jesu Salvator Saeculi; O nata lux de lumine;Salvator mundi Domine.*

(M) ** Van. 08.5062 71 [id.]. Deller Consort (with Wilfred Brown, Gerald English, Eileen McLoughlin (in hymns)), Maurice Bevan, Deller.

Alfred Deller pioneered so much repertoire on LP, and even today Tallis's settings of the *Lamentations of Jeremiah* are not generously represented on disc. They are here given poised, expressive performances and the motets are presented with their alternating plainsong. However, there is comparatively little difference in dynamic range between the plainsong and the hymns, and the closely balanced recording robs the *Lamentations* of much of their atmosphere, while no real pianissimos are possible. The sound itself is full and truthful.

Mass for four voices; Motets: *Audivi vocem; In manus tuas Domine; Loquebantur variis linguis; O sacrum convivium; Salvator mundi; Sancte Deus; Te lucis ante terminum; Videte miraculum.*
(B) *** Naxos Dig. 8.550576 [id.]. Oxford Camerata, Jeremy Summerly.

The Oxford Camerata with their beautifully blended timbre have their own way with Tallis. Lines are firm, the singing has serenity but also a firm pulse. In the *Mass* (and particularly in the *Sanctus*) the expressive strength is quite strongly communicated, while the *Benedictus* moves on spontaneously at the close. The motets respond particularly well to Jeremy Summerly's degree of intensity. The opening *Loquebantur variis linguis* has much passionate feeling, and this (together with the *Audivi vocem*, and especially the lovely *Sante Deus*) shows this choir of a dozen singers at their most eloquent. The recording, made in the Chapel of Wellington College, is very fine indeed, and there is a brief musical note provided by the conductor. Excellent value.

Mass: Puer natus est nobis (for seven voices).
(M) *** EMI Dig. CDM5 65211-2. King's College, Cambridge, Ch., Ledger – BYRD: *Mass for 5 voices;* TYE: *Mass: Euge Bone.* ***

The magnificent seven-part writing in the *Mass* (a work assembled in recent years from a variety of sources – see below) contrasts well with the Byrd and Tye *Masses*, both masterpieces, with which it is coupled. The choir, at its finest, is beautifully recorded (digitally, in 1981, whereas the two couplings are analogue) against the ample acoustic of the King's Chapel.

Mass Puer natus est; Motets: *Salvatore mundi; Suscipe quaeso Dominus.*
✿ (B) *** Cal. CAL 6623 [(M) id.]. Clerkes of Oxenford, David Wulstan – WHITE: *Motets.* ***

A quite outstanding reissue, made the more desirable by the inclusion of the four very beautiful motets by the neglected Elizabethan contemporary of Tallis, Robert White. The Tallis *Mass* was reconstructed by David Wulstan and Sally Dunkley, prompted by the researches and speculations of Joseph Kerman and Jeremy Noble. The details are too complex to be outlined here, and the *Credo* exists only as a fragment, but the results are so beautiful that readers should on no account miss this record. The *Mass* is among the finest Tallis – and, for that matter, the finest music of the period – and it is performed with dedication and authority by these singers. There is no need to hesitate here: this is one of the most important recent reissues of early English choral music, and it is also one of the most successful artistically and technically, for the analogue recording could hardly be bettered.

Missa Salve intemerata Virgo.
(B) *** CfP Dig. CD-CFP 4654 [(M) id.]. St John's College, Cambridge, Ch., George Guest – TAVERNER: *Western wynde mass & song.* ***

Taverner's Mass, *The Western wynde*, with which this is coupled, is based on the celebrated popular tune of the day, while the Tallis derives from an earlier motet of the same name. But the *Missa Salve intemerata Virgo* does in fact rework more of the original than is customary in parody Masses; only about a quarter is completely new. The Choir of St John's College, Cambridge, under George Guest is very well recorded and they give a very spirited account of themselves, very different from the small, chamber-like performances which are prevalent nowadays, but musically no less satisfying. At this price, a splendid bargain.

Taneyev, Sergei (1856–1915)

Suite de concert (for violin and orchestra), *Op. 28.*
(M) *** EMI CDM5 65419-2 [id.]. David Oistrakh, Philh. O, Malko – MIASKOVSKY: *Cello concerto.* *** ✿

David Oistrakh's superb account of Taneyev's attractively diverse *Suite*, ranging from rhapsodic ardour in the first (of five movements) to sparkling virtuosity in the *Tarantella* finale, has been available only rarely, even on LP. The early (1956) stereo is of high quality and few would guess the age of the recording from the present CD transfer, which is full-bodied and admirable.

Tartini, Giuseppe (1692–1770)

Concerti grossi Nos. 3 in C; 5 in E min. (trans. by Giulietto Menghini from *Sonatas, Op. 1/3 & 5*); (i) *Cello concerto in D. Violin concertos:* (ii) *in A min.;* (iii) *in G.*
(B) *** HM Dig. HMX 290853.55 (3) [(M) id.]. (i) Roel Dieltiens; (ii) Enrico Gatti; (iii) Chiara Banchieri; Ens. 315 – CORELLI: *Trio sonatas, Op. 5/1–6.* VIVALDI: *Chamber sonatas.* ***

Here Banchieri's flexible Ensemble 315 expands to become a chamber orchestra (8;2;2;2) and in the *Cello concerto* horns are added. All three works have eloquent slow movements and they are played admirably, using period instruments very persuasively. The concertos are framed by a pair of *Concerti grossi* effectively arranged from two of Tartini's *Trio sonatas*. Warmly resonant sound ensures that orchestral textures are not wanting in body. The disc comes at bargain price in a slip-case in harness with *Sonatas* of Corelli and Vivaldi.

Cello concerto in A.
(B) *** DG Double 437 952-2 (2) [id.]. Rostropovich, Zurich Coll. Mus., Sacher – BERNSTEIN: *3 Meditations;* BOCCHERINI: *Cello concerto No. 2;* GLAZUNOV: *Chant du Ménestrel;* SHOSTAKOVICH: *Cello concerto No. 2;* TCHAIKOVSKY: *Andante cantabile* etc.; VIVALDI: *Cello concertos.* ***

As with the other works in this fine 1978 collection, Rostropovich's view of Tartini's *A major Concerto* is larger than life; but the eloquence of the playing disarms criticism, even when the cellist plays cadenzas of his own that are not exactly in period. This is part of a first-class Double DG anthology which can be recommended almost without reservation.

Violin concertos in C, D.2; F, D.67; A, D.96; A min., D.115; B min, D.125.
(M) ** Erato/Warner 0630 12988-2. Piero Toso, Sol. Ven., Claudio Scimone.

These are all attractive concertos. Toso plays them elegantly and is given smooth, warm and polished accompaniments. This is pleasing enough, but the end effect is a bit bland.

Violin concertos: in E min., D.56; in A, D.96; in A min., D.113.
(M) *** Erato/Warner 4509 92188-2. Uto Ughi, Sol. Ven.

Tartini is a composer of unfailing originality, and the three violin concertos on this record are all very rewarding. The *Concerto in A major*, which comes last on the disc, has an additional (probably) alternative slow movement, a *Largo Andante* which is particularly beautiful. Uto Ughi's performances are distinguished by excellent taste and refinement of tone, and I Solisti Veneti are hardly less polished. The harpsichord continuo is somewhat reticent, but otherwise the recording is exemplary. Highly recommended.

Tavener, John (born 1944)

The Protecting veil.
(M) ** Carlton Dig. 30366 01092 [id.]. Josephine Knight, E. Sinfonia, Bramwell Tovey – NYMAN: *Strong on Oaks, strong on the causes of Oaks.* **

John Tavener's meditation for cello and strings, *The Protecting veil*, was inspired by the miraculous appearance of the Virgin Mary in Constantinople in the tenth century. After its first performance in 1989 and subsequent recording with Steven Isserlis as soloist, it had an extraordinary popular success, intensely devotional music, spacious and seamless. It takes a magnetic performance for it fully to sustain its length, and here Josephine Knight with Tovey and the English Sinfonia cannot match the original performers, adopting as they do even broader speeds for a work here lasting over 50 minutes. Nor is the sound quite as beautiful as it should be. The original, full-priced Virgin/EMI issue is well worth the extra cost (VC7 59052-2).

Taverner, John (c. 1495–1545)

Mass: The Western wynde; Song: The Western wynde.
(B) *** CfP Dig. CD-CFP 4654 [(M) id.]. St John's Coll., Cambridge, Ch., George Guest – TALLIS: *Missa Salve intemerata Virgo.* ***

This St John's performance of John Taverner's mass, *The Western wynde*, is prefaced by the song on which both it and the motet of the same name are based. It also attracted both Tye and Sheppard. The Mass is basically a sequence of 36 variations of much subtlety and ingenuity on the theme and is one of the key works of the period. This spirited and robust performance by the Choir of St John's College, Cambridge, under George Guest is very well recorded; it is very different in style from the small, chamber-like, vibrato-free performances to which we are becoming accustomed (and by which we are becoming beguiled), but is every bit as valid. An admirable and, at this price, very economical introduction to the composer.

Mass: The Western Wynde; Christe Jesu pastor bone; Dum transisset Sabbatum; Kyrie Le Roy; Mater Christie.
(B) *** Decca Double 452 170-2 (2) [id.]. King's College, Cambridge, Ch., Willcocks – BYRD: *Masses for 3, 4 and 5 voices* etc. ***

John Taverner's remarkable individuality is admirably shown by this excellent King's concert. The *Western Wynde Mass* (so called because of its use of this secular tune as a constantly recurring ground) is a masterpiece of the highest order. Its lines soar to express rich expressive feeling, particularly in the *Sanctus*, and overall it is hauntingly memorable. The other music here also shows the composer's wide range of expressive power: the motets are by no means dwarfed by the Mass and are works of great beauty in their own right. With first-class King's performances, appropriately more extrovert in feeling than the coupled music of Byrd, this makes an outstanding collection, with the highly evocative 1961 (originally Argo) recording giving the trebles an abundant body of tone.

Tchaikovsky, Peter (1840–93)

Complete orchestral works

Volume I: (i) *Capriccio italien, Op. 45;* (ii) *Piano concerto Nos. 1–3, Opp. 23, 44 & 75; Andante and finale for piano and orchestra, Op. 79* (orch. Taneyev); *Concert fantasy for piano and orchestra, Op. 56.* (iii–iv) *Violin concerto, Op. 35.* (v; vii) *Francesca da Rimini, Op. 32.* (vi–vii) *Manfred symphony, Op. 58;* (i) *Marche slave, Op. 31;* (viii) *Pezzo capriccioso* (for cello and orchestra), *Op. 62;* (i) *Romeo and Juliet (fantasy overture);* (iii–iv) *Sérénade mélancolique* (for violin and orchestra), *Op. 62;* (vi–vii) *Symphonies Nos. 1–6;* (viii) *Variations on a Rococo theme (for cello and orchestra), Op. 33;* (iii–iv) *Valse scherzo* (for violin and orchestra), *Op. 34.*
(B) **(*) Ph. 456 187-2 (8) [(M) id. import]. (i) Concg. O, Haitink; (ii) Werner Haas, Monte Carlo Op. O, Inbal; (iii) Salvatore Accardo; (iv) BBC SO, C. Davis; (v) New Philh. O; (vi) LSO; (vii) Markevitch; (viii) Maurice Gendron, VSO, Dohnányi.

At the heart of Volume I of the Philips survey of Tchaikovsky's orchestral music is the first-class Markevitch set of the symphonies from the early 1960s. The layout involves a break after the first two movements of the *Fifth* which should not have been necessary, but the new CD transfers are otherwise admirable. The analogue sound is suitably resonant and full-bodied, brilliant without harshness. The CDs retain the bloom on the strings and provide a fine weight and sonority for the brass. Markevitch is a genuine Tchaikovskian and his readings are unidiosyncratic, without lacking personality or firmness of grip. There is fine momentum and plenty of ardour. For the *First Symphony* he finds the Mendelssohnian lightness in his fast pacing of the opening movement. In the *Little Russian* (No. 2) the opening horn solo is full of character and the allegro tautly rhythmic. The finale is striking for its bustling energy rather than its charm. The *Polish Symphony* (No. 3) has a comparably dynamic first movement, but the central movements are expansively warm, the ballet-music associations not missed. Nos. 4 to 6 are also available on a Duo (see below). No. 4 is totally compulsive. The close of the first movement, like the coda of the finale, brings the highest degree of tension and a real sense of triumph over adversity. No. 5 has a less flexible first movement, and some might feel that here the forward momentum is too hard pressed to let the secondary material really blossom, but the listener is carried along with the tide. The Waltz also is swift but does not lack grace. The finale by comparison has a firm momentum but is broadened uncharacteristically for its closing rhetoric. Markevitch is fully back on form in the *Pathétique*. There is no lack of passion or depth of feeling, and the third movement is a genuine Scherzo, but with the march culmination very satisfyingly handled. The close of the symphony has an elegiac quality, to complete a reading which has a wide emotional range and is gripping from first to last.

Manfred is rather less successful. Markevitch's account was the pioneering stereo recording in the mid-1960s, but with so ardently romantic a subject a more uninhibited approach is required, one that will provide the driving force in the fast movements and the coaxing delicacy in more relaxed moments. On neither count does Markevitch measure up to the finest versions, although the playing is of high quality and there are moments of drama in the outer movements. The recording is well up to standard and sounds much better here than on its original LP incarnation. Markevitch's *Francesca da Rimini* is certainly exciting. But soon after the opening the reading moves forward rather frenetically and feels too hard-driven to be completely convincing. Haitink could not be more different in the *Capriccio italien*, a warm-blooded account with the Concertegebouw string-playing elegantly turned. The restatement of the main theme at the end is given tremendous weight and – to be honest – sounds a bit phlegmatic; it also means that the coda gets under way rather too slowly. But within the rich Concertgebouw acoustic this is still distinctly enjoyable, as is the sombre yet vivid *Marche slave*, which benefits greatly from the spacious ambience. *Romeo and Juliet*, too, is a passionate account. But Haitink does not wear his heart on his sleeve and characteristically the reading has an element of nobility, with very fine string-playing in the love theme. The recording, if not sharply defined, has breadth and impact.

The collection of *Piano concertos* is notable for including the *Andante and finale*, put together and orchestrated by Taneyev. Werner Haas proves a brilliant and responsive soloist and dominates the performances. But he is let down by the comparatively inadequate orchestral playing of the Monte Carlo orchestra. These performances are not a write-off, for they have plenty of life, but they detract from the appeal of the box as a whole. They are discussed in detail under their separate, Duo issue, below.

Absolutely no reservations about Accardo's memorable account of the *Violin concerto* (which is given without cuts), and he is equally persuasive in the touching *Sérénade mélancholique* and the elegant *morceau* which Tchaikovsky designated a *Valse scherzo*. His is not a virtuoso display, but the playing has both poise and freshness, and plenty of flair. In the concerto there is a keen lyricism and a fine sense of line, and there is refinement and restraint in the slow movement that is ravishing in its gentle reverie. He is sensitively accompanied by Sir Colin Davis and the BBC Symphony Orchestra. The mid-1970s analogue recording is very good indeed. Maurice Gendron does not disappoint in the two concertante cello works. He plays both exceedingly well and, if his impetuous, romantic verve misses some of the elegance of the *Variations*, the lightweight *Pezzo capriccio* has considerable charm. Again natural recording (from the early 1960s). As with the *Violin concerto*, the solo balance is close. Overall this inexpensive box will give considerable satisfaction to any keen Tchaikovskian, and above all it underlines what an extraordinary tunesmith this greatest of Russian composers was.

Volume II:(i–ii) *1812 overture, Op. 49;* (iii) *Fatum, Op. 77;* (iv; ii) *Hamlet (fantasy overture), Op. 67a;* (i; v–vi) *Nutcracker* (complete ballet), *Op. 71;* (vii) *Serenade for strings in C, Op. 48;* (i; v) *Sleeping Beauty* (complete ballet), *Op. 66;* (vii) *Souvenir de Florence in D min., Op. 70;* (iii) *The Storm, Op. 76;* (iv–v) *Suites Nos. 1–3, Opp. 43, 53 & 55; 4 (Mozartiana), Op. 61;* (viii) *Swan Lake* (ballet): slightly abridged version *Op. 20;* (iii) *The Tempest, Op. 18*. Opera excerpts: (ix) *Cherevichi (The Caprices of Oxana): Introduction; Danse russe; Danse des cosaques. Eugene Onegin: Polonaise; Waltz; Ecossaise. The Maid of Orleans: Entr'acte; Danse des bohémiens; Danse de polichinelles et des histrions. The Oprichnik: Danses. The Sorceress: Introduction; Danse des histrions et scène.*

(B) **(*) Ph. Analogue/Dig. 456 188-2 (9) [(M) id. import]. (i) Concg. O; (ii) Markevitch; (iii) Frankfurt RSO, Inbal; (iv) New Philh. O; (v) Dorati; (vi) with Boys' Ch. of St Bavo Cathedral; (vii) Netherlands CO, Zinman; (viii) SRO, Ansermet; (ix) ROHCG O, Sir Colin Davis.

For the first of the three major ballet scores, Philips have turned to Dorati's dramatically vivid (1975) complete *Nutcracker*, gloriously played by the Concertgebouw Orchestra, as fine as any version in the catalogue, and also available separately on a Philips Duo – see below. However, in the present box the layout is less than ideal, with nearly all the ballet accommodated on the fourth disc, but involving a change to the fifth CD for the final *Waltz and Apotheosis*. The Dorati/Concertgebouw partnership provides an almost equally magnetic account of the great *Sleeping Beauty* score, where the Amsterdam recording is even fuller, if less sparkling, although digital. The orchestral playing here is again first class (especially in the last Act, which gives the orchestral wind soloists many chances to shine); but, although this is polished, finely detailed and enjoyable, the result is not as consistently vibrant as the *Nutcracker*. For *Swan Lake* Philips turned to the Decca catalogue and Ansermet's 1959 recording, which still sounds extremely vivid, if not sumptuous. The Suisse Romande Orchestra is no match for the Concertgebouw Orchestra, and the ballet is not absolutely complete (Ansermet uses the Drigo edition of the score). But little of importance is left out, and Ansermet's charismatic direction ensures that the music-making is consistently alive. This is discussed more fully in its separate issue as a Double Decca. Dorati and the New Philharmonia return to give us the four underrated *Orchestral Suites* – and very enjoyable they are. They, too, are available separately, as a Philips Duo (see below), as are the little-known and rewarding symphonic poems, *Fatum*, *The Storm* and *The Tempest*, in excellent performances from Inbal and the Frankfurt Radio Symphony Orchestra. Curiously, the companion performance of *The Voyevoda* is omitted here, even though it is mentioned both on the outside of the box and in the accompanying notes! However, Markevitch's *Hamlet* is included, a fervent account, lacking subtlety but opening and closing with powerfully sonorous evocation. *1812*, too, is a good rousing version, resonantly recorded. The highly inspired *String serenade* and the equally endearing *Souvenir de Florence* are entrusted to the Netherlands Chamber Orchestra under David Zinman. His reading of the *Serenade* proves to be rather laid-back, lacking charm and sparkle in the waltz and expressive fervour in the main melody of the *Elegy*; the

Souvenir is fresher and more immediate; both are helped by warm, full string recording from the mid- to late-1970s. Finally comes a most engaging collection of rare Tchaikovsky dances, drawn from his operas, revealing no new masterpieces but again showing the composer's vigorous melodic resource and his brilliant use of the orchestral palette. The opening items from *Eugene Onegin* tend to overshadow what follows in their tuneful inspiration, especially when they are played with such brio and commitment; but there are no disappointments in the rest of the programme. Lively, characterful playing from the Royal Opera House, Covent Garden, Orchestra, directed by Sir Colin Davis, is matched by lavishly sumptuous sound.

(i) *Andante cantabile* (from *String quartet No. 1*); (ii) *Capriccio italien;* (i; iii) *Piano concerto No. 1 in B flat min., Op. 23;* (ii) *Symphony No. 5 in E min., Op. 64.*
(BB) ** Carlton LSO Double Dig. 30368 01227 (2) [(B) id.]. LSO; (i) James Judd; (ii) Rozhdestvensky; (iii) with John Lill.

John Lill is powerful and authoritative in Tchaikovsky's most famous concerto, but his orchestral support from the LSO under James Judd is not very strongly characterized, and the recording-balance seeks brilliance rather than weight. This certainly displays Lill's dexterity in the finale, which has plenty of excitement, but overall this is not very competitive, when only the *Andante cantabile*, sweetly played, is used to fill up the first disc (playing time: 43 minutes). Though less brightly recorded than its two companions (see below) in Rozhdestvensky's Carlton LSO series of Tchaikovsky symphonies, with strings a little cloudy, this version of the *Fifth* brings a strong, passionate performance, with the middle movements in particular beautifully done. The *Capriccio italien* is also given a sunny and relaxed reading at relatively spacious speeds. But this CD has not gained by being paired with its less attractive companion.

Andante cantabile, Op. 11; Nocturne in D min., Op. 19/4; Pezzo capriccioso in B min., Op. 62; Variations on a rococo theme for cello and orchestra, Op. 33.
(M) **(*) BMG/Melodiya 74321 40724-2 [id.]. Valentin Feighin, Estonian State SO, Neeme Järvi – HAYDN: *Cello concerto.* **(*)

This is one of the half-dozen CDs devoted to Neeme Järvi's early recordings made in the USSR that BMG/Melodiya have issued to mark his sixtieth birthday. Most were made in the mid-1960s, but these are the last recordings he made in 1978 in Tallinn with the Estonian State Orchestra before he left for Sweden and the USA. It comprises Tchaikovsky's major output for cello and orchestra and features Valentin Feighin, a player of great naturalness and expressive eloquence, little known in the West. These are glorious performances, a worthy companion to Daniil Shafran's Haydn concerto with which they are coupled.

Andante cantabile for cello and orchestra, Op. posth; (i) *Variations on a rococo theme, Op. 33.*
(B) *** DG Double 437 952-2 (2) [id.]. Rostropovich, BPO; (i) cond. Karajan – BERNSTEIN: *3 Meditations;* BOCCHERINI: *Cello concerto No. 2;* GLAZUNOV: *Chant du Ménestrel;* SHOSTAKOVICH: *Cello concerto No. 2;* TARTINI: *Cello concerto;* VIVALDI: *Cello concertos.* ***

Rostropovich indulges himself affectionately in the composer's arrangement of the *Andante cantabile*, and the balance – all cello with a discreet orchestral backing – reflects his approach. Rostropovich's famous and much-praised account of the *Rococo variations* with Karajan (see below) has been added as part of a highly desirable anthology – a real bargain in DG's Double-CD series with two discs offered for the price of one.

Andante cantabile, Op. 11; Nocturne, Op. 19/4 (both arr. for cello & orchestra); *Pezzo capriccioso, Op. 62; Variations on a rococo theme, Op. 33* (original versions).
(M) **(*) Virgin/EMI Dig. CUV5 61225-2. Isserlis, COE, Gardiner (with GLAZUNOV: *2 Pieces, Op. 20; Chant du ménestrel, Op. 71;* RIMSKY-KORSAKOV: *Serenade, Op. 37;* CUI: *2 Morceaux, Op. 36* ***).

Isserlis's playing has slight reserve but also an elegant delicacy which is appealing, although it suits Glazunov and Cui rather better than it does Tchaikovsky's *Andante cantabile*. John Eliot Gardiner provides gracefully lightweight accompaniments and the Virgin recording is faithfully balanced, fresh in texture and warm in ambience.

(i–ii) *Capriccio italien, Op. 45;* (iii) *Piano concerto No. 1 in B flat min., Op. 23;* (iv–vi) *Violin concerto in D, Op. 35;* (v; vii) *1812 Overture, Op. 49;* (i–ii) *The Nutcracker* (ballet): *Waltz of the flowers;* (viii; ii) *Serenade for strings in C, Op. 48;* (viii–x) *Valse-scherzo* (for violin and orchestra), *Op. 34;* (v; xi) *The Sleeping Beauty* (ballet): *Rose adagio;* (viii; xii) *Swan Lake* (ballet): Act II: *Pas d'action.*
(B) ** Ph. Duo 438 386-2 (2) [(M) id. import]. (i) LPO; (ii) Stokowski; (iii) Haas, Monte-Carlo Opéra O, Inbal; (iv) Szeryng; (v) Concg. O; (vi) Haitink; (vii) Markevitch; (viii) LSO; (ix) Midori; (x) Slatkin; (xi) Dorati; (xii) Monteux.

Described somewhat over-optimistically as 'The best of Tchaikovsky', this Duo bargain double-album nevertheless offers a generous and enjoyable programme. Stokowski's contribution derives from a series of recordings he made in London for Philips in the mid-1970s, preceding the conductor's Indian summer in the CBS recording studios just before he died. *Capriccio italien* has much excitement, especially at the close, and many characteristic touches of detail before that, but the *Serenade for strings* is surprisingly straight, as if Stokowski were seeking to acknowledge the music's Mozartian ancestry, with unsumptuous sound to match. There is some very neat playing from the LSO violins, the *Waltz* has elegance and the *Elegy* unexaggerated fervour. The finale is lively enough but does not unleash the degree of bustle one might have expected. The *Waltz of the flowers* is more characteristic, with a sudden dramatic fortissimo towards the end. Haas's account of the *B flat minor Concerto* has plenty of excitement; the orchestra is less impressive, but these players rise to the adrenalin of the soloist in the finale, and Haas's own contribution is first rate throughout. Szeryng is luckier in having the Concertgebouw Orchestra in the *Violin concerto*, but Haitink is rather slack in directing the accompaniment in the outer movements. Szeryng is warmly sensitive, and the relaxed manner of the performance may appeal to some listeners; but, while the solo playing in the finale is spirited, the end result fails to catch fire. The recording is excellent. Midori plays the *Valse-scherzo* with a delightfully light touch, and there are no complaints about the other performances. Markevitch's *1812* is lively enough, but it has a resonantly boomy bass drum instead of cannon in the final climax.

Capriccio italien; 1812 overture; Francesca da Rimini; Romeo and Juliet.
(M) ** DG Dig. 445 523-2 [id.]. Chicago SO, Barenboim.
(M) ** DG Dig./Analogue 439 983-2. Israel PO, Bernstein.

Barenboim is too ready to let the tension relax to be entirely convincing throughout this programme, although his affection for the music is never in doubt. He is slinkily persuasive in the *Capriccio*, but by the finest Chicago standards *1812* is much less impressively played, though not without excitement. The recording could expand more and the violin sound has a distinct digital edge. The *Capriccio* is more agreeable overall. In *Romeo and Juliet* Barenboim conveys a sensuous quality in the love theme, but the ardour of the performance is sporadic, though there is a burst of excitement in the feud music. The middle section of *Francesca da Rimini* yields some fine solo wind playing, notably from the clarinet; but the full nervous tension of the outer sections is partly subdued by the conductor's partiality for breadth, although the coda is exciting enough. The sound is always vivid.

Bernstein's approach to *Francesca* certainly conveys the passion of the story, but the Israel Philharmonic does not play the central section as idyllically as one might hope; moreover Bernstein's pacing is idiosyncratic and unconvincing here. *Romeo and Juliet* is only moderately exciting, in spite of a brilliant sound-balance. The Tel Aviv acoustic is too dry for music which needs a warmly expansive resonance. With the extra presence and definition in the digitally recorded works (the *Capriccio* and *1812*), the ear can accept – though not revel in – the chosen ambience. At the end of *1812* the cannon make a spectacular effect, though the sudden peal of bells near the end seems contrived. Overall, this cannot be recommended with any great enthusiasm.

Capriccio italien, Op. 45; 1812 overture; Marche slave, Op. 31; Romeo and Juliet (fantasy overture).
(BB) *** Naxos Dig. 8.550500; *4550500* [id.]. RPO, Adrian Leaper.

Like Sian Edwards, Adrian Leaper is a natural Tchaikovskian; whether in the colourful extravagance of the composer's memento of his Italian holiday, the romantic ardour and passionate conflict of *Romeo and Juliet*, the sombre expansiveness of *Marche slave* with its surge of adrenalin at the close, or in the extrovert celebration of *1812*, he produces playing from the RPO that is spontaneously committed and exciting. The brilliantly spectacular recording, with plenty of weight for the brass, was made in Watford Town Hall, with realistic cannon and an impressively resonant imported carillon to add to the very exciting climax of *1812*. A splendid disc that would still be recommendable if it cost far more.

(i) *Capriccio italien, Op. 45; 1812 overture, Op. 49;* (ii) *Fatum, Op. 77; Francesca da Rimini, Op. 32 ; Hamlet, Op. 67;* (i) *Marche slave;* (ii) *Romeo and Juliet* (fantasy overture); *The Tempest, Op. 18; The Voyevoda, Op. 78.*
(B) **(*) Decca Double 443 003-2 (2) [id.]. (i) National SO of Washington, DC; (ii) Detroit SO; Antal Dorati.

Dorati made his recordings of the symphonic poems in Washington in the early 1970s, while the triptych of *Capriccio italien, 1812* and *Marche slave* marked the return of the Detroit orchestra to the recording scene at the beginning of 1979. The recording has the benefit of the splendid Detroit acoustics, although *1812*, rather endearingly, has a spectacular laminated eruption of American Civil War cannon and bells – including Philadelphia's Liberty Bell! – at the end. The result is unbelievable but certainly spectacular, and clearly was aimed at the hi-fi demonstration market of the time. The performance of the *Capriccio* is not without elegance, but *Marche slave* seems almost excessively sombre until the change of mood at the coda, which is taken briskly. *Fatum* is quite successful, but Dorati's accounts of *Francesca da Rimini* and *Hamlet* are rather underpowered compared with Stokowski, but they are spacious readings, not without individuality, and the central section of *Francesca* is sensitively done. *Romeo and Juliet* takes a while to warm up. When it does, Dorati gives the love theme a distinctive sweep, and the closing pages are very convincing. *The Tempest* obviously excited the conductor's imagination and is vividly done, while the rapturous love theme is played with tingling ardour. *The Voyevoda* is hardly one of the composer's more inspired pieces, although its scoring is sophisticated. Dorati makes the most of its melancholy and dark wind colouring which matches the sombre lower strings.

(i) *Capriccio italien; 1812 overture; Romeo and Juliet;* (ii) Song: *None but the lonely heart; Eugene Onegin: Lensky's aria.*
(B) *** [EMI Red Line Dig. CDR5 69844]. (i) Philh. O, Domingo; (ii) Domingo, Philh. O, Behr.

Here we have Domingo in his newest role as conductor giving heartfelt, somewhat idiosyncratic and quite individual readings of three popular orchestral favourites, with plenty of drama and with the passion worn on the sleeve. *1812* is ceremonially measured, with the organ adding breadth and spectacle at the close. The recording is appropriately spacious and resonant. Any lack of sharp co-ordination of ensemble is surely compensated for by the impact throughout. The vocal items show that Domingo can still tug at the emotions in his more familiar role. The recording, made in All Saints', Tooting, London, provides an expansively resonant panoply of Tchaikovskian hyperbole.

(i) *Capriccio italien, Op. 45;* (ii) *Francesca da Rimini, Op. 32;* (i) *Nutcracker suite, Op. 71a;* (ii) *Serenade for strings;* (i) *Eugene Onegin: Polonaise and Waltz.*
(M) **(*) Ph. 442 735-2 (2). (i) LPO; (ii) LSO; Leopold Stokowski.

Curiously entitled '*The Early Years*' this Philips box instead includes some of Stokowski's last recordings, made in 1973 (when he was 91) and 1974; he died three years later in September 1977. The performances certainly show his charisma and there are moments of magic, but there is wilful egotism too. *Capriccio italien* brings genuine panache, and the infectiously vigorous *Eugene Onegin* dances have characteristic flair. But in the *Nutcracker suite* (which he played so beautifully for Disney in *Fantasia*), the *Marche* is presented at such a hard-driven pace that the middle section sounds gabbled; then, after introducing the *Sugar Plum Fairy* with a string tremolando, his phrasing is so mannered (with repeated tenutos on the falling clarinet phrase) that few will find this comfortable to live with, even if later the *Waltz of the flowers* is exhilarating. The 1974 account of *Francesca da Rimini*, although not as well controlled as his classic early stereo version with the New York Stadium Orchestra, is very exciting; indeed there is no doubt about the temperament of the reading: the music races off (not entirely convincingly) almost as soon as the performance begins. But the middle section is beautifully played and Stokowski generates a tremendous emotional thrust at the climax. There is no possible doubt about the moment when the lovers are slain, and the ferocious return to Dante's inferno leads to a cataclysmic close, with the cymbals echoing into silence. The *String serenade* is characteristically bold and romantic, with sumptuous tone from the LSO strings – a real 'Stokowski sound' – and, after the characteristically luscious Waltz, the *Elégie* is ardent and the finale full of energy. The recordings, although resonant, have been splendidly remastered; on LP the quality was never as full-bodied as it is now.

Capriccio italien, Op. 45; Manfred Symphony, Op. 58; Romeo and Juliet (fantasy overture); Serenade for strings in C, Op. 48; The Tempest, Op. 18.
(B) *** BMG/Melodiya Twofer 74321 34164-2 (2) [id.]. USSR SO, Svetlanov.

Svetlanov's recordings of the major Tchaikovsky orchestral works, made in the late 1960s, still stand up well to current competition; the remastering for CD is highly successful, retaining the vividness and colour and minimizing any coarseness. Their reissue on three 'Twofers' (as BMG/Melodiya have designated their two-for-the-price-of-one double-CD packs) makes a genuine bargain. The vibrant brass-playing opening of *Capriccio italien* immediately establishes the very Russian credentials of these performances, yet the strings bring both panache and warmth too, while the final tarantella generates a sudden burst of adrenalin at the close. But the key work here is *Manfred*, and Svetlanov provides a superb account, strong and uninhibited, among the finest available: the orchestral playing has splendid colour and urgency, with plenty of passion from the strings. The full-blooded Russian recording is entirely appropriate and, while the work's weaker moments are not totally disguised, this is altogether very satisfying. *Romeo and Juliet* has similar red-blooded romanticism, and *The Tempest*, too, with its memorably ecstatic love theme, is passionate in a characteristically Russian way. This emphasizes the melodrama of the piece – better this, however, than undercharacterization – and the opening and closing sections depicting Prospero's magic island are evocatively done, with thrustful horn playing. The *Serenade for strings* is a spacious account; Svetlanov seeks Mozartian elegance in the first movement by not pressing too hard. The *Waltz* is beautifully turned, and in the *Elegy* the Slavonic ardour preserves a deep melancholy rather than seeking extrovert passion. The finale has plenty of vigour but the breadth of the reading is preserved, and with fine string playing this is a most attractive performance.

Piano concertos Nos. 1–3.

(B) ** EMI forte CZS5 68637-2 (2) [CDFB 68637]. Gilels, New Philh. O, Maazel – BARTOK: *Piano concerto No. 2;* PROKOFIEV: *Piano concerto No. 5.* *(*)

It is a pity that Gilels elects to play the truncated Siloti edition of the *Second Piano concerto*, for it effectively diminishes the claim that this inexpensive forte set has on the collector's allegiance. His playing is of the highest order of mastery and has the virtue of presenting the works with the freshness of new discovery. The (1972) Abbey Road recording is very good and the New Philharmonia under Maazel provide admirable support. However, this conductor formed a much less fruitful partnership with Richter and the couplings are disappointing.

(i) *Piano concertos Nos. 1–3;* (ii) *Violin concerto.*

(B) *(*) Decca Double Dig. 448 107-2 (2) [id.]. (i) Victoria Postnikova, VSO, Rozhdestvensky; (ii) Kyung-Wha Chung, Montreal SO, Dutoit.

The Postnikova/Rozhdestvensky performance of the *First Concerto* is unconvincing with its very measured tempos (see below). These artists choose the complete original score of the *Second Concerto*, but again, with slow speeds, the performance hangs fire. The long single movement of the *Third Concerto* also needs more consistently persuasive treatment, though the dactylic dance-theme is delectably pointed. Close balance for the piano in a firm, clear recording, enhanced on CD – but the performances remain unenticing. Even at Decca Double price this set cannot be recommended, not even with the inclusion of Chung's splendid account of the *Violin concerto*, which is in a wholly different and higher league.

Piano concertos Nos. (i) *1 in B flat min.;* (ii) *2 in G;* (iii) *3 in E flat;* (iv) *Violin concerto in D;* (v) *Variations on a rococo theme for cello and orchestra.*

(B) **(*) EMI Rouge et Noir Analogue/Dig. CZS5 69695-2 (2) [CDZB 69695]. (i) Georges Cziffra, Philh. O, Vandernoot; (ii) Sylvia Kersenbaum, Fr. R. O, Martinon; (iii) Peter Donohoe, Bournemouth SO, Barshai; (iv) Leonid Kogan, Paris Conservatoire O, Silvestri; (v) Pierre Fournier, Philh. O, Sargent.

This is one of the most worthwhile of French EMI's Rouge et Noir compilations in which different groups of artists play the music of a single composer for, although Cziffra's *B flat minor Piano concerto* is disappointingly idiosyncratic, everything else is very valuable indeed, notably Kogan's splendid account of the *Violin concerto* and Fournier's distinctive and stylish *Rococo variations*. Cziffra always displays a prodigious technique, but his partnership with Vandernoot shows little feeling of symbiosis in the concerto's first movement. Although the concerto opens excitingly enough, conductor and soloist are not wholly agreed on the degree of forward thrust the music needs: sometimes one presses on, sometimes the other, producing sporadic bursts of bravura. In the finale Vandernoot's reprise of the big tune is pulled right back, almost losing the music's impetus, and only the pianist's final burst of energy saves the day. Despite the use of Kingsway Hall, the 1958 recording is artificially balanced, and the strings tend to shrillness. Sylvia Kersenbaum's 1972 account of the *Second Piano concerto* with Martinon is a different matter. It is absolutely complete, and it was the finest to have appeared on LP at the time. The chosen tempo for the opening movement is perfect, and Martinon's opening has a sweep to compare with that of the *B flat minor Concerto*. The violin and cello soloists in the slow movement play most sensitively, as does the pianist, and she is splendidly ebullient in the finale. One's only slight reservation concerns the recording, made in the Salle Wagram, full but very resonant; in the CD transfer, while the piano is convincingly placed, the orchestral tuttis are not quite sharp. But this is still very enjoyable, and the performance itself is upstaged only marginally by the much-praised, full-price version by Peter Donohoe. It is he who provides a totally satisfying account of the *Third Concerto*, in an excellent, modern, digital recording.

For the *Violin concerto* we turn to Leonid Kogan (in 1959) who gives a wonderful performance. Enjoyment, warmth and spontaneity are written into every bar of his interpretation, individual from his very first entry. His tone is gloriously rich and, if he rarely achieves a pianissimo, that may be the fault of the close solo balance which is nevertheless truthful in timbre, while the orchestra is still well in the picture. The songful *Andante* is most sensitively done, and the finale especially infectious. Kogan really makes it dance, with a fine lift to the rhythm, to evoke something of the Russian festival atmosphere of *Petrushka*. In the first movement both Kogan and Silvestri are more concerned with the architecture, and the interpretation is steadier: the build-up of tension where the main theme is developed is most exciting through their very refusal to slacken the basic speed.

Finally comes Fournier's aristocratic and elegant reading of the delightful *Rococo versions*, a performance which in its sheer style has never been surpassed, with Sargent and the Philharmonia providing an immaculate accompaniment of great finesse. This was the work's stereo début in 1956 (on the Columbia label) and it was given high praise by us in volume one of the hardback *Stereo Record Guide*. Fournier's fine tone is well caught by the engineers and he is very well balanced with the orchestra. Both are given a warm, analogue recording which still approaches demonstration standard; indeed it does not sound in the least dated.

Piano concertos Nos. 1–3; Andante and finale, Op. 79 (orch. Taneyev); *Concert fantasia*.
(B) ** Ph. Duo 438 329-2 (2) [(M) id. import]. Werner Haas, Monte-Carlo Opéra O, Inbal.

Piano concertos Nos. 1–3; Concert fantasy, Op. 56.
(BB) **(*) Virgin Classics Dig. Double VBD5 61463-2 (2) [CDVB 61462]. Mikhail Pletnev, Philh. O, Fedoseyev.

Mikhail Pletnev's masterful account of the *First Concerto* has all the qualities we associate with his remarkable pianism. This high-voltage account, together with that of the *Concert fantasy*, is among the very finest of modern recordings in the catalogue. Vladimir Fedoseyev and the Philharmonia Orchestra give excellent support and the production by Andrew Keener is exemplary. However, while the *Second Concerto* brings comparably commanding playing from Pletnev, whose exceptional affinity with this composer is much in evidence, unfortunately it also brings a small cut in the slow movement. (Why do artists detract from the attractiveness of a recording in this way?) Even so, Pletnev has the advantage of totally idiomatic string soloists and his handling of the second group of the first movement has great tenderness. Elsewhere his seemingly effortless virtuosity is little short of breathtaking. It would be difficult to improve on the *Third Concerto*, which is characterized strongly and interestingly. Not only does the pianism again generate great electricity, but the orchestral playing too is highly charged. The recording is very good, but not in the demonstration bracket. Nevertheless admirers of this pianist will count this Virgin Double (two CDs for the cost of one mid-priced disc) a very real bargain.

Werner Haas is an intelligent and masterly player, and moreover he is a true Tchaikovskian. His enviable technical command means that the many passages of pianistic rhetoric can be thrown off powerfully. He is very impressive in the *B flat minor* (the central section of the *Andante* scintillates), and the finale of the *Second Piano concerto* – which is presented in its original version, uncut – brings a burst of exhilarating bravura to compare with Donahue's famous recording. The solo passages for violin and cello in the *Andante* of that work are played with fair competence and a modest degree of ardour by Franco Ferrari and Jean-Max Clement, but no more than that. Poetry is consistently at Haas's fingertips, however; Inbal, though not always the most imaginative accompanist, directs all the music with enthusiastic vigour and often with real passion. The *Third Concerto* and *Concert fantasia* have no lack of excitement. The nub is the orchestral playing. The fullest sonority which the Monte Carlo orchestra possessed in 1970–71, when these recordings were made, lacks the body of the major European orchestras and, although Inbal often shows a fine ear for detail (the opening of the *Concert fantasia*, with its charming *Nutcracker* overtones, sparkles as it should), the accompaniments here are no more than adequate. Fortunately these players can sometimes rise to the occasion, and the gentle opening of the rare *Andante*, Op. 79 (completed by Taneyev), is affectionately done, until the entry of the lacklustre cello and violin solos. This is a rather repetitive movement, and the *Allegro maestoso* finale is laboured (not entirely the fault of the players), but this rare example of Tchaikovsky's concertante style is still worth having on disc. The recording balance allows Haas to dominate easily, and the orchestral sound itself has a truthful amount of body. The resonance occasionally clouds the more complex orchestral tuttis, notably in the *Third Concerto*, but that is not necessarily disadvantageous in hiding some of the sins of ensemble. But with Haas's contribution so consistently musical and technically reliable, there is more here to enjoy than to cavil at, and these discs are not expensive.

Piano concerto No. 1 in B flat min., Op. 23.
✿ (M) (***) RCA mono GD 60321 [09026 60321-2]. Horowitz, NBC SO, Toscanini – MUSSORGSKY: *Pictures*. (***)
(M) *** RCA 09026 61961-2. Van Cliburn, RCA SO, Kondrashin – BEETHOVEN: *Piano concerto No. 5*. ***
(M) *** Decca 417 750-2 [id.]. Ashkenazy, LSO, Maazel – CHOPIN: *Concerto No. 2*. ***
(M) *** [RCA Basic 100 09026 68404-2]. Artur Rubinstein, Boston SO, Leinsdorf – SCHUMANN: *Piano concerto*. **
(M) **(*) Mercury 432 011-2 [id.]. Byron Janis, LSO, Menges – SCHUMANN: *Concerto*. ***

(M) **(*) BMG/Melodiya 74321 40721-2 [id.]. Grigori Sokolov, USSR SO, Neeme Järvi – SAINT-SAENS: *Piano concerto No. 2*. **(*)

(M) (***) RCA mono GD 60449 [60449-2-RG]. Horowitz, NBC SO, Toscanini – MUSSORGSKY: *Pictures* etc. (***)

(M) (**) DG 447 420-2 [id.]. Sviatoslav Richter, VSO, Karajan – RACHMANINOV: *Piano concerto No. 2*. ***

(B) *(*) EMI CfP CD-CFP 6045. Peter Katin, LPO, Pritchard – LITOLFF: *Concerto symphonique: Scherzo*. ***

(B) *(*) Decca Eclipse Dig. 448 221-2; *448 221-4*. Victoria Postnikova, VSO, Rozhdestvensky – RACHMANINOV: *Piano concerto No. 2*. ***

(i) *Piano concerto No. 1. The Seasons, Op. 37: January; February; April; May; August; October; November; December*.

(B) *** Tring. Dig. TRP 023 [(M) id.]. Ronan O'Hora, (i) with RPO, James Judd.

(i) *Piano concerto No. 1. Theme and variations, Op. 19/6*.

(M) *** EMI CDM7 64329-2 [id.]. Gavrilov, (i) Philh. O, Muti – BALAKIREV: *Islamey*; PROKOFIEV: *Concerto No. 1*. ***

Horowitz's famous record of the *B flat minor Concerto*, recorded at a concert in Carnegie Hall in 1943 with his father-in-law conducting (GD 60321), has achieved legendary status and has dwarfed almost every record of the work made since. The sheer power of the playing means that within seconds the ear makes allowances for the sonic limitations. This performance has now been reissued as part of the Toscanini Edition with a more attractive coupling than in its last incarnation. A record not to be missed on any account. (Readers should note that this live concert version of the Tchaikovsky *Concerto* is still also available coupled with Horowitz's 1952 recording, conducted by Reiner, of Beethoven's *Emperor Piano concerto*, on RCA GD 87992.)

Van Cliburn and the Soviet conductor Kondrashin give an inspired performance with as much warmth as glitter. The 1958 recording is forward and could do with more atmosphere, but the digital remastering has brought a firmer orchestral image, and the piano timbre is also improved. Coupled with an outstanding version of the *Emperor concerto*, this is a very distinguished reissue indeed, even if the piano timbre here is shallower than in the coupling.

Having already given us an outstanding version of the Grieg *Concerto*, Ronan O'Hora and James Judd repeat their success with a memorably fresh, new look at Tchaikovsky's *B flat minor Concerto*. The very opening is gloriously arresting, and then O'Hora sets off with a crisp, sparkling duplet rhythm for the main theme of the allegro, pulling back naturally and poetically for his gentle introduction of the lovely secondary group. The *Andante semplice* brings contrasting delicacy, and in the central section O'Hora's chimerical lightness is like a will-o'-the-wisp. Then the finale makes a fitting culmination, with the joyful spirit of Russian dance paramount, rather than any barnstorming; but the exciting final reprise of the big tune is capped with a stormy bravura flourish from the soloist. The whole performance has the spontaneous feel of a live occasion, and the recording balance is just about ideal, with a bold, natural piano-image set against a richly spacious orchestral tapestry. As with his Grieg record, the pianist chooses a coupling of solo pieces, in this case eight out of the twelve 'months' which make up *The Seasons*. They are presented with an agreeable, impulsive charm and plenty of colour. *May night*, the November *Troika* and the warmly lyrical October *Autumn song* are particularly successful.

Ashkenazy refuses to be stampeded by Tchaikovsky's rhetoric, and the biggest climaxes of the first movement are made to grow naturally out of the music. In the *Andantino* too, Ashkenazy refuses to play flashily. The finale is very fast and brilliant, yet the big tune is broadened at the end in the most convincing way. The remastering is highly successful: the piano sounds splendidly bold and clear while the orchestral balance is realistic.

Rubinstein re-recorded the work for RCA in stereo in 1963 and is hardly less dashing than Horowitz. Yet, as before, there is a mercurial quality here, not only in the central section of the slow movement but also in the finale. The result, if perhaps not as overwhelming as with Horowitz, is hardly less magnetic, with fine bravura in the outer movements and a poetic *Andante*. Leinsdorf is obviously caught up in the music-making and the Boston Symphony opens the work splendidly and provides plenty of excitement throughout. The sound is remarkably good in its new CD incarnation. This coupling with Schumann is currently not available in the UK.

Byron Janis's account is in many ways as dazzling as his Rachmaninov recordings. Menges is not as strong an accompanist as Dorati, most noticeably so in the finale. But this remains a memorable performance, with much dash and power from the soloist in the outer movements and the *Andantino* agreeably delicate. The Mercury sound is excellent, full and resonant, with a big piano image up front.

Grigory Sokolov was only sixteen when he won the Tchaikovsky Piano Competition in 1966 with a dazzling account of the Saint-Saëns *G minor Concerto*, with which the Tchaikovsky *B flat minor Concerto* is coupled. The Tchaikovsky performance from the following year is no less remarkable, and not just for virtuosic display but also for poetic depth. Remarkable playing, not just from the young soloist but also from the USSR Symphony Orchestra and Neeme Järvi. The recording may be pretty rough-and-ready but, given the excitement generated by this young performer, few will be greatly worried.

Horowitz's earlier version, also coupled with Mussorgsky, was made in Carnegie Hall, in 1941, under studio conditions. The recording is altogether better balanced than the live performance by the same artists, and the orchestral sound is much fuller; indeed the quality brooks no real criticism. But throughout one feels that Toscanini – with his soloist responding readily – is forcing the pace, creating enormous urgency. This is an exhilarating listening experience; but the sense of occasion of the live performance created a really great performance which is undoubtedly more satisfying despite its sonic limitations.

Gavrilov is stunning in the finale of the *Concerto*; however, the final statement of the big tune is broadened so positively that one is not entirely convinced. Similarly in the first movement, contrasts of dynamic and tempo are extreme, and the element of self-consciousness is apparent. The *Andante* is full of tenderness and the *prestissimo* middle section goes like quicksilver, displaying the vein of spontaneous imagination that we recognize in Gavrilov's other records. The recording is full and sumptuous. In the *Variations*, Op. 19, Tchaikovsky's invention has great felicity. Gavrilov's playing is stylishly sympathetic here, and the Balakirev and Prokofiev couplings are dazzling.

The element of struggle for which this work is famous is all too clear in the Richter/Karajan performance; not surprisingly, these two musical giants do not always agree: each chooses a different tempo for the second subject of the finale and maintains it, despite the other. However, in both the dramatic opening and the closing pages of the work they are agreed in a hugely mannered, bland stylization which is not easy to enjoy. Clearly two major artists are at work, but it is difficult to praise the end-product as a convincing reading. The recording is full-blooded, with a firm piano image.

Peter Katin's Classics for Pleasure version is given a fine recording and is basically quite a strong, musical reading. But there is somehow a lack of drama and flair, and the absence of extrovert bravura from the soloist (especially in the middle section of the slow movement) produces an impression of facelessness. Even at bargain price the coupling is short on playing time but it remains the best thing on the record.

The collaboration of wife and husband in the Postnikova/Rozhdestvensky performance makes for a very personal reading, marked by spacious speeds. The very introduction is disconcertingly slow and so is the basic tempo for the central *Andante*, while in other places Postnikova's expressive fluctuations sound studied, even if the clarity of articulation is remarkable.

(i) *Piano concerto No. 1 in B flat min., Op. 23;* (ii) *Violin concerto in D, Op. 35;* (iii) *Hamlet (fantasy overture);* (iv) *Overture, The Storm, Op. 76;* (v) *Romeo and Juliet (fantasy overture);* (vi) *Serenade for strings in C, Op. 48: Waltz and finale. Symphonies Nos. 4 in F min., Op. 36;* (vii) *5 in E min., Op. 64;* (viii) *6 in B min. (Pathétique), Op. 74;* (ix) *Variations on a rococo theme, Op. 33;* (x) *Eugene Onegin:* Act I: *Tatiana's letter scene;* (iii) Act II: *Waltz;* Act III: *Polonaise.*

✿ (M) (***) EMI mono CHS7 64855-2 (4) [ZDMD 64855]. (i) Solomon, Philh. O, Issay Dobrowen; (ii) Bronislaw Huberman, Staatskapelle Berlin, William Steinberg; (iii) Philh. O, Dobrowen; (iv) Philh. O, Lovro von Matačić; (v) VPO, Karajan; (vi) VPO, Furtwängler; (vii) La Scala, Milan, O, Cantelli; (viii) BPO, Furtwängler; (ix) Tortelier, Philh. O, Menges; (x) Ljuba Welitsch, Philh. O, Walter Susskind.

This is *the* indispensable Tchaikovsky box. It collects great performances, mainly from the late 1940s, including the aristocratic (1949) Solomon account of the *B flat minor concerto* which, in terms of poetry, finesse and virtuosity, can hold its own with any in the catalogue. The two great pre-war records are the wonderfully pure Huberman (1928) account of the *Violin concerto* with the youthful William Steinberg conducting and the electrifying (1938) *Pathétique* from Furtwängler and the Berlin Philharmonic. Collectors will not need reminding of the dramatic intensity of Ljuba Welitsch's Letter scene from *Eugene Onegin*, recorded in 1948, or of Karajan's superb 1946 *Romeo and Juliet* with the Vienna Philharmonic (possibly never surpassed in his later recordings). Re-hearing the Cantelli La Scala performance of the *Fifth Symphony*, recorded at the EMI Abbey Road studios immediately after their appearance at the 1950 Edinburgh Festival, makes one realize why it has become legendary. It is absolutely straight, classical in its proportions, restrained yet totally authentic in feeling, and played marvellously. Furtwängler's account of the *Fourth* with the Vienna Philharmonic is the only performance that could possibly excite controversy, for it does not have the intensity of his *Pathétique*. Tortelier made his first version of the *Rococo variations* with Beecham in 1947. As this is available separately, coupled with Strauss's *Don Quixote*, the choice here was of his later (1955) version with Menges and the Philharmonia. Apart from their excellence artistically, the *Hamlet* and *The Storm* Overture which the Philharmonia recorded with Lovro von Matačić in 1956 pay testimony to the splendid ears of the production team, Lawrance Collingwood and Douglas Larter. Excellent transfers too.

(i) *Piano concerto No. 1;* (ii) *Violin concerto in D, Op. 35.*

(B) *** DG Classikon 439 420-2; *439 420-4* [431 609-2]. (i) Martha Argerich, RPO, Dutoit; (ii) Milstein, VPO, Abbado.

(BB) *** RCA Navigator 74321 17900-2 [Silver Seal 60491-2-RV]. (i) John Browning; (ii) Erick Friedman; LSO, Ozawa.

(B) ** [EMI Red Line Dig. CDR5 69845]. (i) Andrei Gavrilov, BPO, Ashkenazy; (ii) Augustin Dumay, LSO, Tchakarov.

(M) *(*) Ph. 446 203-2. (i) Rafael Orozco, Rotterdam PO, Edo de Waart; (ii) Henryk Szeryng, Concg. O, Haitink.

Argerich's 1971 version of the *First Piano concerto* with Dutoit has long been among the top recommendations. The sound is firm, with excellent presence, and its ambience is more attractive than the later version. The weight of the opening immediately sets the mood for a big, broad performance, with the kind of music-making in which the personalities of both artists are complementary. Argerich's conception encompasses the widest range of tonal shading. In the finale she often produces a scherzando-like effect; then the orchestra thunders in with the Russian dance-theme to create a real contrast. The tempo of the first movement is comparatively measured, but satisfyingly so; the slow movement is strikingly atmospheric, yet delicate, its romanticism light-hearted. Milstein's 1973 performance of the *Violin concerto* is equally impressive, undoubtedly one of the finest available, while Abbado secures playing of genuine sensitivity and scale from the Vienna Philharmonic, with a recording that is also well balanced.

Browning's mid-1960s interpretation of the solo role in the *Piano concerto* is remarkable, not only for power and bravura but for wit and point in the many *scherzando* passages, and in the finale he adopts a fast and furious tempo to compare with Horowitz. Erick Friedman, Heifetz's pupil, is a thoughtful violinist who gives a keenly intelligent performance of the companion work, imbued with a glowing lyricism and with a particularly poetic and beautiful account of the slow movement. There is plenty of dash and fire in the finale, and Ozawa gives first-rate support to both soloists. The recording is excellent. Two performances to match those of almost any rival; moreover this disc is in the lowest price-range.

For Gavrilov's digital remake of the *B flat minor Concerto*, EMI teamed him up with Ashkenazy and recorded the Berlin Philharmonic in their old analogue venue, the Jesus-Christus-Kirche. The balance is not entirely convincing, with the orchestra often sounding rather recessed. After opening impressively, the first movement flows rather more convincingly than before, but the alternation of gentle poetry with sudden bursts of pianistic bravura still fails to sound entirely spontaneous. The slow movement has a scintillating middle section, but the finale was even more gripping in the analogue version. Dumay plays with some flair and gives a highly musical account of the *Violin concerto*, but there are more magnetic accounts of this coupling.

The Philips alternative is uncompetitive. Orozco's version of the *First Piano concerto* is flamboyant enough but, despite the bravura and good (mid-1970s) recording, it fails to be memorable. The *prestissimo* central section of the slow movement is certainly intended by the composer as an opportunity for the soloist to show his mettle, but the lack of refinement here is unattractive. Szeryng is sweetly lyrical in the *Violin concerto*, but he is not helped by Haitink, who provides a rather slack accompaniment. The relaxed manner of the performance of the first movement fails to generate enough impulse and the finale too fails to ignite. This cannot match Szeryng's early stereo version of the work with the Boston Symphony and Munch.

(i) *Piano concerto No. 1 in B flat min., Op. 23. Nutcracker* (ballet): excerpts.

(M) **(*) RCA 09026 68530-2 [id.]. (i) Emil Gilels; Chicago SO, Reiner.

Gilels's early (1955) RCA recording is somewhat over-reverberant, with the sound less refined than usual from this source; indeed it is almost coarse. The *Nutcracker* ballet music also seems a bit inflated, although it is very well played (if without much charm). The performance of the concerto, however, is very exciting and full-blooded and may be spoken of in the same breath as the famous Horowitz/Toscanini version, while Gilels gives a beautifully gentle account of the outer sections of the slow movement.

(i) *Piano concerto No. 1 in B flat min., Op. 23. Dumka, Op. 59.*

(M) *** BMG/Melodiya 74321 33219-2 [id.]. Ashkenazy; (i) USSR State SO, Konstantin Ivanov – LISZT: *Piano concerto No. 1* etc. **(*)

(BB) *(*) Discover Dig. DICD 920118 [id.]. David Lively, (i) Slovak R., New PO, Rahbari (with BALAKIREV: *Islamey* *).

Ashkenazy's Russian recording was made in 1962, immediately after he had been awarded joint first prize in the Tchaikovsky competition with John Ogdon, whom we hear in equally impressive form playing the Liszt couplings. The notes reveal that Ashkenazy was out of sympathy with the Tchaikovsky concerto, and he comments: 'To play all that bravura which I actually detest, you have to believe in it passionately . . . And that type of octave playing was not really my thing – that was really for John Ogdon, Van Cliburn and Horowitz.' Yet he gives a remarkably fine account of the work, exciting without barnstorming, and with the middle section of the slow movement particularly appealing in its buoyant lyrical flow. With Ivanov an obviously sympathetic partner, and a vividly Russian orchestral backcloth, the outer movements have no lack of power or adrenalin, yet there is an underlying concern with musical values that is even more impressive here than in Ashkenazy's later version with Maazel for Decca. The studio recording is splendidly full-blooded. The solo encore was played in front of a Moscow audience, so perhaps one should not be surprised at their audible bronchial contributions.

Although agreeable enough and unexceptionally recorded, the David Lively/Rahbari performance of the Tchaikovsky concerto on Discover emphasizes its lyrical nature at the expense of exuberance and dash: the rhetoric is played down even in the grand finale, where the final statement of the tune is broad rather than arresting. The Balakirev coupling is quite well played but not distinctive, and the piano timbre here is shallow.

Violin concerto in D, Op. 35.

(M) *** Decca 425 080-2 [id.]. Kyung-Wha Chung, LSO, Previn – SIBELIUS: *Violin concerto.* ***

(BB) *** Naxos Dig. 8.550153; *4550153* [id.]. Takako Nishizaki, Slovak PO, Kenneth Jean – MENDELSSOHN: *Concerto.* ***

(B) *** DG Double 453 142-2 (2) [id.]. Nathan Milstein, VPO, Abbado – BEETHOVEN: *Concerto* ***; BRAHMS: *Concerto* **(*); MENDELSSOHN: *Concerto.* ***

(M) *** Sony Stern Edition I SMK 66829 [id.]. Stern, Phd. O, Ormandy – SIBELIUS: *Violin concerto.* ***

(M) (***) EMI mono CDH7 64030-2 [id.]. Heifetz, LPO, Barbirolli – GLAZUNOV: *Violin concerto* (***) ✿; SIBELIUS: *Violin concerto.* (**)

(M) ** BMG/Melodiya 74321 40720-2 [id.]. Victor Tretyakov, Moscow PO, Neeme Järvi – PAGANINI: *Violin concerto No. 1.* **

(BB) ** Discover Dig. DICD 920122 [id.]. Evgeny Bushkov, Slovak R. New PO, Rahbari – MENDELSSOHN: *Concerto.* **(*)

Violin concerto in D; Sérénade mélancolique. String serenade: Waltz.

(M) **(*) RCA 09026 61743-2 [id.]. Heifetz, Chicago SO, Reiner – MENDELSSOHN: *Concerto.* ***

Chung's earlier recording of the Tchaikovsky *Concerto* with Previn conducting has remained one of the strongest recommendations for a much-recorded work ever since it was made, right at the beginning of her career. Although she recorded it later with Dutoit, anyone should be well satisfied with Chung's 1970 version with its Sibelius coupling. Her technique is impeccable and her musicianship of the highest order, and Previn's accompanying is highly sympathetic and responsive. This has warmth, spontaneity and discipline, every detail is beautifully shaped and turned without a trace of sentimentality. The recording is well balanced and detail is clean, though the acoustic is warm. This is a very distinguished record, very suitable for reissue in Decca's Classic Sound series.

There can be no real reservations about the sound of the present remastering of Heifetz's 1957 stereo recording, with the Chicago acoustics ensuring a full ambience to support the brilliance of the orchestra. Heifetz is closely balanced, but the magic of his playing can be fully enjoyed. There is some gorgeous lyrical phrasing, and the slow movement marries deep feeling and tenderness in an ideal performance. The finale is dazzling but is never driven too hard. Reiner always accompanies understandingly, producing fierily positive tuttis. The Mendelssohn coupling is equally desirable, and the *Sérénade mélancolique* makes a splendid bonus.

Takako Nishizaki gives a warm and colourful reading, tender but purposeful and full of temperament. As in the Mendelssohn with which this is coupled, the central slow movement is on the measured side but flows sweetly, while the finale has all the necessary bravura, even at a speed that avoids breathlessness. Unlike many, Nishizaki opens out the little cuts which had become traditional. With excellent playing and recording, this makes a first-rate recommendation in the super-bargain bracket.

Milstein's fine (1973) version with Abbado remains among the more satisfying recordings. It now comes as part of a DG Double with three other concertos, although it is Zukermann rather than Milstein who plays the Beethoven (and very impressively too).

Stern was on peak form when he made his first stereo recording with Ormandy, and it is a powerfully lyrical reading, rich in timbre and technically immaculate. The playing has undoubted poetry, but it is not helped by the very close balance of the soloist, so that *pianissimos* consistently become *mezzo fortes*. The orchestral sound is vivid but lacks amplitude.

Heifetz's first (mono) recording of the Tchaikovsky *Violin concerto*, made in 1937, has tremendous virtuosity and warmth. The sound is opaque by modern standards but the ear quickly adjusts, and the performance is special even by Heifetz's own standards. The transfer, too, is very good and, coming as it does with a classic account of the Glazunov and a fascinating Sibelius, this is a real bargain.

The Tchaikovsky *Concerto* was recorded in 1966 when the nineteen-year-old soloist, Viktor Tretyakov, had just triumphed at the Tchaikovsky Competition. Tretyakov has had relatively little exposure in the West and he plays with brilliance and virtuosity of the very highest order. The finale is quite breathtaking. Alas, the sound is not particularly good for its period and the recording engineers have placed the young soloist far too forward. All the same, this is well worth hearing.

Surprisingly, the other young Russian soloist Evgeny Bushkov is less successful in the Tchaikovsky concerto than in the coupled Mendelssohn. He and Rahbari take the first movement in a fairly relaxed manner, with bursts of energy, but towards the end the spontaneity slips, although the playing of both soloist and orchestra is of a high standard and the recording is full and well balanced.

Violin concerto; Sérénade mélancolique, Op. 35; Souvenir d'un lieu cher, Op. 42 (*Méditation; Scherzo; Mélodie;* orch. Glazunov).
(BB) *(**) Naxos Dig. 8.550124. Mariko Honda, Slovak PO or CSR SO, Keith Clark.

It was an excellent idea for Naxos to put all Tchaikovsky's music for violin and orchestra on a single super-bargain CD. In fact the *Souvenir d'un lieu cher* includes the *D minor Méditation*, originally intended as the slow movement for the *Concerto*, plus two other pieces, a *Scherzo* and a *Mélodie*, here orchestrated by Glazunov. Together they almost form another miniature concerto (though with the fast movement at the centre). Mariko Honda is wholly in sympathy with the specifically Tchaikovskian melancholy which permeates these shorter, lyrical pieces, and even in the *Concerto* her account of the slow movement and the lyrical episodes of the finale bring a darker colouring than with many soloists. Yet her playing can sparkle too, though overall her chosen tempi are comparatively relaxed. These are all performances of considerable intensity, well accompanied, and it is a pity that the brilliant digital recording balances her so closely, so the microphones do not always flatter her tone in the more histrionic upper tessitura. The orchestral sound is also brightly vivid.

(i) *1812 overture; Capriccio italien.*
✿ (M) *** Mercury 434 360-2 [id.]. (i) Bronze French cannon, bells of Laura Spelman Rockefeller Memorial Carillon, Riverside Church, New York City; Minneapolis SO, Dorati (with separate descriptive commentary by Deems Taylor) – BEETHOVEN: *Wellington's victory*. *** ✿

Just as in our listing of this famous Mercury record we have placed *1812* first, so in the credits the cannon and the glorious sounds of the Laura Spelman Carillon take precedence, for in the riveting climax of Tchaikovsky's most famous work the effects completely upstage the orchestra. This is not to suggest that Dorati's performance is in any way lacking. Indeed he makes a great deal of the character and colour of the Russian folk material on which the composer draws so tellingly. But at the end, when the carillon floods into the listener's room and the cannon open fire, the effect is quite overwhelming – far more so than it ever was in its original, LP format, when the narrow grooves could not contain the full amplitude of the sound without some degree of congestion. On this remastered CD the balance is managed spectacularly and the timing of the 'shots' nicely arranged by Wilma Cozart Fine's skilful editing, while the Minneapolis orchestra, who are clearly enjoying themselves both in *1812* and in the brilliant account of *Capriccio italien*, give of their best – even if the (early 1958) stereo is not entirely flattering to the violins. Deems Taylor provides an avuncular commentary on the technical background to the original recording. But heed the cautionary warning on the CD packaging, for before he begins to speak the cannon reopen fire!

1812 overture; Francesca da Rimini; Marche slave; Romeo and Juliet (fantasy overture).
(B) *** EMI Dig. CD-EMX 2152 [(M) id.]. RLPO, Sian Edwards.

The control of the emotional ebb and flow of *Francesca da Rimini* shows Sian Edwards as an instinctive Tchaikovskian. Francesca's clarinet entry is melting and the work's middle section has a Beechamesque sense of colour. The passionate climax, representing the discovery of the lovers, falls only just short of the vehement force of the Stokowski version, while the spectacular recording gives great impact to the closing whirlwind sequence and the despair-laden final chords, where the tam-tam makes its presence felt very pungently. *1812* is also very enjoyable indeed, full of vigour and flair, a majestic final sequence with superbly resounding cannon. In *Romeo and Juliet*, the love-theme is ushered in very naturally and blossoms with the fullest ardour, while the feud music combined with the Friar Lawrence theme reaches a very dramatic climax. *Marche slave*, resplendently high-spirited and exhilarating, makes a perfect foil. The full-bodied recording is well balanced and thrilling in the proper Tchaikovskian way.

(i) *1812 overture;* (ii) *Marche slave.*

(M) **(*) Decca Phase Four 443 896-2 [id.]. (i) Welsh Nat. Op. Ch., Band of Grenadier Guards, RPO Ch., RPO; (ii) LSO; Stokowski – MUSSORGSKY: *Night on the bare mountain* etc. **; BORODIN: *Prince Igor: Polovtsian dances.* **

Stokowski's very eccentric *1812* certainly does not lack spectacle, although it is coarsely recorded. The pyrotechnic effects in the closing pages are accompanied by an overwhelming carillon, then suddenly the chorus appears out of nowhere to sing the Russian hymn. Similarly in *Marche slave* there are gross manipulations of balance to bring out certain instruments (the heavy brass especially) and effects. But it is a powerful performance with a whimsical beginning to the coda.

(i) *1812 overture, Op. 49; Marche slave, Op. 91;* (ii) *Nutcracker suite, Op. 71a;* (i) *Romeo and Juliet* (fantasy overture); (ii) *Swan Lake* (ballet): *suite, Op. 20; Sleeping Beauty* (ballet): *Introduction and Lilac Fairy; Adagio; Waltz.*

(BB) ** Carlton LSO Double Dig. 30368 01147 (2) [(B) id.]. LSO, (i) Yuri Ahronovitch; (ii) Richard Williams.

Yuri Ahronovich's readings are extremely wilful. He moulds the lyrical music idiosyncratically and drives on the allegros with the acceleration in constant flux. The LSO ensemble suffers, but the thrust is undeniable. There is no doubt that this music-making creates bursts of excitement, and the sound is physically very involving. The recording is very spectacular and the balance is truthful, the ambience a little dry but with a convincing perspective. The dynamic range is wide and the fusillade of cannon at the end of *1812* impressively realistic, without ruining the musical focus. In the coupled ballet suites, the LSO respond well to Richard Williams's direct approach, and both playing and sound make a vivid if slightly anonymous impression. The characteristic dances from the *Nutcracker* bring less individual characterization than usual, but the *Waltz of the flowers* has a nice lilt.

1812 overture; Nutcracker suite; Romeo and Juliet (fantasy overture); Swan Lake suite; Symphony No. 6 (Pathétique).

(B) *(*) Decca Double 455 810-2 (2) [(M) id. import]. Chicago SO, Solti.

It is a pity these two CDs were paired, for their appeal is uneven. Characteristically Solti provides an exciting and spectacular *1812*, and the bold immediacy of the Chicago sound brings compulsive music-making throughout. At the end the cannon shots are placed precisely, but the bells are curiously blurred. *Romeo and Juliet* has an unexpected element of restraint. The stuctural symmetry is underlined by the mirroring in the coda of the elegiac melancholy of the opening; and the love theme, very gentle and tender when it first appears on the cor anglais, finds a yearning passion, yet in the battle music the violins bite hard and at the climax the trumpets ring out resplendently. The overall effect is highly individual if not wholly spontaneous. The *Nutcracker suite* also produces characterful solo playing and much subtle detail from Solti, while the ear is struck by the vivid colours of Tchaikovsky's scoring when the sound of the individual instruments is so very tangible. The *Swan Lake suite* is also played splendidly, but there is some lack of charm, except at the entry of the cygnets. However, the key work here is the *Pathétique Symphony*, and this is not a success. With dangerously fast tempi throughout the first and third movements, the element of hysteria is never far away in Solti's intense reading; and the element of nobility, so necessary to provide emotional balance, is missing. The Scherzo/march loses all charm at this hectic pace; indeed the march element virtually disappears altogether. The finale is more controlled in feeling but does not resolve the performance in any satisfactory way. The brilliantly clear recording does not help by making the violins sound excessively bright.

(i) *1812 overture;* (ii) *Romeo and Juliet* (fantasy overture); (iii) *Serenade for strings in C, Op. 48.*

(M) **(*) DG Classikon Dig. 439 468-2; *439 468-4*. (i) Gothenburg SO, Järvi; (ii) Philh. O, Sinopoli; (iii) Orpheus CO.

Järvi's *1812* is exciting – and not just for the added Gothenburg brass and artillery or for the fervour of the orchestra at the opening. Järvi clearly knows how to structure the piece, and he obviously enjoys the histrionics, and so do we. Sinopoli's reading of *Romeo and Juliet*, however, is also very appealing, if with a hint of self-consciousness at the first entry of the big love theme; however, there is plenty of uninhibited passion on the later repeats. In the *Serenade for strings* no one could accuse the Orpheus Chamber Orchestra of lack of energy in the outer movements. Overall it is an impressive performance, even if the problems of rubato without a conductor are not always easily solved. The sound is first class, with the acoustics of the Performing Arts Center at New York State University providing plenty of warmth as well as clarity and a full, firm bass-line, very important in this work.

(i) *Fatum* (symphonic poem), *Op. 77;* (ii; iii) *Francesca da Rimini* (fantasy after Dante), *Op. 32;* (ii; iii) *Hamlet* (fantasy overture), *Op 67a;* (iv; v) *Romeo and Juliet* (fantasy overture); (i) *The Storm, Op. 76; The Tempest, Op. 18; The Voyevoda, Op. 78* (symphonic poems);(iv; iii) *1812 Overture, Op. 49.*
(B) **(*) Ph. Duo 442 586-2 (2) [(M) id. import]. (i) Frankfurt RSO, Eliahu Inbal; (ii) New Philh. O; (iii) Igor Markevitch; (iv) Concg. O; (v) Bernard Haitink.

On this two-for-the-price-of-one Duo set come finely committed performances of four of Tchaikovsky's little-known symphonic poems in excellent recordings from the mid-1970s with the right kind of sonority and ambience. The most remarkable piece (which is superbly performed by Inbal and the Frankfurt orchestra) is *The Storm*, a surprisingly coherent structure in sonata form which suddenly appeared in 1864 as Tchaikovsky's first fully fledged orchestral composition (after various student efforts). It has all the fingerprints of the later masterpieces: individual and attractive melodic and harmonic content and an astonishing orchestral flair. Yet the composer never published it. In his splendid biography of the composer, David Brown comments: 'Much of *The Storm* has the familiar and individual sound of Tchaikovsky's own mature orchestration. Already he is showing that natural facility of conceiving his ideas directly in terms of orchestral textures and colour.' *The Voyevoda* is a very late work which is unconnected with the opera of the same name (they are based on different subjects). If not entirely successful, it has some good ideas and characteristic orchestration. But it so dissatisfied its composer – though not the press and public – at its first performance that he tore up the score in anger and despair. Fortunately the orchestral parts survived. *Fatum*, written four years after *The Storm*, is a much less successful and less assured piece and rests completely in the shade of the composer's first great masterpiece, *Romeo and Juliet*, which followed in 1869 (although it was revised twice, in 1870 and 1880). *The Tempest* is notable for its memorably passionate love theme and the atmospheric opening and close depicting Prospero's island and the sea. Here the performance is very ardent, but the reverberant acoustic makes Tchaikovsky's climaxes a bit noisy. Markevitch's accounts of *Francesca da Rimini* and *Hamlet* have characteristic intensity and drive, but are weaker in dealing with the lyrical passages, although there are no complaints about the orchestral playing. Haitink's *Romeo and Juliet* is full of atmosphere and is spaciously conceived, although it builds up a full head of passion rather slowly. *1812* makes a lively bonus, rather individual in its pacing, but not unconvincingly so. But it is for the four novelties that this set is worthwhile.

Francesca da Rimini.
(M) *** DG 453 988-2 [id.]. Leningrad PO, Rozhdestvensky – SHOSTAKOVICH: *Symphony No. 5.* **(*)
(M) ** Virgin/EMI Dig. CUV5 61124-2 [id.]. Houston SO, Christoph Eschenbach – DVORAK: *Symphony No. 9.* **

Rozhdestvensky's *Francesca da Rimini* is a *tour de force* and can almost be spoken of in the same breath as Beecham's electrifying pre-war recording with the LPO (now available in a superb Dutton transfer – see Concerts, below). As with Beecham, the inferno music is breathtakingly done and the music for the lovers' passion, which with Beecham is deeply felt and poignant, is conveyed with enormous intensity by the Leningrad orchestra. Yet the idyllic central section is relaxed, Tchaikovsky's glowingly imaginative writing for the woodwind nicely pointed. The 1959 recording, made in Wembley Town Hall, is reverberant and not completely refined – the Russian brass playing is somewhat blatant in the climaxes; but such is the excitement and spontaneity of the performance that one is swept along uncomplaining.

Eschenbach's performance of *Francesca da Rimini* has similar qualities to those in the Dvořák symphony with which it is coupled. With clean textures and ensemble, with rhythms crisply resilient and with the brass section gloriously ripe, it is a refreshing performance which yet lacks Tchaikovskian passion. It makes a generous and unusual fill-up for the *New World Symphony*.

Manfred Symphony, Op. 58 (see also above, under *Capriccio italien*).
(M) *** EMI Dig. CDM7 64872-2. Philh. O, Muti.

Muti's reading is forceful and boldly dramatic throughout. His Scherzo has a quality of exhilarating bravura, rather than concentrating on delicacy; the lovely central melody is given a sense of joyous vigour. The *Andante*, after a refined opening, soon develops a passionate forward sweep; in the finale the amplitude and brilliant detail of the recording, combined with magnificent playing from the Philharmonia Orchestra, brings a massively compulsive projection of Tchaikovsky's bacchanale and a richly satisfying dénouement. The CD adds to the weight and definition of the recording and, if the effect is slightly less than sumptuous, the Kingsway Hall ambience adds plenty of warmth and colour. Recommended.

Manfred Symphony, Op. 58; Marche slave, Op. 31; Romeo and Juliet: fantasy overture.
(B) ** EMI forte CZS5 69776-2 (2) [(M) id. import]. LSO, Previn – RACHMANINOV: *Symphony No. 2.* **

Previn's 1973 version of *Manfred* with the LSO is outstandingly well recorded, one of the finest of all analogue recordings of the work, made in the Kingsway Hall, with vivid sound balanced in the most natural way. But the performance is disappointing. The best movement is the Scherzo, which is charmingly done, but the outer movements, spaciously conceived, are less convincing and without the strong forward impulse this score must have if it is to succeed. *Marche slave* and *Romeo and Juliet* are altogether more successful, even if the latter is less romantic than some performances. Previn takes a clear-headed, totally unsentimental view; as a result, the music emerges more strongly in design and no less vivid than usual. The 1972 recordings, made at Abbey Road, have a hint of studio ambience rather than the concert hall.

The Nutcracker (ballet), *Op. 71* (complete).
(B) *** BMG/Melodiya Twofer 74321 40067-2 (2). Bolshoi Theatre Children's Ch., Bolshoi Theatre O, Rozhdestvensky.
(B) *** CfP CD-CFPD 4706 (2) [CDCB 47267]. Amb. S., LSO, Previn.
(B) *** Decca Double 444 827-2 (2) [id.]. Nat. PO, Bonynge – OFFENBACH: *Le Papillon*. ***
(BB) ** Naxos Dig. 8.550324/5 [id.]. Slovak RSO (Bratislava), Lenárd – CHOPIN/GLAZUNOV: *Chopinina*. **

(i) *The Nutcracker* (complete); (ii) *Serenade for strings in C, Op. 48*.
(M) **(*) Mercury 432 750-2 (2). (i) LSO; (ii) Philharmonia Hungarica, Antal Dorati.

(i) *The Nutcracker* (ballet): complete; (ii) *Sleeping Beauty* (ballet): highlights.
(B) *** Ph. Duo 442 562-2 (2) [(M) id. import]. (i) Concg. O, with boys' Ch., Dorati; (ii) LSO, Fistoulari.

Dorati's 1975 complete *Nutcracker* with the Concertgebouw Orchestra now makes a clear first choice in the bargain category, more particularly as it is coupled with Fistoulari's equally outstanding 1962 set of highlights from the *Sleeping Beauty*. In the former the playing of the Concertgebouw Orchestra is immensely refined yet often very dramatic. Dorati's conception is both vivid and strong. Its vitality is noticeable from the *Miniature overture* onwards with an engaging rhythmic spring and no forcing of accents. The pine forest journey has seldom sounded more ardent and is built to a tremendous climax. Then the *Waltz of the Snowflakes* produces the most delightfully fresh choral quality from the Boys' Choir of St Bravo Cathedral, Haarlem. Dorati's attention to detail is affectionate, and in the dances which make up Act II his characterization is sure, although the *Waltz of the flowers* could ideally have more lilt. The CD transfer brings less sumptuous sound than on the old LPs, but the Concertgebouw ambience ensures body as well as vividness. Fistoulari's greatness as a ballet conductor is well celebrated by the *Sleeping Beauty* selection, which was extremely well recorded in its day and has transferred to CD with striking amplitude and brilliance. He conducted Tchaikovsky without hysteria yet generated great excitement, as the breadth and power of the *Rose adagio* immediately demonstrates, while the delightful *Panorama* is admirably relaxed and glowing. The selection is well made and satisfying, with plenty of charm and sparkling colours from the LSO wind players.

We enthused about Rozhdestvensky's recording when it originally appeared on HMV in the mid-1970s, and it remains among the most vital accounts of the ballet in the catalogue. It has a very strong Russian colouring, nowhere more strikingly different from a Western approach than in the *Waltz of the snowflakes*, with the children's voices singing lustily. The timbres of woodwind and brass are robustly textured, the colouring bold. The *March* has a more military brassiness than usual – and very arresting it is, quite unlike the more piquant stylization one normally expects. In fortissimos the trombones make a strong impression. The strings have added bite yet are expansive too, but there is never the slightest hint of sentimentalizing the music, while the opening party scene conveys the rumbustious character of adults and children enjoying themselves. The big climaxes have plenty of excitement, and in the characteristic dances of the *Divertissement* the orchestral palette has never glowed more vividly. The result is refreshingly spontaneous and full of character. Every point of Tchaikovsky's music tells, and the sheer life of the playing disarms any criticism. The excellent recording actually dates from 1960 and the present transfer brings a consistently lively projection without detracting from the theatrical atmosphere.

With Dorati's LSO *Nutcracker* the Mercury engineering is sophisticated, with a natural balance; the hall ambience provides warmth and bloom, yet detail is characteristically refined. Dorati relishes every detail, his characterization is strong, and the playing is full of life and elegance. The *Journey through the pine forest* expands magnificently while the choral delicacy of the *Waltz of the snowflakes* is full of charm. In Act II the characteristic dances have much colour and vitality. Altogether a great success. However, the *Serenade for strings* is less compelling. The slightly dry effect does not capture quite enough of the hall ambience and turns a close scrutiny on ensemble from the Philharmonia Hungarica, who could at times be more polished. It is an affectionate performance, but not an especially vital one.

Previn's earlier (1972) analogue set with the LSO has been freshly remastered. As in his later, digital version (only available combined with the other two ballets), the famous dances in Act II are played with much sophistication, and indeed the orchestral playing throughout is of very high quality. With Act I sounding brighter and more dramatic than in its original LP format, this CfP reissue makes a fine bargain alternative to Dorati's mid-priced Mercury set with the LSO.

Bonynge's set is made the more attractive by its rare and substantial Offenbach coupling. His approach is sympathetic and the orchestral playing is polished, even if in the opening scene he misses some of the atmosphere. With the beginning of the magic, as the Christmas tree expands, the performance becomes more dramatically involving and Bonynge is at his best in the latter part of the ballet, with fine passion in the Act II *Pas de deux* and plenty of colour in the characteristic dances. The Decca Kingsway Hall recording is brilliant on top, yet has a glowing ambient warmth.

The Naxos super-bargain *Nutcracker* is played with great zest in Bratislava, and there is no lack of polish either. There is never a dull moment here, and the famous 'characteristic dances' of the Act II *Divertissement* emerge vividly. The digital recording has the brightest colouring and the effect overall could never be described as dull. But there are snags: there is a relative absence of charm and the *Waltz of the snowflakes* is minus its children's chorus. The Bolshoi Ballet did it that way at a London performance, but the omission of a highly engaging and appealingly innocent effect from a record is not easy to forgive. The *Waltz of the flowers*, too, lilts much more persuasively in Rostropovich's hands – see below – even though he takes liberties with it. The break between the two Naxos CDs is at an awkward spot, just before the arrival of the Spanish dancers in the *Divertissement*, and the listener is left 'in mid-air' until the second disc continues the music.

The Nutcracker (ballet), *Op. 71:* excerpts.
(B) ** Millennium MCD 80402 [id.]. RPO, Artur Rodzinski – DELIBES: *Coppélia, Sylvia:* excerpts. **

A lively, well-characterized set of excerpts, as one would expect from this fine conductor, but the RPO strings do not sound as well nourished as they do in some of Sir Thomas's recordings. The CD offers 12 numbers – about 50 minutes of music. The recording was made in 1956 and sounds very natural and well balanced, save for the celesta in the *Sugar plum fairy*, which is rather too upfront. All the same, given the rich stock of alternatives, many equally cheap and much better recorded and even better played, this is not particularly competitive.

Nutcracker suite, Op. 71a.
(M) *** Decca Phase Four 455 154-2 [id.]. Boston Pops O, Fiedler – J. STRAUSS: *Waltzes.* **
(M) **(*) Sony SBK 46550; *SBT 46550* [id.]. Phd. O, Ormandy – CHOPIN: *Les Sylphides;* DELIBES: *Coppélia; Sylvia: Suites.* ***

Fiedler's Phase Four performance has marvellous spirit and vigour; the music is played with striking élan and colour. The vividly coloured recording helps to project the music-making and, while it is the spontaneity and life of the playing itself that are so striking, this is a demonstration of Phase Four at its very best.

The Philadelphia Orchestra made this wonderful music universally famous in Walt Disney's *Fantasia* and they know how to play it just as well under Ormandy in 1963 as they did under Stokowski. Perhaps there is less individuality in the characteristic dances, but the music-making has suitable moments of reticence (as in the neat *Ouverture miniature*) as well as plenty of flair. In the *Waltz of the flowers* Ormandy blots his copybook by taking the soaring violin tune an octave up on its second appearance.

(i) *Nutcracker suite;* (ii) *Sleeping Beauty* (excerpts); (iii) *Swan Lake* (excerpts).
(B) **(*) EMI CZS7 62816-2 (2) [CDZB 61816]. LSO, André Previn, (i) with Amb. S.
(B) ** Ph. Virtuoso 426 975-2 [(M) id. import]. LSO; (i) Dorati; (ii) Fistoulari; (iii) Monteux.

By the use of two CDs, offering some 148 minutes of music, this EMI set (issued in the 'two for the price of one' series) covers a substantial proportion of the key numbers from all three ballets. *The Nutcracker* selection is particularly generous in including, besides virtually all the most famous characteristic dances, the 13-minute episode in Act I starting with the Battle sequence, continuing with the magical pine forest journey and finishing with the delightful choral *Waltz of the snowflakes*. Previn and the LSO provide vivacious, charismatic playing and the recording is full, bright and vivid. The remastering, however, loses some of the smoothness and refinement of focus of the original, analogue recordings in the interest of a lively upper range. But this remains very enjoyable and excellent value.

There is some fine music-making here, especially under Fistoulari and Monteux. Dorati is lively, but his *Waltz of the flowers*, though rhythmically neat, lacks something in glamour. However, apart from the *Nutcracker*, the selections are arbitrary and not particularly generous. To have a *Swan Lake* 'suite' without *the* oboe tune seems extraordinarily bad planning. On DG, costing only a little more, Rostropovich offers nine more minutes of music, and he secures superlative playing from the Berlin Philharmonic, while the DG engineers enhance his very special music-making with recording that is both lustrous and spectacular.

Nutcracker suite; Sleeping Beauty: suite; Swan Lake: suite.
❀ (M) *** DG 449 726-2 [id.]. BPO, Rostropovich.
(M) *** EMI (SIS) CDM7 64332-2. LSO, Previn.

Rostropovich's triptych of Tchaikovsky ballet suites is very special. His account of the *Nutcracker suite* is enchanting: the *Sugar plum fairy* is introduced with ethereal gentleness, the *Russian dance* has marvellous zest and the *Waltz of the flowers* combines warmth and elegance with an exhilarating vigour. The *Sleeping Beauty* and *Swan Lake* selections are hardly less distinguished, and in the former the *Panorama* is gloriously played. The CD remastering (for inclusion in DG's 'Legendary Recordings' series), which was always outstanding, now approaches demonstration standard, combining bloom with enhanced detail. 69 minutes of sheer joy, and at mid-price too.

The digital remastering has been very successful on the EMI disc, freshening the sound of the excellent recordings, taken from Previn's analogue complete sets (which means that the *Dance of the sugar plum fairy* in *The Nutcracker* has the longer coda rather than the ending Tchaikovsky devised for the *Suite*). The performances are at once vivid and elegant, warm and exciting. Previn's *Panorama* from *Sleeping Beauty* is hardly less beguiling than Rostropovich's and the recording has comparable warmth. There is nearly 73 minutes of music here, and this version can be strongly recommended alongside the DG disc; it is a most enjoyable record.

Nutcracker suite, Op. 71a; Sleeping Beauty: excerpts; *Swan Lake: suite.*
(M) ** [RCA Basic 100 09026 61711-2]. Phd. O, Ormandy.

Ormandy's suites, sumptuously recorded in the 1960s, are ripely spectacular, full of life but not refined or subtle, although the orchestral playing – with plenty of rhythmic life – is polished as well as enthusiastic. The music is enjoyable in an opulently colourful way.

Ballet highlights (with narrative) from: *The Nutcracker; Sleeping Beauty; Swan Lake.*
(M) * Conifer Dig. 75605 55018 (*Nutcracker*); 75605 55019 (*Sleeping Beauty*); 75605 55017 (*Swan Lake*). Tony Scotland, ROHCG O, Mark Ermler.

This is a misguided enterprise, and it is difficult to discover at which age-group Tony Scotland's narratives – which he has written himself – are aimed. His manner seems too avuncular for really young children, and older listeners will find there is far, far too much text. Moreover it doesn't bear repetition. In *The Nutcracker*, the background to the events of Petipa's scenario concerning the enigmatic Herr Drosselmeyer is of some interest, but in *Sleeping Beauty*, because the story is so simple and the action limited, every number is described to no advantage at all. Tchaikovsky's music says it all, and that is very well played and recorded here. The three CDs are available separately.

Romeo and Juliet (fantasy overture).
(B) ** EMI CfP CD-CFP 6043 [(M) id. import]. LPO, Sir Charles Mackerras – Richard STRAUSS: *Don Juan; Till Eulenspiegel.* **
(BB) *(*) ASV CDQS 6040. Sydney SO, Serebrier – SIBELIUS: *Symphony No. 1.* *(*)

Mackerras's account has plenty of surface excitement, but emotionally it is rather laid back and, although sensitively played and well recorded, it lacks panache.

José Serebrier's account of *Romeo and Juliet* with the Sydney Symphony Orchestra is respectable and comes with an acceptable account of the *First Symphony* of Sibelius. An odd coupling, given the competition in both works, even at the bargain end of the catalogue, and not a strong contender in either. Looking at it in cold, commercial terms, there is better value to be had elsewhere, even if the Sydney account is not lacking in merit.

(i) *Romeo and Juliet* (fantasy overture, ed. Stokowski). (ii) *Sleeping Beauty* (ballet), *Op. 66* (excerpts); *Swan Lake* (ballet), *Op. 20* (excerpts).
(M) *(**) Decca Phase Four 448 950-2 [id.]. (i) SRO; (ii) New Philh. O; Stokowski.

Stokowski plays both ballet suites with great panache, generating a consistently high level of adrenalin. The orchestral playing under his direction is characteristically fine, and no one knew better than he how to shape a Tchaikovsky melody or indeed (and here he uses the possibilities of artificial balancing unashamedly) how to reveal a felicitous detail of scoring. It is a pity that the Phase Four techniques have contributed a gloss of artificial brilliance to reduce the naturalness of the strings, but this music-making remains utterly magnetic and often thrilling (witness the finale of *Swan Lake* or the introduction to the *Sleeping Beauty*). The selections are not predictable; indeed the *Panorama* from *Sleeping Beauty* is a surprising omission. However, for Stokowski aficionados the collector's item here is *Romeo and Juliet*. Stokowski held the view that Tchaikovsky wanted to finish his fantasy overture in a gently elegiac mood and that the final loud orchestral chords were a sop to public taste. So, being a law unto himself, he recorded the overture without the ending indicated in the score, adding an emphasized percussive crash before the funeral procession. The performance itself has a languorously passionate climax, but the brightly lit Phase Four sound is not refined enough to please the ear consistently.

Serenade for strings in C, Op. 48.
(BB) *** ASV CDQS 6094 [(M) id.]. Polish R. CO, Duczmal – SUK: *Serenade* ***; GRIEG: *Holberg suite* etc. **(*)

The Polish Radio Chamber Orchestra is a first-class body of players, and they give a highly individual reading, full of subtlety and grace. The conductor's imaginative nuancing of dynamic shading is most winning, and this account often finds a rare quality of tenderness alongside its vigour and expansiveness. The Waltz is relaxed and gentle; later there is a wistful delicacy in the *Elégie* as Tchaikovsky's lovely cantilena is floated over gentle pizzicatos. The finale is exquisitely prepared, then the allegro is off with the wind, very fast, light and balletic, again with engagingly crisp articulation. Altogether this is the kind of performance that makes one appreciate this as one of the composer's greatest works, with its Mozartian elegance and perfection of form. The recording is excellent, full, transparent, yet with a fine overall bloom.

Serenade for strings; Souvenir de Florence, Op. 70.
(BB) **(*) Naxos Dig. 8.550404 [id.]. Vienna CO, Philippe Entremont.

Entremont's performances of Tchaikovsky's two major string works communicate above all a feeling of passionate thrust and energy. The *Waltz*, with its neatly managed tenutos, has a nice touch of romantic feeling and, after the ardour of the *Elégie*, the finale steals in persuasively, again producing an unflagging impetus, with dance-rhythms bracing and strong. The unaccountably neglected *Souvenir de Florence* has comparable momentum and eagerness. The dashing main theme of the first movement swings along infectiously, while the wistful secondary idea also takes wing. Entremont brings out the charm and responds easily to the variety of mood, both here and in the *Allegretto*, permeated with a flavour of Russian folksong. Throughout, the commitment and ensemble of the VCO bring the most persuasive advocacy and make one wonder why the *Souvenir* does not have a more central place in the string repertoire.

The Sleeping Beauty (ballet), *Op. 66* (complete).
(BB) *** Naxos Dig. 8.550490/2 [id.]. Slovak State PO (Košice), Andrew Mogrelia.
(M) **(*) Decca (IMS) 425 468-2 (3). Nat. PO, Richard Bonynge – MEYERBEER: *Les Patineurs*. ***
(M) **(*) EMI CMS7 64840-2 (2) [CDQB 54814]. LSO, Previn.
(B) ** Ph. Duo 446 166-2 (2) [id.]. Concg. O, Dorati.

Andrew Mongrelia conducts Tchaikovsky's score with an ideal combination of warmth, grace and vitality. Moreover the Slovak State Philharmonic prove to be an excellent orchestra for this repertoire, with fine wind-players and equally impressive string principals for the important violin and cello solos. Mogrelia relishes the orchestral detail – and there is much inspired Tchaikovskian scoring here – and he moves the music on with a natural sense of pacing and generates plenty of excitement in the big set-pieces: the climaxes which come at the ends of Acts I and II are splendidly expansive. The Naxos digital recording is full and brilliant without being overlit, and the acoustics of the House of Arts in Košice bring a spacious ambience so that the spectacular moments have sufficient room to expand, and the orchestral colours are vivid. A clear first choice among all available recordings, irrespective of cost.

Bonynge secures brilliant and often elegant playing from the National Philharmonic Orchestra and his rhythmic pointing is always characterful. As recorded, however, the upper strings lack sumptuousness; otherwise, the sound is excellent and there is much to give pleasure, notably the drama of the awakening scene and the Act III *Divertissement*. The Decca sound has a fine sparkle here, and the solo violin (Mincho Minchev) and cello (Francisco Gabarro) provide most appealing solo contributions.

In Previn's 1974 complete set the analogue EMI recording is less brilliant than some, the balance slightly recessed so that the sound is sumptuous with a richly resonant bass. But there is a distinct absence of glitter. With warm, polished orchestral playing, Previn conveys his affection throughout, but too often – in the famous *Waltz*, for instance – there is a lack of vitality, and in the *Entr'acte* between Scenes i and ii of Act II, with its elegant violin solo from John Brown, the atmosphere is so cosy that the style hovers perilously near that of the salon. On the other hand, the *Panorama* which comes immediately before this shows Previn and his orchestra at their very best, the tune floating over its rocking bass in the most magical way. With Previn's tempi sometimes indulgently relaxed, it has been impossible to get the complete recording on to a pair of CDs, and the *Pas berrichon* and *Sarabande* included in the original (three-disc) LP issue have been cut.

Dorati's complete *Sleeping Beauty* was recorded over a period between May 1979 and January 1981. It is a consistently vibrant and dramatic account, supported by firm, rich recording and splendid orchestral playing (especially in the last Act, which gives the orchestral wind soloists many chances to shine). Yet this is a score that – for all its melodic inspiration – can momentarily disengage the listener's attention; and here, in spite of the drama, this does happen. Everything is well characterized, but at times there is a lack of magic.

Sleeping Beauty (ballet): highlights.
(M) ** Sony SBK 46340; *SBT 46340* [id.]. Phd. O, Ormandy – ROSSINI: *Boutique fantasque*. **(*)

Ormandy provides a sumptuously glossy selection, with nearly an hour's music (the CD plays for 76 minutes overall). Superbly polished and often exciting playing but, with a forward balance, the effect is somewhat overwhelming. The sound is opulently brilliant rather than refined.

Sleeping Beauty (ballet): *suite*.
(BB) ** Naxos Dig. 8.550079; *4550079* [id.]. Czech RSO (Bratislava), Ondrej Lenárd – GLAZUNOV: *The Seasons*. **(*)

The Czech Radio Orchestra under Ondrej Lenárd play Tchaikovsky's ballet suite with spirit and colour, and the recording has plenty of weight and ambience and no lack of brilliance but the *Panorama* is disappointing, taken fast and with a lack of subtlety in the rocking bass rhythm.

Sleeping Beauty (ballet): *suite; Swan Lake* (ballet): *suite*.
(B) **(*) [EMI Red Line Dig. CDR5 69871]. Phd. O, Muti.

This is one of the first recordings made by the Philadelphia Orchestra in the Fairmount Hall, which provides a flattering ambience for this great orchestra. There is a very wide dynamic range, however, which means that when one achieves a satisfactory level for the violin/cello duet the spectacular climaxes are almost overwhelming. Muti's approach is essentially spacious and he concentrates on the elegance of the music, achieving an excellent response from his orchestra.

(i) *Souvenir d'un lieu cher (Méditation), Op. 42/1;* (ii) *Sérénade mélancolique for violin and orchestra, Op. 26*.
(M) *** Sony Stern Edition I SMK 66830 [id.]. Isaac Stern, with (i) Nat. SO, Rostropovich; (ii) Columbia SO, Brieff – BRUCH: *Violin concerto No. 1*; WIENIAWSKI: *Violin concerto No. 2*. **(*)

Glorious playing from Stern. He is recorded too closely (as is the Columbia Symphony in the *Sérénade*) but his warm timbre is caught lusciously and he knows just how to catch the composer's nostalgic feeling. Both accompaniments are sympathetic.

Suites Nos. 1 in D min., Op. 43; 2 in C (Caractéristique); 3 in G, Op. 55; 4 in G (Mozartiana), Op. 61.
(B) *** Ph. Duo 454 253-2 (2) [(M) id. import]. New Philh. O, Antal Dorati.

Dorati's highly distinguished set of the four underrated *Orchestral suites* of Tchaikovsky come from the late 1960s. They have never sounded better than in the present CD transfer: the sound has some lack of transparency and ultimate vividness, but it is pleasingly naturally balanced. Dorati was a masterly ballet conductor and he brings out the balletic feeling, in the first two suites especially, and revels in the infinitely inventive orchestral detail which shows the composer consistently seeking subtle new orchestral colourings, not least in the *Scherzo burlesque* of the *Second Suite* with its folksy accordions, while in the final wild *Danse baroque* there is even an anticipation of Stravinsky's *Petrushka*. *Mozartiana* is also neatly and stylishly done. In the *Third Suite* Svetlanov's Russian recording demonstrates more Slavic temperament, but Dorati is thoroughly at home in the justly famous *Theme and variations*, capped by a splendid closing *Polacca*: the Philips recording expands impressively here and rises to the occasion. At Philips Duo price this is very recommendable indeed and is a source of much enjoyment.

Suites Nos. 1 in D min., Op. 43; 2 in C (Caractéristique) Op. 53.
(M) *** Melodiya/BMG Dig. 74321 17099-2 [id.]. USSR SO, Svetlanov.
(BB) *** Naxos Dig. 8.550644. [id.]. Nat. SO of Ireland, Stefan Sanderling.

Tchaikovsky's *Orchestral suites* are directly descended from the dance suites of the baroque era; Svetlanov brings to them an appropriately light touch. The highlight of the *First Suite* is the deliciously orchestrated *Marche miniature* which tends to dwarf everything else in sheer memorability – except perhaps the *Introduction*, where Tchaikovsky's innate melancholy at the opening is effectively dispersed by the following fugato. But the other movements are also immediately attractive, especially the closing *Gavotte*. Svetlanov's inspirational reading of the *Second Suite* is doubly distinctive for making the listener realize that this is a far more substantial and attractive work than was previously thought. The *Scherzo burlesque* has a part for accordions in its central section, but here they are mixed in with folksy woodwind sounds and the effect is highly piquant. In the final *Danse baroque* the Russian energy of the performance bubbles right over. With such sympathetic playing and first-class digital recording this is a prime recommendation at mid-price.

Stefan Sanderling (son of Kurt) also shows how well he understands the music's baroque ancestry in nicely turned performances of works which are neglected on record and almost never heard in the concert hall. The playing of the excellent National Symphony Orchestra of Ireland – another Naxos discovery – is polished and sympathetic to the Tchaikovskian ardour that wells up every now and then. Each of the movements (six in No. 1; five in No. 2) is neatly characterized, and there is much charm and colour. In the *Scherzo burlesque* of No. 2 the four interpolated accordions come through well in the middle section, and the suite's closing *Danse baroque* is very spirited indeed. The recording, made in Dublin's National Concert Hall, is spacious yet allows the intimate detail of the orchestration to emerge vividly. A fine, super-bargain alternative to Svetlanov.

Suites Nos. 3 in G, Op. 55; 4 in G (Mozartiana), Op. 61.
(M) *** Melodiya/BMG Dig. 74321 17100-2 [id.]. USSR SO, Svetlanov.
(BB) **(*) Naxos Dig. 8.550728 [id.]. Nat. SO of Ireland, Stefan Sanderling.

Svetlanov treats Tchaikovsky's finest suite, the *Third*, very freely, supported by the most eloquent response from one of the premier Soviet orchestras. In the *Theme and variations*, some of Svetlanov's tempi are unexpected, and the finale *Polacca* is less overwhelming than in some previous versions, Svetlanov emphasizing its dance rhythms rather than seeking to be grandiose. Svetlanov is hardly less successful in the *Fourth Suite* (*Mozartiana*), where Tchaikovsky's neat scoring is always respectful of the original music. Even so, the *Preghiera*, based on Mozart's *Ave verum*, can sometimes sound too opulent, but not here. The closing *Variations* (where Mozart used Gluck's '*Unser dummer Pöbel meint*' suite) are a delight. With excellent digital recording in both works and an attractive concert-hall ambience this is very recommendable, particularly at mid-price.

Sanderling shows much delicacy of feeling both in the opening *Gigue* of *Mozartiana* and in the *Elégie*, the first movement of the *Third suite*, where he is warm without being carried away; in No. 4, the *Preghiera* is touching without the climax becoming too lavish. The orchestral playing is of the highest quality in terms of sensitivity and polish, and it is a pity that one has reservations about the performances of the sets of variations which Tchaikovsky uses for each finale. In *Mozartiana* Sanderling is very romantic and, although orchestral detail is nicely observed, his affectionate rubato affects the directness of manner with which Mozart's original piano variations would have been presented. The masterly *Theme and variations* which end the *Third suite* are superbly done until the finale, when Sanderling is just that bit too grandiloquent and measured. With such richly expansive recording it cannot fail to make its effect but, with a little more pace and a touch more rhythmic lift, it could have been the overwhelming culmination the composer intended.

Swan Lake (ballet), *Op. 20* (complete).
(B) *** CfP Dig. CD-CFPD 4727 (2) [(M) id. import]. Philh. O, John Lanchbery.
(B) **(*) DG Double 453 055-2 (2) [(M) id. import]. Boston SO, Ozawa.
(M) **(*) Melodiya/BMG 74321 17082-2 (3) [id.]. Russian State SO, Svetlanov.
(BB) ** Naxos Dig. 8.550246/7 [id.]. Slovak RSO (Bratislava), Ondrej Lenárd.

Lanchbery's 1982 *Swan Lake* makes a superb bargain. The CfP reissue on a pair of CDs, which play for 79 minutes and 75 minutes respectively, accommodates Acts I and II on the first disc and Acts III and IV on the second. Though two numbers are cut, the set includes the extra music (a *Pas de deux*) which Tchaikovsky wrote to follow the *Pas de six* in Act III, when Siegfried dances with Odile, mistakenly believing her to be Odette. The EMI recording, made at Abbey Road, is very fine indeed: spacious, vividly coloured and full, with natural perspective and a wide (but not uncomfortably wide) dynamic range. The orchestral playing is first class, with polished, elegant string phrasing matched by felicitous wind solos. Lanchbery's rhythmic spring is a constant pleasure; everything is alert and there is plenty of excitement at climaxes.

Ozawa's version omits the Act III *Pas de deux* but otherwise plays the complete original score. His performance is certainly alive and often vigorous (as at the opening *Allegro giusto*). But it has not quite the verve of Lanchbery's CfP version; Ozawa's approach is more serious, less flexible. Yet the playing of the Boston orchestra is strikingly polished and sympathetic, and there are many impressive and enjoyable things here, with wind (and violin) solos always giving pleasure. The end result is a little faceless, in spite of a spectacular, wide-ranging analogue recording, as vivid as it is powerful, and admirably transferred to CD.

Swan Lake is easily the most successful of Svetlanov's recordings of the three great Tchaikovsky ballets and, were it on two discs instead of three, it would be very competitive. Svetlanov is often exhilarating in his lively pacing, very Slavonic in impetus. Yet all the famous numbers relax glowingly and emerge with flying colours. The opening of Act II with its famous oboe swan theme is ideally paced and the climax is unspoiled by brass blatancy, though they certainly are given their head. Later, the *Danses des cygnes* are very persuasive (with excellent violin and cello soloists) and the Act III *Divertissement* brings vivid solo wind playing. At the end, the spectacular finale has great excitement and passion. The digital recording is admirably full-blooded and the strings have plenty of amplitude.

Recorded in the Concert Hall of the Slovak Radio (Bratislava) in 1989, Lenárd's complete *Swan Lake* is both exhilarating and full-blooded and does not lack refinement or colour either. The sound is wide-ranging and full, and the very quality of racy excitement which makes his complete *Nutcracker* seem too hard-driven, here, more appropriately adds zest, although at times tempi are very fast indeed. This emphasizes the lyrical contrasts (as does the very wide dynamic range of the recording) and the famous oboe tune is always presented gracefully. Wind and brass playing is vivid, and altogether this makes a lively entertainment and, with the whole ballet offered on two discs, very economic too.

Swan Lake (ballet), *Op. 20* (slightly abridged recording of the European score).
(B) **(*) Decca Double 440 630-2 (2) [id.]. SRO, Ansermet – PROKOFIEV: *Romeo and Juliet*. **

Returning to Ansermet's 1959 recording of *Swan Lake*, one is amazed by the vigour of the playing and the excellence of the recording. The Drigo version of the score, which Ansermet uses, dates from 1895; Drigo added orchestrations of his own, taken from Tchaikovsky's piano music (Op. 72), yet he left out some 1,600 bars of the original score. Ansermet offers the Act I introduction and Nos. 1–2, 4, 7 and 8; Act II, Nos. 10–13; Act III, Nos. 15, 17–18 and 20–23, with No. 5 (the *Pas de deux)* then interpolated before Nos. 28 and 29 from Act IV. Despite the obvious gaps, most of the familiar favourites are included here, and the music-making has such zest and colour that one cannot but revel in every bar. The solo wind playing is not always as sweet-timbred as in some other versions, but the violin and cello solos are well done, and there is not a dull moment throughout. The transfer is well managed, full-blooded and bright, and there is not too much wrong with the timbre of the upper strings. It was a happy idea to couple this on its Double Decca reissue with a selection of 15 items from the two suites from Prokofiev's *Romeo and Juliet* ballet, even if here the orchestral playing is less impressive.

SYMPHONIES

Symphonies Nos. 1–6.
(M) *** DG 429 675-2 (4). BPO, Karajan.

Symphonies Nos. 1–6; Andante cantabile; Capriccio italien; Fatum; Francesca da Rimini, Op. 22; Romeo and Juliet (fantasy overture); *Serenade for strings, Op. 48; The Tempest; Voyevoda.*
(B) **(*) BMG/Melodiya 74321 17101-2 (6). USSR SO, Svetlanov.

Symphonies Nos. 1–6; Capriccio italien; Manfred Symphony.
❀ (M) *** Chandos Dig. CHAN 8672/8 [id.]. Oslo PO, Jansons.

Symphonies Nos. 1–3; Francesca da Rimini, Op. 32.
(B) **(*) BMG/Melodiya Twofer 74321 34163-2 (2) [id.]. USSR SO, Svetlanov.

Symphonies Nos. 4–6 (Pathétique); Andante cantabile in B flat, Op. 11; The Voyevoda, Op. 78.
(B) **(*) BMG/Melodiya Twofer 74321 40066-2 [id.]. USSR SO, Svetlanov.

Symphonies Nos. 1–6; Manfred Symphony; Francesca da Rimini; Romeo and Juliet (fantasy overture).
(M) *** EMI CMS5 65709-2 [CDME 65709] (5) [id.]. LPO, Mstislav Rostropovich.

Symphonies Nos. 1–6; Romeo and Juliet (fantasy overture).
(B) *** EMI CZS7 67314-2 (4) [(M) id. import]. Philh. O, Riccardo Muti.
(B) *** Decca 430 787-2 (4) [(M) id. import]. VPO, Lorin Maazel.

Jansons's Tchaikovsky series, which includes *Manfred*, is self-recommending. The full romantic power of the music is consistently conveyed and, above all, the music-making is urgently spontaneous throughout, with the Oslo Philharmonic Orchestra always committed and fresh, helped by the richly atmospheric Chandos sound. The seven separate CDs offered here are packaged in a box priced as for five premium discs.

Muti's outstanding set of the Tchaikovsky symphonies is made the more attractive by the addition of his superb analogue *Romeo and Juliet*, one of the finest available and full of imaginative touches, offered on four CDs. He recorded his cycle of the numbered symphonies over a period of six years in the late 1970s. It represented not only the high point of his recording partnership with the Philharmonia Orchestra but also the peak of his interpretative career. It is a measure of Muti's success that even the first of the series to be recorded, No. 1, brings a performance as refined and persuasive as it is exciting, and the three early symphonies all bring orchestral playing which is both sophisticated and colourful. Throughout the cycle, and especially in the strong and urgent No. 4, Muti's view is brisk and dramatically direct, yet never lacking in feeling or imagination. In No. 5 he underlines the symphonic strength of the first movement rather than the immediate excitement. The finale then presents a sharp contrast, with its fast tempo and controlled excitement. In the *Pathétique* tempi are again characteristically fast, yet the result is fresh and youthful, with the flowing first-movement second subject given an easy expressiveness. The March, for all its urgency, never sounds brutal and the finale has satisfying depth and power. The sound generally is well up to EMI's best analogue standard of this period, and it has been transferred to CD very impressively, with the focus firm and no lack of body and weight.

Rostropovich recorded the Tchaikovsky symphonies in the Kingsway Hall in 1977 concurrently with live performances at the Royal Festival Hall; though at certain points (as in some of the *fugato* development sections) the ensemble could be a shade crisper, this is a minor point when the performances have not only passion and electricity but also great charm and refinement. The first three symphonies are done superbly in every way – Rostropovich manages to choose his tempi most persuasively and his rhythmic pointing is consistently delectable – outshining here most of the opposition. Symphonies Nos. 4 to 6 are all characterized by relatively slow but well-pointed accounts of the first movements, and only in No. 5 is there any suspicion of the argument dragging. Otherwise these are sensitive, deeply felt readings which should be easy to live with. The recording is outstandingly warm and full-bodied. The pianissimo string-tone is particularly beautiful. *Manfred* too is most persuasive, with a Scherzo of Berliozian refinement. *Francesca da Rimini* and *Romeo and Juliet* were recorded the following year at Abbey Road. The readings are intensely individual and full of poetic feeling, with the love-theme in *Romeo and Juliet* introduced with the greatest tenderness. Yet although Rostropovich's pacing is as free as his moulding of the melodic lines, the listener is carried along by the expressive vitality of the orchestral playing. *Francesca da Rimini* has an epic scale, with a breathtaking finale, yet again there is touching delicacy in the work's central section, with radiant sounds from the LPO woodwind. The sound remains resonant and spacious, with great body and impact, and the CD remastering loses nothing of the richness, in fact adding to its dramatic profile. To fit the music on to five CDs, the third and sixth symphonies have had to be split across discs, which is a less than ideal arrangement; but in all other respects this set can be recommended with the utmost enthusiasm.

Karajan offers the six symphonies fitted on to four mid-priced CDs, the only drawback being that Nos. 2 and 5 are split between discs. From both a performance and a technical point of view, the accounts of the last three symphonies are in every way preferable to his later, VPO digital versions; all offer peerless playing from the Berlin Philharmonic which the Oslo Philharmonic cannot always quite match, for all their excellence.

Maazel's performances from the mid-1960s have been remastered and reissued on four CDs, necessitating a break only at the centre of No. 4. The recordings come from a vintage Decca period and are remarkably full and vivid. In the early symphonies the hint of edge in the digital remastering (and it is very minimal) increases the bite and sense of urgency at the expense of charm (this is not a strong feature of Nos. 2 and 3 anyway). But in Nos. 4–6 (and especially in No. 4) the performances, always grippingly spontaneous, sound newly minted, helped by the freshness of the VPO playing. Perhaps No. 5 lacks the fullest expansive qualities, but there are few more effective accounts of the March/Scherzo from the *Pathétique*. *Romeo and Juliet* is exciting too, with plenty of romantic flair.

Evgeny Svetlanov's Tchaikovsky cycle of the symphonies comes from 1967; most of the additional orchestral items date from 1970. *Voyedova*, the *Andante cantabile* and the *Capriccio italien* are later: the late 1980s. The merits of these performances are well known: full-blooded, intense and thoroughly idiomatic, without being in the aristocratic, Mravinsky class. However, they are well worth considering at this price: the boxed package of six CDs is offered at bargain price. Svetlanov's are performances of much temperament and fire, though the orchestral playing is a little variable. With fast tempi in the outer movements the *First Symphony* comes fully alive, with the atmosphere of the Russian winter felt in the *Adagio*. The Scherzo is beautifully managed and the finale – after the noble and restrained opening – has the quality of genuine Russian dance so that one can imagine the Cossack boots kicking. The *Little Russian* has plenty of character too. Svetlanov takes the *Andantino* very slowly but retains the charm, and he does not let the finale get out of hand. The *Polish Symphony* is a performance of strong contrasts between the inner and outer movements. The orchestral playing is somewhat variable and ensemble is less than perfect. The *Alla tedesca* is a little slow and slightly ponderous, but everywhere else the music's characterization is apt and the rhetoric of the finale is again well handled. The *Fourth*, bold and direct, stands out among the last three symphonies, very well held together. In the finale Svetlanov makes no pause each time the second subject appears. The *Fifth*, however, while it has a fine lyrical impulse, is surprisingly undramatic. When the motto theme should storm into the middle of the slow movement it makes its entrance and there is comparatively little impact. The Waltz is elegantly done, but the opening of the finale languishes a bit and the movement really comes to life only when the allegro proper begins. The *Pathétique* is much more convincing, with a beautifully moulded second subject. The Scherzo-march is somewhat relaxed but the finale is powerfully controlled and eloquent. The extra items are well worth having, especially the rare *Voyevoda*, while the middle section of *Francesca da Rimini* has a unique lyrical fervour. The sound throughout is bright and full-blooded to match the performances and, even taking our reservations into account, this set is worth its modest asking price. In the USA the layout for the last three symphonies (on three separate CDs) is as follows: *Symphony No. 4; String serenade* (74321 37878-2); *Symphony No. 5; Capriccio italien* (74321 37879-2); *Symphony No. 6; Francesca da Rimini* (74321 37880-2).

Symphonies Nos. 1 in G min. (Winter daydreams), Op. 13; 2 in C min. (Little Russian), Op. 17.
(BB) **(*) Belart 461 322-2 [(M) id. import]. VPO, Lorin Maazel.

It is good news that, having restored Maazel's Sibelius symphonies to the catalogue, Polygram's super-bargain Belart label is now beginning on his hardly less successful Tchaikovsky cycle, also made with the VPO in the 1960s. In the first two symphonies Maazel's performances clearly look forward to the emotional tautness of the mature symphonies from the *Fourth* onwards, rather than seeking to bring out the charm of the young composer's earliest essays in symphonic form. But if the first movement of the *Winter daydreams Symphony* is driven hard and the Mendelssohnian quality of the opening is not as warmly evocative as with Rostropovich, Maazel is altogether happier with the rhetoric than the Russian conductor, and the finale is particularly successful: even Tchaikovsky's somewhat academic fugato section is made to come off, with short stabbing emphases of each entry of the theme. There is also evidence of the care with which Maazel has studied the score. Much felicitous detail emerges afresh and the delightful Scherzo comes to life splendidly, with a real feeling displayed for the line of the waltz which forms its centrepiece, and the movement's coda is delectably neat. The slow movement is not as dreamy as one might ask, but it is not without atmosphere, and the style of the playing, with strong, thrusting horns for the final statement of the main theme, is convincing enough in the context of the other movements. The *Little Russian Symphony* is presented with similar hard-driving brio. The charming *Andantino marziale* is nicely done, but the Scherzo is vivid rather than gay, and the finale is exciting without being genial. The performance is not helped by the spectacularly resonant (and brilliantly engineered) analogue recording, which has a degree of harshness and tends to prevent the music from smiling. Excellent value just the same: a disc that is well worth trying when it costs so little.

Symphonies Nos. 1 (Winter daydreams); 2 (Little Russian); 3 (Polish).
❀ (B) *** Mercury Double 434 391-2 (2) [id.]. LSO, Dorati – ARENSKY: *Variations on a theme by Tchaikovsky*. *(*)

Dorati recorded the first three Tchaikovsky symphonies between the 26th and the 30th July 1965 in Watford Town Hall, not long before Mercury ceased to be an independent company. The set was briefly available in America but, so far as we can trace, only the *First Symphony* was ever issued in the UK – a decade later on a thin-sounding Philips Universo LP which was poorly received. Dorati had clearly thought deeply about each symphony, for each of his interpretations is individual and all three have a striking freshness. After its comparatively mellow beginning, the opening movement of the *First Symphony* generates great thrust and excitement, while the lovely, wistful *Adagio* expands romantically to its powerful climax on the horns, before the touchingly nostalgic closing section. The Scherzo (marked *Giocoso*) is surprisingly relaxed, treated very like ballet music and played with much elegance. When the central waltz arrives, it is warmly languorous so that the gentle reprise of the outer section then falls nicely into place. Dorati's tempo here may seem idiosyncratic, but it is very close to that suggested by the composer. The solemn melancholy of the introduction to the finale follows on naturally, and the allegro immediately gathers pace, sharply rhythmic, with its stabbing fugato entries crisply pointed. The desolate preparation for the coda builds to an eloquent *maestoso* climax, and only in the repetitive final peroration does Dorati fail to convince completely. But he is not alone in this, and Tchaikovsky must take a share of the blame.

The horn solo which introduces and closes the first movement of the *Little Russian Symphony* is not bold but hauntingly evocative, and the following allegro is crisp and energetic with a powerful recapitulation. The *Andante marciale* is deliciously neat and gentle and is built to a fine climax, after which the diminuendo is handled equally deftly. After a sparkling Scherzo, rhythmically crisp and sparkling, Tchaikovsky's superb finale – one of the composer's very finest inspirations – does not disappoint, with the ever-alert LSO strings dancing lightly and vigorously in the main theme, the brass sumptuous at the climax and richly capping the brilliantly played coda.

Again in No. 3 Dorati catches the full character of the music's Russian melancholy which dominates the introduction, and he infuses the *Allegro vivo* with great thrust and rhythmic strength. The three central movements are the heart of the symphony and they are beautifully played, full of doleful colouring and nostalgia, with the *Andante elegiaco* producing a heartfelt climax and the Scherzo rustling with nicely observed detail. The final *Polacca*, which gives the symphony its name, is carried by the energetic thrust Dorati generates, and the grandiloquent coda concludes the piece in a final burst of excitement. The brilliant, spacious and full-blooded recording is just right for this music. There is a touch of fierceness at times, but it adds to the bite, and altogether these performances are remarkably satisfying. The Arensky coupling is apt, but in the event somewhat disappointing.

(i) *Symphonies Nos. 1 in G min. (Winter daydreams); 2 in C min. (Little Russian); 3 in D (Polish);* (ii) *Francesca da Rimini.*
(B) *** Ph. Duo 446 148-2 (2) [id.]. (i) LSO; (ii) New Philh. O; Markevitch.

Markevitch is a genuine Tchaikovskian and his readings have fine momentum and plenty of ardour. In the *First Symphony* he finds the Mendelssohnian lightness in his fast pacing of the opening movement, while there is real evocation in the *Adagio* and a sense of desolation at the reprise of the *Andante lugubre*, before the final rousing peroration. In the *Little Russian Symphony* the opening horn solo is full of character and the allegro tautly rhythmic. The *marziale* marking of the *Andantino* is taken literally, but its precise rhythmic beat is well lifted. The finale is striking for its bustling energy rather than its charm. The *Polish Symphony* has a comparably dynamic first movement, but the central movements are expansively warm, the ballet-music associations not missed. The finale is strongly full-blooded. *Francesca da Rimini* is very exciting too, and there is some lovely wind playing from the New Philharmonia in the central section. Excellent sound, warmly resonant and full-bodied.

Symphony No. 1 (Winter Daydreams); Hamlet (fantasy overture), *Op. 67.*
(BB) *** Naxos Dig. 8.550517 [id.]. Polish Nat. RSO, Adrian Leaper.

Leaper conducts a taut and sympathetic reading of *Winter Daydreams*, with excellent playing from the Polish orchestra enhanced by vivid recording, fresh and clear, with plenty of body and with refined pianissimo playing from the strings in the slow movement. This is among the finest Tchaikovsky recordings on the Naxos list, with all four movements sharply characterized. The overture too comes in a tautly dramatic reading. An outstanding bargain.

Symphonies Nos. (i) *2 (Little Russian), Op. 17;* (ii) *4 in F min.*
✿ (B) *** DG Classikon 429 527-2; *429 527-4* [(M) id. import]. (i) New Philh. O; (ii) VPO; Claudio Abbado.

Abbado's coupling of Tchaikovsky's *Second* and *Fourth Symphonies* is one of the supreme bargains of the current catalogue. His account of the *Little Russian Symphony* is very enjoyable, although the first movement concentrates on refinement of detail. The *Andantino* is very nicely done and the Scherzo is admirably crisp and sparkling. The finale is superb, with fine colour and thrust and a memorably spectacular stroke on the tam-tam before the exhilarating coda. The 1967 recording still sounds excellent. But this is merely a bonus for an unforgettable account of the *Fourth Symphony*, unsurpassed on record. Abbado's control of the structure of the first movement is masterly. The *Andantino*, with its gentle oboe solo, really takes wing in its central section, followed by a wittily crisp Scherzo, while the finale has sparkle as well as power, epitomizing the Russian dance spirit which was Tchaikovsky's inspiration. It was recorded in 1975 in the Musikverein and still sounds very good indeed.

Symphony No. 3 (Polish); The Tempest, Op. 18.
(BB) **(*) Naxos Dig. 8.550518 [id.]. Polish Nat. RSO, Antoni Wit.

Though Wit cannot match Leaper with the same orchestra in the *Symphony No. 1*, with playing a degree less alert and the recording not so full and forward, his *Little Russian Symphony* is still an attractive reading. The first and last movements both have a fine swagger, and if the ensemble could be crisper in the middle movements, Wit characterizes them well. *The Tempest*, an extended fantasia based on Shakespeare, not to be confused with *The Storm*, makes an attractive and unusual coupling and is again given a fine if not distinctive performance.

Symphonies Nos. (i) *4 in F min., Op. 36;* (ii) *5 in E min., Op. 64; 6 in B min. (Pathétique).*
(B) *** DG Double 453 088-2 [id.]. BPO, Karajan.
(B) *** Decca Double 443 844-2 (2) [(M) id. import]. Philh. O, Ashkenazy.
(M) (***) DG mono 447 423-2 (2). Leningrad PO; (i) Kurt Sanderling; (ii) Mravinsky.
(B) **(*) Ph. Duo 438 335-2 (2) [id.]. LSO, Markevitch.
(B) *(*) Teldec/Warner Ultima Dig. 0630 18966-2 (2) [(M) 95981-2]. Leipzig GO, Masur.

Symphony No. 4 in F min., Op. 36; Romeo and Juliet (fantasy overture).
(BB) *(*) RCA Navigator 74321 29252-2 [(M) id. import]. Phd. O, Eugene Ormandy.

Symphony No. 5 in E min., Op. 64; 1812 overture; Marche slave.
(BB) ** RCA Navigator 74321 21291-2 [(d.) 09026 61853-2]. Phd. O, Eugene Ormandy.

(i) *Symphony No. 6 in B min. (Pathétique)*; (ii) *Serenade for strings in C, Op. 48.*
(BB) **(*) RCA Navigator 74321 24210-2 [(d.) 09026 60908-2]. (i) Phd. O, Ormandy; (ii) Moscow Soloists, Yuri Bashmet.

Who would have thought in the early days of CD that one day we would be offered Karajan's outstanding Berlin Philharmonic performances of the three last symphonies for the cost of one premium-priced CD! Karajan's 1977 analogue version of No. 4 (the most atmospherically recorded of the three) is undoubtedly more compelling than his previous recordings and also is in most respects preferable to the newer, digital, Vienna version. It is the vitality and drive of the performance as a whole that one remembers, although the beauty of the wind-playing at the opening and close of the slow movement can give nothing but pleasure. Similarly the 1976 reading of the *Fifth* stands out from his other recordings. The first movement is unerringly paced and has great romantic flair; in Karajan's hands the climax of the slow movement is grippingly intense, though with a touchingly elegiac preparation for the horn solo at the opening. The Waltz has character and charm too – the Berlin Philharmonic string-playing is peerless – and in the finale Karajan drives hard, creating a riveting forward thrust. Karajan had a special affinity with Tchaikovsky's *Pathétique symphony* (and – remembering Furtwängler's famous 78-r.p.m. set – so has the Berlin Philharmonic Orchestra). He has recorded it five times in stereo. For many the 1977 version is the finest. With a brilliant – even too brilliant – recording of the widest dynamic range (though not an especially sumptuous lower resonance) the impact of Tchaikovsky's climaxes – notably those of the first and third movements – is tremendously powerful, the articulation of the Berlin players precise and strong. The climactic peaks are created with fierce bursts of tension, and the effect on the listener is almost overwhelming. In the 5/4 movement Karajan allows the middle section to increase the elegiac feeling, against a background of remorseless but distanced drum-beats, like a tolling bell. The finale has great passion and eloquence, with two gentle sforzandos at the very end to emphasize the finality of the closing phrase. The digital remastering of the analogue recordings is eminently satisfactory.

Ashkenazy's set makes a genuine alternative bargain on Double Decca, although the layout splits No. 5 across the two discs between the second and third movements. Apart from the emotional power and strong Russian feeling of the readings, the special quality which Ashkenazy conveys is spontaneity. The freshness of his approach, his natural feeling for lyricism on the one hand and drama on the other, is consistently compelling, even if at times the orchestral ensemble is not always immaculate. The late-1970s Kingsway Hall recording quality is full and atmospheric, with the strings full, the brass sonorous and a satisfyingly resonant, Tchaikovskian ambience. This could be a best buy for those wanting all three symphonies in modern stereo (but not digital) versions, as the sound is more sumptuous than that provided by DG for Karajan.

Mravinsky re-recorded the three last symphonies of Tchaikovsky with his Leningrad orchestra for DG in stereo, but these legendary earlier, mono performances (No. 4 conducted by Kurt Sanderling) from the mid-1950s were even more satisfying, and they sound marvellously vivid. The earlier readings, without loss of concentration, were less exaggeratedly histrionic, and Sanderling's speeds for the finale of the *Fourth Symphony* particularly, but also Mravinsky's for the *Fifth*, were not as frenetic as in the latter's stereo versions. The opening of the *Fifth* again brings an added dimension of Russian melancholy, and Mravinsky sustains a lyrical intensity throughout the symphony characteristic of all his Tchaikovsky readings. The composer's marking for the slow movement 'con alcuna licenza' is taken very literally: this is a performance of great dramatic extremes, the only drawback for Western ears being the solo horn with his undeniable wobble. The finale has great zest, with blazing perorations from the brass. The emotional power of Mravinsky's *Pathétique* has been equalled elsewhere but never surpassed. The climax of the first movement has tremendous passion, the Scherzo/march is brilliantly pointed yet has plenty of weight, and the finale is deeply eloquent, genuinely touching rather than hysterical. The special rasp of the Russian trombones, which the composer would have recognized, is very telling here, as elsewhere.

There are many collectors who count Markevitch's Philips recordings from the 1960s as having a similar distinction. Certainly Markevitch's *Fourth* is as exciting as almost any available. It has a superb thrusting first-movement Allegro and, while throughout Markevitch allows himself a degree of rubato in the rocking crescendo passage, as with Monteux it is the forward momentum of the performance that captures the listener. After a less evocative opening than Monteux, Markevitch applies to the first movement of the *Fifth* the forthright, highly charged approach which was so effective in the *Fourth*. He makes no concessions to the second-subject group, which is presented with no let-up on the fast pace at which he takes the main *Allegro*. Tchaikovsky's romanticism is turned into energy and the intended contrast is lost, and in the vigorous finale the final statement of the big tune is slow and rather stolid. In the *Pathétique* Markevitch provides great intensity in his account of the first movement; some might feel that he is too aggressive, even though the performance is always under emotional control. The second movement has both warmth and elegance – more so than with Monteux – and the march is treated broadly, providing suitable contrast before a deeply felt performance of the finale, where the second subject is introduced with great tenderness. With three symphonies offered for the cost of one premium-priced CD, this is certainly worth considering, for all the reservations about the *Fifth*.

Ormandy made his recordings of the *Fourth* and *Fifth Symphonies* in 1973–4, towards the end of his long tenure at Philadelphia and when he himself was in his seventies. The orchestra is still in glorious form, but the readings bring an element of routine, of going through the motions, and the electricity flickers only fitfully. In the first movement of the *Fourth* there are a few individual touches to suggest Ormandy's involvement and, after a somewhat lukewarm *Andantino*, its finale cannot help but make an effect with such magnificent playing; but the *Fifth* brings moments of blandness throughout and here the finale loses its impetus soon after it begins. *Romeo and Juliet* similarly brings relatively subdued passions. This is the coupling for both the *Fourth* and *Fifth Symphonies*, offered at mid-price, in the USA, which is a pity, for Ormandy's *1812* is presented with panache, with a resonant chorus to sing the Russian hymn, as well as some impressive cannon and a carillon at the close. *Marche slave* is very slow and pontifical.

When one turns to the *Pathétique*, recorded some six years earlier in 1968, the transformation is remarkable. This is a vintage Ormandy performance of a work with which he obviously identified closely, and it has even greater individuality and passion than his earlier (1960) account for Sony (see below). The introduction of the beautiful second subject of the first movement is wonderfully tender and, after the riveting development section, its return brings the fullest possible sense of apotheosis. The 5/4 movement winningly combines both warmth and a touch of melancholy, and the March/Scherzo is powerfully arresting. The finale is ardent yet also has dignity, and at the very end Ormandy conveys a touching resignation – all passion spent. The orchestra is on its toes throughout, and the only snag is the very brightly lit sound, much shallower than the later recordings; but this is not enough to detract seriously from the involvement of the performance. Moreover RCA have found a highly appropriate coupling for this Navigator reissue. Yuri Bashmet's account of the *String serenade* with the Moscow Soloists has matching energy and fire, and great finesse in the matter of light and shade. The *Waltz* is light and airy, the tenutos observed without voluptuous emphasis. The *Elégie* opens gently and delicately but develops a volatile ardour at its climax, and the finale is highly animated, its dance-rhythms bursting with energy. The virtuosity of the playing is emphasized by another brightly lit (digital) recording, made two decades later, which has plenty of ambience and a very wide dynamic range. A thoroughly collectable disc, especially at the inexpensive asking price.

Masur and the Leipzig Gewandhaus Orchestra give a rich and refined reading of the *Fourth Symphony* which reflects the German symphonic tradition rather than anything Russian. Looking at Tchaikovsky without a hint of hysteria underlines the symphonic strength, as it did with both Klemperer and Boehm; but, unlike those Germanic predecessors, Masur is warm and smooth rather than rugged. The rounded, bass-heavy recording underlines that. Masur's reading of the *Fifth Symphony* is refined and detailed, spacious in many of the speeds as well as in the characteristically distanced recording, well blended with woodwind behind the strings. It is a reading in the German tradition, with a major snag in the ponderousness of the slow introductions to the outer movements. Masur's reading of the *Pathétique* is well laid out but with a very low level of tension despite consistently fine playing from the Leipzig orchestra. The recording is rich and natural, but the Leipzig acoustics do not provide the necessary brilliance and projection, and it has to be said that, overall, this set is difficult to recommend.

Symphony No. 4 in F min., Op. 36.
(M) *(**) Van. Everyman 08 6162 71 [id.]. American SO, Stokowski (with SCRIABIN: *Etude in C sharp min., Op. 2/1* **(*)).

Symphony No. 4; Capriccio italien.
(M) *** DG 419 872-2. BPO, Karajan.

(i) *Symphony No. 4;* (ii) *Francesca da Rimini, Op. 32.*
(M) ** Mercury 434 373-2 [id.]. (i) LSO; (ii) Minneapolis SO; Antal Dorati – BORODIN: *Prince Igor: Overture.* **

In Karajan's 1977 analogue recording it is the vitality and drive of the performance as a whole that one remembers, although the beauty of the wind playing at the opening and close of the slow movement can give nothing but pleasure. The CD transfer is extremely vivid. The ubiquitous *Capriccio italien* is offered as a filler.

Dorati's performance of the *Fourth Symphony* is assured and often exciting but sounds a little cut and dried. The climaxes are tense but, like the accelerandos, well controlled. The finale comes off very well indeed. If you like your Tchaikovsky not too frenetic, you may enjoy this very much, and it is certainly a performance to live with, especially when the 1960 Mercury recording, made in Wembley Town Hall, is so full-blooded and with the right kind of ambience. However, *Francesca da Rimini* was recorded (two years earlier) in Minneapolis, and the evocative, sustained writing of the middle section is not helped by the dry, lustreless acoustic. The climax is exciting but without the coloration of resonance. Tchaikovsky's method of building up a climax by throwing short repeated figures at great speed into an orchestral maelstrom loses all its effect and tends to become just a pointless succession of notes. The coupled *Prince Igor* overture is much more successful.

Stokowski's is a fascinating but exasperatingly eccentric performance. The pity is that the magnetism and basic understanding are in no doubt. Without the numerous minor interferences with the conductor's score and the constant fluctuations in the music's rhythmic flow this could have been a great performance. Even as it is, it has splendid moments. The *Andantino* with its thrilling central climax and wonderfully touching coda is really memorable. But immediately at the opening of the first movement Stokowski makes his intentions clear. At the end of the third bar the trombones are added to the horns, anticipating the brass tutti Tchaikovsky has so carefully prepared for the seventh bar. Then, when the *Moderato con anima* begins, there is a flagrant tenuto on the opening phrase, and this kind of rhythmic distortion is used in both the principal tunes of the first movement. Indeed tenutos are sprinkled around freely, and Stokowski has also re-written the drum parts. Only the Scherzo (brilliantly done) is comparatively free from interference, whereas the end of the finale is grotesque. The amazing thing is that, through all these excesses, Stokowski carries the orchestra with him and at the same time maintains the tension at a higher pitch than almost any other recorded performance. The early stereo is suitably spectacular, spacious and full, with the harshness present on the old LPs now completely tamed. As a fill-up Stokowksi offers a richly indulgent orchestration of Scriabin's piano *Etude in C sharp minor*.

Symphonies Nos. 4 in F min., Op. 36; 6 in B min. (Pathétique), Op. 74; Marche slave, Op. 31; The Storm Overture, Op. 76.
(BB) **(*) Carlton LSO Double Dig. 30368 01237 (2) [(B) id.]. LSO, Rozhdestvensky.

After the fanfare, Rozhdestvensky's performance of the *Fourth Symphony* takes a little while to warm up, but, when the first climax arrives, it is very impressive. The lyrical secondary material is presented very beguilingly and the rocking string theme at the *ben sostenuto* is positively sensuous. The slow movement is basically simple, although Rozhdestvensky allows himself a mannered emphasis at its climax. The Scherzo, light and gentle, has the feeling of an arabesque, and the finale is strongly articulated and expansive. First-class digital recording and a powerful response from the LSO in both the symphony and the *Marche slave*. Rozhdestvensky's passionate reading of the *Pathétique* fails to match the finest in precision of ensemble – the slow finale is warm rather than tense or tragic – but the sense of spontaneity is most compelling.

Symphony No. 5 in E min., Op. 64.
(M) **(*) Decca Phase Four 455 157-2 [id.]. New Philh. O, Stokowski – GLAZUNOV: *Violin concerto*. **

Symphony No. 5; Capriccio italien.
(BB) * Naxos Dig. 8.550191 [id.]. Slovak PO, Stephen Gunzenhauser.

Symphony No. 5 in E min.; Francesca da Rimini, Op. 32.
(B) **(*) [EMI Red Line Dig. CDR5 69842]. Phd. O, Muti.

Symphony No. 5 in E min.; Marche slave.
(M) *** DG 419 066-2. BPO, Karajan.

(i) *Symphony No. 5;* (ii) *Nutcracker suite, Op. 71a.*
(B) *** DG Classikon 439 434-2; *439 434-4* [(M) id. import]. (i) Leningrad PO, Mravinsky; (ii) BPO, Karajan.

Symphony No. 5; Serenade for strings in C, Op. 48.
(B) *** Sony SBK 46538; *SBT 46538* [id.]. Phd. O, Ormandy.

Symphony No. 5; (i) *Eugene Onegin: Tatiana's letter scene.*
✿ (B) *** EMI Dig. CD-EMX 2187 [(M) id.]. LPO, Sian Edwards; (i) with Eilene Hannan.

Sian Edwards conducts an electrifying and warm-hearted reading of Tchaikovsky's *Fifth*, which matches any version in the catalogue, particularly when it comes with an unusual and exceptionally attractive fill-up, Tchaikovsky's greatest inspiration for soprano, *Tatiana's letter scene*. That is freshly and dramatically sung, in a convincingly girlish impersonation, by the Australian, Eilene Hannan. Sian Edwards's control of rubato is exceptionally persuasive, notably so in moulding the different sections of the first movement of the symphony, while the great horn solo of the slow movement is played with exquisite delicacy by

Richard Bissell. The Waltz third movement is most tenderly done, while the finale brings a very fast and exciting allegro, challenging the orchestra to brilliant, incisive playing.

Mravinsky's earlier stereo version of the *Fifth* with the Leningrad Philharmonic on DG would occupy a distinguished place in any collection. The performance is full of Slavonic vitality and the reading is romantic as well as red-blooded (the second subject of the first movement is both warm and graceful). The solo horn has a faint wobble in the famous solo in the slow movement, and the trumpets in the final peroration of an exhilaratingly fast finale also have a vibrato, but these details are unimportant when the reading has such fire and individuality. The recording, made in Watford Town Hall in 1960, is resonant and full, if not always absolutely clean in focus. By comparison Karajan's 1966 *Nutcracker suite* sounds a little cool, but it is marvellously polished and vivid, and the *Waltz of the flowers* has the most agreeable elegance.

Karajan's 1976 recording stands out from his other recordings of the *Fifth*. The first movement is unerringly paced and has great romantic flair; in Karajan's hands the climax of the slow movement is grippingly intense, though with a touchingly elegiac preparation for the horn solo at the opening. The Waltz has character and charm too – the Berlin Philharmonic string playing is peerless – and in the finale Karajan drives hard, creating a riveting forward thrust. The remastered recording brings a remarkable improvement.

The oddity of Muti's Philadelphia version is that, though the first two movements have the disappointingly over-relaxed manners that marked his *Pathétique* earlier, often with surprisingly slack ensemble, the last two movements are played with the high voltage one expects of this conductor and orchestra at their finest. The fill-up is also played at white heat, a powerful performance. It makes a rare and worthwhile coupling. The sound, not as clear as it might be, has warmth and weight beyond most recent Philadelphia issues.

Ormandy's *Fifth*, splendidly recorded in the spacious acoustics of Philadelphia's Broadwood Hotel, is early (1959) stereo and is one of his very finest Tchaikovsky performances. There is not a suspicion of routine here; indeed the reading has tremendous grip and excitement, and the Philadephia strings play gloriously, particularly in the *Andante cantabile*, which generates great passion. The breadth of the introduction to the finale is arresting, and the reading has enormous confidence. In the first movement Ormandy indulges himself in upwards portamenti in the second-subject group, which some listeners may resist, but the powerful surge forward afterwards is engulfing. Again the weight of string-tone at the opening of the *Serenade* (recorded the following year) establishes the full-blooded character of Ormandy's approach; in the allegro the Mozartian pastiche is minimized, but the bouncing rhythmic figure is vigorously pointed. The *Waltz* is sumptuously elegant, with radiant violin *tenutos*, the *Elegy* deeply felt, beautifully phrased and spread over the widest canvas. The finale opens delicately but soon generates great bustle. Overall this coupling is a magnificent demonstration of the Ormandy regime in Philadelphia at its very peak.

Stokowski is spectacularly recorded (in Stuttgart in 1966). But the conductor's concern with tonal grandeur has its drawbacks, and his cuts make the end result controversial. He tends to languish rather than press forward and, although tension is well maintained, the speeds for the main allegros of the first and last movements are essentially spacious and in consequence there is some sacrifice of vitality. Yet with the flick of the wrist, as it were, Stokowski can create some fine blazes of excitement, as in the coda of the opening movement, the climax of the *Andante cantabile* or the closing moments of the symphony. The vivid impact of every department of the orchestra lights up every detail of Tchaikovsky's inspired orchestration. However, there are a number of cuts (four bars, twice, in the first movement, two bars in the introduction to the finale, and a longer cut later), but the most noticeable effect to anyone without a score is that Stokowski dispenses with the pause before the final coda.

Stephen Gunzenhauser's account with the Slovak Philharmonic is less refined and detailed as an interpretation than the best of its competitors. Rhythms sometimes grow heavy and not all Western ears will adjust to the fruity horn solo, while the finale lacks a little in tension. It has good, warm, digital sound.

Symphony No. 6 in B min. (Pathétique), Op. 74.

(M) (***) RCA mono GD 60312 [60312-2-RG]. Phd. O, Toscanini – R. STRAUSS: *Death and transfiguration.* (***)

(B) * [EMI Red Line Dig. CDR5 69843]. Phd. O, Muti – SCRIABIN: *Le poème de l'extase.* ***

Symphony No. 6 (Pathétique); Capriccio italien; Eugene Onegin: Waltz & Polonaise.

(B) **(*) Sony SBK 47657; *SBT 47657* [id.]. Phd O, Ormandy.

Symphony No. 6 (Pathétique); 1812 overture.

(M) **(*) RCA 09026 61246-2 [id.]. Chicago SO, Reiner – LISZT: *Mephisto waltz.* ***

Symphony No. 6 (Pathétique); Francesca da Rimini.
(BB) ** Naxos Dig. 8.550097 [id.]. Slovak RSO (Bratislava), Ondrej Lenárd.

Symphony No. 6 in B min. (Pathétique); Marche slave, Op. 31.
(BB) ** Tring Dig. TRP 011 [id.]. RPO, Sir Yehudi Menuhin.

Symphony No. 6 (Pathétique); Nutcracker suite, Op. 71a.
(M) (**) RCA mono GD 60297. NBC SO, Toscanini.

Symphony No. 6 (Pathétique); Romeo and Juliet (fantasy overture).
(M) *** Virgin/EMI Dig. CUV5 61267-2 [id.]. Bournemouth SO, Andrew Litton.
(M) *** DG Masters (IMS) Dig. 445 601-2. Philh. O, Sinopoli.
(M) **(*) Mercury 434 352-2 [id.]. LSO, Antal Dorati.

Symphony No. 6 (Pathétique); Romeo and Juliet (fantasy overture); The Voyevoda, Op. 78.
(M) *(*) Sony Theta Dig. SMK 60126 [id.]. Chicago SO, Abbado.

(i) *Symphony No. 6 (Pathétique);* (ii) *Swan Lake* (ballet): *suite.*
(B) *** DG Classikon 439 456-2; *439 456-4*. (i) Leningrad PO, Mravinsky; (ii) BPO, Karajan.
(BB) **(*) ASV Dig. CDQS 6091 [(M) id. import]. (i) LPO; (ii) RPO, Bátiz.

Litton's is an outstanding performance, full of temperament, not just fiery but tender too, arguably the finest of the whole Litton cycle. The Bournemouth playing has never been neater, with the sound bringing out the fine clarity of articulation. The only idiosyncrasy is that in the big second-subject melodies of the outer movements Litton prefers speeds broader than usual, but with no hint of self-indulgence in the finely moulded phrasing. With an account of *Romeo and Juliet* that builds up powerfully from a restrained start, the disc makes a splendid culmination, a match even for the earlier, Virgin version with Pletnev, and more fully and cleanly recorded. It also gains in practical terms even over the Pletnev issue when the coupling is so much more generous.

If one divides interpreters of this *Symphony* into those who tend to press ahead in stringendo and those who hold back in ritenuto, Sinopoli – perhaps surprisingly after his Elgar *Second* – is firmly in the former group. What is striking here is the passion of the playing of the Philharmonia, recorded with the most satisfying opulence. Sinopoli's reading of the opening movement is beautifully shaped, with the second subject introduced very tenderly. He adopts slow speeds for the middle two movements but sustains them well, with the 5/8 rhythm of the second brought even closer than is common to the feeling of a waltz. In the march of the third movement, many will prefer Sinopoli's broader view, with a slight easing on the big, swaggering, fortissimo entries leading to a satisfying culmination. The finale brings a highly eloquent response from the Philharmonia strings and the result is very moving. The big advantage that Sinopoli has in this mid-priced reissue is that it is generously coupled with *Romeo and Juliet*, which is also very exciting. Even if there is a hint of self-consciousness at the first entry of the love theme, there is plenty of uninhibited passion in the later repeats. In short this is one of the finest of recent versions of the *Pathétique*, and it is highly recommendable. Excellent recording.

Mravinsky's very Russian (stereo) account of the *Pathétique* is justly renowned. It is deeply passionate, yet the second subject of the first movement is introduced with much tenderness. The last two movements are very fine indeed; the Scherzo/march is brilliantly pointed, yet has plenty of weight, and the finale is very moving without ever letting the control slip. The present transfer of the 1960 recording (made in Wembley Town Hall) maintains the agreeable ambience, even if at times the Russian brass comes over raucously at climaxes. Karajan's *Swan Lake suite* has characteristic charisma and excitement, with polished BPO playing seemingly aiming for brilliance, and the recording, made a decade after the symphony, has somewhat less allure in the matter of string sonority. But no one could complain of lack of vividness.

Ormandy's fine 1960 performance is a reading of impressive breadth, dignity and power, with no suggestion of routine in a single bar. The orchestra makes much of the first-movement climax and plays with considerable passion and impressive body of tone in both outer movements; yet there is an element of restraint in the finale which prevents any feeling of hysteria. In short, this is most satisfying, a performance to live with; the CD transfer, while brightly lit, avoids glare in the upper range. Ormandy's panache and gusto give the *Capriccio italien* plenty of life without driving too hard, and the dances are rhythmically infectious.

Reiner is given full-blooded 1957 sound but his *Pathétique* – although it has some bursts of excitement in the first movement, and the Chicago ambience adds much to the lively Scherzo/march – as a whole does not completely convince. The last movement is tender rather than producing the intensity and anguish inherent in a Russian performance. *1812* is without cannon but is very enjoyable nevertheless. What makes this reissue distinctive is Reiner's superb account of Liszt's *Mephisto waltz*, perhaps the finest on record.

Dorati's 1960 recording of the *Pathétique* is much better focused on CD than it seemed to be in its rather indifferent Philips LP pressing. Now there is much brilliance, underpinned by the weight and resonance of Watford Town Hall. The reading has plenty of dynamism in the first movement and the 5/4 movement, unusually brisk, is exhilarating, if hardly a conventional reading. There are some minor eccentricities of tempi in the Scherzo/march but the climax is thrilling, and the finale, as so often with this symphony, is finely done, volatile, but grippingly so. *Romeo and Juliet* opens with dignity, is tender in the love music and brings plenty of excitement at the climax. Not a first choice, but there is nothing routine about this music-making.

Toscanini's Philadelphia version of the *Pathétique* glows with the special magic that developed between him and the orchestra over the winter season of 1941–2. Though far more disciplined than most readings, it is altogether warmer than his NBC recording, with the great second-subject melody of the first movement tender in its emotions, not rigid in its easy rubato. He even eases the tempo sympathetically for the fortissimo entries of the march in the third movement. Alongside a magnificent account of the Strauss – an apt link, with death the theme – it makes a superb historical document.

Bátiz's (1982) reading of the *Pathétique* is distinctly enjoyable, attractively fresh and direct, with the great second-subject melody the more telling for being understated and with transitions just a little perfunctory. The Scherzo/march comes off especially well. The brass are set rather forward, but this makes for a very exciting climax. Otherwise the balance is good and the sound is generally excellent. It is even better in the *Swan Lake suite*, recorded five years later. The RPO playing is very good indeed, polished, warm and alert. Barry Griffiths and Françoise Rive are sensitive string soloists in the *Danse des cygnes*. The suite ends with the great tune near the end of the ballet where the violins are echoed powerfully by the four horns in unison. An excellent super-bargain coupling.

Menuhin's performance has its moments of excitement but in the last resort does not leave a very deep impression. The central movements go best, the third more Scherzo than march. Throughout, ensemble could be crisper and, although the very end of the finale is moving, with an eloquent contribution from the RPO brass, the movement's earlier climax is slightly mannered. There is a proper pause before *Marche slave* and this sparklingly alive and spontaneous performance, despite somewhat over-brilliant sound, demonstrates what is missing in the symphony. Recording good, but artificially balanced and rather two-dimensional.

On Naxos, Ondrej Lenárd conducts a relatively low-key account of the *Pathétique* which yet, with generally neat playing from the Slovak Radio Symphony Orchestra, is sympathetically refreshing. Even if the fortissimo entries of the march in the third movement lack a sense of drama, the crispness of the approach at a relatively relaxed speed is attractive, and Lenárd moulds the great melodies of the outer movements with natural sympathy. *Francesca da Rimini* brings a more keenly dramatic performance, a generous fill-up for a disc at super-bargain price, warmly and atmospherically recorded.

The 1947 NBC recording for Toscanini, dry and unhelpful, also has high 78 surface hiss, which detracts from a characteristically powerful and intense performance. Speeds are all on the fast side, but only in the first movement do the results ever sound perfunctory, and the middle movements are delectably pointed in rhythm, while the slow finale at a flowing speed is both noble and passionate. The sound for the *Nutcracker* is far clearer, a crisp, bright interpretation, even if the Sugar Plum Fairy is heavy-footed.

Abbado's Sony version, bringing the benefit of generous couplings, notably the rare *Voyevoda* (which the composer rejected), still is unsuccessful in the relative lack of tension, and less-than-pinpoint precision in ensemble. It cannot match Abbado's own earlier, Vienna version for DG. The recorded sound is a little muffled, lacking full bite.

Muti's Philadelphia version does not begin to match his much earlier Philharmonia recording. This one is uncharacteristically slack and lacking in dramatic tension, and the digital recording is poorly focused. The coupling is generous, but hardly allows a recommendation.

(i) *Symphony No. 6 (Pathétique); Romeo and Juliet (fantasy overture);* (ii) *The Nutcracker; Sleeping Beauty; Swan Lake:* excerpts.

(BB) *** EMI Seraphim CES5 68537-2 (2) [CDEB 68537]. Philh. O, with (i) Carlo Maria Giulini; (ii) Erfrem Kurtz; with Y. Menuhin.

Giulini's EMI performance of the *Pathétique* was recorded with the Philharmonia on top form in 1959, and this reissue still sounds excellent in the CD transfer. Giulini takes a spacious view of the symphony. There is a degree of restraint in the way he interprets the big melodies of the first and last movements, which are given an almost Elgarian nobility. Yet passionate intensity is conveyed by the purity and concentration of the playing, which equally builds up electric tension and excitement without hysteria. It now comes coupled with his equally fine performance of *Romeo and Juliet*, recorded two years later, a not dissimilar reading and equally superbly played. The work's climax is dramatically very powerful. The second of the two CDs in this inexpensive package also shows the Philharmonia Orchestra at its absolute peak. The early (late 1950s) stereo sounds astonishingly full, and the performances combine elegance and finesse with sparkle and colour. Here all of the *Nutcracker suite* is included except the *Chinese dance*, an inexplicable omission that would have nicely fitted on, as the programme plays for 77 minutes 39 seconds. A splendid super-bargain compilation.

Variations on a rococo theme for cello and orchestra, Op. 33.
❀ (M) *** DG 447 413-2 [id.]. Rostropovich, BPO, Karajan – DVORAK: *Cello concerto.* *** ❀
(BB) *** CfP Silver Double CDCFPSD 4775 (2) [(B) id.]. Robert Cohen, LPO, Macal – BEETHOVEN: *Triple concerto;* DVORAK: *Cello concerto;* ELGAR: *Cello concerto.* ***
(BB) *** EMI Seraphim CES5 68521-2 (2). (i) Paul Tortelier, N. Sinfonia, Yan Pascal Tortelier – DVORAK: *Cello concerto* etc. ***
(B) *** Sony SBK 48278; *SBT 48278* [id.]. Leonard Rose, Phd. O, Ormandy – BLOCH: *Schelomo* ***; FAURE: *Élégie* ***; LALO: *Concerto.* **(*)
(M) *** Carlton Dig. 30366 0011-2 [id.]. Tortelier, RPO, Groves – DVORAK: *Rondo in G min.* ***; ELGAR: *Cello concerto in E min.* **(*)
(M) *** [RCA Basic 100 09026 68086-2; *68086-4*]. Ofra Harnoy, LPO, Mackerras – DVORAK: *Cello concerto.* ***

Rostropovich uses the published score rather than the original version which more accurately reflects the composer's intentions. But this account, with Karajan's glowing support, is so superbly structured in its control of emotional light and shade that one is readily convinced that this is the work Tchaikovsky conceived. The recording (made in the Jesus-Christus-Kirche) is beautifully balanced and is surely one of the most perfect examples of DG's analogue techniques. It sounds remarkably real and present in this superb remastering and well deserves its place at the head of DG's 'Legendary Recordings' series.

As in the Dvořák concerto, with which his performance of the *Rococo variations* is coupled, Robert Cohen tends to avoid pronounced rubato, yet the result is warmly expressive as well as strong. The 1978 recording is first rate, and anyone fancying the other three works included on this Classics for Pleasure Silver Double will find Cohen's artistry is consistently rewarding.

A finely wrought account from Tortelier *père*, accompanied by the Northern Sinfonia under Tortelier *fils*. This is very enjoyable, if perhaps not quite so distinguished as Rostropovich on DG. Well worth considering when the Dvořák couplings are so generous.

Leonard Rose's warm and elegant – yet at times quite ardent – account of these splendid variations is balm to the senses, and Ormandy provides admirable support. The recording is forwardly balanced but the dynamic range remains reasonably wide, and the cello is firmly and realistically focused.

Tortelier's version on the Carlton label is warm and red-blooded, if technically not as flawless as his earlier reading, but the recording is pleasantly atmospheric, slightly distanced so that the tenderness of the performance is brought out the more.

Ofra Harnoy plays the *Rococo variations* with lightness and grace. Hers is an individual view, but a diverting one, for she uses the very widest range of dynamic, and Mackerras offers her sensitive support. The recording balance is excellent within an agreeably warm acoustic. This particular coupling is available only in the USA.

CHAMBER AND INSTRUMENTAL MUSIC

String quartet in B flat; String quartets Nos. 1–3; (i) *Souvenir de Florence.*
(M) *** BMG/Melodiya 74321 18290-2 (2). Borodin Qt, (i) with Rostropovich, Talalyan.

On the mid-priced BMG/Melodiya set, the *Souvenir de Florence* with Rostropovich and Talalyan comes from 1965, whereas the three *Quartets* plus the student *Quartet movement* that Tchaikovsky wrote in 1865 were all recorded at roughly the same time (1979–80). This version is superb and without peer, and makes an unassailable recommendation. One need look no further.

(i) *String quartets Nos. 1–3*; (ii) *Souvenir de Florence, Op. 70.*
(B) ** Decca Double 452 614-2 (2) [id.]. (i) Gabrieli Qt; (ii) ASMF, Marriner.

The Gabrielis give finely conceived performances of the three *String quartets*, producing well-blended tone-quality. Their ensemble is excellent, and they are completely inside the music. The recordings are clean and alive, but ideally the upper range could be projected less forcefully, and the CD transfer emphasizes the fierceness. While first choice inevitably rests with the Borodin Quartet (a mid-priced set which includes the *Souvenir de Florence*), this is recommendable as an inexpensive Double Decca alternative. Certainly the *Souvenir de Florence* is an attractive proposition, played by a full body of strings, especially when they are an ensemble of the calibre of the Academy of St Martin-in-the-Fields; the one snag is that their version has been subjected to some tactful cutting.

String quartet No. 1 in D, Op. 11.
(B) *** Cal. CAL 6202 [(M) id.]. Talich Qt – BORODIN: *Quartet No. 2.* **(*)
(M) **(*) Decca 425 541-2. Gabrieli Qt – BORODIN; SHOSTAKOVICH: *Quartets.* **(*)
(M) *(*) DG (IMS) Dig. 445 551-2 [id.]. Emerson Qt – BORODIN: *String quartet No. 2* *(*); DVORAK: *String quartet No. 12 (American).* **

A glorious account of Tchaikovsky's best-loved quartet from the Talich group. They play the opening movement with an unassertive, lyrical feeling that is quite disarming, while the famous *Andante cantabile* has never sounded more beautiful on record, shaped with a combination of delicacy of feeling and warmth that is wholly persuasive. The Scherzo has plenty of verve, and the finale winningly balances the music's joyful vigour and its underlying hint of melancholy with the same lightness of touch that makes the first movement so enjoyable. The 1987 digital recording is beautifully balanced, not too brightly lit but well integrated, with a natural presence. Very highly recommended.

The Gabrielis give a finely conceived performance, producing well-blended tone-quality, and the 1977 recording is clean and alive; but ideally the upper range could be less forcefully projected.

The Emerson Quartet are immaculate in terms of technical address, but they do not allow the music to speak for itself. We are rarely unaware of their virtuosity. The DG recording is very clean and present.

PIANO MUSIC

Solo piano music

Capriccioso in B flat, Op. 19; Danse russe in A min., Op. 40; Dialogue in B, Op. 72; Dumka in C min., Op. 59; L'espiègle in E, Op. 72; Humoresque in E min., Op. 10; Mazurka in D, Op. 40; Nocturne in F, Op. 10; Polacca de concert in E flat, Op. 72; Polka in B min., Op. 52; Rêverie in D, Op. 9; Rêverie du soir in G min., Op. 19; Romances in F min., Op. 5; in F, Op. 51; Scherzo in F, Op. 2; Tendre reproches in C sharp min., Op. 72.
(BB) *(*) Naxos Dig. 8.550504 [id.]. Ilona Prunyi.

Ilona Prunyi is recorded in the same acoustic as, but with a different team and three years later than, her *Seasons*. The sound is not quite so oppressively close, though it is still forward and shallow. She plays this much-underrated repertoire with great vitality and musical intelligence; but anyone who has heard some of these miniatures played by a great pianist will know how much more there is to this music.

The Seasons, Op. 37b; Chanson triste in G min.; Nocturne in C sharp min.; Songs without words in A min.; in F.
(BB) (*) Naxos Dig. 8.550233 [id.]. Ilona Prunyi.

No quarrels here with Ilona Prunyi's musical response in *The Seasons* and other Tchaikovsky pieces, which she plays with evident sympathy. Every quarrel with the dreadfully close balance, which makes it difficult to get very far into the year. This upfront, two-dimensional sound gives no pleasure.

Piano sonata No. 2 in G, Op. 37; 6 Morceaux, Op. 51.
(BB) ** ASV Quicksilva Dig. CDQS 6153 [(M) id. import]. Alma Petchersky – SCRIABIN: *Piano sonata No. 3* etc. **
(BB) * Naxos Dig. 8.553063 [id.]. Oxana Yablonskaya.

The Tchaikovsky *G major Sonata* calls for the most commanding virtuosity and, while Alma Petchersky's account is a brave attempt, she faces formidable competition from the likes of Richter and Pletnev. Her playing is not in that class.

Tchaikovsky's piano music is much patronized and underrated. Played by a Richter or a Pletnev, the *G major Sonata* can sound masterly. Oxana Yablonskaya is not the most subtle of artists, given to grand gestures and over-free use of rubato. The price is competitive but it is better to spend more and buy this often endearing music in a performance of greater stature. Postnikova's Erato version will do well enough, although it is coupled with *The Seasons*, and for that one must turn to Pletnev.

VOCAL MUSIC

Liturgy of St John Chrysostum, Op. 41; Liturgical hymns: *Blessed are they who Thou hast chosen; The hymn of the Cherubim; It is meet; Now the angels are with us; Our Father; To Thee we sing.*
(B) *** EMI forte (SIS) CZS5 68661-2 (2) [CDFB 68661]. Grigorov-Teres, Spasov, Manolov, Nikolov, Svetoslav, Obretenov, Bulgarian A Capella Ch., Georgi Robev.

One does not think of Tchaikovsky as a composer of religious music. Yet, listening to these ardent and moving performances by this splendid Bulgarian choir – not only of the *Liturgy* but also the simple hymns – one realizes that, like most Russians, he found a religious dimension within himself and was clearly moved by the words he was setting. Much of the music here is simple and traditionally homophonic (for that was essential if it was to achieve church performance) but Tchaikovsky's ready melodic gift brought its own individuality, as in the beauty of the simple downward scale at the opening of the *Cherubic hymn*; as in the comparable Rachmaninov work, this is a lyrical highlight. Elsewhere he tries a little imitative polyphony all his own with his 'Alleluias', as in *Praise ye the Lord*. There are moments of high drama too in the postlude for the Creed (and elsewhere), while the closing section of *Thine own of Thine own* is gloriously serene. Tchaikovsky was again obviously deeply touched by the words beginning 'Especially for our most holy', and his music for the Lord's Prayer is directly appealing. The Bulgarian singing has great intensity of feeling and, aided by the cathedral acoustic, the effect is wonderfully spacious. Indeed, all this music could hardly be performed more convincingly, and the recording is superb.

The Snow Maiden, Op. 12 (complete incidental music).
(M) *** Chant du Monde Dig. RUS 788090. Natalia Erasova, Alexander Arkipov, Nikolai Vassiliev, Sveshnikov Russian State Ch., Bolshoi Theatre O, Andrey Chistiakov.
(BB) **(*) Naxos Dig. 8.553856 [id.]. Elena Okolysheva, Arkady Mishenkin, Moscow Capella, Moscow SO, Golovschin.

Ostrovsky's play, *The Snow Maiden*, based on a Russian folk-tale, prompted Tchaikovsky to compose incidental music, no fewer than 19 numbers, lasting 80 minutes. Much of it is vintage material, very delightful, bringing reminders of *Eugene Onegin* in the peasant choruses and some of the folk-based songs, and of the later Tchaikovskian world of *The Nutcracker* in some of the dances. He himself thought so well of the music that he wanted to develop it into an opera, but was frustrated when Rimsky-Korsakov wrote one first. The ideas are consistently fresh and charming, and this is a cherishable rarity. Chistiakov's fine 1994 performance, now reissued on Chant du Monde's mid-priced Russian label, is in every way highly recommendable. The three excellent soloists are characterfully Slavonic, rather too forwardly balanced but well caught by the recording, and the fine singing of the chorus is given both sonority and plenty of bite. The orchestral playing is highly persuasive, and there is a pleasingly atmospheric ambience.

Tchaikovsky's engaging score also inspires Golovschin and his Moscow forces to a warmly idiomatic performance on Naxos, richly and colourfully recorded, if without quite the same degree of vividness. This may not match the Chant du Monde version in vitality, which at generally faster speeds sparkles more and offers crisper ensemble, but it is similarly persuasive. The conductor's affection is obvious. There are only two soloists to share the vocal music, but they are convincingly Slavonic and they are balanced slightly less forwardly, which is not a disadvantage. This Naxos disc is well worth its more modest cost. Both recordings offer full translations.

OPERA

Eugene Onegin (complete).
(M) (**) BMG/Melodiya mono 74321 17090-2 (2). Belov, Vishnevskaya, Lemeshev, Avdeyeva, Bolshoi Theatre Ch. & O, Khaikin.

The BMG transfer of the 1955 Bolshoi recording clarifies the sound, with voices focused well forward, even though big ensembles bring serious distortion. With Boris Khaikin a deeply sympathetic conductor, this is a powerfully idiomatic performance which captures the authentic Russian tradition more persuasively than most recordings from the Soviet period, with the genre numbers crisply sprung and with some first-rate playing from some of the Bolshoi instrumentalists, even if the horn adopts a typical howling tone. Though the mono sound is limited, the voices are not constricted, and the off-stage choruses, so important in this work, are well balanced to make them as atmospheric as possible. As Onegin, Evgeni Belov is clear and forthright, while Galina Vishnevskaya, near the beginning of her Bolshoi career, is firm and bright, if rarely able to convey subtler half-tones, partly thanks to the close-up recording. Also very Russian-sounding, but clear and not whining, is the Lensky of Sergei Lemeshev. A historic set, worth investigating. Only brief notes are provided, with no libretto or translation.

Eugene Onegin: highlights.
(M) **(*) DG Dig. 445 467-2 (from complete set, with Allen, Freni, Von Otter, Shicoff, Burchuladze, Sénéchal, Alldis Ch., Dresden State O, Levine).

Even though the (full-price) Levine set is not our first choice for the complete opera, this 75-minute selection brings out the superb qualities of the singing. It includes the Letter scene (with Freni a freshly charming Tatiana), the Waltz and Polonaise scenes (with the excellent Leipzig Radio Chorus), also the Act II Duel scene and other key arias, all strongly characterized, and the entire closing scene (11 minutes). The recording, made in the Dresden Lukaskirche, is too closely balanced and unatmospheric; but as a sampler this is clearly valuable.

The Queen of Spades (Pique Dame) (complete).
(M) ** BMG/Melodia 74321 17091-2 (3). Atlantov, Milashkina, Levko, Fedosseiev, Borisova, Valaitis, Bolshoi Theatre Soloists, Ch. & O, Mark Ermler.

This Bolshoi version was recorded in 1974 and now passes from the Philips label to RCA. The sense of presence and atmosphere makes up for shortcomings in the singing, with Vladimir Atlantov as Herman too taut and strained, singing consistently loudly, and with Tamara Milashkina producing curdled tone at the top, not at all girlish. Both those singers, for all their faults, are archetypally Russian, and so – in a much more controlled way – is Valentina Levko, a magnificent Countess, firm and sinister.

Yolanta (complete).
(B) ** CPO Dig. CPO 999 456-2 (2) [id.]. Gurevich, Katchinian, Ben, Denolfo, ECOV Ch., Warsaw PO, Rotman.

Tchaikovsky's imagination was obviously touched by the fairy-tale story of a blind princess in medieval Provence who is finally cured by the arrival of the knight who falls in love with her. The libretto may be flawed but the lyrical invention is a delight. The CPO version, with two discs offered for the price of one, makes a fair recommendation, brightly recorded in upfront sound, with a good cast. Under Hans Rotman the performance, well played, brings out the passion of the score, but less subtly, less idiomatically than is ideal. As Iolanta, Michaela Gurevich sings tenderly but with some edge. Ian Denolfo as Vaudémont is warm and firm but is strained on top; Alexander Ben as Robert is strong and urgent, while Arutiun Katchinian is on the light side as the King.

Teixeira, António (1707– after 1759)

Motet: *Gaudate, astra.*
(M) *** DG Codex 453 182-2 [id.]. Jennifer Smith, Fernando Serafim, Calabrese, Ferreira, De Macedo, Fernandes – ALMEIDA: *Beatus vir* etc.; CARVALHO: *Te Deum*. SEIXAS: *Adebat Vincentius* etc. ***

Teixeira's non-liturgical, Italianate motet, *Rejoice, stars, rejoice*, alternates tenor recitative with a pair of delightful soprano arias, gracefully and – in the case of the second – brilliantly sung by Jennifer Smith. The continuo support here is excellent, and the recording is fresh and pleasing. Most enjoyable.

Telemann, Georg Philipp (1681–1767)

(i) *Concert sonata for trumpet & strings in D;* (ii) *Trumpet concertos: in E min.; in G;* (iii) *Triple concerto for trumpet & 2 oboes in D;* (iv) *Concerto for 3 trumpets, 2 oboes, timpani & strings in D.*
(M) *** Erato/Warner Dig./Analogue 0630 13743-2. Maurice André, (i) Vienna Soloists; (ii) Franz Liszt CO, Budapest, Frigyes Sándor; (iii) Pierlot, Chambon, Hogne, Jean-François Paillard CO, Paillard; (iv) Touvron, Lionel André, Arrignon, Chavana, Ens. O, Jean-Pierre Wallez.

The concerto for three trumpets, two oboes and strings (recorded digitally in 1982) has some very attractive textures and the invention is fresh; the companion work for trumpet and a pair of oboes (which have the *Siciliano* third movement to themselves) is scored in a similarly imaginative way, with the accompaniment reduced to a single bassoon (which at times is almost an additional soloist) and continuo. André scales down his tone where necessary to balance with the woodwind. Both this and the rest of the programme is analogue, from the 1970s. The *Concert sonata* (here reconstructed by Fernand Oubradous) has a highly expressive, very Italianate *Largo* (the harpsichord just about peeps in here) and a joyous finale, which André relishes, but with plenty of necessary light and shade. The remaining works are true solo concertos of high calibre: the cantabile line of the melancholy *Andante* of the *G major* is played very touchingly; the rondo finale is simultaneously *galant* and regal. The mood then changes again for the warmly expressive *Andante* which opens the *E minor Concerto*; its second movement is a catchy *moto perpetuo*. André negotiates it skilfully – and particularly so the recitativo by which it is interrupted in the middle. After the noble following *Largo*, the work is capped by a crisply buoyant finale, by no means predictable in its progress. These are all memorable works, showing their composer to be a leading figure in baroque trumpet repertoire. In the multiple concerto, Wallez's accompaniment is not strong in personality, but all the other concertos are given excellent support. Highly recommended.

(i) *Concerto for 2 flutes, 2 oboes and strings in B flat;* (ii) *Triple concerto for flute, oboe d'amore, violin and strings in E; Oboe d'amore concerto in D; Trumpet concerto in D;* (iii) *Concerto for trumpet, 2 oboes in D;* (ii) *Double viola concerto in G;* (i) *Concerto for 3 trumpets, 2 oboes, timpani and strings in D;* (iv) *Double concerto for violin, trumpet and strings in D;* (i) *Suite in G (La Putain); Tafelmusik, Part I: Conclusion in E min. for 2 flutes and strings.*

(M) *** Van. 08.9138.72 (2) [id.]. (i) Soloists, Esterhazy O, David Blum; (ii) Soloists, I Solisti di Zagreb, Antonio Janigro; (iii) Peter Masseurs, Amsterdam Bach Soloists; (iv) Mincho Minchev, Nikolai Chochev, Sofia Soloists, Vasil Kazandiev.

The sheer interest of the repertoire here outweighs any minor reservations about the recording, which comes from the 1960s. However, the sound, particularly in the Esterhazy recordings, is warm and full and the performances are expert. The diversity of Telemann's inexhaustible invention is well demonstrated. In the *Concerto for two violas* the soloists interweave inseparably from the orchestral texture, a device borrowed from Vivaldi who named it 'violette all'inglese'. The solo *Oboe d'amore concerto* and *Trumpet concerto* are both fine, four-movement works, but it is the collective concertos that offer the greatest interest. The *Concerto for two flutes, two oboes and strings* begins elegantly with richly mellifluous blending; then, after a busy *Presto*, the two oboes open the *Cantabile* unaccompanied in a gravely Handelian melody. The *Triple concerto for flute, oboe d'amore and violin in E major* opens with an imposingly spacious *Andante*, very like an introduction to an aria or a chorus from an oratorio; then, after a lively allegro, comes a particularly fine *Siciliano*. The *Concerto for three trumpets, two oboes and timpani* brings a sprightly Handelian fugue, including trumpets and oboes within the part-writing. The oboes gently dominate the gravely expressive *Largo* arietta, and the piece ends with more rollicking interplay between all concerned. The result is an irresistible masterpiece. The suite, *La Putain* ('The Prostitute'), contains an invitation by way of a folksong (*Ich bin so lang nicht bei dir g'west*) to 'Come up and see me sometime'. The suite of strongly characterized dances which follow reminds one not a little of the incidental music of Lully and Rameau in its feeling for colour. The *Concerto for trumpet and two oboes in D* is added on to the end of the first CD, and the performance by the Amsterdam Bach Soloists (with Peter Masseurs a splendid soloist) appears to use original instruments. The second CD closes the programme with a brief contribution from Sofia, the *Concerto for violin, trumpet and strings in D*, vividly played but rather thinly recorded. But overall this highly stimulating set must receive the warmest possible welcome.

Oboe concertos: in D min.; E min.; F min.

(M) *** Virgin Veritas/EMI Dig. VER5 61152-2 [id.]. Hans de Vries, Alma Musica Amsterdam, Bob van Asperen – ALBINONI: *Concertos from Op. 9.* ***

Hans de Vries is a very fine player and he produces an attractively full yet refined timbre from his baroque oboe (which dates from 1735). Apart from the stylishness of his phrasing, there are absolutely no intonation problems and the bravura articulation in the *moto perpetuo Allegro molto* second movement of the *E minor Concerto* is astonishingly clean. The authentic accompaniments are alert and stylish and not in the least vinegary. The solo balance seems excessively forward, but that may be partly the result of the acoustic, and the accompanying strings remain well in the picture.

Concerto for 3 oboes & 3 violins in B flat, TWV 44:43; (i) *Concerto for recorder, bassoon & strings in F; Concerto for 4 violins in G, TWV 40:201; Overture (Suite) in F for 2 horns, violins & continuo, TWV 44:7.*

(M) *** Teldec/Warner 0630 12320-2. VCM, Harnoncourt, (i) with Frans Brüggen, Otto Fleischmann.

One of the best Telemann discs currently available. The five-movement Overture or Suite featuring a pair of horns shows the composer at his most characteristic (natural horns are used), and the performances are most persuasive. The oboes also sound splendidly in tune, which is not always the case with the baroque instrument, and phrasing is alive and sensitive. Indeed these performances are extremely fine, and only the *Concerto for recorder and bassoon* lets the disc down a little; it is also not as well played as the others. The quality is good and the digital remastering has not tried to clarify artificially what is basically a resonant recording with inner detail mellowed by the ambience. Outlines, however, are cleaner and one would not guess that this dates from 1966.

Recorder concerto in G min.; Double concerto in A min. for recorder, viola da gamba and strings; Double concerto in A for 2 violins in scordatura; Concertos for 4 violins: in C and D.
(B) **(*) DG Classikon 439 444-2; *439 444-4* [(M) id. import]. Soloists, Col. Mus. Ant., Goebel.

These are chamber concertos rather than solo concertos such as we associate with Vivaldi. They are diverting and inventive, without at any point reaching any great depths: like so much of Telemann, they are pleasing without being memorable. Nevertheless they are eminently well served by these artists and well recorded. There is an edge on the sound of the string ripieno which not all ears will enjoy, but any reservations are almost forgotten when one looks at the price of this CD.

(i–iii) *Double concerto in E min. for recorder and transverse flute;* (iv) *Viola concerto in G;* (i; v) *Suite in A min. for flute and strings;* (iii) *Overture des Nations anciens et modernes in G.*
(M) *** Teldec/Warner 9031 77620-2 [id.]. (i) Frans Brüggen, (ii) Franz Vester, (iii) Amsterdam CO, André Rieu; (iv) Paul Doctor, Concerto Amsterdam, Brüggen; (v) SW German CO, Friedrich.

All these works show Telemann as an original and often inspired craftsman. His use of contrasting timbres in the *Double concerto* has considerable charm; the *Overture des Nations anciens et modernes* is slighter but is consistently and agreeably inventive, and the *Suite in A minor*, one of his best-known works, is worthy of Handel or Bach. Frans Brüggen and Franz Vester are expert soloists and Brüggen shows himself equally impressive on the conductor's podium accompanying Paul Doctor, the rich-timbred soloist in the engaging *Viola concerto*. The sound, splendidly remastered, is unbelievably good, with fine body and presence: it is difficult to believe that these recordings are now three decades old.

(i) *Viola concerto in G;* (ii) *Suite in A min. for recorder and strings; Tafelmusik,* Part 2: (iii) *Triple violin concerto in F;* Part 3: (iv) *Double horn concerto in E flat.*
❁ (BB) *** Naxos Dig. 8.550156; *4550156* [id.]. (i) Kyselak; (ii) Stivín; (iii) Hoelblingova, Hoelbling, Jablokov; (iv) Z. & B. Tylšar, Capella Istropolitana, Richard Edlinger.

Our Rosette is awarded for enterprise and good planning – to say nothing of good music-making. It is difficult to conceive of a better Telemann programme for anyone encountering this versatile composer for the first time and coming fresh to this repertoire, having bought the inexpensive Naxos CD on impulse. Ladislav Kyselak is a fine violist and is thoroughly at home in Telemann's splendid four-movement concerto; Jiři Stivín is an equally personable recorder soloist in the masterly *Suite in A minor*; his decoration is a special joy. The *Triple violin concerto* with its memorable *Vivace* finale and the *Double horn concerto* also show the finesse which these musicians readily display. Richard Edlinger provides polished and alert accompaniments throughout. The digital sound is first class.

Darmstadt overtures (suites), TWV 55/C6 (complete).
(M) *** Teldec/Warner 4509 93772-2 (2). VCM, Harnoncourt.

What strikes one with renewed force while listening to these once again is the sheer fertility and quality of invention that these works exhibit. This is music of unfailing intelligence and wit and, although Telemann rarely touches the depths of Bach, there is no lack of expressive eloquence either. The performances are light in touch and can be recommended with real enthusiasm. This would make an excellent start to any Telemann collection.

Overture (Suite) in B flat (La Bourse); Suites in C and G.
(M) *** Vanguard/Passacaille Dig. 99710. Il Fondamento, Paul Dombrecht.

Paul Dombrecht and Il Fondamento follow up the success of their *Water music* coupling (see below) with characterful period-instrument performances of three more of Telemann's suites. Each is in its usual form: French overture followed by various dances, sometimes given epithets. The *C major Suite* (which comes last on this CD) is one of the most sprightly and its third number (*Les étudiants galliards*) is something of a hit. There is also a fine *Sarabande*, while the penultimate *Canaries* and closing *Air Italien* also have much charm. The *Overture in B flat* is also a suite of dances, and every number is given a sobriquet, such as the charming *Le repos interrompu*, *La guerre en la paix* and, more remarkably, *L'Espérance de Mississippi*. Its overall title, *La Bourse*, is associated with the ground floor of the composer's mansion, where he lived between 1712 and 1721, which at that time housed the Hamburg Stock Exchange. Excellent recording, but a collection to be played just one suite at a time!

Tafelmusik (Productions 1–3) complete.
(M) *** Teldec/Warner 4509 95519-2 (4). Concerto Amsterdam, Frans Brüggen.

Brüggen's Teldec set was made in the mid-1960s. The playing is very good indeed, and the recorded quality, like so many of these Das Alte Werk reissues, is first rate, with the usual proviso that the balance is forward, reducing the range of dynamic. The solo playing is expert (Hermann Baumann and Adriaan van Woudenberg are the impressive horn players in the *Double concerto* in the Third Book). The performances have vitality throughout, the sound is full yet has a spicing of astringency, and this mid-priced reissue compares very favourably with the premium-priced sets.

Tafelmusik: Production 1: *Quartet in G for flute, oboe, violin & continuo; Trio in E flat for 2 violins & continuo;* Production 2: *Quartet in D min. for 2 flutes, cello &harpsichord; Trio in E min. for flute, oboe & continuo;* Production 3: *Quartet in E min. for flute, violin, cello & continuo; Trio in D for 2 flutes & continuo.*
(M) *** DG Dig. 447 296-2. Col. Mus. Ant., Goebel.

Only in the *String trio* from Production 1 could there be any reservation about Reinhard Goebel's meagre period-violin timbre, and that relatively minor; the wind quartets and trios here are sheer delight and are played with the lightest touch. The recording is closely balanced but the ambience is warm, making this an excellent entertainment (nearly 70 minutes) to accompany a dinner party.

Tafelmusik, Production 2: *Triple Violin concerto in F; Double concerto in A for flute and violin;* Production III: *Double horn concerto in E flat.* (i) *Suite in D for viola da gamba and strings.*
(BB) ** BMG/DHM Baroque Esprit 0542 77467-2 [id.]. Coll. Aur.; (i) with Johannes Koch.

Collegium Aureum use original instruments, but while the recording does not lack clarity any possible abrasiveness is mellowed by the warm acoustic. The hand horns have some technical problems in their double concerto, but otherwise the performances are accomplished and lively, if not distinctive. In the *Suite in D* Johannes Koch's solo viola does not stand out greatly from the texture; otherwise this attractive work is well projected.

Water music (Hamburger Ebb' und Fluth).
(M) *** Van./Passacaille Dig. 99713. Il Fondamento, Paul Dombrecht – HANDEL: *Water music.* ***

Telemann's *Water music* is rightly one of his most popular works, and it is good to have a thoroughly recommendable period-instrument performance available at mid-price and aptly coupled with Handel. The playing is of a high standard and the reed instruments of Il Fondamento are characterful. Telemann's invention is of a very high standard, not only for the vivacious numbers but also for the expressive writing: the Loure (*Der Verliebte Neptunes*) is quite memorable. But most striking of all is the Gigue entitled *Ebbe und Fluth*, which ingeniously suggests the shifting currents of the Alster. The recording is excellent.

CHAMBER MUSIC

Frans Brüggen Edition, Volume 1: *Essercizii musici: Sonata in C, TWV 41:c5; in D min., TWV 41:d4. Fantasias: in C, TWV 40:2; in D min., TWV 40:4; in F, TWV 40:8; in G min., TWV 40:9; in A min., TWV 40:11; in B flat, TWV 40:12. Der getreue Music-Meister: Canonic sonata in B flat, TWV 41:b3; Sonatas in C, TWV 41:c2; in F, TWV 41:F2; in F min., TWV 41:f1.*
(M) *** Teldec/Warner 4509 93688-2. Frans Brüggen, Anner Bylsma, Gustav Leonhardt.

In this single-disc anthology of Telemann's chamber music Brüggen plays with his usual mastery and, as one would expect from Gustav Leonhardt's ensemble, the performances have polish and authority, and they are excellently recorded. The music itself is highly inventive and entertaining.

12 Fantasias for unaccompanied violin (complete).
(M) *** Maya Dig. MCD 9302. Maya Homburger.

Telemann's *12 Fantasias* for solo violin are a decade later than Bach's *Partitas* and *Sonatas,* and they are less ambitious and demanding. Each is in either three or four movements, usually opening with a *Largo* or *Grave*, alternating with *Allegros*. Their invention is of high quality and they make very enjoyable listening, especially when played with such life and style. Maya Homburger uses a baroque violin and has joined in recordings with the Academy of Ancient Music, English Baroque Soloists and the English Concert, so she has thoroughly absorbed and mastered period-instrument techniques. This is cheerful music and it would be difficult to imagine these works being played more freshly or with a more sensitive espressivo. Homburger is recorded most naturally against a warm but not too resonant acoustic, and there is not a trace of vinegar in her timbre.

Der getreue Music-Meister (complete).
❀ (B) *** DG 447 722-2 (4) [(M) id. import]. Mathis, Töpper, Haefliger, Unger, McDaniel, Würzburg Bach Ch., Instrumental soloists, including Linde, Tarr, Melkus, Schäffer, Elza van der Ven, Ulsamer.

We award a Rosette for sheer enterprise to DG's Archiv division in recording (in 1966–7) a 'complete' version of Telemann's *Der getreue Music-Meister* ('The constant Music Master') which has been called the first musical periodical. Telemann published 25 issues or 'lessons' in all, resourcefully serializing works so that, in order to collect a multi-movement sonata, subscribers would have to wait over three or four issues until publication was complete. (Needless to say, each work is performed here with the movements gathered together.) Other composers were invited to contribute, although Telemann stipulated that they should pay their own postage in sending manuscripts to him for inclusion! Thus the present box includes a lute piece by Weiss, a *Gigue sans basse* by Pisandel and an ingenious choral canon by Zelenka. There is also a great deal of refreshing instrumental music of Telemann with the widest variety of instrumentation, with various combinations of recorder, flute, oboe, chalumeau, bassoon, trumpet and various stringed instruments, including a *Burlesque suite* for 2 violins ingeniously depicting scenes from *Gulliver's Travels*. The operatic arias from *Eginhard*, *Belsazar* and *Sacio* are of considerable interest, while the comic fable from *Aesopus* concerns 'The she-goat's wooing of the lion'. Among the other vocal items there is an aria about 'The woman who is going out of tune'. Sixty-two pieces are recorded here, spread over four CDs (originally five LPs). Performances are almost invariably of excellent quality, and Edith Mathis and Ernst Haefliger stand out among the vocal soloists. Excellent documentation includes full vocal texts. The recording sounds delightfully fresh and natural.

(i) *6 Paris quartets (Nouveaux quatuors en six suites)* (1738): *Nos. 1 in D min.; 2 in A min.; 3 in G; 4 in B min.; 5 in A; 6 in E min.;* (ii) (Orchestral) *Suites: in E flat (La Lyra) for strings;* (iii) *in F for solo violin, 2 flutes, 2 oboes, 2 horns, strings & timpani.*

✾ (M) *** Teldec/Warner 4509 92177-2 (2). (i) Quadro Amsterdam (Frans Brüggen, Jaap Schröder, Anner Bylsma, Gustav Leonhardt); (ii) Concerto Amsterdam, Frans Brüggen; (iii) with Schröder.

In 1730 Telemann published a set of six quartets for violin, flauto traverso, viola da gamba and bass continuo, and these were sufficiently popular to be pirated by the French publishing house, Le Clerk, and reprinted in 1736 – without the composer's permission. Telemann learned by this experience. During a long and fruitful visit to Paris in 1737/8, by virtue of a *Privilège du Roi*, he was able himself to publish a new and even finer set. When these records first appeared, we commented: 'The performances are of such a high order of virtuosity that they silence criticism, and Frans Brüggen in particular dazzles the listener.' Moreover the recording is of the very first class, beautifully balanced and tremendously alive (like the performances themselves), and the CD transfer, as is invariably the case with these Das Alte Werk reissues, is immaculate. To fill out the space on the second CD, we are offered a pair of orchestral suites. The *Suite in F* is the more ambitious and probably dates from the beginning of the 1730s; the autograph score was found in Dresden, and this was almost certainly one of the works '*per molti strumenti*' written (and not only by Telemann), for the local orchestra, so famous at the time. The *La Lyra Suite in E flat major* is much earlier, but its invention is hardly less resourceful and in the third movement, *La Vielle*, Telemann gives a more than passable imitation of a hurdy-gurdy.

Thomas, Ambroise (1811–96)

Overtures: *Mignon; Raymond.*

(M) *** Mercury (IMS) 434 321-2 [id.]. Detroit SO, Paray – BIZET: *L'Arlésienne; Carmen: suites.* **(*)

These justly famous overtures are almost never heard in the concert hall nowadays. *Mignon*, opening with a delightful series of lyrical ideas on flute, clarinet and then horn, is matched by the ebullience of *Raymond*, perhaps more of a bandstand piece. The Detroit orchestra play both with wonderful finesse and Gallic spirit: this is repertoire which Paray directs as to the manner born, like his Auber overtures on the same label. The excellent (1960) recording was made in the Cass Technical High School Auditorium.

Hamlet (complete).

(M) *** Decca (IMS) Dig. 433 857-2 (3). Milnes, Sutherland, Morris, Winbergh, Conrad, Tomlinson, WNO Ch. & O, Bonynge.

Thomas's *Hamlet* may be an unashamed travesty of Shakespeare, complete with happy ending (in its original form), but it remains a strong and enjoyable example of French opera of its period. So much was evident from Richard Bonynge's 1983 Decca set. Here, Ophélie has priority vocally in brilliant and beautiful numbers, with Sutherland taking all the challenges commandingly. Ophelia's famous Mad scene was one of the finest of her early recordings, and here, 24 years later, she still gives a triumphant display, tender and gentle as well as brilliant in coloratura. The heroine's primacy is reinforced when the role of Hamlet is for baritone, here taken strongly if with some roughness by Sherrill Milnes. Outstanding among the others is Gösta Winbergh as Laërte (in French without the final 's'), heady and clear in the only major tenor role. John Tomlinson as Le Spectre sings the necessary monotones resonantly, James Morris is a gruff Claudius and Barbara Conrad a fruity Gertrude. The compelling success of the whole performance of a long, complex opera is sealed by Bonynge's vigorous and sympathetic conducting of first-rate Welsh

National Opera forces, brilliantly and atmospherically recorded. The layout, with Act I on the first CD and the other four Acts, two apiece, on the other two, is surely ideal, and the documentation is good.

Thomson, Virgil (1896–1989)

Film scores: *The Plow that broke the Plains; The River* (suites).
(M) *** Van. 08.8013.71 [OVC 8013]. Symphony of the Air, Leopold Stokowski – STRAVINSKY: *Soldier's Tale*. ***

Virgil Thomson's orchestral music may be sub-Copland (he too uses cowboy tunes like *Old paint*), but in Stokowski's charismatic hands these two film scores emerge with colours glowing and their rhythmic, folksy geniality readily communicating. The recording is resonantly atmospheric, but vivid too. Most enjoyable, and with a worthwhile coupling. This is at upper mid-price in the USA.

Tippett, Michael (1905–98)

(i) *Concerto for double string orchestra;* (ii–iv) *Piano concerto;* (i) *Fantasia concertante on a theme of Corelli; Little music for strings;* (v; iv) *Praeludium for brass, bells and percussion; Suite for the birthday of Prince Charles;* (vi; iii–iv) *Triple concerto for violin, viola, cello and orchestra;* (vii) *The blue guitar* (sonata for solo guitar). Vocal music: (viii–ix) *Bonny at morn* (Northumbrian folksong for unison voices and 3 recorders); (viii) *A Child of our time: 5 Negro spirituals.* (viii; x) *Crown of the year* (cantata); (viii) *Dance, Clarion air* (madrigal); (xi) *Evening canticles;* (viii) *Music* (unison song); *Plebs Angelica* (motet for double choir); *The weeping Babe* (motet for soprano and choir). *The Midsummer Marriage:* (v; iv) *Ritual dances;* (xii) *Sosostris's aria*.
(BB) *** Nimbus Dig. NI 1759 (4) [id.]. (i) English String O, William Boughton; (ii) Martino Tirimo; (iii) BBC PO; (iv) cond. composer; (v) E. N. Philh. O; (vi) Ernest Kovacic, Gerard Causé, Alexander Baillie; (vii) Craig Ogden; (viii) Christ Church Cathedral Ch., Oxford (members), Stephen Darlington; (ix) Michael Copley, Maurice Hodges, Evelyn Nallen; (x) Medici Qt, with wind soloists, Martin Jones (piano) and percussion; (xi) St John's College, Cambridge, Ch., George Guest; (xii) Alfreda Hodgson.

This bargain collection of Tippett, issued to mark the composer's death in 1998, is specially valuable for containing two discs of recordings made by Tippett himself. When he did them, he was already in his late eighties, and the performance of the *Ritual dances* from *A Midsummer marriage* is not as incisive as most other versions, but the warmth of expressiveness and the sense of occasion conveyed are most compelling, the more so in Alfreda Hodgson's rich and resonant performance of Sorostris's aria from the same opera, even though the voice is backwardly balanced. It is good too to have Tippett offering a rare example of his occasional music in the uncomplicated *Prince Charles suite*. Even more valuable is the concerto disc, again more relaxed at more spacious speeds than rival versions, but with outstanding soloists revealing Tippett at his most warmly magnetic. Martino Tirimo is particularly impressive in the elaborate figuration of the *Piano concerto* which can easily sound empty. Broad speeds, well sustained, also mark William Boughton's readings of the string pieces on the fourth disc; the *Guitar sonata*, tautly played by Craig Ogden, and *Evening canticles* sung by the St John's College Choir under George Guest (for whom they were written) make a splendid supplement. The choral singing from Christ Church Cathedral Choir on the second disc is also excellent, with the school cantata, *The Crown of the year*, revealing the composer at his most open and least enigmatic. Warm, atmospheric sound, characteristic of Nimbus.

Concerto for double string orchestra; Fantasia concertante on a theme of Corelli; (i) *Songs for Dov*.
(M) *** Virgin/EMI Ultraviolet Dig. CUV5 61326-2. SCO, composer, (i) with Nigel Robson.

It is particularly valuable to have the *Concerto for double string orchestra*, which Tippett had never previously recorded himself. Interpreting his own youthful inspiration, the nonogenarian gives delightfully pointed readings of the outer movements, bringing out the jazzy implications of the cross-rhythms, not taking them too literally, while the lovely melody of the slow movement has never sounded more warmly expressive. The Scottish Chamber Orchestra plays with comparable passion in the *Fantasia concertante*, a related work from Tippett's middle period, while Nigel Robson is a wonderfully idiomatic and convincing tenor soloist in the difficult vocal lines of the three *Songs for Dov*. Warm, full recording.

Little music for string orchestra.
(M) **(*) Chandos Dig. CHAN 6576 [id.]. Soloists of Australia, Ronald Thomas – BLISS: *Checkmate*; RUBBRA: *Symphony No. 5*. ***

Tippett's *Little music* was written in 1946 for the Jacques Orchestra. Its contrapuntal style is stimulating but the music is more inconsequential than the *Concerto for double string orchestra*. It receives a good if not distinctive performance here, truthfully recorded.

VOCAL MUSIC

A Child of our time (oratorio).
(M) **(*) Carlton Dig. 30367 0205-2 [(M) id. import]. Armstrong, Palmer, Langridge, Shirley-Quirk, Brighton Festival Ch., RPO, Previn.

(i) *A Child of our time* (oratorio); (ii) *The Weeping Babe*.
(BB) **(*) Belart 461 123-2 [(M) id. import]. (i) Morison, Bowden, Lewis, Standen, RLPO Ch. & O, Pritchard; (ii) Cantelo, John Alldis Ch., Sir Colin Davis.

Previn's is a colourful and winning performance, warmer and more expressive than Davis's, predictably helped by the conductor's natural understanding of jazz rhythms. This is a reading which leaves you in no doubt as to the depth of emotion felt by the composer; but ensemble is not always ideally crisp, the chorus is set rather backwardly and the soloists, a less polished if just as characterful team as Davis's, have uneven moments. The digital recording is unobtrusively natural, if slightly recessed.

It is good to have a super-bargain version of Tippett's oratorio, and if the (originally Argo) recording is not modern – it dates from the late 1950s – it sounds remarkably clear in its CD format and is not without atmosphere. There is even a case for preferring this Pritchard performance, despite the less crisp ensemble, to Sir Colin Davis's Philips version, coupled at premium price with *The Knot Garden* (446 331-2). Pritchard's approach is more feeling and sympathetic, and after all this is music which speaks of deep emotion. Elsie Morison and Richard Lewis both sing most beautifully. The brief fill-up, *The Weeping Babe*, was recorded a decade later. It is a setting of some Edith Sitwell poems, a wartime piece of lyrical simplicity, and is excellently sung by the Alldis Choir. This is highly recommendable.

Toch, Ernst (1887-1964)

Symphony No. 3.
(M) *** EMI CDM5 65868-2. Pittsburgh SO, Steinberg – HINDEMITH: *Mathis der Maler;* MARTIN: *Petite symphonie concertante.* **(*)

Until 1950, when he was sixty-three, Ernst Toch, the expatriate German composer who settled in America, had not written a symphony; then, in a sudden burst of creative energy, he produced three in quick succession. This one, first performed in 1955, was commissioned by the American Jewish Tercentenary Committee of Chicago, and the composer himself attaches to it a quotation from Goethe – 'Certainly I am but a wanderer on the earth, a pilgrim – are you anything more?' Toch linked this in his mind with the idea of the Wandering Jew and, though there is no specific programme for the symphony, this was the idea which lay beneath his thoughts during the writing of it. It is an impressive work, thoughtful and exciting by turns, with the central *Andante tranquillo–Allegro* (slow movement and Scherzo combined) especially appealing. Toch adopts no conventional form and links the whole work together with a striking motto theme. But, while the symphony is essentially rhapsodic in feeling, it is the sense of continuity, of musical arguments following naturally after one another in what seems a spontaneous flow, which marks it out. In Steinberg's superb performance it makes a powerful impression as a work which is deeply sincere and serious, but readily approachable. The early stereo (1957) is remarkably atmospheric and clear; only a degree of thinness on top dates the sound. Toch's exotic orchestration – steam valve and all – is beautifully caught, and one is even reconciled to the idea of a Hammond organ in the score, when it is made to sound so effective. A highly recommendable reissue, with intelligent couplings.

Tomkins, Thomas (1572–1656)

Music for viols: *Almain in F* (for 4 viols); *Fantasias 1, 12 & 14* (for 3 viols); *Fantasia* (for 6 viols); *Galliard: Thomas Simpson* (5 viols & organ); *In Nomine II* (for 3 viols); *Pavane in A min.* (for 5 viols & organ); *Pavane in F; Ut re mi (Hexachord fantasia)* (both for 4 viols); (Keyboard) (i) *Fancy for two to play. Pavan and galliard: Earl Strafford*. (Organ) *In nomine; Miserere; Voluntary;* Verse anthems: *Above the stars; O Lord, let me know mine end; Thou art my King.*
✿ (BB) *** Naxos Dig. 8.550602 [id.]. Rose Consort of Viols, Red Byrd; Thomas Roberts; (i) with John Bryan.

This well-planned Naxos programme is carefully laid out in two parts, each of viol music interspersed with harpsichord and organ pieces and ending with an anthem. It gives collectors an admirable opportunity to sample, very inexpensively, the wider output of Thomas Tomkins, an outstandingly fine Elizabethan musician whose music is still too little known. Born in Gloucester, he spent his career both as 'instructor choristarum' at Worcester Cathedral and as a member of the Chapel Royal, helping to supervise the music at the coronation of Charles I. But with the arrival of Cromwell he withdrew from public life. (The organ he installed at Worcester was removed.) Best known for his magnificent church music, it is refreshing to discover what he could do with viols, experimenting with different combinations of sizes of instrument, usually writing with the polyphony subservient to expressive harmonic feeling, as in the splendid and touching *Fantasia for 6 voices*. Perhaps the most remarkable piece here is the *Hexachord fantasia*, where the scurrying part-writing ornaments a rising and falling six-note scale (hexachord). Tomkins's keyboard and organ music is similarly full of character (the *Fancy for two to play* especially so). His *Pavans* are solemn, even stately, yet his *In nomine* setting for viols is quite lively. The performances here are expert and warmly musical, and they make very enjoyable listening. The two five-part verse anthems and *Above the stars*, which is in six parts, are accompanied by five viols; they are performed colloquially, with counter-tenor lead for *Above the stars* and a bass soloist in *Thou art my King*; both parts are demanding and are attractively sung here. This well-recorded collection, like Naxos's early Telemann collection (8.550156), earns its Rosette not just for the stimulation it brings, but for the enterprise shown.

Tosti, Francesco (1846–1916)

Songs: *L'alba sepàra della luce l'ombra; Aprile; 'A vucchella; Chanson de L'adieu; Goodbye; Ideale; Malia; Marechiare; Non t'amo; Segreto; La serenata; Sogno; L'ultima canzone; Vorrei morire.*
(M) *** Ph. (IMS) 426 372-2. José Carreras, ECO, Muller.

Tosti (knighted by Queen Victoria for his services to music) had a gently charming lyric gift in songs like these, and it is good to have a tenor with such musical intelligence – not to mention such a fine, pure voice – tackling once-popular trifles like *Marechiare* and *Goodbye*. The arrangements are sweetly done, and the recording is excellent.

Turina, Joaquin (1882–1949)

Rapsodia sinfónica (arr. Halfter).
(B) *** Decca Eclipse Dig. 448 243-2; *448 243-4* [(M) id. import]. Alicia de Larrocha, LPO, Frühbeck de Burgos – ALBENIZ: *Rapsodia española;* RODRIGO: *Concierto de Aranjuez* etc. ***
(M) (***) Dutton Lab. mono CDCLP 4000 [id. full price]. Moura Lympany, Philh. O, Susskind (with ALBENIZ: *Tango;* GRANADOS: *Goyescas No. 4;* CHOPIN: *Fantasie-Impromptu*) – MOZART: *Piano concertos Nos. 12 & 21.* (***)

Turina's *Rapsodia sinfónica* has been recorded by others, but in the hands of Alicia de Larrocha it is played with such éclat that it becomes almost memorable and thoroughly entertaining. Excellent, vivid sound.

Turina's *Rapsodia sinfonica* enjoyed great popularity in the days of 78-r.p.m. records, and far greater than its present-day profile would suggest. In her 1949 recording Moura Lympany despatches it with all the lightness and delicacy you could wish for. Her Albéniz, Chopin and Granados encores all come from 1953, when HMV were still issuing shellac records, and they have great charm and style. Excellent transfers.

GUITAR MUSIC

Fandanguillo, Op. 36; Homenaje a Tarréga; Ráfaga, Op. 53; Sevillana (Fantasia), Op. 29; Sonata, Op. 61.
(M) *** EMI Dig. CDM5 66574-2 [id.]. Manuel Barrueco – ALBENIZ: *Suite española, Op. 47.* ***

It was Segovia who prompted Turina to write these vibrantly colourful pieces which are now central to any classical guitarist's repertoire. The *Fandanguillo* (its percussive thumping imitates the stamping feet of the zapateado) and *Sevillana* are vibrant with flamenco rhythms, while the spectacular and evocative *Ráfaga* translates as 'gust of wind'. They are played here with panache and glittering virtuosity. The *Sonata* requires a more subtle palette, and a sense of structure. Barrueco's account is masterly, seducing the ear in the gentle, seemingly improvisatory central *Andante* and then creating a flashing pulse for the chimerical finale. The recording is intimate, yet with a fine sense of presence.

Canto a Sevilla

(BB) *** Arte Nova Dig. 74321 51624-2 [id.]. Ana Rodrigo, Gran Canaria PO, Leaper – RODRIGO: *Concierto di Aranjuez.* **

Turina's cantata in tribute to the city of Seville is among his finest and most attractive works, a 40-minute piece in seven atmospheric movements, here given a warm and colourful reading with Ana Rodrigo a youthfully fresh and clear soprano soloist. Excellent sound. It is a pity that a more imaginative coupling was not chosen, for the Rodrigo *Concierto de Aranjuez*, though perfectly acceptable, cannot be numbered among the more memorable accounts on CD.

Tye, Christopher (*c.* 1505–*c.* 1572)

Mass: Euge bone (in 6 parts).

(M) *** EMI CDM5 65211-2. King's College, Cambridge, Ch., Ledger – BYRD: *Mass for 5 voices;* TALLIS: *Mass: Puer natus est nobis.* ***

Christopher Tye's *Mass for six voices* is one of the glories of early Tudor music, amazingly rich and complex. This fine (1980) recording – attractively coupled with Byrd's masterpiece and the wonderfully reconstructed Tallis work – is well balanced between clarity and atmosphere, and the quality of the singing is a fine tribute to Ledger's work with this unique choir.

Urbanner, Erich (born 1936)

String quartet No. 3.

(M) *** Teldec/Warner 3984 21967-2. Alban Berg Qt – BERG: *Lyric suite* etc.; WEBERN: *6 Bagatelles* etc. ***

Urbanner's avant-garde *Third Quartet* is expertly played, but its single-movement form, Schoenbergian in ancestry, does not yield music of real memorability. The Berg and Webern couplings are what make this finely recorded reissue a desirable acquisition.

Ustvolskaya, Galina (born 1919)

(i) *Piano concerto* (for piano, string orchestra and timpani); (ii–iii) *Grand duet* (for cello and piano); (iv) *Octet* (for 2 oboes, 4 violins, timpani and piano); (iii) *Piano sonata No. 3.*

(M) ** BMG Melodiya 74321 49956-2 [id.]. (i) Pavel Serebryakov, Leningrad State Philharmonic Soc. CO; (ii) Oleg Stolpner, (iii) Oleg Malov; (iv) Kosoyan, Chinakov & Ens.

Galina Ustvolskaya was first a pupil of Shostakovich at the Leningrad Conservatoire and then became his assistant until the Zhdanov decree resulted in their dismissal along with Shebalin and others. Despite Shostakovich's support, her music remained in the shadows during the Soviet years, and it is only in the present decade that she has come into her own. The *Piano concerto* comes from 1946, the period of her studies with Shostakovich, whose imprint it bears; and this 1970 performance by Pavel Serebryakov and the Leningrad Chamber Orchestra was its première. The *Octet*, a strong piece with some of the heiratic feeling of Stravinsky, was composed in 1949–50 and not premièred until the 1970s. There are six piano sonatas, composed between 1947 and 1988, and the *Third* from 1952 has a spare, uncompromising angularity that is extraordinarily radical for the early 1950s, astonishingly so for the Soviet Union. It has a certain aridity; there is a lack of rhythmic variety and it asserts and repeats its ideas rather than developing them. The *Cello duet* was composed in the 1960s for Rostropovich: this is the only mid-price account. For many it will be a tough nut to crack, but there is no doubt that, like so much of the music of this reclusive figure, it springs from a genuine vision. An interesting and worthwhile issue, though (with the exception of the *Cello duet*) the recordings come from the 1970s and are not top-drawer.

Vaňhal, Jan (1739–1813)

Violin concerto in B.

(BBB) *** Discover Dig. DICD 920265 [id.]. Ivan Zenaty, Virtuosi di Praga, Oldrich Vlček – MYSLIVECEK: *Violin concerto.* ***

Like his Bohemian contemporary, Mysliveček, Vaňhal was born in Bohemia almost a generation before Mozart; he similarly wrote inventive, lively music, of which this violin concerto is an appealing example, with the central slow movement a nostalgic intermezzo. On this well-recorded bargain issue Ivan Zenaty with his clean, full tone again proves an outstanding advocate, with the Virtuosi di Praga providing lively support on modern instruments. Excellent recording.

Varèse, Edgar (1883–1965)

Amériques; (i; ii) *Ecuatorial;* (ii) *Nocturnal* (ed. & completed Chou Wen-Chung).
(M) **(*) Van. 08 4031-71 [OVC 4031]. (i) Ariel Bybee; (ii) University Civic Choral Bass Ens.; Utah SO, Abravanel (with HONEGGER: *Pacific 231* **).

Amériques was written when the composer was still under the spell of his first impressions of New York. Its rhythms are unpredictable and its cross-currents and dissonant colourings suggest the organized chaos of the metropolitan civilization of the twentieth century. The *Nocturnal* was commissioned by the Koussevitzky Foundation, and the composer began it in 1961. But Varèse did not live to finish his music, and it was first performed in an incomplete state. However, the composer also left notes about intended changes, although these are sometimes ambiguous. Chou Wen-Chung has bravely edited the completed portion of the piece and added closing material from the composer's sketches. The result is surprisingly convincing and, although we know where Chou Wen-Chung's section begins, the ear does not detect any sudden drop in intensity or quality. Like the account of *Amériques*, the performance is not lacking in exuberance and even humour (even if perhaps this is not all intentional). *Ecuatorial* is a stronger and more directly emotional work, mystical, and based on a high-flown but poetic text by Miguel Asturias. The music in some ways recalls Milhaud's *L'homme et son désir* in creating a background atmosphere suggestive of a tropical jungle. The voices are used with great colouristic imagination. All these performances are most convincing, with the orchestra plainly enjoying themselves, and the characteristically atmospheric Utah acoustic seems ideal for these scores; even if Honegger's picture of a railway engine, which is added as a fill-up, is less well-focused, the sound is never ugly. An important reissue, with texts included.

Vaughan Williams, Ralph (1872–1958)

Oboe concerto.
(M) *** Carlton Dig. 30366 0065-2 [id.]. Pamela Pecha, Moscow PO, Paul Freeman – R. STRAUSS: *Oboe concerto;* SCHICKELE: *Oboe concerto.* ***

Pamela Pecha gives a particularly attractive account of this sometimes elusive concerto, managing its opening cantilena with pleasing spontaneity and revelling in its folksong element. The effect is both fresh and warm-hearted. She is accompanied excellently, and the recording has a glowing ambience which flatters all concerned.

(i) *Oboe concerto. English folksongs suite; Fantasia on Greensleeves; Fantasia on a theme by Thomas Tallis; Partita for double string orchestra.*
(B) **(*) EMI Eminence Dig. CD-EMX 2179 [(M) id.]. (i) Jonathan Small; RLPO, Vernon Handley.

The charmingly lyrical *Oboe concerto* is given a delectable performance here by Jonathan Small, the flowing pastoralism of its first movement perfectly caught and the more demanding finale impressively handled by conductor and soloist alike. The rarer *Partita for string orchestra* (one without double-basses) is more ambitious even than the *Tallis fantasia* and is some five minutes longer. This is also very well played and sonorously recorded. It is chiefly remembered for the *Intermezzo* headed 'Homage to Henry Hall', a unique tribute to the 1940s' leader of a dance-band whose signature-tune, 'Here's to the next time', is hinted at in the first string group, while the second provides a jazzy pizzicato bass. The work is attractive, but elsewhere it is not as catchy as one always hopes. Handley gives an essentially rhapsodic account of the *Tallis fantasia*, relaxing in its central section and then creating an accelerando to the climax. The inner string group creates radiantly ethereal textures, but ideally the recording needs just a little more resonance – the work was written to be first performed in Gloucester Cathedral – although it is rich-textured and truthful.

(i) *Oboe concerto. Fantasia on Greensleeves;* (ii) *The Lark ascending.*
(M) *** DG 439 529-2. (i) Neil Black; (ii) Zukerman, ECO, Barenboim – DELIUS: *Aquarelles* etc.; WALTON: *Henry V.* ***

Neil Black's creamy tone is very well suited to Vaughan Williams's *Oboe concerto* and he gives a wholly persuasive performance. Zukerman's account of *The Lark ascending* is full of pastoral rapture – even if perhaps not totally idiomatic, the effect is ravishing. The recordings from the late 1970s have not lost their allure or atmospheric warmth in the digital remastering.

(i) *Oboe concerto. Fantasia on Greensleeves; Fantasia on a theme of Thomas Tallis; Five variants of Dives and Lazarus; The Lark ascending; The Wasps: Overture.*
(M) *** Nimbus Dig. NI 7013 [id.]. (i) Maurice Bourgue; English String O or SO, William Boughton.

Opening with an exuberant account of *The Wasps overture*, this is a very attractive and generous 70-minute collection of favourite Vaughan Williams orchestral pieces, most sympathetically played under William Boughton and presented amply and atmospherically. The spacious acoustic of the Great Hall of Birmingham University ensures that the lyrical string-tune in the overture is properly expansive without robbing the piece of bite, and that both the deeply felt *Tallis fantasia*, with its passionate climax, and *Dives and Lazarus* have a rich amplitude of string-sound. Michael Bochmann, the sympathetic soloist in *The Lark ascending*, playing simply yet with persuasive lyrical freedom is nicely integrated with the warm orchestral backing. More questionable is the *Oboe concerto*, with the superb French soloist, Maurice Bourgue, balanced too close. Nevertheless Bourgue's playing, sharply rhythmical and with a rich, pastoral timbre, makes a good case for an (until recently) comparatively neglected piece.

Piano concerto in C.
(B) *** EMI Dig. CD-EMX 2239 [(M) id.]. Piers Lane, RLPO, Handley – DELIUS: *Piano concerto;* FINZI: *Eclogue.* ***

Piers Lane defies the old idea of this as a grittily unpianistic work, giving it a powerful, refreshing reading, helped by fine playing from the RLPO under Handley, always a sympathetic Vaughan Williams interpreter. Though this hardly outshines Howard Shelley's full-price Lyrita version with its more involving, less distant recording, the apt and unusual coupling can be warmly recommended.

English folksongs suite; Fantasia on Greensleeves; In the Fen Country; (i) *The Lark ascending; Norfolk rhapsody No. 1;* (ii) *Serenade to music.*
(M) *** EMI CDM7 64022-2 [id.]. LPO, LSO or New Philh. O, Sir Adrian Boult; (i) with Hugh Bean; (ii) 16 soloists.

All the music here is beautifully performed and recorded. Hugh Bean understands the spirit of *The Lark ascending* perfectly and his performance is wonderfully serene. The transfers are fresh and pleasing; in the lovely *Serenade* (which Boult does in the original version for 16 soloists) the voices are given greater presence.

English folksongs suite; Fantasia on a theme by Thomas Tallis; Fantasia on Greensleeves; (i) *The Lark ascending. The Wasps: Overture; Entr'acte No. 1; March of Kitchen Utensils.*
(B) ** Tring Dig. TRP 031 [(M) id.]. (i) Jonathan Carney; RPO, Christopher Seaman.

The highlight here is a rapt account of the idyllic *Lark ascending*, with Jonathan Carney, the highly sensitive soloist, often sustaining a haunting pianissimo solo line. The *Tallis fantasia* is also a fine performance, both ethereal and passionate; but this, like the whole programme, is affected by too close microphones in a reverberant acoustic. The dynamic range of the recording is realistically wide, but fortissimos inevitably bring fierceness, even though the basic ambience is spacious.

English folksongs suite; Toccata marziale.
(BB) *** ASV CDQS 6021 [(M) id.]. London Wind O, Denis Wick – HOLST: *Military band suites* etc. ***

As in the Holst suites, the pace of these performances of the original scores is attractively zestful, and if the slow movement of the *English folksongs suite* could have been played more reflectively, the bounce of *Seventeen come Sunday* is irresistible.

Fantasia on Greensleeves; (i) *Fantasia on a theme of Thomas Tallis.*
(BB) **(*) RCA Navigator 74321 17905-2 [(B) Basic 100 09026 61724-2]. Phd. Ch. & O, Ormandy – HOLST: *The Planets.* (***)
(BB) (*(*)) Belart mono 461 362-2 [(M) id. import]. New SO of L., Anthony Collins – DELIUS: *Brigg Fair* etc. (**); ELGAR: *Introduction and allegro; Serenade.* (*(*))
(B) *(*) Millennium MCD 80099. V. State Op. O, Sir Adrian Boult – HOLST: *The Planets.* *
(M) * DG (IMS) Dig. 445 561-2. Orpheus CO (with BRITTEN: *Simple symphony* ***) – ELGAR: *Elegy* etc. *(*)

Gloriously ripe performances of both works from Ormandy and the Philadelphia strings, recorded in 1970 and 1972 respectively. Subtlety is not the strong point and the second orchestra in the *Tallis fantasia* is made to seem too close; but the warm intensity of the playing confounds such criticism and there is a gravity in the way Ormandy presents the famous *Greensleeves* melody that is very endearing. There are few recordings that in their resonant opulence show the body of tone the Philadelphia strings could command at that time.

As well as being a distinguished Sibelian, Anthony Collins was a fine conductor of English music, and he reads deeply into Vaughan Williams's masterly *Tallis fantasia*. Furthermore the small second orchestra offers an impressive sense of recession, and conveys well the ethereal quality of the writing in the more serene sections of the score. *Greensleeves* is very successful too. The snag is the pinched upper-string fortissimos, which do not fall easily on the ear. If your equipment can produce a fairly strong treble roll-off (which is what the Decca engineers provided on the original, full-priced LP), this can be made to sound acceptable.

Recorded in 1959, the players of the Vienna State Opera Orchestra find hardly more affinity with the music of Vaughan Williams than they do with Holst, although the ensemble is better. Despite Boult's special efforts, the solo string quartet in the *Tallis fantasia* fail to respond to the hushed, ethereal quality of the writing (especially the cellist, whose phrasing is awkwardly angular). *Greensleeves*, too, is comparatively graceless.

Even more than in the coupled Elgar, the Orpheus performance of the *Tallis fantasia* suggests a lack of the kind of familiarity and innate understanding of the music which comes with frequent performance. Though there are moments of passion, they are short-lived and the overall pacing is unconvincing. The bright, vividly clear recording confirms the need for a greater weight and body of tone to help the work to expand emotionally.

Fantasia on Greensleeves; Fantasia on a theme by Thomas Tallis; (i) *The Lark ascending.*

(M) *** Virgin/EMI Dig. CUV5 61126-2 [id.]. (i) Christopher Warren-Green; LCO, Warren-Green – ELGAR: *Introduction and allegro* etc. ***

(B) *** Sony SBK 62645; *SBT 62645* [id.]. (i) Phd. O, Ormandy; (ii) Rafael Druian; Cleveland Sinf., Louis Lane – DELIUS: *Brigg Fair; Dance Rhapsody No. 2* etc. ***

Fantasia on Greensleeves; Fantasia on a theme of Thomas Tallis; Five variants of Dives and Lazarus; (i) *Flos Campi.*

(M) *** Van. 08.4053.71 [OVC 4071]. (i) Sally Peck, Utah University Ch.; Utah SO, Maurice Abravanel.

Christopher Warren-Green and his London Chamber Orchestra give a radiant account of *The Lark ascending*, in which Warren-Green makes a charismatic solo contribution, very free and soaring in its flight and with beautifully sustained true pianissimo playing at the opening and close. For the *Tallis fantasia*, the second orchestra (2.2.2.2.1) contrasts with the main group (5.4.2.2.1) and here, though the effect is beautifully serene, Warren-Green does not quite match the ethereal, other-worldly pianissimo that made Barbirolli's full-price reading unforgettable. But that is a minor quibble; the performance overall has great ardour and breadth, almost to match the coupled *Introduction and allegro* of Elgar in its intensity. The recording, made at All Saints' Church, Petersham, is quite ideal in its resonant warmth and atmosphere, yet has good definition. This is an altogether superb disc.

These thoroughly recommendable performances from 1963 on Sony demonstrate the special feeling American musicians can find for English music. In the *Tallis fantasia* Ormandy (like Barbirolli) characteristically underlines the drama of a work that is often regarded as delicate and atmospheric. Some listeners might object to the lustiness of the first climax, but it is utterly convincing in its passionate richness. Moreover the smaller contrasting string group is better balanced here and makes a more ethereal contrast than in Ormandy's later, RCA version (see above). The recording of *The Lark ascending* was made during the period when Louis Lane was a colleague of George Szell at Cleveland and the orchestra was at the peak of its form. Rafael Druian is the highly poetic violin soloist, a performance that has never been surpassed for its delicate sustained pianissimos, even though the balance is fairly close. The orchestral playing, besides being polished, has both character and atmosphere. The CD transfers have expanded the original sound most strikingly. With highly romantic Delius performances as coupling, this is one of the most desirable of Sony's 'Esssential Classics'.

On Vanguard *Greensleeves* is slow and gracious, and there are more passionate versions of the *Tallis fantasia* available; but the noteworthy point is the way Abravanel catches the inner feeling of the music. Both here and in *Dives and Lazarus* the full strings create a gloriously rich sonority. Sally Peck, the violist, is placed with her colleagues rather than as a soloist in *Flos Campi* (following the composer's expressed intention), yet her personality still emerges well. Abravanel, always a warm, energetic conductor, displays real understanding, allowing the music to relax as it should in this evocation of the Song of Solomon, but never letting it drag either. The CD transfer is excellent, retaining the naturalness of the original recording.

Fantasia on Greensleeves; (i) *The Lark ascending.*

(B) *** DG Classikon 439 464-2; *439 464-4* [(M) id. import]. (i) Zukerman; ECO, Barenboim – BRITTEN: *Serenade*; DELIUS: *On hearing the first cuckoo in spring* etc. ***

This DG Classikon bargain CD makes a most attractive anthology. Zukerman's account of *The Lark ascending* has a uniquely rapturous pastoralism and it is beautifully played and recorded.

Fantasia on a theme by Thomas Tallis.

(M) *** EMI CDM5 66760-2. RPO, Stokowski – DVORAK: *String serenade;* PURCELL: *Dido and Aneas: Dido's lament.* ***

❀ (M) (***) EMI mono CDM5 66601-2. Philh. O, Karajan – BRITTEN: *Variations on a theme of Frank Bridge* (***) ❀; STRAVINSKY: *Jeu de cartes.* (**)

Stokowski's care with tonal balance brings radiant antiphonal effects as the various string-groups are contrasted. Surprisingly, the performance is unusually straightforward; there is less variation of speed than is common and there is little *stringendo* at the approach to the main climax. Stokowski is comparatively serene, yet his restraint does not in any way interfere with the music's forward momentum. He conjures the ripest string playing from the RPO and some lovely, refined instrumental solos. The 1975 Abbey Road sound has fine body and a wide dynamic range, and this glorious performance takes its place among the finest ever recorded.

Karajan's version of the *Tallis fantasia*, coupled with Britten's *Variations on a theme of Frank Bridge*, is one of the outstanding records of the 1950s, sounding as fresh and sonorous today as it did then. Sonically it is little short of amazing, and artistically it is no less impressive. The playing of the Philharmonia strings is altogether superlative, and the *Tallis fantasia* sounds both idiomatic and vivid, rather like a newly cleaned painting. Recordings of the work are legion, and stereo undoubtedly brings an added dimension, but this mono CD ranks among the very best, from the early Boyd Neel and Boult sets of 78s, through such memorable accounts as that of Mitropoulos, to the more recent supreme version from Barbirolli (still at full price).

(i) *Fantasia on a theme by Thomas Tallis; Five variants of Dives and Lazarus; Norfolk rhapsody No. 1;* (ii) *In Windsor Forest;* (i; iii) *Toward the Unknown Region.*

(M) *** EMI CDM5 65131-2. (i) CBSO; (ii) Bournemouth Symphony Ch. & Sinf.; (iii) with CBSO Ch.; Norman Del Mar.

Norman Del Mar's strong and deeply felt account of the *Tallis fantasia* is given a splendid digital recording, with the second orchestral group creating radiant textures. The direct approach, however, lacks something in mystery, and not all of the ethereal resonance of this haunting work is conveyed. The early (1907) cantata, *Toward the Unknown Region*, set to words of Walt Whitman, and *In Windsor Forest*, which the composer adapted from his Falstaff opera, *Sir John in love*, make a perfect coupling. The movements are not always exact transcriptions from the opera, for the composer rethought and amplified certain passages. Norman Del Mar directs warmly sympathetic performances, given excellent sound.

Five variants of Dives and Lazarus; (i) *The Lark ascending; The Wasps: Overture and suite.*

(B) *** EMI Dig. CD-EMX 9508 [(M) id.]. (i) David Nolan; LPO, Handley.

The immediacy of the recording allows no mistiness in *The Lark ascending*, but it is still a warm, understanding performance. The overture is spaciously conceived and it leads to charming, colourful accounts of the other, less well-known pieces in the suite, tuneful and lively. The *Five Variants of Dives and Lazarus* is superbly played and recorded. The sound is fresh and clear, if rather brightly lit.

Job (A masque for dancing); (i) *The Lark ascending.*

(BB) *** Naxos Dig. 8.553955 [id.]. E. N. Philh., Lloyd-Jones, (i) with David Greed.

Job (A masque for dancing); The Wasps overture.

(BB) (***) Belart mono 461 122-2 [(M) id. import]. LPO, Boult.

In this splendid account of Vaughan Williams's masterly ballet score, David Lloyd-Jones – at super-budget price on Naxos – virtually upstages the competition. He gives a performance tingling with drama, yet with much delicacy of feeling. The opening scene is particularly atmospheric and the *Saraband of the Sons of God* brings a noble dignity, especially when it returns expansively on the full brass. There is much fine orchestral playing: the principal oboe's contributions throughout and the solo violin in scene vii are touchingly fragile, while Job's comforters are portrayed with delectably oily saxophone-playing. The big climaxes bring a superb brass contribution; indeed the brass almost submerge the organ at the vision of Satan. The dance rhythms are caught superbly – bitingly so in *Satan's dance of triumph*, genially Holstian in the *Galliard of the Sons of the Morning*. The Epilogue is touchingly ethereal. The recording, made in Leeds Town Hall, has an ideal spaciousness, yet combines vivid detail with glowing textures. For an encore the orchestral leader, David Greed, provides an exquisitely delicate portrayal of the *Ascending lark*, not as charismatic perhaps as Iona Brown's version (see Concerts section), but with a remarkably sustained closing *piano-pianissimo*.

Boult made four LP recordings of *Job*, and this Belart/Decca mono version has a special kind of warmth and freshness. No apologies need be made for the mono recording, which sounds fuller and more atmospheric than some early digital stereo discs; and the same comment might apply to the delightful incidental music for *The Wasps*, with the lovely string-tune in the *Overture* as spacious as one could ask and the delicious *March past of the kitchen utensils* comparably piquant.

(i) *Suite for viola and orchestra;* (ii) *Flos campi;* (iii) *Hymn-tune preludes Nos. 1 & 2; Overture: The poisoned kiss; The running set.*
(M) **(*) Chandos CHAN 6545 [id.]. Bournemouth Sinf., (i) with Riddle, cond. Del Mar, (ii) with Ch.; (iii) cond. Hurst.

The *Suite* is lightweight but engaging, unpretentious music to be enjoyed, with its charming *Carol* and quirky *Polka mélancolique*. Frederick Riddle is an eloquent soloist, even if the playing is not always technically immaculate, and Norman Del Mar directs sympathetically. The overture to the opera *The poisoned kiss* is merely a pot-pourri, but it is presented most persuasively here. *The running set* is an exhilarating fantasy on jig rhythms. Fine performances under George Hurst.

SYMPHONIES

Symphonies Nos. 1–9 (complete); *Fantasia on Greensleeves; Fantasia on a theme of Tallis; Norfolk rhapsody No. 1; 5 Variants of Dives and Lazarus.*
(M) **(*) RCA 09026 61460-2 (6) [id.]. Philh. O, Slatkin.

Symphonies Nos. 1–9; Fantasia on a theme by Thomas Tallis; Job; (i) *The Lark ascending.*
(M) ** Teldec/Warner Dig. 0630 17047-2 (6). Soloists, BBC Ch. & SO, Andrew Davis; (i) with Tasmin Little.

Symphonies Nos. 1–9; (i) *Flos campi; Serenade to music.*
(M) *** EMI Dig./Analogue CD-BOXVW 1 (6) [CDCFP VW1]. Soloists, Liverpool Philharmonic Ch., RLPO, Vernon Handley; (i) with Christopher Balmer.

Handley's set consists of the six individual CDs in a handsome blue slipcase, and it will especially suit those needing both economy and modern, digital sound; only the *Sinfonia Antartica* is analogue – and that is still a fine modern recording, offering also the orchestral version of the *Serenade to music* as a fill-up. In all his Vaughan Williams recordings Handley shows a natural feeling for expressive rubato and is totally sympathetic. Many of his performances are first or near-first choices and No. 5 is outstanding in every way. This disc also includes a very successful account of *Flos campi*.

Leonard Slatkin, following in the footsteps of André Previn in the earlier VW cycle for RCA, shows consistent sympathy for the idiom. Like the composer himself in his surviving recordings, Slatkin prefers speeds faster than usual, and that makes the central symphonies of the cycle less warmly expressive and less atmospheric than some rivals, but the earliest and, notably, the last symphonies find Slatkin at his finest. His achievement in this cycle is above all to demonstrate that the last three symphonies make a worthy conclusion, unconventionally but tellingly symphonic. Fine playing and generally full, atmospheric recording. The six CDs are offered for the price of four.

The coupling of the *Pastoral Symphony* and *Sinfonia Antartica* was the last to be recorded (in 1996) in Andrew Davis's Vaughan Williams cycle. The *Pastoral Symphony* is beautifully played, with the lyrical, idiomatic feeling naturally sustained. The *Antartica*, too, is consistently evocative rather than electrically tense, although the superb recording certainly creates a massively dramatic effect for the organ entry in the slow movement. The splendid Teldec sound is consistent throughout the series, but the *Sea Symphony*, finely sung as it is, fails quite to add up to the sum of its parts. It is a degree too literal and one is less involved than with the finest rival versions. The *London Symphony* has some impressive moments – in particular the Scherzo – as has the *Eighth*, but again this is without the grip and concentration of its most notable competitors, and the lack of dramatic tension in the violent No. 4 prevents the performance from catching fire, while the *Fifth*, warmly played as it is, is a shade too mellow. The *Sixth*, however, provides just the degree of tautness and urgency that the music needs, yet with emotions kept under firm control. Teldec's wide-ranging recording, setting the orchestra at a slight distance, somewhat blunts the impact in the first three movements, then works beautifully in the chill of the hushed pianissimo meditation of the finale, as it does in the two shorter works which act as fill-ups. They are more warmly expresssive, with Tasmin Little an immaculate soloist in *The Lark ascending*. The *Ninth Symphony*, coupled with a very successful account of *Job*, also has a similarly expansive recording (and again the organ entry is a spectacular moment); but the ultimate sharpness of concentration is missing, and it is the serene closing music of the ballet that lingers in the memory.

Symphonies Nos. 1–8; Partita for double string orchestra.
(BB) (***) Belart mono 461 422-2 (5) [(M) id. import]. Baillie, Cameron, Ritchie, Gielgud, LPO Ch., LPO, Boult.

In some ways Boult's mono set of the Vaughan Williams *Symphonies* (No. 8 is in stereo) is unsurpassed, and the recording still sounds amazingly realistic, especially in the *Sea Symphony*, a demonstration LP in its day. The composer was present at the recording sessions and the orchestral playing was notable for its inspirational intensity. The five discs are handsomely packaged in a strong cardboard box with an engaging portrait of the young composer on the front. A set which is as indispensable as it is inexpensive. The discs are all available separately as follows: the *Sea Symphony* (450 144-2); the *London Symphony* (461 008-2); the *Pastoral Symphony* and No. 5 (461 118-2); Nos. 4 and 6 (461 117-2); and Nos. 7 and 8 (see below) on 461 116-2. Boult's first recording of No. 9 is on Everest (EVC 9001).

A Sea Symphony (No. 1).
(B) **(*) EMI Dig. CD-EMX 2142 [(M) id.]. Rodgers, Shimell, Liverpool PO Ch., RLPO, Handley.
(BB) (***) Belart mono 450 144-2 [(M) id. import]. Baillie, Cameron, LPO Ch. & O, Boult.
(M) *** RCA GD 90500 [60580-2-RG]. Harper, Shirley-Quirk, London Symphony Ch., LSO, Previn.
(M) *** EMI CDM7 64016-2 [id.]. Armstrong, Carol Case, LPO Ch., LPO, Boult.

Vernon Handley conducts a warmly idiomatic performance, which sustains relatively slow speeds masterfully. The reading is crowned by Handley's rapt account of the slow movement, *On the beach at night alone*, as well as by the long duet in the finale, leading on through the exciting final ensemble, *Sail forth*, to a deeply satisfying culmination in *O my brave Soul!* Joan Rodgers makes an outstandingly beautiful soprano soloist, with William Shimell drier-toned but expressive. The recording, full and warm, presents problems in its extreme dynamic range, while placing the two soloists rather distantly. Yet to have such a performance in modern digital sound on a mid-price issue is self-recommending.

As a performance, Boult's (early 1952) Decca mono recording with outstanding soloists and incisive and sympathetic singing from the LPO Choir has never been surpassed. However diffuse the argument may be, conveyed here is the kind of urgency one normally gets only at a live performance. The realistic presence of the dramatic opening has not lost its power to astonish. Boult was at his most inspired. This newly transferred Belart CD makes the very most of the master tape, and only the lack of body of the massed upper strings betrays the age of the original. The choral sound is full and well focused and the Kingsway Hall acoustic spacious and warm; the closing section, *Away O soul*, is particularly beautiful.

Previn does not always relax, even where, as in the slow movement, he takes a rather measured tempo. The finale similarly is built up over a longer span, with less deliberate expressiveness. The *Epilogue* may not be so deliberately expressive, but it is purer in its tenderness and exact control of dynamics. Previn has clear advantages in his baritone soloist and his choir. The rich ambience remains, with the performers set slightly back.

Boult's stereo version demonstrates his affectionate style, drawing consistently expressive but never sentimental phrasing from his singers and players. John Carol Case's baritone does not sound well on disc with his rather plaintive tone-colour, but his style is right, and Sheila Armstrong sings most beautifully. The set has been remastered with outstanding success.

A London Symphony (No. 2).
(M) **(*) EMI CDM5 65109-2. Hallé O, Barbirolli – IRELAND: *London overture*. ***
(BB) ** ASV Dig. CDQS 6162 [(M) id.]. Philh. O, Arwel Hughes – ELGAR: *Cockaigne*. **

A London Symphony; (i) *Concerto accademico; The Wasps: Overture.*
(M) *** RCA GD 90501 [60581-2-RG]. LSO, Previn; (i) with James Buswell.

A London Symphony; Fantasia on a theme of Thomas Tallis.
(M) *** EMI CDM7 64017-2. LPO, Boult.

A London Symphony; Partita for double string orchestra.
(BB) *** Belart mono/stereo 461 008-2 [(M) id. import]. LPO, Sir Adrian Boult.

A London symphony; The Wasps: Overture.
(BB) *** Naxos Dig. 8.550734. Bournemouth SO, Kees Bakels.

On RCA, though the actual sonorities are subtly and beautifully realized by Previn, the architecture is presented equally convincingly, with the great climaxes of the first and last movements powerful and incisive. Most remarkable of all are the pianissimos which here have great intensity, a quality of frisson as in a live performance. The LSO play superbly and the digitally remastered recording, made in Kingsway Hall, still sounds well with its wide range of dynamic. The fill-ups are welcome, especially James Buswell's fine account of the *Concerto*.

The sound remains spacious on Boult's splendid 1970 version and the orchestral playing is outstandingly fine. The orchestra produces lovely sounds, the playing deeply committed; and criticism is disarmed. With Boult's noble, gravely intense account of the *Tallis fantasia* offered as a coupling, this remains an attractive alternative to Previn. The new CD transfer is remarkably successful.

The Naxos version of Vaughan Williams's *London Symphony*, coupled with the *Wasps overture*, is powerful and dedicated. Kees Bakels draws ravishing sounds from the Bournemouth Symphony Orchestra, notably the strings, with the slow movement both warm-hearted and refined, and with pianissimos that have you catching the breath. The problem is the extraordinary range of dynamic in the recording. If you adjust the volume-level for the pianissimo at the start, you are quickly blasted out of your seat by the first fortissimo. A thrilling experience none the less, and throughout this is a performance to stimulate the ear, not least the Scherzo, which is full of atmosphere with VW's clever scoring very nicely realized.

In his 1968 EMI recording of the *London Symphony*, Barbirolli did not quite achieve the intensity of his earlier, Pye version (currently not available), choosing a more relaxed and spacious approach. In many places this brings a feeling of added authority, as at the end of the first movement where the threads are drawn together with striking breadth. The slow movement gains from the fuller recording but has less passion, while the Scherzo, taken relatively slowly, is more controversial. The powerful finale and finely graduated pages of the Epilogue make considerable amends, and this remains an impressive account.

Boult's 1952 recording of the *London Symphony* has great atmosphere and intensity. His later, EMI performance is warmer, but the voltage of this first LP version is very compelling, bringing the feeling of a live performance. The mono sound is spacious and basically full, but the violins sound very thin above the stave, and the remastering has not improved matters, especially in the glorious slow movement. But such is the magnetism of the music-making that the ear readily adjusts. The *Partita* was recorded in the earliest days of stereo in 1956. It is not one of the composer's most remarkable works (it was originally a double string trio) and it does not inspire Boult as does the symphony; but it is well played and the string sound here is more agreeable, if not outstanding.

Owain Arwel Hughes's version comes as the main component in a musical celebration of London, coupled with Elgar's *Cockaigne*. The orchestral sound is admirably refined but, with consistently slow speeds and rhythms often rather heavy, it cannot compare with the finest available. Recommendable to those who fancy the package.

(i) *A London Symphony (No. 2); Fantasia on Greensleeves; The Wasps overture;* (ii) *Serenade to music*.
(M) (***) Dutton Laboratories mono CDAX 8004 [id. full price]. (i) Queen's Hall O; (ii) Isobel Baillie, Stiles Allen, Elsie Suddaby, Eva Turner, Margaret Balfour, Astra Desmond, Muriel Brunskill, Mary Jarred, Heddle Nash, Walter Widdop, Parry Jones, Frank Titterton, Roy Henderson, Robert Easton, Harold Williams, Norman Allin, BBC SO; Sir Henry Wood.

The historic Decca recording of Vaughan Williams's *London Symphony*, with the specially assembled group of musicians designated as the 'Queen's Hall Orchestra', conducted by Sir Henry Wood, brings a most striking discrepancy of pace with modern performances. The first movement alone takes over three minutes less than in most latter-day recordings. The not-so-slow introduction may lack mystery but there has never been a more passionate account of the work than this on record, and even with limited dynamic range – no true pianissimo is caught – the hushed intensity of the slow movement is tellingly conveyed in a way that only Barbirolli has since matched in his early stereo recording for Pye. The *Symphony* comes coupled with shorter Vaughan Williams works, *The Wasps overture*, *Greensleeves* and, best of all, the original (1938) Columbia recording of the *Serenade to music*, with the 16 soloists specified in the score, a stellar group of quite remarkable distinction. The gently soaring phrase 'of sweet harmony' has never sounded so sweetly angelic as when sung here by Isobel Baillie. The Dutton Laboratory transfers are outstandingly true to the originals.

A London Symphony (No. 2); Symphony No. 8 in G min.
(M) *** EMI Dig. CD-EMX 2209; *TC-EMX 2209*. RLPO, Handley.

Vernon Handley gives a beautifully paced and well-sprung reading of the *London Symphony*, not as crisp in ensemble as some and with the sound diffused rather than sharply focused. The result is warmly sympathetic and can be strongly recommended, if the generous coupling of the *Eighth Symphony*, an underestimated work, is preferred.

(i) *A Pastoral Symphony (No. 3); Symphony No. 4 in F min.*
(M) *** RCA GD 90503 [60583-2-RG]. (i) Heather Harper; LSO, Previn.
(B) *** EMI Dig. CD-EMX 2192 [(M) id. import]. (i) Barlow; RLPO, Vernon Handley.

Previn draws an outstandingly beautiful and refined performance from the LSO, the bare textures sounding austere but never thin, the few climaxes emerging at full force with purity undiminished. In the *F minor Symphony* only the somewhat ponderous tempo Previn adopts for the first movement lets it down. But on the whole this is a powerful reading, and it is vividly recorded.

Although Vernon Handley's speeds are relatively fast – as those of his mentor, Boult, tended to be – he has the benefit of refined modern digital recording to help bring out the element of mystery in the *Pastoral Symphony*. The extra bite and warmth of expressiveness in Previn's view brings even greater dividends in the *Fourth Symphony*, when he sustains generally slower speeds. Handley's approach is lighter and less violent. But in a symphony that is less brutal than was originally thought, there is a case for this sympathetic alternative approach.

(i) *A Pastoral Symphony (No. 3);* (ii) *Symphony No. 5 in D.*
(M) **(*) EMI CDM7 64018-2 [id.]. (i) Margaret Price, New Philh. O; (ii) LPO, Sir Adrian Boult.
(BB) (***) Belart mono 461 118-2 [(M) id. import]. (i) Margaret Ritchie; LPO, Boult.

On EMI, in the *Pastoral Symphony* Boult is not entirely successful in controlling the tension of the short but elusive first movement, although it is beautifully played. The opening of the *Lento moderato*, however, is very fine, and its close is sustained with a perfect blend of restraint and intensity. Boult gives a loving and gentle performance of No. 5, easier and more flowing than most rivals', and some may prefer it for that reason, but the emotional involvement is a degree less intense, particularly in the slow movement. Both recordings have been very successfully remastered.

It is good to have the earlier, Kingsway Hall recordings back in the catalogue. They were made in 1952/3 with the composer present; although some allowances have to be made for the lack of amplitude in the upper string climaxes, the present transfer is impressively full and the recording is basically full and luminous. The translucent textures Boult creates in the *Pastoral Symphony* (the opening is hauntingly ethereal) and his essential delicacy of approach are balanced by his intensity in the *Fifth*, where the climax of the first movement has wonderful breadth and passion. The LPO play with great sympathy and warmth in music that was still new, the *Fifth* only a decade old, at the time this record was made.

Symphonies Nos. (i) *3 (Pastoral). 6 in E min.*
(BB) **(*) Naxos Dig. 8.550733 [id.]. Bournemouth SO, Kees Bakels.

Kees Bakels' serenely expressive account of the *Pastoral* has moments of drama to heighten its quiet intensity of atmosphere. There is much lovely orchestral playing, with the soloists in the Bournemouth Symphony Orchestra very sympathetic to the music's subtle, lyrical resonance. The account of the *Sixth* does not catch the degree of underlying menace in the *Lento* second movement that seemed so prophetic at the symphony's broadcast première (under Boult) but the performance overall has plenty of life and vigour, and Bakels sustains the epilogue with an ethereal, glowing pianissimo. First-rate Naxos recording in both works.

(i–ii) *Symphony No. 4 in F min.;* (ii–iv) *Oboe concerto;* (iii; v) *Fantasia on a theme of Tallis; The Wasps: overture*.
(M) **(*) EMI CDM5 66539-2. (i) RPO; (ii) Berglund; (iii) Bournemouth SO; (iv) with John Williams; (v) Silvestri.

Berglund directs a rugged, purposeful account of the *Fourth Symphony*, one which refuses to relax even in the more lyrical passages. Berglund follows the composer himself in preferring an unusually fast speed in the first movement, while the second movement is superbly sustained at a very slow tempo. The playing of the RPO may not match that of the Previn and Boult versions in polish, but Berglund's extra bite is fair compensation, not to mention his more modern (1979) recording. Silvestri's account of the *Tallis fantasia* is quite different in character and just as individual. His approach is more brilliant, less expansive, with remarkable tension in the opening and closing pages and a touch of restraint in handling the second orchestra. But the central climax of the work is tremendously passionate, taut, highly charged. The string playing is excellent, the recording very good with a touch of graininess in the fortissimo textures. Silvestri's account of *The Wasps overture* emphasizes the brio, with the expansiveness of the great lyrical melody not allowed to interfere with the forward momentum. The vivacity of the playing is certainly well projected by the vivid recording. The *Oboe concerto*, beautifully played by the Bournemouth orchestra's principal in the mide-1970s, makes a delightful pastoral interlude between the two major works.

Symphony No. 4 in F min.; Fantasia on Greensleeves; Fantasia on a theme of Thomas Tallis; (i) *Serenade to music.*
(M) *** Sony SMK 47638 [id.]. NYPO, Bernstein; (i) with Addison, Amara, Farrell, Chookasian, Tourel, Verrett-Carter, Bressler, Tucker, Vickers, London, Flagello, Bell.

This is one of the most rewarding of the reissues in the Bernstein Edition. The account of the *Fourth Symphony* is strangely impressive. Bernstein's first movement is slower than usual but powerful and very well controlled; he captures the flavour and intensity of the score as well as the brooding intensity of the slow movement. The New York orchestra play very well indeed, particularly in the extremely characterful Scherzo. This is a thoroughly competitive reading, freshly thought out and with a compelling integrity to commend it. The 1965 Avery Fisher recording, though not first class, is very well transferred. The *Tallis fantasia*, spacious and essentially serene, is just short of being romantic but retains its elegiac atmosphere. Here the venue is the more resonant Manhattan Center, and the 1976 sound is full and rich-textured. The *Greensleeves fantasia*, also taken expansively, uses a solo violin in its central section. The performance of the *Serenade* features a star-studded cast and, though they are rather forwardly balanced, the ambience has agreeable warmth and the performance catches the work's radiance, with Adele Addison singing Portia's closing solo quite beautifully.

Symphonies Nos. (i) *4 in F min.;* (ii) *5 in D.*
(M) (***) Dutton Lab. mono CDAX 8011 [id. full price]. (i) BBC SO, composer; (ii) Hallé O, Barbirolli.

In 1937 Vaughan Williams recorded his violent *Fourth Symphony* with the BBC Symphony Orchestra, then at its pre-war peak, and he proved a bitingly urgent inspirer. This historic recording has been transferred to CD by Michael Dutton in astonishingly full-bodied sound, bringing out the high voltage of the playing, never quite matched since on record. Aiming to shock, RVW said he wasn't sure he liked the piece, but it was what he meant. After that, the *Fifth Symphony*, inspired by Bunyan, held no shocks; but, more than anyone, Sir John Barbirolli in this première recording of 1944, made in the year following its first performance, brings out a rare passion behind the seamless pastoral idiom. The great climaxes in the first and third movements are more red-blooded than in any recordings since. Though the string-playing of the wartime Hallé may not be as immaculate as one would expect today, this inspired performance, vividly transferred, has one consistently magnetized.

Symphonies Nos. 4 in F min.; 6 in E min.
(M) **(*) EMI CDM7 64019-2. New Philh. O, Sir Adrian Boult.
(BB) (**(*)) Belart mono 461 117-2 [(M) id. import]. LPO, Boult (with speech by the composer).

Symphony Nos. (i) *4 in F min.;* (ii) *6 in E min.;* (i) *Fantasia on a theme by Thomas Tallis.*
(B) (***) Sony mono SBK 62754; *SBT 62754* [id.]. NYPO, (i) Mitropoulos; (ii) Stokowski.

The recordings of Vaughan Williams's two apocalyptic symphonies made by the New York Philharmonic – No. 4 conducted in 1956 by Dmitri Mitropoulos (in a reading approved by the composer himself) and No. 6 in 1949 by Stokowski (directing with unsentimental thrust) – make a fascinating coupling. As transferred to CD they sound far better than they ever did on LP. Both demonstrate what idiomatic power and brilliance American players could bring to the composer's two most abrasive symphonies. Stokowski's reading is the more controversial, disconcertingly fast in the slow movement and unpointed in the slow, visionary finale. Mitropoulos in a generous fill-up shows equal understanding of the rarefied *Tallis Fantasia*. Not to be missed – truly an 'Essential Classic'.

In the *Fourth Symphony* Sir Adrian procures orchestral playing of the highest quality from the New Philharmonia, and the slow movement is particularly successful. The recording, too, is first class, and this increases the sense of attack in the first movement of the powerful *Sixth Symphony*. Here, the strange finale is played beautifully, and the atmosphere is not without a sense of mystery, but a greater degree of underlying tension is needed

On Belart, Boult, as ever, shows himself to be a master interpreter of Vaughan Williams, but in the tearingly dramatic *Fourth Symphony* the age of the recording and its relative lack of amplitude blunt the fullness of the work's impact, powerful as it still is. The performance of the *Sixth* is another matter: it drew from Boult and the LPO some of the very finest and most committed playing in the whole cycle; certainly Boult never matched it in his later recording for EMI. After the ebullience of the first movement comes the frightening warning of the slow movement, with its slow triplet rhythm built into a climax of the utmost menace. Following the brash and popular Scherzo the work closes in a mood of almost complete desolation which is wonderfully sustained here and brings a spoken eulogy of praise from the composer, who was present at the sessions. Here the Decca mono recording is very impressive indeed.

Symphony No. 5 in D; The England of Elizabeth: 3 Portraits (arr. Mathieson).
(M) *** RCA GD 90506 [60586-2-RG]. LSO, Previn.

Symphony No. 5 in D; (i) *Flos campi* (suite).
✿ (B) *** EMI Dig. CD-EMX 9512; TC-EMX 2112 [(M) id. import]. RLPO, Handley; (i) with Christopher Balmer & Liverpool Philharmonic Ch.

Vernon Handley's disc is outstanding in every way, a spacious yet concentrated reading, superbly played and recorded, which masterfully holds the broad structure of this symphony together, building to massive climaxes. The warmth and poetry of the work are also beautifully caught. The rare and evocative *Flos campi*, inspired by the Song of Solomon, makes a generous and attractive coupling, equally well played, though the viola solo is rather closely balanced. The sound is outstandingly full, giving fine clarity of texture.

Previn refuses to be lured into pastoral byways. His tempi may be consistently on the slow side, but the purity of tone he draws from the LSO, the precise shading of dynamic and phrasing, and the sustaining of tension through the longest, most hushed passages produce an outstanding performance, very well transferred to CD. Previn's later, full-price Telarc version with the RPO does not match this in raptness and emotional thrust. The *England of Elizabeth suite* is a film score of no great musical interest but is undoubtedly pleasant to listen to.

Symphonies Nos. 6 in E min.; 9 in E min.
(B) *** EMI Dig. CD-EMX 2230; *TC-EMX 2230* [(M) id. import]. RLPO, Vernon Handley.
(M) *** [RCA 60588-2-RG]. LSO, Previn.

Handley, with rich, full recording, gives warm-hearted readings of Nos. 6 and 9, two works that in their layout – both ending on measured, visionary slow movements – can be seen as related, quite apart from sharing the same key. Next to Previn in the same coupling, Handley lacks some of the darker, sharper qualities implied. Though his speeds are consistently faster, he is more comfortable, and the recording adds to that impression. Handley's approach is a valid one, when the slow pianissimo finale, here presented as mysterious rather than desolate, was inspired not by a world laid waste by nuclear war, but by Prospero's 'cloud-capp'd towers' in Shakespeare's *The Tempest*.

In the first three movements Previn's performance is superbly dramatic, clear-headed and direct, with natural understanding. His account of the mystical final movement with its endless pianissimo is not, however, on the same level, for the playing is not quite hushed enough, and the tempo is a little too fast. The *Ninth* stimulates Previn to show a freshness and sense of poetry which prove particularly thought-provoking and rewarding. The RCA recording is highly successful.

(i) *Sinfonia Antartica (No. 7); Serenade to music.*
(B) *** EMI Dig. CD-EMX 2173 [(M) id. import]. (i) Alison Hargan; RLPO and Ch., Vernon Handley.

(i) *Sinfonia Antartica (No. 7); The Wasps* (incidental music): *Overture and suite.*
(M) **(*) EMI CDM7 64020-2 [id.]. (i) Sheila Armstrong; LPO, Sir Adrian Boult.

As in his other Vaughan Williams recordings, Handley shows a natural feeling for expressive rubato and draws refined playing from the Liverpool orchestra. At the end of the epilogue Alison Hargan makes a notable first appearance on disc, a soprano with an exceptionally sweet and pure voice. In well-balanced digital sound it makes an outstanding bargain, particularly when it offers an excellent fill-up, the *Serenade to music*, though in this lovely score a chorus never sounds as characterful as a group of well-chosen soloists.

Sir Adrian gives a stirring account and is well served by the EMI engineers. The inclusion of Vaughan Williams's Aristophanic suite, *The Wasps*, with its endearing participation of the kitchen utensils plus its indelibly tuneful *Overture*, is a bonus, although in the *Overture* the upper strings sound a bit thin.

Sinfonia Antartica (No. 7).
(BB) *** RCA Navigator 74321 29248-2 [(M) id. import]. Heather Harper, Sir Ralph Richardson, London Symphony Ch., LSO, André Previn – WALTON: *Cello concerto.* ***

(i) *Sinfonia Antartica (No. 7); Symphony No. 8 in D min.*
(BB) *** Belart mono/stereo 461 116-2 [(M) id. import]. LPO, Boult; (i) with Margaret Ritchie, LPO Ch.; superscriptions spoken by Sir John Gielgud.
(M) *** RCA GD 90510 [60590-2-RG]. (i) Harper, Richardson, London Symphony Ch.; LSO, Previn.

Boult's 1953 performance of the *Sinfonia Antartica* has never been surpassed; the superbly atmospheric mono recording, with its translucent icy vistas and Margaret Ritchie's floating, wordless soprano voice sounding quite ethereal, remains a model of balancing. Boult and the LPO achieve the highest level of concentration throughout, and the evocation of the frozen landscapes and the shifting ice-floes is as compelling as his control of the structure of a work that is never easy to hold together, while the organ entry at the climax of *Landscape* is a truly engulfing moment. Sir John Gielgud's superscriptions (from the score) act as moving preludes. The *Eighth Symphony*, summoned as it were by bells, is early stereo (1956). Only the first and last movements make use of the full orchestra (which includes a remarkable array of tonal percussion) while the middle two movements are scored for wind instruments alone (Scherzo) and strings alone (*Cavatina*). The LPO plays beautifully, and the Decca engineers seem to have relished the challenge of balancing these unusual sounds of glissando tubular bells, tuned gongs, vibraphone, xylophone, and all the other exotic ingredients. The string-tone sounds far fuller and more expansive than it did when this recording last appeared, on a Decca Ace of Diamonds CD; and altogether this caps this remarkably successful series of Belart super-bargain reissues.

In the *Sinfonia Antartica* Previn's interpretation concentrates on atmosphere rather than drama in a performance that is sensitive and literal. Because of the recessed effect of the sound, the portrayal of the ice-fall (represented by the sudden entry of the organ) has a good deal less impact than on Vernon Handley's version. Before each movement Sir Ralph Richardson speaks the superscription written by the composer on his score. Previn's account of the *Eighth* brings no reservations, with finely pointed playing, the most precise control of dynamic shading, and a delightfully Stravinskian account of the bouncing Scherzo for woodwind alone. Excellent recording, which has been opened up by the digital remastering and made to sound more expansive. As can be seen, Previn's *Sinfonia Antartica* is also available coupled with Walton's *Cello concerto* – a real bargain on RCA's super-budget Navigator label.

Symphonies Nos. 8 in D min.; 9 in E min.
(M) *** EMI CDM7 64021-2. LPO, Sir Adrian Boult.

Boult's account of the *Eighth* may not be as sharply pointed as some other versions, but some will prefer the extra warmth of the Boult interpretation with its rather more lyrical approach. The *Ninth* contains much noble and arresting invention, and Boult's performance is fully worthy of it. He draws most committed playing from the LPO, and the recording is splendidly firm in tone. The digital remastering is well up to the high standard EMI have set with these reissues of Boult's recordings.

CHAMBER MUSIC

Fantasia on Greensleeves; The Lark ascending; 2 Pieces; 6 Studies in English folksong (all for violin and piano); *Violin sonata.*
(M) *** Carlton Classics Dig. 30366 00132 [id.]. Lydia Mordkovitch, Julian Milford.

Vaughan Williams's violin-writing can seem wayward and elusive; but in Lydia Mordkovitch, always inspired in English music, it finds an ideal interpreter. It is especially good to have the rarely heard *Violin sonata* in which Mordkovitch establishes a fine partnership with Julian Milford, and he also proves an outstanding accompanist when she provides a fascinating new slant, given with deep feeling, on *The Lark ascending* in its version with piano, rather than orchestra. An offbeat but attractive issue, and excellent, well-balanced recording.

(i) *Phantasy quintet* (for 2 violins, 2 violas & cello); *String quartet No. 2 in A min. (For Jean on her birthday);* (ii; iii) *6 Studies in English folk-song for cello and piano;* (iii; iv) *Violin sonata in A.*
(M) *** EMI CDM5 65100-2. (i) Music Group of London; (ii) Eileen Croxford; (iii) David Parkhouse; (iv) Hugh Bean.

This collection of relatively little-known chamber works, very well performed and recorded at Abbey Road in 1972/3, can be recommended strongly – and not only to devotees of Vaughan Williams. The *Phantasy quintet* dates from the composer's full maturity in 1912. It is conceived in a compressed one-movement form but falls into four distinct sections: these to be played (attacca) without a break, as advocated by W. W. Cobbett. The ethereal opening is Vaughan Williams at his most ecstatically pastoral in feeling, and the *Alla Sarabanda* third section is also very beautiful. The *Six studies in English folk-song* are highly characteristic, while the *Violin sonata* (1954) is a relatively gawky work but one which, like much later Vaughan Williams, has a tangily distinctive flavour, especially in a performance as fine as this. The *Second quartet*, written between the *Fifth* and *Sixth Symphonies*, was offered as a birthday present to a viola player friend of the composer, Jean Stewart. It contains some strikingly original ideas, notably in the purposefully sombre but bleakly haunting *Largo* with its harmonium-like textures and, in the plangent Scherzo, with its *tremolandos* and *sul ponticello* devices. The performances by the Music Group of London bring out the deeper qualities of both this and the richly scored *Quintet*.

Violin sonata in A min.

(M) **(*) EMI CDM5 66122-2. Yehudi Menuhin, Hephzibah Menuhin – ELGAR: *Sonata* **(*); WALTON: *Sonata*. (**)

The late Vaughan Williams *Sonata* is an unexpected piece for the Menuhins to record and, though in the first movement (as in the Elgar) their tempo is controversially slow, giving the music unexpected weight, the whole performance makes a fine illumination of an elusive piece, not least from the pianist, who copes splendidly with the often awkward piano-writing. The recording is first rate.

VOCAL MUSIC

(i) *10 Blake songs* (for voice and oboe); (ii) *Songs of travel*. Songs: *Linden Lea; Orpheus with his lute; The water mill; Silent noon*.

(M) *** Decca 430 368-2. Robert Tear; (i) Neil Black; (ii) Philip Ledger – BUTTERWORTH: *Shropshire lad*. ***

Songs of travel; Linden Lea.

(BB) *** Belart 461 493-2. Robert Tear, Philip Ledger – PARRY: *English lyrics*. **(*)

Robert Tear, recorded in 1972, cannot match Ian Partridge in his wonderfully sensitive account (currently withdrawn) of the *Blake songs*, but his rougher-grained voice brings out a different kind of expressiveness, helped by Neil Black's fine oboe playing. The *Songs of travel*, here presented complete with the five extra songs published later, are also most welcome, as are the other four songs, notably *Silent noon*, added for this reissue. Ledger is a most perceptive accompanist.

Robert Tear's set of the nine *Songs of travel* plus the favourite among the others, *Linden Lea*, all of which are vividly sung and recorded, are also available on a super-bargain Belart CD which couples them with 20 rarely heard songs of Parry.

arr. of traditional carols: *As it fell one May morning (The holy well); Behold the great Creator (This endris night); Come all you faithful Christians (Hereford carol); From far away we come to you (Snow in the street); How far is it to Bethlehem? (Children's song of the nativity); It was on Christmas Day (All in the morning); Joseph dearest, Joseph mine (Song of the crib); Nowell, this is the salutation (Salutation carol); O little town of Bethlehem; Now blessed be thou, Christ Jesu (Coverdale's carol); Now is Christmas y-come (Golden carol); On Christmas night (Sussex carol); Rise up, rise up, you merry men all! (The miraculous harvest); Shepherds left their flocks a-straying (Quem pastores); Sweet baby, sleep! (Wither's rocking hymn); Sweet dreams, form a shade o'er my lovely infant's head (Blake's cradle song); This is the truth sent from above; Wassail (Gloucestershire Wassail).*

(B) **(*) Carlton Dig. 30367 01212 [(M) id.]. Cardiff Festival Ch., Owain Arwel Hughes; Robert Court.

Many of Vaughan Williams's arrangements of traditional carols are designed for congregational use, admirably straightforward strophic settings with organ. There are obvious highlights. *Wither's rocking hymn* and *Coverdale's carol* are rightly famous, and the simplicity of *Blake's cradle song* is beautifully caught here, with trebles alternating with the fuller choir. VW remembered that early carols were often dance-songs and *Now is Christmas y-come*, and *Nowell, this is the salutation*, similarly treated, are rhythmically vigorous. *Joseph dearest, Joseph mine* also swings along joyfully, quite different from the more restrained German version we usually hear. The much more elaborate setting of the *Gloucestershire Wassail* is the obvious highlight, and the concert ends with a boldly extrovert *Susssex carol*, with a strong contribution from the organist, Robert Court. The singing is of high calibre and the recording warmly atmospheric, but the predominance of hymn-like settings makes this progamme less appealing than some carol collections with a much wider variety of style.

(i) *3 Choral hymns (Easter hymn; Christmas hymn; Whitsunday hymn);* (ii) *Communion service in G min.: Sanctus*. (i) *Come down, O love divine*. (ii) *Festival Te deum*. (i) *For all the Saints; O taste and see; Prayer to the Father; Te deum in G; Valiant for truth; We've been awhile a-wandering; Wither's Rocking hymn*.

(M) ** Chandos CHAN 6550 [id.]. (i) Worcester Cathedral Ch., Christopher Robinson; H. Bramma; (ii) Westminster Abbey Ch., Douglas Guest.

A useful if not distinctive collection of Vaughan Williams's shorter choral works. Besides the short *Te Deum* and the *Festival Te Deum*, among the more striking settings is *Valiant for truth*, a much subtler piece than its Salvation Army-like title would suggest. The three *Choral hymns* are spaciously conceived but would have benefited from a recording with more bite. As it is, the sound is atmospheric but not very clear in detail. The performances generally are of a good standard. The documentation provides all the words but no comments about the settings.

(i) *Epithalamion;* (ii) *Merciless Beauty.*
(M) *** EMI Dig./Analogue CDM7 64730-2. (i) Roberts, Shelley, Bach Ch., LPO, Willcocks; (ii) Langridge, Endellion Qt – *Riders to the sea.* ***

Vaughan Williams's setting of *Epithalamion* began life as a masque in the late 1930s and, only a year before he died, he expanded it into the coolly lyrical cantata recorded here. Scored for baritone and small orchestra with piano (Howard Shelley quite superb) and solo parts for flute and viola, it is an eloquent and thoroughly characteristic piece. Stephen Roberts gives a beautiful account of it, and Philip Langridge is hardly less impressive in *Merciless beauty*, three much earlier settings for voice and string trio. *Riders to the sea* is also indispensable – see below. This reissue makes a most valuable addition to the Vaughan Williams discography. The first two works were recorded digitally; *Riders to the sea* is analogue (1970) but sounds equally vivid and well focused. Splendid performances throughout.

(i) *Fantasia on Christmas carols.* arr. of carols: *And all in the morning; Wassail song* (also includes: TRAD., arr. Warlock: *Adam lay y-bounden; Bethlehem down*).
(M) ** EMI CDM7 64131-2. Guildford Cathedral Ch., Pro Arte O, Barry Rose; (i) with Barrow – HELY-HUTCHINSON: *Carol Symphony;* QUILTER: *Children's overture.* **

Vaughan Williams's joyful *Fantasia on Christmas carols* is comparatively short. It was written for performance in 1912 in Hereford Cathedral, so the acoustic at Guildford Cathedral is well chosen. The performance here is suitably exuberant, and John Barrow is a good soloist, but not everyone will respond to his timbre and style, and the King's performance with Hervey Alan is marginally preferable (however, that is currently unavailable). But the Christmas carol arrangements are delightful, beautifully sung and recorded, and this reissue is worthwhile for its interesting couplings.

Alfred Deller Edition: Arrangements of folksongs (with Deller Consort, Desmond Dupré, lute): *An acre of land; Bushes and briars; Ca' the yowes; The cuckoo and the nightingale; The dark-eyed sailor; Down by the riverside; A farmer's son so sweet; Greensleeves; John Dory; Just as the tide was flowing; The jolly ploughboy; Loch Lomond; The lover's ghost; My boy Billy; The painful plough; The spring time of the year; The turtle dove; Ward the pirate; Wassail song.*
(M) ** Van. 08.5073.71 [id.].

These highly artistic folksong settings can be effectively performed either by choir or by soloists. Although basically Deller allocates one voice to each part, there are some doublings where – for example – the two voices do not blend well. The spirit in which these settings are performed is, however, admirable. Deller himself sings *Down by the riverside* as a solo, with lute accompaniment, and this is effectively followed by the gentle choral version of *Bushes and briars*. Similarly, Deller's *My boy Billy* is followed by the atmospheric *The spring time of the year*, and the solo *The cuckoo and the nightingale* by the choral *Loch Lomond*, one of the most enjoyable arrangements here. The recording is a little dry, but the stereo adds to the sense of atmosphere.

Folksong arrangements: *An acre of land; Bushes and briars* (2 versions); *Ca' the yowes; Early in the spring; 5 English folksongs (The dark-eyed sailor; The spring time of the year; Just as the tide was flowing; The lover's ghost; Wassail song* (2 versions)); *Greensleeves; John Dory; Loch Lomond; The seeds of love; The turtle dove; The unquiet grave; Ward the pirate.*
(M) *** EMI CMS5 65123-2 (2). London Madrigal Singers, Bishop – HOLST: *Choral songs;* ELGAR: *Part-songs* etc. ***

As recording manager, Christopher Bishop has supervised many fine records of Vaughan Williams's music (as well as much else); here, with a choir of hand-picked singers, he shows that he is a first-rate interpreter of the composer in his own right. This is a delightful collection of part-songs, far more varied than one might expect. There is nothing at all pretentious about the settings and each one shows subtly the distinction of RVW's mind, never falling into mere routine. The singing of the London Madrigal Singers is admirably lithe and sensitive, and this is altogether a lovely recital, beautifully engineered. Additional performances of *Bushes and briars* and the *Wassail song* in their versions for men's voices (the latter arranged by Herbert Pierce) come as part of the second half of this collection. This includes music by Elgar, Howells, Bax, Delius, Britten and Warlock, sung no less impressively by the Baccholian Singers of London. An invaluable reissue.

Mass in G min.
(M) *** EMI CDM5 65595-2. King's College, Cambridge, Ch., Willcocks – BAX; FINZI: *Choral music.* ***

Here with the finest band of trebles in the country Sir David Willcocks captures the beauty of the Vaughan Williams *Mass* more completely than any rival, helped by the fine, atmospheric, analogue recording. This is a work which, on the one hand, can easily seem too tense and lose its magic or, on the other, fall apart in a meandering style; Willcocks admirably finds the middle course. Although recorded two decades before the Bax and Finzi couplings, the remastered analogue sound is by no means second best.

5 Mystical songs; O clap your hands.

(M) *** EMI CDM5 65588-2. John Shirley-Quirk, King's College, Cambridge, Ch., ECO, Willcocks – FINZI: *Dies natalis;* HOLST: *Choral fantasia; Psalm 86.* ***

In the *Five Mystical songs* to words by George Herbert, John Shirley-Quirk sings admirably, and the motet, *O clap your hands*, makes a fine bonus for a recommendable triptych of English vocal works.

(i) *On Wenlock Edge;* (ii) *Songs of travel* (song-cycles).

(M) *** EMI Dig. CDM7 64731-2. (i) Robert Tear; (ii) Thomas Allen, CBSO, Rattle – BUTTERWORTH; ELGAR: *Songs.* ***

Vaughan Williams's own orchestration of his famous song-cycle, made in the early 1920s, has been curiously neglected. It lacks something of the apt, ghostly quality of the version for piano and string quartet, but some will prefer the bigger scale. The orchestral version brings home the aptness of treating the nine songs as a cycle, particularly when the soloist is as characterful and understanding a singer as Thomas Allen. The Housman settings in the other cycle are far better-known, and Robert Tear – who earlier recorded this same orchestral version with Vernon Handley and the Birmingham orchestra – again proves a deeply perceptive soloist, with his sense of atmosphere, feeling for detailed word-meaning and flawless breath control. Warm, understanding conducting and playing, and excellent sound.

On Wenlock Edge (song-cycle from A. E. Housman's *A Shropshire Lad*); (i) *10 Blake songs for voice and oboe. 4 Hymns: (Lord, come away!; Who is this fair one?; Come love, come Lord; Evening hymn);* Songs: *Merciless beauty;* (ii) *The new ghost; The water mill.*

(M) *** EMI CDM5 65589-2. Ian Partridge, (i) Janet Craxton, Music Group of London; (ii) Jennifer Partridge.

The EMI mid-priced CD is an outstandingly beautiful record, with Ian Partridge's intense artistry and lovely individual tone-colour used with compelling success in Vaughan Williams songs both early and late. The Housman cycle has an accompaniment for piano and string quartet which can sound ungainly but which here, with playing from the Music Group of London, matches the soloist's sensitivity; the result is atmospheric and moving. The *Ten Blake songs* come from just before the composer's death: bald, direct settings that with the artistry of Partridge and Craxton are darkly moving. The tenor's sister accompanies with fine understanding in two favourite songs as a welcome extra. The other (much rarer) items make an attractive bonus, with the *Four Hymns* distinctively accompanied by viola and piano.

(i) *5 Tudor portraits;* (ii) *Benedicite;* (iii) *5 variants of Dives and Lazarus.*

(M) *** EMI CDM7 64722-2. (i) Bainbridge, Carol Case, Bach Ch., New Philh. O; (ii) Harper, Bach Ch., LSO; (iii) Jacques O; Willcocks.

Ursula Vaughan Williams reports in her biography of the composer that the first performance of the *Five Tudor portraits* – in Norwich in 1936 – was remarkable for shocking many of the audience. The composer deliberately chose bawdy words by the early Tudor poet, John Skelton, and set them in his most rumbustious style. This is a good, strong performance, but the soloists are not earthy enough for such music. It is a pity that the humour was not underlined more strongly, but the musical invention is still more than enough to sustain compelling interest, and the digital remastering has brought splendid bite and projection to the chorus without losing too much of the original ambience. The *Benedicite* is another strong work, compressed in its intensity, too brief to be accepted easily into the choral repertory, but a fine addition to the RVW discography. The *Five variants of Dives and Lazarus* is beautifully played and warmly recorded and adds a touch of serenity and balm after the vigour of the vocal works.

OPERA

The Pilgrim's Progress.

(M) *** EMI CMS7 64212-2 (2) [ZDMB 64212]. Noble, Burrowes, Armstrong, Herincx, Carol Case, Shirley-Quirk, Keyte, LPO Ch., LPO, Boult.

(M) **(*) RNCM PP1/2 (2). Richard Whitehouse, Wyn Griffiths & soloists, Ch. & O of Royal N. Coll. of Music, Igor Kennaway.

The Pilgrim's Progress is crammed full of delectable ideas. John Noble gives a dedicated performance in the central role of Pilgrim, and the large supporting cast is consistently strong. Vanity Fair may not sound evil here, but Vaughan Williams's own recoil is vividly expressed, and the jaunty passage of Mr and Mrs By-Ends brings the most delightful light relief. Boult underlines the virility of his performance with a fascinating and revealing half-hour collection of rehearsal excerpts, placed at the end of the second CD. The outstanding recording quality is confirmed by the CD transfer, which shows few signs of the passing of two decades.

Enterprisingly, in 1992 the Royal Northern College of Music in Manchester presented a staging which effectively brought out the operatic qualities of a work too often dismissed as an oratorio. Obviously student voices cannot match those of the front-rank singers of the 1970s who appear on the earlier recording, but the vitality is what matters. Richard Whitehouse as the Pilgrim boldly shoulders the weightiest individual burden, but this is an opera in which good teamwork is more important than individual performances, and under Igor Kennaway the young singers and players perform with a dedication that could hardly be more compelling. The two CDs can be obtained direct from the College and are in the mid-price range.

Riders to the sea (opera) complete.

(M) *** EMI CDM7 64730-2. Burrowes, M. Price, Watts, Luxon, Amb. S., L. O Nova, Meredith Davies – *Epithalamion; Merciless Beauty.* ***

The one-Act opera, *Riders to the sea*, is among Vaughan Williams's supreme masterpieces, a word-by-word setting of J. M. Synge's one-act play which heightens an already darkly intense drama. The EMI recording is beautifully recorded, though there is too much wind machine. The analogue recording, clear yet wonderfully atmospheric, approaches the demonstration bracket in its CD format and, with its equally rare couplings, this can be strongly recommended. All who care about this composer should investigate this work.

Sir John in Love (complete).

(M) *** EMI CMS5 66123 [CDMB 66123] (2). Herincx, Bainbridge, Watts, English, Eathorne, Tear, John Alldis Ch., New Philh. O, Meredith Davies.

'He wrote it for his own enjoyment,' commented Ursula Vaughan Williams when talking of her husband's project to compose a Falstaff opera, fully appreciating the obvious comparisons with Verdi, not to mention Nicolai and Holst. That love comes out from first to last in a rich and delightful score, tricked out with musical plums in almost every scene, not just the famous arrangement of *Greensleeves*, but also in delectable settings of Elizabethan lyrics (no fewer than 18 of them), and folksong themes that are superbly integrated in the score. Though the libretto does not begin to match Boito's Verdi, it has its own felicities, and the minor characters are more fully presented. Except for the final scene (one of the few passages that directly mirrors Verdi) and its conclusion on a Merrie England-style jig, there are few disappointing passages. On record any dramatic weaknesses tend to be minimized, particularly in a vigorous and well-sung performance like this one, with Meredith Davies relishing the colourfulness of the score. Raimund Herincx is a positive and sympathetic Falstaff; and Helen Watts as Mrs Quickly and Elizabeth Bainbridge as Mrs Ford rise ripely to the occasion. Wendy Eathorne as Anne Page and Robert Tear as Fenton make a delightful pair of lovers (helped in Act I by some lovely oboe-playing), and such singers as Gerald English as Dr Caius add to the stylishness. The 1974 Abbey Road recording is vivid and warmly atmospheric and beautifully balanced. It is admirably transferred to CD, and the booklet includes both the libretto and a cued synopsis. Highly recommended.

COLLECTIONS

'The ultimate collection': Fantasia on Greensleeves; Fantasia on a theme by Thomas Tallis; (i) *The Lark ascending.* (ii) *A Sea Symphony: Scherzo: The Waves. Symphony No. 3: Moderato pesante. Symphony No. 5: Romanza (Lento). Symphony No. 6:* lst movement: *Allegro. The Wasps: Overture.*

(M) ** Teldec/Warner Dig. 3984 22125-2 [id.]. BBC SO, Andrew Davis, with (i) Tasmin Little; (ii) BBC Ch.

Any attractions this might have had as a sampler are negated by the totally inadequate documentation, which gives virtually no information about the symphonies from which these individual movements are drawn and does not even mention the name of the violin soloist in *The lark ascending* – Tasmin Little, who plays with such refined delicacy. Having said that, the music itself makes quite an enjoyable ongoing concert. The programme opens with *The Wasps overture* and closes with a very relaxed *Greensleeves fantasia*, both of which are new recordings; the other excerpts are drawn from Andrew Davis's full-priced cycle of the symphonies, among which the *Sixth* is especially impressive. The first movement here has great thrust and excitement, and the great lyrical string-tune is gloriously played. The choral Scherzo from the *Sea Symphony* has plenty of life, but the choice of the *Moderato pesante* from the *Pastoral Symphony* was curious, and the slow movement from the *Fifth Symphony* and the *Tallis fantasia*, although warmly serene, are ultimately somewhat lacking in tension. The recording throughout is of high quality.

Vecchi, Orazio (1550–1605)

L'Amfiparnaso (commedia harmonica); *Il Convito musicale* (musical banquet: excerpts): *O Giardiniero; Lunghi danni; Bando del asino.*
(B) *** HM Dig. HMC 90856.58 (3) [(M) id. import]. Ens. Clément Jannequin, Dominique Visse – BANCHIERO: *Barca di Venetia per Padova* ***; MARENZIO: *Madrigals* **(*); LASSUS: *Madrigal comedies.* ***

Orazio Vecchi is the least familiar of the four Italian composers, each of whom contributes a collection of (usually) dramatized madrigals to Harmonia Mundi's CD Trio of *'Comédies madrigalesques'*. Unlike Lassus, Vecchi, although earning his living as a *maestro di capella* in the church, leaned in his own music towards the secular. *L'Amfiparnaso* is a series of linked scenas, sung rather than acted. The comedy is introduced by a Prologue, and the characters include an old man, a courtesan who has no wish to oblige him, an amorous doctor who serenades his betrothed and a heroine who teases a Spanish captain and then tries to kill herself when she fears her younger lover is dead. Fortunately she is interrupted and the two lovers then meet by chance and pledge undying faithfulness, so that everything can end happily. It is all slight but well crafted and is brought vividly to life by the solo and ensemble singing here. *Il Convito musicale* (of which we are given only excerpts) is an innocent pastoral sequence set in the garden, where first the taste of grapes is extolled, then the pleasures of Venetian wine. A touching lament, *Lunghi danni*, follows; but it is the closing section, with its engaging vocal imitations of instruments and animals croaking all together, which makes the piece memorable. The recording is first class and so is the documentation.

L'Amfiparnaso (madrigal comedy).
(BB) *** Naxos Dig. 8.553312 [id.]. Cappella Musicale di Petronio di Bologna, Vartolo.

Described as a 'madrigal comedy', Vecchi's *L'Amfiparnaso*, first performed in 1594, fascinatingly points forward to the development of opera as a new genre in the following decade. The text in a Prologue and three brief Acts develops a comic plot stocked with *commedia dell'arte* characters, but, instead of solo voices representing different characters, hereeach scene is set as a madrigal for a small group of voices. Each madrigal, three in the first Act, five in both the other two, is preceded by a brief spoken summary, the whole making up a taut entertainment that still sounds fresh and charming after 400 years. Much is owed to the liveliness of the Naxos performance, using a first-rate ensemble from Bologna under Sergio Vartolo. With splendidly crisp ensemble the singers consistently bring out the sharply rhythmic quality of Vecchi's writing, with clear, well-balanced sound. Full texts and an English translation are provided.

Verdi, Giuseppe (1813–1901)

(i) *Ballet music from: Aida (including Triumphal march); Macbeth; Otello.* (ii) Overtures: *Aroldo; La forza del destino; Giovanna d'Arco; Luisa Miller; Nabucco; Oberto, conte di San Bonifacio; I vespri siciliani.*
(B) *** Decca Eclipse Dig. 448 238-2; *448 238-4* [(M) id. import]. (i) Bologna Teatro Comunale O; (ii) Nat. PO; Chailly.

Chailly's version enjoys brilliant Decca recording. Besides the ballet music, which is presented with gusto and style, he offers the four most obviously desirable overtures plus three rarities, including the overture to Verdi's very first opera, *Oberto*, and the most substantial of the early ones, *Aroldo*. Crisp and incisive, Chailly draws vigorous and polished playing from the excellent National Philharmonic.

The Lady and the fool (ballet suite; arr. Mackerras).
(B) *** CfP CD-CFP 4618 [(M) id. import]. LPO, Mackerras – SULLIVAN: *Pineapple Poll.* ***

Mackerras's arrangement of Verdi has not caught the public fancy in quite the way of the coupled *Pineapple Poll*, but the scoring is witty and the music vivacious, and it is very well played and recorded here.

Overtures and Preludes: *Aida* (Prelude); *Alzira; Aroldo* (Overtures); *Attila; Un ballo in maschera* (Preludes); *La battaglia di Legnano; Il Corsaro* (Sinfonias); *Ernani* (Prelude); *La forza del destino* (Overture); *Un giorno di regno; Giovanna d'Arco* (Sinfonias); *Luisa Miller* (Overture); *Macbeth; I Masnadieri* (Preludes); *Nabucco* (Overture); *Oberto, Conte di San Bonifacio* (Sinfonia); *Rigoletto; La Traviata* (Preludes); *I vespri siciliani* (Overture).
(B) *** DG Double 453 058-2 (2) [id.]. BPO, Karajan.

It is good to have Karajan's complete set of Overtures and Preludes back in the catalogue. The 1975 recording was one of the very best made in the Philharmonie: the sound combines vividness with a natural balance and an attractive ambience. As we have commented before, the performances have an electricity, refinement and authority that sweep all before them. The little-known overtures, *Alzira*, *Aroldo* and *La battaglia de Legnano*, are all given with tremendous panache and virtuosity. Every bar of this music is alive and, with all the exuberance, Karajan skirts any suggestion of vulgarity. Try the splendid *Nabucco* or the surprisingly extended (8-minute) *Giovanna d'Arco* to discover the colour and spirit of this music-making, with every bar spontaneously alive, while there is not the faintest suggestion of routine in the more familiar items. As a DG Double this is even more strongly recommendable.

Overtures and Preludes: *Aida: Prelude. Alzira: Sinfonia. Aroldo: Sinfonia. Attila: Prelude. Un ballo in maschera: Prelude. Il Corsaro: Prelude. Luisa Miller: Sinfonia. Oberto, Conte di San Bonifacio: Sinfonia. La Traviata: Preludes to Acts I & III. I vespri siciliani: Sinfonia.*
(BB) **(*) Naxos Dig. 8.553018 [id.]. Hung. State Op. O, Pier Giorgio Morandi.

Overtures and Preludes: *La battaglia di Legnano: Sinfonia. Don Carlo: Prelude to Act III. I due Foscari: Prelude. Ernani: Prelude. La forza del destino: Sinfonia. Un giorno di regno: Sinfonia. Giovanna d'Arco: Sinfonia. Macbeth: Sinfonia. I Masnadieri: Prelude. Nabucco: Overture. Rigoletto: Prelude.*
(BB) **(*) Naxos Dig. 8.553089 [id.]. Hung. State Op. O, Pier Giorgio Morandi.

Morandi has served his time conducting at La Scala and he gives ripely robust accounts of these colourful overtures and sinfonias, with excellent playing from his Hungarian musicians, notably from the strings in the *Traviata* and *Aida Preludes* and from the brass in *Nabucco*. *La forza del destino* ends the second disc strongly. Full-bloodedly resonant sound (with the second collection at times marginally sharper in definition) means that this pair of bargain discs is worth anyone's money, even if the readings are not as dramatically individual as those of Chailly and Karajan.

Overtures: *La forza del destino; Nabucco; I vespri siciliani. La Traviata: Preludes, Acts I & III.*
(M) ** Mercury 434 345-2 [id.]. LSO, Antal Dorati – ROSSINI: *Overtures*. (*)

Dorati is an unexpected conductor in Verdi, and these performances are red-blooded as well as fresh and clear, if not distinctive. The LSO playing is good and the dramatic passages in the earlier overtures have both power and brilliance. The *Traviata Preludes*, however, are somewhat lacking in tension and Italianate warmth. The 1957 recording, made at Watford Town Hall, is far superior to the lustreless Rossini coupling with which these performances are saddled.

Requiem Mass.

(B) *** EMI forte CZS5 68613-2 (2) [CDFB 68613]. Scotto, Baltsa, Luchetti, Nesterenko, Amb. Ch., Philh. O, Muti – CHERUBINI: *Requiem in C min.* ***

✿ (B) (***) DG Double mono 439 684-2 (2) [(M) id. import]. Stader, Dominguez, Carelli, Sardi, St Hedwig's Cathedral Ch., Berlin RIAS SO, Fricsay – ROSSINI: *Stabat Mater*. (***)

(M) (***) DG mono 447 442-2 [id.]. Stader, Radev, Krebs, Borg, St Hedwig's Cathedral Ch., Berlin RIAS O, Fricsay.

(M) (***) Dutton Lab. mono CDLX 7010 [id. full price]. Caniglia, Gigli, Stignani, Pinza, Rome Opera Ch. & O, Serafin.

(M) (**(*)) EMI mono CMS5 65506-2 (2) [CDHB 65506]. Schwarzkopf, Dominguez, Di Stefano, Siepi, La Scala, Milan, Ch. & O, De Sabata (with: VERDI: *La Traviata: Preludes to Acts I & III. I vespri siciliani: overture*. WOLF-FERRARI: *Susanna's secret: Overture and Intermezzo*. RESPIGHI: *The Fountains of Rome*. ROSSINI: *William Tell overture* **(*)).

(M) **(*) RCA 09026 61403-2 (2) [id.]. L. Price, J. Baker, V. Luchetti, Van Dam, Chicago Symphony Ch. & SO, Solti.

(B) **(*) EMI Eminence Dig. CD-EMXD 2503 (2) [(M) id. import]. Elizabeth Connell, Ameral Gunson, Edmund Barham, John Tomlinson, Brighton Festival Ch., Royal Choral Soc., RPO, Owain Arwel Hughes.

(B) **(*) DG Double 453 091-2 (2) [(M) id. import]. Freni, Ludwig, Cossutta, Ghiaurov, V. Singverein, VPO, Karajan – BRUCKNER: *Te Deum*. **(*)

(M) **(*) Sony SM2K 47639 (2) [S2K 47639]. Arroyo, Veasey, Domingo, Raimondi, L. Symphony Ch., LSO, Bernstein.

(B) ** Sony SB2K 53252 (2) [S2K 53252]. Amara, Forrester, Tucker, London, Westminster Ch., Phd. O, Ormandy – ROSSINI: *Stabat Mater*. **

(i) *Requiem Mass;* (ii) *4 Sacred pieces*.

(BB) **(*) Naxos Dig. 8.550944/5 (2) [id.]. Filipova, Scalchi, Hernández, Colombara, Hungarian State Op. Ch. & O, Pier Giorgio Morandi.

(B) **(*) Decca Double 444 833-2 (2) [id.]. (i) L. Price, Elias, Bjoerling, Tozzi, V. Musikverein, VPO, Reiner; (ii) Minton, Los Angeles Master Ch., LAPO, Mehta.

With spectacular analogue sound – not always perfectly balanced, but vividly wide in its tonal spectrum – Muti's 1979 Kingsway Hall performance makes a tremendous impact and is in almost all respects preferable to his later version, recorded live eight years later at La Scala. Characteristically he prefers fast speeds, and in the *Dies irae* he rushes the singers dangerously, making the music breathless in its excitement rather than grandly dramatic in its portrayal of the Day of Wrath. It is not surprising that Muti opted for a professional choir, and the engineers are able to give it fine impact. Unashamedly, from first to last this is an operatic performance, with a passionately committed quartet of soloists, underpinned by Nesterenko in glorious voice, giving priestly authority to the *Confutatis*. Scotto is not always sweet on top, but Baltsa is superb, and Luchetti sings freshly. Now offered very inexpensively, and aptly coupled with a splendid (digital) account of Cherubini's *C minor Requiem*, so admired by Berlioz, this readily goes to the top of the list of bargain recommendations.

Fricsay's superb mono studio recording of Verdi's *Requiem* caused a sensation when it first appeared on LP in 1954. Its tingling drama anticipated the later version, and though tempi are generally faster than in that live account there is marginal extra precision and polish. This makes a worthy reissue in DG's 'Legendary Recordings' series, with the full, spacious mono recording already showing that the DG engineers, using mono techniques, could achieve a combination of clarity and atmosphere – especially in recording the big choral climaxes – to anticipate their later stereo records. The solo team is first class with the contribution of Kim Borg standing out, although in the latter part of the work the solo ensembles are at times even more eloquent in the live performance. But this earlier version makes an equally astonishing impact.

Fricsay's second recording, which DG have now reissued on a bargain Double coupled with Rossini, is of a live performance given in 1960, the very last he conducted before his untimely death. In biting drama it has never been surpassed, and even though speeds are often measured when compared with his fine studio recording (which DG have also currently reissued on a single disc as an 'Original'), such is the voltage of this later performance that it doesn't sound slower. Moreover it is underpinned by a commanding gravity that plainly reflects the conductor's own emotions during his last illness. Like him, the two male soloists are Hungarian, and both are first rate, with the tenor, Gabor Carelli, pleasingly Italianate of tone (his *Ingemisco* is ravishing). Maria Stader, the soprano soloist, is common to both performances; here she sings with clear, pure tone, if very occasionally suffering intonation problems, which did not trouble her in the earlier version. Oralia Dominguez is the rich mezzo. The chorus is superbly disciplined, yet ardent: the *Dies irae* is electrifying, the *Sanctus* is wonderfully light and joyful and the closing *Lux aeterna* raptly beautiful, for Fricsay's concentration never falters. The CD transfer enhances the bite of the choral projection without losing the atmospheric warmth of a recording which. even today, can startle by its immediacy of sound.

Well recorded, with first-rate Hungarian chorus and orchestra, the Naxos version offers an enjoyable account of Verdi's *Requiem* which may lack something in dramatic intensity but which consistently brings out the work's lyrical warmth. Though the tenor, César Hernández, is at times coarse, straining in the upper register, the other three soloists are very good, notably the Bulgarian soprano, Elena Filipova, with her opulent tone. This is a performance which gains in intensity as it progresses and, if anything, the *Four Sacred pieces*, an apt fill-up, bring performances even more dedicated, with refined choral singing. Though the chorus is set slightly behind the orchestra, this can be recommended as a good bargain version, though it is worth remembering that Richard Hickox's outstanding Chandos version of the *Requiem*, coming on a single full-priced disc, is also a bargain, and the Chandos recording has a much more sharply detailed recording of the chorus. It is well worth the relatively small extra cost (CHAN 9490).

Reiner's opening of the *Requiem* is very slow and atmospheric. He takes the music at something like half the speed of Toscanini and shapes everything very carefully. Yet as the work proceeds the performance quickly sparks into life, and there is some superb and memorable singing from a distinguished team of soloists. The recording has a spectacularly wide dynamic range, enhanced by the CD format, and, with the chorus singing fervently, the *Dies irae* is almost overwhelming. Mehta's performance of the *Sacred pieces* has much more brilliant, sharply focused recording than Giulini's, but in every other way Giulini's performance of Verdi's last work (or group of works) provides a deeper, more searching experience. However, that is at full price.

The Dutton Sound transfer of Serafin's historic recording of 1939 relates the work to the Verdian operatic tradition more closely than most latter-day versions. The beefy, Italianate sound of the chorus is what Verdi himself no doubt had in mind, and the team of soloists is characterfully representative of the finest Italian singing at that period. The recording was built round Beniamino Gigli, singing with his most golden tone. Though his tendency to aspirate the vocal line and to bring his half-tone down to a gentle croon may upset the purists, few performances are as winning as his, and both Ebe Stignani and Ezio Pinza are at their supreme best, rarely matched since. The soprano, Maria Caniglia, is more variable but, always dramatic, she rises splendidly to the challenge of the final *Libera me*. Whether because of co-ordination problems between such distinguished soloists, a brief *a cappella* passage of 11 bars for mezzo, tenor and bass soloists is omitted towards the end of the *Lux aeterna*.

Victor de Sabata's legendary 1954 recording unashamedly adopts the most spacious speeds and a deeply devotional manner, helped by a starry quartet of soloists. When it came out, it was not well received by many, who found the slow speeds self-indulgent, the very opposite of those adopted by Tullio Serafin, whose early recording made an obvious comparison, lasting a full 22 minutes less. Also this de Sabata version, master-minded by Walter Legge, was due to be superseded ten years later by Giulini's stereo version, ensuring that it never reappeared on LP, making this CD transfer very welcome, limited in sound but with fine dynamic contrasts. Unlike the Fricsay version, the electrical urgency – well illustrated in some of the orchestral fill-ups on the set – flashes out only occasionally in sudden dynamic bursts, as in the *Dies irae*. Otherwise dedication is the keynote. Far more than the later (full price) Giulini set, de Sabata's is a performance of extremes, totally concentrated but very personal in its new look, often with underlining that draws attention to itself, as in *Te decet hymnus*. Where de Sabata rides triumphant is in his spine-tingling authority, however controversial he may be, and the four superb soloists respond with total commitment, Schwarzkopf most of all, in radiant voice. Oralia Dominguez excels herself, as cleanly focused as Schwarzkopf, with her rapid flicker-vibrato adding character to the firm mezzo timbre. Giuseppe di Stefano sings with headily fresh tone and de Sabata even woos the occasional *mezza voce* from him, while Siepi, not quite as rock-like or imaginative as Pinza for Serafin, is splendid too. The chorus sing lustily but with characteristic Italian reluctance to match in an ensemble. The fill-ups complete the picture of de Sabata: the *Traviata Preludes*, rapt and finely shaded, the Respighi sensuously atmospheric, the *William Tell overture* given surprising refinement. Best of all are the two little Wolf-Ferrari items, in their point and sparkle deliciously witty in a way one might not have expected from de Sabata. For all one's reservations, this remains a revelatory set.

On RCA, with an unusually sensitive and pure-toned quartet of soloists – Luchetti perhaps not as characterful as the others, Leontyne Price occasionally showing strain – and with superb choral singing and orchestral playing, Solti's 1977 Chicago version has all the ingredients for success. The set is well worth having for Janet Baker's deeply sensitive singing, but the remastered recording – less than ideally balanced – tends to be fierce on climaxes and in sound; and in other ways too, Solti's earlier, Decca/Vienna set is preferable.

Recorded live in St Paul's Cathedral in March 1994, the Eminence version under Owain Arwel Hughes brings a concentrated and warmly atmospheric performance, with recording that captures far more detail than one would ever have expected in such a reverberant venue. The acoustic does not inhibit Hughes from adopting a grippingly fast speed for the *Dies irae*, and any flaws of ensemble are compensated by the biting intensity inspired by this live event. Both Elizabeth Connell and Ameral Gunson under pressure have their vibratos exaggerated by the microphone, but the operatic flavour of their singing is most persuasive. John Tomlinson is also a degree less steady than he has usually been on disc, but he sings with great character and thrilling tone. Best of all is the tenor, Edmund Barham, singing with clear, fresh tone and with finely shaded contrasts of expression, as in the great *Ingemisco*. The weight of the choral sound is vividly caught. Without a coupling, even at bargain price, this is hardly a definitive choice, but it is a warmly individual one.

Karajan's earlier recording of the *Requiem* has been greatly enhanced in its CD transfer, with the whole effect given greater presence and immediacy. He has a fine team of soloists, too. However, Karajan's reading still smooths over the lines of Verdi's masterpiece. The result is often beautiful, but, apart from the obvious climaxes, such as the *Dies irae*, there is a lack of dramatic bite. However, with two discs offered for the price of one, many collectors may be tempted to try this.

Bernstein's 1970 *Requiem* was recorded in the Royal Albert Hall. By rights, the daring of that decision should have paid off; but with close balancing of microphones the result is not as full and free as one would have expected. Bernstein's interpretation remains marvellously persuasive in its drama, exaggerated at times, maybe, but red-blooded in a way that is hard to resist. The quartet of soloists is particularly strong.

Ormandy's is a sincere, warm-blooded performance, with ardent choral singing and plenty of drama. The snag lies with the soloists, who all fall far short of their rivals on other bargain sets (notably Fricsay's). One has only to sample their contribution to the *Kyrie* to hear that this is not really distinguished singing.

(i; ii) *Requiem Mass;* (iii; iv) *Inno delle nazione;* (ii) *Te Deum;* (iii) *Luisa Miller: Quando le sere al placido*. (iv) *Nabucco: Va pensiero*.

(M) (***) RCA mono GD 60299; *GK 60299* (2) [60299-RG-2; *60299-RG-4*]. (i) Nelli, Barbieri, Di Stefano, Siepi; (ii) Robert Shaw Ch.; (iii) Jan Peerce; (iv) Westminster Ch.; NBC SO, Toscanini.

Toscanini's account of the *Requiem* brings a supreme performance, searingly intense. The opening of the *Dies irae* has never sounded more hair-raising, with the bass-drum thrillingly caught, despite the limitation of dry mono recording. And rarely has the chorus shone so brightly in this work on record, while the soloists are near-ideal, a vintage team. The other works make fascinating listening, too. The *Te Deum* was one of Toscanini's very last recordings, a performance more intense than usual with this work, and it is good to have the extraordinary wartime recording of the potboiling *Hymn of the Nations*. The *Internationale* is added to Verdi's original catalogue of national anthems, to represent the ally, the USSR.

OPERA

Aida (complete).

(M) *** EMI CMS7 69300-2 (3) [Ang. CDMC 69300 full price]. Freni, Carreras, Baltsa, Cappuccilli, Raimondi, Van Dam, V. State Op. Ch., VPO, Karajan.

(M) *** Decca 414 087-2 (3) [id.]. Tebaldi, Simionato, Bergonzi, MacNeil, Van Mill, Corena, V. Singverein, VPO, Karajan.

(M) (***) RCA mono GD 86652 (3) [6652-2-RG]. Milanov, Bjoerling, Barbieri, Warren, Christoff, Rome Op. Ch. & O, Perlea.

(M) ** RCA 74321 39498-2 (3) [6198-2-RC full price]. Leontyne Price, Bumbry, Domingo, Milnes, Raimondi, Sotin, Alldis Ch., LSO, Leinsdorf.

(M) (**) [RCA mono 60300-RG-2 (3)]. Nelli, Gustavson, Tucker, Valdengo, Robert Shaw Ch., NBC SO, Toscanini.

On EMI, Karajan's is a performance of *Aida* that carries splendour and pageantry to the point of exaltation. Yet Karajan's fundamental approach is lyrical. On record at least, there can be little question of Freni lacking power in a role normally given to a larger voice, and there is ample gain in the tender beauty of her singing. Carreras makes a fresh, sensitive Radames, Raimondi a darkly intense Ramphis and Van Dam a cleanly focused King, his relative lightness no drawback. Cappuccilli here gives a more detailed performance than he did for Muti on EMI, while Baltsa as Amneris crowns the whole performance with her fine, incisive singing. Despite some over-brightness on cymbals and trumpet, the Berlin sound for Karajan, as transferred to CD, is richly and involvingly atmospheric, both in the intimate scenes and, most strikingly, in the scenes of pageant, which have rarely been presented on record in greater splendour. The set has been attractively re-packaged and remains first choice for the opera, irrespective of price.

On Decca, as on EMI, Karajan was helped by having a Viennese orchestra and chorus; but most important of all is the musicianship and musical teamwork of his soloists. Bergonzi in particular emerges here as a model among tenors, with a rare feeling for the shaping of phrases and attention to detail. Cornell MacNeil too is splendid. Tebaldi's creamy tone-colour rides beautifully over the phrases and she too acquires a new depth of imagination. Among the other soloists Arnold van Mill and Fernando Corena are both superb, and Simionato provides one of the very finest portrayals of Amneris we have ever had in a complete *Aida*. The recording has long been famous for its technical bravura and flair. CD enhances the overall projection, but the brightness on top at times strikes the ear rather too forcibly. Nevertheless this remains a remarkable technical achievement.

All four principals on the historic RCA set are at their very finest, notably Milanov, whose poise and control in *O patria mia* are a marvel. Barbieri as Amneris is even finer here than in the Callas set, and it is good to hear the young Christoff resonant as Ramphis. Perlea conducts with great panache.

There is much to commend in Leontyne Price's 1971 recording of *Aida*, reissued at mid-price in RCA's Opera Treasury series, though currently remaining at full price in the USA; with a fine cast, it is a set that might be worth considering. But inevitably it comes into direct comparison with Price's earlier set on Decca and by that standard it is a little disappointing. Price's voice is not as glowing as it was and, though there are moments when she shows added insight, it is the earlier performance which generates more electricity and has more dramatic urgency. Domingo makes a warm and stylish Radames, Milnes a strong if hardly electrifying Amonasro and Bumbry a superb, imaginative Amneris. It is a pity that the recording, by the most recent standards, does not capture the glamour of the score. Most of the earlier sets are more impressive in sound.

Toscanini's 1949 performance of *Aida* is the least satisfying of his New York opera recordings. Richard Tucker sings well but makes a relatively colourless Radames, and Herva Nelli lacks weight as Aida, neatly though she sings and with some touching moments. Nancy Gustavson's Amneris lacks all menace, and Valdengo as Amonasro is the only fully satisfying principal. Yet Toscanini is so electrifying from first to last that his admirers will accept the limited, painfully dry recording. The set is no longer available in the UK.

Aida: highlights.

(M) *** Decca 458 206-2 [id.] (from complete recording, with Leontyne Price, Jon Vickers, Rita Gorr, Robert Merrill, Giorgio Tozzi, Rome Op. Ch. & O, cond. Solti).

(M) *** Decca 452 733-2 [id.] (from above complete set, with Tebaldi, Bergonzi, Simionato, MacNeil, V. Singverein, VPO, cond. Karajan).

(B) **(*) DG Classikon Dig. 439 482-2 [(M) id. import](from complete recording, with Ricciarelli, Obraztsova, Domingo, Nucci, Ghiaurov; cond. Abbado).

(B) **(*) [EMI Red Seal CDR5 72562]. Caballé, Domingo, Cossotto, Ghiaurov, ROHCG Ch., New Philh. O, Muti.

(M) ** [RCA Basic 100 09026 62676-2] (from above complete set with Leontyne Price, Domingo, Bumbry, Milnes, Raimondi; cond. Leinsdorf).

(M) *(*) Sony Dig. SMK 53506 [id.] (from complete recording, with Millo, Domingo, Zajick, Morris, Ramey, Met Op. Ch. & O; cond. Levine).

(B) * EMI CfP CD-CFP 6019 (from complete recording, with Birgit Nilsson, Franco Corelli, Grace Bumbry, Mario Sereni, Rome Op. Ch. & O, Mehta).

The selection from Solti's full-price recording is generous (71 minutes) and makes an obvious first choice, for not only is it handsomely packaged in a slipcase in Decca's Opera Gala series but it comes with full translation.

Most collectors will probably have the alternative Karajan set, made later for EMI with Freni and Carreras, so the Decca sampler of John Culshaw's famously spectacular, early (1959) stereo version is also very welcome, for Tebaldi and Bergonzi were both on top form and the supporting cast is impressive. The timing is 61 minutes, and a cued synopsis is included.

In Abbado's 1981 La Scala *Aida*, it was the men who stood out, Domingo a superb Radames, Ghiaurov as Ramphis, Nucci a dramatic Amonasro, and Raimondi as the King. Ricciarelli is an appealing Aida, but her legato line is at times impure above the stave, and Elena Obraztsova produces too much curdled tone as Amneris. The recording is bright and fresh, but not ideally expansive in the ceremonial scenes. As is usual with DG's bargain Classikon series, the documentation is good, though without translations. The selection offers 64 minutes of music.

On Muti's set of highlights, Caballé's portrait of the heroine is superb, full of detailed insight into the character and with plenty of examples of superlative singing, while Cossotto makes a fine Amneris. Domingo produces glorious sound, but this is not one of his most imaginative recordings. However, the sound is relatively small-scale, underlining the fierceness of Muti's reading.

The selection from Leontyne Price's 1971 RCA recording is enjoyable enough, and those tempted by the cast-list – Domingo an impressive Radames, with Milnes and Bumbry both in good voice – should find this selection acceptable enough. But Price is in even finer voice on the Decca set.

Levine's 1990 recording of *Aida*, made with Met. forces in the limited acoustic of the Manhattan Center, is hardly among the most successful versions of this much-recorded opera. Both Aprile Millo in the title-role and Dolora Zajick as Amneris are disappointing in the unevenness of their vocal production and, though Plácido Domingo again makes a commanding Radames and the selection is generous (75 minutes), the recording is not expansive enough to do full justice to the grand spectacle of Verdi's score.

Mehta's 1967 *Aida*, made in Rome, was his first complete opera recording and it was not surprising that he failed to measure up to the standards of his rivals, including Karajan and Solti. That might not have mattered had the singing cast been outstandingly imaginative but, apart from Birgit Nilsson in the title-role, there is nothing special to recommend this bargain set of highlights. Bumbry fails to convey much depth of feeling, Corelli and Sereni give routine performances and even the sound fails to make one really sit up.

Attila (complete).

(M) *** Ph. 426 115-2 (2). Raimondi, Deutekom, Bergonzi, Milnes, Amb. S., Finchley Children's Music Group, RPO, Gardelli.

With its dramatic anticipations of *Macbeth*, the musical anticipations of *Rigoletto* and the compression which (on record if not on the stage) becomes a positive merit – all these qualities, helped by a fine performance under Gardelli, make this Philips version of *Attila* an intensely enjoyable set. Deutekom, not the most sweet-toned of sopranos, has never sung better on record, and the rest of the cast is outstandingly good. The 1973 recording is well balanced and atmospheric.

Un ballo in maschera (complete).

(M) *** DG Dig. 449 588-2 (2). Domingo, Barstow, Nucci, Quivar, Sumi Jo, V. State Op. Konzerthhvereinigung, VPO, Karajan.

(B) *** DG Double 453 148-2 (2) [id.]. Ricciarelli, Domingo, Bruson, Obraztsova, Gruberová, Raimondi, La Scala, Milan, Ch. & O, Abbado.

(M) *** RCA GD 86645 (2) [6645-2-RG]. L. Price, Bergonzi, Merrill, Grist, Verrett, Flagello, RCA Italiana Op. Ch. & O, Leinsdorf.

(M) *** EMI (SIS) CMS5 66510-2 (2) [Angel CDMB 66510]. Arroyo, Domingo, Cappuccilli, Grist, Cossotto, Howell, ROHCG Ch., New Philh. O, Muti.

(M) **(*) Decca (IMS) 440 042-2 (2). Tebaldi, Pavarotti, Milnes, Donath, Regina Resnik, Santa Cecilia Academy, Rome, Ch. & O, Bartoletti.

(M) (***) [RCA mono 60301-2-RG (2)]. Herva Nelli, Jan Peerce, Robert Merrill, Virginia Haskins, Claramae Turner, Nicola Moscona, NBC Ch. & SO, Toscanini.

(B) ** Ph. Duo 456 316-2 (2) [id.]. Montserrat Caballé, José Carreras, Patricia Payne, Sona Gazarian, Ingvar Wixell, Robert Lloyd, Ch. & O of ROHCG, Sir Colin Davis.

Recorded in Vienna early in 1989, *Un ballo in maschera* was Karajan's last opera recording and it makes a fitting memorial, characteristically rich and spacious, with a cast – if not ideal – which still makes a fine team, responding to the conductor's single-minded vision. Standing out vocally is the Gustavo of Plácido Domingo, strong and imaginative, dominating the whole cast. He may not have the sparkle of Pavarotti in this role, but the singing is richer, more refined and more thoughtful. Amelia is Josephine Barstow's finest achievement on record, and dramatically she is most compelling. Leo Nucci, though not as rough in tone as in some of his other recent recordings, is over-emphatic, with poor legato in his great solo, *Eri tu*. Sumi Jo, a Karajan discovery, gives a delicious performance as Oscar the page, coping splendidly with Karajan's slow speed for her Act I solo. Florence Quivar produces satisfyingly rich tone as Ulrica. Though the sound is not as cleanly focused as in the full-price Decca recording for Solti, it is warm and full.

Abbado's powerful reading, admirably paced and with a splendid feeling for the sparkle of the comedy, remains highly recommendable, especially at its new price. The cast is very strong, with Ricciarelli at her very finest and Domingo sweeter of tone and more deft of characterization than on the Muti set of five years earlier. Bruson as the wronged husband Renato (a role he also takes for Solti) sings magnificently, and only Obraztsova as Ulrica and Gruberová as Oscar are less consistently convincing. The analogue recording clearly separates the voices and instruments in different acoustics, which on CD is distracting only initially and after that brings the drama closer.

The reissued RCA set makes a fine bargain. Leontyne Price is a natural for the part of Amelia, spontaneous-sounding and full of dramatic temperament. Only in the two big arias does Price for a moment grow self-conscious. Robert Merrill here seems to have acquired all sorts of dramatic, Gobbi-like overtones to add to the flow of firm, satisfying tone. Bergonzi is a model of sensitivity, while Reri Grist makes a light, bright Oscar, and the Ulrica of Shirley Verrett has a range of power, richness and delicacy coupled with unparalleled firmness that makes this one of her most memorable recorded performances. Excellent recording, hardly showing its age, with the voices rather forward.

On EMI the quintet of principals is also unusually strong, but it is the conductor who takes first honours in a warmly dramatic reading. Muti's rhythmic resilience and consideration for the singers go with keen concentration, holding each Act together in a way he did not quite achieve in his earlier recording for EMI of *Aida*. Arroyo, rich of voice, is not always imaginative in her big solos, and Domingo rarely produces a half-tone, though the recording balance may be partly to blame. The sound is full and vivid, and for the present reissue a new booklet has been provided with full translation.

The main interest in the Decca set rests in the pairing of Tebaldi and Pavarotti. The latter was in young, vibrant voice, but Tebaldi made her recording in the full maturity of her career. Much of her singing is very fine indeed, but there is no mistaking that her voice here is nowhere near as even as it once was. For the command of her performance this is a version well worth hearing and the supporting cast is strong, not only Milnes as Renato and Donath as Oscar, but Resnik a dark-voiced Ulrica. Bartoletti directs the proceedings dramatically, and the (1970) Decca recording remains strikingly vivid and atmospheric.

Un ballo was the very last of the complete operas that Toscanini conducted in New York in concert performance. It was given in Carnegie Hall in January 1954, just three months before the maestro finally retired. Though the performance cannot match in exhilaration his unique reading of *Falstaff*, it stands as one of the most cherishable mementoes of his conducting of Verdi. Speeds are often fast and the control characteristically taut, but it is wrong to think of the performance as rigid, when rubato is often so freely expressive. Peerce misses some of the lightness of the role, clear in diction but not very characterful, yet Herva Nelli here gives one of her finest performances, with a beautiful, finely moulded line in her big numbers, including the two arias. Robert Merrill is superb as Renato, singing magnificently in *Eri tu*, while Claramae Turner is firm as a rock as Ulrica. The sound is typically dry, not at all atmospheric, but clean and well detailed. The set is not currently available in the UK.

Keen opera collectors will feel that Davis's version, based on a Covent Garden production, is worth having as an inexpensive Duo set, particularly as Davis is good at bringing out the ironic humour in Verdi's score. Caballé and Carreras match Davis's lightness of touch, but the dramatic power is diminished. Despite fine recording (dating from 1978–9), this is less satisfying than most of the competing versions.

Un ballo in maschera: highlights.

(M) *** DG (IMS) Dig. 445 468-2 (from above complete set, with Ricciarelli, Domingo, Bruson, Gruberová, Raimondi, La Scala, Milan, Ch. & O, Abbado).

The 68-minute selection from the full-price Abbado version, which includes the *Prelude* and opens brightly with *S'avanza il conte*, makes a good mid-priced choice, with a cued synopsis of the narrative for the listener to follow the action. The excerpts are well chosen to represent Domingo, but Ricciarelli's splendid contribution is not neglected. The CD transfer faithfully reflects the qualities of the complete set which costs little more than the present single disc.

La Battaglia di Legnano (complete).

(M) *** Ph. 422 435-2 (2). Ricciarelli, Carreras, Manuguerra, Ghiuselev, Austrian R. Ch. & O, Gardelli.

La Battaglia di Legnano is a compact, sharply conceived piece, made the more intense by the subject's obvious relationship with the situation in Verdi's own time. One weakness is that the villainy is not effectively personalized, but the juxtaposition of the individual drama of supposed infidelity against a patriotic theme brings most effective musical contrasts. Gardelli directs a fine performance, helped by a strong cast of principals, with Carreras, Ricciarelli and Manuguerra all at their finest. Excellent recording.

Il Corsaro (complete).

(M) *** Ph. 426 118-2 (2). Norman, Caballé, Carreras, Grant, Mastromei, Noble, Amb. S., New Philh. O, Gardelli.

In *Il Corsaro*, though the characterization is rudimentary, the contrast between the two heroines is effective, with Gulnara, the Pasha's slave, carrying conviction in the *coup de foudre* which has her promptly worshipping the Corsair, an early example of the Rudolph Valentino figure. The rival heroines are taken splendidly here, with Jessye Norman as the faithful wife, Medora, actually upstaging Montserrat Caballé as Gulnara. Gardelli directs a vivid performance, with fine singing from the hero, portrayed by José Carreras. Gian-Piero Mastromei, not rich in tone, still rises to the challenge of the Pasha's music. Excellent, firmly focused and well-balanced Philips sound.

Don Carlos (complete).

(M) *** EMI CMS7 69304-2 (3) [Ang. CDMC 69304 full price]. Carreras, Freni, Ghiaurov, Baltsa, Cappuccilli, Raimondi, German Op. Ch., Berlin, BPO, Karajan.

(M) (**(*)) EMI mono CMS7 64642-2 [CDMC 64642 full price] (3). Christoff, Stella, Nicolai, Mario Filippeschi, Gobbi, Neri, Rome Op. Ch. & O, Santini.

(M) (**) DG mono 447 655-2 (2). Fernandi, Siepi, Bastianini, Jurinac, Simionato, Steffanoni, V. State Op. Ch., VPO, Karajan.

Karajan opts firmly for the later, four-Act version of the opera on EMI, merely opening out the cuts he adopted on stage. The *Auto da fé* scene is here superb, while Karajan's characteristic choice of singers for refinement of voice rather than sheer size consistently pays off. Both Carreras and Freni are most moving, even if *Tu che le vanità* has its raw moments. Baltsa is a superlative Eboli and Cappuccilli an affecting Rodrigo, though neither Carreras nor Cappuccilli is at his finest in the famous oath duet. Raimondi and Ghiaurov as the Grand Inquisitor and Philip II provide the most powerful confrontation. The sound is both rich and atmospheric and is made to seem even firmer and more vivid in its current remastering, giving great power to Karajan's uniquely taut account of the four-Act version. The set's presentation has also been attractively redesigned, and this set remains at the top of the recommended list.

The vintage EMI mono recording offers a seriously cut version of the four-Act score, indifferently conducted by Gabriele Santini, but it is still an indispensable set, with performances from Tito Gobbi as Rodrigo and Boris Christoff as Philip which have never been remotely matched. Gobbi's singing in the Death scene is arguably the finest recorded performance that even this glorious artist ever made, with a wonderful range of tone and feeling for words. The bitingly dark tone of Christoff as the King also goes with intense feeling for the dramatic situation, making his big monologue one of the peaks of the performance. Antonietta Stella, never a very distinctive artist, gives one of her finest recorded performances as Elisabetta, only occasionally squally. As Eboli, Elena Nicolai controls her fruity mezzo well, even if the vibrato becomes obtrusive; and the most serious blot is the singing of the tenor, Mario Filippeschi, and even that is not as coarse or strained as we have often had latterly.

Karajan's DG set of the four-Act version was recorded live at the Salzburg Festival in 1958 and, despite the lovely singing of Sena Jurinac as the Queen, it cannot compare with his Berlin performance of 20 years later on EMI, recorded in the studio but with the Salzburg Festival cast of that year. Simionato, Bastianini and Siepi were all among the finest Italian singers of their day, but in this opera their performances are generalized rather than illuminating. For a live recording of its period the sound is good.

Don Carlos: highlights.

(M) *** EMI (SIS) CDM7 63089-2 (from complete recording, with Domingo, Caballé, Raimondi, Verrett, Milnes, Amb. Op. Ch., ROHCG O, Giulini).

(M) **(*) Sony Dig. SMK 53507 [id.] (from complete recording, with Furlanetto, Millo, Zajick, Sylvester, Chernov, Ramey, Battle, NY Met. Ch. & O, Levine).

Giulini's disc of highlights can be highly recommended. In selecting from such a long opera, serious omissions are inevitable; nothing is included here from Act III, to make room for the *Auto da fé* scene from Act IV – some 37 minutes of the disc is given to this Act. With vivid sound, this is most stimulating; the only reservation concerns Caballé's *Tu che le vanità*, which ends the selection disappointingly.

Although, like Levine's *Aida*, his Met. *Don Carlos* highlights was recorded in the Manhattan Center, the sound is comparatively full and vivid. Michael Sylvester (as Don Carlos) and Aprile Millo (as Elisabetta) are both well cast and, if the rest of the team are more uneven and Ferruccio Furlanetto is a less than ideal King Philip, this 74-minute selection makes a more than acceptable mid-priced sampler.

I due Foscari (complete).

(M) *** Ph. 422 426-2 (2). Ricciarelli, Carreras, Cappuccilli, Ramey, Austrian R. Ch. & SO, Gardelli.

I due Foscari brings Verdian high spirits in plenty, erupting in swinging cabalettas and much writing that anticipates operas as late as *Simon Boccanegra* and *La forza del destino*. The cast here is first rate, with Ricciarelli giving one of her finest performances in the recording studio to date and with Carreras singing tastefully as well as powerfully. The crispness of discipline among the Austrian Radio forces is admirable, but there is less sense of atmosphere here than in the earlier, London-made recordings in the series.

Ernani (complete).

(M) *** RCA GD 86503 (2) [6503-2-RG]. Leontyne Price, Bergonzi, Sereni, Flagello, RCA Italiana Op. Ch. & O, Schippers.

(M) **(*) Ph. Dig. 446 669-2. Lamberti, Sass, Kovats, Miller, Takacs, Hungarian State Op. Ch. & O, Gardelli.

At mid-price, Schippers' set, recorded in Rome in 1967, is an outstanding bargain. Leontyne Price may take the most celebrated aria, *Ernani involami*, rather cautiously, but the voice is gloriously firm and rich, and Bergonzi is comparably strong and vivid, though Mario Sereni, vocally reliable, is dull, and Ezio Flagello gritty-toned. Nevertheless, with Schippers drawing the team powerfully together, it is a highly enjoyable set, with the digital transfer making voices and orchestra sound full and vivid.

Originally issued on Hungaraton, this early digital set now returns to the catalogue on Philips at mid-price with full libretto and translation. Gardelli's conducting is most sympathetic and idiomatic in the Hungarian version and, like Muti's, it is strong on ensembles. Sylvia Sass is a sharply characterful Elvira, Callas-like in places, and Lamberti a bold Ernani, but their vocal flaws prevent this from being a first choice. Capable rather than inspired or idiomatic singing from the rest. The digital recording is bright and well balanced, although the CD transfer brings out the fact that the recording acoustics are very resonant. An enjoyable set all the same.

Falstaff (complete).

(M) **(*) Decca 417 168-2 (2) [id.]. Sir Geraint Evans, Ligabue, Freni, Kraus, Elias, Simionato, RCA Italiana Op. Ch. & O, Solti.

(M) (***) RCA mono GD 60251 (2) [60251-RG-2]. Valdengo, Nelli, Merriman, Elmo, Guarrera, Stich-Randall, Robert Shaw Ch., NBC SO, Toscanini.

(M) **(*) DG Dig. 447 686-2 (2). Giuseppe Taddei, Raina Kabaivanska, Janet Perry, Christa Ludwig, Rolando Panerai, Francisco Araiza, Piero de Palma, Heinz Zednik, V. State Op. Ch., VPO, Karajan.

We owe an apology to the late Sir Geraint Evans in previously missing Decca's reissue of his assumption of the role of Verdi's Falstaff, in partnership with Sir Georg Solti. Their set, originally issued by RCA, comes up as sparkling as ever on a pair of mid-priced CDs. There is an energy, a sense of fun, a sparkle that outshines rival versions, outstanding as they may be. Evans never sounded better on record, and the rest of the cast live up to his example admirably. Solti drives hard, and almost any comparison with the ancient Toscanini set will show his shortcomings, but it is still an exciting and well-pointed performance, the rest of the cast well contrasted. Although Giulini still leads the premium-priced versions (DG 410 503-2) the Decca set is still very much worth considering.

Toscanini's fizzing account of Verdi's last masterpiece has never been matched on record, the most high-spirited performance ever, beautifully paced for comedy. Even without stereo, and recorded with typical dryness, the clarity and sense of presence in this live concert performance set the story in relief. The cast is excellent, led by the ripe, firm baritone, Giuseppe Valdengo. Such singers as Nan Merriman as Mistress Page, Cloe Elmo as a wonderfully fruity Mistress Quickly and Frank Guarrera as Ford match or outshine any more recent interpreters. Toscanini's favourite soprano in his last years, Herva Nelli, is less characterful as Mistress Ford, rather over-parted but still fresh and reliable.

Karajan's second (1980) recording of Verdi's last opera, made over 20 years after his classic EMI Philharmonia version with Gobbi and Schwarzkopf (still at full price), has lower standards of precision, yet it conveys a relaxed and genial atmosphere. With the exception of Kabaivanska, whose voice is not steady enough for the role of Alice, it is a good cast, with Ludwig fascinating as Mistress Quickly. Most astonishing of all is Taddei's performance as Falstaff himself, full, characterful and vocally astonishing from a man in his sixties. The digital sound is faithful and wide-ranging, and the CD transfer captures the bloom of the original reverberant recording so vividly that one worries less about any oddities of balance.

La forza del destino (complete).

(M) *** RCA 74321 39502-2 (3) [full price RCD3 1864]. Leontyne Price, Domingo, Milnes, Cossotto, Giaiotti, Bacquier, Alldis Ch., LSO, Levine.

(M) *** RCA GD 87971 (3) [4515-2-RG]. Leontyne Price, Tucker, Merrill, Tozzi, Verrett, Flagello, Foiani, RCA Italiana Op. Ch. & O, Schippers.

(M) **(*) EMI CMS7 64646-2 (3) [CDMC 64646 full price]. Arroyo, Bergonzi, Cappuccilli, Raimondi, Casoni, Evans, Amb. Op. Ch., RPO, Gardelli.

(M) * Decca 443 678-2 (3) [id.]. Milanov, Di Stefano, Warren, Elias, Tozzi, Santa Cecilia, Rome, Ch. and O, Previtali.

James Levine directs a superb performance. The results are electrifying. Leontyne Price recorded the role of Leonora in an earlier RCA version made in Rome in 1956, but the years have hardly touched her voice, and details of the reading have been refined. The roles of Don Alvaro and Don Carlo are ideally suited to the regular team of Plácido Domingo and Sherrill Milnes so that their confrontations are the cornerstones of the dramatic structure. Fiorenza Cossotto makes a formidable rather than a jolly Preziosilla, while on the male side the line-up of Bonaldo Giaiotti, Gabriel Bacquier, Kurt Moll and Michel Sénéchal is far stronger than on rival sets. In a good, vivid transfer of the mid-1970s sound, this is a strong, well-paced version with an exceptionally good and consistent cast. Now reissued at mid-price in RCA's UK Opera Treasury series, and quite stylishly re-packaged, it makes an unmissable bargain, although for the moment it remains at full price in the USA.

On RCA, Leontyne Price's voice (in 1964) was fresher and more open; on balance this is a more tender and delicate performance than the weightier one she recorded with Levine. Richard Tucker as Alvaro is here far less lachrymose and more stylish than he was earlier in the Callas set, producing ample, heroic tone, if not with the finesse of a Domingo. Robert Merrill as Carlo also sings with heroic strength, consistently firm and dark of tone; while Shirley Verrett, Giorgio Tozzi and Ezio Flagello stand up well against any rivalry. The sound is remarkably full and vivid.

Gardelli, normally a reliable recording conductor in Italian opera, here gives a disappointing account of a vividly dramatic score. The cast is vocally strong and each member of it lives up to expectations. Moreover the recording – made in 1969 in Watford Town Hall – is first rate, vivid, full and atmospheric. But it is vital in so long and episodic a work that overall dramatic control should be firm. Gardelli's contribution prevents this from being a first choice at mid-price when the Schippers set is available on RCA, although admirers of the individual artists in the EMI cast will find much to enjoy when the sound is so flattering to the voices. The layout places Acts I and II on the first disc, while Acts III and IV are each allotted a CD apiece.

Decca must be scraping the bottom of the barrel to bring out Previtali's early stero set (originally issued on RCA) which, even when it first appeared, was compared adversely to its main competitor, dominated by Tebaldi and conducted by Molinari-Pradelli – which itself has long been outclassed by subsequent recordings. In Rome, Milanov as Leonora was beginning to show her age, with occasional gusty swoops, her performance hardly comparable with Tebaldi's exquiste *mezza voce*; and Di Stefano, a relatively pale Alvaro, still was not entirely free of crudeness. Rosalind Elias as Preziosilla sounds fruity and bosomy. Perhaps the set may be regarded as a memorial to Leonard Warren, a fine Don Carlo; but with uninspired conducting from Previtali this reissue has little to recommend it.

La forza del destino: highlights.

(M) **(*) Decca 452 736-2 [id.] (from complete set, with Renata Tebaldi, Mario del Monaco, Cesare Siepi, Ettore Bastianini, Guilietta Simionato, St Cecilia Ac., Rome, Ch. & O, cond. Molinari-Pradelli).

An excellent if ungenerous (58 minutes) set of highlights from one of Decca's early-stereo opera sets, made in Rome in July 1955. As can be heard in the glorious opening *Madre, Madre, pietosa Vergine*, Tebaldi is on her finest form: her *mezza voce* here is exquisite. The stereo recording of the chorus is also amazingly atmospheric. Alas, as in so many of these early Decca Italian opera sets, Mario del Monaco never matches this. His voice is not in question, but the unrelievedly stentorian style is wearing. The supporting cast is more impressive, especially Simionato's Preziosilla, with a sparkling *Rataplan*, brilliantly recorded. As Molinari-Pradelli's conducting is not one of the set's strongest features, a highlights disc is the best way to approach this recording. There is a cued synopsis.

Un giorno di regno (complete).

(M) *** Ph. 422 429-2 (2). Cossotto, Norman, Carreras, Wixell, Sardinero, Ganzarolli, Amb. S., RPO, Gardelli.

Un giorno di regno may not be the greatest comic opera of the period, but this scintillating performance under Gardelli clearly reveals the young Verdi as more than an imitator of Rossini and Donizetti, and there are striking passages which clearly give a foretaste of such numbers as the duet *Si vendetta* from *Rigoletto*. Despite the absurd plot, this is as light and frothy an entertainment as anyone could want. Excellent singing from a fine team, with Jessye Norman and José Carreras outstanding. The recorded sound is vivid.

Giovanni d'Arco (complete).

(M) **(*) EMI CMS7 63226-2 (2) [CDMB 632262]. Cabbalé, Domingo, Milnes, Amb. Ch., LSO, Levine.

The seventh of Verdi's operas, based very loosely indeed on Schiller's drama, is an archetype of the works which the master was writing during his 'years in the galleys'. 'Melodic generosity and youthful resilience' are the qualities singled out by Charles Osborne in his study of the Verdi operas, and the score certainly confirms that. The pity is that James Levine, here a youthful whirlwind, does not respond to the resilience more effectively. Though the ensemble is superb, he consistently presses on too hard in fast music, with the rum-ti-tum hammered home. He is far more sympathetic in passages of 'melodic generosity', particularly when Caballé is singing. What had become a standard trio of principals for the 1970s here gives far more than a routine performance. With fine recording there is much to enjoy, even when the plot – whittled down to Joan, her father (who betrays her) and the King – is so naïve.

I Lombardi (complete).

(M) *** Ph. 422 420-2 (2). Deutekom, Domingo, Raimondi, Amb. S., RPO, Gardelli.

I Lombardi reaches its apotheosis in the famous *Trio*, well known from the days of 78-r.p.m. recordings. By those standards, Cristina Deutekom is not an ideal Verdi singer: her tone is sometimes hard and her voice is not always perfectly under control, yet there are also some glorious moments and the phrasing is often impressive. Domingo as Oronte is in superb voice, and the villain Pagano is well characterized by Raimondi. Among the supporting cast Stafford Dean and Clifford Grant must be mentioned. Gardelli conducts dramatically and the action projects vividly.

(i) *I Lombardi, Act III: Trio*. (ii) *Rigoletto, Act IV* (complete).

(M) (**) RCA mono GD 60276 (2) [60276-2-RG]. (i) Della Chiesa, Peerce, Moscona; (ii) Warren, Milanov, Peerce, Moscona, Merriman, All City Highschool Ch. & Glee Clubs, NBC SO, Toscanini – BOITO: *Mefistofele: Prologue*. (***)

It is interesting to find a little-known singer, Vivian della Chiesa, emerging strongly alongside Jan Peerce and Nicola Moscona. The last Act of *Rigoletto* was given in a wartime fund-raising concert in Madison Square Garden and, though the brittleness of sound is at times almost comic and the tautness of Toscanini's control was unrelenting, the performances of the principals are formidable, with Zinka Milanov at her most radiant. With Toscanini's searing account of the *Mefistofele Prologue*, this makes a generous compilation.

Luisa Miller (complete).

(M) *** [RCA 6646-2-RG (2)]. Moffo, Bergonzi, Verrett, MacNeil, Tozzi, Flagello, RCA Italiana Op. Ch. & O, Cleva.

In many ways the Cleva RCA set provides a performance to compete with the full-price versions and is just as stylish, with Moffo at her very peak, singing superbly, Carlo Bergonzi unfailingly intelligent and stylish, and Verrett nothing less than magnificent in her role as a quasi-Amneris. MacNeil and Tozzi are also satisfyingly resonant, and Fausto Cleva tellingly reveals his experience directing the opera at the Met. Good recording.

Macbeth (complete).

(M) *** DG 449 732-2 (2) [id.]. Cappuccilli, Verrett, Ghiaurov, Domingo, La Scala, Milan, Ch. & O, Abbado.

(M) *** EMI (SIS) CMS7 64339-2 (2) [Ang. CDMB 64339]. Milnes, Cossotto, Raimondi, Carreras, Amb. Op. Ch., New Philh. O, Muti.

(M) **(*) Decca 440 048-2 (2). Fischer-Dieskau, Suliotis, Ghiaurov, Pavarotti, Amb. Op. Ch., LPO, Gardelli.

(M) **(*) RCA GD 84516 (2) [4516-2-RG]. Warren, Rysanek, Bergonzi, Hines, Met. Op. Ch. & O, Leinsdorf.

(M) (*(**)) EMI mono CMS5 66447-2 (2) [CDMB 64944]. Callas, Mascherini, Tajo, Penno, Della Pergola, La Scala, Milan, Ch. & O, Victor de Sabata.

At times Abbado's tempi are unconventional, but with slow speeds he springs the rhythm so infectiously that the results are the more compelling. The whole performance gains from superb teamwork, for each of the principals – far more than is common – is meticulous about observing Verdi's detailed markings, above all those for *pianissimo* and *sotto voce*. Verrett, hardly powerful above the stave, yet makes a virtue out of necessity in floating glorious half-tones, and with so firm and characterful a voice she makes a highly individual, not at all conventional Lady Macbeth. As for Cappuccilli, he has never sung with such fine range of tone and imagination on record as here, and Plácido Domingo makes a real, sensitive character out of the small role of Macduff. Excellent recording, splendidly remastered as one of the first operas to be included in DG's 'Legendary Recordings' series, and now at mid-price and on two discs.

Muti's 1976 version of *Macbeth*, made at Abbey Road, appeared within weeks of Abbado's, confirming that, in this opera, new standards were being set on record. Though Muti and his team do not quite match the supreme distinction of Abbado and, later, Sinopoli, they provide a valid alternative. Both Milnes and Cossotto sing warmly and are richly convincing in their relatively conventional views of their roles, while the comfortable reverberation and warmth of the EMI recording conceal any slight shortcomings of ensemble. The reissue therefore provides a firm mid-priced recommendation for this opera, and it fits neatly on to a pair of CDs.

Fischer-Dieskau does not give a traditional performance in this great tragic role, for characteristically he points the words in full Lieder-style. Nor is he in his freshest voice, growing gritty in some climaxes; but it is still a marvellous, compelling performance which stands repeated hearing. Suliotis is – to put it kindly – a variable Lady Macbeth. In the first aria there are moments when her voice runs completely out of control, but she still has imagination, and her 'voice of a she-devil' (Verdi's words) is arguably the precise sound needed. Certainly she settles down into giving a striking and individual performance, while Ghiaurov as Banquo and Pavarotti as MacDuff sing with admirable poise. Gardelli and the LPO are treated to specially vivid recording which has transferred vibrantly to CD.

Leinsdorf's version brings a large-scale performance featuring three favourite principals from the Met. Leonie Rysanek here gives one of her finest performances on record, producing her firmest, creamiest sound for the Sleepwalking scene, even though the coloratura taxes her severely. Leonard Warren, much admired in this part before his untimely death (on stage, singing Don Carlo in *La forza del destino*), gives a strong, thoughtful reading, marred by the way the microphone exaggerates his vibrato. Carlo Bergonzi is a stylish, clear-toned Macduff. Good sound for its period.

The role of Lady Macbeth could hardly have been more perfectly suited to Maria Callas, and though there are serious flaws in this live recording of 1952 – evidently taken off a radio relay – the commanding presence, the magnetic musical imagination and the actual vocal quality abrasive enough to qualify as the 'she-wolf' Verdi wanted, make this a unique experience. In 1952 the vocal flaws that beset Callas were largely in the future, with thrilling sound in every register. Also Victor de Sabata, despite some odd misjudgements like his brisk tempo for the Sleepwalking scene, is comparably incisive as a conductor. Sadly, nothing else in the performance matches such mastery, with Enzo Mascherini a dull, uncharacterful Macbeth and only the resonant Italo Tajo as Banquo otherwise commanding attention. Scrubby, limited sound which most ears will still accommodate for the sake of such a performance.

I Masnadieri (complete).

(M) *** Ph. 422 423-2 (2). Caballé, Bergonzi, Raimondi, Cappuccilli, Amb. S., New Philh. O, Gardelli.

(M) **(*) Decca (IMS) Dig. 433 854-2 (2). Sutherland, Bonisolli, Manuguerra, Ramey, WNO Ch. & O, Bonynge.

Few will seriously identify with the hero-turned-brigand of *I Masnadieri* who stabs his beloved rather than lead her into a life of shame; but, on record, flaws of motivation are of far less moment than on stage.

The melodies may only fitfully be of Verdi's more memorable quality, but the musical structure and argument often look forward to a much later period with hints of *Forza*, *Don Carlo* and even *Otello*. With Gardelli as ever an urgently sympathetic Verdian, and a team of four excellent principals, splendidly recorded, the set can be warmly welcomed.

Sutherland's is a weightier view than Caballé took in the earlier, Philips recording, conveying more light and shade. The cabaletta for her great Act II aria brings a coloratura display, with Sutherland still at her very peak. Though Bonisolli sings with less refinement than Bergonzi on the rival set, he has great flair, as in his extra flourishes in the final ensemble of Act II. Manuguerra sings strongly too. He may not be as refined as his rival, Cappuccilli, but he sounds more darkly villainous. Ramey as Massimiliano sings with fine clarity, but the voice does not sound old enough for a father. The Welsh National Opera Chorus projects with the lustiness of stage experience, even if the Kingsway Hall acoustic clouds some choral detail slightly. Even so, the digital sound is very impressive in its fullness and depth, and at mid-price this is certainly worth considering, especially by Sutherland fans.

Nabucco: highlights.

(M) *** Decca 421 867-2; *421 867-4* (from complete recording with Gobbi, Suliotis, Cava, Previdi, V. State Op. Ch. & O, Gardelli).

(M) ** EMI CDM7 63092-2. Manuguerra, Scotto, Ghiaurov, Luchetti, Obraztsova, Amb. Op. Ch., Philh. O, Muti.

Suliotis's impressive contribution is well represented on the Decca highlights disc, and there are fine contributions too from Gobbi. Needless to say, the chorus *Va, pensiero* is given its place of honour and the selection runs for 58 minutes.

Though the EMI disc offers fairly generous measure (nearly 65 minutes) and has an impressive cast-list, it is much less involving, although the famous chorus, *Va, pensiero*, sounds well enough.

Otello (complete).

(M) *** RCA 74321 39501-2 (2) [RCD2-2951 full price]. Domingo, Scotto, Milnes, Amb. Op. Ch., Nat. PO, Levine.

(M) *** RCA GD 81969 (2) [1969-2-RG]. Vickers, Rysanek, Gobbi, Rome Op. Ch. & O, Serafin.

(M) *** EMI (SIS) CMS7 69308-2 (2) [Ang. CDMB 69308]. Vickers, Freni, Glossop, Ch. of German Op., Berlin, BPO, Karajan.

(M) (***) EMI mono CHS5 65751-2 (2) [CDMB 65751]. Vinay, Martinis, Schoefler, Dermota, V. State Op. Ch., VPO, Furtwängler.

(M) **(*) Decca (IMS) 440 045-2 (2). Cossutta, M. Price, Bacquier, V. Boys' Ch., V. State Op. Ch., VPO, Solti.

(M) (**(*)) RCA mono GD 60302 (2) [60302-2-RG]. Vinay, Valdengo, Nelli, Merriman, Assandri, NBC Ch. & SO, Toscanini.

On RCA, Domingo as Otello combines glorious heroic tone with lyrical tenderness. Scotto is not always sweet-toned in the upper register, and the big ensemble at the end of Act III brings obvious strain; nevertheless, it is a deeply felt performance which culminates in a most beautiful account of the all-important Act IV solos, the *Willow song* and *Ave Maria*, most affecting. Milnes too is challenged by his role: this Iago is a handsome, virile creature beset by the biggest of chips on the shoulder. In the transfer of the 1977 analogue original the voices are caught vividly and immediately, and the orchestral sound too is fuller and cleaner than in many more recent versions. Now reissued in RCA's Opera Treasury series, this becomes really competitive and is a clear first choice among mid-priced versions. In the USA it remains at full price for the moment.

No conductor is more understanding of Verdian pacing than Serafin and, with sound that hardly begins to show its age (1960), this presents two of the finest solo performances on any *Otello* recording of whatever period: the Iago of Tito Gobbi has never been surpassed for vividness of characterization and tonal subtlety; while the young Jon Vickers, with a voice naturally suited to this role, was in his prime as the Moor. Leonie Rysanek is a warm and sympathetic Desdemona, not always ideally pure-toned but tender and touching in one of her very finest recorded performances. The sense of presence in the open, well-balanced recording is the more vivid on CD, thanks to a first-rate transfer.

Karajan directs a big, bold and brilliant account, for the most part splendidly sung and with all the dramatic contrasts strongly underlined. There are several tiny, but irritating, statutory cuts, but otherwise on two mid-price CDs this is well worth considering. Freni's Desdemona is delightful, delicate and beautiful, while Vickers and Glossop are both positive and characterful, only occasionally forcing their tone and losing focus. The recording is clarified on CD.

Furtwängler, dedicated to the German repertory, at the 1951 Salzburg Festival broke with tradition by presenting Verdi's masterpiece, no doubt intending to rival the pre-war Toscanini. The result is incandescent, a performance of extremes. Set against rapt concentration and tender expressiveness in such passages as the Act I love duet and Desdemona's final scene, the fierily dramatic attack of the main drama is heightened all the more. So the oath duet of Otello and Iago in Act II is thrilling, and the clarity of both Ramon Vinay in the title-role and of Paul Schoeffler as a clean-cut, rather Germanic Iago adds to the bite. Vinay, who recorded the role with Toscanini four years earlier, has a focus and power ideally suited to the role, even if the voice is rarely beautiful. It matters surprisingly little that the Austrian Radio recording of the stage production often balances him distantly. Dragica Martinis, whose career was sadly short, is here revealed as a tender and charming Desdemona, every bit a match for her more celebrated colleagues. The orchestral sound is limited and dim, with intrusive stage-noises, but the electricity and atmosphere still come over well.

The warmth and tenderness of Solti's Vienna reading of *Otello* as well as its incisive sense of drama take one freshly by surprise. The recording is bright and atmospheric to match, which leaves the vocal contributions as a third and more debatable deciding point. Of the very finest quality is the singing of Margaret Price as Desdemona, a ravishing performance, with the most beautiful and varied tonal quality allied to deep imagination. Carlo Cossutta as Otello is not so characterful a singer but, more than most rivals, he sings with clear, incisive tone and obvious concern for musical qualities. Gabriel Bacquier gives a thoughtful, highly intelligent performance as Iago, but his relative weakness in the upper register brings obvious disappointment. The Decca recording, however, has a sense of spectacle (notably in the opening scene) and perspective which is particularly appealing.

Toscanini's historic 1947 reading suffers more than usual from dry, limited sound but in magnetic intensity it is irresistible, bringing home the biting power of Verdi's score as few other recorded performances ever have. Ramon Vinay makes a commanding Otello, baritonal in vocal colouring but firm and clear, with a fine feeling for words. Giuseppe Valdengo had few rivals among baritones of the time in this role, strong, animated and clean in attack, though the vocal differentiation between hero and villain is less marked than usual. Herva Nelli is sweet and pure if a little colourless as Desdemona. The recording prevents her from achieving a really gentle pianissimo, and Toscanini, for all his flowing lines, fails to allow the full repose needed.

Otello: highlights.

(M) *** EMI CDM7 63454-2 (from above recording, cond. Karajan.).

(B) **(*) [EMI Red Line Dig. CDR5 72105]. Domingo, Ricciarelli, Diaz, La Scala, Milan, Ch. & O, Maazel.

The Karajan highlights disc offers a generally well-managed selection (though of less than an hour), including excerpts from all four Acts, with a substantial excerpt from Act IV including Freni's touching *Willow song* and *Ave Maria*, then moving on to the tragic finale. The sound is full, appropriately weighty in the score's more spectacular moments.

On EMI Red Line comes a fine performance from Domingo and taut, subtle control from Maazel, particularly good in the spacious, tenderly emotional treatment of the final scene. The unsinister Iago of Justino Diaz is disappointingly negative. Ricciarelli as Desdemona sings most affectingly, with pianissimos beautifully caught in the *Willow song* and *Ave Maria*. One snag is the sound, which is curiously recessed, with the voices often not quite in focus and with little sense of presence.

Rigoletto (complete).

(B) *** Ph. Dig. Duo 462 158-2 (2) [id.]. Bruson, Gruberová, Shicoff, Fassbaender, Lloyd, St Cecilia Ac., Rome, Ch. & O, Sinopoli.

(M) **(*) RCA GD 86506 (2) [6506-2-RG]. Merrill, Moffo, Kraus, Elias, Flagello, RCA Italiana Op. Ch. & O, Solti.

(B) ** Decca Double 443 853-2 (2) [id.]. MacNeil, Sutherland, Cioni, Siepi, Malagu, Academy of Santa Cecilia, Rome, Ch. & O, Sanzogno.

(BB) ** Naxos Dig. 8.660013/4 (2) [id.]. Tumagian, Ferrarini, Ramiro, Ch. & Slovak RSO (Bratislava), Rahbari.

(M) *(*) EMI (SIS) CMS5 66037-2 (2) [Ang. CDMB 66037]. Milnes, Sills, Kraus, Ramey, Amb. Op. Ch., Philh. O, Rudel.

(B) *(*) Arte Nova/BMG Dig. 74321 46499-2 (2) [id.]. Tichy, Komov, DeFeis, Besenyei, Monarcha, Romanian Nat. Op. Ch., Europa SO, Gröhs.

Edita Gruberová might have been considered an unexpected choice for Gilda, remarkable for her brilliant coloratura rather than for deeper expression, yet here she makes the heroine a tender, feeling creature, emotionally vulnerable yet vocally immaculate. Similarly, Renato Bruson as Rigoletto does far more than produce a stream of velvety tone, detailed and intense, responding to the conductor and combining beauty with dramatic bite. Even more remarkable is the brilliant success of Neil Shicoff as the Duke, more than a match for his most distinguished rivals. Here the *Quartet* becomes a genuine climax. Brigitte Fassbaender as Maddalena is sharply unconventional but vocally most satisfying. Sinopoli's speeds, too, are unconventional at times, but the fresh look he provides makes this one of the most exciting Verdi operas on disc, helped by full and vivid recording, consistently well balanced. This is a first choice for this opera, irrespective of price.

Anna Moffo makes a charming Gilda in the Solti set of 1963. Solti at times presses too hard, but this is a strong and dramatic reading, with Robert Merrill producing a glorious flow of dark, firm tone in the name-part. Alfredo Kraus is as stylish as ever as the Duke, and this rare example of his voice at its freshest should not be missed. A good bargain, though there are statutory cuts in the text.

The earlier Sutherland recording came a decade before her triumphant partnership with Pavarotti. Cornell MacNeil was a resonant but uncharacterful Rigoletto, although Cioni, if conventional, sings well enough as the Duke of Mantova. Sutherland's own performance epitomizes her soft-grained style at its most extreme. The result is often intensely beautiful, particularly in *Caro nome*, but as a dramatic experience it cannot compare with the later Decca set. Nino Sanzogno jogs through everything very neatly, but it is the fine technical quality of the recording and the reliability of the singing that engage the attention, rather than the drama.

Rahbari conducts a neat but rather underpowered account of *Rigoletto*, well played and recorded but lacking full Verdian bite. Though Eduard Tumagian is young-sounding baritone for the title-role of the hunchback jester, lacking dramatic weight, he sings cleanly and with feeling. The Gilda of Alida Ferrarini is bright and fresh, agile in *Caro nome* with a tight trill at the end. There and elsewhere her singing is slightly marred by an overfondness for under-the-note coloration which, with so precise a voice, often sounds flat. Yordy Ramiro is over-parted as the Count, with much of his singing crisp and clean, though often strained on top. The quartet in the final Act is made the more attractive by having four fresh young voices.

Rudel's late-1970s version on EMI, well recorded, can be recommended to devotees of Beverly Sills but not really to anyone else. This was her last major opera recording before her retirement, and the voice as recorded was no longer beautiful, the tone shallow and often tremulous. Milnes as Rigoletto is just as strong as in the earlier Sutherland/Bonynge set on Decca, and Kraus also effectively repeats the success of his singing on two earlier sets. But with Rudel's refreshing direction at times marred by excessive tensions, this is a reissue of limited value.

Recorded in Vienna – not live but on stage in a theatre, which brings some odd recording balances – the Arte Nova set offers an enjoyable ensemble performance with young-sounding principals but which yet lacks dramatic bite. The Viennese baritone, Georg Tichy, has a splendid voice, and his phrasing is generally sensitive, but when it comes to the big moments – as for example the aria, *Cortigiani, vil razza dannata*, or the final duet – he fails to give more than a superficial idea of the emotions involved. As Gilda the young American coloratura, Doreen DeFeis, sings very sweetly in lyrical music, as for example *Tutte le feste*, but she grows shrill at the top under pressure, and her coloratura is not always quite agile enough. The Bulgarian, Sergei Komov, has a powerful tenor that too readily grows coarse, with excessive underlining distorting the melodies. Among the others, the bass, Janusz Monarcha, sings most resonantly as both Monterone and Sparafucile. None of the principals is helped by the tendency of the conductor, Wolfgang Gröhs, to rush in vigorous music, though by contrast he is most considerate of the singers elsewhere. A libretto is provided in Italian and German with only a synopsis in English.

Rigoletto: highlights.

(M) *(*) Teldec/Warner Dig. 0630 15807-9 (from complete recording, with Leech, Agache, Vaduva, Ramey, Larmore, Welsh Nat. Op. Ch. & O, Rizzi).

This is not one of Carlo Rizzi's more impressive opera recordings. In the title-role Alexander Agache has the benefit of a glorious voice, but his characterization of the hunchback is sketchy, lacking bite and conviction. Richard Leech sings strongly as the Duke, but without charm. As Gilda, Leontina Vaduva uses her light, sweet, pretty voice very capably, poised as well as agile, but she is not helped by the general slackness.

Simon Boccanegra (complete).

✿ (M) *** DG Originals 449 752-2 (2) [id.]. Freni, Cappuccilli, Ghiaurov, Van Dam, Carreras, La Scala, Milan, Ch. and O, Abbado.

(M) (***) EMI mono CMS7 63513-2 (2). Gobbi, Christoff, De los Angeles, Campora, Monachesi, Dari, Rome Op. Chor & O, Santini.

(BB) **(*) Discover Dig. DICD 920225/6 [id.]. Tumagian, Gauci, Aragall, Mikulas, Sardinero, BRTN Philharmonic Ch. and O, Alexander Rahbari.

Abbado's 1977 recording of *Simon Boccanegra* is one of the most beautiful Verdi sets ever made. Under

Abbado the playing of the orchestra is brilliantly incisive as well as refined, so that the drama is underlined by extra sharpness of focus. The cursing of Paolo after the great Council Chamber scene makes the scalp prickle, with the chorus muttering in horror and the bass clarinet adding a sinister comment, here beautifully moulded. Cappuccilli, always intelligent, gives a far more intense and illuminating performance than the one he recorded for RCA earlier in his career. He may not match Gobbi in range of colour and detail, but he too gives focus to the performance; and Ghiaurov as Fiesco sings beautifully too. Freni as Maria Boccanegra sings with freshness and clarity, while Van Dam is an impressive Paolo. With electrically intense choral singing as well, this is a set to outshine even Abbado's superb *Macbeth* with the same company, superbly transferred to CD (see above). The set is now all the more desirable at mid-price.

Tito Gobbi's portrait of the tragic Doge of Genoa is one of his greatest on record, and it emerges all the more impressively when it is set against equally memorable performances by Boris Christoff as Fiesco and Victoria de los Angeles as Amelia. The Recognition scene between father and daughter has never been done more movingly on record; nor has the great ensemble, which crowns the Council Chamber scene, been so powerfully and movingly presented, and that without the help of stereo recording. The transfer is full and immediate, giving a vivid sense of presence to the voices, though tape-hiss is on the high side.

On the Discover bargain label Rahbari's well-paced reading is newly recorded in good digital sound with strong casting. Excellent East European principals are joined by the long-established Spanish tenor, Giacomo Aragall, and the baritone, Vincente Sardinero. Miriam Gauci is a vibrant, sympathetic Amelia, and though Eduard Tumagian is not the most characterful Boccanegra and Peter Mikulas could be darker-toned in the bass role of Fiesco, their voices are clear and well-focused, despite backward balance. Libretto in Italian only. Good value.

Stiffelio (complete).

(M) *** Ph. 422 432-2 (2). Carreras, Sass, Manuguerra, Ganzarolli, Austrian R. Ch. & SO, Gardelli.

Coming just before the great trio of masterpieces, *Rigoletto*, *Il Trovatore* and *La Traviata*, *Stiffelio* is still a sharply telling work, largely because of the originality of the relationships and the superb final scene in which Stiffelio reads from the pulpit the parable of the woman taken in adultery. Gardelli directs a fresh performance, at times less lively than Queler's of *Aroldo* but with more consistent singing, notably from Carreras and Manuguerra. First-rate recording from Philips, typical of this fine series.

La Traviata (complete).

(B) **(*) CfP CD-CFPD 4450 (2) [(M) id. import]. De los Angeles, Del Monte, Sereni, Rome Op. Ch. & O, Serafin.

(M) **(*) Decca 411 877-2 (2) [id.]. Sutherland, Bergonzi, Merrill, Ch. & O of Maggio Musicale Fiorentino, Pritchard.

(B) **(*) DG Double 453 115-2 (2) [id.]. Scotto, Raimondi, Bastianini, La Scala, Milan, Ch. & O, Votto.

(M) **(*) RCA 09026 68885-2 (2) [id.]. Anna Moffo, Richard Tucker, Robert Merrill, Rome Op. Ch. & O, Previtali.

(M) (*(**)) EMI mono CMS5 66450-2 (2) [CDMB 66450-2]. Callas, Di Stefano, Bastianini, La Scala Ch. & O, Giulini.

(M) (**) RCA mono GD 60303 (2) [60303-2-RG]. Albanese, Peerce, Merrill, NBC Ch. & SO, Toscanini.

(BB) *(*) Naxos 8.660011/2 (2) [id.]. Krause, Ramiro, Tichy, Ch. & Slovak RSO (Bratislava), Rahbari.

Even when Victoria de los Angeles made this EMI recording in the late 1950s, the role of Violetta lay rather high for her voice. Nevertheless it drew from her much beautiful singing, not least in the coloratura display at the end of Act I which, though it may lack easily ringing top notes, has delightful sparkle and flexibility. As to the characterization, De los Angeles was a far more sympathetically tender heroine than is common; though neither the tenor nor the baritone begins to match her in artistry, their performances are both sympathetic and feeling, thanks in part to the masterly conducting of Serafin. All the traditional cuts are made, not just the second stanzas. The CD transfer is vivid and clear and at bargain price this is worth any collector's money, though only a synopsis is provided.

In Sutherland's 1963 recording of *La Traviata*, it is true that her diction is poor, but it is also true that she has rarely sung on record with such deep feeling as in the final scene. The *Addio del passato* (both stanzas included and sung with an unexpected lilt) merely provides a beginning, for the duet with Bergonzi is most winning, and the final death scene, *Se una pudica vergine*, is overwhelmingly beautiful. This is not a sparkling Violetta, true, but it is vocally closer to perfection than almost any other in a complete set. Bergonzi is an attractive Alfredo and Merrill an efficient Germont.

It is worth having the 1962 DG La Scala set just for the moving and deeply considered singing of Renata Scotto as Violetta, fresher in voice than in her later, HMV set. In a role which has usually eluded the efforts of prima donnas on record, she gives one of the most complete portraits, with thrilling coloratura in Act I and with the closing scene unforgettably moving. It is sad that the rest of the cast is largely undistinguished. Gianni Raimondi as Alfredo is stirring if not refined, and Bastianini is a coarse Germont *père*. The conductor, Anonino Votto, gives routine direction but certainly keeps the music alive. The usual stage cuts are observed, but the recording is vividly atmospheric and, reissued on a DG Double, this should not be dismissed. There are good notes and a more-than-adequate cued synopsis.

Anna Moffo makes a most beautiful Violetta in a performance that is never less than sympathetic. She is not as assured as she might be in the coloratura of Act I, but everywhere else her unaffected manner and care for phrasing and tonal nuances make for a performance to match almost any in the catalogue at whatever price. Richard Tucker too makes a strong and on the whole not coarse Alfred and, though Robert Merrill is not as understanding a Germont here as he was in the earlier Sutherland set, the casting is more consistent than in many full-priced versions. The conducting of Previtali could be more colourful and the performing cuts usual at that time are made, but the recording has come up excellently, and this is certainly well worth considering.

Callas's version with Giulini was recorded in 1955, three years before the Ghione Lisbon set, when the voice was fresher. There is no more vividly dramatic a performance on record than this, unmatchable in conveying Violetta's agony; sadly, the sound, always limited, grows crumbly towards the end. It is sad too that Bastianini sings so lumpishly as Germont *père*, even in the great duet of Act II, while di Stefano also fails to match his partner in the supreme test of the final scene. The transfer is fair.

Toscanini's live recording, made in December 1946, was one of the first he made of complete operas in his final years in New York, following after *La Bohème* in the previous February. Here, even more than in the Puccini and certainly more than in his later Verdi recordings, his speeds are not just fast but relentless. Even so, the high tension of the drama is hair-raising, and both Licia Albanese and Jan Peerce respond impressively, not letting the strict discipline mar their vocal production. The sound, as always with Toscanini recordings of this period, is painfully dry but very clear and forward.

Like the parallel recording of *Rigoletto*, the Naxos version of *La Traviata* is often underpowered and lacks bite but offers an attractive performance from Monika Krause as Violetta. The big test of *Ah dita alla giovine* in her duet with Germont in Act II brings an exquisitely shaded pianissimo, and her *Addio del passato* in Act III is no less touching for being taken at a genuine andante, with less rhythmic freedom than usual. As in *Rigoletto*, Yordy Ramiro sounds over-parted as Alfredo, with a flutter in the voice occasionally becoming intrusive, but he generally sings cleanly. The Germont of Georg Tichy is among the most prosaic on disc, wooden and unresponsive even to Krause's most exquisite singing. The sound, as in other Bratislava recordings, is clean and atmospheric. As in other Naxos operas, copious tracking is linked to a detailed synopsis and full Italian text.

La Traviata: highlights.

(M) *** Decca 458 211-2 [id.] (from above complete set, with Sutherland, Bergonzi, Merrill; cond. Pritchard).

(M) *** EMI CDM5 65573-2 (from complete set, with Scotto, Kraus, Bruson; cond. Muti).

(B) **(*) DG Classikon 439 421-2; *439 421-4* [(M) id. import]. Cotrubas, Domingo, Milnes, Bav. State Op. Ch. & State O, Carlos Kleiber.

(M) ** Decca 452 734-2 [id.] (from complete set, with Renata Tebaldi, Gianni Poggi, Aldo Protti, St Cecilia Ac., Rome, Ch. & O, cond. Molinari-Pradelli).

Decca's highlights from Sutherland's first (1963) recording make a clear first choice. They come handsomely packaged in Decca's Opera Gala series, with a generous selection (73 minutes) and including a full translation. Sutherland is in ravishing voice, and Bergonzi is also in excellent form. The set is discussed more fully above.

Muti's complete set is at full price and it isn't a first choice, so many will be glad to have this 61-minute, mid-price disc of highlights, including both the Act I and Act III *Preludes* and a well-balanced selection from each of the three Acts, with most of the key numbers included.

For many, Cotrubas makes an ideal star in *Traviata*, but unfortunately the microphone-placing in Carlos Kleiber's complete set (DG 415 132-2) exaggerates technical flaws and the vibrato becomes too obvious at times. Such is her magic that some will forgive the faults, for her characterization combines strength with vulnerability, but Kleiber's direction is equally controversial with more than a hint of Toscanini-like rigidity in the party music and an occasionally uncomfortable insistence on discipline. However, the strong contributions of Domingo and Milnes make this bargain-priced Classikon highlights CD very worthwhile, as it contains 71 minutes of music, including the two *Preludes*. The documentation is well thought out, except that it omits a track-by-track synopsis of the narrative.

Even earlier than Decca's Santa Cecilia *Forza del destino*, this 1954 Tebaldi *La Traviata* emerges on CD in astonishingly vivid and atmospheric stereo. Though Violetta was not Tebaldi's ideal role, there is much superb singing from her here. The delicacy of her phrasing is a delight, bringing a most tender portrait. Her refinement contrasts with the relative coarseness of Gianni Poggi as Alfredo and the lack of imagination of Aldo Protti as Germont. Yet this CD is well worth hearing for Tebaldi in her early prime.

La Traviata (complete, in English).

(BB) **(*) CfP Silver Double CDCFPSD 4799 (2) [(B) id.]. Masterson, Brecknock, Du Plessis, E. Nat. Op. Ch. & O, Mackerras.

Mackerras directs a vigorous, colourful reading which brings out the drama, and Valerie Masterson is at last given the chance on record she has so long deserved. The voice is caught beautifully, if not always very characterfully, and John Brecknock makes a fine Alfredo, most effective in the final scene. Christian Du Plessis' baritone is less suitable for recording. The conviction of the whole enterprise is infectious – but be warned, Verdi in English has a way of sounding on record rather like Gilbert and Sullivan.

Il Trovatore (complete).

❁ (M) *** RCA 74321 39504-2 (2) [6194-2-RC full price]. Leontyne Price, Domingo, Milnes, Cossotto, Amb. Op. Ch., New Philh. O, Mehta.

(M) (***) RCA mono GD 86643 (2) [6643-2-RG]. Milanov, Bjoerling, Warren, Barbieri, Robert Shaw Ch., RCA Victor O, Cellini.

(B) *** DG Double 453 118-2 (2) [(M) id. import]. Stella, Bergonzi, Cossotto, Bastianini, La Scala, Milan, Ch. & O, Serafin.

(M) **(*) EMI CMS7 69311-2 (2). Price, Bonisolli, Cappucilli, Obraztsova, Raimondi, German Op. Ch., Berlin Ch., BPO, Karajan.

(B) ** Ph. Duo Dig. 446 151-2 [id.]. Carreras, Ricciarelli, Mazurok, Toczyska, Lloyd, ROHCG Ch. & O, C. Davis.

(M) ** EMI CMS7 63640-2 (2). Corelli, Tucci, Simionato, Merrill, Rome Op. Ch. & O, Schippers.

(B) * Decca Double 448 743-2 (2). Tebaldi, Del Monaco, Savarese, Simionato, Maggio Musicale Fiorentino Ch. & O, Erede.

(B) * Naxos Dig. 8.660023/4 [id.]. Frusoni, Longhi, Tschistiakova, Servile, Budapest Festival Ch., Hungarian State Op. O, Will Humburg.

The soaring curve of Leontyne Price's rich vocal line is immediately thrilling in her famous Act I aria, and it sets the style of the RCA performance, full-bodied and with the tension consistently held at the highest levels. The choral contribution is superb; the famous *Soldiers'* and *Anvil choruses* are marvellously fresh and dramatic. When *Di quella pira* comes, the orchestra opens with tremendous gusto and Domingo sings with a ringing, heroic quality worthy of Caruso himself. There are many dramatic felicities, and Sherrill Milnes is in fine voice throughout; but perhaps the highlight of the set is the opening section of Act III, when Azucena finds her way to Conte di Luna's camp. The ensuing scene with Fiorenza Cossotto is vocally and dramatically quite electrifying.

Though dating from 1952, using a cut text as in the Met. production, the Cellini version brings a vivid reminder of that great opera house at a key period. Milanov, though at times a little raw in Leonora's coloratura, gives a glorious, commanding performance, never surpassed on record, with the voice at its fullest. Bjoerling and Warren too are in ringing voice, and Barbieri is a superb Azucena, with Cellini – rarely heard on record – proving an outstanding Verdian.

There is room in the catalogue for a really recommendable bargain set of *Il Trovatore*, and Serafin's DG Double La Scala set fits the bill nicely. For the present DG Double reissue, the documentation has been improved with the synopsis well cued, and the absence of a libretto/translation matters less in such a popular opera where the narrative is easy enough to follow from the very basic synopsis. The performance itself is immensely enjoyable, with the contributions of Cossotto as Azucena and Carlo Bergonzi, splendid as Manrico, as satisfying in those roles as almost any on record. Stella and Bastianini give flawed performances, but they have many impressive moments; as Leonora's opening aria readily demonstrates, Stella is in full voice and identifies strongly with the heroine. The conducting of Serafin is crisp and stylish, and the 1963 recording is transferred to CD with fine vividness, yet has plenty of atmosphere. Indeed this splendidly red-blooded performance often vies with the famous Mehta RCA set in dramatic impact. Excellent value.

The later Karajan set with Leontyne Price promised much but proved disappointing, largely because of the thickness and strange balances of the recording, the product of multi-channel techniques exploited over-enthusiastically. So the introduction to Manrico's aria, *Di quella pira*, provides full-blooded orchestral sound, but then the orchestra fades down for the entry of the tenor, who in any case is in coarse voice. In other places he sings more sensitively, but at no point does this version match that of Mehta on RCA. CD clarifies the sound but makes the flaws in the original recording all the more evident.

Sir Colin Davis offers a fresh and direct, slightly understated reading. The refinement of the digital recording makes for a wide, clean separation but, with the backward placing of the orchestra, the result does not have the dramatic impact of the Mehta RCA version. The *Anvil chorus* sounds rather clinical and other important numbers lack the necessary swagger. Ricciarelli's Leonora is most moving, conveying an element of vulnerability in the character, but Carreras lacks the full confidence of a natural Manrico. He is less effective in the big, extrovert moments, best in such inward-looking numbers as *Ah si ben mio*. Toczyska's voice is presented rather grittily in the role of Azucena. Mazurok similarly is not flattered by the microphones but, with clean, refined ensemble, this emerges as the opposite of a hackneyed opera.

The Schippers set of *Il Trovatore* is a long way short of the ideal, but Merrill's Conte di Luna is characterful and firmly sung, if sometimes ungainly. Simionato is an excellent Azucena; Tucci, though less assured than her colleagues, sings very beautifully. Corelli is at his powerful best as Manrico, a really heroic, if not always subtle, tenor. His *Di quella pira* displays rather crude histrionics, but its gutsiness is welcome when Schippers' conducting is inclined to be rigid, somewhat preventing the temperature from rising; otherwise Schippers' incisiveness is compelling in an atmospheric recording that is characteristic of the Rome Opera House.

Even at Double Decca price this Tebaldi/Del Monaco *Trovatore* is a non-starter. Del Monaco has exactly the right heroic tone-colour for Manrico, and it was a great pity that he failed so lamentably to do much more than bawl away. It is all very exciting for a few minutes but so wearing after a time. Tebaldi, as always, has some lovely moments, but in the last resort there is some lack of imagination in her interpretation. Her singing generally is technically flawless, but one rarely feels that new insight into the meaning of a phrase which many less reliable singers sometimes give. About the best singing in the set comes from Simionato. The conducting too does not have quite the lift and dramatic tension this opera above all calls for, although the early stereo (1956) is effective enough in conveying atmosphere. There is no libretto, merely an uncued synopsis.

The Naxos version brings a direct and alert reading from the conductor, Will Humburg, with excellent playing from the Hungarian orchestra. By contrast, the singing hardly rises above the routine, which in this opera is a fatal disadvantage. Though Maurizio Frusoni as Manrico has ample power, the voice is often unsteady, and Daniela Longhi as Leonora loses focus at the top. More impressive is Roberto Servile as di Luna, with firm, clear tone, though it is hardly a characterful voice. The recording has been produced with a fair attempt at simulating stage noises and movement, though the acoustic is too washy.

COLLECTIONS

Arias & excerpts (recorded 1906–16, with Gadski, Hempel, Scotti, Alda, Ruffo, Tetrazzini, Jacoby, Amato, Gluck, Schumann-Heink) from: *Requiem; Aida; Un ballo in maschera; Don Carlo; La forza del destino; I Lombardi; Macbeth; Otello; Rigoletto; La Traviata; Il Trovatore*.
(M) (***) RCA mono 09026 61242-2 [id.]. Enrico Caruso.

Like the miscellaneous Caruso collections transferred at the same time, these recordings were restored by Thomas Stockham using the Soundstream digital process which removes unwanted horn resonances; the improvement in sound is phenomenal. The voice often sounds pristine, and only the heavily scored accompaniments serve to remind the listener of the early recording dates. There are many famous recordings here and it is good that other singers are featured too, Gadski in *La fatal pietra* from *Aida*, Hemel in *La rivedrà nell'estasi* from *Un ballo in maschera*, Scotti in the excerpts from Act I of *Don Carlo* and Act III of *La forza del destino*, and so on. The version of the *Quartet* from *Rigoletto* (*Bella figlia*) includes Tetrazzini, Josephine Jacoby and Amato. The programme is well chosen and the sound revelatory. Sample the superbly stylish *Questa o quella* or *La donna è mobile* (from *Rigoletto*), or the soaring *Ah sì, ben mio* (*Il Trovatore*), all recorded in 1908, which sound amazingly free from the mechanical problems of the early recording process. Surface noise is reduced, but still present; yet the ear soon programmes it out.

Arias, Volume I: *Don Carlos: Tu che la vanità. Ernani: Surta è la notte . . . Ernani! Ernani, involami. Macbeth: Nel di della vittoria . . . Vieni!, t'affretta; La luce langue; Una machia è qui tuttora! (Sleepwalking scene). Nabucco: Ben io t'invenni . . . Anch'io dischiuso un giorno.*
(M) *** EMI CDM5 66460-2 [id.]. Maria Callas, Philh. O, Nicola Rescigno.

Originally issued with the sobriquet, 'Verdi heroines', this recital marked Callas's only visit to record at Abbey Road, in September 1958. Much of its content shows the great diva at her very finest. Dismiss the top-note wobbles from your mind, and the rest has you enthralled by the vividness of characterization as well as the musical imagination. It is sad that Callas did not record the role of Lady Macbeth complete. Here *La luce langue* is not as intense as the Act I aria and the Sleepwalking scene, which are both unforgettable, while she holds the tension masterfully in the long Don Carlos scene. Abigaille, Elvira and Elisabetta all come out as real figures, sharply individual. Finely balanced recording, with the CD transfer well up to the high standard of the Callas Edition. This is the disc to choose from three collections of Verdi arias.

Arias, Volume II: *Aroldo: Ciel ch'io respir!. . . Salvami, salvami tu gran Dio! O Cielo! Dove son io. Don Carlo: Non pianger, mia compagna; O don fatale. Otello: Mia madre aveva una povera ancella . . . Piangea cantando . . . Ave Maria piena di grazia.*
(M) **(*) EMI CDM5 66461-2 [id.]. Maria Callas, Paris Conservatoire O, Nicola Rescigno.

Arias, Volume III: *Aida: Ritorna vincitor. Attila: Liberamente or piangi!. . . Oh! ne! fuggente nuvolo. Un ballo in maschera: Ecco l'orrido campo; Morrò, ma prima in grazia. Il Corsaro: Egli non riede ancor . . . Non so le tetre immagini; Né sulla terra . . . Vola talor dal carcere . . . Verrò . . . Ah conforto è sol la speme. Il Trovatore: Tacea la notte placida . . . Di tale amor. I vespri siciliani: Arrigo! ah parli a un core.*
(M) **(*) CDM5 66462-2 [id.]. Maria Callas, Paris Conservatoire O or Paris Opéra O, Resigno.

For her second and third collections of Verdi arias, Callas went to Paris in December 1963 and February 1964 (Volume II); and then she began a third compilation in April 1964, returning in 1965 and 1969. She approved some of the tracks for release in 1972, and the rest first appeared in 1978. In the second volume, the Shakespearean challenge of the Desdemona sequence from *Otello* is commandingly taken, very distinctive, and all the singing is dramatic. Allowances have to be made, but there is much here to cherish. The third is much more uneven, with the later items coming from a period when the voice had detriorated, particularly in the items recorded as late as 1969. There are exceptions, of course: Aida's *Ritorna vincitor*, vehemently done, is magnificent, and the two arias from *Il Corsaro*, although among her last recordings, show the vocal technique at its most assured (particularly in the legato phrasing) and the artistry at its most commanding. So this third disc is essential for Callas devotees; it can be recommended to others only with some reservations.

Arias: *Aida: Ritorna vincitor!; Qui Radamès verrà! O patria mia. Il Trovatore: Che più t'arresti; Tacea la notte;* (i) *Di tale amor. Timor di me?; D'amor sull'ali rosee.*
(M) *** RCA 09026 68883-2 [id.]. Leontyne Price, Rome Opera O, Oliviero de Fabritiis or Artur Basile; (i) with Laura Londi – PUCCINI: *Arias*. **(*)

When this record was first issued, in 1961, we commented that, compared with her complete set, the singing of the *Aida* arias was less successful here and that Leontyne Price was obviously relaxing more there so that her natural sense of drama came across magnificently. In the *Trovatore* arias, too, we noted a certain reluctance to soften the voice in the way we had heard often enough in the opera house. Since then this recital, known as the 'blue album' (the colour of the original LP is reproduced on the CD), has justly become a collectors' item; listening to the glorious flow of tone, one can understand why. The recording was always excellent and the CD brings added bloom to the sound.

Arias & duets: *Un ballo in maschera: Teco io sto. Il Corsaro: Egli non riede ancora! Don Carlos: Non pianger, mia compagna. Giovanna d'Arco: Qui! Qui! Dove più s'apre libero il ciela; O fatidica foresta. Jérusalem: Ave Maria. I Masnadieri: Dall'infame banchetto io m'involai; Tu del mio; Carlo vive. Otello: Già nella notte densa; Ave Maria. Il Trovatore: Timor di me; D'amor sull'ali rosee; Tu vedrai che amor in terr. I vespri siciliani: Arrigo! Ah, parli a un cor.*
(M) *** RCA GD 86534 [6534-2-RG]. Katia Ricciarelli, Plácido Domingo, Rome PO or St Cecilia Ac. O, Gavazzeni.

At mid-price this collection of Verdi arias and duets from two star singers, both in fresh voice, makes a good bargain. The inclusion of rarities adds to the attractions, and though the sound is not the most modern, it is more than acceptable in the bright digital transfer.

Choruses from: *Aida; La Battaglia di Legnano; Don Carlo; Ernani; La forza del destino; Macbeth; Nabucco; Otello; La Traviata; Il Trovatore.*
(BB) *** Naxos Dig. 8.550241; *4.550241* [id.]. Slovak Philharmonic Ch. & RSO, Oliver Dohnányi.

The super-bargain Naxos collection by the excellent Slovak Philharmonic Choir brings very realistic sound and the slightly recessed choral balance in the Bratislava Radio Concert Hall is very natural: it certainly does not lack impact and, in the *Fire chorus* from *Otello*, detail registers admirably. Under Oliver Dohnányi's lively direction the chorus sings with admirable fervour. The collection ends resplendently with the Triumphal scene from *Aida*, omitting the ballet but with the fanfare trumpets blazing out on either side most tellingly. With a playing time of 56 minutes this is excellent value in every respect.

Choruses: *Aida: Gloria all'Egitto. Don Carlos: Spuntato ecco il dì. I Lombardi: Gerusalem!; O Signore, dal tetto natio. Macbeth: Patria oppressa! Nabucco: Va, pensiero; Gli arredi festivi. Otello: Fuoco di gioia! Il Trovatore: Vedi! le fosche; Or co' dadi . . . Squilli, echeggi.*
(M) **(*) Ph. 462 064-2. Dresden State Op. Ch. & O, Varviso.

Varviso's collection of choruses brings polished and full-bodied but at times soft-grained performances, beautifully supported by the magnificent Dresden orchestra. Gentler choruses are excellent, but the dramatic ones lack something in bite. One of the highlights is the *Fire chorus* from *Otello*, in which the choral and woodwind detail suggests the flickering flames of bonfires burning in Otello's honour. The recording is warmly atmospheric and natural, and with any reservations this is still very enjoyable. But the selection is short measure at barely 46 minutes.

Choruses: *I due Foscari: Tace il vento. Ernani: Evviva! beviam! beviam!; Un patto! . . . Si ridesti. I Lombardi: Gerusalem. Luisa Miller: Ti desta, Luisa. Macbeth: Patria opressa!; Che faceste? dite su! (Witches' chorus). Nabucco: Va, pensiero (Chorus of Hebrew slaves; Gli arredi festivi. Il Trovatore: Vedi le fosche (Anvil chorus). I vespri siciliani: Si celebri alfine tra canti, tra fior.*
(B) **(*) EMI Eminence CD-EMX 2272 [(M) id. import]. Welsh Nat. Op. Ch. & O, Richard Armstrong.

The Welsh National Opera made its initial reputation by the strength of its chorus work and, while these performances are not always refined, they are for the most part vivid and lusty, with plenty of character and rhythmic feeling. The natural eloquence of the Welsh often surfaces in lyrical moments, but the famous *Va, pensiero* from *Nabucco*, although effective, is not as memorable as one have might expected. The witches in *Macbeth*, however, are rather quaintly characterized to provide a moment of light relief. Excellent (1979) analogue recording, full and clear, but it is surprising, when the overall programme timing is only 46 minutes, that space was not found for the famous Triumphal scene from *Aida*.

'The world of Verdi': (i) *Aida: Celeste Aida;* (ii) *Grand march and ballet*. (iii) *La forza del destino: Pace, pace mio Dio*. (iv) *Luisa Miller: O! Fede negar potessi ... Quando le sere al placido*. (v) *Nabucco: Va pensiero*. (vi) *Otello: Credo. Rigoletto:* (vii) *Caro nome;* (viii) *La donna è mobile;* (vii; viii; ix) Quartet: *Belle figlia dell'amore*. (x) *La Traviata: Prelude, Act I;* (vii; xi) *Brindisi: Libiamo ne'lieti calici. Il Trovatore:* (xii) *Anvil chorus;* (xiii) *Strida la vampa;* (viii) *Di quella pira. I vespri siciliani:* (xiv) *Mercè, diletti amiche*.
(M) *** Decca 433 221-1; *433 221-4*. (i) Vickers; (ii) Rome Op. Ch. & O, Solti; (iii) G. Jones; (iv) Bergonzi; (v) Amb. S., LSO, Abbado; (vi) Evans; (vii) Sutherland; (viii) Pavarotti; (ix) Tourangeau, Milnes; (x) Maggio Musicale O, Fiorentino, Pritchard; (xi) Bergonzi; (xii) L. Op. Ch., Bonynge; (xiii) Horne; (xiv) Chiara.

Opening with the *Chorus of the Hebrew slaves* from *Nabucco* and closing with Pavarotti's *Di quella pira* from *Il Trovatore*, this quite outstandingly red-blooded Verdi compilation should surely tempt any novice to explore further into Verdi's world, yet at the same time it provides a superbly arranged 74-minute concert in its own right. The choice of items and performances demonstrates a shrewd knowledge of both popular Verdi and the Decca catalogue, for not a single performance disappoints. Joan Sutherland's melting 1971 *Caro nome* with its exquisite trills is the first of three splendid excerpts from *Rigoletto*, ending with the famous Quartet, and other highlights include Dame Gwyneth Jones's glorious *Pace, pace, mio Dio*, introduced of course by the sinisterly scurrying *Forza del destino* motif, Sir Geraint Evans's superb account of Iago's evil *Credo* from *Otello* – here the Decca sound adds to the riveting impact – and Marilyn Horne's dark-timbred *Strida la vampa* from *Trovatore*. Solti, too, is at his most electric in the great March scene from *Aida*. The stereo throughout is splendidly vivid, and this mid-priced collection is worth every penny of its modest cost.

Victoria, Tomás Luis de (*c*. 1548–1611)

Mass and Motet: *O magnum mysterium*. Mass and Motet: *O quam gloriosum. Ardens est cor meum; Ave Maria*.
(BB) *** Naxos Dig. 8.550575 [id.]. Oxford Camerata, Jeremy Summerly (with Alonso LOBO: *Versa est in luctum* ***).

These Masses are already familiar from recordings by David Hill's Westminster Cathedral Choir. But this Naxos coupling is by no means second best. Like David Hill, Jeremy Summerly moves the music of each Mass on fairly briskly until the *Sanctus* and *Agnus Dei*, when the spacious *espressivo* of the singing makes a poignant contrast. The two motets on which the Masses are based are sung as postludes and very beautiful they are, especially the idyllic *O magnum mysterium*. Finally the short *Versa est in luctum* (a setting of a section of the Requiem Mass) by Alonso Lobo, a Spanish contemporary, ends the concert serenely. The recording is excellent and this is a fine bargain.

Mass and Motet: *O quam gloriosum*.
(BB) *** Belart 461 018-2 [(M) id. import]. Mary Thomas, Jean Allister, Edgar Fleet, Christopher Keyte, Carmelite Priory Ch., London, John McCartney – PALESTRINA: Masses: *Ecce ego Joannes; Sine nomine*. ***

Like the Palestrina couplings, this paired Mass and motet are exceptionally distinguished performances, and they are made the more attractive (in all three cases) by this ideal recorded presentation which couples the motet which is musically connected with each Mass, something which we expect these days as a matter of course but which happened less frequently in the early 1960s, when these recordings first appeared. The sound is remarkably fine, for the microphone placing has been well calculated to the acoustic so that, while the part-writing can be heard clearly, the overall blend is tonally beautiful.

Vieuxtemps, Henri (1820–81)

Violin concertos Nos. 2 in F sharp min., Op. 19; 3 in A, Op. 25.

(BB) *** Naxos Dig. 8.554114 [id.]. Misha Keylin, Janáček PO, Dennis Burkh.

Vieuxtemps wrote seven violin concertos and, on the evidence of this fine Naxos coupling, Nos. 2 and 3 are by no means inferior to the better-known Nos. 4 and 5. They are full of good tunes, both slow movements are warmly touching and finales have lyrical as well as histrionic appeal. Misha Keylin (Russian by birth but now an American émigré) gives highly persuasive performances that are technically dazzling and constantly tickle the ear in their subtlety of bowing and colour, easy rubato and imaginative dynamic shading. Dennis Burkh provides the strongest backing: his spirited introductions for both works (and especially the *Third*, with its throbbing drama) are arresting, and the orchestral playing, somewhat leonine in timbre, is excellent. So too is the recording, made in the Janáček Concert Hall, Ostrava, with the soloist not too close for comfort in his Paganinian flights into the stratosphere. Most enjoyable, and a real bargain by any standards.

Violin concertos Nos. 4 in D min., Op. 31; 5 in A min. (Grétry), Op. 37.

(M) *** EMI (SIS) CDM5 66058-2. Itzhak Perlman, O de Paris, Barenboim – RAVEL: *Tzigane;* SAINT-SAENS: *Havanaise.* ***

Violin concerto No. 4 in D min., Op. 31.

(M) (***) EMI mono CDH7 64251-2 [id.]. Heifetz, LPO, Barbirolli – SAINT-SAENS: *Havanaise* etc.; SARASATE: *Zigeunerweisen;* WIENIAWSKI: *Concerto No. 2.* (***)

Violin concerto No. 5 in A min., Op. 37.

(M) (***) EMI mono CDH5 65191-2 [id.]. Heifetz, LSO, Sargent – MENDELSSOHN: *Concerto* (**(*)); MOZART: *Concerto No. 5.* (***)

This coupling of the two best-known Vieuxtemps violin concertos is not only apt; it presents superbly stylish readings, with Perlman both aristocratically pure of tone and intonation and passionate of expression. In his accompaniments Barenboim draws warmly romantic playing from the Paris orchestra. The 1976–7 recording, as usual with Perlman, balancing the soloist well forward, now sounds a little dated, with a touch of shrillness on the upper range of the violin. However, this remains a three-star record, the more so for its inclusion of two of Perlman's very finest recordings as couplings.

The Vieuxtemps concertos are not great music, but, when played like this by Heifetz, one is almost convinced that they are. His account of *No. 4 in D minor* with Barbirolli, made in 1935, is coupled with other dazzling performances. Heifetz and Barbirolli had a good rapport when they first collaborated the previous year – which was just as well, as Barbirolli only learnt at 11 o'clock on the morning of the recording that he was due to record the Vieuxtemps *Fourth Concerto* (which he had not directed before) that very afternoon. The results are pretty amazing.

Heifetz's recording of the *Fifth Concerto in A minor* was made in London just after the war with Sir Malcolm Sargent. This comes together with Heifetz's celebrated account of the Mendelssohn (made with Beecham and the RPO in 1949) and the 1934 recording with Barbirolli and the LPO of Mozart's *Turkish Concerto*. There are some cuts, but Heifetz's playing is glorious and the sound excellent for its period.

Violin concerto No. 5 in A min., Op. 37.

(M) *** Sony Dig. SMK 64250 [id.]. Cho-Liang Lin, Minnesota O, Marriner – BRUCH; MENDELSSOHN: *Concertos.* ***

(M) *** DG Dig. 457 896-2 [id.]. Mintz, Israel PO, Mehta – LALO: *Symphonie espagnole;* SAINT-SAENS: *Introduction & Rondo capriccioso.* ***

(M) *** RCA 09026 61745-2 [id.]. Heifetz, New SO of L, Sargent – BRUCH: *Violin concerto No. 1* etc. ***

(M) *** Decca Dig. 460 007-2 [id.]. Kyung Wha Chung, LSO, Foster – LALO: *Symphonie espagnole;* RAVEL: *Tzigane.* ***

(M) **(*) Sony SBK 48274 [id.]. Zukerman, LSO, Mackerras – BRUCH: *Concerto No. 1;* LALO: *Symphonie espagnole.* **(*)

Cho-Liang Lin plays with flair and zest and is well supported by Sir Neville Marriner and the Minnesota Orchestra. The recording is first class, and the couplings of the more famous concertos of Bruch and Mendelssohn could not be more appropriate.

Mintz's performance has enormous dash and also real lyrical magic. Mehta, obviously caught up in the inspiration of the solo playing, provides an excellent accompaniment. This is another example of a memorable live performance 'recorded on the wing' and, if the acoustic is not especially flattering, the sound is obviously truthful and well balanced.

The quicksilver of Heifetz is well suited to the modest but attractive *Fifth Concerto* of Vieuxtemps, and Sir Malcolm again provides a musical and well-recorded accompaniment. The balance of the soloist is rather close but the digital remastering is successful, and the couplings are both attractive and generous.

Even more than the Lalo *Symphonie espagnole* which forms the major coupling, the Vieuxtemps No. 5 needs persuasive advocacy, and that is certainly what Kyung Wha Chung provides, not just in her passionate commitment in the bravura sections but also in the tender expressiveness of the slow movement, so much more compelling than the usual, more extrovert manner. The 1974 Kingsway Hall recording has perhaps lost a little of its original allure in the matter of the solo violin timbre but is otherwise very satisfactory.

Zukerman provides here an enjoyable bonus to his dazzling accounts of the Bruch and Lalo works. There is comparable dash for Vieuxtemps, yet he coaxes the *Adagio* tenderly. Again a very forward balance, but the ear adjusts.

Villa-Lobos, Heitor (1887–1959)

Alvorada na floresta tropical (Dawn in a tropical rainforest); Bachianas brasileiras No. 2 (for orchestra) includes: *The little train of the Caipira. Dança frenética;* (i) *Mômoprecóce (fantasy for piano and orchestra).*

(BB) *** Arte Nova Dig. 73421 54465-2 [id.]. (i) Marco Antonio de Almeida; Jena PO, David Montgomery.

Once again the enterprising Arte Nova label almost upstages the competition with a super-budget collection that is in every way recommendable. Like Cristina Ortiz (below), Marco Antonio de Almeida is Brazilian born, and he and Montgomery give a clamorously invigorating and atmospherically persuasive account of the *Mômoprecóce* ('Carnival King'). If the Jena Philharmonic strings have not the body of tone of the New Philharmonia, the often glittering detail is very effectively projected by the modern digital recording, and the notes with the disc give useful programmatic detail of its picaresque content. The exotic sounds of the tropical rainforest are also vividly caught, and the energetic toccata rhythms have plenty of energy. The sultry, jazzy atmosphere of *The song of the vagabond*, the first movement of the *Bachianas brasileiras No. 2*, is seductive, and the catchy trombone tune of the fourth (*Song of the desert*) is equally engaging. But of course this piece is famous mainly for its charming portrayal of *The little train of the Caipira*, which is brought to life most winningly. The *Dança frenética* which ends the concert is spirited enough but is as much warmly colourful as frenetic.

Bachianas brasileiras Nos. 1–9; Chôros Nos. 2 (for flute & orchestra); *5* (for piano, Alma Brasileira); *10* (for chorus & orchestra); (i) *11* (for piano & orchestra). *2 Chôros (bis)* (for violin & cello); (i) *Piano concerto No. 5; Descobrimento do Brasil; Invocação em defesa da Patria;* (i) *Momoprecoce* (fantasy for piano & orchestra); *Symphony No. 4. Qu'est-ce qu'un Chôros?* (Villa-Lobos speaking).

(M) (**(*)) EMI mono CZS7 67229-2 (6) [CDZF 67229]. De los Angeles, Kareska, Basrentzen, Braune, Tagliaferro, Du Frene, Plessier, Cliquennois, Bronschwak, Neilz, Benedetti; (i) Blumental; Chorale des Jeunesses Musicales de France, Fr. Nat. R. & TV Ch. & O, cond. composer.

This six-CD box is a colourful, warm-hearted collection, not helped by dull mono recordings and ill-disciplined performances, but full of a passionately surging intensity that plainly reflects the personality of a composer of obvious charisma, if of limited ability as a conductor. Endearingly, there is a 10-minute track spoken in French by Villa-Lobos himself. All nine of the *Bachianas brasileiras* are recorded here, including the celebrated No. 5 for soprano and eight cellos, with Victoria de los Angeles a radiant soloist. That recording is already well known, but most of the others have had very limited circulation. They make an enjoyable collection for, despite the dull sound, the warmth of the writing never fails to come over.

Bachianas brasileiras Nos. 1; 2 (includes *The little train of the Caipira*); (i) *5* (for soprano & 8 cellos); (ii) *6* (for flute & bassoon); *9*.

(M) (**) EMI mono CDH7 61015-2 [id.]. French Nat. R. O, composer, with (i) De los Angeles; (ii) Fernand Dufrêne, René Plessier.

It is good to have on EMI's historic Références label this generous collection of the composer's own recordings, not immaculate in performance and with depressingly dry and boxy recording, but full of colour and life. Though even Victoria de los Angeles' golden voice loses some of its bloom, her account of the famous No. 5 is ravishing, and no one has been more persuasive than the composer himself in the other favourite, the *Little train of the Caipira*.

(i–ii) *Bachianas brasileiras No. 3;* (iii) *Guitar concerto;* (iv) *Fantasia for soprano saxophone and chamber orchestra;* (i) Piano music: *A próle do bébé No. 1* (suite); *A lenda de caboclo; Alma brasiliera (Chorus No. 5); Cicio brasileiro: Festa no sertão; Impressões seresteiras.*

(B) *** EMI forte CZS5 72670-2 (2) [(M) id. import]. (i) Cristina Ortiz; (ii) New Philh. O, Ashkenazy; (iii) Angel Romero, LPO, Jésus López-Cobos; (iv) John Harle, ASMF, Marriner.

In many ways this is the finest Villa-Lobos collection in the catalogue, and it is certainly the most varied. His rather melancholy piano piece, *A lenda de caboclo* ('Legend of a half-caste') gives a clue to the unique identity of this music, for the composer's mother was Hispanic, his father of Indian descent. No. 3 of the *Bachianas brasileiras*, which dates from 1938, is the only one of the series to involve the piano. The *Mômoprecóce* began life in 1920 (while the composer was living in Paris) as the set of piano pieces called *Carnaval das Crianças*, and it was reworked in its concertante form later. Like so much of Villa-Lobos's music, the score is rowdy and colourful. It is not music of great substance, and its sheer zest for life and unrelieved cheerfulness may be too much for some listeners. Cristina Ortiz, herself Brazilian, is a natural choice for this repertoire. She plays with appropriate vigour, reflective feeling and colour, and Ashkenazy gives splendid support. The late-1970s recording approaches the demonstration bracket of its time. The CD transfer adds a hint of edge to the high violins but is otherwise excellent. Ortiz is equally impressive in the solo piano pieces (again very well recorded), which she plays with flair and at times with touching tenderness, as in Villa-Lobos's portaits of the *Clay* and *Rag dolls*, the third and and sixth members of *A próle do bébé* ('Baby's family'); she then dazzles with scintillating virtuosity in the scherzando closing *Polincinelle*. This music, written in 1918, exhibits strong French influences (Debussy, Poulenc, Satie), but the impressionistic genre pieces which end the recital have more local colour. Angel Romero makes the very most of the comparatively slight *Guitar concerto*, bringing out its Latin feeling (especially in the cadenza at the end of the *Andantino e andante*), and Marriner subtly relishes the score's exotic colouring. The *Fantasia for soprano saxophone* is a more substantial piece with three well-defined movements, each inventive in a different way. John Harle is a perceptive soloist with a most appealing timbre; both he and Jésus López-Cobos are fully at home in the Villa-Lobos sound-world and their performance is one of the highlights of the set. The recordings in both these concertante works (made in 1984 and 1990 respectively) are well up to the best Abbey Road analogue standards.

Guitar concerto.

(M) *** Sony SMK 60022 [id.]. John Williams, ECO, Barenboim – CASTELNUOVO-TEDESCO: *Guitar concerto;* RODRIGO: *Concierto de Aranjuez.* ***

(BB) *** Naxos Dig. 8.550729 [id.]. Norbert Kraft, Northern CO, Nicholas Ward – CASTELNUOVO-TEDESCO: *Concerto* ***; RODRIGO: *Concierto de Aranjuez.* ***

John Williams's compulsive performance makes the very most of the finer points of Villa-Lobos's comparatively slight concerto, and especially the rhapsodic quality of the *Andantino*. The recording is bright and fresh, the soloist characteristically close, but the effect is vividly present.

An excellent account from Norbert Kraft, spontaneous and catching well the music's colour and atmosphere. If it is not quite as individual as Bream's version, it has the advantage of vivid, well-balanced, modern, digital recording and excellent couplings. Another genuine Naxos bargain.

(i) *Guitar concerto. 12 Etudes; 5 Preludes.*

(M) *** RCA 09026 61604-2. Julian Bream, (i) LSO, André Previn.

A highly distinguished account of the *Guitar concerto* from Bream, magnetic and full of atmosphere in the slow movement and finale. Previn accompanies sympathetically and with spirit. The rest of the programme also shows Bream in inspirational form. He engages the listener's attention from the opening of the first study and holds it to the last. The recording has a nice intimacy in the concerto and the solo items have fine presence against an attractive ambience.

Piano concertos Nos. 1-5.
(B) *** Decca Double Dig. 452 617-2 (2) [(M) id. import]. Cristina Ortiz, RPO, Miguel Gómez-Martínez.

What emerges from the series of concertos, as played by Cristina Ortiz here, is that the first two are the most immediately identifiable as Brazilian in their warm colouring and sense of atmosphere, even though the eclectic borrowings are often more unashamed than later, with many passages suggesting Rachmaninov with a Brazilian accent. No. 3, the work Villa-Lobos found it hard to complete, tends to sound bitty in its changes of direction. No. 4, more crisply conceived, has one or two splendid tunes, but it is in No. 5 that Villa-Lobos becomes most warmly convincing again, returning unashamedly to more echoes of Rachmaninov. With Ortiz articulating crisply, there is much to enjoy from such colourful, undemanding music, brilliantly recorded and sympathetically performed. Now at Double Decca price, this entertaining set is worthy of a place in all but the smallest collections.

CHAMBER MUSIC

5 Preludes for guitar.
(B) *** Sony SBK 62425; *SBT 62425* [id.]. John Williams (guitar) – GIULIANI: *Variations on a theme by Handel;* PAGANINI: *Caprice No. 24; Grand sonata;* D. SCARLATTI: *Sonatas.* ***

Although John Williams is balanced a shade too closely, he is very well recorded; his playing, improvisationally spontaneous and full of magical evocation, is of the highest level of mastery. A lower-level setting compensates for the balance and enables this artist's playing to register effectively. These are as perfect and as finely turned as any performances in the catalogue.

Suite populaire brésilienne; Etudes Nos. 5 in C; 7 in E.
(M) *** RCA 09026 61596-2. Julian Bream – Recital: *'Twentieth-century guitar II'.* ***

The *Suite populaire brésilienne* is deservedly among Villa-Lobos's most popular music. The composer disclaims the idea that these four chôros (pieces in the style of Brazilian street-bands) were intended as a suite, but they fit together remarkably well. Bream plays them with his usual flair and brings out all their vivid colouring. The two contrasted *Etudes* are also fine pieces. Excellent late-1970s recording.

VOCAL MUSIC

Bachianas brasileiras No. 5 for soprano and cellos.
(B) *** Decca Double Dig. 444 995-2 (2) [id.]; *444 995-4.* Kiri Te Kanawa, Lynn Harrell and instrumental ens. – CANTELOUBE: *Songs of the Auvergne.* ***
(M) *** RCA 09026 62600-2 [id.]. Anna Moffo, American SO, Stokowski – CANTELOUBE: *Chants d'Auvergne;* RACHMANINOV: *Vocalise.* ***

The Villa-Lobos piece makes an apt fill-up for the Canteloube songs, completing Kiri Te Kanawa's recording of all five books. It is, if anything, even more sensuously done, well sustained at a speed far slower than one would normally expect. Rich recording to match.

Anna Moffo gives a seductive performance of the most famous of the *Bachianas brasileiras*, adopting a highly romantic style (matching the conductor) and warm tone-colour.

Vivaldi, Antonio (1675–1741)

Philips Vivaldi Edition, Volume 1: Concertos: (i) *L'Estro armonico, Op. 3;* (ii) *La Stravaganza, Op. 4;* (iii) *6 Violin concertos, Op. 6.* Chamber music: (iv) *12 Sonatas for 2 violins, Op. 1;* (v) *12 Violin sonatas, Op. 2;* (vi) *6 Sonatas for 1 or 2 violins, Op. 5.*
(B) *** Ph. 456 185-2 (10) [id.]. (i) Michelucci; (ii) Ayo; (iii) Carmirelli; (i–iii) I Musici; (iv–vi) Accardo, Canino, De Saram; (iv) Gulli; (vi) Gazeau.

Philips's Vivaldi Edition is very competitively priced, and any reservations tend to be swept aside when the coverage is so uniquely comprehensive and the music-making so warmly enjoyable. *L'Estro armonico* is also available separately on a Duo (see below). *La Stravaganza* is the earlier, analogue version, which is generally preferable to I Musici's later, digital set. Both concertos draw on recordings made (mostly in the highly suitable acoustics of La Chaux-de-Fonds, Switzerland) in 1962–3. These are refreshing and lively performances, and the current transfers offer gleaming tuttis, while the soloists are realisically placed and cleanly focused. Maria Teresa Garatti's continuo features a chamber organ as well as harpsichord in Op. 4, and there is much delicacy of feeling in slow movements to balance the spirited buoyancy of allegros. The half-dozen concertos of Opus 6 are much rarer and this was their stereo debut, made at the same venue more than a decade later, in 1977. Curiously, tuttis are heavier and more opaque, and Vivaldi's invention here is more uneven than in the named sets. But their rarity will undoubtedly tempt keen Vivaldians and there are some particularly fine slow movements, such as the *Grave* centrepiece of the *Second Concerto in G minor* with its solemn duo between violin and cello. The performances, with Pina Carmirelli a stylish soloist, are polished and responsive, with well-judged tempi.

The reissue of the chamber music is particularly welcome, as these sonatas are not otherwise readily obtainable. In any case it is unlikely that Accardo's performances, so ably supported by Franco Gulli (in Opus 1), Rohan de Saram (cello) and Bruno Canino (harpsichord) could be surpassed in terms of fluency, musicianship and sheer beauty of tone. The shadow of Corelli still hangs over Op. 1, but much of the invention is characteristically Vivaldian, and the final sonata (*No. 12 in D minor*) is an engaging set of variations on *La Follia*. The solo sonatas of Op. 2, with continuo, are particularly fine, particularly the last two, with the opening *Preludio* of the penultimate work (in D major) a haunting duet between violin and cello. Four of Opus 5 (dating from 1716–17) are solo sonatas with continuo, the remainder being trio sonatas in which the violinist Sylvie Gazeau joins the group. The recording is excellent and collectors will find unexpected rewards in these stimulating works.

Philips Vivaldi Edition, Volume 2: Concertos: (i–ii) *12 Concertos for oboe or violin, Op. 7;* (iii) *Il Cimento dell'armonia e dell'inventione* (*The Trial between harmony and invention,* including *The Four Seasons*), *Op. 8; La Cetra, Op. 9;* (iv) *6 Flute concertos, Op. 10;* (i) *6 Violin concertos, Op. 11; 6 Violin concertos, Op. 12.*
(B) *** Ph. 456 186-2 (9) [id.]. I Musici, with (i) Accardo; (ii) Holliger; (iii) Ayo; (iv) Gazzelloni.

Although it includes Felix Ayo's pioneering stereo recording of Op. 8 (including *The Four Seasons*) which is also available separately as a Duo (see below), *La Cetra* and the very familiar Op. 10 *Flute concertos*, the remainder of the content of Volume II of this bargain Vivaldi edition is almost as rare as Volume I. *La Cetra* dates from 1964 and was again recorded at La Chaux-de-Fonds, as was Opus 7, a decade later, thus ensuring a realistic and pleasing sound-balance. With Ayo again the principal soloist, the playing is spirited, characterful and expressively rich, though the overall effect is less individual than in some of the competing versions. One drawback is that solo passages are given no continuo support, though Maria Teresa Garatti provides an organ continuo for the ripieno. Opus 7 is much less familiar but is certainly very rewarding. One has only to sample the finale of *No. 4 in A minor*, with its pungent clashes in the ripieno, to find the composer at his most dashing, resourcefully re-using a theme from the opening movement. The playing of Accardo (who has the lion's share of these concertos) and Holliger is altogether masterly; they have fine rapport with their fellow musicians of I Musici, and the 1975 sound-balance is first class.

Severino Gazzeloni's version of the Op. 10 *Flute concertos* (which include three named masterpieces, *La tempesta di mare*, the hauntingly atmospheric *La notte* and the chirping *Il gardellino*) has been in circulation throughout the last three decades and has stood the test of time. Its merits are well established and it remains a safe recommendation for the general collector, even alongside its authentic rivals, for the timbre of the soloist's modern instrument is very appealing. This too is available on a Duo within a collection of other flute concertos and is discussed below.

The Opp. 11 and 12 *Violin concertos* were recorded in 1974–5. The best of them are very rewarding indeed and, played superlatively by Salvatore Accardo, they are likely to beguile the most reluctant listener. Again one especially remembers the slow movements. *Op. 11/2 in E minor* is separately familar as *Il favorito*, rightly named for its exquisite slow-movement cantilena over a pizzicato accompaniment. But the expressive *Aria* which forms the Andante of *Op. 11/3 in A major*, and the gentle central *Largo cantabile* of *No. 4 in G* are hardly less touching. Equally the *Largo* and *Larghetto* movements of Op. 12 have a moving serenity on Accardo's bow. *No. 1 in G minor* brings a poignant *espressivo* and in *No. 6 in B flat* Vivaldi again floats a lovely melody over gentle pizzicatos. Tuttis are ample in sound, the balance is virtually ideal and the CD transfers are among the best in the series. As it so happens, Oiseau-Lyre have recently issued a full-priced set of Op. 12 on period instruments from Hogwood's Academy of Ancient Music and the result is much less beguiling, with the timbre of the soloist, Pavlo Beznosiuk, unattractively meagre. Hogwood's tempi are consistently much faster, and this is most striking in slow movements. In the case of the central *Largos* of Nos. 4 and 6, Hogwood's overall timing is just about half as long as that of I Musici, totally altering the character of the *espressivo*.

L'Estro armonico (12 Concertos), Op. 3.
(B) **(*) Ph. Duo 446 169-2 (2) [id.]. Garatti, Altobelli, Colandrea, Cotogni, Gallozzi, Michelucci, Vicari, I Musici.
(B) ** EMI forte CZS5 69376-2 (2) [CDFB 69376]. Virtuosi di Roma, Fasano.

L'estro armonico, Op. 3; (i) *Bassoon concerto in A min., RV 498;* (ii) *Flute concerto in C min., RV 441;* (iii) *Oboe concerto in F, RV 456;* (i; iii; iv) *Concerto in F for 2 oboes, bassoon, 2 horns and violin, RV 574.*

(B) *** Decca Double 443 476-2 (2) [id.]. ASMF, Marriner; with (i) Martin Gatt; (ii) William Bennett; (iii) Neil Black; (iv) Celia Nicklin, Timothy Brown, Robin Davis, Iona Brown.

Vivaldi's *L'Estro armonico* includes some of his finest music and had great influence. Those who have not been won over to the more abrasive sound of original instruments will find Marriner's set no less stylish. As so often, he directs the Academy in radiant and imaginative performances of baroque music and yet observes scholarly good manners. The delightful use of continuo – lute and organ as well as harpsichord – the sharing of solo honours and the consistently resilient string playing of the ensemble make for compelling listening. The 1972 recording, made in St John's, Smith Square, is immaculately transferred, and as a bonus we are offered four of Vivaldi's most inventive concertos which occupied a whole LP to themselves when first issued in 1977. Each work has its own individuality and its own special effects. The *A minor Bassoon concerto* has a delightful sense of humour and in RV 441 the flute chortles like a bird. The work for oboes and horns is agreeably robust but has an imaginatively scored slow movement. The recording is a model of clarity and definition and has plenty of warmth and atmosphere.

The Philips Duo offers fresh and lovely performances; melodies are finely drawn and there is little hint of the routine which occasionally surfaces in I Musici – and, for that matter, in Vivaldi himself. However, in making comparisons this group often yields to St Martin-in-the-Fields, who have crisper textures and convey greater enthusiasm. Even so, I Musici are a good choice and are certainly recommendable. However, whereas the Decca Marriner set (at the same cost) offers extra works as a bonus, this Philips reissue, with its overall playing time of just two hours, offers none.

Fasano's performances are certainly musically fresh and enjoyable, but the contrasts between orchestra and solo groups, and between first and second violins in the orchestra, lose some of their effect through being minimized by the recording balance. These contrasts are the very stuff of which concerti grossi are made, and it is a pity when the chance is missed to make the most of this. One can, of course, identify when the concertino and the ripieno are playing, but here the dynamic result is not as stimulating as it should be. The recording, from the beginning of the 1960s, now sounds a little dated in the matter of the smoothness of the string-timbre, and this cannot compare with Marriner's ASMF set.

L'Estro armonico, Op. 3/1, 2, 4, 7, 8 & 10–11.

(BB) *** Naxos Dig. 8.550160 [id.]. Capella Istropolitana, Jozef Kopelman.

Jozef Kopelman and the Capella Istropolitana enter hotly contested territory and enjoy a strongly competitive edge, given the price-tag. The performances here are eminently satisfactory, being both lively and musical, and the recording has warmth and presence. There are so many excellent rival versions of Op. 3, but this selection is certainly enjoyable in its own right. Suffice it to say that it is good value for money.

L'Estro armonico: Double violin concerto in A min.; Quadruple violin concerto in B min.; Triple concerto in D min., for 2 violins and cello, Op. 3/8, 10–11. Triple violin concerto in F.

(B) ** Carlton IMP Dig. 30367 02352 [(M) id.]. Soloists, SCO, Laredo.

The three concertos from *L'Estro armonico* are among Vivaldi's finest; they receive vigorous performances from members of the Scottish Chamber Orchestra, with their director, Jaime Laredo, again creating the lively spontaneity which informs his successful version of *The Four Seasons*. While the solo playing occasionally lacks the last touch of polish, there is excellent team-spirit, and the phrasing has more light and shade than in Laredo's companion collection of wind concertos (see below). The recording is a shade over-bright, but there is a firm supporting bass-line and the acoustic is attractive, adding ambience and warmth without blurring detail. This is distinctly enjoyable, but the playing time of 41 minutes precludes a strong recommendation, even at bargain price.

La Stravaganza (12 concertos), *Op. 4* (complete).

❀ (B) *** Decca Double 444 821-2 (2) [430 566-2]. Soloists, ASMF, Marriner.

Marriner's performances make the music irresistible. The solo playing of Carmel Kaine and Alan Loveday is superb and, when the Academy's rhythms have such splendid buoyancy and lift, it is easy enough to accept Marriner's preference for a relatively sweet style in the often heavenly slow movements. As usual, the contribution of an imaginatively varied continuo (which includes cello and bassoon, in addition to harpsichord, theorbo and organ) adds much to the colour of Vivaldi's score. The recording, made in St John's, Smith Square, in 1973/4, is of the very highest quality and the CD transfers are in the demonstration class.

The Trial between harmony and invention (12 Concertos), Op. 8.
(B) **(*) Ph. Duo 438 344-2 (2). Felix Ayo, I Musici.
(B) ** Erato/Warner Ultima 0630 18968-2 (2) [id.]. Sol. Ven., Scimone.

Felix Ayo recorded the first four concertos (*The Four Seasons*) in 1959 and his was one of the finest of the early versions, although the recording was rather resonant. The remaining concertos in the set – full of typically Vivaldian touches which stamp these works as among the best of their time – date from 1961/2 and the recording, though still full-bodied, is less reverberant. The solo playing is very good and an undoubted freshness pervades the music-making here, although Maria Teresa Garatti's continuo fails to come through adequately. Good value.

Scimone directs energetic readings of the 12 concertos, very enjoyable in their way, with the 1971 recording (actually made in Italy) nicely balanced except for backward continuo. But stylish as these performances are for their period, with Piero Toso an excellent soloist, they are not quite as fine as other versions listed here.

The Trial between harmony and invention, Op. 8: Concertos Nos. 5–12.
(B) *** Sony SBK 53513; *SBT 53513* [id.]. Pinchas Zukerman, Neil Black, ECO, Philip Ledger.

Zukerman's solo playing is distinguished throughout, and the ECO provide unfailingly alert and resilient accompaniments. In *Concerto No. 9 in D min.* oboist Neil Black takes the solo position and provides a welcome contrast of timbre – Vivaldi designed this concerto as optionally for violin or oboe, but it probably sounds more effective on the wind instrument. The recording throughout is lively, with a close balance for the soloists. The sound is attractive and does not lack fullness. This 77-minute CD encapsulates all the concertos from Op. 8 except the first four and includes such favourites as *La tempesta di mare* (RV 253), *Il piacere* (RV 108) and *La Caccia* (RV 362).

The Four Seasons, Op. 8/1–4.
(M) **(*) Carlton Classics Dig. PCD 2000 [id.]. Jaime Laredo, SCO.
(B) **(*) EMI Eminence Dig. CD-EMX 2009 [(M) id.]. Krzysztof Jakowicz, Polish CO, Maksymiuk.

(i) *The Four Seasons, Op. 8/1–4;* (ii) *Violin concerto in E flat, RV 253 (La tempesta di mare), Op. 8/5;* (iii) *Flute concerto in D (Il gardellino), RV 428, Op. 10/3; Concerto for strings in A.*
(B) ** EMI forte CZS5 68625-2 (2) [CDFB 68625]. (i) Ferro, Mozzato; (ii) Malanotte; (iii) Rispoli; Virtuosi di Roma, Fasano – CORELLI: *Concerti grossi.* **

(i; ii) *The Four Seasons, Op. 8/1–4;* (i; iii) *Violin concerto in E flat (La tempesta di mare), Op. 8/5, RV 253;* (iv) *Triple concerto in F for flute, oboe and bassoon, RV 570; Double concerto in G min. for flute and bassoon (La notte), RV 104.*
(BB) *** ASV Dig. CDQS 6148 [(M) id.]. (i) José-Luis Garcia; (ii) ECO; (iii) Fort Worth CO, Giordano; (iv) William Bennett, Neil Black, Robin O'Neill, ECO, Malcolm.

(i) *The Four Seasons, Op. 8/1–4;* (ii) *Violin concertos: L'Estro armonico: in A min., Op. 3/6. La Stravaganza: in A, Op. 4/5. Concerto in C min. (Il sospetto), RV 199.*
(M) *** EMI CDM7 64333-2 [id.]. Perlman, (i) LPO; (ii) Israel PO.

(i) *The Four Seasons. L'Estro armonico: Double violin concerto in A min., RV 522; Quadruple violin concerto in B min., RV 580, Op. 3/8 & 10; Bassoon concerto in B flat, RV 502; Cello concerto in C min., RV 401; Oboe concerto in C, RV 447; Double trumpet concerto in C, RV 537; Triple violin concerto in F, RV 551.*
(BB) *** Virgin Classics Dig. Double VBD5 61466-2 (2) [CDVB 61465]. (i) Christopher Warren-Green; Soloists; LCO.

The Four Seasons; (i) *L'Estro armonico: Quadruple violin concerto in B min., RV 580, Op. 3/10.*
(BB) *** Discover Dig. DICD 920202 [id.]. Oldřich Vlček; (i) with Hessová, Kaudersová, Nováková; Virtuosi di Praga.

(i) *The Four Seasons, Op. 8/1–4;* (ii) *Violin concertos: in E flat (La tempesta di mare), Op. 8/5, RV 253; in E (L'amoroso), RV 271.*
(BB) ** RCA Navigator 74321 17884-2 [(M) 09026 60542-2]. (i) Salvatore Accardo, Camera Italiana O; (ii) Patrice Fontanarosa, I Nuovi Virtuosi di Roma.

The Four Seasons; Concerto for strings (Alla rustica) in G, RV 151.
(BB) ** Naxos Dig. 8.550056 [id.]. Takako Nishizaki, Capella Istropolitana, Gunzenhauser.

(i) *The Four Seasons; Concerto for strings in G (Alla rustica), RV 151;* (ii) *Violin concerto in E (L'amoroso), RV 271; Sinfonia in B min. (Al Santo Sepolcro), RV 169.*
(B) *** DG Classikon 439 422-2; *439 422-4* [(M) 415 301-2]. (i) Michel Schwalbé; (ii) Thomas Brandis; BPO, Karajan.

(i) *The Four Seasons. Concerto funèbre; Concerto per l'orchestra di Dresda; Concerto per la Solennità di San Lorenzo.*
(B) **(*) Decca Eclipse Dig. 448 225-2; *448 225-4* [(M) id. import]. (i) Franco Gulli; I Filarmonici de Teatro Comunale di Bologna, Chailly.

(i) *The Four Seasons, Op. 8/1–4;* (ii) *Mandolin concerto in C, RV 425*; (iii) *Double mandolin concerto in G, RV 532; (iv) Double trumpet concerto in C, RV 537.*
(M) *** Ph. Dig/Analogue 442 393-2. (i) Salvatore Accardo, I Solisti delle Settimane Internazionali di Napoli; (ii) Parisi; (iii) Del Vescovo, Ruta; (iv) Adelbrecht, Mathez; (ii-iv) I Musici.

Christopher Warren-Green makes a brilliantly charismatic soloist, with the London Chamber Orchestra providing delectably pointed bird-imitations in *Spring* and *Summer*. Tempi of allegros are very brisk, but the effect is tinglingly exhilarating when the soloist's bravura is so readily matched by the accompanying ensemble. Slow movements offer the widest contrast, with delicate textures and a subtle use of the continuo, as in *Winter* where Leslie Pearson makes a delightful surprise contribution to the finale, having already embroidered the opening allegro and prevented it from being too chilly. The recording, made in All Saints' Church, Wallington, has plenty of ambient fullness but remains bright and fresh. Dashing and vital, and yet imaginatively pictorial at the same time, this will be regarded by many collectors as a best buy in its new Virgin Double format (two CDs for the cost of one medium-priced disc) as the coupling is a group of seven of Vivaldi's most appealing concertos which offer further examples of the vividly spontaneous music-making characteristics of the London Chamber Orchestra in their heyday at the beginning of the 1990s.

The second disc opens brightly with the *Double trumpet concerto* and, in the works for oboe and bassoon both soloists (Gordon Hunt and Merrick Alexander respectively) play with much character and elegance and, in the case of the latter, also a touch of humour. The lovely slow movement of the *C minor Cello concerto* is warmly sympathetic on Andrew Schulman's bow. For some reason, a continuo is used only in the two woodwind concertos. The harpsichord swirls are rather effective in the first movement of the *Oboe concerto*, and in the *Largo* of the *Bassoon concerto* a chamber organ piquantly introduces the solo entry. The excerpts from *L'Estro armonico* are gleamingly strong and expressive, and again one senses an added energy, possibly deriving from the musicians standing while they play. The excellence of the recording is again very striking.

The super-bargain ASV version of *The Four Seasons*, with José-Luis Garcia as soloist and musical director, is particularly pleasing, with the violins of the accompanying group sweetly fresh and the soloist nicely balanced. The overall pacing is beautifully judged, and each movement takes its place naturally and spontaneously in relation to its companions. The effects are well made, but there are no histrionics and, although the continuo does not always come through strongly, the unnamed player makes a useful contribution to a performance that is very easy to live with. The one drawback to this issue is that there is only one track for each of the *Four Seasons*. The new couplings add two versions of *La tempesta del mare*, both the one with solo violin (from Op. 8) and the even more engaging triple concerto arrangement for flute, oboe and bassoon. The equally attractive flute/bassoon version of *La notte* completes the listener's pleasure. The wind soloists are illustrious and George Malcolm's accompaniments are a model of baroque style.

Salvatore Accardo's version is of particular interest in that he uses a different Stradivarius for each of the four concertos – period instruments with a difference! Thanks to this aristocrat of violinists, the sounds are of exceptional beauty. The performances are much enhanced, too, by the imaginative continuo playing of Bruno Canino, who is not given a credit in the booklet provided with this reissue. The notes also neglect to say that these were live performances, recorded digitally at the Cremona Festival in 1987. They have all the virtues of live music-making but none of the drawbacks. The other concertos are excellently played, and the analogue recording is first class.

Perlman's imagination holds the sequence together superbly, and there are many passages of pure magic, as in the central *Adagio* of *Summer*. The digital remastering of the 1976 recording is managed admirably, the sound firm, clear and well balanced, with plenty of detail. Now this record has been made much more competitive by the addition of three extra violin concertos, all fine works. Although the acoustic is somewhat dryish, this does not prevent these extra works from sounding very good.

Karajan's 1972 recording of *The Four Seasons* was an undoubted success and remains very enjoyable. Its tonal beauty is not achieved at the expense of vitality and, although the harpsichord hardly ever comes through, the overall scale is acceptable. Michel Schwalbé is a memorable soloist; his playing is neat, precise and very musical, with a touch of Italian sunshine in the tone. The current remastering for DG's bargain label, Classikon, has restored the body and breadth of the original, and in the additional works (recorded in the St Moritz Französische Kirche in Switzerland two years earlier) the string-sound is glorious. The sheer charisma of the BPO playing, notably in the *Sinfonia al Santa Sepolcro*, where the first movement is presented with great expressive depth, is difficult to resist, and the *Concerto alla rustica* sounds wonderfully sumptuous. Vivaldi would surely have been amazed!

An excellent alternative super-bargain version from the Virtuosi di Praga, fresh, bright and clean, with a strong, highly responsive soloist in Oldřich Vlček. *Spring* is immediately vivacious and the viola produces a nice little rasp for the shepherd's dog. *Autumn* is delicately somnambulant, and the opening of *Winter* is well below zero and is decorated with a clink from the continuo. The *Concerto for four violins* makes for a popular encore. Excellent sound and very good value.

Jaime Laredo's performance has great spontaneity and vitality, emphasized by the forward balance which is nevertheless admirably truthful. The bright upper range is balanced by a firm, resonant bass. Laredo plays with bravura and directs polished, strongly characterized accompaniments. Pacing tends to be on the fast side; although the reading is extrovert and the lyrical music – played responsively – is made to offer a series of interludes to the vigour of the allegros, the effect is exhilarating rather than aggressive. However, there is no extra music.

The digital Decca Eclipse version from Chailly, with an assured and highly musical soloist in Franco Gulli, has the advantage of top-drawer sound and brings performances that are warmly animated and well characterized (without exaggeration), using modern instruments to pleasing effect. The Bologna Philharmonic accompanies spiritedly, if without the very last degree of polish. *The Four Seasons* starts at band 8 of the CD, and the programme opens with the three other works, as imaginative as anything in the vast Vivaldi repertory. They are very well played too. Enjoyable though this is, it cannot rise to the very top of a crowded list.

The performance by Krzysztof Jakowicz and the Polish Chamber Orchestra characteristically bustles with vigour, with strong dynamic contrasts and a balance between the fast, energetic allegros – rhythms crisp and incisive – and the gentle sostenuto of the lyrical music. However, the fast tempi at times bring the feeling that the music is driven very hard. The solo playing offers arresting bravura but is also sensitive, so that the gentle breezes and summer languor are as readily communicated as the violent storms and the icy briskness of what is plainly seen as a harsh Polish winter. The 1980 recording is bright, not edgy, but somewhat dry in timbre.

The super-bargain Naxos version is given first-class digital sound, warm, fresh and well balanced (though the continuo does not come through very impressively). Takako Nishizaki plays beautifully, displaying an appropriate degree of bravura, and the accompaniment under Stephen Gunzenhauser is modest in scale and pleasingly finished. These are amiably musical performances, but Vivaldi's pictorial imagery is understated: the shepherd's dog has obviously just returned from an exhausting spring walk and *Winter* has seemingly been mellowed by the depletion of the ozone layer.

The version by the Virtuosi di Roma features two different soloists (Luigi Ferro and Guido Mozzato) who interchange and play two concertos each. Renato Fasano directs a straightforward and enjoyable but in no way distinctive set, and the early (1959) sound is acceptable enough. Of the other concertos, the unidentified work for strings is played freshly enough, but *Il gardellino* is probably the best of the bunch; in it the flautist, Pasquale Rispoli, demonstrates musicianly phrasing and excellent breath control in his notably spacious account of the central *Largo*. The rest of this rather pot-luck baroque collection is discussed under the main Corelli coupling.

Not unexpectedly, Accardo on his earlier, RCA Navigator version makes an accomplished and appealing soloist and the Orchestra de Camera Italiana offer full, bright supporting textures. The programmatic drama is conveyed well, but musical values are paramount and this is enjoyable in its fresh, direct manner, if not especially memorable. The sound is vivid, and this might be considered at bargain price, especially as the two couplings are brightly and vigorously done and digitally recorded; but there are many other more striking versions.

'The world of Vivaldi': (i) *The Four Seasons, Op. 8/1–4;* (ii) *Guitar concerto in D, RV 43;* (iii) *Piccolo concerto in C, RV 443;* (iv) *Concerto for strings in G (alla rustica), RV 151;* (v) *Double trumpet concerto in C, RV 537.*

(M) **(*) Decca 433 866-2. (i) Kulka, Stuttgart CO, Münchinger; (ii) Fernández, ECO, Malcolm; (iii) Bennett, ASMF, Marriner; (iv) Lucerne Festival Strings, Baumgartner; (v) Wilbraham, Jones, ASMF, Marriner.

Konstanty Kulka's performance of *The Four Seasons* from the early 1970s has stood the test of time. The solo playing is first class and Münchinger's accompaniment is stylish and lively. It was Münchinger who, with a different soloist, put this famous concertante work on the map with his first mono LP recording in the 1950s (the first in the UK – though Scherchen pioneered the work in the USA in the late 1940s) and so it is good to have the present reminder of his Vivaldi sympathies. The sound is a little astringent on top but does not lack body, and its brightness adds to the freshness. The quartet of concertos now offered as ballast certainly give a good cross-section of Vivaldi's world, all played with expertise and well recorded. The *Concerto for guitar* is digital; the *Double trumpet concerto* sounds a shade over-bright.

The Four Seasons, Op. 8/1–4 (arr. for flute and strings).
(M) *** RCA GD 60748 [60748-2-RG]. James Galway, Zagreb Soloists.

James Galway's transcription is thoroughly musical and so convincing that at times one is tempted to believe that the work was conceived in this form. The playing itself is marvellous, full of detail and imagination, and the recording is excellent, even if the flute is given a forward balance, the more striking on CD.

The Four Seasons, Op. 8/1–4; L'Estro armonico: Concerto in B min. (originally for 4 violins), *Op. 3/10, RV 580. Concerto in D* (originally for lute), *RV 83* (all arr. Goss for guitar quartet).
(M) ** Carlton Classics Dig. 30366 00692 [id.]. Tetra Guitar Quartet.

Vivaldi's *Four Seasons* seems indestructible, whatever soloist or combination – here four guitars – it is arranged for. The snag in this instance is the lack of variety of timbre, and it cannot be said that the composer's special effects make much of an impression, with the opening of *Winter* failing to register a low temperature. Moreover the playing here is affectionately easy-going rather than conveying the bravura and solo virtuosity which Vivaldi's original certainly intended. The other two concertos transcribe agreeably enough, and the concert makes amiable listening. But this is a disc to recommend solely to guitar enthusiasts.

The Trial between harmony and invention: Violin concertos Nos. 5 (La tempesta di mare); 6 (Il piacere); 7–8; 10 (La caccia); 11–12, Op. 8/5–8, 10–12.
(BB) **(*) Naxos Dig. 8.550189 [id.]. Béla Bánfalvi, Budapest Strings.

Béla Bánfalvi is not a household name outside Hungary but he is a fine player with a good sense of style, and he leads the Budapest Strings to good effect. The first four of the Op. 8 set, namely *The Four Seasons*, have already been recorded in the Naxos Vivaldi series by Takako Nishizaki and the Capella Istropolitana. The playing in this sequel is unfailingly musical and fresh, and the recorded sound is very good. It is not to be preferred to, say, Marriner (Decca) but, taken in its own right, it is perfectly recommendable.

La Cetra (12 Violin concertos), Op. 9.
(M) *** Virgin Veritas/EMI Dig. VED5 61246-2 (2) [ZDMB 61246]. Monica Huggett, Raglan Bar. Players, Kraemer.

(i) *La Cetra;* (ii) *Double oboe concerto in D min., RV 535;* (iii) *Piccolo concerto in C, RV 443.*
❁ (B) *** Decca Double 448 110-2 (2) [id.]. (i) Iona Brown, ASMF; (ii) Neil Black; (iii) Celia Nicklin; both with ASMF, Marriner.

La Cetra (The Lyre) was the last set of violin concertos Vivaldi published. Iona Brown, for some years the leader of St Martin's Academy, here acts as director in the place of Sir Neville Marriner. So resilient and imaginative are the results that one hardly detects any difference from the immaculate and stylish Vivaldi playing in earlier Academy Vivaldi sets. There is some wonderful music here; the later concertos are every bit the equal of anything in *The Trial between harmony and invention*, and they are played gloriously. The recording too is outstandingly rich and vivid, even by earlier Argo standards with this group, and the Decca transfer to CD retains the demonstration excellence of the original analogue LPs, with a yet greater sense of body and presence. For the Double Decca reissue, two of Vivaldi's most engaging wind concertos have been added, winningly played by two estimable Academy soloists and made the more attractive in slow movements by the imaginative continuo from Kenneth Heath (cello), Christopher Hogwood (harpsichord) and Colin Tilney (organ). The sound is every bit as good as in the concertos for violin.

Monica Huggett and the Raglan Baroque Players offer performances so accomplished and in such good style that they are unlikely to be surpassed in authentic-instrument versions of *La Cetra*. She is in excellent form and her virtuosity always appears effortless. The Raglan Baroque Players are of the same size as the Academy of Ancient Music and some players are common to both groups. First-class recording.

6 Flute concertos, Op. 10.
(M) *** Carlton Dig. 30367 0021-2 [id.]. Judith Hall, Divertimenti of L., Paul Barritt.
(M) **(*) RCA 09026 61351-2. James Galway, New Irish CO.

Judith Hall's record of the Op. 10 *Flute concertos* is fresh and brightly recorded. She plays with considerable virtuosity and a great deal of taste. The Divertimenti of London is a modern-instrument group and the players are both sensitive and alert.

James Galway directs the New Irish Chamber Orchestra from the flute – and to generally good effect. The playing is predictably brilliant and the goldfinch imitations in *Il Gardellino* (which comes first on the disc) are enticing. Slow movements demonstrate Galway's beauty of timbre and sense of line to consistently good effect, although some may find the sweet vibrato a bit too much for baroque repertoire. No complaints about the recording quality.

6 Flute concertos, Op. 10; Flute concertos: in A min., RV 108; in D, RV 429; in G, RV 438; in A min., RV 440; in C min., RV 441; (i) *Double flute concerto in C, RV 533. Piccolo concerto in A min., RV 445.*
(B) *** Ph. Duo 454 256-2 (2) [(M) id. import]. Severino Gazzelloni, I Musici; (i) with Marja Steinberg.

This Duo set purports to contain Vivaldi's 'complete flute concertos', but it is an unlikely claim: the works for sopranino recorder, RV 443 and 444, are not here, nor is the arrangement of *La notte* (RV 104) which includes also a bassoon. However, the solo flute version is (Op. 10/2) and, with its movements representing ghosts (*Fantasmi*) and sleep (*Il sonno*), is a masterpiece by any standards. A Duo collection entirely made up of concertante works for flute might be thought a rather daunting prospect, but Gazzelloni is an artist of such quality and poetry that such doubts are banished. And it must be added that these concertos all show Vivaldi in the best light, not only in the best-known, *La tempesta di mare* and *Il gardellino*, from Op. 10, but in many of the miscellaneous concertos, too: witness the delicate slow movement of the *A minor*, RV 440, the touching *Largo* of the *C minor*, RV 441, or the lively opening movements of the *D major*, RV 429, and *A minor*, RV 108, which also brings another pensive central *Largo* and a gaily dancing finale. These modern-instrument performances have elegance, and Gazzelloni's playing is masterly: his tone is admirably fresh and clean, while I Musici give him splendid support. Indeed the accompaniments have splendid life and detail, and the balance and analogue recordings (from the 1960s and 1970s) are of a high order.

Complete bassoon concertos

Bassoon concertos: in C, RV 466; in C, RV 467; in C, RV 469; in C, RV 470; in C, RV 471; in C, RV 472; in C, RV 473; in C, RV 474; in C, RV 475; in C, RV 476; in C, RV 477; in C, RV 478; in C, RV 479; in C min., RV 480; in D min., RV 481; in E flat, RV 483; in E min., RV 484; in F, RV 485; in F, RV 486; in F, RV 487; in F, RV 488; in F, RV 489; in F, RV 490; in F, RV 491; in G, RV 492; in G, RV 493; in G, RV 494; in G min., RV 495; in G min., RV 496; in A min., RV 497; in A min., RV 498; in A min., RV 499; in A min., RV 500; in B flat (La notte), RV 501; in B flat, RV 502; in B flat, RV 503; in B flat, RV 504.
(M) *** ASV Dig. CDDCX 625 (6). Daniel Smith, ECO, Ledger; Zagreb Soloists, Ninic.

The bassoon seems to have uncovered a particularly generous fund of inspiration in Vivaldi, for few of his 37 concertos for that instrument are in any way routine. Daniel Smith's achievement in recording them all is considerable, for he plays with constant freshness and enthusiasm. His woody tone is very attractive and he is very well caught by the engineers. This set can be welcomed almost without reservation and, dipped into, the various recordings will always give pleasure. We have listened to every one of these concertos and have come up smiling. Daniel Smith is a genial and personable player and he has considerable facility; even if some of the more complicated roulades are not executed with exact precision, his playing has undoubted flair. He is balanced well forward, but the orchestral accompaniment has plenty of personality and registers well enough.

For the last three CDs of the series the Zagreb Soloists take over the accompaniments and offer alert, vivacious playing that adds to the pleasure of the performances. Daniel Smith, too, responds with more vigour and polish, and overall there is plenty of affectionate warmth.

Complete cello concertos

Volume 1: *Cello concertos: in C, RV 398; in C, RV 399; in D, RV 404; in D min., RV 406; in F, RV 410; in F, RV 412; in A min., RV 419.*
(BB) *** Naxos Dig. 8.550907 [id.]. Raphael Wallfisch, City of L. Sinfonia, Nicholas Kraemer.

Volume 2: *Cello concertos: in C, RV 400; in C min., RV 401; in E flat, RV 408; in G, RV 413; in A min., RV 422;* (i) *Double cello concerto in G min., RV 531.*
(BB) *** Naxos Dig. 8.550908 [id.]. Raphael Wallfisch, (i) with Keith Harvey; City of L. Sinfonia, Nicholas Kraemer.

Volume 3: *Cello concertos: in C min., RV 402; in D, RV 403; in D min., RV 407;* (i) *in E min., RV 409; in A min., RV 418; in B flat, RV 423; in B min., RV 424.*
✿ (BB) *** Naxos Dig. 8.550909 [id.]. Raphael Wallfisch, (i) with Johanna Graham; City of L. Sinfonia, Nicholas Kraemer.

Volume 4: *Cello concertos: in D min., RV 405; in F, RV 411; in G, RV 414; in G min., RV 416 & RV 417; in A min., RV 420 & RV 421.*
(BB) *** Naxos Dig. 8. 550910 [id.]. Raphael Wallfisch, City of L. Sinfonia, Nicholas Kraemer.

Vivaldi liked to write for instruments playing in the middle to lower register, and he left 27 solo concertos for the cello, all of which are here. This Naxos series is part of an overall survey, with plans eventually to record every one of the Vivaldi concertos! Certainly the company has begun admirably and the choice of Raphael Wallfisch as soloist could hardly have been bettered. He forms an admirable partnership with the City of London Sinfonia, directed from the harpsichord or chamber organ by Nicholas Kraemer. The first concerto of Volume 1, the fine *F major*, RV 412, sets off with great energy and produces a characteristically atmospheric central *Larghetto*. Wallfisch plays with restrained use of vibrato and a nicely judged expressive feeling. In the *A minor* work which follows (RV 419), Kraemer effectively uses an organ continuo to enliven the opening tutti and underpin the singing cello line in the *Andante*. The alert, resilient orchestral string-playing in the allegros is a pleasure in itself.

Besides several very striking solo works, Volume 2 of the Naxos series includes Vivaldi's only *Double cello concerto*, with much bustling interchange in the outer movements and the soloists answering each other eloquently in the *Largo*. In the *G major* solo *Concerto*, RV 413, there is a brilliantly articulated *moto perpetuo* semiquaver theme which alternates between soloist and orchestra; then follows a thoughtful slow movement, somewhat improvisatory in feeling, in which Wallfisch is in his element, suspended over Kraemer's gentle organ continuo. Bravura passage-work returns in the finale. Throughout these performances one admires the soloist's subtle use of light and shade and his partnership with the accompanying group and Nicholas Kraemer's continuo.

Volume 3 is a particularly fine collection and as good a place to start as any. The soloist's bravura staccato playing at the opening on the *B flat major*, RV 423, commands the listener's attention at the very beginning of the disc, and this work has a matching good-humoured finale. The *Concerto in D minor*, RV 407, is one of Vivaldi's very best, and its central *Largo e sempre piano* again brings a touching solo response. Vivaldi is never predictable, and perhaps the most striking work of all here is the *E minor Concerto*, RV 409, where the cello is joined by a subservient and somewhat doleful solo bassoon. In the *Adagio–Allegro molto* opening movement, the two soloists wind their way through a melancholy recitativo, regularly interrupted by modest bursts of energy from the string tutti, reminding one of *The Four Seasons*; then in the much briefer *Allegro–Adagio* slow movement the procedure is reversed: the orchestral strings are gently sustained and the soloists busy. The finale is more conventional in manner, but the presence of the bassoon ensures that the effect is still aurally intriguing.

Volume 4 brings a further batch of concertos notable for their vitality and the vigorous bravura demanded from the soloist. Throughout these four discs there is never a hint of routine. Wallfisch's playing has extraordinary precision, and both he and the accompanying group continually communicate their enthusiasm for this endlessly inventive music. The recording is vividly realistic and the balance seems very well judged indeed within the warm but never clouding ambience of All Saints' Church or Conway Hall, London. A remarkable achievement, standing very high indeed in the Vivaldi discography. We award a token Rosette to Volume 3, but the final volume is hardly less stimulating, and our accolade could surely apply to either of the other two.

Cello concertos: in C, RV 398; in G, RV 413.
(B) *** DG Double 437 952-2 (2) [id.]. Rostropovich, Zurich Coll. Mus., Sacher – BERNSTEIN: *3 Meditations;* BOCCHERINI: *Cello concerto No. 2;* GLAZUNOV: *Chant du Ménestrel;* SHOSTAKOVICH: *Cello concerto No. 2;* TARTINI: *Cello concerto;* TCHAIKOVSKY: *Andante cantabile* etc. ***

Performances of great vigour and projection from Rostropovich; every bar comes fully to life. Spendidly lively accompaniments and excellent CD transfers, bright and clean with no lack of depth. Rostropovich's performances come as part of a very generous Double DG compilation, with the two discs offered for the price of one.

Cello concertos: in G, RV 413; in G min., RV 417.
(M) **(*) EMI CDM7 64326-2 [id.]. Lynn Harrell, ECO, Zukerman – HAYDN: *Concertos.* **(*)

Though Lynn Harrell is hardly a classical stylist among cellists (as he shows in the Haydn coupling), he gives lively, imaginative performances of two fine Vivaldi concertos (the *G major* particularly attractive) and is well accompanied by Zukerman. The sound is lively and full, if not as smooth as on the Haydn concertos, which are interspersed with Vivaldi on the generous (74-minute) CD.

Flute concertos, Volume 1: *Chamber concertos: in C, for flute, oboe, violin, bassoon & continuo, RV 88; in D, for flute & 2 violins, RV 89; in D, for flute, violin, bassoon & continuo (Il gardellino), RV 90; in D, RV 91; in D min., RV 96 (both for flute, violin, bassoon & continuo); in F, RV 99; in G min., RV 107 (both for flute, oboe, violin, bassoon & continuo).*
(BB) *** Naxos Dig. 8.553365 [id.]. Béla Drahos and soloists, Nicolaus Esterházy Sinf.

The first of a forthcoming series, this Naxos disc collects multiple concertos, but with a continuo instead of an orchestra. Although not to be played at a single sitting, these works offer a great deal of pleasure stemming from their rich textural interplay with plenty of imitation among the soloists. The quality of invention is astonishingly high. *Il gardellino* (which opens the programme) is justly famous, but the G minor work, RV 107, is also remarkable, with a touching *Siciliano* slow movement; it ends with a chaconne which maintains the minor key. Here as elsewhere Vivaldi's use of the bassoon ornamentation is felicitous. RV 88 has a strikingly cheerful opening movement, then gives prominence to the flute both in its central *Largo cantabile* and in another chirping finale. RV 89 effectively brings a change of colour in the use of a pair of violins in juxtaposition to the flute. The performances here are admirable and the recording is most effectively balanced. Another Naxos winner.

Flute concerto in G min. (La notte), Op. 10/2, RV 439; Concertos for strings: in D min. (Madrigalesco), RV 129; in G (Alla rustica), RV 151. Violin concertos: in D (L'Inquietudine), RV 234; in E (L'Amoroso), RV 271. Double violin concerto in A, RV 523; Sinfonia in B min. (Al Santo Sepolcro), RV 169.
(B) **(*) DG Classikon 449 851-2 [(M) id. import]. Soloists, BPO, Karajan.

This collection dates from 1971 (except for the *Flute concerto*, which was recorded a decade later) and shows Karajan indulging himself in repertoire which he clearly loves but for which he does not have the stylistic credentials. Yet the sheer charisma of the playing and the glorious body of tone the orchestra creates within a resonant acoustic, notably in the extraordinary *Sinfonia al Santo Sepolcro*, is difficult to resist. The orchestra dominates even the solo concertos and the soloists seem to float, concertante style, within the resonantly glowing ambience.

Flute concertos: in A min., RV 108; in F, RV 434; Double flute concerto in C, RV 533; Sopranino recorder concertos: in C, RV 443 & RV 444; in A min., RV 445.
(BB) *** Naxos Dig. 8.550385; *4550385* [id.]. Jálek, Novotny, Stivin, Capella Istropolitana, Oliver Dohnányi.

The Capella Istropolitana, who are drawn from the excellent Slovak Philharmonic, play with vitality and sensitivity for Oliver Dohnányi and the soloists show appropriate virtuosity and flair. As always, there are rewards and surprises in this music, revealed by Jiři Stivin's undoubted artistry. The sound is very good indeed, and so is the balance.

Double flute concerto in C, RV 533; Double oboe concerto in D min., RV 535; Double horn concerto in F, RV 539; Double trumpet concerto in C, RV 537; Concerto for 2 oboes, 2 clarinets and strings, RV 560.
(B) ** Carlton IMP Dig. 30367 02252 [(M) id.]. Soloists, SCO, Laredo.

An attractive bargain-priced compilation, with soloists and orchestra set back in a good perspective in a believable acoustic. The resonance tends to make the trumpet timbre spread, but otherwise the sound is very good. The solo playing is accomplished, although rather more light and shade between phrases would have made the performances even more enticing, while Jaime Laredo's direction of the slow movements is not especially imaginative. However, the main drawback to this reissued collection is the short playing time (41 minutes 27 seconds), and Carlton would have been better advised to couple the contents of this CD with Laredo's companion collection of string concertos (see above), cutting out a single concerto if necessary.

Guitar concertos in C, RV 82; in D, RV 93.
(M) **(*) DG (IMS) 439 984-2. Siegfried Behrend, I Musici – CARULLI: *Concerto in A;* GIULIANI: *Concerto in A, Op. 30.* ***

Both these concertos are transcriptions of chamber works intended for the lute. They work well enough on guitar and are most elegantly played here. Although – as the opening of the *D major* shows – there is no lack of life in the performances, their predominating characteristic is of smooth elegance, and a more robust and sinewy effect can be more telling in this repertoire.

Guitar concerto in D, RV 93.

(B) *** Sony SBK 58168; *SBT 58168* [id.]. John Williams, ECO – GIULIANI: *Concerto, Op. 30;* RODRIGO: *Concierto de Aranjuez* etc. ***

This is a familiar work but none the less delightful for that. It is played with predictable liveliness and artistry and, although the balance (as so often with this solo instrument) places the soloist too forward, the orchestra is well in the picture and the ambience is pleasing.

Guitar concertos: in D, RV 93 (arr. Malipiero); *in A* (arr. Pujol from *Trio sonata in C, RV 82*); (i) *Double concerto for guitar and viola d'amore in D min., RV 540* (arr. Malipiero).

(B) **(*) Decca Eclipse 448 709-2; *448 709-4* [(M) id. import]. Eduardo Fernández, ECO, Malcolm, (i) with Norbert Blume – GIULIANI: *Concerto;* PAGANINI: *Sonata.* **(*)

Eduardo Fernández is a musician's guitarist whose playing is consistently refined and sensitive, always responsive to the composer's needs, if at times perhaps a little too self-effacing. Yet the performance of the *Double concerto for guitar and viola d'amore* is winningly intimate, particularly in the very gentle central *Largo*, in which Fernández is perfectly balanced with Norbert Blume. The solo concertos are enjoyable in a similarly refined manner, with bravura unexaggerated and Malcolm always providing the most understanding and polished accompaniments, the recording is first class and beautifully balanced.

Fourteen concertos: Disc 1: (i–ii) *Lute concerto in D, RV 93; Double concerto for 2 mandolins in G, RV 532;* (i; iii) *Recorder concertos: in A min., RV. 108; in G min. (La notte);* (iv) *Violin concerto in D (Grosso Mogull), RV 208.* Disc 2: Double concertos: (v) *Double concertos: for 2 cellos in G min., RV 531; 2 flutes in C, RV 533; 2 trumpets in C, RV 537. Concerto for Flautino (sopranino recorder) in C, RV 443; Concertos for strings: in D min. (Madrigalesco), RV 129; in G (Alla rustica), RV 151; in G min., RV 153; Quadruple concerto for 2 violins & 2 cellos in D, RV 564; L'Estro armonico: Quadruple violin concerto in B min., Op. 3/10, RV 580.*

(B) *** O-L Double Dig./Analogue 455 703-2 [id.]. (i) New London Cons., Pickett, with (ii) Tom Finucane; (iii) Philip Pickett; (iv) Stanley Ritchie, Bach Ens., Rifkin; (v) Soloists, AAM, Hogwood.

The 14 concertos on this Oiseau-Lyre Double readily demonstrate the extraordinary diversity of Vivaldi's concertos and in many cases his originality too. None more so than the remarkable *Violin concerto*, RV 208 (written about 1710), nicknamed – probably not by the composer – '*Grosso Mogull*'. The outer movements with their *moto perpetuo* arpeggios demand great virtuosity from the soloist, and the slow movement is a long Recitativo, more like an improvisation. The remarkable seven-minute finale, perhaps the longest in any Vivaldi concerto, has a bravura central cadenza which demands and is given a performance of dazzling virtuosity by the soloist here, Stanley Ritchie. An unforgettable performance, very well recorded. The concertos for lute, mandolin and recorder are also expertly and pleasingly played by Philip Pickett and his group, whose brand of authenticity is rather less abrasive than Hogwood's. The digital sound is first class. But the colour and tang of the Academy of Ancient Music remains enticing in its own way. Not everything in this issue is of equal substance: the invention in the *Double trumpet concerto*, for example, is not particularly strong; but for the most part it is a rewarding and varied programme. It is especially appealing in that authenticity is allied to musical spontaneity. The *Concerto for two flutes* has great charm and is dispatched with vigour and aplomb. Performances and recording alike are first rate. For the reissue, three extra works have been added (giving an overall playing time of 70 minutes), most notably the famous *Quadruple violin concerto* from *L'Estro armonico*, taken from the Academy's splendid complete set, with John Holloway, Monica Huggett, Catherine Mackintosh and Elizabeth Wilcock the excellent soloists.

Oboe concertos: in C, RV 447 & RV 451; in F, RV 455 & RV 457; in A min., RV 461 & RV 463.

(BB) *** Naxos Dig. 8.550860 [id.]. Stefan Schilli, Budapest Failoni CO, Béla Nagy.

Oboe concertos: in C, RV 450 & RV 452; in D, RV 453; in D min., RV 454; (i) *Double oboe concertos: in C, RV 534; D min., RV 535; A min., RV 536.*

(BB) *** Naxos Dig. 8.550859 [id.]. Stefan Schilli; (i) with Diethelm Jonas; Budapest Failoni CO, Béla Nagy.

Excellent playing from these Budapest musicians, who seem set to provide us with a survey of Vivaldi's concertante works for oboe. The second of these two discs offers the three *Double concertos*, and the two CDs between them include half the solo works. They are often surprisingly florid, requiring considerable bravura from the soloist. A good example is the Minuet finale of RV 447, which is a cross between a Rondo and a theme and variations. Vivaldi is never entirely predictable, except that his invention never seems to flag, and many of the simple *Grave*, *Larghetto* and *Largo* slow movements are very pleasing indeed.

Oboe concertos: in A min., RV 461; in D min., RV 454.
(B) ** EMI CfP CD-CFP 6048 [(M) id. import]. Sydney Sutcliffe, Virtuosi of England, Arthur Davison – ALBINONI: *Concerti a cinque.* **

The other half of an attractive coupling with Albinoni (the concertos of the two composers alternate effectively), these performances are admirably alive and sensitive in matters of style. Sydney Sutcliffe is an excellent soloist, but Davison's direction is characteristically straight. He is rather unbending in Vivaldi's slow movements, as if to contrast them with the more beguilingly tender *Adagios* of Albinoni. The sound is crisp and clean, but this collection plays for only 35 minutes!

(i) *Oboe concertos: in C, RV 540; in D min., RV 454; in F, RV 457;* (i–ii) *Double oboe concerto in D min., RV 535;* (i; iii) *Double concerto for oboe, bassoon and orchestra in G, RV 545;* (i–iii) *Concerto for 2 oboes, 2 violins, bassoon and orchestra, RV 557;* (i) *Recorder concerto in F, RV 442.*
(B) *** HM Dig. HMA 1903018 [id.]. (i) Marie Wolf (oboe or recorder); (ii) Márton Brandisz; (iii) Paul Tognon; Capella Savaria, Pál Németh.

While two of the solo oboe concertos here were conceived for bassoon, Marie Wolf with her warm phrasing and clean tonguing makes them all sound custom-made for her principal instrument. Indeed she creates robust yet creamy tone on her baroque oboe, especially in the *Largo* of RV 454, while the chromatic 'slides' in the work's first movement are most seductively managed. In the double concertos the other wind soloists produce equally characterful timbres: the two oboes blend well together, yet have individuality, while the combination of oboe and the chortling, woody bassoon must surely make the listener smile at the genial exchanges. Then Marie Wolf turns to her recorder and charms us yet again. The delightful slow movement of RV 442 is made the more fragile by the use of muted strings in the orchestra and the accompaniments have finesse and transparency. Indeed there are few more appealing bargain collections of Vivaldi wind concertos played on original instruments than this. The recording is beautifully balanced and truthful.

Concertos for strings: in C, RV 113 & RV 114; in D min., RV 127; in F, RV 138; in G (Alla Rustica), RV 151; in G min., RV 153, RV 156 & RV 157; in A min., RV 161; in B flat, RV 167.
(BB) **(*) Naxos Dig. 8.553742 [id.]. Accademia I Filarmonici, Alberto Martini.

The Accademia I Filarmonici is Italy's equivalent of the North American Orpheus group, a conductorless chamber orchestra, to some extent led from the bow by Alberto Martini. They do not use period instruments, but their style, brisk and athletic, with comparatively lean textures, is well removed from that of I Musici. They make the most of this group of Vivaldi's string concertos – which might equally well have been called sinfonias. The only famous one is *Alla Rustica*, which is vigorously done. Slow movements are delicate in texture with the harpsichord continuo coming through naturally. Not all this music is equally appealing, but the best movements are quite indelible, for instance the jogging opening allegro of RV 113 and its minor-key *Grave* slow movement, and the gay, *moto perpetuo* finale of the *D minor* work, RV 127, which ends the programme. Excellent recording, but a disc to be dipped into rather than played through.

Violin concertos, Op. 8, Nos. 5 in E flat (La Tempesta di mare), RV 253; 6 in C (Il Piacere), RV 180; 10 in B flat (La Caccia), RV 362; 11 in D, RV 210; in C min. (Il Sospetto), RV 199.
(B) *** CfP Dig. CD-CFP 4522 [(M) id. import]. Sir Yehudi Menuhin, Polish CO, Jerzy Maksymiuk.

Menuhin's collection of five concertos – four of them with nicknames and particularly delightful – brings some of his freshest, most intense playing in recent years. Particularly in slow movements – notably that of *Il Piacere* ('Pleasure') – he shows afresh his unique insight in shaping a phrase. Fresh, alert accompaniment and full digital recording.

Violin concertos: (i) *in C min. (Il Sospetto), RV 199;* (ii) *in D (Grosso Mogul), RV 208; in D (L'inquietudine), RV 234;* (i) *in E (Il Ripososo), RV 270; in E (L'Amoroso), RV 271; in B flat (O sia il corneto da posta), RV 363;* (i; iii) *Quadruple violin concerto in B flat, RV 553.*
(M) ** Erato/Warner Analogue/Dig. 4509 97415-2. (i) Piero Toso; (ii) Marco Fornaciari; (iii) with Sasaki, Bartagnin, Scalabrin; Sol. Ven., Scimone.

Piero Toso is a first-rate Vivaldi soloist and his playing in the lovely *Cantabile* of *L'Amoroso*, the *Andante* of *Il Sospetto* and the *Largo* of the *Posthorn concerto* is ravishing in tone and phrase. Incidentally, the nickname of the latter comes from the dotted rhythms and fanfare effects (with double-stopping) in the first movement. Marco Fornaciari is also a fine player and he makes a good deal of the *Grave-Recitativo* of the *Grosso Mongol concerto* (another puzzling Vivaldi sobriquet), even if he is a bit romantic in his lyrical style. The snag is that, while Scimone's accompaniments are lively and stylish, the resonant acoustic combined with the CD remastering coarsens the string tuttis. The quality is cleaner in the digital

L'Inquietudine and *Quadruple violin concerto*, which latter work comes off here with some charm.

Miscellaneous Concerto Collections

(i) *The Trial between harmony and invention: Violin concertos Nos. 5 in E flat (La tempesta di mare); 6 in C (Il piacere), Op. 8/5–6;* (ii) *Bassoon concertos: in C, RV 472; in C min., RV 480; in A min., RV 498; in B flat, RV 504.*
(M) *** Chan. CHAN 6529 [id.]. (i) Ronald Thomas, Bournemouth Sinf.; (ii) Robert Thompson, L. Mozart Players, Ledger.

The two concertos included here from *The Trial between harmony and invention* were among the best of the complete set recorded by Ronald Thomas in 1980. The use of modern instruments does not preclude a keen sense of style, and the balance is convincing. The bassoonist Robert Thompson turns a genial eye on his four concertos. He is rather forwardly projected but the performances are direct and personable and, like the sound, agreeably fresh, among the most attractive accounts of Vivaldi's bassoon concertos available on CD. An enjoyable collection.

Concerti 'con molti instromenti': Bassoon concerto in E min., RV 484; Flute concerto in G min. (La notte), Op. 10/2, RV 439; Double mandolin concerto in G, RV 532; Concerto con multi instromenti in C, RV 558; Double concerto for oboe and violin in B flat, RV 548; Concerto for strings (alla rustica), RV 151; Concerto for 2 violins and two cellos in G, RV 575; L'estro armonico: Concerto for 4 violins in D, Op. 3/1, RV 549.
(M) *** DG Dig. 447 301-2; *447 301-4* [id.]. Soloists, E. Concert, Pinnock.

This extremely generous 72-minute collection of very varied works is very enticing at mid-price, showing Pinnock and the English Concert at their liveliest and most refreshing, although not always so strong on charm. (The account of the *Bassoon concerto* is perhaps an unintentional exception, for the solo timbre has a certain bovine character.) The *Concerto for four violins* is very lithe, and throughout the concert the solo playing is predictably expert. The orchestral concerto, RV 558, involves an astonishing array of instruments.

Bassoon concerto in A min., RV 498; Flute concerto in C min., RV 108; Double horn concerto in F, RV 539; Oboe concerto in F, RV 456; Double oboe concerto in D min., RV 535; 2 Concertos for 2 oboes, bassoon, 2 horns & violin in F, RV 569 & RV 574; Piccolo concerto in C, RV 208.
(B) *** Decca Double 452 943-2 (2) [id.]. Soloists, ASMF, Marriner – BELLINI: *Oboe concerto in E flat;* HANDEL: *Oboe concertos* etc. ***

Marriner's modern-instrument performances of favourite Vivaldi wind concertos, made between 1965 and 1977, have long been praised by us. The soloists are all distinguished and the playing here is splendidly alive and alert, with crisp, clean articulation and well-pointed phrasing, full of imagination, yet free from over-emphasis. The *A minor Bassoon concerto* has a delightful sense of humour. Although the musical substance may not be very weighty, Vivaldi was never more engaging than when writing for wind instruments, particularly if he had more than one in his team of soloists, as in the two attractive composite works included in the programme. The vintage recordings remain in the demonstration bracket.

Bassoon concertos: in A min., RV 497; in B flat (La notte), RV 501; Double mandolin concerto in G, RV 532; Piccolo concerto in C, RV 443; Viola d'amore concerto in D min., RV 394; Double violin concerto for violin and violin per eco lontano in A, RV 552.
(M) *** Pierre Vernay Dig. PV 730052. Soloists, Paul Kuentz CO, Kuentz.

Although described as 'six rare concertos', this most enjoyable, 71-minute collection is made up entirely of favourites, all played with much character. The two mandolinists, Takashi and Sylvia Ochi, are as personable as the sprightly bassoonist, Fernand Corbillon, with his woody French timbre, while the *Echo violin concerto* (the echoes feature in the ripieno as well as the solo writing) comes off to great effect. Fine accompaniments from Kuentz and first-rate digital sound, naturally balanced.

Double concertos: for 2 cellos in G min., RV 531; 2 flutes in C, RV 533; 2 oboes in D min., RV 535; 2 mandolins in G, RV 532; 2 trumpets in C, RV 537; 2 violins, RV 523.
(M) *** Ph. 426 086-2. I Musici.

This makes an attractively diverse collection. Most of these concertos are admirably inventive and the performances show I Musici at their very best, on sparkling form. The sound is good too.

Double cello concerto in G min., RV 531; Lute concerto in G, RV 93; Double mandolin concerto in G, RV 532; Recorder concertos: in C min., RV 441; in C, RV 443. Trio for violin, lute & continuo in G min., RV 85.
(M) *** DG Dig. 445 602-2. Demenga, Häusler, Söllscher, Copley, Camerata Bern, Füri.

An excellent mid-priced digital collection, assembled from various records made by the Camerata Bern, which will especially suit those who like their Vivaldi on original instruments. Söllscher's account of the *Duet concerto* for mandolins (in which he takes both solo roles) is quite outstanding, and there is some breathtaking virtuosity from Michael Copley in the *Recorder concertos*. Further variety is provided by the *Trio*, which is also an attractive work. The well-balanced recording has splendid presence and realism.

Double cello concerto in G min., RV 531; Lute (Guitar) concerto in D, RV 93; Oboe concerto in F, F.VII, No. 2 (R.455); Double concerto for oboe and violin; Trumpet concerto in D (trans. Jean Thilde); *Violin concerto in G min., Op. 12/1; RV 317.*
(BB) *** Naxos Dig. 8.550384; *4550384* [id.]. Capella Istropolitana, Jaroslav Krechek.

This is a recommendable disc from which to set out to explore the Vivaldi concertos, especially if you are beginning a collection. Gabriela Krcková makes a sensitive contribution to the delightful *Oboe concerto in F major*, F.VII, No. 2 (R.455), and the other soloists are pretty good too. Should this programme meet your particular needs, there is no need for hesitation.

Double concertos: for 2 cellos in G min., RV 531; 2 flutes in C, RV 533; 2 trumpets in C, RV 537; Concerto for Flautino (sopranino recorder) in C, RV 443; Concertos for strings: in D min. (Madrigalesco), RV 129; in G (Alla rustica), RV 151; in G min., RV 153; Quadruple concerto for 2 violins & 2 cellos in D, RV 564; L'Estro armonico: Quadruple violin concerto in B min., Op. 3/10, RV 580.
(M) *** O-L 443 198-2 [id.]. Soloists, AAM, Hogwood.

Not everything in this issue is of equal substance: the invention in the *Double trumpet concerto*, for example, is not particularly strong; but for the most part it is a rewarding and varied programme. It is especially appealing in that authenticity is allied to musical spontaneity. Performances and recording alike are first rate. As can be seen above, this collection is also available as part of a Oiseau-Lyre Double, containing 14 concertos in all, which costs only a little more than the present single disc.

Flute concerto in G min. (La notte), Op. 10/2, RV 439; Oboe concerto in A min., RV 463; Concertos for strings: in G min., RV 156; in D min. (Madrigalesco), RV 329; Double trumpet concerto in C, RV 537; Violin concerto in G, Op. 11/4, RV 308; Quadruple violin concerto in B min., Op. 3/10, RV 580.
(B) ** EMI Eminence Dig. CD-EMX 2210 [(M) id. import]. Soloists, Hanover Band, Anthony Halstead.

An attractive clutch of concertos, including several of Vivaldi's best, although it is a pity that the version of *La notte* was not chosen which includes also a bassoon. The period performances are lively, spick and span but are a little lacking in individuality of personality. The recording is excellent.

Double concertos: for 2 flutes in C, RV 533; for 2 horns in F, RV 538 & RV 539; for 2 trumpets in C, RV 537; for oboe and bassoon in G, RV 545; Concerto (Sinfonia in D) for strings, RV 122; Quadruple concerto for 2 oboes and 2 clarinets, RV 560.
(BB) *** Naxos Dig. 8.553204 [id.]. Soloists, City of L. Sinfonia, Nicholas Kraemer.

An enjoyably lively clutch of concertos, very well recorded in All Saints' Church, East Finchley. The opening double concertos for two horns, RV 539, two flutes, RV 533, and two trumpets, RV 537, all go well enough and offer expert solo contributions, but then at the arrival of the *Quadruple concerto for two oboes and two clarinets* the playing suddenly sparks into extra exuberance, and one senses the musicians' enjoyment of one of Vivaldi's most imaginatively scored multiple works. The *Concerto for two horns* which follows (RV 538) has a similar (bold) ebullience, and the concert is rounded off by a captivating account of RV 545, where both the oboe and bassoon clearly relish every bar of their engaging dialogue. Throughout, Kraemer's accompaniments are polished and spirited.

Concerto for 2 flutes, 2 oboes, 2 clarinets, bassoon, 2 violins & strings in C (Per la Solennità di San Lorenzo), RV 556; Violin concertos: in D (Fatto per la Solennità della S. Lingua di S. Antonio), RV 212; in F (per la Solennità di San Lorenzo), RV 286; in C (in due cori, Per la S.S. ma Assontione di Maria Vergine), RV 581; Double concerto for violin, oboe & strings in B flat (Funèbre), RV 579.
(M) *** Erato/Warner 0630 13744-2. Sol. Ven., Claudio Scimone.

Although the presentation of this CD describes it as a collection of 'solemn concertos' and there is much of the composer's finest expressive writing here, there is also a great deal that is vivid and lively too. Indeed this is an exceptionally stimulating collection of music written for performance on various religious feast-days, and all these works have the composer's imagination working at full stretch. The *Violin concerto in C*, RV 581, is for two string orchestras with echo effects. The *Concerto funèbre* is atmospheric in a darkly expressive way. Using muted strings in the acompaniments plus additional instruments, it is one of the composer's most strikingly original works. The *Violin concerto in D*, RV 212, brings remarkable violin cadenzas in the outer movements, with the soloist soaring up like a bird in the finale. The multiple concerto, RV 556, which is listed first, ends the concert in a blaze of florid colour, with the clarinets standing out – they were novel instruments at the time of composition – in the *Allegro molto*, and they are featured again in the finale; but, more strikingly, in the slow movement the principal clarinet has an important cantilena solo over pizzicato strings. The modern-instrument performances under the ever-reliable Claudio Scimone are excellent, with first-rate solo playing, and the balance is always well managed. The sound too is pleasingly warm yet not clouded.

Concerto per l'Orchestra di Dresda in G min. (for 2 recorders, 2 oboes & bassoon), RV 577; Concerto per la Solennità di S. Lorenzo in C, RV 556; Chamber concerto for recorder, oboe, violin, bassoon & continuo in D (La pastorella), RV 95; Flute concerto in G min. (La notte), Op. 10/2, RV 439; Concerto for strings (Sinfonia) in C, RV 114; Quadruple concerto for 2 violins and 2 cellos in G, RV 575.
(M) *** Virgin Veritas/EMI Dig. VER5 61275-2. Soloists, Taverner Players, Andrew Parrott.

This is a particularly winning collection – an hour of Vivaldi at his most creative. The opening Dresden concerto with its interplay between the wind groups, but including also solo violin obbligati, is particularly original; then comes the delightful pastoral chamber concerto, with its rustic woodwind charm. This has a particularly engaging siciliano for the solo recorder as its central *Largo*, so nicely played (and decorated) here by Marion Verbruggen, while the imitative finale is hardly less endearing. The two-movement 'Sinfonia', RV 114, is also notable for its inventive finale – in the form of a ciaconna. *La notte* is (by common consent) among Vivaldi's most imaginative works for flute; its descriptive evocations are atmospherically caught by the Taverner Players, notably '*Ghosts*' and '*Sleep*' which is so reminiscent of the *Four Seasons*. The following concerto for a pair each of violins and echoing cellos at times sounds more like a concerto grosso. The grand opening of the *Concerto for S. Lorenzo* is Handelian, but Vivaldi's own personality reasserts itself firmly in the following allegro. The work is richly scored and, apart from the main protagonists – a pair of solo violins – features recorders, oboes and (a great novelty at that time) clarinets, with ear-catching results. This is its first recording in its original form; Vivaldi, for practical reasons, later dispensed with the clarinets. It makes a splendid conclusion to an outstanding concert, very well laid out, beautifully and authentically played, and excellently recorded.

CHAMBER MUSIC

2 Chamber sonatas for 2 violins and continuo in D min., Op. 1/8 & 12 (La Follia), RV 63 & RV 64; 4 Chamber sonatas for 2 violins: in F, RV 68 & RV 70; in G, RV 71; in E flat, RV 77.
(B) *** HM Dig. HMX 290853.55 (3) [(M) id.]. Ens. 315 (Chiara Banchieri, Véronique Méjean, Käthi Gohl, Jesper Christensen) – CORELLI: *Trio sonatas, Op. 5/1–6.* TARTINI: *Concerti grossi* etc. ***

This is the most winning of the three CDs of baroque music gathered together in a slip-case in Harmonia Mundi's bargain-price Trio format. Vivaldi's variations on *La Follia* extend to 11 minutes and are highly inventive, while Op. 1/12 also includes an extended set of variations, all in the key of D minor, with the two violins sometimes in dialogue with each other. The remaining four *Chamber sonatas* were not published until after the composer's death. They are genuine duet sonatas, written in the three-movement format which Vivaldi favoured in his concertos, with the interplay between the two violins often demanding considerable bravura as well as indulging in all kinds of imaginatively exuberant devices and effects. Vivaldi indicated the bass line as optional, and it is omitted here. It is not missed and these works might be compared (if not quite in the same breath) with Bach's sonatas for a single, unaccompanied violin. These works by Vivaldi are not programmatic, yet they have a life and spirit which place them among the composer's finest music. They are splendidly played on period instruments, and these expert musicians certainly convey their enjoyment of this rewarding music. The recording has striking presence and realism.

VOCAL MUSIC

Beatus vir, RV 597; Credo, RV 592; Magnificat, RV 610.
(M) *** Ph. (IMS) 420 651-2. Soloists, Alldis Ch., ECO, Negri.

Beatus vir, RV 598; Dixit Dominus in D, RV 594; Introduzione al Dixit: Canta in prato in G, RV 636 (ed. Geigling); *Magnificat in G min., RV 611* (ed. Negri).
(M) *** Ph. (IMS) 420 649-2. Lott, Burgess, Murray, Daniels, Finnie, Collins, Rolfe Johnson, Holl, Alldis Ch., ECO, Negri.

Crediti propter quod, RV 105; Credo, RV 591; Introduction to Gloria, RV 639; Gloria, RV 588; Kyrie, RV 587; Laetatus sum, RV 607.
(M) *** Ph. (IMS) 420 650-2. M. Marshall, Lott, Finnie, Rolfe Johnson, Alldis Ch., ECO, Negri.

Dixit dominus, RV 595; In exitu Israel, RV 604; Sacrum, RV 586.
(M) *** Ph. (IMS) 420 652-2. Alldis Ch., ECO, Negri.

Introduction to Gloria, RV 642; Gloria in D, RV 589; Lauda Jerusalem in E min., RV 609; Laudate Dominum in D min., RV 606; Laudati pueri Dominum in A, RV 602.
(M) *** Ph. (IMS) 420 648-2. Marshall, Lott, Collins, Finnilä, Alldis Ch., ECO, Negri.

These Philips recordings come from the late 1970s. Vittorio Negri does not make use of period instruments, but he penetrates as deeply into the spirit of this music as many who do, and they come up splendidly in their new format, digitally refurbished. Any lover of Vivaldi is likely to be astonished that not only the well-known works but the rarities show him writing with the keenest originality and intensity. There is nothing routine about any of this music, nor any of the performances either.

(i–v) *Beatus vir in G, RV 597;* (vi) *Introduction to Gloria, RV 639;* (i; iv; vi–vii) *Gloria in D, RV 588;* (i–ii; viii) *Gloria in D, RV 589;* (i; iii; vi–vii; ix) *Magnificat in G min., RV 611;* (x) *Nulla in mundo pax sincera, RV 630;* (xi) *Stabat Mater, RV 621.*
(B) *** Ph. Duo 462 170-2 (2) [id.]. (i) Margaret Marshall; (ii) Ann Murray; (iii) Anne Collins; (iv) Anthony Rolfe Johnson; (v) Robert Holl; (vi) Linda Finnie; (vii) Felicity Lott; (viii) Birgit Finnilä; (ix) Sally Burgess; (x) Elly Ameling; (xi) Jochen Kowalski; Alldis Ch., ECO, Negri.

This Philips Duo is drawn from the four CDs above and can be strongly recommended in its own right. It includes the two *Glorias* and the double-choir version of the *Magnificat*, while the *Beatus vir*, also for two choirs, is a similarly stirring piece. The collection opens with striking vocal bravura from Linda Finnie, who sings the *Introduction to Gloria*, K.639, with spectacular virtuosity; later there is a comparable display from Elly Ameling in *Nulla in mundo pax sincera*, with the brilliant upper tessitura of the closing *Alleluia* stressing her to the limit of her powers. Jochen Kowalski is the fine soloist in the touching *Stabat Mater*. The other soloists are also splendid, while the choir, vividly recorded, captures the dark, Bach-like intensity of many passages, contrasted with more typical Vivaldian brilliance. The analogue recordings are transferred to CD most impressively. A splendid point of entry into Vivaldi's vocal and choral sound-world, where there is no question of routine inspiration, as there can sometimes be in his concertos.

Beatus vir, RV 597; Canta in Prato; Credo in E min., RV 591; Gloria in D, RV 589; In Furore; Kyrie in G min., RV 587; Lauda Jerusalem, RV 609; Magnificat in G min., RV 610; Nulla in mundo pax sincera.
(B) **(*) Erato/Ultima 0630 18969-2 (2) [(M) id. import]. Jennifer Smith, Wally Staempfli, Verena Schweizer, Uta Spreckelsen, Nicole Rossier, Hanna Schaer, Jean-Pierre Maurer, Philippe Huttenlocher, Lausanne Vocal Ens. & CO, Corboz.

About the time Negri was making his Vivaldi recordings for Philips, Michel Corboz, an equally fine choral conductor, was working in Lausanne. Modern instruments are used to produce a warm, well-focused sound; the acoustic is spacious and the performances vital and musical. The professional singers of the Lausanne Choir are generally admirable, and the soloists are sweet-toned. The programme opens with a lively performance of the more famous *Gloria*, and the first CD closes with the *Magnificat* given in its simpler first version on a relatively small scale, with the chorus singing the alto solo, *Fecit potentiam*. The *Kyrie in G minor* with its double chorus, double string orchestra, plus four soloists makes a fine contrast in its magnificence. The *Beatus vir* is another stirring piece, used to open the second disc. The acoustic is spacious but not cavernous and the performances are vital and musical. There is much to enjoy on this pair of CDs and, if the Negri survey is stylistically the more satisfying investment, it involves a great deal more outlay; the Ultima Double is a recommendably inexpensive way to get to know some of Vivaldi's finest choral music.

Beatus vir, RV 597; Gloria in D, RV 589.
(BB) **(*) Naxos 8.550687 [id.]. Anna Crookes, Jayne Quitaker, Carys-Anne Lane, Caroline Trevor, Oxford Schola Cantorum, N. CO, Ward.

This Naxos coupling of what are probably the two favourite Vivaldi choral works is beautifully recorded and well worth its modest cost. Although some listeners will want greater attack in the famous opening and closing sections of the *Gloria* and in the *Potens in terra* in the companion work, these spacious performances, directed by Nicholas Ward, are still warmly enjoyable, partly because of the freshness of the solo contributions, but also because the choral singing has considerable intensity, especially in the continual return of the haunting *Beatus vir* chorale ('Blessed is the man that feareth the Lord; He hath great delight in his commandments') in RV 589. The *Paratum cor eius*, too, brings a surge of choral feeling, and the chorus rises to the occasion for the splendid closing *Gloria Patri*. Full translations are included; full marks, Naxos!

Cantatas: (i) *All'ombra di sospetto, RV 678;* (ii–iii) *Amor hai vinto, RV 651;* (i) *Lungi dal vago volto, RV 680; Vengo a voi, luci adorate, RV 682.* (iv) *Gloria in D, RV 589;* (v; iii) *Nisi Dominus (Psalm 127), RV 608;* (ii–iii) *Nulla in mundo pax sincera, RV 630.* (vi) *Trio sonata (La Folia), RV 63.*

(B) *** O-L Double Analogue/Dig. 455 727-2 (2) [id.]. (i) Catherine Bott, New London Cons., Pickett; (ii) Emma Kirkby; (iii) AAM, Hogwood (iv) Judith Nelson, Kirkby, Carolyn Watkinson, Christ Church Cathedral Ch., AAM, Preston; (v) James Bowman; (vi) Simon Standage, Catherine Mackintosh, Christopher Hogwood.

Vivaldi's secular cantatas are lightweight but have much charm. The present group were written in Mantua between 1718 and 1720. Combining recitative and a pair of arias, they usually express the dolours of unrequited love in an Arcadian setting. The exception here is *Lungi dal vago volta*, in which the lovers are apart; but they are reunited before the end. In each case the words are written from the male point of view, yet here they are treated as soprano solos – delightfully so, for, after Emma Kirby has opened the programme with a characteristically fresh-voiced *Amor, hai vento*, Catherine Bott takes over with her softer focus and more plaintive style. As a central instrumental interlude we are offered a lively and stylish account of the *Trio sonata* which Vivaldi based on *La Folia*, in essence a set of variations, almost a chaconne, following closely after Corelli's similar exercise which ends his Opus 5. The first CD opens with the familiar *Gloria*, and the freshness and point of the Christ Church performance are irresistible; anyone who doubts the attractiveness of authentic string techniques should sample this, for the absence of vibrato adds a tang exactly in keeping with the performance. The soloists too keep vibrato to the minimum, adding to the freshness, yet Carolyn Wilkinson rivals even Dame Janet Baker (the soloist in the Willcocks/King's version) in the dark intensity of the Bach-like central aria for contralto, *Dominus Deus, Agnus Deus*. The choristers of Christ Church Cathedral excel themselves and the recording is remarkably fine. The solo motet, *Nulla in mundo pax sincera*, brings back Emma Kirkby, who copes splendidly with the bravura writing for soprano. James Bowman is also a persuasive soloist in the more extended, operatic-styled setting of Psalm 127. But since Vivaldi probably wrote *Nisi Dominus* for the Pietà, a Venetian orphanage for girls, there is a case here for preferring a soprano voice.

Motets: *Canto in prato, RV 623; In furore giustissimae irae, RV 626; Longa mala umbrae tertores, RV 640; Vos aurae per montes (per la solennita di S. Antonio), RV 634.*

(M) *** Erato/Warner Dig. 4509 96966-2. Cecilia Gasdia, Sol. Ven., Scimone.

Though the booklet for this collection of Vivaldi rarities fails to provide texts for these four solo motets, they make a delightful collection, also displaying the formidable talent of a rising star among Italian sopranos, Cecilia Gasdia. Vivaldi's solo motets might be described structurally as concertos for voice, but generally with a recitative between first movement and slow movement. *Canto in prato* is the exception, with three jolly, rustic allegros in succession. Lively performances and well-balanced recording.

(i) *Dixit Dominus in D, RV 594;* (ii) *Stabat Mater, RV 621.*

(B) **(*) Sony SBK 48282; *SBT 48282* [id.]. (i) Hill Smith, Bernardin, Partridge, Caddy; (i–ii) Watts; E. Bach Festival ((i) Ch.) O, Malgoire – D. SCARLATTI: *Stabat Mater.* **(*)

Malgoire's overemphatic style of baroque playing, with first beats of bars heavily underlined, is inclined to be wearing, but these fine works make an excellent coupling, and the singing is first rate, from both the chorus and the soloists in the better-known setting of *Dixit Dominus*, and particularly from Helen Watts in the moving sequence of solo items that makes up the *Stabat Mater*. Reverberant, church-like acoustic.

(i) *Gloria in D, RV 588; Gloria in D, RV 589;* (ii) *Concerto for guitar and viola d'amore, RV 540.*

(B) *** Decca Eclipse Dig. 448 223-2; *448 223-4* [(M) id. import]. (i) Russell, Kwella, Wilkens, St John's College, Cambridge, Ch., Wren O, Guest; (ii) Fernández, Blume, ECO, Malcolm.

(i) *Gloria in D, RV 588; Gloria in D, RV 589;* (ii; iii) *Beatus vir in C, RV 597; Dixit dominus in D, RV 594;* (iv; iii) *Magnificat in G min., RV 610.*

(B) *** Decca Double Dig./Analogue 443 455-2 (2) [id.]. (i) Russell, Kwella, Wilkens, Bowen, St John's College, Cambridge, Ch., Wren O, Guest; (ii) Jennifer Smith, Buchanan, Watts, Partridge, Shirley-Quirk, ECO, Cleobury; (iii) King's College, Cambridge, Ch.; (iv) Castle, Cockerham, King, ASMF, Ledger.

The two settings of the *Gloria* make an apt and illuminating pairing. Both in D major, they have many points in common, presenting fascinating comparisons, when RV 588 is as inspired as its better-known companion. Guest directs strong and well-paced readings, with RV 588 the more lively. Good, warm recording to match the performances. *Dixit dominus* cannot fail to attract those who have enjoyed the better-known *Gloria*. Both works are powerfully inspired and are here given vigorous and sparkling performances with King's College Choir in excellent form under its latest choirmaster. The soloists are a fine team, fresh, stylish and nimble, nicely projected in the CD format. But what caps this outstanding Vivaldi compilation is the earlier King's account of the inspired *Magnificat in G minor*. Ledger uses the small-scale setting and opts for boys' voices in the solos such as the beautiful duet (*Esurientes*) which is most winning. The performance overall is very compelling and moving, and the singing has all the accustomed beauty of the King's records. The transfer of an outstanding (1976) analogue recording to CD is admirable, even richer than its digital companions.

As can be seen, those seeking an inexpensive disc of the two *Glorias* will find the Eclipse CD a satisfactory alternative, and the *Concerto for guitar and viola d'amore* makes an attractively lightweight interlude between the two choral works.

Gloria in D, RV 589.

(M) *** Decca 421 146-2. Vaughan, J. Baker, King's College, Cambridge, Ch., ASMF, Willcocks – HAYDN: *Nelson Mass*. ***

(M) *** O-L 443 178-2 [id.]. Nelson, Kirkby, Watkinson, Ch. of Christ Church Cathedral, Oxford, AAM, Simon Preston – HANDEL: *Utrecht Te Deum and Jubilate*. ***

(BB) *** Naxos Dig. 8.554056 [id.]. Oxford Schola Cantorum, N. CO, Nicholas Ward – BACH: *Magnificat*. ***

The CD remastering of the stylish 1962 Willcocks recording of Vivaldi's *Gloria* is strikingly vivid and, with excellent choral and solo singing, this makes a fine and generous bonus for the Haydn *Nelson Mass*.

The freshness and point of the Christ Church performance of the *Gloria* are irresistible; anyone who normally doubts the attractiveness of authentic string technique should sample this, for the absence of vibrato adds a tang exactly in keeping with the performance. The soloists too keep vibrato to the minimum, adding to the freshness, yet Carolyn Watkinson rivals even Dame Janet Baker in the dark intensity of the Bach-like central aria for contralto, *Domine Deus, Agnus Dei*. The choristers of Christ Church Cathedral excel themselves, and the recording is outstandingly fine. This now comes generously coupled with Handel, making a total playing time of 74 minutes.

On Naxos it is most refreshing to have a performance of Vivaldi's most popular choral work that with modern instruments and a relatively small choir clarifies textures, revealing inner detail usually obscured. With Jeremy Summerly directing the choir and Nicholas Ward conducting the orchestra, the rhythmic point of the writing is reinforced, helped by superb sound, fresh, clear and immediate.

Stabat mater, RV 621.

(M) **(*) Ph. Dig. 462 054-2 [id.]. Kowalski, Concg. CO, Negri – PERGOLESI: *Stabat mater*. **(*)

The coupling here is undoubtedly apt, but it was a curious decision to pair Maazel's highly romantic performance of Pergolesi with a much more authentic approach to Vivaldi's setting from a counter-tenor. Negri's accompaniment also uses modern instruments, and what appears to be a chamber-organ continuo; but it is altogether more restrained and stylish, though still matching the warmth of the soloist. Jochen Kowakski is a highly expressive singer with a rich timbre. There is a tiny lapse of pitching in the brief *Fac ut ardeat*, but otherwise this performance cannot be faulted. The recording is excellent, but as this reissue comes as part of the Philips Choral Collection, there are no texts.

OPERA

L'Incoronazione di Dario (complete).

(B) **(*) HM Musique d'Abord Dig. HMA 1901235/7 [id.]. Elwes, Visse, Lesne, Ledroit, Verschaeve, Poulenard, Mellon, Nice Bar. Ens., Bezzina.

Set in the fifth century BC at the Persian court, this Vivaldi opera involves the conflict which followed the death of King Cyrus and the succession of Darius. Written in 1717, it is one of Vivaldi's earlier operas, in places reflecting the great oratorio he had written the year before, *Juditha triumphans*, reworking three numbers. The opera here receives a lively performance, generally well sung. John Elwes as Darius himself, though stylish, does not sound as involved as some of the others, notably the male alto, Dominique Visse, who is superb both vocally and dramatically as the female confidante, Flora. Reliable singing from the whole cast, and first-rate recording. The full libretto is provided only in Italian, with translated summaries of the plot in English, French and German. However, this reissue on Harmonia Mundi's bargain Musique d'Abord label is very tempting.

Tito Manlio (complete).
(M) **(*) Ph. 446 332-2 (4). Luccardi, Wagemann, Hamari, Finnnilä, Marshall, Trimarchi, Lerer, Ahnsjö, Berlin R. Ch. & CO, Negri.

Vivaldi claimed that he wrote this massive score in a mere five days – which sounds improbable, even for him. The inspiration of the set numbers, most of them short, simple arias, is generally lively, and they are attractively spiced with obbligato solos. The overture sets the classical scene well, with its pomposo, trumpet-full style; the main snag for the modern listener is the sheer length, which achieves Wagnerian proportions. First issued on LP in the tercentenary year, the opera is given here uncut except for some snipping of *secco* recitatives, which still make up a very substantial proportion of the whole. The performance, using modern instruments, is crisp and stylish, sympathetically directed by Negri and with generally excellent solo singing, though (with women taking three male parts) it is hard to follow the story, since the timbres are not as distinct as they might be. The recording quality has an attractive bloom on it which has not been lost in the CD transfer, and for the dedicated Vivaldian this will undoubtedly give pleasure.

Voříšek, Jan Vaclav (1791–1825)

Impromptus Nos. 1–6, Op. 7.
(M) ** Carlton IMP Classics Dig. 30367 00902 [id.]. Dirk Joeres – SCHUBERT: *Impromptus* etc. **

It was an intelligent idea to couple these *Impromptus*, which inspired the whole genre, with Schubert's better-known and more searching pieces. The German pianist, Dirk Joeres, is a sensitive and imaginative player, and his playing will give pleasure, though his recording is just a shade bass-heavy.

Wagner, Richard (1813–83)

(i) *A Faust overture; Overtures: Der fliegende Holländer; Rienzi; Lohengrin: Prelude to Act I;* (ii) *Prelude to Act III. Tannhäuser: Overture and Grand march.*
(B) *** Sony SBK 62403; *SBT 62403* [id.]. (i) Cleveland O, Szell; (ii) Phd. O, Ormandy.

Szell's Wagner collection, recorded in Severance Hall in 1965, remains one of his most impressive records and is worthy to rank alongside his electrifying programme of excerpts from the *Ring* (SBK/*SBT* 48175 – see below). The inclusion of the still rarely heard *Faust overture* is most welcome. Hearing this searingly dramatic and intense work, one again wonders why it has not become a repertory piece. It was conceived in 1840 at the time of the *Dutchman* – which is also included here – and rewritten in 1855 during the composition of the *Ring*. To describe the playing of the Cleveland Orchestra as brilliant is inadequate, for the precision and beauty of tone clothe deeper understanding. Though, characteristically, the pianissimos are not always as hushed as they might be, the body of orchestral tone is gloriously expansive. However, there is one fascinating anomaly in the *Faust overture* for which there seems no feasible explanation. As a reader (Douglas Bertram) has pointed out, in the chord on the first beat after figure 'F' in the score, the violins clearly play E natural, when it should surely be E flat. Toscanini plays E flat and that sounds correct and logical when related to what follows. But then why did Szell, so meticulous in matters of detail, get it wrong? Of course it hardly affects the overall validity of the performance, yet it remains a fascinating musical conundrum. The concert opens with Ormandy's physically thrilling account of the *Tannhäuser overture*, followed by the *Grand march* (sumptuous Philadelphia strings), and he also contributes an ebullient *Lohengrin* Act III *Prelude*. The Philadelphia recordings are less refined but the concert overall makes for a rich experience.

Siegfried idyll.
(M) *** DG 449 725-2 [id.]. BPO, Karajan – R. STRAUSS: *Ein Heldenleben.* ***
(M) *** DG (IMS) 439 969-2 (2). BPO, Karajan – BRUCKNER: *Symphony No. 8.* ***
(M) *** Carlton IMP Classics Dig. 30367 0029-2 [(M) id.]. SCO, Jaime Laredo – DVORAK: *String serenade* etc. ***
(M) **(*) EMI CMS7 63277-2 (2). Philh. O, Klemperer – MAHLER: *Symphony No. 9.* ***

Karajan's account of Wagner's wonderful birthday present to Cosima is unsurpassed; it has never sounded better than in this new transfer for DG's series of 'Legendary Recordings', aptly coupled with Strauss's *Ein Heldenleben*, Karajan's very first stereo recording for DG.

A beautiful performance from Jaime Laredo and the Scottish Chamber Orchestra, warm and poised and ending serenely, yet moving to a strong central climax. The recording, made in Glasgow City Hall, has a pleasingly expansive ambience, yet textures are clear.

Klemperer favours the original chamber-orchestra scoring and the Philharmonia players are very persuasive, especially in the score's gentler moments. However, the balance is forward and, although the sound is warm, the ear craves a greater breadth of string tone at the climax.

(i; ii) *Siegfried idyll.* (iii; iv) *Overture: Der fliegende Holländer.* (i; v) *Götterdämmerung: Siegfried's Rhine journey. Lohengrin:* (i; ii) *Prelude to Act I;* (vi; iv) *Prelude to Act III. Die Meistersinger:* (vi; iv) *Overture;* (vii; viii) *Prelude to Act III.* (ix; viii) *Parsifal: Prelude & Good Friday music. Overtures:* (vi; iv) *Rienzi;* (vii; x) *Tannhäuser. Tristan:* (iii; iv) *Preludes to Acts I & III;* (vi; iv) *Death of Isolde.* (i; v) *Die Walküre: Ride of the Valkyries.*

(B) *** DG Double 439 687-2 (2) [id.]. (i) BPO; (ii) Kubelik; (iii) Bayreuth Festival O; (iv) Karl Boehm; (v) Karajan; (vi) VPO; (vii) Deutsche Op., Berlin, O; (viii) Jochum; (ix) Bav. RSO; (x) Otto Gerdes.

The *Siegfried idyll* is beautifully shaped by Kubelik and equally beautifully played by the Berlin Philharmonic. He also conducts an impressive *Lohengrin Act I Prelude*, again with the BPO, who have played it under everyone who matters, including, of course, Furtwängler. Boehm not only provides a richly sustained opening for *Rienzi* but is pretty exciting in *Der fliegende Holländer* and at his finest in the *Tristan Preludes* – taken from his 1966 Bayreuth complete set – which glow with intensity. Surprisingly, Karajan contributes only two items, but both bring plenty of adrenalin. But the highlight of the set comes last, Jochum's electrifying and Rosette-worthy performance of the *Prelude and Good Friday* music from *Parsifal*. Recorded in the Munich Herculessaal, it is not only a demonstration record from the earliest days of stereo, but the playing has a spiritual intensity that has never been surpassed. Elsewhere the recordings, dating from the late 1950s to the early 1980s, have all been transferred vividly, with some sounding fuller and more refined than others. The documentation, as with the rest of this series, is totally inadequate.

Siegfried idyll. Die fliegende Holländer: Overture. Lohengrin: Prelude to Act III. Rienzi: Overture. Tannhäuser: Overture.

(B) *** Tring Dig. TRP 008 [(M) id. import]. RPO, Vernon Handley.

The *Siegfried idyll* is beautifully played and radiantly recorded, but the highlight is Handley's excitingly rumbustious account of the *Rienzi overture* with thrilling brass and an exuberant contribution from the side-drum, snares a-rattling. This is a demonstration item. The heavy brass also makes a splendidly weighty contribution to the famous *Lohengrin Act III Prelude* and is hardly less effective at the climax of the *Ride of the Valkyries*. Handley uses the concert ending in both these pieces, and his spacious treatment of the reprise of the Pilgrim's chorale at the close of the *Tannhäuser overture* makes a satisfying close to a programme which is played as well as it is recorded (in the suitable resonance of St Augustine's Church, Kilburn).

Siegfried idyll (with rehearsal); *Der fliegende Holländer: Overture; Die Meistersinger: Prelude to Act I; Lohengrin: Prelude to Act I; Parsifal: Prelude to Act I and Good Friday music; Tannhäuser:* (i) *Overture and Venusberg music.*

(M) *** Sony SMK 64456 (2) [id.]. (i) Occidental College Ch.; Columbia SO, Bruno Walter.

Walter's is above all a gentle performance of the *Siegfried idyll*; the opening is quite lovely. The 1963 recording seems fuller than before, with more ambient warmth, especially at the climax – which has no lack of ardour – while the rapt quality of the closing ritenuto is magical. Before the performance, we hear an extended rehearsal sequence lasting three-quarters of an hour, which most listeners will find fascinating. The rest of the programme was recorded in 1959. Highlights include the glowing *Parsifal Prelude* and *Good Friday music*, matching Jochum in its simple intensity, and the superb account of the *Tannhäuser Overture* and *Venusberg music* with its thrillingly sensuous climax, and the closing pages – the Occidental College Choir distantly balanced – bringing a radiant hush. The years have not diminished its impact, and again one notices that both here and in the *Flying Dutchman* and *Meistersinger overtures* the orchestra has more body and weight, while the *Lohengrin Prelude*, relaxed but beautifully controlled, sounds radiant.

Siegfried idyll; Overtures: Der fliegende Holländer; Rienzi. Die Meistersinger: Prelude to Act III; Dance of the Apprentices; Entry of the Masters.

(B) ** EMI CfP CD-CFP 6049 [(M) id. import]. LPO, Sir Edward Downes.

Sir Edward Downes was the first British conductor in the post-war period to conduct a *Ring* cycle at Covent Garden. As a Wagnerian he may at times lack a little in tension and excitement, but here (as in the opera house) he conducts fresh and direct performances. The *Siegfried idyll* is especially successful, and there is some fine brass playing in the Act III *Prelude* of *Die Meistersinger. Rienzi* gains from Downes's slight degree of reticence, yet the opening string-tune sounds gloriously ripe. The 1976 recording, made in the Henry Wood Hall, is warm and atmospheric,

Siegfried idyll. Lohengrin: Preludes to Acts I & III. Die Meistersinger: Prelude to Act I. Parsifal: Prelude to Act I. Tristan und Isolde: Prelude and Liebestod.
(B) *** Ph. Virtuoso 420 886-2 [(M) id. import]. Concg. O, Haitink.

The addition of Haitink's simple, unaffected reading of the *Siegfried idyll* to his 1975 collection of *Preludes* enhances the appeal of a particularly attractive concert. The rich acoustics of the Concertgebouw are surely ideal for *Die Meistersinger*, given a memorably spacious performance, and Haitink's restraint adds to the noble dignity of *Parsifal*. The *Lohengrin* excerpts are splendidly played. The digital remastering is almost entirely beneficial.

ORCHESTRAL EXCERPTS FROM THE OPERAS

Overture: Der fliegende Holländer. Lohengrin: Preludes to Acts I & III. Die Meistersinger: Overture; Dance of the apprentices; Entry of the Masters. Overtures: Rienzi; Tannhauser.
(M) *** EMI CDM5 66805-2 [id.]. Philh. O, Klemperer.

Götterdämmerung: Siegfried's funeral music and Rhine journey. Parsifal: Prelude. Das Rheingold: Entry of the Gods into Valhalla. Siegfried: Forest murmurs. Tannhäuser: Prelude to Act III. Tristan und Isolde: Prelude and Liebestod. Die Walküre: Ride of the Valkyries.
(M) *** EMI CDM5 66806-2 [id.]. Philh. O, Klemperer.

It is good to have Klemperer's view of Wagner. Most of the performances reissued here as part of EMI's 'Klemperer legacy' have the kind of incandescent glow found only in interpretations of really great conductors, and the Philharmonia Orchestra plays immaculately. If, judged by the very highest standards, Klemperer falls just a degree short, and the *Tristan Prelude* and *Liebestod* do not have the sense of wonder that Toscanini and Furtwängler brought, the feeling of ennobled passion at the climax cannot fail to communicate. The characteristically spacious and superbly shaped *Parsifal and Lohengrin Preludes* are a highlight for similar reasons. Elsewhere, if the level of tension is more variable, Klemperer's readings are always solidly concentrated, even if this means that the plodding *Meistersingers* seem a bit too full of German pudding. Yet there is no lack of zest in the *Lohengrin Prelude to Act III*. The *Ride of the Valkyries*, however, without the concert coda, ends rather abruptly. The remastering for CD has brought a gloriously full sound-picture, yet clearer than on the original LPs, the quality admirably truthful and almost in the demonstration bracket.

Der fliegende Holländer: Overture. Götterdämmerung: Siegfried's funeral music; Finale. Die Meistersinger: Overture. Tristan und Isolde: Preludes, Acts I & III; Liebestod. Die Walküre: Ride of the Valkyries.
(M) ** DG Dig. 445 571-2. O de Paris, Barenboim.

Barenboim's 1982 Wagner collection was rather successful. He achieved fairly idiomatic playing from the French orchestra and there is no lack of warmth or tension, particularly in the excerpts from *Tristan*. The three excerpts from the *Ring*, recorded the following year, are less telling. Here the orchestra – particularly the brass section – does not sound authentic, and the recording acoustic is not helpful, failing to give the necessary resonance to the brass sounds.

(i) *Der fliegende Höllander: Overture*. (ii) *Lohengrin: Prelude to Act I. Die Meistersinger: Overture*. (iii) *Parsifal: Prelude and Good Friday music*. (iv) *Tannhäuser: Overture*.
(B) **(*) DG Classikon 439 445-2; *439 445-4* [(M) id. import]. (i) Bayreuth (1971) Festival O, Boehm; (ii) BPO, Kubelik; (iii) Bav. RSO, Jochum; (iv) German Op. O, Berlin, Otto Gerdes.

Most of these performances are duplicated in a particularly attractive DG Double set of Wagner's orchestral excerpts mentioned above, but this shorter, Classikon bargain collection includes Jochum's superb account of the *Parsifal* excerpts and is quite worthwhile in its own right.

Der fliegende Holländer: Overture. Lohengrin: Prelude to Act I. Die Meistersinger: Overture. (i) *Tannhäuser: Overture and Venusberg music. Tristan: Prelude and Liebestod.*
(M) *** EMI (SIS) CDM7 64334-2. BPO, Karajan; (i) with German Op. Ch.

All the music here is played excellently, but the *Overture and Venusberg music* from *Tannhäuser* (Paris version, using chorus) and the *Prelude and Liebestod* from *Tristan* are superb. In the *Liebestod* the climactic culmination is overwhelming in its sentient power, while *Tannhäuser* has comparable spaciousness and grip. There is an urgency and edge to the *Flying Dutchman overture*, and *Die Meistersinger* has weight and dignity, but the last degree of tension is missing.

Overtures and Preludes: *Der fliegende Holländer: Overture. Lohengrin: Preludes to Acts I & III; Parsifal: Prelude. Rienzi: Overture. Tannhäuser: Overture* (original version).
(M) *** DG 453 989-2 [id.]. VPO, Karl Boehm.

Under Boehm, the Vienna Philharmonic Orchestra plays beautifully in a choice of overtures and preludes spanning Wagner's full career, from *Rienzi* to *Parsifal* – in which the performance of the *Prelude* is superbly eloquent. Above all, Boehm's approach is spacious with speeds broad rather than urgent, yet there is no lack of concentration, and the account of *Rienzi* has striking life and vigour. Indeed all the performances – and especially the *Lohengrin Prelude to Act I* and the *Tannhäuser overture* – show a compulsive inevitability in their forward flow. The recording is full and vivid; but not all the balances seem quite natural, and there is a slight tendency (not serious enough to spoil enjoyment) to aggressiveness in the fortissimo brass. The recordings were made in the Musikverein between 1975 and 1980, and they include two items from the very end of Boehm's recording career. The collection offers a splendid reminder of his greatness as a Wagnerian, but the playing time is only just over 64 minutes; there would have been room for the *Meistersinger overture* or the *Prelude and Liebestod* from *Tristan*, which Boehm recorded at the same sessions. This collection is an obvious candidate for DG's 'Originals' series, and perhaps that will offer another chance to include one or other of these items.

Der fliegende Holländer: Overture. Lohengrin: Prelude to Act III. Die Meistersinger: Overture. Rienzi: Overture. Tannhäuser: Overture. Die Walküre: Ride of the Valkyries.
(BB) *(*) Carlton LSO Double Dig. 30368 01217 (2) [(B) id.] . LSO, Tuckwell – BERLIOZ: *Symphonie fantastique*. *

An enjoyable concert, well played and given excellent digital recording. But the performances, although polished and not lacking spontaneity, are in no way distinctive.

Overtures: (i) *Der fliegende Holländer;* (ii) *Die Meistersinger. Lohengrin: Prelude to Act I. Overtures:* (i) *Rienzi;* (ii) *Tannhäuser*. (i) *Prelude: Tristan und Isolde*. (ii) *Die Walküre: Ride of the Valkyries*.
(M) **(*) Decca 458 214-2 [id.]. (i) VPO; (ii) Chicago SO; Solti.

Recorded between 1960 (*Rienzi*) and 1986 (the *Lohengrin Prelude*) these performances were newly made in the studio, not taken from complete opera sets. So this is the self-contained *Tannhäuser overture* from the Dresden version, and very exciting it is, with brilliant sound. The following *Meistersinger Prelude* is noticeably fuller and more expansive. But all the music-making here demonstrates Solti's characteristic Wagnerian flair and brings a high degree of tension. In *Der fliegende Holländer* the VPO are driven too hard and the effect is fierce, but *Rienzi* is mellower, with the big tune at the opening obviously relished. The CD transfers are vivid but not always absolutely refined.

Der fliegende Holländer: Overture. Parsifal: Preludes to Acts I & III.
(M) *** EMI CDM5 66108-2 [id.]. BPO, Karajan – R. STRAUSS: *Ein Heldenleben*. ***

These recordings come from 1974 and are magnificently played and sumptuously recorded. There is urgency and edge in *The Flying Dutchman*, which is very exciting, and the string playing in the *Parsifal Preludes* is nobly shaped; if here perhaps the very last degree of tension is missing, the Berlin strings create a glorious sound.

Götterdämmerung: Dawn and Siegfried's Rhine journey. Lohengrin: Preludes to Acts I & III. Die Meistersinger: Prelude to Act I. Das Rheingold: Entry of the Gods into Valhalla. Rienzi: Overture. Siegfried: Forest murmurs. Tannhäuser: Overture. Die Walküre: Ride of the Valkyries; Wotan's farewell and Magic fire music.
(B) *** EMI forte (SIS) Dig. CZS5 68616-2 (2) [CDFB 68616]. BPO, Tennstedt.

This EMI forte double combines two highly successful collections from the early days of the digital era. The recordings were made in the Philharmonie between 1981 and 1983; they could ideally be more opulent in the middle and bass, but the brilliance is demonstrable, and there is weight, too, and fine detail, especially in the atmospheric *Forest murmurs*. Moreover the orchestral playing is superb and the sense of spectacle is in no doubt. Tennstedt amalgamates something from the combined Furtwängler and Klemperer traditions with his broad, spacious readings, yet the voltage is consistently high. The opening and closing sections of the *Tannhäuser overture* are given a restrained nobility of feeling without any loss of power or impact. Similarly the gorgeous string melody at the opening of *Rienzi* is elegiacally moulded, and later when the brass enter in the allegro there is no suggestion of the bandstand. In the Act I *Lohengrin Prelude*, Tennstedt lingers in the pianissimo sections, creating radiant detail, then presses on just before the climax. The Berlin Philharmonic are on top form throughout.

(i) *Götterdämmerung: Siegfried's Rhine journey and Funeral music.* (ii) *Lohengrin: Prelude to Act III.* (i) *Die Meistersinger: Overture; Prelude to Act III; Dance of the apprentices; Procession of the Masters.* (ii) *Tannhäuser: Grand march.*
(M) ** RCA (i) stereo / (ii) mono 09026 61792-2 [id.]. (i) Chicago SO; (ii) RCA Victor O; Fritz Reiner.

It is rare that one has to complain about the stereo sound achieved by the RCA engineers in Chicago's Orchestral Hall in the late 1950s, but in the stereo Wagner sessions included here the sound is too sumptuously inflated: all amplitude, with no sparkle in the treble. It makes Reiner's spacious account of the *Die Meistersinger overture* seem too weighty and overblown, although the close of the *Procession of the Masters* is more effective. However, there is some glorious playing from the horns in the great *Prelude to Act III* from the same opera, and the opening of *Siegfried's Rhine journey* has plenty of tension and atmosphere. The other three items use an East Coast pick-up orchestra and were recorded in mono in New York's Manhattan Center in 1950.

Götterdämmerung: Dawn and Siegfried's Rhine journey; Funeral march. Lohengrin: Preludes to Acts I & III. Die Meistersinger: Overture; Dance of the apprentices. Die Walküre: Ride of the Valkyries.
(B) *** CfP Dig. CD-CFP 9008 [(M) id. import]. LPO, Rickenbacher.

Karl Anton Rickenbacher secures first-class playing from the LPO with the strings at their peak in the radiant opening of the *Lohengrin Prelude*. Some might feel that his pacing of the *Die Meistersinger overture* is fractionally fast. The CD sound is firm and full; indeed the *Prelude to Act III* of *Lohengrin* makes a splendid demonstration recording; an exciting performance, particularly vividly projected.

Götterdämmerung: Dawn and Siegfried's Rhine journey; Siegfried's death and funeral march. Lohengrin: Prelude to Act I. Tannhäuser: Overture and Venusberg music. Tristan und Isolde: Liebestod. Die Walküre: Ride of the Valkyries.
(M) (***) RCA mono GD 60306 [09026 60306-2]. NBC SO, Toscanini.

Götterdämmerung: Dawn; (i; ii) *Zu neuen Taten; Willst du mir Minne schenken; O heilige Götter; Siegfried's Rhine journey; Brünnhilde's immolation:* (i) *Starke Scheite schichtet mir dort; Wie Sonne lauter strahlt mir sein Licht; Mein Erbe nun nehm'ich zu eigen; Fliegt heim ihr Raben!; Grane, Mein Ross, sei mir gegrüsst. Siegfried: Forest murmurs.*
(M) (***) RCA mono GD 60304 [09026 60304-2]. (i) Helen Traubel; (ii) Lauritz Melchior; NBC SO, Toscanini.

Toscanini's special brand of electricity comes over vividly in these characteristic Wagner performances. The *Lohengrin Prelude* and the soaring *Tristan Liebestod* have typical intensity and, although the dynamic range is compressed, the sound is surprisingly good, as it is in the tenderly sensuous *Venusberg* sequence in *Tannhäuser*. One is offered a choice here of the *Götterdämmerung Dawn* sequence with or without the vocal contribution in which both Helen Traubel and Melchior are strong enough musical personalities to stand up against Toscanini. The recordings date from the 1940s and 1950s and, as transferred, are surprisingly full, with something of a concert-hall effect in the Carnegie Hall *Immolation* sequence of 1941. Traubel rides over the orchestra with considerable dominance.

Götterdämmerung: Dawn and Siegfried's Rhine journey; Siegfried's death and funeral music. Die Meistersinger: Prelude. Das Rheingold: Entry of the Gods into Valhalla. Siegfried: Forest murmurs. Tristan und Isolde: Prelude & Liebestod. Die Walküre: Wotan's farewell and Magic fire music.
❀ (M) *** SBK 48175; *SBT 48175* [id.]. Cleveland O, Szell.

The orchestral playing here is in a very special class. Its virtuosity is breathtaking. Szell generates the greatest tension, particularly in the two scenes from *Götterdämmerung*, while the *Liebestod* from *Tristan* has never been played on record with more passion and fire. The *Tristan* and *Meistersinger* excerpts (from 1962) have been added to the contents of the original LP, which contained the *Ring* sequences made later (in 1968), and the improvement in quality with the latest remastering for CD is little short of miraculous. Like the similarly remastered Dvořák *Slavonic dances*, this is reasonably worthy of Szell's extraordinary achievement in Cleveland in the 1960s, even if the forward balance of the recording places a limit on the dynamic range.

Götterdämmerung: Dawn and Siegfried's Rhine journey; Siegfried's death and funeral music. Die Meistersinger: Prelude. Das Rheingold: Entrance of the gods into Valhalla. Siegfried: Forest murmurs. Die Walküre: The Ride of the Valkyries.
(M) *(**) Decca Phase Four (IMS) 443 901-2 [id.]. LSO, Stokowski.

This collection of *Ring* excerpts was first issued in 1966 and was not one of Decca's most successful Phase Four recordings. There is a shrill, superficial brilliance and patches of roughness in the highly modulated recording – but no matter, this is vintage Stokowski. He is at his most electrifying in *Siegfried's*

Rhine journey, while the gods enter Valhalla like a procession of Roman juggernauts. The opening *Ride of the Valkyries* is especially affected by the top-heavy balance (though the flute and piccolo detail is aurally fascinating), but *Forest murmurs* with its chirruping birds has never sounded more atmospherically potent. The *Mastersingers prelude* was recorded 'live' at the London Festival Hall in 1972 and, if the orchestra is made to seem much too close, the overall balance is better and the sound somewhat more refined. The performance is full of adrenalin but has warmth and grandeur too, with some glorious playing from the LSO strings. The applause is justified.

Gotterdämmerüng: Dawn and Siegfried's Rhine journey; Siegfried's funeral music. Tristan und Isolde: Prelude to Act I; (i) *Isolde's narration and curse;* Act III: *Liebestod.*
(M) ** Decca 452 896-2 [id.]. VPO, Knappertsbusch; (i) with Birgit Nilsson and Grace Hoffman.

The excerpts from *Tristan* were made in 1959, before Nilsson recorded her first complete set under Solti, and the performance displays less extrovert feeling than might be expected. But the end result is in many ways made the more impressive with the emotion of the moment conveyed by reticence and controlled power. Knappertsbusch characterstically feels for the sublime lengths of Wagner rather than seeking the dramatic cutting edge of a Solti, but with spacious recording the result is persuasive. The Act I duet (with Grace Hoffman) extends from the passage where Isolde sends Brangäne to fetch Tristan to the fateful moment when she selects the death potion. For the orchestral extracts from *Götterdämmerung* Knappertsbusch returns to his usual duller style, but the early stereo ensures that unexceptional playing is still enjoyable. Even so, this is hardly a candidate for Decca's Classic Sound series.

Lohengrin: Preludes to Acts I & III; Die Meistersinger: Prelude. Parsifal: Good Friday music. Tannhauser: Overture and Venusberg music. Tristan und Isolde: Prelude & Liebestod.
(M) ** Mercury 434 342-2 [id.]. LSO, Dorati.

These are vibrantly direct performances, and no one could deny the moments of excitement or the competence of the LSO playing. But there is no incandescence in the *Parsifal* music or in the *Lohengrin Prelude to Act I*. Like other Mercury recordings made in London (in this case, at Wembley or Watford Town Halls) at this period (1959–60), the sound is very immediate and faithful for its time, but the acoustic is not really ideal for the music.

Lohengrin: Preludes to Acts I & III. Parsifal: Preludes to Acts I & III.
(BB) *** EMI Seraphim CES5 69092 (2) [CDEB 69092]. BPO, Karajan – BRUCKNER: *Symphony No. 8.* ***

Karajan's Act I *Lohengrin Prelude* is graduated superbly; the *Parsifal* excerpts, too, are nobly shaped, yet here the tension is held at a marginally lower level. The *Parsifal* excerpts bring rapt serenity. This is magnificent playing, and the 1975 recording has an attractively wide amplitude.

Lohengrin: Preludes to Acts I & III. Tristan und Isolde: Prelude & Liebestod.
(M) *** EMI CDM5 66107-2 [id.]. BPO, Karajan – R. STRAUSS: *Sinfonia domestica.* ***

These Karajan performances (again from 1974) are in a class of their own. The body of tone produced by the Berlin Philharmonic gives a breathtaking richness to the climaxes. That of the first *Lohengrin Prelude* is superbly graded, and in the *Tristan Liebestod* the orgasmic culmination is quite overwhelming, as is the thrilling brass playing in the famous *Lohengrin* Act III *Prelude*.

Die Meistersinger: Overture. (i) *Tannhäuser: Overture and Venusberg music.*
(M) *** EMI CDM5 66106-2 [id.]. BPO, Karajan, (i) with German Op. Ch. – R. STRAUSS: *Don Quixote.* ***

Further excerpts from Karajan's outstanding (1974) sessions: a superb sense of timing and spaciousness is applied to the *Tannhäuser* excerpts, and the *Die Meistersinger Prelude* has a similar imposing breadth. The sound is excellent.

Die Meistersinger: suite from Act III (arr. Barbirolli) (*Prelude; Dance of the apprentices; Entry of the Masters*).
(B) (***) Dutton Lab. mono CDEA 5504 [(M) id.]. Hallé O, Barbirolli – BERLIOZ: *Symphonie fantastique.* (***)

Barbirolli's own suite from *Meistersinger*, Act III, was a favourite work with him, and this recording, made in 1944, just over a year after he took over the Hallé, brings out the warmth and resonance of the playing under his guidance. The sound is astonishingly full and rich for the period, as transferred by Dutton, a cherishable coupling for Barbirolli's fine 1947 version of the *Symphonie fantastique*.

VOCAL MUSIC

Wesendonk Lieder: Der Engel; Stehe still; Im Treibhaus; Schmerzen; Träume. Götterdämmerung: Starke Scheite schichet mir dort. Siegfried: Ewig war ich. Tristan: Doch nun von Tristan?; Mild und leise.
(M) (***) EMI mono CDH7 63030-2 [id.]. Kirsten Flagstad, Philh. O, Furtwängler, Dobrowen.

Recorded in the late 1940s and early '50s, a year or so before Flagstad did *Tristan* complete with Furtwängler, these performances show her at her very peak, with the voice magnificent in power as well as beautiful and distinctive in every register. The *Liebestod* (with rather heavy surface noise) may be less rapt and intense in this version with Dobrowen than with Furtwängler but is just as expansive. For the *Wesendonk Lieder* she shades the voice down very beautifully, but this is still monumental and noble rather than intimate Lieder-singing.

OPERA

Der fliegende Holländer (complete).
(M) *** Ph. Dig. 434 599-2 (2) [id.]. Estes, Balslev, Salminen, Schunk, Bayreuth Festival (1985) Ch. & O, Nelsson.
(B) *** Naxos Dig. 8.660025/6 [id.]. Muff, Haubold, Knodt, Seiffert, Budapest R. Ch., Vienna ORF SO, Steinberg.
(M) **(*) EMI Dig. CMS7 64650-2 (2) [Ang. CDMB 64650]. Van Dam, Vejzovic, Moll, Hofmann, Moser, Borris, V. State Op. Ch., BPO, Karajan.
(M) **(*) Decca (IMS) 417 319-2 (2) [id.]. London, Rysanek, Tozzi, ROHCG Ch. & O, Dorati.
(B) (*(*)) Teldec/Warner mono 4509 97491-2 (2). Uhde, Weber, Varnay, Lustig, Schärtel, Traxel, Bayreuth Ch. & O, Keilberth.

Woldemar Nelsson, with the team he had worked with intensively through the season, conducts a performance even more glowing and responsively paced than those of his starrier rivals. The cast is more consistent than any, with Lisbeth Balslev as Senta firmer, sweeter and more secure than any current rival, raw only occasionally, and Simon Estes a strong, ringing Dutchman, clear and noble of tone. Matti Salminen is a dark and equally secure Daland and Robert Schunk an ardent, idiomatic Erik. The veteran, Anny Schlemm, as Mary, though vocally overstressed, adds pointful character, and the chorus is superb, wonderfully drilled and passionate with it. Though inevitably stage noises are obtrusive at times, the recording is exceptionally vivid and atmospheric. On two mid-priced discs only, it makes an admirable first choice.

Pinchas Steinberg, who has been outstandingly successful as music director of the ORF Orchestra and who was responsible for RCA's brilliant recording of Massenet's *Cherubin*, here proves a warmly sympathetic Wagnerian. More than most rivals, he brings out the light and shade of this earliest of the regular Wagner canon, helped by the refined, well-balanced recording, and by brilliant, sharply dramatic playing from the orchestra. His speeds are more urgent than most, with rhythms well sprung and melodic lines understandingly moulded. The chorus too sings with a bite and precision to match any rival. The cast of soloists may not be in that league, but they sing clearly and on the whole freshly, avoiding most of the cardinal faults of Wagner singers today. Alfred Muff as the Dutchman attacks the notes cleanly, with vibrato only occasionally intrusive. The vibrato of Ingrid Haubold is more of a problem but, except under pressure, it is well controlled, and she begins *Senta's Ballad* with a meditative pianissimo, a rare achievement. Both tenors are excellent, Peter Seiffert as Erik and Joerg Hering as the Steersman, and though Erich Knodt with rather a gritty baritone is an uncharacterful Daland, his Act II aria is light and refreshing, thanks to Steinberg's fine rhythmic pointing. The recording is both atmospheric and clear, and the set comes with libretto, translation, notes and very detailed synopsis, an outstanding bargain.

The extreme range of dynamics in EMI's recording for Karajan, not ideally clear but rich, matches the larger-than-life quality of the conductor's reading. He firmly and convincingly relates this early work to later Wagner, *Tristan* above all. His choice of José van Dam as the Dutchman, thoughtful, finely detailed and lyrical, strong but not at all blustering, goes well with this. Van Dam is superbly matched and contrasted with the finest Daland on record, Kurt Moll, gloriously biting and dark in tone, yet detailed in his characterization. Neither the Erik of Peter Hofmann, nor – more seriously – the Senta of Dunja Vejzovic matches this standard; nevertheless, for all her variability, Vejzovic is wonderfully intense in *Senta's Ballad* and she matches even Van Dam's fine legato in the Act II duet. The CD transfer underlines the heavyweight quality of the recording, with the *Sailors' chorus* for example made massive, but effectively so, when Karajan conducts it with such fine spring.

Dorati, with rhythms well sprung, draws strong and alert playing and singing from his Covent Garden forces in a consistently purposeful performance, helped by Culshaw-style sound-effects. The well-spread recording is full and atmospheric and, like the Philips set, the reissue is offered on two mid-price

CDs. George London's Dutchman brings one of his most powerful performances on disc, occasionally rough-toned but positive. Leonie Rysanek may sound too mature for Senta, but as a great Wagnerian she brings a commanding presence and the most persuasive sense of line. There is no weak link in the rest of the cast, well set up at the start by the characterful Richard Lewis as the Steersman.

Recorded live at the 1955 Bayreuth Festival, Keilberth's version, very well cast, is electrically intense and purposeful, but it is seriously marred in this CD reissue by a poor transfer. It is far worse than the last LP transfer that appeared on Decca, with the orchestral sound distressingly fizzy and ill-focused. It is astonishing that the 1955 sound here can be so poor, when the same company's transfer of Knappertsbusch's 1951 *Parsifal* is far fuller. Happily, voices come out far better than the orchestra, with Hermann Uhde a dark, firm Dutchman and Astrid Varnay a powerful Senta, singing with high tonal and dynamic contrasts, and with Ludwig Weber an incisve Daland. As Erik, Rudolf Lustig is undistinguished, strained at times. It is time that Fricsay's superb DG version with Josef Metternich in the title-role, also made in 1955, was reissued.

Der fliegende Holländer: highlights.

(M) **(*) Ph. (IMS) Dig. 446 618-2 [id.] (from above complete (1985) Bayreuth set, with Estes, Balslev, Salminen, Schunk; cond. Nelsson).

(M) **(*) EMI (SIS) Dig. CDM5 66052-2 (from above complete set with Van Dam, Vejzovic, Moll, Hofmann; cond. Karajan).

(M) **(*) Decca 452 731-2 [id.] (from above set, with London, Rysanek, Tozzi; cond. Dorati).

A generous (76 minutes) and well-chosen selection from the outstanding Philips set is let down by the absence of any documentation, save a list of the 12 excerpts.

This EMI highlights disc is only slightly more generous than most of the rest of the series (67 minutes) but will be useful for those wanting to sample Karajan's 1983 recording, particularly as José Van Dam as the Dutchman and Kurt Moll as Daland are both so impressive, and Senta's ballad (Dunja Vejzovic) is very movingly sung. The synopsis relates each excerpt to the narrative.

Dorati's Decca CD is another vintage set of highlights (recorded at Walthamstow in 1960) which is well worth considering, where the complete set from which it is taken would no longer be a top choice. Yet the recording is splendid and Dorati certainly keeps the performance alive.

Götterdämmerung (complete).

(M) *** Ph. 412 488-2 (4). Nilsson, Windgassen, Greindl, Mödl, Stewart, Neidlinger, Dvořáková, Bayreuth (1967) Festival Ch. & O, Boehm.

(B) *** RCA Dig. 74321 45421-2 (4). Kollo, Altmeyer, Salminen, Wenkel, Nocker, Nimsgern, Sharp, Popp, Leipzig R. Ch., Berlin R. Ch., Dresden State Op. Ch., Dresden State O, Janowski.

(M) *** Ph. 434 424-2 (4) [id.]. G. Jones, Jung, Hübner, Becht, Mazura, Altmeyer, Killebrew, (1979) Bayreuth Festival Ch. & O, Boulez.

Boehm's urgently involving reading of *Götterdämmerung*, very well cast, is crowned by an incandescent performance of the final Immolation scene from Birgit Nilsson as Brünnhilde. It is an astonishing achievement that she could sing with such biting power and accuracy in a live performance, coming to it at the very end of a long evening. The excitement of that is matched by much else in the performance so that incidental stage-noises and the occasional inaccuracy, almost inevitable in live music-making, matter hardly at all. Josef Greindl is rather unpleasantly nasal in tone as Hagen, and Martha Mödl as Waltraute is unsteady; but both are dramatically involving. Thomas Stewart is a gruff but convincing Gunther and Dvořáková, as Gutrune, strong if not ideally pure-toned. Neidlinger as ever is a superb Alberich. In its new mid-price format this can be strongly recommended.

With sharply focused yet warmly ambient sound, Janowski's *Götterdämmerung* hits refreshingly hard, at least as much so as in the earlier operas in the cycle. Speeds rarely linger but, with some excellent casting – consistent with the earlier operas – the result is rarely lightweight. Jeannine Altmeyer as Brünnhilde rises to the challenge, not so much in strength as in feeling, and here, as throughout the series, she consistently avoids the kind of squally and ill-focused – if powerful – tone-production that puts some listeners off Wagner altogether. Yet she is ecstatic in Act I, bitter in Act II, dedicated in the Immolation scene. Kollo is a fine Siegfried, only occasionally raw-toned, and Salminen a magnificent Hagen, with Nimsgern again an incisive Alberich on his brief appearances. Despite an indifferent Günther and Gutrune and a wobbly if characterful Waltraute, the impression is of clean, strong vocalization matched by finely disciplined and dedicated playing, all recorded in faithful stereo, with very good detail. A remarkable achievement and an undoubted bargain.

Boulez's 1979 analogue recording is warm and urgent. The passion of the performance is established in the Dawn music before the second scene of the Prologue and, with a strong if not ideal cast, it has a clear place as a first-rate mid-price recommendation. Manfred Jung as Siegfried gives a fresh, clean-cut performance. Jeannine Altmeyer sings Gutrune, sweet but not always ideally clean of attack; Fritz Hübner is a weighty Hagen, Franz Mazura a powerful Gunther and Gwendoline Killebrew a rich, firm Waltraute. Dame Gwyneth Jones as Brünnhilde, always very variable, has some splendid moments, notably at the close of the Immolation scene. The sound is aptly atmospheric but lacks something in weight in the brass, though there is no lack of excitement at the end of Act II.

Götterdämmerung: scenes (sung in German): *Dawn; Brünnhilde and Siegfried's entrance; Siegfried's Rhine journey; Siegfried's funeral march; Brünnhilde's immolation.*
(B) *** CfP CD-CFP 4670 [(M) id.]. Rita Hunter, Alberto Remedios, LPO, Mackerras.

This Classics for Pleasure disc of highlights was made in 1972, six years before the classic complete set in English by the same artists. Vocally what stands out in Hunter's performance is the pinging precision of even the most formidable exposed notes. Here she revealed herself to be a natural competitor in the international league, and her simple, fresh manner in the most intense moment of the *Immolation*, the hushed farewell of *Ruhe, du Gott*, is caught most affectingly. Remedios is also in splendid form, and Mackerras draws dedicated and dramatic playing from the LPO. The recording still sounds very impressive indeed, full-blooded and present, with the closing scene magnificently vivid. An outstanding bargain.

Götterdämmerung: highlights.
(M) *** Teldec/Warner Dig. 0630 13823-9 (from complete set, with Jerusalem, Anne Evans, Kang, Von Kannen, Bundschuh, Meier, Turner, Bayreuth (1991) Festival Ch. & O, Barenboim).
(M) **(*) Ph. (IMS) 446 616-2 (from above complete (1979) Bayreuth set, with Jones, Jung; cond. Boulez).

The 73 minutes of highlights are satisfactorily chosen from the excellent Barenboim full-price set and a synopsis is provided though not keyed directly to the 18 excerpts.

Many collectors will want to sample the Boulez set, and this CD offering 78 minutes of highlights should serve admirably, except for the lack of either translation or synopsis – or, indeed, any kind of documentation at all except for detailing the 16 excerpts. They include *Siegfried's Rhine journey* and *Funeral march* and the final Immolation scene, so telling here.

The Twilight of the Gods (*Götterdämmerung:* complete; in English).
(M) *** EMI CMS7 64244-2 (5). Hunter, Remedios, Welsby, Haugland, Hammond-Stroud, Curphey, Pring, E. Nat. Op. Ch. & O, Goodall.

Goodall's account heightens the epic scale. The few slight imprecisions and the occasional rawness of wind tone actually seem to enhance the earthiness of Goodall's view. Both Rita Hunter and Alberto Remedios give performances which are magnificent in every way. In particular the golden beauty of Remedios's tenor is consistently superb, with no Heldentenor barking at all, while Aage Haugland's Hagen is giant-sounding to focus the evil, with Gunther and Gutrune mere pawns. The voices on stage are in a different, drier acoustic from that for the orchestra, but considering the problems the sound is impressive. As for Goodall, with his consistently expansive tempi he carries total concentration – except, curiously, in the scene with the Rhinemaidens, whose music (as in Goodall's *Rhinegold* too) lumbers along heavily.

The Twilight of the Gods (Götterdämmerung): Act III: excerpts (in English).
(M) *** Chandos CHAN 6593 [id.]. Rita Hunter, Alberto Remedios, Norman Bailey, Clifford Grant, Margaret Curphey, Sadler's Wells Opera Ch. & O, Goodall.

Originally recorded by Unicorn in the early 1970s, even before the Sadler's Wells company had changed its name to the English National Opera, this single Chandos CD brings an invaluable reminder of Reginald Goodall's performance of the *Ring* cycle when it was in its first flush of success. The two-LP set is here transferred on to a single CD, lasting 66 minutes and covering the closing two scenes. In many ways it possesses an advantage over even the complete live recording of the opera, made at the Coliseum five years later, when Rita Hunter and Alberto Remedios are here obviously fresher and less stressed than at the end of a full evening's performance. It is good too to have this sample, however brief, of Clifford Grant's Hagen and Norman Bailey's Gunther, fine performances both. Fresh, clear recording, not as full as it might be. But at mid-price this CD is well worth investigating.

Lohengrin (complete).
(M) *** RCA 74321 50164-2 (3). Kónya, Amara, Dooley, Gorr, Hines, Boston Pro Musica Ch. & SO, Leinsdorf.
(M) **(*) EMI CMS5 66519-2 (3) [CDMD 693142]. René Kollo, Anna Tomowa-Sintow, Dunja Vejzovic, Siegmund Nimsgern, Karl Ridderbusch, German Op. Ch., Berlin, BPO, Karajan.
(M) **(*) Ph. 446 337-2 (3). Jess Thomas, Silja, Vinay, Varnay, Crass, Krause, Bayreuth Festival Ch. & O, Sawallisch.

(M) ** DG 449 591-2 (3). James King, Janowitz, Thomas Stewart, Gwyneth Jones, Bav. R. Ch. & SO, Kubelik.

When Leinsdorf's Boston version of *Lohengrin* was recorded in August 1965, it was the first complete opera set to be made in America for many years, and at the time the ambitiousness of that project (associated with the Tanglewood Festival) injected the performers – not just the the singers but also the chorus and the orchestra, which here plays radiantly, thanks to direction from Leindorf that is far warmer than was common from him in his Boston period. Though the solo contributions cannot quite match those of the glorious full-price Kempe set on EMI, it has one important advantage in the splendid singing of Sándor Kónya in the name part, wonderfully true and heroic-sounding. It is good too to hear the second part of the *Narration*, even though Wagner himself suggested its exclusion from stage performances. The set's other great asset is the atmospheric acoustic of Symphony Hall, which makes the big ensembles sound superbly expansive, as at the end of Act I after the clashing swords of the duel between Lohengrin and Telramund have been impressively simulated. The CD transfer is highly successful in all respects, losing nothing of the analogue atmosphere and clearer, better focused than the competing (full-priced) EMI Kempe version, making this an obvious first choice in the medium-price range. The documentation for this reissue in RCA's Golden Treasury series is admirable. The set is not available in the USA.

Karajan, whose DG recording of *Parsifal* is so naturally intense, fails in this earlier but related opera to capture comparable spiritual depth. So some of the big melodies sound a degree over-inflected and the result, though warm and expressive and dramatically powerful, with wide-ranging recording, misses an important dimension. Nor is much of the singing as pure-toned as it might be, with René Kollo too often straining and Tomowa-Sintow not always able to scale down in the necessary purity her big, dramatic voice. Even so, with strong and beautiful playing from the Berlin Philharmonic, it remains a powerful performance, and it makes a fair mid-priced version on three CDs.

The Sawallisch recording was of a live performance at Bayreuth in 1962 and has a propulsive thrust over Wagner's expansive paragraphs through the presence of an audience. For this dramatic tension one naturally has to pay in stage-noises, occasional slips and odd balances, but the recording captures the unique flavour of the Festspielhaus splendidly. What above all will dictate a listener's response is his reaction to the voices of Anja Silja as Elsa and of Astrid Varnay as Ortrud. Though Silja has been far less steady on record in other sets, this is often not a pretty sound, and Varnay was firmer in her earlier Bayreuth recording for Decca in mono. Jess Thomas is here not as reliable as he has been in other performances; but Sawallisch's direction is superb, fresh and direct, never intrusive. Considering the problems of recording, on CD the sound is marvellously refined as well as atmospheric. The opera fits neatly on three discs, with each Act complete and unbroken.

In Kubelik's DG set, the performance of Gundula Janowitz as Elsa is ravishing, with a constant stream of glorious tone over the widest range, and deeply expressive phrasing. For her alone this set is one for Wagnerians to hear. James King is an imaginative Lohengrin, but Thomas Stewart's Telramund has nothing like the dramatic intensity one ideally requires. Gwyneth Jones as the wicked Ortrud provides a sad showing. The pain of her performance, with many passages completely out of control, would be enough to turn most collectors away, and, though Kubelik's interpretation begins dramatically and is often dedicated and thoughtful, it cannot compare with Kempe's, which glows with expressive conviction. A vivid CD transfer makes the most of the lively 1971 recording.

Die Meistersinger von Nürnberg (complete).

(M) (***) EMI mono CMS7 64154-2 [CDMD 641542]. Ferdinand Frantz, Rudolf Schock, Elisabeth Grümmer, Gottlob Frick, Benno Kusche, Gerhard Unger, Marga Höffgen, St Hedwig's Cathedral Ch., German Op., Berlin, Ch., BPO, Kempe.

(M) (***) EMI mono CHS7 63500-2 (4) [CDHD 63500]. Schwarzkopf, Edelmann, Kunz, Hopf, Unger, Bayreuth Festival Ch. & O, Karajan.

(M) (*(**)) Decca mono 440 057-2 (4). Schoeffler, Gueden, Treptow, Edelmann, Dönch, Poell, Dermota, Schürhoff, V. State Op. Ch., VPO, Knappertsbusch.

Though Kempe's classic EMI set is in mono only, one misses stereo surprisingly little when, with closely balanced voices, there is such clarity and sharpness of focus. The orchestra rather loses out, sounding relatively thin; but with such an incandescent performance – not quite as intense as Karajan's live Bayreuth version of 1951 but consistently inspired – one quickly adjusts. The cast has no weak link. Elisabeth Grümmer is a meltingly beautiful Eva, pure and girlish, not least in the great Act III Quintet, and Rudolf Schock gives the finest of all his recorded performances as Walther, with his distinctive timbre between lyric and heroic well suited to the role. Ferdinand Frantz is a weighty, dark-toned Sachs, Gottlob Frick a commanding Pogner, Benno Kusche a clear-toned Beckmesser and Gerhard Unger an aptly light David.

Recorded live at the 1951 Bayreuth Festival, Karajan's EMI version has never quite been matched since for its involving intensity. The mono sound may be thin and the stage noises often distracting, but, with clean CD transfers, the sense of being present at a great event is irresistible, with the great emotional moments – both between Eva and Walther and, even more strikingly, between Eva and Sachs – bringing a gulp in the throat. The young Elisabeth Schwarzkopf makes the most radiant Eva, singing her Act III solo *O Sachs, mein Freund!* with touching ardour before beginning the Quintet with flawless legato. Hans Hopf is here less gritty than in his other recordings, an attractive hero; while Otto Edelmann makes a superb Sachs, firm and virile, the more moving for not sounding old. There are inconsistencies among the others but, in a performance of such electricity generated by the conductor in his early prime, they are of minimal importance. The four mid-price CDs are generously indexed and come with a libretto but no translation. EMI should have indicated the index points not just in the libretto, but in the English synopsis as well.

Knappertsbusch takes a characteristically spacious view, but one which brings out the comedy as well as the poignancy of the piece. Maybe in reflection of the order of recording, Act II stands out as one of the most moving on disc, matched since but not surpassed. Paul Schoeffler with his dark, slightly metallic tone makes a searching Hans Sachs, wise and benevolent but unsentimental. Hilde Gueden is an enchanting Eva, with her unmistakable golden tone making the heroine provocative, even minxish. Her duet with Sachs is a high point, touching rare depths of emotion when Sachs remembers the wife and family who died, while then selflessly refusing to push himself forward as Eva's partner. The rest of the cast, though not so characterful, is still very strong, notably Anton Dermota as David and Karl Dönch as Beckmesser, with Günther Treptow not too strenuous as Walther. Sadly, the Decca transfer is edgy, with string-tone far more acid-sounding than on the original LP, even if voices come over well.

Die Meistersinger: highlights.

(M) *** DG 445 470-2 (from complete set, with Fischer-Dieskau, Domingo, Ligendza, Lagger, Hermann, Laubenthal, Ludwig, German Op. Ch. & O, Berlin, Jochum).

(B) (***) EMI mono CD-EMX 2228 [(M) id. import]. Frantz, Schock, Grümmer, Frick, Kusche, Unger, Höffgen, St Hedwig's Cathedral Ch., German Op., Berlin, Ch., Berlin State Op. Ch., BPO, Kempe.

(M) **(*) EMI CDM7 63455-2 (from complete set, with Adam, Evans, Kelemen, Ridderbusch, Kollo, Schreier, Donath, Hess, Leipzig R. Ch., Dresden State Op. Ch. & State O, Karajan).

(M) ** Ph. 446 621-2 [id.]. Ridderbusch, Bode, Sotin, Hirte, Cox, Stricker, (1974) Bayreuth Festival Ch. & O, Varviso.

Jochum's DG excerpts are especially valuable for giving fair samples of the two most individual performances: Fischer-Dieskau as a sharply incisive Sachs, his every nuance of mood clearly interpreted, and Domingo a golden-toned if hardly idiomatic Walther. Needless to say, the 76-minute selection, opening with the *Overture*, includes the Act III Quintet, also the opera's closing scene. The recording, made in March 1976 in the Berlin Jesus-Christus Kirche with the voices placed rather closely, matches the fine quality of the complete set.

The 72-minute selection from Kempe's classic EMI mono set is not dissimilar, this time demonstrating Ferdinand Frantz's comparatively weighty, dark-toned Sachs, while Rudolph Schock, with his distinctive timbre between lyrical and heroic, is ideally suited to the role of Walther. Elisabeth Grümmer is a meltingly beautiful Eva, particularly so in the great Act III Quintet. Again voices are closely balanced and there is striking clarity of focus so that, although the orchestra sounds relatively thin, one soon adjusts when the singing is so fine and there is good ambience.

Many will prefer to have a sampler rather than investing in the complete Karajan stereo set, which is let down by the casting of Theo Adam as Sachs. The selection runs to nearly 68 minutes.

The 1974 Bayreuth performance is flawed (and the big crowd scenes bring obtrusive stage-noises), but the Swiss conductor, Silvio Varviso, is a persuasive Wagnerian, one who inspires the authentic ebb and flow of tension. With the exception of Hannelore Bode's disappointing Eva, much of the singing here is very enjoyable, with Karl Ridderbusch a firmly resonant Hans Sachs and the other Masters really singing their parts. But this set of highlights (nearly 78 minutes) is let down, like the others in this Philips series, by the absence of a synopsis to relate the excerpts to the narrative.

Parsifal (complete).

(M) (***) Teldec/Warner mono 9031 76047-2 (4). Windgassen, Mödl, Weber, London, Uhde, Van Mill, 1951 Bayreuth Festival Ch. & O, Knappertsbusch

(M) **(*) EMI CMS5 65665-2 (4) [CDMD 65665]. Ellsworth, Joll, McIntyre, Meier, Gwynne, Folwell, Welsh Nat. O Ch. & O, Goodall.

Hans Knappertsbusch was the inspired choice of conductor made by Wagner's grandsons for the first revivals of *Parsifal* after the war. The Teldec historic reissue is taken from the first season in 1951 and makes a striking contrast with the later Knappertsbusch recording, made in stereo for Philips 11 years later. The 1951 performance is no less than 20 minutes longer overall, with Knappertsbusch, always expansive, even more dedicated than in his later reading. The cast is even finer, with Wolfgang Windgassen making other Heldentenors seem rough by comparison, singing with warmth as well as power. Ludwig Weber is magnificently dark-toned as Gurnemanz, much more an understanding human being than his successor, Hans Hotter, less of a conventionally noble figure. Martha Mödl is both wild and abrasive in her first scenes and sensuously seductive in the long Act II duet with Parsifal, and Hermann Uhde is bitingly firm as Klingsor. Though the limited mono sound is not nearly as immediate or atmospheric as the later stereo, with much thinner orchestral texture, the voices come over well, and the chorus is well caught.

EMI have reissued the Goodall version at mid-price and on four CDs instead of the original five, which brings considerable savings on the original cost. There are no complaints about the sound, which is admirably full and vivid. Goodall in his plain, unvarnished, patiently expansive reading characteristically finds deep intensity in a strong, rough-hewn way. He may lack the ethereal beauties of Karajan, for here *Parsifal* is brought down to earth, thanks not just to Goodall but to the cast which with one exception stands up well to international competition. It was plainly a help that these same singers had appeared together under Goodall on stage in the Welsh National Opera production. Donald McIntyre gives one of his very finest performances as Gurnemanz, with more bloom than usual. Waltraud Meier's powerful, penetrating voice suits the role of Kundry well, while the American, Warren Ellsworth, has power and precision, if little beauty, as Parsifal. Only the ill-focused Amfortas of Phillip Joll is disappointing, too gritty of tone, though he too makes the drama compelling.

Parsifal: highlights.

(M) ** Ph. Dig. 446 622-2. Hofmann, Meier, Estes, Salminen, Sotin, (1985) Bayreuth Festival Ch. & O, Levine.

The (75 minutes) Philips selection from Levine's earlier Bayreuth recording includes the Act I Prelude only. The singing of Peter Hofmann as Parsifal is flawed, although Waltraud Meier is an outstanding Kundry. Perhaps surprisingly, the contribution of Hans Sotin as Gurnemanz is strongly featured when he is vocally less reliable than usual. In any case, these highlights are hardly enticing when the meagre back-up documentation fails to relate the excerpts to a plot synopsis.

Das Rheingold (complete).

(M) *** Ph. 434 421-2 (2) [id.]. McIntyre, Schwarz, Zednik, Pampuch, Becht, (1980) Bayreuth Festival O, Boulez.

(M) **(*) Ph. 412 475-2 (2). Adam, Nienstedt, Windgassen, Neidlinger, Talvela, Böhme, Silja, Soukupová, Bayreuth (1966) Festival O, Boehm.

(B) **(*) RCA Dig. 74321 45418-2 (2). Adam, Nimsgern, Stryczek, Schreier, Bracht, Salminen, Vogel, Büchner, Minton, Popp, Priew, Schwarz, Dresden State O & Ch., Janowski.

The Boulez version is taken from the 1980 Festival. The early digital sound has plenty of air round it, giving a fine impression of a performance in the Festspielhaus with all its excitement, though voices are not caught as immediately as on the Boehm set. Sir Donald McIntyre here gives a memorable and noble performance, far firmer than his rival for Boehm, Theo Adam. Heinz Zednik is splendid as Loge and Hanna Schwarz is a powerful Fricka, while Siegfried Jerusalem brings beauty of tone as well as distinction to the small role of Froh. Hermann Becht is a weighty rather than incisive Alberich, and the only weak link is Martin Egel's unsteady Donner. Though not as bitingly intense as Boehm, Boulez, with speeds almost as fast, shatters the old idea of him as a chilly conductor.

Boehm's preference for fast speeds here brought the benefit that his was one of the first CD sets in which the whole of the *Vorabend* could be contained on two CDs. The pity is that the performance is marred by the casting of Theo Adam as Wotan, keenly intelligent but rarely agreeable on the ear, at times here far too wobbly. On the other hand, Gustav Neidlinger as Alberich is superb, even more involving here than he is for Solti, with the curse made spine-chilling. It is also good to have Wolfgang Windgassen as Loge; among the others, Anja Silja makes an attractively urgent Freia.

Janowski's distinguished *Rheingold* is now the least expensive digital set on CD. The studio sound, though not without ambience, has the voices close and vivid, with the orchestra in the background. If the result lacks the atmospheric qualities which make the Solti *Rheingold* still the most compelling in sound, thanks to the detailed production of the late John Culshaw, the effect still grips the listener, even if Donner's hammer-blow is let down by the effects department with only a very ordinary anvil stroke. Theo Adam, in spite of some grittiness of tone, makes a fine Wotan and the set is consistently well cast, including Peter Schreier, Matti Salminen, Yvonne Minton and Lucia Popp, as well as East German singers of high calibre. The current transfer is very impressive and the set is very well documented.

Das Rheingold: highlights.
(M) (***) Teldec/Warner Dig. 0630 13820-9 (from complete set, with Tomlinson, Finnie, Brinkmann, Schreibmeyer, Clark, Johansson, Svendén, Von Kannen, Pampuch, Hölle, Kang, Leidland, Küttenbaum, Turner, (1991) Bayreuth Festival O, Barenboim).

It is difficult to recommend a set of highlights which contains barely 51 minutes of music, with John Tomlinson's magnificent Wotan not as well represented as he might be; although the Barenboim Teldec recording is highly enjoyable, collectors would do better to go for the complete (full-price) set.

The Rheingold (complete, in English).
(M) **(*) EMI CMS7 64110-2 (3). Bailey, Hammond-Stroud, Pring, Belcourt, Attfield, Collins, McDonnall, Lloyd, Grant, English Nat. Op. O, Goodall.

Goodall's slow tempi in *Rheingold* bring an opening section where the temperature is low, reflecting hardly at all the tensions of a live performance, even though this was taken from a series of Coliseum presentations. Nevertheless the momentum of Wagner gradually builds up so that, by the final scenes, both the overall teamwork and the individual contributions of such singers as Norman Bailey, Derek Hammond-Stroud and Clifford Grant come together impressively. Hammond-Stroud's powerful representation of Alberich culminates in a superb account of the curse. The spectacular orchestral effects (with the horns sounding glorious) are vividly caught by the engineers and impressively transferred to CD, even if balances (inevitably) are sometimes less than ideal.

Rienzi (complete).
(M) ** EMI CMS7 63980-2 (3). Kollo, Wennberg, Martin, Adam, Hillebrand, Vogel, Schreier, Leipzig R. Ch., Dresden State Op. Ch., Dresden State O, Hollreiser.

It is sad that the flaws in this ambitious opera prevent the unwieldy piece from having its full dramatic impact. This recording is not quite complete, but the cuts are unimportant and most of the set numbers make plain the youthful, uncritical exuberance of the ambitious composer. Except in the recitative, Heinrich Hollreiser's direction is strong and purposeful, but much of the singing is disappointing. René Kollo at least sounds heroic, but the two women principals are poor. Janis Martin in the breeches role of Adriano produces tone that does not record very sweetly, while Siv Wennberg as the heroine, Rienzi's sister, slides most unpleasantly between notes in the florid passages. Despite good recording, this can only be regarded as a stop-gap.

Der Ring des Nibelungen: an introduction to *The Ring* by Deryck Cooke, with 193 music examples.
(M) *** Decca 443 581-2 (2) [id.]. VPO, Solti.

The reissue in Decca's Classic Sound series of Deryck Cooke's fascinating and scholarly lecture is most welcome. Even though the CD reissue omits the printed text, the principal musical motives are all printed out in the accompanying booklet and they demonstrate just how the many leading ideas in *The Ring* develop from one another, springing from an original germ. The discourse is riveting, though even dedicated Wagnerians may not want to hear it many times over. The music examples, many of them specially prepared, are not always inserted with the skill one is accustomed to on BBC Radio 3, but this is still a thoroughly worthwhile acquisition for those who already have recordings of the operas.

Der Ring des Nibelungen (complete).
✿ (M) *** Decca 455 555-2 (14) [id.]. Nilsson, Windgassen, Flagstad, Fischer-Dieskau, Hotter, London, Ludwig, Neidlinger, Frick, Svanholm, Stolze, Böhme, Hoffgen, Sutherland, Crespin, King, Watson, Ch. & VPO, Solti.
(B) *** Ph. 446 057-2 (14) [(M) 420 325-2]. Nilsson, Windgassen, Neidlinger, Adam, Rysanek, King, Nienstedt, Esser, Talvela, Böhme, Silja, Dernesch, Stewart, Hoeffgen, (1967) Bayreuth Festival Ch. & O, Boehm.
(B) *** EMI CZS 72731-2 (14) [id.]. Behrens, Varady, Lipovšek, Schwarz, Hale, Kollo, Wlaschiha, Schunk, Tear, Rootering, Bav. State Opera Ch. & O, Sawallisch.
(B) *** RCA Dig. 74321 45417-2 (14). Jeannine Altmeyer, René Kollo, Theo Adam, Peter Schreier, Siegmund Nimsgern, Siegfried Vogel, Yvonne Minton, Ortrun Wenkel, Matti Salminen, Lucia Popp, Siegfried Jerusalem, Jessye Norman, Kurt Moll, Cheryl Studer, Leipzig R. Ch., Dresden State Op. Ch. & O, Janowski.
(M) *** DG 435 211-2 (15). Veasey, Fischer-Dieskau, Stolze, Kelemen, Dernesch, Dominguez, Jess Thomas, Stewart, Crespin, Janowitz, Vickers, Talvela, Brilioth, Ludwig, Ridderbusch, BPO, Karajan.
(M) **(*) EMI Dig. CMS7 64775-2 (14). Eva Marton, James Morris, Marjana Lipovšek, Heinz Sednik, Theo Adam, Peter Haage, Siegfried Jerusalem, Kiri Te Kanawa, Kurt Rydl, Jadwiga Rappé, Cheryl

Studer, Reiner Goldberg, Waldtraud Meier, Matti Salminen, Thomas Hampson, John Tomlinson, Eva-Maria Bundschuh, Bav. R. Ch. & SO, Haitink.

(M) (***) EMI (SIS) mono CZS7 67123-2 (13) [Ang. CDZM 67123]. Suthaus, Mödl, Frantz, Patzak, Neidlinger, Windgassen, Konetzni, Streich, Jurinac, Frick, RAI Ch. & Rome SO, Furtwängler.

(M) ** DG Dig. 445 354-2 (14) [id.]. Behrens, Goldberg, Morris, Norman, Ludwig, Moll, Met. Op. O, Levine.

Solti's was the first recorded *Ring* cycle to be issued. Whether in performance or in vividness of sound, it remains the most electrifying account of the tetralogy on disc, sharply focused if not always as warmly expressive as some. Solti himself developed in the process of making the recording, and *Götterdämmerung* represents a peak of achievement for him, commanding and magnificent. Though CD occasionally reveals bumps and bangs inaudible on the original LPs, this is a historic set that remains as central today as when it first appeared.

Anyone who prefers the idea of a live recording of the *Ring* cycle can be warmly recommended to Boehm's fine set, more immediately involving than any. Recorded at the 1967 Bayreuth Festival, it captures the unique atmosphere and acoustic of the Festspielhaus very vividly. Birgit Nilsson as Brünnhilde and Wolfgang Windgassen as Siegfried are both a degree more volatile and passionate than they were in the Solti cycle. Gustav Neidlinger as Alberich is also superb, as he was too in the Solti set; and the only major reservation concerns the Wotan of Theo Adam, in a performance searchingly intense and finely detailed but often unsteady of tone even at that period. The sound, only occasionally constricted, has been vividly transferred. In the UK Philips are currently offering this version of the *Ring* in a 14-disc limited edition (which means in effect for a limited time) at bargain price. Waverers should snap this up while it is still around and before it returns to mid-price under its earlier catalogue number (420 325-2).

On 14 discs at bargain price, the Sawallisch version of the *Ring* makes an excellent recommendation. This is the sound-track of the Bavarian State Opera production by Nikolaus Lehnhoff, as recorded in 1989 for television. The cast is as fine as any in rival versions of the digital age, the performances gain in dramatic momentum and expressive spontaneity from being recorded live, and – rather surprisingly – the sound is outstandingly rich, warm and spaciously atmospheric, in many ways outshining rival digital recordings. Sawallisch conducts with a thrust and energy not always present in his studio recordings, with speeds often faster than have become common. One minor quibble is that both *Walküre* and *Siegfried* could each have been fitted easily on to three CDs instead of four, even if *Siegfried* gains from being presented one disc per Act. As to the casting, Robert Hale proves a noble Wotan, virile and strong. The voice may not be beautiful, but the range of expression is great, so that in *Walküre* the final moment of his kissing Brünnhilde's godhead away could hardly be more tender.

Ekkekhard Wlaschiha, as in rival sets, is a magnificent Alberich, darkly sinister, with firm focus; and Kurt Moll is also superb in the roles of Fafner, Hunding and Hagen. Hildegard Behrens may not be a weighty Brünnhilde, with some unevenness of production, but, as in Levine's DG *Ring* cycle from the Met., she rises superbly to the big challenges at the end of both *Siegfried* and *Götterdammerung*. Other outstanding contributions come from Marjana Lipovšek as Fricka, Robert Tear as Loge, Julia Varady as Sieglinde, Waltraud Meier as Waltraute, and Hanna Schwarz as Erda, with such excellent singers as Nancy Gustafson in minor roles. The only notable reservations come over the two Heldentenor roles, with Robert Schunk rather gritty as Siegmund, failing to respond to the lyrical writing, and – more particularly – René Kollo as Siegfried. A few years earlier the voice would have been ideal, but here it regularly frays into unevenness under pressure, though his acting remains very convincing. No libretto is provided, but the synopses are linked to plentiful cue-points. An excellent, keenly enjoyable set.

Dedication and consistency are the hallmarks of the (originally Eurodisc) *Ring*, a series of studio recordings made between 1980 and 1983 with German thoroughness by the then East German record company, Eurodisc. It is now reissued by RCA on 14 budget-priced CDs, to make it a highly attractive bargain. Voices tend to be balanced well forward of the orchestra, but the digital sound is admirably full as well as clear. Indeed the clarity has one concentrating on the words, helped by Janowski's vividly direct approach to the score. One can enter the set at any point to sense the ongoing tension. Overall this is a good deal more rewarding than many of the individual sets that have been issued at full price over the years since it first appeared. The documentation is first class. The set is not yet available in the USA.

Karajan's recording of *The Ring* followed close on the heels of Solti's for Decca, providing a good alternative studio version which equally stands the test of time. The manner is smoother, the speeds generally broader, yet the tension and concentration of the performances are maintained more consistently than in most modern studio recordings. Casting is not quite consistent between the operas, with Régine Crespin as Brünnhilde in *Walküre*, but Helga Dernesch at her very peak in the last two operas. The casting of Siegfried is changed between *Siegfried* and *Götterdämmerung*, from Jess Thomas to Helge Brilioth, just as strong but sweeter of tone. The original CD transfers are used without change for this mid-price compilation.

Haitink recorded the *Ring* cycle in the years when he was emerging as an inspired Wagner conductor. Strong and purposeful, he takes a thoughtful view which in each music-drama nevertheless builds up unerringly in tension and power, with the beauty of Wagner's orchestration consistently brought out. The recordings are warm and full, if not as sharply defined as they might be, and the principal snags lie in some of the casting, notably with Eva Marton as Brünnhilde, too often gusty and ill-focused. Theo Adam too is a disappointing Alberich, dramatically intense but unable any longer to sustain a steady line. James Morris as Wotan is here more sympathetic than in the Levine set, dating from the same period, but he yields to other singers in the role. For the rest, a strong and compelling issue, still (arguably) technically the best studio recording of the *Ring* in digital sound, the more welcome in this 14-disc package at mid-price.

When in 1972 EMI first transferred the Italian Radio tapes of Furtwängler's studio performances of 1953, the sound was disagreeably harsh, making sustained listening unpleasant. In this digital transfer, the boxiness of the studio sound and the closeness of the voices still take away some of the unique Furtwängler glow in Wagner, but the sound is acceptable and actually benefits in some ways from extra clarity. Furtwängler gives each opera a commanding sense of unity, musically and dramatically, with hand-picked casts including Martha Mödl as a formidable Brünnhilde, Ferdinand Frantz a firm-voiced Wotan and Ludwig Suthaus (Tristan in Furtwängler's recording) a reliable Siegfried. In smaller roles you have stars like Wolfgang Windgassen, Julius Patzak, Rita Streich, Sena Jurinac and Gottlob Frick.

DG have sensibly repackaged Levine's New York *Ring* cycle on 14 discs at a special mid-price, and some listeners will welcome so strongly cast a recording in up-front studio sound, even though aggressively digital and not always kind to voices. The glory of the cycle is the conclusion, Levine's powerful reading of *Götterdämmerung*, with the sound rather fuller than in the earlier operas. Yet overall this is a set with too many flaws and disappointments, best recommended to those who have enjoyed Levine's spacious reading at the Met. or relayed on television.

'The best of The Ring': excerpts from *Das Rheingold; Die Walküre; Siegfried; Götterdämmerung.*
(B) *** Ph. Duo 454 020-2 (2) (from (1967) Bayreuth Festival recordings; cond. Karl Boehm).

The Ring 'Great scenes': Das Rheingold: Entry of the Gods into Valhalla. Die Walküre: Ride of the Valkyries; Magic fire music. Siegfried: Forging scene; Forest murmurs. Götterdämmerung: Siegfried's funeral march; Brünnhilde's Immolation scene.
(M) *** Decca 458 210-2 [421 313-2]. Nilsson, Windgassen, Hotter, Stolzel, VPO, Solti.

Although the Solti and Karajan single-disc selections have their own appeal – and, of course, there are more extended highlights available from each opera – as potted 'Rings' go, this Philips Duo is probably the best buy. The only snag is that Bernard Jacobson's very brief synopsis of the narrative fails to relate each track to the story. However, since not too much happens in each of the four operas, and what does isn't too complicated, this Philips Duo set, taken from Boehm's outstanding complete recording, can certainly be enjoyed as a summary of Wagner's intentions, and virtually all the key scenes are included.

The excerpts from Solti's *Ring* are often quite extended – the *Entry of the Gods into Valhalla* offers some ten minutes of music, and the *Forest murmurs* from *Siegfried* starts well before the orchestral interlude. Only *Siegfried's funeral march* is in any sense a 'bleeding chunk' which has to be faded at the end; and the disc closes with 20 minutes of Brünnhilde's Immolation scene. The reissue in Decca's Opera Gala series comes handsomely packaged in an additonal slip-case and is complete with good documentation, full translations and nostalgic pictures of the young Georg Solti, Birgit Nilsson and the producer, John Culshaw. This appears to be available only in the UK.

The Ring: highlights: *Das Rheingold: Lugt, Schwestern! Die Wenken lacht in den Grund; Zur Burg führt die Brücke. Die Walküre: Der Männer Sippe sass hier im Saal; Ride of the Valkyries; Wotan's farewell and Magic fire music. Siegfried: Forest murmurs; Aber, wie sah meine Mutter wohl aus?; Nun sing! Ich lausche dem Gesang; Heil dir, Sonne! Heil dir, Licht!. Götterdämmerung: Funeral music; Fliegt heim, ihr Raben!.*
(B) *** DG Classikon 439 423-2 [(M) id. import] (from above complete recording; cond. Karajan).

The task of selecting highlights to fit on a single disc, taken from the whole of the *Ring* cycle, is daunting. But the DG producer of this Classikon super-bargain issue has extended the previous selection to 77 minutes and managed to assemble many key items, either very well tailored or ending satisfactorily. The whole of Wotan's great *Farewell* scene with the *Magic Fire music* is included, and much else besides. Moreover the *Funeral music* from *Götterdämmerung* (where the previous CD ended) is now followed by *Brünnhilde's Immolation* and continues to the end of the opera. The transfers are extremely brilliant (the

Ride of the Valkyries is given an edge of excitement) and this makes a magnificent bargain reissue. It seems carping to complain that the notes do not find space to detail what happens in each excerpt. But sonically this should surely tempt any novice in this repertoire to want to go on and explore Wagner's masterly cycle still further.

Siegfried (complete).

(M) *** Ph. Dig. 434 423-2 (3) [id.]. Jung, G. Jones, McIntyre, Zednik, Becht, Wenkel, Hübner, Sharp, (1980) Bayreuth Festival O, Boulez.

(M) *** Ph. 412 483-2 (4). Windgassen, Nilsson, Adam, Neidlinger, Soukupová, Köth, Böhme, Bayreuth (1967) Festival Ch. & O, Boehm.

(B) *** RCA Dig. 74321 45420-2 (4). Kollo, Altmeyer, Adam Schreier, Nimsgern, Wenkel, Salminen, Sharp, Dresden State O, Janowski.

Like the first two music-dramas in his Bayreuth *Ring* cycle, Boulez's version takes a disc less than usual and comes at mid-price in the Philips Bayreuth series. Here the advantage is even greater when each Act is complete on a single disc. It was recorded in 1980. If anything, Boulez is even more warmly expressive than in *Rheingold* or *Walküre*, directing a most poetic account of the *Forest murmurs* episode and leading in each Act to thrillingly intense conclusions. Manfred Jung is an underrated Siegfried, forthright and, by latterday standards, unusually clean-focused, and Heinz Zednik is a characterful Mime. As in the rest of the cycle, Sir Donald McIntyre is a noble Wotan, though Hermann Becht's weighty Alberich is not as strongly contrasted as it might be. Norma Sharp as the Woodbird enunciates her words with exceptional clarity and, though Gwyneth Jones as Brünnhilde has a few squally moments, she sings with honeyed beauty when the Idyll theme emerges, towards the end of the love duet. The digital sound is full and atmospheric, though it is a pity that the brass is not caught as weightily as it might be.

The natural-sounding quality of Boehm's live recording from Bayreuth, coupled with his determination not to let the music lag, makes his account of *Siegfried* as satisfying as the rest of his cycle, vividly capturing the atmosphere of the Festspielhaus, with voices well ahead of the orchestra. Windgassen is at his peak here, if anything more poetic in Acts II and III than he is in Solti's studio recording, and vocally just as fine. Nilsson, as in *Götterdämmerung*, gains over her studio recording from the extra flow of adrenalin in a live performance; and Gustav Neidlinger is unmatchable as Alberich. Erika Köth is disappointing as the woodbird, not sweet enough, and Soukupová is a positive, characterful Erda. Theo Adam is at his finest as the Wanderer, less wobbly than usual, clean and incisive.

Janowski's *Siegfried* is in almost every way impressive. The singing is generally first rate with Kollo fine in the name role, hardly ever strained, and Peter Schreier a superb Mime, using Lieder-like qualities in detailed characterization. Siegmund Nimsgern is a less characterful Alberich, but the voice is excellent, and Theo Adam concludes his portrayal of Wotan/Wanderer with his finest performance of the series. There are a few less effective moments (Act II rather scurries to a close with Siegfried in pursuit of a rather shrill woodbird in Norma Sharp), but this is a small blot on a performance that brings cumulative tension in the splendid final scene. The relative lightness of Jeannine Altmeyer's Brünnhilde comes out in this love duet (which of course includes music famous in the *Siegfried idyll*) more strikingly than in *Walküre*, but this matters far less on record than it would in the theatre. The tenderness and femininity are most affecting, as at the entry of the idyll motif, where Janowski in his dedicated simplicity is also at his most compelling, so that the opera moves to a thrilling close, with both singers at their finest. Clear, beautifully balanced, digital sound with voices and orchestra firmly placed, and an agreeable ambience add to the listener's pleasure. At bargain price this is splendid value.

Siegfried: highlights.

(M) (***) Teldec/Warner Dig. 0630 13822-9 (from complete set, with Jerusalem, Clark, Tomlinson, Anne Evans, Von Kannen, Philip King, Svendén, Leidland, (1992) Bayreuth Festival Ch. & O, Barenboim).

(M) *(**) Ph. Dig. 446 615-2 [id.] (from above set, with Jung, Zednik, Gwyneth Jones; cond. Boulez).

The Teldec selection from *Siegfried* (46 minutes 30 seconds) is even less generous than the companion highlights CD from *Das Rheingold*, but it does at least include the Act I dialogue between John Tomlinson's memorable Wanderer and Graham Clark's unforgettable portrayal of Mime. Sir Donald McIntyre's noble contribution is omitted altogether from the Philips selection, which concentrates on the Mime/Siegfried duologues in Act I, then on Siegfried entirely in Act II (apart from the Woodbird), and on the Siegfried/Brünnhilde interchanges in Act III. As usual in this Philips series, the snag is that neither a translation nor a cued synopsis is provided, only a list of excerpts and participants.

Siegfried (complete, in English).

(M) *** EMI CMS7 63595-2 (4). Remedios, Hunter, Bailey, Dempsey, Hammond-Stroud, Grant, Collins, London, Sadler's Wells Op. O, Goodall.

More tellingly than in almost any other Wagner opera recording, Goodall's spacious direction here conveys the genuine dramatic crunch that gives the experience of hearing Wagner in the opera house its unique power, its overwhelming force; this is unmistakably a great interpretation caught on the wing. Remedios, more than any rival on record, conveys not only heroic strength but clear-ringing youthfulness, caressing the ear as well as exciting it. Norman Bailey makes a magnificently noble Wanderer, steady of tone, and Gregory Dempsey is a characterful Mime, even if his deliberate whining tone is not well caught on record. The sound is superbly realistic, even making no allowances for the conditions. Lovers of opera in English should grasp the opportunity of hearing this unique set.

Tannhäuser (Dresden version; complete).
(M) **(*) EMI CMS7 63214-2 (3) [CDMC 634214-2]. Hans Hopf, Elisabeth Grümmer, Dietrich Fischer-Dieskau, Marianne Schech, Gottlob Frick, German State Op., Berlin, Ch. & O, Konwitschny.

The Konwitschny set is a fine one, marred by one serious flaw: the coarse singing of Hans Hopf in the name role; he fails to convey the joyous lyricism of the part, straining much of the time and with plenty of intrusive aitches. The opening scene with Venus is particularly daunting since Marianne Schech is the other comparatively weak member of the cast and, when they go a-wobbling together, the result is not far from comic. But happily things improve rapidly. Elisabeth Grümmer, Fischer-Dieskau and Gottlob Frick are all magnificent, and Konwitschny draws enthusiastic playing and singing from everyone. The chorus, important in this opera, is especially good, and the atmospheric recording adds to the warmth of the performance.

Tannhäuser (Dresden version): highlights.
(M) *(**) Ph. (IMS) 446 620-2 (from complete set, with Windgassen, Silja, Waechter, Stolze, Bumbry, (1962) Bayreuth Festival Ch. & O, Sawallisch).

With a generally good cast, and with Bumbry's sensuous Venus getting the opera off to an impressive start, many collectors will be glad to have these extensive (78 minutes) excerpts from Sawallisch's dedicated performance of the Dresden version of *Tannhäuser*; once again, the considerable drawback is the lack of a cued synopsis.

Tannhäuser (Paris version; complete).
(M) (**(*)) DG mono 457 682-2 (3) [id.]. Hans Beirer, Eberhard Wächter, Gottlob Frick, Gré Brouwenstijn, Waldemar Kmentt, Christa Ludwig, Gundula Janowitz, V. State Op. Ch. & O, Karajan.

Tannhauser was the one Wagner opera in the central canon which Karajan did not record for a regular record company, failing in that to match his rival, Sir Georg Solti. That makes this Austrian Radio recording in mono the more valuable, dry and limited in sound as it is, with voices well forward but with little bloom on either voices or instruments. Using the revised and expanded Paris version of the score, the recording dates from January 1963, revealing how Karajan varied his approach to each Act. With a hectic account of the *Venusberg music* he is urgent and passionate in Act I, but that leads to a more measured manner in Act II, and an unusually spacious one in the tragedy of Act III. In the title-role the Heldentenor, Hans Beirer, is variable, with no bark in his powerful voice but with some juddery unevenness to spoil the focus, more happily cast in Acts II and III than in Act I. As in her later recording for Solti, Christa Ludwig is a magnificent Vernus, and the Dutch soprano, Gré Brouwenstijn, too little recorded, an impressive Elisabeth. Gottlob Frick is a powerful, dark-toned Hermann, and Eberhard Wächter a lyrical Wolfram, with fine legato in *O star of Eve*.

Tristan und Isolde (complete).
(M) *** EMI CMS7 69319-2 (4) [Ang. CDMD 69319]. Vickers, Dernesch, Ludwig, Berry, Ridderbusch, German Op. Ch., Berlin, BPO, Karajan.
(M) *** DG 449 772-2 (3) [id.]. Windgassen, Nilsson, Ludwig, Talvela, Waechter, Bayreuth Festival (1966) Ch. & O, Boehm.
(M) *** Decca (IMS) 430 234-2 (4) [id.]. Uhl, Nilsson, Resnik, Van Mill, Krause, VPO, Solti.
(M) *** Decca 443 682-2 (4). Mitchinson, Gray, Howell, Joll, Wilkens, Folwell, Welsh Nat. Op. Ch. & O, Goodall.
(M) (**) Naxos mono 8.110008/10 [id.]. Melchior, Traubel, Thorborg, Huehn, Kipnis, Gurney, NY Met. Op. Ch. & O, Erich Leinsdorf.

Karajan's is a sensual performance of Wagner's masterpiece, caressingly beautiful and with superbly refined playing from the Berlin Philharmonic. Dernesch as Isolde is seductively feminine, not as noble as Flagstad, not as tough and unflinching as Nilsson; but the human quality makes this account if anything more moving still, helped by glorious tone-colour through every range. Jon Vickers matches her in what is arguably his finest performance on record, allowing himself true pianissimo shading. The rest of the cast is excellent too. The recording has been remastered again for the present reissue and the 1972 sound has plenty of body, making this an excellent first choice, with inspired conducting and the most satisfactory cast of all. The set has also been attractively repackaged with cleanly printed documentation.

Boehm's Bayreuth performance offers one enormous benefit in presenting one of the big Wagner operas for the first time on disc without any breaks at all, with each Act uninterrupted. Boehm is on the urgent side in this opera and the orchestral ensemble is not always immaculate; but the performance glows with intensity from beginning to end, carried through in the longest spans. Birgit Nilsson sings the *Liebestod* at the end of the long evening as though she was starting out afresh, radiant and with not a hint of tiredness, rising to an orgasmic climax and bringing a heavenly pianissimo on the final rising octave to F sharp. Opposite Nilsson is Wolfgang Windgassen, the most mellifluous of Heldentenoren; though the microphone balance sometimes puts him at a disadvantage to his Isolde, the realism and sense of presence of the whole set bathes you in the authentic atmosphere of Bayreuth. Making up an almost unmatchable cast are Christa Ludwig as Brangaene, Eberhard Waechter as Kurwenal, and Martti Talvela as King Mark, with the young Peter Schreier as the Young Sailor. The remastering for DG's 'Originals' series has further refined the CD transfer, and for many this will be first choice as it comes on three CDs against Karajan's four.

Solti's performance is less flexible and sensuous than Karajan's, but he shows himself ready to relax in Wagner's more expansive periods. On the other hand the end of Act I and the opening of the Love duet have a knife-edged dramatic tension. Nilsson is masterly in her conviction and – it cannot be emphasized too strongly – she never attacks below the note as Flagstad did, so that miraculously, at the end of the Love duet the impossibly difficult top Cs come out and hit the listener crisply and cleanly, dead on the note; and the *Liebestod* is all the more moving for having no soupy swerves at the climax. Fritz Uhl is a really musical Heldentenor. Dramatically he leaves the centre of the stage to Isolde, but his long solo passages in Act III are superb and make that sometimes tedious Act into something genuinely gripping. The Kurwenal of Tom Krause and the King Mark of Arnold van Mill are both excellent and it is only Regina Resnik as Brangäne who gives any disappointment. The production has the usual Decca/Culshaw imaginative touch, and the recording matches brilliance and clarity with satisfying co-ordination and richness.

Based on the much-praised production of the Welsh National Opera company, Goodall's recording of *Tristan* was made in 1980/81, not on stage but at Brangwyn Hall, Swansea, just when the cast was steamed up for stage performances. Typically from Goodall, it is measured and steady, but the speeds are not all exceptionally slow and, with rhythms sharply defined and textures made transparent, he keeps the momentum going. The WNO orchestra is not sumptuous, but the playing is well-tuned and responsive. Neither Linda Esther Gray nor John Mitchinson is as sweet on the ear as the finest rivals, for the microphone exaggerates vibrato in both. But Mitchinson never barks, Heldentenor-style, and Gray provides a formidable combination of qualities: feminine vulnerability alongside commanding power. Gwynne Howell is arguably the finest King Mark on record, making his monologue at the end of Act II, so often an anti-climax, into one of the noblest passages of all. This may not have the smoothness of the best international sets but, with its vivid digital sound, it is certainly compelling, and a libretto in three languages is an additional bonus.

Recorded live at the Met. in New York in February 1943, the historic Naxos set offers a performance which vividly conveys the atmosphere of a big occasion on stage despite very limited and variable sound. Act I fares best, with the voices forward and well focused, working up to a thrilling, almost frenzied climax at the end of the Act. Lauritz Melchior gives a performance very similar to that in the EMI recording from Covent Garden in the 1930s (conducted partly by Beecham, partly by Reiner), establishing him as arguably the finest exponent of the role this century. Helen Traubel may not have the total security of Kirsten Flagstad, whether in that earlier historic recording or in Furtwängler's studio set, and in the love duet she misses out the difficult top C's, but it is a rich, warmly expressive performance. Sadly, the glowing account of the *Liebestod* at the end is marred by some of the worst recording in the whole set. Acts II and III (both slightly cut, following the custom of the time) bring crumbly orchestral sound, and as a rule the voices are not as clear and fresh as in Act I, yet one can readily sense the stage atmosphere. The rest of the cast make a strong team, with Alexander Kipnis outstanding as King Mark, making his monologue, so often boring, into a magnetic experience.

Tristan und Isolde (slightly abridged).

(M) (***) EMI mono CHS7 64037-2 (3) [Ang. CDHC 64037]. Melchior, Flagstad, Herbert Janssen, Margarete Klose/Sabine Kalter, Sven Nilsson/Emanuel List, ROHCG Ch., LPO, Beecham/Reiner.

In both recordings used here, Melchior and Flagstad take the title-roles, with Herbert Janssen as Kurwenal, three legendary singers in those roles, but the parts of King Mark and Brangäne were sung by different singers – and, above all, Fritz Reiner was the conductor in the 1936 recordings. It is astonishing to find that the warmly expansive account of Act I is the work of Reiner, while it is Beecham who is responsible for the urgent view of Act II with its great love duet – part of it cut following the manner of the day. Act III is divided between Beecham in the first part, Reiner in the second. Whatever the inconsistencies, the result is a thrilling experience, with Flagstad fresher and even more incisive than in her studio recording with Furtwängler of 15 years later, and with Melchior a passionate vocal actor, not just the possessor of the most freely ringing of all Heldentenor voices.

Tristan und Isolde: highlights.
(M) *** Ph. (IMS) 446 617-2 (from above (1966) Bayreuth Festival recording, with Windgassen, Nilsson, Talvela; cond. Boehm).

Tristan with its seamless flow is less suitable than most of Wagner's operas for selecting excerpts from an ongoing performance but, with 77 minutes included, these highlights from the 1966 Boehm Bayreuth set, including the Act I Prelude, are excellent value save for the absence of a proper documented synopsis.

Die Walküre (complete).
(M) *** Ph. 412 478-2 (4). King, Rysanek, Nienstedt, Nilsson, Adam, Burmeister, Bayreuth (1967) Festival Ch. & O, Boehm.
(M) (***) EMI mono CHS7 63045-2 (3). Mödl, Rysanek, Frantz, Suthaus, Klose, Frick, VPO, Furtwängler.
(B) *** RCA Dig. 74321 45419-2 (4). Altmeyer, Norman, Minton, Jerusalem, Adam, Moll, Dresden State O, Janowski.
(M) **(*) Ph. 434 422-2 (3). Hofmann, Altmeyer, G. Jones, McIntyre, Schwarz, Salminen, (1980) Bayreuth Festival O, Boulez.

Boehm's performance has claims to be considered a first choice for this opera, irrespective of cost, and at mid-price it is unsurpassed. Rarely if ever does his preference for fast speeds undermine the music; on the contrary, it adds to the involvement of the performance, which never loses its concentration. Theo Adam is in firmer voice here as Wotan than he is in *Rheingold*, hardly sweet of tone but always singing with keen intelligence. As ever, Nilsson is in superb voice as Brünnhilde. Though the inevitable noises of a live performance occasionally intrude, this presents a more involving experience than any rival complete recording. The CD transfer transforms what on LP seemed a rough recording, even if passages of heavy orchestration still bring some constriction of sound.

Furtwängler, an excellent cast and the Vienna Philharmonic in radiant form match any of their successors. Ludwig Suthaus proves a satisfyingly clear-toned Heldentenor, never strained, with the lyricism of *Wintersturme* superbly sustained. Neither Léonie Rysanek as Sieglinde nor Martha Mödl as Brünnhilde is ideally steady, but the intensity and involvement of each is irresistible, classic performances both. Similarly, the mezzo of Margarete Klose may not be very beautiful, but the projection of words and the fire-eating character match the conductor's intensity. Gottlob Frick is as near an ideal Hunding as one will find, sinister but with the right streak of arrogant sexuality; while the Wotan of Ferdinand Frantz may not be as deeply perceptive as some, but to hear the sweep of Wagner's melodic lines so gloriously sung is a rare joy. The 1954 sound is amazingly full and vivid, with voices cleanly balanced against the inspired orchestra. The only snag of the set is that, to fit the whole piece on to only three CDs, breaks between discs come in mid-Act.

Once again in *Die Walküre* Janowski's direct approach matches the clarity of the recording, with voices well forward of the orchestra but not aggressively so. The balance allows full glory for the singing from a satisfyingly consistent cast. Jessye Norman might not seem an obvious choice for Sieglinde, but the sound is glorious, the expression intense and detailed, making her a fine match for the good if rather less imaginative Siegmund of Siegfried Jerusalem. They are well matched in the passionate close of Act I and Janowski rises to the occasion. The one snag from so commanding a Sieglinde is that she dramatically overtops the Brünnhilde of Jeannine Altmeyer, who yet conveys a touching measure of feminine vulnerability in the leading Valkyrie, even in her godhead days. The beauty and the frequent sensuousness of her singing are the more telling against the strong, gritty Wotan of Theo Adam, and the illumination of the narrative is consistent and intense, well supported by Janowski with surges of orchestral tone, especially in the great closing duet with the fire music which ends the opera, in which Adam sings so tenderly that one almost forgets his slow vibrato (which can be a problem under pressure). Kurt Moll is a gloriously firm Hunding, and Yvonne Minton a searingly effective Fricka, and altogether this reissue, most satisfyingly transferred to CD, makes a splendid bargain.

The major advantage of the Boulez Bayreuth version of 1980 is that it comes at mid-price on only three discs, with atmospheric digital sound and a strong, if flawed, cast. Jeannine Altmeyer is a generally reliable Sieglinde, but Peter Hofmann's tenor had already grown rather gritty for Siegmund and in Act I is not as mellifluous as he should be. Donald McIntyre makes a commanding Wotan, Hanna Schwarz a firm, biting Fricka and Gwyneth Jones is at her least abrasive, producing beautiful, gentle tone in lyrical passages. Boulez's fervour will surprise many, even if he does not match Boehm's passionate urgency in this second instalment of the tetralogy.

Die Walküre: Act I (complete).

(M) *** Ph. (IMS) 442 640-2 [id.]. Leonie Rysanek, James King, Gerd Nienstedt, (1967) Bayreuth Festival O, Boehm.

(M) (***) EMI (SIS) mono CDH7 61020-2. Lehmann, Melchior, List, VPO, Bruno Walter.

It seems not unusual to have Act I of *Die Walküre* offered alone on disc, and indeed the sequence of events between Siegmund, Sieglinde and Hunding make a miniature opera in their own right, so collectors who have the Solti *Ring* will welcome this well-transferred CD as a sampler of a highly involving performance from 1967.

One is consistently gripped by the continuity and sustained lines of Walter's reading, and by the intensity and beauty of the playing of the Vienna Philharmonic. Lotte Lehmann's portrait of Sieglinde, arguably her finest role, has a depth and beauty never surpassed since, and Lauritz Melchior's heroic Siegmund brings singing of a scale and variety – not to mention beauty – that no Heldentenor today begins to match. Emanuel List as Hunding is satisfactory enough, but his achievement at least has latterly been surpassed.

Die Walküre: Act III (complete).

(M) *** Decca 448 575-2 [id.]. Flagstad, Edelmann, Schech, VPO, Solti.

(M) (***) EMI mono CDH7 64704-2. Varnay, Rysanek, Bjoerling, (1951) Bayreuth Festival O, Karajan.

The Solti recording was made in 1957. Flagstad came out of retirement to make it, and Decca put us eternally in their debt for urging her to do so. She sings radiantly. The meticulousness needed in the recording studio obviously brought out all her finest qualities, and there is no more than a touch of hardness on some of the top notes to show that the voice was no longer as young as it had been. Edelmann is not the ideal Wotan, but he has a particularly well-focused voice and when he sings straight, without sliding up or sitting under the note, the result is superb, and he is never wobbly. But it is Solti's conducting that prevents any slight blemishes from mattering. Not surprisingly, the recording too is remarkably vivid, anticipating the excellence of the great *Ring* project which was to follow, and so makes an obvious choice for reissue in Decca's 'Classic Sound' series.

Recorded in 1951, the first season after the war, Karajan's Bayreuth version of Act III shows the still-young conductor working at white heat. Speeds are far faster than in his DG studio recording, and very close to those in his live recording made at the Met. in 1969 (Nuova Era). Ensemble inevitably is not as taut as it was in the studio performance, but the electricity is far keener, and his cast is a characterful one. Astrid Varnay is an abrasive Brünnhilde, presenting the Valkyrie as a forceful figure, even in penitence prepared to stand up against her father. Leonie Rysanek is a warm Sieglinde, powerful rather than pure, with a rather obtrusive vibrato even at that date. Sigurd Bjoerling by contrast, the least-known of the principals, proves a magnificently virile Wotan, steady as a rock in the *Farewell*, but colouring the voice with a near-shout at the command, '*Loge, hier!*' The mono sound is transferred with bright immediacy, with some harshness on top but plenty of weight in the bass. This makes a splendid supplement to Karajan's superb Bayreuth *Meistersinger*, also recorded live in 1951.

Die Walküre: highlights.

(M) *** Teldec/Warner Dig. 0630 13821-9 (from complete set, with Elming, Hölle, Tomlinson, Secunde, Anne Evans, Finnie, Johansson, Floeren, Close, (1992) Bayreuth Festival O, Barenboim).

(M) *** Ph. (IMS) 446 614-2 (from above (1980) Bayreuth Festival recording, with Hofmann, Altmeyer, G. Jones; cond. Boulez).

With *Die Walküre*, Teldec are back on form in offering a well-planned 75-minutes selection following the opera's narrative line admirably (though, as usual, the synopsis is not cued).

As with the others in this otherwise excellent Philips series of Wagnerian highlights, the documentation is totally inadequate, with the excerpts listed baldly and with no synopsis provided to relate each to the narrative. But as this is by no means a first choice among recordings of this opera, many collectors will be interested in such a generous sampler (78 minutes) rather than the complete recording.

The Valkyrie (complete; in English).

(M) *** EMI CMS7 63918-2 (4). Hunter, Remedios, Curphey, Bailey, Grant, Howard, E. Nat. Op. Ch. & O, Goodall.

The glory of the ENO performance lies not just in Goodall's spacious direction but in the magnificent Wotan of Norman Bailey, noble in the broadest span but very human in his illumination of detail. Rita Hunter sings nobly too, and though she is not as commanding as Nilsson in the Solti cycle she is often more lyrically tender. Alberto Remedios as Siegmund is more taxed than he was as Siegfried in the later opera (lower tessituras are not quite so comfortable for him) but his sweetly ringing top register is superb. If others, such as Ann Howard as Fricka, are not always treated kindly by the microphone, the total dramatic compulsion is irresistible. The CD transfer increases the sense of presence and at the same time confirms the relative lack of sumptuousness.

VOCAL COLLECTIONS

Arias: *Götterdämmerung:* (i) *Zu neuen Taten; Starke Scheite schichtet mir dort. Lohengrin: Euch Lüften mein Klagen. Parsifal:* (i) *Ich sah' das King. Tristan: Mild und leise. Die Walküre: Du bist der Lenz; Ho-jo-ho!.*

(M) (***) RCA mono GD 87915 [87915-2-RG]. Flagstad, (i) with Melchior, San Francisco Op. O, or Victor SO (both cond. Edwin McArthur); Phd. O, Ormandy.

Recorded for RCA in America between 1935 and 1940, this first generation of Wagner recordings by Flagstad reveals the voice at its noblest and freshest, the more exposed in consistently close balance on the 78s of the period. It is a pity that only two of the shortest items – from *Lohengrin* and *Walküre* – have Ormandy conducting. Most of the rest are conducted by Flagstad's protégé, Edwin McArthur, including the two longest, the big duet for Parsifal and Kundry and Brünnhilde's Immolation scene. Yet the grandeur of Flagstad's singing is never in doubt, the commanding sureness, and, though the orchestral sound is unflatteringly dry, the voice is gloriously caught in clean transfers.

Choruses from: *Der fliegende Holländer; Lohengrin; Die Meistersinger; Parsifal; Tannhäuser.*

(M) *** Decca (IMS) 421 865-2 [id.] (from complete sets, cond. Solti).

Solti's choral collection is superb, with an added sophistication in both performance and recording. The collection opens with a blazing account of the *Lohengrin* Act III *Prelude*, since of course the *Bridal chorus* grows naturally out of it. But the *Pilgrims' chorus*, which comes next, creates an electrifying pianissimo and expands gloriously, while the excerpts from *Die Meistersinger* and *Parsifal* show Solti's characteristic intensity at its most potent.

Waldteufel, Emil (1837–1915)

Waltzes: *Acclamations; España; Estudiantina; Les Patineurs.*

(M) *** EMI CDM7 63136-2. Monte Carlo Nat. Op. O, Boskovsky – OFFENBACH: *Gaîté parisienne.* **

Boskovsky's collection has the advantage of including, besides the three favourites, *Acclamations*, which he opens very invitingly. His manner is *echt*-Viennese, but *The Skaters* responds well to his warmth and there is no lack of sparkle here. The remastering of the mid-1970s recording is admirably fresh.

Walton, William (1902–83)

'Walton edition': (i; ii) *Viola concerto;* (i; iii) *Violin concerto;* (iv) *Coronation marches: Crown imperial; Orb and sceptre; Façade (suites Nos. 1–2); Hamlet: Funeral march. Henry V* (scenes from the film with Sir Laurence Olivier & chorus; suite, arr. Mathieson); *Johannesburg festival overture; Partita for orchestra; Portsmouth Point overture; Richard III: Prelude & suite. Spitfire prelude and fugue; Symphony No. 1 in B flat min.;* (v) *The Wise Virgins (ballet suite)* & (iv) *Sheep may safely graze;* (iv; vi) *Belshazzar's Feast.*

(M) *** EMI stereo/mono CHS5 65003-2 (4). (i) Sir Yehudi Menuhin; (ii) New Philh. O; (iii) LSO; (iv) Philh. O; (v) Sadler's Wells O; (vi) with Donald Bell, Philh. Ch.; all cond. composer.

EMI follows up its revelatory Elgar Edition with this handsome Walton Edition, bringing together the composer's own EMI recordings not previously available on CD, with some of the most important dating from the mono interregnum before stereo arrived. The big revelation is Walton's own recording of the *First Symphony*, made in mono in October 1951, and here presented with far more bite and body than ever it had on the long-deleted LP. It emerges as among the most exciting versions ever, consistently displaying the Walton characteristic – faithfully observed later by such devotees as Previn – of treating the persistent syncopated rhythms with a jazzy freedom. The passion behind the performance is intense, most of all in the slow movement, which gains from superb woodwind playing from the Philharmonia soloists. Comparing Walton's 1959 stereo version of *Belshazzar's Feast* here with his earlier one of 1943 is fascinating, with speeds consistently more spacious, but with tensions just as keen and ensemble consistently crisper, though with less mystery conveyed. The one snag is the soloist, Donald Bell, clean of attack but uncharacterful.

Belshazzar and the *Symphony* make up the first disc, very generous measure, and all four discs are very well filled indeed. The second disc, entirely stereo, couples Menuhin's recordings of the *Violin* and *Viola concertos* with his version of the *Partita*, made in 1959. The new transfer of that last, fuller than before, reveals what extra fun Walton himself finds, bouncing the rhythms. Though Menuhin's account of the *Viola concerto* is a little effortful, not always flowing as it should, his viola sound is gloriously rich and true, and when it comes to the *Violin concerto*, recorded in July 1969, this is a vintage Menuhin performance, marked by his very distinctive tone and poignantly tender phrasing.

The third disc, mono except for Walton's scintillating account of the *Johannesburg festival overture* and the *Hamlet Funeral march*, brings together the shorter pieces. This 1955 account of the *Façade suites* lacks the tautness of Walton's consistently brisker pre-war versions, not helped by less immediate recording. The *Coronation marches* and *Portsmouth Point*, recorded in 1953 to celebrate the Queen's coronation, have a beefy strength, with Walton as conductor bringing out not just the swagger but also the full-throated emotion behind the marches. The 1953 sessions also produced a new version of the Bach arrangement, *Sheep may safely graze*, warmer and more refined than the one in the original (1940) recording of *The Wise Virgins*. That was made with the Sadler's Wells Orchestra in July 1940, bright and vigorous, even if the ensemble is not of the crispest.

The final disc contains the film music – the *Spitfire Prelude and fugue*, the *Richard III Prelude* and *Suite* and the *Henry V Suite*, all made in 1963 as a package. Most important is the belated restoration of the complete Henry V sequence with Laurence Olivier, recorded in 1946 on four 78-r.p.m. records, but reissued on LP by RCA with seven minutes of cuts from the opening and closing scenes. The transfer is again first rate, with the atmospheric quality of the writing vividly caught, even if the mono sound lacks a little in body. The sound of arrows at the climax of the Agincourt charge has never been matched on subsequent recordings. What consistently comes out throughout the set is that in his seemingly reticent way Walton was just as inspired a conductor of his own music as Elgar was of his.

Cello concerto.

(M) *** Sony Dig. SMK 53333 [id.]. Yo-Yo Ma, LSO, Previn – ELGAR: *Cello concerto*. ***

(BB) *** RCA Navigator 74321 29248-2 [(M) id. import]. Piatigorsky, Boston SO, Munch – VAUGHAN WILLIAMS: *Sinfonia Antartica*. ***

(M) *** RCA 09026 61498-2 [id.]. Piatigorsky, Boston SO, Munch – DVORAK: *Concerto*. **(*)

Yo-Yo Ma and Previn give a sensuously beautiful performance. With speeds markedly slower than usual in the outer movements, the meditation is intensified to bring a mood of ecstasy, quite distinct from other Walton, with the central allegro becoming the symphonic kernel of the work, far more than just a scherzo. In the excellent CBS recording, the soloist is less forwardly and more faithfully balanced than is common.

The *Cello concerto* was written for Piatigorsky and he plays it with a gripping combination of full-blooded eloquence and subtlety of feeling, readily capturing the bitter-sweet melancholy of its flowing lyrical lines. The closing pages of the final variations are particularly haunting. Munch provides a totally understanding accompaniment, with the strings of the Boston Symphony finding that special quality of lyrical ecstasy which is such a distinctive part of this concerto. The 1957 recording is a bit close, but the improvement of the CD over the old LP is enormous, and the ambience of Symphony Hall is much more apparent than before. As can be seen, this performance is also available coupled to Previn's fine account of Vaughan Williams's *Sinfonia Antartica* on RCA's bargain-basement Navigator label.

(i) *Viola concerto. Johannesburg festival overture; Symphony No. 2.*

(BB) *** Naxos Dig. 8.553402 [id.]. (i) Tomter; E. N. Philh. O, Paul Daniel.

With Paul Daniel drawing brilliantly pointed, keenly idiomatic playing from the English Northern Philharmonia, this first of the Naxos Walton series could not be more promising, helped by warm, clear and well-balanced recording. Pride of place goes to the thoughtful, deeply felt reading of the *Viola concerto* with the Norwegian viola-player, Lars Anders Tomter. Though Tomter's tight vibrato is at times obtrusive, he brings out the tender poetry of this most elusive of Walton's string concertos, with its mixture of melancholy and wit. More than others, Tomter observes pianissimo markings, and rightly he adopts a flowing speed for the first movement while refusing to be rushed in the Scherzo and finale, which with delectable pointing acquire extra scherzando sparkle. The overture is given the most exuberant performance, rivalling the composer's own, with the orchestra's soloists playing brilliantly. In the *Symphony No. 2* Daniel gives extra transparency to the often heavy orchestration, making the work less weighty than usual but just as warmly expressive. A superb bargain.

(i) *Viola concerto;* (ii) *Symphony No. 1;* (iii) *3 Songs from Façade.*

✿ (M) (***) Dutton Laboratories mono CDAX 8003 [id. full price]. (i) Riddle, LSO, composer; (ii) LSO, Harty; (iii) Dora Stevens, Foss.

This first ever recording of the *Viola concerto*, made for Decca in December 1937 with Walton conducting the LSO and with Frederick Riddle as soloist, puts a totally different complexion on the piece from usual. Riddle's performance has never been surpassed by even the starriest viola-players since for, unlike almost every rival today, he takes the first movement, *Andante comodo*, at a flowing speed that avoids over-romanticizing the yearning melody at the start. Yet Riddle finds a poignant tenderness in the concerto. In the central Scherzo he is more relaxed, with wittily sprung rhythms, while after a fast, spiky account of the finale the epilogue is wistful rather than tragic. Amazingly, this historic recording was never transferred to LP, making the superb transfer from Dutton Laboratories doubly welcome. It is coupled ideally with the very first recording of Walton's *First Symphony*, made in 1935 by the LSO under Sir Hamilton Harty. Though the playing is not always as polished as in modern versions, the emotional thrust under Harty has never been surpassed. Again the sound is beefy and full, amazingly so when you think that Decca's improvised studio was in a warehouse building near Cannon Street station. The songs, with Dora Stevens accompanied by her husband, Hubert Foss, Walton's publisher from OUP, are a charming makeweight.

Violin concerto.

(M) *** Decca 460 014-2 [id.]. Kyung Wha Chung, LSO, André Previn – BEETHOVEN: *Violin concerto.* **

(M) *** EMI CDM7 64202-2. Ida Haendel, Bournemouth SO, Berglund – BRITTEN: *Violin concerto.* ***

In the brooding intensity of the opening evocation, Kyung Wha Chung presents the first melody with a depth of expression, tender and hushed, that has never been matched on record, not even by Heifetz. With Previn as guide and with the composer himself a sympathetic observer at the recording sessions, Chung then builds up a performance which must remain a classic, showing the *Concerto* as one of the greatest of the century in this genre. Outstandingly fine recording, sounding the more vivid in its CD format. This now comes coupled with the Beethoven *Concerto*, an unfortunate choice, as it is one of Chung's relatively unsuccessful major recordings.

A sunny, glowing, Mediterranean-like view of the concerto from Ida Haendel, with brilliant playing from the soloist and eloquent orchestral support from the Bournemouth orchestra under Paavo Berglund. The CD transfer of the fine (1977) recording, made in the Guildhall, Southampton, brings a brilliant orchestral tapestry to provide the necessary contrast and, given the quality of the playing (as well as the interest of the equally successful Britten coupling), this is an eminently desirable reissue.

(i) *Violin concerto;* (ii; iii) *Capriccio burlesco;* (iv; iii) *Façade suite No. 1; Johannesburg festival overture.*

(B) *** Sony SBK 62749; *SBT 62749* [id.]. (i) Francescatti, Phd. O, Ormandy; (ii) Orchestra; (iii) André Kostelanetz; (iv) NYPO.

Zino Francescatti's 1959 recording of the Walton *Violin concerto* with Eugene Ormandy and the Philadelphia Orchestra comes close to matching the power and thrust of both the Heifetz versions that preceded it. In a first-rate transfer to CD in Sony's British Heritage series, it is very well coupled with the Walton recordings made in New York by André Kostelanetz, far more than a light-music specialist. These include the characteristically bustling showpiece that Walton dedicated to him, the *Capriccio burlesco*, given a performance of tremendous brio, the ever-delectable *Façade* pieces as well as the most lovable and exuberant of Walton's three witty overtures, the *Johannesburg festival*, stunningly done. Forward, larger-than-life recording.

Coronation marches: Crown imperial; Orb and Sceptre; Façade suites Nos. 1 & 2; (i; ii) *Gloria;* (ii) *Te Deum.*

(M) *** EMI CDM7 64201-2. (i) Robothom, Rolfe Johnson, Rayner Cook, CBSO Ch.; (ii) Choristers of Worcester Cathedral; CBSO, Frémaux.

The three Walton works inspired by coronations are here splendidly coupled with the grand setting of the *Gloria*. Frémaux directs a highly enjoyable performance but it rather pales before the Coronation *Te Deum*, which may use some of the same formulas but has Walton electrically inspired, exploiting every tonal and atmospheric effect imaginable between double choirs and semi-choruses. The two splendid marches are marvellously done too. The rich, resonant recording is apt for the music, spacious and with excellent perspectives, and it has transferred splendidly to CD, with the brass both sonorous and biting and the choral sound fresh as well as with plenty of weight. The *Façade suites* have been added for the CD and here the remastering is even more telling, adding point to playing which is already affectionately witty. Frémaux's rhythmic control gives a fresh, new look to familiar music: his jaunty jazz inflexions in *Old Sir Faulk* are deliciously whimsical.

Façade (original version; complete).
(B) *** Sony SBK 62400; *SBT 62400* [id.]. Vera Zorina, Phd. O, Ormandy – HOLST: *Planets*. **
(BB) ** Belart 450 136-2 [(M) id. import]. Dame Peggy Ashcroft, Paul Scofield, L. Sinf., composer.

Façade (absolutely complete).
(BB) *** Discover Dig. DICD 920125 [id.]. Hunter, Melologos Ens., Van den Broeck.

Enterprisingly the Discover International label at bargain price offers the most complete version of Walton's Entertainment yet, using a group of Belgian instrumentalists, the Melologos Ensemble, under Silveer van den Broeck. When the reciter, Pamela Hunter, has made a speciality of reciting these Edith Sitwell poems, not exactly imitating Dame Edith herself but observing the strictly stylized, rhythmically crisp manner originally laid down, it makes a welcome and delightful disc. Five items appear here for the first time, adding to those resurrected by Walton himself in *Façade 2*. What one registers here, even more than with *Façade 2* alone, is that the early settings are more experimental and less sharply parodistic than the later, well-known ones, though in the accompaniment to one of them, *Aubade* ('Jane, Jane, tall as a crane'), there is a clear tongue-in-cheek reference to Stravinsky's *Rite of spring*. The recording is cleanly focused, balanced with the voice in front of the players yet obviously in the same acoustic, not superimposed; and the clarity and point of the solo playing, notably from the flute and clarinet, are splendid. Pamela Hunter is excellent too, happily characterizing with a minimum of 'funny voices'. At the price, a disc to recommend to all.

Ormandy's version of 16 movements from Walton's entertainment comes as a refreshingly unexpected coupling for Bernstein's colourful reading of *The Planets* which is hardly a first choice for this much-recorded work. But at bargain price the Walton recording is thoroughly worthwhile in its own right. It is a pity that all 21 movements were not recorded, for Vera Zorina, who recorded *Façade* as a bravado solo act in 1961, is an infectious, pointedly rhythmic reciter, her words sharply and often wittily projected, while under Ormandy the chamber group from the Philadelphia Orchestra plays with a brilliance, clarity and precision rarely matched. Their narrator is no less seductive in the cooler evocations (*En famille*; *Through gilded trellises*; *By the lake*) than in the captivating *Country dance*, *Polka* and *Waltz*. The *Jodelling song* is delightfully crisp, and the *Popular song* has a light-hearted insouciance. The integration of the vocal line and accompaniment in these later numbers is remarkable, while the closing *Sir Beelzebub* has striking panache from all concerned. Admirably vivid recording. It is a pity that the coupling is not more imaginative, but this is a real collector's item.

Walton's own stereo version from the early 1970s makes a fascinating supplement. Peggy Ashcroft is aptly characterful. She often lags behind the beat, but this adds to the sense of magnetic idiosyncrasy, and she is recorded so close that her breath is constantly in one's ear. Paul Scofield is the slowest and least rhythmic of reciters, but the composer keeps the music going as a subtle, quiet commentary in the background, and the effect is unique. The stereo is both atmospheric and immediate, and you can hear every word. Not a first choice, but an interesting bargain supplement to the essential Discover version.

(i) *Façade;* (ii) *Belshazzar's Feast*.
(M) ** Sony mono/stereo SMK 46685 [id.]. (i) Edith Sitwell, David Horner, CO, Frederick Prausnitz; (ii) Walter Cassel, Rutgers University Ch., Phd. O, Ormandy.

Dame Edith Sitwell made this flawed New York recording of the *Façade* entertainment in January 1949, and though as ever her ripely characterful voice is magnetic, it was not agile enough to cope with the rhythmic complexities or even to get the words right. In one number, *Tango-Pasodoble*, she is helped out by David Horner. A fascinating supplement to the classic recording with Peter Pears as well as Dame Edith, but no replacement. Ormandy directs a strong and purposeful, if not always idiomatic account of *Belshazzar's Feast*, recorded in upfront stereo sound, making a generous coupling.

Film scores

As You Like It: suite. The Battle of Britain: suite. Henry V: suite. History of the English speaking peoples: March. Troilus and Cressida (opera): *Interlude*.
(M) *** EMI Dig. CDM5 65585-2. LPO Ch. & O, Carl Davis.

The Battle of Britain suite presents the music that (for trumpery reasons) was rejected for the original film, including a Wagnerian send-up and a splendid final march. Another vintage Walton march here was written for a television series based on Churchill's history, but again was never used. It is a pity that the *Henry V suite* does not include the Agincourt charge, but it is good to have the choral contributions to the opening and closing sequences. Best of all, perhaps, is the long-buried music for the 1926 Paul Czinner film of *As You Like It*. If only he had allowed himself to throw off music like this rather more often, we would all have gained by it. Warm, opulent recording.

Scenes from Shakespeare (compiled Christopher Palmer): *As You Like It; Hamlet; Henry V; Richard III*.
(M) **(*) Chandos Dig. CHAN 7041 [id.]. Sir John Gielgud, Christopher Plummer, ASMF, Marriner.

This makes an apt and attractive compilation, putting together well-chosen selections from the recordings of Walton's Shakespeare film-music, first issued in the complete Chandos edition, not just the three masterly films directed by Laurence Olivier, but also the pre-war *As You Like It*. Roughly two-thirds of the *Henry V* music is included here, and about half of each of the other three. However, many collectors will opt to have more music and will prefer to hear the Shakespearean text in the theatre or cinema.

Henry V: A Shakespeare scenario (after music from the 1944 film; arr. Christopher Palmer).
(BB) ** Naxos Dig. 8.553343 [id.]. Michael Sheen and Anton Lesser (nar.), Dublin RTE Concert O, Andrew Penny.

Using virtually all the music which Walton wrote for Laurence Olivier's Shakespeare film, Christopher Palmer has here devised a compelling sequence of over 50 minutes, including the evocative opening and closing sequences with their exhilarating choruses. Andrew Penny draws warmly committed, refined playing from the Irish orchestra, with some excellent solo work. The recorded sound is warmly atmospheric; but what undermines the impact of the performance is the balance, with the backward positioning of the orchestra exaggerated in relation to the spoken voices, which are placed very close. The manner of Michael Sheen (as the King) and Anton Lesser (in the other roles, including narrator), both of whom have worked very successfully with the Royal Shakespeare Company, is rather stagey and high-flown for a recording. While a bargain version is very welcome, the Chandos version at full price, conducted by Sir Neville Marriner and with Christopher Plummer as narrator, has a far keener impact and is well worth the extra cost (CHAN 8892).

Henry V: Passacaglia; The Death of Falstaff; Touch her soft lips and part.
(M) *** DG 439 529-2. ECO, Barenboim – DELIUS: *Aquarelles* etc.; VAUGHAN WILLIAMS: *Oboe concerto* etc. ***

These two fine Walton string pieces make an admirable complement to a sensuously beautiful collection of English music, with Barenboim at his most affectionately inspirational and the ECO very responsive, and with the 1975 recording retaining its warmth and bloom.

Symphonies Nos. 1–2.
(B) *** EMI Dig. CD-EMX 2206 [(M) id. import]. (i) LPO; (ii) LSO; Sir Charles Mackerras.

Where too often No. 2 has been dismissed as Walton imitating himself, saying nothing new, Mackerras firmly establishes the work's distinction, above all in its control of argument and its brilliant use of a very large orchestra. The thematic material may not be as striking as in the high-voltage *First Symphony*, with its eruption of youthful inspiration, but there is consistent lyrical warmth. Mackerras's reading of No. 1, using the LPO, adopts broader speeds than usual. It may not be as bitingly dramatic as the very finest versions, but the richness and strength of the symphony, one of the key British works of its period, come over powerfully. Warm, full recording in both symphonies. An outstanding bargain.

Symphony No. 1; Partita for orchestra.
(BB) *** Naxos Dig. 8.553180 [id.]. E. N. PO, Paul Daniel.

Symphony No. 1; Portsmouth Point overture.
(M) **(*) Virgin/EMI Dig. CUV5 61146-2. LPO, Slatkin.

Symphony No.1; Overture Scapino; Siesta.
(B) ** Arte Nova/BMG Dig. 74321 39124-2 [id.]. Gran Canaria PO, Adrian Leaper.

If anything even more clearly than on his first Naxos disc of Walton, Paul Daniel demonstrates his natural affinity with this composer's music. In the *First Symphony* he knows unerringly how to build up tension to breaking point before resolving it and then building again. He is also freer than many in his use of rubato, as well as in the degree of elbow-room he allows for jazzy syncopations, always idiomatic. The *Scherzo* is sparkily witty, not just full of malice. In the slow movement, after the poised opening, Daniel tends to press ahead slightly for the sections which follow, agonizingly intense. The finale with its brassy, more extrovert manner has plenty of panache, and though textures could be more transparent – largely a question of the reverberant Leeds Town Hall acoustic – the weight and bite of the sound are excellent. This is a version that vies with even the finest at whatever price, and it outshines most. Daniel's reading of the *Partita* brings out above all the work's joyfulness, with the outer movements relaxed in their brilliance and the central slow movement warmly expressive.

The brilliance, bite and clarity of sound in Slatkin's version of the *First Symphony* reinforce the tautness of the performance, nagging the mind with repetitive rhythms and tension piled on tension. Slatkin does not have quite the rhythmic mastery in giving a jazzy lift to syncopations or in moulding Waltonian melody that you find in both Previn's versions, and the Scherzo is almost breathlessly fast. But the finale is magnificent, bringing thrust and power, and culminating superbly in the uninhibited triple timpani passage near the end. Slatkin takes an equally electric view of the *Overture*, again played brilliantly by the LPO.

Very well played and recorded, with crisp ensemble and clean separation, Leaper's version of the *First Symphony* is warmly sympathetic and surprisingly idiomatic for a non-British orchestra. The gentler moments are particularly impressive, but Leaper hardly compares with Daniel on his rival Naxos version, also at super-bargain price, when it comes to building tension. For all its many fine qualities, it is a performance at a far lower voltage.

Symphony No. 2; Partita for orchestra; Variations on a theme by Hindemith.
❁ (B) *** Sony SBK 62753; *SBT 62753* [id.]. Cleveland O, Szell.

In a letter to the conductor, Walton expressed himself greatly pleased with Szell's performance of the *Second Symphony*: 'It is a quite fantastic and stupendous performance from every point of view. Firstly it is absolutely right musically speaking, and the virtuosity is quite staggering, especially the Fugato; but everything is phrased and balanced in an unbelievable way.' Listening to the splendidly remastered CD of this 1961 recording, one cannot but join the composer in responding to the wonderfully luminous detail in the orchestra. Szell's performance of the *Hindemith variations* is no less praiseworthy. Finally comes the *Partita*, which was commissioned by the Cleveland Orchestra and given its première a year before the recording was made. The recordings are bright, in the CBS manner, but the ambience of Severance Hall brings a backing warmth and depth, and these are technically among the finest of Szell's recordings in this venue.

The Wise virgins (ballet suite arr. from Bach).
(M) *** EMI CDM5 65911-2 [id.]. Concert Arts O, Robert Irving – GLAZUNOV: *The Seasons;* SCARLATTI/TOMMASINI: *Good humoured ladies.* ***

Walton's orchestral arrangements of Bach created a score for the Sadler's Wells ballet in 1940. All the music except the second piece, a chorale-prelude, is extracted from cantatas, and the delightful '*Sheep may safely graze*' (richly presented here) is a highlight, alongside the tranquil '*See what His love can do*' from Cantata No. 85. However, some of the flamboyant brass writing and Walton's unashamedly anachronistic treatment brought the score into critical disfavour in the 1960s; and only recently has public opinion (after acknowledging the very real pleasures of Stokowski's Bach transcriptions) taken Walton's ballet excursion back into favour. It could not be better presented than it is here, and the resonant recording emphasizes the ebullience of the uninhibited moments, especially the robust finale.

CHAMBER MUSIC

Violin sonata.
(BB) *** ASV Quicksilva CDQS 6191 [(M) id.]. McAslan, Blakely – ELGAR: *Violin sonata.* ***
(M) (**) EMI mono CDM5 66122-2. Yehudi Menuhin, Louis Kentner – ELGAR; WALTON: *Sonatas.* **(*)

Lorraine McAslan gives a warmly committed performance of Walton's often wayward *Sonata*, coping well with the sharp and difficult changes of mood in both of the two long movements. The romantic melancholy of the piece suits her well and, though the recording does not make her tone as rounded as it should be, she produces some exquisite pianissimo playing, making this a very impressive début recording. John Blakely is a most sympathetic partner, particularly impressive in crisply articulated scherzando passages. At its modest cost this is very highly recommendable.

The Menuhins commissioned this sonata to be premièred by the present performers, and it was dedicated jointly to their wives. It was completed in 1940 but the composer withdrew it, and the present two-movement version was recorded in 1950. First recordings are always special, and this one is no exception; but it is a pity that the very forward recording tends to treble emphasis, which is unflattering to Menuhin's upper register in its CD transfer.

CHORAL MUSIC

Anon in love (song-cycle).
(M) *** RCA 09026 61601-2. Peter Pears, Julian Bream (guitar) – BRITTEN: *Songs from the Chinese* etc.; SEIBER: *Four French folk songs.* ***

Walton wrote his cycle, *Anon in love*, for Pears and Bream, and the melisma of the opening song, *Fain would I change that note*, soars aloft in a way that Pears made his own. The other songs progress from nostalgia and romantic feeling to jolly revelry (*I gave her cakes and ale*) and consummation (*To couple is a custom*), with the closing number in the form of a brilliantly earthy scherzando. With attractive couplings this (Volume 18) is one of the most attractive and valuable reissues in the Julian Bream Edition, providing an entire programme played and sung by the artists who inspired the music.

Belshazzar's Feast.
(B) *** Sony SBK 63039 [id.]. Walter Cassel, Rutgers University Ch., Phd. O, Ormandy – MAHLER: *Kindertotenlieder; 3 Rückert Lieder.* ***

(i) *Belshazzar's Feast. Improvisations on an impromptu of Benjamin Britten; Overtures: Portsmouth Point; Scapino.*
(M) *** EMI CDM7 64723-2. LSO, Previn, (i) with John Shirley-Quirk, L. Symphony Ch.

(i) *Belshazzar's Feast. In honour of the City of London.*
(B) *** EMI Dig. CD-EMX 2225 [(M) id.]. (i) David Wilson-Johnson; L. Symphony Ch., LSO, Hickox.

Richard Hickox not only conducts one of the most sharply dramatic accounts of *Belshazzar's Feast* currently available, even crisper and keener (if less jazzy) than Previn's superb (1971) EMI version; but he couples it with the one major work of Walton left unrecorded: his cantata, *In honour of the City of London*. With forces almost as lavish as those in the oratorio, its vitality and atmospheric colour come over on this record to a degree generally impossible in live performance. As for *Belshazzar* under Hickox, its voltage has never seemed higher on record, thanks not just to the LSO and Chorus – in far sharper form than for Previn, 17 years earlier – but also to the full and brilliant digital recording. The dramatic soloist is David Wilson-Johnson, colouring his voice with chilling menace in the writing-on-the-wall sequence. Now reissued on EMI's mid-priced Eminence label, this makes a very strong recommendation.

Previn's EMI version of *Belshazzar's Feast* remains among the most spectacular yet recorded. The digital remastering has not lost the body and atmosphere of the sound but has increased its impact. This fine performance was recorded with Walton present on his seventieth birthday and, though Previn's tempi are occasionally slower than those set by Walton himself in his two recordings, the authenticity is clear, with consistently sharp attack and with dynamic markings meticulously observed down to the tiniest hairpin markings. Chorus and orchestra are challenged to their finest standards, and John Shirley-Quirk proves a searching and imaginative soloist. The *Improvisations*, given a first recording, make a generous fill-up alongside the two overtures in which Previn, the shrewdest and most perceptive of Waltonians, finds more light and shade than usual. Again the remastered sound is excellent.

The 1961 Ormandy account has great fervour and atmosphere. The choral singing may not be absolutely refined but it has enormous enthusiasm, the words are clear and the effect is highly invigorating, often thrilling. Walter Cassel makes an attractively robust contribution (he sounds a bit like Owen Brannigan) and he also projects his words well. The balance has the orchestra well forward – although not at the expense of the choral bite – and the orchestral and percussive detail is fully and tinglingly conveyed. The spaciousness of the recording is also impressive; altogether, if not an obvious first choice, this is very enjoyable indeed. The coupling is hardly apt, but it offers some memorable singing from Jennie Tourel on her finest form.

OPERA

Troilus and Cressida (complete).
(M) **(*) EMI CMS5 65550-2 (2). Cassilly, J. Baker, Bainbridge, English, Luxon, Van Allan, Rivers, Lloyd, ROHCG Ch. and O, Lawrence Foster.

Few operas since Puccini have such a rich store of memorable tunes as *Troilus and Cressida*. This red-bloodedly romantic opera on a big classical subject deserves to enter the regular repertory. The great glory of EMI's live recording, made at Covent Garden during the 1976 revival, is the singing of Dame Janet Baker in the role of Cressida. Though the dry acoustic takes some of the bloom away from the voice, the glorious variety of her tonal colourings still gives a superb idea of Dame Janet's masterly singing in opera at the very peak of her career: the weight, beauty and heartfelt expressiveness are wonderfully telling, giving a distinctive slant to the whole opera. It is good to have this historic document on CD, even if in face of the magnificent Chandos recording, based on the Opera North production, it inevitably remains second best, not helped by intrusive audience noises. The one compensation of the very dry Covent Garden sound is that the dramatic bite is often enhanced. Otherwise the beauty of Walton's writing, for voices and orchestra alike, is minimized and the voices are never flattered. Richard Cassilly as Troilus uses his powerful Heldentenor tone intelligently, but the lower register is often gritty. The bite and purposefulness of Lawrence Foster's conducting come over well.

Warlock, Peter (1894–1930)

'Centenary collection': (i) *Capriol suite;* (ii) *Serenade to Frederick Delius on his 60th birthday*. Songs: (iii) *Adam lay ybounden;* (iv) *Autumn twilight;* (v) *Balulalow;* (vi) *Bethlehem Down;* (vii) *Captain Stratton's fancy;* (viii) *The Curlew* (song-cycle); (ix) *I saw a fair maiden;* (x) *The Lady's birthday* (arrangement); (v) *Pretty ring time;* (x) *The shrouding of the Duchess of Malfi;* (xi) *Where riches is everlasting;* (xii) *Yarmouth Fair*.

(M) *** EMI CDM5 65101-2 [id.]. (i) E. Sinf., Neville Dilkes; (ii) Bournemouth Sinf., Norman Del Mar; (iii) Robert Hammersley, Gavin Williams; (iv) Frederick Harvey, Gerald Moore; (v) Janet Baker, Philip Ledger; (vi) Guildford Cathedral Ch., Barry Rose; (vii) Robert Lloyd, Nina Walker; (viii) Ian Partridge, Music Group of London; (ix) Westminster Abbey Ch., Douglas Guest; (x) Baccholian Singers, Jennifer Partridge; (xi) King's College, Cambridge, Ch., Willcocks; (xii) Owen Brannigan, Ernest Lush.

A splendid anthology of Warlock – less well-known as the music critic, Peter Heseltine. Opening with one of our favourite versions of the *Capriol suite* from the English Sinfonia under Neville Dilkes, brightly coloured and full of vigour, followed by Warlock's touchingly tender tribute to Delius, the selection ranges over a well-chosen selection of favourite songs, solo and choral. The other key item is *The Curlew*, Warlock's most striking and ambitious work, a continuous setting of a sequence of poems by Yeats which reflect the darker side of his complex personality. Ian Partridge, with the subtlest shading of tone-colour and the most sensitive response to word-meanings, gives an intensely poetic performance, beautifully recorded. Among other performances those of Dame Janet Baker stand out, but many of the songs here are persuasively beautiful. At the very close of the recital Owen Brannigan restores our high spirits with his characteristically ebullient delivery of *Yarmouth Fair*. The transfers are consistently well managed.

(i) *Capriol suite; 6 English tunes; 6 Italian dance tunes; Serenade for strings;* (ii) *The Curlew* (song-cycle).

(BB) *** Arte Nova Dig. 74321 37868-2 [id.]. (i) L. Festival O, Ross Pople; (ii) Martyn Hill, Edward Beckett, Alison Alty, Robert Gibbs, Amanda Smith, Peter Stevens, Ferenc Szucs.

Warlock's two most important works, not just the colourful *Capriol suite* but also the extended and searchingly intense setting of Yeats's *The Curlew*, are here very well coupled with three others, two of them – not three as the booklet suggests – in première recordings. The *Six English tunes* and the *Six Italian dance tunes* are both miniature suites on the lines of *Capriol*, setting dances from the Elizabethan period in warmly sympathetic arrangements. Each is even more compact than *Capriol*, with movements barely a minute long unpretentiously making colourful points and moving on. The *Serenade* – which has been recorded many times already – is quite different, lusciously echoing Delius in its string writing. Ross Pople directs clean-cut, consciously small-scale readings that rightly bring out the emotion of the writing. The tenor, Martyn Hill, placed well forward in *The Curlew*, similarly brings out the emotional thrust of the words with commendably clear diction. Warm recording to match.

(i) *Capriol suite;* (ii) *The Curlew* (song-cycle); *5 Nursery jingles. The Birds; Chopcherry; Fairest May; Mourn no moe; My gostly fader; Sleep; The water lilly.*

(BB) **(*) ASV CDQS 6143 [(M) id.]. (i) RPO, Barlow; (ii) James Griffett, Haffner Qt; Mary Murdoch, Mary Ryan.

Though Griffett's performance of *The Curlew* is not so beautiful or so imaginative as Ian Partridge's, it is good to have a bargain record of songs by a composer with a strikingly distinctive feeling for English verse. Each one of these songs is a miniature of fine sensitivity, and James Griffett sings them with keen insight, pointing the words admirably. The instrumental playing is most sensitive, and the recording, made in Christ Church, Chelsea, is warmly atmospheric yet clear. The performance of the *Capriol suite* is also a very good one, and the digital recording is first rate. This CD is well worth its modest cost.

Weber, Carl Maria von (1786–1826)

(i) *Bassoon concerto in F, Op. 75;* (ii–iii) *Clarinet concerto No. 1 in F min., Op. 73;* (ii; iv) *Clarinet quintet in B flat, Op. 34.*

(M) ** DG 453 990-2 [id.]. (i) Milan Turkovic, Bamberg SO, Schneidt; (ii) Karl Leister; (iii) BPO, Kubelik; (iv) Vienna Chamber Music Ens. (members).

Karl Leister is the principal soloist of the BPO and the CD begins with the *Clarinet concerto*. Kubelik opens the work boldly and the orchestra is splendidly recorded. The balance with the soloist is just about right and Karl Leister plays eloquently, if without the extra flair and sense of bravura that Kubelik demonstrates. Yet the finale has an engagingly light, rhythmic touch. The same urbane, slightly reticent approach works better in the *Quintet*, which is beautifully if slightly suavely played, and again it is in the giocoso *Rondo* that the soloist is heard obviously relishing Weber's jaunty rhythms. Milan Turkovic then comes on stage to show how it should be done, and he plays with much spirit throughout, relishing equally the bassoon's dolorous lyricism in the *Adagio* and not overdoing the hints of buffoonery. The delicately coloured timbre of his French bassoon adds to the listener's pleasure, and again the recording balance is realistic.

Clarinet concertos Nos. 1 in F min., Op. 73; 2 in E flat, Op. 74; Clarinet concertino in E flat, Op. 26.
(M) *** Classic fM Dig. 75605 57019-2. Colin Lawson, Hanover Band, Goodman – SPOHR: *Clarinet concerto No. 1.* ***
(BB) *** Naxos Dig. 8.550378 [id.]. Ernst Ottensamer, Slovak State PO (Košice), Johannes Wildner.

Stylish and imaginative period performances from Colin Lawson with the Hanover Band, vividly recorded, of Weber's three concertante works for clarinet make an attractive grouping, particularly when generously supplemented by the Spohr *First Concerto*. With his attractively reedy tone Lawson is a most persuasive soloist, moulding Weber's melodies seductively and pointing rhythms jauntily, with brilliant feats of tonguing, in the light-hearted finales of each work.

Ernst Ottensamer is a highly sensitive clarinettist, who has played with the major Viennese orchestras and is a member of the Vienna Wind Ensemble. His account of the two *Clarinet concertos* can hold its own against nearly all the competition in the current catalogue in any price category. The Košice orchestra also responds well to Johannes Wildner's direction, and the recorded sound is very natural and well balanced. A real bargain.

Piano concertos Nos. 1 in C, Op. 11; 2 in E flat, Op. 32; Konzertstück, Op. 79.
(BB) **(*) Discover Dig. DICD 920222 [id.]. Dana Protopopescu, Belgian R. & TV O, Rahbari.

(i) *Piano concerto Nos. 1 in C, Op. 11;* (ii) *2 in E flat, Op. 32;* (i) *Konzertstück in F min., Op. 79; Polacca brillante (L'Hilarité), Op. 72.*
(BB) *** Naxos Dig. 8.550959 [id.]. Benjamin Frith, Dublin R. & TV Sinf., Prionnsias O'Duinn.

The young Hungarian pianist, Dana Protopopescu, plays all three works with striking freshness and an almost Chopinesque feeling in the lyrical music. Her sparkling passage-work and the chimerical changes of tempo and character of the *Konzertstück* are deftly managed. She is persuasively partnered by Alexander Rahbari, who enters fully into the spirit of her romantic style, convincing the listener that these works gain much from the added colour of a modern piano. Excellent recording.

However, Benjamin Frith's accounts are even finer and he receives splendid support from O'Duinn and the excellent Dublin Sinfonietta. In consequence, these performances all have more depth (the *Konzertstück* is particularly fine). Both slow movements in the concertos bring rapt concentration; Frith's playing has plenty of dash, yet its impetuosity is never inclined to run away with itself (as from time to time it almost does with Dana Protopopescu). The Naxos CD is not only better recorded, it also includes the appropriately named *L'hilarité Polacca brillante*, which Frith plays with attractive panache.

Symphonies Nos. 1 in C; 2 in C, J.50/51. Die Drei Pintos: Entr'acte. Silvana: Dance of the young nobles; Torch dance. Turandot: Overture; Act II: *March;* Act V: *Funeral march.*
❀ (BB) *** Naxos Dig. 8.550928 [id.]. Queensland PO, John Georgiadis.

Weber wrote his two symphonies in the same year (1807) and, though both are in C major, each has its own individuality. The witty orchestration and operatic character of the writing are splendidly caught in these sparkling Queensland performances, while in the slow movements the orchestral soloists (notably the languishing viola in the *Adagio* of No. 2) relish their solos, for all the world like vocal cantilenas. Weber's scoring is often adventurous and he finds plentiful opportunities for the horns to shine, especially in the playful main theme of the *Presto* finale of No. 1. Weber's writing is frequently unpredictable, not least in the surprising closing bars of No. 2; and Georgiadis and his players present both works with striking freshness and spontaneity. The Naxos recording is in the demonstration class, and the disc is made the more attractive for the inclusion of orchestral excerpts from two little-known operas and incidental music from *Turandot*. The *Entr'acte* from the incomplete *Die Drei Pintos* was put together by Mahler from Weber's sketches.

CHAMBER AND INSTRUMENTAL MUSIC

Clarinet quintet in B flat, Op. 34.
(M) *** O-L 444 167-2. Alan Hacker, The Music Party – HUMMEL: *Clarinet quartet.* ***
(M) **(*) EMI CDM5 65995-2. Gervase de Peyer, Melos Ens. – BERWALD: *Septet* ***; SPOHR: *Double quartet.* **

(i) *Clarinet quintet; Introduction, theme and variations for clarinet and string quartet, Op. posth.;* (ii) *Grand duo concertante in E flat, Op. 48; 7 Variations on a theme from Silvana in B flat, Op. 33* (both for clarinet and piano).
(BB) *** Naxos Dig. 8.553122 [id.]. Kálmán Berkes, with (i) Auer Qt; (ii) Jenö Jandó.

If you want to hear how Weber's *Clarinet quintet* must have sounded during his lifetime, Alan Hacker and the Music Party will probably be your first choice. The Gerock clarinet Hacker uses is from 1804, eleven years before the first complete performance of the *Quintet*. Hacker plays with his customary artistry and sensitivity, and with lots of bite and sparkle in the bravura passages. The recording is clear and vivid. Hacker has a price advantage and an ideal coupling.

Naxos conveniently gather together expert and winning performances of Weber's major chamber works featuring the clarinet. If the *Introduction, theme and variations* is now considered spurious, it is still an agreeably amiable piece. The *Quintet* is particularly successful. Berkes leads a lusciously appealing account af the *Adagio* and then sets off, chortling with great zest, in the *Capriccio presto* Minuet; the finale is no less infectious in its sparkling virtuosity. With Jandó an admirable partner, the *Grand duo concertante* is hardly less successful, and the two sets of variations are presented with both elegance and panache. The recording, made in the Scottish Church, Budapest, is realistic if too resonant, but the charisma and spontaneity of this Hungarian music-making carry the day in spite of this.

The Melos performance, with its extrovert dotted rhythms in the first movement and almost bucolic Scherzo, is very assured, and Gervase de Peyer's bravura playing in the finale is memorable. However, there is a slight lack of warmth here, caused partly by the recording acoustic, which is vivid but slightly dry.

PIANO MUSIC

Piano sonata No. 1 in C, Op. 24 (J.138); Invitation to the dance, Op. 65 (J.260); 6 Variations on an original theme, Op. 40 (J.7); 9 Variations on a Russian theme: 'Schöne Minka', Op. 40 (J.179).
(BB) ** Naxos Dig. 8.550988 [id.]. Alexander Paley.

Piano sonata No. 2 in A flat, Op. 39 (J.199); Grande Polonaise, Op. 21 (J.59); 6 Variations on Naga's aria: 'Woher mag dies wohl kommen?' from Vogler's opera, Samori, Op. 6 (J.43); 7 Variations on a gypsy song, Op. 55 (J.219).
(BB) ** Naxos Dig. 8.550989 [id.]. Alexander Paley.

Piano sonata No. 3 in D min., Op. 49 (J.206); Momento capriccioso, Op. 12 (J.56); 7 Variations on an original theme, Op. 9 (J.55); 7 Variations on Binchi's air: 'Vien quà, Dorina bella', Op. 7 (J.53); 8 Variations on the Air de ballet from Castore e Polluce by Abbé Vogler, Op. 5 (J.40).
(BB) ** Naxos Dig. 550990 [id.]. Alexander Paley.

Piano sonata No. 4 in E min., Op. 70 (J.287); Les Adieux, Op. 81 posth.; Polacca brillante (L'hilarité), Op. 72 (J.268); Rondo brillante (La gaîté), Op. 62 (J.252); 7 Variations on a theme from Méhul's opera, Joseph, Op. 28 (J.141).
(BB) **(*) Naxos Dig. 8.553006 [id.]. Alexander Paley.

Alexander Paley's survey of Weber's piano output is certainly comprehensive. His playing has finesse and polish and is often thoughtful, but it tends to reveal relatively little below the surface of the music. The result is generally pleasing, although at times Paley's rubato in Weber's secondary lyrical ideas is a little fussy and in the sets of variations, after announcing each theme characterfully, the playing seems to slip back into routine as if Paley were not really involved with Weber's invention. What does fire him is the bravura writing, and the Mendelssohnian *Momento capriccioso* on the third disc is vivaciously done. For some reason, the *Fourth E minor Sonata* also excites a strong response and this is easily the most compelling performance of the four. Then the closing *Rondo* and *Polacca* are thrown off infectiously. So disc four is the place to start if you are tempted by these inexpensive discs, which are all well recorded.

OPERA

Overtures: *Abu Hassan; Beherrscher der Geister (Ruler of the spirits); Euryanthe; Der Freischütz; Jubel; Oberon; Preciosa.*
(M) ** CDM7 69572-2 [id.]. Philh. O, Sawallisch.

Needless to say, the Philharmonia Orchestra play brilliantly and sympathetically for Sawallisch, and his collection also includes novelties in *Jubel* and *Preciosa*. However, the effect of the remastered recording is somewhat brash.

Abu Hassan (opera; complete).
(M) *** CPO/EMI CPO 999 551-2 [id.]. Forster, Gedda, Edda Moser, Moll, Bav. State Op. Ch. & O, Sawallisch.
(M) *** RCA 74321 40577-2. Schreier, Hallstein, Adam, Dresden State Op. Ch., Dresden State O, Heinz Rogner.

Written in 1810 at the height of the Napoleonic Wars, this frothy little farce completely belies that background, reflecting the then-current fashion for 'Turkish' themes and providing an unexpected slant on Weber's genius in the realm of opera. The overture is fizzingly brilliant, leading to a sequence of ten numbers, only three of them arias, including two for Abu Hassan's wife, Fatime. The plot involves the machinations of Abu Hassan to get himself out of debt, with the Caliph (one of three speaking roles) finally awarding him a thousand gold pieces. Sawallisch conducts a brilliant performance, with Nicolai Gedda in the title-role pointing his music lightly, with Edda Moser vibrantly expressive as his wife, and with Kurt Moll superb as the grasping money-lender, Omar. First-rate sound, engineered in 1975 by an EMI–Electrola team.

The alternative Eurodisc version, reissued on BMG/RCA, dates from three years earlier and has a similarly light-hearted presentation. It is not as starrily cast as its CPO/EMI competitor, but the singing of soloists and chorus is consistently pleasing. As with the reissued EMI set, the narrative and dialogue are often cued separately and can be omitted at will. The RCA libretto with translation omits this dialogue, assuming that the non-German listener will dispense with it. The 1971 recording is transferred smoothly and pleasingly; it lacks something in sparkle, but that is no real deterrent when the performance is well characterized, to bring out the almost Mozartian wit.

Die drei Pintos (complete; adapted Mahler).
(M) *** RCA 74321 32246-2 (2) [id.]. Popp, Hollweg, Prey, Scovotti, Moll, Munich PO, Bertini.

A valuable addition to the catalogue, even though the assurance on the box, 'libretto enclosed', is misleading for there is only the German text. *Die drei Pintos* was left unfinished by Weber; he started work on it in 1820 but managed to sketch only seven numbers. Mahler completed it in the 1880s, adding 15 more, 11 of which were rearrangements of other Weber. The performance here is recorded complete with the spoken dialogue separately cued so that one can bypass it if necessary. The soloists are excellent and the whole production is lively and dramatic, while the orchestral support under Gary Bertini is first rate. So is the chorus, and you will need to sample only the engaging opening *Auf Wiedersehn* ensemble, with Werner Hollweg a fresh-voiced Gaston, to be won over immediately. The sound is excellent, warmly atmospheric and with cleaner detail than on the original LPs.

Der Freischütz (complete).
(M) *** EMI CMS7 69342-2 (2). Grümmer, Otto, Schock, Prey, Wiemann, Kohn, Frick, German Op. Ch., Berlin, BPO, Keilberth.
(M) **(*) EMI CMS5 65757-2 (2) [CDMB 65757]. Nilsson, Köth, Gedda, Berry, Ch. & O of Bav. State Op., Heger.
(M) ** Decca 443 672-2id.]. Behrens, Donath, Meven, Kollo, Moll, Brendel, Grumbach, Bav. R. Ch. & SO, Kubelik.

Keilberth's is a warm, exciting account of Weber's masterpiece which makes all the dated conventions of the work seem fresh and new. In particular the Wolf's glen scene on CD acquires something of the genuine terror that must have struck the earliest audiences and which is far more impressive than any mere scene-setting with wood and cardboard in the opera house. The casting of the magic bullets with each one numbered in turn, at first in eerie quiet and then in crescendo amid the howling of demons, is superbly conveyed. The bite of the orchestra and the proper balance of the voices in relation to it, with the effect of space and distance, helps also to create the illusion. Elisabeth Grümmer sings more sweetly and sensitively than one ever remembers before, with Agathe's prayer exquisitely done. Lisa Otto is really in character, with genuine coquettishness. Schock is not an ideal tenor, but he sings ably enough. The

Kaspar of Karl Kohn is generally well focused, and the playing of the Berlin Philharmonic has plenty of polish. The overall effect is immensely atmospheric and enjoyable.

Heger's EMI set, recorded in Munich in 1969, cannot match Keilberth's earlier EMI version of 1958 in atmospheric intensity, with the Wolf's Glen scene markedly less chilling in its dramatic impact. Yet otherwise, with warm, open sound, there is a nice feeling for a stage performance, with an excellent team of soloists from the Bavarian State Opera. Heger is an understanding interpreter, springing rhythms infectiously, drawing fine playing from the orchestra and supporting his cast well. Nicolai Gedda as Max is stylish, even if he tends to bluster, while Birgit Nilsson masterfully scales her massive Wagnerian voice down, to produce pure, sweet tone and smooth legato in Agathe's two sublime arias. Erika Koth is a light, bright, agile Annchen, and the chorus sing splendidly. An enjoyable set, if not the finest version at mid-price. Helpfully, the dialogue is put on separate tracks.

Kubelik takes a direct view of Weber's high romanticism. The result has freshness but lacks something in dramatic bite and atmosphere. There is far less tension than in the finest earlier versions, not least in the Wolf's Glen scene, which in spite of full-ranging, brilliant recording seems rather tame. The singing is generally good – René Kollo as Max giving one of his best performances on record – but Hildegard Behrens, superbly dramatic in later German operas, here as Agathe seems clumsy in music that often requires a pure lyrical line. The sound has been successfully remastered; but this cannot compare with Keilberth's early EMI set.

Der Freischütz: highlights.

(B) *** DG Classikon 439 440-2 [(M) id. import] (from complete recording, with Janowitz, Mathis, Schreier, Adam, Vogel, Crass, Leipzig R. Ch., Dresden State O, Carlos Kleiber).

Anyone looking for a set of highlights from *Der Freischütz* cannot better this bargain Classikon disc, taken from a compelling performance which is consistently well sung and dramatically conducted by Carlos Kleiber. The 73-minute selection includes the full Wolf's Glen scene at the end of Act II, and the 1973 recording still sounds very well indeed.

Oberon (complete).

(M) *** DG 419 038-2 (2) [id.]. Grobe, Nilsson, Domingo, Prey, Hamari, Schiml, Bav. R. Ch. & SO, Kubelik.

Weber's delicately conceived score is a sequence of illogical arias, scenas and ensembles strung together by an absurd pantomime plot. Although, even on record, the result is slacker because of that loose construction, one can appreciate the contribution of Weber, in a performance as stylish and refined as on DG. The original issue included dialogue and a narrative spoken by one of Oberon's fairy characters. In the reissue this is omitted, cutting the number of discs from three to two, yet leaving the music untouched. With Birgit Nilsson commanding in *Ocean, thou mighty monster*, and excellent singing from the other principals, helped by Kubelik's ethereally light handling of the orchestra, the set can be recommended without reservation, for the recording remains of excellent quality.

Webern, Anton (1883–1945)

(i) *Concerto for nine instruments, Op. 24; 5 Movements for string quartet* (orchestral version), *Op. 5; Passacaglia, Op. 1; 6 Pieces for large orchestra, Op. 6; 5 Pieces for orchestra, Op. 10; Symphony, Op. 21; Variations for orchestra, Op. 30*. Arrangements of: BACH: *Musical offering: Fugue* (1935). (ii) SCHUBERT: *German dances* (for small orchestra), *Op. posth*. Chamber music: (iii) *6 Bagatelles for string quartet, Op. 9; 5 Movements for string quartet, Op. 5;* (iv; v) *4 Pieces for violin and piano, Op. 7;* (v; vi) *3 Small pieces for cello and piano, Op. 11;* (v; vii) *Quartet, Op. 22* (for piano, violin, clarinet & saxophone); (iii) *String quartet, Op. 28; String trio, Op. 20;* (v) *Variations for piano, Op. 27*. (Vocal) (viii; i) *Das Augenlicht, Op. 26;* (ix; x) *5 Canons on Latin texts, Op. 16;* (viii; ix; i) *Cantata No. 1, Op. 29;* (viii; ix; xi; i) *Cantata No. 2, Op. 31;* (viii) *Entflieht auf leichten Kähnen, Op. 2;* (ix; x) *5 Sacred songs, Op. 15;* (xii; v) *5 Songs, Op. 3; 5 Songs, Op. 4;* (xii; x) *2 Songs, Op. 8;* (xii; v) *4 Songs, Op. 12;* (xii; x) *4 Songs, Op. 13; 6 Songs, Op. 14;* (ix; x; xiii) *3 Songs, Op. 18;* (viii; i) *2 Songs, Op. 19;* (xii; v) *3 Songs, Op. 23;* (ix; v) *3 Songs, Op. 25;* (ix; x) *3 Traditional rhymes, Op. 17*.

(M) *** Sony SM3K 45845 (3) [S3K 45845]. (i) LSO (or members), Pierre Boulez; (ii) Frankfurt R. O, composer (recorded December 1932); (iii) Juilliard Qt (or members); (iv) Stern; (v) Rosen; (vi) Piatigorsky; (vii) Majeske, Marcellus, Weinstein; (viii) John Alldis Ch.; (ix) Lukomska; (x) with Ens., Boulez; (xi) McDaniel; (xii) Harper; (xiii) with John Williams. Overall musical direction: Boulez.

These three CDs contain all Webern's works with opus numbers, as well as the string orchestra arrangements of Op. 5 and the orchestration of the *Fugue* from Bach's *Musical offering*. A rare recording of Webern himself conducting his arrangement of Schubert dances is also included. What Pierre Boulez above all demonstrates in the orchestral works (including those with chorus) is that, for all his seeming asceticism, Webern was working on human emotions. The Juilliard Quartet and the John Alldis Choir convey comparable commitment; though neither Heather Harper nor Halina Lukomska is ideally cast in the solo vocal music, Boulez brings out the best in both of them in the works with orchestra. Rarely can a major composer's whole *oeuvre* be appreciated in so compact a span. There are excellent notes, every item is cued, and perhaps it is carping to regret that the *Passacaglia* and *Variations for orchestra* were not indexed.

Concerto for 9 instruments, Op. 24.

(M) *** Chandos CHAN 6534 [id.]. Nash Ens., Simon Rattle – SCHOENBERG: *Pierrot Lunaire.* ***

This late Webern piece, tough, spare and uncompromising, makes a valuable fill-up for Jane Manning's outstanding version of Schoenberg's *Pierrot Lunaire*, a 1977 recording originally made for the Open University. First-rate sound and a beautifully clean CD transfer.

5 Movements, Op. 5; Passacaglia, Op. 1; 6 Pieces for orchestra, Op. 6; Symphony, Op. 21.

(M) *** DG 427 424-2 (3). BPO, Karajan – BERG: *Lyric suite; 3 Pieces;* SCHOENBERG: *Pelleas und Melisande; Variations; Verklaerte Nacht.* ***

(M) *** DG (IMS) 423 254-2. BPO, Karajan.

Available either separately or within Karajan's three-CD compilation, this collection, devoted to four compact and chiselled Webern works, is in many ways the most remarkable of all. Karajan's expressive refinement reveals the emotional undertones behind this seemingly austere music, and the results are riveting. Karajan secures a highly sensitive response from the Berlin Philharmonic, who produce sonorities as seductive as Debussy. Incidentally, he plays the 1928 version of Op. 6. A strong recommendation, with excellent sound.

Passacaglia for orchestra.

(BB) *** RCA Navigator 74321 29243-2 [(M) id. import]. Cologne RSO, Wakasugi – BERG: *Violin concerto;* SCHOENBERG: *Verklaerte Nacht.* ***

The Cologne Radio Symphony Orchestra understand what this music is about and under Hiroshi Wakasugi give a powerfully committed and very well-played account of Webern's most spectacular orchestral work. The 1977 recording is full and atmospheric, and the couplings on this inexpensive CD of key twentieth-century works are equally recommendable, despite inadequate documentation.

5 Pieces for orchestra, Op. 10.

(M) *** Mercury (IMS) 432 006-2 [id.]. LSO, Dorati – BERG: *3 Pieces* etc.; SCHOENBERG: *5 Pieces.* ***

Webern's *Five pieces*, Op. 10, written between 1911 and 1913, mark a radical point in his early development. Their compression is extreme. The couplings could hardly be more fitting, and the whole record can be strongly recommended to anyone wanting to explore the early work of Schoenberg and his followers before they formalized their ideas in twelve-note technique. Bright, clear, 1962 recording to match the precision of the writing.

6 Bagatelles, Op. 9; 5 Movements, Op. 5 for string quartet.

(B) *** DG Classikon 439 470-2 [(M) id. import]. LaSalle Qt – SCHOENBERG: *Verklaerte Nacht* etc. **(*)

Webern's six *Bagatelles*, written between 1911 and 1913, are characteristic of his brevity and density of expression; the earlier (1909) *Five Movements*, although succinct, are slightly more expansive. They are superbly played here and, while this is not easy music, it is certainly atmospheric and as arresting in impact as on the day it was written.

6 Bagatelles, Op. 9; 5 Movements, Op. 5; Quartet, Op. 28.

(M) *** Teldec/Warner 3984 21967-2 [id.]. Alban Berg Qt – BERG: *Lyric suite* etc.; URBANNER: *String quartet No. 3.* ***

Really outstanding playing of the Webern pieces by the Berg Quartet makes this a disc to be heard, a first choice in this repertoire as the recording is impeccable and the LaSalle CD above omits the Op. 28 *Quartet*. The Berg couplings are hardly less fine, although the somewhat Schoenbergian quartet by the Austrian composer, Erich Urbanner, is less memorable.

Weill, Kurt (1900–1950)

Kleine Dreigroschenmusik.

(M) *** DG 439 488-2. L. Sinf., David Atherton – BUSONI: *Doktor Faust:* excerpt; HINDEMITH: *Mathis der Maler (Symphony)*; PFITZNER: *Palestrina: 3 Preludes.* **

The London Sinfonietta and David Atherton give a lively and idiomatic account of this popular score. This is thoroughly recommendable, and the 1975 recording sounds very good indeed. The interesting couplings undoubtedly enhance the value of this CD.

Symphonies Nos. 1–2.

(M) ** EMI CDM5 65869-2 [id.]. BBC SO, Gary Bertini – BUSONI: *Berceuse élégiaque* ***; SCHOENBERG: *Chamber Symphony No. 2.* **(*)

Kurt Weill's unpredictable symphonies are fascinating, the first a student piece written in Berlin in 1921 when Weill was still a Busoni pupil. However, the influences were mainly from Mahler and Schoenberg, and the youthful urgency and imagination of the argument in a complex interlinked form carries the work off most successfully. No. 2 (1933–4) is obviously a more mature work, with three colourful and effective movements that are nearer to the idiom of Shostakovich and Kabalevsky. Behind the characteristic ostinatos and near-vulgar melodies there is a lurking seriousness. The performances are committed but could be better disciplined. No complaints about the late-1960s recording.

Happy End (play by Brecht with songs); *Die sieben Todsünden (The Seven deadly sins).*

(M) *** Sony mono/stereo MPK 45886 [id.]. Lotte Lenya, male quartet & O, Ch. & O, Brückner-Rüggeberg.

The Sony/CBS performance of *The Seven deadly sins*, with the composer's widow as principal singer, underlines the status of this distinctive mixture of ballet and song-cycle as one of Weill's most concentrated inspirations. The rhythmic verve is irresistible and, though Lenya had to have the music transposed down, her understanding of the idiom is unique. The recording is forward and slightly harsh, though Lenya's voice is not hardened, and the effect is undoubtedly vivid. *Happy end* was made in Hamburg-Harburg in 1960. Lenya turned the songs into a kind of cycle (following a hint from her husband), again transposing where necessary, and her renderings in her individual brand of vocalizing are so compelling they make the scalp tingle.

Die sieben Todsünden (The Seven deadly sins) complete.

(M) *** EMI Dig. CDM7 64739-2. Ross, Rolfe Johnson, Caley, Rippon, Tomlinson, CBSO, Rattle – STRAVINSKY: *Pulcinella.* ***

(i) *Die sieben Todsünden (The Seven deadly sins); Kleine Dreigroschenmusik.*

(M) *** Sony Dig. SMK 44529 [id.]. (i) Migenes, Tear, Kale, Opie, Kennedy; LSO, Tilson Thomas.

Rattle's moving account of this Brecht–Weill collaboration gives it a tender but refreshing new look. The key point is the casting of Elsie Ross as the two Annas, the one idealistic, the other practical, who in this sharply drawn sequence visit various American cities and their respective deadly sins. It was the first version to use the original soprano pitch (as does the newer account with Fassbaender on Harmonia Mundi). The higher pitch makes it easier for Elsie to contrast the singing of Anna I with the speaking of Anna II. The final epilogue brings them back to where they started, beside the Mississippi in Louisiana; and the agony of disillusion is presented with total heartache, thanks to Miss Ross's acting. Her singing is sweet and tender, rather than a more abrasive cabaret style: she is far less aggressive than Lotte Lenya's version (see above, under *Happy end*), and though Rattle's direction is sharp and analytical the spring in the rhythm and nicely judged expressiveness of phrase give a warmth which is very attractive and also brings out the work's often Mahlerian intensity. Rattle's speeds – nearer to Tilson Thomas's fast ones than to Mauceri's slow – have the dramatic bite of the one and the poignancy of the other, and the vocal quartet has the best voices of all, but loses some impact from being balanced (like the soprano) relatively distantly. But with such a generous coupling and at mid-price, it must be our primary recommendation. The digital recording has plenty of theatrical atmosphere.

In Tilson Thomas's performance with the LSO, Julia Migenes also uses the lower version of the score, colouring the voice even more boldly than Ute Lemper, echoing, even imitating, Lenya closely. With voices and instruments forwardly focused in the same consistent acoustic, the bite of the writing and its tangy beauty are put over powerfully, with Tilson Thomas's relatively brisk speeds adding to the power rather than to the poignancy. This makes a formidable mid-priced alternative to the Rattle version, in some ways more forceful, but with a coupling, apt as it is, rather less generous.

Weinberger, Jaromír (1896–1967)

Schwanda the Bagpiper: Polka and fugue.

(M) *** RCA 09026 62587-2 [id.]. Chicago SO, Fritz Reiner – DVORAK: *Symphony No. 9* etc.; SMETANA: *Bartered Bride: overture.* ***

This infectious orchestral display-piece was better known in the days of 78s. Reiner and his fine orchestra give a bravura performance, building to a huge climax. The Chicago recording is excellent and this CD overall is most attractive.

Wert, Giaches de (1535–96)

Il settimo libro de madrigali.

(M) *** Virgin Veritas/EMI Dig. VER5 61177-2. Consort of Musicke, Anthony Rooley.

Giaches de Wert was Monteverdi's predecessor in Mantua at the court of Count Alfonso Gonzaga. He was fairly prolific: this is the seventh of twelve books of madrigals, published in 1581 to celebrate the nuptials of the Duke's son, Vincenzo, and the final dialogue madrigal, *In qual parte sì ratto* ('Where are his swift pinions'), cleverly embroiders the elements of the bridegroom's family (an eagle) and those of his bride (the hyacinth: 'A flawless white pearl'). The opening madrigal is celebratory: *Sorgi e rischiara* ('Arise, light up the sky with thy approach, Holy Mother of love, lead in the day'), but many of the other varied settings are concerned with the trials and disappointments of love. De Wert certainly emerges here as a composer of expressive depth and personality and with a fine feeling for words. He is not another Monteverdi but his art is well worth knowing, and the singing here is persuasive, expressively responsive and beautifully blended, even if it does not always make the music project irresistibly. The recording is well up to the high standard of this stimulating Veritas series.

White, Robert (*c.* 1538–74)

Motets: *Christe qui lux es; Domine quis habitavit; Portio mea Domine; Regina coeli.*

✽ (B) *** Cal. CAL 6623 [(M) id.]. Clerkes of Oxenford, David Wulstan – TALLIS: *Mass Puer natus est* etc. *** ✽

Robert White, another neglected master of Elizabethan polyphony, married the daughter of Christopher Tye while based at Ely Cathedral; he then moved on to Chester, ending his days as choirmaster of St Peter's Cathedral in Westminster. His style of writing has a basic restraint and often shows a gentle, Dowland-like melancholy, so striking at the opening of *Domine quis habitavit*. But this is often offset by the soaring trebles, especially in the ravishing *Portio mea Domine*, while *Christe qui lux es*, the last motet on this record, is very touching indeed. Glorious performances by Wulstan and the Clerkes of Oxenford, who have the full measure of this repertoire. The analogue recording could hardly be bettered. Not to be missed.

Widor, Charles-Marie (1844–1937)

Organ symphonies Nos. 5 in F min., Op. 42/1 (complete); *6 in B, Op. 42/2: 1st movt; 8 in B, Op. 42/4: 4th movt (Prelude).*

(M) *** Saga EC 3363-2. David Sanger (organ of St Peter's Church, Clerkenwell, London).

David Sanger's account of the Widor *Symphony No. 5* is first class in every respect and is recorded with fine bloom and clarity. His restraint in registering the central movements prevents Widor's cosy melodic inspiration from sounding sentimental, and the finale is exciting without being overblown. The other symphonic movements are well done but serve to confirm the conclusion that the famous *Toccata* from No. 5 was Widor's masterpiece. The Clerkenwell organ has a pleasingly wide palette of colour, perhaps surprisingly well suited to this repertoire.

Symphony No. 5 in F minor, Op. 42/1: Toccata.

(B) **(*) EMI forte (SIS) CZS5 69328-2 (2) [CDFB 69328]. Fernando Germani – BACH: *Concertos* etc. **; FRANCK: *Chorales* etc. *(*)

The kind of tonal opulence obtained from the Selby Abbey organ suits the Widor showpiece better than Franck, and the delightful *Toccata* fairly bounces along. Those wanting the complete symphony from which the *Toccata* is extracted should turn to David Sanger on Saga.

Wieniawski, Henryk (1835–80)

Violin concertos Nos. 1 in F sharp min., Op. 14; 2 in D min., Op. 22; Fantaisie brillante on themes from Gounod's Faust, Op. 20.
(BB) ** Naxos 8.553517 [id.]. Marat Bisengaliev, Polish Nat. RSO, Wit.

(i) *Violin concertos Nos. 1–2;* (ii) *Caprice in A min.* (arr. Kreisler); *Obertass-Mazurka, Op. 19/1; Polonaise de concert No. 1 in D, Op. 4; Polonaise brillante No. 2, Op. 21; Scherzo–tarantelle, Op. 16.*
(M) *** EMI CDM5 66059-2. Itzhak Perlman; (i) LPO, Ozawa; (ii) Samuel Sanders.

Those who have enjoyed the relatively well-known *Second Concerto* of this contemporary of Tchaikovsky should investigate this coupling of his two concertos. The *First* may not be as consistently memorable as the *Second*, but the central *Preghiera* is darkly intense, and the finale is full of the showmanship that was the mark of the composer's own virtuosity on the violin. Perlman gives scintillating performances, full of flair, and is excellently accompanied. The recording, from 1973, has similar admirable qualities to the companion remastered CD, from the same period, of Paganini's *First Concerto*. The sound is warm, vivid and well balanced, and all the clearer and more realistic in its compact disc format. It is preferable to Perlman's digital re-make of the *Second Concerto*. The mid-priced reissue includes a mini-recital of shorter pieces. The *Caprice* and *Scherzo-tarantelle* are both dazzling, but lose some of their appeal from Perlman's insistence on a microphone spotlight. There is both charm and panache in the account of the *Obertass-Mazurka*, and Samuel Sanders comes more into the picture in the introductions for the two *Polonaises*, although the violin still remains far too near the microphone.

Though Bisengaliev's initial entry in the *First Concerto* on high double stopping is dauntingly edgy and abrasive, that is happily not typical of the performances as a whole. Born in Kazakhstan in 1962 and a Leipzig prizewinner in 1988, he may not be quite as imaginative or individual as rivals like Perlman or Shaham, and he is less bold in bravura, but the security of his technique is formidable, with a fine tonal range. His gentle half-tones in the slow movements of both works are strikingly beautiful, magically caught in the full and vivid Polish recording. The *Faust Fantaisie brillante*, like most such pot-pourris, is charming but rather outstays its welcome. The shuffling of themes, not usually the obvious ones, is most skilful, prompting deftly pointed playing from Bisengaliev. Wit and the Katowice orchestra provide most sympathetic support. Good value, but with Perlman now available at mid-price this is very much a bargain choice.

Violin concerto No. 2 in D min., Op. 22.
(M) (***) EMI mono CDH7 64251-2 [id.]. Heifetz, LPO, Barbirolli – SAINT-SAENS: *Havanaise* etc.; SARASATE: *Zigeunerweisen;* VIEUXTEMPS: *Concerto No. 4.* (***)
(M) **(*) Sony Stern Edition I SMK 66830 [id.]. Stern, Phd. O, Ormandy – BRUCH: *Violin concerto No. 1* **(*); TCHAIKOVSKY: *Méditation; Sérénade mélancolique.* ***

Everything that Heifetz touched turned to gold. He is as much in a class of his own here as he is elsewhere on this CD. The concerto was recorded in 1935 with the young John Barbirolli, with whom Heifetz formed a strong rapport. It is doubtful that this performance has ever been bettered on record. The sound is perhaps less vivid than the best recordings of the day, but the transfers are very good.

Stern's recording comes from 1957, and the very close balance is not flattering to his upper range (although of course this playing can stand any kind of scrutiny). The songful slow movement is played simply and beautifully, and the finale is very *energico* indeed. Stern's virtuosity is both thrilling and astonishing in its clean articulation. Ormandy, as usual, provides fine support and the orchestra, though also balanced artificially, plays against a warm ambience.

Capriccio-waltz, Op. 7; Gigue in E min., Op. 27; Kujawiak in A min.; Légende, Op. 17; Mazurka in G min., Op. 12/2; 2 Mazurkas, Op. 19; Polonaise No. 1 in D, Op. 4; Russian carnival, Op. 11; Saltarello (arr. Lenehan); *Scherzo-tarantelle in G min., Op. 16; Souvenir de Moscou, Op. 6; Variations on an original theme, Op. 15.*
(BB) **(*) Naxos Dig. 8.550744 [id.]. Marat Bisengaliev, John Lenehan.

All the dazzling violin fireworks are ready to bow here, from left-hand pizzicatos in the *Russian carnival* to multiple stopping (and some lovely, warm lyricism) in the *Variations on an original theme*, plus all the dash you could ask for in the closing *Scherzo-tarantelle*. The four *Mazurkas* have plenty of animated folk feeling and local colour, while the beautiful *Légende* (which Wieniawski dedicated to his wife as a nuptial gift) is both touchingly gentle and passionately brilliant. Marat Bisengaliev is without the larger-than-life personality of a Perlman, but he is a remarkably fine player and a stylist, as well as being able to produce a sparkling moto perpetuo at will, as in the Neapolitan *Saltarello*, arranged by the pianist, John Lenehan, who provides his partner with admirable support throughout. The snag is the very reverberant acoustic of the Rosslyn Hill Chapel, Hampstead – so obviously empty. One adjusts to this (with some reluctance); otherwise the sound and balance are natural enough.

Williamson, Malcolm (born 1931)

Violin concerto.

(M) *** EMI CDM5 66121-2. Yehudi Menuhin, LPO, Adrian Boult – L. BERKELEY: *Concerto;* PANUFNIK: *Concerto*. ***

An eloquent work with much greater expressive power and depth than one usually associates with this sometimes facile Australian composer. Menuhin plays it beautifully and the LPO under Boult give generous support. The 1971 Abbey Road recording is admirably full, yet clear and detailed. A satisfying and thoughtful concerto, completing a triptych which is well worth exploring.

Wirén, Dag (1905–86)

Serenade for strings in G, Op. 11.

(BB) *** Naxos Dig. 8.553106 [id.]. Bournemouth Sinf., Richard Studt – Concert: *Scandinavian string music*. ***

The engaging *String serenade* is Dag Wirén's one claim to international fame, and it is good to welcome an outstanding super-bargain version. The natural impetus and lyrical charm of the first movement is most winning and the Scherzo brings fizzing bravura, while the colour and mood of the *Andante* is aptly caught. The finale certainly earns its hit status, full of spontaneous, lilting energy. First-rate recording within an entirely recommendable concert of Scandinavian string music, not all of it familiar.

Wolf, Hugo (1860–1903)

Italian serenade in G.

(B) **(*) Ph. Duo 456 330-2 (2) [id.]. I Musici – BOTTESINI: *Grand duo concertante* **; MENDELSSOHN: *Octet* **(*); ROSSINI: *String sonatas*. **.

The *Italian serenade* is an infectiously gay and high-spirited miniature, without doubt a masterpiece, and one whose popularity is by no means as great as it should be. I Musici play it extremely well, even if (as with the principal Rossini coupling) they do not do full justice to its effervescent spirits and sheer *joie de vivre*. They are vividly recorded, but there is a hint of edge on the CD transfer.

String quartet in D min.

(M) ** DG (IMS) 437 128-2 (2) LaSalle Qt (with BRAHMS: *Quartets Nos. 1–2* *(*)).

The *String quartet* was written when Wolf was only twenty. The finale was added later. It is an ambitious work (41 minutes long), original in its metric flow, and the music has all the direct passion of youth. It suits the LaSalle Quartet better than the Brahms couplings (which are much less recommendable). Though they press hard at times, the long slow movement is eloquent and often beautifully played and the finale has plenty of impetus. Bright, immediate, 1967 sound. We hope this may be reissued, differently coupled.

6 Lieder für eine Frauenstimme. Goethe-Lieder: Die Bekehrte; Ganymed; Kennst du das Land?; Mignon I, II & III; Philine; Die Spröde. Lieder: *An eine Aeolsharfe; Auf einer Wanderung; Begegnung; Denk es, o Seele; Elfenlied; Im Frühling; Sonne der Schlummerlosen; Wenn du zu den Blumen gehst; Wie glänzt der helle Mond; Die Zigeunerin.*

(M) **(*) EMI CDM7 63653-2. Elisabeth Schwarzkopf, Gerald Moore or Geoffrey Parsons.

This is a superb collection, representing the peak of Schwarzkopf's achievement as a Lieder singer. It is disgraceful that no texts or translations are provided as this will seriously reduce its appeal for some collectors; but the selection of items could hardly be better, including many songs inseparably associated with Schwarzkopf's voice, like *Mausfallen spruchlein* and, above all, *Kennst du das Land?*.

Eichendorf Lieder: *Nachtzauber; Die Zigeunerin. Mörike Lieder: Elfenlied; Der Genesene an die Hoffnung; Lebewohl; Storchenbotschaft.* Lieder from *Italienisches Liederbuch: Du sagst mir; Ich esse nun mein Brot; Ich hab' in Penna; Nein, junger Herr; Nur lass uns Frieden schliessen; O wär' dein Haus durchsichtig; Schweig' einmal still; Verschling' der Abgrund; Wer rief dich denn?*. Lieder from *Spanisches Liederbuch: Bedeckt mich mit Blumen; Geh', Geliebter, geh' jetzt; Herr, was trägt der Boden hier; In dem Schatten*

meiner Locken; Klinge klinge mein Pandero; Mögen alle bösen Zungen; Sie blasen zum Abmrarsch. Encores: *Trau' nicht der Liebe. Mörike Lieder: Der Knabe und das Immelein; Nimmersatte Liebe; Selbstgeständnis.*
(M) (***) EMI mono CDH5 65749-2. Elisabeth Schwarzkopf, Gerald Moore.

This Wolf collection, recorded live at Salfurg recitals in 1957 and 1963, is a most valuable supplement to Schwarzkopf's searching and intense studio recordings of Wolf. In many ways the extra degree of freedom in the live performances adds to the intensity of the experience, both in weighty songs and in lighter ones such as *Wer rief dich denn?* (uniquely vehement) and *Ich hab' in Penna*. The recordings, originally made by Austrian Radio, capture the voice beautifully, with words crystal clear. Texts are given but no translation.

Goethe Lieder: *Anakreons Grab; Blumengruss; Erschaffen und Beleben; Gleich und gleich; Harfenspieler I, II & III; Ob der Koran von Ewigkeit sei?; Phänomen; Der Rattenfänger; Sie haben wegen der Trunkenheit; So lang man nüchtern ist; Spottlied; Trunken müssen wir alle sein!; Was in der Schenke waren heute.* Mörike Lieder: *Abschied; An die Geliebte; An eine Aolsharfe; Auf ein altes Bild; Bei einer Trauung; Elfenlied; Er ist's; Fussreise; Der Gärtner; Gebet; Gesang Weylas; Heimweh; Jägerlied; Nimmersatte Liebe; Der Tambour; Verborgenheit.*
(BB) *** Virgin Classics Dig. Double VBD5 61418-2 (2) [CVBD 61418]. Thomas Allen, Geoffrey Parsons – BRAHMS: *Lieder.* ***

It was a particularly happy idea to combine Thomas Allen's splendid recital of relatively familiar Brahms songs with an exceptionally generous (74-minute) collection of Wolf's Goethe and Mörike settings, which are much rarer, both on disc and in the recital room. Allen enters fully into the spirit of each song, and Geoffrey Parsons accompanies with characteristic imagination. Whether the words convey ardour (as in one of the best known, *An die Geliebte*), are hauntingly evocative (as in the remarkable *Harfenspieler* settings) or are exuberantly extrovert (*Der Rattenfänger*), these artists unerringly project their mood. Alas, this inexpensive reissue includes neither translations nor song summaries; the documentation of this otherwise remarkable series is consistently inadequate. But the vocal treasure offered here and the excellence both of performances and of Andrew Keener's recording balance at Abbey Road carries the day.

Italienisches Liederbuch (complete).
(M) *** EMI CDM7 63732-2 [id.]. Elisabeth Schwarzkopf, Dietrich Fischer-Dieskau, Gerald Moore.
(M) *** Ph. (IMS) 442 744-2 (2). Elly Ameling, Gérard Souzay, Dalton Baldwin – R. STRAUSS: *Lieder.* ***

All 46 songs of Wolf's *Italienisches Liederbuch* are here, sung by Schwarzkopf and Fischer-Dieskau on an EMI CD playing for two seconds over 79 minutes, generous measure indeed at mid-price! These songs show the composer at his most captivatingly individual. Many of them are very brief fragments of fantasy, which call for the most intense artistry if their point is to be fully made. No one today can match the searching perception of these two great singers in this music, with Fischer-Dieskau using his sweetest tones and Schwarzkopf ranging through all the many emotions inspired by love. Note particularly the little vignette, *Wer rief dich denn?*, which Schwarzkopf interprets more vividly than anyone else: scorn mingling with hidden heartbreak. Gerald Moore is at his finest, and Walter Legge's translations will help bring the magic of these unique songs even to the newcomer. The well-balanced 1969 recording has been admirably transferred, giving the artists a fine presence.

Elly Ameling, delicately sweet and precise, contrasts well with Souzay, with his fine-drawn sense of line. The charm and point of these brief but intensely imaginative songs are well presented, with perceptive accompaniment from Dalton Baldwin. The coupled Richard Strauss recital also shows Souzay at his most perceptive. However, the unforgettable 1969 version with Schwarzkopf and Fischer-Dieskau has the advantage of being offered uncoupled, on a single, mid-priced CD.

(i; ii) *Italienisches Liederbuch* (complete). (ii) Eichendorf Lieder: *Erwartung; Der Freund; Der Glücksritter; Heimweh; Lieber Alles; Liebesglück; Der Musikant; Die Nacht; Nachtzauber; Der Schreckenberger; Der Scholar; Seemanns Abschied; Der Soldat I & II; Das Ständchen; Unfall; Verschwiegene Liebe; Der verzweifelte Liebhaber. In der Fremde I, II & IV; Nachruf; Rückkehr.* Michelangelo Lieder: *Alles endet, was entstehet; Fühlt meine Seele das ersehnte Licht; Wohl denk'ich oft an mein vergangnes Leben.*
(M) *** DG (IMS) 439 975-2 (2) (i) Christa Ludwig; (ii) Dietrich Fischer-Dieskau; Daniel Barenboim.

Fischer-Dieskau is superb in these varied items from the *Italian Song Book*, always underlining the word-meanings with the inflexion of a born actor, helped by the understanding accompaniment of Barenboim. In the women's songs, Christa Ludwig is less uninhibited and, after Schwarzkopf's accounts of such jewels as *Wer rief dich denn*, these may seem undercharacterized, with the voice not always perfectly steady; but Ludwig too has natural compulsion in her singing and responds splendidly to the pointed playing of Barenboim. The *Eichendorf* and *Michelangelo Lieder* make a splendid supplement for the CD issue, and the mid-1970s recording gives an entirely natural effect.

Mörike Lieder: Michelangelo Lieder: Alles endet, was entstehet; Fühlt meine Seele; Wohl denk' ich oft. Mörike Lieder: Abschied; An de Schlaf; An die Geliebte; Auf eine altes Bild; Auf eine Christblume I & II; Auf einer Wanderung; Auftrag; Begegnung; Bei einer Trauung; Denk' es, o Seele!; Der Feuerreiter; Füssreise; Der Gärtner; Gebet; Die Geister am Mummelsee; Der Genesene an die Hoffnung; Gesang Weyla's; Heimwek; Im Frühling; In der Fru'he; Der Jäger; Jägerlieg; Karwoche; Der König bei der Krönung; Lebe wohl; Lied eines Verliebten; Neue Liebe; Nimmersatte Liebe; Peregrina I & II; Schlafendes Jesuskind; Selbstgeständnis; Seufzer; Storchenbotschaft; Der Tambour; Um Mitternacht; Wo find' ich Trost; Verborgenheit; Zitronnenfalter im April; Zur Warnung.
(M) (***) EMI mono/stereo CMS7 63563-2 (2). Dietrich Fischer-Dieskau, Gerald Moore.

This collection of Wolf's settings of Mörike, 44 songs, was recorded in 1957, with four songs completing the collection, added two years later. Those four are in stereo but, so compelling is Fischer-Dieskau's singing, one hardly worries that the others are all in mono only. The experience is the more vivid thanks to the close placing of the singer, as though face to face. Texts and translations are given.

Spanisches Liederbuch (complete).
(M) *** DG 457 726-2 (2) [id.]. Schwarzkopf, Fischer-Dieskau, Moore.

In this superb DG reissue as part of DG's series of Originals, the sacred songs provide a dark, intense prelude, with Fischer-Dieskau at his very finest, sustaining slow tempi impeccably. Schwarzkopf's dedication comes out in the three songs suitable for a woman's voice; but it is in the secular songs, particularly those which contain laughter in the music, where she is at her most memorable. Gerald Moore is balanced rather too backwardly – something the transfer cannot correct – but gives superb support. In all other respects the 1968 recording sounds first rate, the voices beautifully caught. A classic set.

Wolpe, Stefan (1902–72)

(i) *Symphony No. 1;* (ii) *Chamber pieces Nos. 1–2;* (iii) *Yigdal cantata.*
(BB) *** Arte Nova Dig. 74321 46508-2. (i) NDR SO, Johannes Kalitzke; (ii) Instrumental Ens.; (iii) NDR Ch., H. Neumann.

This valuable collection, superbly played and vividly recorded, gives an excellent conspectus of the work of Stefan Wolpe, one of Webern's most distinguished pupils. Born in Berlin, he went to Palestine in 1934, working as a music-teacher, before emigrating to the United States four years later. One of the first pieces he wrote on arrival was the *Yigdal cantata*, settings of Hebrew texts which brilliantly reconcile a serial technique with traditional Jewish music, warm and expressive. The purely instrumental works are far tougher, with the *Symphony* crisp and purposeful, culminating in the longest and most energetic movement of the three. The two *Chamber pieces*, each for 14 instruments, very much in the manner of Webern, are among Wolpe's last works, even more compressed, with the second ending in a powerful timpani solo, but each seeming to reflect his frustration and defiance over suffering from Parkinson's disease. At Arte Nova price, well worth investigating by the adventurous.

Zandonai, Riccardo (1883–1944)

Francesca da Rimini: excerpts from Acts II, III & IV.
(M) **(*) Decca 433 033-2 (2). Olivero, Del Monaco, Monte Carlo Op. O, Rescigno – GIORDANO: *Fedora*. **(*)

Magda Olivero is a fine artist who has not been represented nearly enough on record, and this rare Zandonai selection, like the coupled set of Giordano's *Fedora*, does her some belated justice. Decca opted to have three substantial scenes recorded rather than snippets and, though Mario del Monaco as Paolo is predictably coarse in style, his tone is rich and strong and he does not detract from the achievement, unfailingly perceptive and musicianly, of Olivero as Francesca herself. Excellent, vintage 1969, Decca sound.

Zelenka, Jan (1679–1745)

Hippocondrie à 7 in A, ZWV 187; Overture à 7 concertanti in F, ZWV 188; Sonata No. 2 in G min. for 2 oboes, bassoon and continuo, ZWV 181.
(M) **(*) Teldec/Warner 0630 17386-2. VCM, Harnoncourt.

No one could accuse Harnoncourt of a lack of vitality in his performances of this lively, inventive and often unpredictable music by one of Bach's most remarkable contemporaries. There is some fine oboe-playing too, and the strings are brightly alert throughout. As usual with this conductor, accents are strong and rhythms bounce firmly, yet there is also some fine, expressive playing. The five-movement *Overture* (or suite), which shows well the diversity of Zelenka's invention, is particularly characterful. Recording (dating from 1980) is characteristically bright and forward, yet the range of dynamic is wide.

Zemlinsky, Alexander von (1871–1942)

Lyric symphony, Op. 18.

(BB) *** Arte Nova Dig. 74321 27768-2 [id.]. Vlatka Orsanic, James Johnson, SWFSO, Gielen – BERG: *Lyric suite: 3 Pieces* etc. ***

At speeds markedly faster than usual, Michael Gielen conducts an exceptionally powerful and purposeful account of Zemlinsky's *Lyric symphony*. If generally one is all too aware of the composer's debt to Mahler and the example of *Das Lied von der Erde*, here the work emerges as very fresh and distinctive in its own right, echoing Mahlerian neurosis only in the last two linked movements. The playing of the orchestra is outstanding and the two soloists are ideal, singing with clean attack and fresh tone. First-rate recording too. An outstanding bargain, well coupled with the Berg works, including the *Lyric suite* with its quotations from Zemlinsky. The only snag is that the booklet is totally inadequate, with poor notes and no texts or translations, and not even any identification of the seven Tagore poems used by Zemlinsky in the symphony.

6 Maeterlinck Lieder, Op. 13.

(B) *** Decca Double (IMS) 444 871-2 (2) [id.]. Concg. O, Chailly – MAHLER: *Symphony No. 6*. ***

Beautifully sung by Jard van Nes in her finest recording to date, these ripely romantic settings of Maeterlinck make an unusual but valuable fill-up for Chailly's rugged and purposeful reading of the Mahler *Symphony*. This is very much the world of medieval chivalry which inspired *Pelléas et Mélisande*, and Zemlinsky responds wholeheartedly. The rich, vivid recording captures van Nes's full-throated singing with new firmness.

Concerts of Orchestral and Concertante Music

'The Art of conducting: Great conductors of the past' (Barbirolli; Beecham; Bernstein; Busch; Furtwängler; Karajan; Klemperer; Koussevitzky; Nikisch; Reiner; Stokowski; Richard Strauss; Szell; Toscanini; Walter; Weingartner): WEBER: *Der Freischütz overture* (LSO, Arthur Nikisch). BRAHMS: *Symphony No. 4* (LSO, Felix Weingartner). Richard STRAUSS: *Der Rosenkavalier*: suite of film music (Augmented L. Tivoli Theatre O, Richard Strauss). BRAHMS: *Tragic overture.* WAGNER: *Parsifal: Prelude and Good Friday music* (BBC SO, Arturo Toscanini). BEETHOVEN: *Fidelio overture*. SCHUBERT: *Symphony No. 8 in B min. (Unfinished)* (both VPO). WAGNER: *Tristan und Isolde: Prelude, Act III* (Philh. O; all conducted Wilhelm Furtwängler). MOZART: *Così fan tutte overture* (Glyndebourne Festival O, Fritz Busch). MOZART: *Serenade: Eine kleine Nachtmusik.* WAGNER: *Siegfried idyll.* MAHLER: *Symphony No. 5: Adagietto* (VPO, Bruno Walter). WAGNER: *Tristan und Isolde: Prelude, Act I* (LPO, Fritz Reiner). SIBELIUS: *Symphony No. 7* (BBC SO, Serge Koussevitzky). CHABRIER: *Joyeuse marche*. DELIUS: *Irmelin Prelude*. SIBELIUS: *Tapiola* (RPO, Sir Thomas Beecham). ELGAR: *Introduction and allegro for strings* (L. Sinfonia, Sir John Barbirolli). DVORAK: *Symphony No. 8 in G* (Cleveland O, George Szell). BEETHOVEN: *Symphony No. 7* (Philh. O, Otto Klemperer). *Symphony No. 8*. SMETANA: *Má Vlast: Vltava* (BPO, Herbert von Karajan). BACH/STOKOWSKI: *Toccata and fugue in D min*. RESPIGHI: *The Pines of Rome* (Symphony O or Symphony of the Air, Leopold Stokowski). BERLIOZ: *Harold in Italy* (O Nat. de France, Leonard Bernstein, with Donald McInnes, viola). Comparisons: BEETHOVEN: *Symphony No. 5:* first movt (BPO, Nikisch; VPO, Furtwängler; Philh. O, Karajan; Philh. O, Klemperer). Rehearsal sequences (excerpts): BEETHOVEN: *Symphony No. 5*. MOZART: *Die Entführung aus dem Serail* (with Gottlob Frick). HAYDN: *Symphony No. 100 (Military)* (all RPO, Beecham). BEETHOVEN: *Overture Leonora No. 3* (Stockholm PO, Furtwängler). TCHAIKOVSKY: *Symphony No. 4*: Finale (Hallé O, Barbirolli).
(M)(***) EMI (SIS) CMS5 65915-2 (7) [CDMG 65915].

EMI have issued this carefully prepared seven-disc set to offer examples of the art of some of the most famous musicians of the twentieth century. There is much here that is treasurable. Now we can hear Nikisch in Weber; Felix Weingartner conducts a glowingly lyrical account of Brahms's *Fourth Symphony* which shows his natural mastery of Brahmsian phrasing and line; Koussevitzky is heard in Sibelius, Furtwängler in Beethoven, Wagner and Schubert, Beecham in Delius and Chabrier, and Barbirolli is uniquely warm-blooded in Elgar. We have both Klemperer and Karajan in complete performances of Beethoven symphonies and, after various rehearsal sequences, we are given the chance to compare Nikisch, Furtwängler, Karajan, Klemperer and Beecham in the first movement of the Beethoven *Fifth Symphony*.

Academy of Ancient Music, Christopher Hogwood

PACHELBEL: *Canon & Gigue*. HANDEL: *Water music: Air. Berenice: Overture; Minuet; Gigue*. VIVALDI: *Flute concerto in G min. (La notte), Op. 10/2*. BACH: *Christmas oratorio, BWV 248: Sinfonia. Quadruple harpsichord concerto in A min., BWV 1065*. CORELLI: *Concerto grosso (Christmas concerto), Op. 6/8*. A. MARCELLO: *Oboe concerto in D min.*
(M) **(*) O-L Analogue/Dig. 443 201-2.

It seems a curious idea to play popular baroque repertoire in a severe manner; Pachelbel's *Canon* here sounds rather abrasive and lacking in charm. But those who combine a taste for these pieces with a desire for authenticity should be satisfied. The selection for this reissue has been expanded and altered. Handel's Queen of Sheba no longer arrives – and she is not missed (for she was much more seductive in Beecham's hands) – and the highlight of the original, full-priced compilation (a pair of Gluck dances) is no longer present! Instead, we get several new items taken from another Academy of Ancient Music compilation of baroque music associated with Christmas, notably Corelli's splendid Op. 6/8, in which the playing has a suitably light touch, and Vivaldi's engaging *La notte Flute concerto*, while Bach's *Quadruple harpsichord concerto* substitutes for the famous Vivaldi work for four violins (Op. 3/10). On the whole an enjoyable mix. The new playing time is 67 minutes.

Academy of St Martin-in-the-Fields, Sir Neville Marriner

SUPPE: Overture: *Light cavalry*. GRIEG: *2 Elegiac melodies, Op. 34; Holberg suite, Op. 40: Prelude*. TCHAIKOVSKY: *Andante cantabile* (from *String quartet No. 1)*. DVORAK: *Nocturne in B, Op. 40*. PONCHIELLI: *La Gioconda: Dance of the hours*. NICOLAI: *The Merry Wives of Windsor* (overture). FAURE: *Pavane, Op. 50*. BOCCHERINI: *String quintet in E, Op. 13/5: Minuet*. WAGNER: *Siegfried idyll*. HANDEL: *Solomon: Arrival of the Queen of Sheba*. J. S. BACH: *Cantata No. 208: Sheep may safely graze; Cantata No. 147: Jesu, joy of man's desiring; Christmas oratorio: Pastoral symphony*. HANDEL: *Berenice: Minuet. Messiah: Pastoral symphony*. SCHUBERT: *Rosamunde: Entr'acte No. 3 in B flat*. GLUCK: *Orfeo ed Euridice: Dance of the blessed spirits*. BORODIN: *String quartet No. 2 in D: Nocturne*. SHOSTAKOVICH: *The Gadfly: Romance*. MUSSORGSKY/RIMSKY-KORSAKOV: *Khovanshchina: Dance of the Persian slaves*. RIMSKY-KORSAKOV: *Tsar Saltan: The Flight of the bumble bee. The Snow Maiden: Dance of the tumblers*.
(BB) *** CfP Silver Double Dig. CD-CFPSD 4811 (2) [(B) id.].

This CfP Silver Double draws on the contents of three different (HMV) digital collections, recorded between 1980 and 1987. The first included the *Siegfried idyll*, in which Marriner uses solo strings for the gentler passages, a fuller ensemble for the climaxes, here passionately convincing. Delicately introduced by the harp and the gentle striking of the morning hour, the account of the *Dance of the hours* has characteristic finesse and colour, while there is comparably gracious phrasing in *The Merry Wives of Windsor overture*. The other, mainly gentle, pieces by Tchaikovsky, Fauré, Boccherini and Grieg are given radiant performances. To open the second disc, Handel's *Queen of Sheba* trots in very briskly and here the noble contour of Handel's famous *Berenice* melody is the first thing to strike the ear; but it is the Schubert *Entr'acte* from *Rosamunde* and the passionately expressive Borodin *Nocturne* that resonate in the memory. With the Shostakovich *Barrel organ waltz* providing a touch of piquancy and Mussorgsky's *Persian slaves* suitably sinuous and sentient, this makes a most agreeable entertainment, ending with gusto with Rimsky's *Tumblers*. The digital sound is excellent throughout.

'Academy Favourites': HANDEL: *Solomon: Arrival of the Queen of Sheba. Berenice: Minuet. Water music: suite*. VIVALDI: *Concerto for 4 violins, Op. 3/10* (with Alan Loveday, Carmel Kaine, Iona Brown, Roy Gillard). BACH: *Suite No.3 in D, BWV 1069*. MOZART: *Serenade: Eine kleine Nachtmusik*.
(M) *** Decca 436 999-2; *436 999-4*.

Here is an archetypal programme of baroque favourites: repertoire in which Marriner and his Academy made their name. Every performance here is fresh, and the recordings (made between 1964 and 1974) are smoothly transferred and still sound first class.

'Fantasia on Greensleeves': VAUGHAN WILLIAMS: *Fantasia on Greensleeves; The Lark ascending* (with Iona Brown); *English folksong suite*. WARLOCK: *Serenade; Capriol suite*. BUTTERWORTH: *A Shropshire lad; Two English idylls; The Banks of green willow*. DELIUS: *A Village Romeo and Juliet: The walk to the Paradise Garden. Hassan: Intermezzo and serenade. A song before sunrise; On hearing the first cuckoo in spring; Summer night on the river; La Calinda*. ELGAR: *Serenade for strings, Op. 20; Sospiri for strings, harp and organ; Elegy for strings, Op. 58; The Spanish Lady (suite); Introduction and Allegro, Op. 47*.
(B) *** Decca Double 452 707-2 (2) [(M) id. import].

This exceptionally generous programme, mainly of English pastoral evocations but including Iona Brown's Elysian account of *The Lark ascending* and Elgar's two string masterpieces in not wholly idiomatic but very characterful performances, is self-recommending, for the Academy are thoroughly at home here and play with consistent warmth and finesse, while the vintage Decca sound never disappoints. Marvellous value for money.

American masterpieces

'American masterpieces' (with (i) Cleveland O, Louis Lane; (ii) Phd. O, Eugene Ormandy; (iii) NYPO, André Kostelanetz): (i) BERNSTEIN: *Candide overture*. (ii) IVES: *Variations on 'America'*. (iii) William SCHUMAN: *New England triptych*. (ii) BARBER: *Adagio for strings*. GOULD: *American salute*. (iii) GRIFFES: *The pleasure dome of Kubla Khan*. (ii) MACDOWELL: *Woodland sketches: To a wild rose*. (iii) GERSHWIN: *Promenade*. (ii) GOTTSCHALK: *Cakewalk: Grand walkaround* (arr. Hershy Kay). (i) BENJAMIN: *Jamaican rumba*. RODGERS: *On Your Toes: Slaughter on 10th Avenue*. Virgil THOMSON: *Louisiana Story* (film score): *Arcadian songs and dances*.
(B) **(*) Sony SBK 63034; *SBT 63034* [id.].

Not everything here is a masterpiece, and Arthur Benjamin, who makes the wittiest contribution, was an

Australian! But there are some obvious favourites included and one or two novelties, among them the attractively folksy *Arcadian songs and dances* of Virgil Thomson, affectionately directed in Cleveland by Louis Lane. He is well recorded, and so, on the whole, is Ormandy, who presents the Ives *Variations* with charm as well as panache, while the Philadelphia strings are powerfully eloquent in Barber's *Adagio* and warmly persuasive in MacDowell's engaging *To a wild rose*. Kostelanetz conducts with plenty of personality and zest and is at his best in the Gershwin *Promenade* and the touching central movement of Schuman's *New England triptych*. But here the up-front recording of the NYPO is overlit and the climaxes of the otherwise atmospheric *Kubla Khan* sound aggressive. A stimulating programme, just the same.

(i) American Symphony Orchestra Wind Group or (ii) Orchestra, Leopold Stokowski

(i) MOZART: *Serenade No. 10 for 13 wind instruments in B flat, K.361*. (ii) VIVALDI: *L'Estro armonico: Concerto grosso in D min., Op. 3/11*. BACH: *Jesu, joy of man's desiring* (arr. SCHICKELE); *Sheep may safely graze* (arr. STOKOWSKI). CORELLI: *Concerto grosso in G min. (Christmas), Op. 6/8*.
(M) *** Van. 08 8009 71 [id.].

Stokowski's expressive exaggerations – inevitable even in Mozart – are never extreme, so that they do not get in the way of enjoyment of this highly characterful performance of the *Wind serenade*. The solo work in the lovely *Adagio* third movement is exceptionally sensitive in its flexibility, and the sprung rhythms of the fast movements are infectiously controlled. The Bach transcriptions, too, are warmly enjoyable, but it is the baroque *concerti grossi* that show the Stokowski magnetism at its most telling. In the Corelli, Igor Kipnis provides the continuo and he is nicely balanced. Allegros sparkle and the famous *Pastorale* is expressively beautiful. In the Vivaldi, the continuo is almost inaudible, but again the string playing is buoyant and joyful in allegros, while the third-movement *Largo* is quite ravishing. The 1966–7 recordings are excellent and the transfers first rate.

Anderson, John (oboe), Philharmonia Orchestra, Simon Wright

'Venetian oboe concertos': ALBINONI: *Concertos in B flat, Op. 7/3; in D, Op. 7/6*. MARCELLO: *Concerto in D min*. VIVALDI: *Concertos in D, RV 453; in F, RV 455; in A min., RV 461*. CIMAROSA/BENJAMIN: *Concerto in C min*.
(M) **(*) Nimbus Dig. NI 7027 [id.].

John Anderson is principal oboist of the Philharmonia and he plays these concertos with warmth, elegance and grace. The one slight drawback is the rather plushy tuttis from the resonantly recorded Philharmonia Orchestra. Although they give delicate support in the Marcello *Adagio*, the orchestral touch is heavier in the *Larghetto* of the Vivaldi *A minor*, RV 461. The concerto arranged by Arthur Benjamin from the music of Cimarosa is a highlight, the *Introduction* delicately tender and the second movement deliciously pointed.

André, Maurice (trumpet)

Trumpet concertos (with LPO, Jesús López-Cobos): HAYDN: *Concerto in E flat*. TELEMANN: *Concerto in F*. ALBINONI: *Concerto in D min*. MARCELLO: *Concerto in C min*.
(M) *** EMI CDM7 69189-2.

Maurice André's cultured playing gives much pleasure throughout this collection. Slow movements are elegantly phrased and communicate an appealing, expressive warmth. The stylishness and easy execution ensure a welcome for the Albinoni and Marcello works, which are transcriptions but are made thoroughly convincing in this format. Excellent, lively accompaniments from the LPO under López-Cobos, and good sound, the more vivid on CD.

Trumpet concertos (with (i) ECO, Mackerras; (ii) Munich Bach O, Karl Richter; (iii) Munich CO, Stadlmair): (i) VIVIANI: *Sonata for trumpet & organ in C* (with Hedwig Bilgram). VIVALDI: *Double trumpet concerto in C, RV 537*. TELEMANN: *Concerto-Sonata in D*. (ii) HANDEL: *Concerto in G min*. (arr. from *Oboe concerto No. 3*). (iii) M. HAYDN: *Trumpet concerto in D*. J. HAYDN: *Trumpet concerto in E flat*.
(M) *** DG 419 874-2 [id.].

This DG collection (well recorded in the late 1960s and late 1970s) represents Maurice André's art most impressively. The only transcription included is from a Handel *Oboe concerto*, and that is reasonably effective. Michael Haydn's *Concerto*, a concertante section of a seven-movement *Serenade*, has incredibly high tessitura, with the D trumpet taken up to high A (the fourth ledger-line above the treble stave), the highest note in any classical trumpet concerto. It is just a peep but, characteristically, Maurice André reaches up for it with consummate ease. He is completely at home in all this repertoire: his version of the Joseph Haydn *Concerto* is stylish and elegant, with a memorably eloquent account of the slow movement, the line gracious and warmly serene. The *Sonata for trumpet and organ* by Giovanni Buonaventura Viviani (1638–*c*. 1692) is also an attractive piece, comprising five brief but striking miniatures, each only a minute or so in length. In the Vivaldi *Double concerto* André plays both solo parts.

Argerich, Martha (piano) with other artists

Martha Argerich Collection.
(M) **(*) DG Analogue/Dig. 453 566-2 (11) [id.].

Volume I: Concertos: BEETHOVEN: *Piano concertos Nos. 1 in C, Op. 15; 2 in B flat, Op. 19* (with Philh. O, Sinopoli). CHOPIN: *Piano concertos Nos. 1 in E min., Op. 11* (with LSO, Abbado); *2 in F min., Op. 21.* SCHUMANN: *Piano concerto in A min., Op. 54* (both with Nat. SO, Rostropovich). TCHAIKOVSKY: *Piano concerto No. 1 in B flat min., Op. 23* (with RPO, Dutoit). LISZT: *Piano concerto No. 1 in E flat* (with LSO). PROKOFIEV: *Piano concerto No. 3 in C, Op. 26.* RAVEL: *Piano concerto in G* (with BPO; both cond. Abbado).
(M) **(*) DG Analogue/Dig. 453 567-2 (4) [id.].

The chimerical volatility of Martha Argerich's musical personality comes out again and again in this impressive survey of her recorded repertory. Her ability in concertos to strike sparks in a musical partnership with the right conductor (Giuseppe Sinopoli in Beethoven and Abbado in Chopin's *First Concerto*) brings characteristically spontaneous music-making, bursting with inner life. If the same composer's *F minor Concerto*, recorded ten years later in 1978, is rather less successful, she is back on form again in Tchaikovsky (with Dutoit), to produce a performance which has a genuine sense of scale and which balances poetry with excitement. Her temperament takes less readily to the Schumann *Concerto* (here with Rostropovich), a performance which has dynamism, vigour and colour, and delicacy in the slow movement, but which does not quite capture the work's more refined romantic feeling in the outer movements. Yet her Liszt *E flat Concerto* is surprisingly restrained, gripping without any barnstorming. She is perhaps at her very finest in Prokofiev's *Third Concerto* and hardly less impressive in the Ravel *G major*, a performance full of subtlety, but vigorous and outgoing too. Abbado was again her partner in the three last-mentioned works and together they found a rare musical symbiosis. DG have generally given Argerich's concertos excellent recording, and there is nothing here which will not provide stimulating repeated listening. All these performances (except the Chopin *Second Concerto*) are discussed in greater depth under their composer entries above.

Volume II: Chopin and Bach: CHOPIN: *Piano sonatas Nos. 2 in B flat min., Op. 35; 3 in B min., Op. 58; Barcarolle in F sharp, Op. 60; Scherzos Nos. 2 in B flat min., Op. 31; 3 in C sharp min., Op. 39; 24 Preludes, Op. 28; Preludes in C sharp min., Op. 45; in A flat, Op. posth.; Andante spianato & Grande Polonaise brillante, Op. 22; Polonaise No. 6 in A flat, Op. 53; Polonaise-Fantaisie in A flat, Op. 61; 3 Mazurkas, Op. 59.* BACH: *Toccata in C min., BWV 911; Partita No. 2 in C min., BWV 826; English suite No. 2 in A min., BWV 807.*
(M) **(*) DG 453 572-2 (3) [id.].

Argerich's accounts of the two Chopin *Sonatas* are fiery, impetuous and brilliant, with no want of poetic vision to commend them. Both, however, have a highly strung quality that will not be to all tastes. The *Preludes* show Argerich at her finest, full of individual insights. The *Scherzo No. 3* and *Barcarolle* are taken from her remarkable début LP recital of 1961 and are very impetuous indeed, and are also less easy to live with. She seems not to want to provide a firm musical control, but is carried away on a breath of wind. Many of the other pieces are played splendidly, with the *Scherzo No. 2* impressively demonstrating her technical command. Her Bach, too, is lively but well conceived. The digital remastering gives the piano-image striking presence, and the recording is resonant and full in timbre, although at fortissimo levels the timbre becomes hard.

Volume III: Music for piano solo and duo: SCHUMANN: *Kinderszenen, Op. 15; Kreisleriana, Op. 16; Piano sonata No. 2 in G min., Op. 22.* LISZT: *Piano sonata in B min.; Hungarian rhapsody No. 6.* BRAHMS: *Rhapsodies, Op. 79/1–2.* PROKOFIEV: *Toccata, Op. 11.* RAVEL: *Gaspard de la nuit; Jeux d'eau; Sonatine; Valses nobles et sentimentales. Ma mère l'oye; Rapsodie espagnole* (arr. 2 pianos & percussion). BARTOK: *Sonata for 2 pianos & percussion* (with Freire, Sadlo, Guggeis). TCHAIKOVSKY: *Nutcracker suite, Op.*

71a (arr. 2 pianos). RACHMANINOV: *Symphonic dances for 2 pianos, Op. 45* (with Economou).
(M) **(*) DG Analogue/Dig. 453 576-2 (4) [id.].

The third box contains much of interest. There is no doubting the instinctive flair or her intuitive feeling for Schumann. However, she is let down by an unpleasingly close recording of *Kinderszenen* and *Kreisleriana*. Her Ravel again shows her playing at its most subtle and perceptive, yet with a vivid palette, even if at times a little more poise would be welcome. Taken from her début recital of 1961, the Brahms *First Rhapsody* is explosively fast; then suddenly she puts the brakes on and provides most poetic playing in the central section. Such a barnstorming approach is more readily at home in the Prokofiev *Toccata*, and she goes over the top in the Liszt *Hungarian rhapsody* with a certain panache. In the Liszt *Sonata*, although the playing demonstrates an impressively responsive temperament, the work's lyrical feeling is all but submerged by the brilliantly impulsive virtuosity. Good but not exceptional recordings, a bit hard in the Liszt, though that may well reflect faithfully the percussive attack of Argerich's powerful hands. The Ravel arrangements (with percussion!) are done with eminently good taste, restraint and musical imagination but, all the same, is there a need for them at all? They are more interesting to hear once or twice than to repeat. The Bartók, though, has tremendous fire and intensity. The aural image is very good and discreetly balanced. The Tchaikovsky *Nutcracker* arrangement of Nicolas Economou works well. The playing is of a very high order. The Rachmaninov *Dances* are played with great temperament, and everything is marvellously alive and well thought out. There is much sensitivity and a lively sense of enjoyment in evidence, as well as great virtuosity. The recording is good.

CHOPIN: *Scherzo No. 3 in C sharp min., Op. 39; Barcarolle in F sharp min., Op. 60.* BRAHMS: *2 Rhapsodies, Op. 79.* PROKOFIEV: *Toccata, Op. 11.* RAVEL: *Jeux d'eau.* LISZT: *Hungarian rhapsody No. 6; Piano sonata in B min.*
(M) (**) DG 447 430-2 [id.].

This particular 'Legendary Recording' in DG's series of 'Originals' presents Argerich's remarkable début LP recital, recorded for DG in 1961. The phenomenal technique (she was twenty-one at the time) is as astonishing as the performances are musically exasperating. This artist's charismatic impulsiveness is well known, but in presenting Chopin and Brahms she is too impetuous by half, although *Jeux d'eau* brings a certain Ravelian magic. The Liszt *Sonata* has been added on; it dates from a decade later and yet again, although the bravura is breathtaking and there is no lack of spontaneity, the work's architecture and indeed its breadth are to some extent sacrificed to the insistent forward impulse of the playing. Good but not exceptional recording, a bit hard in the Liszt, though that may well reflect faithfully the percussive attack of Argerich's powerful hands.

'Duo Piano Extravaganza': MOZART: *Andante with 5 variations, K.501.* DEBUSSY: *En blanc et noir* (both with Stephen Kovacevich). BARTOK: *Sonata for 2 pianos and percussion* (with Kovacevich, Goudswaard, De Roo). RACHMANINOV: *Suite No. 2 for 2 pianos, Op. 17.* LUTOSLAWSKI: *Variations on a theme of Paganini.* RAVEL: *La valse* (all with Nelson Freire). BARTOK: *Concerto for 2 pianos and percussion* (with Freire, Labordus, Pustjens, Concg. O, Zinman). SAINT-SAENS: *Carnival of the animals* (with Freire, Kremer, Van Keulen, T. Zimmermann, Maisky, Hörtnagel, Grafenauer, Brunner, Steckeler & Salmen-Weber).
(B) *** Ph. Duo Dig./Analogue 446 557-2 (2) [(M) id. import].

Mozart's charming *Andante and variations* is here taken at a rather brisker tempo than usual, but the playing of Argerich and Kovacevich is unfailingly sensitive and vital, and they are equally imaginative in Debussy's *En blanc et noir*, which comes from the last years of his life and is full of unexpected touches. Then, joined by Willy Goudswaard and Michel de Roo, they give a strongly atmospheric and finely characterized performance of Bartók's *Sonata for two pianos and percussion*. At that point Argerich changes keyboard partners and, with Nelson Freire, two more percussionists and the Concertgebouw Orchestra under Zinman, offers us the *Concerto* which Bartók drew from his sonata. Comparing the two, one might wonder why a full orchestra was necessary, to add relatively little. Argerich and Freire continue with a dazzling virtuoso account of Rachmaninov's *Second Suite*, rushing the waltzes off their feet (the movement is marked *presto*, but they play it *prestissimo*). Their virtuosity is further tested by Lutoslawski's *Variations* for piano duo (based wittily on that famous Paganini tune), dating from 1941, and they are not found wanting: the result is exhilarating. Their contribution concludes charismatically with Ravel's own transcription of *La valse*. The recital ends with an affectionate but distinctly eccentric account of Saint-Saëns's *Carnival des animaux* presented in the composer's own original chamber version. From the very beginning, pacing is deliberately slow, the approach essentially refined (but with the instrumentalists adding a few jocular individual comments), and the *Tortoises* nearly grind to a halt. The *Kangaroos*, however, are very light on their feet, the *Aquarium* ethereally transparent, the *Cuckoo in the woods* mistily atmospheric, and the *Birds* flit about daintily. The self-consciously clumsy *Pianists* bring us back to the human world, and after the *Fossils* have had their witty gamble the *Swan* glides in very gently and gracefully on Mischa Maisky's elegant cello. The finale springs to life with sparkling rhythmic pointing and dashing roulades from the piano duo. This is perhaps not a *Carnival* for all seasons, but it is refreshingly different and, like the rest of this superb collection, it is very well recorded.

'Ballet gala', cond. Sir Georg Solti

'Ballet gala' (with (i) ROHCG O; (ii) BPO; (iii) L. Symphony Ch., LSO; (iv) Israel PO): (i) PONCHIELLI: *La Gioconda: Dance of the hours.* GOUNOD: *Faust: ballet music.* OFFENBACH (arr. Rosenthal): *Gaîté parisienne ballet music.* GLUCK: *Orfeo ed Euridice: Dance of the Furies; Dance of the Blessed Spirits.* (ii) MUSSORGSKY: *Khovanshchina: Dance of the Persian Slaves.* (iii) BORODIN: *Prince Igor: Polovtsian dances* (both ed. Rimsky-Korsakov). (iv) ROSSINI–RESPIGHI: *La Boutique fantasque* (complete ballet).
(B) **(*) Decca Double 448 942-2 (2) [(M) id. import].

Scintillating performances of high polish and prodigious vitality, recorded with great brilliance, mostly in the late 1950s. At times one might feel that the strings are overlit, although there is glowing woodwind colour and plenty of ambience, even if the Israel recording of *La Boutique fantasque* is drier than the rest. Yet they play very well, the strings are on very good form indeed, there are moments of affectionate charm, and this is easy to enjoy. The bright, intense Solti style suits the *Faust ballet music* less well (compared, say, with Beecham's affectionate coaxing) but the sparkle is in no doubt. Solti drives Offenbach's *Gaîté parisienne ballet music* hard, with strongly accented rhythms. But the Covent Garden Orchestra respond vivaciously (as they do in Ponchielli's *Dance of the hours*) and give a virtuoso performance: their bravura is certainly infectious, if sometimes a little breathless. Solti seldom recorded with the Berlin Philharmonic, and this great orchestra seems to have had a slight softening effect on his vibrant musical nature: the sensuously sinuous playing in the Mussorgsky/Rimsky-Korsakov *Dance of the Persian slaves* is certainly seductive. This derives from a 1959 concert called '*Romantic Russia*' which is surely a candidate for reissue in Decca's 'Classic Sound' series. The characterful Gluck dances come from the complete set of a decade later. Overall this programme is highly stimulating – Solti couldn't be dull even if he tried.

Bamberg Symphony Orchestra, Rudolf Kempe

'In memoriam': BRAHMS: *Symphony No. 2 in D, Op. 73; Variations on a theme of Haydn, Op. 56a.* SCHUBERT: *Symphony No. 8 (Unfinished).* SMETANA: *Má Vlast: From Bohemia's woods and fields.* MOZART: *Serenade No. 13 (Eine kleine Nachtmusik), K.525.* BIZET: *L'Arlésienne: suites 1–2.*
(B) *** RCA 74321 32771-2 (2) [(M) id. import].

A first-class tribute to a fine conductor, with the single proviso that the Bamberg violins in this 1963 recording are made to seem a bit emaciated above the stave; otherwise the sound is full and nicely resonant. The Brahms *Second* is a splendidly alive reading with a strong lyrical impetus, and the *Variations* are comparably successful. But it is the electrifying account of Schubert's *Unfinished* that resonates in the memory, immensely dramatic, yet with the opening and close of the second movement radiantly beautiful in its contrasting repose. The shorter works all go well, the Bizet the least individual, but still played with affection and style.

Baroque Music

'Music of the Baroque' (played by: (i) Orpheus CO; (ii) Simon Standage; (iii) David Reichenberg; (iv) Trevor Pinnock (harpsichord); (v) English Concert Ch.; (vi) English Concert, Trevor Pinnock; (vii) Söllscher (guitar), Camerata Bern, Füri; (viii) Hannes, Wolfgang & Bernhard Läubin, Simon Preston, Norbert Schmitt): (i) HANDEL: *Solomon: Arrival of the Queen of Sheba.* (vi) *Water Music: Allegro – Andante; Air; Bourrée; Hornpipe.* (i) *Xerxes: Largo.* (v, vi) *Messiah: Hallelujah chorus.* (vi) *Music for the royal fireworks: La Réjouissance.* (iii; iv; vi) *Oboe concerto No. 1 (Adagio; Allegro).* (vi) *Concerto grosso, Op. 6/12 in B min. (Aria; Larghetto e piano).* (i) PACHELBEL: *Canon in D.* (viii) MOURET: *Rondeau.* J. S. BACH: (i) *Jesu, joy of man's desiring.* (vi) *Brandenburg concerto No. 3 in G (Allegro).* PURCELL: *Sound the trumpet, sound.* (ii; vi) VIVALDI: *The Four seasons: Winter (Largo).* (vii) *Lute concerto in D (Largo).* (i) ALBINONI (arr. GIAZOTTO): *Adagio in G min.* CORELLI: *Christmas concerto, Op. 6/8 (Allegro; Pastorale; Largo).* (iv) DAQUIN: *Le Coucou.*
(B) *** DG Classikon Dig. 449 842-2; *449 842-4* [(M) id. import].

This 75-minute concert draws on various digital recordings made during the 1980s to make a most agreeable entertainment. The various items have all been issued previously, and their performance pedigrees, on either modern or original instruments, cannot be gainsaid. The opening *Arrival of the Queen of Sheba* and the elegantly played Pachelbel *Canon* feature the Orpheus Chamber Orchestra, but Pinnock's suite from the Handel *Water music* is equally persuasive in demonstrating the advantages of period instruments in baroque repertoire. Such contrasts are aurally stimulating and, with plenty of favourite items included, this makes a very successful bargain sampler, when all the music is consistently well played and recorded. However, the lack of proper documentation is a drawback: the two excellent vocal soloists in Purcell's *Sound the trumpet* are unnamed.

BBC Concert Orchestra, Vernon Handley

'The essential British light music': GOODWIN: *633 Squadron* (film theme). ELLIS: *Coronation Scot.* FARNON: *Westminster waltz; Jumping bean.* COATES: *London suite: Knightsbridge march; Covent Garden. By the sleepy lagoon. Dam busters march.* ANCLIFFE: *Nights of gladness (waltz).* HOPE: *Mexican hat dance.* BINGE: *Sailing by; Elizabethan serenade.* HAYDN WOOD: *The Horse Guards, Whitehall.* DUNCAN: *Little suite: March.* BENJAMIN: *Jamaican rumba.* TOMLINSON: *Concert jig.* WHITE: *Puffin' Billy.* COLLINS: *Vanity Fair.* BUCALOSSI: *Grasshopper's dance.* Arthur WOOD: *Barwick Green.*
(M) *** Classic fM Dig. 76505 57003-2 [id.].

There are now several nostalgic CD collections of these delightfully tuneful musical lollipops, many associated with radio or TV programmes as signature tunes, but none better than this. Ernest Bucalossi's *Grasshopper's dance*, for instance, a novelty number from a bygone age, now unexpectedly conjures up dancing milk-bottles in a TV commercial. Vernon Handley conducts everything with zest. Indeed some might feel that his pacing of Ron Goodwin's *633 Squadron* title-sequence (perhaps the most memorable horn-theme since Richard Strauss) is a fraction too fast; yet it is thrilling when played with such panache. However, Robert Farnon's *Westminster waltz* brings a relaxed charm, and Peter Hope's *Mexican hat dance* has an oboe interlude as its centrepiece, played most delectably here. Handley presents Ronald Binge's *Sailing by* with seductive languor, while the *Elizabethan serenade* has winning delicacy, as has Anthony Collins's *Vanity Fair*. Arthur Wood's *Barwick Green*, indelibly associated with 'The Archers', begins with an introductory fanfare and is re-scored for woodwind. The middle section is omitted, and not all will respond to this new arrangement. The Eric Coates marches are perhaps most famous of all. Handley's alert vigour (particularly in the *Dam busters*) is infectious, yet his vivacity doesn't prevent him from a grand broadening for the final presentation of the big tune at the close.

BBC Symphony Orchestra

'BBC Proms Centenary 1895–1995': BERLIOZ: *Symphonie funèbre et triomphale:* 3rd movt: *Apothéose* (cond. Sir John Pritchard). TCHAIKOVSKY: *Nutcracker suite* (cond. Sir Malcolm Sargent). ELGAR: *Symphony No. 1 in A flat* (cond. Sir Adrian Boult). GLUCK: *Orfeo ed Euridice: Che disse? ch'ascolta . . . Addio, addio, o miei sospiri* (J. Baker; cond. Raymond Leppard). WAGNER: *Tannhäuser: Overture & Venusberg music* (with BBC Women's Chorus; cond. Sir Thomas Beecham). JANACEK: *Sinfonietta* (cond. Rudolf Kempe). SHOSTAKOVICH: *Tahiti trot* (arr. of YOUMANS: *Tea for two*; cond. Gennady Rozhdestvensky). R. STRAUSS: *Der Rosenkavalier: suite* (Hallé O, Sir John Barbirolli).
(M) *(**) Carlton Classics DMCD 98 (2) [id.].

Though this collection of broadcast performances from the Proms on two generously filled CDs has a number of recordings to cherish, the choice of items is unrepresentative to the point of being bizarre. Why no recordings of Sir Henry Wood, when Beecham – hardly a conductor much associated with the Proms – is included with the *Tannhäuser overture* and *Venusburg music*? Dating from 1954, it comes with atmospheric chorus. Surely Sir Colin Davis and Basil Cameron, for long Prom associates of Wood, should also be here? Yet there is much to enjoy, even if the upper-mid-price (£19.99 suggested price) is rather high for such a mixed bag.

The gem of the collection is Boult's 1976 Prom performance of Elgar's *First Symphony*. The tape-hiss may be high, but it is not enough to get in the way of one of the most passionate performances of Elgar on disc, with the weight of brass vividly caught. The great melodies of the slow movement are warmly flexible, moulded with more loving rubato than Boult ever allowed himself in the studio, while the finale surges to a thrilling close that brings a gulp to the throat, fully justifying the wild Prom cheer at the end. The Pritchard Berlioz, dating from 1983, is most atmospheric, and though Sargent's 1966 account of Tchaikovsky's *Nutcracker suite* (surely inappropriate representation) is winningly fresh, the audience is maddeningly intrusive and noisy. The '*Addio*' aria from Gluck's *Orfeo* draws from Dame Janet Baker not just her characteristic intensity but a dazzling display of crisply defined coloratura. The Beecham *Tannhäuser* item (with offstage women's chorus included in the *Venusberg music*) has obvious magic, and is aptly set against Barbirolli's ripely flamboyant account with the Hallé of Strauss's *Rosenkavalier suite*. Rudolf Kempe in Janáček's *Sinfonietta* is welcome too, a most sympathetic reading, even if this music needs sharper focus. The selection ends with a gem, Rozhdestvensky's scintillating account – allegedly the first British performance – of Shostakovich's arrangement of *Tea for two*, a vintage Prom event. Recordings are of good BBC quality.

BBC Symphony Orchestra, or (i) Light Symphony Orchestra, Sir Adrian Boult

'English gramophone premières': BLISS: *Music for strings*. VAUGHAN WILLIAMS: *Job: A Masque for dancing*. (i) Ethel SMYTH: *2 Interlinked French folk melodies; Interlude from Entente Cordiale*.
(M) (***) Dutton Lab. mono CDAX 8016 [id. full price].

Here are two key works in the Boult discography: the Bliss *Music for strings* and Vaughan Williams's *Job*, sounding better than they have ever done before. The Bliss was premièred at the Salzburg Festival in 1935, and Boult and the strings of the BBC Symphony Orchestra recorded it two years later at the Abbey Road Studios. While later stereo recordings have improved on the sound of Bliss's string sonorities, no one has surpassed the intensity of the playing here. Doubtless the war held up the recording of *Job*, written in 1930, which Vaughan Williams had dedicated to Sir Adrian, for it was not committed to disc until 1946, the first of four recordings Boult made of it, and in some ways the freshest. A selfrecommending issue for all admirers of this fine British conductor.

BBC Symphony Orchestra and Chorus, BBC Singers, James Loughran

'The last night of the Proms': SULLIVAN/MACKERRAS: *Pineapple Poll: suite*. LAMBERT: *The Rio Grande* (with Peter Donohoe, piano). IBERT: *Divertissement*. ELGAR: *Pomp and circumstance march No. 1*. WOOD: *Fantasia on British Sea Songs*. ARNE: *Rule Brittania*. PARRY: *Jerusalem* (both with Benjamin Luxon). TRAD.: *Auld Lang Syne*.
(B) *** BBC Radio Classics 15656 9191-2 [(M) id.].

If you want a memento of 'The last night of the Proms', this is the one to go for. It is in fact drawn from four 'Last nights', all conducted by James Loughran, in 1977, 1979, 1982 and 1984. At that period the Promenaders were still well behaved and they don't spoil any of the music. There is a 'peep' at the end of the opening number of *Pineapple Poll* and a whistle after *Belaye's hornpipe*, but it adds a bit of spice to Loughran's performance, which lacks something in panache. However, *The Rio Grande*, Constant Lambert's masterly concoction for piano, female soloist (here unnamed), chorus and orchestra is highly successful, with Peter Donohoe just the man to relish the work's jazzy inflexions. In Ibert's *Divertissment* the brass rightly camp it up and the result at the end with the unexpected obbligato police whistle (Ibert's own idea) causes great hilarity. Benjamin Luxon is the excellent male soloist in the famous vocal pieces in which the audience participate with unrestrained fervour, from *Land of hope and glory* to a thrilling *Jerusalem*. There is unexplained laughter at the end of the first verse of the former, but this CD spectacularly captures the spirit of the occasion. *Auld Lang Syne* is throat-catching, but the most touching moment of all is when in the Wood *Fantasia* everyone hums very gently to '*There's no place like home*'.

Belgian Radio & TV Philharmonic Orchestra, Brussels, Alexander Rahbari

Romantic symphonic music from Antwerp: MORTELMANS: *Spring idyll*. ALPAERTS: *Pallieter: Wedding feast*. VAN HOOF: *1st Symphonic suite*. BLOCKX: *Milenka: Flemish Fair*. STERNFIELD: *Song and dance at the court of Mary from Burgundy*.
(BB) ** Discover Dig. DICD 920100 [id.].

Flemish rhapsodies: BRUSSELMANS: *Flemish rhapsody*. SCHOEMAKER: *Flemish rhapsody*. DE JONG: *Flemish rhapsody*. ABSILL: *Flemish rhapsody*. ROUSSEL: *Flemish rhapsody*. DE BOECK: *Flemish rhapsody*.
(BB) **(*) Discover DICD 920101 [id.].

This is all unknown repertoire – easy-going late nineteenth- or twentieth-century music from Belgium. On the first CD, Mortelmans' *Spring idyll* is lyrically appealing but perhaps a shade extended for its thematic content, the Jef Van Hoof and Jan Blockx suites agreeably inventive but innocuous. By far the most attractive music comes in the suite of *Song and dance from Burgundy*, nicely scored and piquantly harmonized dances by Susato and his sixteenth-century contemporaries, somewhat comparable with Respighi's *Ancient airs and dances*.

The Flemish rhapsodies all use folk material very effectively, although Brusselmans employs themes of his own invention, written in folk style. All these works are colourfully orchestrated and make agreeable listening, using jolly tunes which in flavour are often like Christmas carols. By far the most striking is the work by the Frenchman, Albert Roussel, which has a characteristic touch of harmonic astringency to tickle the ear. The playing of the Brussels orchestra under Rahbari is enthusiastic yet does not lack finesse, and the recording has an attractive concert-hall ambience and balance. It is not always too sharply defined in some of the more elaborately scored climaxes of the rhapsodies, but the effect is natural. The documentation is excellent.

Berlin Philharmonic Orchestra, Herbert von Karajan

'Meditation' (Overtures and Intermezzi): J. STRAUSS Jr: *Der Zigeunerbaron overture*. MASSENET: *Thaïs: Méditation* (with Anne-Sophie Mutter). CHERUBINI: *Anacréon overture*. WEBER: *Der Freischütz overture*. SCHMIDT: *Notre Dame: Intermezzo*. PUCCINI: *Intermezzi: Suor Angelica; Manon Lescaut*. MASCAGNI: *L'amico Fritz: Intermezzo*. HUMPERDINCK: *Hansel and Gretel overture*. MENDELSSOHN: *Hebrides overture (Fingal's Cave), Op. 26*
(M) *(*) EMI Dig./Analogue CDM7 64629-2.

A curiously planned if generous (78 minutes) programme, deriving from three different sources. It opens with a rather weighty analogue account of Strauss's *Zigeunerbaron overture*, then moves on to the digital items, first the *Méditation* from *Thaïs* (with Anne-Sophie Mutter a gently restrained soloist), immediately followed by the *Anacréon overture*, with textures reminiscent of plum pudding. The Weber and Humperdinck overtures, too, are disappointing, the first lacking electricity, the second charm. The *Intermezzi* are much more successful, played very passionately and sumptuously, with the ample recording providing somewhat over-nourished string-textures with a touch of grit in the treble. The best piece by far is the closing *Hebrides overture*, recorded much earlier (in 1960) and beautifully managed.

LISZT: *Les Préludes, G.97*. SIBELIUS: *Finlandia, Op. 26; Pélleas et Mélisande: suite*. SMETANA: *Má vlast: Vltava*.
(M) *** DG (IMS) Dig. 445 550-2.

This is an outstanding concert, showing Karajan at his most charismatic; and the orchestral playing is certainly in a class of its own. In the performance of *Pelléas et Mélisande* we have a version of Sibelius's subtle and atmospheric score that can compare with the classic Beecham version, originally dating from 1957. Indeed in certain movements, *Spring in the park* and the *Pastorale*, it not only matches Sir Thomas but almost surpasses him. The *Pastorale* is altogether magical, and there is plenty of mystery in the third movement, *At the seashore*, omitted from the Beecham version. Some may find the opening movement, *At the castle gate*, a little too imposing, but the fervour and eloquence of the playing should win over most listeners. The recording is very striking, with great clarity and presence. Karajan is also at his finest in this performance of *Vltava*, and there is some radiant playing from the Berlin orchestra in the moonlit stillness before the river approaches the St John's Rapids. *Les Préludes* is vibrant but a little brash. *Finlandia* reinforces the feeling that this Berlin Philharmonic/Karajan partnership has never been equalled, not even by Toscanini and the NBC Symphony Orchestra.

(i) Berlin Philharmonic Orchestra; (ii) Berlin RIAS Symphony Orchestra; (iii) Berlin Radio Symphony Orchestra; (iv) Vienna Philharmonic Orchestra; (v) South German Radio Symphony Orchestra, Ferenc Fricsay

'Ferenc Fricsay Portrait': (i) BEETHOVEN: *Symphony No. 9* (with Irmgard Seefried, Maureen Forrester, Ernst Haefliger, Dietrich Fischer-Dieskau, St Hedwig's Cathedral Ch.) (stereo; 445 401-2).

BARTOK: *Violin concerto No. 2* (with Tibor Varga); (ii) *Dance suite; Cantata profana* (with Helmut Krebs, Dietrich Fischer-Dieskau, RIAS Chamber Ch., St Hedwig's Cathedral Ch.) (mono; 445 402-2).

(ii) R. STRAUSS: *Don Juan, Op. 20; Duet-Concertino for clarinet, bassoon, strings and harp* (with Heinrich Geuser, Willi Fugmann); *Burleske, Op. 11* (with Margrit Weber); (i) *Till Eulenspiegel, Op. 28* (mono; 445 403-2).

(ii) LIEBERMANN: *Furioso*. BLACHER: *Paganini variations, Op. 26*. EGK: *French suite*. (iii) VON EINEM: *Piano concerto, Op. 20* (with Gerty Herzog); *Ballade for orchestra, Op. 23* (mono/stereo; 445 404-2).

STRAVINSKY: (ii) *The Rite of spring; Petrushka* (1947 version); (iii) *Movements for piano and orchestra* (with Margrit Weber) (mono/stereo; 445 405-2).

(ii) ROSSINI: *Overtures: Il barbiere di Siviglia; Tancredi; Il Signor Bruschino; La gazza ladra; Semiramide*. VERDI: *Overtures: Nabucco; La traviata* (Preludes to Acts I & III); *La forza del destino; Aida; I vespri siciliani* (mono; 445 406-2).

BRAHMS: (iv) *Symphony No. 2 in D, Op. 73;* (iii) *Variations on a theme of Haydn, Op. 56a; Alto rhapsody, Op. 53* (with Maureen Forrester, RIAS Chamber Ch.) (mono; 445 407-2).

MOZART: (ii) *Requiem Mass No. 19 in D min., K.626* (with Elisabeth Grümmer, Gertrude Pitzinger, Helmut Krebs, Hans Hotter, RIAS Chamber Ch., St Hedwig's Cathedral Ch.); (iii) *Adagio and fugue in C min., K.546* (mono/stereo; 445 408-2).

TCHAIKOVSKY: (i) *Symphony No. 6 (Pathétique);* (ii) *Violin concerto in D, Op. 35* (with Yehudi Menuhin) (mono; 445 409-2).

KODALY: (ii) *Dances of Marosszék;* (iii) *Symphony; Psalmus hungaricus, Op. 13* (with Ernst Haefliger, St Hedwig's Cathedral Ch.) (mono/stereo 445 410-2).

Bonus CD: (v) SMETANA: *Má Vlast* (extracts): *Vltava* (rehearsal and concert performance) (mono; 445 411-2).
❁ (M) *** DG mono/stereo 445 400-2 (10).

Although many younger collectors know their Furtwängler, Beecham and Monteux, the Hungarian conductor, Ferenc Fricsay, never enjoyed cult status. The appearance of this ten-CD box offers an excellent opportunity to evaluate him, and DG deserve congratulations on its planning and presentation – and originally on making each disc separately available as well – although, alas, this no longer applies. To many, we are sure, it will come as something of a revelation: indeed, although we admired and respected Fricsay in the 1950s and '60s, coming back to these performances (or, in some cases, hearing them for the first time) serves afresh to reaffirm his stature.

One striking feature of the collection is the sheer quality of the sound produced by the DG engineers of the 1950s. One thing is quite self-evident: that the original mono pressings did scant justice to their achievement. The original LPs did not reproduce such vivid detail, such presence or body. Among the riches that are assembled here, one of the surprises is *The Rite of spring* (445 405-2), far removed from any vestige of the current view of the work as some kind of sanitized orchestral showpiece. This brings this score alive with a freshness and ferocity that remind one of the first encounter with this extraordinary score. *The Rite* is far more savage and powerful than Markevitch's celebrated account with the Philharmonia that came out at the same time. Alas, it is not now available separately.

Naturally the contemporary music with which Fricsay was specially associated must have first claim. The DG Dokumente version of the Bartók *Divertimento* and *Music for strings, percussion and celeste* does not prepare you for the excellence of the Bartók disc here (445 402-2). His *Dance suite* is one of the best ever committed to disc, wonderfully idiomatic, vital and yet relaxed; the *Cantata profana* too is excellent, though Tibor Varga's account of the *Violin concerto* does not displace Menuhin. Of particular value is the disc coupling Rolf Liebermann's *Furioso*, Werner Egk's *French suite*, two von Einem works, and Boris Blacher's *Paganini variations* (445 404-2). The Blacher was almost a popular warhorse in the

1950s, so frequently did it appear; it is a resourceful and diverting piece which, like his engaging *Concertante musik*, should be a popular repertory piece. Apart from these and the Kodály (445 410-2), which are effortlessly idiomatic and thrillingly alive, Fricsay is no less impressive in the mainstream repertoire.

In Richard Strauss he is hardly less persuasive, and the disc devoted to that master is particularly welcome for a delightful performance of the *Duet-Concertino for clarinet, bassoon, strings and harp*. We remember what an enormous impact his splendid Tchaikovsky *Pathétique* made on collectors when it first appeared: it remains one of the most vital and intense of all recorded performances and should now be reissued in DG's 'Originals' series of Legendary Performances. The Brahms *Second Symphony*, one of his later recordings (1961), which has not appeared before in Britain, has a rich, lyrical warmth and a sense of forward movement worthy of Bruno Walter. Needless to say, the box is not comprehensive: there are Mozart symphonies and operas, now in currency separately, and the three Bartók *Piano concertos* with Géza Anda reappear among DG's 'Originals'. Those buying the ten CDs as a package get a bonus disc, which includes a 1960 performance of Smetana's *Vltava*, made with the orchestra of Süddeutsches Rundfunk, with an hour-long rehearsal in their Stuttgart studios. It is easy to follow but there is a précis of his remarks in both English and French. We do not normally give rosettes for this kind of compilation, but this should certainly have one in recognition of the care lavished on it, and the artistic and technical excellence of these performances. The only CD now available separately is Beethoven's *Choral Symphony*.

Berlin Philharmonic Orchestra, Paris Conservatoire Orchestra or Belgian Radio & TV Orchestra, André Cluytens

'Artist profile': BEETHOVEN: *Symphony No. 6 in F (Pastoral), Op. 68.* BERLIOZ: *L'enfance du Christ: La fuite en Egypte: Overture; Shepherds' farewell* (with René Duclos Ch.). DEBUSSY: *Jeux.* FRANCK: *Le chasseur maudit.* PIERNE: *Concertstück, Op. 39, for harp and orchestra* (with Annie Challan). ROUSSEL: *Bacchus et Ariane, Op. 43: suite No. 2; Sinfonietta, Op. 52; Le festin de l'araignée (fragments symphoniques), Op. 17.*

✿ (B) *** EMI (SIS) CZS5 68220-2 (2) [(M) id. import].

There is something special about this compilation. André Cluytens was a much-underrated conductor and, though his account of the *Pastoral Symphony* with the Berlin Philharmonic was highly acclaimed on its first appearance, he was generally taken for granted during his lifetime. His 1957 recording of the *Pastoral* with the same orchestra was in mono, and some would say it was even more inspired. In any event it made a sufficient impression to encourage EMI to re-record it in 1960 and then to go on to do a complete cycle. The stereo version (offered here) is radiant and glowing – as good as any made during the 1960s, and better than many that followed. His account of *Jeux* with the Orchestre de la Société des Concerts du Conservatoire was vastly more atmospheric than the Boulez account with the Philharmonia (CBS) which came out at much the same period, though some of the subtlety, delicacy and the slight haze of the old LPs have been lost in the transfer. (The original opens out and has much greater range, but the present disc is still very good and reproduces smoothly on most machines.) The Pierné rarity is also beautifully done and makes a welcome addition to the catalogue. The second *Bacchus et Ariane* suite is both exhilarating and atmospheric, and never has Roussel's spider feasted so sumptuously and in such an exotic ambience as it does here. Let us hope that EMI will restore Cluytens' account of Debussy's *Images* and the Roussel *Third* and *Fourth Symphonies*. At full price these two discs would be well worth having, but for so modest an outlay they represent an altogether outstanding bargain. One of the most rewarding issues of the year.

(i) Berlin Philharmonic, (ii) Royal Philharmonic, (iii) Vienna Philharmonic or (iv) Philharmonia Orchestra, Rudolf Kempe

R. STRAUSS: (i) *Till Eulenspiegels lustige Streiche; Don Quixote* (with Paul Tortelier). (ii) SMETANA: *The Bartered Bride: Overture and suite.* HUMPERDINCK: *Hänsel und Gretel: Overture and suite.* (iii) LEHAR: *Gold and Silver waltz.* Josef STRAUSS: *Sphärenklänge waltz.* WEBER: *Oberon overture.* (iv) HAYDN: *Symphony No. 104 in D (London).*

(B) *** EMI (SIS) CZS5 68736-2 (2) [(M) id. import].

Kempe's recording of *Don Quixote* with Tortelier, recorded as early as 1958 but sounding remarkably full and fresh, is one of the great classics of the gramophone. *Till Eulenspiegel*, more than almost any other recorded performance, conveys the wit and sparkle of the music in playing that is brilliant but never forced. And the rest of the programme here is hardly less treasurable, the *Bartered Bride* music played with plenty of Slavonic sparkle balanced by Kempe's characteristic warmth, which latter quality also suits the rare Humperdinck suite so readily. The two *Waltzes* are affectionately mannered but still most enjoyable, and Weber's *Oberon overture*, with its romantic opening horn solo, comes from another area of repertoire in which Kempe is thoroughly at home. The Haydn symphony is a heavyweight account by today's standards but the orchestral playing is first class: outer movements are rhythmically buoyant and the lovely slow movement is attractively mellow. Excellent sound throughout.

Boskovsky Ensemble, Willi Boskovsky

'Viennese bonbons': J. STRAUSS, Sr: *Chinese galop; Kettenbrücke Waltz; Eisele und Beisele Sprünge. Cachucha galop.* J. STRAUSS, Jr: *Weine Gemüths waltz; Champagne galop; Salon polka.* LANNER: *Styrian dances; Die Werber & Marien waltzes; Bruder halt galop.* MOZART: *3 Contredanses, K.462; 4 German dances, K.600/1 & 3; K.605/1; K.611.* SCHUBERT: *8 Waltzes & Ländler.*
(M) *** Van. 8.8015.71 [OVC 8015].

This is a captivating selection of the most delightful musical confectionery imaginable. The ensemble is a small chamber group, similar to that led by the Strausses, and the playing has an appropriately intimate Viennese atmosphere. The transfer is impeccable and the recording from the early 1960s, made in the Baumgarten Hall, Vienna, is fresh, smooth and clear, with a nice bloom on sound which is never too inflated.

'Rare old Vienna dances, Vol. 2: *The charm of old Vienna':* Johann STRAUSS Sr: *Gitana galop; Annen polka; Hofball-Tänze; Seufzer galop.* MAYER: *Schnofler-Tanz'.* HAYDN: *Zingarese Nos. 1, 6 & 8; Katherinen Tänze Nos. 4, 6, 8 & 12.* SCHUBERT: *Tänze from Opp. 9, 18, 67, 77 & 127; Ecossaisen, Op. 49.* LANNER: *Abendsterner waltz; Cerrito polka; Neue Wiener Ländler, Op. 1.* STELZMULLER: *Stelzmüller Tanz'.*
(M) **(*) Van. 08 8016.71 [OVC 8016].

Boskovsky's series of recordings of Viennese light music continues to intoxicate with their lightness of touch and transparency of texture. The style is not so far removed from a Schrammeln orchestra, and the recording is warm and lively throughout. However, the present disc is a little below the very high standard of Volumes 1 and 3, containing a certain amount of wallpaper music, while the CD transfers are not always too smooth, occasionally bringing a touch of edge to Boskovsky's violin, with textures not cleanly focused in the Schubert *Ecossaisen* and Haydn *Katherinen Tänze*. Even so, there are some delectable lollipops here, notably the opening *Gitana galop* of Johann Strauss Senior with its horn obbligato, and his very catchy *Annen polka* (not to be confused with his son's piece of the same name). Lanner's *Cerrito polka*, too, is most engaging, and Mayer's *Schnofler-Tanz'* have an almost decadent touch of schmalz.

'Rare old Vienna dances, Vol. 3: *Greetings from old Vienna':* SCHUBERT: *Gratzer galop; Ecossaisen; Galop.* LANNER: *2 Mazurkas; Malapou galop. Hansjörgel polka.* Johann STRAUSS Sr: *Badjaderen Waltz, Op. 53.* Johann STRAUSS Jr: *Scherz polka, Op. 72.* Josef STRAUSS: *Marien-Klänge waltz, Op. 214.* PAYER: *Galanterie Waltz.* BEETHOVEN: *6 Contredanses. Four 'Dances of old Vienna'* by STELZMULLER, GRUBER and ANON.
(M) *** Van. 08.8017.71 [OVC 8017].

This is just as delightful as the first issue in Boskovsky's delectable series. The opening Schubert *Gratzer galop* will entice anyone, played as lightly as this, and Lanner's pieces are equally sparkling. Hieronymus Payer's *Galanterie waltz* is aptly named and quite charming, as are the four brief '*Dances of old Vienna*', with two included from the composer of the carol, *Silent night*. Even with this intimate group of strings, Boskovsky manages the authentically silky Viennese lilt, notably in the *Marien-Klänge waltz* of Josef Strauss, but father Johann's *Badjaderen* is hardly less winning. Wonderfully natural and transparent sound, immaculately transferred to CD.

Boston Pops Orchestra, Arthur Fiedler

'The Collection'.
(M) *** RCA 09026 68011-2 (3).

'Marches in Hi-Fi': VERDI: *Aida: Grand march.* HERBERT: *March of the toys.* SOUSA: *Semper fidelis; The Stars and stripes forever.* TCHAIKOVSKY: *Marche miniature.* TRAD.: *Yankee doodle.* MORSE: *Up the street.* BERLIOZ: *Rákóczy march.* RODGERS: *March of the Siamese children.* IPPOLITOV-IVANOV: *Procession of the Sardar.* PLANQUETTE: *Le régiment de Sambre-et-Meuse.* BEETHOVEN: *Turkish march.*

ALFORD: *Colonel Bogey*. EMMETT: *Dixie*. GOULD: *American salute*. GERSHWIN: *Strike up the band!*. MENDELSSOHN: *War march of the priests*. SIBELIUS: *Alla marcia*. ROZSA: *March of the charioteers*. (09026 61249-2).

'Hi-Fi Arthur Fiedler': RIMSKY-KORSAKOV: *Le coq d'or* (suite). ROSSINI: *Overture: William Tell*. TCHAIKOVSKY: *Marche slave*. CHABRIER: *España*. LISZT: *Hungarian rhapsody No. 2; Rákóczy march*. (09026 61497-2).

OFFENBACH: *Gaîté parisienne* (ballet, arr. Rosenthal) complete. ROSSINI/RESPIGHI: *La boutique fantasque*. (09026 61847-2).

These three 'Living Stereo' CDs come in a slipcase to celebrate the work of a conductor, much liked by the American musical public, who was in some ways the Boston equivalent of Sir Henry Wood in England. Over several decades he did much to promote the kind of popular concerts that would introduce new generations of potential music-lovers to enter Symphony Hall, knowing they would enjoy themselves. His musical flair was never better celebrated than in his sparkling coupling of ballet music by Offenbach/ Rosenthal and Rossini/Respighi, and that CD is available separately (as are the others). The exuberant and colourful collection of marches of all kinds is also very well programmed and most enjoyable, and it is a pity that RCA have chosen '*Hi-Fi Arthur Fiedler*' to make up the triptych. The opening *Coq d'or suite*, although atmospheric, generates only a low level of tension and, while the other pot-boilers included are vivid enough, there is nothing here in any way strikingly individual, although the orchestral playing is consistently alert. The remastering is impressively managed, for these recordings all come from the early years of stereo, mainly from the late 1950s.

'Classics for children': SAINT-SAENS: *Carnival of the animals* (with verses by Ogden Nash, spoken by Hugh Downs; Leo Litwin & Samuel Lipman, pianos). BRITTEN: *Young person's guide to the orchestra* (with commentary by Eric Crozier, spoken by Hugh Downs). GRIEG: *Peer Gynt suite No. 1, Op. 46; Suite No. 2: Solveig's song* (with Eileen Farrell). LOESSER: *Hans Christian Andersen* (film music): Medley, arr. HAYMAN: *Kid stuff* (suite).
(M) **(*) RCA 09026 68131-2 [id.].

A very successful collection, well designed to appeal to quite young children. Hugh Downs, speaking directly and with no suggestion of precociousness, makes Ogden Nash's witticisms concerning the Saint-Saëns menagerie seem less contrived than usual and occasionally raises a smile. He is also excellent with Crozier's description of Britten's orchestra. Both works are very well played, the Saint-Saëns with vigour and enthusiasm and bringing a fine cello solo in *Le Cygne* from Martin Hoherman. The only reservation is the resonant empty-hall sound, which is flattering at modest levels but becomes a bit harsh in fortissimos, with the famous Boston acoustics not always tamed. But children are unlikely to mind, and we enjoyed the programme throughout, not least the string of good tunes at the end (Hayman's suite includes the *Children's marching song* from Rodgers' *The King and I*, *Mary had a little lamb* and *Alouette*). The only orchestral blot is the playing of the solo horn in *Morning* from *Peer Gynt*, which sounds nervous and wobbly: clearly a sub-principal had taken over for the recording. Otherwise almost full marks.

'Pops Caviar': BORODIN: *In the Steppes of Central Asia; Prince Igor: Overture; Polovtsian dances*. RIMSKY-KORSAKOV: *Russian Easter Festival overture; Flight of the bumble bee*. KHACHATURIAN: *Gayaneh: suite. Masquerade: galop*. TCHAIKOVSKY: *Eugene Onegin: Polonaise. Sleeping Beauty: waltz*.
(M) **(*) RCA 09026 68132-2 [id.].

Vibrant performances, with the Khachaturian *Gayaneh suite* (Fiedler at his most ebullient) and Tchaikovsky items standing out. The Borodin pieces could be more romantic, but they are certainly alive and very well played. The 'Living stereo' from the late 1950s is extremely vivid.

'Pops Christmas party': Leroy ANDERSON: *A Christmas festival; Sleigh ride*. TCHAIKOVSKY: *Nutcracker* (ballet): extended excerpts. SCOTT: *Toy trumpet*. HUMPERDINCK: *Hänsel und Gretel: Dream pantomime*. MOZART: *Sleigh ride*. MARKS: *Rudolph the red-nosed reindeer*. COOTS: *Santa Claus is coming to town*.
(M) ** RCA 09026 61685-2 [id.].

Introduced with Leroy Anderson's brightly scored Christmas pot-pourri, this 72-minute selection centres on Fiedler's extremely vivid 1956 set of highlights from the *Nutcracker*, as seasonal an offering as you could wish. The early stereo lacks something in opulence, but the zest and character of the playing compensates. Some of the other items are less repeatable, but they are presented with plenty of spirit.

'Fiedler encores': SIBELIUS: *Finlandia*. GRIEG: *Peer Gynt suite No. 1; Suite No. 2: Solveig's song*. DVORAK: *Slavonic Dance, Op. 46/1*. SMETANA: *Má vlast: Vltava*. VAUGHAN WILLIAMS: *English folk song suite*. IVES: *Variations on 'America'*.
(M) **(*) Decca Phase Four 448 952-2 [id.].

These recordings derive from a pair of LPs originally published in 1975 and 1978. The 1975 performance of the *Peer Gynt* excerpts is direct, alive and spontaneous. It is recorded with exceptional life and vividness and is very enjoyable indeed. There are more tender accounts of *Solveig's song* available, but that is the only reservation. The other items make a characteristically lively concert. Fiedler always keeps the pot boiling, even if his balance of various ingredients lacks subtlety at times. The outer movements of the *English folksongs suite* come off with robust vigour, and he gives a splendidly rumbustious account of Ives's *Variations on 'America'*. The overall balance is forward, which precludes wide dynamic contrasts but ensures good projection and detail if not the last degree of refinement.

'Slaughter on 10th Ave': RODGERS: *On Your Toes: Slaughter on 10th Avenue*. GOULD: *Interplay (Gavotte; Blues)*. BERNSTEIN: *Fancy Free (Galop; Waltz; Danzon)*. FALLA: *Three Cornered Hat: 3 Dances*. SHOSTAKOVICH: *Age of Gold: Polka*. COPLAND: *Rodeo: Hoe-down*. GINASTERA: *Estancia: Malambo*. KHACHATURIAN: *Gayaneh: Sabre dance*.
(M) **(*) RCA 09026 68550-2 [id.].

'Boston Tea Party': NICOLAI: *The Merry Wives of Windsor: overture*. VAUGHAN WILLIAMS: *Fantasia on Greensleeves*. BOLZONI: *Minuet*. LEHAR: *The Count of Luxemburg: Waltzes; The Merry Widow: Waltz*. arr. HAYMAN: *Moonglow* and *Theme from 'Picnic'; The Pajama Game: Hernando's hideway*. BALFE: *The Bohemian Girl: Overture*.
(M) ** RCA 09026 68793-2 [id.].

These two 'Pops' concerts both date from 1958 and '*The Boston Tea Party*' found its way into our very first hardback (1960) *Stereo Record Guide*. We commented then that *Greensleeves* is played at a very much slower tempo than is usual in England, revealing an unexpected dignity which is endearing, but that the highlight of the disc is Balfe's attractive (and seldom heard) *Bohemian Girl overture*, which comes up as bright as a new pin, as indeed does *The Merry Wives*. The programme is indelibly dated by the inclusion of the hits of the time – *Moonglow*, the *Theme from 'Picnic'* and *Hernando's hideway* – but none of these has the charisma of Fiedler's pre-war 78 disc of Jacob Gade's *Jealousy*, the first RCA record by a 'classical' orchestra to sell a million copies. (This title was curiously appropriate in suggesting the reason for Koussevitzky's unsympathetically discourteous treatment of his colleague.)

The second collection is more aptly named, for Fiedler and his players give a superb account of Rodgers's miniature ballet, *Slaughter on 10th Avenue* which, with its sound effects (pistol-shots and police whistle), is integrated into the plot of the musical from which it is derived. Within its brief compass it has a trio of good tunes, and Fiedler makes a splendid climax out of the bouncing syncopated theme which is the most memorable of the three. The rest of the programme is well devised and the performances are equally lively, particularly the colourful dances from Falla's *The Three-cornered Hat*, although some might find that Ginastera's *Malambo* repeats its slender musical idea once too often. On both discs the bright-eyed recording, with its backing Symphony Hall ambience, comes up well in the new 'Living Stereo' transfers – but, with only 44 minutes' playing time on each CD, it would have been a better idea to pair them as a two-for-the-price-of-one Double.

Boston Symphony Orchestra, Serge Koussevitzky

COPLAND: *El Salón México*. FOOTE: *Suite in E min., Op. 63*. HARRIS: *Symphony (1933); Symphony No. 3*. MCDONALD: *San Juan Capistrano – Two Evening Pictures*.
(M) (***) Pearl mono GEMMCD 9492.

Koussevitzky's performance of the Roy Harris *Third Symphony* has never been equalled in intensity and fire – even by Toscanini or Bernstein – and Copland himself never produced as exhilarating an *El Salón México*. The Arthur Foote *Suite* is unpretentious and has great charm. Sonic limitations are soon forgotten, for these performances have exceptional power and should not be missed.

Boston Symphony Orchestra, Chicago Symphony Orchestra or San Francisco Symphony Orchestra, Pierre Monteux

'Pierre Monteux Edition': BEETHOVEN: *Symphonies Nos. 4, Op. 60; 8, Op. 93; Overture: The Ruins of Athens.* BACH: *Passacaglia & fugue in C min.* (09026 61892-2). BERLIOZ: *Symphonie fantastique; Benevenuto Cellini overture; Les Troyens: Act II Prelude. La damnation de Faust: Rákóczy march* (09026 61894-2). BRAHMS: *Symphony No. 2, Op. 73; Schicksalslied, Op. 54.* MAHLER: *Kindertotenlieder* (with Gladys Swarthout) (09026 61891-2). CHAUSSON: *Symphony, Op. 20; Poème de l'amour et de la mer.* CHABRIER: *Le roi malgré lui: Fête-polonaise* (09026 61899-2). DEBUSSY: *Images; Sarabande; Nocturnes* (09026 61900-2). LISZT: *Les Préludes.* SCRIABIN: *Poème de l'extase, Op. 54.* SAINT-SAENS: *Havanaise, Op. 83.* DEBUSSY: *La mer* (09026 61890-2). DELIBES: *Coppélia: suite; Sylvia: suite.* GOUNOD: *Faust: ballet music* (09026 61975-2). FRANCK: *Symphony in D min; Pièce héroïque.* D'INDY: *Istar* (symphonic variations), *Op. 42* (09026 61967-2). D'INDY: *Symphony on a French mountain air (cévenole), Op. 25; Fervaal, Op. 40; Symphony No. 2, Op. 57* (09026 61888-2). RIMSKY-KORSAKOV: *Scheherazade* (symphonic suite), *Op. 35; Sadko, Op. 5; Symphony No. 2 (Antar), Op. 9* (09026 61897-2). R. STRAUSS: *Ein Heldenleben, Op. 40; Death and transfiguration, Op. 24* (09026 61889-2). STRAVINSKY: *Petrushka; The Rite of spring* (09026 61898-2). TCHAIKOVSKY: *Symphonies Nos. 4, 5 & 6 (Pathétique)* (09026 61901-2).
(M) (***) RCA 09026 61893-2 (15) [id.].

Monteux was born in 1875, 13 years after Debussy and seven before Stravinsky, and the great French conductor's career was to co-exist and readily adapt to the enormous changes that came in music in the first half of the twentieth century. He made recordings from the 1920s onwards and, while he obviously brought special insights to French music, there is universal agreement that his repertoire had no geographical limitations and his interpretative versatility was extraordinary: everything was made to sound fresh. He loved the German repertoire and hated to be type-cast as a French specialist. His insights were as compelling in a Beethoven or Brahms symphony as in Stravinsky's *Rite of spring*, of which he conducted the 1913 world première in the city of his birth. (Noting the dismayed fury of the public at the *Rite of Spring*'s début, he confessed with great candour that 'At that time I did not understand one note!') Later, of course, he came to know every note and worked with the composer on the score before it entered his concert repertoire. He also directed the opening performances of *Petrushka*, *Daphnis et Chloé* and *Jeux* for Diaghilev's Ballets Russes.

For Americans, his name will always be associated with the San Francisco Symphony, whose musical director he became in 1936 and where he stayed for 16 years, until 1952. From 1951, he also conducted regularly at Boston, where he recorded both French and Russian repertory. In the mid-1950s he also came regularly to London, where he made some of his finest later recordings with the LSO for Decca. Yet his San Francisco coupling of the Beethoven *Fourth* and *Eighth Symphonies* has all the exuberant freshness one associates with his Beethoven.

In his 1945 *Symphonie fantastique*, one of the finest ever recorded, the volatile manipulation of tempo in the first movement grows naturally out of the music and, with the sparkling waltz providing a pleasingly elegant interlude, the slow movement combines Byronic romanticism with intensity. The last two movements generate great excitement and the clipped rhythms of the *March to the scaffold* are full of Gallic character. The close balance of the mono recording also means that not only are the strings given plenty of body in their slow-movement cantilena but remarkable detail also registers in the finale.

Monteux had a very special place in his heart for Brahms and he recorded the *Second Symphony* four times. In many ways his later, VPO version is the finest and it includes the first-movement exposition repeat. But the present San Franciso performance is unerringly paced and has great warmth and energy. The Chausson *Symphony* is warm, fresh and subtly coloured in the first movement, the *très lent*, darker, more intense without neurosis, while the finale is certainly exuberantly *animé*. A refreshing reading, remarkably well recorded. In Debussy's *Images*, the *Gigues* has every bit as strong an atmosphere as one remembered; so, too, has the middle movement of *Ibéria* (*Parfums dans la nuit*), which never appeared in the UK (according to W.E.R.M., the complete set appeared on LP in France). The *Sarabande* (orchestrated by Ravel), recorded in 1946, is masterly and elegant. The 1955 *Nuages* is a great improvement in sound and is marvellously paced, with sumptuous string sonority – one of the best *Nuages* ever! It has the advantage of the ambience of Boston's Symphony Hall. So has *La Mer*, another performance showing Monteux's ear for detail and atmosphere, the *Dialogue du vent et de la mer* exciting without going over the top.

The performance of Liszt's *Les Préludes* has tremendous panache and gusto. Scriabin's *Poème de l'extase* has refined, translucent detail and a passionate climax, achieved in spite of the comparatively limited dynamic range of the recording. These performances were made in Carnegie Hall and are close-miked, but for Saint-Saëns's *Havanaise* we return to Boston and join Leonid Kogan, who gives a sparkling and deliciously sultry account (with the advantage of stereo). This piece, like many of the other orchestral works, has individual sections banded, so one can isolate the coda and enjoy Kogan's wonderfully chimerical closing bars.

Monteux's ballet experience was not confined to twentieth-century scores and he knew just how to bring a sparkle to the eyes and a bloom to the cheeks of *Coppélia* and *Sylvia*. The Boston acoustics add bloom and this 1953 recording sounds almost like stereo; Gounod's ballet suite from *Faust* was recorded in San Francisco six years earlier, and the Opera House acoustics are also pleasing.

The stereo César Franck *Symphony*, dating from 1961, is masterly – perhaps Monteux's very finest recording. The addition of Charles O'Donnell's orchestration of the *Pièce héroïque* is a distinct bonus. Its chromatic links with the *Symphony* are the more obvious in its orchestral format: it sounds rather like a symphonic poem with a brassy dénouement. The 1941 mono recording (like the *Faust* ballet music) shows the excellence of the acoustics of San Francisco's War Memorial Opera House. Vincent d'Indy's *Istar* (from 1945) completes Volume 8. It is a colourful and increasingly energetic piece. Although the sound is boxier, the strings have plenty of middle sonority and the performance is unlikely to be bettered, since Monteux was a friend of the composer and took special care with recordings of his music (as did Beecham with Delius).

Volume 9, devoted entirely to the music of d'Indy, is an especially valuable disc, since the *Second Symphony* held a special place in Monteux's affections. This was its first commercial recording and it remained the only one for the best part of 40 years. The 1941 recording of the *Symphonie sur un chant montagnard français* is splendidly paced and comes up sounding very fresh, even though there is some distortion in the lower end of the range and the piano tone calls for some tolerance. The Russian-born pianist, Maxim Schapiro, relatively little known nowadays, is very good indeed. The *Second Symphony* is a marvellous performance, though this transfer is a bit flat. Checked against the LP (RCA LCT 1125) and a tuning fork, we made it over half a semitone down!

Monteux made his complete recording of *Daphnis et Chloé* for Decca, but the *First suite* (initially described as 'symphonic fragments') has remarkable allure, even if the sound is not quite secure at the opening. It includes not only a chorus but also a wind-machine. The other Ravel pieces are distinctive (some of the *Valses nobles* have captivating delicacy), but Lalo's melodramatic overture and Ibert's translucent *Escales* suffer from the restricted mono sound. No such complaints about the 1942 *Scheherazade*, where once more the resonance of the San Francisco Opera House provides mono sound of unexpected warmth and allure. With the orchestra's concertmaster, Naoum Blinder (very well balanced), taking the role of the heroine with panache this is a tremendously compelling performance. The orchestra produces sumptuous tone and in the finale the playing is so riveting that the ear hardly notices that there is any dynamic restriction: the final climax is truly magnificent. In many ways this is even finer than Monteux's later, stereo, Decca record. *Sadko* is hardly less intoxicating and *Antar* has plenty of exotic colour and impetus, but here the sound is two-dimensional.

As a recording, the 1947 *Ein Heldenleben* must be counted a virtual failure. In spite of the use of the San Francisco Opera House, the engineers obviously sought brilliance above all and the violins are made to sound paper-thin and shrill. However, Monteux's glorious 1960 *Death and transfiguration*, recorded in California Hall, ranks with the very finest, as gripping as – and even more sumptuous than – Szell's Cleveland version. Like his Brahms, it shows just how well this extraordinarily versatile conductor could handle main-line German repertoire, with the San Francisco brass sounding like Reiner's Chicago players and the transformation scene at the end both radiant and thrillingly voluptuous.

The Stravinsky coupling offers the finer of Monteux's two stereo *Petrushkas*, coupled with a remarkably fine mono *Rite of spring* from 1951. *Petrushka* is much better played here than the later, Decca version with the Paris Conservatoire Orchestra: vivid throughout, with the tension especially high in the final scene, and all the bustle of the Shrovetide Carnival brilliantly conveyed. *The Rite* is marvellously played and, because of the Boston ambience, sounds remarkably like stereo. There is plenty of rhythmic vehemence and the closing *Danse de la terre* of Part 1 brings thrillingly menacing articulation. Although the balance is close, the *Cercles mystérieux des adolescentes* is hauntingly evocative and the final *Sacrificial dance* with its snarling brass brings a powerful climax and a quickening of tension in the very last bars.

The three great Tchaikovsky *Symphonies* were recorded in Boston between 1955 and 1959 and are among Monteux's finest records. The *Fourth* is a most compulsive reading which sweeps through the score with its momentum sustained from first to last. The *Fifth* (1958) is direct, full-blooded and exciting, still among the finest versions available. The remastered recording is a revelation: strings and brass sound wonderfully rich and this is one of the best of all the RCA recordings made in Boston in the early stereo era. There are a few minor eccentricities of tempo, and in the finale Monteux makes a few agogic distortions, but the performance has such panache that he convinces the listener in all he does.

The *Pathétique* is a mono recording, but the ear would hardly guess when the Boston sound has such amplitude and depth. The reading is essentially dignified, except in the *Allegro con grazia*, which has a curious feeling of urgency, even of hurry. The finale, the apex of the reading, is heartfelt and spontaneously passionate without ever gushing. The orchestra responds nobly, especially in the restrained, dignified coda.

Bournemouth Sinfonietta, Richard Studt

English string music: BRITTEN: *Variations on a theme of Frank Bridge, Op. 10.* HOLST: *St Paul's suite, Op. 29/1.* DELIUS: *2 Aquarelles.* VAUGHAN WILLIAMS: *5 Variants of Dives and Lazarus.* WARLOCK: *Capriol suite.*
(BB) *** Naxos Dig. 8.550823 [id.].

This is the finest of the concerts of string music recorded for Naxos by Richard Studt and the excellent Bournemouth Sinfonietta. The Britten *Frank Bridge variations* is particularly memorable, showing easy virtuosity yet often achieving the lightest touch, so that the *Vienna waltz* movement sparkles in its delicacy. The *Funeral march* may not be so desperately intense as Karajan's famous mono version with the Philharmonia, but it is still very touching; and the following *Chant* is ethereal in its bleakly refined atmosphere. The sprightly Holst *St Paul's suite* and Warlock's *Capriol*, agreeably robust, could hardly be better played, while Vaughan Williams's *Dives and Lazarus* is especially fresh and conveys the famous biblical story of the rich man and the beggar most evocatively, especially in the very beautiful closing section, when Lazarus finds himself in heaven. The recording, made in St Peter's Church, Parkstone, is full-bodied, immediate and real – very much in the demonstration bracket.

20th-Century string music: BARTOK: *Divertimento.* BRITTEN: *Simple symphony, Op. 4.* WALTON: *2 Pieces from Henry V: Death of Falstaff (Passacaglia); Touch her soft lips and part.* STRAVINSKY: *Concerto in D.*
(BB) ** Naxos Dig. 8.550979 [id.].

This is the least successful of the three concerts of string music recorded by Naxos in Bournemouth. The Sinfonietta players do not sound completely at ease in the shifting moods of the Bartók *Divertimento* and their ensemble could be crisper in the Stravinsky *Concerto*. The *Simple Symphony* comes off brightly, with a gently nostalgic *Sentimental sarabande* and a brisk, alert finale, but the *Playful pizzicato* could be more exuberant, especially in its famous trio which the composer wrote so joyously. The two Walton pieces are warmly atmospheric, and there are no complaints about the sound.

Scandinavian string music: GRIEG: *Holberg suite.* Dag WIREN: *Serenade, Op. 11.* SVENDSEN: *2 Icelandic melodies; Norwegian folksong; 2 Swedish folksongs, Op. 27.* NIELSEN: *Little suite in A min., Op. 1.*
(BB) *** Naxos Dig. 8.553106 [id.].

The liltingly spontaneous account of the Dag Wirén *Serenade* ensures a welcome for this enjoyable collection of Scandinavian music. The performance of Grieg's perennially fresh *Holberg suite* is hardly less successful in its combination of energy and polish, folksy charm and touching serenity in the famous *Air*. Nielsen's *Little suite* also has plenty of style and impetus, the changing moods of the finale neatly encompassed. The Svendsen folksong arrangements belong to the 1870s. The two *Icelandic melodies* are melodically robust but the *Norwegian folksong* is gentler and quite lovely. Yet it is the second of the two *Swedish folksongs* that most reminds the listener of Grieg. All are played with a natural expressive feeling, and the recording, made in the Winter Gardens, Bournemouth, has a fine, full sonority to balance its natural brilliance.

Brendel, Alfred (piano)

'The Art of Alfred Brendel' (complete)
(B) *** Ph. Analogue/Dig. 446 920-2 (25) [id.] (includes bonus CD).

'The Art of Alfred Brendel' Volume 1: HAYDN: *Andante con variazione in F min., Hob. XVII/6; Piano sonatas in E flat, Hob. XVI/49; in C, Hob. XVI/50; Sonata in E flat, Hob. XVI/52.* MOZART: *Piano concertos Nos. 14 in E flat, K.449; 15 in B flat, K.450; 19 in F, K.459; 21 in C, K.467; 26 in D (Coronation), K.537; 27 in B flat, K.595; Double piano concerto in E flat, K.365* (with ASMF, Marriner; K.365 with Imogen Cooper). *Adagio in B min., K.540; Piano sonatas Nos. 8 in A min., K.310; 11 in A, K.331; 13 in B flat, K.333; 14 in C min., K.457; Fantasia in C min., K.475; Rondo in A min., K.511.*
(M) *** Ph. Analogue/Dig. 446 921-2 (5) [id.].

Volume 2: BEETHOVEN: *Piano concertos Nos. 4 in G, Op. 58; 5 in E flat (Emperor), Op. 73* (with Chicago SO, Levine). *Andante in F (Andante favori), WoO 57; Bagatelle in A min. (Für Elise), WoO 59; 6 Bagatelles, Op. 126; 6 Ecossaises, WoO 83; Piano sonatas Nos. 3 in C, Op. 2/3; 11 in B flat, Op. 22;*

18 in E flat, Op. 31/3; 23 in F min. (Appassionata), Op. 57; 24 in F sharp, Op. 78; 29 in B flat (Hammerklavier), Op. 106; 30 in E, Op. 109; 5 Variations on 'Rule Britannia', WoO 79; 6 Variations in F, Op. 34; 15 Variations and fugue on a theme of Prometheus (Eroica), Op. 35; 33 Variations on a waltz by Diabelli, Op. 120.
(M) **(*) Ph. Dig./Analogue 446 922-2 (5).

Volume 3: SCHUBERT: *Sonatas Nos. 4 in A min., D.537; 13 in A, D.664; 14 in A min., D.784; 15 in C, D.840; 16 in A min. (Relique), D.845; 19 in C min., D.958; 20 in A, D.959; 21 in B flat, D.960; Allegretto in C min., D.915; 11 Ecossaises, D.781; Fantasy in C (Wanderer), D.760; 12 German dances, D.790; 16 German dances, D.783; Hungarian melody in B min., D.817; 6 Moments musicaux, D.780.*
(M) *** Ph. Analogue/Dig. 446 923-2 (5).

Volume 4: LISZT: *Piano concertos Nos. 1–2; Totentanz* (paraphrase on the *Dies irae*) (with LPO, Haitink); *Années de Pèlerinage: Book 1: 1st year: Italy; Book 2: 2nd & 3rd years: Italy; Sonata in B min.* Concert paraphrase: WAGNER: *Tristan: Isoldes Liebestod; Csárdás macabre; En rêve (Nocturne); Harmonies poétiques et religieuses: Invocations; Bénédiction de Dieu dans la solitude; Pensée des morts; Funérailles. Klavierstück in F sharp; Légendes; La lugubre gondola Nos. 1–2; Mosonyis Grabgeleit; RW (Venezia); Schlaflos! Frage und Antwort; Trübe Wolken (Nuages gris); Unstern: Sinistre; Valse oubliée No. 1; Vexilla regis Prodeunt; Weinachtsbaum (Christmas tree/Arbre de Noël) suite* (excerpts); *Weinen, Klagen, Sorgen Zagen.*
(M) *** Ph. Analogue/Dig. 446 924-2 (5).

Volume 5: BRAHMS: *Piano concertos Nos. 1–2* (with BPO, Abbado). *4 Ballades, Op. 10; Theme and variations in D min.* (from *String sextet, Op. 18*). SCHUMANN: (i) *Piano concerto in A min., Op. 54* (with LSO, Abbado). (ii) *Abendlied, Op. 85/12; Adagio and Allegro in A flat, Op. 70; Fantasiestücke, Op. 73; 3 Romances, Op. 94; 5 Stücke im Volkston, Op. 102* (with Heinz Holliger). *Etudes symphoniques, Op. 13. Fantasia in C, Op. 17; Fantasiestücke, Op. 12; Kinderszenen, Op. 15; Kreisleriana, Op. 16.*
(M) *** Ph. Analogue/Dig. 446 925-2 (5).

Weihnachtsbaum (A Christmas tree) (suite).
(***) Ph. mono 454 140-2 [id.] (bonus disc).

'The Art of Alfred Brendel' subdivides into five boxes, each of five CDs, and we have surveyed them in some depth under their composer entries. Brendel aficionados will have to decide whether to invest in the complete set (with the five individual boxes in a slip-case), which offers some saving in cost, or to pick and choose. Brendel's overall achievement in a wide breadth of repertoire is quite remarkable, as indeed is the consistency of the Philips engineering: few (if any) artists have enjoyed such reliably truthful recording. However, while the Haydn/Mozart, the Liszt and the Schubert boxes can be recommended almost without serious reservation, the Beethoven collection is slightly marred by the inclusion of Brendel's digital recordings of the *Fourth* and *Emperor Piano concertos*, which are considerably inferior on almost all counts to his earlier, analogue versions. Perversely, the problem with the Brahms collection is the inclusion of Brendel's recent digital versions of both concertos, which are outstandingly fine and thus will probably have already found their way into the collections of most of his admirers! The choice for Volume 4 of his most recent 1991 recording of the Liszt *Sonata* is also difficult to fathom when, by general consensus, both his earlier versions are superior in almost all respects. But the rest of the Liszt package is very impressive indeed, as is the Schubert box, which offers many of his analogue recordings not otherwise available.

With the complete set comes a bonus disc of Liszt's *Christmas tree suite*, a mono recording from 1951–2. While it is unique, its appeal is limited by its poor technical quality: a blurred focus at higher dynamic levels, and moments of distortion. The music itself, written by Liszt for his granddaughter to play, is of relatively limited interest. Only the complete set is available in the USA.

British light music

'British light music' (with (i) Light Music Society O, Sir Vivian Dunn; (ii) Pro Arte O, George Weldon; (iii) Studio Two Concert O, Reginald Kilbey; (iv) Eric Coates and his O): (i) DUNCAN: *Little suite: March.* CURZON: *The Boulevardier.* BINGE: *The Watermill.* DOCKER: *Tabarinage.* HOPE: *The Ring of Kerry suite: The jaunting car.* (ii) COATES: *Springtime suite: Dance in the twilight.* COLLINS: *Vanity Fair.* CURZON: *Punchinello: miniature overture.* TOMLINSON: *Little serenade.* BINGE: *Miss Melanie.* Alan LANGFORD: *Waltz.* BAYCO: *Elizabethan masque.* DEXTER: *Siciliano.* HAYDN WOOD: *Moods suite: Joyousness.* (iii) *Paris suite: Montmartre.* BINGE: *Elizabethan serenade.* VINTER: *Portuguese party.* OSBORNE: *Lullaby for*

Penelope. FARNON: *Portrait of a flirt.* HARTLEY: *Rouge et noir.* (iv) COATES: *Impression of a Princess; Wood nymphs; The Dam Busters march.*
(M) *** EMI CDM5 66537-2.

Obviously inspired by the great success of the two programme of British light music recorded (at premium price) by Ronald Corp for Hyperion, EMI have delved into their archives and brought out this equally attractive selection, drawing on four different sources, all of the highest quality. Moreover this EMI CD is offered at mid-price and includes 76 minutes of ear-catching melody. The obvious favourites are here, from Ronald Binge's famous *Elizabethan serenade* to his delectable vignette evoking *The Watermill*, Anthony Collins's *Vanity Fair* (the popularity of which he valued above his fame as a conductor) and Robert Farnon's witty *Portrait of a flirt*. But also included are many more novelties of equal charm: Bayco's winning pastiche, *Elizabethan masque*, Binge's wistful portrait of *Miss Melanie*, Alan Langford's pastel-shaded *Waltz*, Harry Dexter's lilting *Siciliano*, Leslie Osborne's gently touching *Lullaby for Penelope*, and the delicious Irish whimsy of Peter Hope's *Jaunting car*. To bring lively contrast come Robert Docker's roisterous *Tabarinage* and Gilbert Vinter's equally vivacious *Portuguese party*. The stereo recordings, made at Abbey Road between 1963 and 1970, are excellent and very pleasingly transferred. Appropriately, the programme opens and closes with the music of Eric Coates, and the last four items are conducted by the composer, ending with a vigorous account of *The Dam Busters march*. These are mono recordings, but of high quality.

'Proms favourites': (iv) COATES: *London suite; London Bridge march.* GRAINGER: (i) *Molly on the shore; Mock Morris.* (iv) *Handel in the Strand.* (iv) WAGNER: *The Ride of the Valkyries.* (v) BERLIOZ: *Roman carnival overture.* (v) GOUNOD: *Funeral march of a marionette.* ELGAR: (v) *Pomp and circumstance marches Nos. 1 in D (Land of hope and glory); 4 in G.* (ii) *Fantasia on British sea songs* (arr. Wood). (iii) JARNEFELT: *Praeludium.*
(M) (**(*)) Dutton Laboratories mono CDAX 8008 [id. full price].

In the early days, the Proms were the exact opposite of what they have become under the BBC's current programming policy, and this collection of 'pops' is representative of the kind of music Wood introduced, especially on Saturday evenings, to draw in the widest audience. It includes the famous *Sea-songs* which became a staple of the 'Last night' celebrations, put together in 1905 to celebrate the centenary of the Battle of Trafalgar. It sounds incredibly vivid here, especially the famous *Sailor's hornpipe*, where one is immediately tempted to clap and which works up into such a zestful frenzy at the end that the listener is left breathless. Wood conducts everything with aplomb. The programme is slight and, for all the skill of the transfer engineers, one needs modern stereo for the shorter lollipops to sound their best; even so, the *Carnaval romain overture* (from 1940) has a strikingly convincing ambience. The early Decca recordings included here sound rather dry and studio-ish, especially the unexpansive *Ride of the Valkyries* (not Wood's fault). But the lollipop which leaps off the original shellac is track 7, Wood's own re-orchestration of Grainger's *Handel in the Strand*, and this is surely the demonstration item. This record was issued to coincide with Arthur Jacobs' splendid biography, *Henry J. Wood, Maker of the Proms*.

(i) **Brymer, Jack** (clarinet), **Vienna State Opera Orchestra, Felix Prohaska;** (ii) **David Glazer** (clarinet), **Würtemberg CO, Faerber;** (iii) **Joža Ostrack** (clarinet), **Mozart Festival Orchestra, Lizzio**

Clarinet concertos: (i) KROMMER: *Concerto in E flat.* WAGNER (BAERMANN): *Adagio for clarinet and strings.* DEBUSSY: *Première rapsodie.* (ii) WEBER: *Clarinet concerto No. 1 in F min.; Clarinet concertino, Op. 26.* STAMITZ: *Concerto No. 3.* (iii) MOZART: *Concerto in A, K.622.*
(M) *** Van. 08.9176.72 (2).

Jack Brymer's performance of the Krommer *Concerto* with its melting *Adagio* and delightful, chortling finale is a joy, while the Baermann *Adagio* (once attributed to Wagner) and the Debussy *Rapsodie* are also superbly poised. David Glazer's Weber (the *First concerto* and the engaging *Concertino*) is most elegant, with the slow movement of the concerto beautifully phrased and both finales winningly jocular – the close of the *Concertino* chirrups just as it should. The Stamitz is plainer but still very agreeable. Joza Ostrack's performance of the greatest work of all, by Mozart, agreeably combines warmth and finesse; so altogether this makes a worthwhile anthology. Accompaniments are well managed and the recordings are all fully acceptable, if not absolutely refined; but the interest of the repertoire – so conveniently gathered together – more than compensates. No recording dates are given.

Camden, Anthony (oboe), City of London Sinfonia, Nicholas Ward

Italian oboe concertos: CIMAROSA, arr. Arthur BENJAMIN: *Concerto in C.* BELLINI: *Concerto in E flat.* RIGHINI: *Concerto in C.* FIORILLO: *Sinfonia concertante in F* (with Julia Girdwood). CORELLI, arr. BARBIROLLI: *Concerto in A.* PERGOLESI/BARBIROLLI: *Concerto in C min.*
(BB) **(*) Naxos Dig. 8.553433 [id.].

This collection recalls the series of outstanding recordings made by Evelyn Rothwell for Pye/PRT with her husband, Sir John Barbirolli, conducting. He specially arranged the highly engaging pastiche works of Corelli and Pergolesi for her to play and put his signature firmly on the *Sarabanda* of the Corelli *Concerto*, which he scored as a duet for oboe and cello, his own instrument. Lady Barbirolli's recordings have just been restored to the catalogue. Meanwhile these sympathetic and stylishly played performances from Anthony Camden will suffice admirably, particularly at Naxos price. He has a most attractive timbre, and Nicholas Ward's accompaniments are impeccable. There are two very small reservations. The Fiorillo *Sinfonia concertante*, which features a pair of oboes (the second part is neatly managed by Julia Girdwood), although nicely written for the two soloists, is very conventional in its material and the first movement is a shade too long. The other point concerns the delightful five-note opening phrase of Arthur Benjamin's delicious Cimarosa confection, which Camden plays curiously lethargically, echoed by Ward. It is a small point, but Lady Barbirolli's account still lingers in the memory. The Naxos recording is excellently balanced and truthful.

Capella Istropolitana, Adrian Leaper

'English string festival': DOWLAND: *Galliard a 5.* ELGAR: *Elegy, Op. 58; Introduction and allegro, Op. 47; Serenade, Op. 20.* BRIDGE: *Lament.* PARRY: *An English suite; Lady Radnor's suite.*
(BB) **(*) Naxos Dig. 8.550331 [id.].

It is fascinating and rewarding to hear these excellent Slovak players turn their attention to essentially English repertoire, and with a considerable degree of success. The brief Dowland *Galliard* makes a strong introduction, and the attractive pair of neo-Baroque Parry suites of dance movements, played with warmth, finesse and spirit, are given bright and lively sound. In the Elgar *Introduction and allegro* the violins above the stave have their upper partials over-brilliantly lit by the digital recording, the focus not quite sharp; but otherwise the sound is full, with plenty of resonant ambience. The playing is strongly felt, but the fugue is a bit too measured, and the great striding theme, played in unison on the G string, could also do with more pace, especially when it returns. Otherwise this is persuasive, and the *Serenade* is presented simply, combining warmth and finish. At super-bargain price, this is worth exploring.

(i) Casadesus, Jean or (ii) Robert (piano), with (iii) Paris Conservatoire Orchestra, (iv) Pierre Dervaux, or (v) André Vandernoot

(i; iii–iv) RAVEL: *Piano concerto in G; Piano concerto for the left hand.* (i; iii; v) BACH: *Piano concerto in D min., BWV 1052.* (i) Pièces de clavecin: RAMEAU: *Les Tricolets; La Joyeuse; L'enharmonique; L'Egyptienne; Menuets I & II; La Triomphante.* F. COUPERIN: *La Bandoline; Les Moissonneurs; Le Dodo, ou l'amour au berceau; Les Tricoteuses; Le tici toc choc, ou les maillotins; La Favorite.* Piano music: POULENC: *Improvisation No. 5 in A min.* FRANCAIX: *Portraits de jeunes filles: La Tendre; La Moderne.* TAILLEFERRE: *Valse lente; Larghetto.* Robert CASADESUS: *Sardane; Résonances (sur le nom de Claude Pasquier); Toccata, Op. 40.* (ii) Domenico SCARLATTI: *Keyboard sonatas, Kk. 9, 13–14, 23, 27, 125, 198, 377, 430 & 533.*
(B) (***) EMI Rouge et Noir (SIS) mono CZS5 69467-2 (2) [CDZB 69467].

This handsome two-CD package mainly celebrates the work of Jean Casadesus, *le fils oublié*, as Jean-Charles Hoffelé's excellent note calls him; only the 11 Scarlatti sonatas are played by Casadesus *père*. (Jean Casadesus died in Canada in 1972 when he was 44, his father a few months later in Paris.) The only one of the performances to have appeared in the UK before is the Bach concerto. When it was reviewed alongside a Glenn Gould version in 1959, William Mann spoke of 'the French boy having the inestimable advantage of not singing'. The 1956 recording of Ravel's *G major Concerto* with Pierre Dervaux and the Conservatoire Orchestra shows the then 28-year-old to be an artist of considerable taste and refinement. His Couperin and Rameau have style and elegance, and he plays two of Jean Françaix's five *Portraits de jeunes filles* with great charm. Robert's Scarlatti sonatas are a delight, as are Jean's 1954 recordings of three of his father's compositions. The transfers come up very well indeed.

Casals, Pablo (conductor & cello)

Casals Edition (orchestral and concertante recordings)

BACH (with Prades Festival O): *Brandenburg concerto No. 5 in D, BWV 1050* (with Eugene Istomin, Joseph Szigeti, John Wummer); *Piano concerto in F min., BWV 1056* (with Clara Haskil); *Violin concerto in A min., BWV 1041* (with Isaac Stern); *Violin and oboe concerto in C min., BWV 1061* (with Isaac Stern, Marcel Tabuteau).
(M) (**(*)) Sony mono SMK 58982-2 [id.].

All these recordings come from the early 1950s, when Casals directed festivals at Prades and Perpignan and assembled some of the greatest artists of the day for these summer nights of music-making. The Bach disc comes from Prades and all the performances date from the first festival in 1950. The *Brandenburg concerto No. 5* with Istomin as pianist, Szigeti and the flautist John Wummer is a rarity – and, if Sony's publicity is to be believed, has not appeared before. It is let down by Szigeti's (at times) scrawny tone, and the orchestral playing is a bit heavy-footed. Clara Haskil's playing in the *F minor Concerto*, BWV 1056, is as eloquent and sensitive as one would expect, and Isaac Stern's account of the *A minor Violin concerto* is hardly less impressive. Perhaps the most moving thing on the disc is the slow movement of the *C minor Violin and Oboe concerto*, where the oboist is the legendary Marcel Tabuteau. Music-making from another age.

MOZART (with Perpignan Festival O): *Violin concerto No. 5 in A (Turkish), K.219* (with Erica Morini); *Sinfonia concertante in E flat, K.364* (with Isaac Stern, William Primrose).
(M) (**(*)) Sony mono SMK 58983-2 [id.].

The Mozart performances come from Perpignan and July 1951. The *A major Violin concerto*, K.219, is played superbly by Erica Morini (who also gives a totally memorable account of the Brahms *Concerto* on Millennium – see above in the Composer index). Her Mozart playing is classically lithe and free from any striving after effect. The *Sinfonia concertante* (with Stern and Primrose) is also fine but is rather measured, and really needs to be a little lighter in touch.

MOZART (with Perpignan Festival O): *Piano concertos Nos. 14 in E flat, K.449; 27 in B flat, K.595* (with Eugene Istomin); Concert aria: *Ch'io mi scordi di te?* (with Jennie Tourel, Mieczyslaw Horszowski).
(M) (**) Sony mono SMK 58984-2 [id.].

Horszowski's playing in the *B flat Concerto*, K.595, is a model of style and elegance, though Casals gives him robust rather than discreet support. But neither the Istomin account of the *E flat*, K.449, nor the Mozart *Ch'io mi scordi* with Jennie Tourel is well served by the engineers – though nor, for that matter, is Horszowksi.

SCHUBERT (with Prades Festival O): *Symphony No. 5 in B flat. String quintet in C, Op. 163, D.956* (with Isaac Stern, Alexander Schneider, Milton Katims, Paul Tortelier).
(M) (***) Sony mono SMK 58992-2 [id.].

The Schubert *Fifth Symphony*, recorded in 1953, omits the first-movement exposition repeat but, as with everything this great musician does, is full of musical interest. It has not been issued in the UK before, eclipsed by the later (and perhaps even finer) performance by the 1970 Marlboro Orchestra in stereo. However, this earlier account boasts a particularly eloquent reading of the slow movement. The Casals account of the sublime Schubert *C major String quintet* has rarely been absent from the catalogue: it first appeared on Philips and then CBS, and is too familiar to require detailed comment. Recorded in 1952, it sounds as marvellous as ever. This coupling is surely a must for all Casals admirers.

SCHUMANN (with Prades Festival O, Ormandy): *Cello concerto in A min., Op. 129. Piano trio in D min., Op. 63* (with Mieczyslaw Horszowski, Alexander Schneider). *5 Stücke im Volkston* (with Leopold Mannes).
(M) (**(*)) Sony mono SMK 58993-2 [id.].

The Schumann *Cello concerto* was recorded in Prades in 1953 with Ormandy conducting the Prades Festival Orchestra, while the Op. 63 *Trio* and the *Fünf Stücke im Volkston* date from the previous year. Although one leading magazine claimed that the *Trio* had not appeared in the UK before, it was in fact released in a CBS commemorative box. The sound naturally calls for tolerance but that should be enthusiastically extended. Casals once said that 'In Schumann . . . every note is so much from the heart.' Casals plays it for all it is worth, and some might wish for slightly more subdued and restrained emotions. Casals recorded the *D minor Trio* for HMV with Thibaud and Cortot in 1928, and this 1952 Prades performance with Schneider and Horszowski is, if anything, even finer. A performance of stature, with less of the heart-on-sleeve approach which distinguishes the *Concerto*, this was again listed in one source as 'new to the UK', but it has appeared both on LP and on CD. The sensitive and imaginative phrasing is a model of its kind. Whatever reservations one might have, these are all performances to be reckoned with.

Chicago Symphony Orchestra, Fritz Reiner

'The Reiner sound': RAVEL: *Rapsodie espagnole; Pavane pour une enfante défunte.* LISZT: *Totentanz* (with Byron Janis). WEBER/BERLIOZ: *Invitation to the dance.* RACHMANINOV: *The Isle of the dead, Op. 29.*
(M) *** BMG/RCA 09026 61250-2.

'*The Reiner sound*', a combination of marvellous orchestral playing and the glorious acoustics of Chicago's Orchestra Hall, recorded with the simplest stereo microphone techniques, is heard at its finest and most distinctive in the superb Ravel items. The Liszt *Totentanz* brings an exciting bravura contribution from Byron Janis, and the Weber is agreeably polished and spirited. The microphone balance in *The Isle of the dead* is a shade close, but this, too, is one of the finest of Reiner's Chicago recordings.

'Russian showpieces': MUSSORGSKY: *Pictures at an exhibition* (orch. Ravel); *Night on a bare mountain* (arr. RIMSKY-KORSAKOV). TCHAIKOVSKY: *Marche slave; Suite No. 1: Marche miniature.* BORODIN: *Polovtsian march.* KABALEVSKY: *Colas Breugnon overture.* GLINKA: *Ruslan and Ludmilla overture.*
(M) *** BMG/RCA 09026 61958-2 [id.].

Reiner's famous (1957) recording of the *Pictures* (discussed in the composer section) is linked with a powerful *Night on a bare mountain* within a 1959 concert of shorter Russian pieces, all brilliantly played and spectacularly recorded. Reiner's account of the *Ruslan and Ludmilla overture* is not quite as taut as Solti's famous LSO version, but its racy geniality is very attractive. *Colas Breugnon* with its syncopated cross-rhythms has plenty of gusto; the *Polovtsian march* is robustly rhythmic and Tchaikovsky's *Marche slave* suitably sombre, yet with an exciting coda.

Chicago Symphony Orchestra, Frederick Stock

WAGNER: *Die Meistersinger Overture.* BRAHMS: *Hungarian dances Nos. 17–21.* GOLDMARK: *In the springtime Overture.* SUK: *Fairy tales: Folkdance (polka).* GLAZUNOV: *Les ruses d'amour: Introduction and waltz.* TCHAIKOVSKY: *Symphony No. 5 in E min.* PAGANINI: *Moto perpetuo, Op. 11* (orch. Stock). WALTON: *Scapino: comedy overture.* DOHNANYI: *Suite for orchestra, Op. 19.* R. STRAUSS: *Also sprach Zarathustra.* STOCK: *Symphonic waltz. Op. 8.*
❁ (M) (***) Biddulph mono WHL 021/22 [id.].

Frederick Stock, born in Germany in 1872, studied composition and violin at the Cologne Conservatoire; among his teachers was Humperdinck, and Mengelberg was a fellow student. He began his career as an orchestral violinist, and in 1895 he emigrated to America to join the ranks of the Chicago Symphony as a viola player. The orchestra was then four years old. In 1905 he was hired on a temporary basis as its musical director; but he stayed on for nearly 40 years until he died in October 1942. He built the orchestra into the splendid ensemble which Fritz Reiner was eventually to inherit and established its world reputation, especially for its brass playing, although (on the evidence of these recordings) the strings were equally impressive. Like Reiner, he had the advantage of the marvellous acoustics of Chicago's Symphony Hall in which to make his records which, alongside Stokowski's Philadelphia recordings, are technically among the finest to come out of America in the late 1920s. Indeed the sound in Tchaikovsky's *Fifth* (1927) is so warm and full-bodied that in no time at all one forgets one is listening to an old recording and simply revels in the rich string patina and fine woodwind colours (heard at their finest in the elegantly played waltz movement). The brass come fully into their own in the finale. Stock's interpretation is endearingly wilful, very like Mengelberg's more famous reading, which was made only six months later. Stock pulls back at the entry of the secondary group in the first movement. The effect is emphasized because of a side change but is consistent in the recapitulation. The slow movement is very much *con alcuna licenza* (Tchaikovsky's marking) and the horn soloist must have needed great nerve to sustain his great solo at the chosen spacious tempo. But Stock has that supreme gift of being able to create the feeling of a live performance while making a recording, and this *Fifth*, for all its eccentricities, is very enjoyable. The finale has the traditional cut which was so often observed at that time, but the effect is seamless and the final brass peroration has only ever been topped by Stokowski's 78-r.p.m. Philadelphia set. The programme opens with a thrillingly sonorous account of *Die Meistersinger overture* (1926), with the tension held right to the end, in spite of the big rallentando at the majestic reprise of the introductory 'fanfare'. The Brahms dances, played with virtuosity and considerable panache, were recorded in 1925 but never issued, and both the Suk *Polka* (1926) and the charming Glazunov *Waltz* (1929) show the colourful palette of Stock's Chicago woodwind section, while Goldmark's *In the springtime overture* sounds uncommonly fresh in this early (1925) performance. The Dohnányi suite too (1928) is stylishly and pleasingly done, with nice touches of wit and plenty of lilt in the waltz featured in the closing movement, where Stock handles the tempo changes with affectionate sophistication. But here for some reason the recording is very closely miked and dry; was it actually recorded in Symphony Hall, one wonders, for there is little ambient effect?

Stock's most famous record is of Walton's *Scapino overture*, which he commissioned for the orchestra's fiftieth anniversary celebrations. It is played here with fizzing virtuosity and much élan and is particularly valuable in being the only existing recording of Walton's original score before the composer made his revisions. This and an equally brilliant account of Paganini's *Moto perpetuo*, deftly played in unison by the orchestral violins, were recorded in 1941, the sound brightly lit (the violins are closely miked in the Paganini) but retaining underlying warmth. The set ends appropriately with a work indelibly associated with Chicago because of Reiner's superb, later, stereo version: Strauss's *Also sprach Zarathustra*. But Stock's account certainly does not come under its shadow. The spectacular opening is remarkably well caught and the passion of the violins is thrilling. This was made in 1940, and here the Columbia engineers made a compromise between brilliance and richness of timbre, with the hall ambience adding a natural breadth. The range of dynamic is striking, and Stock's reading must be placed among the finest, for it is seemingly completely spontaneous, yet splendidly controlled and shaped. The orchestral concentration is held at the highest level throughout, and particularly so during the darkly dormant section of the score on the lower strings associated with 'Science' and the later passage on the high violins; Stock then follows with an exciting accelerando to reach the spectacular climax in 'The Convalescent'. He maintains this thrust through to the closing pages, with the tolling bell coming through plangently, and the coda very touching. Then for an encore the conductor provides a charmingly tuneful *Symphonic waltz* of his own composition, endearingly inflated but not boring when presented with such zest, and sumptuously recorded in 1930. Yet there is nothing 'historic' about live music-making of this calibre, and this fascinating set is very highly recommended. It certainly does Stock's reputation full justice.

Chung, Kyung Wha (violin)

'The Great violin concertos': MENDELSSOHN: *Concerto in E min., Op. 64* (with Montreal SO, Dutoit). BEETHOVEN: *Concerto in D, Op. 61* (with VPO, Kondrashin). TCHAIKOVSKY: *Concerto in D, Op. 35*. SIBELIUS: *Concerto in D min., Op. 47* (both with LSO, Previn).
(B) **(*) Decca Double Analogue/Dig. 452 325-2 (2) [(M) id. import].

This Double Decca begs comparison with Grumiaux's Philips Duo called, more sensibly, '*Favourite violin concertos*' (see below). But Grumiaux offers Brahms instead of Sibelius and concentrates on repertoire in which his refined, poetic style produces satisfying results in all four works. Chung only scores three out of four. Her collection is let down by the 1979 account of the Beethoven which, measured and thoughtful, lacks the compulsion one would have predicted, due largely to the often prosaic conducting of Kondrashin. There is poetry in individual movements – the minor-key episode of the finale, for example, which alone justifies the unusually slow tempo – but, with too little of the soloist's natural electricity conveyed and none of her volatile imagination, it must be counted a disappointment, despite the first-class digital sound.

The Mendelssohn, made two years later, could not be more different. Chung favours speeds faster than usual in all three movements and the result is sparkling and happy, with the lovely slow movement fresh and songful, not at all sentimental. With warmly sympathetic accompaniment from Dutoit and the Montreal orchestra, amply recorded, the result was one of her happiest recordings.

The Sibelius/Tchaikovsky pairing (from 1970) has already been successfully reissued at mid-price as part of Decca's Classic Sound series (425 080-2) and is highly praised in our main volume. She brings an equally sympathetic and idiomatic response to both concertos, and Previn's accompaniments are of the highest order. The latter is a much better investment than the latest format, unless the Mendelssohn is essential.

Kyung Wha Chung Edition (complete).
(M) **(*) Decca Analogue/Dig. 460 016-2 (10).

PROKOFIEV: *Violin concertos Nos. 1 in D, Op. 19; 2 in G min., Op. 63;* STRAVINSKY: *Violin concerto* (with LSO, André Previn) (425 003-2 [id.]).

BARTOK: *Violin concertos Nos. 1, Op. posth*: (with Chicago SO); *2 in B min.* (with LPO; both cond. Sir Georg Solti) (425 015-2 [id.]).

SIBELIUS: *Violin concerto in D min, Op. 47;* TCHAIKOVSKY: *Violin concerto in D, Op. 35* (with LSO, Anré Previn) (425 080-2 [id.]).

BRUCH: *Violin concerto No. 1 in G min., Op. 26; Scottish fantasia for violin and orchestra* (with RPO, Rudolph Kempe) (448 597-2 [id.]).

BERG: *Violin concerto* (with Chicago SO, Sir Georg Solti). BACH: (Unaccompanied) *Violin partita No. 2 in D min.; Sonata No. 3 in C* (460 005-2 [id.]).

FRANCK: *Violin sonata in A.* DEBUSSY: *Violin sonata in G min.* (both with Radu Lupu). CHAUSSON: *Poème for violin and orchestra, Op. 25* (with RPO, Charles Dutoit) (460 006-2 [id.]).

LALO: *Symphonie espagnole, Op. 21* (with Montreal SO, Dutoit). VIEUXTEMPS: *Violin concerto No. 5 in A, Op. 37* (with LSO, Lawrence Foster). RAVEL: *Tzigane* (with RPO, Dutoit) (460 007-2 [id.]).

SAINT-SAENS: *Violin concertos Nos. 1 in A, Op. 20* (with Montreal SO, Charles Dutoit); *3 in B min., Op. 61* (with LSO, Lawrence Foster); *Havanaise, Op. 83; Introduction and Rondo capriccioso* (with Montreal SO, Dutoit) (460 008-2 [id.]).

BEETHOVEN: *Violin concerto in D, Op. 61* (with VPO, Kirill Kondrashin). WALTON: *Violin concerto* (with LSO, André Previn) (460 014-2 [id.]).

ELGAR: *Violin concerto in B min., Op. 61* (with LPO, Sir Georg Solti). MENDELSSOHN: *Violin concerto in E min., Op. 64* (with Montreal SO, Charles Dutoit) (460 015-2 [id.]).

This mid-priced set celebrates Kyung Wha Chung's remarkable achievement during her highly successful recording period with Decca between 1970 and 1983, beginning with her – in many ways still unsurpassed – coupling of the Sibelius and Tchaikovsky *Concertos* with André Previn. The great majority of her Decca records were inspirational and all were given the benefit of first-class sound – first analogue, then digital. The exceptions are the disappointing partnership with Kondrashin in the Beethoven *Concerto*, and her over-romantic approach to Bach's works for unaccompanied violin – here rather inappropriately coupled with Berg. The ten CDs are offered for the price of nine in a slipcase, but most collectors will prefer to pick from the separate issues – all discussed under their composer entries.

Columbia Symphony Orchestra or New York Philharmonic Orchestra, Bruno Walter

Bruno Walter Edition Volume 1 (complete)
(M) **(*) Sony stereo/mono SX10K 66246 (10).

MAHLER: *Symphonies Nos.* (i) *1 (Titan)* (with Columbia SO); (ii) *2 (Resurrection)* (with Emilia Cundari, Maureen Forrester, Westminster Ch., NYPO); (iii) *Lieder eines fahrenden Gesellen* (with Mildred Miller, Columbia SO) (SMK 64447) (2) [id.].

MAHLER: *Symphony No. 4* (with Desi Halban, NYPO); (ii) *Lieder und Gesänge: Frühlingsmorgen; Erinnerung; Hans und Grethe; Ich ging mit Lust durch einen grünen Wald; Starke Einbildungskraft; Ablösung im Sommer; Scheiden und Meiden; Nicht wiedersehen* (Halban & Walter, piano) (mono SMK 64450) [id.].

MAHLER: (i) *Symphony No. 5* (with NYPO) (mono SMK 64451) [id.].

MAHLER: *Symphony No. 9* (with rehearsal & conversation between Bruno Walter and Arnold Michaelis) (with Columbia SO) (SMK 64452) (2) [id.].

MAHLER : *Das Lied von der Erde* (with Mildred Miller, Ernst Haefliger, NYPO) (SMK 64455) [id.].

WAGNER: *Siegfried idyll* (with rehearsal); *Der fliegende Holländer: Overture; Die Meistersinger: Prelude to Act I; Lohengrin: Prelude to Act I; Parsifal: Prelude to Act I; Tannhäuser: Overture and Venusberg music* (with Columbia SO) (SMK 64456) (2) [id.].

BEETHOVEN: *Violin concerto* (with Joseph Szigeti, NYPO). MENDELSSOHN: *Violin concerto* (with Nathan Milstein, NYPO) (mono SMK 64459) [id.].

The first volume of Sony's Bruno Walter Edition understandably concentrates on Mahler, with the recordings of the *First*, *Second* and *Ninth Symphonies* and, to a lesser extent, *Das Lied von der Erde*, an indispensable part of the catalogue. Nos. 4 and 5 are mono, but Walter aficionados will want these too although, for all the conductor's magnetism, the orchestral playing in New York is less refined. In the first movement of the *Fifth*, Walter's seamless and seeminglyspontaneous control of the Funeral march is memorable, as of course is the glowing *Adagietto*. The Lieder recital, which is a makeweight to the glorious mono version of the *Fourth Symphony*, is made special by his piano accompaniments for Desi Halban, reticent as it is. Walter's Wagner orchestral recordings also show him at his finest, and here the ear notices the greater amplitude and weight with which the Sony engineers have enhanced the sound. Szigeti's account of Beethoven's *Violin concerto* comes from New York in 1947. His classical purity of line is still evident, but the loss of bloom on his timbre and the moments of disturbing vibrato which troubled the great violinist in the last decade of his career had already begun to surface. Milstein's patrician account of the Mendelssohn *Concerto* was recorded two years earlier and is undoubtedly distinguished, although he re-recorded the work in stereo with Abbado for DG with equal success. All these recordings are available separately, and the stereo CDs are discussed in greater detail under the appropriate composer listing. The rehearsal recordings add to the value and interest of these important reissues.

Columbia Symphony Orchestra, Bruno Walter

Bruno Walter Edition, Volume 2 (complete)
(M) **(*) Sony stereo/mono SX10K 66247 (10).

BEETHOVEN: *Symphonies Nos. 1 in C, Op. 21; 2 in D, Op. 36; Coriolan Overture* (SMK 64460).

BEETHOVEN: *Symphonies Nos. 3 in E flat (Eroica), Op. 55; 8 in F* (SMK 64461).

BEETHOVEN: *Symphonies Nos. 4 in B flat, Op. 60; 6 in F (Pastoral), Op. 68* (SMK 64462).

BEETHOVEN: *Symphonies Nos. 5 in C min., Op. 67; 7 in A, Op. 92* (SMK 64463).

BEETHOVEN: *Symphony No. 9 in D min., Op. 125* (with Cundari, Rankin, Da Costa, Wilderman, Westminster Ch. (SMK 64464)).

BEETHOVEN: *Symphonies Nos. 4, 5, 7 & 9* (rehearsals) (SMK 64465).

BARBER: *Symphony No. 1, Op. 9*. Richard STRAUSS: *Don Juan; Death and transfiguration*. DVORAK: *Slavonic Dance, Op. 46/1* ((mono) SMK 64466).

Johann STRAUSS Jr: Waltzes: *An der schönen blauen Donau; Geschichten aus dem Wiener Wald; Kaiser Weiner Blut;* Overtures: *Die Fledermaus; Der Zigeunerbaron*. BRAHMS: *Hungarian dances Nos. 1, 3, 10 & 17*. SMETANA: *Vltava* (both with NYPO) ((mono) SMK 64467).

MOZART: (i) *Violin concertos Nos. 3 in G, K.216; 4 in D, K.218; Serenade No. 13 (Eine kleine Nachtmusik), K.525* ((i) with Zino Francescatti (SMK 64468)).

BRAHMS: (i) *German Requiem;* (ii) *Alto rhapsody, Op. 53* (with (i) Seefried, London, Westminster Ch., NYPO; (ii) Mildred Miller, Occidental College Concert Ch., Columbia SO ((mono/stereo) SMK 64469)).

Although he enjoyed a position of pre-eminence in the 1930s, Bruno Walter was never invited to record a Beethoven cycle. Duplication was less frequent then than it is now, and Weingartner and Toscanini dominated the field. (Walter's glorious pre-war records of the *Pastoral Symphony* with the Vienna Philharmonic give some idea of how good it might have been.) After he settled in the United States he recorded all nine symphonies with the New York Philharmonic and Philadelphia orchestras, but the set offered here is with the Columbia Symphony, made in California in 1958/9, not long before he died, and by general consent the finer of the two by a considerable margin. These performances embody the humane, songful approach which characterized his finest work, their warmth standing out in contrast against the gaunt, often matter-of-fact approach of Klemperer. Tempi are not exaggerated and, although Walter may not have had the electricity and fiery qualities that distinguish Toscanini's NBC Beethoven, there is no lack of either rhythmic vitality or lyrical intensity. There is also a rehearsal disc (available as part of the set) which shows his courteous, gentle, yet firm approach to music-making in the slow movement of the *Fourth*, the first movements of the *Fifth* and *Seventh* and the Scherzo of the *Ninth*. All these recordings are discussed more fully under their individual entries, as they are all available separately. Of particular interest in the present set is the 1945 version of Barber's *First Symphony*, which makes its first appearance since the two blue-label 78-r.p.m. discs were withdrawn in the early 1950s. Not only is this the only *American* symphony, it is the only *contemporary* symphony Walter recorded: his repertoire never embraced much modern music (though he did conduct Wellesz's *Prospero's spell*). Like the two Strauss tone-poems with which it is coupled, it is a mono disc and, though the resulting transfer produces cleaner and better-focused sound than the originals, it still calls for some tolerance. Walter's Mozart was particularly notable for its humane qualities, and he gives admirable support to Francescatti, his soloist in the two best-known violin concertos, who is at times over-tense – what the French would call *nerveux*. The Brahms *Requiem* with the youthful Irmgard Seefried and George London comes from 1954 and is also in mono. Its companion, the *Alto Rhapsody*, with Mildred Miller comes from 1962, the year of his death, and is less successful. However, this is a collection which serious collectors will want to have.

Columbia Symphony Orchestra or New York Philharmonic Orchestra, Bruno Walter

Bruno Walter Edition, Volume 3 (complete)
(M) **(*) Sony stereo/mono SX10K 66248 (10).

BRAHMS: *Symphony No. 1 in C min., Op. 68; Variations on a theme of Haydn, Op. 56a; Academic festival overture.*
(M) *** Sony SMK 64470 [id.]. Columbia SO, Walter.

BRAHMS: *Symphonies Nos. 2 in D, Op. 73; 3 in F, Op. 90.*
(M) *** Sony SMK 64471 [id.]. Columbia SO, Walter.

BRAHMS: *Symphony No. 4 in E min., Tragic overture;* (i) *Song of Destiny (Schicksalslied), Op. 54.*
(M) *** Sony SMK 64472 [id.]. Columbia SO, Walter; (i) with Occidental College Concert Ch.

MOZART: (i) *Symphonies Nos. 25 in G min., K.183; 28 in C, K.200; 29 in A, K.201;* (ii) *35 in D (Haffner), K.385.*
(M) (***) Sony mono SMK 64473 [id.]. (i) Columbia SO; (ii) NYPO, Walter.

MOZART: *'The birth of a performance':* (recorded rehearsals of *Symphony No. 36*); (i) *Symphonies Nos. 36 in C (Linz), K.425;* (ii) *38 in D (Prague), K.504.*
(M) *** Sony mono SM2K 64474 (2) [S2K 64474]. (i) Columbia SO; (ii) NYPO, Walter.

MOZART: *Symphonies Nos. 39 in E flat, K. 543; 40 in G min., K.550; 41 in C (Jupiter), K.551.*
(M) (**) Sony mono SMK 64477 [id.]. NYPO, Walter.

SCHUBERT: *Symphony No. 9 in C (Great); Rosamunde: Overture; Ballet music; Entr'acte No. 3.*
(M) **(*) Sony SMK 64478 [id.]. Columbia SO, Walter.

BEETHOVEN: (i) *Triple concerto for piano, violin and cello in C, Op. 56.* (ii) BRAHMS: *Double concerto for violin, cello and orchestra in C, Op. 102.*
(M) *(**) Sony mono/stereo SMK 64479 [id.]. (i) Walter Hendl, John Corigliano, Leonard Rose, NYPO; (ii) Francescatti, Fournier, Columbia SO, Walter.

(i) BRUCKNER: *Te Deum.* (ii) MOZART: *Requiem mass in D min., K.626.*
(M) ** Sony mono 64480 [id.]. (i) Yeend, Lipton, Lloyd, Harrel; (ii) Seefried, Tourel, Simoneau, Warfield; Westminster Ch., NYPO, Walter.

Walter's set of the Brahms symphonies is self-recommending, still standing high on the list of recommendations. The present remastering has improved detail, with a very slight loss of bloom on the violins. His Schubert *Ninth* is also endearing, and the mono Mozart recordings from the 1950s also bring much refreshment – although, surprisingly, the last three symphonies are less successful than the earlier ones. The rehearsal sequence for the *Linz Symphony* remains as fascinating as ever. All these recordings are discussed fully under their composer entries. The relative disappointments are the Beethoven *Triple concerto*, which is unattractively balanced, and the two choral works. Both are spaciously dramatic performances (and the Mozart *Requiem* has a splendid solo team), but the choral singing, although ardent, is not as polished as we would expect today.

Bruno Walter Edition Volume 4 (complete).
(B) **(*) Sony stereo/mono SX9K 66249 (9).

BRUCKNER: *Symphony No. 4 in E flat (Romantic)* (SMK 64481) [id.].

BRUCKNER: *Symphony No. 7 in E* (SMK 64481) [id.].

BRUCKNER: *Symphony No. 9 in D min.* (❀ SMK 64483) [id.].

DVORAK: *Symphonies Nos. 8 in G; 9 in E min. (New World)* (SMK 64484) [id.].
(all above with Columbia SO)

HAYDN: *Symphonies Nos. 88 in G; 100 in G (Military)* (with Columbia SO); *102 in B flat* (with NYPO) (stereo/mono SMK 64485) [id.].

HAYDN: *Symphony No. 96 in D (Miracle)* (with NYPO). MOZART: *3 German dances, K.605/1–3; Masonic funeral music, K.477; Minuets, K.568 & 599; Overtures: Così fan tutte; The Impresario; Le nozze di Figaro; Die Zauberflöte* (with Columbia SO) (mono/stereo SMK 64486) [id.].

SCHUBERT: *Symphonies Nos. 5 in B flat, D.485; 8 in B min. (Unfinished)*. BEETHOVEN: *Overture: Leonora No. 3* (with Columbia SO or NYPO) (stereo/mono SMK 64487) [id.].

SCHUMANN: *Symphony No. 3 in E flat (Rhenish)* (with NYPO). BEETHOVEN: *Overtures: Egmont; Leonora No. 2* (with Columbia SO) (mono/stereo SMK 64488) [id.].

BEETHOVEN: *Piano concerto No. 5 (Emperor)* (with Serkin, NYPO). SCHUMANN: *Piano concerto in A min.* (with Eugene Istomin, Columbia SO) (mono/stereo SMK 64489) [id.].

The highlights of this set are Bruckner's *Fourth* and (especially) the *Ninth Symphony*; by their side the *Seventh* is comparatively disappointing. The coupling of Dvořák's *Eighth* and *New World Symphonies* is also very special, and Walter's way with Schubert has an endearing grace and warmth. The Haydn symphonies are of more mixed appeal. Only Nos. 88 and 100 are stereo (made in 1961) and the glorious slow movement of the former drags, while similarly slow tempi in the *Military Symphony* also bring heaviness. The finales of both works are the most successful movements; overall, the effect is more of a rehearsal than live performances. The Mozart programme is much more characteristic. Walter's tempi in the overtures are unerringly apt, but readers should note that these are not Walter's more recent, stereo recordings but his earlier, mono versions made in 1954. The account of the *Masonic funeral music* is particularly fine. Good sound, too. The performance of Schumann's *Rhenish Symphony* is impressive, although this is mono; of the Beethoven overtures, *Leonora No. 2* is really outstanding. This is stereo; the other two are mono. However, neither of the concertos could be placed among the more remarkable versions of these works in the current catalogue, although Serkin's mono *Emperor* is more memorable than Istomin's Schumann (which is early stereo).

(i) **Concertgebouw Orchestra;** (ii) **LSO, Pierre Monteux**

(i) BEETHOVEN: *Symphony No. 3 in E flat (Eroica)*. SCHUBERT: *Symphony No. 8 (Unfinished)*. (ii) TCHAIKOVSKY: *Swan Lake* (ballet): *highlights*. BRAHMS: *Symphony No. 2 in D, Op. 73; Tragic overture, Op. 81; Academic festival overture, Op. 80*. RAVEL: *Boléro; La valse; Ma Mère l'Oye*. DEBUSSY: *Images; Le martyre de Saint Sébastien*.
(M) ** Ph. (IMS) 442 544-2 (5).

This Philips box, celebrating Monteux's recordings in London and Amsterdam during the early 1960s, is rather a mixed offering. Monteux's 1962 Concertgebouw *Eroica* is better played (though not better recorded) than his Vienna Philharmonic version for Decca of five years earlier (see above, under its composer entry). But in any case that Vienna performance is much more satisfying interpretatively; the Philips version is let down by the absence of real weight in the *Funeral march*. Monteux's *Unfinished* is also disappointing. In the first movement there is an unashamed speed-change between the first and second subjects, while Monteux believes in treating the second movement in leisurely fashion and obtaining the maximum contrast. This is not among his more alert performances, although the recording is full and well balanced. The Concertgebouw Orchestra seemed to inspire him less than the LSO. However, much the same comments must be made about his London account of Brahms's *Second Symphony*, which offers relaxed idiomatic playing and an eminently sound reading; yet the performance fails to resound in the memory in quite the way of his earlier Decca records of the Beethoven symphonies. Incidentally, the *Tragic overture*, recorded at the same time, which has rather more drama, has not been issued before.

Monteux's complete 1964 version of Ravel's *Ma Mère l'Oye* is a poetic, unforced reading given characteristically refined and naturally balanced sound by the Philips engineers, though the effect is not as translucent as Paray's Mercury version (434 343-2 – see under the composer). *La Valse* goes well too, but *Boléro* brings a slight quickening of tempo in the closing pages.

The 59-minute selection from Tchaikovsky's *Swan Lake*, often reissued in the days of LP, was one of Monteux's Philips successes. The spacious acoustic means that the 1962 recording hardly sounds dated, and it suits the conductor's approach to the finale, which he takes slowly – some might feel too slowly – and grandly, supported by rich-toned brass. Throughout, the LSO playing is beautifully turned. Hugh Maguire is the only individual to be named (for his violin solo in the Dance of Odette and the Prince), but the comparably fine contribution of the principal oboe is also worth noting.

Undoubtedly the best of the five discs included here is the classic Monteux coupling of *Images* and the orchestral version of *Le martyre de Saint Sébastien*, and this needs restoring to the catalogue as an individual issue. Monteux's performance of *Images* was notable for its freshness and impetus (although this is achieved by the concentration of the playing rather than by fast tempi). The 1963 recording is another tribute to the Philips engineering of the time, for there is a fine sheen of warmth and sensuousness to the strings (especially in *Les parfums de la nuit*), while the woodwind is delicately hued. This vivid yet refined feeling for colour is carried through into the orchestral sections from *Le martyre*. The fragility of texture of Debussy's exquisite scoring is marvellously balanced by Monteux, and he never lets the music become static.

Concertgebouw Orchestra, George Szell

'The Concertgebouw recordings': SCHUBERT: *Rosamunde: Overture; Ballet music No. 2; Entr'actes Nos. 1 & 3.* MENDELSSOHN: *A Midsummer Night's Dream: Overture; Scherzo; Nocturne; Wedding march.* MOZART: *Symphony No. 34 in C, K.338.* BEETHOVEN: *Symphony No. 5 in C min., Op. 67.* SIBELIUS: *Symphony No. 2 in D, Op. 43.*
(M) *** Ph. 442 727-2 (2).

George Szell was musical director of the Cleveland Orchestra from 1946 until his death in 1970, and he turned his players into an ensemble of the most remarkable virtuosity. But he also occasionally guest-conducted other orchestras with great success, and the present anthology spans the decade from 1957 to 1966. Probably the most striking performance here is the Sibelius *D major Symphony*. Szell's reading is marvellously taut and well held together, and its merits are well known: great tension and power. The remastered sound is a great improvement on the earlier CD reissue. Beethoven's *Fifth* is hardly less thrilling; if not quite as intense as his Cleveland version, that is not necessarily a drawback, with such fine playing. The Schubert and Mendelssohn incidental music is hardly less impressive. The *Rosamunde overture* has a strikingly resilient spring and the *Ballet music* and *Entr'actes* match polish and charm. Particularly attractive is the way Szell quickens the pace of the middle section of the *B flat Entr'acte* so that the effect of the reprise of the famous principal melody is heightened. The lightness and clean, sweet articulation of the violins in the Mendelssohn *Midsummer Night's Dream overture* are a delight: the wonderfully nimble wind-playing in the *Scherzo* is no less engaging, and there is a fine horn solo in the *Nocturne*. Szell, as usual, offers big-band Mozart, but the playing in the *Andante* has refinement as well as warmth, and the finale brings a bustle achieved from articulation of great precision.

Detroit Symphony Orchestra, Paul Paray

'French opera highlights': HEROLD: *Overture: Zampa.* AUBER: *Overture: The Crown diamonds.* GOUNOD: *Faust: ballet suite; Waltz* (from Act II). SAINT-SAENS: *Samson et Dalila: Bacchanale.* BIZET: *Carmen: Danse bohème.* BERLIOZ: *Les Troyens: Royal hunt and storm.* MASSENET: *Phèdre overture.* THOMAS: *Mignon: Gavotte.*
(M) *** [Mercury 432 014-2].

Paul Paray's reign at Detroit tempted the Mercury producers to record a good deal of French music under his baton, and here is a good example of the Gallic verve and sparkle that were achieved. The only disappointment is the unslurred horn phrasing at the magical opening and close of the *Royal hunt and storm*.

'Marches and overtures à la Française': MEYERBEER: *Le Prophète: Coronation march.* GOUNOD: *Funeral march for a marionette.* SAINT-SAENS: *Marche militaire française; Marche héroïque.* DE LISLE: *La Marseillaise.* Overtures: ADAM: *Si j'étais roi.* BOIELDIEU: *La Dame blanche.* ROSSINI: *William Tell.* OFFENBACH: *La belle Hélène; Orpheus in the Underworld. Contes d'Hoffmann: Barcarolle* etc.
(M) **(*) Mercury (IMS) 434 332-2 [id.].

A generous and flavourful Gallic concert, recorded in three different Detroit venues, with acoustics not entirely flattering to the orchestra, who nevertheless always play splendidly. The Adam and Boieldieu overtures need the glow of Kingsway Hall: here the resonance of Cass Technical High School slightly clouds detail. The marches and the Offenbach items were recorded in 1959 in Old Orchestral Hall, and the sound is more expansive. The most memorable pieces are the wittily engaging Gounod (always to be remembered as Alfred Hitchcock's TV signature-tune) and the spirited *Belle Hélène overture*, not put together by the composer, but none the worse for that. Throughout, the élan of the playing always brings enjoyment, and the virtuosity of the fiddles in the *William Tell galop* is exhilarating.

Dichter, Misha (piano), Philharmonia Orchestra, Sir Neville Marriner

Concertante works: ADDINSELL: *Warsaw concerto*. GERSHWIN: *Rhapsody in blue*. LITOLFF: *Concerto symphonique, Op. 102: Scherzo*. CHOPIN: *Fantasia on Polish airs, Op. 13*. LISZT: *Polonaise brillante* (arr. of WEBER: *Polacca brillante, Op. 72*).
(B) *** Ph. Virtuoso Dig. 411 123-2; *411 123-4* [(M) id. import].

Never before has the orchestral detail of Addinsell's indelible pastiche emerged so beguilingly on record as it does here under Marriner; he and Misha Dichter combine to give the music genuine romantic memorability, within a warmly sympathetic acoustic. Gershwin's famous *Rhapsody* is hardly less successful, the performance spirited yet glowing. To make a foil, the Litolff *Scherzo* is taken at a sparkingly brisk tempo and projected with great flair. The Chopin *Fantasia* has a lower voltage, but the closing Liszt arrangement of Weber glitters admirably. The sound is first rate and is very believable in its CD format.

Driessche, André van (horn), Belgian Radio & TV Orchestra, Rahbari

'Flemish Romantic Horn concertos' by MEULEMANS; DE JONG. HERBERIGS: *Cyrano de Bergerac*; EECHAUTE: *Night poem*.
(BB) *** Koch/Discover Dig. DICD 920299 [id.].

Four Flemish composers, very little known outside Belgium, here offer a series of richly enjoyable works, very well recorded, all with solo horn brilliantly played by André van Driessche. The most striking is the Straussian symphonic poem, *Cyrano de Bergerac*, by Robert Herberigs, inspired by Rostand's play, with heroic outer sections and love music in the middle. The *Horn concertos* of Arthur Meulemans and Marinus De Jong, each in three compact movements, also have ripe Straussian echoes, as well as anticipations of Hollywood film music, while Prosper van Eechaute's *Night poem* brings the most sensuous music of all. At super-bargain price, this is well worth investigating.

Du Pré, Jacqueline (cello)

'The Art of Jaqueline Du Pré': (with (i) LSO, Sir John Barbirolli; (ii) RPO, Sir Malcolm Sargent; (iii) New Philh. O; (iv) Chicago SO; (v) ECO; (vi) Daniel Barenboim; (vii) Valda Aveling; (viii) Gerald Moore; (ix) Ernest Lush; (x) Steven Bishop). (i) ELGAR: *Cello concerto in E min., Op. 85*. (ii) DELIUS: *Cello concerto*. (iii; vi) SAINT-SAENS: *Cello concerto No. 1 in A min., Op. 33*. (iv; vi) DVORAK: *Cello concerto in B min., Op. 104; Waldesruhe, Op. 68*. (iii; vi) SCHUMANN: *Cello concerto in A min., Op. 129*. (i; vii) MONN: *Cello concerto in G min*. HAYDN: *Cello concertos in* (i) *C and* (v; vi) *D, Hob VIIb/1–2*. (vi) CHOPIN: *Cello sonata in G min., Op. 65*. (vi) FRANCK: *Cello sonata in A*. (viii) FAURE: *Elégie in C min., Op. 24*. (viii) BRUCH: *Kol nidrei, Op. 47*. BACH: *(Unaccompanied) Cello suites Nos. 1–2, BWV 1007/8*. (ix) HANDEL: *Cello sonata in G min*. BEETHOVEN: (vi) *Variations in G min, WoO 45; on Judas Maccabeus: See the conqu'ring hero comes;* (x) *Cello sonatas Nos. 3, in A, Op. 69; 5 in D, Op. 102/2*. (vi) *Variations on themes from 'The Magic Flute': 7 variations in D, WoO 46 (Bei Männern, welche Liebe fühlen); 12 variations in F, WoO 66 (Ein Mädchen oder Weibchen)*.
(B) *** EMI CZS5 68132-2 (6) [(M) id. import].

Admirers of this remarkably gifted artist, whose career ended so tragically, will welcome this survey of her major recordings, made over the incredibly brief period of a single decade. Her first recordings (1961) have a BBC source and her last (the Chopin and Franck *Sonatas*) were made at Abbey Road in 1971. But of course she made her real breakthrough in 1965 with the justly famous Kingsway Hall recording of the Elgar *Concerto* with Barbirolli. Some items included here are not otherwise currently available (including the *Concerto* by Matthias Georg Monn) and, with excellent transfers, this set is an admirable and economical way of exploring her art. There are good if brief notes and some heart-rending photographs showing this young prodigy playing with characteristic concentration and joyously in conversation with her equally young husband, Daniel Barenboim.

'A Lasting inspiration' (with Daniel Barenboim, cond. or piano): BOCCHERINI: *Cello concerto in B flat* (arr. GRUTZMACHER). DVORAK: *Cello concerto (Adagio); Silent woods, Op. 68/5*. HAYDN: *Cello concerto in C*. BEETHOVEN: *Piano trio No. 5 in D (Ghost), Op. 70/1; 7 Variations on 'Bei Männern'* (both with Pinchas Zukerman). BRAHMS: *Cello sonata No. 1 in E min., Op. 38*. FRANCK: *Sonata in A* (arr. DELSART) *(Allegro ben moderato)*.
(M) **(*) EMI CMS5 66350-2 (2) [(M) id. import].

A medium-priced anthology that is self-recommending if the mixed programme is of appeal. The chamber-music performances have the same qualities of spontaneity and inspiration that have made Du Pré's account with Barbirolli of Elgar's *Cello concerto* come to be treasured above all others. Any tendency to self-indulgence, plus a certain leaning towards romantic expressiveness, is counterbalanced by the urgency and intensity of the playing. In the Brahms *Sonata* it is hard to accept the blatant change of tempo between first and second subjects, but here too there is warmth and flair. If some find Du Pré's approach to Haydn too romantic, it is nevertheless difficult to resist in its ready warmth. The Beethoven *Ghost Trio* is comparably individual and inspirational. The sound-quality is fairly consistent, for all the remastered transfers are successful.

Eastman-Rochester Orchestra, Howard Hanson

American orchestral music: BARBER: *Capricorn concerto, Op. 21* (with Joseph Mariano (flute), Robert Sprenkle (oboe), Sidney Mear (trumpet)). PISTON: *The Incredible flutist* (ballet suite). GRIFFES: *Poem for flute and orchestra.* KENNAN: *3 Pieces.* MCCAULEY: *5 Miniatures for flute and strings* (all with Joseph Mariano (flute)). BERGSMA: *Gold and the Señor Commandante* (ballet suite).
(M) *** [Mercury 434 307-2].

A first-rate concert of pioneering recordings, made between 1957 and 1963. The collection is worth having for Barber's *Capricorn concerto* alone, a less characteristic work than, say, any of the *Essays for orchestra*, or the solo concertos. Walter Piston's ballet *The Incredible flutist* comes from 1938 and the suite is one of the most refreshing and imaginative of all American scores. Griffes' *Poem* with its gentle, shimmering textures is French in feeling but is thoroughly worthwhile in its own right. Joseph Mariano is an excellent soloist as he is in the more simplistic but engaging *Miniatures* of the Canadian, William McCauley (born 1917). Kent Kennan's *Three Pieces* are clearly influenced by the ballet music of Stravinsky. Bergsma's ballet is rather noisy at times, and fails to be memorable, though brightly scored. Excellent performances throughout and typically vivid Eastman-Rochester sound.

American orchestral music II: MCPHEE: *Tabuh-Tabuhan (Toccata for orchestra).* SESSIONS: *The Black maskers (suite).* Virgil THOMSON: *Symphony on a hymn tune; The Feast of love* (with David Clatworthy).
(M) *** [Mercury 434 310-2].

McPhee's *Tabuh-Tabuhan*, written in 1936, uses Balinese music for its main colouring and rhythmic background. Roger Sessions' *Black maskers suite* was written as incidental music for a play by Andreyev about devil worship and the Black Mass, but it is not in the same class as, say, Prokofiev's *Scythian suite*. This is no fault of the performance or recording. The Virgil Thomson *Symphony*, although based on hymn-like material, is attractively quirky (reflecting the composer's Parisian years, the influence of Les Six, and Satie in particular). The cantata could hardly be more contrasted in its warmly flowing lyricism, a heady setting of an anonymous Latin love poem. The poet revels in the erotic joys of love, and the composer and his excellent soloist are obviously delighted by the voluptuous feeling of the words. As always the vintage Mercury sound is vivid with colour.

American music: MOORE: *Pageant of P. T. Barnum.* CARPENTER: *Adventures in a perambulator.* Bernard ROGERS: *Once upon a time (5 Fairy tales).* Burrill PHILLIPS: *Selection from McGuffey's Reader.*
(M) *** [Mercury 434 319-2].

John Alden Carpenter's suite was a favourite of American audiences before the Second World War and is diverting and often charming. The idiom is amiably innocuous but surprisingly seductive, not least the closing number, *Dreams*. Douglas Moore's *Pageant of P. T. Barnum* is hardly less accessible, with its engaging portraits of *Jenny Lind*, *General and Mrs Tom Thumb* and *Joice Heth*, a negress who was supposedly 160 years old! Bernard Rogers's set of *Five Fairy tales* is scored with whimsical charm. William Holmes McGuffey's *Readers* formed the staple textbook diet of schoolchildren in mid-nineteenth-century America. The gently nostalgic second movement pictures *John Alden and Priscilla* (who sailed on the *Mayflower*), and the noisy finale depicts *Paul Revere's midnight ride*. If this is perhaps the least memorable of the four works included here, its composer sums up rather succinctly the ethos of the whole programme. The performances are affectionate and committed throughout and the early stereo (1956–8) remarkably truthful.

(i) Eastman Rochester Orchestra or (ii) Eastman Philharmonia; Howard Hanson; (iii)Robert Sprenkle (oboe), Francis Tursi (viola), Armand Basile (piano)

'Music for quiet listening': (i) John LA MONTAINE: *Birds of paradise, Op. 34.* (ii) GRIEG: *Elegiac melody: The last spring.* LIADOV: *The enchanted lake; Kikimora.* (iii) Charles Martin LOEFFLER: *2 Rhapsodies: L'Etang (The pool); La Cornemuse (The bagpipe).* (i) HANSON: *Fantasy variations on a theme of youth* (with David Burge, piano).
(M) *** Mercury 434 390-2 [id.].

Under a rather deceptive title, Wilma Cozart-Fine, the Mercury producer, has gathered together an exceptionally imaginative compilation which is considerably more than the sum of its individual musical components. John La Montaine's *Birds of paradise* is eclectic but ear-tickling, and it is recorded with that glittering sharpness of focus and bold colouring for which the Mercury engineers were justly famous. With the composer at the (concertante) piano, its opening evokes Messiaen and its close Debussy. Prefaced by a quotation from Wilfred Owen, it is artfully crafted and imaginatively scored, and not too long. A particularly eloquent account of Grieg's most beautiful *Elegiac melody* is then followed by vividly atmospheric accounts of two of Liadov's most memorable orchestral miniatures. The orchestra then stays silent while Robert Sprenkle (a piquant-timbred oboist), Francis Tursi and Armand Basile present Charles Martin Loeffler's engaging – indeed haunting – pair of rhapsodic miniatures. Loeffler was concertmaster of the Boston Symphony but resigned from his first desk in 1903 to devote himself to composition. (He was born in Alsace and before his Boston appointment had played as a member of the court orchestra of a Russian nobleman, wintering in Nice and spending the summers at Lake Lugano!) His elegantly fastidious style is undoubtedly Gallic, and these two pieces are more subtly written and offer a far wider range of invention than their titles suggest. The programme ends with a set of variations for piano and orchestra by Howard Hanson, full of lyrical warmth and imbued with that strongly personal, nostalgically Nordic melodic imprint which makes this splendid composer's music so striking. It is gloriously played and richly recorded.

Eastman Wind Ensemble, Frederick Fennell

American wind band music: Morton GOULD: *West Point (Symphony for band).* GIANNINI: *Symphony No. 3.* HOVHANESS: *Symphony No. 4, Op. 165* (cond. A. Clyde Roller).
(M) ** Mercury 434 320-2 [id.].

Fine playing, but the music here is often too inflated to give pleasure on repetition. Gould's *West Point Symphony* is in two movements, *Epitaphs* (which at 11 minutes 55 seconds is far too long) and *Marches.* The *Symphony No. 3* of Vittorio Giannini improves as it proceeds: the Scherzo and finale are the most interesting movements and the most attractively scored. Best by far is the Hovhaness *Symphony No. 4* (admirably directed by A. Clyde Roller) with its bold, rich, brass sonorities in the slower outer movements contrasting with marimba, vibraphone and other tuned percussion instruments in the central *Allegro.* Splendid sound, too.

Music from ballet and opera: SULLIVAN/MACKERRAS: *Pineapple Poll: suite* (arr. DUTHOIT). ROSSINI/RESPIGHI: *La boutique fantasque: suite* (arr. Dan GODFREY). GOUNOD: *Faust: ballet suite* (arr. WINTERBOTTOM). WAGNER: *Lohengrin: Prelude to Act III; Bridal chorus* (arr. WINTERBOTTOM); *Elsa's procession* (arr. CAILLIET). *Das Rheingold* (arr. Dan GODFREY).
(M) ** Mercury 434 322-2 [id.].

Although played with characteristic Eastman verve, this is essentially a programme for admirers of wind band transcriptions – here mostly traditional scorings by prominent British military band arrangers. Little of this music gains from its loss of string textures, and the famous Rossini/Respighi *Boutique fantasque* lacks sumptuousness. All this would be entertaining on the bandstand, but at home the ear craves the full orchestra.

'Hands across the sea – Marches from around the world': SOUSA: *Hands across the sea; The US Field Artillery; The Thunderer; Washington Post; King Cotton; El Capitan; The Stars and Stripes forever.* GANNE: *Father of victory (Père de la victoire).* Mariano SAN MIGUEL: *The golden ear.* TIEKE: *Old comrades.* PROKOFIEV: *March, Op. 99.* HANSSEN: *Valdres march.* Davide DELLE CESE: *Inglesina.* COATES: *Knightsbridge.* MEACHAM: *American patrol.* GOLDMAN: *On the Mall.* MCCOY: *Lights out.* KING: *Barnum and Bailey's favourite.* ALFORD: *Colonel Bogey.* KLOHR: *The Billboard.*

(M) *** Mercury (IMS) 434 334-2 [id.].

March records don't come any better than this, and nor does military/concert-band recording. The sparkling transients at the opening of *Hands across the sea* and the peppy spirit of the playing (as with all the Sousa items, and especially *The Stars and Stripes forever*) give the listener a real lift, while the French *Father of victory* and German *Old comrades* are just as full of character. The Prokofiev is as witty as you like, and Fennell shows he understands the more relaxed swagger of the British way in *Colonel Bogey*. First rate – but, with a 65-minute programme, this needs to be taken a march or two at a time, unless you want to fall out with the neighbours – this is not a CD to reproduce gently!

Elizabethan Serenade

'Elizabethan Serenade' (played by (i) Slovak RSO, Andrew Penny; (ii) Czecho-Slovak RSO, Adrian Leaper; (iii) RTE Concert O or Czecho-Slovak or Slovak RSO, Ernest Tomlinson; (iv) Slovak RSO, Gary Carpenter): (i) COATES: *By the sleepy lagoon;* (ii) *London suite: Knightsbridge march. Dam Busters march.* CURZON: *Robin Hood suite: March of the bowmen.* KETELBEY: *Bells across the meadows; In a monastery garden; In a Persian market* (both with chorus). (iii) ELLIS: *Coronation Scot.* (ii) HAYDN WOOD: *Sketch of a dandy;* (iii) *Roses of Picardy.* (ii) FARNON: *Westminster waltz.* (i) DUNCAN: *Little suite: March.* (iii) BINGE: *Sailing by; Elizabethan serenade.* BENJAMIN: *Jamaican rumba.* TOMLINSON: *Little serenade.* WHITE: *Puffin' Billy.* (ii) GERMAN: *Tom Jones: Waltz.* (iii) COLLINS: *Vanity Fair.* (iv) MAYERL: *Marigold.*
(BB) *** Naxos Dig. 8.553515 [id.].

The Naxos collection is in effect a super-bargain sampler for a worthwhile (full-priced) Marco Polo Light Music composer series, and it inexpensively duplicates a great deal of the repertoire included on other similar programmes by various orchestras (see above and below). Our allegiance to their excellence remains, but the strong appeal of the present collection is obvious. The performances are a little more variable but are always very good, and those conducted by Ernest Tomlinson, who includes his own delightful *Little serenade*, are excellent, notably Edward White's *Puffin' Billy*, Arthur Benjamin's *Jamaican rumba* and the morceau by Anthony Collins. There are no complaints about the recording either. Excellent value.

English Chamber Orchestra, Daniel Barenboim

English music (with (i) Neil Black; (ii) Pinchas Zukerman): DELIUS: *On hearing the first cuckoo in spring; Summer night on the river; 2 Aquarelles; Fennimore and Gerda: Intermezzo.* VAUGHAN WILLIAMS: *Fantasia on Greensleeves;* (i) *Oboe concerto;* (ii) *The Lark ascending.* WALTON: *Henry V* (film incidental music): *Passacaglia: The death of Falstaff; Touch her soft lips and part.*
(M) *** DG 439 529-2 [id.].

We have always had a soft spot for Barenboim's warmly evocative ECO collection of atmospheric English music. Even if the effect is not always totally idiomatic, the recordings have a warmth and allure that are wholly seductive.

English Chamber Orchestra, Benjamin Britten

'English music for strings': PURCELL (ed. Britten): *Chacony in G min.* ELGAR: *Introduction and allegro, Op. 47.* BRITTEN: *Prelude and fugue for strings, Op. 47; Simple Symphony, Op. 4.* DELIUS: *2 Aquarelles.* BRIDGE: *Sir Roger de Coverley for string orchestra.*
❀ (M) *** Decca 448 569-2 [id.].

This rich-toned recording, still sounding extraordinarily real and vivid, was surely a prime candidate for reissue in Decca's 'Classic Sound' series. It was one of the first made at The Maltings, Snape, in 1968 (although the *Prelude and fugue*, which has been added to fill out the CD, dates from three years later). The warm acoustic gives the strings of the English Chamber Orchestra far greater weight than you would expect from their numbers. Britten drew comparably red-blooded playing from his band, whether in his own *Simple Symphony* (a performance unsurpassed on disc), the engaging Bridge dance or the magnificent Purcell *Chacony*, which has never sounded more imposing. It is good to find him treating his own music so expressively. In the Delius the delicacy of evocation is delightful, while the Elgar is in some ways the most interesting performance of all, moving in its ardour yet with the structure of the piece brought out far more clearly than is common. An indispensable reissue to set alongside Barbirolli's coupling of the string music of Elgar and Vaughan Williams.

English Chamber Orchestra, Raymond Leppard

'Music of the Baroque': Marc-Antoine CHARPENTIER: *Te Deum in D: Introduction*. ALBINONI (arr. GIAZOTTO): *Adagio in G min.* (played by La Grand Ecurie et la Chambre du Roy, Jean-Claude Malgoire). PACHELBEL: *Canon and Gigue in D*. HANDEL: *Solomon: Arrival of the Queen of Sheba. Berenice: Minuet*. GLUCK: *Orfeo ed Euridice: Dance of the Blessed Spirits*. BACH: *Orchestral suites: No. 2 in B min., BWV 1067: Badinerie; No. 3 in D, BWV 1068: Air. Cantata No. 78: Wir eilen mit schwachen* (duet; arr. Leppard). MARCELLO: *Oboe concerto in D min.: Adagio*. VIVALDI: *L'Estro armonico: Violin concerto in D, Op. 3/ 9: Larghetto* (with Jose-Luis Garcia). PURCELL: *Abdelazar: orchestral suite. The Old Bachelor: suite*.
(M) *** Sony Theta SMK 60161.

Although it contains a number of favourite baroque lollipops which are presented by the ECO with characteristic elegance and finish, the major items here are two suites of Purcell's theatre music. The writing is consistently inventive, and *Abdelazar* includes the tune (a *Rondeau*) – taken briskly here – which Britten made famous in his variations. Leppard ensures that rhythms are keenly resilient and the expressive playing is nicely judged. The elaborately decorated account of Pachelbel's *Canon* is also very attractive, opening and closing gently but with a fine central climax, while Leppard's arrangement of the jolly *Duetto* from Bach's cantata, *Jesu der du meine Seele*, is equally winning. William Bennett is the highly musical flute soloist in Gluck's *Dance of the Blessed Spirits*. The forward balance and resonant acoustic produce agreeably warm sound-quality, but this may seem too well upholstered to ears used to the Academy of Ancient music, with the harpsichord artificially balanced and only just audible in the quieter lyrical music. However, the bright violin timbre more than compensates. The programme opens with Charpentier's fanfare *Introduction* for his *Te Deum* which is instantly familiar as the signature tune of European television. La Grand Ecurie et la Chambre du Roy, directed by Jean-Claude Malgoire, ends the 74-minute concert with a memorably fresh version of the Albinoni/Giazotto *Adagio*. Altogether this is a superior collection of its kind.

English Sinfonia, Sir Charles Groves

'Entente cordiale': FAURE: *Masques et bergamasques, Op. 112; Pavane, Op. 50*. ELGAR: *Chanson de nuit; Chanson de matin, Op. 15/1–2*. DELIUS: *On hearing the first cuckoo in spring*. RAVEL: *Pavane pour une infante défunte*. WARLOCK: *Capriol suite*. BUTTERWORTH: *The Banks of green willow*. SATIE: *Gymnopédies Nos. 1 & 3* (orch. Debussy).
(B) *** Carlton Dig. PCD 2017 [(M) id.].

Having given us some attractive Haydn and Schubert recordings with the English Sinfonia, Sir Charles Groves then offered a happy juxtaposition of French and British music. He opens with a performance of Fauré's *Masques et bergamasques* which is sheer delight in its airy grace, and later he finds passion as well as delicacy in the Butterworth rhapsody, very effectively followed by Debussy's languorous orchestrations of the Satie *Gymnopédies*. Groves's approach to Warlock's *Capriol* dances is essentially genial (Marriner's version has more zest); but all this music-making is easy to enjoy. The playing is polished and spontaneous and the recording, made at Abbey Road, quite splendid.

English String Orchestra or English Symphony Orchestra, William Boughton

'The spirit of England': ELGAR: *Overture Cockaigne; Introduction and allegro, Op. 47; Sospiri, Op. 70*. DELIUS: *Summer evening*. BUTTERWORTH: *The banks of green willow; A Shropshire lad*. FINZI: *Suite from Love's Labour's Lost; Clarinet concerto* (with Alan Hacker). VAUGHAN WILLIAMS: *The lark ascending* (with Michael Bochmann); *Oboe concerto* (with Maurice Bourgue); *Fantasia on a theme of Thomas Tallis; Fantasia on Greensleeves*. PARRY: *Lady Radnor's suite*. BRIDGE: *Suite for string orchestra*. HOLST: *St Paul's suite*. WARLOCK: *Capriol suite*. BRITTEN: *Variations on a theme of Frank Bridge, Op. 10*.
✿ (B) *** Nimbus Dig. NI 5210/3 [id.].

The Birmingham-based English String and Symphony Orchestras under William Boughton are completely at home in this repertoire. One has only to sample the excitingly animated account of Holst's *St Paul's suite* (which also has much delicacy of feeling), the ideally paced Warlock *Capriol suite*, or the vibrant account of Britten's *Frank Bridge variations*, to discover the calibre of this music-making. The recordings were made in the Great Hall of Birmingham University which, with its warm reverberation, gives the strings a gloriously rich body of tone, supported by sumptuous cello and bass sonorities. The Elgar *Introduction and allegro* expands wonderfully at its climax (yet the fugue is not blurred) and in Vaughan Williams's *Lark ascending*, where the violin solo is exquisitely played with wonderful purity of tone by Michael Bochmann, the closing pianissimo seems to float in the still air. The work most suited to such an expansive acoustic is Vaughan Williams's *Tallis fantasia*, a deeply expressive performance which gives the listener the impression of sitting in a cathedral, with the solo string group, perfectly matched and blended in timbre, evoking a distant, ethereal organ. The lovely Butterworth pieces are tenderly sympathetic, and Alan Hacker's rhapsodically improvisatory account of Finzi's *Clarinet concerto* is full of colour and warmth. Perhaps Maurice Bourgue's oboe is balanced a little too closely in Vaughan Williams's *Oboe concerto* but the ear adjusts. On the other hand, the flutes melt magically into the strings in the famous *Greensleeves fantasia*. Delius's *Summer evening*, an early work, is quite memorable, and the suites of Parry and Finzi are full of colourful invention. The Bridge *Suite for strings* brings a lively response, with sumptuous textures. Only the opening *Cockaigne overture* of Elgar is a little lacking in profile and drama – and even here Boughton's relaxed, lyrical approach is enjoyable, for he broadens the final climax very satisfyingly. Very inexpensively priced indeed, this box makes an outstanding bargain.

English Symphony Orchestra; English String Orchestra; Philharmonia Orchestra, William Boughton

'The Spirit of England' Volume II: HOLST: *The Planets, Op. 32; The Perfect Fool* (ballet music), *Op. 39.* ELGAR: *Enigma variations, Op. 36. The Wand of Youth suite No. 2, Op. 1b.* PARRY: *An English suite.* FINZI: *Eclogue* (with Martin Jones, piano). BRIDGE: *There is a willow grows aslant a brook.* DELIUS: *Florida suite.* VAUGHAN WILLIAMS: *The Wasps: Overture.* IRELAND: *Downland suite: Minuet.* BERKELEY: *Serenade for strings.* BRITTEN: *Peter Grimes: 4 Sea interludes. Young person's guide to the orchestra.*
(B) **(*) Nimbus Dig. NI 5450/3 [id.].

An enjoyable enough bargain collection, warmly and often vividly played and given characteristically spacious and resonant sound which is always pleasing to the ear. However, it is much too richly upholstered for Elgar's *Wand of Youth* (and why offer the second suite and not the first?), although it suits Boughton's enjoyably expansive account of *Enigma*, even if *Nimrod*, paced very slowly, lacks something in ultimate tension. *The Planets* is well played by the Philharmonia Orchestra, but *Mars* fails the malignancy test and Boughton's reading overall is somewhat undercharacterized (except in the strikingly poignant *Saturn*); the use of the Royal Albert Hall for this recording has meant close microphones, which have produced a surprisingly small-scale effect for such a spectacular venue. The Finzi *Eclogue* (with Martin Jones the sympathetic soloist), the Delius *Florida suite*, Parry's *English suite* and the Berkeley *String serenade* are very successful, as are the shorter pieces, by Bridge, Ireland and Walton; but the Britten performances, though evocative (notably the first *Sea interlude*), are lacking something in dramatic profile and bite, and the *Young person's guide to the orchestra* ideally needs a sharper definition.

European Community Chamber Orchestra, Eivind Aadland

HINDEMITH: *5 Pieces for strings, Op. 11.* BARBER: *Adagio, Op. 11.* BRITTEN: *Simple symphony, Op. 4.* WARLOCK: *Capriol suite.* BARTOK: *Romanian folk dances.*
(B) ** Carlton IMP Dig. PCD 2044 [(M) id.].

Excellent playing from this fine group of European musicians. However, they cannot make Hindemith's rather austere set of string pieces (written for student performance) sound much more than utility music, and they miss the final degree of passion at the climax of Barber's *Adagio*, which is otherwise eloquently played. Some of the tempi in the *Capriol suite* seem slightly eccentric, but the Bartók dances are vibrant and, apart from a lack of a nursery-rhyme exuberance in the *Playful pizzicato*, the account of the Britten *Simple symphony* has comparable liveliness and crispness of ensemble.

Fernández, Eduardo (guitar), English Chamber Orchestra

Guitar concertos: RODRIGO: *Concierto de Aranjuez.* CASTELNUOVO-TEDESCO: *Concerto No. 1 in D, Op. 99* (both cond. Miguel Gómez Martinez). GIULIANI: *Concerto in A, Op. 30.* VIVALDI: *Concerto in D, RV*

93 (both cond. George Malcolm). PONCE: *Concierto del sur*. VILLA-LOBOS: *Concerto* (both cond. Enrique Garcia Asensio). ARNOLD: *Concerto*.
(B) **(*) Decca Double Dig. 455 364-2 (2) [(M) id. import].

There are few guitar concertos to match the effectiveness of the jazz-inflected piece by Malcolm Arnold. Fernández is in his element in this work, making the haunting melody of the first movement's second subject warm and not sentimental, echoed by the glowing ECO strings, while the full depth of the blues-inspired slow movement is also movingly conveyed. Yet outer movements are fizzingly vital, the playing spikily incisive in bringing out the jazz overtones. As we have said elsewhere, Fernández is a musician's guitarist whose playing is consistently refined and sensitive, and he is again at his most inspired in the concertos by Ponce and Villa-Lobos, creating magical evocation in the atmospheric slow movements, where Enrique Garcia Asensio is a persuasive partner. The Giuliani and Castelnuovo-Tedesco concertos are presented with warm, refined elegance; the *Andantino* of the latter is made to sound charmingly ingenuous, and the Vivaldi too brings refinement rather than extrovert brilliance. It is in the most famous concerto of all, the Rodrigo *Concierto de Aranjuez*, that some listeners may feel Fernández falls short in his total unwillingness to treat the music as a vehicle for extrovert display. The beautiful *Adagio* is unusually ruminative, but the outer movements, too, are comparatively laid back, delicate in feeling, yet by no means lacking in vitality. We found all the music-making here most refreshing, and certainly the Decca digital recording is consistently well balanced and of the highest quality.

Février, Jacques (piano)

(with (i) Fr. Nat. R. & TV O, Georges Tzipine; (ii) Francis Poulenc, Paris Conservatoire O, Georges Prêtre): (i) RAVEL: *Piano concerto for the left hand*. DEBUSSY: *Fantaisie for piano and orchestra*. (ii) POULENC: *Double piano concerto. Les soirées de Nazelles; Improvisations; Thème varié; Napoli*. MILHAUD: *Saudades do Brazil; Printemps*.
(B) (**) EMI Rouge et Noir (SIS) mono/stereo CZS5 69464-2 (2) [CDZB 69464].

Jacques Février was a much-respected pianinst in his day; he was Ravel's own choice in the 1930s as interpreter of the *Concert pour la main gauche*. By the time he actually came to record it with Tzipine and the Orchestre National in 1957, he had lost some of the freshness and sensitivity that he must have had. He also recorded the *D minor Concerto* of Poulenc with the composer himself in stereo in 1962, the last year of Poulenc's life. Février was no virtuoso pianist, and his technique and variety of tonal gradation were not exceptional. But the character of the Poulenc piano pieces come across well, though the Debussy *Fantaisie* is not particulaly distinguished.

Fowke, Philip (piano), **Dublin RTE Concert Orchestra, Proinnsías O Duinn**

'Piano concertos from the movies': ADDINSELL: *Warsaw concerto*. BEAVER: *Portrait of Isla*. ROZSA: *Spellbound concerto*. ROTA: *Legend of the Glass Mountain*. Richard RODNEY BENNETT: *Murder on the Orient Express: Theme and Waltz*. BATH: *Cornish rhapsody*. HERRMANN: *Concerto macabre*. Charles WILLIAMS: *The Dream of Olwen*. PENNARIO: *Midnight on the Cliffs*.
(BB) * Naxos Dig. 8.554323 [id.].

The net is spread widely here, but most of these movie concertos now sound very cheap and more than a little faded. The only real success is the *Warsaw concerto*, designed as a Rachmaninov pastiche when (reputedly) that composer turned down the commission. Richard Addinsell provided one good and one really memorable theme, Lionel Salter had a hand in the structure, and Roy Douglas put the final pieces together and skilfully orchestrated the score in the style of the great Russian composer. It is well played by Philip Fowke, but the orchestral support is hardly sparkling. The only other piece of note – although some ears find the *Dream of Olwen* melody rather endearing – is Bernard Herrmann's *Concerto macabre* which is too long but is characteristically inventive. Miklós Rózsa's *Spellbound 'concerto'* was composed to accompany a Dali-designed dream sequence and featured an electronic theremin. This is ineffectively replaced here by a synthesizer, and the music's impact is severely diluted without its essential colouristic ingredient.

French National Radio Orchestra, Igor Markevitch

'Les Introuvables d'Igor Markevitch': J. S. BACH: *Musical offering, BWV 1079 (orch. Markevitch).* HAYDN: *Symphonies Nos. 101 in D (Clock); 102 in B flat.* MENDELSSOHN: *Symphony No. 4 in A (Italian), Op. 90.* ROSSINI: Overtures: *The Barber of Seville; La scala di seta; William Tell; La gazza ladra; The Italian girl in Algiers; Cenerentola.* SCHUBERT: *Symphony No. 8 in B min. (Unfinished).* SHOSTAKOVICH: *Symphony No. 1 in F min., Op. 10.* R. STRAUSS: *Le Bourgeois Gentilhomme suite.* TCHAIKOVSKY: *Symphony No. 4 in F min., Op. 36.*
(B) (**) EMI mono CMS5 69212-2 (4).

Markevitch was, relatively speaking, a latecomer to conducting. Before the war he concentrated on a career as pianist and composer. As a sixteen-year-old he had been the soloist in a performance of his own *Piano concerto* in Diaghilev's last London season in 1929. Four years later, in 1933, he took lessons from Monteux and, subsequently, Scherchen to prepare him for performances of his own works. It was only after the Second World War that his conducting career took off. He held numerous conducting posts in Stockholm (hence his subsequent recordings of the Berwald *Symphonies* for DG), Madrid, Montreal, Paris and Rome. The present recordings with the Orchestre National de la Radiodiffusion Française were made between 1954 and 1957, and they show the orchestra in splendid shape. Markevitch's arrangement of Bach's *Musical offering* is for a small ensemble of flute, violin, cello and harpsichord, though the six-part *Ricercare* is for full strings. Whether it be Haydn or Schubert, the playing is meticulously prepared and finely shaped, though the 'emotional detachment' of which Jeremy Siepmann's note speaks is to be noted even in Tchaikovsky's *Fourth symphony*. (Markevitch's later account in the 1960s with the LSO is to be preferred.) The Rossini overtures and Strauss's *Le bourgeois gentilhomme* have a certain sparkle and elegance, though they do not eclipse Giulini in the former or Kempe and Reiner in the latter. Good mono sound.

(i) French National Radio Orchestra; (ii) London Symphony Orchestra, Leopold Stokowski

DEBUSSY: (i) *Images:* (ii) *Ibéria. Nocturnes* (with BBC Women's Chorus). RAVEL: *Rapsodie espagnole.* (i) IBERT: *Escales.*
(M) *** EMI CDM5 65422-2 [id.].

This brings together two separate LPs, with the *Nocturnes* and the Ravel *Rapsodie*, brilliantly done by the LSO, representing one of the very finest of Stokowski's Capitol records, made at Abbey Road in 1957. Here is 'full dimensional sound' with the microphones less close than in most of the American recordings on this label, and there is atmosphere as well as brilliance. The second of the *Nocturnes*, *Fêtes*, is taken fast, giving it electric intensity. *Sirènes* is then sensuously evocative, leading on to the thrillingly high-powered reading of the Ravel. In the French recordings, made in the Salle Wagram in 1958, the sound is brightly lit, but there is still plenty of ambience. The playing of the French National Radio Orchestra is warmly persuasive but with ensemble less crisp. Stokowski's panache and his feeling for colour are consistently magnetic, with the opening evocation of *Palermo* in *Escales* bringing some unforgettably languorous playing from the strings, while the combination of Mediterranean warmth and passion in *Valencia* is even more highly charged. Though the 1957/8 recordings do not convey a true pianissimo, the dynamic range is still impressive and the sound is wonderfully vivid and immediate.

(i) French Radio Orchestra, (ii) Philharmonia Orchestra; Igor Markevitch

PROKOFIEV: (i) *Love for 3 Oranges (suite), Op. 33;* (ii) *Le pas d'acier (suite), Op. 41;* (i) *Scythian suite, Op. 20.* STRAVINSKY: (i) *Le baisir de la fée (Divertimento);* (ii) *Petrushka: suite;* (i) *Pulcinella (suite);* (ii) *The Rite of spring.*
(B) (**(*)) EMI Rouge et Noir mono/stereo CZS5 69674-2 (2) [CDZB 69674].

Igor Markevitch was the last and most unusual of Diaghilev's protégés and married the daughter of his first, Nijinsky. Markevitch's career initally took off as a composer and pianist. However, after the end of the Second World War, during which he served in the Italian resistance, he gave up composition to concentrate on conducting full time. He was an excellent ballet conductor whose cool elegance can be readily observed in these recordings. His mono (1952) account of *Le Sacre* with the Philharmonia Orchestra caused quite a stir in its day, but this 1959 stereo re-make, undertaken at very short notice when Klemperer was taken ill, has much to recommend it, even if the former has perhaps the greater atmosphere. Markevitch gets good results from the Philharmonia Orchestra throughout and a very professional response from the French Radio Orchestra, which was in better shape than the Conservatoire Orchestra at this period. *Le pas d'acier* is a rarity these days and is hardly ever encountered in the concert hall; it sounds to excellent effect here. The Paris recordings come from 1954–5 and the Philharmonia *Petrushka* and *Pas d'acier* from 1954. Only the 1959 *Le sacre* is in stereo.

Gilels, Emil (piano)

'Gilels Edition'

(M) (**) BMG/ Melodiya 74321 40116-2 (5) [id.].

BEETHOVEN: *Piano sonatas Nos. 8 (Pathétique), Op. 13; 14 (Moonlight), Op. 27/2.* SCHUBERT: *Impromptu, D.935/1.* RAVEL: *Pavane pour une Infante défunte; Jeux d'eau.* MEDTNER: *Sonata-reminiscenza, Op. 38/1.* CHOPIN: *Etude, Op. 25/2.* PROKOFIEV: *The Love for 3 oranges: Scherzo; March* (74321 40117-2).

CHOPIN: *Piano concerto No. 1.* POULENC: *Concert champêtre in D* (with Moscow PO, Kondrashin) (74321 40118-2).

MOZART: *Piano sonatas, K.281 & K.310; Fantasia, K.397; 6 Variations, K.398; 10 Variations, K.455* (74321 40119-2).

SCHUBERT: *Moments musicaux, D. 780.* SHOSTAKOVICH: *Sonata No. 2, Op. 64.* SCHUMANN: *Arabeske.* CHOPIN: *Ballade No. 1* (74321 40120-2).

SCRIABIN: *Piano sonata No. 3; 5 Preludes, Op. 74.* BEETHOVEN: *Sonata No. 29 (Hammerklavier), Op. 106* (74321 40121-2).

These five CDs are available as a boxed set (and separately, in the UK only); wisely so, since it puts the collector in a position to pick and choose. Nothing by Gilels is less than distinguished. As one American critic wrote at about the time of this recital, 'With the very first notes anyone with half an ear must realize he is in the presence of one of the greatest of pianists.' But the quality of sound of these recordings is so variable as to justify detailed comment and grading.

The first disc (74321 40117-2) comes from a recital Gilels gave in the Grand Hall of the Moscow Conservatoire just before Christmas 1968, in front of a very attentive audience. The programme is close to a Carnegie recital which HMV recorded in February 1969, including the *Moonlight Sonata* and an incomparable performance of the Medtner *Sonata-reminiscenza*. The present recital includes some particularly beautiful Ravel and a no less eloquent account of the Medtner sonata. The short Prokofiev excerpts from *Love for three oranges* are much to be relished. The recording calls for tolerance: it is shallow and in no way does justice to the sheer beauty of sound one recalls Gilels making in the flesh. Three stars for the playing, one for the sound.

The next CD (74321 40118-2) couples the Chopin *Piano concerto No. 1* with the Poulenc *Concert champêtre*, played on the piano, not the harpsichord, with Kondrashin and the Moscow Philharmonic. Here the recordings, which are from 1962, present more serious problems. The Chopin is pretty rough and climaxes are distinctly coarse. Gilels makes the *Concert champêtre* sound convincing enough, such is the extraordinary range of colour he commanded.

The Mozart disc (74321 40119-2) comes from a live recital given in January 1970 in the Grand Hall of the Moscow Conservatoire. According to BMG/Melodiya's documentation, none of the performances has been available before. From the early *B flat sonata*, K.281, whose finale is delivered with such wit, through to the marvellously characterized *A minor*, K.310, this finds Gilels at his most individual and sublime, exquisite in every detail, without the slightest trace of preciosity. The sound is not as distinguished as the playing but is perfectly acceptable. The performances are certainly three-star and Rosette-worthy, but the sound rates two stars.

The Schubert *Moments musicaux*, D.780, and Shostakovich *Sonata No. 2* (74321 40120-2) together with the Schumann and Chopin pieces come from a recital given in March 1965. Gilels recorded the Schubert and the Shostakovich for HMV and RCA respectively in the West not long afterwards, both in marginally better sound. The present performances are every bit as fine, and the recording is perfectly acceptable. Gilels's account of the Shostakovich *Sonata* has never been surpassed on disc.

The Scriabin *Sonata No. 3* and the *Preludes*, Op. 74, and Beethoven's *Hammerklavier Sonata* (74321 40121-2) are the highlights of the set. Recorded at a 1984 recital, only a fortnight before he gave much the same programme at London's Festival Hall, they offer eminently satisfactory sound – though again it does not do full justice to the range of colour or delicacy of touch Gilels commanded in real life. But then, nor does his DG *Hammerklavier* (410 527-2), which has great presence and clarity but is marred by a certain glare. This live recording comes closer to capturing what those who attended his London recital will recall. One of the most impressive *Hammerklavier*s now available.

Gould, Glenn (piano)

Glenn Gould Edition

BACH: *Harpsichord concertos Nos. 1–5; 7, BWV 1052/6 & BWV 1058* (with Columbia SO, Bernstein (No. 1) or Golschmann).
(M) (**) Sony mono (No. 1)/stereo SM2K 52591 (2) [S2K 52591].

BACH: *Fugues, BWV 953 & BWV 961; Fughettas, BWV 961 & BWV 902; 6 Little Preludes, BWV 933/938; 6 Partitas, BWV 825/830; Preludes, BWV 902 & 902/1a; Prelude and fugue, BWV 895; 2 Preludes & fughettas, BWV 899/900.*
(M) (**) Sony SM2K 52597 (2) [S2K 52597].

BACH: *Goldberg variations, BWV 988; Three-part Inventions, BWV 788/801.*
(M) (**) Sony SMK 52685 [id.] (live recordings from Salzburg and Moscow).

BACH: *Goldberg variations, BWV 988; Well-tempered Clavier: Fugues in E, BWV 878; F sharp min., BWV 883.*
(M) (**(*)) Sony mono SMK 52594 [id.] (1955 recording).
(M) (**) Sony Dig. SMK 52619 [id. (*Variations* only)].

BACH: *15 Two-part Inventions; 15 Three-part Inventions, BWV 772/801.*
(M) (**) Sony SMK 52596 [id.].

BACH: *Well-tempered Clavier, Book I, Preludes and fugues Nos. 1–24, BWV 858/869.*
(M) (**) Sony SM2K 52600 (2) [S2K 52600].

BACH: *Well-tempered Clavier, Book II, Preludes and Fugues Nos. 25–48, BWV 882/893.*
(M) (**) Sony SM2K 52603 (2) [S2K 52603].

BACH: *Well-tempered Clavier: Preludes and fugues: in E, BWV 878; in F sharp min., BWV 883.* HANDEL: *Harpsichord suites Nos. 1–4, HWV 426/9.*
(M) (**) Sony mono/stereo SMK 52590 [id.].

BACH: *Sonata for violin and harpsichord No. 4 in C min. BWV 1017.* BEETHOVEN: *Violin sonata No. 10 in G, Op. 96.* SCHOENBERG: *Phantasy for violin and piano, Op. 47* (all with Yehudi Menuhin).
(M) (**) Sony mono SMK 52688 [id.].

BEETHOVEN: *Piano concertos Nos. 1–5* (with Columbia SO, Golschmann (No.1); Columbia SO, Bernstein (Nos. 2–3); NYPO, Bernstein (No. 4); America SO, Stokowski (No. 5)).
(M) (***) Sony SM3K 52632 (3) [S3K 52632].

BEETHOVEN: *7 Bagatelles, Op. 33; 6 Bagatelles, Op. 126; 6 Variations in F, Op. 34; 15 Variations with fugue in E flat (Eroica), Op. 35; 32 Variations on an original theme in C min., WoO 80.*
(M) (**) Sony SM2K 52646 (2) [S2K 52646].

BEETHOVEN: *Piano sonatas Nos. 24 in F sharp, Op. 78; 29 in B flat (Hammerklavier).*
(M) (**) Sony SMK 52645 [id.].

BIZET: *Nocturne No. 1 in F; Variations chromatiques.* GRIEG: *Piano sonata in E min., Op. 7.* SIBELIUS: *Kyllikki (3 Lyric pieces), Op. 41; Sonatines Nos. 1–3, Op. 67/1–3.*
(M) (**(*)) Sony SM2K 52654 (2) [S2K 52654].

BRAHMS: (i) *Piano quintet in F min., Op. 34.* SCHUMANN: (i) *Piano quartet in E flat, Op. 47* (with (i) Montreal Qt; (ii) Juilliard Qt (members)).
(M) (**) Sony SMK 52684 [id.].

BRAHMS: *4 Ballades, Op. 10; Intermezzi, Op. 76/6–7; Op. 116/4; Op. 117/1–3; Op. 118/1, 2 & 6; Op. 119/1; 2 Rhapsodies, Op. 79.*
(M) (**) Sony Analogue/Dig. SM2K 52651 (2) [S2K 52651].

HAYDN: *Piano sonata in E flat, Hob XVI:49.* MOZART: *Piano concerto No. 24 in C min., K.491* (with CBC SO, Walter Süsskind); *Fantasia (Prelude) and fugue in C, K.394; Sonata in C, K.330.*
(M) (**) Sony SMK 52626 [id.].

HINDEMITH: (i) *Alto horn sonata in E flat;* (ii) *Bass tuba sonata;* (i) *Horn sonata;* (iii) *Trombone sonata;* (iv) *Trumpet sonata* (with: (i) Mason Jones; (ii) Abe Torchinsky; (iii) Henry Charles Smith; (iv) Gilbert Johnson).
(M) (**) Sony SM2K 52671 (2) [S2K 52671].

HINDEMITH: *Piano sonatas Nos. 1–3.*
(M) (**(*)) Sony SMK 52670 [id.].

LISZT: *Concert paraphrases* of Beethoven's *Symphonies Nos. 5 in C min.; 6 in F (Pastoral): 1st movt.*
(M) (**) Sony SMK 52636 [id.].

LISZT: *Concert paraphrase* of Beethoven's *Symphony No. 6 in F (Pastoral).*
(M) (*) Sony SMK 52637 [id.].

Richard STRAUSS: *Piano sonata in B min., Op. 5; Enoch Arden, Op. 38; 5 Pieces, Op. 3;* (i) *Ophelia Lieder, Op. 67* (with Elisabeth Schwarzkopf).
(M) (**(*)) Sony Dig./Analogue SM2K 52657 (2) [S2K 52657].

Contemporary music: MORAWETZ: *Fantasy in D min.* ANHALT: *Fantasia.* HETU: *Variations, Op. 8.* PENTLAND: *Ombres.* VALEN: *Piano sonata No. 2.*
(M) (**) Sony SMK 52677 [id.].

Consort music: BYRD: *1st Pavane & Galliard.* GIBBONS: *Fantasy in C min.; Allemande; Lord Salisbury's pavane & galliard.* BYRD: *Hugh Ashton's ground; 6th Pavane & galliard; A Voluntary; Selliger's round.* SWEELINCK: *Fantasia in D (Fantasia cromatica).*
(M) (**) Sony stereo/mono SMK 52589 [id.].

GOULD: *Lieberson madrigal; So you want to write a fugue* (McFadden, Keller, Fouchécourt, Van Kamp, Naoumoff, Ens., Rivvenq); *String quartet No. 1* (Monsaingeon, Apap, Caussé, Meunier); *2 Pieces for piano; Piano sonata* (unfinished) (Naoumoff); *Sonata for bassoon and piano* (Marchese, Naoumoff).
(M) (**) Sony Dig. SMK 47814 [id.].

Glenn Gould is an artist who excites such strong passions that guidance is almost superfluous. For his host of admirers these discs are self-recommending; those who do not respond to his pianism will not be greatly interested in this edition. For long he enjoyed cult status, enhanced rather than diminished by his absence from the concert hall. There is too much that is wilful and eccentric in these performances for any of them to rank as a sole first recommendation. Yet if for his devotees virtually all his recordings are indispensable, for the unconverted a judicious approach is called for.

Generally speaking, his earlier recordings are to be recommended to those who are sceptical as to his gifts. There is nothing eccentric about the early recordings. His 1957 performances of the Beethoven *Second Piano concerto* with Ladislav Slovák in Leningrad and Bernstein in New York are first rate in every respect. He leaves everything to his fingers rather than his head, and his performance is eminently sensitive. We have commented on these individually and on the set of Beethoven concertos, made with Golschmann, Bernstein and Stokowski. (The *C major Concerto*, with Vladimir Golschmann, is particularly exhilarating, and both this and the *C minor* with Bernstein command admiration.) There is no questioning Gould's keyboard wizardry or his miraculous control of part-writing in Bach, for which he had much intuitive feeling. The majority of his Bach discs evince strong personality and commitment throughout, even though the tiresome vocalise (which became an increasing source of frustration, particularly later in his recording career) is a strain. The famous 1955 38-minute repeatless mono recording of the *Goldberg* sounds more of a curiosity nowadays, but it is nothing if not a remarkable feat of digital prestidigitation.

Gould possessed a fine and inquiring mind and both a sharp and an original intellect, as readers of the strongly recommended collection of his writings on music, *The Glenn Gould Reader*, will know. (Judging from the sampler Sony CD, widely available also on videocassette and laserdisc and containing *So you want to write a fugue* and some of his CBC television appearances, his sense of humour was less sophisticated, in fact pretty cringe-making.) His enterprise and intellectual curiosity, however, inspire respect. Everything he does is the result of artistic conviction, whether it is championing Bizet's *Nocturne* and *Variations chromatiques* ('a giddy mix of Chopin and Chabrier') or Schoenberg. He had great feeling for Hindemith and championed this composer at a time when he had become comparatively unfashionable, and likewise *Kyllikki* and the three *Sonatinas* of Sibelius. In fact his tastes are always unpredictable: Strauss's *Enoch Arden*, Grieg's early *Sonata*, and the *Second Piano sonata* of the Norwegian 12-note master, Fartein Valen. And who, nowadays, would dare to play Byrd and Gibbons on the piano?

Sony deserve congratulations on this formidable enterprise, and collectors will note that the sound-quality of the originals has in the main been much improved – as indeed it needed to be. However, the sound generally has insufficient freshness and bloom, and the eccentricity (some might say egocentricity) of some of Gould's readings and the accompanying vocalise are often quite insupportable.

Grumiaux, Arthur (violin)

'Favourite violin concertos' (with (i) Concg. O; (ii) New Philh. O; (iii) Sir Colin Davis; (iv) Bernard Haitink; (v) Jan Krenz): BEETHOVEN: (i; iii) *Concerto in D;* (i; iv) *Romance No. 2 in F.* BRAHMS: (ii; iii) *Concerto in D.* (ii; v) MENDELSSOHN: *Concerto in E min.* TCHAIKOVSKY: *Concerto in D.*
✿ (B) *** Ph. Duo 442 287-2 (2) [(M) id. import].

Another extraordinary Duo bargain set from Philips, containing some of the great Belgian violinist's very finest performances. He recorded the Beethoven twice for Philips, and this is the later account from the mid-1970s with Sir Colin Davis. Grumiaux imbues this glorious concerto with a spirit of classical serenity and receives outstanding support from Davis. If we remember correctly, the earlier account with Galliera had slightly more of a sense of repose and spontaneous magic in the slow movement, but the balance of advantage between the two versions is very difficult to resolve as the Concertgebouw recording is fuller and richer and (even if there is not absolute orchestral clarity) there is less background noise. The performance of the Brahms, it goes without saying, is full of insight and lyrical eloquence, and again Sir Colin Davis lends his soloist the most sympathetic support. The (1973) account of the Mendelssohn is characteristically polished and refined, and Grumiaux, even if he does not wear his heart on his sleeve, plays very beautifully throughout: the pure poetry of the playing not only lights up the *Andante* but is heard at its most magical in the key moment of the downward arpeggio which introduces the second subject of the first movement. In the Tchaikovsky his playing similarly – if less overtly emotional than some – has the usual aristocratic refinement and purity of tone to recommend it. His reading is beautifully paced and has a particularly fine slow movement; both here and in the brilliant finale he shows superb aplomb and taste. With excellent accompaniments in both works from Krenz, this adds to the attractions of the set, for the 1970s recording has a wide range and is firmly focused in its CD format.

Hälsingborg Symphony Orchestra, Okko Kamu

'Swedish orchestral favourites': SODERMAN: *Swedish festival music.* STENHAMMAR: *The Song* (cantata): *Interlude.* LARSSON: *Pastoral suite; A Winter's Tale: Epilogue.* PETERSON-BERGER: *Frösöblomster: 4 Pieces.* ALFVEN: *Roslagspolka; Midsummer vigil; Gustavus Adolphus II suite.* WIREN: *Serenade for strings: Marcia.*
(BB) *** Naxos Dig. 8.553115 [id.].

A useful anthology of popular favourites from the Swedish repertory, nicely played by the Hälsingborg orchestra and Okko Kamu, which should have wide appeal, not only in but outside Sweden. The playing is lively, the performances of the Alfvén and Lars-Erik Larsson pieces are as good as any in the catalogue, the recording is excellent and the price is right.

Harle, John (saxophone), **Academy of St Martin-in-the Fields, Sir Neville Marriner**

DEBUSSY: *Rapsodie for alto saxophone and orchestra.* IBERT: *Concertino da camera.* GLAZUNOV: *Concerto.* Richard Rodney BENNETT: *Concerto.* HEATH: *Out of the cool.* VILLA-LOBOS: *Fantasia.*
(B) *** [EMI Red Line CDR5 72109].

A first-class disc in every way. These are all attractive and well written for their instrument, and John Harle is its master. The Debussy, Ibert and Glazunov are all works well worth getting to know. The recording is excellent.

Harnoy, Ofra (cello)

'Portrait': DVORAK: *Silent woods; Cello concerto in B min., Op. 104: Finale* (with Prague SO, Mackerras). SAINT-SAENS: *The Swan.* ELGAR: *Salut d'amour.* FOSS: *Capriccio.* FAURE: *Après un rêve.* DEBUSSY: *La*

fille aux cheveux de lin (with Michael Dussek, piano). VIVALDI: *Double concerto for violin and cello in F, RV 544* (with Igor Oistrakh); *Cello concerto in B min., RV 424*. HAYDN: *Cello concerto in C: Allegro molto* (all with Toronto CO, Paul Robinson). TCHAIKOVSKY: *Variations on a rococo theme, Op. 33; Andante cantabile*. BRUCH: *Kol Nidrei* (with LPO, Mackerras). LALO: *Cello concerto in D min.: Intermezzo*. OFFENBACH: *Andante for cello and orchestra* (both with Bournemouth SO, Antonio de Almeida). BOCCHERINI: *Cello concerto in B flat: Allegro moderato*. RIMSKY-KORSAKOV: *Flight of the bumble-bee*. FALLA: *El amor brujo: Ritual fire dance*. GERSHWIN: *Summertime* (with Catherine Wilson, piano). SARASATE: *Zapateado* (with Helena Bowkun, piano). FRANCK: *Cello sonata* (arr. from *Violin sonata*): *Allegro poco mosso* (with Cyprien Katsaris, piano).
(B) *** RCA Twofer Dig. 74321 46574-2 (2) [id.].

This programme is very well planned to show the talents of a cellist who has too often been underrated because her CDs have usually been adorned by glamorous portraits. But she plays beautifully too! Although the collection contains a few individual movements from complete works, they all stand up well on their own, notably Lalo's delightful *Intermezzo*, the highlight of the concerto from which it is drawn, and the Dvořák finale ends the concert spiritedly. Ofra Harnoy sustains this collection from beginning to end with playing which is unfailingly stylish, beautifully phrased and warm in tone. She can produce sparkling fireworks too, as in the Foss *Capriccio* and the fizzing Sarasate *Zapateado*, but for the most part she ravishes the ear with her delicacy of timbre and feeling, notably so in the Bruch *Kol Nidrei*, the Tchaikovsky *Rococo variations*, the lollipop *Andante for cello and orchestra* of Offenbach and Debussy's delicate evocation of *The maid with the flaxen hair*. She is consistently well accompanied and always flatteringly recorded in a warm acoustic, yet she puts on an equally persuasive baroque mantle for her lively and cultured accounts of the two Vivaldi concertos, both of which have memorable slow movements. Highly recommended for late evening listening.

Harp concertos

Harp concertos (played by: (i) Marisa Robles; (ii) ASMF, Iona Brown; (iii) Osian Ellis, LSO, Bonynge; (iv) Werner Tripp, Hubert Jellinek, VPO, Münchinger; (v) Philh. O, Dutoit): (i; ii) BOIELDIEU: *Harp concerto in C*. DITTERSDORF: *Harp concerto in A* (arr. PILLEY). (iii) GLIERE: *Harp concerto, Op. 74*. (i; ii) HANDEL: *Harp concerto, Op. 4/6*. (iv) MOZART: *Flute and harp concerto in C, K.299*. (i; v) RODRIGO: *Concierto de Aranjuez*.
(B) *** Decca Double 452 585-2 (2) [(M) id. import].

Boieldieu's *Harp concerto* has been recorded elsewhere but never more attractively. The (originally Argo) recording is still in the demonstration class and very sweet on the ear. Dittersdorf's *Harp concerto* is a transcription of an unfinished keyboard concerto with additional wind parts. It is an elegant piece, thematically not quite as memorable as Boieldieu's, but captivating when played with such style. Glière's is an unpretentious and tuneful work, with Osian Ellis performing brilliantly. Excellent (1968) Kingsway Hall recording. Handel's Op. 4/6 is well known in both organ and harp versions. Marisa Robles and Iona Brown make an unforgettable case for the latter by creating the most delightful textures while never letting the work sound insubstantial. The ASMF accompaniment, so stylish and beautifully balanced, is a treat in itself, and the recording is well-nigh perfect. The much earlier Vienna recording of Mozart's *Flute and harp concerto* is played stylishly and has stood the test of time, the recording smooth, full, nicely reverberant and with good detail. Refinement and beauty of tone and phrase are a hallmark throughout, and Münchinger provides most sensitive accompaniments. The glowing acoustic of St Barnabas Church, London, creates an attractively romantic aura for Marisa Robles's magnetic and highly atmospheric account of the composer's own arrangement for harp of his *Concierto de Aranjuez*. Robles is so convincing an advocate that for the moment the guitar original is all but forgotten, particularly when, with inspirational freedom, she makes the beautful slow movement sound like a rhapsodic improvisation. It is a haunting performance, and the digital sound is first rate. Altogether an excellent anthology; however, the Boieldieu, Dittersdorf and Handel concertos on the first disc are also available separately at mid-price, and we gave a Rosette to this disc in our main volume (Decca 425 723-2; *425 723-4*).

Haskil, Clara (piano)

Clara Haskil: The Legacy: Volume II: Concertos

(for Volumes I & III, see below, under Instrumental recitals)

BEETHOVEN: *Piano concerto No. 3 in C min., Op. 37.* CHOPIN: *Piano concerto No. 2 in F min., Op. 21.* FALLA: *Nights in the gardens of Spain* (all with LOP, Markevitch). MOZART: *Piano concertos Nos. 9 in E flat (Jeunehomme), K.271; 23 in A, K.488; Concert rondo in A, K.386* (with VSO, Sacher or Paumgartner); *20 in D min., K.466* (two versions, with VSO, Paumgartner or LOP, Markevitch); *24 in C min., K.491* (with LOP, Markevitch). SCHUMANN: *Piano concerto in A min., Op. 54* (with Hague PO, van Otterloo).
(M) **(*) Ph. mono/stereo 442 631-2 (4) [id.].

This second box of recordings, issued in the Philips 12-disc 'Clara Haskil Legacy', is of concertante works. The earliest of Haskil's concerto records is the Schumann (1951) and is not quite as poetic as that of her compatriot, Lipatti (Haskil was born in Bucharest), though there are some wonderful things, such as the reposeful development section of the first movement and the slow movement. The Hague orchestra's oboe has a surprisingly wide vibrato. Haskil's refinement and grace are to be heard at their best in the Mozart concertos (K.466 and K.491 were recorded in the month before her death), and her fire and temperament, albeit beautifully controlled, in the Falla *Nights in the gardens of Spain*. Her family had originally come from Spain. One snag about the set is that the Beethoven is split over two CDs.

Heifetz, Jascha (violin)

'The Heifetz Collection'

RCA's '*Heifetz collection*' celebrates an extraordinary legacy of recordings, extending to 65 CDs in 46 volumes, representing a supreme artist who, by common consent among his peers, was the most gifted violinist of the twentieth century, and probably of all time. His recorded repertoire was remarkably wide and quite adventurous, although he did not seek to interpret experimental, avant-garde works. He made many first recordings and always had something fresh to contribute to established masterpieces. Often his unmatched technical facility encouraged him to choose tempi faster than usual, but never simply for the sake of display: he always put the composer first. This collection was originally issued as an unwieldy if reasonably priced complete set, but the discs are currently being reissued separately, or in groups, at mid-price. The whole series should be available during the lifetime of this book, but we have listed only the CDs we have been able to lisen to. John Pfeifer has obviously done his best with sometimes recalcitrant originals, often unflatteringly closely balanced, while some background noise remains on the 78 transfers.

Volume 1: *'The Acoustic Recordings 1917–1924'* (with André Benoist; Samuel Chotzinoff; O, Pasternak): SCHUBERT: *Ave Maria.* DRIGO: *Valse bluette.* ELGAR: *La Capricieuse, Op. 17.* SARASATE: *Malagueña, Habanera, Op. 21/1 & 2; Introduction and tarantelle, Op. 43; Zapateado, Op. 23/2; Zigeunerweisen, Op. 20/1; Carmen fantasy, Op. 25.* BAZZINI: *La ronde des lutins.* BEETHOVEN: *Ruins of Athens: Chorus of Dervishes; Turkish march.* WIENIAWSKI: *Scherzo-Tarantelle, Op. 16; Concerto No. 2, Op. 22: Romance.* ACHRON: *Hebrew melody, Op. 33; Hebrew lullaby, Hebrew dance, Op. 35; Stimmung, Op. 32.* PAGANINI: *Moto perpetuo; Caprices, Nos. 13 & 20.* KREISLER: *Minuet; Sicilienne et Rigaudon.* GLAZUNOV: *Meditation; Valse.* MOSZKOWSKI: *Guitarre, Op. 45/2.* CHOPIN: *Nocturnes, Op. 9/2; Op. 27/2.* TCHAIKOVSKY: *Souvenir d'un lieu cher: Scherzo, Op. 42/2. Serenade: Valse, Op. 48/2. Concerto, Op. 35: Canzonetta. Sérénade mélancolique, Op. 26.* MENDELSSOHN: *On wings of song, Op. 34/2; Concerto in E min.: finale.* DVORAK: *Slavonic dances, Op. 46/2; Op. 72/2 & 8.* SCHUMANN: *Myrthen: Widmung, Op. 25/1.* LALO: *Symphonie espagnole, Op. 21: Andante.* MOZART: *Divertimento No. 17, K.334: Minuet. Haffner Serenade, K.250: Rondo.* D'AMBROSIO: *Serenade, Op. 4.* JUON: *Berceuse, Op. 28/3.* GOLDMARK: *Concerto in A min., Op. 28: Andante.* GODOWSKY: *Waltz in D.* BRAHMS: *Hungarian dance No. 1 in G min.* HAYDN: *Quartet (Lark), Op. 64/5: Vivace.* GRANADOS: *Danzas españolas, Op. 37/5; Andaluza.* BOULANGER: *Nocturne in F; Cortège.* SCOTT: *The gentle maiden.* SAINT-SAENS: *Havanaise, Op. 83.*
(M) (***) RCA mono 09026 61732-2 [61732-2-RG] (3).

These recordings serve as a salutary reminder of Heifetz's extraordinary powers. The earliest records come from the year of the Russian Revolution, when Heifetz was still sixteen and only five years after he had made his début in St Petersburg. As always with Heifetz, even the highest expectations are surpassed: his effortless technical mastery is dazzling, the golden tone strong and pure, the accuracy of his intonation almost beyond belief and his taste impeccable. The collector will also be agreeably surprised by the quality of sound; the earliest was made only two weeks after his Carnegie Hall début, when the art of recording was still relatively primitive, and the original 78-r.p.m. disc was single-sided. Seventy or more years later, his brilliance remains undimmed. The recordings are arranged in chronological order, though the differences during the period are relatively small. This set is a mandatory purchase for all who care about the art of violin playing.

Volume 3: GLAZUNOV: *Méditation*. PAGANINI: *Caprice No. 20* (both with Arpád Sándor). VIEUXTEMPS: *Violin concerto No. 4 in D min., Op. 314*. WIENIAWSKI: *Violin concerto No. 2 in D min., Op. 22* (both with LPO, Barbirolli); *Polonaise brillante No. 1 in D, Op. 4*. CYRIL SCOTT: *Tallahassee suite*. FALLA: *Danza española No. 1*. GRIEG: *Violin sonata No. 2 in G, Op. 13* (all with Emanuel Bay). POULENC: *Mouvement perpétuel*. DINICU: *Hora staccato*. SZYMANOWSKI: *Roxana's song*. BAZZINI: *La ronde des lutins*. BACH: (Unaccompanied) *Violin sonatas Nos. 1, BWV 1001; 3, BWV 1005*.
(M) (**) RCA mono 09026 61734-2 (2) [id.].

The very first item here (persuasively recorded in 1934) offers a tenderly romantic performance of the Glazunov *Méditation* and establishes not only the sophistication of detail but also the warmth and beauty of Heifetz's lyricism, and this is borne out in the Wieniawski and Vieuxtemps *Concertos*, recorded a year later. The Wieniawski *Andante* is ravishing and the first violin entry in the Vieuxtemps quite magical. Although the solo instrument is far too close, it is caught fairly truthfully, if sounding a bit scratchy at times (notably in the Vieuxtemps dashing Scherzo), and it is a pity that Barbirolli's fine accompaniments are made to sound so papery, except in the slow movements. Among the other encores, Poulenc's *Mouvement perpétuel* has charm but is a shade too schmaltzy; the brilliant *Hora staccato* (1935) and the transcribed Szymanowski song both sound as if the microphone was inside the solo instrument! Bazzini's *La ronde des lutins* is also right up front, but the sound is cleaner (1937). Cyril Scott's *Tallahassee suite* is a novelty these days, with only the *Danse nègre* remembered. Heifetz makes both the last two movements memorable by playing the tune lyrically in harmonics. The two Bach unaccompanied *Violin sonatas* are remarkably consistent with the later versions (in Volume 17), but the sound is understandably rougher. The Grieg *G major Sonata* is a delightful performance but suffers from a degree of wow; otherwise the sound is good, apart from the exaggerated violin balance.

Volume 4: FAURE: *Violin sonata No. 1 in A, Op. 13*. BRAHMS: *Violin sonata No. 2 in A, Op. 100* (both with Emanuel Bay); *Violin concerto in D, Op. 77*. PROKOFIEV: *Violin concerto No. 2 in G min., Op. 63* (both with Boston SO, Koussevitzky). SAINT-SAENS: *Introduction and rondo capriccioso, Op. 28* (with LPO, Barbirolli); *Havanaise, Op. 83*. SARASATE: *Zigeunerweisen, Op. 20* (both with LSO, Barbirolli).
(M) (**) RCA mono 09026 61735-2 (2) [id.].

The piano introduces the Fauré *Sonata* with timbre which is dry and uningratiating, then almost immediately Emanuel Bay becomes subservient to the very bright, forward violin-sound and the overall effect robs the work of much of its charm, although the lyrical finale comes off well. The Brahms *Sonata* (also from 1936) is ill-focused at the opening, but the warmth of the performance means one is willing to make allowances for the technical disabilities. The *Introduction and rondo capriccioso* of Saint-Säens (1935), the *Havanaise* and Sarasate's *Zigeunerweisen* (both 1937) were recorded at Abbey Road. They are all ravishingly played (Heifetz at his finest), with scintillating finales (especially the Sarasate) and, provided one accepts an orchestra which makes less impact than the violin, the sound is quite acceptable. Again the solo violin dominates the Prokofiev (1937) and Brahms (1937) *Concertos* (with Koussevitzky), and in the former the close microphones negate the Symphony Hall ambience, so it is the slow movement which makes the strongest impression. The Brahms *Concerto* is sonically very much more successful, with the Boston Symphony shrill-sounding but effectively in the picture, and one can respond to what is undoubtedly an outstanding performance, with a thrilling finale.

Volume 5: BRAHMS: *Double concerto for violin, cello and orchestra, Op. 102* (with Feuermann, Phd. O, Ormandy). BEETHOVEN: *Violin concerto in D, Op. 61* (with NBC SO, Toscanini). WALTON: *Violin concerto in B min.* (with Cincinnati SO, Goossens). CHAUSSON: *Concert for violin, piano and string quartet, Op. 21* (with Sanromá, Musical Art Qt). PROKOFIEV: *Gavotte, Op. 32/3; March, Op. 12/1*. RACHMANINOV: *Etude-tableau, Op. 39/2; Daisies; Oriental sketch* (all with Emanuel Bay).
(M) (***) RCA mono 09026 61736-2 (2) [id.].

The Heifetz–Feuermann partnership was justly celebrated in their 1939 recording of the Brahms *Double concerto*, especially for the eloquence of the *Andante*. Ormandy, already proving himself a natural accompanist, provides passionately committed support, and the acoustic of the Philadelphia Academy helps the orchestra to sound relatively expansive. The overall balance is surprisingly well managed. The 1940 set of the Beethoven *Violin concerto* used the notorious NBC Studio 8-H but, although dry, the sound is not thin, and again the balance is very convincing for this is a partnership of equals (the only time these two great musicians recorded together) and Toscanini makes sure the orchestra is well in the picture. The slow movement is Elysian and the finale sparkles, the pacing just about perfect. It was Heifetz who commissioned the Walton *Concerto* and who gave the first performance, as well as making this inspirational wartime recording of the original score, which has never been surpassed, in 1941. Heifetz's contribution is glorious and the partnership with Goossens (one of the most underrated of conductors) produces the feeling of total spontaneity. The Scherzo is dazzling, but it is the work's bitter-sweet lyricism that the soloist captures so seductively. The sound, using the Music Hall in Cincinnati, is worthy of the playing, by the standards of those days. The atmospheric Chausson *Concert* is well chosen to make a foil for the Walton, the delicacy of the central movements well observed. The latter recording, made in the appropriately named Lotus Club (in New York), is confined but suitably intimate. The encores are agreeable, with the song-transcription, *Daisies*, the most striking. But altogether this compilation is indispensable.

Volume 6: Transcriptions/arrangements: BACH: *Concerto for two violins, BWV 1043* (with RCA Victor CO, Waxman); *English suite No. 6: Gavottes*. CASTELNUOVO-TEDESCO: *Sea Murmurs; Tango*. RAVEL: *Valses nobles et sentimentales, Nos. 6, 7*. MEDTNER: *Fairy tale, Op. 20/1*. DEBUSSY: *La chevelure; La fille aux cheveux de lin; Il pleure dans mon coeur*. FALLA: *Jota; Pantomime*. NIN: *Cantilène asturienne*. MILHAUD: *Corcovado*. BAX: *Mediterranean*. HALFFTER: *Danza de la gitana*. POLDOWSKI: *Tango*. BEETHOVEN: *German dance No. 6*. MENDELSSOHN: *Piano trio in D min., Op. 49: Scherzo. Song without words, Op. 19/1*. CHOPIN: *Nocturne, Op. 72/1*. ARENSKY: *Concerto in A min.: Tempo di valse* (with Emanuel Bay). RIMSKY-KORSAKOV: *Flight of the bumblebee*. MOZART: *Divertimento No. 17, K.334: Minuet*. KORNGOLD: *Much Ado About Nothing: Garden scene; Holzapfel und Schlehwein (March)* (all with Emanuel Bay). SARASATE: *Romanza andaluza*. SCHUBERT: *Piano sonata, D.850: Rondo*. TANSMAN: *Mouvement perpétuel* (all with Emanuel Bay). BRUCH: *Scottish fantasy* (with RCA Victor SO, Steinberg). VIEUXTEMPS: *Violin concerto No. 5, Op. 37* (with LSO, Sargent).
(M) (***) RCA mono 09026 61737-2 (2) [id.].

The outer movements of the Bach *Double concerto* are pretty fast. Heifetz plays both solo parts, and to have him twice in the slow movement, so to speak, singing his cantabile line with an equally ravishing response, forestalls any criticism about lack of contrast. This was achieved by recording the principal solo part on film and adding the second part to the recording with the soloist using earphones (Heifetz never repeated the exercise). Franz Waxman, the Hollywood composer, conducts the accompaniments with real zest. Castelnuovo-Tedesco's *Tango* falls less easily on the ear than it might when it follows so closely on the heels of the Bach finale but, once one has adjusted, the following series of sweetmeats will surely titillate even the most jaded palate, especially Debussy's haunting *Il pleure dans mon coeur* and the seductive *Pantomime* from Falla's *El amor brujo* (later, the same composer's glittering *Jota* ends the programme). Mendelssohn's *Scherzo* from the *D minor Piano trio* and the Arensky *Tempo di valse* bring delightful contrasting insouciance, while Rimsky's *Bumblebee* has seldom buzzed so vociferously or flown at such velocity. All these items were recorded with the faithful Emmanuel Bay in October 1946, and the sound is generally quite sophisticated. The second disc opens with a further batch of encores. Heifetz is equally charismatic and elegant when playing the familiar *Minuet* from Mozart's *Divertimento*, K.334, as in the lesser-known but no less catchy *Rondo* from Schubert's *D major Piano sonata*, D.850. Debussy's *La fille aux cheveux de lin* brings a bewitching interlude, and Heifetz demonstrates his fondness for Korngold by including two utterly different but equally characteristic transcriptions from *Much Ado About Nothing*. Again the 1946–7 sound is a great improvement on comparable earlier recordings. This applies equally to the pair of concertante works which end the programme, Bruch's *Scottish fantasia* and Vieuxtemps's *Concerto No. 5 in A minor*, where the 1947 orchestral accompaniment is at last beginning to sound full-bodied and realistic. Needless to say, Heifetz's presentation of Bruch's endearing Scottish melodies is a special delight, while the finale is joyously rhythmic. The brief *Adagio* of the Vieuxtemps is also played superbly, with the reprise quite magical. This may be a lightweight programme but it could surely not be better presented.

Volume 7: ELGAR: *Violin concerto in B min., Op. 61* (with LSO, Sargent). SAINT-SAENS: *Violin sonata No. 1 in D min., Op. 75* (with Emanuel Bay). TCHAIKOVSKY: *Violin concerto in D, Op. 35* (with Philh. O, Susskind). BEETHOVEN: *Violin sonata No. 9 in A (Kreutzer), Op. 47* (with Moiseiwitsch).
(M) (***) RCA mono 09026 61738-2 (2) [id.].

These were all works that Heifetz was to record again, but not with greater freshness, and by the 1950s he was being given recording of excellent quality. With Sargent in top form underpinning the performance, he provides an inspirational reading of the Elgar *Concerto*, notable for its natural volatility; yet the tenderness and warmth are never in doubt and the slow movement is deeply felt. The finale has an impulsive freedom and sense of fantasy which make the long cadenza sound completely spontaneous, especially as earlier themes are recalled. Heifetz had a soft spot for the lighthearted Saint-Saëns *Sonata* which follows and makes it seem to be a minor masterpiece. How elegantly he plays the delicious *Allegretto moderato*, almost a waltz, which takes the place of the Scherzo, and the finale, a fizzing *moto perpetuo*, is played with breathtaking agility. The 1950 recording of the Tchaikovsky *Concerto* is first class in every way and Susskind makes an ideal partner – his springing of the polacca tutti of the first movement is a joy. The work's opening is beautifully managed and Heifetz's entry and his presentation of the main themes are wonderfully warm and affectionate. The finale has great dash and sparkle. In the *Kreutzer Sonata* Moiseiwitsch is immediately commanding, and this is a superbly authoritative and alive account – as fine as any ever recorded. The slow-movement variations are glorious and full of imaginative touches from both artists; in every way this is preferable to Heifetz's stereo remake with Brooks Smith (see below), and certainly the mono recording (made at Abbey Road) is in the demonstration bracket.

Volume 8: BRAHMS: *Violin sonata No. 3 in D min., Op. 108* (with William Kapell). BEETHOVEN: *Romances Nos. 1, 2* (with RCA Victor SO, Steinberg). BRUCH: *Violin concerto No. 1 in G min., Op. 26* (with LSO, Sargent). WIENIAWSKI: *Polonaise brillante No. 1, Op. 4*. HANDEL: *Sonata in D, Op. 1/13*. SCHUBERT: *Violin sonatina in G min., D.408* (all three with Emanuel Bay). BLOCH: *Sonatas Nos. 1* (with Emanuel Bay); *2 (Poème mystique)* (with Brooks Smith). RAVEL: *Tzigane* (with LAPO, Wallenstein).
(M) (**(*)) RCA mono 09026 61739-2 (2) [id.].

William Kapell rather takes a back seat in the opening Brahms *Sonata*, which is nevertheless given a warmly passionate reading. But the 1950 recording (made in Hollywood) has returned to the up-front sound-balance which makes the violin's upper range somewhat fierce. Heifetz's first version of the Max Bruch *Concerto* (1951) is also a bit top-heavy, although the glowing warmth of the slow movement is impossible to resist and the finale has great zest. Sargent again proves a fine partner. So does William Steinberg in the two *Romances*, which are presented with appealing simplicity. Heifetz's Handel is stylishly dignified, with a nobly shaped *Larghetto*. He treats the Schubert *Sonatina* very classically and is perhaps too emphatic for so innocent a piece. But the veiled tone at the opening of Bloch's *First Sonata* and his subtle changes of colour demonstrate his natural affinity with this composer, and although later fortissimos register rather fiercely the music's special atmosphere is sensitively caught. The *Second Sonata* (*Poème mystique*) is in essence a series of eight brief vignettes with connecting material; its diversity of mood is imaginatively explored, with the *Più lento* ('*Gloria in excelsis Deo*') particularly touching. The finale is marked *Molto quieto* yet produces a final outburst of extraordinary passion. The Ravel *Tzigane* (Heifetz's only recording) is pretty intense, too. The solo playing becomes dazzling at the close but is let down by the thin, brash orchestral tuttis.

Volume 9: MOZART: *Violin sonatas in B flat, K.378; K.454* (with Emanuel Bay); *Duo in B flat, K.424; Divertimento in E flat, K.563* (with Emanuel Feuermann). HANDEL: *Harpsichord suite No. 7 in G min.: Passacaglia* (trans. Johan Halvorsen) (all three with William Primrose); *Sonata in E, Op. 1/15* (with Emanuel Bay). GRIEG: *Violin sonata No. 2 in G, Op. 13* (with Brooks Smith). SINDING: *Suite in A min., Op. 10* (with LAPO, Wallenstein).
(M) (**) RCA mono 09026 61740-2 (2) [id.].

These Mozart performances (from 1941), in which Heifetz is joined by William Primrose and (in the *E flat Divertimento* for string trio) also by Feuermann, are at times curiously stiff rhythmically, almost as if regulated by clockwork. Felicitous playing, of course, and immaculate ensemble, but the bright forward sound does not help to give the feeling that these artists are relaxing and enjoying themselves. The two *Violin sonatas* (1936) are more communicative and lively but still a bit literal. However, the Handel *Passacaglia* (1941), very effectively arranged as a *Duo*, is splendidly done and is most diverting. The *Sonata* from Op. 1, recorded a decade later, is even more spontaneous; Heifetz clearly relishes the noble *Largo* and perhaps overdoes the intensity here. But the result, if distinctly out of period style, is persuasive when the tune itself is so appealing. The early Grieg *Sonata* is the highlight of the set. It is both played and recorded beautifully (1955). The interpretation is very little different from his 78-r.p.m. version of 1936, but the sound is vastly superior and the result is sheer delight. The first movement of the Sinding *Suite* brings another dazzling *moto perpetuo* at which Heifetz was so adept, and he follows it with a G-string soliloquy to open the slow movement. The finale is inconsequential but with a folksy flavour. Good (1953) recording; but this is not one of the more memorable programmes, and it is a pity that the Grieg *Sonata* was included here instead of within one of the more enticing compilations.

Volume 10: BEETHOVEN: *String trios Opp. 3; 9/1, 3* (with Primrose, Piatigorsky); *Violin sonatas Nos. 3 in E flat; 8 in G.* MOZART: *Violin sonata in C, K.296* (all three with Emanuel Bay); *Violin concerto No. 5 in A (Turkish), K.219* (with LSO, Sargent).
(M) (**) RCA mono 09026 61741-2 (2) [id.].

The two Beethoven *Violin sonatas* which open Volume 10 bring consistently felicitous playing from Heifetz, especially the two closing movements of Op. 10/3. But Emanuel Bay is backwardly placed and his personality fails to come through. These performances are no match for the later, stereo set with Brooks Smith. The last of Mozart's five *Violin concertos* was a favourite with Heifetz and he recorded it three times. This is the second version, with Sargent making a strong partner. The first movement has great verve, the *Adagio* much intensity – perhaps a shade too much – but the finale has lots of character. The three Beethoven *String trios* are together on the second disc. The (1957) recording is rather dry and studio-bound but faithful enough, and this is real chamber-music playing, the music intimately shared among three musicians of the highest calibre. There is shared virtuosity, too, of course, notably in the *Presto* finale of Op. 9/1, but no ostentatious self-seeking. The Op. 3 *Trio in E flat*, with its two slow movements, is presented with disarming simplicity.

Volumes 11–15: BEETHOVEN: *Violin concerto in D, Op. 61.* MENDELSSOHN: *Violin concerto in E min., Op. 64.* PROKOFIEV: *Violin concerto No. 2 in G min., Op. 63* (all three with Boston SO, Munch). BRAHMS: *Double concerto for violin, cello and orchestra, Op. 102* (with Piatigorsky, RCA Victor SO, Wallenstein); *Violin concerto in D, Op. 77.* TCHAIKOVSKY: *Violin concerto in D, Op. 35* (both with Chicago SO, Reiner); *Sérénade mélancolique, Op. 26; Serenade in C, Op. 48: Waltz* (with CO). SIBELIUS: *Violin concerto in D min., Op. 47* (with Chicago SO, Hendl). GLAZUNOV: *Violin concerto in A min., Op. 82* (with RCA Victor SO, Hendl). BRUCH: *Violin concerto No. 1 in G min., Op. 26; Scottish fantasy, Op. 46* (with Osian Ellis). VIEUXTEMPS: *Violin concerto No. 5 in A min., Op. 37* (all with New SO of London, Sargent). MOZART: *Sinfonia concertante, K.364* (with William Primrose, RCA Victor SO, I. Solomon). BACH: *Double violin concerto* (with Erick Friedman, Thornton Lofthouse, New SO of London, Sargent).
(M) *** RCA 09026 61779-2 (5) [id.].

With Volumes 11–15 we at last come to the stereo recordings, and it is a great pity that the five discs are packaged together in this way, rather than being offered separately. The remastering for CD is consistently impressive, but many collectors could already have one or more of the recordings included in what is undoubtedly a very impressive first collection.

RCA's digital transfer of the early (1955) Beethoven recording has a remarkable sense of realism and presence, with the soloist only a little closer than is natural. The performance may adopt fast speeds but it never sounds rushed, finding time for individuality and imagination in every phrase. For some listeners the comparative lack of serenity in the first movement (though not in the *Larghetto*) will be a drawback, but the drama of the reading is unforgettable. Heifetz's unique timbre is captured marvellously; the assured aristocracy of the playing confounds criticism.

As with the Beethoven, so the transfer of the Brahms *Violin concerto* (recorded ten months earlier) makes vivid and fresh what was originally a rather harsh Chicago recording, more aggressive than the Boston sound. The speeds for all three movements may be fast, but Heifetz's ease and detailed imagination make them more than just dazzling, while the central *Andante*, at a flowing speed, is delectably songful.

The stereo remake of the Tchaikovsky *Concerto*, fine though it is, has not quite the simplicity and glow of the earlier, mono set with Susskind (see above). But with the upper range of the 1957 recording smoothed and the orchestral presence enhanced, the magic of Heifetz can now be enjoyed more fully. There is some gorgeous lyrical playing and the slow movement marries deep feeling and tenderness in ideal proportions, while the finale scintillates. Reiner accompanies positively, producing fierily positive tuttis. A fine performance of the *Sérénade mélancolique* and an arrangement of the *Waltz* make attractive encores.

As one might expect, Heifetz then gives a fabulous performance of the Mendelssohn *Concerto*. His speeds are consistently fast, yet in the slow movement his flexible phrasing sounds so inevitable and easy that it is hard not to be convinced. The finale is a *tour de force*, light and sparkling, with every note in place. The recording remains brightly vivid, but the sound is smoother than before.

Heifetz's 1959 stereo performance of the Sibelius *Concerto* with the Chicago Symphony Orchestra under Walter Hendl set the standard by which all other versions have come to be judged. It is also one of his finest recordings; in remastered form the sound is vivid, with the Chicago ambience making an apt setting for the finely focused violin-line. The purity and luminous beauty of the violin-tone at the opening put the seal on this as an interpretation of unusual depth, consummate technique and supreme artistry.

In the *arioso*-like slow movement of the Prokofiev No. 2, Heifetz chooses a faster speed than is usual, but there is nothing unresponsive about his playing, for his expressive rubato has an unfailing inevitability.

In the spiky finale he is superb, and indeed his playing is glorious throughout. The 1959 recording has been further improved by the current remastering, which is smoother and richer than ever before, with a fine glow of resonance and plenty of bloom in the slow movement.

Heifetz is incomparable in the Glazunov *Violin concerto*. His account is the strongest and most passionate (as well as the most perfectly played) in the catalogue. In his hands, the work's sweetness is tempered with strength. The RCA Orchestra under Hendl gives splendid support and again the current remastering of the (1963) sound has added lustre to the quality.

In the Bruch *Violin concerto*, Heifetz plays with supreme assurance. The slow movement shows him in top romantic form. He then follows on with the *Scottish fantasia*, and the panache and subtlety of his bowing and control of colour bring a wonderful freshness to Bruch's charming Scottish whimsy. Sargent accompanies sympathetically and it is noticeable that, though the soloist is balanced much too closely, there is never any doubt that Heifetz can still produce a true pianissimo.

The quicksilver of Heifetz is just as well suited to the modest but attractive *Fifth Concerto* of Vieuxtemps, and Sir Malcolm provides a musical and well-recorded accompaniment. The balance of the soloist is rather close, but the digital remastering is again very successful in adding to the warmth and bloom of the 1961 sound.

The last three performances are new to CD. Although Wallenstein is not as fine an accompanist as Ormandy, he provides a sympathetic backcloth for the Heifetz–Piatigorsky partnership in the Brahms *Double concerto* which, if it does not quite match Heifetz's earlier version with Feuermann, is still a strong, warm-hearted account with a strikingly brilliant finale. The 1960 recording has been improved out of all recognition upon the harsh quality of the LP, and there is certainly no lack of warmth here.

The Mozart *Sinfonia concertante* dates from 1956 and brings a quite fruitful partnership between Heifetz and Primrose. If other performances are fresher and more inspirational in the slow movement, this is still warmly enjoyable, although the brisk pace for the finale is not entirely convincing. The recording is remarkably successful, with a freshly detailed orchestral backcloth.

For his second recording of the Bach *Double concerto*, recorded in Walthamstow Town Hall in 1961, Heifetz is joined by his pupil, Erick Friedman, a fine soloist in his own right. Once again outer movements are brisk, but in the slow movement the interchange, although warmly musical, does not match Heifetz's earlier, mono version, where he played both solo parts so memorably.

Volume 16: BEETHOVEN: *Violin sonatas Nos. 1–10*.
(M) (**(*)) RCA mono/stereo 09026 61747-2 (3) [id.]. with Emanuel Bay, Brooks Smith.

Although recorded in unflatteringly dry sound with the violin balanced very close, and despite the fact that Heifetz sometimes takes his preference for fast speeds to extremes, his flair and imagination shine through in the whole cycle. The bold assurance of the playing tends to work against any deeper, darker qualities emerging, but nevertheless these performances consistently give the lie to the idea that Heifetz was a cold player. Even when he chooses a fast tempo and sticks firmly to it, the individuality of phrasing and expression is magnetic. Each movement becomes a refreshing voyage of discovery. Not that Emanuel Bay (Brooks Smith in the *Kreutzer*) is allowed to be an equal partner. Deft and responsive, he simply follows and supports the great virtuoso. The *Kreutzer*, one of the last works to be recorded, is offered in stereo.

Volume 17. BACH: (Unaccompanied) *Violin sonatas Nos. 1–3, BWV 1001, 1003 & 1005; Violin partitas Nos. 1–3, BWV 1002, 1004 & 1006*.
(M) (***) RCA mono 09026 61748-2 (2) [id.].

The dry and limited mono sound of Heifetz's classic set, dating from the 1950s, does not prevent one being thrilled by the astonishing bravura of his playing. Speeds are often extremely fast – phenomenally so in the fugues – yet rhythms are controlled superbly. Though the power of the performances is overwhelming, the closeness and dryness of the acoustic give a kind of drawing-room intimacy, as if the master-violinist was in your own room. With slow movements as well as fast taken faster than usual, these are not meditative readings – but nor are they cold, for Heifetz's creative imagination in his phrasing has one consistently registering the music afresh.

Volume 20: BRUCH: *Violin concerto No. 2 in D min., Op. 44*. CONUS: *Violin concerto in E min.* WIENIAWSKI: *Violin concerto No. 2 in D min., Op. 22* (all three with RCA Victor SO, I. Solomon). TCHAIKOVSKY: *Sérénade mélancolique, Op. 26* (with LAPO, Wallenstein).
(M) (***) RCA mono 09026 61751-2 [id.].

Bruch's *Second Concerto* has always been underrated because of the fame of the first, but, as Heifetz demonstrates here, in the work's first (1954) recording, it has no lack of fine ideas and the finale is very jolly. Both this and the Conus *Concerto* have since been taken up by Perlman. But Heifetz's 1952 account was the first to reveal the latter's appealingly simple brand of lyricism. However, Wieniawski's *Second D minor Concerto* is the highlight of the collection, with its winsome central *Romanze* and twinkling *moto perpetuo* finale (*à la* zingara), where Heifetz is in his element. Tchaikovsky's *Sérénade mélancolique* makes a touching encore. The mono sound is very good throughout, apart from the usual very forward balance for the soloist.

Volume 21: KORNGOLD: *Violin concerto in D, Op. 35* (with LAPO, Wallenstein). ROZSA: *Violin concerto, Op. 24* (with Dallas SO, Hendl); *Sinfonia concertante, Op. 29 (Theme with variations)* (with Piatigorsky, CO). WAXMAN: *Carmen fantasy* (with RCA Victor SO, Voorhees).
(M) **(*) RCA mono/stereo 09026 61752-2 [id.].

It was Heifetz who established the Korngold *Violin concerto* in the recorded repertoire. It is quite familiar now from more recent versions, but the playing in this 1953 mono recording is dazzling: the lyrical music sounds gorgeous and the material, drawn from film scores, is always appealing – and especially when presented like this. The Rózsa *Concerto*, which has the advantage of stereo, is slightly less memorable but is still worth hearing in such a performance. The *Theme with variations* is inventive but not melodically memorable. Here Heifetz is joined by Piatigorsky, also in very good form, and they work very hard to make something of this relatively intractable piece. Waxman's *Carmen fantasy* (mono, 1946) is simply a string of Bizet's hit tunes, and they are presented with a panache that is little short of astonishing. Few reservations have to be made about the recording.

Volume 22: CHAUSSON: *Poème, Op. 25* (with RCA Victor SO, cond. Izler Solomon). LALO: *Symphonie espagnole, Op. 21*. SAINT-SAENS: *Havanaise; Introduction and Rondo capriccioso* (with RCA Victor SO, Steinberg). SARASATE: *Zigeunerweisen* (all cond. Steinberg).
(M) (***) RCA mono 09026 61753-2 [id.].

In the Chausson *Poème*, Heifetz, as usual, is much too close to the microphone, which affects this subtle piece more than most. But the playing is masterly. The performances of the Saint-Saëns *morceaux de concert* have extraordinary charisma: Heifetz's chimerical bowing in the coda of the *Havanaise* is captivating. Similarly the 1951 account of the Lalo *Symphonie espagnole* has superb panache, and there are no complaints about the mono recording, except that it omitted the *Intermezzo* (a practice curiously common at that time); the playing is dazzling. The Sarasate *Zigeunerweisen* scintillates in the fireworks, while the lyrical melody brings the most luscious tone and sophisticated colouring. Apart from the balance, this collection has satisfactory sound and makes a marvellous sampler for Heifetz's great artistry and supreme command of his instrument.

Volume 23: WALTON: *Violin concerto in B min.* (with Philh. O, composer). GRUENBERG: *Violin concerto, Op. 47* (with San Francisco SO, Monteux).
(M) (**(*)) RCA mono 09026 61754-2 [id.].

This is the later version of the Walton *Violin concerto*, first issued in 1951, which Heifetz made with the composer conducting, using the revised score. Speeds are often hair-raisingly fast, but few Heifetz records convey as much passion as this, in music which he inspired and helped to edit, as Joachim did with Brahms. The mono recording is dry, but it seems warmer with more bloom in this new transfer, and the high-voltage electricity has never been matched in this radiant music. However, the earlier mono recording of the original score has an inspirational quality not quite equalled by this later recording. Moreover the coupled Gruenberg *Concerto*, also commissioned by Heifetz, is not a work of any great individuality, even if its songful slow movement (based on fragments from spirituals) is well sustained by the Heifetz bow, and the lively dance finale invites and receives much brilliance from the soloist.

Volume 24: BACH: *Violin concertos Nos. 1–2* (with LAPO, Wallenstein). MOZART: *Violin sonata in B flat, K.454*. PAGANINI: *Caprices Nos. 13, 20* (arr. KREISLER) (with Brooks Smith). VITALI: *Chaconne in G min.* (with Ellsasser (organ)).
(M) (**) RCA mono 09026 61755-2 [id.].

Wallenstein is hardly a Bach stylist, although he uses a reduced-size orchestra; but outer movements are quite lively and Heifetz invests each slow movement, and especially that from the *A minor Concerto*, with his own special charisma, and there is no denying the lyrical beauty of the playing. The Mozart *Sonata* is crisp and clean; again the slow movement is not entirely in style but is still enjoyable. The two Kreisler-arranged Paganini *Caprices* are slow and luscious, while the once-famous Vitali *Chaconne* is heard in Respighi's arrangement with a superfluous organ part which undermines the effect of the violin variants. This is one of the least rewarding issues in the Heifetz Edition.

Volume 25: SPOHR: *Violin concerto No. 8 in A min., Op. 47* (with RCA Victor SO, I. Solomon); *Double quartet, Op. 65* (with Baker, Thomas, Piatigorsky, Amoyal, Rosenthal, Harshman, Lesser). BEETHOVEN: *Serenade, Op. 8* (with Primrose, Piatigorsky).
(M) (***) RCA mono/stereo 09026 61756-2 [id.].

Spohr's *Gesangszenekonsert* is in mono and dates from 1954. A dazzling performance which, in sheer beauty and refinement of tone, remains unsurpassed. Although the recording acoustic could with advantage have been more ample, this is still good sound for its period, and in some ways it is more appealing than the dryish (1968) stereo recording of the *D minor Double quartet*. The first violin dominates the texture, a reminder both of Spohr's prowess as a violinist and – certainly – of Heifetz's. His distinctive timbre and glorious tone shine through. The Beethoven *String serenade* is neatly played by this illustrious trio, but the confining effect of the studio acoustic make the music sound dry in both senses of the word. The result is often spirited but curiously uningratiating.

Volume 26: MOZART: *Violin concerto No. 5 in A (Turkish), K.219* (with CO). *Violin sonata in B flat, K.378* (with Brooks Smith). *String quintet in G min., K.516* (with Baker, Primrose, Majewski, Piatigorsky).
(M) (**(*)) RCA mono/stereo 09026 61757-2 [id.].

A marvellously exhilarating account of the *A Major Concerto* from Heifetz, while his actual entry in the first movement is quite ethereal. He directs the accompanying group himself. The early-1960s stereo is fully acceptable and the performance memorable, with the crystalline clarity of articulation matched by warmth of timbre and aristocratic phrasing. The *String quintet* suffers from an over-stressed urgency in the first movement, which is surely too fast and which robs the music of much of its underlying melancholy. There is nevertheless much to admire in the rest of the work, for the playing itself is very fine. The studio recording is pleasing, the stereo natural although closely balanced. The *Sonata* is a 1954 mono recording of good quality, and the performance comes off rather well.

Volume 27: ARENSKY: *Piano trio No. 1 in D min., Op. 32*. TURINA: *Piano trio No. 1, Op. 35* (both with Pennario). KODALY: *Duo, Op. 7* (all three with Piatigorsky).
(M) (**) RCA 09026 61758-2 [id.].

The Arensky *Trio* is a fine work in the Russian romantic chamber tradition, music which can verge on the Palm Court if it is played in a simpering way but which is richly rewarding if played full-bloodedly. It has a splendid lollipop Scherzo with a virtuoso part for the pianist. This Pennario throws off with aplomb, and his companions are fully equal to the surge of emotionalism elsewhere. After a strong opening, the Turina *Trio* turns out to be quite lightweight and not strikingly Spanish in atmosphere. Unfortunately, in both works the dry recording militates against the music's effect, and this also applies to the Kodály *Duo*, which nevertheless brings some ethereal playing in the central *Adagio*. A picture on the leaflet shows the bare studio in which these recordings were made: no wonder the effect lacks ambience and warmth.

Volume 28: BRAHMS: *String quintet No. 2 in G, Op. 111* (with Baker, Thomas, Rosenthal). BEETHOVEN: *Piano trio in E flat, Op. 70/2* (with Pennario). BOCCHERINI: *Violin sonata in D* (all three with Piatigorsky). MOZART: *Serenade No. 7 in D (Haffner): Rondo* (with Brooks Smith).
(M) (**) RCA 09026 61759-2 [id.].

Although there is not the richness of string blend one might expect in the first movement of the Brahms *Quintet*, the inner movements bring a compensating transparency of texture and the sound itself is quite acceptable. It is a fine performance, as is the lively account of the Beethoven *Piano trio*. The Boccherini *Sonata*, a duo for violin and cello, is an inventive work, and the interplay between Heifetz and Piatigorsky is appealing. The *Rondo* from the Mozart *Haffner Serenade* is then played by Heifetz with great brilliance as a breathtaking encore. But overall this does not gel as a particularly distinctive concert.

Volume 29: BEETHOVEN: *Piano trio No. 7 in B flat (Archduke), Op. 97*. SCHUBERT: *Piano trio in B flat, D.898* (both with Rubinstein, Feuermann)
(M) (***) RCA mono 09026 61760-2 [id.].

These two glorious performances were studio recordings made in 1941. The sound is remarkably good and, although there are a few tiny clicks, otherwise the background noise is not too intrusive. The balance is forward, but the three instruments are more sonorously captured here than in some of the later Heifetz–Piatigorsky stereo records. The playing in the *Archduke* has tremendous life and warmth, while the *Andante* of the Schubert *Trio* is wonderfully simple in its lyrical flow, with Feuermann and Heifetz opening the movement with a magical dialogue. The Scherzo sparkles, without being taken too fast, and the finale has a splendid, natural impetus; here it is Rubinstein who catches the ear, even though he is placed more backwardly. This is one of the finest CDs of the series.

Volume 30: MOZART: *Violin concerto No. 4 in D, K.218* (with New SO of London, Sargent). BEETHOVEN: *Piano trio in E flat, Op. 1/1* (with Lateiner). VIVALDI: *Double concerto for violin and cello in B flat, RV 547* (with CO). HANDEL: *Passacaglia* from *Harpsichord suite No. 7* (trans. Halvorsen) (all three with Piatigorsky).
(M) (**) RCA 09026 61761-2 [id.].

Heifetz takes a brisk view of the first movement of the Mozart *D major Concerto* but plays his runs with crystal clarity and typical verve. This is very much Mozart *à la* Heifetz, and this is a distinct gain in the *Finale*, though something lyrical is lost in the slow movement. Sargent's accompaniment matches the solo line perfectly. The Beethoven *Piano trio* is crisp and neat; the recording is a little dry, but the players convey their pleasure in the music and the finale is winningly spirited. Although a chamber orchestra is used in the Vivaldi *Concerto*, the effect is heavy and a bit gruff in the outer movements and the ear craves more transparency. The *Andante*, however, brings a winning interplay between the two illustrious soloists. The *Passacaglia* from the *G minor Harpsichord suite* of Handel sits uneasily on the instrumental combination of violin and cello; although the playing is of high quality, the end result is ineffective.

Volume 31: A. BENJAMIN: *Romantic fantasy* (with Primrose, RCA Victor O, I. Solomon). STRAVINSKY: *Suite italienne*. GLIERE: *Prelude, Op. 39/1* (both with Piatigorsky). WIENIAWSKI: *Capriccio-valse, Op. 7*. FALLA: *Jota; Nana (Berceuse)*. SGAMBATI: *Serenata napoletana* (all three with Brooks Smith). CASTELNUOVO-TEDESCO: *The Lark* (with Emanuel Bay). BRAHMS: *Hungarian dance No. 7* (with LAPO, Wallenstein).
(M) (***) RCA mono/stereo 09026 61762-2 [id.].

Heifetz didn't like Bartók, and Arthur Benjamin was his idea of a modern composer who wrote music which was enjoyable to play. He wasn't far wrong (about Benjamin) and the *Romantic fantasy* is a very winning triptych, with a horn soloist (Joseph Eger) to catch the ear as the first-movement *Nocturne* opens. Heifetz and Piatigorsky are a bit rough and angular with the opening of Stravinsky's *Suite italienne* (arranged as a duo for violin and cello), but after that they titillate the ear, both spikily and tenderly. The rest of the programme is a series of utterly seductive encores, played with a brilliance and panache that are justly legendary. The sound is good, and the closing *Hungarian dance* is irresistible in its quixotic rubato.

Volume 32: BRAHMS: *Piano trio No. 1 in B, Op. 8* (with Feuermann and Rubinstein). DOHNANYI: *Serenade in C for string trio, Op. 10* (with Primrose and Feuermann). R. STRAUSS: *Violin sonata in E flat, Op. 18* (with Brooks Smith).
(M) (***) RCA mono 09026 61763-2 [id.].

Another of the very finest records of the series, so much so that each performance has been listed and discussed under its composer. The performance of the Richard Strauss *Sonata* has never been surpassed.

Volume 33: FRANCK: *Piano quintet in F min.* (with Pennario, Baker, Primrose and Piatigorsky). DVORAK: *Piano trio (Dumky), Op. 90* (with Lateiner and Piatigorsky). SIBELIUS: *Nocturne* (with Brooks Smith).
(M) *(**) RCA 09026 61764-2 [id.].

Leonard Pennario leads a dramatic and intelligent reading of the Franck *Piano quintet*, excelling in fine phrasing and a sensitive use of timbre. But the one who steals the show time and time again is Heifetz: his way of playing those many wistful and passionate sentences is irresistible. Indeed, although the piano is well in the picture, the violin dominates throughout and Israel Baker and William Primrose are quite outbalanced. The stereo is two-dimensional. The internal balance is much better in the *Dumky Trio*, and Piatigorsky's singing line often dominates. Not surprisingly, it is a sparkling performance, but Heifetz plays with wonderful tenderness too. It is a pity that the artists are placed so forwardly; one might relish the presence, but it reduces the dynamic range and tends to make Heifetz sound shrill when he is being forceful. But this is magnificent music-making, and the Sibelius *Nocturne* makes a charismatic encore.

Volume 34: MOZART: *String quintet (No. 5) in C, K.515* (with Baker, Primrose, Majewski, Piatigorsky). BACH: *Partita No. 2, BWV 1004: Chaconne*. MENDELSSOHN: *Piano trio No. 2 in C min., Op. 66* (with Pennario, Piatigorsky).
(M) (**(*)) RCA 09026 61765-2 [id.].

The Mendelssohn and Mozart recordings were part of the Heifetz–Piatigorsky concerts series of recordings, dating from 1963 and 1964 respectively. Both recordings are dry and closely balanced, but the Mozart performance, although its technical efficiency is somehow emphasized by the acoustic, is strongly projected and has an underlying warmth. The finale sparkles and there is less of the feeling of intense pressure which adversely affected the opening movement of this group's earlier recording of the *G minor Quintet*. The two-dimensional studio recording of the Mendelssohn *Trio* does not help its intimacy, but it remains a fine performance, especially the *Andante* and dazzling Scherzo. The compelling account of the Bach *Chaconne* was recorded for a Heifetz TV special.

Volume 35: MENDELSSOHN: *Octet, Op. 20* (with Baker, Belnick, Stepansky, Primrose, Majewski, Rejto). TOCH: *Divertimento, Op. 37/2* (both with Piatigorsky). RACHMANINOV: *Daisies*. Robert Russell BENNETT: *A Song sonata*. SHULMAN: *Cod liver 'ile*. GERSHWIN: *It ain't necessarily so* (all with Brooks Smith). STRAVINSKY: *Berceuse*. SHOSTAKOVICH: *Danse fantastique, Op. 5/2* (both with Emanuel Bay). Heifetz on music (talk).
(M) (**(*)) RCA mono/stereo 09026 61766-2 [id.].

The Mendelssohn *Octet*, like the Franck *Quintet* above, was recorded in conjunction with a series of Pilgrimage Theatre Concerts, given at Hollywood in the autumn of 1961 by a star cast of musicians, most of them resident in California. With Heifetz and Piatigorsky as the twin props of this enterprise, excitement was guaranteed, but the playing brings reservations too. The *Octet* of Mendelssohn certainly responds to this galaxy of virtuoso string-players. Heifetz, leading the ensemble, is very much in evidence, but if now and then the work sounds like a violin concerto, this is due not only to the vigour of Heifetz's playing but also to the way this brilliant piece is scored. The lightness and grace of the famous *Scherzo* is unforgettable. But the close balance prevents full enjoyment. The Toch *Divertimento* (a duo) is a fine piece, and the bravura of these virtuosi is extraordinary in the closing *Vivace molto*. The sound improves considerably in the Rachmaninov song and the other novelty, an engaging *Song sonata* by Robert Russell Bennett, a radio recording from 1955 sounding unexpectedly good. Its three movements are marked *Belligerent*, *Slow and lonely* – with haunting, veiled tone from Heifetz – and *Madly dancing*, which is rhythmically catchy and a chance for the letting down of hair, which is well taken. Stravinsky's *Berceuse* (wonderfully warm-toned) makes a good foil for the vibrant Shostakovich miniature. Before the final *It ain't necessarily so*, Heifetz offers some homely advice – to students on practising, about his purchase of an electric car as a symbol of the need to fight against Californian smog, and some homespun philosophy too. (Self-) Discipline, he suggests, is important for enjoying life, while he is sure that 'We have too many comforts – actually they are not conducive for dreaming.'

Volume 36: TCHAIKOVSKY: *Piano trio in A min., Op. 50*. MENDELSSOHN: *Piano trio in D min., Op. 49* (both with Rubinstein, Piatigorsky).
(M) (**) RCA mono 09026 61767-2 [id.].

These recordings date from 1950. They were made in a very dry acoustic and allowances have to be made for their two-dimensional quality and lack of range, particularly so far as the piano timbre is concerned. The playing is high-powered and at times a bit hard-driven, particularly the *Scherzo* of the Mendelssohn. Nevertheless the golden tone of Heifetz and Piatigorsky is a joy in itself (as is the digital dexterity of Rubinstein); the playing is marvellously authoritative and much of it is *con amore*, but it is public, 'big-time' playing, not chamber-music-making. There is a substantial cut in the finale of the Tchaikovsky.

Volume 37: SCHUBERT: *String quintet in C, D.956* (with Israel Baker, William Primrose, Gregor Piatigorsky, Gabor Rejto); *String trio No. 2 in B flat, D.581*. BACH: *Sinfonias: BWV 790, 795 & 789* (all with Primrose, Piatigorsky). SCHUBERT: *Ave Maria* (with Emanuel Bay)
(M) ** RCA stereo/mono 09026 61768-2 [id.].

The Heifetz team play magnificently in the Schubert *Quintet*; their blend and beauty of tone is remarkable, though allegros are fast and streamlined. The recording is very close, which inevitably means a reduction of dynamic range, but there is a hushed quality in the great slow movement and one can feel that these players are genuinely moved by the music, even if the effect cannot be said to be ethereal. In the *String trio* the playing, as playing, is altogether marvellous, of course, and there is a degree of intimacy, almost charm here. The closing *Rondo* is neatly articulated and ensemble is amazingly clean, while the brief Bach *Sinfonias* are rather attractive and obviously serious in intention. But the close balance does not help. The transfers are excellent. Only the *Ave Maria* is in mono; Heifetz plays it with touching restraint, but Emanuel Bay's piano accompaniment is very much in the background – even when he opens alone.

Volume 38: SCHUBERT: *Piano trio No. 2 in E flat, D.929* (with Jacob Lateiner, Piatigorsky). BRAHMS: *Piano trio No. 2 in C, Op. 87* (with Leonard Pennario, Piatigorsky).
(M) **(*) RCA 09026 61769-2 [id.].

Although closely balanced, the stereo from 1963 and 1965 adds a certain bloom to the studio sound, and Heifetz and Piatigorsky make the most of their Schubertian dialoue in the *E flat Trio*. They are certainly stylish and almost affectionate, but perhaps not disarming. Leonard Pennario comes over more strongly than his piano colleague in the passionate Brahms *Trio*; indeed he is often able to dominate the music-making and, while the remarkable symbiosis between Heifetz and Piatiorsky remains, the three artists are on more or less equal terms and are at one in their interpretation, which has the strongest lyrical impulse. Bravura playing from all concerned in the brilliant Scherzo, and even the *giocoso* finale is moved on very briskly. The remastering gives a very clean, slightly dry but very truthful sound-picture and, once one adjusts, it is easy to respond to such unique ensemble playing.

Volume 39: TCHAIKOVSKY: *Souvenir de Florence, Op. 70* (with Israel Baker, Milton Thomas, Paul Rosenthal, Piatigorsky, Laurence Lesser). DVORAK: *Piano trio No. 3 in F min., Op. 65* (with Pennario, Piatigorsky).
(M) ** RCA 09026 61770-2 [id.].

The *Souvenir de Florence* is a performance of strong, extrovert feeling. It seems likely that these artists had not played the work before they got together to rehearse for one of the famed Heifetz–Piatigorsky concerts in Los Angeles in 1968. Certainly, for all their vigour they don't quite catch the infectious buoyancy of the rhythmic swing of the first movement and, although they do better with the finale, the effect is still very forceful. Although the somewhat dry recording (not as close as usual) may have something to do with it, the rather grainy timbre of the ensemble has more to do with unsuccessful linear tonal matching. The Russian charm of the *Allegretto* hardly survives a tempo that is pressed on so positively, and these artists seem mainly concerned with expressing vehement passion in this very Slavic music and they miss its mellower side. The Dvořák *Trio* is shared by Leonard Pennario, so we know that it will be more or less a trio of equals. However, the bright Heifetz violin-sound still dominates. Again charm is not a strong point, but Piatigorsky's introductory solo in the *Adagio* ensures that there will be a memorable interplay with the great violinist. The finale has great verve and impetus. The 1963 recording is too close, but truthful.

Volume 40: GERSHWIN: *Preludes; Porgy and Bess selection.* KORNGOLD: *Much Ado about Nothing: Garden scene.* RACHMANINOV: *Oriental sketch, Op. 2/2; Daisies, Op. 38/3.* PROKOFIEV: *The Love for 3 oranges: March.* KHACHATURIAN: *Gayaneh: Sabre dance* (all with Brooks Smith). SCHUBERT: *Ave Maria, D.839.* GODOWSKY: *Alt Wien.* MENDELSSOHN: *On wings of song, Op. 34/2.* DINICU: *Hora staccato.* DEBUSSY: *La plus que lente.* DRIGO: *Valse bluette.* POULENC: *Presto in B flat.* PONCE: *Estrellita.* SARASATE: *Zapateado, Op. 23/2.* RACHMANINOV: *Vocalise, Op. 34/14.* KROLL: *Banjo and fiddle.* J. ACHRON: *Hebrew melody, Op. 33.* WIENIAWSKI: *Scherzo-tarantelle* (all with Emanuel Bay).
(M) *** RCA mono/stereo 09026 61771-2 [id.].

This collection of lollipops opens with the Gershwin collection, played with winning style and sophistication – Heifetz at his most charismatic. Moreover the ear is immediately aware of unusually good and well-balanced sound, with the pianist (here Brooks Smith) not relegated to the background, and well recorded too. Heifetz is in his element in the witty Prokofiev march, while the Khachaturian *Sabre dance* and Dinicu's *Hora staccato* bring some fabulous bowing, and the luscious G-string tone in Mendelssohn's *On wings of song* is very little short of being schmaltzy. Sarasate's *Zapateado* takes immediate wing and leads into a series of bravura pieces which are all quite breath-taking. Even though the content is lightweight, few of Heifetz's records show his consummate musical and technical mastery to better effect, and the Rachmaninov *Vocalise*, which acts as an interlude, is gently ravishing. The recordings date from between 1946 and 1970, but the splendid transfers are remarkable in disguising the age of the earlier ones. Not to be missed.

Volume 41: DVORAK: *Piano quintet in A, Op. 81* (with Lateiner, Baker, Joseph de Pasquale, Piatigorsky). BRAHMS: *Sextet in G, Op. 36* (with Baker, Primrose, Virginia Majewski, Piatigorsky, Rejto); *Hungarian dances Nos. 11 in D min.; 17 in F min.; 20 in D min.* (with Brooks Smith).
(M) *** RCA mono/stereo 09026 61772-2 [id.].

The performance of the Dvořák *Quintet* is glorious, one of the very finest and most spontaneous examples of the collaboration of these remarkable musicians. The recording may be too close, the interpretation romantically high-powered, but they achieve a total partnership. Here the pianist, Jacob Lateiner, is never upstaged by his companions, and the overall result is splendid. These artists are clearly in love with Dvořák's music: they play the second-movement *Dumka* with both delicacy and élan, the central section of the Scherzo is warm and touching, and the finale has the kind of sparkle and lyrical intensity one might expect. The recording dates from 1964 and, though it is inclined to be dryish, the piano-tone is fully acceptable. The Brahms *Sextet* was recorded in 1961. The acoustic is again rather dry and does not do full justice to the rich-textured sounds made. But its fine-spun melodies, rhetorical polyphony and engaging rhythms and colours are certainly realized from a musical point of view. The finale brings a light-hearted brilliance of execution that shows the team at their best. Though made a few years earlier (in mono in 1956), the transcriptions by Joachim and Kreisler of the Brahms *Hungarian dances* sound fresh enough. Heifetz is of course incomparable, and here he is accompanied sensitively and discreetly by Brooks Smith.

Volume 42: UBERT: *Fantasie in C, D.934* (with Brooks Smith). BRAHMS: *Piano quartet No. 3 in C min., Op. 60* (with Lateiner, Schonbach, Piatigorsky). BEETHOVEN: *String trio No. 2 in D, Op. 9/2* (with Primrose, Piatigorsky).
(M) *(**) RCA 09026 61773-2 [id.].

Heifetz's account of the *C major Fantasy* was recorded in 1968, though the dry studio acoustic almost suggests an earlier provenance. Brooks Smith is a fine player and he is well recorded; Heifetz is his incomparable self and he plays sweeetly and appealingly. The Brahms *Piano quartet* is given a powerful, big-boned performance (at times perhaps a bit too high-powered, but let that pass). However, although the ear adjusts, the dry, boxed-in acoustic diminishes the pleasure these players give. The performance of the Beethoven *D major Trio* comes from 1960 and is the earliest of the recordings in this volume. The dryish sound remains a handicap but, as one would expect from these artists, the playing is magisterial and, like the Schubert, there is much to delight musically. The transfers are first class.

Volume 43: CASTELNUOVO-TEDESCO: *Violin concerto No. 2 (I Profeti), Op. 66* (with LAPO, Wallenstein). FERGUSON: *Violin sonata No. 1, Op. 2* (with Lillian Steuber). FRANCAIX: *String trio in C* (with de Pasquale, Piatigorsky). Karen KHACHATURIAN: *Violin sonata in G min., Op. 1* (with Steuber).
(M) **(*) RCA mono/stereo 09026 61774-2 [id.].

In his violin concerto, subtitled *The Prophets*, Castelnuovo-Tedesco sought to represent the fiery eloquence of the ancient prophets among the surrounding voices of the people and the voices of nature. It is an appealing neo-romantic piece whose opening suggests Bloch or Vaughan Williams; but the idiom is predominantly sunny. The thematic substance has a strong Hebrew flavour, especially in the slow movement. Heifetz plays with glorious, full-throated tone and the Los Angeles orchestra under Wallenstein give excellent support. The 1954 mono recording places the soloist far forward but is otherwise quite spacious and is generally very acceptable as remastered here. Howard Ferguson's *First Violin sonata* was written when the composer was in his early twenties. It is beautifully crafted and, though not strongly individual (it springs from the tradition of Brahms and Elgar), is a satisfying musical experience. The dryish acoustic of the stereo recording does not flatter the pianist, but Heifetz's fine playing rises eloquently above such limitations. Jean Françaix's debonair *String trio* of 1933 is a delight, full of sophistication and tenderness. Recorded in 1964, it is marvellously played. Karen is the nephew of Aram Khachaturian and studied with Miaskovsky and Shostakovich in the late 1940s. Their tutelage shows in every bar of this eminently well-fashioned but not particularly individual piece. The work is beautifully played by Heifetz, though Lillian Steuber is not the most poetic of pianists. Good (1966) recording and excellent transfers. This is among the more rewarding of these Heifetz compilations.

Volume 44: DEBUSSY: *Violin sonata in G min.; La fille aux cheveux de lin*. RESPIGHI: *Violin sonata in B min*. RAVEL: *Sonatine; Menuet* (all with Emanuel Bay); *Piano trio in A min*. (with Rubinstein, Piatigorsky). MARTINU: *Duo for violin and cello* (with Piatigorsky).
(M) **(*) RCA mono/stereo 09026 61775-2 [id.].

Heifetz's immaculately played account of the Debussy *Violin sonata* was recorded in 1950 and the golden tone is glorious; some allowances have to be made for the dryish piano-timbre – though not, of course, for Emanuel Bay's playing. *La fille aux cheveux de lin* makes a ravishing encore. The Respighi *Sonata* was recorded the day before, and the quality of the performance has never been surpassed. The inspired opening of the Ravel *Piano trio* is curiously lacking in magic and atmosphere. Peerless though the playing is, this is not a version to which one would be tempted to return often. Martinu composed two duos for violin and cello, this short but powerful piece dating from 1927. It is the only stereo recording (1964) on this disc, but the acoustic is still on the dry side. Fabulous playing. The remastering has once again brought an improvement in the sound, particularly that of the piano, and this is another of the most valuable Heifetz reissues.

Volume 45: SAINT-SAENS: *Violin sonata No. 1 in D min., Op. 75; Le cygne*. FAURE: *Violin sonata No. 1 in A, Op. 13*. DEBUSSY: *Beau soir; Golliwog's cakewalk; La chevelure; La fille aux cheveux de lin*. IBERT: *Le petit âne blanc*. RAVEL: *Valses nobles et sentimentales, Nos. 6–7*. POULENC: *Mouvement perpétuel* (all with Brooks Smith).
(M) *** RCA mono/stereo 09026 61776-2 [id.].

Heifetz opens the Saint-Saëns *Sonata* like a whirlwind, but Brooks Smith matches his bravura and they are equally at home in the rather lovely *Adagio* and the feather-light *Allegretto* and scintillating *moto perpetuo* finale. The 1965 stereo is very good. The Fauré *Sonata* is a decade earlier but the mono sound is pleasing, though the piano is placed comparatively backwardly. The playing itself is properly delicate in feeling. Then follow a chimerical (stereo) series of shorter pieces, many of them transcriptions and all played wonderfully. Heifetz's subtly bowed portrayal of Saint-Saëns's *Swan* upstages many a cellist's performance.

Selections from 'The Heifetz Collection': DEBUSSY: *Preludes, Book 1: La fille aux cheveux de lin* (with Isidor Achron). RIMSKY-KORSAKOV: *Tsar Saltan: Flight of the bumble-bee* (with Arpad Sandor). PROKOFIEV: *Violin concerto No. 2 in G min., Op. 36: 2nd movt* (with Boston SO, Koussevitzky). HANDEL: *Harpsichord suite No. 7 in G min.: Passacaglia* (with William Primrose). RACHMANINOV: *Daisies, Op. 38/3* (with Emanuel Bay). BACH: *Double violin concerto in D min., BWV 1043: Vivace* (with RCA Victor SO, Steinberg); *Partita No. 3 in E, BWV 1006: Preludio.* BEETHOVEN: *Violin sonata No. 5 in F (Spring), Op. 24: Allegro* (with Bay). DINICU: *Hora staccato* (with Bay). SAINT-SAENS: *Introduction and rondo capriccioso in A min., Op. 28* (with RCA Victor SO, Steinberg). SINDING: *Suite for violin and orchestra, Op. 10: 3rd movt* (with LAPO, Wallenstein). MENDELSSOHN: *Octet in E flat, Op. 20: Scherzo; Allegro leggierissimo* (with I. Baker, A. Belnick, J. Stepansky, Primrose, V. Majewski, G. Piatigorsky, G. Rejto). GERSHWIN: *Porgy and Bess: Summertime; It ain't necessarily so* (with Brooks Smith). FALLA: *7 Canciones populares españolas: No. 4 (Jota): 'Nana' (Berceuse)* (with Brooks Smith). TCHAIKOVSKY: *Violin concerto in D, Op. 35: Allegro vivacissimo* (with Chicago SO, Reiner).
(M) (***) BMG/RCA 09026 62645-2 [id.].

A good sampler of Heifetz's astonishing wizardry, ranging from the pioneering record of Prokofiev's *G minor Concerto* with the legendary Koussevitzky, recorded not long after its composition, to snatches from his vast post-war output.

Horowitz, Vladimir (piano)

The '*Horowitz Editions*'

Obviously these expensive compilations are designed for libraries and ambitious private collectors. The RCA set includes concertos, so is listed here under Orchestral Collections. The smaller Sony (CBS) set consists entirely of solo piano music and is listed below in our Recitals section. In one sense, both sets are highly desirable and to choose between them is almost impossible.

'The Vladimir Horowitz Edition': (complete RCA recordings with var. orchestras & conductors): BEETHOVEN: *Sonatas Nos. 14 (Moonlight); 21 (Waldstein); 23 (Appassionata)* (GD 60375). CHOPIN: *Sonata No. 2; Nocturnes, Op. 9/2; 55/1; Impromptu No. 1, Op. 29; Etudes, Op. 10/3–4; Ballade No. 1, Op. 23; Mazurka, Op. 30/4; Scherzo No. 1, Op. 20* (GD 60376). PROKOFIEV: *Sonata No. 7, Op. 83; Toccata, Op. 11.* BARBER: *Sonata, Op. 26.* KABALEVSKY: *Sonata No. 3, Op. 46.* FAURE: *Nocturne No. 13.* POULENC: *Presto in B flat* (GD 60377). MUSSORGSKY: *Pictures at an exhibition; By the water.* TCHAIKOVSKY: *Concerto No. 1* (with NBC SO, Toscanini) (GD 60449). CZERNY: *La Ricordanza (Variations on a theme by Rode), Op. 33.* MOZART: *Sonata, K.332.* MENDELSSOHN: *Variations sérieuses, Op. 54.* SCHUBERT: *Sonata, D.960* (GD 60451). SCARLATTI: *Sonata, Kk.380.* BACH (arr. Busoni): *Nun komm' der Heiden Heiland (Come Redeemer).* HAYDN: *Sonata, Hob XVI/52.* BEETHOVEN: *Sonata No. 14 (Moonlight).* BRAHMS: *Violin sonata No. 3* (with Nathan Milstein). SCHUMANN: *Träumerei* (GD 60461). SCHUMANN: *Kinderszenen; Clara Wieck variations.* LISZT: *Valse oublié No. 1; Hungarian rhapsody No. 6.* DEBUSSY: *Sérénade à la poupée.* FAURE: *Impromptu No. 5.* MENDELSSOHN: *Songs without words: May breezes.* BRAHMS: *Waltz in A flat.* CHOPIN: *Barcarolle; Nocturne, Op. 15/2; Mazurkas Opp. 24/4; 30/4; Scherzo No. 3.* LISZT/BUSONI: *Etude No. 2* (GD 60463). BRAHMS: *Concerto No. 2, Op. 83* (with NBC SO, Toscanini); *Intermezzo, Op. 117/2.* SCHUBERT: *Impromptu, D.899.* LISZT: *Au bord d'une source; Sonetto No. 4 del Petrarca; Hungarian rhapsody No. 2* (GD 60523). MUSSORGSKY: *Pictures at an exhibition.* SCRIABIN: *Etude, Op. 2/1; Preludes Nos. 11/5; 22/1; Sonata No. 9.* HOROWITZ: *Danse excentrique.* TCHAIKOVSKY: *Dumka.* BIZET/HOROWITZ: *Carmen variations.* PROKOFIEV: *Sonata No. 7: III.* RACHMANINOV: *Humoresque; Barcarolle.* DEBUSSY: *Sérénade à la poupée.* SOUSA/HOROWITZ: *The Stars and stripes forever* (GD 60526). SCRIABIN: *Sonatas Nos. 3, Op. 23; 5, Op. 53; Preludes, Op. 11/1, 3, 9–10, 13–14, 16; 13/6; 15/2; 16/1, 4; 27/1; 48/3; 51/2; 59/2; 67/1; Etudes, Op. 8/7, 12; 42/5* (GD 86215). SCHUMANN: *Sonata No. 3 (Concerto without orchestra); Humoresque, Op. 20; Fantasiestücke, Op. 111; Nachtstücke, Op. 23* (GD 86680). CHOPIN: *Polonaise-Fantaisie, Op. 61; Ballades Nos. 1, Op. 23; 4, Op. 52; Barcarolle, Op. 60; Etudes, Opp. 10/5; 25/7; Waltz, Op. 69/1; Andante spinato & grande polonaise, Op. 22* (GD 87752). CLEMENTI: *Sonatas, Opp. 14/3; 26/2; 33/3 (Sonata quasi concerto); 34/2; 47/2 (rondo)* (GD 87753). RACHMANINOV: *Sonata No. 2, Op. 36; Moment musical, Op. 16/2; Prelude, Op. 32/5; Polka V. R.; Concerto No. 3* (with RCA Victor SO, Fritz Reiner) (GD 87754). BIZET/HOROWITZ: *Carmen variations.* SAINT-SAENS/LISZT/HOROWITZ: *Danse macabre.* MOZART: *Rondo alla turka.* MENDELSSOHN/LISZT/HOROWITZ: *Wedding march & variations.* MENDELSSOHN: *Songs without words: Elégie; Spring*

song; The Shepherd's complaint. DEBUSSY: *Sérénade à la poupée*. MOSZKOWSKI: *Etudes in A flat; in F; Etincelles*. CHOPIN: *Polonaise, Op. 53*. SCHUMANN: *Träumerei*. MENDELSSOHN: *Scherzo a capriccio*. LISZT/HOROWITZ: *Rakóczy march*. RACHMANINOV: *Prelude in G min*. SOUSA/HOROWITZ: *The Stars and stripes forever* (GD 87755). TCHAIKOVSKY: *Concerto No. 1* (with NBC SO, Toscanini). BEETHOVEN: *Concerto No. 5 (Emperor)* (with RCA Victor SO, Fritz Reiner) (GD 87992). SCARLATTI: *Sonatas, Kk.46; 87; 322; 380; 455; 531*. SCARLATTI/TAUSIG: *Capriccio (Sonata, K.20/L.375)*. BEETHOVEN: *Sonata No. 7*. CHOPIN: *Mazurka, Op. 30/3; Nocturnes, Opp. 27/1; 72/1; Waltzes, Opp. 34/2; 64/2; Ballade No. 3, Op. 47*. VON DOHNANYI: *Concert étude, Op. 28/6 (Capriccio)* (09026 60986-2). CHOPIN: *Scherzos Nos. 1–2; Mazurkas, Opp. 7/3; 41/1; 50/3; 59/3; 63/2–3* (09026 60987-2). *God save the queen*. CHOPIN: *Polonaise-fantaisie, Op. 61; Ballade No. 1*. SCHUMANN: *Kinderszenen, Op. 15*. SCRIABIN: *Etude, Op. 8/12* (09026 61414-2). LISZT: *Sonata in B min.; Ballade No. 2; Consolation No. 3; Funerailles; Mephisto waltz No. 1* (09026 61415-2). SCARLATTI: *Sonatas, L.33; 118; 186; 189; 224; 494*. CHOPIN: *Ballade No. 4; Waltz (L'adieu), Op. 69/1*. LISZT: *Ballade No. 2*. RACHMANINOV: *Prelude, Op. 23/5* (09026 61416-2). RACHMANINOV: *Concerto No. 3* (with NYPO, Ormandy) (09026 61564-2).
(M) (***) RCA Dig./analogue mono/stereo 09026 61655-2 (22) [id.].

The RCA set comprises 22 CDs, ranging from the 1940s through to the 1980s before he was lured to DG – and omitting the period when he was out of the public eye or with the CBS label. Included in the survey are the two accounts of the Rachmaninov *Third Piano concerto*, the 1951 account with Reiner (which is to be preferred) and the 1978 account with Ormandy. There are two versions of the *Pictures at an exhibition*, one from 1947 and the other from a Carnegie Hall recital in 1951. Not to be missed in the RCA set are the epoch-making Barber *Sonata* and Prokofiev *Seventh*, his Clementi sonata disc and his Scriabin *Third* and *Fifth sonatas*, as well as the electrifying Tchaikovsky *B flat minor Concerto* with Toscanini. His 1951 *Emperor concerto* with Reiner has been consistently underrated and has a splendid authority; his Brahms *Second* with Toscanini is less compelling and lacks spontaneity and, in the slow movement, warmth. His Liszt *Sonata* is magnificent but not as breathtaking as the 1933 version, included in the EMI set. The recordings vary greatly: many are an improvement on the originals – though in many cases they needed to be. Alas, they are no longer available separately.

Hungarian State Orchestra, Mátyás Antal

'Hungarian festival': KODALY: *Háry János: suite*. LISZT: *Hungarian rhapsodies for orchestra Nos. 1, 2 & 6* (arr. DOEPPLER). HUBAY: *Hejre Kati* (with Ferenc Balogh). BERLIOZ: *Damnation de Faust: Rákóczy march*.
(BB) *** Naxos Dig. 8.550142; *4550142* [id.].

The Hungarian State Orchestra are in their element in this programme of colourful music for which they have a natural affinity. There is no more characterful version of the *Háry János suite* (we have already mentioned it in the Composer index) and Hubay's concertante violin piece, with its gypsy flair, is similarly successful, even if the violin soloist is not a particularly strong personality. The special interest of the Liszt *Hungarian rhapsodies* lies in the use of the Doeppler orchestrations, which are comparatively earthy, with greater use of brass solos than the more sophisticated scoring most often used in the West. The performances are suitably robust and certainly have plenty of charisma. The brilliant digital recording is strong on primary colours but has atmosphere too, and produces plenty of spectacle in the Berlioz *Rákóczy march*.

Järvi, Neeme, with various orchestras

'The early Melodiya recordings'

BRAHMS: *Symphonies Nos. 2 in D, Op. 73; 3 in F, Op. 90* (with Moscow PO).
(M) *(*) BMG/Melodiya 74321 40719-2.

PAGANINI: *Violin concerto No. 1 in D, Op. 6;* TCHAIKOVSKY: *Violin concerto in D, Op. 35* (with Viktor Tretyakov, Moscow PO).
(M) ** BMG/Melodiya 74321 40720-2.

SAINT-SAENS: *Piano concerto No. 2 in G min., Op. 22;* TCHAIKOVSKY: *Piano concerto No. 1 in B flat min., Op. 23* (with Grigory Sokolov, USSR SO).
(M) **(*) BMG/Melodiya 74321 40721-2.

BEETHOVEN*Piano concerto No. 4 in G, Op. 58* (with Maria Grinberg, USSR SO). Richard STRAUSS: *Don Juan; Till Eulenspiegel* (with USSR TV and R. Large SO).
✿ (M) ** BMG/Melodiya 74321 40722-2.

CHERUBINI: *Requiem Mass No. 2 in D min.;* SHOSTAKOVICH: *Loyalty, Op. 135* (with Estonian State Ac. Male Ch., Estonian RSO).
(M) ** BMG/Melodiya 74321 40723-2.

HAYDN: *Cello concerto No. 2 in D, Hob. VIIb/2* (with Daniil Shafran, USSR SO). TCHAIKOVSKY: *Variations on a rococo theme, Op. 33; Pezzo capriccioso in B min., Op. 62; Andante cantabile, Op. 11; Nocturne in D min., Op. 19/4* (with Valentin Feighin, Estonian State SO).
(M) **(*) BMG/Melodiya 74321 40724-2.

These six issues of some of his first Melodiya recordings, made mostly in the 1960s, have been issued to mark Neeme Järvi's sixtieth birthday and have been chosen by him. They are offered in a slipcase at a highly competitive price but are also available separately and are discussed individually in the main body of the text. Technically they are variable, though the age of the recordings is by no means an indication of quality. Daniil Shafran's marvellous Haydn concerto from 1962 is superior to the coarse and unpleasing sound the engineers produce in the brilliant performances of the Strauss tone-poems recorded in 1974. The Brahms symphonies, recorded with the Moscow Philharmonic in 1966, do not rise much above the routine; but there are some outstanding things that makes the set well worth having. Dazzling accounts of the Paganini *D major* and Tchaikovsky *Violin concertos* from the nineteen-year-old Viktor Tretyakov and a hardly less impressive Tchaikovsky *B flat minor Concerto* from the sixteen-year-old Grigory Sokolov. But perhaps the greatest finds are Maria Grinburg's seraphic Beethoven *G major Concerto* and Daniil Shafran's Haydn.

Karajan Edition (EMI)

The Berlin years, Vol. 1

BEETHOVEN: *Piano concertos Nos. 1 in C, Op. 15; 2 in B flat, Op. 19.*
Alexis Weissenberg, BPO (CDM5 66090-2).

BEETHOVEN: *Piano concertos Nos. 3 in C min., Op. 37; 5 in E flat (Emperor), Op. 73.*
Alexis Weissenberg, BPO (CDM5 66091-2).

BEETHOVEN: (i) *Piano concerto No. 4 in G, Op. 58;* (ii) *Triple concerto in C, Op. 56.*
(i) Alexis Weissenberg; (ii) David Oistrakh, Rostropovich, Richter; BPO (CDM5 66092-2).

BRAHMS: *Variations on a theme of Haydn, Op. 56a;* (i) *Piano concerto No. 2 in B flat, Op. 83.*
BPO, (i) with Hans Richter-Haaser (CDM5 66093-2).

BRUCKNER: *Symphony No. 4 in E flat (Romantic).*
BPO (CDM5 66094-2).

BRUCKNER: *Symphony No. 7 in E.*
BPO (CDM5 66095-2).

HAYDN: *Symphonies Nos. 83 in G min. (The Hen); 101 in D (Clock); 104 in D (London).*
BPO (CDM5 66097-2).

MOZART: *Symphonies Nos. 29; 35 (Haffner); 36 (Linz); 38 (Prague); 39; 40; 41 (Jupiter). Rehearsal extracts.*
BPO (CMS5 66113-2 (3)). Also available separately: *Nos. 29, 35 & 36* (CDM5 66098-2); *Nos. 38 & 39* (with rehearsal extracts) (CDM5 66099-2); *Nos. 40 & 41* (with rehearsal extracts) (CDM5 66100-2).

MOZART: (i) *Sinfonia concertante in E flat, K.297b.* BRAHMS: (ii) *Violin concerto in D, Op. 77.*
(i) Steins, Stähr, Hauptmann, Braun; (ii) Kremer; (i–ii) BPO (CDM5 66101-2).

SCHUBERT: *Symphonies Nos. 1–2* (with WEBER: *Der Freischütz: overture*) (CDMS5 66102-2); *Nos. 3–4* (with *Rosamunde ballet music, D.797*) (CDMS5 66103-2); *Nos. 5–6* (with *Overture (Die Zauberharfe), D.644*) (CDMS5 66104-2); *Nos. 8–9* (CDM5 66105-2).

R. STRAUSS: *Don Quixote, Op. 35.* WAGNER: *Tannhäuser:* (i) *Overture and Venusberg music. Die Meistersinger: Overture.*
BPO, (i) with German Op. Ch. (CDM5 66106-2).

R. STRAUSS: *Sinfonia domestica, Op. 53.* WAGNER: *Tristan und Isolde: Prelude & Liebestod; Lohengrin: Preludes to Acts I & III.*
BPO (CDM5 66107-2).

R. STRAUSS: *Ein Heldenleben, Op. 40.* WAGNER: *Der fliegende Holländer: Overture; Parsifal: Preludes to Acts I & III.*
BPO (CDM5 66108-2).

BRAHMS: *Tragic Overture, Op. 81.* HINDEMITH: *Mathis der Maler* (symphony). BRUCKNER: *Symphony No. 8 in C min.*
BPO (CMS5 66109-2 (2)).

Karajan's period with EMI, after he had left Decca, was less consistently successful than his later, DG era, when he probably reached the peak of his recording career. Some collectors will resist the sumptuous orchestral sound he was given in the works of Haydn and Mozart and also perhaps in Schubert too, where we are now accustomed to more transparent textures. In the Beethoven concertos he was not well partnered by Weissenberg, but in the Brahms *B flat Concerto* it was surely Karajan, rather than his soloist, Hans Richter-Haaser, who was responsible for the waywardness of the interpretation. Not surprisingly, he is heard at his finest in the music of Bruckner, Richard Strauss, Wagner and Hindemith. All these recordings are separate issues.

King, Thea (clarinet)

'The clarinet in concert': BRUCH: *Double concerto in E min., for clarinet, viola and orchestra, Op. 88* (with Nobuko Imai). MENDELSSOHN: *2 Concert pieces for clarinet and basset horn: in F min., Op. 113; in D min., Op. 114* (with Georgina Dobrée). CRUSELL: *Introduction and variations on a Swedish air, Op. 12* (all 4 works with LSO, Alun Francis). SPOHR: *Variations in B flat for clarinet and orchestra in a theme from Alruna.* RIETZ: *Clarinet concerto in G min., Op. 29.* SOLERE: *Sinfonie concertante in F for 2 clarinets* (with Georgina Dobrée). HEINZE: *Konzertstück in F* (all with ECO, James Judd or Andrew Litton).
(B) *** Hyperion Dyad Dig. CDD 22017 (2) [id.].

A thoroughly engaging programme of forgotten music (the Bruch is not even listed in the *New Grove*), all played with skill and real charm, and excellently recorded. The Bruch *Double concerto* is particularly individual, but the two attractive Mendelssohn concert pieces (each in three brief movements) and the quixotic Crusell *Variations* are by no means insubstantial. They are discussed more fully under their composer entries. The novelties on the second disc are slighter but no less entertaining: the jaunty Spohr *Variations* followed by the *galant* concerto by Julius Rietz (1812–77) with its engaging lyrical flow. One cannot help but smile at the garrulous chatter between the two solo instruments, which evokes the clinking of tea-cups, in Etienne Solère's *Sinfonie concertante*, while Gustav Heinz's warmly tuneful *Konzertstück* has a jocular, Hummelian finale to match the bouncing closing Rondeau of the Solère. The playing brings many chortling roulades and a seductive timbre from the ever-stylish Thea King, and Georgina Dobrée is a nimble partner in the *Sinfonie concertante*. The accompaniments are excellent too, while the recording has fine range and presence.

Koussevitzky, Serge (double-bass and conductor)

Collections (with (i) Pierre Luboshutz; (ii) Boston SO; (iii) Bernhard Zighera, Pierre Luboshutz): BEETHOVEN: (i) *Minuet in G* (arr. Koussevitzky): (ii) *Symphony No. 6 in F (Pastoral).* (iii) ECCLES: *Largo.* (i) LASKA: *Wiegenlied.* KOUSSEVITZKY: *Concerto, Op. 3: Andante; Valse miniature.* (ii) Johann STRAUSS Sr: *Wiener Blut; Frühlingstimmen.*
(M) (***) Biddulph mono WHL 019 [id.].

In his youth and before he was established as a conductor of international celebrity, Koussevitzky was regarded as the greatest double-bass virtuoso of the age. In 1928–9, in his mid-fifties, he was enticed into the New York Studios to record the above with the pianist, Bernard Zighera, but he then re-recorded everything with Pierre Luboshutz the following year. These performances confirm that he brought to the double-bass the same lyrical intensity and feeling for line and sonority that distinguished his conducting. Judging from the two concerto movements included here, he was no great composer, but the 1928 recording of the *Pastoral Symphony* with the Boston Symphony Orchestra is little short of a revelation. As an interpretation it feels just right; generally speaking, it is brisk but totally unhurried, each phrase wonderfully shaped. Given the fact that he never lingers, the paradox is that this performance seems strangely spacious. One young and knowledgeable collector to whom we played this thought it quite simply 'among the best *Pastorals* ever'; moreover the recorded sound is remarkable for its age and comes up very freshly. This disc, though comparatively expensive, is worth it.

Lefébure, Yvonne (piano)

MOZART: *Piano concerto No. 20 in D min., K.466* (with BPO, Furtwängler). BACH/LISZT: *Prelude and fugue in A min., BWV 543; Fantasia and fugue in G min., BWV 542.* BACH/BUSONI: *Chorale: Ich rufe zu dir, BWV 639.* BACH, arr. Hess: *Chorale: Jesu, joy of man's desiring, BWV 147.* BEETHOVEN: *Piano sonatas Nos. 30 in E, Op. 109; 31 in A flat, Op. 110. 32 Variations on a theme of Diabelli, Op. 120.*
(B) (**) EMI Rouge et Noir mono CZS5 69473-2 (2) [CDZB 69473].

Yvonne Lefébure belongs to the generation of French pianists who came into their own in the early days of LP, like Jacqueline Blancard and Monique Haas. She was much admired as a child for her Beethoven playing, which earned the approval of Fauré no less and which is represented here by two of the late sonatas plus a lightning survey of the *Diabelli variations*, shorn of repeats so that they run to only half an hour – a non-starter. The *E major Sonata*, Op. 109, is very impressive. Of particular interest is her Mozart *D minor Concerto*, K.466, recorded with Furtwängler in 1954 at Lugano, playing full of fervour and intensity. Her cadenzas are unusual, too, by the conductor, Fred Goldbeck. All the recordings are mono and from the mid-1950s.

Leningrad Philharmonic Orchestra, Yevgeni Mravinsky

The Mravinsky Edition (complete)

(M) **(*) RCA 74321 25189-2 (10) [id.].

Volume 1: BRAHMS: *Symphony No. 2 in D, Op. 73.* SCHUBERT: *Symphony No. 8 in B min. (Unfinished), D.759.* WEBER: *Oberon: Overture.*
(M) **(*) RCA 74321 25190-2 [id.].

Volume 2: MOZART: *Overture: The Marriage of Figaro; Symphony No. 39 in E flat, K.543.* MUSSORGSKY: *Khovanshchina: Prelude to Act I.* SIBELIUS: *Legend: The Swan of Tuonela, Op. 22/2; Symphony No. 7 in C, Op. 105.*
(M) **(*) RCA 74321 25191-2 [id.].

Volume 3: STRAVINSKY: *Agon* (complete). SHOSTAKOVICH: *Symphony No. 15 in A, Op. 141.*
(M) **(*) RCA 74321 25192-2 [id.].

Volume 4: BRUCKNER: *Symphony No. 9 in D min.*
(M) ** RCA 74321 25193-2 [id.].

Volume 5: TCHAIKOVSKY: *The Nutcracker:* excerpts. PROKOFIEV: *Romeo and Juliet: suite No. 2.*
(M) *** RCA 74321 25194-2 [id.].

Volume 6: HINDEMITH: *Symphony, Die Harmonie der Welt.* HONEGGER: *Symphony No. 3 (Symphonie liturgique).*
(M) *** RCA 74321 25195-2 [id.].

Volume 7: BEETHOVEN: *Symphony No. 4 in B flat, Op. 60.* TCHAIKOVSKY: *Symphony No. 5 in E min.*
(M) **(*) RCA 74321 25196-2 [id.].

Volume 8: BARTOK: *Music for strings, percussion and celeste.* DEBUSSY: *Prélude à l'après-midi d'un faune.* STRAVINSKY: *Apollo* (ballet; complete).
(M) **(*) RCA 74321 25197-2 [id.].

Volume 9: SHOSTAKOVICH: *Symphonies Nos. 6 in B min., Op. 54; 10 in E min., Op. 93.*
(M) **(*) RCA 74321 25198-2 [id.].

Volume 10: WAGNER: *Götterdämmerung: Siegfried's Funeral march. Lohengrin: Preludes to Acts I & III. Die Meistersinger: Overture. Tannhäuser: Overture. Tristan und Isolde: Prelude & Liebestod. Die Walküre: Ride of the Valkyries.*
(M) **(*) RCA 74321 25199-2 [id.].

Yevgeni Mravinsky's stature has gained increasing recognition among the wider musical public outside his native country since his death in 1988. Mravinsky did not make many commercial records: the derisory terms offered to the Leningrad orchestra during the days of the Soviet Union were not conducive to recording. Moreover Mravinsky did not like recording under studio conditions, and so the bulk of his legacy derives from the concert hall. The discs are available both separately and as a ten-CD set.

(Volume 1: 74321 25190-2) Mravinsky's accounts of the Brahms *Second Symphony* and the Schubert *Unfinished Symphony*, together with the Weber *Oberon Overture*, come from concerts given at the end of April 1978. They should not be confused with the performances he gave at the Vienna *Festwochen* later that summer (for which they were obviously preparation) and which appeared briefly on a four-LP EMI/ Melodiya set in the early 1980s, including also the *Fifth Symphonies* of Tchaikovsky and Shostakovich. (Then the Vienna *Oberon*, at under 9 minutes, occupied a whole LP side!) Generally speaking these performances are, if anything, finer, with a moving *Unfinished* and a lyrical but vital Brahms.

(Volume 2: 74321 25191-2) The Mozart pieces, the *Figaro overture* and the *Symphony No. 39 in E flat*, come from the same 1965 concert as the two Sibelius works, *The Swan of Tuonela* and the *Seventh Symphony*. The Mussorgsky *Dawn on the Moscow river*, the evocative *Prelude* to the first Act of *Khovanshchina*, was given two days earlier. The *Seventh* is a performance of stature. Even if Mravinsky rushes the very opening ascent in the cellos and the trombone does have a wide vibrato, it has that intensity this score must have. Although the characterful account of the *Figaro overture* has been available before on Olympia, the Mozart symphony has not; it is a performance of the old school, with great power and again much lyrical intensity. There is a slight drop in pitch at 5 minutes 15 seconds into the slow movement.

(Volume 3: 74321 25192-2) That same intensity is to be found in the 1965 performance of Stravinsky's *Agon*, even if it is evident that the players are not completely inside this particular score; some of the jewelled, hard-edged sound-world Stravinsky evokes is missing. The sound is perfectly acceptable without being in the first flight. Shostakovich's *Fifteenth Symphony* comes from May 1976. Authenticity of feeling and dramatic power compensate for imperfections of execution – and generally rough recording – and the darkness and intensity of the slow movement come over superbly in Mravinsky's hands. There is no doubting the special insights he brings to the work. The new transfer has perhaps a fractionally sharper image.

(Volume 4: 74321 25193-2) Bruckner's *Ninth Symphony* comes from a public performance in 1980, though, for all the skill of the RCA team, the sound still remains fairly coarse and rough-grained. The performance has tremendous grip and strong personality, though Mravinsky moves things on sometimes where greater breadth might be better, and there are some idiosyncratic touches (excessive slowness at letter R in the Novak Edition, track 1, 15 minutes 50 seconds), but sonic limitations do inhibit a strong recommendation.

(Volume 5: 74321 25194-2) The excerpts from Tchaikovsky's *Nutcracker* and the *Second suite* from Prokofiev's *Romeo and Juliet* are identical with the performances that previously appeared on Philips in 1988. The Tchaikovsky is quite magical, possessing all the warmth and enchantment one could wish for, and the sound is every bit as good as the Philips transfer. The Prokofiev, too, is music-making of real stature. As we said first time round, 'phrases breathe and textures glow; detail stands in the proper relation to the whole. There is drama and poetry, and wonderfully rapt *pianissimi*.' However, the fourth movement, the *Dance* in the printed score, is omitted from this recording.

(Volume 6: 74321 25195-2) Both the Hindemith *Symphony*, *Die Harmonie der Welt*, and Honegger's masterly *Symphonie liturgique* come from 1965. Both are performances of stature and few allowances need to be made for the sonic limitations of either work. Sonically this is infinitely superior to the 1980 Bruckner *Ninth* or the 1976 Shostakovich *Tenth*. In fact the CD is among the most desirable of the present set. Mravinsky maintains a tremendous grip on the Hindemith and his *Liturgique* is a very distinguished and imaginative performance.

(Volume 7: 74321 25196-2) The Beethoven *Fourth Symphony* dates from 29 April 1973. It is a performance that calls only the most exalted comparisons to mind – Weingartner, Toscanini's pre-war BBC performances. The Tchaikovsky *Fifth Symphony* comes from the same concert – and what a concert it must have been! The performance is even more electrifying than either of the earlier DG versions, though climaxes are somewhat rough. RCA's advanced technology has managed to tame them a little, and this account can certainly be recommended alongside the DG versions – and the coupling certainly makes it highly recommendable.

(Volume 8: 74321 25197-2) The performance of Bartók's *Music for strings, percussion and celeste*, the Debussy *Prélude à l'après-midi d'un faune* and Stravinsky's *Apollo* all come from 1965, which would seem to be a good vintage for Leningrad recordings and, in the Bartók at least, an unbronchial time for audiences. Even the pianissimo introduction to the Bartók is relatively (though not completely) undisturbed. The Stravinsky, which is new to UK catalogues, finds the Leningrad strings in splendid form, although Mravinsky rather favours a more heavily accented articulation and less seductive tone-quality than we find in Markevitch's 1963 LSO recording. The balance is closer than in the Bartók. There are some extraneous audience noises here, too, which will irritate some listeners.

(Volume 9: 74321 25198-2) Mravinsky's account of the Shostakovich *Sixth* comes from 1972. Though its first movement is not in fact slower than his 1965, it is not quite as intense in feeling. The *Tenth Symphony* was among the symphonies Mravinsky conducted in 1976 to mark what would have been the composer's seventieth birthday. The opening bars suffer from an intrusively restive audience (and the microphones do not capture the very first note). The performance (31 March 1976) is tremendously intense and of great documentary interest. The recording is mono; though this is not stated on the disc, it certainly sounds as if it is. Generally speaking, the recording is not as good as its 1972 companion.

(Volume 10: 74321 25199-2) Mravinsky's Wagner is of stature and breadth, and the anthology of pieces collected here ranges from 1965 to 1982, the year of his retirement. Variable quality but invariably fine playing from the Leningrad orchestra, and decent transfers. Incidentally, the complete set comes in a very flimsy cardboard slipcase – ours came unstuck within the first few minutes' use!

The Mravinsky Edition: Volumes 11–20

(M) (**) mono/stereo BMG/Melodiya 74321 29459-2 (10) [id.].

BEETHOVEN: *Symphonies Nos. 5 in C min., Op. 67; 7 in A, Op. 92.*
❁ (M) (**) BMG Melodiya mono 74321 29400-2 [id.].

BRAHMS: *Symphonies Nos. 3 in F, Op. 90; 4 in E min., Op. 98.*
(M) *(*) BMG/Melodiya 74321 29401-2 [id.].

BRUCKNER: *Symphony No. 8 in C min.*
(M) (**) BMG/Melodiya mono 74321 29402-2 [id.].

Richard STRAUSS: *An Alpine Symphony;* (i) *Horn concerto No. 1 in E flat, Op. 11.*
(M) (**) BMG/Melodiya mono/stereo 74321 29403-2 [id.]. (i) with Vitaly Buyanovsky.

OVSYANIKO-KUILIKOVSKY: *Symphony No. 21 in G min.* SHOSTAKOVICH: *Symphony No. 5 in D min., Op. 74.*
(M) (**) BMG/Melodiya mono 74321 29404-2 [id.].

SHOSTAKOVICH: *Symphony No. 7 in C (Leningrad), Op. 60.*
(M) (**) BMG/Melodiya mono 74321 29405-2 [id.].

SHOSTAKOVICH: *Symphony No. 8 in C min., Op. 65.*
(M) (**) BMG/Melodiya mono 74321 29406-2 [id.].

TCHAIKOVSKY: *Symphony No. 4 in F min., Op. 36.* GLAZUNOV: *Symphony No. 4 in E flat, Op. 48.*
(M) (*(*)) BMG/Melodiya mono 74321 29407-2 [id.].

TCHAIKOVSKY: *Symphony No. 6 in B min. (Pathétique).* RIMSKY-KORSAKOV: *Tale of the invisble city of Kitezh.*
(M) (*(*)) BMG/Melodiya mono 74321 29408-2 [id.].

TCHAIKOVSKY: *Capriccio italien, Op. 45; Francesca da Rimini, Op. 32; Serenade for strings, Op. 48.*
(M) (*) BMG/Melodiya mono 74321 29409-2 [id.].

As with the earlier edition (discussed above), the ten CDs are available either as a set (priced at a discount) or individually at mid-price. Inevitably they are variable in quality and readers will probably want to make their own choice. The Beethoven symphonies (on 74321 29400-2) are of early provenance; the *Fifth* comes from 1949 and is a powerful, tremendously concentrated account, and it is obvious that the BMG engineers have taken great trouble over it. The *Seventh* is a later account, dating from 1958, and from the very first note there is no doubt that it is a performance of stature. The listener is immediately gripped and held, as if in a vice, until the last bar, as one is by Toscanini's celebated New York Philharmonic account. The sound has a good deal more space than the *Fifth*, though some allowances have to be made (there is some discoloration and roughness in climaxes) but the performance is of stature – as fine as (if not finer than) such Western classics of the period as Cantelli, Klemperer, Colin Davis, Karajan and Konwitschny. It deserves classic status.

The two Brahms symphonies come from 1972 and 1973. Mravinsky's Brahms is relatively little known in the West: recordings of a *First Symphony* from 1950, a *Second* from 1978 (this was also included in the Vienna *Festwochen* programmes the same year), a *Third Symphony* from 1965 and the present 1973 account of the *Fourth Symphony* have appeared on Melodiya. The *Third* was recorded while the orchestra was on a visit to Moscow in 1972. There is, as always, a certain grandeur about Mravinsky, though the *Third Symphony* suffers from rough recording-quality. The aural image in the *Fourth* is set further back and the overall sound is more pleasing, though definition is not ideal in either recording. The reading is a distinguished one without having the commanding stature of Mravinsky at his greatest.

Mravinsky's account of Bruckner's *Eighth Symphony* comes from 1959, and Melodiya copies were briefly available in specialist outlets in the late 1960s. It is a noble performance, much tauter than, say, Furtwängler – whose Testament issue runs to nearly 79 minutes as opposed to Mravinsky's 73 minutes 42 seconds. There is breadth and dignity, and the slow movement is very spacious and beautiful.

The 1962 performance of Strauss's *Alpine Symphony* was first discussed in our 1989 *Yearbook*, when it appeared on the Olympia label along with *Siegfried's funeral music* from *Götterdämmerung*. We wrote then that it is 'marvellously concentrated in feeling and spacious in conception; if only the recording were rich enough to do it full justice, it would be a strong recommendation . . . it is obviously a performance of grandeur and almost transcends the limitations of the recording'. The superb orchestral response still remains a source of wonder and Mravinsky's control is pretty awesome. It is difficult to discern any significant improvement in the mono sound. Their excellent notes tell us that Mravinsky conducted the *Alpine symphony* five times, as many times as he did *Till Eulenspiegel*. This and the *First Horn concerto* consitituted his entire Strauss repertory. Vitaly Buyanovsky was first horn in the Leningrad orchestra, and Shostakovich must have had his virtuosity in mind when writing his *First Cello concerto*. His vibrato will be a little too wide for many tastes, but he is a wonderfully musical player all the same. Again, the recording, made in 1964 though in stereo, calls for tolerance.

The name of the Ukraine composer Nikolai Ovsyaniko-Kuilikovsky (1768–1848) will not be found in *Grove* or in any other dictionary. His *Twenty-first Symphony* was said to have been written for the opening of the Odessa Theatre in 1809. The work was published by the State Opera House in 1951 but is in fact by Mikhail Goldstein and belongs with the hoaxes of Kreisler, Henri Casadesus, Klenovsky and others. This elegant four-movement pastiche, to which Mravinsky and the Leningrad orchestra lent their names, is engaging and is played with great delicacy and lightness of touch. Like the Shostakovich *Fifth Symphony*, with which it is coupled, it was recorded at a concert in April 1954.

Mravinsky's association with the Shostakovich symphonies was closer than almost any other maestro's. He conducted the first performances of the *Fifth*, *Sixth*, *Seventh*, *Eleventh* and *Twelfth Symphonies*, and went on to conduct the *Fifth* more than 100 times: there are four other Mravinsky performances in the catalogue – all, of course, with the Leningrad orchestra – from 1965 (Russian Disc, coupled with No. 6 – at full price), 1966 (again Russian Disc, with Salmanov's *Symphony No. 2*), 1967 (Praga, with No. 9), an LP from the Vienna Festwochen of 1978 and 1984 (Erato – no coupling). The present version is the earliest, and fewer allowances need be made for the (mono) sound than one might expect. Mravinsky's authority is everywhere in evidence and the slow movement is particularly intense.

Mravinsky's account of the *Leningrad Symphony* (74321 29405-2) is the 1953 recording, at various times available on Melodiya LP, but the *Eighth Symphony* (74321 29406-2) is a newcomer. There are several accounts in circulation, including his 1960 performance at the Festival Hall (which appeared on Melodiya LPs) and his 1982 account on Philips (which was more accurately transferred on Russian Disc). The present version is in some ways the most intense of all. It comes from 1947, when the scars of wartime suffering and privations were fresh in every Russian mind. This Moscow performance was given just before the Leningrad orchestra set out on their visit to Prague where the *Eighth Symphony* made so deep an impression, conquering an initially hostile audience. Its intensity is extreme and almost painful. The listener is gripped as in a vice, and in its expressive power and anguish the symphony makes an overwhelming effect. Those who fear that the actual sound will resemble the soundtrack of wartime Russian films, with masses of distortion, can be reassured. Given the fact that it is over 50 years old, the sound is remarkably good. The upper strings are uncomfortably hard, but such is the quality of this great performance that such things are soon forgotten.

Those who have Mravinsky's 1960 Tchaikovsky *Fourth Symphony* (in the DG stereo set – the 1956 mono *Fourth* was with Sanderling) will probably opt to skip this Melodiya performance, taut and dramatic though it is, in favour of the finer DG sound. It is coupled with a superb, highly persuasive account of Glazunov's *Fourth Symphony*. The BMG/Melodiya engineers have enormous skill, but the 1947 sound resists even their expertise. Similar qualifications apply to the suite from Rimsky-Korsakov's *Tale of the Invisible City of Kitezh* and the Tchaikovsky *Sixth Symphony*, both of which come from the spring of 1949. Pretty fabulous playing, of course, and there are superb things in the *Pathétique*; but for the non-specialist collector Mravinsky's 1956 or 1960 DG recordings will – and, indeed, should – take priority.

The other Tchaikovsky recordings (74321 29409-2) come from 1948–1950, though BMG have done a good job on the transfers. The earliest of them, *Francesca da Rimini*, has an electrifying opening and tremendous dramatic intensity. The upper strings, however, sound a little wanting in opulence at the top end of the spectrum (no doubt the microphone placement was in some measure to blame), and there is some execrable brass intonation (at about 12 minutes in). The playing in the *Serenade for strings* has an impressive eloquence, but the majority of collectors may find the quality of sound here and in the *Capriccio italien* an inhibiting factor.

Leningrad Symphony Orchestra, Yuri Temirkanov

STRAVINSKY: *Petrushka*. Andrei PETROV: *La création du monde*. RAVEL: *Daphnis et Chloé: suite No. 2*.
(M) ** BMG/Melodiya 74321 32044-2.

The *Petrushka* was issued in the UK in 1979 and the *Daphnis et Chloé* comes from 1970. The performances are decent though not by any means among first recommendations. Andrei Petrov's *Creation of the world* from 1971 is approachable, with jazzy, aleatoric and folkish ingredients, but it is hardly a patch on Milhaud's *La création du monde* in either wit or character.

Leonhardt, Gustav ((i) harpsichord; (ii) cond. Orchestra of Age of Enlightenment)

'Portrait': BACH: (i) *English suite No. 3, BWV 808; Partita No. 1, BWV 825;* (ii) *Double harpsichord concerto No. 2 in C, BWV 1061* (with Bob van Asperen, Melante Amsterdam). C. P. E. BACH: *Hamburg Sinfonia, Wq. 183/2*. PURCELL: *Ode for Queen Mary: Love's goddess sure was blind* (with Julia Gooding, James Bowman, Christopher Robson, David Wilson-Johnson and OAE Chorus).
(M) **(*) Virgin/Veritas EMI Dig. VM5 61400-2 [id.].

Leonhardt opens ebulliently with the *G minor English suite* and he is also at his thoughtful best in the *B flat Partita*. The *Double harpsichord concerto* is lively too, although here the resonant acoustic means that the overall sound-picture is less than ideally clear in focus. The other highlight is the lively C. P. E. Bach *Sinfonia*, with its remarkably colourful, though brief, central *Adagio*. The single vocal item, the Purcell *Ode*, brings distinguished solo singing and refined detail, but could ideally be more robust in feeling. Readers wanting to sample Leonhardt's special contribution to the world of baroque music would do better to choose from his own Teldec Edition, below, under Instrumental Recitals.

Light Music Classics

'The Great British musical experience – 50 Light music classics': WILLIAMS: *Devil's galop; Girls in grey; A Quiet stroll* (Charles Williams & O); *The Young ballerina*. Jack BEAVER: *Cavalcade of Youth* (Queen's Hall Light O, David King). COATES: *March: Calling all workers; By the sleepy lagoon; March: Knightsbridge; March: Sound and vision* (SO or Concert O, composer). FARNON: *Westminster waltz* (Robert Farnon & O); *Jumping bean* (O, Sidney Torch). WHITE: *Puffin' Billy* (Melodi Light O, Hubert Clifford); *Runaway rocking horse*. RICHARDSON: *Melody on the move* (Queen's Hall Light O, Williams). HAYDN WOOD: *Horse Guards – Whitehall*. ELLIS: *Coronation Scot*. Philip GREEN: *Horse feathers*. Frederick CURZON: *Dance of an ostracised imp* (Queen's Hall Light O, Sidney Torch). STRACHEY: *In party mood* (West End Celebrity O). YORKE: *Saphires and sables* (Concert O, Peter Yorke); *Silks and satins*. John MALCOLM: *Non stop* (L'Orchestre Devereux). Donald PHILLIPS: *Skyscraper fantasy* (Charles Williams & O). Geoffrey TOYE: *The haunted ballroom*. Trevor DUNCAN: *Little suite: March* (Light Music Society O, Sir Vivian Dunn); *High heels* (O, Sidney Torch); *Smile of a smile* (SO, Carl Anderson); *The girl from Corsica*. GOODWIN: *The Headless Horseman* (Concert O, Ron Goodwin). WOOD: *Barwick Green*. MORLEY: *A Canadian in Mayfair*. TORCH: *On a spring note; All strings and fancy free* (O, Sidney Torch). Woolfe PHILLIPS: *Parisian mode* (O, composer). VAUGHAN WILLIAMS: *Sea songs* (New Concert O, Nat Nyll). Ronald HAMMER: *PC 49 theme* (New Century O, Torch). John FORTIS: *Dancer at the fair* (O, Charles Shadwell). Laurie JOHNSON: *Las Vegas* (Group Forty O). MELACHRINO: *Starlight Roof waltz; Winter sunshine* (George Melachrino O). Easthope MARTIN: *Evensong*. Ray MARTIN: *Marching strings* (Concert O, composer). Ronald BINGE: *Sailing by* (Percy Grainger O). Ernest TOMLINSON: *Concert jig*. Jack COLES: *Parakeets and Peacocks* (O, Jack Coles). Clive RICHARDSON: *Running off the rails* (Columbia O); *Beachcomber*. Archibald JOYCE: *Dreaming* (O, Sidney Torch). Malcolm ARNOLD: *Little suite: March* (Pro Arte O, Gilbert Vinter).
(B) (***) EMI mono/stereo CDGB 50 (2).

This generous two-disc anthology (148 minutes) stands out from all other current bargain collections of British light music for its sense of historical perspective. Its frontispiece depicts HMV's Nipper looking at Vivian Ellis's *Coronation Scot* steaming out from a pre-war radio set, a musical vignette that celebrated one of the most famous of all BBC Radio's fictional characters. He was the hero of Francis Durbridge's stylish and well-plotted detective series from the 1940s, the novelist-turned-sleuth, Paul Temple. The collection, which includes 50 tunes in total, opens with the *Devil's galop* (which served to introduce the more ingenuous series, *Dick Barton – Special Agent*) and closes with music by Malcolm Arnold, not a signature-tune but a lively march, brilliantly orchestrated and with a most engaging string-melody as its centrepiece. The most famous marches were of course by Eric Coates (who conducts them himself in mono recordings taken from 78-r.p.m. discs). Apart from such vivid reminders of *In Town Tonight* and *Music While You Work*, there is much more nostalgia, and older readers will recall once hugely popular programmes like *Housewives' Choice*, *Down Your Way* and, of course, that great survivor, *The Archers*, whose introductory *Barwick Green* is seldom heard played in full, and many others. Early TV is again represented by Coates, who wrote the almost forgotten *Sound and Vision* to introduce ATV in 1955. The original series of *Dr Finlay's Casebook*, *Emergency – Ward 10* and *What's My Line?* are all represented, but also included is Charles Williams's *Young Ballerina*, which was used as background music for a short film called 'The Potter's Wheel', shown as a 'restful' interlude between early TV programmes, but which also came in handy in the event of a breakdown. One of the other memorable survivors among the radio themes is Ronald Binge's delightfully lyrical *Sailing by*, which is still heard before the late-night shipping forecasts listened to by professionals on land and sea alike. The second disc includes a number of pieces which are not directly connected with radio or TV programmes but which are representative of an era when a great deal of popular music was orchestral and did not involve electric guitars. All in all, this is an imaginatively chosen collection which will stir many memories. The performers feature a cross-section of musicians who made their careers in the field, including many famous names, but also some that are now forgotten. All are lively and sympathetic advocates of music, which may be insubstantial but which always catches the ear. The EMI transfers are excellent and so is the documentation, with a paragraph for every item. Highly recommended.

Lipatti, Dinu (piano)

(with Nadia Boulanger; Philh. O, Zürich Tonhalle O, Lucerne Festival O; Galliera, Ackermann, Karajan): BACH: *Chorale, Jesu, joy of man's desiring* (arr. HESS, from BWV 147); *Chorale preludes, BWV 599 & 639* (both arr. BUSONI); *Partita No. 1, BWV 825; Siciliana* (arr. KEMPFF, from BWV 1031). D. SCARLATTI: *Sonatas, Kk. 9 & 380*. MOZART: *Piano concerto No. 21 in C, K.467; Piano sonata No. 8 in A min., K.310*. SCHUBERT: *Impromptus Nos. 2–3, D.899/2 & 3*. SCHUMANN: *Piano concerto in A min., Op. 54*. GRIEG: *Piano concerto in A min., Op. 16*. CHOPIN: *Piano concerto No. 1 in E min., Op. 11; Barcarolle, Op. 60; Etudes, Op. 10/5 & 25/5; Mazurka No. 32, Op. 50/3; Nocturne No. 8, Op. 27/2; Piano sonata No. 3 in B min., Op. 58; Waltzes Nos. 1–14*. LISZT: *Années de pèlerinage, 2nd Year: Sonnetto 104 del Petrarca*. RAVEL: *Alborada del gracioso*. BRAHMS: *Waltzes* (4 hands), *Op. 39/1–2, 5–6, 10, 14–15*. ENESCU: *Piano sonata No. 3 in D, Op. 25*.

❁ (M) (***) EMI CZS7 67163-2 (5) [partly included in CDH 630382, CDH 698002].

This set represents Lipatti's major recording achievements. Whether in Bach (*Jesu, joy of man's desiring* is unforgettable) or Chopin – his *Waltzes* seem to have grown in wisdom and subtlety over the years – Scarlatti or Mozart, these performances are very special indeed. The remastering is done well, and this is a must for anyone with an interest in the piano.

London Gabrieli Brass Ensemble

'The splendour of baroque brass': SUSATO: *La Danserye: suite*. G. GABRIELI: *Canzona per sonare a 4: La Spiritata*. SCHEIDT: *Suite*. PEZEL: *Ceremonial brass music*. BACH: *The Art of fugue: Contrapunctus IX*. CHARPENTIER: *Te Deum: Prelude in D*. arr. JAMES: *An Elizabethan suite*. CLARKE: *The Prince of Denmark's march*. HOLBORNE: *5 Dances*. STANLEY: *Trumpet tune*. LOCKE: *Music for His Majesty's sackbutts and cornetts*. PURCELL: *Trumpet tune and ayre. Music for the funeral of Queen Mary* (with Chorus).

❁ (BB) *** ASV CDQS 6013 [(M) id.].

This is one of the really outstanding brass anthologies, and the digitally remastered analogue recording is very realistic. The brass group is comparatively small: two trumpets, two trombones, horn and tuba; and that brings internal clarity, while the ambience adds fine sonority. The opening Susato *Danserye* is splendid music, and the Scheidt *Suite* is similarly inventive. Pezel's *Ceremonial brass music* is also in effect a suite – it includes a particularly memorable *Sarabande*; while Matthew Locke's *Music for His Majesty's sackbutts and cornetts* opens with a very striking *Air* and offers six diverse movements overall. With the Gabrieli *Canzona*, Purcell's *Trumpet tune and ayre* and the Jeremiah Clarke *Prince of Denmark's march* (better known as the *Trumpet voluntary*) all familiar, this makes a superb entertainment to be dipped into at will. The closing *Music for the funeral of Queen Mary* brings an eloquent choral contribution. Introduced by solemn drum-beats, it is one of Purcell's finest short works and the performance here is very moving. The arrangements throughout the concert (usually made by Crispian Steele-Perkins, who leads the group both sensitively and resplendently) are felicitous and the documentation is excellent. This is a very real bargain.

London Philharmonic Orchestra, Sir Thomas Beecham

'Vintage Beecham': HANDEL: *Solomon: Arrival of the Queen of Sheba.* DVORAK: *Legend, Op. 59/3.* BIZET: *Carmen suite.* DELIUS (arr. Fenby): *Koanga: La Calinda.* MENDELSSOHN: *A Midsummer Night's Dream: Incidental music, Op. 61.* J. STRAUSS Jnr: *Waltz: Voices of spring.* BORODIN: *Prince Igor* (excerpts).
(M) (***) Dutton Laboratories mono CDLX 7003 [id. full price].

The quality of Michael Dutton's transfers here is remarkable. All the repertoire comes from the 1930s, yet for most of the time the ear has to make few concessions to enjoy this music-making, almost as if it had been put on disc yesterday. The opening *Arrival of the Queen of Sheba* has remarkable tangibility and profile, and no one ever 'magicked' the *Barcarolle* from the *Tales of Hoffmann* as did Beecham. But it is the *Carmen* excerpts which help to make this collection indispensable, played with such glowing, lyrical feeling and colour – the cultivated way Beecham builds up the climax of the *Danse bohème* is an object lesson in combining orchestral finish with a steadily increasing spontaneous surge of energy. The Borodin *Polovtsian dances* (a famous recording from the 1934 Leeds Festival) is a tribute to Walter Legge's skill with location recording – something much less easy to manage then than now – and the result is breathtaking. Even Beecham's later stereo version does not quite achieve the sheer abandon at the end, yet the Leeds performance was not recorded 'live'. Detail is less than perfect, but the full-bodied choral sound, topped by the percussion, yet with plenty of weight in the bass, makes a glorious impact, and the final accelerando is breathtaking. The the 73-minute concert concludes with a bitingly Russian *Polovtsian march.*

'Beecham favourites': BIZET: *L'Arlésienne: suite No. 1: Prélude; Minuet; Adagietto; suite No. 2: Minuet* (from *The Fair Maid of Perth*); *Farandole.* GRIEG: *Peer Gynt: suite No. 1, Op. 46.* TCHAIKOVSKY: *Francesca da Rimini, Op. 32.* GRETRY: *Zémire et Azor: Air de ballet.* CHABRIER: *España (rhapsody).*
❀ (B) (***) Dutton Lab. mono CDEA 5017 [(M) id.].

Beecham re-recorded both the *L'Arlésienne* and *Peer Gynt suites* with the RPO in stereo, but he did not surpass these earlier, LPO performances, recorded for the Columbia label in the late 1930s. The sound was remarkably good for its time, but in these fine Dutton transfers it is better than ever, glowing and warm yet with plenty of brightness for the violins, so that the earthily rumbustious *In the Hall of the Mountain King* unleashes a thrilling climax. But (even if the upper woodwind harmonics are not absolutely clean) it is perhaps the gentler evocations which remain most firmly in the memory and it is the oboist, Leon Goossens, who makes *Morning* from *Peer Gynt* unforgettable and who points the delicate rhythm of the famous Grétry *Air de ballet* so exquisitely. The Bizet and Grieg suites were recorded at Abbey Road, except for the *Death of Ase*, for which Beecham chose Kingsway Hall, with warmly ravishing results, especially at the moving closing section; and Anitra has never danced with more alluring delicacy. Kingsway Hall was also used for *Francesca da Rimini* and *España.* In *Francesca*, Bernard Walton's clarinet solo which introduces the heroine in the middle section is delectably seductive and (in the words of Neville Cardus) Beecham's baton seems 'to bring the hell-fire outer sections of the work visually before us'. The closing pages have great ferocity, with a superb final burst from the timpani which all but drowns the tam-tam. *España* was perhaps the most famous of all Beecham's 78s and was cherished by all three of the authors of this book. It always sounded marvellous, and so it does here. Beecham's combination of swagger and *joie de vivre* is balanced by Gallic elegance. He recorded the two 78 sides at two separate sessions, three weeks apart, but one would never guess that this sparkling performance was not played continuously. This CD offers one Beecham anthology that no admirer of this greatest of English conductors should miss. It has splendid notes by Lyndon Jenkins, and it is ridiculously inexpensive.

London Philharmonic Orchestra, Sir Adrian Boult

'The Boult historic collection'

BUTTERWORTH: *A Shropshire lad* (rhapsody); *The Banks of green willow* (idyll). BAX: *Tintagel* (tone-poem). HOLST: *The perfect fool* (ballet suite). VAUGHAN WILLIAMS: *Old King Cole* (ballet). ELGAR: *Chanson de nuit; Chanson de matin, Op. 51/1–2.*
(BB) (***) Belart mono 461 354-2.

ARNOLD: *English dances Nos. 1–8, Sets 1 (Op. 27) & 2 (Op. 33).* WALTON/BACH: *The Wise Virgins (ballet). Siesta; Overtures: Portsmouth Point; Scapino.* ELGAR: *3 Bavarian dances, Op. 27.*
(BB) (***) Belart mono 461 359-2.

Apart from his major Elgar recordings for EMI, Boult's special skills as an interpreter of English music have never been heard to better effect on record than in this pair of Belart collections, deriving from the Decca mono catalogue of the 1950s. Both programmes are played superbly by the London Philharmonic Orchestra in sparkling and sensitive form and are given vintage Decca recording of very high quality. Butterworth's two beautiful evocations of the English countryside have wonderful delicacy of texture and feeling, while Bax's *Tingagel* is both evocative and passionately full-blooded at its climax. Holst's *Perfect fool* ballet suite sounds remarkably fresh and vivid, and Vaughan Williams's *Old King Cole* (taken from another ballet of 1923) is both jolly and boisterous, as befits the image of that famous nursery-rhyme monarch. Elgar's paired miniatures of morning and night have characteristically affectionate warmth, and here the full ambience of the recording might almost be mistaken for stereo. The second disc includes more amiable Elgar and Walton's ballet based on the music of Bach where, without loss of character, Boult merges the spirit of the two musical eras with great success. Of the two Walton overtures, *Portsmouth Point* is vigorous enough but has not quite the rhythmic bite of Boult's earlier, HMV recording (first issued on a ten-inch 78-r.p.m. disc); *Scapino*, however, effervesces brilliantly. Finest of all is Boult's pioneering set of Malcolm Arnold's *English dances*, never surpassed in subtlety of characterization or indeed vividness. The exquisite fragility of the first dance (*Andantino*) and the haunting nostalgia of the third (*Mesto*) are set in bold relief by the ebullience of the *Vivace* which comes in between. Here the Decca Kingsway Hall recording remains in the demonstration bracket it occupied from the day the music first appeared, on a Decca medium-play 10-inch LP.

London Philharmonic Orchestra, Sir Hamilton Harty

'The art of Sir Hamilton Harty' (recordings from 1933 and 1935): BAX: *Overture to a picaresque comedy.* BERLIOZ: *Roméo et Juliette, Op. 7: Romeo's reverie and Feast of the Capulets. Funeral march for the last scene of Hamlet, Op. 18/3.* HANDEL, arr. HARTY: *Royal Fireworks music: suite; Water music: suite.* SCHUBERT: *Marche militaire.* SIBELIUS: *Valse triste.* SMETANA: *Overture: The Bartered Bride.*
(M) (***) Dutton Lab. mono CDLX 7016 [id. full price].

These early recordings Sir Hamilton Harty made for Columbia come up sounding better than ever. No later recording has come anywhere near Harty's pioneering account of Bax's *Overture to a picaresque comedy*, which has great character and sparkle. It is a marvellous piece, and this alone would be worth the price of the record. But Harty's Berlioz was unsurpassed in its day. His *Romeo's reverie and Feast of the Capulets*, which featured in Percy Scholes's 'Columbia History of Music' on two 10-inch 78s (which RL still treasures) combines atmosphere and magic, and not even Colin Davis's *Funeral march for the last scene of Hamlet* erases the memory of this 1937 version. All the other items give unalloyed pleasure, and the Dutton transfers are of the highest quality.

London Symphony Orchestra, Yuri Ahronovitch

'Russian Spectacular': KHACHATURIAN: *Gayaneh: Sabre Dance. Spartacus: Adagio of Spartacus and Phrygia. Masquerade: Waltz.* PROKOFIEV: *Lieutenant Kijé: Troika. Love for 3 oranges: March.* BORODIN: *Prince Igor: Polovtsian dances.* GLINKA: *Ruslan and Ludmilla overture.* MUSSORGSKY: *Night on the bare mountain.* SHOSTAKOVICH: *The Gadfly: Folk festival.*
(B) **(*) Carlton LSO Double Dig. 30368 01247 (2) – RIMSKY-KORSAKOV: *Scheherazade.* **(*)

An excellent collection of characteristically vivid Russian orchestral genre pieces, played with plenty of spirit and polish by the LSO, who are in excellent form. Yuri Ahronovitch may not be a subtle conductor, but his pacing here is notably convincing in Mussorgsky's *Night on the bare mountain*, while the piquant Prokofiev *March* is crisply rhythmic and nicely pointed. The *Sabre dance* and *Polovtsian dances* have no lack of energy or fire. The recording combines brilliance with weight, though the ambience is a little dry.

London Symphony Orchestra, Ataulfo Argenta

'España': CHABRIER: *España*. RIMSKY-KORSAKOV: *Capriccio espagnol, Op. 34*. GRANADOS: *Spanish dance No. 5 (Andaluza), Op. 37*. MOSZKOWSKI: *5 Spanish dances, Book I, Op. 12*. DEBUSSY: *Images* (with SRO).
(M) *** Decca (IMS) 443 580-2 [id.].

Ataulfo Argenta (about whom the documentation of this reissue in Decca's 'Classic Sound' series says nothing) was one of the more promising stars on the Decca roster in the late 1950s, but sadly he died before the promise could fully be realized. Nevertheless this brightly recorded mixture of Spanishry, mostly from the pens of non-Spaniards, readily displays his flair, not least in the sparkling account of Chabrier's title-piece. The slight but endearingly dated Moszkowski dances are beautifully played, and the last three are especially successful. But the highlight of the disc is Rimsky's *Capriccio* which (alongside Maazel's DG Berlin Philharmonic version from the same period) has never been surpassed for its brilliance and Mediterranean colour, with superb virtuosity from the LSO. The 1957 Kingsway Hall recording with its glittering percussion is dazzling in this CD transfer and only a slight tightness in the upper range of the violins prevents the highest technical accolade. The fullness and range are astonishing for their time, and the Decca recording team can well be proud of the early stereo. The Debussy *Images* (recorded in Victoria Hall, Geneva, the same year) show the conductor's fine ear for intricate detail, so well etched by the recording, but the response of the Suisse Romande Orchestra (used to playing this work under Ansermet) has less body of tone than that produced by the LSO. A fascinating collector's CD, just the same.

London Symphony Orchestra, Antal Dorati

ENESCU: *Romanian rhapsody No. 2*. BRAHMS: *Hungarian dances Nos. 1–7; 10–12; 15; 17–21; Variations on a theme of Haydn, Op. 56a*.
(M) ** Mercury (IMS) 434 326-2 [id.].

Dorati is completely at home in the Enescu *Second Rhapsody* (played passionately – but, as music, not nearly as memorable as No. 1) and the Brahms *Hungarian dances*, where he captures a true Hungarian spirit. When he takes a piece faster than expected, one does not feel he is being wilful or intent on showing off, but simply that he and his players are enjoying themselves. If the delicious rubato in No. 7 does not spell enjoyment, one would be very surprised. The recording, made at either Watford or Wembley, sounds firmer and cleaner than on LP. The *Variations* are enjoyable but not distinctive.

London Symphony Orchestra, Roderick Dunk

'That's entertainment': SCHWARTZ–DIETZ: *That's entertainment*. GERSHWIN: *Girl Crazy overture*. LOEWE: *My Fair Lady: symphonic suite*. LLOYD WEBBER: *Evita interlude*. STYNE–MERRILL: *Funny Girl: Don't rain on my parade*. BOCK: *Fiddler on the roof overture*. NOEL GAY: *Me and my girl*: selection. KERN: *Showboat*: selection. HERMAN: *Mack and Mabel overture*. SONDHEIM–STYNE: *Gypsy: Everything's coming up roses*.
(B) *** Carlton LSO Double Dig. 30368 01257 (2) [(M) id.] – GERSHWIN: *An American in Paris; Piano concerto; Rhapsody in blue*. ***

This group of selections from famous musicals is brightly and warmly played and very well recorded. It is perhaps not distinctive music-making, but it is very professionally presented and easy to enjoy. However, tuneful as it all is (particularly the suite from *My Fair Lady*), it is not a CD that most collectors would want to replay too often, while the splendid Gershwin coupling certainly is.

London Symphony Orchestra, Sir Charles Mackerras

'Kaleidoscope – An orchestral extravaganza': SMETANA: *The Bartered Bride: Dance of the comedians*. NICOLAI: *Overture: The Merry Wives of Windsor*. Johann STRAUSS Sr: *Radetzky march*. WEBER: *Overture: Abu Hassan*. MEYERBEER: *Le Prophète: Coronation march*. BRAHMS: *Hungarian dance No. 1*. THOMAS: *Overture: Mignon*. TCHAIKOVSKY: *Mazeppa: Cossack dance*. SUPPE: *Overture: The Jolly robbers*.

OFFENBACH: *Overture: Orpheus in the Underworld*. WEBER (arr. BERLIOZ): *Invitation to the dance*. GLINKA: *Jota aragonesa*.
(M) *** Mercury (IMS) 434 352-2 [id.].

The insert-note for this zestful concert is illustrated with a picture of Mackerras taken 35 years ago, before he became Sir Charles, for – almost unbelievably – these recordings were made at Walthamstow in July 1961. The performances sparkle with life and vivacity: the opening *Dance of the comedians* is matched in exhilaration by the highlight of the concert, the fizzingly crisp *Cossack dance* from Tchaikovsky's *Mazeppa*. The orchestra is obviously enjoying itself in the series of bandstand overtures, with responsive playing in all departments, and the lollipops are hardly less effervescent. The one snag is that the violin timbre above the stave is thin, at times to the point of shrillness; but many will readily adjust to this when otherwise the sound approaches demonstration bracket in its colour, sonority and presence, so that Glinka's glittering *Jota aragonesa* makes a spectacular final item. Containing the contents of a pair of LPs (originally published in the UK on the Philips label) the playing time is enticingly generous (75 minutes).

London Symphony Orchestra, Leopold Stokowski

'Orchestral transcriptions': BYRD: *The Earl of Salisbury and Galliard pavan*. CLARKE: *Trumpet voluntary*. SCHUBERT: *Moment musical No. 3 in F min*. CHOPIN: *Mazurka in A min., Op. 17/4*. TCHAIKOVSKY: *Chant sans paroles*. DUPARC: *Extase*. RACHMANINOV: *Prelude in C sharp min., Op. 3/2* (with Czech PO: BACH arrangements: *Chorale prelude: Wir glauben all' an einen Gott ('Giant fugue'), BWV 680; Easter cantata, BWV 4: Chorale; Geistliches Lied No. 51: Mein Jesu, BWV 487; Passacaglia and fugue in C min., BWV 582; Toccata and fugue in D min., BWV 565; Well-tempered Clavier, Book 1: Prelude No. 8 in E flat min., BWV 853*).
(M) *** Decca Phase Four 448 946-2 [id.].

Sumptuously recorded, with the LSO on top form in 1974, these lollipops are often flagrantly far removed from their composer's original conceptions, becoming virtually newly composed in their vivid, Stokowskian orchestral flamboyance. The *Trumpet voluntary* is surely a collectors' item, with its sweetly anachronistic violins in the middle section, and the Chopin *Mazurka* is hardly less extraordinary in its transformation, opening mysteriously with *sul ponticello* strings, and turning into a dreamy rhapsody with its indulgent flute solo. The Byrd *Pavan* is treated as romantically and seductively as the *Song without words* of Tchaikovsky, yet the Schubert *Moment musical* has a bouncing charm. There are plenty of bold histrionics in the scoring of Rachmaninov's most famous *Prelude*, but imaginative touches too, and the LSO respond passionately. With its collection of Bach transcriptions, recorded two years earlier in Czechoslovakia, this is a treasurably unique stereo sampler of Stokowski's orchestral magic – his persistent search for the warmest *espressivo* and sonorously rich beauty of texture, irrespective of any other considerations. The CD transfers are highly successful.

London Symphony Orchestra, or (i) Philharmonia Orchestra, George Weldon

English music: VAUGHAN WILLIAMS: *Overture and Aristophanic suite: The Wasps*. BAX: *Tintagel*. HOLST: *The Perfect Fool* (ballet music); *A Somerset rhapsody, Op. 21; Marching song, Op. 22/2;* (i) *St Paul's suite*.
(M) (***) Dutton Lab. mono CDCLP 4002 [id. full price].

George Weldon began his career with the pre-war Hastings Municipal Orchestra. Then in 1947 he succeeded Leslie Heward as musical director of the City of Birmingham Symphony Orchestra, where he stayed until 1951. Suddenly dismissed, he was subsequently invited by Barbirolli to join him as associate conductor with the Hallé, which proved to be the peak of Weldon's career. He was perhaps not a great conductor, but his performances were always polished and vivid, stylish and unegocentric. Above all he had that special gift (not always given to greater musicians) of being able to bring music consistently to life within the bare walls of the recording studio. This gift was recognized by Walter Legge, and from 1944 onwards he made a series of recordings in London, specializing in English music, which are admirably represented here. All are tingling with life and are splendidly played. The finest is Holst's *St Paul's suite*, for which Weldon had a special affection, and its *Intermezzo* has never been played on record with more intensity of feeling, with a splendid violin solo from the leader of the Philharmonia (in 1953), Manoug Parikian. The Kingsway Hall recording remains demonstration-worthy. Perhaps Weldon treats the *Marching song* with too much Elgarian regality, but the result has greater impact than usual; Bax's *Tingagel*, if without quite the overall sweep of Boult's Decca LPO account of the same period (see above), still generates plenty of excitement and is vividly detailed. The attractive Vaughan Williams *Wasps* incidental music suits the bright-eyed Weldon manner perfectly. The recordings (from either 1953 or 1955), whether made at Kingsway Hall or Abbey Road are all excellent and certainly do not sound dated. Indeed in these remarkable Dutton transfers the sound is spacious enough almost to suggest stereo, and one realizes that the EMI engineers of that time were setting standards of realism to match their Decca colleagues at West Hampstead.

(i) London Symphony Orchestra, Gaston Poulet; (ii) Philharmonia Orchestra, William Schüchter

'Spanish favourites': (i) ALBENIZ: *Iberia* (orch. Arbos). GRANADOS: *Goyescas: Intermezzo.* FALLA: *La vida breve: Intermezzo and Dance.* TURINA: *La procesión del Rocio, Op. 9;* (ii) *Danzas fantásticas.* GRANADOS: *Spanish dances, Op. 37: Oriental; Andaluza; Rondall aragonesa.*
(B) *** Dutton Lab. mono CDEA 5502 [(M) id.].

This colourful repertoire calls for superb recording, and this is exactly what it received in 1954. Indeed it is so fine that it stands up surprisingly well to present-day standards, though of course the frequency range and timbre are not as wide-ranging as we expect from later stereo recordings. But the sound of all these Parlophone LPs from the 1950s was remarkably natural and lifelike, and most people to whom we have played this disc have heard it with amazement. If no apology need be made for the recording, the performances are also of quality. Gaston Poulet's account of the Arbos transcription of *Iberia* is captivating and thoroughly idiomatic, and so, too, are the Turina *Danzas fantásticas* under Schuchter.

(i) London Symphony Orchestra; (ii) Royal Philharmonic Orchestra; (iii) Anatole Fistourlari; (iv) Gaston Poulet

'French favourites': (i; iii) POULENC: *Les Biches (ballet suite).* (ii–iii) *Aubade* (choreographic concerto for piano and 18 instruments). DEBUSSY: *Fantaisie for piano and orchestra* (both with Fabienne Jacquinot, piano). (i; iv) RAVEL: *Alborada del gracioso; Une barque sur l'océan.*
(B) *** Dutton Lab. mono CDEA 5501 [(M) id.].

Here are some more splendidly fresh performances from the early-1950s' Parlophone label. Expert and attractive accounts of *Alborada del gracioso* and *Une barque sur l'océan* from the LSO under Gaston Poulet are coupled with two Poulenc works; a sparkling and vivacious *Les biches* from Fistoulari and the same orchestra, and a captivating *Aubade* with Fabienne Jacquinot. She is hardly less persuasive in Debussy's neglected *Fantaisie*, both with the RPO (billed on the LP at the time, as older collectors will remember, as the Westminster Symphony Orchestra for contractual reasons). In any event, these are thoroughly delightful performances and few allowances need be made, for the recorded sound is little short of amazing.

Los Angeles Philharmonic Orchestra, Zubin Mehta

Spectacular orchestral showpieces: HOLST: *The Planets.* Richard STRAUSS: *Also sprach Zarathustra.* John WILLIAMS: Film scores: *Close Encounters of the Third Kind (suite); Star Wars (suite).*
(B) **(*) Decca Double 452 910-2 (2) [(M) id. import].

Zuhbin Mehta's set of *Planets* ranks high in stellar splendour and has been a demonstration record since it was first issued on LP in 1971. The performance is strongly characterized and splendidly played. It is discussed more fully under its composer entry, where it is paired with Holst's *Perfect fool* suite. However, hi-fi buffs will surely think this Double Decca set well worth considering with such appropriate couplings. In the never-to-be-forgotten opening of *Also sprach Zarathustra* Mehta has the distinction of stretching those famous first pages longer than any rival. From the start, this 1969 recording was also plainly intended for demonstration with its extrovert sonic brilliance, and as such it succeeds well; but other versions are more interesting interpretatively. Mehta is a good, even a passionate Straussian, but he is a forceful rather than an affectionate one. The two John Williams film scores were recorded later, in 1977, and again offer a spectacular sound-stage. However eclectic the inspiration, both scores are undeniably attractive and each draws considerable appeal from the imaginative orchestration. The music from *Star Wars* forms a definite suite of six movements; the shorter piece from *Close Encounters* is continuous and essentially atmospheric.

Both are very well played in Los Angeles and, if Mehta's approach has an element of hyperbole, in *Star Wars* the Hollywoodian theme picturing Princess Leia includes a horn solo which is played quite gorgeously, while the closing section has an appropriate swagger.

Ma, Yo-Yo (cello)

'Great cello concertos': HAYDN: *Concerto in D, Hob VIIb/2* (with ECO, Garcia). SAINT-SAENS: *Concerto No. 1, Op. 33* (with O Nat. de France, Maazel). SCHUMANN: *Concerto in A min., Op. 129* (with Bav. RSO, C. Davis). DVORAK: *Concerto in B min., Op. 104* (with BPO, Maazel). ELGAR: *Concerto in E min., Op. 85* (with LSO, Previn).
(M) *** Sony Dig./Analogue M2K 44562 (2) [id.].

An enticing mid-priced package, offering at least two of the greatest of all cello concertos, in Yo-Yo Ma's characteristic and imaginatively refined manner. Only the performance of the Haydn gives cause for reservations and these are slight; many will enjoy Ma's elegance here. He is also lucky in his accompanists, and the CBS sound gives no reasons for complaint.

Milstein, Nathan (violin)

'The art of Nathan Milstein' (with (i) Pittsburgh SO, Steinberg; (ii) New Philh. O, Frühbeck de Burgos; (iii) Philh. O, Fistoulari, or (iv) Leinsdorf; (v) Erica Morini & CO; (vi) O, Robert Irving; (vii) Leon Pommers; (viii) Artur Balsam; (ix) Rudolf Firkušný): (i) GLAZUNOV: *Violin concerto in A min., Op. 90.* (ii) PROKOFIEV: *Violin concerto No. 2, Op. 63.* (iii) SAINT-SAENS: *Violin concerto No. 3, Op. 61.* (i) TCHAIKOVSKY: *Violin concerto in D, Op. 35.* (iii) BRAHMS: *Violin concerto in D, Op. 77.* (iv) BEETHOVEN: *Violin concerto in D, Op. 61.* (i) DVORAK: *Violin concerto in A min., Op. 53.* (v) VIVALDI: *Double violin concerto in D min., Op. 3/11.* (vi) RACHMANINOV: *Vocalise, Op. 34/14.* MUSSORGSKY: *Sorochintsky Fair: Gopak.* GLAZUNOV: *Meditation, Op. 32.* TCHAIKOVSKY: *Waltz-scherzo, Op. 34; Souvenir d'un lieu cher, Op. 42.* RIMSKY-KORSAKOV: *Fantasia on Russian themes, Op. 33* (arr. KREISLER). (vii) VIVALDI: *Violin sonata No. 2 in A.* HANDEL (arr. HUBAY): *Larghetto.* CORELLI: *La Follia, Op. 5/12.* TARTINI: *Violin sonata in G min. (Devil's trill).* BACH: *Air from Suite No. 3, BWV 1068.* MOZART: *Violin sonatas: in C, K.296; in E min., K.304.* RIMSKY-KORSAKOV: *Tsar Saltan: Flight of the bumble bee.* GLUCK: *Orfeo: Dance of the Blessed spirits.* BRAHMS: *Hungarian dance No. 2.* MASSENET: *Thaïs: Méditation.* CHOPIN: *Nocturne No. 20 in C min.* FALLA: *Jota.* WIENIAWSKI: *Scherzo-Tarantelle, Op. 16.* DEBUSSY: *Minstrels.* SARASATE: *Introduction and tarantella, Op. 43.* KREISLER: *Prelude and allegro in the style of Pugnani.* (viii) HANDEL: *Violin sonata in D, Op. 1/4.* VITALI: *Chaconne.* PROKOFIEV: *Violin sonata No. 2 in D.* (ix) BEETHOVEN: *Violin sonata No. 5 in F (Spring).*
(M) **(*) EMI stereo/mono ZDMF7 64830-2 (6) [id.].

BACH: (Unaccompanied) *Violin sonatas and partitas, BWV 1001/6* (complete).
✿ (M) (***) EMI mono ZDS7 64793-2 (2) [id.].

Milstein recorded for companies other than EMI, and his career went on long after the mid-1960s, when this survey ends. But certainly the recordings here often show him at his freshest and in fine technical form. In 1960 he played the Tchaikovsky *Concerto* with glitter and panache, with Steinberg absolutely on the ball with the matching accompaniment. He also found the warmth to do justice to the romanticism of the Glazunov and the scintillating technique to bring off the fireworks in the finale; he was pretty impressive, too, in the Saint-Saëns No. 3. His Dvořák, however, was efficient and clean rather than particularly beguiling, and the Prokofiev No. 2 does not find him at his best either. The Brahms *Concerto* was a straightforwardly lyrical reading, with the slow movement particularly beautiful. It is most satisfying; but he treated the Beethoven *Concerto* at that time as a relatively lightweight and intimate tonal edifice and played his own cadenzas to prove he had an individual view. The set also includes an impressive *Spring Sonata* with Firkušný, but why no Kreutzer? Many of the shorter pieces come off with the flair we associate with Perlman, and in the classical chamber works Milstein is always impressive. With generally excellent transfers, admirers of this artist should find much to relish here, even if he was to go on to record finer versions of some of the key works later.

As an appendix, EMI have reissued Milstein's superb early mono set of the Bach *Sonatas and partitas* for solo violin. With brisker tempi than in his later, DG, stereo recording (see under the composer), the result is exhilaratingly fresh and spontaneous, and the vivid recording has remarkable presence.

Minneapolis Symphony Orchestra, Antal Dorati

Concert: GERSHWIN: *An American in Paris*. COPLAND: *Rodeo (4 Dance episodes)*. SCHULLER: *7 Studies on themes of Paul Klee*. BLOCH: *Sinfonia breve*.
(M) ** [Mercury 434 329-2].

This is a disappointing collection, a rare occurrence for this label, but you can't win them all! Dorati's *Rodeo* lacks the incandescent vitality of Bernstein's electrifying New York version, and Gershwin's *American in Paris* doesn't suit the Hungarian conductor too well either (try the big blues tune at its trumpet entry). The almost over-detailed recording does not help, either here or in Bloch's rather dry *Sinfonia breve*, which needs richer string textures. It is highly suitable for Schuller's sharply etched *Seven studies on themes of Paul Klee* but, brilliantly though this is played, the music itself does not live up to the promise of titles like *The twittering machine* and *Little blue devil*.

ALBENIZ: *Iberia* (suite, orch. Arbós). FALLA: *La Vida breve: Interlude and dance*. MUSSORGSKY: *Khovanshchina: Prelude; Dance of the Persian slaves*. SMETANA: *The Bartered Bride: Overture and 3 Dances*.
(M) ** Mercury 434 388-2 [id.].

The Northrop Auditorium in Minnesota never proved an ideal venue acoustically for the Mercury recording team. Although the sound is not without warmth and the woodwind have bloom, there is an underlying acoustic dryness. Using the favoured M56 Telefunken microphones, closely placed, this produced an unattractive glare, even a fierceness in fortissimos, an artificial brilliance likely to appeal only to hi-fi buffs. Of course the somewhat brash Arbós scoring in *Iberia* does not help, and certainly Dorati catches the sinuous Spanishry of this music. He is equally vital in the rest of the programme, which is all brilliantly played; but easily the highlight here is Mussorgsky's highly atmospheric *Khovanshchina Prelude*. With its orchestration expertly touched in by Rimsky-Korsakov, it magically pictures the sun rising over the Kremlin. Although the timbre of the orchestra's principal oboe is not opulent, this is one of the most evocative accounts in the CD catalogue, and here the recording cannot be faulted.

Mutter, Anne-Sophie (violin)

'Modern': STRAVINSKY: *Violin concerto in D* (with Philh. O, Sacher). LUTOSLAWSKI: *Partita for Anne-Sophie Mutter* (with Philip Moll, piano); *Chain II* (with BBC SO, composer). BARTOK: *Violin concerto No. 2*. MORET: *En rêve* (with Boston SO, Ozawa). BERG: *Violin concerto*. RIHM: *Time chant* (with Chicago SO, Levine).
(M) *** DG Dig. 445 487-2 (3).

Here is an unexpected portrait of an outstanding young artist linked with the attractions of inexpensively cutting one's teeth on twentieth-century violin repertoire, offered in brilliant, modern, digital recordings. The Stravinsky *Concerto* makes a splendid opener: there is no more recommendable version, with wit and feeling nicely balanced and excellent, sharply defined sound. The Berg is hardly less successful. Mutter opens with the most delicate pianissimo and her reading is intensely passionate. Her Bartók is more controversial, played with stunning virtuosity and brilliance but at times overcharacterized, even glossy in its brilliance, and in the scherzando section of the second movement she is much faster than the metronome marking; indeed the performance tends to sensationalize the concerto, although the playing is not unfelt and the bravura is astonishing. The Lutoslawski pieces are among the best of his recent compositions and evoke a powerful response from their dedicatee. The Moret is a slight but enticing piece with plenty of shimmering sonorities and a dazzling solo part. The finale erupts suddenly but the introspective musing of the earlier writing returns with sporadic bursts of energy from the soloist which bring the piece to a lively conclusion. The Rihm concerto is a rhapsodical, meditative piece, its effect heightened by the orchestral backing. It is played with superb concentration.

Nat, Yves (piano)

FRANCK: *Symphonic variations for piano and orchestra* (with Paris Conservatoire O, Gaston Poulet). SCHUBERT: *6 Moments musicaux, D.780*. CHOPIN: *Piano sonata No. 2 (Funeral march), Op. 35; Fantasy in F min., Op. 49; Barcarolle, Op. 60; Waltz No. 14 in E min., Op. posth*. BRAHMS: *2 Rhapsodies, Op. 79; Variatons and fugue on a theme of Handel; 3 Intermezzi, Op. 117; Intermezzo, Op. 117/2*. LISZT: *Hungarian rhapsody No. 2*. STRAVINSKY: *Petrushka: Danse russe*. NAT: *Pour un petit moujik*.
(B) (**) EMI Rouge et Noir mono CZS5 69461-2 [CDZB 69461-2] (2).

Yves Nat enjoyed great esteem in French musical circles in the early years of the century. He was an unostentatious player, but he retired from active performance in the 1930s to devote himself to teaching and composition. A selfless performer whose art prompted Proust to say that when Nat played, he 'disappears from view and is no more than a window giving on to the masterpiece itself'. He emerged from retirement to make some recordings in the 1950s and justifies the high regard in which he was held. Among his contemporaries there were artists with greater polish and virtuosity, but he had great integrity and serves the music well. None of the performances in this set was issued in the UK during the 1950s (Nat died in 1956 in his mid-sixties); all are recorded in good though not spectacular mono sound. The set is primarily for piano buffs with a special interest in the French tradition.

National Symphony Orchestra

'This is full frequency range recording' (cond. (i) Sydney Beer; (ii) Anatole Fistoulari; (iii) Boyd Neel; (iv) Victor Olof): (i) BIZET: *L'Arlésienne: suite No. 1.* (ii) BERLIOZ: *Damnation de Faust: Hungarian march.* GLIERE: *The Red Poppy: Russian sailors' dance.* TCHAIKOVSKY: *Marche slave; The Oprichnik: Overture.* (i) WAGNER: *Götterdämmerung: Siegfried's Rhine Journey.* (iii) SAINT-SAENS: *Danse macabre.* WOLF-FERRARI: *The Jewels of the Madonna: Intermezzos, Acts I and II.* (i) DELIUS: *Irmelin prelude.* (iv) CHABRIER: *ña.*

(M) (***) Dutton mono CDK 1200 [id. full price].

Made by the National Symphony Orchestra between June and November 1944, these recordings represented the full emergence of Decca's newly developed recording process with an extended range. The founder of the orchestra, using his wealth benevolently, was Sidney Beer, who persuaded many star players to join him. Particularly impressive are his readings of the Bizet suite and the Wagner, with wind and brass superbly caught. Boyd Neel steps away from his usual image as a chamber conductor in a crisp, flamboyant account of *Danse macabre* with Leonard Hirsch, the NSO leader, a prominent and firm soloist. The Wolf-Ferrari interludes are less successful, with higher hiss and violins less sweet. Fistoulari's bright, rhythmically alert contributions inspire recordings of such vividness one can hardly believe they are over 50 years old; the rare *Oprichnik Overture* is specially welcome. Most spectacular of all is the final item, Chabrier's *España*, with Victor Olof, best known as recording producer for both EMI and Decca, here whizzing the players thrillingly through the showpiece. The occasion prompted his engineering colleague, Arthur Haddy, to produce sound that is so vivid, with a remarkably wide dynamic range, one could almost swear it is in stereo. Malcolm Walker provides a model note, not just outlining the background of *ffrr* but giving an impressively detailed history of the Decca company from 1929 onwards

NBC Symphony Orchestra, Arturo Toscanini

Concert: WALDTEUFEL: *Les Patineurs waltz.* Leopold MOZART: *Toy Symphony.* Johann STRAUSS Jr: *Tristsch-Tratsch polka; Waltz: An der schönen blauen Donau.* SUPPE: *Overture: Poet and peasant.* PONCHIELLI: *La Gioconda: Dance of the hours.* BACH: *Suite No. 3 in D: Air.* WEBER/BERLIOZ: *Invitation to the dance.* GLINKA: *Jota aragonesa.*

(M) (**) [RCA (mono) 09026 60308-2].

It was one of the tragedies of the history of recording that no one at RCA had the nerve to tell Toscanini that this kind of beautifully orchestrated light music needed a warmer ambient effect rather than the close-microphoned sharpness of detail he favoured. Just the same, the Waldteufel and Strauss waltzes, if not very idiomatic, are full of character and zest, and the maestro finds real Italianate charm in the *Dance of the hours*, in 1952. Otherwise these are all Carnegie Hall recordings from the 1940s, as is the brilliant *Tritsch-Tratsch polka.* But the 8-H Studio broadcast of Leopold Mozart's *Toy Symphony* brings the most grotesque pips and squeaks as special effects – one wants to laugh for the wrong reasons. The star item here is Paganini's *Moto perpetuo*, where the incredibly crisp, clean bravura of the NBC violin section survives the closest Studio 8-H scrutiny – a *tour de force* of virtuosity. Glinka's *Jota aragonesa* is nearly as brilliant but suffers badly from the unglamorous dryness.

Overtures: HEROLD: *Zampa.* HUMPERDINCK: *Hänsel und Gretel.* KABALEVSKY: *Colas Breugnon.* MOZART: *Die Zauberflöte.* ROSSINI: *William Tell.* SMETANA: *The Bartered Bride.* THOMAS: *Mignon.* VERDI: *La forza del destino.* WEBER: *Der Freischütz.*

(M) (**) RCA (mono) GD 60310.

The most famous recording here is *William Tell*, available on two ten-inch 78 discs before the war with a badly managed 'hanging in the air' side-break, after the pastoral section and before the exhilarating final galop. It is Toscanini at his best; although made in Studio 8-H, the sound has body and is more than acceptable. *Die Zauberflöte* (made in the same venue) is brisk and amazingly precise, but the violins sound fierce under pressure. The opening *Zampa* also has great zest, and 'hi-fi' cymbals, but here the close balance is very intrusive. It quite spoils *Colas Breugnon*, which is flat and thin, and it robs *Mignon* of the necessary bloom on the woodwind. *La forza del destino*, however, is characteristically vibrant. These four recordings were all made in Carnegie Hall, but one would hardly recognize the ambience, although *Hansel and Gretel* is rather more agreeable. In *The Bartered Bride* Toscanini's stabbing fugato entries for the strings are highly characteristic, but this is another Studio 8-H record and very clinical sounding.

New Philharmonia Orchestra, Raymond Leppard

'18th Century Overtures': J. C. BACH: *Catone in Utica.* RAMEAU: *Les Paladins. Zaïs; Pygmalion.* BOYCE: *Cambridge Installation Ode.* Alessandro SCARLATTI: *Il giardino di rose.* CIMAROSA: *I traci amanti.* PERGOLESI: *L'Olimpiade.* HANDEL: *Il pastor fido.* GRETRY: *Le jugement de Midas.* BONONCINI: *Polifemo.* SACCHINI: *Oedipe à Colone.* MEHUL: *La chasse du jeune Henri.*
(M) *** Ph. 446 569-2.

This is a winning collection if ever there was one, with half as many items again as in the original LP collection, all extremely interesting and tuneful music – much of it little-known – and full of surprises. Rameau's *Les Paladins* and *Pygmalion* are a delight, while *Zaïs* is remarkably dramatic with its unusual timpani contributions. Boyce's *Cambridge Installation Ode*, a considerable piece, opens with proper dignity but later offers some neat contrapuntal writing. Scarlatti's *Il giardino di rose* opens delicately, then introduces a lively allegro featuring dueting trumpets. Cimarosa's *I traci amanti* has the strings dancing gaily; Sacchini's *Oedipe à Colone* is another charmer, and the rest of the programme is hardly less diverting. Best of all is Méhul's *La chasse du jeune Henri* with its splendid echoing horn-calls, justly a favourite of Sir Thomas Beecham's; and the artistry and lightness of touch that distinguish Raymond Leppard's direction of the New Philharmonic is at times worthy of Sir Thomas. The late-1960s recording is full and lifelike; textures are less transparent than we would expect today, but many will respond to the lithe beauty of the modern string-sound.

New York Philharmonic Orchestra, Sir John Barbirolli

Barbirolli in America (1938–9): DEBUSSY: *Images: Ibéria.* TCHAIKOVSKY: *Francesca da Rimini.* SCHUBERT: *Symphony No. 4 in C min. (Tragic).*
(B) (***) Dutton Laboratories mono CDEA 5000 [(M) id.].

Along with Beecham in Mozart, Walter in Haydn and Schubert, and Casals and Szell in Dvořák, this is one of many vividly transferred historic issues from Dutton Laboratories being offered at bargain price. Barbirolli's brilliant recordings of 1938–9, made with the New York Philharmonic Symphony, here totally refute the myth that Barbirolli as successor to Toscanini was a failure. All three of these works were rarities on disc at the time – even the Schubert, which comes in a forceful, high-powered reading which yet has a Schubertian smile. The crisp attack in the Tchaikovsky is thrillingly caught too, though sadly some cuts are made – common practice at the time. The Debussy brings a white-hot performance and the most vivid sound of all, weighty and full, with castanets and brass leaping out from the speakers. Not to be missed by fans of this remarkably volatile and inspirational conductor.

'Barbirolli conducts the NYPO': RESPIGHI: *The Fountains of Rome; Ancient airs and dances: Suite 3: Arie de corte.* PURCELL, arr. Barbirolli: *Suite for strings with horns, flutes and cor anglais.* SCHUBERT: *5 German dances & 7 Trios, D.90.* CRESTON: *Threnody.* MENOTTI: *Overture: The Old Maid and the Thief.*
(B) (**) Dutton Lab. mono CDEA 5019 [(M) id.].

Barbirolli was appointed Toscanini's successor as principal conductor with the New York Philharmonic in 1936, and the Purcell *Suite* was his first commercial recording with the orchestra in 1938; the Respighi and Schubert followed in 1938–9. The Purcell arrangement now sounds inflated, except for the very touching *Largo* ('Dido's Lament'), an exquisite cor anglais solo from Englebert Brenner. The Respighi *Pines* show the warmth of the Carnegie Hall ambience in a way that Toscanini's records almost never did; indeed the Italianate allure that Barbirolli brings, especially to the closing evocation of the Villa Medici fountain at sunset, is beautifully caught in this fine Dutton transfer, though overall the recording suffers from a lack of a really dramatic dynamic range. The other highlight here is the touching *Threnody* of Paul Creston, its opening radiantly caught. The Menotti *Overture* is mainly of documentary interest. Both these recordings were apparently made non-commercially for the American Office for War Information (Music Division).

Oistrakh, David (violin)

David Oistrakh Edition (complete)
(M) **(*) BMG/Melodiya 74321 40710-2 (5) [id.]. Details as below.

Volume 1: TCHAIKOVSKY: *Violin concerto in D, Op. 35* (with Moscow PO, Rozhdestvensky). SIBELIUS: *Violin concerto in D min., Op. 47; 2 Humoresques, Op. 87* (with USSR R. Large SO, Rozhdestvensky).
(M) *** BMG/Melodiya 74321 34178-2.

Volume 2: BRAHMS: *Violin concerto in D, Op. 77* (with USSR R. Large SO, Kondrashin). DVORAK: *Violin concerto in A min., Op. 53* (with USSR SO, Kondrashin).
(M) (**) BMG/Melodiya mono 74321 34179-2.

Volume 3: VITALI: *Ciacona in G min.* GLUCK: *Melody* from *Orfeo ed Euridice*. BRAHMS: *Hungarian dances Nos. 5, 8 & 20.* FALLA: *6 canciones populares españolas: El paño moruno; Nana; Cancón; Polo; Asturiana; Jota.* ALBENIZ: *Love song.* RACHMANINOV: *Vocalise, Op. 34/14* (all with Vladimir Yampolski, piano). SCHUMANN: *Widmung, Op. 25/1.* GLAZUNOV: *Raymonda: Entr'acte.* RACHMANINOV: *Daisies* (all with Inna Kollegorskay, piano). SCHUMANN: *Romance in A, Op. 94/2.* GRANADOS: *Danzas españolas No. 5.* DEBUSSY: *Suite bergaasque: Passepied. Beau soir* (with Abram Makarov, piano).
(M) (**) BMG/Melodiya 74321 34180-2.

Volume 4: BRAHMS: *Violin sonatas Nos. 2, Op. 100; 3, Op. 108.* FRANCK: *Violin sonata in A* (all with Sviatoslav Richter, piano).
(M) *** BMG/Melodiya 74321 34181-2.

Volume 5: BARTOK: *Violin sonata No. 1.* SHOSTAKOVICH: *Violin sonata, Op. 34* (both with Sviatoslav Richter, piano).
(M) *** BMG/Melodiya 74321 34182-2.

The five CDs of the BMG/Melodiya set are available singly (in the UK only) or packaged in a slipcase at a discount. The first disc (BMG/Melodiya 74321 34178-2) couples the 1968 account of the Tchaikovksy *Violin concerto* with the Sibelius and the two Op. 87 *Humoresques*, recorded three years earlier at the time of the Sibelius centenary. Oistrakh probably played the Tchaikovsky more often than any other concerto, and on one occasion surprised Shostakovich by the intensive practising he overheard coming from the neighbouring hotel room. When Shostakovich asked him why such arduous practice was still necessary after more than a hundred performances, Oistrakh gave his oft-quoted reply: 'But that is exactly why! It has to be just as fresh and new as though it were the very first performance . . . I am trying to track down its melodic elements even in pure mechanical episodes.' It certainly sounds as fresh as ever here in a performance given to mark the great violinist's sixtieth birthday. The Sibelius, which Oistrakh had recorded in Stockholm with Sixten Ehrling in 1953 (now reissued on the Testament label), is a marvellous, golden-toned account that stands the test of time.

The Brahms and Dvořák *Concertos* share the second disc (BMG/Melodiya 74321 34179-2), both with the conductor Kyrill Kondrashin. The Brahms comes from 1952 and the Dvořák from 1949, so that the sound calls for tolerance. Superb though this playing is, the great majority of collectors will prefer to have either Oistrakh's 1954 Dresden recording with Konwitschny (DG), coupled with his no less superb version of the Tchaikovsky, or the later Orchestre National de l'ORTF under Klemperer. The quality in the Dvořák is moderately excruciating on climaxes but, if you can make allowances, the performance is absolutely terrific. Never has the work sounded more brilliant yet radiated more repose. The sleeve and label bear the legend 'stereo' but such stereo transcription as there may be eludes these ears.

The shorter pieces listed on the third disc (BMG/Melodiya 74321 34181-2) are also incomparable as playing but they too were recorded between 1946 and 1952, so the sound again calls for tolerance. Nothing else does and, to be fair, the remastering engineers have taken the greatest care to get the best sound they can.

The fourth disc (BMG/Melodiya 74321 34181-2) offers more familiar Oistrakh material: the Brahms

A major and *D minor Sonatas* and the Franck, with Richter as pianist. The Franck and the *D minor* Brahms come from 1968 and the *A major* was recorded four years later. The Franck has been issued in a Vox transfer, coupled with the Sibelius *Concerto* on Volume 1 and the Shostakovich *Sonata* (included in Volume 5) plus the Khachaturian *Concerto*. The BMG/Melodiya team have taken rather more trouble over the production, though it is only on critical equipment that these differences really matter.

The last disc includes the Bartók *First Sonata*, which dates from 1972 and is arguably the finest account of the work ever recorded (matching Menuhin's superb mono version from the 1950s with his sister, Hephzibah). The Shostakovich *Sonata*, Op. 134, was composed for Oistrakh's sixtieth birthday in 1968 and remains the definitive performance (if a performance logically could ever be called definitive).

'The Originals' (with (i) VSO; (ii) Igor Oistrakh; (iii) RPO, Goossens; (iv) Dresden State O, Konwitschny): (i) BACH: (i) *Violin concertos Nos. 1 in E; 2 in A min;* (ii–iii) *Double violin concerto in D min., BWV 1041–3.* BEETHOVEN: (iii) *Romances Nos. 1 in G, 2 in F, Opp. 40 & 50.* BRAHMS: (iv) *Violin concerto, Op. 77.* TCHAIKOVSKY: *Violin concerto, Op. 35.*
(M) (***) DG stereo/mono 447 427-2 (2) [id.].

In 'The Originals' series at mid-price, DG here offers reissues of classic Oistrakh recordings unavailable for years in any format. Rarest are the 1954 mono recordings of the Brahms and Tchaikovsky *Concertos*, more relaxed, more volatile readings than those Oistrakh recorded later in stereo. Oistrakh moves effortlessly from dashing bravura to the sweetest lyricism, the complete master. The Bach and Beethoven offerings are hardly less welcome. Allowing for the practice of the time, these Bach performances are all strong and resilient, consistently bringing out the sweetness and purity of Oistrakh's playing, not least in the rapt accounts of the slow movements. Directing the Vienna Symphoniker from the violin, Oistrakh may make the tuttis in the two Bach solo concertos rather heavy, but he then transforms everything the moment he starts playing. The Bach *Double concerto* with Oistrakh father and son, accompanied by Goossens and the RPO, is more magnetic still, and they accompany him no less sympathetically in the warm, poised readings of the two Beethoven *Romances*.

Orchestra of St John's, Smith Square, John Lubbock

'On hearing the first cuckoo in spring': VAUGHAN WILLIAMS: *Fantasia on Greensleeves. Rhosymedre.* GRIEG: *Peer Gynt: Morning.* RAVEL: *Pavane.* DELIUS: *On hearing the first cuckoo in spring.* FAURE: *Masques et bergamasques: Overture. Berceuse, Op. 56.* SCHUBERT: *Rosamunde: Entr'acte No. 2; Ballet music No. 2.* MOZART: *Divertimento in D, K.136: Presto.*
(BB) **(*) ASV Dig. CDQS 6007 [(M) id.].

An enjoyable bargain collection of essentially atmospheric music for late evening. Fine playing throughout: tempi are very relaxed, notably in the Grieg, Fauré and Schubert items, but the evocation is persuasive. The digital recording is first class, full and clear, yet not too clinical in its detail. Some might feel that the music-making here verges on the somnolent in its consistently easy-going manner – the Delius piece is indicative of the conductor's style – but the closing Mozart *Presto* ends the concert with a sparkle.

Osipov State Russian Folk Orchestra, Vitaly Gnutov

'Balalaika favourites': BUDASHIN: *Fantasy on two folk songs.* arr. GORODOVSKAYA: *At sunrise.* KULIKOV: *The Linden tree.* OSIPOV: *Kamarinskaya.* MIKHAILOV/SHALAYEV: *Fantasy on Volga melodies.* ANDREYEV: *In the moonlight; Under the apple tree; Waltz of the faun.* SOLOVIEV/SEDOY: *Midnight in Moscow.* TCHAIKOVSKY: *Dance of the comedians.* SHISHAKOV: *The living room.* arr. MOSSOLOV: *Evening bells.* arr. POPONOV: *My dear friend, please visit me.* RIMSKY-KORSAKOV: *Flight of the bumble-bee.*
✿ (M) *** Mercury 432 000-2 [id.].

The Mercury recording team visited Moscow in 1962 in order to make the first recordings produced in the Soviet Union by Western engineers since the Revolution. The spirit of that unique occasion is captured wonderfully here – analogue atmosphere at its best. The rippling waves of balalaika sound, the accordion solos, the exhilarating accelerandos and crescendos that mark the style of this music-making: all are recorded with wonderful immediacy. Whether in the shimmering web of sound of *The Linden tree* or *Evening bells*, the sparkle of the folksongs or the sheer bravura of items like *In the moonlight*, which gets steadily faster and louder, or in Rimsky's famous piece (sounding like a hive full of bumble-bees), this is irresistible, and the recording is superbly real in its CD format.

Perlman, Itzhak (violin)

'Great Romantic Violin Concertos' (with (i) Chicago SO or (ii) Philh. O, Giulini; (iii) Concg. O, Haitink; (iv) RPO, Lawrence Foster; (v) Phd. O, Ormandy): (i) BRAHMS: *Concerto in D, Op. 77.* (iii) BRUCH: *Concerto No. 1 in G min., Op. 26.* (ii) BEETHOVEN: *Concerto in D, Op. 61.* (iv) PAGANINI: *Concerto No. 1 in D, Op. 6.* (iii) MENDELSSOHN: *Concerto in E min., Op. 64.* (v) TCHAIKOVSKY: *Concerto in D, Op. 35.*
(M) **(*) EMI Analogue/ Dig. CMS7 64922-2 (3) [ZDMC 64922].

These major Perlman recordings include his earlier (1980) studio recording of the Beethoven *Concerto*; it is among the most commanding of his readings and the element of slight understatement, the refusal to adopt too romantically expressive a style, makes for a compelling strength, perfectly matched by Giulini's thoughtful, direct accompaniment. The (1976) Brahms is also a distinguished performance, again finely supported by Giulini, this time with the Chicago orchestra, a reading of darker hue than is customary, with a thoughtful and searching slow movement rather than the autumnal rhapsody which it so often becomes. The (1983) Bruch *G minor concerto* must be counted a disappointment, however, not helped by the harsh, early digital recording which gives an edge to the solo timbre. The performance is heavily expressive and, like the Mendelssohn (recorded at the same time), is not nearly as spontaneous as Perlman's earlier, analogue recording with Previn. The Paganini (1971) is one of Perlman's very finest records and, although the traditional cuts are observed, the performance has irresistible panache and has been transferred to CD very well. In the Tchaikovsky (1978) the soloist is placed less aggressively forward than is usual. Perlman's expressive warmth goes with a very bold orchestral texture from Ormandy and the Philadelphia Orchestra. However, admirers of these artists are unlikely to be disappointed.

'The Art of Itzhak Perlman' (with Israel PO, Mehta; Pittsburgh SO, Previn; LPO, Ozawa; RPO, Foster; also Ashkenazy, Bruno Canino, Samuel Sanders, Previn (piano) and other artists): BACH: *Concerto, BWV 1056; Partita No. 3, BWV 1006.* VIVALDI: *Concerto, RV 199.* MOZART: *Oboe quartet, K.370.* BRAHMS: *Sonata No. 3; Hungarian dances 1–2, 7 & 9.* SINDING: *Suite, Op. 10.* WIENIAWSKI: *Concerto No. 1.* SIBELIUS: *Concerto.* KHACHATURIAN: *Concerto.* KORNGOLD: *Concerto.* STRAVINSKY: *Suite italienne.* ANON.: *Doyna.* YELLEN/POLLACK: *My Yiddishe Momma.* FOSTER (arr. HEIFETZ): *The Old folks at home.* PONCE (arr. HEIFETZ): *Estrellita.* JOPLIN: *The Rag-time dance; Pineapple rag.* SMETANA: *Z domoviny.* KREISLER: *Liebesfreud; Liebesleid.* RACHMANINOV (arr. PRESS/GINGOLD): *Vocalise.* GRAINGER: *Molly on the shore.* PREVIN: *Look at him; Bowing and scraping.* TRAD. (arr. KREISLER): *Londonderry air.* SARASATE: *Carmen fantasy.*
(M) *** EMI Analogue/Dig. CMS7 64617-2 (4) [ZDMD 64617].

This box contains a feast of this great violinist's recordings. He made the choice himself and, while the concertos, particularly the Wieniawski, Sibelius, Khachaturian, and Korngold (and not forgetting the dazzling concertante *Carmen fantasy* of Sarasate or the *Suite* of Sinding) are all indispensable, the shorter pieces on the last disc just as readily display the Perlman magic. They include the delectable jazz collaboration with Previn, the beautifully played Kreisler encores, and many popular items which are readily turned into lollipops. The stylish account of the Stravinsky *Suite italienne* which ends disc three is also one of the highlights of the set. For the most part the recordings have the violin very forwardly balanced, but that was Perlman's own choice; the sound is otherwise generally excellent.

Petri, Michaela (recorder)

'The ultimate recorder collection': VIVALDI: *The Four Seasons: Spring* (with Guildhall String Ens., George Malcolm). *Concerto in D (Il gardellino), Op. 10/3: Finale. Concerto in G min. (La Notte), Op. 10/2, RV 439.* SAMMARTINI: *Recorder concerto in F* (all with Moscow Virtuosi, Vladimir Spivakov). SATIE: *Gymnopédie No. 1.* GLUCK: *Orfeo: Melody & Dance of the Blessed Spirits.* BACH: *Suite in D, BWV 1067: Air.* SCHEINDIENST: *Variations.* TARTINI: *Sonata in G min. (Devil's trill).* KOPPEL: *Nele's dances Nos. 15–18.* JACOB: *An encore for Michaela* (all with Lars Hannibal, arr. for recorder and guitar). GRIEG: *Peer Gynt: Solveig's song; Anitra's dance. Lyric pieces: Butterfly; Little bird, Op. 43/1 & 4; March of the Trolls, Op. 54/3; Once upon a time, Op. 71/1. 2 Norwegian dances, Op. 35/1–2* (all arr. Langford). KOPPEL: *Moonchild's dream: conclusion.* ARNOLD: *Recorder concerto, Op. 133: Lento.*

CHRISTIANSEN: *Dance suite, Op. 29: Molto vivace* (all with ECO, Okko Kamu). HANDEL: *Sonata in G min., Op. 1/2.* BACH: *Sonata in E flat* (transposed G), *BWV 1031* (with Keith Jarrett, harpsichord). TELEMANN: *Trio sonata No. 3 in F min.* (with Hanne Petri, harpsichord, David Petri, cello). *Sonata No. 5 in D min. for 2 recorders* (with Elisabeth Selin). CORELLI: *Concerto grosso, Op. 6/8 (Christmas): Finale* including *Pastorale* (with Nat. PO, Martin Neary). BACH: *Cantata No. 140: Chorale: Wachet auf* (with Westminster Abbey Ch., Alistair Ross, organ; cond. Neary).
(B) ** RCA Twofer 74321 48020-2 (2); *74321 48020-4* [id.].

This is a collection that will best appeal to amateur recorder players, and might make a good birthday present for a young beginner, who will surely be impressed by Michaela Petri's easy virtuosity and will respond to a string of such famous melodies. Even if not all of them transcribe too well, and many are far more effective on the instruments for which they were written. Vivaldi's *Spring* from *The Four Seasons* is indestructible, but Bach's famous *Air* sounds puny, while Grieg's *Second Norwegian dance* is much better suited to the oboe. However, there is quite a lot of genuine recorder repertoire here, stylishly presented, which hopefully should tempt any budding young soloist to explore further. The recording balance is generally well managed and the effect is truthful and not overblown.

Philadelphia Orchestra, Leopold Stokowski (see also under Stokowski RCA Edition)

'Fantasia': BACH, orch. Stokowski: *Toccata and Fugue in D min.* DUKAS: *L'apprenti sorcier.* MUSSORGSKY, arr. Stokowski: *A Night on the Bare Mountain.* STRAVINSKY: *The Rite of spring.* TCHAIKOVSKY: *Nutcracker Suite.*
(M) (***) Pearl mono GEMMCD 4988.

A self-recommending disc. *The Rite of spring* comes from 1929–30 and the *Nutcracker* from as early as 1926, though one would never believe it. Everything Stokowski did at this period was full of character, and the engineers obviously performed miracles. The latest recording is Stokowski's amazing arrangement of *A Night on the Bare Mountain*, which dates from 1940. Such is the colour and richness of sonority Stokowski evokes from the fabulous Philadelphians that surface noise and other limitations are completely forgotten. The transfers are very good.

'Philadelphia rarities' (1928–1937): arr. STOKOWSKI: *2 Ancient liturgical melodies: Veni, Creator Spiritus; Veni, Emmanuel.* FALLA: *La vida breve: Spanish dance.* TURINA: *Gypsy dance, Op. 55/5.* DUBENSKY: *Edgar Allan Poe's 'The Raven'* (narr. Benjamin DE LOACHE). arr. KONOYE: *Etenraku: Ceremonial Japanese prelude.* MCDONALD: *The legend of the Arkansas traveller; The Festival of the workers (suite): Dance of the workers. Double piano concerto* (with Jeanne Behrend & Alexander Kelberine). EICHHEIM: *Oriental impressions: Japanese nocturne. Symphonic variations: Bali.* SOUSA: *Manhattan Beach; El Capitan.*
(M) (***) Cala mono CACD 0501 [id.].

All these recordings show what splendid recorded sound Stokowski was achieving in Philadelphia as early as 1929. The opening Stokowski liturgical arrangements show how that master of orchestral sonority could make liturgical chants his very own, with a discreet tolling bell to indicate their source. Falla's *Spanish dance* shows him at his most sparklingly chimerical. Dubensky's music does not add a great deal to Edgar Allan Poe, but the narrator, Benjamin de Loache, certainly does, presenting the narrative with the essentially genial, melodramatic lubricity of Vincent Price. Hidemaro Konoye and Stokowski and his players conspire between them to provide an extraordinarily authentic Japanese sound in *Etenraku*, and then in *The legend of the Arkansas traveller* we have a complete change of local colour for Alexander Hilsberg's folksy, sub-country-and-western violin solo. Henry Eichheim's Japanese and Balinese impressions are suitably exotic, but not music one would wish to return to. As for Harl McDonald's *Double piano concerto*, the piano writing is splashy and the finale is spectacularly based on the *Juarezca*, a jazzy Mexican dance. The two soloists provide convincing, extrovert dash, and Stokowski obviously revels in what Noël Coward might have described as 'potent cheap music' if with nothing like the melodic appeal of Coward's own work. The two Sousa marches have both poise and élan, but here the sound is barely adequate – not the fault of the CD transfer. The programme lasts for 78 minutes and Stokowksi aficionados need not hesitate.

Philharmonia Orchestra or (i) La Scala, Milan, Orchestra, Lovro von Matačić

'Artist profile': BRUCKNER: *Symphony No. '0' in D min.: Scherzo* (only). GLAZUNOV: *Raymonda* (ballet), *Op. 57: suite.* RIMSKY-KORSAKOV: *Scheherazade, Op. 35.* TCHAIKOVSKY: *Suite No. 3 in G, Op. 55: Theme and variations. Hamlet: (fantasy overture), Op. 67a; The Storm, Overture, Op. 76;* (i) *Eugene Onegin: Introduction; Waltz; Polonaise.*
(B) **(*) EMI CZS5 68739-2 (2) [CDCB 68739].

Lovro von Matačić was one of the most admired conductors of the late 1950s and '60s; he made a number of memorable recordings of Slavonic repertoire for the English Columbia (EMI) label. Although his 1959 *Scheherazade* does not surpass the Beecham or Reiner versions from the same period, it is still a very fine performance, meticulously prepared and finely shaped, and the familiar (1956) accounts of *Hamlet* and the overture to Ostrovsky's *The Storm* with the Philharmonia Orchestra sound as fresh as they did when they were coupled together on mono LP.

Philharmonia Orchestra or NBC Symphony Orchestra, Guido Cantelli

'Artist profile': MOZART: *A musical joke, K.522; Symphony No. 29 in A, K.201.* BEETHOVEN: *Symphony No. 7 in A, Op. 92.* SCHUBERT: *Symphony No. 8 in B min. (Unfinished).* FRANCK: *Symphony in D min.*
(B) *** EMI CZS5 68217-2 (2) [(M) id. import].

Not only do Cantelli's classic accounts have the authority of a master-conductor, they also have a perfect sense of proportion, phrasing that is alive and supple, and a natural elegance. The Mozart *A major Symphony*, K.201, blends style and an expressive freedom which seems totally spontaneous yet which is beautifully shaped and controlled. This is music-making of an order of which period-instrument groups should be envious. The Beethoven *Seventh Symphony* is well held together without being in the least overdriven, and the Schubert *Unfinished* is also a selfless reading, free of idiosyncrasy and all the more full of character for being so. The Franck *Symphony*, recorded with the NBC Symphony for which he was being groomed after Toscanini, is also a performance of some stature. The recordings wear their years lightly: they are now 40 years old and are still going strong.

Philharmonia Orchestra or Royal Philharmonic Orchestra, Efrem Kurtz

'Artist profile': RIMSKY-KORSAKOV: *The snow maiden: suite. Le Coq d'or: suite; Dubinushka, Op. 62.* LIADOV: *Kikimora, Op. 63; Baba-Yaga, Op. 56; The enchanted lake, Op. 62; A musical snuffbox, Op. 32.* SHOSTAKOVICH: *Symphony No. 1 in F, Op. 10.* KHACHATURIAN: *Masquerade: Waltz; Galop.* GLINKA: *A life for the Tsar* (ballet music). KABALEVSKY: *The Comedians: suite, Op. 26.* PROKOFIEV: *Symphony No. 1 in D (Classical), Op. 25.*
(B) *** EMI CZS7 67729-2 (2) [CDZB 67729].

These Kurtz recordings were made between 1957 and 1963, but the sound has dated hardly at all and on CD sounds both colourful and lustrous. The playing of the Philharmonia in the Prokofiev and Shostakovich symphonies is superbly polished and responsive and the performances combine wit and high spirits with much character; the Rimsky-Korsakov suites and Liadov tone-poems (with the RPO playing in the latter) bring comparable finesse and plenty of atmosphere. The effect in *Le Coq d'or* is vividly refined rather than sultry, but *The snow maiden* sparkles, and the Kabalevsky *Comedians suite* has ebullience without vulgarity. Glinka's attractive dances from *A life for the Tsar* show why he was regarded as the 'father' of Russian orchestral music. It is good to have Kurtz's distinguished contribution to the early EMI stereo catalogue properly represented in what is one of the very best of EMI's 'Artist profile' series: this is well worth its modest cost.

Philharmonia Orchestra or Royal Philharmonic Orchestra, Artur Rodzinski

'Artist profile': FALLA: *El amor brujo: Ritual fire dance. Three-cornered Hat: suites Nos. 1–2.* GRANADOS: *Danzas españolas: Andaluza.* ALBENIZ (orch. Arbos): *Navarra; Iberia: El Corpus en Seville; Triana.* GLINKA: *Ruslan and Ludmilla overture.* MUSSORGSKY: *Khovanshchina: Prelude.* RIMSKY-KORSAKOV: *Russian Easter festival overture.* TCHAIKOVSKY: *Romeo and Juliet* (fantasy overture). R. STRAUSS: *Salome: Dance of the seven veils* (with Philharmonia Orchestra): *Dance suite from pieces by Couperin; Death and transfiguration, Op. 24.*
(B) *** EMI CZS5 68742-2 (2) [CDZB 68742].

Rodzinski gives striking and high-voltage accounts of the Spanish repertoire and gets brilliant playing from the Royal Philharmonic, who are most in evidence here. He is hardly less characterful elsewhere with the Philharmonia. What a vintage period this was, too, for good, well-balanced recorded sound. Strongly recommended.

Pierlot, Pierre (oboe)

'The magic of the oboe' (with Sol. Ven., Scimone; or Paillard CO, Jean-François Paillard): VIVALDI: *Concertos in C, RV 452; F, RV 455.* ALBINONI: *Concerto a cinque in D min., Op. 9/2.* CIMAROSA: *Concerto* (arr. BENJAMIN). ZIPOLI: *Adagio for oboe, cello, organ and strings* (arr. GIOVANNINI). MARCELLO: *Concerto in C min.* BELLINI: *Concerto.*
(M) *** Erato/Warner 4509 92130.

For once, a record company's sobriquet for a collection does not disappoint: this is indeed a magical and very generous (74 minutes) collection, well recorded. One might say the cream of baroque oboe concertos are included here, and Benjamin's arrangement of movements by Cimarosa with its delightful central *Siciliano* and spiccato finale is as engaging as any. The Albinoni and Marcello concertos have memorable slow movements, too, and the Bellini a catchy Polacca finale. The novelty is Zipoli's *Adagio*, sumptuously arranged by Francesco Giovannini after the manner of Giazotto's 'Albinoni *Adagio*'. It doesn't quite come off, but it is a very near miss. Throughout, Pierlot's sweet, finely focused timbre and graceful phrasing are a constant pleasure.

Rampal, Jean-Pierre (flute)

'20th century flute masterpieces' (with (i) LOP, Froment; (ii) O de l'ORTF, Martinon; (iii) LOP, Jolivet; (iv) Robert Veyron-Lacroix): (i) IBERT: *Concerto.* (ii) KHACHATURIAN: *Concerto* (arr. from *Violin concerto*). (ii) JOLIVET: *Concerto.* (iii) MARTINU: *Sonata.* HINDEMITH: *Sonata.* PROKOFIEV: *Sonata in D.* POULENC: *Sonata.*
(M) **(*) Erato/Warner 2292 45839-2 (2) [id.].

The concertos on the first CD have less than perfectly focused orchestral strings, and the Khachaturian arrangement is dispensable. But the Ibert *Concerto* is winning and the more plangent Jolivet not inconsiderable. The highlights of the collection are all on the second disc, three out of four of them inspired works delightfully written for the instrument and marvellously played. Only the first movement of the Hindemith is a bit below par in its utilitarian austerity; the cool slow movement and more vigorous finale have something approaching charm. The Prokofiev *Sonata* (also heard in a version for violin – but the flute is the original) is a masterpiece, and Rampal makes the very most of it. Then comes the delightful Poulenc piece with its disarmingly easy-flowing opening, delicious central cantilena and scintillating finale with hints of *Les Biches*. The recording of the sonatas, made in 1978, is vividly firm and realistic. If this set is reissued later on a Bonsai Duo, it will be well worth seeking out.

(i) RCA Victor Symphony Orchestra; (ii) Symphony of the Air, Leopold Stokowski

'Rhapsodies': (i) LISZT: *Hungarian rhapsody No. 2*. ENESCU: *Romanian rhapsody No. 1*. SMETANA: *Má Vlast: Vltava. The Bartered Bride overture*. (ii) WAGNER: *Tannhäuser: Overture and Venusberg music* (with chorus). *Tristan und Isolde: Prelude to Act III*.
(M) *** BMG/RCA 09026 61503-2 [id.].

Recorded in 1960 and 1961, this collection shows the great orchestral magician at his most uninhibitedly voluptuous. The opening tutti of the Liszt *Hungarian rhapsody* with full-throated horns and richly sonorous double basses makes a huge impact, and the Enescu is comparably sumptuous in its glowing colours. *Vltava* is romanticized, with an expansive treatment of the main lyrical theme, but *The Bartered Bride Overture* is bursting with energy, with the stereo clearly defining the emphatic string entries of the opening fugato. The *Overture and Venusberg music* from *Tannhäuser* combines sensuousness with frenetic excitement, and then a sentient relaxation appears in the *Tristan Prelude* to Act III. This is over-the-top Stokowski at his most compulsive, but is not for musical puritans. The CD transfers encompass the breadth of amplitude of the forwardly balanced recordings without problems.

Rostropovich, Mstislav (cello)

'The Rostropovich Edition': Cello concertos: DVORAK: *Concerto in B min., Op. 104* (with LPO, Giulini). BRAHMS: *Double concerto for violin and cello in A min., Op. 102* (with David Oistrakh, Cleveland O, Szell). HAYDN: *Cello concertos in C & D, Hob VIIb/1–2* (with ASMF, Marriner). BLOCH: *Schelomo* (with O Nat. de France, Bernstein). Richard STRAUSS: *Don Quixote, Op. 35* (with BPO, Karajan). MIASKOVSKY: *Cello concerto in C min., Op. 66* (with Philh. O, Sargent).
(M) **(*) EMI (SIS) CMS5 65701-2 (3) [ZDMC 65701].

Rostropovich recorded the Dvořák *Concerto* three times before this version (with Talich, Boult and Karajan), and this 1977 EMI performance is his least successful on record. He makes heavy weather of most of the concerto, and his unrelieved emotional intensity is matched by Giulini, who focuses attention on beauty of detail rather than structural cohesion. Even so, there are many incidental beauties that compel admiration, and the engineering is impressive. The Brahms *Double concerto* (recorded eight years earlier in Cleveland with David Oistrakh and Szell) is a different matter altogether and can be counted among the most powerful and eloquent performances on record (in the same league as Heifetz/Feuermann and Thibaud/Casals). In Bloch's *Hebrew rhapsody* the collaboration of Rostropovich and Bernstein is a triumph. The ripe expressiveness of both artists blends superbly, so that the rhapsodic flow conveys total concentration from the deeply meditative opening phrases (*con somma espressione*) onwards. The recording is ripe to match, but spotlights the soloist. The two solo Haydn *Concertos*, which date from 1975, are more controversial. Rostropovich's earlier recording of the *C major Concerto* with Britten was brilliant enough but, at even faster speeds in the outer movements, his virtuosity in the EMI performance is astonishing. However, apart from the extra haste (which brings its moments of breathless phrasing) both here and in the more familiar *D major Concerto*, there is a degree of self-indulgence in the warmth of expressiveness. However, the Karajan/Rostropovich *Don Quixote*, which came a year later, rights the balance. It is predictably fine and its only failing is a tendency for Rostropovich to dominate the aural picture. He dominates artistically too. His Don is superbly characterized and the expressiveness and richness of tone he commands are a joy in themselves. There are moments when one wonders whether the intensity of his response does not lead to over-emphatic tone, but in general both the cello and viola soloists and the Berlin orchestra under Karajan silence criticism. In many ways the Miaskovsky *Concerto*, the earliest recording here (1956), is the most valuable item of all, and Rostropovich's recording with Sir Malcolm Sargent remains unsurpassed. Fortunately it is also available separately – see under its composer listing.

'Masterpieces for cello' (with various orchestras and conductors): BERNSTEIN: *3 Meditations for cello and orchestra* (from *Mass*). BOCCHERINI: *Cello concerto No. 2*. GLAZUNOV: *Chant du Ménestrel*. SHOSTAKOVICH: *Cello concerto No. 2*. TARTINI: *Cello concerto*. TCHAIKOVSKY: *Andante cantabile; Variations on a rococo theme*. VIVALDI: *Cello concertos, RV 398 and RV 413*.
(B) *** DG Double 437 952-2 (2) [id.].

A self-recommending set, with two CDs for the price of one. Each of the works included is discussed under its composer entry. The only drawback is the inadequate documentation.

(i) Royal Opera House, Covent Garden, Orchestra, John Hollingsworth; (ii) London Philharmonic Orchestra, Basil Cameron

'Scandinavian favourites': (i) ALFVEN: *Midsummer vigil, Op. 19 (Swedish rhapsody No. 1); Gustav Adolf II: suite: Elegy.* SVENDSEN: *Carnival in Paris, Op. 9.* GRIEG: *Sigurd Jorsalfar suite, Op. 56; 2 Elegiac melodies, Op. 34.* NIELSEN: *Maskarade: Dance of the cockerels.* (ii) SIBELIUS: *Karelia suite: Alla marcia; King Christian II suite: Musette; Kuolema: Valse triste; Romance in C for strings, Op. 42.*
(B) (***) Dutton Lab mono CDEA 5500 [(M) id.].

Expert transfers of recordings from the very first years of LP, mainstays of this repertoire in the early 1950s. While few of these performances are 'great', all of them are much better than they were thought to be at the time and they give enormous pleasure now. The Svendsen *Carnival in Paris* goes with a real swing, and so, too, does the perennially fresh Alfvén *Midsummer vigil*.

Rousseau, Eugene (saxophone), Paul Kuentz Chamber Orchestra, Kuentz

Saxophone concertos: IBERT: *Concertino da camera for alto saxophone and 11 instruments.* GLAZUNOV: *Alto saxophone concerto in E, Op. 109.* VILLA-LOBOS: *Fantasia for soprano saxophone, 3 horns and string orchestra.* DUBOIS: *Concerto for alto saxophone and string orchestra.*
(M) *** DG 453 991-2 [id.].

An enterprising anthology. The Glazunov is a late work and the best-known and most often recorded of the pieces here. However, both the Villa-Lobos *Fantasia* and the Ibert *Concertino da camera* are as appealing and exotic, and there is much to give pleasure. The longest work is the *Concerto for alto sax* by Max-Pierre Dubois, a pupil of Milhaud: fluent, well crafted and civilized. Eugene Rousseau is an expert and persuasive soloist and the recording, which dates from the early 1970s, is first class.

Royal Philharmonic Orchestra, Sir Thomas Beecham

French music: BIZET: *Carmen suite No. 1.* FAURE: *Pavane, Op. 60; Dolly suite, Op. 56.* DEBUSSY: *Prélude à l'après-midi d'un faune.* SAINT-SAENS: *Le rouet d'Omphale.* DELIBES: *Le Roi s'amuse* (ballet suite).
❀ (M) *** EMI CDM7 63379-2.

No one conducts the *Carmen Prelude* with quite the flair of Sir Thomas, while the last movement of the *Dolly suite*, *Le pas espagnole* (in Rabaud's orchestration) has the kind of dash we associate with Beecham's Chabrier. But for the most part the ear is beguiled by the consistently imaginative and poetic phrasing that distinguished his very best performances. Delibes' pastiche ballet-score, *Le Roi s'amuse*, is given the special elegance that Sir Thomas reserved for music from the past unashamedly rescored to please the ear of later generations. The remastering is marvellously managed.

'Lollipops': TCHAIKOVSKY: *Eugene Onegin: Waltz.* SIBELIUS: *Kuolema: Valse triste.* BERLIOZ: *Damnation of Faust: Menuet des follets; Danses des sylphes. Les Troyens: Marche.* DVORAK: *Legend in G min., Op. 59/3.* DEBUSSY: *L'enfant prodigue: Cortège et Air de danse.* CHABRIER: *Marche joyeuse.* GOUNOD: *Roméo et Juliette: Le sommeil de Juliette.* VIDAL: *Zino-Zina: Gavotte.* GRIEG: *Symphonic dance No. 2 in A, Op. 64/2.* DELIUS: *Summer evening.* SAINT-SAENS: *Samson et Dalila: Danse des prêtresses de Dagon; Bacchanale.* MOZART: *Thamos, King of Egypt: Entr'acte. Divertimento in D, K.131: Minuet. March in D (Haffner), K.249.*
(M) **(*) EMI (SIS) CDM7 63412-2.

It was Beecham who first used the word 'lollipop' to describe his brand of succulent encore pieces. In this selection of 17 examples, Beecham's devotion to French music shines out, with over half of the items by French composers; but the account of the *Waltz* from Tchaikovsky's *Eugene Onegin* chosen to start the disc is totally untypical of Beecham, with its metrical, unlilting rhythms. The transfers generally convey a good sense of presence but tend to emphasize an edge on top, which is an unfortunate addition to previous incarnations of this music on disc.

BACH: *Christmas Oratorio: Sinfonia.* BERLIOZ: *Overture, Le Corsaire.* CHABRIER: *Marche joyeuse.* DEBUSSY: *Printemps.* MUSSORGSKY: *Khovanshchina: Dance of the Persian slaves.* SIBELIUS: *Tapiola, Op. 112.* SMETANA: *The Bartered Bride: Overture; Polka; Dance of the Comedians.*
(M) (***) Dutton Lab mono CDLX 57027 [id. full price].

An exciting reissue which restores two great Beecham recordings to circulation, first his 1946 accounts of Debussy's *Printemps* – a performance that has never been surpassed on records in terms of its naturalness of phrasing and unforced sense of pace – and Sibelius's *Tapiola*, only the third recording of it ever made. Berlioz's *Le Corsaire* and Chabrier's *Marche joyeuse* were the RPO's first commercial recording, made within two months of the orchestra's foundation. Throughout these records the wind playing is distinguished by both eloquence and elegance. Everything here is new to CD – wonderfully transferred.

Royal Philharmonic Orchestra, Per Dreier

'Norwegian rhapsody': GRIEG: *Peer Gynt suite No. 1. Elegiac melody: The last spring. Norwegian dance No. 2.* SVENDSEN: *Polonaise; Variations on a Norwegian folk tune; Norwegian artists' carnival.* KJERULF: *The Wedding in Hardanger.* BULL: *Solitude.* NORDRAAK: *Maria Stuart: Purpose; Valse caprice. Olav Trygvason; National anthem.* HALVORSEN: *Entry of the Boyars; Danse visionnaire.*
(M) *** Carlton Dig. 30367 0083-2 [id.].

A cheap and cheerful CD of popular Scandinavian repertoire, presented with character and charm by the late Per Dreier and the RPO. The novelties by Kjerulf and Nordraak are just as appealing as the better-known items. Thoroughly recommendable performances, and good recording.

Royal Philharmonic Orchestra, Sir Charles Groves

'An English celebration': ELGAR: *Serenade for strings, Op. 20.* BRITTEN: *Variations on a theme of Frank Bridge, Op. 10.* VAUGHAN WILLIAMS: *Fantasia on a theme by Thomas Tallis.* TIPPETT: *Fantasia concertante on a theme of Corelli.*
✿ (B) *** Carlton Dig. 30367 0068-2 [(M) id.].

With gloriously full and real recording, providing the most beautiful string textures, this is one of Sir Charles Groves's very finest records and it makes a worthy memorial to the achievement of the closing decade of his long career. The RPO players give deeply felt, vibrant accounts of four great masterpieces of English string music.

Royal Philharmonic Orchestra, Adrian Leaper

'Orchestral spectacular': CHABRIER: *España.* RIMSKY-KORSAKOV: *Capriccio espagnol.* MUSSORGSKY: *Night on the bare mountain* (arr. Rimsky-Korsakov). BORODIN: *Prince Igor: Polovtsian dances.* RAVEL: *Boléro.*
(BB) *** Naxos Dig. 8.550501 [id.].

Recorded in Watford Town Hall by Brian Culverhouse, this concert would be highly recommendable even if it cost far more. All these performances spring to life, and the brilliant, full-bodied sound certainly earns the record its title. The brass in the Mussorgsky/Rimsky-Korsakov *Night on the bare mountain* has splendid sonority and bite, and in the *Polovtsian dances* the orchestra 'sings' the lyrical melodies with such warmth of colour that the chorus is hardly missed. Leaper allows the *Capriccio espagnol* to relax in the colourful central variations, but the performance gathers pace towards the close. Chabrier's *España* has an attractive rhythmic lilt, and in Ravel's ubiquitous *Boléro* there is a strong impetus towards the climax, with much impressive playing on the way (the trombone solo, with a French-style vibrato, is particularly strong).

(i) Royal Philharmonic Orchestra or (ii) Philharmonia Orchestra, Vladimir Ashkenazy

'Russian delights': (i) TCHAIKOVSKY: *Capriccio italien, Op. 45; Francesca da Rimini, Op. 32.* (ii) RIMSKY-KORSAKOV: *The Tale of Tsar Saltan: suite, Op. 57; Flight of the bumblebee.* BORODIN: *Prince Igor: Polovtsian dances* (with Matthew Best, L. Opera Ch.).
(B) *** Decca Eclipse Dig. 448 989-2; *448 989-4* [(M) id. import].

This Ashkenazy compilation is first class in every respect, and the recordings (made between 1983 and

1988) are of Decca's finest vintage. *Capriccio italien* is superb, spectacular, elegant and possessed of exhilarating impetus. *Francesca da Rimini* is very exciting too, with much fine wind-playing from the RPO in the lyrical central section. Ashkenazy is also in his element in the dazzlingly scored *Tsar Saltan suite*, and the Philharmonia players obviously relish the good tunes, sonorous brass writing and glittering effects. In the *Polovtsian dances* the singing of the London Opera Chorus has striking fervour, with solo interjections from Matthew Best (normally not included) to bring an added edge of excitement, although it is a pity that the percussion-led opening dance is omitted.

(i) Royal Philharmonic Orchestra; (ii) Vienna Philharmonic Orchestra, Rafael Kubelik

'Artist profile': (i) BRAHMS: *Hungarian dances Nos. 17–21.* (ii) BORODIN: *Symphony No. 2 in B min.* TCHAIKOVSKY: *Symphony No. 4 in F min., Op. 36.* MARTINU: *Les fresques de Piero della Francesca.* JANACEK: *Taras Bulba.* BARTOK: *Concerto for orchestra.*
(B) *** EMI CZS5 68223-2 (2) [(M) id. import].

Kubelik's concert opens well. In the Brahms *Hungarian dances* he sounds as if he is enjoying himself, and the RPO responds with good-humoured virtuosity, while in the 1960 Borodin *Second* there is an agreeable warmth. The finale bursts with colour and makes a satisfying culmination. Kubelik's Tchaikovsky *Fourth* is a fine and often brilliant reading. If not electrifying, it has very real qualities of understanding and sympathy for the composer's intentions, plus a remarkable freedom from idiosyncrasies, notably in the first movement which offers both drama and excitement in a way that makes it a fine performance to live with. The finale is splendid, not rushed but with plenty of adrenalin, the well-prepared coda among the most exciting on record, helped by a 1960 recording of substantial weight as well as brilliance.

The Bartók *Concerto for orchestra* (1958) offers first-rate playing and apt tempi, and the vigour of the intepretation reflects the music's inherent virtuosity, especially in the outer movements, without going over the top. One could say the same for *Taras Bulba*, recorded at the same time. Indeed it is difficult to credit the recording date, so vivid and full-blooded is the quality. No less persuasive is the pioneering stereo account of the *Frescoes of Piero della Francesca*, inspired by the fifteenth-century frescoes by the Umbrian painter of that name in the church of San Francesco at Arezzo in Italy, depicting 'The History of the True Cross'. Kubelik conducted its première only two years before making this recording, which is vivid and full of intensity.

Sakonov, Josef (violin), London Festival Orchestra

'Violin encores': HUBAY: *Hejre Kati.* GODARD: *Berceuse de Jocelyn.* TCHAIKOVSKY: *Valse sentimentale; None but the lonely heart.* STERNHOLD: *Fêtes tziganes.* MASSENET: *Thaïs: Méditation.* HEUBERGER: *Opernball: Im chambre séparée.* KORNGOLD: *Garden scene.* MONTI: *Czárdás*
(M) *** Decca Phase Four 444 786-2 [id.] (with miscellaneous works by KETELBEY ***).

This collection makes an admirable coupling for Decca's Ketèlby collection. Josef Sakonov is a specialist in Hungarian fireworks and Zigeuner melodies. He plays on one of a pair of Guarnerius violins dating from 1735 and he certainly produces a sumptuous tone, helped by the very forward balance of the Phase Four recording. Heuberger's *Im chambre séparée* is used to show off the luscious effects possible on the lower strings of this superb instrument, while there are some dazzling fireworks in the bravura items (Sternhold's *Fêtes tziganes* a real highlight). There is taste as well as flamboyance here, and the opening melody and Tchaikovsky's *Valse* are very nicely done. With vivid sound, this is most enjoyable when presented with such flair.

Scottish Chamber Orchestra, Laredo

'String masterpieces': ALBINONI: *Adagio in G min.* (arr. GIAZOTTO). HANDEL: *Berenice: Overture. Solomon: Arrival of the Queen of Sheba.* BACH: *Suite No. 3, BWV 1068: Air. Violin concerto No. 1 in A min., BWV 1041: Finale.* PACHELBEL: *Canon.* PURCELL: *Abdelazar: Rondo. Chacony in G min.*
(B) *** Carlton Dig. PCD 2001 [(M) id. import].

An excellent issue. The playing is alive, alert, stylish and committed without being overly expressive, yet the Bach *Air* has warmth and Pachelbel's *Canon* is fresh and unconventional in approach. The sound is first class, especially spacious and convincing on CD, well detailed without any clinical feeling. The

Purcell *Rondo* is the tune made familiar by Britten's orchestral guide; the *Chaconne* is played with telling simplicity.

Serenades: 'Favourite Serenades'

'Favourite Serenades' (played by (i) Netherlands CO, Zinman; (ii) ECO, Leppard; (iii) I Musici; (iv) ASMF, Marriner; (v) Accardo, Leipzig GO, Masur; (vi) Netherlands Wind Ens., Edo de Waart; (vii) Catherine Michel, Monte Carlo Op. O, Almeida): (i) TCHAIKOVSKY: *String serenade, Op. 48*. (ii) DVORAK: *Serenade for strings, Op. 22*. (iii) MOZART: *Eine kleine Nachtmusik*. (iv) HOFFSTETTER/HAYDN: *Serenade from String quartet in F, Op. 3/5*. (v) BRUCH: *Serenade for violin and orchestra, Op. 75*. (iii) WOLF: *Italian serenade in G*. (vi) R. STRAUSS: *Serenade for wind, Op. 7*. (vii) RODRIGO: *Concierto serenade for harp and orchestra*.
(B) **(*) Ph. 438 748-2 (2) [(M) id. import].

A generous 156-minute anthology about which there are few reservations. Zinman's account of the Tchaikovsky *Serenade* has not the very strongest profile, but it is polished and warmly recorded. I Musici play Wolf's infectiously gay little masterpiece extremely well, even if perhaps they do not do full justice to its effervescent spirit and sheer *joie de vivre*. Everything else here will certainly give pleasure, especially the rare Max Bruch concertante serenade, so enticingly tuneful with Accardo in ravishing form. Catherine Michel's account of Rodrigo's *Serenade concerto* for harp is not quite as enticing as Zabaleta's famous DG version, but the spicy harmonies are made to catch the ear with piquant abrasiveness. Excellent sound (mostly from the 1970s) and smooth remastering ensure aural pleasure throughout.

Silvestri, Constantin

'Artist profile' (with (i) Philh. O; (ii) VPO; (iii) Bournemouth SO; (iv) LPO; (v) Paris Conservatoire O): (i) RIMSKY-KORSAKOV: *May night overture*. (ii) RAVEL: *Rapsodie espagnole*. (iii) ELGAR: *Overture: In the South (Alassio), Op. 50*. (iv) DVORAK: *Symphony No. 8 in G, Op. 88*. (v) GLINKA: *Overture Ruslan and Ludmilla*. (i) BORODIN: *Prince Igor: Overture; Polovtsian dances*. TCHAIKOVSKY: *Symphony No. 5 in E min., Op.64*.
(B) **(*) EMI CZS5 68229-2 (2) [(M) id. import].

Undoubtedly the highlight of this concert is the electrifying account of Elgar's *In the South overture*, a performance never surpassed in its ongoing intensity, recorded with the Bournemouth Symphony Orchestra in 1967, only two years before Silvestri's death. The introspective temperament of Tchaikovsky's *Fifth Symphony* also suits Silvestri and, in spite of the characteristic eccentricities of rubato (which are not always quite spontaneous), he builds up the climaxes in the first two movements with great excitement. The *Andante* is very telling, and the horn solo is quite lovely; the waltz, too, is given real elegance. The finale opens with dignity and then the *Allegro vivace* goes with the wind, with brilliant Philharmonia virtuosity carrying the day. Here the early-1957 Kingsway Hall recording, though full-bodied, has a degree of harshness. The Borodin *Prince Igor overture* generates similar romantic feeling (with another superb horn solo) and thrust, and the *Polovtsian dances* glow with colour and sweep to their close with explosive energy. Silvestri's LPO recording of Dvořák's *Eighth* is also enjoyable: at times wilful, at others warm and genial, full of verve, but never eccentric. Rimsky-Korsakov's *May night* has a particularly enticing blend of rich colours and vivid detail while the Glinka *Ruslan and Ludmilla* generates exciting bravura from the Philharmonia strings, without being pressed too hard. The glitteringly extrovert account by the VPO of Ravel's *Rapsodie espagnole*, if not particularly subtle, brings plenty of excitement.

Slovak Philharmonic Orchestra

'Russian Fireworks' (cond. (i) Richard Hayman; (ii) Kenneth Jean; (iii) Stephen Gunzenhauser; (iv) Michael Halász): (i) IPPOLITOV-IVANOV: *Caucasian sketches: Procession of the Sardar*. (ii) LIADOV: *8 Russian folksongs*. KABALEVSKY: *Comedian's galop*. MUSSORGSKY: *Sorochinski Fair: Gopak. Khovanshchina: Dance of the Persian slaves*. (iii) LIADOV: *Baba Yaga; The enchanted lake; Kikimora*. (iv) RUBINSTEIN: *Feramor: Dance of the Bayaderes; Bridal procession. The Demon: Lesginka*. (ii) HALVORSEN: *Entry of the Boyars*.
(BB) *** Naxos Dig. 8.550328 [id.].

A vividly sparkling concert with spectacular digital sound, more than making up in vigour and spontaneity for any lack of finesse. The Liadov tone-poems are especially attractive and, besides the very familiar pieces by Ippolitov-Ivanov, Halvorsen and Mussorgsky, it is good to have the Rubinstein items, especially the *Lesginka* which has a rather attractive tune.

Solomon (piano), Philharmonia Orchestra, Herbert Menges

'Solomon Profile': BEETHOVEN: *Concertos Nos. 1 in C, Op. 15; 3 in C min., Op. 37; Sonata No. 27 in E min., Op. 90.* GRIEG: *Concerto in A min., Op. 16.* SCHUMANN: *Concerto in A min., Op. 54.*
(B) *** EMI CZS7 67735-2 (2) [CDZB 67735].

Solomon is at his most inspired throughout. The Beethoven *Concertos* are particularly fresh and spontaneous, and his Grieg/Schumann coupling has been highly praised by us since the earliest days of stereo. The Op. 90 *Sonata* is unsurpassed in wisdom. The (1956) Abbey Road recordings have never sounded better, and Solomon's wide range of colour is faithfully caught.

South West German Radio Orchestra, Baden-Baden, Ernest Bour

'L'Oeuvre du XX siècle' Vol. 1: DEBUSSY: *La Mer; Khamma; Jeux.* RAVEL: *Rapsodie espagnole; Ma Mère l'Oye (suite); Valses nobles et sentimentales; Le tombeau de Couperin.* STRAVINSKY: *The Rite of spring; Le chant du rossignol.* ROUSSEL: *Suite in F, Op. 33; Symphonies Nos. 3 in G min., Op. 42; 4 in A, Op. 53.*
❀ (B) **(*) Astrée Audivis E 7800 (4) [id.].

Ernest Bour was a champion of the new music both of the French and Viennese schools, though his sympathies were wide. He even conducted the première outside Denmark of Holmboe's *Seventh Symphony*. He is probably best known for the miraculously stylish première mono recording of Ravel's *L'Enfant et les sortilèges* – given a Rosette in our main edition and re-listed above, under the composer (Testament SBT 1044). He was a true musician wholly unconcerned with building a career or hype. The bulk of his career was spent in Strasbourg, Hilversum and Baden-Baden. Four bargain CDs, each nicely packaged with a splendid booklet. The recordings derive from the archives of the Südwestfunk, Baden-Baden, and vary in quality – not surprisingly, given the fact that they range from 1965 to 1987. They are all made in the Hans Rosbaud Studio and a few of them sound studio-bound and insufficiently transparent. Roussel's marvellously spirited *Suite en F* (1965) is a case in point, but fortunately the two symphonies, recorded in 1967 (No. 3) and 1977 (No. 4) are very good indeed without being in the demonstration bracket. There is an atmospheric *Le sacre* (1969) and, on the same disc, *Le chant du rossignol* (1972) offers splendid sound; the performance, while it does not quite match the Chicago version under Reiner (see under Stravinsky in our composer index), runs it pretty close.

The Debussy performances have a very idiomatic and natural feel to them. There is a finely paced account of *La Mer* (1968) with good sound, a very persuasive version of *Khamma* (1987) with excellent sound, and an outstanding *Jeux* (1984), worthy to rank alongside the finest now before the public. The Ravel performances are all recorded between 1967 and 1974 and show Bour's natural affinity for this composer. The *Fería* from *Rapsodie espagnole* may not be as intoxicating as the Reiner but it comes a close second; the *Ma Mère l'Oye* suite (1972) shows great tenderness and panache, and there is much tenderness and real style in the *Valses nobles*, though the 1967 recording is less transparent than the *Jeux* or, for that matter, *Le tombeau de Couperin*. This set cannot be a three-star recommendation as it is uneven, but it really deserves a Rosette for the special interpretative qualities Bour brings to much of this music. Like Fricsay now (though not in his lifetime), Bour was underrated and deserves some long-overdue recognition.

'L'Oeuvre du XX siècle' Vol. 2: SCHOENBERG: *5 Orchestral pieces, Op. 16; Variations for orchestra, Op. 31; Accompaniment to a motion picture scene, Op. 34; Theme and variations for orchestra, Op. 43b.* BERG: *3 Orchestral pieces, Op. 6; Altenberg Lieder, Op. 4* (with Halina Lukomska); *Violin concerto* (with Salvatore Accardo). WEBERN: *6 Pieces for orchestra, Op. 6; 5 Pieces for orchestra, Op. 15; 4 Lieder, Op. 13* (with Halina Lukomska); *Symphony, Op. 21; Variations, Op. 30.* BARTOK: *The Wooden prince (suite); Dance suite; Divertimento.*
(B) **(*) Astrée Audivis E 7805 (4) [id.].

Ernest Bour was a champion of the Second Viennese School and, judging by these discs, one of its outstanding exponents. These performances have much greater warmth than Boulez or Gielen bring to this repertoire. The Webern items speak far more naturally than in Boulez's hands, for all the latter's clarity and refinement. As with the French music listed above, the recordings derive from the archives of the Südwestfunk, Baden-Baden, and were all made in the Hans Rosbaud Studio. The *Five Orchestral pieces*, Op. 16, of Schoenberg are among the earliest (1962) and the Berg *Violin concerto* and Webern *5 Pieces*, Op. 10, among the latest (1976). Two of the highlights here are the Berg *Concerto* with Salvatore Accardo as soloist and the Webern, Op. 10, as well as the Schoenberg five *Orchestral pieces* and *Variations*, Op. 31, but the Bartók is no less idiomatic. Those who find Karajan's Schoenberg and Berg too beautified, and Boulez's too clinical, will welcome this highly persuasive music-making. Recordings are not quite three-star but the performances are. Bour was obviously a selfless and dedicated music-maker, and readers wanting a suitable entry point into this world need look no further.

Starker, Janos (cello), Philharmonia Orchestra, Giulini or Susskind

'Artist profile': BOCCHERINI: *Cello concerto in B flat* (cond. Carlo Maria Giulini). FAURE: *Elégie, Op. 24*. DVORAK: *Cello concerto in B min*. DOHNANYI: *Konzertstück, Op. 12*. PROKOFIEV: *Cello concerto in E min., Op. 58*. MILHAUD: *Cello concerto No. 1* (all cond. Walter Susskind).
(B) *** EMI (SIS) CZS5 68745-2 (2) [CDZB 68745].

These are excellent performances, all made in the late 1950s or early 1960s when Starker was in his prime. His account of Milhaud's delightful *First Cello concerto* is quite captivating, and he makes out a strong case for the Dohnányi *Konzertstücke*, still something of a rarity on record. It is good to have the original version of Prokofiev's *Cello concerto*, which he reworked later in life with the collaboration of Rostropovich as the *Sinfonia concertante*, Op. 125. The original is by no means the inferior and does not deserve to be wholly supplanted. The *Elegie* is played rather straightforwardly, always with beautiful tone and a firm line but lacking the quiet reflection which is part of its character. A similar approach is taken with the Dvořák *Concerto*, but there is plenty of vitality and warmth and often sensitive playing. Totally distinguished and very well-transferred, vintage, EMI recordings.

Steele-Perkins, Crispian (trumpet)

Six Trumpet concertos (with ECO, Anthony Halstead): J. HAYDN: *Concerto in E flat*. TORELLI: *Concerto in D*. M. HAYDN: *Concerto No. 2 in C*. TELEMANN: *Concerto for trumpet, two oboes and strings*. NERUDA: *Concerto in E flat*. HUMPHRIES: *Concerto in D, Op. 10/12*.
(M) *** Carlton 30366 0066-2 [id.].

Collectors who have relished Håkan Hardenberger's famous full-price collection of trumpet concertos might well go on to this equally admirable concert, which duplicates only the Joseph Haydn – and that in a performance hardly less distinguished. Crispian Steele-Perkins has a bright, gleaming, beautifully focused timbre and crisp articulation, with easy command of the high tessitura of the Michael Haydn work and all the bravura necessary for the sprightly finales of all these concertos. His phrasing in the slow movement of Joseph Haydn's shapely *Andante* is matched by his playing of the *Largo* of the Neruda and the *Adagio–Presto–Adagio* of the Torelli, another fine work. Anthony Halstead with the ECO gives him warmly sympathetic support. The recording balance gives the soloist plenty of presence, but the orchestra is recorded rather reverberantly, an effect similar to that on the Hardenberger record.

Stern, Isaac (violin)

'A Life in Music': Boxes I–II (for Boxes III–IV, see under Instrumental Recitals)

'A Life in music': Box I
(M) *** Sony Analogue/Dig. SX11K 67193 (11) [SXK 67193].

Volume 1: VIVALDI: *The Four Seasons, Op. 8/1–4* (with Jerusalem Music Centre CO); *Concertos for 2 violins, RV 516, 524* (arr. RAMPAL) (with Jean-Pierre Rampal (flute), Franz Liszt CO); *Concerto for 3 violins, RV 551* (with Pinchas Zukerman, Itzhak Perlman, NYPO, Mehta); *L'estro armonico: Double concerto in A min., Op. 3/8* (arr. FRANKO); *Concertos for 2 violins, RV 514, 517, 509, 512* (with David Oistrakh, Phd. O, Ormandy). Carl STAMITZ: *Sinfonia concertante in D* (with Pinchas Zukerman (viola), ECO, Barenboim) (SM2K 66472 (2)) [S2K 66472].

Volume 2: BACH: *Violin concertos 1–2, BWV 1041–2* (with ECO, Schneider); *Concerto for 2 violins, BWV 1043* (with Itzhak Perlman, NYPO, Mehta); *Concerto for oboe & violin in C min., BWV 1060* (with Harold Gomberg, NYPO, Bernstein) (SMK 66471) [id.].

Volume 3: MOZART: (i) *Violin concertos No. 1, K.207;* (ii) *No. 2, K.211;* (iii) *No. 3, K.216;* (ii) *No. 4, K.218;* (i) *No. 5, K.219;* (ii) *Adagio in E, K.261; Rondo in C, K.373.* (iv) *Concertone for 2 violins in C, K.190;* (v) *Sinfonia concertante for violin & viola, K.364.* (i) Columbia SO, Szell; (ii) ECO, Schneider; (iii) Cleveland O (members), Szell; (iv; v) Pinchas Zukerman, ECO; (iv) Schneider; (v) Barenboim (SM3K 66475 (3)) [S3K 66475].

Volume 4: BEETHOVEN: *Violin concerto in D, Op. 61* (with NYPO, Barenboim); (i) *Triple concerto in C, Op. 56* (with Eugene Istomin (piano)); BRAHMS: *Double concerto in A min., Op. 102* (i) (with Leonard Rose (cello), Phd. O, Ormandy); *Violin concerto in D, Op. 77* (with NYPO, Mehta) (SM2K 66941 (2)) [S2K 66941].

Volume 5: MENDELSSOHN: *Violin concerto in E min., Op. 64.* DVORAK: *Violin concerto in A min., Op. 53; Romance in F min., Op. 11* (with Phd. O, Ormandy) (SMK 66827) [id.].

Volume 6: TCHAIKOVSKY: *Violin concerto in D, Op. 35.* SIBELIUS: *Violin concerto in D min., Op. 47* (with Phd. O, Ormandy) (SMK 66829) [id.].

Volume 7: WIENIAWSKI: *Violin concerto No. 2 in D min., Op. 22.* BRUCH: *Violin concerto No. 1 in G min., Op. 26* (with Phd. O, Ormandy). TCHAIKOVSKY: *Méditation, Op. 42/1* (orch. Glazunov) (with Nat. SO, Rostropovich); *Sérénade mélancolique, Op. 26* (with Columbia SO, Brieff) (SMK 66830) [id.].

There is a feast of superb playing here. It is a pity that the choice of the Beethoven and Brahms *Concertos* features Stern's recent versions instead of his more inspired, earlier accounts (with Bernstein and Ormandy respectively) and the Dvořák *Concerto*, too, is something of a disappointment. But the Bruch, Mendelssohn, Sibelius and Tchaikovsky are glorious, and both the Bach *Double concerto* and Mozart *Sinfonia concertante* bring comparably inspirational music-making. The solo Mozart *Concertos* also give much pleasure, while in the Vivaldi collection, where Stern's partner is David Oistrakh, there are some more marvellous performances of baroque double concertos, and the results are very compelling indeed. Although too often recordings are balanced very forwardly, the remastered sound is a very great and consistent improvement on the old LPs.

'A Life in music': Box II
(M) **(*) Sony SX9K 67194 (9) [SXK 67194].

Volume 9: BARTOK: *Violin concertos Nos.* (i) *1;* (ii) *2* ((i) with Phd. O, Ormandy; (ii) with NYPO, Bernstein) (SMK 64502) [id.].

Volume 10: PROKOFIEV: *Violin concertos Nos. 1–2* (with NYPO, Mehta). BARTOK: *2 Rhapsodies for violin and orchestra* (with NYPO, Bernstein) (SMK 64503) [id.].

Volume 11: BERG: *Violin concerto* (with NYPO, Bernstein); *Chamber concerto for piano, violin & 13 wind* (with Peter Serkin, LSO (members), Abbado) (SMK 64504) [id.].

Volume 12: STRAVINSKY: *Violin concerto in D* (with Columbia SO, cond. composer). ROCHBERG: *Violin concerto* (with Pittsburgh SO, Previn) (SMK 64505) [id.].

Volume 13: BARBER: *Violin concerto, Op. 14* (with NYPO, Bernstein). MAXWELL DAVIES: *Violin concerto* (with RPO, Previn) (SMK 64506) [id.].

Volume 14: HINDEMITH: *Violin concerto* (with NYPO, Bernstein). PENDERECKI: *Violin concerto* (with Minnesota O, Skrowaczewski) (SMK 64507) [id.].

Volume 15: BERNSTEIN: *Serenade for violin, strings, harp and percussion, after Plato's Symposium* (with Symphony of the Air, cond. composer). DUTILLEUX: *Violin concerto 'L'Arbre des songes'* (with O Nat. de France, Maazel) (SMK 64508) [id.].

Although there are a few more reservations here than with Box I, there are some unforgettable performances too. The Barber *Concerto* remains unsurpassed and unsurpassable, as does the Stravinsky, recorded in mono with the composer, while the Dutilleux and Hindemith works are almost as fine. In the Stravinsky, no apology need be made for the sound and the performance is electrifying. The two-disc set which includes music of Lalo, Saint-Saëns, Chausson and others is particularly enticing and makes a good sample of the sheer calibre and remarkable charisma of Stern's playing; unfortunately Sony have withdrawn it.

(Leopold) Stokowski Symphony Orchestra, Leopold Stokowski

'Music for strings': PURCELL: *King Arthur suite: Hornpipe*. J. S. BACH: *Suite No. 3: Air; Mein Jesu, was für Seelenweh befällt dich in Gethsemane; Partita in E: Preludio*. HANDEL: *Alcina: Tamburino*. GLUCK: *Orpheus and Eurydice: Dance of the blessed spirits. Iphigenia in Aulis: Lento. Armide: Musette*. BOCCHERINI: *Minuet*. PAGANINI: *Moto perpetuo*. BORODIN: *Quartet No. 2: Nocturne*. TCHAIKOVSKY: *Quartet No. 1: Andante cantabile*. RACHMANINOV: *Vocalise*. TURINA: *La Oracion del Torero*. T. BERGER: *Rondino giocoso*.
(M) ** EMI CDM5 65912-2 [id.].

These recordings, which date from 1957–8 and which appeared originally on the Capitol label, have never before sounded so full and lustrous, and together make a most pleasant compilation of string arrangements. Tempi are generally leisured, and Stokowski's Bach has seldom sounded more indulgent, especially the famous *Air* from the *Third Orchestral Suite*. The violin *Preludio*, however, has plenty of dash, brilliantly played after the fashion of the equally successful Paganini display-piece. However, the Borodin and Tchaikovsky *Quartet* slow movements are again slow and sumptuous almost to the point of lethargy, and it is in the Turina *Oracion* that the Stokowskian magic ravishes the senses by its sheer sonic radiance.

Stokowski, Leopold

'Stokowski Stereo Collection'.
(M) *** [RCA 09026 68443-2] (14).

Disc 1: (i) BACH: *Transcriptions*. (ii) HANDEL: *Music for the Royal Fireworks* – with (i) LSO; (ii) RCA Victor SO (09026 62605-2).

Disc 2: (i) BEETHOVEN: *Symphony No. 3 in E flat (Eroica), Op. 55; Overture Coriolan*. (ii) BRAHMS: *Academic festival overture* – with (i) LSO; (ii) New Philh. O (09026 62514-2).

Disc 3: CANTELOUBE: *Songs of the Auvergne*. VILLA-LOBOS: *Bachianas Brasileiras No. 5*. RACHMANINOV: *Vocalise* – all with Anna Moffo, American SO (09026 62600-2).

Disc 4: (i) DVORAK: *Symphony No 9 in E min. (From the New World), Op. 95*. (ii) SMETANA: *Vltava; Overture: The Bartered bride* – with (i) New Philh. O; (ii) RCA Victor SO (09026 62601-2).

Disc 5: MAHLER: *Symphony No. 2 in C min. (Resurrection)*. BRAHMS: *Symphony No. 4 in E min., Op. 98* – with (i) Brigitte Fassbaender, Margaret Price, LSO and Ch.; (ii) New Philh. O (09026 62606-2 (2)).

Disc 6: RIMSKY-KORSAKOV: (i) *Scheherazade;* (ii) *Russian Easter Festival overture* – with (i) RPO; (ii) Chicago SO (09026 62604-2).

Disc 7: SHOSTAKOVICH: *Symphony No. 6 in B min., Op. 54; The age of gold: suite*. KHACHATURIAN: *Symphony No. 3 (Symphonic poem)* – all with Chicago SO (09026 62516-2).

Disc 8: PROKOFIEV: *Romeo and Juliet* (excerpts). MENOTTI: *Sebastian: suite* – both with members of NBC SO (09026 62517-2).

Disc 9: (i) TCHAIKOVSKY: *Symphony No. 6 in B min. (Pathétique), Op. 74*. (ii) ENESCU: *Roumanian rhapsody No. 1*. LISZT: *Hungarian rhapsody No. 2* – with (i) LSO; (ii) RCA Victor SO (09026 62602-2).

Disc 10: WAGNER: Volume 1: excerpts from *Das Rheingold; Die Walküre; Rienzi; Tannhaüser; Tristan und Isolde* – with Symphony of the Air; soloists, RPO (09026 62597-2).

Disc 11: WAGNER: Volume 2: orchestral excerpts from: *Tristan und Isolde; Die Meistersinger; Götterdämmerung* – with RPO, LSO (09026 62598-2).

Disc 12: *'Inspiration'*: BACH, BEETHOVEN, HANDEL, GLUCK, TCHAIKOVSKY, WAGNER, RACHMANINOV, etc., with Norman Luboff Ch., N. SO of L., RCA SO (09026 62599-2).

Disc 13: *'The Final Bach Toccata and fugue; rehearsals and sessions'*: BACH, BEETHOVEN, MAHLER, WAGNER, LSO, RPO, NBC SO (members) (09026 62560-2).

RCA's Stokowski Collection arrived just as we were going to press so they are discussed together below, rather than in the composer index. However they are all available separately.

The first disc contains characteristic Bach transcriptions (from 1974), richly played and warmly expressive at slow tempi. The opening *Chaconne* from the *Violin partita No. 3 in E major* (which in turn is based on Busoni's piano transcription) is very spacious indeed, running to nearly 18 minutes, which must be a record. But the LSO make a glorious string-sound, helped by the ample acoustics of St Giles, Cripplegate. Bach's famous *Air* and the chorale, *Ein feste Burg*, have never sounded more opulent, yet (except for purists) the effect can still be moving, for the playing is obviously deeply felt. In the *Royal Fireworks music* (dating from 1961) Stokowski uses a very large group of wind (to follow Handel's original scoring) plus strings. Tempi are again very grand and measured, and at the end (reasonably enough, but only Stokowski would dare do it) the sounds of real fireworks and enthusiastic crowd-noises are introduced momentarily, laminated to the closing tutti.

Stokowski's *Eroica* comes from 1974. He was 93, but this didn't inhibit his energy. Indeed he is electrifying in the outer movements, strong and superbly controlled with a sense of forward movement that never loses its grip. The *Funeral march* is spontaneously lyrical rather than hushed and intense, not a weighty reading, to match the rest. The Scherzo is superbly resilient at high speed. The Walthamstow recording is full and well balanced. This disc also includes the conductor's brief but touchingly sincere 'thank you' to the orchestra: 'You make the music sound profound,' he tells them, 'and that's not easy.'

The warmly sensuous triptych of Canteloube's *Chants d'Auvergne* and the *Bachianas brasileiras No. 3* of Villa-Lobos (with Anna Moffo singing creamily and seductively) was completed by the *Vocalise* of Rachmaninov with Moffo's wordless melisma quite seamless, and this has been one of the conductor's enduring successes. It has stayed fairly permanently in the catalogue and is still there now, so it is listed and discussed above.

Above all, Stokowski's 1960 *New World Symphony* reveals the maestro's genius for moulding phrases and tempi, for pointing the drama of such music as this. There are one or two Stokowskian idiosyncrasies – trumpet-trills at the end of the first movement, for example – and almost every repeat is omitted; but as a document of a great musician at a vintage period it provides a warming experience. Sharp stereo separation and particularly vivid reproduction of timpani and brass.

In 1974 Stokowski recorded a Mahler symphony for the first time, presenting a youthful and surprisingly direct view. The crisp attack and relatively fast tempi of the first three movements, with dotted rhythms sharply pointed, are the hallmark of a youthful approach. Though his mezzo soloist Brigitte Fassbaender's singing in *Urlicht* is less hushed than it should be (partly a question of balance), the massive finale erupts superbly, with the final passage with its vision of heaven very telling indeed. That same year the veteran Brahmsian recorded a wonderfully vigorous account of his *Fourth Symphony*, its urgency tempered with a glowingly warm lyricism, so effective within the spacious Walthamstow ambience. This was the last performance Stokowski was to give of this work, and the CD provides a fitting Brahmsian swan-song. The glorious slow movement is at the heart of a superbly controlled reading that, with its surging *Passacaglia* finale, is very satisfying indeed.

Stokowski recorded *Scheherazade* more than once, but his 1975 version is characteristic of his warmly sensuous approach. The RPO make some alluringly beautiful orchestral sound, recorded in a warmly resonant acoustic (achieved at Abbey Road), which at the climax of the last movement could be more sharply defined (and here the bass drum adds to the weight). With Erich Gruenberg in the title-role providing a sweet-toned commentary, the first and second movements are almost linked. Stokowski is at his most charismatic in the slow movement, and his nudgings of rubato are not always spontaneous, despite the rich sheen of tone he creates. Although there is no lack of drama, in the last analysis this reading does not show him at his most vital, although the coupled *Russian Easter festival overture* (another Rimsky piece he made very much his own) is as vivid and colourful as one could wish.

Khachaturian's *Third Symphony* might almost have been designed to demonstrate how not to write symphonically. The composer's chronic tendency to repeat a phrase *ad nauseam*, his refusal to appreciate that enough is enough – there is a truly terrible organ passage in mad triplets early in this symphony – are the antithesis of true development. Even so, Stokowski's richly expressive direction and the virtuoso playing of the Chicago Symphony Orchestra in 1968 almost make the results tolerable, particularly when the recording is so spectacular. He recorded the Shostakovich *Sixth* at the same time, a wholly different approach to symphonic writing. Though Stokowski's is essentially a romantic view, finding little bitterness, the underlying poignancy of feeling is not lost when expressed in a more optimistic way. His expressive moulding of the composer's long-breathed melodic lines is naturally spontaneous, and the powerful first movement makes a memorable impression. The control of tempo throughout is wholly convincing – flexible without being over-indulgent – and the finale has a fine rhythmic point and sparkle. The characterization of the *Age of Gold suite* is no less vivid, the *Adagio* richly expansive to contrast with the famous *Polka*, which has never sounded wittier. Excellent recording, atmospheric and with a wide dynamic range.

The curious pairing in 1954 of Prokofiev and Menotti was among Stokowski's first stereo recordings for RCA (although he had already recorded in stereo for the soundtrack of Walt Disney's *Fantasia*). The selection from *Romeo and Juliet* (still comparatively little known at that time) concentrated on the score's lyrical and passionate movements and endowed them with ardent romantic feeling. The coupling is colourful and surprisingly tuneful music from Menotti's ballet, *Sebastian*; indeed the *Barcarolle* and *Sebastian's dance* (a delicate, pastel-shaded waltz) are equally charming, helped by Stokowski's affectionate warmth.

Stokowski's *Pathétique*, however, is for aficionados only: it is very wayward. Impressively played and recorded, at Walthamstow in 1973, the performance shows too much evidence of Stokowski's desire to regard his interpretation as a personal document, and to impose his own personality on the music. The two famous rhapsodies (and Stokowski was always closely associated with the *Second Hungarian rhapsody* of Liszt) are played with characteristic charisma and zest.

The pair of Wagner CDs bring a truly Stokowskian approach. In the highly dramatic *Ring* sequences the voices are very noticeably absent; but when he does use singers, as in his programme with the Symphony of the Air, they are kept totally subservient to the conductor's luxuriantly rich orchestral conception. That is the only possible description of the string playing in the *Tristan Prelude*. This kind of approach – dedicated to sensuous beauty of sound alone – misses the inner quality of the music, and the closing pages of the *Venusberg music*, wonderfully rich though they are, have little feeling of spirituality. But with exciting performances of both the *Tannhäuser overture* (with vivid detail in the middle section) and the *Ride of the Valkyries*, this is still recommendable for Stokowski's unique treatment of Wagner.

The penultimate CD offers Stokowski's inflated orchestration of his own selected suite from Handel's *Water music*, plus a series of choral lollipops, beautifully sung by the Norman Luboff Choir, ranging from Bach's *Jesu, joy of man's desiring* and *Sheep may safely graze* to Wagner's *Pilgrims' chorus* from *Tannhäuser* and the spiritual, *Deep river*. The concert opens with a surprisingly successful choral arrangement of a Beethoven song called 'The heav'ns are telling' and closes with Gluck's *Dance of the Blessed Spirits*, which is treated similarly.

The final disc includes Stokowski's last recording of his most celebrated Bach transcription, plus excerpts from Wagner's *Rienzi overture* (including rehearsal sequences) and the Mahler *Second*. A brief but vivid 7-minute extract from the finale of Beethoven's *Pastoral Symphony*, played by members of the NBC Symphony Orchestra and taken from a very early stereo session, comes as a bonus. The standard of transfers throughought the series can reflect only credit on the current RCA engineering team. The notes by the well-known Stokowskian expert, Edward Johnson, are brief but always interestingly informative.

Stuttgart Chamber Orchestra, Münchinger

'Baroque concert': PACHELBEL: *Canon.* GLUCK: *Orfeo: Dance of the Blessed Spirits.* HANDEL: *Water music: suite No. 3; Organ concerto in F* (*Cuckoo and the nightingale;* with M. Haselböck); *Oboe concerto No. 3 in G min.* (with L. Koch). L. MOZART: *Toy Symphony.* ALBINONI: *Adagio in G min.* (arr. GIAZOTTO). BACH: *Suite No. 3, BMV 1068: Air.* BOCCHERINI: *Minuet* (from *String quintet in E. Op. 13/5*).

(B) **(*) Decca Dig. 448 239-2; *448 239-4* [(M) id. import].

Beautifully recorded – the CD is particularly fine – this is an attractive concert with a very well-played suite from Handel's *Water music*, and the engaging *Cuckoo and the nightingale Organ concerto* (with Martin Haselböck an excellent soloist) to give a little ballast. The performance of Pachelbel's *Canon* is a little heavy-handed, but the strongly expressive account of Albinoni's *Adagio* is convincing. The *Toy Symphony* has some piquant special effects, and the shorter lollipops are played quite elegantly. The overall mood is a trifle serious, but that is Münchinger's way. For the Eclipse reissue, an elegant performance of a Handel *Oboe concerto* has been added.

Symphony of the Air, Leopold Stokowski

RESPIGHI: *The Pines of Rome.* KHACHATURIAN: *Symphony No. 2 (The Bell).* SHOSTAKOVICH: *Symphony No. 1 in F min., Op. 10; Prelude in E flat* (orch. Stokowski); *Lady Macbeth of Mtsensk: Entr'acte.* BLOCH: *Schelomo (Hebrew rhapsody)* (with Georg Neikrug, cello). FRESCOBALDI: *Gagliarda.* PALESTRINA: *Adoramus te.* CESTI: *Tu mancavi a tormentarmi, crudelussima speranza* (all 3 orch. Stokowski). GABRIELI: *Sonata pian' e forte*

(M) *** EMI (SIS) ZMS5 65427-2 (2) [ZDMB 565427].

This brings together a varied group of recordings made by Stokowski with the Symphony of the Air (formerly NBC Symphony Orchestra) on the United Artists label. Nearly all were made at Carnegie Hall in 1958/9 and, if the playing is variable, Stokowski's readings are all characterful and compelling. He conducts the Respighi with characteristic flair and intensity so that, quite apart from the panache of the outer movements, the clarinet solo in the third movement leading up to the nightingale sounds has rarely been more evocative. He plays the bombastic Khachaturian symphony, inspired by the Second World

War, for all it is worth and a lot more besides. In these two works the sound is less full and open than on the Capitol recordings that Stokowski made in London and Paris during the same period. But the Shostakovich *First Symphony* has a convincing concert-hall balance and is pointedly done, an outstanding performance even if the first movement is relatively relaxed, slacker than the rest. *Schelomo* (forwardly but not too dryly recorded in the Manhattan Towers Hotel, New York City) has Neikrug as a satisfyingly firm and expressive cello soloist, even if he hardly matches Feuermann on Stokowski's classic Philadelphia recording. The maestro's own arrangements of sixteenth- and seventeenth-century Italian pieces may be as unauthentic as could be, but the performances are magnetic, especially the accounts of the richly scored Palestrina piece and the infinitely touching *Aria* of Pietro Cesti, played most beautifully. The brass in the solemn Gabrieli *Sonata* is thrilling, with the Carnegie Hall acoustic adding to the sonority.

Tortelier, Paul (cello)

'The early HMV Recordings' (1947–8) (with (i) Gerald Moore; (ii) RPO, Del Mar, or (iii) Beecham): (i) DEBUSSY: *Sonata*; (ii) FAURE: *Elégie;* (iii) R. STRAUSS: *Don Quixote, Op. 35*. (ii) TCHAIKOVSKY: *Variations on a Rococo theme, Op. 33*. (i) TORTELIER: *Le pitre*.
(M) (***) EMI mono CDH5 65502-2.

Tortelier's first record of *Don Quixote* comes from 1947 and was recorded in the presence of Strauss himself. It was reissued some years ago with Beecham's account of the suite from *Le bourgeois gentilhomme*. When this *Don Quixote* first appeared, the authors of *The Record Guide* (1951) called it 'one of the finest orchestral recordings ever made; the performance is noble in proportions and full of exquisite detail'; and it still sounds pretty impressive, nearly half a century later. The emphasis in the present issue is on the young Tortelier, and his eloquent Tchaikovsky *Rococo variations* with Norman Del Mar conducting the RPO is first class. The Fauré *Elégie* was never issued (there is a rather sour orchestral chord at the beginning), but Tortelier's contribution is as splendid here as it is in the Debussy *Sonata*. Admirers of the great French cellist – and those interested in *Don Quixote* – should not miss these splendid transfers.

Trumpet: 'The sound of the trumpet'

'The sound of the trumpet': CLARKE: *Trumpet voluntary*. M.-A. CHARPENTIER: *Te Deum: Prelude* (arr. Hazel). PURCELL: *Trumpet tune and air* (arr. Hurford; all with Peter Hurford, organ, Michael Laird Brass Ens.). HAYDN: *Trumpet concerto in E flat* (Alan Stringer, trumpet, ASMF, Marriner). BACH: *Christmas oratorio: Nun seid ihr wohl gerochen* (arr. Reeve). SCHEIDT: *Galliard battaglia*. HANDEL: *Occasional oratorio: March* (arr. Hazel); *Royal Fireworks music: Overture* (arr. & cond. Howarth) (all with Philip Jones Brass Ens.); *Messiah: The trumpet shall sound* (with Gwynne Howell, bass). VIVALDI: *Double trumpet concerto in C, RV 537* (with John Wilbraham, Philip Jones, trumpets). HUMMEL: *Trumpet concerto in E* (with John Wilbraham, trumpet; all three with ASMF, Marriner). STANLEY: *Trumpet tune in D* (arr. Pearson; with Leslie Pearson, organ). ARBAN: *Carnival of Venice* (arr. & cond. Camarata; L. Festival O; both with John Wilbraham).
✿ (M) *** Decca Analogue/Dig. 458 194-2 [id.].

The Decca production team are particularly adept at compiling an anthology like this, and there is simply no better single-disc recommendation for those who enjoy the sound of trumpets – regal and exciting – on the lips of true virtuosi. Such indeed are John Wilbraham and the individual players of the Alan Laird and Philip Jones Ensembles (especially in Elgar Howarth's highly effective brass arrangement of the *Overture* from Handel's *Royal Fireworks music*). The popular favourites by Jeremiah Clarke, once attributed to Purcell, and Purcell's own *Trumpet tune and air* are equally appealing. Wilbraham's account of the Hummel *Concerto* is among the finest ever recorded, elegant in the slow movement and with the finale sparkling irresistibly. Marriner and the ASMF, during their vintage period, accompany with comparable polish, as they do Alan Stringer, who plays the Haydn *Concerto* excellently, with a bolder and more forthright open timbre which is undoubtedly authentic. Peter Hurford, when he participates, is similarly stylish. Almost every item here is a winner, and the stereo interplay in Scheidt's *Galliard battaglia* is indicative of the demonstration standard of many of the recordings included. The programme ends with a dazzling display from John Wilbraham in Camarata's lollipop arrangement of the most famous of all cornet solos, Arban's variations on the *Carnival of Venice*. The CD has good documentation and a particularly enticing frontispiece, with the title of the anthology embossed in gold lettering on the jewel-case – truly worthy of our Rosette.

Tuckwell, Barry (horn), **Academy of St Martin-in-the-Fields, Sir Neville Marriner** or (i) with **English Chamber Orchestra**

Horn concertos: TELEMANN: *Concerto in D.* CHERUBINI: *Sonata No. 2 in F for horn and strings.* Christoph FORSTER: *Concerto in E flat.* WEBER: *Concertino in E min., Op. 45.* Leopold MOZART: *Concerto in D.* Giovanni PUNTO: *Concertos Nos. 5 in F; 6 in E flat; 10 in F; 11 in E.* (i) Michael HAYDN: *Concertino in D* (arr. SHERMAN). Joseph HAYDN: *Concerto No. 1 in D.*
✿ (B) *** EMI forte CZS5 69395-2 (2) [CDFB 69395].

Barry Tuckwell readily inherited Dennis Brain's mantle and held his place as Britain's pre-eminent horn player for several decades before finally retiring in 1997. This EMI forte double-CD celebrates his supreme achievement in nearly a dozen of the finest concertos for his instrument; the Tuckwell recordings of the key works by Wolfgang Amadeus and Richard Strauss are of course available elsewhere. His supreme mastery and ease of execution, his natural musicality and warm lyricism of line – to say nothing of his consistent beauty of tone – make every performance here memorable, and he has the advantage of polished, graceful accompaniments from the ASMF under Marriner, except in the works by Michael and Joseph Haydn in which he directs the ECO himself with comparable elegance. The concerto of Telemann opens with a catchy *moto perpetuo*, despatched with aplomb; then comes a fine *Adagio* which often moves to the very top of the horn's upper range before the tension is released in the buoyant finale. The Cherubini *Sonata* opens with a melancholy *Largo*, then erupts into joyous high spirits, while the racing opening arpeggios of the concerto by Leopold Mozart and the tight trills in the finale (with harpsichord echoes) are managed with comparable exuberance. The Weber is an attractively diverse and extensive (17 minutes) set of variations and includes a good example of horn 'chords', where the soloist plays one note and hums another; it also has an exceptionally joyful finale. One of the novelties is a delightful concerto by the virtually unknown Christoph Forster (1693–1745) with its amiably jogging first movement marked *Con discrezione* and its brief, disconsolate *Adagio* followed by a closing Rondo in which, though the clouds clear away, the lyrical feeling remains. In some ways most striking of all is the collection of four concertos by the Bohemian virtuoso, Giovanni Punto, a successful and highly cultivated composer whose music is enjoyably distinctive, a mixture of Mozartian influences and Hummelian *galanterie*. The individual CD of these four works was issued to celebrate Barry Tuckwell's fiftieth birthday, and the performances show him at his finest. The recording throughout is of EMI's finest analogue quality, and the remastering retains the warmth and beauty of the originals.

Udagawa, Hideko (violin)

Concertante works (with LPO, Klein): GLAZUNOV: *Violin concerto in A min., Op. 82.* TCHAIKOVSKY: *Souvenir d'un lieu cher, Op. 42.* CHAUSSON: *Poème, Op. 25.* SARASATE: *Romanze andaluza, Op. 22/1.* SAINT-SAENS: *Caprice, Op. 52.*
(B) *** Carlton Dig. 30367 0031-2 [(M) id.].

With the violin balanced forward, the Glazunov receives a heartfelt performance which rivals almost any, even if the finale does not offer quite such bravura fireworks as Itzhak Perlman (at full price). It is valuable to have all three of the haunting pieces which Tchaikovsky called *Souvenirs d'un lieu cher* – the *Méditation* and *Mélodie*, much better known than the central *Scherzo*. They are here done in Glazunov's orchestral arrangements. The Chausson *Poème* is warmly convincing if a little heavy-handed, the Sarasate Andalusian *Romanze* dances delightfully, and only in the final Saint-Saëns *Caprice* does Udagawa's playing sound a little effortful in its virtuosity. Warm, full recording to match.

Ulsamer Collegium, Josef Ulsamer with **Konrad Ragossnig** (lute) and Eduard Melkus Ensemble

'Dance music through the ages'

I: Renaissance dance music: ANON.: *Lamento di Tristano; Trotto; Istampita Ghaetta; Instampita Comincia-mento di gioia; Saltarello; Bassa danza à 2; Bassa danza à 3.* GULIELMUS: *Bassa danza à 2.* DE LA TORRE: *Alta danza à 3.* ATTAIGNANT: *Basse danses: La brosse – Tripla – Tourdion; La gatta; La Magdelena.* DALZA: *Calata ala Spagnola.* NEUSIEDLER: *Der Judentanz; Welscher Tanz.* MILAN: *Pavana I/II.* MUDARRA: *Romanesca guarda me las vacas.* PHALESE: *Passamezzo – Saltarello; Passamezzo d'Italye*

– Reprise – Gallarde. LE ROY: *Branle de Bourgogne*. B. SCHMIDT: *Englischer Tanz; Tanz: Du hast mich wollen nemmen*. PAIX: *Schiarazula Marazula; Ungaresca – Saltarello*. SUSATO: *Ronde*. GERVAISE: *Branle de Bourgogne; Branle de Champagne*.

II: Early Baroque dance music: MAINERIO: *Schiarazula Marazula; Tedesca – Saltarella; Ungaresca – Saltarella*. BESARDO: *Branle – Branle gay*. MOLINARO: *Saltarello; Ballo detto Il Conte Orlando: Saltarello*. GESUALDO: *Gagliarda del Princippe di Venosa*. CAROSO: *Barriera (Balletto in lode della Serenissima D. Verginia Medici d'Este, Duchessa di Modena); Celeste Giglio (Balletto in lode delli Serenissimi Signori Don Ranuccio Farnese, e Donna Margarita Aldobrandina Duca, e Duchessa di Parma e idi Piacenza etc.)*. CAROUBEL: *Pavana de Spaigne; 2 Courantes; 2 Voltes*. HOLBORNE: *Pavane: The Funerals; Noel's galliard; Coranto: Heigh ho holiday*. ANON.: *Kempe's jig*. DOWLAND: *Queen Elizabeth her galliard; Mrs Winter's jump*. SIMPSON: *Alman*. GIBBONS: *Galliard*. PRAETORIUS: *Galliarde de la guerre; Reprise*. HAUSSMANN: *Tanz; Paduan; Galliard; Catkanei*.

III: High Baroque dance music: ANON.: *Country dances: Running footman; Greensleeves and Pudding eyes; Cobler's jigg; How can I keep my maiden head*. SANZ: *Canarios*. CORRETTE: *Menuet I/II*. HOTTETERRE: *Bourrée*. BOUIN: *La Montauban*. SANZ: *Pasacalle de la Cavalleria de Napoles; Españoletas; Gallarda y Villano*. CHEDEVILLE: *Musette*. REUSNER: *Suite Paduan (Allemande; Courantel Sarabande; Gavotte; Gigue)*. POGLIETTI: *Balletto (Allemande; Amener; Gavotte; Sarabande; Gavotte)*. DESMARETS: *Menuet; Passe-pied*. FISCHER: *Bourrée; Gigue*. ANON.: *Gavotte*. LOEILLET II DE GANT: *Corente; Sarabande; Gigue*. LULLY: *L'Amour malade* (opéra ballet): Conclusion; *Une Noce de Village* (dance suite).

IV Rococo dance music (Eduard Melkus Ensemble): C. P. E. BACH: *5 Polonaises, Wq.190; 2 Menuets with 3 Trios, Wq.189*. RAMEAU: *Zoroastre: Dances (Air tendre en Rondeau; Loure; Tambourin en Rondeau; Sarabande; Gavotte gaye avec Trio; Premier Rigaudon; Air en Chaconne*). STARZER: *Contredanse; Gavotte mit Trio; Pas de deux; Menuet; Gavotte mit Trio; Moderato; Gavotte; Menuet mit Trio; Gavotte mit Trio; Passe-pied mit Trio*.

V: Viennese classical dance music: EYBLER: *Polonaise*. HAYDN: *2 Menuets, Hob IX/11:4 & IX/16:12*. GLUCK: *Orfeo ed Euridice: Ballet: Don Juan (Allegretto)*. MOZART: *6 Landerische, K.606; 5 Kontretänze, K.609*. ZEHN: *Deutsche*. BEETHOVEN: *4 Kontretänze, WoO 14/4, 5, 7 & 12*. SALIERI: *Menuetto*. WRANITZKY: *Quodlibet*.

VI: Viennese dance music from the Biedermeier period (1815–48): PALMER: *Waltz in E*. BEETHOVEN: *Mödlinger Tänze Nos. 1–8, WoO 17*. MOSCHELES: *German dances with trios and coda*. SCHUBERT: *5 Minuets with Trios, D.89; 4 komische Ländler, D.354*. ANON.: *Linzer Tanz; Vienna polka*. LANNER: *Hungarian galop in F*.
❀ (B) *** DG 439 964-2 (4) [(M) id. import].

This collection, on four well-filled CDs (recorded between 1972 and 1974), explores the history of European dance music from the beginning of the fifteenth century right through to the first three decades of the nineteenth century, just about the time when Johann Strauss Senior was making his début. The members of the Ulsamer Collegium play an extraordinary range of authentic period instruments. Keyboards, strings, wind and plucked vihuela, as well as guitar, lute and hurdy-gurdy, are used with the greatest imagination, always to seduce the ear with variety of colour. There is not a whiff of pedantry or of abrasiveness of the kind that too often accompanies 'authentic' performances, yet the documentation is characteristically and fascinatingly thorough. The consistent tunefulness of the music is a continual source of pleasure and surprise. Among the composers of early baroque dance music, Pierre Francisque Caroubel and Mario Fabrizio Caroso stand out: the suite of dances by the former, played variously on gambas and recorder consort, is most diverting. On the second CD, the keyboard, gamba and lute pieces from the English Elizabethan school hardly need advocacy, but they are beautifully played (the lute and guitar solos of Konrad Ragossnig are most distinguished throughout the set) as is the jolly suite of dances by Valentin Haussman – another unfamiliar name to turn up trumps. Among the high baroque composers Esaias Reusner (1636–79) provides another diverting dance suite which, like the ballet music of Alessandro Poglietti, proves as elegant and finished as the ballet suite of Lully. In the Rococo era, Carl Philipp Emanuel Bach contributes five spirited *Polonaises*, and after a gracious interlude from Rameau there is a set of more robust and extrovert dances from Josef Starzer (1726–87). We enter the Viennese classical period with a clash of cymbals enlivening a *Polonaise* by Joseph Eybler (1764–1846), who sounds ahead of his time; but the two *Minuets* of Haydn stay well in period. As this stage of the proceedings the excellent Eduard Melkus Ensemble take over. The first of the Mozart *Contredanses*, K.609, which opens the fourth CD makes reference to a famous tune from *Figaro*, and Paul Wranitzky quotes from the same opera in his *Quodlibet*. Beethoven produced irresistible music. Moscheles and Schubert follow his example, the latter providing some deliciously flimsy *Ländler*, while the delicate *E major Waltz* of Michael Palmer

(1782–1827), the two anonymous dances from Linz and Vienna and the *Hungarian galop* of Joseph Lanner (which ends the programme) point onwards to the heyday of Viennese dance music, when Johann Strauss Junior was to reign supreme. Overall, this is a most stimulating and rewarding survey.

USSR Symphony Orchestra, Evgeny Svetlanov

'Waltzes and Polonaises by Russian composers': LIADOV: *Polonaise in C, Op. 49.* ARENSKY: *Suite No. 3, Op. 33: Polonaise in D; Waltz.* NAPRAVNIK: *Dubrovsky: Polonaise.* GLINKA: *A Life for the Tsar: Waltz and Polonaise.* TCHAIKOVSKY: *Swan Lake: Polonaise and Waltz. Sleeping Beauty: Polonaise and Waltz. The Nutcracker: Waltz of the flowers. Eugene Onegin: Polonaise and Waltz. Cherevicki: Polonaise.* LYAPUNOV: *Polonaise in D min., Op. 16.* GLAZUNOV: *Raymonda: Grand waltz. Les ruses d'amour: Waltz. Scènes de ballet: Waltz and Polonaise.* RUBINSTEIN: *Valse caprice, Op. 86.* RIMSKY-KORSAKOV: *Christmas Eve: Polonaise. Pan Voyevoda: Polonaise.* MUSSORGSKY: *Boris Godunov: Introduction and Polonaise.*
(B) ** BMG/Melodiya Twofer 74321 53456-2 (2) [(M) id. import].

Although the polonaise is a Polish dance-form, Russian composers have virtually adopted the style for themselves. Tchaikovsky wrote the best of them, but Rimsky too brought the polacca rhythm to life with brilliant orchestral colouring, and Mussorgky's *Polonaise* in *Boris Godunov* is predictably individual. Those by Liadov which open the collection are a bit pompous here but have pleasingly lyrical middle sections; the piece by Napravnik sparkles more. When it comes to waltzes, Tchaikovsky again leads the field, but Glazunov could charm the ear too, as the three ballet waltzes on the second disc demonstrate. Rubinstein's *Valse-caprice* is rather cheap. The performances are warm, lively and polished, but at times the recording, generally very good, is a bit over-brilliant on top, with fierce percussion.

Vienna Philharmonic Orchestra, Herbert von Karajan

'The great Decca recordings': BRAHMS: *Symphonies Nos. 1 in C min., Op. 68; 3 in F, Op. 90; Tragic overture, Op. 81.* HAYDN: *Symphonies Nos. 103 in E flat (Drumroll); 104 in D (London).* MOZART: *Symphonies Nos. 40 in G min., K.550; 41 in C (Jupiter), K.551.* TCHAIKOVSKY: *Romeo and Juliet* (fantasy overture); *Nutcracker suite; Swan Lake* (ballet): *suite; Sleeping Beauty* (ballet) *suite.* ADAM: *Giselle* (ballet; abridged). BEETHOVEN: *Symphony No. 7 in A, Op. 92.* DVORAK: *Symphony No. 8 in G, Op. 88.* GRIEG: *Peer Gynt* (incidental music): *suite No. 1; suite No. 2: Ingrid's lament; Solveig's song.* HOLST: *The Planets* (suite), *Op. 31.* Johann STRAUSS Jnr: *Die Fledermaus: Overture and ballet music. Der Zigeunerbaron: Overture.* Polkas: *Annen; Auf der Jagd.* Waltz: *Geschichten aus dem Wiener Wald.* Josef STRAUSS: *Delirien waltz.* Richard STRAUSS: *Till Eulenspiegel; Salome: Dance of the 7 veils. Don Juan, Op. 20; Also sprach Zarathustra, Op. 30.*
(B) **(*) Decca 448 042 (9) [(M) id. import].

Following directly on after his EMI Philharmonia recordings with Walter Legge, Karajan's five-year Decca period with the Vienna Philharmonic – master-minded by producers John Culshaw and Erik Smith – lasted from 1959 until 1964. Though the epithet 'great' can be applied to only a handful of the recordings in this box, almost all of them have far more character and musical appeal than many of the more anonymous records flooding the present-day CD market. Certainly Karajan's 1960 *Romeo and Juliet* stands the test of time, not only for its passion but also for its delicacy of feeling in the 'moonlight' music, and his virtually complete (1961) recording of Adam's *Giselle* (with sumptuous sound still approaching demonstration standard) shows what a fine ballet conductor he was, the playing combining affectionate warmth, elegance and drama. The suites from the three Tchaikovsky ballets have comparable panache and generate considerable excitement; apart from the rather plangent timbre of the VPO's principal oboe, they have plenty of glowing colour, with the *Panorama* from *Sleeping Beauty* endearingly suave and the final climax from *Swan Lake* riveting in its histrionic power. The *Nutcracker suite* has more vivid characterization than the later, Berlin Philharmonic account, with the *Waltz of the flowers* lilting agreeably. The remastering scores over the analogue DG versions in its greater ambient depth.

The excerpts from *Peer Gynt* bring the freshest reponse from the VPO, with gutsy Trolls galloping into the *Hall of the Mountain King*, and *Solveig's song* radiantly beautiful. Again, the 1961 Decca recording stands up well alongside the later DG analogue version (which we count as marginally the most alluring of his three stereo accounts) and in many ways is superior in body and naturalness. As for *The Planets*, dating from that same vintage year, this is certainly a great performance, with *Mars* among the most thrilling ever put on disc. With whining Wagnerian tubas it makes a terrifying impact; then *Venus* follows, transmuted into sensuous balm – the *Venus* of gentle ardour rather than mysticism. *Jupiter* is bucolic and breezy, the Vienna strings bringing their own characteristic tone-colour to the big central tune. *Saturn* with its slow, sad march and *Uranus* with superb VPO brass are no less outstanding, and the wordless chorus at the end of *Neptune* is more atmospheric than in almost any other version. The analogue recording is so stunningly vivid that it could have been made yesterday.

Karajan never surpassed his 1960 VPO collection of overtures, polkas and waltzes by Johann and Josef Strauss until he came to make his wonderful (DG) 1987 New Year concert with the same orchestra. His later, BPO records sound glossy by comparison, yet here his rhythmic touch is unerring in the two overtures, while the polkas have all the flair you could ask for. However, the highlight is the highly seductive account of *Tales from the Vienna woods*, played most beautifully, an account which may have been equalled, but has never been surpassed.

The superlative performances of Richard Strauss tone-poems are hardly less remarkable, and they sound wonderfully fresh. In this repertoire no one can quite match Karajan in the panache and point of his conducting. This programme is available separately in Decca's 'Classic Sound' series and is discussed above under its composer entry.

In the symphonic repertoire the results are less even. Of the two Haydn symphonies, No. 103 is more urbane than No. 104, though both offer enjoyably polished VPO playing: there is plenty of robust vigour in the latter and both slow movements are beautifully shaped. The same comments might apply to Mozart's *Fortieth* and *Jupiter Symphonies*. In the *G minor* every detail remains beautifully in place, each phrase nicely contoured and in perspective. Beautifully articulate, this performance has genuine dramatic power, even though one feels that it all moves within carefully regulated limits. The reading of the *Jupiter* is strong and direct and has breadth as well as warmth. Exposition repeats are observed in the first movements of each symphony, but not in the finale of the *Jupiter*. Of the two Brahms symphonies, No. 3 is more successful than No. 1, which gives the impression of being over-rehearsed. Its pacing does not always seem spontaneous, with an overall lack of tension; though towards the end of the finale Karajan cannot help creating genuine excitement, this is dissipated in a very slow chorale reference in the coda. The *Third* is much more successful. Here is another case in which the Vienna performance rivals the quality of the later, DG Berlin version. In both, Karajan takes the opening expansively; in both, he omits the exposition repeat. The third movement, too, is very slow, but the overall reading has plenty of grip and tension, and the Decca recording has a fuller and more resonant bass than the DG, and this well suits Brahms. The recording of Beethoven's *Seventh* is also full-bodied, though not as fine as that for the Dvořák *Eighth*. 1961 was certainly a vintage year for the Decca engineers. The Beethoven performance is massive rather than incandescent and refuses to catch fire or grip the listener emotionally. The Dvořák is another matter, a most winning performance with superb orchestral playing. There are moments of slight self-indulgence in the Trio of the Scherzo, but the result is delectable when the Vienna strings are at their creamiest; overall, this account blends polish and spontaneity in almost equal measure. The orchestra sound as if they are enjoying themselves and so do we.

Vienna Philharmonic Orchestra, Hans Knappertsbusch

'Orchestral favourites': J. STRAUSS Sr: *Radetzky march*. KAREL KOMZAK: Waltz: *Bad'ner Mad'ln*. J. STRAUSS Jr: Polkas: *Annen polka; Tritsch-Tratsch polka; Leichtes Blut*. Waltzes: *Accelerationen. G'schichten aus dem Wienerwald*. ZIEHRER: Waltz: *Wiener Bürger*. WEBER/BERLIOZ: *Invitation to the dance*. NICOLAI: Overture *The Merry wives of Windsor*. TCHAIKOVSKY: *Nutcracker suite*. BRAHMS: *Variations on a theme of Haydn; Academic festival overture*. SCHUBERT: *Marche militaire, Op. 51/1*.
(B) ** Decca Double 440 624-2 (2) [(M) id. import].

Hans Knappertsbusch has earned a gramophone reputation for rather slow and sometimes lethargic tempi, but the Strauss performances are lively enough, if without real magic. However, the *Nutcracker suite* is given rather a po-faced account. The Weber/Berlioz *Invitation to the dance*, although a little stiff, has something of a swing, and the overture goes quite well. The recordings are fair for their day: the Strauss items (1957) sound a bit dated, but the later part of the programme (1960) is quite vividly focused. However, this set does not show the conductor in his very best light.

Virtuosi di Praga, Oldřich Vlček

Music for strings: GRIEG: *Holberg suite.* RESPIGHI: *Ancient airs and dances: Suite No. 3.* ELGAR: *Serenade in E min., Op. 20.* ROUSSEL: *Sinfonietta, Op. 52.*
(BB) **(*) Discover Dig. DICD 920236 [id.].

The Prague Virtuosi are an expert body of soloists who command an impressive sonority in spite of their modest size (here eleven players). Some ears might feel that the Elgar *Serenade* lacks ripeness of Elgarian feeling, yet the *Larghetto* is tenderly affecting. Equally, the Respighi suite of *Ancient airs* sounds fresher, less anachronistically voluptuous than usual. The chamber scale suits the *Holberg suite* admirably, with plenty of energy and bite. But undoubtedly the most effective performance here is the Roussel *Sinfonietta*, bracingly astringent and grippingly vital.

Yepes, Narciso (guitar)

'Guitarra española' (with Spanish R. & TV O, Odón Alonso; LSO, Rafael Frühbeck de Burgos): SANZ: *Suite española.* MUDARRA: *Fantasia que contrahaza la harpa en la manera de Ludovico.* NARVAEZ: *Diferencias sobre 'Guárdame las vacas'.* SOLER: *Sonata in E.* SOR: *10 Etudes; Theme and variations, Op. 9.* ALBENIZ: *Suite española: Asturias (Leyenda). Recuerdos de viaje: Rumores de la caleta. Piezas caracteristicas: Torre bermeja (Serenata). Malagueña, Op. 165.* GRANADOS: *Danza española No. 4 (Villanesca).* TARREGA: *Alborada (Capriccio); Danza mora; Sueño; Recuerdos de la Alhambra; Marieta (Mazurka); Capricho árabe (Serenata); Tango.* FALLA: *El amor brujo: El círculo mágico; Canción del fuego fatuo. Three-cornered hat: Danza del molinaro (Farruca). Homenaje: Le tombeau de Claude Debussy.* TURINA: *Sonata, Op. 61. Fandanguillo, Op. 36; Garrotín y soleares; Ráfaga.* BACARISSE: *Passapie; Concertino in A min. for guitar and orchestra, Op. 72.* YEPES: *Catarina d'Alió.* RODRIGO: *En los trigales; Concierto de Aranjuez; Fantasia para un gentilhombre; Concierto madrigal for 2 guitars and orchestra* (with Godelieve Monden, Phil. O, Garcia Navarro). PUJOL: *El abejorro; Estudios.* TORROBA: *Madroños.* MONTSALVATGE: *Habanera.* OHANA: *Tiento; Concierto tres gráficos for guitar and orchestra.* RUIZ-PIPO: *Canción y danza No. 1; Tablas para guitarra y orquestra.* ANON:. *Jeux interdits (Romance); Canciones populares catalanes: La filla del marxant; La filadora; El mestre; La cançó del lladre.*
(M) *** DG (IMS) 435 841-2 (5) [id.].

Narciso Yepes died just as we were going to print, and this collection celebrates his long-lived and distinguished recording achievement in music from his own country. It was inevitable that the three most famous concertante works of Rodrigo would be included, which will involve duplication for many collectors, but the other concertante works, by Barcarisse, Ruiz-Pipó and Ohana are less familiar and very welcome. Among the more ambitious solo pieces are the *Suite* of Sanz and Soler *Sonatas*, plus the *Studies* of Sor. But many of the miniatures are equally memorable in their atmospheric potency (not least the Falla transcriptions), when Yepes's performances – with their vivid palette and high level of concentration – constantly remind us of Beethoven's assertion that a guitar is an orchestra all by itself. Generally excellent sound.

Zabaleta, Nicanor (harp)

'Great concertante works for harp': MOZART: *Flute and harp concerto, K.299* (with Karlheinz Zöller, BPO). BOIELDIEU: *Harp concerto.* RODRIGO: *Concierto serenata* (with Berlin RSO, Märzendorfer). HANDEL: *Harp concerto, Op. 4/6.* ALBRECHTSBERGER: *Harp concerto in C.* DITTERSDORF: *Harp concerto in A.* DEBUSSY: *Danse sacrée et danse profane.* RAVEL: *Introduction and allegro for harp, string quartet, flute and clarinet* (all with members of Paul Kuentz CO).
(B) *** DG Double (IMS) 439 693-2 (2) [(M) id. import].

Zabaleta was an absolute master of his instrument and all these performances are touched with distinction. Johann Albrechtsberger taught Hummel and Beethoven, and his lightweight concerto is very pleasing when played with such flair and delicacy. The same might be said of the charming Boieldieu and Dittersdorf works, both of which display invention of some character, while the Handel and Mozart concertos are acknowledged masterpieces. In the latter, Karlheinz Zöller makes a distinguished partner. When it was first issued on LP, we gave Zabaleta's version of Rodrigo's delectable *Concierto serenata* a Rosette. In the outer movements especially, the delicate yet colourful orchestration tickles the ear in contrast to the beautifully focused harp timbre. Zabaleta is marvellous too in Ravel's *Introduction and allegro*, with sensitive support from members of the Paul Kuentz Chamber Orchestra, and warmly atmospheric sound. The Mozart and Boieldieu works come from the early 1960s; the others are later and, with excellent transfers, this 145 minutes of concertante harp music will surely offer much refreshment, though these are obviously not CDs to be played all at once.

Alain, Marie-Claire (organ)

'A Celebration'.
(M) *** Erato/Warner Analogue/Dig. 0630 15343-2 (6) [id.].

CD1: *J. S. Bach and his predecessors:* LEBEGUE: *Magnificat du premier ton; Noël: Où s'en vont ces gais bergers; Pour l'amour de Marie.* TUNDER: *Choral-fantasia: Jesu Christus, wahr' Gottes Sohn.* BRUHNS: *Prelude and fugue in E min.* BUXTEHUDE: *Chorales: In dulci jubilo, BuxWV 197; Der Tag, der ist so freudenreich, BuxWV 182; Magnificat primi toni, BuxWV 203.* BOHM: *Chorale: Gelobet seist du, Jesu Christ.* BACH: *Fuga sopra il Magnificat, BWV 733; Canonic variations on Vom Himmel hoch, BWV 769; Prelude and fugue in C, BWV 547*

CD2: *The late baroque:* BACH: *Toccata and fugue in D min., BWV 565; Trio sonata in C, BWV 529; Fugue in G min., BWV 578; Trio (Adagio) (after BWV 1027); (Allegro) BWV 1027a; Concerto in D min. (after Vivaldi), BWV 596.* HANDEL: *Concerto in B flat, Op. 4/6.* C. P. E. BACH: *Concerto in E flat, Wq. 35* (both with Paillard CO).

CD3: *The 19th century:* BOELY: *Fantasia and fugue in B flat, Op. 18.* MENDELSSOHN: *Prelude and fugue in C min.* LISZT: *Prelude and fugue on B-A-C-H.* BOELLMAN: *Gothic suite, Op. 25.* WIDOR: *Symphony No. 5: Allegro cantabile; Toccata.* FRANCK: *Prélude, fugue et variation, Op. 18.* GUILMANT: *Sonata in D min. (Allegro assai).*

CD4: *The 20th century:* VIERNE: *Suite No. 2, Op. 53: Toccata in B flat.* A. ALAIN: *Scherzo in E min.; Toccata on l'Antienne 'Cantemus Domino'.* J. ALAIN: *2 Danses à Agni Yavishta; Intermezzo; Litanies; Aria.* POULENC: *Concerto in G min. for organ, strings and timpani* (with ORTF, Martinon). MESSIAEN: *La Nativité du Seigneur: Les bergers; Dieu parmi nous*

CD5: *Rare recordings: from Pachelbel to Mozart:* BACH: *Cantata No. 35: Sinfonia No. 2* (with Paillard CO); *14 Canons on the Goldberg bass* (with O. Alain). PACHELBEL: *Toccata in C; Prelude in D min.; Chorals: Vom Himmel hoch; Chaconne in F min.* BACH: *10 Canons from The Musical offering, BWV 1079.* VIVALDI: *Concerto in D min. for violin, organ and strings, RV 541* (with Toso, Sol. Ven., Scimone). MOZART: *Fantasia for mechanical organ in F min., K.608; Sonata in C, K.336 (Allegro).*

Bonus disc: BACH: *Prelude and fugue in G, BWV 541; Chorale, BWV 721; Aria, BWV 587; Canzona, BWV 588.* C. P. E. BACH: *Sonata No. 6 in G min., Wq.70/6.*

Marie-Claire Alain's recording career is justly celebrated here by Erato, for she has been making recordings for this label since 1953. The sixth (bonus) CD offered here includes four works which were on that first Bach LP, plus a sampler of her latest recording of organ sonatas by Bach's son, Carl Philipp Emanuel, made in 1996. The other five discs survey her achievement over the intervening 40 or so years. There is very little here that is not of high calibre and the range is remarkable, always using organs suitable for the repertoire. The five recitals are arranged in historical order, beginning with Johann Sebastian and his predecessors, followed by a second disc of Bach but with concertos by Carl Philipp Emanuel and Handel. Then comes the nineteenth century, ranging from Boëly, Mendelssohn and Liszt to the French School – Boëllman, Widor, Franck and Guilmant. Compact disc 4 moves on to the twentieth century but stays in France, and all of it is real music, by Vierne, Poulenc, Alain and – of course – Messiaen. The fifth CD purports to be 'rare recordings', but they are not really so very rare, including Bach *Canons* and a Vivaldi *Concerto for violin, organ and strings* which is not one of the plums. But overall this set is well worth considering, especially by those who want some basic organ repertoire for a modest-sized collection. The reproduction is of a high standard.

Amsterdam Loeki Stardust Quartet: Daniel Brüggen, Bertho Driever, Paul Leenhouts, Karel van Steenhoven (recorders)

'Capriccio di flauti': MERULA: *Canzon: La Lusignuola.* JOHNSON: *The Temporiser.* BYRD: *Sermone blando.* ANON.: *Istampa: Tre fontane; Prince Edward's pavan; The Queen of England's pavan.* J. S. BACH: *Contrapunctus I. Fuge alla breve e staccato, BWV 550; Brandenburg concerto No. 3, BWV 1048:* Finale. SWEELINCK: *Mein juges Leben hat ein end.* FRESCOBALDI: *Capriccio V sopra la Bassa Fiamenga; Canzon prima.* CONFORTI: *Ricercar del quarto tono.* PALESTRINA: *Lamentationes Hieremiae.* TRABACI: *Canzon Franzesa terza.* ASTON: *Hugh Ashton's maske.* TAVERNER: *In nomine.* SHOTT: *Aan de Amsterdamse Grachten.*
(M) *** O-L (IMS) 440 207-2.

The Amsterdam Loeki Stardust Quartet are superbly expert players: their blend is rich in colour and their ensemble wonderfully blended and polished. They can also be heard in an outstanding collection of concertos for recorders in consort with the Academy of Ancient Music – see above – but here they are in holiday mood, presenting an enticing series of lollipops. Not that everything is frivolous. There are moments of solemnity, and the pieces by Conforti and Palestrina (among others) bring an appropriate touch of gravitas, while the *Sermone blande* of Byrd is aptly named. But it is the piquant bravura one returns to most readily. *The Temporiser* of Johnson is a delicious *tour de force* and Bach's *Fuga alla breve e staccato* and the sparkling finale of the *Third Brandenburg concerto* are a joy. After a remarkable variety of mood and colour, the concert ends with the winningly florid *Aan de Amsterdamse Grachten,* which readily conjures up a picture of a Dutch carousel. The recording has striking presence and realism.

Anderson, John (oboe), Gordon Back (piano)

'Capriccio': PONCHIELLI: *Capriccio.* HUE: *Petite pièce.* PALADILHE: *Solo.* KALLIWODA: *Morceau de salon, Op. 228.* PASCULLI: *Concerto sopra motivi dell'opera 'La Favorita' di Donizetti.* FAURE: *Pièce.* DONIZETTI: *Solo.* SCHUMANN: *3 Romances, Op. 94.* FRANCK: *Pièce No. 5.* SINIGAGLIA: *Variations on a theme of Schubert, Op. 19.*
(M) **(*) ASV Dig. CDWHL 2100 [id.].

The three *Romances* by Schumann are the highlight of the programme: they have more substance than the rest and are beautifully played, while Sinigaglia's ingenuous variations on one of Schubert's most charming melodies makes for an engaging finale. The decoratively florid *Capriccio* of Ponchielli which opens the recital receives the most stylish bravura from the soloist; but it is completely inconsequential. The *Petite pièce* of Georges Hue is more distinctive and Paladilhe's *Solo* (in fact a duo with piano) is amiable too, as is the Kalliwoda *Morceau,* although it is rather longer than a morceau. When we come to Pasculli's cleverly contrived fantasia on Donizetti's *La favorita,* the tunes are more indelible, and the resulting virtuosity is impressive. Donizetti's own *Solo* is another attractive miniature, as is the lilting Franck *Pièce.* John Anderson is a first-rate oboist and he is persuasively supported throughout by Gordon Back. The recording is very real and immediate. But this lightweight 75-minute concert needs to be dipped into rather than taken all at once.

Andreasen, Henri Wenzel (flute), Anna Oland (piano)

Flute music of the Danish Golden Age: HARTMANN: *Sonata in B flat, Op. 1; Prelude in G min.* FROLICH: *Sonata in A min.* WEYSE: *Rondeau in D min.* KUHLAU: *Duo brillant, Op. 110/1.*
(BB) *** Naxos Dig. 8.553333 [id.].

The Danish Golden Age is, roughly speaking, the period of the artists C. W. Eckersberg and Christen Købke (the first half of the nineteenth century) and it was then that the present repertoire was composed. It is best summarized as slight but pleasing music, and the performances are alert and fresh with good, bright – but not overbright – sound.

Barrueco, Manuel (guitar)

VILLA-LOBOS: *Preludes Nos. 1–5; Choros No. 1 in E min.* BROUWER: *Danza caracteristica. Canticum; Canción de cuna (Berceuse); Elogio de la danza; Ojos brujos; Guajira criolla.* Julián ORBON: *Preludio y danza.*
(M) *** EMI Dig. CDM5 66576-2 [id.].

The Cuban guitarist, Manuel Barrueco, is the lastest star in the line of great guitarists which began with Segovia and includes, of course, both John Williams and Julian Bream. His breadth of repertoire is remarkable and his playing is often electrifying, yet showing the most subtly imaginative touches in the control of rhythm, colour and dynamics. Barrueco is naturally at home in the music of his compatriots, Leo Brouwer and the young Julián Orbon. The latter was a pupil of Aaron Copland, but his *Preludio y danza* comes nearer to the world of Villa-Lobos, with which Barrueco also has a ready affinity. The Brouwer pieces, including the *Canticum* (dazzlingly vibrant and evocative by turns), the deliciously seductive *Canción de cuna*, the haunting *Elogio de la danza* and the *Guajira criolla* with its enticing opening pizzzicatos (violin style), are all marvellously done. Barrueco is perhaps not quite as winningly flexible as Bream in the famous *Third Prelude* of Villa-Lobos, but he makes No. 4 totally his own with a magical vibrato on the repeated *tenutos*. The *Choros* is played with engaging intimacy. the recording cannot be faulted.

FALLA: *The Three-cornered hat: Night; Miller's dance; Dance of the Corregidor; Dance of the Miller's wife. Omaggio per chitarra (Scritto per le tombeau de Debussy).* PONCE: *Sonatina meridional.* RODRIGO: *Invocación y danza (Homeaje a Manuel de Falla); 3 Piezas españolas.*
(M) *** EMI Dig. CDM5 66577-2 [id.].

What comes over here is not just the (often unostentatious) dazzling bravura and the evocative feeling, but the appealingly warm intimacy with which Barrueco communicates so directly to the listener. He finds all the colour and flamenco rhythms in Falla's *Three-cornered hat* ballet music without ever going over the top; but he is at his very finest in the delicate nocturnal evocation of Rodrigo's very personal tribute to Falla. Falla's own *Homenaje for Debussy* flashes vibrantly, as does the *Zapateado* finale of the Rodrigo *Spanish pieces*; but, for all the astonishing technical mastery of this playing, one always feels that Barrueco is looking beneath the music's surface and seeking to find added depth and atmosphere. If you enjoy Spanish guitar music, this recital is unmissable.

Bate, Jennifer (various organs)

British organ music: ELGAR: *Sonata No. 1 in G, Op. 28* (Royal Albert Hall organ). Samuel WESLEY: *Air with variations (composed for Holsworthy church bells); Introduction and fugue in C sharp min.* STANFORD: *Prelude and postlude on a theme of Orlando Gibbons, Op. 105/2; 2 Short preludes and postludes, Op. 101/2 & 4.* PARRY: *Fantasia and fugue in G min.* (organ of St James's Church, Muswell Hill). WALFORD DAVIES: *Solemn melody.* VAUGHAN WILLIAMS: *Prelude on a Welsh hymn tune No. 2: Rhosymedre.* ELGAR: *Imperial march, Op. 32* (arr. MARTIN) (organ of St Andrew's Church, Plymouth).
(BB) **(*) ASV Dig./Analogue CDQS 6160 [id.].

As can be seen from the organs used, this 75-minute recital draws on three different sources. The Elgar *Sonata* features the Royal Albert Hall organ, used impressively and flamboyantly, although quieter passages recede. The recordings made at Muswell Hill draw on a recital originally published on the Hyperion label which we greeted enthusiastically with the comment that the offered programme could stand alongside many more fashionable French compilations for quality and variety of invention. Samuel Sebastian Wesley's rather gentle *Variations* on *Holsworthy church bells* have charm, and his *Introduction and fugue* is strongly argued and well structured, but less flamboyant than the comparable piece by Parry. Other items in the original programme (by Wesley's father, Samuel, and by Russell, Stanley and Charles Wood) have been replaced by three more obviously popular pieces, by Walford Davies and Vaughan Williams, and by Elgar's *Imperial march*, which could use more uninhibited panache than is offered here. However, generally speaking Jennifer Bate's choice of tempi and registration is admirable, and the organs seem well chosen for the repertoire.

Beaux Arts Trio

'A Celebration (1955–1995)': RAVEL: *Piano trio in A min.* HAYDN: *Piano trio in G, Hob XV/25.* FAURE: *Piano trio in D min., Op. 120.* BEETHOVEN: *Piano trio No. 7 (Archduke).* SCHUMANN: *Piano trio No. 2 in F, Op. 80.* MENDELSSOHN: *Piano trio No. 1 in D min., Op. 49.* HAYDN: *Piano trio in F sharp min., Hob XV/26.* SCHUBERT: *Piano quintet in A (Trout), D.667* (with Samuel Rhodes & Georg Hörtnagel); *Piano trio No. 1 in B flat, D.898.* BRAHMS: *Piano trio No. 1 in B, Op. 8.* TCHAIKOVSKY: *Piano trio in A min., Op. 50.* ROREM: *Spring music.*
(M) *** Ph. (IMS) Analogue/Dig. 446 360-2 (4 1).

As can be seen, the present set celebrates the fiftieth anniversary of the Beaux Arts Trio, and even if over the years there have been changes in personnel the character of their playing (with its immaculate ensemble and spontaneity of feeling) has been stimulated and masterminded throughout by the unostentatious dominance of the pianist, Menahem Pressler, always sharply imaginative, who remains as influential as ever. The earliest recordings here (the Ravel, Haydn *G major Trio*, Hob XV/25, and the Fauré) are offered on a separate bonus disc which comes in a separate cardboard sleeve, inside the slipcase. Daniel Guilet's violin is somewhat meagre in timbre, especially in the Ravel and Fauré, but the cello and piano are naturally focused. Some recording dates for the other works are not stated at all and so we have listed the works in approximate order of recording. Rightly, the earlier (1965) account of the *Archduke Trio* is included; it has more spontaneity than the later version, and the overall feeling is of lightness and grace. The Scherzo is a delight, and elsewhere there is an attractive pervading lyricism, so typical of the Beaux Arts style. Some of the other works have been re-recorded digitally with even greater success, notably the Ravel (where originally we noted a lack of charm on the part of Daniel Guilet). But the earlier versions remain thoroughly worthwhile. The playing in the Mendelssohn *D minor Trio* is thoroughly alive and musical, and the Schubert *Trout* is delightfully fresh. Every phrase is splendidly alive, there is no want of vitality and sensitivity; the *B flat Piano trio*, however, is the later, digital version from the mid-1980s, and the performance, though enjoyable, is not quite as spontaneous as the earlier, analogue version. The Brahms, also digital, shows the later group (including Cohen) at its finest, the playing always vital and sensitive, as does the Tchaikovsky *Trio*. This is a another case where the later version is distinctly superior to the earlier, analogue account. The fugue (originally omitted) is now restored, although there is still a sizeable cut in the final coda. But this remains a fine reading, and the recording is very vivid and present.

Belgian Wind Quintet

'Summer music': BEETHOVEN: *Wind quintet in E flat.* HOLST: *Wind quintet in A flat, Op. 14.* BARBER: *Summer music, Op. 31.* ARRIEU: *Quintet in C.*
(BB) *** Discovery Dig. DICD 920322 [id.].

A delightful collection, well worth its modest price. The many felicities of the Barber *Summer music* are matched by those of the much less familiar work of Holst, contemporary with the *Military band suites*. Claude Arrieu (born 1903) also writes very engagingly: her *Quintet* is both elegant and witty. The playing of the Belgian group is polished and spontaneous, and they are very well recorded.

Alban Berg Quartet

Music of the twentieth century: BERG: *Lyric suite.* BARTOK: *String quartet No. 6.* RIHM: *String quartet No. 4.* SCHNITTKE: *String quartet No. 4.* STRAVINSKY: *3 Pieces; Concertino; Double canon.* HAUBENSTOCK-RAMATI: *String quartet No. 2 (In memoriam).* VON EINEM: *String quartet No. 1.* JANACEK: *String quartets Nos. 1–2.*
(M) *** EMI Dig. CMS5 65765-2 (4) [CDMD 65675].

EMI have assembled a four-CD set of the less approachable contemporary music in the repertoire of the Alban Berg Quartet. These range from classics like the Berg *Lyric suite*, the Bartók *Sixth* and the two Janáček quartets to more unfamiliar but by no means uninteresting or intractable works by Wolfgang Rihm and Gottfried von Einem. This is a valuable set which anyone with an inquiring mind will find rewarding. The playing of the Alban Berg Quartet is beyond criticism and the recordings are of high quality.

Berman, Lazar (piano)

Live recital – 27th June 1992: SCHUBERT: *Piano sonata No. 21 in B flat, D960.* LISZT: *Concert paraphrases of Schubert Lieder: Der Leiermann; Täuschung; Gretchen am Spinnrade; Die junge Nonne; Ave Maria; Erlkönig. Mephisto waltz; Années de pèlerinage, 1st Year: Chapelle de Guillaume Tell.* BEETHOVEN/RACHMANINOV: *Extract from The Ruins of Athens.*
(BB) ** Discovery DICD 920164/5 (2) [id.].

Berman's 1992 recital is uncommonly well recorded for a live occasion and the presence of the artist is in no doubt; indeed we have to wait a full half-minute for him to start after the introductory applause. His account of Schubert's last, greatest sonata is obviously both felt and considered. It is certainly dramatic but also wayward, and not all will respond to Berman's agogic distortions of the flow, particularly in the first movement. The Liszt items provide repertoire for which he is famous and the *Mephisto waltz* shows him at his most commanding. Some of the Schubert song transcriptions may be felt to be over-dramatized, though no one could complain about the *Erl-King*. The Beethoven/Rachmaninov encore is properly piquant.

Bowyer, Kevin (organ)

Blackburn Cathedral organ: *'A feast of organ exuberance'*: WOLF–G. LEIDEL: *Toccata Delectatione, Op. 5/35.* SWAYNE: *Riff-Raff.* BERVEILLER: *Suite; Cadence.*
(M) *** Priory Dig. 001.

The spectacular sound made by the magnificent 1969 Walker organ in Blackburn Cathedral is well demonstrated by this first-rate recital. Leidel is from the former East Germany, and his acknowledged influences from Messiaen and Scriabin are well absorbed into his own style. The *Toccata for pleasure* is titillating in its colouring and certainly exuberant in its extravagant treatment of its basic idea, which goes far beyond the minimalism achieved by many of his contemporaries. Giles Swayne is Liverpool-born and his quirky *Riff-Raff*, in the words of the performer, suggest 'isolated flashes of light of varying intensity'. Berveiller comes from the traditional French school of Dupré. His *Suite* is eminently approachable music, with a whimsical second-movement *Intermezzo* to remain in the memory, and a smoothly rich *Adagio*, before the Widorian finale. His *Cadence* provides a lightweight but by no means trivial encore. What one remembers most of all from this concert is the magnificent sonority of the organ, beautifully captured within its natural ambience, and that in itself shows how well composers and performer have combined their talents.

Bream, Julian (guitar or lute)

SOR: *Sonata, Op. 22: Minuetto & Rondo Allegretto. Andante Largo, Op. 5/5; Estudios Nos. 5, 19 & 12; Largo from Fantasie.* TURINA: *Homanaje a Tarrega, Op. 69: Garrotin; Soleares. Fandanguillo, Op. 36; Rafaga, Op. 53.* FALLA: *Le tombeau de Claude Debussy.* VILLA-LOBOS: *Preludes Nos. 1–5.* TORROBA: *Preludio in E. Sonatina in A: Andante & Allegro. Burgalesa.*
(B) *** Millennium MCD 80113 [id.].

This early recital by Julian Bream dates from 1956, but it shows him with an already prodigious technique, a musician-interpreter of the highest calibre. Indeed, following after the last of the Sor items, the lively neo-classical *Rondo Allegretto* (played with crisp flair), the four highly evocative Turina pieces show Bream's characteristically inspirational way with Spanish repertoire, which he plays as colloquially and spontaneously as any Mediterranean-born guitarist. The middle section of the *Fandanguillo* is haunting and the piece ends magically. Bream was to record the Villa-Lobos *Preludes* again, for RCA, but the playing here is already freely inspirational, especially the evocative *E minor Prelude*, made to sound like distant bells tolling. Everything here springs vividly to life: how engaging is the Torroba *Preludio in E major*, while the subtle atmosphere of the closing *Burgalesa* is beautifully caught. We are not sure whether the recording is stereo or mono (the guitar is central and very realistically projected), but there is a most convincing ambience.

❁ *'The Julian Bream Edition'*

The Julian Bream Edition runs to some 30 CDs (available as a boxed set in the USA: 09026 61583-2), representing three decades of a remarkably distinguished recording career. Bream has now moved over to EMI, so this edition is essentially retrospective. The miscellaneous recitals are considered below, although many of the individual volumes have now been withdrawn. The concertante collections are listed as composer entries in our main volume, and the Elizabethan lute songs are listed under Peter Pears among Vocal Recitals. The whole is an astonishing achievement overall, but we especially recommend Volumes 1–2, 8, 13 and 26–27.

Bream, Julian (lute)

Volume 1. '*The golden age of English lute music*': Robert JOHNSON: *2 Almaines; Carman's whistle.* John JOHNSON: *Fantasia.* CUTTING: *Walsingham; Almaine; Greensleeves.* DOWLAND: *Mignarda; Galliard upon a galliard of Daniel Bachelar; Batell galliard; Captain Piper's galliard; Queen Elizabeth's galliard; Sir John Langton's pavan; Tarleton's resurrection; Lady Clifton's spirit.* ROSSETER: *Galliard.* MORLEY: *Pavan.* BULMAN: *Pavan.* BACHELAR: *Monsieur's almaine.* HOLBORNE: *Pavan; Galliard.* BYRD: *Pavana Bray; Galliard; Pavan; My Lord Willoughby's welcome home.*
(M) *** BMG/RCA 09026 61584-2 [id.].

Bream is a natural lutenist and a marvellously sensitive artist in this repertoire, and here he conjures up a wide range of colour, matched by expressive feeling. Here Dowland is shown in more extrovert mood than in many of his lute songs, and overall the programme has plenty of variety. The CD combines two recitals, the first 15 items recorded by Decca in London in September 1963, and the rest of the programme in New York City 2 years later. The recording is exemplary and hiss is minimal.

Volume 2. '*Lute music from the Royal Courts of Europe*': LANDGRAVE OF HESSE: *Pavan.* MOLINARO: *2 Saltarelli; Ballet detto Il Conte Orlando; Fantasia.* PHILLIPS: *Chromatic pavan and galliard.* DOWLAND: *Fantasia; Queen Elizabeth's galliard.* HOWLETT: *Fantasia.* DLUGORAJ: *Fantasia; Finale; Villanellas Nos. 1–2; Finale.* FERRABOSCO II: *Pavan.* NEUSIDLER: *Mein Herz hat sich mit Lieb' verpflicht; Hie' folget ein welscher Tanz; Ich klag' den Tag; Der Juden Tanz.* BAKFARK: *Fantasia.* BESARD: *Air de cour; Branle; Guillemette; Volte.* DOWLAND: *Forlorn hope fancy; My Lord Willoughby's welcome home* (for 2 lutes).
(M) *** BMG/RCA 09026 61585-2.

Molinaro's music has a disconsolate, nostalgic quality: its atmosphere attracted Respighi, who included *Il Conte Orlando* when he orchestrated his suite of *Ancient airs and dances.* Wojciech Dlugoraj's two *Villanella* are equally touching and his busy *Finale* (which we hear in two versions) gives Bream a chance to display some crisply articulated bravura. Hans Neusidler, a leading German lutenist of the period, offers an equally varied group, with each piece curiously titled, ending with an exotic so-called 'Jewish dance'. The Burgundian Jean-Baptiste Besard's music is hardly less characterful, again bringing contrast between the doleful *Air de cour* and *Guillemette* and the two lively dances. Phillips's *Chromatic pavan and galliard* is strongly written, and the Dowland *Fantasia* and his splendidly regal *Galliard* for Queen Elizabeth are at the end of the programme with *Forlorn hope fancy*, before Lord Willoughby rides in vigorously in an arrangement for two lutes, both, of course, played by Bream.

Bream, Julian (guitar)

Volume 8. '*Popular classics for the Spanish guitar*': VILLA-LOBOS: *Chôros No. 1; Etudes in E min. & C sharp min.; Prelude in E min.; Suite popolar brasileira: Schottische-chôro.* TORROBA: *Madraños.* FALLA: *Homenaje pour le tombeau de Debussy. Three-cornered Hat: Miller's dance* (arr. BREAM). TURINA: *Fandanguillo.* arr. LLOBET: *El testament d'Amelia.* SANZ: *Canarios.* M. ALBENIZ: *Sonata* (arr. PUJOL). RODRIGO: *En los trigales.* MOZART: *Larghetto and Allegro, K.229.* GIULIANI: *Sonata in C, Op. 15: Allegro. Rossiniana No. 1, Op. 119* (both ed. Bream).
(M) *** BMG/RCA Analogue/Dig. 09026 61591-2 [id.].

This collection in itself admirably scans Bream's RCA recording career, opening with material from an outstanding early recital made at Kenwood House in 1962, to which other items have been judiciously added from as early as 1959, and from 1965–8 and 1971, plus the two digital Falla pieces which are as late as 1983. Not surprisingly, the tension is a little variable, though the recital makes a very satisfactory whole. The highest voltage comes in the Villa-Lobos pieces which, though often thoughtful and ruminative, sound wonderfully spontaneous, and the Turina *Fandanguillo* is also very fine. The Mozart and Giuliani excerpts are appropriately mellow. Very real recording, with the various acoustics always well managed.

Volume 9. *'Baroque guitar':* SANZ: *Pavanas; Galliardas; Passacalles; Canarios.* GUERAU: *Villano; Canario.* J. S. BACH: *Prelude in D min., BWV 999; Fugue in A min., BWV 1000.* WEISS: *Passacaille; Fantasie; Tombeau sur la mort de M. Comte de Logy.* VISEE: *Suite in D min.* FRESCOBALDI: *Aria con variazione detta la Frescobalda* (arr. SEGOVIA). D. SCARLATTI: *Sonata in E min., K.11* (arr. BREAM); *Sonata in E min., K.87* (arr. SEGOVIA). CIMAROSA: *Sonata in C min., Sonata in A* (both arr. BREAM).
(M) *** BMG/RCA 09026 61592-2.

The four Sanz pieces are strong in colour and atmosphere, and Sylvius Weiss also emerges with an individual voice. The eight-movement *Suite* by Robert Visée, a French court lutenist who lived from about 1650 until 1725, has the most attractive invention. The famous 'La Folia' emerges seductively as the *Sarabande* (it is beautifully played); and the *Gavotte*, two *Minuets*, *Bourrée* and *Gigue* which follow are all loosely based on its melodic contour. Frescobaldi's *Aria con variazione* is another memorable work. Scarlatti's keyboard sonatas transcribe well enough for guitar and the two sonatas of Cimarosa, though not strictly baroque music, are very personable.

Volume 11. *'Romantic guitar':* PAGANINI: *Grand sonata in A.* SCHUBERT: *Sonata in G, D.894: Menuetto.* MENDELSSOHN: *Venetian boating song; Canzonetta* (all 3 ed. Bream). FALLA: *Homenaje pour le tombeau de Debussy.* RAVEL: *Pavane pour une infante défunte.* ALBENIZ: *Suite española: Granada; Leyenda (Asturias)* (arr. BREAM). TARREGA: *Lagrima (Prelude); 3 Mazurkas.*
(M) ** BMG/RCA 09026 61594-2 [id.].

A pleasant but uneven recital. The opening Paganini *Grand sonata* (21 minutes) is a trifle inflated and the Schubert arrangement is not a great success, while the Mendelssohn *Song without words* comes off much better than the *Canzonetta* (arranged from the *String quartet*, Op. 72). Of the other items, the Tarrega pieces have the greatest memorability. The recordings come from three different sources and there is an uncomfortably awkward tape-join between the very relaxed account of the Ravel *Pavane* and the first of the Albéniz pieces.

Volume 12. *'Twentieth-century guitar I':* BERKELEY: *Sonatina, Op. 52/1; Theme and variations.* ROUSSEL: *Segovia, Op. 29.* SMITH BRINDLE: *El polifemo de oro (4 Fragments).* MARTIN: *4 Pièces brèves.* HENZE: *Kammermusik: 3 Tentos.* RAWSTHORNE: *Elegy.* WALTON: *5 Bagatelles.*
(M) *** BMG/RCA 09026 61595-2 [id.].

The finest works here are the Walton *Bagatelles* – dedicated to Bream – and Henze's *Drei Tentos*, interludes from a larger work, which are very attractive in their picturesque impressionism. Lennox Berkeley's *Sonatina*, too, is an enjoyably amiable piece; the *Theme and variations* is more ambiguous thematically and harmonically. Roussel's *Segovia* has a characteristic touch of acerbity. Reginald Smith Brindle's *Fragments* provides four musical invocations of the poetry of Lorca, while in his *Four Pièces* Frank Martin re-creates for the guitar with characteristic finesse the world of the eighteenth-century lute suite. Bream makes the most of all his opportunities and where the music can charm the ear he does not miss a trick. He concludes the Rawsthorne *Elegy*, which the composer did not live to complete, by reprising the restrained opening section. Overall, however, the work remains emotionally uncompromising. Excellent recording.

Volume 13. *'Twentieth-century guitar II':* MOMPOU: *Suite compostellana.* OHANA: *Tiento.* TORROBA: *Sonatina.* GERHARD: *Fantasía.* VILLA-LOBOS: *Suite populaire brésilienne; Etudes Nos. 5 in C; 7 in E.*
(M) *** Dig./Analogue BMG/RCA 09026 61596-2.

This is an exceptionally rewarding recital of one of the very finest of the many reissues in the Julian Bream Edition. Mompou's six-movement *Suite compostellana* is sheer delight with its muted flamenco feeling and air of wistful melancholy. Ohana's *Tiento*, a considerable piece which looks back to the sixteenth century, opens by musing over the famous *La Folia*, and Gerhard's almost equally striking *Fantasía* is similarly improvisational in feeling. Bream plays both pieces marvellously and is quite melting in the *Andante* of Torroba's *Sonatina* – a more ambitious piece than the name would suggest and the composer's finest work for guitar. To this digital collection the attractive, lighter Villa-Lobos suite is added, recorded two decades earlier, but impressively real and present.

Volume 26. Music of Spain: *'La guitarra romántica':* TARREGA: *Mazurka in G; Etude in A; Marieta; Capricho árabe; Prelude in A min.; Recuerdos de la Alhambra.* MALATS: *Serenata.* PUJOL: *Tango Espagñol; Guajira.* LLOBET: *Canciones populares catalanas.* TURINA: *Fandanguillo, Op. 36; Sevillana, Op. 29; Homenaje a Tárrega.*
(M) *** BMG/RCA Dig./Analogue 09026 61609-2.

A mainly digital recital of Spanish music opens with an attractive, lightweight Tárrega group including the *Capricho árabe* and his most famous evocation, the *Recuerdos de la Alhambra*, which in Bream's hands is curiously muted and withdrawn. Then after works by Malats and Pujol (his *Guajira* has some fine special effects) there follows the delightful Llobet suite of nine *Canciones populares catalanas*. The programme ends with vibrant flamenco-inspired music of Turina, including the composer's last (two-part) guitar work, the *Homenaje a Tárrega*. Bream's dynamism in these performances makes one almost believe he was Spanish-born. The final work (consisting of a *Garrotín* and *Soleares*) was recorded at Kenwood House in 1962 and is exceptional in that here the resonance inflates the guitar image; for the rest of the recital the recording is ideal in all respects.

Volume 27. *'Guitarra'* (Music of Spain): MUDARRA: *Fantasias X & XIV*. Luis DE MILAN: *Fantasia XXII*. Luis DE NARVAEZ: *La canción del Emperador; Conde claros*. Santiago DE MURCIA: *Prelude & Allegro*. BOCCHERINI: *Guitar quintet in D, G. 448* (arr. for 2 guitars): *Fandango*. SOR: *Grand solo, Op. 14; Variations on a theme of Mozart, Op. 9; Fantasie, Op. 7; Sonata, Op. 25: Minuet*. AGUADO: *Rondo in A min., Op. 2/3*. TARREGA: *Study in A; Prelude in A min.; Recuerdos de la Alhambra*.
(M) *** BMG/RCA Dig./Analogue 09026 61610-2.

An admirable survey covering 400 years and featuring several different instruments, all especially built by José Ramanillos and including a Renaissance guitar and a modern classical guitar. Bream's natural dexterity is matched by a remarkable control of colour and unerring sense of style. Many of the earlier pieces are quite simple but have considerable magnetism. The basic recital was recorded digitally in 1983 at Bream's favourite venue, Wardour Chapel, Windsor, and is laid out chronologically. Two additional Sor items, the *Fantasie*, Op. 7, and the *Minuet* from Op. 25, were made 18 years earlier in New York and, as they are analogue, have sensibly been added at the end.

Other collections

'Popular classics for Spanish guitar': VILLA-LOBOS: *Chôros No. 1; Etude in E min*. TORROBA: *Madroños*. TURINA: *Homenaje a Tárrega, Op. 69: Garrotín; Solearas. Fandanguillo*. ALBENIZ: *Suite española, Op. 47: Granada; Leyenda (Asturias)*. FALLA: *Homenaje pour le tombeau de Debussy*. TRAD., arr. LLOBET: *Canciones populares catalanas: El testament d'Amelia*.
(M) **(*) RCA 09026 68814-2 [id.].

This outstanding early recital, recorded at Kenwood House in 1962, was one of Bream's very finest LP collections. The electricity of the music-making is consistently communicated, and all Bream's resources of colour and technical bravura are brought into play. The Villa-Lobos pieces are particularly fine, as is the Turina *Fandanguillo* (which comes at the end), and the Albéniz *Leyenda* is a *tour de force* and makes an almost orchestral effect. The recording (originally produced by James Burnett, with Bob Auger the engineer) has been splendidly remastered for RCA's 'Living Stereo' series (the equivalent of Decca's Classic Sound) and Bream is given a remarkable presence, with the analogue background noise all but vanquished. However, the playing time is only 42 minutes, and while Volume 8 of '*The Julian Bream Edition*' (RCA 09026 61591-2) remains available (see above), this must take second place. That earlier reissue includes most of the present items, plus a great deal more music.

'Baroque guitar': SANZ: *Pavanos; Canarios*. J. S. BACH: *Prelude in D min., BWV 999; Fugue in A min., BWV 1000; Lute suite in E min., BWV 996*. SOR: *Fantasy and Minuet*. WEISS: *Passacaille; Fantaisie; Tombeau sur la morte de M. Comte de Logy*. VISEE: *Suite in D min*.
(BB) *** RCA Navigator 74321 24195-2.

This is a shorter version of the baroque recital which forms Volume 9 of the Julian Bream Edition. It still includes well over an hour of music as Bream's superb account of Bach's *E minor Lute suite* has been added. The recording is very natural, and this makes a fine recital in its own right, realistically recorded. A very real bargain in RCA's bargain-basement Navigator series.

Bream, Julian (guitar and lute)

'The ultimate guitar collection' ((i) with Monteverdi O, Gardiner): (i) VIVALDI: *Lute concerto in D, RV 93* (ed. Bream). Lute pieces: CUTTING: *Packington's round; Greensleeves*. DOWLAND: *A Fancy (Fantasia)*. Guitar pieces: SANZ: *Canarios*. Matéo ALBENIZ: *Sonata in D* (arr. PUJOL). Isaac ALBENIZ: *Suite española, Op. 47: Cataluna; Granada; Sevilla; Cádiz; Leyenda (Asturias). Mallorca, Op. 202. Cantos de España: Cordoba, Op. 232/4*. FALLA: *Three-cornered Hat: Miller's dance*. TARREGA: *Recuerdos de la Alhambra*. VILLA-LOBOS: *Chôros No. 1; Preludes Nos. 1 in E min.; 2 in D*. RODRIGO: *En los trigales;* (i) *Concierto de Aranjuez. Tres piezas espanolas*. GRANADOS: *Cuentos para la juventud: Dedicatoria. Tonadilla: La Maja de Goya. Danzas españolas Nos. 4 (Villanesca); 5 (Valses poéticos)*.
❀ (B) *** RCA Dig./Analogue 74321 33705-2 (2).

The extraordinary achievement of RCA's 'Juliam Bream Edition' is admirably summed up by this inexpensive pair of CDs which include two and a half hours of the most popular repertoire for guitar, plus a small group of lute pieces for good measure. There is not a single item here that is not strong in musical personality, and every performance springs vividly and spontaneously to life. John Eliot Gardiner provides highly distinguished accompaniments for the two justly famous concertos, by Vivaldi (for lute) and Rodrigo (for guitar). The first of the two CDs provides a well-planned historical survey, opening with Elizabethan lute music and progressing through to include three magnetic pieces by Villa-Lobos. Highlights include an electrifying performance of Falla's *Miller's dance* from *The Three-cornered Hat* and, of course the most famous guitar piece of all, the *Recuerdos de la Alhambra* of Tárrega. The second collection, which is entirely digital (from 1982–3), concentrates mainly on Isaac Albéniz and Granados (not forgetting the superb accounts of the *Cordoba* by the former and the *Danza espanola No. 5* by the latter, which are highly praised in our composer section). It ends appropriately with Rodrigo's *Tres piezas españolas*, with its remarkable central *Passacaglia*. The recordings are of the highest quality and are excellently transferred to CD.

Bream, Julian and **John Williams** (guitar duo)

'Together': Disc 1: CARULLI: *Serenade in A, Op. 96.* GRANADOS: *Danzas españolas: Rodella aragonesa; Zambra, Op. 37/6 & 11.* ALBENIZ: *Cantos de España: Bajo la palmera, Op. 232/3. Ibéria: Evocación.* GIULIANI: *Variazioni concertanti, Op. 130.* JOHNSON: *Pavan & Galliard* (arr. BREAM). TELEMANN: *Partie polonaise.* DEBUSSY: *Rêverie; Children's corner: Golliwog's cakewalk. Suite bergamasque: Clair de lune.*

Disc 2: LAWES: *Suite for 2 guitars* (arr. BREAM). CARULLI: *Duo in G, Op. 34.* SOR: *L'encouragement, Op. 34.* ALBENIZ: *Cantos de España: Córdoba, Op. 232/4; Suite española: Castilla (Seguidillas).* GRANADOS: *Goyescas: Intermezzo* (arr. PUJOL). *Danzas españolas: Oriental, Op. 37/2.* FALLA: *La vida breve: Spanish dance No. 1.* RAVEL: *Pavane pour une infante défunte.* FAURE: *Dolly* (suite), *Op. 56* (both arr. BREAM).
(B) *** RCA 74321 20134-2 (2).

The rare combination of Julian Bream and John Williams was achieved by RCA in the studio on two separate occasions, in 1971 and 1973, providing the basic contents of these two recitals. Further recordings were made live in Boston and New York in 1978, during a North American concert tour. Curiously, it is the studio programmes which seem the more spontaneous, and Fauré's *Dolly suite*, which sounds a little cosy, is the only disappointment (it also brings some audience noises). Highlights are the music of Albéniz and Granados (notably the former's haunting *Evocación* from *Iberia*, and *Cordoba*, which Bream also included on a very successful solo recital). The transcription of the *Goyescas Intermezzo* is also very successful, as is Debussy's *Golliwog's cakewalk* in a quite different way. Giuliani's *Variazioni concertanti*, actually written for guitar duo, brings some intimately gentle playing, as does the *Theme and variations* which forms the second movement of Sor's *L'encouragement*; while the *Cantabile* which begins this triptych is delightful in its simple lyricism. The Carulli *Serenade* opens the second recital very strikingly, while on the first disc the performance of Ravel's *Pavane*, very slow and stately, is memorable. The Elizabethan lute music by Johnson and Lawes and the Telemann *Partie polonaise* (written for a pair of lutes) bring a refreshing change of style in what is predominantly a programme of Spanish music. The concert ends with Albéniz's *Seguidillas*, and an appropriately enthusiatic response from the audience. With the overall timing at a very generous 149 minutes, the pair of discs comes for the cost of a single premium-priced CD and can be recommended very strongly indeed. This is music-making of the very highest order, and the CD transfers bring fine presence and a natural balance.

Brendel, Alfred (piano)

Vanguard 'Alfred Brendel Collection'

Volume 1: MOZART: *Piano concertos Nos. 9 in E flat, K.271; 14 in E flat, K.449* (with I Solisti di Zagreb, Janigro). *Piano sonata No. 8 in A min., K.310; Fantasia in C min., K.396; Rondo in A min., K.511; 9 Variations on a Minuet by Duport, K.573.*
(M) *** Van. 08 9161 71 (2).

Volume 2: CHOPIN: *Andante spianato et Grande polonaise brillante, Op. 22; Polonaises Nos. 4 in C min., Op. 40/2; 5 in F sharp min., Op. 44; 6 in A flat, Op. 53; 7 (Polonaise-fantasie), Op. 61.* LISZT: *Hungarian rhapsodies Nos. 2–3, 8, 13, 15 (Rákóczy march); Csárdás obstinée.*
(M) **(*) Van. 08 9163 72 (2) .

Volume 3: SCHUBERT: *Piano sonatas Nos. 15 in C (Unfinished), D.840; 19 in C min., D.958; 16 German dances, D. 783.* SCHUMANN: *Etudes symphoniques; Fantasia in C.*
(M) *** Van. 08 9165 72 (2).

Vanguard have now produced their own 'Alfred Brendel collection' from recordings made in the 1960s. Each set of two CDs is offered in a slip-case but with no price saving. The separate discs are discussed above, under their composer headings.

Britton, Harold (organ)

Organ of Royal Albert Hall: *'Organ spectacular'*: SUPPE: *Light Cavalry overture.* LEMARE: *Andantino in D flat.* VERDI: *Aida: Grand march.* ALBINONI: *Adagio* (arr. Giazotto). WAGNER: *Ride of the Valkyries.* BACH: *Toccata and fugue in D min., BWV 565.* TCHAIKOVSKY: *None but the lonely heart.* ELGAR: *Pomp and circumstance march No. 1.* SOUSA: *Liberty Bell.* WIDOR: *Symphony No. 5: Toccata.*
(BB) *** ASV CDQS 6028 [(M) id. import].

If one is to have a collection mainly of arrangements of orchestral lollipops on an organ, the instrument at the Royal Albert Hall is surely an ideal choice: it offers the widest dynamic range, including an effective recession of quieter passages readily at the player's command – used to good purpose in *Light Cavalry* – but can also produce truly spectacular fortissimos, with a wide amplitude and a blaze of colour from its multitude of stops. Harold Britton is obviously fully at home on the instrument and plays in an aptly extrovert style for such a recital, obviously enjoying himself. The CD is in the demonstration class – there are few problems of muddying from reverberation.

Byzantine, Julian (guitar)

Recital: VILLA-LOBOS: *5 Preludes; Chôros No. 1.* PONCE: *Sonatina meridional: Campo.* Eduardo SAINZ DE LA MAZA: *Homenaje a la guitara.* LAURO: *Suite venezolana: Danza negra; Valse. Valse No. 3 (Natalia).*
(B) ** EMI CfP CD-CFP 6046 [(M) id. import].

Julian Byzantine is an expert guitarist and obviously a master of colour. But he is recorded very closely here, and not only does this make his instrument sound larger than life, but it also cuts down on the dynamic range of his playing. His rubato is often freely convincing, but at times the forward balance also gives the impression of deliberation, most strikingly in the five Villa-Lobos *Preludes*, and especially in No. 3. He creates some magical sounds in the *Homenaje a la guitara*, but the finest playing here comes in the pieces of Antonio Lauro, for whom Byzantine obviously has a personal affinity.

Cann, Claire and Antoinette (piano duo)

'Romantic favourites on 2 pianos': SAINT-SAENS: *Danse macabre.* DEBUSSY: *Petite suite.* TCHAIKOVSKY (arr. CANN): *Nutcracker suite:* excerpts. BRAHMS: *Variations on a theme of Haydn (St Antoni chorale), Op. 56b; Waltzes, Op. 39/1–2, 5–6, 9–11 & 15.* MACDOWELL (arr. NIEMANN): *Hexentanz.* LISZT (arr. BRENDEL): *Hungarian rhapsody No. 2.*
❀ (M) *** Apollo Recordings Dig. ARCD 961.

We are glad to welcome the début recital of the Cann duo back to the catalogue. With the demise of the Pianissimo label it was unavailable for some time but now returns on the Apollo label, distributed in the UK by Canterbury Classics. It is difficult to imagine a more scintillating piano duet record than this. Saint-Saëns's skeletons – summoned by an evocative midnight bell – dance as vigorously as do MacDowell's witches in the brilliant *Hexameron*, while Debussy's delightful *Petite suite* – played here very effectively on two pianos, rather than with four hands on one – is full of charm. The Cann sisters then produce a rich-textured fullness of tone for the Brahms *Haydn variations*, which are every bit as enjoyable here as in their orchestral dress. Most remarkable of all are the excerpts from the *Nutcracker suite*, conceived entirely pianistically and glittering with colour. Indeed the *Sugar plum fairy* has a much stronger profile than usual and the *Chinese dance* an irresistible oriental glitter. The *Hungarian dances* bring beguiling variety of mood and texture and display an easy bravura, ending with a lovely performance of the famous *Cradle song* (*No. 15 in A flat*), while the dazzling Liszt *Hungarian rhapsody* ends the recital with great exuberance and much digital panache. The recording, made in Rosslyn Hill Chapel, is exceptionally real and vivid and is ideally balanced.

Casadesus, Robert and Gaby (piano)

'Two pianos and piano four hands': DEBUSSY: *Petite suite; En blanc et noir*. FAURE: *Dolly*. CASADESUS: *3 Danses Méditerranéennes*. SATIE: *3 Morceaux en forme de poire*.
(M) **(*) Sony stereo/mono MPK 52527 [id.].

These accounts come from 1959, save for Robert Casadesus's *Trois Danses Méditerranéennes*, which were recorded in 1950 and are in mono, and *En blanc et noir*, which is from 1963. Although the recording is not in the top bracket (the sound is a bit synthetic and hardens in fortissimo passages), the playing of Robert and Gaby Casadesus has such style and panache that technical limitations should not deter anyone with a taste for this repertoire. They have perfect unanimity and control, as well as wonderfully articulated rhythm. Casadesus's own *Danses Méditerranéennes* are inventive and attractive, distinctly Gallic though not highly personal, and the recording, though shallow, is perfectly acceptable. Fauré's *Dolly Suite* is given with charm, and the Satie *Trois morceaux en forme de poire* are also a delight. Some of the octave unisons in *En blanc et noir* are out of tune, but it is a fine performance for all that.

Casals, Pablo (cello)

Casals Edition (instrumental and chamber music)

BEETHOVEN: *Cello sonatas Nos. 1–5, Op. 5/1–2; Op. 69; Op. 102/1–2; 7 Variations on 'Bei Männern' (from Mozart's 'Die Zauberflöte'), WoO. 45; 12 Variations on 'Ein Mädchen' (from Mozart's 'Die Zauberflöte'), WoO. 66.*
(M) (**) Sony mono SM2K 58985 [id.]. Pablo Casals, Rudolf Serkin.

These Casals accounts of the Beethoven *Cello sonatas* come from 1953 and 1958 and exhibit strong personality but less finish, understandably so when one considers that by the latter date Casals was approaching eighty. In spite of the keyboard expertise of Serkin, these performances do not match his performances with Horszowski, made between 1931 and 1938 and now reissued on EMI, coupled with the Brahms *Second Cello sonata*, in which the pianist is Otto Schulhof. This is an altogether excellent set. ((M) (***) CHS5 65185-2).

BEETHOVEN: *Piano trio No. 1 in E flat, Op. 1/1* (with Eugene Istomin, Joseph Fuchs). SCHUBERT: *Piano trio No. 2 in E flat, D.929* (with Mieczyslaw Horszowski, Alexander Schneider).
(M) (***) Sony mono SMK 58988. [id.].

The *E flat piano trio*, Op. 1, No. 1, with the much and rightly admired Joseph Fuchs and Eugene Istomin is first class, and the Schubert *E flat trio* with Horszowski and Schneider is a commanding account that is well worth considering.

BEETHOVEN: *Piano trio No. 2 in G, Op. 1/2*. SCHUBERT *Piano trio No. 1 in B flat, D.898* (with Eugene Istomin, Alexander Schneider).
(M) (**) Sony mono SMK 58989. [id.].

BEETHOVEN: *Piano trios Nos. 4 in B flat, Op. 11; 7 in B flat (Archduke), Op. 97* (with Eugene Istomin, Alexander Schneider).
(M) (**) Sony mono SMK 58990 [id.].

The Schubert *B flat Trio* on SMK 58989 has its impressive insights, but the *Archduke* on the companion disc does not extinguish memories of the famous pre-war set with Thibaud and Cortot; but there are, as one might expect, perceptive and felicitous and touching phrasing. It comes with the *B flat trio*, Op. 11, the transcription of the *Clarinet trio*.

BEETHOVEN: *Piano trios Nos. 5 in D, (Ghost), Op. 70/1* (with Eugene Istomin, Joseph Fuchs); *6 in E flat, Op. 70/2* (with Eugene Istomin, Alexander Schneider); *12 Variations on a theme from Handel's 'Judas Maccabeus', WoO 46* (with Rudolf Serkin).
(M) (***) Sony mono SMK 58991 [id.].

The two Op. 70 *Trios*, the '*Ghost*' with Fuchs and Istomin and the *E flat* with Alexander Schneider, are given with great spirit and are arguably superior to Casals's later (1958) version with Végh and Engel.

BRAHMS: *Piano trio No. 1 in B, Op. 8* (with Dame Myra Hess, Isaac Stern); *String sextet No. 1 in B flat, Op. 18* (with Isaac Stern, Alexander Schneider, Milton Katims, Milton Thomas, Madeline Foley).
(M) (***) Sony mono SMK 58994. [id.].

The Brahms performances, the *B major Trio*, Op. 8, and the *B flat Sextet*, Op. 18, are hardly less celebrated. The *Trio* with Isaac Stern and Myra Hess is a noble and beautifully phrased performance. The majestic and passionate account of the *Sextet* enjoyed cult status in France and elsewhere when it was used in Louis Malle's 1958 film *Les amants*; and it remains a classic of the gramophone – one of the artistic peaks of the Casals Edition.

Crabb, James, and Geir Draugsvoll (accordions)

Début recital: STRAVINSKY: *Petrushka* (ballet; complete). MUSSORGSKY: *Pictures at an exhibition* (both arr. CRABB/DRAUGSVOLL).
(B) **(*) EMI Debut CDZ5 69705-2 [(M) id.].

It seems impossible to believe that Stravinsky's brilliantly scored ballet, played on a pair of piano accordions, could sound remarkably like the orchestral version; but this phenomenal transcription brings all the colours of the Stravinskian palette vividly before the listener. Only the bold sound of unison horns and the bite of massed strings eludes these virtuosi, and they bring the ballet's drama and pathos fully to life. This is an extraordinary listening experience. Mussorsky's *Pictures from an exhibition* is equally ingenious but is far less consistently effective, for one's ear is used to bold brass sonorities and spectacle. *Catacombes* and the big finale do not really come off, although the grotesque *Baba-Yaga* certainly does, played with proper rhythmic venom; otherwise the most effective pictures are those in which we normally expect woodwind chattering: *Tuileries*, *Limoges* and the cheeping chicks. Nevertheless it's a good try, and the playing itself has astonishing bravura. Well worth sampling on EMI's bargain Debut label. The recording cannot be faulted.

Claude Debussy Wind Quintet

'The new interpreters': LIGETI: *6 Bagatelles; 10 Pieces*. JANACEK: *Mládi; Concertino* (with Philipe Cassard, piano, Bruno Martinez & members of Parish Qt).
(B) *** HM Dig. HMN 911624 [id.].

Anyone who thinks of Ligeti as a 'difficult' composer should sample this infectious performance of the *Six Bagatelles*, especially the riotous élan of the opening *Allegro con spirito* and the more wry wit of the finale. There is unexpected melodic charm too in the *Allegro grazioso* (No. 3), and the sombre tribute to Bartók is darkly memorable. The *Ten Pieces* are thornier, but still stimulating. The penultimate number is marked *Sostenuto stridente* and the finale *Presto bizzare*, but the music remains ear-catching. The two better-known Janáček works are also played with keen rhythmic feeling and, although this is in essence a sampler, it makes a highly enjoyable concert; the recording gives these excellent players a very tangible presence within a nicely judged acoustic.

Duchable, François-René (piano)

Recital: CHOPIN: *Scherzi Nos. 1–4; Fantasie in F min., Op. 49*. LISZT: *Etudes d'exécution transcendente: Nos. 5, Feux follets; 10, Appassionata. Années de Pèlerinage, 2nd Year (Italy): Petrarch Sonnnet No. 104. Grand Etude de Paganini: La Campanella. Nocturne No. 3 (Rêve d'amour); Polonaise No. 2 in E. Mephisto waltz. Consolation No. 3. Harmonies poètiques et religieuses: Funérailles. Concert paraphrase of* BERLIOZ: *Symphonie fantastique* (revised Duchable). DUKAS: *Sonata in B flat min*. SAINT-SAENS: *Etude en forme de valse, Op. 52/6; 6 Etudes, Op. 111; Allegro appassionato; Mazurka, Op. 66*.
(B) *** EMI CES5 72356-2 (3).

François-René Duchable's three-CD set is worth having, not so much for the Liszt – though that is brilliant enough – but for his commanding account of the Saint-Saëns rarities and, above all, for his magisterial Dukas *Sonata*. A pity that the French planners did not include *La plainte, au loin, du faune* and the *Prélude élégiaque sur le thème proposé Haydn*, which was on the original Dukas LP. Judged by modern standards, the 1978 sound is a bit synthetic. There is much to admire here, including an impressive *Symphonie fantastique*.

Duo Reine Elisabeth (Wolfgang Manz and Rolf Plagge)

Russian music for two pianos: STRAVINSKY: *Petrushka*. SCRIABIN: *Romance in A min*. SHOSTAKOVICH: *Concertino, Op. 94*. RACHMANINOV: *6 Morceaux, Op. 11*.
(BB) *** Discover Dig. DICD 920150 [id.].

Petrushka has plenty of colour and a surprising degree of charm; the finale swings along infectiously. The melodically lavish, early Scriabin *Romance* then contrasts aptly with the wittily audacious Shostakovich *Concertino*, which has the temerity to open with an echo of the slow movement of Beethoven's *G major Piano concerto*. The six Rachmaninov *Morceaux* are strongly and colourfully characterized, and their diversity gives much pleasure. In short, Wolfgang Manz and Rolf Plagge create an impressive artistic symbiosis, playing with spontaneity as well as commanding impressive technical resource. Very good recording too – not too reverberant. A bargain.

Du Pré, Jacqueline (cello)

Early BBC recordings, Vol. 1 (with Stephen Kovacevich, Ernest Lush): BACH: (Unaccompanied) *Cello suites Nos. 1 in G; 2 in D min., BWV 1007/8*. BRITTEN: *Cello sonata in C, Op. 65; Scherzo; Marcia*. FALLA: *Suite populaire espagnole* (arr. MARECHAL).
(M) (***) EMI mono CDM7 63165-2.

Early BBC recordings, Vol. 2 (with Ernest Lush, (i) William Pleeth): BRAHMS: *Cello sonata No. 2 in F, Op. 99*. F. COUPERIN: (i) *13th Concert à 2 instruments* (*Les Goûts-réunis*). HANDEL: *Cello sonata in G min.* (arr. SLATTER).
(M) (***) EMI mono CDM7 63166-2.

These two discs gather together some of the radio performances which Jacqueline du Pré gave in her inspired teens. Her 1962 recordings of the first two Bach *Cello suites* may not be immaculate, but her impulsive vitality makes phrase after phrase at once totally individual and seemingly inevitable. In two movements from Britten's *Cello sonata in C*, with Stephen Kovacevich as her partner, the sheer wit is deliciously infectious, fruit of youthful exuberance in both players. The first of the two discs is completed by Falla's *Suite populaire espagnole*, with the cello matching any singer in expressive range and rhythmic flair. The second has fascinating Couperin duets played with her teacher, William Pleeth; the Handel *Sonata* is equally warm and giving. Best of all is the Brahms *Cello sonata No. 2*, recorded at the 1962 Edinburgh Festival.

Fergus-Thompson, Gordon (piano)

'Reverie': DEBUSSY: *Rêverie; Arabesque No. 1; Suite bergamasque: Clair de lune*. SCRIABIN: *Etude, Op. 42/4*. BACH: *Chorales: Wachet auf* (trans. Busoni); *Jesu, joy of man's desiring* (trans. Hess). GLINKA: *The Lark* (trans. Balakirev). GODOWSKY: *Alt Wien*. SAINT-SAENS: *The Swan* (arr. GODOWSKY). SCHUMANN: *Arabeske in C, Op. 18; Kinderszenen: Träumerei*. BRAHMS: *Intermezzo in A, Op. 118*. GRIEG: *Lyric pieces: Butterfly, Op. 43/1; Nocturne, Op. 54/4*. RAVEL: *Le tombeau de Couperin: Forlane. Pavane pour une infante défunte*.
(M) *** ASV Dig. CDWHL 2066 [id.].

This 76-minute recital fills a real need for a high-quality recital of piano music for the late evening, where the mood of reverie is sustained without blandness. Gordon Fergus-Thompson's performances are of high sensibility throughout, from the atmospheric opening Debussy items to the closing Ravel *Pavane*. Perhaps his Bach is a little studied but the rest is admirably paced, and the two favourite Grieg *Lyric pieces* are particularly fresh. Excellent recording.

Fernández, Eduardo (guitar)

'The World of the Spanish guitar': ALBENIZ: *Sevilla; Tango; Asturias*. LLOBET: *6 Catalan folksongs*. GRANADOS: *Andaluza; Danza triste*. TARREGA: *Estudio brillante; 5 Preludes; Minuetto; 3 Mazurkas; Recuerdos de la Alhambra*. SEGOVIA: *Estudio sin luz; Neblina; Estudio*. TURINA: *Fandanguillo; Ráfaga*.
(M) *** Decca Dig 433 820-2; *433 820-4*.

Fernández is most naturally recorded in the Henry Wood Hall. His programme is essentially an intimate one and centres on the highly rewarding music of Tárrega, although opening colourfully with items from

Albéniz's *Suite española*. The Llobet group of *Folksongs*, and Segovia's hauntingly atmospheric *Neblina* ('Mist') make further highlights. Later there is bravura from Turina, notably the spectacular *Ráfaga* ('Gust of wind') but even here, though the playing is vibrant, there is no flashiness. With an hour of music and digital sound, this well-chosen programme is excellent value.

Fierens, Guillermo (guitar)

'Spanish guitar music': VILLA-LOBOS: *Preludes Nos. 1–3.* PONCE: *Preludio, Balletto & Giga.* CASTELNUOVO-TEDESCO: *Capriccio diabolico; Sonata.* ALBENIZ: *Asturias.* TURINA: *Fandanguillo.* SOR: *Introduction and allegro (Gran solo), Op. 14.*
(B) *** ASV Quicksilva Dig. CDQS 6190 [(M) id.].

Argentinian-born Guillermo Fierens studied under Segovia and has won several international prizes, including a First at Rio de Janeiro's Villa-Lobos competition. He is thoroughly sympathetic to that composer's music, and he presents this whole programme brightly and sympathetically, with plenty of personality and character. His technique is commandingly immaculate, his rubato nicely judged. He is very personable in the lively Ponce triptych (pastiche pieces of some charm) and the attractively spontaneous *Sonata* by Castelnuovo-Tedesco, particularly the two engaging central movements, and he finds plenty of bravura for the same composer's *Capriccio diabolico*. (Although it hardly matches Paganini in diabolism, it still makes a strong impression.) The *Gran solo* of Sor is equally appealing, but the highlight of a well-balanced programme is a magically evocative account of the famous *Asturias* of Albéniz. The recording has a vivid presence without being on top of the listener. Excellent value on all counts.

Fischer, Annie (piano)

BARTOK: *Piano concerto No. 3* (with LSO, Markevitch). BEETHOVEN: *Piano sonatas Nos. 8 in C min. (Pathétique), Op. 13; 14 in C sharp min. (Moonlight), Op. 27/2; 32 in C min., Op. 111.* SCHUBERT: *Impromptus: in A flat; F min., D.935/2 & 4.* SCHUMANN: *Kinderszenen, Op. 15; Kreisleriana, Op. 16.*
(B) **(*) EMI Rouge et Noir Double CZ5 68733-2 (2) [CDZB 68733].

Les Introuvables d'Annie Fischer: BEETHOVEN: *Piano sonatas Nos. 8 in C min. (Pathétique), Op. 13; 14 in C sharp min. (Moonlight), Op. 27/2; 18 in E flat, Op. 31/3; 24 in F sharp, Op. 78; 21 in C (Waldstein), Op. 53; 30 in E, Op. 109; 32 in C min., Op. 111.* SCHUBERT: *Impromptus: in A flat; F min., D. 935/2 & 4; Piano sonata in B flat, D.960.* SCHUMANN: *Fantaisie in C, Op. 17; Carnaval, Op. 9; Kinderszenen, Op. 15; Kreisleriana, Op. 16.*
(B) **(*) EMI stereo/mono CZS5 69217-2 (4).

The first disc of the EMI Rouge et Noir Double couples Annie Fischer's two Schubert *Impromptus* and the Beethoven *Pathétique* and *Moonlight* with her Op. 111, while the second includes *Kinderszenen* and the *Kreisleriana*, along with the Bartók *Third Piano concerto*, previously unissued in its stereo form. The performances are identical with those contained in the four-CD set, *Les Introuvables d'Annie Fischer*, also listed above. The Bartók was recorded in the EMI Abbey Road Studio in 1955 but it places the soloist so far forward that orchestral detail is masked. She indulges in some strange (and, despite her Hungarian birth, perhaps not wholly idiomatic) rubato. However, her Schumann is a different matter, remarkably fine. *Kreisleriana*, recorded in Vienna in 1965 in a smallish studio, is magnificent, impassioned and full of fire, though one wishes that the sound had room in which to expand. Her Beethoven is perhaps less impressive and commanding – particularly the *Pathétique* which, despite much sensitivity, suffers from a certain want of depth and sweep. Nevertheless whatever she does is distinguished by unfailing musicality.

There are four CDs in *Les Introuvables d'Annie Fischer*, involving duplication of the three Beethoven sonatas and Schumann's *Kinderszenen* and *Kreisleriana*, albeit not the Bartók *Concerto*. There is much to admire here, but for the general collector the two-disc set is the one to go for.

Fretwork

'Portrait: Music for viols' ((i) with Michael Chance (counter-tenor); Christopher Wilson (lute), Paul Nicholson (organ)): BYRD: *Pavan a 6; Galliard a 6;* (i) *Come to me, grief for ever; Ye sacred muses.* BEVIN: *Browning a 3.* GIBBONS: *Go from my window a 6; Fantasy a 6; In nomine a 5.* DOWLAND: *Lachrimae antiquae; Lachrimae Coacte; Mr John Langtons Pavan; The Earl of Essex galliard; Mr Henry Noell his galliard.* (i) *Lasso vita mia.* LAWES: *Pavan a 5 in C min.; Fantasy a 6 in F; Aire a 6 in F min.* GIBBONS: *Fantasy a 6.* HOLBORNE: *The Honie-suckle; The Fairie-round.*
(M) *** Virgin/Veritas EMI VM5 61402-2.

A quite outstanding concert, with the consort music nicely leavened by three vocal solos. Much of the atmosphere is melancholy, but with the arrival of the two dances by Holborne the mood (and timbre) changes completely, while the following Dowland *Galliards*, if less upbeat, bring yet another change of character. The two vocal highlights are by Byrd, *Come to me, grief for ever*, in which he outflanks Dowland in dolour, and the beautiful *Ye sacred muses*, both sung ravishingly by Michael Chance. Lawes's *Pavan a 5 in C minor* which follows embroiders a particularly memorable theme and features the use of the chamber organ to subtly fill out the sonority, as it does the touching Gibbons *In nomine a 5*, while in the Lawes *Fantasy a 6* the organ has a delicate contrapuntal role. Excellent – if close – recording.

Fromentin, Lawrence, and Domenique Plancade (piano duo)

Debut: 'French piano duets': POULENC: *Sonata.* DEBUSSY: *Petite suite.* RAVEL: *Ma Mère l'Oye suite.* FAURE: *Dolly (suite), Op. 56.* BIZET: *Jeux d'enfants* (complete).
(B) *** EMI Debut CDZ5 72526-2 [id.].

Lawrence Fromentin and Domenique Plancade, both Gold Medal winners at the Paris Conservatoire and pupils of Pascal Devoyon, decided to join together as a duo in 1992, and this is their recording début. The results are very impressive indeed. They encompass the wide stylistic contrasts of their programme with sympathy and panache, from the brittle wit of Poulenc and its underlying innocence, to the exquistely delicate Ravelian atmosphere of *Ma Mère l'Oye* and the gentle charm of Fauré's *Dolly*. Debussy's *Petite suite* is winningly spontaneous, while the perceptively characterized *Jeux d'enfants* of Bizet is the more valuable for being complete, including all 12 movements, not just those familiar in the orchestral suite. The recording is excellent. A genuine bargain in every sense.

Gendron, Maurice (cello)

'The early years (1960–67)' (with (i) Jean Françaix; (ii) Peter Gallion, piano): (i) SCHUBERT: *Arpeggione sonata, D.821.* BEETHOVEN: *Variations: on Mozart's 'Ein Mädchen', Op. 66; 'Bei Männern', WoO 46* (both from *Die Zauberflöte*); *Variations on Handel's 'See the conqu'ring hero comes' from Judas Maccabaeus, WoO 45.* DEBUSSY: *Sonata in D min.* FAURE: *Sonata No. 2 in D min., Op. 117.* FRANCAIX: *Berceuse; Rondino staccato; Nocturne; Sérénade* (all arr. GENDRON); *Mouvement perpétuel.* MESSIAEN: *Quatuor pour la fin du temps: Louange à l'éternité de Jésus.* (ii) POPPER: *Serenade, Op. 54/2.* HANDEL: *Xerxes: Largo* (arr. GENDRON). SAINT-SAENS: *Carnival of the animals: Le cygne.* SCHUMANN: *Kinderszenen: Träumerei.* RIMSKY-KORSAKOV: *Flight of the bumble-bee.* PAGANINI: *Variations on a theme of Rossini* (*Moses fantasy*, arr. GENDRON). MOSZKOWSKI: *Guitare, Op. 45/2* (arr. GENDRON). KREISLER: *Liebesleid.* FALLA: *La vida breve: Spanish dance No. 1.* BACH: *Chorale: Ich ruf' zu dir, Herr Jesu Christ, BWV 639* (arr. GENDRON). CHOPIN: *Introduction and Polonaise brillante in C, Op. 3.* FITZENHAGEN: *Moto perpetuo* (arr. GENDRON). GRANADOS: *Andaluza, Op. 37/5.* DVORAK: *Humoresque, Op. 101/7.*
(M) *** Ph. (IMS) 438 960-2 (3).

The elegant French cellist, Maurice Gendron, has always been well served by the Philips recording engineers who consistently catch his urbane, polished timbre in perfect focus. He does not readily wear his heart on his sleeve, yet while he shows himself a naturally debonair Schubertian in the *Arpeggione sonata* he can also rise with ardour to the expressive feeling of the Debussy and Fauré sonatas which are played with discerning eloquence. His slightly recessive solo personality is surely ideal for the engaging Françaix miniatures, and it is this composer himself who provides a remarkably sympathetic partnership for the diverse programme on the first two CDs – just sample the cultivated way the pair of them introduce Handel's fine melody in Beethoven's *Judas Maccabaeus variations*. The second CD ends with a characteristically intimate account of the famous cello soliloquy from Messiaen's *Quartet for the end of time*. The immaculately played lollipops on the third disc are given a slightly more forward balance.

Yet perhaps one needs a more extrovert approach to some of these items. Rimsky's bumble-bee buzzes comparatively gently and the neat bravura of Fitzenhagen's *Moto perpetuo* is a more suitable example of Gendron's virtuosity, though he readily demonstrates his easy command in the high tessitura of the Paganini variations, where his timbre is always sweet. Perhaps overall this collection is a rather lightweight representation of a great artist, but the polish of Gendron's playing is always a pleasure in itself.

Green, Gareth (organ of Chesterfield Parish Church)

English organ music: LANG: *Tuba tune, Op. 15.* HOWELLS: *3 Psalm preludes, Op. 32.* ELGAR: *Sonata No. 1, Op. 28.* VAUGHAN WILLIAMS: *Rhosymedre (Hymn prelude).* WHITLOCK: *Hymn Preludes: on Darwell's 148th; on Song 13.* COCKER: *Tuba tune.*
(BB) *(*) Naxos Dig. 8.550582 [id.].

The organ as recorded here has no clarity of profile, and even the two characterful *Tuba tunes* fail to make their full effect. The sound in the *Hymn* and *Psalm Preludes* is washy and indistinct. Gareth Green obviously plays the early Elgar *Sonata* very well but it makes an impact only in its more powerful moments, and it is difficult to find a volume level which reveals the unfocused, quieter detail while not having the climaxes too loud.

Griffiths, Ann (harp)

'Virtuoso harp': RESPIGHI: *Ancient airs and dances: Siciliana.* DUSSEK: *Sonata in E flat, Op. 34/1.* ALVARS: *Serenade, Op. 83.* CAPLET: *Divertissement à la française.* TEMPLETON: *Sicilienne.* MORTARI: *Sonatina prodigio.* RUBBRA: *Pezzo ostinato, Op. 102.* Gareth WALTERS: *Little suite.*
(B) *** EMI CfP CD-CFP 6047 [(M) id. import].

A quite delectable recital, with the very atmospheric recording creating a perfect late-evening atmosphere. Ann Griffiths's range of colour is remarkable, and she also uses the widest range of dynamic to beguile the ear, often playing with magical delicacy or dazzling the listener with a sudden burst of virtuosity. She does both in the witty *Divertissement* of André Caplet. After opening with the lovely *Siciliana* from Respighi's *Ancient airs and dances*, she captivates with the charmingly ingenuous *Sonata* of Dussek. Alec Templeton's *Sicilienne* is quite haunting in its evocation of the spirit of Ravel, while the opening movement of Mortari's *Sonata prodigo* offers a more robust, neo-classical style. Rubbra's *Pezzo ostinato* subtly insinuates itself into the listener's consciousness, and the programme ends light-heartedly with the *Little suite* of Gareth Walters, with its bluesy finale. Those who want something more substantial must look elsewhere, but in her feminine way Miss Griffiths is a most sensitive artist and a musical seductress to her fingertips.

Grumiaux, Arthur (violin), **Riccardo Castagnone** (piano)

'The early years': DEBUSSY: *Sonata in G min.* LEKEU: *Sonata in G.* SCHUBERT: *3 Sonatinas; Duo sonata in A.* KREISLER: *Liebesleid; Liebesfreud; Schön Rosmarin; Caprice viennois; Tambourin chinoise.* TARTINI: *Sonata in G min. (Devil's trill), Op. 1/4.* CORELLI: *Sonata in D min., Op. 5/12.* VITALI: *Ciaccona.* VERACINI: *Sonata in A, Op. 1/7.* PAGANINI: *I Palpiti, Op. 13; La Treghe, Op. 8.*
(M) *** Ph. (IMS) 438 516-2 (3).

Here are three CDs of beautifully natural and unaffected music-making. The Debussy and Lekeu sonatas occupy the first CD and come from 1956, as does the Tartini *Devil's Trill sonata* and its companions. The Schubert *Sonatinas* and *Duo* were made two years later but the sound is amazingly fresh. These performances have an aristocratic finesse that will delight all connoisseurs of violin playing. Not to be missed.

Grumiaux, Arthur (violin), **István Hajdu** (piano)

'Favourite violin encores': PARADIS: *Sicilienne.* MOZART: *Rondo, K.250; Divertimento in D, K.334: Minuet.* GLUCK: *Mélodie.* GRANADOS: *Danza española No. 5.* KREISLER: *Schön Rosmarin; Liebesleid; Liebesfreud; Rondino on a theme of Beethoven; Andantino in the style of Padre Martini.* VERACINI: *Allegro; Largo* (arr. CORTI). VIVALDI: *Siciliano* (arr. from *Op. 3/11*). LECLAIR: *Tambourin.* BEETHOVEN: *Minuet in G.* SCHUBERT: *Ave Maria; Ständchen.* DVORAK: *Humoresque in G flat, Op. 101/7; Songs my mother taught me, Op. 55/4; Sonatine in G, Op. 100: Larghetto.* MASSENET: *Thaïs: Méditation.* TCHAIKOVSKY: *Valse sentimentale, Op. 51/6.* ELGAR: *La Capricieuse.* FAURE: *Après un rêve, Op. 7/1;*

Les berceaux, Op. 23/1. ALBENIZ: *Tango, Op. 165/2.* PONCE: *Estrellita.* SIBELIUS: *Nocturne, Op. 51/3.* PERGOLESI: *Andantino.* SCHUMANN: *Kinderszenen: Träumerei.* BACH/GOUNOD: *Ave Maria.* PAGANINI: *Sonata No. 12 in E min., Op. 3/6.* WIENIAWSKI: *Souvenir de Moscou, Op. 6.* RAVEL: *Pièce en forme de habanera; Tzigane.* SARASATE: *Zigeunerweisen, Op. 20/1.* FIOCCO: *Allegro.* BLOCH: *Baal Shem: Nigun.* KODALY: *Adagio.*
(B) *** Ph. Duo 446 560-2 (2) [(M) id. import].

Marvellous fiddler as he is, Grumiaux is not an extrovert in the manner of a Perlman who likes to dazzle and be right on top of the microphones; instead, these are essentially intimate performances. Yet when fire is needed it is certainly forthcoming, as in the superb account of Ravel's *Tzigane*. But Grumiaux is completely at home in what are mostly elegant *morceaux de concert*, and especially the Kreisler encores. He brings a particularly nice touch of rubato to *Schön Rosmarin* and produces a ravishingly stylish *Liebesleid*, while the *Andantino in the style of Martini* is engagingly ingenuous. Schumann's *Träumerei* is made to sound as if originally conceived as a violin solo. The *Méditation* from *Thaïs* is delectably romantic without being oversweet, and the following *Valse sentimentale* of Tchaikovsky has just the right degree of restraint. But Grumiaux's simplicity of style is heard at its most appealing in Wieniawski's *Souvenir de Moscou*, with its warm melody elegantly decorated and then let loose in a burst of Paganinian fireworks. István Hajdu accompanies with comparable taste, notably in Bach's unwitting contribution to Gounod's *Ave Maria*, while his simple introduction to Elgar's *La Capricieuse* is a model of how to set the scene for a salon piece of this kind. He is equally helpful in echoing Grumiaux in Schubert's lovely *Serenade* and in his discreet backing for Ponce's gently voluptuous *Estrellita*. The recording is most natural, without any edginess on the violin-tone, and the piano is pleasingly balanced within a warm acoustic.

Haskil, Clara (piano)

Clara Haskil: The Legacy: Volume 1: Chamber music (with Arthur Grumiaux): BEETHOVEN: *Violin sonatas Nos. 1–10.* MOZART: *Violin sonatas Nos. 18; 21; 24; 26; 32; 34.*
(M) (***) Ph. (IMS) mono 442 625-2 (5).

Volume 3: Solo piano music: BEETHOVEN: *Sonatas Nos. 17 in D min. (Tempest), Op. 31/2; 18 in E flat Op. 31/3* (two versions). MOZART: *Sonata in C, K.330; 9 Variations on a minuet by Jean-Pierre Duport, K.573.* RAVEL: *Sonatine.* Domenico SCARLATTI: *Sonatas in E flat, Kk.193; B min., Kk.87; F min., Kk.386.* SCHUBERT: *Sonata No. 21 in B flat, D.960.* SCHUMANN: *Abegg variations, Op. 1; Bunte Blätter, Op. 99; Kinderszenen, Op. 15; Waldszenen, Op. 82.*
(M) **(*) Ph. (IMS) mono/stereo 442 635-2 (3).

Clara Haskil is a much-venerated pianist, as the very appearance of this 12-CD set shows. Each of the three volumes is available separately but single discs from the collection are not. The first volume (five CDs) is devoted to the Beethoven and Mozart sonatas with her long-standing partner, Arthur Grumiaux; the second (see above), of four CDs, is devoted to her various concerto recordings, including two of the Mozart *D minor*, K.466, one with the Wiener Symfoniker and Paul Sacher in mono (1954), the second with the Lamoureux Orchestra and Markevitch (1960); the third volume (three CDs) collects her solo repertoire, including two different accounts of the Beethoven sonatas (1955 and 1960).

The earliest recordings, the three Scarlatti sonatas, Ravel's *Sonatine* and the Schumann *Abegg variations* and the *Piano concerto in A minor* (with Willem van Otterloo conducting the Hague Orchestra) come from 1951, and the last, the Mozart *Piano concertos in D minor*, K.466, and *C minor*, K.491, and the Beethoven *C minor concerto*, from 1960, the year of her death. Although it is doubtless a truism, her playing is more private than public; hers is a reflective, inward-looking sensibility with nothing of the virtuoso or showman. Her musical dedication is total. Her Schumann is particularly searching and penetrating. And there is an innocence about her Mozart which makes it wonderfully fresh and immediate.

Perhaps part of the success of her partnership with Arthur Grumiaux in the cycle of Beethoven and Mozart sonatas may spring from the understanding she gained of the violin as well as the experience of her earlier partnerships with Enescu, Szigeti and Francescatti. Philips are reticent in disclosing whether they are mono or stereo: they are in fact mono. Notwithstanding, the sound is very pleasing indeed and the playing is beautifully natural yet innately aristocratic.

The solo recordings are equally self-recommending and her Schumann in particular is of exceptional insight. The set is accompanied by very perceptive notes by Max Harrison.

Hill–Wiltschinsky Guitar Duo

Recital: D. SCARLATTI: *Sonata, Kk 141.* SOR: *Fantaisie, Op. 54.* ANON.: *Jota.* HILL: *Rondo for 2 guitars; Canzone.* arr. *The lark in the morning.* MENDELSSOHN: *Song without words, Op. 19/1.* DOWLAND: *2 Elizabethan lute duets: Le rossignol; My Lord Chamberlaine, his galliard.* WILTSCHINSKY: *Nocturne.* PETIT: *Toccata.* KOMPTER: *Milan suite.* CASTELNUOVO-TEDESCO: *Prelude and fugue in F sharp min.* GIULIANI: *Variazioni concertanti, Op. 130.* FAMPAS: *Fantasie.* FALLA: *Three-cornered hat: Ritual fire dance.*
(M) *** Carlton IMP Dig. 30367 00612 [id.].

Here is an attractively intimate, late-evening recital of music for guitar duo that could too easily be passed by. The only item which does not suit the laid-back evening mood of this well-matched pair (Robin Hill and Peter Wiltschinsky) is the vibrant *Ritual fire dance* of Manuel de Falla, which is far more electrifying in Bream's solo performance. But this still leaves an enticing hour-long programme in which every number has a distinct appeal. The Sor 'Introduction, theme and variations' which make up his *Fantaisie*, Op. 54 (wrongly attributed here to Scarlatti) and the equally agreeable Giuliani *Variazioni concertante* are well matched by Hill's own *Rondo*, and his *Canzone* is charming, as is his colleague's *Nocturne*. The Mendelssohn *Song without words* flows winningly and the novelties by Petit and Fampas are very striking. Then the amateur Jan Marten Kompter (the managing director of a Dutch chemical firm) provides four beguiling pastiches which look backward in time. The playing is spontaneously immaculate, and the duo is beautifully recorded.

Hilton, Janet (clarinet), Keith Swallow (piano)

'Rhapsodie': POULENC: *Clarinet sonata.* RAVEL: *Pièce en forme d'habanera.* DEBUSSY: *Première Rhapsodie.* SAINT-SAENS: *Clarinet sonata, Op. 167.* ROUSSEL: *Aria.* MILHAUD: *Duet concertante, Op. 351.*
(M) ** Chandos Dig. CHAN 6589 [id.].

There are some highly beguiling sounds here, and the languorous style adopted throughout is emphasized by the reverberant acoustic, which is less than ideal in creating the feeling of an empty hall. The Ravel and Debussy are given an evocative sentience and the Poulenc comes off very well too; overall, however, there is a feeling that a little more vitality and a more sharply focused sound-picture would have been advantageous.

Horowitz, Vladimir (piano)

'The Horowitz Edition': CHOPIN: *Sonata No. 2; Etudes, Opp. 10/12; 25/7; Scherzo No. 1.* RACHMANINOV: *Etudes-tableaux, Opp. 33/2; 39/5.* SCHUMANN: *Arabesque, Op. 18; Kinderszenen, Op. 15; Toccata, Op. 7.* LISZT: *Hungarian rhapsody No. 19* (trans. Horowitz). D. SCARLATTI: *Sonatas, Kk. 322, 455, 531.* BEETHOVEN: *Sonata No. 8.* SCHUBERT: *Impromptu No. 3.* DEBUSSY: *3 Préludes, Book II.* SCRIABIN: *Poème, Op. 32/1; Etudes, Opp. 2/1; 8/12* (S2K 53457). SCARLATTI: *Sonatas, Kk. 25, 33, 39, 52, 54, 96, 146, 162, 197, 198, 201, 303, 466, 474, 481, 491, 525, 547* (SK 53460). BACH/BUSONI: *Toccata, Adagio & Fugue, BWV 564.* SCHUMANN: *Fantaisie, Op. 17; Träumerei, Op. 15/7; Blumenstück, Op. 19.* SCRIABIN: *Sonatas Nos. 9–10; Poème, Op. 32/1; Etude in C sharp min., Op. 2/1.* CHOPIN: *Mazurkas, Opp. 30/4; 33/4; Etude, Op. 10/8; Ballade No. 1; Polonaise-fantaisie, Op. 61; Nocturne, Op. 72/1.* DEBUSSY: *Serenade for the doll; L'Isle joyeuse.* MOSZKOWSKI: *Etude in A flat, Op. 72/11.* MOZART: *Sonata No. 11, K.331.* HAYDN: *Sonata, Hob XVI/23.* LISZT: *Vallée d'Obermann.* (S3K 53461). CHOPIN: *Ballade No. 1; Nocturne, Op. 55/1; Polonaise, Op. 44.* D. SCARLATTI: *Sonatas, Kk. 55; 380.* SCHUMANN: *Arabeske, Op. 18; Traümerei.* SCRIABIN: *Etude, Op. 8/12.* HOROWITZ: *Variations on a theme from Carmen.* (SK 53465). CLEMENTI: Excerpts from: *Sonatas, Opp. 12/2; 25/3; 50/1. Adagio sostenuto in F, from Gradis ad Parnassum, Book I/14.* J. S. BACH: *Chorale prelude: 'Ich ruf zu dir, Herr Jesu Christ'.* D. SCARLATTI: *Sonatas, Kk. 260; 319.* HAYDN: *Sonata, Hob XVI/48.* BEETHOVEN: *Sonata No. 28, Op. 101.* (SK 53466). BEETHOVEN: *Sonatas Nos. 14, Op. 27/2 (Moonlight); 21, Op. 53 (Waldstein); 23, Op. 57 (Appassionata).* (SK 53467). CHOPIN: *Mazurkas, Opp. 7/3; 17/4; 30/3; 33/2; 41/2; 50/3; 59/3; Etudes, Op. 10/3–6, 12; 3 Nouvelles études, No. 2; Introduction & rondo, Op. 16; Waltzes, Op. 34/2; 64/2; Polonaises, Opp. 40/1; 53; Prélude, Op. 28/6, 15.* SCHUMANN: *Variations on a theme by Clara Wieck; Kreisleriana, Op. 16.* (S2K 53468). SCHUBERT: *Impromptus, D.899/2, 4; D.935/1–2.* LISZT: *Consolation No. 2; Scherzo & Marsch.* DEBUSSY: *Pour les arpèges composées; La terrasse des audiences du clair de lune.* MENDELSSOHN: *Etude, Op. 104b/3.* (SK 53471). SCRIABIN: *Feuillets d'album Opp. 45/1; 58; Etudes, Opp. 8/2, 8, 10–11;*

42, 3–5; 65/3; 2 Poèmes, Op. 69; Vers la flamme. MEDTNER: *Fairy tale, Op. 51/3.* RACHMANINOV: *Sonata No. 2; Prélude, Op. 32/12; Moment musical, Op. 16/3; Etudes-tableaux, Opp. 33/2, 5; 39/9.*
(M) (***) Sony mono SX13K 53456 (13) [id.].

The strength of the Sony box which runs to 13 CDs and includes all Horowitz's recordings from 1962–73 resides in the fact that nearly all these discs are essential repertory for Horowitz collectors but in any case are not now obtainable separately in the UK. Hardly any of these performances can be passed over, whether it be the Scarlatti sonatas or the stunning accounts of Scriabin's *Ninth* and *Tenth*. There is almost nothing that does not show him in top form – and the sound, though not ideal, is greatly improved. Advice for those considering the boxes rather than individual releases would be to buy the Sony and choose liberally from among the CDs singled out for special mention in the RCA set. However, that is no longer possible as neither collection offers its contents available separately in the UK.

'In London': God save the Queen (arr. Horowitz). CHOPIN: *Ballade No. 1 in G min., Op. 23; Polonaise No. 7 in A flat (Polonaise-Fantaisie), Op. 61.* SCHUMANN: *Kinderszenen, Op. 15.* SCRIABIN: *Étude in D sharp min., Op. 8/12.*
(M) *** RCA 09026 61414-2 [id.].

Horowitz's London and New York recitals were both recorded live by RCA and now reappear at mid-price. The highlights from the memorable 1982 London recital omit the elegant Scarlatti sonatas he played on that occasion, doubtless because it would duplicate '*Horowitz at the Met.*' – see below. However, room could surely have been found for the Rachmaninov *Sonata* or for his encores, as the CD is not generously filled. As those who attended this electrifying recital will know, there were idiosyncratic touches, particularly in the *Kinderszenen* (and also in the Chopin *Ballade*), but this is remarkable testimony to his wide dynamic range and his refined *pianopianissimo*. There are many fascinating points of detail in both works (but notably in the Chopin) which give one the feeling of hearing the music for the first time.

'At the Met.': D. SCARLATTI: *Sonatas: in A flat, Kk. 127; in F min., Kk. 184 & 466; in A, Kk. 101; in B min., Kk. 87; in E, Kk. 135.* CHOPIN: *Ballade No. 4 in F min., Op. 52; Waltz No. 9 in A flat, Op. 69/1.* LISZT: *Ballade No. 2 in B min., G. 171.* RACHMANINOV: *Prelude No. 6 in G min., Op. 23/5.*
(M) *** RCA 09026 61416-2 [id.].

The playing is in a class of its own, and all one needs to know is that this recording reproduces the highly distinctive tone-quality Horowitz commanded. This recital, given at the Metropolitan Opera House and issued here at the time of his London Festival Hall appearance in 1982, comes closer to the real thing than anything else on record, except his DG recitals. The quality of the playing is quite extraordinary.

'Encores': BIZET/HOROWITZ: *Variations on a theme from Carmen.* SAINT-SAENS /LISZT/HOROWITZ: *Danse macabre.* MOZART: *Sonata No. 11, K.331: Rondo alla turca.* MENDELSSOHN/LISZT/HOROWITZ: *Wedding march and variations.* MENDELSSOHN: *Elégie, Op. 85/4; Spring song, Op. 62/6; The shepherd's complaint, Op. 67/5; Scherzo a capriccio: Presto.* DEBUSSY: *Children's corner: Serenade of a doll.* MOSZKOWSKI: *Etudes, Op. 72/6 & 11; Etincelles, Op. 36/6.* CHOPIN: *Polonaise in A flat, Op. 53.* SCHUMANN: *Kinderszenen: Träumerei.* LISZT: *Hungarian rhapsody No. 15; Valse oubliée No. 1.* RACHMANINOV: *Prelude in G min., Op. 23/5.* SOUSA/HOROWITZ: *The Stars and Stripes forever.*
(M) (***) BMG/RCA mono GD 87755 [7755-2-RG].

These encore pieces have been around for some time and, apart from the Rachmaninov *Prelude* and the Mendelssohn, derive from the days of the 78-r.p.m. record and the mono LP. Allowances have to be made for the quality which, as one would expect in this kind of compilation, is variable. So in its different way is the playing, which varies from dazzling to stunning!

Hunt, Donald (organ of Worcester Cathedral)

English organ music 2: ELGAR: *Sonata No. 2, Op. 87a; Cantique, Op. 3.* PARRY: *Choral fantasia on an old English tune.* HOWELLS: *Siciliano for a High Ceremony.* WHITLOCK: *Plymouth suite.* VAUGHAN WILLIAMS: *3 Preludes on Welsh hymn tunes.* SUMSION: *Intermezzo; Ceremonial march.*
(BB) * Naxos Dig. 8.550773 [id.].

The organ loft of Worcester Cathedral would seem in principle to be the right place to record Elgar, but the Naxos engineers seem to have been unable to control the resonance and everything here is unattractively diffuse in outline. The amiable miniatures which make up the Whitlock *Plymouth suite* come off best, notably the *Chanty*, but the Howells and Vaughan Williams pieces are very misty. Donald Hunt's account of the Elgar *Sonata* is flabby and the memorable tune with its associations with the *Severn suite* lacks any kind of swinging exuberance.

Hurford, Peter (organ)

'Organ favourites': Sydney Opera House organ: BACH: *Toccata and fugue in D min., BWV 565; Jesu, joy of man's desiring*. ALBINONI: *Adagio* (arr. GIAZOTTO). PURCELL: *Trumpet tune in D*. MENDELSSOHN: *A Midsummer Night's Dream: Wedding march*. FRANCK: *Chorale No. 2 in B min*. MURRILL: *Carillon*. WALFORD DAVIES: *Solemn melody*. WIDOR: *Organ symphony No. 5: Toccata*. Royal Festival Hall organ: FRANCK: *Pièce héroïque*. Ratzeburg Cathedral organ: BOELLMANN: *Suite gothique*.
(B) **(*) Decca Eclipse Dig. 452 166-2; *452 166-4* [(M) id. import].

Superb sound here, wonderfully free and never oppressive, even in the most spectacular moments. The Widor is spiritedly genial when played within the somewhat mellower registration of the magnificent Sydney instrument (as contrasted with the Ratzeburg Cathedral organ), and the pedals have great sonority and power. The Murrill *Carillon* is equally engaging alongside the Purcell *Trumpet tune*, while Mendelssohn's wedding music has never sounded more resplendent. The Bach is less memorable, and the Albinoni *Adagio*, without the strings, is not an asset to the collection either. The *Pièce héroïque* and the *Suite gothique* have been added for the Eclipse reissue.

Isoir, André (Koenig organ at Bon Pasteur, Angers)

French Renaissance organ music: Bransles; Galliards and other dances by GERVAIS; FRANCISQUE; ATTAIGNANT. JANEQUIN: *Allez my fault*. SANDRIN: *Quand ien congneu*. Eustache du CAURROY: *Fantaisie sur une jeune fillette*. ATTAIGNANT: *3 Versets du Te Deum; Prélude aux treize motets; Kyrie cunctipotens. Fantaisies* by GUILLET; LE JEUNE; RACQUET. RICHARD: *Prélude in D min*. THOMELIN: *Duo*. LA BARRE: *Sarabande*. Henri du MONT: *Prélude No. 10 in D min.; Pavane in D min*. ANON.: *Fantaisie; Ave Maris Stella*. ROBERDAY: *Fugue et caprice No. 3 in C; Fugues Nos. 10 in G min.; 12 in D*.
(M) *** Cal. CAL 6901 [id.].

The Angers organ has a spicy régale stop which is used tellingly in several of the dance movements included in the programme, notably Gervaise's *Bransle de Bourgogne* and a *Basse dance*, *Bransle* and *Gaillarde* of Attaignant and also in Sandrin's *Quand ien congneu*. A warmer palette is found for Eustache du Caurroy's agreeable *Fantaisie sur une jeune fillette*. This is a French equivalent to the divisions found in Elizabethan music, whereas the piquant *Fantaisie sur orgue ou espinette* of Guillaume Costeley is very succinct. Attaignant's *Kyrie cunctipotens* and the *Third Fantaisie* of Charles Guillet are essentially chorale preludes, as is the more elaborate *Fantaisie* of Charles Racquet, but the *Second Fantaisie* of Claude le Jeune, a remarkable piece, anticipates the chorale variations of Bach, but using two different fugal subjects. Joseph Thomelin's (two-part) *Duo* is a winning miniature and Joseph de la Barre's *Sarabande* also has a gentle charm, while the three *Fugues* of François Roberday show impressive craftsmanship. No. 12, which ends the recital resplendently, is a good example of Isoir's imaginative registrations, which find ear-tickling contrasts between the plangent and mellow timbres that this organ offers, while the music is kept very much alive. A generous (76 minutes) and stimulating recital, although not to be played all at one sitting.

(i) **Jackson, Francis** (organ of York Minster); (ii) **Michael Austin** (organ of Birmingham Town Hall)

'Pipes of splendour': (i) COCKER: *Tuba tune*. PURCELL: *Trumpet tune and almand*. JACKSON: *Division on 'Nun Danket'*. LEIGHTON: *Paean*. DUBOIS: *Toccata in G*. GUILMANT: *Allegretto in B min., Op. 19*. GIGOUT: *Scherzo in E*. MULET: *Carillon-Sortie*. (ii) REGER: *Toccata and fugue in D min./major, Op. 59/5–6*. DUPRE: *Prelude and fugue in B, Op. 7*. FRANCK: *Final in B flat*.
(M) *** Chandos CHAN 6602 [id.].

It was Francis Jackson who made Cocker's *Tuba tune* (with its boisterous, brassy, principal tune) justly famous, and it makes a splendid opener. But the entire programme shows that it is possible to play and record an English organ without the result sounding flabby. The *Toccata* of Dubois is very winning and, in its quieter central section, detail is beautifully clear, as it is in the charming Guilmant *Allegretto* and the lightly articulated Gigout *Scherzo*. Mulet's *Carillon-Sortie* rings out gloriously and Leighton's *Paean* brings a blaze of tone. The items played in Birmingham by Michael Austin are no less stimulating, especially the two French pieces which have a fine piquant bite, while the Reger isn't in the least dull. Superb transfers of demonstration-standard analogue recording from the early 1970s.

John, Keith (organ)

Organ of St Mary's, Woodford: *'Toccata!'*: BACH/BUSONI: *Partita No. 2 in D min., BWV 1004: Chaconne* (trans. K. John). BACH/RACHMANINOV: *Partita No. 3 in E, BWV 1006: suite* (trans. K. John). GUILLOU: *Sinfonietta*. HEILLER: *Tanz-Toccata*.
(M) *** Priory Dig. PRCD 002.

It was a most imaginative idea to use Busoni's arrangement of Bach's famous *D minor Partita for unaccompanied violin* as a basis for an organ transcription, and the result is like nothing you have ever heard before – especially when Keith John gets cracking on the pedals. The three excerpts from the *E major Partita* (as originally transcribed by Rachmaninov) are hardly less successful: how well the opening *Prelude* sounds on the organ, and one can forgive Keith John's affectionately mannered touch on the famous *Gavotte*. We then have a dramatic, almost bizarre change of mood and colour from Jean Guillou's 'neoclassical' (more 'neo' than 'classical') *Sinfonietta*. Even though it opens with a Bachian flourish, its colouring and atmosphere are highly exotic, the austere central *Allegretto* leading to a somewhat jazzy but naggingly insistent, partly contrapuntal and plangent *Gigue*. Heiller's *Tanz-Toccata*, with its complex rhythms and chimerical changes of time-signature, finally brings a positive link with Stravinsky's *Rite of spring* during the insistent motoric final pages. After his remarkable Bach performances, Keith John's kaleidoscopic registration here shows how adaptable and versatile is the modern (1972) organ at St Mary's, Woodford.

Juilliard String Quartet

'50 Years': Volume 1: BARTOK: *String quartets Nos. 3–4; 6*.
(M) *** Sony mono/stereo SMK 62705 [id.].

This CD collects three Bartók performances, one from each of the Juilliard's cycles, in 1949, 1963 and 1981. It is discussed under the composer.

'50 Years': Volume 2: BACH: *The Art of fugue: Contrapuncti 1–4*. BEETHOVEN: *String quartets Nos. 9 in C (Rasumovsky), Op. 59/3; 16 in F, Op. 135*. HAYDN: *String quartet in D, Op. 76/5: Largo* (only).
(M) ** Sony mono/stereo SMK 62706 [id.].

The first four *Contrapuncti* of *The Art of Fugue* come from the impressive set the Juilliards, made in 1987, to which we awarded three stars. The two Beethoven *Quartets* are drawn from different cycles: the *C major Rasumovsky*, Op. 59, No. 3, comes from 1964 and its companion, the *F major*, Op. 135, from 1982. Both are played with the formidable technical address the Juilliards command, but the acoustic in neither the CBS Studios nor the Coolidge Auditorium of the Library of Congress is ideal. One thinks longingly of the transparency and warmth of the old Quartetto Italiano set on Philips.

'50 Years': Volume 3: MOZART: *String quartet No. 19 in C (Dissonance), K.465*. SCHUBERT: *String quartet No. 15 in G, D.887*.
(M) ** Sony SMK 62707 [id.].

The Mozart was recorded in the CBS Studios in New York in 1977 and the Schubert two years later. Perhaps owing to the group's generous vibrato, the opening of the Mozart is not as mysterious as it could be, though the playing is of the highest order of accomplishment. Tempi are well judged and the first-movement exposition repeat is observed. The Schubert is high-powered and at times sounds too well-upholstered in tone, perhaps the fault of the closer balance; but there are many sympathetic and imaginative moments and much to admire. However, there are deeper and more penetrating accounts on disc.

'50 Years': 'The scherzo through time': Minuets and Scherzi by HAYDN; BEETHOVEN; SCHUBERT; MENDELSSOHN; BRAHMS; FRANCK; RAVEL; SIBELIUS; BARTOK; SCHOENBERG; BERG; CARTER.
(M) * Sony SMK 62712 [id.].

There is some splendid playing here, but it is difficult to imagine any but a few collectors wanting isolated scherzos from great string quartets, however superbly they are played.

'50 Years': Volume 4: DEBUSSY: *String quartet in G min*. HAYDN: *String quartet in D (Frog), Op. 50/6*. VERDI: *String quartet in E min*.
(M) ** Sony SMK 62708 [id.].

Sony have chosen the 1970 performance of the Debussy rather than the 1989. It is immaculate technically but a trifle overblown; the upfront recording renders the aural image oversized rather than intimate. However, the slow movement is wonderful and manages to shake off the impression of 'public' music-making rather than music played in the home. The Haydn quartet is new to the catalogue and was recorded in 1985, again in a rather resonant acoustic; a very enjoyable performance, though again it is almost symphonic and some will want a greater lightness of touch. The Verdi, recorded in 1989 (and previously coupled with the Sibelius *Voces intimae*), is impeccable in technical address – perhaps less winning in terms of charm. All the same, those wanting this particular coupling will find much to reward them.

'50 Years': Volume 5: DVORAK: *Piano quintet in A, Op. 81* (with Rudolf Firkušný, piano). BARBER: *Dover Beach, Op. 3* (with Dietrich Fischer-Dieskau). SCHOENBERG: *Verklaerte Nacht* (with Walter Trampler, viola). SCHUMANN: *Piano quintet in E flat, Op. 44* (with Leonard Bernstein, piano). COPLAND: *Sextet for clarinet, piano and string quartet* (with Harold Wright (clarinet), and the composer, piano). FRANCK: *Piano quintet in F min.* (with Jorge Bolet, piano).
(M) ** Sony SM2K 62709 (2) [S2K 62709].

Apart from the Bartók, this is probably the most desirable of the Juilliard's fiftieth anniversery set. The Dvořák *Piano quintet* is marvellously played by Rudolf Firkušný (recorded in 1975), and so, too, is the magnificent Franck *Piano quintet* with Jorge Bolet (recorded in 1978), which this fine pianist plays with a restrained ardour that is impressive, though at times the Juilliard emote rather too much for comfort. The Copland *Sextet* with the composer himself (1966) and Samuel Barber's absurdly neglected and noble setting of *Dover Beach* with Fischer-Dieskau (1967) are valuable additions to the current catalogue and sound considerably better than on LP. The 1991 *Verklaerte Nacht* is a little too over-heated to be ideal, with rather too much vibrato, but it still gives pleasure, while the 1964 version of the Schumann *Quintet* with Bernstein as pianist is coarsely recorded.

Kang, Dong-Suk (violin), **Pascal Devoyon** (piano)

French violin sonatas: DEBUSSY: *Sonata in G min.* RAVEL: *Sonata in G.* POULENC: *Violin sonata.* SAINT-SAENS: *Sonata No. 1 in D min.*
(BB) *** Naxos Dig. 8.550276; *4550276* [id.].

One of the jewels of the Naxos catalogue, this collection of four of the finest violin sonatas in the French repertoire is self-recommending. The stylistic range of this partnership is evident throughout: they seem equally attuned to all four composers. This is warm, freshly spontaneous playing, given vivid and realistic digital recording in a spacious acoustic. A very real bargain.

Kayath, Marcelo (guitar)

'Guitar classics from Latin America': PONCE: *Valse.* PIAZZOLA: *La muerte del angel.* BARRIOS: *Vals, Op. 8/3; Choro de saudade; Julia florida.* LAURO: *Vals venezolanos No. 2; El negrito; El marabino.* BROUWER: *Canción de cuna; Ojos brujos.* PERNAMBUCO: *Sons de carrilhões; Interrogando; Sono de maghia.* REIS: *Si ela perguntar.* VILLA-LOBOS: *5 Preludes.*
(B) *** Carlton Dig. PCD 2012 [(M) id.].

Marcelo Kayath's inspirational accounts of the Villa-Lobos *Preludes* can stand comparison with the finest performances on record. He plays everything here with consummate technical ease and the most appealing spontaneity. His rubato in the Barrios *Vals* is particularly effective, and he is a fine advocate too of the engaging Lauro pieces and the picaresque writing of João Pernambuco, a friend of Villa-Lobos. The recording, made in a warm but not too resonant acoustic, is first class.

'Guitar classics from Spain': TARREGA: *Prelude in A min.; Capricho arabe; Recuerdos de la Alhambra.* GRANADOS: *La Maja de Goya.* ALBENIZ: *Granada; Zambra; Grandina; Sevilla; Mallorca.* TORROBA: *Prelude in E; Sonatina; Nocturno.* RODRIGO: *Zapateado.* TRAD.: *El Noy de la mare.*
(B) *** Carlton IMP Dig. PCD 2037 [(M) id.].

Following the success of his first, Latin-American recital, Marcelo Kayath gives us an equally enjoyable Spanish collection, full of colour and spontaneity. By grouping music by several major composers, he provides a particularly revealing mix. The two opening Tarrega pieces are predominantly lyrical, to bring an effective contrast with the famous fluttering *Recuerdos de la Alhambra*, played strongly. Then after the Granados come five of Albéniz's most colourful and tuneful geographical evocations, while the Torroba group includes the *Sonatina*, a splendid piece. After Rodrigo he closes with the hauntingly memorable *El Noy de la mare*. There is over an hour of music and the recording has a most realistic presence; but take care not to set the volume level too high.

Kazakevich, Mikhail (piano)

'More piano moods': RACHMANINOV: *Preludes: in E flat min. (1887); F (1891); in C sharp min., Op. 3/2; in D min.; C sharp min.; G flat, Op. 23/3, 7 & 10; in B min.; G sharp min., Op. 32/10 & 12.* Domenico SCARLATTI: *Sonatas: Kk. 73; in D, Kk. 96; in C, Kk. 513.* CHOPIN: *Nocturne in E min., Op. 72/1; Polonaise in C sharp min., Op. 26/1; Sonata No. 3 in B min., Op. 58: Largo.* LISZT: *Concert paraphrase of Schubert's 'Gretchen am Spinnrade'.* BACH: *Italian concerto, BWV 971: Andante.* MAHLER (arr. Kazakevich): *Antonius von Padua.* SCHUMANN: *Kinderszenen* (excerpts): *Träumerei; Fast zu ernst; Kind im Einschlummern. Blumenstücke in D flat, Op. 19. Etudes symphoniques, Op. 13: Variations V & VII.* BRAHMS: *Intermezzi: in A min.; E, Op. 116/2 & 4; in A; in E flat min., Op. 118/2 & 6.* SCHUBERT: *Sonata No. 13 in A, D.664: Finale: Allegro. Moment musical in A flat, D.780; Sonata No. 21 in B flat, D.960: Andante.*
(B) *** BMG/Conifer Dig. 75605 51310-2 (2) [(M) id.].

Although we are not usually enamoured of a 'mood music' collection which features odd movements rather than complete works, this recital works very well because of the distinctive and spontaneous quality of Mikhail Kazakevich's playing which is remakably 'live' and communicative. While much of the programme is reflective, this is far from a continuing reverie of romantic lollipops. Indeed the programme is well planned to give constant variety of mood and style. There is a good deal of Brahms and Rachmaninov (although each piece is usually followed by another from a different composer), and Kazakevich proves equally at home in their quite different sound-worlds, as he does with Scarlatti and Schumann. The first disc ends with the finale from Schubert's *A major Sonata*, D.664, played with the lightest touch, but the recital closes with Rachmaninov's extended *Prelude in B minor* and so ends comparatively sombrely, yet leaves the listener wanting more. Most enjoyable for the late evening, and well recorded too.

King, Thea (clarinet), **Clifford Benson** (piano)

English clarinet music: STANFORD: *Sonata, Op. 29.* FERGUSON: *4 Short pieces, Op. 6.* FINZI: *5 Bagatelles, Op. 23.* HURLSTONE: *4 Characteristic pieces.* HOWELLS: *Sonata.* BLISS: *Pastoral.* REIZENSTEIN: *Arabesques.* COOKE: *Sonata in B flat.*
(B) *** Hyperion Dyad CDD 22027 (2) [id.].

This Hyperion Dyad aptly combines two separate recitals, now offered for the price of one. They were recorded at the beginning of the 1980s and are in many ways complementary. Stanford's *Clarinet sonata* is clearly influenced by Brahms but has plenty of character of its own. The other works on the first disc are all appealingly communicative, lighter in texture and content, but well crafted. The second CD opens with the Howells *Sonata*, among the finest written since Brahms, a warmly lyrical piece in two extended movements that bring out the instrument's varied colourings. Bliss's early *Pastoral* follows, thoughtful and unassuming, improvisatory in feeling. Reizenstein's short piece then acts as an interlude before the Cooke *Sonata*, strong but undemanding, with a darkly nostalgic *Adagio* and a chirpy finale. Thea King's warm, naturally expressive playing makes her an ideal advocate, not only for the music, but for her instrument; and her partner, Clifford Benson, is no less eloquent. Smooth, natural, analogue recording.

Kocsis, Zoltán (piano)

'Children's corner': MOZART: *Piano sonata No. 15 in C, K.545.* BEETHOVEN: *Sonatinas in F & G.* SCHUMANN: *Kinderszenen, Op. 15.* DEBUSSY: *Children's corner.* BARTOK: *Microcosmos Nos. 58, 77, 94, 97, 100, 116, 120, 126, 129–32 & 137.*
(B) HM Musique d'Abord Dig. HMA 190 3006 [id.].

A well-planned and potentially attractive recital is spoiled here by Kocsis's propensity for fast tempi. He dashes off the first movement of Mozart's famous *C major Sonata* at the speed of a stagecoach being pursued by highwaymen, and he is similarly unrelenting in his approach to the Beethoven *Sonatinas*. When the charming opening movement, *Von fremden Ländern und Menschen*, of Schumann's *Kinderszenen* is so lacking in affectionate poise, one's patience evaporates. Not recommended.

Kudo, Shigenori (flute), **Rachel Talitman** (harp)

BOIELDIEU: *Sonata.* RAVEL: *Pavane pour une infante défunte.* BIZET: *Carmen: Intermezzo.* FRANCAIX: *5 Piccoli duetti.* DAMASE: *Sonata.*
(BB) ** Discovery Dig. DICD 920141 [id.].

This recital fails to get off to a good start. The harp is balanced forwardly and the resonant sound robs the ingenuous Boieldieu *Sonata* of freshness, while the famous Bizet *Intermezzo* sounds clumsy when the robust harp accompaniment outbalances the flute. However, things improve in the five *Piccoli duetti* of Jean Françaix, delightful *morceaux* of much individuality, and in Jean-Michel Damase's much more ambitious *Sonata*, which yet has comparable subtlety alongside its direct melodic appeal. These artists are thoroughly at home here, and even the recording sounds more effective.

Kynaston, Nicholas (organ)

'Great organ music' (played on organ of (i) Clifton Cathedral; (ii) Royal Albert Hall): (i) J. S. BACH: *Fantasia and fugue in G min., BWV 542; Fugue in G (Alla gigue), BWV 577; Prelude and fugue in B min, BWV 544; Toccata and fugue in F, BWV 540; Concerto No. 2 in A min., BWV 593* (after Vivaldi); (ii) *Toccata and fugue in D min., BWV 565.* SCHUMANN: *Canon in B min., Op. 56/5.* MENDELSSOHN (arr. BEST): *Athalie: War march of the priests.* SAINT-SAENS: *Fantasie in E flat; Fantasie II in D flat, Op. 101.* GIGOUT: *Grand choeur dialogue; Toccata in B min.* WIDOR: *Symphonies: Nos. 1 in C min., Op. 13/1: Marche pontificale. 4 in F min., Op. 13/4: Andante cantabile. 5 in F min., Op. 42/1: Toccata. 6 in C min, Op. 42/2: Allegro. 9 in C min. (Gothique), Op. 70: Andante sostenuto.* BONNET: *Etude de concert.* MULET: *Carillon-sortie.*
(BB) **(*) CfP Silver Double CDCFPSD 4760 (2) [(B) id.].

Nicholas Kynaston's recital (drawing on three LPs, recorded between 1970 and 1975) uses two organs. The opening *Toccata and fugue in D minor* is played on the Royal Albert Hall organ, with its resonant sonority and wide dynamic range effectively demonstrated but not exaggerated. The change of timbre with the second Bach piece, the *Fantasia and fugue in G minor*, is disconcerting, for this, like the rest of the Bach items, is played on the organ of Clifton Cathedral, beautifully recorded with clean, brilliant treble and a clear yet ample bass response sounding very like a baroque organ. Kynaston's performance is buoyant, as is the lively *Fugue à la gigue* (which may not be authentic but is most enjoyable when registered so piquantly). The other works are more considered and didactic, while in the attractively registered Vivaldi transcription (derived from the eighth concerto in *L'Estro armonico*) the central *Adagio* is rather subdued. Using the Royal Albert Hall organ for the French repertoire is perhaps more controversial but the two Gigout pieces are very colourful and effective, and the movements from the Widor symphonies come off well too, with the grandiose opening of the *Allegro* of the *Sixth Symphony* matched by the climaxes of the *Marche pontificale* of the *First*, while the swirling figurations of the famous *Toccata* from the *Fifth* are balanced by the massive effects from the pedals. In the Saint-Saëns and Liszt pieces, the exaggeratedly wide dynamic contrasts characteristic of this instrument are at the very heart of Kynaston's interpretations, and some might find the gentler music seems too recessed. But overall this is an impressive achievement.

Landowska, Wanda (harpsichord)

'Portrait': F. COUPERIN: *La favorite; Les moissonneurs; Les Langueurs-Tendres; Le gazouillement; La commère; Le moucheron; Les bergeries; Les tambourins; Les fastes de la grande ménestrandise; Le dodo, ou l'amour au berceau; Musette de Taverny; Les folies françaises ou les Dominos; Les calotins et les calotines; Les vergers fleuris; Soeur Monique.* RAMEAU: *Suite in G min.* BACH: *Goldberg variations, BWV 988.* HANDEL: *Suites Nos. 2 in F, HWV 427; 5 in E, HWV 430; 7 in G min., HWV 432.*
(M) (***) Grammofono 2000 mono AB 78715/6 [id.].

It is good to have a representative collection of the art of Wanda Landowska, who put the harpsichord back on the musical map in the twentieth century. She was not the first to do so; Violet Gordon Wood actually made earlier acoustic recordings of some distinction, but it was Landowska's larger-than-life personality that soon made her a star. She gave her first performances on this instrument in 1903, and she toured Europe over the next two decades, visiting the United States from 1923 onwards. She persuaded Falla and Poulenc to write concertos (in 1926 and 1927 respectively) and had Pleyel build a large, modern instrument especially for her concerts. Yet, as is readily apparent here, in the music of Couperin and Rameau she could articulate with the greatest delicacy (*La Poule* is delightful), and she kept her big guns in reserve for appropriate moments. Her *Goldberg variations* was rightly celebrated, the playing robust when required but suitably restrained at other times. Her overall timing is surprisingly close to Leonhardt's but her approach, without any loss of seriousness of purpose, is freer and more imaginative, and her reprise of the *Aria* reminds one of Rosalyn Tureck in its delicacy of feeling.

The recordings of French music were made in 1934, the *Goldberg* in 1933, and the quality is excellent, although in the French *pièces de clavecin* there are pitch differences between some items. The Handel *Suites* are a little more variable in sound, but still impressive, and *The Harmonious Blacksmith* (1935) strikes his anvil at first robustly but later with varying degrees of delicacy: there is no more spontaneous account in the catalogue. In the *Overture* which opens Handel's *Seventh Suite*, Landowska flamboyantly sounds like a full orchestra, and she plays the closing *Passacaglia* with similar satisfying weight, but in between there is a wider range of dynamic. Above all, this great artist communicated her joy in everything she played, and these excellent transfers ensure that we fully share it.

Leonard Consort, Gustav Leonhardt (director, and playing: harpsichord, organ, virginal, viol)

Leonhardt Edition
(B) **(*) Teldec/Warner 3984 21349-2 (21) [(M) id.].

Gustav Leonhardt has made an exceptionally distinguished contribution to period-instrument performances of baroque music. During the 1960s he directed and performed in many first recordings for Das Alte Werk label, and it is appropriate that Teldec should celebrate the fortieth anniversary of that label with a 21-disc Leonhardt Edition. The excellent Ensemble which bears his name always sought to make a sound which, although transparent, also had body, as well as being in believable period style. Similarly for his own many keyboard recordings, he chose instruments which would colour the music pleasingly as well as authentically. Leonhardt's scholarship, his understanding of the finer points of baroque performance detail, not least ornamentation, showed a remarkable combination of musicality and scholarship. If his readings sometimes erred on the side of literal directness and sobriety, he could never be accused of self-regarding eccentricity, and it is apt that these reissued records should carry with their documentation printed tributes from such current experts in the period-instrument field as Bob van Asperen and Ton Koopman. Although we have reservations about recommending the set as a whole, certain of these CDs are very desirable indeed, for the technical stadard of the recordings is remarkably high. All these discs are available separately.

BACH: *Harpsichord concertos* (with (i) Frans Brüggen (flute), Marie Leonhardt (violin); (ii) Eduard Müller; (iii) Anneke Uittenbosch; (iv) Alan Curtis; (v) Janny van Wering). *Concertos*: (i) *in A min., for flute, violin and harpsichord, BWV 1044; for solo harpsichord: Nos. 2 in E; 3 in D; 4 in A; 5 in F min., BWV 1053–6; 6 for harpsichord and 2 recorders in F, BWV 1057; 7 for harpsichord in G min.; 8 in D min., BWV 1058–9; Double harpsichord concertos: Nos.* (ii) *1 in C min., BWV 1060;* (iii) *2 in C, BWV 1061;* (ii) *3 in C min., BWV 1062;* (iii–iv) *Triple harpsichord concertos Nos. 1 in D min.; 2 in C, BWV 1063–4;* (ii–iii; v) *Quadruple harpsichord concerto in A min., BWV 1065* ((M) *(*) Teldec/Warner 3984 21350-2 (3)).

The one clear drawback to this Edition as a complete set (apart from the curious omission of the *First Concerto*, BWV 1052) is Leonhardt's set of *Harpsichord concertos*; this has many fine qualities, including Brüggen's contribution (immediately apparent in the *A minor Concerto*, BWV 1044), but it is surprisingly lacking in imagination and spontaneity. The recording is warm and resonant (comparable with the sound we usually expect from the Collegium Aureum) and reproduces smoothly, but inner clarity leaves much to be desired and the keyboard reproduction in the multiple concertos is much too opaque. In the solo works Leonhardt's steady – at times seemingly unrelenting – progress in allegros wearies the ear and, although he can be sensitive enough in slow movements (witness the famous *Largo* of the *F minor Concerto*), this is very disappointing, all things considered. The set is discussed, rather more fully, under its composer entry (above). This does include the *First Concerto*, but not played by Leonhardt.

BACH: *Goldberg variations, BWV 988* ((M) ** Teldec/Warner 3984 21351-2).

There are no complaints about the recording of the *Goldberg variations* (from 1965, using Leonhardt's favourite copy of a Dulcken harpsichord), which sounds fresh and vivid in its present incarnation. The reading is clear and direct, if not producing any specially individual resonances. Leonhardt was to re-record the work later for Deutsche Harmonia Mundi, and that version has a more spontaneous feeling; but it is not currently available.

BACH: Works for harpsichord: *Chromatic fantasia and fugue in D min., BWV 903; Sonata in D min., BWV 964; Sonata in G, BWV 1005; Suite in E min., BWV 996; Toccata in G, BWV 916* ((M) ** Teldec/Warner 3984 21352-2).

It has to be said that Bach's music does not always show Leonhardt at his very best. His miscellaneous recital is played on a modern harpsichord, but one which is a reproduction of a mid-eighteenth-century Dulcken. The sounds are authentic and attractive; unquestionably Leonhardt's playing reflects what would have been possible in Bach's time and, with judicious ornamentation of repeated sections, the scholarship behind the playing is impeccable. The opening *Chromatic fantasia and fugue* brings exciting dexterity, and so does the *Allegro assai* finale of the *Sonata in G*, which is an arrangement of the work for unaccompanied violin in C, BWV 1005. In between, however, a good deal of the playing is rather metronomic, and the *Suite in E minor* (which Bach probably intended for the (now obsolete) lute-harpsichord) could do with a lighter touch. The recording is rather close, but the CD transfer cannot be faulted.

BACH: *Violin sonatas* (for violin and harpsichord) *Nos. 1–6, BWV 1014–9* (with Lars Frydén) ((M) **(*) Teldec/Warner 3984 21353-2 (2)).

The six *Sonatas for violin and piano* are far less well known than the works for unaccompanied violin or cello, and their relative obscurity is quite undeserved. They contain music of great character and beauty: who can forget the beautful *Siciliana* which opens No. 4 (played most persuasively here by Lars Frydén) or the more solemn dignity of the first movement of the *B minor Sonata*, which Leonhardt opens very simply and which glows with life at the violin entry. Frydén proves to be a most stylish and sympathetic exponent. He uses a baroque violin, made in London in 1767, and lets it sing and dance, just as Bach intended. Although he is balanced fairly closely, if not at the expense of his partner, his timbre is full and cleanly formed and never sounds scratchy – witness his *Dolce* opening of the *A major Sonata*. Throughout these works the polyphony of the allegros is always engagingly fresh, and the continuo offers plenty of opportunities to the imaginative harpsichordist. Alas, Leonhardt does not always take them, for the most part being content to provide ongoing background support. When he is on his own (as again at the opening of No. *5 in F minor*) he proceeds uneventfully onwards until the warm entry of the solo violin transforms the music. In a flowing Andante, as in the *A major* work, he is content to provide a straightforward accompaniment and let his partner soar above him. However, better this than eccentric rubato, and in the jolly second movement of the *E major*, the players work well together, while the finale sparkles with energy. An excellent transfer to CD, but don't play the disc at too high a volume.

BACH: *Quodlibet*, Canons, Chorales, Songs and keyboard works (with Anner Bylsma (cello), Agnes Giebel, Marie Luise Gilles, Bert van t'Hoff, Peter Christoph Runge): *Canon in 2 parts, BWV 1075; in 7 (8) parts, BWV 1078; in 4 parts, BWV 1073; in 4 (5) parts, BWV 1077;* (Keyboard) *Capriccio in B flat (sopra la lontananza del suo fratello dilettissimo), BWV 992; Preludes: in F, BWV 927; in E, BWV 937; in G min., BWV 929; in D, BWV 925; in C, BWV 939; Fugue in C, BWV 952; Prelude and Fugue in A min., BWV 895; Prelude and Fughetta in D min., BWV 899; Suite in F min., BWV 823. Quodlibet, BWV 524*. Arias: *Erbauliche Gedanken eines Tobackrauchers, BWV 515a; Gieb dich zufrieden und sie stille, BWV 511; Vergiss mein nicht, mein allerliebster Gott! BWV 505*. Chorales: *O Herzensangst, o Bangigkeit und Zagen! BWV 400; Nicht so traurig, nicht so sehr, BWV 384; Dir, dir Jehova, will ich singen, BWV 452; Was betrübst du dich, mein Herze, BWV 423; Wer nur den lieben Gott lässt walten* (3 versions), *BWV 691 BWV 434* ((M) *** Teldec/Warner 3984 21354-2).

Much of this material comes from Anna Magdelena's *Clavier-Büchlein*, intended for use by Bach's sons: keyboard pieces, together with simple chorales and songs for domestic entertainment rather than public performance. They show another side of Bach, as a genial but painstaking family man, and the music brings out the best in Leonhardt, who plays the brief keyboard pieces in an appropriately light-hearted manner. He gives a colourful account of the designedly programmatic *Capriccio in B flat* ('*On the departure of a beloved brother*'), personally announcing the title of each section in German. The brief *Canon in 2 parts* wittily introduces a recorder, while the *Canon in 7 (8) parts* fills out quickly and ends in mid-air. The arias and chorales are agreeably outgoing. In *So oft ich meine Tobacks-Pfeife* (subtitled 'The edifying thoughts of a tobacco-smoker') Bert van t'Hoff (or Peter Runge – it is not quite clear which) genially reflects on Bach's 'contented puffing on my small pipe', while the serene *Gieb dich zufrieden und sei stille* ('Be of good cheer and hold your peace') is sung delightfully by Agnes Giebel. The chorale, *Was betrübst du dich, mein Herz* ('Why are you sad, my heart?'), touchingly appears to reflect on a family crisis. But the highlight of the concert is the *Quodlibet* ('As you wish') for vocal quartet, which by definition is an informal, light-hearted piece, but here is a true musical joke, originally intended for performance at a wedding. The manuscript is incomplete (both the beginning and the end are missing) but what there is (about 10 minutes) is set to outrageous words which flit from image to image, not unlike Gilbert's famous Nightmare song, and ending with the observation, 'Oh what a delightful fugue this is!' The whole piece is captivating, especially when sung so freshly. To end the collection, Leonhardt returns to his more didactic Bach keyboard style for BWV 823, BWV 895 and BWV 899, but the closing *Fughetta* of the latter work is pleasingly jaunty. The recording throughout is excellent, and altogether this is a most entertaining concert.

English consort and keyboard music: DOWLAND: *Pavan in C.* LAWES: *Suites Nos. 1 in C min.; 2 in F; Sonata No. 7 in D min.; Suite No. 3 in B flat: In nomine.* COPRARIO: *Fantasia; Suite.* BYRD: *Pavan; Galliard. Fantasia No. 3.* Thomas SIMPSON: *Ricercar: Bonny sweet robin.* Thomas LUPO: *Fantasia.* BYRD: *Pavan; Galliard; Miserere.* MORLEY: *Nancie; Fantasia.* John BULL: *Hexachord fantasia; The Duchesse of Brunswick's toye.* William RANDALL: *Dowland's Lachrymae; Galliard Can't she excuse my wrongs.* TOMKINS: *Pavan; Galliard; A sad pavan for these distracted times.* GIBBONS: *Pavan.* FARNABY: *Fantasia; Spagnioletta.* William TISDALE: *Mrs Katherin Tregians pavan.* ANON.: *A toye* ((M) *** Teldec/Warner 3984 21760-2 (2)).

This two-CD compilation draws on three Das Alte Werk LPs from 1965–6 and 1970, and the result is an unusually comprehensive survey which gives an excellent overall picture of the various composers writing music in Elizabethan and Jacobean England. The programme opens appropriately with Byrd, a consort *Pavane*, and later we are to have a harpsichord *Pavane and Galliard* and two consort *Fantasias*. In between come the highly individual *Suites* of William Lawes, who was a member of the Chapel Royal and a very considerable contributor to early seventeenth-century consort music. His *In nomine* (taken from the *Third Suite*) is particularly eloquent. But the surprise is perhaps the music of William Coprario (Cooper), whose *Fantasia* (for two violins, viola, viol and cello) is very striking indeed, to be followed by a tuneful and light-hearted *Suite in three parts* and the equally engaging *Ricercar on Bonny sweet Robin* by Thomas Simpson. The first CD ends with Lupo's *Fantasia*, another piece of real quality. There could perhaps be more ornamentation in these performances, but on the whole they are in excellent taste and style. There is nothing anaemic about the string textures, nor are they edgy, while the playing itself has plenty of life and spirit. The recording is impeccable. The music of Byrd again opens the second disc with a consort pavane and galliard to introduce his beautiful *Miserere*, which is most touchingly played by Leonhardt on a chamber organ. He continues with a series of keyboard pieces, alternating harpsichord (choosing between two different instruments) and virginal. All come from the Fitzwilliam Virginal Book, except for the Gibbons *Pavane* and the two pieces by Randall. Predictably fine are the Bull *Fantasia* and the three pieces by Thomas Tomkins: here Leonhardt changes instruments for the third, *A sad pavane for these distracted times*. Farnaby's jolly *Spagioletta* makes a spirited contrast and the programme ends with an encore – a brief, anonymous *Toye*.

Consort music: BIBER: *Harmonia artificiosa-ariosa: diversi mode accordata: Partita in A; Mensa sonora: Part 3; Fidicinium sacro-profanum: Sonatas 3–6.* MUFFAT: *Armonico tributo: Sonata 2 in G min.* ROSENMULLER: *Sonata No. 7 a 4.* SCHEIDT: *Paduan a 4.* SCHMELZER: *Sacro-profanus concentus musicus: Sonatas Nos. 7, 9* ((M) *** Teldec/Warner 3984 21761-2).

It was Leonhardt who introduced us (in the late 1960s) to much of Biber's instrumental music, the excellence of which is only now being fully explored. The best-known set is the *Harmonia artificiosa-ariosa*, a collection of seven *Partitas* or suites for strings (published posthumously), and here we are offered the *Third* with its remarkable finale, an elaborately decorated *Chaconne/Canon*. The *Mensa sonora* sonatas (from 1680) are – as the title suggests – essentially homophonic, more concerned with richness of texture and harmony than with contrapuntal ingenuity. Again we are offered Partita III, in five movements, written for a modest chamber ensemble and continuo. The music is warmly expresssive: even the fourth-movement *Chaconne* is mellow. Four of the twelve *Fidicinium sacro-profanum* sonatas follow. They were published three years later and are scored for 2 violins, 2 violas, 2 cellos, and continuo. As their title suggests, contrast is the order of the day, with the expressive movements quite dolorous, while allegros are lively and light-hearted. The *Sixth Sonata* (the last here) opens quite solemnly, and Leonhardt fills out the texture with an organ continuo. The following Muffat *Sonata* opens even more sombrely, but it becomes an inventive series of linked movements alternating Grave slow sections with buoyant allegros. The two Schmelzer *Sonatas* (1662) for two violins, viola and continuo seek contrast in the same way as Biber's music and are similarly entitled *Sacro-profanus concentus musicus*. They are of high quality, as is the briefer work by Johann Rosenmüller and the stately *Paduan* (Pavane) of Samuel Scheidt. As can be seen, all this music, much of which is well off the beaten track, comes from the same fertile period, and Leonhardt and his players (six in all) are persuasive advocates. They use period instruments and are tuned to seventeenth-century pitch, but the sounds they make are full-timbred, and expressive phrasing is not eccentric but is warmly musical.

FROBERGER: Organ and harpsichord works: Organ: *Capriccio II; Fantasia III; Toccata XI alla levazione; Ricercar II; Canzona II*. Harpsichord: *Toccata IX; Suite XVIII; Toccata XVIII; Suite XII* ((M) *** Teldec/Warner 3984 21762-2).

Froberger was a pupil of Frescobaldi and one of the most exploratory and inward-looking composers of the seventeenth century. Leonhardt, who is an authoritative guide, offers here two groups of pieces, the first five played on the now familiar eighteenth-century organ (at the Waalse Kerk, Amsterdam), and the second group on a modern harpsichord, copied from an Italian instrument from the same period. The opening organ *Capriccio* is joyously buoyant, but the *Chorale fantasia* is more thoughtful and in its steady progress anticipates Bach. The *Toccata alla levazione* has much of Frescobaldi's improvisatory feeling, while the *Ricercar II* brings a remarkably solemn profundity. The *Harpsichord suites*, skilfully decorated, are more lively and outgoing and readily show the composer's resourceful melodic and harmonic flare. Most striking is the opening movement of the *Twelfth Suite*, which laments the death of King Ferdinand IV in 1654. The closing *Sarabande* has comparable regal dignity. Excellent recording of both instruments.

KUHNAU: *Musikalische Vorstellung einiger biblischer Historien: Sonatas 1–6 (1: The combat between David and Goliath; 2: Saul healed by David with the help of music; 3: Jacob's marriage; 4, Hezekiah is mortally ill and restored to health; 5: Gideon, the saviour of Israel; 6: The death and burial of Jacob)* (Teldec/Warner (M) *(*) 3984 21763-2 (2)).

Johann Kuhnau was Bach's predecessor at St Thomas's, Leipzig, and this is his fourth and last keyboard work. The *Musical depiction of some biblical stories* (in six *Sonatas*) dates from 1700. Each programatically illustrates a story from the Old Testament, which is filled out by a narrative – an introduction at the beginning of each work, plus titles for each section, the latter usually spoken over the music. Here these introductions, recounting each biblical story in full, given in German – and, fortunately, separately banded on the CDs – are written and spoken by Leonhardt himself, and they are very subjective. Alas, Kuhnau's musical resources are not equal to the pictorial task he has set himself: they are most striking for their naïvety and seldom show much descriptive skill: *The combat between David and Goliath* is depicted with singular lack of imagination. However, when Gideon leads the Israelites into battle, the 'blast of trombones and trumpets' is more tellingly depicted, and the scalic flight of pursued enemy forces, both here and earlier in the David/Goliath narrative, is effective enough. Kuhnau is also rather better at portraying melancholy, as in Saul's rather extended bout of it, before David's not very believable musical cure, and again during Hezekiah's mournful sickness before God relents and restores him to health. In the most intriguing story of all, *Jacob's marriage*, the devious Laban, using the cover of darkness, places his elder ugly daughter, Leah, in the bridal bed instead of the younger, the beautiful Rachel (whom Jacob is expecting). Such duplicity is represented with melodramatically florid flourishes. Then, in a section lasting two minutes, Jacob's relishing of the wedding night consummation is depicted with an amiable little theme, until 'his heart tells him something is amiss'. But in the dim light his misgivings cannot be confirmed and he 'finally falls asleep' – to a single chord. The next morning he discovers his mistake and is none too pleased about it. However, he agrees to keep Leah after the promise that in seven years he can have Rachel too; so the piece ends with a second wedding and repeated celebrations! The organ is used for *Sonatas Nos. 1*, *2* and *4*, the harpsichord for the remainder. Generally it is the latter instrument which works best in the primitive narrative detail, as Leonhardt brings a certain improvisational feeling to the disconsolate music. But to claim this as a 'great work', as Lothar Hoffmann-Erbrecht does in his accompanying note, is singularly misguided. It has historical interest, to be sure, but little else, although one wonders whether a more extrovert account would bring it more fully to life. The documentation is good, if a little unwieldy, with full narrative translations, and the titles given for each section.

MONDONVILLE: (with Lars Frydén): *Violin sonatas Op. 3, Nos. 1 in G min.; 2 in F; 3 in B; 4 in C; 5 in G; 6 in A* ((M) **(*) Teldec/Warner 3984 21765-2).

Mondonville's *Violin sonatas* are important in that they helped the development away from the violin-plus-continuo style to the form as we know it today. Thus both instruments are given proper 'solo' parts to play, and they are often very florid parts. One might be forgiven for occasionally thinking that the composer had forgotten himself and allotted two accompaniment parts instead! But generally the music is inventive enough, and the disc has real historical interest in demonstrating the duet sonata when ideas concerning the marriage of two instruments were very much in the melting pot. Opus 3 dates from about 1734 and predates by 14 years the fascinating Opus 5 set, which also includes the human voice and which is listed and discussed in the composer index above. The recording here, made in 1966, is good but is rather more forward than the earlier (1963) recording by these same artists of the Bach *Violin and harpsichord sonatas*. This means that the full timbre of Lars Frydén's baroque violin is less flattered, although he can still be serenely expressive in the *Arias* which form the slow movements – witness the fine flowing melody of

No. 4 in C major – and Leonhardt's harpsichord (a Kirckman, made in London in 1766) is little sharp-toned. But the two instruments are generally well balanced – and the players seem pretty sure of themselves. Tempi are often brisk and very lively (try the infectious *Giga* finale of that same *C major Sonata*).

Organ and harpsichord music: F. COUPERIN: *Mass à l'usage ordinaire des paroisses: Offertoire sur les grands jeux. L'art de toucher le clavecin: 8 Preludes*. Alessandro POGLIETTI: *Ricercar primi toni*. Nicolas de GRIGNY: *Cromorne en taille à deux parties*. RAMEAU: *Pièces de clavecin*. ANON.: *Daphne; Resonet in laudibus* ((M) **(*) Teldec/Warner 3984 21766-2).

This collection creates a stimulating variety of timbres and textures from the various keyboard instruments which Leonhardt chooses. He first seeks a French association rather than a specific French accent in presenting the Couperin *Offertoire* rather grandly on the Müller organ at Waalse Kerk (or French church) in Amsterdam, which dates originally from 1680. The instrument has clarity and all the necessary bite in the reeds. He then plays eight *Préludes* from *L'art de toucher de clavecin* very stylishly and pleasingly on a copy of a Rück harpsichord by an eighteenth-century Dresden maker, C. A. Gräbner, which works equally well. The solemn *Ricercar* by Alessandro Poglietti, an influential Italian who became organist at the Viennese Imperial Chapel, follows on yet another organ, which it suits admirably. Leonhardt then returns to Amsterdam to find an engaging registration for Nicolas de Grigny's gentle *Cromorne en taille*. According to the documentation, the same Rück/Gräbner harpsichord is used for the six *Pièces de clavecin* of Rameau as for the Couperin *Préludes*, but the recordings were made two years apart and the Rameau (from 1962) is mono, and is less easy on the ear: brighter, harsher and at times even clattery. But one soon adjusts, and the effect is certainly lively and characterful. The anonymous portrait of *Daphne* has a gentle melancholy, and for this Leonhardt uses a noticeably mellower 1648 Ruckers, a stereo recording of five years later, closing with the divisions on *Resonet in laudibus* played on the deliciously reedy Arp Schnitger organ at Noordbroek, Gronigen. Most entertaining.

RAMEAU: *Pièces de clavecin en concerts: Premier concert; Deuxième concert; Troisième concert; Quatrième concert; Cinquième concert* (with Frans Brüggen, Wieland and Sigiswald Kuijken) ((M) *** Teldec/ Warner 3984 21767-2).

These ensemble versions of the *Pièces de clavecin en concerts*, published in 1741, were not pioneered by Leonhardt on LP: there were two previous recordings by Rampal, one on Nonesuch with Robert Veyron-Lacroix and the other on Fontana with Ruggiero Gerlin. But the present (1971) performance trumped its predecessors: it has a surer sense of style and a deeper understanding of the niceties of the period. It is a period-instrument performance, but a thoroughly stimulating and enjoyable one, beautifully recorded.

PURCELL: Anthems, Instrumental music and Songs (with Leonhardt Consort); *Anthems:* (with James Bowman, Nigel Rogers, Max van Egmond, King's College, Cambridge, Choir, Willcocks); *Rejoice in the Lord alway; Blow up the trumpet in Sion; O God, thou art my God; O God, thou hast cast us out; My heart is inditing; Remember not, Lord, our offences*. (Consort) *Chacony in G min.; Overture in D min.; Pavan in B flat; Overture (with Suite) in G; Pavan in A min.; Fantasia (Chaconne): 3 Parts on a ground in D; Overture in G min.; Pavan of 4 parts in G min.; Sonata in A min.; Ground in D min.* (Harpsichord) *Suite in D; Sefauchi's farewell in D min.; A new ground in E min.* Songs: *Fly swift, ye hours; The Father brave; Return, revolting rebels* (with Max van Egmond, Leonhardt Consort). (iv) *Fantasia a 4 No. 7* (Brüggen Consort) ❁ ((M) *** Teldec/Warner 3984 21768-2 (2)).

The Purcell collection is the pick of the bunch and should not be missed. The anthems are all very well sung indeed, with the King's penchant for tonal breadth and beauty. Not all of them have instrumental accompaniments, but those that do enjoy a distinctive sound, using period instruments in such a way that the performances overall happily blend scholarship and vigour, warmth and spontaneity. The recordings were not made at King's College, but in Holland, in 1969, and the acoustic is ideal, not too resonant, so that the effect is uncommonly fresh and clear. The delightful *Blow up the trumpet in Zion* has splendid antiphonal effects which remind one of Purcell's famous directional chorus in *King Arthur*. But the highlight must be *My heart is inditing*, an extended work, also for double chorus, in which the polyphony is a thing of wonder. It is superbly integrated and the choir conclude with a very beautiful performance of the unaccompanied *Remember not, Lord, our offences*.

Leonhardt's excellent Dutch ensemble experiences no difficulty in getting right inside the sprit of Purcell's instrumental music, which they perform with admirable taste and finesse of style. the *Fantasia on a ground*, a brilliant work exploiting the special sound of three violins above a repeated bass motive, is one of the best recorded versions of this piece, as is that of the famous *Chacony in minor*. The two *Overtures* are less familiar; while they may not rank, like the *Pavans* and *Sonatas* here, among Purcell's best music, it is good to have them in such neat and sparkling performances, and Leonhardt's intepretations of the harpsichord solos leaves little to be desired. The stereo sound from the late 1960s is warm and lively, and very successfully transferred.

Organ and harpsichord music: Organ: REINCKEN: *An den Wasserflüssen Babylon*. Heinrich SCHEIDEMANN: *Praeambulum in D.* BACH: *Prelude and fugue in D, BWV 539*. Harpsichord: BOEHM: *Suites Nos. 6 in E flat; 8–9 in F min.* HANDEL: *Suite No. 8 in F min.* J. C. BACH: *Sonata in D, Op. 5/2* ((M) *** Teldec/Warner 3984 21769-2).

Johann Adam Reincken was a famed improviser, and Bach travelled to Hamburg to hear him play. Not surprisingly, his *Chorale fantasia* on *An den Wasserflüssen* is an ingeniously crafted work that projects readily in Leonhardt's fine performance. The following *D minor Prelude and fugue* of Bach might have been moved on a little more swiftly, yet Leonhardt certainly holds the listener's attention at his chosen pace. He then turns to the harpsichord for the three attractive suites of Georg Böhm (French in form and layout, but German in sensibility) and the splendid work of Handel, and he closes with a remarkably modern-sounding *D major Sonata* of J. C. Bach, with its pair of *Allegro di molto* movements (played with great flair), followed by a closing minuet. Leonhardt uses two different organs and (more importantly) three different harpsichords: two copies and, for the J. C. Bach work, an original instrument made in London in 1775. The basic sound of each is quite different (the Böhm and Handel suites appear to be very good mono recordings), and Leonhardt makes the most of his colouristic opportunities. The balance is close but otherwise the CD transfer produces first-class results. Very stimulating.

Harpsichord and Consort Music: FRESCOBALDI: *Toccata settima; Toccata undecima in C; Canzona terza; Toccata in G; Fantasia sesta sopra doi soggetti; 5 Galliards*. Francesco TURINI: *Sonata in A*. CACCINI: *Amarilli mia bella*. Biagio MARINI: *Balletto secondo a tre & a quattro*. D. SCARLATTI: *Sonatas in A min., Kk. 3: Presto; in D min., Kk. 52: Andante moderato; in E, Kk. 215: Andante; in E, Kk. 216: Allegro* ((M) *** Teldec/Warner 3984 21770-2).

Another very enjoyable recital in which Leonhardt uses four different early harpsichords. Frescobaldi's music suits him admirably, for he obviously relishes its improvisational freedom of style and its ability to take the listener by surprise. Alternating an Italian instrument and a sonorous London Kirkman, he plays the *Toccatas* with an entirely appropriate freedom and is equally appealing in the *Canzona*; it is only in the *Fantasia* that he progresses somewhat deliberately. But he finds an appropriately buoyant rhythmic touch for the five brief *Galliards*. Turini's *Trio sonata*, alternately expressive and vigorous, makes a strong contrast, played with elegance and spirit, while the following *Amarilli mia bella* of Cacccini has a certain lovelorn air when played so responsively on a fine Ruckers. The Ensemble returns for Marini's ballet suite, which has a surprisingly grave concluding *Pretirata*. The programme ends with nicely turned performances of four choice keyboard sonatas of Scarlatti, using a characterful instrument made by R. Schütz of Heidelberg. These appear to be more mono recordings (from 1962) but of high quality. The closing work in *E major*, Kk. 216, with its swirling bravura scales is particularly engaging.

Lipatti, Dinu (piano)

CHOPIN: *Sonata No. 3 in B min., Op. 58*. LISZT: *Années de pèlerinage: Sonetto del Petrarca, No. 104*. RAVEL: *Miroirs: Alborada del gracioso*. BRAHMS: *Waltzes, Op. 39/1, 2, 5, 6, 10, 14 & 15* (with Nadia Boulanger). ENESCU: *Sonata No. 3 in D, Op. 25*.
(M) (***) EMI mono CDH7 63038-2 [id.].

The Chopin is one of the classics of the gramophone, and it is good to have it on CD in this excellent-sounding transfer. The Brahms *Waltzes* are played deliciously with tremendous sparkle and tenderness; they sound every bit as realistic as the post-war records. The Enescu *Sonata* is an accessible piece, with an exuberant first movement and a rather atmospheric *Andantino*, but the sound is not as fresh as the rest of the music on this valuable CD. A must for all with an interest in the piano.

'Last recital – Besançon, 16 November 1950': J. S. BACH: *Partita No. 1 in B flat min., BWV 825*. MOZART: *Sonata No. 8 in A min., K.310*. SCHUBERT: *Impromptus in E flat; in G flat, D.899/2–3*. CHOPIN: *Waltzes Nos. 1, 3–14*.
(M) (***) EMI mono CDH5 65166-2.

No collector should overlook this excellent 73-minute recital, originally issued on a pair of LPs. Most of these performances have scarcely been out of circulation since their first appearance: the haunting account of the Mozart *A minor Sonata* and the Bach *B flat Partita* have had more than one incarnation: the collection of Chopin *Waltzes* is perhaps most famous of all, and its legendary reputation is well earned.

The remastering is expertly done, and the ear notices that among his other subtleties Lipatti creates a different timbre for the music of each composer.

Little, Tasmin (violin), Piers Lane (piano)

'Virtuoso violin': KREISLER: *Prelude and allegro in the style of Pugnani; Caprice viennois.* BRAHMS: *Hungarian dance Nos. 1 & 5.* SHOSTAKOVICH: *The Gadfly: Romance.* DRIGO: *Valse bluette.* FIBICH: *Poème.* FALLA: *La vida breve: Spanish dance.* WIENIAWSKI: *Légende, Op. 17.* SARASATE: *Introduction and Tarantelle, Op. 43.* BLOCH: *Baal Sheem: Nigum.* DEBUSSY: *Beau soir.* RIMSKY-KORSAKOV: *Flight of the bumble-bee* (both arr. HEIFETZ). DELIUS: *Hassan: Serenade* (arr. TERTIS). KROLL: *Banjo and fiddle.* RAVEL: *Tzigane.*
(B) *** CfP Dig. CD-CFP 4675 [(M) id. import].

A pretty dazzling display of violin fireworks from a brilliant young fiddler who conveys her delight in her own easy virtuosity The opening Kreisler pastiche, *Prelude and allegro*, is presented with real style, and later the *Caprice viennois* has comparable panache and relaxed charm. The schmaltzy daintiness of Drigo's *Valse bluette* is followed by an unexaggerated but full-timbred warmth in Fibich's *Poème*. The gypsy temperament of the Falla and the ready sparkle of Sarasate's *Tarantella* and Kroll's *Banjo and fiddle* are offset by the lyrical appeal of the more atmospheric piece. The violin is very present – perhaps the microphones are a fraction too close, but the balance with the piano is satisfactory and there is not the exaggerated spotlight here which virtually ruins Perlman's comparable 1994 collection with Samuel Sanders called '*Bits and Pieces*' (EMI CDC7 54882-2), where immediately in the opening Corelli Op. 5 *La Folia* chaconne, as arranged by Kreisler, the violin-timbre is made to sound aggressive, even harsh.

Malcolm, George (harpsichord)

'The world of the harpsichord': BACH: *Italian concerto, BWV 971; Chromatic fantasia and fugue in D min., BWV 903; French suite No. 5 in G, BWV 816; Toccata in D, BWV 912.* PARADIES: *Toccata.* DAQUIN: *The cuckoo.* RIMSKY-KORSAKOV: *Flight of the bumble-bee* (arr. MALCOLM). RAMEAU: *Pièces de clavecin: La Poule; Le rappel des oiseaux; Tambourin.* François COUPERIN: *Pièces de clavecin: Le rossignol-en-amour; Le carillon de Cithère.* TEMPLETON: *Bach goes to town.* MALCOLM: *Bach before the mast.*
✿ (M) *** Decca 444 390-2.

This is a delectable collection, a CD of harpsichord music that should be in even the smallest collection, spanning as it does the gamut of the late George Malcolm's wide repertory. His Bach performances are very considerable indeed; the *Chromatic fantasia* has an appropriate improvisatory element, the *Italian concerto* is full of vitality, and the best known of the *French suites* has a genial, lyrical intimacy to offset the buoyant *Toccata in D*. The comparative gravitas of Bach goes well with the charm of Rameau and Couperin, with their descriptive pieces realized with flair, notably *Le rappel des oiseaux* and *Le carillon de Cithère*. The two witty Bach imitations make a tempting hors d'oeuvre and the Rimsky-Korsakov is similarly a fun piece, played with great bravura; but no one should dismiss the mixture, for there is plenty of real substance here and playing of great distinction. The 1960s recording of the harpsichord (unnamed, but almost certainly a modern copy of a fine baroque instrument) is in the demonstration class, beautifully balanced – not too close – and natural within an airy but not over-resonant acoustic.

Melos Ensemble

18th- and 19th-Century chamber music: MOZART: *Piano and wind quintet in E flat, K.452.* BEETHOVEN: *Piano and wind quintet in E flat, Op. 16; Sextet in E flat for 2 horns, 2 violins, viola & cello, Op. 81b; March for wind sextet in B flat, WoO 29; Rondino for in E flat, WoO 25; Duo No. 1 for clarinet and bassoon, WoO 27.* SCHUMANN: *Fantasiestücke for clarinet and piano, Op. 73. Märchenerzählungen, Op. 132.* BRAHMS: *Clarinet quintet in B min., Op. 115.* REGER: *Clarinet quintet in A:* 2nd movement: *Vivace.*
(B) *** EMI forte CZS5 72643-2 (2) [(M) id. import].

This collection, like its companion below, dates from the late 1960s when the Melos Ensemble gathered together some of London's finest orchestral musicians to make a series of recordings for EMI. There is plenty of individual personality in the music-making here, but how beautifully these fine musicians blend together as a group! The polished elegance and charm of their playing cannot be heard to better effect than in the Mozart *Piano and wind quintet*, dominated by the splendid musicianship of the pianist, Lamar Crowson, and with some particularly felicitous oboe playing from Peter Graeme. Its Beethoven successor follows on naturally, played with a lighter touch than usual to emphasize the Mozartian influences. The *Sextet* which follows brings some splendid bravura from the two horn players, Neil Sanders and James Buck, while the *March* (for wind alone) is very jolly. The *Duo* for clarinet and bassoon is now thought not to be by Beethoven but is very agreeable nevertheless. Schumann's rarely heard *Märchenerzählungen* ('Fairy-tales') is late (1953) and is almost unique in being scored for the same combination as Mozart's *Trio* for clarinet, viola (here Gervase de Peyer and Cecil Aronowitz) and piano. The *Fantasiestücke*, for clarinet and piano, was written four years earlier. Both performances are persuasively warm and mellow, although Lamar Crowson again achieves a strong backing profile. For all their lyricism, these artists don't miss Schumann's marking, '*mit Feuer*', in the finale of Op. 73, and the second movement of Op. 132 is strongly accented to make a bold contrast with the flowingly romantic third, before the similarly bold finale. Gervase de Peyer then relaxes completely to present an essentially lyrical view of the Brahms *Clarinet quintet*. It is a lovely performance, achieving a wistful nostalgia in the slow movement, but it is perhaps in the rippling execution of the arpeggios of the finale that his playing is particularly individual. The Reger lollipop Scherzo, which acts as an encore, may be as light as thistledown, but its central trio has a beguiling richness of style in the post-Brahms tradition. All the recordings were made at Abbey Road, and the sound is excellent throughout; only in the Beethoven *Sextet* is there a hint of thinness in the violins. Overall this will give much refreshment and pleasure.

20th-Century chamber music: RAVEL: *Introduction and allegro for flute, clarinet, harp and string quartet.* POULENC: *Trio for oboe, bassoon and piano; Sonata for clarinet and bassoon.* FRANCAIX: *Divertissement for oboe, clarinet and bassoon; Divertissement for bassoon and string quintet.* MILHAUD: *Suite for violin, clarinet and piano.* BARTOK: *Contrasts for violin, clarinet and piano.* SKALKOTTAS: *Octet; 8 Variations on a Greek tune.* KHACHATURIAN: *Trio for clarinet, violin and piano.* PROKOFIEV: *Overture on Hebrew themes.*
(B) *** EMI forte CZS5 72646-2 (2) [(M) id. import].

If anything, the Melos survey of twentieth-century music is even more enjoyable than their classical programme. It opens with Ravel's sublime *Septet* (with Richard Adeney, Gervase de Peyer and Osian Ellis in the lead). The performance is very fine indeed, and the 1967 Abbey Road recording is that bit warmer and smoother than their earlier version for Oiseau-Lyre/Decca, even if that might have a degree more subtlety (see under Ravel in the composer section). Both the Poulenc pieces are delightful, particularly the delicious *Trio for oboe, bassoon and piano*, which has an admirably dry wit and unfailing inventiveness; the playing is above reproach. The two *Divertissements* of the always elegant Jean Françaix have much inconsequential charm, and the *Ouverture* and *Final* of the irrepressible Milhaud *Suite* sparkle lustrously, while the inner movements produce an engaging, gentle melancholy. The other masterpiece here is the Bartók *Contrasts*, for the same combination as the Milhaud but of altogether stronger fibre. Both are played superbly. The works by the neglected Greek composer, Nikolaos Skalcottas (a Schoenberg pupil who died not long after the Second World War), show a fairly strong personality, the *Octet* abrasively neo-classical, and both pieces revelling in a mordant harmonic dissonance. The surprise is Khachaturian's remarkably cultivated *Trio*, laced with attractively sinuous Armenian ideas. Finally comes Prokofiev's *Overture on Hebrew themes*, another highly spontaneous piece, presented with real style. The recording is excellent throughout.

Navarra, André (cello), **Erika Kilcher** (piano)

Recital: *Sonatas* by: LOCATELLI; VALENTINI; BOCCHERINI: *in A & G.* GRANADOS: *Goyescas: Intermezzo.* FALLA: *Suite populaire espagnole* (arr. Maurice MARECHAL). NIN: *Chants d'Espagne: Saeta; Andalousie.*
(M) *** Cal. CAL 6673 [id.].

Navarra's recital dates from 1981 and shows this fine cellist in top form. He is splendidly partnered by Erika Kilcher who, although she is backwardly balanced in relation to the up-front cello (recorded somewhat dryly), makes a highly artistic contribution with her sympathetic accompaniments. This is immediately noticeable in the splendid opening sonata of Locatelli. But it is the four-movement work by Giuseppe Valentini which is the highlight of the Italian repertoire, a most engaging piece with an elegant *Gavotte* and an aria-like *Largo*, framed by two energetic outer movements in which Navarra's spiccato-like articulation of *moto perpeptuo* allegros is most infectious. He is equally at home in the Spanish half of the programme, and Kilcher joins him in providing colourful characterization of the five miniatures which make up the Falla suite. In the second of the two Nin pieces, *Andalousie*, Navarra sounds like a larger-than-life Spanish guitar. However, it is a pity that the documentation does not identify the Italian sonatas more positively.

Nettle and Markham (two-piano duo)

'In England': CARMICHAEL: *Puppet overture*. GRAINGER: *Country gardens; Lisbon; The brisk young sailor; The lost lady found; Handel in the Strand; English waltz*. VAUGHAN WILLIAMS: *Fantasia on Greensleeves*. WALTON: *Façade: Popular song; Tango pasodoble; Old Sir Faulk; Swiss yodelling song; Polka*. NICHOLAS: *Quiet peace No. 1*. DRING: *Fantastic variations on Lillibulero*. BRIDGE: *Sally in our alley*. COATES: *By the sleepy lagoon*. BLAKE: *Slow ragtime; Folk ballad*. GAY: *Lambeth Walk*. SCOTT: *Lotus Land*. LAMBERT: *3 Pièces nègres: Siesta*. WARLOCK: *Capriol suite: Pavane*. BRITTEN: *Mazurka elegiaca, Op. 23/2*. HOLST: *The Planets: Jupiter*.
(M) *** Carlton 30367 0017-2 [id.].

A recital of mostly brief lollipops lasting nearly 78 minutes might seem too much of a good thing, but Nettle and Markham play with such spirit that the result is almost always diverting. Perhaps they languish a bit in some of the slower pieces, *Greensleeves* and Warlock's *Pavane*, for instance; but for the most part the effect is highly spontaneous, and especially so in the Grainger items which are nicely sprinkled around the programme. *Lisbon*, *The brisk young sailor* and *The lost lady found* all come together, following neatly after Cyril Scott's *Lotus Land*, to make a winning triptych. The recording is excellent.

Nishizaki, Takako (violin)

'Romantic violin favourites' trans. Fritz Kreisler (with Wolf Harden, piano): SCHUBERT: *Rosamunde: Ballet music*. BIZET: *L'Arlésienne: Adagietto*. RIMSKY-KORSAKOV: *Le coq d'or: Hymn to the sun. Sadko: Hindu song. Scheherazade: Oriental dance*. DVORAK: *Songs my mother taught me*. GLUCK: *Orfeo ed Eurydice: Dance of the blessed spirits*. HAYDN: *Piano trio in G: Hungarian rondo. Austrian imperial hymn*. MOZART: *Haffner serenade: Rondo*. SCHUMANN: *Romance, Op. 94*. GRIEG: *Lyric piece: To the spring*. RAMEAU: *Tambourin*. GRAINGER: *Molly on the shore*. TRAD.: *Song of the Volga boatmen; Londonderry air*.
(BB) **(*) Naxos Dig. 8.550125 [id.].

'Violin miniatures' (with Jenö Jandó, piano): KREISLER: *Schön Rosmarin; Rondino; Liebesleid; Liebesfreud; Caprice viennoise*. RACHMANINOV: *Rhapsody on a theme by Paganini: Variation No. 18*. FIBICH: *Poème*. ELGAR: *Salut d'amour*. GRANADOS: *Spanish dance: Andaluza, Op. 37/5*. BRAHMS: *Hungarian dance No. 1*. SCHUBERT: *Moment musical in F min*. DVORAK: *Humoresque, Op. 101/7; Slavonic dance No. 1 in G min*. (all trans. Kreisler). BOCCHERINI: *Minuet*. DEBUSSY: *Clair de lune*. MASSENET: *Thaïs: Méditation*. TCHAIKOVSKY: *Chant sans paroles, Op. 2/3; Chanson triste, Op. 40/2*.
(BB) **(*) Naxos Dig. 8.550306 [id.].

Takako Nishizaki is a highly accomplished player who has recorded prolifically on the Marco Polo and Naxos labels. She has recorded Mozart sonatas with Jenö Jandó and a host of rare works, from Respighi's *Concerto gregoriano* to César Cui's *Suite concertante*. She delivers these miniatures with considerable charm and aplomb. Good recording – no one investing in these CDs is likely to be disappointed and, were there not even more virtuosic and authoritative versions in the catalogue, they would warrant an unqualified three stars.

Ogdon, John and **Brenda Lucas** (pianos)

RACHMANINOV: *Suites for 2 pianos Nos. 1 (Fantasy), Op. 5; 2 in C, Op. 17; Six pieces for piano duet, Op. 11; Polka italienne*. ARENSKY: *Suite for 2 pianos, Op. 15*. KHACHATURIAN: *Sabre dance*. SHOSTAKOVICH: *Concertino, Op. 94*. DEBUSSY: *Petite suite; Fêtes*. BIZET: *Jeux d'enfants*.
(B) **(*) EMI forte CZS5 69386-2 (2) [CDFB 69386].

John Ogdon and Brenda Lucas's readings of the two Rachmaninov *Suites*, not ideally imaginative but enjoyable nevertheless, are aptly coupled with other duet recordings made by them, including the delightful Arensky *Suite* which includes the famous waltz. It is good too to have the long-neglected *Concertino* of Shostakovich and the anything-but-neglected *Sabre dance*, which is rather heavy-going here. However, the Debussy *Petite suite* is very engaging, and most valuable of all is the complete recording of Bizet's *Jeux d'enfants* – all twelve movements. Only the five included by the composer in his orchestral suite are at all well known, and many of the others are equally charming, not least the opening *Rêverie* (*L'Escarpolette*), the Scherzo (*Les chevaux de bois*) and the *Nocturne* (*Colin-Mainard* – 'Blind man's buff'). Fine ensemble and sparkling fingerwork, but just occasionally a touch of rhythmic inflexibility. Good, mid-1970s recording.

Oslo Wind Ensemble

Scandinavian wind quintets: FERNSTROM: *Wind quintet, Op. 59.* KVANDAL: *Wind quintet, Op. 34; 3 Sacred Folktunes.* NIELSEN: *Wind quintet, Op. 43.*
(BB) ** Naxos Dig. 8.553050 [id.].

A super-bargain account of the Nielsen *Quintet*, more relaxed in its tempi and measured in approach than the account by the Scandinavian Quintet on Marco Polo. Very decently recorded, too. The Swedish musician, John Fernström, was a prolific composer whose output runs to twelve symphonies and much else besides. (He was for years solely represented in the catalogue by a *Concertino for flute, women's choir and small orchestra*). This *Wind quintet* is not quite so charming, but is well worth hearing – as, for that matter, is the *Wind quintet* by the Norwegian, Johan Kvandal, a thoughtful figure who is a composer of imagination and substance.

Paderewski, Ignace Jan (piano)

BEETHOVEN: *Sonata in C sharp min. (Moonlight), Op. 27/2.* CHOPIN: *Etudes: in E, Op. 10/3; in D flat, Op. 25/8; in G flat (Butterfly), Op. 25/9. Sonata No. 2 in B flat min. (Funeral march), Op. 35 (movts 3–4); Nocturne in F sharp, Op. 15/2; Polonaise in A flat (Heroic), Op. 53.* SCHUMANN: *Nachtstücke in F, Op. 23/4.* LISZT: *Grandes études de Paganini (La campanella), G.141/3; Hungarian rhapsody No. 10.* WAGNER: *Tristan und Isolde (prelude).* RACHMANINOV: *Prelude in C sharp min., Op. 32/12.* J. STRAUSS Jr: *Man lebt nur einmal, Op. 167.* PADEREWSKI: *Minuet in G, Op. 14/1.*
(M) (**) BMG/RCA mono GD 60923 [id.].

These famous recordings of popular repertoire which used to be found in so many pre-war homes come up pretty cleanly in these transfers. Although there is relatively little interest in Paderewski's recorded legacy these days – and it would be interesting to have heard him in his prime – his musicianship and finesse are never in question.

Pahud, Emmanuel (flute), Eric Le Sage (piano)

'The Romantic flute': BEETHOVEN: *Flute sonatas: in B flat* (attrib.); *in F, Op. 17* (arr. of *Horn sonata*). *Serenade (Trio) in D, Op. 25* (arr. for flute & piano). SCHUBERT: *Introduction and variations on a theme from 'La Belle Meunière' in D min., D.802. Arpeggione sonata, D.821. Sonatina in A min., D.385* (arr. for flute & piano). WEBER: *6 Sonatas for flute and piano, Op. 10; Piano sonata No. 2, Op. 39* (arr. for flute & piano).
(M) ** Audivis Valois Dig. V 4812 (3) [id.].

Emmanuel Pahud is an excellent player who has a pleasing timbre, who phrases most musically and shows considerable subtlety in the matter of light and shade. Eric le Sage is on the whole a good partner, except that at times his *forte* playing tends to overwhelm the flute, partly the fault of the recording. They are heard at their best in the six amiable but lightweight *Sonatas* of Weber (of which the composer thought very little), intended for violin; but in the companion arranged piano sonata, the resonant sound, a problem throughout this third disc, creates an almost ugly effect and certainly clouds the argument. The *Arpeggione Sonata* of Schubert works well in this combination: it is beautifully played. But one wonders why so much of this programme had to feature arrangements, when there is such a huge literature written for the flute. The stature of Beethoven's *Horn sonata* is sadly diminished and his engaging *Serenade Trio* loses much of its charm when a sometimes too-loud piano replaces the original violin and viola.

Payne, Joseph (organ of Vermont University)

Early French organ music: MARCHAND: *11 Pièces d'orgue, Livre II.* COMPERE: *Ave Maria gratia plena; Paranimphus salutat virginem.* JAPART: *Fortuna d'un grand tempo.* CORRETTE: *Messe du huitième ton* (complete). DE GRIGNY: *Hymns: Ave maris stella; A solis ortus (Crudelis Herodes); Fugue à 5.*
(BB) ** Naxos 8.553214 [id.].

This is an enterprising and generous (77 minutes) programme covering a wide range of music. Loyset Compère and Jean Japart lived in the latter half of the fifteenth century and their organ works must be among the earliest to have survived. Both the Marchand *Pièces* and the Corrette *Messe* bring plenty of colour and variety, and Joseph Payne registers everything effectively with a reedy tang which makes it sound French. The sound is full and clearly focused. The snag is the lack of an ecclesiastical ambience, something which is surely essential in a record of this kind, while less important at a live recital. André Isoir's recital on the organ at Bon Pasteur, Angers, is a far better choice for this repertoire (see above).

Perahia, Murray (piano)

25th Birthday Edition: Domenico SCARLATTI: *Sonatas in B min., Kk 27; A, Kk 212.* MOZART: *6 German dances, K.509; Adagio, K.540. Piano concerto No. 27 in B flat, K.595* (with COE). SCHUBERT: *Impromptu in A flat, D.899/4.* SCHUMANN: *Papillons, Op. 2.* CHOPIN: *Ballade No. 1 in G min., Op. 23; Piano concerto No. 2 in F min., Op. 21* (with Israel PO, Zubin Mehta). LISZT: *Gnomenreigen.* RACHMANINOV: *Etudes-tableaux: Nos. 5 in E flat; 6 in A min., Op. 39/5–6.* BARTOK: *Suite, Op. 14; Improvisations on Hungarian peasant songs, Op. 20; Out of doors suite.* BERG: *Sonata, Op. 1.* TIPPETT: *Sonata No. 1.* BEETHOVEN: *Piano and wind quintet in E flat, Op. 16* (with members of ECO). SCHUMANN: *5 Lieder, Op. 40.* BRAHMS: *Piano quartet No. 1 in G min., Op. 25* (with members of Amadeus Qt).
(M) *** Sony Dig./Analogue SX4K 63380 (4) [id.].

This 1997 anthology effectively celebrates Murray Perahia's fiftieth birthday and his 25-year recording association with CBS/Sony. Opening delightfully with two Scarlatti sonatas, the variety of music here readily confims Perahia's pianistic and artistic mastery over the widest musical range, with the Berg *Sonata* (attractively lyrical) and the Tippett (with its haunting *Andante tranquillo*) new to the catalogue. The recordings are technically a little variable but always good, often excellent, notably those made at the Maltings: the Mozart solo works, Liszt and Rachmaninov and the Beethoven *Piano and wind quintet*. The inclusion of the latter makes one wish that its Mozartian predecessor had also been featured, for that omission highlights the problem for many collectors: that, attractive as this mid-priced compilation is, it cuts across other issues which admirers of this great pianist may already possess.

Petri, Michala (recorder or flute)

'Recorder favourites' (with Hanne Petri, harpsichord, David Petri, cello): ANON.: *Greensleeves to a grounde; Divisions on an Italian ground.* Jacob VAN EYCK: *Prins Robberts Masco; Philis Schoon Herderinne; Wat Zal Men op den Avond Doen; Engels Nachtegaeltje.* CORELLI: *Sonata, Op. 15/5: La Folia.* HANDEL: *Andante.* LECLAIR: *Tambourin.* F. COUPERIN: *Le rossignol vainqueur; Le rossignol en amour.* J. S. BACH: *Siciliano.* TELEMANN: *Rondino.* GOSSEC: *Tambourin.* PAGANINI: *Moto perpetuo, Op. 11.* BRUGGEN: *2 Studies.* CHRISTIANSEN: *Satie auf hoher See.* HENRIQUES: *Dance of the midges.* SCHUBERT: *The Bee.* MONTI: *Czárdás.* HERBERLE: *Rondo presto.* RIMSKY-KORSAKOV: *Flight of the bumble-bee.*
(B) *** Ph. Virtuoso Dig. 420 897-2 [id.].

Marvellously nimble playing from Michala Petri, and 71 minutes, digitally recorded at bargain price, so one can afford to pick and choose. Some of the music opening the recital is less than distinctive, but the Couperin transcriptions are a delight and Paganini's *Moto perpetuo* vies with Henriques' *Dance of the midges* for sparkling bravura. There are some attractively familiar melodies by Bach and Handel, among others, to provide contrast, and Henning Christiansen's *Satie auf hoher See* is an unexpected treat. Monti's *Czárdás* ends the programme infectiously.

Pollini, Maurizio (piano)

STRAVINSKY: *3 movements from Petrushka.* PROKOFIEV: *Piano sonata No. 7 in B flat, Op. 83.* WEBERN: *Variations for piano, Op. 27.* BOULEZ: *Piano sonata No. 2.*
(M) *** DG 447 431-2 [id.].

The Prokofiev is a great performance, one of the finest ever committed to disc; and the Stravinsky *Petrushka* is electrifying. Not all those responding to this music will do so quite so readily to the Boulez, fine though the playing is; but the Webern also makes a very strong impression. This is the equivalent of two LPs and is outstanding value. It is a natural candidate for reissue in DG's set of 'Originals' of legendary performances.

Preston, Simon (organ)

'The world of the organ' (organ of Westminster Abbey): WIDOR: *Symphony No. 5: Toccata.* BACH: *Chorale prelude, Wachet auf, BWV 645.* MOZART: *Fantasia in F min., K.608.* WALTON: *Crown imperial* (arr. MURRILL). CLARKE: *Prince of Denmark's march* (arr. PRESTON). HANDEL: *Saul: Dead march.* PURCELL: *Trumpet tune* (arr. TREVOR). ELGAR: *Imperial march* (arr. MARTIN). VIERNE: *Symphony No. 1: Finale.* WAGNER: *Tannhäuser: Pilgrims' chorus.* GUILMANT: *March on a theme of Handel.* SCHUMANN: *Study No. 5* (arr. WEST). KARG-ELERT: *Marche triomphale (Now thank we all our God).*
(M) *** Decca 430 091-2; *430 091-4.*

A splendid compilation from the Argo catalogue of the early to mid-1960s, spectacularly recorded, which offers 69 minutes of music and is in every sense a resounding success. Simon Preston's account of the Widor *Toccata* is second to none, and both the Vierne *Finale* and the Karg-Elert *March triomphale* lend themselves admirably to Preston's unashamed flamboyance and the tonal splendour afforded by the Westminster acoustics. Walton's *Crown imperial*, too, brings a panoply of sound which compares very favourably with an orchestral recording. The organ has a splendid trumpet stop which makes both the Purcell piece and Clarke's *Prince of Denmark's march*, better known as the '*Trumpet voluntary*', sound crisply regal.

Puyana, Rafael (harpsichord)

'The Golden Age of harpsichord music': ANON.: *My Lady Carey's Dompe.* BULL: *Les Buffons; The King's hunt.* PEERSON: *The Primerose; The fall of the leafe.* BYRD: *La Volta.* PHILIPS: *Pavana dolorosa; Galliard dolorosa.* BESARD: *Branle gay.* Louis COUPERIN: *Tombeau de M. de Blancrocher; Pavane.* Antoine FRANCISQUE: *Branle de Montiradé.* BACH: *Keyboard concerto in D min., after Marcello.* FREIXANET: *Sonata in A.* Mateo ALBENIZ: *Sonata in D.* CHAMBONNIERS: *Le Moutier* (after Louis Couperin). RAMEAU: *Gavotte et Doubles.* DIEUPART: *Passepied.* François COUPERIN: *La Pantomime.*
❀ (M) *** [Mercury 434 364-2].

If you think you don't enjoy listening to the harpsichord, Rafael Puyana, who was a pupil of Landowska, will surely persuade you otherwise in this remarkably diverse, 75-minute recital, for he is a supreme master of his instrument. He plays a large, modern, double-keyboard Pleyel harpsichord (replicating one of Landowska's own instruments). In his bravura hands it produces an astonishingly wide range of dynamic, colour and sonority, no better demonstrated than in the *Gavotte et Doubles* of Rameau, which is a continuously inventive set of variations, running on for about ten minutes. Puyana effectively uses every possible device to divert his listeners, to say nothing of demonstrating his own dexterity, which he does again more simply in the engagingly brief *Passepied* of Charles Dieupart (who died in 1740). Martin Peerson's modest variations on a popular song of the period, *The Primerose*, and the more dolorous evocation of *The fall of the leafe* both feature the highly effective dynamic contrasts which this instrument can provide.

The programme opens with the piquant *My Lady Carey's Dompe*, a lollipop if ever there was one, presented with great panache. John Bull's divisions on *Les Buffons* and *The King's Hunt* have never sounded more vital, while Puyana's account of the charming *La Volta* of William Byrd makes one appreciate why it was reputedly a favourite dance of Queen Elizabeth I. Perhaps Puyana goes over the top a bit in his robust presentation of the pieces by Peter Philips, and he plays Bach's *Concerto in D minor* (supposedly after Alessandro Marcello, but sounding more like Vivaldi) in such a robust manner that it is almost if he were sitting at the keyboard of an organ. But the crisply articulated *Sonata* of Freixanet is very effective indeed, and the *Sonata* of Mateo Albéniz is a *tour de force*. The instrument's resonant lower octave is really made to tell in Louis Couperin's *Tombeau*; while the elegant *Le Moutier* of Jacques Champion de Chambonnières brings a nice sonic contrast on three different levels, within a time period of just over two minutes. The Mercury recording is real and vivid, but please don't set the volume level too high. This is one of two harpsichord compilations that deserve a place in every collection: the other is George Malcolm's Decca anthology, '*The World of the harpsichord*', utterly different but equally rewarding – see above. Alas, the Puyana disc has now been withdrawn in the UK.

Richter, Sviatoslav (piano)

'Sviatoslav Richter in the 1950s', Volume 1: PROKOFIEV: *Cinderella: 5 Pieces; Visions fugitives, Op. 22: excerpts; Piano sonata No. 7 in B flat, Op. 83*. SCHUMANN: *Toccata in C, Op. 7*. DEBUSSY: *Images, Book II: Cloches à travers les feuilles* (2 performances). CHOPIN: *Etudes: in C & E* (2 performances), *Op. 10/1 & 3*. RACHMANINOV: *Preludes: in F sharp min., Op. 23/1; in B flat, Op. 23/2; in D, Op. 23/4; in G min., Op. 23/5; in C min., Op. 23/7; in A flat, Op. 23/8; in A, Op. 31/9; in C, Op. 32/1; in B flat min., Op. 32/2; in F, Op. 32/7; in B min., Op 32/10; in G sharp min., Op. 32/12; in G sharp min., Op. 32/15*. TCHAIKOVSKY: *Piano sonata in G, Op. 37*. LISZT: *Valse oubliée No. 1*.
(M) (***) Parnassus mono PACD 96–001/2 [id.].

We owe this double-pack of Richter to the dedication of some enthusiasts who have tracked down a considerable number of live performances from the 1950s which have never been issued before, before his star had risen in the West. The unsigned liner-note claims that Richter was 'perhaps even more of a virtuoso than the more mature artist' and that 'he was more willing to dazzle audiences with his facility'. Another claim the producer makes, and one that must be upheld, is that 'the recorded sound while not the ultimate in fidelity is superior to what we might have expected from early Russian tapes'. The first CD brings some dazzling Prokofiev, recorded in Moscow in April 1958. The transcriptions from *Cinderella*, *Visions fugitives* and the *Seventh Sonata* are little short of amazing. (The sonata was recorded two months before the BMG/Melodiya version made at a recital in the Great Hall of the Moscow Conservatoire, which is every bit as electrifying, though the BMG is better recorded.) The producer's claim that Richter took more risks in this concert performance of the Schumann *Toccata* than in the safer but still stunning DG studio recording later the same year is also on target.

The Tchaikovsky *G major Sonata*, Op. 37, comes from another Moscow recital from December 1954, two years before the BMG account, which also includes two of the pieces from his later recital (the *Cloches à travers les feuilles* and the Chopin *E major study*, Op. 10, No. 3). Richter also recorded the Tchaikovsky sonata in the studio in the mid-1950s (it was issued in the UK on Parlophone). We would not wish to choose between the two presently before the public; what is undeniable is that both are pretty sensational. (There are some barely discernible bumps in the slow movement but the transfers are otherwise excellent.) So, for that matter, are the 11 Rachmaninov *Preludes* in this recital. What pianisim!

'Sviatoslav Richter in the 1950s', Volume 2: MUSSORGSKY: *Pictures at an exhibition*. SCHUMANN: *Abegg variations, Op. 1; 3 Fantasiestücke, Op. 12; Humoreske in B flat, Op. 20*. SCRIABIN: *12 Preludes, Op. 11; Sonatas Nos. 2 in G sharp min., Op. 19; 6, Op. 62*. TCHAIKOVSKY: *Piano concerto No. 1 in B flat min., Op. 23* (with USSR State SO, Nathan Rachlin).
(M) (**(*)) Parnassus mono PACD 96–003/4 [id.].

The earliest performances here are the Mussorgsky *Pictures* and the Scriabin *Sixth Sonata*, which come from a 1952 Moscow recital. The BMG/Melodiya account comes from 1958, the same year as the famous Sofia recital, while their recording of the Scriabin comes three years later, in 1955. The other Scriabin repertoire, along with the Schumann pieces, come from June 1955 and the Tchaikovsky concerto with Nathan Rachlin from 1957. Though the playing is again dazzling, the orchestral recording is coarse and climaxes discolour, and in the climaxes the engineers can be heard reducing the level to avoid overloading. Apart from this, Richter is in a class of his own, and aficianados will surely want this.

DEBUSSY: *Estampes; Préludes, Book I: Voiles; Le vent dans la plaine; Les collines d'Anacapri*. PROKOFIEV: *Visions fugitives, Op. 22, Nos. 3, 6 & 9; Sonata No. 8 in B flat, Op. 84*. SCRIABIN: *Sonata No. 5 in F sharp, Op. 53*.
(M) *** DG 423 573-2.

The Debussy *Préludes* and the Prokofiev *Sonata* were recorded at concerts during an Italian tour in 1962, while the remainder were made the previous year in Wembley Town Hall. The former sound more open than the rather confined studio acoustic – but what playing! The Scriabin is demonic and the Debussy could not be more atmospheric. The performance of the Prokofiev *Sonata* is, like the legendary Gilels account, a classic of the gramophone. But these performances and much more are now available on the DG Double below.

Recital: BACH: *Well-tempered Klavier: Preludes and fugues Nos. 1–6, BWV 846–53.* HAYDN: *Piano sonata in G min.* SCHUBERT: *Allegretto in C min., D.915; Ländler in A, D.366.* CHOPIN: *Polonaise-fantaisie, Op. 61; Etudes: in C; C min. (Revolutionary), Op. 10/7 & 12.* SCHUMANN: *Abegg variations, Op. 1.* DEBUSSY: *Estampes; Préludes: Voiles; Le vent dans la plaine; Les collines d'Anacapri.* SCRIABIN: *Sonata No. 5 in F sharp min., Op. 53.* RACHMANINOV: *Prelude in G sharp min., Op. 32/12.* PROKOFIEV: *Visions fugitives, Op. 22/3, 6 & 9; Sonata No. 8 in B flat, Op. 84.*
❀ (B) *** DG Double 447 355-2 [id.].

This remarkable Richter treasury collects many of the stereo recordings he made for DG (or which were licensed to DG) between 1962 and 1965, including those on the single disc listed above. They are all of good quality and often the sound is excellent, if a little dry. The recordings, taken from live recitals during his Italian tour, bring a cough or two. The opening Bach *Preludes and fugues* immediately bring rapt concentration. The Chopin selection opens with a wonderfully poetic account of the *Polonaise-fantaisie*, and the *Revolutionary study* is almost overwhelming in its excitement. The audience noises may be found intrusive both here and in the superb Debussy performances, yet *Jardins sous la pluie* is quite magical, as is the gentle exoticism of *Pagodes* (both from *Estampes*). Richter's Schumann is no less special, and in the delicious account of the Schubert *Ländler* one can sense the smile in his eyes. Both in the Scriabin and Prokofiev *Sonatas* it is the powerful dynamism of Richter's technique that projects the music so vividly, but of course there is much poetic feeling too. As an inexpensive cross-section of his art, this could hardly be bettered.

'In Memoriam – Legendary recordings (1959–1962)': BACH: *Well-tempered Klavier, Book I: Preludes and fugues Nos. 1, 4–6 & 8, BWV 846, 849/51 & 853.* HAYDN: *Sonata in G min., Hob XVI: 44.* CHOPIN: *Ballades Nos. 3 in A flat, Op. 47; 4 in F min., Op. 52; Polonaise-fantaisie in A flat, Op. 61; Etudes: in C; C min. (Revolutionary), Op. 10/1 & 12.* SCHUBERT: *Allegretto in C min., D.915. Ländler, D.366/1, 3 & 4–5.* SCHUMANN: *Abegg variations, Op. 1.* DEBUSSY: *Estampes; Préludes, Book I: Voiles; Le vent dans la plaine; Les collines d'Anacapri.* RACHMANINOV: *Preludes Nos. 3 in B flat; 5 in D; 6 in G min.; 8 in C min., Op. 23/2, 4–5 & 7; 12 in C; 13 in B flat; 23 in G sharp min., Op. 32/1–2 & 12.* PROKOFIEV: *Visions fugitives, Op. 22/3, 6 & 9.*
(B) *** DG Double 457 667-2 (2) [id.].

Over the years DG have made a number of different collections from the recordings Richter made at live recitals while on tour in Europe between 1959 and 1962. The present programme extends the Chopin coverage to include two *Ballades*, volatile, highly individual performances; the number of Rachmaninov *Preludes* is also increased to cover virtually all the favourites. The remastered recordings – the quality varies somewhat between items – are for the most part very good, though audience noises inevitably intrude at times. The compelling accounts of the Scriabin and Prokofiev *Sonatas* previously included are here omitted. Each disc is generously full and the set is highly recommendable. The discography details are as follows: Rachmaninov *Preludes* (except Op. 32/12): Warsaw, 1959; Haydn *Sonata*, Chopin Op. 47, Debussy *Préludes*: Wembley Town Hall, 1961; Bach, Prokofiev, Chopin (except Op. 47), Debussy *Estampes*, Rachmaninov Op. 32/12, Schubert, Schumann: Italian tour, 1962.

Melodiya Richter Edition (complete)

(M) (*(**)) RCA mono 74321 29460-2 (10) [id.].

Volume 1: BACH: *English suite No. 3 in G min., BWV 808. Piano concerto in D min., BWV 1052* (with USSR SO, Kurt Sanderling). *Double piano concerto in C, BWV 1061* (with Anatoly Vedernikov, Moscow CO, Barshai).
(M) (**) RCA mono 74321 29461-2 [id.].

Volume 2: BEETHOVEN: *Piano sonatas Nos. 8 in C min. (Pathétique); 23 in F min. (Appassionata), Op. 57; Bagatelles, Op. 33/3 & 5; Op. 119/ 2, 7 & 9; Op. 126/1, 4 & 6.*
(M) (**(*)) RCA mono 74321 29462-2 [id.].

Volume 3: SCHUBERT: *Piano sonatas Nos. 16 in A min., D.845; 17 in D, D.850.*
(M) (***) RCA mono 74321 29463-2 [id.].

Volume 4: SCHUMANN: *Fantasiestücke, Op. 12; Humoreske in B flat, Op. 20; Novelleten, Op. 21.*
(M) (***) RCA mono 74321 29464-2 [id.].

Volume 5: SCHUBERT: *Moments musicaux, D.780/1, 3 & 6.* CHOPIN: *Etudes: in E, Op. 10/3; in E min., Op. 25/5. Polonaise No. 1 in C sharp min., Op. 26/1.* FRANCK: *Prélude, choral et fugue.* BARTOK: *15 Hungarian peasant songs.*
(M) (**(*)) RCA mono 74321 29465-2 [id.].

Volume 6: CHOPIN: *Piano concerto No. 2 in F min., Op. 21* (with USSR SO, Svetlanov). SAINT-SAENS: *Piano concerto No. 5 in F, Op. 103.* FRANCK: *Les Djinns* (both with Moscow Youth O, Kondrashin).
(M) (*(**)) RCA mono 74321 29466-2 [id.].

Volume 7: RACHMANINOV: *Piano concertos Nos. 1 in F sharp min., Op. 1; 2 in C min., Op. 18* (with USSR R. & TV Large SO or Leningrad PO, both cond. Kurt Sanderling).
(M) (***) RCA mono 74321 29467-2 [id.].

Volume 8: RIMSKY-KORSAKOV: *Piano concerto in C sharp min., Op. 30.* GLAZUNOV: *Piano concerto No. 1 in F min., Op. 92.* PROKOFIEV: *Piano concerto No. 1 in D flat, Op. 10* (with Moscow Youth O, Kondrashin).
(M) ((***)) RCA mono 74321 29468-2 [id.].

Volume 9: TCHAIKOVSKY: *Piano sonata in G, Op. 37.* MUSSORGSKY: *Pictures at an exhibition.*
(M) (**(*)) RCA mono 74321 29469-2 [id.].

Volume 10: SCRIABIN: *12 Etudes: Op. 2/1; Op. 8/5 & 11; Op. 42/2–6 & 8; Op. 65/1–3; Piano sonata No. 6, Op. 62.* MIASKOVSKY: *Piano sonata No. 3 in C min., Op. 19.* PROKOFIEV: *Piano sonata No. 7 in B flat, Op. 83.*
(M) ((***)) RCA mono 74321 29470-2 [id.].

All these discs which Richter made for the Melodiya label are available separately; the only gain in acquiring them all is a sturdy slipcase. Each disc is annotated separately, and the annotations are all authoritative and full of interest. Most of these recordings will be familiar to collectors of the older generation, but not all of them were issued on Western labels. The oldest of the recordings is of the *G minor English Suite*, which comes from 1948 when Richter would have been in his early thirties and, for all its sonic limitations, it is wonderfully alive. The *Bach D minor Concerto*, made in 1955 with Kurt Sanderling, originally appeared in the UK in a Parlophone series called 'Music from the USSR' not long after Richter's breakthrough Schumann recital on DG. At that time it was coupled with his Rachmaninov *First* from the same year – a dazzling performance, which here appears more logically coupled in the seventh volume of the set with the *Second*, made in 1959 (not as well recorded as his DG set with Stanislaw Wislocki and the Warsaw Philharmonic the following year); but some feel the 1959 version to be a stronger performance, and certainly the orchestral support is impressive.

The Beethoven performances are of early provenance and call for some tolerance as far as the actual sound is concerned, though they are a great improvement on such original Melodiya LPs as we have. The *Pathétique* and the *Bagatelles* come from 1948 and 1955, and the recordings are shallow and a bit clangorous at climaxes. The *Appassionata* was recorded at a public concert in 1960 and was Richter's own preferred version. (He was not satisfied with the studio performance he made with RCA in America.) These are all performances of stature. The *Choral Fantasy*, sung in Russian, comes from 1952 and, although the sound calls for some tolerance, the performance is tremendously compelling.

The Schubert *Sonata in A minor*, D.845, had a disc to itself (with an *Impromptu* as fill-up) when it appeared on blue-label Melodiya LPs, complete with wow, swish and fairly heavy background noise, and it is good to renew its acquaintance in more acceptable sound. (These LPs were never officially issued here but were obtainable in an austere, sleeveless presentation for a derisory sum.) Although Richter made later Schubert recordings for EMI, this *A minor* is in a class of its own for sheer depth of feeling. The two Schubert sonatas were recorded in mono in 1957–8.

Like Perahia, Richter has a special feeling for Schumann. The *Humoreske* in this set is the 1956 account mentioned above, and the *Fantasiestücke* come from roughly the same period as the famous DG LP, which was also recorded in 1956 while Richter was in Prague. If you have the DG disc, there is no need to add the present issue to your library except for the sake of the magisterial *Humoreske*.

The Schubert and Chopin on the next disc are of early provenance (1952), and again the recording is wanting in freshness and bloom – but not the playing! The Franck was made four years later and the Bartók comes from 1972. Like so much in this collection, it is self-recommending.

The Chopin *Concerto No. 2 in F minor* and the Saint-Saëns *Fifth Concerto*, the so-called *Egyptian*, are much less well-known and the dated sound-quality of the Saint-Saëns and Franck couplings, which come from 1952–3, may perhaps have limited their wider dissemination, though the RCA engineers have freshened them up considerably – and many will tolerate the shallowness and distortion of the climaxes for the sake of the performance. The *F minor Concerto* is of much later provenance (1966) and, though the sound is hardly the 'highest of fi', it is serviceable.

The Russian concertos on Volume 6 have all been available at one time or another in the 1950s and '60s though the recordings sounded execrable. The Glazunov, recorded way back in 1952, has never been better played, and the same probably holds for the Rimsky-Korsakov, which Richter made with Kondrashin in 1950. The Prokofiev from 1952 is simply dazzling and is perhaps even more remarkable than the later (and better-recorded) version he made in Prague with Karel Ančerl. However, while the RCA engineers have improved the sound, there are limits to what even they can do with the shrill, hollow orchestral climaxes which suffer from distortion.

The famous 1956 account of the Tchaikovsky *Sonata in G major* shared a Parlophone disc with the Schumann *Humoreske* and is one (if not *the*) classic account of the piece on disc. The 1958 *Pictures at an exhibition* is not to be confused with the live performance Richter gave in Sofia, which was released on Philips. The Melodiya recording might at best be described as 'so-so'. (The notes remind us that Richter is an accomplished painter himself.)

The Scriabin *Etudes* come from 1952, and the *Sixth Sonata* was recorded three years later; he penetrates this music as few artists do. The Miaskovsky *Third Sonata*, recorded in 1953, is an interesting work and it is difficult to envisage more sympathetic advocacy. Much the same must be said of the stunning, demonic account Richter gives of the *Seventh Sonata* which makes most other pianists sound quite tame. Richter had given the first Moscow performance of this sonata in 1943 and this 1958 account finds him at the height of his powers. This extraordinary performance comes over in spite of all the distortion.

To sum up: despite the skill and dedication of those concerned with this project, considerable allowances have to be made for shallow sound-quality, and sometimes distortion too, while the occasional cough can disturb the listener in the live performances. However, allowances are worth making, as most of these performances find Richter in his youthful prime. For those who do not want the whole box, prime recommendations lie with the Schubert sonatas (Volume 3), the Rachmaninov concertos (7), the Tchaikovsky *G major Sonata* and the *Pictures* (9), and the stunning Prokofiev *Seventh Sonata* (10).

Robles, Marisa (harp)

'The world of the harp': FALLA: *Three-cornered Hat: Danza del corregidor*. ALBENIZ: *Rumores de Caleta; Torre bermeja*. BIDAOLA: *Viejo zortzico*. EBERL (attrib. Mozart): *Theme, variations and rondo pastorale*. BEETHOVEN: *Variations on a Swiss song*. BRITTEN: *Ceremony of carols: Interlude*. FAURE: *Impromptu, Op. 86*. PIERNE: *Impromptu-caprice, Op. 9*. SALZEDO: *Chanson de la nuit*. BRAHMS: *Lullaby*. BACH: *Well-tempered Clavier: Prelude No. 1*. CHOPIN: *Mazurka, Op. 7/1; Prelude, Op. 28/15 (Raindrop)*. HASSELMANS: *La source*.
(M) *** Decca 433 869-2 [436 293-2].

The artistry of Marisa Robles ensures that this is a highly attractive anthology and the programme is as well chosen as it is beautifully played. As ex-Professor of the harp at the Madrid Conservatory, Miss Robles has a natural affinity for the Spanish music that opens her programme, and other highlights include a magnetic account of the Britten *Interlude* and the Salzedo *Chanson de la nuit* with its bell-like evocations. The Eberl *Variations* are highly engaging. The excellent recordings derive from the Argo catalogue of the 1960s and '70s, except for the Chopin, Brahms, Bach and Hasselmans pieces, which have been added to fill out the present reissue (75 minutes). The delicious Hasselmans roulades are the epitome of nineteenth-century harp writing. The CD has a most realistic presence.

Romantic piano sonatas

'Great Romantic piano sonatas': CHOPIN: *Sonata No. 2 in B flat min. (Funeral march), Op. 35*. LISZT: *Sonata in B min.* (Rafael Orozco); *Années de pèlerinage: Sonetto 104 del Petrarca* (Claudio Arrau). SCHUMANN: *Sonata No. 2 in G min., Op. 22* (Dinorah Varsi). SCHUBERT: *Sonata No. 21 in B flat, D.960* (Ingrid Haebler). TCHAIKOVSKY: *Sonata in G, Op. 37* (Paul Crossley). SCRIABIN: *Sonata No. 4, Op. 30* (Jean Louis Steuerman).
(B) ** Ph. Duo 442 617-2 (2).

Philips do not always field their first team for this admittedly generous 151 minutes of Romantic piano music. Ingrid Haebler gives a relatively intimate reading of Schubert's greatest piano work; but if the scale is small, the playing is appealing and she makes the finale very much her own. Dinorah Varsi gives a good account of herself in Schumann, but this performance does not really take pride of place in the catalogue. Rafael Orozco is direct and musical in Chopin, but this performance becomes really special only in the central section of the slow movement. His Liszt *Sonata* is another matter: bold, ambitious in scale and very commanding indeed, and strikingly well recorded. Arrau follows with the *Petrarch Sonnet*, which has a finely calculated atmosphere and is remarkably gripping. But he is no more arresting than Orozco. Paul Crossley does not quite catch the grand manner of the Tchaikovsky, but he plays the work spontaneously and musically, with a finely shaped slow movement. Steuerman opens Scriabin's Op. 30 impressively, but the *Prestissimo volando* is less firmly controlled, not helped by a very resonant recording.

Romero, Pepe (guitar)

Spanish music (with (i) Celín Romero): ANON.: *Jeux interdits*. ALBENIZ: *Suite española, Op. 47: Sevilla; Granada. Recuerdos de viaje, Op. 71: Rumores de la caleta. Mallorca* (barcarolle), *Op. 202. España (6 hojas de álbum), Op. 165: Asturias;* (i) *Tango*. GRANADOS: (i) *Danzas españolas, Op. 37: Andaluza; Goyescas: Intermezzo*. Celedonio ROMERO: *Malagueña; Romantico*. TARREGA: *Capricho arabe; Pavana*. SOR: *Introduction & variations on a theme by Mozart, Op. 9*.
(M) **(*) Ph. (IMS) Dig. 434 727-2.

A thoroughly professional and immaculately played collection of favourites. The effect is intimate, pleasing rather than electrifying – the virtuoso showing his paces in familiar pieces. The flamenco-based pieces by the performer's father, Celedonio, bring a sudden hint of fire. For the reissue Celín Romero joins his brother for three duets, and this brings added spontaneity, although the intimate mood remains – witness the Granados *Spanish dance* which does not have the electricity of Julian Bream's solo version. The recording is very natural, but no information is provided about the music (except titles).

Rosenberger, Carol (piano)

'Such stuff as dreams – A Lullaby album for children and adults': Disc I: SCHUMANN: *Scenes from childhood: About faraway lands and people*. KABALEVSKY: *A little tale; Dance on the lawn, Op. 27, Book I/1 & 15; Cradle song, Book II/5*. SCHUBERT: *Impromptus: in B flat, D.899/3: Andante* (only); *in A flat, D.899/2*. BARTOK: *For children: Lost loves; Rose garden, Op. 42/3 & 26*. MOZART: *Sonata in A, K.331: Andante grazioso* (excerpt); *Sonata in F, K.332: Adagio*. BEETHOVEN: *Sonata in E, Op. 109: Andante molto cantable* (excerpt). GRIEG: *In my homeland, Op. 43/3*. RAVEL: *Sonatine: Minuet*. DEBUSSY: *Prélude: La fille aux cheveux de lin*. BRAHMS: *Waltzes in E and A flat, Op. 39/2 & 15* (excerpts). *Intermezzo in A, Op. 8/2*. SATIE: *Gymnopédie No. 1*. MENDELSSOHN: *Songs without words: in A, Op. 19/4; in E flat, Op. 67/1; in D, Op. 85/4; in D, Op. 102/4*. Disc II: SCHUBERT: *Impromptu in B flat, D.899/2*. MOZART: *Sonata No. 11 in A, K.331*. BEETHOVEN: *Sonata No. 30 in E, Op. 109*.
(B) * Delos Dig. Double DE 3230 [id.].

Many many be tempted by the title of this collection and by its pretty frontispiece. However, many of the pieces on the first disc are merely snippets and, with the chosen tempi consistently slow – often to the point of deliberation – the effect soon becomes enervating. One of the most enjoyable performances here is of the Brahms *Intermezzo*, which is not cut, but Debussy's portrait of *The girl with the flaxen hair*, the essence of simplicity, is spoilt by unnecessary rubato. The performances of the major works on the second disc are acceptable but insubstantial, particularly the Beethoven, where the closing slow movement is very near to being sentimentalized. The recording is very real and truthful.

Rubinstein, Artur (piano)

'Carnegie Hall highlights': DEBUSSY: *Préludes, Book I: La cathédral engloutie; Book II: Ondine. Images, Book I: Hommage à Rameau; Book II: Poissons d'or*. SZYMANOWSKI: *Mazurkas, Op. 50/1–4*. PROKOFIEV: *12 Visions fugitives from Op 22*. VILLA-LOBOS: *Prole do bebê*. SCHUMANN: *Arabesque, Op. 18*. ALBENIZ: *Navarra*.
(M) *** BMG/RCA 09026 61445-2 [id.].

Rubinstein was still at his technical peak when these recordings were made during a series of recitals at Carnegie Hall in October, November and December 1961. The performances are wonderfully poised and spontaneous, and the technical accuracy is little short of amazing when one realizes there were no tape splices here. The Debussy pieces are musically outstanding (Rubinstein announces *Ondine* himself, so it must have been an encore, and he plays it beautifully). The Szymanowski *Mazurkas* have wonderful style and the Prokofiev miniatures show an amazing range of colour and sharp characterization. The titles (*Con eleganza – Pittoresco*; *Ridicolosamente*; *Con vivacità*; *Con una dolce lentezza*; *Dolente*; *Feroce* and the slightly misleading *Allegretto tranquillo*) all speak for themselves. The Villa-Lobos suite of dolls is delightful and the closing *Clown doll* (*Polichinelle*) brings fabulous articulation. After the Schumann *Arabesque*, Rubinstein finds a closing burst of passion for Albéniz's *Navarra*, and the audience's response confirms that this was a closing item. But apart from the applause, the audience is remarkably unobtrusive.

'The music of France': (a) RAVEL: *Valses nobles et sentimentales; Le tombeau de Couperin: Forlane. Miroirs: La vallée des cloches.* POULENC: *3 Mouvements perpétuels; Intermezzi: in A flat; in D flat.* FAURE: *Nocturne in A flat, Op. 33/3.* CHABRIER: *Pièce pittoresque No. 10: Scherzo-valse.* (b) DEBUSSY: *Estampes: La soirée dans Grenade; Jardins sous la pluie; Images, Book I: Hommage à Rameau; Reflets dans l'eau; Book 2: Poissons d'or. La plus que lente; Préludes, Book I: Minstrels.*
(M) *** BMG/RCA (a) stereo / (b) mono 09026 61446-2 [id.].

The main part of this recital dates from 1963. The playing is eminently aristocratic and full of insights. The Ravel pieces and the Poulenc could hardly be bettered. The recording has been further enhanced in the present transfer and has both sonority and presence – it is finer than the Carnegie Hall recordings listed above. The Debussy programme derives from 78s made in 1945 and a 1952 mono LP (*Minstrels* is a very striking account). Indeed all the performances are well worth having, especially *Reflets dans l'eau* where the sound is remarkably open.

Russian Baroque Ensemble

'Chamber music from the court of St Petersburg': STARTZER: *Divertimento in A min.* TITZ: *String quartet in G; Violin sonata in F sharp min.* BAILLOT: *Russian air.* MADONIS: *12 Diverse symphonies.* BEREZOVSKY: *Violin sonata in C.* STEIBELT: *Variations on 2 Russian folksongs.*
(BB) **(*) Arte Nova Dig. 74321 51626-2 (2) [id.].

All but one of these still obscure composers came from outside the Russian empire but gravitated to the court in St Petersburg, writing attractive and civilized, if hardly original, music like this. The exception, Maxim Berezovsky, represented here by a fresh, lively *Violin sonata*, came from the Ukraine. In this two-disc collection, much the longest and most ambitious work is the *Quartet in G* by the German, Anton Titz (1742–1810), with an extraordinarily ambitious first movement which alone lasts 20 minutes. He is also represented by a fine *Violin sonata in F sharp minor*. The only signs of ethnic Russian influence come in three sets of variations on Russian themes, and they are just as completely translated to the Viennese tradition as those in Beethoven's *Rasumovsky Quartets*. The performances on period instruments are lusty and heartfelt rather than subtle, given close recording to match. A fascinating, unusual offering.

Russian Piano School

Russian Piano School: *'The great pianists'* Volumes 1–10.

RCA/Melodiya are currently offering eleven CDs that survey the Russian piano tradition from the generation of Goldenweiser and Neuheus, whose pianistic pedigree goes back to the nineteenth-century masters, through to such younger virtuosi as Pletnev and Kissin. All of them have been digitally remastered with great care with 20-bit technology and NoNoise processing and, though the results are inevitably variable (particularly in the earlier recordings), the series affords an invaluable opportunity to steep oneself in the Russian pianistic tradition. Although the set is available in a slipcase, with a small saving in cost (74321 25172-2), the discs are also available separately at mid-price.

Goldenweiser, Alexander Borisovich

Volume 1: ARENSKY: *Forgotten rhythms: Sari, Op. 28/4.* BORODIN: *Petite suite: Mazurka.* GOLDENWEISER: *Song and dance.* MEDTNER: *Novella in C min., Op. 17/2.* RACHMANINOV: *Morceaux de salon: Barcarolle in G min., Op. 10/3. Suite No. 2, Op. 17* (with Grigori Ginsburg). TCHAIKOVSKY: *Dialogue in B, Op. 72/8; Meditation, Op. 72/5; Romance in F, Op. 51/5; Valse sentimentale in F min., Op 51/6.*
(M) (***) RCA mono 74321 25173-2 [id.].

Alexander Goldenweiser (1875–1961) was a pupil of Siloti, Rachmaninov's cousin and himself a pupil of Liszt, and his class-mates at the Moscow Conservatoire included Scriabin, Rachmaninov and Medtner. His composition studies were with Arensky, Ippolitov-Ivanov and Taneyev, all pupils of Tchaikovsky. He lived to be eighty-six and recorded these pieces between 1946 and 1955, when he would have been in his seventies. His own pupils included Tatiana Nikolayeva, Lazar Berman, Dmitri Bashkirov and the composer Kabalevsky. Of particular interest is his powerful 1948 recording of the Rachmaninov *Second*

Suite (with Grigori Ginsburg as the second pianist), since the composer dedicated the piece to him. He wears his virtuosity lightly and, like all the greatest pianists, his lightness of touch leaves one unaware of hammers. The Tchaikovsky pieces of Op. 72 have a particularly touching quality. The recordings come up surprisingly well, given their age.

Neuhaus, Heinrich

Volume 2: MOZART: *Rondo in A min., K.511; Sonata in D for two pianos, K.448* (with Stanislav Neuhaus). DEBUSSY: *Préludes, Books I & II: Danseuses de Delphes; La sérénade interrompue; La puerta del vino; Des pas sur la neige; Les sons et les parfums tournent dans l'air du soir; Les collines d'Anacapri; Bruyères; Minstrels.* PROKOFIEV: *Visions fugitives, Op. 22.*
(M) (***) RCA mono 74321 25174-2 [id.].

Heinrich Neuheus (1888–1964) is one of the most legendary figures among Russian pianists, the teacher of Richter and Gilels among others, a cousin of Szymanowski, much spoken of but scarcely glimpsed on a record label. He studied with Tausig and Godowsky before going on to become an influential teacher, as was his son, Stanislav (1927–80), with whom he recorded the Mozart *Sonata in D major*, K.488, in 1950. The eight Debussy *Préludes*, recorded in 1946 and 1948, have a powerful atmosphere and a refined sense of colour. Acceptable sound, though with not a great deal of top. It is difficult to imagine the *Visions fugitives*, recorded in 1956 when Neuheus was in his late sixties, being played with greater character.

Feinberg, Samuil

Volume 3: BACH, trans. Feinberg: *Sonata No. 5 in C, BWV 529: Largo. Chorale preludes: Allein Gott in der Höh sei Ehr, BWV 711; Allein Gott in der Höh sei Ehr, BWV 662* (two versions); *Wer nur den lieben Gott lässt walten, BWV 647; Allein Gott in der Höh sei Ehr, BWV 663.* MOZART: *Piano sonatas Nos. 4 in E flat, K.282; 18 in D, K.576; Fantasia and fugue in C, K.394; 12 Variations on an allegretto in B flat, K.500.*
(M) (***) RCA mono/stereo 74321 25175-2 [id.].

Samuil Yevgenyevich Feinberg (1890–1972) was a pupil of Goldenweiser and will be one of the discoveries of this collection for many non-specialist collectors. So wide a range of colour and sonority does he command that one is at times tempted to believe that there is more than one pianist playing. His style has a melting lyricism, a limpid tone-quality and a miraculous *pianissimo*; his sonority is of exceptional richness and finesse. He is the opposite of the modern jet-setting virtuoso, and the transcriptions of the Bach organ works and the Mozart are of altogether exceptional beauty. The recordings date from 1951 to 1953, with the exception of four of his Bach transcriptions, which date from 1962. The recordings are very acceptable indeed: playing of this artistry deserves the widest dissemination.

Yudina, Maria

Volume 4: BARTOK: *Mikrokosmos, Books 5 & 6:* excerpts. BERG: *Sonata, Op. 1.* HINDEMITH: *Sonata No. 3.* KRENEK: *Sonata No. 2, Op. 59.* STRAVINSKY: *Serenade in A.*
(M) (***) RCA mono/stereo 74321 25176-2 [id.].

Maria Yudina (1899–1970) studied at first with the legendary Essipova, herself a Leschetizky pupil, and, after her death, was a fellow-student at Leningrad with Sofronitsky; Glazunov appointed her to a teaching post on the spot during her graduation recital. Her openness to modern developments in the West is well illustrated by the recordings assembled here. She carried on a long correspondence with Stravinsky, with whom she is pictured (in the sleeve-note) on his visit to Russia in 1962. These are impressive records: she makes Hindemith's *Sonata No. 3* sound more compelling than almost any other artist who has recorded it, and she succeeds in making Krenek's *Second Sonata* sound like music – no mean achievement! The recordings date from 1960–64 and are of eminently acceptable quality.

Sofronitsky, Vladimir

Volume 5: CHOPIN: *Nocturnes in F & F sharp, Op. 15/1–2; Scherzo No. 1 in B min., Op. 20.* MOZART: *Fantasia in C min., K.475.* PROKOFIEV: *Grandmother's Tales, Op. 31; Pieces for piano, Op. 12/2, 3 & 6–9; Sarcasm, Op. 17/3; Vision fugitive, Op. 22/7.* RACHMANINOV: *Moments musicaux, Op. 16/2 & 5.* SCHUBERT: *Impromptus, D.899/3 & 4.* SCHUMANN: *Sonata No. 1 in F sharp min., Op. 11.* SCRIABIN: *Sonata No. 4 in F sharp, Op. 30; Poème tragique, Op. 34; Valse in A flat, Op. 38; Etude in B flat min., Op. 8/11.*
(M) (**(*)) RCA mono 74321 25177-2 (2) [id.].

Vladimir Sofronitsky (1901–61) is best remembered as a Scriabin interpreter (he married the composer's daughter and was hailed by Tatiana Schloezer, Scriabin's widow, as the finest interpreter of her husband's music). He studied in Warsaw and had attracted the attention of Glazunov, who sent him to study with Alexander Michalowski. In the late 1920s he spent some time in Warsaw and Paris, where he earned the admiration of Prokofiev, whose friendship he enjoyed after his return to the Soviet Union. Sofronitsky was never cultivated by the Soviet regime and rarely appeared in the West, eventually succumbing to drink and drugs. All except the Prokofiev pieces come from a recital at the Small Hall of the Tchaikovsky Conservatoire in the year before his death. The Prokofiev Op. 31 comes from 1946 and the remainder of the group from 1953, recorded in the Scriabin Museum. In the fullness of time RCA will doubtless get round to reissuing all his Scriabin. In the meantime the *Fourth Sonata* gives a good idea why he is so much admired in this composer.

Richter, Sviatoslav

Volume 6: BACH: *Concerto in F in the Italian style, BWV 971.* BEETHOVEN: *Sonata No. 12 in A flat, Op. 26.* CHOPIN: *Ballades Nos. 1 in G min., Op. 23; 2 in F, Op. 38.* HAYDN: *Sonata No. 50 in C, Hob. XVI:50.*
(M) (*(*)) RCA mono 74321 25178-2 [id.].

The Bach *Italian concerto* was recorded in 1948, though it is difficult to credit it, given the excellence of its sound and the relative indifference (to put it mildly) of the later recordings offered here. It is much superior to the 1960 Haydn or Beethoven. Like most of the repertoire on this disc, it is given a performance of much distinction. The Haydn, Beethoven and Chopin items were recorded at recitals in 1960–63, but if the sound is shallow and poor in quality the playing is not. Richter recorded these pieces in the West, and older readers will doubtless recall the various CBS, RCA and EMI LP issues. Perhaps the first movement of the Haydn is too fast for comfort – but still, what playing! The Beethoven sounds very papery in tone and, though the playing is magisterial, the unpleasing sound makes its claims less pressing than many of the other discs in this collection.

Gilels, Emil

Volume 7: BACH: *Prelude and fugue in D, BWV 532.* BEETHOVEN: *32 Variations on an original theme, WoO 80.* LISZT: *Rapsodie espagnole.* PROKOFIEV: *Visions fugitives, Op. 22/1, 3, 5 & 11.* WEBER: *Sonata No. 2 in A flat, Op. 39.*
(M) (**(*)) RCA mono 74321 25179-2 [id.].

Gilels is represented by a recital given in the Grand Hall of the Philharmonic in Leningrad in January 1968. Such is the quality of his pianism that the (very much less than state-of-the-art) recording does not make this anything other than a highly recommendable issue. There are some smudges (as was often the case with Gilels in the concert hall) but they are of little account, given the musical insights and the beauty of sound he produced. The Liszt *Rapsodie espagnole* is pretty breathtaking and the Weber *Sonata No. 2 in A flat* is played with elegance and finesse. Despite the fact that it was January in Leningrad, the audience is very quiet, warmed no doubt by the white-hot, risk-taking pianism which confronted them.

Berman, Lazar

Volume 8: LISZT: *Etudes d'exécution transcendante; Hungarian Rhapsody No. 9 in E flat.*
(M) (**(*)) RCA mono 74321 25180-2 [id.].

The recordings of the *Etudes d'exécution transcendante* were made in the early part of 1959 and the *Hungarian rhapsody* (*Pesther Carneval*) two years later – and they leave something to be desired in terms of presence. However, the sound is vastly superior to the Richter CD reviewed above. As with the latter, no quarrels with the playing, which is absolutely stunning. Effortlessly virtuosic and brilliant, yet poetic and tender when required, and obviously with an immense dynamic range, only partly captured by the engineers. Pianistically this is without question a three-star recommendation.

Pletnev, Mikhail

Volume 9: MOZART: *Sonata No. 16 in B flat, K.570.* PROKOFIEV: *Sonata No. 7 in B flat, Op. 83.* SHCHEDRIN, arr. Pletnev: *Prologue and Horse-racing from Anna Karenina.* TCHAIKOVSKY, arr. Pletnev: *Nutcracker suite.*
❀ (M) *** RCA Analogue/Dig. 74321 25181-2 [id.].

We have long been urging the reissue of Mikhail Pletnev's astonishing transcription of the *Nutcracker suite* which he recorded when he was twenty-one. (EMI originally issued this, but they never promoted it with vigour and, as a result, it disappeared within a couple of years.) Pletnev produces a wider range of colour from the keyboard than most orchestras command, and in the Shchedrin *Anna Karenina* an extraordinarily wide dynamic range. Small wonder that he has become so effective a conductor. Like the Prokofiev *Seventh Sonata*, these were all recorded after he won the Tchaikovsky Competition in 1978. The Mozart is later (1984) and completes a recital which is pre-eminent even in this remarkable series.

Kissin, Yevgeni

Volume 10: PROKOFIEV: *Visions fugitives, Op. 22/10, 11, 16 & 17; Dance in F sharp min., Op. 32/1.* RACHMANINOV: *Etudes-Tableaux, Op. 39/1–6, 9; Preludes: in G flat, Op. 23/10; A min., Op. 32/8. Lilacs, Op. 21/5* (trans. Kissin). SCRIABIN: *Preludes, Opp. 27/1–2; 37/1–4; Etude in C sharp min., Op. 42/5; 4 Pieces, Op. 51.* KISSIN: *2 Inventions.*
(M) *** RCA 74321 25182-2 [id.].

These recordings were made at recitals given at the Grand Hall of Moscow Conservatoire in 1984 and 1986 when Kissin was twelve and fourteen respectively. (He had, after all, played both the Chopin *Concertos* when he was thirteen!) What is there left to say about this remarkable youngster, save that the playing has extraordinary assurance, dazzling technical address and splendid taste. This listener was left spellbound by the sheer passion and brilliance of the playing. The acoustic is a bit reverberant but, given this youth's poetic insight and artistry, technical reservations are of minimal importance.

Russian Piano School: '*The great pianists*' Volumes 11–20.
(M) **(*) BMG/Melodiya 74321 33230-2 (10) [id.].

We have already covered the first ten CDs of the *Russian Piano School*, and now RCA have followed it up with another set of ten. As with the first, they have wisely made them available separately and have also priced them competitively. The artists represented in this second set are less well known (some of them are barely even names outside Russia), but the same astonishing standards of pianistic wizardry and poetic insight prevail. There are some splendid things in this box; but this is another case where the collector is best advised to pick and choose among the separate issues. Yelena Bekman-Shcherbina is hardly known in the West, yet her recital is unforgettable, and there are other little-known but not less distinguished pianists to be discovered here, notably Edvard Syomin and, the youngest artist on the present roster (at the time of making the recordings), Yekaterina Ervy-Novitskaya. Readers will observe that we have given Grigory Ginsburg's remarkable collection of Liszt's *Concert paraphrases* a Rosette (BMG/ Melodiya mono 64321 33210-2 – see below).

Bekman-Shcherbina, Yelena

Volume 11: GLINKA/BALAKIREV: *The Lark.* BALAKIREV: *Au jardin (Etude-idylle in D flat).* GLINKA: *Souvenir de mazurka.* TITOV: *Waltzes: in F min.; G; E min.* LISZT: *Concert paraphrase of Alyabiev's 'The Nightingale'.* RUBINSTEIN: *Waltzes: in A flat, Op. 14/1; in F, Op. 82/5; Barcarolle in A min., Op. 93/3.* TCHAIKOVSKY: *Scherzo humoristique in D, Op. 19/2.* LIADOV: *Mazurkas: in D min., Op. 15/2; in G (Rustique), Op. 31/1.* GLAZUNOV: *Etude in E (Night), Op. 31/3.* ARENSKY: *Le ruisseau dans la forêt, Op. 36/15; Etude in F sharp, Op. 36/13.* SCRIABIN: *Preludes: in A; in F sharp min., Op. 15/1–2; Waltz in A flat, Op. 38.* RACHMANINOV: *Prelude in G, Op. 32/5; Etudes-tableaux: in E flat min.; E flat, Op. 33/ 6–7.*
(M) (***) BMG/Melodiya mono 74321 33209-2 [id.].

Yelena Bekman-Shcherbina is one of the least familiar names and, in the words of Christoph Rueger, her playing 'breathed the elegant, sentimental and patriotic atmosphere of the Russian salon at the turn of the century'. The Balakirev transcription of Glinka's *The Lark*, a transcription of one of the songs from *Farewell to St Petersburg*, is an ideal example of this, and so are the Arensky *Le ruisseau dans la forêt* and Balakirev's *Au jardin* (*Etude-idylle in D flat*). Born in 1882, the same year as Stravinsky, Bekman-Shcherbina studied with Paul Pabst, a teacher of Goldenweiser and Vasily Safonov. She gave the first performances of a number of Scriabin pieces and championed the music of Debussy, Roger-Ducasse and Sibelius. She possessed a wonderful cantabile touch and a melting lyricism. Listen to her Rachmaninov *G major Prelude*! These recordings were all made in 1948 and 1950, not long before her death, and few allowances need to be made for their quality (we have heard worse recordings from the 1970s!). A find!

Ginsburg, Grigory

Volume 12: LISZT: Concert paraphrases: *Fantasia on two themes from Mozart's Nozze di Figaro'* (completed Busoni); *Reminiscences from: Mozart's 'Don Giovanni'; Bellini's 'Norma'; Verdi's 'Rigoletto'; Gounod's 'Faust'*. GINSBURG: *Transcription of 'Largo al factotum' from Rossini's 'Barbiere di Siviglia'*.
✿ (M) (***) BMG/Melodiya mono 64321 33210-2 [id.].

Grigory Ginsburg featured in the earlier ten-CD collection in partnership with his teacher, Alexander Goldenweiser, but his solo recordings are quite dazzling. He was a celebrated Liszt performer and this disc is one of the highlights of a set that is itself all highlights! The *Fantasia on two themes from Mozart's 'Nozze di Figaro'* completed by Busoni beggars description for its lightness of touch and sheer virtuosity. Ginsburg's own transcription of the *Largo al factotum* from Rossini's *Barbiere di Siviglia* has enormous sparkle and humour – not to mention virtuosity. Ginsburg died in 1961 and these recordings, which are of varying quality, come from 1948–58 (the earliest are by no means the most frail). In any event, such is the magnetism of the playing that any sonic limitations are forgotten.

Oborin, Lev

Volume 13: BEETHOVEN: *Sonata No. 31 in A flat, Op. 110*. CHOPIN: *Sonata No. 3 in B min., Op. 58*. BRAHMS: *4 Pieces, Op. 119*. SCRIABIN: *Sonata No. 2 in G sharp min. (Sonata-fantaisie), Op. 19*.
(M) (**) BMG/Melodiya mono 74321 33211-2 [id.].

Lev Oborin belongs to the same generation as Ginsburg and is best remembered in the West as a marvellous chamber-music partner who recorded with Oistrakh and Knushevitzky, though he made relatively few solo appearances. He won the Chopin Competition in 1927, where he won the special accolade of Szymanowski, who is reported to have said, 'It is no shame to bow before him. He creates beauty.' The Beethoven *Sonata in A flat*, Op. 110, recorded in 1952, is an immaculately classical and selfless account, handicapped by an instrument which needs the ministrations of a technician. It is nevertheless a distinguished performance, more so than the Chopin *B minor Sonata*, recorded the previous year. Both the Brahms *Pieces*, Op. 119, and the Scriabin *Second Sonata*, recorded in 1953 and 1955 respectively, are refined and musicianly without perhaps being outstanding.

Grinberg, Maria

Volume 14: SEIXAS: *Minuet in F min.; Toccata in F min.* SOLER: *Sonatas Nos. 2 in C sharp min.; 11 in G min.; 12 in F sharp min.* Domentico SCARLATTI: *Sonatas, Kk.11, 22, 69 & 113*. MOZART: *Fantasia in C min., K.396* (completed Stadler). SCHUMANN: *Bunte Blätter, Op. 99*, excerpts: *Nos. 1–8; 10 & 13*. BRAHMS: *Variations on a theme of Schumann in F sharp min., Op. 11; Waltzes Op. 39/1, 3, 6–7, 15–16*.
(M) **(*) BMG/Melodiya stereo/mono 74321 33212-2 [id.].

Maria Grinberg was born in Odessa in 1908 (the birthplace of so many Russian musicians from Horowitz to Oistrakh) and made some appearances outside the then Soviet Union, including Holland, but did not make a lasting impression. She is obviously an artist of remarkable quality and the pieces by Seixas, Soler and Domenico Scarlatti, recorded in 1967, show an astonishing elegance and style. These are marvellous and subtle performances, alone worth the price of the disc. The Schumann *Bunte Blätter*, Op. 99, are played superbly but the 1947 recording is clangorous and messy. The Brahms *Variations on a theme of Schumann*, recorded in 1964 in decent sound, are quite masterly – among the best accounts of the piece to have been put on record.

Nikolayeva, Tatiana Petrovna

Volume 15: SCHUMANN: *3 Romances, Op. 28; Variations on an original theme in E flat*. PROKOFIEV: *Sonata No. 8 in B flat, Op. 84; Peter and the wolf, Op. 69* (music only; freely transcribed Nikolayeva).
(M) **(*) BMG/Melodiya 74321 33213-2 [id.].

Tatiana Nikolayeva has enjoyed celebrity in the West, thanks to her recordings of the Shostakovich *Preludes and fugues*, which were dedicated to her. The Schumann was recorded in 1983 (the sound is airless and close), the Prokofiev in the early 1960s. She certainly makes the Prokofiev *Eighth Sonata* very much her own and holds the listener in thrall in much the same ways as did Gilels and Richter. Her own transcription of *Peter and the wolf* is as imaginative as its execution. Performances of stature.

Zhukov, Igor

Volume 16: BACH: *Passacaglia in C min., BWV 582* (arr. ZHUKOV). SCHUMANN: *Waldszenen, Op. 82.* TCHAIKOVSKY: *Souvenir de Hapsal, Op. 2.* RACHMANINOV: *Barcarolle in G min., Op. 10/3.* PROKOFIEV: *Children's music (12 easy pieces), Op. 65.*
(M) ** BMG/Melodiya stereo/mono 74321 33214 [id.].

Ashkenazy, Vladimir

Volume 17: CHOPIN: *24 Etudes, Op. 10/1–12; Op. 25/1–12.* LISZT: *Mephisto waltz No. 1.*
(M) (***) BMG/Melodiya mono 74321 33215 [id.].

The two pianists featured in the pair of CDs listed above are familiar in the West, Igor Zhukov less so than Vladimir Ashkenazy. Zhukov has recorded concertos by, among others, Medtner (No. 1), Rimsky-Korsakov and Balakirev, which have been in and out of the catalogue here. In them his virtuosity is pretty electrifying. By the exalted standards of this set as a whole, however, he is, relatively speaking, average – but that is no mean compliment in this context! If you are collecting individual discs rather than the whole box, this is not one to which you need give the highest priority. The Schumann *Waldszenen* and the Tchaikovsky and Rachmaninov items come off well, and the Prokofiev *Children's music*, Op. 65, is a rarity. The Ashkenazy recital is the familiar set of the *Etudes*, Opp. 10 and 25, from 1959–60, once available on Chant du Monde, and is one of the classics of the piano discography; the *Mephisto waltz No. 1* makes an admirable bonus. The sound is quite respectable.

Virsaladze, Eliso

Volume 18: CHOPIN: *Sonata No. 3 in B min., Op. 58; Ballade No. 3 in A flat, Op. 47; Mazurkas Nos. 21 in C sharp min., Op. 30/4; 23 in D, Op. 33/2; Waltzes Nos. 2 in A flat, Op. 34/1; 9 in A flat, Op. 69/1; Nocturne No. 8 in D flat, Op. 27/2; Polonaises Nos. 6 in A flat (Heroic), Op. 53; 7 (Polonaise-fantaisie), Op. 61.*
(M) ** BMG/Melodiya 74321 33216-2 [id.].

Syomin, Edvard

Volume 19: GODOWSKY: *Renaissance* (free arrangements after Rameau), *Nos. 1, 3 & 6.* CHOPIN: *Souvenir de Paganini; Berceuse in D flat, Op. 57.* STANCHINSKY: *3 Preludes* (1907); *5 Preludes* (1907–12). MEDTNER: *Fairy-tales, Op. 20.* EIGES: *Sonata-Toccata No. 4, Op. 15.* ALBENIZ: *Navarra; Tango in D, Op. 165/2.* BUSONI: *Chamber fantasia on Bizet's opera 'Carmen'.* GODOWSKY: *Künsterleben (symphonic metamorphoses on Johann Strauss's waltz).*
(M) *** BMG/Melodiya stereo/mono 74321 33217-2 [id.].

Eliso Virsaladze's Chopin is admirable but not special, certainly not as extraordinary as Edvard Syomin's recital. Nikolayeva spoke of Syomin's 'profound musical culture, virtuosity and freedom of self-expression'. Born in Moscow in 1945, he remains virtually unknown outside his native country, and the development of his career was, so Christoph Rueger's notes tell us, handicapped by a family tragedy and hindered by the Soviet regime. Fortunately he enjoyed the patronage of Melodiya and the Soviet Radio, and it is from their archives that the present recordings come. The recordings range from 1969 through to 1985 and are of variable quality, but the playing in the Busoni *Carmen fantasy* is astonishing. The *Preludes* by Alexei Stanchinsky (1888–1914) are quite touching and, apart from Daniel Blumenthal's record of the *Piano sonatas* for Marco Polo, his only current representation in the catalogue.

Ervy-Novitskaya, Yekaterina

Volume 20: PROKOFIEV: *Sarcasms, Op. 17; Visions fugitives, Op. 22; Romeo and Juliet: 10 Pieces, Op. 75.*
(M) *** BMG/Melodiya 74321 33218-2 [id.].

The youngest of the pianists in this collection (at the time of making her recordings) is Yekaterina Ervy-Novitskaya, who was born in 1951. She received much encouragement from Lev Oborin, whose post-graduate assistant she became. When she was seventeen she won the first prize at the *Concours Musicale Reine Elisabeth* in Brussels. But the acclaim of such keyboard luminaries as Neuhaus and Rubinstein did not prevent her from retiring from the platform to settle in Brussels and devote herself to bringing up a family and to teaching. She made a comeback in Moscow in 1995; but these recordings come from 1969, when she was eighteen, save for the *Romeo and Juliet Pieces*, Op. 75, recorded in 1975.

In any event she obviously has great affinity for the composer, and her account both of the *Fifth Sonata* (in its post-war, revised version) and of the *Visions fugitives* are impressively characterized.

Schiller, Allan (piano)

'Für Elise': Popular piano pieces: BEETHOVEN: *Für Elise*. FIELD: *Nocturne in E (Noontide)*. CHOPIN: *Mazurka in B flat, Op. 7/1; Waltz in A, Op. 34/2. 3 Ecossaisen, Op. 72/3; Fantaisie-impromptu, Op. 66*. MENDELSSOHN: *Songs without words: Venetian gondola song, Op. 19; Bees' wedding, Op. 67*. LISZT: *Consolation No. 3 in D flat*. DE SEVERAC: *The music box*. DEBUSSY: *Suite bergamasque: Clair de lune. Arabesques Nos. 1 and 2. Prélude: The girl with the flaxen hair*. GRIEG: *Wedding day at Troldhaugen; March of the dwarfs*. ALBENIZ: *Granada; Tango; Asturias*.
(BB) *** ASV CDQS 6032 [(M) id.].

A particularly attractive recital, diverse in mood, spontaneous in feeling and very well recorded. The acoustic is resonant, but the effect is highly realistic. There are many favourites here, with Allan Schiller at his most personable in the engaging Field *Nocturne*, De Severac's piquant *Music box* and the closing *Asturias* of Albéniz, played with fine bravura. The Chopin group, too, is most successful, with the Scottish rhythmic snap of the *Ecossaisen* neatly articulated and the famous *B flat Mazurka* presented most persuasively.

Stern, Isaac (violin)

'A Life in Music': Boxes III–IV (for Boxes I–II, see under Orchestral and Concertante Music)

'A Life in music': Box III
(M) **(*) Sony Analogue/Dig. SX12K 67195 (12) [S12K 67195].

Volume 16: (i) BACH: *Trio sonatas in G, BWV 1038; in C min., BWV 1079*. W. F. BACH: *Trio sonata in A min*. (ii) J. C. BACH: *Trio sonata in C*. (iii) *Sonata in C*. (ii) TELEMANN: *Quartet (Trio sonata) in E min*. (with (i; ii; iii) Jean-Pierre Rampal (flute); (i) Leslie Parnas (cello); (ii) Mstislav Rostropovich (cello); (i; iii) John Steele Ritter ((i) harpsichord; (iii) fortepiano); (ii) Matthias Spaeter (lute)) (Dig. SMK 64509) [id.].

Volume 17: BEETHOVEN: *Piano trios Nos. 1–3, Op. 1/1–3; 8, WoO 38; 10 (Variations in E flat), Op. 44*; (with Leonard Rose (cello), Eugene Istomin (piano)) (SM2K 64510) [S2K 64510].

Volume 18: BEETHOVEN: *Piano trios Nos. 4 in B flat, Op. 11; 5 in D (Ghost), Op. 70/1; 6 in E flat, Op. 70/2; 7 in B flat (Archduke), Op. 97; 9 in B flat, WoO 39; 11 (Variations on 'Ich bin der Schneider Kakadu'), Op. 121a* (with Leonard Rose (cello), Eugene Istomin (piano)) (SM2K 64513) [S2K 64513].

Volume 19: (i) SCHUBERT: *Piano trios Nos. 1–2, Op. 99, 100*. (ii) MOZART: *Piano quartet No. 2 in E flat, K.493*. (i) HAYDN: *Piano trio in E flat, Hob XV/10* ((i) with Leonard Rose (cello); (ii) with Milton Katims (viola), Mischa Schneider (cello); (i; ii) with Eugene Istomin (piano)) (SM2K 64516 (2)) [S2K 64516].

Volume 20: MENDELSSOHN: *Piano trios Nos. 1 in D min., Op. 49; 2 in C min., Op. 66* (with Leonard Rose (cello), Eugene Istomin (piano)) (SMK 64519) [id.].

Volume 21: BRAHMS: *Piano trios Nos. 1 in B, Op. 8; 2 in C, Op. 87; 3 in C min., Op. 101* (with Leonard Rose (cello), Eugene Istomin (piano)); *Piano quartets Nos. 1 in G min., Op. 25; 2 in A, Op. 26; 3 in C min., Op. 60* (with Jaime Laredo (viola), Yo-Yo Ma (cello), Emanuel Ax (piano)) (SM3K 64520 (3)) [S3K 64520].

Volume 22: (i) ANON.: *Greensleeves*. FOSTER: *I dream of Jeannie with the light brown hair*. KREISLER: *Liebesleid*. SCHUBERT: *Ave Maria*. (ii) MENDELSSOHN: *On wings of song*. (i) BRAHMS: *Hungarian Dance No. 5*. DVORAK: *Humoresque*. RIMSKY-KORSAKOV: *Flight of the bumble-bee*. (ii) RACHMANINOV: *Vocalise*. (i) TCHAIKOVSKY: *None but the lonely heart*. (ii) BORODIN: *Nocturne*. (i) BENJAMIN: *Jamaican Rumba*. (ii) SATIE: *Gymnopédie No. 3*. (i) GERSHWIN: *Bess, you is my woman now*. COPLAND: *Hoedown* (with (i, ii) Columbia SO; (i) Milton Katims; (ii) Frank Brieff) (SMK 64537) [id.].

With Box III it is perhaps better to pick and choose rather than to go for the complete box. The *Trio sonatas* by Bach and his sons plus an attractive work of Telemann offer some very distinguished playing (especially in the performances featuring Rostropovich) and one can adjust to the up-front balance. The

Beethoven and Brahms *Piano trios* and *Quartets* are indispensable, but the Schubert and Mendelssohn are not. Many will enjoy the final selection of lollipops, sumptuously recorded, although the effect is a bit schmaltzy and they are best taken in small doses. Superb playing, of course, as throughout all three Boxes. All the records (or smaller compilations) are available separately and most are discussed in detail under their composer entries. Overall this is a remarkable achievement.

'A Life in music': Box IV: Chamber and instrumental music
(M) **(*) Sony Analogue/Dig. SX12K 67196 (12) [S12K 67196].

Box IV completes Sony's Isaac Stern Edition and in many ways it is one of the most attractive collections in the survey. Each issue is available separately.

Volume 23: C. P. E. BACH or J. S. BACH: *Sonata in G min., BWV 1020.* J. S. BACH: *Violin sonata* (for violin and harpsichord) *No. 3, BWV 1016; Sonata for violin and continuo, BWV 1023.* HANDEL: *Sonata in D, Op. 1/3.* TARTINI: *Sonata in G min. (Dido Abbandonata), Op. 1/10* (with Alexander Zakin) (mono SMK 68361) [id.].

These recordings come from 1952–3 and, although the violin is balanced rather forwardly, in all other respects the mono recording is first class. Stern shows himself thoroughly at home in baroque repertoire; even though he uses a minimum of embellishments, the style is impeccable. The *Adagio* of the *G minor Sonata*, now thought to be by C. P. E. Bach, is glorious. Alexander Zakin is a splendid partner, playing simply and directly and making one feel for the moment that these works were intended to be heard in a violin/piano partnership, even the continuo sonata, BWV 1023. Similarly in Handel, Stern plays the noble line of the *D major Sonata* with natural sympathy and unexaggerated warmth. The (originally three-movement) Tartini *Sonata* is heard in an arrangement by Leopold Auer, who added a *Largo* taken from the fifth sonata of the same opus, which makes a suitably dramatic interlude to lead into the lively finale. The connection of the work with Metastasio's libretto about Dido (set to music by at least four composers) is obscure, but it served to keep the sonata in the repertoire.

Volume 24: BEETHOVEN: *Violin sonatas Nos. 1–10* (with Eugene Istomin) (Dig./Analogue SM3K 64524 (3)) [S3K 64524].

Stern and Istomin make an inspirational partnership, obviously striking sparks off each other in performances that are brimming with zest and vitality. The performances have striking rhythmic strengths as well as lyrical appeal and are discussed more fully under their composer entry.

Volume 25: SCHUBERT: *Violin sonatinas Nos. 1–3; Rondo in B min. (Rondeau brillant), D.895; Duo in A (Grand duo), D.574; Fantaisie in C, D.934* (all with Daniel Barenboim). HAYDN: *Violin concerto in C, Hob VIIa/1* (with Columbia CO) (Dig./Analogue (mono) SM2K 64528 (2)) [S2K 64528].

Stern and Barenboim find an ideal partnership: the performances have a natural warmth and plenty of character, yet there is an unaffected simplicity and directness of style which especially suits the three early *Sonatinas*. The Haydn *Concerto*, excellently recorded in mono in 1947, is a very acceptable bonus.

Volume 26: BRAHMS: *Violin sonatas Nos. 1–3* (with Alexander Zakin) (SMK 64531) [id.].

Stern and Zakin give splendidly vital and characterful performances of the Brahms *Sonatas*. They have genuine power and conviction, but the 1960 recording brings the usual CBS problem of that period: Stern was far too close to the microphones. The original LP produced far from comfortable tone-quality, but the improvement in the CD remastering is very striking; his tone now emerges, closely scrutinized but unscathed and despite the balance Alexander Zakin's contribution is not submerged. Admirers of these artists will still consider this disc worth its cost.

Volume 27: FRANCK: *Violin sonata in A.* DEBUSSY: *Violin sonata.* ENESCU: *Violin sonata No 3 in A min., Op. 25* (all with Alexander Zakin) (SMK 64532) [id.].

Stern recorded the Franck *Sonata* in 1959. It is a work which suits him especially well and he gives a performance of heartfelt, extrovert feeling, especially in the slow movement, although some might not care for the portamento in its closing bars. Throughout there is much subtlety of detail too. As ever in that period, he was too closely recorded, but the projection suits the intensity of the finale. In some way the Debussy *Sonata* suits him less well; but this is still a commanding performance, impossible not to enjoy, even if one which rather wears its heart on its sleeve. The Enescu *Third Sonata* (1926) is a remarkable work of great vitality and interest, strongly influenced by Romanian folklore, but through its harmonic flavours and rhythmic influences and styles rather than by quoting folksong. The exotic *Andante sostenuto e misterio* even suggests oriental influences from further east and has an improvisatory quality which Stern captures superbly, while the dashing finale throws off sparks of every kind. Its upper tessitura harmonics and histrionics are flawlessly managed, the glissando lyrical spurts given a gypsy passion. In this instance the very close microphones add to the bite, even though, at those times when Stern is pressing hard on the strings, the sound is not quite comfortable.

Volume 28: HINDEMITH: *Violin sonata*. BLOCH: *Violin sonata; Baal shem: Three pictures of Chassidic life* (all with Alexander Zakin). COPLAND: *Violin sonata* (with composer) (mono/stereo SMK 64533) [id.].

The Hindemith *Sonata* (1939) is neither intimidating nor dull. It begins with a friendly if busy melodic flow, and there is a touching melody for the opening and close of the central movement. Stern obviously relishes its engaging *moto perpetuo* central section, and his dainty, light, bravura articulation is spellbinding as the introductory material is reintroduced. The fugal finale again opens simply and, even if its harmonic progressions seem devious at first hearing, their Hindemithian logic soon falls into place. The mono recording, from 1946, is just a little confined but is otherwise very good. Bloch has to be presented with whole-hearted conviction if his music is to make any contact at all, and this performance has just that quality. Stern's playing could hardly be more committed or full of passion and, despite a somewhat forward balance, we would recommend these most persuasive performances of both works, which have never been surpassed.

The Copland recording, which is new to us, is the highlight of the disc. It was made in 1967, with the composer at the piano, and is clearly definitive, for although Stern is still very forward the piano is very much in the picture. The lively central section of the first movement is framed by an *Andante semplice* in which the piano coolly repeats a chordal duplet whose harmonic flavour is instantly identifiable by anyone who has heard the famous Copland ballets. The haunting central *Lento* has a comparable simplicity, and Stern's G-string re-statement of the main theme near the close is particularly telling. The sharply rhythmic finale with its dancing syncopations introduces material we have heard before, notably the coda (which recalls the opening), yet, with the piano chords transformed, the effect is much more upbeat. A marvellously compelling performance, and if Stern is again too near the microphones – as Klemperer once said about something entirely different – 'You will get used to it!'

Volume 29: PROKOFIEV: *Violin sonatas Nos. 1–2* (with Alexander Zakin) (SMK 64534) [id.].

Stern's performances with Zakin are of high quality, the *Andante* of the *F minor* memorably atmospheric, especially after the extrovert bravura of the *Allegro brusco*. But here, more than in most of these reissues, the close balance makes Stern's fortissimo timbre sound unnecessarily acerbic.

Volume 30: BARTOK: *Violin sonatas Nos. 1–2* (with Alexander Zakin). WEBERN: *4 Pieces for violin and piano, Op. 7* (with Charles Rosen) (SMK 64535) [id.].

Stern and Zakin are completely involved in the Bartók *Sonatas*, and the cantabile melisma which opens the *Adagio* of the *First Sonata* can never have sounded more lyrically beautiful on record, while the gutsy bravura of the finale is equally compelling. The rapt opening of the *Second Sonata* is comparably concentrated. The four brief, sharply focused Webern *Pieces* are presented with comparable intensity and authority. Once again one must complain about the too-close balance of the recordings, made in 1967 and 1971 respectively, but the effect is not destructive.

Volume 31: 'Encores with piano': SARASATE: *Caprice basque*. PUGNANI: *Sonata in D: Largo espressivo*. NOVACEK: *Perpetuum mobile*. BLOCH: *Baal shem: Nigun (Improvisation)*. LECLAIR: *Sarabande et tambourin*. MOZART: *Haffner Serenade: Rondo allegro*. GLUCK: *Orpheus and Euridyce: Mélodie*. TCHAIKOVSKY: *Valse sentimentale*. SCHUMANN: *Waldszenen: Bird as prophet*. KREISLER: *Schön Rosmarin*. DVORAK: *Slavonic dance, Op. 46/2*. SZYMANOWSKI: *Chant de Roxane; La Fontaine d'Arethuse*. STRAVINSKY: *Firebird: Berceuse*. DINICU: *Hora staccato*. MILHAUD: *Saudades do Brasil: Tijuca*. PROKOFIEV: *Romeo and Juliet: Danse des jeunes filles des Antilles; Masques*. FALLA: *Suite after 7 Spanish popular songs* (with Alexander Zakin) (mono SMK 64536) [id.].

Marvellous playing from Stern throughout: he is quite dazzling in the arrangement of the Rondo from Mozart's *Haffner Serenade*, while the Kreisler transcription of Gluck's most famous *Mélodie* from *Orféo et Euridice* is played with ravishing delicacy. Tchaikovsky's *Valse sentimentale* and Schumann's *Prophet bird* (from *Waldszenen*), arranged by Leopold Auer, are presented with comparable exquisite grace. If elegant flair is what you are looking for, try Kreisler's *Schön Rosmarin*, while Szymanowski's *Chant de Roxane* and *La fontaine d'Arethuse* are ethereally sensuous, helped by Zakin's atmospheric backing. The *Berceuse* from Stravinsky's *Firebird* is infinitely gentle and touching, while for sparkling, easy bravura the Dinicu *Hora staccato* takes some beating. The two excerpts from Prokofiev's *Romeo and Juliet* are indelibly characterized, although they are not less seductive than the exotic closing Falla suite. The recordings are all mono, made in either 1947 or 1952, but the effect is faithful, if a little dry: the opening Sarasate *Caprice basque* ideally needs a more flatteringly sumptuous acoustic.

Swiss Wind Quintet

20th Century wind quintets: JANACEK: *Mládi*. NIELSEN: *Wind quintet, Op. 43*. HINDEMITH: *Kleine Kammermusik, Op. 24/2*. LIGETI: *6 Bagatelles*.
(BB) *** Koch Discover Dig. DICD 920395 [id.].

Mládi isn't, strictly speaking, a quintet as it has an additional bass clarinet part. But it is uncommonly well played by this excellent Swiss group, and they give an equally sympathetic account of the Nielsen *Quintet*, most winning in the *Minuet* as well as in the third-movement *Theme and variations*. The Hindemith *Kleine Kammermusik* is hardly less successful, notably the dolorous *Waltz* which hints at Walton's *Façade*, and the pensive nostalgia of the third movement, although there is plenty of sparkling vitality elsewhere. The riotously witty opening movment of Ligeti's *Six Bagatelles* is splendidly done. There is little to choose between this performance of an unexpectedly entertaining work and that by the competing Claude Debussy Quintet on Harmonia Mundi (see above). In some ways the programme on this excellently recorded Discovery disc is the more tempting, but both CDs are equally recommendable.

Tagliaferro, Magda (piano)

((i) with Fr. Nat. R. & TV O, Heitor Villa-Lobos): VILLA-LOBOS: (i) *Momoprecoce* (for piano and orchestra). *A Lenda do caboclo. A prole de bebê: O Polichinele. Carnaval das crianças: A gaita de um precoce fantasiado. Ciclo brasileiro: Impressões seresteiras; Festa no sertão. Choros tipico: Alma brasileira. Cirandas: Vamos atrâs de serra. Danças caracteristicas Africanas; Farrapós. Guia pratica: Rosa amarela; A maré encheu*. FALLA: *La vida brêve: Danza española. Three-cornered hat: Miller's dance*. GRANADOS: *Goyescas: The maiden and the nightingale. Danzas españolas Nos. 2 (Oriental) & 5 (Andaluza)*. ALBENIZ: *Cantos de España: Seguidillas; Cordoba. Suite española: Sevilla. Iberia: Evocation; Triana*. MOMPOU: *Scènes d'enfants*. DEBUSSY: *Suite bergamasque: Clair de lune*. CHOPIN: *Andante spianato & grande polonaise brillante, Op. 22; Waltz No. 5 in B flat, Op. 42*. SCHUMANN: *Piano sonata No. 1 in F sharp min., Op. 11*.
(B) *** EMI Rouge et Noir (SIS) stereo/mono CZS5 69476-2 (2).

The Brazilian pianist Magda Tagliaferro was a remarkable artist who was still playing in public well into her late eighties. She was a pupil of Cortot and possessed something of the latter's fantasy and poetic fire. None of these recordings has appeared in the UK before and readers who have not encountered her can be assured that she is an artist of strong personality. The Mompou, Chopin, Debussy and Schumann were recorded in Paris in 1951, *Momprecoce* with the composer in 1954, and most of the other pieces in Paris in 1960, and the remainding Villa-Lobos items in Rio de Janeiro as recently as 1972. The Villa-Lobos pieces have exceptional authority and the set is worth having on their account alone.

Thurston Clarinet Quartet

'Clarinet masquerade': FARKAS: *Ancient Hungarian dances from the 17th century*. MOZART (arr. WHEWELL): *Divertimento No. 2*. TOMASI: *3 Divertissements*. GARNER (arr. BLAND): *Misty*. JOBIM (arr. BLAND): *The Girl from Ipanema*. DESPORTES: *French suite*. ALBINONI (arr. THILDE): *Sonata in G min*. STARK: *Serenade*. GERSHWIN (arr. BLAND): *Rhapsody: Summertime*. PHILLIPS (arr. HARVEY): *Cadenza;* (arr. FERNANDEZ): *Muskrat Sousa*.
(M) *** ASV Dig. CDWHL 2076 [id.].

A light-hearted concert, but an entertaining one which will especially appeal to those who like the clarinet's sonority, reedier than the flute's and with more character. The opening suite of Hungarian folk dances (with the chirps and cheeps in the finale very engaging) leads on to a Mozart *Divertimento* for basset horns. The other pieces, the insouciant Tomasi and the Desportes suite (full of Ravelian elegance) are all amiable, and the arrangement of Gershwin's *Summertime* has the famous opening swerve of *Rhapsody in blue* as its introduction. Finally there is the exuberant *Muskrat Sousa* which features a combination of *12th Street Rag* and *South Rampart Street Parade*. The recording is immaculately vivid.

Vieaux, Jason (guitar)

Recital: MERLIN: *Suite del recuerdo.* PUJOL: *Preludios Nos. 2, 3 , & 5.* ORBON (de SOTO): *Preludio y Danza.* KROUSE: *Variations on a Moldavian hora.* BARRIOS: *Valses, Op. 8/3 & 4; Julia Florida: Barcarola.* MOREL: *Chôro; Danza Brasileira; Danza in E min.* BUSTAMENTE: *Misionera.*
❀ (BB) *** Naxos Dig. 8.553449 [id.].

This is the finest début guitar recital we have heard for some years. Jason Vieaux is a young American musician, already a prize-winner – and no wonder. This Latin-American repertoire is unfailingly diverting in his hands: there are no familiar names here except that of Barrios, yet almost every item is either memorably evocative or it makes the pulse quicken. Vieaux's completely natural rubato at the opening *Evocación* of José Luis Merlin's *Suite del recuerdo* is quite masterly and the slow crescendos in the final *Carnavalito* are thrilling; then there is a complete change of mood and the *Evocación* makes a haunting return before the final *Joropo*. The *Preludios* of Pujol are quite magical; Vieaux then lets his hair down for the *Candombe*. The two *Valses* of Barrios are deliciously fragile, with the central *Barcarola* hardly less subtle, while the more robust Brazilian dances of Jorge Morel have real panache. The Naxos recording has good ambience and is present yet not too closely balanced. Unforgettable.

Wild, Earl (piano)

'The virtuoso piano': HERZ: *Variations on 'Non più mesta' from Rossini's La Cenerentola.* THALBERG: *Don Pasquale fantasy, Op. 67.* GODOWSKY: *Symphonic metamorphosis on themes from Johann Strauss's Künsterleben (Artist's life).* RUBINSTEIN: *Etude (Staccato), Op. 23/2.* HUMMEL: *Rondo in E flat, Op. 11.* PADEREWSKI: *Theme and variations, Op. 16/3.*
(M) *** Van. 08.4033.71 [OVC 4033].

Earl Wild's famous performances from the late 1960s re-emerge on CD with their scintillating brilliance given even greater projection by the digital remastering. Wild's technique is prodigious and his glittering bravura in the engaging Herz *Rossini variations* and Thalberg's equally entertaining *Don Pasquale fantasy* is among the finest modern examples of the grand tradition of virtuoso pianism. Godowsky's piece may have a heavy title, but in Earl Wild's hands, for all the decorative complexities, the lilting waltz-rhythms are still paramount.

Williams, John (guitar)

'Spanish guitar music': I. ALBENIZ: *Asturias; Tango; Cordoba; Sevilla.* SANZ: *Canarios.* TORROBA: *Nocturno; Madroños.* SAGRERAS: *El Colibri.* M. ALBENIZ: *Sonata in D.* FALLA: *Homenaje; Three-cornered hat: Corregidor's dance; Miller's dance. El amor brujo: Fisherman's song.* CATALAN FOLKSONGS: *La Nit de Nadal; El noy de la mare; El testamen de Amelia.* GRANADOS: *La maja de Goya. Spanish dance No. 5.* TARREGA: *Recuerdos de la Alhambra.* VILLA-LOBOS: *Prelude No. 4 in E min.* MUDARRA: *Fantasia.* TURINA: *Fandanguillo, Op. 36.*
(M) *** Sony SBK 46347; *SBT 46347* [id.].

John Williams can show strong Latin feeling, as in the vibrant *Farruca* of the *Miller's dance* from Falla's *Three-cornered hat*, or create a magically atmospheric mood, as in the hauntingly registered transcription of the *Fisherman's song* from *El amor brujo*. He can play with thoughtful improvisatory freedom, as in the Villa-Lobos *Prelude*, with its pianissimo evocation, or be dramatically spontaneous, as in the memorable performance of Turina's *Fandanguillo*, which ends the recital magnetically. The instinctive control of atmosphere and dynamic is constantly rewarding throughout a varied programme, and the technique is phenomenal, yet never flashy, always at the service of the music. The remastering brings a clean and truthful, if very immediate, image. Background is minimal and never intrusive.

Yepes, Narciso (guitar)

'Spanish guitar music': ALBENIZ: *Malagueña; Asturias; Leyenda.* SOR: *Tema con variaciones, Op. 9; Studies, Op. 35/14, 16, 22 & 21.* TARREGA: *Recuerdos de la Alhambra.* SANZ: *Suite española.* MUDARRA: *Fantasia que contrahaze la harpa en la manera de Ludovico.* SOLER: *Sonata in E.* FALLA: *El sombrero de tres picos: Danza del molinero/Farruca.*
(BB) *** Belart 461 276-2 [(M) id. import].

Narciso Yepes was not only an outstanding exponent of this repertoire, he also had that rare gift of constantly creating electrity in the recording studio, and all this music springs vividly to life. In popular favourites like the Tarrega *Recuerdos de la Alhambra*, the exciting transcription of Falla's *Miller's dance*, the earlier baroque repertoire (the Sanz *Suite* is particularly appealing) Yepes's assured, vibrant and always stylish advocacy brings consistent pleasure. He is recorded extremely vividly, and this disc can be recommended alongside the RCA Navigator Julian Bream recital to anyone wanting an inexpensive and representative programme of Spanish guitar music.

Zabaleta, Nicanor (harp)

'Arpa española': ALBENIZ: *Managueña, Op. 165/3; Suite española: Granada (Serenata); Zaragoza (Capricho); Asturias (Leyenda). Mallorca, Op. 202; Tango español.* FALLA: *Serenata andaluza.* TURINA: *Ciclo pianistico No. 1: Tocata y fuga.* GOMBAU: *Apunte bético.* GRANADOS: *Danza española No. 5.* HALFFTER: *Sonatina* (ballet): *Danza de la pastora.* LOPEZ-CHAVARRI: *El viejo castillo moro.*
❁ (M) *** DG (IMS) 435 847-2 [id.].

A good deal of the music here belongs to the guitar (or piano) rather than the harp, but Nicanor Zabaleta, with his superb artistry and sense of atmosphere, makes it all his own. Throughout this delightful programme, Zabaleta gives each piece strong individuality of character. In the Granados *Spanish dance No. 5* he matches the magnetism of Julian Bream's famous recording, and Manuel de Falla's *Serenata andaluza* is hardly less captivating. DG's sound balance is near perfection, as is the choice of acoustic, and the magic distilled by Zabaleta's concentration, often at the gentlest levels of dynamic, is unforgettable.

Vocal Recitals and Choral Collections

Angeles, Victoria de los (soprano)

'The fabulous Victoria de Los Angeles'

Disc 1: RAVEL: *Shéhérazade; 5 Mélodies populaires grecques; 2 Mélodies hébraïques.* DUPARC: *L'invitation au voyage; Phidylé.* DEBUSSY: *L'Enfant prodigue: L'année en vain chasse l'année.* CHAUSSON: *Poème de l'amour et de la mer.*

Disc 2: MONTSALVATGE: *5 canciones negras.* GRANADOS: *Colección se canciones amatorias; Llorad corazón; Iban al pinar.* RODRIGO: *4 madrigales amatorios; Triptic de Mossèn Cinto.* ESPLA: *5 canciones playeras españolas.* TOLDRA: *4 cançons.* TRAD.: *La Dama d'Aragó; El cant dels ocells; Canço de Sega.* MOMPOU: *El Combat del Somni.*

Disc 3: DEBUSSY: *Chansons de Bilitis; Fêtes galantes; Noël des enfants qui n'ont plus de maisons.* RAVEL: *Chants populaires.* HAHN: *3 jours de vendage; Le rossignol de lilas.* FAURE: *Tristesse; Au bord de l'eau; Les Roses d'Ispahan; Toujours.* FALLA: *7 canciones populares españolas. Psyché; Soneto a Córdoba.* TOLDRA: *12 canciones gallegas: As floriñas dos toxos.* TURINA: *Farruca.* RODRIGO: *Villancicos: Pastorcito santo.*

Disc 4: SACRATI: *Prosperina: E dove t'aggiri.* A. SCARLATTI: *Le violette.* HANDEL: *Joshua: Oh! had I Jubal's lyre.* SCHUBERT: *Der Tod und das Mädchen. Die schöne Müllerin: Wohin?; An die Musik; Mignon und der Harfner.* BRAHMS: *Dein blaue Auge; Vergebliches Ständchen; Sapphische Ode.* FAURE: *Chansons d'amour; Clair de lune; Pleurs d'or.* PURCELL: *Let us wander; Lost is my quiet.* HAYDN: *Schlaf in deiner engen Kammer.* J. C. BACH: *Ah! lamenta, oh bella Irene.* BEETHOVEN: *Irish songs: Oh! would I were but that sweet linnet; He promised me at parting; They bid me slight my Dermot dear. Welsh song: The dream.* BERLIOZ: *Les fleurs des landes: Le Trébuchet.* DVORAK: *Möglichkeit; Der Apfel.* TCHAIKOVSKY: *Scottish ballad.* SAINT-SAENS: *Pastorale.* MOZART: *La Pertenza.*
(M) *** EMI CMS5 65061-2 (4) [ZDMD 65061].

A seventy-fifth-birthday celebration, this well-documented set subdivides into a pair of CDs of French and Spanish repertoire with orchestra, and two more with piano. While the French classics give special delight, it is good that room was made for the two separate Rodrigo song selections, as this composer prized his vocal music above all else and it is too little known. Apart from the mélodies, the third disc includes some especially delightful folk-inspired repertoire from both countries, where de los Angeles was in her element; on the fourth, a wide-ranging programme (in which she has the estimable support of Gerald Moore) shows her remarkable versatility. The recordings were made in the 1960s when the voice was at its freshest. If you are an admirer of this lovely voice, snap the set up quickly, for it is unlikely to be around for very long.

'Diva': Arias from ROSSINI: *Il barbiere di Siviglia.* GOUNOD: *Faust.* VERDI: *La Traviata; Otello.* PUCCINI: *La Bohème; Madama Butterfly; Suor Angelica; Gianni Schicchi.* MASCAGNI: *Cavalleria ruricana.* LEONCAVALLO: *Pagliacci.* CATALANI: *La Wally.* MASSENET: *Manon.* BIZET: *Carmen.* GIMENEZ: *La Tempranica.* CABALLERO: *Gigantes y Cabezudos.* BARBIERI: *Il barberillo de Lavaplés.*
(M) *** EMI mono/stereo CDM5 65579-2 [id.].

This splendid compilation brings it home how many of the classic sets of the 1950s and 1960s have Victoria de los Angeles as a golden-toned heroine, responding with heartfelt expressiveness. These include the two incomparable Beecham sets of Puccini's *La Bohème* and Bizet's *Carmen*, Gui's Glyndebourne-based set of Rossini's *Barbiere*, Monteux's magical set of Massenet's *Manon*, Cluytens's recording of *Faust*, Serafin in Puccini's *Il trittico*, not to mention the RCA New York recording in 1953 of *I Pagliacci*, in which de los Angeles sings charmingly as Nedda communing with the birds – not the role one expects from her. These are well supplemented by two items from her superb (1954) opera recital, including a tenderly beautiful *Ave Maria* from *Otello* and three final numbers from Spanish zarzuelas, making a winning collection overall.

Anonymous 4

'A Portrait': excerpts from *'Miracles of Sant'Iago'; 'The Lily and the lamb'; 'A Star in the East'; 'Love's illusion'; 'An English Ladymass'; 'On Yoolis night'*.
(B) *** HM Dig. HMX 2907210 [id.].

'The Cathedral of Santiago' is the home of a collection of medieval chant and polyphony, designed to be sung by a group of young French boy trebles. It proves ideal repertory for the Anonymous Four, as does the collection called '*The Lily and the Lamb*' which centres on hymns, sequences and motets dedicated to the Virgin Mary. '*A Star in the East*' is a programme of unsophisticated Hungarian Christmas music, much of it in melodic monody. '*Love's illusion*' draws on French motets on courtly texts from the Montepelier Codex, many of which are dolorous; '*An English Ladymass*' offers music again celebrating the Virgin Mary but more formally, and '*On Yoolis Night*' is a delightful collection of medieval carols and motets.

Ars Nova, Bo Holten

Portuguese polyphony: CARDOSO: *Lamentatio; Magnificat secundi toni*. LOBO: *Audivi vocem de caelo; Pater peccavi*. MAGALHAES: *Vidi aquam; Missa O Soberana luz; Commissa mea pavesco*. Manuel da FONSECA: *Beata viscera*. Bartolomeo TROSYLHO: *Circumdederunt*. Pedro de ESCOBAR: *Clamabat autem mulier*.
(BB) *** Naxos Dig. 8.553310 [id.].

In every respect this is an outstanding anthology. Apart from the major items from the Portuguese 'famous three' contemporaries, Cardoso, Lôbo and (the least-known) Filippe de Magalhães, which are discussed above under their respective composer entries, the motets by the earlier figures, Pedro de Escobar (*c*. 1465–1535), Bartolomeo Trosylho (*c*. 1500–*c*. 1567) and Manuel da Fonseca (*maestre da capela* at Braga Cathedral in the mid-sixteenth century), are all touchingly, serenely beautiful, if perhaps less individual. The singing of this Danish Choir is superb and so is the Naxos recording. Texts and translations are provided, although for some reason they are printed separately. A unique bargain of the highest quality.

(i) Bach Choir, Sir David Willcocks; (ii) Philip Jones Brass Ensemble, Philip Jones

'In dulci jubilo – A Festival of Christmas': (i; ii) arr. WILLCOCKS: *Fanfare – O come all ye faithful. Gabriel's message; Angelus ad Virginem; Ding dong! merrily on high; God rest you merry, gentlemen; Unto us a son is born; Once in Royal David's city; Hush my dear, lie still and remember; Away in a manger; Sussex carol*. TRAD.: *A virgin most pure; In dulci jubilo*. RUTTER: *Shepherd's pipe carol; Star carol*. GRUBER: *Stille Nacht*. MENDELSSOHN: *Hark the herald angels sing*. (ii) BACH: *Christmas oratorio: chorales: Nun seid Ihr wohl gerochen; Ach, mein herzliebes Jesulein*. TRAD.: *Lord Jesus hath a garden; Come all ye shepherds; Il est né*. arr. IVESON: *We three kings; Jingle bells – Deck the hall; The holly and the ivy*. arr. RUTTER: *Wassail song. We wish you a merry Christmas*.
(B) **(*) Decca Eclipse Dig. 448 980-2; *448 980-4* [(M) id. import].

The titling and documentation of this otherwise admirable Eclipse collection is misleading. It is basically an early (1980) digital concert by the Bach Choir, colourfully accompanied by the Philip Jones Brass Ensemble, conducted by Sir David Willcocks. Fresh simplicity is the keynote: the brass fanfares bring a touch of splendour, but the accompaniments are not over-scored. *Silent night* has never sounded more serene, and the other carols bring a wide variety of mood, while the two engaging Rutter pieces make a further refreshing contrast. However, as a central interlude there is a selection of ten items taken from a separate collection of Christmas music by Philip Jones and his Brass Ensemble without the choir, recorded two years later, also in the Kingsway Hall. Once again sound and playing are of very high quality. Appropriately framed by two chorales from Bach's *Christmas oratorio*, these arrangements are again effectively varied, with *Jingle bells* and *We wish you a merry Christmas* making a sparkling contrast with the gentler and more solemn music. But it must be said that carols are meant to include the words!

Bach Choir, Jacques Orchestra, Sir David Willcocks

'Unforgettable Christmas carols II': MENDELSSOHN, arr. Willcocks: *Hark! the herald angels*. arr. WILLCOCKS: *I saw three ships; God rest you merry, gentlemen; Infant holy; Masters in this hall; Rocking*.

arr. VAUGHAN WILLIAMS: *We've been awhile a-wandering; Wassail.* arr. WOODWARD: *Up! good Christian folk and listen.* HADLEY: *I sing of a maiden.* KIRKPATRICK, arr. Willcocks: *Away in a manger.* BACH: *O little one sweet.* WOODWARD, arr. Willcocks: *Unto us is born a son.* arr. JACQUES: *When Christ was born.* WOODWARD: *When an angel host entered; Past three-o-clock.* MORRIS: *Born in a manger.* arr. JACQUES: *Patapan.* TATE: *Carol with lullaby.* arr. KODALY: *Christmas carol.* arr. PETTMAN: *Gabriel's message.* SCHEIDT: *A child is born.* arr. SHAW: *Coventry carol.*
(B) *** CfP/EMI CD-CFP 6021 [(M) id.].

The clear, direct style of the Bach Choir is different from the cathedral-like King's tradition but equally effective. The acoustic is warm, but the choir's words are wonderfully clear and their style both buoyant and atmospheric. The familiar carols are simply and beautifully sung, notably the lovely Bach chorale and the *Coventry carol.* But within an imaginatively chosen programme it is the lesser-known carols that are especially memorable, not least Hadley's lovely *I sing of a maiden* and the two Vaughan Williams arrangements, *We've been awhile a-wandering* and *Wassail* with its lively inner part-writing. Phyllis Tate's unpredictable *Carol-Lullaby* and Kodály's arrangement of a traditional Hungarian Christmas melody are further highlights. The accompaniments are nicely balanced so that they support rather than overwhelm the singers, but the Willcocks arrangement of *Unto us is born a son* brings somes dramatic orchestral and percussion effects, and the joyfully vigorous *Masters in this hall* is richly scored, as is Scheidt's *A child is born*, with its resonant *Allelujas!*.

Baillie, Dame Isobel (soprano)

'The unforgettable Isobel Baillie': HANDEL: *Samson: Let the bright Seraphim. Rodelinda: Art thou troubled. Messiah: I know that my Redeemer liveth; If God be with us. Theodora: Angels ever bright and fair. Joshua: Oh! Had I Jubal's lyre.* BACH: *Cantata No. 68: My heart ever faithful; Cantata No. 201: Ah yes, just so* (arr. MOTTL). MOZART: *La finta giardiniera: A maiden's is an evil plight. The marriage of Figaro: O come, do not delay.* HAYDN: *The Creation: With verdure clad.* MENDELSSOHN: *Elijah: Hear ye, Israel.* OFFENBACH: *Tales of Hoffmann: Doll's song.* SCHUBERT: *The shepherd on the rock* (with Charles Draper, clarinet); *To music.* ARNE: *Where the bee sucks.*
✿ (M) (***) Dutton Lab. mono CDLX 7013 [id. full price].

It must be unique for a soprano's recording career to span over half a century, yet over all that time Isobel Baillie rarely if ever let down her maxim which provided the title of her autobiography: 'Never sing louder than lovely'. Handel's *I know that my Redeemer liveth* was certainly her most popular record during the war years. Alan Blyth describes this famous 1941 performance in the accompanying insert leaflet: 'Notes are hit fully and truly in the middle, and they are joined together in a seamless line. At the same time Baillie was able to swell and diminish her tone with total ease.' Like the rest of the programme, it is flawlessly transferred by the miraculous Dutton/CEDAR process, and one can enjoy Leslie Heward's warm Hallé accompaniment alongside the voice. In her duet with the trumpet (Arthur Lockwood) which opens the disc, *Let the bright Seraphim*, her bright, gleaming tone wins out every time, and elsewhere there are dazzling displays of agility (as in the 1930 *Doll's song* and the delightful Arne *Where the bee sucks* from 1943) as well as purity and loveliness (as in the 1941 *Art thou troubled* or Susanna's aria from *The marriage of Figaro*, recorded in 1927). Her simplicity of style was just right for Schubert, and her account of *The Shepherd on the rock*, recorded a year later, shows the bright, fresh timbre, which was uniquely hers, under perfect control. The timbre of Charles Draper, the distinguished clarinettist who plays the obbligato, by comparison seems dry and lustreless. A record to treasure on all counts.

Baker, Dame Janet (mezzo-soprano)

'An Anthology of English song' (with Martin Isepp): VAUGHAN WILLIAMS: *The Call; Youth and Love.* IRELAND: *A Thanksgiving; Her Song.* M. HEAD: *Piper.* C. ARMSTRONG GIBBS: *This is a sacred city; Love is a sickness.* DUNHILL: *The Cloths of Heaven; To the Queen of Heaven.* WARLOCK: *Balulalow; Youth.* HOWELLS: *King David; Come sing and dance.* I. GURNEY: *Sleep; I will go with my father a-ploughing.* FINZI: *Come away, come away, Death; It was a lover and his lass.*
(M) *** Saga EC 3340-2 [id.].

A glorious collection superbly sung. Janet Baker's artistry on one of her earliest records reveals moments of pure enchantment in these unpretentious settings of English lyrics. She herself chose them and, though the majority have not immediate popular appeal, they grow more and more attractive on repetition – the melismatic Alleluias in Howells's *Come sing and dance*, the golden simplicity of Gurney's *I will go with my father a-ploughing.* Martin Isepp is an outstanding accompanist, always sympathetic, and the recording is completely natural and very well balanced. The CD transfer brings an astonishing sense of presence and realism. There are good notes, and if the playing time is merely 45 minutes every one of them is treasurable.

Lieder (with Martin Isepp, piano): SCHUMANN: *Frauenliebe und Leben* (song-cycle), *Op. 42* *** ❁. SCHUBERT: *Heimliches Lieben; Minnelied; Die Abgeblühte Linde. Der Musensohn*. BRAHMS: *Die Mainacht; Das Mädchen spricht; Nachtigall; Von ewiger Liebe*.
(M)*** Saga EC 3361-2 [id.].

Janet Baker's inspirational account of *Frauenliebe und Leben*, part of this early Lieder recital for Saga, has never been surpassed. The Schubert songs are not quite on this level (*Der Musensohn* a little jerky), but the Brahms are beyond praise. This is singing of a quality that you find only once or twice in a generation and – whatever the price – this CD is a collector's piece. The stereo on the original LP was curiously balanced, with voice and piano unnaturally separated, but the CD transfer transforms the sound, with oddities ironed out. Set in a dryish acoustic, the quality is now full-bodied, with a vivid sense of presence to make the transcendental performances even more involving.

'Grandi voci': RAVEL: *3 Poèmes de Stéphane Mallarmé; Chansons madécasses*. CHAUSSON: *Chanson perpétuelle, Op. 37*. DELAGE: *4 Poèmes hindous* (with the Melos Ensemble). Arias from: PURCELL: *Dido and Aeneas*. RAMEAU: *Hippolyte et Aricie* (with ECO, Lewis). BACH: *Cantata, BWV 170* (with ASMF, Marriner). CAVALLI: *La Calisto* (with LPO, Leppard).
❁ (M) *** Decca 440 413-2.

The performances of French mélodies included on this record are very beautiful indeed. Chausson's extended cantilena about a deserted lover has a direct communication which Dame Janet contrasts with the subtler beauties of the Ravel songs. She shows great depth of feeling for the poetry here and an equally evocative sensitivity to the songs about India, written in 1912 by Ravel's pupil, Maurice Delage, which are by no means inferior to the songs by his more famous contemporaries. With superb, atmospheric playing by the Melos group and an outstanding 1966 (originally Oiseau-Lyre) recording, this ravishing collection must be placed among Dame Janet's most outstanding recordings. For the current reissue, more remarkable examples of her art have been generously added, not least the lovely Bach aria, *Vergnügte Ruh'*, the dramatic excerpt from Cavalli's *La Calisto* in Raymond Leppard's imaginative realization, and, of course, her heartrending account of Dido's lament, *When I am laid in earth*.

RAVEL: *Shéhérazade* (with New Philh. O, Barbirolli). CHAUSSON: *Poème de l'amour et de la mer*. DUPARC: *Phidylé; La vie antérieure; Le manoir de Rosamonde; Au pays où se fait la guerre; L'invitation au voyage* (with LSO, Previn). SCHUMANN: *Frauenliebe und Leben* (with Barenboim). BRAHMS: *Vier ernste Gesänge, Op. 121; 2 Lieder, with viola, Op. 91* (with Aronowitz, Previn); *4 Duets, Op. 28* (with Fischer-Dieskau, Barenboim).
(B) *** EMI forte CZS5 68667-2 (2) [CDFB 68667].

Dame Janet Baker was always at her finest in French music, and with her 1967 performance of *Shéhérazade* she inspired Barbirolli to one of his most glowing performances in this atmospherically scored music; her range of tone and her natural sympathy for the French language make for heartwarming singing which has a natural intensity. The account of Chausson's *Poème de l'amour et de la mer* is comparably glorious and heart-felt, both radiant and searching, so that this picture of love in two aspects, first emergent, then past, has a sharpness of focus often denied it; in this she is superbly supported by Previn and the LSO. Their partnership is hardly less persuasive in the five Duparc mélodies which the composer orchestrated himself – each a jewelled miniature of breathtaking beauty, with the extra richness and colour of the orchestral accompaniment adding to the depth and intensity of the exceptionally sensitive word-settings, especially in the greatest of them all, *Phidylé*. It was Schumann's *Frauenliebe und Leben* that helped to establish Baker's early reputation, and she returned to this favourite cycle in early maturity with renewed freshness in the light of deeper experience. Where on her Saga record (see above) she transposed most of the earlier songs down a full tone, the later version keeps them in the original keys. Then by contrast it is the later songs which she transposes, reserving her warmer tones for those expressions of motherhood. The wonder, the inwardness, are even more intense, while the final song in some ways brings the most remarkable performance of all (*'Now you have hurt me'*), not at all a conventional expression of mourning. With Barenboim an endlessly imaginative – if sometimes reticent – accompanist, this is another classic example of Baker's art. The Brahms Lieder were the last to be recorded, in 1977, and the gravity and nobility of her singing in the *Four Serious Songs* underlines the weight of the biblical words while presenting them with a far wider and more beautiful range of tone-colour than is common. André Previn's piano is placed rather backwardly, but his rhythmic control provides fine support, and in the two viola songs, which are ravishingly sung and played, these artists are partnered by the late Cecil Aronowitz, making his last appearance on record. To cap the recital come the four varied duets of Op. 28, in which Baker is joined by Dietrich Fischer-Dieskau, recorded at a live recital at London's Queen Elizabeth Hall in 1969. The vivacious closing *Der Jäger und sein Liebchen* makes a spiritedly vivacious coda to a collection which could hardly be bettered. Even if the presentation here omits texts and translations, this set still makes an amazing bargain.

'Arie amarose' (with ASMF, Marriner): GIORDANO: *Caro mio ben*. CACCINI: *Amarilli mia bella*. STRADELLA: *Ragion sempra addita*. SARRI: *Sen corre l'agnelletta*. CESTI: *Intorno all'idol mio*. LOTTI: *Pur dicesti, o bocca bella*. Alessandro SCARLATTI: *Spesso vibra per suo gioco; Già il sole dal gange; Sento nel core*. CALDARA: *Come raggio del Sol; Sebben crudele me fai languir'; Selve amiche*. BONONCINI: *Del più a me non v'ascondete*. DURANTE: *Danza fanciulla gentile*. PERGOLESI: *Ogni pena più spietata*. MARTINI: *Plaisir d'amour*. PICCINI: *O notte o dea del mistero*. PAISIELLO: *Nel cor più non mi sento*.
(M) *** Ph. 434 173-2.

A delightful recital of classical arias, marred only by the absence of libretti. However, unlike the original (1978) LP, the CD has good supporting notes by Lionel Salter, which are essential for proper enjoyment of this repertoire. The programme is cleverly arranged to contrast expressive with sprightly music and the wide range of tonal graduation and beautiful phrasing is matched by an artless lightness of touch in the slighter numbers. The accompaniments are intimate and tasteful; there is no more fetching example than Pergolesi's *Ogni pena più spietata*, with its deft bassoon obbligato (which Stravinsky used for *Pulcinella*) or the short closing song with harpsichord, Paisiello's *Nel cor più non mi sento*. Caldara's *Come raggio del Sol* and *Selve amiche* are most touching, while Scarlatti is there to lighten the mood with *Già il sole dal gange*. The recording has a warm acoustic and the resonance is kind to the voice without loss of orchestral detail. The CD transfer is pleasingly vivid and natural.

'Janet Baker sings' (with Gerald Moore, piano): FAURE: *Automne; Prison; Soir; Fleur jetée; En sourdine; Notre amour; Mai; Chanson du pêcheur; Clair de lune*. STANFORD: *La belle dame sans merci*. PARRY: *Proud Masie; O mistress mine*. William BUSCH: *Rest*. WARLOCK: *Pretty ringtime*. VAUGHAN WILLIAMS: *Linden Lea*. GURNEY: *Fields are full*. BRITTEN: *Corpus Christi carol*. IRELAND: *Sally Gardens*. QUILTER: *Love's Philosophy*. SCHUBERT: *Am Grabe; Anselmos; Abendstern; Die Vögel; Strophe aus Die Götte; Griechenlands; Gondelfahrer; Auflösung*. Richard STRAUSS: *Morgen!; Befreit*.
❀ (M) *** EMI CDM5 65009-2.

Just after he had officially retired, in the late 1960s Gerald Moore returned to the recording studio to accompany Janet Baker, an artist whom he counted high among the many great singers he had accompanied in his career. This recital brings together a sequence of magical perfomances of songs especially dear to Dame Janet, with the voice consistently golden in tone. The Fauré group brings out her intense love of singing in French, and her devotion to the German Lied shines out equally in Schubert and Strauss. The group of ten English songs demonstrates that this neglected genre has comparable claims in beauty and intensity, with such favourite items as Vaughan Williams's *Linden Lea* and Quilter's *Love's philosophy* given heartfelt performances. Even this singer rarely sang with more beauty than here.

Baroque Opera: 'Treasures of Baroque Opera'

'Treasures of Baroque Opera': MONTEVERDI: *L'Orfeo: Toccata* (New London Consort, Pickett); *Prologo: Ritornello . . . Dal mio Permesso amato* (Catherine Bott). ARNE: *Rosamond: Rise, glory, rise* (Emma Kirkby). *Artaxerxes: The soldier tir'd*. PICCINI: *La buona figliuola: Furia di donna*. HANDEL: *Alcina: Tormami a vagheggiar* (Dame Joan Sutherland). *Rinaldo: March and Battle* (ECO, Bonynge); *Armida dispietatat! . . . Lascia ch'io pianga* (Bernadette Greevy). *Rodelinda: Vivi, tiranno* (Marilyn Horne). *Atalanta: Care selve* (Luciano Pavarotti). PURCELL: *Dido and Aeneas: Dido's lament*. CAVALLI: *La Calisto: Ardo, sospiro e piango* (Dame Janet Baker). RAMEAU: *Hippolyte et Arice: Puisque Pluton est inflexible* (John Shirley-Quirk). *Le Temple de la gloire: Overture* (ECO, Raymond Leppard). *Les Indes galantes: Soleil on a détruit tes superbes asiles* (Gérard Souzay). PERGOLESI: *La serva padrona: Stizzoso, mio stizzoso* (Teresa Berganza).
❀ (M) *** Decca Analogue/Dig. 458 217-2 [id.].

This is truly a treasure-chest – one of the finest collections of baroque arias ever assembled on disc, and certainly the most generous, with 16 excerpts, all sung superbly. The overall standard is astonishingly high, with almost every item a plum. After Philip Pickett's dramatic opening *Toccata*, Catherine Bott is in glorious voice as La Musica in *Orfeo* and Emma Kirkby's Arne is equally fresh. The inclusion of Dame Janet Baker's achingly vulnerable portrayal of the betrayed Dido is predictable, but her account of Diana's *Ardo, sospiro e piano* from Cavalli's *La Calisto* is hardly less moving. On a lighter note comes Teresa

Berganza's deliciously coquettish *Stizzoso, mio stizzoso* from Pergolesi's *La Serva Padrona*. Richard Bonynge introduces the Handelian sequence with the *March and Battle* from *Rinaldo* which is more familiar as 'Let us take the road' in *The Beggar's Opera*, and then Bernadette Greevy richly reminds us that Almirena's *Lascia ch'io pianga* is as noble a melody as Handel ever wrote (undecorated, but none the worse for that). She is followed by Marilyn Horne's astounding demonstration of vocal bravura as she leaps from one register to another and back again in *Vivi, tiranno* from *Rodelinda*. The art of Joan Sutherland is well represented (with all the recordings coming from the early 1960s, when the voice was at its sweetest) and it is she who ends the programme with sparkling virtuosity in *Tornami a vagheggiar*. The recording throughout is brilliant and atmospheric in Decca's best manner; the disc is handsomely packaged and full translations are included. Not to be missed!

Battle, Kathleen (soprano), **Plácido Domingo** (tenor)

'Battle and Domingo Live' (with Metropolitan Opera O, Levine): Arias & duets from: VERDI: *La traviata*. DONIZETTI: *Don Pasquale; Lucia di Lammermoor; L'elisir d'amore*. GOUNOD: *Roméo et Juliette*. MOZART: *Don Giovanni*. LEHAR: *Die lustige Witwe*. Overtures to: VERDI: *La forza del destino*. ROSSINI: *L'Italiana in Algeri*.

(M) *** DG (IMS) Dig. 445 552-2 [id.].

These gala occasions can often be very stimulating for the audience, but only very occasionally do they produce an outstanding record. The present recital is surely the exception that proves the rule. From Levine's vibrant *La forza del destino overture* onwards, the 'live' communication of these performances comes across readily. The *La Traviata* duet has great charm, with Domingo obviously matching his voice to the smaller but lovely sound which Battle naturally commands. The lesser-known duet from *Romeo and Juliet* is hardly less delightful, and *Là ci darem la mano* is engagingly relaxed and elegant: who wouldn't be seduced by this Don? No complaints about the solo arias either, but the unforgettable charmer is the final ravishing Waltz duet from *The Merry widow* which is (quite rightly) sung in English. The ringing final cadence is breathtaking. Few hours of operatic excerpts are as magical as this one, and the recording is splendid.

Berganza, Teresa (mezzo-soprano)

'Canciones españolas' (with Narciso Yepes, guitar, Félix Lavilla, piano): SABIO: *Rosa das rosas; Santa Maria*. FUENLLANA: *Pérdida de Antequera*. ANON.: *Dindirindin; Nuaves te traygo, carillo; Los hombres con gran plazer*. MUDARRA: *Triste estava el rey David; Si me llaman a mí; Claros y frescos rios; Ysabel, perdiste la tu faxa*. TORRE: *Dime, triste corazón; Pámpano verde*. VALDERRABANO: *De dónde venis, amore?* MILAN: *Toda mi vida os amé; Aquel caballero, madre*. TRIANA: *Dínos, madre del donsel*. ENCINA: *Romerico*. VAZQUEZ: *Vos me matastes; En la fuente del rosel*. NARVAEZ: *Con qué la lavaré?* ANCHIETA: *Con amores, la mi madre*. ESTEVE: *Alma sintamos*. GRANADOS: *La maja dolorosa: Oh, muerte cruel!; Ay, majo de mi vida!; De aquel majo amante. El majo discreto; El tra la lá y el punteado; El majo timido*. GURIDI: *Canciones castellanas: Llámale con el pañuelo; No quiero tus avellanas; Cómo quieres que adivine!* FALLA: *7 Canciones populares españolas*. LORCA: *13 Canciones españolas antiquas*. TURINA: *Saeta en forma de Salve a la Virgen de la Esperanza; Canto a Sevilla: El fantasma. Poema en forma de canciones: Cantares*. MONTSALVATGE: *5 Canciones negras*.

(M) *** DG (IMS) 435 848-2 (2).

This collection dates from the mid-1970s when Berganza was at her peak, the voice fresh, her artistry mature. In essence she provides here a history of Spanish song, opening with two pieces taken from the *Cantigas de Santa Maria*, dating from the thirteenth century, and moving on through Renaissance repertory and, with only one song from the eighteenth century, to the nineteenth and twentieth, traditional settings by Lorca, Falla's *7 Spanish popular songs* and the engaging *Canciones negras* of Montsalvatge. The collaboration with Narciso Yepes seems ideal, for he is an inspirational artist, while her husband, Félix Lavilla, provides the later piano accompaniments. This is not a specialist recital: the music communicates readily in the most direct way, and excellent notes and translations are provided. The balance is very natural and the CD transfers are immaculately managed. This is repertoire one first associates with Victoria de los Angeles, but Berganza makes it her own and there are not many more attractive Spanish song-recitals than this.

'Grandi voci': MOZART: Concert arias: *Ombra felice! . . . lo ti lascio, K.255; Misero me! . . . Misero pargoletto, K.77; Se ardire e speranza, K.82; Conserati fedel, K.23. Nozze di Figaro:* (alternative aria): *Giunse alfin il momento . . . Al desio do chi t'adora, K.577* (all with VCO, György Fischer); *Ch'io mi scordi di te? . . . None temer, amato bene, K.505* (with Geoffrey Parsons, piano, LSO, Pritchard). HAYDN: *Arianna a Naxos* (cantata; with Félix Lavilla, piano.)
(M) *** Decca 448 246-2.

These Mozart arias were originally issued in the early 1980s within a Decca set gathering together all the arias for soprano, in which Berganza was joined by a number of other singers. It is good to hear her voice still remarkably fresh in 1981 and the singing as stylish as ever (notably so in the opening *Ombra felice! . . . lo ti lascio* and the long alternative aria for Susanna in Act IV of *Figaro*, which was to be replaced by the less taxing *Deh vieni*) and then make a comparison with the superb account of *Ch'io mi scordi di te?* which she recorded with Pritchard (with Geoffrey Parsons playing the piano solo) 19 years earlier in 1962, when the voice had a ravishing youthful bloom. The recital concludes with a highly dramatic and lyrically persuasive account of the ambitious Haydn cantata, *Arianna a Naxos*, made in 1977 with her husband at the piano.

Bergonzi, Carlo (tenor)

'Grandi voci' (arias from): VERDI: *Aida; Luisa Miller; La forza del destino; Il trovatore; Un ballo in maschera; Don Carlo; La Traviata.* MEYERBEER: *L'africana.* GIORDANO: *Andrea Chénier.* CILEA: *Adriana Lecouvreur.* PUCCINI: *Tosca; Manon Lescaut; La Bohème.* PONCHIELLI: *La Gioconda.*
(M) **(*) Decca 440 417-2 [id.].

This recital, consisting mainly of Bergonzi's early stereo recordings, a dozen arias recorded with the Orchestra of the Santa Cecilia Academy, Rome, under Gavazenni in 1957, shows him on consistently peak form. He does not attempt the rare pianissimo at the end of *Celeste Aida*; but here among Italian tenors is a thinking musical artist who never resorts to vulgarity. The lovely account of *Che gelida manina* (with Serafin) comes from two years later. The early stereo has transferred well and retains a bloom on the voice. The other recordings also derive from sets: *La Traviata* (1962), *Un ballo* (1960–61), *Don Carlo* (1965), both with Solti, while the stirring *Cielo e mar* from *La Gioconda* (1967) shows that Bergonzi's tone retained its quality. These added items help to make up a generous playing time of 71 minutes, besides adding variety to what was originally essentially a collection of favourites. Everything sounds fresh.

Bjoerling, Jussi (tenor)

Bjoerling Edition: (Studio recordings 1930–59; with O, Nils Grevillius): Disc 1 (1936–41): Arias from VERDI: *Aida; Rigoletto; Requiem; La Traviata; Il Trovatore.* PUCCINI: *La Bohème; Tosca; La fanciulla del West.* PONCHIELLI: *La Gioconda.* MEYERBEER: *L'Africaine.* MASSENET: *Manon.* BIZET: *Carmen.* GOUNOD: *Faust.* FLOTOW: *Martha.* ROSSINI: *Stabat Mater.* FRIML: *The Vagabond King.* Songs by TOSTI; DI CAPUA; GEEHL. Disc 2 (1941–50): Arias from: PUCCINI: *La Bohème; Turandot; Manon Lescaut; Tosca.* VERDI: *Rigoletto; Un ballo in maschera.* GIORDANO: *Andrea Chénier; Fedora.* MASCAGNI: *Cavalleria rusticana.* LEONCAVALLO: *Pagliacci* (also song: *Mattinata*). DONIZETTI: *L'elisir d'amore.* BIZET: *Les Pêcheurs de perles.* GOUNOD: *Roméo et Juliette.* MASSENET: *Manon.* CILEA: *L'arlesiana.* GODARD: *Jocelyn (Berceuse).* Song: TOSTI: *L'alba separa.* Disc 3: Arias (sung in Swedish) from: GOUNOD: *Roméo et Juliette.* VERDI: *Rigoletto; Il Trovatore.* LAPARRA: *L'illustre Fregona.* BORODIN: *Prince Igor.* PUCCINI: *Tosca; La fanciulla del West.* LEONCAVALLO: *Pagliacci.* MASCAGNI: *Cavalleria rusticana.* ATTERBERG: *Fanal.* RIMSKY-KORSAKOV: *Sadko.* OFFENBACH: *La belle Hélène.* Johann STRAUSS Jr: *Der Zigeunerbaron.* MILLOCKER: *Der Bettelstudent.* Traditional songs (in Swedish) and by PETERSON-BERGER; SJOBERG; SCHRADER; STENHAMMAR; ALTHEN; WIDE. Disc 4: Lieder and songs (1939–59): BEETHOVEN: *Adelaide.* R. STRAUSS: *Morgen; Cäcile.* RACHMANINOV: *In the silence of the night; Lilacs.* FOSTER: *Jeannie with the light brown hair.* D'HARDELOT: *Because.* SPEAKS: *Sylvia.* CAMPBELL-TIPTON: *A spirit flower.* BEACH: *Ah, love but a day.* SJOBERG: *I bless ev'ry hour.* SIBELIUS: *The diamond in the March snow.* ADAM: *O holy night.* Songs by NORDQVIST; SALEN; PETERSON-BERGER; SODERMAN; ALFVEN.
(M) (***) EMI ZDMS5 66306-2 (4) [ZDMD 666306].

All admirers of the great Swedish tenor should consider this comprehensive compilation, 89 items chosen by Harald Henrysson from EMI's Swedish archives and admirably remastered at Abbey Road. The voice is caught freshly and truthfully. Bjoerling's wife, Anna-Lisa, also participates in duets from *La Bohème* and *Roméo et Juliette*, towards the end of the second disc. The selection of arias is almost entirely predictable (and none the worse for that); a number of the key items are offered twice, and sometimes again in Swedish (where they sound surprisingly effective, even an excerpt from Offenbach's *La belle Hélène*). All the songs have a direct popular appeal. Bjoerling opens Disc 4 with a winning account of Beethoven's *Adelaide*, and many will welcome the lighter songs, and particularly the English ballads. However, the closing group of eight Scandinavian songs is memorable: romantic and dramatic by turns, and closing with a bold final contrast, *The diamond in the March snow* of Sibelius, which is capped by Bjoerling's ardent version of Adam's *Cantique de Noël* in Swedish. Excellent documentation, with photographs and full translations.

Operatic recital: Arias from: PONCHIELLI: *La Gioconda*. PUCCINI: *La Fanciulla del West; Manon Lescaut*. GIORDANO: *Fedora*. CILEA: *L'Arlesiana*. VERDI: *Un ballo in maschera; Requiem*. MASCAGNI: *Cavalleria Rusticana* (with Tebaldi). LEHAR: *Das Land des Lächelns*.
(M) *** Decca 443 930-2.

Jussi Bjoerling provides here a flow of headily beautiful, finely focused tenor tone. These may not be the most characterful renderings of each aria, but they are all among the most compellingly musical. The recordings are excellent for their period (1959–60). The Lehár was the last solo recording he made before he died in 1960. The transfers to CD are admirably lively and present.

Bjoerling, Jussi, Enrico Caruso, Beniamino Gigli (tenors)

'Three legendary tenors in opera and song'

Caruso: Arias from: BIZET: *Carmen*. MASSENET: *Manon*. VERDI: *Otello; La forza del destino; Aida*. GIORDANO: *Andrea Chénier*. PUCCINI: *Tosca*.

Gigli: Arias from: LEONCAVALLO: *I Pagliacci* (also Song: *Mattinata*) BIZET: *Les pêcheurs de perles* (also Duet: *Del tempo al limitar;* with Giuseppe de Luca). VERDI: *La Traviata*. PUCCINI: *Tosca*. Song: DI CAPUA: *O sole mio*.

Bjoerling: Arias from VERDI: *Rigoletto*. PUCCINI: *La Bohème; Turandot*. RIMSKY-KORSAKOV: *Sadko*. MEYERBEER: *L'Africana*. MASSENET: *Manon*. Song: TOSTI: *Ideale*.
(M) (***) Nimbus mono NI 1434 [id.].

Nimbus caught on to the idea of promoting a selection from three legendary tenors from their archives and they decided that a single disc (75 minutes) would be the best proposition. Their system of playing back 78-r.p.m. originals through a big fibre horn and re-recording them works very well here with the three voices naturally caught, but the orchestral backing more variable. The documentation is poor and no recording dates are given, but the excerpts are obviously hand-picked and recorded over a fairly wide time-span. Items which obviously stand out are: Caruso's *Un dì, all'azzurro spazio* from *Andrea Chénier* and of course *Celeste Aida* (with a remarkably believable brass fanfare); Gigli's honeyed *E lucevan le stelle* from *Tosca* and his thrilling *O sole mio*; and Bjoerling's *Che gelida manina* from *Bohème*, the seductive *Sadko* 'Song of India' and his glorious *Nessun dorma*. The collection ends splendidly with Caruso and De Luca matching their voices sensationally in the frisson-creating *Pearl fishers* duet.

Bowman, James (counter-tenor)

'The James Bowman collection' (with The King's Consort, Robert King): BACH: *Erbarme dich; Stirb in mir*. HANDEL: *Almighty power; Crueltà nè lontananza; Impious mortal; Tune your harps; Welcome as the dawn of day; Thou shalt bring them in; Or la tromba; Eternal source of light*. PURCELL: *Britain, thou now art great; O solitude; By beauteous softness mixed; An Evening hymn; On the brow of Richmond Hill; Vouchsafe, O Lord*. ANON.: *Come tread the paths*. GABRIELI: *O magnum mysterium*. FORD: *Since I saw your face*. COUPERIN: *Jerusalem, convertere*.
(B) *** Hyperion Dig. KING 3 [(M) id.].

Apart from the opening Bach item, which has not previously been published and which is not entirely flattering, this admirable 78-minute sampler will delight fans of James Bowman as it shows his art and fine vocal control over a wide range of repertoire at which he excelled. Robert King and his Consort provide admirable support.

Caballé, Montserrat (soprano)

'Rossini, Donizetti and Verdi rarities' (with RCA Italiana Ch. & O, (i) Cillario; (ii) Guadagno; (iii) Amb. Op. Ch., LSO Cillario): Arias & excerpts from: (i) ROSSINI: *La Donna del lago; Otello; Stabat Mater; Armida; Tancredi; L'assedio di Corinto.* (ii) DONIZETTI: *Belisario; Parisina d'este* (with M. Elkins, T. McDonnell). *Torquato Tasso; Gemma di Vergy.* (iii) VERDI: *Un giorno di regno; I Lombardi; I due Foscari* (with M. Sunara); *Alzira; Attila; Il Corsaro; Aroldo* (with. L. Kozma).
(M) *** BMG/RCA GD 60941 (2) [09026 60941-2].

Caballé's conviction as well as her technical assurance make for highly dramatic results in scenas that not many years ago would have been laughed out of court. It makes these rarities more attractively convincing that the arias are presented with surrounding detail from a group of well-chosen supporting artists. The Rossini selection is no less rewarding, though the aria from the *Stabat Mater* hardly qualifies as a rarity. The Verdi arias, taken from operas of the early years when the composer was working 'in the galleys', make a further commandingly brilliant recital when sung with such assurance. Caballé is again at her finest, challenged by the technical difficulties as well as by the need to convey the drama. She makes one forget that between the big, memorable tunes there are often less-than-inspired passages. Fine accompaniments throughout and splendidly smooth and vivid CD transfers ensure the success of these two discs, between them offering 144 minutes of music.

Operatic excerpts (with Pavarotti, Milnes, Baltsa) from VERDI: *Luisa Miller*. BELLINI: *Norma*. BOITO: *Mefistofele*. PUCCINI: *Turandot*. GIORDANO: *Andrea Chénier*. PONCHIELLI: *La Gioconda*.
(M) *** Decca 443 928-2.

Although the disc centres on Caballé and is described as 'Operatic arias', there are in fact plenty of duets, and ensembles too. All the excerpts come from highly recommended complete sets, and Pavarotti figures often and strongly. In Bellini, Giordano or Boito, and especially as Liù in *Turandot*, Caballé is often vocally ravishing and she finds plenty of drama and power for Verdi and Ponchielli. There are at least two and sometimes three or four items from each opera, admirably chosen to make consistently involving entertainment. Alas, the back-up notes are inadequate, concentrating on Caballé's association with each of the operas included.

'Diva': Arias from: PUCCINI: *Madama Butterfly; Tosca; Manon Lescaut; La Bohème; Turandot; La Rondine*. ROSSINI: *William Tell*. BELLINI: *Il Pirata; I Puritani*. VERDI: *Giovanna d'Arco; Macbeth; Don Carlo; Aida*. BOITO: *Mefistofele*. MASCAGNI: *Cavalleria rusticana*.
(M) *** EMI CDM5 65575-2 [id.].

This fine compilation is framed by items from Caballé's 1970 Puccini recital in which she impersonates Mimì, Tosca and Butterfly, singing more impressively than she characterizes. Otherwise these are items from complete sets made between 1970 (Giulini's *Don Carlo*) and 1980 (Muti's *I Puritani*). The items are not always the obvious choices from each opera but from first to last they demonstrate the consistent beauty of her singing at that period, responding to a wide range of conductors.

'Great voice': excerpts from: GOUNOD: *Faust; Roméo et Juliette*. MEYERBEER: *Les Huguenots*. CHARPENTIER: *Louise*. BIZET: *Carmen*. PUCCINI: *Manon Lescaut* (with Domingo). R. STRAUSS: *Salome* (Closing scene).
(B) ** DG 431 103-2 [(M) id. import].

Most of the content of Caballé's contribution to DG's '*Grosse Stimmen*' series is drawn from a 1971 recital of French arias. Although the quality of the voice is in no doubt, this was not in fact one of this artist's more distinctive recitals. The vocal line is sometimes not perfectly judged (her earlier, RCA recording of Charpentier's *Depuis le jour* was finer; here the aria's key moments are managed confidently but the performance as a whole is simply less beautiful). In the Gounod numbers the style is not fined down enough: the voice seems a trifle unwieldy. The Meyerbeer item is the most convincing. DG's recording is warm, with a resonant acoustic, kind to both the voice and the superb orchestral playing from the New Philharmonia under Reynald Giovaninetti. The duet from *Manon Lescaut* (*Tu, tu amore?*) with Domingo is vibrantly exciting, but the recording, made at a live performance, is somewhat less flattering. (It is included also on Domingo's recital in this series.) The highlight here is the final scene from *Salome*, recorded with Leonard Bernstein in 1978, although the orchestral sound could ideally be more sumptuous. But the performance is imaginatively full of contrasts, the sweet innocent girl still observable next to the bloodthirsty fiend. The disc is poorly presented, with nothing about music or artist, only titles and recording dates.

Callas, Maria (soprano)

'La Divina I': Arias from: PUCCINI: *Madama Butterfly; La Bohème; Gianni Schicchi; Turandot; Tosca.* BIZET: *Carmen.* CATALANI: *La Wally.* ROSSINI: *Il barbiere di Siviglia.* BELLINI: *Norma.* SAINT-SAENS: *Samson et Dalila.* VERDI: *Rigoletto; La Traviata.* GOUNOD: *Roméo et Juliette.* MOZART: *Don Giovanni.* MASCAGNI: *Cavalleria rusticana.* PONCHIELLI: *La Gioconda.*
**(*) EMI stereo/mono CDC7 54702-2 [id.].

'La Divina II': Arias from: GLUCK: *Alceste; Orphée et Eurydice.* BIZET: *Carmen.* VERDI: *Ernani; Aida; I vespri siciliani; La Traviata; Don Carlo.* PUCCINI: *Manon Lescaut; La Bohème.* CHARPENTIER: *Louise.* THOMAS: *Mignon.* SAINT-SAENS: *Samson et Dalila.* BELLINI: *La sonnambula.* CILEA: *Adriana Lecouvreur.* DONIZETTI: *Lucia di Lammermoor.*
*(*) EMI stereo/mono CDC5 55016-2 [id.].

'La Divina III': Arias and duets from: GIORDANO: *Andrea Chénier.* SPONTINI: *La vestale.* MASSENET: *Manon.* PUCCINI: *Manon Lescaut; La Bohème* (with Giuseppe di Stefano); *Madama Butterfly* (with Nicolai Gedda); *Turandot.* BIZET: *Carmen* (with Nicolai Gedda). ROSSINI: *Il barbiere di Siviglia* (with Tito Gobbi). DELIBES: *Lakmé.* VERDI: *Aida; Il Trovatore.* LEONCAVALLO: *Pagliacci.* MEYERBEER: *Dinorah.*
*** EMI stereo/mono CDC5 55216-2 [id.].

'La Divina' I–III; Maria Callas in conversation with Edward Downes'.
(M) **(*) EMI CMS5 65746-2 (4) [ZDMD 65746].

This handsome (limited-edition) box is clearly aimed primarily at the Callas aficionado, as the back-up documentation includes three separate photographs as well as a liberally illustrated booklet giving a year-by-year biography, beginning with her birth in December 1923. It details her career and personal life through to her tragic final three years as a disillusioned recluse in her Paris apartment, where she died in 1977. The three recital discs (with nearly four hours of music) cover her recording career pretty thoroughly, although the first two are inadequately documented, giving only the date each recording was *published.* '*Divina III*', however, provides both the actual dates and venues of the recordings and details of the other artists involved. A fourth CD offers a conversation between Callas and Edward Downes as broadcast in the USA in two parts – in the intervals of Metropolitan Opera performances in December 1967 and in January 1968. Throughout the three programmes, results are inevitably uneven and if at times the rawness of exposed top-notes mars the lyrical beauty of her singing, equally often her dramatic magnetism is such that many phrases stay indelibly in the memory. Each disc has its share of highlights, with the earlier recordings usually the more memorable. What is perhaps surprising are the omissions: nothing, for instance, from the collection of 'Mad scenes' she recorded with Rescigno. However, many of the choices are apt. '*La Divina I*', for instance, includes her sharply characterful, early 1954 recording of *Una voce poco fa* from Rossini's *Barbiere*, yet '*La Divina III*' draws on the later, complete set for the duet *Dunque io son*, with Tito Gobbi. La Divina II consistently shows her at her finest or near it. The recordings cover a decade from 1954 to 1964 and include much that is arrestingly dramatic (Gluck and Verdi) and ravishing (Puccini and Cilea), while everything shows that special degree of imagination which Callas brought to almost everything she did. The *Mignon Polonaise* is not ideally elegant but it has a distinctive character and charm, and it is almost irrelevant to criticize Callas on detail when her sense of presence is so powerful. The excerpt from *La Traviata* was recorded live in Lisbon in 1958 and even the audience noises cannot detract from its magnetism. All three recital discs are available separately at full price, with the third certainly the place to start, as it centres on early recordings, including the excerpt from *La Vestale*, and opens with the movingly intense *La mamma morta* from *Andrea Chénier*. However, it is astonishing that, having provided so much information about the singer, EMI chose not to include any translations, resting content with a brief synopsis of each aria.

Callas Edition

'Lyric and coloratura arias' (with Philh. O, Tullio Serafin): CILEA: *Adriana Lecouvreur: Ecco, respiro appena . . . Io son l'umile; Poveri fiori.* GIORDANO: *Andrea Chénier: La mamma morta.* CATALANI: *La Wally: Ebben? Ne andrò lontana.* BOITO: *Mefistofele: L'altra notte.* ROSSINI: *Il barbiere di Siviglia: Una voce poco fa.* MEYERBEER: *Dinorah: Shadow song.* DELIBES: *Lakmé: Bell song.* VERDI: *I vespri siciliani: Bolero: Mercè, dilette amiche.*
(M) (***) EMI mono CDM5 66458-2 [id.].

Recorded at the same group of sessions in September 1954 as her very first (Puccini) recital for EMI – see above – this another of the classic early Callas records, ranging extraordinarily widely in its repertory and revealing in every item the uniquely intense musical imagination that set musicians of every kind listening and learning. Coloratura flexibility here goes with dramatic weight. Not all the items are equally successful: the *Shadow song* from *Dinorah*, for example, reveals some strain and lacks charm, but these are all unforgettable performances. Callas's portrait of Rosina in *Una voce poco fa* was never more viperish than here, and she never surpassed the heart-felt intensity of such numbers as *La mamma morta* and *Poveri fiori*. This mono reissue is well balanced and cleanly transferred with the voice vividly projected against a convincing orchestral backdrop.

'Callas at La Scala' (with La Scala, Milan, O, Tullio Serafin): CHERUBINI: *Medea: Dei tuoi figli.* SPONTINI: *La Vestale: Tu che invoco; O nume tutelar; Caro oggetto.* BELLINI: *La Sonnambula: Compagne, teneri amici . . . Come per me sereno; Oh! se una volta solo . . . Ah! non credea mirati.*
(M) (***) EMI mono CDM5 66457-2 [id.].

These recordings were made at La Scala in June 1955 and feature extracts from three operas which at the time Callas had made all her own. However, for some unexplained reason, the diva refused to sanction publication of the *Sonnambula* items, so the original LP was released in 1958 with substituted performances, taken from her complete set, made the previous year. Yet, with Callas in her prime, if anything more relaxed than in those later versions, the remarkable quality is the total consistency: most details are identical in both performances. Aficionados will surely be delighted that the original performances have been restored alongside the Cherubini and Spontini arias. Throughout, Callas is heard at her most magnetic. As usual in this series, the CD transfers are very impressive.

'Mad scenes' (with Philh. Ch. & O, Micola Rescigno): DONIZETTI: *Anna Bolena: Piangete voi?. . . Al dolce guidami castel natio.* THOMAS: *Hamlet: A vos jeux . . . Partagez-vous mes fleurs . . . Et maintenant écoutez ma chanson.* BELLINI: *Il Pirata: Oh! s'io potessi . . . Cor sorriso d'innocenza.*
(M) *** EMI CDM5 66459-2 [id.].

Recorded in the Kingsway Hall in September 1958, this is the record which, Desmond Shawe-Taylor suggested, more than any other summed up the essence of Callas's genius. If the rawness of exposed top notes mars the sheer beauty of the singing, few recital records ever made can match – let alone outshine – this collection of mad scenes in vocal and dramatic imagination.

'Callas à Paris': Volume I (with Fr. Nat. R. O, Georges Prêtre): GLUCK: *Orphée et Euridice: J'ai perdu mon Euridice. Alceste: Divinités du Styx.* BIZET: *Carmen: Habanera; Seguidilla.* SAINT-SAENS: *Samson et Dalila: Printemps qui commence; Amour! viens aider ma faiblesse! Mon coeur s'ouvre à ta voix.* GOUNOD: *Roméo et Juliette: Ah! je veux vivre dans ce rêve.* THOMAS: *Mignon: Ah, pour ce soir . . . Je suis Titania.* MASSENET: *Le Cid: De cet affreux combt . . . pleurez.* CHARPENTIER: *Louise: Depuis le jour.*
(M) *** EMI CDM5 66466-2 [id.].

'Callas à Paris': Volume II (with Paris Conseratoire O, Georges Prêtre): GLUCK: *Iphigénie en Tauride: O malherureuse Iphigénie.* BERLIOZ: *Damnation de Faust: D'amour l'ardente flamme.* BIZET: *Les Pêcheurs de perles: Me voilà seule . . . Comme autrefois.* MASSENET: *Manon: Je ne suis que faiblesse . . . Adieu notre petite table. Suis-je gentille ainsi?. . . Je marche sur tous les chemins. Werther: Werther! Qui m'aurait dit . . . Des cris joyeuse (Air des lettres).* GOUNOD: *Faust: Il était un Roi de Thulé . . . O Dieu! que de bijoux . . . Ah! je ris.*
(M) ** EMI CDM5 66467-2 [id.].

The first LP collection, *Callas à Paris*, dating from 1961, has the singer at her most commanding and characterful. The sequel disc was recorded two years later when the voice was in decline. The vocal contrast is clear enough, and the need at the time to patch and re-patch the takes in the later sessions makes the results sound less spontaneous and natural. But the earlier portraits of Carmen, Alceste, Dalila and Juliette find Callas still supreme, and her mastery of the French repertoire provides a fascinating slant on her artistry.

Recital (with Paris Conservatoire O, Nicola Rescigno): BEETHOVEN: *Ah! perfido* (scena and aria), *Op. 65.* WEBER: *Oberon: Ocean! thou mighty monster.* MOZART: *Le nozze di Figaro: Porgi amor. Don Giovanni: Or sai chi l'onore; Crudele?. . . Non mi dir; In quali eccessi, O numi! . . . Mi tradi quell'alma ingrate.*
(M) ** EMI CDM5 66465-2 [id.].

The 1963–4 recording sessions in Paris which produced these Beethoven, Mozart and Weber arias also included arias by Verdi which were not to appear until a decade later. They were to be among Callas's very last recordings, and the Beethoven scena immediately exposes the flaws that sadly emerged in the great voice towards the end of her career. Yet her fire-eating manner remains irresistible.

'The EMI rarities': 1953 Test: MOZART: *Don Giovanni: Non mir dir,* takes 1 & 2 (cond. Serafin). VERDI:

Macbeth: Una macchia è qui tuttora! (mono version of Sleepwalking scene with Philh. O, Rescigno). 1960–63 sessions (with Philh. O, Antonio Tonini): ROSSINI: *Semiramide: Bel raggio lusinghier. Guglielmo Tell: S'allontanano alfine . . . Selva opaca. La Cenerentola: Nacqui all'affanno . . . Non più mesta.* VERDI: *I vespri siciliani: Arrigo! ah parli ad un core. Don Carlos: O don fatale.* BELLINI: *Il Pirata: Sorgete . . . Lo sognai ferito, esangue* (with Monica Sinclair, Alexander Young). DONIZETTI: *Lucrezia Borgia: Tranquillo ei posa . . . Com'è bello.* WEBER: *Ocean! thou mighty monster.* 1964 sessions (with Franco Corelli, Paris Opéra O, Prêtre): VERDI: *Aida: Pur ti riveggo, mia dolce Aidau.* 1964–5 sessions (with Paris Conservatoire O, Rescigno): VERDI: *I lombardi: Te, Vergin santa. Il Trovatore: Vanne . . . D'amor sull' ali rosee.* 1969 sessions (with Paris Opéra O, Rescigno): VERDI: *I vespri siciliani: Arrigo! ah parli a un core. Attila: Liberamente or piangi! I lombardi: Te, Verfin santa.*
(M) **(*) EMI mono/stereo CMS5 66468-2 (2) [(B) ZDMB5 664682].

The fear was that a collection of Maria Callas's unreleased recordings would include too many items that never appeared because of all-too-obvious vocal shortcomings. In fact, many of the arias here are richly enjoyable. The set brings together the results of all the EMI studio sessions that were previously made available at premium price in earlier published LP collections, '*The Unknown recordings*' and '*Rarities*', and fascinatingly includes also the 1953 test of Mozart's *Non mi dir*. It has long been common knowledge that right at the end of her career Callas made recordings with other artists; included here is the 1964 *Nile* duet from *Aida* with Franco Corelli. Another novelty is the mono version of the Sleepwalking scene from *Macbeth* in which at the end (following Walter Legge's suggestion) the solo voice can be heard moving away to suggest the stage action. In the event this effect was not featured in the finale of the published stereo recording. The rest of the programme consists of alternative recordings of arias which had appeared before in other versions. Even if these are artistically uneven, the early Verdi, Rossini and Bellini excerpts are all most cherishable. The set is available at medium price in the UK but (more sensibly) at bargain price in the USA.

'Live in concert': PUCCINI: *Madama Butterfly: Un bel dì vedremo* (sung by 'Nina Foresti'). PROCH: *Deh! torna mio bene (Air and variations;* with Turin R. O, Manno Wolf-Ferrari). VERDI: *Macbeth: Vieni! t'affretta . . . Or tutte suggete. Nabucco: Ben io t'invenni . . . Anch'io dischiuso un giorno.* DONIZETTI: *Lucia di Lammermoor: Il dolce suono . . . Ardon gli incensi.* DELIBES: *Lakmé: Dov'é l'indiana bruna?* (with Turin R. O, Oliviero de Fabritiis). MOZART: *Die Entführung aus dem Serail: Tutte le torture.* MEYERBEER: *Dinorah: Ahimè! che notte oscura . . . Ombra leggiera.* CHARPENTIER: *Louise: Depuis le jour.* ROSSINI: *Armida: D'amore al dolce impero.* THOMAS: *Hamlet: Ai vostri giochi . . . Ed ora a voi* (with Milan R. O, Alfredo Simonetto). WAGNER: *Tristan und Isolde: Dolce e calmo* (with Athens Festival O, Antonio Votto). SPONTINI: *La vestale: Tu che invoco.* VERDI: *Ernani: Surta è la notte, Ernani, involami. Don Carlos: Tu che le vanità.* BELLINI: *Il Pirata: Oh, s'io potessi . . . Cor sorriso d'innocenza* (with Concg. O, Nicola Rescigno).
(B) (**(*)) EMI mono/stereo CZS5 73030-2 (2) [CDZB5 720302).

This final budget two-CD collection includes all the live 'Unknown recordings' and 'Rarities', and much else besides, derived from radio broadcasts in Turin, Milan, Athens and Holland. The programme opens with a collectors' item, a truncated version of *One fine day* from *Madame Butterfly*, sung on the Major Bowes American Amateur Hour on 7 April 1935, by one Nina Foresti. Callas later revealed her own identity, as a young girl. Just as fascinating in a quite different way is her very early Athens account of Isolde's *Liebestod* in Italian and her 1959 Holland Festival performances of passages from Bellini's *Il Pirata* and Verdi's *Don Carlos*. These bring the fresh illumination of a supreme artist who was both deeply thoughtful and spontaneous in that she never merely repeated herself. Other items have been previously available on a pair of super-budget LaserLight CDs, including an impressive (1959) *Vieni t'affretta* from *Macbeth*. There is also a wild but exciting performance in Italian of Constanze's Act II aria from Mozart's *Il Seraglio*. The technical quality of these excerpts is, of course, variable, but their presntation has been helped by skilled EMI transfers.

'Romantic arias': PUCCINI: *Gianni Schicchi: O mio babbino caro. Manon Lescaut: In quelle trine morbide. La Bohème: Donde lieta uscì. Madama Butterfly: Un bel dì vedremo.* VERDI: *Rigoletto: Caro nome. Il Trovatore: D'amor sull'ali rosee. Otello: Ave Maria.* BELLINI: *La Sonnambula: Come per me sereno.* MEYERBEER: *Dinorah: Ombra leggiera (Shadow song).* DELIBES: *Lakmé: Bell song.* MOZART: *Le nozze di Figaro: Porgi amor.* DONIZETTI: *L'elisir d'amore: Prendi, per me sei libro. Lucia di Lammermoor: Spargi d'amaro piano* (excerpt from *Mad scene*).
(B) *** EMI Eminence CD-EMX 2243.

A comparatively recent bargain assembly of Callas arias, attractively designed to show her lyrical gifts. The Puccini, Verdi and Meyerbeer recordings date from the 1950s, except for the *Ave Maria* from *Otello* which, like the *Nozze di Figaro* and *L'elisir d'amore* arias, comes from a decade later. The brief excerpt from the *Lucia* Mad scene is drawn from the 1960 complete set, and the Bellini *La Sonnambula* excerpt, although originally recorded in 1955, was not passed for publication by Callas until 1978.

Cambridge Singers, John Rutter

'Portrait': BYRD: *Sing joyfully; Non vos relinquam.* FAURE: *Cantique de Jean Racine; Requiem: Sanctus.* RUTTER: *O be joyful in the Lord; All things bright and beautiful; Shepherd's pipe carol; Open thou mine eyes; Requiem: Out of the deep.* PURCELL: *Hear my prayer, O Lord.* STANFORD: *Beati quorum via; The Bluebird.* TRAD.: *This joyful Eastertide; In dulci jubilo.* HANDEL: *Messiah: For unto us a child is born.* FARMER: *A pretty bonny lass.* MORLEY: *Now is the month of maying.* DELIUS: *To be sung of a summer night on the water.* VICTORIA: *O magnum mysterium.* TERRY: *Myn lyking.*
(M) *** Coll. Dig./Analogue CSCD 500 [id.].

John Rutter has arranged the items here with great skill so that serene music always makes a contrast with the many exuberant expressions of joy, his own engaging hymn-settings among them. Thus the bright-eyed hey-nonny songs of John Farmer and Thomas Morley are aptly followed by the lovely wordless *To be sung of a summer night on the water* of Delius, and Stanford's beautiful evocation of *The Bluebird* (one of Rutter's own special favourites). The sound, vivid and atmospheric, suits the colour and mood of the music quite admirably. Not to be missed!

'The Cambridge Singers Collection' (with Wayne Marshall, City of L. Sinf.): DEBUSSY: *3 Chansons d'Orléans.* Folksongs (arr. RUTTER): *The Keel row; The Willow tree.* Gregorian Chant: *Regina caeli laetare.* BRUCKNER: *Ave Maria.* VERDI: *Laudi alla Vergine Maria.* STANFORD: *Magnificat in D; Te Deum in C.* PURCELL: *Remember not, Lord, our offences.* TAVERNER: *Christe Jesu, pastor bone.* PHILIPS: *O Beatum et sacrosanctum diem.* PEARSALL: *Lay a garland.* RUTTER: *Riddle song; Waltz; Magnificat* (1st movement); *The Wind in the Willows* (excerpt, with The King's Singers, Richard Baker, Richard Hickox). TRAD. (arr. RUTTER): *Sing a song of sixpence.*
(M) **(*) Coll. Dig. CSCD 501 [id.].

Here is another attractively chosen, 64-minute sampler, including a wide range of tempting repertoire from arrangements of folksongs to Stanford and Verdi. The Taverner and Philips items are particularly welcome. Rutter includes a fair proportion of his own music, but the opening (only) from his setting of *The Wind in the Willows* will not be something one would want to return to very often.

Cerquetti, Anita (soprano)

'Grandi voci' (arias from): VERDI: *Aida; I vespri siciliani; Nabucco; Ernani; La forza del destino.* BELLINI: *Norma.* SPONTINI: *Agnes von Hohenstaufen.* PUCCINI: *Tosca.* PONCHIELLI: *La Gioconda* (with Giulietta Simionato, Mario del Monaco, Ettore Bastianini, Florence Festival Ch. & O, Gianandrea Gavazzeni).
(M) ** Decca 440 411-2.

This recital sports a really fearsome portrait of Madame Cerquetti with raspberry lips pouting furiously – a Casta diva indeed! In the aria of that name, Cerquetti's entrance is rather marred by an unforgivably flat flute obbligato. Cerquetti's half-tone at the beginning of the aria is most ingratiating (if not entirely free of squelching in toothpaste bursts), but the voice hardens when pressed. With such a big voice the degree of flexibility is credible, but ideally Bellini requires even greater sense of style. The rare aria, *O re dei cieli*, from Spontini's *Agnes von Hohenstaufen* also brings shrill fortissimo attack, but the *Nabucco* excerpt shows up Cerquetti's voice more impressively, with a fine sense of attack in the dramatic recitative, and her richly spun *Vissi d'arte* suggests she was a formidable Tosca. The most impressive items here come from her 1957 complete set of *La Gioconda*; they are rather fine and certainly powerful. The recording is spacious and free without being markedly brilliant. In 1961 Cerquetti withdrew from the operatic stage (temporarily, as she thought) but her attempts to return were thwarted by the pre-eminence of Callas and Tebaldi.

Christ Church Cathedral Choir, Oxford, Stephen Darlington

'English choral music 1514–1682'.
(BB) *** Nimbus Dig. NI 1762 (8) [(B) id.].

This is a superb set, offered at a ridiculously low price. The only disc about which there can be reservations is the collection of anthems, in itself an essential component in any comprehensive survey of early English cathedral choral music. Unfortunately the choice is this instance has been less than ideally representative, and the solo singing is uneven. But this is only one disc out of eight, and it is certainly not to be dismissed. Preparation, and the scholarship behind all these performances, cannot be faulted, nor can the high standard of both the choral singing and the recordings, made (between 1989 and 1995) not in Christ Church Cathedral, but at Dorchester Abbey, also in Oxfordshire, which proves to be an ideal choice acoustically.

John TAVERNER:(*c.* 1490–1545): *Audivi vocem sabbatum de caelo; Kyrie le Roy; Alleluya V. Veni electa mea; Magnificat a 5; Ave Dei Patris filia. Ex eius tumba: sospitati dedit aegros; Dum transisset sabbatum* (2 versions) (Nimbus Dig. NI 5360).

John Taverner was himself Director of the choristers at Christ Church Cathedral. Appointed in 1526, he was there for only four years before moving on to a lesser post at Boston, Lincolnshire. Most of his music was composed during the 1520s, and its rich tapestries of sound reflect great spiritual confidence. The first work here, *Ex eius tumba*, is gloriously full-textured and surges forward splendidly; the *Magnificat* setting, too, is particularly fine – but then so is the *Ave Dei Patris filia*, an early work which opens radiantly, with the trebles soaring. *Dum transisset sabbatum* is heard in two different settings, both equally impressive. For *Audivi vocem sabbatum de caeli* the choral polyphony from the trebles is distanced, while the men sing the plainsong nearer at hand, a ravishing and indeed mystical effect. The recording, full and spacious, is of very high quality.

John TAVERNER: *Missa Mater Christi;* Antiphons: *O Wilhelme, pastor bone; Mater Christi sanctissima* (Nimbus Dig. NI 5218).

This is a liturgical reconstruction by Andrew Carwood for the Feast of the Annunciation of Our Lady, at Eastertide, which intersperses Taverner's *Missa Mater Christi* with the appropriate chant. The disc also includes the motet, *Mater Christi*, on which the Mass itself is built, and the antiphon, *O Wilhelme, pastor bone*. The singing under Stephen Darlington is first class, and the recording (of both this disc and the one above) is difficult to fault: it is well focused and excellently balanced, with a firm image.

John SHEPPARD (*c.* 1515–59): *The Lord's prayer; The Second service: Magnificat & Nunc dimittis. Gaude, gaude, gaude Maria; Filiae Ierusalem; Reges Tharsis et insule; Spiritus sanctus procedens; Laudem dicite Deo nostro; Hec dies; Impetum fecerunt unanimes; Libera nos, salva nos* (Nimbus Dig. NI 5480).

This fine collection duplicates much that is already offered on the pair of Hyperion Dyads of Sheppard's music from Harry Christophers and The Sixteen, discussed in our composer section. But that means that Stephen Darlington has chosen a great deal of the composer's finest music, and the effect here, from a traditional cathedral men's and boys' choir, gives a different and equally inspiring slant on the music. Moreover Darlington has chosen to open his programme with Sheppard's setting of *The Lord's Prayer*, followed by the *Magnificat* and *Nunc dimittis* from the *Second Service*, also sung in English. Both these works were almost certainly written within a week or two of the composer's death and, while their climbing phrases readily identify the composer, their relatively simple harmonic style contrasts with the much more complex and daring polyphony of *Gaude, gaude, gaude Maria*, one of the composer's masterpieces, here including some impressive solo treble contributions. *Filiae Ierusalem* which follows also has a wonderfully rich forward flow, with a memorable rocking melisma and again those momentary touches of dissonance which make this composer's music so individual. *Reges Tharsis et insule* features a constant soaring of the treble line which is thrilling. Two responds bring contrast in being for men's voices alone. *Laudem dicite Deo nostro* is comparatively sombre, while *Impetum fecerunt unanimes* is more lofty in feeling. Splendidly recorded, this expansively ardent singing, with its striking unanimity of ensemble, does full justice to a still under-appreciated composer.

William BYRD (1543–1623): *Mass for 5 voices: Mass Propers for All Saints' Day: Gaudeamus omnes; Timete Dominum; Justorum animae; Beati mundo corde.* Motets: *Laudibus in sanctis; Laudate pueri Dominum; Laudate Dominum* (Nimbus Dig. NI 5237).

BYRD: *Mass for 4 voices: Mass Propers for the Feast of Corpus Christi: Cibavit eos; Oculi omnium; Lauda Sion salvatorem; Sacerdotes Domini; Quotiescunque manducabitis.* Motets: *Pange lingua gloriosi; Ave verum corpus; O salutaris hostia* (Nimbus Dig. NI 5287).

BYRD: *Mass for 3 voices: Mass Propers for the Nativity: Puer natus est nobis; Viderunt omnes fines terrae; Dies sanctificatus; Tui sunt coeli; Viderunt omnes fines terrae.* Motets: *Hodie Christus natus est; Christe redemptor omnium; O admirabile Commertium; A solis ortus cardine; O magnum misterium* (Nimbus Dig. NI 5302).

These recordings have followed the approach pioneered by Harry Christophers and the Sixteen, in that each of the three Masses is interspersed with Mass Propers from the *Gradualia* and the performance placed at a key point in the Church year. The other motets or Psalm settings included on each disc reflect that choice, so that the *Mass for three voices*, for instance, includes suitable Christmas music. The performances are in the traditional English cathedral manner but are of high quality, the music's flowing lines bringing poise and serenity, but they are in no way dramatic: the choir is set back and the cathedral ambience is very telling.

Thomas WEELKES (*c.* 1576–1623): *Alleluja, I heard a voice; Give ear O Lord; Evening service for 5 voices: Magnificat; Nunc Dimittis; Hosanna to the Son of David; When David heard; O Lord, grant the King a long life; Give the King Thy judgements; Gloria in excelsis Deo; Ninth service: Magnificat; Nunc Dimittis* (Nimbus Dig. NI 5125).

Thomas Weelkes was the odd man out among his contemporaries. He was what Colin Wilson would, centuries later, define as an 'outsider'. He fell out with his ecclesiatical superiors and then the religious authorities in general, and he ended his career in disgrace, notorious as a drunkard and for his unholy language. Yet he wrote some of the most original and inspired music in Christendom, music that is contrantly stimulating for its wayward, even wild part-writing, with extraordinary passing dissonances which sound so modern to today's ears. He was wonderfully good at endings, and especially at elaborately decorated '*Amens*'. Here the opening *Alleluja*, although gloriously impassioned, is relatively straight-forward, but *Give ear O Lord* brings a fine example of one of those beautiful extended '*Amens*'. Even so, it is capped by *Amen* which closes the *Magnificat* from the *Evening service for five voices*. The Christ Church choristers are obviously continually caught up in this passionate polyphony, and they sing *Hosanna to the Son of David*, and the moving setting of *When David heard* with the greatest commitment and fervour. But most extraordinary of all is the closing *Magnificat* and *Nunc Dimittis* from the *Ninth Service*. Weelkes surpasses himself with his plangent harmonic progressions towards the end of the *Magnificat* (from '*Glory be to the Father*' onwards) and then in the *Nunc Dimittis*, after opening with deceptive calm, he moves forward with constantly repeated overlapping phrases and audacious clashes which are momentarily almost bizarre. In many ways his writing here anticipates a twentieth-century work in the minimalistic style. In the event, this is the most thrilling collection in this whole anthology.

Chapel Royal anthems: BLOW: *The Lord even the most mighty; O Lord, thou hast searched me.* PURCELL: *I will love Thee; O Lord our Governor; Blessed is he whose righteousness; Who hath believed; Out of the deep; Hear me O Lord.* LOCKE: *How doth the city.* HUMFREY: *Hear, O Heav'ns* (Nimbus Dig. NI 5454).

On the face of it, this collection of anthems seems well chosen and quite representative, but the overall effect is curiously doleful, and a few more robust items would certainly have been welcome. The Purcell anthems are touchingly expressive and bring the best of the solo ensemble singing, but there is too little variety in the music itself; when one turns to the marvellous King's collection within the Harnoncourt Edition (see above), one discovers a vitality that is less obvious here. The opening Blow anthems make virtuoso demands on the bass soloists (Robert MacDonald and William Clements), and they fail to rise – or, rather, lower themselves – to the occasion: the descent to a bottom C and a low trill are negotiated cautiously. There are good things here, of course, not least the choral singing, which is fresh enough; if one takes each anthem individually, the fairly consistent use of the minor mode is less noticeable.

Christ Church Cathedral Choir, Oxford, Francis Grier

'Carols from Christchurch' (with Harry Bicket, organ): GARDNER: *Tomorrow shall be my dancing day.* TRAD.: *O thou man; In dulci jubilo.* HADLEY: *I sing of a maiden.* HOWELLS: *Sing lullaby; Here is the little door.* WARLOCK: *Bethlehem Down.* MATHIAS: *Sir Christèmas.* arr. BACH: *O little one sweet.* TCHAIKOVSKY: *The crown of roses.* HOWELLS: *A spotless rose.* WISHART: *Alleluya, a new work is come on hand.* BRITTEN: *A ceremony of carols* (with Frances Kelly harp): *Shepherd's carol; A Boy was born: Jesu, as Thou art our Saviour.*
(M) *** ASV CDWHL 2097 [id.].

This is among the most attractive of recent mid-priced reissues of carol collections, the more particularly as it includes not only a first-class account of Britten's *Ceremony of carols*, plus *Jesu, as Thou art our Saviour*, with its piercing momentary dissonances, but also the dialogue *Shepherd's carol*, so effectively featuring four soloists. The dozen other carols also bring some radiantly expressive singing, particularly in the three inspired Howells works; the Hadley carol, too, is delightful. They are framed by the admirably lively items by Gardner and Wishart, with Mathias's buoyant *Sir Christèmas* as a centrepiece. Generally good, analogue sound from the early 1980s.

Christoff, Boris (bass)

'Russian songs' (with LOP, Tzipine; Paris Conservatoire O, Cluytens; Alexandre Labinsky, Alexandre Tcherepnine, Janine Reiss, Serge Zapolsky, or Nadia Gedda-Nova (piano); Gaston Marchesini, Maud-Martin Tortelier (cello)): GLINKA: *The Midnight review; Cradle song; What, young beauty; Where is our rose?; The Lark; Ah, you darling, lovely girl; Doubt; Grandpa, the girls once told me; How sweet to be with thee; Do not say the heart is sick; Hebrew song; Elegy; I remember the wonderful moment.* BORODIN: *Those folk; Song of the dark forest; From my tears; The Sea princess; The Pretty girl no longer loves me; The Magic garden; Arabian melody; The false note; The fishermaiden. Listen to my song, little friend; The Sleeping princess; Pride; For the shores of thy far native land; The sea; Why art thou so early, dawn?; My songs are poisoned.* CUI: *Songs, Op. 44: Le Hun; Berceuse; Le ciel est transi; Les songeants. Ici-bas; The tomb and the rose; The Love of a departed one; A Recent dream; Pardon!; Desire; Conspiracy; Song of Mary; The Imprisoned knight; Album leaf; The Prophet; The Statue of Tsarskoïe; In Memory of V. S. Stassov.* BALAKIREV: *Prologue; Song of Selim; Song: The Yellow leaf trembles; The Pine tree; Nocturne; Starless midnight, coldly breathed; The Putting-right; November the 7th; Dawn; Hebrew melody; The Wilderness; The Knight; The Dream; Look, my friend.* RIMSKY-KORSAKOV: *The Pine and the palm; On the hills of Georgia; The Messenger; Quietly evening falls; Hebrew song; Zuleika's song; Across the midnight sky; I waited for thee in the grotto at the appointed hour; The sea is tossing; The Upas tree; The Prophet; Quiet is the blue sea; Slowly drag my days; Withered flower; The rainy day has waned.* TCHAIKOVSKY: *Don Juan's serenade; The Mild stars shone for us; Child's song; Cradle song; Night; Do not ask; As they kept on saying, 'Fool'; To sleep; Disappointment; the canary; None but the weary heart; Again, as before, alone; A Legend.* RACHMANINOV: *Fate; How fair is this spot; When yesterday we met; All once I gladly owned; Morning; All things depart; Thy pity I implore; Christ is risen; Loneliness; O never sing to me again; The dream; The soldier's wife; The Harvest of sorrow; Oh stay, my love; The world would see thee smile; Night is mournful.* Folksongs: arr. SEROV: *The Evil power.* TRAD.: *Doubinouchka: Song of the Volga; The Bandore; Down Peterskaya Street; Going down the Volga; Notchenka* (Folksongs with Russian Ch., Potorjinsky).
(B) *** EMI mono CZS7 67496-2 (5) [CDZE 67496].

This survey covers recordings by the great Bulgarian bass made between 1954 and 1969. The great majority come from the 1960s, the earliest are the Russian folksongs recorded in 1954 and the Rachmaninov and Rimsky-Korsakov (1959). But throughout this remarkably extensive programme, the magnificent voice is in perfect shape and the recordings are faithfully transferred. Some might think a big voice like Christoff's would be unsuitable for art songs, but his sensitivity is never in question and, whenever necessary, he scales it down, especially (for instance) in several of the Glinka songs where he has a cello obbligato. This repertoire is enormously rich in melody and, just as in the opera house, Christoff's art demonstrates the widest emotional range. Characterization is always strong and his feeling for words is just as striking here as in his performances of the stage repertory. Most of the songs are piano accompanied (with a whole range of excellent accompanists) but occasionally orchestral versions are used, as in Rimsky-Korsakov's *The prophet* or Balakirev's *Prologue*, when the orchestra is vividly balanced. The collection ends with an exhilarating half-dozen traditional Russian folksongs in which Christoff is joined by an enthusiastic (if backwardly balanced) Russian chorus and balalaika ensemble. The result is irresistible, with melancholy and joy side by side in a wonderfully Slavonic way. These five well-filled discs not only demonstrate some of the riches hitherto hidden in EMI's international vaults; they also give us unique performances of repertoire most of which is otherwise totally inaccessible. The snag lies in the documentation. As this derives from EMI's French stable, even the song-titles are given in French. (It was a major task identifying and translating them!) No texts are provided, simply a 2-page biographical note.

The City Waites

'The Musicians of Grope Lane': Music of brothels and bawdy houses of Purcell's England: *Diddle diddle or The kind country lovers; The fair maid of Islington; Green stockings; The jovial lass or Dol and Roger; Mundanga was; Lady of pleasure; The old wife; The beehive; Blue petticoats or green garters; The Gelding of the Devil; The maid's complaint for want of a dil doul; Oyster Nan; The frolic; The husband who met his match; The jovial broom man; The disappointment; The lusty young smith; Greensleeves and yellow lace; The jolly brown turd;* Two rounds: *Tom making a manteau; When Celia was learning. Lady lie near me; Oh how you protest; A ditty delightful of Mother Watkin's ale; Miss Nelly*
(M) *** Musica Oscura Dig. 070969.

There really was a Grope Lane, which meant exactly what it says. Apart from a lubricious woodcut at the front of the booklet, illustrating the gelding of the Devil (taken from a broadsheet in the Samuel Pepys Library), it is the words that count here rather than the music, for it is no good having lewd words that one cannot hear, even if they are all included in the booklet. And ballads like *The jovial lass* and *The lusty young smith* are unequivocally lewd; others use metaphor more tastefully and also have a touch of wit, like the 'Ditty delightful', in which the young maid tells her lover, 'I am afraid to die a maid'. He promises to give her Watson's ale and when, after her first draught, she innocently asks for a second, she is disconcerted when she has to wait a little. 'Let us talk a little while,' he suggests. So full marks for the diction of the City Waites and also their swinging dialect style with ballads that usually fall far short of being art songs. The items here are sometimes accompanied, sometimes not, but they are made into a lively entertainment by being interwoven with instrumental pieces from Playford's *Dancing Master*.

Clare College, Cambridge, Choir and Orchestra, John Rutter

'The Holly and the ivy' (Carols): RUTTER: *Donkey carol; Mary's lullaby*. TRAD., arr. RUTTER: *King Jesus hath a garden; Wexford carol;* (Flemish) *Cradle song; Child in a manger; In dulci jubilo; I saw three ships; The holly and the ivy*. TRAD., arr. WOODWARD: *Up! Good Christian folk*. TRAD., arr. WILLCOCKS: *Gabriel's message; Ding! dong! merrily on high; Quelle est cette odeur agréable*. TRAD., arr. PETTMAN: *I saw a maiden*. DARKE: *In the bleak mid-winter*. PRAETORIUS: *The noble stem of Jesse; Omnis mundus jocundetur*. TCHAIKOVSKY: *The crown of roses*. POSTON: *Jesus Christ the apple tree*. TRAD., arr. VAUGHAN WILLIAMS: *Wassail song*.
❁ (M) *** Decca 425 500-2.

This outstanding collection, recorded by Argo in the Lady Chapel at Ely Cathedral in 1979, is a model of its kind. Rutter's admirers, among whom we can be counted, will surely want this disc for the Christmas season. The opening arrangement of *King Jesus hath a garden*, using a traditional Dutch melody, immediately sets the mood with its pretty flute decorations. Moreover Rutter's own gentle syncopated *Donkey carol*, which comes fourth, is indispensable to any Christmas celebration. The whole programme is a delight – not always especially ecclesiastical in feeling, but permeated throughout by the spirit of Christmas joy.

Codex

Codex: 'Treasures from the DG Archiv Catalogue'.
(M) **(*) DG mono/stereo 453 161-2 (10).

The word 'Codex' originally described a quire of manuscript pages held together by stitching – the earliest format of a book; it went on to mean a collection of rare and valuable documents. So the term is used here, appropriately enough, to encapsulate what DG suggest are 'rare documents in sound from 50 years of pioneering recording, ranging from the serene counterpoint of a Machaut, the intensely spiritual polyphony of a Victoria to the imposing state music of a Handel'. The majority of these recordings have never before appeared on CD, and the only snag from the collector's point of view is that authentic styles of performance have changed greatly during the last half-century, as scholarship has re-researched its sources and re-determined the stylistic parameters. The highlight of the collection is Emilio De'Cavaleri's *Rappresentatione di Anima, et di Corpo*, which is well worth seeking out independently. All the discs are currently available separately (in the UK only).

Disc 1 (with Brussels Pro Musica Antiqua, Safford Cape): LEONIN: *Judaea et Jerusalem*. PEROTINUS: *Sederunt principes*. MACHAUT: *Messe de Nostre Dame*. DU FAY: *Vergine bella. Vexilla Regis. Flos florum. Veni creator spiritus. Alma redemtoris mater* (DG mono 453 162-2).

The first disc here opens with an organum duplum, *Judaea et Jerusalem*, of Léonin, and an organum quadruplum, *Sederunt principes* of Pérotinus. The singers of Safford Cape's Pro Musica Antiqua are expertly matched and balanced, and their austere style, slow and deliberate, is not inappropriate. But one would have expected rather more vitality conveyed in Machaut's *Messe de Nostre Dame* (the first known complete polyphonic setting of the Ordinary of the Mass); here the approach is very pure and literal, and the accompaniment (for recorder, fiddles and lute) highly conjectural. All three alternative performances, listed above under the composer, are more stimulating. When one moves on to the selection of hymns, motets and antiphons by Du Fay, the singing suddenly springs to expressive life. The opening accompanied alto solo, *Vergine bella* (a setting of the first verse of an Italian canzona by Petrarch), is justly famous, while *Flos florum*, for mixed voices and fiddles, is both complex and beautiful, as is the account of the (unaccompanied) three-voiced setting of the ninth-century Pentecostal hymn, *Veni creator spiritus*; while the glorious *Alma redemptoris mater* (for accompanied alto, tenor and bass), which paraphrases an eleventh-century Marian antiphon, caps the collection eloquently.

Disc 2 (with Schola Cantorum, Francesco Coradini, Fosco Corti; (i) with Arnoldo Foà): ANON.: Marian Antiphons: *Alma redemptoris mater; Ave regina caelorum; Regina caeli laetare; Salve regina*. Francesco CORTECCIA: (i) *Passione secondo Giovanni (St John Passion)* (453 163-2).

The Florentine composer, Francesco Corteccia (1502–71), took holy orders in 1526 and became organist at the Church of San Lorenzo in 1531; he ended his career as chapel master at Florence Cathedral and he also supervised the music at the Medici Court. His *St John Passion* dates from 1527. The choral writing is simple and touchingly serene. The snag here is that the commentary of the Evangelist is not sung but spoken, and the cueing does not separate the spoken part of the performance, which will be frustrating for non-Italian-speaking listeners, seeking to hear the music without the narrative. Nevetheless the various uninterrupted set-pieces for the choir, including *Tristis est anima mea unsque ad mortem*, the exquisite *Tenebrae factae sunt* and notably *Caligaverunt oculi mei* (which we hear again, below, in Victoria's setting), are very moving, none more so than the desolate closing Evangelicum: *Post haec autem rogavit Pilatum Joseph ab Arimathea*, which is sung here very gently, with a superbly sustained closing pianissimo dying away in the closing fall. Arnoldo Foà speaks the part of the Evangelist with admirable simplicity, and the singing and recording could hardly be bettered. The disc opens with four Marian antiphons, which are also beautifully presented.

Disc 3: Thomás Luis de VICTORIA (with Regensburger Domchor, Hans Schrems): *Missa Vidi speciosam*. Motets and Responsories: *Vidi speciosam; Tamquam ad latronen; O Domine Jesu Christe; Amicus meus; Unus ex discipulis meis; Caligaverunt oculi mei; Dum complerentur; Surrexit Pastor Bonus. Lamentations of Jeremiah: Aleph. Ego vir didens paupertam meam* (453 164-2).

Victoria's *Missa Vidi speciosam* is a parody Mass based on a *Canticum canticorum* motet, also included here, whose words have a distinctly pantheistic character ('I have seen what was like a beautiful dove, rising above the rivers of water, whose fragrance was beyond value in its vestments; and, like spring days, flowers of roses and lilies of the valley surrounded it'). The perfumed symbolism of these words invaded the Mass and, although Victoria modified his musical style somewhat for his ecclesiastical setting, it gives the work an expressive richness which makes it suitable for performance by the mixed voices of Regensburg Choir, even though their expressive manner and their use of vibrato are somewhat anachronistic. The recording brings a limited dynamic range and the plangent Latin ardour of Victoria's writing is elusive, although the closing *Agnus Dei* is heartfelt. The choir are happier in the motets and responsories: the motet on which the Mass is based is beautifully sung, as is the deeply expressive *Caligaverunt occuli mei* ('My eyes have been stitched shut from my weeping'), and the excerpt from the *Lamentations of Jeremiah* is appealingly serene. The choir blends well, but the resonance prevents the clearest focus of inner detail and occasionally intonation is slightly suspect.

Disc 4: Emilio DE'CAVALIERI: *Rappresentatione di Anima, et di Corpo* (with Tatiana Troyanos, Hermann Prey, Kurt Equiluz, Herbert Lackner, Theo Adam, Teresa Zylis-Gara, Edda Moser, V. Chamber Ch., V. Capella Academica, Ens. Wolfgang von Karajan, Mackerras) (453 165-2).

We have not previously encountered this fine (1970) recording of Cavalieri's *The Dialogue of Soul and Body*, not an opera, but much more theatrical than an oratorio. It was not produced for Lent but, more appropriately, at carnival time in February 1600. Cavalieri was in charge of music at the Court of Grand Duke Ferdinand I of Tuscany, and he developed a novel kind of pastoral play in which dialogue, songs and choruses were all sung. The libretto philosophizes on the conflicting demands of hedonistic pleasures and the necessity of spiritual preparation for life's inevitable end. Act I opens with the prudent consideration that time flies, and Time (the excellent Theo Adam) suggests that the audience had better make every moment count, before the sounding of the Last Trump. Good Counsel (the dry-voiced Herbert Lackner) opens Act II with the warning that 'Life is nothing but a battle', and at its close Earthly Life is disrobed and found to be death in disguise; Act III counts the blessings of Heaven and offers a dramatically explicit warning of Hell. At its close, all take the righteous path and glorify the Lord and virtue's victory. With fine, animated choral singing as a backcloth – their first entry, *Questa vita mortale, per fuggir presto ha l'ale* ('This mortal life has wings to fly so fast'), is delightful – the principals bring the piece vividly to life. Tatiana Troyanos is in splendid voice as Anima, Soul. 'I did not fashion myself', she sings, 'And how can I calm these desires of mine'; and Hermann Prey is appropriately dark-voiced and commanding, even gruff, as Corpo (Body). In the small parts, Paul Esswood represents Pleasure, and Kurt Equiluz proves an ardently light-hearted Intellect when he points out in scene iii that 'Every heart loves happiness' (*Ogni cor ama il bene*), while in Act II Teresa Zylis-Gara is a fine Guardian Angel. Anima has an engaging echo dialogue with heaven when she asks if the world should shun all pleasures, and receives an unequivocal reply. Later, the same echo device is used even more effectively when the four-part chorus are echoed in reply by a two-part chorus as they seek to confirm mankind's ultimate destiny in heaven. All in all, this is a most attractive entertainment, with the most uplifting moral purpose to set against its hedonsitic celebrations of human enjoyment. Mackerras was just the man for it: the performance swings along vivaciously, and it is excellently recorded. A real find.

Disc 5: Orlando GIBBONS: *Fantasias for viols Nos. I & II a 3; II a 4; In nomine a 5; O Lord I lift my heart to Thee; Thus Angels sung; Almighty and everlasting God; O my love, how comely now; O Lord, increase my faith; This is the record of John; What is our life? The silver swan; The Cries of London: God give you good morrow; A good sausage* (with Alfred Deller, Deller Consort, Consort of Viols of Schola Cantorum Basiliensis, Wenzinger). MORLEY: *Good love, then fly thou to her; Farewell disdainful; Hark, jolly shepherds, hark; Now is the gentle season; My lovely wanton pearl; Sweet nymph, come to thy lover; Stay heart, run not so fast; O grief, even on the bud* (with Ambrosian Singers, Denis Stevens) (mono/stereo 453 166-2).

The Gibbons programme (from the mid-1950s) provides variety by effectively interspersing the vocal numbers with Fantasias for viols which are played impeccably by Wenzinger and his Schola Cantorum Basiliensis. Deller leads his well-matched vocal group in a series of anthems and hymns that are expressively sung but, with consistently leisured tempi and a limited dynamic range, lack variety. The highlight is the fine verse anthem, *This is the record of John. The Cries of London* are more lively, but they come off even more effectively when the style is more vernacular. The mono recording is full but closely balanced. The Denis Stevens collection of songs and madrigals of Thomas Morley dates from a decade later and is sung by small groups of soloists with great charm and and impeccable style. *Farewell disdainful* and *O grief, even on the bud* are particularly touching. The original collection from which these items are drawn had added variety from the inclusion of harpsichord pieces, admirably played by Valda Aveling. Unaccountably, they are here omitted and are a great loss, especially when there was plenty of room for them, for the overall playing time here is 63 minutes.

Disc 6: HANDEL: *Utrecht Te Deum and Jubilate; Coronation anthem: Zadok the Priest* (with Ilse Wolf, Helen Watts, Wilfred Brown, Edgar Fleet, Thomas Hemsley, Geraint Jones Singers & O, Jones) (453 167-2).

Handel's *Utrecht Te Deum and Jubilate*, first performed in 1713, shows how rapidly he absorbed the style of English cathedral music, improving on it, yet suggesting by his use of soloists and chorus the verse anthem style that goes back to Purcell and Gibbons. As a writer of occasional music Handel had few equals, and these works show him at his best and most brilliant. Nobody now, apart from the historians, cares about the Peace of Utrecht, but the music Handel wrote for the happy year is still vividly before us in this lively performance by Geraint Jones. Ilse Wolf, Edgar Fleet and Thomas Hemsley sing with excellent tone and style; Helen Watts brings her artistry to bear on what is really music for a counter-tenor. Wilfred Brown is a little below his usual high standard. There is adequate depth, even though small resources are used and, though the most famous coronation anthem is not as overwhelming as some like it to be, the 1959 sound remains very impressive and hardly dated.

Disc 7: Carl Philipp Emanuel BACH: *Keyboard fantasias: in C Wq 61/6; in C min. (Probestücke), Wq 63/6* (with Colin Tilney); Lieder: *Uber die Finsternis kurz vor dem Tod, Jesu; Der Frühling; Prüfung am Abend; Morgengesang; Bitten; Trost der Erlösung; Passionslied; Die Güte Gottes; Abendlied; Wider den Ubermut; Demut; Weihnachtslied; Jesus in Gethsemane; Der Tag des Weltgerichts. Psalms: 19, 130 & 148* (with Dietrich Fischer-Diekau, Joerg Demus) (453 168-2).

On the evidence of this collection, Carl Philipp Emanuel was not a true songsmith. Fischer-Dieskau makes the very most of these mainly brief items, but few are melodically memorable. The most attractive are *Trost der Erlösung* and *Die Güte Gottes*, although *Abendlied* and *Wider den Unbermut* are quite pleasing. The Psalms are altogether more striking, all three quite memorable, No. 19 surprisingly lively, and the minuscule No. 148 most engagingly light-hearted. The Christmas Lied is also very attractive. Fisher-Dieskau's voice was at its warmest and freshest at the beginning of the 1970s, and Demus accompanies him sensitively, if rather distantly on a Tangentenflügel (a somewhat advanced fortepiano). The two rhythmically quirky *Fantasias* are attributed to Colin Tilney's clavichord, but it is recorded much too closely and the result is ugly: indeed the instrument is difficult to recognize.

Disc 8: Michel-Richard DELALANDE: *Simphonies pour les souper du roi: Quatrième suite; Sixième suite – Premier Caprice*. Jean-Joseph MOURET: *Fanfares: Première suite. Simphonies: Seconde suite*. PHILIDOR: *Marche à quatre timbales*. LULLY: *Airs de trompettes, timbales et hautbois*. Marc-Antoine CHARPENTIER: *Te Deum: Prélude* (with soloists, Paul Kuentz CO, Kuentz) (453 169-2).

The composer Lalande (or Delalande, all in one word, like Debussy) provided table music of considerable charm for the formal dinners of two French monarchs, Louis XIV and Louis XV, and in 1745 a definitive edition appeared in Paris. It is this score that Paul Kuentz uses as a basis for the two *Suites* recorded here. Mouret, a contemporary of Delalande, captivated the Parisian public for many years with his stage and symphonic music, but his last years were clouded by insanity, due largely to a rapid loss of reputation which coincided with the ascendancy of Rameau. As a musical servant of the French court and nobility, Mouret earned his title of '*le musicien des graces*', and the urbane charm of his symphonies evokes the spirit of the age in an inimitable and even forceful manner. His two attractive suites, the first featuring a solo trumpet and the second a pair of horns, both give their soloists attractive music to play while providing plenty of interest in the overall texture. The Lully set of *Airs* is consistently heavily scored and becomes a bit wearing to the ear, while Philidor uses drums alone; the Charpentier *Prélude* to the celebrated *Te Deum* makes a brief coda, playing for only a minute and a half. Paul Kuentz and his chamber orchestra, topped by the clear, high roulades of Adolf Scherbaum's trumpet, strive manfully to reproduce the spacious ambience at Versailles. If they fall short of their mark, it is due to acoustical rather than musical deficiences, for a Paris studio was used for the sessions and as a result the sound is a little tight and unresponsive. Nevertheless there is much to enjoy here, and the one vocal item in Delalande's fourth suite (*Quitte ici tes ailes*) is well sung by Edith Selig.

Disc 9: TARTINI: *Violin concertos: in D; in G*. NARDINI: *Violin concerto in E flat* (with Eduard Melkus, violin, Vienna Capella Academica, Wenzinger); *Violin sonata in G* (with Lionel Salter, harpsichord) (453 170-2).

Perhaps surprisingly, the DG Archivists have been unable to identify these two Tartini concertos very clearly, and the notes merely tell us that the *G major* dates from the middle period of the composer's creative career and may have been first heard in Prague in 1724, while the *D major* is most probably a late work. Like the Nardini with which they are coupled, both concertos are typical of their composer; because Tartini was a more individual musical personality, they come alive fully as individual works. With their Italianate melodic warmth, in some ways this pair of concertos looks forward to the nineteenth century, but if the florid virtuoso writing in the outer movements holds a balance between the classical style and the grander manner of the future, the slow movements are embroidered with an ornamentation that is essentially baroque in implication. Both concertos are played with sensitivity and musical confidence, and in every respect the music-making here (both solo and orchestral) has both warmth and charm . But to come off in the spirit in which they were written, they need more of the Heifetz and less of the scholar. They were primarily meant to entertain and perhaps astonish, and to do this they need to be thrown off like quicksilver. Nardini's concerto is more conventional, with long cadenza-like interpolations like those in Locatelli's *Art of the Violin*. Edward Melkus plays the fireworks confidently. Yet somehow, as with Tartini, the result fails to convey the excitement – the *raison d'être* of the music – which was obviously generated for listeners of 200 years ago. The *Sonata*, an agreeable little three-movement duo, is again devised to display the soloist, and here the backwardly balanced Lionel Salter makes the most of an indifferent supporting keyboard part. Excellent recording throughout.

Disc 10: SOLER: *Concertos for 2 keyboard instruments Nos. 1–6* (with Kenneth Gilbert and Trevor Pinnock (harpsichords or fortepianos)) (453 171-2).

These Soler concertos are described in the surviving autograph as intended for two organs, but Kenneth Gilbert and Trevor Pinnock use either two harpsichords (copies of Florentine instruments after Vincenzio Sodi, 1782) or two fortepianos (copies by Adlam Burnett of Heilmann, *c*. 1785) – and very attractive they sound too. The music itself is not very substantial and does not possess the character of some of Soler's solo harpsichord music. Most of the concertos are in two movements, the second being minuets plus variations. These are highly skilful performances, well recorded; if the music is not of outsize personality, it is far from unpleasing.

Deller, Alfred (counter-tenor)

Alfred Deller Edition

'Western wind and other English folksongs and ballads' (with Desmond Dupré, lute & guitar, John Southcott, recorder): *Western wind; Early one morning; Black is the colour; All the pretty little horses; Lowlands; The Sally gardens; Bendemeer's Stream; Annie Laurie; The Miller of the Dee; Cockles and mussels; Drink to me only; The foggy, foggy dew; The frog went a-courtin'; The turtle dove; Pretty Polly Oliver; The carrion crow; The wife of Usher's Well; Henry Martin; I am a poor wayfaring stranger; Cold blows the wind; Skye boat song; Every night the sun goes down; Song of a wedding.*
(M) *** Van. 08.5032.71 [id.].

A ravishing collection of folksongs, recorded in 1958 when the great counter-tenor was at the very peak of his form. The early stereo gives a lovely bloom to his voice, and here, as throughout this fine series, the CD transfers are of a high calibre. The opening *Western wind* is justly another of Deller's 'hits', but *Lowlands* is hardly less beautiful, and many other items here show the magic of his tonal nuancing and his natural, spontaneous musicianship. *Annie Laurie* is wonderfully fresh and brings a frisson as he soars up to the top of his range, while the irrepressible *Miller of Dee*, the petite *Pretty Polly Oliver*, and jaunty *Foggy dew* show him well able to lighten his presentation in the most sparkling manner. *Every night when the sun goes down* brings an almost Gershwinesque, bluesy feeling. In the charming *All the pretty little horses*, *The Frog went a'courtin'* and the *Skye boat song*, John Southcott touches in discreet obbligati on the recorder, and throughout Desmond Dupré provides persuasive lute accompaniments. The last four songs listed appear on record for the very first time in any format.

Tavern songs: *'Catches, glees and other divers entertainments'* (with the Deller Consort): PURCELL: *Man is for woman made; Sir Walter; To thee and to the maid; Chiding catch; Once, twice, thrice; When the cock begins to crow; Epitaph, Under this stone; An ape, a lion, a fox, and an ass; True Englishmen; Young Collin; If all be true.* Earl of MORNINGTON: *'Twas you, sir.* SAVILE: *Had she not care enough.* TURNER: *Young Anthony.* TRAD.: *Amo amas, I love a lass.* CORNYSHE: *Ah, Robin; Hoyda, jolly Rutherkin.* LAWES: *Bess Black; Sing fair Clorinda; The captive lover.* ANON.: *I am athirst; Troll the bowl; We be soldiers three; He that will an alehouse keep; Inigo Jones; Summer is icumen in.* ECCLES: *Wine does wonders.* TRAVERS: *Fair and ugly, false and true.* BENNET: *Lure, falconers lure.* ROGERS: *In the merry month of May.* SPOFFORTH: *L'ape e la serpe.* HILTON: *Call George again.* ATTERBURY: *As t'other day.* ARNE: *The street intrigue; Which is the properest way to drink.* BLOW: *Bartholomew Fair; The self banished; Galloping Joan.* BOYCE: *John Cooper.* BARNABY: *Sweet and low.*
(M) **(*) Van. 08.5039.71 [id.].

In this extraordinarily generous 78-minute collection from 1956, 40 items in all, the Deller Consort consisted of Gerald English, Wilfred Brown, Maurice Bevan, Edgar Fleet and Owen Grundy, and they sing, unaccompanied, various catches and glees, part-songs, rounds (of which *Summer is icumen in* is a prime example) and semi-madrigals from both Elizabethan and Restoration England, right up to the pre-Victorian period. The opening 'Choice collection of the most diverting catches', attributed to Purcell, are mainly bawdy, explicitly about the joys of love-making in an age of frankness. The Elizabethan romantic lute-songs had an essential finesse and delicacy of feeling, so the more robust dialogue pieces acted as a healthy counter-balance. The popular ballads could also be restrained, and this opening group ends with a touching glee, *Under this stone*, about the late-lamented Gabriel John. There are many other part-songs intended to charm with their vivacity, and *Young Anthony peeping through the keyhole*, by William Turner (1651–1740) becomes more complex as its hero eagerly joins the two ladies he has overheard discussing their probity. *Ah, Robin*, a lovely glee by William Cornyshe, is better known today, slightly altered in rhythm, as *Sing we Nowell*, while the music for the glee/madrigal *Amo, amas, I love a lass*, with its naughty Latin parody text, could have come straight out of *HMS Pinafore*. Purcell's 'patter' trio, *True Englishmen*, also shows how much Sullivan borrowed from this fertile source. *We be soldiers three* even quotes doggerel French in the way of British soldiers who, in this instance, have returned from the Flemish wars, while *L'ape e la serpe*, a late-eighteenth-century glee by Reginald Spofforth, is sung in Italian. The performances are suitably direct, never prissy, and this especially applies to the robust drinking songs, although occasionally one would have welcomed a more spontaneously earthy bite. The recording is clear and immediate, the ambience dry but pleasing.

PURCELL (with the Deller Consort, (i) Oriana Concert Choir & O; (ii) L. Kalmar O, Walter Bermann, harpsichord)): (i) *Come ye sons of art (Ode on Queen Mary's birthday, 1694); Rejoice in the Lord alway (Bell anthem);* (ii) *My beloved spake; Welcome to all pleasures (Ode on St Cecilia's Day, 1683).*
(M) **(*) Van. 08.5060.71 [id.].

These Purcell performances convey much joy in the music-making, even if for some ears the warmly upholstered (and tonally beautiful) overtures may sound slightly anachronistic. It is good to hear Deller in the famous solos, notably *Strike the viol*, with its intertwining flute obbligato (in *Come ye sons of art*), and *Here the Deities approve* in *Welcome to all the pleasures*, while in the former he is joined by his son, Mark – who sounds more like a treble – for the 'counter-tenor' duet, *Sound the trumpet.* The Deller Consort almost turns *My beloved spake* into a series of madrigals. Pleasingly full sound from 1962.

'Madrigal masterpieces': The Renaissance in France, Italy and England (with Eileen Pouler, Mary Thomas, Wilfred Brown, Gerald English, Maurice Bevan, Geoffrey Coleby, Deller Consort): JANEQUIN: *Ce moys de may; La bataille de Marignan; Au joly boys.* LASSUS: *Mon coeur se recommande à vous; Matona mia cara.* MARENZIA: *Scaldava il sol.* MONTEVERDI: *Baci, soavi, e cari; Ecco mormorar l'onde; A'un giro sol bell'occhi; Non piu guerra!; Sfogava con le stelle.* BYRD: *My sweet little baby* (lullaby). MORLEY: *Now is the month of maying.* GESUALDO: *Ecco moriro dunque/Hai gia mi disco loro.* TOMKINS: *When David heard that Absolom was slain.*
(M) ** Van. 08.5061.71 [id.].

We have moved on in the style of performance of Italian madrigals since this collection was (excellently, if closely) recorded in 1959. The Deller Consort are entirely happy in the English repertoire. Morley's *Now is the month of maying* almost explodes with spring-like vitality, and the Byrd and Tomkins items are beautiful. The Lassus *Mon coeur se recommande à vous* is touchingly serene in the same way, and *Matona mia cara* is freshly presented, but the Janequin and Monteverdi items are less successful, although *Baci, soavi, e cari* has an appealing simplicity.

TALLIS (with Wilfred Brown, Gerald English, Eileen McLoughlin, Maurice Bevan, Deller Consort): *Lamentations of Jeremiah the Prophet.* 5 hymns alternating plainchant and polyphony: *Deus tuorum militum; Jam Christus astra ascenderat; Jesu Salvator Saeculi; O nata lux de lumine; Salvator mundi Domine.*
(M) ** Van. 08.5062.71 [id.].

Alfred Deller pioneered so much repertoire on LP, and even today Tallis's settings of the *Lamentations of Jeremiah* are not generously represented on disc. They are given poised, expressive performances and the motets are presented with their alternating plainsong, but the close recording robs the music-making of atmosphere and the dynamic range is very limited.

MONTEVERDI: *Il ballo delle Ingrate* (with Eileen McLoughlin, David Ward, April Cantelo, Amb. S., L. Chamber Players, Denis Stevens); *Lamento d'Arianna* (with Honor Sheppard, Sally le Sage, Max Worthley, Philip Todd, Maurice Bevan, Deller Consort).
(M)**(*) Van. 08.5063.71 [id.].

Deller's pioneering 1956 stereo recording of Monteverdi's *Il ballo delle Ingrate* would not, perhaps, be a first choice today, but at the time he had the advantage of Denis Stevens's scholarly assistance, and the performance has remarkable authenticity as well as considerable dramatic life. The famous *Lamento d'Arianna* is slightly less successful.

'The three ravens': Elizabethan folk and minstrel songs (with Desmond Dupré, guitar & lute): *The three ravens; Cuckoo; How should I your true love know; Sweet nightingale; I will give my love an apple; The oak and the ash;* (Lute) *Go from my window; King Henry; Coventry carol; Barbara Allen; Heigh ho, the wind and the rain; Waly, waly; Down in yon forest; Matthew, Mark, Luke and John;* (Lute) *A Toye; The Tailor and the mouse; Greensleeves; The Wraggle Taggle Gipsies; Lord Rendall; Sweet Jane; The frog and the mouse; The seeds of love; Near London town; Who's going to shoe your pretty little foot?; Blow away the morning dew; Searching for lambs; Sweet England; Dabbling in the dew; Just as the tide was flowing.*
(M) **(*) Van. 08.5064.71 [id.].

Opening charismatically with *The three ravens*, this very early (1956) recital contains some outstanding performances, notably of *Barbara Allen*, the delightful *Tailor and the mouse*, *The frog and the mouse*, and the captivating *Who's going to shoe your pretty little foot?*. *Searching for lambs* brings another favourite melody, and Deller's inimitable *Greensleeves* is certainly memorable. As before, Desmond Dupré provides highly sympathetic accompaniments, and here he also has a couple of solo opportunities in which to shine. But although the mono recording is admirably truthful, this collection is not quite so spontaneously appealing as the stereo recital listed above, even if it is comparably generous (73 minutes).

'The holly and the ivy': Christmas carols of old England (with April Cantelo, Gerald English, Maurice Bevan, Deller Consort, Stanley Taylor, recorder, Desmond Dupré, lute): *Patapan; We three kings of orient are; I saw three ships; The Coventry carol; It came upon the midnight clear; Good King Wenceslas; Once in Royal David's city; Rocking; The first nowell; God rest you merry gentlemen; Wither's Rocking hymn; Silent night; Wassail song; Dormi Jesus; Boar's head carol; Past three o'clock; Lullay my liking; Adam lay ybounden; Herrick's carol; Angelus ad Virginem; The holly and the ivy; O little one sweet; Song of the Nuns of Chester; Winter-Rose; In dulci jubilo.*
(M) **(*) Van. 08.5065.71 [id.].

Opening vivaciously with *Patapan*, this Christmas collection, simulating a visit from a village group of waits, often has a pleasing simplicity, although at times its madrigalesque style may strike some ears as lacking robustness. The Consort is heard at its best in *I saw three ships*, *Good King Wenceslas* and *The holly and the ivy*. But the highlights are all from Deller himself, and he is in magical form in the *Angelus ad Virginem*, *Winter-Rose* (with a delicate recorder obbligato from Stanley Taylor) and *O little one sweet*, more robust in *Adam lay ybounden*, but again displaying his unique nuancing of colour and dynamic. His serene account of the *Coventry carol* is heard here on disc for the first time.

François COUPERIN: *Leçons de ténèbres I–III* (excerpts) (with Wifred Brown, Desmond Dupré, viola da gamba, Harry Gabb, organ).
(M) *(*) Van. 08.5066.71 [id.].

Although there is some remarkable singing here, Deller cannot compare with Gérard Lesne in this repertoire – his manner is curiously histrionic and self-aware, unusually so for this artist. Harry Gabb's discreet organ accompaniment is to be commended, but Dupré's viola da gamba is too backwardly balanced.

'Duets for counter-tenors' (with Mark Deller & Bar. Ens.): MORLEY: *Sweet nymph, come to thy lover; Miraculous love's wounding; I go before my darling.* PURCELL: *Sweetness of nature.* SCHUTZ: *Erhöre mich wenn ich; Der Herr ist gross.* JONES: *Sweet Kate.* ANON.: *Ah, my dear son.* MONTEVERDI: *Currite populi; Angelus ad pastores ait; Fugge, fugge, anima mea; Salve Regina.* BLOW: *If my Celia could persuade; Ah, heaven, what is't I hear.* DEERING: *O bone Jesu; In coelis.*
(M) *(*) Van. 08.5067.71 [id.].

Deller's style needs no advocacy, and he has trained his son well to follow faithfully in his footsteps. But although Mark has a fine (treble rather than alto) voice, he does not have his father's subtle instinct for light and shade. So in this case a succession of duets for counter-tenors proves far from ideal planning for a whole recital. Moreover the voices are placed very forwardly, somewhat edgily recorded, and robbed of a convincing dynamic range; there are no possibilities for pianissimo singing here.

William BYRD: *'Byrd and his age'* (with Wenzinger Consort of Viols of Schola Cantorum Basiliensis, August Wenzinger): *My sweet little darling; Lullaby, my sweet little baby* (both arr. FELLOWES); *Fantasia for viols in G min.; Ye sacred muses (Elegy on the death of Thomas Tallis); Come pretty babe* (arr. Peter LE HURAY & Thurston DART). ANON.: *Guishardo; Ah, silly poor Joas; O Death, rock me asleep.* WHYTHORNE: *Buy new broom.* Richard NICHOLSON: *In a merry May morn.* Robert PARSONS: *Pandolpho* (all six arr. Peter WARLOCK). William CORKINE: *What booteth love?* (arr. Thurston DART). FERRABOSCO: *Fantasias for viols: in F & G.*
(M) ** Van. 08.5068.71 [id.].

The advantage of accompaniments from the excellent Schola Cantorum Basiliensis under Wenzinger is reduced by the rather forward balance of the voice in relation to the string group, and when the viols play alone the effect is rather dry. It is on the whole a melancholy programme, although *Buy new brooms* comes centrally as a bright diversion. But it is *Ah, silly poor Joas*, the Byrd *Lullaby*, and especially the very touching *Pandolpho* that are memorable, while the closing *O Death, rock me asleep* shows Deller at his most moving.

BACH and HANDEL: BACH: *Cantata No. 170: Vergnügte Ruh', beliebte Seelenlust* (with Leonhardt Bar. Ens.); *Cantata No. 54: Widerstehe doch: Aria: Widerstehe doch; Recitative: Die Art verruchter Sünden; Aria: Wer Sünde tut, der ust vom Teufel. Mass in B min.: Agnus Dei.* HANDEL: Arias: *Orlando: Ah! stigie larve* (Mad scene). *Jepthe: Tis heav'ns all ruling power. Theodora: Kind heaven; Sweet rose and lily.*
(M) ** Van. 08.5069.71 [id.].

These are among Deller's earliest recordings for Vanguard, dating from 1954. In the Bach cantatas Leonhardt provides dull, plodding accompaniments, and his ensemble of original instruments is uninspiringly meagre. The interest of this collection then centres on Deller himself, and he rises to the occasion, especially in the *Agnus Dei* from the *Mass in B minor*, which is most beautifully sung. The Handel accompaniments are more robust and it is good to hear Deller in these operatic excerpts, especially in Orlando's mad scene, but he is also at his finest in both the excerpts from *Theodora*.

'The Cries of London and English Ballads and folksongs': The Cries of London (with April Cantelo, Wilfred Brown, Amb. S., Deller Consort, L. Chamber Players): John COBB: *These are the cries of London*. RAVENSCROFT: *New oysters; Bellman's song; The painter's song; Brooms for old shoes*. DERING: *The cries of London* (all ed. Stevens); *Country cries* (ed. Revell). ANON.: *A quart a penny; I can mend your tubs and pails*. NELHAM: *Have you any work for the tinker?* (all ed. Stevens). WEELKES: *The cries of London* (ed. Noble). English ballads and folksongs (with Deller Consort; Desmond Dupré, lute): *When cockleshells turn silver bells; An Eriskay love lilt; Peggy Ramsay* (arr. Gerard WILLIAMS); *Bushes and briars; Brigg Fair; The cruel mother; A sweet country life* (arr. Imogen HOLST); *The bitter withy; Lang a-growing; The lover's ghost; Lovely Joan; She moved through the fair; A brisk young lad he courted me* (arr. Norman STONE); *Geordie*.
(M) **(*) Van. 08.5072.71 [id.].

Richard Dering's *Fantasia* is sophisticated and creates a continuous ten-minute musical kaleidoscope, ingeniously linking the airs in a seemingly natural sequence, ending with a melodious apotheosis on the words 'and so good night'. Weelkes's selection is little more than half as long, using one soloist, here the fresh-voiced April Cantelo. Even so, she gets through a great many lyrical exhortations to buy, ending with a gentle *Alleluia*. The second half of the recital brings Deller back (in 1959) to the world of ballads and folksongs, opening with a bewitchingly gentle account of *When cockleshells turn silver bells*. Both *The lover's ghost* and the *Eriskay love lilt* take him soaringly upwards, rapturously comparable with *Annie Laurie* on an earlier recital. He is effectively joined by the Consort in *Peggy Ramsay* and they bring variety to the collection with characteristic accounts of *A sweet country life* and *A brisk young lad*. Dupré and his lute set the scene for the lovely *Bushes and briars*. *The cruel mother*, which tells a dreadful story of infanticide, also shows him imaginatively stretched, while *Lang a-growing* with its neat Scottish snap is most effectively done.

VAUGHAN WILLIAMS: Arrangements of folksongs (with Deller Consort, Desmond Dupré, lute): *An acre of land; Bushes and briars; Ca' the yowes; The cuckoo and the nightingale; The dark-eyed sailor; Down by the riverside; A farmer's son so sweet; Greensleeves; John Dory; Just as the tide was flowing; The jolly ploughboy; Loch Lomond; The lover's ghost; My boy Billy; The painful plough; The spring time of the year; The turtle dove; Ward the Pirate; Wassail song*.
(M) ** Van. 08.5073.71 [id.].

These highly artistic folksong settings can be effectively performed either by choir or by soloists, and here Deller often alternates his own estimable solo contributions with choral versions. The recording is a little dry, but the stereo adds to the sense of atmosphere. An enjoyable collection, but not one of the finest of the series. It is discussed more fully under its composer listing, above.

Divas

'Prima voce': Divas 1906–35 (Tetrazzini; Melba; Patti; Hempel; Galli-Curci; Ponselle; Lehmann; Turner; Koshetz; Norena; Nemeth; Muzio): Arias from: VERDI: *Un ballo in maschera; Rigoletto; Aida; Il Trovatore*. THOMAS: *Mignon*. MOZART: *Die Zauberflöte*. ROSSINI: *Il Barbiere di Siviglia*. MASSENET: *Manon*. PUCCINI: *Madama Butterfly*. BEETHOVEN: *Fidelio*. RIMSKY-KORSAKOV: *Sadko*. BORODIN: *Prince Igor*. GOUNOD: *Roméo et Juliette*. BOITO: *Mefistofele*. Songs: YRADIER: *La Calesera*. DENAUDY: *O del mio amato ben*.
(M) (***) Nimbus mono NI 7802 [id.].

The six supreme prima donnas on this compilation are all very well represented. The soprano voice benefits more than most from the Nimbus process, so that with extra bloom Tetrazzini's vocal 'gear-change' down to the chest register is no longer obtrusive. She is represented by three recordings of 1911, including Gilda's *Caro nome* from *Rigoletto*; and Galli-Curci has three items too, including Rosina's *Una voce poco fa* from *Il Barbiere di Siviglia*. The tragically short-lived Claudia Muzio and the Russian, Nina Koshetz, have two each, while the others are each represented by a single, well-chosen item. They include Melba in *Mimi's farewell*, the 60-year-old Patti irresistibly vivacious in a Spanish folksong, *La calesera*, and Frieda Hempel in what is probably the most dazzling of all recordings of the Queen of the Night's second aria from *Zauberflöte*.

'Prima Voce': Divas Volume 2, 1909–40 (Hempel, Galli-Curci, Farrar, Kurz, Garrison, Gluck, Ivogün, Onegin, Schoene, Norena, Ponselle, Leider, Vallin, Teyte, Koshetz, Flagstad, Favero): Arias from: BELLINI: *I Puritani*. MOZART: *Le nozze di Figaro; Die Entführung aus dem Serail*. PUCCINI: *Tosca*. VERDI:

Rigoletto; La forza del destino. OFFENBACH: *Les contes d'Hoffmann; La Périchole.* GODARD: *Jocelyn.* BIZET: *Carmen.* J. STRAUSS Jr: *Die Fledermaus.* THOMAS: *Hamlet.* WAGNER: *Tristan und Isolde; Die Walküre.* MASSENET: *Werther.* PONCE: *Estrellita.* MASCAGNI: *Lodoletta.*
(M) (***) Nimbus mono NI 7818 [id.].

As in the first *Divas* volume, the choice of items will delight any lover of fine singing, a most discriminating choice. Maria Ivogün, the teacher of Schwarzkopf, contributes a wonderfully pure and incisive *Martern aller Arten* (*Entführung*) dating from 1923, and Lotte Schoene is unusually and characterfully represented by Adele's *Mein Herr Marquis* from *Fledermaus*. Frida Leider's *Liebestod* is nobly sung but is surprisingly fast by latterday standards. Maggie Teyte sings delectably in an aria from *La Périchole*; and though some of the pre-electric items in Nimbus's resonant transfers suggest an echo-chamber, the voices are warm and full.

Domingo, Plácido (tenor)

'Domingo favourites'; Arias from: DONIZETTI: *L'elisir d'amore.* VERDI: *Ernani; Il trovatore; Aida; Nabucco; Don Carlos.* HALEVY: *La Juive.* MEYERBEER: *L'Africaine.* BIZET: *Les Pêcheurs de perles; Carmen.* PUCCINI: *Tosca; Manon Lescaut.*
(M) *** DG Dig. 445 525-2; *445 525-4.*

The greater part of this collection is taken from a 1980 digital recital, recorded in connection with yet another gala in San Francisco. The result is as noble and resplendent a tenor recital as you will find. Domingo improves in detail even on the fine versions of some of these arias he had recorded earlier, and the finesse of the whole gains greatly from the sensitive direction of Giulini. Though the orchestra is a little backward, the honeyed beauty of the voice is given the greatest immediacy. The other items are taken from Domingo's complete sets of *Don Carlos* (with Abbado), *Nabucco*, *Manon Lescaut* and *Tosca* (with Sinopoli), and are well up to the high standards this great tenor consistently sets for himself.

'Great voice': Excerpts from: BIZET: *Carmen* (with Berganza). PUCCINI: *Manon Lescaut* (with Caballé); *Fanciulla del West.* VERDI: *La Traviata* (with Cotrubas); *Macbeth.* WAGNER: *Tannhäuser.* Songs: CATARI: *Core'ngrato.* LARA: *Granada.* LEONCAVALLO: *Mattinata.* FREIRE: *Ay, ay, ay.* CURTIS: *Non ti scordar di me.*
(B) **(*) DG 431 104-2 [(M) id. import].

Opening with the *Flower song* from *Carmen* (noble in line rather than melting), it includes also the vibrant 'live' *Manon Lescaut* duet which is also featured on the companion Caballé recital (only this time, curiously, the applause is cut off at the end). Stylish in Verdi and warmly moving in Walther's *Prize song* from *Die Meistersinger*, with resonant choral backing, the disc ends with a few top Italian pops, over-recorded but certainly making an impact. But the selection (59 minutes) is not as generous as other CDs in this series and, as usual, there is no documentation other than titles. At bargain price, however, many will be tempted.

'Domingo sings Caruso': Arias from LEONCAVALLO: *La Bohème; Pagliacci.* DONIZETTI: *L'elisir d'amore.* MASSENET: *Manon; Le Cid.* CILEA: *L'Arlesiana.* FLOTOW: *Martha.* PUCCINI: *La Fanciulla del West; La Bohème.* VERDI: *Rigoletto; Aida.* MEYERBEER: *L'Africana.* GOUNOD: *Faust.* HALEVY: *La juive.* MASCAGNI: *Cavalleria rusticana.*
(M) **(*) BMG/RCA 09026 61356-2 [id.].

Domingo's heroic stage presence comes over well, the ringing tone able to impress in a lyrical phrase, even though more fining down of the tone and a willingness to sing really softly more often would enhance the listener's pleasure. But in the theatre this is obviously a voice to thrill, and the engineers have captured it directly and realistically, from the sobbing verismo of *Pagliacci* to the crisp aristocracy in *Rigoletto*. The selection is an interesting one – the opening aria from Leoncavallo's *Bohème* suggests that this opera is worth reviving.

'Grandi voci' (arias from): BIZET: *Carmen.* WAGNER: *Lohengrin.* R. STRAUSS: *Die Frau ohne Schatten* (with LPO or VPO, Solti). OFFENBACH: *Les Contes d'Hoffmann* (with SRO, Bonynge). MEYERBEER: *L'Africaine.*
(M) *** Decca (IMS) Analogue/Dig. 440 410-2 [id.].

All but one of these recordings come from distinguished complete sets in which Domingo played a major part in ensuring their excellence. Whether as a superb Lohengrin or as the Emperor in Solti's more recent *Die Frau ohne Schatten,* there is no mistaking the nobility of this singing, and the great tenor readily shows his range in the excerpts from *Carmen* and the sparkling *Legend of Kleinzach* from *Contes d'Hoffmann*, all given vintage Decca sound. *O paradis* was recorded live in Rome in 1990.

Early Music Consort of London, David Munrow

Music of the Gothic era: LEONIN: *Viderunt omnes; Alleluya Pascha nostrum; Gaude Maria Virgo; Locus iste.* PEROTIN: *Viderunt omnes; Sederunt principes.* ANON.: *Alle, psallite cum luya; Amor potest; S'on me regarde; In mari miserie; On parole de batre; En mai, quant rosier sont flouri; Dominator Domine; El mois de mai; O mitissima; Hoquetus I–VII; La mesnie fauveline; Quant je le voi; Zelus familie; Quasi non ministerium; Clap, clap, par un matin; Lés l'ormel a la turelle; O Philippe, Franci qui generis; Febus mundo oriens; Degentis vita; Inter densas deserti meditans.* PETRUS DE CRUCE: *Aucun ont trouvé.* ADAM DE LA HALLE: *De ma dame vient; J'os bien a m'amie parler.* PHILIPPE DE VITRY: *Impudenter circumivi; Cum statua.* BERNARD DE CLUNY: *Pantheon abluitur.* HENRI GILLES DE PUSIEUX: *Rachel plorat filios.* MACHAUT: *Lasse! comment oublieray; Qui es promesses; Hoquetus David; Christe, qui lux es.* ROYLLART: *Rex Karole, Johannis genite*
(M) *** DG 453 185-2 (2) [id.].

This curiously named collection, 'Music of the Gothic era', is particularly valuable in providing a remarkably lively survey of medieval music during the two centuries when it was developing at a comparatively swift rate from early organa to the thirteenth-century motet, 'from the monumental to the miniature', as David Munrow says in his notes. So the choice of music moves from Léonin's organum to the *Rex Karole* of Philippe Royllart, dating from the second half of the fourteenth century. The set was originally on three LPs (now reduced to a pair of CDs), so the music comes in three groupings: I, Notre Dame period; II, Ars Antiqua Motetti; and III, Ars Nova Motetti, although there are instrumental items included among the vocal works. Munrow projects this music with characteristically buoyant rhythms and expressive liveliness. Its presentation is essentially conjectural, but to bring the music back to life is the most important thing, and Munrow certainly does that, and most entertainingly too. The recording is excellent.

The David Munrow Edition

'The Art of courtly love' (with James Bowman, Charles Brett, Martyn Hill, Geoffrey Shaw): I: 'Guillaume de Machaut and his age': Jehan de LESCUREL: *A vous douce debonaire* (chanson). MACHAUT: *Amours me fait desirer; Dame se vous m'estés lointeinne; De Bon Espoir – Puis que la douce rousee; De toutes flours; Douce dame jolie; Hareu! hareu! le feu; Ma fin est mon commencement; Mes esperis se combat; Phyton le mervilleus serpent; Quant j'ay l'espart; Quant je suis mis au retour; Quant Theseus – Ne quier veoir; Se ma dame m'a guerpy; Se je souspir; Trop plus est belle – Biauté paree – Je ne sui mie certeins.* P. des MOLINS: *Amis tout dous vis.* ANON.: *La Septime estampie real.* F. ANDRIEU: *Armes amours – O flour des flours.* II: *'Late 14th century avant-garde'*: GRIMACE: *A l'arme a l'arme.* FRANCISCUS: *Phiton Phiton.* BORLET: *2 Variants on the tenor 'Roussignoulet du bois'; Ma tedol rosignol.* SOLAGE: *Fumeux fume; Helas! je voy mon cuer.* Johannes de MERUCO: *De home vray.* ANON.: *Istampitta Tre fontane; Tribum quem; Contre le temps; Restoés restoés.* HASPROIS: *Ma douce amour.* VAILLANT: *Trés doulz amis – Ma dame – Cent mille fois.* PYKINI: *Plasanche or tost.* Anthonello de CASERTA: *Amour m'a le cuer mis.* Matteo da PERUGIA: *Andray soulet; Le greygnour bien.* III: *'The Court of Burgundy'*: DU FAY: *Ce moys de may; La belle se siet; Navré ju sui d'un dart penetratif; Lamention Sanctae Matris Ecclesiae Constantinopolitaine (O tres piteulx – Omnes amici); Par droit je puis bien complaindre. Donnés l'assault; Helas mon dueil; Vergine bella.* BINCHOIS: *Je ne fai tousjours que penser; Files a marier; Amoreux suy et me vient toute joye; Je loe Amours et ma dame mercye; Vostre très doulx regart; Bien puist.* ANON.: *La Spagna* (bass danse) *Variants I & II.*
(M) *** Virgin Veritas/EMI VED5 61284-2 (2) [ZDMB 61284].

David Munrow's two-disc set '*The Art of courtly love*' spans the period 1300–1475 in some depth. The survey is divided into three sections: '*Gaullaume de Machaut and his age*', '*Late fourteenth-century avant-garde*' and '*The Court of Burgundy*'. The first section is introduced arrestingly by two cornetts and an alto shawm, who accompany a striking chanson of Jehan de Lescurel (died 1304) which must have had 'hit' status in its time (*A vous douce debonaire*). The bare harmonies give a real tang to the tune. Then comes the first of many numbers by the justly famous Guillaume de Machaut (*Hareu! hareu! le feu . . . le feu d'ardant desir*) which one hardly needs to translate, and it is certainly ardent! But it is the expressive romantic chansons of Du Fay that make one appreciate how readily the composer came to dominate the combination of lyric poetry and music in fourteenth-century France and to epitomize the title, '*The art of courtly love*'. The virelais, *Se ma dame m'a guerpy* ('If my lady has left me') and *Quant je suis mis au retour*, for solo tenor and chorus, with its sad introductory bass rebec solo, surely anticipate the melancholy eloquence of Dowland, while Machaut could also be attractively lighthearted as in *Se je souspir* ('If I sigh'), or robustly jolly and spiritedly extrovert (*Douce dame jolie*). The second CD opens with a particularly lovely vocal trio by Jehan Vaillant (?1360–90) which anticipates *The first nowell* in its vocal line, and a following ballade, *Amour m'a la cuer mis*, by Anthonello de Caserta (whose career spanned the turn of the century) demonstrates how forward-looking were other composers of 'the late fourteenth-century avante-garde', while Solage is no less enterprising (flourished 1370–90) in providing lugubrious humour with his baritone solo *Fumeux fume* ('He who fumes and lets off steam provokes hot air') with its unlikely melodic line. (Not surprisingly, Munrow gives this rondeau an appropriately bizarre instrumental backing.) 'A man's true worth' (*De home vray*), a ballade by the late-fourteenth-century Johannes de Meruco, also brings lively melodic twists and turns. Gilles Binchois (*c.* 1400–1460) was another leading figure of the time, well represented here, and, like Machaut, he had a wide range. But it is the lovely rondeau duet, *Amoreux suy et me vient toute joye* ('Filled with love, I am overjoyed, hoping that your kindness might bring sweet comfort'), that one specially remembers. With its expressive pleading so direct in its appeal, it is one of the set's highlights and is ravishingly sung here. With the music from 'The Court of Burgundy' we meet the remarkable Guillaume Du Fay with his exhilarating rondeau, *Ce moys de may*, so different in mood from his Masses, followed by an engagingly melancholy echoing duet for two counter-tenors, *La belle se siet au piet de la tour* ('The maiden sits . . . weeping, sighing and venting her grief'), while the virelai, *Helas mon dueil*, a rejected lover's lament, is infinitely touching. However, the collection ends in lively fashion with the anonymous basse danse, *La Spagna*, and here (as in the other instrumental items) Munrow's choice of colour brings an extra dimension to what is basically a very simple dance. All the soloists are distinguished and at their finest. Incidentally, although the translations are not affected, the documentation for this set has the list of titles for the second disc mixed up, starting with bands 12–15, then following with 1–11, but they are all there.

'Monteverdi's contemporaries' (with James Bowman, Martyn Hill and Paul Elliott): MAINERIO: *Il primo libro di balli: 10 Dances.* GUAMI: *Canzoni per sonar: Canzona a 8.* LAPPI: *Canzoni per sonar: La negrona.* PRIULI: *Sacrorum Concentuum: Canzona prima a 12.* PORTA: *Sacro convito musicale: Corda Deo dabimus.* BUSATTI: *Compago ecclesiastico: Surrexit Pastor bonus.* DONATI: *Concerti ecclesiastici, Op. 4: In te Domine speravi.* D'INDIA: *Novi concentus ecclesiastici; Isti sunt duae olivae.* GRANDI: *Motetti con sinfonie, Libro I: O vos omnes; Libro III: O beate Benedicte.*
✿ (M) *** Virgin Veritas/EMI VER5 61288-2 [CDM 61288].

Munrow's art is shown to even greater advantage in his collection of music by Monteverdi's contemporaries which has a comparatively short time-span (1535–1644). Opening with five dances from Giorgio Mainerio's *Il primo libro di balli*, vividly scored, mainly for wind and brass, but unexpectedly bringing a xylophone solo in the *Ballo francese*, the programme continues with other impressive instrumental pieces by Gioseffo Guami, Pietro Lappi and Giovanni Priuli. Then come five more of the Mainerio dances, two of which are solos for the cittern, notably the brilliant and catchy *Schiarazula marazula*, which is as intricately titillating as its title suggests. But this all serves to act as a prelude to a superb collection of vocal music, nearly all of which is entirely unknown. Ercole Porta's sonorous setting of *Corda Deo dabimus* has the counter-tenor (James Bowman) and tenor (Martyn Hill) sonorously underpinned by sackbutts; Cherubino Busatti's *Surrexit Pastor bonus* which follows (James Bowman at his most inspired) is unforgettable. The setting of this short but deeply poignant motet dramatically alternates moods: bright and lighthearted for '*The good shepherd is risen – Alleluia*' and then (with a sudden change) movingly eloquent in telling of the crucifixion, with a despairing downward scale for the word '*mori*' (die) which is infinitely touching. Ignazio Donati's tenor duet, *In te Domine speravi* (Martyn Hill and Paul Elliott) is almost equally eloquent. There is a fine motet from Sigismondo d'India, then comes the other highlight, Alessando Grandi's tragically beautiful *O vos omnes*, gloriously sung by Bowman. This is unforgettable. The concert ends happily in celebration with Grandi's *O beate Benedicte*, with counter-tenor and tenor duetting happily, sometimes in harmony, at others in felicitous imitation with the accompaniment for cornett, tenor sackbutt, organ and bass violin adding to the simple polyphony. Here as elsewhere Munrow's instrumentation has an imaginative flair matched by no other exponent of this repertoire. The recording is superb and this collection, including several out-and-out masterpieces among much else that is rewarding, is on no account to be missed

(i) Early Music Consort of London, David Munrow; (ii) Musica Reservata, John Beckett

'Early music festival': (i) *Florentine music of the fourteenth century* (with James Bowman, counter-tenor, Nigel Rogers and Martyn Hill, tenors): LANDINI: *Ecco la primavera; Giunta vaga biltà; Questa fanciull' amor; De! dinmi tu; Cara mie donna; La bionda treçça; Donna 'l tuo partimento.* ANON.: *Lamento di Tristano; Trotto; Due saltarelli; Quan ye voy le duç; La Manfredini; Istampita Ghaetta; Biance flour.*

PIERO: *Con dolce brama.* TERAMO: *Rosetta.* Lorenzo di FIRENZE: *Chon brachi assai; Dà, dà, a chi avaregia.* Jacobo de BOLOGNA: *Fenice fu' e vissi.* (ii) *Florentine music of the sixteenth century* (with Jantina Noorman, mezzo-soprano, Grayston Burgess, counter-tenor, Nigel Rogers, tenor, John Frost, bass baritone): MONTEVERDI: *Orfeo: Toccata.* Music for Ferdinando de' Medici (incidental music for the play, *La Pellegrina*): MARENZIO: *Second Intermedio.* MALVEZZI & CAVALIERI: *Sesto Intermedio.* FESTA: *Quando ritova.* ANON.: *Allemana-ripresa: Quando ritrova; Pavana: La cornetta; Gagliarda Giorgio; Ahimè sospiri; Pavana: Forze d'Ercole; Orsù, orsù, car'Signori; Pavana: El colognese.* Dance songs (vocal and keyboard settings): *Era di Maggio; El marchesse di Salluzzo; In questo ballo; Non ci vogliam' partire; Bussa la porta; La pastorella; E su quel monte; Maggio valente; Sorella mi piacente.* TROMBONCINO: *Frottola: Io son l'occello.* NOLA: *Tri ciechi siamo.* CARA: *Frottola: Io non compro.*
(B) *** Decca Double 452 967-2 (2) [id.].

This Double Decca happily combines two collections of Florentine music from two different authentic groups recording for the Argo label in the late 1960s and early 1970s. The repertoire may be a century apart, but this means that the contrast is the more striking. The fourteenth-century collection has a wide general appeal. Its key figure, Francesco Landini, has an immediate approachability, and this extends to much else here, especially when the variety of presentation, both vocal and instrumental, is so stimulating. No one knows exactly how or on what instruments accompaniments would have been performed, but David Munrow and his Early Music Consort solve the problems with their usual combination of scholarship and imagination. The singers include artists of the distinction of James Bowman, and the players are quite first rate. David Munrow's recorder playing is virtuosic, and Andrea Zachara da Teramo's *Rosetta*, played on a chamber organ, is most piquant. Attractive music, expertly transcribed and beautifully recorded.

The sixteenth-century collection from Musica Reservata opens with a *Toccata* from Monteverdi's *Orfeo*, vigorously played on a colourful combination of baroque trumpet, sackbuts and percussion, which shows how much more elaborate musical presentation had become in the intervening century. The earthy style of Musica Reservata may be typified by the throaty roaring of the unforgettable Janita Noorman, but the opening vocal number from Luca Marenzio's *Second Intermedio* (incidental music for the play, *La Pellegrina*) is charmingly presented by three boy trebles, accompanied by lyra, viol and harp, and later the choruses (sometimes for double or triple choirs) are both expansive and beautiful. The collection ranges wide in mood among vigorous dances, popular songs and ceremonial music, all of it refreshing to the modern ear. Full translations are included and both programmes can be highly recommended to anyone who wants to explore painlessly and with delight a rich period of musical history. Again the recording is excellent, and the only possible criticism about this straight reissue of a pair of highly recommended LPs is to mention that other explorations were made by Argo at that time; with 51 minutes' playing time on the first disc and 53 on the second, there would have been room to include more music from the intervening period. But each concert here is self-sufficient in itself, and this Double is still worth its cost.

Emmanuel College, Cambridge, Chapel Choir, Timothy Prosser

'Carols from Cambridge': TRAD.: *Veni, veni Emmanuel; The Angel Gabriel; In dulci jubilo.* RUTTER: *What sweeter music.* GAUNTLETT: *Once in Royal David's city.* arr. WILLCOCKS: *Ding dong! merrily upon high; O come all ye faithful.* BRITTEN: *A Hymn to the virgin; Friday afternoons, Op. 7: New year carol.* arr. JACKSON: *Noël nouvelet.* arr. VAUGHAN WILLIAMS: *This is the truth sent from above; Wither's Rocking hymn.* MATHIAS: *Sir Christèmas.* WARLOCK: *Bethlehem Down; Benedicamus Domino.* arr. HAMMOND: *Swete was the song the Virgin Soong.* GARDNER: *Tomorrow shall be my dancing day.* BERLIOZ: *L'enfance du Christ: Shepherds' farewell.* LEIGHTON: *Lully, lulla, thou tiny Child.* RAVENSCROFT: *Remember, O thou man.* HOPKINS: *We three kings.* ORD: *Adam lay y-bounden.* GRUBER: *Stille Nacht.* arr. RUTTER: *Wexford carol.*
(M) *** ASV Dig. CDWHL 2104 [id.].

Opening with the famous melodic chant, *Veni, veni Emmanuel* which turns out to be medieval in origin and not a Victorian hymn, this is a particularly appealing mid-priced collection, beautifully recorded. Although it includes (as the third item) *Once in Royal David's city*, sung in crescendo in the Willcocks arrangement, a strongly expressed *O come all ye faithful*, and Mathias's jovial *Sir Christèmas*, as outgoing and vigorous as one could wish, the style of performance, as befits a smaller chapel choir, is for the most part a pleasingly intimate one. Unlike King's College, Emmanuel uses women's voices, but they are as sweet and pure as any boy trebles, the overall blending and ensemble are nigh perfect and the effect is disarmingly simple, notably so in the lovely *Shepherds' farewell* from Berlioz's *L'Enfance du Christ.* Anna Dennis is a pleasingly fragile soloist in Vaughan Williams's setting of *Wither's rocking hymn*; Rutter's *What sweeter music* and Warlock's *Bethlehem down* are especially touching. Enterprisingly, the famous *Stille Nacht* is presented in its charming original version for two solo voices (Julia Caddick and Sarah Fisher) and guitar. Grüber hastily scored it in this fashion when the organ broke down just before its first performance on Christmas Eve 1818 – in the appropriately named Church of St Nicholas (Oberndorf, Austria). Not all the choices are obvious, and Britten's *New Year carol*, taken from *Friday afternoons*, is an engaging novelty. Prosser and his splendid singers are equally impressive in the livelier carols: the rhythmic syncopations of Gardner's *Tomorrow shall be my dancing day* are as sparkling as the bounce of *We three kings*, and the choir's lightness of touch is equally appealing in Warlock's *Benedicamus Domino* which ends the concert joyfully.

English Opera: 'Stars of English opera'

Arias and excerpts from: HANDEL: *Alessandro* (Isobel Baillie). VERDI: *Simon Boccanegra* (Joyce Gartside; James Johnston; Arnold Matters; Frederick Sharp; Howell Glynne); *Un ballo in maschera* (Jean Watson). GOUNOD: *Faust* (Joan Hammond; Owen Brannigan; Heddle Nash); *La reine de Saba* (Norman Allin). PUCCINI: *La Bohème* (Lisa Perli (Dora Labbette); Gerald Davies). MOZART: *Le nozze di Figaro* (Miriam Licette). TCHAIKOVSKY: *The Maid of Orleans* (Maggie Teyte). GLUCK: *Orfeo ed Euridice* (Kathleen Ferrier). CILEA: *L'Arlesiana*. MASSENET: *Werther* (Tano Ferendinos). DONIZETTI: *L'elisir d'amore* (Hedddle Nash).
(M) (***) Dutton mono CDLX 7024 [id. full price].

The 16 tracks here – including three devoted to a rare 1948 recording, celebrating the first British production of Verdi's *Simon Boccanegra* at Sadler's Wells – demonstrate what outstanding singers, almost all of them technically immaculate, were active in the years immediately after the Second World War. It is striking what clarity of focus marks almost all the singing, with hardly a wobble throughout and with words exceptionally clear, usually but not always involving an English text. Isobel Baillie was never strictly an opera-singer, but it is good to hear her in an aria from Handel's *Alessandro*. The Ferrier recording of Orfeo's great aria, *What is life?*, from Gluck's opera was from a test disc she made with Gerald Moore at the piano, anticipating her Decca recordings, and the *Boccanegra* excerpts feature an excellent team of singers whose careers centred on Sadler's Wells: Joyce Gartside, James Johnston, Arnold Matters and Frederick Sharp, with Michael Mudie conducting, as in the theatre. Another fine ensemble recording of 1948 has Joan Hammond, Heddle Nash and Owen Brannigan in the garden scene from Gounod's *Faust*, and two tracks celebrate the superb voice of the long-neglected Greek-Welsh tenor, Tano Ferendinos. Perhaps most striking of all is the pure, bright singing of Lisa Perli (pseudonym of Dora Labbette) with Beecham conducting in *Mimi's Farewell* from Puccini's *La Bohème*. Transfers are vivid, full and immediate.

Estampie, John Bryan

'Under the greenwood tree' (with Deborah Catterall, Graham Derrick): Walther von VOGELWEIDE: *Palästinalied*. Richard COEUR DE LION: *Ja nuis homs pris*. BLONDEL DE NESLE: *A l'entrant d'este*. Raimbault DE VAQUERIAS: *Kalenda Maya*. CORNYSHE: *Ah! Robin*. STONINGES: *Browning my dear* (on the theme *The leaves be green*). GERVAISE: *4th Livre de Danceries: La Venissienne. 6th Livre de Danceries: Gailliarde*. PLAYFORD: *The Dancing Master: Greenwood; Nottingham Castle; Green Goose Fair; The green man*. SIMPSON: *Ricercar on Bonny sweet Robin*. WEELKES: *When Kempe did dance alone or Robin Hood, Maid Marian and Little John are gone*. ANON.: *Novus miles sequitur; Estampie; Clap, clap un matin s'en aloit Robin; Robin Hood; The Wedding of Robin Hood; Under the greenwood tree; Sellenger's round; Greensleeves* (lute and vocal versions); *Robin Hood and the Curtal Friar; Robin Hood and the Tanner; Robin Hood and Maid Marian; Sweet angel of England* (to the tune *Bonny sweet Robin*); *O lusty May*.
(BB) ** Naxos Dig. 8.553442 [id.].

With John Bryan as music director and Graham Derrick as arranger and main performer, the early-music group, Estampie, here offer a well-devised group of dances and instrumental pieces, interspersed with songs, broadly inspired by the legend of Robin Hood and the ballad, *Robin is to the greenwood gone* in its various forms. That in turn leads to celebrations in song and dance of Maytime and the annual revival of the Green Man. Items range from a song attributed to King Richard Lionheart in the twelfth century to four items drawn (in arrangements by Graham Derrick) from John Playford's collection, *The Dancing Master*, in the seventeenth. The sequence is most illuminating, but the performances, always tasteful, rather lack the bite and earthiness which can make medieval music so invigorating. The final item, a

Scottish song, *O lusty May*, is anything but that, though there and in the other songs the mezzo, Deborah Catterall, sings with fresh, clear tone. Aptly intimate recorded sound.

Evans, Sir Geraint (baritone)

'Arias and sacred songs' (with (i) SRO, Balkwill; (ii) Shelley Singers, Lyrian Singers, Glendower Singers, BBC Welsh SO, Mansel Thomas). (i) HANDEL: *Berenice: Si trai ceppi. Semele: Leave me radiant light.* MOZART: *Le nozze di Figaro: Non piu andrai. Don Giovanni: Madamina, il catalogo. L'oca del Cairo: Ogni momento. Die Zauberflöte: Der Vogelfänger.* BEETHOVEN: *Fidelio: Ha! welch'ein Augenblick!.* LEONCAVALLO: *Prologue.* DONIZETTI: *Don Pasquale: Un fuoco insolito.* VERDI: *Otello: Credo. Falstaff: Ehi! Paggio . . . l'onore! Ladri.* BRITTEN: *A Midsummer Night's Dream: Bottom's dream.* MUSSORGSKY: *Boris Godunov: Tchelkalov's aria.* (ii) MENDELSSOHN: *Elijah: Lord God of Abraham; Is not His word like a fire?.* HANDEL: *Judas Maccabeus: Arm, arm ye brave. Messiah: The Trumpet shall sound.* ROSSINI: *Requiem: Pro peccatis.*
(BB) *** Belart 461 492-2 [(M) id. import].

This is a marvellous display of wide-ranging virtuosity, of artisic bravura such as we know from almost any performance that this ebullient and lovable singer gave. Part of Evans's mastery lay in the way he could convey the purest comedy, even drawing laughs without ever endangering the musical line through excessive buffoonery. His Mozart characters are almost unmatchable – Figaro, Leporello, Papageno – while it is good to be reminded that here is a singer who could be a formidable Iago as well as the most complete Falstaff of his day. Good accompaniment and recording, with a richly atmospheric orchestral backing, of one of Britain's greatest singers at the peak of his form.

Evans, Rebecca (soprano), **Michael Pollock** (piano)

'Debut': BELLINI: *6 Ariette da camera.* VERDI: *Stornella.* RESPIGHI: *Notturno; Storia breve; Tanto bella; Lagrime; L'ultima ebbrezza; Luce.* ROSSINI: *Serate musicale, Vol. 1: L'invito; La pastorella delle Alpi; La promessa.* DONIZETTI: *Ah! rammenta, o bella Irene; A mazzanotte; La ninn-nanna.* WOLF-FERRARI: *4 Rispetti, Op. 11.*
(B) **(*) EMI Dig. CDZ5 69706-2 [id.].

The young Welsh soprano, Rebecca Evans, makes an excellent choice of artist for the EMI Debut series. This programme, devised by the excellent accompanist, Michael Pollock, a specialist in this area, consists almost entirely of miniatures, chips off the workbenches of great opera-composers, which consistently flaunt the Italian love of lyricism. It is striking how, after the opening Bellini group, Verdi immediately has one listening with new attention, when his two lively songs make the singer sparkle. The three Rossini items too – from the *Serate musicale* – bring extra vigour and striking tunes. Two of the Donizetti songs are longer and much closer to operatic models, but the Wolf-Ferrari group brings a charming conclusion, ending with a tiny squib of a tarantella. The recording is bright and forward, even if it does not quite catch the full beauty of Rebecca Evans's voice.

Ferrier, Kathleen (contralto)

'The world of Kathleen Ferrier': TRAD.: *Blow the wind southerly; The Keel Row; Ma bonny lad; Kitty my love.* arr. BRITTEN: *Come you not from Newcastle.* HANDEL: *Rodelinda: Art thou troubled? Serse: Ombra mai fu.* GLUCK: *Orfeo: What is life?* MENDELSSOHN: *Elijah: Woe unto them; O rest in the Lord.* BACH: *St Matthew Passion: Have mercy, Lord, on me.* SCHUBERT: *An die Musik; Gretchen am Spinnrade; Die junge Nonne; Der Musensohn.* BRAHMS: *Sapphische Ode; Botschaft.* MAHLER: *Rückert Lieder: Um Mitternacht.*
❁ (M) (***) Decca mono 430 096-2; *430 096-4.*

This selection, revised and expanded from the original LP issue, admirably displays Kathleen Ferrier's range, from the delightfully fresh folksongs to Mahler's *Um Mitternacht* in her celebrated recording with Bruno Walter and the VPO. The noble account of *O rest in the Lord* is one of the essential items now added, together with an expansion of the Schubert items (*Die junge Nonne* and *An die Musik* are especially moving). The CD transfers are remarkably trouble-free and the opening unaccompanied *Blow the wind southerly* has uncanny presence. The recital plays for 65 minutes and fortunately there are few if any technical reservations to be made here about the sound quality.

'The world of Kathleen Ferrier' Volume 2: TRAD.: *Ye banks and braes; Drink to me only* (both arr.

QUILTER); *I have a bonnet trimmmed with blue; Down by the Sally Gardens; The stuttering lovers* (all arr. Hughes). PURCELL: *The Fairy Queen: Hark! the echoing air.* HANDEL: *Atalanta: Like the love-lorn turtle.* GLUCK: *Orfeo: Che puro ciel.* MAHLER: *Rückert Lieder: Ich bin der Welt abhanden gekommen.* SCHUMANN: *Frauenliebe und Leben: Er, der Herrlichste von allen.* BRAHMS: *Geistliches Wiegenlied; Von ewiger Liebe.* SCHUBERT: *Du bist die Ruh; Rosamunde: Romance.* BACH: *Mass in B min.: Agnus Dei.* HANDEL: *Messiah: He was despised.*
(M) *** Decca mono 448 055-2; *448 055-4.*

Volume II offers a comparable mixture, opening with more delightful folksongs, notably the charming '*stuttering lovers*', although it is *Ye banks and braes* and *Drink to me only* that show the full richness of this glorious voice. *Che puro ciel* stands out among the opera arias for its simple eloquence, and the Brahms *Geistliches Wiegenlied*, with its somewhat wan viola obbligato, is gently ravishing. The passionate *Du bist die Ruh*, the *Rosamunde Romance* and *Von ewiger Liebe* come from a BBC acetate disc of her 1949 Edinburgh Festival recital with Bruno Walter at the piano, and here there is some uneven background noise and the quality deteriorates in the Brahms song. But the CD closes with one of her very last recordings, her unforgettably poignant *He was despised*, with those words given an uncanny presence.

Fischer-Dieskau, Dietrich (baritone)

'Fischer Dieskau Lieder Edition' (complete).
✿ (BB) *** DG 447 500-2 (44) [(M) id. import].

To celebrate the seventieth birthday of the great German baritone, DG published a justifiably extravagant Lieder Edition, summing up the astonishing achievement of the greatest male Lieder singer of our time – although, in making such a claim, one must not forget Gérard Souzay's inestimable contribution in the area of French art-song. The set is offered at budget price, with two discs thrown in for good measure (44 CDs for the price of 42).

Each individual composer grouping is also available separately, still very competitively priced. With consistent artistry from all concerned and with first-class transfers, these CDs are self-recommending. We have discussed the Schubert in previous volumes, and much else, too, in individual issues. Fischer-Dieskau's mastery never ceases to amaze. Sample this set at almost any point and the same virtues emerge: characteristic beauty of vocal tone and an extraordinarily vivid power of characterization and vocal colouring. No less remarkable are his accompanists, including the incomparable Gerald Moore and Daniel Barenboim, whose sensitivity and command of keyboard colour make for consistently memorable results. The Liszt collection is especially valuable. As in a number of other fields, Liszt has been severely under-appreciated as a song composer. This collection of 43 songs plus an accompanied declamation should do much to right the balance. The sheer originality of thought and the ease of the lyricism are a regular delight. Fischer-Dieskau's concentration and inspiration never seem to falter, especially in the most famous of the songs, the *Petrarch Sonnets*, and Barenboim's accompaniments could hardly be more understanding.

SCHUBERT: Lieder (with Gerald Moore, piano): Volume 1 (1811–17); Volume 2 (1817–28). Song-cycles: *Die schöne Müllerin; Schwanengesang; Die Winterreise.*
(B) *** DG 437 214-2 (21) [(M) id. import].

Lieder, Volume I (1811–17): *Ein Leichenfantasie; Der Vatermörder* (1811); *Der Jüngling am Bache* (1812); *Totengräberlied; Die Schatten; Sehnsucht; Verklärung; Pensa, che questo istante* (1813); *Der Taucher* (1813–15); *Andenken; Geisternähe; Erinnerung; Trost, An Elisa; Die Betende; Lied aus der Ferne; Der Abend; Lied der Liebe; Erinnerungen; Adelaide; An Emma; Romanze: Ein Fräulein klagt' im finstern Turm; An Laura, als sie Klopstocks Auferstehungslied sang; Der Geistertanz; Das Mädchen aus der Fremde; Nachtgesang; Trost in Tränen; Schäfers Klagelied; Sehnsucht; Am See* (1814); *Auf einen Kirchhof; Als ich sie erröten sah; Das Bild; Der Mondabend* (1815); *Lodas Gespenst* (1816); *Der Sänger* (1815); *Die Erwartung* (1816); *Am Flusse; An Mignon; Nähe des Geliebten; Sängers Morgenlied; Amphiaraos; Das war ich; Die Sterne; Vergebliche Liebe; Liebesrausch; Sehnsucht der Liebe; Die erste Liebe; Trinklied; Stimme der Liebe; Naturgenuss; An die Freude; Der Jüngling am Bache; An den Mond; Die Mainacht; An die Nachtigall; An die Apfelbäume; Seufzer; Liebeständelei; Der Liebende; Der Traum; Die Laube; Meeres Stille; Grablied; Das Finden; Wandrers Nachtlied; Der Fischer; Erster Verlust; Die Erscheinung; Die Täuschung; Der Abend; Geist der Liebe; Tischlied; Der Liedler; Ballade; Abends unter der Linde; Die Mondnacht; Huldigung; Alles um Liebe; Das Geheimnis; An den Frühling; Die Bürgschaft; Der Rattenfänger; Der Schatzgräber; Heidenröslein; Bundeslied; An den Mond; Wonne der Wehmut; Wer kauft Liebesgötter?* (1815); *Der Goldschmiedsgesell* (1817); *Der Morgenkuss; Abendständchen: An*

Lina; Morgenlied: Willkommen, rotes Morgenlicht; Der Weiberfreund; An die Sonne; Tischlerlied; Totenkranz für ein Kind; Abendlied; Die Fröhlichkeit; Lob des Tokayers; Furcht der Geliebten; Das Rosenband; An Sie; Die Sommernacht; Die frühen Gräber; Dem Unendlichen; Ossians Lied nach dem Falle Nathos; Das Mädchen von Inistore; Labetrank der Liebe; An die Geliebte; Mein Gruss an den Mai; Skolie – Lasst im Morgenstrahl des Mai'n; Die Sternenwelten; Die Macht der Liebe; Das gestörte Glück; Die Sterne; Nachtgesang; An Rosa I: Warum bist du nicht hier?; An Rosa II: Rosa, denkst du an mich?; Schwanengesang; Der Zufriedene; Liane; Augenlied; Geistes-Gruss; Hoffnung; An den Mond; Rastlose Liebe; Erlkönig (1815); *Der Schmetterling; Die Berge* (1819); *Genügsamkeit; An die Natur* (1815); *Klage; Morgenlied; Abendlied; Der Flüchtling; Laura am Klavier; Entzückung an Laura; Die vier Weltalter; Pflügerlied; Die Einsiedelei; An die Harmonie; Die Herbstnacht; Lied: Ins stille Land; Der Herbstabend; Der Entfernten; Fischerlied; Sprache der Liebe; Abschied von der Harfe; Stimme der Liebe; Entzückung; Geist der Liebe; Klage: Der Sonne steigt; Julius an Theone; Klage: Dein Silber schien durch Eichengrün; Frühlingslied; Auf den Tod einer Nachtigall; Die Knabenzeit; Winterlied; Minnelied; Die frühe Liebe; Blumenlied; Der Leidende; Seligkeit; Erntelied; Das grosse Halleluja; Die Gestirne; Die Liebesgötter; An den Schlaf; Gott im Frühling; Der gute Hirt; Die Nacht; Fragment aus dem Aeschylus* (1816); *An die untergehende Sonne* (1816/17); *An mein Klavier; Freude der Kinderjahre; Das Heimweh; An den Mond; An Chloen; Hochzeitlied; In der Mitternacht; Trauer der Liebe; Die Perle; Liedesend; Orpheus; Abschied; Rückweg; Alte Liebe rostet nie; Gesänge des Harfners aus Goethes Wilhelm Meister: Harfenspieler I: Wer sich der Einsamkeit ergibt; Harfenspieler II: An die Türen will ich schleichen; Harfenspieler III: Wer nie sein Brot mit Tränen ass. Der König in Thule; Jägers Abendlied; An Schwager Kronos; Der Sänger am Felsen; Lied: Ferne von der grossen Stadt; Der Wanderer; Der Hirt; Lied eines Schiffers an die Dioskuren; Geheimnis; Zum Punsche; Am Bach im Frühling* (1816); *An eine Quelle* (1817); *Bei dem Grabe, meines Vaters; Am Grabe Anselmos; Abendlied; Zufriedenheit; Herbstlied; Skolie: Mädchen entsiegelten; Lebenslied; Lieden der Trennung* (1816); *Alinde; An die Laute* (1827); *Frohsinn; Die Liebe; Trost; Der Schäfer und der Reiter* (1817); *Lob der Tränen* (1821); *Der Alpenjäger; Wie Ulfru fischt; Fahrt zum Hades; Schlaflied; Die Blumensprache; Die abgeblühte Linde; Der Flug der Zeit; Der Tod und das Mädchen; Das Lied vom Reifen; Täglich zu singen; Am Strome; Philoktet; Memnon; Auf dem See; Ganymed; Der Jüngling und der Tod; Trost im Liede* (1817).
(B) *** DG 437 215-2 (9) [(M) id. import].

Lieder, Volume II (1817–28): *An die Musik; Pax vobiscum; Hänflings Liebeswerbung; Auf der Donau; Der Schiffer; Nach einem Gewitter; Fischerlied; Das Grab; Der Strom; An den Tod; Abschied; Die Forelle; Gruppe aus dem Tartarus; Elysium; Atys; Erlafsee; Der Alpenjäger; Der Kampf; Der Knabe in der Wiege* (1817); *Auf der Riesenkoppe; An den Mond in einer Herbstnacht; Grablied für die Mutter; Einsamkeit; Der Blumenbrief; Das Marienbild* (1818); *Litanei auf das Fest Allerseelen* (1816); *Blondel zu Marien; Das Abendrot; Sonett I: Apollo, lebet noch dein Hold verlangen; Sonett II: Allein, nachdenken wie gelähmt vom Krampfe; Sonett III: Nunmehr, da Himmel, Erde schweigt; Vom Mitleiden Mariä* (1818) ; *Die Gebüsche; Der Wanderer; Abendbilder; Himmelsfunken; An die Freunde; Sehnsucht; Hoffnung; Der Jüngling am Bache; Hymne I: Wenige wissen das Geheimnis der Liebe; Hymne II: Wenn ich ihn nur hab; Hymne III: Wenn alle untreu werden; Hymne IV: Ich sag es jedem; Marie; Beim Winde; Die Sternennächte; Trost; Nachtstück; Prometheus; Strophe aus Die Götter Griechenlands* (1819); *Nachthymne; Die Vögel; Der Knabe; Der Fluss; Abendröte; Der Schiffer; Die Sterne; Morgenlied* (1820); *Frühlingsglaube* (1822); *Des Fräuleins Liebeslauschen* (1820); *Orest auf Tauris* (1817); *Der entsühnte Orest; Freiwilliges Versinken; Der Jüngling auf dem Hügel* (1820); *Sehnsucht* (1817); *Der zürnenden Diana; Im Walde* (1820); *Die gefangenen Sänger; Der Unglückliche; Versunken; Geheimes; Grenzen der Menschheit* (1821); *Der Jüngling an der Quelle* (1815); *Der Blumen Schmerz* (1821); *Sei mir gegrüsst; Herr Josef Spaun, Assessor in Linz; Der Wachtelschlag Ihr Grab; Nachtviolen; Heliopolis I: Im kalten, rauhen Norden; Heliopolis II: Fels auf Felsen hingewälzet; Selige Welt; Schwanengesang: Wie klage'ich's aus; Du liebst mich nicht; Die Liebe hat gelogen; Todesmusik; Schatzgräbers Begehr; An die Leier; Im Haine; Der Musensohn; An die Entfernte; Am Flusse; Willkommen und Abschied* (1822); *Wandrers Nachtlied: Ein Gleiches; Der zürnende Barde* (1823); *Am See* (1822/3); *Viola; Drang in die Ferne; Der Zwerg; Wehmut; Lied: Die Mutter Erde; Auf dem Wasser zu singen; Pilgerweise; Das Geheimnis; Der Pilgrim; Dass sie hier gewesen; Du bist die Ruh; Lachen und Weinen; Greisengesang* (1823); *Dithyrambe; Der Sieg; Abendstern; Auflösung; Gondelfahrer* (1824); *Glaube, Hoffnung und Liebe* (1828); *Im Abendrot; Der Einsame* (1824); *Des Sängers Habe; Totengräbers Heimwehe; Der blinde Knabe; Nacht und Träume; Normans Gesang; Lied des gefangenen Jägers; Im Walde; Auf der Bruck; Das Heimweh; Die Allmacht; Fülle der Liebe; Wiedersehn; Abendlied für die Entfernte; Szene I aus dem Schauspiel Lacrimas; Am mein Herz; Der liebliche Stern* (1825); *Im Jänner 1817 (Tiefes Leid); Am Fenster; Sehnsucht; Im Freien; Fischerweise; Totengräberweise; Im Frühling; Lebensmut; Um Mitternacht; Über Wildemann* (1826); *Romanze des Richard Löwenherz* (1827); *Trinklied; Ständchen; Hippolits Lied; Gesang (An Silvia); Der*

Wanderer an den Mond; Das Zügenglöcklein; Bei dir allein; Irdisches Glück; Wiegenlied (1826); *Der Vater mit dem Kind; Jägers Liebeslied; Schiffers Scheidelied; L'incanto degli occhi; Il traditor deluso; Il modo di prender moglie; Das Lied im Grünen; Das Weinen; Vor meiner Wiege; Der Wallensteiner Lanznecht beim Trunk; Der Kreuzzug; Das Fischers Liebesglück* (1827); *Der Winterabend; Die Sterne; Herbst; Widerschein* (1828); *Abschied von der Erde* (1825/6).
(B) *** DG 437 225-2 (9) [(M) id. import].

Lieder, Volume III: Song-cycles: *Die schöne Müllerin; Schwanengesang; Die Winterreise.*
(M) *** DG 437 235-2 (3).

SCHUMANN: Lieder (with Christoph Eschenbach, piano): *Myrten, Op. 25/1–3; 5–8; 13; 15–19; 21–2; 25–6. Lieder und Gesänge, Op. 27/1–5; Op. 51/4; Op. 77/1 & 5; Op. 96/1–3; Op. 98/2, 4, 6 & 8; Op. 127/2–3. Gedichte, Op. 30/1–3; Op. 119/2. Gesänge, Op. 31/1 & 3; Op. 83/1 & 3; Op. 89/1–5; Op. 95/2; Op. 107/3 & 6; Op. 142/1, 2 & 4; Schön Hedwig, Op. 106. 6 Gedichte aus dem Liederbuch eines Malers, Op. 36. 12 Gedichte aus Rückerts Liebesfrühling, Op. 37. Liederkreis, Op. 39. 5 Lieder, Op. 40. Romanzen und Balladen, Op. 45/1–3; Op. 49/1–2; Op. 53/1–3; Op. 64/3; Belsatzar, Op. 57. Liederkreis, Op. 24. 12 Gedichte, Op. 35. Dichterliebe, Op. 48. Spanisches Liederspiel, Op. 74/6, 7 & 10. Liederalbum für die Jugend, Op. 79; Der Handschuh, Op. 87. 6 Gedichte von Nikolaus Lenau und Requiem (Anhang, No. 7), Op. 90. Minnnespiel, Op. 101. 4 Husarenlieder, Op. 117. Heitere Gesänge, Op. 125/1–3. Spanische Liebeslieder, Op. 138/2, 3, 5 & 7. Balladen, Op. 122/1–2. Sechs frühe Lieder, Op. posth. (WoO 21).*
(B) *** DG 445 660-2 (6) [(M) id. import].

BRAHMS: Lieder (with Daniel Barenboim, piano): *Gesänge, Op. 3/2–6; Op. 6/2–6; Mondnacht, Op. 7/1–4 & 6; Op. 43/1–4; Op. 46/1–4; Op. 70/1–4; Op. 71/1–5; Op. 72/2–5. Lieder und Romanzen, Op. 14/1–8; Gedichte, Op. 19/1–2, 3 & 5; Lieder und Gesänge, Op. 32/1–9; Op. 57/2–8; Op. 58/1–8; Op. 59/1–4, 6–7; Op. 63/1–9; Romanzen, Op. 33/1–15; Lieder, Op. 47/1–4; Op. 48/1, 2, 5–7; Op. 49/1–5; Op. 85/1–2, 4–6; Op. 86/2–5; Op. 94/1–3 & 5; Op. 95/2, 3 & 7; Op. 96/1–4; Op. 97/1–3, 5–6; Op. 105/4–5; Op. 106/1–5; Op. 107/1–2 & 4. Neuen Gesänge, Op. 69/3, 5 & 7. Vier ernste Gesänge, Op. 121.*
(B) *** DG 447 501-2 (6) [(M) id. import].

LISZT: Lieder (with Daniel Barenboim, piano): *Der Alpenjäger; Anfangs wollt' ich fast verzagen; Angiolin dal biondo crin; Blume und Duft; Comment, disaient-ils; Die drei Zigeuner; Du bist wie eine Blume; Der du von dem Himmel bist; Enfant, si j'étais roi; Eine Fichtenbaum steht einsam; Es muss ein Wunderbares sein; Es rauschen die Winde; Der Fischerknabe; Gastibelza; Gestorben war ich; Der Hirt; Hohe Liebe; Ich möchte hingehn; Ihr Glocken von Marling; Im Rhein, im schönen Strome; In Liebeslust; J'ai perdu ma force et ma vie; Klinge leise, mein Lied; Lasst mich ruhen; Die Lorelei; Morgens steh' ich auf und frage; Oh! quand je dors; O Lieb, so lang du lieben kannst; Petrarch sonnets Nos. 1–3; Schwebe, schwebe blaues Auge; S'il est un charmant gazon; Die stille Wasserrose; Des Tages laute Stimmen schweigen; La tombe et la rose; Der traurige Mönch; Uber allen Gipfeln ist Ruh; Die Vätergruft; Vergiftet sind meine Lieder; Le vieux vagabond; Wer nie sein Brot mit Tränen ass; Wieder möcht' ich dir Begegnen; Wie singt die Lerche schön.*
(M) *** DG (IMS) 447 508-2 (3).

Richard STRAUSS: Lieder (with Wolfgang Sawallisch, piano): *5 kleine Lieder, Op. 69; Lieder, Op. 10/2–7; Op. 15/2 & 5; Op. 17/2; Op. 19/1–6; Op. 26/1–2; Op. 27/1, 3 & 4; Op. 29/1 & 3; Op. 31/4; Op. 32/1–5; Op. 36/1 & 4; Op. 37/1–2, 5–6; Op. 49/6; Op. 56/1 & 3; Op. 67/6. Schlichte Weisen, Op. 21; Vier Gesang, Op. 87.*
(M) *** DG (IMS) 447 512-2 (2).

WOLF: Lieder (with Daniel Barenboim, piano): *23 Eichendorf Lieder; 42 Goethe Lieder; 7 Heine Lieder; 4 Lenau Lieder; 3 Gedichte von Michelangelo; Mörike Lieder* (complete); *6 Reinick Lieder; 4 Gedichte von Robert Reinick. 3 Gedichte nach Shakespeare und Lord Byron.* Miscellaneous Lieder by Peitl; Von Matthisson; Körner; Herlossohn; Hebbel; Von Fallersleben; Sturm; Von Scheffel.
(B) *** DG 447 515-2 (6) [(M) id. import].

Flagstad, Kirsten (soprano)

Kirsten Flagstad Edition

Kirsten Flagstad Edition (complete).
(M) **(*) Decca stereo/mono 440 490-2 (5).

MAHLER: *Kindertotenlieder; Lieder eines fahrenden Gesellen* (with VPO, Boult). WAGNER: *Wesendonck Lieder* (with VPO, Knappertsbusch) (440 491-2).

SIBELIUS: Songs: *Arioso; Autumn evening (Höstkväll); Black roses (Svata rosor); But my bird is nowhere to be seen (Men min fagel märks dock icke); Come away, death (Komm nu hit, död!); The diamond on the March snow (Diamanten pa Marssnön); Did I dream? (Var det en dröm); The first kiss (Den första kyssne); The girl returned from meeting her lover (Flickan kom ifran sin älsklings möte); On a veranda by the sea (Pa verandan vit havet); Sigh, rushes, sigh (Säv, säv, susa); Since then I have stopped asking (Se'n har jag ej fragat mera); Spring fleets fast (Varen flyktar hastigt); To the night (Til kvällen).* GRIEG: *Autumn storms (Efterasstormen); I give my song to the spring (Jeg giver mit digt til varen); I would like a waistcoat of silk (Og jeg vil ha mig en silkevest); To you (Til én) I & II.* Arne EGGEN: *Praise to the eternal spring of life (Aere det evige forar i livet).* Eyvind ALNAES: *About love (Nu brister alle de kløfter); A February morning at the Gulf (Februarmorgen ved Golfen); A hundred violins (De hundrede fioliner); Yearnings of spring (Varlængsler).* Harald LIE: *The key (Nykelen); The letter (Skinnvengbrev)* (with LSO, Oivin Fjeldstad) (440 492-2).

GRIEG: Haugtussa (*The Mountain maid;* song-cycle), *Op. 67;* Songs: *Ambition (Der ærgjerrige); Among roses (Millom rosor); At Gjaetle Brook (Ved Gjætle-Bekken); Blueberry slope (Blabær-Li); Children's dance (A hipp og hoppe); A dream (En drøm); The encounter (Møte); Enticement (Det syng); Eros; The first meeting (Det første møte); Fra Monte Pincio (from Monte Pincio); High up in the leafy hills (I liden højt der oppe); I give my song to the spring (Jeg giver mit digt til varen); I love you (Jeg elsker Dig); In the boat (Der gynger en Bad pa Bølge); The little hut (Hytten); Little Kirsten (Liten Kirsten); The little maiden (Veslemøy); Love (Elsk); Sorrowful day (Vond Dag); The water-lily (Med en vanlilje); With a primrose (Med en primulaveris)* (with Edwin McArthur) (mono 440 493-2).

BRAHMS: *Vier ernste Gesänge (4 Serious songs);* Lieder: *Alte Liebe; Am dem Kirchhofe; Am Sonntag Morgen; Bei dir sind meine Gedanken; Dein blaues Auge; Treue Liebe; Wie Melodien zieht es mir; Wir waldelten.* SCHUBERT: *Am Grabe Anselmos; An Der Erlkönig; Ave Maria; Das Mädchens Klage; Dem Unendlichen* (with Edwin McArthur) (mono 440 494-2).

WAGNER: (with (i) Oslo PO or Norwegian State RO, Fjeldstad; (ii) VPO, Knappertsbusch; (iii) VPO, Solti): (i) *Götterdämmerung: Starke Scheite schichtet mir dort (Immolation scene);* (ii) *Lohengrin: Einsam in trüben Tagen. Parsifal: Ich sah das Kind. Die Walküre, Act I: Der Männer Sippe; Du bist der Lenz;* (iii) Act II: *Siegmund! Sieh' auf mich! (Todesverkündigung)* (stereo/mono 440 495-2).

The Decca producer John Culshaw was (understandably) a great admirer of the art of Kirsten Flagstad and it was he who persuaded her to come out of retirement in the mid-1950s. Not only did she contribute to Solti's great *Ring* cycle, singing the part of Fricka (for the first time) in *Das Rheingold*, but other recordings were planned, and most of them are here. She had recorded some of this repertoire earlier for EMI when she was in her prime in the mid-1940s, notably the Grieg and Norwegian songs. Yet the later, Decca recordings, which have more faithful sound, demonstrate again her masterly sense of pacing and of vocal colour and her command of evocation.

In Lieder, Flagstad may not have the evenness of line or bring the perception of word-meanings of the greatest German Lieder singers, but her voice is admirably suited to the *Four Serious songs* of Brahms, of which the third, *O Tod, O Tod, wie bitter bist du*, is most deeply felt, while among the other Brahms songs *Am Sonntag Morgen* brings wonderfully radiant tone and *Dein blaues Auge* is very touching. In Schubert, although the voice at times seems less than wieldy, the operatic drama of *Der Erlkönig* is as memorable as the gently ravishing cantilena of *Am Grabe Anselmos* and the hardly less sympathetic *Alte Liebe*. Here, as elsewhere, Edwin McArthur's accompaniments are a model of support for the great voice and make a sensitive and imaginative impression in their own right. The mono recordings, made at Decca's West Hampstead studios in the spring and late autumn of 1956, are naturally atmospheric, and the ear would hardly guess the sound was not early stereo. The stereo Wagner recordings with Knappertsbusch are uneven, although Flagstad was a superb Sieglinde, and her glorious voice is perfectly suited to the rich inspiration of the *Wesendonk Lieder*. Moreover the excerpt from Solti's partial recording of Act II of *Die Walküre* and the earlier (mono) Immolation scene from Fjeldstad's 1956 *Götterdämmerung* provide an outstanding reminder of one of the finest Brünnhildes of our time. Throughout this set (which presents the five individual CDs in a slipcase) the transfers are consistently vivid, and the documentation is good, with translations provided thoughout. The discs are not now available separately.

'Prima voce' (with Edwin McArthur, piano): GRIEG: *Haugtussa* (song-cycle). Songs by ALNAES; BEETHOVEN; BRIDGE; CHARLES; DVORAK; GRIEG; ROGERS; SCOTT; R. STRAUSS.
(M) (**) Nimbus mono NI 7871 [id.].

Flagstad recorded Grieg's masterpiece, *Haugtussa* ('The Troll maiden'), no fewer than three times, and each time with the same pianist, Edwin McArthur. The first was in 1940; then she recorded it again ten years later – though it is the 1956 LP, when the voice was past its prime, that is the best known. The 1940 version is included here, along with a number of 78s she made in the mid-1930s when her voice was at its glorious best. The Nimbus transfer gives it an added ambience, as if one is picking up another, added acoustic. This proves a little tiring on the ear.

'Great sacred songs' (with LPO, Boult) (sung in English): MENDELSSOHN: *Hear my prayer – O for the wings of a dove. St Paul: Jerusalem.* GRUBER: *Silent night.* GOUNOD: *Ah, turn me not away . . . O divine Redeemer.* PARRY: *Jerusalem.* BORTNYANSKY: *Jubilate.* TRAD.: *O come, all ye faithful.* LIDDLE: *Abide with me.* BACH: *St Matthew Passion: Break in grief; Cantata No. 147: Jesu, joy of man's desiring; If thou be near.* HANDEL: *Messiah: He shall feed His flock; I know that my Redeemer liveth; Praise ye the Lord.*
(M) ** Decca 452 066-2.

In recording *Abide with me* Flagstad was following famous footsteps and this whole 1957 collection of what might be called 'sacred pops' has had deserved popularity over the years. It is very well recorded, with a particularly vivid projection of the voice. Flagstad sings with great majesty and weight, but her swoops and slides are quite out of keeping with what we now expect in such repertoire. Maybe those who will buy this CD will not be troubled by the stylistic considerations – but why, oh why, did Madame Flagstad have to give us that switch-back ride in *Hear my prayer*? Leslie Woodgate's arrangements are sugary – but here again popular demand will have its say. This is at least preferable to the latest manifestation of over-arranging on the comparable CD from Alagna (see above).

Freni, Mirella (soprano)

'Grandi voci' (arias from): PUCCINI: *La Bohème; Tosca; Madama Butterfly.* ROSSINI: *Guglielmo Tell.* VERDI: *Falstaff.* LEONCAVALLO: *Pagliacci.* BOITO: *Mefistofele.* BELLINI: *Bianca e Fernando.* Folksongs, arr. BALILA PRATELLA: *Ninnananna di Modigliana; Ninnananna romagnola.*
(M) *** Decca (IMS) Analogue/Dig. 440 412-2 [id.].

Since making most of these recordings – many of them taken from complete Decca sets made between 1963 and 1980, including her superb Mimi and Butterfly with Karajan – Freni has expanded to even more dramatic roles, but her purity, clarity and sweetness in these mainly lyric roles are a constant delight, nicely varied. The recital ends with two delightful lullabies, essentially folksongs, arranged by Francesco Balila Pratella. The sound is consistently fresh.

'Verismo arias' (with O del Teatro La Fenice, Robert Abbado) from: CILEA: *L'Arlesiana; Adriana Lecouvreur.* GIORDANO: *Andrea Chénier.* CATALANI: *La Wally; Loreley.* ALFANO: *Risurrezione.* MASCAGNI: *Cavalleria Rusticana; Lodoletta; Iris.* ZANDONAI: *Francesca da Rimini.* PUCCINI: *Gianni Schicchi.*
(M) ** Decca (IMS) Dig. 433 316-2 [id.].

An interesting and enterprising collection, recorded in 1990. But Freni should have tackled this very demanding programme earlier in her long career. This is singing which would readily pass muster in the opera house and which is potentially beautiful and always characterful. But, even with the very experienced Christopher Raeburn producing the sessions, the voice is not flattered by the microphones and, too often under stress, the singing is strained and approaching squalliness. Otherwise the recording is first class, and the accompaniments are very sympathetic.

Fretwork

'The English Viol' (with Catherine Bott, soprano, Jeremy Budd, treble, Michael Chance, counter-tenor and (i) Red Byrd): ANON.: *The dark is my delight; Allemande and Galliard* (from *Lumley Books*); *In paradise.* FERRABOSCO I: *In Nomine a 5.* HOLBORNE: *Pavan and Galliard.* BYRD: *Christe redemptor a 4; In nomine a 5 No. 4; Ah silly soul.* DOWLAND: *Lachrimae gementes; Semper Dowland, semper dolens; M. Bucton his Galiard.* FERRABOSCO II: *Pavan and Alman.* GIBBONS: *Fantasia a 6 No. 2; Fantasia a 3 for the 'Great dooble bass'; The silver swan; Fantasia a 2. The cry of London, Part II.* LAWES: *Fantazy a 5 on the playnesong in G min.; Gather ye rosebuds; Aire a 6 in G min.* LOCKE: *Consort of 4 parts in F.* PURCELL: *Fantasia a 4 in B flat No. 5; In nomine a 6.*
✿ (M) *** Virgin Veritas/EMI Dig. VER5 61173-2 [CDM 61173].

Fretwork was one of the really outstanding groups of artists which Virgin Records promoted from their inception and they offer viol playing which is in a class of its own. This superb 77-minute anthology draws on recordings made between 1988 and 1994: the excellence is unvarying: these players catch perfectly the spirit of the later-Tudor and early-Stuart periods. The playing itself has immaculate ensemble and intonation, restrained feeling and great freshness. Much of the music is relatively austere but the effect on the listener is hypnotic. The special character of Elizabethan romantic melancholy is well caught by Dowland (especially in his autobiographical *Semper Dowland, semper dolens*), but there is lively part-writing too, notably from Lawes and Locke. Lawes's *Fantasy a 5 'on the playnesong'* is touchingly expressive, the music's sonority coloured subtly by an (uncredited) chamber organ continuo, while the two pieces by Purcell are also quietly moving. The instrumental music is sprinkled with brief, cheerful, vocal items, delightfully sung, and the selection includes an excerpt from *The Cry of London*, where the vocal group, Red Byrd, offer every conceivable commodity for sale, from a pair of oars and a good sausage to bread and meat 'for the prisoners of the Marshalsea'. Altogether an ideal introduction to a period in English history which was musically very productive. The recording could hardly be bettered.

Galli-Curci, Amelita (soprano)

'Prima voce': Arias from: AUBER: *Manon Lescaut*. BELLINI: *I Puritani; La Sonnambula*. DONIZETTI: *Don Pasquale; Linda di Chamounix; Lucia di Lammermoor*. GOUNOD: *Roméo et Juliette*. MEYERBEER: *Dinorah*. ROSSINI: *Il Barbiere di Siviglia*. THOMAS: *Mignon*. VERDI: *Rigoletto; La Traviata*.
(M) (***) Nimbus mono NI 7806 [id.].

'Like a nightingale half-asleep,' said Philip Hope-Wallace in a memorable description of Galli-Curci's voice, but this vivid Nimbus transfer makes it much more like a nightingale very wide-awake. More than in most of these transfers made via an acoustic horn gramophone, the resonance of the horn itself can be detected, and the results are full and forward. Galli-Curci's perfection in these pre-electric recordings, made between 1917 and 1924, is a thing of wonder, almost too accurate for comfort, but tenderness is there too, as in the Act II duet from *La Traviata* (with Giuseppe de Luca) and the *Addio del passato*, complete with introductory recitative, but with only a single stanza. Yet brilliant coloratura is what lies at the root of Galli-Curci's magic, and that comes in abundance.

Galway, James (flute) with chorus and orchestra

'The James Galway Christmas collection'
(M) *** RCA 74321 41197-2 (2) [id.].

Disc 1: *'James Galway's Christmas carol'* (with BBC Singers, King's School, Canterbury, Choristers, RPO, cond. Galway): GRUBER: *Silent night*. RUTTER: *Shepherd's pipe carol*. BACH: *Suite No. 3: Air. Christmas oratorio: Sinfonia and Chorale. Sheep may safely graze*. OVERTON: *Fantasia on I saw three ships*. TRAD.: *Greensleeves; Zither carol; Patapan; Past three o'clock; I wonder as I wander*. IRELAND: *The holy boy*. BACH/GOUNOD: *Ave Maria*. POSTON: *Jesus Christ the apple tree*. RYAN: *We wish you a merry Christmas*.
(M) *** RCA Dig. 09026 61233-2 [id.].

Disc 2: *'In dulci jubilo'* (with Regensburger Domspätzen, Munich R. O, John Georgiadis): OVERTON: *Fantasia on 'In dulci jubilo'*. TRAD.: *Il est né le divin enfant; Kling Glöckchen Klingeling; O Jesulein süss; Ein Kindlein in der Wiegen; O Tannenbaum; Adeste fidelis; O du Fröliche*. arr. PRAETORIUS: *Es ist ein Ros' entsprungen*. BRAHMS: *Prelude on 'Es ist ein Ros' entsprungen'*. HANDEL: *Messiah: Pastoral symphony*. ALBINONI: *Adagio* (arr. Giazotto/Galway). FISCHER: *Prelude on 'O Jesulein süss'*. MENDELSSOHN: *6 Weihnachtsstücke (Christmas pieces)*. BACH/GOUNOD: *Ave Maria*. arr. LEHRNDORFER: *Bethlehem geboren; In dulci jubilo*. BACH: *Prelude on 'In dulci jubilo'; Cantata No. 147: Jesu, joy of man's desiring*. Arr. BIEBL: *Still, still, still*. PACHELBEL, arr. Galway: *Canon*. GRUBER, arr. Miesner: *Silent night*.
(M) *** RCA RD 60736 [id.].

In the first of these paired collections James Galway's silvery timbre introduces Grüber's *Silent night* unaccompanied before the choir joins in and he later adds an obbligato descant. These are all effectively simple arrangements in which Galway both directs chorus and orchestra and makes regular and attractive solo contributions. John Rutter's engaging *Shepherd's pipe carol* was an obvious choice in a programme that has a happy freshness about its presentation throughout. The interspersed orchestral numbers bring an effective degree of contrast. With clear yet full recorded sound, the ambience mellow but not too ecclesiastical, this is a Christmas compilation that will give a great deal of pleasure.

The second collection, recorded in Munich in 1991, is even more winning. It opens with a charming concertante fantasia on *In dulci jubilo* in which another famous chorale is introduced to lend variety. Galway displays his lightest touch, and the nicely scored variants do not outstay their welcome. The choral items from the Regensburg and Munich choirs have a pleasing simplicity of presentation, and the German traditional carols are particularly welcome, the orchestrations both atmospheric and tasteful. Some items (notably the lovely *O Tannebaum*) are unaccompanied, as is the first verse of *Adeste fidelis*. But here James Galway later adds his own descant, as he does for the closing *Silent night*. The *Pastoral Symphony* from *Messiah* sounds a little like Gluck when flute-dominated, but Galway's florid decoration of Pachelbel's *Canon* is remarkably inventive. The Bach/Gound *Ave Maria* is presented as a flute solo with a delicate harp accompaniment, while the six brief concertante *Christmas pieces* of Mendelssohn are deliciously scored, like a box of Christmas bonbons. Warmly atmospheric recording, with the flute nicely balanced, adds to the appeal of this second highly enjoyable programme. Packaged in a slip-case, these two compilations work well together.

Ghiaurov, Nicolai (bass)

'Russian songs' (with (i) Zlatina Ghiaurov (piano), or (ii) Kaval Ch. & O): (i) TCHAIKOVSKY: *None but the lonely heart; Not a word, O my love; Don Juan's serenade; It was in the early spring; Mid the noisy stir of the ball; I bless you, woods.* BORODIN: *For the shores of your far-off native land.* GLINKA: *Midnight review.* RUBINSTEIN: *Melody.* DARGOMIZHSKY: *The worm; Nocturnal breeze; The old corporal.* (ii) Folksongs: *The cliff; The Volga boatmen; The little oak cudgel; Bandura; Stenka Razin; Along Petersburg Street; In the dark forest; Dark eyes; Dear little night; The Twelve brigands; Farewell, joy.*
(B) *** Decca Double (IMS) 443 024-2 (2) [id.].

One of the problems of producing a record of Russian songs is the inherent danger of monotony of dark colouring and Slavic melancholy. This difficulty is not entirely avoided in Ghiaurov's 1971 recital, as the Tchaikovsky songs have (understandably) been grouped together and have a recognizably similar idiom. Even so, there is some splendid music, and *It was in early spring* and *I bless you, woods* are particularly memorable for their characteristically yearning melodic lines. With the appearance of Glinka's colourful *Midnight review* the mood lightens (even though this is a descriptive piece about old soldiers rising from their graves for a ghostly parade). The three Dargomizhsky songs are notably fine.

For the reissue, the solo recital has been paired with a vibrantly authentic collection of folksongs with the Kaval Chorus and Orchestra – plentifully spiced with balalaikas. Favourite items like the *Volga Boatmen* and *Dubinushka* ('The little oak cudgel'), *Dark eyes* ('Ochi chorni') cannot fail when sung so vividly and presented so atmospherically.

'Grandi voci': Russian and Italian arias (with LSO Ch., LSO, Edward Downes) from: RIMSKY-KORSAKOV: *Sadko.* MUSSORGSKY: *Boris Godunov.* TCHAIKOVSKY: *Eugene Onegin; Iolanta.* RACHMANINOV: *Aleko.* GLINKA: *A Life for the Tsar.* RUBINSTEIN: *The Demon.* BORODIN: *Prince Igor.* BIZET: *Carmen.* VERDI: *Don Carlo; Nabucco. I vespri siciliani* (the latter cond. Abbado).
(M) **(*) Decca 448 248-2 [id.].

Nicolai Ghiaurov's 76-minute recital in Decca's *Grandi voci* is in the main compiled from two previous collections, recorded in 1962 and 1964, although it has now been extended to include Procida's aria from Verdi's *I vespri siciliani*, taken from a Verdi collection of 'Great scenes', admirably directed by Claudio Abbado. In the Russian repertoire Ghiaurov has to yield to his fellow Bulgarian, Boris Christoff, in sheer artistry, particularly on detail. He is best in the comparatively straightforward arias but the vocal quality is what matters, and this is all magnificent singing. The recording too is of Decca's most vivid and flatters Ghiaurov's lyrical line.

Gigli, Beniamino (tenor)

'Prima voce': Vol. 1 (1918–24): Arias from: BOITO: *Mefistofele.* CATALANI: *Loreley.* DONIZETTI: *La Favorita.* FLOTOW: *Martha.* GIORDANO: *Andrea Chénier.* GOUNOD: *Faust.* LALO: *Le roi d'Ys.* LEONCAVALLO: *Pagliacci.* MASCAGNI: *Iris.* MEYERBEER: *L'Africana.* PONCHIELLI: *La Gioconda.* PUCCINI: *Tosca.* Songs.
(M) (***) Nimbus mono NI 7807 [id.].

Gigli's career went on so long, right through the electrical 78-r.p.m. era, that his pre-electric recordings have tended to get forgotten. This collection of 22 items recorded between 1918 and 1924 shows the voice at its most honeyed, even lighter and more lyrical than it became later, with the singer indulging in fewer of the mannerisms that came to decorate his ever-mellifluous singing. In aria after aria he spins a flawless legato line. Few tenor voices have ever matched Gigli's in rounded, golden beauty, and the Nimbus transfers capture its bloom in a way that makes one forget pre-electric limitations. In the one item sung in French, by Lalo, he sounds less at home, a little too heavy; but the ease of manner in even the most taxing arias elsewhere is remarkable, and such a number as the *Serenade* from Mascagni's *Iris* is irresistible in its sparkle, as are the Neapolitan songs, notably the galloping *Povero Pulcinella* by Buzzi-Peccia. One oddity is a tenor arrangement of Saint-Saëns's *The Swan*.

'Prima Voce': Volume 2 (1925–40). Arias from: DONIZETTI: *L'elisir d'amore; Lucia di Lammermoor.* PUCCINI: *Manon Lescaut; La Bohème; Tosca.* VERDI: *La forza del destino; La Traviata; Rigoletto.* THOMAS: *Mignon.* BIZET: *I pescatori di perle.* PONCIELLI: *La Gioconda.* MASSENET: *Manon.* GOUNOD: *Faust.* RIMSKY-KORSAKOV: *Sadko.* GLUCK: *Paride ed Elena.* CILEA: *L'Arlesiana.* CACCINI: Song: *Amarilli.*
(M) (***) Nimbus mono NI 7817 [id.].

Issued to celebrate the Gigli centenary in 1990, the Nimbus selection concentrates on recordings he made in the very early years of electrical recording up to 1931, when his voice was at its very peak, the most golden instrument, ideally suited to recording. The items are very well chosen and are by no means the obvious choices, though it is good to have such favourites as the *Pearlfishers duet* with de Luca and the 1931 version of Rodolfo's *Che gelida manina*. The Nimbus transfers are at their best, with relatively little reverberation.

Glyndebourne Opera

'Glyndebourne Festival Opera' (1934–1994): Excerpts from MOZART: *Le nozze di Figaro* (Audrey Mildmay, Aulikki Rautawaara; Monica Sinclair; Sesto Bruscantini; Ian Wallace; Daniel McCoshan; Franco Calabrese; Graziella Sciutti; Claudio Desderi; Gianna Rolandi; Glyndebourne Festival Ch.); *Così fan tutte* (Heddle Nash; Erich Kunz; Delores Ziegler; Claudio Desderi; Carol Vaness); *Don Giovanni* (Luise Helletsgruber, Audrey Mildmay; Koloman von Pataky; Roy Henderson, Ina Souez; Salvatore Bassaloni; Thomas Allen; Elizabeth Gale); *Idomeneo* (Richard Lewis; Sena Jurinac; Léopold Simoneau); *Die Entführung aus dem Serail* (Margaret Price). GAY: *The Beggar's opera* (Constance Willis; Michael Redgrave; Audrey Mildmay). ROSSINI: *La Cenerentola* (Juan Oncina); *Le Comte Ory* (Cora Canne-Meijer; Juan Oncina; Sari Barabas); *Il barbiere di Siviglia* (Victoria de los Angeles; Lugi Alva; Sesto Bruscantini). MONTEVERDI: *L'Incoronazione di Poppea* (Magda László; Richard Lewis). GERSHWIN: *Porgy and Bess* (Willard White; Cynthia Haymon).
(M) (***) EMI (SIS) stereo/mono; Analogue/Dig. CDH5 65072-2.

Issued to celebrate the opening of the new opera house at Glyndebourne in May 1994, exactly 50 years after the original theatre, this delightful compilation of 20 items ranges wide, starting with the original *Figaro* recording of 1934 conducted by Fritz Busch and concluding with Gershwin's *Porgy and Bess* conducted by Simon Rattle. In his choice of items Paul Campion has opted for some less predictable numbers, even from the obvious classic recordings, like the pre-war Busch sets or the Haitink recordings of recent years. Even more welcome are the rarities. The 1940 recording of *The Beggar's Opera* is a period piece, with Audrey Mildmay, wife of John Christie, the founder, opposite Michael Redgrave as singer. The recordings from the immediate post-war period were of excerpts only and have had very limited currency over the years. The samples here come out very freshly, with Busch conducting for Erich Kunz and Blanche Thebom in *Così fan tutte* and for Richard Lewis in *Idomeneo*. The Vittorio Gui period is well represented in Rossini as well as in Mozart, even if Victoria de los Angeles never actually sang Rosina at Glyndebourne but only recorded it with the company. It is good too to have the sensuously beautiful final duet from Monteverdi's *Poppea* in the Raymond Leppard version, and a rare CfP recording of *Entführung* with the young Margaret Price as Constanze. A treasury of singing to capture the unique flavour of opera at Glyndebourne.

Gomez, Jill (soprano)

'A recital of French songs': BIZET: *Chanson d'Avril; Adieux de l'hôtesse arabe; Vous ne priez pas; La chanson de la rose.* BERLIOZ: *Irlande, Op. 2,* excerpts: *Le coucher du soleil; L'origine de la harpe; La belle voyageuse.* DEBUSSY: *Proses lyriques: De rêve; De grève; De fleurs; De soir. Noël des enfants qui n'ont plus de maisons.*
(M) *** Saga EC 3333-2 [id.].

As in her companion Saga recital of Spanish songs (which still awaits reissue), Jill Gomez consistently captivates the ear in this perceptively chosen collection of French mélodies. Her vividly understanding characterization of the music from the three composers represented means that each emerges with complete individuality. The simple charm of Bizet is conveyed without bringing the slightest suggestion of triviality. The close of his most famous song, *Adieux de l'hôtesse arabe*, is managed very adroitly, and *Vous ne priez pas* is given just the right degree of ardour; she then brings the lightest touch to *La chanson de la rose*. Her soaring line in Berlioz evokes plenty of atmosphere and there is a nicely judged hint of ecstasy, while the languor of Debussy's four *Proses lyriques* brings an instant change of mood and evocation, reflected by John Constable's highly sensitive accompaniments. The passion of *De grève* is matched by the rich colouring of *De fleurs*, and the ardent vigour of *De soir*. Perhaps most memorable of all is the closing song, which Debussy wrote during the First World War, vividly and touchingly depicting a homeless child's plea to Santa Claus. The recording is generally faithful and the playing time (50 minutes) more generous than with most of the companion Saga reissues. However, although Felix Aprahamian's notes are indispensable, it ought to have been possible to include translations on a mid-priced reissue.

'Gramophone Greats'

'20 Gramophone All-time Greats' (original mono recordings from 1907–1935): LEONCAVALLO: *Pagliacci: Vesti la giubba* (Caruso); *Mattinata* (Gigli). BISHOP: *Lo here the gentle lark* (Galli-Curci with flute obbligato by Manuel Beringuer). PURCELL: *Nymphs and shepherds* (Manchester Schools Children's Choir (Choir Mistress: Gertrude Riall), Hallé O, Harty). MENDELSSOHN: *Hear my prayer – O for the wings of a dove* (Ernest Lough, Temple Church Ch., Thalben Ball). MARSHALL: *I hear you calling me* (John McCormack). ELGAR: *Salut d'amour* (New SO, composer). J. STRAUSS: *Casanova: Nuns' Chorus* (Ch. & O of Grossen Schauspielhauses, Berlin, Ernst Hauke). RACHMANINOV: *Prelude in C sharp min., Op. 3/2* (composer). TRAD.: *Song of the Volga Boatmen* (Chaliapin). KREISLER: *Liebesfreud* (composer, Carl Lamson). MOSS: *The floral dance* (Peter Dawson, Gerald Moore). BACH: *Chorale: Jesu, joy of man's desiring* (arr. & played Dame Myra Hess). HANDEL: *Messiah: Come unto Him* (Dora Labette, O, Beecham). SAINT-SAENS: *Samson and Delilah: Softly awakes my heart* (Marian Anderson). BIZET: *Fair Maid of Perth: Serenade* (Heddle Nash). CHOPIN: *Waltz in C sharp min., Op. 64/2* (Cortot). LEHAR: *Land of Smiles: You are my heart's delight* (Richard Tauber). KERN: *Showboat: Ol' man river* (Paul Robeson). SULLIVAN: *The lost chord* (Dame Clara Butt).
(M) (***) ASV mono CDAJA 5112 [id.].

It seems strange and somewhat sad that this marvellous collection of classical 78-r.p.m. hit records, covering a period of three decades, should be coming from ASV rather than HMV (EMI), who are responsible for so many of the actual recordings. Their amazing technical excellence means that they can be enjoyed today as they were then, with occasional clicks and generally not too intrusive background 'surface' noise to create the right ambience. Caruso still projects vividly from a 1907 acoustic master and Amelita Galli-Curci's soprano is as clear and sweet as the day it was made (1919). Other highlights (for us) include the Manchester School Children's choir of 250 voices, electrically recorded in Manchester's Free Trade Hall in 1929. The story goes that, just before the record was made, Sir Hamilton Harty bought cream buns and pop for every child, and that accounts for the warm smile in the singing. Master Ernest Lough's *O for the wings of a dove* is another miracle of perfection from a young boy treble, and Peter Dawson's exuberant *Floral dance* has astonishing diction – you can hear every word – and here Gerald Moore's bravura accompaniment is a key part of the sheer pleasure this performance still gives. Finally, Dame Clara Butt with her deep masculine contralto, clanging like a bell in its lowest register, delivers the sacred piece so beloved by Victorians: Sullivan's *Lost chord*. The transfers are all good (except perhaps for Dame Myra Hess's *Jesu, joy of man's desiring*, where the background surely could have been cut back a bit more).

Great Singers

'Prima voce': Great singers 1909–38 (Tetrazzini; Caruso; Schumann-Heink; McCormack; Galli-Curci; Stracciari; Ponselle; Lauri-Volpi; Turner; Tibbett; Supervia; Gigli; Anderson; Schipa; Muzio; Tauber): Arias from: BELLINI: *La Sonnambula; I Puritani; Norma.* LEONCAVALLO: *Pagliacci.* MOZART: *Don Giovanni; Die Zauberflöte.* ROSSINI: *Il Barbiere di Siviglia.* PUCCINI: *Turandot.* VERDI: *Un ballo in maschera.* BIZET: *Carmen.* PUCCINI: *La Bohème.* SAINT-SAENS: *Samson et Dalila.* MASCAGNI: *L'amico Fritz.* Song: REFICE: *Ombra di Nube.*
(M) (***) Nimbus mono NI 7801 [id.].

This was the first of Nimbus's series of archive recordings, taking a radical new view of the problem of transferring ancient 78-r.p.m. vocal recordings to CD. The best possible copies of shellac originals have been played on an acoustic machine with an enormous horn, one of the hand-made Rolls-Royces among non-electric gramophones of the 1930s, with thorn needles reducing still further the need to filter the sound electronically. The results have been recorded in a small hall, and the sound reproduced removes any feeling of boxy closeness. Those who have resisted the bottled or tinny sound of many historic recordings will find the Nimbus transfers more friendly and sympathetic, even if technically there is an inevitable loss of recorded information at both ends of the spectrum because of the absolute limitations of the possible frequency range on this kind of reproducer.

This compilation makes a good starting point, even if the method still does not provide the ideal answer. The Tetrazzini item with which the selection opens, *Ah non giunge* from Bellini's *La Sonnambula*, is one of the supreme demonstrations of coloratura on record, and the programme goes on to a magnificent Caruso of 1910 and an unforgettable performance of the coloratura drinking-song from Donizetti's *Lucrezia Borgia* by the most formidable of contraltos, Ernestine Schumann-Heink. Then follows John McCormack's famous account of *Il mio tesoro* from Mozart's *Don Giovanni*, with the central passage-work amazingly done in a single breath. Other vintage items include Galli-Curci's dazzling account of *Son vergin vezzosa* from Bellini's *I Puritani*, Eva Turner in her incomparable 1928 account of Turandot's aria, Gigli amiably golden-toned in *Che gelida manina* from *La Bohème*, and a delectable performance of the *Cherry duet* from Mascagni's *L'amico Fritz* by Tito Schipa and Mafalda Favero, riches indeed!

Gruberová, Edita (soprano)

'French and Italian opera arias' (with Munich R. O, Kuhn): DELIBES: *Lakmé: Bell song.* MEYERBEER: *Les Huguenots: Nobles seigneurs, salut!* GOUNOD: *Roméo et Juliette: Waltz song.* THOMAS: *Hamlet: Mad scene.* DONIZETTI: *Lucia di Lammermoor: Mad scene.* ROSSINI: *Semiramide: Bel raggio lusinghier. Il barbiere di Siviglia: Una voce poco fa.*
(B) *** EMI Dig. CD-EMX 2234 [(M) id. import].

Gruberová, for long type-cast in the roles of Queen of the Night and Zerbinetta, here formidably extends her range of repertory in a dazzling display of coloratura, impressive not only in the Italian repertory but in the French too, notably the *Hamlet* mad scene. The agility is astonishing, but the tone as recorded often hardens on top, although the CD provides extra fullness and clarity.

Huddersfield Choral Society, Brian Kay; Phillip McCann; Simon Lindley

'A Christmas celebration' (with Sellers Engineering Band): TRAD.: *Ding dong merrily on high; Kwmbaya; Joys seven; Away in a manger; Deck the hall; O Christmas tree (Tannenbaum); Coventry carol.* JAMES: *An Australian Christmas.* GRUBER: *Silent night.* BACH: *Cantata No. 140: Zion hears the watchmen's voices.* GARDNER: *The holly and the ivy.* arr. RICHARDS: *A merry little Christmas.* HOLST: *In the bleak mid-winter.* arr. WILLCOCKS: *Tomorrow shall be my dancing day.* BRAHMS: *Lullaby.* arr. SMITH: *Santa Claus-Trophobia.* MATHIAS: *Sir Christèmas.* LANGFORD: *A Christmas fantasy.*
(M) *** Chandos Dig. CHAN 4530 [id.].

Sumptuously recorded in the generous acoustic of Huddersfield Town Hall, opening with a spectacular arrangement of *Ding dong merrily* and closing with Gordon Langford's colourful pot-pourri *Fantasy*, this CD offers rich choral tone, well laced with opulent brass. There are simple choral arrangements too, beautifully sung by the Huddersfield choir, like Stephen Cleobury's *Joys seven*, Langford's *Deck the hall* and David Willcocks's slightly more elaborate *Tomorrow shall be my dancing day*, while Grüber's *Silent night* remains the loveliest of all serene carols. In other favourites the brass is nicely intertwined, as in

Away in a manger and the *Coventry carol*, or it provides a sonorous introduction, as in Holst's *In the bleak mid-winter*. Mathias's rhythmically energetic *Sir Christèmas* provides a little spice. The brass are given their head in a solo spot, an effective novelty number, *Santa Claus-Trophobia*, arranged by Sandy Smith, which brings an impressive contribution from the solo tuba. Undoubtedly the brass contribution adds much to the entertainment value of this superbly recorded and well-presented 70-minute concert.

Kanawa, Dame Kiri Te (soprano)

'Classics': Arias from: MOZART: *Die Entführung aus dem Serail; Idomeneo; Don Giovanni; Vesperae solennes de Confessore; Die Zauberflöte; Exsultate, jubilate*. HANDEL: *Samson*. GOUNOD: *Messe solennelle de Saint Cécile; Faust*. SCHUBERT: *Ave Maria*. J. STRAUSS Jnr: *Die Fledermaus*.
(M) *** Ph. Dig. 434 725-2; *434 725-4*.

Admirers of Dame Kiri will find this a pretty good sampler of her diverse talents, including as it does Mozart's *Exsultate, jubilate* with its famous *Alleluia* and the similarly beautiful *Laudate dominum* from the *Solemn Vespers*, plus Handel's brilliant *Let the bright seraphim*. An excellent 74-minute selection from recordings made over two decades from the early 1970s onwards. The notes, however, concentrate on the singer rather than the music.

'Diva': Arias from: CHARPENTIER: *Louise*. MASSENET: *Manon; Hérodiade*. BERLIOZ: *La Damnation de Faust*. GLUCK: *Iphigénie en Tauride*. PUCCINI: *Suor Angelica*. LEONCAVALLO: *Pagliacci*. GIORDANO: *Andrea Chénier*. CILEA: *Adriana Lecouvreur*. Richard STRAUSS: *Der Rosenkavalier*. TCHAIKOVSKY: *Eugene Onegin*.
(M) *** EMI Dig. CDM 65578-2 [id.].

Like others in EMI's Diva series of compilations, this selection has been shrewdly drawn from the limited number of recordings Dame Kiri has made for that company, principally a recital of French opera arias recorded in 1988 and an Italian opera recital made in 1989. These provide a fruitful source for the first nine items, but they are crowned by excerpts from two complete opera sets, the Marschallin's monologue and final solo from Act I of *Der Rosenkavalier* and (in English) *Tatiana's Letter scene* from *Eugene Onegin*, a recording made with Welsh National Opera forces. The beauty of the voice is beautifully caught.

King's College, Cambridge, Choir, Sir David Willcocks

'A Festival of Lessons and carols' (recorded live in the Chapel, Christmas Eve 1958, with Simon Preston, organ): *Once in Royal David's City*. BACH: *Christmas Oratorio: Invitatory*. Lesson I. *Adam lay ybounden*. Lesson II. *I saw three ships*. Lesson III. *Gabriel's message. God rest you merry, gentlemen; Sussex carol*. Lesson IV. *In dulci jubilo*. Lesson V. *Away in a manger; While shepherds watched*. Lesson. VI. *O come, all ye faithful*. Lesson VII. *Hark! the herald angels sing*.
(B) *** Decca 436 646-2; *436 646-4* [(M) id. import].

It was the early mono recording of the King's Christmas Eve service of lessons and carols which – together with the BBC recording of Dylan Thomas's *Under Milk Wood* – brought initial success to the Argo label before it became part of the Decca group. With the coming of stereo the Festival was re-recorded to provide what only stereo can provide: an imaginary seat in the Chapel. The present CD offers that early stereo venture and shows the remarkable success with which the Argo engineers captured the magic of the chapel acoustic – the opening processional remains demonstration-worthy today. Seven of the nine lessons are interspersed with the favourite carols to remind us indelibly what Christmas is really about.

'Noël': Disc 1: MENDELSSOHN: *Hark the herald angels sing*. TRAD.: *The first Nowell; While shepherds watched; I saw three ships; Ding dong! merrily on high; King Jesus hath a garden; Unto us a son is born; O come all ye faithful; Away in a manger; The holly and the ivy; God rest ye merry, gentlemen; See amid the winter's snow; Past three o'clock*. arr. BACH: *In dulci jubilo*. arr. VAUGHAN WILLIAMS: *O little town of Bethlehem*.

Disc 2: TRAD.: *Once in Royal David's city; Sussex carol; Rocking; Rejoice and be merry; Joseph was an old man; As with gladness men of old; The infant King; Christ was born on Christmas day; Blessed be that maid Mary; Lute-book lullaby; Personent hodie; In the bleak midwinter; Coventry carol; Shepherds, in the field abiding*. CORNELIUS: *The three kings; A great and mighty wonder*. WARLOCK: *Balulalow*. TCHAIKOVSKY: *The crown of roses*. TERRY: *Myn lyking*. JOUBERT: *Torches*. VAUGHAN WILLIAMS: *Fantasia on Christmas carols* (with Hervey Alan & LSO).
(B) **(*) Decca Double 444 848-2 (2) [id.].

This Double Decca is essentially a combined reissue of a pair of bargain-priced LP collections, made over a span of eight years at the end of the 1950s and the beginning of the 1960s. They were counted excellent value when they first appeared in Decca's 'World of' series. The 50-minute programme on the first disc concentrates on established King's favourites; the second is not only more generous (66 minutes), but also includes novelties which are designed to get the listener inquiring further, such as Warlock's *Balulalow*, the engaging *Lute-book lullaby* and Joubert's *Torches*. This collection opens with the famous processional version of *Once in Royal David's city* and closes with a superbly joyful performance of Vaughan Williams's *Fantasia on Christmas carols*, very well recorded, with Hervey Alan the excellent soloist. Otherwise the sound is always pleasingly full and atmospheric, but with some of the earlier recordings from the late 1950s not quite as clean in focus as those made in the mid-1960s.

'Great choral classics': ALLEGRI: *Miserere* (with Roy Goodman, treble). PALESTRINA: *Stabat Mater*. TALLIS: *Spem in alium* (40-part motet; with Cambridge University Musical Society); *Sancte Deus*. BYRD: *Ave verum corpus*. VIVALDI: *Gloria in D, RV 589* (with Elizabeth Vaughan, Dame Janet Baker, Roger Lord, ASMF). GIBBONS: *This is the record of John* (with unnamed soloist and Jacobean Consort of Viols). BACH: *Jesu, priceless treasure (Jesu meine Freude), BWV 227*. HANDEL: *4 Coronation anthems: (Zadok the Priest; My heart is inditing; Let thy hand be strengthened; The King shall rejoice;* with ECO).
(B) *** Decca Double 452 949-2 (2) [id.].

An admirably chosen group of choral masterpieces spanning the riches of the sixteenth and seventeenth centuries and the first half of the eighteenth, opening with Allegri's *Miserere* with its soaring treble solo, so confidently sung here by the same Roy Goodman who was later to make his mark as a conductor. Palestrina's *Stabat Mater* which follows is no less arresting in its bold contrasts, and the richness of texture of Tallis's *Spem in alium* is little short of astonishing. The resonant King's acoustic prevents sharp linear clarity, but it underlines the work's spiritual power and extraordinarily expansive sonority. Byrd's beautiful *Ave verum corpus* then brings a serene simplicity, with Vivaldi's exuberant *Gloria* rounding off the first CD. The second programme opens with music by Orlando Gibbons, himself a chorister at King's, a delightfully intimate viol-accompanied solo motet with brief choral echoes. Bach's most famous motet follows, sung in English (none too clearly, because of the reverberation), and the concert closes resplendently with Handel's four *Coronation anthems*, including the most famous, *Zadok the Priest*. Here the sound is quite excellent.

King's College, Cambridge, Choir, Willcocks or Philip Ledger

'Favourite carols from Kings': GAUNTLETT: *Once in Royal David's city*. TRAD., arr. VAUGHAN WILLIAMS: *O little town of Bethlehem*. TRAD., arr. STAINER: *The first nowell*. TRAD., arr. LEDGER: *I saw three ships*. TRAD. German, arr. HOLST: *Personent hodie*. TERRY: *Myn Lyking*. HOWELLS: *A spotless rose*. KIRKPATRICK: *Away in a manger*. HADLEY: *I sing of a maiden*. TRAD. French, arr. WILLCOCKS: *O come, o come Emmanuel*. TRAD., arr. WILLCOCKS: *While shepherds watched; On Christmas night*. arr. WOODWARD: *Up! Good Christian folk and listen*. DARKE: *In the bleak midwinter*. GRUBER: *Silent night*. TRAD., arr. WALFORD DAVIES: *The holly and the ivy*. TRAD., arr. SULLIVAN: *It came upon the midnight clear*. CORNELIUS: *Three kings*. SCHEIDT: *A Child is born in Bethlehem*. TRAD. German, arr. PEARSALL: *In dulci jubilo*. WADE: *O come, all ye faithful*. MENDELSSOHN: *Hark! the herald angels sing*.
(M) *** EMI CDM5 66241-2.

With 71 minutes of music and 22 carols included, this collection, covering the regimes of both Sir David Willcocks and Philip Ledger, could hardly be bettered as a representative sampler of the King's tradition. Opening with the famous processional of *Once in Royal David's city*, to which Willcocks contributes a descant (as he also does in *While shepherds watched*), the programme is wide-ranging in its historical sources, from the fourteenth century to the present day, while the arrangements feature many famous musicians. The recordings were made between 1969 and 1976, and the CD transfers are first class. The two closing carols, featuring the Philip Jones Brass Ensemble, are made particularly resplendent.

'A Festival of Lessons and Carols from King's' (1979) includes: TRAD.: *Once in Royal David's city; Sussex carol; Joseph and Mary; A maiden most gentle; Chester carol; Angels, from the realms of glory*. HANDEL: *Resonet in laudibus*. ORD: *Adam lay ybounden*. GRUBER: *Stille Nacht*. MATHIAS: *A babe is born*. WADE: *O come all ye faithful*. MENDELSSOHN: *Hark! the herald angels sing*.
(M) *** EMI CDM5 66242-2 [CDM 63180].

This 1979 version of the annual King's College ceremony has the benefit of fine analogue stereo, even more atmospheric than before. Under Philip Ledger the famous choir keeps its beauty of tone and incisive attack. The opening processional, *Once in Royal David's city*, is even more effective heard against the background quiet of CD, and this remains a unique blend of liturgy and music.

'Procession with carols on Advent Sunday' includes: PALESTRINA (arr. from): *I look from afar; Judah and Jerusalem, fear not.* PRAETORIUS: *Come, thou Redeemer of the earth.* TRAD.: *O come, o come, Emmanuel!; Up, awake and away!; 'Twas in the year; Cherry tree carol; King Jesus hath a garden; On Jordan's bank the Baptist's cry; Gabriel's message; I wonder as I wander; My dancing day; Lo! he comes with clouds descending.* BYRT: *All and some.* P. NICOLAI, arr. BACH: *Wake, o wake! with tidings thrilling.* BACH: *Nun komm' der Heiden Heiland.*
(M) *** EMI CDM5 66243-2.

This makes an attractive variant to the specifically Christmas-based service, though the carols themselves are not quite so memorable. Beautiful singing and richly atmospheric recording; the wide dynamic range is demonstrated equally effectively by the atmospheric opening and processional and the sumptuous closing hymn.

'Christmas music from King's' (with Andrew Davis, organ, D. Whittaker, flute, Christopher van Kampen, cello and Robert Spencer, lute): SWEELINCK: *Hodie Christus natus est.* PALESTRINA: *Hodie Christus natus est.* VICTORIA: *O magnum mysterium; Senex puerum portabat.* BYRD: *Senex puerum portabat; Hodie beata virgo.* GIBBONS: *Hosanna to the Son of David.* WEELKES: *Hosanna to the Son of David; Gloria in excelsis Deo.* ECCARD: *When to the temple Mary went.* MACONCHY: *Nowell! Nowell!.* arr. BRITTEN: *The holly and the ivy.* PHILIP (The Chancellor): *Angelus ad virginem.* arr. POSTON: *Angelus ad virginem; My dancing day.* POSTON: *Jesus Christ the apple tree.* BERKELEY: *I sing of a maiden.* TAYLOR: *Watts's cradle song.* CAMPION: *Sing a song of joy.* PEERSON: *Most glorious Lord of life.* Imogen HOLST: *That Lord that lay in Assë stall.* WARLOCK: *Where riches is everlastingly.*
(M) *** EMI CDM5 66244-2.

A happily chosen survey of music (63 minutes), inspired by the Nativity, from the fifteenth century to the present day. As might be expected, the King's choir confidently encompasses the wide variety of styles from the spiritual serenity of the music of Victoria to the attractive arrangements of traditional carols by modern composers, in which an instrumental accompaniment is added. These items are quite delightful and they are beautifully recorded (in 1965). The motets, from a year earlier, were among the first recording sessions made by the EMI engineers in King's College Chapel, and at the time they had not solved all the problems associated with the long reverberation period, so the focus is less than sharp. Even so, this group demonstrates the unique virtuosity of the Cambridge choir, exploiting its subtlety of tone and flexibility of phrase.

Psalms of David, Volume 1: *Psalms Nos. 15, 23–4, 42–3, 46, 61, 84, 104, 121–2, 137, 147–50.*
(M) *** EMI CDM5 66784-2.

Psalms of David, Volume 2: *Psalms Nos. 12, 22, 65–7, 78, 81, 114–15, 126, 133–4.*
(M) *** EMI CDM5 66785-2.

Psalms of David, Volume 3: *Psalms Nos. 37, 45, 49, 53, 93–4, 107, 130–31.*
(M) *** EMI CDM5 66786-2.

In pioneer days the early Christians took over the Psalter along with the Old Testament teachings from the Hebrew Temple, and the Psalms have always been an integral part of Anglican liturgy. Although they are called the 'Psalms of David', it has long been recognized that the original Hebrew collection (some 150 strong) was gathered together over a period of several hundred years, and the writings are from many different, anonymous hands. The Anglican settings used on these recordings have offered their composers a fairly wide range of expressive potential, yet the music itself, perhaps because of the stylized metre and the ritual nature of its use, seldom approaches the depth and resonance which are found in the music of the great composers of the Roman Catholic faith: Palestrina, Victoria and so on. Beginning in 1968, the King's College Choir, conducted by Sir David Willcocks from the organ, give an eloquent cross-section of the Psalter on the first two discs, and on the third (in 1974) Philip Ledger continues the series with Francis Grier at the organ. They are beautifully recorded and are well transferred to CD.

'Choral favourites from King's': HANDEL: *Messiah: Hallelujah chorus.* BACH: *Cantata 147: Jesu, joy of man's desiring.* HAYDN: *The Creation: The heavens are telling.* PURCELL: *Rejoice in the Lord alway.* BRITTEN: *Saint Nicholas: The birth of Nicholas* (all three excerpts with soloists). FAURE: *Requiem: Sanctus* (all seven excerpts with ASMF). SCHUBERT: *Psalm 23: Gott ist mein Hirt* (with Philip Ledger, piano). ELGAR: *Coronation Ode: Land of hope and glory* (with soloists, Band of Royal Military School of Music, Cambridge University Musical Society). DELIUS: *To be sung of a summer night on the water* (with Robert Tear). BRITTEN: *Ceremony of carols: There is no rose* (with Osian Ellis, harp). William HARRIS: *Faire*

is the heaven. Charles WOOD: *Hail, gladdening light.* John DYKES: *Holy, holy, holy* (with Philip Jones Brass Ens.; Ian Hare, organ).
(M) *** EMI CDM5 72812-2.

Even more than the comparable budget sampler from Harry Christophers and his Sixteen on Collins (see below), this King's collection makes a satisfying concert in its own right, besides tempting the listener to explore further. Opening with a joyful version of the *Hallelujah chorus*, with the radiant treble contribution very striking, the coverage is wide-ranging. Schubert's delightful setting of the *23rd Psalm* (with Philip Ledger's piano accompaniment) makes an ideal foil for the preceding Purcell anthem and the following excerpt from the Fauré *Requiem*. Similarly the introduction of *Land of hope and Glory* into Elgar's *Coronation ode* begins a delightful sequence of music by Delius and Britten. The concert then closes with three fine examples of the continuing Anglican choral tradition from William Harris, Charles Wood and, ending more conventionally, John Dykes's familiar hymn, *Holy, holy, holy*, but in Willcocks's imaginative arrangement with a descant. The warmly atmospheric King's ambience adds much to the music throughout; only in *The Heavens are telling* from *The Creation* might one have liked a bit more choral bite.

King's College, Cambridge, Choir, (i) Stephen Cleobury (with David Briggs, organ); (ii) Sir David Willcocks; (iii) Anthony Way (treble), St Paul's Cathedral Ch. and CO, John Scott

'The ultimate carol collection': (i) GAUNTLETT, arr. Ledger: *Once in Royal David's city.* arr. WILLCOCKS: *O come all ye faithful; The first nowell;* (ii) *Unto us is born a son;* (i) *God rest ye merry, gentlemen; I saw three ships;* (ii) *See amid the winter's snow; Rocking;* (i) *The infant King.* (i) MENDELSSOHN, arr. Ledger: *Hark! the Herald Angels sing.* DARKE: *In the bleak midwinter.* arr. VAUGHAN WILLIAMS: *O little town of Bethlehem.* (ii) arr. PEARSAL: *In dulci jubilo.* PRAETORIUS: *A great and mighty wonder.* (i) arr. LEDGER: *Sussex carol.* (ii) TATE: *While shepherds watched.* (i) arr. CLEOBURY: *Away in a manger.* arr. WOOD: *Ding dong! Merrily on high;* (ii) *King Jesus hath a garden; Shepherds in the field abiding.* arr. WALFORD DAVIES: *The Holly and the ivy.* arr. WOODWARD: *Up, good Christian folk.* (ii) arr. SHAW: *Coventry carol.* (i) GRUBER, arr. Cleobury: *Silent night.* (iii) SHANE, arr. Alexander: *Do you hear what I hear?.*
(M) **(*) Decca 458 863-2.

Decca's 'Ultimate' carol collection (issued in 1997) is hardly that, but it will suit those looking for an essentially atmospheric concert of tested favourites for Christmas Day. It centres on a 1984 compilation directed by Stephen Cleobury with *Once in Royal David's city* presented not as a processional but as an interplay between treble soloist (Robin Barter) and full choir. The choir is backwardly placed and the atmosphere overall is slightly subdued. However, the organ contribution from David Briggs (uncredited in the documentation) always makes its presence felt and is strongly featured in Willcocks's dramatic arrangement of *Unto us is born a son* and the powerful close of *God rest ye merry, gentlemen.* Philip Ledger's version of *Hark the Herald Angels* also has a spectacular climax. However, in general the recording does not seek to clarify textures but concentrates on capturing the ambient atmosphere. Thus the older recordings conducted by Willcocks, which are interspersed, match up well to the later collection. The modern carol, *Do you hear what I hear*, featuring the eloquent Anthony Way and opulently presented with orchestral accompaniment, while it may be a highlight for some listeners, fits rather uneasily in the middle of the programme (following after the *Sussex carol*), and not everyone will respond to Cleobury's elaboration of the closing *Silent night*, which takes an original turn after the opening verse.

Kirkby, Emma (soprano)

'A Portrait' (with AAM, Hogwood): HANDEL: *Disseratevi, o porte d'Averno; Gentle Morpheus, son of night.* PURCELL: *Bess of Bedlam; From rosie bow'rs.* ARNE: *Where the bee sucks there lurk I; Rise, Glory, rise.* DOWLAND: *I saw the lady weepe.* D'INDIA: *Odi quel rosignuolo.* TROMBONCINO: *Se ben hor non scopro il foco.* VIVALDI: *Passo di pena in pena.* J. S. BACH: *Ei! wie schmeckt der Coffee süsse.* HAYDN: *With verdure clad.* MOZART: *Laudate Dominum; Exsultate, jubilate, K.165.*
✿ (M) *** O-L Dig. 443 200-2.

Admirers of Emma Kirkby's style in early and baroque music will delight (as we did) in this well-chosen 76-minute sampler of her work. L'Oiseau-Lyre have altered and expanded the orginal issue and the excerpt from Handel's *Messiah* has been replaced by the remarkable Angel's aria, *Disseratevi, o porte d'Averno*, from Part I of *La Resurrezione* (calling on the gates of the Underworld to be unbarred to yield to God's glory). It opens with joyous baroque trumpets and oboes, and Emma Kirkby shows with her florid vocal line that anything they can do, she can do better. This is rather effectively followed by Purcell's melancholy mad song, *Bess of Bedlam*, and the equally touching *From rosie bow'rs*. Music by Arne lightens the mood and later there are excerpts from Bach's *Coffee cantata* and popular solos by Haydn and Mozart. This recital is as well planned as it is enjoyable, and Hogwood ensures that accompaniments are consistently fresh and stylish. First-class sound.

Larmore, Jennifer (mezzo-soprano)

'A Portrait': excerpts from MONTEVERDI: *L'incoronazione di Poppea; L'Orfeo*. HANDEL: *Giulio Cesare*. MOZART: *Mass in C min.*
(B) *** HM Dig. HMT 7901575 [(M) id. import].

An excellent reminder of the art of an outstandingly fine mezzo. Five excerpts are offered from her recording of Handel's *Giulio Cesare*, in which she took the principal role with distinction. But she is heard to equal effect as Monteverdi's *Ottavio*, especially in her very touching *Addio Roma*. Her contribution to the Mozart *C minor Mass* is hardly less impressive. This is in essence a sampler, but a well-planned and enjoyable one.

Legge, Walter (producer)

'Les introuvables de Walter Legge': Disc 1: Lieder: WOLF: *Eichendorf Lieder: Der Freund; Der Musikant* (Herbert Janssen with Gerald Moore; 1937); *Mörike Lieder: In der Frühe; Mausfallen-Sprüchlein. Spanish Liederbuch: In dem Schatten meiner Locken. Italienisches Liederbuch: Auch kleine Dinge; Und willst du deinen Liebsten. Wie glänzt der helle Mond*. HAYDN: *Canzonetta: She never told her love; Sailor's song*. MOZART: *Das Veichen* (Elisabeth Schumann with Gerald Moore; 1945/6). SCHUBERT: *Der Musensohn*. Yryö KILPINEN: *6 Lieder um den Tod, Op. 62* (Gerhard Hüsch with Hanns Udo Müller or Margaret Kilpinen; 1934/5). BRAHMS: *2 Lieder with viola, Op. 91* (Kirsten Flagstad with Herbert Downes and Gerald Moore; 1949). WOLF: *Goethe Lieder: Mignon II: Nur wer die Sehnsucht kennt*. SCHUMANN: *Die Kartenlegerin* (Elisabeth Höngen with Hans Zipper; 1946). SCHUBERT: *Der Wanderer* (Hans Hotter with Hermann von Nordberg; 1947). BRAHMS: *Feldeinsamkeit* (Tiana Lemnitz with Herta Klust; 1948). R. STRAUSS: *Cäcile* (Hilde Konetzni with Hermann von Nordberg; 1948).

Disc 2: Voices: O'CONNOR: *The old house*. THAYER: *A child's prayer* (John McCormack with Gerald Moore; 1939). Adrian BEECHAM: *The willow song; O mistress mine* (Nancy Evans, Sir Thomas Beecham; 1940). PURCELL: *The Blessed Virgin's expostulation* (Isobel Baillie with Arnold Goldsbrough, organ; 1941). GLUCK: *Orpheus and Eurydice: What is life to me without thee?* BRAHMS: *Liebestreu; Deutsche Volkslieder: Feinsliebchen* (sung in English). ELGAR: *The Dream of Gerontius: My work is done . . . It is because then thou didst fear*. Maurice GREENE: *I will lay me down in peace; O praise the Lord* (Kathleen Ferrier with Gerald Moore; 1944). GOUNOD: *Au rossignol* (Pierre Bernac with Francis Poulenc; 1945). R. STRAUSS: *Ariadne aux Naxos: Es gibt ein Reich . . . In den Schönen Feierkleidern* (Maria Cebotari, VPO, Karajan; 1948); *Salome:* Final scene, excerpt: *Sie ist ein Ungeheuer* (Ljuba Welitsch, Gertrud Schuster, Josef Witt, VPO, Karajan; 1948). WAGNER: *Tristan und Isolde: Tod denn Alles!* (Ludwig Weber, Elisabeth Schwarzkopf, Philh. O, Schüchter; 1951); *Die Meistersinger: Fliedermonologue* (Hans Hotter, VPO, Karajan; 1948). BOITO: *Mefistofele: L'altra notte* (Renata Scotto, Philh. O, Manno Wolf-Ferrari; 1958). MOZART: *Il rè pastore: L'amerò, sarò costante* (Anna Moffo, Philh. O, Galliera; 1958).

Disc 3: Instruments: BACH: *Toccata and fugue in D min., BWV 565* (Albert Schweitzer, organ of All Hallows by the Tower, Barking, Essex; 1935). MENDELSSOHN, arr. RACHMANINOV: *A Midsummer Night's Dream: Scherzo* (Moiseiwitch; 1939). SARASATE: *Danzas españolas: Playera; Zapateado* (Josef Hassid with Gerald Moore; 1940). SHOSTAKOVICH: *Prelude No. 24, Op. 34/24* (Harriet Cohen; 1942). SCHUBERT: *String quartet No. 14 (Death and the Maiden): Andante* (Philharmonia Qt; 1942). SZYMANOWSKI: *Notturno e Tarantella, Op. 28: Tarantella* (Arthur Grumiaux, Gerald Moore; 1945). WEBER: *Invitation to the dance*. BACH: *Chromatic fantasia and fugue, BWV 903* (Artur Schnabel; 1947/8). Domenico SCARLATTI: *Sonata in F, Kk 7*. BACH/BUSONI: *Cantata No. 140: Chorale: Wachet auf* (Solomon; 1948). Domenico SCARLATTI: *Sonatas: in D min., Kk 9; in D, Kk 33*. HANDEL: *Suite No. 5: The Harmonious blacksmith* (Walter Gieseking; 1951).

Disc 4: Orchestral: BEETHOVEN: *Overture: The Ruins of Athens* (LSO, Weingartner; 1940). LISZT: *Fantasia on a theme from Beethoven's 'Ruins of Athens'* (Egon Petri, LPO, Leslie Heward; 1938). WALTON: *Henry V* (film score): *Passacaglia: The death of Falstaff; Touch her soft lips and part* (Philh.

O strings, composer; 1945). BLISS: March: *The Phoenix* (Philh. O, Constant Lambert; 1946). DVORAK: *Carnaval overture, Op. 9* (Czech PO, Kubelik; 1946). MOZART: *Serenade No. 7 (Haffner): Rondo* (Willi Boskovsky, VPO, Karl Boehm; 1947). BORODIN: *Overture: Prince Igor* (Philh. O, Issay Dobrowen; 1949). PROKOFIEV: *Symphony No. 1 in D (Classical), Op. 25* (BPO, Sergiu Celibidache; 1948).
(B) (***) EMI mono CZS5 69743-2 (4) [(M) id. import].

Many of the items here may be so offbeat as to seem perverse in celebration of the work of the greatest of recording producers. The key word is '*introuvables*', recordings so rare that hardly anyone knows of them. It is surprising for example to have Legge's second wife, Elisabeth Schwarzkopf – she as much an inspiration to him as he always was to her – celebrated with an odd fragment from Wagner's *Tristan*. In the passage leading up to the final *Liebestod*, she acts as foil for the bass, Ludwig Weber, in the brief poignant duet, *Tod denn alles*, between King Mark and Brangäne, a touching performance. It is good to have Legge's first wife also remembered, a lovely singer far less celebrated but much loved, Nancy Evans, who, accompanied at the piano by Sir Thomas Beecham, sings two Shakespeare settings by Beecham's son, Adrian.

Each of the four CDs is devoted to a different category: Lieder, Voices, Instruments and Orchestral. Rightly, the first disc begins with some of the Hugo Wolf recordings, part of the Hugo Wolf Society Edition – the project which first made Legge's reputation – with Herbert Janssen and Elisabeth Schumann the singers chosen here. One might have expected some songs from Elena Gerhardt, but maybe her recordings were counted too '*trouvable*'. A fascinating rarity follows, reminding us that, along with the most prominent Society editions promoted by Legge, covering Beethoven, Bach, Mozart, Sibelius, Delius and others, there was a celebration of a most sensitive Finnish composer, still largely unappreciated, the Yrjo Kilpinen Society, with his songs recorded by the great Lieder-singer, Gerhard Husch, the central figure in Legge's Lieder projects in the 1930s.

The Voices disc ranges from John McCormack to Anna Moffo (enchanting in Mozart's *Il rè pastore*) by way of Ferrier, Cebotari and many others; and the Instrumental disc goes from Albert Schweitzer in Bach to Walter Gieseking in Handel, by way of such neglected artists as the violinist, Josef Hassid. The Orchestral disc then ranges from Weingartner in Beethoven's *Ruins of Athens* and Egon Petri's recording of Liszt's *Variations* on a theme from that work to Celibidache doing Prokofiev's *Classical Symphony* in a typically idiosyncratic way. Karajan, one supposes, was also too '*trouvable*' to be included – though, as he always resisted being anthologized next to others on disc, maybe that rule still applies. In the booklet Alan Sanders writes a searching and informative (if brief) essay on Legge, and there are some delightful photos, though no texts of vocal items. An offbeat, very enjoyable tribute, though nothing could adequately convey a full portrait of such a figure.

London Symphony Chorus and Orchestra, Richard Hickox

'Great opera choruses': BIZET: *Carmen: Toreador chorus.* VERDI: *Il Trovatore: Anvil chorus. Nabucco: Gli arredi festivi; Va pensiero. Macbeth: Che faceste?. Aida: Grand march.* GOUNOD: *Faust: Soldiers' chorus.* BORODIN: *Prince Igor: Polovtsian dances.*
(BB) *** Carlton LSO Double Dig. 30368 01167 (2) [(B) id.] – BIZET: *L'Arlésienne* and *Carmen suites.* **(*)

Most collections of opera choruses are taken from sets, but this is a freshly minted, digital collection of favourites, sung with fine fervour and discipline. The opening *Toreador chorus* from *Carmen* is zestfully infectious, and the *Soldiers' chorus* from *Faust* is equally buoyant. The noble line of Verdi's *Va pensiero* is shaped beautifully by Hickox, with the balance between voices and orchestra particularly good. In *Gli arredi festivi* from *Nabucco* and the famous Triumphal scene from *Aida* the orchestral brass sound resonantly sonorous, even if the fanfare trumpets could have been more widely separated in the latter piece. The concert ends with Borodin's *Polovtsian dances* most excitingly done. The recording, made at the EMI Abbey Road studio, has the atmosphere of an idealized opera house, and the result is in the demonstration bracket, with a projection and presence fully worthy of this polished but uninhibited singing. This is now reissued as an LSO Double, with colourful music by Bizet, also very well recorded.

Lorengar, Pilar (soprano)

'Grandi voci': Arias from: PUCCINI: *La Bohème; La rondine; Madama Butterfly; Turandot; Gianni Schicchi.* DVORAK: *Rusalka.* CHARPENTIER: *Louise.* BIZET: *Carmen; Les Pêcheurs de perles.* MASSENET: *Manon* (with St Cecilia Ac. O, Patanè). MOZART: *Le nozze di Figaro.* BEETHOVEN: *Fidelio.* WEBER: *Der Freischütz.* WAGNER: *Tannhäuser.* KORNGOLD: *Die tote Stadt* (with Vienna Op. O, Walter Weller).

(M) *(*) Decca 443 931-2.

It was a mistake for Pilar Lorengar to open this collection – compiled from two separate, earlier recitals, recorded in 1966 and 1970 – with *They call me Mimi*. Hers is a vocal personality of strong character and temperament, but the style of her singing fails to convince here, and a surer legato is needed in this aria. She is much better as Butterfly and is impressive in Liù's aria. In the German repertoire her vibrato is troublesome in almost every item, with the trills in *Dove sono* barely distinguishable from sustained notes and the throat occasionally constricting to produce something not far from a yodel. The highlight of the collection is the famous *Invocation to the moon* from Dvořák's *Rusalka*.

Lott, Felicity (soprano), Graham Johnson (piano)

Mélodies on Victor Hugo poems: GOUNOD: *Sérénade*. BIZET: *Feuilles d'album: Guitare. Adieux de l'hôtesse arabe*. LALO: *Guitare*. DELIBES: *Eclogue*. FRANCK: *S'il est un charmant gazon*. FAURE: *L'absent; Le papillon et la fleur; Puisqu'ici bas*. WAGNER: *L'attente*. LISZT: *O quand je dors; Comment, disaint-ils*. SAINT-SAENS: *Soirée en mer; La fiancée du timbalier*. M. V. WHITE: *Chantez, chantez jeune inspirée*. HAHN: *Si mes vers avaient des ailes; Rêverie*.
(B) *** HM Musique d'Abord HMA 901138 [(M) id. import].

Felicity Lott's collection of Hugo settings relies mainly on sweet and charming songs, freshly and unsentimentally done, with Graham Johnson an ideally sympathetic accompanist. The recital is then given welcome stiffening with fine songs by Wagner and Liszt, as well as two by Saint-Saëns that have a bite worthy of Berlioz. It makes a headily enjoyable cocktail. Now reissued in the Musique d'Abord series, this is a bargain not to be missed.

Luca, Giuseppe de (baritone)

'Prima voce': Arias from: VERDI: *Don Carlos, Ernani, Il Trovatore, La Traviata, Rigoletto*. ROSSINI: *Il Barbiere di Siviglia*. DONIZETTI: *L'elisir d'amore*. BELLINI: *I Puritani*. DIAZ: *Benvenuto Cellini*. PUCCINI: *La Bohème*. PONCHIELLI: *La Gioconda*. WOLF-FERRARI: *I gioielli della madonna*. Songs: DE LEVA: *Pastorale*. ROMILLI: *Marietta*.
(M) (***) Nimbus mono NI 7815 [id.].

There has never been a more involving account on record of the Act IV Marcello–Rodolfo duet than the one here with de Luca and Gigli, a model of characterization and vocal art. The baritone's mastery emerges vividly in item after item, whether in the power and wit of his pre-electric version of *Largo al factotum* (1917) or the five superb items (including the *Bohème* duet and the *Rigoletto* numbers, flawlessly controlled) which were recorded in the vintage year of 1927. Warm Nimbus transfers.

Ludwig, Christa (mezzo-soprano)

'The Art of Christa Ludwig' (with Gerald Moore or Geoffrey Parsons (piano) & (i) Herbert Downes (viola); (ii) Philh. O, Klemperer; (iii) Berlin SO, Stein or Forster): BRAHMS: *Sapphische Ode; Liebestreu; Der Schmied; Die Mainacht. 8 Zigeunerlieder. 4 Deutsche Volkslieder: Och mod'r ich well en Ding han!; We kumm ich dann de Pooz erenn?; In stiller Nacht; Schwesterlein*. Lieder: *Dein blaues Auge; Von ewiger Liebe; Das Mädchen spricht; O wüsst ich doch; Wie Melodien zieht es mir; Mädchenlied; Vergebliches Ständchen; Der Tod, das ist die kühle Nacht; Auf dem See; Waldeinsamkeit; Immer leiser word mein Schlummer; Ständchen; Gestillte Sehnsucht;* (i) *Geistliches Wiegenlied*. MAHLER: *Hans und Grete; Frühlingsmorgen; Des Knaben Wunderhorn: Ich ging mit Lust durch einen grünen Wald; Wo die schönen Trompeten blasen; Der Schildwache Nachtlied; Um schlimme Kinder; Das irdische Leben; Wer hat dies Liedlein erdacht; Lob des hohen Verstandes;Des Antonius von Padua Fischpredigt; Rheinlegendchen*. Rückert Lieder: *Ich atmet' einen linden Duft; Liebst du um Schönheit; Um Mitternacht; Ich bin der Welt abhanden gekommen*. SCHUMANN: *Frauenliebe und -Leben, Op. 42*. REGER: *Der Brief; Waldeinsamkeit*. SCHUBERT: *Die Allmacht; Fischerweise; An die Musik; Der Musensohn; Ganymed; Auf dem Wasser zu singen; Ave Maria; Die Forelle; Gretchen am Spinnrade; Frühlingsglaube; Der Tod und das Mädchen; Lachen und Weinen; Litanei auf das Fest Aller Seelen; Erlkönig; Der Hirt auf dem Felsen*. WOLF: *Gesang Weylas; Auf einer Wanderung*. R. STRAUSS: *Die Nacht; Allerseelen; Schlechtes Wetter*. RAVEL: *3 Chansons madécasses*. SAINT-SAENS: *Une flûte invisible*. RACHMANINOV: *Chanson géorgienne; Moisson de tristesse*. ROSSINI: *La regata veneziana* (3 canzonettas). (ii) WAGNER: *Wesendonk Lieder*. (iii) HANDEL: *Giulio*

Cesare: Cleopatra's aria. BACH: *St John Passion: Aria: Es ist vollbracht!.* (ii) WAGNER: *Tristan und Isolde: Mild und leise.*
(M) *** EMI CMS7 64074-2 (4) [ZDMD 64074].

Christa Ludwig is an extraordinarily versatile artist with a ravishing voice, readily matched by fine intelligence and natural musical sensitivity to place her among the special singers of our time, including De los Angeles and Schwarzkopf (to name two from the same EMI stable). She was as impressive in Schubert as she was in Strauss and Brahms, and her Mahler is very special indeed. This compensates for the below-par Schumann song-cycle. Her voice took naturally to the microphone, so this four-disc set is another source of infinite musical pleasure to be snapped up quickly before it disappears. The recordings come from the 1950s and 1960s and are very well transferred indeed.

Maurane, Camille (baritone)

Portrait (with Pierrette Alarie, Janine Micheau, Elizabeth Brasseur Ch., Maurice Duruflé, Lily Bienvenu, LOP; (i) Jean Fournet; (ii) Paul Sacher): FAURE: *Requiem, Op. 48; La bonne chanson.* DUPARC: Mélodies: *L'invitation au voyage; Soupir; Testament; Sérénade florentine; La vague et la cloche; Lamento; La vie antérieure; Phidylé; Extase; Elégie; Le manoir de Rosemonde; Chanson triste.* (ii) BRITTEN: *Les Illuminations.* (i) RAVEL: *Don Quichotte à Dulcinée; Shéhérazade.* DEBUSSY: *3 Ballades de François Villon.*
(M) (***) Ph. mono 438 970-2 (2).

Camille Maurane will be familiar to most collectors as the Pelléas in Ansermet's second recording of Debussy's opera and, a decade earlier, in Jean Fournet's 1954 version with Janine Micheau as Mélisande. He was born in Rouen in 1911 as Camille Moreau to parents who were both singers of quality. He was for many years a mainstay of the Opéra-Comique and an expert interpreter of Hahn, Messager and Delibes, and he took part in Maazel's DG recording of *L'Enfant et les sortilèges*. A celebrated Debussy interpreter (he was a pupil of Croiza), one can see why he was so admired when one listens to his *Ballades de François Villon*; and the Duparc group, split over the two discs, also shows his light but affecting baritone and superb diction to splendid advantage. Maurane shares the honours with Janine Micheau, one of the greatest coloratura singers of the period: her account of *Shéhérazade* is excellent, though it does not banish memories of Suzanne Danco's record with Ansermet, also from 1955. Micheau's version of Britten's *Les illuminations* with Paul Sacher is a rarity and has great style – but then most things on this set have. The least desirable performance, perhaps, is of the Fauré *Requiem*, recorded in June 1953, which does not wear its years lightly and sounds distinctly congested. That apart, this is a most valuable set.

McCormack, John (tenor)

'Prima voce': Arias and excerpts from: DONIZETTI: *Lucia di Lammermoor; L'elisir d'amore; La figlia del reggimento.* VERDI: *La Traviata; Rigoletto.* PUCCINI: *La Bohème.* BIZET. *Carmen; I pescatore di perle.* DELIBES: *Lakmé.* GOUNOD: *Faust.* PONCHIELLI: *La gioconda.* BOITO: *Mefistofele.* MASSENET: *Manon.* MOZART: *Don Giovanni.* WAGNER: *Die Meistersinger.* HERBERT: *Natomah.* HANDEL: *Semele; Atalanta.*
(M) (***) Nimbus mono NI 7820 [id.].

With the operas represented ranging from Handel's *Atalanta* and *Semele* to *Natomah*, by Victor Herbert, the heady beauty of McCormack's voice, his ease of production and perfect control are amply illustrated in these 21 items. His now legendary 1916 account of *Il mio tesoro* from *Don Giovanni*, with its astonishing breath control, is an essential item; but there are many others less celebrated which help to explain his special niche, even in a generation that included Caruso and Schipa. Characteristic Nimbus transfers.

'Songs of my heart': TRAD.: *The garden where the praties grow; Terence's farewell to Kathleen; Believe me if all those endearing young charms; The star of the County Down; Oft in the stilly night; The meeting of the waters; The Bard of Armagh; Down by the Salley Gardens; She moved thro' the fair; The green bushes.* BALFE: *The harp that once through Tara's halls.* ROECKEL: *The green isle of Erin.* SCHNEIDER: *O Mary dear.* LAMBERT: *She is far from the land.* HAYNES: *Off to Philadelphia.* MOLLOY: *The Kerry dance; Bantry Bay.* MARSHALL: *I hear you calling me.* E. PURCELL: *Passing by.* WOODFORD-FINDEN: *Kashmiri song.* CLUTSAM: *I know of two bright eyes.* FOSTER: *Jeannie with the light brown hair; Sweetly she sleeps, my Alice fair.*
(M) (***) EMI mono CDM7 64654-2 [id.].

In Irish repertoire like *The star of the County Down* McCormack is irresistible, but in lighter concert songs he could also spin the utmost magic. *Down by the Salley Gardens* and Stephen Foster's *Jeannie with the light brown hair* are superb examples, while in a ballad like *I hear you calling me* (an early pre-electric recording from 1908) the golden bloom of the vocal timbre combining with an artless line brings a ravishing frisson on the closing pianissimo. Many of the accompaniments are by Gerald Moore, who proves a splendid partner. Occasionally there is a hint of unsteadiness in the sustained *piano* tone, but otherwise no apology need be made for the recorded sound which is first class, while the lack of 78-r.p.m. background noise is remarkable.

'(RCA) Met. 100 Singing Years'

Disc 1: Excerpts from: DONIZETTI: *Lucia di Lammermoor* (Marcella Sembrich); *L'elisir d'amore* (Antonio Scotto). PUCCINI: *Tosca* (Emma Eames); *La bohème* (Marcel Journet). BERLIOZ: *Damnation de Faust* (Pol Plançon). BIZET: *Carmen* (Emma Calvé). THOMAS: *Hamlet* (Nellie Melba). MEYERBEER: *L'africana* (Giuseppe Campanari); *Le prophète* (Ernestine Schumann-Heink). WAGNER: *Der fliegende Holländer* (Johanna Gadski); *Parsifal* (Clarence Whitehill). PONCHIELLI: *La Gioconda* (Louise Homer). HALEVY: *La juive* (Enrico Caruso). WOLF-FERRARI: *Le donne curiose* (Geraldine Farrar, Hermann Jadlowker). TCHAIKOVSKY: *Pique dame* (Emmy Destinn). VERDI: *Un ballo in maschera* (Pasquale Amato). GIORDANO: *La cena delle beffe* (Frances Alda).

Disc 2: Excerpts from: LEONCAVALLO: *I Pagliacci* (Alma Gluck). VERDI: *La traviata* (John McCormack; Giuseppe de Luca); *Rigoletto* (Luisa Tetrazzini); *La forza del destino* (Rosa Ponselle). MASCAGNI: *L'amico Fritz* (Miguel Fleta, Lucrezia Bori). TCHAIKOVSKY: *Eugene Onegin* (Giovanni Martelli). MUSSORGSKY: *Boris Godunov* (Paul Althouse, Margarete Ober). MEYERBEER: *L'africana* (Beniamino Gigli); *Dinorah* (Amelita Galli-Curci). KORNGOLD: *Die tote Stadt* (Maria Jeritza). ROSSINI: *Il barbiere di Siviglia* (Tito Ruffo). PUCCINI: *La fanciulla del West* (Edward Johnson). WAGNER: *Die Meistersinger* (Friedrich Schorr, Elisabeth Rethberg).

Disc 3: Excerpts from: BELLINI: *Norma* (Giacomo Lauri-Volpi). TAYLOR: *The King's henchman* (Lawrence Tibbett). DONIZETTI: *Lucia di Lammermoor* (Toti dal Monte); *L'elisir d'amore* (Tito Schipa). WAGNER: *Tannhäuser* (Lauritz Melchior); *Tristan und Isolde* (Kirsten Flagstad); *Die Walküre* (Kerstin Thorborg); *Lohengrin* (Helen Traubel). MOZART: *Don Giovanni* (Ezio Pinza). CHARPENTIER: *Louise* (Grace Moore). GOUNOD: *Roméo et Juliette* (Gladys Swarthout). RIMSKY-KORSAKOV: *Le coq d'or* (Lily Pons). GLUCK: *Alceste* (Rose Bampton). MASSENET: *Manon* (Richard Crooks). HAGEMAN: *Caponsacchi* (Helen Jepson). BIZET: *Carmen* (Bruna Castagna). MOZART: *Le nozze di Figaro* (Bidú Sayão).

Disc 4: Excerpts from: GIORDANO: *Andrea Chénier* (Zinka Milanov). PUCCINI: *Manon Lescaut* (Jussi Bjoerling, Enrico Caruso; Dorothy Kirsten); *Madama Butterfly* (Licia Albanese). R. STRAUSS: *Der Rosenkavalier* (Risë Stevens, Erna Berber). GOUNOD: *Faust* (Leonard Warren). MUSSORGSKY: *Boris Godunov* (Alexander Kipnis). OFFENBACH: *Les contes d'Hoffmann* (Jarmila Novotna). BARBER: *Vanessa* (Steber, Elias, Resnik, Gedda, Tozzi, Cehanovsky). DONIZETTI: *Lucia di Lammermoor* (Jan Peerce). THOMAS: *Mignon* (Patrice Munsel). VERDI: *Aida* (Richard Tucker); *Don Carlo* (Robert Merrill); *Otello* (Ramón Vinay, Giuseppe Valdengo).

Disc 5: Excerpts from: WAGNER: *Die Meistersinger* (Set Svanholm). VERDI: *Macbeth* (Jerome Hines); *Un ballo in maschera* (Marian Anderson); *Otello* (Tito Gobbi); *Macbeth* (Carlo Bergonzi); *La traviata* (Anna Moffo). PUCCINI: *La bohème* (Giuseppe di Stefano); *Turandot* (Birgit Nilsson, Jussi Bjoerling). BELLINI: *La sonnambula* (Roberta Peters). ROSSINI: *Il barbiere di Siviglia* (Cesare Valletti). LEONCAVALLO: *I Pagliacci* (Jon Vickers). BARBER: *Antony and Cleopatra* (Leontyne Price).

Disc 6: BIZET: *Carmen* (Franco Corelli, Mirella Freni). WAGNER: *Lohengrin* (Sándor Kónya). VERDI: *Aida* (Grace Bumbry, Plácido Domingo); *Otello* (Renata Scotto, Katia Ricciarelli); *Rigoletto* (Alfredo Kraus); *Il Trovatore* (Fiorenza Cossotto). LEVY: *Mourning becomes Electra* (Sherrill Milnes). PUCCINI: *La bohème* (Montserrat Caballé). DONIZETTI: *La favorita* (Shirley Verrett). CILEA: *Adriana Lecouvreur* (Domingo). MOZART: *Die Zauberflöte* (Martti Talvela); *Così fan tutte* (Kiri te Kanawa). ROSSINI: *L'italiana in Algeri* (Marilyn Horne).
(M) (***) [BMG/RCA mono/stereo 09026 61580-2 (6)].

With all the singers represented in roles they appeared in at the Met., this lavishly presented collection offers a rich storehouse of fine singing, as well as a fascinating account of that opera house's history over 100 years. Starting with Marcella Sembrich in part of the mad scene from Donizetti's *Lucia di Lammermoor*, each singer is represented only once, with no duplication of items. Even Caruso is represented with only one item, an aria from Halévy's *La Juive*, his last role at the Met. It also means that such a singer as

Nicolai Gedda is represented only in an ensemble number from Barber's *Vanessa*. Even so, the variety and unexpectedness of some of the choices is refreshing, as for example having Sherrill Milnes in an aria from Marvin David Levy's *Mourning becomes Electra*. With such a wide coverage it is impossible to comment on more than a fraction of the content but for lovers of fine singing there is little here to disappoint.

Melchior, Lauritz (tenor)

'Prima voce': Arias from: WAGNER: *Siegfried; Tannhäuser; Tristan und Isolde; Die Walküre; Die Meistersinger; Götterdämmerung.* LEONCAVALLO: *Pagliacci.* MEYERBEER: *L'Africana.* VERDI: *Otello.*
(M) (***) Nimbus mono NI 7816 [id.].

The Nimbus disc of Melchior, issued to celebrate his centenary in 1990, demonstrates above all the total consistency of the voice between the pre-electric recordings of *Siegfried* and *Tannhäuser*, made for Polydor in 1924, and the *Meistersinger* and *Götterdämmerung* extracts, recorded in 1939. Of those, the Siegfried–Brünnhilde duet from the *Prologue* of *Götterdämmerung* is particularly valuable. It is fascinating too to hear the four recordings that Melchior made with Barbirolli and the LSO in 1930–31: arias by Verdi, Leoncavallo and Meyerbeer translated into German. As a character, Otello is made to sound far more prickly. Characteristic Nimbus transfers.

Muzio, Claudia (soprano)

'Prima voce': Arias from: MASCAGNI: *Cavalleria Rusticana.* VERDI: *La forza del destino; Otello; Il Trovatore; La Traviata.* PUCCINI: *Tosca; La Bohème.* GIORDANO: *Andrea Chénier.* BOITO: *Mefistofele.* CILEA: *Adriana Lecouvreur; L'Arlesiana.* BELLINI: *La Sonnambula.* Songs by BUZZI-PECCIA; PERGOLESI; REGER; DELIBES; REFICE.
(M) (***) Nimbus mono NI 7814 [id.].

This Nimbus collection of recordings by the sadly short-lived Claudia Muzio duplicates much that is contained on the EMI Références CD of her. The main addition here is the Act III duet from *Otello* with Francesco Merli, but some cherishable items are omitted. The Nimbus acoustic transfer process sets the voice more distantly as well as more reverberantly than the EMI, with its distinctive tang less sharply conveyed.

Nash, Heddle (tenor)

'The incomparable Heddle Nash': PUCCINI: *La Bohème, Act IV* (complete; with Lisa Perli, Brownlee, Alva, Andreva, LPO, Beecham). Arias from: MOZART: *Così fan tutte* (with Ina Souez); *Don Giovanni* (all in Italian). ROSSINI: *The Barber of Seville.* VERDI: *Rigoletto.* BIZET: *The Fair Maid of Perth.* Johann STRAUSS Jr: *Die Fledermaus* (with Denis Noble) (all in English).
(M) (***) Dutton Lab. mono CDLX 7012 [id. full price].

Once again Dutton Laboratories provide incomparable transfers from 78s – of such quality that Beecham's extraordinarily theatrical (1935) Act IV of *La Bohème*, sung in Italian, communicates like a modern recording. Heddle Nash sings ardently, but Lisa Perli (Dora Labette) as Mimi is equally touching and, if the rest of the cast are less distinctive, Beecham's direction carries the day. Nash's four Mozart recordings (also sung in Italian) are included, notably the 1929 *Il mio tesoro*. Most cherishable of all is the *Serenade* from *The Fair Maid of Perth* from 1932, but there is some very striking Verdi in English, full of flair (in spite of awkward words) and a sparkling Johann Strauss duet with Dennis Noble. It seems carping to criticize that, with only 69 minutes, there would have been room for more. But what there is is technically state of the art.

Norman, Jessye (soprano)

'Great moments of Jessye Norman'.

Disc 1: WAGNER: *Tristan: Prelude and Liebestod. Tannhäuser: Dich, teure Halle; Allmächt'ge Jungfrau. Der fliegende Holländer: Johohoe! Götterdämmerung: Brünnhilde's immolation scene.*

Disc 2: WAGNER: *Wesendonk Lieder.* SCHUBERT: *Dem Unendlichen; Der Winterabend; Auflosung.* POULENC: *Tu vois le feu du soir; La fraîcheur et le feu* (1–7). RAVEL: *Chansons madécasses* (1–3); *Chanson du rouet; Si morne.*

Disc 3: BRAHMS: *German Requiem: Ihr habt nun Traurigkeit*. BERLIOZ: *Roméo et Juliette: Premiers transports que nu n'oublie*. OFFENBACH: *Les Contes d'Hoffmann:* excerpts. *La belle Hélène*: excerpts.
(M) **(*) EMI (SIS) Analogue/Dig. CMS5 65526-2 (3).

One snag for the EMI compilers is having only a limited range of recordings to draw from, which means that each issue overlaps with the others. This three-disc collection is the most comprehensive, with the complete Wagner recital with Tennstedt on the first disc, the second including Wagner's *Wesendonklieder* (with piano) and songs by Schubert, Poulenc and Ravel, and the third a curious mixture of Brahms (from Tennstedt's version of the *German Requiem*), Berlioz (the usual Juliet aria) and Offenbach, a more generous selection from *Contes d'Hoffmann* (five items, including more material unearthed in the Oeser Edition) and *La belle Hélène* (six) than on the *Diva* disc. There are many treasures here, but the mixture is hardly more widely representative than the *Diva* compilation, and here too no texts are given.

'Diva' (from above): Arias from WAGNER: *Tannhäuser; Der fliegende Holländer; Tristan und Isolde*. OFFENBACH: *Contes d'Hoffmann; La belle Hélene*. BERLIOZ: *Roméo et Juliette*.
(M) *** EMI (SIS) CDM5 65576-2 [id.].

This is a magnificent compilation, framed by four items from Jessye Norman's Wagner recital of 1987 with Klaus Tennstedt: Elisabeth's two arias from *Tannhäuser*, *Senta's Ballad* from *Der fliegende Holländer* and *Isolde's Liebestod*, all superb. Her formidable powers of characterization in tragedy and comedy alike are illustrated in the sequence of excerpts from Offenbach's *Contes d'Hoffmann* (four, including long-buried material from the Oeser Edition) and *La belle Hélène* (three), vocally flawless too. It is also good to have her Juliet represented, taken from Muti's otherwise flawed version of Berlioz's *Roméo et Juliette*. More than with most issues in this well-planned series, it is a snag to have no texts provided.

Opera choruses

'Grand opera choruses': VERDI: *Nabucco: Va pensiero (Chorus of the Hebrew slaves). Il trovatore: Vedi! le fosche (Anvil chorus)*. BEETHOVEN: *Fidelio: O welche Lust (Prisoners' chorus)* (Chicago Ch. & SO, Solti). BELLINI: *Norma: Squilla il bronzo del dio! . . . Guerra, guerra!* (Welsh Nat. Op. Ch. & O, Bonynge). WAGNER: *Lohengrin: Prelude to Act III and Bridal chorus. Tannhäuser: Pilgrims' chorus* (V. State Op. Konzertvereinigung or V. State Op. Ch., VPO, Solti). GOUNOD: *Faust: Soldiers' chorus* (Ambrosian Op. Ch., LSO, Bonynge). PUCCINI: *Madama Butterfly: Humming chorus* (V. State Op. Ch., VPO, Karajan). LEONCAVALLO: *Pagliacci: I zampognari! . . . Don, din, don (Bell chorus)* (Santa Cecilia, Rome, Ac. Ch. & O, Gardelli). BIZET: *Carmen: Toreador chorus* (John Aldiss Ch., LPO, Solti). WEBER: *Der Freischütz: Huntsmen's chorus*. NICOLAI: *Die lustigen Weiber von Windsor: O süsser Mond* (Bav. R. Ch. & O, Kubelik). BERLIOZ: *Les Troyens: Dieux protecteurs de la ville éternelle* (Montreal Schubert Ch. & SO, Dutoit). MUSSORGSKY: *Boris Godunov: Coronation scene* (Ghiaurov, V. Boys' Ch., Sofia R. Ch., V. State Op. Ch., VPO, Karajan).
(M) *** Decca Dig./Analogue 458 205-2.

This 75-minute collection re-assembled for reissue in Decca's Opera Gala series is exceptional value and offers vivid, and often demonstration-worthy sound throughout. Most of the excerpts come from distinguished complete sets, notably the *Pilgrims' chorus* from Solti's *Tannhäuser*, which has a memorable sense of perspective, while the *Lohengrin* excerpt is hardly less impressive. However, that also means that they are not always cleanly tailored and sometimes there are soloists too. A high proportion of the items are from Solti, but other highlights include Karajan's *Humming chorus* from *Madama Butterfly*, which is so warmly atmospheric, and the expansive *Coronation scene* from *Boris Godunov*. Bonynge conducts the *War chorus* from *Norma* and the *Soldiers' chorus* from *Faust*. Since the disc's previous issue additional items have been added, notably the excerpts from *Der Freischütz* and Nicolai's *Merry wives of Windor* (from Kubelik) and the *Hymn of deliverance* from *Les Troyens* (Dutoit). Good documentation and translations are provided, an exception rather than the rule for this kind of operatic collection.

Opera Love Songs

'Amor – Opera's great love songs': VERDI: *Aida: Celeste Aida. Luisa Miller: Quando le sere al placido* (Pavarotti). *Rigoletto: Caro nome* (Sutherland). PUCCINI: *Gianni Schicchi: O mio babbino caro* (Tebaldi). *Manon Lescaut: Donna non vidi mai* (Carreras). *Tosca: Recondita armonia* (Corelli). *Tosca: Vissi d'arte* (Kiri Te Kanawa); *E lucevan le stelle* (Domingo). *La Bohème: Musetta's waltz song* (Elizabeth Harwood). *Madama Butterfly: Un bel dì* (Mirella Freni); *Turandot: Signore ascolta!* (Caballé); *Nessun dorma* (Pavarotti). DONIZETTI: *La Favorita: O mio Fernando* (Cossotto). *L'elisir d'amore: Una furtiva lagrima.*

Fedora: Amor ti vieta. PONCHIELLI: *Cielo e mar.* MASSENET: *Werther: Pourquoi me réveiller* (all Pavarotti). BIZET: *Carmen: Habanera* (Troyanos); *Flower song* (Domingo). MOZART: *Nozze di Figaro: Voi che sapete* (Fredrica von Stade).
(M) *** Decca 458 201-2.

Brimming over with stellar performances, this generous (76-minute) collection is a true 'Opera gala'. Pavarotti dominates and seldom lets us down, and he ends the disc with a thrilling performance of his great showpiece, *Nessun dorma*, from his complete set conducted by Mehta. Many of the other excerpts too are drawn from outstanding sets, including Caballé's beautiful *Signore ascolta!* (taken from the same source), Freni's passionately expansive *Un bel dì* from Karajan's *Madama Butterfly*, Domingo's outstanding *Flower song* and Troyanos's *Habanera*, both from Solti's *Carmen*, and Fredrica von Stade's delightful *Voi che sapete*, taken from the same conductor's highly successful *Nozze di Figaro*. Tebaldi's ravishing *O mio babbino caro* dates from 1962 when the voice still had all its bloom, while Marilyn Horne's dark-voiced *Softly awakes my heart* comes from a 1967 recital. Nicely packaged in a slip case, the documentation includes full translations.

Oxford Camerata, Jeremy Summerly

'Lamentations': WHITE: *Lamentations.* TALLIS: *Lamentations, Sets I & II.* PALESTRINA: *Lesson I for Maundy Thursday.* LASSUS: *Lessons I & III for Maundy Thursday.* Estâvão DE BRITO: *Lesson I for Good Friday.*
✽ (BB) *** Naxos Dig. 8.550572 [id.].

On the bargain Naxos label come nearly 70 minutes of sublime polyphony, beautifully sung by the fresh-toned Oxford Camerata under Jeremy Summerly. All these *Lamentations* (*Lessons* simply means collection of verses) are settings from the Old Testament book, *The Lamentations of Jeremiah*. They were intended for nocturnal use and are usually darkly intense in feeling. The English and Italian *Lamentations* have their own individuality, but the most striking of all is the *Good Friday Lesson* by the Portuguese composer, Estâvão de Brito. This is very direct and strong in feeling for, as the anonymous insert-note writer points out, Portugal was under Spanish subjugation at the time and de Brito effectively uses dissonance at the words *non est lex* ('there is no law') to assert his nationalistic defiance. The recorded sound is vividly beautiful within an ideal ambience.

Palmer, Felicity (soprano), John Constable (piano)

'Love's old sweet song': Victorian and Edwardian ballads: SULLIVAN: *My dearest heart.* HAYDN WOOD: *A Brown bird singing; Bird of love divine.* EDEN: *What's in the air today.* TRAVERS: *A Mood.* MOIR: *Down the vale.* SQUIRE: *If I might come to you.* BRAHE: *Two little words.* D'HARDELOT: *Three green bonnets.* EVERARD: *It's all right in the summertime.* MOLLOY: *Love's old sweet song.* SPEAKS: *Morning.* MURRAY: *I'll walk beside you.* SANDERSON: *The valley of laughter.* Lao SILESU: *Love, here is my heart.* LEHR: *Whatever is – is best.* BEHREND: *Daddy.*
(BB) *** Belart 461 4902 [(M) id. import].

The ear-catching item here is Everard's *It's all right in the summertime*, which Felicity Palmer delivers in true music-hall style with a cor-blimey Cockney accent. Even if the off-key piano postlude is also offkey (not matching the humour of the rest at all), the result is a glorious *tour de force* and sets the tone for one of the most warmly characterful recitals of its kind. These were all drawing-room songs which for decades were despised; now, in performances like these, their overtly sentimental charm can be enjoyed afresh as a delightful period offering, superbly accompanied by John Constable. The acoustic is reverberant, not like a drawing-room at all, but the sound is full and vivid.

Patti, Adelina (soprano)

'The Era of Adelina Patti' ((i) Adelina Patti, (ii) Victor Maurel; (iii) Pol Plançon; (iv) Mattia Battistini; (v) Mario Ancona; (vi) Lucien Fugère; (vii) Francisco Vignas; (viii) Emma Calvé; (ix) Maurice Renaud; (x) Fernando de Lucia; (xi) Francesco Tamagno; (xii) Nellie Melba; (xiii) Félia Litvinne; (xiv) Wilhelm Hesch; (xv) Lillian Nordica; (xvi) Mario Ancona; (xvii) Edouard de Reszke; (xviii) Marcella Sembrich; (xix) Francesco Marconi; (xx) Mattia Battistini; (xxi) Lilli Lehmann; (xxii) Sir Charles Santley): Arias from: VERDI: (ii) *Falstaff;* (i, iii) *Don Carlos;* (iv, xx) *Ernani;* (v, xiv) *Otello.* ADAM: (iii) *Le Chalet.* GLUCK: (vi) *Les Pèlerins de la Mecque.* MOZART: (i, ii, xx) *Don Giovanni;* (i, vii, xxi) *Le nozze di Figaro.*

MEYERBEER: (vii) *Le Prophète*. BIZET: (viii) *Carmen*. MASSENET: (ix, xi) *Hérodiade;* (x) *Manon*. THOMAS: (xii) *Hamlet*. WAGNER: (xiii) *Lohengrin;* (xiv) *Die Meistersinger von Nürnberg*. ERKEL: (xv) *Hunyadi László*. DONIZETTI: (xvi) *La favorita;* (xix) *Lucrezia Borgia;* (xii) *Lucia*. BELLINI: (i) *La Sonnambula;* (xviii) *I Puritani*. FLOTOW: (xvii) *Martha*. ROSSINI: (x) *Il barbiere di Siviglia*. GOMES: (xx) *Il Guarany*. Songs by TOSTI; (vi) RAMEAU; (i, vi) YRADIER; (i) HOOK; (i) BISHOP; (ix) GOUNOD; (xv) R. STRAUSS; (xxii) HATTON.
(M) (***) Nimbus mono NI 7840/41 [id.].

The very first item on this wide-ranging collection of historic recordings has one sitting up at once. The voice ringing out from the loudspeakers prompts cheering from the singer's little audience. The clear-toned baritone is singing *Quand'ero paggio* from Verdi's *Falstaff* and, encouraged, he repeats it. More cheering and a third performance, this time in French, to cap the occasion. The singer is Victor Maurel, the baritone whom Verdi chose as his first Falstaff in 1893 and, before that, his first Iago in *Otello*. The recording dates from 1907, and many lovers of historic vocal issues will remember it well. Yet hearing it on the Nimbus transfer to CD brings a sense of presence as never before.

That company's controversial technique of playing an ancient 78 disc with a thorn needle on the best possible acoustic horn gramophone is at its most effective here, with exceptionally vivid results on these acoustic recordings. They not only convey astonishing presence but also a sense of how beautiful the voices were, getting behind the tinny and squawky sounds often heard on old 78s. This is an ideal set for anyone not already committed to historic vocals who simply wants to investigate how great singing could be 90 years ago, providing such an unexpected mix of well-known items and rarities, to delight specialists and newcomers alike.

The first of the two discs offers recordings that Nimbus regards as technically the finest of their day, including Patti in 1906, not just singing but shouting enthusiastically in a Spanish folksong, *La Calesera*, '*Vivan los españoles!*' Recorded much later in 1928 comes the French baritone, Lucien Fugère, eighty at the time but singing with a firm focus that you might not find today in a baritone in his twenties.

The second of the two discs has just as fascinating a mixture, but the recordings 'have not survived the decades so well'. Even so, it is thrilling to hear Sir Charles Santley, born in 1834, the year after Brahms, singing *Simon the Cellarer* with tremendous flair at the age of seventy-nine, and the coloratura, Marcella Sembrich, sounding even sweeter in Bellini than on previous transfers.

Pavarotti, Luciano (tenor)

'Tutto Pavarotti': VERDI: *Aida: Celeste Aida. Luisa Miller: Quando le sere al placido. La Traviata: De' miei bollenti spiriti. Il Trovatore: Ah si ben mio; Di quella pira. Rigoletto: La donna è mobile. Un ballo in maschera: La rivedrà nell'estasi.* DONIZETTI: *L'elisir d'amore: Una furtiva lagrima. Don Pasquale: Com'è gentil.* PONCHIELLI: *La Gioconda: Cielo e mar.* FLOTOW: *Martha: M'appari.* BIZET: *Carmen: Flower song.* MASSENET: *Werther: Pourquoi me réveiller.* MEYERBEER: *L'Africana: O paradiso.* BOITO: *Mefistofele: Dai campi dai prati.* LEONCAVALLO: *Pagliacci: Vesti la giubba.* MASCAGNI: *Cavalleria Rusticana: Addio alla madre.* GIORDANO: *Fedora: Amor ti vieta.* PUCCINI: *La Fanciulla del West: Ch'ella mi creda. Tosca: E lucevan le stelle. Manon Lescaut: Donna non vidi mai. La Bohème: Che gelida manina. Turandot: Nessun dorma.* ROSSINI: *Stabat Mater: Cuius animam.* BIZET: *Agnus Dei.* ADAM: *O holy night.* DI PAPUA: *O sole mio.* TOSTI: *A vucchella.* CARDILLO: *Core 'ngrato.* TAGLIAFERRI: *Passione.* CHERUBINI: *Mamma.* DALLA: *Caruso.*
(M) *** Decca 425 681-2; *425 681-4* (2) [id.].

Opening with Dalla's *Caruso*, a popular song in the Neapolitan tradition, certainly effective, and no more vulgar than many earlier examples of the genre, this selection goes on through favourites like *O sole mio* and *Core 'ngrato* and one or two religious items, notably Adam's *Cantique de Noël*, to the hard core of operatic repertoire. Beginning with *Celeste Aida*, recorded in 1972, the selection of some 22 arias from complete sets covers Pavarotti's distinguished recording career with Decca from 1969 (*Cielo e mar* and the *Il Trovatore* excerpts) to 1985, although the opening song was, of course, recorded digitally in 1988. The rest is a mixture of brilliantly transferred analogue originals and a smaller number of digital masters, all or nearly all showing the great tenor in sparkling form. The records are at mid-price, but there are no translations or musical notes.

'The greatest ever Pavarotti' (with various orchestras and conductors): Arias from: VERDI: *Rigoletto; Il Trovatore; La Traviata; Aida.* PUCCINI: *La Bohème; Turandot; Tosca; Fanciulla del West; Manon Lescaut.* DONIZETTI: *L'elisir d'amore.* FLOTOW: *Martha.* BIZET: *Carmen.* LEONCAVALLO: *I Pagliacci.* GIORDANO: *Fedora.* MEYERBEER: *L'Africana.* MASSENET: *Werther.* Songs: DALLA: *Caruso.* LEONCAVALLO: *Mattinata.* TOSTI: *Aprile; Marechiare; La Serenata.* CARDILLO: *Core 'ngrato.* ROSSINI: *La Danza.* MODUGNO:

Volare. DENZA: *Funiculì, funiculà*. DI CURTIS: *Torna a Surriento*. DI CAPUA: *O sole mio!* SCHUBERT: *Ave Maria*. FRANCK: *Panis angelicus*. MANCINI: *In un palco della Scala* (with apologies to Pink Panther). GIORDANO: *Caro mio ben*. BIXIO: *Mamma*.
(M) *** Decca Analogue/Dig. 436 173-2; *436 173-4* (2).

Such a collection as this is self-recommending and scarcely needs a review from us, merely a listing. The first disc opens with *La donna è mobile* (*Rigoletto*), *Che gelida manina* (*La Bohème*), *Nessun dorma* (*Tosca*), all taken from outstandingly successful complete recordings, and the rest of the programme, with many favourite lighter songs also given the golden touch, is hardly less appealing. The second CD includes Pavarotti's tribute to the Pink Panther and ends with a tingling live version of *Nessun dorma*, to compare with the studio version on disc one. Vivid, vintage Decca recording throughout.

'Grandi voci' (with Nat. PO, Chailly or Fabrittis): GIORDANO: *Fedora: Amor ti vieta. Andrea Chénier: Colpito qui m'avete . . . Un di all'azzuro spazio; Come un bel dì di maggio; Si, fui soldata.* BOITO: *Mefistofele: Dai campi, dai prati; Ogni mortal . . . Giunto sul passo estremo.* CILEA: *Adriana Lecouvreur: La dolcissima effigie; L'anima ho stanca.* MASCAGNI: *Iris: Apri la tua finestra!* MEYERBEER: *L'Africana: Mi batti il cor . . . O Paradiso.* MASSENET: *Werther: Pourquoi me réveiller.* PUCCINI: *La Fanciulla del West: Ch'ella mi creda. Manon Lescaut: Tra voi belle; Donna non vidi mai; Ah! non v'avvicinate! . . . No! No! pazzo son!* (with Howlett).
(M) **(*) Decca (IMS) Dig. 440 400-2 [id.].

This first digital recital record from Pavarotti had the voice more resplendent than ever. The passion with which he tackles Des Grieux's Act III plea from *Manon Lescaut* is devastating, and the big breast-beating numbers are all splendid, imaginative as well as heroic. But the slight pieces, Des Grieux's *Tra voi belle* and the *Iris Serenade*, could be lighter and more charming. The CD gives the voice even greater projection, with its full resonance and brilliance admirably caught, but it does also make the listener more aware of the occasional lack of subtlety of the presentation.

'Live': Recital 1: Arias and duets from: VERDI: *La Traviata; I vespri siciliani; Aida.* MASSENET: *Werther.* PONCHIELLI: *La Gioconda.* DONIZETTI: *La figlia del reggimento; L'elisir d'amore.* MEYERBEER: *L'Africana.* BOITO: *Mefistofele.* MASCAGNI: *L'amico Fritz.* PUCCINI: *Tosca.* Recital 2 (with Katia Ricciarelli and Mirella Freni): Arias from VERDI: *La Traviata; Aïda; Macbeth; La forza del destino; I Lombardi; Il Corsaro; Falstaff; Un ballo in maschera;* Duet from *Otello (Già nella notte densa)*. Arias from PUCCINI: *Turandot.*
(B) **(*) Decca Double (IMS) 443 018-2 (2) [(M) id. import].

Here are two Pavarotti recitals for the price of one, although in the second, mainly a Verdi collection, Katia Ricciarelli, in splendid voice, gets the lion's share of the arias and she and Pavarotti join for only a single duet – from *Otello*. Pavarotti rounds off the programme as usual with *Nessun dorma*, to tumultuous applause. However, applause is not really a problem on the second disc, whereas it is often intrusive on the first. Artistically, however, the partnership of Pavarotti and Freni works well (as we know from their complete recordings). The *Werther* and *Africana* items were new to Pavarotti's repertory at the time; sweet singing from Freni, too, though her delivery at times could be more characterful. Vividly robust recording.

Pears, Sir Peter (tenor)

'The Land of lost content': Twentieth-century English songs (with (i) Benjamin Britten; (ii) Alan Bush; (iii) Viola Tunnard): (i) IRELAND: *The Land of lost content; The Trellis.* BRIDGE: *'Tis but a week; Goldenhair; When you are old; So perverse; Journey's end.* TIPPETT: *Songs for Ariel.* (ii) Alan BUSH: *Voices of the prophets.* (iii) DELIUS: *To daffodils.* MOERAN: *The merry month of May.* VAN DIEREN: *Dream pedlary; Take, o take those lips away.* WARLOCK: *Piggensie; Along the stream.* GRAINGER: *Bold William Taylor.* William BUSCH: *The echoing green; The Shepherd; If thou wilt ease thine heart; Come, o come, my life's delight.*
(BB) ** Belart 461 550-2 [(M) id. import].

This is a well-produced and interesting collection, but it contains little that is really memorable. Sir Michael Tippett's rhapsodical lyricism seems almost too free to pin down the words and Alan Bush's *Voices of the prophets*, for all its passion, is let down by the poem for the fourth section which sounds uncomfortably like Communist propaganda. The yearning quality of the idiom of the songs by William Busch is quite striking, especially coming after the pert Grainger folksong.

Pears, Peter (tenor), **Julian Bream** (lute)

Julian Bream Edition, Volume 19. *Elizabethan lute songs*: MORLEY: *Absence; It was a lover and his lass; Who is is?*. ROSSETER: *What then is love?; If she forsake me; When Laura smiles*. DOWLAND: *I saw my lady weep; Dear, if you change; Stay, Time; Weep you no more; Shall I sue?; Sweet, stay awhile; Can she excuse?; Come, heavy sleep; Wilt thou unkind, thus leave me?; Sorrow stay; The lowest trees have tops; Time's eldest son, Old Age; In darkness let me dwell; Say, love, if ever thou didst find*. FORD: *Come Phyllis; Fair, sweet, cruel*.
(M) *** BMG/RCA 09026 61609-2.

This vintage collection was recorded between 1963 and 1969 when Pears was at the peak of his form. The Dowland songs are particularly fine, sung with Pears's usual blend of intelligence and lyrical feeling, their nostalgic melancholy tenderly caught. Excellent, vivid, well-balanced recording, with Bream's expert accompaniments well in the picture. Most refreshing.

Ponselle, Rosa (soprano)

'Prima voce': Arias from: BELLINI: *Norma*. PONCHIELLI: *La Gioconda*. SPONTINI: *La vestale*. VERDI: *Aida; Ernani; La forza del destino; Otello*. Songs by: ARENSKY; RIMSKY-KORSAKOV; DE CURTIS; DI CAPUA; JACOBS-BOND.
(M) (***) Nimbus mono NI 7805.

One of the most exciting American sopranos ever, Rosa Ponselle tantalizingly cut short her career when she was still at her peak. Only the Arensky and Rimsky songs represent her after her official retirement, and the rest make a superb collection, including her classic accounts of *Casta diva* from Bellini's *Norma* and the duet, *Mira o Norma*, with Marion Telva. The six Verdi items include her earlier version of *Ernani involami*, not quite so commanding as her classic 1928 recording, but fascinating for its rarity. Equally cherishable is her duet from *La forza del destino* with Ezio Pinza.

Price, Leontyne (soprano)

'The Prima Donna Collection' (with RCA Italiana Op. O, Molinari-Pradelli; New Philh. O, Santi; LSO, Downes; or Philh. O, Henry Lewis): Disc 1: Arias from: PURCELL: *Dido and Aeneas*. MOZART: *Le nozze di Figaro*. VERDI: *La Traviata; Otello* (with C.Vozza). MEYERBEER: *L'Africaine*. MASSENET: *Manon*. CILEA: *Adriana Lecouvreur*. Gustave CHARPENTIER: *Louise*. PUCCINI: *Turandot* (with D. Barioni, Amb. Op. Ch.). KORNGOLD: *Die tote Stadt*. BARBER: *Vanessa*.

Disc 2: HANDEL: *Atalanta*. MOZART: *Don Giovanni*. WEBER: *Der Freischütz*. WAGNER: *Tannhäuser*. VERDI: *Macbeth* (with C. Vozza, E.El Hage). BOITO: *Mefistofele*. DVORAK: *Rusalka*. DEBUSSY: *L'enfant prodigue*. GIORDANO: *Andrea Chénier*. ZANDONAI: *Francesca da Rimini*. PUCCINI: *Suor Angelica*. MENOTTI: *Amelia goes to the ball*.

Disc 3: GLUCK: *Alceste*. MOZART: *Don Giovanni*. VERDI: *I Lombardi; Simon Boccanegra*. FLOTOW: *Martha*. OFFENBACH: *La Périchole*. WAGNER: *Die Walküre*. Johann STRAUSS Jr: *Die Fledermaus*. BIZET: *Carmen*. MASCAGNI: *Cavalleria rusticana*. MASSENET: *Thaïs*. PUCCINI: *Gianni Schicchi*. POULENC: *Les dialogues des Carmélites*.

Disc 4: HANDEL: *Semele*. MOZART: *Idomeneo*. BERLIOZ: *La Damnation de Faust*. WEBER: *Oberon*. BELLINI: *Norma* (with B. Martinovich, Amb. Op. Ch.). VERDI: *Rigoletto*. WAGNER: *Tristan und Isolde*. LEONCAVALLO: *I Pagliacci*. CILEA: *Adriana Lecouvreur*. BRITTEN: *Gloriana*.
(M) *** BMG/RCA 09026 61236-2 (4) [id.].

This anthology is drawn from a series of recitals which Leontyne Price recorded for RCA in London and Rome between 1965 and 1979, including many items made when she was at the very peak of her form. Some of the very finest performances come on Disc 1. The famous *Lament* from Purcell's *Dido and Aeneas* makes a moving opener, the voice is wonderfully fresh; and the following performances are all gloriously sung – clearly these early sessions with Molinari-Pradelli in Rome were highly productive. But there are many fine things elsewhere. The Sleep-walking scene from Verdi's *Macbeth* on Disc 2 is a disappointment (Lady Macbeth is plainly not one of her best parts), but her *Come in quest' ora bruna* from *Simon Boccanegra* is very fine, and she finds unusual expressive depth in Offenbach's Act III Prison aria from *La Périchole*. She is, not unexpectedly, superb in *Voi lo sapete* from *Cavalleria rusticana* (disc 3), and a highlight from the final disc is the passionately felt *D'amour l'ardente flamme* from Berlioz's

Damnation de Faust. The languorously played cor anglais solo here is characteristic of the consistent excellence of the accompaniments and, like the voice, they are beautifully recorded. Care has been taken with detail, so that in the long scene from Act I of *Norma* (with *Casta diva* at its centre) there is support from the Ambrosian Chorus, recorded in fine perspective. As she has already recorded a complete *Carmen*, it is good to hear Miss Price singing richly in the subsidiary role of Micaëla, and the programme includes a fair sprinkling of novelties, not least a rare excerpt from Britten's *Gloriana*. In a programme as long as this (approaching five hours of music) there are bound to be minor vocal flaws, but they are surprisingly few, and vocally the performances are amazingly consistent. A feast of opera, very well ordered – each disc makes a satisfying solo recital.

'The essential Leontyne Price'

Discs 1–2: *'Her greatest opera roles'*: Arias from: VERDI: *Aida; Il trovatore; Ernani; La forza del destino*. MOZART: *Così fan tutte Don Giovanni*. PUCCINI: *Madama Butterfly; Tosca; Manon Lescaut; Turandot*. POULENC: *Dialogue des Carmélites*. R. STRAUSS: *Ariadne auf Naxos*. BARBER: *Antony and Cleopatra*.

Discs 3–4: *'Great opera scenes'* from: VERDI: *Otello; Macbeth; Don Carlo*. BEETHOVEN: *Fidelio*. PUCCINI: *Suor Angelica; La Rondine; La Bohème*. BIZET: *Carmen*. VERDI: *La Traviata*. MOZART: *Le nozze di Figaro*. R. STRAUSS: *Die ägyptische Helena; Salome; Die Frau ohne Schatten*. TCHAIKOVSKY: *Eugene Onegin*. BARBER: *Vanessa*. MASSENET: *Manon*. PURCELL: *Dido and Aeneas*.

Discs 5–6: *'Leontyne Price and Friends'*: Excerpts from: VERDI: *Otello; Aida* (with Plácido Domingo; Sherrill Milnes; Marilyn Horne); *Un ballo in maschera; Ernani* (both with Carlo Bergonzi); *Requiem* (with Janet Baker); *Il Trovatore* (with Milnes). MOZART: *Così fan tutte* (with Horne; Tatiana Troyanos). BELLINI: *Norma*. PUCCINI: *Madama Butterfly* (both with Horne). GERSHWIN: *Porgy and Bess* (with William Warfield). BIZET: *Carmen* (with Franco Corelli).

Discs 7–8: *'Leontyne Price in song'*: BERLIOZ: *Nuits d'été*. R. STRAUSS: *Vier letzte Lieder*. FAURE: *Clair de lune; Notre amour; Au cimetière; Au bord de l'eau; Mandoline*. POULENC: *Main dominée par le coeur. Miroirs brûlants: Je nommerai ton front; Tu vois le feu du soir. Ce doux petit visage*. BARBER: *Knoxville, Summer of 1915*. SCHUMANN: *Frauenliebe und -leben, Op. 42; Widmung (Myrthen); Mignon; Volksliedchen; Schöne Wiege meiner Leiden; Er ist's; Heiss mich nicht reden; Lust der Sturmnacht*. R. STRAUSS: *Allerseelen; Schlagendes Herzen; Freundliche Vision; Wie sollten wir geheim*. WOLF: *Der Gärtner; Lebe wohl; Morgentau; Geh, Geliebter, geh jetzt*.

Discs 9–10: *'Spirituals, hymns, & Sacred songs': Ev'ry time I feel the spirit; Let us break bread together; His name so sweet; 'Round about de mountain; Swing low, sweet chariot; Sit down, servant; He's got the whole world in his hands; Deep river; My soul's been anchored in de Lord; On ma journey; A city called Heaven; Ride on, King Jesus; I wish I knew how it would feel to be free; Sinner, please don't let this harvest pass; Sweet little Jesus boy; There is a Balm in Gilead; Let us cheer the weary traveller; Ev'ry time I feel the spirit; My way is cloudy; Nobody knows the trouble I've seen; I couldn't hear nobody pray*. DYKES: *Holy, holy, holy; Lead kindly light*. KNAPP: *Blessed assurance*. SCHUBERT: *Ave Maria*. CONVERSE: *What a friend we have in Jesus*. TRAD.: *Amazing grace; Fairest Lord Jesus; I wonder as I wander*. MALOTTE: *The Lord's prayer*. DOANE: *Pass me not, O gentle Saviour*. Samuel S. WESLEY: *The Church's one foundation*. BRAHE: *Bless this house*. LOWRY: *I need Thee every hour*. BACH/GOUNOD: *Ave Maria*. GERSHWIN: *Porgy and Bess: Summertime*. WARD: *America the beautiful*. JOHNSON: *Lift ev'ry voice and sing*. LUTHER: *A mighty fortress is our God*. HOWE: *Battle hymn of the Republic*.

Disc 11: *'In recital and Interview'*: BRAHMS: *Zigeunerlieder, Op. 103*. CILEA: *Adriana Lecouvreur: Io son l'umile ancella*. TRAD.: *This little light of mine*. Interview with John Pfeiffer (recorded in April 1995).
(M) *** RCA 09026 68153-2 (11) [id.].

'The essential Leontyne Price': Arias and excerpts from: VERDI: *La forza del destino; Il Trovatore; Otello* (with Plácido Domingo). PUCCINI: *Madama Butterfly; La Rondine*. BIZET: *Carmen*. MOZART: *Così fan tutte* (with Marilyn Horne). Songs: BERLIOZ: *Nuits d'été: Absence*. R. STRAUSS: *Vier Letzte Lieder: Beim Schlafengehen*. MALOTTE: *The Lord's prayer*. GERSHWIN: *Porgy and Bess: Summertime. Spiritual: Swing low sweet chariot; Ride on King Jesus*.
(M) *** RCA 09026 68152-2 [id.].

To celebrate the seventieth birthday in February 1997 of this commanding American soprano, RCA have compiled this formidable collection of 11 discs, presenting them in the most extravagant format, with a fully bound, well-illustrated book – including full texts – to match a substantial album in similar format containing the discs. The presentation is among the most impressive we have seen since the coming of CD, and the choice of items lives up to its lavishness, with the first two discs devoted to Price's 'Greatest opera roles', mainly of Mozart, Verdi, Puccini and Strauss, but also including the role of the heroine in Barber's *Antony and Cleopatra*, specially written for her. The next two discs containing 'Great opera scenes' range wider still, concentrating on the same composers but also including unexpected items from Purcell's *Dido and Aeneas* and Tchaikovsky's *Eugene Onegin*. The two discs, 'Price and friends', have her in duet with such artists as Carlo Bergonzi, Franco Corelli, Plácido Domingo, Dame Janet Baker and her one-time husband, William Warfield. The two discs of song then include such substantial items as Barber's *Knoxville* – one of her most magical recordings – Schumann's *Frauenliebe*, Strauss's *Four Last songs* and Berlioz's *Les nuits d'été*. Spirituals, hymns and sacred songs make up the next two discs, leaving a final one of miscellaneous items, Brahms's *Zigeunerlieder*, and the heroine's artistic credo from Cilea's *Adriana Lecouvreur*, all rounded off with an interview conducted by the late John Pfeiffer who master-minded the whole presentation just before he died.

What this rich collection repeatedly brings home is the glorious consistency of Price in her singing over the longest period, with barely any signs of wear in the voice even in the later recordings, and with every note firmly and surely in place, with golden tone pouring forth. There may be some operatic roles which she personally did not enjoy – Verdi's Lady Macbeth for one, as she makes clear in her interview – but the quality of her singing was seldom impaired. It is good too to have it brought home how wide her sympathies have been, readily encompassing such genres as German Lieder. A timely summary of a great career, with a well-chosen sampler disc for those not wanting to stretch to the whole survey. This single CD, however, does not include translations.

Ramey, Samuel (bass)

'Grandi voci': Arias from: MOZART: *Le nozze di Figaro*. HANDEL: *Rodelinda*. DONIZETTI: *Anna Bolena*. VERDI: *I masnadieri; Macbeth*. BELLINI: *Norma*. STRAVINSKY: *The Rake's progress*. WEILL: *Street scene*. arr. COPLAND: *Old American songs – Set No. 1*.
(M) *** Decca Dig. 448 251-2.

Instead of centring on a studio recital, Decca's 'Grandi Voci' collection celebrating the achievement of Samuel Ramey selects excerpts from various complete recordings in which he has participated with distinction during the 1980s, beginning with excerpts from Solti's sparkling *Nozze di Figaro* (in which he took the name-role with distinction, making Figaro a more romantic figure than usual) and ending with his fine set of Copland's *Old American songs*, recorded with Warren Jones in 1990. With consistently vivid Decca sound, this gives a rounded picture of one of the finest basses of our time, whose range was remarkable.

Rolfe Johnson, Anthony (tenor), **David Willison** (piano)

English songs: VAUGHAN WILLIAMS: *Songs of travel*. BUTTERWORTH: *A Shropshire Lad*. IRELAND: *The land of lost content*. GURNEY: *Down by the Salley Gardens; An Epitaph; Desire in spring; Black Stitchel*. WARLOCK: *My own country; Passing by; Pretty ring time*.
(B) *** Carlton 30367 02032 [(M) id. import].

It would be hard to design a better programme of twentieth-century English songs than this, providing one accepts the omission of Britten, and it is a surprise to discover that this nearly-70-minutes-long programme derives from two (Polygram) Polydor LPs from the mid-1970s. At that time this label was not exactly famous for this kind of repertoire but there is hidden treasure here. The performances of the Vaughan Williams and Butterworth cycles are full of life and colour (and are splendidly accompanied), and it is especially good to have the far lesser-known Gurney songs. The recordings have transferred well. A bargain.

Royal Opera House, Covent Garden

Royal Opera House Covent Garden (An early history on record). Singers included are: Melba, Caruso, Tetrazzini, McCormack, Destin, Gadski, Schorr, Turner, Zanelli, Lehmann, Schumann, Olczewska, Chaliapin, Gigli, Supervia, Tibbett, Tauber, Flagstad, Melchior. Arias from: GOUNOD: *Faust*. VERDI: *Rigoletto, Otello*. DONIZETTI: *Lucia di Lammermoor*. VERDI: *La Traviata*. PUCCINI: *Madama Butterfly; Tosca*. WAGNER: *Götterdämmerung; Die Meistersinger; Tristan und Isolde*. R. STRAUSS: *Der Rosenkavalier*. MUSSORGSKY: *Boris Godunov*. GIORDANO: *Andrea Chénier*. BIZET: *Carmen*. MOZART: *Don Giovanni*.
(M) (***) Nimbus mono NI 7819 [id.].

Nimbus's survey of great singers at Covent Garden ranges from Caruso's 1904 recording of *Questa o quella* from *Rigoletto* to the recording of the second half of the *Tristan* love duet, which Kirsten Flagstad and Lauritz Melchior made in San Francisco in November 1939, a magnificent recording, never issued in Britain and little known, which repeated the partnership initiated during the 1937 Coronation season at Covent Garden. The Vienna recording of the *Rosenkavalier* Trio with Lehmann, Schumann and Olczewska similarly reproduces a classic partnership at Covent Garden, while Chaliapin's 1928 recording of the *Prayer* and *Death of Boris* was actually recorded live at Covent Garden, with the transfer giving an amazingly vivid sense of presence. Those who like Nimbus's acoustic method of transfer will enjoy the whole disc, though the reverberation round some of the early offerings – like the very first, Melba's *Jewel song* from *Faust* – is cavernous. Particularly interesting is the 1909 recording of part of Brünnhilde's Immolation scene, with Johanna Gadski commandingly strong.

Russian opera: 'The splendours of Russian opera'

'The splendours of Russian opera': GLINKA: *Overture: Ruslan and Ludmilla.* BORODIN: *Prince Igor: Polovtsian dances* (with London Symphony Chorus; both LSO, Solti); *Galitzky's aria.* RIMSKY-KORSAKOV: *Sadko: Song of the Viking Guest.* RACHMANINOV: *Aleko: Aleko's cavatina* (all three, Nicolai Ghiaurov). TCHAIKOVSKY: *Eugene Onegin: Tatiana's letter scene* (Teresa Kubiak); *Entr'acte and Waltz scene* (Soloists, ROHCG Ch. & O, Solti). *The Maid of Orleans: Farewell to the forests* (Regina Resnik). MUSSORGSKY: *Boris Godunov: Coronation scene* (Ghiaurov, V. State Op. Ch., VPO, Karajan).
(M) **(*) Decca 458 216-2 [id.].

Issued at the same time as Decca's outstanding Baroque opera collection, this Russian compilation cannot match it, either in imaginative choice of items (here rather predictable) or in the consistent excellence of the performances. Solti opens the proceedings with his famous dashing account of the *Ruslan and Ludmilla* overture (although the transfer isn't very glamorous), and Ghiaurov's three arias certainly show the richness of his magnificent voice. But it is Teresa Kubiak's memorable account of *Tatiana's letter scene* from *Eugene Onegin* that is the highlight of the concert, and this is neatly linked to the opera's Waltz scene by the *Entr'acte* based on Tatiana's music. It is good also to have Regina Resnik's fine Farewell aria from *The Maid of Orleans* (which musically has much in common with *Eugene Onegin*). But the present transfer of the choral Coronation scene from *Boris Godunov* seems to have lost some of the rich amplitude of Karajan's 1970 complete recording from which it is taken. As with the rest of Decca's current Opera Gala releases, the presentation is attractive, and full translations are included.

Schipa, Tito (tenor)

'Prima voce': Arias from: MASCAGNI: *Cavalleria Rusticana. L'amico Fritz.* VERDI: *Rigoletto; Luisa Miller.* DONIZETTI: *Lucia di Lammermoor; Don Pasquale; L'elisir d'amore.* LEONCAVALLO: *Pagliacci.* MASSENET: *Manon; Werther.* ROSSINI: *Il barbiere di Siviglia.* THOMAS: *Mignon.* FLOTOW: *Martha.* CILEA: *L'Arlesiana.*
(M) (***) Nimbus mono NI 7813 [id.].

The first nine items on this well-chosen selection of Schipa's recordings date from the pre-electric era. The voice is totally consistent, heady and light and perfectly controlled, between the *Siciliana* from Mascagni's *Cavalleria*, recorded with piano in 1913, to the incomparable account of more Mascagni, the *Cherry duet* from *L'amico Fritz*, made with Mafalda Favero in 1937. It says much for his art that Schipa's career continued at full strength for decades after that. The Nimbus transfers put the voice at a slight distance, with the electrical recordings made to sound the more natural.

Schmidt, Joseph (tenor)

Complete EMI recordings: Arias (sung in German) from: MEYERBEER: *L'africaine.* FLOTOW: *Martha; Alessandro Stradella.* KIENZL: *Der Evangelimann.* KORNGOLD: *Die tote Stadt.* ADAM: *Der Postillon von Longjumeau.* MASSENET: *Manon; Der Cid.* TCHAIKOVSKY: *Eugene Onegin.* MORY: *La Vallière.* GOTZE: *Der Page des Königs.* Johann STRAUSS Jr: *1001 Nacht; Der Zigeunerbaron; Simplicus.* LEHAR: *Zigeunerliebe.* TAUBER: *Der Singende Traume.* DONIZETTI: *Der Liebestrank (L'elisir d'amore).* VERDI: *Rigoletto; Der Troubadour (Il trovatore).* LEONCAVALLO: *Der Bajazzo (Pagliacci).* PUCCINI: *La Bohème; Tosca; Das Mädchen aus dem Goldenen Westen (Fanciulla del West); Turandot.* SERRANO: *El Trust de Los Tenorios.* SPOLIANSKY: *Das Lied einer Nacht* (film). Lieder & Songs: SCHUBERT: *Ständchen;*

Ungeduld. BENATZKY: *Wenn du treulos bist*. NIEDERBERGER: *Buona notte, schöne Signorina*. LEONCAVALLO: *Morgenständchen*. LABRIOLA: *Serenata*. BISCARDI: *L'ariatella*. DENZA: *Funiculì, funiculà*. BUZZI-PECCIA: *Lolita*. DI CAPUA: *O sole mio*.
(M) (***) EMI mono CHS7 64676-2 (2) [id.].

Joseph Schmidt, born in 1904 in what is now Romania, studied in Berlin, and developed what by any standards is one of the most beautiful German tenor voices ever recorded, less distinctive than that of Richard Tauber, but even more consistently honeyed and velvety in the upper registers, exceptionally free on top, so that the stratospheric top notes in *Le Postillon de Longjumeau* have never sounded so beautiful and unstrained. This is the ideal lyric tenor voice, not just for the German repertory, including operetta, but for the Italian; it was tragic that, standing less than five foot high, he was precluded from having an operatic career. Nevertheless, he was most successful in his concert work as well as in his recording career, as this glowing collection demonstrates. He even had a brilliantly successful American tour in 1937; but sadly, as a Jew, he got caught up in Europe during the Second World War, and died from a chest complaint in a Swiss refugee camp in 1942. The records – with informative notes – make a superb memorial, here at last given full prominence in excellent transfers.

The Scholars of London

French chansons: JOSQUIN: *Faute d'argent; Mille regretz*. JANNEQUIN: *Le chant des oiseaux; Or vien ça*. SANDRIN: *Je ne le croy*. GOMBERT: *Aime qui vouldra; Quand je suis aupres*. SERMISY: *Tant que vivrai; Venez regrets; La, la, maistre Pierre*. ARCADELT: *En ce mois délicieux; Margot, labourez les vignes; Du temps que j'estois amoureux; Sa grand beauté*. TABOUROT: *Belle qui tiens ma vie*. VASSAL: *Vray Dieu*. CLEMENS: *Prière devant le repas; Action des Graces*. PASSEREAU: *Il est bel et bon*. LE JEUNE: *Ce n'est que fiel*. LASSUS: *Bonjour mon coeur; Si je suis brun; Beau le cristal; La nuit froide; Un jeune moine*. BERTRAND: *De nuit, le bien*. COSTELY: *Arrête un peu mon coeur*.
(BB) *** Naxos Dig. 8.550880 [id.].

This disc offers a representative selection from the thousands of sixteenth-century French polyphonic chansons, and ranges from the devotional to the amorous, the bawdy and the bucolic. It includes some of the best known, such as the ubiquitous Jannequin *Le chant des oiseaux*, and features such familiar masters as Josquin, Sermisy and Claude Le Jeune. It encompasses Flemish masters writing in the language such as Gombert and Lassus. The Scholars of London are expressive and persuasive guides in this repertoire and are decently recorded at St Silas the Martyr in Kentish Town. There is an all-too-short but thoughtful introduction, and the booklet then reproduces texts and translations. What more can you ask from a disc that would undoubtedly cost less than admission to a concert plus the programme?

Schumann-Heink, Ernestine (contralto)

'Prima voce': Arias from: DONIZETTI: *Lucrezia Borgia*. MEYERBEER: *Le Prophète*. WAGNER: *Das Rheingold; Rienzi; Götterdämmerung*. HANDEL: *Rinaldo*. Songs by: ARDITTI; BECKER; SCHUBERT; WAGNER; REIMANN; MOLLOY; BRAHMS; BOEHM; TRAD.
(M) (***) Nimbus mono NI 7811 [id.].

Ernestine Schumann-Heink was a formidable personality in the musical life of her time, notably in New York, as well as a great singer. 'I am looking for my successor,' she is reported as saying well before she retired, adding, 'She must be *the* contralto.' Schumann-Heink combines to an astonishing degree a full contralto weight and richness with the most delicate flexibility, as in the *Brindisi* from Donizetti's *Lucrezia Borgia*. This wide-ranging collection, resonantly transferred by the Nimbus acoustic method, presents a vivid portrait of a very great singer.

Schwarzkopf, Dame Elisabeth (soprano)

'Diva': Arias from: MOZART: *Nozze di Figaro; Don Giovanni; Così fan tutte*. BEETHOVEN: *Fidelio*. WEBER: *Der Freischütz*. WAGNER: *Lohengrin*. SMETANA: *The Bartered Bride*. R. STRAUSS: *Der Rosenkavalier; Ariadne auf Naxos; Arabella*. HEUBERGER: *Der Opernball*. Johann STRAUSS Jr: *Die Fledermaus*.
(M) *** EMI stereo/mono CDM5 65577-2 [id.].

This single CD in EMI's 'Diva' series offers an excellent and shrewdly selected survey of Schwarzkopf's opera and operetta recordings. Mozart is very well represented, with Schwarzkopf as both Susanna and the Countess in *Figaro*, as Donna Elvira in *Don Giovanni* (from the masterly Giulini recording) and as

Fiordiligi in *Così fan tutte* (commanding in *Come scoglio* under Boehm). From Richard Strauss there is not only the Marschallin's monologue (from the Karajan recording of *Rosenkavalier*) but also Ariadne's lament and Arabella's final solo, another of her most compelling Strauss performances. Immaculate accounts of Weber (Agathe's *Leise, leise* from *Freischütz*) and of Wagner (Elsa's Dream from *Lohengrin*) have been drawn from one of the finest of all her discs, with Heuberger's *Im chambre séparée* as an enchanting operetta tailpiece. Excellent transfers.

'Schwarzkopf Songbook' (with Gerald Moore, Geoffrey Parsons, Nicolas Medtner, Cyril Skalkiewicz (piano)): MOZART: *Warnung; Der Zauberer; Das Veilchen; Der Zauberer.* SCHUBERT: *Ungeduld; Liebe schwärmt.* MENDELSSOHN: *Auf Flügeln des Gesanges.* SCHUMANN: *6 Lieder from Liederkreis, Op. 39; Aufträge; Widmung.* LISZT: *Die drei Zigeuner.* BRAHMS: *Vergebliches Ständchen; Immer leiser; Wie Melodien; Der Jäger; Liebestreu; Ständchen.* JENSEN: *Murmelndes Lüftchen.* MAHLER: *Lob des hohen Verstandes.* R. STRAUSS: *Ach, was Kummer; Wer lieben will; 3 Ophelia Lieder.* WOLF: *25 Lieder from the Italienisches Liederbuch; 8 Goethe Lieder; 4 Mörike Lieder; Keine gleicht von allen Schönen; Wienlied (Im Sommer); Mausfallensprüchlein; In dem Schatten meiner Locken.* GRIEG: *Farmyard song; Ich liebe dich; Mit einer Wasserlilie; Letzter Frühling; Erstes Begegnen; Zu Rosenzeit; Mit einer Primula veris; Lauf der Welt.* DVORAK: *Songs my mother taught me.* TCHAIKOVSKY: *Nur wer die Sehnsucht kennt.* MUSSORGSKY: *In den Pilzen.* MEDTNER: *The muse; The rose; The waltz; When roses fade; 7 Goethe Lieder; Praeludium; Winternacht; Die Quelle.* SIBELIUS: *Die Echo-Nymph; Der Norden; Hundert Wege; Schiff, Schiff, säusle; Der Kuss; Der erste Kuss; War es ein Traum?; Schwarze Rosen.*
(M) *** EMI (SIS) mono/stereo CHS5 65860-2 (3) [CDHC 65860].

Issued to celebrate Schwarzkopf's eightieth birthday in December 1995, these three discs offer many rarities selected from many different periods in her career. So the second of the three, devoted entirely to Wolf, has 25 songs from the *Italian Songbook* in the mono recordings she made in 1959, four more than she contributed to the joint recording of that cycle, much better known, which she made with Fischer-Dieskau ten years later. These earlier examples are more intimate and often more intense. The Mozart song recordings range from a girlish account of *Warnung*, recorded in 1947, and of *Der Zauberer*, recorded in 1951, to a 1970 recording of that second song, warmer, more positive and with more detail. Similarly in the Schumann selection, a 1951 recording of *Aufträge* is set against six songs from the Opus 39 *Liederkreis*, recorded as late as 1974. Brahms is generously represented, mainly from 1970 sessions, with an alternative version of *Vergebliches Ständchen* from 1954, lighter and fresher if less dramatic. Liszt's *Three gypsies* prompt aptly throaty tone, while a song by Adolf Jensen brings one of the loveliest performances of all. The first disc is rounded off with a Strauss group, including a previously unpublished radio recording of the Ophelia songs, compellingly characterized. The third disc is devoted to songs outside the German repertory, mainly done in German, as for example the eight Grieg songs. Medtner is the accompanist in 11 of his own tenderly lyrical songs, while the greatest treasure of all is the final group of eight Sibelius songs, recorded live in 1955 by Finnish Radio in inspired performances, never previously published.

'Encores' (with Gerald Moore or Geoffrey Parsons): BACH: *Bist du bei mir.* GLUCK: *Einem Bach der fliesst.* BEETHOVEN: *Wonne der Wehmut.* LOEWE: *Kleiner Haushalt.* WAGNER: *Träume.* BRAHMS: *Ständchen; 3 Deutsche Volkslieder.* MAHLER: *Um schlimme Kinder artig zu machen; Ich atmet' einen linden Duft; Des Antonius von Padua Fischpredigt.* TCHAIKOVSKY: *Pimpernella.* arr. WOLF-FERRARI: *7 Italian songs.* MARTINI: *Plaisir d'amour.* HAHN: *Si mes vers avaient des ailes.* DEBUSSY: *Mandoline.* arr. QUILTER: *Drink to me only with thine eyes.* ARNE: *When daisies pied; Where the bee sucks.* arr. GUND: *3 Swiss folk songs.* arr. WEATHERLY: *Danny Boy.* J. STRAUSS, Jnr: *Frühlingsstimmen* (with VPO, Joseph Krips).
(M) *** EMI stereo/mono CDM7 63654-2.

Schwarzkopf herself has on occasion nominated this charming account of *Danny Boy* as her own favourite recording of her singing, but it is only one of a whole sequence of lightweight songs which vividly capture the charm and intensity that made her recitals so memorable, particularly in the extra items at the end. As a rule she would announce and explain each beforehand, adding to the magic. The range here is wide, from Bach's heavenly *Bist du bei mir* to the innocent lilt of the Swiss folksong, *Gsätzli*, and Strauss's *Voices of spring.*

'Unpublished recordings' (with (i) Philh. O, Thurston Dart; (ii) Kathleen Ferrier, VPO, Karajan; (iii) Philh. O, Galliera; (iv) Walter Gieseking, Philh. O, Karajan): J. S. BACH: (i) *Cantata No. 199: Mein Herze schwimmt im Blut: Auf diese Schmerzens Reu; Doch Gott muss mir genädig sein; Mein Herze schwimmt im Blut.* (ii) *Mass in B min.: Christe eleison; Et in unum Dominum; Laudamus te.* (iii) MOZART: *Nehmt meinen Dank, K.383.* (iv) GIESEKING: *Kinderlieder.* R. STRAUSS: *4 Last songs.*
(M) (**(*)) EMI CDM7 63655-2.

Long-buried treasure here includes Bach duets with Kathleen Ferrier conducted by Karajan, a collection of charming children's songs by Gieseking, recorded almost impromptu, and, best of all, a live performance of Strauss's *Four Last songs* given under Karajan at the Festival Hall in 1956, a vintage year for Schwarzkopf. Sound quality varies, but the voice is gloriously caught.

'Lieder recital' (with Gerald Moore, piano): BACH: *Bist du bei mir*. PERGOLESI: *Se tu m'ami, se tu sospiri*. HANDEL: *Atalanta: Care selve*. GLUCK: *Die Pilger von Mekka: Einam Bach der fliesst*. BEETHOVEN: *Wonne de Wehmut*. SCHUBERT: *An Sylvia; Romanze aus Rosamunde; Die Vögel; Der Einsame; Vedi quanto adoro*. WOLF: *Kennst du das Land; Philine; Nachtzauber; Die Zigeunerin*. Richard STRAUSS: *Ruhe meine Seele; Wiegenlied; Schlechters Wetter; Hat's gesang, bleibt's nicht dabei*. Encores: MOZART: *Warnung*. SCHUMANN: *Der Nüssbaum*. SCHUBERT: *Ungeduld*.
(M) (**(*)) EMI mono CDH5 66084-2.

Schwarzkopf's 1956 Salzburg recital with Gerald Moore is the third to have appeared on CD, more varied than the earlier two, another great occasion caught on the wing. It ranges from Bach and Handel arias, expansive and poised, through a Schubert-like Gluck song and rare Beethoven to Schwarzkopf's regular repertory of Schubert, Wolf and Strauss, delectably done. Wolf's *Kennst du das Land*, greatest of all Lieder for a woman, here comes not as a climax but at the start of a group, building up with biting intensity. No texts are provided.

Sciutti, Graziella (soprano)

'The early years' (with (i) VSO, Moralt; (ii) LOP, Dervaux; (iii) Jaqueline Bonneau, piano): Excerpts from (i) MOZART: *Così fan tutte; Don Giovanni*. (ii) BELLINI: *La Sonnambula; I Puritani*. DONIZETTI: *Don Pasquale; Linda di Chamounix*. ROSSINI: *Semiramide*. (iii) FAURE: *Rencontre; Toujours; Adieu*. RAVEL: *5 Mélodies populaires grecques*. DEBUSSY: *Ariettes oubliées*.
(M) (**) Ph. mono 442 750-2.

Graziella Sciutti, a singer of great charm, made a later, Decca stereo recital, which showed off her vocal talents much more effectively than this Philips collection. Easily the most impressive items here are the Mozart arias, taken from Moralt's 1956 mono set of *Così fan tutte* in which her Despina shone out from the rest of the cast. She proves a no less charming Zerlina in *Don Giovanni*, recorded the previous year, when, apart from her two solos, she joins with George London in *Là ci darem la mano*. The other arias come from an earlier (1953) mono recital, where she proves not well suited to the Bellini arias but sounds nearer her best as *Linda di Chamounix* and (especially) *Semiramide*, where the touch of flutter in her timbre adds to the vocal character. The French song-recital is transferred from an LP pressing, as the master tape has become lost or degraded, and here the highlight is the *Cinq mélodies populaires grecques*, in which she sings with great charm.

Shirley-Quirk, John (baritone)

'A Recital of English songs' (with Martin Isepp (harpsichord and piano), Nona Liddell and Ivor McMahon (violins), Ambrose Gauntlett (viola da gamba)): PURCELL: *Man is for woman made; Music for a while; 'Twas within a furlong of Edinborough Town; Cantata: When night her purple veil* (arr. BRITTEN). HUMFREY: *A hymne to God the Father*. BUTTERWORTH: *A Shropshire lad* (song-cycle). MOERAN: *Three songs from Ludlow Town*.
(M) *** Saga EC 3336-2 [id.].

A splendid collection of seventeenth- and twentieth-century English songs, with John Shirley-Quirk at his finest. The Housman settings by Butterworth and Moeran are particularly affecting in their lyrical directness. The Purcell and Humfrey items too are very well done, with stylish accompaniment. The recording is not as clean as it might be, but it is acceptable at the price. There is little hint of its age in the presentation, the only date mentioned being 1996.

'Songs of travel' (with Viola Tunnard): VAUGHAN WILLIAMS: *Songs of travel; Linden Lea; Silent noon*. IRELAND: *Sea fever*. STANFORD: *Drake's drum; The Old Superb*. KEEL: *Trade winds*. WARLOCK: *Captain Stratton's fancy*.
(M) *** Saga EC 3338-2 [id.].

With really sensitive singing, John Shirley-Quirk makes it abundantly clear how completely the best of British songs stand comparison with the mainstream of German Lieder. Some of the Vaughan Williams cycle (like *The Roadside Fire*) have a freshness and simplicity that put them close to Schubert, and this complete recording includes an epilogue written with the other songs in the early years of the century but kept in a drawer for years and published only after the composer's death. The other items are among the best known of all British songs. Some of them might be described as school songs, but Shirley-Quirk's singing turns a simple but beautifully wrought song like Keel's *Trade winds* into something extraordinarily moving, while Stanford's *The Old Superb* is unforgettable in its rumbustious vigour. The recording, over 30 years old, is marginally a little restricted in the treble, but the overall effect is most convincing. The name of the accompanist is mis-spelt on the CD and in the notes, which include such gems as '. . . the cycle, full of music as youthfull, frech and beautifull as on the day it was written . . .' Only the year 1996 is mentioned as a date of publication. But this is an unmissable disc.

Simoneau, Léopold (tenor), Pierrette Alarie (soprano)

'The early years': Arias and duets from: MOZART: *Idomeneo; Don Giovanni; Così fan tutte; La clemenza di Tito* (with VPO, Paumgartner). VERDI: *La Traviata* (with Maria Moralès, LOP, Dervaux). GOUNOD: *Roméo et Juliette; Mireille.* THOMAS: *Mignon.* BIZET: *Les pêcheurs de perles.* OFFENBACH: *Les contes d'Hoffman.* BIZET: *Carmen.* DELIBES: *Lakmé* (with LOP, Dervaux or Jouve).
(M) (***) Ph. mono 438 953-2 (2).

The Canadian-born Léopold Simoneau made his début during the war as Hadji in *Lakmé*, excerpts from which are the highlights on the present set. After appearing at New York, he sang at the Opéra-Comique in 1949 in Gounod's *Mireille* and remained in Europe to establish a reputation at Glyndebourne and Aix-en-Provence as a great Mozart interpreter. He married the soprano Pierrette Alarie in 1946 and the musical fruits of their partnership can be sampled here. All these recordings come from 1953–4, and some have not been available in the UK before. Simoneau's phrasing has a seamless elegance and his tone a sweet, lustrous quality that is quite special. His Mozart is handicapped by some pedestrian accompanying by Paumgartner and the Vienna orchestra, but his singing is pretty flawless. The recordings occasionally show signs of discoloration, but the overall quality is good for its age. The Bizet and Gounod arias and duets are well nigh perfect.

The Sixteen, Harry Christophers

'Gloria': VIVALDI: *Gloria in D, RV 589: Gloria.* BACH: *Magnificat in D, BWV 243: Magnificat. Mass in B min.: Gloria; Et in terra pax. Cantata No. 147: Jesu, joy of man's desiring.* CALDARA: *Stabat Mater: Virgo Virginium. Crucifixus à 16.* TAVENER: *The Lamb.* BRITTEN: *Hymn to the Virgin.* LOTTI: *Crucifixus à 8.* ALLEGRI: *Miserere.* BARBER: *Agnus Dei.* TIPPETT: *A Child of our Time: Spiritus: Deep river.* HANDEL: *Samson: Let the bright seraphim.*
(B) **(*) Collins Dig. 1605-2 [id.].

Although this is essentially a sampler, the excerpts all stand up well independently and the 58-minute programme as a whole works admirably in demonstrating the freshness of approach of Harry Christophers and his Sixteen to the wide range of music here. Highlights include Barber's *Agnus Dei* (a choral transcription of his famous *Adagio for strings*) which is radiantly done, Allegri's *Miserere*, with its confident treble soloist, a lively *Jesu, joy of man's desiring* and the lovely spiritual from Tippett's *A Child of our Time*. The drawback is the lack of documentation (apart from the list of full-priced Collins discs from which these excerpts are taken); the exultant soprano soloist in the closing *Let the bright seraphim* (almost certainly Lynne Dawson) from Handel's *Solomon* isn't even named.

The Christmas collection

'A Traditional Christmas collection': The First Nowell; Once in royal David's city; The Sussex carol; While shepherds watched their flocks by night; I saw three ships; Angels from the realms of glory; O little town of Bethlehem; Silent night; Away in a manger; Rocking; In dulci jubilo; Ding dong merrily on high; In the bleak midwinter; Good King Wenceslas; Deck the halls with boughs of holly; The Holly and the ivy; God rest you merry, gentlemen; See amid the winter's snow; Coventry carol; O come all ye faithful; Hark the herald angels sing.

'An Early English Christmas collection': Verbum caro (plainchant); Salutation carol; Nowell sing we, both all and some; Gaudete; Hail Mary full of grace; Gloria in excelsis; There is no rose; Nowell, nowell: Out of your sleep; Remember O thou man; Quid petis, o fili?; Sweet was the song the virgin sang; Lullaby my sweet little babe; Ave rex angelorum; Drive the cold winter away; Nowell, nowell: The Boares head; The Old year now has passed away; Angelus ad virginem; Nowell, nowell: Dieu vous garde; Make we joy; Verbum caro.

'A Twentieth-century Christmas collection: WALTON: *Make we joy now in this fest.* LEIGHTON: *Coventry carol.* FRICKER: *A Babe is born.* RUBBRA: *The Virgin's cradle song.* BRITTEN: *A Hymn to the Virgin.* TAVENER: *The Lamb.* MAXWELL DAVIES: *O magnum mysterium.* HOWELLS: *Sing lullaby; A Spotless rose.* Peter HAYWARD: *Lute book lullaby.* WARLOCK: *Corpus Christi; Balulalow; Benedicamus Domino.* John GARDINER: *Tomorrow shall be my dancing day.*
(M) **(*) Collins Dig. 7045-2 (3) [id.].

With the help of splendidly stylish and always sympathetic singing from The Sixteen, this Collins box surveys the widest range of Christmas music in three distinct collections. Early medieval carols were often joyous song-dances, with the vigour of the dance more important to the participants than the melody. *The Salutation carol* is a fine monodic example, while the Northern European *Audate*, with its infectious cross-rhythms, and the rousing *Nowell, nowell: Out of your sleep* are hardly less enthusiastic. But of course there are lyrical carols too, notably *There is no rose*, while the works of Sheppard included here (*Gloria in excelsis*, *Verbum caro*) and Byrd's *Lullaby my sweet little babe* are spiritually serene. The performances could hardly be bettered, rich in sonority and feeling, and always aptly paced.

The traditional collection is also beautifully sung, the style laid back and atmospheric, ideal for late in the evening of Christmas Day. Few favourites are missing. When one turns to the modern carols, there are plenty of well-chosen examples: by Howells, Walton, Rubbra, Britten, John Tavener and especially Peter Warlock, to reassure any doubter that present-day carol composition has not diminished in quality. What is more controversial is the inclusion of Peter Maxwell Davies's *O magnum mysterium*, in which the sung carols are vibrantly fresh, but the instrumental pieces are uninvitingly avant-garde, almost to the ultimate degree. With a CD player one can of course programme them out if one wishes. Again the performances are first class, and so is the recording.

Sopranos

'Great sopranos of our time' ((i) Scotto; (ii) Schwarzkopf; (iii) Sutherland; (iv) Gruberová; (v) De los Angeles; (vi) Freni; (vii) Callas; (viii) Cotrubas; (ix) Caballé): (i) PUCCINI: *Madama Butterfly: Un bel dì.* (vi) *La Bohème: Sì, mi chiamano Mimì.* (ii) MOZART: *Così fan tutte: Come scoglio.* (iii) *Don Giovanni: Troppo mi spiace . . . Non mi dir.* (iv) DELIBES: *Lakmé: Bell song.* (v) ROSSINI: *Il barbiere di Siviglia: Una voce poco fa.* (vii) DONIZETTI: *Lucia di Lammermoor: Sparsa è di rose . . . Il dolce suono . . . Spargi d'amaro.* (viii) BIZET: *Les Pêcheurs de perles: Comme autrefois.* (ix) VERDI: *Aida: Qui Radames . . . O patria mia.*
(B) *** EMI Eminence CD-EMX 9519 [(M) id. import].

An impressive collection, drawn from a wide variety of sources. It is good to have Schwarzkopf's commanding account of *Come scoglio*, not to mention the formidable contributions of Callas and the early Sutherland reading of *Non mi dir*, taken from Giulini's complete set of *Giovanni.* For the present reissue (under the same Eminence catalogue number) Gruberová's bravura account of the *Bell song* has been substituted for Nilsson's early recording of the key aria from Weber's *Oberon.* The CD transfers are bright and vivid, and this makes a fascinating mid-priced anthology.

Souzay, Gérard (baritone), Dalton Baldwin (piano)

Mélodies françaises: FAURE: *Chanson du pêcheur; Poème d'un jour, Op. 21; Les berceaux; Le secret; Aurore; Fleur jetée; La rose; Madrigal; 5 Mélodies de Venise, Op. 58; La bonne chanson, Op. 61; Le parfum impérissable; Arpège; Prison; Soir; Dans la forêt de septembre; La fleur qui va sur l'eau; Le don silencieux; La chanson d'Eve, Op. 95,* excerpts *(Eau vivante; O mort, poussière d'étoiles). Le jardin clos, Op. 106,* excerpts *(Exaucement; Je me poserai sur ton coeur). Mirages, Op. 113; L'horizon chimérique, Op. 118.* POULENC: *Chansons villageoises; Calligrammes; Le travail du peintre; La fraîcheur et le feu; Airs chantés: Air vif. La grenouillère; Métamorphoses: Reine des mouettes. Priez pour paix.* RAVEL: *5 Mélodies populaires grecques; Epigrammes de Clément Marot; Histoires naturelles; Chansons madécasses; 2 Mélodies hébraïques; Don Quichotte à Dulcinée; Les grands vents venus d'outre-mer; Sainte; Sur l'herbe.* LEGUERNEY: *20 Poèmes de la Pléiade,* excerpts (*Ma douce jouvence est passée; A son page).* HAHN: *L'heure exquise.* DUPARC: *L'invitation au voyage; Sérénade florentine; La vague et la cloche; Extase; Le manoir de Rosemonde; Lamento; La vie antérieure; Testament; Phidylé; Chanson triste; Elégie; Soupir.* GOUNOD: *L'absent; Sérénade.* CHABRIER: *Les cigales; Chanson pour Jeanne.* BIZET: *Chanson d'avril.* FRANCK: *Nocturne.* ROUSSEL: *Le jardin mouillé; Le bachelier de Salamanque.*
❀ (M) *** Ph. 438 964-2 (4).

Now here is something to make the pulse quicken: Gérard Souzay, recorded while still in his prime and in repertoire in which he was unmatched in his day. Only Bernac had as refined an interpretative intelligence and, of an older generation, only Panzera commanded an equal authority and tonal beauty. Souzay's 1963 recording of Fauré's *La bonne chanson* is one of the classics of the gramophone and has been extensively discussed in the *Stereo Record Guide* over the years. It was chosen by RL as one of his 'desert-island' discs in 'The Great Records' ('rich in artistry, imagination and insight'). The recording of the *Deux mélodies hébraïques* is captivating, though Souzay made an even more haunting version for French EMI in the late 1950s; and one is hard pressed to choose between his *Don Quichotte à Dulcinée* and those of Panzera and Bernac. After Souzay's Philips disc with *La bonne chanson* came further recordings of Fauré, an anthology of other French *mélodies* and an LP of the Duparc songs, in every way superior to his later, EMI re-make in the early 1970s. This is treasure-trove which no lover of the French repertoire should be without. It is as essential an acquisition for Souzay admirers as the Schumann *Dichterliebe* – see above, under the composer). Not everyone can afford four CDs all at one go, even at mid-price, and Philips would be wise to re-package the Fauré songs as part of their bargain Duo series, and issue the Duparc separately as well.

Stefano, Giuseppe di (tenor)

'Grandi voci': Arias and excerpts from: GIORDANO: *Andrea Chénier.* PUCCINI: *Tosca; Turandot.* MASSENET: *Werther; Manon.* BIZET: *Carmen; Les Pêcheurs de perles.* GOUNOD: *Faust.* DONIZETTI: *L'elisir d'amore.* PONCHIELLI: *La Gioconda.* VERDI: *La forza del destino.* BOITO: *Mefistofele* (with Cesare Siepi).
(M) *** Decca 440 403-2 [id.].

Flamboyance rarely goes with keen discipline. As Rudolf Bing (among others) has said, if those qualities had been matched in di Stefano, we should have had a tenor to rival Caruso. As it is, a cross-section taken from Decca recordings made between 1955 and 1959 gives a splendid idea not just of his beauty of voice but of his power to project character and feelings. But do not look for stylish restraint in *Una furtiva lagrima* – the tear is anything but furtive – and do not seek a French tenorissimo in *En fermant les yeux* from Massenet's *Manon* but ardour and full timbre. The Puccini excerpts, notably Calaf's *Nessun dorma* and the ringing *Recondita armonia* from *Tosca*, demonstrate there was life before Pavarotti, while the tender opening of *E lucevan le stelle* from the same opera shows that di Stefano could fine his tone down in the most ravishing manner when he needed to. The Decca recordings offer early examples of stereo, but the transfers are remarkably full and vivid.

'Torna a Surrienta' (songs of Italy and Sicily): CD 1 (with London New SO, Iller Pattacini): DE CURTIS: *Torna a Surriento; Tu ca' nun chiagne; Sonta chitarra!* BUONGIOVANNI: *Lacreme napulitane.* TAGLIAFERRI: *Napule canta; Pusilleco ...* CALIFANO: *O 'surdato 'nnammurato.* CARDILLO: *Catari, Catari.* COSTA: *Era di maggio matenata; Scetate.* VALENTE: *Addio mia bella.* CD 2 (with Orchestra, Dino Olivieri): BIXIO: *Parlami d'amore Mariù.* BARBERIS: *Munasterio 'e Santa-Chiara.* CESARINI: *Firenze sogna.* DE CURTIS: *Canta pe'me; 'A canzone 'e Napule; Ti voglio tanto bene.* NARDELLA: *Che t'aggia di!* SIMI: *Come è bello far l'amore quanno è serra.* VANCHERI: *Sicilia bedda.* BUONGIOVANNI: *Fili d'oro.* DI LAZZARO: *Chitarra romana.* RIVI: *Addio, sogni di gloria.* TRAD., arr. FAVARA: *A la barcillunisi; Nota di li lavannari; A la vallelunghisa; Muttètti di lu pàliu; Chiovu 'abattallati'; Cantu a timùni.*
(B) *** Decca Double 455 482-2 (2) [id.].

Giuseppe di Stefano was still in magnificent voice when, in the summer of 1964, he recorded the collection of popular Italian songs assembled on the first disc of this Double Decca. He projects the ardent numbers such as the title-song with characteristic lustiness but less subtlety; despite the inevitable touches of vulgarity, the singing is rich-toned and often charming, and a famous Neapolitan hit like *Catari, Catari* is winningly done. Pattacini's accompaniments are vividly idiomatic. The second collection is even more generous, offering 18 songs (against 11 on the first disc). This dates from 1958, when the voice was even more honeyed, so that Bixio's opening *Parlami d'amore Mariù* sounds almost like operetta and brings an engaging pianissimo ending. The luscious Mantovani-styled accompaniments are certainly seductive, and very well recorded, while in *Come è bello far l'amore quanno è sera* the use of the mandolin is particularly atmospheric. Besides the popular Neapolitan numbers, there are many comparative rarities here, often coming from Venice, Florence or Sicily, with their respective dialects. There are no translations, but none are really needed. As Frank Granville Barker observes in his note: 'Strong emotions are the concern of all these songs, expressed in no less straightforward melodies. The mood is intense, the singer declaring his devotion to his loved one, or despairing when it is not returned. Parting from home inspires as much anguish as parting from the loved one, as we hear in *Addio mia bella Napoli*.' The group of six traditional songs arranged by Favara, which close the recital, are particularly fine; *Muttètti di lu pàliu* (introduced by a fine horn solo) is really memorable, with di Stefano responding to its plaintive melancholy with a very gentle closing cadence. He then follows with a sparkling tarantella, *Chiovu 'abballati'*. This is not a collection to play all at once (and memories of Gigli in this repertory are not vanquished), but in its field it is currently unsurpassed.

Sutherland, Dame Joan (soprano)

'The art of the prima donna' (with ROHCG Ch. & O, Francesco Molinari-Pradelli): ARNE: *Artaxerxes: The soldier tir'd.* HANDEL: *Samson: Let the bright seraphim.* BELLINI: *Norma: Casta diva. I Puritani: Son vergin vezzosa; Qui la voce. La Sonnambula: Come per me sereno.* ROSSINI: *Semiramide: Bel raggio lusinghier.* GOUNOD: *Faust: Jewel song. Roméo et Juliette: Waltz song.* VERDI: *Otello: Willow song. Rigoletto: Caro nome. La Traviata: Ah fors' è lui; Sempre libera.* MOZART: *Die Entführung aus dem Serail: Marten aller Arten.* THOMAS: *Hamlet: Mad scene.* DELIBES: *Lakmé: Bell song.* MEYERBEER: *Les Huguenots: O beau pays.*
✿ (M) *** Decca 452 298-2; *452 298-4* (2) [id.].

This ambitious early two-disc recital (from 1960) has now, rather appropriately, been reissued in Decca's Classic Sound series, for the recording on CD is amazingly full and realistic, far more believable than many new digital recordings. It remains one of Dame Joan Sutherland's outstanding gramophone achievements, and it is a matter of speculation whether even Melba or Tetrazzini in their heyday managed to provide sixteen consecutive recordings quite as dazzling as these performances. Indeed, it is the Golden Age that one naturally turns to rather than to current singers when making any comparisons. Sutherland herself, by electing to sing each one of these fabulously difficult arias in tribute to a particular soprano of the past, from Mrs Billington in the eighteenth century, through Grisi, Malibran, Pasta and Jenny Lind in the nineteenth century, to Lilli Lehmann, Melba, Tetrazzini and Galli-Curci in this, is asking to be judged by the standards of the Golden Age. On the basis of recorded reminders she comes out with flying colours, showing a greater consistency and certainly a wider range of sympathy than even the greatest Golden Agers possessed. The sparkle and delicacy of the *Puritani Polonaise*, the freshness and lightness of the Mad scene from Thomas's *Hamlet*, the commanding power of the *Entführung* aria and the breathtaking brilliance of the Queen's aria from *Les Huguenots* are all among the high spots here, while the arias which Sutherland later recorded in her complete opera sets regularly bring performances just as fine – and often finer – than the later versions.

'The age of Bel canto' (with Marilyn Horne (mezzo-soprano), Richard Conrad (tenor), New SO of London, LSO and Chorus, Bonynge): PICCINNI: *La buona figliuola: Furia di donna irata.* HANDEL: *Atalanta: Care selve. Samson: With plaintive notes. Semele: Iris, hence away.* LAMPUGNANI: *Meraspe: Superbo di me stesso.* BONONCINI: *Astarto: Mio caro ben.* ARNE: *Artaxerxes: Oh! too lovely!* SHIELD: *Rosina: Light as thistledown; When William at eve.* MOZART: *Il rè pastore: Voi che fausti ognor donate. Die Zauberflöte: O zittre nicht. Die Entführung aus dem Serail: Ich baue ganz auf deine Stärke.* BOIELDIEU: *Angéla: Ma Fanchette est charmante.* ROSSINI: *Semiramide: Serbami ognor sì fido. Il barbiere di Siviglia: Ecco, ridente.* AUBER: *La Muette de Portici: Ferme tes yeux.* WEBER: *Der Freischütz: Und ob die Wolke sie verhülle.* BELLINI: *Beatrice di Tenda: Angiol di pace. La straniera: Un ritratto? . . . Sventurato il cor che fida.* DONIZETTI: *Don Pasquale: Tornami a dir che m'ami. Lucrezia Borgia: Il segreto per esser felici.* VERDI: *Attila: Santo di patria . . . Allor che i forti corrono.* ARDITI: *Bolero.*
(M) *** Decca 448 594-2(2) [id.].

For some reason this 1963 set has never been issued on CD before in its original complete form. Now it also reappears in Decca's Classic Sound series. In this famous early recital Sutherland generously shared the honours with other singers who, like herself, have a deep concern for restoring the Bel canto tradition. The tenor, Richard Conrad, sings far more tastefully than most of his tenor colleagues, with a pleasing lightness, but it is Marilyn Horne who firmly establishes her claim to stand beside Sutherland as a singer, often outshining her. It is enormously to Sutherland's credit that she welcomes such competition instead of trying to exaggerate her own merits by picking nonentities. Sutherland can easily afford such generosity, and the style of singing throughout the recital has a consistency obviously guided by Richard Bonynge. One may sometimes object to his insistence on a basically mannered style, but in this recital it is generally less obtrusive than hitherto. It is good to be reminded what a fine Mozartian Sutherland is, in the Queen of the Night's aria, and the delightful point of Shield's *Light as thistledown* is irresistible. Her *Semiramide* duet brings a performance of equal mastery. An essential set for all lovers of the art of singing. Full texts and translations are included.

'Grandi voci': BELLINI: *Norma: Sediziose voci . . . Casta diva . . . Ah! bello a me ritorna. I Puritani: Qui la voce sua soave . . . Vien, diletto* (with ROHCG O, Molinari-Pradelli). VERDI: *Attila: Santo di patria . . . Allor che i forti corrono . . . Da te questo or m'è concesso* (with LSO, Bonynge). DONIZETTI: *Lucia di Lammermoor: Ancor non giunse! . . . Regnava nel silenzio; Il dolce suono mi colpi di sua voce! . . . Ardon gl'incensi* (Mad scene). *Linda di Chamounix: Ah! tardai troppo . . . O luce di quest'anima.* VERDI: *Ernani: Surta è la notte . . . Ernani! Ernani, involami. I vespri siciliani: Mercè, dilette amiche* (*Boléro*).
❁ (M) *** Decca 440 404-2 [id.].

Sutherland's 'Grandi voci' disc is one of the most cherishable of all operatic recital records, bringing together the glorious, exuberant items from her very first recital disc, made within weeks of her first Covent Garden success in 1959, and – as a valuable supplement – the poised accounts of *Casta diva* and *Vien, diletto* she recorded the following year as part of the 'Art of the Prima Donna'. It was this 1959 recital which at once put Sutherland firmly on the map among the great recording artists of all time. Even she has never surpassed the freshness of these versions of the two big arias from *Lucia di Lammermoor*, sparkling in immaculate coloratura, while the lightness and point of the jaunty *Linda di Chamounix* aria and the *Boléro* from *I vespri siciliani* are just as winning. The aria from *Attila* comes from 'The age of bel canto' (1963). The sound is exceptionally vivid and immediate, though the accompaniments under Nello Santi are sometimes rough in ensemble.

'Greatest hits': Excerpts from: HANDEL: *Samson.* PICCINNI: *La buona figliuola.* BELLINI: *Norma; I Puritani.* DONIZETTI: *La fille du régiment; Lucia di Lammermoor: Mad scene.* DELIBES: *Lakmé.* VERDI: *Rigoletto; La Traviata.* GOUNOD: *Faust.* OFFENBACH: *Contes d'Hoffmann.*
(M) *** Decca 458 209-2.

A 76-minute collection like this, well chosen to entertain, is self-recommending at mid-price. It has been nicely repackaged in a slip-case for this reissue in Decca's Opera Gala series, and translations are now included. The chosen recordings have been slightly amended since the previous issue but all come from the period when the voice was at its freshest: *Let the bright seraphim*, the delectable *Caro nome* and the vivacious *Jewel song* from *Faust* all come from 1960, but here the justly famous 1959 *Mad scene* from *Lucia di Lammermoor* has been substituted for the performance in the complete set under Pritchard. The lively excerpt from *La fille du régiment* (1967) and the *Doll song* from *Contes d'Hoffmann* (1972) come from the complete sets, as does the famous Act I *La Traviata* scena (1962), which is now added. The sound is consistently vivid.

Sutherland, Joan (soprano), Marilyn Horne (mezzo-soprano), Luciano Pavarotti (tenor)

'Live from the Lincoln Center, New York' (Duets and trios): VERDI: *Ernani: Solingo, errante e misero. Otello: Già nella notte densa. Il Trovatore: Madre non dormi?* BELLINI: *Norma: Adalgisa! . . . Oh! rimembranza! Ma di' . . . Oh non tremare.* PONCHIELLI: *La Gioconda: Ecco la barca . . . addio; Deh! non turbare.*
(M) *** Decca Dig. 458 207-2 [id.].

Not all gala concerts make good records, but this 1981 occasion is an exception; almost every item here puts an important gloss on the achievements of the three stars, not least in the concerted numbers which have been separated off for this single-disc reissue in Decca's Opera Gala series. It is good to have a sample not only of Sutherland's Desdemona, but also of Pavarotti's Otello (not at that time heard, either on stage or in the studio) in their account of the Act I duet. The final scene from *Il Trovatore* is more compelling here than on the complete set made by the same soloists five years earlier. At times the microphones catch a beat in the voices of both Sutherland and Horne, but not as obtrusively as on some studio discs. Lively accompaniments under Bonynge, bright, vivid, digital recording, but over-loud applause. The documentation includes full translations and a picture of the celebrated occasion.

Tallis Scholars, Peter Phillips

'A Tudor collection': CORNYSH: *Salve regina; Ave Maria, mater Dei; Gaude virgo; Magnificat; Ah, Robin; Adieu, adieu, my heartes lust; Adieu, corage; Woefully arrayed; Stabat mater.* ANON.: *Westron wynde.* TAVERNER: *Western wind Mass; Leroy kyrie; Missa gloria tibi trinitas; Dum transisset Sabbatum.*

TALLIS: *If ye love me; Hear the voice and prayer; A New commandment; O Lord, give thy Holy Spirit; Purge me, O Lord; Verily, verily I say unto you; Remember not, O Lord God; Tunes for Archbishop Parker's Psalter; Out from the deep, O Lord, in thee is all my trust; Blessed are those that be undefiled; Spem in alium; Sancte Deus; Salvator mundi I & II; Gaude gloriosa; Miserere nostri; Loquebantur variis linguis.* BYRD: *Mass for five voices; Mass for four voices; Mass for three voices; Ave verum corpus; Infelix ego.*
(M) *** Gimell/Philips Dig. 454 895-2 (4).

This handsomely produced box collects together four of the CDs made by the Tallis Scholars between 1984 and 1988 when they were pioneering authentic performances of repertory which was later to be taken up by other groups. However, the excellence of their singing and the stylish expressiveness of their approach earned the group several *Gramophone* awards in the first few years of their recording career. The nine Cornysh pieces issued here all derive from the Eton Choir Book and will surely come as a revelation to collectors unfamiliar with this period and a joy to those who are. Much of Cornysh's music has disappeared, including several Masses, and even the opening section of the *Stabat mater* lacks treble, counter-tenor and tenor parts (Peter Phillips uses Frank Lloyd Harrison's reconstruction). The music is quite unlike much other polyphony of the time and is florid, wild, complex and, at times, grave. The Tallis Scholars give magnificent, totally committed accounts of these glorious pieces – as usual their attack, ensemble and true intonation and blend are remarkable. Excellent recording. The Taverner six-part setting of the Mass is one of the great glories of Tudor music, richly varied in its invention (not least in rhythm) and expressive in a deeply personal way very rare for its period. Here it is given an intensely involving performance. Peter Phillips rejects all idea of reserve or cautiousness of expression; the result reflects the emotional basis of the inspiration the more compellingly. The motet, *Dum transisset Sabbatum*, is then presented more reflectively, another rich inspiration. The Tallis disc collects the complete English anthems of the composer. Women's voices are used instead of boys', but the purity of the sound they produce is not in question, and the performances could hardly be more committed or more totally inside this repertoire. Peter Phillips is no less a master of the Byrd repertoire; undoubtedly these performances have great eloquence and variety of expression so that, when the drama is varied with a gentler mood, the contrast is the more striking. The sound made by the Scholars in Merton College chapel is beautiful, both warm and fresh. The account of *Ave verum* is movingly simple.

Tauber, Richard (tenor)

'Opera arias and duos' (with (i) Elisabeth Rethberg; (ii) Lotte Lehmann) from: MOZART: *Don Giovanni.* MEHUL: *Joseph.* OFFENBACH: *Contes d'Hoffmann.* THOMAS: *Mignon.* TCHAIKOVSKY: *Eugene Onegin.* SMETANA: (i) *The Bartered Bride.* WAGNER: *Die Meistersinger.* PUCCINI: *Turandot;* (i) *Madama Butterfly.* KORNGOLD: (ii) *Die tote Stadt.*
(M) (***) EMI mono CDH7 64029-2.

Starting as early as 1922 with Mozart's *Dalla sua pace* from *Don Giovanni*, then immediately following with the 1939 *Il mio tesoro*, this recital charts Tauber's recording career as far as 1945 with the Méhul *Champs paternels* from *Joseph*. Elisabeth Rethberg joins him now and then, notably in the *Butterfly* excerpt, sung in German. The voice is well caught by the transfers, but there are occasionally some noises off. Yet the standard of singing here is so consistently high that one can readily make allowances. For a sampler, try the glorious *Hoffmann* excerpts (1929) or *Lensky's aria* from *Eugene Onegin* (1923).

MOZART: *Don Giovanni: Il mio tesoro. Die Zauberflöte: Dies Bildnis.* Arias from: PUCCINI: *La Bohème; Madama Butterfly; Tosca; Turandot.* LEONCAVALLO: *Pagliacci.* VERDI: *Il Trovatore.* MEHUL: *Joseph in Aegypten.* OFFENBACH: *Contes d'Hoffmann.* THOMAS: *Mignon.* TCHAIKOVSKY: *Eugene Onegin.* SMETANA: *Bartered bride* (all sung in German). WEBER: *Der Freischütz.* LORTZING: *Undine.* KIENZL: *Der Evangelimann.* WAGNER: *Die Meistersinger.* R. STRAUSS: *Der Rosenkavlier.* KORNGOLD: *Die tote Stadt.* LEHAR: *Die lustige Witwe (Lippen schweigen; Vilja-Lied); Paganini; Friederike (O Mädchen, mein Mädchen); Das Land des Lächelns* (4 excerpts, including *Dein ist mein ganzes Herz*). *Giuditta; Die Zarewitsch.* KALMAN: *Die Zirkusprinzessin; Gräfin Mariza.* HEUBERGER: *Der Opernball (Im chambre séparée).* STOLZ: *Adieu, mein kleiner Gardeoffizier; Im Prater blühn wieder die Bäume.* SIECZYNSKI: *Wien, du Stadt meiner Träume.* Johann STRAUSS Jr: *Geschichten aus dem Wienerwald; Rosen aus dem Süden.* ZELLER: *Der Vogelhändler.* DOELLE: *Wenn der weisse Flieder wider blüht.* ERWIN: *Ich küsse Ihre Hand, Madame.* Lieder: SCHUBERT: *Ständchen; Der Lindenbaum.*
(M) (*(**)) EMI mono CMS5 66692-2 (2) [id.].

If one begins with the second of these two CDs, it becomes immediately obvious why Tauber established his reputation with the wider public largely in the field of operetta. The uniquely honeyed voice makes simple melodies like *Lippen schweigen* from *The Merry Widow*, with its magical final cadence, or the *Vilja-Lied* utterly seductive, and that despite often inadequate transfers, with thin, whistly orchestral sound and plenty of distortion, even on the voice itself. One wonders why Tauber, more than most singers of his generation, so regularly suffers from this problem. It isn't that the basic recordings are bad, except for the thin orchestra (though there are frequent moments of blasting); usually the magic and power of the voice are well conveyed; yet the original sources too often seem prone to distortion. The first disc concentrates on opera and opens with a glowingly lyrical 1939 *Il mio tesoro*, but again there is distortion. *Dies Bildnis* (from *Die Zauberflöte*) is acoustic (1922) and rather better, and Tauber then makes *Your tiny hand is frozen* sound beguiling even in German! – the chosen language for most of his records. There are many remarkable performances here, from the lilting *Legend of Kleinsach* (1928) to a stirring *Di quella pira* (1926) with a comic wind band accompaniment, and equally moving versions of Lenski's aria from *Eugene Onegin* (1923), when the band is less clumsy, and the ardent *On with the motley* (recorded in London in 1936 and sung in English). It is a pity the recordings are technically so inadequate, but the voice still enthrals the listener.

Tear, Robert (tenor)

'English baroque recital' (with Iona Brown, violin, Kenneth Heath, cello, Simon Preston and Colin Tilney, harpsichord continuo, ASMF, Marriner): HANDEL: *Look down, harmonious Saint; Meine Seele hört im Sehen; Süsse Stille.* ARNE: *Bacchus and Ariadne:* excerpts; *Fair Caelia love pretended:* excerpts. BOYCE: *Song of Momus to Mars.* James HOOK: *The Lass of Richmond Hill.*
(B) *** Decca Double 452 973-2 (2) [id.]. (with HANDEL: *Acis and Galatea* ***).

Robert Tear's 1969 recital offers a rare Handel cantata and two of his German songs, followed by an even rarer and certainly delightful collection of music by his English successors. This may in essence be a scholarly compilation, but it is one which imparts its learning in the most painless way, including as it does the vigorous Boyce song and the original bouncing setting of *The Lass of Richmond Hill*, beautifully pointed. The *harmonious saint* of the Handel cantata is of course St Cecilia, while Arne too is in Italianate mood in *Bacchus and Ariadne* – until he ends with a galumphing final number with ripe horn parts – very English. Robert Tear is in excellent voice and the recording has all the atmospheric warmth one associates with Argo's recordings of the ASMF in St John's, Smith Square.

Tebaldi, Renata (soprano)

'Grandi voci': Arias and excerpts from: PUCCINI: *Madama Butterfly; La Bohème* (with Carlo Bergonzi); *Turandot* (with Mario del Monaco); *Tosca; Gianni Schicchi; Suor Angelica; La Fanciulla del West* (with Cornell MacNeil); *Manon Lescaut.* VERDI: *Aida; Otello* (with Luisa Ribacci); *La forza del destino.* CILEA: *Adriana Lecouvreur.* GIORDANO: *Andrea Chénier.* BOITO: *Mefistofele.* CATALANI: *La Wally.*
(M) *** Decca (IMS) 440 408-2 [id.].

Those wanting a single-disc, stereo representation of Tebaldi's vocal art could hardly do better than this. It is good that her early mono complete sets of *La Bohème* and *Madama Butterfly* are now again available, and the selection here rightly concentrates on her stereo remakes of the key Puccini operas in the late 1950s, when the voice was still creamily fresh. *Vissi d'arte* (1959) is particularly beautiful. She could be thrilling in Verdi too, as the splendid *Ritorna vincitor!* vibrantly demonstrates, taken from Karajan's complete *Aida*, made in the same year. With a playing time of 75 minutes, this recital should disappoint no one, for the Decca recordings come up as vividly as ever.

'A Tebaldi festival' (with (i) New Philh. O, cond. (ii) Anton Guadago; or (iii) Richard Bonynge; (iv) Monte Carlo Op. O, Fausto Cleva): (i; ii) WAGNER: *Tannhäuser: Salve d'amor, recinto eletto! (Dich teure Halle); Elisabeth's prayer. Lohengrin: Elsa's dream. Tristan und Isolde: Liebestod.* BIZET: *Carmen: Habanera* (with Ambrosian Ch.); *Card scene* (all sung in Italian). SAINT-SAENS: *Samson et Dalila: Amor! i mieie fini proteggi (Amor, viens m'aider); S'apre per te il mio cor (Mon coeur s'ouvre à ta voix).* MASSENET: *Manon: Addio, o nostro piccolo desco (Adieu, notre petite table); La tua non è mano che mi tocca? (N'est-ce plus ma main?).* (i; iii) VERDI: *Aida: Ritorna vincitor!.* PUCCINI: *La Bohème: Musetta's waltz song.* (iv) BELLINI: *Norma: Sediziose voci . . . Casta diva* (with Alfredo Mariotti & Turin Ch.); *I Puritani: Qui la voce . . . Vien, diletto. La Sonnambula: Ah! non credea mirarti.* VERDI: *Nabucco: Ben io t'invenni . . . Salgo già del trono. Don Carlo: O don fatale.* Songs: ROSSINI: *Péchés de vieillesse: La regata veneziana* (3 songs in Venetian dialect). LARA: *Granada.* PONCE: *Estrellita.* CARDILLO: *Catari, Catari.* TOSTI: *'A vucchella.* DE CURTIS: *Non ti scordar di me.* RODGERS: *Carousel: If I loved you.*

(M) **(*) Decca 452 456-2 (2) [id.].

What, Wagner in Italian! Tebaldi, for so long a favourite diva, could apparently get away with almost anything during her vintage years with Decca in a collection which ranges into unexpected corners. She amply justifies her choice of language in the rich lyricism of her Wagner, and it is good to hear such a ravishing account of *Musetta's waltz song*, a role she never assumed in the opera house. *Ritorna vincitor!*, too, is unforgettable, both commanding and richly secure – finer than her performance in her complete stereo set (under Karajan). Plainly she has also chosen many of the other items out of sheer affection – the little songs of Lara, Ponce and Tosti – although the dialect songs of Rossini suit her less well. In those lighter items Douglas Gamley's lush arrangements and Bonynge's indulgent accompaniments add to the glamour of the presentation in the warm acoustics of Kingsway Hall. Though all this opening group was recorded as recently as 1969, the voice was still in fine condition, and anyone who has ever responded to the ripe, rich tone of this generous artist should revel in the sweetmeats presented here, not least the lovely melody from Rodgers's *Carousel*. The closing group of Bellini and Verdi excerpts dates from the previous year and was produced by Christopher Raeburn in Monte Carlo. These items have never been issued before and presumably were not passed by Tebaldi herself. Although the two Verdi excerpts (from *Nabucco* and *Don Carlo*) are thrillingly dramatic and in Bellini the singing brings some glorious legato, cabalettas have moments of wildness and intonation is not always secure. Indeed *Ah! non credea mirarti* should not have been issued, for it does the singer no justice. However, for the most part this is an endearing recital, and she is given consistently supportive accompaniments, while the voice never loses its bloom.

Songs and arias (with Giorgio Favaretto, piano): Recital I: Songs: ANON.: *Leggiadri occhi bello.* A. SCARLATTI: *Le violette.* ROSSINI: *Soirées musicales: La promessa.* BELLINI: *Dolente immagine di fille mia; Vanne, o rosa Fortunata.* MARTUCCI: *La canzone dei recordi (Al folto bosco; Cavanta il ruscello; Sul mar la navicella).* TRAD., arr. FAVARA: *A la barcillunisa.* MASETTI: *Passo e non ti vedo.* TURINA: *Poema en forma de canciones: Cantares.* Arias: HANDEL: *Giulio Cesare: Piangerò la sorte mia.* SARTI: *Giulio Sabino: Lungi dal caro bene.*

Recital II: Songs: A. SCARLATTI: *Chi vuole innamorarsi.* ROSSINI: *Péchés de vieillesse: 3 Songs in Venetian dialect (Anzoleta avanti La Regata; Anzoleta co passa la Regata; Anzoleta dopo la Regata).* Arias: A. SCARLATTI: *Il Seddecia, Re di Gerusalemme: Caldo sangue.* HANDEL: *Armadigi de Gaula: Ah! spietato.* MOZART: *Ridente la calma, K.152; Un moto di gioia, K.579.* BELLINI: *Vaga luna che inargenti; Per pietà, bell'idol mio.* MASCAGNI: *M'ama . . . non m'ama.* RESPIGHI: *Notte.* TOSTI: *'A vucchella.* DAVICO: *O luna che fa lum.*
(B) ** Decca Double 452 472-2 (2) [(M) id. import].

Here combined on a Double Decca are a pair of song recitals which Tebaldi recorded fairly early in her career, in 1956 and 1957 respectively, and which have been out of the catalogue for 40 years, although four items – by Scarlatti, Rossini, Mozart and the charming Favara folksong arrangement – were put out on a stereo '45' disc at the beginning of the 1960s. The voice sounds young and fresh but, like many another Italian opera singer, Tebaldi proved hardly a stylist in eighteenth-century music, and the lighter songs do not always suit her big voice. But when she comes to the arias it is a different matter. Cleopatra's lament from the third Act of Handel's *Giulio Cesare* brings a natural, flowing legato, and Sarti's *Lungi dal caro bene* is gently ravishing. The two Bellini ariettas are also appealingly sung, and Verdi's *Stornella* makes a light-hearted contrast, while the three excerpts from Martucci's seven-part mini-cycle about another forsaken maiden, sadly and affectionately remembering past times with her lover, produces a charming and touching response. The following Sicilian folksong, *A la barcillunisa*, soars like a Puccini aria, and the first disc ends seductively with Turina's *Cantares*.

The second recital opens with a vivacious canzonetta, nicely articulated, warning of the dangers of falling in love, and the following Scarlatti and Handel arias do not disappoint. Tebaldi obviously had a soft spot for Rossini's songs in Venetian dialect (which come from his 'Sins of my old age') and she sings them with a lighter touch here than in her later recording (see above). Tebaldi's Mozart singing is freely peppered with intrusive aitches and occasional swerves, but she is back on form in the two Bellini songs and, after a rich-voiced if a very operatic version of Respighi's *Notte*, she finishes in lighter vein with a lilting Tosti favourite – another song she included in her later recital – and a meltingly affectionate account of a colloquial Tuscan song, arranged by Vincenzo Davico. Throughout, Giorgio Favaretto accompanies quite supportively, if without producing a distinctive personality, but the recording balance does not flatter him and the piano sounds rather withdrawn at times.

'Christmas festival' (with Ambrosian Singers, New Philharmonia Orchestra, Anton Guadagno): TRAD.: *Adeste fidelis; What child is this?; Tù scendi dalle stelle.* BACH/GOUNOD: *Ave Maria.* BRAHMS: *Lullaby.*

ADAM: *O holy night.* GRUBER: *Silent night.* FRANCK: *Panis angelicus.* GOUNOD: *O Divine Redeemer.* SCHUBERT: *Mille cherubini in coro; Ave Maria.*
(M) **(*) Decca 425 214-2.

For Tebaldi admirers the rich, well-placed voice will be enough, still sounding quite fresh in 1971, and backed by Douglas Gamley's flattering arrangements. The programme opens and closes with an inflated (trumpet-led) *Adeste fidelis*, with chorus, which then returns only twice more. *What child is this?* is a charming version of *Greensleeves*. This and the gentle items, the Brahms *Lullaby*, *Tù scendi dalle stelle*, with its folksy, drone-like accompaniment, and Schubert's delightful *Mille cherubini in coro* are the highlights. Tebaldi also sings an attractive Italian version of *Silent night*. At times her touch is a shade ungainly, but the singing never lacks memorability. Spacious Kingsway Hall recording.

Tetrazzini, Luisa (soprano)

'Prima voce': Arias from: BELLINI: *La Sonnambula.* DONIZETTI: *Lucia di Lammermoor.* ROSSINI: *Il Barbiere di Siviglia.* THOMAS: *Mignon.* VERACINI: *Rosalinda.* VERDI: *Un ballo in maschera; Rigoletto; La Traviata; Il Trovatore; I vespri siciliani.* Songs.
(M) (***) Nimbus mono NI 7808 [id.].

Tetrazzini was astonishing among coloratura sopranos not just for her phenomenal agility but for the golden warmth that went with tonal purity. The Nimbus transfers add a bloom to the sound, with the singer slightly distanced. Though some EMI transfers make her voice more vividly immediate, one quickly adjusts. Such display arias as *Ah non giunge* from *La Sonnambula* or the *Boléro* from *I vespri siciliani* are incomparably dazzling, but it is worth noting too what tenderness is conveyed through Tetrazzini's simple phrasing and pure tone in such a tragic aria as Violetta's *Addio del passato*, with both verses included. Lieder devotees may gasp in horror, but one of the delightful oddities here is Tetrazzini's bright-eyed performance, with ragged orchestral accompaniment, of what is described as *La serenata inutile* by Brahms – in fact *Vergebliches Ständchen*, sung with a triumphant if highly inauthentic top A at the end, implying no closure of the lady's window!

Tibbett, Lawrence (baritone)

'Tibbett in opera': excerpts from: LEONCAVALLO: *Pagliacci.* BIZET: *Carmen.* PUCCINI: *Tosca.* VERDI: *Un ballo in maschera; Simon Boccanegra; Rigoletto; Otello.* ROSSINI: *Il barbiere di Siviglia.* GOUNOD: *Faust.* WAGNER: *Tannhäuser, Die Walküre.*
(M) (***) Nimbus mono NI 7825 [id.].

The scale and resonance of Lawrence Tibbett's voice come over vividly in this fine selection of his recordings made between 1926 and 1939. The Nimbus process allows the rapid vibrato in his voice to emerge naturally, giving the sound a thrilling richness in all these varied items. Particularly interesting is the longest, the whole of *Wotan's farewell*, with Stokowski conducting the Philadelphia Orchestra in 1934. It is an over-the-top performance that carries total conviction, even if the sheer volume produces some clangorous resonances in the Nimbus transfer. Also memorable is the celebrated *Boccanegra* Council chamber sequence, recorded in 1939 with Martinelli and Rose Bampton in the ensemble.

Vasari Singers, Jeremy Backhouse

'Twentieth century choral music': PART: *Summa; The Beatitudes* (with John Keys, organ); *7 Magnificat antiphons.* TAVENER: *The Lamb; Funeral ikos; 2 Hymns to the Mother of God. Collegium Regale: Magnificat & Nunc dimittis.* RIDOUT: *Litany* (with Andrew Angus, bass). GORECKI: *Totus tuus.*
(B) *** CfP Dig. CD-CFP 6076 [(M) id. import].

This splendidly sung concert makes an ideal introduction to the admirable twentieth-century school of choral music, written by a group of composers who have not only returned to melody and tonality but have all linked their inspiration to the great ecclesiastical choral traditions of the past. What is so readily demonstrated here is the musical common ground shared by all this vocal repertoire (written between 1977 and 1991). Here serenity and beauty are joined with lavishly blending sonorities and telling use of dynamic contrast. The Estonian composer Avro Pärt's *Summa* (a fresh and carol-like setting of the Creed) is followed by John Tavener's justly famous and haunting carol, *The Lamb*, which Jeremy Backhouse enhances with an effective ritardando at the end of each verse. The music's serenity is interrupted by stabs of dissonance, a device Pärt is to use even more readily in his set of *Beatitudes*, which ends dramatically with a powerful organ epilogue (John Keys). Similarly, the melancholy simplicity of Tavener's *Funeral ikos* links to Alan Ridout's *Litany*, where a solo cantor alternates with bursts of richly harmonized choral tone. The ethereality of Tavener's two *Hymns to the Mother of God* then leads naturally into Pärt's brief but concentrated *Magnificat Antiphons*, with the seventh the longest and most telling. Tavener's *Magnificat* not only brings an exotic oriental influence, but its rocking momentum makes a striking foil for the following more tranquil *Nunc dimittis*. Finally, Górecki's exultant *Totus tuus*, written to celebrate the visit of Pope John Paul to Poland in 1987, ends the programme with exultant feeling, with the diminuendo on the repeated word *Maria* at the close of the piece wonderfully poignant. Indeed the performances here of what is consistently inspired music could surely not be bettered, nor could the recording, atmospheric yet clear, made in the Church of St Giles, Cripplegate, London, in 1995, and superbly balanced by Mike Clements.

Vishnevskaya, Galina (soprano)

Russian songs (with (i) Mstislav Rostropovich, piano; (ii) Russian State SO, Igor Markevitch): (i) TCHAIKOVSKY: *None but the lonely heart; Not a word, beloved; Heed not, my love.* PROKOFIEV: *5 Poems of Anna Akhmatova.* MUSSORGSKY: *Songs and dances of death;* (ii) orch. Markevitch: *Cradle song; The dazzling lassie; Night; Where are you, dear star?; Scallywag; The Dnieper.*
(M) *** Ph. 446 212-2.

The young Vishnevskaya sang many of these songs when she came to the Aldeburgh Festival in 1961 and there is the same intensity here as there was in the Jubilee Hall for that suddenly arranged and most exciting concert. Vishnevskaya even overcomes what one would have imagined were impossible difficulties of transferring the Mussorgsky *Songs and dances of death* from bass to soprano. The result is not always what one imagines the composer intended – but no one could miss how compelling it is. Only occasionally under pressure does the voice grow hard. The singer's mastery of vocal characterization comes out repeatedly. *None but the lonely heart* shows Vishnevskaya at her most impressive, recognizably Russian in her timbre but steadier than most. Her sensitive singing of the Prokofiev songs shows how completely they follow the broad Russian tradition. The recording is rather reverberant, with the piano sounding unusually close for a song recital. Rostropovich, as at Aldeburgh, seems just as much at home accompanying his wife on the piano as playing his cello, and certainly there is the same consummate artistry. The other Mussorgsky songs, including the composer's very first, *Where are you, dear star?*, and the *Cradle song*, a lullaby sung to a dying child, were recorded in Russia a year later with orchestrations by Markevitch, who accompanies with the Russian State Symphony Orchestra. They are hardly less compulsive.

Walker, Norman (bass)

'A portrait of Norman Walker': HANDEL: *Acis and Galatea: I rage, I melt, I burn . . . O ruddier than the cherry. Judas Maccabeaus: I feel the deity within . . . Arm, arm ye brave. Messiah: Why do the nations; The trumpet shall sound.* HAYDN: *The Creation: And God said; Now heav'n in fullest glory.* ELGAR: *Dream of Gerontius: Jesu by that shuddering dread.* HOLBROOKE: *Dylan: Sea King's song; The Children of Don: Noden's song.* GOUNOD: *Faust: Then leave her* (final trio; with Joan Cross, Webster Booth). MARCELLO: *Le quattro Stagioni: Dalle cime del'Api . . . Venti olà.* LANDI: *La morte d'Orfeo: Bevi, bevi.* PURCELL: *What can be done* (trio; with Aldred Deller, Richard Lewis). STORACE: *The pretty creature.* LANE WILSON: *False Phyllis.* HAYNES: *Off to Philadelphia.* CAPEL: *Love could I only tell thee!* MOZART: *The Magic Flute: O Isis and Osiris; The Abduction from the Seraglio: Ah, my pretty brace of fellows.*
✽ (M) (***) Dutton mono CDLX 7021 [id. full price].

Born in 1907, Norman Walker was by training one of the last of the great pre-war British basses, but his sense of style, his clean focus and his technical finesse gave him in many ways a linking role, ushering in a new generation of British singers. This splendid compilation, prepared in collaboration with Walker's record-archivist son, Malcolm, gives a vivid idea of a singer whose career was sadly cut short when he was still in his forties. The earliest recording, never previously published, is of *O Isis and Osiris* from *The Magic Flute*, made when he was only 21, with the voice already fully formed, but in an old-fashioned, rallentando style. Three of the recordings date from the 1930s – two excerpts from rare Holbrooke operas and the glorious *Trio* from Gounod's *Faust* with Joan Cross and Webster Booth – but most are from the early post-war period, when Walker contributed to such classic recordings as Sargent's pioneering version of Elgar's *Dream of Gerontius* (thrillingly represented here in one of the most vivid transfers) and both of his *Messiah* recordings, as well as the HMV 'History of Music in Sound'. Full and dark as the voice is, Walker's agility in ornaments and rapid divisions is phenomenal, not least in another, previously unpublished recording, a witty account of Osmin's aria from *The Seraglio*, done in English with Gerald Moore accompanying. What is remarkable is not only the charisma and vocal richness but also the clarity of the diction. The splendid Dutton transfers are among his finest yet, with plenty of body in the sound and the voice often given an extraordinarily real presence.

Wedding music

'The world of wedding music': WAGNER: *Lohengrin: Wedding march.* BACH: *Suite No. 3: Air* (Stephen Cleobury). CLARKE: *Prince of Denmark's march (Trumpet voluntary).* PURCELL: *Trumpet tune* (Simon Preston). BACH/GOUNOD: *Ave Maria* (Kiri Te Kanawa). SCHUBERT: *Ave Maria.* MOZART: *Alleluja* (Leontyne Price). *Vespers: Laudate dominum* (Felicity Palmer). KARG-ELERT: *Marche triomphale: Nun danket alle Gott.* BRAHMS: *Chorale prelude: Es ist ein Ros entsprungen.* WIDOR: *Symphony No. 5: Toccata.* MENDELSSOHN: *Midsummer Night's Dream: Wedding march* (Peter Hurford). WALFORD DAVIES: *God be in my head.* Hymn: *The Lord's my shepherd* (Huddersfield Choral Soc., Morris). STAINER: *Love divine.* Hymn: *Praise my soul, the King of heaven* (King's College Ch., Cleobury). BACH: *Cantata No. 147: Jesu, joy of man's desiring.* Hymn: *Lead us, Heavenly Father, lead us* (St John's College Ch., Guest). HANDEL: *Samson: Let the bright seraphim* (Joan Sutherland).
(B) ** Decca 436 402-2; *436 402-4* [(M) id. import].

An inexpensive present for any bride-to-be, with many traditional suggestions, well played and sung, though it would have been better to have omitted the Karg-Elert *Marche-triomphale* in favour of Handel's *Arrival of the Queen of Sheba*, to which many a contemporary bride trips down the aisle. Good sound.

Winchester Cathedral Choir, Martin Neary

'A solemn musick' (with Baroque Brass of London): PURCELL: *Funeral music for Queen Mary and Motets; Jehova, quam multi sunt hostes.* CROFT: *Burial service.* BACH: *O Jesu Christ, mein Lebens Licht, BWV 118.* BLOW: *Salvator mundi.* HUMFREY: *Hymne to God the Father.* GREENE: *Lord, let me know mine end.* BATTISHILL: *O Lord, look down from heaven.*
(M) *** EMI Dig. CDM5 66683-2 [id.].

Martin Neary's splendid version of Purcell's *Funeral music* is discussed under its composer entry. The rest of the programme, music with similar associations by other composers, is also very rewarding, usually elegiac in mood but sometimes with dramatic contrasts, as in Croft's *Burial service*. Particularly fine are Greene's *Let me know mine end* and Pelham Humfrey's *Hymne to God the Father*, with the solo beautifully sung by the counter-tenor, David Hurley. The recording is diffuse but pleasingly atmospheric.

Wunderlich, Fritz (tenor)

'Great voice': Arias and excerpts from: MOZART: *Die Zauberflöte; Die Entführung aus dem Serail.* VERDI: *La Traviata* (with Hilde Gueden); *Rigoletto* (with Erika Köth); *Don Carlos* (with Hermann Prey). TCHAIKOVSKY: *Eugene Onegin.* LORTZING: *Zar und Zimmermann; Der Waffenschmied.* ROSSINI: *Il barbiere di Siviglia.* PUCCINI: *La Bohème* (with Hermann Prey). *Tosca.* Lieder: SCHUBERT: *Heidenröslein.* BEETHOVEN: *Ich liebe dich.* TRAD.: *Funiculi-funicula; Ein Lied geht um die Welt* (with R. Lamy Ch.).
(B) *** DG Classikon 431 110-2 [(M) id. import].

Here is 70 minutes of gloriously heady tenor singing from one of the golden voices of the 1960s. Mozart's *Dies Bildnis* makes a ravishing opener, and *Hier soll ich dich denn sehen* from *Die Entführung* is equally beautiful. Then come two sparkling excerpts from *La Traviata* with Hilde Gueden and some memorable Tchaikovsky, like all the Italian repertoire, sung in German. The Rossini excerpt is wonderfully crisp and stylish. Wunderlich is joined by the charming Erika Köth in *Rigoletto* and by Hermann Prey for the rousing *Don Carlos* duet (*Sie ist verloren . . . Er ist's! Carlos!*) and the excerpt from *Bohème*. Last in the operatic group comes the most famous *Tosca* aria, *Und es blitzen die Sterne* (not too difficult to identify in Italian) sung without excessive histrionics. The Schubert and Beethoven Lieder are lovely and, if the two final popular songs (with chorus) bring more fervour than they deserve, one can revel in everything else. Excellent recording throughout. It is a pity there are no translations or notes, but with singing like this one can manage without them. A splendid bargain.